Author-Title Index
to
Joseph Sabin's

Dictionary of Books Relating to America

compiled by

JOHN EDGAR MOLNAR

The Scarecrow Press, Inc.
Metuchen, N.J.   1974

Key to original volumes of Sabin

v. 1.	A - Bedford, Pennsylvania.
v. 2.	Bedinger - Brownell, H. H.
v. 3.	Brownell, H. H. - Chesbrough
v. 4.	Cheshire, New Hampshire - Costa Pereira
v. 5.	Costa Rica - Dumorter
v. 6.	Du Moulin - Franklin, A. W.
v. 7.	Franklin, Benjamin - Hall, Joseph
v. 8.	Hall, Joseph - Huntington, Jedediah V.
v. 9.	Huntington, Joseph - Lacroix, Francois J. P. de.
v. 10.	Lacroix, Frederic - M'Clary
v. 11.	McClean - Memoire justificatif
v. 12.	Memoire justificatif des hommes - Nederland (Articulen)
v. 13.	Nederland (Besoignes) - Omai
v. 14.	Omana y Sotomayor - Philadelphia City Tract Society
v. 15.	Philadelphia Club - Providence, Rhode Island (Measures)
v. 16.	Providence Mechanics' and Apprentices' Library - Remarks relative
v. 17.	Remarks respecting - Ross, C. K.
v. 18.	Ross, D. B. - Schedae
v. 19.	Schedel - Simms, W. G.
v. 20.	Simms, W. G. - Smith, Seba.
v. 21.	Smith, Sebastian Bach - Solis y Valenzuela, Bruno de.
v. 22.	Solis y Valenzuela, Pedro de - Spiritual manifestations
v. 23.	Spiritual maxims - Storrs, R. S.
v. 24.	Storrs, R. S. - Ternaux-Compans, H.
v. 25.	Ternaux-Compans, H. - Tucker, J.
v. 26.	Tucker, J. - Vindex, pseud.
v. 27.	Vindex, pseud. - Weeks, Levi.
v. 28.	Weeks, William Raymond - Witherspoon, J.
v. 29.	Witherspoon, J. - Z.

Key to numbered entries in Sabin

A	1 - 2546	N	51671 - 56364
B	2547 - 9740	O	56365 - (58050)
C	9741 - (18220)	P	58051 - 66883
D	18221 - 21607	Q	(66884) - 67372
E	21608 - 23576	R	67373 - (74601)
F	(23577) - 26265	S	74602 - 94141
G	26266 - 29387	T	94142 - 97659
H	(29388) - 34140	U	97660 - 98253
I	34141 - 35325	V	98254 - 100860
J	(35326) - 36967	W	100861 - 105711
K	36968 - 38373	X	105712 - 105742
L	(38374) - 42894	Y	105743 - 106228A
M	42895 - 51670	Z	106229 - 106413

G. pseud. see F. and G. pseud.
G. pseud. Sumner controversy. 93721
G***. pseud. Beautes de l'historique
d'Amerique. (4202)
G——t. pseud. tr. see Gouriet, ------.
tr.
G . . . y. pseud. Torts apparens. see
Gorjy, Jean Claude.
G., B. J. pseud. Memoria sobre las
principaes causes. 26266
G., C. pseud. Little looking-glass for the
times. 9743
G., C. pseud. ed. 49184
G., C. J. pseud. Ansdale Hall. 26267
G., E. pseud. Compromise, the constitution,
and the union. 26268
G., E. pseud. Triall of tabacco. see
Gardiner, Edmund.
G., E. pseud. tr. see Grimestone, Edward.
supposed tr.
G., E. B. pseud. Addenda. see Greene,
Edward Burnaby.
G., E. C. pseud. ed. 79485
G . . . . . , Ernest. pseud. Lettres edifiantes
et curieuses. 40702
G., F. pseud. Nomenclatura brevis Anglo-
Latino in usum scholarum. 55413
G., F. pseud. Two sermons. see Adair,
James Makittrick. supposed author
G——, F. D. pseud. Manual guide des
voyageurs. see Fernagus de Gelone,
-------.
G——, G. pseud. Shunammite. see
Green, G.
G., G. A. pseud. Nachrichten und
Erfahrungen. 97922
G., I. pseud. Cartas. see Martiniano de
Alencar, J.
G., I. A. pseud. Breeden Raedt. 20596,
23521, 26272, note after 98474, note after
99310
G., J. pseud. City of Washington. see Green-
leaf, James.
G., J. pseud. Receipt to make a speech. see
Galloway, Joseph, 1729?-1803.
G., J. pseud. Some remarks upon A second
letter. see Graham, John.
G., J. pseud. White acre vs. black acre.
26269
G., J. pseud. Widowed mourner. see
Gardiner, John.
G., J. C. pseud. Lee's last campaign. see
Gorman, J. C.
G., J. J. S. P. pseud. Gedancken uber die
Burnuck Kunfft. (26271)
G., J. L. F. V. D. pseud. tr. 33732
G., J. S. pseud. Detector detected. 73769
G., J. V. pseud. Revista literaria. see
Gonzalez, Juan Vicente.
G., J. V. pseud. Venezuela y los Monagas.
see Gonzalez, Juan Vicente.
G., L. pseud. tr. 71685
G., L. C. D. L. pseud. Amerique delivree.
1290, 38759
G., M. pseud. A Monseignevr Monseignevr
dv Vair. see Gobert, M.
G., M. pseud. ed. and tr. Neue Reise nach
Cayenne. 11622
G., M. pseud. Plan of a society. see Gordon,
William.

G., M. pseud. Supplement to the Negro's and
Indian's advocate. see Godwyn, Morgan.
G., M. R. pseud. Respuesta a las cartas.
26273
G., N. pseud. Reys-boeck. see Geelkercken,
Nic. van. supposed author
G., P. pseud. Some stray recollections. see
Gates, Philip.
G., R. pseud. Good speed to Virginia. see
Gray, Robert.
G., R. pseud. Virginia's cure. see Gray,
Robert, 17th cent. supposed author
Greene, Robert. supposed author
Greene, Roger, 17th cent. supposed
author
G., S. pseud. Glass for the people of New-
England. see Groome, S.
G., S. pseud. tr. see Goulard, Simon.
G., T. pseud. Remarks on the Reverend
Mr. Whitefield's journal. see Gib, T.
G., W. pseud. Letter of W. G. (26275)
G., W. pseud. Remarks on a certain publica-
tion. see Gauntley, William.
G., W. pseud. Sketches of Newfoundland and
Labrador. (26276)
G., W. D. pseud. ed. Selections from the
poetical literature of the west. see
Gallagher, William D. ed.
G. D., B. pseud. see Gerbier, Sir Balthazar,
1952?-1667.
G. Y. M., D. G. H. V. D. pseud. tr. see
Guzman y Manrique, Joaquim de.
G. A. pseud. see A., G. pseud.
G. A. A. pseud. see Aynge, G. A. supposed
author
G. A. C. pseud. tr. see C., G. A. pseud.
tr.
G. A. G. pseud. see G., G. A. pseud.
G. A. R. pseud. see Wheeler, W. A.
G. A. T. pseud. see T., G. A. pseud.
G. A. y N. pseud. see A. y N., G. pseud.
G. B. pseud. see G., B. pseud.
G. B. D. B. pseud. see Boileau de Bouillon,
Gilles, 16th cent.
G. B. S. pseud. see Stebbins, Giles Badger.
G. C. pseud. see C., G. pseud.
G. C. pseud. see Cartwright, George.
G. C. W. pseud. see Weygandt, G. C.
G. D. T. pseud. see Gautier du Tronchoy,
----------.
G . . . n F . . . . . . n. pseud. see
F . . . . . . n, G . . . n. pseud.
G. F. pseud. see Fox, George, 1624-1691.
G. F. V. M. pseud. see M., G. F. V. pseud.
tr.
G. G——. pseud. see Green, G.
G. G. D. M. pseud. see Montpleinchamp,
J. Chr. B. de.
G. H. pseud. see H., G. pseud.
G. H. B. pseud. see Bates, G. H.
G. H. D. pseud. see D., G. H. pseud.
G——H——S——. pseud. see Spierin,
George Heartwell.
G. J. pseud. see J., G. pseud.
G. J. V. D. G. Y. M. pseud. tr. see Guzman
y Manrique, Joaquim de.
G. K. pseud. see Keith, George, 1638?-1716.
G. L. pseud. see L., G. pseud.
G. L. H. pseud. see Hammekin, George L.

Gallerie aller merkwurdigen Menschen. 101819
Gallerie der Nationen. 30861
Gallerie von Darstellungen der merkwurdigsten menschlichen Wohnplatze. 38864
Gallern, Hieronymo. (8784)
Gallery of American portraits. 102160
Gallery of British and foreign portraits. 26414
Gallery of famous English and American poets. 16700
Gallery of geography. 49127
Gallery of illustrious Americans. 26415, (40221)
Gallery of nature. 49127
Gallery of the Fine Arts, New York. see New York Gallery of the Fine Arts, New York.
Galles, Ed. (26416)
Galli, -------. 35072
Gallia Christiana. 24834
Gallio perfidy: a poem. 47155
Gallic pride humbled. (65526)
Gallica fides. (25887)
Gallichon, F. C. de la Roche. see La Roche Gallichon, F. C. de.
Galliffet, Gaston Alexandre Auguste, Marquis de, 1830-1909. 5662, 26417
Galligher, ------. (45240)
Gallison, John. (26418)-(26419)
Gallius, C. illus. (73192)
Gallois, ------. 41646
Gallo pitagorico. 50499
Gallon de Villeneuve, Gabrielle Suzanne Barbot. see Villeneuve, Gabrille Suzanne Barbot Gallon de.
Gallop among American scenery. 81029
Galloway, Joseph, 1729?-1803. 11882, 16590-16591, 20051, 20270, 23499, 26420-26445, 33327, (33338), (33339), (33342), 34943, (46918), 59820, (61934), 63798, 68742, 68968, 93593, 97340, 99558, 102645-102646, note after 102651, note after 102652, 2d note after 103119, 104455 see also Great Britain. Army. Garrison, Philadelphia. Superintendent General.
Galloway, Joseph, 1729?-1803. petitioner 3d note after 105598-9 [sic]
Galloway, Joseph, 1729?-1803. supposed author 10671, 15526, (33341), 40506, 46928, 63244, 84642, 4th note after 95742
Galloway, Samuel. What think ye of Congress now? see Galloway, Joseph, 1729?-1803.
Galloway, Samuel, 1811-1872. 26446
Gallows, the prison, and the poorhouse. 67177
Gallucci, Giovanni Paolo, 1538?-1621? tr 124, 69132
Gallucci, Jose Maria. 26447
Gallup, Albert. 96736 see also U. S. Commissioner to the Stockbridge and Munsee Indians.
Gallup, J. 15665
Gallup, Joseph A. 26448
Galphin Claim. Speech . . . May 17, 1850. 8348
Galphin claim. Speech of Mr. E. Stanly. 90322
Galpin case. 26449
Galpine, Calvin. 26450
Galpine, Calvin. defendant 26451
Galt, Alexander Tilloch. 26452-26454
Galt, John, 1779-1839. 26455-(26458), 28419, (62619)-(62620), 95610, 102716
Galt, John M. 26459-(26460), 63774
Galt prize eassy. 71967
Galton, Francis. 26461-26462
Galusha, ------. 92869
Galusha, Jonas, 1753-1834. 33150, 99199 see also Vermont. Governor, 1809-1813 (Galusha) Vermont. Governor, 1815-1820 (Galusha)

Galuski, Ch. see Galusky, Ch.
Galusky, Ch. tr. 33705-33706, 33730
Galvan, Francisco. 87245
Galvan Rivera, Mariano. 26463-26466, (48374), 71627-71628
Galvao, Antonio, d. 1557 13419, 26467-26471, 57765, 66686
Galvano, Antonio. see Galvao, Antonio, d. 1557.
Galvery, Francis R. petitioner 27556
Galveston, Texas. Articles of Association. see Galveston, Texas. Charter.
Galveston, Texas. Charter. 26472
Galveston, Texas. Historical Society. see Galveston Historical Society.
Galveston, Texas. Public Schools. 26473
Galveston Bay and Texas Land Company. 16084, 26474, 93710, 94946, 95086-95087, 105111
Galveston Bay and Texas Land Company. Trustees. 26474, 93710, 105111
Galveston City Company. defendant 90724
Galveston-Dallas news. 84099
Galveston Historical Society. see 82346
Galvez, Bernardo de. 26475-26478
Galvez, Francisca de Paula de Perez. 26479
Galvez, Jose de, Marques de Sonora. (48499) see also Mexico (Viceroyalty) Visitador General.
Galvez, Josef de. 26481-26483, 56260
Galvez, Joseph Joaquin Granados y. see Granados y Galvez, Joseph Joaquin.
Galvez, Mariano. 26484
Galuez, Pedro de. 73042
Galway, N. Y. Second Baptist Church. 26485
Galway, N. Y. Washington Benevolent Society. see Washington Benevolent Society. New York. Galway.
Gama, A. L. see Leon y Gama, Antonio de.
Gama, Antonio, ed. 4216
Gama, Antonio de Leon y. see Leon y Gama, Antonio de.
Gama, Antonio Pinto Chichorra da. 60989 see also Pernambuco. Presidente (Gama)
Gama, Jose Basilio da. 26487
Gama, Jose Bern. Fern. 26489
Gama, Jose da Saldanha da. see Saldanha da Gama, Jose da.
Gama, Jose Vicente da. (26488)
Gama, Leonarda Gil de. see Gil de Gama, Leonarda.
Gama, Manuel Jacinto Mogueira da. 26491
Gama, Nicolau Antonio Mogueira Valle da. 26492
Gama, Vasco da, 1469-1524. 16963, 20518, 26874-26875, 31553, 48490, 50050-50064, (58261), 65402, 66686, 67730, 67743, 1st-5th notes after 106378
Gama e Castro, Jose de. 26493, 47608
Gama Lobo, Ovidio da. 26494-26496, 41713
Gamage, W. 26497
Gamarra, Agustin, Pres. Peru, 1785-1841. 61147 see also Peru. Presidente, 1839-1841 (Gamarra)
Gamba, B. (50598)
Gambara, Laurentius. (26500)-26503
Gambia i Compania. firm see Pereira Gambia i Compania. firm publishers
Gambier, James Gambier, 1st Baron, 1756-1833. 26504
Gambier, Ohio. Kenyon College. see Kenyon College, Gambier, Ohio.
Gambier, Ohio. Ohio Theological Seminary. see Kenyon College, Gambier, Ohio.
Gambino, Pedro J. tr. 26506
Gamble, Archibald. ed. 80347

Gaston, Marie-Madeleine. 47509, 72330
Gaston, William, 1778-1844. 26752, 101280, 101972, 105118
Gaston, William, 1820-1894. 84961, 85212
  see also Massachusetts. Governor, 1875-1876 (Gaston)
Gaston de Segur, Louis. see Segur, Louis Gaston de.
Gatchel, Elisha. 59957, note after 94466
Gatchel, Samuel. 26753-26754
Gatchell, Increase. 62743
Gatchell, Joseph. 26755
Gatchell, William H. 3042
Gate of the Pacific. 62872
Gaterau, Armand. 67089, 75181
Gatereau, -------. 10753, 26756, 75092
Gates, Hezekiah. 26757
Gates, Horatio, 1728?-1806. 50185, 71301, 82379, 87291
Gates, J. ed. 95608
Gates, Philip. 86765
Gates, Theophilus R. (26758)
Gates, Sir Thomas, d. 1621. 99866
Gates, Thomas, fl. 1783. petitioner 22337, 99771
Gates, W. defendant at court martial 26759
Gates, William E. ed. 94355
Gateshead observer. 95502
Gatford, Lionel. 26760, 2d note after 100516
Gathered fragments. (20180)
Gathered leaves. 18409
Gathered sketches from the early history of New Hampshire. (12175)
"Gathered to his people." 26065
Gathering of descendants of Nathan Griffin. 28822
Gatherings from a pastor's drawer. 52315
Gatherings of the west. 38541
Gatica Cerda, -----. 48608
Gatine, Adolphe Ambroise Alexandre. 26761
Gatonbe, John. 13015
Gattel, C. M. tr. 63913
Gatterer, J. Chr. 26762, 31665
Gaubertin, Pierre Boitel, Sieur de. see Boitel, Pierre, Sieur de Gaubertin.
Gaubil, ------. 58549
Gaubit, ------. 40698
Gaucher, -------. illus. 28193
Gaucho. 79128
Gauci, P. lithographer 103829
Gaudet, ------, fl. 1792. 75135
Gaudet, Joseph. 21119-21120
Gaudichaud, ------. 25916
Gaudichaud-Beaupre, C. 98298
Gaudy, -----, fl. 1603. 67545
Gauging epitomized. 105474
Gauld, George. 26763-26764
Gauld, Joseph. cartographer 26763, 42070
Gault, William. defendant 6712, note after 96867
Gaume, J. A. 26765
Gaunt Gurley; or, the trappers of Umbagog. 95477
Gauntley, William. (26766)
Gaussoin, Eugene. 26767-26768
Gautier, -------, fl. 1794. 26769
Gautier, -------, fl. 1859. engr. (63475)
Gautier du Tronchoy, ------. 26770, note after 84151
Gauttier, G. A. 26771
Gauville,----, Vicomte de. 75041
Gavarni, -------. illus. 92536
Gavel: a monthly periodical. 26773
Gavel, and freemason's journal. 26672
Gavelli, Nicolo. 92202-92203
Gavet, D. 6842, (26774)
Gavilan, Alonso Ramos. see Ramos Gavilan, Alonso.

Gavock, Randall W. see MacGavock, Randall W.
Gawrila Sarytschew's Ruszisch-Kaiserlichen Generalmajors von der Flotte. 77125
Gay, Mr. Elegy written in a country church yard. see Gray, Thomas, 1716-1771.
Gay, Bunker. (26776)-26777
Gay, Claude. 26778-(26779)
Gay, Ebenezer, 1696-1787. 18110, 26780-26785
Gay, Ebenezer, 1718-1796. 26785
Gay, Ebenezer, 1766-1837. 26786
Gay, Frederick A. 9970, 26787
Gay, John. 26788
Gay, M. M. 26789
Gay life in New-York! 54286
Gayangos y Arce, Pascual de, 1809-1897. 14637, 16942, 16955, (48317)
Gayarre, Charles. 26790-26797
Gayle, John, 1792-1859. 26798
Gayler, C. 26799
Gayley, James F. (26800)
Gaylor, W. ed. (17869)
Gaylord, N. M. 26801
Gaylord, William L. 26802
Gaylord, Willis. 26803
Gayna, Juan Camacho. ed. 17735, note after 34687
Gayoso, Jose de Souza. see Souza Gayoso, Raymundo Jose de.
Gaytan de Torres, Manuel. (26805)
Gaywood, R. illus. 13448
Gazaignes, Jean Antoine. 26806
Gazelle, a true tale of the great rebellion. 26807
Gazer, Gilse. pseud. Frederick de Algeroy. 26808
Gazeta de Colombia. 26809
Gazeta de gobierno, Madrid. 11099
Gazeta de Guatemala, de 1797. (29078)
Gazeta de Lima. 97660
Gazeta de Lima desde primero de Diciembre de 1743 hasta Mayo 1763. (41110)
Gazeta de literatura. 40059
Gazeta de Mexico. 74944
Gazeta de Mexico, compendio de noticias Mexicanas. 48483
Gazeta de noticias. 82720
Gazeta del gobierno [de Peru.] 98311
Gazeta de tribunaes. (26593)
Gazeta extraordinaria de Montevideo. (50128)
Gazeta mensal de medicina. 38953
Gazeta mercantil. 86786
Gazetas de Mexico. 48484, 98320
Gazette, London. see Great Britain.
Gazette, New York. see New York gazette.
Gazette, Philadelphia. see Philadelphia gazette.
Gazette de Leyde. Nouvelles de livers endroits. 26810
Gazette de Quebec. 10338, 27136, 43858, 84701, 99776
Gazette de Saint-Domingue. (75044), 75073, 75123
Gazette de Saint-Domingue, politique, civile, economique et litteraire. 75124
Gazette du jour. 75165
Gazette extraordinary. (73803)
Gazette for authors, readers, and publishers. 41499
Gazette of legal medicine. 55804
Gazette of literature, art, dramatic criticism, fashion and novelty. 16923
Gazette of the United States. 239, 10889, 23994, 26811, 29982, 84820, 84831-84832, 2d note after 104983

Gazette of the United States, and daily evening advertiser. 26811

Gazette of the United States, and Philadelphia daily advertiser. 101577

Gazette officielle de Saint-Domingue. (75125)

Gazette publications. 7188

Gazette series. Vol. I. 18936

Gazetteer. 28751, 78127

Gazetteer and directory of Jefferson County, N. Y. 35943

Gazetteer and directory of the county of Grey. 84917

Gazetteer and map of the United States. 83926

Gazetteer, directory and business advertiser of Rock County, Wisconsin. 72378

Gazetteer for citizens, and a hand-book for immigrants. 58720

Gazetteer of all the towns on the western waters. 15123, (53393)

Gazetteer of Georgia. 80433

Gazetteer of Illinois. 59483

Gazetteer of Madison County. 43723

Gazetteer of Massachusets: containing a general view of the state. 89563

Gazetteer of Massachusetts, containing descriptions of all the counties. 31068

Gazetteer of Massachusetts proper. 20071

Gazetteer of Michigan, including a history of that state. 48732

Gazetteer of New Hampshire; containing a description of all the counties. 31071

Gazetteer of New Hampshire; containing a particular description of the several towns. 12147

Gazetteer of New-York. 88849

Gazetteer of . . . New York: comprising its topography. 32534, 53677

Gazetteer of the border and southern states. (41885)

Gazetteer of the county of Washington, N. Y. 16783

Gazetteer of the manufacturers and manufacturing towns of the United States. 7303

Gazetteer of the New-England states. Concise and comprehensive. 31634, 96481A

Gazetteer of the New York Central Railroad and general railway index. 53676

Gazetteer of the places named in the letters. 22500, 40594, 86187, 2d note after 98076

Gazetteer of the province of Upper Canada. 85204

Gazetteer of the state of Georgia. (80430)-80432

Gazetteer of the state of Maryland. 24488

Gazetteer of the state of Michigan. 5962

Gazetteer of the state of Missouri. 103064

Gazetteer of the state of New-Hampshire. 23839

Gazetteer of the state of New Hampshire, in three parts. (47996)

Gazetteer of the state of New-Jersey. 27996, 28001

Gazetteer of the state of New-York. 88844-88846, 88848

Gazetteer of the state of New York: comprehending its colonial history. (27997)

Gazetteer of the state of New-York: embracing a comprehensive view of the geography. 25862

Gazetteer of the state of New York, with the census of 1840. 32534, 53677

Gazetteer of the state of Pennsylvania. 27998

Gazetteer of the state of Vermont. 95546, 95550-95551

Gazetteer of the states of Connecticut and Rhode-Island. 59466

Gazetteer of the states of Illinois and Missouri. 4231

Gazetteer of the United Kingdom and its colonies. 38104

Gazetteer of the United States abstracted from the Universal gazetteer. 105237

Gazetteer of the United States, comprising a series of gazetteers. 31069

Gazetteer of the United States, concise and comprehensive. 96481A

Gazetteer of the United States: . . . with valuable statistical tables. 31070

Gazetteer of the world. 26812

Gazetteer of Vermont; affording a summary description. 19023

Gazetteer of Vermont: containing descriptions of all the countries. 31072

Gazetteer's, or, newsman's interpreter. 21761

Gaztelu, Antonio Vazquez. see Vazquez Gaztelu, Antonio.

Gazitua, Joanne de. 61074

Gazlay, Allan W. (67387)

Gazlay, James. reporter 96880

Gazlay (David M.) firm publishers 26813, 76092

Gazlay's business directory of the five great cities of California and Oregon. 26813

Gazlay's San Francisco business directory, for 1863. 76092

Gazofilacio real de Peru. 520, 22819

Gazophilacium regium Perubicum. 520, 22820

Gazophilatium Perubicum. 22819

Gazophylacium Divinae dilectionis. 47357

Gaztelu, Dominico de. tr. 105721-105722

Gazzam, Audley W. ed. 51937

Gazettiere Americano. (1090), 26814

Geaiouajin igiu anishinabeg enumiajig. (57086)

Geamplieerde octroy van de Oost-Indische Compagnie. 26815

Gear, A. S. 26816

Gear, D. L. 26817

Geare, Allen. 26818

Geary, John White, 1819-1873. 26819, 37042
see also Kansas (Territory) Governor, 1856-1857 (Geary) Pennsylvania. Governor, 1867-1873 (Geary)

Geary and Kansas. 27338

Gebauer, August. (4858)

Gebbie & Barrie. firm publishers 84493

Gebedt, van den Ridder Balthazer Gerbier. 27124

Gebel Teir. 97406

Gebelin, Antoine Court de. see Court de Gebelin, Antoine, 1725-1784.

Gebhard, F. see Gerhard, Frederick.

Gebhardt, A. G. 147, 26821-26822

Gecommitteerdens van de Groenlandsche en Straat Davidsche Vischeryen. petitioners 70052

Gecommitteerdens uyt de Hollandsche Raden en Ministers in de Collegien ter Admiraliteyt in Holland. 47767, 4th note after 102895

Gedachten en wenken over de kolonisatie. 59767

Gedachten over de belangens en plichten der onzydige mogentheden. 100626

Gedachten over de emancipatie der Negerslaven 39269

Gedachten over den Afrikaanschen Slaavenhandel 55077

Gedachten ten gunste der Planters en Lands-Ambtenaren te Suriname. 52349, 5th note after 93855

Gedancken uber das Emigrations-Recht. 25487

Gedancken uber die Burnuck Kunfft der Franzosischen Escadren. (26271)

Gedanken uber das Buch Daniel. 84477

Gedanken uber die Bestimung [sic] des Menschen. 95698

Gedanken uber die zukunftige Politik Amerikas.
20899
Gedankwaerdige zee en landreizen. (55278)
Geddes, Alexander. 26823, 81868
Geddes, George. 26824
Geddes, James. 26825
Geddes, Michael. tr. 32164
Geddie, John. 26826
Geddings, E. 88019 see also South Carolina
Medical Association. Committee on the
Medical Topography of the State of South
Carolina. Chairman.
Gedenckwaerdighe voyage naer West-Indiae.
9086
Gedenkschriften der omwenteling in het rijk
van Mexico. 72205
Gedenkschriften van Benjamin Franklin. 25553
Gedenkschriften van Konkhr. Alexander van
der Capellen. (10737)
Gedenkwaardige en al-om beroemde voyagien
der Spanjaarden. 86428
Gedenkwaardige reizen. 12556
Gedenkwaardige reizen vanden beroemden
Capiteyn John Smith na Virginien. 82822,
82838
Gedenkwaardige scheeps-togten na Rio de la
Plata. 77683
Gedenkwaardige voyagie van Andries Battel van
Leigh in Essex. 3960
Gedenkwaardige West-Indie Voyagien. 4806,
31362
Gedenkzuil, ter gelegenheid der vry-verklaaring
van Noord-Amerika. 41963
Gedeporteerde geestelyken, uyt de Fransche
Guyane in America. pseud. Verzaemelinge
van eenige brieven. 99322
Gedeputeerde Heeren Bewinthebberen vande
Geoctroyeerde West-Indische Compagnie.
see Nederlandsche West-Indische Com-
pagnie. Bewinthebberen. Gedeputeerde.
Gedichten den Zeitlauften gemas. 101901
Gedichten op de overheerlijke papiere
snijkunst. 38208
Gedrangte Erzahlung seiner Wanderungen.
33745
Gedrangtes Gemalde des Zustandes von Mexico.
73892, 101301
Gedurige onlusten. 102889A
Gee, Ernest R. ed. 89639-89640
Gee, Joshua. 952, 26827-26829, 37244,
59688, 66015, 86745, note after 96426,
97575
Gee, Joshua, 1689-1748. 17675, 20057,
(20271), 23585, (26830)-(26832), (30173)
65237, 92671
Geelkercken, Nic. van. supposed author
7633
Geer, Asa. 105364
Geer, George P. 26833, 28702, 30660
Geer, J. J. 26835
Geer, James. 26834
Geer's express directory, and railway
forwarder's guide. 26833, 28702
Geer's Hartford directory for 1842. 30660
Geest van het politiek systema van de
Regeering van Amsterdam. 98508
Geeup, Jeru, of Jackass Alley. pseud.
North and south. 82025
Gefahr bey unbekehrten Predigern. 94689
Gefahren der Wildness. (5557)
Gefangene unter des Wilden in Nord Amerika.
33922
Gefe del Estado a los pueblos de su mando.
29079
Geffeken, M. F. H. ed. 44831
Geffrey, Charles Fitz. see Fitz-Geffrey,
Charles.

Gefuhrten Protocoll bey der Funften
Versammlung der Gemeine Gottes im
Geist. 51292, 4th note after 97845
Gegeneinanderstellung ihrer Revolutionen.
106337
Gegenwart und Zukanft der Plata-Lander.
26836
Gegenwartige Krieg in Nord-Amerika. 28182
Gegenwartiger Zustand der Colonie von St.
Domingo. 26838
Gegenwartiger Zustand deree Finantzen von
Franckreich. 26837
Gegenwartiger Zustand von Peru. 81616
Geheime Anecdotes. 26839
Geheime Geschichte der Revolution in Colombia.
6184, 21068
Geheime Zamenspraken van Lord North.
55517
Geheimnisse des Tages. 89424
Geijer, ------. 26840
Geikie, John C. 26841, note after 90307
Geinitz, H. B. (26842)
Geiser, ----- Sommer. see Sommer-
Geiser, ------.
Geisler, Adam Friedrich, ca. 1757-1800.
26843, 101877
Geisterhaus in New-York. Ein Roman.
(1598)
Geistliche Magazin. 77506
Geisweiler, Constantin. tr. 38282
Gekruicigde Christus. 73073
Gelashmin, Hattain. Indian name see James,
George.
Gelays, Melin de Saint. see Saint-Gelays,
Melin de.
Geldard, James. (26844)
Gelderland (Dutch Province) Laws, statutes,
etc. 93934
Gelderschman. pseud. Hollanders in Iowa.
32520
Gelehrte England oder Lexikon der jetzlebenden
Schfiftsteller. 70153
Gelieven in de Woestigen. 12248
Gellatly, A. 26845, 83796
Gellibrand, Henry. 35711-35712, note after
92708
Gelline, P. L. 26846
Gelobte-Land. 99534
Gelone, ----- Fernagus de. see Fernagus de
Gelone, ------.
Gelpi y Ferro, ----- Gil. see Gil Gelpi y
Ferro, ------.
Gelston, David. appellant 96868-96869
Gelston, David. plaintiff 96869
Geluckwenschinghe aen de West Indische vlote.
26847
Geluk op reis. (28680)
Gelves, ------, Marques de. supposed author
69212
Gem of the western world, for all seasons.
26848, 91033
Gem of the western world, for 1851. 26848,
91033
Gem, or fashionable business directory. 54288
Gemaelde von dem Freystaate Columbia.
14595
Gemalde der Entdeckung und Colonisirung.
19539
Gemalde der Lander und Volker mit Gezung
auf ihre Geschichte. 26848A
Gemalde der Nord-Amerikanischen Freistaaten.
(55456)
Gemalde des Bundsstaates von Nordamerika.
7450
Gemalde von Columbien und Guyana. 23769
Gemalde von Jamaica. 91691
Gemalde von Nord-Amerika in allen
Beziehungen. 8204

Gemebunda Maya. 75608

Gemeenzaame leerwyze om het basterd of
Neger-Engelsch. 103083

Gemeenzame zamenspraken behoorende bij
behovest. Proeve. 48227

Gemeenzame zamenspraken behoorende by
de: Proeve eeuer Hollandsche spraakkunst. 66747

Gemeine Gottes im Geist. see Congregation
of God in the Spirit.

Gemeine Recht (Common law) der Vereinigten
Staaten von Amerika. 20922

Gemeling, Joh. George. (26849)

Gemelli Careri, Giovanni Francesco, 1651-
1725. 10820-10821, 13015, 20518,
26850-26851, 30483, 80987

Gemelli Carreri's voyage round the world.
13015, 26851

Gemidos e suspiros do Brazil. 81097

Gemidos poeticos sobre os tumulos. 81299

Gemino Liminari Toleto ac Navarrea. 61129

Gemistus, Georgius. ed. 66470

Gemma, Reinerus, frisius, 1508-1555. 1739,
1742, 1744-1756, (26852)-(26856), 27724,
62588, 77801

Gemma Phrysius. see Gemma, Reinerus,
frisius, 1508-1555.

Gemma Phrysivs De principiis astronomiae
& cosmographiae; de usu globi. 26853,
62588

Gemma Phrysius De principijs astronomiae
& cosmographiae, deq3 vsu globi ab
eodem editi. 26855

Gemma Phrysius de principiis astronomiae et
cosmographiae deque usu globi ab eodem
editi. (26852)

Gemma Phrsivs De principiis astronomiae et
cosmographiae, deqve vsv globi cosmo-
graphici ab eodem editu. (26856)

Gemman Phrysium, apud Louanienses Medicum
ac Mathematicum insignen, restituta.
(26854)

Gems for you. 50374

Gems from Abraham Lincoln. 41149

Gems from American female poets. 28894

Gems from Greenwood. 29822

Gems from the American poets. 26857

Gems from the tailings, or the sluice club.
83974

Gems of female biography. 82426

Gems of Japonicadom. 36664

Gems of poetry. 105184

Gems of Rocky Mountain scenery. 46823

Gems of the western world. 31643

Genand, J. A. tr. 40132

Genandte relationes curiosae. (30277)

Genaue Beschreibung fur Auswanderungslustige.
(6014)

Genaue Zusammenstellung. 8221

Genauen Beschreibung von der Entfuhrung des
William Morgan. 36660

Gendron, -------, Sieur. 26858, note after
69259

Genealogia das familias Botelho, Arrunda,
Sampaio. 26492

Genealogia de la noble, y antigva casa, de
Gabeza de Vaca. 59588

Genealogia de los reyes Mexicanos. 80987

Genealogia ducum Burgundiae, Brabantiae,
Flandriae, Hollandiae, etc. (63019)

Genealogias del Nuevo Reyno de Granada. 24835

Genealogical account of the descendants of
Richard Burke. 6943

Genealogical account of the descendants of
Thomas Hastings. 8937

Genealogical account of the family of Alexander.
33826, (51820)

Genealogical account of the Noyes family.
(56216)

Genealogical account of Wigard Levering and
Gerhard Levering. 36509

Genealogical address, giving a brief history of
the parish and founders. 16288

Genealogical address, giving a brief history of
the parishioners. (16287)

Genealogical and biographical. 84734, 84910

Genealogical and biographical account of the
family of Bolton. 6245

Genealogical and biographical account of the
family of Drake. (20870)

Genealogical and biographical history of Kenkuk
County. 85101

Genealogical and biographical record. 27427

Genealogical and biographical sketch of the
name and family of Brackett. 71020

Genealogical and biographical sketch of the
name and family of Richardson. (71019)

Genealogical and biographical sketch of the
name and family of Stetson. 3685

Genealogical and Biographical Society, New
York. see New York Genealogical and
Biographical Society.

Genealogical and historical memoir of the
family of Otis. 57863

Genealogical and historical miscellany. 85589

Genealogical and historical notes of the Bowles
family. 7080

Genealogical and historical record. 59455,
59458

Genealogical and historical reocrd of the
descendants of William Locke. 41729

Genealogical and historical register of the
descendants of John Pease. 59458

Genealogical catalogue. 91030

Genealogical chart of the Bowles family.
95635

Genealogical chart of the Richard Lyman
family. 42794

Genealogical chart of the Royal House of
Stuart. 85244, 85246

Genealogical chart of the Sargent family.
1514

Genealogical chart of the Sill family. 81019

Genealogical circular. 47990

Genealogical cross index of the four volumes.
(77233)

Genealogical dictionary of the first settlers
of New England. (77233)

Genealogical, historical, biographical, and
chronological chart. 32491

Genealogical history of Edward Spalding.
88924

Genealogical history of John and George Steele.
21439

Genealogical history of John Hoyt. (33401)

Genealogical history of the descendants of
Joseph Peck. 59474

Genealogical history of the families of
Robinsons. 72177

Genealogical history of the family of
Montgomery. (50158)

Genealogical history of the Holt family.
21440

Genealogical history of the Lee family. 47220

Genealogical history of the Redfield family.
68505

Genealogical history of the Rice family.
101278

Genealogical history with short sketches and
family records. 8433

Genealogical items of the Kellogg family.
37283

Genealogical list of the Sheldons in America.
80123

Genealogical memoir of the Chase family.
12176

Genealogical memoir of the descendants of
Ambrose Fowler. 25324

Genealogical memoir of the descendants of
Capt. William Fowler. (25303)

Genealogical memoir of the descendants of
Robert Day. (18966)

Genealogical memoir of the descendants of
William Bradford. 24205

Genealogical memoir of the families of
Lawrences. 29644

Genealogical memoir of the family by the
name of Farmer. 23823

Genealogical memoir of the family of Elder
Thomas Leverett. (80776)

Genealogical memoir of the family of John
Lawrence. 39358

Genealogical memoir of the family of Rev.
Nathaniel Rogers. 72613

Genealogical memoir of the family of Richard
Otis. 57864

Genealogical memoir of the Gilbert family.
95636

Genealogical memoir of the Huntington family.
(33954)

Genealogical memoir of the Leonard family.
19070

Genealogical memoir of the Prescott families
in America. 65258

Genealogical memoir of the Wentworth family.
12438

Genealogical memoirs of William Bradford.
(66719)

Genealogical memoranda. 85456, 95458

Genealogical notes. 27949

Genealogical notes and errata. (77233)

Genealogical notes and queries. (58187)

Genealogical notes of the Colden family. 66716

Genealogical notes on the Foot family. (58880)

Genealogical notes on the Provoost family.
66717

Genealogical notes relating to Lieut.-Gov.
Jacob Leisler. (66718)

Genealogical record, from 1630-1873. (72422)

Geneological [sic] record of Captain Stephen
Smith. 84250

Genealogical record of several families.
(50903)

Genealogical record of the Hodges family.
32336

Genealogical record of the Smiths of Oyster
River. 84479

Genealogical record of Thomas Bascom. 30470

Genealogical records of the descendants of
David Mack. 84243

Genealogical register. 20238

Genealogical register [by Joseph Snively.]
85456

Genealogical register of the descendants in the
male line of David Atwater. 26859

Genealogical register of the descendants in the
male line of Robert Day. 18967

Genealogical register of the descendants of
George Abbot. 19

Genealogical register of the descendants of
John Scranton. 78478

Genealogical register of the descendants of
Richard Faxon. 23936

Genealogical register of the descendants of
several ancient puritans. 50905

Genealogical register of the descendants of
the early planters. 50906

Genealogical register of the descendants of
Thomas Flint. 24781, note after 92069

Genealogical register of the first settlers of
New-England. 23824, (77233)

Genealogical register of the inhabitants and
history of the towns. 50907

Genealogical register of the name and family
of Herrick. (31574)

Genealogical register of the name of Bostwick.
6790

Genealogical registry of the United States.
26860

Genealogical reprints, series M, 1919, no. 3.
94815

Genealogical sketch of the Bird family. 5543,
26863

Genealogical sketch of the descendants of
Reinhold and Matthew Marvin. 45033

Genealogical sketch of the descendants of
Thomas Green. 28612

Genealogical sketch of the families of Rev.
Worthington Smith. 84925

Genealogical sketch of the first three
generations of Prebles. 65007

Genealogical sketch of the Preble families.
65018

Genealogical sketch of the Riddell family.
(71156)

Genealogical table of the family and descendants
from Mr. Jacob Leavitt. 39558

Genealogical table of the family of Chauncy's.
12339

Genealogical table of the Lee family. (31868)

Genealogical tables of emperors, kings and
princes. 1398

Genealogie de Jacques Cartier et de sa
famille. 67018

Genealogie de M. le Comte d'Estaing. 94178

Genealogie der regierenden hohen Haupter und
anderer furstlichen Personen. 89755

Genealogie des Bethencourts et Barcquemons.
5073

Genealogies. 74144

Genealogies and biographical sketches of the
ancestry. 78642

Genealogies of Hadley families. 6255

Genealogies of the families and descendants
of the early settlers. (6283)

Genealogies of the first settlers of Passaic
Valley. 41502

Genealogies of the Lymans of Middlefield.
20035

Genealogies of the male descendants of
Daniel Dod. (20484)

Genealogist. pseud. Concise view. see
Cenchar, A. supposed author

Genealogy and biography of the Elmer family.
22357

Genealogy and history of the family of
Williams in America. 104378

Genealogy from Adam to Christ. 31243

Genealogy of a branch of the Metcalf family.
(48164)

Genealogy of a part of the Ripley family.
(71526)

Genealogy of a portion of the Brown family.
8539

Genealogy of a protion of the Pope family.
64126

Genealogy of Consider Smith of New Bedford,
Mass. 83488

Genealogy of descendants of Thomas Oliver,
of . . . Boston. 57204

Genealogy of Ephraim and Sarah Thayer. 95230

Genealogy of fourteen families. 95230

Genealogy of Jesus Christ. 2129

Genealogy of John Thomson. 95569

Genealogy of Mathias Hoffer. 32383

Genealogy of Othniel Phelps. 61386

[Genealogy of] Percival and Ellen Green.
28557

General address to the inhabitants of America. 29956

General advertisement, intended to promote printing. 94439

General advertiser. see New York journal: or the general advertiser.

General advertiser and city directory for 1856. 53348

General Agent for Claimants Before the Board of Commissioners Under Article 6th of the Treaty Between Great Britain and the United States, 1794. 93768 see also American Loyalists. claimants. Board of Commissioners Under Article 6th of the Treaty Between Great Britain and the United States, London, Nov. 19, 1794.

General Aid Society for the Army, Buffalo, N. Y. see United States Sanitary Commission. General Aid Society for the Army, Buffalo.

General Allen's memorial. 99134

General amnesty. 78032

General and field orders. 80413

General and mechanical description. 45721

General and particular description of America. (42744)

General and private laws. 26866

General and public acts of Congress. 15530

General and special laws of the state of Minnesota. 49248

General and statistical description of Pierce County, Wisconsin. 62749

Gen. Andrew Jackson, and the Rev. Ezra Stiles Ely. (35346)

General announcement [of Cornell University.] 16798

General Anti-slavery Convention, London, 1840. 8084, note after (65854), (82082)

General Anti-slavery Convention, London, 1843. 8084, note after (65854)

General argument of the last manifesto. 93605

General Armstrong (Armed Brig) in Admiralty 14391, 69089-(69090)

General Assembly begun and held at the capitol . . . on . . . the first day of June . . . 1775. 99974

General Assembly of 1866. 6069

General Assembly of the province of Nova-Scotia, begun and holden at Halifax. 56108

General Assembly's missionary magazine. (65167), 65185

General Assembly's state of the right of the colony of New York. 792, 20987, 90629, 5th note after 98997

General Association of Baptists in Indiana. see Baptists. Indiana. General Association.

General Association of Baptists in Kentucky. see Baptists. Kentucky. General Association.

General Association of Congregational Ministers and Churches in Kansas. see Congregational Churches in Kansas. General Association.

General Association of Congregational Ministers in Massachusetts. see Congregational Churches in Massachusetts. General Association.

General Association of Connecticut. see Congregational Churches in Connecticut. General Association.

General Association of Illinois. see Congregational Churches in Illinois. General Association.

General Association of Iowa. see Congregational Churches in Iowa. General Association.

General Association of Michigan. see Congregational Churches in Michigan. General Association.

General Association of New-Hampshire. see Congregational Churches in New-Hampshire. General Association.

General Association of New York. see Congregational Churches in New York. General Association.

General Association of . . . New York, . . . at Paris. (53679)

General Association of Philadelphia. see Baptists. Pennsylvania. Philadelphia General Association.

General Association of the Baptists of Missouri. see Baptists. Missouri. General Association.

General Association of the State of Connecticut. see Congregational Churches in Connecticut. General Association.

General atlas. 10858, 79123

General atlas containing distinct maps. (42611)

General atlas, describing the whole universe. 38021

General atlas for the present war. (26868)

General atlas, of all the known countries in the world. 42610

General attacked by a subaltern. 16587-16588, 26867, 39714, 92830-92831, 92850

General aviso. 97686

General banking law [of Illinois.] (34199)

General banking law [of New York.] 55566

General banking law, passed by the Legislature. 97993

General bankrupt law. 90469

General Beauregard's official report. (4198)

General bill of mortality for Dover, N. H. 20743

General biographical dictionary. 5781

General Board of the Young Men's Mutual Improvement Associations. 83500

General brief view of the existing controversy. 93205

General Burgoyne's answer. 39708

General Burgoyne's orders. 9256

General Burgoyne's proclamation. 10304

General business directory for the city of Cleveland. 82242

General business directory, of the cities of Pittsburgh and Allegheny. 63128

General business directory of the city of Cleveland. 82242, note after 91325

General Butler in New Orleans. History of the administration. 58946

General Butler in New Orleans. Von James Parton. 58947

General Butler; the Democratic review. 7671

General Butler's defence. 62784

Gen. Butler's letter to the editor. 9615

Gen. Cass's extra pay. 91633

General catalogue of books, in the various departments. 103698

General catalogue of 1856. (14717)

General catalogue of Jefferson College. 35940

General catalogue of old and new books for 1837. 70887

General catalogue of old and new books, in English. 70887

General catalogue of the Bridgewater State Normal School. 46139

General catalogue of the Central High School. (61529)

General catalogue of the Newton Theological Institution. (55095)

General catalogue of the officers and alumni. 72368

General catalogue of the officers and graduates . . . 1837 to 1865. 48804

General catalogue of the officers and graduates in the Department of Arts. 60758

General catalogue of the officers and graduates of Rutgers College. 74438

General catalogue of the Ohio University. 57015

General catalogue of the Rochester Theological Seminary. 72363

General catalogue of the State Normal School, at West Newton. 46139

General catalogue of the theological department in Yale College. 105889

General catalogue of the Theological Seminary, Bangor, Me. 3158

General catalogue of the Theological Seminary, Princeton, New Jersey. (65657)

General catalogue of the trustees, instructors, and students. 66848

General catalogue [of Union College.] 97775

General causes of all hurtful mistakes. 50659

General censure: or Sampson with a jaw bone in his hand. 2036, 81985

General character, present and future prospects, of Ohio. 2333

General chart of the globe. 97281

General chart of the northern ocean. (66699)

Gen. Chauncey Whittlesey's renunciation of freemasonry. 103825

General chronicle. 26870

General chronological detail of maritime events 91091

General circular to all persons of good character. 26871, 37260, 57551

General collection of the best and most interesting voyages and travels. 2180, 3605, (5051), 5057, 6376, 6870, 9359, 14095, 16275, 16964, 25999, 36496, 36813, (37617), (55278), 57953, 57972, 60999, 62572, 62806, 62957-62958, 82830, 95349, 6th note after 97689

General collection of the best and most interesting voyages and travels in various parts of America. 62958

General collection of treatys, declarations of war, manifestos, and other public papers, relating to peace and war. 26873

General collection of treatys, declarations of war, manifestos, and other publick papers, relating to peace and war, among the potentates of Europe. 26872

General collection of voyages and discoveries. 26875

General collection of voyages and travels, from the discovery of America to the commencement of the nineteenth century. 5910, 22312, 35712, (56980), (58171), 62572, 98444

General collection of voyages and travels, . . . from the discovery of America, . . . to the travels of Lord Valentia. 46981

General collection of voyages, undertaken either for discovery. 26874

General commercial directory. 10257

General Committee Appointed by the World's Temperance Convention, New York, 1853. Meeting, 1st, Albany, 1854. 65850

General Committee of Conference, for the Erection of a Monument to the Memory of Washington. see Pennsylvania. Legislature. General Committee of Conference, for the Erection of a Monument to the Memory of Washington, 1833.

General Committee of Republican Young Men of New York. see Democratic Party. New York. New York City. General Committee of Young Men.

General Committee of the Republicans of Connecticut. see Democratic Party. Connecticut. General Committee. .

General Committee of Whig Young Men, New york. see Whig Party. New York. New York City. General Committee of Whig Young Men.

General Committee Representing the Yearly Meetings of Genesee, New York, Philadelphia, and Baltimore. 34676

General conference. 78345

General Conference of Congregational Churches in Minnesota. see Congregational Churches in Minnesota. General Conferen

General Conference of the Congregational Churches in Maine. see Congregational Churches in Maine. General Conference.

General Conference of the Congregational Churches in Maine. Churches and ministers from 1672-1867. (43935)

General Conference of the Free-Will Baptist Connection in North America. see Free-Will Baptists. North America. General Conference.

General considerations for planting New-England. 106052

General Convention, Washington, Texas, 1836. see Texas (Republic) General Convention, Washington, 1836.

General convention—1865. 66151

General Convention for the Improvement of the Colored Inhabitants of Canada, Amherstburg, Ontario, 1853. 1334

General Convention of Agriculturalists and Manufacturers and Others Friendly to the Encouragement and Support of the Domesti Industry of the United States, Harrisburg, Pa., 1827. see Harrisburg Convention, 1827.

General convention of Baptists, being their second triennial meeting. 3238

General Convention of Congregational and Presbyterian Ministers of Vermont, Middlebury 1807. 99234 see also Congregational Churches in Vermont. General Convention

General Convention of Congregational Ministers and Churches in Vermont. see Congregational Churches in Vermont. Genera Convention.

General Convention of Congregational Ministers and Delegates in the United States, Albany 1852. see Congregational Churches in the U. S.

General Convention of Delegates Held in Washington on the Subject of the Chesapea and Ohio Canal. see Chesapeake and Ohio Canal Convention, Washington, D. C., 1823-1826.

General convention of 1856. 88571

General convention of 1865. 20349

General Convention of the Brotherhood of the Protestant Episcopal Church. 66159 see also Convention of the Mutual Benefit Societies or Brotherhoods of the Protestant Episcopal Church in the United States, New York, 1853.

General Convention of the Christian Church, Marion, N. Y., 1850. see Christian Church. General Convention, Marion, N. Y., 1850.

General Convention of the District of the New-Hampshire Grants, 1777. see Vermont. Convention, 1777.

General Convention of Universalists for the United States of America. see Universalist Church in the United States. General Convention.

General Convention of Western Baptists. 1st, Cincinnati, 1834. 102971

General Conventions in the New Hampshire Grants, 1775-1777. see Vermont. Convention, 1775-1777.

General conventions in the New Hampshire grants, for the independence, organization, and defence of the state of Vermont. 1st note after 98997

General court martial. Cincinnati, O. 82437

Gen. Cowdin and the First Massachusetts Regiment. 17231

General de Division a sus compatriotas. 76731

General description of a plan. 84899

General description of Nova Scotia. 8197, 29686

General description of Nova Scotia, illustrated by a new and correct map. 56133

General description of . . . Ohio. (56916)

General description of the Bahama Islands. 21901

General description of the five great divisions of the globe. (49713)

General description of the Indian tribes of North and South America. 77844

General description of the leading countries. 22492

General description of the provinces. 10463

General description of the West-Indian islands. 81426

General dictionary, historical and critical. 67598

General dictionary of commerce, trade, and manufactures. (50990)

General dictionary of geography, physical, political, statistical, and descriptive. 5692

General digest of the acts of the Legislature of Louisiana, passed from . . . 1804 to 1827. 42228

General digest of the acts of the Legislature of the late territory of Orleans. 42227

General directions for collecting and drying medicinal substances. (15269)

General directory of Biddeford and Saco. 5227

General directory of citizens and a business directory. 10118

General directory . . . of the principal towns east of the Cascade Mountains. (58026)

General directory . . . of the principal towns in the upper country. 58027

General Echenique, Presidente despojado del Peru, en su vindicacion. (21769)

General Emancipation Society of Missouri. (49595)

General English pilot. (22617)

General epistle given forth by the people of the Lord, called, Quakers. (26877), 59703

General epistle given forth by the people of the Lord, called, Quakers, that all may know. (66925)

General epistle of James. 12458

General epistle . . . to the people called Quakers. 46895

General evening post. 40451, 62542, 92694

General examination of the Pacific Ocean. (37621)

General Executive Committee to provide Means to Relieve the Sufferings in Ireland, Philadelphia. see Philadelphia. Town Meeting, 1847. General Executive Committee to Provide Means to Relieve the Sufferings in Ireland.

General exports from the port of Charleston. 87850

General fast. A lyric ode. 26878

General Felipe Mazero al publico. 47204

General Fitz John Porter's reply. 64249

General free banking law. 88304

General Fremont, and the injustice done him. 8396

General Gage's coliloquy. 6571

General Gage's confession. 26319

General Gage's instructions. 26317

General Gage's soliloquy. 6571

General geography, and rudiments of useful knowledge. 88847

General, geological, historical, & statistical review. 7051

Gen. George Washington's account with the United States. 101546A

General George Washington's farewell address. 101627

General Gonzales Ortega and his nine endorsers. 57677

General Gonzalo de Solis, Holguin, dize. 86437

General Grant and his campaigns. 39037

General Grant for a third term. 83575

General Grant's lady detective. 28317

General Grant's views in harmony with Congress. 68010

General Gouverneur von Scholten og Almueskolerne paa St. Croix. 18274

General government and the leaders of the New-England opposition contrasted. 26865, 52945

General guide to the companies formed for working foreign mines. 22603

General H. W. Halleck's report. 29884

General Halleck and General Burnside. (29885)

General Harmer's expedition. 85142

General Harper's speech. 30427

General Harrison in Congress. 30578

Gen'l Harrison's cause vindicated. 104593

General Harrison's Leben und Wirken. 29006

General Hayne, in reply to Mr. Webster, of Massachusetts. 31039

General heads for the natural history of a country great or small. 7139

General hints to emigrants. 26879

General historia de los Indias. (57991)

General history and collection of voyages and travels, arranged in systematic order. 9730, (11608), 16275, 19985, 31558, 37631, 55448, 89452, 91609, note after 99383C

General history and descriptions of the empires. 5727

General history, cyclopedia, and dictionary of freemasonry. 43622

General history of all the important tragic events. 101506

General history of all voyages and travels. (26880), 21351

General history of America. 50937

General history of Connecticut, from its first settlement under George Fenwick, Esq. to its latest period of amity with Great Britain. 61209

General history of Connecticut, from its first settlement under George Fenwick to its latest period of amity with Great Britain. 61210

General history of Duchess County. 83718

General history of earthquakes. 9502

General history of Europe contained in the monthly mercuries. 65319

General history of Europe; or, the historical and political monthly mercury. 65319

General history of Georgiana the Queen-Mother. (26993)

General history of humming-birds, or the
   Trochilidae. (44926)
General history of inland navigation. 62494
General history of land and ocean telegraphs.
   7940
General history of missions throughout the
   world. 11960
General history of New England. 33443
General history of North and South America.
   40023
General history of North and South America,
   including the celebrated work of
   Robertson. 26881, 96144
General history of quadrupeds. 1383
General history of Spain. 44553
General history of the Americans. 59250,
   1st note after 102210
General history of the Baptist denomination in
   America. 4646, 4648
General history of the British empire in
   America. 105682-105682B
General history of the Christian church.
   (65507)
General history of the cruelties and proceedings
   of the inquisition. 26883
General history of the . . . Independent Odd
   Fellows Society. 56690
General history of the late war. 22667, 26882
General history of the lies raised & propagated.
   59867
General history of the lives and adventures.
   36194-(36195)
General history of the most prominent banks
   in Europe. (27641)
General history of the North American Indians.
   77849
General history of the Order of the Independent
   Odd Fellows Society. 70416
General history of the pyrates. 36188-36190
General history of the Quakers. 9072, 17584
General history of the robberies and murders.
   (23477)-23478, (36187)
General history of the Sabbatarian churches.
   18887
General history [of the Soldiers' Aid Society
   of Northern Ohio.] 76663, 86316
General history of the town of Sharon. 78815
General history of the United States of America.
   97186
General history of the United States of America;
   from the discovery in 1482, to 1792.
   97185
General history of the vast continent and
   islands of America. 13015, 31557-31558
General history of the world, being an
   abridgment. (78557)
General history of the world, from the creation
   to the present time. 29328
General history of the world, from the earliest
   period to the year 1840. 73445
General history of the world from the earliest
   times until the year 1831. 73444
General history of trade. 26884
General history of· Virginia, New England, and
   the Summer Isles. 82823
General Hospital, Buffalo. see Buffalo
   General Hospital.
General Hospital Society of Connecticut, New
   Haven. Directors. 15697
General Hospital Society of Connecticut, New
   Haven. President. 15697
General Hunt's letter to Senator Sam Houston.
   33882
General idea of the college of Mirania. 84599-
   84600, 84614, 84678C
General impost considered and defended.
   (32782), 105988

General index of the laws. 53684
General index to the American statesmen
   series. 84335
General index to the colonial records. (31103)
General index to the documents and laws of
   the state. 53681
General index to the documents of the state .
   from 1777 to 1865. 53681
General index to the documents relative to the
   colonial history. (53682)
General index to the first twelve volumes.
   (55316)
General index to the journals of the Legislative
   Assembly of Canada. 10487
General index to the laws of Pennsylvania.
   (60115)
General index to the laws of the state. 53683
General index to the laws of the United States.
   9199, 15531
General index to the North American review.
   55564
General institution of the order. 13130
General instructions for the government of the
   consular and commercial agents. 26885,
   95036
General instructions to sanitary inspectors.
   76548, 76647
General instructions to the Consuls and
   Commercial Agents. 16151
General instructions to the Surveyor General.
   53111
General intelligencer. 88307
General introduction and supplement to the two
   tracts. (65447), 65457
General introduction by Mrs. C. M. Kirkland.
   69013
General introduction to the gold region of
   Nova Scotia. (14686), 81061
General introduction to statistical account of
   Upper Canada. 28138, (28143)
General introduction to the two tracts on civil
   liberty. 65448, 65457
General introductory remarks. 89369
Gen. Israel Putnam. 31818
General Jackson. A sketch. 26797
General Jackson's conduct in the Seminole
   War. 60970
Gen. Jackson's farewell address. 35347
Gen. Jackson's letter to Carter Beverley.
   35348
Gen. Jackson's Negro speculations. 93797
Gen. Jackson's reply to Mr. Clay. 35348
General Jose Tadeo Monagas. 49931
General Joseph Smith's appeal to the Green
   Mountain Boys. 83241
General Lafayette a ses collegues de la
   Chambre des Deputes. 38583
General Lafayette in Amerika. 40736
General Lafayette. Memoires authentiques.
   (12277)
General Land-Kontoret. see U. S. Com-
   missioner of Public Lands.
General Lane's Birgade in central Mexico.
   7196
General laws, and joint resolutions. 14742
General laws and liberties of the Massachusets
   [sic] colony. (45742)
General laws and liberties of the Massachusett
   colony. 45743
General laws and resolves of the Legislature
   of the commonwealth of Massachusetts.
   45747
General laws of Massachusetts, from the
   adoption of the constitution. 45744
General laws of Pennsylvania, from . . . 1700,
   to April 18, 1849. 60016

General laws of Pennsylvania, from . . . 1700, to April 22, 1846. 60016

General laws of Pennsylvania, from . . . 1700, to . . . 1852. 60016

General laws of the commonwealth of Massachusetts. (45745)

General laws of the commonwealth of Massachusetts, passed subsequently to the revised statutes. (45746)

General laws of the corporation of Washington. 20306

General laws [of the Free and Accepted Masons of Maryland.] 45159

General laws of the Improved Order of Red Men. 26886

General lavves of the Massachusetts colony. 45741

General laws of the state of California. 10022, 32276

General laws of the state of Kansas, in force. 37067

General laws of the state of Kansas, passed at the first session. 37066

General laws of the territory of Dakota. 18296

General laws, resolutions, memorials, and private acts. 14741

General Lee and Santa Claus. 13177

Gen. Lee songster. 77975

General Lee's farewell dinner, at New-York. 81529

General Lewis Cass. 11352

General Lopez, the Cuban patriot. (41993)

General McCall's report. 42970

General McClellan and the Army of the Potomac. 65522

General McClellan and the conduct of the war. 34005

General McClellan's letter of acceptance. 10187, 19510

General McClellan's letter of acceptance [together with his West Point oration.] (43021)

General M'Clellan's Peninsula campaign. 37646

General McClellan's record. 43030

Gen. McClellan's report of its operations. (43011)

General McClellan's spy. 69220

General magazine, and historical chronicle. (26887)

General magazine of arts and sciences. 26888

General managers' report [of the Great Central Route Blue Line.] 28439

General Manuel Quesada a las republicas de America. 67120

General Manuel Rincon justificado. 71417

General map and analysis. 23176

General map made onelye for the particular declaration. (29594)

General map of the discoveries of Admiral de Fonte. 28460, 1st note after 94082

General Martin. 44877

General Meeting, Chester, S. C., 1831. see Chester, S. C. General Meeting, 1831.

General Meeting of the Citizens of Philadelphia and Parts Adjacent, 1779. see Philadelphia. General Meeting of the Citizens of Philadelphia and Parts Adjacent, 1779.

General Meeting of the Electors, Westminster, England, 1782. see Westminster, England. General Meeting of the Electors, 1782.

General Meeting of the Merchants and Traders, Philadelphia, 1765. see Philadelphia. General Meeting of the Merchants and Traders, 1765.

General Meeting of the Society of the Cincinnati, Philadelphia, 1784. see Society of the Cincinnati. General Meeting, Philadelphia, 1784.

General mortgage. 55821

General Mosquera al publico de la Nueva Granada. (51075)

General Narcisco Lopez y la isla de Cuba. 41992

Gen. Nathaniel Lyon, and Missouri in 1861. 59499

General offer of the Gospel. 46331

General officer. pseud. Letters. (40584)

General officer. pseud. New system of military discipline. 53405

General officer. pseud. Pope's campaign in Virginia. (64118)

General officer. pseud. Rules, maxims, and observations. 74098

General officer. pseud. Speech. see Burgoyne, John, 1722-1792.

General opposition of the colonies. 26889

General; or, twelve nights in the hunters' camp. 34653

General order no. 45. 51743

General order of the Sanitary Commission for its executive service. 76587, 76647

General order regulating the uniform of the militia. 26890

General orders. 101699

General orders affecting the volunteer force. 26891

General orders. Department of the East. 26893

General orders for the second division of the Massachusetts militia. 95869

General orders from Headquarters Department of the Gulf. 9613

General orders from Adjutant and Inspector-General's Office. 15270, 26895

General orders from the Adjutant and Inspector-General's Office, Confederate States Army, for the year 1863. 26896, 72174

General orders from the Adjutant and Inspector-General's Office, Confederate States Army, from January 1 to June 30, 1864. 15271

General orders from the Adjutant and Inspector-General's Office for 1863. 15272

General orders from the Office of the Adjutant General. 53516

General orders. Head-quarters, Morris Town, January 22, 1777. 101695

General orders. Head-quarters, 2d division, Nashville. 94783

General orders in Wolfe's army during the expedition. 67024

General orders issued by Major-General William Heath. 84904

General orders, no. 20. 51739

General orders of the War Department. (26892), 56435

General orders of the War Department, from January 18, 1861. 26894

General orders. Philadelphia, April 11. 1777. 101698

General orders. Wilmington, September 5, 1777. 101701

General organization for the relief of the poor. (61693)

General outline of the United States of North America. (26897)

General Parkhill (Ship) in Admiralty (58779)

Gen. Perham's platform. 60923

General Pierce's administration and the Nebraska bill. 90422

General plan for a mail communication. 43642

General plan for laying out towns and townships. 26898, (79821)-79822

General plan for the establishment of schools. 28913

General plan of education appointed for the South-Carolina Society's Female Academy. 88034

General plan of education appointed for the South-Carolina Society's Male Academy. 88035

General Pope's Virginia campaign of 1862. 49111

General Porter's appeal, Morristown, N. J. 64249

General practice of the churches of New-England. (17101), 71762

General practice of the churches of New-England, relating to baptism, vindicated. 17100, 71756

General prayer. 79196

General preface. 84677

General Prim, le Senat, les Cortes et la presse Espagnole. 65523

General principles of a constitution. 102722

General principles of English grammar. 68540

General principles of government and commerce. 102367, note after 102396

General Protestant Episcopal Sunday School Union, New York. (66129), 66152

General Protestant Episcopal Sunday School Union, New York. Board. 66152

General Protestant Episcopal Sunday School Union, New York. Executive Committee. 54289

General Protestant Episcopal Sunday-School Union, New York. Pennsylvania Auxiliary. see Protestant Episcopal Sunday-School Society of Pennsylvania.

General Protestant Episcopal Sunday School Union. Proceedings of the third triennial meeting of the society. 66152

General provisions of the law. 10421

General public acts of Congress. 26899

General public statutory law. 45150

General Rail Road Committee. 89246

General Rail Road Committee. Committee to Correspond with the Corporation of Pittsburgh and Allegheny, on the Subject of a Rail Road from Pittsburgh to Cumberland. 89246

General railroad laws of California. 10023

General railroad system for New Jersey. 35439

General railway index. 53676

General reflections occasioned by the Letter to two great men. 26900

General register. 14730-14731

General register, for 1842. 50269

General register of politics and literature. 16045, 26901

General register of the colonial dependencies of Great Britain. (14694)

General register of the Navy and Marine Corps of the United States. 47285

General regulations adopted by the Grand Lodge of Virginia. 100473

General regulations for the army. 26902

General regulations for the army of the United States. 26903

General regulations for the gentlemen of the bar. 99159

General regulations for the government of the army. 95057

General regulations for the government of the Grand Lodge of New Jersey. 53126

General regulations for the military forces of . . . New York. 53126

General regulations for the military forces of . . . New York. 53685

General regulations for the military forces of Ohio. 56917

General regulations for the Navy and Marine Corps. 26904

General regulations for the organizing of congregations. 26905, 72975

General regulations for the Supply Department. 76592, 76647

General remarks on rail-roads. 95746

General remarks on the leading principles of that work. 15523, (19253)

General remarks on the origin of surnames. (74153)

General remarks on the proceedings lately had. 26906

General remarks—reliable documents. 58522

General remarks upon the coleoptera of Lake Superior. 39666

General report. 35308, 69946

General report in relation to the market department. 61694

General report . . . June 1st, 1861. 35030

General report of the British Commissioner. (54494)

General report of the . . . Chesapeake and Delaware Canal Company. 12499

General report of the Colonial Land and Emigration Commissioners. 14689, 26907

General report of the Commissioner of Public Works. (10558)

General report of the Committee on Internal Improvements. 45151

General report of the Emigration Commissioner 22499

General report of the Geological Survey of Newfoundland. 36878

General report of the Orphans' Home of Industry. 57648

General report upon the zoology of the several Pacific Railroad routes. 69946

General repository and review. (26907A)

General repository of history, politics, and literature. (52450)

General repository of history, politics, and science. (1205), 8457

General repository of literature and state papers. 101156

General repository of useful knowledge. 54798

General Republican address. 26908, 100673

General Republican Corresponding Committee of the City of Albany. see Democratic Party. New York. Albany. Corresponding Committee.

General result of Negro apprenticeship. 81986

General review. see Christian examiner and general review.

General review of the African slave trade. (26915)

General Riedesel's official correspondence. 71301

Gen. Rob. E. Lee's report of the battle. 7467, 44444

General Rosas devant la France. 6906

General Rosas et la question de la Plata. 73213, 75486

General rules and regulations for the government of the Grand Lodge. 87847

General rules and specifications for the location and construction of M'Adamized turnpike roads. 104236

General rules for making a large geography. 21760

General rules of the general societies of the Methodist Episcopal Church. 48186

General rules of the United Society. 97887

Gen. S. Smith's speech. 83986

Gen'l Samuel Ryan Curtis. In memoriam. 18065

General Santa-Anna a los Mexicanos. 76733

General Santa-Anna a sus compatriotas. 76732

General Santa-Anna burlandose de la nacion. 93341

General school law of . . . New York. 53686

General Scott and his staff. 78406

Gen. Scott's correspondence with Hon. W. L. Marcy. 78407

Gen. Scott's guide in Mexico. 83680

Gen. Scott's letter of acceptance. 20428

General Sherman's evidence before the Congressional Committee. 80414

General Sherman's Indian spy. (7292)

General Sherman's official account of his great march. 80414

General Simon Bolivar. 56276

General Smith's views on the powers and policy. 83242-83245

General Smyth to the soldiers. 85184

General Society of Mechancis and Tradesmen of the City of New York. 54290, 86075

General Society of Mechanics and Tradesmen of the City of New York. Charter. 54290, 54676, 86075

General Society of Mechanics and Tradesmen of the City of New York. Finance Committee. 54290

General Society of Mechanics and Tradesmen of the City of New York. Library. 54290

General Society of Mechanics and Tradesmen of the City of New York. School Committee. 54290

General Society of Mechanics and Tradesmen of the City of New York. Treasurer. 54290

General Society of the Cincinnati. see Society of the Cincinnati.

General St. Clair's expedition against the Indians in 1791. 85142

General statement [of the Trustees of Burlington College.] 9337

General statements by the Directors to the stockholders. 105451

General statistics of the British empire. (43643)

General statute laws of the state of New York. 85243

General statutes of . . . New Hampshire. 52828

General statutes of the commonwealth of Massachusetts. (54748)

General statutes of the commonwealth . . . relating to the public schools. 54749

General statutes of the state of Connecticut. 15763

General statutes of the state of Kansas. (37068)

General statutes of the state of Minnesota. (49249)

General statutes of the state of Rhode Island. 70700

Gen. Stephen Elliott. 87514

General stud-book, containing pedigrees of stallions. 26909

General stud-book: containing the pedigrees of the most celebrated horses. 21841

General Sullivan's address to the freemen of New-Hampshire. 93509

General survey of that part of the island of St. Christopher's. (42917)

General survey of the antient and modern state of that island. 41871

General survey of the physical phenomena of the universe. 33728

General survey of the political situation of the several powers. 23224

General survey of the present situation of the principal powers. 23224, (23230), (23231), 23235

General Synod of the Evangelical Lutheran Church in the United States of America. 29013, 66467

General Synod of the Evangelical Lutheran Church in the United States of America. Theological Seminary, Gettysburg, Pa. see Gettysburg, Pa. Theological Seminary of the General Synod of the Evangelical Lutheran Church in the United States of America.

General synopsis of North American ornithology. 11369

General synopsis of the business of the city. 12629

General tax laws. 53112

General Taylor. 4787

General Taylor—the war. (77327)

General Theological Seminary of the Protestant Episcopal Church in the United States, New York. see New York (City) General Theological Seminary of the Protestant Episcopal Church in the U. S.

General Theological Seminary . . . its embryo history—beginnings and growth. (66153)

General Theological Seminary of the Protestant Episcopal Church in the United States of America. Proceedings relative to the organization. 26911, (54291)

General theory of the Dudley Observatory in the abstract. 21100

General Tom Thumb's songs. 92729, 92735

General topography of North America. 35953, 35962

General Town Meeting, Philadelphia, 1779. see Philadelphia. Town Meeting, 1779.

General treatise of monies & exchanges. 26912

General treatise of naval trade and commerce. 26913

General treatise of the dominion of the sea. 36946

General treatise on the slavery question. 36571

General treaty of peace, amity, &c. 52776

General Union for Promoting the Observance of the Christian Sabbath. (26914)

General Union for Promoting the Observance of the Christian Sabbath. Pennsylvania Branch. (60305)

General view of colprotage as conduct. (14757)

General view of Kennebec, Me. (6091)

General view of New Hampshire. 12147

General view of the cause. 105566

General view of the coast. 49112

General view of the English colonies. 7473

General view of the origin and nature of the constitution. 2895, 26916

General view of the penitentiary system. (30321)

General view of the principles and design. 51158

General view of the progress of the Unitarian doctrine. 4598

General view of the rise . . . of the American navy. 26917

General view of the state [of Michigan.] 5962

General view of the statistics and condition of the church. 88124

General view of the trade and navigation of the world. 29894

Geneva College, Geneva, N. Y. Medical Institution. 26938, 26940
Geneva College, Geneva, N. Y. Medical Institution. plaintiffs 89386
Geneva College, Geneva, N. Y. Medical Institution. Board of Professors. 26939
Geneva College, Geneva, N. Y. Medical Institution. Trustees. Standing Committee. 89387
Geneva College, Geneva, N. Y. Rutgers Medical College, New York. 74447-74448
Geneva Lake, Wisc. Division no. 26, Sons of Temperance. see Sons of Temperance of North America. Wisconsin. Geneva Lake Division, no. 26.
Geneva Lyceum, Geneva, N. Y. 26941
Geneva pamphlet on the relations between Spain and Cuba. 88853
Geneva, Seneca Falls and Waterloo directory. 26937
Genhardt, Charles de. 8839, 33733
Genial showman. 31959
Genie des hommes. 12264
Genie du Christianisme. 12237, 12269
Genille et de Marly-le-Chatel, Martin Fumee, Seigneur de. see Fumee, Martin, Sieur de Marly-le-Chatel, 16th cent.
Genlin, Sylvester. 26943
Genlin, Thomas Hedges. (26944)
Genio, Arthur. (26945)
Genis, Tadeo. 10803
Genius and mission of the Protestant Episcopal Church. (14772)
Genius and Mission of the Protestant Episcpal Church in the United States of America. 14773
Genius and moral achievements of the spirit of foreign missions. 103379
Genius and posture of America. 757
Genius and spirit of the Hebrew Bible. 67465
Genius of America to General Carleton. 26946, 102041-102042
Genius of Britain to General Howe. (26947)
Genius of Columbia—a poem. (26948)
Genius of ecclesiastical freedom. (22096)
Genius of Erin. 14888, 26949
Genius of Great Britain, an ode. 26950
Genius of masonry. 38074, 76255
Genius of oblivion. 29670
Genius of universal emancipation. 26951
Genlis, Stephanie Felicite Brularet de Sillery, Comtesse de. see Sillery, Stephanie Felicite Brularet de, Comtesse de Genlis, 1746-1830.
Genlis, Stephanie Felicite Ducrest de Saint-Aubin, Comtesse de. see Saint-Aubin, Stephanie Felicite Ducrest de, Comtesse de Genlis.
Genoa, Italy. 89648
Genoa, Italy (Republic) Treaties, etc. 69543
Genoese pilot. pseud. Account. 62806, note after 90319
Genoese pilot's account. 62806, note after 90319
Genois, J. de Saint. see Saint-Genois, J. de.
Genouese. pseud. Prohemio primo, sopra il libro de Messer Marco Polo. 67736
Genouilly, Charles Rigault de. 1701, note after 12285, 73506
Genres des poissons de la faune de Cuba. 63673
Gens de lettres. pseud. Amerique Septentrionale et Meridionale. 1295
Genth, Frederic Augustus. 85072
Gentil de la Barbinais, ------ le. see La Barbinais, ----- Le Gentil de.

Gentilhomme de la suite de Fernand Cortes. pseud. Relation abregee sur la Nouvelle-Espagne. 94854
Gentil-homme de la Ville d'Elvas. pseud. see Knight of Elvas. pseud.
Gentilhomme Francois. pseud. Relation d'vn voyage avx Indes Orientales. 69248
Gentilhomme Portugais. pseud. Lettre. 94621
Gentil-homo. pseud. Relatione di alcvne cose della Nuoua Espagna. 16951, 67740
Gentils Reisen in den Indischen Meeren. 38398
Gentium septentionalium historiae breviarum. 43833
Gentle manners. 106199
Gentle savage. 8421
Gentleman, Francis. ed. 88530
Gentleman. pseud. Account of the French settlements in America. 95, 10330, 12143
Gentleman. pseud. Answer to the committee. 93364
Gentleman. pseud. Compendious history of the rise and progress. see Mather, Samuel, 1706-1785.
Gentleman. pseud. Country and town officer. 45700
Gentleman. pseud. Critical essay concerning marriage. see Salmon, Thomas.
Gentleman. pseud. Description of the Genesee country. see Williamson, Charles. supposed author
Gentleman. pseud. Description of the country of the Mississippi. 26144
Gentleman. pseud. Description of the settlement of the Genesee country. see Williamson, Charles. supposed author
Gentleman. pseud. Drunkard. 84785
Gentleman. pseud. Essay on the merchandize of slaves. see Dudley, Paul.
Gentleman. pseud. Letter. 40282
Gentleman. pseud. Letter from a gentleman to his friend. see Panther, Abraham. pseud.
Gentleman. pseud. Letter from a gentleman to his friend in Dutchess-County. 78553
Gentleman. pseud. Letter from a gentleman to his friend, in England. 10504
Gentleman. pseud. Letter from a gentleman to his friend in New York. 40296
Gentleman. pseud. Letter on toleration. 40374
Gentleman. pseud. Lord N——th condemned. (55516)
Gentleman. pseud. New history of Jamaica. 35585, (35636), 82167
Gentleman. pseud. Philanthropic tour through the United States. 62428
Gentleman. pseud. Plain dealer: number II. see Z., X. Y., Gentleman. pseud.
Gentleman. pseud. Proposals for a tobacco-law. 45295
Gentleman. pseud. Seasonable caveat against popery. see Dudley, Paul.
Gentleman. pseud. Sketches of several distinguished members. 81509, note after 105083
Gentleman. pseud. Some remarks. 103374
Gentleman. pseud. West Indians defended. see White, Edward. Byam, Edward Samuel. supposed author
Gentleman and citizen's pocket almanack. 91386
Gentleman and gardener's kalendar. 95611
Gentleman and ladies musical companion. 91718

Gentleman and lady's musical companion. 91716-91717

Gentleman and lady's pocket almanack. 71688

Gentleman at Barbadoes. pseud. Letter. see Baxter, Thomas.

Gentleman at Elizabeth-Town. pseud. Letter. see P., W. pseud.

Gentleman at Halifax. pseud. Letter. see Howard, Martin, d. 1781.

Gentleman at New-York. pseud. Letter. 16729

Gentleman at New-York. pseud. Voice of truth. (12491), 1st note after 100681

Gentleman at Rome. pseud. Remarks on a proposed canal. (69494)

Gentleman at the bar. pseud. Examination of the rights of the colonies. 23372

Gentleman at the trial. pseud. reporter By authority. The trial of James Hill. 31834

Gentleman bred in his family. pseud. History and life of Robert Blake. 5791

Gentleman educated at Yale College. pseud. Introduction to the study of philosophy. 34950

Gentleman educated at Yale College. pseud. Philosophic solitude. see Livingston, William.

Gentleman emigrant. 90116

Gentleman eminent in that art. pseud. reporter 103580

Gentleman for many years a resident in America. pseud. Letter to Lord George Germaine. 27143

Gentleman, formerly of Boston. pseud. Dangerous vice. see Bourne, Sylvanus. supposed author   Church, Edward. supposed author.

Gentleman formerly of Boston. pseud. Dangers of vice. see Bourne, Sylvanus. supposed author   Church, Edward. supposed author

Gentleman from South Carolina. pseud. Go-between. see Devot, ------. supposed author

Gentleman highly respected in the literary world. pseud. Letter on the maintainance of the clergy. see Franklin, Benjamin, 1706-1790.

Gentleman immediately returned from a tour of that continent. pseud. Historical review of North America. 55525

Gentleman immediately returned from a tour of the continent. pseud. Historical review and directory of North America. 32079

Gentleman in a select society. pseud. Reply. 69672

Gentleman in America. pseud. Extract of a letter. see Cooper, Thomas.

Gentleman in an eminet station on the spot. pseud. Accurate and authentic journal of the siege of Quebec. 66987

Gentleman in Barbadoes. pseud. British empire in America, consider'd. 8099

Gentleman in Barbados. pseud. Some observations on a direct exportation of sugar. see Ashley, John.

Gentleman in black, and tales of other days. 35135, (35148)

Gentleman in Boston. pseud. Enquiry into the state of the bills of credit. 22649

Gentleman in Boston. pseud. Letter from a gentleman in Boston to a Unitarian clergyman. see Tappan, Lewis.

Gentleman in Boston. pseud. Letter from a Gentleman in Boston to his friend in Connecticut. 40283

Gentleman in Boston. pseud. Letter from a gentleman in Boston to Mr. George Wishart. see Chauncy, Charles, 1705-1787.

Gentleman in Boston. pseud. Prize essay. see Tuckerman, Joseph.

Gentleman in Connecticut. pseud. Examiner examined. (23375)

Gentleman in Connecticut. pseud. Letter. 58632

Gentleman in Connecticut. pseud. Letter from a gentleman in Connecticut, relative to a paper currency. 40284

Gentleman in Connecticut. pseud. Regulator for Crazy Will's death-watch. 68969

Gentleman in England. pseud. Letter. 40285, 61773

Gentleman in Guadaloupe. pseud. Copy of a letter. 16723

Gentleman in Guadaloupe. pseud. Reasons for keeping Guadaloupe. (19779), 29044, note after (68267)

Gentleman in Halifax. pseud. Letter from a gentleman in Halifax to his friend in Boston. 40286

Gentleman in Italy. pseud. Some modern directions. 86658

Gentleman in Jamaica. pseud. Answer to the Rev. Mr. Clarkson's essay. see Francklyn, Gilbert.

Gentleman in London. pseud. Claim of the colonies. see Knox, William.

Gentleman in London. pseud. Letter from a gentleman in London, to a merchant. 21419

Gentleman in London. pseud. Letter from a gentleman in London, to his friend in Pennsylvania. see Smith, William, 1727-1803. supposed author

Gentleman in London. pseud. Letter from a gentleman in London to his friend in the country. (18761)

Gentleman in Maryland. pseud. Extract of a letter. 23506

Gentleman in Massachusetts. pseud. Essential rights. see Williams, Elisha.

Gentleman in Mount Hope. pseud. Letter. 40288

Gentleman in New-England. pseud. Animadversions, critical and candid. see Welles, Noah. supposed author

Gentleman in New England. pseud. Letter from a gentleman in New England. (409

Gentleman in New-England. pseud. State of religion in New-England. 69400, 90595-90597, 103594, 3d note after 103650

Gentleman in New-York. pseud. Letter from a gentleman in New-York. 40289, (6968, 86592, note after 96961

Gentleman in Newport. pseud. Brief representation. see B., A. pseud.

Gentleman in North-America. pseud. Information to emigrants. see Smith, William, 1728-1793.

Gentleman in Nova-Scotia. pseud. Letter. see W., J. pseud.

Gentleman in one of the back counties. pseud Conduct of the Paxton men. 1663, (15209), 59268

Gentleman in Philadelphia. pseud. Late regulations. see Dickinson, John, 1732-1808.

Gentleman in Philadelphia. pseud. Letter from a gentleman in Philadelphia, to a freeholder. (61775)

Gentleman in Philadelphia. pseud. Letter from a gentleman in Philadelphia to his friend in Bucks. (61774)

Gentleman in Philadelphia. pseud. Thoughts on emigration. see Cooper, Thomas.

Gentleman in Scotland. pseud. Letter. (40290), note after 103628

Gentleman in South-Carolina. pseud. Letter. 19817

Gentleman in Switzerland. pseud. Enquiries relative to middle Florida. (43612)

Gentleman in that country. pseud. Good news from Virginia. 100478

Gentleman in the city. pseud. Letter. see Penn, William, 1644-1718.

Gentleman in the country. pseud. Letter from a gentleman in the country to a member of Parliament in town. 17610

Gentleman in the country. pseud. Letter from a gentleman in the country, to his friend in Boston. 58897

Gentleman in the country. pseud. Letter from a gentleman in the country, to his friend in Edinburgh. 103629

Gentleman in the country. pseud. Letter from a gentleman in the country to his friend in town. 40293

Gentleman in the country. pseud. Letter from a gentlemen in the country to S——— W———. 40294

Gentleman in the country. pseud. Observations on a late epitaph. 56485, (60284)

Gentleman in the country. pseud. Remarks on a pamphlet. see Ferguson, Adam.

Gentleman in the country. pseud. Remarks upon a discourse. (28006)

Gentleman in the county. pseud. History of the county of Berkshire. 24270

Gentleman in the east. pseud. Letter. see Gale, Benjamin, 1715-1790.

Gentleman in the east. pseud. Present state of the colony of Connecticut considered. see Gale, Benjamin, 1715-1790.

Gentleman in the eastern part of said colony. pseud. Present state of the colony of Connecticut considered. see Gale, Benjamin, 1715-1790.

Gentleman in the Massachusetts-Bay. pseud. Essential rights and liberties. see Williams, Elisha.

Gentleman in the navy lately arrived from there. pseud. Account of the present state of Nova-Scotia. see B., J. pseud.

Gentleman in the town of Boston. pseud. Wonderful appearance of an angel. see W., S. pseud.

Gentleman in the west. pseud. Congratulatory letter. see Hobart, Noah.

Gentleman in the West Indies. pseud. Letter. 47917

Gentleman in the western country. pseud. Captivity & sufferings of Mrs. Mary Smith, &c. 83535

Gentleman in town. pseud. Illuminatio Britannicae. 34329

Gentleman in town. pseud. Observations. 56474

Gentleman in town. pseud. Scribler being a letter. 60605, 78475, 104455

Gentleman in Transilvania. pseud. Letter. see Hunt, Isaac.

Gentleman in Virginia. pseud. Copy of a letter. (16724), (40291), 60716, 2d note after 95968, 3d note after 100449, 2d note after 100483

Gentleman in Virginia. pseud. Letter from a gentleman in Virginia to a merchant in Philadelphia. (16724), (40291), 60716, 2d note after 95968, 3d note after 100449, 2d note after 100483

Gentleman in Virginia. pseud. Letter from a gentleman in Virginia, to the merchants of Great Britain. see Randolph, Peyton, 1721?-1775.

Gentleman in Wethersfield. pseud. Letter. 4102

Gentleman late of Christ's College, Cambridge. pseud. Letter from New Jersey. see Thompson, Thomas, 1708?-1773. supposed author

Gentleman lately arriv'd. pseud. History of Caledonia. (9920), 18556, 78218

Gentleman lately arrived from that colony. pseud. Importance of settling and fortifying Nova Scotia. 56141

Gentleman lately resident on a plantation. pseud. Account of the island of Jamaica. see Marsden, Peter.

Gentleman, lately returned from America. pseud. Letters on emigration. 22502, 40615

Gentleman, long resident in the West Indies. pseud. Account of Jamaica. see Stewart, John, of Jamaica.

Gentleman, may years resident in Canada. pseud. Impartial account of the civil war in the Canadas. 10463

Gentleman, now resident in Jamaica. pseud. True and impartial account. see Houstoun, James. supposed author

Gentleman of America. pseud. Some considerations on the consequences. 86620

Gentleman of Baltimore. pseud. Letter. see Speed, Joseph J.

Gentleman of Baltimore. pseud. Letters entitled, The American commercial claims. 40580

Gentleman of Baltimore. pseud. Miscellany. 49450

Gentleman of Barbadoes. pseud. Barbadoes packet. (3256)

Gentleman of Barbadoes. pseud. Present state of the British sugar colonies considered. (65328), (69514)

Gentleman of Barbadoes. pseud. Proposals offered for the sugar planters redress. (66041)

Gentleman of Boston. pseud. Notes made during an excursion. see Hale, Nathan.

Gentleman of Connecticut. pseud. Democratiad. see Cobbett, William, 1763-1835. supposed author Hopkins, Lemuel. supposed author

Gentleman of Connecticut. pseud. Plea before the ecclesiastical council. see Huntington, Joseph.

Gentleman of distinguished merit in the city of New-York. pseud. [Letters.] (25955)

Gentleman of Elvas. pseud. see Knight of Elvas. pseud.

Gentleman of foreign extraction. pseud. Observations on a variet of subjects. see Duche, Jacob.

Gentleman of Georgetown. pseud. Eulogy on General George Washington. 101806

Gentleman of good worth, now resident in London. pseud. Newes from New-England. 54970

Gentleman of Halifax. pseud. Vindication of Governor Parr and his council. see Parr, John.

Gentleman of his congregation. pseud. Familiar dialogue between a minister & a gentleman of his congregation. 20057

Gentleman of his fleet. pseud. Nevves of Sr. Walter Rauleigh. see M., R. pseud.

Gentleman of Lincoln's Inn. pseud. Free thoughts. 25720

Gentleman of Maryland. pseud. Battle of Bunkers Hill. see Brackenridge, Hugh Henry, 1748-1816. supposed author and Parke, John. supposed author

Gentleman of Massachusetts. pseud. Christian orator. 12919

Gentleman of Massachusetts. pseud. Fayette in prison. see Eliot, James.

Gentleman of Massachusetts. pseud. Writer. see Bradford, Gamaliel, 1795-1839.

Gentleman of Mississippi. pseud. Secession. (78705)

Gentleman of New-Brunswick. pseud. Letter. 52522

Gentleman of N. York. pseud. King's bridge cottage. see Woodworth, Samuel.

Gent. of New York. pseud. Party spirit exposed. 58972

Gentleman of New York. pseud. Remarks on the home squadron. 69465

Gentleman of New-York. pseud. Templar. 94658

Gentleman of North Carolina. pseud. Appendix to Aristides's vindication. 35921, 98530

Gentleman of Northumberland. pseud. Grave answer. see Murray, James, 1732-1782. supposed author

Gentleman of Philadelphia. pseud. Biographia Americana. see French, Benjamin Franklin.

Gentleman of Quebec. pseud. Account of the attack and engagement at Quebec. 36728

Gentleman of Portsmouth, N. H. pseud. Versification. see Sewall, Jonathan Mitchel, 1748-1808.

Gentleman of Richmond. pseud. ed. Southern and south-western sketches. 88291

Gentleman of Rhode Island colony. pseud. Verses on Dr. Mayhew's book. see Goddard, William.

Gentleman of South Carolina. pseud. Southern odes. see Northrop, Clavdian Bird, 1812-1865.

Gentleman of South Carolina. pseud. Description of Brunswick. see Putnam, Henry.

Gentleman of South Carolina. pseud. Story of AEneas and Dido burlesqued. see Rugeley, Rowland. supposed author and Wells, Robert, d. 1794. supposed author

Gentleman of talents. pseud. Notes on the navigation of the Mississippi. 55970

Gentleman of that country. pseud. New-England's faction discovered. see Dove, C.

Gentleman of that island. pseud. Letter. 21400

Gentleman of the army. pseud. Poem. see Humphreys, David.

Gentleman of the Baltimore bar. pseud. Some account of General Jackson. 21732

Gentleman of the bar. pseud. reporter Case of Baptis Irvine. 35112, 3d note after 96883

Gentleman of the bar. pseud. Early history of western Pennsylvania. see Rupp, I. Daniel.

Gentleman of the bar. pseud. Justice's guide. see Thompson, Benjamin Franklin.

Gentleman of the bar. pseud. reporter Report of a case. see Tatham, William. reporter

Gentleman of the bar. pseud. reporter Report of the case of Thomas Graham. see Gazlay, James. reporter

Gentleman of the bar. pseud. reporter Trial of Robert M. Goodwin. 96877

Gentleman of the bar. pseud. reporter Trial of William Stewart. 91710

Gentleman of the bar at Harrisburg. pseud. Observations in a letter. (60283)

Gentleman of the bar of Staunton. pseud. Virginia scrivener. 100565

Gentleman of the city of New-York. pseud. Letter. (40295)

Gentleman of the faculty. pseud. Observations and remarks. see Jackson, Hall.

Gentleman of the Inner Temple. pseud. Dissertation on the political abilities. 4008

Gentleman of the Inner Temple. pseud. Letter to Lord Chatham. see Dawes, Matthew.

Gentleman of the Inner Temple. pseud. ed. Miscellaneous collection. 14642, 29396, 49441

Gentleman of the Inner Temple. pseud. Prospect from Malvern Hill. 66068

Gentleman of the island. pseud. Political account of the island of Trinidad. see M'Callum, P. F. supposed author

Gentleman of the law. pseud. Argument in the case of Ebenezer Smith Platt. 63352

Gentleman of the law. pseud. New conductor generalis. 52581

Gentleman of the law. pseud. Some observations upon the bill now dependening. 86695

Gentleman of the law, in West Jersey. pseud. Introductory preface. 79823

Gentleman of the medical faculty. pseud. Essay on the natural history of Guiana. see Bancroft, Edward.

Gentleman of the profession. pseud. reporter Report of the trial of Henry Bedlow. (69914)

Gentleman of the province. pseud. General history of Connecticut. see Peters, Samuel A.

Gentleman of the province. pseud. Rev. Samuel Peters' LL. D. General history of Connecticut. see Peters, Samuel A.

Gentleman of the said collony. pseud. Trve relation. see Smith, John, 1580-1631.

Gentleman of the south. pseud. Original memoir of the Floridas. (24891)

Gentleman of the town of Elvas. pseud. see Knight of Elvas. pseud.

Gentleman of the University of Oxford. pseud. Political mirror. 63788

Gentleman of undoubted credit. pseud. Letter see Richardson, William.

Gentleman of Virginia. pseud. Poems on several occasions. see Dawson, William, 1705?-1752.

Gentleman of Warrington, England. pseud. Why I have not gone to the south. see Robson, W.

Gentleman of Wilkesbarre. pseud. Appendix. (11986)

Gentlman on board that fleet. pseud. He has kept his word. 99249

Gentleman on Long-Island. pseud. Tour to Cowneck and North Hempstead. 96335

Gentleman on the spot. pseud. reporter Dee of horror! 23673

Gentleman perfectly acquainted with the unfortunate sufferer. pseud. Surprising adventures and sufferings of John Rhodes. 70763-70764, 71709, 93907-93908

Gentleman recently returned from it. pseud. Notes on the Vice Royalty of La Plata. 38999, 2d note after 98174

Gentleman resident at the Sierra Leone. pseud. Two letters on the slave trade. 96956

Gentleman resident in Monte Video. pseud. Rosas and the River Plate. 73219

Gentleman resident in the West Indies. pseud. Montgomery. 50161

Gentleman resident there. pseud. Emigration to America. see Rickman, Thomas Clio.

Gentleman residing in this city. pseud. Picture of New York. see Mitchill, Samuel Latham.

Gentleman residing there. pseud. Groans of Jamaica. 28914

Gentleman some time resident in the United States. pseud. Comparative view of the British and American constitutions. see M'Cormick, Samuel. supposed author

Gentleman that has not seen the foregoing letter. pseud. Some additional considerations. see Blackwell, John.

Gentleman travelling through Bucks County. pseud. Letter. (40297), 61776

Gentleman who accompanied him through his campaigns. pseud. Life and public services of Major-General McClellan. 43023

Gentleman who attended in the said court. pseud. reporter Trial of Mauritius Vale. 98339

Gentleman, who has made shooting his favourite amusement. pseud. Sportsman's companion. see Bell, C. supposed author

Gentleman who has recently visited the United States. pseud. View of the state of parties. see M'Cormack, Samuel.

Gentleman who has resided many years in Pennsylvania. pseud. Brief state of the province of Pennsylvania. see Smith, William, 1727-1803.

Gentleman who has resided several years in Jamaica. pseud. Trade granted to the South Sea-Company. (58160), 96427

Gentleman who has resided there upwards of seven years. pseud. Description of Georgia. 27037

Gentleman who has spent eleven weeks in Florida. pseud. Authentic narrative of the Seminole War. 24901, (79063)-79064, 4th note after 97085

Gentleman who lives there at present. pseud. Letter, giving a description of the isthmus of Darian. (78222)

Gentleman who resided there. pseud. Account of the present state of Nova-Scotia. see M., W. pseud.

Gentleman who resided many years in both kingdoms. pseud. New trade laid open. 53416

Gentleman who resided many years in Jamaica. pseud. Letter to a member of Parliament. 40397

Gentleman who resided many years in those countries. pseud. tr. True and particular relation. see Johnson, Henry. tr.

Gentmena, who resided more than twenty years in Jamaica. pseud. Strictures on the slave-trade. see Othello. pseud.

Gentleman who resided some time in Philadelphia. pseud. Caspipina's letters. see Duche, Jacob.

Gentleman, who resided upwards of fifteen years in that country. pseud. Considerations and remarks on the present state of the trade to Africa. 15942

Gentleman who resides in the country 60 or 70 miles from New-York. pseud. engr. 72992

Gentleman who travelled through those states in the summer of 1820. pseud. Topographical sketches. 96186

Gentleman who was an officer under that general. pseud. History. see Biggs, James. and Bullard, Henry Adams. incorrectly supposed author

Gentleman who was taken in the fleet. pseud. Account of the taking of the East and West-India fleet. 102812

Gentleman's and lady's diary. 90943-90944

Gentleman's and lady's monthly magazine. 15709

Gentleman's and trademan's complete annual account book. 550

Gentleman's complete annual kalendar for . . . 1772. 17172

Gentleman's law magazine. (26955)

Gentleman's magazine. 14456, (26954), 31389, (46925), 66724, (71969), 83423, 83778, 84678C, 91308, 91652, 92853-92854, 101738, 102647

Gentleman's maritime chronology. 91092

Gentleman's monthly companion. 73798

Gentleman's monthly intelligencer. (41859)

Gentleman's parental monitor. 90249

Gentleman's pocket almanac for . . . 1831. 99160

Gentleman's pocket library. 20286, 90249

Gentleman's pocket register, and free-mason's annual anthology. 39190

Gentleman's political and commercial pocket alamnac for 1801. 82378

Gentleman's political pocket-almanac for . . . 1796. 82377

Gentleman's political pocket-almanack, for the year 1795. 82376

Gentlemen! 95925

Gentlemen . . . 95930

Gentlemen, . . . 90346

Gentlemen: . . . 89960

Gentlemen, a list of the pensioners who are still chargeable to the state. 100407

Gentlemen and ladies' complete songster. 81667

Gentlemen and ladies diary. 90938-90940, 90942

Gentlemen and ladies' town and country magazine. 26953

Gentlemen and ladies vocal museum. 86958

Gentlemen, at a time which degenerate Britons are with brutal rage. 104294

Gentlemen at college. pseud. Testimony. see Harvard University. President and Fellows.

Gentlemen, at the sollicitation of a number of my friends. 10089A

Gentlemen. [Circular letter of the governor, Henry Lee.] 100221

Gentlemen employed by the General Assembly. pseud. eds. Grants, concessions, and original constitutions. 39527

Gentlemen, I have in vain used every means. 101297

Gentlemen, I have the honor to transmit to you. 89352

Gentlemen, I last year appeared in print. 101334

Gentlemen, in congratulating you upon the return of peace. 105403

Gentlemen in Dedham, Mass. pseud. Diocesan register and New England calendar. 20207, 52631

Gentlemen in the county, clergymen and laymen. pseud. History of the county of Berkshire, Massachusetts. 19848, 24270, 92912

Gentlemen, inclosed you have a copy of the proceedings. 101121

Gentlemen, it's well known. 86985

Gentlemen, last Sunday monring several letters were received. 100008

Geognostisches Gemalde von Brasilien.
  (22826)
Geografia cioe descrittione vniversale della
  terra partita. 66506, 66508
Geografia de la isla de Cuba, por Don
  Estaban Pinchardo. 62604
Geografia de la isla de Cuba, por Felipe Poey.
  63671
Geografia de las lenguas de Mexico. 57641
Geografia de las lenguas y carta etnografica
  de Mexico. 57641
Geografia de Smith. 72787
Geografia de Venezuela segun Codazi. 72786
Geografia del Peru. 59334
Geografia del Peru, Bolivia y Chile. 9562
Geografia di Cl. Tolomeo. 66506, 66508
Geografia di Clavdio Ptolemeo Alessandrino.
  (66502)
Geografia di Clavdio Tolomeo Alessandrino,
  gia tradotta di Greco in Italiano da
  M. Giero. Rvscelli. 66505
Geografia di Clavdio Tolomeo Alessandrino,
  nuouamente tradotta di Greco in Italiano,
  da Girolamo Rvscelli. 66503
Geografia di Clavdio Tolomeo Alessandrino,
  nuouamente tradotta di Greco in Italiano
  da Ieronimo Rvscelli. 66504
Geografia di Clavdio Tolomeo Alessandrino,
  tradotta di Greco nell' idioma volgare
  Italiano da Girolamo Rvscelli. 66507
Geografia di M. Livio Sanvto distinta in XII
  libri. 76897
Geografia elemental dispuesta para los ninos.
  72787, 83946-83948
Geografia fisica, fisographia y politica del
  Peru. 39066
Geografia fisica y politica de la isla de Cuba.
  (63672)
Geografia general, para el uso de la juventud
  de Venezuela. 14678, note after 98875
Geografia historica, estadistica y local de la
  provincia de Cartagena. (55276)
Geografia politica universal comparada. 39066
Geografia universal. 96235
Geografische bijdragen tot de kennis der
  bezittenen van de Europeanen, in Azie,
  Afrika en Amerika. 26968
Geografisk politisk veskrivelse over de
  forenede Nordamerkanske stater. 6235
Geographia Cl. Ptholemaei. 66475
Geographia Cl. Ptolemaei Alexandrini. (66489)
Geographia di Francesco Berlingeri [sic]
  Fiorentino. 66500-66501
Geographia di Francesco Berlinghieri
  Fiorentino. 66500
Geographia di Francesco Berlinghieri
  Fiorentino in terza rima. 66501
Geographia et cosmographia Blaviana. 5718
Geographia hierarchica, sive status
  ecclesiastici. 77606
Geographia historica, donde se describen los
  reynos. 51448
Geographia Ocvlvs historiarvm theatri
  geographiae. 66497
Geographia universalis. 21486
Geographia vniversalis, vetvs et nova. 66484,
  66486-66487
Geographiae Blavianae pars qvinta. 5714
Geographiae Cl. Ptolemaei. (66476), 66479
Geographiae Cl. Ptolemaei pars secvnda.
  66492-66493, 66495-66496
Geographiae Clavdii Ptolemaei Alexandrini.
  (66488)
Geographiae enarrationis libri octo. 55492-
  55493, 63016, (66482)-(66483), (66496),
  (66890), 73198, 76838
Geographiae et hydrographiae reformatae.
  (70811)-70812

Geographiae libri VIII. 66497
Geographiae libro octo. 66491, 66494
Geographiae tum veteris tum novae absolutissi-
  mum opus. 43822
Geographiae, tum veteris, tum novae, volumina
  duo. 66496
Geographiae vniversae tvm veteris, tvm novae
  absolvtissimvm opus. 66492-66493, 66495
Geographiae universalae, veteries et novae.
  59033
Geographiae veteris tabvlae aliqvot. 66497
Geographic, historical summary. 26969, 101256
Geographica Abrah. Ortelij. 32005, 77901
Geographica historica. 23605
Geographicae enarrationis libri viii. 43822
Geographicae enarrationis libri octo. (66482)-
  (66483), (66485)
Geographicae orbis terrarum veteribus cogniti.
  66498
Geographical account of Upper California.
  25836
Geographical and commercial gazette. 26970
Geographical and comparative list of the birds.
  6265
Geographical and historical description of
  each state and territory. 37429
Geographical and historical description of the
  principal objects of the present war in
  the West-Indies. 26973, 2d note after
  102833
Geographical and historical dictionary of
  America and the West Indies. 683, 95512
Geographical and historical grammar. 20726,
  3d note after 93596
Geographical and historical view of California.
  101210
Geographical and historical view of Texas.
  55319, 99547
Geographical and historical view of the world.
  5338
Geographical & mineralogical notes, to
  accompany Mr. Wyld's map. 105655
Geographical and mineralogical notes to
  accompany Wyld's map. 10004
Geographical and physical account of that
  country. 55251
Geographical and statistical account of the
  province of Louisiana. 42229
Geographical and statistical department. 96481A
Geographical and statistical history of the
  county of Olmstead. 49731
Geographical and statistical history of the
  county of Winnebago. (49664)
Geographical and statistical sketch of . . .
  Wabasha County. (49732)
Geographical and Statistical Society, New York.
  see New York Geographical and
  Statistical Society.
Geographical and statistical view of
  Massachusetts proper. 20073
Geographical and statistical view of the United
  States. 32146, 94232
Geographical and topographical description of
  Wisconsin. 38979
Geographical botany of the United States.
  4232
Geographical catalogue of the mollusca.
  10008, 16575-16576
Geographical catechism of Pennsylvania.
  74156
Geographical chart of the American federal
  republic. 92915
Geographical, commercial, and agricultural
  view. 6007
Geographical, commercial, and historical
  survey. 32147, 106120
Geographical, commercial, and philosophical
  view of the present situation. 104831

Geographical, commercial, and political essays. 26971

Geographical compilations. (17034)

Geographical description, natural and civil history. 94166

Geographical description of all the countries in the known world. 13448

Geographicall [sic] description of all the countries in the known world. (13443)

Geographical description of all the countries in the knowne worlde. 13444

Geographical description of Pennsylvania. 78327

Geographical description of the coasts, harbours, and sea ports. 11030, 27799

Geographical description of the four parts of the world. (5928), 76720

Geographical description of the kingdoms of England, Scotland, and Ireland. (5965)

Geographical description of the state of Louisiana: presenting a view of the soil. 18528

Geographical description of the state of Louisiana, the southern part. 18529

Geographical description of the state; with sketches of its natural history. 4434-4435

Geographical description of the states of Maryland and Delaware. (78328)

Geographical description of the United States. 47430

Geographical description of the United States, with the contiguous British and Spanish possessions. 47431

Geographical description of the western states and territories. 8558

Geographical description of the whole con-tinent of America. 35953

Geographical description of the world. 47437

Geographical description of the world, with a brief account of the several empires, dominions and parts thereof. 47971

Geographical dictionary. 6145

Geographical dictionary. In which are presented the present and antient names. 4930

Geographical dictionary, of all the countries, provinces, remarkable cities, etc., of the world. (26972)

Geographical dictionary of North America and the West Indies. 18692, 18694

Geographical dictionary of the United States of North America. (78329)

Geographical dictionary . . . of the whole world. 6145

Geographical dictionary, or universal gazetteer. 105238

Geographical distribution of animals and plants. 62622

Geographical distribution of consumption in Massachusetts. 19664

Geographical distribution of mammals. 51487

Geographical extracts, forming a general view of earth and nature. 59283

Geographical grammar. 62662

Geographical hand book. 30462

Geographical, historical, and statistical repository. 18530

Geographical, historical and statistical view of the central or middle United States. 94317

Geographical, historical, commercial, and agricultural view of the United States of America. 26974

Geographical, historical, political, philosophical and mechanical essays. Number II. 23176

Geographical, historical, political, philosophical and mechanical essays. The first. 2317

Geographical historie of Africa. 40047

Geographical history of Nova Scotia. (56135), (56137)-(56138)

Geographical keys. 91496

Geographical magazine. (44927)

Geographical memoir upon Upper California. 25837

Geographical narrative, containing a concise description of the several states and provinces of the American continent. 36893

Geographical, natural and civil history of Chili. 49893-49894

Geographical notices of Panama, Nicaragua, &c. 43642

Geographical poem on the state of Vermont. 82749

Geographical question book. 49722

Geographical reader. 49722

Geographical reader, for the Dixie children. 50426

Geographical review. 82832

Geographical sketch of St. Domingo. 13252, 26975, 4th note after 96480

Geographical sketch of that part of North America, called Oregon. 29815, (37261)

Geographical sketch of the state of Georgia. (80814)

Geographical sketches on the western country. 18408

Geographical-spelling-book. 102445-102446

Geographical, statistical and ethical view of the American slaveholders' rebellion. 50966

Geographical, statistical and historical account of Texas. 103114

Geographical survey of Africa. (43643)

Geographical, topographical, and historical view of that country. 10010

Geographical treatise on all within the circuit of the seas. 79350

Geographical view of all the post towns in the United States. 73890

Geographical view of Pennsylvania. 18530

Geographical view of the British possessions. 83617

Geographical view of the British possessions in North America. 83623

Geographical view of the district of Maine. 103306

Geographical view of the province of Upper Canada. 83616, 83618-83622, 83624, 83627

Geographical view of the United States. 26976, 97917

Geographical view of the United States. Embracing their extent and boundaries. 97918

Geograpicis [sic] libris octo orbem totum habitabilem. 66497

Geographicke description of the regions. (47886)

Geographie. 11411, 57457

Geographie ancienne et historique. 85256

Geographie bibliophile. pseud. Martin Hylacomylus Waltzemuller. see Avezac Macaya, Marie Armand Pascal d'.

Geographie, climat et population. 74922

Geographie de l'Amerique. [Par Alexandre de Saillet.] 74968

Geographie de l'Amerique. Par Auguste Jeunesse. 36096

Geographie de l'ile d'Haiti. (1929)

Geographie de Ptoleme. 66508

Geographie de Ptolemee, reproduction photolithographique. 66508
Geographie d'Edrisi. 68443
Geographie du moyen age. (39978)
Geographie du Perou. 59335
Geographie en Estampes. 26977
Geographie generale de l'Amerique. 16930
Geographie, histoire et monuments. 44169
Geographie moderne. 62959
Geographie moderne et universelle. 71868
Geographie, naturgeschichte und topographie von Texas. 37442
Geographie nouiter castigatū & emaculatū additiōibus. 66481
Geographie physique. 46971
Geographie physique de la mer. 46970
Geographie vniverselle. 21482
Geographie universelle, ancienne et moderne. 47870
Geographie universelle de Malte-Brun. 44160
Geographie von Amerika und insbesondere von den Vereinigten Staaten. 29411
Geographisch Handtbuch. 66894
Geographisch-statistische Beschreibung der Argentinischen Republik. 25991
Geographisch-statistische Beschreibung von Britisch Guiana. 77784
Geographisch-statistische Beschreibung von Californien. 30704
Geographisch-statistische Beschreibung von Ober- und Nieder-Peru. 25990
Geograph.-statist.-topographische Beschreibung. (9677)
Geographisch-statisch-topographische Skizze fur Einwanderer und Freunde der Lander und Volkerkunde. 8208
Geograph.-statist.-topographische Skizze fur Einwanderer und Freunde der Lander-und Volkerkunde. 8200
Geographisch-statistische Uebersicht der sammtlichen Hollandischen Besitzungen. 102834
Geographisch-statistische und geschichtliche Beschreibung. 77665
Geographische Belustigungen zur Erlauterung der neuesten Weltgeschichte. 26980
Geographische en historische beschrijving der kusten von Noord-Amerika. 19616, (31357)
Geographische en historische beschryvingh der vier bekende werelds-deelen Europa, Asia, Africa en America. 76722
Geographische landtaffel dess Gebiets des Grossen Torken. 94195
Geographische, natuurkundige en historische berighten. 26978
Geographische Skizzen und Scenen. 38242
Geographische-statistische Beitrage zur kenntniss. 26982
Geographische Tabellen. 5012
Geographische vnd historische Beschreibung. 128, 26981
Geographische und kritische Nachrichten und Anmerkungen. (22570), 22573
Geographische und magnetische Beobachtungen. 25823
Geographische Unterricht uber den Welttheil von Europa. 11656
Geographische Vorstellung eines Globi. 76838
Geographische Wanderungen. 1463
Geographischen Beschreibung der Provinz Pensylvanien. 51690
K. Geographischen Gesellschaft zu London. see Royal Geographical Society, London.
Geographischen Mittheilungen. 71228
Geographischer Anhang. 44996, 89549
Geographischer Anstalt uber wichtige neue Erforschung. 49765

Geographisches Jahrbuch. (26979)
Geographisches Lesebuch fur alle Stande. 52382
Geography anatomiz'd. 27991
Geography and geology of Vermont. 95547
Geography and history of British America. 32347
Geography and history of Lower Canada. 95548
Geography and natural history of Nova Scotia. 18952
Geography and resources of Arizona and Sonora. 51211
Geography [by Busching.] 21748
"Geography" by Daniel Adams. 191
Geography, by R. C. Smith. 83930-83935
Geography [by Sir Richard Phillips.] 99551A
Geography delineated. 10999
Geography, description and resources of central and southern Colorado. (14743)
Geography epitomized. (26983)
Geography epitomized; or a description of the terraqueous globe. 18736
Geography epitomized; or a tour round the world. 18737
Geography for beginners. By J. Russell Smith. 83372
Geography for beginners; or the instructer's [sic] assistant. 104044-104045
Geography for schools, academies, and families. 83936
Geography, history, and resources of the silver regions of North America. 51210
Geography, history, and statistics of America and the West Indies. 10843, (15055)
Geography made easy. 50936
Geography of America and the West Indies. 26984, 41874, w97307
Geography of Boston, County of Suffolk and the adjacent towns. 85488
Geography of British history. 33608
Geography of California for the use of schools. 13262
Geography of Canada. 27322
Geography of Hudson's Bay. 3664, 13833
Geography of Massachusetts. (11118)
Geography of Middlesex County. 11119
Geography of New England. 5936
Geography of New-Hampshire. 11116, 52829
Geography of New Hampshire, with a sketch of its natural history. 101098
Geography of New York state. 83374
Geography of Oregon and California. 28631
Geography of Pennsylvania: containing an account of the history. 96763
Geogfaphy of Pennsylvania for the use of schools. (21738)
Geography of Pottawattamie country. 83649
Geography of South Carolina. 81212
Geography of the British colonies and dependencies. 31640
Geography of the British empire. 38104
Geography of the state of New York. 46766
Geography of the states and territories. 27389
Geography of the United States. 88844
Geography of Vermont, for children. 95551
Geography on the productive system. 83922-83927, 83930-83935, note before 93906
Geography on the productive system for schools. 83927
Geography rectified. 50535
Geography, topography and geology of the shores of Lake Superior. 38672
Geologic reconnaissance in southeastern Seward peninsula. 83721
Geological account of the United States. 47267
Geological and agricultural survey of 100 miles west of Omaha. 1067, (22054)

Geological and agricultural survey of Rensselaer County. 21701, 1st note after 98549

Geological and agricultural survey of the district adjoining the Erie Canal. 21702, (53688), 3d note after 98549

Geological and natural history survey of Minnesota. 49247

Geological and natural history survey of North Carolina. 55620

Geological and phisiological [sic] disquisition. 38866

Geological chart. (36103)

Geological description of the north shore of Lake Superior. 41809

Geological essays. (31008)

Geological evidences of the antiquity of man. 42759

Geological formations of the Burlington limestone. 55337

Geological grammar. 21705

Geological history of Manhattan or New York island. 17326

Geological introduction. 18649

Geological map of the United States. 5808, (44502)

Geological nomenclature for North America, founded upon geological surveys. 21703, 2d note after 98549, 3d note after 103741

Geological observations on coral reefs. 18645

Geological observations on South America. 18646

Geological prodromus. 21703

Geological profile. 21701, 1st note after 98549

Geological ramble. 71255

Geological remarks. 84411

Geological remarks on the maritime parts of the state of New York. 49749

Geological report and description of organic remains. 4257

Geological report by Dr. D. D. Owen. 75789

Geological report . . . by Dr. J. S. Newberry. (34463)

Geological report . . . by G. C. Swallow. 88607

Geological report; by J. S. Newberry. 35308

Geological report (by J. S. Newberry, T. A. Conrad, and E. N. Horsford.) 69946

Geological report . . . By Profs. Wm. F. Roberts and Fred C. Kropff. (71934)

Geological report, by Thomas Antisell. 69946

Geological report, by William P. Blake. 69946

Geological report of an examination made in 1834. 23961

Geological report of Bela Hubbard on survey. 48736

Geological report of Dr. Charles T. Jackson. (71295)

Geological report of lands belonging to the Ridgway Company. (35398)

Geological report of Prof. Henry D. Rogers. 72668

Geological report of the country along the line. 49594

Geological report of the exploration of the Yellowstone and Missouri Rivers. 31004

Geological report of the midland counties of North Carolina. 55616

Geological report of the Potomac Iron Company's property. (64588)

Geological report on the Dauphin and Susquehanna Coal Company's mineral lands. (71931), note after 92907

Geological report on the island of Jamaica. (35584)

Geological report on the Kensington Silver-Lead Mines. 60869

Geological report to the British Association for the Advancement of Science. 72672

Geological report upon the Fourche Cove. 64764

Geological reports, by Dr. C. C. Parry. 22£

Geological reports . . . [by Henry K. Strong. 92912

Geological reports for 1853, 54, 55, 56 [of Canada.] 10546

Geological reports on the location of the Summit Copper Mining Company. 9363£

Geological reports on the Middletown silver-lead mines. 60866

Geological reports on the mineral & timber lands of D. Kingsbury. 58009

Geological researches in China, Mongolia, and Japan. 85072

Geological Society, London. (5358), 18955, 91210

Geological Society of Pennsylvania. 26987, (60117)

Geological structure, organic remains, and mineral resources of Nova Scotia. 189

Geological survey and reports on the propert[of the South Ham Gold and Copper Mining Co. 88130

Geological survey. First and second annual report of progress. 35002

Geological survey in Nova Scotia and Cape Breton. 56187

Geological survey of British Guiana. 77294

Geological survey of California. . . . Geographical catalogue. 16576

Geological survey of California. J. D. Whitr State Geologist. 10007

Geological survey of Canada. Descriptive catalogue of . . . minerals. 26986

Geological survey of Canada. Figures and descriptions of Canadian organic remai⁺ Decade I. 10458

Geological survey of Canada. Figures and descriptions of Canadian organic remai⸱ Decade II. 29805

Geological survey of Canada. Palaeozoic fossils. 5410

Geological survey of Canada. . . . Report o⸲ Dr. T. Sterry Hunt. 33893

Geological survey of Canada. Report of progress, 1842-3 [-1858.] 41809

Geological survey of Canada. Report of progress for the years 1853-54-55-56. 10459

Geological survey of Illinois. 34253

Geological survey [of Indiana.] 34488

Geological survey of Jamaica. (35584)

Geological survey of New York. 1838. 1932

Geological survey of New York. Palaeontolo⸱ 53796

Geological survey of Ohio. 56926

Geological survey of Ohio, its progress in 1869. (56925)

Geological survey of Ohio. Report of progre⸱ in 1870. 56927

Geological survey of the county of Albany. 617, 21710, 26985

Geological survey of the environs of Philade⹊ 97051

Geological survey of the state [of New York. Questions proposed to observers.] 468⸱

Geological survey . . . . Palaeontology. 537⸱

Geological surveys and reports on the property of the Nicolet Mining Co. 552⸱

Geological surveys and reports, . . . w⸱ a statement of the condition. 55407

Geological surveys . . . of the Lennoxville Mining . . . Company. 40037

Geological text-book, prepared for popular lectures on North American geology. 2⸱

Geologie. (5153)

Geologie, mineralogie et botanique. 26330

Geologie du Perou. 17648

Geologie et mineralogie. 98298

Geologie, paleontologie. 57457

Geologie. Voyages geologique dans les republiques de Guatemala et de Salvador. 20542

Geologische Bilder zur Geschichte der Erde und ihrer Bewohner. 9345

Geologischen . . . Urzustand des Erdbodens. 39607

Geology. 69946

Geology and industrial resources of Caligornia. 97652

Geology and metallurgy of the iron ores of Lake Superior. 25247

Geology and mineral resources of the Philippine Islands. 84529

Geology and mineral resources of the Solomon and Casadepaga Quadrangles. 83720

Geology and palaeontology. Geology; by A. H. Worthen. 34253

Geology and palaeontology [of Ohio.] 56928

Geology and physical geography of Brazil. 30714

Geology and recession of the falls. (36213)

Geology. Assistants: Prof. J. D. Whitney, Prof. Leo. Lesquereux, Mr. Henry Englemann. 34253

Geology; by A. H. Worthen. 34253

Geology. By James D. Dana. 18426

Geology, by President E. Hitchcock and Dr. G. C. Shumard. 68476

Geology of Buffalo. 31018

Geology [of Iowa.] (35000)

Geology of Cape May County, New Jersey. 38020

Geology of Georgia. 17036

Geology of New Hampshire. 52833

Geology of New Jersey. 16239, 53123

Geology of New-York. 53790

Geology of North America, by Jules Marcou. 44503

Geology of North America: with two reports on the prairies of Arkansas and Texas. 26988

Geology [of Ohio.] 56928

Geology of Pennsylvania, a government survey. 60119, 72657

Geology of southern California. (1712)

Geology of the county of Cape May. 53116

Geology of the earth. 7049

Geology of the Skykomish Basin, Washington. 84534-84537

Geology of the first geological district [of New York.] 53790

Geology of the voyage of the Beagle. 18645-18646, 18648

Geology of upper Illinois. 80165

Geometrica Euclidis. 74801

Geopp, Charles. 27684

Georg Washington. 101819

Georg Washington. Ein Lebensbild fur Jung und Alt. 77669

Georg Washington's . . . Lebensbeschreibung. 44791

George I, King of Great Britain, 1660-1727. 33686, 99252 see also Great Britain. Sovereigns, etc., 1714-1727 (George I)

George II, King of Great Britain, 1683-1760. (68802), 96544 see also Great Britain. Sovereigns, etc., 1727-1760 (George II)

George III, King of Great Britain, 1738-1820. 451, 19275, 26994, 26996, 26999, 40467, 64572, 88944, 96553, 102499 see also Great Britain. Sovereigns, etc., 1760-1820 (George III)

George III, King of Great Britain, 1738-1820. spurious author 19928, (38916), 67955

George III, King of Great Britain, 1738-1820. spurious defendant 33032

George, A. tr. 51670

George, Mrs. A. Saint. see Saint George, Mrs. A.

George, Cousin. pseud. see Cousin George. pseud.

George, Daniel. 26989

George, John H. 26990

George, Mary Edmond St. see Mary Edmond St. George. sister

George, N. J. T. 26991

George, William. 26992

George (Ship) see May (Ship) in Admiralty

George Alexander Stevens' celebrated lectures on heads. 91500

George Allen, LL. D. 84511

George Allen, the only son. 106141

George B. McClellan as a patriot. 26400

George Beach, and the Northampton town meeting. 4090

George Canning and his times. 90480

George Clinton next president. 17352

George Fox and his first disciples. (33377)

George Fox digg'd out his burrovves. (25355), 25363-(25364), 51773, 104337

George H. Pendleton and the volunteers. 59646

George H. Pendleton, the Copperhead candidate for Vice-President. 59644

George Howard's Esq. Brautfahrt. 64544

George Keith an apostate. 106104

George Keith contradicting himself and his brother Bradford. 59663

George Keith once more brought to the test. 37216, 66738

George Keith varied in fundamentalls. 66740

George Keith's challenge to William Pen and Geor. Whitehead. (37184)

George Keith's eyes opened. 37186

George Keith's fifth narrative. (37191)

George Keith's fourth narrative. (37191)

George Keith's imagined magick of Quakerism confirmed. 103657

George Lunt. 32774

George Mason. 24788

George N. Sanders on the sequences of southern secession. 76385

Geo. P. Rowell & Co.'s American newspaper directory. (47793), 73548, 73551

George P. Rowell & Co's circular to advertisers. 73549

George P. Rowell & Co.'s handbook of news-paper advertising. 73550

George Peabody. A funeral sermon. 29835

George Sandy's journey to the Holy Land. 66686

George Stanley. 26841, note after 90307

George Taletell. pseud. Recreations. see Holmes, Isaac Edward. supposed author

George the Third, his court and family. 26995

George Town, Mass. Indian Conference, 1717. see Massachusetts (Colony) Indian Conference, George Town, 1717.

George Town on Arrowsick Island Aug. 9th, 1717. (15436)-15437, 34654, 80806

George W. Hawes' Indiana state gazetteer. 34535

George W. Hawes' Ohio state gazetteer. 57005

George W. Hawes' state gazetteer and business directory. (37514)

George Washington. 97247

Geo. Washington, a new favourite song. 101815

George Washington Bicentennial Commission. see United States George Washington Bicentennial Commission.

George Washington, crowned by "equality, fraternity, and liberty." 72647

George Washington, le fondateur de la republique. 23800

George Washington, Lierzang. 94163, note after 101819, 3d note after 101888

George Washington, President of the United States. 96605

George Washington, the illustrious owner of Mount Vernon. 101855

George Washington, the most illustrious patiot. 101820

George Washington to the people of the United States. 101599

George Washington University, Washington, D. C. (14860)-14861

George Washington University, Washington, D. C. Enosinian Society. 14862

George Washington University, Washington, D. C. National Medical College. see George Washington University, Washington, D. C. School of Medicine.

George Washington University, Washington, D. C. School of Medicine. 14859, 52006

George Washington's accounts of expenses. 101546A

George Washington's farewel[1] address to the people of the United States. 101565

George Washington's resignation. 101588

George Whitefield; a biography. 4401

George Whitefield; centenary commemoration. 71072

George Wilson and his friend. 104618

Georges, ------ Saint. see Saint-Georges, ---------.

Georgetown, D. C. 74256, 74257, (74270)-74271, 99301, 2d note after 101951

Georgetown, D. C. Charter. 27003-27004

Georgetown, D. C. Committee. 101956

Georgetown, D. C. Lancaster School. 38785

Georgetown, D. C. Monastery of the Visitation. (51839)

Georgetown, D. C. Ordinances, etc. 27003-27004

Georgetown, D. C. Sisters of the Visitation. see Sisters of the Visitation, Georgetown, D. C.

Georgetown, Ky. Georgetown College. see Georgetown College, Georgetown, Ky.

Georgetown, S. C. Citizens. petitioners 47663

Georgetown College, Georgetown, Ky. 27006

Georgetown University. Philodemic Society. Commemoration of the Landing of the Pilgrims of Maryland, 4th, 1855. 11864-11865

Georgi Horni Arca noe sive historia imperiorum et regnorum. 33013

Georgi Horni De originibvs Americanis. 33014-33015

Georgia (Colony) 91305, 91307, 91313, 91315

Georgia (Colony) Agent. 27055, 91307 see also Stephens, Thomas.

Georgia (Colony) Charter. 1069, 12162-12163, (41430), 87376, 94215-94218, 1st note after 99889

Georgia (Colony) General Court and Session of Oyer and Terminer, and General Goal Delivery. Chief Justice. 27041, note after 91992 see also Stokes, Anthony.

Georgia (Colony) General Assembly. 27034

Georgia (Colony) General Assembly. House. 27059

Georgia (Colony) Governor, 1761-1776 (Wright) (27056), 36718 see also Wright, Sir James, Bart., 1714-1785.

Georgia (Colony) Laws, statutes, etc. 39410, 39414, (44475)

Georgia (Colony) Orphan House, Savannah. see Savannah. Bethesda Orpahn House.

Georgia (Colony) Secretary. 27113, 91315 see also Stephens, William, 1671-1753.

Georgia (Colony) Trustees for Establishing the Colony of Georgia. 27008, 27046, 27104, 29673, 50352, 95612

Georgia (Colony) Trustees for Establishing the Colony of Georgia. Common Counil. 91313

Georgia. 27080, 27089, 39144, (49547), 70075 88065, 102963

Georgia. claimant 50934, 104879

Georgia. defendant 11308, 27020, 27048, 27081, 44794-44795, 61206, 90113, 1053

Georiga. Adjutant and Inspector General. 23119, 27094 see also Eustace, Jean Skey.

Georgia. Board of Public Works. 27096

Georgia. Commissariat. 27090

Georgia. Commissioner on Railroads and Canals. 2903

Georgia. Commissioner on Trade With the Indians. 15243, 37838 see also King, Thomas Butler, 1800-1864.

Georgia. Commissioners on Lands Claimed b the State. 27072, 95390

Georgia. Comptroller-General. 27035, 27098

Georgia. Constitution. 1269, 1271, 2071, 5316, 6360, 16086-16090, 16092, 16097, 16099-16103, 16107, 16113, 16118-16120 16133, (19476), 25790, 27032-27033, 27060, 33137, (47188), 59771, (66397), 100342, 104198

Georgia. Convention, 1788. 22233, note after 106022

Georgia. Convention, 1821. 27078

Georgia. Convention, Milledgeville, 1850. 27036

Georgia. Convention, Milledgeville and Savannah, 1861. (27061)

Georgia. Convention, Milledgeville, 1865. 27060

Georgia. Council. 43331

Georgia. General Assembly. 15841, 27030, 27038, 27070-(27071), 27102-27103, 271 34655, 43331, 44029, 46056, 60247, 64808, 69903

Georgia. General Assembly. petitioners 69

Georgia. General Assembly. Committee on Cherokee Lands. 34655

Georgia. General Assembly. Committee on Powers of the General Government and Rights of the State. 64808

Georgia. General Assembly. Joint Committe to Investigate the Condition of the Georgia Penitentiary. 27019

Georgia. General Assembly. Portion of the Members. 27093, 27102, 87436, 87443

Georgia. General Assembly. House of Representatives. 27057-27058, 27107

Georgia. General Assembly. Senate. 27015 27062

Georgia. Geological and Agricultural Survey 17036

Georgia. Governor, 1798-1801 (Jackson) 102 see also Jackson, James, 1757-1806.

Georgia. Governor, 1823-1827 (Troup) 2707 27076, 27080 see also Troup, George Michael, 1780-1856.

Georgia. Governor, 1827-1829 (Forsyth) 64 see also Forsyth, John, 1780-1841.

Georgia. Governor, 1835-1837 (Schley) 27028 34867 see also Schley, William, 1756-18

Georgia. Governor, 1839-1843 (McDonald) 78 see also McDonald, Charles James, 1793-1860.

Georgia, Governor, 1851-1853 (Cobb) 32842, 87548 see also Cobb, Howell, 1815-1868.

Georgia. Governor, 1857-1865 (J. E. Brown) 18841, (27053), (27075), 27110, 33150, 78765 see also Brown, Joseph Emperson, 1821-1894.

Georgia. Governor, 1872-1876 (Smith) 82795 see also Smith, James Milton, 1823-1890.

Georgia. Laws, statutes, etc. 2903, 13574, 13842, 23765, 25150, 25197, (27009)-27012, 27026, 27029, 27030, 27038, 27039, 27040, 27054, 27060, (27061), 27064, 27083, 27088-27089, 27095, 38703, 39414, (44475), 52051, 61206, 69760, 70820-70821, 77652, 82438, 87538, 88054, 89066, note after 106003

Georgia. Penitentiary. 27099

Georgia. Quartermaster's Department. 27090

Georgia. State Library. 27023

Georgia. Supreme Court. 18815, 27020

Georgia. Treasurer. (27101)

Georgia. University. Library. 27021, 27114

Georgia, a poem. To which are added, other metrical compositions. 9087

Georgia. A poem. Tomo chachi. An ode. 27047, note after 102702

Georgia again! 23873

Georgia against Florida. 27048

Georgia almanac, for . . . 1834. (28805)

Georgia analytical repository. 27059

Georgia and Carolina almanac. 27050

Georgia and Ohio again. 91256

Georgia and the Supreme Court. 105321

Georgia argus. 102473

Georgia Association. see Baptists. Georgia. Georgia Association.

Georgia bequest. (69545)

Georgia book, in warp and woof. 27063

Georgia Female College, Macon, Ga. see Wesleyan College, Macon, Ga.

Georgia gazette. 106383

Georgia historical collections. see Georgia Historical Society collections.

Georgia historical quarterly. 83978

Georgia Historical Society. (1397A), (22280), 27027, 27031, 27079, 38978, 39327, 45000-45001, (45003), 50352, (56847), 87900, 91305, 91316, 91572, 94215, 94218, 3d note after 106134

Georgia Historical Society collections. (1397A), 27079, 39327, 45000-45001, (45003), 50352, 91305, 91316, 91572, 3d note after 106134

Georgia home gazette. 88340

Georgia huntsman. pseud. Georgia bequest. see Rembert, W. R.

Georgia illustrated. (70963)

Georgia justice. 27051

Georgia lands occupied by the Cherokee Indians. 34655

Georgia Loyalists. claimants see American Loyalists. claimants

Georgia Mississippi Company. 27054, (27112), note after 90859, 1st-2d notes after 106003

Georgia Mississippi Company. Charter. 27054, 1st note after 106003

Georgia Mississippi Company. Directors. 27054, 1st note after 106003

Georgia Rail Road and Banking Company. Cashier. 95573

Georgia Rail Road and Banking Company. Chief Engineer and General Agent. 95573 see also Thomson, J. Edwar.

Georgia Relief and Hospital Association. 27100

Georgia republican. pseud. Southern question. 88453

Georgia republican. 27052

Georgia republican extra. 27052

Georgia scenes, characters, incidents, &c. 41936

Georgia sketches. 36382

Georgia spec; or, land in the moon. 97618

Georgia speculation unveiled; in two numbers. 5593

Georgia speculations unveiled. In two parts. 5594

Georgia State Association of the Southern and Western States Reform Medical Association. see Southern and Western States Reform Medical Association. Georgia State Association.

Georgia Teachers' Society. see Teachers' Society of Georgia.

Georgian. pseud. Remarks on a volunteer navy. 69406

Georgian Bay canal. 45475

Georgian era. 27115

Georgian Orphan House destroyed. 36234

Georgia's record in the revolution of 1861. 24969

Georgical dictionary. 19056

Georgick papers for 1809. (45896)

Georgii Hornii De originibus Americanis libri quatuor. 33015

Georgii Rithaymeri De orbis terrarvm sitv compendium. 71582

Georgii Washingtonis vita. 38806

Georgivs Interianvs, Aldo Ro. S. 67736

Gepaste aanspraak aan't volt van Nederland. 106045

Geplaagde Hollander of de lastige nabuur. 77513

Geral-Milco. 59278

Gerano, -------. 27117

Gerapporteerde concept der Heeren Gecommitteerden. 69543, 1st note after 102911

Gerard, -----. 62173

Gerard, F. C. tr. 10295, 77895-77896

Gerard, G. 27118

Gerard, James Watson, 1823-1900. 1679, 27119, 86564

Gerard de Braham, William. see Brahm, John Gerar William de.

Gerard de Rayneval, J. M. see Rayneval, J. M. Gerard de.

Gerard Mercator. Sa vie et ses oeuvres. 67432

Gerardi Mercatoris Atlas sivi cosmographicae meditationes. (47881)-47882

Gerardi Mercatoris Rvpelmvndani in tabulas Ptolemaicas a se delineatas annotationes. 66497

Gerber, Henrique. 27121

Gerbier, Balthazar, Baron Douvily. see Gerbier, Sir Balthazar, 1592?-1667.

Gerbier, Sir Balthazar, 1592?-1667. 27122-27132, (37674), 56682, 86845, 1st note after 93596

Gerdart, E. V. (27935)

Geree, John. 80199-80200

Gereformeerden Gemeenten in Pensylvanien. see Reformed Church in the U. S.

Gerhard, Benjamin. 18313

Gerhard, Frederick. 26820, 27133-27134

Geri, Andrea. tr. 95146

Gerin, Elzear. 27136

Gerin-Lajoie, Antoine, 1824-1882. 10455, (12573), 27137, (41510)

Gerke, Heinrich Christian. 27138
Gerling, C. L. 27256
Germ of severe ethical analysis. 27139
Germain, Lord George. see Sackville,
George Sackville Germain, 1st Viscount,
1716-1785.
Germain-Leduc, ------- St. see Saint-
Germain-Leduc, -------.
German airs with English words. 86924
German-American Citizens, New York. see
New York (City) German-American
Citizens.
German Charitable Society's lottery, on Petty's
Island. (27146)
German colony and Lutheran Church in Maine.
(63681)
German commercial gazette. (65339)
German Conversations-Lexicon. 84062
German Democratic Central Club, New York.
Special Committee. 54229
German Democratic Union Party. New York.
New York City. General Committee.
Conference Committee. 54229
German emigrant. 6176, note after 92721
German, English and American Ministers at
Berlin, Germany. 41188
German Evangelical Lutheran Ministerium of
Pennsylvania. see Evangelical Lutheran
Ministerium of Pennsylvania and Adjoining
States.
German Evangelical Lutheran Zion's Church,
Boston. see Boston. German
Evangelical Lutheran Zion's Church.
German freeholder. pseud. German freeholder
to his countrymen. 27147, 61696
German freeholder to his countrymen. 27147,
61696
German in America. (6131)
German letter. 32947, 2d note after 102507
German Lutheran Church, Philadelphia. see
Philadelphia. German Lutheran Church.
German Lutheran Churches, New York. see
United German Lutheran Churches in
New York City.
German Protestant Churches. see United
Brethren.
German psalmody. 66456
German Reformed Church, Baltimore. see
Baltimore. German Reformed Church.
German Reformed Church, in the United States
Army. 27150
German Reformed Church in the United States
of America. see Reformed Church in
the U. S.
German Reformed Congregation, Philadelphia.
see Philadelphia. German Reformed
Congregation.
German sentiment on the Sunday question.
93745
German Society Contributing to the Relief of
Distressed Germans in Pennsylvania.
Library. 27151
German Society of Pennsylvania. see Deutsche
Gesellschaft von Pennsylvanien,
Philadelphia.
German Society of the City of New York.
27152, (54292)
German Society of the City of New York.
Charter. 27152, (54292)
German story. 87170, 87172
Germaniae ex variis scriptoribus perbruis
explcatio. 63016-(63019)
Germaniae inferioris historiae et loca aliquot
declarata. (63019)
Germanicus. pseud. Germanicus. see
Randolph, Edmund.

Germanicus. pseud. Getreue Warnung gegen
die Lockvogel. see Weiss, Lewis.
supposed author
Germanicus. 67812
Germann, W. 78014
Germantown, Pa. American Classical and
Military Academy, Mount Airy. see
American Classical and Military Academy
Mount Airy, Pa.
Germantown, Pa. Contributors for Erecting
and Establishing a School-House and
School. 27156
Germantown, Pa. Dritten Confernz der
Evangelischen Religionen Teutscher
Nation in Pennsylvania, 1742. see Unite
Brethren. Pennsylvania.
Germantown, Pa. Friends' School. see
Friends' School, Germantown, Pa.
Germantown, Pa. Gemeine Gottes im Geist
Funften Versammlung, 1742. see
Congregation of God in the Spirit.
Germantown, Pa. Germantown Club. see
Germantown Club, Germantown, Pa.
Germantown, Pa. Lyceum, Mount Airy. see
Mount Airy Lyceum, Mount Airy, Pa.
Germantown, Pa. Mount Airy Agricultural
Institute. see Mount Airy Agricultural
Institute, Germantown, Pa.
Germantown, Pa. Vierte General-Versammlun
der Kirche Gottes aus allen Evangelische
Religionen in Pennsylvania, 1742. see
United Brethren. Pennsylvania.
Germantown, Pa. Young Men's Christian
Association. see Young Men's Christian
Association, Germantown, Pa.
Germantown: a tale of the Quaker city during
the revolution. 27159
Germantown Academy, Philadelphia. Centennia
Celebration, 1860. 27155
Germantown Club, Germantown, Pa. 61699
Germantown Blues. see Pennsylvania. Militia
Germantown Blues.
Germantown Society for Promoting Domestic
Manufactures. 27157
Germany. Treaties, etc. 51311
Germany; . . . with a preliminary view of the
political condition. 43284
Germs of growth. 21839
Gernsbach, Weil von. 78050
Gerrarld, Joseph. 27164
Gerrat, Thomas. defendant 6326, 1st note
after 96956, 1st note after 97284
Gerrish, J. 3599, 27165, 90592
Gerrish, Joseph. 72691
Gerrish, Martha. (1827), 27166
Gerrish (S.) firm publisher 94107
Gerrish and Barrell. firm publishers 3599
Gerrit Smith and the Vigilant Association of
the City of New York. 82609
Gerrit Smith land auction. 82610
Gerrit Smith land auction. Three quarters of
a million acres. (82611)
Gerrit Smith on McClellan's nomination and
acceptance. 82612-82613
Gerrit Smith on the bailing of Jefferson Davis
82614
Gerrit Smith on the Fort Pillow and Plymouth
massacre. 82615
Gerrit Smith on the presidential question.
82616
Gerrit Smith to C. P. Kirkland. 82517
Gerrit Smith to Doctor Cheever. 82618
Gerrit Smith to Edwin Croswell. 82619
Gerrit Smith to General Lee. 82620
Gerrit Smith to George Thompson. 82621
Gerrit Smith to Governor Seymour. 82622

Gerrit Smith to his constituents. 82623
Gerrit Smith to Horace Greeley. 82624
Gerrit Smith to John A. Gurley. 82625
Gerrit Smith to John Stuart Mill. (82671)
Gerrit Smith to Mr. Garrison. 82626
Gerrit Smith to Montgomery Blair. 82627
Gerrit Smith to Owen Lovejoy. 82628
Gerrit Smith to President Grant. 82629
Gerrit Smith to Professor Lewis. 82648
Gerrit Smith to Senator Sumner. 82630
Gerrit Smith to Thaddeus Stevens. 82631
Gerrit Smith to the rank and file of the
    Democratic Party. 82632
Gerrit Smith to William Lloyd Garrison.
    82633
Gerritsz, Hessel. 5905, 33489-33491, 52359,
    67355, 68346
Gerry, Elbridge, 1744-1814. 2411, 2446,
    44154, 46128, 56809, 99303
    see also Massachusetts. Governor,
    1810-1812 (Gerry)   U. S. Legation.
    France.
Gerry, Elbridge, 1744-1814. incorrectly
    supposed author 56539, note after
    101486
Gerry, Elbridge Thomas, 1837-1927.
    reporter (79837)
Gersdorf, B. de. ed. 66957
Gersen, Giovanni. 10656
Gershom. pseud. Emigration for the million.
    27167
Gerson, -------. ed. 4849
Gerson, Juan. 27168
Gerstacker, Friedrich, 1816-1872. 8353,
    10017, 20130, 27169-27194, (31242),
    41397, 69143, 2d note after 99534,
    1st note after 100641, 102502
Gerstacker's travels. 27179
Gerstner, Clara (von Epplen Hartenstein) von.
    27195
Gerstner, Franz Anton, Ritter von. 27195-
    (27197)
Gertrude of Wyoming. 31719, 29150-29151
Gertrude of Wyoming; a Pennsylvanian tale.
    10268
Gertrude of Wyoming; or, the Pennsylvanian
    cottage. 10269
Gertrudes Magna, Francisco de Paula de
    Sancta. 27198-27200
Gertrudis, Francisco Santa. see Santa
    Gertrudis, Francisco.
Gertrudis, Jose Agustin Santa. see Santa
    Gertrudis, Jose Agustin.
Gervais, -------. petitioner (2765), 75163,
    99242
Gervinus, G. G. ed. 25129, (27201)-27203
Gervoy, -----. 84478
Gesammelt auf einer siebenmonatlichen Tour
    durch die Vereinigten Staaten von Nord-
    Amerika. 49923
Gesammelte Aktenstucke des Vereins zum
    Schutze Deutscher Einwanderer in Texas.
    (554), (27204), 95131
Gesammelte Erzahlungen. 27194
Gesammlete [sic] Nachrichten von den
    Engelischen Kolonien. 27205
Gesammelte Romane. 16564
Gesammelte Werke von Charles Sealsfield.
    64541
Gesammten Vereinigten Staaten von Nord-
    Amerika. (24160)
Geschaft, Verkehr und Arbeit in den
    Vereinigten Staaten. (25663)
Geschichte Allgemeine, du Lander und Volker
    von America. 27206
Geschichte aus dem Kriege. 25835
Geschichte aus dem letzten Amerikanisch-
    Engelischen Kriege. 39869, 64546-64547

Geschichte aus dem Sudamerkianischen
    Revolutionskriege. 100784
Geschichte aus Pensylvanien. 5555
Geschichte der Abiponer. 20413
Geschichte der Amerikanischen Eichen. 48692
Geschichte der Amerikanischen Indianer. 156
Geschichte der Amerikanischen Revolution,
    aus den Acten des Congresses. 67688
Geschichte der Amerikanischen Revolution von
    Georg Bancroft. 3125
Geschichte der Amerikanischen Urreligionen.
    51290
Geschichte der Aufhebung der Skalverei. 70291
Geschichte der Befreiung Nord-Amerika's.
    104596
Geschichte der Besitzungen und Handlung der
    Europaer in Beyden Indien. 68115
Geschichte der Buchdruckerkunst in Meklenburg.
    99334
Geschichte der Christlichen Ansiedler von
    Neu-England. 78976
Geschichte der Colonisation Amerika's. 38277
Geschichte der Colonisation von Neu-England.
    72190, 2d note after 94271
Geschichte der Democratie in dern Vereinigten
    Staaten. 33651
Geschichte der Deutschen 18. Band. 89758
Geschichte der Deutschen Einwanderung in
    Amerika. 37094
Geschichte der Einfuhrung der Sclaverei in
    Amerika. 22782
Geschichte der Englischen Kolonien in
    Nordamerika. 9288, 27209, 32162
Geschichte der Entdeckung Amerika's von
    Columbus bis Franklin. (38213)
Geschichte der Entdeckung und Eroberung
    Peru. 105720
Geschichte der Entdeckung und Eroberung von
    Mexico. (29496)
Geschichte der Entdeckung von Amerika.
    27210, 51555
Geschichte der Entdeckungen und Schiffahrten
    im Norden. 25136
Geschichte der Erfindung, Construktion und
    Fabrikation derselben. 18666
Geschichte der Eroberung Siberiens und des
    Handels. 17311
Geschichte der Eroberung von Florida. 98746
Geschichte der Eroberung von Chili. (49891)
Geschichte der Eroberung von Mexico. 65271
Geschichte der Eroberung von Peru. 65278
Geschichte der Errichtung und des Handels.
    27211
Geschichte der Europaer in Nordamerica.
    89757
Geschichte der Europaischen. 27212
Geschichte der Expedition des Generals Mina
    nach Mexiko 1816. 72206
Geschichte der Flibustier. 1904
Geschichte der Frau von Walwille &c. 101130
Geschichte der Gefangnissreform. 4376
Geschichte der geographischen Entdeckungreisen
    zu Wasser und zu Lande. 104703
Geschichte der grossen Rebellion in den
    Vereinigten Staaten. (28483)
Geschichte der grossen Verschworung. 37118
Geschichte der Insel Dominica. 2345
Geschichte der Insel Hayti. 30219
Geschichte der Insel Hayti oder St. Domingo.
    67532
Geschichte der Insel Hayti und ihres
    Negerstaats. 36655
Geschichte der Katholischen Missionen.
    80013
Geschichte der Kolonisirung der Freyen
    Staaten der Alterthums. 27217
Geschichte der Kriege in und ausser Europa.
    27213

Geschichte und Organization des Katholischen Instituts in Cincinnati, O. 32110

Geschichte und Wesen der Klopfenden Geister. 89424

Geschichte und Zustande der Deutschen in Amerika. 41827

Geschichte von Amerika. 71998

Geschichte von Amerika von dessen Entdeckung. (74384)

Geschichte von Brasilien. Von Dr. Ernst Munch. 51303

Geschichte von Brazilien [von Heinrich Handelmann.] 1715, 30218

Geschichte von Columbia. 51304

Geschichte von dem Ursprung, Zunehmen und Fortgang des Christlichen Volcks. (79616)

Geschichte von der Eroberung Mexico. 86493

Geschichte von Mexico. 13522

Geschichte von der Marterwoche, Auferstehung und Hemmelfahrt unsers Herrn und Heilandes Jesu Christ. 2098, 24423

Geschichte von Paraguay. (22821)

Geschichte von Paraguay und dem Missions-werke der Jesuiten in diesen Lande. 12132

Geschichten aus der Geisterwelt. 4101

Geschichtliche Entwickelung der Nord-Amerikanischen Union. 51715

Geschichtlicher Beweis. 85107

Geschichts-Bibliothek fur's Volk. 25524

Geschichts-Erzahlung. 67632

Geschichts-Repetition. 37164

Geschichtsdrama in drei Theilen. (73877)

Geschied- en aardrijkskundige beschrijving. 6447

Geschied- en handel-kundig tafereel van de Bat. West-Indische Colonien. (27218), 40088, 6th note after 93855

Geschiedenis der Kolonie van Suriname. (40087), 3d note after 93855, 7th note after 93855

Geschiedenis der matigheids-gezelschappen in de Vereenigde Staten van Amerika. 2787

Geschiedenis der Nederlanders buiten Europa. 36992

Geschiedenis der Nederlandsche volkplantingen in Noord-Amerika. 68645

Geschiedenis der scheepvaart in den Atlantischen Ocean. 19793A

Geschiedenis der Staathuishoudkunde in Nederland. (68646), note before 98186

Geschiedenis der Verovering van Peru. 65279

Geschiedenis uit Pensylvanie. 5552

Geschiedenis van Amerika. 71999

Geschiedenis van de Bezittingen en den Koophandel der Europeanen in de Beide Indien. (68114), 68116

Geschiedenis van de Noord-Amerikaansche Staats-omwenteling. 67689

Geschiedenis van de Vereenigde Staaten van Noord Amerika. 31778

Geschiedenis van eergisteren, uit het Maleitsche vertaald. 98510

Geschiedenis van het geschil tusschen Groote-Britannie en Amerika. 244

Geschiedenis van het Nederlandsche zeewezen. 36635

Geschiedkundig aanteekening rakende proeven van Europesche kolonisatie in Suriname. (67411)

Geschiedkundige beschouwing van St. Domingo. (21897)

Geschiedkundige beschouwing van de walvisch-visscherij. 7399

Geschildert auf einer Untersuchungs-Expedition. 90373

Geschildert in Beziehung auf siene geographischen, socialen und ubrigen Verhaltnisse. 86505

Geschildert von einem Reisen. 16488

Geschillen der Engelschen met hinne volkplantingen in America. (27219), 84662

Geschwinde Rechner, oder das Handlers rutzlicher Gehulfe. 27220

Gesellschaft. 85371

Gesellschaft Deutscher Naturforscher und Aerzte. 37105

Gesellschaft fur Anthropologie, Ethnologie und Urgeschichte, Frankfurt a. M. see Frankfurter Gesellschaft fur Anthropologie, Ethnologie und Urgeschichte.

Gesellschaft fur die Deutsch-Evangelische Mission in Amerika, Berlin. see Berliner Gesellschaft fur die Deutsch-Evangelische Mission in Amerika.

Gesellschafft[sic] Jesu bisz zur Vergiessung ihres Blutes. 94331

Gesellschaft zur Verbreitung des Glaubens, Koln. 1579A

Gesellschaft zur Verbreitung Politischer Kenntnisse. see Society for the Diffusion of Political Knowledge, New York.

Gesellschaftsleven und Sitten in der Vereinigten Staaten von Amerika. 105591

Gesenius. 102370

Gesner, Abraham. 27221-27226, 52548

Gesner, George Welten. 27224

Gesner, Konrad, 1516-1565. 27227-27228, (40046)

Gesprach der wandlenden Seelen mit Adam, Noah und Simon Cleophas. 77470

Gessner, L. 27229

Gest, ----. (45494)

Gesta Anglo-Americana scilicet et progymnas-mata. 23964, 80733

Gesta proxime per Portugalenses in India. 99335

Gestandnisse einer Erben. 22845

Gest's anti-masonic almanac. (45494)

Gesuita. pseud. Lettera. 71553

Gesuitas quitados y restituidos al mundo. 76219

Getino, Luis G. Alonso. ed. 100622

Getreue Warnung gegen die Lockvogel. 102512

Getreuester und zuverlassigster Wegweiser und Rathgeber. 68523

Getrou verhaal van den waren toestant der meest herderloze gemeentens in Pensylvanien. (77643)

Getrouw vervaal van de opkomst en tegenwoord. toestand der zo genaamde Methodisten in Engeland. 27230

Getrouwe beschryving de wilden in Noord Amerika. 102511

Getsinvsidv nunadvnelitolvi taline digaleyvtanvhi. 12433

Getter, Charles. defendant 96870

Gettysburg, Pa. Monument. Dedication exercises, 1869. 51019

Gettysburg, Pa. National Cemetery. 23263 see also Soldiers' National Cemetery Associa-tion.

Gettysburg, Pa. National Cemetery. Commis-sioners. see Soldiers' National Cemetery Association. Board of Commissioners.

Gettyburg, Pa. National Cemetery. Dedication Ceremonies, 1863. 23263

Gettysburg, Pa. Pennsylvania College. see Pennsylvania College, Gettysburg, Pa.

Gibson, William, 1788-1868. 4107, (27323), 59151

Gibson & Co. firm auctioneers 66731

Gibson Association of Vermont. (82411)
see also Acting Gibson Association of Vermont.

Gibson Division, no. 21, Dorchester, Mass.
see Sons of Temperance of North America. Massachusetts. Gibson Division, no. 21, Dorchester.

Gibson's guide and directory of the state of Louisiana. 27317

Gibstone, Henri. 27324

Giddinge, George P. 27325

Giddinge, J. R. see Giddings, Joshua Reed, 1795-1864.

Giddings, Joshua Reed, 1795-1864. 3401, 27326-27329

Giddings, Joshua Reed, 1795-1864. supposed author 71381

Giddings, L. 27330, 81574

Giddins, Edward. 27331-27332, (52654), 60301

Giebel, C. 9352

Giesecke, Sir Charles Lewis, 1761-1833. 57576

Giesy, Samuel H. 27333

Gifford, A. (53102), 53131

Gifford, A. supposed author 82023

Gifford, Andrew. ed. 103510

Gifford, Andrew. defendant 96832

Gifford, C. H. 27334

Gifford, George. 27335

Gifford, John. 27336

Gifford, S. N. 21493, 38836, 1st note after 95377

Gift: a tale of the Washington Soldiers' and Sailors' Orphans' Fair. 19837

Gift book for all seasons. 50136

Gift book of American melodies. 50820

Gift for a friend. 85564

Gift for all seasons. 39254

Gift of innocence and beauty. 85568

Gift for scribblers. 85432

Gift for the children of sorrow. 71140-(71141)

Gift for the people. 52038

Gift of friendship. 84139

Gift of friendship, or token of remembrance for 1848. 84143

Gift of gifts. 32848

Gift of the Holy Ghost. 89369

Gifts of the spirit of ministers. 12331

Gigantologia Spagnola vendicata dal M. R. P. Fr. Giuseppe Torrubia. 96310

Gigault de la Bedolliere, Emile. see La Bedolliere, Emile Gigault de.

Giguet, --------. (1534), (27337)

Gignoux, Regis. 100745

Gihon, John H. 27338, 87268

Gijon y Leon, Thomas de. 27339, 27514

Gijsbert, --------. 98973

Gil, Francisco. 27340

Gil, Manuel. 56746

Gil de Gama, Leonarda. 27342

Gil de Jaz, Isid. 27341

Gil Gelpi y Ferro, --------. 27343

Gil Ramirez, Joseph, see Ramirez, Joseph Gil.

Gil y Garces, Martin. 27344, 48807

Gil Blas. 101866

Gil-Blas en Californie. (21180A)

Gil Blas in California. 21181

Gil Gomez el insurgenta. (19975)

Gilaire, Isidore Geoffroy Saint. see Saint-Gilaire, Isidore Geoffroy.

Gilbart, James William. 27345

Gilbert, ------, fl. 1717. 75095

Gilbert, A. G. (27346)

Gilbert, Amos. (25708), 27348

Gilbert, B. 66686

Gilbert, Benjamin. 27348, 42165, note before 101219-101219

Gilbert, Benjamin J. 18632, 1st note after 97087, 2d note after 103214 see also Hanover, N. H. Congregational Church. Committee.

Gilbert, C. N. P. (27350)

Gilbert, Daniel. 105425 see also Democratic Party. Massachusetts. Worcester County. Convention, Worcester, 1812. Secretary.

Gilbert, E. W. ed. 65203

Gilbert, F. (27349)

Gilbert, F. illus. 17936

Gilbert, Sir Humphrey, 1539?-1583. 27351, (29594), 82979

Gilbert, John. illus. 41908-(41909), 41921-41922, 92495

Gilbert, John, Apb. of York, 1693-1761. (27352)

Gilbert, Joseph. cartographer 16277, 35954, (35867), (40141), (55557)

Gilbert, Joseph. 35953-35954, 35962, 35966

Gilbert, Lyman. 27353

Gilbert, Pedro. defendant see Gibert, Pedro. defendant

Gilbert, R. 27354

Gilbert, Thomas. 94806

Gilbert, W. G. 54699

Gilbert, William, 1540-1603. 27356

Gilbert, William, fl. 1796. 27355, 101555

Gilbert against Tennent. 30172, 62419, 94687

Gilbert family. 101219

Gilbert Tennent, harmonius. 94687

Gilberti, Maturino. 27357-27361, 46909, 47342, note just before (71416)

Gilberti Colchestrensis De magnete magneticisque corporibus. 27356

Gilchrist, Adam. 53473, 54042, 83604

Gilchrist, R. B. 85298

Gilchrist, R. C. 15271, 27362

Gilde von Rarop, Symon. see Rarop, Symon Gilde von.

Gildemeister, Charles. 11090

Gildemeister, J. C. F. 27363

Gildersleeve, Mrs. C. H. (32712)

Gildon, Charles, 1665-1724. 4370, 27364

Gilds naar California. 10005

Gilead. 82973

Giles, Amos. plaintiff 12397, 2d note after 97117

Giles, Charles, 1783-1867. 27365-(27366)

Giles, Chauncey. 27367

Giles, J. A. 27368

Giles, Joel. 27369

Giles, John. Memoirs of odd adventures. see Gyles, John, 1678?-1755.

Giles, John, 1755?-1824. 27371

Giles, John Eustace. 21427

Giles, Tomas Suarez de. see Suarez de Giles, Tomas.

Giles, William Branch, 1762-1830. 27372-27377, (56531), 66513), 96015, 100506

Giles, William Fell. 27378, (45211A)

Giles Homespun. pseud. see Homespun, Giles. pseud.

Gilham, W. 27379-27380

Gilij, Filippo Salvadore. see Gilius, Filippo Salvadore.

Gilius, Filippo Salvadore. 27381-27382, 51480, (51482), 99777

Gill, --------, fl. 1748. 101877

Gill, -------, fl. 1780. 86743

Gill, -------, fl. 1852. 20395

Gill, Edward H. 92814, 92816

Gill, John. 27383 see also Bucks County, Pa. Sub-Lieutenant.
Gill, John, 1697-1771. 13350
Gill, Julia. 27387
Gill, Moses. 85864
Gill, Obahiah. 27384, 46517
Gill, R. W. 45078
Gill, Sarah (Prince) 65590, 65594
Gill, Theodore. 82810
Gill, Theodore Nicholas. (27385)-27386
Gill. firm publishers see Edes & Gill. firm publishers
Gillam, Benjamin. 62743
Gillam, Robert. 93598
Gillam Phillips. 92694
Gillandet, -------. illus. 27415
Gilleland, James C. (17904), 27388-27389
Gillelen, F. M. L. 27390
Gilles Gogo. pseud. Olla podrida. see Masson, E.
Gillespie, Alexander. 27391-27393
Gillespie, George. supposed author note before 17046-17046, 2d note after 103852
Gillespie, George L. 84774
Gillespie, Leonard. 27394-27395
Gillespie, William W. 90117
Gillespy, Edward. 27396, 79743
Gillespy, George. 27397
Gillet, -------, fl. 1761. 94390
Gillet, Eliphalet, 1768-1848. 27398-27401
Gillet, Ransom Hooker, 1800-1876. 27402-27403, 96726 see also U.S. Commissioner to the New York Indians.
Gillett, -------, fl. 1793. 28884
Gillett, Eliphalet. see Gillet, Eliphalet, 1768-1848.
Gillett, Ezra Hall, 1823-1875. 12365, 27404
Gillett, Francis. 27405
Gillett, T. S. 53684, 64281
Gillette, A. H. (36270)
Gillette, Abram Dunn, 1807-1882. 27406-27407, 27410, (33170)
Gillette, Charles. 24234, 27408, 28703
Gillette, Francis, 1807-1879. 27409
Gillette, U. B. 27410
Gilley, George. defendant 89626
Gilley, William B. (27411), 57175, 80561
Gilliam, Albert M. (27412)
Gillian, and other poems. 74535
Gillies, John. 27413-27415, 103579, 103611
Gillies, Mary. (27416)
Gilliland, Lyle W. 64386 see also Portland, Oregon. Librarian.
Gilliland, William. 27417
Gillingham. firm see White and Gillingham. firm
Gilliss, James Melville, 1811-1865. 2259, 27256, 27418-27419, 83001, 85072
Gillmor, William. supposed author 89473
Gillmore, Parker. 27420-27421
Gillmore, Q. A. (27422)-27424
Gillmore, Robert H. 27425
Gillpatrick, James. (27426)
Gilly, Matth. Blanc. see Blanc-Gilly, Matth.
Gilman, Arthur. 27427-27428
Gilman, Carolina (Howard) 1794-1888. 27429-27431, 38923, 39859, 57814, 58102, 68397, 85307, 88483, 1st note after 95662, 2d note after 102991, 104023
Gilman, Daniel Coit, 1831-1908. 27432-27433, 54476
Gilman, John Taylor, 1753-1828. 33150, 52896 see also New Hampshire. Governor, 1813-1816 (Gilman)
Gilman, Samuel, 1791-1858. 27429, 27434-(27326), 39777, 47564

Gilman, Tristram. 27437
Gilman, W. S. ed. 2d note before 99889
Gilman, Winthrop S. defendant 27438, 41268, note after 97069
Gilmer, Francis W. (27439)
Gilmer, George R. (27440)
Gilmer, John Adams, 1805-1868. 27441
Gilmer, John H. 27442-27444
Gilmor, Harry. 27445
Gilmore, J. H. 27446
Gilmore, James R. (23026), 27447-(27453), 51623, 68322
Gilmore, Joseph Albree, 1811-1867. 82332 see also New Hampshire. Governor, 1863-1865 (Gilmore)
Gilmore, Patrick S. 27454
Gilmore & Brown. firm see Chipman, Hosmer and Co. firm
Gilpin, Henry Dilworth, 1805-1860 1183, 27455-27458, 43716, 55831, 57405
Gilpin, Henry Dilworth, 1805-1860. petitioner 3189
Gilpin, Mrs Henry D. 27459
Gilpin, J. tr. 24725
Gilpin, J. Bernard. 27460
Gilpin, Johnny. pseud. Toddy-mill. 96098
Gilpin, Joshua. 12494, 27461-27463
Gilpin, Richard A. petitioner 61819
Gilpin, Thomas, 1776-1853. 27464-27466, 55831, 59749
Gilpin, William, 1724-1804. 27467
Gilpin, William, 1813-1894. (27468)-27469
Gimber, -------. illus. 46836
Gimbrede, J. N. illus. 57316
Gimenez Frias, Josef Antonio. see Ximenez y Frias, Jose Antonio.
Ginammi, Marco. tr. 11245-11248
Ginger-snaps. 58961
Ginguene, -------. ed. 11816
Giocondo, Giovanni. tr. 99327-99352, 99360-99361, 99378
Gioja, Flavio. (19793)
Giordan, Jean Francois. 27471-27472, 29099, 44062, 44391
Giordano. A tragedy. 39449
Giorgini, Giovanni. see Giovanni Giorgini da Jesi.
Giornale, overo descrittione del faticosissimo, & trauagliosissimo viaggio. 77964
Giornale politico. 11103
Gioseppe di S. Teresa, Gio. see Santa Teresa, Giovanni Gioseppe di.
Giovagnoli, Anton Francisco. 27475
Giovanni, madame. pseud. see Saint Mars, Gabrielle Anne Cisterne de Courtiras, Vicomtesse de, 1804-1872.
Giovanni Giorgini da Jesi. 27473, note after 36086, 37574
Giovanni Gioseppe di Santa Teresa. see San Teresa, Giovanni Gioseppe di.
Giovio, Paolo, Bp. of Nocera, 1483-1552. 25994, 27478, 34100-34107, 36773-36776, 67736, 79345
Gipsy Smith. His life and work. 83894-83895
Gispy Smith in Brooklyn. 83896
Gipsy Smith's best sermons. 83896
Giraldo, Josef. 27479
Girard, Charles. 2808, 23083, 27419, (27480), 27481-27484, 68476, 69946, 81472-81473, 85072
Girard, Fr. illus. 92526
Girard, James Watson. 80148
Girard, Just. pseud. Excursion d'un touriste au Mexique. see Roy, J. J. E.
Girard, M. P. S. 67929

Girard, Stephen, 1750-1831. 1939-1940, 27486-27488, 47561, 62284, 81371, 82979, 101199
Girard, Stephen, fl. 1844. 27489
Girard de Propiac, Catherine Joseph Ferdinand. see Propiac, Catherine Joseph Ferdinand Girard de, 1759-1822.
Girard and his college. (68793)
Girard Bank, Philadelphia. 27490
Girard Bank, Philadelphia. claimants 50152
Girard College, Philadelphia. 1939, 27491, (27494), 40975, 83793
Girard College, Philadelphia. Board of Directors. 1939, (27494)
Girard College, Philadelphia. Board of Trustees. (27494)
Girard College, Philadelphia. Building Committee. 27493, 101199
Girard College, Philadelphia. Building Committee and Architect. (27494)
Girard College, Philadelphia. Charter. 1939
Girard College, Philadelphia. Magnetic and Meteorological Observatory. (56465), 85072
Girard College and its founder. 1940, (27494)
Girard Estate. Commissioners. 27488
Girard Estate. Commissioners. Special Committee. (27494)
Girard Life Insurance, Annuity and Trust Company of Philadelphia. Charter. 61700
Girard Trust. (27494)
Girard Trust. Managers. (27494)
Girardeau, John L. 27495, 85323
Girardin, Elile de. 33618
Girardin, Louis Hue. 9273, 104878
Girardot, Auguste Theodore, Baron de. 27496
Girard's will. 62284
Giraud, ------, fl. 1862. 27497
Giraud, A. tr. 77070
Giraud, C. F. F. J. ed. 27499-(27500), 29178, 99458
Giraud, Charles. 22538
Giraud, J. P. (27498)
Giraud, Octave. 27501
Giraudiere, H. de Chavannes de la. see Chavannes de la Giraudiere, H. de.
Girault, A. N. 27502-27503, 89831, 1st note after 99504, 101888
Girault's French teacher, No. II. 101888
Girava, Hieronymo. 27504
Gird, H. H. 27505
Girdlestone, Thomas. 27506
Girdwood, John. 27507
Girelli, B. tr. 76757
Girl. pseud. Letter from a girl to her sweetheart in the army. 93040
Girlhood and womanhood. 28345
Girls' High School, Providence, R. I. see Providence, R. I. Girls' High School.
Girls' Industrial Home, Rathbone, O. see Ohio. Girls' Industrial Home, Rathbone.
Girls' Industrial School Association, New York. see Association of the Girls' Industrial School, New York.
Girl's reading-book. 80920
Giro del mundo. 10820, 26850
Girod, Amury. 27508
Girod, John Francis. 27509
Girod-Chantrans, Justin. 27510, 100812
Gironde (French Department) 75042
Gironde (French Department) Directoire. 75189
Giros. see Queiros, Pedro Fernandes de, d. 1615.

Girot-Pouzol, -------. 27511 see also France. Corps Legislatif. Conseil des Anciens. Commission.
Gisborne, Lionel, 1823-1861. 27319, (27512)
Gisborne, Thomas. 27513
Gisements de metaux precieux des etats. 87295
Gisson y Leon, Thomas. see Gijon y Leon, Thomas de.
Gist, Christopher. (27515), (64735)
Gist, States R. 87371 see also South Carolina. Adjutant and Inspector General.
Gist, William Henry, 1809-1874. 33150, 87471 see also South Carolina. Department of Construction and Manufacture. Chief. South Carolina. Governor, 1858-1860 (Gist)
Gitche spirit of the red man. 83485
Gitt, Joseph S. 45396
Gittermann, J. C. H. 27516
Gituerrez, ------. 20548
Givnti, Tommaso. 67731-67739
Giuntini, F. note after 99383C
Giuseppe della Madre di Dio. see Jose de la Madre di Dios.
Giuseppe Sallusti. Storia delle missioni apostoliche. (75805)
Giustiniani, Agostini, Bp. of Nebio. 27518, (66468)
Giustiniani, L. (27519)
Give Caesar his due. 22137
Giver more blessed than the receiver. 21977, 22525
Givre, Gaston Demousseaux de. see Demousseaux de Givre, Gaston.
Givry, M. (27520)
Gjengangeren. note after 96061
Glacers of the Canadian Rockies and Selkirks. 85072
Glackmeyer, Charles. 50246
Glackmeyer, E. 27521
Glad tidings. (27522), 65122
Glad tidings for the Democrats. 14032, 85597, 94025
Glad tidings for the hospital. 31307
Gladden, S. W. 86944
Gladden, Washington. 27523
Gladman, G. 10590
Gladstone, John. 27524-27526
Gladstone, Thomas H. 27527-27529
Gladstone, William Ewart, 1809-1898. (27530), 83876
Glance at a few of our literary progenies. 42434
Glance at Illinois, her lands, and their comparative values. 10208
Glance at John Wilbur's book. 10082
Glance at New York. 28583
Glance at New York. A local drama. 54293
Glance at New York: embracing the city government. 54294
Glance at one of Mr. Barrett's "Spiritual tornadoes." (77442)
Glance at philosophy. 27913
Glance at private libraries. 23864
Glance at state rights. 27531, note before 90644
Glance at the Baptists. 48925
Glance at the British islands. 47045
Glance at the currency and resources generally. 95088
Glance at the eccelsiastical councils of New England. 19896
Glance at the Iroquois. 97489
Glance at the leading measures. 24057

Glimpse of Iowa in 1846. 54997

Glimpse of the American victories. 13890, 14011

Glimpse of the far-west. 80294

Glimpse of the field of victory. 64797

Glimpse of the great western republic. 17969

Glimpse of the state of the nation. 101787

Glimpses of New York City. (27582), 2d note after 88112

Glimpses of the supernatural. 22258

Glimpses of western life. (37991)

Globe, Toronto. 74582

Globe, Toronto. defendant 8077

Globe, Washington (1831-1864) see Daily globe.

Globe. By T. O'Connor. (27582)

Globe Village, Mass. Evangelical Free Church. see Southbridge, Mass. Evangelical Free Church.

Globensky, Charles Auguste Maximilien, 1830-58495, 94638

Globi astronomici canones vsum & expedita parxim eiusde exprometes. (77799), 77808

Globi Stelliferi, sive sphoerae stellarum fixaru usus. 77801

Globi stelliferi . . . vsus. 77805

Globo y estandarte Mejicano. 36963

Globo y estandarte Mejicano. Editores. 36963

Globus mundi declaratio. 27583, 102623

Glocester, Mass. see Gloucester, Mass.

Glocken. 63547

Gloire de S. Vrsvle divisee en devx parties. 38619, 98167

Gloire des guerrieurs ne sauroit etre complete. 49398

Gloria Britannorum. 27586

Gloria de la nacion por su rey y por su union. 99679

Gloria de loz Pizarros. (49898)

Gloria Dei Church, Wiccacoe, Pa. see Wiccacoe, Pa. Gloria Dei Church.

Gloria especial de Christo. 86254

Gloria majorum, posteris lumen. 30872

Glorias Argentinas y recuerdos historicos. (35067)

Glorias de Espana deduc. de su restauracion milagrosa. 26413

Glorias de Queretaro. 80972, 80982

Glorias de Queretaro [sic] en la foundacion de la Congregacion. (27786)

Glorias de Queretaro, en la fundacion y admirables progresos. 80974, 1st note after 106302

Glorias de Queretaro en la Nueva Congregacion Eclesiastica. 80973

Glorias del segundo siglo de la Compania de Jesus. 11360

Glorias Dominicanas en su esclarecido. 31728

Glories of the Lord of Hosts. 9711

Glorifying God in the fire. 103510

Glorifying God in the fires. 89744

Gloriosa coroa d'esforcados religiosos da Companhia de Jesu. 27587, 29127

Gloriosos desempenos de las mas ardiente caridad. 86546

Gloriosus Franciscus redivivus. 44556

Glorious church. 20391

Glorious espousal. 46335

Glorious 14th of December, 1782. (23123), 34969

Glorious glimmerings of the life, love, unity and pure joy. 58058

Glorious Hartford convention. 98835

Glorious manifestation of the further progress of the Gospel among the Indians in New-England. 72696, 96297-97301, note after 103689

Glorious message, to all citizens of the United States. 85113, 85122

Glorious message, commanded to be sent to Abraham Lincoln. 35706

Glorious news. 7847, 27588

Glorious news from the West-Indies. 102835

Glorious progress of the Gospel amongst the Indians in New England. (22152), note before 92797, note after 104794

Glorious things of the city of God. 20391

Glorious throne. A short view of our great Lord-Redeemer. 46336

Glorious throne: or, a sermon concerning the glory of the throne. 46694

Glory and shame of America. 62781

Glory and the shame of England. 8543, 40223

Glory be to God on High. 30699, 1st note after 100518

Glory of a house of worship. 13656

Glory of America. A century sermon. 706

Glory of America; comprising memoirs. 27589, 95442

Glory of Boston. A poem. 56378

Glory of Colombia; her yeomanry. (21298)

Glory of Columbia her yeomanry! (21299)

Glory of God in the firmament of His power. (14525)

Glory of God's house. 28743

Glory of goodness. 46337

Glory of New York. 72631

Glory of soldiers cannot be completed without acting well the part of citizens. 49398

Glory of the latter house. A centennial plea for presbyterian election. 89254

Glory of the latter house: a discourse. (31806)

Glory of the latter house. A sermon, on the dedication of the First Presbyterian Church. 74722

Glory of the Lord filling his house. 92251

Glory which adorns the daughters of God. 46234

Glorying in the cross. 74723

Glossaria linguarum Brasiliensium. 44999

Glossario dos termos usuaes de Caca. 7546

Glossarium Azteco-Latinum. 74948

Glossarium Azteco-Latinum et Latino-Aztecum. 74948

Glossary and the life of the author. 79729

Glossary of botanical terms. 5297

Glossary of Philippine mining terms. 84529

Glossary of supposed Americanisms. (22374)

Glossary of words and phrases. 3737

Glossary to Say's entomology. 77386

Glossbrenner, ------. 11126

Glosser. A poem. 36880

Gloster, Archibald. 27590

Gloster, Henry. 83487 see also British Guiana. Court of Policy. Secretary.

Gloucester, Bishop of. see Beadon, Richard, successively Bp. of Gloucester, and Bath and Wells, 1737-1824.
Benson, Martin, Bp. of Gloucester, 1689-1752.
Johnson, James, successively Bp. of Gloucester, and Worcester, 1705-1774.
Warburton, William, Bp. of Gloucester, 1698-1779.
Wilcocks, Joseph, successively bp. of Gloucester, and Rochester, 1673-1756.
Yorke, James, successively Bp. of Gloucester, and Ely, d. 1808.

Gloucester, Dean of. see Sherlock, Thomas, successively Bp. of Salisbury, and London, 1678-1761.
Tucker, Josiah, 1712-1799.
Waugh, John.
Gloucester, England. Court of Assize. 103500
Gloucester, Eng. Methodists. plaintiffs see Methodist Church (England) Gloucester. plaintiffs
Gloucester, Mass. Board of Health. (27596)
Gloucester, Mass. First Church. 7268, 27584, 103399
Gloucester, Mass. First Church. Pastor. 27584, 103399 see also White, John, 1677-1760.
Gloucester, Mass. Masonic Fire Society. see Masonic Fire Society, Gloucester, Mass.
Gloucester, Mass. Ordinances, etc. 27593
Gloucester, Mass. Society of Christian Independents. see Society of Christian Independents, Gloucester, Mass.
Gloucester, Mass. Universalist Centennial, 1870. see Universalist Centennial, Gloucester, Mass., 1870.
Gloucester, Mass. Wingaersheek Division, no. 183. see Sons of Temperance of North America. Massachusetts. Wingaersheek Division no. 183, Gloucester.
Gloucester County, England. Court of Assize. see Gloucester, England. Court of Assize.
Gloucester County, N. J. Democratic Association. see Democratic Association, Gloucester County, N. J.
Gloucester County, N. J. Washington Benevolent Society. see Washington Benevolent Society. New Jersey. Gloucester County.
Gloucester and Rockport directory for 1869. 27595
Gloucester directory . . . 1859. (27594)
Gloucester fisherman, Gloucester, Massachusetts. (84324)
Gloucester Fox Hunting Club. 27600
Gloucester hoax. 78541
Gloucester times. 84323
Glover, Anna. (27601)
Glover, E. 14894
Glover, G. illus. 71906
Glover, Habakkuk. (27602)
Glover, John William, 1815-1899. 17936
Glover, Joseph. 27603
Glover, L. M. 27604-27605
Glover, Richard. 23302, (27606)-(27610), 4th note after 102788
Glover, Richard. incorrectly supposed author 1783, (39697)-39698
Glover, Samuel T. 27611-27614, 41150
Glover, Samuel T. defendant (27613), 75407
Glover, Sir Thomas. 66686
Glover, Thomas W. 87534
Glover memorials and genealogies. (27601)
Glover rescue trials. 6394
Gloverville: or, the model village. 89674
Gluckliche Christenthum in Paraguay. (51421)
Glucks- und Unglucksfalle Martin Speelhovens. 89242-89243
Glyndon, Howard. pseud. Idyls of battle and poems of rebellion. see Redden, Laura C.
Glynn, ------. 25595, 34579-34580, 99584, note just before 103108
Glynn, James. defendant at court martial 96872
Gnaw-wood; New England life in a village. 12432

Go ahead, and a few other poems. (41038)
Go-ahead Louisiana and Texas almanac for 1839. 27617
"Go ahead!" no. 4. (17576)
Go-between, or two edged sword. 19827, 27619
Go wana gwa ih sat hah yon de-yas hah gwah. (28168), 105547
Goa, Reinoldo Guisco de. 70787
Goad, Christopher. 104335-104336
Goadby, John. 27616
Goadby, Robert. 27615
Goadby, Robert. supposed author 93889
Goat Island as a railway terminus at San Francisco. 90212
Gobat, Georgio. tr. (67494)
Gobble, Ezekiel, and Co. pseud. see Ezekiel Gobble and Co. pseud.
Gobeo de Victoria, Pedro. see Victoria, Pedro Gobeo de.
Gobernador de la provincia y el excelentisimo cabildo. (9015)
Gobernantes de Mexico. (71625)
Gobert, M. 77952
Gobien, ------ le. see Le Gobien, ---------
Gobierno. 99482
Gobierno de las haciendas de Cacoo. 10778
Gobierno de los regulares de la America. (58841)
Gobierno de Manuel de Amat por Miguel Feijoo de Sosa. 71450
Gobierno de General Comonfort. 64332
Gobierno del Salvador y la Cura Eclesiastica. 76202
Gobierno Espanol en sus colonias y en las republicas Americanas. 67338
Gobierno gentil y Catolico. 28255
Gobierno supremo de la republica a los Mexicanos. 48485
Gobierno vindicado. 98876
Gobineau, Joseph Arthur de, Comte. 27620
Gobright, John C. 27621-27623
Gobirght, L. A. 27624
Gock, Carl. 27625
Gockelius, Christophorus Ludovicus. 27626
Gocking, G. G. G. 27627
God, a believer's glory. 103510
God a refuge, &c. (24774)
God acknowledged in the nation's bereavement. 32263
God against slavery. 12400
God always right. 57891
God and our country. (7008), 66782
God and the nation. 33405
God arising and pleading his people's cause. 37649
God bless Abraham Lincoln! 41189
God brings to the desired haven. (65600)
God by his power causes the earth and its inhabitants to tremble. 25369
God dealing with slavery. 71149
God deals with us as rational creatures. (14525)
God destroyeth the hope of man! 65601
God determines the rise and fall of princes. 92252
God gives, and takes away. 62082
God glorified in his wroks. 42009
God glorified in the work of redemption. 21944
God glorious in the scenes of the winter. (9717)
God hiding himself in times of trouble. (38779)
God in civil government. 2326
God in no sense the author of sin. 80393
God in the camp. 104259

God in the pestilence. 22788
God in the pestilence and the fire. 64692
God in the storm. 84296
God in the war. 82700
God is a great King. (14525)
God is to be praised. 97187
God of our fathers. 21140
God of tempest and earthquake. 9714
God of the Bible against slavery. (4298)
God or our country. (7008)
God our protector. 6517, 20238, 39183
"God our refuge in trouble." (76474)
God pleading with America. 90361
God round about his people. 62831
God ruling the nations for the most glorious
    end. 33972
God save our noble union! 65398
God save the king. 86880, 89434
God seen above all. 27406
God sometimes answers his people. 200
God speaketh. (43338)
God the author of human greatness. 89796
God the dwelling place of the righteous in all
    generations. 19830
God the glorious, holy, wonder-working God.
    104724
God the judge, putting down one, and setting
    up another. 25394
God the perpetual renewer. 68059
God the protector and hope of the nation.
    39569
God, the refuge of his people. 84543
God the strength and portion of his people.
    (9717)
God the strength and salvation of his people.
    (25041)
God the strength of rulers and people. 104407
God the supreme ruler and governour of the
    world. 68128
God to be glorified in the fires. (39694)
God with the aged. 26074
God with us. 9646
Godar, M. tr. 3255C
Godard-Lange, ------. 27630
Goddard, Delano A. (27631)
Goddard, Edward. 27632
Goddard, Francis W. ed. 27649
Goddard, Frederick B. (27633)
Goddard, Josiah. 27635-27636
Goddard, Kingston. 27634, 60336
Goddard, M. K. 45251
Goddard, N. 27637
Goddard, Samuel A. 27638-27640
Goddard, Thomas A. see Goddard, Thomas H.
Goddard, Thomas H. (27641)
Goddard, William. 27642-27645, 47142,
    (60310), 66327, note after 99295, 2d note
    after 97091, note after 103264
Goddard, William. supposed author 55104,
    2d note after 97091
Goddard, William Augustus. 27646
Goddard, William Giles. 27647-27648
Godefroy, F. see Godefroy, M.
Godefroy, M. 27650, (63966), 68421
Godefroy, Marie-Anne. see Burgogne, Marie-
    Anne (Godefroy) du Vivier-.
Godefory et Augustin. (21025)
Goden, Julius. see Soden, Julius, Graf von,
    1754-1831.
Goderich, Frederick James Robinson,
    Viscount. see Ripon, Frederick James
    Robinson, Earl of, 1782-1859.
Godet, J. A. 27652
Godet, Theodore L. 27653

Godey, Louis Antoine, 1804-1878. ed. (38549),
    83513, 84162
Godey's lady's book. (38549), 83513, 84162
Godfrey, of Bullen. 66686
Godfrey, A. W. 27654
Godfrey, John A. (70769)
Godfrey, Mary. (27655), 79064
Godfrey, Samuel E. defendant 96873
Godfrey, Thomas, 1704-1749. 27656-27657,
    (60298)
Godfrey, Thomas, 1736-1763. (27658), 84610,
    84678C
Godfrey, William C. 27659, 43043
Godfrey Greylock. pseud. Taghconic. see
    Smith, Joseph Edward Adams, 1822-1896.
Godfrey's narrative of the last Grinnell Arctic
    Exploring Expedition. 27659, 43043
Godin, -----. 16930, 27660, (38482), 38485,
    38489
Godines. see Bendenius, Cornelius.
Godinez y San Pablo, Miguel. 27661
Godley, John Robert. 27662
Godliness excludes slavery. 2632
Godly and faithful man characterized. 15216
"Godly and faithful man" delineated. 28199
Godly fathers, and a defence of their people.
    11968
Godly minister. pseud. Choice dialogues.
    see Checkley, John.
Godly pastor. 105751
Godly sorrow described. 7300
Godman, John D. 27663-27665, 40735, 56706,
    79471, note after 101863
Godman, Stuart Adair. 27666
Godoi, Diego de. see Godoy, Diego de,
    16th cent.
Godoy, Diego de, 16th cent. 2250, 16936-16937,
    16951, 67740, 94854
Godoy, Manuel de. see Godoy Alvarez de
    Faria Rios Sanchez y Zarzosa, Manuel
    de, Principe de la Paz, 1767-1851.
Godoy, Nicholas de. 27670
Godoy Alvarez de Faria Rios Sanchez y
    Zarzosa, Manuel de, Principe de la
    Paz, 1767-1851. 27667-27669
God's awful determination against a people.
    (17094)
God's blessing of peace. 43184
God's blessing on his own institutions. 105989
God's call to his people to turn unto Him.
    18706
God's call to his people . . . . Two sermons
    preached at Plymouth. 17102
God's care of the New-England colonies.
    92893
God's challenge. 39199
God's concern for a Godly seed: sermon.
    16603
God's concern for a Godly seed. Sermon on
    a day of prayer. 16640
God's controversy with the people of the
    United States. 43340
God's culture in His vineyard. 13838
God's conduct of His church through the
    wilderness. (80188)
God's counsel and purpose. 82729
God's design in sending sickness upon men.
    32826
God's discipline of nations. 55909
God's doings, and man's duty. 61196
God's doings for the nation. 63424
God's eye on the contrite. 347
God's face set against an incorrigible people.
    25408

Gomes da Rocha, Jose. see Rocha, Jose Gomes da.

Gomes da Silva Gerford, Sebastiao. see Silva Gerford, Sebastiao Gomes da.

Gomes Davila, Beatriz. see Davila, Beatriz Gomes.

Gomes de Brito, Bernardo. 23027, 27754, 94595

Gomes de Castro, Jose Constantino. see Castro, Jose Constantino Gomes de.

Gomes Freire, Manuel. see Santa Maria, Agostinho de.

Gomez, Alfonso. (75565)

Gomez, Duarte. (27759)

Gomez, E. J. ed. and tr. 92730

Gomez, Francisco. defendant (36943)

Gomez, J. 27761

Gomez, J. B. 27766

Gomez, J. M. 27767

Gomez, Jose. (48440)

Gomez, M. M. 27768

Gomez, Manuel. 27769

Gomez, Vicente. defendant 43255

Gomez Brizeno, Juan. see Brizeno, Juan Gomez.

Gomez da Silva, Francisco. see Silva, Francisco Gomez da, 1791-1852.

Gomez de Avellaneda, Gertrudis. 27755-27757, (47979)

Gomez de Cervantes, Nic. 27762

Gomez de la Cortina, Jose. see Cortina, Jose Gomez de la.

Gomez de la Cortina, Jose Justo. see Cortina, Jose Justo Gomez de la Cortina, Conde de la, 1799-1860.

Gomez de la Parra, Jose. 27763-27764, 58840

Gomez de Mora, Juan. 27765

Gomez de Ocampo, Diego. see Ocampo, Diego Gomez de.

Gomez de Solis, Luis. see Solis, Luis Gomez de.

Gomez de Vidaurre, Felipe. see Vidaurre, Felipe Gomez de.

Gomez Fariaz, Benito. defendant 36872

Gomez Imaz, Manuel. ed. 98861

Gomez Navarrete, Juan. see Navarrete, Juan Gomez.

Gomez Parada, Vicente. 27771

Gomez Pedraza, Manuel. see Pedraza, Manuel Gomez.

Gomez Rendon, Sebastian. plaintiff 86422

Gomez Roubaud, Rafael. see Roubaud, Rafael Gomez.

Gomez Tonel de Sotomayor, Juan. see Tonel de Sotomayor, Juan Gomez.

Gomez y Anaya, Cirilo. 27755, 27758, 52253

Gomont, H. tr. (41928)

Gon Netscher, A. D. van der. see Netscher, A. D. van der Gon.

Goncaga, Francisco. see Gonzaga, Francesco, Bp.

Goncalez, Antonio. see Gonsales, Antonio.

Goncalez de Acuna, Antonio. see Acuna, Antonio Gonzalez de.

Goncalez de Cueto, Damiano. 27772

Goncalez de Eslava, Fernan. see Gonzalez de Estava, Fernan.

Goncalez de Guemes, Pedro. see Guemes, Pedro Goncalez de.

Goncalez de Mendoca, Juan. see Gonzalez de Mendoza, Juan, Abp., 1571-1639.

Goncalez de Nagera, Alonzo. 12799, 27785

Goncalez de Poueda, Bartholome. 64742
see also Chuquisaca, Bolivia. Real Audiencia. Presidente.

Goncalez de Santalla, Thirso. 105716

Goncalez del Campillo, Manuel Ignacio. see Gonzalez del Campillo, Manuel Ignacio, Bp., 1740-1813.

Goncalez Holguin, Diego. see Gonzalez Holguin, Diego, d. 1552.

Goncalez Molguin, Diego de. see Gonzalez Holguin, Diego, d. 1552.

Goncalves, Jose Vicente. defendant 97697

Goncalves de Magalhanes, Domingos Jose, Visconde de Araguaya, 1811-1882. 43792-43793

Goncalves Dias, Antonio, 1823-1864. (19962)-19963, 70320

Goncalves dos Sanctos, Luis. see Sanctos, Luis Goncalves dos.

Goncalves Zarco, Joao. see Zarco, Joao Goncalves, 15th cent.

Goncalves & Corea. firm. see Oliveira Goncalves & Correa. firm

Gondomar appearing in the likeness of Matchiauell in a Spanish parliament. 78377, 100801

Gondra, D. G. M. de. tr. 44463

Gongara y Lujan, Pedro Jimenez de. see Almodovar del Rio, Pedro Jimenez de Gongara y Lujan, Duque de, d. 1794

Gongara y Siguenza, --------. see Siguenza y Gongora, Carlos de, 1634-1700.

Gongora, ------, fl. 1803. (27786)

Gongora, Carlos de Siguenza y. see Siguenza y Gongora, Carlos de, 1645-1700.

Gongora, Ignacia Cruzat y. see Cruzat y Gongora, Ignacia.

Gongora Marmolejo, Alonso de. see Marmolejo, Alonso de Gongora.

Gonnein, ------. 76838

Gonneville, Jean Binot Paulmyer de. see Paulmier, Jean, d. ca. 1669.

Gonsalves da Cruz, Antonio. 68331-68332

Gontaut, Armand Louis de. see Biron Armand Louis de Gontaut, Duc de Lauzun afterwards Duc de, 1747-1793.

Gontran le chercheur d'or. 86388

Gonzaga, Annibale. see Gonzaga, Francesco Bp.

Gonzaga, Francesco, Bp. 25934, 27790, 4455 48464, 57469, 76105-76106 see also Franciscans. Master General, 1579-158 (Gonzaga)

Gonzaga, Juan Perez de Guzman y. see Guzman y Gonzaga, Juan Perez de.

Gonzaga, Luigi. 27791

Gonzaga, Luis. 27792

Gonzaga Cuevas, Luis. see Cuevas, Luis Gonzaga.

Gonzaga de la Encina, Luis. see La Encina Luis Gonzaga de.

Gonzaga Vieyra, Luis. see Vieyra, Luis Gonzaga.

Gonzaga Fair, Washington, D. C., 1865. 898

Gonzales, Antonio. 70098 see also Nueva Granada (Viceroyalty) Virrey, 1590-1597 (Gonzales)

Gonzales, Antonio. tr. 27794, 71490-(71491)

Gonzales, Antonio Teran de. see Teran de Gonzales, Antonio.

Gonzales, M. E. ed. (70366)

Gonzales Carranza, Domingo. tr. 11030, 27799

Gonzales de Mendoza, Juan. see Gonzalez de Mendoza, Juan, Abp., 1571-1639.

Gonzales de Merchado, Luigi. (63179)

Gonzales de Quiroga, Diego. see Quiroga, Diego Gonzales de.

Gonzales de Valdeosera, Miguel. (26933)

Gonzales Ortega, Jesus. see Ortega, Jesus Gonzales.

Gonzalez, Antonio. 27794

Gonzalez, Antonius, fl. 1655. 27792, 73178

Gonzalez, Cabrera Bueno. 27797

Gonzalez, Florentino. 27801

Gonzalez, J. 27803-27804

Gonzalez, Jose. 27807

Gonzalez, Joseph. ed. 98713

Gonzalez, Juan. 27810, 73008, 85742

Gonzalez, Juan Francisco. 27813

Gonzalez, Juan Vicente. 27815-(27817)

Gonzalez, M. Amparo Fernandez y. see Fernandez y Gonzalez, M. Amparo.

Gonzalez, Manuel Dionisio. 27820

Gonzalez, Miguel. plaintiff 86410

Gonzalez, P. 27821

Gonzalez, Salvador. tr. (58281)

Gonzalez, Tomas. (27824)

Gonzalez, Tomas. supposed author 86555

Gonzalez Aravia, Miguel. see Aravia, Miguel Gonzalez.

Gonzalez Arnao, Vicente. see Arnao, Vicente Gonzalez.

Gonzalez Barcia, Andres. see Barcia, Andres Gonzalez.

Gonzalez Bustillo, Juan. 27811

Gonzalez Ciaparro, Giov. see Ciaparro, Giov. Gonzalez.

Gonzalez Carranza, Domingo. see Gonzales Carranza, Domingo.

Gonzalez Davila, Gil. see Davila, Gil Gonzalez.

Gonzalez de Acuna, Antonio. see Acuna, Antonio Gonzalez de.

Gonzalez de Aguero, Juan Francisco de Castaniza. 11393, 27814

Gonzalez Araujo, Pedro. 27823

Gonzalez de Agueros, Pedro. 524, 27822, 49894

Gonzalez de Barcia Carballido y Zuniga, Andres. see Barcia Carballido y Zuniga, Andres Gonzalez de, 1673-1743.

Gonzalez de Bustos, Francisco. 9600, (27798)

Gonzalez de Camdano, -------. 27795

Gonzalez de Castro, Juan. 75890

Gonzalez de Doblas, ------. see Doblas, ------ Gonzalez de.

Gonzalez de Estava, Fernan. 27773, 27800

Gonzalez de Carcia, And. see Garcia, And. Gonzalez de.

Gonzalez de la Puenta, Juan. 27808

Gonzalez de la Rosa, Manuel Toribio. see Rosa, Manuel Toribio Gonzalez de la.

Gonzalez de la Vega, -------. 27795

Gonzalez de la Vega, Jose Maria. tr. (65266)

Gonzalez del Campillo, Manuel Ignacio, Bp., 1740-1813. 10312, 34190, 66555, 66562 see also Puebla, Mex. (Archdiocese) Bishop (Gonzalez del Campillo)

Gonzalez del Pino, Joseph. 27805

Gonzalez del Valle, Jose Z. 48162

Gonzalez de Mendoza, Juan, Abp., 1571-1639. 27775-27785, 47826-47829, 66686, 69210

Gonzalez di Mendozza, Giouanni. see Gonzalez de Mendozza, Juan, Abp., 1571-1639.

Gonzalez Holguin, Diego, d. 1552. 27774, 32493-(32495)

Gonzalez Holguin, Diego, d. 1552. supposed author 5020, 10710, 20565, 32492, (67160), 100643

Gonzalez Laguna, Francisco. see Laguna, Francisco Gonzalez.

Gonzalez Maldonado, Eugenio. see Maldonado, Eugenio Gonzalez.

Gonzalez Olivares, Ignacio. see Olivares, Ignacio Gonzalez.

Gonzalez Sancha, Francisco. see Sancha, Francisco Gonzalez.

Gonzalez Sancha, Lorenzo. see Sancha, Lorenzo Gonzalez.

Gonzalez Saravia, Miguel. see Saravia, Miguel Gonzalez.

Gonzalez y Montoya, Josef. 27806

Gonzalo Moron, Fermin. see Moron, Fermin Gonzalo.

Gonzalo Pinero, --------. 27825, (62939)

Gonzalo, Victoriano Lopez, Bp. 27826 see also Puebla, Mex. (Archdiocese) Bishop (Gonzalo)

Gonzalve Grand d'Hauteville, Paul Daniel. see D'Hauteville, Paul Daniel Gonzalve Grand.

Gooch, Daniel Wheelwright, 1820-1891. 27827-27828, 84956

Gooch, Sir Thomas, Bart., Successively Bishop of Bristol, Norwich, and Ely, d. 1754. 55917

Gooch, Sir William, Bart., 1681-1751. 99975, 99977-99988, 100458 see also Virginia (Colony) Governor, 1727-1749 (Gooch)

Gooch, Sir William, Bart., 1681-1751. defendant 99894 see also Virginia (Colony) Governor, 1727-1749 (Gooch) defendant

Good advice to youth. 80460

Good and faithful servant: a sermon . . . June 30, 1872. (66761)

Good and faithful servant. A sermon preached at Milton. 14137

Good and faithful servant: and the joy awarded to him. (18188)

Good believers' character. 106198

Good book, and amenities of nature. 67452

Good cause of President Lincoln. A lecture. 55008

Good centurion. 85470

Good character. (46340)

Good child's book. 82509

Good conversation. 44078

Good counsel how to close savingly with Christ. (30358)

Good devised. 89141

Good evening for the best of dayes. (46341)

Good faith and union. 33890

Good fetch'd out of evil; a collection of memorables. 46342, 104260

Good fetch'd out of evil, in three short essays. 104261

Good government of Christian families recommended. 32736

Good gray poet. 56659

Good humour. (27830), 96075

Good Indian missionary. (27829)

Good Intent Beneficial Society, Philadelphia. 61702

Good investment, a story of the upper Ohio. 24655

Good land in which we live. 6957

Good land we live in. (28906)

Good lessons for children. 46343

Good man. 93078

Good man making a good end. 46344

Good man useful in life. 96093

Good master well served. (46345)

Good men described, and good things propounded. 46440

Good men described, and the glories of their goodness, declared. 46231

Good men the treasure of earth. 7347
Good men, under God, the strength and defence of a people. (54947)
Good merchant. 106056
Good minister. A discourse preached at Hollis, N. H. 18859
Good minister. A sermon preach'd at Stonington. 40772
Good minister . . . exemplified in the life and character. 35416
Good minister of Jesus Christ. A sermon, preached in Boston. 91795
Good minister of Jesus Christ, nourished by the words of faith. (82416)
Good missionary. 60963
Good moral principles of the government of the United States. 94491
Good natured credulity. 86825
Good news from a far country. A sermon preached at Boston. 91796
Good news from a far country. In seven discourses. 58892
Good news from home. 27831, 42548
Good nevves from New-England: or a true relation of things. 66686, 104795, 106053
Good news from Nevv-England: with an exact relation. 27832
Good news from Pensilvania. 37186
"Good news from Virginia, sent from James his town by a gentleman." 100478
Good newes from Virginia. Sent to the Covnsell and Company of Virginia. 103313
Good news! Good news from home. 27831, 42548
Good newes of the day-breaking. (56742), (80815)
Good news to the Iroquois nation. 104211
Good of Great Britain, Ireland, and British North America identified. 4905
Good of the community impartially considered. 27833, 74420, 3d note after 97116
Good old age, a brief essay. (27834), 46346
Good old age. A sermon occasioned by the death of Hon. John Davis. 26536
Good old Virginia Almanac. 27835
Good old way. (46347)
Good order established in Pennsylvania and New Jersey. 8952, 17510, 56650
Good patriot's security in the time of public distress. 99249
Good people marked in their foreheads. 92062
Good people of this commonwealth . . . having ratified the constitution. 100055
Good president. 91067
Good public roads. (27836)
Good reason . . . congregational priests are federal! ! ! 95572
Good republican. 90907
Good reward of a faithful servant. 46259
Good rulers a choice blessing. 46207
Good rulers the fathers of their people. 40789
Good Samaritan: a sermon, delivered in . . . New-York. (73052)
Good Samaritan. An oration delivered . . . May 22d, 1796. 70471
Good Samaritans. A poem. 68175
Good shepherd. 103510
Good soldier. Extracted from a sermon. 18760, 18763
Good souldiers [sic] a great blessing. 100910
Good soldiers described, and animated. 94106
Good speed to Virginia. (27837)
Good subject's wish. 24529
Good Templars. Grand Lodge. 91053
Good the author of promotion. 43474

Good time coming. 49003
Good twelve cents worth of political love powder. 102492
Good twenty-five cents worth of political love powder. 102492
Good Will Division, no. 17, Sons of Temperance. see Sons of Temperance of North America. Massachusetts. Good Will Division. no. 17, New Bedford.
Good wives. (12716)-(12717)
Good words, June, 1865. 41240
Good work for a good magistrate. 61193
Goodale, Ebenezer. defendant at court martial 27838, 96874
Goodale, John. (27839)
Goodale, M. S. (27840)-27841
Goodale, S. L. 43908
Goodale, Baptist. 27842
Goode, George Brown. 84986, 84988, 85072, 85091-85092, 85097 see also Smithsonian Institution. Assistant Secretary.
Goode, S. 86580
Goode, Thomas. 27843
Goode, Thomas F. 86580
Goode, William O. 27844
Goode raad voor landverhuizers naar de Vereenigde Staten. 4375
Goodell, C. L. (27845)
Goodell, William, 1792-1878. (27846)-27850, 88295
Goodenow, John M. 27851-27853
Goodenow, Stirling. 27854-27855, 53550
Goodere, Samuel. defendant 86587
Goodfellow, William. 27856, 41235, 6th note after 96964
Goodhue, Josiah F. (27857)
Goodhue, Samuel. (27858)
Goodhue, Sarah. 27859
Goodloe, Daniel R. (27860)-(27864), 34802, (81962), 81997, 92867
Goodly heritage of Connecticut. (2667)
Goodly heritage of Jerseymen. 20391
Goodman, -------, fl. 1834. 62231
Goodman, Charles Holmes. 90006
Goodman, D. ed. (49814)
Goodman, H. H. 89304
Goodman, John D. ed. 62010
Goodman, John R. (27865)
Goodman, R. 105055
Goodman, Richard. 27866
Goodman, W. F. 27868
Goodman, William. 27867
Goodnatured hint about California. 25120
Goodness of God in restoring peace. 82887
Goodness of God in the conversion of youth. 90200
Goodness of God learned from the Bible. 8429
Goodrich, -------, fl. 1823. (76380)
Goodrich, C. R. ed. 81066
Goodrich, Charles Augustus, 1790-1862. 4714, 10262, (22449), 27869-27875, 39586, 105800, 105842
Goodrich, Charles Augustus, 1790-1862. supposed author 15721, 36334, note after 101998, note before 101999, 105720
Goodrich, Charles Augustus, 1790-1862. Incorrectly supposed author 15720, (69512), note after 101998, 103169
Goodrich, Charles Augustus, 1790-1862. defendant before church council 57602, 1st note after 105357, 105358
Goodrich, Charles B. 27876-27877
Goodrich, Chauncey, 1759-1815. 27878-(27879) (69843)
Goodrich, Chauncy Allen, 1790-1860. 27880
Goodrich, Chauncy E. (27881)

Goodrich, Elizur. 27882-27884, 105796
Goodrich, Frank B. 27885-(27887), 1st note after 96962
Goodrich, James W. 27888
Goodrich, John Z., b. 1801. 27889-27892, 67222
Goodrich, Samuel. (27893)
Goodrich, Samuel Griswold, 1793-1860. 17329, 17359, 24632, 27894-27906, (27908)-27922, 36123, 48028, 52278, 85431, note before 92205, 92343, 94243, 94248, 94559, 3d note after 96106, 97918, 97927, 101844, 104311
Goodrich, Samuel Griswold, 1793-1860. supposed author 27907, 27923, 41024
Goodrich, Samuel Griswold, 1793-1860. incorrectly supposed author (25539), 27924, 94242
Goodrich, William H. 27925
Goodricke, Henry. 27926-(27928), 89191
Goodridge, Charles Medyett. 27929.
Goodridge, Elijah Putnam. (27930)
Goodsell, N. ed. 26922
Goodsir, Robert Anstruther. 27931
Goodson, John. 83039
Goodspeed, E. J. 27932
Goodwell, Godek. pseud. Currency; the evil and the remedy. see Kellogg, Edward, 1790-1858.
Goodwin, -------, fl. 1862. (27935)
Goodwin, B. 27934
Goodwin, Daniel. ed. 27949
Goodwin, Daniel R. 27936
Goodwin, Edward C. (27937)
Goodwin, Ezra Shaw. (27938)
Goodwin, Frederick J. 27939
Goodwin, H. C. (27941)-(27942)
Goodwin, H. M. (27943)
Goodwin, Hezekiah. 27940, 100595, 2d note after 105939
Goodwin, Ichabod. 52902
Goodwin, Isaac. 27944-27945, 95377
Goodwin, John, 1594?-1665. (74457), 50773
Goodwin, John, 1594?-1665. supposed author (69679), 74624, 91382-91383
Goodwin, John A. 39506
Goodwin, L. S. 27946
Goodwin, Nathaniel. 27947-27949
Goodwin, Philo A. 27950
Goodwin, Robert M. defendant 27951, 96875-96878
Goodwin, Thomas, 1600-1680. (17066)-17067, 21991, 27952-27954, 32838, 32832, 32860, 55888, (69679), 74624, 80205, 91383 see also Church of Scotland. General Assembly. Commission.
Goodwin, Thomas Shepard. 27955
Goodwin, William, fl. 1648. 32860
Goodwin, William, 1790 or 91-1872. (15739), 27956
Goodwin, William A. (15739)
Goodwin, William F. 68409
Goowdin's annual legislative statistics. (15739)
Goodwin's town officer. 27945, 95377
Goodwish, Mr. pseud. Curious and interesting dialogue. see Valiniere, Pierre Huet de la.
Goodyear, Charles, 1804-1876. 27957
Gookin, Charles. 60399 see also Pennsylvania (Colony) Governor, 1709-1717 (Gookin)
Gookin, Daniel, 1612?-1687. 27413, 27958-27959
Gookin, Nathaniel. 27960, 30153, note after 95748
Goold, Thomas. 27961

Goos, P. 27962, 106290
Gopsill, William. (36068)
Gopsill (James) firm publisher 27963-(27964), (36068), (54874), 61606
Gopsill's directory of Reading. 27963
Gopsill's Newark city directory. (54874)
Gopsill's Philadelphia city and business directory. 61606
Gopsill's Westchester County directory. (27964)
Goram, Robert. see Coram, Robert.
Gordian knot untied. (51378)
Gordillo, Antonio Murillo y. see Murillo ·y Gordillo, Antonio.
Gordoa, J. (27966)
Gordon, A. H. see Stanmore, Arthur Charles Hamilton-Gordon, 1st Baron, 1829-1912.
Gordon, A. J., fl. 1845. 12200, 27969
Gordon, Adoniram Judson, 1836-1895. 27970-27971
Gordon, Alexander. (41354)
Gordon, Arthur Hamilton. see Stanmore, Arthur Charles Hamilton-Gordon, 1st Baron, 1828-1912.
Gordon, Charles. defendant 3644
Gordon, Cosmo. defendant at court martial 27972
Gordon, G. A. 27974
Gordon, G. W. 27977
Gordon, George. petitioner 27973, 36413
Gordon, George F. 27976
Gordon, George Hamilton. see Aberdeen, George Hamilton Gordon, 4th Earl of, 1784-1860.
Gordon, George Henry, 1825?-1886. 27975
Gordon, George William. (27978)
Gordon, Harry. (64835)
Gordon, J. D. reporter 65627
Gordon, J. W. 27988-27989
Gordon, James Bentley. 27979
Gordon, James D. 27980
Gordon, John, 1717-1790. (27980A)
Gordon, John, fl. 1772. petitioner 27981, 101042
Gordon, John, fl. 1791. 94806
Gordon, Sir John, fl. 1793. supposed author 96992
Gordon, John, fl. 1804. defendant at court martial 27982
Gordon, John, d. 1845. defendant (27983)-27987
Gordon, John Hamilton. see Stanmore, Arthur Charles Hamilton-Gordon, 1st Baron, 1829-1912.
Gordon, Leonard. plaintiff 81325
Gordon, Mary Jane. 9957
Gordon, N. M. 27990
Gordon, P. supposed author 27992, (32193), (32226)
Gordon, Patrick, 1644-1736. 59931-59934, 60124-60125, (60627), 67561 see also Pennsylvania (Colony) Governor, 1726-1737 (Gordon)
Gordon, Patrick, fl. 1700. 27991
Gordon, Sir Robert, of Lochinvar, d. 1627? 27967, 41715
Gordon, S. 27993
Gordon, Samuel. 92979
Gordon, Thomas, d. 1750. (34453), 86631, 96767, note after 96768
Gordon, Thomas F. 27994-28003, 1st note after 101265
Gordon, W. 28004
Gordon, W. R. 28013-28015
Gordon, William. defendant (27983)-27986
Gordon, William, 1728-1807. 21963, 28005-28011, 90943, 95642

Gordon, William A. (28012)
Gore, -------. RN 25142
Gore, Christopher. 28016-28017, (79012)
Gore, Francis, 1769-1852. 85205 see also
    Ontario. Lieutenant Governor, 1806-1817
    (Gore)
Gore, Montague. 28018-28019
Gorgas, Josiah, 1818-1883. 15333 see also
    Confederate States of America. Ordnance
    Department.
Gorges, ---------, fl. 1797. (28021)
Gorges, Sir Arthur. 66686
Gorges, Sir Fernando, 1565?-1647. 28020,
    (36203)-note after 36203
Gorges, Fernando, 1630-1718. ed. 28020,
    (36203)-note after 36203
Gorgues, --------. 39236
Gorham, George C. 28022
Gorham, John. (28023)
Gorham, Robert. see Coram, Robert.
Gorham, Me. Seminary. see Gorham
    Seminary, Gorham, Me.
Gorham, Me. Soldier's Monument. 28025
Gorham Seminary, Gorham, Me. (28026)
Gorigos, Hetorum, Prince of. see Hethum,
    Prince of Korghos, d. 1308.
Gorisito, Fr. de. 28027
Gorjy, Jean Claude. 96312
Gorling, Adolph. 28028
Gorman, -------. plaintiff (5576)
Gorman, Charles O. 28029
Gorman, Edward. defendant 95557
Gorman, J. C. 26270, 28031
Gorman, John B. 28030
Gorman, Willis A. 89203
Gorman. firm publishers see Nichols &
    Gorman. firm publishers
Gorostiaga, Jose B. 25104
Gorostiza, Manuel Eduardo de, 1789-1851.
    28032, 63309, 102205 see also Mexico.
    Legation. U. S.
Gorostiza, R. J. Argote y. see Argote y
    Gorostiza, R. J.
Gorrie, P. Douglass. 28033-28037
Gorringe, Henry H. 28038
Gorriti, Juana Manuela. 28039
Gortari, Mathias de Angles y. see Agnles y
    Gortari, Mathias de.
Gorton, Benjamin. 28040
Gorton, John. 5791
Gorton, Samuel. 28041-(28046), 70719, 104796
Gortz, C. C. von. (28047)
Gosche, Richard. (64601)
Goschen, Georg Joachim. 1279, 28049
Gosh, Josiah Ludwig, d. 1811. 28048, 42168-
    42171, 101896-note after 101898
Gosnold, Bartholomew, d. 1607. 66686
Gospel. 50738
Gospel, a dying saint's triumph. 103510
Gospel . . . a sermon . . . Portland, Nov. 9,
    1825. 21525
Gospel, according to John, in the Creek
    language. 8942
Gospel according to John. Ωpωnvkv hera
    chanichωyvten. (17460)
Gospel . . . according to John. Translated
    into the Cherokee language. 12461
Gospel according to John. Translated into the
    Ottawa language. 47377
Gospel according to Luke. 67765
Gospel according to Mark. 67765
Gospel according to Mark, and extracts from
    some other books. 69648
Gospel according to Mathew in the Charibbean
    language. 31304

Gospel according to Matthew in the Ojibwa
    language. 57083
Gospel according to Matthew. Translated into
    the Cherokee language. 12460
Gospel according to Matthew, translated into
    the Choctaw language. (12873)
Gospel according to Matthew. Translated into
    the Muskokee language. 51582
Gospel according to Matthew, translated into
    the Nez Perces language. 88875
Gospel according to Saint John. By Teyonin-
    hokarawen. 49846, 95145
Gospel according to St. John, in Esquimaux
    and English. 22850
Gospel according to St. John in the language
    of the Malliseet Indians. 67758
Gospel according to St. John. Translated into
    the Chippeway tongue. (12832)
Gospel according to Saint Luke, translated
    into the Seneca tongue. 79121
Gospel according to Saint Mark. 85452
Gospel according to St. Mark, into the Mohaw
    tongue. 49845
Gospel according to St. Mark; translated into
    the language of the Cree Indians. 17454
Gospel according to St. Matthew, and the Acts
    of the Apostles. 42770
Gospel according to Saint Matthew, in the
    Micmac language. 67756
Gospel, . . . according to St. Matthew,
    translated into the Mohawk language.
    49844
Gospel according to Saint Matthew translated
    into the Shawanoe language. (79977)
Gospel according to Saint Matthew. Translate
    into the Whawannoe language. 42769
Gospel akording tu Sent Luk. 67757
Gospel among the Dakotas. 71343
Gospel applied to the fugitive slave law. 909
Gospel call. 79933
Gospel church portrayed. 30642
Gospel-covenant; or the covenant of grace
    opened. (9096)-9097
Gospel-doctrine of justification by faith. 625
Gospel doctrine. Selections from the sermons
    and writings. 83347
Gospel family-order. 25351
Gospel for the poor. (46348)
Gospel harvest and Christian's duty. 19877
Gospel harvest, illustrated in a sermon at
    Boston. (50953)
Gospel herald. 92683, 92687
Gospel hidden to them that are lost. 5916
Gospel in a nut shell. 83114
Gospel in Canada, and its relation to Huron
    College. 5574, 34009
Gospel in Central America. 17691
Gospel in New-England. 59655
Gospel, in the church. 20391
Gospel in the far west. 21264, 47174
Gospel incense. 13868
Gospel magazine. (30395), 97269
Gospel minister. 103344
Gospel-minister described. (46210)
Gospel-ministers . . . a sermon preached to
    the ministers. (67767)
Gospel-ministers are the servants of Christ-
    Jesus. 62511
Gospel ministers, Christ's ambassadors.
    (62819)
Gospel ministers considered under the similit
    of fishers of men. 24574
Gospel ministers exhibited under the motion o
    stars. 80795

Gospel minister's farewell. 88887
Gospel ministers must be fit. 1831
Gospel-ministers to preach Christ to their people. 18110
Gospel-ministry a warfare. 75845
Gospel ministry the rich gift. (14525)
Gospel ministry vindicated from contempt. 91482
Gospel music. 28050
Gospel of Christ preached to the poor. 19362
Gospel of justification by the righteousness of God. 46310, 46349
Gospel of St. John. 67765
Gospel of St. John in the language of the Esquimaux. 22850
Gospel of St. Matthew; translated into the Ojibwa language. 57081
Gospel of slavery. A primer of freedom. 28051, 35090, 1st note after 95375
Gospel of the brazen serpent. (46617), note after 106242
Gospel of the city explained. 46260
Gospel of the manna, to be gathered in the morning. 46395
Gospel of the rainbow. 46551
Gospel of the typical servitude. 17686
Gospel of to-day. 11932
Gospel of the church. 20391
Gospel order revived. 28052, 28506, 65689, 91945, note after 105090
Gospel ordinance. 78281
Gospel ordinances. 50660
Gospel preachers and preaching. 14426
Gospel rangers. 47994
Gospel reflector. 50739
Gospel reminiscences in the West Indies. 28053, 92941-92943
Gospel sonnets, or spiritual songs. (22794)
Gospel summons. 84626
Gospel supper. 103515, 103593
Gospel, the power of God unto salvation. 81626
Gospel the wisdom of God. 89744
Gospel-times, or oaths forbidden under the Gospel. 66926
Gospel to be preached to all men. 102521
Gospel to be published and applied against all sin. (12406)
Gospel tract no. IV. 92683
Gospel tracts.—No. IV. 92684
Gospel treasure in earthen vessels. 103398
Gospel treasury. 89517
Gospel-truth stated and vindicated. 12333, 104184
Gospel-truths. 59691
Gospel visiter. see Southern pioneer and Gospel visiter.
Gospels according to St. Matthew, St. Luke, St. Mark and St. John. 18292
Gospels and epistles in the Greenland language. 22853
Gospels of Luke and John. 18292
Gospels of Matthew and John in Arrawak. 2100
Gospels of St. Matthew and St. John in the language of the Ojibwa Indians. 57981
Gospels, written in the Negro patois of English. (32372), 52257
Goss, C. C. (28054)
Goss, Elbridge H. 28056
Goss, Ephraim. (28055)
Goss, Thomas. 360, 6254, 11968, 3d note after after 96741
Goss, Warren Lee. 28057
Goss, William. 92308

Gosse, Edmund. ed. 83021
Gosse, L. A. 28058-28059
Gosse, Philip Henry. 28060-28064
Gosselman, Carl August. 28065-28068
Gossip, or a laugh with the ladies. (13435)
Gossips of Rivertown. (52139)
Gossom, Stephen. 27752
Gostling, George. 28069
Goswell, William. 75626 see also Salem, Mass. Mayor, 1869-1870. (Goswell)
Got, Bertrand de. see Clement V, Pope, 1264-1314.
Gotham and the Gothamites. 36287
Gothardt Arthes, M. see Arthes, M. Gothardt.
Goths in New-England. (44736)
Gottfried, Johann Ludwig. see Abelin, Jean Philippe.
Gottfriedt. see Abelin, Jean Philippe.
Gottingisches historisches Magazin. 47412
Gottlieb Gottsoock. (65066)
Gottlieb Mittelberger's Reise nach Pennsylvanien im Jahr 1750. 49761
Gottschalk, P. 96515
Gottsched, J. C. 100720
Gottsched, Luis. Adelg. Vict. tr. 100720
Gottsliche liebes. 100775
Gotzen, J. G. tr. 43781
Gotzler, J. E. ed. (68215)
Goubert, Eugene. 63545
Goudy, Thomas. ed. 94883
Gouge, W. note before 92797-92797
Gouge, William M. (28071)-28074
Gougenot des Mousseaux, Henry Roger. 28075
Gough, James. 28076
Gough, John. (28077)-28078
Gough, John B. 28079-28083, 69095
Gough, Thomas. tr. 25149
Gough, William. see Goffe, William, d. ca. 1679.
Gough Division, No. 2, Quebec. see Sons of Temperance of North America. Quebec. Gough Division, no. 2, Quebec (City)
Goujard, Aime Jacques Alexandre. see Bonpland, Aime Jacques Alexandre, 1773-1858.
Goulain de Laudonniere, Rene. see Laudonniere, Rene Goulaine de.
Goulard, Simon. tr. 57805
Gould, ----------. defendant 92333
Gould, ----------. ed. (28116) ᴄ
Gould, A. B. 46082
Gould, Albert P. 28084
Gould, Augustus Addison, 1805-1866. 5467, 27419, (28085)-28090 see also Massachusetts. Zoological and Botanical Survey.
Gould, Benjamin Apthorp. 28091-28097, 42706, 85072, 89533 see also Committee on Spiritualism, Boston, 1857.
Gould, Benjamin Apthorp. supposed author 94136
Gould, Charles. defendant 28098
Gould, Cahrles. petitioner 24561
Gould, Sir Charles, Bart. see Morgan, Sir Charles Gould, Bart., 1726-1806.
Gould, Daniel, d. 1716. 28099
Gould, David. 28100
Gould, Edward S. 28101-28102
Gould, Elijah. petitioner 28103
Gould, G. H. 28104
Gould, Hannah Flagg. (28105)
Gould, J. plaintiff 102448
Gould, James. 28106-28107
Gould, Jay. 28108

Gould, John, 1804-1881. 18649, 28109-(28112), 31945, (44926)

Gould, John Stanton. (28113)-(28114)

Gould, John W. (28116)

Gould, Josiah. 28115

Gould, Levi S. (28117)

Gould, Marcus T. C. defendant 15617

Gould, Marcus T. C. reporter 8466, 28118-28121, 31715, (43001), 45471, 53945, 66931, 91226, 91566, note after 92151, 96901, note after 96937, 96938, note after 96948, 103059

Gould, N. 28122

Gould, Nathaniel D. 28123

Gould, Roland F. 28124

Gould, Thomas B. 28125, (32371)

Gould, Vinson. (28126)-28127, 55388, 104528

Gould, W. see Guild, William.

Gould, William. 28128

Goulding, F. R. 28130

Goulding, Henry. 59688

Goulding, John. supposed author 90824

Gould's stenographic reporter. 91226

Gouley, George Frank. ed. 25802

Gouley, J. W. S. 84277

Goulty, J. N. 28131

Goulu, Ferd. engr. 85819

Gouly, B. 28132

Goupil, Rene. 80018

Gouraud, Francois Fauvel. see Fauvel-Gouraud, Francois.

Gouraud, J. B. G. Fauvel. see Fauvel Gouraud, J. B. G.

Gourdin, ------. 47929

Gourdin, Theodore S. 28135

Gourdon, William. 66686

Gourgues, D. de. 24902, 39234-39236, note before 99284

Gouriet, --------. tr. 100836

Gourlay, Robert. see Gourlay, Robert Fleming.

Gourlay, Robert Fleming. (28136)-(28143), 98086

Gourlay, William. 28144

Gourlie, John H. 28145

Gouroff, --------. 28146

Gouve, ------ le. see Le Gouve, ---------.

Gouvernement des colonies Francaises. 14709, 61252

Gouverneur. pseud. Remarks on the life insurance laws of New-York. 28149

Gouverneur, Abraham. petitioner 90020

Gouverneur, Isaac. defendant 39877

Gouverneur, Isaac. plaintiff 28147

Gouverneur, J. J. A. tr. 74165

Gouverneur, Lorenzo D. 28148, (28951), 79699

Gouverneur, Samuel L. 50019

Gouverneur, N. Y. Riverside Cemetery. 71654

Gouverneur Wesleyan Seminary, Ogdensburgh, N. Y. 28150

Gouvest, J. H. Maubert de. see Maubert de Gouvest, J. H.

Goux, --------. 28151

Gouy d'Argy, -------, Marquis de. see Gouy d'Arsy, Louis Henri Marthe, Marquis de, 1753-1794.

Gouy d'Arsy, Louis Henri Marthe, Marquis de, 1753-1794. 8039, 28152-28155, 47519, 75081, 75149 see also Santo Domingo (French Colony) Commissaires. Rapporteur. Santo Domingo (French Colony) Deputes a l'Assemblee Nationale.

Gov. pseud. Rhymed tactics. see Godfrey, John A.

Govantes, Agustin. 72523

Goveo de Victoria, Pedro. see Victoria, Pedro Gobeo de.

Gouernador Don Bernardo de Tejada. 94596

Governess. 94556

Governing principles and evils to be avoided. 89669

Governing race. 28156, 67376

Government. 44909, 106079

Government a divine institution. 14321

Government a divine ordinance. 68997

Government aid to American shipping interests 48018

Government and administration. 542

Government and Christianity. 78939

Government and improvement of mirth. (14528

Government and laws of every country. (56622

Government and liberty described. 2630

Government and rebellion. (192)

Government and the currency. (48863)

Government, and the right of revolution. 86132

Government bound to protect from the dram-ship. 82634

Government commission of enquiry. 67720

Government contracts. Report of the special committee. 28157, 69907

Government contracts. Speech . . . in the House. 18918

Government expenditures. 43

Government finances and the currency. 26401

Government gazette, St. Croix. see St. Croix

Government House, Halifax, N. S. 17th September, 1863. 56195

Government is an effect, not a cause. (56367)

Government is of God. (39263)

Government of Canada. (11601), 2d note after 105598-9 [sic]

Government of Christ considered and applied. 102219

Government of cities. (78018)

Government of God. 39720

Government of God desirable. 4332

Government of God universal. 64792

Government of laws, not despotism. (39130)

Government of Sir Edmund Andros over New England. (8177)

Government of the Army of the republic of Texas. 95058

Government of the church of Christ. 5760

Government of the church of Christ, and the authority of church judicatories established. 95580

Government of the Methodist Episcopal Church An examination of Dr. Bond's rejoinder. (33569)

Government of the Methodist Episcopal Church anti-republican and despotic. 43573

Government of the Methodist Episcopal Church —Its origin. 91476

Government of the rebellious states. 73349

Government of the second Adam. (82499)

Government of the territories. 8180

Government of the United States. 57596

Government, or no government. 28158

Government paper money. 96396

Government sale. 28159

Government . . . Sermon . . . before the Congress. 38872

Government specie-paying bank of issue. 8841

Government survey. 60119

Government survey with a general view. 7268

Government telegraphs. 57729

Governor's speech. (13743), (43942), 60123
Governour's speech at the prorouging the
    Assembly. 35633
Governour's speech to the Assembly. 60125
Govierno eclesiastico pacifico. 99668
Govin, Carlos Manuel Trelles y. see Trelles
    y Govan, Carlos Manuel, 1866-
Govin, D. Joseph. 28161-28162
Gow, Daniel. 28163
Gow, Mrs. L. B. 12730, 42690
Gowahas. indian name see Wright, Asher.
Gowahas Goyadoh. 28164
Gowan, --------- 28167
Gowan, James. 28165
Gowan, Ogle R. 28166
Gowan (William) firm publisher 8953, 19612,
    49026, note after 28166
Go-wana Gwo-ih sat'hat yon de yas dah' gwah.
    (28168)
Gowanas Hotel and Wharf Company. 28169
Gowan's bibliotheca Americana. 8953, 19612,
    49026, note after 28166
Gowen, A. C. 28170
Gowen, James. 28171
Gower, E. 28172
Gower, Sir Erasmus, 1742-1814. (59572),
    90843
Gower, Granville Leveson. see Stafford,
    Granville Leveson-Gower, 1st Marquis
    of, 1721-1803.
Goycoechea, Jose Antonio. 28173, 51224
Goyena, P. ed. 70298
Goyeneche, J. Sebastian, Abp. 28174
Goyeneche, Juan de. 86448, 86453
Gozlan, Leon, d. 1866. 21368
Gozman, Francisco del Valle y. see Valle y
    Gozman, Francisco del.
Gozo del Mexicano imperio por su indepen-
    dencia y libertad. 77115
Gozosa descripcion de las gestibus demon-
    straciones. 28175
Gozzi, C. Gaspare. tr. 92204
Gra, Barry. pseud. Cakes and ale at Wood-
    biney. see Coffin, Robert Barry.
Graaf, Johannes de. 49560, 102897 see also
    St. Eustatius (Dutch Colony) Commandeur,
    1776-1781 (Graaf)
Graaff, Nicolaus de. 28176
Graah, Wilhelm August. 28177-28179, 62945
Grabe, ---------. 28180
Graberg, Jacopo. (28181), 67484
Grabhorn Press rare American series. 103893
Grabowski, Stanislaus. 28182-28183
Gracchus. pseud. Address to the electors of
    New Hampshire. 52941
Grace. a slave appellant 29517, 1st note
    after 92630
Grace, --------- de. 38710
Grace, Henry. (28184)
Grace, J. supposed author 28185, 47584
Grace and glory. (51518)
Grace and truth. 22240
Grace Barclay's diary. 64461
Grace Church, Albany. see Albany. Grace
    Church.
Grace Church, Jamaica, N. Y. see Jamaica,
    N. Y. Grace Church.
Grace Church, Newton, Mass. see Newton,
    Mass. Grace Church.
Grace Church, San Francisco. see San
    Francisco. Grace Church.
Grace Church Charity School, New York. see
    New York (City) Grace Church Charity
    School.

Grace Church Education Society, New York.
    see New York (City) Grace Church
    Education Society.
Grace defended. A censure on . . . ungodline
    (46350)
Grace defended. . . . In which the doctrine
    original sin. (47125)
Grace displayed: an interesting narrative.
    44714
Grace displayed in the conversion of Mr.
    Studley. 105178
Grace Dudley. 61231
Grace Greenwood. pseud. see Lippincott,
    Sarah J. (Clarke)
Grace of the Gospel. 105252
Grace Parish, New York. see New York
    (City) Grace Parish.
Gracerie, -------- de la. 28187
Gracey, S. L. (28188)
Gracia concedida por S. M. a los habitantes
    la isla. 56747
Gracia triunfante en la vida de Catharina
    Tegakovita. 98172
Gracias (Honduras Department) 32759, 5514
Gracias singulares del C. Coronel J. M.
    Tornel. 97202
Gracie, Pierre, called Ferrande, ca. 1435-ca
    1520. 28189
Gracie's Alabama Brigade. (79889)
Gracious presence of God. 22272
Graded course of instruction. (52483)
Gradin, A. (28190)
Gradual abolition of slavery. 28191
Gradual western march to the Pacific Ocean
    94384
Graduate, late an officer in the United State
    Army. pseud. Letter to the Honorable
    Mr. Hawes. 40484, 102946
Graduate of '69. pseud. Four years at Yale
    (25286)
Graduate of the U. S. Naval Academy. pseu
    United States Naval and Military Acade
    see Smith, Oscar, 1887-
Graduate of Yale College, of the class of 18
    pseud. Reminiscences of scenes. see
    Mitchell, John.
Graduated tables, showing the comparative
    amount of money. 45757
Graduated Tax Association, New York. 904
Graduated taxation upon accumulated wealth.
    90489
Graduating exercises of the class of 1856.
    69641
Graduel Romain a l'usage du Diocese de
    Quebec. 67004
Graef, H. A. 8290
Graenlandz saga. 2058, (28646), 74880
Graf, -------. illus. (66483)
Grafen N. L. von Zinzendorf Leben und
    Charakter. 88929
Grafen von Mirabeau Sammlung einiger phi
    phischen und politischen Schriften. 49
Graff, George. 38802, 55774 see also La
    caster County, Pa. Collector of Excis
    Northampton County, Pa. Collector of
    Excise.
Graffarel, P. ed. 95339
Graffenried, Friedrich von. 7859
Graffigny, Francoise (d'Isembourg d'Happon
    court) de. see Grafigny, Francoise
    (d'Isembourg d'Happoncourt) de, 1695-
Graffort, Thomas. 6474, 95946
Grafigny, Francoise (d'Isembourg d'Happonc
    de, 1695-1758. 28192-28193, 28197,
    40560, 40692, (40693)

Grammar of the Pima or Nevome. 2124, 84380

Grammar School Board, Boston. see Boston. School Committee. Grammar School Board.

Grammar School in the Eastern Part of the Town of Roxbury, Mass. see Roxbury, Mass. Eastern Grammar School.

Grammar school system of Ontario. 28253

Grammarians funeral. 96153

Grammatic, vor Diejenigen, Welche in andern Sprachen und deren Fundamenten erfahren sind. 56353, 77197, 88825-88827

Grammatica construccion de los hymnos ecclesiasticos. 29036

Grammatica da lingua geral dos Indios do Brasil. 24314

Grammatica de la lengua-Chilena. 23971

Grammatica de la lengua Mexicana. 29372

Grammatica della lingua Otomi. 52412

Grammatica et lexicon linguae Mexicanae. 57233

Grammatica Gronlandica Danico-Latina. (22038)

Grammatica Latina. 46909

Grammatica linguae Selicae. 47861

Grammatica ober de Creoolske sprog på de Danske eilande i America. 42910

Grammatica y vocabulario de la lengua Otomi. 10953

Grammatical institute of the English language. 102336-102337, 102355-102357, 102359, 102367, 102377

Grammatical institutes in verse. 33799

Grammatical sketch of the Heve language. 28252, 84381

Grammatical sketch of the language spoken by the Indians. 17028

Grammatici in Cosmographiae libros intro-ductorium. 52206

Grammatik der Dakota Sprache. 26279

Grammatik der Gronlandischen Sprache. (38042)

Grammatik der Kiriri-Sprache. 44180

Grammatik der Sonorischen Sprachen. 9523

Grammatische Bau der Algonkin-Sprachen. 51283

Grammell, William. incorrectly supposed author 20403, 50806

Gran almanaque y directorio del comercio. 48486

Gran artista y la gran senora. 71310

Gran cuestion fiscal de Venezuela. 7797

Gran fee del centurion Espanol. 20136

Gran piscator de las Nueva-Espana. 26573

Granada. Laws, statutes, etc. 86236

Granada (Nueva Granada) see Colombia.

Granada (Province) Director Supremo. 62931 see also Pineda, Jose Laureano.

Granada, Nicaragua. 28254

Granada, Spain (Archdiocese) 86443

Granadino. pseud. General Simon Bolivar en la campana. 56276

Granadino. pseud. Opinion de un Granadino sobre la division. 14559

Granados y Galvez, Joseph Joaquin. 28255

Granate Granadino-Americano i Catolica. 76700

Granbery, J. C. 84992

Granby, Charles Manners, 2d Marquis of. see Rutland, Charles Manners, 4th Duke of, 1754-1787.

Grand, J. C. le. see Le Grand, J. C.

Grand, Jean Baptiste Bernard le. see Le Grand, Jean Baptiste Bernard.

Grand d'Hauteville, Ellen (Sears) see D'Hauteville, Ellen (Sears) Grand.

Grand d'Hauteville, Paul Daniel Gonsalve. see D'Hauteville, Paul Daniel Gonsalve Grand.

Grand Pierre, -------- Dralse de. see Dralse de Grandpierre, -------.

Grand Pierre, J. H. 28274-28276

Grand American Hall, . . . Leicester Square. 83011

Grand and imposiing celebration. 64711

Grand appeal to the nation. 60925

Grand arcanum detected. 28548

Grand army. 31169

Grand Army of the Republic. 17417, 48751, 74088 see also Soldier's friend and Grand Army of the Republic.

Grand Army of the Republic. National Encampment, Washington, D. C., 1870. 65888

Grand Army of the Republic. Department of Massachusetts. 45758

Grand Army of the Republic. Department of Michigan. 17427, 48751

Grand Army of the Republic. Department of Minnesota. 49298

Grand Army of the Republic. Department of New Jersey. 53100

Grand Army of the Republic. Department of New York. Alexander Hamilton Post no. 182. 84423

Grand atlas. 5715, 5718

Grand ballad of Cora. 8137, 80342

Grand California tree. 10012

Grand Canyon of Arizona. 84488

Grand celebration in honor of the passage of the ordinance of emancipation. 28256

Grand celebration in the city of St. Paul. (28257)

Grand Chaplain of the Grand Lodge of New Hampshire. see Freemasons. New Hampshire. Grand Lodge. Grand Chaplain.

Grand chef des Seminoles. 69057

Grand chorus. 28258

Grand civic and military procession in Philadelphia. 101821

Grand Committee of Twenty, Augusta, Ga. see Augusta, Ga. Grand Committee of Twe

Grand Consistory of the State of Massachuset Valley of Boston. (45759)

Grand conspiration du pillage. 77747

Grand Council U. L. A. State of California, San Francisco. April 20th, 1865. 1001

Grand coureurs d'aventures. 12561

Grand debat entre Duffay et consorts. 75126, 87116

Grand Democratic Republican Meeting, New York, 1838. see Democratic Party. I York. New York City.

Grand Division of the Sons of Temperance of Indiana. see Sons of Temperance of North America. Indiana. Grand Divisi

Grand elixir. 88164

Grand encampment of Knights Templar, and appendant orders. (28259)

Grand encampment of Knights Templar . . . Massachusetts. 38133

Grand era of ruin. (1526)

Grand Federal Procession, Philadelphia, 1788 see Philadelphia. Grand Federal Proc sion, July 4, 1788.

Grand funeral march. 64286

Grand gazetteer. 7791

Grand Gulf Rail Road and Banking Company. 49491

Grand illustrated encyclopaedia of animated nature. (26054)

Grand issues of the war. 24435

Grand jurors duty considered. (28260)

Grand jury report. 53326

Grand list of the state of Connecticut for the first of October, 1854. 15746

Grand Lodge . . . extra quarterly communication. 60129

Grand Lodge jurisdictionary claim. 31010

Grand Lodge of Free and Accepted Masons of . . . Louisiana. 42259

Grand Lodge . . . of Free and Accepted Masons, of . . . Massachusetts. 45760

Grand Lodge . . . of Free and Accepted Masons of . . . Massachusetts, in union with the . . . Grand Lodges in Europe and America. 72179

Grand Lodge . . . of . . . Maine. (53992)

Grand Lodge of South Carolina, October 4th 5808. 87846

Grand Lodge of the Most Ancient and Honorable Society of Free & Accepted Masons of the State of Vermont. 99189

Grand Lodge of the State of Louisiana. Grand annual communication. 42259

Grand Lodge of the State of Louisiana. Report of the committee. 45503

Grand Lodge of the United States. Adjourned session. 45504

Grand lodges of Alabama. 28261

Grand Mass Meeting of the Citizens of San Francisco, 1863. see Republican Party. California. San Francisco.

Grand Miscellaneous Concert, For the Benefit of the Orphan Asylum, New York, 1844. see New York (City) Grand Miscellaneous Concert, for the Benefit of the Orphan Asylum, 1844.

Grand miscellaneous concert, for the benefit of the Orphan Asylum, to be performed at Washington Hall. 54296

Grand mistakes. 28262

Grand moving mirror of American scenery. 2852, 7764

Grand national peace jubilee. 28263

Grand National Republican Meeting, New York, 1830. see National Republican Party. New York. New York (City)

Grand Ohio Company. see Ohio Company.

Grand-ouest des Etats-Unis. (81309)

Grand Pawnee Indians. see Pawnee Indians.

Grand peristrephic panorama of the polar regions. 89541

Grand peuple qui se relevo. 26728

Grand point of solicitude. 46351

Grand preparations. 85122

Grand preparations for the promised peaceable reign of Christ. 85114

Grand pyrate. (18078)

Grand question, whether war or no war. 28264, 57395, note after 101144-101145

Grand Ralley of the Workingmen of Charlestown, Mass. 3d, 1840. 12125

Grand Rapids, Mich. First Congregational Church. Committee. 83364

Grand Rapids city directory for 1867-68. 28265

Grand Reception Extended by the Pupils of the Public Grammar Schools . . . to Peter Cooper, New York, 1858. (54604)

Grand review of the dead. (51756)

Grand revival in old Edgefield in 1809. 102466

Grand, romantic, cabalistic, melo drama, in three acts. 97466

Grand rovtier de mer, de Iean Hvgves de Linschot. 41371, (41373)

Grand routier de mer qu'il convient tenir. (28266)

Grand Royal Arch Chapter of Maine. 43993

Grand Royal Arch Chapter of Massachusetts. 45761

Grand scheme . . . under the names of the Atlantic Telegraph Company. (37349)

Grand State Fair of the Mechanics and Agricultural Fair Association of Louisiana. see Mechanics and Agricultural Fair Association of Louisiana. Grand State Fair.

Grand Statement of the funds of Yale College. 105858

Grand theatre historique. 3

Grand trio. Fuller, Jeter, Yates. 84852

Grand trio. Jeter, Fuller, Yates. 84853

Grand-tronciade ou itineraire de Quebec a la Riviere-du-Loup. 11364

Grand Trunk Railway Company of Canada. (28269)

Grand Trunk Railway Company of Canada. defendants 85421

Grand Trunk Railway Company of Canada. petitioners (28269)

Grand Trunk Railway Company of Canada. Celebration Committee. Sub-Committee. 50264

Grand Trunk Railway Company of Canada. Managing Directors. (28268)

Grand Trunk Railway Company of Canada. Vice-President. (28268)

Grant Trunk Railway of Canada. Proceedings of the preference bondholders historically, legally and financially considered. 85219

Grand voyage dv pays des Hurons. 74883, 74885

Grand voyage du pays des Hurons situe en l'Amerique. 74881-74882, 74884

Grande miseno en la America. 28270

Grande poder dos vates. 27199

Grand vipre fer-de-lance de la Martinique. 50557

Grandes bailes y maromas en casa de Dona Prudencia de Mendiola. 99705

Grandes chasses. 48224

Grandes chroniques de St. Denis du tems de Charles V. 76838

Grandes viahes clasicos. 99380

Grandeur et avenir des Etats-Unis. 11046, 26700

Grandeur of the struggle and its responsibilities. 24406

Grandeza Mexicana. 2862, 1st note after 98300

Grandeza o decadencia del Peru. 3640

Grandezas del poder en la concepcion de Maria. 87232

Grandfather's story of the first settlers of New England. 32196

Grandguillot, A. 28271

Grandidier, Ernest. (28272)

Grandma Smith. pseud. Soldier's friend. see Smith, Susan E. (Drake) 1817-

Grandmaison, Millin de. tr. 105627

Grandmother's grandmother. 83486

Grandmottet, --------. tr. 72232

Grandpierre, -------- Dralse de. see Dralse de Grandpierre, --------.

Grandpre, L. de. tr. 44120

Grandy, Moses. 28277, note after 95499

Grange, ------- La. see La Grange, --------.

Grange, Jules, 21216

Grange de Checieux, G. A. F. Simon de la
   see Lagrange de Checieux, G. A. F.
   Simon de.
Granger, A. H. (28279)
Granger, Amos Phelps, 1789-1866. (28280)
Granger, Arthur. 28278
Granger, Arthur. supposed author 27698
Granger, Gideon, 1767-1822. 22679, 28118,
   (28281)-(28283), (39911), 53477, (64487)-
   64491, 80854, 80856, 99810 see also
   U. S. Post Office Department.
Granger, James, 1723-1776. 82823
Granger, James N. 28284
Granier, J. E. (28285)-28286
Granier de Cassagnac, Adolphe de. 28287
Granite Club, Boston. 28288
Granite dry docks. 93148
Granite monthly. 102254
Granite State Lincoln Club, Washington, D. C.
   444, 52797 see also Republican Party.
   Washington, D. C.
Granite state magazine. 103200
Graniteville Manufacturing Company.
   President. 28289
Graniteville Manufacturing Company.
   Treasurer. 28289
Gransboerna eller Wish-Ton-Wish's Klagan.
   16558
Granskeren. (18240)
Grant, --------. 74484
Grant, Mrs. see Grant, Anne (MacVicar)
   1755-1838.
Grant, A. 28295
Grant, Abraham Phineas, 1804-1871. 28290
Grant, Andrew. (2712), 28291-28293
Grant, Anne (MacVicar) 1755-1838. (28296)-
   28297
Grant, Charles. see Glenelg, Charles Grant,
   Baron, 1778-1866.
Grant, Charles, Vicomte de Vaux. 28298-
   28299
Grant, David. (28302)
Grant, E. B. 28303
Grant, Francis. 70110
Grant, J. 3606
Grant, J. M. 28305
Grant, J. P. ed. 28297
Grant, Sir J. P. 35605
Grant, J. W. 28308
Grant, James, fl. 1764-1771. 72848 see also
   East Florida. Governor, 1764-1771
   (Grant)
Grant, James, 1771 or 2-1833. 28306
Grant, James, fl. 1776. (28304)
Grant, Jeremiah. 28307
Grant, Matthew. 28309, 91754
Grant, Robert. defendant 72620, note after
   96880
Grant, T. 28320
Grant, Ulysses Simpson, Pres. U. S., 1822-
   1885. 19515, 28311, 28315-28317,
   31164, 40611, 41157, (48141), 53362,
   68010, (70984), 78036, 80417-(80418),
   84774 see also U. S. Army. General
   of the Army.   U. S. President, 1869-
   1877 (Grant)
Grant, William H. (28321)
Grant, William R. 28322
Grant & Co. firm see Fordyce, Grant &
   Co. firm
Grant against Greeley. 65348
Grant and Colfax. 8155
Grant and his campaigns. 16701
Grant and release of one eighth part of
   Carolina. 10971
Grant and Sherman. 31150

Grant: and why he should be elected president.
   50836
Grant as a soldier and statesman. 33381
Grant campaign songster. 28317
Grant from the state of New York to Robert
   Livingston and Robert Fulton. 71349
Grant of King Charles the First, to Sir
   Edmund Plowden. 98637
Grant of the Northern Neck in Virginia to Lord
   Culpepper. 99889
Grant routier et pilotage. 28189
Grant sends United States troops to carry the
   election. 84808
Grant, Sherman, Thomas, Sheridan, and Far-
   ragut. 8160, 57925, 85153
Grant songster. 28317
Grant songster. A collection of campaign
   songs for 1868. 28317
Grant, the man of mystery. 83671
Grant to the Georgia Mississippi Company.
   27054, note after 106003
Grantees of New Hampshire. see Proprietors
   of the New Hampshire Grants.
Grantham, Sir Thomas. 28323
Grantland, Seaton, 1782-1864. 28324
Grant's Attorney General exposes the false-
   hoods of Senator Morton. 84808
Grants by the Governor of South Carolina.
   72848
Grants, concessions, and original constitutions.
   39527, 89425
Grants to Messrs. Wilson and Exeter. 16084,
   94946
Grants to the Van Rensselaer and Livingston
   families. 65486
Granville, J. 28325
Granville, John Carteret, 1st Earl, 1690-1763.
   10979, 93911
Granville, John Carteret, 1st Earl, 1690-1763.
   supposed author 90617-90619
Granville, Mass. Jubilee, 1845. 28327
Granville, Ohio. Denison University. see
   Denison University, Granville, Ohio.
Granville, Ohio. Female Seminary. 28329
Granville, Ohio. Literary and Theological
   Institution. see Denison University,
   Granville, Ohio.
Granville Jubilee, Granville, Mass., 1845. see
   Granville, Mass. Jubilee, 1845.
Granville Jubilee, celebrated at Granville,
   Mass. 28327
Granville Literary and Theological Institution.
   see Denison University, Granville, Ohio
Granzbauer und der Kohlen-Toni in Amerika.
   91219
Graphaeus, Corn. Scribon. ed. 43833-43834
Graphic account of the alarming riots. 61703
Graphic scenes of the Japanese Expedition.
   (31242)
Graphic sketches from old and authentic works.
   103394
Graphic sketches. Part I. The natives of
   Virginia. 103394
Graphtolites of the Quebec group. 10458,
   29805
Graple with abstractionists. 88488
Grason, William, 1786-1868. 2992, (45141),
   45260 see also Maryland. Governor,
   1838-1841 (Grason)
"Grasping the promises." 86265, 88050
Grass River Division, no. 368, Sons of Temper-
   ance. see Sons of Temperance of North
   America. New York. Grass River
   Division, no. 368.
Grasse-Tilly, Alexandre Francois Auguste,
   Comte de. 28330

Grasse-Tilly, Francois Joseph Paul, Marquis de, 1722-1788. 28330-28333

Grasse Tilly, Francois Joseph Paul, Marquis de 1722-1788. supposed author 23034, 28331

Grasset de Saint Sauveur, Jacques. 16808, 28334-28335, 75487-75488

Grassi, Giovanni. (28336)

Graswinkel, Dirk. supposed author 7504

Grata brevitas. 46352

Grateful reflections on the divine goodness. 28337, 86895, 2d note after 104986

Grateful reflexions on the signal appearances. 25395

Grateful sacrifice. 77569

Gratien, Henri. see Bertrand, Henri Gratien, Comte de.

Gratissimo et inclito Mexicano mvseo. 86445

Gratitude and obedience to the Preserver of Men. 104963

Gratitude for individual and national blessings. 22009

Gratitudes de un exercitanto a las misericordias de Dios. 11462

Grattan, Peachy R. 28338

Grattan, Thomas Colley. 28339-28340

Gratton, John. (28341), 103703

Gratulatory address. 13120, 28342, 97403

Graty, Alfred M. du. see Du Graty, Alfred M.

Grau, J. (28343)

Graue, ------ du Pont. see Pont-Graue, ------ du.

Grauert, W. tr. (28483)

Graues, ------. 31740

Graun, --------. 86969

Grave, John. 28344

Grave van Nassau la Leck, L. Th. see Nassau la Leck, L. Th. Grave van.

Grave and death destroyed. 65602

Grave answer to Mr. Wesley's calm address. 102647

Grave-mounds and their contents. (36124)

Grave of the heart. 79713

Grave, without any order. 83450

Graveairs, a deacon. pseud. Americans roused. see Sewall, Jonathan, 1728-1796.

Graveairs, a deacon. pseud. Cure for the spleen. see Sewall, Jonathan, 1728-1796.

Gravendonc, Jean. tr. 4638, 76813

Graves, --------. tr. 87172

Graves, Mrs. A. J. 28345-28346

Graves, Allen T. 28347

Graves, H. C. note after 102109

Graves, Henry W. 89888, note after 94615 see also Springfield, N. J. Centennial Celebration, July 4, 1876. Committee of Publication.

Graves, J. (28349)

Graves, J. R. 28350

Graves, John. (28348), 80583

Graves, John. supposed author 80583, 105673

Graves, John Boonen. plaintiff 37475, 100777

Graves, Louisa Carolina. claimant (28352)

Graves, R. claimant (28352)

Graves, Richard Stanford. 28351

Graves, Samuel Colleton. supposed author 97701

Graves, Thomas Graves, 1st Baron, 1725?-1802. 13751

Graves, William, 1724?-1801. 28354-(28355), 86565

Graves, William, fl. 1807-1810. (28353)

Graves of the Indians. 28356

Gravesend, N. Y. (28357)

Gravi, ------. tr. 100725

Gravier, -------. (80003)

Gravier, -------, Comte de Malet du. see Malet du Gravier, -------, Comte de.

Gravier, Gabriel. 28358, 29471, 69285, 98171

Gravier, Jacques. 28259-28361

Gravier, Jean. 20481, 28362

Gravier, Jean. Plaintiff (28363)

Graville, B. C. Graillard de. see Graillard de Graville, B. C.

Graviora Manent. pseud. Letters on the College of Physicians and Surgeons. see Manley, James R.

Gravisi, --------, Marquis. (10914)

Gravities and gaieties. 27575

Gray, --------, fl. 1866. 90416

Gray, A. B. 28375-28376, 88431

Gray, Alonzo. 28364-28365

Gray, Asa, 1810-1888. 1120, 27419, 28366-28374, 35308, 96293, 96297, 69946, 85072

Gray, B. G. 28378

Gray, Bunker. (28377)

Gray, Church. petitioner 46092

Gray, David. 28379

Gray, E. H. (28380)

Gray, Edward. 28381

Gray, Edward. printer 93021

Gray, Edwin, b. 1743. 28382, 68198

Gray, Ellis. (28383)

Gray, Francis Calley, 1790-1856. 17042, (28384)-(28387), 45652, 60953, 102294-102295 see also Boston. Committee of Merchants and Others, 1820.

Gray Frederick Turell. (28388)-28390, 51592, note after 93744

Gray, George Robert, 1808-1872. 28401, 71032

Gray, Harrison. 15529, 15597, 28391, 2d note after 97553

Gray, Horace. (45746)

Gray, Horatio. 28392

Gray, Hugh. (28393)

Gray, Iron. pseud. Gospel of slavery. see Thomas, Abel Charles.

Gray, J. see Smith, J. Gray.

Gray, J. B. 7003

Gray, J. E. 31945

Gray, J. W. D. 28394

Gray, James, fl. 1809. 28396

Gray, James, fl. 1821. 28395

Gray, John, fl. 1777. (28397)

Gray, John, fl. 1865. 85361

Gray, John Chipman, 1839-1915. 28399, 85212

Gray, John Edward, 1800-1875. 28400-28401, 71031-71032

Gray, M. W. (28402)

Gray, Robert, 17th cent. supposed author 26274, 2d note after 100571

Gray, Robert, fl. 1609. (27837)

Gray, Robert, 1761-1822. (28403)-28405

Gray, Robert A. 28406

Gray, S. Brownlow. 28407

Gray, Thomas, 1716-1771. 100663

Gray, Thomas, 1772-1847. 28409-28412

Gray, Thomas, 1803-1849. (28413)

Gray, Thomas, fl. 1861. 28408

Gray, Thomas R. 97487

Gray, W. H. 28416

Gray, W. S. 28417

Gray, William C. (28414)

Gray, William Fairfax. petitioner 95101-95102

Gray, William Farley. (28415)
Gray, Zackary. (28393), (79238)
Gray. firm publishers see Crouch & Gray.
firm publishers
Gray Reserve, Philadelphia. see Pennsylvania.
Militia. First Regiment, Company A.
(Gray Reserve, Philadelphia)
Gray substance of the medulla oblongata and
trapezium. 85072
Graydon, Alexander. 28418-28420
Graydon, William. 28421
Gray's narrative. 28379
Grayson, Edwin T. defendant at court martial
28422
Grayson, Eldred. pseud. Standish, the puritan.
see Hare, Robert. supposed author
Grayson, William. petitioner 90731
Grayson, William John, 1788-1863. (28424)-
28427, 31990, (32330), 68274
Great admirer of his worth, and true mourner
for his death. pseud. Elegy upon the
death of the Reverend Mr. Thomas
Shepard. see Oakes, Urian.
Great advantages accruing to Great Britain.
33198-33199
Great advantages of our colonies and planta-
tions. 105078
Great advantages of trade in general. 105078
Great agricultural & mineral west. 10254
Great and solemn obligations to early piety.
65603
Great American battle. (11063)
Great American crisis. 83476
Great American nation. 2970
Great American novel. 92498
Great American question, with personal
reminiscences. 21230
Great American scout and spy. 73940
Great and grave questions for American
politicians. 8375
Great and happy doctrine of liberty. (47448)
Great and important meeting of Democratic
Republicans. 28428
Great and Little Osage Indians. see Osage
Indians.
Great Anti-slavery Meeting, Birmingham,
Eng., 1835. 69893
Great Anti-tariff Meeting of the People of
Abbeville District, S. C., 1828. see
Abbeville District, S. C. Anti-tariff
Meeting, 1828.
Great Arctic mystery. 28429
Great assize. 83975
Great auction sale of slaves. 28430, 37331,
81987, 95593, note after 95596, 2d note
after 103115
Great awakening. 85144
Great awakening. A history of the revival of
religion. 96419
Great Balcombe. A novel. 97373
Great Barrington Academy. 28431
Great battle between slavery and freedom.
(58746)
Great battle year. (72146)
Great bear hunt. (69024)
Great blessing, of primitive counsellors.
46689
Great blessing of stable times. 10682
Great Britain. 573-576, (774), 1014, 1660,
1662, (5571), 5943, (7056), 8115, 9159,
10514, 11766, 13686, 15201, 15205,
15265, 16023, 16852. 16853. 16856-
16858, 16862, (16890)-16892, 16895,
16897-(16898), 16900-16901, 16903,
17365, 20461, (20464), (22626), 23561,

24630, 25497, 26150, (26252), 26438,
30930, (32223), 33687, 34388, 34399,
34852-34853, 34859, 36956, (37130)-
(37131), 37701, 40576, (41650), 42267,
44046, 42443-42444, 44605, 45451,
45622, 46195, 46762, (46918), 46919,
(47511)-47512, 47516-47517, (47547),
(47548), 48095, (48137), 46560, 51082,
51661, 51818, 52579. 53975. 55148.
55158, (55528), (55530)-55534, 55538,
55709, (55710), 55712, 56765, 56768,
56776, 58446, (58465), 58473-58474,
58483, 64938, 69530, 70070, 70143,
74337, 74344, 75952, 79888, 81933,
86730, 88829, 89991, 90000, 90639,
note before 90764, 1st note after 93806,
93853, 2d note after 99911, 101710,
101924, 102876, 102883, 102897, 104005
Great Britain. claimants 21914, 70143, 8193
97911
Great Britain. defendants 99894
Great Britain. Admiralty. 3606, 3664, 4045,
4349, 17610, 22796, 28401, 31945,
32121, 34415, 37701, 38152, 49343,
(49933), (58464), 58471, 58860, 58864,
58867, 71031-71033, 74713, 74966,
78865, 87315, 100546, 101906
Great Britain. Admiralty. Board of Longitude
see Great Britain. Admiralty. Commis-
sioners of Longitude.
Great Britain. Admiralty. Commissioners of
Longitude. (74699), 101020-101030
Great Britain. Admiralty. Committee to
Inquire and Report on the Recent Arctic
Expeditions in Search of Sir John
Franklin. 1920, 25633
Great Britain. Admiralty. Hydrographic
Office. see Great Britain. Hydrograp
Office.
Great Britain. Advocate General. 45276,
44690 see also Marriott, James.
Great Britain. Agent in the Antilles. 3884-
3885, 36956-(36957) see also Basket,
Sir James.
Great Britain. Agents to Manage the Capture
of St. Eustatius. 23415, (75201)
Great Britain. Antarctic Naval Expedition.
74711
Great Britain. Anti-slavery and Abolition
Societies. see Anti-slavery and Abolit
Societies of the United Kingdom.
Great Britain. Arctic Land Expedition, 1833-
1835. 2613
Great Britain. Army. 2455-2456, 2309,
(9253), 9256, 10699, 11131-11132, 1113
11485, 11487, 13755, (14987)-(14988),
15056, 30771, 30930, (36740), 38164,
41429, 41432, 41450, 41451, 41456,
42860. 44792, 47433, 53270, 53271,
567-56768, 57490, 57500, 67024,
(68802), 74053, 82975-82976, 95299,
note after 96144, 1st note after 99245,
100010, 102861, 104987-104989, 105602-
105605
Great Britain. Army. Articles of War.
53045, 78665
Great Britain. Army. Commission. 85234
Great Britain. Army. Commission on the
North American Provinces. 85234
Great Britain. Army. Commissioners for
Settling a Cartel for the Exchange of
Prisoners With the United States, 1779.
69750 see also Andre, John, 1751-178
and Hyde, West.

82904 see also Ripon, Frederick James Robinson, <u>Earl</u> of, 1782-1859.

Great Britain. Colonial Office. Commission to Assertain the Truth of the Narrative of James Williams. 104239

Great Britain. Commission Appointed to Enquire into the Losses of American Loyalists, 1783-1789. 85247

Great Britain. Commission for the Trial of William Kidd and Nine of His Men, 1701. 37701-37702, 37705

Great Britain. Commission of Claims Under the Convention of February 8, 1853, between the United States and Great Britain. <u>see</u> Commission of Claims Under the Convention of February 8, 1853, Between the United States and Great Britain.

Great Britain. Commission of Inquiry into the Destruction of the Gaspee. 3740

Great Britain. Commissioner Appointed to Inquire into the Cultivation and Supply of Cotton in South America. 17123

Great Britain. Commissioner of Inquiry into the Administration of Civil and Criminal Justice in the West Indies. see Great Britain. Commissioner on Civil and Criminal Justice in West Indies.

Great Britain. Commissioner on Civil and Criminal Justice in West Indies. 21509, 102869 <u>see also</u> Dwarris, <u>Sir</u> Fortunatus.

Great Britain. Commissioners for Emigration. (22504), (34704), 98075

Great Britain. Commissioners for Inquiring into the Administration and Practical Operation of the Poor Laws. 23527

Great Britain. Commissioners for Managing and Causing to Be Levied His Majesty's Customs and Other Duties in America. <u>see</u> Great Britain. Customs Establishment. and Great Britain. Commissioners of Customs in America.

Great Britain. Commissioners for Maryland. 100546-100547

Great Britain. Commissioners for Taking, Examining, and Stating the Public Accounts. 26260, 88204

Great Britain. Commissioners for the Sale of Lands in Tobago. (25309), 1st note after 93591, 1st note after 96048

Great Britain. Commissioners for Virginia. 4th note after 99888

Great Britain. Commissioners of Appeals in Prize Causes. <u>see</u> Great Britain. High Court of Appeals for Prizes.

Great Britain. Commissioners of Customs. see Great Britain. Customs Establishment.

Great Britain. Commissioners of Customs in America. (4923), 34846-(34849)

Great Britain. Commissioners of Inquiry Into the Administration of Civil and Criminal Justice in the West Indies. see Great Britain. Commissioner on Civil and Criminal Justice in West Indies.

Great Britain. Commissioners of Review. see Great Britain. Board of Trade.

Great Britain. Commissioners of the Customs, Boston. see Great Britain. Commissioners of Customs in America.

Great Britain. Commissioners on the Limits of St. Lucia and Nova Scotia. (774), 16023, (47546)-(47547), note after (47740)-47742, (56129), 62694, 69671, note after 96403 <u>see also</u> Mildmay, William. <u>and</u> Shirley, W.

Great Britain. Commissioners to Enquire Into the State of Canada. 10584

Great Britain. Commissioners to Explore and Survey the Territory in Dispute Between the Government of Great Britain and the United States of America, 1839. 69777

Great Britain. Commissioners to Inquire Into the Grievances Complained of in Lower Canada. 10582

Great Britain. Commissioners to Settle and Determine the Boundary Line Between the Colonies of New York and New Jersey see Great Britain. Royal Commissioners for Settling the Boundary Line Between the Colonies of New York and New Jersey

Great Britain. Commissioners to Settle the Boundary Line Between New Hampshire and Massachusetts. see Great Britain. Royal Commissioners for Settling the Boundary Between New Hampshire and Massachusetts.

Great Britain. Commissioners to the New York Industrial Exhibition, 1854. (54494) see also Wilson, ----------.

Great Britain. Commissioners, to Treat, Consult, and Agree Upon the Means of Quieting the Disorders Now Subsisting in Certain of the Colonies, 1778. (10924)-(10925), (14380) <u>see also</u> Auckland, William Eden, <u>1st</u> <u>Baron</u>, 1744-1814. Carlisle, Frederick Howard 5th <u>Earl</u> of, 1748-1825. Clinton, Sir Henry, 1738?-1795. Johnstone, George 1730-1787.

Great Britain. Commissioners to Try the Conspirators in Antigua. 1698

Great Britain. Commissioners Under the 4th Article of the Treaty of Ghent. see Commissioners Under the 4th Article of the Treaty of Ghent, Dec. 24, 1814.

Great Britain. Consulate. Belize, Honduras. 65811 see also Codd, ---------.

Great Britain. Consulate. Charleston, S. C. 9159, 16887, 87501, 87856 <u>see also</u> Bunch, ——. Mathew, George.

Great Britain. Consulate. Freetown, Sierra Leone. 58819

Great Britain. Consulate. Havana. 58819

Great Britain. Consulate. Paramaribo. 588

Great Britain. Consulate. Rio de Janeiro. 58819

Great Britain. Continental Naval Board. see Massachusetts (Colony) Continental Naval Board.

Great Britain. Council. 3282, 45929, 57494 57501-(57502), (78149), 99252

Great Britain. Council. Secretary. (78149) see also Scobel, Henry.

Great Britain. Council for New England. se Council for New England.

Great Britain. Council for Virginia. (36286 53249, 55946, note after 99867, 99877, 99879, 99882 <u>see also</u> Virginia Comp of London.

Great Britain. Court of Chancery. 34416, 81387

Great Britain. Court of Common Pleas. Chief Justice. (14087) <u>see also</u> Cockburn, <u>Sir</u> Alexander James Edmund, 1802-188

Great Britain. Court of Exchequer. 34419

Great Britain. Court of King's Bench. 6912 23561, 24371, (23479), 30374, 40490, 63352, 67545, 67560, (67567), 67569, 67590, 69175, 68176, 96910-96918, 98500, 102784

Great Britain. Court of King's Bench. Chief Justice. 24368

32760, 33548, (36755), 38747, 39629,
49353, 53287, 57400, 58463, (58485),
58817, 65025, 65861-65862, 67744,
70077, 71318-71319, 75410, 78114-78116,
79092, 79369, 81569, (81854), 81932,
(81949), 82899, 82902-82906, 82909,
85232, 88190, 88195, 88196, 88204,
89172, 89209, 2d note after 92693, 93367,
93371, note after 95491, 96091, 96191,
98073, 99249, 101300, 103958-103959,
104987, 104989, 2d note after 105598-9
[sic]

Great Britain. Parliament. House of Commons. Committee of Secrecy. 26260, 79374

Great Britain. Parliament. House of Commons. Committee of Secrecy on the Investigation of the Conduct of the Earl of Orford. 26260, 57581, 58031, (69729), 101148

Great Britain. Parliament. House of Commons. Committee of the Whole House to Consider the Slave Trade. 81736-81738

Great Britain. Parliament. House of Commons. Committee on Canada. 10600, 95373, 95474

Great Britain. Parliament. House of Commons. Committee on Colonial Laws. 14690

Great Britain. Parliament. House of Commons. Committee on Petition of Peter Soumans, of New Jersey, and Jos. Ormstone. 53221

Great Britain. Parliament. House of Commons. Committee on Petition of the Deputies of the United Moravian Churches. 69731, 1st note after 97845

Great Britain. Parliament. House of Commons. Committee on Petition of the Merchants of London. 69938

Great Britain. Parliament. House of Commons. Committee on Petition of the Sierra Leone Company. 80887

Great Britain. Parliament. House of Commons. Committee on Petition of William Paterson. 18565

Great Britain. Parliament. House of Commons. Committee on Petition on Sugar Refineries of London. 4823, 95700

Great Britain. Parliament. House of Commons. Committee on State of British Fisheries. 23740

Great Britain. Parliament. House of Commons. Committee on the American Papers. 16813, 26427-(26428), 34943

Great Britain. Parliament. House of Commons. Committee on the Sugar Duties. 4823

Great Britain. Parliament. House of Commons. Committee on the Trade to Newfoundland. 54989

Great Britain. Parliament. House of Commons. Committee on Yellow Fever in Bermuda. 4909

Great Britain. Parliament. House of Commons. Committee to Enquire into the State and Condition of the Countries Adjoining Hudson's Bay. 33548, 58462, 2d note after 92693

Great Britain. Parliament. House of Commons. Minority. 41453

Great Britain. Parliament. House of Commons. Secret Committee on South Sea Company. 88168, 88187, 88197, 88204

Great Britain. Parliament. House of Commons. Select Committee on Aboriginal Tribes. 34675, 34705

Great Britain. Parliament. House of Commons. Select Committee on Arctic Expedition. 25633

Great Britain. Parliament. Select Committee on Ceylon and British Guiana. 89472

Great Britain. Parliament. House of Commons. Select Committee on Colonial Military Expenditures. 373

Great Britain. Parliament. House of Commons. Select Committee on Emigration. 22503, 69905

Great Britain. Parliament. House of Commons. Select Committee on Foreign Trade. 31685

Great Britain. Parliament. House of Commons. Select Committee on Negro Apprenticeship. 52260

Great Britain. Parliament. House of Commons. Select Committee on Sugar and Coffee Plantations. 58818, 93457

Great Britain. Parliament. House of Commons. Select Committee on the Accounts. (69733)

Great Britain. Parliament. House of Commons. Select Committee on the Extinction of Slavery Throughout the British Dominions. 81848, 82046

Great Britain. Parliament. House of Commons. Select Committee on the Civil Government of Canada. 10562, 10576

Great Britain. Parliament. House of Commons. Select Committee on the Hudson's Bay Company. 33549

Great Britain. Parliament. House of Commons. Select Committee on the Slave Trade. (49370), (80593), 81735, 81745-81746, 81898

Great Britain. Parliament. House of Commons. Select Committee on Treatment of Slaves in the West Indies. 102851

Great Britain. Parliament. House of Commons. Select Committee on West Indies. 17617, 58470, 70259, 102841, 3d note after 102863

Great Britain. Parliament. House of Commons. Speaker. 60629, 91307

Great Britain. Parliament. House of Lords. 10967, 10872, (11193)-11194, 11307, 15053, (19091), 19098-19099, 19687, 21315, 28294, 33032, 33686, 33689, (33690), 33693, 36756, 39450, 40467, 42053-42054, 43591, 49353, (49370), 56560, (56802), 62457, 65862, 69087, 79092, 80084, 80329, 87359, 87805, 88190, 91849, 93369-93370, 99249, 104145, 105082

Great Britain. Parliament. House of Lords. Committee on Colonial Slavery. (81747)

Great Britain. Parliament. House of Lords. Committee to Enquire into the Proceedings in the Colony of Massachusetts Bay, 1774. 69877

Great Britain. Peace Commissioners, Ghent, 1814. 53975, 90739

Great Britain. Peace Commissioners, Paris, 1782-1783. 66394 see also Oswald, Richard, 1705-1784.

Great Britain. Privy Council. 24744, 34072, 50015, 59962, 59972, 65773, 72687, 73459, note before 90598, 2d note after 98664, 99774, 103331, 103894, 104595

56582, 65044-65046, (68711), 75534,
86077, 88944, 90598, 93427, 96553,
100010, 100667, 100756, 2d note after
101545, 102499, 104005, 104459 see
also George III, King of Great Britain,
1738-1820.
Great Britain. Sovereigns, etc., 1830-1837
(William IV) (28300) see also William
IV, King of Great Britain, 1765-1837.
Great Britain. Sovereigns, etc., 1837-1901
(Victoria) see also Victoria, Queen
of Great Britain, 1819-1901.
Great Britain. Sovereigns, etc., 1901-1910
(Edward VII) 658, 69284 see also
Edward VII, King of Great Britain,
1841-1910.
Great Britain. Stamp Paper Office, London.
5195, 11490, 53058, 59963, 61246,
88005, note before 91508, 94172
Great Britain. State Record Office, London.
see Great Britain. Public Record
Office, London.
Great Britain. Treasury. (35584)
Great Britain. Treasury. Commissioners on
the Public Accounts. 13750, 90591,
101150, note after 103106
Great Britain. Treaties, etc. 276-277, (469),
775-776, 1059, 2144-2151, 2154, 2154C,
2155-2156, 2158, 2227, 2447-2449, 2461,
3357, (6361), (6582), (7164), 7877,
7904-7905, 8126-8127, 9021, 10481,
10663, 10883, (11759), (12830), 13400,
13578, (13895), (14009), 14273-14275,
14371-14372, 14389, 14396-14399, 14566,
(14989), 15493, 15770, (16088), 16195,
(16197), (16202), 17184, (17531), 18875,
19124, 19186, 19273-19275, (20464),
20825, (21123), (22015), 23422, 23535,
23962, 23966, 25074, 25640, 25729,
(26388), 26872-26873, 28069, 28292, 30335,
30825, 31594, (32223), (32768), 32773,
33854, (34614), 35779, 35849, 39155,
39383, 40319, 42054, 42889, (43282)-
43283, 44046, 47515-47516, (47531),
48073, (48107), 50016, 50018, 51079,
51083, 52843, 53913, 56163, 56475,
56502, 56530, 56569, 62455, (64480),
64517, 64837, 65044, 66394, 68441,
68934, 69440, 69443, (69476), note after
69528, 72044, 74337, 75240, 78919,
79375, 80700-80701, 82008, 83609,
84819, 84842, 86742, 89991, 91091-
91093, note after 92002, 93129, 94070,
94777, 95655, 96516, note before 96521-
96521, 96525-96545, 96548-96553, 96557-
96558, 96560-96564, note before 96570,
96572-96578, 96580-96585, 97298, 97545,
2d note after 97583, 98926, 2d note after
99216, 99585, 100039, 101144, 101147,
101167, note after 101847, 102401, 1st
note after 102785, 2d note after 102806
Great Britain. War Office. 9251, 9260,
85243
Great Britain and America. 81401
Great Britain and the United States. (21847)
Great Britain and the United States, with a
view to their future commercial connection. 28434
Great Britain oppressing America. (51432)
Great Britain successfully vindicated. 91681
Great Britain undeceived in the conduct of
government. 28435
Great Britain vs. Edward John Eyre. 24371
Gt. Brit. vs. John Hatchard. 30841
Great Britain vs. Nelson and Brand. (13087)

Great-Britain's commercial interest explained.
64562, 64564
Great Britain's complaints against Spain.
28436
Great Britain's right to tax her colonies.
28437, 1st note after 94085, note after
106386
Great Britain's speediest sinking fund is a
powerful maritime war. 28438
Great-Britain's true system. 64565
Great calamity! 79617
Great care and concern of men under Gospel-
light. 44752
Great cave of Dry Fork of Cheat River,
Virginia. 36645
Great caverns of Kentucky. (2731)
Great Central Fair, Philadelphia, 1864. see
Philadelphia. Great Central Fair, 1864.
Great Central Fair for the Benefit of the
United States Sanitary Commission,
Philadelphia, 1864. see Philadelphia.
Great Central Fair, 1864.
Great Central Route. Blue Line. 28439
Great Christian doctrine of original sin
defended. 21942
Great commercial prize. 14167
Great commission. 90908
Great Commoner. sobriquet see Pitt,
William, 1st Earl of Chatham, 1708-
1778
Great concern of a watchman for souls. 21943
Great concern of New-England. 102220
Great concern of parents. 3471
Great conference and its lessons. 72632
Great conflagration. (80031)
Great conflict of the day. 33964
Great conflict; or cause and cure of secession.
(49035)
Great conflict, what has been gained, and what
remains to be done. (39041)
Great consolations. 46353
Great conspiracy. An address delivered at
Mt. Kisco. 35843
Great conspiracy. Full account of the assassi-
nation plot. 28440
Great constitutional right of petition violated.
66938
Great controversy of states and people. (28441)
Great convention. Description of the Convention
of the People of Ohio. 56930
Great cotton question. 28442
Great country. 73241
Great crime of our civilization. 36670
Great day. 83450
Great day of judgment. 39795
Great debate! 85122, 85124
Great deliverance. A sermon . . . in . . .
Davenport. 39761
Great deliverance and the new career. 7680
Great deliverance at sea, by W. Johnson.
23723, 100846
Great demonstration at New Haven. 37644
Great design and the scope of the Gospel
opened. 24679
Great difficulty, and distinguishing reward.
(28443)
Great disclosure of spiritual wickedness!! in
high places. 58105
Great discussion! 64953
Great divorce case. 35817
Great drama; an appeal to Maryland. (37423)
Great drama of human progress. 43841
Great duellist. 39562
Great Dutch flat swindle!! 28444
Great duty of charity. 2200

Great duty of family religion. 103524
Great duty of Gospel ministers to preach. 84351
Great duty of ministers. (16295)
Great duty of offending and offended brethren. 65104
Great duty of propagating the truth. 91224
Great duty of public worship. 84615
Great duty of waiting on God. (14525)
Great encouragement to ministerial effort. 84408
Great encyclic epistle. 85115, 85118
Great effects result from little causes. (64233)
Great end and interests of New-England. (49658)
Great error of American agriculture exposed. 50444
Great events in modern history. (26054)
Great evil in New York and Brooklyn. 13365
Great evil of sin. 4489
Great exhibition of the Works of Industry of All Nations, London, 1851. see London. Great Exhibition of the Works of Industry of all Nations, 1851
Great Falls, N. H. see Somersworth, N. H.
Great Falls directory. 20745
Great Falls Manufacturing Company. 28446
Great Falls Manufacturing Company. Investigating Committee. 28447
Great Fillmore Meeting, . . . New York. Also, a message from President Fillmore. 24333
Great fire. 61706
Great first cause. 64954
Great funeral oration on Abraham Lincoln. 30341
Great future of America and Africa. (19840)
Great God has magnified His word to the children of men. (14525)
Great gold fields of Cariboo. 31126
Great Gospel priviledge of having Christ exhibited to sinfull men. 79444, (79448), 91940, note after 98054, 104082-104083
Great healing springs on the battle-field. 43118
Great highway. 26191
Great impeachment and trial of Andrew Johnson. 36172
Great importance of Cape-Breton. (10730), 28448
Great importance of the Havanna. 863
Great in goodness. 70974
Great Inaugural Mass Meeting of the Loyal National League, New York, 1863. see Loyal National League of the State of New York.
Great Indian chief of the west. 5677, 28449
Great iron wheel. 28350
Great issue. An address delivered before the Union Campaign Club. 35849
Great issue in a nutshell. 81988
Great issue, or rebellion against democracy. 21475, 28451, (35097)
Great issue, or the rebellion against democracy. 28451
Great issue; or, the three presidential candidates. 26626
Great issue to be decided in November next! 28450
Great issues. 8285
Great issues before the country. 23253
Great issues of the day. 24467
Great Jackson Meeting in Baltimore. No. I. 35391
Great Kentucky statesmen. 11049

Great lakes. (20319)
Great lamentation. 90985
Great libel case. (57388)
Great man fallen! A discourse on the death of Abraham Lincoln. 58130
Great man fallen. A sermon preached in the Methodist Church, Baton Rouge, La. 7363
Great man fallen in Israel. A sermon preach at Cambridge. (1834), 95737
Great man fallen, in Israel; the sermon, the next after the death, of Zachary Taylor. 20391
Great man in Israel. (77980)
Great Mass Meeting in Favor of the Union, San Francisco, 1861. see San Francisco. Great Mass Meeting in Favor of the Union, 1861.
Great Mass Meeting of Loyal Citizens, at Cooper Institute, . . . March 6, 1863. 28452
Great match race over the Pennsylvania course. 89631
Great meeting at Philadelphia. 90411
Great Meeting of Irishmen at Philadelphia. . . . August 6, 1832. 35391
Great Meeting of Irishmen, to Prevent the Re-election of Andrew Jackson Philadelphia, 1832. see Philadelphia. Great Meeting of Irishmen, to Prevent the Re-election of Andrew Jackson, 1832
Great Meeting of the Friends of Civil and Religious Liberty, Baltimore, 1837. 45289
Great Meeting on Texas, New York, 1836. 95114
Great Men are God's gift. 37971
Great men: their characteristics, influence, and destiny. 41387
Great message to all governments and all nations. 85116
Great metropolis; a mirror of New York. (8667)
Great metropolis; or guide to New York for 1846. 20527, 54298
Great metropolis: or New-York almanac for 1850. 54298
Great metropolis: or New York in 1845. 54298
Great metropolis. Tracts for cities, no. 1. 54297
Great moral duties of a free and independent people. 74724
Great mystery of Foxcraft discovered. 28453, 39817, 66735, 66743
Great national deliverance. (39694)
Great national object. 28454, (38470)
Great national painting. Professor Risley's original gigantic moving panorama. 83010
Great national painting, Sheridan's ride. (68986)
Great national painting! The original voyage down the Mississippi! 83010
Great National Peace Jubilee and Musical Festival, Boston, 1869. 56772
Great national question. 95775
Great national thoroughfare from the west and south-west. 28455
Great necessity & use of the Holy Sacraments 37197
Great news for the friends of progression in truth. 85117
Great news from Barbadoes. 3270
Great news from Jamaica in the West Indies. 28456

Great news from the Barbadoes. 3270
Great north-west, her material resources. 47899
Great northern conspiracy of the O. S. L. 28457
Great Northern Turnpike Company. Charter. 28458
Great northwest. 64384
Great northwestern conspiracy in all its startling details. 2513
Great number of their constituents. 12547, 40513
Great number of your constituents. 12547, 40513
Great paper bubble. 19449
Great Peace Convention, New York, 1863. (65860)
Great pestilence in Virginia. 25117
Great Piqua murder. 51208
Great plot discovered. 28459
Great principles associated with Plymouth Rock. 5723
Great principles involved in the present controversy. (78742), 100582
Great probability of a north west passage. 28460, 1st note after 94082
Great providences toward the loyal part of this nation. 5435
Great Public Meeting at the Tabernacle, New York, 1854. see New York (City) Great Public Meeting at the Tabernacle, 1854.
Great Public Meeting on the Ship Pennsylvania and the Navy Yard, Philadelphia, 1837. see Philadelphia. Great Public Meeting on the Ship Pennsylvania and the Navy Yard, 1837.
Great public meeting. Ship Philadelphia—Navy Yard. 61707
Great question answered. (82159)
Great question of the day. 19834
Great question to be considered by the King. 59704
Great questions of national and state politics. 3206
Great questions of the times, discussed in a brief report. 28461
Great questions of the times, exemplified in the antagonistic principles involved in the slaveholder's rebellion. 80445
Great railway enterprise. (9596)
Great rebellion. 50630
Great rebellion: a history of the civil war in the United States. 31151
Great rebellion. An address delivered in the Methodist Episcopal Church. 87266
Great rebellion. By the Rev. R. Fisher. (24482)
Great rebellion: causes, progress, and remedy. 32458
Great rebellion, in the light of Christianity. 75848
Great rebellion; its history, biography and incidents. 8156
Great rebellion: its secret history, rise, progress, and disastrous failure. (6828)
Great rebellion of 1861. 9471
Great republic. Description of the largest ship in the world. (28462), 43360
Great republic monthly. 28463, 84162
Great resources, and superior advantages of the city of Joliet. 73552
Great revival of 1800. 89255
Great revolution, calculated to save the approaching downfall of the American republic. 104064

Great rising and breaking of a bubble. 53387
Great Salt Lake County, Utah. see Salt Lake County, Utah.
Great salvation revealed and offered in the Gospel explained. 104401
Great Sanitary Fair, New York, 1864. see New York (City) Metropolitan Fair, 1864.
Great sin of formality in God's worship. 50297
Great Sodus Bay, and the Sodus Canal. 86204
Great solar eclipse of the 16th of June, 1806. 18580
Great Southern Co-operation and Anti-secession Meeting, Charleston, 1851. see Southern Rights and Co-operation Meeting, Charleston, S. C., 1851.
Great southwest or plain guide for emigrants and capitalists. (55165)
Great speech of Hon. William H. Seward. 79524
Great speech of Maj.-Gen. Kilpatrick. (37743)
Great speech of the Hon. George Mifflin Dallas. 18318
Great speech to the Democracy in mass meeting. 20031
Great State Convention of Friends of the Administration, Concord, N. H., 1828. see National Republican Party. New Hampshire. Convention, Concord, 1828.
Great steam-duck. 28465
Great struggle between democracy and absolutism impending. 28466
Great surrender to the rebels in arms. 28467
Great Temperance Meeting in Tremont Temple, Boston, 1867. see Boston. Great Temperance Meeting, 1867.
Great Temperance Meeting in Tremont Temple, Monday evening, April 15th, 1867. Reception of Senator Wilson. 89627
Great thoroughfares and their national aspects. 78877
Great town meeting, . . . [in favor of] Van Buren and Johnson. 62018
Great Town Meeting, Philadelphia, 1840. see Democratic Party. Pennsylvania. Philadelphia.
Great trans-continental railroad guide. 17587, 28468
Great trans-continental tourists' guide. 28469
Great Union Meeting, New York, 1859. see New York (City) Union Meeting, Dec. 19, 1859.
Great Union Meeting, Philadelphia, 1850. see Philadelphia. Great Union Meeting, 1850.
Great Union Meeting, Philadelphia, 1851. see Philadelphia. Great Union Meeting, 1851.
Great Union Meeting, Philadelphia. December 7, 1859. 28471
Great Union Meeting in Philadelphia, . . . November, 1851. 61708
Great Union Meeting, New York, December 19th, 1859. 28470
Great Union speech . . . in Chicago. 41801
Great union war ratification meeting, at the Cooper Institute. 28472, 56238
Great utility of inland navigation. 28473
Great Valley, Pa. St. Peter's Church. 62219
Great victory obtained by the English against the Dutch. (28474)
Great west and her commercial metropolis. (21987)
Great west: containing narratives. 33298, 33300

Great west. Emigrants', settlers', and travellers' guide. 29761
Great west; its history, its wealth, its natural advantages, and its future. 18398, (26603)
Great west; railroad, steamboat, and stage guide. 29759
Great west: travellers', miners', and emigrants' guide. (29758)
Great Western (Ship) 13528
Great western almanac, 1842. 28475
Great western business guide. 18816
Great Western Iron Company. 28476, (35091)
Great Western Iron Company. Charter. 28476, (35091)
Great western magazine and Anglo-American journal. 28477, (28518)
Great Western Railroad Company, Canada. Board of Directors. 28478
Great Western Railroad Company, Canada. Chief Engineer. 28478, note after 93149 see also Stuart, Charles Beebe.
Great Western Railroad Company, Canada. Committee of American Friends. 28478
Great Western Railroad Company of Illinois. (34316)
Great Western Railway of Canada, Buffalo and Lake Huron. 10639
Great Western Sanitary Fair, Cincinnati, 1863. see Cincinnati. Great Western Sanitary Fair, 1863.
Great Western Turnpike Road. First Company. see First Company of the Great Western Turnpike Road.
Great Whig Festival, Baltimore, 1835. see Whig Party. Maryland. Baltimore.
Great Whig Meeting, Boston, 1838. see Whig Party. Massachusetts. Boston.
Great Whig Meeting of Citizens of Boston, 1838. see Whig Party. Massachusetts. Boston.
Great work. 82758
Great work of Christ's spirit, &c. (40421), 103068
Great work of salvation opened and pressed. 24682
Great wrong! and how it may be remedied. 67852
Greater Britain. 20155
Greater prosperity through greater foreign trade. 83369
Greatest concern in the world. 46354
Greatest discovery of the age! 84441, 84446
Greatest sermon that was ever preached. 104382
Greatest sinners exhorted and encouraged. 46690
Greatest sufferers not always the grestest sinners. 83441
Greatness and sovereignty of God. 104363
Greatness of sin improv'd by the penitent. 102221
Greatness the result of goodness. 102746
Greatrakes, Valentine. 93755
Greaves, Thomas. 9095
Grece, Charles Frederick. 28479-(28480)
Grecian wreath of victory. (28481)
Grediaga, J. G. 981, 54300
Greek Committee, New York. see New York Greek Committee.
Greek exile. 11392
Greek girl; a tale. 81176
Greek slave. 38599, 72706
Greeley, Horace, 1811-1872. 7072, (13509), 13536, (15463), 22513, 22981, 24182, 28482-28494, 35949, 37092, 40575,

55558, 57816, 58944, 76957, 82605, 84162, 87019, 93347, 94799
Greeley, Horace, 1811-1872. defendant (16421), 17641, 41548
Greeley, W. A. 83810, 83991
Greeley and Bennett. 28496
Greeley, Beecher, Garrison, etc. 28495
Greeley, Allen. (28497)
Green, --------, fl. 1731. 16234
Green, --------. plaintiff (73530)
Green, A. ed. 12899A
Green, Aaron. (28498)
Green, Alexander L. P. complainant 84738
Green, Andrew H. (28499)
Green, Ashbel, 1762-1848. 28500-(28505), 89736
Green, Ashbel, 1762-1848. defendant 65221, 72741
Green, Bartholomew. 28052, 28506, 65689, 88506, 91945, 97421, note after 105090
Green, Benjamin. 28507-28509
Green, Benjamin C. petitioner (28519)
Green, Beriah. (28510)-28512
Green, Calvin. 28513, (79721)-79722, note before 93610, note after 97880, 5th note after 102601
Green, Calvin. supposed author 79723-79727, note after 94924, note after 97880, note after 106196
Green, Charles. 101029
Green, D. petitioner (28519)
Green, David. (28592)
Green, Duff, 1791-1875. 14898, 28414-(28518) 68817, 97990, 1st-2d notes after 101931, note after 101967
Green, Enoch. 28521
Green, Francis H. 28522-28523
Green, Francis H. supposed author 48898
Green, Henry G. defendant 28524
Green, Isaiah. defendant 4771, 44898
Green, Isaiah L. (28525)
Green, J. (45286)
Green, J. H., fl. 1862. 28536
Green, J. H. see Greene, Jonathan Harrington, b. 1812.
Green, J. W. see Greene, J. W.
Green, Jacob. 28526-28527
Green, Jacob. supposed author 56558, 98573 99543, 104266
Green, James. defendant 104663
Green, James D. 28530
Green, James Diman, 1798-1882. 28528-28529, 43060
Green, James Stephen, 1817-1870. 28531-28533, 37041, 90678
Green, John. (28537)-28530, (35963), 65406, 84559, 84560, 84562
Green, John, Bp. of Lincoln, 1706?-1779. (28540)
Green, John, 1835-1913. 28541
Green, John A. 28542
Green, John B. 28543
Green, John C. 86155
Green, John O. 28544-28545
Green, Jonathan. defendant 105353
Green, Joseph, Jr. 28550
Green, Joseph, 1706-1780. 28546-(28549)
Green, Joseph C. 28551
Green, Lewis Warner. 29922
Green, Matthew. 28552
Green, Nathaniel, fl. 1768. 63476
Green, Nathaniel, fl. 1775. 101690
Green, Nelson Winch. 28553-28554, 83550-83554
Green, Roger, 17th cent. supposed author 26274, 2d note after 100571

Greene, S. S. 86618
Green, Samuel, 1615-1701 or 2. 102181
Green, Samuel, 1793-1834. 28555, 92259
Green, Samuel, d. 1822. (28556)
Green, Samuel Abbott, 1830-1918. 19801
    28557, 94172, 95192, 95820, 96153-
    96154, 104110-104111, 104653
Green, Samuel B. 28558
Green, Sanford M. 28559, 48794
Green, Seth. 73107 see also New York
    (State) Commissioners of Fisheries.
Green, Thomas. petitioner 95101
Green, Thomas, successively Bishop of
    Norwich, and Ely, 1658-1738. 28614
Green, Thomas, J. 28561-28562
Green, Timothy. 28052, 28506, 65689
Green William. miscellaneous writer
    (28564)
Green, William. supposed author 85206-
    85207
Green, William. slave 28565
Green, William, fl. 1774. 28563
Green, William, 1806-1880. 81703, 100230
Green, William, fl. 1848. 28566
Green, William Henry. 28567-28568
Green, William L. (28569)
Green, William N. 96936
Green, Willis. 93380, 96362, 101069 see also
    Whig Congressional Committee, 1844.
    Chairman.
Green (Samuel) firm publishers 15668
    (15829), 28560
Green (T.) firm publishers 28560
Green & Co. firm. see Truscott, Green &
    Co. firm
Green, Brown & Co. firm 90742
Green-back. pseud. Green-back to his
    country friends. (28570)
Green-back to his country friends. (28570)
Green Bank, Burlington, N. J. St. Mary's
    Hall. see St. Mary's Hall, Burlington,
    N. J.
Green Bay, Wisconsin. Division no. 2., Sons
    of Temperance. see Sons of Temper-
    ance of North America. Wisconsin.
    Green Bay Division, no. 2.
Green Bay (Diocese) 72943
Green Bay (Diocese) Bishop (Krautbauer)
    72944 see also Krautbauer, Francis
    Xavier, Bp.
Green Bay (Diocese) Synod, 1876. 72944
Green Bay and Lake Superior Railroad
    Company. 28573
Green Bay and Mississippi Canal Company.
    defendant 37679
Green Bay Division, no. 2. see Sons of
    Temperance of North America.
    Wisconsin. Green Bay Division, no. 2.
Green box of Monsieur de Sartine. 95796
Green hand. pseud. Green hand's first
    cruise. see Yoncker. pseud.
Green hand; a "short" yarn. (28574)
Green hand's first cruise. 28575
Green Mount Cemetery, Montpelier, Vt. see
    Montpelier, Vt. Green Mount
    Cemetery.
Green mountain. 105970, 106050
Green mountain boys. 95475-95476, 95478-
    95479, 95484-95485
Green mountain boys: or Vermont and the
    New York land jobbers. 83717,
    83719
Green mountain girl. pseud. Experience of a
    Green mountain girl. 99175
Green Mountain Liberal Institute, South Wood-
    stock, Vt. 28576, 88220

Green Mountain Mining Company of Vermont.
    28577
Green Mountain repository for the year 1832.
    28578, note after 95548
Green Mountain Slate and File Company.
    28579
Green Mountain spring. 43343
Green mountain tale. 95483
Green mountain traveler. 3517
Green peas, picked from the patch of Invisible
    Green. 17509
Green Spring, Ohio, with the analysis of its
    water. 89693
Green-Wood; a directory for visitors. (13607)
Green-Wood cemetery, its rules, rgeulations,
    &c. 28694
Greenback movement. 91117
Greenbacks forever. 51938
"Greenbacks;" or, the evils and the remedy.
    (56598)
Greenbacks; the evils and remedy for using
    promises to pay. 28571
Greenbank (T. K.) firm publishers 10937,
    (28572), 79323
Greenbank's periodical library. 10937, (28572),
    79323
Greenbush, N. Y. Charter. 28580
Greencastle, Ind. De Pauw University. see
    De Pauw University, Greencastle,
    Indiana.
Greene. pseud. Strictures upon the letter.
    see Coxe, Tench.
Green, A. L. P. 48191
Greene, Albert C. (2482)
Greene, Albert Gorton, 1802-1868. 8620,
    20948-(20949), 28581-28582, 41489,
    66239, 66250, note just before 68379
Greene, Alfred G. see Greene, Albert Gorton,
    1802-1868.
Greene, Asa. 28583-28586, 2d note after
    96495, note after 105956
Greene, Asa. supposed author 54294
Greene, B. F. 69638
Greene, Benjamin. (28587)-28589
Greene, Charles G. 30663, 103290
Greene, Charles G. defendant 4111
Greene, Charles S. 28591
Greene, Christopher R. 28590
Greene, Edward Burnaby. 28593, (66008),
    96174, 101754-101756
Greene, Frances. 28594, 79691
Greene, Frances Harriet (Whipple) see
    McDougall, Frances Harriet (Whipple)
    Greene.
Greene, George Washington. 28595-(28601),
    35221
Greene, H. 40575, 94799
Greene, H. W. (28603)
Greene, Hiram. 28602
Greene, Hugh W. 31051, 46130, 1st note after
    89210
Greene, J. 28539, 65402
Greene, J. M. 84961
Greene, J. W. (24034), 46109
Greene, Jerome B. (28604)
Greene, John P. 28606
Greene, Jonas. 28605
Greene, Jonathan Harrington, b. 1812. 28534-
    28535
Green, Max. 28607
Greene, Nathaniel, 1742-1786. 4758, 36343-
    36344, 35723, 74870
Greene, Nathaniel, 1797-1877. 28608,
    (57637)
Greene, Rhodom A. 27051

Greene, Richard Henry. (28609)
Greene, Richard Ward, 1792-1875. 35680, 66276
Greene, Robert. supposed author 26274, 2d note after 100571
Greene, Roger. supposed author 26274, note after 100571
Greene, Samuel D. appellant (28610)-(28611)
Greene, Samuel S. 28612
Greene, Talbot. 28613
Greene, Thomas, Bp. see Green, Thomas, successively Bishop of Norwich, and Ely, 1658-1738.
Greene, Thomas A. 28615
Greene, William. 28616-28617
Greene, William B. 28618-(28620)
Greene, William H. plaintiff 28621
Greene County, N. Y. Agricultural Society. see Greene County Agricultural Society.
Greene County, N. Y. Board of Supervisors. (28623)
Greene County, N. Y. Washington Benevolent Society. see Washington Benevolent Society. New York. Green County.
Greene and Delaware Society for the Promotion of Good Morals. 28624
Greene County Agricultural Society. 28622
Greene Foundation, New York. see New York (City) Trinity Church. Greene Foundation.
Greene Street Synagogue, New York. see New York (City) Greene Street Synagogue.
Greeneville, Tenn. Constitutional Convention, 1785. see Tennessee (Franklin Governmental District) Constitutional Convention, Greenville, 1785.
Greenfield, William. 28625
Greenfield, Mass. Boarding School. see Boarding School, Greenfield, Mass.
Greenfield, Mass. Ecclesiastical Council, 1753. see Congregational Churches in Massachusetts. Ecclesiastical Council, Greenfield, 1753.
Greenfield, Mass. Ecclesiastical Councils, 1813. see Congregational Churches in Massachusetts. Ecclesiastical Councils, Greenfield, 1813.
Greenfield, Mass. Fellenberg Academy. see Fellenberg Academy, Greenfield, Mass.
Greenfield, Mass. High School for Young Ladies. 28626
Greenfield, Mass. St. James' Church. Committee of Publication. 93079
Greenfield hill: a poem. 21554
Greenhalgh, T. 28629
Greenhill, William. 80199-80200, 80205, 80212, 80252
Greenhill, William. petitioner 27954
Greenhough, J. G. 83507
Greenhow, Robert, 1800-1854. 4889A, 23725, 23728, (28630)-28633, 41460, 86544-86545, 95370 see also U. S. Department of State. Translator of Foreign Languages.
Greenhow, Rose O'Neill. 28634
Greenhow, W. 71578
Greenland, Commandeurerne og Mandskabet, Skibene. 28636
Greenland and Iceland. (28647)
Greenland, and other poems. 50144
Greenland: being extracts from a journal. 74646
Greenland-Eskimo vocabulary. 101906

Greenland family. 28648
Greenland Family School, Plainfield, N. J. 63250
Greenland minstrel. 5693
Greenland missions. 28649
Greenland tale. 36295A, 60793
Greenland, the adjacent seas, and the northwest passage. 57576
Greenlanders. 100984
Greenlander's travels in Europe. 24944
Greenlandic Psalm-book. 28644
Greenlandish folklore. 22854
Greenleaf, Abner. 28660
Greenleaf, James. 100929
Greenleaf, John. ed. 73781-73782
Greenleaf, Jonathan, 1785-1865. 28661-28663
Greenleaf, Lawrence N. 28664
Greenleaf, Moses. (28665)-28666
Greenleaf, P. H. 28667
Greenleaf, Simon, 1783-1853. 28669-(28670), 40925
Greenleaf, Thomas. 45599, 67205, 103783 see also Massachusetts. Meeting of Citizens From Every Part of the State, Boston, 1815. Secretary.
Greenleaf, Thomas, 1755-1798. ed. 83604
Greenleaf, William. 105372 see also Worcester County, Mass. Sheriff.
Greenleaf's New-York, Connecticut & New-Jersey almanack. 28671
Greenough, ------. 60496
Greenough, Horatio. 28672
Greenough, William Bates. 83760
Greenough, William Whitwell, d. 1899. 26652 28673-28674
Greenough. firm publishers see Dudley & Greenough. firm publishers
Greenough (W. A.) & Co. firm publishers 30909, (51860), 64426
Greenough & Deved. firm publishers see Edwards, Greenough & Deved. firm publishers
Green's almanack and register. 15668, (15829)
Green's register for the state of Connecticut. 28560
Greensboro, Ala. Southern University. see Southern University, Greensboro, Ala.
Greensboro, Vt. Congregational Church. 92066
Greensburg, Pa. Friends of the General Administration Meeting, 1827. see National Republican Party. Pennsylvania. Greensburg.
Greenville, S. C. Southern Baptist Theological Seminary. see Southern Baptist Theological Seminary, Greenville, S. C.
Greenville Court House, S. C. Temperance Convention, 1842. see Temperance Convention, Greenville Court House, S. 1842.
Greenwich, N. Y. Congregational Church. 28678
Greenwich Reformed Dutch Church, New York see New York (City) Greenwich Reform Dutch Church.
Greenwood, ---------. illus. 95405
Greenwood, Andrew. 28679
Greenwood, F. (28680)
Greenwood, F. W. ed. 28685
Greenwood, Francis William Pitt, 1797-1843. 26098, 28681-28688, (49063), 88970, 88972, 88975, 89002, 89006, 89009, 89014, 95190-95191, 97833

Greenwood, Grace. pseud. see Lippincott, Sarah J. (Clarke)
Greenwood, Isaac. 28689
Greenwood, Isaac. supposed author 101195
Greenwood, Isaac. defendant 96829
Greenwood, James, d. 1737. 28690
Greenwood, James, fl. 1864. 28691
Greenwood, John. 28692
Greenwood, Miles. defendant 90145
Greenwood Cemetery, N. Y. see New York (City) Greenwood Cemetery.
Greenwood cemetery: a history of the institution. (13608)
Greenwood cemetery, and other poems. 12539
Greenwood cemetery. Surveyed by E. Boyle. (28693)
Greenwood illustrated. 13606, (28695), 74169
Greenwood in 1846. 13606, (28695), 74169
Greenwood leaves, a collection of sketches and letters. 13461, note after (41404)
Greenwood tragedy. 37896
Greepe, Thomas. 28701, 97103
Greer, George P. incorrectly supposed author 26833, 28702
Greer, John. appellant 86356
Greer, Sarah D. 66934, 70284
Greeshian Poette. pseud. Scheepe-thiefe. see Moore, John C.
"Greeting to America" of Jenny Lind. 1308
Greevous grones for the poore. 88961, 1st note after 100478
Gregg, ----------, fl. 1790. supposed author 106327
Gregg, Alexander, Bp., 1819-1893. 24234, 27408, 28703-28704
Gregg, Andrew, 1755-1835. 28705
Gregg, Daniel H. (28706)
Gregg, G. Ormsby. (28707), 63130
Gregg, J. 44698
Gregg, James. 28708
Gregg, Jarvis. 28709-28710
Gregg, Josiah. 28712-18716
Gregg, Marcy. 87793
Gregg, Samuel. 28717
Gregg, T. Chandler. 28718
Gregg, W. H. (28721)
Gregg, W. P. 28722
Gregg, William. 28719-28720
Greggs, --------. 91849
Gregoire, -------- 75540 see also France. Corps Legislatif. Conseil des Cinq-Cents. Commission des Colonies.
Gregoire, Henri, Bp., 1750-1851. (3421), 4933, 13477, (17167), 17507, 28723-28737, 38911, 40666, (81947), 97507
Gregorii Picchae Oratio ad Sixtum V. Pont. Max. 62602
Gregorio de Argaiz. 1944, 28739
Gregorio Valvins. 87296
Gregorius XIII, Pope, 1502-1585. 75884, 93589 see also Catholic Church. Pope, 1572-1585 (Gregorius XIII)
Gregorius XVI, Pope, 1765-1846. 22587, 28747, (56653) see also Catholic Church. Pope, 1831-1846 (Gregorius XVI)
Gregorius Nazianzensus, Saint, Patriarch of Constantinople. 57983
Gregorius, S. G. 28738
Gregory, J. M. 28742
Gregory, John. 98339 see also Jamaica. Supreme Court of Judicature, St. Jago de la Vega. Chief Justice.
Gregory, John, 1724-1773. 90234, 90238, 90240, 90244

Gregory, John, fl. 1853. 28740
Gregory, John, fl. 1860. 28741
Gregory, John Goadby. 84862
Gregory, John M. ed. 48766
Gregory, Olinthus Gilbert, 1774-1841. 9353
Gregory, Oscar H. 28743
Gregory, Samuel. 28744-28745
Gregory, William. 28746
Gregory Gold Mining Company. 66081
Gregory Gryphon. pseud. see Gryphon, Gregory. pseud.
Gregory Seaworthy. pseud. see Seaworthy, Gregory. pseud.
Gregory's guide to California. 28744
Gregory's history of Mexico. 28744
Greiff, B. (69369)
Greig, John. 104441
Greiner, Meinrad. (42209), 42251
Greipel, E. W. von. tr. 44162
Grellet, Stephen. 28748
Gremio de Jente de Mar, San Juan, Puerto Rico. Charter. 66596
Gremio de los Azogveros, Potosi, Peru. defendants 98358
Gremio de los Azogveros, Potosi, Peru. petitioners (64595)
Gremio de los Azogveros de la villa imperial de Potosi del Peru, suplica a V. M. y por el Geronimo Garbita. (64595)
Gremio de Mineros Administradores de la Real Mina, Oropeza, Bolivia. 56293
Gremio de Navieros de Peru. defendants 79146
Gremio de Panaderes, Vera Cruz, Mexico. 98905
Gremio de Panaderes, Vera Cruz, Mexico. Thesorero Veedor y Diputado. 98905 see also Lebrixa y Pruna, Manuel de.
Gremio de Panaderos de Mexico. 48644
Gremio de Plateros, Puebla, Mexico. 56410, 66566
Gremio de Abastos, Lima. see Lima. Gremios de Abastos.
Grenada, West Indies. Agent. 42720 see also Lushington, William.
Grenada, West Indies. Assembly. 104904
Grenada, West Indies. Laws, statutes, etc. 28750, 28753-28756, 85362
Grenada Agricultural Society. 28761
Grenada planter. pseud. Brief enquiry. 7865, 104904
Grenada planter. pseud. Letter. 7865, 104904
Grenada planter. 28751
Grenard, Leo. 28762
Grenell, G. St. Leger. defendant before military commission 9381
Grenier, --------. 28763
Grennell, George. 28764, (28869)
Grenville, George, 1712-1770. 9294, (15052), 15202-15023, 15928, 28767-28769, (28772), 28776, 38180, 46928, 63064, note just before 65329, 69436, 2d note after 89184, 90287, 2d note after 94663, 95750, 103123
Grenville, George, 1712-1770. supposed author (15202)-(15203), 95750
Grenville, George, 1712-1770. incorrectly supposed author (5859), 10243, 28770-28771, 3d note after 103122
Grenville, George, 1712-1770. spirit author 19947, note after 96403
Grenville, R. K. 51501
Grenville, Sir Richard, 1541?-1591. (8784)
Grenville, Richard, 1711-1799. see Temple, Richard Temple Grenville-Temple, Earl, 1711-1779.

Grenville, William Wyndham Grenville, <u>Baron</u>, 1759-1834. 105679
Grenville papers. 28776, 2d note after 94663
Greto de alarma en los Indios contra los blancos y cartas. 56365
Gretry, ---------. 44656, 100745
Grety, Andre. 100745
Grevelink, A. H., <u>Bp</u>. 28777-(28779)
Grew, Henry. 28780-28781
Grew, Mary. 28782
Grew, Theophilus. 28783
Grewingk, C. , 28784-(28785)
Grey, Benjamin Edwards. 28786
Grey, Sir Charles Edward, 1785-1865. 10574, 28787
Grey, Charles Grey, 2d <u>Earl</u>, 1764-1845. 33365
Grey, George. 60675 see also Pennsylvania. General Assembly. House of Representatives. Speaker.
Grey, <u>Sir</u> George, 1812-1898. 28788
Grey, Henry George Grey, 3d <u>Earl</u>, 1802-1894. (28789)
Grey, Isaac. 28790, 79243
Grey, Richard, 1694-1771. 42873, 79458
Grey, Robert. 28791
Grey, Zackary. 28792-28794
Grey-bay mare. 39966
Grey Town, Mosquito Shore. <u>see</u> San Juan del Norte, Nicaragua.
Greyjackets, and how they lived. 28795
Greylock, Godfrey. <u>pseud</u>. Taghconic. <u>see</u> Smith, Joseph Edward Adams, 1822-1896.
Greyslaer: a romance of the Mohawk. 32385
Gribble, Charles B. (28800)
Gribelin, --------. <u>engr</u>. 5112
Gricom, John H. 28876-28878
Grider, Henry, 1796-1866. 28801
Gridiron. 105848
Gridley, Jeremy. <u>incorrectly supposed author</u> 240, 32551, 7th note after 97146, 97147
Gridley, John. 28802
Gridely, Philo. (28803)
Gridley, Samuel H. (70947)
Grieb, Chr. Fr. <u>tr</u>. 4539, 8520
Grieben, A. H. 28804
Grief a-la-mode. A comedy. 91152
Grief and duty. (18584)
Griefs d'appel. 99598
Griendlief, Thomas. <u>supposed author</u> 64163-64164
Grier, Robert. (28805)-28806
Grier, Robert Cooper, 1794-1870. 51456, 84728
Grier's southern almanac for the states of Georgia. 28806
Griesinger, Theodor. 28807-28808
Griestetter, Vuolffgang. <u>ed</u>. 11237, 39118
Grievances of the American colonies candidly examined. 32967
Grieve, James. <u>tr</u>. 38301, (38303)
Grievous, Peter, <u>A</u>. B. C. D. E. <u>pseud</u>. Pretty story. <u>see</u> Hopkinson, Francis, 1739-1791.
Grievous, Peter, Junr. <u>pseud</u>. Congratulatory epistle. 14025
Griffen, --------. <u>defendant</u> 36136
Griffen, Phebe. 28810
Griffen, Solomon. <u>complainant</u> 104500 <u>see also</u> Friends, Society of. New York Monthly Meeting. Property Committee. complainants
Griffet de Labeaume, A.-G. <u>tr</u>. 68746

Griffin, Appleton P. C. <u>ed</u>. 85375, 88964
Griffin, Augustus. (28811)
Griffin, Benjamin. 28812
Griffin, Cornelius. 28813
Griffin, Ebenezer. 28814
Griffin, Esther. 28815
Griffin, Edmund D. (28816)
Griffin, Edward Dorr, 1770-1837. 28817-28818, 89716, 89740, 92835
Griffin, Francis. <u>ed</u>. (28816)
Griffin, Frederick. (28819)
Griffin, G. W. 65065
Griffin, George. 54593
Griffin, John. 28820, note after 104633
Griffin, John Quincy Adams. (5541), 28821
Griffin's journal. (28811)
Griffing, Josephine L. <u>petitioner</u> 80404
Griffith, Mrs. -------. <u>tr</u>. 21020, 99415, 99418, 99420
Griffith, David. (28823)
Griffith, Francis P. 28824
Griffith, George. 3213, note before 92797, note after 92800, 3d note after 103687
Griffith, J. (69154), 83665
Griffith, James F. (28826)
Griffith, John. (28825)
Griffith, Maurice. 34896
Griffith, Owen. <u>plaintiff</u> 40855
Griffith, Richard. 91342
Griffith, Thomas W. 28827-(28828)
Griffith, William. 28829-28832
Griffiths, D. 28833
Griffiths, John Willis, 1809?-1882. 28834
Griffiths, Julia. 28835, 92395, 92452
Griffiths, Mattie. 28836
Griffiths, Samuel P. 99822, 99825
Grigg, -------. <u>defendant</u> 103160
Grigg, John. 28837
Grigg (John) <u>firm publisher</u> 28838, 88300
Griggs, ---------. 28840
Griggs, William N. 28839
Grigg's southern and western songster. 28838, 88300
Grignion, -------. <u>illus</u>. 77467
Grigori Schelechof Ruszischen Kaufmanns erste und zewyte Reise. (77539)
Grigsby, Hugh Blair. (28842)-(28844)
Grigsby, John. (58935)
Grijalua, Joan de, 1559?-1627. 22086, (28845)
Grijalva, Hernando de. 84379
Grilley, Jean, 1624-1677. 151-152, 52380, 72757, (72759), note after 93778, 1st note after 100824
Grim, Charles Frederic. (28847)
Grim, Dick, the one-eyed robber. 28848
Grimaldi, Heronimo, <u>Marques</u> de, 1720-1786. 28846
Grimas de Lima. 64573
Grimes, G. 28849
Grimes, J. S. 28850
Grimes, James Wilson, 1816-1872. (28851)-(28852), 52127
Grimes, William H. 95126
Grimestone, Edward. <u>tr</u>. 131, 47118
Grimke, Angelina Emily, 1805-1879. 28853-28854
Grimke, Frederick. 28855
Grimke, John Faucheraud, 1752-1819. 86134, 87450, note before 87563, 87706, 88013-88014
Grimke, Sarah. 102550
Grimke, Sarah Moore, 1792-1873. (28856)
Grimke, Thomas Smith, 1786-1834. 21606, 28857-28862, 87453, 87468, 87531, 88085 <u>see also</u> South Carolina.

Legislature. Senate. Committee to Examine the Bank of the State. Chairman.

Grimm, Wilhelm. tr. (2772)

Grimoult, ------. 28863

Grimshaw, A. H. ed. 28867

Grimshaw, William, 1782-1852. 2774, 28864-28867, 67695

Grin with the gentlemen. (13435)

Grindrod, R. B. 28868

Grineus, Simon. 32682

Gringo. 18900

Gringos oder Ansichten aus dem Innern von Mexico und Californien. 104891

Gringos: or, an inside view of Mexico and California. 104892-104893

Grinnell, George. see Grennel, George.

Grinnell, Joseph, 1789-1885. 28870-28871, (52746)

Grinnell, Josiah Bushnell, 1821-1891. 28872

Grinnell, William T. 70662

Grinnell Land. 25055

Griscom, John, 1774-1852. 28873-28875

Griscom, John Hoskins, 1808-1874. 28876-28878

Grisebach, A. H. R. 28879

Girssomn, Wilhelm. 28880

Griswold, A. (18939)

Griswold, Alexander Viets, Bp. (28881), 92077

Griswold, C. D. 28883

Griswold, Charles. (28882)

Griswold, E. 28884

Griswold, F. (28885), 35715

Griswold, George. plaintiff 96881

Griswold, J. 35715

Griswold, John. 28886

Griswold, John Augustus, 1822-1872. 19515, 52127

Griswold, Matthew, 1714-1799. 15744 see also Connecticut. Governor, 1784-1786 (Griswold)

Griswold, Nathaniel L. plaintiff 96881

Griswold, Roger, 1762-1812. 15831-15832, 15744, 28888-28890 see also Connecticut. Governor, 1811-1813 (Griswold)

Griswold, Rufus Wilmot, 1815-1857. 1199, 5509, 28891-28901, 34932, (63522), 63570-63571, 66967, 77982, 84156, 85433, 97380

Griswold, S. O. 28902

Griswold, Samuel B. 42813

Griswold, Stanley. 5592, 28903-(28908), 90761, 93066

Griswold, Whiting. 28909

Griswold, Rev. Whiting. (28910)

Griswold & Co. firm publishers 61606

Griswold (Thomas) & Co. firm defendants 18970-18971

Griswold College, Davenport, Iowa. Preparatory Department. 28911

Griswold vs. Griswold. 28899

Gritos contra el Investigador Don Guillermo del Rio o Beque. 105953A

Grizzly Jake. 28912

Groam, Robert. see Coram, Robert.

Groans of a saint. 91223

Groans of Europe at the prospect of the present posture of affairs. 21208

Groans of Jamaica. 28914

Groans of Missouri: a poem. 77858, 77879, 3d note after 96452

Groans of the plantations. 3271, 20242, note after 28914

Gorans of the protestant church. 81435

Groben, J. Van der. tr. 73386

Grocer, J. R. 28915

Groenlandische Gesellschafft, Copenhagen. see Koppenhagen-Groenlandische Gesellschafft.

Groenlandische Reise Beschreibung. 44834

Groenlandsch Geselschap te Koppenhagen. see Koppenhagen-Groenlandische Gesellschafft.

Groenlandsk A. B. D. Bog. 28645

Groenwall, And. 28916

Groesbeck, Herman J. 28917

Groesbeck, Mary W. defendant 83638

Groesbeck, William Slocum, 1815-1897. 28918

Grolier, P. N. tr. 35131

Grondergenaar in die kolonie. pseud. Slaven-emancipatie en slaven-arbeid in Suriname. 93864

Grondich discours.—Naerder bedenckingen.—Vertoogh. 98201

Grondich discours over desen aen-staeden vrede-handel. 98195

Grondig bewijs dat syne Roomsch-Keiz. Maj. in zijne Oostenr. (4848)

Grondige ende waerachtige beschrijvinge. (14958), 37691, 67558

Grondlycke onderrricht van sekere voorname hoofd-stricken. 23719

Grondwet van de Vereenigde Staten van Noord-Amerika. 28921

Grone, A. C. E. von. 28919

Groneweg, L. 28920

Groenwall, And. 5664, 28916

Groningen (Dutch Province) Laws, statutes, etc. 93834

Groningen (Dutch Province) Staten Generael. 78000-78002

Gronland. see Greenland.

Gronland, berbeitet von Johannes Russwurm. 75767

Gronland geografisk og statistik beskrevet. 71433, 71435

Gronland geographisch und statistisch Besch-reiben. 23099, (71434)

Gronlandia antiqva. 96192

Gronlandia edur Graenland saga. 2058, 74880

Gronlandia, edur Groenlands saga. (28646)

Gronlandia, eller historie om Gronland. 36637

Gronlands amfipoder beskrevne. (38321)

Gronlands annulata dorsibranchiata. 57659

Gronlands beskrivelse. (4819)

Gronlands historiske mindesmaerker. (28650), (67467)

Gronlandsche Gesellschaft, Copenhagen. see Koppenhagen Groenlandishe Gesellschafft.

Gronlandske chronica. 42882

Gronlandske handel og Gronlands colonisation. 46850

Gronlandske ordbog. 23604

Gronlandske relationer. 18298

Gronnoiosaw, James Albert Ukawsaw. 28922

Gronovius, Johann Friedrich, 1690-1760. (3808), 3809, 28923-28924

Gronow, Lewis. 28925 see also Chester County, Pa. Sub-Lieutenant.

Groome, S. 28926

Groot, Jeldert Jansz. 28927

Groot, Jose M. 28928

Groot, Olaus de. see Magnus, Olaus, Abp. of Upsala, 1490-1558.

Groot placcaetboek inhoudende de placaten ende ordonnantien. 28930

Groot volk dat zich verheft. (26733)

Groote journael vande wonderlijcke ende groote reyse. 55432

Groote schrijf-almanach. (28931)

Groote tafereel der dwaasheid. 28932

Groote wonderlijcke wereldt. (36639)-36640
Grooten atlas oft wereltbeschrijving. 5716
Grootmoedige en heldhaftige Hollandsche
　　Amasoon. 95322
Gropings after truth. 33975
Gros, C. 39125
Gros, John Daniel. (28933)
Gros mosqueton diplomatique. 13884
Grosbeck, David. defendant 83638
Grose, Francis. 482, 28934
Grosett, J. R. 28935
Grosourdy, Rene de. 28942, 69601-69602
Gross, ---------, fl. 1792. 75132
Gross, Charles H. 2486, (28936)
Gross, Charles H. supposed author 4586
Gross, Eugene L. 34283
Gross, Ezra Carter, 1787-1829. 28940
Gross, Samuel David, 1805-1884. 28937-
　　28939, 55552
Gross, William. (28941)
Gross, William L. 34283
Gross Britanniens und der Vereinigten Staaten
　　neuere Handels-politik. 20218
Gross-Britaanische Scepter in der Neuen Welt.
　　57159
Gross-Brittannisches America nach seiner
　　Erfindung. 57158, note after (28941)
Gross errours and hypocrisie detected in
　　George Whitehead. 37198, 59663
Gross representation of the public documents.
　　91633
Grosse Conflikt in Amerika. (28483)
Grosse Erweckung in den Vereinigten Staaten.
　　29530
Grosse Feuersbrunst zu New-York. (14299)
Grosse Rebellion. (31152)
Grosser Eisenbahn-Post und Reise-Karte.
　　8209
Grosseste Denkwurdigkeiten der Welt. (30277)
Grossherzoglichen Bibliothek zu Weimar. see
　　Weimar. Grossherzogliche Bibliothek.
Grosvenor, Cyrus Pitt. 28943-28944
Grosvenor, Cyrus Pitt. supposed author
　　13133, 28944
Grosvenor, Daniel. 28945
Grosvenor, David A. 28946
Grosvenor, Ebenezer. 28947
Grosvenor, L. 28948-28950
Grosvenor, Lorenzo D. see Gouverneur,
　　Lorenzo D.
Grosvenor, Thomas Peabody, 1778-1817. 9944,
　　(28952)-28953
Grosvenor, W. M. 28954
Grosvenor, a tragedy. 29670
Grosze Tour. 64541, (64549), 64550
Grote, Augustus Radcliffe. 28955
Grote, George, 1794-1871. 56424
Grote, J. C. 72229
Grote, Olaus de. see Magnus, Olaus, Abp.
　　of Upsala, 1490-1558.
Grote nieuw bereisde wereld. 49792
Grotius. pseud. Pill for the delegates.
　　28958
Grotius. pseud. Vindication of Thomas
　　Jefferson. see Clinton, De Witt,
　　1769-1828.
Grotius, Hugo, 1583-1645. 28956-(28957),
　　33015, 38561-38562, 61293, (73771),
　　(78971)
Groton, Mass. 28968, 28971
Groton, Mass. Committee on a High School.
　　(28972)
Groton, Mass. Ecclesiastical Council, 1826.
　　see Congregational Churches in
　　Massachusetts. Ecclesiastical Council,
　　Groton, 1826.

Groton, Mass. First Church. 28967
Groton, Mass. First Parish Library. 28962
Groton, Mass. Lawrence Academy. see
　　Lawrence Academy, Groton, Mass.
Groton, Mass. Lodge no. 71, Independent
　　Order of Odd Fellows. see Odd Fellows
　　Independent Order of. Massachusetts.
　　Groton Lodge, no. 71.
Groton, Mass. Ordinances, etc. 28959-(28960
　　28969
Groton, Mass. Overseers of the Poor. (2897
Groton, Mass. Public Library. (28961)
Groton, Mass. School Committee. (28960),
　　28973
Groton, Mass. Selectmen. (28974)
Groton, Mass. Superintending School Committe
　　28975
Groton, Mass. Union Church. Congregational
　　Library. 28963
Groton Academy, Groton, Mass. 28964
Groton Centre, Mass. North Middlesex Cir-
　　culating Library. see North Middlesex
　　Circulating Library, Groton Centre, Mas
Groton in the witchcraft times. 104111
Groton Invincible Club. (28966)
Groton Junction post office. 8479
Groton Lodge, no. 71, Independent Order of
　　Odd Fellows. see Odd Fellows, Indepen
　　dent Order of. Massachusetts. Groton
　　Lodge, no. 71.
Groton Soapstone Quarry and Manufactory.
　　28970
Groton Union Conference. see Baptists.
　　Connecticut. Stonington Union Conference
Grouchy, Nicolas de. tr. 11387
Grouchy, Sophie de. see Condorcet, Sophie
　　de Grouchy, Marquise de. tr. 82308,
　　82317
Ground of confidence in foreign missions.
　　(71269)
Ground of national consolation and hope.
　　(82388)
Grovnds and ends of the baptisme of the
　　children of the faithfvll. (17066)
Grounds and principles of Christian religion.
　　46775
Grounds and rules of musick explained. 10119
Grounds for gratitude. 70934
Grounds of ministerial fellowship, discussed
　　in a series of pamphlets. 28628, 104118
Grounds of opposition to Mr. Seward. 8346
Grovnds of plantations examined, and vsuall
　　objections answered. 17075, 103396-
　　103397
Grounds of secession from the M. E. Church.
　　78346
Group. 13695
Group, a farce. 101483
Group, as lately acted. 2160, 101482
Group of poems touching that river. 101342
Group; or, an elegant representation illustrate
　　28977
Grouped thoughts and scattered fancies. 81215
Grout, Henry M. 28979
Grout, Jonathan. 28978
Grout, Moses W. 105363
Grout, Thomas J. 90449, note after 92355
Grout, William W. (28980)
Grouvel, --------. 28981
Groulx, L. T. 28984
Groux, Daniel E. 28982-28983
Grova, Manuel de. 3350
Grove, Miss -------. 28986
Grove, Burley. alias see Allen, James.
　　defendant
Grove, James P. (28985)

Grove, Joseph, fl. 1703. 5631, note after
103702
Grove, Joseph, d. 1764. 28987
Grove, P. V. tr. 92518
Grove, Silvanus. 59688
Groveland, Mass. Auditors. 28988
Grover, La Fayette, 1823-1911. 28989, 57558
see also Oregon (Territory) Commis-
sioner to Collect the Laws and Anchives
of Oregon.
Grover, Martin, 1811-1875. 28990
Grover, S. T. supposed author 69462
Grover, William. 28991
Groves, K. 64962
Groves, Robert. 28992
Grow, Galusha Aaron, 1823-1907. 28993-
28997
Growler Gruff, Esquire. pseud. Cynick.
18216
Growler's income tax. 2136
Growth and influence of Christianity in the
world. 105502
Growth and manufacture of silk. (26931),
81010
Growth and prospects of the University of the
City of New York. (45429)
Growth of civil and religious liberty in
America. (47092)
Growth of individualism. 43631
Growth of New York. 28998
Growth of the New York Conference. 3168
Grua Talamanca, Miguel de la, Marques de
Branciforte. 76861 see also Mexico
(Viceroyalty) Virrey, 1794-1798 (Grua
Talamanca)
Grubb, Sarah. 86577-86578
Grube, August Wilhelm. 28999
Gruber, J. A. 23094, 29010, 4th note after
97845, note after 106352, 106355
Gruber, Jacob. defendant 29000
Gruber, Johann Adam, fl. 1730-1750. 2462, 4th
note after 97845
Gruber, Johann Gottfried, 1774-1851. (29001)
Grudon, Juan Luis de. 39215
Grue, Thomas la. see La Grue, Thomas.
Gruff, Growler. pseud. see Growler Gruff,
Esquire. pseud.
Gruget, Claude. tr. (48243)-48244
Grumbler, Anthony, of Grumbleton Hall.
pseud. Miscellaneous thoughts. see
Hoffman, David.
Grund, Francis J. 29002-(29009)
Grund, Francis J. supposed author 62715
Grundlage von Vortragen im geographischen
Verein zu Frankfort a. M. 68492
Grundliche An- und Aufforderung an die
ehmahlig Erwerckte. 29010, 4th note
after 97845, 106355
Grundliche History von Erfundung der Grossen
Landschafft. 40177
Grundliche Nachrichten uber die Verfassung
der Landschaft. 51480, (51482), 98777
Grundliche vnd sattsame Beschreibung desz
Newen Engellands. (33673), 103332
Grundliche, vnd vmbstandliche fernere
Beschreibung. 4567, (4585), 33674
Grundliche vnd warhaffte Beschreibung aller
Mitternachtingen vnd Nortwerts gelegenen
Landen und Insulen. 47383
Grundliche vnd warhaffte Beschreibung desz
neuwen Engellandts. 33667, 82819
Grundliche und wahrhaffte Reise-Beschreibung.
5905, 52359
Grundlichen Nachricht von dem Bakkeljau-und
Stockfischfang bey Terreneuf. 106377

Grundlicher Bericht des in America zwischen
dem Rio Orinoco. 11337
Grundlicher Bericht von Beschaffenheit und
Eigenschaft. 28011
Grundlicher Bericht von dem jetzigen Zustand.
(8784), note after 99383C
Grundlicher Unterricht von den Metallen.
(67375)
Grundliche An- und Aufforderung an die
Ehmahlig erweckte hier. 29010
Grundlicke Erweisung dass Ihro K. Kais. Maj.
in Dero Oesterreichischen Niederlanden.
4847A
Grundlicke Nachrichten uber die Verfassung
der Landschaft. 98777
Grundlinien der Ethnographie. (4858)
Grundlinien der physikalischen Erdbeschreibung.
4857A
Grundriss der Geographie. 4857A
Grundriss von Nordamerika. 29012
Grund's speech from the "North American."
(29009)
Grundtliche Erklarung. 33663
Grundtliche Relation oder Beschreibung. 101423
Grundung von New-Switzerland im Staate
Illinois. 75372
Grundverfassung der Evangelischen-Lutherischen
General-Synode. 29013
Grundy, Felix, 1777-1840. 29014-(29016), 89216,
note after 102276
Grundy, Robert C. 29017
Grunewald, Ernst. 3327
Grunwald, Charles. illus. 83556
Gruterus, Jacobus. 66494
Gruvel, --------. tr. 49890
Grymes, Philip. supposed author 98977
Grynaeus, Simon, 1493-1541. 16961, note after
16965, 30482-30483, 34100-34107, 40960,
50050-50064, 62803, 63960, 74803, note
after 99383C, 1st-5th notes after 106378
Gryphon, Gregory. pseud. Theatrical censor.
95286
Guadalara, J. E. 29018
Guadalajara y Xabierr, Marco de. (34196)
Guadalajara (Mexican State) 65976
Guadalajara (Mexican State) Ministro de
Hacienda. 56442
Guadalajara (City) Catedral. 22363, 29025
Guadalajara (City) Consulado. Charter. 29028
Guadalajara (City) Junto de Comercio. see
Jalisco (State) Junto de Comercio de
Guadalajara.
Guadalajara (City) Sagrario. 57719
Guadalajara (City) Santa Iglesia Catedral. see
Guadalajara (City) Catedral.
Guadalajara (Archdiocese) 15081, 29021,
29031, 29032, 44275
Guadalajara (Archdiocese) petitioners 48518
Guadalajara (Archdiocese) Archbishop (Espinosa)
22903-22904, 56454 see also Espinosa,
Pedro, Abp., 1793-1866.
Guadalajara (Archdiocese) Bishop [ca 1859]
29019-29020, 44276
Guadalajara (Archdiocese) Bishop (Rivas)
71613 see also Rivas, Diego Rodriguez,
Bp.
Guadalajara (Archdiocese) Cabildo. 29021-
(29023), 22904, 56454, 68681
Guadalajara (Archdiocese) Cabildo. defendants
(29024)
Guadalajara (Archdiocese) Governador de la
Mitra. (29026)
Guadalcazar, Diego Fernandez de Cordova, 1.
Marques de. see Fernandez de Cordova,
Diego, 1. Marques de Guadalcazar.

Guatemala. Supremo Tribunal de Justicia.
86518
Guatemala. Treaties, etc. 32762
Guatemala (City) (29081)
Guatemala (City) Ayuntamiento. 29096,
(34838), (75770), 76860
Guatemala (City) Ayuntamiento. Archivo.
29072
Guatemala (City) Catedral. Cabildo. 29083
Guatemala (City) Catedral. Dean. 19043
Guatemala (City) Ordinances, etc. 76860
Guatemala (City) Secretario de la Municipali-
dad. 29072, 76860 see also Arevalo,
Rafael de.
Guatemala (City) Seminario. Observatorio.
(41677)
Guatemala (City) Sociedad de Geografia e
Historia. see Sociedad de Geografia e
Historia de Guatemala.
Guatemala (City) Sociedad Economica. see
Sociedad Economica de Guatemala.
Guatemala (City) Sociedad Economica de
Amantes de la Patria. see Sociedad
Economica de Amantes de la Patria de
Guatemala.
Guatemala (City) Sociedad Economica de
Amigos. see Sociedad Economica de
Amigos de Guatemala.
Guatemala (City) Universidad de San Carlos.
(76933)
Guatemala (City) Universidad Nacional.
Library. (77618)
Guatemala (Archdiocese) 29083, 34836
Guatemala (Archdiocese) Bishop (Alvarez de
Toledo) see also Alvarez de Toledo,
Juan Baptista, Bp.
Guatemala (Arhcdiocese) Archbishop (Cortes y
Larraz) 16969 see also Cortes y
Larraz, Pedro, Abp.
Guatemala (Archdiocese) Bishop (Ribera) see
also Ribera, Payo Henriquez de, Abp.
Vera Paz (Diocese) Bishop (Ribera)
Mexico (Archdicoese) Archbishop (Ribera)
Mexico (Viceroyalty) Virrey, 1673-1680
(Ribera)
Guatemala (Archdiocese) Bishop (Rodriguez
de Ribas) 29074, 72541-72542 see also
Rodriguez de Ribas, Diego, Bp., d. 1771.
Guatemala (Archdiocese) Provisor y Vicario
General. plaintiff 26587 see also
Garcia de Gastizabal, Martin. plaintiff
Guatemala; goegraphical, historical and
topographical. 29080
Guatemalensis ecclesiae in optimi sui parentis
orbitate lugubris lamentatio. 10709
Guatemalensis ecclesiae monumenta. 39524
Guatemalteco. pseud. Memorias para la
historia de la revolucion. see Marure,
Alejandro. supposed author and
Montufar, Manuel. incorrectly supposed
author and Paul, Manuel. supposed
author
Guatimala, [sic] or, the republic of Central
America. 21320
Guatimozin uber die Welt. 71597
Guatimozin, ultimo Emperador de Mejico.
27756
Guay-Trouin, -------- du. 29098
Guayana. Presidente. 47601
Guayaquil. Concejo Municipal. 29097
Guaxaca (Diocese) Bishop [ca 1631] 106003A
Guaxara (Diocese) 34836
Guazacoalco, colonie de MM. Laisne de
Villeveque et Giordan. 21023
Guazzo, Marco. see Montovano, Marco.

Gudelig barna-catekes till ungdomens tjenst i
de Svenska Forsamleingar i Pensylvanien.
94035
Guds nades rikedom emot syndare. 105517
Guelen, Auguste de. 29100-(29101)
Guelfos y Gibelinos, drama en cuatro actos.
29058
Guell y Rente, Jose. 29102-(29103)
Guemes, Pedro Goncalez de. 29105
Guemes Pacheo de Podilla, Juan Vicente de,
Conde de Revillagigedo. 56254, 70285-
70288 see also Mexico (Viceroyalty)
Virrey, 1789-1794 (Guemes Pacheo de
Podilla)
Guemes y Horcasitas, Juan Francisco de.
29104 see also Mexico (Viceroyalty)
Virrey, 1746-1755 (Guemes y Horcasitas)
Guen, Genaro. 29107
Guen, Lewis le. see Le Guen, Lewis.
Guenebault, J. H. 29108
Guennes da Silva Mello, Joaquim. see Silva
Mello, Joaquim Guennes da.
Guenot, G. ed. 12273
Guepes Canadiennes. 39985, note after 94187
Guerard, Benjamin, d. 1789. 87536 see also
South Carolina. Governor, 1783-1785
(Guerard)
Guerard, Jean. cartographer 76838
Guerilla chief. 51039
Guerilla chief, and other tales. (69047)
Guerilla spy. 29482
Guerillas of the Osage. 32625
Guerin, H. C. defendant at court martial
(48147)
Guerin, Leon. 29109
Guerin, M. E. ed. 78689
Guerin-Meneville, F. E. 21353, 29110-29111,
74921-74922
Guerini, Aloise. see Alvise, Querini.
Guernsey, Alfred H. 29113
Guernsey, Clara Florida. 29114, 85370
Guernsey, Egbert. 29115-29116
Guernsey, Orrin. 29117
Guernsey County (Ohio) meteorites. 82993
Guerra, Fermin Aurelio de Tagle Cossio y.
see Tagle Cossio y Guerra, Fermin
Aurelio de.
Guerra, Joan. 29118-29119
Guerra, Jose. 29120
Guerra, Jose de Bustamante y. see
Bustamante y Guerra, Jose de.
Guerra, Jose Martin, Bp. 29121 see also
Yucatan (Diocese) Bishop (Guerra)
Guerra, Jose Servando Teresa de Mier Noriega
y. see Mier Noriega y Guerra, Jose
Servando Teresa, de 1765-1827.
Guerra, Rosa. 29122
Guerra Manzanares, Ignacio. see Manzanares,
Ignacio Guerra.
Guerra Servando, Jose de Mier y. see Mier
y Guerra Servando, Jose de.
Guerra y Morales, Christoval Ruiz. see Ruiz
Guerra y Morales, Christoval.
Guerra de Chile cavsas de sv dvracion medios
para sv fin. 94898
Guerra de Espana con Mejico. 29125
Guerra de religion. 56401
Guerra de Tejas sin mascara. 95089, 95130
Guerra do Paraguay. 29123, 88736
Guerra es el supremo de los males. 97717
Guerras ciuiles que huuo entre Picarros, y
Almagros. 98755
Guerras y conuersion de la nacion del Rio
Hiaqui. 70789
Guerre, Chr. 31553

Guerre a mort de l'opposition contre le Cit. Cabet. (9780)

Guerre Americaine son origine et ses vraies causes. 19766

Guerre aux Etats-Unis. 18495

Guerre civile, aux Etats Unis. 18224, 29124

Guerre civile aux Etats-Unis d'Amerique. 77534

Guerre civile aux Etats-Unis 1861-1863. 39239

Guerre civile en Amerique et l'esclavage. 9741

Guerre d'Amerique. Campagne du Potomac. 36408, 1st note after 97024

Guerre d'Amerique. 1860-65. (20096)

Guerre d'Amerique et la mediation. (48032)

Guerre d'Amerique et les hospitaliers. 11644

Guerre d'Amerique recit d'un soldat du sud. 24991

Guerre d'Amerique. Resume des operations militaires et maritimes. (38306)

Guerre dans la Plata en 1865. 38997

Guerre de la secession. 39658

Guerre de l'independance Americaine Washington. 5406

Guerre de l'independance et republique. 51408

Guerre des colonies d'Amerique 1764-83. 98983

Guerre des Etats-Unis d'Amerique. (39660)

Guerre des freres par Alfred des Essarts. 19732

Guerre d'Espagne. (12253)

Guerre du Mexique de 1862 a 1866. 39262

Guerre du Mexique 1861-1867. (40162)

Guerre et l'humanite aux XIXe siecle. 11644

Guerre noire. 2389

Guerreiro, Bartholomeu. 27587, 29126-29128, 69162

Guerreiro, Bartholamey. see Guerreiro, Bartholomeu.

Guerreiro, Fernam. see Guerreiro, Bartholomeu.

Guerrera, Antonio de. (8784)

Guerrero, B. Sanchez. 29129

Guerrero, Bartholome Lobo, Abp. 16065, 16071, (29131), note after 41711 see also Lima (Archdiocese) Archbishop (Guerrero)

Guerrero, Cosma Enriquez. 29130

Guerrero, Felipe Ignacio de Truxillo y. see Truxillo y Guerrero, Felipe Ignacio de, Bp.

Guerrero, Jose. (55154), 55159 see also Nicaragua. Supremo Director, 1847-1849 (Guerrero)

Guerrero, Jose Maria. 29132, 99687

Guerrero, Juan. petitioner 86412

Guerrero, Teodoro. (29133)

Guerrero, Vicente, Pres. Mexico, 1783?-1831. 29136 see also Mexico. Presidente, 1829 (Guerrero)

Guerrero, Vicente, Pres. Mexico, 1783?-1831. defendant 29138

Gverrero de la Cueba, Juan Diego. plaintiff 98156

Guerrero Martinez Rubio, Nicolas Antonio. see Rubio, Nicolas Antonio Guerrero Martinez.

Guerrero y Davila Urrutia y Arana, Juan Antonio. ed. 93349

Gverres civiles des Espagnols dans le Peru. 98750

Guerrico, Jose P. de. tr. 14207

Guerrilla parties considered. 40985

Guerrillas: an original domestic drama. 42962

Guers, -------. 91222

Guesada, Vicente G. 9040

Guess, George, or Sequoya, Cherokee Indian, 1770?-1843. 34481

Guesses by a Yankee in London. 31518

Guest, Moses. 29139

Guest, Richard. 29140

Guest of the "Community," near Watervliet, New York. pseud. Revelation of the extraordinary visitation. 70159

Guests of Brazil. 33965-33966

Guette, S. de Broe, Seigneur de Citry et de la see Broe, S. de, Seigneur de Citry et de la Guette.

Gueudeville, -------. 29141

Gueudeville, Nicolas, ca. 1654-ca. 1721. 2914? 38637, (38643)

Gueullette, Thomas Simon, 1683-1766. 29143

Guevara, Ant. Ladron de. (29144)

Guevara, Baltasar Ladron de. see Ladron de Guevara, Baltasar.

Guevara, Baltasar Pardo de Figueroa y. see Pardo de Figueroa y Guevara, Baltasar.

Guevara, Cristoval Sanchez de. see Sanchez de Guevara, Cristoval.

Guevara, Diego Ladron de, Bp. 29145 see also Quito (Diocese) Bishop (Guevara)

Guevara, J. de Arroyo Ladron de. see Ladron de Guevara, J. de Arroyo.

Guevara, Joseph Augustin de Aldama y. see Aldama y Guevara, Joseph Augustin de.

Gueuara, Ioan Ladron de. 76110 see also Franciscans. Province of San Francisco de Quito. Visitador.

Guevara, Luis Velez de. see Velez de Guevara, Luis.

Guevara, Miguel de. 29146

Guevara, Miguel Thadeo de. 29146-29148

Guevara, P. (29149), 29379

Guevara y Salamanca, Juan Velez de. see Velez de Guevara y Salamanca, Juan.

Guezenac, Alfred, 1823-1866. 29151

Gugy, A. A. 86651

Guia de forasteros de Guatemala. (29086)

Guia de forasteros de la isla de Cuba. (1775?

Guia de forasteros de la Nueva Granada. 56266

Guia de forasteros de la republica Boliviana. 6191

Guia de forasteros de Lima. (41081)

Guia de forasteros de Lima, correjida para el ano de 1822. 41111

Guia de forasteros de Mexico, para el ano de 1791. 106404

Guia de forasteros del Departemento del Cuzco 24836

Guia de forasteros en la siempre fiel isla de Cuba. 17777

Guia de forasteros en Mexico, para el ano de 1811. 48314, 106404

Guia de forasteros pora 1867. 6134

Guia de forasteros politico-commercial de la ciudad de Mexico. 71627

Guia de forasteros y repertorio de conocimien utiles. (956)

Guia de hacienda de la republica Mexicana. 23049

Guia de la ciudad de Caracas. 10770

Guia de la ciudad de Nueva York. 42902

Guia de la hacienda de la republica Mexicana. (48487)

Guia de los forasteros de Mexico de 1788. 48488

Guia de los frac-mazones utilisimo. 102244

Guia de Nueva York. 981, 54300

Guia de Nueva York y los Estados Unidos. (29152)

Guia de Nueva York y los Estados Unidos. Conteniendo un plano. 84768

Guia del estado ecclesiastico, seglar, y regular. 29153

Guia del estado eclesiastico de Espana. 26121

Guia del viajero en los Estados Unidos. 29154

Guia do correio do Brasil. (79308)

Guia do Rio de Janeiro. 71457

Guia geographica de Medrano. 47359

Guia geographica, y hydrographica. 47358

Guia historico-discriptiva-administrativa, judicial y de domicilio de Lima. (26116)

Guia judicial. 72545, 72548

Guia politica eclesiastica y militar del Peru. 9777

Guia politica, eclesiastica y militar del Virreynato del Peru. 61130, 97718

Guia politica, eclesiastica y militar del Virreynato del Peru [para los anos de 1794-1797.] 61130, 97718

Guiana. see British Guiana. French Guiana. Surinam.

Guiana, Bishop of. see Percy, William, Bp. of Guiana.

Guiana in 1772. 93408

Guiane. 101350

Guiane Franciase. see French Guiana.

Guichenot, A. 74921-74922

Guida generale della navigazione per le coste settentrionali ed orientali. 72507

Guida per la navigazione dello stretto di Gibilterra. 92862

Guide. 16490

Guide Americain. (73456)

Guide and directory for the state of Louisiana. 42231

Guide and directory for Virginia City. (14431)

Guide and directory of the state of Louisiana. 27317

Guide between Washington, Baltimore, Philadelphia, New York, and Boston. 20325

Guide-book. 62007

Guide book and pocket map. 16282

Guide book for British Columbia. 8094

Guide-book for investments in petroleum stocks. 29201

Guide book for the use of the guests of the Equinox House. 44224

Guide book of the Atlantic and St. Lawrence, and St. Lawrence and Atlantic Rail Roads. 4247, (29198)

Guide-book of the Central Railroad of New-Jersey. 29199

Guide book to Mr. Washington Friend's great American tour. 25952

Guide book to the Central Park. 54158

Guide book to the gold regions of Fraser River. 29200

Guide book to the scenery of western North Carolina. 14791

Guide de la conversation en trois langues. (1933)

Guide de l'emigrant. 9994

Guide de l'observateur. 23568, 55357, 93480

Guide . . . des Antilles et des regions intertropicales. (40730)

Guide des emigrants aux Etats-Unis. 29203

Guide des emigrants Francais dans les etats de Kentucky et d'Indiana. 29204

Guide des emigres au Texas. 29202

Guide du commerce de l'Amerique. 11813

Guide du navigateur dans l'ocean Atlantique. 6027

Guide for all. 80763

Guide for claimants of deceased soldiers. (25331)

Guide for emigrants. (59484)

Guide for emigrants to Minnesota. (49250)

Guide for invalids. 55522

Guide for the distributing reservoir. 54301

Guide for the emigrant. 10254

Guide for the Pennsylvania Railroad. 60358

Guide for the road to California. 91127

Guide from Montreal and Quebec to the eastern townships of Lower Canada and to Portland. 29205

Guide, gazetteer, and directory of the Dubuque and Sioux City Railroad. 21042

Guide medical des Antilles. (40730)

Guide on the North Pennsylvania Rail Road. 55724

Guide, or counsellor, of human life. 29206

Guide politique pour la campagne presidentielle de 1860. 29207

Guide pour les voyageurs. 74986

Guide pratique des emigrants en Californie. 73423

Guide santiaire des voyageurs aux colonies. (19694)

Guide through Mount Auburn. A hand-book for passengers. (10146), 30209, note after 91550

Guide through Mount Auburn . . . . By Nathaniel Dearborn. 19079

Guide through Mount Auburn Cemetery. (51147)

Guide through Mount Auburn Cemetery, in Cambridge, Mass. 10145

Guide through Nahant. 40779

Guide through the Albany Rural Cemetery, [sic] 13023

Guide through the city and environs [of Boston.] 19080

Guide through the middle, northern, and eastern states. 20318

Guide through the United States. 94311

Guide to American politics. 2649

Guide to Boston and vicinity. 66635

Guide to Burr's map of New-York. 9439

Guide to California. 28744

Guide to capitalists and emigrants. (55653)

Guide to Central Park and mercantile directory. (54406)

Guide to Christ. 91950-91953

Guide to emigrants proceeding to Australia and the Canadas. 29208

Guide to Fraser River. 25686

Guide to government situations. 29209

Guide to Havana, Mexico and New York. 84768

Guide to Haiti. 68525

Guide to Heaven from the word. (30358)

Guide to Illinois. 14795

Guide to inventors. 50409

Guide to knowledge. 71809

Guide to Lake George and Lake Champlain. 52322

Guide to Lake George, Lake Champlain, Montreal and Quebec. 95549

Guide to Laurel Hill Cemetery. 61709

Guide to Laurel Hill Cemetery, near Philadelphia. 39255, 82987

Guide to Minnesota. 49251

Guide to Montreal and its environs. 50252

Guide to national improvement. 36110

Guide to New Rochelle and its vicinity. 6246

Guide to New York City. (61379)

Guide to . . . New York, containing a list of all the streets. 54302

Guide to New-York for 1846. 20527, 54298

Guide to New York, its public buildings. (54303)

Guide to New York; its public buildings, places of amusement. 54304

Guide to Niagara Falls and its scenery. (36213)

Guide to northern archaeology. 29211

Guide to northern Illinois. 29760

Guide to Philadelphia. 83783

Guide to Pike's Peak. 49212

Guide to Plymouth, and recollections of the pilgrims. (74404)-(74405)

Guide to Pomerade's original panorama. 17185

Guide to Providence River and Narragansett Bay. 3227

Guide to rambles from the Catskill Mountain House. 11552

Guide to reason. 91818

Guide to Saratoga Springs and vicinity. 70965

Guide to South Bend, Notre Dame du Lac, and Saint Mary's, Indiana. 29212

Guide to Texas. 57349

Guide to Texas emigrants. 26474, 93710, 95086, 105111

Guide to the . . . British and foreign West Indies. (57763)

Guide to the Canadas. 28144

Guide to the capitol and to the national executive offices. 49115

Guide to the capitol of the United States. 49114

Guide to the Central Park. 54158

Guide to the Central Park. Illustrated. 70964

Guide to the city of Chicago. 12655

Guide to the city of New York and its neighborhood. 52322

Guide to the environs of . . . New York. 54305

Guide to the falls of Niagara. (19781)

Guide to the fortifications and battlefields around Petersburg. 61217

Guide to the geology of New York and the state geological cabinet. 41145

Guide to the gold country of California. 105656

Guide to the gold mines of Kansas. 64985

Guide to the gold region of California. (10013)

Guide to the gold regions. 103893

Guide to the handwriting of distinguished men and women. 52346

Guide to the Hudson River by railroad and steamboat. (33510), 51369

Guide to the lakes and mountains of New-Hampshire. 29213

Guide to the lions of Philadelphia. 61710

Guide to the new gold region of western Kansas and Nebraska. (29210)

Guide to the North Pennsylvania Rail Road. 55724

Guide to the Northern Pacific Railroad lands. 55822

Guide to the orchard and fruit garden. 41291

Guide to the Philadelphia Museum. 61711

Guide to the places of interest in Philadelphia. 61712

Guide to the presidential election of 1864. (41203)

Guide to the principal places of interest in Newport. 55041

Guide to the principles and practice of the Congregational Churches of New England. 49697-49698

Guide to the "prize grant" in Venezuelan Guayana. 59155

Guide to the right understanding of our political union. 36160

Guide to the sculpture, paintings, coins, and other objects of art. 75359

Guide to the Smithsonian Institution and National Museum. 85090

Guide to the South Pacific Rail Road lands. 88151

Guide to the southwest. 83737

Guide to the springs. 59208, 59192, 53289

Guide to the springs, and trip to the lakes. 94661

Guide to the study of insects. 58098

Guide to the upper Mississippi River. (20319)

Guide to the value of California gold. (21822)

Guide to the Virginia springs; . . . a description. 29214, 2d note after 100478

Guide to the Virginia springs and natural curiosities. 50470

Guide to the White Mountains and lakes of New Hampshire. 29215

Guide to those about to visit that country [i. California.] 9969

Guide to travelers visiting the falls of Niagara. 55119

Guide to travellers through the northern and middle states. 18909

Guide to travellers visiting the middle and northern states. (28903)

Guide to Upper Canada. 98076

Guide to wealth. 82241

Guide to West-Point. (14794)

Guide to Wisconsin. 25777

Guide with a treatise on the mineral waters. 76921

Guidee, Archolle. 29216

Guido, Antonio de Quintana y. see Quintana y Guido, Antonio de.

Guide, T. J. 49757

Guido, Tomas. 96231

Guidonis Pancirolli Rerum memorabilium sive deperditarum. 58412

Guignard, Alexis de. see Saint-Priest, Alexis de Guignard, Comte de 1805-1851

Guignard, Ph. 29217

Guignas, ------. (80003)

Guigon, A. B. ed. 66961

Guijo, Gregorio Martin de. (48440)

Guilbert, Edmund. (29218)

Guilbert de Pixerecourt, R. C. see Pixerecourt, R. C. Guilbert de.

Guild, ------. illus. 29219

Guild, Benjamin. ed. 80286

Guild, Calvin. (29220)

Guild, Curtis. 84062

Guild, Reuben Aldridge. 8624, 17069, 29221, (29224), 36109, 51773, 55871, 82723, 90478, 104341, 104343

Guild, Samuel Eliot. 29225

Guild, W. H. illus. 54154

Guild, William. 28129, 29226-29227

Guilday, Peter Keenan, 1884- 85257

Guilding, J. 29228

Guileless Isralite. 82336

Guilford, John North, Earl of, 1732-1792. 42, 25341, 26994, 55518, 64572, 85243

Guilford Mineral Spring water. 29229

Guilhelmo, ------, Coronel. see William, ------. RA

Gurney, Joseph John, 1788-1847. supposed
    author 82097
Gurney, Samuel. 29317, (55655)
Gurney (J.) and Son. photographers (66155),
    (75444)
Gurney Evening School, Philadelphia.
    Managers. 61713
Gurowski, Adam, hrabia, 1805-1866. 29318-
    29321
Gus Shaw's comic song and recitation book.
    79908
Gus Shaw's new comic songs. 79908
Gus Shaw's original comic songs. 79908
Gusmao, Alexandre de. 29322
Gvsman, Nvnno di. see Guzman, Nuno de,
    16th cent.
Guss, A. L. 29323
Gussefeld, F. L. engr. 89762
Gussew, M. tr. 33726
Gusta, Francisco. supposed author 63912-
    63913
Gustaf II Adolf, King of Sweden, 1594-1632.
    (68983), 98186, 98199, 98202-98205,
    note after 98207, 98210 see also
    Sweden. Sovereigns, etc., 1611-1632
    (Gustaf II Adolf)
Gustafson, Zadel Barnes. ed. 106372
Gustave Lambert au Pole Nord. (14942)
Gustavus Adolphus. see Gustaf II Adolf,
    King of Sweden, 1594-1632.
Gustavus Vasa. see Equiano, Olauhah.
Gustavus Vasa, the deliverer of his country.
    (8242)
Gutch, -------. 67599
Guter Rath an Einswanderer in die Vereinigten
    Staaten von Nord-Amerika. 19868
Guter Rath fur Auswanderer nach den Vereinig-
    ten Staaten von Nordamerika. 4374
Guter Swatzman. pseud. tr. see Giocondo,
    Giovanni.
Gutheiseen der Hochwurdigsten Herrn Pfarrers
    der Heilihen Kreuzkirche. 75472
Guthrie, -------, fl. 1860. (12406)
Guthrie, Abelard. 29324-29325
Guthrie, G. J. 30113, 76536, 76657 see also
    Great Britain. Army. Surgeon General.
Guthrie, James, 1792-1869. 21782, 29326,
    63005, 72675 see also U. S. Secretary
    of the Treasury.
Guthrie, W. E. (29329)
Guthrie, William, 1708-1770. 1060, 10858,
    (29327)-29328, (78330)
Gutierre Coronel, Juan. see Gutierrez
    Coronel, Juan.
Gutierres Coronel, Ricardo Josef. see
    Gutierrez Coronel, Ricardo Joseph.
Gutierrez, -------. 29336
Gutierrez, Alonzo. 29331-(29332), 57517,
    68936, note after 68936, note before
    89152, note before 98912-98919
Gutierrez, Alonzo. supposed author (48387),
    98919
Gutierrez, Bonifacio. 48454 see also
    Mexico. Ministerio de Hacienda.
Gutierrez, Diego. 86555
Gutierrez, Diego Cano. 29334
Gutierrez, Eusebio. (29335)
Gutierrez, F. M. 49757
Gutierrez, J. J. 29337
Gutierrez, J. M. ed. (70311)
Gutierrez, Joaquin Posada. see Posada
    Gutierrez, Joaquin.
Gutierrez, Jose Maria. 29338-29340
Gutierrez, Jose Ygnacio. 69978
Gutierrez, Juan Maria. 29341-29348, 35536,
    38443

Gutierrez, Manuel Agustin. 99783
Gutierrez, Ricardo, 1836-1896. (29350)-29355
Gutierrez Coronel, Juan. 99730
Gutierrez Coronel, Ricardo Joseph. 29330,
    47952, 50611
Gutierrez Cosio, Pedro. plaintiff 61136
Gutierrez Davila, Julian. see Davila, Julian
    Gutierrez.
Gutierrez de Alba, Jose M. 29352
Gutierrez de la Concha y de Irigoyen, Jose.
    see Habana, Jose Gutierrez de la
    Concha e Irigoyen, Marquis de la,
    1809-1895.
Gutierrez de la Fuente, Ant. see La Fuente,
    Ant. Gutierrez de.
Gutierrez de la Huerta, Francisco. (29358)
Gutierrez de Medina, Cristobal. 99400
Gutierrez de Pineres, Tomas. see Pineres,
    Tomas Gutierrez de.
Gutierrez de Rubalcava, Joseph. see
    Rubalcava, Joseph Gutierrez de.
Gutierrez y Estrada, Jose Maria, 1800-1867.
    29262, 29353-29357
Guts-Muths, J. Ch. F. 29361-29363
Guttle and gulpit. A farce. 70464
Guttrie, W. 9763
Guy, Francis. 86655
Guy Hamilton: a story of our civil war.
    (46846)
Guy Livingstone. 39351
Guy Rivers. 81190, 81197, 81199, 81204-
    81205, 81245, 81264, 81275, 81278-
    81279
Guy Rivers; a tale of Georgia. 81216, (81217?
Guy Rivers, the outlaw. 81217
Guyana. 19539
Guyane. see French Guiana.
Guyane, civilisation et barbarie. 11700
Guyane en 1772. 93411
Guyane Francaise. see French Guiana.
Guyane Francaise. 6982
Guyane Francaise en 1865. 71686
Guyane Francaise et l'ordre de Saint-Joseph
    de Cluny. 4938
Guyane Francaise, ses limites vers l'Amazo
    75478
Guyane Francaise, ses mines d'or et ses
    autres richesses. 74987
Guyane, ou histoire, moeurs, usages et
    coutumes des habitants. 19546
Guyart, Marie. see Marie de l'Incarnation,
    Mere, 1599-1672.
Guyer, E. reporter 60032
Guyer, I. D. 29365
Guyho, M. Corentin. 29364
Guyon, -------. (29366)
Guyot, Arnold Henry, 1807-1884. (71338),
    85019
Guyot's elementary geography in the Dakota
    language. (71338)
Guyse, -------. 21939
Guyton de Morveau, Louis Bernard, Baron,
    1737-1816 88905
Guzman, ------- Fuentes y. see Fuentes y
    Guzman, ---------.
Guzman, Alonzo Enriquez de. 29367
Guzman, Antoine de Saavedra. 29380
Guzman, Antonio Leoncadio. 29368-29371
    see also Venezuela. Ministerio del
    Interior, Justicia, y Relaciones Exterio
Guzman, Diego de Galdo. 29372
Guzman, Diego Holgado de. 98150
Guzman, Diego Rodriguez. 29373
Guzman, Domingo de. defendant 27309,
    (51797), 69915, 93808, 96948

Guzman, Felix Hernandez de. plaintiff 94629
Guzman, Francisco del Valle y. see Valle
  y Guzman, Francisco del.
Guzman, Gaspar de. see Olivares, Gaspar de
  Guzman, Conde Duque de, 1587-1645.
Guzman, Jos. Javier. 29374
Guzman, Jose Maria Torres y. see Torres y
  Guzman, Jose Maria.
Guzman, Jose Maria Vaca de. see Vaca de
  Guzman y Manrique, Jose Maria.
Guzman, Jose Martin y. see Martin y
  Guzman, Jose.
Guzman, Juan. (48665), 98823, 1st note after
  99783
Guzman, Juan de Texada y. see Texada y
  Guzman, Juan de.
Guzman, Juan Pablo Viscado y. see Viscado
  y Guzman, Juan Pablo.
Guzman, Luis Henriquez de. see Henriquez
  de Guzman, Luis, Conde de Alva de
  Aliste y de Villaflor.
Guzman, Maria Tello de. plaintiff 94629
Guzman, Miguel. 99786
Guzman, Nuno de, 16th cent. 16951, 66686,
  97740
Guzman, Nuno de, 16th cent. defendant 67646
Guzman, Pedro Jose. (29377)
Guzman, Rui Diaz de. see Diaz de Guzman,
  Rui, 1558?-1629.
Guzman, Sebastian. 80987
Guzman, Sebastian de Sandoval y. see
  Sandoval y Guzman, Sebastian de.
Guzman Sotomayor y Mendoza, Baltazar de
  Zuniga. see Zuniga Guzman Sotomayor
  y Mendoza, Baltazar de, Marques de
  Valero.
Guzman y Ayala, Sebastian Lopez de. see
  Lopez de Guzman y Ayala, Sebastian.
Guzman y Cordova, Seb. de. ed. 80976
Guzman y Gonzaga, Juan Perez de. 79781
  see also Panama (Province) Gobernador,
  1669-1671 (Guzman y Gonzaga)
Guzman y Manrique, Joaquin de. tr. 79230-
  79232, note after 99404, note after
  101248, 101249
Guzman y Medina, Juan Tello de. see Tello
  de Guzman y Medina, Juan.
Gwatkin, John. 29381
Gwatkin, Thomas. 95977
Gwin, William McKendree, 1805-1885. 29383
Gwinett, Ambrose. pseud. Candide Anglois.
  see Bickerstaff, Isaac, d. 1812?
  supposed author
Gwinett, Ambrose, pseud. Life and adven-
  tures. see Bickerstaff, Isaac, d. 1812?
  supposed author
Gwinett, Ambrose. pseud. Life, strange
  voyages, and uncommon adventures. see
  Bickerstaff, Isaac, d. 1812? supposed
  author
Gwinism in California. 62670
Gwinn, C. J. M. (29382), 45271
Gwinnett, Ambrose. pseud. Wunderbare
  Geschichte. see Bickerstaff, Isaac, d.
  1812? supposed author
Gwynn, Stuart. 2840, 42868
Gyermekek szamara. 92584
Gyles, John, 1678?-1755. 27370, 29387
Gymnasium, New Haven, Conn. see New
  Haven Gymnasium, New Haven, Conn.
Gymnasium, Pittsfield, Mass. see Pitts-
  field, Mass. Gymnasium.
Gymnasium, Utica, N. Y. see Utica
  Gymnasium, Utica, N. Y.
Gymnasium Vosagense. 101018

Gymnast, Christopher. pseud. Paxtoniade.
  59272
Gyroscope. 85386
Gysius. 11256

H

H. pseud. Confederate. see South Caroli-
  na. pseud.
H——s. pseud. Defence of the Scots
  abdicating Darien. see Harris,
  Walter. supposed author (18552),
  78206, 78209, (78215)
H. pseud. Divine cosmographer. see Hodson,
  William, fl. 1640.
H. pseud. Early days at Racine, Wisconsin.
  67391
H. pseud. ed. History of the life and times
  of John Wesley. see Heylin, ------.
  ed.
H. pseud. Letter on the subject of raising
  money. see Huidekooper, -------.
  supposed author
H. pseud. Lyrics by the letter H. see
  Halpine, Charles Grahame.
H. pseud. Theatrum victoriae. see
  Herckmans, Elias. supposed author
H., Mrs. pseud. Three years in field
  hospitals. see Holstein, Anna M.
H. pseud. Truth and falsehood. 97260
H., A. pseud. Dedication. see Holmes,
  Alexander. supposed author
H., A. pseud. General censure. 2036, 81985
H——son, A——ld. pseud. Reports of the
  Honourable the Committee of Secrecy.
  see Hutcheson, Archibald.
H., A. B. pseud. Contributions to the rhymes
  of the war. see Hasson, Alexander
  Breckinbridge, d. 1877.
H., A. J. pseud. Foederal monthly. see
  Hamilton, Andrew Jackson.
H . . . . , Ch . . . . D. pseud. tr. 25504
H., E. pseud. Jamaica viewed. see
  Hickeringill, Edmond.
H., E. pseud. Paper. see Harrison, Edward.
H., E. A. W. pseud. Ella Lincoln. (29388)
H., G. pseud. American mines. 29390
H., G. pseud. World surveyed. 29389
H., G. L. pseud. tr. 24323
H., G. L. pseud. Brief remarks. see
  Hammekin, George L. supposed author
H., H., Anglo Britannoae. pseud. Herwologia
  anglica. see Holland, Henry.
H., H. E. pseud. Remarks on the language.
  see Hale, Horatio.
H., I. pseud. ed. 82844-82850, 3d note after
  100533
H., I. pseud. Faction, a sketch. 29391
H., J. pseud. tr. 78974
H., J. pseud. Common apologie of the Chvrch
  of England. see Hall, Joseph.
H., J. pseud. Description of the last voyage
  to Bermudas. see Hardy, John.
H., J. pseud. Liberlismo y sus efectos.
  (29392), 40920
H., J. pseud. ed. Life and adventures of
  John Nicol. 55241
H., J. pseud. Morgan Lewis. (29393)
H., J. pseud. Reise naar Guatemala. see
  Haefkens, J.
H., J. pseud. ed. Two broad-sides against
  tobacco. 97551
H., J. A. pseud. Examination of the power of
  the President to remove from office. see
  Hamilton, James Alexander, 1788-1878.
  supposed author

Habakkuk O. Westman. pseud. see Ewbank,
Thomas. supposed author
Habana, Jose Gutierrez de la Concha y de
Irigoyen, Marques de la, 1809-1895.
(15104), 67141
Habana. see Havana.
Habana. Lyrisch-epische Dichtung. 6825
Habanero. pseud. Manifiesto. see Arango,
Jose de.
Habanero. pseud. Reflexiones de un
Habanero. 17804
Habanero. 17802, 29416
Habeas corpus. 29461
Habeas corpus. A response to Mr. Binney.
55173
Habeas corpus and martial law. A review of
the opinion of Chief Justice Taney.
58696
Habeas corpus and martial law. By Robert L.
Breck. 7665
Habeas corpus. By J. Heermans. 31234
Habeas corpus for the custody of an infant
child. 19915, 49067
Habeas corpus. Its death, and how it came
by it. 29462
Habeas corpus, the law of war, and confiscation
tion. 55174
Habeas corpus. The proceedings in the case
of John Merryman of Baltimore County.
(29463)
Habel, S. 85072
Habersham, A. W. (29466)
Habersham, James, 1712 or 13-1775. 29468,
103640 see also Savannah. Bethesda
Orphan House. Superintendent of Tem-
poral Affairs.
Habersham, Richard Wylly, 1786-1842. 29467,
79009
Habersham, S. E. 29469
Habes in hac pagina. Amice lector Alberti
Magni Germani principis philosophi. 673
Habes in hac paginis. Amice lectori Alberti
Magni Germani principis philosophi. 671
Habes lector: hoc libello. 98283
Habicht & Co. firm see Clews, Habicht &
Co. firm
Habiendo llegado a mis manos un periodico
sedicioso. 98853
Habiendo tenido los rebeldes Cura Don Jose
Maria Cos y Prebendado. 98852
Habit and its slaves. 85103
Habitans & Negocians de la Louisiane.
petitioners see Louisiana (Province)
Habitans et Negocians. petitioners
Habitans de Guadeloupe, Charges de l'Adminis-
tration Provisoire. see Guadeloupe.
Administration Provisoire.
Habitans de la Partie du Nord de Saint-
Domingue. see Santo Domingo (French
Colony) Habitans de la Partie du Nord.
Habitans des Colonies Francaises. petitioners
47514
Habitans du desert. 12239
Habitant de la Pennsylvanie. pseud. Reponse
aux principales questions. see Bonnet,
M. E.
Habitant de Louisbourg. pseud. Lettre.
40671
Habitant de Saint-Domingue. pseud. Testament
de mort d'ogre. 94901
Habitant des Antilles. pseud. Memoire en
reponse a M. M. les soi-disant philan-
tropes. 82013
Habitant des colonies. pseud. Observations.
see Gregoire, Henri, Bp., 1750-1831.

Habitant du Cap-Francais, Saint Domingue.
pseud. "J'ai vu." 10756
Habitant obscur de l'ancien hemisphere. pseud.
De l'influence de la revolution d'Amerique
sur l'Europe. see Condorcet, Marie
Jean Antoine Nicolas Caritat, Marquis de.
Habitantes de esta America. 105987B
Habitantes de la isla de Cuba. 100634
Habitantes de la Nueva Galicia. 98854
Habitants de la Caroline du Nord. see North
Carolina. Citizens.
Habitants de la Guadeloupe. see Guadeloupe.
Habitants.
Habitants de Russelltown. see Russelltown,
Quebec. Citizens.
Habitants du Pais de Canada, Dit la Nouvelle
France. see New France. Habitants.
Habitation du desert. 69048
Habiti antichi, et moderni di tutto il mondo.
98732
Habituum, seu disciplinarum omnium. 69131
Habrichti, J. 29470
Hacendado. pseud. Llamamiento de la isla
de Cuba. see Madan, Cristobal.
Hacendados de los Llanos de Apam, Mexico.
petitioners 69969
Hachard, Marie Madeleine. 29471, 69285,
98171
Hachette, -------- Fourquet d'. see Fourquet
d'Hachette, ---------.
Hachin-wakanda. 83684
Hacienda publica. 29472
Hack, Johannes. tr. 16532
Hack, John. respondent 99975
Hack, Wilhelm. 56681, note after 93841
Hacke, William. 18373, 29473
Hacke, William. cartographer (9920), 19556,
78218
Hackelton, Maria W. 29474
Hacket, Thomas. 70792, 95338
Hackett, Horatio B. (29475)
Hackett, James. 29476-29477
Hackley, Richard S. (29478)-29480
Hackley, Richard S. claimant 24900
Hackney, D. D. 104237
Haco, Dion. 29481-29482
Hadden, William. ed. 52692
Haddock, Charles B. 29483-(29484)
Haddock, T. M. 77258
Haddock's Savannah, Ga. directory. 77258
Haddy and Duval's magazine. (30587)
Hadelich, -------. 29485
Hades look'd into. 46355
Hadfield, William. 29486-29487
Hadley, Amos. 29488
Hadley, J. V. 79357
Hadley, Samuel A. 29489
Hadley, W. Hobart. 1073, 29490-29491
Hadley, Mass. Hopkins Academy. see
Hopkins Academy, Hadley, Mass.
Hadley, Mass. Two Hundredth Anniversary
Celebration, 1859. 29492
Hadley Falls Company. Committee Appointed
By the Stockholders. 29493
Hadley Falls Company. Directors. 29493
Hadot, Marie Adele Barthelemy. see
Barthelemy-Hadot, Marie Adele.
Hadriani Relandi Dissertationum miscellanearum
69242
Haeberlin, Carl Ludwig. 29494-(29496), note
after 95070
Haec sunt acta Capitali Generalis Bononiae.
(20580), 29497
Haec sunt provisiones pro bono regimine
Provincialium Indiarum. 20581, 29497

Haiti sa fertilite, ses ressources commer-
cials. 29572

Haiti, ses progres. (6309)

Haitiade, poeme epique en huit chants. 75127

Haizelwood republic. 71323

Hake, firm publishers see Bennet en Hake.
firm publishers

Haken, J. Ch. L. 29590

Hakewill, James. 29591

Haclvyt, R. see Hakluyt, Richard, 1552?-
1616.

Hakluyt, Richard, 1552?-1616. (1552), 1564,
(5051), 9759, 11604, (11608), 20856,
24858, (24864), (24896), 24897, (25854),
25999, 26469, 26470, 27351, 29559,
29592-29601, note after 29601, 30377,
30482-30483, 30954, 31095, note after
36681, 37686, 38212, 39236, 40175,
1st note after 45010, 45011, 53286,
57765, 59498, note after 65395, 66683,
67554, (67585), 69210, 70792, 77289,
79342, 80349, 87206, 95333, 97145,
99281, 99366, 3d note after 99856,
100460, 2d note after 102836, 1st note
after 105510, 106330

Hakluyt Society. 3664, 13833, 26000, 29367,
29593, 47171, 62806, 67552, 67554-
67555, (74131), 82862, 87206, 89452,
90060, 92664, 98738, 98757, 99363,
99375, 99376, 100940, 105720

Hakluyt's collection of early voyages. 9759,
note after 36681, 100460

Haklvytus posthumus or Pvrchas his pilgrimes.
66683

Halbert, Henry. defendant 29602

Halberstadt, A. 29603

Halbindianer. 49911

Halcyon cabala; containing the fundamental
principles. 98123, 100670

Halcyon cabala containing the platform. 98123,
100670

Halcyon Church of Christ in Columbia. 98123,
100670

Halcyon luminary and theological repository.
29604

Halde, ------- du. see Du Halde, ----------.

Haldeman, R. J. 29605-29606, (81814)

Haldeman, S. Stehman. (29607)-29610, 47469,
60319

Haldeman's zoological contributions. 29608

Haldimand, Sir Frederick, 1718-1791. 52579
see also Canada. Governor General,
1778-1786 (Haldimand)

Haldrich, ---------. 29611

Haldrick, ---------. supposed author 29611,
(31775)

Hale, Captain. 22500, 40594, 86187, 2d note
after 98076

Hale, Judge. 59699

Hale, Albert. 29612

Hale, Alden. 92675

Hale, B. E. 29616

Hale, B. F. (29617)

Hale, Benjamin. (29613)-29615

Hale, Mrs. C. L. 29621

Hale, C. S. (29622)

Hale, Charles. 29618, 29620, (45703)

Hale, Charles. reporter (29619), 45704

Hale, Daniel. supposed author 25000, 89297

Hale, David. 29623

Hale, Edward Everett, 1822-1909. (29624)-
29632, 44526, 57112, 85071, 86341,
93163, note after 95129, 2d note after
96410

Hale, Enoch, 1753-1837. 29633

Hale, Enoch, 1790-1848. 29634

Hale, George. 38007

Hale, Henry M. 76033 see also San
Francisco. Auditor.

Hale, Horatio Emmons, 1817-1896. 29635-
29636, 104970

Hale, J. 29639

Hale, James R. 85954

Hale, John, 1636-1700. 29637

Hale, John, d. 1796? 29638, 1st note after
90723

Hale, John Parker, 1806-1873. 20428, 29640-
29641, 63347, 79584

Hale, Jonathan. 4074, 7269, 99830

Hale, M. P. 29646

Hale, Sir Matthew, 1609-1676. 15215, 29642,
58682, 86659-86661

Hale, Mercy, b. 1805. 29644

Hale, Moses. 29643, (29645), (54680)

Hale, Nathan, 1784-1863. 3186, 6499, 6785,
29648, 29650-29656, 45781, (66586),
93163, 94073, note after 104786

Hale, Nathan, 1784-1863. supposed author
18681, 33647, 55713, note after 100780,
101507

Hale, Nathan, 1784-1863. incorrectly supposed
author 29649, note after 97923

Hale, Nathan, fl. 1864. 29657

Hale, Nathaniel. incorrectly supposed author
29657, 29828

Hale, Robert S. 88829

Hale, Robert Ward. 29658

Hale, Salma. 29660, 29662-29665

Hale, Salma. supposed author 272, 29659,
52798, 80855

Hale, Salma. incorrectly supposed author
(29661), 32218, 65082, 93554, note
before 97919

Hale, Sarah Josepha (Buell) 1788-1879.
29666-29670, 50232, (57384)

Hale, William. 29671

Hale Monument Association. 29647

Halen, Oseam. tr. (8784)

Hales, John G. 29672

Hales, M. 42596

Hales, Sir Matthew. see Hale, Sir Matthew,
1609-1676.

Hales, Stephen. 29673, 83978

Haley, Thomas. 25454, 29674, 29930

Haley, William D. ed. (62565)

Half a century's labors in the Gospel. 80034

Half a million dollars to be given away.
88015

Half century. 18812

Half century celebration of the Presbytery of
Rochester. 72342

Half-century discourse. A sermon, delivered
in Warwick. 83730

Half-century discourse . . . Billerica, Feb. 21,
1813. (17892)

Half-century discourse . . . . Delivered at
Norwich. (42010)

Half century discourse, delivered in Hadley.
32956

Half-century discourse, delivered in North-
Hampton, N. H. 25874

Half century discourse, delivered November
16, 1828. (71507)

Half century discourse delivered . . . Oct. 19,
1818. 39773

Half-century discourse. History of the Church
in Newington. 7159

Half-century discourse; on occasion of the
fiftieth anniversary. 64294

Half-century discourse. The First Church in
Buffalo. 13468

Hamilton, Walter. 84563 see also Leeward
Islands. Governor (Hamilton)

Hamilton, William. of New York 30038

Hamilton, William. reporter (30039), note
after 57236, (60037), 60041-60042,
note before 96910, 1st note after 96927

Hamilton, William, fl. 1661. tr. 68142

Hamilton, William, 1811-1891. 30040-30041,
35107

Hamilton, William, d. 1820. ed. 36361,
84115, note after 101900

Hamilton, William, d. 1856. 30043

Hamilton, William, fl. 1863. 30042

Hamilton, William J. 30044

Hamilton, William R. 30045

Hamilton, William T. 30046-30047

Hamilton-Gordon, Arthur. see Stanmore,
Arthur Hamilton-Gordon, 1st Baron.

Hamilton, N. Y. Madison University. see
Madison University, Hamilton, N. Y.

Hamilton, Ohio. Buckeye Celebration, 1835.
see Buckeye Celebration, Hamilton,
Ohio, 1835.

Hamilton, Ohio. Meeting of the Citizens on
the Subject of a Western National Armory,
1841. see Meeting of the Citizens of
Hamilton and Rossville, Ohio, on the
Subject of a Western National Armory,
1841.

Hamilton County, N. Y. Board of Supervisors.
30066

Hamilton County, Ohio. Agricultural Society.
see Hamilton County Agricultural
Society.

Hamilton County, Ohio. Bar. 27852

Hamilton County, Ohio. Court of Common
Pleas. 27852

Hamilton County, Ohio. Farmer's College.
see Farmer's College, College Hill,
Ohio.

Hamilton County, Ohio. Longview Hospital,
Carthage. Board of Trustees. (41938)

Hamilton County, Ohio. Longview Hospital,
Carthage. Officers. (41938)

Hamilton County, Ohio. Ohio Female College.
see Ohio Female College, College Hill,
Ohio.

Hamilton County, Ohio. Sabbath School
Association. see Hamilton County
Sabbath School Association.

Hamilton; and other poems. 91317

Hamilton Club series. 10065, 29970, 104279

Hamilton College, Clinton, N. Y. 24502,
30060-(30061), 30063-30064

Hamilton College, Clinton, N. Y. Semi-
Centennial Celebration, 1862. 30062

Hamilton College, Clinton, N. Y. Union
Society. 30065

Hamilton College, Clinton, N. Y. Union
Society. Library. 30065

Hamilton County Agricultural Society. 102962

Hamilton County Auxiliary Bible Society. see
Auxiliary Bible Society of the Counties
of Montgomery, Fulton and Hamilton,
N. Y.

Hamilton County Sabbath School Asosciation.
30067

Hamilton daily spectator. 86823

Hamilton directory for 1866-7. 30070

Hamilton. Eleventh series. 10867

Hamilton Female Seminary, Utica, N. Y.
30068

Hamilton gazette. 9354

Hamilton Literary and Theological Institution.
30069

Hamilton spectator. 86824

"Hamilton" to the friends of peace and good
order. 10889, 30052

Hamilton vs. Eaton. 30048

Hamiltoniad: or, an extinguisher for the roya'
faction of New-England. (23979), 10427

Hamiltoniad: or, the effects of discord. 300

Hamlet, a dramatic prelude. 74251

Hamlet, prince of Denmark, in three acts.
70830

Hamlin, Augustus C. 30073

Hamlin, Edward Stone, 1808-1894. 30074

Hamlin, Hannibal, 1809-1891. 30075, 33354,
(43944) see also Maine. Governor,
1857-1858 (Hamlin)

Hamlin, William E. 70682 see also U. S.
Provost Marshall of Rhode Island.

Hamline, Leonidas L. 30076-30077, 58382

Hammekin, George L. supposed author 1191
95141

Hammen y Leon, Lorenzo Vander. 30079

Hammer and rapier. 16323

Hammerdorfer, Karl. 30080, 87292

Hammerer defeated. 106101

Hammett, Edward. 92713

Hammett, John. 30081

Hammitt, Samuel Adams. 30082-30084, 9275
3d note after 95112

Hammett, Samuel Adams. see Hammett,
Samuel Adams.

Hammon, Jupiter. 30085-30086, 103142

Hammon, William. (43241)

Hammond, Abijah. 30087

Hammond, Abram Adams, 1814-1874. 35024
see also Indiana. Governor, 1860-186'
(Hammond)

Hammond, Anthony. (53632)

Hammond, Charles. 30088

Hammond, Charles, 1779-1840. 30090, note
after 90601, 99545

Hammond, Charles, 1779-1840. reporter
(30089), note after 96853

Hammond, Charles, 1813-1878. 30091-30092,
50041, 92272

Hammond, George, 1763-1853. 16866, 25911,
34900, 35911, 35881, (59479), 62908,
2d note after 101709 see also Great
Britain. Legation. United States.

Hammond, H. L. ed. 93744

Hammond, Isaac Weare, 1831-1890. ed. 527
61280, 66514, 1st-2d notes after 98997,
note after 98998, 1st note after 99003,
103894

Hammond, J. Pinkney. (30103)

Hammond, J. T. cartographer 83928

Hammond, J. W. 30104, 60659

Hammond, Jabez D. 30094-30097, 36011,
(47418), 65098

Hammond, James. 30093

Hammond, James Hamilton. (30098)-30101,
82096, note after 97063

Hammond, James Henry, 1807-1864. 19836,
22263, 30101, (36415), 65736, 80006,
81240, 82091, 82096, 88058, 7th note
after 88114 see also South Carolina.
Governor, 1842-1844 (Hammond)

Hammond, John, fl. 1655. 30102, 82976

Hammond, John W. (60657), 60659

Hammond, Judah. (5982)

Hammond, Laurence. 6474, 95946

Hammond, M. B. ed. 103756

Hammond, M. C. M. 30106

Hammond, M. M. 30105

Hammond, Otis Grant, 1869- ed. 52791, 61'
66514, 93510, 1st-2d notes after 98997,
note after 98998, 1st note after 99003,
103894

Hammond, Samuel H. 30107-30110
Hammond, Wells S. 30111
Hammond, William Alexander, 1828-1900.
    30113, 30114, 30116, (43241), 57853,
    69954, 76565, 76647, 84268 see also
    U. S. Surgeon General's Office.
Hammond, William Alexander, 1828-1900.
    defendant at court martial (30112),
    30115-30116, 2d note after 90723
Hammond, William G. 30117
Hammond's Circulating Library, Newport, R. I.
    see James Hammond's Circulating
    Library, Newport, R. I.
Hamon, --------. supposed author 33556
Hamon, Amedee. 30118
Hamon, Henry. 30119
Hamond, Aime Tome de. see Tome de
    Hamond, Aime.
Hamor, Ralph. (8784), (30120)-30122, 66686,
    note before 90030, 92665, note after
    99872
Hampden. pseud. [fl. 1796] 84832
Hampden. pseud. [fl. 1798] 23453, 2d note
    after 100462
Hampden. pseud. Genuine book of nullification.
    30124, (56314)
Hampden. pseud. Letter to the President of
    the United States. 30125
Hampden. pseud. Letters addressed to the
    friends of freedom. see Jervis, John B.
Hampden. pseud. Vindication of the petition.
    99816
Hampden, Allen. 30123
Hampden, Augustus Charles Hobart. see
    Hobart-Hampden, Augustus Charles,
    1822-1886.
Hampden, Mass. Mechanic Association. see
    Hampden Mechanic Association.
Hampden, Mass. Missionary Society. see
    Missionary Society, Hampden, Mass.
Hampden County, Mass. Benevolent Associa-
    tion. see Benevolent Association of
    Hampden County, Mass.
Hampden County, Mass. Washington Benevolent
    Society. see Washington Benevolent
    Society. Massachusetts. Hampden
    County.
Hampden County Agricultural Society. 30131
    see also Hampshire, Franklin and
    Hampden Agricultural Society.
Hampden County Agricultural Society.
    Committees. 30131
Hampden County Society. 30128
Hampden District Medical Society. 30132
Hampden federalist. 94719
Hampden letter. 18829, 18833
Hampden Mechanic Association. 30126
Hampden-Sidney [sic] Academy, Knoxville,
    Tenn. see Tennessee. University.
Hampden Sydney College, Hampden Sydney,
    Va. 30133-(30134)
Hampshire County, Conn. Some of the
    Ministers. see Some of the Ministers
    in the County of Hampshire, Conn..
Hampshire County, Mass. Court. 102587
Hampshire County, Mass. Ministers. see
    Congregational Churches in Massachusetts.
    Hampshire County Association.
Hampshire County, Mass. Washington
    Benevolent Society. see Washington
    Benevolent Society. Massachusetts.
    Hampshire County.
Hampshire Agricultural Society. 30138 see
    also Hampshire, Franklin and Hampden
    Agricultural Society.
Hampshire and Hampden Canal Company.
    Agents. 86734A

Hampshire and Hampden Canal Company.
    Engineer. 30144
Hampshire Association Charitable Association.
    30140
Hampshire Central Association. see Con-
    gregational Churches in Massachusetts.
    Hampshire Central Association.
Hampshire Convention of the Friends of the
    Licence Law, 1838. (30135)
Hampshire County Central Association. see
    Congregational Churches in Massachusetts.
    Hampshire Central Association.
Hampshire County Charitable Society. see
    Charitable Society of Hampshire County,
    Mass.
Hampshire County Northern Association. see
    Congregational Churches in Massachusetts.
    Hampshire Northern Association.
Hampshire Education Society. (30143)
Hampshire Education Society. Directors.
    (30143)
Hampshire, Franklin and Hampden Agricultural
    Society. 30145-30146
Hampshire, Franklin, and Hampden Convention,
    1812. see Convention of Delegates from
    the Counties of Hampshire, Franklin, and
    Hampden, Northampton, Mass., 1812.
Hampshire Missionary Society. Trustees.
    (30137), 63926, 94206
Hampshire narrative. (30136)
Hampshire, ss. Between J. Bardwell et al.,
    plaintiffs in equity 102587
Hampson, John, 1760-1817? (30147)-(30149),
    68708
Hampton, George. 30150
Hampton, Moses, 1803-1878. 30151
Hampton, Wade, 1752?-1835. 87733
Hampton, Wade, 1818-1902. 87791, 87817,
    88111
Hampton, Va. Hampton Normal and Agricultural
    Institute. see Hampton Normal and
    Agricultural Institute, Hampton, Va.
Hampton Academy, N. H. 30154
Hampton Normal and Agricultural Institute,
    Hampton, Va. 30155, 88517
Hampton Normal and Agricultural Institute,
    Hampton, Va. President. 30155 see also
    Hopkins, ---------.
Hanaford, Jeremiah Lyford. 30156
Hanaford, Phebe Ann (Coffin) 1829-1921.
    30157-30162
Hanaford, W. G. 6494
Hanau, Friedrich Casimir, Graf zu. see
    Casimir, Friedrich, Graf zu Hanau.
Hanbury, B. 30163
Hanby, William. 89059
Hanchett, ---------. 49247
Hanckel, Thomas M. 22283, 30164, 86132
Hancock. pseud. Essays on Texas. 30194,
    note after 95080
Hancock. pseud. Essex Junta exposed.
    (30196)
Hancock. pseud. Letter to the Hon. Samuel
    A. Eliot. see Dexter, Franklin.
Hancock. pseud. Whole truth. see Russell,
    Jonathan.
Hancock, a citizen of Massachusetts. pseud.
    Whole truth. see Russell, Jonathan.
Hancock, ---------. 8103
Hancock, Dorothy (Quincy) see Scott, Dorothy
    (Quincy) Hancock.
Hancock, J. W. 30189
Hancock, John. pseud. De Witt Clinton and the
    late war. 13729, 30187
Hancock, John. M. D. (8104), (30182)-30183
Hancock, John, 1671-1752. (30165)-(30169)

Hancock, John, 1702-1744. 30170-30175, 62419, 64687, 94687

Hancock, John, 1737-1793. (6737), 10364, 15597, 25583, 30176-30179, (45953), 64028, 78114, 79369, 82979, 85865, 97533, 99007 see also Massachusetts. Governor, 1780-1785 (Hancock) Massachusetts. Governor, 1788-1793 (Hancock) U. S. Continental Congress, 1775. President.

Hancock, John, 1824-1893. 30184-30186

Hancock, Philo. pseud. see Philo-Hancock. pseud.

Hancock, Sallie J. 30190-(30191)

Hancock, T., fl. 1733. 98696

Hancock, Thomas. 102820

Hancock, William. 30192

Hancock, Winfield Scott, 1824-1886. 30193, 80411

Hancock (J.) firm publisher (30188)

Hancock Division, Centerville, Conn. see Sons of Temperance of North America. Connecticut. Hancock Division, Centerville (Hamden)

Hancock Mining Company. Directors. 30197

Hancock's fifth of March oration. 16603

Hand, William M. 30198

["Hand-bill formed by the Committee of the Cornish Convention."] 99003

Hand-boeck; of cort begryp der caerten ende beschrijvinghen. 38881, note after 100632

Hand book. see Handbook.

Hand-in-Hand Fire Company, Philadelphia. (61719)

Hand of God as seen in the fall of Richmond. 78684

Hand of God, as seen in the present great rebellion. 79142

Hand of God in American history. 5308

Hand of God in history. 68152

Hand of God in the great man. 3792

Hand of God in the overthrow of slavery. 32355, 52037

Hand of God in the reformation of drunkards. (44749)

Hand of God recognized. 80121

Hand of God with the black race. 43271

Hand of God visible in the overthrow of slavery. 32355, 52037

Hand- und Reisebuch fur Auswanderer. 8206, 8210-8211

Handasyd, --------. petitioner 104926

Handbills. 99049

Hand book. 85596

Hand-book almanac for the Pacific states. (30200), 38131

Hand-book almanach for the Pacific states. (30200), 38131

Hand-book and guide to Philadelphia. 84983

Handbook, descriptive of the route to Ogdensburgh. 56828

Hand-book exhibiting the development, variety, and statistics. 25731

Hand-book for active service. 30199

Hand-book for county officers. (55218)

Handbook for emigrants to Brazil. 7587

Hand book for emigrants to the province of New Brunswick. (30205)

Hand-book for immigrants to the United States. 30206

Hand book for infantry. 20994

Handbook for overland expeditions. (44514)

Hand-book for passengers over the Cambridge Railroad. (10146), 30209, note after 91550

Hand-book for readers and students. 64612

Hand book for riflemen. 20994

Handbook for settlers. 12552

Handbook for strangers, June 17, 1857. (3021

Hand-book for the Democracy for 1863 & 64. 58451, 85887

Hand-book for the practice of war. 36436

Hand-book for the rank and file of the army. (37119)

Hand-book for the stranger in Philadelphia. 30212, 61714

Hand-book for the visiter [sic] to Lowell. 30215, 42481

Hand-book for the war. (30216)

Hand-book for travelers to Niagara Falls. 30214

Hand-book for travellers through the United States. 82930

Hand-book for visitors. (48874)

Hand-book, giving the history and position of each company. (7289)

Handbook of agricultural, horticultural, and landscape gardening. 16659

Hand book of American literature. 11800

Handbook of American travel. 29755-29756

Hand-book of American travel, northern and eastern tour. 70962

Hand-book of artillery. 71901

Hand-book of artillery, for the service of the United States. 71900, (71902)

Handbook of Baptist history. 68023

Hand book of British Columbia. 8095, 13507

Hand-book of business in Lowell, Mass. 1724

Handbook of Central Park. 2893

Hand book of Chicago. 30202

Hand-book of Cincinnati. 13068

Hand-book of civil rights. 30203

Handbook of contemporary biography. 44875

Hand-book of geographical statistics. 19449

Hand book of geography and natural history of Nova Scotia. 18953

Hand-book of heraldry. 44453

Handbook of history and chronology. 28742

Hand-book of Illinois. 14259

Handbook of information for emigrants to New-Brunswick. (60983)

Hand-book of information for emigrants to Nova Scotia. 57965

Hand-book of information for soldiers, sailor marines, &c. 86835

Hand-book of Iowa. 5836

Handbook of literature and the fine arts. 715

Hand-book of Montreal, Quebec, and Ottawa. 50460

Hand-book of military organization for office of the line. 37120

Hand-book of Minnesota. 5837, 49252

Hand-book of Newport and Rhode Island. 203

Handbook of newspaper advertising. 73550

Hand-book of northern pleasure travel. 8559

Handbook of politics for 1868. 43628

Hand book of practical receipts. 30210

Handbook of Quebec. 67005

Hand book of Rhode Island. 70585

Hand-book of Saratoga, and strangers' guide. 76916

Hand book of statistical and general informat 8116

Hand-book of statistics for 1863. 9980

Handbook of statistics of the United States. 89054

Handbook of Stevens Point. 30211, 91584

Hand book of streets and distances. 54306, note before 94435

Hand-book of surgical operations. 84276

Hand-book of the Albany Rural Cemetery. 24611

Hand-book of the cotton trade. (22338)
Hand-book of the Democracy, for 1863-64.
  30204, (32928), 36262, (36267), 58451,
  85887
Handbook of the General Convention of the
  Protestant Episcopal Church. 61052
Handbook of the history of the United States.
  69011
Hand-book of the internal revenue. 22422
Hand-book of the Kansas Pacific Railway.
  37037
Hand-book of the Kansas State Agricultural
  College. (37036)
Hand-book of the nation. (31397)
Handbook of the new gold fields. 2951
Handbook of the north-west. 80295
Hand-book of the Oneida Community. (30208)
Handbook of the River Plate. 51268
Hand book of the River Plate republics. 51268
Hand-book of the St. Lawrence River. 75320
Hand-book of the sulphur-cure. 24656
Handbook of the traveling exhibit of graphic
  arts. 83739
Hand-book of the United States Navy. 57742
Hand-book of the U. S. tax law. 68497
Handbook of tobacco culture. 77350
Hand-book of travel. 43836
Hand-book of universal biography. 27672
Hand book of Wisconsin. (12000)
Handbook on cotton manufacture. (26844)
Hand book, or annual record of horticultural
  and agricultural statistics. 80329
Hand-book to all the chief water-falls. 52322,
  57940
Hand-book to autographs. 52346
Hand-book to Canada and the United States.
  (30201)
Handbook to California. 45421
Hand book to Ogdensburgh, Montreal, Quebec.
  30207
Hand-book to Kansas Territory and the Rocky
  Mountains' gold region. (68526)
Hand-book to the gold fields of Nebraska and
  Kansas. 9707
Handbook to the Museum of the Academy of
  Natural Sciences. 81672
Hand book to the Pacific and California. 95510
Hand-book with route list. (38664)
Handbuch der Geographie und Statistik. 19436,
  91197
Handbuch der Geschichte des Europaischen
  Staatensystems. 31230
Handbuch der Lander- und Staaten-Kunde.
  38055
Handbuch der Parliamentarischen Praxis.
  18116
Handbuch der regionalen Geologie. 84531
Handbuch fur Ansiedler in den Vereinigten
  Staaten. 24696
Handbuch . . . fur Auswanderer. (33011)
Handbuch fur Auswanderer nach Texas.
  10898
Handbuch fur Deutsche Auswanderer. (30216)
Handbuch fur meine Freunde. 74130
Handbuch und Wegweiser fur Auswanderer.
  29007
Handbuch von Californien. 102506
Handbuchlein, der gantzen Welt gelegenheit.
  66891
Handtbuchlin, der gantzen Welt genlegenheit.
  (66890)
Handcuffs for white men! (81727)
Handel New York's im Jahre 1855. 48676
Handelmann, Heinrich. 1715. 30218-30220
Handelsverkehr zwischen England und
  Russland. 29940

Handerson, H. E. 95192
Handey, William H. 30221
Handfield, J. 9353
Handful of mountain corn. 104696
Handjeri, Prince Vlangali-. see Vlangali-
  Handjeri. Prince
Handkerchiefs from Paul. 104653, 104655
Handle for the battle axe. 102087
Handleidinge tot eene Hervormde Geloovs-
  Belydenis. 98585
Handlin, W. W. (30222)
Handschrift Pauke's. (59173)
Handschriften van den Vader Quesnel. 100746
Handwercksmann in Philadelphia. pseud.
  Lautere Wahrheit. see Franklin,
  Benjamin, 1706-1790.
Handwerksmann in Germanton. pseud.
  Verschiedene Christliche Wahrheiten.
  see Sower, Christopher, 1693-1758.
Handy, George. (30223)
Handy, George. defendant 60111
Handy, Isaac W. K. 30224
Handy, M. P. supposed author (71211)
Handy, William W. 30225
Handy-book about books. 74674
Hand book about books which relate to books.
  74674
Hanes Caban f'Ewythr Tomos. 92620
Hanes caethwas Crist'nogol. 92624
Hanes o fasnach y Caethglud yn Africa. 3514
Hanes wedi ei ysgrifenu gan law Mormon.
  83146
Hanes y gwrthyfel mawr yn y Talaethan
  Vnedig. (36574)
Haney, John. 60290
Haney. firm publishers see Levison & Haney.
  firm publishers
Hanger, George. see Coleraine, George
  Hanger, 4th Baron, 1751?-1824.
Hanger, Thomas Holme. 29521
Hanging Rock and Lawrence Furnace Railroad
  Company. Engineer. 104293 see also
  Williams, John S.
Hank Jasper, the spy of the Delaware. 72078
Hankey, William Alers. 93261
Hankins, Marie L. 30228
Hanks, S. W. supposed author 89486
Hanly, Peter. 30229
Hann, Nancy van. see Van Haun, Nancy.
Hanna, J. M. 30230
Hanna, John Smith. 30231
Hanna, S. W. 30232
Hannaford, Edwin Ebenezer. 30233
Hannah, John. ed. 36137, 67599
Hannah Corcoran. 9892
Hannah Logan. Memoirs of her husband. 41791
Hannah Logan's courtship. 82873, 83984
Hannah More Academy, Philadelphia. 61715
Hannah Penn's letter of instructions. 59673
Hannah Swanton, the Casco captive. 94022
Hannay, Charles J. J. 30234
Hannay, James. 63535, (63538)
Hannay, Robert. 30235
Hannegan, Edward A. 30236
Hannibal, 247-183 B. C. 92802
Hannibal, Julius Caesar. pseud. Black
  diamonds. 30237
Hannibal, Mo. Convention of Presbyterian
  Ministers and Elders, 1841. see
  Presbyterian Church in the U. S. Synod
  of Missouri.
Hannibal and St. Joseph Rail Road Company.
  30238
Hannibal's speech to the Senate of Carthage.
  92802
Hanning, John. 30239

Hanno. (70046), 67730, 67743

Hanno, Joseph, d. 1721. defendant 46559, 69766

Hannon. see Hanno.

Hannon Carthaginensius. see Hanno.

Hannone. see Hanno.

Hannoverischen Offizier. pseud. Aus Columbien an seine Freunde. 14557

Hannoverischen Offizier. pseud. Briefe aus Columbien an seine Freunde. 7922

Hannum, John. 12546

Hanover. Treaties, etc. 65935

Hanover, Indiana. Hanover College. see Hanover College, Hanover, Indiana.

Hanover, Mass. Church. 32115

Hanover, Mass. Educational Meeting, 1838. see Plymouth County Association for the Improvement of Common Schools. Education Meeting, Hanover, Mass., 1838.

Hanover, Mass. School Committee. (30244)

Hanover, Mass. Selectmen. 30243

Hanover, N. H. Citizens. 52791, note after 98998

Hanover, H. N. Congregational Church. Committee. 18632, 1st note after 97087, 2d note after 103214 see also Dewey, Benoni. Gilbert, Benjamin J. Wheelock, James.

Hanover, N. H. Dartmouth Church. 18612

Hanover, N. H. Dartmouth College. see Dartmouth College.

Hanover County, Va. 100071

Hanover County, Va. Clergymen. see Clergymen of Hanover County, Va. pseud.

Hanover Academy, South Hanover, Ind. see Hanover College, Hanover, Ind.

Hanover Academy and Indiana Theological Seminary. see Hanover College, Hanover, Ind.

Hanover College, Hanover, Ind. 30240-30242, 88132-88134, 88138

Hanover College, Hanover, Ind. petitioners 88135-88136

Hanover College, Hanover, Ind. Trustees. 88131, 88136

Hanover Street Christian Church, Boston. see Boston. Hanover Street Christian Church.

Hanoverian. pseud. Old fox tarr'd and feather'd. see Toplady, Augustus Montague.

Hannum, John. 12546 see also Chester County, Pa. Sub-Lieutenant.

Hans Breitmann about town. (39963)

Hans Breitmann and his philosopede. (39963)

Hans Breitmann as a politician. (39963)

Hans Breitmann in church. (39963)

Hans Breitmann in politics. (39963)

Hans Breitmann's ballads. (39963)

Hans Breitmann's Christmas. (39963)

Hans Breitmann's party. (39963)

Hans Egade, der Apostel der Gronlander. 6110

Hans Egedes levnet. 61227

Hans Staden van Homborgs Beschrijvinge van America. 90054-90055

Hans Staden van Homborgs Beschrijvinghe van America. 90043

Hans Staden van Homborgs Beschryvinge van America. 90050-90051, 90058

Hans Staden van Homborghs Beschrijvinge van America. 90052-90053

Hans Staden von Hamburg's Reise. 25472

Hans Staden von Homborgs Beschrijvinghe van America. 90044-90049

Hansard, Thomas Curson, 1776-1833. 9223, 30245-30246

Hansard Knollys Society. see Hanserd Knollys Society for the Publication of the Works of Early Engilish and Other Baptist Writers.

Hansard's analytical Parliamentary digest. 30246

Hanscom, S. P. 30247

Hansen, Christian. 30248

Hansen, Leonard. 27793, 30249-30252, (42056 73176-(73180), 73188, (73189), (73193), 100612

Hansen, Paul Botten. see Botten-Hansen, Paul.

Hansen, Peter O. 83115, 83215, 83216-83218

Hansen, T. 30253

Hanserd Knollys Society for the Publication of the Works of Early English and Other Baptist Writers. 17069, 104332, 104341

Hansford, ------. 102346

Hanson, Alexander Contee, 1786-1819. 1975, 16006, 30255-30260, (56525)

Hanson, Alexander Contee, 1786-1819. defend at court martial (30261)

Hanson, Alexander Contee, 1786-1819. report 30254, 3d note after 96883

Hanson, C. 30268

Hanson, Charles W. 30262

Hanson, Elizabeth. 30263-30266, 69376

Hanson, Francis. (35624)

Hanson, H. C. 24906

Hanson, John H. 30267-30268, 104213

Hanson, John W. 30269-30272

Hanway, Jonas. 100, 30276

Hanson, Samuel. appellant 30273

Hanson, Thomas. 30275

Hanway, Castner. defendant 2202, 7724, 30274, (71820)

Hanway, Jonas. 30276

Happel, Everhard Gverner. (30277)-30279

Happiness and pleasure of unity in Christian societies. 364

Happiness of a free government. 39196

Happiness of a holy life. 27166

Happiness of a long and useful life. 71834

Happiness of a people, having God for their ally. 32315

Happiness of a people illustrated and explaine 2868

Happiness of a people in the wisdome of their rulers. (33444)

Happiness of being ready. 59479

Happiness of man the glory of God. 8725

Happiness of rewarding the enemies of our religion. 94692

Happiness of the Godly at death. 103746

Happoldt, C. 12041

Happoncourt, Francoise d'Isembourg d'. see Grafigny, Francoise (d'Isembourg d'Happoncourt) de, 1695-1758.

Happy Briton. 30280

Happy dismission, of the holy believer. 4643

Happy effects of diligence and self-control. 102808

Happy effects of keeping a good conscience. 93222-93223

Happy effects of union. (33958)

Happy harvest. 90201

Happy home and good society all the year round. 29670

Happy nation. 42806

Happy new year. 66762

Happy new year! 66898

Happy reconciliation. 97014

Happy voyage compleated, and the sure anchor cast. (51518)

Hargrave, Francis, 1741?-1821. 30374, 67590
Hargrove, John. 30375
Haring, Carlos Guilherme. ed. 71457
Hariot, Thomas. see Harriot, Thomas, 1560-1621.
Harison, Francis. see Harrison, Francis.
Harison, Richard. 30566, (34385), note after 53697, (68287), note after 83791
Harison, W. H. 30381, 2d note after 96986
Harizon, Antonio de. supposed author (30382) 41985, (44529)
Harker, Samuel. 30383, 66911, 94127
Harkness, Edson. (30384)
Harkness, William. 85072
Harlaem River. 30385
Harlakenden, Richard. 80209
Harlan, James. (37531) see also Kentucky. Commissioners on the Code of Practice in Civil and Criminal Cases.
Harlan, James, 1820-1899. 30386
Harlan, Mary B. 30387
Harlan, Richard. 27665, (30388)-30393), (35460) see also Commission Appointed to Visit Canada, For the Investigation of the Epidemic Cholera, 1832.
Harland, Marion. pseud. Alone. see Terhune, Mary Virginia (Hawes)
Harlaquin Doctor Faustus. 93890
Harleian collection of voyages and travels. 57765
Harleian miscellany. 7854, 30297, 30394, 34800, 52041, 67550, (67586), 67590, 67599, 71899, 74616, 78366, 78369, 78994, 89383, 99557, note after 100901
Harlean tracts. (28474), 32056, 66027, 73788, 2d note after 95377, 1st note after 102836
Harlem, N. Y. Friendly Society. see Friendly Society of the Town of Harlem, N. Y.
Harlem, N. Y. General Synod of the Reformed Dutch Church in North America. see Reformed Dutch Church in North America. General Synod, Harlem, N. Y., 1807.
Harlem (City of New York): its origin and early annals. 71388
Harlequin have at all. 39512
Harlequin sauvage. 13616, 2d note after 96139
Harlete, Henry. 26314
Harley, Thomas. 95711
Harlow, Laurence. (30395), 97269
Harlow, Samuel R. 30396-(30397)
Harm watch harm catch. 3961
Harman, John. (30398)-30399
Harmans, J. Smith. (32698), 47910, 47911
Harmansen, Wolphart. 68455
Harmanson, John H. 30400
Harmar, Josiah, 1753-1813. (74155)
Harmar, Josiah, 1753-1813. defendant at court of inquiry 30401
Harmer, John. (30402)
Harmer (Joseph) publisher 89135
Harmon, Daniel Williams, 1778-1845. 30404
Harmon, Henry Clay, 1833-1892. 30403
Harmon, John. (30405)
Harmonia Americana. 32675
Harmonia coelestis. 4697
Harmonia sacra. 91718
Harmonia Sacred Music Society, Philadelphia. (61716)
Harmoniae, Philos. pseud. Selection of hymns and poems. see MacNemar, Richard.
Harmonial Benevolent Association. 89514
Harmonial man: or, thoughts for the age. 18791

Harmonic minstrelsy. (35746)
Harmonie Gesellschaft. see Harmony Society in Indiana.
Harmonies of nature. 30720
Harmonius action. 49017
Harmoniten zu Oeconomie im Staate Pensylvanien. 67917
Harmony. 32496
Harmony and connexion of the various acts of Divine providence. 83803
Harmony Division, no. 5, New Haven, Conn. see Sons of Temperance of North America. Connecticut. Harmony Division, no. 5, New Haven.
Harmony Grove Cemetery, Salem, Mass. see Salem, Mass. Harmony Grove Cemetery
Harmony of interests. 10831
Harmony of the Gospels. 22153
Harmony of wisdom and felicity in relation. 30406
Harmony Society in Indiana. 95698
Harnden, Harvey. 30407
Harney, E. E. 30408
Harney, J. A. 35032 see also Iowa. State Land Office. Registrar.
Harney, William S. 30409
Harney, William S. USA 48132, 101922
Harnisch, W. tr. 73380
Haro, Cristoffel de. (7559)-7560
Haro, Damian Lopez de. 30410
Haro, Marcelino de Solis y. see Solis y Haro Marcelino de.
Haro y Peralta, Alonzo Nunez de. see Nunez de Haro y Peralta, Alonzo, Abp., 1729-1800.
Haro y Tamariz, Antonio de. 30412
Harold. pseud. Bridle on the heart. see Smith, Tom Wash.
Harold, John. plaintiff before presbytery 30413
Harold, William Vincent. 10899, 30414, 34759, 47236
Haroldus, Franciscus. 30415-30417, 49836
Harp, and other poems. (30986)
Harp and the hickory tree. 32619
Harp and the plow. 10694
Harp of a thousand strings. 7412
Harp of Acadia. pseud. Poems descriptive and moral. see McPherson, John.
Harp of Acushnet. 30917
Harp of freedom. (13288)
Harp of Israel. 41572
Harp of nature. 8576
Harp of Sylva. 36489
Harp of the beech woods. 30417, note after 97486
Harp of the west. 69007
Harp of the west: a volume of poems. 102616
Harp of Zion. 50740
Harpe, ----- la. see La Harpe, ----------.
Harpe, Benard de la. see La Harpe, Benard de.
Harpe, Jean Francois de la. see La Harpe, Jean Francois de.
Harper, Charles C. 30419, 77448
Harper, Ida Husted. ed. 90405
Harper, J. A. 52884, 97988
Harper, James, 1797-1875. 54594 see also New York (City) Mayor, 1844-1845 (Harper)
Harper, Joseph M. 30420
Harper, Lewis. 30421, 49502
Harper, R. D. 30422
Harper, Robert Goodloe, 1765-1825. (30423)-30444, 45096, 50020, 55166, 101161

Harper, Robert Goodloe, 1765-1825. supposed
   author 87733
Harper, William, 1790-1847. 19836, 22263,
   30099, 30418, 30445-30446, 46140, 48097,
   65736, 81240, 82091, 82096, 83854, 87423,
   87461-87462, 87970, 88041, 88058, 7th
   note after 88114, note after 90638 see
   also South Carolina. State Reporter.
Harper. firm publishers 18448, 29113,
   82726-82727, 95216, 95217, 97725, note
   after 97587, note after 99383C, 100482
Harper & Brothers. firm publishers 9188,
   30447-30449, 43545, 74390, 90656
Harper & Calvo. firm publishers 87532
Harper & Brothers. School District Library.
   97725
Harper establishment. 30448
Harper's encyclopaedia of United States history.
   note after 99383C
Harper's family library. 18448, 32050, 82726,
   94216, note after 97587
Harper's Ferry insurrection. 3401
Harper's Ferry. Its lessons. 70825
Harper's Ferry outbreak and its lesson. 2932
Harper's Ferry tragedy. 14901
Harper's Franklin Square library. 100482
Harper's magazine. 1262, 5679, 16163,
   20691, 20693, 24655, (48985), 62490,
   (81907)
Harper's miscellany for young persons.
   95216
Harper's monthly. (4021)
Harper's new monthly magazine. 30447,
   54695, 93092, note after 95734, 1st note
   after 100557
Harper's New York and Erie Rail-Road guide
   book. 30449, 43545
Harper's New-York class-book. 74390
Harper's pictorial history of the great
   rebellion. 29113
Harper's school district library. 1036
Harper's statistical gazetteer of the world.
   82927
Harper's stereotype edition. ,95217
Harper's stereotype edition. Festivals, games,
   and amusements. 82726
Harper's stereotype edition. Tales from
   American history. 71807-71809, 5th note
   after 94244
Harper's stereotype edition, with engravings.
   71983
Harper's weekly. (9663A), 19301
Harpe's head. 29786
Harpocrates. pseud. Preface. see Hollis,
   Thomas.
Harponville, Vicomte Gustave d'Hespel d'.
   see Hespel d'Harponville, Vicomte
   Gustave d'.
Harrich, Raimundo Pascual. 17754
Harries, Walter. see Harris, Walter.
Harring, Paul Harro. see Harro-Harring,
   Paul.
Harrington, Miss --------. 30452
Harrington, E. B. 48794
Harrington, George F. 30453
Harrington, Henry F. 30454-30455
Harrington, Joseph. (30456)
Harrington, Leicester Fitzgerald Charles
   Stanhope, 5th Earl of, 1784-1862.
   39895
Harrington, Timothy. (30457)-(30459), 73591,
   89050
Harrington, William H. (30460)
Harrington, William Stanhope, 1st Earl of,
   d. 1756. 38955, 59332, 90292 see also
   Great Britain. Legation. Spain.

Harrington's directory of the city of Austin.
   2429
Harrington's oration. (30460)
Harriot, Thomas, 1560-1621. 5112, (8784),
   20926, 30376-30377, 82823, 84162,
   91860, 103395
Harriott, John. (30461)
Harris, --------, 18th cent. 30489
Harris, --------, fl. 1854. 66301, 70757
Harris, --------, fl. 1856. 76092
Harris, Alexander. 30462
Harris, B. W. 30465
Harris, Benjamin. ed. 66526
Harris, Benjamin, fl. 1681. defendant (30463)
Harris, Benjamin, fl. 1792. defendant 105702
Harris, Benjamin Gwinn, 1806-1895. 30464
Harris, Carey A. 96722-96724, 96729 see
   also U. S. Commissioner to the First
   Christian and Orchard Parties of the
   Oneida Indians.
   U. S. Commissioner to the Sauks and
   Foxes of Missouri. U. S. Commissioner
   to the Winnebago Indians. U. S. Com-
   missioner to the Yankton Indians.
Harris, Caroline. 30466, 63462
Harris, Charles H. (30467)
Harris, D. L. 30468, 30859
Harris, Edward Doubleday. (30469)-30471,
   30536
Harris, Elisha. (30472), (69001), 76653,
   76664, 90788
Harris, George. of Baltimore (30473)
Harris, George, 1844-1922. defendant 85212
Harris, Henry, 1689-1729. 30494-30495
Harris, I. (30474)
Harris, Ira, 1802-1875. 30475-30476
Harris, Isaac. 63128
Harris, Isham Green, 1818-1897. 23372,
   33150, 37577, 69859 see also Tennessee.
   Governor, 1857-1862 (Harris)
Harris, J. B. 89630
Harris, J. Dennis. 30477
Harris, James D. 60750, note after 97766
   see also Union Canal Company of
   Pennsylvania. Engineer.
Harris, James H. (30478)
Harris, James Howard. see Malmesbury,
   James Howard Harris, 3d Earl of,
   1807-1889.
Harris, Rev. James H. (30479), 85853
Harris, James Morrison, 1818-1898. 30480-
   (30481), (45211A)
Harris, John, 1667?-1719. 1629, 5057, (11609),
   16964, 30482-20483, 55448, 60234, 77963,
   89452
Harris, John B. 85234
Harris, John O. (30484)
Harris, John S. 30485, 70570
Harris, Jonathan S. 30486
Harris, Luther M. 30487-30488
Harris, Mary. defendant (30490), 67065
Harris, Miriam (Cole) 30502
Harris, N. S. (30491)
Harris, Nicholas. 103939
Harris, Raymond. 18504, (30492), (33606),
   67714, (79498)
Harris, Robert William. 30493
Harris, Sampson Willis, 1809-1857. 30497,
   30503
Harris, Samuel. illus. 63894
Harris, Samuel, 1814-1899. (30498)-30500
Harris, Samuel F. 30501
Harris, Mrs. Sidney S. see Harris, Miriam
   (Cole)
Harris, T. 30525, 57126
Harris, T. S. tr. 79118

Harris, Thaddeus Mason, 1768-1842. 20623,
25798, 30504-30521, 2d note after
69442, 93243, 95175, 95176, 1st note
after 97014, 1st note after 100877,
101471, 101810, 101870
Harris, Thaddeus William, 1795-1856. 30522-
(30524), 30729-30730, 46082 see also
Massachusetts. Zoological and Botanical
Survey.
Harris, Thomas, fl. 1745-1750. 30525, 39120,
64130
Harris, Thomas, 1784-1861. 30526
Harris, Thomas L. (30527)
Harris, Thompson S. (26277), 105546
Harris, W. T. 90763
Harris, Walter. supposed author 18551-
(18552), 18571, 78206, 78209-78210,
(78215), 78234, 7th note after 95843
Harris, Walter, fl. 1809-1812. 30528
Harris, Wiley Pope, 1818-1891. (23627),
30529
Harris, William, 1720-1770. 61194
Harris, William, 1765-1829. 30530
Harris, William Alexander, 1805-1864. 30496,
30538
Harris, William C. 30531
Harris, William L. 30532
Harris, William Tell. 30533-30534
Harris, William Thaddeus. 30535-(30537)
Harris, William W. 30539
Harris, William Wager. defendant 105702
Harris (Isaac) firm publishers 63128
Harris, Bogardus & Labatt. firm publishers
76092
Harris collection of American poetry. 91873
Harris' general business directory. 63128
Harris' Pittsburgh & Allegheny directory.
63128
Harris' Pittsburgh business directory. 63128
Harrisburg, Pa. Agricultural Convention,
1851. see Agricultural Convention,
Harrisburg, Pa., 1851.
Harrisburg, Pa. American Party Convention,
1845. see American Party. Pennsyl-
vania. Convention, Harrisburg, 1845.
Harrisburg, Pa. Anti-masonic Party Con-
vention, 1832. see Anti-masonic Party.
Pennsylvania. Convention, Harrisburg,
1832.
Harrisburg, Pa. Canal Convention, 1824. see
Pennsylvania Canal Convention, Harris-
burg, 1824.
Harrisburg, Pa. Convention, Held for the
Promotion of Agriculture and Manufacture,
1827. see Convention, Held for the
Promotion of Agriculture and Manufacture,
Harrisburg, 1827.
Harrisburg, Pa. Constitutional Convention,
1837-1838. see Pennsylvania. Con-
stitutional Convention, Harrisburg, 1837-
1838.
Harrisburg, Pa. Convention of Delegates
From Several Counties of the Common-
wealth, on the Swatara Mining District,
1839. see Swatara Mining District
Convention, Harrisburg, Pa., 1839.
Harrisburg, Pa. Convention of Delegates
Opposed to Executive Usurpation and
Abuse, 1834. (60403)
Harrisburg, Pa. Convention of Democratic
Republican Young Men, 1836. see
Democratic Party. Pennsylvania.
Convention of Young Men, Harrisburg,
1836.

Harrisburg, Pa. Convention to Organize a
State Anti-slavery Society, 1837. see
Pennsylvania Convention to Organize a
State Anti-slavery Society, Harrisburg,
1837.
Harrisburg, Pa. Convention to Propose
Amendments to the Constitution, 1837.
see Pennsylvania. Constitutional
Convention, Harrisburg, 1837.
Harrisburg, Pa. Democratic Party Convention
1824. see Democratic Party. Pennsylvania. Convention, Harrisburg, 1824.
Harrisburg, Pa. Democratic Party Convention
1828. see Democratic Party. Pennsylvania. Convention, Harrisburg, 1828.
Harrisburg, Pa. Democratic Party Convention
1832. see Democratic Party. Pennsylvania. Convention, Harrisburg, 1832.
Harrisburg, Pa. Democratic Party Convention
1835. see Democratic Party. Pensylvania. Convention, Harrisburg, 1835.
Harrisburg, Pa. Democratic Party Convention,
1856. see Democratic Party. Pennsylvania. Convention, Harrisburg, 1856.
Harrisburg, Pa. Democratic Party Convention
1859. see Democratic Party. Pennsylvania. Convention, Harrisburg, 1859.
Harrisburg, Pa. Democratic Party Convention,
1866. see Democratic Party. Pennsylvania. Convention, Harrisburg, 1866.
Harrisburg, Pa. Democratic Whig National
Convention, 1839. see Whig Party.
National Convention, Harrisburg, Pa.,
1839.
Harrisburg, Pa. Female College. see
Pennsylvania Female College, Harrisburg
Harrisburg, Pa. General Convention of
Agriculturists and Manufacturers and
Others Friendly to the Encouragement
and Support of the Domestic Industry of
of the United States, 1827. see Harris-
burg Convention, 1827.
Harrisburg, Pa. Military Convention, 1832.
see Military Convention, Harrisburg,
Pa., 1832.
Harrisburg, Pa. National Convention of the
Whig Party, 1839. see Whig Party.
National Convention, Harrisburg, Pa.,
1839.
Harrisburg, Pa. Pennsylvania State Conventio
to Promote Common School Education,
1850. see Pennsylvania State Conventic
to Promote Common School Education,
Harrisburg, 1850.
Harrisburg, Pa. Railroad Convention, 1838.
see Railroad Convention, Harrisburg,
Pa., 1838.
Harrisburg, Pa. State Convention of Coloured
Citizens, 1848. see State Convention of
Coloured Citizens of Pennsylvania,
Harrisburg, 1848.
Harrisburg, Pa. State Hospital. see Pennsy
vania. State Hospital, Harrisburg.
Harrisburg, Pa. State Rights Democratic
Party Convention, 1859. see State
Rights Democratic Party. Pennsylvania.
Convention, Harrisburg, 1859.
Harrisburg, Pa. State Sabbath Convention,
1844. see State Sabbath Convention,
Harrisburg, Pa., 1844.
Harrisburg, Pa. State Temperance Conventior
1842. see State Temperance Conventio
Harrisburg, Pa., 1842.

Harrisburg, Pa. Swatara Mining District Convention, 1839. see Swatara Mining District Convention, Harrisburg, Pa., 1839.
Harrisburg, Pa. Town Council. 30549
Harrisburg, Pa. Union Canal Convention, 1838. see Union Canal Convention, Harrisburg, Pa., 1838.
Harrisburg, Pa. Western Pennsylvania Hospital. see Dixmont, Pa. Western Pennsylvania Hospital.
Harrisburg, Pa. Whig Party National Convention, 1839. see Whig Party. National Convention, Harrisburg, Pa., 1839.
Harrisburg and Hamburg Railroad. 30542
Harrisburg and Hamburg Railroad. Chief Engineer. 60131
Harrisburg and Hamburg Railroad. President. 60131
Harrisburg and Lancaster Railroad Company. 30543, 60072
Harrisburg and Lancaster Railroad Company. Chief Engineer. 60132 see also Roberts, William Milnor.
Harrisburg business directory, and stranger's guide. (30540)
Harrisburg Cemetery Association. 30544, 85172
Harrisburg Cemetery Association. Charter. 30544, 85172
Harrisburg Cemetery Association; charter, history and by-laws. 30544
Harrisburg Convention, 1827. (16198), 26876
Harrisburg convention. Proceedings fo the Democratic Whig National Convention. 30545, 60416, 65841, note after 103268
Harrisburg directory, and a business directory. 30541
Harrisburg directory, and stranger's guide. 93283
Harrisburg insurrection. 30546
Harrisburg National Democratic Union Club. 30547 see also Democratic Party. Pennsylvania. Harrisburg.
Harrisburg, Portsmouth, Mountjoy and Lancaster Railroad Company. 60133
Harrisburg, Portsmouth, Mountjoy and Lancaster Railroad Company. Directors. 30548, 60133
Harrisburg, Portsmouth, Mountjoy and Lancaster Railroad Company. President. 30548, 60133
Harrisburg Presbytery. see Presbyterian Church in the U. S. A. Presbytery of Harrisburg.
Harrisburg water works. 30549
Harrish, Raimundo Pascual. 17754, (26701)
Harrison, --------, fl. 1804. 17677, (29986)
Harrison, --------, fl. 1806. 30563
Harrison, --------, fl. 1815. 30564
Harrison, Benjamin, 1726?-1791. 100210 see also Virginia. Governor, 1781-1784 (Benjamin Harrison)
Harrison, David. 30551-30552
Harrison, Edward. 30553
Harrison, Elias. (30554)
Harrison, Francis. 30379
Harrison, Francis. defendant 731, 30380, 84558, 84778
Harrison, Francis. supposed author 95900
Harrison, George. 30555-30556, 78722, 81895

Harrison, H. 30557
Harrison, Henry B. 30558, 89199
Harrison, Henry W. 30559
Harrison, J. F. 54582
Harrison, J. Scott. 30562
Harrison, Jesse Burton, 1805-1841. (30561)
Harrison, Jesse Burton, 1805-1841. supposed author 70270, 2d note after 100580
Harrison, John. incorrectly supposed author 30560, 33366
Harrison, Josiah. 53090
Harrison, P. cartographer 87349
Harrison, R. 30565
Harrison, R. H. 15323, 18775, 69750 see also U. S. Commissioners for Settling a Cartel for the Exchange of Prisoners With Great Britain, 1779.
Harrison, Richard. see Harison, Richard.
Harrison, Richard Almgill, 1824-1904. 30567-30568
Harrison, Robert H. (11731), 18775, 101700
Harrison, Susannah. (30569)
Harrison, Thomas. 87409 see also South Carolina. Comptroller General.
Harrison, Walter. 30570
Harrison, William Henry, Pres. U. S., 1773-1841. 447, 448, 18005, 25876, 30571-30574, 36503, (41630), 63811, 78647, 104204-104205 see also U. S. President, 1841 (William Henry Harrison)
Harrison almanac. 30579
Harrison and log cabin song book. 30580
Harrison Democrat. pseud. Word in season 105456
Harrison medal. 18090
Harrison medal minstrel. 30581
Harrison melodies, original and selected. 30582
Harrison's Bar letter of Gen. McClellan. (43013)
Harris's Circulating Library, Worcester, Mass. see Clarendon Harris's Circulating Library, Worcester, Mass.
Harris's Ferry, Pa. Indian Conference, 1757. see Pennsylvania (Colony) Indian Conference, Harris's Ferry, 1757.
Harriss, Julia Mildred. 30598
Harrisse, Henry, 1830-1910. 4565, 4918, 19741, 24130, 24933, 30599-30604, 63180, 87988, 99363
Harrison, David. 30605
Harro-Harring, Paul. 30606
Harrodsburg, Ky. University. see Kentucky. University, Harrodsburg.
Harrower, David. (30607)
Harry, James Spencer, tr. 12241
Harry Burnham, the young continental. (8891)
Harry Harson. 35117
Harry Nimrod. pseud. ed. see Nimrod, Harry. pseud. ed.
Harry Penciller. pseud. see Penciller, Harry. pseud.
Harry Quillem. pseud. see Quillem, Harry. pseud.
Harry Wandsworth Shortfellow. pseud. see Clarke, Mary Cowden-, 1809-1898.
Harsha, David A. 30608-30610, 39648
Harsnet, Samuel, Abp. of York, 1561-1631. 103331
Hart, Miss ----------. 30639
Hart, A. B. (79284)
Hart, Abram. 30611
Hart, Adolphus M. 30612-30616, note after 92624
Hart, Albert Bushnell, 1854-1943. 82850, 84340

Hart, Alfred A. 30617
Hart, Arthur Wellington. 30618
Hart, Burdett. 30619-30620
Hart, Charles Henry. 30621-30622, 41176
Hart, Cheney. 30623
Hart, H. L. 50797, note after 92778
Hart, Frederic W. (23455), 30624-(30625)
Hart, George. 27113, 91315
Hart, George. defendant 30626
Hart, J. 105017
Hart, John. 8956-8957, 86068, note after 94918
Hart, John Seely, 1810-1887. 30627-30628, 32618, 53195, 59993
Hart, Joseph. 30629 see also Bucks County, Pa. Lieutenant.
Hart, Joseph C. 30630
Hart, Julia Catharina Beckwith. 96166, 96169
Hart, Levi. (30631)-30637
Hart, Luther. 30638
Hart, Nathaniel C. 30640
Hart, O. B. 30641
Hart, Oliver. 30642
Hart, Robert. illus. 73385
Hart, Roswell. 30643
Hart, Samuel. 78561
Hart, Samuel. supposed author 63606, 3d note after 88114
Hart, Seth. 30645
Hart, William. plaintiff 67822
Hart, William, 1713-1784. 30646-(30648), (32953), 32955, 79272, 96092, 96094, note after 102754, 103327
Hart, William, 1713-1784. supposed author 105932
Hart, William, fl. 1865. 30649
Hart, William Chetwood de. see De Hart, William Chetwood, 1800-1884.
Hart, William T. plaintiff (74472), 91108
Hart (Ship) 59584, 93383
Harte, Francis Bret, 1836-1902. 30650
Harte, Walter. 30651
Hartegan, James. defendant 32362, 96946, 96951, 2d—3d notes after 102623
Harte, William. see Hart, William, 1713-1784.
Harten, Gerard von. see Von Harten, Gerard. defendant
Hartenstein, Clara von Epplen. see Gerstner, Clara (von Epplen Hartenstein) von.
Hartford (J.) & Co. firm publishers 54459
Hartford, Conn. Acorn Club. see Acorn Club, Hartford, Conn.
Hartford, Conn. African Mission School Society. see African Mission-School Society, Hartford, Conn.
Hartford, Conn. American Asylum for the Education and Instruction of the Deaf and Dumb. see American Asylum for the Education and Instruction of the Deaf and Dumb, Hartford, Conn.
Hartford, Conn. American School for the Deaf. see American School for the Deaf, Hartford, Conn.
Hartford, Conn. Anti-masonic State Convention, 1830. see Anti-masonic State Convention of Connecticut, Hartford, 1830.
Hartford, Conn. Asylum for the Education and Instruction of Deaf and Dumb Persons. see American School for the Deaf, Hartford, Conn.
Hartford, Conn. Centennial Celebration of the First Company Governor's Foot Guard, 1871. 65764
Hartford, Conn. Charter. 30657

Hartford, Conn. Charter Oak Hall. (12161), 14763, 30669, 65765
Hartford, Conn. Committee. 90770
Hartford, Conn. Connecticut Historical Society. see Connecticut Historical Society, Hartford.
Hartford, Conn. Connecticut State Agricultural Society's Second Annual Cattle Show and Fair, 1855. see Connecticut State Agricultural Society. Cattle Show and Fair, 2d, Hartford, 1865.
Hartford, Conn. Convention, 1814. see Hartford Convention, 1814.
Hartford, Conn. Evangelical Tract Society. see Hartford Evangelical Tract Society.
Hartford, Conn. Female Beneficient Society, see Female Beneficient Society, Hartford, Conn.
Hartford, Conn. Fire Department. 30655
Hartford, Conn. First School Society. see First School Society, Hartford, Conn.
Hartford, Conn. Fourth Congregational Church. 30646
Hartford, Conn. Governor's Foot Guard. see Connecticut. Governor's Foot Guard. 1st Company, Hartford.
Hartford, Conn. Hartford Female Seminary. see Hartford Female Seminary, Hartford, Conn.
Hartford, Conn. High School. (30661)
Hartford, Conn. Hospital. 30652
Hartford, Conn. Hospital. Executive Committee. 30652
Hartford, Conn. Meeting of the Republican Party, 1856. see Republican Party. Connecticut. Meeting, Hartford, 1856.
Hartford, Conn. Meeting to Consider the Propriety of Forming the Protestant Episcopal Historical Society, 1850. see Protestant Episcopal Historical Society.
Hartford, Conn. Natural History Society. see Natural History Society of Hartford, Conn.
Hartford, Conn. North Church. (30656)
Hartford, Conn. Ordinances, etc. 30655, 30657
Hartford, Conn. Putnam Phalanx. 13248, 23384, 66849
Hartford, Conn. Republican Party Convention 1856. see Republican Party. Connecticut. cut. Convention, Hartford, 1856.
Hartford, Conn. Retreat for the Insane. see Retreat for the Insane, Hartford, Conn.
Hartford, Conn. Second Church. 65771
Hartford, Conn. Society for Savings. see Society for Savings, Hartford, Conn.
Hartford, Conn. Society for Affording Relief to the Families of Deceased Ministers. see Society for Affording Relief to the Families of Deceased Ministers, Hartford, Conn.
Hartford, Conn. Society for the Relief of the Insane. see Society for the Relief of the Insane, Hartford, Conn.
Hartford, Conn. Society of Young Men. see Society of Young Men, Hartford, Conn.
Hartford, Conn. Soldiers' Aid Association. see Soldiers' Aid Association, Hartford, Conn.
Hartford, Conn. Special Committee on War Debts. 30667
Hartford, Conn. State Convention of National Republican Young Men, 1832. see National Republican Party. Connecticut. Convention of Young Men, Hartford, 1832.

Hartford, Conn. State Convention of Sabbath School Teachers, 1st, 1857. see State Convention of Sabbath School Teachers, 1st, Hartford, Conn., 1857.

Hartford, Conn. State Convention of the Whig Young Men of Connecticut, 1840. see Whig Party. Connecticut. State Convention of Whig Young Men, Hartford, 1840.

Hartford, Conn. Theological Seminary. see Hartford Theological Seminary.

Hartford, Conn. Theological Seminary of the Protestant Episcopal Church in the United States. see Theological Seminary of the Protestant Episcopal Church in the United States, Hartford, Conn.

Hartford, Conn. Trinity College. see Trinity College, Hartford, Conn.

Hartford, Conn. Washington Benevolent Society. see Washington Benevolent Society. Connecticut. Hartford.

Hartford, Conn. Washington College. see Trinity College, Hartford, Conn.

Hartford, Conn. Young Men's Institute. see Young Men's Institute, Hartford, Conn.

Hartford, N. Y. Antimasonic Convention of the Young Men of the County of Washington, 1830. see Antimasonic Convention of the Young Men of the County of Washington, Hartford, N. Y., 1830.

Hartford, N. Y. Convention of the Young Men of the County of Washington, 1830. see Antimasonic Convention of the Young Men of the County of Washington, Hartford, N. Y., 1830.

Hartford, N. Y. Convention of Young Men of the County of Washington, Opposed to the Masonic Institution, 1830. see Antimasonic Convention of the Young Men of the County of Washington, Hartford, N. Y., 1830.

Hartford County, Conn. Jail. 69875

Hartford County, Conn. Court. 69875

Hartford County, Conn. Northern Association. see Congregational Churches in Connecticut. Hartford County North Association.

Hartford County, Conn. Superior Court. 95557

Hartford American mercury. see American mercury.

Hartford and New Haven Railroad Company. petitioners 30671

Hartford and New Haven Railroad Company. Engineer. 97542 see also Twining, Alexander Catlin.

Hartford and Springfield Railroad. Engineer. 30670, 58357 see also Palmer, J. N.

Hartford Argillo Manufacturing Company. petitioners 30664

Hartford, August 27, 1777. The following is a narrative. 104136

Hartford Auxiliary of the American Colonization Society. see Hartford Colonization Society.

Hartford-Bridge Company. petitioners 30672

Hartford city directory. 30660

Hartford Colonization Society. 30659

Hartford compact. see Connecticut (Colony) Constitution.

Hartford Convention, 1814. 9799, 42802, 45959, 65785, 80587

Hartford Convention, 1814. Commissioners to Washington. 45959

Hartford Convention in an uproar! 30662, note after 101993

Hartford County Agricultural Society. (30679), 93162

Hartford County North Association. see Congregational Churches in Connecticut. Hartford County North Association.

Hartford County Peace Society. 103166

Hartford courant. 30665, 86690, note after 93162

Hartford daily post. (18939)

Hartford directory. 30660

Hartford Evangelical Tract Society. 30654

Hartford Female Seminary, Hartford, Conn. (30661)

Hartford Female Seminary. Prospectus. (30661)

Hartford Hospital, Hartford, Conn. see Hartford, Conn. Hospital.

Hartford, in 1640. 64324

Hartford in the olden time. 30665, note after 93162

Hartford selection of hymns. 92958

Hartford Theological Seminary. 15802, 23528, 97593

Hartford Theological Seminary. Trustees. 105891-105892

Hartford Tract Society. (30666)

Hartford war debt bonds. 30667

Hartgers, Joost. see Hartgerts or Hartgers, Joost.

Hartgerts or Hartgers, Joost. 30680, 31505, 55442, (74830), 77933, 89448, 98739

Hartley, Cecil B. 30681-30684

Hartley, David, 1732-1813. 9247, 30685-30693, 89210

Hartley, David. supposed author 1659, 8964, 30688, 101118, 103123

Hartley, Oliver C. 30694

Hartley, Robert M. 30695

Hartley, Thomas. 50697, 56576

Hartley, Thomas, 1709?-1784. 8192, 14373, 30696

Hartley, Thomas, 1748-1800. 30697

Hartley, W. M. B. 30665, 30698, 86973, note after 93162

Hartley Norman. A tale of the times. 30123

Hartlib, Samuel, d. ca. 1670. 30699-30702, 1st note after 100518

Hartman, G. W. (30703)

Hartman, H. G. 4353

Hartman, John. 104289

Hartmann, --------. 30706

Hartmann, C. 30704

Hartmann, Johann Adolph. 30705

Hartnel, Richard. 95118

Hartpence, A. 30707

Hartranft, Frederick Berg. ed. 97190

Hartroerende, stigtelyke bespiegeling behelzende de memorie van Ridder Yorke. 30708

Hart's pathfinder. 30617

Hartshorn, C. W. (30709)

Hartshorne, R. T. 30711

Hartshorne, Richard. 26245, 30710

Hartsinck, Jan Jacob. 30712-(30713)

Hartsville, Pa. Ladies' Aid Society. see Soldiers Aid Society, Hartsville, Pa.

Hartsville, Pa. Soldiers Aid Society. see Soldiers Aid Society, Hartsville, Pa.

Hartt, Charles Frederick. 2743, 30714

Hartwell, Abraham. 30715

Hartwell, Henry. 30716, note after 104154

Hartwick, George. (30719)-30720

Hartwick, N. Y. Evangelical Lutheran Synod. see Hartwick Synod of the Evangelical Lutheran Church in the State of New York.

Hartwick Seminary, Albany, N. Y. see
   Hartwick Theological and Classical
   Seminary, Albany, N. Y.
Hartwick Synod of the Evangelical Lutheran
   Church in the State of New York.
   20422, 30718, 53658 see also
   Evangelical Lutheran Ministerium of
   the State of New York and Adjacent
   States and Counties.
Hartwick Theological and Classical Seminary,
   Albany, N. Y. 30717
Hartwood politician. 13788
Hartwell, Jonas. 34585
Harvard, W. M. (30721)
Harvard College. see Harvard University.
Harvard University. 8471, 10156, 14407-
   (14408), 22130, 23272, (24040), 30722,
   (30724), 30727, 30733, 30736-30740,
   (30749), 30754, (30759A)-(30761), 30765,
   52758-52759, 65572, 67208, (67240),
   67244, (80827), 101056, 103901, 103905
Harvard University. petitioners 23271, 30765,
   (42447), 45990
Harvard University. Astronomical Observatory.
   30725
Harvard University. Board of Overseers.
   (30749), (30752), (30759A), 30765, 69399
Harvard University. Board of Overseers.
   petitioners 30751
Harvard University. Board of Overseers.
   Committee, 1824. (30757), 2d note after
   69405
Harvard University. Board of Overseers.
   Committee, 1824. One Lately a Member.
   pseud. see One Lately a Member. pseud.
Harvard University. Board of Overseers.
   Committee, 1825. (30759A)
Harvard University. Board of Overseers.
   Committee of Visitation. Minority. 67244
Harvard University. Board of Overseers.
   Committee on a New Organization, 1824.
   (30759A)
Harvard University. Board of Overseers.
   Committee on Requirements of Admission.
   (30759A)
Harvard University. Board of Overseers.
   Committee on the State of the University,
   1823. (20759A)
Harvard University. Board of Overseers.
   Committee on the State of the University,
   1824. 30758
Harvard University. Board of Overseers.
   Committee on the Theological School.
   (30759A)
Harvard University. Board of Overseers.
   Committee to Confer With a Like
   Committee of the President and Fellows,
   1857. (30749)
Harvard University. Board of Overseers.
   Committee to Consider What Measures,
   if Any, May be Adobted to Reduce the
   Expenses Incident to a Residence at
   Cambridge. (30759A)
Harvard University. Board of Overseers.
   Committee to Procure a Perfect Copy
   of the College Charter, 1862. (30759A)
Harvard University. Board of Overseers.
   Committee To Revise the By-laws and
   Rules. (30749)
Harvard University. Board of Overseers.
   Committee to Visit the Law School,
   1849. 93671
Harvard University. Board of Overseers.
   Committee to Visit the Lawrence
   Scientific School, 1849. (30759A)

Harvard University. Board of Overseers.
   Committee to Visit the Library, 1805.
   36035
Harvard University. Board of Overseers.
   Committee to Visit the Library, 1850.
   30730
Harvard University. Board of Overseers.
   Committee to Visit the Library, 1857.
   30730
Harvard University. Board of Overseers.
   Committee to Visit the Library, 1861.
   30730
Harvard University. Board of Overseers.
   Committee to Visit the University, 1849.
   (30759A)
Harvard University. Boylston Medical School.
   7144-7145, 30738, 45874
Harvard University. Boylston Medical Society
   7144, 9899, 30735, 30765, 32621, 79871
Harvard University. Charter. (30749)
Harvard University. Class of 1642. 52758,
   note before 92797
Harvard University. Class of 1811. 30765
Harvard University. Class of 1834. (30752),
   30765
Harvard University. Class of 1846. 71516
Harvard University. Class of 1851. 59197
Harvard University. Class of 1862. 59346
Harvard University. Class of 1864. 59346
Harvard University. Class of 1865. 59346
Harvard University. Class of 1867. 59346
Harvard University. Class of 1869. 59346
Harvard University. Class of 1870. 59354
Harvard University. Commencement, 1773.
   25075
Harvard University. Commencement, 1813.
   30765
Harvard University. Corporation. 8471,
   (30749), (30752), 30765
Harvard University. Corporation. petitioners
   30751, (30759A)
Harvard University. Department of History
   and Government. 84338
Harvard University. Divinity School. (30749).
   30765
Harvard University. Divinity School. Directo
   30765
Harvard University. Dudleian Lecture. see
   Dudleian Lecture, Harvard University.
Harvard University. Faculty. (30752)-30753,
   30765, 95158
Harvard University. Festival of the Alumni,
   1860. (24040)
Harvard University. Hasty-Pudding Club.
   30734
Harvard University. Hasty-Pudding Club.
   Library. 30734
Harvard University. Hebrew Instructor. (307
   1st note after 94928, 103566
Harvard University. Henry Warren Torey
   Fund. 84338
Harvard University. Law Institution. see
   Harvard University. Law School.
Harvard University. Law Library. see
   Harvard University. Library. Law
   Library.
Harvard University. Law School. 30735,
   30765
Harvard University. Lawrence Scientific
   School. 30765
Harvard University. Librarian. 30730, 82739
   see also Smith, Isaac, 1749-1829.
Harvard University. Library. 30728-30730,
   82739, 88965-88966
Harvard University. Library. Law Library.
   (30731)-30732, note after 93645

Harvard University. Library. Law Library.
Librarian. 30732, note after 93645
see also Sumner, Charles, 1811-1874.
Woodward, William R.
Harvard University. Massachusetts Pro-
fessorship of Natural History. 30765
Harvard University. Museum of Comparative
Zoology. 503, 30748, 42803, (51572)
Harvard University. Museum of Comparative
Zoology. Trustees. (51572)
Harvard University. Natural History Society.
30735
Harvard University. Observatory. 6288
Harvard University. Phi Beta Kappa. see
Phi Beta Kappa. Massachusetts Alpha,
Harvard University.
Harvard University. Pi Tau. eds. 30755,
59539
Harvard University. Pierian Sodality. 30735
Harvard University. Porcellian Club. 30735
Harvard University. Procellian Club. Library.
30735
Harvard University. President. 17675,
(30724), 30726, 30730, (30752), (30759A),
(30764), 67209, 67244, 88994-88996,
88999, 89014, 1st note after 94928,
103566, 103901 see also Holyoke,
Edward, 1689-1769. Quincy, Josiah,
1772-1864. Sparks, Jared, 1789-1866.
Harvard University. President and Fellows.
(30759A), 67239, 99827
Harvard University. President and Fellows.
petitioners (30750)-30751, (30759A),
45918, (45991), 88994-88996
Harvard University. President and Fellows.
Committee. (30749)
Harvard University. President, Professors,
Tutors, and Hebrew Instructor. 30764,
103556
Harvard University. Professors and Tutors.
23271, (30749), 30756, (30764)-30765,
(42458)
Harvard University. Professors and Tutors.
petitioners 30751, 101385
Harvard University. Public Lecture. 103906,
103910
Harvard University. Resident Instructors.
petitioners (30759A)
Harvard University. Rumford Society. 30735
Harvard University. Society for the Promotion
of Theological Education. see Society
for the Promotion of Theological
Education in Harvard University.
Harvard University. Society of Christian
Brethren. 30765
Harvard University. Steward. 80825
Harvard University. Students, 1807. publishers
30762, 90699, note after 103460
Harvard University. Theological School. see
Harvard University. Divinity School.
Harvard University. Treasurer. 30765
Harvard University. Tuesday Lecture. 103899,
103898
Harvard University. Tutors. (30764), 1st
note after 94928, 103566
Harvard University. Tutorships. 30765
Harvard University. Undergraduates. 30746
Harvard University. Undergraduates.
petitioners 30751
Harvard University. Warren Anatomical
Museum. 30741
Harbard Bible class. 86567
Harvard College and its benefactors. 30742
Harvard College triennial catalogue. 17107
Harvard-Columbia Freshman Boat Race, New
London, Conn., 1895. 83492

Harvard graduates' magazine. 84041
Harvard historical studies. 84338
Harvard Lyceum. 30743
Harvard magazine. 30744
Harvard memorial biographies. (30745)
Harvard register. 30746
Harvard Silver Mining Association. 30766
Harvard student. pseud. Poems. see Ward,
H. D. supposed author
Harvard-Yale Boat Race, New London, Conn.,
1895. see Yale-Harvard Boat Race,
New London, Conn., 1895.
Harvardiana. 30747
Harvardine. pseud. New-England almanack.
see Danforth, Samuel. supposed author
Harvard's ephemeris, or almanack. 55009,
62743
Harve de Grace, Md. Meeting of Sundry
Citizens of Harford County, 1836. see
Harford County, Md. Meeting of Sundry
Citizens, Harve de Grace, 1836.
Harvest, George. 30767, 83978
Harvest and the reapers. 54932
Harvest home. 80125
Harvest Home Meeting of Chester and
Montgomery Counties at Valley Forge,
July 28, 1828. 30768
Harvest of counterfeiters. 57634
Harvey, Arthur. 30769
Harvey, Arthur. reporter (74581)
Harvey, C. T. 30770, 75423
Harvey, Edward. 30771, 81142, 100010
Harvey, Gabriel. 94165
Harvey, George. 30772-30773, 92495
Harvey, Gideon. 30774
Harvey, H. 30776
Harvey, Henry. 30775
Harvey, James. 30777
Harvey, Joseph. 58654
Harvey, M. 30778
Harvey, R. J. 30779
Harvey, Thomas. 30780, 93261, 93264
Harvey, W. W. 30782
Harvey, William. illus. 60936-69037, 60946,
69064, 69085
Harvey, William Henry. 30781-30782, 85072
Harvey's illustrations of our country. 30773
Harvey's scenes of the primitive forest of
America. 30772
Harvie (Henry A.) firm publisher 30784
Harvie's Prince Edward Island almanack.
30784
Harward, Thomas. 30785
Harwood, A. A. 30786
Harwood, Edwin. 30787
Harwood, John Edmund. (30788)
Has not constitutional monarchy in Brazil more
tended to prosperity? 7606
Has religion anything to do with our colleges.
30789
Has the Chief Justice a casting vote? 79136
Has the revolt destroyed the union. 22101
Has the Society for the Promotion of
Collegiate and Theological Education at
the West or has it not, fulfilled it whole
mission? 85917
Has theses ex universa theologia depromptas
in perillustri. (94225A)
Has this administration done any thing to put
down the rebellion? 30790
Hasbrouck, A. Bruyn. 30791
Hasbrouck, John W. 48873
Hase, Theodor de. supposed author 72769,
2d note after 100873
Haseltine, Ebenezer. 30792

Haseme ma[n]dado, q[ue] assi como represente a Su Magestad. 74031
Hasenclever, Peter. 30793
Haske, John. see Huske, John, 1721?-1773.
Haskel, Daniel, 1784-1848. 30796, 43127, 43130
Haskell, Abraham. 30797
Haskell, Caleb Niles. ed. 54915
Haskell, Daniel. 30404, 30798-30799, 99227
Haskell, Daniel Noyes, 1818-1874. (30800)
Haskell, Ezra. defendant 96882
Haskell, T. N. 30801
Haskett, William J. 30803
Haskell (William O.) & Son. firm 30802
Haskin, John B. see Haskins, John B.
Haskins, Elizabeth (Ladd) ed. 38519
Haskins, John B. 30804
Haskins, R. W. (30805)
Haskins, S. M. 30806
Hass, Charles de. see De Hass, Charles.
Hass, Wills de. see De Hass, Wills, 1818?-1910.
Hassall, Miss ---------. 30807, note after 78746
Hassan Bashaw, Dey of Algiers. 96486
    see also Algiers. Sovereigns, etc. (Hassan Bashaw)
Hassan, A. B. see Hasson, Alexander Breckinridge, d. 1877.
Hassan Straight-Shanks. pseud. illus. 50692
Hassar of de Negers. 35269
Hassard, John R. G. (30810)
Hassard, Samuel. (30811)
Hassaurek, F. 30812
Hasse, Adelaide Rosalie, 1868- note before 87347
Hassel, Johann Georg Heinrich. 30813-30815
Hassert, Luke. 87057
Hassler, F. R. 13821, 30816-30819, 65661, 71854
Hasson, Alexander Breckinridge, d. 1877. 30808-30309, (34112)
Hasta que ahorcaron al frayle; y a todos los coyotitos. 89414
Haste and waste. 57126
Hasted, Frederick. 30820
Hasting, Ebenezer. 105364
Hasting to be rich. 13589
Hastings, David K. defendant at court martial 30821
Hastings, G. E. 84678C
Hastings, Hiram P. 30822
Hastings, John, 1778-1854. 30823
Hastings, Lansford W. 30824-30825
Hastings, Sally. 30826
Hastings, Samuel D. 30827
Hastings, Selina. see Huntingdon, Selina Hastings, Countess of, 1707-1791.
Hastings, Susannah Johnson. 34469, 36324-36327
Hastings, T. 14999
Hastings, W. S. 30828
Hastings Circulating Library, Utica, N. Y. see Merrill & Hastings Circulating Library, Utica, N. Y.
Hastings memorial. 8937
Hasty Pudding; a poem. 3420, note just before 30829
Hasty Pudding Club, Harvard University. see Harvard University. Hasty-Pudding Club.
Hasty recognition of rebel belligerency. 4625
Hasty sketch humbly offered by way of introduction. 101899
Haswell, Anthony. 30829, 101827
Haswell, Charles H. 30830

Haswell, R. reporter 87511
Hat, Rene. defendant 47349
Hatak Yoshuba Uhleha hut Chihowa Anukhobela ya Ibbak Toyuka. 21960
Hatboro, Pa. Monument. 30832
Hatboro, Pa. Union Library Company. 30831, note after 97808
Hatboro, Pa. Union Library Company. Charte 30831, note after 97808
Hatch, ---------. illus. (70963)
Hatch, Arthur. 66686
Hatch, C. B. 24522-24523
Hatch, Mrs. C. L. V. 30833, 58750
Hatch, David. petitioner 33253
Hatch, Israel Thompson, 1808-1875. 31022, 39834
Hatch, J. jr. 30836
Hatch, John. 66686
Hatch, Nathaniel. 30837-30838
Hatch, Reuben. 30839
Hatch, William Stanley. 30840
Hatchard, John. defendant 30841
Hatcher, of Salisbury. pseud.?? tr. (41981)
Hatchets to hew down the tree of sin. 39409, 96105
Hate, Caleb. defendant 96884
Hate-Smoke, William. pseud. see William Hate-Smoke. pseud.
Hatfield, Edwin F. 30842-30843, 81624, 89905
Hatfield, Julia. 30844
Hatfield, Mass. Trustees to Receive Contributions for the Ransom of the Captives Taken by the Indians. 91929
Hathaway, G. W. 30845
Hathaway, Levi. 30846
Hathaway, Silas. petitioner 65098, 69392
Hathaway, Silas. defendant 65098, 69392, 98610
Hathaway, Warren. 30847
Hatheway, Calvin. 30848
Hatin, Eugene. 30849
Hattain Gelashmin. Indian name see James, George.
Hattersley, John. 30850
Hattie Silver Mining Company. 52405
Hatton, -----------. RA 43431, 94397
Hatton, Ann Julia. 30851
Hatzar-Maveth. 46356
Hauch, John Carsten. 30852-30853
Hauck, W. 5421
Hauckesworth, John. see Hawkesworth, John.
Haud immemor. 68606
Hauff, Hermann. 33738, 105720
Haughton, James. 30854
Haughton, R. B. 30855
Haughwout & Co. firm 30856
Haun, Nancy Van. see Van Haun, Nancy.
Haunted hearts. 17934
Haunted wood. 22297
Haunts of vice in New York. 62708
Haupt, Herman. 85775 see also Sociedade Internacional de Immigracao, Rio de Janeiro. Director.
Haupt, Herman, 1817-1905. 30857-30859, 32890, 60358, 88458 see also Southern Railroad Company. Chief Engineer.
Haupt, Marie Guerrier de. tr. (16431), 16503
Haupt (Herman) & Co. firm 30859
Hauptbegebenheiten der Amerikanischen Geschichte. 3327
Hauptconservatorium der K. Bayerischen Armee. see Bavaria. Armee. Hauptconservatorium.

Hauptmann, I. G. 30860
Hauranne, Ernest Duvergier de. see
　Duvergier de Hauranne, Ernest.
Haus, im Comite des Ganzen, hatte den
　Finanz-Entwurf unter Berathung. 32877
Hausbibliothek der Jugend. 92580
Hausbibliothek fur Lander- und Volkerkunde.
　1462, 89997
Haushaltung oder Gallerie von Darstellungen.
　38864
Hausleutner, Ph. W. G. 30861
Hausleutner, W. G. tr. 61000
Hausted, Peter. tr. 95621
Haut, Marc de. (30862)
Haute-Vienne Jourdan, ------ de la. see
　Jourdan, ------ de la Haute-Vienne.
Haute politique du jour des deux gouvernements.
　28133
Hautefeuille, L. B. 30863-30865
Hauterive, -------, Comte d'. 30866
Hauteur de quelques sommites de Alpes.
　68443
Hauteville, Ellen (Sears) Grand d'. see
　D'Hauteville, Ellen (Sears) Grand.
Hauteville, Paul Daniel Gonzalve Grand d'.
　see D'Hauteville, Paul Daniel Gonzalve
　Grand.
Hauthal, Luise. tr. 37008
Havana. 29421
Havana. petitioners 29456
Havana. Ayuntamiento. 17747, 29434, 59290,
　68244
Havana. Ayuntamiento. Comision Sobre
　Poblacion Blanca. (34715), 44983
Havana. Banco Espanol. (29457)
Havana. British Commissioner. see Great
　Britain. Consulate. Havana.
Havana. Carcel. 17806
Havana. Casa de Beneficencia. 29448, 69227
　see also Comisiones Reunidas de la
　Real Sociedad Economica, Casa de
　Beneficencia y Demas Dependencias de
　Aquel Cuerpo, Havana.
Havana. Casa de Beneficencia. Junta de
　Gobierno. 20217
Havana. Casa de Education de Buenavista.
　17803
Havana. Cemeterio General. 29433
Havana. Colegio de San Carlos. 72523
Havana. Comisarios de Barrio. 29447
Havana. Compania de Tobaco. Charter.
　29422
Havana. Consulado. see Cuba. Consulado,
　Havana.
Havana. Cuerpo de Serenos. 68858
Havana. Institucion Agronoma. see
　Institucion Agronoma, Havana.
Havana. Intendente de Exercito. see Cuba.
　Intendente de Exercito, Havana.
Havana. Junta Censoria Interina. 1886
Havana. Junta de Generales. see Cuba.
　Junta de Generales.
Havana. Junta Proyestada. (1871)
Havana. Junta Superior de Hacienda. 19968,
　(23415), 29432
Havana. Ordinances, etc. 17747, 17806, 17809,
　29432, 29433, 29447, 29453, 29454,
　59290, 68858
Havana. Parroquia de Santo Angel Custodia.
　see Santo Angel Custodia (Parroquia),
　Havana.
Havana. Policia. 29454
Havana. Real Aduana de Mar. see Cuba.
　Real Aduana de Mar.
Havana. Real Audiencia. see Cuba. Real
　Audiencia.

Havana. Real Audiencia de Cuentas. see
　Cuba. Real Audiencia de Cuentas.
Havana. Real Sociedad Economica de la
　Havana. see Sociedad Economica de
　Amigos del Pais de la Havana.
Havana. Real Sociedad Economica de Amigos
　del Pais. see Sociedad Economica
　de Amigos del Pais de la Havana.
Havana. Real Sociedad Patriotica. see
　Sociedad Economica de Amigos del Pais
　de la Havana.
Havana. Real y Conciliar Colegio Seminario.
　plaintiff 29441
Havana. Regidor. 67329 see also Quintana
　Warnes, Jose Maria.
Havana. Regidores. plaintiffs 99437-99438
Havana. Sociedad Anonima Denominada Banco
　Industrial. see Sociedad Anonima
　Denominada Banco Industrial, Havana.
Havana. Sociedad Anonima "La Colonizadora."
　see Sociedad Anonima "La Colonizadora,"
　Havana.
Havana. Sociedad de Credito Industrial. see
　Sociedad de Credito Industrial, Havana.
Havana. Sociedad Economica. see Sociedad
　Economica de Amigos del Pais de la
　Havana.
Havana. Sociedad Economica de Amigos del
　Pais. see Sociedad Economica de
　Amigos del Pais de la Havana.
Havana. Sociedad Filarmonica de Santa Cecilia.
　see Sociedad Filarmonica de Santa
　Cecilia, Havana.
Havana. Tribunal del Consulado. 11292, 73008,
　85742
Havana, Tribunal del Protomedicato. 98382
Havana. Tribunal y Real Audiencia de
　Cuentas. see Cuba. Real Audiencia
　de Cuentas.
Havana. Univesidad. 17768
Havana (Province) Diputacion. (34712), 62937
Havana (Diocese) Bishop (ca. 1805) 29433
Havana (Diocese) Bishop (Tres-Palacios y
　Verdeja) 96781 see also Tres-Palacios
　y Verdeja, Felipe Jose de, Bp.
Havana, N. Y. People's College. see
　Montour Falls, N. Y. People's College.
Havana Ice-House controversy. 18365
Havane. Extrait du dictionnaire du comerce
　et des marchandises. 74918
Havanero. pseud. Carta. see F., D. B. P.
　pseud.
Havanne. 47978
Have, L. J. ten. (30869)
Have faith in God and the people. 37272
Have the people of Missouri the right to
　prescribe the qualifications? 20817
Have the people of the District of Columbia
　any rights? 37729
Have we a national standard of English
　lexicography? 47983
Have we the best possible ambulance system?
　30870
Have we, the people of the United States, an
　infidel or a heathen system of government?
　43141
Haven, -------- de. see De Haven, --------.
Haven, --------, fl. 1858. 15485
Haven, Alice B. (30871)
Haven, C. C. 30872-30874
Haven, C. W. (30875)
Haven, D. W. (52975), 91756, 103618
Haven, E. O. 30877
Haven, Elias. 30878
Haven, Erastus Otis, Bp., 1820-1881. (30876),
　41215, 43852, 48804

Haven, Gilbert, jr. 30883
Haven, Gilbert, Bp., 1821-1880. 30879-30882
Haven, Jason, 1733-1803. (30884)-30888
Haven, Joseph, 1816-1874. 30889
Haven, Nathaniel Appleton. 30890, 95806
Haven, Nicodemus. 105013
Haven, Samuel. 30891-30892
Haven, Samuel. supposed author 19221,
  38776, note after 90752
Haven, Samuel Foster, 1806-1881. 30893-
  30896, 49340, 85071, 85072, 86917, 89542,
  95406
Haven, Solomon George, 1810-1861. 30897
Haven, Thomas. 30898
Havens, Henry H. 53684
Havens, J. S. 30900
Havens, Palmer E. 30901-(30902)
Haven's Nicodemus. 30899
Haverford, Pa. Haverford School. see
  Haverford School, Haverford, Pa.
Haverford, Pa. Loganian Library. 30906
Haverford School, Haverford, Pa. 30904-
  30905, (30907)
Haverford School, Haverford, Pa. Managers.
  30905
Haverford revisited. (30907)
Haverhill, Mass. Society for the Promotion
  of Temperance. see Society for the
  Promotion of Temperance in Haverhill
  and Vicinity.
Haverhill, N. H. Citizens. 52791, note after
  98998
Harverhill, N. H. Ecclesiastical Council,
  1858. see Congregational Churches in
  New Hampshire. Ecclesiastical Council,
  Haverhill, 1758.
Haverhill, N. H. Ecclesiastical Council, 1759.
  see Congregational Churches in New
  Hampshire. Ecclesiastical Council,
  Haverhill, 1759.
Haverhill and Bradford directory for 1867.
  (30910)
Haverhill Aqueduct Company. petitioners
  51615
Haverhill directory for 1865. 30909
Haverhill journal. 100595
Haverhill; or, memoirs of an officer in the
  army of Wolfe. 36519
Haversack. 30911
Havestadt, Bernard. (30912)
Havfruen eller Soskummeren, en fortaelling.
  (16509)
Haviendo a sv tiempo dado parte a V. R. del
  dichoso tra[n]sito. 87246
Haviendo dado cuenta a V. Mag. en 13. de
  Febrero. 86439
Haviland, John de. 30913
Havre de refuge. 82786
Haw, William. 30914
Haw-ho-noo. 38919
Hawaiian Islands: their progress and condition.
  1419, 90107
Hawes, --------, fl. 1646. petitioner (44055),
  100439, 4th note after 102831
Hawes, --------; fl. 1836. 40484, 102949
Hawes, Mrs. A. H. 30915
Hawes, Barbara. 30916
Hawes, Elizabeth. 30917
Hawes, George W. 34535, (37514), (45247),
  57005, 57065
Hawes, George Whitefield. supposed author
  2948, 21156, (31631)
Hawes, J. H. (30919)
Hawes, Joel, 1789-1867. (1418), 30920-30925,
  (47077), (65855), 89736

Hawes, Mrs. Joel. 30926
Hawes, Mary Virginia. see Terhune, Mary
  Virginia (Hawes)
Hawes, Richard. 30927-30928
Hawes, Roger. 66686
Hawes, William Post. 30929
Hawes (G. B.) firm publishers 30918
Hawes-Place Congregational Church, Boston.
  see Boston. Hawes-Place Congregation
  Church.
Hawk Chief: a tale of the Indian country.
  35115
Hawk-Eye Pioneer Association, Des Moines
  County, Iowa. 19746
Hawke, Edward Hawke, 1st Baron, 1705-1781.
  2459, 30930
Hawke, W. defendant 99742
Hawker, Peter. 30931
Hawkes, J. supposed author 6778, 70137
Hawkes, John. 30932
Hawkes, T. H. 30933
Hawkesbury, Charles Jenkinson, 1st Baron.
  see Liverpool, Charles Jenkinson, 1st
  Earl of, 1727-1808.
Hawkesworth, John. 16267, 16275, 30934-
  30945, (69276), 78097, 88528, 88532
Hawkesworth, John. incorrectly supposed
  author 4246, 16242, note after 36695
Hawkesworth, Richard. tr. 96501
Hawkhurst, J. W. 82348
Hawkins, Alfred. 30946, 67045
Hawkins, Archibald. 90369
Hawkins, Benjamin. 27027, 30947, 96600-
  96601, 96607 see also U. S. Com-
  missioners to the Cherokee Indians.
  U. S. Commissioners to the Chickasaw
  Indians. U. S. Commissioners to the
  Choctaw Indians.
Hawkins, Christopher. (30948)-30949
Hawkins, E. W. defendant 30950
Hawkins, Ernest. 30951-30952
Hawkins, James. 30953
Hawkins, Sir John, 1532-1595. (8784), 30954,
  66686
Hawkins, John, fl. 1779. 99052, 99075
Hawkins, John, fl. 1796. 30955
Hawkins, Joseph. 30956
Hawkins, Joseph. ed. 14876, 1st note after
  101785
Hawkins, M. T. 90338
Hawkins, Mary. defendant 36994, 94411, note
  after 96882, 3d note after 96891
Hawkins, Sir Richard, 1562?-1622. 30957-
  30958, 66686
Hawkins, Rush C. (30959)
Hawkins, W. 66686
Hawkins, William George. 30960-(30961)
Hawkins's picture of Quebec. 30946
Hawkins Zouaves. (30959)
Hawkridge, ---------. (74131)
Hawks, Francis Lister, 1798-1866. 1798,
  13009, 16352, 24986, 28652, 29971,
  30957, 30962-30971, 30973, (36285),
  38284-(38285), 41073-41075, 45315,
  (66172), (66973), (70868), 71645, 82858,
  92343, 1st note after 97724, 3d note afte
  97724, 97725, 2d note after 97725, 97726
  2d note after 97726, 1st note after 99856
  2d note after 100461, 2d note after 10046
  1st note after 100494, 100513
Hawks, Francis Lister, 1798-1866. supposed
  author (6372)
Hawks, Micajah. defendant 96895, 101475
Hawks about the devecote. 81277
Hawks of Hawk Hallow. 5551

Haywarde, Richard. pseud. Prismatics.
  31082
Hayward's New England gazetteer. 31075
Hayward's history of all religions. 31066
Haywood, Edward Graham. (31083)
Haywood, John, 1753?-1826. 30571, 31084-
  31087, 55645, 94733, 94737-94739,
  94774, 94775, 94780-94782, 93805
Haywood, John, 1753?-1826. supposed author
  94814
Haywood, John H. 31088
Haywood, Peter, 35660, 105080 see also
  Jamaica. Governor, 1716-1718
  (Haywood)
Haywood, William Henry, 1801-1852. 31089
Haywood, William S. (31090)
Hazard, Benjamin, 1770-1841. 31091-(31093),
  42730, 66240, 70450 see also
  Providence Bank, Providence, R. I.
  Counsel.
Hazard, Charles T. 31094
Hazard, Charles T. defendant 1310, 5785,
  31094, 35314
Hazard, Charles T. petitioner 31094
Hazard, Ebenezer. 28790, 31095, 45708,
  51017, 51774, 79243, 98637
Hazard, Erskine. 31096
Hazard, George S. 73959, (58595) see also
  U. S. Commission to the Universal
  Exposition, Paris, 1867.
Hazard, Joseph, b. 1751? 31097
Hazard, Joseph, 1757-1817. 31098
Hazard, Mumford. defendant 35314
Hazard, Nathaniel. 8986
Hazard, Rowland G. (31099)-31101, (57938)
Hazard, S. H. 31108
Hazard, Samuel. (6107), 19163, (31102)-31107,
  note after 60301, 62651, 83983, 84604,
  91869, note after 95562, 101219, 102508
Hazard, Thomas R. 23623, 31110-31112,
  70687
Hazard, Thomas R. defendant 5785-5786,
  31109, 31112
Hazard, Thomas R. petitioner 31112
Hazard, Willis Pope, 1825-1913. 1094, 31113
Hazard's Pennsylvania register. (6107)
Hazard's register. 62651
Hazard's United States commercial and
  statistical register. 31107
Hazart, Cornelius. 31114-31115
Haze, J. de. 94576
Hazel, Harry. pseud. Flying artillerist. see
  Jones, J.
Hazel, Harry. pseud. Yankee Jack. see
  Jones, J.
Hazel Green Collegiate Institute. 31116
Hazelius, Ernest L. 31117
Hazeltine, Lieut. Col. -----. (31118), 67299
Hazeltine, A. 35736
Hazeltine, Silas Wood. 31119
Hazelton, Harry. 31120
Hazen, Jacob A. (31121)
Hazen, Moses. claimant 103369, 103439
Hazen, Nathan W. 31122
Hazlitt, William, 1737-1820. (31123)
Hazlitt, William, 1778-1830. 19284, (31124)-
  31125, 61337, 72191, 81217, 2d note
  after 94271
Hazlitt, William Carew, 1831-1913. 31126,
  97139
Hazzard, Charles I. S. 90200
Hazzi, ------ de. 47270
He being dead, yet speaketh. 64785
He has kept his word. 99249
He hoikehonua, he mea is e hoakaka'i i ke
  ano a ka honua nei a me na nea maluna
  iho. 105096

He mau mea i wae ia mailoko mai o na
  Hoikeana a me na Unuhina a Iosepa
  Kamika. 83276
He mea tango mai i nga whakakitenga. 83277
He mooolelo i kakauia e ka lima o Moramona
  83131
He mooolelo i kakuia ma ka lima o Moramona
  iho o na Papa i Laweia Mailoko mai o
  na Papa o Nepai. 83133
He ni ya' wah syoh no' nah jih. 105547A
He of the iron arm. 20584
He pasa Ekklesia. 74157
He that would keep God's commandments must
  renounce the society of evil doers.
  79418
He tuhituhinga i tuhithuhia e te Ringa o
  Moromana. 83136-83137
He tuwe he. 71334
He wou'd be a poet. 96324
Heacock, Grosvenor W. 31127
Heacock, J. W. (31128)
Heacock family. 31129
Head, Edward Francis. 31130, 63891, 93647
Head, Sir Edmund Walker, Bart., 1805-1868.
  33551 see also Canada. Governor
  General, 1854-1861 (Head)
Head, Sir Francis Bond, Bart., 1793-1875.
  9191, 10528, 31131-31142, 71718, 98067
  see also Ontario. Lieutenant Governor
  1836-1838 (Head)
Head, Sir Francis Bond, Bart., 1793-1875.
  supposed author 8420, 3d note after
  95742
Head, Sir Francis Bond, Bart., 1793-1875.
  defendant 72871
Head, George, 25082, 31143-31144, 50115
Head, Joseph. jr. 31145
Head Quarters, Middle Brook, March 10, 1778
  101705
Head-Quarters, Morris-Town, 8th May, 1777.
  101699
Head-Quarters, Morris Town, January 22, 177
  101695
Head Quarters, Newtown, 27th Dec. 1776.
  101693
Head-quarters, 2d Division, Nashville, May 24
  1814. 94783
Headington, J. N. 90555
Headlam, John. 31146
Headlands in the life of Henry Clay. (13561)
Headless horseman. 69049
Headley, Joel Tyler, 1813-1897. 28900, 3114
  31161
Headley, Phineas Camp, 1819-1903. (31162)-
  31169
Heads of a course of lectures on natural
  history. 102065
Heads of a sermon. 69660
Heads of agreement assented to by the United
  Ministers. (77391)
Heads of articles of complaint by Rip Vandam
  (53693), 98435
Heads of articles of complaint, made by Rip
  Van Dam, Esq. 98432
Heads of inquiry relative to the present state
  16747
Heads of the Christian religion. 46497
Headsman. 16437-16438
Heady, Morrison. 31170
Heald, Henry. supposed author 103020
Heald, Joseph G. 31171
Healed one's prophulacticon. 829
Healey, John. tr. 29820
Healing and slavation for our country from
  God alone. (6071)
Healing art. 91620-91621
Healing of the nations. 43866

Healing question propounded and resolved. 98498-98499
Health almanac, for 1832. 64254
Health and education. 66267
Health and profit. 29469
Health and wealth of the city of Wheeling. 68670
Health law. An act for establishing an Health Office. 61717
Health laws of the city of New York. 54308
Health laws of the state of Delaware. 19387
Health laws of the state of Pennsylvania. 60134
Health officer's annual report for the year 1867. (72343)
Health of Caledonia. 78217
Healthful diet. 829
Healy, --------. illus. 31172
Healy, J. D. 95602
Healy, Joseph. 31173
Healy, T. W. 52399
Healy, William. 31174
Heap, Gwinn Harris, 1817-1887. 4106, 31175
Hear both sides. 104657A
Hear both sides; being a statement of the controversy. 102723
Hear both sides. Document and papers. (31177), note after 91895
Hear both sides, or an address to all impartial men. (31176)
Hear him and his neighbours. 40575, 94799
Hear Hon. Geo. H. Pendleton. 59645
Hear the voices of O'Connell and Emmett!!! (33288)
Heard, Isaac V. D. 31178
Heard, Jared M. (31179)
Heard, John T. 31180
Heard, Nathan. 47987
Hearer. pseud. Remarks on the immediate abolition lecture. 69466
Hearer of them. pseud. ed. Some theological conclusions. 91962
Hearing before the Committee on Banks and Banking. (29851)
Hearn, Thomas, 1678-1735. 10157
Hearne, Samuel. 31181-31186, 43808, 97707
Heart, Jonathan. (34358)
Heart garrisoned. 104084
Heart-in-Hand Fire Company, New York. 54309
Heart of New England hardned through Wickedness, 33360, (33362)
Heart of N-England rent at the blasphemies of the present generation. 55883
Heart of New England rent at the blasphemies of the present generation. 22359, 33360, (33362), 55883, 59659
Heart of sensibility. 91340-91341
Heart of the Andes. 55382
Heart of the commonwealth. 33382
Heart of the continent. (42649)
Heart of the world. 46840
Heart-melting exhortation. 46780
Heart-purity encourag'd and press'd. 22438
Heart whisperings, or echoes of song. 81392
Heart whispers. 2321
Hearth-stone. 57791
Heartman, Charles Frederick, 1883- 15043, 83427, 93232, 97207. 98998, 99006, 100448, 100449, 103126, 103135, 103140-103142, 2d note after 105927, note after 105928
Heartman's historical series. 15043, 83427, 93232, 97207, 98998, 100448-100449, 2d note after 105927, note after 105928
Hearts forever. 35089

Hearts of oak. 86898
Hearts of war! 85200
Heartt, H. G. (3838)
Hearty well-wisher to publick credit. pseud. South-Sea scheme examined. 88201-88202
Heat and thirst. 78339, 96128
Heath, --------. illus. 67695
Heath, C. A. supposed author 15940, 16019, 1st note after 102825, 102826-102827
Heath, H. H. 31187
Heath, J. E. ed. 88393
Heath, James Ewell. 21848, 4th note after 100577, 103291
Heath, James P. 31188
Heath, John. 31189
Heath, John. defendant at court martial 61047
Heath, Labaw. (31190)
Heath, Nathaniel H. 69618
Heath, Upton S. 31191
Heath, William, 1737-1814. 14162-14163, 31192, 84904, 2d note after 104027
Heathcote, George. 31193
Heathcote, Sir Gilbert, 1651?-1733. 65865, 88192
Heathcotes. 16441
Heather, William. (31194)
Heatherington, A. 31195
Heathfield, Richard. tr. 26510
Heaton, David, 1823-1870. 27863
Heautonaparnumenos. 32840
Heaven given only to saints. (51518)
Heaven ready for the saints. 64801
Heaven shut against Arminians and Antinomians. 17675
Heaven the best country. 96157
Heaven the residence of the saints. 59606, 103131
Heavenly attractions. 80323
Heavenly conversation. 46357
Heavenly doctrine of man's justification. 17675
Heavenly merchandize. 104085
Heavenly mission to all governments. 85115
Heavens. 89438
Heavens alarm to the world. 46691, 46696
Heaven's treasury opened. 32939
Heaviside, J. T. C. (31196)
Hebb, George. 45126
Hebbard, William Wallace. 31197
Hebbe, Gustave C. tr. 41018, 64545
Heberden, William. 31198, 34792
Heberer, Johann Michael. 72227
Hebert, Paul Octave, 1818-1880. 42268 see also Louisiana. Governor, 1853-1856 (Hebert)
Herbert, William. 31199, 31474
Hebler, Sharpless John. plaintiff 58441
Hebreus Psalmboeck. 66454
Hebrew Benevolent Society, New York. 54310
Hebrew Charitable Fund, Philadelphia. Annual Dinner, 1st, 1853. 61718
Hebrew grammar. 42873, 79458
Hebrew lexicon. 102370
Hebrew servitude, and American slavery. 37401, (81990)
Hebrew Young Men's Literary Association, New York. 54310
Heb. XII: 6. 84288
Hebron, Conn. Washington Benevolent Society. see Washington Benevolent Society. Connecticut. Hebron.
Hechavarria, Santiago Joseph de, Bp. 31201, 59014 see also Cuba (Diocese) Bishop (Hechavarria)
Hecho es notorio a V. M. 93317

Heirs at Law of William James. Agent. 90762

Heirs of Caron de Beaumarchais. petitioners 69804

Heirs of Gen. Thadeus Kosciusko. (36269)

Heirs of Gen. Thomas Nelson. petitioners 61273

Heirs of —————— Halsey. plaintiffs. 17966

Heirs of James Parish. appellants 58611

Heirs of John Poultney. plaintiffs 96920

Heirs of John Poultney versus William Cecil's executor. 96920

Heirs of Robert Morris. 50869

Heirs of Robert Morris to Robert S. Paschall. 50869

Heirs of Stephen Girard. plaintiffs 27488, 58857, 60043

Heising, A. 31247

Helba, chef de la tribu des Nemchas. 5512

Helden des Sudens. 4528

Helden van het zuiden. 4528A

Helderberg war. 95417

Helderbergia. 77848

Heldin von Tennessee. (70449)

Heldring, O. G. 4375, 31248

Helen Dhu. pseud. see Black, Helen. supposed author Lester, Charles Edward. supposed author

Helen Halsey. (81279)

Helen Lason. 31249

Heley, W. 66686

Helf, Josephine Lebassu d'. see Lebassu d'Helf, Josephine.

Helfenstein, Ernest. pseud. Hugo. see Smith, Elizabeth (Oakes) 1806-

Helfenstein, Ernest. pseud. Salamander. see Smith, Elizabeth (Oakes) 1806-

Hell broke loose. 97736

Hellenbrock, Abraham. (31250), 94697

Heller, Carl Bartholomaeus. 31251

Heller, G. P. ed. 6277

Hellier, Henry R. 61606

Hellier & Co. firm publishers 31253, 53349, 75346

Hellier & Co.'s Chicago business directory. 31253

Hellier & Co.'s Saint Louis business directory. 75346

Hellier's New Orleans business directory. 53349

Hellimer, Regis. (31254)

Helling, Jacob. defendant 95643

Hellman, Andrew. alias see Horn, Adam.

Hellmuth, Isaac, Bp. of Huron. 31255

Hello, J. M. 31256

Hellrigle (R. C.) & Co. firm publishers 89892

Hellwald, Friedrich von. 31257-(31258)

Helm, James I. 31260

Helm, John Larue, 1802-1867. (70981)

Helme, Elizabeth. tr. 10284-10285, (10304), (14651)

Helmer, C. D. 31262

Helmersen, Gr. v. (2711)

Helmig van der Vegt, A. 31263

Helms, Anton Zacharius. (31264)-(31266), 62506

Helmuth, J. Henry C. 31267-31268

Helmuth, J. Henry C. supposed author 101829

Heloise. 72189

Helot, ——————. 98682

Help for distressed parents. (46358)

Help of the Lord, in signal deliverances. 105164

Help to a national reformation. 31269

Help to the language of the natives in that part of America. 104339-104340

Help vs. helplessness. 89378

Helper, Hinton Rowan, 1829-1909. 27516, (31270)-31274, 59563, 84721, 97763

"Helperism" annihilated! (77492)

Helping hand: . . . an account of the Home for Discharged Female Convicts. 37989

Helping hand for town and country. 20902

Helpless hand. 69050

Helps, Sir Arthur, 1813-1875. 31276-31280, note after 92624

Helps to education in the homes of our country. 9506

Helps to the study of the Book of Mormon. 83105

Helter von Scelter. pseud. Schemer. see Ridley, J.

Helvetischen Societet Erkaufte, 33. 21829

Helvetius, ——————. 96413

Helvidius. pseud. Letters. see Madison, James, Pres. U. S., 1751-1836.

Helvington; a dramatic story in five acts. 31281

Helvvisse, Thomas. see Helwys, Thomas, 1550?-1616?

Helwys, Thomas, 1550?-1616? 72106

Helyot, Pierre, 1660-1716. 31282

Hemel-sang. 91166

Hemenway, Abby Maria. 31283-31284, 86941, 1st note after 99199

Hemenway, Samuel. 99143

Hemisphere. 31286

Hemmen i nya verlden. 7709

Hemmenway, Moses. 2632, 31287-31288

Hemmersam, Michael. 31289-31290, (38244), 2d note after 102842

Hemorrhage from gun-shot wounds. 30113, 76657

Hemphill, John, 1803-1862. 31291

Hemphill, Joseph. (38292)

Hemphill, Samuel. 25591, 31293, 31295, 31296, (36017)

Hemphill, Samuel. defendant before Synod 31293-(31294), 31297, (36017), 2d note after 99826

Hempstead, Stephen. (2489), (31298), (67952)

Hempstead, N. Y. respondents (31300), 55717

Hempstead, N. Y. Christ's First Church. Session. defendant before Presbytery 30413

Hempstead, N. Y. Hempstead Institute. see Bryant School, Roslyn, N. Y.

Hempstead case. 31299-(31300)

Hempstead Institute, Hempstead, N. Y. see Bryant School, Roslyn, N. Y.

Hempstead sentinel. 95470

Henchman, Daniel. 86917, 98696

Henchman, Nathaniel. 31302

Henden, ——————. 17051

Henderson, A. W. 31307

Henderson, Alexander. of Belize, Honduras. 31303-31305

Henderson, Alexander, fl. 1641. 11397

Henderson, Alexander, II. 1866. 31306

Henderson, George, fl. 1802. 31310

Henderson, George. RA 31308-31309

Henderson, George D. 31311

Henderson, H. 31312

Henderson, J. 31320

Henderson, J. B. 85061

Henderson, J. Stanley. 31324

Henderson, Jacob. 31313

Henderson, James. 31314-31316

Henderson, James Henry Dickey, 1810-1885. (31322)

Henderson, John, 1795-1866. 31321

Henderson, John Brooks, 1826-1913. 31317-31319

Henderson, John H. 31323
Henderson, Marc Antony. pseud. Song of
   Milgenwater. see Strong, George
   Augustus.
Henderson, Mathew H. 31326
Henderson, Samuel. 29945
Henderson, Stewart. (31327)
Henderson, Thomas, 1789-1854. 31328,
   101961
Henderson, Thomas J. reporter 35341
Henderson, W. 14894
Hendree, John. 98099
Hendrick Pannebecker. 60746, 1st note after
   97529
Hendricks, Harmon. appellant 100997
Hendricks, Thomas Andrew, 1819-1885.
   (31330)
Hendricks, William, d. 1776. supposed author
   36728
Hendricks, William, 1782-1850. 31329
Hendrickson, John. defendant 31331, (39716)
Hendrickson, Joseph. complainant (31332)
Hendrickson, Joseph. defendant (31332),
   80737, 80738, 105025, 105026
Hendrickson, Joseph. plaintiff 19205, 23321,
   88244
Hendrik, Hans. 71440
Hendschel, Thomas. 31333
Hendy, James. 31334-31336
Heney, H. 31337
Henfrey, Benjamin. 31338
Henfield Division, no. 2, Salem, Mass. see
   Sons of Temperance of North America.
   Massachusetts. Henfield Division, no.
   2, Salem.
Hengist Hobnail. pseud. see Hobnail,
   Hengist. pseud.
Henick, M. B. ed. 55748
Henin de Cuvillers, Etienne Felix, Baron d'.
   1755-1841. tr. 25095
Hening, William Waller. 31339-31340, 80283,
   2d note before 99889, note before 99927,
   100013, 100015, 100026, 1000231, note
   before 100232, 100406, 100464
Henley, Morton Eden, 1st Baron, 1752-1830.
   99585
Henis, Tadeo Xavier. 31341, 58513
Henisson, ---------. illus. 16262
Henker. 16440
Henkle, Moses Montgomery. 31342, 88384
Henley, David. 1749-1823. defendant at court
   martial (31343)-31344
Henley, Samuel. 31345-31346, 95977
Henlin, Peter. see Henlyn, Peter.
Henlyn, Peter. 31653-(31657)
Hennebo, R. tr. 36193
Hennepin, Johannes. see Hennepin, Louis,
   1640-1701?
Hennepin, Louis, 1640-1701? 4806, 4936,
   19616, (20247), 25853, (31347)-31374,
   69299, (79995), 80002, (80023), 91139,
   95332, 98752
Hennequin, Joseph Francois Gabriel, 1775-
   1842. 18331
Henni, J. M., Bp. 31375, 56883
Hennig, Christian Gottfried. tr. (10914),
   31376, (36957)
Henning, Thomas. 31377
Henningio, Marco. tr. 27781
Henningsen, C. F. (31378)
Henri, Chanoine de Mayence. cartographer
   76838
Henri IV, King of France, 1553-1610.
   (14991), 50223 see also France.
   Sovereigns, etc., 1589-1610 (Henri IV)

Henri, C. tr. 58789
Henri le chancelier. 93416
Henrici Glareani Helvetii, poetae lavreati, De
   geographia liber vnvs. 27537, 27539-
   27540, (27542)-27544, 27546
Henrici Glareani poetae lavreati De geographi
   liber vnvs. 27538
Henrion, D. 33563
Henrion, Mathieu R. A., Baron. 31379-31380
Henrion de Flozelles, --------. 8015
Henriques Leal, Antonio. see Leal, Antonio
   Henriques.
Henriquez, Francisco. 31382
Henriquez, Leonardo. 94351
Henriquez de Guzman, Luis, Conde de Alva
   de Aliste y de Villaflor. 61135, 99617
   see also Peru (Viceroyalty) Virrey,
   1655-1661 (Henriquez de Guzman)
Henriquez de Ribera, Payo. see Ribera,
   Payo Henriquez de, Abp.
Henry VI, King of England, 1421-1771. suppo
   author 84584
Henry VII, King of England, 1457-1509. 2959
   see also Great Britain. Sovereigns,
   etc., 1485-1509 (Henry VII)
Henry VIII, King of England, 1491-1547.
   (55249) see also Great Britain.
   Sovereigns, etc., 1509-1547 (Henry VIII)
Henry VIII, King of England, 1491-1547.
   spirit author 78374-78375, 100799
Henry, Prince of England. spirit author
   78374-78375, 100799
Henry, ------------. tr. 5208, 6970, 31406
Henry, ------------. fl. 1812. 31405
Henry, A. G., d. 1865. 84483
Henry, Alexander. 31383
Henry, Angel Antonio. 31384
Henry, Caleb Sprague, 1804-1884. 31385-
   (31388), 54846, 77257
Henry, David. 16303, 31389, (54897)
Henry, George. 31390
Henry, George. tr. 36589
Henry, George W. 31391
Henry, Gustavus Adolphus, 1804-1880. 31392
Henry, Guy V. 31393
Henry, Isaac S. 83230
Henry, J. 10171, 10441, (31394)
Henry, James. 31395
Henry, James. jr. (31396)
Henry, John, British spy. 48068, 69819 see
   also Great Britain. Secret Agent for
   Effecting a Separation of the United
   States.
Henry, John, fl. 1812. 23020, (31399)
Henry, John, fl. 1821. 31398
Henry, John, fl. 1852. (31397)
Henry, John Joseph. 31400-31401
Henry, Joseph, 1799-1878. 31403, 53434,
   70474, 85002, 85005, 85024, 85026,
   85076, 85084, 85090 see also
   Smithsonian Institution. Secretary.
Henry, Jospeh, 1799-1878. petitioner 85039
Henry, Joseph, fl. 1839. 31402
Henry, M. S. 31404, 39880
Henry, P. 89220
Henry, P. F. 31407, (81617), 91081-91082,
   91083, 98442
Henry, Patrick, 1736-1799. 11005, 25595,
   31408, 34579-34580, (39521), (78388),
   99584, 100003, 100192, 100211-100212,
   note just before 103108 see also
   Virginia. Governor, 1776-1779 (Henry)
   Virginia. Governor, 1784-1786 (Henry)
   Virginia. Committee of Safety.
Henry, Robert. 31409

Henry, Robert P. 31410
Henry, Robert R. 31411
Henry, Samuel. (31412)
Henry, Symmes C. 31413-(31414)
Henry, T. Charlton. 31415
Henry, T. F. tr. (44793)
Henry, W. A. 56189
Henry, Walter. 31416-(31417), note after 96968
Henry, William. (62280) see also Philadelphia County, Pa. Lieutenant.
Henry, William S. (31418)
Henry, William Wirt. 31419
Henry, Ill. North Illinois University. see North Illinois University, Henry, Ill.
Henry Adams as a historian. 84787
Henry and Frances. 99418
Henry B. Fearon's narrative. 84304-84306, 84320-84321
Henry Boynton Smith: his life and work. (82712)
Henry C. Carey on national matters. 10842
Henry Clay and the administration. 13557
Henry County; past and present. 63406
Henry VIII. and his court. 51245
Henry Franklin. pseud. see Wakefield, Priscilla (Bell)
Henry H. Leeds & Minor. firm see Leeds (Henry H) & Minor. firm
Henry H. Leeds & Minor Auctioneers, office No. 93 Liberty Street. 83842
Henry Hedgehog. pseud. see Hedgehog, Henry. pseud.
Henry Homespun, Jr. pseud. see Southwick, Solomon.
Henry Hudson. note before 100436
Henry Hudson in Holland. (51463)
Henry Hudson, the navigator. 2184
Henry J. Raymond and the New York Press. 46979
Henry Kingsbury and his descendants. 19032
Henry; or, the juvenile traveller. 31420
Henry Oxnard Preble, 1847-1871. 65008
Henry Roberts; or, Incidents of the war of 1861-62-63. (31421)
Henry St. John, gentleman. 16315
Henry W. Rogers on the rebellion. (72677)
Henry Ward Beecher and Theodore Parker. 4315, 26706
Henry Wheaton, & al. versus Richard Peters, & al. 103162
Henshaw, David, 1791-1852. 31422-(31425), (57637), 103003
Henshaw, David, 1791-1852. supposed author 100662
Henshaw, J. Sidney. 2095, (31430)
Henshaw, John C. defendant at court martial 31426
Henshaw, John Prentis Hewley, Bp. 16312, 31427-31429, 51262, note before 90694
Henshaw, Josiah. defendant before church council 90691
Henshaw, Sarah Edwards. (31431)
Henson, Gravenor. 31434
Henson, Josiah. 31432-31433, note after 92624
Hensseir, -------. 31435
Hentz, Caroline Lee. 31436
Hentz, N. M. 31437-31438, 94196
Hentz, N. M. incorrectly supposed author 31439, 97306
Heny, G. A. 31440
Henz, Rath. ed. 4643
Hepburn, David. 26621
Hepburn, John. 31441
Hepburn, Robert S. E. 31442
Heptameron des nouvelles de tres illustre et tres excellente Princesse Marguerite de Valois. 44535

Hepworth, George Hughes, 1833-1902. 31443-31446
Her bereaved consort. pseud. Discourse . . . [on] the death of Mrs. Elizabeth Howard. see Howard, Simeon.
Her curse and her cure. 68154
Her daughter. pseud. ed. Journal and correspondence of Miss Adams. see De Windt, Carolina Amelia (Smith)
Her dying words. 105467
Her father. pseud. Discourse on the sabbath following the funeral of Miss Elizabeth P. Hooker. see Hooker, Edward W.
Her father. pseud. Silentiarius. see Mather, Cotton, 1663-1728.
Her husband. pseud. Elegy to the memory of Mrs. Mary Wharton. see Wharton, Charles Henry.
Her husband. pseud. Sketches of the religious life and faith of Mrs. Lydia Hale Keep. see Keep, John.
Her mother. pseud. Brief memoir of Harriet [M. Gardiner.] see Gardiner, Mrs. William.
Her mother, H. L. M. pseud. Florence Murray. see Murray, H. L.
Her pastor. pseud. Close of a sermon. see Sprague, William Buell.
Her sister. pseud. Memoir of the author. see Erma, ---------.
Her trials and interests in connection with the war. 45253
Hera, Jose Santos de la. 31447
Herald (Brig) in Admiralty 63405
Herald almanac for the United States, for 1849. 31448
Herald of freedom extra. 105032
Herald of Gospel liberty. 31449, (82485)
Herald of internal improvement. see Civil engineer and herald of internal improvement.
Herald of knowledge. 96285
Herald of life & immortality. 92486
Herald of peace. 99799
Herald of peace and truth to all saints. 57190
Herald of progress. see Social pioneer, and herald of progress.
Herald of salvation. 84281
Herald of the American Temperance Society. 89491
Herald of the New Jerusalem. 31450
(Herald of the times) 23623, 31111
Herald of the union. 31451
Heraldic journal. 31452, 86790
Heraldo Espanol. 87162
Heraldo, periodico politico, literario y comercial. 31453
Herald-Dumesle, -------. 31454
Heras, Bartolome Maria de. see Maria de Heras, Bartolome, Abp.
Herbarium florae Brasiliensis. 44990
Herbemont, N. 87744
Herbermann, C. G. tr. 96193
Herberstein, Sigmund, Freiherr von, 1486-1566. (67737)
Herbert, Charles. 31456
Herbert, Francis. pseud. Talisman. see Bryant, William Cullen, 1794-1878. Sands, Robert Chares, 1799-1832. Verplanck, Gulian Crommelin.
Herbert, George. (31457)
Herbert, Henry Howard Molyneux. see Carnarvon, Henry Howard Molyneux Herbert, 4th Earl of, 1831-1890.
Herbert, Henry John George. see Carnarvon, Henry John George Herbert, 3d Earl of, 1800-1849.

Hermit, Lunar. pseud. see Lunar Hermit. pseud.

Hermit. (1133), 84585

Hermit; a poem. 73543

Hermit [by Oliver Goldsmith.] 100804

Hermit in America on a visit to Philadelphia. 101136-101137

Hermit in New-Jersey. pseud. Liberty, a poem. 40933

Hermit in Philadelphia. Second Series. 101138

Hermit of New Jersey. 53127

Hermit of Philadelphia. Second series. 101140

Hermit of St. Eirene. pseud. Ocean waves. see Schaad, J. Christian.

Hermit of the Colorado hills. 9552

Hermit, or an account of Francis Adam Joseph Phyle. (2283), 31920, 62589

Hermit: or the unparalleled sufferings and surprising adventures of Philip Quarll. 66949-(66950)

Hermit; or, the wonderful lamp. 82973

Hermitage. pseud. Life of Gen. Frank Pierce. (31511)

Hermitage, and other poems. (81016)

Hermite, Bernard l'. see L'Hermite, Bernard.

Hermite, Jacques l'. (8784), 11607, 14957-14960, 19152, 31501-31510, 33675, 43760, 67355, 68455, 1st note after 97141, 100932

Hermite de la Guiane. (36769)

Hermit's observations about the fair at Meadville. 89271

Hermosa, J. 31512

Hermosa y Salcedo, Francisco Ugarte de la. see Ugarte de la Hermosa y Salcedo, Francisco.

Hermoso, Fusastino de S. Juan. 48391

Hermosvra de Angelica. 98769

Hernaiz, Francisco. 23445

Hernan Cortes. Narracion familiar. 16946

Hernan Cortez en Tobasco. 24122, 24402

Hernandes de Ovideo, Gonzalo. see Ovideo, Gonzalo Hernandes de.

Hernandez, Ant. de Valle. 31513

Hernandez, Benito. 72811

Hernandez, Francisco. 31514-31517, 68027, 105727

Hernandez, James. 31518

Hernandez, Jose de la Luz. (31523)

Hernandez, Jose Maria Perez y. 31521-31522

Hernandez, Juan Jose. 31520

Hernandez, Juan Jose. defendant 31519

Hernandez, Marcos Reinel. see Santa Maria, Miguel de.

Hernandez, Pascual. tr. 38708

Hernandez, Pero. 9768

Hernandez, Roque. ed. 93579

Hernandez, Tome. 77094

Hernandez de Biedma, Luis. see Biedma, Luis Hernandez de.

Hernandez de Cordova, Francisco. see Cordova, Francisco Hernandez de.

Hernandez de Guzman, Felix. see Guzman, Felix Hernandez de.

Hernandez de Oviedo y Valdez, Gonzalo. see Oviedo y Valdes, Gonzalo Fernandez de, 1478-1557.

Hernandez de Quir, Pedro. see Queiros, Pedro Fernandes de, d. 1516.

Hernandez i Caldaza, Antonio. 23969-23971

Hernandez y Davalos, J. E. ed. 98806

Hernandia. 74025

Herndon, William Lewis. 31524

Hero and the slave. 44887

Hero boy. (31162)

Hero missionary. (59157)

Hero of Lake George. 55375

Hero of Medfield. 37880

Hero of no fiction. 3534, (39840)

Hero of two flights. 20653

Hero of western Virginia! 43024

Hero series, no. 3. 84064

Herod, John and Jesus. 47176

Heroe. Historia contemporanea. (31525)

Heroes and battles of the American revolution. 31526, 92215

Heroes and hunters of the west. 31527

Heroes and martyrs. (50358), (50361)

Heroes and martyrs of Georgia. 24969

Heroes and martyrs of the modern missionary enterprise. 83495

Heroes and patriots of the south. 30681

Heroes are historic men. 22259

Heroes Brazileiros na campanha do sul em 1865. 74641

Heroes of Albany. (13361)

Heroes of discovery. 51092

Heroes of the XVIIIth century. 34367

Heroes of the lake. 31528, note after 105184

Heroes of the last lustre. 49217

Heroes of the nineteenth century. 31529

Heroes of the north, or the battles of Lake Eire, and Champlain. 103721

Heroes of the "rank and file." 32428

Heroes of the revolution. 26029

Heroes of the west. (4724)

Heroi-comico-serious-parodical-pindaric ode. 6511

Heroi-satiri didactic poem. 35088

Heroic address, for the fourth of July, 1813. 31530, 36410

Heroic incidents of the civil war in America. 31531

Heroic patriotism. 43393

Heroic periods of a nation's history. (40853)

Heroic poem. 37062

Heroic poem, from the taking of Minorca, by the French. 101257, 104110-104111

Heroic poem on the taking of Gen. Burgoyne, &c. 63626

Heroic poem: to which is annexed a thanksgiving epistle of electioneering success. 96324

Heroic poem. With notes critical and explanatory. 78473

Heroic speech, at the head of her army against the Spaniards. 68259

Heroic succession. 21156

Heroic women of the west. 26030

Heroical poem. 36566

Heroicidad del espiritu de S. Francisco de Assis. 72516

Heroicvm. 25994, 79345

Heroina diligente, corona de su esposo. (73078)

Heroine Chretienne du Canada. 23650, 39588

Heroine de Chateauguay. (12573)

Heroine du Texas. (23581), 31532, note before 95090

Heroine of Fort Laramie. 67299

Heroine of Tennessee. 70448

Heroine of the Confederacy. 56655

Heroine of the rebellion. 36862

Heroines of history. 31642

Heroines of Methodism. 14328

Heroines of sacred history. 91116

Heroines of the missionary enterprise. 21808

Heroism and adventure in the nineteenth century. 31533, 90026

Heywood, Peter. 31674, 94199
Heywood, William S. 103035
Hezekiah. A Christian armed with strength.
46359, 46622
Hezekiah Hectic. pseud. see Hectic,
Hezekiah. pseud.
Hiatt, J. M. 31675
Hiawatha. 41922, (46832)
Hiawatha; poeme Indo-Americain. (41928)
Hiawatha: rendered into Latin. 41929, 55008
Hibbard, Augustine George, 1833- 31676,
104126
Hibbard, Billy. 31677, 86636, 104522
Hibbard, F. G. ed. 30077
Hibbard, Harry. 31678
Hibbard, J. R. 31679
Hibbard, Rufus T. 31680
Hibbert, Edward. 31681
Hibbert, George. 7891, 31682, (81914), 98836
Hibbert, Mary. 31683
Hibbert, N. 31684-31685
Hibbert, Robert. 16624, (16626), 81972, 1st
note after 102803
Hibernia (Brig) in Admiralty 60180, 60582,
94236
Hibernia Fire Company, Philadelphia. 31686,
(61719)
Hibernia Fire Engine Company, no. 1. 31686
Hibernian chronicle. 79743
Hibernian Provident Society, New York. 54311
Hibernian Provident Society, Philadelphia.
see Society of the Friendly Sons of
St. Patrick, Philadelphia.
Hibernian Provident Society of New York.
31687
Hibernian Society, Philadelphia. see Society
of the Friendly Sons of St. Patrick,
Philadelphia.
Hibernian Society For the Relief of Emigrants
From Ireland, Philadelphia. see Society
of the Friendly Sons of St. Patrick,
Philadelphia.
Hibernicus. pseud. Letters on the natural
history. see Clinton, De Witt, 1769-
1828.
Hibernicus. pseud. Sketch of the life of
Samuel Neilson. 52298
Hibernus, or memoirs of an Irishman. 31688
Hic recens accedit Hannonis Carthaginensium.
(40046)
Hichborn, Benjamin. (6737), 31689-41690
Hickcox, John H. (31691)-31692
Hickeringill, Edmond. 31693-31695
Hickey, --------. defendant 49386, note
after 101854
Hickey, William. 16111, 20798, (31696), 2d
note after 98079
Hickling, --------, fl. 1854. 93608
Hickman, Edward. ed. 21974
Hickman, Edward C. 31697
Hickman, George H. 11356, 31698-31700,
(63839)
Hickman, Harris Hampden. 31701
Hickman, J. G. 31702
Hickman, John, 1810-1875. 31703, (37053)
Hickman, N. 3025, 13158, 31704-31705
Hickman, William. (31706)
Hickok, H. C. 59994
Hickok, Laurens P. (31707)
Hickok, M. J. (31708)
Hickory Hall; or, the outcast. 88662
Hickory series. 85370
Hicks, Albert W. defendant 31709
Hicks, E. (53692)
Hicks, Edward. 31715

Hicks, Elias, 1748-1830. 31710-31715, 56566
103059, 104521
Hicks, G. E. 31719
Hicks, Jennie E. supposed author 88962
Hicks, R. 31720
Hicks, Robert. defendant (16776)
Hicks, Rosanna. 104175
Hicks, Samuel. defendant (16787)
Hicks, Thomas, fl. 1673-1674. 59718, 59728
Hicks, Thomas, 1823-1890. 31721-31722
Hicks, Thomas Holliday, 1798-1865. 33150,
45120, 45329 see also Maryland.
Governor, 1858-1862 (Hicks)
Hicks, Whitehead, 1728-1780. 53630, 97291
see also New York (City) Mayor, 176
1776 (Hicks)
Hicks, Whitehead. complainant (16787)
Hicks. firm publishers see Mills and Hick
firm publishers Robertson, Mills and
Hicks. firm publishers
Hidalga, L. 31724
Hidalgo, Ignacio Xavier. 31725
Hidalgo, Jose. 31726-31727
Hidalgo, Jose Maria Zelaa e. see Zelaa e
Hidalgo, Jose Maria.
Hidalgo, Miguel. 31728-31730
Hidatsa-English dictionary. 80015
Hidatsa grammar. 80015
Hidatsa (Minnetaree) English dictionary. 800
Hidden life of a Christian. 97382
Hidden orgies of Mormonism practised in
Nauvoo and its temple. 98494
Hidden things brought to light. 70894-(70895)
Hide and Leather Trade Dinner, New York,
1859. see Annual Dinner of the Hide
and Leather Trade of the City of New
York, 1859.
Hiemalis. pseud. Officia propria. 56756
Hiemcke, A. H. 31731
Hier komt Paul Jones aan Het is soon aardig
ventje. 36564
Hierarchy of the American Scientific, Educa-
tional and Philosophical Society. 18725
Hierarchy of the Catholic Church in the Unit
States. 80008
Hieronymus. pseud. Essay. 99610, note aft
105324
Hieronymus, Saint, ca. 340-420. 23114, 7683
99365, 106294, 106330-106331
Hierophant. 31732
Hiesler, William M. 31733
Higbee, Jeremiah. 31734
Higby, William. 31735
Higgenson, Francis. see Higginson, Francis
1587?-1630.
Higgins, B. 3632
Higgins, Dryan. 31736
Higgins, George. 60806, 85618 see also
Snyder, Cook and Co. firm
Higgins, Godfrey. 31737
Higgins, J. T. 52305, 57942, 76692
Higgins, James. 45374
Higgins, Thomas W. (31738)
Higginson, Francis, 1587?-1630. 31739-3174
106052
Higginson, Francis, fl. 1847. 31741
Higginson, Francis John, 1806-1872. 31742,
69428
Higginson, John, d. 1720. 31743-31746, (465
(46789), 49657-(49658), 51012, 67164,
92351, 94932, 104900
Higginson, John, d. 1720. supposed author
(19639)
Higginson, Nathaniel. (79447)
Higginson, S. 31750, 42450

Higginson, Stephen, 1743-1828. 31748-(31749), note after 94676, 1st note after 105630

Higginson, Stephen, 1743-1828. supposed author (29954), (31747)

Higginson, Stephen, Jr. 31751

Higginson, Thomas Wentworth, 1823-1911. (30745), 31752-31755, 84037

Higginson's journal of his voyage to New-England. 106052

High and Mighty, the Burgesses of the Royal State of Virginia, to the people of the non-slave-holding states. (31888), 63502, 100509

High attainment. 46360

High churchman vindicated." (32305)

High civilization the moral duty of Georgians. 22278

High Clifford. 97520

High court of justice. 11569

High Court of Justiciary, Edinburgh. see Edinburgh. High Court of Justiciary.

High esteem which God hath of the death of his saints. 104086

High-flying church-man stript of his legal robe, appears a Yaho. 39969-39970

High license and prohibition. 83701

High life in New York. 82134-(82135), 91282

High life in New-York and Saratoga. 64551

High private. pseud. Original poem. 57615

High private." 31756

High probability. 80911

High Street Baptist Church, Charlestown, Mass. see Charlestown, Mass. High Street Baptist Church.

High Street Congregational Sabbath School, Providence, R. I. see Providence, R. I. High Street Congregational Sabbath School.

High school magazine. 70586

High school policy of Massachusetts. 3676

High School Society, New York. 54312

High School Society, New York. Committee to Prepare a Plan of Instruction and Articles of Subscription. 54312

High School Society, New York. Trustees. 54312

High-School Synod, Newburgh, N. Y. 17270, 90007, note before 96989

High treason. 99096

High-waies of God and the king. (78365), 78379

High-ways of God and the king. 78378

Highdays and holydays in Old England and New England. 41735

Higher Christian education. 21512

Higher law. 31757

Higher law . . . . A discourse. 71936

Higher law: a lecture 47181

Higher law: a sermon for the times. 21266

Higher law" in its application to the fugitive slave bill. 42030

Higher law, in its relations to civil government. 33113

Higher law, tried by reason and authority. 31758, note after 89554A

Highest and lowest prices of gold for four years. 27708

Highest civilization a result of Christianity. 58369

Highest law. 32331

Highest use of learning. 32250

Highland brigade. 22275

Highland County, N. Y. 31759

Highlands, Mass. see Worcester, Mass.

Highlands. A tale of the Hudson. 31760, note after 101036

Highly important communication to all governments and nations. 85118

Highly important public epistle. 85119

Hightstown, N. J. Classical and Scientific Institute. see New Jersey Classical and Scientific Institute, Hightstown, N. J.

Highway from the Mississippi to the Pacific Ocean. 4787

Highway of all nations. (24999)

Highway of the seas in time of war. 42027

Higinson, John. 104900

Higuera y Amarilla, Bernabe de la. (69218)

Hija del crimen o la loca. 63725

Hija del medico. (19975)

Hijas de flora. 98118

Hijo de Tamaulipas. pseud. Apologia del Cuarto Congreso Constitucional. 94277

Hijo del pueblo. pseud. Dos palabras a los Espanoles de Cuba. see Soler y Gabarda, Geronimo.

Hijo del pueblo. (75916)

Hijos de Hernan Cortez. 22842

Hijos de los conquistadores. pseud. Noticias relatives a el primer plan de independencia. 56013

Hijos del Difunto S. D. Miguel Antonio Bravo de Saravia Irarrazabul. defendants 35049

Hijos y Herederos de Danres Arias Tenorio. plaintiffs 86408

Hilaire, August Francois Cesar Prouvencal de Saint. see Saint-Hilaire, Auguste Francois Cesar Prouvencal de, 1779-1853.

Hilaire, Edme Jean Hilaire Filleau de Saint. see Filleau de Saint Hilaire, Edme Jean Hilaire.

Hilaire, Isidore Geoffroy Saint. see Geoffroy Saint Hilaire, Isidore, 1805-1861.

Hildago, Joseph Maria Zelaa e. see Zelaa e Hildago, Joseph Maria.

Hildago, Miguel. (66521)

Hildago Costilla, Miguel. see Costilla, Miguel Hildago.

Hildago, Mexico. Ayuntamiento. 66114

Hildagos de Medellin. 98026

Hildebrand, Samuel S. 31761

Hildebrandt, Christoph. ed. 38284

Hildeburn, Charles Swift Riche, 1855-1901. 85249

Hildreth, F. A. 31762

Hildreth, Hosea. (31763)-31768

Hildreth, Hosea. supposed author (45654)

Hildreth, James. 31769

Hildreth, Richard, 1807-1865. 30589, 31770-(31792), 32129, 82065, 92476, 92494, 92528, 98425

Hildreth, Richard, 1807-1865. supposed author 16181, 29611, 30677, (31775)

Hildreth, Richard, 1807-1865. reporter (31792), 96818

Hildreth, Samuel Prescott, 1783-1863. (31793)-(31800), 77911, 82072, 84617

Hildrop, John. 31801

Hildt, John. ed. 54940

Hilfsquellen der Vereinigten Staaten von Nord-Amerika. 8051

Hilgard, Eugene W. 42230, (49501), (49503)-49504, 85072 see also Mississippi. State Geologist.

Hilgard, T. C. 69946

Hilhouse, William. 31802

Hill, A. F. (31803)

Hill, Aaron, 1685-1750. ed. 100719

Hill, Ambrose Powell, 1825-1865. 15367

Hill, Alonzo, 1800-1871. 31804-(31806), 39902, 105441 see also Worcester Sunday School Society. Secretary-Treasurer.

Hill, Anthony. (31807)

Hill, Benjamin Harvey, 1823-1882. 31808, 69861
Hill, Benjamin M. 31809
Hill, Benjamin Thomas. ed. 2d note after 95414
Hill, Benson Earle. 31810
Hill, Bradbury C. 84974
Hill, Charles W. 31811
Hill, Clement Hugh. 31812
Hill, D. H. ed. 38821
Hill, Ebenezer, 1766-1854. 31813, 31845
Hill, Elizabeth. (31814)
Hill, G. 31815
Hill, George. (73989), 2d note after 100820
Hill, George Canning. 31816-31819
Hill, George W. (31820)-31821
Hill, H. A. tr. 49837, (49839), 49841, 49844, 49848, 49850-49851, 3d note after 97291
Hill, H. R. 31827
Hill, Hamilton A. 31822-(31825)
Hill, Hannah. 31826
Hill, Herbert. ed. 88565
Hill, Ira. (31828)
Hill, Isaac. USN 79925
Hill, Isaac, 1788-1851. 3830, (23856), (31829)-(31832), 64621
Hill, J. J. 31833
Hill, James, called John the Painter. see Aitken, James, 1752-1777. defendant
Hill, Jeremiah. defendant before church council 31842
Hill, John, called John the Painter. see Aitken, James, 1752-1777. defendant
Hill, John. tr. 6352
Hill, John, 1716?-1775. supposed author note before 90250-90286
Hill, John, d. 1735. 31843
Hill, John, fl. 1816-1820. engr. 33529, 79935, note after 101087, 101742-101743
Hill, John Boynton. 31844-31846
Hill, Joshua. (31847)
Hill, Levi L. 86855, 93622
Hill, Mark Langdon. (20226), 20476, (31848)-31849, (37852)-(37853), 37856, 104779
Hill, N. N. 85144
Hill, Nicholas. 31850-(31851)
Hill, Pascoe Grenfell. (31852)
Hill, Philip Carteret. 31853
Hill, R. (31854)
Hill, Ralph, 1827-1899. 31855
Hill, Richard. 31858, 82987
Hill, Richard, 1795-1872. 28060, 28063, 31856-(31857)
Hill, Robert W. 31859
Hill, Rowland. 85250
Hill, S. S. 31860-31862
Hill, T. (81929)
Hill, Theophilus H. 31863
Hill, Thomas. 31865
Hill, Thomas, 1818-1891. 31864, 84013, 91049
Hill, Uri K. 99225
Hill, W. B. 31867
Hill, William. 31866
Hill, William H. (31868)
Hill, Wills. see Devonshire, Wills Hill, 1st Marquis of, 1718-1793.
Hill, Yankee. (55759)
Hill & Co. firm publishers 31870
Hill & Barton. firm publishers defendants 98052-98053
Hill and Moore. firm publishers 52885
Hill & Savage. firm publisher 31869
Hill & Co.'s Confederate States railroad guide. 31870

Hill and Moore's improved edition of the New Hampshire register. 52885
Hill & Savage's Confederate railroad guide. 31869
Hill difficulty. (12406)
Hillard, E. B. 31871
Hillard, George Stillman. 6488, (13660), 202 29263, 31872-31875, 45711, (69709)
Hillard, Isaac, b. 1737. 19608, 31891-31892 31915, 52628, 96011
Hillard, J. E. 13821
Hillary, Wilhelm, fl. 1788. 31336
Hillary, William, d. 1763. 31876-31877
Hille, ---------. 628, 66062
Hiller, Joseph. 31878
Hiller, O. Prescott. 31879-31880
Hillhouse, Augustus L. tr. 48694-48695
Hillhouse, James, 1687?-1740. 31881
Hillhouse, James, 1687?-1740. defendant be church council 19946, 53253
Hillhouse, James, 1754-1832. (31176), 31882 31884, (41688), 89207, 94745, 105796
Hillhouse, James, fl. 1822. 89346 see also Connecticut. School Fund Commissione
Hillhouse, James Abraham, 1789-1841. (318 31886, 74747
Hillhouse, Thomas. 31887
Hillhouse, William, 1757-1833. 17537, (3188 (31889), 63502, 81944, 100509
Hilliard, Henry Washington, 1808-1892. 238 (31890)
Hilliard, Isaac. see Hillard, Isaac, b. 1737
Hilliard, Joseph, d. 1843. (31893)
Hilliard, Richard. 8956-8957
Hilliard, Timothy, 1746-1790. (31894)-(31895 103350
Hilliard, William. 31896
Hilliard d'Auberteuil, Michel Rene, 1751-178 999, 9082, (21038), 31897-31904, 7506 75074
Hillier, Richard. 31905
Hilliger, G. tr. (77074)
Hillock, ---------. cartographer 35953-35954, 35962, (40141)
Hills, Alfred C. (31906)-31907
Hills, George. 31908
Hills, George Morgan. 31909
Hills, John. 31910
Hills, R. ed. 47315
Hills, lakes, and forest streams. 30107
Hillsboro, Oregon. Referee Sale of Real Estate, 1869. 84764
Hillsboro' farms. 13855
Hillsborough, Wills Hill, 1st Earl of. see Devonshire, Wills Hill, 1st Marquis of 1718-1793.
Hillsborough, Ill. First Congregational Chu 31913
Hillsborough, N. C. Convention, 1788. see North Carolina. Convention, Hillsboro 1788.
Hillsborough, Ohio. Oakland Female Semina see Oakland Female Seminary, Hills-borough, Ohio.
Hillsdale, Mich. Hillsdale College. see dale College, Hillsdale, Mich.
Hillsdale College, Hillsdale, Mich. 48760
Hillsdale College, Hillsdale, Mich. Ladie Literary Union. 88684
Hillside church. 12678
Hillyard, Isaac. see Hillard, Isaac.
Hillyer, Asa. (31916)
Hillyer, George S. defendant 70257 see a Kansas. Auditor. defendant
Hilt to hilt. 16316

Hiltell, Theodore H. 10022, 32276
Hilten, Janszoon Jan van. tr. 44268
Hiltner, Joannis. 77804
Hilton, John T. (6765), (31917), 74313, note
   after 97006
Hilton, R. B. (31917)
Hilton, W. 56056
Hilton, William, d. 1675. (31919)
Hiltzheimer, B. supposed author (2283),
   31920, 62589
Hime, Humphrey Lloyd. 31921
Himes, Joshua V. 10206, 31922, 49076
Himno de la guerra de la America. 31923
Himno de riego. 31923
Himno nacional Argentino. 31923
Himno nacional oriental. 31923
Himnos patrioticos. 31923
Himself. pseud. Memoirs of a nullifier.
   47565
Himson, Samuel. defendant 96939
Hinblick auf Deutsche Emigration und Deut-
   schen Handel. 77624
Hincheta, Jose. 31924
Hinchliff, Thomas Woodbine. 31925
Hinchliffe, Henry J. 31926
Hinchliffe, John, Bishop of Peterborough,
   1731-1794. 31927
Hinchman, Morgan. plaintiff 8466, 89212
Hinchman conspiracy case. 31928
Hinchman's trial considered in its relation to
   the public. 91816
Hinckley, ---------. illus. 89765
Hinckley, A. 31929
Hinckley, Frederic. 31930
Hinckley family. 48154
Hincks, Edward W. 31960
Hincks, Edward Y. 85212
Hincks, Sir Francis, 1807-1885. 10418, 10612,
   31931-31932, (33315), 82684-82685 see
   also Canada. Inspector General.
Hincks, John. defendant 96888
Hincks, Thomas. defendant 96888
Hind, James. alias see Aitken, James,
   1752-1777. defendant
Hind, Henry Youle. 10590, 10630, 31921,
   31933-31939
Hinde, William. 31946
Hinderances to a successful ministry. 78639
Hinderson, -------. 50231
Hindes, Samuel. defendant 31940, 45313
Hindman, Thomas Carmichael, 1828-1868.
   15368, 31941
Hindobro, Francisco Garcia de. 31942
Hinds, Ebenezer. 31943
Hinds, Richard Brinsley. 31944-31945
Hine, ---------. 17936
Hine, Homer. 31947
Hine, L. A. 31948-31949
Hines, David Theodore. 31950
Hines, Gustavus. (31951)-31953
Hine's progress pamphlets. 31949
Hingeley, E. 31954
Hingerle, A. (31955)
Hingham, William. 96935
Hingham, Mass. plaintiffs 88163
Hingham, Mass. Agricultural and Horticultural
   Society. see Agricultural and Horticul-
   tural Society, Hingham, Mass.
Hingham, Mass. Committee on the Financial
   Affairs. 31957
Hingham, Mass. Corner Stone Division, no.
   165. see Sons of Temperance of North
   America. Massachusetts. Corner Stone
   Division, no. 165, Hingham.
Hingham, Mass. First Church of Christ.
   101381

Hingham, Mass. Horticultural Society. see
   Agricultural and Horticultural Society,
   Hingham, Mass.
Hingham and Quincy bridges. 67289
Hingham patriot. 63494
Hingston, Edward P. 8646, 31959
Hinkley, Edward Otis. 45114-45115, 45117
Hinkley, Samuel. petitioner 13738, 31884
Hinman, Royal R. 6010, 15776, 39161-31963
Hinman, S. D. 31964
Hinojosa, ------- Ortiz de. see Ortiz de
   Hinojosa, --------.
Hinojoso, Alonso Lopez de. see Lopez de
   Hinojoso, Alonso.
Hinrichs, Gustavus. 35002, 77821
Hinsdale, Theodore. 25232, 73562, 102947
Hinslop, --------. 31995 see also Trinidad.
   Governor (Hinslop)
Hinssen, L. tr. 82270
Hint at the case. 63206
Hint of what may be said in opposition. 105664
Hint to the public. 20757
Hint to the south. 77631
Hinterlassenen Schriften. 89014
Hinton, John Howard. 31965-31968, 32220
Hinton, Richard J. 31969, (68526)
Hinton, William. 82835
Hints addressed to the public. 81396
Hints addressed to wise men. (31970), 42449,
   94678, 4th note after 98684
Hints and criticisms on the follies of the day.
   63931
Hints and information for the use of emigrants.
   62842
Hints and queries. (59756)
Hints and suggestions to intending emigrants.
   5917
Hints and suggestions to the tourist. 8224,
   41760
Hints by the Shamrock Society, New York.
   47436
Hints concerning Greenwood. (13609)
Hints for a specific plan for the abolition of
   the slave trade. 31971, 1st note after
   102835
Hints for American husbandmen. (31972),
   60296
Hints for Australian emigrants. 17967
Hints for Buncombe. (18366)
Hints for entering the River Saguenay. (74938)
Hints for essays. 8641
Hints for naval officers. 3860
Hints for our young people. 78795
Hints for relief. (22293)
Hints for some new regulations in the sugar
   trade. 31973
Hints for the control and prevention of
   infectious diseases. 30113, 76657
Hints for the people, &c. 24413
Hints for the people; with some thoughts on
   the presidential election. (74424)
Hints for the representatives of the country.
   60136
Hints on a cheap mode of purchasing the liberty.
   (31974)
Hints on a system of popular education. 104772
Hints on banking. 31975, 43676
Hints on colonization and abolition. 7693
Hints on dress and beauty. 82510
Hints on early rising. 86587A
Hints on emigration to Upper Canada. 20798,
   2d note after 98079
Hints on extemporaneous preaching. 71525
Hints on female education. 44626
Hints on female education, with an outline.
   44627

His friend. pseud. Letter to a clergyman.
see Catholicus. pseud.

His friend. pseud. Remains of Maynard
Davis Richardson. 71075

His friend. pseud. Yamoyden. see Sands,
Robert Charles, 1799-1832.

His friend in London. pseud. Letter to an
American planter. 40425

His guardian. pseud. Narrative of the early
days. see Welch, Andrew.

His Highness the Prince of Orange, his letter
to the Lords Spiritual and Temporal.
104144-104146

His Highness the Prince of Orange, his speech
to the Scots Lords and gentlemen.
104146

His Highness's additional declaration. 104143

His Honour the Prests proclamation. 98058B

His intimate friend. pseud. Biographical
notice of the late Hon. Dudley Atkins
Tyng, Jr. see Lowell, John.

His jewels. (31996)

His kinsman. pseud. Dialogue between an
uncle and his kinsman. 97723

His last message. 83291

His loving sister, Bull-a. pseud. Beauties
of Brother Bull-us. 4205

His Majesties gracious letter to the Earle
of Sovth-Hampton. 31998, 35676,
99886

His Majestie's letter to the Earle of Southampton. 31998, 35676, 99886

His majesties letter to the Lords Leifetenants.
90110

His Majesties propriety and dominion on the
Brittish seas asserted. 13514

His Majesty having been pleased, by his two
several orders. 99252

His Majesty Leopold I. King of the Belgians.
(36119)

His Majesty's declaration of war against the
King of Spain. 31997

His Majesty's explanatory notes on the new
treaty. 8127

His Majesty's Loyal Associated Refugees
Assembled at Newport, R. I. petitioners
(19156), 42563 see also American
Loyalists.

His Majesty's Loyal Subjects, Late West
Florida. petitioners 24847, 102767
see also American Loyalists.

His Majesty's most gracious letter to the
government of the Massathusets [sic]
Colony in New-England. 104147

His Majesty's most gracious speech to both
houses of Parliament, on Friday, October,
27, 1775. 32002

His Majesty's most gracious speech to both
houses of Parliament on Thursday,
October 26, 1775. 32001

His Majesty's most gracious speech to both
houses of Parliament, on Wednesday,
November 30, 1774. 32000

His Majesty's most gracious speech to
Parliament. 31999

His Majesty's proposals. 56134

His Majesty's royal commission to William
Cosby. (53693A)

His Majesty's royal decree. 68227

His Majesty's Ship Liverpool. 32003

His Majesty's . . . speech to both houses of
Parliament, October 26, 1775. 26996

His Majesty's Subjects Having Property In
and Lately Established Upon the Mosquito
Shore in America. petitioners see
British Honduras. Citizens. petitioners

His Majesty's Subjects, Settled on the Coast
of Yucatan, in the Bay of Honduras.
Petitioners see British Honduras.
Citizens. petitioners

His Majesty's Subjects, the Principal Inhabitants
of the Mosquito Shore. see British
Honduras. Citizens.

His Majesty's Suffering Loyalists. petitioners
see American Loyalists. petitioners

His parents. pseud. Memoir of Robert
Troup Paine. see Paine, Martyn.

His parishioner. pseud. Second dialogue,
between a minister and his parishioner.
see Bellamy, Joseph. and Taylor,
Nathaniel. supposed author

His peoples deliverance in times of danger.
(17064)

His recantation. 50696, 105629

His sister. pseud. Writings of Hugh Swinton
Legare. see Bullen, Mary Swinton
(Legare)

His son. pseud. ed. Short compilation of the
extraordinary life and writings of Thomas
Say. see Say, Benjamin. ed.

His son-in-law. pseud. Memoir of Dr. Thomas
Henderson. see Smith, Francis Henney,
1812-1890.

His spouse. pseud. Dialogue between a
southern delegate, and his spouce. 19933,
4th note after 98269

His successor. pseud. Memoir of Rev.
Thomas Sumner Winn. 104785

His supercargo. pseud. Wild achievements,
and romantic voyages, of Captain John
Francis Knapp. see S., J. W. pseud.

His ten wives. 85535

His voice to us in the terrible earthquake.
14496

His whole civil life. (25845)

His wife. pseud. Memoir of Daniel Safford.
see Safford, A. E.

His youngest son. pseud. ed. Autobiography
of Levi Hutchins. see Hutchins, Samuel,
1806-1884.

Hiscox, E. T. 31994

Hispania Damiani a Goes, Eqvitis Lvsitani.
(27689)

Hispania sive de regis Hispaniae-regnis et
optibus commentarius. 38560

Hispania victrix. 27725

Hispaniae bibliotheca. 77900

Hispaniae illvstratae sev rervm in Hispania et
praesertim in Aragonia gestarum scriptores varii. (77903)

Hispaniae illvstratae sev rervm vrbivmque
Hispaniae, Lvsitaniae, AEthiopiae et
Indiae scriptores varii. 32005, 77901-
77902

Hispaniae illvstratae sev vrbivm rervmque
Hispanicarvm, academiarvm, bibliothe-
carvm, clarorvm deniqve in omni
disciplinarvm genere scriptorum auctores
varii. 44545, 77904

Hispaniae veteris descriptio. 32005, 77901

Hispanic American historical review. 57959,
note after 95644

Hispanicae dominationis Arcana. 102504

Hispanicarum rerum scriptores aliquot ex
bibliotheca clarissimi viri Domini
Roberti Beli Angli. 4477, (32004)

Hispaniola, a poem. 103335

Hispaniola, Hayti, Saint Domingo. 3956

Hispanorum in America & India crudelitates
& barbaries. 102504

Hispanorum in Nouam Indiae continentis
Hispaniam. (8784)

Histoire de la mission des Peres Capvcins.
4, 106227
Histoire de la nation Juive. (40086), (51894),
3d note after 93855
Histoire de la navigation. 13419, 41368-
(41370), (41373), note after 41727
Histoire de la navigation, son commencement,
son progres. 13018
Histoire de la negociation de la France.
32014
Histoire de la Nouvelle-France. 40172,
40177, 99728
Histoire de la Novvelle-France. Contenant
les navigations, decouvertes, & habitations
faites par les Francois es Indes Occidentales & Nouvelle-France. 40173
Histoire de la Novvelle France contenant les
navigations, decouvertes, & habitations
faites par les Francois es Indes Occidentales & Nouvelle-France souz l'avoue &
authorite de noz Rois Tres-Chretiens.
(40169)-40171
Histoire de la Nouvelle-York. 84573
Histoire de la paix entre les Roys de France
et d'Espagne. 32015
Histoire de la persecution de deux saints
eveques. 10804
Histoire de la premiere decovverte et con-
qveste des Canaries. 32016
Histoire de la presse en Angleterre et aux
Etats Unis. (17828)
Histoire de la Princesse Jaiven Reine du
Mexique. (32017)
Histoire de la province de Sancta-Cruz.
(43795)
Histoire de la republique des Etats-Unis.
2247
Histoire de la republique d'Haiti. 96332
Histoire de la revolution d'Amerique. 67692-
67693
Histoire de la revolution de 1868. 67624
Histoire de la revolution de Saint-Domingue.
18333
Histoire de la Terre Nevve dv Peru en l'Inde
Occidentale. 32018, 57994
Histoire de la traite & de l'esclavage des
Negres. 26013
Histoire de la tribu des Osages. 100607
Histoire de la vie et des voyages de Christophe
Colomb. 35174
Histoire de la Virginie. 5115-5117, (74605)-
74606, note after 91491, 2d note after
100478, 2d note after 100518
Histoire de l'abolition de l'esclavage. 39045
Histoire de l'Academie des Sciences. 3604
Histoire de l'administration de Lord North.
(31901), 99561
Histoire de l'administration du Sieur Bigot.
(38696), 47528
Histoire de l'Amerique. 44477, 71990-71995
Histoire de l'Amerique Meridionale. (11741)
Histoire de l'Amerique Septentrionale. 2692,
100808
Histoire de l'eau-de-vie en Canada. 67020
Histoire de l'emigration Europeenne. 21480
Histoire de l'empire du Bresil. 101359
Histoire de l'esclavage pendant les deux
dernieres annees. 77748
Histoire de l'etablissement des Francais.
17156
Histoire de l'expedition aux Rivieres d'Orenoque
et d'Apure. 31989
Histoire de l'expedition de trois vaisseaux.
4379
Histoire de l'expedition des Francais, a Saint-
Domingue. 48211

Histoire de l'expedition des Francais au
Mexique. 22564
Histoire de l'Exposition Universelle de 1855.
72030
Histoire de l'Hotel-Dieu de Quebec. 36825
Histoire de l'ile de Cuba. 17786
Histoire de l'ile de Saint-Domingue, depuis
l'epoque de sa decouverte. 3885, 36956-
(36957)
Histoire de l'ile Saint-Domingue. 21896
Histoire de l'Indie. 11387
Histoire de l'inoculation preservative de la
fievre jaune. (44443)
Histoire de l'insurrection du Canada. 58489
Histoire de l'intervention Francaise au Mexique.
(39838), 47036
Histoire de l'intervention Francaise au Mexique
1862-1867. 21490
Histoire de l'isle de Barbades. 36944, 68430
Histoire de l'isle de Saint-Domingue. 44140
Histoire de l'isle Espagnole ou de S. Domingue.
12127
Histoire de Mademoiselle Villars. 12554,
note after 99431, 1st note after 100838
Histoire de Miss Montague. 50047
Histoire de Moncade. (32019)
Histoire de Mgr. de Laval. (7430)
Histoire de M. Cleveland, fils naturel de
Cromwel. 65408
Histoire de Monsieur Cleveland, fils naturel de
Cromwel. 65409
Histoire de New-York. (35166)
Histoire de Nicaragua. 57996
Histoire de Nicolas I. Roy du Paraguai. 32020,
92200
Histoire de nouvelles decouvertes. 25914
Histoire de Philippe II. 94854
Histoire de Philippe Emmanuel de Lorraine.
50220
Histoire de Portvgal. 57805
Histoire de premier, second et troisieme
voyages. 16262
Histoire de sa vie et de ses voyages. (73266)
Histoire de S. Domingue. 12128
Histoire de St. Domingue, republique d'Haiti.
75128
Histoire de Samuel. 100791
Histoire de ses revolutions. 75195
Histoire de Toussaint-Louverture. (17189),
(42351)
Histoire del islande. 26330
Histoire del S. D. Fernando Colombo. 97682
Histoire der beroerten van Engelandt. (42757)
Histoire der Boecaniers. (23469)
Histoire der Engelsche zee-roovers. 36193
Histoire der Reisen oder Sammlung von
Reisebeschreibungen. 32095
Histoire der Sevarambes. 74822
Histoire des Abenakis. 46948
Histoire des Amazones anciennes et modernes.
(29366)
Histoire des Antilles et des colonies Francaises.
(68924)
Histoire des arbes forestiers. 48693
Histoire des avanturiers filibustiers. (23477)-
23478, 36192, 67985
Histoire des avanturiers que se sont signalez
dans les Indes. (23475)-(23476)
Histoire des caciques d'Haiti. 52057
Histoire des Canaries. 4850
Histoire des chenes de l'Amerique, ou descrip-
tions et figures. 48691
Histoire des chenes de l'Amerique Septentrionale.
48701
Histoire des chenes de l'Amerique Septentrionale,
consideres principalment sous les rapports
de leur usage. 48696

Histoire des Chichimeques ou des anciens rois de Tezcuco. 35320
Histoire des choses et des hommes de Juillet. (77096)
Histoire des choses memorables advenves en la terre dv Bresil. 99728
Histoire des choses plus memorables aduenes en Maragnan. 106227
Histoire des choses plus memorables advenues tant ez Indes Orientales. (35790)
Histoire des colonies Europeennes. 9284
Histoire des colonies fondees par les Anglais. (44793)
Histoire des colonies Francaises. 39651
Histoire des decouvertes des Europeens. 3656
Histoire des decouvertes et conquestes des Portugais. (38591)-(38592)
Histoire des decouvertes et des voyages faits dans le nord. (25137)
Histoire des decouvertes faites par divers savans voyageurs. (58329)
Histoire des decouvertes geographiques des Hollandais. 19647
Histoire des demoiselles de Saint-Javier. 58063
Histoire des dernieres trovbles dv Bresil. (50579), 50724
Histoire des derniers mois de l'empire Mexicain. 31484
Histoire des desastres de Saint-Domingue, ouvrage ou l'on expose les causes de ces evenemens. 11108, 75130
Histoire des desastres de Saint-Domingue, precedee d'un tableau. 3312, 75129
Histoire des deux conquerans tartares. 4936
Histoire des deux voyages entrepris par ordre du gouvernement Anglais. 25631
Histoire des differens peuples du monde. 57730
Histoire des drogues. 115, 14355
Histoire des etablissements . . . des Europeens. 68081
Histoire des etats et des territoires. 23557
Histoire des Etats-Unis. 35874
Histoire des Etats-Unis d'Amerique. Par Charles Oge Barbaroux. 3298
Histoire des Etats-Unis d'Amerique. [Par Samuel G. Goodrich.] 27899
Histoire des Etats-Unis d'Amerique. Par Theophile Maynard. 47169
Histoire des Etats-Unis d'Amerique; par Theophile Menard. 47796
Histoire des Etats-Unis de l'Amerique Septentrionale. 77531
Histoire des Etats-Unis depuis la decouverte du continent Americain. 3123
Histoire des Etats-Unis, racontee aux enfants. 39935
Histoire des finances. (21147)
Histoire des flibustiers. 1905
Histoire des gverres civiles des Espagnols dans les Indes. 98750
Histoire des hommes de couleur dans les colonies Francaises. (47421)
Histoire des Incas. 98751
Histoire des Incas, rois du Perou. 98751
Histoire des Indes, de. J. P. Maffei. (43782)
Histoire des Indes de Portugal. 11388
Histoire des Indes Orientales. (19447)
Histoire des Indes Orientales et Occidentales. (43783)
Histoire des Indiens de l'Amerique Septentrionale. 3246
Histoire des Indiens des Etats-Unis. 49962

Histoire des Indies Occidentales. 11272
Histoire des Isles Sandwich et de la mission Americaine. (32021)
Histoire des joyavx. 12010, 32022
Histoire des Lepidopteres les plus rares de Georgie. (82789A)
Histoire des loix principales. 9601
Histoire des maladies de S. Domingue. 64730
Histoire des martyrs. 45015
Histoire des missions. 12294
Histoire des nations civilisees. 7429
Histoire des naufrages. 19619, 19621, 23567, note after 32002
Histoire des navigations aux terres australes. (8388), 89444, 89451, note after 99383C
Histoire des negociations commerciales et naritimes. 78918
Histoire des nouvelles decouvertes faites dans la mer du Sud. 25913
Histoire des oiseaux du Bresil. 19692
Histoire des ordres monastiques. 31282
Histoire des pays septentrionaux. 43834
Histoire des peches. 70100, 101231-note after 101231, 1st note after 106377
Histoire des peuples Americains. 49862
Histoire des peuples du nord. 103157
Histoire des Picea. 8753
Histoire des pins et des sapins de l'Amerique Septentrionale. 48697
Histoire des pirates Anglois. 36192
Histoire des plantes de la Guiane Francaise. 2348
Histoire des plantes de l'Europe. 32023
Histoire des plantes les plus remarquables du Bresil et du Paraguay. (75216), 75220
Histoire des plantes, novvellement trouuees en l'isle Virginie. 32024, 72042
Histoire des plus illustres et scavans hommes de leurs siecles. 95341
Histoire des progres de la puissance navale et l'Angleterre. (75532)-75533
Histoire des progres de l'un des Etats-Unis d'Amerique. 25969
Histoire des pyramides de Quito. (38478)
Histoire des relations commerciales entre la France et le Bresil. 77353
Histoire des relations des Hurons et des Abnaquis du Canada. 47977
Histoire des religions. 4933
Histoire des religions de tous les royaumes du monde. 36770
Histoire des revolutions d'Haiti. 74984
Histoire des revolutions politiques et litteraire de l'Europe. (77657)
Histoire des Sevarambes. 98299
Histoire des societes du temperance des Etats Unis. 2785
Histoire des simples medicamens apportes de l'A-merique. [sic] 49948
Histoire des simples medicamens apportes des terres neuves. 49947
Histoire des terres novvellement descovvertes. 69210
Histoire des Tolteques. 9561
Histoire des traites de paix entre les puissanc de l'Europe. 38201
Histoire des traites de paix, et autres negotiations. 75477
Histoire des tremblemens de terre. 42596
Histoire des trembleurs. 32025
Histoire des troubles de l'Amerique Anglaise. 87291
Histoire des troubles de l'Amerique Anglaise, ecrite sur les memoires. 87290
Histoire des troubles de St. Domingue. 26756

Histoire des voyages et decouvertes des compagnons de Christophe Colomb. (35209)

Histoire des Wahabis. 57222

Histoire des Yncas. 98743, 98748

Histoire des Yncas du Perou. 36812, 2d and 4th notes after 97689

Histoire des Yncas, rois du Perou. 98752

Histoire des Yncas, roys dv Perv. 98743

Histoire descriptive et pittoresque de Saint Domingo. 44638

Histoire d'Ethiopie. 36944, 68430

Histoire d'Haiti. 43704

Histoire d'Haiti (Ile de Saint-Domingue). 44141

Histoire diplomatique du Chevalier Portugais Martin Behaim. 51479

Histoire du Baron de Pufendorff. (8783)

Histoire du Bresil. 28292

Histoire du Bresil, depuis sa decouverte en 1500. 4154

Histoire du Bresil Francais au seizieme siecle. 99728

Histoire du Canada. 61006

Histoire du Canada, a l'usage des ecoles et des familles. 73745

Histoire du Canada de F. X. Garneau. (5147)

Histoire du Canada, de son eglise et de ses missions. 7431, 24110

Histoire du Canada depuis sa decouverte jusqu'a nos jours. (26675)-26676

Histoire du Canada en tableaux. 38884

Histoire du Canada et des Canadiens. 5160

Histoire du Canada et coyages. 74881-74882, 74885-74886

Histoire du Canada par l'Honorable William Smith. 43858, 84701, 99776

Histoire du Canada, par M. l'Abbe de Belmont. 67020

Histoire du Canada, sous la domination Francaise. 5159

Histoire du Christianisme des Indes. 38510

Histoire du commerce de toutes les nations. 77607

Histoire du commerce et de la civilization au nord. 73466

Histoire du commerce et de la navigation des peuples anciens. 32026

Histoire du commerce et de l'industrie. 7432

Histoure du commerce homicide appele traite des noirs. 13477

Histoire du conflit Americain de ses causes. 87144

Histoire du 18 Fructidor. (39107)

Histoire du XIXe siecle. 27202

Histoire du fanatisme. 32025

Histoire du fleuve Amur. (51287)

Histoire du General de Lafayette. 95803

Histoire du General Lafayette en Amerique. 68926

Histoire du General Moreau. (12277)

Histoire du grand marais maudit. 92399

Histoire dv grand royavme de la Chine. 27780, 47828-47829

Histoire du Groenland. 14374

Histoire du Japon et du Paraguay. 12134

Histoire du massacre. 24319

Histoire dv massacre de plvsievrs religievx. 32027

Histoire du Mexique. 95146

Histoire du Mexique. Juarez et Maximilien. 20548

Histoire du monde. (12606)

Histoire du Montreal 1640-1672. 67023

Histoire dv Nouveau Monde. (38558)

Histoire du Paraguay. 12129-12130

Histoire du Paraguay: Par Mlle Celliez. 11660

Histoire du Paraguay sous les Jesuites. (21763)

Histoire du passe, du present et de l'avenir probable du Haut-Saguenay. (62863), 74941

Histoire du pays nomme Spitsberghe. (32028)

Histoire du Pere Sahagun. 35319

Histoire du Perou. Par le P. Anello Oliva. (57186)

Histoire du Perou. Par Miguel Cavello Balboa. 2860

Histoire du Peru, partie principale des Antipodes. 9873

Histoire du peuple Americain. 10917

Histoire du Pierre Soule. 47924

Histoire du Portugal et de ses colonies. 6852

Histoire du premier etablissement dans la Virginie. 5115-5117, 2d note after 100478

Histoire du regne de Ferdinand et d'Isabelle. 65286

Histoire du regne de Philippe II. 65293

Histoire du royaume de Chili. 35757

Histoire du royaume de Quito. 98793

Histoire du tabac. 2758, 64875

Histoire du temps de l'empire. 93412

Hisoire du temps du Christophe Colomb. 16480

Histoire du voyage. 11411

Histoire du voyage, par Dumont-Durville. 21216

Histoire du voyage, par P. Gaimard et E. Robert. 26330

Histoire du voyage por Capitaine J. Ribault. 24894, note after 94854, 94856

Histoire d'un pou Francois. 32029, 32119

Histoire d'un traite de paix. 78919

Histoire d'un voyage aux Isles Malouines. 60996

Histoire d'vn voyage faict en la terre dv Bresil. 40149-40150

Histoire d'vn voyage fait en la terre dv Bresil. 40148, (40151)

Histoire d'vn voyage fait en la terre dv Bresil, dite Amerique. 40152

Histoire d'une juene Creole de la Guateloupe. 10327

Histoire d'une jeune fille sauvage. 34141

Histoire d'une persucution fait au Japon. 68455

Histoire ecclesiastique, politique et litteraire du Chili. (23573)

Histoire ende het leven van den . . . Keyser Caerle V. 97678

Histoire et commerce des Antilles Angloises. 9601

Histoire et commerce des colonies Angloises. 9602, 30794-30795, 34027, 2d note after 65324

Histoire et decouvertes de l'Amerique. 10296

Histoire et description de toutes les plantes. (75219)

Histoire et description des voies de communica-tion. 12583

Histoire et description du Kamtschatka. (38304)

Histoire et description generale de la Nouvelle France. 12135-12136

Histoire et geographie par Malte-Brun. 44161

Histoire et la geographie illustrees des Etats-Unis. 44161

Histoire & martyre de onze mille vierges. 38619, 98167

Histoire et voyages des Indes Occidentales. 16710

Histoire generale botanique. 97508

Histoire generale, civile, naturelle, politique, et religieuse. 38731
Histoire generale de la marine. 6158
Histoire generale de l'Amerique. 96337
Histoire generale de l'Asie. 73453
Histoire generale de l'etablissement du Christianisme. 6019
Histoire generale de l'origine et progrez des Freres Mineurs. 67915
Histoire generale de l'Univers. 38710
Histoire generale de Portugal. 38468
Histoire generale de Portugal. Par Mr. Legeuen de la Nevfville. (38862)
Histoire generale des Antilles. 19763-19764
Histoire generale des Antilles, habitees par la Francais. 21458, 72314
Histoire generale des ceremonies. (4932)
Histoire generale des choses de la Nouvelle-Espagne. 74951
Histoire generale des divers etats d'Europe. 32030
Histoire generale des insectes de Surinam. 47961
Histoire generale, des isles de S. Christophe. 21457
Histoire generale des missions Catholiques. 31379
Histoire generale des peches anciennes et modernes. 55406
Histoire generale des races humaines ou philosophie ethnographique. 75804
Histoire generale des traites de paix. 26601
Histoire generale des voyages. 3656, (16952), 16963, 28539, 48490, 52370, 65402, 85380, 92204
Histoire generale des voyages et conqvetes des Castillans. 31547-31550
Histoire generale des voyages et decouvertes maritimes et continentales. 16368
Histoire generale des voyages ou nouvelle collection. 65403-65404
Histoire generale d'Espagne, comprinse en XXVII liures. 47117
Histoire generale d'Espagne, du P. Jean de Mariana. 44554
Histoire generale et iconographique de lepidopteres. 6155
Histoire generale et raisonnee de la diplomatie Francaise. 24675
Histoire generalle des Indes Occidentales & terres nuues. 27746-27749, 102836
Histoire geographique de la Nouvelle Ecosse. (38564)-(38565), (56137)
Histoire geographique du Bresil. 19547
Histoire impartiale des evenemens militaires et politiques. 38389, 41905
Histoire interessante du naufrage du R. P. Crespel. 17477
Histoire maritime de France et des colonies. 29109
Histoire maritime des Provinces Unies. 7406
Histoire medicale de l'armee Francaise. (27350)
Histoire memorable du derniere voyage eux Indes. 39634
Histoire moderne des Chinois. (44825)
Histoire moeurs et coutumes des nations Indiennes. 31206
Histoire, moeurs, usages et coutumes des habitans. 94416
Histoire morale des iles Antilles de l'Ameriqve. (72317)
Histoire morale des peuples sauvages. 2580, 70904
Histoire naturelle, agricole et economique du mais. 6263

Histoire naturelle, civile et geographique de l'Orenoque. (29277)
Histoire naturelle de la Caroline, de la Floride et des isles de Bahama. (11513)
Histoire naturelle de la Caroline, Floride. 11514
Histoire naturelle de la cochenille. 74500
Histoire naturelle de la Hollande Equinoxile. 24114
Histoire naturelle de l'homme. 65478
Histoire naturelle de l'ile de Cuba. 29110
Histoire naturelle de l'island du Groenland. 1408A
Histoire naturelle de l'islande et du Groenland. 1408
Histoire naturelle des colibris. 40215
Histoire naturelle des oiseaux de paradis. 40215
Histoire naturelle des oiseaux de paradis et des rolliers. 40731
Histoire naturelle des oiseaux du Paraguay et de la Plata. 2541
Histoire naturelle des oiseaux-mouches. 40215
Histoire naturelle des orthopteres du Mexique. (77209)
Histoire naturelle des peoples. 19615
Histoire naturelle . . . des picides. (44121)
Histoire naturelle des volcans. 57505
Histoire naturelle du pais. 19615
Histoire naturelle du sucre et du cacao. 67091
Histoire naturelle d'une partie d'oiseaux nouveaux et rares. 40731, 1st note after 98298
Histoire naturelle et agricole de cette cereale. 6262
Histoire naturelle et civile de la Californie. 98843
Histoire natvrelle et generalle des Indes. 57992-(57993)
Histoire naturelle et morale des Antilles. 72323
Histoire naturelle et morale des Isles Antilles. 72314-72319
Histoire natvrelle et moralle des Indes. 125
Histoire naturelle et politique de la Pensylvanie 36991, 73490
Histoire naturelle, generale et particuliere. (41054)
Histoire naturelle-histoire-theologie Moeurs et coutumes. (69595)
Histoire naturelle, morale, civile et politique de l'Asie. 73491
Histoire notable de la Floride. 39234-39235
Histoire novvelle dv Novveav Monde. 4795
Histoire ofte larlijck verhael. 38556
Histoire ov commentaires advenues depuit LXX ans. 93887
Histoire philosophique et politique des etablissemens et du commerce des Europeens dans l'Afrique Septentrionale. 68082
Histoire philosophique et politique des etablissemens et du commerce des Europeens dans les deux Indes. 11824, 47206, 58239, (61313), (68072)-(68075), 68077-68078, 68080-68085, 68097-68103, 68110-68111, 68013, 92197
Histoire philosophique et politique des isles Francoises. 68083
Histoire physique des Antilles Francaises. 50555
Histoire physique, economique et politique du Paraguay. 19473
Histoire physique, politique et naturelle de l'ile de Cuba. 29110, 74922
Histoire pittoresque des voyages dans les cing parties du monde. 30849

Historia natvrele, e morale delle Indie. 124
Historia natvralis Brasiliae. 7588, 63028
Historia naturalis Palmarum, opus tripartitum. 44991
Historia navalis, sive celeberrimorum Praeliorum. 95777
Historia navigationis anno 1577. 5053
Historia navigationis australis. (14350)-(14351), 31539-31543
Historia navigationis in Brasiliam quae et American dicitvr. 6118, 32041, 40153-(40154), 94273
Historia navigationis Martini Frobisseri. (25995), 79346
Historia nova e completa da America. 62955
Historia of avontuurlyke reize. 35134
Historia Olai Magni Gothi. 43831
Historia om forenta Amerikas sjelfstandighet. 89760
Historia om Gronland. 17416
Historia orbis terrarum. 4255
Historia orientalis. 59231
Historia original de este escritor. 74945
Historia, over cronica del gran regno del Perv. 13053
Historia panegyrica de tribus martyribus eiusdem Societatis. 55267
Historia panegyrica y vida prodigiosa de Santa Rosa. 27342
Historia Paraguaiensis. 12131, 1st note after 98488
Historia plantarum rarorum. 45004
Historia plantarum species hactenus editas. 68027
Historia politica de los establecimientos ultramarinos. (68084)
Historia politica y natural de la isla de Cuba. 74913
Historia pontifical y Catholica. (34196)
Historia popular. 57579
Historia prodigiosa de la admirable aparicion. 9789
Historia provinciae Paraquariae Societatis Jesv. 94575
Historia Quakeriana. 17583
Historia razonada de Josefa de la Torre. 98597
Historia rela sagrada. (58295)
Historia relacion del reyno de Chile. 62957
Historia relatio. 24137, 31535, 1st note after 98488
Historia secreta. (32042)
Historia secreta de la corte. 75028
Historia Siciliana. (9193)
Historia synopsi. 74665
Ἱστορία τῆς Ἀμερικῆς. 72002
Historia totius orbis antiquis. 33018
Historia tragico-maritima. 23027, 27754, 94595
Historia universal de la primitiva, y milagrosa imagen de Nª. Sª. de Guadalupe. (76126)
Historia universal de la primitiva, y milagroso imagen de Nuestra Senora de Guadalupe. 25458
Historia universal desde os tempos mas remotos ate os nossos dias. 32039
Historia van een reyse ghedaen inden lande van Bresillien. (40155)
Historia vera circa l'origine, e nascita di Cristoforo Colombo. 10311
Historia verdadera de la conquista de la Nueva Espana. 19978-19981
Historia, viages, historia natural, historia religiosa. 51563
Historia Vinlandiae antiqvae. 96193

Historia y conquistada esperitual de Yucatan. 40961
Historia y descripcion de Mejico. 22818
Historia, y descubrimiento de el Rio de la Plata. 3350, 77684
Historia, y viage del mvndo. 57525
Historiadores primitivos de las Indias Occidentales. 3350, (14676), 16937, 27733, 32043, 57987, 77684, 105720, 106269
Historiae ab Hieronymo Benzono Mediolanense scripta. (8784)
Historiae Americanae secunda pars continens navigationes Gallorum in Floridam. (8784)
Historiae Americae sivi Novi Orbis. (8784)
Historiae animalium. 27227
Historiae animalium et mineralium Novae Hispaniae. 31516
Historiae antipodum sivi Novi Orbis partis nonae liber tertius. (8784)
Historiae antipodum, sivi Novi Orbis qui vulgo Americae et Indiae Occidentalis nomine usurpatur. (8784)
Historiae Belgiae. 13033
Historiae Canadensis. (21072)
Historiae de rebus Hispaniae. (44543)-44544
Historiae des drogues. 13801
Historiae Hispanicae appendix. 44545, 77904
Historiae luctuosae expeditionis. (8784)
Historiae Mennonitarum plenior deducto. 78107
Historiae per Saturan ex Novi Orbis scriptoribus. 5942
Historiae periculorum Petri de Victoria ac Sociorum eius. 99443-99444
Historiae Peruvanae Ordinis Eremitarvm S. P. Avgvstini libri octodecim. 8740
Historiae plantarum Novae Hispaniae. 31517
Historiae regum septentrionalium. 85484
Historiae rerum natrualium Brasiliae. 1371, 7588, 63028
Historiae Soc. Jersu. Lib. XV. part V. note after 69259
Historiae Societatis Jesu pars quinta. (36765)
Historiae Venetiae. 4619
Historiale beschrijvinghe der goudtrycke landen in Chili ende Arauco. 22728
Historiale description de l'Afrique. (40044)-(40045), note after 99383C
Historiam Baeticam. 72023
Historian of times in the west. 102977
Historian's guide. (32044)
Historiarum Indicarum. 43769-43774, (43784)
Historiarum regum septentrionalium. 85484
Historias del origen de los Indios. 32045, 105727
Historias ecclesiasticas y seculares de Aragon. 38949
Historias estraordinarias. 63563
Historias extraordinarias de Edgard Poe. 63564
Historias sagradas, y eclesiasticas morales. 99760
Historias varias canonicas moralizadas en sermones. 19430
Historic Americans. 58747
Historic and antiquarian scenes in Brooklyn and its vicinity. 24295
Historic annals of the National Academy of Design New York Drawing Association, etc. 17923
Historic certainties respecting the early history of America. 32046, 32048
Historic defence of experimental religion. 104379
Historic discourse. 39798

Historic doubt respecting Shakespeare. 85170
Historic doubts relative to Napoleon Buona-
parte. 32048, 90024
Historic doubts relative to the American war.
90024
Historic fire. 4299
Historic-Genealogical Society of New England,
Boston. see New England Historic-
Genealogical Society, Boston.
Historic lessons for civil war. (17271)
Historic progress and American democracy.
51107
Historic progress of civil and rational liberty.
103309
Historic records of the Fifth New York
Cavalry. 6292, 6861
Historic significance of the southern revolution.
(29860)
Historic sketch by M. W. Hackelton. 29474
Historic tale of the Puritans and the Baptists.
3231
Historic tales of olden times. 102141-102142
Historic tree of British North America.
48021
Historica narracion de los naufragios. 3350
Historica relatio. 31535
Historica relacion del reyno de Chile. 57972-
57973, 57974, 98374
Historica relacione del regno di Cile. (57971),
57974, 98376
Historical abridgement of discoveries in the
north of America. 27722
Historical abridgement of the voyages and
discoveries of the Spaniards in the same
seas. 24749
Historical account of all taxes. (73808)
Historical account of all the voyages round
the world. 16303, 31389, (54897)
Historical account of American coinage.
(31691)
Historical account of Bouquet's expedition
against the Ohio Indians. 84619
Historical account of Christ Church, Boston.
(21711)
Historical account of Christ Church, Phila-
delphia. (20636)
Historical account of coffee. 22317
Historical account of Columbia Lodge of Free
and Accepted Masons of Boston, Mass.
31180
Historical account of earthquakes. 33931
Historical account of English money. 56316
Historicall account of hurricanes. 6146
Historical account of Kentucky. 43821
Historical account of Massachusetts currency.
24032
Historical accout [sic] of matters of fact in that
affair. 9926
Historical account of my own life. (9867)
Historical account of naval and maritime
affairs. (67602)
Historical account of St. Thomas, W. I.
(38170)
Historical account of signal naval victories.
8073
Historical account of some memorable actions.
28323
Historical account of some of the most signal
naval victories. (63699)
Historical account of the attempts hitherto
made. 22312
Historical account of the black empire of
Hayti. 67531
Historical account of the circumnavigation of
the globe. 32050

Historical account of the climates and diseases
of the United States. 17999
Historical account of the Connecticut currency.
8231
Historical account of the discoveries and
travels in North America. 51500
Historical account of the discovery of the
island of Madeira. 679, 32051, 69287
Historical account of the doings of the Christian
Indians. 27958
Historical account of the establishment of the
colony of Jamaica. 35630
Historical account of the expedition against
the Ohio Indians, in the year MDCCLXIV.
72726-72727, 84617-84618, 85254
Historical account of the expedition against the
Ohio Indians, in the year 1764. 84616
Historical account of the First Church [in
Marblehead.] 3488
Historical account of the First Presbyterian
Church and Society in Newburyport,
Massachusetts. 104353
Historical account of the First Presbyterian
Church of Princeton. 77588
Historical account of the first settlement of
Salem. (36281)
Historical account of the first three business
tokens. 9540
Historical account of the French King's breach.
26872
Historical account of the Incorporated Society
for the Propagation of the Gospel in
Foreign Parts. 33800-(33801)
Historical account of the interment of the
remains. 32052
Historical account of the island of Saint
Vincent. (80271)
Historical account, of the late disturbance,
between the inhabitants of the back
settlements of Pennsylvania, and the
Philadelphians, &c. 32053, 60137-(60138),
60145, 97714, 2d note after 102552
Historical account of the life and adventures of
the Botocudo chieftan. 11725
Historical account of the life, travels and
Christian experiences of that antient,
faithful servant of Jesus Christ, Thomas
Chalkley. 11749
Historical account of the life, travels, sufferings
Christian experiences, and labour of love,
in the work of the ministy. 25352
Historical account of the many signal naval
achievements. 32054
Historical account of the marriage rites and
ceremonies. 17551, 75821-75822
Historical account of the military operations of
the late war. (7048)
Historical account of the most celebrated
voyages. (46982), 46984, 102540
Historical account of the most remarkable
earthquakes. (8720)
Historical account of the naval power of France
46182
Historical account of the old court and new
court controversy. 4160
Historical account of the origin, customs and
traditions of the Indians at the missionary
establishment of St. Juan Capistrano.
(10031), 72048
Historical account of the origin, customs, and
traditions, of the Indians of Alta-California
(10031), 72048
Historical account of the Protestant Episcopal
Church. (18299), 87928
Historical account of the Providence stage.
(5764)

Historical account, of the recovery of one from the dangerous errors of Quakerism. 64973, 72688

Historical account of the rise and establishment of the people call'd Quakers. 32055

Historical account of the rise and growth of the West-India collonies. 32056, 2d note after 95377, 1st note after 102836

Historical account of the rise and progress of the colonies of South Carolina and Georgia. 11067, 31630, 1st note after 87851

Historical account of the rise, progress and present state of the canal navigation in Pennsylvania. 50865, 84620-84621

Historical account of the sessions of Assembly. 35586

Historical account of the several plagues that have appeared. 34779

Historical account of the Siamese twin brothers. 80811

Historical account of the small-pox inoculated in New England. (7141)

Historical account of the Society, drawn up by order of the members. 85980

Historical account of the Sturbridge and Bury fairs. 32049

Historical account of the Virgin Islands. 93398

Historical account of the voyages and adventures of Sir Walter Raleigh. 67559

Historical account of the Washington Monument, in the capitol square. 71182

Historical account of the Washington Monument, with biographical sketches. (32057)

Historical account of those individuals who have been distinguished. 95216

Historical account of those persons who have been distinguished. 4429

Historical account touching the succession of the crown. 9372, 81492

Historical address and poem. (24776), 68207

Historical address at Conway centennial celebration. 16224, 70818

Historical address at the dedication of a monument in Charlestown, N. H. 38400

Historical address, . . . at the semi-centennial anniversary. (63982)

Historical address before the Congregational Church. 68998

Historical address by Charles B. Rice. (70819)

Historical address, by Charles Seymour. 79639

Historical address by . . . Charles W. Slack. 45859

Historical address by Hon. Julius Rockwell. (72442)

Historical address, by Rev. Edward Lathrop. 90117

Historical address, by Rev. Samuel Souther, of Worcester, Mass. 26104, 88268

Historical address by the pastor. 88127

Historical address. Commemorative of the graduating class of 1837. 83389

Historical address, delivered at Hampton, New Hampshire. 20750

Historical address delivered at Holden, Mass. 18369

Historical address delivered at Hubbardton, Vt. 13295

Historical address, delivered at the centennial celebration. 91041

Historical address, delivered before Morton Encampment, no. 4. 81324

Historical address delivered before the Church of Christ, in North Coventry. 9929

Historical address, delivered before the citizens of the town of Dedham. 30894

Historical address delivered before the First Baptist Church. 89310

Historical address delivered by J. J. Pringle Smith. 87931

Historical address delivered in Monticello, Illinois. 2912

Historical address delivered in the First Congregational Church. 988

Historical address, delivered on the fourth of July, 1839. 84404

Historical address delivered on the one hundredth anniversary of the first town meeting. 12994

Historical address delivered to the Liberty Independent Troop. 36469

Historical address . . . July 4, 1876. 93092

Historical address, of the city of Newport. 80098

Historical address on the two hundredth anniversary. 84758

Historical address pronounced before the House of Convocation. 4132

Historical address to the graduating class of 1868. (7089)

Historical address to the sabbath schools. 18959, 84414

Historical and bibliographical preface. 18135

Historical and biographical address. 7249

Historical and biographical genealogy of the Cushmans. (18128)

Historical and biographical papers. 84091, 84969

Historical and biographical tracts. 17105

Historical and centennial discourses. 85391

Historical and centennial romance of the revolution. 89924

Historical and chronological account of the origin and progress of the city. (54579)

Historical and chronological deduction of the origin of commerce. 1382

Historical and critical account of Hugh Peters. 61194

Historical and critical account of the lives. 25851

Historical and descriptive account of British America. 51501

Historical and descriptive account of the four species. 101221-101222

Historical and descriptive account of the Peruvian sheep. 101223

Historical and descriptive illustrations. (33520)

Historical and descriptive lessons. 32059

Historical and descriptive narrative of the Mammoth Cave. (25183)

Historical and descriptive narrative of twenty years' residence. 91611

Historical and descriptive sketches of Norfolk and vicinity. (25118)

Historical and descriptive sketches of the maritime colonies. 43285

Historical and explanatory notes on every article. 9437

Historical and genealogical register. 90505

Historical . . . and genealogical register of . . . West Boylston. 37676

Historical and genealogical researches and recorder of passing events of Merrimack Valley. (32060), (64051)-64052

Historical and geneological [sic] record. 72454

Historical and geographical account of Algiers. 91534-91535

Historical and geographical account of the province and country of Pensilvania [sic]. 95395-95396

Historical and geographical description of the British empire. 22668

Historical & geographical description of the great country. 58142

Historical and geographical memoir of the North American continent. 27979

Historical and geographical notes. 63960

Historical and Geological Society of Wyoming. see Wyoming Historical and Geological Society, Wilkes Barre, Pa.

Historical and legal examination. 4785

Historical and literary curiosities. 82400

Historical and local illustrations. 51199

Historical and miscellaneous works. 100479

Historical and mythological traditions. 89965

Historical and philosophical considerations on religion. (70843)

Historical and Philosophical Society of Missouri. see Missouri Historical and Philosophical Society.

Historical and Philosophical Society of New York. 8526

Historical and Philosophical Society of Ohio. (56931)-(56932), 86620, 94103, 94356, 101080, 105499, note after 106203 see also Ohio State Archaeological and Historical Society.

Historical and Philosophical Society of Virginia. see Virginia Historical and Philosophical Society.

Historical and physical sketch of a malignant epidemick. 32061, 45160, 105625

Historical and political account of the southern and northern states. 77499, 79685

Historical and political dissertations. 8405

Historical and political monthly mercury. (50184), 65319

Historical and political reflections on the rise and progress of the American rebellion. 26431

Historical and political survey of the losses sustained by the French nation. 35302

Historical and political view of the present and ancient state of the colony of Suriname. 24118, 8th note after 93855

Historical and practical essay on the culture and commerce of tobacco. 94409

Historical & prophetical print in the year 1770. 63769

Historical and scientific sketches of Michigan. 32062, 103692

Historical and statistical account [of Chicago.] (12639)

Historical and statistical account of New Brunswick. (2288)

Historical and statistical account of Nova-Scotia. 29687

Historical and statistical account of the foreign commerce. (32696)

Historical and statistical gazetteer of Massachusetts. 89564

Historical and statistical information, respecting the history. 77849, (77856)

Historical and statistical register. (35421)

Historical and statistical review of Austin. 2429

Historical and statistical sketch of Croydon, N. H. 16579

Historical and statistical sketch of the Railroad City. 32562

Historical and statistical sketches of Buffalo. (32063)

Historical and statistical sketches of Lake County. 29554

Historical and topographical sketch of Bunker Hill battle. (12696), 19075, 33805, 94058

Historical anecdote translated from the French. 14000, note after 97538

Historical anecdotes, civil and military. (32064)

Historical annals of Dedham. 44316

Historical appendix, by Rev. Thomas Boutelle. 93952

Historical appendix, by Wm. Carter. 34297

Historical Association of New York. see New York State Historical Association.

Historical Association of Texas. see Texas State Historical Association.

Historical ballad, in eleven bleats. 77530

Historical beauties for young ladies. 62852

Historical biography. 36930

Historical cabinet. (21276)

Historical catalogue of the paintings in the Philadelphia Museum. 61722

Historical catalogue of the St. Andrew's Society of Philadelphia. 84745

Historical catechism. 97514

Historical century sermon. 78332

Historical characters. 94260

Historical chart. (42775)

Historical, chemical and therapeutical analysis. 861

Historical Club of the Methodist Episcopal Church. see Methodist Episcopal Church. Historical Club.

Historical collection comprising important and interesting items. 97514

Historical collection, from official records, files, &c. 31962

Historical collection of the several voyages and discoveries. 18334, (18338)

Historical collection of the state of New York. 3331

Historical collections; being a general collectio of interesting facts. 3319

Historical collections [by Rushworth.] 31095

Historical collections. By W. C. Sharpe. 79855

Historical collections; consisting of state papers. 31095, 45706, 51017, 51774, 98637

Historical collections of all nations. 26031

Historical collections of Louisiana. 9116, (9605), 11824, 24852-24854, (24896), 80002, 87205-87206, 95332, 96172, note after 99605, 3d note after 99856, 1st note after 105510

Historical collections of Louisiana and Florida. (25854), 70792

Historical collections of Ohio. 33299

Historical collections of South Carolina. 11067 11766, 27572, 31630, 49086, 57157, 66724, 87349, 1st note after 87851, 104685, 106015

Historical collections of the Essex Institute. 23014, 88922

Historical collections of the great west. 33298 33300

Historical collections of the Indians in New England. 27959

Historical collections of the Junior Pioneer Association. 101291

Historical collections of the Protestant Episcopal Church. 37199

Historical collections of the Protestant Episcopal Society. 53883

Historical collections of the state of New Jerse 3330

Historical collections of the state of Pennsylvania. 18979

Historical collections of Virginia. 33301

Historical collections relating to remarkable periods of the success of the Gospel. 27413-27414

Historical collections relating to the American colonial church. 61053, 61057-(61059)

Historical considerations on the siege and defence of Fort Stanwix. (77850)

Historicall description of the most famous kingdomes and common-weales therein. 105491

Historicall description of the most famous kingdomes and commonweales in the worlde. 6801, (36282), 1st note after 96483

Historicall description of the most famous kingdomes in the world, relating their situation, manners, customes, and civil government. 36287, 1st note after 96483

Historical description of the place. 13676

Historical description of the province and country of West-New-Jersey. 95395

Historical details, having relation to the campaign of the North-Western Army. 32047, 104738

Historical dictionary. 75931

Historical discourse. 49041

Historical discourse . . . at Brookfield. 25006

Historical discourse at Montgomery, N. Y. 43547

Historical discourse at North Leverett. (1496)

Historical discourse at the centennial celebration. (52975), 91756, 103618

Historical discourse, at the hundredth anniversary. 63977

Historical discourse before the General Association of New Hampshire. 76239

Historical discourse . . . before the Schoharie County Bible Society. 41384

Historical discourse by Chas. P. Bush. 72342

Historical discourse by Prof. Albert Hopkins. 32905

Historical discourse. By Rev. Dr. G. Duffield. (21137)

Historical discourse, by Rev. Edward Lathrop. 90117

Historical discourse by, Rev. John M. McLeod. 43540

Historical discourse, by Rev. John Wheeler. 99213

Historical discourse by the President, Rev. J. M. Sturtevant. 93281

Historical discourse by the Rev. Dr. Cowley. 28327

Historical discourse, commemorative of the organization of the First Presbyterian Church. 90909

Historical discourse concerning the prevalency of prayer. 46692, 46726-56727

Historical discourse, containing an account of the rise and progress. 94570

Historical discourse, deliverd at Chelsea, Mass. 38905

Historical discourse delivered at Malden, Mass. 105622

Historical discourse, delivered at Newbury. (13605)

Historical discourse, delivered at Norwich. 92153

Historical discourse delivered at St. Peter's Church. (12519)

Historical discourse, delivered at Springfield. 89897

Historical discourse delivered at the celebration of the one hundred and fiftieth anniversary of the First Reformed Dutch Church. 91158

Historical discourse delivered at the celebration of the one hundredth anniversary of the erection of the Congregational Church. (64301)

Historical discourse; delivered at the celebration of the second centennial anniversary. 29529

Historical discourse delivered at the closing of the Old Episcopal (St. Paul's) Church, Dedham. 2576

Historical discourse, delivered at the hundredth anniversary of the organization of the Second Congregational Church. (6274)

Historical discourse delivered at the last service held in the Reformed Protestant Dutch Church. 93117

Historical discourse delivered at the one hundred and fiftieth anniversary of the formation of the church in Green's Farms. 69367

Historical discourse delivered at the semi-centennial celebration. 78056

Historical discourse delivered at the 250th anniversary of the first Baptist church in America. 35415

Historical discourse delivered at West Brookfield, Massachusetts, November 27, 1828. 25007, 103200

Historical discourse delivered at West Brookfield, Mass., on occasion of the one hundred and fiftieth anniversary of the First Church. 21286

Historical discourse, delivered at West Springfield. 89735

Historical discourse delivered at Worcester. 2668

Historical discourse, delivered before the Bible Society of the County of Greene. 72418

Historical discourse, delivered before the citizens of Concord. 22456

Historical discourse delivered . . . before the citizens of Farmington. 64300

Historical discourse, delivered . . . before the citizens of New Haven. 37891

Historical discourse delivered before the Connecticut Historical Society. 18991

Historical discourse delivered before the Pennsylvania Historical Society. (21381), 85877

Historical discourse delivered before the Society for the Commemoration of the Landing of William Penn, 24 October 1832. (21381), 85877

Historical discourse, delivered by Hon. Joseph P. Bradley. 74437

Historical discourse, delivered by the pastor. 67884

Historical discourse, delivered . . . Dec. 2, 1860. 21807

Historical discourse delivered December 3, 1865. 50816

Historical discourse delivered in Abington. 82693

Historical discourse, delivered in Dorchester. 893

Historical discourse, delivered in Norwich. 27432

Historical discourse, delivered in the Central Baptist Meeting House. 35416

Historical discourse, delivered in the First Presbyterian Church in Galena. 89266

Historical discourse, delivered in the First Universalist Meeting-House. 81070

Historical discourse, delivered in the New North Church. 26157

Historical discourse delivered July 26, 1876. 71952

Historical discourse, delivered March 29, 1839. 18891

Historical discourse, delivered . . . November 4, 1866. 64238

Historical discourse, delivered November 29, 1840. 105089

Historical discourse delivered on occasion of the re-opening and dedication of the First Reformed (Dutch) Church. (73060)

Historical discourse delivered on the fiftieth anniversary of the formation of the First Baptist Church. 49119

Historical discourse delivered on the fiftieth anniversary of the organization of the Baptist Church, Webster, Mass. 68518

Historical discourse, delivered on the fiftieth anniversary of the organization of the First Baptist Church, in Bristol, R. I. (33426)

Historical discourse delivered on the fortieth anniversary of his pastorate. 9393

Historical discourse delivered on the occasion of the one hundred and twenty-fourth anniversary of the Congregational Church. 70865

Historical discourse . . . February 26, 1855. 22259

Historical discourse, First Church Marblehead. 7309

Historical discourse for the Jubilee of the Society for the Propagation of the Gospel. 16810

Historical discourse from Psalm XLVIII. 12, 13. 80265

Historical discourse given on the fiftieth anniversary of the Baptist Church. 85490

Historical discourse, Hamilton College. 24503

Historical discourse in commemoration of the one hundredth anniversary of the formation of the First Congregational Church in Templeton. 194

Historical discourse in commemoration of the two-hundredth anniversary of the settlement of Norwalk, Ct. 6958

Historical discourse, . . . in . . . Stratford, Conn. 58129

Historical discourse, in two parts. 70915

Historical discourse, May 6, 1862. 18859

Historical discourse. New year's sermon. 80529

Historical discourse, November 24th, 1864. (21135)

Historical discourse of the Presbyterian Church. 27841

Historical discourse on occasion of the fiftieth anniversary. 47252

Historical discourse on taking leave of the old church edifice. 2633

Historical discourse on the centennial anniversary of the Reformed Dutch Church. 16982

Historical discourse on the civil and religious affairs of the colony of Rhode-Island. (10076), 70719

Historical discourse on the civil and religious affairs of the colony of Rhode-Island and Providence Plantations in New-England. (10075)

Historical discourse on the fiftieth anniversary of the First Baptist Church in Worcester, Mass. 18835

Historical discourse on the first invention of navigation. (62448)

Historical discourse on the life, deeds and character of Sir Mathew Cradock. (71888)

Historical discourse on the Reformed Prot. Dutch Church of Albany. 72633

Historical discourse on the rise and progress of the First Congregational Church, of St. Albans, Vermont. 21452

Historical discourse on the ruling elders. (72195)

Historical discourse, on the two hundredth anniversary. (2677)

Historical discourse, preached before the General Association of N. H. (6956)

Historical discourse preached in, May 16, 1855. (13432)

Historical discourse, preached in Plymouth, Mass. 13327

Historical discourse, preached January 12, 1862. 5788

Historical discourse, preached on the first Sabbath in January. 89315

Historical discourse prepared for the semi-centenary Sabbath. 35750

Historical discourse relating to the origin and history. 83322

Historical discourse, . . . respecting the progress of Presbyterianism. 36372

Historical discourse . . . to the South Evangelical Church. 39264

Historical discourse, Ware, Mass. 14044

Historical discourses of Hon. E. N. Sill, and Rev. L. Bacon. 94271

Historical discourses, relating to the First Presbyterian Church in Newark. 90906

Historical disquisition concerning the knowledge 72003

Historical disquisition on the mammoth. 59425

Historical documents and incidents. 70497

Historical documents from 1678-1691. 25852

Historical documents [issued by the Institut Francaise de Washington.] 1st note after 100572, 100837

Historical documents from the Old Dominion. (9722), 40785

Historical drama. By George H. Calvert. (10084)

Historical drama, in five acts. 43365, (58021), note after 100508

Historical drama, in three acts. (7653)

Historical episode. 14041

Historical epitome of the state of Louisiana. 42232

Historical essay and notes. 78747

Historical essay. By Brantz Mayer. 47105

Historical essay. By J. Lothrop Motley. 51105

Historical essay. By Rev. H. Darling. 18586

Historical essay concerning witchcraft. 34063

Historical essay on President Reed. (68620)

Historical essay on the English constitution. (67675), 67677

Historical essay, read before the General Association of Illinois. 73746

Historical estimate of the state. 9547

Historical eulogium on Don Hipp. Ruiz Lopez. (41981)

Historical events relating to the north and south lines. 70497

Historical exposition and legal opinion upon the title. 103425

Historical facts . . . relating to Newfane. 94466

Historical fancy. In two acts. 70830

Historical genealogy of the Lawrence family. 39371

Historical, geographical and statistical view of New York City. 54314

Historical geographical, commercial, and philosophical view of the American United States. 104830, 104832

Historical, geographical, commercial, and philosophical view of the United States of America. 104833

Historical, geographical, political, and natural history of North America. 32065

Historical, geographical, political, statistical and social account. 47100

Historical, geographical . . . sketches of Evansville, 23198

Historical inquiry, anterior to Dunlap's history. 18358

Historical inquiry concerning Henry Hudson. 68170

Historical inquiry into the ancient and present state of medicine. 48866

Historical inquiry into the production and consumption of the precious metals. 35492

Historical introduction. 52025

Historical introduction and an index. 36205

Historical introduction by Daniel Neal. 14502

Historical introduction by Henry B. Dawson. 74433

Historical introduction, by Rev. H. Humphrey. 52723, note after 65546

Historical investigation into the first appearance of the venereal disease in Europe. 76270

Historical, Israel-Indian tragedy. 36503

Historical journal. see Worcester magazine and historical journal.

Historical journal [of Dom Pernety.] 6870, 60997

Historical journal of the American war. 45853, 59619

Historical journal of the campaigns in North-America. 38164

Historical journal of the expeditions by sea and land. 17020

Historical journal of the war in America. 15056, 105602-105605

Historical journal written in French. 6870

Historical legend of Georgia, from 1717. 51193

Historical letters. 100480

Historical letters, including a brief but general view. 14904

Historical letters on the first charter of Massachusetts government. (18079)

Historical magazine. 7209, 9095, 11787, 18938, 18943, 19634, 25161, 31312, (32066), 50381, 50535, 53079, 65298, (65618), 69291, (73981), 74692, 74898, 79350, 79446, (80023), 83423, 84678C, 85144, 86758, 89391, 94096, 95697, 95819, 98039, 1st note after 98997, 100999, 103223, 103353

Historical manual of the Congregational Church, in Springfield, Vt. 89895

Historical manual of the South Church of Andover, Mass. (50293)

Historical map of Pennslyvania. 80026

Historical, medical, and economical display of the vegetable kingdom. 80066

Historical memoir of Billerica. 23825

Historical memoir of Christopher Columbus and his discoveries. 14666

Historical memoir of the Boston Episcopal Charitable Society. 6700, 7138

Historical memoir of the colony of New Plymouth. 4064, (20871)

Historical memoir of the colony of New Plymouth, from the flight of the pilgrims into Holland. 4065

Historical memoir of the House of Brunswick. (33629)

Historical memoir of the past and present condition. 3143

Historical memoir of the Pennsylvania Society, for Pomoting [sic] the Abolition of Slavery. 52235

Historical memoir of the Springfield Cemetery. (5920), note after 89877

Historical memoir of the war in West Florida. (39214)

Historical memoir of the western railroad. (5921), 103010

Historical memoir of Washington Territory. 8662

Historical memoirs of Admiral Charles Stirling. 91842

Historical memoirs of Louisiana. 25853

Historical memoirs of shipwrecks. 13421

Historical memoirs of the battle of Piggwacket. 94107

Historical memoirs of the fight at Piggwacket, &c. 94108

Historical memoirs of the late fight at Piggwacket. 94111

Historical memoirs of the late fight at Piggwackett. 94108

Historical memoirs of the life of Tom Gard'ner. 26654-26655, 93828

Historical memoirs of the province of New York. 84570

Historical memoirs of the United States. 10062

Historical memoirs, relating to the Housatunnuk Indians. 32945-32946

Historical memoirs, relating to the Housatunnuk, or Stockbridge Indians. 32947, 2d note after 102507

Historical memorial of the negotiation of France and England. 10514, 47517, 69530

Historical memorials relating to the independents. 30163

Historical miscellany. 32069

Historical miscellany of the curiosities and rarities in nature and art. 32068

Historicall narration of Gods wonderfull workings upon sundry of the Indians. 80205, note before 92797

Historical narration of the dangerous pernicious practices and opinions. 104794

Historical narrative, and declaration. 92825

Historical narrative and topographical description of Louisiana. 34056, (34358)

Historical narrative, containing a brief sketch of work of God. 92826

Historical narrative: explanation and vindication of the course pursued by the Grand Lodge of New York. (53692)

Historical narrative, explanation, and vindication of the course pursued by the Grand Lodge of the State of New York. 32067

Historical narrative from the death of La Salle. (9605)

Historical narrative of the civil and military services. 18956

Historical narratives of the most noted calamities. 80537

Historical notes. (28830)

Historical notes and documents. 61054, (66173)

Historical notes, in reference to the Crawford County Sabbath School Union. 707

Historical notes of the American colonies and revolution. (28831)

Historical notes of the First Presbyterian Church. 61665

Historical notes on Kentucky. 91838

Historical notes on slavery and colonization. 32070

Historical notes on the Canadian colony of Detroit. 32071

Historical notes on the employment of Negroes in the American army. (50379)

Historical notes, relating to the Pennsylvania Reformed Church. 27160, 101420

Historical notes respecting the Indians of North America. (29708)

Historical notice of Joseph Mygatt. 51644

Historical notice of the Essex Institute. 23015

Historical notices. 98140

Historical notices by Henry Onderdonk, Jr. 67069

Historical notices, confession of faith, and covenant. 86803

Historical notices of Connecticut. 64324

Historical notices of Hartford. (30668)

Historical notices of St. Ann's Parish. 809

Historical notices of St. James' Parish. 20887

Historical notices of Saint John's Church. 73881

Historical notices of Saint Peter's Church, in the city of Perth-Amboy. 11989

Historical notices of St. Peter's Church, Perth Amboy, New Jersey. 12524

Historical notices of St. Domingo. 9270

Historical notices of the First Congregational Church at Canterbury. 32072

Historical notices of the First Congregational Church in Braintree. 7355

Historical notices of the First Congregational Church in Canterbury, Conn. 39539

Historical notices of the missions of the Church of England. 30952

Historical notices of the New North Religious Society. 6660, 22132

Historical notices of the . . . Parish [of St. Matthew's Church.] 3682

Historical notices of the Piscataqua Association. 25873

Historical notices of Thomas Fuller and his descendants. (26182)

Historical novel. 34875, 41398

Historical novel. By Charles J. Peterson. 61231

Historical novel. By J. B. Jones. 36530

Historical novel. By John Carsten Hauch. 30853

Historical novel, by L. Muhlbach. 51245

Historical novel. By Melville. 805, (47484)

Historical novel, exhibiting a view. 18849, 100467, 101204

Historical nuggets. 91508

Historical nuggets. Bibliotheca Americana. (5199), 25567, 91510-91511

Historical or rather conjectural poem. 75264

Historical oration . . . fourth of July, 1860. 55020

Historical outline of Lower California. 93834

Historical outline of the American Colonization Society. 88971, 88973

Historical outlines for the use of schools. 6791

Historical papers [of the Trinity College Historical Society.] 104450

Historical parallel between him [i. e. Heister Clymer] and Major-General John W. Geary. (31808)

Historicall perspective. 67591

Historical picture, death of President Lincoln. 71555

Historical picture gallery. (11950)

Historical picture of the Mississippi by DeSoto. 93161

Historical play. 51029

Historical play of Columbus. 53397

Historical poem. By Henry F. King. 37803

Historical poem, . . . dedication of the Soldiers' Monument. 59500

Historical poem. Delivered at the public commencement. 105785

Historical poem. In sixteen elegies. 85243-85244

Historical poem, with notes and appendix. 101903

Historical, poetical and pictorial American scenes. 3321

Historical, political and military sketch of the black republic. 67534

Historical preface. 6839

Historical preface, life and pedigree of the author. 33453

Historical preface, or memoirs of the battle, at Piggwackett. 94107

Historical Printing Club. publishers 93611

Historical reader. 33855

Historical reader, designed for the use of schools. (32073)

Historical recollections, discourse delivered at Lebanon, N. H. 16341

Historical recollections of St. Paul's Chapel, New York. 20348

Historical record of the city of Savannah. 39733

Historical record of the First, or King's Regiment of Dragoon Guards. 32074

Historical record of the proceedings of the Court of Common Pleas. 27852

Historical record of the Royal Marine Forces. (55250)

Historical records and studies of the United States Catholic Historical Society. 99362

Historical records of the British Army. 10699

Historical records of the Fifth New York Cavalry. 6861

Historical reference lists. (80565)

Historical register. 32075

Historical register, and Confederate's assistant to national independence. 35420

Historical register from the creation to the close of the year 1825. 75419

Historical register of the United States. 32076, 58379

Historical relation of New England to the English commonwealth. 95637

Historical relation of the first discovery of the isle of Madera. 680

Historical relation of the first planting of the English. (36204)

Historical relation of the kingdom of Chili. 13015, 57972

Historical relics of the White Mountains. 32077, 89047-89048

Historical remarks, and moral reflections. 73559

Historical remarks on the taxation of free states. (47944)

Historical reminiscences of Camden. 10160

Historical reminiscences of Summit County. 5263

Historical reminiscences of the city of Albany. 32078

Historical research respecting the opinions of the founders. (41564)-41565

Historical researches by John Ranking. (28181)
Historical researches on the conquest of Peru. 67891-(67892)
Historical review. 95632
Historical review and directory of North America. 32079
Historical review of North America. 55525
Historical review of Pennsylvania, from its origin. 25513
Historical review of the constitution and government of Pennsylvania. 25512
Historical review of the New-York and Erie Railroad. (42023)
Historical review of the Puritan government in Massachusetts. 57212
Historical review of the Royal Marine Corps. 27393
Historical romance. 9425, 106048
Historical romance, and other poems. 79987
Historical romance. By G. H. Hollister. 32553
Historical romance. By T. C. M. 42919
Historical romance. By the author of "Guy Rivers." 81204
Historical romance, embracing the periods of the Texas revolution. 13617
Historical romance, founded on the events of 1814-15. (13845)
Historical romance, founded on the events of the late war. 25877
Historical romance in three chapters. 33647, 101507
Historical romance of America. 18920
Historical romance of border life. (4724)
Historical romance of 1775. 67042
Historical romance of the Fenian invasion of Canada. 78108
Historical romance of the maritime British provinces. 29744
Historical romance of the Old Dominion. (11172), 100443
Historical romance of the revolution in Carolina. 81223-81224
Historical scenes in the United States. 3320
Historical series (Heartman's) 15043, 93232, 97207, 2d note after 105927
Historical series (Munsell's) 1311, 7301, (9253), 11597, 19788, 21694, 33138, (33148), 51370, 57496, (72725), 74496, (80003), 90375
Historical series (Woodward's) 20867, 20884, 33453, 62489, (68405)
Historical sermon. 91622
Historical sermon before the Presbytery of Ontario. 58155
Historical sermon . . . before the Reformed Protestant Dutch Church of Deerpark, Port Jervis, N. Y. 81711
Historical sermon delivered at Brimfield, January 7, 1821. 98297
Historical sermon, delivered at Deerfield, Mass. 11852
Historical sermon delivered in St. Peter's Church, Cheshire. 4131C
Historical sermon discussed as a memorial. 37014
Historical sermon, giving a concise history of the First Baptist Church. 58781
Historical sermon preached at Shiloh Baptist Church. 83863
Historical sermon, preached in the Coates' Street Presbyterian Church. 21140
Historical sermon . . . St. Paul's Cathedral, Buffalo. (80155)

Historical sketch. 59065, 83559
Historical sketch and an address by A. Hazeltine. 35736
Historical sketch and essay on the resources of Montana. 43853
Historical sketch and genealogy of George and Thomas Geer. 26834
Historical sketch and notes by the Rev. Samuel Hart. 78561
Historical sketch, articles of faith and covenant, and regulations of the first Church of Christ, Springfield, Mass. 89862
Historical sketch, articles of faith and covenant, principles and rules, and catalogue of members. (63496)
Historical sketch. By Andrew Wright. 105542
Historical sketch by G. J. Abbot. (11866)
Historical sketch, by Rev. G. Henry Manderville. 44230
Historical sketch, by Rev. Theophilus Packard, Jr. 70936
Historical sketch [by William B. Smith.] 43314, 84750
Historical sketch compiled from various sources. 83505
Historical sketch, covenant and articles of faith, of the Fifth Congregational Church. (66269)
Historical sketch, delivered . . . in St. Stephen's Church. 65440
"Historical sketch," etc. 3940
Historical sketch, general description, plan and extent of the city. 6033
Historical sketch of Abingdon, Plymouth County, Massachusetts. (32289)
Historical sketch of and remarks upon congressional caucusus. 10889
Historical sketch of Amherst, in the county of Hillsborough, in New-Hampshire. 23827
Historical sketch of Amherst, in the county of Hillsborough, N. H. 23828
Historical sketch of Amherst, N. H. 23826
Historical sketch, of ancient agriculture. 57315
Historical sketch of and an account of the McCormick family. 84330
Historical sketch of Bedford, N. H. 77247
Historical sketch of Beechwood Church. 14228
Historical sketch of Block Island. 80099
Historical sketch of Brown University. 8623
Historical sketch of Charlestown. 3763
Historical sketch of Col. Benjamin Bellows. 4570
Historical sketch of Columbia College. 14842
Historical sketch of Columbia College, in the city of New-York. 50429
Historical sketch of commerce and navigation. 14193
Historical sketch of continental paper money. 1183, 7668
Historical sketch of Deerfield. 104270
Historical sketch of Dr. Elisha Perkins. 83392
Historical sketch of East Greenwich Seminary. 21647
Historical sketch of Easthampton, Mass. 105617
Historical sketch of Fall River. (25314)
Historical sketch [of George Washington.] 33945
Historical sketch of Grass Valley. 9728
Historical sketch of Gy-ant-wa-chia, and of the Six Nations of Indians. 16807, 85580
Historical sketch of Gy-ant-wa-chia—the Cornplanter, and of the Six Nations of Indians. 16807, 85580
Historical sketch of Haverhill. 75857
Historical sketch of Iowa College. 43843

Historical sketches of the First Church in
Hartford. 30921, 30925

Historical sketches of the Indians. (26032)

Historical sketches of the late war. 95590

Historical sketches of the missions of the
United Brethren for propagating the
Gospel among the heathen. 32606

Historical sketches of the missions of the
United Brethren for propagating the
Gospel among the heathen, from their
commencement to the year 1817. 32607

Historical sketches of the mound builders.
26357

Historical sketches of the origin and progress
of the Massachusetts Medical Society.
694

Historical sketches of the paper currency of
the American colonies. 62488

Historical sketches of the parish of Trinity
Church. (8843)

Historical sketches of the . . . Philadelphia
Hose Company. 62004

Historical sketches of the Presbyterian Church
(O. S.), in Licking County, Ohio. 31606

Historical sketches of the principles and
maxims of American jurisprudence.
(32088)

Historical sketches of the revolution, the
foreign and civil wars. (75131)

Historical sketches of the revolutions, and
the foreign and civl wars. 12356

Historical sketches of the sacred relics.
4437

Historical sketches of the slave trade. 51302

Historical sketches of the spirit of orthodoxy.
24281

Historical sketches of the Tabernacle. (79299),
92272

Historical sketches of the ten miles square.
22236

Historical sketches of the town [of Alstead, N.
H.] 2085

Historical sketches of the town of Leicester.
101520

Historical sketches of the townships of Licking,
Bowling Green, Franklin and Hopewell.
13573, (40970), 85133

Historical sketches of the United States.
60971

Historical sketches of Wesleyan Methodism.
85207

Historical sketches of western Presbyterianism.
83305

Historical Society of Buffalo. see Buffalo
Historical Society.

Historical Society of Chicago. see Chicago
Historical Society.

Historical Society of Cincinnati. see Cincinnati Historical Society.

Historical Society of Connecticut. see
Connecticut Historical Society, Hartford.

Historical Society of Delaware. see Delaware
Historical Society.

Historical Society of Dorchester, Mass. see
Dorchester Historical Society.

Historical Society of Florida. see Florida
Historical Society, St. Augustine.

Historical Society of Florida: organized in
St. Augustine, 1856. Constitution. 24867

Historical Society of Galveston. see Galveston
Historical Society.

Historical Society of Galveston. Series no. I.
82346

Historical Society of Georgia. see Georgia
Historical Society.

Historical Society of Iowa. see Iowa State
Historical Society.

Historical Society of Ipswich. see Ipswich
Historical Society.

Historical Society of Kansas. see Kansas
State Historical Society.

Historical Society of Kentucky. see Kentucky
State Historical Society.

Historical Society of Maine. see Maine
Historical Society.

Historical Society of Maryland. see Maryland
Historical Society.

Historical Society of Michigan. see Michigan
Historical Society.

Historical Society of Minnesota. see Minnesota
Historical Society.

Historical Society of Mississippi. see Mississippi Historical Society.

Historical Society of Montana. see Montana
Historical Society.

Historical Society of Montreal. see Societe
Historique de Montreal.

Historical Society of New Hampshire. see
New Hampshire Historical Society,
Concord.

Historical Society of New Haven Colony. see
New Haven Colony Historical Society.

Historical Society of New Jersey. see New
Jersey Historical Society.

Historical Society of New York. see New
York Historical Society.

Historical Society of Nova Scotia. see Nova
Scotia Historical Society.

Historical Society of Ohio. see Ohio State
Archaeological and Historical Society.

Historical Society of Orleans County, Vt. see
Orleans County Historical Society.

Historical Society of Pennsylvania. see
Pennsylvania. Historical Society.

Historical Society of Pennsylvania. [Preamble
and resolutions signed] Joseph R. Ingersoll, President. 60144

Historical Society of Philadelphia. see
Philadelphia Historical Society.

Historical Society of Rhode Island. see Rhode
Island Historical Society.

Historical Society of St. Louis. see St. Louis
Historical Society.

Historical Society of South Carolina. see
South Carolina Historical Society.

Historical Society of the Protestant Episcopal
Church. see Protestant Episcopal
Historical Society.

Historical Society of the University of North
Carolina. see North Carolina Historical
Society.

Historical Society of Vermont. see Vermont
Historical Society.

Historical Society of Virginia. see Virginia
Historical Society.

Historical Society of Westchester County.
see Westchester County Historical
Society.

Historical Society of Wisconsin. see
Wisconsin. State Historical Society.

Historical Society of Worcester, Mass. see
Worcester Historical Society.

Historical statement of the Evangelical Lutheran
Synod of New York. 53659

Historical studies. (28597)

Historical study. By John Morley. 50725

Historical study. By the Hon. George Shea.
79983-79984

Historical study. By William Henry Trescot.
96783

Historical summary of Lower California. 8662

Historical summary of naval and maritime events, from the time of the Romans to the treaty of peace, 1802. 77778

Historical summary of naval and maritime events, including authentic accounts of the most remarkable engagements. 77779

Historical summary of the five years' search for Sir John Franklin. 61182

Historical summary of the several attacks that have been made upon the city of New York. (49743)

Historical survey of the foreign affairs of Great Britain. 39645

Historical survey of the French colony in the island of St. Domingo. (21894), 21905, 98837

Historical survey of the island of Saint Domingo. (21895)

Historical survey of the relation of the early Methodists to slavery. 19821

Historical tale. 31438, 94196, 105691

Historical tale; after the manner of John Gilpin. 97377

Historical tale of the early settlement of Vermont. 95479

Historical tales for youth. 39777

Historical, topographical and critical illustrations. 54712, note before 99588

Historical, topographical, and descriptive view of the United States of America. (43428)

Historical, topographical and statistical view of the United States. 104833

Historical tract by Judge Green. 81703

Historical tragedy. 59288

Historical tragedy in five acts. 106135

Historical tragedy, in three acts. 83024

Historical tragedy. Of five acts. 14109

Historical tragedy Paetus Coecinna in five acts. 64990

Historical treatice [sic] of the practice of the Court of Chancery. 5765

Historical view of heresies. (43239)

Historical view of Roman Catholic missions. 84359

Historical view of the American revolution. 28598

Historical view of the Commission for Enquiring Into the Losses, Services, and Claims, of the American Loyalists. 104591

Historical view of the first planters of New-England. 71846-71847

Historical view of the government of Maryland. 43561

Historical view of the progress of discovery. 97657, 97658

Historical view of the public celebrations of the Washington Society. (32089), 102034

Historical view of the rise and progress of the sect. 37706

Historical view of the roman imperial laws against libels. 6214, 24748, 93387

Historical view of the world. 67708

Historical vindication of the abrogation. 8491

Historical vindications. 18205

Historicall . . . see Historical . . .

Historici fidelissimi justa ac praestantissimi, De religionibus orientalibus libri III. 59231

Historick recital, of the different occurrences. 75132

Historico da Companhia Industrial da Estrada de Ferro de Mangaratiba. 85627

Historico da fabrica de papel de Orianda. 85628

Historico-dramatico ambrosial eclogues. 32090

Historico e analyse esthetigraphica do quadro de um episodio. 24315, 85628A

Historico juridico del derecho. 50106

Historico-political geography. (58987)

Historico-political memoir. 32911

Historico, y sagrado novenario de la milagrosa imagen de Nuestra Senora del Pueblito. 99613

Historicus. pseud. Additional letters. see Harcourt, Sir William George Granville Venables Vernon, 1827-1904.

Historicus. pseud. American neutrality. see Harcourt, Sir William George Granville Venables Vernon, 1827-1904.

Historicus. pseud. Belligerent rights. see Harcourt, Sir William George Granville Venables Vernon, 1827-1904.

Historicus. pseud. Letter. see Harcourt, Sir William George Granville Venables Vernon, 1827-1904.

Historicus. pseud. Letters of Historicus. see Harcourt, Sir William George Granville Venables Vernon, 1827-1904.

Historicus. pseud. Sham-patriot unmasked. see Sampson, Ezra.

Historie antigua de Megico. 13520

Historie booke. 83468

Historie de Nederland oorlogen. 6398

Historie del Sig. Agostino di Zarate. 106270-106271

Historie del Sig. Don. Fernando Colombo. (14674)-14675

Historie dell' Indie. 13049, 13052

Historie der bereorten van Engelandt. 32092

Historie der inquisitie tot Goa. 32093

Historie der Martelaren. 32094

Historie der Nederlandschen en haar nabueren oorlogen. 48176

Historie der Neue Welt. (4800)

Historie der Sevarimbes. 98299

Historie di M. Marco Gvazzo. 44402

Historie di quattro principali citta del mondo. 106255

Historie di tvtte le cose degne di memoria qval del anno M. D. XXIIII. 44401

Historie memorabili [di] Alessandro Zilioli. 106333

Historie naturael ende morael van de Westersche Indien. 126-127, note after (41373)

Historie nelle quali s'ha particolare & vera relatione. (14676)

Historie õ Americe. (3798)

Historie of America or Brasill. 6120

Historie of Cambria, now called Wales. 40914

Historie of Lopez Vaz. 66686

Historie of man. 66677

Historie of the discouerie and conquest of the East Indies. 11391

Historie of the great and mightie kingdome of China. 27783

Historie of the Mexican nation. 66686

Historie of the West-Indies. 1563, 29600, 45011, 2d note after 102836

Historie of the world. 73312, (73325)

Historie of travaile into Virginia Britannia. 92664

Historie om conqvesten af Mexico. 86492

Historie om Gronland. 17420

History and antiquities of New Haven, Conn.,
from its earliest settlement to the
present time. With biographical
sketches. 3334
History and antiquities of the city of St.
Augustine. 23670
History and antiquities of the name and
family of Kilbourn. 37735
History and business guide of Stark Co. O.
73438
History and character of American revivals
of religion. (14774)
History and characteristics of the Reformed
Protestant Dutch Church. 19460
History and chemical investigation of maize
or Indian corn. 75793
History and condition of common schools.
(3466)
History and condition of the legislation of
Rhode Island. 70587
History and condition of the Portland Society
of Natural History. 64369
History and confession of the young felon.
30950
History and cultivation of cotton and tobacco.
19189
History and debates of the Convention of the
People of Alabama. 84877
History and description of America. (32122),
94396
History and description of an epidemic fever.
29634
History and description of New England.
(16369)
History and description of the Astronomical
Observatory. 6288
History and description of the Baltimore and
Ohio Rail Road. 2992, 84847
History and description of the Canadas. 10462
History and description of the Opera House.
61888
History and description of the republic of
Buenos Ayres. 103962
History and design of the American Institute
of Instruction. 22429
History and development of races. 57726
History and directory of Nevada County,
California. 81063
History and directory of Yates County. 104032
History and doctrine of the millennium. 101299
History and evidence of the passage of Abraham
Lincoln. 41190
History and gazetteer of Vermont. 96649
History and genealogy of Fenwick's colony.
(80739)
History and genealogy f the Davenport family.
18691
History and genealogy of the Kilbourn family.
37734
History and genealogy of the Prentice of
Prentiss family. 5469
History and general description of New France.
(80023)
History and general views of the Sandwich
Islands Mission. 19991
History and geography of the Mississippi
Valley. 24789
History and government of the Phoenix Social
Club. 62585
History and honorary role of the Twelfth
Regiment Infantry, N. G. S. N. Y. 20766
History and horrors of the Delderberg war.
32108
History and its philosophy. 31386
History and its sources. 7754

History and law of the writ of habeas corpus.
34740
History and life of Robert Blake, Esq. 5791
History and lives of distinguished characters
in the British navy. 52074
History and lives of the most notorious pirates.
32109
History and location of Fort Nassau on the
Delaware. 2019
History and manual of the Congregational
Church of Dubuque, Iowa. 21041
History and mystery of Methodist Episcopacy.
42966
History and new gazetteer. 18692
History and organization of the Catholic
Institute in Cincinnati, O. 32110
History and origin of the missionary societies.
84357
History and philosophy of earthquakes. 32111
History and political science. 40985
History and practice of the art of photography.
85415
History and present attitude of the temperance
cause. 4618
History and present condition of St. Domingo.
8530
History and present state of the town of
Newburyport. 18088
History and present state of Virginia. 5112,
(74605)-74606, note after 91491, 97111,
1st note after 100480
History and progress of the electric telegraph.
74738
History and progress of the four Indian
kings. 32113
History and progress of the missionary
societies. 84358
History and progress of the temperance
reformation. 8897
History and prospects of the Publication
Committee. 65168
History and records of the Elephant Club.
95594
History and remarkable life of the truely
Honourable Colonel Jacque. 19279
History and repository of pulpit eloquence.
24432-24433
History and statistics of the state of Maryland.
(37426)
History and theory of revolutions. 13320
History and topography of Dauphin, Cumberland,
Franklin, Bedford, Adams, and Perry
Counties. 74158
History and topography of New York. 79650
History and topography of Northumberland,
Huntingdon, Mifflin, Centre, Union,
Columbia, Juniata and Clinton Counties,
Pa. (74159)
History and topography of the United States of
America. 31965, 32220
History and topography of the United States of
North America. 31966
History and vindication of the doctrines. 18587
History and vision of Clio. 44890, 1st note
after 97010
History, articles of faith and covenant of the
Congregational Church in South Woburn.
88219
History, articles of faith and covenants, together
with the rules. 88218
History, articles of faith, etc., of the Hanover
Church. 32114
History, articles of faith . . . of the Mariner's
Church. (44589)
History. By A. Rooker. 73089

History by Charles Emory Stevens. 91490

History. By W. C. Martyn. 45008

History, catalogue and arrangements of the Theological Seminary of the Associate Reformed Synod of New-York, at Newburgh. 95313

History, character, and results, of the Westminster Assembly of Divines. 85297

History, charter and by-laws of the Massachusetts Lodge. 45849

History, civil and commercial, of the British colonies in the West Indies. 21894-(21895), 21901, (21904), 65382, 106128

History, confession of faith, etc., of the Mount Vernon Congregational Church in Boston. (51179)

History, correspondence, and pedigrees of the Mendenhalls of England. 47800

History, debates, and proceedings of both houses of Parliament. 32112

History, description, and statistics of the Bloomingdale Asylum for the Insane. 21628

History, diagnosis and treatment of the fevers of the United States. 3728

History from original sources by associated scholars. 84340

History, geography, and statistics of British North America. 50006

History, given by himself [i. e. Josiah White.] 103437

History, government, doctrines, customs, and prospects of the Latter-Day Saints. 24184

History, laws and ordinances of San Luis Obispo. 76140

History, manners and customs, of the North America Indians. 32115

History, objects and principles of the Order of the Sons of Temperance. 24710

History, order, confession of faith and covenant of the Congregational Church in Southbridge, Mass. 88260

History of a Bible. 103985

History of a brigade of South Carolinians. 9916

History of a case of discipline. 32116

History of a cavalry company. 34136

History of a Christian slave. 92487, 92489

History of a corporation of servants. (32117), 104938

History of a cotton bale. 32118

History of a dreadful catastrophy. 12967, 61198, 84400

History of a family as told by themselves. 31858, 82987

History of a French louse. 32029, 32119

History of a law suit in the republic of Ecuador. 20171

History of a long war with Indian salvages [sic]. 46289

History of a porcupine. 14003

History of a session of the General Assembly of . . . Maryland. 45161

History of a struggle for justice between the two. 12408

History of a tatterdemalion. 12967, 61198, 84400

History of a voyage of the China Sea. 103411

History of a voyage to the coast of Africa. 30956

History of a voyage to the Malouine (or Falkland) Islands. 6870, 60997

History of a young puritan. 33969

History of a zoological temperance convention. 32250

History of Abraham. 26409

History of Abraham Lincoln and the overthrow of slavery. 2069

History of Acadie, Penobscot Bay and river. 103307

History of Acton, Me. 26190

History of Acworth, N. H. 47998

History of Adjutant Trowel and Bluster. 102

History of agricultural societies on the mode Berkshire system. 32120, 102130

History of Alabama. 62668

History of Alabama and dictionary of Alabam biography. 83004

History of all nations. 27900

History of all regiments and batteries. 2436

History of all religions. 77701-77702, note after 85148-85150, 85154

History of all religions. By David Benedict. 4650

History of all religions in the United States and Europe. 31066

History of all the engagements by sea and land. 32121

History of all the teachers' associations. 39

History of America. By Thomas F. Gordon. 27999

History of America. [By William Robertson. 71973-71974, 71976, 71978, (71982), 71985-(71987), 71989, 72008, (72012), 85593, 96333

History of America; containing the geographi political and commercial state of the c tinent. 21021

History of America. Containing the history Virginia. 71975

History of America, from its discovery by Columbus to the conclusion of the late war. (74383)

History of America, from the earliest settle ment to the present time. 55520

History . . . of America, from the first discovery to the fourth of March, 1825. 27871

History . . . of America, from the first discovery to the present time. 27871

History . . . of America, from the first discovery to the year 1827. 27871

History of America, in two books. 32123, 40024, 50937, 57181

History of America: including the history of Virginia. 71977

History of America. . . . Report . . . [on] th expediency of adopting measures to procure from the different public office in England, copies of papers. 23268

History of American abolitionism. 24985

History of American contributions to the English language and literature. 11801

History of American manufactures from 1608 to 1860. 5606

History of American missions to the heathen 32124, 96418

History of American slavery and Methodism. 46865

History of American socialisms. 56226

History of American taxation, from the year 1763. 32125

History of Amherst, N. H. 83897

History of an expatriated family. 34353

History of an expedition against Fort Du Que 7211, (77042)

History of an Italian captive. 99431, note af 100822

History of an old fringed petticoat. 32126

History of an unjust and improper trial. 741

History of ancient America. (36502)
History of ancient Mexico. 28000
History of ancient Weathersfield, Connecticut. 91754
History of ancient Windsor, Connecticut. 5635, 28309, 31009, 91752-91754
History of ancient Woodbury, Connecticut. 17029
History of Andover. From its first settlement. 13, 32127
History of animals. 27228
History of animals; being the fourth volume of Elements of useful knowledge. 102350
History of Anti-Christ. (82499)
History of Antietam National Cemetery. 32128
History of Antigua. 84539
History of Antonio Alvares. 99429, note after 100822
History of Arizona and New Mexico. (76810)
History of Armstrong County, Pennsylvania. 83880
History of Auburn. (29778)
History of Bacon in Virginia. 4372
History of Bacon's and Ingram's rebellion. 19051, 51810, 2d note after 100494
History of Baltimore city and county. (77508)
History of banking in America. 27345
History of banks. (31775), 32129
History of baptism. 72170-(72171)
History of baptism; or, one faith, one baptism. 75445
History of Baptist Indian missions. 43112
History of Barbadoes, from the discovery of the island. 64853
History of Barbados. 77785
History of Barnet, a converted Indian. 54933
History of Bedford, New-Hampshire. (4279)
History of Belfast. 103476
History of Berkshire County, Massachusetts. 83324
History of Beverly. 92043
History of Black Hawk. 82460
History of Block Island. (4264)
History of Boston. By Robert Carver. 11195
History of Boston, from its origin to the present period. 32908
History of Boston, from 1630 to 1857. 32130
History of Boston, from 1630 to 1856. 6522, 32697
History of Boston, the metropolis of Massachusetts. 85488-85489
History of Bradford, Mass. 61030-61031
History of Brazil; by Robert Southey. (4155)-4156, 88552-88553
History of Brazil, comprising a geographical account. 28291
History of Brazil; comprising its geography. 31314
History of Brazil, from the period of the arrival of the Braganza family. 2008
History of Breed's (commonly called) Bunker's Hill battle. 50976
History of Bridgewater. (11202)
History of Bristol Parish. 81704
History of Bristol Parish, Va. 81705
History of British Guiana. (18350)
History of Broome County, N. Y. 32131
History of Brown University, with illustrative documents. 29222
History of Bucks County from its earliest settlement. 8884
History of Bunker Hill battle. 94059-94061
History of Bunker Hill battle and monument. 9178
History of Caledonia. (9920), 18556, 78218

History of California. By Franklin Tuthill. 97510
History of California. [By George Wilkes.] 103996
History of California, from its discovery to the present time. (10764)
History of Cambridge. (32581)
History of Canada for the use of schools and families. 73743
History of Canada, from its first discovery, comprehending an account. 31488
History of Canada; from its first discovery, to the peace of 1763. 43858, 84701, 99776
History of Canada, from its first discovery to the present time. (43581)
History of Canada, from the time of its first discovery until the union year 1840-41. 26676
History of Canada to the treaty of Utrecht, in 1713. 10625
History of Candia. 21720
History of Cape Cod. (25760)
History of Captain Thomas Parismas. 58615
History of Carausius. 19633
History of Carolina. 7800, 39452
History of changes that have taken place. 18812
History of Charles Careful, and Harry Heedless. 100587-100591
History of Charles P. 54933
History of Charles V. (72012)
History of Chares the Vth. (76429)
History of Charlestown in New Hampshire. 17638
History of Charlestown, Massachusetts. (26081)
History of Charlestown, New-Hampshire, the old no. 4. 77195
History of Charlotte Temple. (73605)
History of Chatham, Massachusetts. 84759-84760
History of Chelmsford. 883
History of Chenango County. (13296)
History of Chesterville, Maine. 79436
History of Chicago. 29365
History of Chile. 973
History of Christ's Church, West Haven. 11940
History of church music in America. 28123
History of civilization. 43464
History of Clear Creek and Boulder Valleys, Colorado. 82752
History of Clear Creek Church. 94481
History of clock and watchmaking in America. 6391
History of Colonel Doniphan's campaign to Chihuahua. 15888
History of Col. Parke's administration. 25859-25860
History of commerce, and a chronological table. 6348
History of commerce from the earliest times. 26265
History of Commodore Anson's voyage round the world. 1636, 32132, 101190
History of Commodore Nutt. 56345
History of Concord. 6959
History of congregationalism from about A. D. 250 to 1616. 66657
History of congregationalism from about A. D. 250 to the present time. 66658
History of Congress; exhibiting a classification of the proceedings of the Senate and House of Representatives. 15888
History of Congress; exhibiting a classification of the proceedings of the Senate, and the House of Representatives. (15532)

History of Connecticut. 61213
History of Connecticut, designed for schools. 27875
History of Connecticut, from the earliest settlement to the present time. (11011)
History of Connecticut, from the first settlement of the colony. 32552
History of Connecticut from the first settlement to the present time. 21536
History of constitutional reform in New Jersey. 5302
History of cosmopolite. (20753)
History of Crown Point, N. Y. 89055
History of Crusonia. 72224, note before 93805
History of Cuba. 2972
History of Cumberland. 20832
History of Dartmouth College. 82351
History of Davenport's invention. 18719
History of deaf-mute instruction and institutions. 3469
History of Dedham. 105500
History of defection in New-England. 32133
History of De Kalb County, Ill. 32134
History of Delaware County and border wars of New York. 28108
History of Delaware County, Pennsylvania. (82584)
History of democracy in the United States. 10745, 32135
History of Dickinson County, Iowa. 83882
History of discoveries made by Europeans. 3654
History of dissenters, from the revolution in 1688. 6137
History of Don Francisco de Miranda's attempt to affect a revolution in South America. 5333-5334, 9117
History of Dublin, N. H. 40114
History of Duchess County. 83719
History of Dungeon Rock. 22565, (48149)
History of Durham, Connecticut. 25325
History of Duryee's Brigade. 33139
History of earthquakes. 32136
History of East Boston. 93711
History of Eastern Vermont. 29735
History of Eastport, and vicinity. 103048
History of ecclesiastical affairs in Pepperell. 1492, 60842
History of ecclesiastical proceedings relative to the Third Presbyterian Church in Philadelphia. 22384, 99126
History of education, ancient and modern. 77674
History of education in New Hampshire. 6960
History of Edwin Forrest. (25107)
History of Egyptian mummies. 61298
History of Eliza Wharton. 25229, 103731
History of . . . Elizabeth. 10158
History of Elizabeth, New Jersey. 30842
History of Elmira, Horseheads, and the Chemung Valley. 26343
History of Emily. Montague. 8240
History of England [by Frederick Guest Tomlins.] 96144
History of England [by Thomas Babington Macaulay.] 23659, 25146, 32491, 42949
History of England during the reign of George III. 78349
History of England during the reign of George the Third. 46178
History of England: during the reigns of K. William, Q. Anne, and K. George I. 67608

History of England from the accession of James I. to that of the Brunswick line. 42946
History of England, from the accession of George III., 1760, to . . . 1837. 33604
History of England, from the accession of George the Third, to the conclusion of the peace in the year 1783. 466
History of England, from the earliest times to the peace of 1783. 27336
History of England from the peace of Utrecht. 90287
History of England from the peace of Utrecht to the peace of Aix-la-Chapelle. 90287-90288
History of England from the peace of Utrecht to the peace of Paris. 90289
History of England from the peace of Utrecht to the peace of Versailles. 58325, 8900 90287, 90290
History of England, from the revolution to the end of the American war. 32163, 85105
History of England; or the memorials of the English affairs. 59715, note after 10367
History of England . . . to the death of the King. 466
History of epidemic cholera. 8917
History of episcopacy. 29253
History of Erie County, Pennsylvania. 76493
History of every attempt at resistance. (3213
History of facts in relation to Ebenezer Hinds 31943
History of facts. Writ[t]en by a friend to truth. 95435
History of Fall River. 25315
History of Farmington, Me. 58772
History of Fayette County, Pennsylvania. 987
History of Ferdinand and Isabella. 76381
History of Fillmore County, Minnesota. 5612
History of Florence, &c. 78992
History of Florida from its discovery. (23669
History of Fort Halifax, Me. 58254
History of four months. 100899
History of Framingham and Holliston. 5345
History of Framingham, Massachusetts. (3691
History of Franklin County. (44929)
History of freemasonry and masonic digests. 49705
History of freemasonry; . . . discourse . . . in Bridgewater. (57653)
History of freemasonry from the year 1829 to 1841. 57203
History of freemasonry in Kentucky. 50871
History of freemasonry in New York. 33576
History of freemasonry, with additions, notes, critical and historical. (39403)
History of French influence in the United State 32138
History of friends. 21593
History of Gans Egede. 22031
History of Gardiner, Pittston, and West Gardiner. (30270)
History of Gardner, Massachusetts. (27557)
History of General Tom Thumb. 92731
History of Geneva, Wisconsin. 81166
History of Georgia, containing brief sketches. (42973)
History of Georgia, from its earliest settleme 2132
History of Georgia, from its first discovery. (36505), 91574
History of Gilmanton. (38783)

History of gold as a commodity and as a measure of value. 101306

History of grain-elevators. 9056, note after 95451

History of Grand Ligne Mission, Canada East. 18219

History of grants under the Great Council of New England. 30895

History of Great Britain from the death of George II. 49034

History of Great Britain, 1688-1802. 4600

History of Greenfield. 104040

History of Greenland: containing a description of the country. 17417

History of Greenland: including an account of the mission. 17418

History of Greensboro' and the Congregational Church. 92066

History of governments. 21154

History of Grant's campaign for the capture of Richmond. 10697

History of Guilford, Connecticut. 83742

History of Hadley, including the early history of Hatfield. 6255, 36843

History of Harrison County, Iowa. 83351

History of Harvard University. 67214

History of Harvard University, from its foundation. (59540)

History of Harwinton, Connecticut. 12827

History of Haverhill, Massachusetts. 49422, 103819

History of Haverhill, Massachusetts, from its first settlement. 12177

History of Henry Villars. 106142

History of her regiments, and other military organizations. (69092)

History of Herkimer County. 4782

History of Hernando Cortes. 37

History of Hernando de Soto and Florida. 80533, 98745

History of Hertfordshire. 12339

History of Humboldt County. 105053

History of his [i. e. Columbus's] previous life. 4218

History of his [i. e. Lincoln's] eventful administration. (3617)

History of Holden. 18368

History of Illinois, from its commencement as a state. 25070

History of Illinois, from its earliest settlement. 11008

History of Illinois from its first discovery and settlement. (8484)

History of Illinois. My own times. 70420

History of Illinois, 1775-1833. (21984)

History of immigration to the United States. 8226

History of Independence Hall. 4427

History of Indiana. 84793, 84795-84796

History of Indiana, from its earliest exploration by Europeans. 20172

History of Indiana, from its earliest exploration by Europeans to the close of the Territorial government. 20173

History of Indianapolis, from 1818 to 1868. 8489, 34582

History of infant baptism. 69522

History of Ipswich, Essex, and Hamilton. 24033

History of its [i. e. Springfield, N. J.'s] centennial fourth. 89888, note after 94615

History of its [i. e. the American Pharmaceutical Association's] foundation. 1192

History of Jacobism. 14021, 63374

History of Jamaica & Barbadoes. (32139)

History of Jamaica. Or, general survey of the antient and modern state of that island. 41871

History of Jamaica. With observations on the climate. (69620)

History of James Morgan. (50670)

History of Jay County, Indiana. 50154

History of Jefferson College. 83304

History of Jefferson County in the state of New York. 33140

History of Jefferson County, N. Y. 95825

History of Jemima Wilkinson. 33484, 104033

History of jewels. 12011, 32140

History of Jim Crow. 7954

History of Job. 83480

History of John Smith's picture. 32141

History of John Vandelure. 103225

History of Joseph. 26409

History of Joseph. A poem. 73542-73543

History of Joseph and his brethren. 21168

History of Joseph, in the language of the Dakota or Sioux Indians. 18290, 63995

History of Joseph Smith. 83242, 83245-83246, 83252, 83255, 83289, 83292

History of Kamtschatka. 38301

History of Kansas. 32559

History of Kennebunk Port. 7204

History of Kentucky [by Connelly and Coulter.] 85376

History of Kentucky. Exhibiting an account of the modern discovery. 44780, (67442)

History of Kentucky. From its earliest discovery and settlement. 84934, 84936-84937

History of Kentucky, from its earliest settlement to the present time. 2133

History of Kentucky; including an account of the discovery. 44779

History of King Philip. 39

History of King Philip's War. By Benjamin Church. (12976)

History of King Philip's War. By the Rev. Increase Mather, D. D. 46280, 46693

History of King Philip's War, commonly called the Great Indian War. 12998, 91750

History of King's Chapel in Boston. 28684

History of Knox College and Galesburgh. 26358

History of Knox County, Illinois. 84247

History of Knox County, Ohio. 55858

History of Lake Champlain. 58367

History of Lancaster County. 74160, 89175

History of land titles in Massachusetts. 93498

History of legal tender paper money. 89033

History of Leicester, Mass. (39898)

History of Lexington Kentucky. (67745)

History of Lewis County. 33142

History of Lewy's Island Lodge. 77031

History of liberty and slavery. 77351

History of Lincoln Lodge, in Wiscasset. 79438

History of Licking County, O. 85144

History of Lockport. 41743

History of Lodge Francaise No. 53. 85464

History of Londonderry. 58663

History of Long Island. 95468-95469

History of Long Island, from its first settlement. (65533)

History of Lope de Aguirre. 88550

History of Lord North's administration. 55515, 99561

History of Louise, daughter of a Canadian nun. 6919, (42069)

History of Louisiana, from its first discovery and settlement. 9188

History of Louisiana, from the earliest period. 44871

History of New-York [by William Smith.]
54472, 84570

History of New York City. 92149

History of New York, for schools. 21302

History of New York, from the beginning of
the world. 35149, 35162

History of New York from its earliest settlement. 2134

History of New-York, from the first discovery
to the year M.DCC.XXXIII. 84569, note
after 105999

History of Newbury, Vt. 83869

History of Newburyport. 82547

History of Newfoundland from the earliest
times. 59513

History of Newgate of Connecticut. 61390

History of Newton, Massachusetts. 84046

History of Nicholas I. 85153, 85164

History of Nicholas I. and the Crimean War.
85151-85152

History of Norridgewock, Maine. (894)

History of North America and its United
States. 57181

History of North America; comprising, a
geographical and statistical view. 32146,
94232

History of North America. Containing, a
review of the customs and manners. 16583

History of North America. Containing an
exact account. (32145)

History of North-America, from the first-
discovery thereof. 32144, 94099

History of North and South America, containing,
an account of the first discoveries of the
New World. 32148, 106120

History of North and South America. From
its discovery to the death of General
Washington. 85593-85594

History of North and South America, with an
account of the West Indies. 106121

History of North Bridgewater. (37867)

History of North Brookfield. 103200

History of North Carolina. By Hugh Williamson. 104449

History of North Carolina, from the earliest
period. 44872

History of North Carolina: with mapes and
illustrations. 30965

History of Northampton, Lehigh, Monroe,
Carbon, and Schuylkill Counties. 74162

History of Northumberland Co. 84851

History of Norway. 56213

History of Norwich, Connecticut. 11573

History of Norwich, Connecticut, from its
settlement in 1660. (11572)

History of Nova Scotia, Cape Breton, the Sable
Islands, New Brunswick. 44912

History of Nova Scotia, or Acadie. (51433)

History of Oberlin. 82430

History of Ohio. 11013

History of "Old Abe." 3615

History of Old Chester. (12167)

History of Olive Branch Lodge. 83698

History of Oregon. 103999-104000

History of Oregon and California. (28630),
(28632)

History of Oregon, containing a condensed
account. 97298

History of Oregon, geographical and political.
103997

History of Oregon, 1792-1849. 28416

History of Oregon Territory. 23866

History of Our Blessed Saviour. 84553

History of our country. 70979

History of our flag. (77088)

History of our lake commerce. 9056, note
after 95451

History of Our Lord and Saviour Jesus Christ.
(19376), (40989), note after 106301

History of Our Lord and Saviour Jesus Christ
epitomiz'd. 62517

History of our own times. 10270

History of Our Saviour. 22059

History of paper. 83325

History of paper making. 83328

History of Paraguay. 12133

History of party. 16309

History of Pekin. (59566)

History of Pennsylvania. 28002

History of Pennsylvania, from its earliest
settlement to the present time. (11014)

History of Pennsylvania Hall. 103804

History of Pennsylvania Hall, which was
destroyed by a mob. 102228

History of Pennsylvania, in North America.
66223, 89175, 97288

History of Perry's expedition to Japan. 7754

History of persecution. (74429)

History of persecution, in four parts. 11870

History of Peru. 59250

History of Peter and John Hay. 102475-102476

History of Philadelphia. 83783

History of Philadelphia, 1609-1884. 75510,
83793

History of Philadelphia, with a notice of
villages. (7048)

History of Phoenix Lodge. 41731

History of Pickens County, Ala. 83670

History of pirates. (32148)

History of pithole. (40095)

History of Pittsburgh. 17363

History of Pittsfield. 83334, 83336

History of Pittsfield, (Berkshire County,)
Massachusetts, from the year 1800 to the
year 1876. 83327

History of Pittsfield, (Berkshire County,)
Massachusetts, from the year 1734 to the
year 1800. 83326

History of Plymouth Plantation. 7262-7263,
19051, 51017, 106053

History of political parties in the state of
New-York. 36003

History of political religion. 2876

History of Pomfret. 33843

History of Pompey the Little. 32149

History of Poor Sarah. 67765

History of Portland, from its first settlement.
104525

History of preliminary experimental proceedings.
2301

History of preliminary proceedings of Third
Presbytery. 43191

History of presidential elections. 90460

History of prime ministers and favourites in
England. 32150

History of Prince Lee Boo. 32151

History of Princeton, Worcester County,
Massachusetts, civil and ecclesiastical.
30156

History of Princeton, Worcester County, Mass.
from its first settlement. 74311

History of printing in America. 95405-95406

History of proceedings, and debates of the
fifth session. 32155

History of propellers and steam navigation.
43251

History of prostitution. (76512)

History of Providence County, Rhode Island.
84977

History of public health. 84276

History of the American Jacobins. 14021
History of the American Lutheran Church. 31117
History of the American Medical Association. 18872
History of the American mission to the Pawnee Indians. 97518
History of the American Missionary Association. note after 94370
History of the American Missionary Society. 1149A
History of the American privateers. 14194
History of the American revolution, and biographical sketches. 61232
History of the American revolution. By David Ramsay. 67687
History of the American revolution. By George Bancroft. 3118
History of the American revolution. [By J. L. Blake.] 5783
History of the American revolution. By Michael Doheny. 20532
History of the American revolution. By the Rev. Dr. Shepherd. 80285-80287
History of the American revolution; comprehending all the principal events. 854, note after 102121
History of the American revolution; in scriptural style. 85595
History of the American revolution; including an impartial examination of the causes. 32156
History of the American revolution, including the most important events and resolutions of the Honourable Continental Congress. 33473
History of the American revolution: intended as a reading-book for schools. 92194, 104347
History of the American revolution, with a preliminary view of the character and principles of the colonies. 104687
History of the American telegraph. 24277
History of the American theatre. 18328, 21300
History of the American theatre; and anecdotes of the principal actors. 21300
History of the American Tract Society. 90461
History of the American troops. 32157, 103452
History of the American trotting horse. 82192
History of the American union. 37474
History of the American war. (24722)
History of the American war of 1812. 32158
History of the American wars. 95443
History of the Amistad captives. 3324
History of the Ancient and Honorable Artillery Company. 103751
History of the ancient Penacooks. 6959
History of the Anglo-Americans. (41234)
History of the annexation of Texas. 52200, 84463, 93663
History of the Argentine Republic. 20571
History of the arts of design. 98481
History of the Asiatic cholera in Providence. 85496
History of the assassination of James King. 23798
History of the author's life. 33920
History of the Babylonish cabal. 91183
History of the backwoods. 59132
History of the bank-rupt court. 89489
History of the banking system. 28074
History of the Baptist Association in Wales. 95431

History of the Baptist Association of New London. 53256
History of the Baptist Church, Brookline, Mass. 8254
History of the Baptist churches. 32160, note after 93254
History of the Baptist Indian missions in North America. 62446
History of the Baptists in Maine. 49082
History of the Baptists in New England. 93632
History of the Baptists in the western states. 83463
History of the battle at Lexington. 33109, 62568
History of the battle of Breed's Hill. 14162-14163, 2d note after 104027
History of the battle of Lake Erie. 13678
History of the battle of Lexington. 71508
History of the battle of the crooked billet. 18901
History of the Belville Settlement. 31799
History of the Bill family. 5372A
History of the bills of credit. 31692
History of the Black Hawk War. 100978
History of the Book of Common Prayer. 65947
History of the Boston-Athenaeum. (67215)
History of the Boston Dispensary. (39385)
History of the Boston massacre. 37712, 96946
History of the Brazils. 7589
History of the British colonies. (44910)
History . . . of the British colonies in the West Indies. 94565
History of the British dominions in North America. (32161)
History of the British empire, from the accession of James I. 43286
History of the British empire, from the year 1765. 32163, 85105
History of the British empire in America. 105682
History of the British plantations in America. (37240)
History of the British United Empire Loyalists of America. 74560
History of the Broadway Tabernacle Church. (54136)
History of the Brooklyn and Long Island Fair. 8294
History of the Brown's Ferry operation in 1863. 84772
History of the bucaniers. (23479)-23480
History of the bucaniers of America. 23483-23486, 23488-23484, (67986)
History of the buccaneers. 29473
History of the buccaneers of America. 9388
History of the buccaniers of America. 20182
History of the Buffalo public schools. 91135
History of the Bunker Hill Monument. 58096
History of the Bunker Hill Monument Association. 101465
History of the business and business men of Boston. 6479
History of the cabinet of the United States. 84796
History of the cabinet of the United States of America. 84793
History of the campaign of 1805, &c. (9314)
History of the campaign of 1812. (10263)
History of the campaign of Mobile. 1489
History of the campaigns, and associations in the field. 30233
History of the campaigns of 1780 and 1781. 30226, 43431, 94397
History of the canal policy of . . . New-York. 53660

History of the conquest of Peru, by the Spaniards. 97162

History of the conquest of Peru, with a preliminary view. 65272-(65274)

History of the conspiracy of Pontiac. 58803

History of the consolidation of the city of Philadelphia. 65428

History of the constitution [of Vermont] during his administration. (12821)

History of the Consumptives' Home. (17863)

History of the controversy in the University of the City of New York. 14827, 54706

History of the convention of the Leeward Islands. 9849

History of the Cooper Shop Volunteer Refreshment Saloon. 50402

History of the copper mines. (61385)

History of the cotton famine. 2078

History of the cotton manufacture in Great Britain. 2776

History of the counties of Berks and Lebanon. 74163

History of the county of Berkshire, Massachusetts. 19848, 24270, 92912

History of the county of Fond du Lac, Wis. 49663

History of the county of Orange. 75493

History of the county of Westchester. 6247

History of the county of Worcester. 130769

History of the criminal law of Rhode Island. 90477

History of the cruelties of the inquisition. (5988)

History of the Cumberland Presbyterian Church. 82783

History of the Cutter family of New England. 18192

History of the Davenport family. 74613

History of the Delaware and Iroquois Indians. (32165)

History of the Delaware Department of the Great Central Fair. (19388)

History of the Democratic Party. 36630

History of the descendants of Elder John Strong. 21513

History of the destruction of His Britannic Majesty's Schooner Gaspee. 3740

History of the detection, conviction, life and designs of John A. Murrel [sic.] 51552, note before 91708, 101209

History of the devil and Dr. Faustus. 93890

History of the De Witt Guard. 19881

History of the discovery and conquest of America. (71980), 71988

History of the discovery and conquest of India. 23802

History of the discovery and conquest of the Canary Islands. 79

History of the discovery and settlement of America. 71979, 71981, 71983-71984

History of the discovery and settlement of the valley of the Mississippi. 49966

History of the discovery and settlement to the present time. 46983

History of the discovery of America. 82808, 97193-97196, 97201

History of the discovery of America, written for children. 24756

History of the discovery of Maine. (43971)

History of the discovery of the valley of the Mississippi. 30612

History of the disease usually called typhoid fever. 93977

History of the dispute with America. 243

History of the district of Maine. 93499

History of the dividing line. (9721)

History of the dividing line and other tracts. (9722)

History of the division of the First Baptist Church, In Southbridge. 88262

History of the division of the Presbyterian Church. (32166), (36833)

History of the Doans. 8243

History of the Donatists. note after 102109

History of the Dudley Street Baptist Church. 73639

History of the Dutch war in 1672. 14390

History of the early adventures of Washington among the Indians.

History of the early policy of the Presbyterian Church. 2802

History of the early puritans. 44711

History of the early settlement and Indian wars. 19308

History of the early settlement of Bridgewater. 49707

History of the early settlement of the Juniata Valley. 36618

History of the early settlers of Sagamon County, Illinois. (64772)

History of the eastern expeditions of 1689, 1690, 1692, 1696, and 1704. 12977

History of the Eastern Penitentiary. 60080

History of the ecclesiastical affairs of Pepperell. 60842

History of the effort to secure representation of the educational institutions of Ohio. 77889

History of the eighteenth century. 77656

History of the 86th Regiment Illinois Volunteer Infantry. (37927)

History of the Eighty-Third Regiment Pennsylvania Volunteers. 36858

History of the Eleventh Regiment Ohio Volunteer Infantry. 56934

History of the Eleventh Wisconsin Veteran Volunteer Infantry. 43588

History of the emigration and settlement of our predecessors. 28128

History of the English language and literature. 11801

History of the English puritans. 45008

History of the epidemic yellow fever. 24067

History of the Episcopal Church in Connecticut. 4133

History of the Episcopal Church, in Narragansett, Rhode-Island. 98029

History of the erection of the monument on the grave of Myron Holley. 32532

History of the establishment and progress of the Christian religion. 32167

History of the evangelical churches in New York. (25848)

History of the evangelical churches of Boston. 50420

History of the events and men of July, 1830. 77097

History of the events which transpired during the Navy Island campaign. 41303

History of the excise law of the state of New-York. 31221

History of the Exhibition . . . of 1857. 50030

History of the expedition conducted by William Hull. (33641), 57071

History of the expedition under the command of Captains Lewis and Clarke. (40828), 40833

History of the Exposition of Textile Fabrics. (47055)

History of the express business. 91826

History of the express companies. 91827

History of the extra session of Congress, convened by proclamation, September 4, and terminated October 4, 1832. (15533)

History of the extra session of Congress, convened in Washington, by proclamation. 32168

History of the fabulous deities of the ancients. 50038

History of the fallen angels of the scriptures. 65496

History of the family (ancestral and descendant) of the Hon. William Fiske. 24540

History of the family (ancestral and descendant) of William Fiske. (24541)

History of the Federal and Democratic parties. (32169)

History of the federal government. 25766

History of the federal government for fifty years. 7224

History of the female sex. 46411

History of the 51st Regiment of P. V. and V. V. 58773

History of the Fifty-Ninth Regiment Illinois Volunteers. 39173

History of the fight at Concord. 33109, 71508

History of the fight of the intrepid Captain John Loveell. [sic] 94109

History of the first attempt of the Huguenots to colonize Florida. (25854)

History of the first Church and Paris in Dedham. 38773

History of the First Church and Society in Raynham. 76479

History of the First Church, Charlestown. 8969

History of the First Congregational Church and Society, of Woodstock, Conn. 28949

History of the first discovery and settlement of Virginia. 76456, 91860-91862, 1st note before 99889

History of the First Independent Church, Philadelphia. 11797

History of the First New Hampshire Regiment. 37713

History of the First New Jersey Cavalry. 66873

History of the First Presbyterian Church, Edgewater, Staten Island. 72423

History of the First Presbyterian Church of Frankfort, Indiana. 83700

History of the First Presbyterian Church, Orange, N. J. 33406

History of the First Regiment (Massachusetts Infantry.) 17832

History of the first settlement of Virginia. 5112-5113, 1st and 3d notes after 100480

History of the first steamship pioneers. 86019

History of the first ten years of the reign of George the Third. 26997, 43249

History of the First Universalist Church. 85522

History of the Five Indian Nations depending on the province of New York. 14270, 84566

History of the Five Indian Nations of Canada. 14273-14275

History of the Five Indian Nations of the province of New York. 14271, (80023)

History of the flag. 65012

History of the flag, by a distinguished historian. 37693

History of the Floridas. 99607

History of the formation of the Ladies' Society. 38542

History of the formation of the Newsboys' Lodging House. 7158

History of the foundation and endowment of the Lane Theological Seminary. 38861

History of the founders of the Federal Street Church. (54916)

History of the four Georges, Kings of England. 77705, 85156, 85157

History of the fourteenth century. 35743

History of the Fourteenth Regiment Alabama Vols. 34013

History of the freebooters of the Antilles. 79354, 105692

History of the French revolution. 20988

History of the fur trade. 10537

History of the gallant adventures, 20587, note after 97428

History of the gaols of this state. 45763

History of the garret &c. &c. (32170), 63650

History of the General or Six Principle Baptists. 38122

History of the German Reformed Church. 47112

History of the gift book business. 32171

History of the gigantic headed boy of Georgia. 20765

History of the government of the island of Newfoundland. (68671)

History of the gold regions. (23868)

History of the grammar school. 20160

History of the Grand Chicago and North-Western "ring," etc. 58958

History of the Grand Trunk Railway. 8569

History of the great Albany Constitutional Convention of 1821. 92134

History of the great and mighty kingdom of China. 27784

History of the great Atlantic cable. 7940

History of the great express robbery of Livingston & Wells. (41653)

History of the great international contest between Heenan and Sayers. (77403)

History of the great massacre by the Sioux Indians in Minnesota. 8803

History of the great railroad adventure. 6310

History of the great rebellion. (6319), note after 42135

History of the great rebellion, from its commencement to its close. (37657)

History of the great rebellion in the United States of America. 28482

History of the great Republic. 59478

History of the great secession from the Methodist Episcopal Church. 22255

History of the great struggle in both hemispheres. 27849

History of the Great Western Sanitary Fair. 32172

History of the Half Breed Tract. 13622

History of the Hallech Guard. 70970

History of the Hampshire Bar. 5918

History of the Harrisburg Cemetery Association. 85172

History of the Hart Family. 18902

History of the Hartford Convention. 21537

History of the Hartsville Ladies' Aid Society. 86313

History of the haunted caverns of Magdelana. 36365

History of the Hawaiian or Sandwich Islands. 35796

History of the head-longs and the long-heads. 27364

History of the hen fever. 9394

History of the High St. Baptist Church in Charleston, Ms. 12111
History of the Holland Purchase. 97489
History of the Holy Jesus. 84553
History of the House of Medici. 85170
History of the Huguenots. [By W. Carlos Martyn.] 45008
History of the Huguenots. [By Anne Marsh.] 44722
History of the Humane Society of Massachusetts. 32173, (33680), 45765
History of the Hutchinson family. 34093
History of the illegal arrests and imprisonments of American citizens. 44798
History of the Independent or Congregational Church in Charleston. (67690), 94719
History of the Indian tribes of Hudson's River. 74495
History of the Indian tribes of North America. 43410A-(43411)
History of the Indian tribes of the United States. 77849
History of the Indian wars. 82808, 85254, 97196
History of the Indian wars in New England. 33453
History of the Indian wars with the first settlers of the United States, particularly in New-England. 76366, 94252
History of the Indian wars with the first settlers of the United States to the commencement of the late war. 32174, 76367
History of the Indians. 27913
History of the Indians of Connecticut. 19292
History of the Indians of North and South America. (27902)
History of the Indies. Second part. 27731
History of the institution [i. e. the Boston Mercantile Library Association.] 6745
History of the institution [i. e. the Greenwood Cemetery] from 1838 to 1864. (13608)
History of the institution of the Sabbath day. (24510)
History of the insurrection, in the four western counties. (24360)
History of the insurrections, in Massachusetts. 49324
History of the introduction and use of Scutelleria Lateriflora. 88903
History of the introduction of pure water into the city. 7277
History of the introduction of state normal schools in America. 8340
History of the Irish settlers in North America. (43262)
History of the iron trade. 78503
History of the island of Dominica. 2343
History of the island of Newfoundland. 1644
History of the island of St. Domingo. Abridged from the history of Bryan Edwards. 21900
History of the island of St. Domingo, from its first discovery by Columbus. 3884, 75133
History of the island of St. Domingo from its first discovery by the Portuguese to 1823. 8369
History of the islands of Cape Breton and St. Johns. 32175
History of the issues of paper-money in the American colonies. 30613
History of the isthmus of Panama. 78866
History of the Italian Opera Company imported to America. 64011-64012

History of the Jamaica case. 24369
History of the Jefferson Medical College of Philadelphia. (26800)
History of the Jesuits. 91213
History of the Jewish nation. 84062
History of the Jews. 36666
History of the kingdom of Basaruah. 96482
History of the kingdoms and states of Asia, Africa and America. 32176
History of the kings and queens of England. 84994
History of the Knights Templar of the state·of Pennsylvania. 17465
History of the labors of the Rev. Eugenio Kincaid. (59156)
History of the Ladies' Temperance Benevolent Societies. (36252)
History of the last session of Congress. (15534), 84075
History of the late ecclesiastical oppressions in New England and Vermont. 32178, 80634, 2d note after 99205
History of the late minority. 953, 32177
History of the late persecution inflicted by the state of Missouri. 64965
History of the late province of Lower Canada. 12936
History of the late province of New-York. 84571-84572
History of the late rebellion from 1860 to 1865. 86319
History of the late war, between Great Britain and the United States. 95487
History of the late war between the United States and Great Britain: containing a brief recapitulation. 32179
History of the late war, between the United States and Great-Britain. Containing a minute account. 7163-(7164), 18333
History of the late war between the United States and Great Britain. Containing an accurate account. 27388
History of the late war between the United States and Great Britain, with a critical appendix. 2775, 17925
History of the late war, from the commencement of hostilities after the peace of Aix-la-Chapelle. 72880
History of the late war in North-America. 44396
History of the late war in the plantations. (18916), 20651, 70574
History of the late war in the western country. 42929
History of the late war, or annual register of its rise, progress and events. 32180
History of the later puritans. 44712
History of the law of shipping and navigation. 68672
History of the laws of Massachusetts respecting paupers. 57980
History of the legal tender paper money. 89040
History of the legislation of Congress upon the American fisheries. 25262
History of the Lehigh Coal and Navigation Company. (39878)
History of the Lehigh Valley. 31404, 39880
History of the life and adventures of Henry Grace. (28184)
History of the life and adventures of J. Plummer. 63464
History of the life and adventures of Mr. Anderson. 1380
History of the life and death of Hugh Peters. 61197

History of the life and death of John W. Stephens. 91055

History of the life and death, virtues and exploits, of General George Washington. 102483-102484

History of the life and public services of Major General Andrew Jackson. 35366

History of the life and services of Captain Samuel Dewees. 30231

History of the life and times of Edmund Burke. (43477)

History of the life and times of James Madison. (71663)

History of the life and times of John Wesley. 91477

History of the life and voyages of Christopher Columbus. (35169)-(35171), (35173)

History of the life of Thomas Ellwood. 22352, 105653

History of the life of William Pitt. 63093

History of the life, very strange adventures, and works of Captain John Macpherson. 43635

History of the little Frenchman and his bank notes. 32183

History of the lives and bloody exploits of the most noted pirates. 32182, (32197)

History of the lives and exploits of the most remarkable pirates. (36196)

History of the lives, last words, and dying confessions of three most noted criminals. 1066

History of the lives of the most notorious pirates and their crews. 32181

History of the loan of 1864. 21699

History of the Loco-Foco or Equal Rights Party. 9723

History of the "man after God's own heart!" 86635

History of the Maroons. 18322

History of the martyrs epitomized. 44124

History of the Massachusetts General Hospital. 6999, 45846

History of the Massachusetts Normal Art School. 84499

History of the massacre at Indian Keys in Florida. 32184

History of the Medical Department of Harvard University. 30765

History of the Medical Department of the University of Pennsylvania. 11086

History of the medical education and institutions in the United States. 18871

History of the medicinal springs at Saratoga and Ballstown. 76917

History of the mercantile, political, and official career of our "model" mayor! (54317)

History of the Methodist Church in Hartford. 17435

History of the Methodist Church within the territories embraced in the late Conference of Eastern North America. 84421

History of the Methodist Episcopal Church. note after 91480

History of the Methodist Episcopal Church, from its origin in 1776. 3166

History of the Methodist Episcopal Church in the United States and Canada. 28036

History of the Methodist Protestant Church. 58592

History of the Mexican war. (50317)

History of the Miami Baptist Association. 21311

History of the middle states. 41073

History of the mild yellow fever. 92033

History of the Mission House of the Protestant Episcopal Church. 66154

History of the mission of the Secession Church. 71955

History of the mission of the United Brethren among the Indians in North America. (42110)

History of the mission of the United Brethren's Church to the Negroes. 8874

History of the missions in Japan and Paraguay. (9822)

History of the missions of the Methodist Episcopal Church. 92819

History of the Missisco Valley. 93709

History of the Missouri compromise. 52200, 84463, 93663

History of the Mobile dumping ground. 84777

History of the modern Jews. 85154

History of the Mohammedan dynasties of Spain. 16942

History of the Moravian Church in Philadelphia. 71591

History of the Moravian missions among the Indians. 32185, 2d note after 97850

History of the Moravian missions in Ohio. 85136

History of the Moravians. 71405-71406

History of the Moravians, from their first settlement. 50521

History of the Mormons. 85145-85146

History of the Mormons, or Latter Day Saints. 11477

History of the Morristown Ghost! 72721, 106070

History of the most interesting events in the rise and progress of Methodism. 106201

History of the most remarkable voyages. 33628

History of the Most Worshipful Grand Lodge of Virginia. 20739

History of the names of men, nations, and places. (50530), (75878)

History of the Narragansett Church. 43662

History of the nation, from its earliest period. 11066

History of the national flag of the United States of America. 30032

History of the national peace jubilee and great musical festival. 27454

History of the national political conventions. 29924

History of the nature of the excise laws. 32186

History of the navy during the rebellion. (7149)

History of the navy of the United States of America. 16442

History of the navy of the United States of America. Abridged. 16444

History of the navy of the United States of America. Continued to 1853. 16443

History of the negotiations in reference to the eastern and north western boundary of the United States in 1841. 32187, 39380

History of the Negro plot. (33060)

History of the Negro slave trade. 5646

History of the New Bedford churches. 37264

History of the New Brick Church. 71777

History of the New-England Emigrant Aid Company. 32188

History of the New Netherlands. 21301

History of the New World, by Don Juan Baptista Munoz. 51345

History of the New World, by Girolamo Benzoni. 4805, 85347

History of the New World, called America. 32194

History of the New York African Free Schools. 1487

History of the New-York Kappa Lambda conspiracy. 32189, (54789)

History of the New York National Guard. 32190

History of the newly discovered islands of Canaria. 34107

History of the 99th Indiana Infantry. 42608

History of the Ninth Regiment Illinois Volunteer Infantry. (50894)

History of the Ninth Regiment of Volunteers of New Jersey Infantry. 23295

History of the North Church, New Haven. 21471

History of the North-Western Soldiers' Fair. 12656

History of the northern campaign of 1777. (78052)

History of the Northmen, or Danes and Normans. 103157

History of the Oberlin-Wellington rescue. 80503

History of the Ohio canals. 56935

History of the oil regions of Venango, [sic] County Pa. 21740

History of the Ojebway Indians. (36590)

History of the Old and New Testament, illustrated with notes, and adorned with cuts, for use of children. 5167

History of the Old and New Testament. Illustrated with notes and adorned with cuts. For the use of children, &c. 5169

History of the Old and New Testament, interspersed with moral and instructive reflections. 68665

History of the old buildings on the corner School and Washington Street, Boston. 80777

History of the old Cheraws. 28704

History of the old folks' concerts. (37336)

History of the old men of the montain. 65490

History of the old Second Division of the Army of the Cumberland. 20515, 32159

History of the Old South Church in Boston, in four sermons. 104907

History of the Old South Church of Boston. 86212

History of the old towns Norridgewock and Canaan. 30271

History of the old township of Dunstable. 25342

History of the One Hundred and Eighty-Ninth Regiment of New-York Volunteers. (72749)

History of the 104th Pennsylvania Regiment. 18903

History of the 114th Regiment, New York Volunteers. 59580

History of the 102d Illinois Infantry Volunteers. 24691

History of the One Hundred and Seventeenth Regiment, N. Y. Volunteers. 51209

History of the One Hundred and Thirty-Eighth Regiment, Pennsylvania Volunteer Infantry. 40842

History of the One Hundred and Twelfth Regiment N. Y. Volunteers. (34127)

History of the Onondaga Historical Association. 57361

History of the operations of a partisan corps. 81135

History of the operations of the British troops in that country. 38999

History of the operations of the Society for the Promotion of Collegiate and Theological Education at the West. 85918

History of the order, by J. Wadsworth. 36140

History of the Order of the Sons of Temperance. (22328)

History of the ordinance of 1787. 14327

History of the Oregon Territory and British North-American fur trade. 21321

History of the Oregon Territory: containing the laws of Oregon. 77349

History of the organization and movements of the Fourth Regiment of Infantry, United States Army. (64766)

History of the organization of the Methodist Episcopal Church South. 48187

History of the origin and design of the . . . [Massachusetts Congregational Charitable] Society. 95178

History of the origin and progress of adult schools. 96286

History of the origin and progress of the late war from its commencement. 32191

History of the origin, formation, and adoption of the constitution. (18038)

History of the origin, progress, and termination of the American war. 13753, 91057, 95606

History of the origin, rise, and progress of the Masonic Order in Texas. 74462

History of the origin, rise and progress of the war in America. (32192)

History of the original settlements on the Delaware. 24183

History of the oyster. 23570

History of the Parish of St. Thomas' Church. 49084

History of the parish registers of England. 9357

History of the passage of the act increasing the salaries of members of Congress. (72215)

History of the past fifty years. 20349

History of the Patagonians. 59250, 1st note after 102210

History of the peace with France. (32195)

History of the Penobscott Indians. 93506

History of the people called Quakers. 28078

History of the people called Quakers, from their first rise. (28077)

History of the peopling of the several parts of the world. 30482

History of the Pequot War. [By Charles Orr.] 97733, 99766

History of the Pequot War. By Lieut. Lion Gardiner. (26625)

History of the personal adventures, heroic exploits, and romantic incidents. 9158

History of the Peruvian syrup. 13341

History of the pestilence, commonly called yellow fever. 15179

History of the Pigwackett Baptists. 24925, 83790

History of the pilgrims. 32196

History of the pioneer and modern times of Ashland County. 38062

History of the pioneer settlement of Phelps and Gorham's Purchase. 97489-97490

History of the pious Indian convert. 100992

History of the pirates, containing the lives of those noted pirate captains. 32182, (32197), (36191)

History of the reign of George the Third, from his accession to the throne. 71946

History of the reign of George the Third, King of Great-Britain &c. 32203

History of the reign of George III. to the termination of the late war. 5647

History of the reign of George III. to the termination of the late war. Second edition, completed to the death of the king. 5647

History of the reign of Philip the Second. 65289-65291

History of the reign of the Emperor Charles the Fifth. 65295

History of the relation of the pastor to the "Christian Church" of Nashville. 24094

History of the religious denominations in the United States. 83289

History of the religious movement of the eighteenth century. 91477

History of the religious society of Friends. 35760

History of the republic of Texas. 43886

History of the republic of the United States of America. (30021)

History of the Republican Party in Ohio. 83365

History of the Rev. Hugh Peters. 61221

History of the revisions of the discipline of the Methodist Episcopal Church. 80355

History of the revival of religion in the time of Edwards. 96419

History of the revolution in Texas. 32204, 54948, note after 95091

History of the revolution in the southern states. (23927)

History of the revolution of Caraccas. 24800

History of the revolution of South Carolina. 67688, (67691)

History of the revolution of the 18th Fructidor. 32205

History of the revolutionary debt of Rhode Island. 71148

History of the revolutionary war between Great Britain and the United States. 81603

History of the revolutionary war with England. 7792

History of the rise and fall of the South Sea Stock. (32206)

History of the rise and progress of the arts of design. 21303

History of the rise and progress of the Baptists in America. 23465

History of the rise and progress of the Baptists in Virginia. 79089

History of the rise and progress of the iron trade. 25855

History of the rise and progress of the Pennsylvania chronicle. 27642-(27643), 27645, 2d note after 97091

History of the rise & progress of the rebellion. 88468

History of the rise and progress of the United States of North America. 28243

History of the rise and progress of the war in North-America. (32192)

History of the rise, difficulties & suspension of Antioch College. 69157

History of the rise, increase, and progress of the Christian people called Quakers. 12913, (66917), 79602-79611, (79613)-79615, note after 103655

History of the rise, increase, and progress of the Society of Friends. 79612

History of the rise of Methodism in America. 39684

History of the rise, progress and accomplishment of the abolition of the African slave-trade. 13486

History of the rise, progress, and destiny of the American Party. (32207), 87110

History of the rise, progress, and establishment, of the independence of the United States of America. 28011

History of the rise, progress, and existing condition of the western canals. 102130

History of the rise, progress, and existing state of the Berkshire Agricultural Society, in Massachusetts. 102131

History of the rise, progress, and present condition of the Bethlehem Female Seminary. 68989

History of the rise, progress, and present condition of the Moravian Seminary for Young Ladies. 68990

History of the rise, progress, and suppression of rebellious insurrections. 32208

History of the rise, progress, and termination of the American revolution. 101484

History of the rise, progress, genius, and character of American Presbyterianism. 31866

History of the Sabbatarians or Seventh Day Baptists in America. 13403

History of the sacred scriptures in every language and dialect. 5186

History of the St. Albans Raid. 88830

History of the Saints. (4733)

History of the Salem and Danvers Aqueduct. 22561

History of the same war. 46693

History of the San Juan water boundary question. 24630

History of the Sandwich Islands. By Lahainaluna. (19992)

History of the Sandwich Islands: with an account of the American mission. (32209)

History of the Sandy Creek Baptist Association. (66707)

History of the school of the Reformed Protestant Dutch Church. 21338

History of the Second Baptist Church, Cambridge, Mass. 20592

History of the Second Company of the Seventh Regiment. 13273

History of the Second Church, or Old North, in Boston. 71777

History of the Second Congregational Church, New Haven. 29904

History of the Second Iowa Cavalry. 62736

History of the Second Massachusetts Regiment of Infantry. (67276)

History of the Second Presbyterian Church, Newark, N. J. 83339

History of the Second Presbyterian Congregation in Newark, N. J. 15182

History of the . . . [Second Presbyterian] Church, two discourses. 85300

History of the second ten years of the reign of George the Third. 26998, (32210), 43249

History of the second war between the United States and Great Britain. 95590

History of the self-styled Perfectionists. 21677

History of the separation in Indiana Yearly Meeting of Friends. 21851

History of the services of the troops and people of New Jersey. 25251

History of the settlement and Indian wars of Tazewell County, Virginia. 5226

History of the settlement by the whites, of north-western Virginia. 104928

History of the settlement of Oregon. 37262

History of the settlement of Stueben County, N. Y. 43570

History of the Sevarites or Sevarambi. 98299

History of the seven years war. 41301

History of the Seventh-Day Baptist General Conference. 2733

History of the 75th Illinois Infantry. 20516

History of the Seventy-Sixth Regiment New York Volunteers. (82295)

History of the Shakers. 30803

History of the Shawnee Indians. 30775

History of the Shuey family in America. 80756

History of the siege of Boston. 26080, (26082)

History of the silk bill. 21383

History of the Sioux or Dakota Indian mission. (32211), 97519

History of the Sioux war and massacres of 1862 and 1863. 31178

History of the Six Nations. 92137

History of the Six Nations. David Cusick's sketches. 18142

History of the 16th Regiment Pennsylvania Cavalry. 28711, 32212

History of the Sixtieth Alabama Regiment. (79889)

History of the Sixtieth Regiment New York State Volunteers. 21810

History of the Smithsonian exchanges. 85093

History of the Society of Friends in America. 6986

History of the Society of Jesus in North America. 103353

History of the South Carolina College. 38428, 87978

History of the Southern Confederacy. 24985

History of the Southern Iowa Soldiers' Fair. 32213

History of the southern rebellion. 32220

History of the Spaniards proceedings in America. 28020

History of the Spanish discoveries prior to 1520. 27999

History of the Spirit Lake Massacre. 32214, note after 89469

History of the spirit-rappers. (14203)

History of the Stafford projectiles. 90080

History of the Stanton Street Baptist Church. 90449, note after 92355

History of the state during the war. (69092)

History of the state of California. 26033

History of the state of Indiana. 84794-84794A

History of the state of Maine. 104493

History of the state of New York. First period, 1609-1664. 8178

History of the state of New York. For the use of common schools. 67804

History of the state of New York, from the first discovery. (21675)

History of the state of New-York including its aboriginal and colonial annals. 51130, 102920, note after 105999

History of the state of New York, political and governmental. 83738

History of the state of Ohio, natural and civil. 2334

History of the state of Rhode Island and Providence Plantations. 2083

History of the state of Vermont. 95551

History of the state of Vermont, from its discovery and settlement. 33096

History of the state of Vermont, from its earliest settlement. 95550

History of the state prison in Charlestown. 88222

History of the steamboat case. 32215, note after 91888

History of the strange adventures, and signal deliverances. 2207

History of the strange sounds or rappings. 19849

History of the struggle for slavery extention or restriction. 28488

History of the sufferings and wrongs of Mr. Sylvester Brown. 8563

History of the supernatural in all ages and nations. 33378

History of the temperance reform in America. 32217

History of the temperance reform in Concord. 6961

History of the temperance reformation. 94641

History of the temperance reformation. [By Cyrus Mann.] 44312

History of the Tenth Regiment, Vermont Volunteers. 31049

History of the Territory of Wisconsin. 92950

History of the Texas conspiracy. 12701

History of the Third Georgia Regiment. 85373

History of the 13th Infantry Regiment of Connecticut Volunteers. 89671

History of the thirty-ninth Congress. 3532

History of the Tontine Building. 19624

History of the town of Abingdon. 32290

History of the town of Antrim. 103781

History of the town of Berkley. 76481

History of the town of Concord. 334, (79878)

History of the town of Cornwall. 46890

History of the town of Danvers. 30272

History of the town of Dorcester. (20619)

History of the town of Dumbarten. 90517

History of the town of Essex. (17697)

History of the town of Essex from 1634 to 1868. 17698

History of the town of Exeter. 84704

History of the town of Fitchburg, Massachusetts. 96300

History of the town of Flatbush. 93073

History of the town of Gloucester. (2582)

History of the town of Gorham. 62735

History of the town of Goshen. [By Augustine George Hibbard.] 104126

History of the town of Goshen. [By Hiram Barrus.] 83541

History of the town of Greenwich. 47219

History of the town of Groton. 9624

History of the town of Hampstead. 82747

History of the town of Hingham. 41264

History of the town of Lee. 26347

History of the town of Lexington. 33478

History of the town of Marlborough. 33479

History of the town of Mason. 31844

History of the town of Medford. 8377

History of the town of Middlefield, Massachusetts. 84342

History of the town of Montpelier. 95480

History of the town of Natick, Mass. 5346

History of the town of Norton. 13284

History of the town of Newburgh. 74494

History of the town of Peterborough. 82322

History of the town of Pittsfield. 19848, 24270, 92912

History of the town of Pittsfield, in Berkshire County, Mass. (24271)

History of the town of Plymouth. 95150-95151
History of the town of Rindge. 90884
History of the town of Rochester, Vt. 104393
History of the town of Sharon. 78816
History of the town of Shoreham. (27857)
History of the town of Shrewsbury, furnished for the Worcester magazine and historical journal. 101277
History of the town of Shrewsbury, Massachusetts. 101278
History of the town of Townsend. 77297
History of the town of Union. 80826, 80828
History of the town of Westminster. 33480
History of the town of Windham. 84405
History of the town of Worthington. 70838
History of the towns of Haddam and East Haddam. 24272
History of the township of Bridgewater, Mass. 33947
History of the townships of Byberry and Moreland. (44934)
History of the trial of Castner Hanway and others. 30274
History of the transactions and commerce between Russia and China. 17309
History of the translations . . . of the scriptures. (44738)
History of the tread mill. (30321)
History of the troops furnished by the state of Iowa. 34751
History of the troubles in Kansas. 62532
History of the turf in South Carolina. 88012
History of the 12th Regiment of New Hampshire Volunteers. 83969
History of the 28th Regt. Massachusetts Vols. 18127
History of the 23d. Iowa Infantry Volunteer Regiment. 89404
History of the Twenty-Second United States Infantry. 83699
History of the ungrateful conduct of Enoch Brian. 95858
History of the union. 9436
History of the United Netherlands. 51109
History of the United States. (32221)
History of the United States, and biography of the signers. 32220
History of the United States before the revolution. (76484)
History of the United States. [By Avery.] 84616-84617, 84647
History of the United States. [By George Bancroft.] 3122, 28600, (41600), 67221
History of the United States. [By George Tucker.] 97307
History of the United States. By J. W. Barber. 3325
History of the United States, by John Inman. 46940
History of the United States . . . by Samuel R. Hall and A. R. Baker. 29844
History of the United States Cavalry. 7195
History of the United States, compiled from American and other sources. 32219
History of the United States for families and libraries. 42116
History of the United States for 1796. (10064)
History of the United States, for the use of schools. 18693
History of the United States, for the year 1796. (29969)-29970
History of the United States from 1492 to 1866. 44935
History of the United States, from the discovery of America to the close of the great rebellion. 71929

History of the United States, from the discovery of America to the close of the year 1862. 71928
History of the United States, from the discovery of America to the inauguration of President Lincoln. 71927
History of the United States, from the discovery of the American continent. 3117
History of the United States, from the discovery of the American continent to the present time. 3116
History of the United States from the discovery of the American continent to the war of independence. 3119
History of the United States. From the earliest period to the administration of James Buchanan. 89338
History of the United States, from the earliest period to the administration of President Johnson. 89340
History of the United States, from their first settlement as colonies, to the close of the administration of Mr. Madison. 29663, note before 97919
History of the United States, from their first settlement as colonies to the close of Mr. Tyler's administration in 1845. 29664
History of the United States, from their first settlement as colonies, to the close of the war with Great Britain. 29662, 32218, note before 97919
History of the United States, from their first settlement as English colonies, in 1607, to the year 1808. (67694), 84123
History of the United States from their first settlement. For the use of schools. 32222
History of the United States, from their first settlement to the peace of Ghent. 28866
History of the United States Naval Academy. 44770
History of the United States navy. 83960
History of the United States. No. I. 30970, 2d note after 97726, 2d note after 100480
History of the United States. No. 2. (30966), 3d note after 97724
History of the United States: N°. III. 97725
History of the United States of America. By a citizen of Massachusetts. (29661), 65082, 93554, note before 97919
History of the United States of America. By Harvey Prindle Peet. 59535
History of the United States of America. [By Henry Adams.] 84787
History of the United States of America. By J. A. Spencer. 89341
History of the United States of America . . . . By John Lord. 42028
History of the United States of America. By Rev. Charles A. Goodrich. (22449), 27871
History of the United States of America. [By Richard Hildreth.] (31777)
History of the United States of America, designed for schools. 29115
History of the United States of America, from the adoption of the federal constitution. (31777)
History of the United States of America, from the discovery of the continent by Columbus to the present time. 27903
History of the United States of America, from the discovery of the continent in 1492. 93757
History of the United States of America, from the discovery of the continent, to the close of the first session of the thirty-fifth Congress. 59160

History of the United States of America, from the discovery of the continent to the organization of the government. 31776

History of the United States of America: from the earliest period to the present time. 79682

History of the United States of America, from the period of the discovery to the present time. (74341)

History of the United States of America under the constitution. 77916

History of the United States of America; with a brief account of some of the principal empires & states. (29661), 65082, 93554

History of the United States of America. With a continuation. 43354

History of the United States of America. Written in accordance with the principles of peace. 51535

History of the United States of North America. 26034

History of the United States of North America; from the discovery of the western world to the present day. 3788

History of the United States of North America, from the plantation of the British colonies till their assumption of national independence. 28245

History of the United States of North America, from the plantation of the British colonies till their revolt and declaration of independence. 28244

History of the United States, on a new plan. 57248

History of the United States, or republic of America. 104046

History of the United States Sanitary Commission. 91785

History of the United States Secret Service. 2841

History of the United States . . . to the cession of Florida. 28867

History of the United States . . . to the fifth census. 28867

History of the United States . . . to the peace with Mexico. 28867

History of the United States . . . to the sixth census. 28867

History of the United States; to which is prefixed a brief historical account. 102358

History of the University of Pennsylvania. 84585, 84597, 84608, 84611, 84622, 84641, 84643, 84678C

History of the University of Pennsylvania, from its origin to the year 1827. 105029

History of the upper country of South Carolina. 41802

History of the usury laws. 16712

History of the valley of the Mississippi. 30614

History of the valley of Virginia. 20490, 37611, 44258, 97611, note after 105690

History of the Venango oil regions. (30467)

History of the Viceroyalty of Buenos Ayres. 103963

History of the Vigilance Committee of San Francisco. 76048

History of the Virginia Company of London. 52285

History . . . of the visitation of yellow fever. 28876

History of the voyages and adventures of John Van Delure. 98466-98467, 98470

History of the voyages and discoveries made in the north. 25138

History of the voyages and travels of Capt. Nathaniel Uring. 98124-98126

History of the voyages of Christopher Columbus 14656

History of the war between Great Britain and the United States of America. 2356

History of the war between Mexico and the United States. 47097

History of the war, between the United States and Great Britain. (32223), 74337

History of the war between the United States and Mexico. (32224)

History of the war between the United States and Mexico, from the commencement of hostilities. (36004)

History of the war between the United States and the Sac and Fox nations of Indians. 100978

History of the war between the United States and Tripoli, and other Barbary powers. (6050), 32225, 3d note after 96993

History of the war debt of England. 37254

History of the war in America between Great Britain and her colonies. (32193), (32226)

History of the war in America, from its commencement to the conclusion of 1783. 27992

History of the war in America, Germany, and the East-Indies. 85106

History of the war, in which the Son of God engaged with all the powers of darkness. (80392)

History of the war of the independence. 6820-6821

History of the war of the union. 21497

History of the war of the United States and Great Britain. 95590

History of the war, 1755-1763. 67680

History of the war with America, France, Spain and Holland. 1501, 32227

History of the wars occasioned by the French revolution. 27334

History of the wars of New-England, with the Eastern Indians. (26625), 52872, 59654-59655

History of the wars of the French revolution. 2774

History of the wars of the United States. 95590

History of the wars of the United States. Containing a history of the revolution. 61233

History of the wars with the British and Indians on our north western frontier. 30586, 35422

History of the Welsh settlements in Licking County, Ohio. 85137

History of the Wesleyan Methodist connection of America. 46865

History of the West Branch Valley of the Susquehanna. 47382

History of the West Indies. Comprising Jamaica, Honduras, Trinidad, Tobago. (44913)

History of the West Indies, containing the natural, civil, and ecclesiastical history of each island. 14244

History of the western country. 94415

History of the western insurrection. 7166

History of the western states. (41074)

History of the western world. 24087

History of the Whig Party. (57633)

History of the whiskey insurrection. 17362

History of the white mountains. 17441

History of the wood lease case. (22774), 60945

History of the work of redemption. 21967

History of the working of American politicians for thirty years. 84151

History of the working of the American government for thirty years. 4787, 84151, note after 95362

History of the works, and annual report of the Chief Engineer. 62370

History of the works of the learned. 32228

History of the world: . . . by Samuel Maunder. 46941

History of the world, ecclesiastical and civil. 12607

History [of the world] from 1831 to 1840. 36497

History of the world. In five books. 67542-67544, 67554, 67560, (67570), 67599

History of the world; or, an account of time. 61175

History of the world: the second part. 73312

History of the world written by Sir Walter Rawleighe. 67560

History of the world's correspondence. (68639)

History of the Wyandott mission at Upper Sandusky. 24379

History of the yellow fever, as it appeared in the city of Natchez. 96180

History of the yellow fever, as it appeared in the city of New York. 33081

History of the yellow fever. By Dr. John Lining. 41333

History of the yellow fever. By Joseph Mackrill. 43480

History of the yellow fever in New Orleans. 53328

History of the yellow fever which prevailed at Philadelphia. 10871

History of the . . . [Young Men's Missionary Society of New York.] 106177

History of their [i. e. the Shakers'] rise and progress. (8567)

History of Thomaston, Rockland, and South Thomaston, Maine. (21714)

History of three of the judges of King Charles I. 91742

History of Threefingered Jack. 56420, 4th note after 95756

History of Tom Sayers and John C. Heenan. 77402

History of Thomas Thumb. 96132

History of Torrington, Ct. 76249

History of Toussaint Louverture. 91239

History of Toussaint Louverture. A new edition. 42352, 91235

History of Toussaint Louverture, the African hero. 42349, 91235

History of trauayle in the West and East Indies, and other countreys lying eyther way. 1562, 62803, 102837, 2d note after 104134, 106330

History of Trinidad. (36662)

History of twenty years. 21735

History of universalism in the United States 103799

History of Upper and Lower California. 25035

History of Upper Canada. (73744)

History of Venezuela. 83640

History of Vermont, from its discovery to its admission into the union. 29780

History of Vermont, from its earliest settlement. (11015)

History of Vermont, natural, civil and statistical. 7286, 56386, 95544, 95546, 95552-95553, 4th note after 99005

History of Vermont . . . with a geographical account of the country. 21676

History of Vermont; with descriptions, physical and topographical. (4252)

History of Virgil A. Stewart. 33250, note before 91708

History of Virginia. 30970, 2d note after 99726, 2d note after 100480

History of Virginia, commenced by John Burk. 9273

History of Virginia, from its discovery and settlement. (33370)

History of Virginia, from its discovery till the year 1781. 10259

History of Virginia, from its earliest settlement to the present time. (2135)

History of Virginia, from its first settlement to the present day. 9272-9273, 10216

History of Virginia, from its first settlement to the year 1754. 44894

History of Virginia, in four parts. 5113-5114, 3d note after 100480

History of Virginia, New England and the Summer Isles. 62957

History of voyages and travels. 102204

History of Wales. 64746

History of Wales: containing some interesting facts. 102618

History of Wallingford, Conn. 18808

History of Warren; a mountain hamlet. (41529)

History of Warren, Rhode Island. 24206

History of wars and fightings. 89684

History of Waterbury, Connecticut. (8232)

Histroy of Wells, Vermont. 59174

History of Wenham. 853

History of Wesleyan Methodism. 82582-28583

History of Wesleyan Methodists. 17713

History of West Boylston, Mass. 17628

History of West Point. (7150)

History of western Massachusetts. 32511

History of William Pe[n]n's conversion from a gentleman to a Quaker. 97693

History of William Stephens. 91306

History of . . . Winchendon, from the grant of the township. (34121)

History of . . . Winchendon (Worcester Co., Mass.) (45025)

History of Wisconsin. 84861

History of Wiskonsin [sic]. 43537

History of witches. 43039, 43543

History of witches and wizards. 32229, 58066

History of Woburn, Middlesex County, Mass. 79452

History of woman. 26191

History of woman suffrage. 90405

History of Worcester in the war of the rebellion. 45026

History of Worcester, Massachusetts. 31587

History of Worcester, Massachusetts, from its earliest settlement. 41267

History of Wyoming, in a series of letters. 49200

History of Yale College. (13212), 105760

History of York County from its erection. 11126

History of York County, from one thousand seven hundred and nineteen. 74161

History of Yucatan. 23775

History, organization and transactions of the Ohio Editorial Association. 56981

History, possessions and prospects of the Maryland Historical Society. (45211A), (47096)

Holmes, Francis Simmons, 1815-1882. 32599-
32600, 87532
Holmes, George F. 32601
Holmes, Isaac. 32602
Holmes, Isaac Edward, 1796-1867. 32603
Holmes, Isaac Edward, 1796-1867. supposed
author 94254
Holmes, J. S. 6519
Holmes, James G. (32604)
Holmes, John, master of Holt Grammar School
73398-73400, (32402), 81848
Holmes, John, 1686?-1734. 32608
Holmes, John, 1773-1843. 32605, 32609-
(32611)
Holmes, John, fl. 1818-1830. 32606-32607
Holmes, John McClellan. 32612
Holmes, John Milton. 32613
Holmes, John S. 32614
Holmes, Joseph T. 32615
Holmes, Mary J. 32616-32617
Holmes, Mary (Stiles) 23766, 91750, 91778
Holmes, Mead. 32618
Holmes, Nathaniel, 1599-1678. 17091, 28050
Holmes, Oliver Wendell, 1809-1894. 23271,
30290, 32619-32621, 45874, (52746),
63156, 64034, 83330, 84185, note after
89212, 90070, 106207
Holmes, S. 32622
Holmes, Samuel N. (32632)
Holmes, Sidney T. 32624
Holmes, Stephen. 32625
Holmes, Sylvester. 32626-32627
Holmes, Thomas H. 15367
Holmes, W. 32628
Holmes, William. defendant 96949
Holmes, Sir William Henry. (32629)
Holmes' patriotic songs. (32623)
Holmesburg Public School, Philadelphia. see
Philadelphia. Holmesburg Public School.
Holmesby, John. 32630
Holmfeld, Carl Dirckinck. see Dirckinck-
Holmfeld, Carl.
Holman, ------. 93382
Holman, ------. defendant 104413
Holroyd, John Baker. see Sheffield, John
Baker Holroyd, 1st Earl of.
Holstein, Anna M. supposed author 29399,
2d note after 95756
Holstein, H. la Fayette Villaume Ducoudray.
see Ducoudray-Holstein, H. la Fayette
Villaume, 1763-1839.
Holt, ---------, fl. 1768. ed. 100788
Holt, ---------, fl. 1773. 22126
Holt, ---------, fl. 1780. 82303
Holt, Charles. 32645
Holt, Edward. 32646
Holt, Edwin. (32647)
Holt, Henry. 32649
Holt, John. ed. and publisher (25955),
77413, 86868, 95988, 100788, 102046-
102048
Holt, Joseph, 1807-1894. 19904-19905, 32650-
32655, 36262, (36267), (56973), 56099,
(64475), 69874 see also U. S. Judge
Advocate General's Office (Army)
U. S. Post Office Department.
Holt, Peter. 32656
Holt, Thomas. 32657
Holt. firm publishers 32648
Holton, David P. 86699
Holton, Frances K. 86699
Holton, Hart B. petitioner 32659
Holton, Hart B. plaintiff 32658, 32660

Holton, Isaac F. 32661
Holton, William C. 32662, 57742
Holt's New-York register, for 1804. 32648
Holwarda, Joannes Phocylides, 1618-1651. ed.
25473
Holwell, --------. 32663
Holy, D. Muys van. see Muys van Holy,
Nicolaes.
Holy, Nicolaes Muys van. see Muys van Holy
Nicolaes.
Holy and profane state. (26181)
Holy & useful life recommended from the
happy end of it. 14488
Holy Bible. 5168, 5170-5171, 5174-5176,
(5177A), 5180-5181
Holy Bible abridged. 84553
Holy Bible abridged; or, the history of the
Old and New Testament. 5167, 5169
Holy Bible . . . and the Apocrypha: with
marginal references. 5178
Holy Bible containing the Old and New
Testaments. 5165
Holy Bible: containing the Old Testament and
the New. (22154)
Holy Bible abridged, &c. With cuts. 5179
Holy Bible translated from the Latin Vulgate.
(5166)
Holy Bible . . . with the Apocrypha. 5177,
5182
Holy Bible . . . with the Apocrypha . . .
and . . . an index. 5173
Holy Bible . . . with the Apocrypha . . . .
With an index. 5172
Holy connexion. 24579
Holy fear of God, and his judgments. 17095
Holy land. 34100-34107
Holy life of Gregory Lopez. 42854
Holy life, pilgrimage, and blessed death of
Gregory Lopez. 42585
Holy living and dying. 83975
Holy meditations for sea-men. 105040A
Holy men engaged in unholy work. 50846
Holy, sacred and divine roll and book. 32664,
79706-79708, note after 91701
Holy scriptures. 79254
Holy scriptures of the New Testament. 83247-
83250
Holy scriptures, translated and corrected by
the spirit of revelation. 83247-83249
Holy spirit convincing the world of sin. 10357
Holy spirit convincing the world of sin, of
righteousness, and of judgment. 79420
Holy spirit convincing the world of sin, of
righteousness, and of judgment, considered
in four sermons. 79419
Holy spirit the gift of God. 79421
Holy table, name, and thing. 31653
Holy time. (66872)
Holy voice. 18367
Holy walk and glorious translation of Blessed
Enocy. (14489), 46798
Holy walk with God. (14490)
Holy wars against ministers by their people.
72419
Holyoake, G. J. 32665, 58250
Holyoke, Edward, d. 1660. (32666)
Holyoke, Edward, 1689-1769. 32667-32672, 370
62743, 103901 see also Harvard
University. President.
Holyoke, Edward Augustus, 1728-1829. 32673
Holyoke, Samuel, 1762-1820. 32674-32675,
54921, 1st note after 101856
Holywood, John. see Sacro Bosco, Joannes
de, fl. 1230.

Holzwarth, J. 32685
Homann, J. B. 32686
Homans, Benjamin. 2043, 32687-32690
Homans, Isaac Smith, 1807-1874. 6484, 6522,
  32691-32692, 32695, 32697-32699, 47910,
  72589, 1st note after 91552
Homans, Isaac Smith, jr. 3190, 32693-(32696),
  51965
Homans, John. 45874, note after 89212
Homar, a hermit of the east. pseud.
  Consolation of Homar. 84684-84685
Homberg, E. (32700)
Hombre reconocido. 94631
Hombres celebres de Chile. 93299
Hombres utiles de todos los paises. 72789
Hombron, Jacques Bernard. 21216, 32701
Home, Henry, Lord Kames. see Kames,
  Henry Home, Lord, 1696-1782.
Home, John. supposed author 14096, 14098,
  32703, note after 97744
Home. 16434
Home. A sermon. 45029
Home, a thanksgiving sermon. 34742
Home and Coast Guard, New Bedford, Mass.
  Company C. see Massachusetts.
  Militia. New Bedford Home and Coast
  Guard. Company C.
Home and college. 33964
Home and colonial review of commerce,
  manufactures, and general politics.
  23377
Home and foreign record. 32704
Home and politics. (12727)
Home and the nation. 1422
Home and the world. (32705)
Home as found. 16434, 16447
Home Association. 32706
Home authors and home artists. 32707
Home ballads. 916, 11113
Home book of the picturesque. 32707
Home. By Miss Sedgwick. 78773, 78774
Home. By the author of "Redwood." 78772
Home cyclopaedia. 71523
Home evangelization. 32708
Home folks. 83372
Home for Aged and Infirm Colored Persons,
  Philadelphia. 61724
Home for Aged Females, Roxbury, Mass.
  see Roxbury Home for Children and
  Aged Females, Roxbury, Mass.
Home for Aged Women, Providence, R. I.
  66271
Home for Aged Women, Providence, R. I.
  Charter. 66271
Home for Children, Roxbury, Mass. see
  Roxbury Home for Children and Aged
  Females, Roxbury, Mass.
Home for Destitute Children. see Brooklyn.
  Industrial School Association, and Home
  for Destitute Children.
Home for Destitute Colored Children, Philadel-
  phia. (61725)
Home for Friendless Children, Newport, R. I.
  55036
Home for Friendless Women and Children,
  Springfield, Mass. see Springfield
  Home for Friendless Women and
  Children, Springfield, Mass.
Home for immigrants. 1986
Home for immigrants, being a treatise on the
  resources of Iowa. 35011
Home of Jewish Widows and Orphans of New
  Orleans. 53329
Home for Little Wanderers, Philadelphia.
  61795

Home for the Friendless, New Haven, Conn.
  52979
Home for the Friendless, New York. see
  American Female Guardian Society,
  New York. Home for the Friendless.
Home for the Industrious Blind, Philadelphia.
  Managers. 60339 see also Pennsylvania
  Institution for the Instruction of the
  Blind, Philadelphia.
Home for the industrious immigrant. 87391,
  87405
Home gazette. 88340
Home Guard, Philadelphia. see Philadelphia.
  Home Guard.
Home harmonies. 63933
Home here, &c. 82329
Home heroes, saints and martyrs. 2137
Home in New Brunswick. 19558
Home in the New World. 32617
Home in the west. A novel. 32616
Home in the west, a poem. (32709), note
  after 98049
Home League. 399, 32710
Home League. Committee on the Tariff Laws.
  32710
Home life. 87264
Home missionary. (73750)
Home missionary, and American pastor's
  journal. 32711, 59026
Home missionary life. 80069
Home missionary magazine. 94369
Home Missionary Society of Massachusetts.
  see Massachusetts Home Missionary
  Society.
Home Missionary Society of Philadelphia.
  see Philadelphia Home Missionary
  Society.
Home Missionary Society of Rhode Island.
  see Congregational Churches in Rhode
  Island. Home Missionary Society.
Home Missionary Society of Strafford County,
  N. H. see Strafford Home Missionary
  Society.
Home Missionary Society of the Congregational
  Churches in Rhode Island. see Congrega-
  tional Churches in Rhode Island. Rhode
  Island Home Missionary Society.
Home Missionary Union. see New Hampshire
  Female Cent Institution and Home
  Missionary Union.
Home missions. A sermon . . . Boston, May
  31, 1826. 14137
Home missions; a sermon in behalf of the
  American Home Missionary Society.
  3502
Home missions and slavery. 82340
Home missions: as connected with Christ's
  dominion. 92254
Home missions. First annual report to the
  Trustees. 18307
Home missions in Illinois. 73746
Home missions. [First] annual report of the
  Presbyterian Board of Home Missions.
  65169
Home monthly. (32712)
Home of the ancient dead restored. 55893
Home of the badgers: comprising an early
  history of Wisconsin. 81581
Home of the badgers, or a sketch of the early
  history of Wisconsin. (56683)
Home of the mutineers. 32713, 51541
Home of the wanderers. (7094)
Home of Washington after the war. 73425
Home of Washington and its associations.
  42117, 42125

Home scenes and home sounds. 91292
Home scenes told by old travellers. 61376
Home-sketches of Essex County. (16236)
Home Squadron . . . July 7, 1841. (37841)
Home, sweet home. (59006), 83677
Home, the arms, and the armory of Samuel Colt. 14763
Home, the basis of the state. (79638)
Home, the school, and the church. 32714
Home tourist. 81210
Home views of the picturesque and beautiful. 32715
Home words for the soldier. (32716)
Home University library of modern knowledge. 84341-84342
Home work of foreign missions in Ohio. 91533
Homenagem aos heroes Brasileiros. 52415
Homenaje de gratitud a la memoria del benemerito ministro Don Diego Portales. 86251
Homens, Francisco da Mae dos. 32717
Homer. see Homerus.
Homer, Arthur. (5198), (32720)
Homer, Harriet. 47798
Homer, James Lloyd. 32721-32724, 33648, 34803, 80642
Homer, James Lloyd. supposed author 32699, 1st note after 81552
Homer, John. 32725
Homer, Jonathan. 32726-32729
Homer, William Bradford. (32730)
Homer, N. Y. Congregational Church. 37162
Homer, N. Y. Cortland Academy. see Cortland Academy, Homer, N. Y.
Homergue, Jean d'. tr. 21378, 32731
Homeri Ilias. 32718-32719
Homerus. 32718-32719, 84896, 104998
Homes, Henry Augustus, 1812-1887. (32732)-32733, 53830 see also New York (State) Librarian.
Homes, John. 32734
Homes, Nathaniel. see Holmes, Nathaniel, 1599-1678.
Homes, William, 1663-1746. (32735)-32737
Homes, William, fl. 1854-1855. (32738)
Homes abroad. 44938
Homes and fortunes in the boundless west. (27633)
Homes for all. Published by the North Missouri R. R. Co. 32739
Homes for all. Southern Railway Emigrant Association prospectus. 88462
Homes for all. Speech of Gerrit Smith. (82635)
Homes of American authors. (32740), (38848)
Homes of American statesmen. 32741
Homes of the New World. 7712
Homes of the New World. Impressions of America. 7713
Homes of the west. 32742
Homes, vines, and fig-trees for all. (9797)
Homespun, Giles. pseud. Negro emancipation. 52261
Homespun, Henry, jr. pseud. ed. Plough boy. see Southwick, Solomon. ed.
Homespun; or, five and twenty years ago. 38464
Homestead architecture. 82163
Homestead Association, Quincy, Mass. see Quincy Homestead Association.
Homestead Association of West Philadelphia. see West Philadelphia Homestead Association.

Homestead bill. Speech on Hon. H. H. Sibley. 80820
Homestead bill. Speech of Hon. John Kelley. 37313
Homestead Bill—the state of parties—and the presidency. 91257
Homestead on the hillside. 32617
Homesteads for actual setlters. (32743)
Homesteads for city poor. (32744)
Homesteads for soldiers and sailors. 930
Homesteads for soldiers—who are their friends? 36885
Homesteads, the Republicans and settlers. (32745)
Homeward bound. 16447-(16448)
Homework for all. 54932
Homilia que pronuncio. 51217
Homily for the times. 80364
Homme. 6438
Homme Americain. 57457
Homme Americain. Notes sur les Indiens. 81310
Homme Americaine (de l'Amerique Meridionale (57455)
Homme aux cent femmes. 21368
Homme dans la foule. (69035)
Homme de la nature. 2580
Homme de la nature, histoire des peuples sauvages. 70904
Homme de la race Latine. pseud. Lettre a Sa Majeste l'Empereur Napoleon III. 6130, 40663
Homme de lettres. pseud. Amerique, d'apres les voyageurs les plus celebres. 1289, 38758
Homme de sa couleur. pseud. Vie privee politique et militaire de Toussaint-Louverture. 96350
Homme du Sud. 72827
Homme impartial. pseud. Observations. 56095, 56470, (62991)
Homme ou singe. 64731
Homme, sa haute antiquite. 75538
Hommes de couleur. pseud. Memoires. (47553)
Hommes de Couleur de la Martinique. petitioners 5653, (57421)
Hommes d'etat de la France constitutionalle. 24677, 28133
Hommes et les moeurs aux Etats-Unis d'Amerique. 30036
Hommes rouges de l'Amerique du Nord. (32746), (44438)
Hommes volans. note after 104017
Hommius, Festus. 72110
Homo. psued. Few suggestions on the slave trade. 81978
Homo. pseud. Financiers A, B, C. 32748
Homo. pseud. Interim. 32747
Homo. pseud. Lettre . . . to the Chairman of the Committee. 45802
Homo. pseud. Signs of the times. 32749
Homo, Aquae. pseud. Sermon. see Waterman, Joyham.
Homo attritus. (76031)
Homoeopathic directory. 82717
Homoeopathic directory of New York and vicinity. 82719
Homoeopathic dispensary Association, New York. see New-York Homoeopathic Dispensary Association.
Homoeopathic Medical College of Pennsylvania. 60147

Homoeopathic Medical College of Pennsylvania. Charter. 60147
Homoeopathic Medical College of Pennsylvania. Professor Morgan's Valedictory. 60147
Homoeopathic Medical Society of the State of New York. (53695)
Homoeopathic Society of Rhode Island. see Rhode Island Homoeopathic Society.
Ho-na-ya-wus. Indian name see Farmer's Brother. Seneca Indian Chief
Hondius, Cornelis. 5714
Hondius, Jodocus, 1546-1611. 5014, 5714, 32750, 32751, 33562, 33658-33659, 38880, 47885, (47887)-47889, 66494, 66683-66684, 67546, (67562)-67566, 82816, 82823, 82829, 95757, note after 100632
Hondivs his map of the Christian world. 66683
Hondivs his mape of France. 66684
Hondt, Joos de. see Hondius, Jodocus, 1546-1611.
Hondt, P. de. ed. 65404
Honduras. 32753, (32768), 32773, 51083
Honduras. British Legation. see Great Britain. Legation. Honduras.
Honduras. Citizens. 32760
Honduras. Comisionados. (76204), (76208)
Honduras. Constitution. 32757
Honduras. Laws, statutes, etc. 32755
Honduras. Legation. Great Britain. 55148
Honduras. Ministro Jeneral. 32770-32771 see also Alvarado, Francisco. Rugama, Laenciado da Jose Maria.
Honduras. Patriotas. see Patriotas de Honduras. petitioners
Honduras. President, 1845. 32764
Honduras. President, 1852-1855 (Cabanas) 32772 see also Cabanas, Trinidad, Pres. Honduras, d. 1871.
Honduras. Treaties, etc. 32762, (32768), 32773, (76204), (76208), 89971
Honduras. Vice-President. 68788
Honduras (Diocese) 32761, 34836
Honduras: a record of facts. 55912
Honduras almanack for 1829. (32766)
Honduras and British Honduras. 89966
Honduras and Guatemala. 89967
Honduras; descriptive, historical, and statistical. 89968
Honduras et ses ports. 59583
Honduras Interoceanic Railway. 89969
Honduras Interoceanic Railway Company. 89970, 89988
Honduras Interoceanic Railway Company. Agent and Attorney of the Grantees and Proprietors of the Charter. 89960 see also Squier, Ephraim George, 1821-1888.
Honduras Interoceanic Railway Company. Charter. 89971
Honduras Interoceanic Railway. Concluded, June 23, 1853. 32755
Honduras Interoceanic Railway. Preliminary report. 32767, note after 89969
Honduras Interoceanic Railway. Supplementary report. 89970
Honduras Interoceanic Railway: with maps of the line and ports. 89971
Hondureno. pseud. tr. see Alvarado, Leon. tr.
Hondvius his map of the world. 66683
Hondy, J. see Hondius, Jodocus, 1546-1611.
Hone, John. 12386
Hone, Philip. 32774

Hone, William. 89471
Honest American. pseud. To the respectable public. 96023
Honest clergyman. pseud. Choice dialogues. see Checkley, John.
Honest exposure of the honest manner. 94436
Honest free-holder of West-Chester County. pseud. No placemen. 102953
Honest grief of a tory. 32775
Honest John Smith. pseud. see Smith, John. pseud.
"Honest John's" farmer's almanack. 82914
Honest laugh at "honest" people. 52588
Honest man. pseud. Honest man's reason's for declining. see Lloyd, Charles.
Honest man. pseud. President Lincoln's views. 41159
Honest man. pseud. Reply to Mr. Heathcote's letter. 33193
Honest man's almanack. 32776
Honest man's interest as he claims any lands in the counties of New-Castle, Kent, or Sussex in Delaware. 59957, note after 94466
Honest man's interest, as he claims any lands in the counties of New-Castle, Kent, or Sussex, on Delaware. 52567
Honest man's reasons for declining. 41681
Honest politician. (32777), note after 99774
Honest sailor. pseud. Duel and no duel. (21101)
Honest servant's advice to his master. (49449)
Honest the best policy. 63218
Honest the best policy. By E. A. 80389
Honest welch-cobler. 32778
Honesta parsimonia. 46361
Honestus. pseud. Observations on the pernicious practice of law. see Austin, Benjamin.
Honestus. pseud. Expose of the Baltimore Custom House frauds. 3035
Honestus. pseud. Seventeenth jewel. 79361
Honestus. pseud. Thoughts of the actual settlers. 95724
Honestus. pseud. Vindication of the land agent. 32779, 43947-(43948)
Honesty, Obadiah. pseud. Remonstrance of Obadiah Honesty. 69581
Honesty, Obadiah. pseud. Reverend Mr. Smith vindicated. (32780)
Honesty, Obadiah. pseud. Second edition, with additions, of, A remonstrance. 32781
Honesty shewed to be the true policy. (32782), 105988
Honesty the best policy. 33960
Honesty the best policy in the worst times. 5639
Honey-moon. 96057
Honeycomb, William. pseud. Bee, no. 1. 4285
Honeyman, David, 1817- 56187
Honeyman, James. 32783
Honeywood, St. John. 32784-32785, 63587-63588, 1st-3d notes after 101872
Hongkong daily press. 56354, 86608-86609
Honig, Jacob, 1816-1870. 32787
Honig Janszoon, Jacob. see Honig, Jacob, 1818-1870.
Honiger, Nicolaus. tr. 1762-1762A, 4797-4798
Honolulu, Bishop of. see Stanley, Thomas Nettleship, Bishop of Honolulu, 1823-1898.
Honolulu (Diocese) (19922), 76454, 96419

Hoog Mogende Heeren! Vertoonen met behoorlyk respect Bewinthebberen. 102889A

Hooge, ------- Romyn de. see Romyn de Hooge, ---------.

Hooge regeeringe ingedient. 102919

Hoogerduin, D. E. (32804)

Hooghe or Hooge, Romain de. see Romyn de Hooge, --------.

Hooghe, T. Romain de. see Romyn de Hooge, --------.

Hoogland, Edward. (37081)

Hoogstraten, F. van. tr. 57806

Hook, ---------, fl. 1701. 85933A

Hook, ---------, fl. 1914. 84518-84519

Hook, W. H. (32808)

Hook, Walter Farquhar. 32806-32807, 43675

Hook, William. defendant 3644

Hooke, Nathanael. ed. 86489-86491

Hooke, William. (32809)-32811, 52959

Hooker, Asahel. 32812

Hooker, E. C. 32813

Hooker, Edward W. (32814)-(32816), 32847, 41599, note after 84134, note after 95556, 99161

Hooker, George. 90681

Hooker, Herman. 32818

Hooker, Isabella Beecher. petitioner 90404

Hooker, John, 1729-1777. 32819

Hooker, John, 1816-1901. 15776, 32820

Hooker, Mrs. John. ed. 89882

Hooker, Joseph, 1814-1879. 2052, 43030, 80427-(80418)

Hooker, Joseph Dalton. 28401, 32822-32823, 55303, 71032

Hooker, M. 11615

Hooker, Mary Anne. (32824)

Hooker, Nathanael. 32825-32826

Hooker, Samuel. 32827

Hooker, Thomas, 1586?-1647. 32828-32862, 33496, (74460), 92113

Hooker, Thomas, 1586?-1647. supposed author 87293

Hooker, Sir William Jackson. 32863-32866, 67461

Hooker, Worthington. 32867

Hooker (H. E.) & Co. (32817)

Hookes, Ellis. 89501

Hoole, E. 32868

Hoop Scheffer, J. G. de. see Scheffer, J. G. de Hoop.

Hoop petticoats. (32869)

Hoop-pole band. 95603

Hoop-pole law. 45162

Hooper, --------. 42465

Hooper, E. J. 32870, 102979

Hooper, Isaac T. 32995-32996

Hooper, Johnson J. 86589

Hooper, Josiah. 32871

Hooper, Lucy. 32872-32873

Hooper, Richard. ed. (76455), (76468)

Hooper, Samuel. 3191, 17992, 26403, 27892, 32874-32877, 42465, 86807-86808, note after 89113, 93269

Hooper, Thomas. 32878

Hooper, Thomas W. 32879

Hooper, William. defendant 90145

Hooper, William, 1674-1767. 32880

Hooper, William, 1792-1876. 32881

Hooper, William Henry, 1813-1882. (32882)

Hooper, William Hulme, 1827-1854. (32883)

Hooper & Co. firm engravers see Bobbett, Hooper & Co. firm engravers

Hooper's western fruit-book. 32870

Hoorn, Jan ten. 6341, 32884, (57377), 98930

Hoornbeek, Jacob. 32887

Hoornbeek, Johannis. (32437), 32885-32886

Hoosac mountain tunnel. 4288

Hoosac tunnel and Troy and Greenfield Rail Road. 30468

Hoosac tunnel. Appeal to the people of Massachusetts. 30858

Hoosac tunnel: its condition and prospects. 5535

Hoosac tunnel: our financial maelstrom. 5536

Hoosac tunnel . . . reply . . . to . . . Legislature of Massachusetts. 30859

Hoosac tunnel route compared with the Western Railroad. 24264

Hooasc Tunnel. Speech of Hon. H. G. Parker of Greenfield. 58674

Hoosick Falls, N. Y. Washington Birth Day Celebration, 1862. 32891

Hooton, Charles. 32892

Hooton, Elizabeth. 25171, 81375

Hooton, Oliver. 25171, 81375

Hooten, Robert Treat. 32893

Hoover, David. 32894

Hope, Alexander James Beresford Berseford-, 1820-1887. 32895-32899, 66122

Hope, Henry. 32900

Hope, James Barron. 32901-32903, 86161

Hope, Thomas. 82832, note after 92664, 2d note after 100510

Hope en Compagnie. firm petitioners 47762

Hope (Brig) in Admiralty 96930A, 96935

Hope, a poem. (44381)

Hope and have. 57216

Hope deferred not lost. 19752

Hope Division, No. 3, Sons of Temperance. see Sons of Temperance of North America. Pennsylvania. Hope Division, No. 3.

Hope for my country. (35751)

Hope for our country. A sermon preached in the Second Presbyterian Church. 83342

Hope for our country. A sermon preached, . . . October 19, 1862. 21572

Hope for the heathen. 45463

Hope in death. 68592

Hope Leslie. 78769, 78775-78777, (78780), 78784, 78786, 78790, 78798, 78804-(78805)

Hope of immortality. 103910

Hope of Israel newly extant and printed in Amsterdam. 44193

Hope of Israel; presumptive evidence. 81282

Hope of Israel, written by Menasseh Ben—Israel. 44194

Hope of manking. 38307

Hope of the righteous in their death. (14492)

Hopedale, Ohio. McNeely Normal School. see Hopedale Normal College, Hopedale, Ohio.

Hopedale Community. 32904

Hopedale Normal College, Hopedale, Ohio. 43597

Hopedale Normal College, Hopedale, Ohio. Union Institute. 43597

Hopeful view of national affairs. 36484

Hopefully waiting and other verses. 67810

Hopewell, M. (21987)

Hopfengartner, P. Fr. tr. (74209)

Hopfner, Eduard. tr. 89957

Hopkins, --------. 30155 see also Hampton Normal and Agricultural Institute, Hampton, Va. President.

Hopkins, --------, fl. 1721. 65865, 88192

Horn, -------- van. see Van Horn, -------.

Horn, Adam. defendant 33012

Horn, George, 1620-1670. 33013-33018

Horn, George, fl. 1781. 33019

Horn, H. J. (33020)

Horn, Hosea B. (33021)

Horn, John. 21872, 33022

Horn, W. O. von. pseud. Benjamin Franklin. see Oertel, Philipp Friedrich.

Horn, W. O. von. pseud. Lesensgang Georg Washingtons. see Oertel, Philipp Friedrich.

Hornbeck, H. B. 33026

Hornblower, Joseph Coerten, 1777-1864. 72162

Hornblower, Josiah. (33027)

Hornblower, W. H. 33028-33029

Hornby, Edward. 33030

Hornby. firm see Pultney and Hornby. firm.

Horne, Augustus V. van. see Van Horne, Augustus V.

Horne, David van. see Van Horne, David.

Horne, Henry. 33031

Horne, John. see Tooke, John Horne, 1736-1812

Horne, John van. see Van Horne, John.

Horne, Thomas Hartwell. (33033)

Horneck, --------. RA 94569

Hornell, N. Y. Library Association. 33034

Horner, F. 95659

Horner, Gustavus R. B. (33035)

Horner, J. M. 33036

Horner, William Edmonds, 1793-1853. 33037-33038, 56533, 60756, 60758, 1st note after 100506

Hornet. 97799

Hornot, Ant. 33039

Horn's overland guide. (33021)

Hornsnell, William. 33062

Horologgi, Giuseppe. tr. 95336-95337

Horores de Cortes. (9577)

Horozco, Nuno Nunez de Villavicencio y. see Villavicencio y Horozco, Nuno Nunez de.

Horr, H. 43853

Horrebow, Niels. 1407

Horrey, William J. 27034

Horrible confession of the pirate and murdered. 27294, 101243

Horrible disclosures. 38341

Horrible doctrines!! 73728

Horrible Greasy. pseud. Negroleum. 52276

Horrible ley mercantil y sus ejecutores. 98877

Horrible massacre of the Deitz family. 7792

Horribles crueldades de los conquistadores. (9576), 35318

Horrid Indian cruelties. 105689

Horrid massacre at Dartmoor Prison, England. 100890

Horrid massacre in Virginia. 97487

Horrible murder of Mrs. Ellen Lynch. 89765

Horrid nature and enormous guilt of murder. 12331

Horrocks, James. 33040

Horrors of Napoleon's campaign in Russia. 105260

Horrors of St. Domingo. 30807, note after 78746

Horrors of secession. 33837

Horrors of slavery. 103670

Horrors of slavery. By John Kenrick. 37461

Horrors of slavery; exemplified in the life . . . of . . . Robert Wedderburn. 102438

Horrors of slavery: or, the American tars in Tripoli. 68034

Horrors of the first of May. 105178, 105194

Horrors of the Negro apprenticeship system. 93259

Horrors of the Negro slavery. (33041), note after 102837

Horrors of the Queen City. (19107)-19108

Horrors of the slave trade. 33042

Horrors of the slave-trade. Stranding of the slaver. 81991

Horrors of the Virginian slave trade. (81361)

Horrors of West India slavery. 102838-102839

Horry, Charles Lucas Pinckney. 58228, 101809

Horry, Elias. 33043

Horry, P. 33044-(33046), 102489

Horsburgh, James. 33047

Horschelmann, Fred. 19436, 91197

Horse and horsemanship of the United States. 31465

Horse not originally imported. 32600

Horse portraiture. 81364

Horse-shoe: a poem. 24042

Horse Shoe Robinson. 37413, (37423)

Horse story. (36456)

Horsey, Sir Jerome. 66682

Horsey, John R. 33049

Horsfield, Thomas. (33049A)

Horsford, Eben Norton, 1818-1893. 33050-33052, 42706, 79946, 89533, note after 106301 see also Committee on Spiritualism, Boston, 1857.

Horsford, Jerediah, 1791-1875. 33054

Horsford, John. (33053)

Horsford, Mary Gardiner. 33055

Horsley, Samuel, successively Bishop of St. Davids, Rochester, and St. Asaph, 1733-1806. 33056-33057, 69478, 72333

Horsmanden, Daniel. (33058)-33061 see also New York (City) Recorder.

Hort, William P. 71254

Horta, Garcia da. see Orta, Garcia de.

Hortega, Jose Diaz de. see Diaz de Hortega, Jose.

Hortelano, ---------. 98147

Hortensius. pseud. Essay on the liberty of the press. see Hay, George, 1765-1830.

Hortensius. pseud. Fugitive public essays. 26123

Horticosa, Petrius di. 33063

Horticultural Association of Monroe, Mich. 50032

Horticultural embellishment of school-house grounds. 33411

Horticultural Exhibition, Salem, Mass., 1850. 75689

Horticultural Fair, New Haven, Conn., 1838. Managers. 52994

Horticultural journal. 24906

Horticultural register, and gardiner's [sic] magazine. 33064

Horticultural repository. 54772

Horticultural Society, Buffalo, N. Y. see Buffalo Horticultural Society.

Horticultural Society of Cincinnati. see Cincinnati Horticultural Society.

Horticultural Society of Hingham, Mass. see Agricultural and Horticultural Society, Hingham, Mass.

Horticultural Society of Indiana. see Indiana State Horticultural Society.

Horticultural Society of Kansas. see Kansas Horticultural Society.

Horticultural Society of London. see Royal Horticultural Society, London.

Horticultural Society of Massachusetts. see
    Massachusetts Horticultural Society.
Horticultural Society of Minnesota. see
    Minnesota Horticultural Society.
Horticultural Society of Montreal. see
    Montreal Horticultural Society.
Horticultural Society of New Bedford, Mass.
    see New Bedford Horticultural Society.
Horticultural Society of New Haven, Conn.
    see New Haven Horticultural Society.
Horticultural Society of New Haven County,
    Conn. see New Haven County
    Horticultural Society.
Horticultural Society of New York. see New
    York Horticultural Society.
Horticultural Society of Northern Illinois. see
    Northern Illinois Horticultural Society.
Horticultural Society of Ohio. see Ohio
    State Horticultural Society.
Horticultural Society of Pennsylvania. see
    Pennsylvania Horticultural Society,
    Philadelphia.
Horticultural Society of Pittsburgh. see
    Pittsburgh Horticultural Society.
Horticultural Society of Rhode Island. see
    Rhode Island Horticultural Society.
Horticultural Society of the State of New York.
    see New York State Horticultural
    Society.
Horticultural Society of the Valley of Genesee.
    33065
Horticulturist. 3869
Horticulturist, and journal of rural art and
    rural taste. (33066)
Hortigosa, Fran. Antonio. 33067
Hortigosa, Tomas Lopez de. 44244
Horto, Garcia ab. see Orta, Garcia de.
Horton, Francis. 33069
Horton, George M. 33070
Horton, H. P. 33071
Horton, John M. 12672
Horton, N. S. 33072
Horton, R. G. 94290
Horton, Sir Robert John Wilmot. see Wilmot-
    Horton, Sir Robert John, Bart., 1784-
    1841.
Horton, Rushmore G. 33077-33078
Horton, Sanford J. 33079
Horton, Valentine Baxter, 1802-1888. 33080
Hortons; or American life at home. 11363
Hortulanus, Nicolaus. 77804
Hortus Americanus. (3376)
Hortus Britanno Americanus. 11506
Hortus Castensis. 8422
Hortus Elginensis. (33086)
Hortus Europae Americanus. 11507
Hortus Floridus. 58996
Hortus Jamaicensis. 42683
Hortus Oestensis. 21901
Hortus Peruvianus medicinalis. 61288
Hortus Sanitatis. 40122
Horwitz, -----. 102370
Hosack, Alexander. 33081
Hosack, Alexander Eddy, 1805-1871. 33082
Hosack, David, 1769-1835. 12482, 13645,
    (29481), 33083-33089, 54362, 84571,
    84572
Hosack, John. 33090
Hosannah of Zion's children very pleasing to
    Zion's King. 62517
Hosea Sprague's register of the weather.
    89676
Hosemann, Theodor. illus. 20122, 27182
Hosford, B. F. 33091
Hosford, Hocum. 42483 see also Lowell,
    Mass. Mayor, 1864 (Hosford)

Hosford's calendar. (33092)
Hoskens, Jane. 33093
Hoskins, Bradford S. 33094
Hoskins, James. 6108, 6122, 33095, 92322,
    92329
Hoskins, Nathan. 33096-33097
Hosmer, Albert N. 92675
Hosmer, C. Lawton. 33098
Hosmer, George W. 9056, 9058, 9063, 33099-
    (33100), note after 95451
Hosmer, H. P. 33103
Hosmer, Harriet. 33101, 47798, 55958
Hosmer, Hezekiah L. 33102
Hosmer, James B. (33104)
Hosmer, James Kendall, 1834-1927. 33105-
    33106, 104845
Hosmer, Margaret. 33107-33108
Hosmer, Rufus. 33109
Hosmer, S. D. 33110
Hosmer, Stephen. 33111-33112
Hosmer, William, 33113-33114
Hosmer, William H. C. 33115-(33116), 77833
Hosmer and Co. firm see Chipman, Hosmer
    and Co. firm
Hosmot, Hyton. pseud. Saturniad. see Bake
    W. D.
Hospicio de Pobres, Mexico City. see Mexico
    (City) Hospicio de Pobres.
Hospital, Albany, N. Y. see Albany. Hospita
Hospital, Hartford, Conn. see Hartford, Conn
    Hospital.
Hospital, New York. see New York Hospital.
Hospital and Almshouse, New York. see
    New York (City) Hospital and Almshouse
Hospital Association, Lowell, Mass. see
    Lowell Hospital Association, Lowell, Mas
Hospital days. 105213
Hospital de la Misericorde, Quebec. see
    Quebec (City) Hospital de la Misericord
Hospital de los Indios, Mexico City. see
    Mexico (City) Hospital de los Indios.
Hospital de Todos Santos, Lisbon. see Lisbo
    Hospital de Todos Santos.
Hospital for the Insane, Boston. see
    Massachusetts. Hospital for the Insane,
    Boston.
Hospital for the Insane, Jacksonville, Ill. see
    Illinois. Hospital for the Insane,
    Jacksonville.
Hospital for the Insane, Philadelphia. see
    Philadelphia. Pennsylvania Hospital for
    the Insane.
Hosptial for the Insane, St. Peter, Minn. see
    Minnesota. State Hospital, St. Peter.
Hospital gazette. (53355)
Hospital life; being incidents from the prayer
    meeting and hospital. 33117
Hospital life in the Army of the Potomac.
    (68626)
Hospital of the Protestant Episcopal Church,
    Philadelphia. see Philadelphia. Hospita
    of the Protestant Episcopal Church.
Hospital of the Protestant Episcopal Church,
    Philadelphia. 61726
Hospital-prison-ship. 25891
Hospital Real y General de los Indios. see
    Mexcio (City) Hospital de los Indios.
Hospital scenes after the battle of Gettysburg,
    July, 1863. 27237
Hospital sketches. 690
Hospital transports. (33118)
Hospitales. 33119
Hospitalidad De S. Juan de Dios. see
    Hospitallers of St. John of God.
Hospitalieres. Quebec. defendants and
    petitioners 67035

Hospitalieres. Quebec. Mere Superieure. 67011-67014, (67496) see also Marie de Saint Bonaventure. Mere Superieure

Hospitallers of St. John of God. (68842)

Hospitallers of Saint John of God. Guatemala. 29076

Hospitallers of Saint John of God. Province of the Archangel San Rafael de los Reynos del Peru y Chile. Comissario General. 61165, (75986) see also Alfaro, Diego de.

Hospitals and the church. 91575

Hospitals, British, French, and America. 47045

Hospitals of the United States. 2016

Hoste, Sir George. 85234

Hostilities by Mexico. (48493)

Hostilities with Creek Indians. 33120

Hostmann, F. W. 33121-33122

Hot corn. 72182

Hot Springs, Bath County, Virginia. 33123

Hotaling, Samuel. (33124)

Hotchkin, James H. (20158), 33125

Hotchkin, Samuel Finch, 1833-1912. 57749

Hotchkiss, A. S. 90531

Hotchkiss, Frederick William. 33126-33129

Hotchkiss, G. B. ed. 103192-103193

Hotchkiss, Giles W. 33130

Hotchkiss, Jed. 33131

Hotchkiss, William A. (27026)

Hotel folly. 33132

Hotel guide. 10473

Hotel rooms business directory. 61606

Hotham, Sir Beaumont. 31834

Hotham, Sir Charles. illus. 29486

Hotten, J. C. 23788

Houbloup. pseud. Museo pintoresco Mejicano. (51567)

Houbraken, -------. engr. 9343, 93459

Houckgeest, E. van Braam. (33133)

Houdin, Michael Gabriel. 33134

Houdin's last respects to George Washington. 33134

Hough, Franklin Benjamin, 1822-1885. 1452, 1457, 5899, 6543, (12089), 19788, 21694, 25063, 33136-33154, 42543-(42544), 53577, 53805, 64708, (72725), 80873, 84484, 92304, 95825

Hough, John. (33155)

Hough, John, successively Bishop of Oxford, Litchfield and Coventry, and Worcester, 1651-1743. 33135

Hough, Joseph. reporter 95643

Hough, Lewis S. 33156

Hough, Sabin. ed. 52572

Hough, William Jervis, 1795-1869. 33157

Houghton, Asa. 33158

Houghton, Douglass. 48733 see also Michigan. State Geologist.

Houghton, Edwin B. (33159)

Houghton, G. H. (33161)

Houghton, George Frederick. 9645, 33160

Houghton, J. jr. 9486, 38676

Houghton, J. F. 10001

Houghton, Joab. 33162

Houghton, John C. 90451

Houghton, S. O. 88428

Houghton, Thomas. 33163-33164

Houghton, William A. 33165-33166

Houghton Association. Agent to England. 33167, 82412 see also Smith, Columbus.

Houghton Association. Meeting, Worcester, Mass., 1847. 33167, 82412

Houghton's genuine almanac. 33158

Houk, George W. 33168

Houldbrooke, ------. (80593)

Houmas land claim. 33169

Hour, and the man! 52480

Hour and the man. A romance of Hayti. 44937

Hour of patriotism. 5436

Hour of peril. 3718

Hour; the peril; the duty. 11059

Houre glasse of Indian news. (55183)

Hour which cometh, and now is. 13418

Hour with the pilgrim fathers. 78244

Hours at home. (33170)

Hours, etc. 55382

Hours with my pupils. (61354)

Housatonic. pseud. Case of hereditary bias. see Smith, William Henry, 1833-1896.

Housatonic Agricultural Society. (33171)

Housatonic Canal Company. 33172

Housatonic Indians. see Stockbridge Indians.

Housatonic Railroad Commissioners. see Massachusetts. Commissioners on the Housatonic Railroad.

Housatonic Railroad Company. Board of Directors. 33174

House, according to the order of the day, resolved itself. 100099

House and home. (87804)

House and School of Industry, New York. see New York House and School of Industry.

House by the sea. 68176

House documents, second session, thirteenth Congress. 15535

House holder. pseud. Letters concerning the general health. see Hopkins, Samuel Miles. supposed author and Romayne, Nicholas. supposed author

House-hunting and home-sickness. 84150

House journal of the Legislative Assembly of the state of Kansas. (37048)

House journal of the State Legislature of the state of Nebraska. 52188

House-keeper's guide and everybody's hand-book. 64405, 83477, 84953

House lots for sale. 105368

House . . . memorial of the Senators and Representatives. 37038, 37070

House no. 19. Papers relating to the coal mines. 45764

House no. 37. Commonwealth of Massachusetts. 37934

House of Bishops of the Protestant Episcopal Church of the United States. (66155)

House of bondage. (71959)

House of Christ. 83520

House of Clerical and Lay Deputies. Order of the day. 66156

House of Correction, Essex County, Mass. see Essex County, Mass. House of Correction.

House of Correction and Employment, Philadelphia. see Philadelphia. House of Correction and Employment.

House of Delegates . . . Baltimore . . . Contested election. 45163

House of God: a discourse delivered. 78397

House of God. A sermon, delivered at the opening of the Branch Church. 88888

House of Hope Presbyterian Church, St. Paul, Minn. see St. Paul, Minn. House of Hope Presbyterian Church.

House of Mercy, New York. see New York House of Mercy.

House of Reformation, Boston. see Boston. House of Reformation.

House of Reformation, Providence, R. I.
see Providence, R. I. House of
Reformation.
House of Reformation for Juvenile and Female
Offenders, Manchester, N. H. see New
Hampshire. Industrial School.
House of Refuge, Boston. see Boston.
House of Refuge.
House of Refuge, Cincinnati. see Cincinnati.
House of Refuge.
House of Refuge, New York. see Society
for the Reformation of Juvenile
Delinquents, New York. House of
Refuge.
House of Refuge, Philadelphia. see Philadel-
phia. House of Refuge.
House of Refuge, St. Louis. see St. Louis
House of Refuge.
House of Refuge for Coloured Juvenile
Delinquents, Philadelphia. see Philadel-
phia. House of Refuge for Coloured
Juvenile Delinquents.
House of Refuge for Western Pennsylvania,
Pittsburgh. see Pennsylvania. House
of Refuge for Western Pennsylvania,
Pittsburgh.
House of Refuge of the City of New York.
Reply of the Managers. 33175
House of Representatives, May 15th, 1830.
92233
House of Representatives. Speech of William
P. Sheffield. 80100
House of Representatives. Wednesday, Jan.
26, 1820. 60150
House of the Lord. 90926
House of the seven gables. 30994
House of wisdom in a bustle. 96325
House Old Nick built. 33175
House surgeon and physician. 30198
House that Jeff built. 33176, (68565)
House that Tweed built. 33177
Household library. (82267)
Household mysteries. 61254
Household of Bouverie. 101417
Household poems. (41932)
Household story of the American conflict.
(72145)-72148
Householders' Mutual Insurance Company.
54318
Housekeeper's companion. 61759
Houseman, Abraham. plaintiff 96886
Houser, Henry. 33178
Houses of refuge and schools of reform.
33179
Houseworth, T. 9977
Houseworth (T.) & Co. firm publishers
33180
Housewrights, Salem, Mass. see Association
of Housewrights, Salem, Mass.
Houssatonuoc Indians. see Stockbridge
Indians.
Houston, A. B. 33181
Houston, F. L. 91146
Houston, George. 23855, 49215
Houston, George Smith, 1811-1879. 33182-
(33184)
Houston, James Alexander. 15584, 33185-
33186
Houston, John W. 33187
Houston, M. H. 33188
Houston, Robert W. plaintiff 64251, 2d note
after 96883

Houston, Samuel, 1793-1863. 15888, (19093)
33189, 33190, 33193-33195, 33902,
(33881), 94720, 94951, 94961, 95000,
95005-95017, 95028-95034 see also
Texas (Republic) Army. Commander in
Chief. Texas (Republic) President,
1836-1838 (Houston) Texas (Republic)
President, 1841-1844 (Houston) Texas.
Governor, 1859-1861 (Houston)
Houston's Senate debates. (19093), 33195
Houstoun, James, b. ca. 1690. 15962, (33197)-
33199
Houstoun, James, b. ca. 1690. supposed author
97095
Houstoun, Matilda Charlotte (Jesse) Fraser,
1815?-1892. 33200-33202
Houstoun, William, 1695?-1733. 33196
Hout, L. tr. (30037)
Houtman, Cornelis de, ca. 1540-1599. 14349,
14957-14960, 74833
Houtman, Frederick. 74841
Houton de Labillardiere, Jacques Julien. see
Labillardiere, Jacques Julien Houton de,
1755-1834.
Hove, ------ van. see Van Hove, ---------.
Hove, Michiel Ten. see Ten Hove, Michiel.
Hovel of the rocks. 104462
Hoven, --------- (van Uitenhage de Mist) de.
33355, 69250, note after 97676
Hovey, Alvah. (33203), 84045
Hovey, Alvin Peterson, 1821-1891. 33484
Hovey, Charles Mason, 1810-1887. 1089, 33205
33208, 43809
Hovey, Horace C. 33209-33210
Hovey, Ivory. 33211-33213
Hovey, P. B. 1089, 33207
Hovey, Sylvester. (33214)
Hovey, William. petitioner 33215
Hovey, William A. 33216
How, David. 33217
How, Henry. (33218)
How, Henry R. 33219
How, Nehemiah. 33220
How, Samuel. 93424
How, Samuel B. (33221)-(33223)
How, Thomas Yardley. 12921, 14349, (14375),
32294, (33224)-(33226), 40570
How a bride was won. 27194
How and when our war debt can be paid. 3727.
How and where the money goes. 76687
How and why we give thanks. 22009
How and why young people should cleanse their
way. 16640
How are the heathen to be converted. 85291
How are you, Maximilian? 84849
How are you to be saved.? 67765, 3d note
after 94241
How Ben Franklin made his mark. 25616
How, by whom, and for what was the war
begun? (47166)
How Bull Rull [sic] battle was lost. 33227
"How can I help to abolish slavery?" 11996
How can we best help our camps and
hospitals. 33228
How Christ the Son glorified God. 92064
How do you like our country? 46885
How Douglas Democrats will vote. 40611
How easily the wand of a magician may be
broken by a woman. 37451
How Edmonia Lewis became an artist. 40794
How equal and unjust taxation affects the
interest. (60151)

How every man may become the owner of his home. 84437

How far the Gospel requires believers to aspire after being completely perfect. (79448), note after 98054, 104082

How far the people of the loyal states are responsible for the war. 81167

How General McCall pronounced for peace in Pennsylvania. 40611

How General Sherman proclaimed peace at Atlanta. 40611

How he went to roundout. (36127)

How I came to be governor. 24689

How is the strong staff broken, and the beautiful rod. 18182

How Massachusetts reigns and has reigned. 8348

How McClellan took Manassas. 43022

How New York City is governed. (58948)

How one church went through a war. 84901

How our national debt can be paid. 22097

How our national debts can be paid. (33229)

How patriotic services are rewarded in Canada. 38463

How protection, increase of public and private revenues. 10842

How shall I govern my school. 104776

How shall the lawyers be paid? 78840

How shall we vote on the water act? note after 6785, 79879

How slavery injures the free working man. (55459)

How specie payments may be resumed. 70992

How the people's constitution was made for Rhode Island. 70588

How the Sanitary [Commission] does its work. 5994

How the south rejected compromise. 12200, 33230

How the story books are made. 30448

How the war commenced. (33231)

How the western states can become the imperial power. 22097

How they act in Baltimore. 2988

How they win. 83587-83589

How this administration condusts this war. 42164

How to abolish slavery in America. 33233

How to avoid losses in Wall Street. 83647

How to be happy. 80922

How to conquer Texas. 29626, note after 95129, 2d note after 96410

How to deal with it. 82094

How to develop a national literature. (71741)

How to emigrate. 37903

How to extinguish the one and establish the other. 81634

How to get a farm. 50814

How to get in and out of the metropolis. 54693

How to get rich. 41620

How to get rich, or a key to honest wealth. 82348

How to get, save, spend, give, lend, and bequeath money. (25733)

How to have cheap iron. 10842

How to kill three birds with one stone. 33234

How to live in hard times. 46448

How to live in hard times. By a poor man. 97727

How to make small gas bills! 62336

How to make sugar. 57397

How to make sun-dials fitting for all those places. 5972

How to make the war short and the peace righteous. 105579

How to manage horses. 98633

How to meet the events of 1862. 65093

How to organize a national bank. 16313

How to pay it: or, a method of discharging the national debt. 39534

How to pay the debt of cities. 20206

How to raise an efficient army. (48977)

How to renew our national strength. 33235

How to resume specie payments. 36885

How to save the nation. 90143

How to see the New York Chrystal Palace. 54319

How to settle the Texas question. 33236, 95092

How to strengthen our army and crush the rebellion. (20512)

How to test precious metals. (9991)

How tobacco is raised and prepared for market. 88355

How we farm, mine, and live generally. 23861

How we may relieve ourselves from taxation. 9615

How will nullification work? (67132)

How will you answer it? 48973

Howard. pseud. Disquisition on imprisonment for debt. see Fay, Joseph Dewey, 1779-1825.

Howard, pseud. Essays of Howard. see Fay, Joseph Dewey, 1779-1825.

Howard, ----------. defendant 104413

Howard, ----------. ed. 41481

Howard, ----------, fl. 1795. 86653

Howard, B. 89883

Howard, Benjamin Chew, 1791-1872. 33240-(33241), 33268-33269, 45110, (78261)

Howard, Bezaleel. 33238-33239

Howard, C. (33280)

Howard, C. W. 33243-33244, 88117

Howard, Charles. (33242)

Howard, Charles. appellant 3042, 8481

Howard, Edward. 33245-33246

Howard, F. K. 25294, (33247)

Howard, Frederick. see Carlisle, Frederick Howard, 5th Earl of.

Howard, George William Frederick. see Carlisle, George William Frederick Howard, 7th Earl of, 1802-1864.

Howard, H. ed. 70700

Howard, H. R. 30364, 33250-33251, note before 91708

Howard, Henry. see Northampton, Henry Howard, Earl of, 1540-1614.

Howard, Henry. see Suffolk, Henry Howard, 12th Earl of, d. 1779.

Howard, J. H. illus. 79914, 90431

Howard, Jacob Merritt, 1805-1871. 33252-33254, (48776) see also Michigan. Attorney General.

Howard, James S. 33255, 2d note after 90696

Howard, John. 33256-33257

Howard, John C. (33258)

Howard, John Eager, 1752-1827. 33259, (45378)

Howard, John Henry. 33260

Howard, John S. (33261)

Howard, Joseph. supposed author 90431

Howard, Joseph P. 33262

Howard, Leonard. (33263)

Howard, Luke. 17754, 33264-33265, 78283, 78289, 105204

Howard, Margaret. defendant 33266

Howard, Mark. 33267

Howard, Martin, d. 1781. supposed author 7889, 19249, 29702, 32968, 40281, 40457, 57868, 69455, 3d note after 99800

Howard, Martin S. 33270-33271
Howard, Middleton. 33272, 58036
Howard, Oliver Otis, 1830-1909. 27239,
(33272)-(33274), 60592, 80420 see also
U. S. Bureau of Refugees, Freedmen,
and Abandoned Lands. Commissioner.
Howard, Percy. 33275
Howard, Richard L. ed. 56990
Howard, Robert. 33277
Howard, Sir Robert. 33276
Howard, S. (33280)
Howard, Simeon. 33278-33279, 95642
Howard, Thomas, 1561-1626. see Suffolk,
Thomas Howard, 1st Earl of, 1561-1626.
Howard, Volney E. 33281-33282, 49548
Howard, W. A. (33285)
Howard, William. engineer 33283, 64593,
87958, 93938 see also Maryland.
Susquehannah Commissioners.
Howard, William, 1817-1891. 33284
Howard, William D. 42538
Howard de Walden, Thomas Howard, 1st
Baron. see Suffolk, Thomas Howard,
1st Earl of, 1561-1626.
Howard Association, Philadelphia. 55483
Howard Association of New Orleans. 53330
Howard Benevolent Society, Boston. 6728,
92021
Howard Division, No. 26, Sons of Temperance.
see Sons of Temperance of North
America. Nova Scotia. Howard
Division, No. 26, Halifax.
Howard Fire Insurance Company. (42482)
Howard Fire Insurance Company. Charter.
(42482)
Howard's gold chart. 33262
Howard Glyndon. pseud. Idyls of battle and
poems of rebellion. see Redden,
Laura C.
Howard Glyndon. pseud. Notable men in
"the House." see Redden, Laura C.
Howard Mission and Home for Little
Wanderers, New York. 86948
Howard Society of New Jersey. see New
Jersey Howard Society.
Howard Street Church, Salem, Mass. see
Salem, Mass. Howard Street Church.
Howard Sunday School, Philadelphia. see
Philadelphia. Howard Sunday School.
Howard University, Washington, D. C. 33287
Howe, Cheney. 49615
Howe, E. D. (33290)
Howe, E. P. 33291
Howe, Ester. (33288)-33289
Howe, George. 33292-33296
Howe, Henry. 33305
Howe, Henry, 1816-1893. 3330-3332, 33297-
33304
Howe, J. 33316
Howe, J. W. 33318
Howe, James. defendant 74372-74373
Howe, James. pseud. tr. 98488
Howe, James B. 33306
Howe, James H. (33307)
Howe, John. (33308)
Howe, John. ed. 56158
Howe, John, jr. 33310
Howe, Joseph, 1804-1873. 30028, 31932,
33311-(33315), (51433)
Howe, Julia (Ward) 1819-1910. 33318-(33319)
Howe, Mark Antony De Wolfe, Bp., 1808-1895.
33320
Howe, Mary A. 33321
Howe, Nathanael. 33322-33324
Howe, R. H. 33325

Howe, Richard Howe, Earl, 1725-1799. 33326
33327, 52069, 94841
Howe, Robert. 100004
Howe, Robert. defendant at court martial
33328
Howe, Samuel Gridley, 1801-1876. 33329-
(33333), (58023), 75191
Howe, Timothy. 76917
Howe, Timothy Otis, 1816-1883. 33334-33337
Howe, Thomas. defendant at court martial
48976, 8th note after 96930A
Howe, Wiliam. (33345)
Howe, William Bell White, Bp., 1823-1894.
(33346), 87931
Howe, William Howe, 5th Viscount, 1725-1814
16813, 20909, 23499, 26429, 26443,
(33338)-(33339), 46919, 68968, 85243,
note after 102651
Howe (J. A.) firm publisher (75013)
Howe (Joseph) firm publisher 29687
Howel, James. see Howell, James.
Howell, Bertram H. claimant 48340
Howell, E. C. 49433
Howell, George Rogers. 33347
Howell, Isaac. petitioner 60723
Howell, James. (33348)
Howell, James B. 33349
Howell, John. 33350
Howell, Reading. 33351, 50865, 60026, 84624
see also Pennsylvania. Commissioners
Appointed to Explore the Head-waters
of the Rivers Delaware, Lehigh, and
Schuylkill, and the North-West Branch
of the Susquehanna.
Howell, Robert Boyle C. (33352)
Howell, S. N. 81416
Howell, Samuel. 61493
Howell, Thomas Bayly, 1768-1815. 67590
Howell, W. T. (25321), 33353
Howell (J. F.) & Co. firm publishers 6821
Howell (J. F.), Martin & Co. firm 53170
Howells, William Dean, 1837-1920. 33354,
62596
Howell's predictions. 32663
Howen, -------- (Uitenhage de Mist) see
Hoven, ------- (van Uitenhage de Mist)
de.
Howes, Frederick. 33357
Howes, Reuben W. 33358
Howes, William B. 33359
Howe's almanac, for 1848. (75013)
Howgill, Francis. 33360-33364, 52756
Howick, Charles Grey, Viscount. see Grey
Charles Grey, 2d Earl, 1764-1845.
Howison, John. 30560, 33366-33367
Howison, N. M. 33368-33369
Howison, Robert R. (33370)-33371
Howitt, Anna Mary. illus. 33373
Howitt, Emanuel. 33372
Howitt, Mary (Botham) 1799-1888. 9452, 7713
33373-33375, 33379
Howitt, William, 1792-1879. 22627, 33376-
33379
Howitz, Orville. 83664, note after 86785
Howland, A. 70740
Howland, C. H. 33380
Howland, Edward. 33381
Howland, Edward Cole. 84505
Howland, G. G. defendant (57622)
Howland, George. petitioner (52497)
Howland, Henry J. 33382
Howland, John. 33383-33385
Howland, S. defendant (57622)
Howland, S. A. (33386), 90853
Howland, Thomas. 99591

Howland, William. 16224
Howlett, Heman. 33387, 73942
Howlett, T. R. 33388
Howly, R. 101211
Hows, E. 33389
Hows, John A. 8816, 33390-33391, 92775
Howse, Joseph. 33392, (62550)
Howson, Henry. 33393
Hoxse, John. 33394
Hoy, Jan. 33395
Hoy va a ser encapillado el criminal Padre Arenas. 89415
Hoyas, E. 32756
Hoyland, J. 33396
Hoyo, Joseph del. 33397
Hoyos, Juan de los. ed. 96977
Hoyos Santillana, Ignacio de. see Santillana, Ignacio de Hoyos.
Hoyt, Mrs. -------. 33411
Hoyt, --------. defendant 76498, 95779, 102207
Hoyt, A. defendant before church conference 33398
Hoyt, Albert Harrison. 33399
Hoyt, Alfred M. 64424
Hoyt, Comfort. (33400)
Hoyt, David W. (33401)
Hoyt, Edmund S. 43988
Hoyt, Epaphras, 1765-1850. 33402-33403, 91607
Hoyt, George H. 33404
Hoyt, Goold. defendant 96869
Hoyt, Goold. respondent 96868-96869
Hoyt, James. 33405-33406
Hoyt, Jesse. (33407), (43437)
Hoyt, John W. 33408 see also U. S. Office of Education.
Hoyt, Joseph G. 33409-33410
Hoyt, Ralph. (33412)-33413
Hoyt. firm publishers see Fox and Hoyt. firm publishers
Huano del Peru. 74924
Huartus, Ioannus. 64450
Hubard, Edmund W. (33416)
Hubard Gallery, New York. 33415
Hubbard, A. C. (33417)
Hubbard, Bela. 9486, 33418, 38676, 48736
Hubbard, David. 33419
Hubbard, Ebenezer. 33420
Hubbard, Elizabeth. 33421
Hubbard, F. M. 4430
Hubbard, Gardiner G. 33422
Hubbard, George H. (33423)
Hubbard, Giles H. reporter 33424, 98405
Hubbard, H. 33425
Hubbard, H. G. (33426)
Hubbard, Henry, 1784-1857. 13653, 33427-33428
Hubbard, J. P. 13385
Hubbard, Jeremiah. 14732, 32351
Hubbard, John, 1703-1773. 33430-33432, 42984, 105926
Hubbard, John, 1703-1773. supposed author 50235, 86781, 105936
Hubbard, John, 1759-1810. 33433-33435
Hubbard, John Niles, b. 1815. (33436), 98428
Hubbard, John W. 33437
Hubbard, Jonathan. 33431, 52984, note after 97187
Hubbard, Lorenzo. 16651
Hubbard, Oliver P. 83654
Hubbard, S. G. 33438
Hubbard, Samuel D. 33439-33440
Hubbard, Samuel M. 33441

Hubbard, Thomas. 15436, (34857), 36737, 62579, 5th note after 102623 see also Massachusetts (Colony) Commissioners to Treat With the Eastern and Penobscot Indians, 1753. Massachusetts (Colony) Commissioners to Treat With the Eastern Indians, 1752.
Hubbard, William, 1621-1704. 16563, 31746, 33442-33453, 46640, (46789), 72691, 84350, 94932, 97190, 104900, 106052
Hubbard, William B. 33454
Hubbard (Thomas) firm publisher 83402
Hubbard Silver Mine . . . in Austin, Nevada. 33455
Hubbard's narrative. 106052
Hubbardston, Mass. Schools. 33456
Hubbell, Horatio. 33458
Hubbell, Isaac. 65487
Hubbell, J. H. 33459
Hubbell, Levi. 33460
Hubbell, Levi. defendant 33461, 37728, 74529
Hubbell, Martha (Stone) 33462
Hubbell, Seth, 1759-1832. 33463
Hubbell, Stephen, 1802-1884. 33464
Hubbell, William Wheeler. (33465)-33468
Hubbell & Patton Gold and Silver Company, established in . . . Philadelphia. 33469
Hubbert, --------. 33470
Hubel, G. A. 89285
Huber, -----------. defendant (20260), 69106
Huber, -----------. tr. 72232
Huber, B. 33471
Huber, V. A. 33472
Hubert, ----------. tr. 15495
Hubert and Ellen. 77009
Hubert and Ellen. With other poems. 77008
Hubley, Adam. 49200
Hubley, Bernard. 33473
Hubner, -------. see Huebner, -----------.
Hubsch Tolmetsch. pseud. see Giocondo, Giovanni.
Huc, ---------. 33474
Huc quicumq3 novas. 67355
Huckens, Ester. 26245, 30710
Hucks, Samuel. defendant 102781
Huddart, R. T. 33475
Hudson, -------, fl. 1848. 33500
Hudson, Agur. defendant 96922
Hudson, C. F. 90567
Hudson, Charles, 1795-1881. 33477-(33482), 41179, 2d note after 96724, 103035
Hudson, Charles, fl. 1823. 33476, 70103
Hudson, Charles, fl. 1857. 33483, 3d note after 96986
Hudson, Damian, 1808-1875. 33486, 68830
Hudson, David. 33484-33485, 104043
Hudson, E. M. 33487, 33488
Hudson, Henry, d. 1611. 33489-33491, (33666), 66686, 67355, 68346, (74131)
Hudson, Henry Norman, 1814-1886. 9618, (33493)
Hudson, Isaac. 33494
Hudson, Samuel. 32861, 33495-33497, 92113
Hudson, Thomas J. 33498
Hudson, Timothy B. (33499)
Hudson, N. H. Old Nutfield Celebration, 1869. see Celebration of the One Hundred and Fiftieth Anniversary of the Settled Part of Old Nutfield, N. H., 1869.
Hudson, N. J. Charter. (33501)
Hudson, N. Y. First Presbyterian Church. (33504)

Hudson, N. Y. First Reformed Dutch Church.
(33504)
Hudson, N. Y. Washington Benevolent Society.
see Washington Benevolent Society. New
York. Hudson.
Hudson, Ohio. Fifty-Sixth Anniversary
Celebration of the Settlement, 1856.
33505
Hudson, Ohio. Western Reserve College.
see Western Reserve University,
Cleveland, Ohio.
Hudson. 33491
Hudson and Delaware Canal Company.
petitioners 33507
Hudson, and its tributary region. (29852)
Hudson, and northern routes from New York
to Montreal. (33511)
Hudson between Sandy Hook and Sandy Hill.
33512
Hudson City and Columbia County directory.
33503
Hudson Female Seminary, New York. (33504)
Hudson, from the wilderness to the sea. 42118
Hudson illustrated with pen and pencil. 33513
Hudson legends. 35186
Hudson remarker. 89499
Hudson River and its vicinity. (33514)
Hudson River, and the Hudson River Railroad.
33516
Hudson River Baptist Association. see
Baptists. New York. Hudson River
Baptist Association.
Hudson River Baptist Association North. see
Baptists. New York. Hudson River
Baptist Association North.
Hudson River Bridge Company at Albany.
defendants 81069
Hudson River guide. 20325, note after 55831
Hudson River guide; containing a description.
33515
Hudson River Industrial School Association.
33533
Hudson River Institute, Claverack, N. Y.
33534
Hudson River portfolio. 33529, note after
101087
Hudson River Railroad. Commissioners.
33535
Hudson River Railroad. Directors. 33535-
33536
Hudson River Railroad. Report on the
location of the line. 36072
Hudson the navigator. 13037
Hudson weekly gazette. 84553
Hudson's Bay and Pacific territories. (50796)
Hudson's Bay Company. 18095, 20404, 33551-
33552, (72259) see also British and
American Joint Commission For the
Final Settlement of the Claims of the
Hudson's Bay and Puget's Sound
Agricultural Companies.
Hudson's Bay Company. plaintiff 90392
Hudson's Bay Company. Charter. 20404,
33545, 33548, 33551
Hudson's Bay Company; what is it? 33544
Hudson's Bay Company's charter. 20404
Hudson's Bay; or, a missionary tour. 74586
Hudson's Bay; or, every-day life in the
wilds. 2952
Hudson's Bay question, from the "Colonial
intelligencer." 33540
Hudson's Bay territories and Vancouver's
Island. 44915
Hudson's Bay territories; a series of letters.
22772

Huebeldinck, Martin. 14349
Huebner, ------. 54941, 77544
Huehuetlapallan, Amerika's grosse Urstadt in
den Konigreiche Guatimala. 71447
Hvehvetlatholli. 36786
Hvei Tlamahvicoltica Omonexiti. 39141, note
after 98362
Huejutla, Mexico. Establecimiento de
Education Publica. Alumnos. 33553
Huelstett, --------. 33554
Huelstett uber die Nordwestliche Durchfahrt.
33554
Huen-Dubourg, J. 33555-33556
Huergo, Palmon. 33558
Huerta, Alonso. 33559-33560
Hverta, Geronomo de. tr. (63421)
Huerta, Juan A., Bp. 33561 see also Pun
(Diocese) Bishop (Huerta)
Hues, R. 33562-33563
Hues O'Neil, Sieur de Beaulieu. pseud. see
Bailley, Adrien, 1649-1706.
Huestis, Jabez W. (33565)
Huestis, Jonathan. 33566
Huet, P. D. 33567-33568
Huet de la Valiniere, Pierre. see Valiniere
Pierre Huet de la.
Huevel, Jacob Adrien van. see Van Huevel,
Jacob Adrien.
Huevel, Jacob Adrien vanden. see Van Huev
Jacob Adrien.
Huey tlamahuicoltica omonexiti 39141, note
after 98362
Huff, J. W. (33569)
Huff, T. D. defendant 97773
Huffington, William. (19384), 33570
Huffman, Abigail. appellant 96762
Huffumborghausen, Baron. pseud. Congress
between the beasts. 33571
Hufidalgo Deluas. pseud. see Knight of
Elvas. pseud.
Huger, Alfred. 33572-(33573)
Hugginiana. (33575)
Huggins, Edward. 33574
Huggins, John Richard Desborus. (33575)
Huggins, William. defendant 105354
Huggins's fantasy. (33575)
Hugh A. Pue, Esq. 66542
Hughan, Thomas. 102777
Hughan, William James. 33576
Hughes, --------, fl. 1765. 84586
Hughes, --------, fl. 1855. 7052
Hughes, Benjamin F. 33577-33578
Hughes, D. L. 33579
Hughes, Edward B. 33580
Hughes, F. W. 60529
Hughes, George W. 1595, 24515, (33581)
Hughes, Griffith. 335182
Hughes, Henry. 33583-(33584)
Hughes, Hugh. 33585
Hughes, James. 33586
Hughes, James M. 30566, (34385), note after
53697, (68287), note after 83791, 10181
101880
Hughes, Jeremiah. 45092, 55314
Hughes, John. 33587, 62743
Hughes, John Joseph, Abp., 1797-1864.
2875, 4326, (8371), 8347, (30810), 3358
33591, 33593-33594, 48934, 61065 see
also New York (Archdiocese) Archbis
(Hughes)
Hughes, John Joseph, Abp., 1797-1864. spirit
author 13167

Hughes, John T. 33595-(33596)
Hughes, John W. defendant (33597)
Hughes, L. B. (33598)-33599
Hvghes, Levves. 96027
Hughes, Mathew. 33600
Hughes, Nimrod. 33601
Hughes, S. R. 33602
Hughes, Samuel. 96442
Hughes, T. S. 33604
Hughes, Thomas, 1822-1896. (33603), (42656)
Hughes, Thomas Aloysius, 1849- 103353
Hughes, W. L. tr. 63559
Hughes, William. tr. (69035)
Hughes, William, fl. 1665-1683. 33605
Hughes, William, fl. 1788. (33606)-33607
Hughes, William, 1817-1876. 33608, 46942
Hughes, Denver and Peck. firm 33609-
  33610, 70244
Hughes High School, Cincinnati. see
  Cincinnati. Hughes High School.
Hughes' Michigan general shippers' guide.
  33602
Hughs, Mary (Robson) 33611-33612
Hugo, Victor Marie, Comte, 1802-1885.
  27692, (31378), (33613)-33620, 39226,
  49399, 47292, note before 91289
Hugo: a legend of Rockland Lake. 82511
Hugo Playfair. pseud. see Playfair, Hugo.
  pseud.
Hvgone, Hermanno. tr. 89460
Hugonis Grotii De origine gentium Americana-
  rum dissertatio. (28957)
Huguenot exile in Virginia. 1st note after
  100572, 100837
Huguenot settlers of New York City and its
  vicinity. 2954
Huguenots. 25027
Huguenots at home in America. 25027
Huguenots in Florida. 81222, (81232)
Huguenots in France and America. (39735)
Huguenots: their settlements, churches, and
  industries in England and Ireland.
  82280, 82281
Huguet Latour, L. A. see Latour, L. A.
  Huguet.
Huhlenberg, W. A. 64642
Huhn, J. B. 33622
Huhn, W. 33623
Huidekoper, Frederic, 1817-1892. (33624)
Huidekoper, H. J. 33625
Huidekoper, H. J. supposed author 60205
Huidekoper, J. H. ed. 97832
Huile de petrole. 79383A
Huish, Robert. 33626-(33629)
Huit, Ephraim. 33630
Huit mois en Amerique. 21489
Hulbert, ------, fl. 1821. (43001), 96901
Hulbert, Archer Butler, 1873-1933. note after
  106203
Hulbert, Charles. 33631
Hulbert, Daniel P. M. 33632
Hulbert, John. 96734-96735 see also U. S.
  Commissioner to the Saganaw Tribe of
  Chippewas. U. S. Superintendent of
  Indian Affairs (Acting)
Hulbert, P. 104719
Hulburd, Calvin T. (33633)
Hulburt, J. Beaufort. (33994)-33995
Hulett, J. engr. 84617
Hulett, T. G. 33634
Hulfsbuch beim Interrichte in der Geographie
  fur Lehrer. 10687
Hulfsquellen und der Krieg Nordamerika's.
  10842
Hull, A. Gerald. 33635

Hull, Isaac, 1773-1843. 25722, 1st note after
  99448
Hull, Isaac, 1773-1843. defendant at court of
  inquiry (33636)
Hull, John. (33637)
Hull, John Simpson. 33638
Hull, Laurens. (33639)
Hull, Morris N. B. (33640)
Hull, William. 1753-1825. (10263), (19074),
  (33642)-33646, 48755, 48780, 85417
  see also Michigan (Territory) Governor,
  1805-1812 (Hull)
Hull, William, 1753-1825. defendant at court
  martial 25045, (33642), 33644-33646
Hull and East Riding Anti-slavery Association.
  93609
Hulme, Thomas. 13982, 84355-84356
Hulot, Henricivs Lvdovicvs. 95251
Hulsemann, Johann Georg. (33650)-33651,
  44518 see also Austria. Charge
  d'Affaires. U. S.
Hulsius, Levinus, d. 1606. 2139, 7567,
  (7585), 8427, (11608), 19152, 30122,
  31476, (33652)-33679, 41659, 55436,
  67355, 67546, (67562)-67566, 67981,
  (77679), 77680-77682, 77686, 77956,
  82819, 82846, 89342, 103332
Hulswit, ------. 36123
Hulton, Henry. 34846
Huma Associacao de Litteratos, Rio de
  Janeiro. 7604
Huma carta para elrey N. Senhor. 99522
Huma noticia biographia de seu autor. 10299
Huma senhora. pseud. Brasil visto pro Cima.
  7530
Human beings not property. 42369
Human comedy. 16323
Human geography. 83373-83374
Human government and the laws. 42032
Human heart discovering itself under trials.
  92777
Human knowledge. 44737
Human liberty against ultra-temperance
  intolerance. 38067
Human life. 79947
Human life a pilgrimage. 21052
Human longevity. 21693
Human slavery in the southern states. 73335
Human sorrow and divine comfort. 83624
Human soul, its migrations and its transmigra-
  tions. 67851
Human sufferings and divine comfort. 83617
Human wisdom inadequate to the world's
  salvation. 71150
Humane Fire Society, Portsmouth, N. H.
  64422
Humane Fire Society, established Febraury
  1796. 64421
Humane impositions proved unscriptural.
  83442
Humane policy, or justice to the aborigines.
  3216
Humane police; or, the civilization of the
  Africans. 3217
Humane Society, Cambridge, Mass. see
  Cambridge Humane Society.
Humane Society of Massachusetts. see
  Humane Society of the Commonwealth
  of Massachusetts.
Humane Society of . . . Massachusetts. 45765
Humane Society of the Commonwealth of
  Masscahusetts. 3734, 30510, 32173,
  (33680)-33681, 45765, 95197, 102061
Humane Society of the Commonwealth of
  Massachusetts. Charter. 3734

Humane Society of the State of New York.
53696, (69742)

Humane Society of the State of New York.
Committee to Inquire Into the Number
of Tavern Licences. 35854, 53696,
(69742)

Humanitas. pseud. New and interesting view
of slavery. 33682

Humanitas. pseud. 33683 Reflections on
slavery. 33683

Humanity in the city. 11947

Humanity pleading for the "Maine law."
(16823)

Humard, -------. see Harvard, James.

Humason, W. L. 33685

Humberger, Johannes. tr. 130, (8784)

Humbert, Alois, 1829-1887. 77213

Humbert, Auguste, tr. 10842

Humble address and earnest appeal. 23079,
97350

Humble address and petition of the merchants.
95945

Humble address of His Majesties Council.
35633

Humble address of the Burgesses. 99916

Humble address of Charles Desborow. 19686

Humble address of divers of the gentry.
6474, 95946

Humble address of Her Majesty's Council.
(52894)

Humble address of the Council. 99899-99904,
99906

Humble address of the Council, in assembly.
99893

Humble address of the Council in assembly,
to the Honourable William Gooch, Esq.
99892, 99896

Humble address of the Council, in assembly,
to the Honourable William Gooch, Esq;
His Majesty's Lieutenant-Governor and
Commander in Chief, of the Colony and
Dominion of Virginia. 99895, 99897-
99898

Humble address of the Council, in assembly,
to the Honourable William Gooch, Esq;
His Majesty's Lieutenant-Governor and
Commander in Chief of the Colony and
Dominion of Virginia. May 19, 1732.
99890

Humble address of the Council in assembly,
to the Honourable William Gooch, Esq;
His Majesty's Lieutenant-Governor of
the Colony and Dominion of Virginia.
99891

Humble address of the gentry. (33688)

Humble address of the "Grand Inquest for the
Body of the Island of Barbadoes." 79008

Humble address of the House of Burgesses.
99904, 99919-99919-99924

Humble address of the House of Burgesses,
to the Honourable William Gooch, Esq.
99915, 99918

Humble address of the House of Burgesses,
to the Honourable William Gooch, Esq;
His Majesty's Lieutenant-Governor.
99912, 99917

Humble address of the House of Lords, to the
King. 33686

Humble address of the inhabitants of Newfoundland. 54976, 94549

Humble address of the Lords to His Majesty.
19678

Humble address of the people of Great Britain.
33687

Humble address of the publicans of New-
England. (33688)

Humble address of the representatives of the
counties of New-Castle, Kent, and Sussex
(52568)

Humble address of the Right Honourable the
Lords Spiritual and Temporal, in Parliament assembled, presented to Her Majes
on Wednesday the thirteenth day of Marc
1705. 10972, 87359, 87805

Humble address of the Right Honourable the
Lords Spiritual & Temporal in Parliamen
assembled, presented to His Majesty,
Feb. 12, 1699. 78219

Humble address of the Right Honourable the
Lords Spiritual and Temporal in Parlia-
ment assembled, presented to His
Majesty, October 27, 1775. (33690)

Humble address of the Right Hon. the Lords
Spiritual and Temporal, presented to His
Majesty on Friday, October 27, 1775.
33689

Humble address to every Christian. 24444,
33691

Humble address to the King. 33692

Humble address to the legislators of the
commonwealth of Virginia. 100501

Humble address to the Parliament and
Assembly. 58510, 104342

Humble address to [sic] the Right Hon. the
Lords Spiritual and Temporal in Parlia-
ment assembled, presented to His Majest
December 1, 1774. 33693

Humble and earnest address of the Third
Church. 103323

Humble apology for the Quakers. 33694

Humble attempt at scurrility. 25637, 84586,
84678C

Humble attempt &c. 2200

Humble attempt to discover the ten lost tribes
of Israel. 6856

Humble attempt to promote . . . visible union.
21945

Humble attempt to support the truth of God.
3955

Humble attempt towards the improvement of
psalmody. 96087

Humble attempts at immortality. 100764

Humble call to Archippus. 97418

Humble confession, declaration, recantation,
and apology of Benjamin Towne. 51511,
104939

Humble conqueror. (2700)

Humble country cousin of Peter Pindar Esq.
pseud. Some very gentle touches. 8678

Humble discourse of the incomprehensibleness
of God. (14525)

Humble, earnest and affectionate address to th
clergy. 39326

Humble effort to promote order. 91359

Humble enquiry into the nature of the de-
pendency. 106387

Humble imitation of a work under a similar
title. 67114

Humble impartial essay upon the peace of
Jerusalem. 94693

Humble importunity and faith, victorious.
42009

Humble inquiry into the rules of the word of
God. 21946

Humble inquiry into the scripture account of
Jesus Christ. 9422, 93820

Humble intercession for the distressed town of
Boston. 86866, 106139

Humble petition and address of the General
Court sitting at Boston in New England,
unto the High and Mighty Prince Charles
the Second. 33696

Humble petition and address of the General
Court sitting at Boston, New England,
unto the High and Mighty Prince Charles
the Second. 33695
Humble petition and declaration of the generall
inhabitants. 101508
Humble petition and information of Sir Lewis
Stucley. 67550, 93235
Humble petition and memorial of the Assembly
of Jamaica. 35587, 35664
Humble petition of Denys Rolle, Esq. 72848
Humble petition of J. Collins. 54976, 94549
Humble petition of many divines. 96029
Humble petition of proprietors of plantations
in Nevis. 33697, 52428
Humble petition of Roger Williams of London.
104344
Humble petition of several planters and others.
96016
Humble petition of several proprietors of
plantations. 33697, 52428
Humble petition of severall that . . . are
willing to adventure. 101443
Humble petition of the House of Delegates of
the Province of Nova Scotia. (56139)
Humble petition of the inhabitants of the
colony. 101508
Humble petition of the merchants. 95938-
95939
Humble petition of the people called Quakers.
100527
Humble petition of His Majesty. 19160
Humble plea, addressed to the Legislature of
California. 89256
Humble proposals of the ministers who
presented the petition. 104336
Humble remonstrance of John Blande of
London. 100529
Humble representation and earnest supplica-
tion. 93814
Humble representation, by William Smith,
D. D. and James Day, M. D. 84623
Humble representation, by William Smith,
D. D. Provosot of the College. 84622,
84674
Humble representation of the Council-General.
(78239)
Humble representation of the Council of the
Company of Scotland. (18557)
Humble request. 106052
Humble reqvest of His Maiesties loyall sub-
jects. (21090), 33698, 78431, 104846
Humble submission of several kings. 33699
Humble submission to divine sovereignty.
26225
Humble supplication of the ministers of
Scotland. 78379
Humble tribute to my country. 22242, 22273
Humble tribute to . . . William Ellery
Channing. note after (58767)
Humble wagoner. pseud. Beginning and the
end. 4364
Humbley, Adam. (38801) see also Lancaster
County, Pa. Lieutenant.
Humboldt, Alexander, Freiherr von, 1769-1859.
162, 1555, 2002A, 4834, 4857, 6334,
8103, 8201, 8839, 9876, 12272, 25131,
(27261), 31593, 33618, 33700-33730,
33732-33745, 33747-33764, 33766-33773,
37256, 38049, 38241, 38728, 40038,
41777, 49913-49915, 50115, 52105,
57458-57459, 58549, (58551), 71995,
(77791), 79051, 81454, note after 94501,
94853, 96501, 98679, 99383B, 105741
Humboldt, Friedrich Heinrich Alexander,
Freiherr von. see Humboldt, Alexander,
Freiherr von, 1769-1859.

Humboldt, Gay. pseud. Poems and letters.
33774
Humboldt Centennial Celebration, Dubuque,
Iowa, 1869. see Iowa Institute of
Science and Arts, Dubuque. Humboldt
Centennial Celebration, 1869.
Humboldt Savings and Loan Society, San
Francisco. 34912, 76050
Humboldt times. 105053
Humboldt's life and character. 91781
Humbug: a look at some popular impositions.
33775
Humbug and the reality. (18993)
Humbug exposed! 94152
Humbug: or, an expose of the operation.
105955
Humbuggiana. 16362
Humbugs of New-York. 68653
Humbugs of the world. 3563
Humbugs of Washington City. (51657)
Hume, David, 1711-1776. 85105, 97331, 97659
Hume, David, 1711-1776. spirit author 19947,
note after 96403
Hume, George Henry. 33776
Hume, Hamilton. 33777
Hume, John, successively Bishop of Bristol,
Oxford, and Salisbury. (33778), 84846
Hume, Joseph, 1777-1855. 33779, 58159
Hume, Sophia. 33780-(33781), 40618
Hume Campbell, Hugh. see Marchmont, Hugh
Hume Campbell, 3d Earl of.
Humeristische Geschichte von New-York.
(35167)
Humes, Gilbert. 17941
Humes, Gilbert. defendant 17941, 30345
Humes, Thomas W. 21656, 33782 see also
East Tennesse Relief Association,
Knoxville. General Agent.
Humiliation and hope. 21134
Humiliations followed with deliverances.
(46363), 94022
Humillis confessio. 25408
Hummel, A. H. reporter (70423)
Hummerich, Franz. 99363
Humming bird. 33783
Humor, satire, and sentiment treated
scientifically. 30237
Humorous account of some of the exploits.
26096
Humourous adventures of Dick Bully. 96098
Humorous description in verse. 91058
Humorous description of the tour of His
Royal Highness. 16778
Humourous history of New York. 35152, 35154
Humorous novel. 78686
Humorous poems. 32621
Humours of Eutopia. 33784
Humors of the west. 71396
Humors of Uncle Abe. 41207
Humours on the border. 16323
Humphrey, -------, fl. 1835. 31595
Humphrey, Asa. 33785, 77885
Humphrey, Edward P. 7695, (33786)-33787
Humphrey, Heman, 1779-1861. 33788-33794,
34474, 52723, note after 65546, 89736
Humphrey, Old. pseud. Indians of North
America. see Mogridge, George.
Humphrey, Old. pseud. North American
Indians. see Mogridge, George.
Humphrey, S. D. ed. 18272
Humphrey, Z. M. (33796), 93744
Humphrey (George P.) firm publisher 99573,
103452
Humphrey Hedgehog. pseud. see Hedgehog,
Humphrey. pseud.
Humphrey Scourge. pseud. see Scourge,
Humphrey. pseud.

Humphreys, Alexander. see Humphreys-
Alexander, Alexander, calling himself
Earl of Stirling, 1783-1859.
Humphreys, Andrew Atkinson, 1810-1883.
(33797), 35308, 69900, 69946
Humphreys, Benjamin Grubb, 1808-1882. 49538
see also Mississippi. Governor, 1865-
1868 (Humphreys)
Humphreys, C. A. 33798, note after 89883
Humphreys, Daniel, 1740-1827. 33799, 92273
Humphreys, David, 1689-1740. 33800-(33801)
Humphreys, David, 1752-1818. 1365, 24022,
(33802)-(33815), 71321, (82501), 86106,
94058, 97204, 105968
Humphreys, David C. (33816)
Humphreys, Edward R. 33817-33820
Humphreys, Francis. 33821
Humphreys, Hector. 33822
Humphreys, Samuel. tr. 29143
Humphreys, W. H. 33823
Humphreys-Alexander, Alexander, calling
himself Earl of Stirling, 1783-1859.
(33824)-33826, (51820), 91840-91841,
93598,
Humphreys-Alexander, Alexander, calling
himself Earl of Stirling, 1783-1859.
defendant 33827-33829, 91841A, 94084,
note after 97471
Humphries, David. see Humphreys, David,
1752-1818.
Humphries (P. L.) & Co. firm publishers
98443
Humphrys, Benjamin. 93598
Hundert Episteln. 106295
Hundertjahrige Bestand des Amerikanischen
Methodismus. 51895
Hundertjahrige Trost-Rede aus Brasilien fur
die Schweigende Gesellschaft Jesu in
Europa. 99526
Hundley, D. R. 33831
Hundred Boston orators. 42089
Hundred cities and large towns of America.
(61379)
Hundred illustrated gems. 27534, 40222
Hundred years ago. (57728)
Hundred years ago, and other poems. 80877
Hundred years of Methodism. 81367
Hunfalvy, P. 33832
Hungarian exile and his adventures. 91189,
91990
Hungary. Treaties, etc. 19274, 96543-96545
Hungerford, James. (33833)
Hungerford, John, d. 1729. 65865, 88192
Hungerford, Orville. 33834
Hunkers and Algerines identified. (20647),
note after 96509
Hunkpapa Indians. Treaties, etc. 96642
Hunn, John S. 33835
Hunn, Nathanael. 33836
Hunnewell, James F. ed. 89274
Hunnicutt, James W. 33837
Hunt, --------, fl. 1833. 89204
Hunt, --------, fl. 1856. 2861
Hunt, --------, fl. 1859. 64985
Hunt, Benjamin Faneuil. (33838)-33839, 92878
Hunt, Benjamin Faneuil. defendant 83854
Hunt, Benjamin S. (33840), (81989)
Hunt, Charles Havens. 33841
Hunt, Cornelius E. (33842)
Hunt, Daniel. 33843
Hunt, E. B. 33844
Hunt, Ebenezer. 92884
Hunt, Ezra M. (33845)-33846
Hunt, F. W. (33847)
Hunt, Freeman. (1816), (2781), (5291), 17109,
11218-11219, 15624, 24483, 24648,
33848-33853, 34907, 35806, 39354, 39564,

43358, 47919, 47920, (64500), (67216),
93270
Hunt, Freeman. supposed author 1043
Hunt, Gaillard, 1862-1924. 83509-83510,
96788, 100081
Hunt, Gilbert J. 33854-33856
Hunt, H. 33861
Hunt, H. W. 38837
Hunt, Harriot K. 33857
Hunt, Henry J. 33858
Hunt, Hiram Paine, 1796-1865. 33859-33860
Hunt, Isaac, 1751-1809. 5219, 16170, 19929,
33862-33866, 84586, 84589, 84678C,
93366, note before 96481A
Hunt, Isaac H. 33867, 92057
Hunt, J. 33870
Hunt, J., jr. (33869)
Hunt, J. Dickinson. (33876)
Hunt, J. G. 33877
Hunt, James. (33868)
Hunt, James H. 50755
Hunt, Jeremiah. 33871
Hunt, John. petitioner (59611), 61671
Hunt, John. plaintiff 5379, 33874, 91855
Hunt, John, 1740?-1824. ed. 6121, 14956,
82873
Hunt, John, 1744-1775. 33872-(33873)
Hunt, John, fl. 1837. 33875
Hunt, John Warren. 33878-33879
Hunt, Jonathan, jr. (33880)
Hunt, Memucan. (33881)-33883
Hunt, Nathan. (33884), 33903
Hunt, Noah H. (33885)
Hunt, R. tr. 17456
Hunt, Randell. 33886
Hunt, Richard M. 33888
Hunt, Richard S. 33887
Hunt, Robert, 1807-1887. 36879
Hunt, Rowland. (33889)
Hunt, Sanford Beebee, 1825-1884. 9063, 78504
Hunt, Theodore Gaillard, 1805-1893. 33890
Hunt, Thomas. 87879
Hunt, Thomas P. 33895
Hunt, Thomas Sterry, 1826-1892. 8755, 33892-
33894, 41818
Hunt, Thornton Leigh. 33891, 72871
Hunt, Timothy Dwight. 33896
Hunt, W. L. G. 33908
Hunt, Washington, 1811-1867. 33897-33898,
53566, 53616, 68959 see also New York
(State) Governor, 1851-1853 (Hunt)
Hunt, William. 601, (33899)-33900
Hunt, William, 1825-1896. (33901)
Hunt, William, fl. 1856. 33902
Hunt, William, fl. 1858. 33903
Hunt, William Gibbes. 25172, 33904-(33907),
45521, 96466
Hunt (John P.) firm publisher (41885)
Hunt (W. H.) firm publisher 88117
Hunt and Adams. firm publishers 89508
Hunt Female Beneficial Society, Philadelphia.
61731
Hunt of the wild horse. 69079
Hunted, transported, and doomed to toil.
46186
Hunter, Alfred. (33909)-33910, note after
64141
Hunter, Daniel J. pseud. Sketch of Chili.
see Vicuna Mackenna, Benjamin.
Hunter, David, 1802-1886. (33913)-33914,
88935
Hunter, Fanny. 23787, 33916
Hunter, Henry. tr. 75474
Hunter, Hiram A. 33917, 34616
Hunter, Mrs. James. tr. 17455
Hunter, James, 1817-1881. tr. 17454, 17456

Hutchinson Division, No. 63, Sons of
Temperance. see Sons of Temperance
of North America. Virginia. Hutchinson
Division, No. 63.
Hutchinson, Krohl & Co. in support of their
right to the possession. 34094
Hutchinson papers. (34070), 65646, 98500
Hutchinson's New Brunswick directory. 52534
Hutchinson's Newburgh directory. (54905)
Hutchinson's Republican songster. (34065)
Huter, Simon. publisher 77677
Huth, Georg Leonhard. tr. (11510), 11515,
22090
Hutson, Mary. 8791, 41605
Hutson, William. 83450
Hutted knoll. 16570
Hutten, Hugo Rudolph. tr. 92555
Hutten, Ulric von. pseud. Appeal to the laity.
34098
Hutten, Ulric von. pseud. Epistle congratula-
tory. 34099
Hutten, Ulrich de, 1488-1523. 34095-(34097)
Huttich, Johann, 1480-1544. 16961, note after
16965, 30482-30483, 34100-34107, 40960,
50050-50064, 62803, 63960, 74803, note
after 99383C, 1st-5th notes after 106378
Hutton, -------. 8582
Hutton, George. 34108
Hutton, Mancius S. 86117
Hutton, Mathew, Abp. of Canterbury, 1693-
1758. 34109
Hutton, William. 10368, 22497, 34110-34111
Hutton & Freligh. firm publishers 88417-
88418
Hutton & Freligh's southern monthly. 88417
Huxley, Thomas Henry, 1825-1895. 83876
Huxon, A. B. see Hasson, Alexander
Breckenridge, d. 1877.
Huygens, C. 104143
Huyghue, Douglas S. (34113)
Huysmann, Roelf. see Agricola, Rudolphus,
1443-1485.
Huzza for the American navy. 21309, 105957
Huzza for the constitution! 21309
Hyacinthe, H. Cordonnier de Saint. see
Cordonnier de Saint Hyacinthe, H.
Hyatt, Alpheus. 85072
Hyatt, Thaddeus. 93643
Hyatt, Thaddeus. defendant 79454
Hyatt, Thaddeus. petitioner 34114
Hybridity in animals and plants. (51024)
Hyde, Alvan. 34115-34117, 98736, 104424-
104425
Hyde, Ann Maria. 34118, 80967
Hyde, C. 84971
Hyde, Charles. 34119
Hyde, Charles. petitioner 82939
Hyde, Eli. 34120
Hyde, Ezra. (34121)
Hyde, J. T. 90559
Hyde, Jabez B. tr. 34122, 79119-79120
Hyde, Jabez B. supposed author 79117
Hyde, James F. C. (34123)
Hyde, John, jr. 34124
Hyde, Nancy Maria. (34125)
Hyde, Thomas. 82833
Hyde, Thomas. tr. 25281, 60934
Hyde, West. 18775, 69750 see also Great
Britain. Army. Commissioners for
Settling a Cartel for the Exchange of
Prisoners, 1779.
Hyde, William. 34126
Hyde, William L. (34127)
Hyde de Neuville, J. G., Baron. 93996
Hyde Park, Mass. 34128
Hyde Park, N. Y. Reformed Dutch Church.
(80452)

Hyde Park historical record. 92875
Hydraulic and nautical observations. 64822
Hydraulicus. 30557
Hydrographia. (24316)
Hydrographia y theoria de planetas. (11718)
Hydrographic report. 35308
Hydrographie. 21216
Hydrographie de la mer du Sud. 25914
Hydrographie du haut San-Francisco. 40915
Hydrographie et physique. 21353
Hydrographie Francoise. 4554
Hydrographie pour l'intelligence du dit voyage.
69248
Hydropathic and Physiological School, New
York. see New York Hydropathic
and Physical School.
Hyenne, Robert. (34129)
Hyer, -------. defendant 64038, 64039
Hyer, W. G. 73154
Hygeden, Ranulphus. 76838
Hygiene des Europeens dans les climats
tropicaux. 75504
Hygienic, medical, and surgical experiences
in the war. 76664
Hygienic observations. 76653
Hyko Silver-Mining Company. 42868, (69955)
Hyko Silver Mining Company, located in the
Pah-Ranagat Lake silver mining district.
42868
Hylacomylus, Martin. see Waldeseemuller,
Martin, 1470-1521?
Hylkes, Reinier. 34130
Hylton, --------. defendant 103854
Hymen; an accurate description of the
ceremonies. (34131)
Hymen's recruiting sergeant, nos. I. and II.
102477
Hymen's recruiting-serjeant. 102477-102478,
102495
Hymn. 32596, 106069
Hymn book. 85507
Hymn book for the use of Ojibwa Indian
congregations. (57082)
Hymn-book in the language of the Sequimaux.
22855
Hymn, by John G. Whittier. 103805
Hymn, composed by the late Reverend Mr.
George Whitefield. 103526
Hymn, composed by the Reverend Mr. George
Whitefield. 103527-103528
Hymn, composed for, and sung on the occasion.
94364
Hymn for the eighty-seventh anniversary of
American independence. 6169
Hymn for the occasion. 93091
Hymn, ode, and dirge. 101822
Hymn, on the death of Gen. Washington.
101823
Hymn, on the melancholy occasion of the death
of George Washington. 101824
Hymn on Washington. 101825
Hymn, sung at the consecration of Union Lodge
in Dorchester. 95176
Hymn to liberty. 92060
Hymn, written at the request of the Committee
of Arrangements. 101868
Hymn written for the simultaneous celebration.
77010
Hymne a la liberte. 34132
Hymno, imperial, e constitucional. 101153
Hymns. (65534), 104976
Hymns adapted and set to music. 54921,
1st note after 101856
Hymns and divine songs. 94893
Hymns and odes, composed on the death of
Gen. George Washington. 70915, 70919,
1st note after 101825

Idea of the English school sketch'd out. 61201
Idea of the reformation in England. 46301, 46790
Idea sucinta de las cortes. 94162
Idea sucinta del probabilismo. (72495)
Idea sucinta del proceso seguido. (22363)
Ideal life. 41007
Idealina. 67173
Ideals of government. 83747
Ideas contra La paz. 94897
Ideas de un comerciante sobre el modo de destruir. 34176
Ideas de virtud. 55269
Ideas importantes acerca del patronato. 34177, 47417, 86398
Ideas necesarias a todo pueblo Americano independente. 34178, 72275
Ideas politicas. 64900
Ideas sobre colonisacao precedidas a uma succinta exposicao. 38454
Ideas sobre de incorporacion de Cuba. (74767)
Ideas de fusion. 4988
Idee de la traite et du traitement des Negres. 34179
Ideen uber die Auswanderung nach Amerika. 7452
Idees sommaires sur la restauration de Saint-Domingue. (28155)
Ideler, Julius Ludwig. tr. 33724
Idem pelo Director Herman Haupt. 85664
Identifier of the ministers and members. 85437
Identity of the old Hartford Convention Federalists. 30663, 103290
Ides, Evert Isbrands. 4936
Ides of March. 34180
Idioma de los Indios. 38381, 56007, (75765)
Idioma de los Yncas. 55397
Idiomas de la America Latina. 85683
Idle man. pseud. Political reveries. (63802)
Idle man. 18439
Idle-poor secluded from the bread of charity. 12331
Idle scholar. pseud. Bryant homestead-book. see Hatfield, Julia.
Idleness in the market-place considered and reproved. (65108)
Idler. 34181
Idlewild: a tale of west Tennessee. 88417
Idolatrous Christian. 86713
Idolatry. (50741)
Idolatry destroyed. 14137
Idolatry of Rome. 78768
Idomen; or, the vale of Yumuri. 106372
Idyl for the people. 34182
Idyl of the great war and other poems. 91060
Idylles Bresiliennes. 94418
Idyllio. 98709
Iets over de emancipatie der slaven. (34183)
Iets over de gevolen van de afschaffing der slavernij. (34184)
If ministers deny Christ, He also will deny them. 92093
Ifanez, Pascual Madoz e. see Madoz e Ifanez, Pascual.
Ifirth, John. defendant (36077)
Iglesia de la SS. Trinidad, Mexico City. see Mexico (City) Iglesia de la SS. Trinidad.
Iglesia Parrochial de la Santa Vera-Cruz, Mexico City see Mexico (City) Iglesia Parrochial de la Santa Vera-Cruz.
Iglesia y el estado considerados en sus relaciones. 11714
Ignace, Francoise Juchereau de St. see Juchereau de St. Ignace, mere Francois.
Ignacia, Margarida. 34186

Ignacio, Jose. 34187-34189
Ignacio, Maria Anna Agueda de San. see San Ignacio, Maria Anna Agueda de.
Ignacio, Martin. 27775
Ignacio de Arena, Thomas. 34192
Ignacio de Castro, Pedro. ed. 56459
Ignatii Loiolae vita. (43771)-43772
Ignatii Loiolae vita postremo recognita. 43770
Ignatius. pseud. Truth, the whole truth, and nothing but the truth. 97267
Ignatius Jones, pseud. see Worth, Gorham A.
Ignipotence abroad. 84878
Ignorance, the parent of crime. (41526)
Ignorantia scientifica. 46365
Ignotus. pseud. Thoughts on trade in general. 95729
Iguain, Jose Felis. (71311)
Ihrie, George. 30409
Ijslandt ende Groenlant. 5904
Ijsze, of de togt ter walvischvangst. 38241
Ikabod Izax. pseud. see Stebbins, George Stanford.
Ike Partington. 90482
Ikins, Arthur. 34194
Ilacomilus, Martinus. see Waldseemuller, Martin, 1470-1521?
Ilay, ----------, Earl of, fl. 1721. 65865, 88192
Ile-Bourbon. 39300
Ile de Cuba. (73274)
Ile de Cuba. Le Comte de Villenueva et le General Tacon. 18667
Ile de Sable. (12573)
Iles de France. 34195
Iles divers des trois oceans. (23767)
Iles Marquises ou Noukahiva. 21223
Iles Taiti. (21124)
Iliad of Homer. 84896
Ilias. 84896
Ill-judged bounties tending to beggary on both sides. 34327
Ill news from New-England. (13865)
Ill newse from New-England. 13307
Ill newse from NewEngland. [sic] 13308
Illegal arrests. 19389
Illegality of slavery. 79896
Illegality of the trial of John W. Webster. 89609
Illegitimate letter. 12358, 59267
Illephonsus a Veracruse. see Gutierrez, Alonzo.
Illerkuksamut imaloneet illuarnermik ajokersou 91170
Illescas, Goncalo de. (34196)
Illingworth, i Compania. see Powles, Illingworth, i Compania. firm
Illinois (Territory) Constitution. 57583
Illinois. 34326
Illinois. plaintiff 20630
Illinois. Adjutant General. 34299-34300, 34306 see also Fuller, Allen C.
Illinois. Asylum for the Education of the Deaf and Dumb. see Illinois. School for the Deaf, Jacksonville.
Illinois. Auditor of Public Accounts. 34250
Illinois. Bank. see Bank of Illinois.
Illinois. Bank Commissioners. 34200
Illinois. Bar. 41186
Illinois. Board of Commissioners of Public Works. 34311
Illinois. Canal Commissioners. 34202, 34208
Illinois. Commissioners of Public Charities. 34217
Illinois. Constitution. 1269, 1271, 2071, 5316 (5563), 6360, 9672, 16103, 16107, 16113, 16133, 22781, 29731, 33137, 34218-34220 (47188), 57583, 59771, (66397), 104198

Illinois. Constitutional Convention, 1847. 34219

Illinois. Constitutional Convention, 1862. 34221

Illinois. Constitutional Convention, 1869. 34222-34223

Illinois. Courts. (3920), 34248

Illinois. Geological Survey. 34252-34253

Illinois. Governor, 1830-1834 (Reynolds) 96673 see also Reynolds, John, 1788-1865.

Illinois. Governor, 1842-1846 (Ford) 83288 see also Ford, Thomas, 1800-1850.

Illinois. Governor, 1857-1860 (Bissell) 33150, 34269 see also Bissell, William Henry, 1811-1860.

Illinois. Governor, 1861-1865 (Yates) 34270, 34298, 34306 see also Yates, Richard, 1818-1873.

Illinois. Governor, 1865-1869 (Oglesby) 34271 see also Oglesby, Richard, 1824-1899.

Illinois. Hospital for the Insane, Jacksonville. 34254-34256

Illinois. Industrial University. see Illinois. University.

Illinois. Institution for Feeble-Minded Children. 34237

Illinois. Institution for Feeble-Minded Children. Experimental School. Directors. 34238

Illinois. Institution for the Blind. 34259

Illinois. Investigating Committee on the Hospital for the Insane. 34257

Illinois. Laws, statutes, etc. (3920), 9859, 9862, 12630, 12650, 12665, 13621, 26363-26364, 23765, 29731, 29553, (34199), 34224, (34236), 34241, 34247-34249, 34278-34290, 36526, 39414, 48761, 48768, 52051, 70820-70821, (73262), 82438, 85598, 89066

Illinois. Legislature. 34277, 34291

Illinois. Legislature. petitioners (34203), 34206

Illinois. Legislature. Joint Select Committee on the State Bank. (34201)

Illinois. Legislature. House of Representatives. (34274), 34276, 34277, 34292

Illinois. Legislature. Senate. (34274)-34275, 34277

Illinois. Legislature. Senate. Committee on Internal Improvements. 34323

Illinois. Militia. 86th Regiment. 34303

Illinois. Militia. Needle Pickets, Quincy. 67280

Illinois. Militia. Volunteers, 1846. 34302

Illinois. Public Schools. (3920), 34248

Illinois. School for the Deaf, Jacksonville. 34230

Illinois. School for the Deaf, Jacksonville. Principal. 34231

Illinois. School for the Deaf, Jacksonville. Trustees. 34231

Illinois. Secretary of State. 34272

Illinois. Southern Insane Asylum. Commissioners. 34258

Illinois. Southern Normal University, Carbondale. 34243

Illinois. State Board of Agriculture. 34198

Illinois. State Board of Equalization. 34315

Illinois. State House Commissioners. 34264

Illinois. State Normal University, Normal. 1605, 34242

Illinois. State Penitentiary. Commissioners. 34309

Illinois. State Penitentiary. Superintendent. 34308

Illinois. State Sanitary Bureau. 34266

Illinois. State Sanitary Commission. 34266

Illinois. State Sanitary Commissioner. 34304, 71732 see also Robb, T. P.

Illinois. State Teachers Institute. 24244

Illinois. State Trustee of the Illinois and Michigan Canal. 56394 see also Illinois and Michigan Canal. Trustees. Oakley, Charles.

Illinois. Superintendent of Common Schools. see Illinois. Superintendent of Public Instruction.

Illinois. Superintendent of Public Instruction. 34225-34226

Illinois. Supreme Court. 41186, 77443, 84346, 89841, 103969

Illinois. Treasurer. (34251)

Illinois. University. 2862, 34235, 84897, 1st note after 98300

Illinois. University. Board of Trustees. 34233, (34236)

Illinois. University. Board of Trustees. Committee on Courses of Study and Faculty. (34236)

Illinois. University. Regent. (34234)

Illinois and Michigan Canal. 34207

Illinois and Michigan Canal. Trustees. 34207 see also Illinois. State Trustee of the Illinois and Michigan Canal.

Illinois and Michigan Canal. Documents relating to the negotiation. 34204

Illinois and Michigan Canal. January, 1852. 34205

Illinois and Missouri state directory. (50049)

Illinois and Ouabache Land Companies. see United Illinois and Wabash Land Companies.

Illinois and St. Louis Bridge Company. Chief Engineer. 34324 see also Eads, James B.

Illinois and the West. 36449

Illinois and Wabash Land Company. see United Illinois and Wabash land Companies.

Illinois Antiquarian and Historical Society. see Antiquarian and Historical Society of Illinois.

Illinois Anti-slavery Convention, Upper Alton, 1837. (34313), 81818

Illinois as it is. 26820, 27133

Illinois Association, Quincy, Ill. see Congregational Churches in Illinois. Illinois Association, Quincy.

Illinois Baptist Pastoral Union. see Baptists. Illinois. Pastoral Union.

Illinois Branch of the American Education Society. see American Education Society. Illinois Branch.

Illinois Central Rail Road Company. 34317, (34320)

Illinois Central Rail Road Company. Committee. 34317

Illinois Central Rail Road Company offer for sale over 2,400,000 acres of selected prairie, farm and wood lands. 34317

[Illinois Central Rail Road Company] offers . . . over 1,000,000 acres. 34317

[Illinois Central Rail Road Company] offers . . . over 1,500,000 acres. 34317

Illinois College, Jacksonville. 34228

Illinois College, Jacksonville. Quarter Century Celebration, 1855. 93281

Illinois Constitutional Convention. Constitution . . . adopted by the convention . . . June 7, 1847. 34219

Illinois Convention of Colored Citizens, Chicago, 1853. see Convention of the Colored Citizens of the State of Illinois, 1st, Chicago, 1853.

Illinois Country [ca 1770] His Britannick Majesty's New Subjects. petitioners see Illinois Country [ca 1770] Inhabitants. petitioners

Illinois Country [ca 1770] Inhabitants. petitioners 104017

Illinois Education Society. see American Education Society. Illinois Branch.

Illinois farmer's almanac. 49615

Illinois farmers' almanac, for . . . 1842. 89573

Illinois gazetteer. 29762

Illinois General Association. Report of Committee of Investigation on the rights of Congregationalists in Knox College. 34214

Illinois Geological Survey. Abstract of a report on Illinois coal. 34252

Illinois in 1837. (34260), 34325

Illinois in 1837 and 1838. (34260)

Illinois Land Company. see United Illinois and Wabash Land Companies.

Illinois monthly magazine. (34261), 102996 see also Western monthly magazine, and literary journal.

Illinois Natural History Society. 1605, (34262)

Illinois, Osage and Otoptata chiefs in Paris, in 1725. 80014

Illinois Soldiers' College, Fulton, Ill. 34239

Illinois State Agricultural Society. 34198

Illinois state business directory. 84945

Illinois State College Association. 34240

Illinois state gazetteer and business directory. 34263

Illinois State Historical Society, Springfield. 96172

Illinois State Medical Society. 34265

Illinois State Medical Society. Annual Meeting, 9th, 1859. 34265

Illinois State Medical Society. Annual Meeting, 10th, 1860. 34265

Illinois State Sanitary Bureau. Report of transactions. 34266

Illinois studies in language and literature. 2862, 1st note after 98300

Illinois teacher. 34244

Illinois: tragedie en cinq actes. 5388, 77221, 87304

Illinois und Missouri. 8205

Illinois Wesleyan University, Bloomington. 34245

Illman & Pilbrow. firm engrs. 84359

Illorar de Courcy; an auto-biographical novel. 101419

Illoraz de Courcy. 101419

Illowy, B. 34328

Illuminated annual for 1846. 39515

Illuminatio Britannicae. 34329

Illuminations for legislators, and for sentimentalists. 4479

Illustracion de la Rosa del Peru. (1897), 73183

Illustracion Mexicana. 96197

Illustrated agriculturist's almanac. 34330

Illustrated American biography. 36450

Illustrated annual register of rural affairs. 34331, note after 95426

Illustrated archaeological and genealogical collections. 21079

Illustrated Artic [sic] news. 23608

Illustrated atlas. 7261

Illustrated biography. 77224

Illustrated catalogue, 1854. 16993

Illustrated catalogue of the Boston School Furniture Manufactory. 30802

Illustrated catalogue of the Museum of Comparative Zoology, at Harvard college. 30748

Illustrated catalogue of the Museum of Comparative Zoology, at Harvard college. . . . No. 1. Ophiuridae and astrophytidae. 42803

Illustrated catalogue of the Museum of Comparative Zoology, at Harvard College. Published by order of the Legislature. 503

Illustrated Catholic family almanac. 34332

Illustrated description of the Broadway Pneumatic Underground Railway. 34333

Illustrated edition. Life and achievements of Gen. Winfield Scott. 78408

Illustrated family Christian almanac. 34334

Illustrated gazetteer of the United States. (23786)

Illustrated gift book for all seasons. 88686

Illustrated guide to and through Laurel Hill Cemetery. 83734

Illustrated guide to the Hudson and its tributaries. 52322

Illustrated guide to the Hudson River. 33530

Illustrated hand-book, a new guide for travellers. 34335, 82928

Illustrated hand-book of American travel. 70960-70961

Illustrated hand-book of the great west. 58719

Illustrated historical gazetteer. 58724

Illustrated historical sketches of the Indians. (26035)

Illustrated history of Lowell. 17248

Illustrated history of the American revolution. 94431

Illustrated history of the New World. (19572)

Illustrated history of the Panama Railroad. 57851

Illustrated history of the successful business houses. 62199

Illustrated history of Washington and his times 26036

Illustrated incidents in the life of William Henry Harrison. 30583

Illustrated journal of art, science, and mechanics. 78120

Illustrated journal of instruction and entertainment. (9313)

Illustrated library of travel, exploration and adventures. 71017

Illustrated life, campaigns, and public services of Lieut.-General Grant. 28310

Illustrated life, campaigns and public services of Philip H. Sheridan. 19561

Illustrated life of General Winfield Scott. (78409), note before 93092

Illustrated life, services, martyrdom, and funeral of Abraham Lincoln. 41191

Illustrated literary periodical. (54783)

Illustrated lives and adventures of the desperadoes. 93618

Illustrated magazine for girls and boys. see Scribner's illustrated magazine for girls and boys.

Illustrated magazine for the people. 78484

Illustrated magazine of entertaining reading. (26345)

Illustrated magazine of tales, travels. (55807)

Illustrated memoir. 98812

Illustrated miners' hand-book. 34336

Illustrated monthly miscellany for the young. 88948

Illustrated Mount Vernon record. 34337

Illustrated national guide. 56233

Illustrated national railway and steam navigation guide. 56223

Illustrated natural history of the animal kingdom. 27904

Illustrated new monthly. 91286

Illustrated new world. (42119)

Illustrated New York. (55193)

Illustrated notes of an expedition. 2372

Illustrated pilgrim almanac. 34338, 80788

Illustrated poems. 80923

Illustrated record of the industry of all nations. 81066

Illustrated religious magazine for the family. 22148, 74655

Illustrated school history of the United States. 66887

Illustrated sporting New Yorker. 89633

Illustrated supplement to paper on "Prehistoric and modern copper mines of Lake Superior." 84082

Illustrated uniform edition of humorous American works. 94822

Illustrated weekly journal of belles-lettres, science and the arts. 88391

Illustration. 50763

Illustration of the advantages, which are likely to result. (69620)

Illustration of the death of the war eagle. 18583

Illustration of the genus cinchona. 38728

Illustration of the work of the holy spirit. 36584

Illustrationen zu Onkel Tom's hutte. 92572

Illustrations and expositions of the principles. 34340

Illustrations and sketches of American character. 64409

Illustrations, by pen and pencil, of the history, biography, scenery, relics, and traditions of the last war for American independence. 42130

Illustrations, by pen and pencil, of the history, biography, scenery, relics, and traditions of the war for independence. 42129

Illustrations illustrated. 2657

Illustrations of Constantinople. 85203

Illustrations of Contra Costa Co. California. 84946

Illustrations of Devonian fossils. 53797

Illustrations of disease with the microscope. 64156

Illustrations of faith, drawn from the word of God. 82389

Illustrations of fossil footprints of the valley of the Connecticut. 19054

Illustrations of free masonry. 50400

Illustrations of masonry. (25810), 102232-102242

Illustrations of masonry, by one of the fraternity. (50676), (50678), 90894

Illustrations of masonry. By William Preston. 65383

Illustrations of medical botany. 11087

Illustrations of Napa County California. 84947

Illustrations of new, rare, and otherwise interesting North-American plants. 28369

Illustrations of our country. 30773

Illustrations of political economy. 44938

Illustrations of popular errors. 69377

Illustrations of Rip Van Winkle. 18582

Illustrations of South American plants. 48891

Illustrations of southern chivalry. 34341, 76651

Illustrations of surface geology. 85072

Illustrations of the algae of the Southern ocean. 30781

Illustrations of the birds of California. 11369

Illustrations of the birds of Jamaica. 28060

Illustrations of the divine government. 84417

Illustrations of the fulfilment of the prediction of Merlin. (39928)

Illustrations of the legend of Sleepy Hollow. 35187

Illustrations of the life and character of Daniel Webster. 3226

Illustrations of the manners, customs, and condition of the North American Indians. 11537

Illustrations of the natural history, by James Nichol. 51503

Illustrations of the natural history, by James Wilson. 51501

Illustrations of the parliamentary history of the reign of George III. 11602

Illustrations of the 'peculiar institution.' 67853

Illustrations of the principal events in the life of Washington. 88974

Illustrations of the West Indies. 1517

Illustrations of Venezuela. 89284

Illustrations on human frailty and vanity. (18419)

Illustrations par MM. Yan' Dargent, Foulquier et Q. Freeman. 44250

Illustrations to Bowen's picture of Boston. 7044

Illustrations to the geological report of Wisconsin, Iowa, and Minnesota. 58009

Illustrations to the researches into the physical history of mankind. 65480

Illustrative anachronisms by Thomas Worth. 54960

Illustrative notes by Henry B. Dawson. 33217

Illustrative notes by Wm. M. Darlington. 47070

Illustrazione della mummua Peruviana. 16791

Illustrerad handbok for emigranter af alla klasser. 93986

Illustres Americains. 16744

Illustres voyageuses. 16930

Illustrious and beloved General Washington, has departed from scenes of mortal life. 101827

Illustrious bigoraphy. 72004

Illustrious guest. A tract, in simple style. 106067

Illustrious men of the United States. 34342

Illustrious personages of the nineteenth century. (34343)

Illustrirte Familien-Bibliothek. 34344

Illustrirte Geographie von Nord- und Sud-Amerika. 67918

Illustrirte Kindererzahlungen fur Sommertage und Winterabende. 92577

Illustrirte Mississippithal. 40807

Illustrische Geschichte der Vereinigten Staaten Amerika's. (26050)

Illvstrissimo atqve Serenissimo Principi ac Domino D. Mavritio Lantgravio Hessiae. 41366

Illvstrissimo. D. D. Lvdovico de Velasco huius noui orbis proregi candidissimo. 96218

Illustrissimo et Reverendissimo D. D. Fr. Ludovico de Velasco. Dei, et Apostolicae Sedis gratia. (94225A)

Illustrissimo Renato Iherusalem & Sicili[a]e regi. 99354-99355

Illustrissimo Senor. Advertencias de danos qve se sigven. 93320

Il^{mo}. Sr. El Dr. D. Fermin Aurelio de
Tagle, Cossio, y Guerra. 94213

Illmo. Senor. El Dr. D. Joseph Xavier de
Tembra, y Simanes. 94635

Illustrissimo Sr * El Licdo. D. Joseph
Balthasar de Somonte, y Velasco. 86862

Illustrium autorum collectanea ad usum
studiosae juventutis facta. 22815

Illvstrivm scriptorvm religionis Iesv catalogvs.
70778

Ilman & Pilbrow. engrs. 12891, 84358-84362,
84365

Ilmestone, -------. 17051

Ilsley, Charles P. 34345

Ilsley, F. 34346

Ilustracion de la derecho que compece a la S.
Iglesia Cathedral de Mexico. 34347

Ilvstracion de la destreza Indiana. 29373

Ilustracion de las pinturas del arco de triunfo.
34348, (40077), 98814

Ilvstracion de la Rosa del Perv. (1897),
73183

Ilustracion del derecho Espanol. 75549-75551

Ilustracion del derecho real de Espana. 75548,
75552

Ilustracion Hispano-Americana. 34349

Ilustracion Mexicana. 34350

Ilustraciones sobre la masoneria. 102243

Ilustrador nacional. 98853

Ilustrados y liberales habitantes de Puerto-
Principe. 11425

Ilustre Archicofradia de San Miguel, Mexico
City. see San Miguel (Parroquia),
Mexico (City) Archicofradia de San
Miguel.

Ilustres Americanas. 34020

Ilmo. Senor. El Lic. D. A. de Souza y
Amador. 88813

Ilustrisimo Senor Obispo de Tricala. 44648

Image du monde de Guathier de Metz. 76838

Image of God in Ebony. 81992

Image of the beast. 84025

Image de la Virgen Maria Madre de Dios de
Gvadalvpe. 76289

Imagen de Maria triunfante de las aguas.
77116

Imagen de N. S. de Copacavana. 76186

Imagen del mundo sobre la espera geografia.
(44108)

Imagen iris de N. Sen. de Valvanera. 44226

Imagen politica del gobierno del Exc.^{mo} Senor
D. Diego Ladron de Guevara. 60850

Imaginary conversation between President
Jackson and the ghost of Jefferson. 34351

Imaginary conversation between Presidents
Jefferson and Jackson. 35928

Imaginary conversations of literary men and
statesmen. 38845

Imaginative biography. 8829

Imaginative story. 81196

Imago mundi, attribue a Mr. Gonnein. 76838

Imago mundi de 1410. 76838

Imago mundi d'Honore d'Autun. 76838

Imago sacris coloribus adumbrata animosi
Philippi V. (39233)

Imaz, Manuel Gomez. see Gomez Imaz,
Manuel.

Imbas, Tuppin. 90040

Imbert, Eloy. (34352)

Imbray (James) & Son. firm 34415

Imgerutit attorekset illagektunnut Labradoreme-
tunnut. 22857

Imitation d'un pamphlet Anglo-Americain.
49393

Imitation of Jesus Christ. 37343, 1st note
after 95453

Imlay, George. 24336-24337, 24338, 34053,
34054, 34056, 34355, (34358), 82422

Imlay, Gilbert. 34353-34359

Imlay, James H. 34360

Immaculado Conceicao, Brazil (Ecclesiastical
Province) 11736, 66386

Immaculado Conceicao, Brazil (Ecclesiastical
Province) Procurador. 11736, 66386
see also Chagas, Antonio das.

Immaculatae Virginis deiparae S. Mariae de
Guadalupe Mexicanae. 34361

Immanuel I, King of Portugal. see Emanuel I
King of Portugal, 1469-1521.

Immanuel: or, a discovery of true religion.
79956-79957

Immediate admission of Kansas as a state.
79525

Immediate abolition lecture. 69466

Immediate abolition of slavery by act of
Congress. 8453

Immediate abolition of slavery compatible.
50987

Immediate concernments of the British empire.
17535

Immediate emancipation. 8408

Immediate emancipation in Maryland. 34362

Immediate emancipation in Missouri. 20817

Immediate emancipation safe and profitable for
masters. 93134

Immediate emancipation would be safe for the
masters. 93144

Immediate, not gradual abolition. 31668, 34363
81993

Immediate revelation. 89369

Immence gathering [of] . . . ten thousand
Democrats. 54130

Immence meeting in favor of the union. 34364

Immensity of God. 1804

Immigracion. 17845

Immigrant Society, Boston. 6729

Immigrant white free labor, or imported black
African slave labor. 79526

Immigrants' Friend Society for the Valley of th
Mississippi. 34365

Immigrant's good Samaritan. 37881

Immigrants' guide to Minnesota in 1856. 34366
49253

Immigration, and the Commissioners of Emigra
tion of the State of New York. 37099,
53697

Immigration Convention, Charleston, S. C., 187
87852

Immigration into the United States. 12676

Immigration into the United States of America.
(77473)

Immigration; its evils and consequences.
(9532)

Immigration of Chinese. 76947

Immigration report. (56140)

Immigration Society of British Guiana. Agent.
10800

Immigration to British North America. 50282

Imminent dangers to the free institutions of th
United States. 50962

Immortal; a . . . romance. 51700

Immortal Washington. 95880

Immortality: a poem, in ten cantos. 72165

"Immortality." A sermon occasioned by the
death of Barnabas Bidwell. 82751

Immortality of the soul. 83450

Immortality of the soule. 32841

Immortals or the heroes of the XVIIIth century
34367

Immutability of divine truth. 85394

Immutable right. 59354

Imparcial. pseud. see S., J. J. pseud.

Imparcial. Periodico politics, cientifies, y
literario. 34368

Imparcial. Revista Hispano-Americana.
70316

Imparciales. pseud. Vindicacion de los
crimenes. 76747, 99784

Impartial. pseud. To the dissenting electors
of all denominations. 95915

Impartial account of a late debate at Lyme.
9105, 103941

Impartial account of Liet. Col. Bradstreet's
expedition. 7301

Impartial account of the civil war in the
Canadas. 10463

Impartial account of the final campaign of
the late war. 20954

Impartial account of the late expedition against
St. Augustine under General Oglethorpe.
9830, 56845-56846, 2d note after 87848,
87853

Impartial account of the life of the Rev. John
N. Maffitt. 22364

Impartial account of the origin and progress
of the difficulties existing between the
Congregational Church in Durham, N. H.
91152A

Impartial account of the proceedings in France.
(12811)

Impartial account of the state of New England
or, the late government there, vindicated.
46731-46732, 58359, (65323), note after
70346, 92350

Impartial account of the trial of Ebenezer
Mason. 45432

Impartial account of the trial of Mr. Levi
Weeks. 102461

Impartial address of the Federal Committee of
Albany. 619, 35929

Impartial address to the citizens of the city
and county of Albany. 619, 35929

Impartial address to the citizens of the United
States. 19827, 27619

Impartial and authentic narrative of the battle.
13422

Impartial and correct history of the late war
between the United States and Great
Britain. 42401

Impartial and correct history of the war between the United States of America, and
Great Britain. 56658

Impartial and hunourous observations. 14023

Impartial and true history of the life and
services of Major General Andrew
Jackson. (35367)-(35368)

Impartial appeal to the reason, interest and
patriotism. 34267

Impartial appeal to the reason, justice, and
patriotism. 81996

Impartial citizen. pseud. Dissertation upon
the constitutional freedom of the press.
see Sullivan, James, 1744-1808.

Impartial citizen. April, 1849. 34369

Impartial collection of essays. 1208

Impartial compendium. 69963

Impartial description of Surinam. 101462

Impartial enquirer. pseud. Some difficulties
proposed for solution. see Worcester,
Noah, 1758-1837.

Impartial enquiry into certain parts of the
conduct. 63828

Impartial enquiry into the present American
disputes. 32147, 106120

Impartial enquiry into the right of the French
King. (34370)

Impartial enquiry into the state and utility of
the province of Georgia. 45001, (60861)

Impartial enquiry into the transactions of the
late directors. (34371)

Impartial enquiry into the value of the South-
Sea stock. 88183

Impartial examination of a judgment. 77648

Impartial examination of Mr. Robert Sandeman's
letters. 76339

Impartial examination of the case of Captain
Isaac Phillips. (62493)

Impartial examination of the dispute between
Spain and her American colonies. 23059

Impartial examination of the right of search.
77646

Impartial examination of the second volume of
Mr. Daniel Neal's history. 28792

Impartial exhibition of the doctrines. (26708)

Impartial Frenchman. pseud. Genuine letters
and memoirs. see Pichon, Thomas.

Impartial hand. pseud. Essay on the management of the present war. 22962

Impartial hand. pseud. ed. Genuine collection.
(63092)

Impartial hand. pseud. Grand pyrate. (18078)

Impartial hand. pseud. Informations concerning
the province of North Carolina. 34708

Impartial hand. pseud. Life and particular
proceedings of the Rev. Mr. George
Whitefield. see Tucker, Josiah, 1712-
1799. supposed author

Impartial hand. pseud. Life of Admiral Vernon.
99249

Impartial hand. pseud. Ruling & ordaining
power of congregational bishops. see
Foxcroft, Thomas, 1697-1769.

Impartial hand. pseud. Some critical observations. 86634

Impartial hand. pseud. Some seasonable
reflections. 37192

Impartial hand. pseud. Vindication of the
proceedings. 35670

Impartial history of abuses in the government.
10066, note after 63795

Impartial history of Great Britain. 34372

Impartial history of religious creeds. (55215)

Impartial history of the late.glorious war in
Europe. 34373

Impartial history of the late war. (34374)

Impartial history of the present war in America;
containing an account of its rise and progress. 51505-51506

Impartial history of the present war in America;
from its commencement. 68094

Impartial history of the proceedings of the
Church and people of Goshen. 103748

Impartial history of the trial of Benjamin Bell.
4448

Impartial history of the war in America,
between Great Britain and her colonies.
(34375)

Impartial history of the war in America, between Great Britain and the United States.
34376

Impartial history of the war in America; from
its first commencement. 51507

Impartial inquirer. 31750, 42450

Impartial inquiries, respecting the progress of
the Baptist denomination. 105267

Impartial inquiry into the elective power of the
people. (67675)

Impartial man. pseud. Hints for some new
regulations. 31973

Impartial member of Parliament. pseud.
Sentiments. 79155

Impartial memoirs of the lives and characters
of the officers. 12155

Impartial narrative of the dispute . . . upon
the case of John Olyphant. 57258
Impartial narraitve of the proceedings of nine
ministers. 78767
Impartial narrative of the reduction of Belle
Isle. 4511, 34378
Impartial narrative of the trial of Luther
Gleason. (27566)
Impartial narrative. 1798. 34377
Impartial observations. 34379
Impartial observer. pseud. Letter to a
member of the British Parliament.
40407
Impartial observer. pseud. Views of Ithaca
and its environs. see Southwick,
Solomon.
Impartial observer. pseud. Vindication of
the character of Mrs. Elizabeth Dana.
18410
Impartial reflections on the conduct of the
late administration. (34380)
Impartial reflections upon the present state
of affairs. 34381
Impartial relation of an open and publick
dispute. (72684)
Impartial relation of the first rise and
cause of the recent differences. 34022
Impartial relation of the hail-storm of the
fifteenth of July. 34382
Impartial repository of public events. 955
Impartial representation of the conduct of the
several powers of Europe. 72881-(72882)
Impartial review. 93205
Impartial review of new books. (63800)
Impartial review of testimonies in favor of the
divinity. 105268
Impartial review of that part of Dr. Rush's
. . . publication. 18000
Impartial review of the causes and principles
of the French Revolution. 93500
Impartial review of the life and writings,
public and private character, of the late
Rev. John Wesley. 14337
Impartial review of the rise and progress of the
the controversy. (34383)
Impartial sentimental letter. 94935
Impartial sketch of the life of Thomas Paine.
58248
Impartial sketch, of the various indulgences.
(34384)
Impartial statement of the controversy respect-
ing the decision of the late committee of
canvassers. 1795, (34385), note after
53697, note after 83791
Impartial statement of the facts in the case
of Rev. George Witherell. 104927
Impartial suffrage. 2191
Impartial summary of the actions fought.
(18847)
Impartial trial of the spirit operating in this
part of the world. 9905-9906
Impartial view. 80543
Impartial view of the conduct of the ministry.
(34386)
Impartial view of the real state of the black
population. (81994)
Impartial view of the respective claims of
Mr. Shulze and Mr. Gregg. 93959
Impartial view of the war in America. (71813)
Impartialis. pseud. Address to the electors
of New-Hampshire. see Plumer,
William. supposed author
Impartialis. pseud. Letters of gratitude.
(34387)
Impartiality. pseud. Impartial observations.
34379

Impartiality of Jehovah vindicated. (71368)-
71369
Impeachment and Correction of Errors. Pres.,
Directors and Co. of the Union Turnpike
Road adms. Thomas Jenkins. 96890,
97822
Impeachment and trial of Andrew Johnson.
36172
Impeachment of Andrew Johnson. His suspen-
sion from office. 36172
Impeachment of James Buchanan, President
of the United States. 8863
Impeachment of Judge Watrous. 91258
Impeachment of Mr. La Fayette. 38583, 98682
Impeachment of the President of the United
States. 90144
Impeachment of the President. Opinion . . .
May 11, 1868. 50791
Impeachment of the President. Opinion of
Mr. Edmunds. 21871
Impeachment of the President. Opinion of
Mr. Howe. 33336
Impeachment of the President. Remarks of
Hon. W. H. Kelsey. 37326
Impeachment of the President. Speech . . .
delivered in the House of Representatives.
9615
Impeachment of the President. Speech . . .
February 24, 1868. 42815
Impeachment of the President. Speech of Hon.
Benjamin M. Boyer. 7131
Impeachment of the President. Speech of Hon.
John A. Nicholson, . . . February 24,
1868. 55228
Impeachment of the President. Speech of Hon.
John V. L. Pruyn, of New York, in the
House . . . February 24, 1868. (66414)
Impeachment of the President. Speech of Hon.
Leonard Myers. 51634
Impeachment of the President. Speech of Hon.
Thomas Laurens Jones. (36614)
Impeachment of the President. Speech of Hon.
William Mungen. 51317
Impeachment of the President. Speech of Hon.
Worthington C. Smith. 84931
Impeachment of the President. Speeches of
Hon. William H. Koontz . . . and Hon.
Green B. Raum. 28236
Impeachment. Speech . . . in the House.
(6977)
Impeachment trials. Robinson, vs. Lorillard.
96923
Impeachments. James Jackson and Caleb Hate.
96884
Impending conflict between Romanism and
protestantism. 83352
Impending contest. The issues of the campaign.
34268
Impending crisis of 1860. 46901
Impending crisis of the south: how to meet it.
(31271), 84721, 97763
Impending crisis. Speech of William S. Holman.
32571
Impending revolutions, an introductory to the
approaching millennial jubilee. 104978
Impenitent sinner disarmed of his plea. 46366
Impenitent sinners warned of their misery.
104087
Imperatrice du Mexique a Paris. 38379
Imperfect list of descendants from Job Lane,
Wm. Lane of Dorchester, and William
Lane of Boston. 38851
Imperfection of the creature. 3471
Imperiaes resolucoes do Conselho de Estado.
85680
Imperial and county annual register. 34388

Imperial and provincial acts, &c. (34389)
Imperial Brazilian Mining Association. see
    Brazilian Mining Association.
Imperial gazetteer. 5692
Imperial Gold and Silver Tunnel Company.
    (34163)
Imperial herald. 86361
Imperial Instituto de Agricultura, Rio de
    Janeiro. Conselho Director. Secretaria.
    85630
Imperial Instituto dos Meninos Cegos, Rio de
    Janeiro. 71466
Imperial magazine. 92837
Imperial orden de Guadalupe. see Orden de
    Guadalupe (Mexico)
Imperialis Mexicana Universitas illustrata.
    48494
Imperio do Brasil considerado nas suas
    relacoes. (76324)
Imperio. Opusculo sobre la situacion actual.
    (17844)
Imperio y clero. 48264
Imperio y el clero Mexicano. 78908
Imperio y la intervencion. 48495
Impiedade confundida. 76325
Impiety in high places. 83580
Implements and machinery adapted to rice
    culture. 87738
Impolicy and injustice of emancipating the
    Negro slaves. 34390
Impolicy of building another rail road. 24045,
    34391
Impolicy of making paper a legal tender. 50791
Impolicy of providing for a family by life
    assurance. 43493
Impolicy . . . of transferring the terminus.
    (54729)
Impolity of protective duties. 48862
Import duties considered in relation to the
    happiness of the people. (34394)
Import tariff, and other revenue laws. (15273)
Importance and advantage of Cape Breton,
    truely stated. 6215
Importance and claims of the Lawrence
    University. 83754
Importance and necessity of His Majesty's
    declaration of war. 104824
Importance de nos colonies occidentales.
    101244
Importance of a faithful execution of law.
    21465
Importance of a purified literature. 18405
Importance of a register law. 34392
Importance of an early and habitual prepared-
    ness for death. 90839
Importance of Canada considered. 39707
Importance of Cape Breton consider'd. 6215,
    10731
Importance of Cape Breton to the British
    nation. 33198-33199
Importance of Cape Breton to the British
    nation. Humbly represented. 2357
Importance of diversified employments. 93119
Importance of duly receiving and hearing the
    ministers of Christ. 92932
Importance of effectually supporting the Royal
    African Company of England. 34393,
    note after 73770
Importance of exalting the intellectual spirit of
    the nation. (31388)
Importance of gaining and preserving the
    friendship of the Indians. (37392)
Importance of God's presence with an army.
    2950
Importance of Jamaica to Great-Britain,
    consider'd. 35588

Importance of keeping the heart. 104916
Importance of liberal tastes. (64646)
Importance of military skill. 13430
Importance of ministers being men of Christ.
    25396
Importance of moderation in civil rulers.
    (14130)
Importance of practical education and useful
    knowledge. 23271
Importance of promoting literary and social
    concert. 20825
Importance of railroads in the south-western
    counties of Pennsylvania. 88155
Importance of religion in the civil ruler,
    considered. 103788
Importance of religion to the legal profession.
    6072
Importance of relying on the efforts of the
    people. 1471
Importance of scientific studies. 91042
Importance of settling and fortifying Nova
    Scotia. 56141
Importance of spiritual knowledge. 14131
Importance of stringent usury laws. 103304
Importance of sustaining the law. 104802
Importance of the African expedition considered.
    (64566)
Importance of the British dominion in India.
    34395
Importance of the British plantations in
    America. (29766)
Importance of the church. 91115
Importance of the colonies of North America,
    and the interest of Great Britain with
    regard to them, considered. 6220,
    (68029)-68032
Importance of the colonies to Great Britain.
    74461
Importance of the divine presence with our
    host. 5559
Importance of the divine presence with the
    armies of God's people. 65530
Importance of the sugar colonies to Great-
    Britain stated. 34396, 80606, note after
    102839
Importance of theological institutions. 38156
Importance of uniting manual labour with
    intellectual attainments. 97626
Importance of usury laws. 103304
Importance of virtue and piety as qualifications
    of rulers. 18405
Importancia de la historia de la marina
    Espanola. 98612
Importancia de Mexico para la emigracion
    Alemana. (77118)
Importancia del restablecimiento de los
    Jesuitas. 34397
Important act of the legislature of South-
    Carolina. 87695
Important and interesting trial of Mortimer J.
    Smith. 83637-83638
Important and interesting trial of Samuel M.
    Fox. 25374
Important correspondence. (44759)
Important correspondence between bank officers
    and the Comptroller. (72141)
Important correspondence on the subject of state
    interposition. 30004, 30014
Important decision for working-men. 95557
Important disclosures. 85120
Important documents, concerning Texas. 95079,
    95093
Important documents in relation to the present
    situation of Venezuela. 58139
Important documents presented to Congress,
    Nov. 29, 1809. 34399

Important documents presented to Congress with the President's message. 83813

Important documents which accompanied the message of the President. 34398, 83812

Important duties and qualifications of Gospel ministers. 103066

Important duty of a timely seeking of God. (22439)

Important duty of children. 3471

Important extracts from . . . letters. (38117)

Important extracts from recent letters from the United States. 34401

Important facts . . . proving . . . that the approaching presidential election is forever to decide the question. 34402

Important facts relating to the lottery privileges. 97768

Important general laws, passed . . . 1864. 60634

Important hints to the inhabitants of the province. (11679), 45864

Important historic Presbyterian events. 83390

Important letter on the principles involved. 41159

Important letter to Henry C. Lowell. note after 42429

Important message to the people. 33025

Important objects of the evangelical ministry considered. 30637

Important opinion of Attorney General Bates. (3928)

Important opinion of Hon. B. R. Curtis. 18028

Important question concerning invasions. 97351

Important question examined. (34403)

Important question: shall the subject of slavery forever prevent all useful legislation? 1780

Important report by Chancellor Lindsley. 51880

Important report of a joint committee. 34404

Important slave case. 26008

Important state papers. 34400, 83814, 83816

Important state papers and public documents. 15587

Important state papers and public documents. 15519

Important state papers. [Correspondence between the British ministers and Mr. Smith.] 35410

Important state papers. Documents accompanying the President's message. 83816

Important state papers. Documents which accompanied the message. 83817

Important state papers. No. 2. 83815

Important statement of facts. (17299)

Important suggestions to laborers. 2829, 30304

Important tenets for the introduction of a new era. 85124

Important to tax-payers. (34405)

Important to the people of Washington County. 103866

Important trial for seduction. 9478, 96842

Important view of the present state of affairs. 15206

Importante voto de un ciudadano. 98658

Importantissimas y verdaderes revoluciones. 58840

Importation de la fievre jaune en Europe. 5030

Imported in the last vessel from England. 29746

Imposition exposed. (72622)

Imposition of inoculation as a duty religiously considered. 34406

Impositions and frauds in Philadelphia. 61732

Imposto sobre os vencimentos. 24129

Impostor detected. (7258), 14026, note after 95800, 12th note after 95843

Impostura desmascarado. 76326

Imposturas del Dr. Felix Maria Alfonzo. 5529

Impostures and calumnies of George Montgomery West. 89348

Impracticability of a North-West passage. 34407

Imprecation against the enemies of God. (1452

Imprecatory psalms viewed in the light of the southern rebellion. 58619

Imprenta Argentina. 94606, 94869

Imprenta asaltada por Armona y su partida. 42106

Imprenta del comercio, Lima. 51068

Imprenta del Siglio. firm publishers 65549

Impresiones de un viage de Mexico a Washington. 39065, (73172)

Impresiones del gaucho Anastasio el Pollo. 10315

Impresiones y cuadros del Parana. 77130

Impress considered as the cause why British seamen desert. 34408

Impressed seamen from Salem. From the Salem gazette of April 27, 1813. 75665

Impressed seamen from Salem. From the Salem gazette of March 30, 1813. 75664

Impressiones de un viaje a los Estados-Unidos de America. (80881)

Impressions and experiences of the West Indie. 2788

Impressions de voyage. 56433

Impressions made on the inhabitants of Haverhill, &c. 17095

Impressions of America and the American churches. 40803

Impressions of America. By Frederika Bremer. 7713

Impressions of America. By George Rose. 73241

Impressions of America, during the years 1833, 1834, and 1835. 64780

Impressions of northern society upon a southerner. 55568

Impressions of prison life in Great Britain. 21586

Impressions of the west and south during a six weeks' holiday. 34410

Impressions of the west and south. . . . Lette which "first appeared in a Toronto newspaper." 37886

Impressoes de viagem. 16838

Imprisoned debtor. pseud. Excursion of the dog cart. (23383)

Imprisonment among the Turks. 9187

Imprisonment and enslavement of British colored seamen. 27549

Improbabilities that the Americans are of that race. (40231)

Impromptu speech of His Excellency Governor Pickens. 87556

Improprieties and errors in the common versie of the scriptures. 102370

Improve your conduct. 94237

Improved almanac. 49221, 84948

Improved calendar, from 1501 to 1900. 55907

Improved chronological summary of the history of the United States of America. 102590

Improved edition of the church covenanty. 97888

Improved edition. Smith's atlas. 83934
Improved McAdamized roads. 104290
Improved mode of defence. (62850)
Improved New-England farmer's almanack. (39555)
Improved New-England primer. 52729
Improved New England double directory. 54459
Improved Order of the Red Men. 26886
Improved railway connections in Philadelphia. (34411)
Improvement Association, Staten Island, N. Y. see Staten Island Improvement Association.
Improvement era. 83500
Improvement in forcing the cultivation of cotton. 64719
Improvement, in two parts. note after 101417
Improvement of government. 34735
Improvement of medical education in the United States. 58193
Improvement of Taunton River. 45487
Improvement of the doctrine of earthquakes. (65604)
Improvement of the Ohio River. (71938)
Improvement of the State House. 45766
Improvement of the tenement house system. 82943
Improvement of the Upper Mississippi River. (67727)
Improvements in agriculture, &c., in the United States. (22346)
Improvements in the military establishments of the United States. (18328)
Improvements of agriculture as an art and a profession. 14535
Improvements of agriculture in Nova Scotia. 18956
Improvements of the Mississippi. 30557
Improvements of universities. 67454
Improvements practicable in American colleges. 3459
Imps o' the prairie. 90009
Impugnacao ao protesto do Sr. Visconde de Jequitinhonha. 88737
Impugnacion a la iniciativa del H. Congreso de Zacatecas. 34412
Impugnacion a la nueva escta. 72276
Impugnacion a la requesta. 9016
Impugnacion a las falsedades. 94864
Impugnacion a las observaciones hechas por varios Yucatecos. 98624, 106224
Impugnacion a las observaciones que en 19 del ultimo Octubre hizo un Yucateco. 34413, 98624
Impugnacion a los articulos publicados. 35080
Impugnacion a los observaciones relativas a la pacificacion de Yucatan. 34413, 98624, 106224
Impugnacion al articulo inserto contra el fundador. 76157
Impugnacion al folleto titulado: Ensayo filosofico-critico. 97696
Impugnacion al impreso que se publico en S. Sanvador. 34414
Impugnacion al informe del General Santa-Anna. (26512)
Impugnacion al algunos errores politicos. 60902
Impugnacion de algunos impios. 27823
Impugnacion de la obra de Fr. Francisco Ayeta. 76776
Impugnacion el articulo inserto contra el fundador. 61132
Impugnacion por D. Jose Antonio Saco. (74768)

Imputed righteousness explained and vindicated. 20059
Imray, J. F. 73417
In a congress, begun and holden at Charles-Town. 87413
In a general convention. Begun and holden at the capitol. 100020
In addition to the laws and facts, stated in the memorial. 25032
In Amerika. 27180
In amico Philalethe. 28043
In Assembly, March 30, 1836. 31595
In chancery. 85421
In chancery, before the Chancellor. 97781
In chancery. Before the Chancellor. In the matter of the New-York Life Insurance and Trust Company. 54793
In chancery: before the Chancellor of the State of New York. 91610
In chancery. Breviate. 34416
In chancery. James D. Doty vs. Stephens T. Mason. 96860
In chancery. The answer of the Trustees of Union College. 97779
In chancery. The joint and several answers of the Trustees. 97780
In Claudii Ptolemei supplementum modernior lustratio terre. (66478)
In committee chamber, May 16, 1776. 61733
In committee chamber, Worcester, Nov. 18, 1776. 105347
In committee, December 14, 1774. 61734
In committee of inspection and observation. 61735
In Congress, May 15, 1776. 106119
In Congress, Thursday, September 22. 1774. 34417
In Congress, Wednesday, April 3, 1776. 15537
In convention, at New-Castle, for the Delaware state. 52569
In convention for the state of Pennsylvania. 60153
In convention. June 12, 1776. 100022
In convention of the representatives of . . . New-York. 53698
In convention. Present 112 members. 100023
In convention. Saturday, March 25, 1775. 100024
In convention . . . the 25th of June, 1788. 100034
In convention. Thursday, April 9, 1782. 105419
In council, April 12, 1781. 100209
In council, December 29, 1788. 100095
In council 8th of June, 1798. 100227
In council, February 20, 1786. 100212
In council, January 19, 1781. 100197
In council, January the 16th, 1797. 100226
In council, January 29, 1787. 100214
In council, January 21, 1790. 100407
In council, June 16, 1779. 100036
In council, March 30, 1781. 100208
In council, March 26, 1781. 100206
In council, May 4, 1781. (68570)
In council, May 20, 1788. 100216
In council, 29th Dec., 1788. 100218
In cvi si tratta le meravgliose cose del mondo. 44498
In defence of the Jewish religion. 78672
In Domini Nortoni librum. 698, (21090), 78431, 104846
In effigiem carmen. 66494
In ejectment: the people of the state of New York vs. the Rector, &c. of Trinity Church. 49046

In error. House of Lords. Between David Ogden. (56802)

In error. The town of North Hempstead, etc., appellants. (31300)

In General Assembly, Saturday, February 13, 1799. 60154

In hoc opera haec continentur noua translatio primi libri geographiae. 66479

In hoc operae haec continetvr Geographia Cl. Ptholemaei. 66475-(66476)

In hoc volvmine continentvr hi libri. 41067

In hoc volumine hec continentur. De imperio militantis ecclesiae. 35264

In honor to the administration. (64566)

In laudem serenissi mi Ferdinandi Hispaniarum Regis. 98923

In luctuosum excessum. 42635

In memoria: David M. Jones, Harry O'Neill, James Newell. 85173

In memoriam. 41193, 41208, 85341

In memoriam. A discourse . . . at the funeral of Elisha Cowles Jones. 64303

In memoriam. A discourse delivered November 18, 1872. (64302)

In memoriam. A discourse on the assassination of Abraham Lincoln. 55163

In memoriam. A discourse preached in Worcester. (31806)

In memoriam. A discourse preached Nov. 1st, 1868. 22051

In memoriam. A tribute of respect offered by the citizens. 39792

In memoriam. Abraham Lincoln, assassinated at Washington. (41192)

In memoriam. Abraham Lincoln. Proceedings at the Athenaeum Club. (51640)

In memoriam. An address. 38544

In memoriam, B. Davis Noxon. 56208

In memoriam. Biographical sketches of Mrs. David Starr. 90546

In memoriam. By a breaved father. 80309

In memoriam. [By A. G. Dana.] 18393

In memoriam. [By Amos Kendall.] 37355

In memoriam. [By Isaac McConihe.] 43084

"In memoriam" by Mr. Henry Cleveland. 2381

In memoriam. [By William F. Morgan.] (50688)

In memoriam . . . . [By William Henry Furness.] 26237

In memoriam. Captain Charles S. Montgomery. 13529

In memoriam celeberrimi viri Domini Francisci Drake. (81440)

In memoriam. Charles C. Jewett. 36109

In memoriam. Charles Redington Mudge. 51232

In memoriam. Calvin Pease. 59459

In memoriam. David L. Seymour. 79642

In memoriam. Discourses in commemoration of Abraham Lincoln. 2342

In memoriam. Eben Caldwell Stanwood. 90458

In memoriam [Edmund Dexter.] 19888

In memoriam. Edwin R. Purple. 66720

In memoriam. Eliza H. Sperry. 89405

In memoriam—Eliza Hale Paine. 58183

In memoriam. Francis W. Sabine. 74717

In memoriam. General Lewis Cass. 11352

In memoriam. Gen. Stepehn Elliott. (22284), 87514

In memoriam, George Duffield. 43098

In memoriam George Ripley. 71523

In memoriam H. L. A. (34418), (58315)

In memoriam. Hugh A. Pue. 66542

In memoriam. J. Lawrence Smith. 83003

In memoriam. J. W. B. (8636)

In memoriam. Jared Sparks. 89014

In memoriam. John A. Roebling. 72577

In memoriam. John Cox, 1795-1871. 65008

In memoriam. John M. Speed. 89231

In memoriam. John Ross Nicols. 84066

In memoriam Joseph Gilbert Totten. 44858

In memoriam. Mr. Amos Sheffield. 80094

In memoriam. Mrs. Lucy Wilder Stearns. 90920

In memoriam. Mrs. Marianne Fitch Stranahan 89091

In memoriam of Rt. Rev. John B. Fitzpatrick. (24623)

In memoriam. Orson Phelps. 61387

In memoriam. Our heroic dead. 85138

In memoriam. Professor John Addison Porter 64277

In memoriam. Rev. Bishop James Osgood Andrew. 84992

In memoriam. Rev. S. F. Smith. 84047

In memoriam Sarah Hills Hall. (29846)

In memoriam. T. Hooper. 32878

In memoriam. Testimonials of the life and character of the late Francis Jackson. 35409

In memoriam. The life and ministry of the Rev. Joseph Morgan Smith. 83364

In memoriam. Thomas Smith. 84374

In memoriam. Thomas Starr King. (37849)

In memory of a beloved husband. 89769

In memory of a beloved wife and mother. 80095

In memory of a mother's love. 83568

In memory of Abraham Lincoln. 31676

In memory of Carlton Edwards. (21911)

In memory of Charles Pelham Curtis. 18030

In memory of Daniel Webster. 13310

In memory of Edwin M. Stanton. 90394

In memory of Edward W. Whelpley. 49097

In memory of Francis Edwin Hoppin. (32998)

In memory of Gen. H. H. Ross. 73394

In memory of George Peabody. 45216

In memory of Henry Coit Perkins. 88922

In memory of Hon. Increase Sumner. 78510

In memory of the ill-thought of, and much disesteem'd W. S. 84678C

In memory of the noble act of Mr. Charles Ridgely. 92003

In Mexico. 27181

In obitum Hookeri. 32860

In obitum magnae spei juvenis, Nathanaelis Smiberti. 5109

In our Independent journal of this morning. 93805

In perils by mine own countrymen. 37039

In provincial congress, Watertown, May 5, 1775. (45767)

In qvesto volvme si contengono septe giornate. 66500-66501

In rapsodiam historiarvm ab orve conditio. 74658

In re: the Southern Railway and Steamship Association. 83860

In rebuttal. By R. A. C. Smith. 83849

In relation to collisions at sea. 53585

In relation to the claims of the officers of the late Texan navy. 8844

In reply to Mr. Webster, of Massachusetts. 31039

In reply to Patrick Henry. 57363

In reply to the speeches of Mr. Webster and Mr. Clay. 9936

In Senate . . . . February 4, 1836. 9936

In Senate, March 20, 1849. 82581

In Senate, March 12, 1834. 88215

In Senate of the United States. February 5, 1834. 102287
In Senate of the United States. January 13, 1808. 82882
In Senate of the United States, Jan. 30, 1851. 80468
In Senate of the United States, March 1st, 1797. 94745
In Senate of the United States. March 4, 1834. 71742
(In Senate of the United States, Wednesday, January 10, 1838.) 102306
In Senate . . . [Report of the Assistant Post-master General.] 64482
In Senate, 21st March, 1811. 63356
In sepulchrum Hookeri. 32860
In sequentes varias geographiae Claudii Ptolemaei lectiones. 66508
In Supreme Court, January term, 1874. 88152
In tabulas Ptolemaicas a se delineatas an-notationes. 66497
In tenebris. 74286
In the administration of His Excellency, the Honourable Robert Monckton. 53705
In the Circuit Court of the United States. 87299
In the Court for the Correction of Errors. Between Lorentz Smith, appellant, and Elisha Adams, respondent. 83493
In the Court for the Correction of Errors. Robert H. Morris, Mayor of . . . New York, plaintiff in error vs. the people. 54320
In the Court for the Correction of Errors. William Williams, survivor of Asahel Seward, plaintiff in error. 104412
In the Court for the Trial of Impeachments and Correction of Errors. Ambrose Spencer, plaintiff. 89298
In the Court for the Trial of Impeachments and Correction of Errors. Ezra White, vs. the people of the state of New York. 103382-103383
In the Court for the Trial of Impeachments and Correction of Errors, President, Directors and Co. of the Union Turnpike Road. 96890, 97822
In the Court for the Trial of Impeachments and the Correction of Errors, between David Gelston and Peter A. Schenck, appellants. 96868
In the Court for the Trial of Impeachments, and the Correction of Errors; between Goold Hoyt, defendant in error. 96869
In the Court for the Trial of Impeachments, and the Correction of Errors; between Goold Hoyt, respondent. 96869
In the Court for the Trial of Impeachments and the Correction of Errors, between Jacob T. Walden and Thomas Walden, defend-ants in error. 100996
In the Court for the Trial of Impeachments and the Correction of Errors. Between James Jackson, ex dem. Brockholst Livingston. 96885
In the Court for the Trial of Impeachments and the Correction of Errors. Between James Jackson ex dem. Brockholst Livinston, and others plaintiffs in error; and John Robins, defendant in error. 96887
In the Court for the Trial of Impeachments, and the Correction of Errors, between John Watts and Herman Le Roy. 102175

In the Court for the Trial of Impeachments and the Correction of Errors, between Justin Lyman & Elias Lyman, appellants. 96896
In the Court for the Trial of Impeachments and the Correction of Errors, between Nathaniel L. Griswold and George Griswold. 96881
In the Court for the Trial of Impeachments and the Correction of Errors. Between Richard Bedell and others. 31299
In the Court for the Trial of Impeachments, and the Correction of Errors, between Thomas Franklin, John I. Staples, and others. 96865
In the Court for the Trial of Impeachments and the Correction of Errors. Effingham H. Warner, and James H. Ray. 101435
In the Court for the Trial of Impeachments and the Correction of Errors. James Jackson ex dem. Abraham Houseman and others. 96886
In the Court for the Trial of Impeachments and the Correction of Errors. John T. Smith, plaintiff in error. 83019
In the Court for the Trial of Impeachments and the Correction of Errors. Levinus Wendell, plaintiff in error. 102625
In the Court for the Trial of Impeachments, and the Correction of Errors. Mac Neven and others, appellants. 96903
In the Court for the Trial of Impeachments, and the Correction of Errors. Philip Van Cortlandt. 98438
In the Court for the Trial of Impeachments and the Correction of Errors, Philip Verplanck impleaded with James Arden. 91365
In the Court for the Trial of Impeachments and the Correction of Errors. Robert Whiteside vs. the people. 103686
In the Court of Appeals the Mayor and City Council of Baltimore. 8481
In the Court of Claims. The Muscogee or Creek Nation of Indians. 51583
In the Court of Exchequer. 34419
"In the days of Tiberus Caesar." 30553
In the District Court of the United States. (58779)
In the eleventh month, on the nineth day of the month. 8654
In the fourteenth year of the reign of George the Third. 98063
In the heart of the Alaskan gold fields. 83599
In the House of Delegates, December 15, 1789. 100097
In the House of Delegates, Friday, January 11, 1799. 100106
In the House of Delegates, Friday the 24th December, 1784. 100082
In the House of Delegates. January 13, 1786. 100088
In the House of Delegates, Monday, the 7th of January, 1788. 100093
In the House of Delegates. November 14, 1785. 100087
In the House of Delegates, Saturday, December 12, 1795. 100099
In the House of Delegates, the 25th of Decem-ber, 1788. 100095
In the House of Delegates . . . the 25th of October, 1787. 100091
In the House of Delegates, Thursday the 30th of December 1784. 100084
In the House of Delegates, Thursday, 28th November, 1793. 100098

In the House of Delegates Tuesday, the 1st of November, 1786. 100089
In the House of Delegates, Tuesday the 28th of December, 1784. 100083
In the House of Delegates, Wednesday, the 29th of November, 1786. 100090
In the House of Lords. 69087
In the House of Representatives, February 8, 1784. 45768
In the House of Representatives, March 10, 1858. 91261
In the House of Representatives, November 29, 1799. 87538
In the House of Representatives of the United States, Tuesday the 8th of May, 1792. 75018
In the matter between Frederick P. Stanton and Hon. Has. H. Lane. 90412
In the matter ex parte, Anson Field. 82206
In the matter of application of Samuel F. B. Mores. 30334
In the matter of certain coin claimed by the Richmond banks, etc. 89232
In the matter of Christ Church, New-Brighton. 52516
In the matter of George Gordon's petition for pardon. 27973, 36413
In the matter of proving the last will and testament of Henry Parish. 58611
In the matter of proving the last will and testament of the late Robert Stewart. 91703
In the matter of proving the will of Henry Parish. 58611
In the matter of proving the will of James R. Wilson. 104643
In the matter of the appeal of Egbert C. Smyth from the Visitors of the Theological Institution in Phillips Academy in Andover. Appellant's brief. 85212
In the matter of the appeal of Egbert C. Smyth from the Visitors of the Theological Institution in Phillips Academy in Andover. Before Hon. George D. Robinson. 85212
In the matter of the appeal of Egbert C. Smyth from the Visitors of the Theological Institution in Phillips Academy in Andover. Brief of Mr. Baldwin. 85212
In the matter of the application of the Philadelphia Society for the Employment and Instruction of the Poor. 62037
In the matter of the award made by the Senate of the United States. 84448
In the matter of the charges against Professors Egbert C. Smyth, William J. Tucker, J. W. Churchill, George Harris, and Edward Y. Hincks. 85212
In the matter of the claim of the Girard Bank. 50152
In the matter of the complaint against Egbert C. Smyth and others, Professors of the Theological Institution in Phillips Academy, Andover. 85212
In the matter of the complaint against Egbert C. Smyth and others, Professors of the Theological Institution in Phillips Academy, Andover. The Andover defence. 85212
In the matter of the complaint against Egbert C. Smyth and others, Professors in the Theological Institution in Phillips Academy in Andover. 85212
In the matter of the contested election from the 1st District of Ohio. (77406)

In the matter of the contested election of District Attorney. (38087)
In the matter of the estate of Charles S. Boker, deceased. 68169
In the matter of the investigation of certain charges against Hon. Wm. B. Smith. 84748
In the matter of the memorial of the owners of the Steamship Meteor. 69767
In the matter of the New-York Life Insurance and Trust Company. 54793
In the matter of the Panoche Grande Rancho. 53022
In the matter of the petition of H. R. Low. 42397
In the matter of the Puget's Sound Agricultural Company. 18083
In the matter of the Schooner Virginia. 100576
In the matter of Thomas Kaine. 21914
In the matter of William Post Sackett. 74759
In the matter of Yerba Buena Island. (63724)
In the name . . . . A Proclamation. 60155
In the Privy Council, Jamaica. 67721
In the Senate, December 21, 1793. 87507
In the Senate . . . . February 18, 1858. . . . Mr. Collamer, 14360
In the Senate . . . February 18, 1858. Mr. Douglas. 20693
In the Senate. . . . February 18, 1858. . . . Mr. Green. 37041
In the Senate, January 28, 1863. 42396
In the Senate of the United States. April 4, 1834. 71742
In the Senate of the United States. August 11, 1856. 37040
In the Senate of the United States. February 2, 1865. 85064
In the Senate of the United States. (February 27, 1877.) 74138
In the Senate of the United States. July 21, 1854. 52189
In the Senate of the United States, March 29, 1830. 83991
In the Senate of the United States. . . . Mr. Douglas made the following report. 20693
In the Senate of the United States, Monday, January 16, 1837. 102302
In the Society of the Cincinnati. 87950
In the Supreme Court of Louisiana. 82145
In the Supreme Court of Ohio. The Cincinnati Southern Railroad. 90145
In the Supreme Court of Ohio. The City Solicitor, vs. the city of Cincinnati. 90140
In the Supreme Court of . . . Pennsylvania . . Motion on behalf of the Southwark Railroad Company. 62267
In the Supreme Court of Pennsylvania. . . [opinion] in the matter of the estate of Charles S. Boker. 68169
In the Supreme Court of the state of Kansas. 37593
In the Supreme Court of the United States, between John L. Sullivan & others, appellants. 93524
In the Supreme Court of the United States, December term, 1854. 78256
In the Supreme Court of the United States, December term, 1852. 83725
In the Supreme Court of the United States. December term, 1864. 89224
In the Supreme Court of the U. States. In prize. 3924
In the Supreme Court. . . . State of Louisiana versus John Cook. 21621
In the track of our emigrants. 71687
In the tropics. 34420

In the United States District Court. 4702
In the woods with Bryant, Longfellow, and
Halleck. 33390
In the year of Our Lord, one thousand seven
hundred and eighty-seven. 85864
In time of war prepare for peace. 24716
In tractatus seguentes prolegomena ad
lectorem. 67355
In uno, plura; e pluribus unum. 20401
In vinculis or the prisoner of war. 34421,
37168
In what sense the heart is deceitful and
wicked. 8506
In what was the convention right? 74611
Ina. pseud. Paragraphs on the subject of
judicial reform. see Price, William.
Inability of the sinner to comply with the
Gospel. 82215
Inadmissible principles of the King of
England's proclamation. 245
Inactive member. pseud. Freemasonry in
New York. 25806
Inana y Torre, Jose Isidro. 11093, 34423
Inasmuch as the Sons of Columbia consider
themselves unrivalled. 101856
Inauguracion de la estatua del Libertador
Simon Bolivar. 34424
Inaugural address, and the charge. (49064)
Inaugural address . . . Ann Arbor, Michigan.
(30876)
Inaugural address as Governor of Delaware.
10700
Inaugural address as President of Middlebury
College. 3941
Inaugural address as Principal of Oneida
Conference Seminary. 39073
Inaugural address as Principal of the Belle-
ville Seminary. 36243
Inaugural address, . . . at Antioch College,
Yellow Springs. 31864
Inaugural address, . . . at Cambridge,
December 11, 1816. 5299
Inaugural address, . . . at Gardiner. 29615
Inaugural address . . . at his [i.e. Lewis
Mayer's] inauguration. 47112
Inaugural address . . . at Mercersburg, Pa.
82320
Inaugural address at Middletown. (24537)
Inaugural address at the opening of Morrison
College. (59533)
Inaugural address. . . at the opening of the
Mercantile Library Hall. (32738)
Inaugural address at the opening of the Quebec
School of Medicine. 50794
Inaugural address, at the opening of the Troy
University. 92922
Inaugural address before . . . Newark College
. . . April 26th, 1836. 45481
Inaugural address, . . . before the . . .
General Synod. 77723
Inaugural address . . . before the Medical
Society of . . . New-York. 44301
Inaugural address . . . before the Medical
Society of the County of New-York.
33089
Inaugural address before the Teachers' In-
stitute. 68654
Inaugural address . . . before . . . Trinity
College. (37613)
Inaugural address by Benjamin Seaver. 78674
Inaugural address, by Henry Ruffner. 73924
Inaugural address by J. B. Crockett. 76049
Inaugural address. . . by John Prescott
Bigelow. (5314)
Inaugural address by President John H.
Lathrop. 34518

Inaugural address, by President O. P. Sutton.
86012
Inaugural address [by Prof. Frisbie.] (55864)
Inaugural address by Rev. J. W. Hall. 42959
Inaugural address. By Rev. Miles P. Squier.
90005
Inaugural address . . . by Samuel Harris.
30499
Inaugural address delivered at the opening of the
University of Kittanning. 24376
Inaugural address delivered . . . before the
Board of Regents. 11021
Inaugural address delivered before the Board
of Trustees of Marion College. 64690
Inaugural address, delivered before the
Directors of Wittenberg College. 89752
Inaugural address delivered before the Medical
Society of the County of New-York. 57319
Inaugural address, delivered before the New-
York Historical Society. (33087)
Inaugural address delivered before the Rhode
Island Homoeopathic Society. 65368
Inaugural address, delivered before the Trustees,
faculty, and students. 19345
Inaugural address delivered by Hon. J. V. C.
Smith. 82807
Inaugural address, delivered February 24,
1857. 90261
Inaugural address delivered 15th May, 1848.
67050
Inaugural address, delivered in Brunswick,
September 9th, 1802. (43391)
Inaugural address, delivered in . . . Connecti-
cut. 26360
Inaugural address, delivered in . . . Harvard
College . . . July 14, 1857. 22309
Inaugural address, delivered in the Chapel of
Geneva College. (29613)
Inaugural address delivered in the Chapel of
Morrison College, November 2, 1849.
18745
Inaugural address delivered in the Chapel of
Morrison College, November 2, 1835.
14238
Inaugural address, delivered in the Chapel of
the University of Cambridge. (25981)
Inaugural address, delivered July 8, 1839.
96395
Inaugural address delivered July 31st, 1849.
84927
Inaugural address, delivered to the law class
of the University of Virginia. 88226
Inaugural address delivered to the tenth General
Assembly. 35006
Inaugural address . . . in . . . Hamilton Literary
and Theological Institution. 43823
Inaugural address . . . in South Carolina Col-
lege. 40985
Inaugural address . . . in the Mercer-Street
Church. 72067
Inaugural address . . . January 8, 1862. 45164
Inaugural address . . . January 11th, 1865.
45164
Inaugural address, Jan. 5, 1857. 70817
Inaugural address . . . January 5, 1864. 85227
Inaugural address, . . . Jan. 7, 1845. 44449
Inaugural address . . . July 27, 1859. 41958
Inaugural address . . . Kalamazoo College.
28742
Inaugural address, Lafayette College. 17969
Inaugural address, March, 1849. 104205
Inaugural address. . . . March 15, 1853. 85227
Inaugural address . . . March 21, 1854. 85227
Inaugural address . . . New-York Academy of
Medicine. (51120)
Inaugural address of Fred'k F. Low. 42395

Inaugural address of Geo. Graham. 28206

Inaugural address of Gov. Davis. 72483

Inaugural address of Governor F. W. Shunk.
60156

Inaugural address of Governor J. W. Geary.
37042

Inaugural address of Governor P. F. Thomas.
45164

Inaugural address of Governor Thomas O.
Moore. 42234

Inaugural address of His Excellency Marcus
Morton. (67260)

Inaugural address of His Honor, George B.
Richmond. 71130

Inaugural address of His Honor, George F.
Richardson. 71007

Inaugural address of His Honor Hocum
Hosford. 42483

Inaugural address of His Honor Samuel B.
Spooner. 89623

Inaugural address of Hon. Augustus W.
Bradford. 7236

Inaugural address of Jacob D. Cox. 17259

Inaugural address of James D. Cox. 56935

Inaugural address of . . . Jedediah Jewett.
64346

Inaugural address . . . of John Gorham.
(28023)

Inaugural address of Leonard J. Sanford.
76494

Inaugural address of Martin Van Buren,
President of the United States. 98411

Inaugural address of Martin Van Buren,
President of the United States, March 4,
1837. 98411

Inaugural address of Mayor Curtis. 13622

Inaugural address of . . . Mayor of . . .
Milwaukee. 49155

Inaugural address of Michael Hahn. (42235)

Inaugural address of Mirabeau B. Lamar.
95018

Inaugural address of Nathaniel B. Shurtleff.
80778

Inaugural address of Ogden N. Rood. 73088

Inaugural address of President Davis. 15274

Inaugural address of President Edward James
Roye. 73837

Inaugural address of President J. H. Fairchild.
(23676)

Inaugural address of R. J. Walker. 37043

Inaugural address of Ralph P. Lowe. 35004

Inaugural address of Rev. Bennet Tyler.
97593

Inaugural address of Rev. E. F. Rockwell.
72421

Inaugural address of Richard J. Oglesby.
34271

Inaugural address of Richard Yates. 34270

Inaugural address of Rodman M. Price.
53129

Inaugural address of Salmon P. Chase. 12200

Inaugural address of the Governor. 48739

Inaugural address of the Hon. Frederick Smyth.
44211, 85227

Inaugural address of the Mayor, April 7, 1854.
37459

Inaugural address of the Mayor delivered April
26th, 1847. 12108

Inaugural address of the . . . Mayor, to the
City Council. 42839

Inaugural address of the President for the
ensuing year. 12672

Inaugural address of the President [of the
Andrew Johnson Club.] 59481

Inaugural address of the President [of the
San Francisco Medical Society]. 76094

Inaugural address of the President of the Unite
States. (63838)

Inaugural address of the President, Reverend
Samuel Hanson Cox. (40147)

Inaugural address of the Rev. Benjamin Labare
48839

Inaugural address of the Rev. George Junkin.
38586

Inaugural address, of the Rev. Gilbert Morgan.
60157

Inaugural address of the Rev. P. J. Sparrow.
89017

Inaugural address of Thomas Jefferson. 35885

Inaugural address of William Cannon. 19389

Inaugural address of William M'Willie. 49506

Inaugural address . . . on taking the chair.
26399

Inaugural address on the nature and advantage
of an English and liberal education.
74562

Inaugural address . . . on the seventeenth of
February, 1858. 40985

Inaugural address, pronounced in Burlington,
July 26th, 1815. 2425

Inaugural address . . . to the City Council.
41248

Inaugural address . . . to the . . . General
Assembly. 35005

Inaugural address to the legislature. 48740

Inaugural address . . . Union Theological
Seminary. 82709

Inaugural addresses and first annual messages
of all the Presidents. 18005, 63811

Inaugural addresses at the opening of the
Presbyterian Theological Seminary of the
North West. (65205)

Inaugural addresses, . . . in the University.
54707

Inaugural addresses of Profs. Haven and Bart
lett. 15485

Inaugural addresses of the Mayors of Boston.
82805, 82807

Inaugural addresses of Theodore W. Dwight an
Geo. P. Marsh. 14828, 21545

Inaugural addresses . . . with the first annual
messages. (14151)

Inaugural botanico-medical dissertation. 8076

Inaugural ceremonies at the opening of the ne
"Pioneer Hall." 86012

Inaugural charge by J. M. Porter, Esq. 3858

Inaugural discourse before the New York
Academy of Medicine. 25448

Inaugural discourse, . . . before the New-Yor
Historical Society. 50828

Inaugural discourse . . . before the New-York
Horticultural Society. 33089

Inaugural discourse, by Sidney H. Marsh.
44760

Inaugural discourse, by William G. T. Shedd.
80081

Inaugural discourse delivered at Andover, Sep
1, 1852. 92393

Inaugural discourse, delivered at the opening
of Rutgers Medical College. 33089

Inaugural discourse, delivered at Williams
College. 32943

Inaugural discourse delivered before the Boa
of Trustees. 70429

Inaugural discourse, delivered before the
University in Cambridge. 55865

Inaugural discourse, delivered before the
University in Cambridge, Massachusetts
September 3, 1831. 24953

Inaugural discourse delivered in . . . Clinton
2622

Inaugural discourse, delivered in the Chapel of Columbia College. 77675

Inaugural discourse, delivered in the Chapel of the University in Cambridge. 11896

Inaugural discourse, delivered in the First Congregational Church, Cincinnati. 16218

Inaugural discourse, delivered June 3, 1837. 21383

Inaugural discourse, delivered on the fourth day of January, 1821. 69653

Inaugural discourse . . . in . . . Antioch College. (33100)

Inaugural discourse . . . July 20th, 1854. (39348)

Inaugural discourse of Brantz Mayer . . . March 7th, 1867. (57096)

Inaugural discourse of collegiate education. 18955

Inaugural discourse of the President . . . July 24th, 1862. 36371

Inaugural discourse on medical education. 20825

Inaugural dissertation: being an attempt to disprove the doctrine of putrefaction of the blood. 79629

Inaugural dissertation, being an attempt to prove that certain substances are conveyed, unchanged, into the circulation. (82446)

Inaugural dissertation on cholera morbus. 33089

Inaugural dissertation on opium. 78617

Inaugural dissertation on opium, embracing its history. 84775

Inaugural dissertation on the bilious malignant fever. 8553

Inaugural dissertation on the chemical and medical history of Septon. 75862

Inaugural dissertation, on the chemical and medical properties of the persimmon tree. 105105

Inaugural dissertation on the principal mineral waters of the states. 47374

Inaugural dissertation on the production of animal heat. 88904

Inaugural dissertation on the puerperal fever. 103077

Inaugural dissertation on the scarlatina anginosa. 94544

Inaugural dissertation, upon the three follwoing subjects. 96161

Inaugural essay on the bilious typhus. (59761)

Inaugural essay on the effects of cold upon the human body. 91870

Inaugural essay on the yellow fever. 33081

Inaugural lecture at the opening of the first session. (37780)

Inaugural lecture before Mechanics' Institute. 106066

Inaugural message of Governor Fletcher. 24741

Inaugural message of Gov. John Hancock. 64028

Inaugural message of Governor Ramsey to the Senate and House of Representatives. 49254

Inaugural message of the Governor of Michigan. 48740

Inaugural message to the General Assembly. 34269

Inaugural oration. 3941

Inaugural oration, delivered in the Chapel of Williams College. (57166)

Inaugural oration, . . . Feb. 21, 1810. 18826

Inaugural oration, on the progress and importance of the mathematical sciences. 49336

Inaugural services; on . . . inducting the first President of the Ingham Collegiate Institute. (40147)

Inaugural sermon of the Right Rev. C. F. Robertson. (71944)

Inaugural sermon to the First Parish in Waltham, January 2, 1870. 42998

Inaugural speech of James Madison. (35886)

Inaugural speech [of R. Y. Hayne.] 87544

Inaugural speech [of Thomas Jefferson.] (23365)

Inaugural speeches and messages of Thomas Jefferson. (35886)

Inaugural speeches of Washington, Adams and Jefferson. 101709

Inaugural thesis. 64157

Inauguration ceremonies and address of Hon. Thomas Swann. 3037

Inauguration ceremonies [at the Caldwell Monument.] 9918

Inauguration of Dudley Observatory. 92774

Inauguration of Governor M. L. Ward, January 16, 1866. 53130

Inauguration of James McCosh. (43103)

Inauguration of James McCosh, D. D., L. L. D. 53088

Inauguration of Mill's equestrial statue. (35369)

Inauguration of the Dudley Observatory. 21098

Inauguration of the equestrian statue of Washington. (71183)

Inauguration of the fourth President of Indiana University. 34518

Inauguration of the Ladies' Home for Sick and Wounded Soldiers. (54327)

Inauguration of the National Union Club. 7772

Inauguration of the Perry statue. 13678

Inauguration of the Rev. Chas. Augustus Aiken. 85483

Inauguration of the Rev. John Maclean. 43515

Inauguration of the Spartansburg Female College. 81266

Inauguration of the statue of Daniel Webster. 102321

Inauguration of the statue of Horace Mann. (44325)

Inauguration of the statue of Warren. (9174)

Inca Garcilasso de la Vega's Commentaries of Peru. 66686

Incarnation, Marie de l'. see Marie de l'Incarnation. Mother Superior

Incarnation. 90927

Incas, o la destruccion del imperio del Peru. 44655

Incas; or, the destruction of the empire of Peru. 44653

Incas, ou la destruction de l'empire du Perou. (44652), 56299

Incendiary spy. 29482

Incendie du Cap. 60929, 96344

Incendie du village, ou les represailles militaires. 31594

Incentives to the study of the ancient period of American history. 77851

Inchanted lady's prophecy. 47980

Inchbald, Elizabeth (Simpson) 1753-1821. 17876, 88540-88541

Inches, ----------. 90612

Inchiquin, the Jesuit's letters. 34732, (50944), 59215

Inciativa de hacienda. (73027)

Incidental notices. 36905

Incidental poems. 20202

Incidental remarks of William H. Seward. 79527

Incidental remarks on masonry. 2929

Incidental remarks on the diseases. (8104), (30182)

Incidental reply to Mr. H. R. Helper's "Compendium of the impending crisis of the south." 59563

Incidents and adventures in rebellion of the border. 5599

Incidents and characters from life in the Baltimore Conference. 24732

Incidents and narratives, and also fragments of sermons. 8302

Incidents and narratives of travel in Europe. (26054)

Incidents and observations connected with the life of John A. Little. 41519

Incidents and scenes on the battle-fields and in Richmond. (44629)

Incidents and sketches connected with the early history of the settlement of the west. 34426

Incidents and sufferings in the Mexican war. (48573)

Incidents from the prayer meeting and the field. 2048

Incidents in American history. (3326)

Incidents in Dixie. 34427

Incidents in the early history of the Northwestern Territory. (14929)

Incidents in the early life of Hawser Martingale. 82118

Incidents in the history of the counties. (48818)

Incidents in the life and conversion of an atheist. 91817

Incidents in the life of a blind girl. 18973

Incidents in the life of a provincial. 86651

Incidents in the life of a slave girl. 7722, note after 12718, 19232, 35501

Incidents in the life of a soldier. 26215

Incidents in the life of George W. Henry. 31391

Incidents in the life of George W. Murray. 51496

Incidents in the life of Jacob Barker of New Orleans. 3392

Incidents in the life of James Gibson. (36249)

Incidents in the life of John Edsall. (21875)

Incidents in the life of Milton W. Streeter. 95848

Incidents in the life of President Dwight. 21564

Incidents in the life of Rev. J. Asher. 2186

Incidents in the life of W. Henry Harrison. 30584

Incidents, marches, battles and camp life. (48764)

Incidents of a cruise in the United States Frigate Congress. 14799

Incidents of a journey from Pennsylvania to Wisconsin Territory. 84862

Incidents of a southern tour. 2337

Incidents of a trip through the Great Platte Valley. 79669

Incidents of a whaling voyage. (57239)

Incidents of adventure in the history of the first settlers. 3230

Incidents of American camp life. 34428

Incidents of American slavery. 63325, 85166

Incidents of border life. Comprising narratives of strange and thrilling adventure. 34429

Incidents of border life, illustrative of the times. 65719

Incidents of field, camp, and hospital life. 22331

Incidents of itinerancy. 68037

Incidents of life and adventures in the Rocky Mountains. 91392

Incidents of my later years. (14329)

Incidents of personal experience. 85519

Incidents of political and exploratory travel. (57184)

Incidents of shipwreck. 16646

Incidents of ten years' itinerancy in the west. 11062

Incidents of the civil war in America. 34430

Incidents of the freshet on the Lehigh River. 39883

Incidents of the Hon. Daniel Webster. 89068

Incidents of the insurrection in the western parts of Pennsylvania. (7189)

Incidents of the slave trade. 28629

Incidents of the United States Christian Commission. 82457

Incidents of the war. 68573

Incidents of the war, humorous, pathetic, and descriptive. 9379

Incidents of the war of 1861-62-63. (31421)

Incidents of travel and adventure in the far west 11180

Incidents of travel and exploration in the land of the Incas. 89987

Incidents of travel in Central America. 91301

Incidents of travel in Central America, Chiapas and Yucatan. 91297-91298

Incidents of travel in Egypt, Arabia Petraea, and the Holy Land. 91297

Incidents of travel in Greece, Turkey, Russia and Poland. 69381

Incidents of travel in the southern states and Cuba. 67374

Incidents of travel in Yucatan. 91299

Incidents of travel to California. 97663

Incidents of western travel. 62718

Incidents on land and water. (3923)

Incidents recalled. 28867

Incidents taken from Mansfield's life of General Scott. 78410

Incidents which happened during the war with America. 1102

Incipit prologus super constitutiones Fratruum Heremitarum. (68936), 98913

Incipit registrum. 66473-(66476)

Incitativa de un Espanol Americano. (34431)

Incitativa del Padre Soto al Pensador Mexicano 87218

Inckel, ---------. 34432

Inclan, L. G. 34433

Incle and Yarico: a tragedy, of three acts. 105986

Incognito. pseud. Reflexiones. (68731)

Incognitus. pseud. Thoughts on the abolition of slavery. 95687

Income and expenditure of the United States of America. 29949

Income record. 54321

Income tax. 89841

Income tax of the residents of Philadelphia and Bucks County. (61736), 62194

Income tax of the residents of Philadelphia, income of 1865 and 1866. 61737

Income tax. Speech of Hon. John Scott, of Pennsylvania, delivered in the Senate of the United States. 78311

Income tax. Speech of Hon. John Scott of Pennsylvania in the Senate of the United States. (78312)

Incomes of the citizens of Boston and other cities and towns in Massachusetts. 6507 45769

Incomenza il libro de la prima navigatione. 41055

Inco[m]parabilis relectiones vndecim. 100619

Incomparable excellency of religion. 2425

Inconnu. pseud. Remarques critiques. see Eberstein et Chion du Bergier, --------, Baron.

Inconnue. pseud. Kenwood. see French, L. Virginia.

Inconsistence of renouncing the half-way covenant. 4492

Inconsistencie of the independent way. 11615

Inconsistencies of Christian professors. (45438)

Inconsistency of the strict constructionists. 102017

Inconstancy of youth. 101236

Inconveniencies that have happened to some persons. 99885, 99887

Incorporated Church Society of the Diocese of Quebec. see Church Society of the Diocese of Quebec. 67006

Incorporated District of the Northern Liberties, Pennsylvania. see Northern Liberties (District), Philadelphia.

Incorporated July 29, 1876. Southwestern Cooperative Association. 88613

Incorporated Proprietors of the Social Library in Salem, Mass. see Social Library, Salem, Mass. Proprietors.

Incorporated Society for the Conversion and Religious Instruction and Education of Negro Slaves. see Society for the Conversion and Religious Instruction and Education of Negro Slaves.

Incorporated Society for the Propagation of the Gospel in Foreign Parts, London. see Society for the Propagation of the Gospel in Foreign Parts, London.

Incorporating act and constitution of the Bible Society of Salem. 75638

Incorporation, by-laws, history, reports and finance statements. 75384

Incorporation laws of Illinois. 34282

Incorporation laws, passed by the General Assembly. 34281

Incorporation of Providence Plantations. see Rhode Island (Colony)

Incorporation of the Five Points House of Industry: articles of incorporation. 54280

Incorporation of the Southern Transportation Company. 88509

Incorporirten Deutschen Gesellschaft zur Unterstutzung Bedrangter Deutschen im Staat Pennsylvanien. see Deutsche Gesellschaft von Pennsylvanien, Philadelphia.

Incorruptible key composed of the cx. Psalm. 28042-28043

Incouragement to coronells by Sir William Alexander. 91853

Increase of banking facilities. 84932

Increase of crime. 70857

Increase of immortality; a sermon. (41577)

Increase of piety. 34434, 44483, 105172

Increase of the kingdom of Christ. 1735

Increase of the ministry. 89105

Inculpations du commerce. 14058

Inc'Wadi Yokuqala Ka-Yowannes Intloko Yokuqala. (34425)

Indagaciones sobre la amonedacion en Nueva Espana. (22119)

Indagaciones sobre las antiguedades Mexicanas. 35070

Indarte, Jose Rivera. 34435-34437, 100789, 105745

Indberetning i anledning af en efter offentlig foranstaltning foretagen reise. 72585

Indebtedness of the city of New York to its university. 20897

Indebtedness of the state. (58620)

Indecision, a tale of the far west. 49702

Indemnite en faveur des colons de Saint-Domingue. 75134

Indemnity bill. (43876)

Indemnity for expenses of war in Florida. 34438

Indenture. 86807-86808

Indenture of agreement 4th July, 1760. 34439

Independance absolue des Americains des Etats-Unis. 23919, (34441)

Independance de l'empire du Bresil. (4157)

Independance pacifique du Canada. 38812

Independence Day Celebration, Philadelphia, 1865. see Philadelphia. Independence Day Celebration, 1865.

Independence Day; or, two modes of spending it. 34442

Independence des Anglo-Americains. (8021)

Independence d'Haiti et la France. 12156

Independence guide. 34443

Independence Jubilee, Spencertown, N. Y. see Spencertown, N. Y. Independence Jubilee, 1846.

Independence, liberty, justice. 105594

Independence of Canada. 33977

Independence of Cuba. 57711

Independence of Hayti. 22175

Independence of the South. 66419

Independence; or, which do you like best? 34970, note after 36638

Independence preserved. 22529

Independence programme for July 4, 1865. 34444

Independence-sermon . . . July 4, 1814. 13267

Independencia de la isla de Cuba. 29107

Independencia de Mexico. (48496)

Independencia de Mexico. Anaversario del primer grito. (34445)

Independencia Mexicana. 34446

Independency on scriptures of the independence of churches. 31496, 46781, note before 96158

Independency the object of the Congress in America. 15538, 34447

Independent. pseud. Discourse on government and religion. 20240

Independent. 63826, 89094, 89101, 89554A

Independent American. (16840)

Independent chronicle. 59443, 95933, 104279

Independent citizen. 34448

Independent Company of Cadets. 34449

Independent courier. (13895), (14009), 25640, 101838, note after 101847

Independent Democratic Party. see Free Soil Party.

Independent Democratic platform. 20428-20429

Independent Democrats in Congress. see Free Soil Party.

Independent Division, No. III, West Amesbury, Mass. see Sons of Temperance of North America. Massachusetts. Independent Division, No. III, West Amesbury.

Independent Free Territory Convention of the People of Ohio, Cincinnati, 1848. see State Independent Free Territory Convention of the People of Ohio, Cincinnati, 1848.

Independent gazetteer. 9836-9837, (68568), 82725, 101838

Independent gazetteer. Editor. defendant 57272, 57828 see also Oswald, Eleazer. defendant

Independent Irishman. pseud. Familiar letters to John B. Fitzpatrick. (24623)

Independent journal. 93795, 93805

Independent journal. see Monthly religious magazine and independent journal.

Independent leger, and lyceum weekly journal. 34450

Independent man. pseud. Occasional letters on taxation. 56626

Independent mechanic. 34451

Independent Medical School of Pennsylvania. 60158

Independent monthly. 25942

Independent nomination! 82355, 104222

Independent Odd Ladies, United Order of. see United Order of Independent Odd Ladies.

Independent ode, dedicated to the illustrious President of the United States. 103145

Independent Order of Odd Fellows. see Odd Fellows, Independent Order of.

Independent Order of Odd Fellows. Journal of the Grand Lodge of Minnesota. (49255)

Independent Order of Rechabites. North America. 68939

Independent Order of the Sons of Malta. 60161

Independent Order of the Sons of Malta. Grand Consistory of Columbia, Philadelphia, 1858. 60161

Independent Order of the Sons of Malta. Grand Convocation and Supreme Grand Council, Washington, D. C., 1860. 86990

Independent Order of the Sons of Malta. Grand Council. 86989

Independent Order of the Sons of Malta. Massachusetts. Lodge of the Iron Cross, Boston. 86991

Independent Order of the Sons of Malta. Pennsylvania. 86993

Independent Order of the Sons of Malta. Pennsylvania. Convention and Supreme Grand Lodge, Philadelphia, 1860. 60161, 86994

Independent Order of the Sons of Malta. Pennsylvania. Minne-ha-ha Lodge, No. 1, Philadelphia. 86994

Independent Order of the Sons of Malta. Pennsylvania. Supreme Grand Lodge. 60161, 86992-86993

Independent Order of the Sons of Malta. Virginia. Grand Convocation and Supreme Grand Lodge, Richmond, 1860. 86996

Independent patriot. pseud. To the real patriots. 96017

Independent patriot. 83302

Independent Presbyterian Church, Savannah, Ga. see Savannah, Ga. Independent Presbyterian Church.

Independent press. 84241

Independent reflector. 34452, (41651), 84576, 90011

Independent Republic of Liberia. 40925

Independent Society for the Culture and Propagation of Learning and Good Manners, Concord, Mass. 95314

Independent Society in Concord. see Independent Society for the Culture and Propagation of Learning and Good Manners, Concord, Mass.

Independent whig. pseud. Letter to the Right Honourable Charles Jenkinson. (40520)

Independent whig (Manchester, Eng.) 89173

Independent whig (New York) (17350), 90011

Independent whig (Philadelphia) (34453), 37175 note after 96767

Independents voyage to New England. (66937)

Independiente. 72797

Indes, Melchior Oyanguren de Santa. see Oyanguren de Santa Ines, Melchior.

Indes orientales et occidentales et autres leiux 32805, 73067

Index. pseud. Individual liberty, legal, moral and licentious. 48987

Index. pseud. Queries about the "Sanitary Commission." 34456

Index. A weekly journal. 34454

Index and maps to Captain Palliser's reports. (58333)

Index des statuts en force des la Bas Canada. 10490

Index for persons in America claiming properties abroad. 82406

Index for persons in America claiming properties abroad, as heirs-at-law. 82405

Index for the 18th-21st Congress. 15539

Index of awards on claims. (53699)

Index of dates. 73412

Index of names and places in Sullivan's District of Maine. 93499

Index of subjects [of the library of Brown University.] 8605

Index of the classified catalogue. 10393

Index of the printed acts and resolves. 3741

Index to advertisements which have appeared. 29278

Index to all the laws and resolutions of . . . Ohio. 56937

Index to all the laws of the state of Illinois. 34283

Index to all the printed committee reports. 15539

Index to American genealogies. 84298

Index to documents relative to North Carolina. 55624

Index to journals of the House of Assembly of Nova Scotia. 56142

Index to J. Ross Browne's report. 8662

Index to Ohio laws. 14204

Index to periodical literature. 64040, (64044), (64045)

Index to the annual monitor. 98705

Index to the bibliotheca sacra and American Biblical repository. 5202

Index [to the Book of Mormon.] 83040

Index to the calendar of Maryland state paper (736)

Index to the catalogue of books in the Upper Hall. 6759

Index to the catalogue of a portion of the Public Library. 6759

Index to the city documents [of Boston.] 6759

Index to the code as amended. 89332

Index to the constitution of . . . New York. (53970)

Index to the documents of the House of Representatives. 34455

Index to the documents of the Legislature of New York. (6128)

Index to the executive communications from 1817-1823. 15539

Index to the executive communications made t the House of Representatives. 15539

Index of the executive documents and reports of committees. 15540

Index to the geology of the northern states, with a transverse section. 21704

Index to the geology of the northern states, with transverse sections. 21705

Index to the Holy Bible. 72608

Indian Conference, Johnson Hall, N. Y., 1765.
see New York (Colony) Indian Con-
ference, Johnson Hall, 1765.
Indian Conference, Lancaster, Pa., 1757. see
Pennsylvania (Colony) Indian Conference,
Lancaster, 1757.
Indian Conference, Lancaster, Pa., 1762. see
Pennsylvania (Colony) Indian Conference,
Lancaster, 1762.
Indian Conference, Philadelphia, 1744. see
Pennsylvania (Colony) Indian Conference,
Philadelphia, 1744.
Indian Conference, Philadelphia, 1756. see
Pennsylvania (Colony) Indian Conference,
Philadelphia, 1756.
Indian conferences at Johnson-Hall, in May,
1765. 25595, 34579-34580, 99584, note
just before 103108
Indian Congress, Fort Stanwix, N. Y., 1768.
see New York (Colony) Indian Congress,
Fort Stanwix, 1768.
Indian converts: or, some account of the lives.
47124-(47125)
Indian converts, Tschoop and Shabasch. 34462
Indian cord. 22566
Indian cottage. 78774
Indian Council, Buffalo Creek Reservation,
N. Y., 1842. see New York (State)
Indian Council, Buffalo Creek Reservation,
1842.
Indian Council, Cattaraugus, N. Y., 1843. see
New York (State) Indian Council, Cat-
taraugus, 1843.
Indian Council, Cattarauhus, N. Y., 1845. see
New York (State) Indian Council, Cat-
tarauhus, 1845.
Indian Council, Ottowa River, 1791. 19103,
(49351)
Indian Council, Walla Walla, Wash., 1855. see
Washington (Territory) Indian Council,
Walla Walla, 1855.
Indian Creek and Jack's Knob Coal, Salt, Lead,
Lumber, Oil, and Manufacturing Company.
(34463)
Indian deed for the town. 88229
Indian department (Canada) return. 34464
Indian dialects of North America. 1049
Indian dialogues. 22160
Indian dictionary. note after 106301
Indian doctor's dispensatory. 83709-83710
Indian emperour. 20979
Indian expedition during the summer of 1863.
80821
Indian fairy book. (46832), 46833
Indian gallery of portraits. 11531
Indian gallows, and other poems. (70767)
Indian gazette. 82976
Indian girl. 34465
Indian girl; and other poems. 25456
Indian grammar begun. 22157, 22158
Indian graves in Floyd and Chickasaw Counties,
Iowa. 85041
Indian guide to health. 43875
Indian hater. (64200)
Indian Hill Cemetery, Middletown, Mass. see
Middletown, Mass. Indian Hill Cemetery.
Indian hygienia. 40916
Indian hymns. 79119
Indian in his wigwam. 77837, 77852, 77867,
77872
Indian Jim. A tale of the Minnesota massacre.
22297
Indian legend of olden times. 34594
Indian legends and other poems. 33055
Indian maiden. 75252
Indian maid's last arrow. 36582

Indian man, a resident in Oneida County. pseu
Experience. 104520
Indian man, a resident in Oneida County. pseu
Religious experience. 104518
Indian massacre in Minnesota. 9327
Indian massacres and war in Minnesota. 4308
Indian melodies. 77853
Indian melodies. By Thomas Commuck. 1499
Indian Mission Association. Annual Meeting,
1st, Louisville, 1843. 34466
Indian missions in Guiana. (7744)
Indian missions in the United States of Americ
(34468), 82261
Indian mummy. 85041
Indian names of Long Island. 54476
Indian names of places in Rhode-Island. 5892(
Indian narratives. 34469
Indian nectar. 93224
Indian notes. 99362
Indian notices. 31802
Indian nullification of the unconstitutional laws
of Massachusetts. 1736, 85433
Indian of New-England, and the north-Eastern
provinces. 94680, 94682
Indian pensioners to the front!! 34459
Indian philosopher. pseud. Telliamed. see
Maillet, B. de.
Indian philosopher. 96036
Indian portraits. 34470, 43410
Indian pottery. 67966
Indian prayer book. 72885
Indian primer. 91295
Indian primer. And Milk for babes. 22161
Indian primer; or, the first book. (34471)
Indian princess an operatic melo-drama.
3393
Indian prophecy, a national drama. 101828
Indian proprietors of Mattebeseck. 94682
Indian queen. 20979
Indian queen. A tragedy. 33276
Indian queen of Chenango: a poem in four
cantos. 93239
Indian queen's revenge. 36582
Indian question. 34472
Indian races of North and South America.
8681
Indian remains, by T. Ewbank. 27419
Indian remains in southern Georgia. (36478)
Indian remains of the Penobscot Valley. 8450(
Indian researches. 82147
Indian reservation Sulphur Springs, near
Buffalo, N. Y. 34473
Indian rights and our duties. 33791, 34474
Indian scalp. 34475
Indian sketches. 82277
Indian sketches, taken during an expedition.
35117
Indian sketches, taken during an expedition to
the Pawnee Tribes. (35116)
Indian-slayer. By J. Springer. 89834
Indian-slayer. By P. Preston. 65376
Indian songs of peace. 17463, 84671, 84673
Indian songs of peace, with a proposal for
erecting Indian schools. 34476, 84624
Indian songs of peace: with a proposal, in a
prefatory epistle. 34476, 84624
Indian speech, delived [sic] before a gentleman
missionary. 68472
Indian speech, in answer to a sermon. 89175
Indian speech. The speech of Sagona Ha.
68473
Indian speeches; delivered by Farmer's Brothe
and Red Jacket. 89187
Indian spirit. 48042
Indian stories. 34477
Indian story. 57426

Indian story; being a narrative of facts. 93077, 104274

Indian summer. 8808

Indian system. 78591

Indian tale. 9821

Indian tale. By C. Sealsfield. 64555, 2d note after 96106

Indian tale. [By Douglas S. Huyghue.] (34113)

Indian tale. [By J. Hunt.] (33869)

Indian tale. [By John Davis.] 18848, 82860, 100438, 100467

Indian tale. [By John Richardson.] 71042-71044

Indian tale. By Samuel Webber. 102252

Indian tale. By the Viscomte de Chateaubriand. 12259

Indian tale. [By Thomas Osmond Summers.] 44537, 93630

Indian tale. In four cantos. 2654, 51026

Indian tale interpreted and told in English verse. 34478

Indian tale of frontier life. 80275

Indian tales and legends. 77835

Indian tales; Keetsea, or the enchanted rock. 75253

Indian Territory. see also Oklahoma.

Indian Territory. General Council, Okmulgee, 1871. 34662

Indian trade. 34479

Indian tradition: a poem. 39187

Indian tradition. No fiction. 34480

Indian tragedy. 18409

Indian traits. 95217

Indian treaties. (30030), 34481, note after 96593

Indian tribes—northwestern frontier. 34482

Indian tribes of Guiana. 7745-7746

Indian tribes of the United States. 77854

Indian tribes. Speech of. Hon. Sam Houston. 33193

Indian vocabulary. 66686

Indian voyages. 25471

Indian wars. 20490

Indian wars and captivities of the United States. 26055

Indian wars, in twenty-eight chapters. 82808, 97196

(Indian wars of America.) 82808, 97196

Indian wars of the United States, from the discovery to the present time. 26039, 50455

Indian wars of the United States, from the earliest period. 26040

Indian wars of the west. 24790

Indian wars. Proposals by Henry Trumbull. 97197

Indian wife of the white hunter. 91284

Indian woman. pseud. see Betty, an Indian Woman.

Indian woman. 6860, 64084-64085, 97859

Indian woman, an Indian character. 6860

Indiana (Territory) petitioners (34555)

Indiana (Territory) Laws, statutes, etc. (34540), 34544

Indiana (Territory) Sundry Inhabitants of the Counties of Randolph and St. Clair. petitioners see Randolph County, Ind. Citizens. petitioners and St. Clair County, Ind. Citizens. petitioners

Indiana. 34509, 34561

Indiana. Adjutant General. (34557), 34562-34563 see also Noble, Laz. Terrell, W. H. H.

Indiana. Agent to Examine the Condition of the State Bank and Branches. 34491

Indiana. Agent to Purchase Arms for the State. 34565 see also Owen, Robert Dale.

Indiana. Allotment Commissioners. 34564

Indiana. Association for the Improvement of Common Schools. see Association for the Improvement of Common Schools in Indiana.

Indiana. Asylum for the Education of the Deaf and Dumb. see Indiana. School for the Deaf, Indianapolis.

Indiana. Auditor. 34526

Indiana. Board of Education. 34508, 84401

Indiana. College. 34516

Indiana. Constitution. 1269, 1271, 2071, 5316, 6360, 9672, 16103, 16107, 16113, 16133, 29731, 33137, 34502, 34542, (34548)-34549, (47188), 59771, (66397), 104198

Indiana. Constitutional Convention, 1851. 34502

Indiana. Courts. 79125

Indiana. Deaf and Dumb Asylum. see Indiana. School For the Deaf, Indianapolis.

Indiana. Draft Commissioner. 34564

Indiana. Financial Secretary. 34526

Indiana. Fund Commissioner. (34524)-34525, 90482 see also Stapp, Milton.

Indiana. General Assembly. 34493, 34504, 34529, 34574-34575

Indiana. General Assembly. Minority Committee. 34526

Indiana. General Assembly. House of Representatives. 34538

Indiana. General Assembly. Senate. 34501, 34503, 34539, 90374

Indiana. Geological Survey. 17254, 34488, 34527-34529

Indiana. Governor, 1837-1840 (Wallace) 34530 see also Wallace, David, 1799-1859.

Indiana. Governor, 1849-1857 (Wright) (34556) see also Wright, Joseph Albert, 1809-1867.

Indiana. Governor, 1857-1860 (Willard) 33150 see also Willard, Ashbel Parsons, 1820-1860.

Indiana. Governor, 1860-1861 (Hammond) 35024 see also Hammond, Abram Adams, 1814-1874.

Indiana. Governor, 1861-1867 (Morton) 22498, (34556), 51018 see also Morton, Oliver Hazard Perry Throck, 1823-1877.

Indiana. Governor, 1867-1873 (Baker) (34556) see also Baker, Conrad, 1817-1885.

Indiana. Hospital for the Insane, Indianapolis. 34536

Indiana. Institution for the Deaf and Dumb. see Indiana. School for the Deaf, Indianapolis.

Indiana. Laws, statutes, etc. 23765, 29731, 39414, 34506, 34519-34521, 34526, (34541)-34543, 34545-34549, 34567, 34572, (34951), 39435, 48761, 48768, 52051, 70820-70821, 82438, 89066, 100879

Indiana. Medical College, Laporte. 34554

Indiana. Militia. 34567

Indiana. Militia. 93d Regiment. 34484

Indiana. Militia. Paymaster. 34564

Indiana. Militia. 66th Regiment. 34484

Indiana. Militia. 34th Regiment. 34484

Indiana. Pay Agents. 34564

Indiana. Quartermaster General. 34565

Indiana. School for the Blind, Indianapolis. Trustees. 34510

Indiana. School for the Deaf, Indianapolis. (21205), 34511

Indiana. School for the Deaf, Indianapolis. Trustees. 34511

Indiana. Special Agents. 34564

Indiana. State Bank. see State Bank of Indiana.

Indiana. State Bank. Bondholders. see Bondholders of the Indiana State Bank for 1844-1845.

Indiana. State Board of Agriculture. 34486-34489

Indiana. State Board of Colonization. 34501

Indiana. State Board of Colonization. Secretary. 34501

Indiana. State Board of Education. see Indiana. Board of Education.

Indiana. State Geologist. 34488, 34527-34529 see also Cox, E. T. Owen, David Dale. Owen, Richard.

Indiana. State Library. 34495

Indiana. State Prison. 34568

Indiana. Superintendent of Common Schools. see Indiana. Superintendent of Public Instruction.

Indiana. Superintendent of Public Instruction. 34507-34508, 82232 see also Smart, James H.

Indiana. Supreme Court. 84403

Indiana. Treasurer. 34526

Indiana. University. 34517-34518

Indiana. University. Board of Trustees. 105658

Indiana. University. Board of Trustees. Committee. 34517

Indiana. University. President. 34518 see also Lathrop, John H.

Indiana. Wabash and Erie Canal Commissioners. see Wabash and Erie Canal. Commissioners.

Indiana. Wabash and Erie Canal Trustees. see Wabash and Erie Canal. Trustees.

Indiana annual register, and pocket manual. 34531

Indiana as a home for emigrants. 22498, 51018

Indiana Asbury University. see De Pauw University, Greencastle, Ind.

Indiana banker. pseud. Michigan first regiment. (48764)

Indiana Branch of the Presbyterian Education Society. see Presbyterian Education Society. Indiana Branch.

Indiana Canal Company. 34494

Indiana Colonization Society. Agent. 34501

Indiana Company. Proprietors. see Proprietors of Indiana.

Indiana Convention to Organize a State Anti-slavery Society, Milton, 1838. 34570

Indiana gazetteer. 34532-34533, 78304-78305

Indiana Harmony Society. see Harmony Society of Indiana.

Indiana: in relation to its geography. 24489

Indiana Infantry. see Indiana. Militia.

Indiana Institute for the Education of the Blind. see Indiana. School for the Blind, Indianapolis.

Indiana Legion. 34558

Indiana Legion and Minutemen. see Indiana Legion.

Indiana masonic state directory and masonic advertiser. 34551

Indiana miscellany. 84753

Indiana railway gazetteer. 34534

Indiana Sanitary Commission. 34566

Indiana Sanitary Convention, Indianapolis, 1864. 34560

Indiana school journal. 34514

Indiana schools, and the men who have worked in them. 82232

Indiana soldier. pseud. Seven months a prisoner. see Hadley, J. V.

Indiana soldiers in the Department of the Cumberland. 34559

Indiana state gazetteer and business directory. 34535

Indiana state gazetteer and shipper's guide. 17242, 34576, 80324

Indiana State Horticultural Society. 34537

Indiana State Medical Society. 93975

Indiana state prison. First annual report. 34568

Indiana State Teachers' Association. 34513-34514

Indiana Theological Seminary, South Hanover, Ind. see Hanover College, Honover, Indiana.

Indiana Yearly Meeting. see Friends, Society of. Indiana Yearly Meeting.

Indianapolis. Bar. 34584, 83695

Indianapolis. Board of Trade. petitioners (34583)

Indianapolis. Christian Convention, 1859. see Christian Convention, Indianapolis, 1859.

Indianapolis. Common Council. petitioners (34583)

Indianapolis. Convention of Freedmen's Commissions, 1864. see Convention of Freedmen's Commissions, Indianapolis, 1864.

Indianapolis. Democratic State Convention, 1836. see Democratic Party. Indiana. Convention, Indianapolis, 1836.

Indianapolis. Hospital for the Insane. see Indiana. Hospital for the Insane, Indianapolis.

Indianapolis. Indiana Sanitary Convention, 1864. see Indiana Sanitary Convention, Indianapolis, 1864.

Indianapolis. National Sunday School Convention, 5th, 1872. see National Sunday School Convention. 5th, Indianapolis, 1872.

Indianapolis. North-Western Christian University. see North-Western Christian University, Indianapolis.

Indianapolis. School for the Blind. see Indiana. School for the Blind, Indianapolis.

Indianapolis. School for the Deaf. see Indianapolis. School for the Deaf, Indianapolis.

Indianapolis. Social Order of Temperance. see Social Order of Temperance, Indianapolis.

Indianapolis. State Convention of the Indiana Democratic Party, 1866. see Democratic Party. Indiana. Convention, Indianapolis, 1866.

Indianapolis. 32562

Indianapolis as it is in 1855. 34581

Indianapolis city directory and business mirror. 93957

Indianapolis city directory for 1865. 34582

Indianapolis directory. 8489

Indianapolis directory, city guide and business mirror. 34581

Indianapolis directory for 1868. 34582

Indianapolis directory for . . . July 1, 1868. 8489, 34582

Indianapolis Presbytery. see Presbyterian Church in the U. S. A. Presbytery of Indianapolis.

Indiana's roll of honor. 78483

Indiane primer Asuh negonneyeuuk. 22161
Indianer in New-Engeland. 54944
Indianer in Nord-America. (62797)
Indianer Nord Amerika's und die wahrend eines achtjahrigen Aufenthalts. 11539
Indianer-Predigt. pseud. see Indian Chief. pseud.
Indianer-Sommer in Nord-Amerika. 43870
Indianer von Santa Catalina Istlavacan. 77617
Indianergeschichte aus dem Jahre 1812. (4724)
Indianian. pseud. Facts for the people. 83690
Indianian. pseud. Inquiry into the equal rights of the states. see Smith, Jeremiah, 1805-1874.
Indianan. pseud. Is slavery as it exists in the southern states, morally wrong? 34587
Indianische historia. 23997
Indianische Reise Iohannis Sortmanni Oester-rodens. 87198
Indianischer Religionstadt der gantzen Newen Welt. 25934
Indians. pseud. Interesting letters. 16794, 41538
Indians, a play, in five acts. 96057
Indians, a tale. 9821, 71088
Indians, a tragedy. 71087, (71089)
Indians and Injin. 16525
Indians and the gold mines. 7093
Indians Charged with Being Engaged in Philip's Designs. defendants 68392
Indians—Cherokee Nation, West. Memorial . . . April 1, 1840. 34657
Indians—Cherokees—May 26, 1840. 34656
Indians—Choctaw citizens of Mississippi. 34658
Indians, friendly and unfriendly. (43102)
Indians killing & scalping, thirty persons. 83535
Indians of Cape Flattery. 85072, 94011
Indians of North America. 49835
Indians of Ohio. see Ohio Indians.
Indians of South Carolina. see South Carolina Indians.
Indians on the battle field and in the wigwam. 26038
Indians. Or narratives of massacres and depredations. 34659
Indians removed to west of the Mississippi from 1789. 34660
Indians, the ten lost tribes. 1735
Indicacion de algunos de los principales objetos. 34681
Indicaciones al Congreso demonstrado las causas fundamentales. 34682
Indicaciones al Congreso Nacional para la mas acertada resolucion. 99657
Indicaciones sobre el origen, vicisitudes y estado. 65516
Indicacoes de utilidade publica. 24172
Indicador. 29082
Indicador administrativo das alfandegas e mesas de rendas. 81077
Indicador de la federacion Mexicana. 48497
Indicarum historiarum librii III. 43229
Indications of the mineral districts in all the New England states. 77762
Indicator alphabetico da morada dos seus principaes habitantes. 71457
Indice alfabetico con los nombres de las calles. (48457)
Indice alfabetico y chronologico de las materias mas notables. 69666

Indice alphabetico das leis da Provincia da Parahyba. 88778
Indice alphabetico das leis, decretos, avisos e consultas. 41713
Indice alphabetico das leis, decretos e avisos. 26495
Indice alphabetico das leis do imperior do Brasil. 88774
Indice alphabetico de materias. 81084
Indice alphabetico nao so' de todas as materias. 81077
Indice de las materias que comprende la ley de administracion. 51673
Indice generale della storia dell' America. 15018
Indictment and trial of Col. Edward Stiff. 91725
Indictment and trial of Sir Richard Rum. 74121
Indictment and tryal of Sir Richard Rum. 34683, (74118), 74120
Indictment for practicing law. 75407
Indiculus universalis. (30912)
Indiens de la Baie d'Hudson. 19428, 37009
Indiens de la Province de Mato-Grosso. (46949), (51196)
Indiens des Etats-Unis. 79045
Indigene de l'Amerique du Sud. pseud. Lettres a M. l'Abbe de Pradt. (40684)
Indigenous races of the earth. 56038
Indigent Widows and Single Women's Society, Philadelphia. 61739
Indigo. 87534
Indio. pseud. Dialogo entre una senorita y un Indio. 19922
Indio. pseud. Historia de la conquista de Mejico. (49434)
Indio. pseud. Tardes Americanas. 28255
Indio. pseud. Ya volvio Santa-Anna. 76747
Indio esclavo. 11241
Indio Moranducara. pseud. Sume. 93587
Indio patriota. pseud. Carta. see Toledo y Dubois, Jose Alvarez de.
Indios bravos. 57735
Indios de los pueblos de Istlaguaca, Iocotitlan. 98593
Indios del Andaqui. (34684)
Indis patriotae. pseud. Carta. see Toledo y Dubois, Jose Alvarez de.
Indische Hutte. (12250)
Indissoluble nature of the American union. (10746)
Individual and associate effort. 82732
Individual and public reform. 3794
Individual liberty, legal, moral and licentious. 48987
Individual of little note. pseud. Appeal to candour. 81874
Individual report and revelation. 63867
Individual reports of the state assessors. 53962
Individual responsibility to the nation. (64639)
Individual y verdadera relacion. (42590)-(42591)
Individuality and obedience. 83302
Individuo del ejercito-unito. pseud. Victoria del Lago-Negro. see Loza, Jose Manuel. supposed author
Indoctum Parliamentum. 79709
Indorum Floridam provinciam inhabitantium eicones. (8784)
Indreniis specimen de Esquimaux. 22856
Inducements to the colored people. 10800
Induction of Professor John S. Hart. 53195
Inductive arithmetic, and federal calculator. note before 83906, 83914

Indulgencias de Nuestra Senora del Carmen. 98724

Indulgencias del Rosario de la Virgen Maria. 94221

Indulgencias perpetuas concedidas a los Congregantes de la Congregacion. 34685

Indulgencias y perdones, co[n]cedidas a las Cofrades di Sanctissimo Sacrame[n]to. 93590

Indus Britannicus. pseud. Remarks on the trial. 106314

Industria agricola. (48274)

Industria y el poder. 60916

Industrial Aid Society for the Prevention of Pauperism, Boston. note just before 85910

Industrial and commercial geography. 83375

Industrial and financial resources of the United States. 29892, (34686)

Industrial art education. 84494

Industrial art education, considered economically. 84499

Industrial art of the International Exhibition. 84493

Industrial Art Union, Mineral Point, Wisc. see Mineral Point Industrial Art Union.

Industrial colleges. 6240

Industrial conflict. 84065

Industrial drawing. 84504

Industrial exchanges and social remedies. 3379

Industrial Exhibition, New York, 1854. see New York Industrial Exhibition, New York, 1854.

Industrial Fair Association, Baton Rouge, La. see Baton Rouge Industrial Fair Association.

Industrial history of free nations. 43121

Industrial Home Association, New York. see New York Industrial Home Association.

Industrial Home for Girls, Philadelphia. see Philadelphia. Industrial Home for Girls.

Industrial Home for the Instruction of Girls in the Arts of Housewifery, Philadelphia. see Philadelphia. Industrial Home for Girls.

Industrial investments and emigration. 78472

Industrial record. see Fisher's magazine and industrial record. National magazine and industrial record.

Industrial resources, etc., of the southern and western states. 19117-19118

Industrial resources of Nova Scotia. 27222

Industrial resources of Wisconsin. 28740

Industrial School, Chelsea, Mass. see Chelsea Industrial School.

Industrial School, Manchester, N. H. see New Hampshire. Industrial School, Manchester.

Industrial School, Rochester, N. Y. see New York (State) State Industrial School, Rochester.

Industrial school advocate and soldier's aid. 26275

Industrial School Association, Brooklyn. see Brooklyn Industrial School Association, and Home for Destitute Children.

Industrial School for Boys, Lansing, Mich. see Michigan. Industrial School for Boys, Lansing.

Industrial School for Girls, Dorchester, Mass. see Massachusetts. Industrial School for Girls, Dorchester.

Industrial School for Girls, Lancaster, Mass. see Massachusetts. Industrial School for Girls, Lancaster.

Industrial School for Girls, Winchester, Mass. see Massachusetts. Industrial School for Girls, Winchester.

Industrial School for Girls of Maryland. see Maryland Industrial School for Girls.

Industrie agricole et miniere du Chili. 6451

Industrie dans le bassin de la Plata. (51202)

Industrie Francaise et l'esclavage des Negres. 39381

Industry. 83703

Industry and diligence in our callings earnestly recommended. 101489

Industry and diligence in the work of religion. (14493)

Industry & frugality proposed as the surest means. 34687

Industry of Massachusetts. 2d note after (19871)

Industry, the only means to render manufactures cheap. 65678, 103121

Indwelling of the spirit. 103516, 103529

Inebriate. 80750

Inebriate Asylum, Binghampton, N. Y. see New York (State) State Hospital, Binghampton.

Inebriate asylum. 45168

Inebriates' Home for Kings County. Superintendent's report. 37876

Inebriate's hut. 88667

Inemigo da desordem. pseud. Tranquillisador dos povos. 96451

Inequality of individual wealth. 100965

Ines de la Cruz, Juana. see Juana Ines de la Cruz, Sister, 1561-1695.

Inexcusableness of a knowing people refusing to be reformed. 104396

Inexcusableness of neglecting the worship of God. 91941, 91954

Inexhaustible Petroleum Company, of New York 66089

Inexorable logic. 34688

Inexpediency of establishing bishops in America 45417

Inez; a tale of the Alamo. (34689)

Infallible cure for political blindness. (34690)

Infallible scheme for the reduction of Canada. 17685

Infallibility of the church tested by the scriptures. 70857

Infallibility of the clergy and officers of the Presbyterian Church. 29305

Infamous letter sent to Mr. John Oldden. 14016

Infamous sentiments. (34691)

Infancy of the union. 68607

Infant Asylum, New York. see New York Infant Asylum.

Infant Asylum of Massachusetts. see Massachusetts Infant Asylum.

Infant baptism from heaven. 82722-82723

Infant-baptism "from heaven," and immersion, as the only mode of baptism. (13597)

Infant baptism vindicated. 24427

Infant bride of Truxillo. (13858)

Infant School Society, Charleston, S. C. 12092

Infant School Society, New York. 54322

Infant School Society, Providence, R. I. see Providence Infant School Society.

Infant School Society of the Northern Liberties and Kensington, Pa. 61741, 103178

Infant schools. 10889

Infant sprinkling proved to be a human traditic 101063

Infantado, Rodrigo Diaz de Vivar, 6. Duque del. defendant 51043

Infante, Joaquin. (70015)

Infantes, Tomas de Portes e. see Portes e Infantes, Tomas de, Abp.

Infantry camp duty. 8888

Infantry exercise of the United States Army. 34692, 64661

Infantry sword exercise. 58562

Infantry tactics. 11328

Infantry-tactics; or rules for the exercise and manoeuvres of the United States Infantry. 78411

Infants die to live. 85325

Infelicia. 47864

Infeliz banqueiro Antonio Jose Domingues Ferreira. 24166

Inferences from the pestilence and the fast. 758

Inferior surface of the trilobite discovered. 28527

Infirmities and comforts of old age. 39199

Infernal conference. (34693)

Infidel. 5553

Infidelity disarmed. 83667

Infidelity of abolitionism. 62528

"Infidelity" of abolitionism. 26712

Infinite importance of the obedience of faith. 2632

Infirmary, Pittsburgh, Pa. see Pittsburgh. Infirmary.

Infirmary for Diseases of the Lungs in Massachusetts. see Massachusetts Infirmary for Diseases of the Lungs.

Infirmary for Women and Children, New York. see New York Infirmary for Women and Children.

Inflexible patriot. 79399, (79402), note after 99292

Influence. 89770

Influence de la decouverte de l' Amerique. (26957)

Influence de la revolution de l'Amerique sur l'Europe. 34694

Influence du despotisme de l'Angleterre sur les deux mondes. 4177, note after 34694

Influence d'un livre. 26739

Influence exerted. 42033

Influence of Catholic Christian doctrines. (24603)

Influence of Christianity of civil society. 104348

Influence of Christianity upon civil liberty. 2790

Influence of climate, and other agents. 2037

Influence of climate, in a commercial, social, sanitary, and humanizing point of view. 20320

Influence of climate in North and South America. (20321)

Influence of democracy. 23311

Influence of education on the quality and pecuniary value of labor. 3469

Influence of education on the quality and value of labor. 15725

Influence of Edwards on the spiritual life of New England. 85222

Influence of freedom on popular and national education. 4618

Influence of history on individual and national action. 11729

Influence of intemperance on the moral sensibility. 92120

Influence of religion on liberty. 104908

Influence of scientific discovery and invention on social and political progress. 21427

Influence of slavery upon the white population. 34697

Influence of Sunday-schools at the west. 4618

Influence of temperance upon intellectual discipline. 80071

Influence of the Germans of the United States. 83962

Influence of the great war on shipping. 83376

Influence of the mechanic arts on the human race. 26797

Influence of the ministry. 76475

Influence of the ministry at large in the city of Boston. 3793

Influence of the railroads of the United States. (34696)

Influence of the United States abroad. 38308

Influence of the war on our national prosperity. 20513

Influence of tropical climates . . . on European constitutions; [being a treatise on the principal diseases.] 36225

Influence of tropical climates on European constitutions; including practical observations. (44886)

Influence of tropical climates on European constitutions. To which is added tropical hygiene. 36224

Influence of truth. 20193

Influence of virtue. 105056

Influence of woman upon the destinies of a people. 12850

Influence without intervention. 20391

Influences of democracy on liberty. 1299

Influences of western civilization of China. 80758

Informa a V. M. de los motivos de su dictamen. 79138

Informa en el pleyto que sigue con la parte. 98609

Informacao dada ao Ministro de Estado dos Negocios da Fazenda. 17953

Informacao, ou descripcao topographico e politica. 11706

Informacoes para servir de base a divisao dos bispados. 98828

Informacion. (63505)

Informacion en derecho. 99636

Informacion en qve se prveva aver sido de la Provincia de San Gabriel. 96978

Informacion para la historia. 34698

Informacion, presupuesto, bases y condiciones de la Compania de Minas. 94634

Informacion sobre reformas en Cuba y Puerto Rico. 66595

Informatie voorde rechtgeleerde. 27125, (37674)

Information about Texas. 7364

Information about the country. (9991)

Information acquired from the best authority. (35534)

Information and advice to emigrants. 47437

Information and direction to such persons. (59707), 102227

Information concernant l'affaire de Darien. 18558

Information concerning the present state of the slave trade. 81995

Information concerning the slave-trade. (34699)

Information exhibited by the Attorney-General. 37600

Information for army meetings, June, 1864. 34700

Inhabitant of the North-Western Territory.
pseud. Observations, on a letter from
George Nicholas. (55167)
Inhabitant of the state of Maryland. pseud.
Poetical epistle. see Wharton, Charles
Henry.
Inhabitant there. pseud. Sad and deplorable
news from New England. 74812-74813
Inhabitant there, a friend to truth and peace.
pseud. Brief narration of the practices.
see Welde, Thomas. supposed author
Inhabitants and Traders to the Aforesaid
Islands [of St. Christophers and Nevis.]
petitioners see Nevis. petitioners
and St. Christophers. petitioners
Inhabitants' Meeting Against the Change of the
Route of the Erie Canal, Schenectady,
1836. see Schenectady, N. Y. Inhabi-
tants' Meeting Against the Change of the
Route of the Erie Canal, 1836.
Inhabitants of Albany. see Albany. Citizens.
Inhabitants of Barbadoes. see Barbadoes.
Citizens.
Inhabitants of Bath, N. H. see Bath, N. H.
Citizens.
Inhabitants of Beaver County, Pa. see Beaver
County, Pa. Citizens.
Inhabitants of Boston and its Vicinity. see
Boston. Citizens.
Inhabitants of Boston, and the Country Adjacent.
see Boston. Citizens.
Inhabitants of Cambridge in New-England. see
Cambridge, Mass. Citizens.
Inhabitants of Canaan, N. H. see Canaan,
N. H. Citizens.
Inhabitants of Cardigan, N. H. see Cardigan,
N. H. Citizens.
Inhabitants of Dutchess County, N. Y. see
Dutchess County, N. Y. Citizens.
Inhabitants of Enfield, N. H. see Enfield,
N. H. Citizens.
Inhabitants of Hanover, N. H. see Hanover,
N. H. Citizens.
Inhabitnats of Haverhill, N. H. see Haverhill,
N. H. Citizens.
Inh[abitant]'s of Hingham vs. the inh[abitant]'s
of South Scituate. 88163
Inhabitants of His Majesty's Leeward-Caribbee-
Islands. pseud. Letter to the Right
Reverend the Lord Bishop of London.
see Robertson, Robert.
Inhabitants of Honduras. see Honduras.
Citizens.
Inhabitants of Landaff, N. H. see Landaff,
N. H. Citizens.
Inhabitants of Lime, N. H. see Lime, N. H.
Citizens.
Inhabitants of Lebanon, N. H. see Lebanon,
N. H. Citizens.
Inhabitants of Louisiana. see Louisiana.
Citizens.
Inhabitants of Machias, Maine. see Machias,
Maine. Citizens.
Inhabitants of Mecklenburg County, Va. see
Mecklenburg County, Va. Citizens.
Inhabitants of Michigan. see Michigan.
Citizens.
Inhabitants of New-Jersey. see New Jersey
(Colony) Citizens.
Inhabitants of New Orleans. see New Orleans.
Citizens.
Inhabitants of New York. see New York
(City) Citizens.
Inhabitants of Newberry District, S. C. see
Newberry District, S. C. Citizens.

Inhabitants of Newfoundland. see Newfound-
land. Citizens.
Inhabitants of Newport, R. Island, Distillers of
Rum and Importers of Molasses.
petitioners 55051
Inhabitants of North Carolina. see North
Carolina. Citizens.
Inhabitants of Northampton, Mass. see
Northampton, Mass. Citizens.
Inahbitants of Northampton County, Pa. see
Northampton County, Pa. Citizens
Inhabitants of Otsego County, N. Y. see
Otsego County, N. Y. Citizens.
Inhabitants of Oxford, N. H. see Oxford,
N. H. Citizens
Inhabitants of Pennsylvania. see Pennsyl-
vania. Citizens.
Inhabitants of Pennsylvania. (61742)
Inhabitants of Pennsylvania Settled on Lands
Claimed by Connecticut. see Penn-
sylvania. Inhabitants, Settled on Lands
Claimed by Connecticut.
Inhabitants of Pernambuco. see Pernambuco.
Citizens.
Inhabitants of Petersburg, Va. see Peters-
burg, Va. Citizens.
Inhabitants of Philadelphia. see Philadelphia.
Citizens.
Inhabitnats of Plainfield, N. H. see Plain-
field, N. H. Citizens.
Inhabitants of Queens County, N. Y. see
Queens County, N. Y. Citizens.
Inhabitants of Richland District, S. C. see
Richland District, S. C. Citizens.
Inhabitants of Rochester, Interested in the Use
of the Waters of the Genesee, for Hy-
draulic Purposes. see Rochester, N. Y.
Inhabitants Interested in the Use of the
Waters of the Genesee, for Hydraulic
Purposes.
Inhabitants of Salem, Mass. see Salem, Mass.
Citizens.
Inhabitants of Schenectady. see Schenectady,
N. Y. Citizens.
Inhabitants of South Carolina. see South
Carolina. Citizens.
Inhabitants of Spanish Town, Jamaica. see
Spanish Town, Jamaica. Citizens.
Inhabitants of Sullivan County, N. Y. see
Sullivan County, N. Y. Citizens.
Inhabitants of the city of New York, having
broke their non-importation agreement.
61922
Inhabitants of the city of Schenectada, [sic]
N. Y. see Schenectady, N. Y. Citizens.
Inhabitants of the District of Niagara. see
Niagara (District), Ontario. Citizens.
Inhabitants of the Mississippi Territory. see
Mississippi (Territory) Citizens
Inhabitants of the Plantation and Colony of the
Sommer-Islands. see Bermuda Com-
pany.
Inhabitants of the Territory of Orleans. see
Louisiana (Territory) Citizens.
Inhabitants of the town of Plainfield, N. H.
see Plainfield, N. H. Citizens.
Inhabitants of the town of Salem, Mass. see
Salem, Mass. Citizens.
Inhabitants of the town of Sutton, Mass. see
Sutton, Mass. Town Meeting, Jan. 27,
1777.
Inhabitants of the town of Sutton, in legal town-
meeting assembled. 93981
Inhabitants of this city are desired. 95975
Inhabitants of Waterford, N. Y. see Water-
ford, N. Y. Citizens.

Inhabitants of West Florida. see Florida (Territory) Citizens.

Inhabitants of Westchester County, N. Y. see Westchester County, N. Y. Citizens.

Inhabitants of Wyoming and others.. see Allen, Ethan, of Pennsylvania, fl. 1786. and Franklin, John, fl. 1786. and Jenkins, John, fl. 1786.

Inhabitants on the Niagara Frontier. see Niagara (District), Ontario. Citizens.

Inheritance of principles. (12406)

Inheritance to children's children. 3795

Inhuman torture!! 62682

Iniciativa del H. Congreso de Zacatecas. 34412

Iniciativa que dirig. al Congreso. 56453

Iniciativa que la Honorable Legislatura de Queretaro. 67106

Iniciativa que para impedir la importacion. 66558

Iniciativa y esposicion que dirigieron la Congreso. 34413, 98624

Iniciativas presentadas a la Camara de Diputados. 48503

Inigo, J. 34781

Inimitable and incomprehensible doggrel poem. 97110

Iniquities of New York. 54096

Iniquity. (29830)

Iniquity abounding. 14043

Iniquity exposed. 103780

Iniquity of licensed injustice. (81839)

Iniquity purged by mercy and truth. 34059

Iniquity unfolded. 23681

Initiate emancipation. 2191

Initiatory discourse. 32531

Initvm. sapiente. Timor. Domini obra compuesta por Lucio Marineo. 44586

Injunction case. 96811

Injurious effects of protective and prohibitory duties. 7255

Injurious effects of slave labour. 81996

Injurious tendency of the proposed slave registry bill. 34782

Injury done them by slavery. 64093

Injustice and cruelty of the slave trade considered. (47818)

Injustice and impolicy of the slave trade. 21968

Injustice and inexpediency of that tax examined. 84443

Injustice in permiting the Rev. John M'Millan to escape. 5529

Injustice towards neutrals. 8514

Inkle and Yarico: an opera. 14526, note after 105986

Inklings: containing sketches of life. 64976

Inklings of adventure. 104507

Inland navigation. 94813

Inland monthly. 85451

Inland sea. 16493

Inleiding van den vertaler. 72205

Inlets and outlets. 82389

Inleydinge van de autheur. (20593), note after 98474

Inleydinghe tot den gunstighen leser. 77934

Inlichting over de huano of guano van Peru en Bolivia. (6452)

Inman, Henry. 34783

Inman, John. 14867, 34784, 46940-46941

Inman. firm publishers see Fisher and Inman. firm publishers

Inmigracion de trabajadores Espanoles. 87249

Inmutable. 79182

Inn of rest. Later poems. 83601

Inner and outer life of Miranda Elliot. 47056

Inner life of Abraham Lincoln. 10989

Inner light and culture. (64668)

Inner life of the V. M. I. cadet. (82554)

Innern Communicationen der Vereinigten Staaten von Nordamerika. (27197)

Innes, John. 34785-34787

Innes, R. Prescott. see Prescott-Innes, R.

Innes, William. (34788)-34789, 50995, 82068, 82204, 2d, 4th notes after 102785

Innocency vindicated. (28044)

Innocent X, Pope, 1574-1655. 7704, 34790, 56265, 58280, (77142) see also Catholic Church. Pope, 1644-1655 (Innocent X)

Innocent XI, Pope, 1611-1689. 23039, 62601, (68842), 68845, 72528, 76275, 93581, 96052 see also Catholic Church. Pope, 1676-1689 (Innocent XI)

Innocent XII, Pope, 1615-1700. 68849 see also Catholic Church. Pope, 1691-1700 (Innocent XII)

Innocent XIII, Pope, 1655-1824. 68249 see also Catholic Church. Pope, 1721-1724 (Innocent XIII)

Innocent amusements. 77310

Innocent blood crying to God. 39184

Innokentii. see Veniaminov, Ioann Yevseyevich.

Innub nangminek isumaliornera Gudib'lo tekkotinera. 91171

Inocencia vindicada. (36797)

Inoculacion de las viruelas. 87150

Inoculation in Antigua. 25685

Inoculation of the small pox as practiced in Boston. 34793, 46744

Inoculation. The abuses and scandals of some late pamphlets. (34791)

Inoffensive ministry described. 25042

Inordinate love of the world inconsistent with the love of God. 22129

Inorganic forces ordained to supersede human slavery. 23312

Inquietudes de los Indios sus naturales. 11424, 50109, note after 96260

Inquirer. 34794

Inquirer after truth. pseud. Letters to Rev. Moses Stuart. see Balfour, Walter.

Inquiries addressed to Parson Brownlow. (33242)

Inquiries by the Agricultural Society. 45774

Inquiries from a friend. 73391

Inquiries into the origin, institution, and proper mode. 93741

Inquiries into the probability that the historical part. (33290)

Inquiries occasioned by the address. (52836), 105328

Inquiries of a freeholder. 26680

Inquiries of an emigrant. 34795, 62640

Inquiries relating to Negro emancipation. 34796

Inquiries respecting the author. 36912

Inquiries, respecting the history, present condition, and future prospects. 34661, (77856)

Inquiries respecting the history, traditions, languages, manners, customs, religion, &c. 11348

Inquiries with reference to the disposition of hospital supplies. 76644

Inquiry after his capacity for self-government. 89784

Inquiry concerning the future state. 32949

Inquiry concerning the trade, commerce, and policy of Jamaica. 35590

Inquiry how to prevent the small-pox. 31031

Inquiry into scriptural and ancient servitude. (82436)

Inquiry into some of the geological phenomena. (31008)

Inquiry into the accordancy of war. 21606

Inquiry into the alleged tendency of the separation of convicts. 34797, 58108

Inquiry into the American Colonization and American Anti-slavery Societies. 68657

Inquiry into the authenticity of documents. 84382

Inquiry into the best mode of supplying the city. 6785

Inquiry into the cause of social evil. 96395

Inquiry into the cause of the prosperity. 88822

Inquiry into the causes and consequences of the Orders in Council. 3384

Inquiry into the causes and cost of corrup [sic] state legislatuion. 34798

Inquiry into the causes and nature of the yellow fever. 102177

Inquiry into the causes and origin of slavery in the United States. 34799

Inquiry into the causes of our naval miscarrages. 34800

Inquiry into the causes of the differences in climate. 22953

Inquiry into the causes of . . . the insurrection in Grenada. (28752)

Inquiry into the causes of the insurrection of the Negroes. 75135

Inquiry into the causes of the present state. 67503

Inquiry into the causes of the public distress. 34801, 39383

Inquiry into the causes of the rise and fall of the lakes. 27332

Inquiry into the causes that have retarded the prosperity. 56956

Inquiry into the causes which have affected the prospects and condition. (54729)

Inquiry into the causes which have retarded the accumulation of wealth. (27860), 34802, 81997

Inquiry into the causes which led to the dissentions. (62214)

Inquiry into the causes which produce and the means of preventing diseases. 4455

Inquiry into the character and tendency of the American Colonization and American Anti-slavery Societies. 35857, (35865)

Inquiry into the colonial policy of the European powers. 8409

Inquiry into the commercial policy of the United States. 32724, 34803, 80642

Inquiry into the comparative moral tendency. 88975

Inquiry into the condition and prospects of the African race. (34804)

Inquiry into the conduct of Great Britain in the present affairs. (34805)

Inquiry into the consequences attending them. 42156

Inquiry into the consequences both of Calvinistic and Armenian principles. 20063

Inquiry into the constitution of the visible Church of Chirst. 46769

Inquiry into the constitutionality of military reserves. 34806

Inquiry into the distinct rights of the officers and people. 55301

Inquiry into the distinctive characteristics of the aboriginal race. 51023

Inquiry into the effects of ardent spirits. note after 74241

Inquiry into the effects of our foreign carrying trade. 50335

Inquiry into the effects of public punishments. 74223

Inquiry into the effects of putting a stop to the African slave trade. 67715

Inquiry into the effects of spirituous liquors. note after 74241

Inquiry into the equal rights of the state. 82802

Inquiry into the evidence relating to the charges brought. 58172-(58173)

Inquiry into the expediency of dispensing with bank agency. 28072

Inquiry into the fitness of attending Parliament. 34807

Inquiry into the formation of Washington's farewell address. 5477

Inquiry into the foundations of government. (31785)

Inquiry into the importance of the militia. 93712

Inquiry into the influence of physical causes upon the moral faculty. (74235)-47236, note after 74241

Inquiry into the itineracy. 32316

Inquiry into the lawfulness of slavery. 106004

Inquiry into the laws of organized societies. 24511

Inquiry into the laws which determine the value 91851

Inquiry into the means of preventing the evils. (71765)

Inquiry into the medical efficacy of a new species. 69366

Inquiry into the merits of the American Colonization Society. 32351, 93132

Inquiry into the merits of the principal naval actions. 35719

Inquiry into the moral and religious character. 101439

Inquiry into the natural history of medicine among the Indians. 74224, (74226)

Inquiry into the natural rights of man. 34808

Inquiry into the nature and benefits of an agricultural survey. 87373

Inquiry into the nature and causes of the great mortality. 43512

Inquiry into the nature and causes of the present disputes. 34809

Inquiry into the nature and causes of the wealth of nations. 64823, 82302-(82305)

Inquiry into the nature and character of ancient and modern slavery. 82203

Inquiry into the nature and design of Christ's temptation. 92161

Inquiry into the nature and results of the slaveholding system. 31773

Inquiry into the nature and tendency of speculative free masonry. 90894, 90896-90897

Inquiry into the nature and treatment of the prevailing epidemic. 104648

Inquiry into the nature and use of political sovereignty. 20174

Inquiry into the nature and uses of money. 20723, 34810, 4th note after 98549

Inquiry into the nature of value and of capital. 36162

Inquiry into the nature, results, and legal basis of the slave-holding system. 31774

Inquiry into the necessity and general principles of reorganization. 56599

Inside out; or, an interior view of the New York State Prison. 14157

Inside out, or rougery exposed. 38999

Inside view. 79174

Inside view of Mexico and California. 104892-104893

Inside view of slavery. 58875

Inside view of the rebellion. 15626

Inside view of the southern sentiment. 4785

Inside view of the W——— inquisition. 105339

Inside views of slavery on southern plantations. 72816

Insidious attack on Mr. Borch. 6399

Insight into the discovery. 50812

Insigne victoria que el Senor Marquez de Guadalcazar. 34819

Insignes missioneros de la Compania de Jesvs. 105716

Insignis & admiranda historia. (8784)

Insinuatie, protestie, ende presentatie. 98544

Insinuator. 97782

Inskip, John S. 34820

Insolvent laws of Massachusetts. 18171

Insolvent register. (34821)

Inspectors of the Free Ports of Gaspe and Sault Ste. Marie. see Canada. Inspectors of the Free Ports of Gaspe and Sault Ste. Marie.

Inspirational discourse. 30340

Inspired translation. 80134

Instability. A poem. 67465, note after 105488

Instability of humane greatness. 30174

Installation address . . . to St. Paul Lodge. 82294

Installation of Reverend Edward Mitchell. 49681

Installation sermon [by Stephen Sanford Smith.] 84293

Installation sermon [by Thomas Wentworth Higginson.] 31755

Installation service. 87008

Installation services of Rev. William J. Hoge. 32435, note after 89770

Installment law. 87645

Instances of navigators who have reached high northern latitudes. 3630

Instances of the effects of sudden joy. 93034

Instellinge ae Generale Compagnie. 7590

Institucion Agronoma, Havana. 74928

Institvcion, modo de rezar, y milagros. 94221

Instituciones de derecho canonico Americano. 20606

Instituciones de derecho real de Castilla y de Indias. 979

Instituciones del derecho civil de Castilla. 103429

Instituicoes de direito civil Lusitano. 42346

Institut Canadien de Quebec. 66997

Institut des Archives Historiques, Paris. see Paris. Institut des Archives Historiques.

Institut des Archives Historiques. Abbot Lawrence. (39344)

Institut Francais de Washington. 1st note after 100572, 100837

Institut Historique, Paris. 69655-69656

Institut National des Sciences et Arts, Paris. see Paris. Institut National des Sciences et Arts.

Institut Royal, Paris. Academie des Sciences. see Academie des Sciences, Paris.

Instituta criminal teorico-practica. 52252

Instituta ordinis Beati Francisci. 34823

Institute, Albany, N. Y. see Albany Institute, Albany, N. Y.

Institute, East Windsor, Conn. see Hartford Theological Seminary.

Institute, Flushing, N. Y. see St. Paul's College, Flushing, N. Y.

Institute, Philadelphia. see Philadelphia Institute.

Institute, West Philadelphia, Pa. see West Philadelphia Institute.

Institute for Colored Youth, Philadelphia. 56425, 61743

Institute for Colored Youth, Philadelphia. Library. 61743

Institute for colored youth. 61743

Institute for Savings, Worcester, Mass. see Worcester County Institute for Savings, Worcester, Mass.

Institute for the Education of the Blind in Indiana. see Indiana. School for the Blind, Indinapolis.

Institute for the Education of the Deaf and Dumb in Maryland. see Maryland. State School for the Deaf, Frederick.

Institute for the Instruction of the Blind in Maryland. see Maryland. School for the Blind, Baltimore.

Institute for the Instruction of the Blind in Ohio. see Ohio State School for the Blind, Columbus.

Institute for the Promotion and Encouragement of the Arts of South Carolina. see South Carolina Institute.

Institute for the Promotion of the Mechanic Arts in Maryland. see Maryland Institute for the Promotion of the Mechanic Arts.

Institute of Education in Maryland. see Maryland Institute of Education

Institute of Education in Rhode Island. see Rhode Island Institute of Education.

Institute of Natural Sciences, Halifax, N. S. see Nova Scotian Institute of Natural Sciences, Halifax.

Institute of Reward for Orphans of Patriots in Rhode Island. see Rhode Island Institute of Reward.

Institute of Science, Delaware County, pa. see Delaware County, Pa. Institute of Science.

Institute of Science and Arts, Dubuque, Iowa. see Iowa Institute of Science and Arts, Dubuque.

Institutes of American law. 6981

Institutes of international law, public and private. 26640

Institutes of the civil law of Spain. 103429

Institution, New York. see New York Institution, New York.

Institution and first proceedings of the Society for the Encouragement of Arts. 34825, 3d note after 85897

Institution and proceedings of the Society of the Cincinnati. 13124

Institution considered in regard to its influence. (73917)

Institution, &c. Published for the use of the members. 86128

Institution for Feeble Minded Children, Syracuse, N. Y. see New York (State) Institution for Feeble Minded Children, Syracuse.

Institution for Feeble-Minded Chilrden in Kentucky. see Kentucky. Institution for the Education of Feeble-Minded Children, Frankfort.

Institution for Savings, Worcester County, Mass. see Worcester County Institute for Savings, Worcester, Mass.

Institution for the Blind, Batavia, N. Y. see New York (State) State School for the Blind, Batavia.

Institution for the Blind, New York. see New York Institution for the Blind.

Institution for the Deaf and Dumb, Fulton, Mo. see Missouri School for the Deaf, Fulton, Mo.

Institution for the Deaf and Dumb, Jackson, Miss. see Mississippi. School for the Deaf, Jackson.

Institution for the Deaf and Dumb and the Blind, Raleigh, N. C. see North Carolina. School for the Deaf and Dumb, Raleigh. and North Carolina. School for the Blind, Raleigh.

Institution for the Deaf and Dumb of Kentucky. see Kentucky. School for the Deaf, Danville.

Institution for the Deaf and Dumb of Minnesota. see Minnesota. School for the Deaf, Farribault.

Institution for the Education of the Deaf and Dumb, Farribault, Minn. see Minnesota. School for the Deaf, Farribault.

Institution for the Education of the Deaf and Dumb in Illinois. see Illinois. School for the Deaf, Jacksonville.

Institution for the Education of the Deaf and Dumb of Ohio. see Ohio State school for the Deaf, Columbus.

Institution for the Instruction of the Blind in Pennsylvania. see Pennsylvania Institution for the Instruction of the Blind.

Institution for the Instruction of the Deaf and Dumb, New York. see New York Institution for the Instruction of the Deaf and Dumb.

Institution of Civil Engineers, London. (41693)

Institution of Civil Engineers of New York State. see New York State Institution of Civil Engineers.

Institution of slavery, viewed in the light of divine truth. 31013

Institution of the Boston Dispensary, for the Medical Relief of the Poor. 6698

Institution of the Humane Society of the Commonwealth of Massachusetts. 33681, 45765

Institution of the Merrimack Humane Society; with the rules. 48012

Institution of the New York State Society of Cincinnati. 86120

Institution of the Society, in New York. 19939, (32948), 81956)

Institution of the Society of the Cincinati, formed by the officers of the American army, at its cantonment. 13126

Institution of the Society of the Cincinnati, formed by the officers of the American army of the revolution. 13125

Institution of the Society of the Cincinnati. Formed by the officers of the army of the United States, for the laudible purposes. (13121)

Institution of the Society of the Cincinnati. Formed by the officers of the army of the United States. Published by order. 13123

Institution of the Society of the Cincinnati. Organization of the state society of Pennsylvania. 86126

Institution of the Society of the Cincinnati. . . . Published by order and for the use of the members. 13122

Institution of the Society of the Cincinnati. Together with the roll. 13127

Institution of the Society of the Cincinnati, with the bye-laws and rules of the New-Jersey State Society. 86116

Institutions de l'histoire du Canada. 5150, (5153)

Institutions geographiques. 71872

Instituto Brasileiro de Historico e Geographico, Rio de Janeiro. see Brazil. Instituto Brasileiro de Historico e Geographico.

Instituto Cubano. 17780, note just before 34721, 42745

Instituto da Ordem dos Advogados Brasileiros. 47754

Instituto historico geographico e ethnographico do Brasil, fundado no Rio de Janeiro. 34826

Instituto Literario, Toluca, Mexico. 47036

Instituto Literario de Mexico. Colegio y Escuelas Lancasterianas, San Agustin de las Cuevas, Mexico. 99623

Instituto Nacional de Geografia y Estadistica Mexicana. see Sociedad Mexicana de Geografica y Estadistica.

Instituto Polytechnico Brasileiro, Rio de Janeiro. Commissao de Redaccao. 70312

Instituto y Hacienda Normal Para la Ensenanza de la Agricultura de la Republica del Peru en Lima. 74816

Instruccao publica. 85652

Instruccion a curas y ecclesiasticos de las Indias. (948)

Instruccion a que deben arreglarse los Senores Gobernadores. 98320

Instruccion aprobada por el Rey. 66596

Instruccion de la lengua Latina. 57578

Instruccion de litigantes. (75770)

Instruccion de los Comisionadores de la Direccion General. 34827

Instruccion del metodo con que repartirse a los Indios. 41114

Instruccion exacta, y util de las derrotas. 21770, (55396)

Instruccion familiar que muestra de que modo se producen. 77355

Instruccion formada en virtud de Real orden se S. M. 48504

Instruccion general para los Capitanes y Tenientes de partido. 17783

Instruccion nautica que acompana a la carta. 34828

Instruccion para el arreglo de conoscer y proceder. (29084)

Instruccion para el gobierno de la Real Aduana de Mar. 34829

Instruccion para el gobierno interior y buen regimen. 34830

Instruccion para formar una linea o cordon. 56252

Instruccion para hacer versos Latinos. 72536

Instruccion para jeneralizar el cultivo de la morera. 74817

Instruccion para las ayuntamientos constitucionales. 34831

Instruccion para que los administradores de aduanas hagan. 99652

Instruccion para que se liquiden las cuentas generales. 34832

Instruccion para reducir facilmente las pesas y medios extrangeras. 34833

Instruccion pastoral del Illmo. Senor Don Francisco Xavier de Lizana y Beaumont. 41662

Instruccion pastoral sobre el metodo practico. 16969

Instruccion pastoral sobre la indulgencia plenaria. 73871

Instruccion practica y provisional en forma de advertencias. 76306

Instruccion previa [sic] sobre el papel periodico. (65556)

Instruccion (primera y segunda), que puede tenerse presente. 12775

Instruccion primaria. 76148

Instruccion que debe observarse para el arreglo. 48505

Instruccion que debia observar el Capitan Hernando de Alarcon. 84379

Instruccion reglamentaria aprobada por S. M. (66597)

Instruccion reservada que el Conde de Revilla Gigedo. 70288

Instruccion sobre caminos. 86818

Instruccion sobre el cultivo del nopal y cria. 34834

Instruccion sobre el remedio de las lagartijas. (40063)-40064

Instruccion y arte para regular el oficio divino. 34853

Instruccion, y doctrina de novicios. 98737

Instruccion y forma que se ha de tener. 34836

Instruccion y metodo con que se ha de establecer el Hospital. 34837

Instruccion, y practica de la navigation. 71632

Instrucciones dogmatico-morales. 71249

Instrucciones para el Jusgado de Bienes de Difuntos. 48506

Instrucciones para la constitucion fundamental. (34838)

Instrucciones para la cria cientifica de ovejas. 28804

Instrucciones para la eleccion de diputados. 93781

Instrucciones que dio el Presidente de los Estados Unidos del Norte America. 63695, 63697, 88939, 97913, 97925

Instrucciones que los Virreyes de Nueva Espana dejaron. 34839

Instrucciones secretas de los Jesuitas. (49981)

Instrucciones y senales para el regimen y maniobras de Escuadra. 75587

Instrucc,oens, que os Padres, que governao os Indios, ihres derao. 63895

Intruccoes para os viajantes e empregados nas colonias. 34840

Instruccoes secretas que devem, guardar todos os Religiosos da Companhia. 49980

Instructer's [sic] assistant. 104045

Instrvctio manvdvctionem prestans in cartam itinerariam Martini Hilacomili. 101025-101026

Instruction a F. de Al. Mendonza. 47823

Instruction familiere. 77354

Instruction for field artillery; compiled from standard military authority. 90511

Instruction for field artillery, extracted from Gilham's memorial. 27379

Instruction for heavy artillery. (34841)

Instruction for naval light artillery. 58776

Instruction for officers on outposts and patrol duty. 34842

Instruction from the grave. 51261

Instruction generale pour ce qui regarde le commerce. (77270)

Instruction nauthica, y vocabulario nautico. 58269

Instruction nautique de los passages a l'isle de Cuba. 17784

Instruction nautique et locale pour les voyages a la Guyane Francaise. 63890

Instruction nautique pour se rendre d'Europe. 34843

Instruction nautique sur les cotes de la Guiane Francaise. 39104

Instruction nautique sur les passages a l'ile de Cuba. 91186

Instruction nouvelle des poincts plus excellentes. (14234)

Instrvction oder Anleitung. 98196

Instruction pour faciliter l'execution de ladite declaration. 19167

Instruction pour les colonies Francoises. 14713, 34844

Instruction pour les isles de Saint Domingue. 75098

Instruction pour leur defence. 93823

Instruction tres-exacte pour ceux qui ont dessein. 102226

Instructions. 100491

Instructions adressees a MM. les Governeurs des colonies. 67154

Instructions and forms for the guidance of post-masters. 94990

Instructions and forms to be observed in applying for army pensions. 34845

Instructions and observations relative to the navigation. 5617

Instructions and tables of the Superintendent of Education. 10433

Instructions by the Commissioners of His Majesty's Customs, for the due collection of His Majesty's Revenue of Customs in America. 34847

Instructions by the Commissioners of His Majesty's Customs in America. 34848

Instructions by the Commissioners of His Majesty's Customs in America, to [blank] who is appointed [blank] of the customs. (34849)

Instructions by the Commissioners of His Majesty's Customs in America to Robert Trail, Esq. 34846

Instructions concerning the tax on legacies. 34850

Instructions de l'Assemblee Generale Coloniale. 95733

Instructions for children. (46211)

Instructions for collecting, testing, melting and assaying gold. (37469)

Instructions for collectors of taxes. 15275

Instructions for colporteurs of the Presbyterian Board of Publication. 65192

Instructions for forming a battalion for review of parade. 98517

Instructions for gentlemen, merchants, students, souldiers, marriners, &c. 36594

Instructions for missionaries to the West India islands. 102840

Instructions for research. (27302)

Instructions for sailing through the several passages. 72996

Instructions for school-masters. 85934

Instructions for taking the census of the state. 53703

Instructions for the agents for collecting subscriptions to the produce loan. (15276), (34851)

Instructions for the better government and organization of common schools. 30981, 53704

Instructions for the cavalry. 98518

Instructions for the clergy. 85934

Instructions for the clergy employ'd by the Society for the Propagation of the Gospel in Foreign Parts. 85937

Instructions for the collectors and comptrollers in America. 34852

Instructions for the collectors of the war tax. 15418

Instructions for the commanders of merchant ships. 34853

Instructions for the cultivating and raising of flax and hemp. 81701

Instructions for the Deputies appointed to meet in General Congress. 100008

Instructions for the expedition towards the North Pole. 72024

Instructions for the government of the armies of the United States. 40985

Instructions for the guidance of Her Majesty's naval officers. 34854

Instructions for the guidance of the medical officers. 34855

Instrvctions for the increasing of mulberie trees. 90110

Instructions for the management of a plantation in Barbadoes. 3272

Instructions for the members of the Unitas Fratrum. 50522

Instructions for the treating with the Indians. (34857)

Instructions for the treatment of Negroes, &c. &c. &c. 34856, 81999

Instructions for the use of public schools. 53132

Instructions for treating with the Eastern Indians. (34857), 62579

Instructions for youth, gentlemen and noblemen. 67599

[Instructions from Executive to naval officers.] 100215

Instructions from the General Assembly of Virginia, to Stephens Thompson Mason. 100078

Instructions from the General Assembly of Virginia, to their Senators in Congress. 15005, 100077

Instructions from the inhabitants of the Territory of Orleans. 53331

Instructions from the Prudential Committee. 34858

Instructions from the Regents of the University of the State of New York, to the several colleges. 30981

Instructions from the Regents of the University to the several academies. (54000)

Instructions from the Secretary of State. 9260

Instructions from the Society, for the Propagation of the Gospel in Foreign Parts. 85938

Instructions generales pour naviguer dans les differents oceans. 46974

Instructions given by M. O. de Santangelo to his counsel. 76831

Instructions given by the President of the United States of America. 56524, 63694, 88939, 97925

Instructions given with a commission for seizing the ships, etc. 34859

Instructions how the piety of singing. 46212

Instructions in preparing soldiers' pay. 34860

Instructions nautiques destinees a accompagner les carts. 46964

Instructions nautiques, relatives aux cartes et plans. 34862

Instructions nautiques sur la cote du Perou. 26558

Instructions nautiques sur les cotes de la Guyane Francaise. 29175

Instructions nautiques sur les cotes de la Platagonie. 27828

Instructions nautiques sur les cotes et les debouquemens de Saint-Domingue. 12236

Instructions nautiques sur les cotes occidentales d'Amerique, de la Riviere Tumbez a Panama. (24627)

Instructions nautiques sur les cotes occidentales d'Amerique, du Golfe de Penas a la Riviere Tumbez. (24628)

Instructions nautiques sur les cotes occidentales de l'Amerique du Sud. 24626

Instructions of a father to his son. 67599

Instructions of May, 1764. 57866

Instructions of the School Committee, 1805. (28960)

Instructions, of 22d February, 1775. 26317

Instructions on how to obtain letters patent for new inventions. 51340

Instructions on the erection of four new Catholic episcopal sees. 34863

Instructions pour naviguer sur le cote meridionale de Terre-Nueve. 34864

Instructions, reports, and journals. 49776

Instructions showing what classes of persons are entitled. 73253

Instructions sur la port de Vera-Cruz et ses environs. 21393

Instructions to and dispatches from the late and present ministers. 34866

Instructions to be observed for the formation. (18748)

Instructions to Charles Cotesworth Pinckney. 34865

Instructions to Citizen Genet. (26931)

Instructions to emigrants. 22500, 40594, 86187, 2d note after 98076

Instructions to emigrants: an attempt to give a correct account. 55379

Instructions to general inspectors. 76577, 76647

Instructions to General Jessup. 34867

Instructions to his [i. e. Sir Walter Raleigh's] son. 67572, 67598

Instructions to his sonne; and the son's advice to his aged father. 67272-67273

Instructions to his sonne: and to posteritie. 67578

Instructions to his sonne; and to posterity. (67579), 57599

Instructions to inspectors on campaign duties. 34868

Instructions to Mr. Slidell. (29856)

Instructions to mustering officers and others. 34869

Instructions to our trusty and vvell-beloved Coll. Vetch. 99390

Instructions to the agent sent out by President Boyer. (16894), (29576)

Instructions to the American Plenipotentiaries. 53975, 90639

Instructions to the Collectors of the Washington National Monument Society. 102033

Instructions to the commanders of private ships of war. 15527

Instructions to the commanders of private ships or vessels of war. 15537

Instructions to the Commissioners. 90709

[Instructions to the delegates representing this commonwealth.] 100086

Interest of the country in laying no duties.
34882-(34884), 97562, 100770, 106314
Interest of the merchants and manufacturers
of Great Britain. 34885
Interest of the nation, as it respects all the
sugar plantations abroad. 34886, note
after 102840
Interest of the state in the health and longevity
of the people. 35803, 46043, 47656
Interest table and counting-house almanack.
8680
Interested members. 45961
Interesting account of Buell's occupation of
Tennessee. 8702
Interesting account of several remarkable
visions. 64955, 64959, 83287
Interesting account of the early voyages.
(34887)
Interesting account of the engagement. 2291
Interesting account of the plague. 34888
Interesting account of the project of France.
34889
Interesting account of the voyages and travels.
24508
Interesting account of this wonderful, newly
discovered animal. 89599
Interesting account of those extraordinary
people. (22858), (34890)
Interesting accounts of prison life. 6292,
6861
Interesting additions by a merchant. 26827,
note after 96426
Interesting and authentic narrative of the
abduction. 97955, note after 103826
Interesting and authentic narrative of the most
remarkable shipwrecks. 95441
Interesting and authentic narratives of the most
remarkable shipwrecks. 95444
Interesting and important correspondence
between the opposition members. 6831,
59004
Interesting and remarkable account of the
terrible sufferings. 14335
Interesting appendix. (2489), (67952)
Interesting appendix to Sir William Blackstone's
Commentaries. 5697
Interesting biographical sketch of the Lilli-
putian king. 78412
Interesting book of tales. 88948
Interesting collection of modern lives. 34891
Interesting controversy between Rev. Clark
Brown. 92785
Interesting correspondence. 88642, 97949
Interesting correspondence, between citizens
of Elizabeth City County. 98413
Interesting correspondence between His Excel-
lency Governour Sullivan and Col.
Pickering. 62650, note before 93501
Interesting correspondence between Lord
Buchan and our illustrious fellow-citizen.
101755
Interesting correspondence between the Rev.
John Johnson. 36235
Interesting correspondence. Letter from Mr.
Richard Rush. 74253
Interesting correspondence. Letter of Com-
modore Stockton. 91896
Interesting debate at the reception of Gov.
Andrew Johnson. 60164
Interesting description of British America.
66418
Interesting description of the city of Buenos
Ayres. 34892
Interesting detail of the operations of the
American fleet. 21743

Interesting documents. Containing an account
of the federal procession. 51471
Interesting essays, chiefly on the subject of
the yellow fever. 62410
Interesting ether cases. 4107
Interesting events in the history of the United
States. (3326)
Interesting experiences while traveling as a
colporteur. 85520
Interesting extracts from Connecticut records.
6010
Interesting extracts, historical and fictitious.
34893
Interesting facts on the subject of taxing.
34901
Interesting history of Charles Mortimer. 98455
Interesting history of the Baron de Lovzinski.
42358
Interesting incidents in the history of several
of the converts. 34894
Interesting journal of Abner Stocking. 91883
Interesting journal of Mr. Charles Le Raye.
18170, 3d note after 96185
Interesting life and adventures of General
Israel Putnam. 66804
Interesting life, travels, voyages, and daring
engagements. 36546
Interesting life, travels, voyages, and daring
engagements of that celebrated and justly
renouned commander Paul Jones. 36548
Interesting life, travels, voyages, and daring
engagements, of the celebrated Paul Jones.
36547
Interesting memoirs and documents relating to
American slavery. 82000
Interesting narrative of Mary Jamison. 105548
Interesting narrative of the captivity and
sufferings of Philip Brigdon. 29767
Interesting narrative of the great success
attending the judicious exertions. 84358
Interesting narrative of the life, and missionary
labours of Joshua Marsden. 44714
Interesting narrative, of the life of John
Marrant. 44677
Interesting narrative of the life of 'Olaudah
Equiano. 22714, 98661
Interesting narrative of the loss of the ship
Milo. 94056
Interesting narrative of the murder of John
Love. 95264
Interesting narrative of the sufferings and
singular adventures of Miss Meonora
Siddons. 80851
Interesting narrative . . . of the sufferings of
Mr. Joseph Barker. 34895
Interesting narrative of the voyage, shipwreck,
and . . . adventures of Mr. Drake Morris.
50809
Interesting narratives and discoveries. 34896
Interesting narratives of extraordinary
sufferings and deliverances. 34897
Interesting official documents. 10775, (34898),
note after 98877
Interesting original letter from General
Washington to his lady. 101738
Interesting papers illustrative of the riots.
34899
Interesting papers relative to the recent riots.
3038
Interesting particulars of the loss of the
American ship Hercules. 92352
Interesting political discussion. 42451
Interesting public documents and official
correspondence. (12937)
Interesting report of the rise and progress of
the Protestant Episcopal Church. 26505

Interesting revolutionary incidents and
sketches of character. 11168
Interesting sketch of the life and death of
Doctor Harry I. Todd. 104645
Interesting sketch of the life of Dr. H[enry]
T[odd.] 104644
Interesting Spanish tales. 105178
Interesting state papers. 34900, 2d note after
101709
Interesting story, founded on fact. 84129-
84130, 1st note after 94758
Interesting story of Mrs. Eliza Williamson.
104447
Interesting tale for children. 85575
Interesting tracts, relating to the island of
Jamaica. 35591
Interesting trial! (60165), 83762
Interesting trial of Edward Jordan. 36643
Interesting trials of the pirates. 41527, 7th
note after 96930A
Interests of agriculture and commerce,
inseparable. 42720
Interests of the country and the prosperity of
the West India planters mutually secured.
17617, 70259, 102841, 3d note after
102863
Interests of the several princes and states of
Europe Consider'd. (34902)
Interet Francaise dans la Plata. 19434
Interets coloniaux envisages dans leur rapport.
38589
Interets coloniaux, souvenirs de voyages.
16802, 38493
Interets des colonies Hollandoises du sud de
l'Amerique. 34903, 38763, 75005
Interets des nations de l'Europe. 14966A,
(79233)-79234
Interets des puissances continentales relative-
ment a l'Angleterre. 95320
Interets des puissances de l'Europe. 73493
Interets Francais et Europeens a Santo-
Domingo. (6310), (75136)
Interets presens et les pretentions des
puissances de l'Europe. 73494
Interference of the British legislature.
(34904), note after 102841, 106285
Interference of the executive in the affairs.
70725
Interference theory of government. 8043
Interiano, Paulo. 34905
Interianus, Gregorius. see Gregorius
Interianus.
Interim. 32747
Interior cabinet laid open. 36936
Interior causes of the war. 34906
Interior view of Port Hudson. 8335
Interior view of the New York State Prison.
14157
Interlocutory exercise at the South Grammar
School. 42378, 78670
Interlude, called "The metamorphosis." 20314,
94403
Intermediate or secondary geography. 49722
Intermediate standard speaker. 76966
Interment of the dead. 17699
Intermittent periodical. (36983)
Internal condition of the American democracy
considered. 43264
Internal evidences of Christianity. 20059
Internal improvement. 10889
Internal Improvement Convention, Baltimore,
1834. 3039, 36726
Internal Improvement Convention, Williamsport,
Pa., 1836. 62082
Internal improvement of South Carolina. 49116

Internal improvement. Proceedings of meeting
22752, 102972
Internal improvement. Rail roads, canals,
bridges, &c. 60166, 92813
Internal improvement system of the state of
Missouri. (49597)
Internal Improvements Convention, Baltimore,
1825. see Convention on Internal
Improvements, Baltimore, 1825.
Internal Improvements Convention, Baltimore,
1836. see Convention on Internal
Improvements of Maryland, Baltimore,
1836.
Internal Improvements Convention, Concord,
N. H., 1825. (15145), 15156, (52825),
note after (52943)
Internal improvements in the state of New
York. 24648, 34907
Internal improvements. Speech of Hon. C. E.
Stuart. 93152
Internal improvements. Speech of Hon. F. P.
Stanton. 90413
Internal improvements. The relation of the
state to the Baltimore and Ohio Rail
Road Company. 45170
Internal relations of the cities, towns, villages
counties, and states. 34908
Internal revenue guide, 1867. 22423
Internal revenue law. Approved, July 13, 186
34911
Internal revenue law as it affects savings bank
in California. 34912, 76050
Internal revenue laws. 20925
Internal revenue record and customs journal.
34919
Internal revenue recorder and excise journal.
34918
Internal revenue—report of the Commissioner
of Internal Revenue. 34913
Internal revenue. Speech . . . June 1, 1868.
37272
Internal revenue statutes now in force. 34914
Internal state of America. 25516
Internal tax bill. 34920
Internal tax. Speech of Hon. Robert C. Schenc
77578
Internal taxation simplified. 5286
Internal witness of the spirit. 71114
Internal work of the wind. 85072
International almanac for 1866. 19449
International Antislavery Conference, Paris,
1867. 70121
International art-union journal. 34921
International Bridge Company. petitioners
34922
International code: address on this subject.
24274
International code of commerce, in connection
with the law of nature and nations.
40754
International coinage. By J. Ross Snowden.
85583
International coinage for Great Britain and the
United States. 737
International coinage. I. Report of Senator
Sherman. 34923
International coinage. Report of Senator
Morgan. 50636
International coinage. Speech . . . April 13,
1870. 37272
International Commercial Convention, Portland
Me., 1868. 34924
International Commercial Convention. Pro-
ceedings . . . in the city of Portland,
Me. 34923

International Committee on Weights, Measures, and Coins. 23534

International Congress, York, England, 1864. Delegate of the New York Chamber of Commerce. 45034 see also Marvin, William.

International Congress Called in 1879 at Paris to Examine the Plans for Constructing an Inter-Oceanic Canal Between the Atlantic and Pacific. see Interoceanic Canal Convention, Paris, 1879.

International Congress of Americanists, 1st, Nancy, France, 1875. 73308

International Copyright Association. 34925

International copyright [by Cornelius Mathews.] 46840

International copyright [by Robert Pearsall Smith.] 83877-83878

International exchange. 34926

International exchange list of the Smithsonian Institution. 85028

International exchange service of the Smithsonian Institution. 85029

International Exhibition, London, 1862. see London. International Exhibition, 1862.

International Exhibition, 1862. Catalogue of Canada products, etc. 34927

International Exhibition, 1862. Catalogue of the Nova Scotian Department. 34928

International Geological Congress. 12th, Toronto, 1913. 84533

International Harvester case. Contents: opinion of the court. 84519

International Harvester case. The opinions of Judges Smith, Hook and Sanborn. 84518

International Harvester Company. 84518-84519

International Harvester Company. defendants 84518-84519

International law. Case of the private armed brig of war. (69090)

International law. Case of the Trent. (58697)

International law; or, rules regulating the intercourse of states. (29881), 39433

International law. War and peace. 34929

International literary exchanges. 34931, 65799

International literary exchanges, with documents relating thereto. 34930

International magazine. 3945

International Medical Congress, 9th, Washington, D. C., 1887. 83367

International monthly magazine of literature, science and art. 34932

International Ocean Telegraph Company. 54830, 69676, 84773

International Ocean Telegraph Company. President. 84773 see also Smith, William Farrar, 1824-1903.

International Ocean Telegraph Company monopoly. 24904

International policy. (34933)

International policy of the great powers. 2746

International relations with Brazil. 7591, 53586

International Show Committee of Nova Scotia. (56181)

International Statistical Congress, London, 1860. (34934)-34935

International Statistical Congress, Berlin, 1863. 22262, 34935

International Statistical Congress, Berlin, 1863. American Delegate. see Ruggles, Samuel B.

International Statistical Congress, The Hague, 1869. American Delegate. see Ruggles, Samuel B.

International Statistical Congress at Berlin. V. Session, from the 6th to the 12th September, 1863. 22262

International Statistical Congress at Berlin. VI. Session. . . . September 11th, 1863. 34935

International Statistical Congress. Programme of the fourth session. (34934)

International Statistical Congress. Report of the proceedings of the fourth session. 34935

International Steamship Company. 40264

International sympathies. 46186

International topographical rail road guide. 34936

International tourist guide. 34937

International Workers of the World. Centralia Publicity Committee. 84489

International Workers of the World. Northwest District Defence Committee. 84489

International Workers of the World. Publishing Bureau, Chicago. 84489

International Workers of the World. Publishing Bureau, New Castle, Pa. 84489

International Workingmen's Association. U. S. Sections Francaises. 85706

Internationality and international congresses. 73954

Inter-oceanic canal. 82994

Interoceanic Canal Convention, Paris, 1879. Representative for San Francisco County and City And Chamber of Commerce. 82994 see also Smith, John Lawrence, 1818-1883.

Inter-oceanic canal for all nations. 34939

Inter-oceanic railways and canals. 34941

Interposicion de la R. N. de C. A. Contestacion del Gobierno Provisorio. 55152

Interposicion de la R. N. de C. A., para al pacifico deseulace. 34942

Interpretacao do acto adicional. 85653

Interpretation des anciens textes Mayas. 73307

Interpretation of baptismal names. (74153)

Interpretation of the Rev. E. S. Ely's dream. 22384

Interrogatoire de M. Franklin. 78115

Interrogatoire de Mr. Franklin Depute de Pensilvania [sic]. 25504

Interrogatoire de Mr. Penn. 78114

Interrogatoire devant la Chambre des Communes. 25585

Interrogatoire que Mr. Francklin [sic] subit au mois de Fevrier. 78114

Interrogatorien van Jos. Galloway. 34943

Interrogatories of J. Preston. 79880

Interrogatories on naval construction. (34944)

Interrogatorio de la vida y virtudes del Ven Hermano Fr. Bartolome de Jesus y Maria. 80833

Inter-state slave-trade. 58325

Intervention Anglo-Francaise dans le Rio de la Plata. 19270

Intervention de la France dans le Rio de la Plata. (39981)

Intervention for freedom. 2730

Intervention Francaise au Mexique, accompagnee de documents inedits. 34945, note after 48507

Intervention Francaise au Mexique 1861-1867. 37606

Interviews memorable and useful. 17270

Intimate acquaintance of the deceased. pseud. see T., J. pseud.

Intimations on manufactures. (6415), (81583)

Intire [sic] new entertainment. (76703), 101487

Introduction by Anson G. Chester. (37255)
Introduction by B. J. Lossing. 28312
Introduction by Bishop Janes. 84756-84756A
Introduction by Bolling A. Pope. 33488
Introduction by C. C. North. 84755
Introduction, by C. E. Stowe. 27415
Introduction by Cassius M. Clay. 68311
Introduction by Charles Elliott. (26284)
Introduction by Charles I. Bushnell. (14160)
Introduction by Clements R. Markham. 81285
Introduction by Cymon. 38079
Introduction by David J. East. 13312
Introduction by Dio Lewis. 91100
Introduction by Dr. J. H. Van Evrie. 78259
Introduction by Edmund Kirke. (23026)
Introduction by Elder D. Millard. 79906
Introduction by Elihu Burritt. 92489
Introduction by Ernest Rhys. 84316
Introduction by F. L. Hawks. 24986
Introduction by Fred. Law Olmsted. 27528
Introduction by George Augustus Sala. 8647,
   30339, 84181, 84183
Introduction by George Bancroft. 33841,
   37098
Introduction by George P. Morris. 51700
Introduction by George William Curtis. 30477
Introduction by Harriet Beecher Stowe.
   (52301)
Introduction, by Henry P. Tappan. (34343)
Introduction by Henry Ward Beecher. 15096
Introduction by Hon. Henry Pirtle. (13287)
Introduction by Hon. R. A. Chapman. 19893
Introduction, by Horace Greeley. 57816
Introduction by Horatio Gates Jones. 25421
Introduction by Hudson Maxim. 84235
Introduction by J. P. Peck. 63917
Introduction by Jacob Mott. 30081
Introduction, by James McCune Smith. 26677
Introduction by John Downing. 31047
Introduction by John S. Hart. 32618
Introduction by Lucias C. Matlack. 5163,
   (46866)
Introduction by M. W. Jacobus. 83456
Introduction by Mark Hopkins. 18812
Introduction, by Mr. C. Churchill. 106040
Introduction by Mrs. H. B. Stowe. 31433,
   note after 92624
Introduction by Mrs. L. H. Sigourney. 13630
Introduction by Mrs. Lucia Gilbert Calhoun.
   49818
Introduction by N. P. Willis. 62965
Introduction by Nathan Bangs. 92823
Introduction by Nathan Brown. 72816
Introduction by Prof. Henry E. Peck. 80503
Introduction by R. D. Turner. (16042)
Introduction by R. H. Major. 27784
Introduction by R. S. Foster. 82427
Introduction by R. Sheldon Mackenzie. 50401
Introduction, by Rev. Alexander Clark. 26835,
   63100
Introduction by Rev. B. F. Tefft. 92819
Introduction by Rev. Bishop E. S. Janes.
   13271
Introduction, by Rev. D. W. Clark. 82424
Introduction by Rev. Dr. Alexander Maclaren.
   83894
Introduction, by Rev. Henry A. Boardman.
   68151
Introduction by Rev. Henry Wilkes. 67872
Introduction by Rev. J. G. Greenhough. 83507
Introduction by Rev. Joseph Cumming. 78524
Introduction by Rev. N. L. Rice. 92818
Introduction by Rev. R. K. Sewell. 79420
Introduction by Rev. S. C. Bartlett. 71339
Introduction by Rev. S. Irenaeus Prime.
   (21423)

Introduction by Rev. T. G. Jones. 36612,
   (68412), note after 88311
Introduction, by Rev. T. R. Birks. 5574,
   34009
Introduction, by Rev. Thomas De Witt. 21338
Introduction, by Rev. William B. Sprague.
   83495
Introduction by Rev. William Dickson. 24461
Introduction by Richard B. Kimball. 75158
Introduction, by Robert Baird. 26734
Introduction, by S. B. Treat. 71343
Introduction, By Samuel B. Smith. 84032
Introduction. By Samuel H. Cox. 17270,
   49478, 89783
Introduction by Samuel Hanson Cox. 30843
Introduction, by Samuel Hanson Cox, D. D.
   37976
Introduction by Samuel M. Smucker. (15761)
Introduction by Samuel S. Smith. 73205
Introduction by Taylor Lewis. 56036
Introduction by the author of "War in disguise."
   67839, 91241
Introduction by the Hon. and Rev. Baptiste Noel.
   73489
Introduction by the Hon. Arthur Kinnaird.
   24416
Introduction, by the Hon. Joseph R. Ingersoll.
   23271
Introduction by the Irish editor. 73238
Introduction, by the Meeting for Sufferings,
   Virginia. 55359
Introduction by the Most Reverend Archbishop
   of New York. (8371)
Introduction by the present publisher. 39912
Introduction by the publisher. 78995
Introduction by the Rev. C. P. Krauth. 73344
Introduction by the Rev. John Angell James.
   65714
Introduction by the Rev. S. W. Christophers.
   92823
Introduction by the Rev. Samuel J. May. 62614
Introduction, by the Rev. T. Brainerd. 78320
Introduction, by the Rev. T. R. Birks. 5574,
   34009
Introduction by the Rev. Thomas De Witt.
   25972
Introduction by the Rev. William Arthur. 48919
Introduction by Thomas M. Eddy. 32428
Introduction by W. P. Strickland. 24832
Introduction [by W. S. Pelletreau.] 88229
Introduction, by W. T. Blair. 17726
Introduction by Whitelaw Reid. 84789
Introduction by Wilberforce Eames. 2d note
   after 103846
Introduction by William R. Williams. 45439
Introduction, comprising a brief historical
   sketch. (35937)
Introduction, containing a brief epitome of the
   most remarkable transactions. 65585
Introduction, containing a brief history of the
   state. (9668)
Introduction, containing notices of routes, &c.
   (33984)
Introduction; containing some accounts. 74646
Introduction de la conversion del piritu. 5853
Introduction, episode, and conclusion of the
   discussion. 82803
Introduction et accompagnee de notes par H.
   Baudrillart. 82317
Introduction et des eclaircissements par M.
   d'Avesac. 27788
Introduction et des notes par Gabriel Gravier.
   29471, 69285, 98171
Introduction et des notes par M. Ferdinand
   Denis. 106227

Introduction, et enrichi de pieces justificatives
et de notes. (9141)

Introduction et un vocabulaire de l'ecriture
hieratique Yucateque. 73301

Introduction, exhibiting . . . the importance of
our colonies. 1382

Introduction, exhibiting the settlement of
western Virginia. 9654

Introduction generale au droit publique.
3903A

Introduction, giving the origin and brief
history of the Society. 88317

Introduction, historical and explanatory.
(41909)

Introduction historique, auquel on a joint
des recherches. 24751, note just
before 44492

Introduction historique . . . par Victor Langois.
66508

Introduction of a full explanation to be
published hereafter. 95600

Introduction of Methodism into Boston. 14198

Introduction of paper money involves the
abolishment of taxation. 34948, 48669

Introduction of religion into politics right and
needed. 31059

Introduction of the matters preceding it.
63073, 2d note after 89187

Introduction of the power loom. (1814)

Introduction of the shorter catechism. 51586

Introduction of Wilberforce Eames. 2d note
after 103856

Introduction of Webster's spelling book.
102998

Introduction on the early history of Catho-
licity. 79998

Introduction on the faculty of the will. 96415

Introduction on the geology of the tertiary
formations. 39905

Introduction on the writ of habeas corpus.
10589

Introduction par Edouard Laboulaye. 36638

Introduction par George Sand. 92534

Introduction . . . par M. V. A. Malte-Brun.
37256

Introduction, poetical address, and appendix.
9902, 101168

Introduction sur le caractere de Washington.
89011-89012

Introduction sur l'influence et le caractere de
Washington. 101747

Introduction to a breviary of the history of
England. 67598-67599

Introduction to a course of lectures. 59419

Introduction to a history of the second
American war. 82001

Introduction to a treatise on civil liberty.
40985

Introduction to American law. 101081

Introduction to American literature. 70829

Introduction to anatomy. 85386

Introduction to arithmetic. (73125)

Introduction to chronology. 84363-84364

Introduction to English grammar. 102359

Introduction to geography. 52769, 79124

Introduction to geography and a natural history
of the earth. 49905

Introduction to his [i. e. Samuel Thomson's]
new guide to health. 95604

Introduction to municipal law. 63925

Introduction to natural philosophy. 85386

Introduction to popular lessons. 71809

Introduction to systematic physiological botany.
56351

Introduction to the American edition by
John C. Lord. 81152

Introduction to the American edition of Mrs.
D. M. Mulock Craik's A woman's thoughts
about women. 85202

Introduction to the art of decyphering. 84563

Introduction to the art of singing. 94014

Introduction to the art of singing by note.
101196

Introduction to the constitutional law of the
United States. 63924

Introduction to the defence of Rev. Abner
Kneeland. 38091

Introduction to the faith and doctrine of the
Church of Jesus Christ. 64972

Introduction to the federalist. 35844

Introduction to the grounds of musick. 94015-
94016

Introduction to the history of America. 34949

Introduction to the history of the colony and
ancient dominion. 10215

Introduction to the history of the nineteenth
century. 27203

Introduction to the history of the revolt. 11762

Introduction to the history of the revolt of the
colonies. 11761

Introduction to the Hon. James Williams' "The
south vindicated." (32924)

Introduction to the Latin tongue. 65650

Introduction to the observations made by the
judges. 66990, 67007

Introduction to the pedagogic methods of Dr.
Maria Montessori. 84333

Introduction to the rush-light, etc. 14015

Introduction to the science of government.
106059

Introduction to the shorter catechism. 17461

Introduction to the singing of psalm-tunes.
97423

Introduction to the singing of psalm-tunes, in
a plain & easy method. 97422

Introduction to the singing of psalm-tunes, in
a plain and easy method. With a
collection of tunes in three parts. 97424
97428

Introduction to the singing of psalm-tunes, with
a collection of tunes. 97419

Introduction to the study of bibliography.
(33033)

Introduction to the study of botany. 15075

Introduction to the study of mathematics.
34951

Introduction to the study of philosophy. 13219

Introduction to the study of philosophy, for the
use of pupils. 34950

Introduction to the United States speaker.
(42381)

Introduction to the water-cure. (55215)

Introduction to the whole. (32953), note after
102754

Introduction to the whole art. 79030

Introduction upon the history of the slave
question. 30274

Introduction, wherein is an account of the
inhabitants. 82169

Introdvctionis in universam geographiam.
13805

Introductions by G. Campbell Morgan and
Alexander McLaren. 83895

Introdvctoria additione. 74801

Introdvctorivm Isagogae in libros geographiae
Ptolemaei. 66481

Introductory. 85443

Introductory account, containing observations.
(21893), note after (35559)

Introductory account of the preceding campaign
72726-72727, 84618

Introductory address . . . April 9th, 1856. 32553

Introductory address . . . at the first meeting. 30016

Introductory address, at the opening of the hall. 20391

Introductory address, by David Everett. 103479

Introductory address by Henry R. Schoolcraft. 77843

Introductory address by I. Rowell. 73553

Introductory address, by Jedediah Morse. 12121, (50948), 91812

Introductory address . . . by . . . R. W. Wilson. 92133

Introductory address by Robert C. Winthrop. 23252

Introductory address, by S. Hanbury Smith. 84070

Introductory address, by several ministers in New-York. 104944

Introductory address by William Betts. 14806

Introductory address delivered at the inauguration of James Clark. 22261

Introductory address, delivered at the opening of the Wesleyan Academy. (24537)

Introductory address, delivered by Frances Wright. 105592

Introductory address, delivered in the Cincinnati Medical Institute. 84071

Introductory address delivered to the students of Washington College. 37807

Introductory address of His Excellency Joseph A. Gilmore. 82332

Introductory address of the Historical Society. 35310

Introductory address of the President [of the American Philosophical Society.] 59143

Introductory. Address, on the causes of the struggle. 50368, note after 68327

Introductory address . . . opening of the General Theological Seminary of the Protestant Episcopal Church. (32301)

Introductory address to the Corps of Cadets at the Virginia Military Institute. (82554)-82555

Introductory address to the course of lectures. 98996

Introductory address to the eighth course of lectures. 70152

Introductory address to the Hon. Thomas Erskine. (64166), 2d note after 96805

Introductory address to the Rt. Hon. John Adams, President of the Continental Congress of America. 51813, 92354

Introductory address to the Rt. Honourable John Adams. 92353

Introductory address to the students . . . of the College of Physicians and Surgeons of the University of . . . New York. 44301

Introductory address to the students . . . of the College of Physicians and Surgeons of the University of the State of New York. 19331

Introductory address, . . . Western Theological Seminary. 22261

Introductory and commendatory notice. 8433

Introductory arithmetic. note before 83906, 83909, 83910, 83922

Introductory chapter, by Francis Fogie. 67982

Introductory chapter, by Hon. Mark Skinner. (31431)

Introductory chapter, by Thomas De. Witt. 37943

Introductory chapter on the history of the American liturgy. 65947

Introductory discourse. 7483

Introductory discourse, . . . and a tribute to the memory. 33089

Introductory discourse . . . before the Chillicothe Lyceum. 40094

Introductory discourse, delivered at New-Haven. 97493

Introductory discourse, delivered before the American Institute of Instruction, at Boston, August 22, 1833. 93555

Introductory discourse, delivered before the American Institute of Instruction, at their annual meeting, in 1839. 67908

Introductory discourse, delivered before the Literary and Philosophical Society of New-York. 13715

Introductory discourse, delivered on the 6th day of November, 1837. 82921

Introductory discourse, delivered to the lunatics in the Asylum. 90202

Introductory discourse on medical education. (39716)

Introductory discourse on the present state of literature. (5198)

Introductory discourse . . . on the state. 40985

Introductory discourse on vital statistics. 2753

Introductory discourse . . . the sixth of November, 1820. 33089

Introductory discourse to an argument in support of the payments made of British debts. 47904, 92841

Introductory discourse to catechitical instruction. 7477

Introductory discourse to the history of North-Carolina. 104451

Introductory dissertation on cannon. 96339

Introductory dissertation on the origin, history and connection of the languages. 102335

Introductory essay and a memoir by Edwards A. Park. (32730)

Introductory essay, and an original poem. 104910

Introductory essay and explanatory notes. 35222

Introductory essay and notes. 43365, (58021), note after 100508

Introductory essay and notes by J. S. Nicholson. 82304

Introductory essay by Clarence H. Vance. 2d note after 99553

Introductory essay, by H. Chapin. (10826)

Introductory essay by J. H. Evans. 104808

Introductory essay by J. Matheson. 14224

Introductory essay by L. Woods. 41954

Introductory essay by Leonard Woods. 89736-89737

Introductory essay by R. Jeffery. 38064

Introductory essay by R. S. Storrs. 66660

Introductory essay by Rev. John Codman. 97382

Introductory essay . . . . By Rev. R. C. Shimeall. 80492

Introductory essay by Rev. W. Reeves. 14346

Introductory essay by Spencer H. Cone. 36848

Introductory essay, by the Rev. George Redford. 89737

Introductory essay. By the Rev. John Dowling. (20752)

Introductory essay by Thomas Chalmers. 78514

Introductory essay on Canadian poetry. 19838

Introductory essay on the constitution and government of the United States. 3307

Introductory geography, for children. 83937-83945

Introductory remarks at St. Mark's Church in the Bowery. 21507

Introductory remarks. By a citizen of Virginia. 13550

Introductory remarks by Hon. Ira M. Barton. 2668

Introductory remarks by J. Sherman. 92497

Introductory remarks by . . . J. Sherman. 92466

Introductory remarks [by John Greenleaf Whittier.] 285, 103819

Introductory remarks by John Lomas. 96939, 101112

Introductory remarks by William B. Sprague. 16366

Introductory remarks on the state of the primitive churches. 14093

Introductory report to the code of evidence. (41617)

Introductory report to the code of prison discipline. (41617)

Introductory report to the code of procedure. (41617)

Introductory report to the code of reform and prison discipline. (41617)

Introductory report to the system of penal law. (41617)

Introductory review of the progress and extent of immigration. 8226

Introductory sermon, delivered in the New Presbyterian Church. 73053

Introductory sermon, delivered in the Presbyterian Church in Vandewater Street. 17910

Introductory sermon, . . . in St. Peter's Church, Albany. (64646)

Introductory sermon . . . January 27, 1867. 43419

Introductory sermon on divine decrees. 91999

Introductory sermon, preached in the Bowery Presbyterian Church. 20069

Introductory sermons. 84293

Introductory sketch of the system of public elementary instruction. 10427

Introductory sketch, with suggestions. 91323

Introductory statement. 8238

Introductory to his [i. e. Samuel Auston's] ministry in Worcester. 2425

Introductory to the approaching millennial jubilee. 104978

Introductory to the fifteenth annual course of lectures. 90524

Invalid. pseud. Winter in the West Indies and Florida. 104829

Invalid at Saratoga. 55523

Invalid instructed. 32826

Invalide; ou, l'ami du jeune age. 98964

Invalidity of John Faldo's vindication of his book. 59708

Invalidity or unwarrantableness of lay ordination. 4259

Invalid's guide to the Virginia Hot Springs. 27843

Invaluable legacy to Americans. 101571, 101601

Invasion de Cardenas. 10811-10812

Invasion de la Vuelta-Abajo. 10812

Invasion of Canada in 1775. A journal of Col. H. Caldwell. 36393

Invasion of Canada, in 1775. [A letter from Col. H. Caldwell.] 67022

Invasion of Canada in 1775. [By E. M. Stone.] 70719

Invasion of Canada in 1775. By Major Henry Caldwell. 9903

Invasion of Harper's Ferry. 36170

Invasion of the Territory of Alabama. 62669

Invasiones Inglesas al Rio de la Plata. 103673

Invasive war. 67587

Inventaire general de plus curieuses recherches. (75557)

Inventeurs et la loi des Etats-Unis modifiee en 1861. 3588

Invention of letters. 58200

Inventis commentarium. 44348

Inventor's and patentee's guide and pocket record. 69099-(69100)

Inventors' Convention, 1845-1847. see Convention of Inventors, 1845-1847.

Inventor's National Institute. 34952

Inventory of property for the various defensive works. 34953

Invertebrates. (47371), 85072

Investigacion de la naturaleza y causas de la riqueza. 82312-(82313)

Investigacion de los medios mas opurtunos. 34956

Investigacion del origin, y privilegios de los ricos hombres. 50106

Investigaciones historicas sobre los principales. (13179)

Investigaciones politico-ecclesiasticas jurisdiccion ecclesiastica. 34957

Investigaciones sobre la naturaleza, causas y prevencion de la fiebre. 34332

Investigacoes historicas e scientificas. 52358, 88783

Investigacoes sobre os recenseamentos da populacao geral. 88805

Investigador del Peru. 34955

Investigador Mexicano. 34954

Investigateur, journal de l'Institut Historique. 69655-69656

Investigation and exposure of the management. (34958)

Investigation by the Police Committee. 74983

Investigation into free-masonry by a Joint Committee. (45505)

Investigation into the affairs of the Delaware and Raritan Canal. 10828, 19412

Investigation into the alleged official misconduct of the late Superintendent. 62051

Investigation into the causes and consequences of the politics. (66072)

Investigation into the charges against Lieut. Bennett H. Young. 4710, 74983

Investigation into the conduct, acts and doings of Harrison Reed. 24868

Investigation into the fifteen gallon law of Massachusetts. 34959

Investigation into the murder of Dr. J. K. Robinson. 72134

Investigation of that false, fabulous and blasphemous misrepresentation. 34960

Investigation of the causes of the explosion. 39023

Investigation of the currents of the Atlantic Ocean. 69617

Investigation of the orbit of Neptune. 85072

Investigation of the orbit of Uranus. 85072

Investigation of the Police Committee of the City Council. 38769

Investigation of the powers vested in the Congress. 89914

Investigation of the present temperance question. 18796

Investigation of the properties of the liriodendron tulipifera. 72719

Investigation: or monarchy and republicanism analyzed. 34963

Investigation upon the survey of the coast. 30817

Iowa College, Davenport, Iowa. 34985, 43844
Iowa Conference Seminary. 34985
Iowa County Agricultural Society. 35042
Iowa County Agricultural Society. Annual Fair, 8th, 1863. 35042
Iowa emigrant. 26383
Iowa frontier during the war of the rebellion. 83882
Iowa hand book for 1856. 58721
Iowa Indians. Treaties, etc. 96632, 96647, 96662, 96708, 96725, 96730 see also Michigan Indians. Treaties, etc.
Iowa Institute of Science and Arts, Dubuque. 34991
Iowa Institute of Science and Arts, Dubuque. Humboldt Centennial Celebration, 1869. 34991
Iowa Institute of Science and Arts. Celebration of the Humboldt centennial and opening. 34991
Iowa instructor and school journal. 34992
Iowa Land Company. (35010)
Iowa Pioneer Lawmakers' Association. see Pioneer Lawmakers' Association of Iowa.
Iowa Railroad Land Company. 34977
Iowa Soldiers' Orphans Home, Davenport. 35030
Iowa Soldiers' Orphans Home, Davenport. Officers. 35030
Iowa State Agricultural Society. (34971)
Iowa State Agricultural Society. Secretary. (34971)
Iowa state gazetteer. 29561
Iowa State Historical Society. (34972)-34973, 83725, 83882
Iowa State Historical Society. Committee of Publication. (34972)
Iowa State Historical Society. Corresponding Secretary. 34973
Iowa State Historical Society. Executive Committee. 34973
Iowa State Historical Society. Librarian. (34972)
Iowa State Horticultural Society. Secretary. (34971)
Iowa: the home for immigrants. 35011
Iowa Wesleyan University, Mount Pleasant. 34995
Ioway grammar. 30041, 35107
Ioway Indians. see Iowa Indians.
Ioway primer. 35107
Ippocrate, Lvoghi d'. see Lvoghi d'Ippocrate.
Ipswich, Mass. 35043
Ipswich, Mass. Convention, 1778. see Essex County, Mass. Convention, Ipswich, 1778.
Ipswich, Mass. Convention, 1812. see Essex County, Mass. Convention, Ipswich, 1812.
Ipswich, Mass. Court of Common Pleas. 79895
Ipswich, Mass. Ecclesiastical Council, 1747-1748. see Congregational Churches in Massachusetts. Ecclesiastical Council, Ipswich, 1747-1748.
Ipswich, Mass. Ecclesiastical Council, 1805. see Congregational Churches in Massachusetts. Ecclesiastical Council, Ipswich, 1805.
Ipswich, Mass. First Church. 35044
Ipswich, Mass. Ordinances, etc. 102629
Ipswich, Mass. School Committee. (35048)
Ipswich, Mass. Second Church. 13592, (35046)-35047
Ipswich, Mass. Seminary for Female Teachers. see Ipswich Seminary for Female Teachers.

Ipswich, Mass. Second Parish. (18435)
Ipswich chronicle. 83316
Ipswich Historical Society. 101326
Ipswich Seminary for Female Teachers. 35045
Iquazafigo, Jacome. 99523
Ira Allen. 99000
Iragnez, --------. 34147
Irasusta y Uranga, Jose Maria Orruno. 35050-(35052)
Irby, J. R. McD. 48985
Iredell, James, 1788-1853. (25961), 43653, (55637), 55648, (55670), 55689, 96866 see also North Carolina. Governor, 1827-1828 (Iredell)
Ireland, John. supposed author 65042, 99778
Ireland, John. defendant before church council 35054-35055
Ireland, John B. (35056)
Ireland, Joseph N. (18231), 24310, 35057-35058
Ireland. Laws, statutes, etc. (18009)
Ireland. Natives. see Natives of Ireland.
Ireland. Natives, Residing Within the United States of America. petitioners. see Natives of Ireland, Residing Within the United States of America. petitioners
Ireland. People. pseud. see People of Ireland. pseud.
Ireland. Public Record Office. 98637
Ireland and America. 35059
Ireland and America, via Galway. (4420), (35060)
Ireland and Canada. (33074), note after 104595
Ireland and Canada; supported by local evidence. 33075, note after 104595
Ireneus Philalethius. pseud. Tweede wachter. see Teelinck, Ewout.
Irenicon. 19663
Irenicvm. 35063
Irenicum ecclesiasticum. 94693
Irhoven van Dam, W. van. 35064
Iriarte, F. 35065
Iriarte, Francisco. plaintiff 103966
Iriarte, Francisco Suarez. see Suarez Iriarte, Francisco.
Iriarte, Maria de la Luz. defendant 103966
Iriarte, Thomas. (35067)-35068
Iriarte y Laza. firm plaintiffs (36943)
Iribarren, Guillermo. 35069
Irigoyen, Jose Gutierre de la Concha y de. see Habana, Jose Gutierrez de la Concha y de Irigoyen, Marques de la, 1809-1895.
Irim, or halcyon cabala. 100670
Irinyia, Jozsef. tr. 92417, 92583
Irion, L. F. B. 35070
Irion, R. A. 94994 see also Texas (Republic) Secretary of State.
Iris. 89492, 95555
Iris Americaine. 35074
Iris de Nueva Espana. 35075
Iris diadema inmortal. 24156
Iris, or literary messenger. 35071
Iris. Periodico critico y literario. 35072
Iris. Periodico quincenal de literatura. 35073
Irisarri, Antonio Jose de. 35076-35080, 94837
Irisarri, Antonio Jose de. supposed author 97694
Irisarri, Fermin de. 35081
Irish, David. 35082
Irish, James. 43953
Irish adopted citizen. pseud. Fifty reasons. 13556
Irish American Relief Association of Portland, Me. 64347
Irish Brigade and its campaigns. 16228

Irish Catholic whig. pseud. Irish Catholic whig to his fellow countrymen. see Gorman, Charles O.

Irish Catholic whig to his fellow countrymen. 28029

Irish Citizens' Central Executive Committee. see Central Executive Committee of Irish Citizens, Washington, D. C.

Irish clergyman. pseud. Missionary geography. 49468

Irish editor. pseud. ed. 73238

Irish Emigrant Association. 56584

Irish Emancipation Society, Baltimore. 68191

Irish Emigrant Association, New York. see New York Irish Emigrant Association.

Irish friend. 8538, 17484, (81880), 93262

Irish gentleman in London. pseud. Letter. 63764

Irish gentleman, now in America. pseud. Poetry. (49452)

Irish girl in America. 74824

Irish in America. 43856, 51207

Irish liberator. pseud. Address. see O'Connell, Daniel, 1775-1847.

Irish Ninth in bivouac and battle. (43594)

Irish-office-hunter-oniad. 35984

Irish patriot. 35085, (56653)

Irish position in British and in republican North America. 43264

Irish race, at home and abroad. 29896

Irish Relief Committee of New York. 54324

Irishman. pseud. British sympathies in the American crisis. see King, A.

Irishman and southern democrat. 9948

Irishman now in America. pseud. Hibernicus. 31688

Irishmen! Hear the voices of O'Connell and Emmett!! (33288)

Irishmen's Meeting, New York, 1825. see New York (City) Meeting of Irishmen, 1825.

Irishmen's Meeting to Prevent the Re-election of Andrew Jackson, Philadelphia, 1832. see Philadelphia. Great Meeting of Irishmen, to Prevent the Re-election of Andrew Jackson, 1832.

Irishmen's petition. 94039

Irkutks, Russia. Chancery. 90063

Irlanda, Antonio de. 86378

Irminger, C. 35086

Irokesische Junhfrau. 35087

Irolo Calar, N. de. see Yrolo Calar, Nicolas de.

Iron, N. C. 35089

Iron age. 52014

Iron clad ships. 35092

Iron-clad songster. 79858

Iron Cliffs Company. 25247

Iron Convention, Pittsburgh, 1849. (35093)

Iron dike. 35094

Iron furnace. 2377

Iron Gray. pseud. Gospel of slavery. see Thomas, Abel C. supposed author

Iron hearted regiment. 13304

Iron is king. 35095

Iron manufacturer's guide to the furnaces. 40187

Iron Manufacturers of Great Britain. (11316)

Iron Manufacturers of New England. petitioners 31026

Iron-moulders' national union. 90164

Iron Mountain Railroad Company. (35096)

Iron Mountain Railroad Company. Directors. petitioners (35096)

Iron mountain region. (13844)

Iron platform. 21475, (28451), (35097)

Iron question. 10842

Iron region. 25249

Iron resources of Michigan. 35098

Iron steamships. 71710

Iron will. (19574)

Iron workers of Philadelphia. petitioners 61830 see also Workers in Iron of Philadelphia. petitioners

Ironico hablador. 98258

Ironicus, Titus. pseud. see Titus Ironicus. pseud.

Ironmasters' Convention, Philadelphia, 1849. 60073

Ironside, Beatice. (56604)

Ironside, J. pseud. Truth. 35100, 1st note after 97259

Ironsides. 76437

Ironton, O. petitioners 35101

Irony, Solomon. pseud. Fashion. 35088

Iroquois Indians. 88733

Ironquois Indians. Treaties, etc. 96559

Iroquois; or, the bright side of Indian character 36183

Iroquois voyageant en Europe. pseud. Letters Iroquoises. see Maubert de Gouvest, J. H.

Irregular ode. 22593

Irremediability of capital punishment. 89067

Irrepressible conflict: a sermon for the times. 42014

Irrepressible conflict. A speech by William H Seward. 79528

"Irrepressible conflict" and its consequences! (77472)

Irrepressible platform. 6928

Irujo y Tacon, Carlos Martinez de. see Casa Yrujo, Carlos Martinez de Yrufo y Tacor Marques de, 1763-1824.

Irvin, Margaret. see Smith, Margaret Irvin, d. 1800.

Irvin, S. M. 30041, 35107

Irvine, A. 35108

Irvine, Baptis. (35109), 35111

Irvine, Baptis. supposed author 7182, 35110 note after 92835

Irvine, Baptis defendant 30254, 35112, 2d note after 96883

Irving, Edward. 35113, 71915

Irving, W. H. pseud. Irving, on Lake Erie, see Willcox, Henry P. supposed author

Irving, John Beaufain. 85307

Irving, John Beaufain. supposed author 88012

Irving, John Treat, 1778-1838. 35114-35117, 48019

Irving, Pierre M. 35118, 35137, 35202, 35210

Irving, Ralph. 35119

Irving, Theodore. 35120-35121

Irving, Thomas. (35122)

Irving, Thomas Pitt. 35123, 101891

Irving, Washington, 1783-1859. 1358, 4741, 4777, (5522), 11553, 18582, 18735, 19642, 25415, 25432, 30000, 32707, 35118, 35124-35218, (35219), 35222-(35225), (40198), 2d note after 44432, 50222, (68468), (70987), 71486, 72417, 72485, 78686, 85536, 92150-92151, note before 94245, note before 94463, note before 96334-96334

Irving, Washington, 1783-1859. supposed author 35124, 105457-8 [sic]

Irving, Washington, 1783-1859. incorrectly supposed author (35191), 101840

Irving, William. 35222-(35225), (68468)

Irving gift. (35219)

Irving Library Institute, Philadelphia. 61744
Irving memorial. 35221
Irving, on Lake Irie. 104127
Irvingiana: a memorial of Washington Irving. 21499
Irwin, Abraham. 82763, 82770B
Irwin, George. 9902, 101168
Irwin, Jared, 1750-1818. 49073
Irwin, John. 89246
Irwin, Richard Biddle, 1839-1892. 7096
Irwin, S. M. 30040-30041
Irwin, Thomas. 35226
Irwin, William. 35227
Irwin, William Wallace, 1803-1856. 35228
Is a law against slavery in the territories necessary? (73952)
Is a member of the legislature, or a justice of the Supreme Court, eligible to the office of United States Senator? 35229
Is a tax on through tonnage constitutional? 60358
Is a whale a fish? (46955), 75851, 2d note after 96891
Is Asiatic cholera contagious? 85497
Is cheap sugar the triumph of free trade? 57268
Is cotton "king?" 17125, 89973
Is cotton our king? 35230
Is Davis a traitor. 5893
Is democracy dishonesty? 73114
Is emancipation the object of the present war? 13807
Is het vertrek der geloovigen in Nederland naar Noord-Amerika een werk van God of uit den booze? 2564
Is it calumny? 35231
Is it expedient that a state convention should be called? 35232
Is it expedient to introduce slavery into Kansas? (27864), 92867
Is it lawful to poison our neighbour? 93226
Is it safe to elect General Blair? 73967
Is Millard Fillmore an abolitionist? 24333
Is Napoleon Antichrist? 80493
Is Ohio to be Africanized? (17271)
Is our prosperity a delusion? 35233
Is she a brigand? 83788
Is slaveholding constitutional and scriptural? 26133
Is slavery a blessing? 5894, 79900
Is slavery a sin in itself? (82159)
Is slavery as it exists in the southern states, morally wrong? 34587
Is slavery condemned by the Bible? 33008
Is slavery consistent with national law? 32467
Is slavery defensible from scripture? 93135
Is slavery sanctioned by the Bible? 82002
Is slavery sinful? 82803
Is the act entitled "an act for enrolling and calling out the national forces, and for other purposes," passed March 3, 1863, constitutional or not? 25735
Is the Alabama a British pirate? 22614, 42534
Is the Diocese of New York vacant? 53706
Is the government of a state, a republic or a despotism? (35234)
Is the harbor of New Bedford of any importance? 52488
Is the Hon. McRoberts more honorable than the Hon. Mitchell? (76826)
Is the north right? 93373
"Is the north right!" 35235
Is the popular voice to be stifled at the ballot-box? 73114

Is the relation of master to servant a sin, per se? 18300
Is the south ready for restoration? (35236)
Is the system of slavery sanctioned or condemned by scripture? 35237
Is there any ground to apprehend the extensive and dangerous prevalence of Romanism in the United States? (6073)
Is West Indian slavery justifiable by the New Testament? 102842
Isaac Adriance, appellant. 89349
Isaac Bickerstaff. pseud. Bickerstaff's Boston almanack. see West, Benjamin, 1730-1813.
Isaac Bickerstaff. pseud. Letter from a gentleman in Transylvania. see Hunt, Isaac.
Isaac Bickerstaff. pseud. New England almanac for 1781. see West, Benjamin, 1730-1813.
Isaac N. Whiting's general catalogue of books. 103698
Isaac T. Hopper: a true life. 12719
Isaac the Scribe. pseud. Some chapters, of the Book of the chronicles. 86610
Isaac Van Pumpkin. pseud. see Van Pumpkin, Isaac. pseud.
Isaac Weld's des jungern Reise durch die Staaten. 102536
Isaacs, M. S. pseud. Jewish pride. see Kraskowski, Thomas.
Isabel. pseud. Pelayo. see Mowatt, Anna Cora (Ogden) 1819-1870.
Isabel I, Queen of Spain, 1451-1504. 22550, note after 40960 see also Spain. Sovereigns, etc., 1749-1516 (Fernando V)
Isabel II, Queen of Spain, 1830-1904. 66593, (66597), 68855, 93303 see also Spain. Sovereigns, etc., 1833-1868 (Isabel II)
Isabel, Gonsalo de Santa. see Santa Isabel, Gonsalo de.
Isabelle, Arsene. (35239)
Isabelle de Verneuil. 85383
Isacii Pontani Discvssionvm historicarvm libri duo. 64001
Isadore or the captives of the Norridgewocks. (51551)
Isaer efter det tydske. 6824
Isaiah Thomas's catalogue of English, Scotch, Irish and American books. 95403
Isaiah's message to the American nation. (43157)
Isaiah's prospect of the church. 20391
Isak T. Hopper. Lebensgeschichte. 12720
Isambert, Francois Andre. 35240
Isasaga, Pedro Matias de Tagle. see Tagle Isasaga, Pedro Matias de.
Isassi, J. D. 35241
Isbell, Thomas M. 35242
Isauria (Diocese) Bishop (Molleda) (55263) see also Molleda, Gregorio de, Bp.
Isbrands Ides, Evert. see Ides, Evert Isbrands.
Isdell, Sarah. supposed author 98341
Isembourg d'Happoncourt, Francoise d'. see Grafigny, Francoise (d'Isembourg d'Happoncourt) de, 1695-1758.
Isert, Paul Erdmann. 35243-(35246)
Isham, Asa Brainerd, 1844- 59168
Isham, Jirah. 35247
Isham, R. N. 76562, 76647
Isham, Warren. ed. 48762
Isherwood, Benjamin Franklin, 1822-1915. (35248)-(35249), 84959 see also U. S. Bureau of Steam Engineering.

Ish-noo-ju-lut-sche. 80067
Isidore of Seville. see Isidorius, Saint,
   Bishop of Seville, d. 636.
Isidorius, Saint, Bishop of Seville, d. 636.
   76838
Isla, Ruiz de. 35250, note after 74024
Isla de Cuba, inmigracion de trabajadores
   Espanoles. 87249
Isla de Cuba, pintoresca, historica, politica.
   1530
Isla de Cuba por Don Urbano F. de Sotomayor.
   87250
Isla de Cuba, sus males y situacion actual.
   (18226)
Isla de Cuba. Tomo I. 99404
Island. 5910
Island home. 75933
Island minstrel. 40121
Island of Anticosti. 39044
Island of Cuba. By Alexander von Humboldt.
   33721
Island of Cuba: its resources, progress, and
   prospects. 43694
Island of Cuba, or Queen of the Antilles. 851
Island of Navassa. 26768
Island of Prince Edward. 96178
Island of St. Domingo. 80163
Island of St. Marguerite. 75243
Island of the giant fairies. 11756
Island Pond Copper Manufacturing Company.
   35251
Island republics of St. Domingo. 57711
Island, the people, and the pastor. 51543
Islandia sive populaorum et mirabilium quae
   in ea isula reperiuntur accuratior
   descriptio. 5902
Islands, &c., of the Pacific Ocean. 24358
Isle, Guillaume de l'. see L'Isle, Guillaume
   de, 1675-1726.
Isle, Guil. Phil. Buache de l'. 35252
Isle, J. N. de l'. see L'Isle, J. N. de.
Isle de Cuba et la Havane. 46173
Isle deserte: comedie. (14412)
Isle of Man. 3485
Isle of Pines. 25255, 82181-82184
Isle of Shoals. 82823
Isle Royale Mining Company. Directors.
   35260
Isle Saint-Christophe. 75014
Isleno. 72990
Isles Espagnoles. 77743
Islip, Adam. 94165
Ismael Ben Kaizer. 19549
Isnard, Achille Nicolas. 35261
Isnardi, Felice. 4565, 35262
Isocrates. 48236
Isocrates. pseud. Question of the Bahama
   jurisdiction. 35263
Isola, Peter Coppo da. see Coppo da Isola,
   Peter.
Isolanis, Isodorus de. 35264
Isolario, . . . con la giunta del Monte dell'
   Oro. (6418)
Isolario di Benedetto Bordone. 6419-6421
Isole piv famose del mondo. 64148-64153
Isonponthouan. 35265
Isqvierdo, Pedro Saenz. see Izqvierdo, Pedro
   Saenz.
Israel, --------. 35267
Israel, Manasseh ben Joseph ben. see
   Manasseh ben Joseph ben Israel,
   1604-1657.
Israel Ben Ader. pseud. see Ben Ader,
   Israel. pseud.
Israel Potter. 47481

Israel vindicated. 35268
Israelite. pseud. Israel vindicated. 35268
Israelite indeed. 93087
Israelite with guile. 18126
Israel's mourning for Aaron's death. (26830)
Israel's true safety. 18470, (19157), 104088
Isselt, E. W. van Dam van. 35269
Isselt, Michaelis ab. 66494, 93884
Issue, and its consequences. (25733)
Issue explained. (35270)
Issue fairly presented. 35271
Issue in California. 11367
Issue of the November election. 14204
Issue, presented in a series of letters on
   slavery. 2751
Issues and duties of the day. 44376
Issues of American politics. 81619
Issues of the campaign. 34268
Issues of the canvass. 68057
Issues of the conflict—terms of peace. 79529
   (79531)
Issues of the contest. 85609
Issues of the day. Speech of William M. Eva
   23203
Issues of the day. Speech . . . St. Louis
   . . . Oct. 21. 31319
Issues of the hour, political and military.
   (14118)
Issues of the presidential election. 85377
Issues of the rebellion. A sermon preached.
   5789
Issues of the rebellion. Speech. . . . in the
   House of Representatives. 24209
Issues of United States notes. 24209
Ist Sclaverei verdammt in der Bible? (33009
Isthme de Panama. 12584
Isthme de Tehuantepec et l'isthme de Panama
   50769
Isthmus line to the Pacific. 46967
Isthmus of Darien in 1852. 27319, (27512)
Isthmus of Darien ship canal. 17860
Isthmus of Nicaragua, Central America. 551
Isthmus of Panama. (35272)
Isthmus of Panama, and what I saw there.
   28883
Isthmus of Panama. By Charles Toll Bidwell
   5257
Isthmus of Panama. History of the Panama
   Railroad. 57851
Isthmus of Tehuantepec; being the results of
   survey. 3480
Isthmus of Thuantepec, Mexico. (81498)
Istlaguaca, Mexico. Indios. see Indios de l
   Pueblos de Istlaguaca, Iocotitlan.
R. Istituto Veneto di Scienze, Lettere ed Arti
   Venice. 47863
Istoria degli Fiorent. Scrittori. 52254
Istoria del governo d'Inghilterra. 44946
Istoria della conquista del Messico. 86486
Istoria della conquista del Mexico. 16951
Istoria della conversione alla nostra Santa
   Fede. 26591
Intoria della guerra fra gli Stati-Uniti
   d'America. 7165
Istoria della vita del Venerabile Monsignore
   Don Giovanni di Palafox e Mendoxa.
   81468
Istoria delle gverre del regno del Brasile.
   27474, 55498, (76793)-76794
Istoria descrizione de' tre' regni Congo,
   Matamba, et Angola. 11592
Istoria o breuissima relatione. 11242-11244
Istoria Veneziana. 4621
Istorie del Peru. 13048-13049
Istorie dell' Indie Orentali. 43780

Istorie delle Indie Orientali. 43777
Istvan, Kozli Prepost. see Prepost, Istvan.
It having been industriously propagated.
 95941
It is a fearful thing. 14494
It is a mad world my masters. 54972, note
 after 94477
Is is desired that the Sons and Daughters of
 Liberty. 86986
Is is not surprising to those who have been
 acquainted with you. 92884
It is now full time for us all to be on our
 guard. 100012
Is is now generally known. 105805
Is is of the Lord's mercies. (14525)
Is is proposed to print. 72994
Is is so unlady-like. 90402
Is is the nature of comparison to associate
 with misfortune. 93776
Is is with extreme pain I have discovered.
 91327
Is is with great reluctance. 98526
It may become necessary. 93470
Itabayana, --------, Visconde de. 35274
Italia sacra. 24834
Italian. pseud. Voyage to Mexico and
 Havana. see Barinetti, Charles. 3383
Italian history or biography of Francisco
 Farnese. 82851
Italian Merchants. petitioners see Portugal,
 Italian, and Spanish Merchants, London.
 petitioners
Italian mercury. 47934
Italian mission. 85526
Italian School, New York. see Children's
 Aid Society, New York. Italian School.
Italian sights and Papal principles. (35797)
Italiano dimorante al servizio del Re Fedel-
 issimo. pseud. Risposto prima. 71553
Italiano profugo in America. pseud. Com-
 ponimenti poetici. (78873)
Itauna, Barao de. 69317 see also San Paulo
 (Brazilian Province) Presidente (Itauna)
Item con dem Frantzosen Schiffarth. 1762-
 1762A
Item, was Gestalt der schone Portus und Hafe
 Totos Los Sanctos. (7585)
Items of abuse in the government. (54188)
Items of church history, the gift of the Holy
 Ghost. 83252
Items of church history, the government of
 God. 83253
Items, on travel. (35275), note after 96084
Items submitted to the consideration. (53622)
Iter extaticum terrestre. 37966
Iter Hispanicum eller resa til Spanska
 landerna. (41772)
Iter in America. 100960
Iter nobilissimi equitis Thomae Candisch.
 (8784)
Ithaca, N. Y. Citizens. 88642
Ithaca, N. Y. Twenty-Six Citizens. see
 Ithaca, N. Y. Citizens.
Ithaca and Oswego Railroad Company. 35276-
 35277, 94073
Ithaca as it was. (27941)
Ithier, Paul. tr. 49678, 65293
Ithuriel. pseud. Ariel dissected. 81894
Itier, Jules. 35281-35282
Itinera filiorum Israel per desertum. 106294,
 106330-106331
Itinera mundi. 60934
Itinera priscorum Scandianorum in Americam.
 103033
Itineraire de Constantinople a la Mecque.
 68443

Itineraire des Francais dans la Louisiane.
 21028
Itineraire du General Lafayette. 38583
Itineraire du Nouueau Monde. 27780
Itineraire du voyage de la flotte du Roi
 Catholique. 94854
Itineraire pittoresque du Flueve Hudson.
 48916
Itineraires de l'Afrique Septentrionale. 68443
Itineraires et coupes geologiques. 11411
Itinerant. 21917
Itineraria dvo Antonini Pii. 66497
Itinerario a las cinco partes de la Europa,
 Africa, Asia, America, y Magalanica.
 57525
Itinerario de Buenos-Aires a Cordoba. 87306
Itinerario de larmata del Re Catholico in India.
 98643
Itinerario de Ludonico [sic] de Varthema.
 98643
Itinerario de Ludouico de Varthema. 98644-
 98647
Itinerario de un camino. 97742
Itinerario del Nuevo Mundo. 27775-27777
Itinerario geographico. 8129
Itinerario para parochos de Indios, en que se
 tratan las materias. (59624)
Itinerario para parochos de Indios, su oficio
 y oblicaciones. 59623
Itinerario, voyage ofte schipvaert. 41356,
 41358-41360
Itinerarios y derroteros de la republica
 Mexicana. 976
Itinerarivm ad regiones svb Aeqvinoctiali
 plaga. 27116
Itinerarvm catholicvm proficientium. (24934)
Itinerarium Hispaniae, vervattende een reys-
 beschryvinghe. 106296
Itinerarium Indiae Occidentalis. (14350)-
 (14351), 31539-31543
Itinerarium Indicum. 37691
Itinerarium ofte schipvaert naer Oost ofte
 Portugaels Indien. 41361-41363, 41366
Itinerariu[m] Portugallesiu[m] e Lusitania in
 India[m]. 50058, note after 99383C, 1st
 note after 106378
Itinerary. 69946
Itinerary [of Ezra Stiles.] 97210
Itinerary of the New World. 27775
Itineribvs describitvr avrifervm et potentissi-
 mum regnum Gviana. (8784)
Itinerum atq$_3$ flvviorvm ortum & aquilonem
 versus e Moscovia in Siberiam . . .
 descriptio. 67355
Its author at the confessional. 14952
Its [i. e. Pennsylvania's] scenery. 7053
Its promises and their failures. 50730
Itself. pseud. Tale of a box. 94238
Itta y Para, Elizalde. 35285
Itta y Para, J. M. G. de. 35286
Itta y Parra, Bartholome Phelipe. see Yta y
 Parra, Bartholome Felipe de.
Iturbide, Augustin de, Emperor of Mexico,
 1783-1824. 7750, 35287-(35296), 48335,
 99708 see also Mexico (Empire, 1822-
 1923) Emperor (Iturbide)
Iturburu, Atilano Calvo. tr. 65285
Iturri, Francisco. 35298
Iturrigary, Jose, Abp. 35299, 65930, 106220A-
 106220B, see also Mexico (Archdiocese)
 Archbishop (Iturrigary) Mexico (Vice-
 royalty) Virrey, 1803-1808 IIturrigary)
Iver Beres Gronlands beskrivelse. 2166
Ivernois, Sir Francis d'. 35300-35302
Iverra, Justo. ed. 68836

J. D. pseud. see Danforth, John, 1660-1730.
J. D. pseud. see Davenport, James, 1597-1670.
J. D. pseud. see Duer, John. supposed author
J. D. pseud. see Dunlop, John.
J. D. C. pseud. see C., J. D. pseud.
J. D. H. L. pseud. see Herlein, J. D.
J. D. L. V. pseud. see V., J. D. L. pseud.
J. D. P. pseud. see P., J. D. pseud.
J. D. R. pseud. see Roussignac, Jacques de.
J. E. pseud. see Elderkin, John.
J. E. pseud. see Eliot, John, 1604-1690.
J. E. pseud. see Ellis, Jonathan.
J———E———g. pseud. see Ewing, John.
J. E. R. pseud. see R., J. E. pseud.
J. E. S. pseud. see S., J. E. pseud.
J. F. pseud. see F., J. pseud.
J. F. pseud. see Foster, John.
J. F. pseud. see Freeman, James.
J. F., Moderator. pseud. see F., J., Moderator. pseud.
J. F. B. pseud. see B., J. F. pseud.
J. F. de L. pseud. see Fernandez de Lizardi, Jose Joaquin, 1776-1827.
J. F. de Surville's Reise im das Sudmeer. 5912
J. F. M. pseud. see Mascarenhas, Jose Freire de Monteroyo.
J. F. M. M. pseud. see M., J. F. M. pseud.
J. F. S. pseud. see Schroter, Jo. Fred.
J. G. pseud. see G., J. pseud.
J. G. pseud. see Galloway, Joseph, 1729-1803.
J. G. pseud. see Gardiner, John.
J. G. pseud. see Graham, John,
J. G. pseud. see Greenleaf, James.
J. G. I. pseud. see Garcia Icazbalceta, Joaquin, 1825-1894.
J. G. J. pseud. see Johnson, John G.
J. G. M. pseud. see M., J. G. pseud.
J. G. R. pseud. see R., J. G. pseud.
J. G. R. pseud. see Roscio, J. G.
J. G. S. pseud. see S., J. G. pseud.
J. G. T. P. pseud. see Torres Palacios, Jose Gregorio de.
J. G. W. pseud. see Whittier, John Greenleaf, 1807-1892.
J. Green, proposes to publish the journals. (45286)
J. H. pseud. see H., J. pseud.
J. H. pseud. see Haefkens, J.
J. H. pseud. see Hall, Joseph.
J. H. pseud. see Hardy, John.
J. H. L. A. pseud. see A., J. H. L. pseud.
J. H. N. pseud. see Nagel, J. H.
J. H. S. pseud. see S., J. H. pseud.
J. H. T. pseud. see T., J. H. pseud.
J. H. W. pseud. see Waddell, John Hunter.
J———I———. pseud. see I———, J———. pseud.
J. I. H. y S. pseud. see Heredia y Sarmiento, Jose Ignacio.
J. I. T. pseud. see T., I. J. pseud.
J. J. pseud. see J., J., a lieutenant in the navy. pseud.
J. J. pseud. see Janeway, James.
J. J. C. pseud. see C., J. J. pseud.
J. J. D. pseud. see D., J. J. pseud.
J. J. L. pseud. see L., J. J. pseud.
J. J. L. pseud. see Lejarza, Juan Jose Martinez de.
J. J. O. pseud. see O., J. J. pseud.
J. J. R. pseud. see R., J. J. pseud.
J. J. R. pseud. see Rousseau, Jean Jacques, 1712-1778. supposed author
J. J. R. pseud. see Wilkes, John, 1727-1797. supposed author

J. J. S. pseud. see S., J. J. pseud.
J. J. S. pseud. see Sheed, J. J.
J. J. S. P. G. pseud. see G., J. J. S. P. pseud.
J. L. pseud. see Lenox, James.
J. L. pseud. see Logan, James.
J. L. F. V. D. G. pseud. see G., J. L. F. V. D. pseud.
J. L. M. pseud. see M., J. L. pseud.
J. L. M. pseud. see Martin, J. L.
J. L. S.** pseud. see Schulze, Johan Ludwig.
J. Lawrence Smith. 83003
J. M. pseud. see M., J. pseud.
J. M. pseud. see Milton, John, 1608-1674.
J. M. pseud. see Mortimer, J.
J. M. A. B. pseud. see B., J. M. A. pseud.
J. M. A. C. pseud. see Castellar, Joao Maria Augusto.
J. M. B. de *****. pseud. see Saint Victor, Jacques Maximilien Benjamin Bins de.
J. M. C. pseud. see C., J. M. pseud.
J. M. J. pseud. see J., J. M. pseud.
J. M. J. Portrait d'un missionnaire apostolique. (13139)
J. M. K. pseud. see K., J. M. pseud.
J. M. L. pseud. see L., J. M. pseud.
J. M. P. pseud. see P., J. M. pseud.
J. M. R. H. pseud. see H., J. M. R. pseud.
J. M. T. pseud. see T., J. M. pseud.
J. M. V. pseud. see V., J. M. pseud.
J. M. V. pseud. see Villasenor Cervantes, Jose Maria.
J. M. V. C. pseud. see Villasenor Cervantes, Jose Maria.
J. M. Y. Y. pseud. see Y., J. M. Y. pseud.
J. Mcl. pseud. see McL., J. pseud.
J. N. pseud. see N., J. pseud.
J. N. L. pseud. see L., J. N. pseud.
J.-N. P. pseud. see P., J.-N. pseud.
J. N. T. pseud. see Troncoso, Juan Nepomuceno.
J. Norberto de S. S. pseud. see Souza Silva, Joaquim Norberto de, 1820-1891.
J. O. pseud. see Ormrod, John.
J. O. pseud. see Oxenbridge, John.
J. O. T. pseud. see Terry, John Orville.
J. O. W. pseud. see W., J. O. pseud.
J. P. pseud. see P., J. pseud.
J. P. pseud. see Pennyman, John.
J. P. pseud. see Phillips, John.
J*** P******. pseud. see Pringle, Sir John.
J. P. pseud. see Purvis, John.
J. P. F. N. A. pseud. see Nabuco de Araujo, Jose Paulo de Figueiroa.
J. P. L. pseud. see L., J. P. pseud.
J. Q. García, Jose de. see García, Jose de J. Q.
J. R. pseud. see R., J. pseud.
J. R********. pseud. see Rivington, James. spurious author
J. R. pseud. see Rogers, John, 1649?-1721.
J. R.***. pseud. see Romanet, J.
J. R. A. pseud. see Ames, Julius Rubens. supposed author
J. R. O. pseud. see O., J. R. pseud.
J. R. Putnam's plan for removing bars. 66828
J. R. W. pseud. see Willson, James Renwick, 1780-1853.
J. R. Y. pseud. see Indarte, Jose Rivera.
J. R. Y. S. pseud. see S., J. R. Y. pseud.
J. S. pseud. see S., J. pseud.
J. S. pseud. see Sabine, James.
J. S. pseud. see Scottow, Joshua.
J. S. pseud. see Sherman, J.
J. S. pseud. see Sullivan, James, 1744-1808.
J. S.—a layman. pseud. see Sullivan, James, 1744-1808.
J. S. C. pseud. see Sierra, Justo.

J. S. de A. pseud. see A., J. S. de.
J. S. G. pseud. see G., J. S. pseud.
J. S. Stoddard's proposed canal. 91935
J. St. N. pseud. see St. Nicholas, John.
J. Sanford's almanac . . . for 1805. 76487
J. Seldeni opera omnia tam edita quam
   inedita. (78975)
J. Smith . . . Cyfieithiad o'r saes'neg. 82901
J Synnerhet evangelista brodra. 17416
J. T. pseud. see T., J. pseud.
J. T. Buckingham acquitted. 43790
J. T. de C. pseud. see C., J. T. de.
J. T. H. pseud. see H., J. T. pseud.
J. T. W. pseud. see W., J. T. pseud.
J. Thornton Randolph. pseud. see Peterson,
   Charles J.
J. Tyrwhitt Brooks. pseud. see Vizetelly,
   Henry.
J. V. pseud. see V., J. pseud.
J. V. pseud. see Vaux, James.
J. V. G. pseud. see Gonzalez, Juan Vicente.
J. van H. pseud. see H., J. van, Patriot
   van't Vaderlandt. pseud.
J. W. pseud. see W., J. pseud.
J. W. pseud. see Wadsworth, James.
J. W. pseud. see Ward, Edward.
J. W. pseud. see Whiting, John, 1656-1722.
J*** W*********. pseud. see Williamson,
   John, d. 1840.
J*** W*******. pseud. see Winthrop, John,
   1714-1779. supposed author
J. W. pseud. see Wise, John.
J. W. pseud. see Wiswall, Ichabod.
J***** W*******. pseud. see Wolcott,
   Josiah. supposed author
J. W. pseud. see Wyeth, Joseph.
J. W. B. pseud. see Barquera, Juan
   Wenceslao.
J. W. D. pseud. see Caspar, F. X. von.
J. W. S. pseud. see S., J. W. pseud.
J. Wesley's Leben. 88554
J. Wilkes Booth, the assassinator of President
   Lincoln. 29481
J. Y. pseud. see Y., J. pseud.
Jaarboekje voor het jaar 1856. 93857
Jaarboekje voor [het jaar] . . . 1857. 93867
Jabez's character and prayer. 16640
Jaboatam, Antonio de Sancta-Maria. 34144,
   35333-35334
Jacinto de Caxica, Fray. 35335
Jack, C. J. 35336
Jack, Canabal. pseud. Ran away from home.
   see Reid, Thomas Mayne, 1818-1883.
Jack, Colonel. pseud. History and remarkable
   life. see Defoe, Daniel, 1659?-1731.
Jack Downing's letters. 84144, 84158
Jack Downing's song book. 84178
Jack Downing's Yankee stories. 84159
Jack Gilmore, Esq. 102473
Jack Halliard. pseud. see Halliard, Jack.
   pseud.
Jack in the forecastle. 82118
Jack Morgan songster. 35338
Jack Mosby, the gurilla chief. 51039
Jack Nips. pseud. see Leland, John. sup-
   posed author
Jack Nothing. pseud. Dialogue between the
   giant Polypheme and his son. 19929
Jack Retort. 35339
Jack Somers in the navy. 57216
Jack Tar, or the Florida reef. 16450
Jack Tar's journals. 59477
Jack the piper. 86894
Jack Tory. pseud. see Walter, Thomas,
   1696-1725.

Jack Traveller. pseud. Letter from a gentle-
   man in Transylvania. see Hunt, Isaac.
Jackman, Benjamin. (35340)
Jackman, W. G. engr. 84141
Jackson, ---------. cartographer 1147
Jackson, ---------. engr. 97657
Jackson, ---------, fl. 1836. plaintiff 84346,
   103969
Jackson, ---------. supposed author 97106
Jackson, Dr. -------, fl. 1803. 96402
Jackson, Mrs. -------, fl. 1803. 96402
Jackson, ----------, fl. 1652. 104336
Jackson, Albert. defendant 35341
Jackson, Andrew, Pres. U. S., 1767-1845.
   445-(448), 3138, 4787, (14151), (14929),
   18005, 20314, 21445, 25429, 25876,
   29932, 31769, 33120, 34607, 34641,
   35342-35345, 35347-35348, 35350-35359,
   35374, 35376, (35378) 35391, 36008,
   40370, 40575, (43589), (44237), 44925,
   47186, 47200, 48096-48104, 48148, 51782
   56758, 56778, 63811, 64585, 65933,
   66067, 69479, (77238), 78647, (79065),
   85070, 87423, 88068, 6th note after 88114
   88496, 94760, 94783, 94799, note after
   95362, 96595, 96659-96662, 96665, 98411
   98425, 102279-102281, 102291, 104204-
   104205 see also U. S. President,
   1829-1837 (Jackson)
Jackson, Andrew, Pres. U. S., 1767-1845.
   supposed author 30883
Jackson, Andrew, Pres. U. S., 1767-1845.
   petitioner 35349
Jackson, Andrew, Pres. U. S., 1767-1845.
   spirit author 34351, 35928, 71149
Jackson, Andrew, b. 1814. 35392-35393,
   51778
Jackson, Charles, 1775-1855. 35394-35395,
   35931
Jackson, Charles David. 35396
Jackson, Charles ,Thomas, 1805-1880. 5804,
   11727, (16172), 18278, 35397-35402,
   35403, 38674, 42006, (43936)-(43938),
   (48737), (49210), 52830-52831, 52834,
   (55750), (70685), (71295), 80027, 82996,
   88362 see also Maine. State Geologis
Jackson, David T. petitioner 35404
Jackson, Ebenezer. 35605-35606
Jackson, Edmund. 62767
Jackson, Edward. 35407, 104972 see also
   Woburn, Mass. First Church. Pastor.
Jackson, F. Wolcott. 90675
Jackson, Francis. 88118-88119 see also
   South Cove Corporation, Boston. Agent.
Jackson, Francis James, 1770-1814. 30257,
   34400, 35410, 42443-42444, 42446, 4245
   83809-83817 see also Great Britain.
   Legation. United States.
Jackson, Frederick. (35411)
Jackson, G. F. tr. 35528
Jackson, H. W. R. 35420-(35421)
Jackson, Hall. 35412
Jackson, Halliday. 35413
Jackson, Henry. 35414-35416
Jackson, Henry R. (35417)-(35419)
Jackson, Isaac R. 30586, 35420-35423
Jackson, Isaac R. supposed author 30594,
   81523-(81524)
Jackson, J. tr. 88927
Jackson, J. B. S. 30741
Jackson, James. defendant 96884, 96888,
   101425, 102625
Jackson, James. plaintiff 88951, 96885-96888
Jackson, James, 1757-1806. 49073, 102116
   see also Georgia. Governor, 1798-
   1801 (Jackson)

Jackson, James, 1777-1867. (35424)-(35429), 45874, note after 89212
Jackson, James, 1810-1834. 35426-35427
Jackson, James, 1819-1887. 84992
Jackson, James C. 35430
Jackson, Jesse W. 35432
Jackson, John, of Philadelphia. (35435)
Jackson, John, fl. 1660. 80212
Jackson, John, d. 1807. (59572)
Jackson, John, fl. 1819. 35433
Jackson, John, fl. 1833. (35434)
Jackson, John Andrew. 89925
Jackson, John C. (35436)
Jackson, John George, 1777-1825. 35437
Jackson, John Mills. 35438, 2d note after 99571
Jackson, John P. 35439, (53185)
Jackson, Jonathan, 1743-1810. 35441, 93506, 3d note after 95720, 95943
Jackson, Jonathan Walker. 35440
Jackson, Joseph C. 35442
Jackson, Joseph H. (35443)
Jackson, Joseph W. 35444
Jackson, Lewis E. 35445, (54444)
Jackson, Margaret. (35446)
Jackson, P. 84641
Jackson, Patrick T. 17127, 35449, 89643
Jackson, Patrick T. petitioner 6498, 17114, (35448)
Jackson, Paul. 23388, 61547, 84595
Jackson, Potter. (35447)
Jackson, R. E. Scoresby. see Scoresby-Jackson, R. E.
Jackson, R. M. S. (35453)
Jackson, Richard. petitioner 101150
Jackson, Richard, fl. 1760. (35450)
Jackson, Richard, 1764-1838. (35451), 70689
Jackson, Robert. 35454-(35456)
Jackson, Samuel. tr. 88932
Jackson, Samuel, 1787-1872. 35458-(35460) see also Commission Appointed to Visit Canada, for the Investigation of the Epidemic Cholera, 1832.
Jackson, Samuel C. 35461
Jackson, Stonewall. see Jackson, Thomas Jonathan, 1824-1863.
Jackson, Tatlow. (35462)-35463
Jackson, Thomas, 1783-1873. 35464-35465, note after 102680, 102702
Jackson, Thomas Jonathan, 1824-1863. 19492, 2d note after 100578
Jackson, William, 1730-1803. (16088)
Jackson, William, Bishop of Oxford, 1751-1815. (35471), 71547
Jackson, William, 1759-1828. (35472)-(35474), 101724, 101748-101749, 101803
Jackson, William, 1759-1828. petitioner (35474), 47696
Jackson, William, 1783-1855. 35475-35476
Jackson, William, 1793-1844. 35483
Jackson, William A. 35477, 35480-(35481)
Jackson, William J. 15330
Jackson, William M. 35482-35483
Jackson, William S. 35484
Jackson, La. Insane Asylum. see Louisiana. Insane Asylum, Jackson.
Jackson, Miss. Institution for the Deaf. see Mississippi. School for the Deaf, Jackson.
Jackson, Miss. School for the Deaf. see Mississippi. School for the Deaf, Jackson.
Jackson, Miss. State Library. see Mississippi. State Library, Jackson.
Jackson, Miss. State Rights' Convention, 1834. see State Rights' Convention, Jackson, Miss., 1834.

Jackson against the father of his country. 101772
Jackson and Burr. (35382)
Jackson and liberty. 32619
Jackson and New Orleans. 35371
Jackson and the generals of the war of 1812. 36005
Jackson and the veto. 61745
Jackson Central Committee of Maryland. 45052 see also Democratic Party. Maryland.
Jackson city directory. 35485, note before 95420
Jackson Club of the City and County of Philadelphia. 103855 see also Democratic Party. Pennsylvania. Philadelphia. Democratic Party. Pennsylvania. Philadelphia County.
Jackson Committee of Cincinnati. 35373 see also Democratic Party. Ohio. Cincinnati.
Jackson Committee of Nashville. 35373 see also Democratic Party. Tennessee. Nashville.
Jackson Convention, Concord, Mass., 1820. (50396)
Jackson Democratic Association, Washington, D. C. 35370 see also Democratic Party. Washington, D. C.
Jackson Democratic Association, Washington, D. C. Committee. see National and Jackson Democratic Association. Committee.
Jackson Democratic Association. Proceedings at the banquet. 35370
Jackson offering. 35372
Jackson wreath. 101164
Jacksonian democrat. pseud. Address to the Democrats of Massachusetts. see Sennott, George.
Jackson's letter on Texas. 88496
Jackson's victory. 3968
Jacksonville, Ill. Asylum for the Education of the Deaf and Dumb. see Illinois. School for the Deaf, Jacksonville.
Jacksonville, Ill. Convention of American Instructors of the Deaf and Dumb, 5th, 1858. see Convention of American Instructors of the Deaf and Dumb. 5th, Jacksonville, Ill., 1858.
Jacksonville, Ill. Hospital for the Insane. see Illinois. Hospital for the Insane, Jacksonville.
Jacksonville, Ill. Illinois College. see Illinois College, Jacksonville, Ill.
Jacksonville, Ill. Morgan County Sabbath School Convention, 1866. see Morgan County Sabbath School Convention, Jacksonville, Ill., 1866.
Jacksonville, Ill. School for the Deaf. see Illinois. School for the Deaf, Jacksonville.
Jacksonville city directory. 35486
Jacksonville city directory. 35487, 1st note after 100816
Jacob, Gerard. 35487, 1st note after 100816
Jacob, John J. 35488-(35489)
Jacob, Joseph. 35490, (46655)
Jacob, Koul. 78672
Jacob, Stephen. 35491
Jacob, William. 35492
Jacob Barker to the electors. (3390)
Jacob Barter to the public. 3392
Jacob Barker's speech. 3392
Jacob Leisler. pseud. see Bradford, Vincent L.
Jacob Lind's . . . Versuch uber die Krankheiten. 41278

Jacob Omnium. pseud. see Omnium, Jacob. pseud.
Jacob Steendam. 91167-91169
Jacob Steendam, noch vaster. 51460, 51464, 91169
Jacob Webster, of Windsor, in Connecticut. 102325
Jacobi, Abraham. 84277
Jacobi, E. 35494
Jacobi, John Christian. 66456
Jacobin looking-glass. 35495
Jacobiniad. (26623)
Jacobinism. 14021
Jacobins of Missouri and Maryland. 5741
Jacobo Philippo. Frate see Foresti, Jacobo Philippo.
Iacobo Sanazaro Patritio Neapolitano et Eqviti Clariss. S. P. D. 67736
Jacobs, Anthony. 91836
Jacobs, Bela, 1786-1836. 35496-35497
Jacobs, Curtis M. (25712), (35497A)-35498
Jacobs, Harriet. 35501
Jacobs, Justin A. 35500
Jacobs, M. 35502
Jacobs, Peter. 35503, (57082), (57094)
Jacobs, Sarah Sprague, b. 1813. ed. 35496, 35505
Jacobs, Thomas Jefferson. 35506
Jacob's address to Laban. 73534
Jacob's ladder. 103510
Jacob's vow upon his leaving his father's house. (14525)
Jacobsen, F. 35507
Jacobus Antiquarius, of Milan. (66468)
Jacobus. pseud. Big bull in a court house. 35509
Jacobus, Melancthon W. 35508, 83456
Jacobus Pylarinus. pseud. see Pylarinus, Jacobus. pseud.
Jacomb, Robert. 35510
Iacomilvs, Martinvs. see Waldseemuller, Martin, 1470?-1518?
Jacott, Francisco Frias y. see Frias y Jacott, Francisco, Conde de Pozos Dulces, 1809-1877.
Jacottet, -------. illus. 48916
Jacquemard, -------. see Jacquemart, N. F.
Jacquemart, Fr. ed. 35512, 73511
Jacquemart, N.-F. 35511, 68739
Jacquemin, -------. 35513-35514
Jacquemont, Victor. (35515)
"Jacques." pseud. Theatrical contributions. 35518, 95289
Jacques, ---------. (17453), 68322
Jacques, A. 35516
Jacques, Francis. 83857
Jacques, John. 50731
Jacques, John W. see Jaques, John Wesley.
Jacques, Moses, defendant 35783, 96908
Jacques de St Albin. pseud. see Collin de Plancy, Jacques A. S.
Iac. Corvti Doctoris Medici Parisiensis. Canadensivm plantarvm. (16809)
Jacquin, Nicolas Joseph, Baron. see Jacquin, Nikolaus Joseph, Freiherr von, 1727-1817.
Jacquin, Nikolaus Joseph, Freiherr von, 1727-1819. 2440, 20942, 35519-(35523)
Jacquinot, -------. 21216
Jaeger, B. 35525-35527
Jaeger, Friedrich Wilhelm, 1796-1848. 35524
Jaeger, G. F. 35528
Jaers 1628 roepende stemme tot de Vereenighde Nederlanden. 89745
Jaffrey, N. H. 35529, 35531

Jaffrey, N. H. Selectmen. 35530
Jaffrey, N. H. Superintending School Committee. 35530
Jagd. (16449)
Jagemann, C. J. 38366, 99469
Jaggar, William. 35532
Jagger, S. H. 35533
Jagger, William. (35534)-35535, note after 93439
Jagt-en reisavonturen in Amerika. 93105
Jaguh nigoages wathah. 47868, 105556
Jahkursoe, an Indian. 105218
Jahnsenykes, Williamson. pseud. Memoir of the northern kingdom. see Jenks, William.
Jahr an den Ufern des Sacramento. 21184
Jahr an den Ufern des San Josquin und des Sacramento. 21187
Jahr in Californien. (21186)
Jahrbuch. 89755
Jahrbuch fur Romanische und Englische Literatur. 35536
Jahrbucher der Gessellschaft zur Verbreitung des Glaubens, Coln. 1579A
Jahrbucher der neuern Geschichte der Englischen Pflanzungen. 9287
Jahresbericht der . . . Canal Commissioners. 59955
Jahresbericht der Deutschen Gesellschaft von Pennsylvanien. 60054
Jahresbericht des Emigranten-Commissare von New York. (59595)
Jahres-Bericht des Direktoren-Rathes der offentlichen Schulen von St. Louis. 75366
Jahresbericht des General-Auditors uber die Finanzen des Staats. 59905
Jahresbericht des Staats Schatzmeisters uber die Finanzen des Staats. 60167
Jahres-Bericht und Mitglieder-Verzeichniss. 54325
Jahres-Bericht von Handel, Manufakturwesen, . . . und Stadt Milwaukee. (49156)
"J'ai vu" d'un habitant du Cap. 10756
Jail Association of Quebec. see Quebec Jail Association.
Jail question. 35537
Jaillot, Charles Hubert Alexis. 35538
Jakare-Ouassou. 6842, (26774)
Jakob Cooks dritte und letzte Reise. 16263
Jakob und Edward Jefferson's Reise nach Californien. 38241
Jalapa (Mexican State) Congreso General, 1824 35541
Jalapa, Mexico (City) Colegio Nacional. 35542
Jalapa, Mexico (City) Conferencias entre el Ministro de Relaciones Exteriores Plenipotenciario y el Contra Almirante Plenipotenciario de Francia, 1838. see Mexico. Conferencias entre el Ministro de Relaciones Exteriores Plenipotenciario y el Contra Almirante Plenipotenciario de Francia Sobre el Arreglo de las Diferencias entre Ambas Naciones, Jalapa, 1838.
Jalisco (Mexican State) (29024), 35546, 48282
Jalisco (Mexican State) petitioners 35554
Jalisco (Mexican State) Asamblea Departmental petitioners 35555
Jalisco (Mexican State) Comandancia General. 35549
Jalisco (Mexican State) Commandante General. 35544, 50118 see also Montenegro, J J. G.
Jalisco (Mexican State) Congreso. 35548, 56453

Jamaica in 1850. 5305
Jamaica in 1866. 30780
Jamaica: its past and present state. 62468
Jamaica lady. (35607)
Jamaica. Letter on promoting immigration into that colony. (41299)
Jamaica magazine. (35598), 35638
Jamaica magistrate's and vestryman's assistant. 35599
Jamaica merchant. pseud. Don John further displayed. 15962, 20586
Jamaica movement. 35600
Jamaica papers. 35597
Jamaica. Papers laid before the Royal Commission of Enquiry. 23562
Jamaica physical journal. 35601
Jamaica Plain, Mass. Massachusetts Infant Asylum. see Massachusetts Infant Asylum, Jamaica Plain.
Jamaica Plain, Mass. Quinohequin Lodge, I. O. O. F. see Odd Fellows, Independent Order of. Massachusetts. Quinohequin Lodge, Jamaica Plain.
Jamaica Plain and West Roxbury directory. 8251
Jamaica planter. pseud. Notes on the two reports. 35640, 35666-35667, 2d note after 97578
Jamaica planter. pseud. Observations upon the African slave trade. 56585
Jamaica planter's guide. (73465)
Jamaica plantership. 43559
Jamaica practice of physic. 18460
Jamaica proprietor. pseud. Letter to the Duke of Wellington. 40463
Jamaica Proprietors, Resident in Great Britain. pseud. Statement of the objections. 90747
Jamaica question. 16692
Jamaica question: papers relative to the condition. (35602)
Jamaica. Respondents case. 35603
Jamaica retraced. 16800
Jamaica. The speech of W. Burge . . . Agent for Jamaica. 9223
Jamaica. The speech of W. Burge . . . at the bar of the House of Commons. 9224
Jamaica under the apprenticeship system. 35604
Jamaica under the new form of government. 35605
Jamaica viewed. 31693-31694
Jamaica; who is to blame? 35606
Jamaica's miseries shew London's mercies. 20607
Jamaika und die Bahamas. (49485)
Jamaique. 101350
James, Duke of york. see James II, King of Great Britain, 1633-1701.
James I, King of Great Britain, 1566-1625. 31998, 35675-35676, 67548-67550, (67592), 90110, 91853, 95638, 97551, 99886 see also Great Britain. Sovereigns, etc., 1603-1625 (James I)
James II, King of Great Britain, 1633-1701. 1521, 35677, 79370, 96529, 96532, 99889 see also Great Britain. Sovereigns, etc., 1685-1688 (James II)
James, ---------, fl. 1865. 41220
James, Benjamin, ed. 87690
James, Charles I. 1203, 35680
James, Charles I. complainant 35680
James, Charles I. plaintiff 35680
James, Charles P. 35678-35679
James, E. M. 35681

James, E. P. 35692-35693
James, Edwin, 1797-1861. 5429, 12833, 35682-(35691), 77390, 94328-94330
James, Elisha. 35694
James, Elizabeth Mary. tr. 26952, 81027
James, George. 100991
James, George Payne Rainsford. 35695-35697
James, Henry. 35698-(35699)
James, Henry F. 35700
James, Horace. 35701-35702
James, I. (35703)
James, Isaac. (35704), 79018
James, James. 35706
James, John Angell. 21937, 35705, 65714, 89737
James, John H. 35707, 43690
James, John Warren. (35708)-35709
James, Joseph. (35710), 94137
James, Joseph. printer 91846
James, Joseph Earl. ed. 89599
James, Mary. tr. 26952, 81027
James, Robert, 1705-1776. tr. 59225
James, T. P. 35713
James, Thomas. 13015, 20518, 35711-35712, (74131), note after 92708
James, Uriah P. (28885), 35714-(35716)
James, W. 87172
James, Wharton. plaintiff 12197
James, William. 26908, 100693 see also Democratic Party. New York. Albany. Corresponding Committee. Chairman.
James, William, d. 1827. 35717-35722, 101366
James, William Dobein. 35723
James, Zillah Fitz. see Fitz-James, Zillah.
James. firm publishers see Kimball & James firm publishers
James (J. A.) & Co. firm publishers 97989
James (J. A. & U. P.) firm publishers (28885), 35714-35715
James (U. P.) firm publishers see James (J. A. & U. P.) firm publishers
James & Williams. firm publishers 87532
James Abram Garfield. Commemorative services. 84413
James Buchanan, his doctrines and policy. 8864
James Carver, plaintiff in error, vs. James Jackson. 96888
James D. Doty vs. Stephens T. Mason. 96860
James Freeman. pseud. see Norris, John.
James G. Holmes, Commission of the City Debt, to the stockholders. (32604)
James Gillespie Blaine. 90460
James Gordon Bennett and the Herald. 96396
James Hammond's Circulating Library, Newport, R. I. 30093
James Jackson and Caleb Hate. 96884
James Jackson ex dem. Abraham Houseman and others. 96886
James Kent Stone. 84510
James Knox Polk, and a history of his administration. 36006
James Louis Petigru, of South Carolina. (28425)
James Madison unmasked. 17352
James McHenry Howard. A memoir. 84467
James Mott: a biographical sketch. 28782
James Monroe, President of the United States of America, to all and singular to whom these presents shall come, Greeting: Whereas a treaty between the United States of America and the Choctaw Nation of Indians. 96625

James Monroe, President of the United
  States of America, to all and singular
  to whom these presents shall come,
  Greeting: Whereas a treaty between the
  United States of America and the Quapaw
  Nation of Indians. 96634
James Monroe, President of the United States
  of America. To all and singular to
  whom these presents shall come,
  Greeting: Whereas a treaty between the
  United States of America and the Sock
  and Fox Tribes of Indians. 96633
James Monroe, President of the United States,
  to all and singular to whom these pre-
  sents shall come, Greeting: Whereas a
  treaty between the United States of
  America and the Ioway Tribe of Indians.
  96632
James Munroe. 38082
James Quicksilver. pseud. see Quicksilver,
  James. pseud.
James' railroad and route book. (28885),
  35715
James' reply to a brief statement on his naval
  history. 35721
James River and Kanawha Company. 35724
James River Company. (35727)
James Sidney Rollins. 84752
James Smith's vindication. 82776
James Smithson. 84988
James Smithson and his bequest. 84985,
  84987
James West Circus. 105343
James, Anna Brownell (Murphy) 1794-1860.
  (35728)-35732, 38914
Jameson, D. D. 93454
Jameson, James. defendant 96889
Jameson, John Alexander. 35733
Jameson, John Franklin, 1859-1937. ed.
  38886, 46731-46732, note after 70346,
  82832, 82950, 92350, 92940, 100547,
  103353, 104845
Jameson, Robert, 1774-1854. 18210, (40201)-
  40202, 51787
Jameson, William H. (35734)
James's rail road and route book. 28885,
  35715
James's river guide. (35716)
James's strange and dangerous voyage. 13015,
  35712
James's travellers' companion. 35714
Jamestown, N. Y. Jamestown Academy. see
  Jamestown Academy, Jamestown, N. Y.
Jamestown, Va. 35737
Jamestown, Va. Second Centennial Anniversary
  Jubilee, 1807. 35739, 1st note after
  100520
Jamestown Academy, Jamestown, N. Y. 35735
Jamestown Exposition 1607-1907. 84970
Jamestown of Pemaquid. 29474
Jamestown Tercentennial Exposition, Norfolk,
  Va., 1907. 85022
Iamet, Denys. note after 69259
Jamie Parker, the fugitive. 62790
Jamieson, -----------. 35742
Jamieson, J. 35740
Jamieson, Milton. 35741
Jamison, D. F. 35743, 87510
Jamison, Jacob. 20330, 105544
Jan Jacob Mauricius, Gouverneur-General van
  Suriname. 80991
Jan woyake ciqon dena eepi. 18291, 71336
Jane Talbot. 8457
Jane and her teacher. 104618
Janes, E. S., Bp. 13271, 84756-84756A

Janes, Edwin L. (35744)
Janes, Frederic. 35745
Janes, Walter. (35746)
Janes, Fowler, Kirkland & Co. firm petitioners
  (35747)
Janes family. 35745
Janesville, Wisc. Board of School Com-
  missioners. (35748)
Janesville democrat. 35749
Janesville: its business, manufactories, water
  power, etc. 35749
Janet, Gustave. illus. 69038
Janet-Lange, --------. illus. 3565, 69075
Janeway, J. 96107
Janeway, J. L. 41187
Janeway, Jacob James. 35750-(35751)
Janeway, James. 35752-35755, 46555, 4th note
  after 96106, 96107-1st note after 96107
Janeway, Richard. comp. 9372, 81492
Janeway, Thomas Leiper. (35756)
Janey, Jean. 35757
Jani Hoyeri De religione Gronlandorum naturali
  dissertationes tres. 33395
Janin, Andre. 35758
Janin, Jules. 1866
Janisch, Joseph. 35759
Janney, Samuel M. 35760-35762, 86030
Janney, Thomas. 35763
Jans, Anneke. 35765-35766, 5th note after
  96979
Janse, Anneke. see Jans, Anneke.
Jansen, H. J. tr. 51479, 62805
Jansen, Jacob. 35767
Jansen, M. H. 35769
Jansen, Martin. (35768)
Jansen, Sir Theodore, Bart., fl. 1721.
  37783, 65865, 88192, 88197
Janson, Charles William. 35770
Janson, Forbin, Bp. (35771) see also Nancy,
  France (Diocese) Bishop (Janson)
Jansonius, Guilielmvs. see Blaeuw, William
  Janszoon.
Janssen, Carl Emil. 35772
Janssen, Sir Theodore, Bart. see Jansen,
  Sir Theodore, Bart., fl. 1721.
Jansson, Juan. 5714, 35773-35774
Jansz, Kees. pseud. Brasilsche breede-byl.
  7534
Jansz, Willem. see Blaeuw, William
  Janszoon.
Janszoon, Jacob Honig. see Honig. Jacob,
  1816-1870.
Janszoon, W. 35775
January, 1873-June, 1878. Public laws. 70700
January 1st, 1863. Eighteenth annual report.
  54792
January 5, 1857. 83568
January 17, 1774. Supplement to the American
  Flint Glass Manufactory, Pettie's Island
  Cash Lottery. (61296)
January 7, 1778. 60168, 103236
January 10, 1826. 95381
January 29, 1831. 105414
Janus. pseud. Critical moment. 35776
Janus. 95192
Janus coelestis. 3471
Janvier, Francis De Haes. 35777-(35778),
  51437
Japan. Treaties, etc. 35779, 58340
Japan and around the world. 88882
Japan: . . . and the expedition fitted out in the
  United States. (43246)
Japan, and the expedition thereto. 877
Japan expedition. 88882
Japanese treaties concluded at Jeddo. 35779

Jeffers, James, d. 1831. defendant 27294-
27295, 96871, 101243
Jefferson. pseud. Both sides. 6816
Jefferson. pseud. Examination of the
Charleston memorial. see Carey,
Mathew, 1760-1839.
Jefferson. pseud. To the people. see
Richardson, J. S.
Jefferson, Edward. 38241
Jefferson, Jacob. 38241
Jefferson, James. petitioner 70659
Jefferson, Thomas, Pres. U. S., 1743-1826.
(445)-449, 856, 1226, 2025, (3211),
3823, 4030, 4037, 5113, (5302), 8127,
(9325), 9428-9429, 11027, 12488, 12877,
(14151), 14312, 16105-(16106), 16117-
16118, 18005, 20449, (20458), (22237),
22797, (23365), 25876, 25911, 26259,
26328, 27072, 28011, 29949, 29953,
29984, 31419, 34544, (35880)-(35919),
(35925), (35930), 35933-(35934), 35936-
(35937), (35961), 36579, (37240), (37656),
39751, (40117), 40696, 40824-40827,
40832-40838, 41427, 41610, 42177-42179,
42192, 42264, 42266, 42291, (43720),
(48057)-48065, 48148, (48755), (49519),
50013, (50137), 50336, 52083, (54024),
(55169), 55968, 56434, 58231, 58478-
(58479), 63811, 64127, 65004, 65340,
65359, (67854), (68117), 68118, 69789,
71995, 72717, 75318, 77360, 78647,
79369, 81857, 82288-82290, 82974,
82976, 82979, 83811, 83818-83823,
84076, 84602, 84787, 84835, 84904,
85198, 85376, 89198, note after 91540,
1st note after 92859, 93553, note after
93610-93611, 93958, 93960, 95390, note
after 95562, note before 95775, 96015,
96413, 96415, 2d note after 96498,
96499, 96576, 96579, 96591-96592,
96613, 96625, 96627, 96691, 96991, 3d
note after 97146, 97302, 97440, 1st note
after 99824, 100040-100041, 100066,
100193-100209, note before 100232,
100326, 100334, 100341-100344, 100451,
1st note after 100461, 2d note after
100504, 2d note after 100506, 100540,
note after 100545A, 101709, 101719-
101720, 101722, 101726, note after
101839, 102017, 103334, 104204-104205,
104647, 105157, see also U. S. Department of State. U. S. President,
1801-1809 (Jefferson) Virginia. Governor, 1779-1781 (Jefferson) Virginia.
University. Rector.
Jefferson, Thomas, pres. U. S., 1743-1826.
supposed author 19933, 35933, 4th note
after 98269
Jefferson, Thomas, Pres. U. S., 1743-1826.
spirit author 34351, 35928
Jefferson, Thomas, Pres. U. S., 1743-1826.
spurious author 89079, 89403
Jefferson against Madison's war. (35930),
3d note after 97146
Jefferson and liberty. 55187
Jefferson at Monticello. 62792
Jefferson Barracks, Mo. 89201
Jefferson City, Mo. Emancipation Convention,
1862. see Emancipation Convention,
Jefferson City, Mo., 1862.
Jefferson City, Mo. Lincoln Institute. see
Lincoln Institute, Jefferson City, Mo.
Jefferson College, Canonsburgh, Pa. 35940
Jefferson College, Canonsburgh, Pa. Board of
Trustees. Committee. 105664

Jefferson College, Canonsburgh, Pa. Franklin
Literary Society. 35940
Jefferson College, Canonsburgh, Pa. Philo
Literary Society. 35939-35940
Jefferson College, Canonsburgh, Pa. Philo
Literary Society. Library. 35939
Jefferson College, Canonsburgh, Pa. President.
102007, 105664 see also Wylie,
Andrew.
Jefferson College, Washington, Miss. (35941),
88616
Jefferson College, Washington, Miss. Board of
Trustees. petitioners 69844
Jefferson College, Washington, Miss. Charter.
(35941)
Jefferson College, Washington, Miss. Library.
(35941)
Jefferson County, N. Y. Agricultural Society.
see Jefferson County Agricultural
Society.
Jefferson County, N. Y. Board of Supervisors.
35944
Jefferson County, N. Y. Institute, Watertown.
see Jefferson County Institute, Water-
town, N. Y.
Jefferson County, Vt. Washington Benevolent
Society. see Washington Benevolent
Society. Vermont. Jefferson County.
Jefferson County Agricultural Society. (35945)
Jefferson County Agricultural Society. Cattle
Show and Fair. 1st, 1818. (35945)
Jefferson County Horticultural Society. see
Louisville and Jefferson County Horti-
cultural Society.
Jefferson County Institute, Watertown, N. Y.
102095
Jefferson Davis, and his complicity in the
assassination. 18838, 68163
Jeff. Davis and the rebels justified. 28495
Jefferson Medical College, Philadelphia.
(35946), 61746
Jefferson Medical College, Philadelphia.
Faculty. 90711
Jefferson Medical College, Philadelphia.
Faculty. petitioners 61746
Jefferson Medical College, Philadelphia.
Trustees. 61746, 90711
Jefferson Medical College. (21278)
Jefferson Medical College . . . in relation to
John Barnes. 3518
Jefferson Medical College. . . . Introductory
lecture. (59154)
Jefferson monument magazine. 35947
Jeffersoniad. 19518
Jeffersonian. pseud. Which will you have as
president? 103261
Jeffersonian democracy defined and vindicated.
9611
Jeffersonian Republican. pseud. Exhibition of
wolves in sheep's clothing. 23401
Jeffersonian Republican. pseud. Life of
William H. Seward. 79598
Jeffersonian Weekly. 35949
Jefferson's manual of parliamentary practice.
16117
Jefferson's memoirs. 232
Jefferson's notes on the state of Virginia.
35899-35900
Jefferson's writings. 93611
Jeffersonville and New-Albany Canal Company.
Charter. (35951)
Jeffersonville and New-Albany Canal Company.
Engineer. (35951)
Jeffrey, R. (35952), 38064
Jeffreys, Robert. 16277, (55557)

Jeffreys, Thomas. 16278, 28460, (28537), 35953-35971, 38302, (40141), 51285, (55557), (64835), 67008, 71926, 1st note after 94082, 102830
Jeffries, B. J. tr. (10919)
Jeffries, C. 35973
Jeffries, James Culbertson. 35972
Jeffries, John. (35974)
Jeffries, John P. (35975)
Jeffries, Thomas Fayette. 35976
Jehan, Louis Francois, b. 1803. 35977
Jehan de St. Clevien, J. F. 35977
Jehovah is the king and saviour of His people. 79422
Jehovah-Jireh. 82950
Jehovah-Shalom. 43155
Jehovah the helper of America. (43154)
Jehovah's character as a man of war. 23
Jehu O'Cataract. pseud. see Neal, John.
Jekyll, N. (35978)
Jeles jorteneti. 89010
Jelly, Thomas. 35979
Jemison, Jacob. tr. 20330, 105544
Jemison, Mary. 78678-(78682)
Jena. Ethnographischen Archiv. see Ethographischen Archiv, Jena.
Jenckes, Joseph, 1656-1740. 2635
Jenckes, Thomas Allen, 1818-1875. 35680, 35980-35982
Jenckins, Charles J. 71214
Jeneral de Brigada Ramon Castilla a sus conciudanos. 12776
Jeneral Santa-Cruz esplica su conducta publica. 76771
Jenifer, Daniel, 1791-1855. 35983
Jenings, Edmund. 35984-(35987), 39258, 64827, 64829
Jenings, Samuel. 37178, 37205, 53083, 66737
Jenio de Rimac. 99611
Jenkin, Griffin. 7919, note just before 53081
Jenkins, Charles. 22595, (35988), 88943
Jenkins, Charles J. 35989
Jenkins, Edward. 35990
Jenkins, Elisha. plaintiff (35991), 98547
Jenkins, Geoffrey. pseud. Legislative sketches. 35992
Jenkins, Howard M. 35993
Jenkins, J. Foster. 35999, 76626, (76673)
Jenkins, James. 35994
Jenkins, John. ed. 88615
Jenkins, Rev. John, of Montreal. 35995-35998
Jenkins, John. petitioner 103404
Jenkins, John, fl. 1786. (59830), 105686A, 105693A
Jenkins, John J. 3600
Jenkins, John S. 36001-36014
Jenkins, John W. 36015
Jenkins, Joseph. 36016
Jenkins, Mary H. 46886
Jenkins, Obadiah. (36017)
Jenkins, Samuel. 36445
Jenkins, Timothy, 1799-1859. (36020)
Jenkins, Thomas. defendant 96890, 97822
Jenkins, Thornton A. 36018-36019
Jenkins, Walworth. 36022
Jenkins, Warren. 36021
Jenkinson, Anthony. 66686
Jenkinson, Charles. see Liverpool, Charles Jenkinson, 1st Earl of, 1727-1808.
Jenkinson, Isaac. 36024
Jenkinson, John Banks, Bishop of St. Davids, 1781-1840. (5006)
Jenkinson, Robert Banks. see Liverpool, Robert Banks Jenkinson, 2d Earl of, 1770-1828.

Jenks, George E. 36028, 90796
Jenks, Joseph. see Jenckes, Joseph, 1656-1740.
Jenks, Samuel H. 36029
Jenks, William. 36030-36035, (43391), 93608
Jenks, family. 36032
Jenkyl, N. petitioner (35978)
Jenner, Edward. 98272
Jenner, Thomas. 103659
Jenness, -------. 82823
Jennings, -------, fl. 1707. 44082
Jennings, Calvin. defendant (8249), note after 91015
Jennings, Clotilda. 36037
Jennings, David. 36028, 46625
Jennings, Ebenezer. 36039, 102755
Jennings, Henry S. 36040
Jennings, Isaac. 36041
Jennings, James. 36042
Jennings, Jonathan. 96678 see also U. S. Commissioners to the Potawatomi Tribe of Indians of the Prairie.
Jennings, Louis J. 36043
Jennings, Needler R. 42205
Jennings, Obadiah. 36044
Jennings, Paul. 36045
Jennings, R. L. ed. (25708)
Jennings, Richard Downing. 36047
Jennings, Samuel. 8956-8957, (36048), 37196
Jennings, Samuel Kennedy, 1771-1854. 36049
Jennings Association. 82413
Jennison, Edwin. 84293
Jenney, -------. lithographer 84774
Jenny Ambrose. 36050
Jenny Lind: her life, her struggles, and her triumphs. 73275
Jenny Lind in America. 73276
Jenny Lind mania in Boston. (41279)
Jenny Wade, of Gettysburg. 27236, 36051
Jennyns, J. Clayton. 36052
Jenseits des Oceans. 20124, 22782
Jenson, Andrew. tr. 83255, 82371-83272
Jenyns, -------, fl. 1810. 95315
Jenyns, Leonard. 18649
Jenyns, Soame. 6218, 35835, 36053, 57865, 68744
Jenyns, Soame. supposed author 9282-9283
Jeografia de Nicaragua. 86963
Jeografia fisica i politica. 56278
Jeografia fisica i politica del estado del Cauca. 60900
Jephson, Ralph. (36054), 103591
Jepphi, Recos. pseud. see Recos Jepphi. pseud.
Jequitinhonha, -------, Visconde de. (36055), 88737
Jequitinhonna, -------, Visconde de. see Jequitinhonha, -------, Visconde de.
Jeremiah, Ezekiel, Daniel, and the Minor Prophets. 71335
Jeremiah, Ezekiel, Daniel, qa wicasta wokcan tokokeca. 71335
Jeremiah Morton's letter. 51002
Jeremiah Saddlebags. pseud. see Read, D. F. and Read, J. A.
Jeremie, John. 36056-36057
Jeremie, Nicolas, 1669?-1732. 4936, 68419
Jeremy Bentham and the usury law. 103304
Jeremy Bentham to the National Convention of France. 4767
"Jeremy Jollyboy" songster. 86221
Jeremy Peters. pseud. see Peters, Jeremy. pseud.
Jerico, Vt. Washington Benevolent Society. see Washington Benevolent Society. Vermont. Jerico.

Job Sass. pseud. see Sass, Job. pseud.
Jobson, David Wemyss. 36136
Jobson, Frederick James, 1821-1881. 36137
Jobson, Richard. 66686
Jocelin, Simeon. 36138, 93802
Jocelyn, George B. 36139-36140
Jocelyn, S. S. engr. 83653
Jocelyn, Simeon. see Jocelin, Simeon.
Jockey Club, Louisville. see Louisville
   Jockey Club.
Jockey Club, Washington, D. C. see
   Washington Jockey Club, Washington,
   D.C.
Jockey Club of Maryland. see Maryland
   Jockey Club.
Jockey Club of South Carolina. see South
   Carolina Jockey Club.
Joco-serious dialogue. 94118
Joco-serious review. 20672
Iocotitlan, Mexico. Indios. see Indios de
   los Pueblos de Istlaguaca, Iocotitlan.
Jocundus. tr. see Giocondo, Giovanni. tr.
Jode, ------- de. see De Jode, ---------.
Joe the 'sarpint. 90009
Joel B. Sutherland or James Gown. 62301
Joel Barlow to his fellow citizens. (3422)
Joerg, E. 7861, 36141
Ioernael. ofte. voyagie vande Groenlandts-
   Vaerders. 34968
Jogues, Isaac. (36142)-36144, 80018, (80023)
Jo-gui-ye-sos. see Gordon, Samuel.
Johann Ayme's Deportationsreise. 2522
Johann Bunians Pilgrims oder Christin Reise.
   62849
Johann Elyot unde sie Familie Mayhew.
   (7445)
Johann Jacob Astor. 56738
Johann Peter Reicharts, eines Hoch-Furstl.
   Brandenburg. 68981
Johann Reinhold Forester's und Georg
   Forester's Reise um die Welt. 25129
Johann Schoner. 77804
Johann Schoner Professor of Mathematics at
   Nuremberg. 77803
Johann Schoner. 77804
Johann Sloane M. D. 82168
Johann Woolman. 105201
Johannes, Count. see Jones, George, 1810-
   1879.
Johannes in Eremo. (46371), 46409
Johannes Scrawlenburgius. pseud. see
   Scrawlenburgius, Johannes. pseud.
Johannis Caroli Spies Archiatri Wolffen-
   buttelensis. 89436
Johannis Caroli Spies Sereniss. Ducis
   Brunsvico. 89437
Johannis Luyts, Philosophiae professoris.
   (42733)
Iohannis Marquardi I. Cᵈ. De iure mercatorum
   et commerciorum. 44661, 98216
Johannis Wolferi, ethic. polit. ac geograph.
   prof. 105632
John. pseud. Amsterdamsche veerman op
   Middelburgh. 1345, note after 102878
John *********. alias see Syllavan, Owen.
   defendant
John of Enon. pseud. Watery war. see
   Benedict, David.
John the Painter. alias see Aitken, James,
   1752-1777. defendant
John, who is called a Quaker. pseud. Beames
   of eternal brightness. 4116
John, Cousin. pseud. see Cousin John.
   pseud.
John, Hector St. see St. John, Hector.

John, Henry Roscoe Saint. see St. John,
   Henry Roscoe.
John, Henry Saint. see Bolingbroke, Henry
   St. John, Viscount, 1678-1751.
John, J. Saint. see St. John, J.
John, James Augustus Saint. see St. John,
   James Augustus.
John, John R. Saint. see St. John, John R.
John, O. Saint. see St. John, O.
John, Orestes Henry Saint. see St. John,
   Orestes Henry.
John, Percey B. St. see St. John, Percy B.
John, Peter Saint. see St. John, Peter.
John, S. J. Saint. see St. John, S. J.
John, Samuel Saint. see St. John, Samuel.
John, T. E. Saint. see St. John, T. E.
John, T. P. Saint. see St. John, Thomas P.
John, Uncle. pseud. see Uncle John. pseud.
John, William Charles St. see St. John,
   William Charles.
John A. Roebling. 72577
John Adams. pseud. see Adams, John.
   pseud.
John Agawam. pseud. see Story, Joseph.
   supposed author
John Allen vs. W. B. Burke. 96811
John Andrew Schulze my Jo, John, &c. 84863
John Arch, a Cherokee young man. 93215
John Asawatomie Brown, der Negerheiland.
   66398
John B. Gough's early history. 64728
John Bean of Hingham. 80779
John Beedle's sleigh-ride. 36145, 43045
John Bradbury's travels. 84304-84306, 84320-
   84321
John Brown. (82636)
John Brown. Condamnation a mort. 12968
John Brown invasion. 8518, 20935
John Brown mort pour l'affranchisement des
   noires. 24125
John Brown, or the true and false philanthropist
   3400
John Brown. Par Victor Hugo. 33616
John Brown Pioneer Radical Republican Club,
   New Orleans. 53318 see also Republi-
   can Party. Louisiana. New Orleans.
John Brown; sa vie. 44659
John Brown, with a photograph representing his
   execution. 33617
John Brown's body. 83677
John Brown's expedition. 58749
John Bull. pseud. see Hamilton, W. R.
John Bull and Brother Jonathan. (59193)
John Bull in America. 59198
John Bull starving. 86077
John Bull the clothier. 4433
John Bryons, sbersten Befehlshaber uber ein
   Englisches Geschwader. 9736
John C. Fremont! "Is he honest? is he
   capable?" (25845)
John C. Fremont! "Ist er Ehrlich? ist er
   Sahig?" (25845)
John Calvin and the influence of his doctrines.
   91767
John Carter Brown Library. see Brown
   University. John Carter Brown Library.
John Chissel. pseud. see Chissel, John.
   pseud.
John Cogitans. pseud. see Morey, Charles.
John Cotton's answer to Roger Williams.
   51773
John Cotton's life and letters. 106052
John Cox, 1795-1871. 65008
John Dickinson, (etc.)*** 20039
John Doe. pseud. see Doe, John. pseud.

John Doe and Richard Doe. 28102

John Dutton's letters from New-England. 21343, 65646

John Eliot, the apostle to the Indians. 106051

John F. Prescott's city and business directory. 97072

John Faustus. pseud. see Walter, Thomas, 1696-1725.

John Filson. 84936

John Foster. 95820

John Gatonbe's voyage. 13015

John Grant. 84422

John Graves Simcoe. Proclamation of George the Third. 98065B

John Gray, of Mount Vernon. 18359

John H. Sheppard,—Register of Probate, 1813-1834. 80313

John H. Smith. August 20, 1842. 82971

John H. Smith. December 29, 1841. 82970

John H. Smith. Memorial of John H. Smith. 82969

John H. Surratt and his mother. 28440

John Hammett's vindication and relation. 30081

John Hopkins' notions on political economy. 36146

John Jacob Astor plan! 88487

John Keese, auctioneer. 84093

John Langdon and Son's . . . directory. 54459

John Law—his body moulders in the ground. 49970

John Law the projector. 546

John Leo, a More. see Leo Africanus, Jean.

John Letcher and his antecedents. (40237)

John Linings Tabelle uber die Aus-und Absonderungen des Korpers. 11773

John M. Clayton and the Nicaragua Canal Treaty. (79532)

John M. Costello. 17022

John M. Spear's labors for the destitute prisoner. 89077

John M. Speed. 89231

John Malcom. 27650, (63966), 68421

John Melish's Reisen durch die Vereinigten-Staaten. 47437

John O'Brien. 72465

John Oldburg, Esq. pseud. see Withington, Leonard.

John P. Branch historical papers. 84743

John Palmer's journal of travels. 84304-84306, 84320-84321

John Poultney's Heirs. plaintiffs see Heirs of John Poultney. plaintiffs

John Presbyter. pseud. see Presbyter, John. pseud.

John Queristicus. pseud. see A., E. H. M. pseud.

John Quincy Adams' disunion letter. 88496

John Quincy Adams, President of the United States of America, to all and singular to whom these presents shall come, Greeting. Treaty between the United States of America and the Cherokee Nation of Indians. 96656

John Quincy Adams, President of the United States of America, to all and singular to whom these presents shall come, Greeting: Whereas, a treaty between the United States of America and the Chippeway, Menomonie and Winnebago Tribes of Indians. 96652

John Quincy Adams, President of the United States of America, to all and singular to whom these presents shall come, Greeting: Whereas a treaty between the United States of America and the Creek Nation of Indians. 96636

John Quincy Adams, President of the United States of America, to all and singular to whom these presents shall come, Greeting: Whereas a treaty between the United States of America and the Crow Tribe of Indians. 96646

John Quincy Adams, President of the United States of America, to all and singular to whom these presents chall come, Greeting: Whereas, a treaty between the United States of America, and the Eel River or Thorntown Party of the Miami Indians. 96655

John Quincy Adams, President of the United States of America, to all and singular to whom these presents shall come, Greeting: Whereas a treaty between the United States of America and the Great and Little Osage Tribes of Indians. 96637

John Quincy Adams, President of the United States of America, to all and singular to whom these presents shall come, Greeking: Whereas a treaty between the United States of America, and the Hunk-papas Bank of the Sioux Tribe of Indians. 96642

John Quincy Adams, President of the United States of America, to all and singular to whom these presents shall come, Greeting: Whereas a treaty between the United States of America and the Kanzas Nation of Indians. 96638

John Quincy Adams, President of the United States of America, to all and singular to whom these presents shall come, Greeting: Whereas a treaty between the United States of America and the Maha Tribe of Indians. 96650

John Quincy, Adams, President of the United States of America, to all and singular to whom these presents shall come, Greeting: Whereas a treaty between the United States of America and the Ottoe and Missouri Tribe of Indians. 96648

John Quincy Adams, President of the United States of America, to all and singular to whom these presents shall come, Greeting: Whereas a treaty between the United States of America and the Pawnee Tribe of Indians. 96649

John Quincy Adams, President of the United States of America, to all and singular to whom these presents shall come, Greeting: Whereas a treaty between the United States of America and the Poncar Tribe of Indians. 96639

John Quincy Adams, President of the United States of America. To all and singular to whom these presents shall come, Greeting: Whereas a treaty between the United States of America, and the Potawatamie Tribe of Indians. 96653

John Quincy Adams, President of the United States of America, to all and singular to whom these presents shall come, Greeting: Whereas a treaty between the United States of America and the Ricara Tribe of Indians. 96643

John Quincy Adams, President of the United States of America, to all and singular to whom these presents shall come, Greeting: Whereas a treaty between the United States of America and the Shawonee Nation of Indians. 96651

John Quincy Adams, President of the United States of America, to all and singular to whom these presents shall come, Greeting: Whereas a treaty between the United States of America and the Sioune and Ogallala Tribes of Indians. 96641

John Quincy Adams, President of the United States of America, to all and singular to whom these presents shall come, Greeting: Whereas a treaty between the United States of America, and the Sioux and the Chippewa, Sac and Fox, Minominie, Ioway, Sioux, Winnebago, and a portion of the Ottawa, Chippewa, and Potawottomie, Tribes of Indians. 96647

John Quincy Adams, President of the United States of America, to all and singular to whom these presents shall come, Greeting: Whereas a treaty between the United States of America and the Teton, Yancton, and Yanctonies Bands of the Sioux Indians. 96640

John Quincy Adams, President of the United States of America. Whereas a treaty between the United States of America and the Creek Nation of Indians. 96654

John Quincy Adams, President of the United States, to all and singular to whom these presents shall come, Greeting: Whereas a treaty between the United States of America and the Belantse-etoa or Minnetaree Tribe of Indians. 96644

John Quincy Adams, President of the United States, to all and singular to whom these presents shall come, Greeting: Whereas a treaty between the United States of America and the Mandan Tribe of Indians. 96645

John Quod. pseud. see Irving, John Treat.

John Randolph, abroad and at home. 36894, 67848, 74254

John Rhea desires to return his thanks. 62327, 70466

John Robinson, Prediker der leidsche Brownisten-Gemeente. 38018

John Rogers, a servant of Jesus Christ, to all my beloved Brethren in Christ. 72686

John Rogers a servant of Jesus Christ, to any of the flock. 72685, 72686

John Rogers; the compiler of the first authorized English Bible. 12541

John Rogers . . . to the Church of Christ at Wester. 72682

John Ross Nicols. 84066

John S. pseud. see Sechla, John.

John Sebastian vs. Covington and Cincinnati Bridge Company. (56999)

John Sidney. pseud. see Sydney, John. pseud.

John Smith. pseud. see Smith, John. pseud.

John Smith of Milford. 83852

John Smith, the faithful, the devoted, the successful missionary. 82908

John Smith's letters. 36147, 84145

John-Street Church, New York. see New York (City) John Street Church.

John Still-Will. pseud. see Still-Will, John. pseud.

John Stirling Esquire. 91849

John Stoddard of Wethersfield, Conn. 59133

John Sydney. pseud. see Sydney, John. pseud.

John Tanner Denkwurdigkeiten. 35685, 94328

John Tatham, New Jersey's missing governor. 83982

John Tell Truth. pseud. see Le Blanc, Jean Bernard. supposed author

John the Painter's ghost. 31835

John, the traitor. (36148)

John Tyler, President of the United States, to all and singular to whom these presents shall come, Greeting. 96737

John Vandike. pseud. see Vandike, John. pseud.

John Viator. pseud. see Peters, Samuel. supposed author

John W. Gould's private journal. (28116)

John Wabash. pseud. see Sharron, J. supposed author

John Wesley's thoughts upon slavery. 102680

John Wheelwright. 65646, 103223

John Woods vindication of himself. 66742

John Wright Stanly's reply. 90351

John Y. Beall. 4110

Johnes, --------, fl. 1806. (50900)

Johnes, Arthur James, 1809-1871. 36149

Johnny Gilpin. pseud. see Gilpin, Johnny. pseud.

Johnny Weston. 44771

Johnny Wright. 32742

Johns, Evan. 36150-36151

Johns, H. V. D. (36153)

Johns, Henry T. 36152

Johns, James. 99221

Johns, John, Bp., 1796-1876. 36155-(36157)

Johns, Kensley, 1791-1857. 36158

Johns, Walter R. 15219

Johns Hopkins Hospital, Baltimore. see Baltimore. Johns Hopkins Hospital.

Johnson, --------. ed. (36232)

Johnson, --------. incorrectly supposed author 36279, 36885

Johnson, Mrs. see Hastings, Susannah Johnson.

Johnson, --------, fl. 1827. 100497

Johnson, --------, fl. 1834. 4411

Johnson, --------, fl. 1857. 66107

Johnson, --------, fl. 1865. 86814

Johnson, A. G. 36166-36167, (36281)

Johnson, A. J. 24486, 36182

Johnson, A. S. supposed author 47565

Johnson, Alfred. (36164)

Johnson, Alfred. Jr. 36165

Johnson, Alexander Bryan, 1786-1867. 16137, 36159-36163

Johnson, Allen. 85433

Johnson, Andrew, Pres. U. S., 1808-1875. 2652, 25253, 36168-36170, 36173-36175, 36181, (41226), (48142)-48145, 51085, 58468-(58469), (69754), 71366, 87445, 96396, 98005 see also U. S. President, 1865-1869 (A. Johnson)

Johnson, Andrew, Pres. U. S., 1808-1875. defendant at impeachment 36172, 36178-36181

Johnson, Anna C. 36183

Johnson, B. R. 36185

Johnson, Ben. 51028

Johnson, Benjamin Pierce, 1793-1869. 28622, (36184) see also New York (City) Agent to Attend the Exhibition of the Industry of All Nations, 1851.

Johnson, C. B. 36198-(36199)

Johnson, Chapman. 36186

Johnson, Charles. (23477)-23478, 32182, (32197), 36187-36197

Johnson, Charles Andrew. 2690

Johnson, Charles P. 36200

Johnson, Cuthbert W. 36201

Johnson, David. 83854, 87970

Johnson, Ebenezer. 36202

Johnson, Edward. 28020, (36203)-36205
Johnson, Edwin. (33274)
Johnson, Edwin F. 36206-36207, 54723
Johnson, Evan M. 36208-36209
Johnson, Ezra R. 36210
Johnson, F. 36211
Johnson, F. H. 36212-36214
Johnson, Francis. defendant 8799-8800
Johnson, Francis. reporter 93241
Johnson, George Washington. 23690, 36215
Johnson, Guy. petitioner 93593, 3d note after
    105598-9 [sic]
Johnson, H. C. Ross. 36216
Johnson, H. S. 36220A
Johnson, Helen Margaret. 36217
Johnson, Henry. tr. (42593)-42594, 97102
Johnson, Herrick, 1832-1913. 36218-(36220)
Johnson, Herschel Vespasian, 1812-1880. 402,
    (20696), 28493, 31808, 33930, 36221,
    (74480), 88335, note after 97063
Johnson, Herzon A. defendant 49545
Johnson, Isaac. (21090), 33698, 78431, 104846
Johnson, Isaac A. 87889
Johnson, J. illus. 102850
Johnson, J. E. 36231
Johnson, J. F. 84739
Johnson, J. P. petitioner (36246)
Johnson, Jacob, 1713-1797. 6225, (36222)
Johnson, James, successively Bishop of
    Gloucester, and Worcester, 1706-1774.
    (36223), 84646
Johnson, James, 1777-1845. 36224-36226
Johnson, James, 1780-1811. defendant
    (36227), (75954), note after 96890
Johnson, James, fl. 1821. claimant 36228
Johnson, James, II. 1835. 36229
Johnson, James A. 36230
Johnson, Jesse Zimmerman. (36232)
Johnson, John. 36237
Johnson, John, 1706-1791. 36233
Johnson, Sir John, 1742-1830. 33144
Johnson, John, 1778-1855. see Johnston,
    John, 1778-1855.
Johnson, John, fl. 1792. 36234
Johnson, John, d. 1824. defendant 36236,
    96891
Johnson, John, fl. 1835. 75284
Johnson, John B. 36238-36241
Johnson, John G. 36242
Johnson, John H. 36243
Johnson, John I. 36244
Johnson, Joseph. (36245)
Johnson, Joseph B. (36246)
Johnson, Joseph E. 15264
Johnson, L. (36248)
Johnson, Laura. 36247
Johnson, Lewis Farley Clogstown. tr. 103429
Johnson, Lorenzo D. (36249)-36254
Johnson, Louisa. 36255
Johnson, Lyman H. (36256)
Johnson, M. C. (37531) see also Kentucky.
    Commissioners on the Code of Practice
    in Civil and Criminal Cases.
Johnson, Maur. 86574
Johnson, Nathan. 25232, 73562, 102947 see
    also West Stafford, Conn. Second
    Church. Committee.
Johnson, Sir Nathaniel, d. 1713. 87359 see
    also South Carolina (Colony) Governor,
    1703-1708 (Johnson)
Johnson, Oliver. 26258-26259
Johnson, Overton. 36250
Johnson, Ovid F. 60065
Johnson, Parish B. comp. (12429)
Johnson, R. U. 85374

Johnson, Reverdy, 1796-1876. 18484, (20696),
    (26250), 36261-36273, 36278, 36280,
    38900, (58709), note after 69421, 70196,
    88323 see also U. S. Commissioner
    to New Orleans.
Johnson, Reverdy, 1796-1876. petitioner
    36265
Johnson, Reverdy, 1796-1876. incorrectly
    supposed author 38900, 76521
Johnson, Richard Mentor, 1780-1850. 36274-
    36278, 41823, 41843, 70196, 98410
Johnson, Robert, fl. 1586-1626. 6811-6812,
    (36282)-36287, 53249, 56098, 1st note
    after 96483, 1st note after 99856, note
    after 99867, 99873, 105491
Johnson, Robert Ward, 1814-1879. 36288-
    36289, 65863
Johnson, Rosa Vertuer. 36290
Johnson, S., fl. 1736. 98433
Johnson, S. M. pseud. see Fulton, John.
    supposed author
Johnson, Samuel, 1696-1772. (10681), 23091,
    (25392), (32311), 36291-(36295), 78732,
    (80536), 84678C, 86750, 86752, 95355,
    103067
Johnson, Samuel, 1709-1784. 106-107, 1657,
    2760, 4091, 4095, 15523, (19253), (20062),
    28250, 36295A-(36312), 50452, 56060,
    58399, 60793, 63216, 63230-63231,
    63771, note after 69480, 69549, 73616,
    78299, 78302, 79729, (80041), 80608-
    80609, 90317, note before 94431, note
    before 94434, 95355, note after 95709,
    96184, 97635, 102360, 102647, 105486
Johnson, Samuel, 1822-1882. 36313-36314
Johnson, Samuel B. 36315
Johnson, Samuel P. 16807, 85580
Johnson, Samuel Roosevelt. (36320)-36321,
    72491 see also New York (City) General
    Theological Seminary of the Protestant
    Episcopal Church in the U. S. Dean.
Johnson, Sidney L. 86356
Johnson, Stephen. 36322-36323
Johnson, Susannah. see Hastings, Susannah
    Johnson.
Johnson, T. W. 36331
Johnson, Theodore T. 36328-36329
Johnson, Thomas. 95005 see also Texas
    (Republic) Navy. Judge Advocate.
Johnson, Thomas C. (36330)
Johnson, W. defendant 96924
Johnson, W. S. 84604
Johnson, Walter Rogers, 1794-1852. 15721,
    (36332)-36334, 84985, 84989, 86811, note
    before 101999
Johnson, William. 23723, 36335-36336, 100846
Johnson, Sir William, Bart., 1715-1774.
    36337-(36339), 38164, 53647, 65759
Johnson, William, 1771-1834. 3200, 4758-
    (4759), (36340)-36344, (39750), 94805
Johnson, William, 1771-1834. supposed author
    55969, 87902
Johnson, William, 1819-1866. see Johnson,
    William, 1819-1866.
Johnson, William Cost, 1806-1860. 36346-
    (36347)
Johnson, William D. 36348
Johnson, William L. 36349
Johnson, William M. 36350
Johnson, William Samuel, 1727-1819. 15748,
    36351, 45454
Johnson, Willis Fletcher. 83738
Johnson & Carey. firm (36257)
Johnson protocol and international good
    neighborhood. (37290)

Joint Committee to Adjust and Mark the Eastern Shore Boundary Between Maryland and Virginia. see Maryland. General Assembly. Joint Committee to Adjust and Mark the Eastern Shore Boundary Between Maryland and Virginia.

Joint Committees on Indian Affairs. see Joint Committee on Indian Affairs, of the Four Yearly Meetings of Friends of Genesee, New York, Philadelphia, and Baltimore.

Joint debates between George Northrop, Esq. 55840

Joint Delegation of the Committee on the Indian Concern of the Yearly Meeting of Baltimore, Philadelphia and New York to Visit the Indians Under the Care of Friends, in the Northern Superintendency, State of Nebraska, 1869. (69871)

Joint Delegation Appointed by the Committee on the Indian Concern of the Yearly Meetings of Ohio and Genesee. (34611)

Joint documents of the Senate and House of Representatives. 48741

Joint education of the sexes. (23677)

Joint letter from the most considerable proprietors. 36405

Joint letter from the proprietors of the island of Barbadoes. 3273

Joint memorial and resolutions of the Nevada Legislature. 52410

Joint reply of the Council and Assembly. 8005

Joint resolution in honor of Louis Kossuth. 79591

"Joint resolution" on the subject of emancipation. 31703

Joint resolution (S. 38) providing quarantine regulations. 85498

Joint resolutions and report to the Ohio Legislature. (56938)

Joint resolutions of the City Council. (64420)

Joint resolutions of the General Assembly of Florida. 34926

Joint resolutions withdrawing the consent of . . . New Jersey. 53134

Joint rules and orders. 70562

Joint rules of the two houses. (16106), 16117

Joint Special Committee of the New York Chamber of Commerce and American Geographical and Statistical Society on the Decimal System. 54643 see also American Geographical Society of New York.

Joint Special Committee on the Back Bay Streets, Boston. see Boston. City Council. Joint Special Committee on the Back Bay Streets.

Joint Special Committee [on] . . . the petition of George Latimer. 39206

Joint Special Committee's report. 73645

Joint Standing Committee on Boston Harbor, Boston. see Boston. City Council. Joint Standing Committee on the Harbor.

Joint Staning Committee on Claims, to which was referred the petition. 44027

Joint Standing Committee on Federal Relations. 45883

Joint stock act of Connecticut. 15764

Joint Stock Mutual Insurance Merchandizing Company. 71919

Joint Watering Committee of Northern Liberties & Spring Garden Water Works. 62371 see also Northern Liberties,

Philadelphia. Watering Committee. Spring. Garden (District), Philadelphia. Water Works.

Joinville, Francois Ferdinand Philippe Louis Marie d'Orleans, Prince de, 1818-1900. 36406-36408, 1st note after 97024

Joke upon joke. 89553

Joker's knapsack. 6346

Jolie fille du Faubourg Quebec. (12573)

Joliet, A. illus. 20554

Joliet, Louis, 1645-1700. 25853, 44666

Joline, John K. 31530, 36410

Jolis, Giuseppe. 36411

Jollet, --------. defendant 47527

Jolliffe, John. 4501, 12283, 27978, (36412)-36413

Jollivet, Adolphe. 36414-36422, 38984, 96071

Jolly, S. J. Ducoeur. see Ducoeur Joly, S. J.

Jolly bear and his friends. 79756

Joly, --------. illus. 48916

Joly, -------- Cretineau. see Cretineau-Joly, ----------.

Joly, --------- de. 36424, (75118)

Joly, --------- de. petitioner 93792

Joly, Jean. (36423)

Joly, S. J. Ducoeur. see Ducoeur Joly, S. J.

Joly de St. Valier, --------, Sieur. (36425)-36430

Jomard, Edme-Francois, 1777-1862. 36431-36435, 52105, 58554, 77804, 85781, 85791, 100990 see also Societe de Geographie, Paris. Commission Speciale.

Jomini, Henri, Baron de. 36436

Jonae, A. see Vidalin, Argrimur Jonsson, 1568-1648.

Jonah: or, the dove in safety. 46608, note after 105465

Jonama, ------- de. 36437

Jonama, Santiago. 36438

Jonas, Arngrimus. see Vidalin, Argrimur Jonsson, 1568-1648.

Jonas Michaelius. 55308

Jonas Poole's voyages to Cherie Island. 66686

Jonathan. pseud. Brieven uit en over de Vereenigde Staaten van Noord-Amerika. 36439, note before 93999

Jonathan. pseud. No mistake. see Hamilton, W. R.

Jonathan. pseud. Reflections of a few friends in the country. 68690-68691

Jonathan, one of the people called Christians. pseud. Prefatory epistle. (13870)

Jonathan, the Jew. pseud. Conversion. (76340)

Jonathan and Ann Heacock. 31129

Jonathan and his neighbours in 1865-6. (81604)

Jonathan Bull and Mary Bull. 43709

Jonathan Corncob. pseud. see Corncob, Jonathan. pseud.

Jonathan Dickerson's erstaunliche Geschichte. 20016

Jonathan Edwards, a retrospect. 85222

Jonathan Edwards' idealism. 85213

Jonathan Jefferson Whitlaw. 97029

Jonathan Pindar, Esq. pseud. see Tucker, St. George. supposed author

Jonathan Punkin. pseud. see Punkin, Jonathan. pseud.

Jonathan Slick. pseud. see Slick, Jonathan. pseud.

Jonathan Slick. pseud. see Stephens, Ann Sophia (Wintherbotham)

Jonathan Steadfast. pseud. see Daggett, David. supposed author

Joncaire-Chabert, Daniel de. 11722, (47522)

Jonceaux, Emile. 36638
Joncourt, Elie de. tr. 1637, 101186-2d note after 101186, 1st note after 101187
Jones, --------. 480, 36440
Jones, --------. ed. 79729
Jones, Captain. see Lloyd, David.
Jones, Major. pseud. see Thompson, William Tappan, 1812-1882.
Jones, Mrs. --------. (36585)
Jones, ----------. USN 25722
Jones, --------, fl. 1837. 48190, 74566
Jones, A. (36443)
Jones, A. A. 36447-36448
Jones, A. D. 36441, 36449-36451
Jones, A. L. 41742
Jones, Absalom. 36442
Jones, Alexander. 36444-36446
Jones, Alexander H. 36452
Jones, Amanda T. 36453
Jones, Anson, 1798-1858. 36454-36455, 95000, 95005, 95035 see also Texas (Republic) President, 1844-1846 (Jones)
Jones, Arthur T. (36456)
Jones, B. M. 36459
Jones, Benjamin, fl. 1754. 36457
Jones, Benjamin, fl. 1863. 36458
Jones, C. C. tr. 66726
Jones, Caleb. 85509
Jones, Calvin. 36460
Jones, Cave, 1769-1829. 32294, (33225), 36461-(36465), 65042, 99778
Jones, Cave, 1769-1829. plaintiff 18867, 1st note after 96891
Jones, Charles, fl. 1812. 36466
Jones, Charles, fl. 1855. 36467
Jones, Charles A. 36468
Jones, Charles Colcock, 1831-1893. 36469-(36481), 80874-80875, 85357, 88370
Jones, Charles J. 36484
Jones, Charles L. S. (36483)
Jones, Charles Lee. (36482)
Jones, D. S. see Jones, William Alfred.
Jones, Daniel W. tr. 83139
Jones, David. petitioner 36485, 73625
Jones, David, 1736-1820. 36486-36488
Jones, E. 36491
Jones, Edward C. 36489, 89814
Jones, Edward E. ed. 89508
Jones, Eleazer. 104886
Jones, Electra F. (36490)
Jones, Elijah. (36492)
Jones, Elizabeth, fl. 1817. 36235
Jones, Elizabeth C. 36494
Jones, Elnathan. 68499
Jones, Ep. 65484
Jones, Ernest. 36495-36496
Jones, Evan. 12446, 12454
Jones, Frederick. 36497, 73444
Jones, Frederick T. 85418
Jones, Gabriel. 98977
Jones, George. see Jones, Seaborn, 1788-1864.
Jones, George, 1800-1870. 36499
Jones, George, 1810-1879. 36500-36503
Jones, George W. 50465
Jones, George Washington, 1806-1884. 36504
Jones, George Wymberley. see De Renne, George Wymberley Jones, 1827-1880.
Jones, Griffith. petitioner 73625
Jones, H. V. 100510
Jones, Rev. Henry, fl. 1830. 50218
Jones, Henry, fl. 1846. (36506)
Jones, Henry W. F. (36507)
Jones, Mrs. Herbert. 82855
Jones, Horatio Gates. (6283), 25421, 36488, 36508-36510

Jones, Hugh. 36511-(36512)
Jones, I. D. 36515
Jones, Ignatius. pseud. Random recollections see Worth, Gorham A.
Jones, Isaac. 36514
Jones, J. 36516-36517
Jones, J. Elizabeth. 36538
Jones, J. H. 28503, 52292, 89744
Jones, J. W. ed. 88334
Jones, James Athearn. 36518-36522, 40429, 94246, note after 101165
Jones, James Chamberlain, 1809-1859. 36523
Jones, Jehu Glancy, 1811-1878. 36542
Jones, Jesse. 55774 see also Northampton County, Pa. Collector of Excise.
Jones, John, missionary tr. (12832)
Jones, John, fl. 1621. 97005
Jones, John, 1729-1791. 36524, 94063
Jones, John, 1772-1837. 36525
Jones, John, fl. 1788. 100055
Jones, John, fl. 1790. 9902, 101168
Jones, John, fl. 1864. 36526
Jones, John B. tr. 12454
Jones, John Blackamp, 1810-1866. (36527)-36528, 36530-36537, (80730)-(80732), note after 89943
Jones, John Blackamp, 1810-1866. incorrectly supposed author 36529, 95543-note after 95543
Jones, John Franklin. 36539
Jones, John G. (36541)
Jones, John Gale. 36540
Jones, John H. defendant 36543
Jones, John Matthew. 36544
Jones, John Paul, 1747-1792. 25722, 36546-36560, note after 94476, 1st note after 99448
Jones, John Pringle. 36571
Jones, John R. 36545
Jones, John Rice. (34540)
Jones, John Richter. 36572
Jones, John William. (36574)
Jones, John Winston, 1791-1848. 36573
Jones, John Winter. ed. 29593
Jones, Joseph. 36575-36577, 85072
Jones, Major Joseph. pseud. see Thompson, William Tappan, 1812-1882.
Jones, Joseph H. 36578
Jones, Joseph Seawell. 36579-(36580)
Jones, Justin. (36581)
Jones, L. Augustus. 36582
Jones, Levi, Jr. 15847, 104980 see also Democratic Party. Massachusetts. General Committee. Clerk.
Jones, Lot. 36583-36584
Jones, Matt Bushnell, 1871- note before 99008, 99131
Jones, Morris Charles. 36586
Jones, Noel. (37492)
Jones, Norris M. 36587, 95398
Jones, Pascal. 36588
Jones, Paul. see Jones, John Paul, 1747-1792.
Jones, Pearson. 101690
Jones, Peter. (12832), 36589-36593, 57081
Jones, Philip. 36594
Jones, Dr. Pleasant. pseud. Slaveholder abroad. see Starnes, Ebenezer. and Thompson, William Tappan, 1812-1882. incorrectly supposed author Thorpe, Thomas Bangs. incorrectly supposed author
Jones, Pomroy. (36596)
Jones, R. 36598
Jones, R. D. 36599

Journal d'un voiage [sic] le long de la cote de la Mer Magellanique. 12129

Journal d'un voyage sur les cotes d'Afrique et aux Indes d'Espagne. 36685

Journal d'un expedition fait dans la Mer Pacique du Sud & du Nord. 16260

Journal during a residence at the Red River Colony. 102737, 102738

Journal, during his [i. e. J. Marsden's] passage from New-York to England. 44713

Journal, during the time he [i. e. George Whitefield] was detained in England by the embargo. 103539-103540

Journal during the time he [i. e. George Whitefield] was detained in England, by the embargo. Vol. II. 103543

Journal embodying a full and impartial enquiry. 102978

Journal es decouvertes de la Nouvelle France. 11841

Journal et impressions de voyage. 93272

Journal. First settlers of Southold. (28811)

Journal for the farm, the garden, and the fireside. 17150, (17869)

Journal for the people. 66100

Journal for the southern farm and fireside. 88485

Journal fra anno 1734 til 1740. (22035)

Journal from a few days after his [i. e. George Whitefield's] arrival at Georgia, to his second return thither from Pennsylvania. 103544

Journal, from a few days after his [i. e. George Whitefield's] arrival at Savannah, June the fourth. 103546

Journal, from a few days after his [i. e. George Whitefield's] return to Georgia to his arrival at Falmouth. 103550

Journal from Bent's Fort to St. Louis. 59

Journal from his [i. e. George Whitefield's] arrival at London, to his departure from thence. 103538-103539

Journal, from his [i. e. George Whitefield's] arrival at Savannah, May 7. 103536

Journal from his [i. e. George Whitefield's] arrival at Savannah, to his return to London. 103535, 103539

Journal from his [i. e. George Whitefield's] embarking after the embargo, to his arrival at Savannah in Georgia. 103542-103543

Journal from his [i. e. George Whitefield's] leaving New-England, October 1740. To his arrival at Falmouth in England. 103548

Journal from his [i. e. George Whitefield's] leaving Stanford in New-England. 103549

Journal, from Savannah, June 15. 1740. to his [i. e. George Whitefield's] arrival at Rhode-Island. 103547

Journal general de medicine. 98353

Journal generale de Saint-Domingue. 75139

Journal hebdomadaire. 85706

Journal historique de la revolution. (29233)

Journal historique de l'establissement des Francais a la Louisiane. 36690, 38631

Journal historique de toutes les Assemblees. 28153, 75149

Journal historique des evenemens arrives a St. Eustache. 58495, 94638

Journal historique du dernier voyage. 36760

Journal historique du voyage a l'equateur. 38490

Journal historique du voyage de M. de Lesseps. (40208)

Journal historique d'un voyage fait aux Isles Malouines. 60997

Journal historique d'un voyage fait par ordre du Roi. 12135-12136

Journal hist. et lit. 24017

Journal-history of the Seventy-Third Ohio Volunteer Infantry. 34014

Journal holden fra 1721 till 1788. 22034

Journal illustre des voyages et des voyaguers. 99383B

Journal in America, 1837-1838. 83427

Journal in jail. (55215)

Journal in minature. 17226

Journal in the Confederate Army of Tennessee. 17911

Journal in the province of Massachusetts Bay. 103807

Journal kept at Nootka Sound. 36122

Journal kept by Count William de Deux-Ponts. 19801

Journal kept by E. Bacon. 81742

Journal kept by Hugh Finlay. 24375

Journal, kept by John Bartram. 92221-92222

Journal kept by Miss Sarah Foote. 84132

Journal kept by order of the Honourable Society (In Scotland) For Propagating Christian Knowledge. (7340), 85994

Journal kept by the author [i. e. Sarah Hoding] in the United States. 32374

Journal kept during a tour to the West Indies. 50430

Journal kept during a voyage from Philadelphia to Calcutta. 35332

Journal kept from London to the Island of St. Maries. 50412

Journal kept from Scotland to New Caledonia in Darien. 49438

Journal kept on board of the ship Rainbow. 19775, note after 96363

Journal litteraire et scientifique. 43799

Journal manuscrit et autres documents. (8754)

Journal mensurel. 70354

Journal, oder Beschreibung der wunderbaren Reise. 33669, 77956

Journal of a boat-voyage through Rupert's Land. 71025

Journal of a botanical excursion. 66729

Journal of a captured missionary. 28746

Journal of a convention, . . . at Wilmington. 66157

Journal of a convention at Windsor, Vt. 15867

Journal of a convention, held for the promotion of Agriculture and Manufacture. 36691

Journal of a convention of delegates from several states. 36692

Journal of a convention of the clergy and laity. 100513

Journal of a convention of the Protestant Episcopal Church. 66157

Journal of a convention . . . Philadelphia, from July 28th to August 8th, 1789. 66157

Journal of a convention . . . Philadelphia, from June 20th to the 26th, 1786. 66157

Journal of a cruise in the Mediterranean and Levant. 104776

Journal of a cruise in the U. S. Ship Delaware. 35267

Journal of a cruise made to the Pacific Ocean. (64218)-64219

Journal of a cruise of the United States Schooner Dolphin. 59186

Journal of a fever. 89147

Journal of a French officer on board the Chezine Frigate. 26630

Journal of a journey performed in . . . 1818. 41799

Journal of a voyage to the northern whale-fishery. (78171)

Journal of a voyage to the polar seas. 4566

Journal of a voyage to the south seas, in His Majesty's Ship the Endeavour. (58787), 58788

Journal of a voyage to the south seas, in the Japan. 35786

Journal of a voyage to the United States. 40735

Journal of a voyage undertaken by order of His Present Majesty. (62573)

Journal of a voyage up the River Missouri. (7168), 7176

Journal of a wanderer. (36698)

Journal of a West India proprietor. 40821

Journal, of a young man of Massachusetts. 102060

Journal of American history. 83462

Journal of an actress reviewed. 37332

Journal of an emigrating party. 8807, 57544

Journal of an excursion made by the Corps of Cadets. 36701

Journal of an excursion to the United States and Canada. 36702

Journal of an excursion to the United States of North America. 101241

Journal of an expedition 1400 miles up the Orinoco. (72125)

Journal of an expedition from Pirara to the Upper Corentyne. 77786

Journal of an expedition made in the autumn of 1794. 25063

Journal of an expedition performed by the forces. 36703

Journal of an exploring tour beyond the Rocky Mountains. 58729

Journal of an officer during the siege of Fort Detroit. 36704

Journal of an unfortunate prisoner on board. 36705

Journal of agriculture (Boston) 36700

Journal of agriculture (New York) 36699

Journal of agriculture and proceedings of the Lower Canada Gricultural Society. 10344

Journal of Alfred Ely. (22378)

Journal of Andrew Ellicott. (22216)-22217

Journal [of Andrew Welck.] 2d note after 102515

Journal [of Anson G. Phelps.] 65093

Journal of banking. 28073

Journal [of Beatty.] 21928

Journal [of Benedict Arnold.] 83467

Journal of Biblical literature and theological science. 65654

Journal of books and opinion. 1927

Journal of both sessions of the convention. 36706

Journal [of Bradford and Winslow.] (51198)-51201, note after 104797, 106053

Journal [of Bulkeley.] (50834)

Journal [of C. Carroll.] (45211A)

Journal [of C. G. von Murr.] 4043

Journal of Capt. A. R. Johnston. 22536

Journal of Captain B. L. E. Bonneville. 35126, 35195

Journal of Capt. Cook's last voyage to the Pacific Ocean, and in quest of a north-west passage. 39691

Journal of Capt. Cook's last voyage to the Pacific Ocean, on discovery. 36707

Journal of Captain Harry Gordon. (64835)

Journal [of Captain Middleton.] 20404

Journal of Charles Carroll of Carrollton. (11068), (45211A)

Journal [of Charles Wesley.] 102643-102644

Journal [of Charlevoix.] 25853

Journal of charity. (64370)

Journal of Christian education. (59533)

Journal of Christian Frederick Post. 64453

Journal of Christopher Gist. (27515)

Journal of Christopher Gist down the Ohio River. (64735)

Journal of commerce. 9638-9639, 29911, (58438), 63826, 84441, 84446, 92035-92036

Journal of commerce (New York) see New York journal of commerce.

Journal [of Commodore Truxton.] 97282

Journal of Company B., 1st O. V. A. 18198

Journal of criticism. 41486

Journal [of Crow.] (19715)

Journal of current literature. 93381

Journal [of D. Stanton.] 97059

Journal of Daniel Coker. (14253)

Journal [of David Branerd.] 21953

Journal of Dr. Coke's third tour through the West Indies. 14246

Journal of Doctor Heremiah Smipleton's [sic] tour of Ohio. 97201

Journal of Dr. Lavagnino. 39275

Journal of E. Bacon. 2641, 81740-81741

Journal of each provincial congress of Massachusetts. 45785

Journal of education. see Minnesota teacher and journal of education.

Journal of education and science. 102961

Journal of education for Lower Canada. (36708)

Journal of education for Ontario. 36709

Journal of education for Upper Canada. 10423

Journal of education, province of Quebec. 36710

Journal of events principally on the Detroit and Niagara frontiers. 48024

Journal of 1855. (45307)

Journal of eighty voyages. (14196)-14197

Journal of facts. 74140

Journal of Fanny A. Kemble. [sic] (36357)

Journal of [Fanny Knight Kemble.] 28430

Journal of five years in Asia, Africa, and Europe. (35056)

Journal of Francis Asbury. 2162

Journal of freedom. 14733

Journal of Gen. William Rudolph Smith. 84862

Journal of geography and collateral sciences. 14790

Journal of geology. 84532, 84537

Journal [of George Croghan.] (74155)

Journal [of George Fox.] 28794, 106101

Journal of George James. 100991

Journal [of George Whitefield.] 27270-27271, 28794, (36750), 103535, 103647

Journal of health. 20358, 29863, 77439

Journal of health. see New York medical gazette, and journal of health.

Journal of health. see Scapel: a journal of health.

Journal of Heber C. Kimball. 95525

Journal [of Henri Bouquet.] (74155)

Journal of his [i. e. George Washington's] expedition to the Ohio, in 1754. (41650), note after 91855

Journal of his [i. e. William Penn's] life. 59690, (59731)

Journal of his [i. e. John Woolman's] life and travels. 33264, 105204

Journal of his [i. e. Thomas Chalkley's] life, travels and Christian experiences. 11747, 11754, 33265

Journal of his [i. e. Sir Walter Raleigh's] second voyage to Guiana. 67555

Journal of his [i. e. M. Joutel's] voyage to Mexico. 25853, 36763

Journal of his [i. e. Francis Higginson's] voyage to New-England. 106052

Journal of history. 83038, 83071, 83147, 83152, 83289, 83302

Journal of humanity. 89491

Journal of incidents. 36711

Journal of instructive and entertaining literature. 54831

Journal of Isaac Norris. 55501

Journal of Isaac Senter. 79148

Journal of Job Scott, an American minister. 78284

Journal of Job Scott, late of North America. 78285

Journal of John Candler. 10674

Journal [of John James Audubon.] 92341

Journal of John Leach. 39508

Journal of John Percival, Earl of Egmont. 91305

Journal [of John R. McDowall.] 43188, (43190), note after 103223

Journal [of John Taylor.] 94478

Journal of John Udell. 97663

Journal of John Wesley. 102652, 102654-102674

Journal [of John Winthrop.] 20884, 24037, 102401

Journal of John Woolman. 105211

Journal of law. 36712

Journal of Lewis and Clarke [sic] to the mouth of the Columbia River. 40832

Journal of Lieut. Simon Stevens. 91557-91558

Journal of Lieut. William Feltman. 24038

Journal of literature, news, politics, the drama, fine arts, etc. 59131

Journal of Llewellen Penrose. 60801

Journal [of Lussan.] (23475), (23477), 23478

Journal of Major George Washington. 15205, 17365, (41650), 14949, (47511)-47512, 51661, (74155), note after 91855, 101710

Journal of Marshal Soult. (38072)

Journal of medicine. (80563)

Journal of medicine and surgery. see Nashville journal of medicine and surgery.

Journal of Mr. James Ray. 68026

Journal of music. 21520

journal of my [i. e. J. Pollard Blanchard's] forty-fifth ascension. 5826

Journal [of Napier.] (19715)

Journal of natural history (Boston) see Boston journal of natural history.

Journal of natural history, agriculture, education and literature. 52047

Journal of natural sciences. 39908

Journal of occurrences. (31793), (47395)

Journal of one of the surviving officers. (20487)

Journal of papers on subjects connected with maritime affairs. 52065

Journal of Peggy Dow. 20759

Journal of political economy. see Examiner and journal of political economy.

Journal of political economy. see Free trade advocate, and journal of political economy.

Journal of prison discipline. 78074

Journal pf proceedings, and a list of the officers [of the American Institute of Instruction, Boston.] 1108, (39668)

Journal of proceedings, and a list of the officers [of the American Institute of Instruction, Providence, R. I.] 66275

Journal of proceedings, and list of the officers [of the American Institute of Instruction, Lowell, Mass.] 42484

Journal of proceedings [of the American Institute of Instruction, New Haven.] 52983

Journal of proceedings [of the American Institute of Instruction, Northampton, Mass.] (55765)

Journal of proceedings [of the American Institute of Instruction, Portland, Me.] 64348

Journal of proceedings of the Commercial Convention. 36713

Journal of proceedings of the Convention of the People. 27060

Journal of proceedings [of the convention of the state of South Carolina]. 87430

Journal of proceedings of the Grand Division of the Sons of Temperance. 53958, 87057

Journal of proceedings of the Grand Division of the state of Massachusetts. 45760

Journal of proceedings of the National Teacher Association. 52029

Journal of proceedings of the Provincial Congress of New-Jersey. 53106, 53139

Journal of proceedings of the Regents of the Smithsonian Institution. 85030

Journal of proceedings of the Right Worthy Grand Lodge. (56691)

Journal of proceedings of the St. Louis Academ of Sciences. 84244

Journal of proceedings of the Senate in the matter of George W. Smith. 82591

Journal of proceedings of the Senate of Maryland. 45176

Journal of proceedings of the Southern Convention. 88330

Journal of progress in literature and education 41498

Journal of public events, from 1753 to 1783. 84570

Journal of Quebec. 67023

Journal of R. J. Meigs. 9538

Journal of real estate. 38822

Journal of reflections and observations. (1985

Journal of reform and literature. 90154

Journal of researches into the natural history and geology. (18647)

Journal of Rev. John Marrant. 44676

Journal of Richard Mather. 46777, 106052

Journal of Richard Smith. 83761

Journal [of Right Rev. Simon Wm. Gabriel Brute.] (4052)

Journal [of Robert Forbes.] 7288

Journal of Roger Wolcott at the siege of Louisbourg. 104986

Journal of rural art and rural taste. (33066)

Journal of Sally Wister. 82979

Journal of school and home education. 88502

Journal [of Scrog.] (19715)

Journal of Seth Crowell. 17701

Journal of several visits to the Indians. 4006

Journal of Sibley's Indian expedition. 80821, 86267

Journal [of Smith.] (19715)

Journal of social science. (36714), 89555

Journal of Solomon Nash. 9538, (51852)

Journal of that faithful servant of Christ, Charles Osborn. 57745

Journal of the Academy of Natural Sciences of Philadelphia. 61404, (77377), 77389, 98579, 103061

Journal of the acts of the General Assembly. 53707

Journal of the Adventure's voyage in 1772, 1773, and 1774. 16247

Journal of the American Baptist Anti-slavery Convention. 36715

Journal of the American Geographical and Statistical Society. (54077), 91521

Journal of the American Institute. 1105, (36716)

Journal of the American Silk Society and rural economist. 36717, 82674

Journal of the annual convention, held in 1859. (37079)

Journal of the annual convention of the Diocese of Central New York. 53875

Journal of the annual convention of the Diocese of Connecticut. (15815), 101999

Journal of the . . . annual convention of the Protestant Episcopal Church in the Diocese of Ohio. 56939

Journal of the annual convention of the Protestant Episcopal Church of the Diocese of Michigan. 48779

Journal of the annual session of the Franckean Evangelic Lutheran Synod. 25475

Journal of the Assembly of the first session of the state of Nevada. 52401

Journal of the Assembly of the state of New York. 53708, 54010

Journal [of the Associates of the Late Doctor Bray.] 83976

Journal of the author. 79371

Journal of the author's [i. e. John Taylor's] life. 94482

Journal of the author's [i. e. an English farmer's] voyage across the Atlantic, in June, 1819. 10447, 10541, note after 98077

Journal of the beginning and proceedings of the English plantation. (51198)

Journal of the Bishop of Montreal. 51186

Journal of the Board of Agriculture. 63428

Journal of the Board of Canal Commissioners of Pennsylvania. 59954

Journal of the Board of Education, December, 1858. 34987

Journal of the Board of Education [of New York City.] 54121

Journal of the Board of Regents. 84395

Journal of the Board of Revenue Commissioners. (59922)

Journal of the Board of Supervisors of Onondaga. (57358)

Journal of the Board of Supervisors of the County of Rensselaer. 69635

Journal of the Boston Society of Natural History. 1796

Journal of the campaign in Canada. 10471

Journal of the campaign of United States Dragoons. 48099

Journal of the campaigns of the 12th Regt. Rhode Island Volunteers. 28308

Journal of the captivity and sufferings of John Foss. (21588)

Journal of the City Convention [of New York.] 54174

Journal of the Committee of the States. 15545

Journal of the Common Council of . . . Philadelphia. 61748

Journal of the Common Council of the city of Schenectady. 77594

Journal of the Congress of the Four Southern Governors. (27056), 36718

Journal of the Congress of the United States of America. 36719

Journal of the Constitutional Convention, 1857. 34983

Journal of the Constitutional Convention, 1869. 34223

Journal of the Constitutional Convention of Illinois, 1862. 34221

Journal of the Constitutional Convention of . . . Massachusetts. (45779)

Journal of the Constitutional Convention [of North Carolina.] 55627

Journal of the Constitutional Convention of the District of Maine. 43945

Journal of the Constitutional Convention, of the Territory of Minnesota. 49256

Journal of the convention assembled November 17, 1845. 49598

Journal of the convention assembled to frame a constitution. 70590

Journal of the convention at its session of 1865. (55629)

Journal of the convention . . . begun . . . the 4th . . . of June, 1867. (53713)

Journal of the convention called for the purpose of re-adopting, amending or changing the constitution of the state of Louisiana. 42240

Journal of the convention for framing a constitution of government. 45780

Journal of the convention . . . held at . . . Albany, . . . June, 1846. (53712)

Journal of the convention . . . held . . . in . . . Albany. 53711

Journal of the convention, holden at Windsor, Vt., January 20, 1836. 99195, 104768

Journal of the convention, holden at Windsor, Vt., Sept. 29th & 30th, 1830. 15868, 99194

Journal of the convention in relation to the charter. 54326

Journal [of the Convention of Delaware, 1776.] 52569

Journal of the Convention, of . . . New-York. 53710

Journal of the Convention of South-Carolina 1860-'61. 27093, 27102, 87436, 87440, 87443

Journal of the Convention . . . [of South Carolina] held in 1860, 1861, and 1862. 87440

Journal of the Convention of the Alabama Territory. 558

Journal of the Convention of the People of North Carolina. 55628

Journal of the Convention of the People of South Carolina: assembled at Columbia. 87424

Journal of the Convention of the People of South Carolina, held in Columbia. 87445-87446

Journal of the Convention of the People of South Carolina, held in 1860-'61. 87432, 87435-87436

Journal of the Convention of the People of South Carolina, held in 1860, 1861 and 1862. 87437

Journal of the Convention of the . . . [Protestant Episcopal] Church, held in Philadelphia. (60438)

Journal of the Convention of the Protestant Episcopal Church in the Diocese of Georgia. 66164

Journal of the Convention of the Protestant-Episcopal Church of Maryland. (45306)

Journal of the Convention of the Protestant Episcopal Church . . . of New York. 53876

Journal of the Convention of the State of New-York. 53709, 100031

Journal of the Convention of the State of
Pennsylvania. (60170)

Journal of the Convention, of the Territory
of the United States North-west of the
Ohio. 94880

Journal of the Convention of Virginia. 100030

Journal of the Convention of Young Men, of
the State of New-York. 53714, 1st note
after 106151

Journal of the Council at the first regular
session. 52190

Journal of the council during the first session.
49257

Journal of the Council of Censors. 36720,
60171

Journal of the Council of Safety. 88005

Journal [of the Council of the Colony of New
York.] 84575

Journal of the Council of the first session.
57552

Journal of the Council of the Legislative
Assembly. 14745

Journal of the Council of the Territory of
Kansas. (37046)

Journal of the Council of the Territory of
Washington. 101917

Journal of the Council of War. 66519

Journal of the Court for the Trial of
Impeachments. 20634

Journal of the cruise of the United States
Ship Susquehanna. 9489

Journal of the debates and proceedings in the
Convention of Delegates. 29654, 45781

Journal of the Elliott Society of Natural
History. 84914

Journal of the Essex-County Natural History
Society. (23010)

Journal of the establishment of the French in
Louisiana. 25853

Journal of the Ethnological Society of London.
36721

Journal of the events. 103997

Journal of the executive proceedings of the
Senate [of New Jersey.] 53137

Journal of the executive proceedings of the
Senate of the United States. 15553

Journal of the expedition against Quebec.
47396

Journal of the expedition against the northern
Indians. 37944

Journal of the expedition of Dragoons. (20497)

Journal of the expedition of E. F. Beale.
31175

Journal of the expedition of enquiry. 27319,
(27512)

Journal of the expedition to Carthagena.
102632

Journal of the expedition to La Guira and
Porto Cavallos. (36722), 1st note after
102842

Journal of the expedition to Quebec, in the
year 1775. note after 7269, 47485-
(47486)

Journal of the expedition up the River St.
Lawrence. (36723), 67022, 67024

Journal of the Federal Convention. 22233,
note after 106002

Journal of the fifty-seventh annual Convention
of the Protestant Episcopal Church in
. . . Connecticut. 66162

Journal of the . . . first annual meeting.
51940

Journal of the first congress of the American
colonies. 17722, 15541

Journal of the first, second, and third voyages
for the discovery. 58869

Journal of the first session of the House of
Representatives. 60172

Journal of the first session of the Legislative
Council of Idaho Territory. (34164)

Journal of the first session of the Senate of
the United States. 15551

Journal of the fourteenth annual convention of
the Protestant Episcopal Church in the
Diocese of California. (66161)

Journal of the fourth session of the Council of
Idaho Territory. (34165)

Journal of the Franklin Institute. 12584,
(25655), (68512), 89118, 93519, 93521,
96480 see also Franklin journal.

Journal of the Free Trade Convention. 36724

Journal [of the Friends Historical Society.]
83315

Journal of the General Assembly of His
Majesty's province of New Jersey. 5313

Journal of the General Assembly [of the
Colony of New York.] 84558, 84566,
90629

Journal of the General Assembly of the state
of South Carolina. 87483

[Journal of the General Assembly of the state
of Vermont at their session at Windsor,
October, 1778.] 99024

Journal of the General Assembly of the state
of Vermont, begun and held at Middlebury
99044

Journal of the General Assembly of the state
of Vermont, begun and held at the city
of Vergennes. 99042

Journal of the General Assembly of the state
of Vermont. Begun and holden at
Windsor. 99043

Journal of the general conventions of the
Protestant Episcopal Church. (66172)

Journal of the General Council of the Indian
Territory. 34662

Journal of the general meeting of the
Cincinnati, in 1784. 77035

Journal of the Geological Society of London.
18955

Journal of the Grand Division, of the Sons of
Temperance. 87032

Journal of the Grand Encampment. 60160

Journal of the Grand Lodge of Minnesota.
(49255)

Journal of the Historical and Philosophical
Society of Ohio. (56931)-(56932), 94356

Journal of the Honorable Council of the
Territory of N. Mexico. (53278)

Journal of the Honourable House of Representatives. 45783

Journal of the Honble House of Representatives
May 1755. 45730

Journal of the Honourable House of Representatives, of His Majesty's province of
the Massachusetts-Bay in New-England.
45782

Journal of the House of Assembly of Lower
Canada. (10491)

Journal of the House of Assembly of Newfoundland. 54982

Journal of the House of Assembly of Prince
Edward Island. 65633

Journal of the House of Assembly of Upper
Canada. 10492

Journal of the House of Assembly of Upper
Canada for the twenty-eighth of May
to the ninth of July, 1901. 98060

Journal of the House of Burgesses. At a
General Assembly. 99928

Journal of the House of Burgesses. General
Assembly begun and held. 99974

Journal of the life, travels, and Gospel labours, of that faithful servant and minister of Christ, Job Scott. 78287, (78291), 78293-78294, (78296)

Journal of the life, travels, and Gospel labours of that faithful servant of Christ, Job Scott. 78288

Journal of the life, travels, and Gospel labours, of William Williams. 104411

Journal of the life, travels, and labour of love. 20033

Journal of the life, travels and labours in the work of the ministry. (28825)

Journal of the life, travels, and religious labours, of William Savery. 23173, 77282

Journal of the life, travels, labors, and religious experience of Isaac Martin. 44882

Journal of the life, travels, sufferings, and a labour of love. 21873, note before 91980

Journal of the Linneaen Association of Pennsylvania College. (41497)

Journal of the manual arts, trades and manufactures. (53833)

Journal of the march of a party of provincials. 36728

Journal of the march of a regiment of mounted riflemen. 17660

Journal of the Massachusetts [Colony] House of Representatives. 88221

Journal of the meetings which led to the institution. (60438)

Journal [of the Methodist Episcopal Church Ohio Conference.] 82776

Journal of the Most Worshipful Grand Lodge of Vermont. 99191

Journal of the National Freedmen's Relief Association. 51981

Journal of the National Republican Convention . . . in . . . Baltimore. 36729

Journal of the New Brunswick Society. (52536)

Journal of the New-York State Agricultural Society. 53811

Journal of the operations of the Queen's Rangers. 81134

Journal of the . . . [Philadelphia] College of Pharmacy. 61984

Journal of the pilgrims at Plymouth. 51199, 51201

Journal of the plantation at Plymouth. 7263, 51200

Journal of the Portland Society of Natural History. 64369

Journal of the Presbyterian Historical Society. 84850, 104533

Journal of the Primary Convention of the Diocese of Albany. (53877)

Journal of the Primary Convention of the Protestant Episcopal Church. 66168

Journal of the principal occurrences during the siege of Quebec. 80734

Journal of the proceedings against the conspirators at New-York. (33060)

Journal of the proceedings and debates. (49508)

Journal of the proceedings at two conferences. 36730

Journal of the proceedings begun to be held at Falmouth. 36730

Journal of the proceedings in Georgia. 27113, 91305, 91313, 91315

Journal of the proceedings in the detection of the conspiracy. (33058)-33059

Journal of the proceedings in the late expedition to Port-Royal. 36731

Journal of the proceedings of a convention, begun and held in Knoxville. 94731

Journal of the proceedings of a convention, composed of delegates. 36732

Journal of the proceedings of a convention, holden at Windsor, Vermont. 99196

Journal of the proceedings of a convention of delegates. (24870)

Journal of the proceedings of a Convention of Literary and Scientific Gentlemen. 19334, 36734

Journal of the proceedings of a convention of the Mutual Benefit Societies or Brotherhoods. 66159

Journal of the proceedings of a convention of the Protestant Episcopal Church in . . . New Jersey. 53208

Journal of the proceedings of a meeting of the Board of Trustees. (36733)

Journal of the proceedings of a meeting of the clergy. 94804

Journal of the proceedings of an adjourned meeting of the Second Triennial Convention 10014

Journal of the proceedings of Congress. Held at Philadelphia, from January to May, 1776. 36739

Journal of the proceedings of Congress, held at Philadelphia, from September 5, 1775 to April 30, 1776. (15547), note after 36738

Journal of the proceedings of Congress, held at Philadelphia, May 10, 1775. 15543, note after 36738

Journal of the proceedings of delegates assembled at Brunswick. 36735, 82577

Journal of the proceedings of His Majesty's forces. 9925

Journal of the proceedings of Jacob Wendell. 36736, 5th note after 102623

Journal of the proceedings of the annual convention . . . Boston. (45957)

Journal of the proceedings of the annual convention of the Protestant Episcopal Church in the Diocese of Connecticut. 66162

Journal of the proceedings of the annual convention of the Protestant Episcopal Church, in the Eastern Diocese. 66163

Journal of the proceedings of the annual convention of the Protestant Episcopal Church of . . . Indiana. 34499

Journal of the proceedings of the annual convention of the Protestant Episcopal Church . . . of New York. 53878

Journal of the proceedings of the annual convention of the Protestant Episcopal Church, of the state of South-Carolina. 87928

Journal of the proceedings of the Baptist State Convention, in Alabama. 563

Journal of the proceedings of the Bishop, clergy and laity of the Protestant Episcopal Church in . . . Connecticut. 66162

Journal of the proceedings of the bishops, clergy and laity . . . at Philadelphia. (60438)

Journal of the proceedings of the bishops, clergy and laity of the Protestant Episcopal Church in the United States. 66158

Journal of the proceedings of the Board of Supervisors of the county of Jefferson. 35944

Journal of the proceedings of the Board of Supervisors of the county of Oneida. (57335)

Journal of the proceedings of the Commissaries of the colony of New York.
36738

Journal of the proceedings of the Commissioners appointed by His Excellency Governor
Shirley. 36737

Journal of the proceedings of the Commissioners appointed for managing a treaty of
peace. 34083

Journal of the proceedings of the Common
Council of the city of Detroit. 19789

Journal of the proceedings of the Commons
House of Assembly. 27059

Journal of the proceedings of the Congress
held at Philadelphia, September 5, 1774.
15542, note after 36738

Journal of the proceedings of the Congress
held at Philadelphia, September 5th,
1774. Containing, the bill of rights.
15544

Journal of the proceedings of the Constitutional
Convention. 24871

Journal of the proceedings of the Convention,
held at Ann Arbor. (48743)

Journal of the proceedings of the Convention
held at . . . Richmond. 100010

Journal of the proceedings of the Convention,
held in New Haven. (15753), 52982

Journal of the proceedings of the Convention
of Delegates assembled at Burnsiwck.
36735, 82577

Journal of the proceedings of the Convention
of the People. 27060

Journal of the proceedings of the convention
of the Protestant Episcopal Church in
the state of Vermont, held at Manchester.
99203

Journal of the proceedings of the convention
of the Protestant Episcopal Church in
the state of Vermont, held at Middlebury.
99204

Journal of the Proceedings of the Convention
of the state of Louisiana. 42242

Journal of the proceedings of the Convention
on Internal Improvements of Maryland.
45172

Journal of the proceedings of the Convention
to Form a Constitution. (53136)

Journal of the proceedings of the Court of
Common Council. 55921

Journal of the proceedings of the eighth
General Convention. 53248

Journal of the proceedings of the fiftieth annual
convention. 66169

Journal of the proceedings of the first annual
convention. 49259

Journal of the proceedings of the first Senate
of . . . New Jersey. 53137

Journal of the proceedings of the forces under
General Maclean. (36740)

Journal of the proceedings of the fourth annual
convention. 66166

Journal of the proceedings of the fourth
convention of the Protestant-Episcopal
Church in Kentucky. 37569

Journal of the proceedings of the [43d] annual
convention. 70624

Journal of the proceedings of the Friends of
Domestic Industry. (55313)

Journal of the proceedings of the General
Assembly of the state of Vermont, at
their adjourned session, held at
Bennington. 99025

Journal of the proceedings of the General
Assembly of the state of Vermont, at
their adjourned session held at Norwich.
99027

Journal of the proceedings of the General
Assembly of the state of Vermont; at
their session at Bennington, January,
1791. 99034

Journal of the proceedings of the General
Assembly of the state of Vermont, at
their session at Rutland, in October one
thousand seven hundred and ninety four.
99038

Journal of the proceedings of the General
Assembly of the state of Vermont; at
their session at Rutland, in October,
1792. 99036

Journal of the proceedings of the General
Assembly of the state of Vermont, at
their session at Windsor, in October.
99037

Journal of the proceedings of the General
Assembly of the state of Vermont, at
their session at Windsor, October 13th,
1791. 99035

Journal of the proceedings of the General
Assembly of the state of Vermont, at
their session, held at Bennington. 99030

Journal of the proceedings of the General
Assembly of the state of Vermont, at
their session, held at Windsor. 99028

Journal of the proceedings of the General
Assembly of the state of Vermont, at
their stated session, held at Castleton.
99033

Journal of the proceedings of the General
Assembly of the state of Vermont, at
their stated session, held at Manchester.
99031

Journal of the proceedings of the General
Assembly of the state of Vermont at
their stated [session held at Rutland,
October, 1786.] 99029

Journal of the proceedings of the General
Assembly of the state of Vermont, at
their stated session, held at Rutland,
the second Thursday of October, 1784.
99026

Journal of the proceedings of the General
Assembly of the state of Vermont, a t
their stated session held at Westminster.
99032

Journal of the proceedings of the General
Assembly of the state of Vermont.
Begun and held at Rutland. 99040

Journal of the proceedings of the General
Assembly of the state of Vermont, begun
and held at Windsor, in the county of
Windsor. 99039

Journal of the proceedings of the General
Assembly of the state of Vermont: begun
and holden at Windsor. 90041

Journal of the proceedings of the General
Council. 15277

Journal of the proceedings of the General
Council of the republic of Texas. 94958

Journal of the proceedings of the Grand
Division of the Sons of Temperance of
the District of Columbia. 87026

Journal of the proceedings of the Grand Division
of the Sons of Temperance of the State
of Massachusetts. 87032

Journal of the proceedings of the Grand
Division of the Sons of Temperance, of
the State of Ohio. 87071

Journal of the proceedings of the Grand
Division of the Sons of Temperance of
the State of Wisconsin. 87099

Journal of the proceedings of the . . . Grand
Lodge of . . . Massachusetts. 56692

Journal of the proceedings of the Grand Lodge of New Hampshire. 52835

Journal of the proceedings of the . . . Grand Lodge . . . of Pennsylvania. 60160

Journal of the proceedings of the Grand Royal Arch Chapter. (56941)

Journal of the proceedings of the Honourable House of Representatives of His Majesty's province of the Massachusetts Bay. (45784)

Journal of the proceedings of the Hon. House of Representatives of the state of New Hampshire. (52839)

Journal of the proceedings of the Honorable Senate. 52841

Journal of the proceedings, of the Honorable the American Continental Congress. 15526, note after 63244, 84642

Journal of the proceedings of the House of Assembly. 10025

Journal of the proceedings of the House of Delegates [of Maryland.] 45173

Journal of the proceedings of the House of Delegates [of Maryland] . . . January session, 1862. 45174

Journal of the proceedings of the House of Representatives of the state of Florida. 24872

Journal of the proceedings of the House of Representatives of the Territory of the United States of America, South of the River Ohio. 94721-94722

Journal of the proceedings of the Legislative Council of . . . New Jersey. 53138

Journal of the proceedings of the Legislative Council of the Territory of Florida. 24873

Journal of the proceedings of the Legislative Council of the Territory of the United States of America, South of the River Ohio. 94723-94724

Journal of the proceedings of the Massachusetts Temperance Convention. 45908, 94645

Journal of the proceedings of the Medical Convention of Ohio. 56942

Journal of the proceedings of the National Division of the Sons of Temperance of North America. 87009

Journal of the proceedings of the National Division of the Sons of Temperance of North America. Twenty-second annual session. 51973

Journal of the proceedings of the National Republican Convention. 36741, 102282

Journal of the proceedings of the ninth annual convention. 66167

Journal of the proceedings of the primary convention. (53879)

Journal of the proceedings of the Provincial Congress of North-Carolina, held at Halifax, on the 4th day of April, 1776. 55631

Journal of the proceedings of the Provincial Congress of North-Carolina, held at Halifax the 12th day of November, 1776. 55632

Journal of the proceedings of the Provincial Synod. 36742

Journal of the proceedings of the second adjourned meeting. (66161)

Journal of the proceedings of the Senate and House of Representatives. 87483

Journal of the proceedings of the Senate of Maryland. 45175

Journal of the proceedings of the Senate of the General Assembly. (24874)

Journal of the proceedings of the Senate of the Territory of Florida. 24875

Journal of the proceedings of the sixteenth annual convention. 66160

Journal of the proceedings of the Sixth General Council. 83520

Journal of the proceedings of the South-western Convention. 88612

Journal of the proceedings of the Special Convention. (66161)

Journal of the proceedings of the third session of the fifth Congress. 15548

Journal of the proceedings of the twenty-ninth convention. 52842

Journal of the Provincial Congress of South Carolina. 87365

Journal of the provision of the Sons of Temperance of . . . New York. 53958, 87057

Journal of the public and secret proceedings of the Convocation of the People of Georgia. (27061)

Journal of the public proceedings of the Convention of the People of South Carolina 87438

Journal of the [Public School] Society. 54615

Journal of the regular and volunteer forces. (2044)

Journal of the Resolution's voyage. 16247

Journal of the Rev. Ammi R. Robbins. 71736

Journal of the Rev. Daniel Shute. (80800)

Journal of the Rev. Dr. Coke's fourth tour. 14247

Journal of the Rev. Dr. Coke from Gravensend to Antigua. 14242

Journal of the Rev. Dr. Coke's visit to Jamaica (14245)

Journal of the Rev. Doctor Stephen Williams. 104378

Journal of the Rev. G. Lewis. 40803

Journal of the Rev. J. B. Cates. 81740

Journal of the Rev. John Wesley. 102681

Journal of the Reverend John Wesley, A. M. 102681

Journal of the Rev'd Mr. Frisbie, Missionary. 103212

Journal of the Reverend Peter Jacobs. 35503

Journal of the Rev. S. D. Hinman. 31964

Journal of the Rev. Thomas Smith. 84352

Journal of the Rev. Timothy Flint. 100998

Journal of the revolution in the French part of St. Domingo. 94307

Journal of the Rhode Island Institute of Instruction. 70635, 70723

Journal of the route from New York to Real del Monte. 36743

Journal of the Royal Geographical Society. 73792, 77793-77794

Journal of the second annual convention of the Protestant Episcopal Church in the Diocese of Illinois. 66165

Journal of the second annual convention of the Protestant Episcopal Church in the Diocese of Michigan. 66170

Journal of the second biennial session of the House of Representatives. 561

Journal of the second biennial session of the Senate of Alabama. 562

Journal of the second Council of Safety. 88005

Journal of the Select Council. 61749

Journal of the Senate and House of . . . Mississippi. 49510

Journal of the Senate and House . . . [of Oregon.] 57554

Journal of the Senate [and] House of Representatives. 49260

Journal of the Senate. Anno Domini, 1776. 100150

Journal of the Senate . . . anno MDCCXC. 60174

Journal of the Senate at the first [-second] session. 94751

Journal of the Senate at the first session of the fourth General Assembly. 94751

Journal of the Senate extra session. 49602

Journal of the Senate. First session of the General Assembly. 35013

Journal of the Senate for 1812. (42243)

Journal of the Senate . . . in cases of impeachments. 56944

Journal of the Senate of Georgia. 27062

Journal of the Senate of Maryland. (45177)

Journal of the Senate of . . . Michigan. 48729

Journal of the Senate of . . . Mississippi.

49509

Journal of the Senate of Minnesota. 49261

Journal of the Senate of . . . Pennsylvania. 84648

Journal of the Senate of the commonwealth of Kentucky. 37517

Journal of the Senate of the first General Assembly. 34275

Journal of the Senate of the first session. 52402

Journal of the Senate of the General Assembly of . . . North Carolina. 55633

Journal of the Senate of the General Assembly of . . . North Carolina at its session 1860-'61. (55634)

Journal of the Senate of the state of California. (10024)

Journal of the Senate of the state of Connecticut. 15741

Journal of the Senate of the state of Deleware. 19390

Journal of the Senate of the state of Indiana. 90374

Journal of the Senate of the state of Indiana, for the first session. 34539

Journal of the Senate of the state of Michigan. 48745

Journal of the Senate of the state of Missouri. 49601

Journal of the Senate of the state of New Hampshire. 52840

Journal of the Senate [of the state of New York.] 54011

Journal of the Senate of the state of New York, at their tenth session. 53716

Journal of the Senate of the state of Ohio. 56943

Journal of the Senate of the state of South-Carolina. 87526

Journal of the Senate of the state of Tennessee. 94749-94750

Journal of the Senate of the United States, in cases of impeachments. 36744

Journal of the Senate of the United States of America. 15552

[Journal of the Senate of Virginia.] 100151-100191

Journal of the session of the House of Representatives. 60175

Journal of the session of the Senate. 60176

Journal of the shipwreck and sufferings of Daniel Foss. 25189

Journal of the siege and blockade of Quebec. 67024

Journal of the siege and surrender of Louisbourg. 42175

Journal of the siege of Louisbourg. 80545-80549

Journal of the siege of Oswego. 48965

Journal of the siege of Quebec. 67008

Journal of the Special Convention. 53208

Journal of the State Convention and ordinances. (49511)

Journal of the State Convention, held at St. Louis. (49603)

Journal of the State Convention of South Carolina. 87431

Journal of the Stated Preacher to the Hospital and Almshouse, in the City of New-York, for a part of the year of Our Lord 1813. 22384

Journal of the Stated Preached to the Hospital and Almshouse in the City of New York, for the year of Our Lord 1811. (22383)

Journal of the taking of Post St Vincents. [sic] (13287)

Journal of the telegraph. 36745

Journal of the Territorial Council of Kansas. 37047

Journal of the Texian Expedition against Mier. 28562

Journal of the third convention of the Protestant Episcopal Church. 41892

Journal of the third session, fifth Congress. 15556

Journal of the third session of the Legislature of the state of California. 10026

Journal of the thirty-first annual convention of the Diocese of Maine. 44005

Journal of the thirty-sixth general convention of the New Church. 52575

Journal of the times. 36746

Journal of the transactions and occurrences in the settlement. 104847

Journal of the travels and sufferings of Daniel Saunders. 77172

Journal of the twelve months campaign. 5625

Journal of the United States Agricultural Society. 36747

Journal of the United States in Congress assembled. 15545

Journal of the visit of H. R. H. the Prince of Wales. 22600

Journal of the votes and proceedings, as well of the Committee of Safety. 53139

Journal of the votes and proceedings . . . of the Committee of Safety. 53106

Journal of the votes & proceedings of the Convention of New-Jersey. (53140)

Journal of the votes and proceedings of the General Assembly of the colony of New-York. Begun the 9th day of April, 1691. (53719)

Journal of the votes and proceedings of the General Assembly of the colony of New-York, begun the 17th of November, 1767. 53721

Journal of the votes and proceedings of the General Assembly of the colony of New York. Begun the twelfth day of Februay February, 1747-8. 53718

Journal of the votes and proceedings of the General Assembly of the colony of New York. [From March 24, to Sept. 22, 1747.] (53717)

Journal of the votes and proceedings of the General Assembly of the colony of New-York, from 1766 to 1776. 53720

Journal of the votes and proceedings of the General Assembly of the colony of New York, 1768[-1775]. 53721

Journal of the votes and proceedings of the General Assembly of the colony of New York, 1766. 84558

Journal of the votes and proceedings of the
House of Assembly of . . . New
Brunswick. 52537
Journal of the votes and proceedings of the
Lower House of Assembly. 45178
Journal of the votes and proceedings of the
. . . representatives. 60177
Journal of the votes of the General Assembly
of the colony of New-York. (53722)
Journal of the voyage from New York, via
Nicaragua, to San Francisco. (10764)
Journal of the voyage of the sloop Mary.
36748
Journal of the voyages and travels of a corps
of discovery. 26741
Journal of the Western Society of Engineers.
84898
Journal of the writer [i. e. a native born
Virginian.] 79371, 88478
Journal of Thomas Chalkley. 11750
Journal of Thomas Hulme. 31982, 84355-
84356
Journal [of Thomas Smith.] 84368
Journal of Thomas Story. 92327
Journal of Thomas Wilson. 20033
Journal of three thousand three hundred miles.
26316
Journal of three years' residence. (9067)
Journal of transactions and correspondence.
1088
Journal of transactions and events. 11150
Journal of travel in different parts of the
United States. (2514)
Journal of travels from New-Hampshire to
Caratuck. 37199, 66193
Journal of travels in . . . 1838. 72067
Journal of travels in England, Holland and
Scotland. (81036)-(81037), 81041-81042
Journal of travels in North America. 768,
38071
Journal of travels in the interior during the
years 1824, 1825, 1826. 81515
Journal of travels in the United States and
Lower Canada in 1817. 58360, 84304-
84306, 84320-84321
Journal of travels into the Arkansa [sic]
Territory. (56348)
Journal of travels over the Rocky Mountains.
(36749)
Journal of travels over the Rocky Mountains,
to the mouth of the Columbia River.
58358
Journal of travels through several towns in the
country. (36750)
Journal of two campaigns of the Fourth
Regiment. 101032
Journal of two visits made to some nations of
Indians. 36488
Journal of useful knowledge. 36751
Journal of useful sciences. 9968
Journal of visitation in Nova Scotia. 34769
Journal of visitation to the western portion.
13004, 92643
Journal of voyages and travels in the interiour.
30404
Journal of voyages and travels through the
north-west continent. (43501)
Journal of voyages; containing an account.
21280
Journal of voyages to Marguaritta, Trinidad,
and Maturin. 167
Journal of walks in the woods. 42072
Journal of Wayne's campaign. (7132), (35489)
Journal of what passed in the expedition of
His Excellency Colonel Benjamin Fletcher.
(24713)

Journal [of William Caton.] 9416
Journal of William H. Richardson, a private
soldier in Col. Doniphan's command.
71093
Journal of William H. Richardson, a private
soldier in the command of new and old
Mexico. 71094
Journal of William Loughton Smith. 84816,
84819, 84824, 84830, 84832, 84835,
84837
Journal of William Scudder, an officer of the
late New York Line. (78533)
Journal [of William Stephens.] 94215
Journal of winds, weather, &c. 18336
Journal [of Zebulon M. Pike.] 62835
Journal officiel de la Convention . . . de la
Louisiane. 42275
Journal officiel de la republique Francaise.
note after 99383C
Journal officiel des travaux de la Convention.
(42276)
Iovrnal ofte beschryvinghe van de wonderlicke
reyse. 68454, 77920
Journal, ofte dagh-register, over de reyse.
23578
Journal ofte historiaelse beschrijvinge. 8184
Journal on board H. M. Ship Cambridge.
74614
Journal on the settlement of St. Louis. 75357
Journal on the western expedition. 49200
Journal or extract, from the logbook of the
voyage. (29594)
Journal: or full account of the late expedition
to Canada. 101050
Journal or historical account of the life,
travels and Christian experiences of that
antient, faithful servant of Jesus Christ,
Thomas Chalkley. 11749
Journal, or historical account of the life,
travels, sufferings, Christian experiences,
and labour of love. 25352
Iovrnal ov description de l'admirable voyage
de Guillaume Schouten Hollandois. 77947
Iovrnal ou description du merveilleux voyage
de Gvilliavme Schovten. 77948-77951
Iovrnal ov relation exacte dv voyage de Gvill.
Schovten. 77952-77954
Journal politique de Saint-Domingue. (75180)
Journal politique et litteraire. 29584
Journal politique, litteraire, maritime. 9126
Journal publie a Mexico. 29261
Journal publie par un autre officier. 23923,
73377
Journal publie par un officier a bord de
l'Alexandre. 23923, 73377
Journal received February 4, 1741. 91305,
91314
Journal redige par un flaneur. 23789
Journal solely devoted to life, fire and marine
insurance. 34874
Journal tres-fidele des observations faites.
(11835)
Journal univ. des sc. med. 4849
Journal up the Illinois River. (34053)-34054,
(34358)
Journal van de reise naar Gronland. (36752)
Journal von Brasilien oder vermischte
Nachrichten. 22828
Journal while among the Indians. 21927
Journal, written by himself [i. e. Samuel
Smith.] 83997
Journal, written during his [i. e. James
Sharan's] voyages and travels. (79772)
Journal written on board of H. M. S. Cambridge.
75879

Journal, written on the coasts of Chili. 29718

Journal zur Kunstgeschichte und zur allgemeiner Litteratur. 51480, (51482), 98777

Iournalen van drie voyagien. 11607, 31503-31504

Iournalier verhael ofte copie van sekeren brief. (7592)

Journalist. pseud. Memoirs of James Gordon Bennett. see Pray, Isaac C.

Journaliste Americain. pseud. Secession aux Etats-Unis. see Mortimer, J.

Journalist's account of the outlaw Rande. 84246

Journals and appendices of the Legislative Assembly of Canada. 36757

Journals and letters of Colonel John Allan. 37715

Journals and proceedings of the General Assembly of the commonwealth of Pennsylvania. 60178

Journals and proceedings of the General Assembly, in Grand Committee. 90023

Journals and proceedings [of the General Assembly of Vt.] 99049

Journals and proceedings of the General Assembly [of Vermont from 1778 to January 1791.] 99024

Journals, &c. [of the Continental Congress.] 15545

Journals for 1773 [of the New York General Assembly.] 90629, 5th note after 98997

Journals kept by the Rev. Thomas Smith. 84350

Journals . . . of Allen Alonzo Kingsbury. 37880

Journals [of Andrew Burn.] 9353

Journals of Assembly [of Vermont.] 99049

Journals of Christian Frederick Post. 66223, (74155)

Journals of Congress. (23526)

Journals of Congress, and of the United States in Congress assembled. 15545

[Journals of Congress. Containing the proceedings] from January 1, 1776. 15545

Journals of Congress. Containing the proceedings from Sept. 5. 1774. 15545

Journals of Congress for the year 1776. 74069

Journals of Congress, from Saturday April 24th to Monday, May 3d, 1779. 15550

Journals of Congress from the first meeting to the adoption of the constitution. 36753

Journals [of Edward Winslow.] 51012

Journals of expeditions to the north of California. 8759

Journals of general conventions . . . 1785-1835. 84693

Journals of John Wesley. 102675

Journals of Madam Knight. 38124

Journals of Major Robert Rogers. (72725)-(72728), 84618

Journals of Major Samuel Shaw. 79959

Journals of Mr. Commissary van Reck. 68369

Journals of the American Congress. (15546)

Journals of the American Convention to Form a Liturgy. 38183

Journals of the annual conventions. 56939

Journals of the Assembly of Jamaica. 35589, 35608

Journals of the Board of Regents. 85080

Journals of the Committee of Safety. 100037

Journals of the Committees on the Revised Statutes. 45786

Journals of the consultation held at San Felipe de Austn [sic]. 94952

Journals of the Continental Congress. 93430

Journals of the convention, assembled at the city of Austin. 94978

Journals of the convention [of the Connecticut Medical Society.] 15783

Journals of the Convention of the Free, Sovereign and Independent People of Texas. 94956

Journals of the Convention of the province of Maryland. (45286)

Journals of the Conventions of the People of South Carolina. 87425

Journals of the Conventions of the Protestant Episcopal Church in the Diocese of New-York. (53880)

Journals of the Conventions of the Protestant Episcopal Church in the Diocese of Rhode Island. 70625

Journals of the Council of State of Virginia. 100037

Journals of the First Branch of the City Council of Baltimore. 63126

Journals of the first Legislative Assembly of the Territory of Arizona. 36754

Journals of the fourth Congress. 94965, 94970

Journals of the General Conference. 48188

Journals of the General Convention of the Protestant Episcopal Church. 84678C

Journals of the General Conventions of the Protestant Episcopal Church, in the United States . . . from . . . 1784. 66171, note after 103462

Journals of the General Conventions of the Protestant Episcopal Church, in the United States, 1785-1835. (66173)

Journals of the Grand Lodge of Vermont. 99190

Journals of the House of Assembly of Nova Scotia. 56142

Journals [of the House of Assembly of South Carolina Colony.] 2d note after 87347

Journals of the House of Commons, 1801-1802. 85232

Journals of the House of Commons from Nov. 8th, 1547 to 1854. (36755)

Journals of the House of Lords. 65862, 88190

Journals of the House of Lords, beginning anno primo Henrici Octavi 1509. 36756

Journals of the House of Representatives of the colony of the Massachusetts-Bay. (45787)

Journals of the House of Representatives of the republic of Texas. 94965

Journals of the Legislative Assembly of Canada. 10487

Journals of the Legislative Assembly of the province of Quebec. (67009)

Journals of the Legislative Council and Legislative Assembly of the province of Canada. 10493

Journals of the lives and travels of Samuel Bownas, and John Richardson. 71024

Journals of the missionaries. 34894

Journals of the ocean. 102206

Journals of the Provincial Congress of South-Carolina. 87353, 87360, 87365

Journals of the Provincial Congress of South Carolina held at Charles-Town. 87361

Journals of the Provincial Congress, Provincial Convention, Committee of Safety and Council of Safety of . . . New-York. 53723

Journals of the Rev. Dr. Coke's five visits to America. 14243

Journals of the Rev. Dr. Coke's three visits to America. 14243

Journals of the Senate and House of Delegates . . . of Maryland. 45165

Journals of the Senate and House of Representatives of the fourth General Assembly. (34274)

Journals of the Senate of the republic of Texas. 94970

Journals of the Senate, when sitting for the purpose of trying an impeachment. 60179

Journals of travels from New Hampshire to Caratuck. 53883

Journals [of William Dunbar and Dr. Hunter.] 40828

Journals relative to the exploration of that portion of British North America between Lake Superior and the Pacific Ocean. 58331

Journee de Lexington. 27650, (63966), 68421

Journee du Chretien sanctifiee par la priere et la meditation. 36758

Journey across the Alleghanies. (7046)

Journey across the American continent. 17267

Journey across the island of Newfoundland. 16789

Journey across the Pampas. 7388

Journey all round the world. (81377)

Journey beyond the Rocky Mountains. (58730), 58375

Journey by wagon from Ohio to Wisconsin Territory. 84132

Journey from Babylon to Jerusalem. 20757

Journey from Buenos Ayres. 1509

Journey from Constantinople. 101153

Journey from Egypt to Jerusalem. 74672

Journey from India, towards England. (59572)

Journey from Philadelphia to New-York. 25893-(25894)

Journey from Prince of Wale's Fort. 31181-31182

Journey in Moravia and Bohemia. (59572)

Journey in North America, containing a survey. 14461

Journey in North America, described in familiar letters. 29310

Journey in the back country. 57241

Journey in the seabord [sic] slave states. 57242

Journey in the West Indies. 18325

Journey of life. 20757

Journey of the Mississippi River. 49551

Journey over land, from the Gulf of Honduras to the Great South-Sea. 14095

Journey over the Isthmus of Darien. 29473

Journey through Illinois and Michigan. 37949

Journey through Kansas. 7151

Journey through Nova Scotia. 72113

Journey through Spain. 96389

Journey through Texas. (57243)

Journey through the United States and part of Canada. 23220

Journey of Great-Salt-Lake-City. (69594)

Iourney to Pvckanokick. (51198), note after 104797

Journey to the ancient capital of Peru. 44613

Journey to the gold diggins. 68157

Iourney to the kingdome of Namaschet. (51198), note after 104797

Journey to the land of Eden. (9721)-(9722)

Journeyings of the Djebel Kumri. 47197

Journeyman printer. pseud. Novellettes of a traveller. see Nott, Henry Junius.

Journeymen cabinet and chair-makers, Philadelphia book of prices. 36759

Journeymen Cordwainers of the City of New York. defendants 75959, (78979), note after 96947

Journeymen House-Carpenters of the City of New York. 41441

Journeymen Printers National Convention, New York, 1850. see National Convention of Journeymen Printers of the United States, New York, 1850.

Journeymen Shipwrights' Society, New York. see New York Journeymen Shipwrights' Society.

Journeymen Shipwrights' Union of Massachusetts. see Massachusetts Journeymen Shipwrights' Union.

Journeymen Tailors, Philadelphia. defendants see Twenty-Four Journeymen Tailors, Philadelphia. defendants

Journeys and explorations in the cotton kingdom. 57240

Journeys of Abraham Lincoln. 14199

Journeys of the children of Israel. 8192

Joutel, Henri, 1640?-1735. 25853, 36760-36763

Jouvency, Joseph. 36764-(36767), note after 69259

Jouy, Victor Joseph Etienne de. (36768)-(36769), 89596

Jove, Manuel Moreno y. see Moreno y Jove, Manuel.

Joven Americano. pseud. Poesias. 63632

Joven de Entonces. pseud. Recuerdos de la invasion Norte-Americana. see Roa Barcena, Jose Maria.

Jovenase, ---------, Duc de. see Chelemar, -------, Prince de.

Jovenaso, ---------, Duque de. see Chelemar, -------, Prince de.

Jovenes orientales. pseud. eds. Recuerdo semanario. 68460

Jovet, Jean. 36770-36771

Jovial companion. 14879

Jovial songster. 36772

Jovio, Paolo. see Giovio, Paolo, Bp., 1483-1552.

Jovius, Paulus. see Giovio, Paolo, Bp., 1483-1552.

Joy, Benjamin. 36778, 1st note after 97160

Joy, Charles A. 14806

Joy, George. 1200, 36779

Joy, James F. 36780-36781

Joy, Thomas. plaintiff 40855

Joy & Co. firm see Donoho, Joy & Co. firm

Joy and gladness. 24517

Joy and gratitude to God. 38872

Joy and salvation by Christ. 30891

Joy days on both sides of the water. 41735

Joy in tribulation. 7456

Joy of children walking in truth. 40773

Joy of faith. 39796

Joy of the saints. 78585

Joy, the duty of survivors. 12331

Joyau, L. 56471

Joyce, J. ed. 82304

Joyce, John. defendant 36782

Joyce, L. E. Elliott. ed. 100940

Joyeuse, Louis Thomas Villaret. see Villaret-Joyeuse, Louis Thomas.

Joyfull newes out of the new found world. (49945)

Ioyfull newes out of the new-found VVorlde. 49946

Ioyfull nevves ovt of the newe found worlde.
49944
Joyful sacrifice of a prosperous nation.
101123
Joyful tidings to the begotten of God in all.
84551

Joynes, Edward S. 21885, (36783)
Joynes, William T. 100462
Joys and sorrows of American life. 31436
Joze, S. 7610
Jozebudre einer, inr Zahre, 1811. 7178
Ju Otoshki-kikindiuin au kitogimaminan.
57090
Ju Otoshki-kikindiuin au tebeniminvng. 57091
Juan Baptista. see San Juan Bautista, Elias
de, d. 1605.
Juan de Alvarado. Fray (36788)
Juan de Angliara. see Anghiera, Pietro
Martire d', 1455-1526.
Juan de Avila. Fray 36790
Juan de la Anunciacion. Fray 1726, (36795)-
36798
Juan de la Concepcion. Fray 36799
Juan de la Cruz. see De la Cruz, Juan.
Juan de la Madalena. see Estrada, Juan.
Juan de la Madre de Dios. 43755
Juan de San Bernàrdo. 36792
Juan de San Jose. Fray (64399), 76121
Juan de San Miguel, fl. 1685. 76173
Juan de San Miguel, fl. 1691-1709. 36793,
76174-76180
Juan de Vargas. see Vargas, Juan de.
Juan, Don --------, fl. 1663. 36784
Juan, Alexandro Bonilla y San. see Bonilla
y San Juan, Alexandro.
Juan, Jorge. see Juan y Santacilia, Jorge,
1713-1773.
Juan, Pedro Antonio Castillo y San. see
Castillo y San Juan, Pedro Antonio.
Juan, Vicente Folch y. see Folch y Juan,
Vicente.
Juan Bautista, Elias de San. see San Juan
Bautista, Elias de, d. 1605.
Juan Bautista, Matias de San. see San Juan
Bautista, Matias de.
Juan de Dios Arias, C. 36791
Juan Hermoso, Faustino de San. see Hermoso,
Faustino de San Juan.
Juan Martinena, Juan Martin de. see
Martinena, Juan Martin de Juan.
Juan y Santacilia, Jorge, 1713-1773. (19702),
36801-36803, 36807-36808, 36812,
57458-47459, note before 97683, 1st note
after 97684, 2d note after 97684, 1st
note after 97687, 2d note after 97689, 4th
note after 97689, 6th note after 97689,
100815
Juan y Santacilia, Jorge. incorrectly supposed
author 36804-(36806), 36809-36811,
36813, 1st-2d notes after 97686, 1st-2d
notes after 97689, 4th note after 97689,
6th note after 97689
Juan Nicot cumple su promesa contraida con
el publico. (55264)
Ivan Recio de Leon . . . haze relacion a V. M.
68362
Ivan Recio de Leon Maesse de Campo, . . .
peligros del dilatado camino. 68355
Juana, Queen of Castile, 1479-1555. 22550,
note after 40960 see also Castile.
Sovereigns, etc., 1504-1506 (Juana) and
Spain. Sovereigns, etc., 1504-1506
(Fernando V)
Juana Ines de la Cruz, sister, 1651-1695.
17333-17335, note after 34687, 36814-
36815, 76264

Juanito le harpiste. 21371
Juarez, Benito Pablo, Pres. Mexico, 1806-
1872. 20548, 26719, 36816, 48518,
56400, 57679 see also Mexico. Presi-
dent, 1857-1872 (Juarez) Oaxaca (Mexican
State) Governador, 1847-1853 (Juarez)
Juarros, Domingo. 36817-(36818)
Juba. pseud. "United we stand; divided we
fall." see Allen, Benjamin. supposed
author
Jubilee; a half-century discourse. (42010)
Jubilee: a sermon, containing a history of the
origin of the First Baptist Church.
58790
Jubilee: a sermon preached . . . on Friday,
August 1st, 1834. 101369
Jubilee at Mount St. Mary's, October 6, 1858.
36823
Jubilee College, Illinois. Agent. 36822, 1st
note after 90670 see also Kellogg,
E. B.
Jubilee: 1817-1867. 9340
Jubilee in Commemoration of the Second
Centennial Anniversary of the Settlement
of Virginia, Jamestown, Va., 1807. see
Jamestown, Va. Second Centennial
Anniversary Jubilee, 1807.
Jubilee memorial of the American Bible
Society. (24191)
Jubilee memorial of the semi-centennial
anniversary of the First Presbyterian
Church. 64436
Jubilee of MDCCCLI, in New-York. 85946
Jubilee of Lawrence Academy. 39389
Jubilee of New England. 105086
Jubilee of the constitution. 281
Jubilee sermon. 20391
Jubilee sermon, containing a history of the
origin. (58791)
Jubilee sermon delivered at the request. 11305
Jubilee sermons. 104718
Jubileo del Ano Santo. (41115)
Jubilos de Lima en la dedicacion de su Santa
Iglesia Cathedral. 74020
Jvbilos de Lima y fiestas feales. 60851
Jubilos de Lima, y glorias del Peru. 36824
Jubilos de Maerica. 79186
Jubinal, Achille. ed. 39858
Juchereau de St. Ignace, Mere Francoise.
36825
Judaeis, Cornelius de. cartographer 36826
Judah, Samuel B. H. 8838, 36827-36829,
94241
Judah, Theodore D. 36830
Judah P. Benjamin's intercepted instructions.
4703, 81812
Judaism. 71852
Judas the traitor hung up in chains. 50301
Judd, A. B. 36831
Judd, David W. 36832
Judd, Eben W. 91970-91973
Judd, Gideon N. (32166), (36833)-(36835)
Judd, H. O. (36836)
Judd, Jonathan. 36837
Judd, Norman Buel, 1815-1878. 36838
Judd, Orange. (36839)
Judd, Orrin B. 36848, 54757
Judd, Samuel. defendant (46955), 75951, 2d
note after 96891
Judd, Sylvester, 1789-1860. 6255, 36843-
36844
Judd, Sylvester, 1813-1853. 36840-36842
Judd, Thomas. 36845
Judd, Willard. 36848
Judd, William. 36846-36847

Judd vs. Trumbull. 36847
Judge, Jonathan J. (36849)
Judge Advocate's vade mecum. 39718
Judge Anderson's speech. 1411
Judge Clayton's review of the report. 13581
Judge Davis and the presidency. 44770
Judge Douglas. 7671
Judge Douglas in reply to Judge Black. 20693
Judge Douglas—the bill of indictment. 78033
Judge Fayette Smith. 83557
Judge Holt's report. (56973)
Judge Jay's portrait at White Plains. 35849
Judge Kelley's views on the Chinese question. 37272
Judge Kent's excellent charge to the jury. 96819
Judge Loring's decision. 6505, 9404
Judge of the covivial court of Dover. pseud. ed. American magazine of wit. (1138)
Judge Redfield's letter to Senator Foot. (68500)
Judge Strong's charge to the Grand Jury. 93069
Judge Symme's [sic] pamphlet. 94104
Judge Todd's answer and the court's decision. 96084
Judges' catalogue of the articles. 45225
Judgment, a vision. (36850)
Judgment and approbation of Dr. James Usher. 7996, 16037
Judgment begun at the House of God. 18470
Judgment, delivered in the Court of Vice-Admiralty. 97747
Judgment given by twenty eight Quakers against George Keith. 37200, 97113
Judgment given forth by twenty-eight Quakers. 37200, 97113
Judgment of Lord Stowell. 29617, 1st note after 92630
Judgment of our worthy brethren of New England. 28050
Judgment of several eminent divines of the congregational vvay. (36851), 46695
Judgment of the Rector and Tutors of Yale-College. 105827
Iudgement [sic] of the Reformed Churches of France. 91384
Judgment of whole kingdoms and nations. (19280), 86795-86798
Judgement [sic] thereupon in answer to a certain printed paper. 5628
Judgment seat; a discourse. (43223)
Judgements [sic] in the Admiralty of Pennsylvania. 60180
Judgments of God, confessed and deprecated. 18006
Judgments of God upon the nations. 36852
Judgments of providence in the hand of Christ. 14496
Ivdices, commentariis literarib[us] com muralib[us]. 99669
Judicial chronicle. (27302)
Judicial decisions on the writ of habeas corpus. 98394
Judicial decisions upon the cases of jabeas corpus. 3189
Judicial power in the United States. 84516
Judicial, practical and mercantile guide of British Guiana. 98480
Judicial record of Hon. Henry W. Williams. 8441
Judicial specimens, and brief explanatory correspondence. 7304
Judiciary. 48913, 1st note after 95515, 95517

Judiciary system. 7087
Judicious and select essays and observations. 67561
Judicious and select observations. 67587
Judicious observation on that dreadful comet. 104922
Judisches Schulwesen in Amerika. 24206
Judith, Esther, and other poems. 36853, 106372
Judith religiossa. 50117
Judson, A. M. 36858
Judson, Adoniram. 36854
Judson, Andrew T. (36855)-36857
Judson, David. 4095, 36859, 78730
Judson, E. 36863
Judson, Edward Z. C., 1822-1886. (36860)-(36862, 88617
Judson, Ephraim. 36864, 73408
Judson, L. Carroll. 36865-36867
Judson, Roswell. 102335
Judson Circulating Library, Stamford Seminary, N. Y. see Stamford Seminary, N. Y. Judson Circulating Library.
Jueces Plenipotenciaros de Castilla y Portugal. see Portugal. Jueces Plenipotenciaros. and Spain. Jueces Plenipotenciaros.
Juago filoarmonico. (76021)
Ivez Conservador de los Religiosos de Santo Domingo de la Provincia de Gvaxaca. 106003A
Juffer in schyn. 36868
Juga jucunda. 46372, 46518
Juge, M. A. 36869
Juge de paix et officier de paroisse. 61005
Jugemann, Bernhard Severin. 36870
Jugement errone de M. Ernest Renan. (17981)
Jugement impartial sur les operations militaires de la campagne. 67020
Jugement rendu souverainement et en dernier ressort. 10472
Jugenbjahre, vom ihm selbst beschrieben. 25517
Jugglers detected. 2669
Juggler's tricks, or legerdemain exposed. 98895
Jugglery. 82637
Jugla y Font, Antonio. ed. 29276
Juglar, Clement. 36871
Juicio critico de los ministerios de la inquisicion. 93348
Juicio critico de sus obras. 9583
Juicio critico sobre el restablecimiento de la Compania de Jesus. 93343
Juicio critico sobre el sistema de hacienda en Mexico. 50510
Juicio de imprenta. 36872
Juicio de imprenta y nuevos abusos de la autoridades hermanas. 93401
Juicio de la obra de Senor Arzobispo Depradt. 99656
Juicio de residencia del Escelentisimo Senor Don M. Tacon. 94193
Juicio historico-canonico-politico. 36873
Juicio imparcial que sirve de respuesta al papel. 44065
Juicio imparcial sobre la exposicion del Senor Obispo de Popayan. 86236
Juicio imparcial sobre las principales causas de la revolucion. (65112)
Juicio imparcial sobre los acontecimientos de Mexico. 36874, 106278
Juicio posesorio de los terrenos del Cenicero. 36875
Juicio sobre el codigo civil. 76702
Juicio sobre la causa seguida contra . . . Andres Pimentel. 62875

Junkin, George. 36931-(36934), 38586, 96822

Junta Civica de Mexico. <u>see</u> Mexico. Junta Civica.

Junta de Fomento, La Guaira, Venezuela. <u>see</u> La Guaira, Venezuela. Junta de Fomento.

Junta de Historia y Numismatica Americana, Buenos Aires. 94606

Junta de Observacion, Buenos Aires. <u>see</u> Buenos Aires. Junta de Observacion, 1815.

Junta Directiva de la Empresa de los Caminos de Hierro de Cardenas y Jucaro. <u>see</u> Cuba. Junta Directiva de la Empresa de los Caminos de Hierro de Cardenas y Jucaro.

Junta Directiva de la Union Americana. <u>see</u> Sociedad de la Union Americana de Santiago de Chile. Junta Directiva de la Union Americana.

Junta General de la Real Compania Guipuz-coana de Caracas del ano de 1772. 10777

Junta Provincial de Censura no desempena las funciones. 62937

Junta Superior de Cadiz a la America Espanola. 36935

Junta Superior Directiva de Hacienda, Havana. <u>see</u> Havana. Junta Superior de Hacienda.

Junta Suprema del Reyno a la nacion Espanola. 48508

Juntas im Thal des Rio de Copiapo. 9352

Junto of Members of the Provincial Parliament of Lower Canada. <u>see</u> Quebec (Province) Assembly.

Junto, or the interior cabinet laid open. 36936

Jupiter's decree. 92409

Jurado, Juan. 36937 <u>see also</u> Cuba. Real Audiencia, Havana. Fiscal.

Ivrado Palomino, Bartolome. <u>see</u> Palomino, Bartolome Ivrado.

Jurado celebre. 36938

Juras Reales, --------, Baron de. 51215

Jure, -------- de. <u>tr.</u> 77647-77648

Jurgensen, Christian August. (36938A)

Jurgensen, Jorgen. 36939

Juridica demonstracion de la justicia. (67401)

Juridical memorial. 22011

Juridicus. <u>pseud.</u> Some additional remarks. (17400)

Juridisk tidsskrift. 26135

Jurien, P., fl. 1687. 101877

Juris allegatio pro Episcopo del Cuzco. 61133

Iuris allegato. 99634

Ivris antecessoris. 86521

Juris Consultus. <u>pseud.</u> Review of the tribute to the pilgrims, &c. 30925

Jurisconsult. <u>pseud.</u> Considerations on the appointment. <u>see</u> Boyd, S. S.

Jurisconsulto. <u>pseud.</u> ed. 88798

Jurisconsultus. <u>pseud.</u> Observations on the reform. 36940

Jurisdiction and powers of the United States courts. (39321)

Jurisdiction of justices of the peace and office and duties of judges of probate. 84882

Jurisdiction of justices of the peace in civil and criminal cases; and the offices and duties. 84881

Jurisdiction of justices of the peace in civil and criminal cases, with forms. 84883

Jurisdiction of our state courts over the violators. 67143

Jurisdiction of the Court of Chancery in Pennsylvania. 60181, note after 97166

Jurisdiction of the lakes. 59159

Jurisdiction of the Privy Council in appeals. 3218

Jurtze Reise Beschreibung. 97662

Jury-institutionen i storbritanien. 72585

Jury of odd fellows. <u>pseud.</u> American magazine of wit. (1138)

Juryman. <u>pseud.</u> Englishman's right. <u>see</u> Hawles, Sir John.

Juryman's guide for the state of New York. 21914

Jusselain, Armand. 36941

Jusserand, J. J. 84997

Jussieu, Antoine Laurent de, 1747-1836. (36942), 51249, 67461, 74005, 82788

Jussieu, Adrien de, 1797-1853. (75218), (75222)

Just account of an Ecclesiastical Council. 28627

Just and cleare refutation. 38886, 92940

Just and impartial account of the transactions. 18601

Just and impartial narrative of the controversy (24533), 75666

Just and modest vindication. 18571, (32340), note after 78219, 78234

Ivst and necessarie apology of certain Christians. 72098-72099, 72110

Just and plain vindication of Sir William Keith. 37243

Just and seasonable vindication. 16305

Just and true account. 61750

Just appreciation of Sir John Ross's character. 7360

Just arrived by express. 100031

Just commemorations. 46373

Just concern of the people of God. 27403

Just confutation of an abusive printed half-sheet. 66735

Just limitation of slavery in the laws of God. 79823, 95530

Just man's prerogative. 104089

Just published and now selling. (61751)

Just rebuke to a dialogue betwixt Simon and Timothy. 67995

Just rebuke to several calumnies. 8954

Just remarks on a late book. (25392), 103067

Just rules of commerce declared. (46381)

Just supremacy of Congress over the Territories. (18039)

Just vindication of the covenant. 13867

Justa defensa de la Academia Cubana de Literatura. 74769

Justa literaria certamen poetico. 13058

Justa literaria palestra metrica. 24154, 72532

Justa represelia en desagravio. (19269)

Justa repulsa contra las horribles calumnias. (36943)

Justa retribuicao dada ao compadre de Lisboa. 76327

Justa vindicacion a las imputaciones. 96219

Justa vindicacion por Fr. Veremundo A Androminas de Cascaliendres. 11298

Justamond, J. O. tr. (68087)-68089

Justas quejas de los Chupadores. 98027

Justas y respetuosas consideraciones. 93303

Justel, Henri. 36944, 68430

Justia. <u>pseud.</u> Our world. <u>see</u> Adams, F. Colburn.

Justice. <u>pseud.</u> Few introductory observations. 58999

Justice. <u>pseud.</u> Reply to Censor. 87936

Justice. pseud. Review of Ellwood Fisher's lecture. see Osgood, Mussey.
Justice, Alexander. 36946
Justice and constables assistant. 28421
Justice and expediency of conciliating the American states. 8512
Justice and expediency; or slavery considered. 103806
Justice and mercy recommended. 59496
Justice and necessity of taxing the American colonies. (36947)
Justice and necessity of the war with our American colonies considered. (36948)
Justice and necessity of the war with our American colonies examined. 10931
Justice and policy. An essay. 36949
Justice and policy of a war with Spain demonstrated. 36950
Justice and policy of the late act of Parliament. 38182
Justice as well as mercy. 12537
Justice en Autriche. 85453
Justice essential to national prosperity. 6395
Justice in the bye ways. 203
Justice Love-Country. pseud. Dialogue. see Gooch, Sir William, Bart., 1681-1751.
Justice of a state. 73955
Justice of God in the damnation of sinners. 21947
Justice of our national cause. 42032
Justice of the peace, and county and township officer. 44800
Justice of the peace; containing a brief treatise. 84880
Justice of the present war against the French. 22322, 36951
Justice to a colonial governor. 24370
Justice to Buck. 8864
Justice to Hiram Powers. 37297
Justice to Jackson. 92007
Justice to the aborigines essential. 3216
Justice to the constitution. 82638
Justice to the land states. 93660
Justice to the living. 59105
Justice to the south! 20643
Justice's guide. 95470
Justicia en defensa de la verdad. 98958
Justicia y la razon. 93294
Justicia y la razon, "los verdaderos imparciales." 76203
Justico literaria y palestra metrica. 24154, 72532
Justificacion de los assientos de Averia. 36952
Justificacion que el Lic. D. Felipe Jauregui. (35822)
Justificatie van de resolutien ende proceduren. (78001)
Justification by faith. 58769
Justification by works. 20059
Justification de la conducta publica seguida. 26579
Justification de la politique Bresilienne dans la Plata. 58545, 81113
Justification de la resistance des colonies Americaines. 36953
Justification de Louis Tousard. 96340
Justification de M. La Fayette. 69716
Justification de plusieurs faits. 6877, 38490
Justification de M. de Luzerne. 17158
Justification des memoires de l'Academie des Sciences de 1744. 6877, 38490
Justification of believers. (51518)

Justification of Commodore Paulding's arrest. (20611)
Justification of his [i. e. Josiah Burchett's] naval memoirs. 9207
Ivstification of separation from the Church of England. 72100-72101, 72110
Justification of the administration of Castro-land. 95825
Justification of the conduct of the ministry. 36954
Justification of the doctrine. (59899)
Justification of the independent churches of Christ. 12687
Justification of the Legislature. 80042
Justification of the present war against the United Netherlands. 93225
Justification of the veto of the late President, &c. 13684
Justification publiee par M. de la Luzerne. 17168
Justificazion de la conducta de Manuel Crecencio Rejon. (69160)
Justifying memorial in answer. 27282
Justin, J. P. (36955)
Justin, ------ Placide. see Placide-Justin, --------.
Justinian. pseud. Currency of the future. (36960)
Justinian. pseud. Relations of the federal government. see Cruger, Lewis.
Justinian. pseud. Remarks on the report. 36958
Justinina. pseud. Sovereign rights of the states. 36959
Justinian. pseud. Statesman's manual. see Cruger, Lewis.
Justinian, of South Carolina. pseud. Sovereign rights of states. see Cruger, Lewis.
Justis belli causis. 79180
Justitia. pseud. Letter. see Graduate, late an officer in the United States Army. pseud.
Justitius. pseud. Remarks on the organization. 36961
Justiz, Francisco Jose. 36962 see also Cuba. Cuerpo Nacional de Ingenieros. Director Subinspector Interno.
Justo Jimenez, Juan. see Jimenez, Juan Justo.
Justo Festivo. pseud. Soliloquio entre Dr. Pineres y Justo Festiov. see Quesada, Rafael.
Justos reclamos. 36963
Justus, --------. ed. 6106, 92322
Justus Strictus Veritas. pseud. Nuevas reflexiones. 56289
Juvenal. pseud. (50137), (55169), 100451
Juvenal Junius. pseud. see Junius, Juvenal. pseud.
Juvencio, J. see Jouvency, Joseph.
Juvencius, Josephus. see Jouvency, Joseph.
Juvenile anti-slavery series [of tracts.] (36964)
Juvenile Asylum, New York. see New York Juvenile Asylum.
Juvenile biography. (36965)
Juvenile cabinet. 90543
Juvenile depravity and crime in our city. (30527)
Juvenile essays. 60840
Juvenile guide. 79712, 106199
Juvenile instructor. 85530
Juvenile Library Company, Richmond, Va. 71164, 3d note after 104862
Juvenile lyre. 84048

K

Kameakua, G. M. tr. 83132
Kames, Henry Home, Lord, 1696-1782.
  32702, 84103-84106, 105254-105255,
  105260
Kamiena di Kroes. 66749
Kampen, N. G. van. 36992-(36993), 40836,
  106334
Kamper, Peter. plaintiff 36994, 94411, note
  after 96882, 3d note after 96891
Kampf der Freiheit am Niagara. 10623
Kampfscenen der Indianer. 38197
Kampner, Peter. see Kamper, Peter.
Kamtschatka, Russia. Chancery. 90063
Kanachchatageng. 55307
Kanachtageng. (34626), 70905, 1st note
  after 94551
Kanawha County, [W.] Va. Citizens.
  petitioners 36995
Kanawha County, [W.] Va. Manufacturers of
  Salt. petitioners see Manfuacturers
  of Salt, Kanawha Co., [W.] Va.
  petitioners
Kane, Elisha Kent, 1820-1857. 25373,
  (36998)-37003, (77905)-(77907), 77912,
  85072, 85145-85146
Kane, John Kent. see Kane, John Kintzing,
  1785-1858.
Kane, John Kintzing, 1785-1858. (1056),
  37006, 69932
Kane, Margaret (Fox) 25373
Kane, Paul. 19428, 37007-37009
Kane, Thomas L. 37010-37011
Kane, William. 37012
Kane County gazetteer. 37013
Kane, der Nordpolfahrer. 36999
Kane Monument Association. 37005
Kanki, Vicente Pazos. see Pazos-Kanki,
  Vicente.
Kannenburch, Hendrick van. supposed author
  66102
Kanouse, Peter. 37014
Kansas. pseud. Shawnee treaty. 79982
Kansas (Territory) 58477
Kansas (Territory) Comptroller. 37089
Kansas (Territory) Constitution. 39654,
  37038, 37070
Kansas (Territory) Delegate Convention,
  Big-Springs, 1855. 37077
Kansas (Territory) Governor, 1854-1855
  (Reeder) 68627-(68629) see also
  Reeder, Andrew Horatio, 1807-1864.
Kansas (Territory) Governor, 1856-1857
  (Geary) 37042 see also Geary, John
  White, 1819-1873.
Kansas (Territory) Governor, 1857 (Walker)
  37043 see also Walker, Robert John,
  1801-1869.
Kansas (Territory) Governor, 1858-1860
  (Medary) 37035, 56877, 57063 see also
  Medary, Samuel, 1801-1864.
Kansas (Territory) Laws, statutes, etc.
  (37030), 37063-(37065)
Kansas (Territory) Legislature. petitioners
  (68629)
Kansas (Territory) Legislature. Council.
  (37046)-37047
Kansas (Territory) Legislature. House of
  Representatives. (37045)
Kansas (Territory) Superintendent of Common
  Schools. 37031
Kansas (Territory) Treasurer. 37089
Kansas. 37078
Kansas. Adjutant General. 37082
Kansas. Asylum for the Deaf and Dumb,
  Olathe. 37052
Kansas. Auditor. 37019

Kansas. Auditor. defendant 70257 see also
  Hillyer, George S. defendant
Kansas. Census, 1865. (37021)
Kansas. Commissioner of Claims. (37081)
Kansas. Constitution. 1269, 16113, 33137,
  37020, 37023-37024, 37038, 37070,
  (66397), 83736
Kansas. Geological Survey. 37032-37033,
  (48685)
Kansas. Governor, 1861-1863 (Robinson)
  37034-37035 see also Robinson, Charles,
  1818-1894.
Kansas. Governor, 1861-1863 (Robinson)
  defendant 72057 see also Robinson,
  Charles, 1818-1894. defendant
Kansas. Laws, statutes, etc. 37027, 37066-
  (37068), 70820-70821, 82438
Kansas. Legislature. House of Representa-
  tives. (37048), 37090
Kansas. Legislature. House of Representa-
  tives. Select Committee on Cherokee
  Neutral Lands. 37084
Kansas. Législature. Senate. 37090-(37091)
Kansas. Secretary of State. 37086
Kansas. Secretary of State. defendant 72057
  see also Robinson, John W. defendant
Kansas. Special Committee on "Claim Bonds."
  37088
Kansas. State Agricultural College, Manhattan.
  (37036)
Kansas. State Board of Agriculture. (37017),
  85514
Kansas. State Geologist. 37032-37033,
  (47371), (48685) see also Mudge, B. F.
  Swallow, G. C.
Kansas. State Penitentiary. Directors.
  37059
Kansas. Superintendent of Public Instruction.
  37028
Kansas. Supreme Court. 37593
Kansas. University. 37029
Kansas. University. Board of Regents.
  37029
Kansas. 27527
Kansas: a description of the country. 58852
Kansas Academy of Science. 85514
Kansas affairs in the Senate. 14360
Kansas affairs. Mr. Howard, from the Select
  Committee. 33269
Kansas affairs. Speech of Hon. Charles
  Sumber. 93661
Kansas aid societies. 37049
Kansas and Nebraska. 10261
Kansas and Nebraska hand-book for 1857-8.
  58722
Kansas and Nebraska—the deed and its results.
  58736
Kansas and Nebraska: the history, geographical
  and physical characteristics. (29624)
Kansas and Nebraska—the Nebraska question.
  37050
Kansas and the constitution. (24456)
Kansas and the country beyond. 16696
Kansas and the Emigrant Aid Company. 84037
Kansas and the Osage swindle. 33404
Kansas and the Supreme Court. 29641
Kansas annual register for the year 1864.
  37051, note after 90516
Kansas Asylum for the Deaf and Dumb,
  Olathe. Annual report for 1865. 37052
Kansas Baptist Convention. see Baptists.
  Kansas. Convention.
Kansas bill. Speech of Hon. J. P. Benjamin.
  (4705)
Kansas City, Mo. College of Physicians and
  Surgeons. 37093

Kaufman, David Spangler, 1813-1851. 37117
Kaufmann, ---------. 24013, 51076
Kaufmann, Gerard. see Mercator, Gerhardus, 1512-1594.
Kaufmann, Peter. 37118
Kautz, August V. (37119)-37120
Kawanio Che Keeteru. 37121, 78535
Kavanagh, a tale. (41932)
Kay, Alexander M. see McKay, Alexander.
Kay, James E. de. see De Kay, James E.
Kay, Joseph. 88909
Kay, Josiah S. 60300
Kaye, John William. 37123, 48168
Kayser, J. C. 37124
Ke-Yu, Seu. see Seu Ke-Yu.
Keach, Benjamin. (37125), 81435, note after 101268
Keach, Horace A. (37126)
Keach, Israel. 37127
Kean, Charles. ed. 80341
Kean, P. reporter 15370
Kean, Peter. 37128
Kearney, John W. petitioner 98516
Kearney, Philip, 1814-1862. 37129, 98516
Kearney, R. 68795
Kearny, -----------. RA 60662
Kearny, J. 12508
Kearsley, G. 37133
Kearsley, John. (37134)
Keath, Sir William. see Keith, Sir William, Bart., 1680-1749.
Keating, --------. (60516)
Keating, Edward. 87208
Keating, Maurice, d. 1784. defendant 37135
Keating, William Hypolitus, 1799-1840. (37136)-(37137)
Keatinge, G. 37138, 45200
Keatinge, George. reporter 100765
Keatinge, Maurice. tr. (19984)-19985
Keber, M. 37139
Kecht, J. Sm. 37140
Keckley, Elizabeth. 36141
Kedar, Obed. 37142-37143
Kedge-anchor. 7316
Keech, B. 37212
Keefer, Justus. 37144
Keefer, Thomas Coltrin, 1821-1914. 31939, (37145)-37146, (50241), 50275
Keehan, Hattia M. 37147
Keel and saddle. 60179
Keeler, John. 37148
Keeler, Ralph. 37149
Keeler, William J. cartographer 37150
Keeler's map of the U. S. territory. 37150
Keeley, P. C. 37152
Keeling, R. J. 37151
Keeling, W. 66686
Keemle, Charles. 75346
Keen, Gregory Bernard, 1844- ed. 98637
Keen, Moses W. defendant 37153
Keene, Sir Benjamin, 1697-1757. 72044
Keene, Edmund, successively Bishop of Chester, and Ely, 1714-1781. 37154
Keene, Richard Raynal, 1779-1839. 37155-37158
Keene, N. H. County Law Reform and Working Men's Convention, 1833-1834. see County Law Reform and Working Men's Convention, Keene, N. H., 1833-1834.
Keene, N. H. School Committee. 37160
Keene, N. H. Superior Court of Judicature. see Cheshire County, N. H. Superior Court of Judicature.
Keene directory and register. 37159
Keep, John. 37161-37162, 57167
Keep cool, a novel. 86785

Keep cool, go ahead, and a few other poems. (41038)
Keep government within its limits. 82639
Keep it constantly before the public. 50742
Keep-sake. 89492
Keeps of Kanphy? 27063
Keepsake, or token of remembrance for 1848. 84139, 84146
Keer, ----------. cartographer 95757
Keere, Pierre du. see Keere, Pieter van der.
Keere, Pieter van der. engr. 77951
Kees Jansz. see Jansz, Kees. psued.
Keese, John. 32873, 37163, 84093
Keese. firm see Cooley & Keese. firm
Keetsea; or, the enchanted rock. 75253-75254
Keeuka, and other poems. 13831, 37931
Kee-way-nay. Potawatomi Indian Chief 96702
Keferstein, Horst. 37164
Keferstein, Wilhelm. 37165
Kegan Paul, Trench, & Co. firm publishers 83876
Kehoe, Lawrence. ed. 33590
Kehukee Association. see Baptists. North Carolina. United Baptist Association.
Kehukee Baptist Association. see Baptists. North Carolina. United Baptist Association.
Kehuky Association. see Baptists. North Carolina. United Baptist Association.
Keijzer, M. tr. 3739, 8593, 31778
Keil, Juan Jorge. ed. (9890)
Keiler vouchers. 37167
Keiley, A. M. 34421, 37168-37169
Keily's brief description and statistical sketch. 37170
Keim, Beverley R. 89109
Keim, De Benneville Randolph. 37171-37172
Keim, William H. 37173
Keimer, Samuel. (6107), (37174)-37176, 60754, 73234, 82869, 96321, 98000
Kein Roman. 101129
Keith, B. (1117)
Keith, Elizabeth. 8956-8957
Keith, George, a Quodlibitarian. pseud. Dialogue. see Young, Samuel, fl. 1690-1700.
Keith, George, 1638?-1716. 828, (1771), 12914, 17584, 19367, 22351, (23894), 24278, 25357, 32025, 37177-(37191), 37193-37228, (44077), 46407, (46466), (46746), 53883, 57908, 59657, 59663, 59665, 59718, 62420, 66193, 66738, 79256, 86057, 1st-2d notes after 99931, 2d note after 96956, 97113, note after 100595, 103657-103658, 103660, 103702-103703, 104070, note after 104098, 104256
Keith, George, 1638?-1716. supposed author 58398
Keith, George B. 37229
Keith, Sir George Mouat. 37230, 62506
Keith, Isaac Stockton. 37231-(37232)
Keith, Israel. 37233
Keith, James. 37234-(37235)
Keith, O. B. 37236
Keith, Thomas. 84129
Keith, Wendell. ed. 31761
Keith, Sir William, Bart., 1680-1749. 952, (37238)-37244, (58936), 59929-59930, 60208, 60626, 60656, (60733), (60748), 66015, 66745, 86783, 94038, 97575 see also Pennsylvania (Colony) Governor, 1717-1726 (Keith)
Keith and Co. firm see Belding, Keith and Co. firm
Keitt, Lawrence. note before 99008

Keitt, Lawrence Massillon, 1824- (16860),
37245, note after 87402, 87436, 87438
see also South Carolina. Commission
to Negociate with the Government of
the United States, 1860-1861.
Kekitchemanitomenahn gahbemakjeinnunk
Jesus Christ. 12833
Kell, Edmund. (37247)
Kelland, --------. 37248
Keller, F.-A.-E. 37249
Keller, Francisco. ed. (52376), 91981
Keller, George. 37250
Keller, M. 37251
Kellet, Alexander. 37252-(37253), (47869)
Kellett, Henry. 1918, (43072), 71033
Kellett, T. P. 37254
Kelley, Daniel G. (37255)'
Kelley, F. 37256
Kelley, Frederick M. 37257-(37258)
Kelley, Hall J. 26871, 29815, 37259-37263,
57551
Kelley, Hall J. petitioner 37263
Kelley, J. Filmore. 37264-37266
Kelley, William Darrah, 1814-1890. 15909,
37267-37274, 51456, 55840, 61445,
84728
Kelley, William H. 83038
Kello, John. 37276
Kellogg, --------. 42303
Kellogg, Allyn S. 37277
Kellogg, Brainerd. 37278
Kellogg, Charles D. (37280)
Kellogg, D. O. 37282-37283
Kellogg, David. 37281
Kellogg, E. B. 36822, 1st note after 90670
see also Jubilee College, Illinois.
Agent.
Kellogg, Edward, 1790-1858. 14770, 26658,
27933, 37284-37287
Kellogg, Elijah. 37288
Kellogg, Ensing H. 37289-(37290)
Kellogg, Ezra B. 37291
Kellogg, Francis William, 1810-1879. 37292
Kellogg, Giles B. 37293
Kellogg, Lewis. 37294
Kellogg, Martin. 37295, 2d note after 90670
Kellogg, Miner K. 37296-37297
Kellogg, Orlando. (37298)-37299
Kellogg, Robert H. (37300)
Kellogg, T. D. 37301
Kellogg, William. 37302
Kellogg, Johnson & Co. firm publishers
37301
Kellogg's United States mercantile register.
37301
Kellom, John H. 9707
Kells, Charles E. supposed author 9969,
3d note after 96480
Kelly, Alfred. 37303
Kelly, Christopher. (37304)
Kelly, Edmond. 37305
Kelly, Ebenezer Beriah. (37306)
Kelly, Fitzroy. 30335
Kelly, George. (37307)
Kelly, George F. 37308
Kelly, Hugh. 77818
Kelly, J. (37311)
Kelly, J. T. 82954
Kelly, J. Wells. 37309
Kelly, James. 37310
Kelly, John, 1763-1848. 37312, 105036
Kelly, John, 1821-1886. 37313
Kelly, John, fl. 1853. 37314
Kelly, Jonathan Falconbridge, 1818-1854.
23722, 37315
Kelly, Patrick. 37316
Kelly, Robert. (37317)-(37318)

Kelly, Samuel. plaintiff 96888
Kelly, Sarah. alias see Willis, Sarah.
defendant
Kelly, T. W. 37319
Kelly, Thomas. illus. 82809
Kelly, William. alias see Webb, William,
d. 1754. defendant
Kelly, William. (37320)-37321
Kelly, William, fl. 1855. 37322
Kelly, William D. 22713, note before 90885
Kelroy, a novel. 37323
Kelsall, Charles. (37324), 3d note after
78761, note after 101786
Kelsey, D. W. (44379)
Kelsey, John. 37325
Kelsey, William H. 37326
Kelso, Isaac. 37327
Kelten in Amerika. (25905)
Kelty, Mary Ann. 37328
Kemble, Frances Anne, 1809-1893. 9632,
9657, 28430, (36357), 37329-37332,
note after 95596, 2d note after 103115
Kemble, Frances Anne, 1803-1893. defendant
9657
Kemble, Peter. defendant 39877
Kemble, Peter. plaintiff 28147
Kemeys, John Gardner. 37333
Kemp, Alexander Ferrie. (37334)
Kemp, Francis Adrian van der. see Van
der Kemp, Francis Adrian, 1752-1829
Kemp, James, Bp. 13186, 37337-37338,
65922
Kemp, Robert H., 1820-1897. (37336)
Kemper College, Mo. 37340, 37342
Kemper College, Mo. Medical Department.
see Missouri Medical College, St.
Louis.
Kempis, Thomas a. 37343, 1st note after
95453
Kempshall, Everard. 37344
Kenckes, Thomas A. 70710, 90828
Kendal, Samuel. 37345-37347
Kendall, Amos. (12457), 12477, 37348-37355,
58958, 90114-90115 see also U. S..
Commissioners to the Cherokee Indians.
Kendall, Amos. claimant 37350, 37354
Kendall, Amos. petitioner 50963
Kendall, B. F. 37356, note after 95797,
10th note after 95843
Kendall, E. D. (37359)
Kendall, Edward A. 37357-37358
Kendall, George Wilkins. 37360-37362, 44698,
67792
Kendall, James. 37364-37366
Kendall, John. 37367, 92325-92326
Kendall, John B. 37369
Kendall, John E. claimant 37350, 37354
Kendall, Jonas. 37368
Kendall, R. C. 37370
Kendall's expositor. (37363)
Kendell, Amos. 37354
Kendrick, Ariel. 37371
Kendrick, Asahel C. 37372-37373
Kendrick, Burton. 37374
Kendrick, Clark. (37375)
Keninon, John. 37376
Kenly, John R. 37377
Kennard, James. 37378
Kennard, Thomas W. 37379
Kennaway, John H. (37380)
Kennebec. 13703
Kennebec County, Me. Teachers' Institute.
37382
Kennebec Conference of Churches. see
Congregational Churches in Maine.
Kennebec Conference.

Kennebec gazette. 103831
Kennebec Locks & Canals Company.
Engineer. 37385 see also Boardman,
William.
Kennebec Purchase Proprietors. see
Plymouth Company, 1749-1816.
Kennebeck River. Survey of Kennebec River.
37387
Kennebeck bridge. 37381
Kennebeck intelligencer. 93899
Kennedy, Rev. Dr. ------, fl. 1842. 640
Kennedy, Andrew, 1810-1847. (37389)
Kennedy, Andrew James. 37390
Kennedy, Anthony. 37391
Kennedy, Archibald. (37392)-37394, 79261
Kennedy, Archibald. defendant 83979
Kennedy, C. M. ed. 37398
Kennedy, Duncan. 640, 37395-37396, 73970,
73977
Kennedy, James, Captain. (37397)
Kennedy, James, d. 1859. 37398-37400
Kennedy, John, 1813-1900. 37401, (81990)
Kennedy, John, fl. 1836. 97989
Kennedy, John, fl. 1861. 37402
Kennedy, John H. 37403
Kennedy, John Pendleton, 1795-1870. (6412),
14771, 19256, 37404, 37406-(37423),
(45211A), 47878, 59390, (68468), 84812,
87275, note after 92624, 5th note after
93998, 99927 see also Peabody
Institute, Baltimore. President.
Kennedy, John Pendleton, 1795-1870.
incorrectly supposed author 37405,
93092
Kennedy, Joseph Camp Griffith, 1813-1887.
11670, 11673-11674, 34725-34733 see
also U. S. Census Office. Superinten-
dent.
Kennedy, Joseph Pulaski. 37435
Kennedy, Joseph Pulaski. defendant (37434)
Kennedy, Lionel H. reporter 37436
Kennedy, Patrick. (34053)-(34055), (34358),
(37437)
Kennedy, Philip Pendleton, 1808?-1864.
37405, 93092
Kennedy, Robert. (37438)
Kennedy, Robert Lenox. 86155
Kennedy, Thomas. 45362, 45390
Kennedy, Thomas, 1776-1832. 37439
Kennedy, William, 1799-1871. 37440-37442,
95118
Kennedy, William, 1813-1890. 37443
Kennedy, William M. 37445
Kennedy, William M. supposed author
65729
Kennedy, William S. (37446)
Kennerly, C. B. R. 09946
Kennet, Lord --------. reporter. 102437
Kennett, White, Bishop of Peterborough, 1660-
1728. 30599, 37447-(37449), 85939
Kenney, Joel. 37450
Kenney, Lucy. 37451, 58401, 98425
Kennicott, Benjamin. (66455)
Kennicott, E. D. 37452
Kennicott, John A. 34198
Kennignham, William. see Cuningham,
William, b. 1531.
Kennion, John W. 37453
Kenniston, Laban. defendant (27930), 37454-
37455
Kenniston, Levi. defendant (27930), 37454-
37455
Kenniston, Seban. defendant (27930)
Kennon, Beverly. defendant at court martial
37456
Kenny, Daniel J. 37457

Kenny, Lucy. 37451, 74141
Kenny, W. defendant at court martial (37458)
Kenosha, Wisc. Mayor, 1854. 37459
Kenosha, Wisc. Ordinances, etc. 37460
Kenrick, Francis Patrick, Bp. 14800, (72960)
see also Philadelphia (Diocese) Bishop
(Kenrick)
Kenrick, John. 37461
Kenrick, Peter Ricardo, Abp. 72971 see also
St. Louis (Archdiocese) Archbishop
(Kenrick)
Kenrick, William, 1725?-1779. 103847
Kenrick, William, 1789-1872. 37462-37463
Kenrick, William, fl. 1846. (37464)
Kenrick Nursery. firm 37463
Kensington, N. H. (20747)
Kensington, Pa. see also Philadelphia.
Kensingtno, Pa. Charter. 59792
Kensington, Pa. Evangelical Home Missionary
Society. see Evangelical Home
Missionary Society of Kensington, Pa.
Kensington, Pa. Infant School Society. see
Infant School Society of the Northern
Liberties and Kensington, Pa.
Kensington, Pa. Ordinances, etc. 59792,
61588
Kensington District of the Northern Liberties.
see Kensington, Pa.
Kensington and Penn Township Rail-Road
Company. Managers. (61752)
Kent, Aratus. 11938, 37466
Kent, Benjamin, fl. 1734. 37467
Kent, Benjamin, fl. 1828. 37468
Kent, Daniel. defendant at court martial
96952, 102153
Kent, Edward, 1802-1877. 43996 see also
Maine. Governor, 1838-1839 (Kent)
Kent, Edward N. (37469)
Kent, George. (37470)
Kent, George A. 84974
Kent, Henry Oakes, 1834— 37471, (52943)
see also New Hampshire. Commissioner
on Eastern Boundary of State, from
Fryeburg to Canada.
Kent, J. tr. 12230
Kent, J., fl. 1785. 10230
Kent, James, 1763-1847. 5657, 36231, (37472)-
37475, 37479, 37926, 54063, 45063,
51133, 53082, 53745, 54115, 54174,
54469, 61206, 69689, 96819, 102277
see also New York (State) Chancellor.
Kent, John. 71114 see also Church.
Editor.
Kent, Joseph, 1779-1837. 37477-37479
Kent, William. 37482, (54666), 54707
Kent County, Del. (37483)
Kent County, R. I. Farmers. petitioners
37484
Kent Academy, Providence, R. I. 37482
Kent's Hill, Me. Wesleyan Seminary and
Female College. see Maine Wesleyan
Seminary and Female College, Kent's
Hill, Me.
Kentuckian. pseud. Biographical sketch. see
Langsworthy, Asahel. supposed author
Kentuckian. pseud. Martial law. see
Nicholas, S. S.
Kentuckian. pseud. Memory of Pocahontas.
63503
Kentuckian. pseud. Plain tale. 63237,
104030
Kentuckian. pseud. Power and policy of
exclusion. 64782
Kentuckian. pseud. Zula. 106395
Kentuckian in New York. (11172), 100443,
5th note after 100577

Kentuckian speech. 32653

Kentuckier's John Tanner Denkwurdigkeiten. 35685, 94328

Kentucky. pseud. 103867

Kentucky. 37577, 69859

Kentucky. Adjutant General. (37551)-37553, 37556

Kentucky. Asylum for Insane, Lexington. Directors. 37490

Kentucky. Asylum for Insane, Lexington. Managers. 37489, (37491)

Kentucky. Asylum for Insane, Lexington. Physician. 37490

Kentucky. Auditor of Public Accounts. 37511, 78965 see also Selby, Benjamin.

Kentucky. Bank. see Bank of Kentucky.

Kentucky. Board of Education. 37504

Kentucky. Board of Internal Improvement. 37572

Kentucky. Commissioners for the Erection of the State Capitol. 37573

Kentucky. Commissioners of the Sinking Fund. 37510

Kentucky. Commissioners on the Boundary Line with Tennessee. 37547

Kentucky. Commissioners on the Code of Practice in Civil and Criminal Cases. (37531) see also Harlan, James. Johnson, M. C. Stevenson, John White, 1812-1886.

Kentucky. Commissioners to Prepare and Report a System of Common Schools. 37507

Kentucky. Commissioners to the Washington Peace Conference, 1861. 37578

Kentucky. Committee on the Sinking Fund. see Kentucky. Commissioners of the Sinking Fund.

Kentucky. Constitution. 1269, 1271, 2071, 5316, 6360, 9672, 16097, 16099-16103, 16107, 16113, 16133, 17099, 25790, 33137, 37499, 37501, 37537, 37540, (47188), 59771, (66397), 104198

Kentucky. Constitutional Convention, 1849. 37500

Kentucky. Court of Appeals. (37536), 37539, 37560, 37561, 37581, 64110, 85376

Kentucky. Courts. 79125

Kentucky. Eastern Lunatic Asylum. see Kentucky. Asylum for Insane, Lexington.

Kentucky. General Assembly. 23382, 37486, 37560, (37564), 37572, 37577, (37579), 56422, 69859, 87538

Kentucky. General Assembly. Committee on Religoin. 37574

Kentucky. General Assembly. Committee on the Biographical Sketch of Hon. John L. Hlem. 31261

Kentucky. General Assembly. Committee on the Coal-Trade and Iron Interests of Kentucky. 37575

Kentucky. General Assembly. Committee on the Official Conduct of the Judges of the Court of Appeals. (37576)

Kentucky. General Assembly. Committee on the Proposed Amendment to the United States Constitution. Minority. 37557

Kentucky. General Assembly. Joint Committee on Banks. 37493, 37495

Kentucky. General Assembly. Joint Committee to Visit the Deaf and Dumb Asylum at Danville. (37491)

Kentucky. General Assembly. Select Committee to Whom was Referred the Response of the Treasurer. 37511

Kentucky. General Assembly. House of Representatives. 7117, 37516, (37541), 37548, 103865

Kentucky. General Assembly. House of Representatives. Committee on Education. 37507

Kentucky. General Assembly. Senate. 7117, 37517, (37541), 85379, 93805

Kentucky. Geological Survey. 37513, 46813, 84936

Kentucky. Governor, 1812-1816 (Shelby) 33150 see also Shelby, Isaac, 1750-1826.

Kentucky. Governor, 1816-1820 (Slaughter) 37547 see also Slaughter, Gabriel, 1767-1830.

Kentucky. Governor, 1824-1828 (Desha) 37548 see also Desha, Joseph, 1768-1842.

Kentucky. Governor, 1828-1832 (Metcalfe) 37507 see also Metcalfe, Thomas, 1780-1855.

Kentucky. Governor, 1832-1834 (Breathitt) 87423 see also Breathitt, John, 1786-1834.

Kentucky. Governor, 1839-1840 (Wickliffe) 37549 see also Wickliffe, Charles Anderson, 1788-1869.

Kentucky. Governor, 1840-1844 (Letcher) 40239 see also Letcher, Robert Perkins, 1788-1861.

Kentucky. Governor, 1851-1855 (Powell) 56422 see also Powell, Lazarus Whitehead, 1812-1867.

Kentucky. Governor, 1855-1859 (Morehead) 33150 see also Morehead, Charles Slaughter, 1802-1868.

Kentucky. Governor, 1859-1862 (Magoffin) 23382, 37577, 69859 see also Magoffin, Beriah, 1815-1885.

Kentucky. Institution for the Deaf and Dumb. see Kentucky. School for the Deaf, Danville.

Kentucky. Institution for the Education of Feeble-Minded Children, Frankfort. Commissioners. 37506

Kentucky. Insurance Bureau. 37515

Kentucky. Keeper of the Penitentiary. see Kentucky. Penitentiary. Keeper.

Kentucky. Laws, statutes, etc. 23765, 34354, 34356-34357, 37492, 37505, 37518, 37521 (37524), (37527)-(37540), 37550, (37564), (37568), 39414, 40881, 42316-(42320), 42323, 42325, 42328, 42336, 52051, 64338, 70820-70821, 82438, 90436, 94080, 2d note after 95313, 96328, 96460, 97892, 100353, 100355, 100356, 100393

Kentucky. Lunatic Asylum. see Kentucky. Asylum for Insane, Lexington.

Kentucky. Military Institute. (37555)

Kentucky. Penitentiary. Keeper. 37570

Kentucky. Quartermaster General. 37554

Kentucky. School for the Deaf, Danville. (37491)

Kentucky. School for the Deaf, Danville. Trustees. (37491)

Kentucky. Second Auditor. 37511

Kentucky. Secretary of State. 37571

Kentucky. State Geologist. 37513 see also Owen, David Dale.

Kentucky. Superintendent of Public Instruction. 37504, 77811

Kentucky. Treasurer. 37511
Kentucky. Union Men. petitioners see
    Union Men of Kentucky. petitioners
Kentucky. University, Harrodsburg. 37508
Kentucky (Confederate Provisional Govern-
    ment) 37503
Kentucky (Confederate Provisional Govern-
    ment) Constitution. 37503
Kentucky (Confederate Provisional Govern-
    ment) Governor. 37503
Kentucky; a tale. 29688
Kentucky Academy. see Transylvania
    University, Lexington, Ky.
Kentucky Agricultural Society. see Kentucky
    State Agricultural Society.
Kentucky and Foreign Bible Society. 37558
Kentucky and Tennessee. (47222)
Kentucky and Virginia Resolutions, 1798.
    9436, 9936, 15005, 19836, 22233,
    (22237), 23453, (23627), (43720),
    (53773), 87538, 89203, 100073, 100077,
    100079-100081, 100105, 2d note after
    100462-100463, note after 100545A,
    note after 106002
Kentucky and Virginia resolutions of 1798 and
    1799. 89203
Kentucky Anti-slavery Society. 37566
Kentucky Association for the Promotion of
    Internal Improvements. see Associa-
    tion for the Promotion of Internal
    Improvements in the State of Kentucky.
Kentucky Branch of the United States Sanitary
    Commission. see United States
    Sanitary Commission. Kentucky Branch.
Kentucky Branch of the U. S. Sanitary Com-
    mission. Report. (76654)
Kentucky Catholic. pseud. Catholic question
    in politics. 37498, 65065
Kentucky Coal Mining Company. (37518)
Kentucky Colonization Society. 37519
Kentucky Colonization Society. Fifth annual
    report. 37519
Kentucky Democrat. pseud. Letters on the
    presidency. see Nicholas, Samuel
    Smith.
Kentucky farmer's almanack. (37520)
Kentucky farmer's almanac for 1810 [-1818,
    1822]. 93230
Kentucky Farmers' Bank. see Farmers'
    Bank of Kentucky.
Kentucky freemason. . . . a masonic monthly
    journal. 37545
Kentucky freemason; an organ of ancient
    craft masonry. 37544
Kentucky gazette. 96469
Kentucky Historical Society. see Kentucky
    State Historical Society.
Kentucky Historical Society register. 105053
Kentucky Improvement Company. 37522
Kentucky Institution for Feeble-Minded
    Children. Report of Commissioners
    for 1864-5. 37506
Kentucky justice. 94080
Kentucky lawyer. pseud. Review of the
    decision. (78262)
Kentucky Mechanics' Institute, Louisville.
    42336
Kentucky Mechanics' Institute, Louisville.
    Exhibition, 2d, 1854. (37523)
Kentucky Medical Society. see Kentucky
    State Medical Society.
Kentucky Mining and Manufacturing Company.
    (37524)
Kentucky protest against slavery. 70827
Kentucky reporter. 93806
Kentucky republican. 84366

Kentucky revival. (43605), (52324), 89893
Kentucky State Agricultural Society. (37488)
Kentucky State Convention of Colored Men,
    Lexington, 1867. see State Convention
    of Colored Men, Lexington, Ky., 1867.
Kentucky State Historical Society. 37521,
    84940, 105053
Kentucky State Historical Society. petitioners
    37512
Kentucky State Medical Society. 37525, 89453
Kentucky state register. 37526, 77498
Kentucky Synod. see Presbyterian Church
    in the U. S. A. Synod of Kentucky.
Kentucky Theological Seminary of the
    Protestant Episcopal Church. see
    Theological Seminary of the Protestant
    Episcopal Church in Kentucky.
Kentucky tragedy. 31200
Kentucky tragedy. A full and particular
    account. 4162
Kentucky tragedy. A sequel to Charlemont.
    (81192)
Kentucky tragedy. A tale of passion. 81191
Kentucky tragedy, letters of Ann Cook. 4161
Kentucky vs. James Morrison. 37561
Kentucky whig. 3198
Kenyon, Archibald. 37582
Kenyon, H. B. 2636, 37583
Kenyon, Lloyd, Lord, 1773-1802. 96910-96918
Kenyon College, Gambier, O. 37584-37585,
    (37587), 57014
Kenyon College, Gambier, O. Board of
    Trustees. 20708, 37589-37590
Kenyon College, Gambier, O. Grammar
    School. 37584
Kenyon College, Gambier, O. Philomathesian
    Sciety. 37586
Kenyon College, Gambier, O. Theological
    Seminary. 37586-(37587)
Kenyon College, in 1828. 12194
Keogh, James. (37592)
Keokuk, Chief of the Sauk and Fox Indians
    defendant 37493
Keokuk, Iowa. Library Association. see
    Keokuk Library Association, Keokuk, Iowa.
Keokuk, Iowa. Mayor, 1856 (Curtis) 13622
    see also Curtis, ------, fl. 1856.
Keokuk, Iowa. Transportation Convention,
    1869. 71619
Keokuk, Iowa. Transportation Convention,
    1869. petitioners 71619
Keokuk general directory. 37594
Keokuk Library Association, Keokuk, Iowa.
    37595
Kepler, Johann. 73294
Keppel, Frederick, Bishop of Exeter, 1729-
    1777. (37596)
Keppel, Thomas. 37597
Keppel, William Coutts. see Bury, William
    Coutts Keppel, Viscount.
Ker, Henry. 37599
Ker, John. 37600-37602
Ker, Leander. 37603
Keralio, -------- Matugene de. see Matugene
    de Keralio, ---------.
Keratry, Emile de, Comte. 9176, 16184,
    (37604)-(37609)
Keraudren, P. F. 37610
Kercheval, Samuel. 20490, 37611, 44258,
    note after 105690
Kerckelycke historie . . . tot 1666. 33017
Kerckelycke historie van de gheheele
    weereldt. 31115
Keredern, Philippe Regis Denis de. see
    Trobriand, Philippe Regis Denis de
    Keredern, Comte, de, 1816-1897.
Kerfoot, John Barret, Bp., 1816-1881. 37612-
    (37613)

Kerfoot, Samuel H. 37614
Kerguelen-Tremarec, Y. J. de. 37615-
37618
Kerhallet, Charles Philippe de. 37619-37622
Kerk, school en wetenschap in de Vereenigde
Staten. 8959
Kerkelijke geschiedenis. 2794
Kerl, Simon. 37623
Kerlerec de Kervasegan, Louis Billouard de,
Marquis. 72330 see also Louisiana
(Province) Governeur, 1752-1763
(Kerlerec de Kervasegan)
Kerlerec de Kervasegan, Louis Billouard de,
Marquis. defendant 47509, 72330
see also Louisiana (Province)
Governeur, 1752-1763 (Kerlerec de
Kervasegan) defendant
Kern, ----------. petitioner 26592
Kern, Richard H. 35764, (37624), 105714
Kern alter und neuer . . . geistreicher Lieder.
60183
Kerner, J. S. tr. 48692
Kerner, Justinus. 4010
Kerney, M. 45137
Kerney, Martin Joseph, 1819-1861. (37625)
Kerney, Michael. 99372-99373
Kernwood. 25877
Kerr, --------. cartographer 38880, 95757,
note after 100632
Kerr, --------. plaintiff 45375
Kerr, Henry T. 37626
Kerr, Hugh. 37627
Kerr, Jacob. 37628
Kerr, Jacob. complaint to Presbytery 79376
Kerr, John Leeds. 45370
Kerr, Lewis. (37629)
Kerr, Lewis. defendant 105484
Kerr, Michael Crawford, 1827-1876. (37630)
Kerr, Orpheus C. pseud. see Newell,
Robert Hasell.
Kerr, Robert. 9730, (11608), 16275, 16984,
19985, 31558, 37631, 55448, 89452,
91609, note after 99383C
Kerr, Thomas. 37632
Kerr, W. C. 55621 see also North
Carolina, Geologist.
Kerr, William Henry. see Lothian, William
Henry Kerr, 4th Marquis of, d. 1755.
Kerr, William Schomberg Robert. see
Lothian, William Schomberg Robert
Kerr, Marquis.
Kerr. firm publishers 53348
Kerr's general advertiser and city directory.
53348
Kersey, Jesse. 37635-37636
Kersfeest in Californie. 37637
Kershaw, Philip G. 37638
Kershaw District, S. C. Citizens. petitioners
37639, 88076, note after 94393
Kershaw Distirct, S. C. State Rights, Union
and Jackson Party. see State Rights,
Union and Jackson Party of Kershaw
District, S. C.
Kershaw District, S. C. Tariff Meeting,
Camden, 1826. 88076, note after 94393
Kershaw District, S. C. Tariff Meeting,
Camden, 1826. Committee to Draft
a Memorial and Resolutions to Congress.
88076, note after 94393
Kershaw Distirct, S. C. Tariff Meeting,
Camden, 1826. Committee to Draft
a Memorial and Resolutions to Congress.
Chairman. 88076, note after 94393
see also Nixon, H. G.
Kerst, S. Gottfried. 37640-37641
Kerstboek voor Kinderen. 37637

Kervasegan, Louis Billouard de Kerlerec de.
see Kerlerec de Kervasegan, Louis
Billouard de, Marquis.
Kerversau, -------. (37642)
Kesukod uttiyen Jehovah kessehtunkup. (46278)
Kesukod uttiyeu Lord Kessehtunkup. 18478
Ketcham, Henry. 85160
Ketchum, Edgar. (33272)
Ketchum, Edward B. petitioner 37643
Ketchum, Hiram. 37644-37646, 104500
Ketchum, Jesse. 98069
Ketchum, Silas. (37647)
Ketchum, William. 37648
Ketel, J. 18273
Keteltas, Abraham. 37649-37650
Keteltas, William. 14897, 37651
Keter der Goddelyke waarheden. 29502
Kettelas, William. 37652
Kettell, G. F. 37653
Kettell, Samuel. (14668), (18916), 20005,
20651, 37654-37655, 70574
Kettell, Samuel. supposed author 95871,
note after 105970
Kettell, Thomas Prentice. (5302), 22085,
(37656)-37658, (55964), 64761
Keulen, Gerard van. 37659
Keulen, J. van. ed. 100766
Keux, ----- le. see Le Keux, -------.
Keuze uit de openbaringen. 83273
Ke-Wa-Ze-Zhig, a son of the chief of the
Chippeways. 37660
Kewen, E. J. C. 37662
Kewley, John. 37663-(37664)
Key, --------. 37669
Key, Astley Cooper. 37665
Key, B. see Key, Francis Scott, 1779-1843.
Key, Francis Scott, 1779-1843. 37666-(37668),
81832, 90497-90500
Key. 37672
Key for exercise on Mitchell's series of outline
maps. 49722
Key into the language of America. 51773,
70719, 104339-104340, 105074
Key-notes of American liberty. 37693
Key opening the way to every common under-
standing. (59709), (59729), 66918, 66928
Key to a chart of the successive geological
formations. 29806
Key to Canada. 10473
Key to honest wealth. 82348
Key to Morse's picture of the House of
Representatives. 50963
Key to our joy. 17369
Key to "practical and mental arithmetic" for
the use of teachers. note before 83906,
83909
Key to practical music. (5419)
Key to Richardson's environs of Boston.
71004
Key to Smith's new arithmetic. note before
83906, 83112
Key to Stearne's exposure of Jamaica justice.
91339
Key to the church-catechism. 37670
Key to the colonies. 7701
Key to the disunion conspiracy. 97374
Key to the English cabinet. 36919
Key to the figurative language. (82540)
Key to the history of the American war.
63878
Key to the Iliad of Homer. 84896
Key to the Iliad of Homer. For the use of
schools. 84896
Key to the Indian language of New-Enyland.
[sic] 94681-94682
Key to the Ku Klux. 63866

Key to the modern bastile! 43275
Key to the orders in council. 37671
Key to the practical and mental arithmetic. 83928
Key to the quarterly catalogues of the . . . young ladies. 54876
Key to the revelation. (82540)
Key to the science of theology. 64960
Key to the post offices. 10473
Key to the six per cent cabinet. 10069
Key to the solution of our political difficulties. 82022
Key to Uncle Tom's cabin. 92411-92412, 92485
Key to universalism. 80104
Key to unlock the door, that leads in. 26058
Keye, Otto. (4196), 9389, 29186, 37673-37675, note after 93852, 1st note after 93879, note after 100935
Keyens, Otto. see Keye, Otto.
Keyes, Benjamin F. 37676
Keyes, Edward L. (37677)-(37678)
Keyes, Elisha W. 37679
Keyes, Emerson W. 37680-37681 see also New York (State) Banking Department. Deputy Superintendent.
Keyes, Frederick J. 37682
Keyes, George L. 85596
Keyes, John G. 37683
Keyes, William. 37684
Keyes' hand-book of northern pleasure travel. 85596
Keyes's hand book. 85596
Keymersant, Michael. 37685
Keymis, Laurens. 4937A, (8784), 14349, 14957, (14958), 37686-37691, 67558, 67595-67597
Keymolen, L. 37692
Keymus, Laurentius. see Keymis, Laurens.
Keynton, John. 37694
Keyport Company. (24804)
Keys of the kingdom. 83755
Keyes [sic] of the kingdom of heaven, and power thereof. 11616, 17067-17068, 17091, note after 99832
Keyser, Charles S. 37695-37696
Keyser, Rudolph. 37697
Keystone. 45527
Keystone agricultural almanac, for 1840. 37698
Keystone Publishing and Manufacturing Company. petitioners 37698
Keystone Watch Case Company. defendant 84519
Keyzer, M. tr. see Keijzer, M. tr.
Khanikoff, Nicolas de. 68443
Ki noh shuh. 103454
Kiana: a tradition of Hawaii. 35799
Kianasa, nana nonedowaga neuwenuda. 34122, 79120
Kick for a bite. 13886, 14032, 85597
Kick for the whipper. 14395
Kickapoo Indians. Treaties, etc. 96679, 99605
Kidd, Adam. 37700
Kidd, H. A. ed. 88617
Kidd, William, 1645?-1701. 16654
Kidd, William, 1645?-1701. defendant 32182, (32197), 37701-37705
Kidder, Daniel P. 14330, 24723, 37706-37709, 42632
Kidder, Frederic. 28090, 37710-37717, 64133, 82852, 94112, 96946
Kidder, J. illus. 63894
Kidder, J. H. 85065 see also Smithsonian Institution. Curator.

Kidder family in England and America. 37714
Kiderlen, William L. J. 37718
Kidnapped and the ransomed. 62614
Kidnapped clergyman. 37719
Kid-napper trapan'd. (37720)
Kidnapping an outrage. (28380)
Kidney, John Steinfort. 37721-37722
Kidwell, Zedekiah, 1814-1872. (33797)
Kiehl, E. J. 37723
Kiernan, J. L. ed. (54812)
Kiersted, C. C. plaintiff 37724
Kierzkowski, A. 37725
Kiesewetter, F. tr. 36999
Kiesselbach, Wilhelm. (37726)
Kiew Neika's return. 86902
Kiewitch, Theodor Jan. (37727)
Kiffin, William. 59718
Kijkje in de hut van oom Tom. 92522
Kilborne, F. L. 84331-84332
Kilbourn, Byron. 37728, 49177
Kilbourn, Hallet. 37729
Kilbourn, John. 37730-37731, (57029), (66515)
Kilbourn Historical and Genealogical Society. 37732
Kilbourne, Payne Kenyon. 37733-(37736)
Kilburn, Joseph. 37737
Kilby, W. H. 103048
Kilgore, Damon Y. 37739-37740
Kilham, Alexander. 37741
Kilian, Wolf. illus. 63367
Killdare, the black scout. 37742
Killinghall, -------. 4395
Killroy, Matthew. defendant 32362, 95946, 96951, 2d-3d notes after 102623
Kilmore and Ardagh, Bishop of. see Wetenhall, Edward, successively Bishop of Cork, and Kilmore and Ardagh, 1636-1713.
Kilpatrick, Judson. (37743)
Kilpatrick and our cavalry. 37744, 50403
Kilty, John. 37745
Kilty, William, 1757-1821. 45107, 45166, 45190, 45320 see also Maryland. Chancellor.
Kilty, William, 1757-1821. supposed author 100598
Kimayer, Thomas. 37746, 52361
Kimball, Charles Otis. (37747)
Kimball, Charles P. 76092
Kimball, Daniel. (37748)-37749
Kimball, David T. 37750-37752
Kimball, Edmund. (37753), 57856
Kimball, G. F. 37754
Kimball, Heber G. 83283, 95525
Kimball, Henry. 37755
Kimball, Horace. supposed author 1165, 2696
Kimball, J. C. 64597
Kimball, J. Horace. 95460
Kimball, J. P. 13810, 25247, 39405, 94948
Kimball, Jacob. 37756
Kimball, Jerome Bonaparte. 37757
Kimball, John. 37762
Kimball, Joseph. 37763
Kimball, M. G. (37764)
Kimball, Moses. 37765
Kimball, Richard Burleigh. 34420, (37766)-37767, 75158
Kimball, Sullivan C. 37768
Kimball, T. J. 37769
Kimball (J. C.) firm publishers 44143
Kimball (John F.) & Co. firm publishers 37758-37759
Kimball & Dodge. comps. (37760)
Kimball & James. firm publishers 37761
Kimball & James' business directory. 37761

Kimball Union Academy, Meriden Village,
N. H. (37770)
Kimball's directory of Malone. 44143
Kimball's directory of Potsdam village.
64597
Kimball's Ohio, Kentucky, and Indiana state
register. 37759
Kimber, John. defendant 96892
Kimber, S. Junior 37771, 2d note after
94129
Kimijser, Arnold. (37772)
Kimyer, Arnold. see Kimijser, Arnold.
Kind relation. pseud. Friendly check. see
Wise, John.
Kindelan, Sebastian. 37773
Kinder, Thomas. petitioner 37774
Kinder meiner Laune. (48912)
Kinderhook, N. Y. Kinderhook Academy.
see Kinderhook Academy, Kinderhook,
N. Y.
Kinderhook Academy, Kinderhook, N. Y.
37775
Kinderhook Division, No. 164, Sons of
Temperance. see Sons of Temperance
of North America. New York. Kinder-
hook Division, No. 164.
Kindermann, F. C. 37776
Kindersley, Mistress. pseud. Briefe von der
Insel Teneriffa. see Kindersley,
Nathaniel E.
Kindersley, Mrs. pseud. Letters from the
island of Teneriffe. see Kindersley,
Nathaniel E.
Kindersley, Nathaniel E. 37777-37778
Kind of poem. 5348
Kind word to the officers of our army.
88047
King, Dr. ---------. 37797
King, -------. illus. 43410-(43411)
King, -------, fl. 1860. 35221
King, A. 8124, 37781
King, Alonzo. 37779
King, Andrew. (37780)
King, Austin Augustus, 1801-1870. 49641,
50734, 83238
King, Barnabas. 37782, 72375
King, C. (21117)
King, Charles, fl. 1721. 37783
King, Charles, 1789-1867. 37784-37789,
40246, 53584, 98534
King, Clarence. 29523
King, Dan. (37790)
King, Daniel Putnam. 37791-37792, 3d note
after 103271
King, David, 1806-1883. 37795
King, David, 1812-1882. (37794)
King, Dexter S. (37796)
King, Edward, 1735?-1807. 37798
King, Edward, 1794-1873. 37799
King, Edward, 1795-1837. see Kingsborough,
Edward King, Viscount, 1795-1837.
King, Edward, fl. 1828-1848. 28120, 25336,
80736, 96938
King, Elizabeth T. 37802
King, Finaly M. ed. 45534
King, H. 49591
King, Henry C. 88012
King, Henry F. 37803
King, Horace. (37804)
King, Horatio. (37805)
King, J. F. H. 30711
King, James, Rector of St. Michael Crooked-
Lane. 37806, 83978
King, James, 1750-1784. 4079, 16250-16251,
(16257), 25142, (59572)
King, James, 1816-1880. 37807

King, James G. 37809
King, Jeb. 37810
King, John. banker 37812
King, John, Bishop of London, 1559?-1621.
37811
King, John, 1813-1893. 37813
King, John Alsop, 1788-1867. 33150, 37816,
53528, 53616 see also New York
(State) Governor, 1857-1859 (King)
King, John Anthony. 37814-37815
King, John B. 37817
King, John Pendleton, 1799-1888. 37818
King, John W. 37819, 37822, 80997
King, Jonas. (37820)
King, Joseph. petitioner 103112
King, Maria M. 37823
King, Matthew. defendant 6326, 1st note after
96956, 1st note after 97284
King, Mitchell. 37824
King, Peter. 37825
King, Philip Parker, 1793-1856. (18647),
37826-37828
King, Preston, 1806-1865. 37829-37830
King, Richard. (37831)
King, Robert. 37832
King, Rufus, 1755-1827. 14837-14838, 37833-
(37835), note after 53697, note after
83791, 84720, 84827
King, Rufus, 1817-1891. 84342
King, Samuel Ward, 1786-1851. 37836, 70577
see also Rhode Island. Governor, 1839-
1843 (King)
King, Thomas. 61064, 94817
King, Mrs. Thomas, d. 1809. 61064, 94817
King, Thomas Butler, 1800-1864. 15243,
37837-(37841), 76045 see also Georgia.
Commissioner. U. S. Customs House,
San Francisco. Collector.
King, Thomas F. 37842
King, Thomas K. 37843
King, Thomas Starr. 37844-37848, 63162
King, Walter. 37850-(37852)
King, William, 1663-1712. 98182
King, William, 1768-1852. (20226), 20476,
31849, 37854-37856, 43995, 70988,
104779 see also Maine. Governor,
1820-1822 (King)
King, William, 1768-1852. defendant at court
martial 37854
King William, 1758-1852. incorrectly supposed
author (37853)
King, William Ross. (37857)
King, William Rufus de Vane, 1786-1853.
8865, 58482
King, William Sterling, 1818-1882. 36700,
37859
King, William W. 42213
King. firm publishers 72340
King (David) and Company. appellants 69087
King (E. D.) firm publishers 51872
King & Smith. firm publishers 48984
King against Picton. 18324
King caucus. A poem. 100957
King-caucus, or "secrets worth knowing."
37860
King Charles II's declaration about religion.
46790
King George's right to the crown. 26757
King Hezekiah's bitterness and relief. 18470
King Jehoshaphat's charge to the judges.
(65070)
King lay musing upon his bed. 95736
King of Angelo. (37861)
King of Denmark's ordinance. 37862
King of pirates. 2487
King of rivers. By Cora Montgomery. 50134

Kitchin, Thomas. 38021-38022
Kite, John L. 38023
Kite (Benjamin and Thomas) firm publishers
    61606, 97732
Kite (Thomas) firm see Kite (Benjamin
    and Thomas) firm publishers
Kite's Philadelphia directory for 1814.
    61606
Kitschi-Gami oder Erzahlungen von Obern-
    See. 38214
Kittera, Thomas. 61703
Kittlitz, Friedrich Heinrich, Freiherr von,
    1799-1874. 38024-38026, (42739)
Kittredge, G. L. ed. 104242
Kittredge, Jonathan. (38027)
Kjer, J. tr. 28544
Klaar en kortbondigh vertoogh. 27120,
    (48910), note after 98990
Klacht van Nieuw-Amsterdam. 91167
Klachte der West-Indische Compagnie. 38028,
    3d note after 102893
Klaer-afmaelende samenspraeck. 55423
Klaer licht. 38029, 102886, 4th note after
    102893
Klaer lichtende noord ster. 41960
Klaer vertooch. 38030
Klaere aenteeckeninge op de negotiatie van
    den Heer Ambassʳ. Downingh. 97063
Klaere aenteeckeninghe op de negotiatie van
    den Heer Ambassʳ Downingh. 97063
Klaes. pseud. Amsterdamsche Vreeman op
    Middelburgh. 1354, note after 102878
Klagen uber den Tod des General
    Waschingtnos. 101829
Klagh-vervolgh vanden Deenschen Koninck.
    38031, 5th note after 102893
Klagreden vom Verfall des Christenthums.
    96793
Klagte over de bedorvene zeden der
    voorgangeren. 38032
Klagte van eenige leeden der Nederduytse
    Hervormde Kerk. 25755, 25974, 98572
Klaproth, Heinrich Julius. 31593, 38033,
    47956, 58549
Klare aenwiksinge. (38034)
Klare besgryving [sic] van Cabo de Bona
    Esperanca. 38035
Klare et waarachtige beschryving. (50580)
Klare und gewisse wahrheit. (38036)
Klauke, ------. 38037
Klausing, Anton Ernst. tr. 9288, 27209,
    32162
Kleefisch, J. H. ed. 90062
Klein, Hermann J. 38038
Klein, L. ed. (27197)
Klein Katechismun. 64913
Kleine, S. M. tr. 98767
Kleine Cosmographia. 38039, 76975
Kleine Davidsche Psalterspiel der Kinder
    Zions. 66467, 93916, 106364
Kleine Goldgraber in Californien. 27194
Kleine Harfe. 66467
Kleine historische Schriften. 1904
Kleine Missionsbibliothek. 9321
Kleine Schriften. 25520
Kleinere Schriften. (33725)
Kleinknecht, C. D. 38040-(38041)
Kleinschmidt, Samuel. (38042)
Klemm, G. 38043
Klencke, H. (38044)
Klencke, P. F. Hermann. (38045)-38047
Klerk, J. de. (38048)-1st note after 38048,
    note after 98472
Kletke, H. 33739, 38049-38050
Klett, J. Davides. (41825), (52385)
Kleyne wonderlijke werelt. 36640

Kleynhovius, C. F. 38051
Klinck, --------. ed. 601
Klinckhardt, C. G. 94639
Kline, A. C. 38052
Klingerder and Co. firm 15003, 55529
Klinkowstron, Axel, Friherre. 38053
Klippart, John H. (38054)
Kloden, Gustav Adolph von. 38055
Kloos, J. H. 38056
Klosterleben Karls V. 65295
Klotzsch, Johann Friedrich, 1805-1860. 4834,
    77780
Klucktspel met Zang. (40033)
Klunzingen, Karl. 38057
Klupfel, Karl. 23999, 90039
Kmoch, George. 36697, 38225
Knaben von neuen Jahren abgelegt Wurde.
    101542
Knapp, Anthony L. 38058
Knapp, Chauncey L. 38059
Knapp, Frederic N. 38060-38061, 76547,
    76553, 76559, 76563, 76584, 76585,
    76603, 76621, 76647
Knapp, H. S. 38062
Knapp, Isaac. 38063
Knapp, J. G. 38979
Knapp, J. J. defendant 17708, 2d note after
    103741
Knapp, Jacob. 38064
Knapp, John Francis. defendant 17708, 38065-
    38066, 96893, 102319, 2d note after
    103741
Knapp, Martin. 38067
Knapp, Moses L. (38068)
Knapp, Samuel Lorenzo, 1783-1838. 768, 12998,
    31966, (33520), 38069-38084, 40952,
    76255, 79687, 91742
Knapp, William H. 38085-38086
Knapsack notes. 79773
Knavery detected. 22182, 59045
Knavery exposed. 50761
Knavery scourged! 81730
Kneass, Horn R. (38088), (60083)
Kneass, Horn R. defendant (38087)
Kneass, Samuel H. 62183
Kneass, Strickland. 60358
Knecht Jesu Christi. pseud. Etliche zu
    dieser Zeit. see Zinzendorf, Nicolaus
    Ludwig, Graf von, 1700-1760.
Kneedler, ------. plaintiff 34727, (38089)
Kneedler vs. David M. Lane & others.
    (38089)
Kneeland, Abner. (38090)-38091, 62048, 92832
Kneeland, Abner. defendant 21293, 38091
Kneeland, Samuel. 82393
Kneeling to God, at parting with friends.
    18470
Knelb, P. H. 38092-38093
Knibb, William. 38094
Knick-knacks from an editor's table. 13331
Knickerbocker. pseud. Wreckmaster. 38095
Knickerbocker, Diedrich. pseud. see Irving,
    Washington, 1783-1859.
Knickerbocker. 37767, 84162, 101338, 101879
Knickerbocker. Contributors. pseud. 38098
Knickerbocker almanac for 1848. 38097
Knickerbocker and Nevada Silver Mining
    Company. 38100
Knickerbocker gallery. 38098
Knickerbocker: or, New York monthly magazine.
    38096
Knickerbocker sketch-book. 38099
Knickerbocker's address. 21339
Knickerbocker's history of New York. 35158,
    35160, 35163, 35165
Knibb, William. 38084

Knight, Dr. 38109-38111, 48166
Knight, Madam. see Knight, Sarah (Kemble) 1666-1727.
Knight, A. R. (38102)
Knight, Ann Cuthbert. (24699), 38101
Knight, C. F. 38106
Knight, Charles, 1793-1873. 17374, 38103-38105
Knight, Daniel. 38107
Knight, D. M. 38108
Knight, Edward. 85619
Knight, Franklin. (38112), 101719-101720, 101722
Knight, Frederick. 38113-38114, note before 93242, 1st note after 95623, note after 97540
Knight, Helen C. 38115
Knight, Henry Cogswell. 38116
Knight, Isaac. 33917
Knight, J., fl. 1818. (38117)
Knight, John. defendant 101521-101522
Knight, John. plaintiff 102435-102437
Knight, John, d. 1606. 66686, (74131)
Knight, John, fl. 1833-1834. 47283
Knight, Jonathan. 2992, 38118, 72157 see also Baltimore and Ohio Railroad Company. Chief Engineer.
Knight, Jonathan, 1789-1864. 38119, 83653-83654
Knight, Joseph. 38120
Knight, Joseph. plaintiff 102434-102437
Knight, Lucian Lamar, 1868- ed. 38978, 91307, 91313, 91315, 94215
Knight, Nehemiah R. (38121)
Knight, Richard. 38122
Knight, Sarah. 38123
Knight, Sarah (Kemble) 1666-1727. 38124-38125
Knight, Thomas Frederick. 38126-(38129)
Knight, Titus. 38130
Knight, William H. 3142, (30200), 38131, 58079
Knight and friars. 97377
Knight and quack. 32236
Knight of Elvas. pseud. (23864), 24858, (24865), 24895-(24896), 27806, 62806, 87206, note after 90319, 3d note after 99856, 1st note after 105510
Knight of the black flag. 50645
Knight of the conquest. (5550)
Knight Russ Ockside. pseud. History and records of the Elephant Club. see Thomson, Mortimer, 1832-1875. and Underhill, Edward Fitch, 1830-1898.
Knights of the frozen sea. (38135)
Knights of the Golden Circle, &c. 78751
Knights of St. Crispin. see Order of the Knights of St. Crispin.
Knights of the Horse-Shoe. 11173, 100482
Knights of the Round Table. see Yale University. Knights of the Round Table.
Knights Templars. see Freemasons.
Knitting-work. 38075
Knivet, Anthonie. 66686
Knolton, ------. 17407
Knopf, D. C. 38138
Knot, G. C. P. (38139)
Knot, Maple. pseud. Life and advnetures of Simon Seek. see Clemo, Ebenezer.
Know all men by these presents that I, John Wood. 105049
Know all men by these presents, that we, John Abbot. 103030
Know all men by these presents, that, whereas. 93563
Know nothing. 38142

Know nothing; a poem for natives and aliens. 38141
Know-nothing almanac and true American's manual. 38140
Know nothing platform. 38143
Know nothingism. 38148
Know-nothingism exposed. 91870
Know nothings cause and effect. 38145
Knowlan, James. 38149
Knowledge and liberty. 92769
Knowledge and practice of Christianity. 104691
Knowledge increased by travelling to and fro. 94206
"Knowledge is power." 62766
Knowledge: its relation to the progress of mankind. 90928
Knowledge, liberty, religion. 63963
Knowledge of Christ indispensable required. (18707)
Knowledge of Christ recommended. 59609
Knowledge of Jesus Christ the best knowledge. 103551
Knowledge of salvation precious. (72892)
Knowledge of the Bible important to youth. 66228
Knowledge of the true God. 71337
Knowles, --------. defendant 40451, 62542, 92695
Knowles, Sir Charles. 17610-17611, 22796, (38152)
Knowles, Sir Charles. supposed author 11128, 1st note after 99245
Knowles, Sir Charles. defendant at court martial 38150-(38152), note after 96893
Knowles, J. P. 70738
Knowles, James. ed. 83876
Knowles, James Davis. (12923), (14882), 38153-38156
Knowles, John P. reporter 70696
Knowles, Newman. 102781
Knowles, William. reporter (27983)
Knowles, William J. 38157
Knowls, John. 105475
Knowlton, Charles. 38158
Knowlton, J. M. 38159
Knowlton Mining Company. Directors. 38160
Known author. pseud. Tale of a New Yorker. 94239
Knox, Alexander. 88559-88560
Knox, Henry. (38161)
Knox, Hugh. 38162
Knox, John. pseud. At a meeting of the True Sons of Liberty. 86983
Knox, John. pseud. Sermon for the times. 38167
Knox, John, 1505-1572. 101877
Knox, John, 1720-1790. 38163, 84617, 84618
Knox, Capt. John, d. 1778. 15056, 38164, 101047, 105602-105605
Knox, John, 1790-1858. 38165
Knox, John P. (38169)-(38170)
Knox, Jonathan Jay. 37762
Knox, Loren L. (38171)
Knox, Robert. (38172)
Knox, Samuel. (38173)-(38174)
Knox, Samuel. supposed author 35900, 35936, 1st note after 99824
Knox, Thomas. 38175
Knox, Thomas P. 38176
Knox, Thomas Wallace. 16293, (38177), 79652
Knox, Vicesimus. 89471-89472
Knox, W. J. 38186

Knox, William, 1732-1810. (1969), 9294, 15928, (23375), (28768)-(28769), 38178-38183, 46928, 56562, note just before 65329, 69436, 95751, 103123

Knox, William, 1732-1810. supposed author (3111), 38180, 81961, 2d note after 103122

Knox, William Eaton, 1820-1883. 38185

Knox County, Ill. Circuit Court. 84246

Knox College, Galesburg, Ill. 2738, (38187)-38188

Knox College, Galesburg, Ill. Knoxiana Publication Society. 38188

Knox College, by whom founded and endowed. 2738

Knox Manual Labor College. see Knox College, Galesburg, Ill.

Knox manuscripts. 81694

Knoxiana. 38188

Knoxiana Publication Society. see Knox College, Galesburg, Ill. Knoxiana Publication Society.

Knoxville, Tenn. Blount College. see Tennessee. University.

Knoxville, Tenn. Constitutional Convention, 1796. see Tennessee. Constitutional Convention, Knoxville, 1796.

Knoxville, Tenn. Division No. 3, Sons of Temperance. see Sons of Temperance of North America. Tennessee. Knoxville Division, No. 3.

Knoxville, Tenn. East Tennessee Relief Association. see East Tennessee Relief Association, Knoxville.

Knoxville, Tenn. Hampden-Sidney Academy. see Tennessee. University.

Knoxville, Tenn. Masonic Convention, 1814. see Masonic Convention, Knoxville, Tenn., 1814.

Knoxville, Tenn. Semi-Centennial Celebration, 1842. (38190)

Knoxville, Tenn. Southern Commercial Convention, 1857. see Southern Commercial Convention, Knoxville, Tenn., 1857.

Knoxville, December 10, 1809. 94758

Knoxville Division, No. 3, Sons of Temperance. see Sons of Temperance of North America. Tennessee. Knoxville Division, No. 3.

Knoxville, May 10th, 1805. 94757

Knoxville, 23d April, 1798. 94754

Knoxville whig. 8702, 8704

Ko nga Akoranga me nga Kawenata. 83228

Ko te parata utu nui. 83277

Ko te pukapuka a Moromona. 83136-83137

Kob, Karl Friedrich. 38191

Kobbe, Peter Ludwig Christian von. 38192

Kobel, H. illus. 36634, 55284, 70100, 101231-note after 101231

Koch, Albert. 5128

Koch, Albert Charles. 38193-38200

Kock, Christophe Guillaume. 26601, 38201

Koch, F. C. L. (38202)-38203

Koch, J. G. F. 38204

Koch, Louis. 5128-5129

Kodresko, T. tr. 92599

Koeler, Hermann. 38205

Koempfer, ------. 69381

Koempfer's account of Japan. 69381

Koenen, H. J. 38206

Koenig, ------. ed. 68443

Koenig, -------, Π. 1805. 38207

Koerber, Philipp. ed. 89548

Koerten, J. 38208

Koffler, John Frederick. 38209

Kohl, Johann Georg, 1808-1878. 19195, 38210-38219, (43917)

Kolb, Carl. tr. 20008

Kohler, Carl. (38220)

Kohler, F. G. 38222

Kohler, Friedrich. 3739, 38221

Kohler, J. tr. 38302

Kohler, Johann Tobias. ed. 38223, 95529, 95836

Kohler, Otto. tr. 38224

Kohlmeister, Benjamin. 36697, 38225

Κοιναι φρασεις και ιδιωματα της νεωτερας ελληνικης διαλεκτου. 105791

Kolb, Johann Ernst. 38226

Kolben, ------. 38163

Kolbing, Friedrich Ludwig. 97854

Kollar, V. (63678)

Kollock, Henry. 38227

Kollock, Shepard. 78581, 85207

Kollock, Shepard. supposed author 72720-72722

Kollock, Shepard K. (38228)

Kollonitz, Paula, Comtesse. (38229)-38230

Koln, German. Gesellschaft zur Verbreitung des Glaubens. see Gelsellschaft zur Verbreitung des Glaubens, Koln.

Kolnische Zeitung. 2052A, 19241, 93103-93104

Kolonisations-Gesellschaft in Konigsberg zur Grundung. 37139

Kolonist, tijdschrift toegewijd aan de welvaart van Suriname. 38232

Κομητογραφια. 46691, 46696

Komiteens navn af M. A. de Tocqueville. 18724

Kongelige Danske Westindiske og Guineiske Compagnies participanters convention. 102939

Konige, A. von. ed. 103032

Konigl. Englischen Dewegen nach Teutschland erlassenen Abmahnung. 2390, 32377, 98990

Koniglich Sachsischen Strafanstalten. 4861

Konigliche Spanische Meerschlacht und Victoria. (76756)

Konigseer, C. M. ed. 97435

Konigshofen, Nicolaus Honiger von. tr. 45012

Konigshofen, Tauber. tr. 1762A

Konigsmarke, or, old times in the new world. 59201

Konigsmarke, the Long Finne. 59200

Konsag, Ferdinand. see Konschak, Ferdinand.

Konschak, Ferdinand. 1768, 38233-38234,. 57680

Kooch, Jeremiah. 38235

Koontz, William H. 38236

Koopman in Amsterdam. pseud. Brief. 7912

Koopman te Londen. pseud. Verhandelung. see Tucker, Josiah, 1712-1799.

Koopman van Sint Eustatius. pseud. Regt der ingezetenen van deezen staat. (68933)

Koort uyttreksel uyt de aanteykeninge van de Baron de Lahontan. (38048)

Kopernik, Mikolaj. see Copernicus, Nicolaus, 1473-1543.

Kopfi, Kaspar. ed. 75372, 93793

Kopfi, Salomon. 75372, 93793

Koplin, Alexander Bernhar. tr. 41773

Koppe, Diogo. ed. 98649

Koppe, F. W. 7925, 16959, 38237-38238

Koppenhagen-Groenlandische Gesellschafft. 25997, (38973)-38974, note after 100853, note after 100854

Koppernigk, Niklas. see Copernicus, Nicolaus, 1473-1543.

Kossuth excitement. 35867
Kossuth: his career; his mission. 80362
Kossuth in New England. 38266
Kossuth or Washington. 6075, 42979
Kossuth . . . speech . . . at the A. S.
   Bazaar . . . Dec. 27th, 1851. 62628
Kost Ka, Bienaventurado Stanislao. 38271
Kostelige Perle. 83271-83272
Koster, Henry. 38272-(38274)
Koster, T. 38275
Kostliche Perle. 83274-83275
Kotte, C. F. 38276
Kottenkamp, Franz Justus, 1806-1858.
   38277-(38278), 90373
Kotzebue, August Friedrich Ferdinand von,
   1761-1819. 8137, 4792, 11817, 38279-
   38283, 80340, 80342, 97573
Kotzebue, Otto von, 1787-1846. 21211-21215,
   38284-38292, 62509
Koul Jacob in defence of the Jewish
   religion. 78672
Kouns, Nathan. 96675-96676, 96679, 96683
   see also U. S. Commissioners to the
   Kaskaskia and Peoria Indians. U. S.
   Commissioners to the Kickapoo Indians.
   U. S. Commissioners to the Piankeshaw
   and Wea Indians. U. S. Commissioners
   to the Shawanoe and Delaware Indians.
Kozmograffia Czieska. 51401
Kracheninnokow, S. P. see Krascheninnokoff,
   Stephan Petrovich.
Krachteloose donder van de Helschen hond.
   (38293)
Kraemer, --------. lithographer 91293
Krafft, Charles L. defendant 45163, 45328
Krafft, F. C. de. see DeKrafft, F. C.
Krafft, Michael. 38294
Krag, Thomas. 92438
Kragh, Petr. (7409), (22851), 22871, 28657-
   (28658), 38295-38296, 40133
Kraitsir, Charles V. 38297
Kramer, John Theophilus. (38298)
Kramern, Matthia. tr. 6441, 7407, note
   after 98470
Krans, Edward H. 21507
Krantzius, Alb. 38299, 106294, 106330
Krascheninnokoff, Stephan Petrovich. 38300-
   (38304)
Kraskowski, Thomas. (38305)
Krater. 16429
Kratz, Arthur. (38306)
Krause, William E. F. 38307-38308
Krauskopp, William. 5434
Krautbauer, Francis Xavier, Bp. 72944
   see also Green Bay (Diocese) Bishop
   (Krautbauer)
Krauth, Charles Porterfield. 23123, (38309)-
   38310, 60313, 73344
Krebs, Charles G. lithographer 84774
Krebs, Ernst Hugo. 38311-38312
Krebs, Henry J. 38313
Krebs, John M. 23435, 38314-38315, note
   after 89770
Kreenen, J. J. 74752
Kreet der Africanen tegen hunne Europeesche
   verdrukkers. 13487
Kreidebildungen von Texas. 72591
Kreil, A. tr. 20413
Kreisig, Friedrich Ludwig. tr. 2982
Kreisphysikus, -------. 24013, 51076
Kreool A B C buk. (37870)
Kretzschmar, A. tr. 1864, 3124, (10933),
   16473, 17936, 72231, 92403, 92444
Kretzschmar, W. 38316
Kreuger, Hendrick. (32804)
Krider, John. 38317

Krieg der Triple-Allianz. 77734
Kriege, Hermann. (25617), 38318
Kriegk, Georg Ludwig. 2586, 38319
Kriegsbilder aus Amerika. 23076
Kries, F. ed. 78183
Krijgsavonturen tijdens den Mexikannsche
   vrikheidsoorlog. 4519A
Krike, ----------. RN 17610, 22796, 38152
Krisis in Nord Amerika. 68994
Kritische Untersuchingen. 33724
Kritischen Abhandlungen. 13522
Kroeger, A. E. 38320
Kroehl. firm see Husted & Kroehl. firm
Krofyt, S. H. de. see De Krofyt, S. H.
Kroff, Mich. ed. 33010
Krohl & Co. firm see Hutchinson, Krohl
   & Co. firm
Kronenberg, M. E. ed. 99365, 99383
Kronfels, L. von. tr. 12263
Kropf, Lewis L. 82851
Kropff, Fred. C. 71933-(71934)
Kroyer, Henrik Niels. (38321)
Kruger, F. 38324
Kruger, F. J. 38323
Kruistogten van de Alabama en de Sumter.
   79079
Krull, W. (38325)
Krummacher, F. A. ed. 88554
Krunitz, D. Joh. Ge. tr. 22025
Kruseman, J. D. 38326
Krusenstern, Adam Johann von. 21211-21215,
   38327-38333
Ku-Klux-Klan. 38342
Ku Klux legislation—bayonet vs. freedom.
   (71941)
Ku Klux legislation. Speech of Hon. Charles
   H. Porter. (64205)
Kuchler, Hans Lorenz. 47115
Kuchler, Jacobo. 38334
Kufahl, Ludwig. 38335, 73907
Kugler, John B. 38336
Kuhn, Adam. 38337
Kuhn, Ernst. 99363
Kuhn, F. A. (38338)
Kuhn, J. M. 38339
Kuhn, William. 38340
Kuhne, H. Th. ed. (38044)
Kuipers, K. J. 38344
Kulb, Phil. Hedw. tr. 21218, 105720
Kulcs Tamás bátya kunykójához. 92417
Kulenkampff, J. S. 77649
Kultuur en de bewerking van het siukerriet.
   (31485)
Kummer, --------. illus. 80369, note after
   96778
Kunddi, A. 4644
Kunftigen Verhaltnisse der civilisirten Welt.
   77687
Kunkel, John Christian, 1816-1870. 38346
Kunnuk og maja elter Gronlaenderne. 36870
Kunst Millionair zu Werden. 1379
Kunstmann, Friedrich. 2313, 38347-38348
Kunth, Charles Sigismond. 33761, 33764-
   33767
Kunze, G. 38349
Kunze, Johann Christoph. 38350-38351
Kunzel, Heinrich. 3327, 16446
Kinziger, ------. 23997
Kunzmann, Joseph. defendant 15097
Kurbe, Augustin. 38972
Kurnberger, F. 38352
Kurtz, Benjamin. (38353)
Kurtz, Hermann. 12251
Kurtz, J. D. (2588), 12081, 87396
Kurtze, F. 38354
Kurtze Aufmunterung. 98135

L. M. pseud. see M., L. pseud.
L. M. pseud. see Montana, Luis. supposed author
L. M. B. pseud. see Barbe-Marbois, Francois de, Marquis, 1745-1837.
L . . . . . M . . . . B . . . . , Armateur. pseud. see Prudhomme, Luis.
L. M. N. pseud. tr. see Lenoble, Eustache. tr.
L. M. S. pseud. see Sargent, Lucius M
L. Marinei Sicvli Regii Historiographi opus. (44585)
L. P. pseud. see P., L. pseud.
L. P., Conseil. pseud. see P., L. pseud.
L. Quincius Cincinnatus. pseud. see Quincy, Edmund, 1703-1788. supposed author
L. S. pseud. see S., L. pseud.
L. S. L. pseud. see Livingston, Luther S.
L. T. pseud. see Tappan, Lewis.
L. Talavera a sus compatriotas. 94225
L. V. pseud. see V., L. pseud.
Laactshures on various subjects. 38391
Laatste der Mohikanen. 16457, 16569
Laatste geldkrisissen in de Vereenigde Staten. 38392
Laatste Irokezen. 12559
Laatste ontdekking van een vierde eiland in Terra Australis. 82189
Labanoff de Rostoff, Alexandre. 38394
Labaothe. 1584
La Bar, George. 38395
La Barbinais, Le Gentil de. 38396-39398
La Barcena, Manuel de. 38399
Labaree, Benjamin. 38400-38401
La Barra, Justo de. 38402
La Barre, Le Febvre de. (38403)
La Barrera y Troncoso, M. de. 38404
La Barreyrie, F. de. 38405
Labarta, Roman Ignacio Mendez y. see Mendez, Ramon Ignacio, Abp., d. 1839.
Labarthe, Charles de. (38406)-38407, 85781, 85791
Labastida y Davalos, Pelagio Antonio de, Abp., 1816-1891. 39283-39284 see also Mexico (Archdiocese) Archbishop (Labastida y Davalos)
La Bastide, Martin de. 38408
Labat, Jean Baptiste. 21437, 30483, 38409-38416, 57458-57459, (64038), 71252
Labatt. firm publishers see Harris, Bogardus & Labatt. firm publishers
Labaume, Jules. (68924)
La-Baye miscellany. 74991
Labbe, Jacob Joseph. 38417
Labeaume, A.-G. Griffet de. see Griffet de Labeaume, A.-G.
La Bedolliere, Emile Gigault de. tr. 16410, 16418, 16423, 16424, (16433), 16435, 16439, 16453, 16466, 16472, 16480, 16482, 16491, 16496, 16503, 16511, (16514), 16526, 16527, 16529, 16531, 16543, 16546, 16550, 16561, (31792), 38418, 69030, 69032, 69038, 69075, 92432, 92519, 92530-92531, 99511
Labelle, M. F. 38419
Labillardiere, Jacques Julien Houton de, 1755-1834. 38420-38423, (59572)
La Bonniniere, Gustave Auguste de Beaumont de. see Beaumont de la Bonniniere, Gustave Auguste de, 1802-1866.
Labor; address, by Hon. S. W. Barker. 87738
Labor and capital. 14775
Labor and other capital. (37285)
Labor and reward. 79948
Labor and wages at home and abroad. 534

Labor; its history and prospects. 58024
Labor, its relations in Europe and the United States compared. 1814A
Labor question. (38424)
Labour question in the West Indies. 55402
Labor Reform League of New England . . . . An address to the members. (38425)
Labour that attends the Gospel-ministry. 8079
Labor the only true source of wealth. 24536
Laboratory duty. 91568
La Borde, Sieur de. 36944, 68430
La Borde, Jean Benjamin de. 31352-31355, (38426)-(38427)
La Borde, Maximilian, 1804-1873. 38428, 87978-87979
Laboria, --------. 38429
Labourer's hand book and true guide. 8111
Labourers in America. pseud. Twenty-four letters. 97536
Laborie, P. J. 38430-38432
Laborien, Th. (12574)-12575
Laborieu, Th. see Laborien, Th.
Laboring classes. 8714
Laboring man. pseud. Facts for the laboring man. see Hazard, Thomas R.
Labors, defeats, triumphs. (44749)
Labors for the destitute prisoner. 89077
Labors for the prisoner. 89078
Labours of John Meyer in British Guiana. 28053, 92943
Labors of love. 13280
Labouderie, --------. 52105
Laboulaye, Edouard Rene Lefebvre de, 1811-1883. 2247, 11915-11916, 15428, 25552, 26734, 36638, (38433)-38446, 100809
Labourie, Theodore. 38447
Labra y Cadrana, Rafael Maria de, 1843-85710
Labrador. (12573)
Labrador; a poetical epistle. 11151
Labrador Argentino. (9018)
Labrador Mission. 69876
Labradores de los Valles Circunvecinos del Peru. plaintiffs 79146
Labre, Benedict Joseph. 95232
Labree, Lawrence. (38448), 73524, 84154
Labricio portundo. 75567, 75568
Labrie, Jacques. (38449)
Lac, F. M. Perrin du. see Perrin du Lac, F. M.
Lac Ontario, ou le guide. 16451, 16490
Lacarriere Latour, Arsenio. see Latour, Arsenio Lacarrier.
La Carrieres, A. C. de. 38450
Lacasa, Pedro. 38451-(38452), 49757
Lacasta, Martin Sese y. see Sese y Lacasta Martin.
Lacedemonia (Archdiocese) Archbishop [ca 1837] 81103
Lacerda, Antonio Francisco de. 59656
La Cerda, Jose de Zuniga y. see Zuniga y La Cerda, Jose de.
La Cerda, Juan Fernandez de Salinas y. see Salinas y La Cerda, Juan Ferdinandez de.
Lacerda Werneck, Luiz Peixoto de. ed. 38453-38454, 59170
La Cerna, D. Jacinto. 38455
Lacey, John. see Lacy, John.
Lacey, William B. 38457
La Chaise, Francois d'Aix de. (38458)
Lachapelle, --------, fl. 1797. 62892
Lachapelle, Alfred, Comte de, b. 1830. 38459, 67910
Lacharriere, --------. 5652
Lachartiere, Andre de. 38460

Ladies' Anti-slavery Society of Bristol and Clifton, Eng. see Bristol and Clifton Ladies' Anti-slavery Society.

Ladies' Association Attached to the Roman Catholic Orphan Asylum, New York. see New York (City) Roman Catholic Orphan Asylum Ladies' Association.

Ladies' Association, Auxiliary to the American Colonization Society, Philadelphia. 61754

Ladies' Association for Soldiers' Relief, Philadelphia. 61755

Ladies' Association, for the Aid of Military Hospitals, Milwaukee. (49157)

Ladies' Auxiliary Emancipation Society, Glasgow. see Glasgow Ladies' Auxiliary Emancipation Society.

Ladies Benevolent Society, Montreal. 50240

Ladies' Benevolent Society, New Orleans. Managers. 53332

Ladies' Bethel Association, Providence, R. I. (66274)

Ladies' Bible and Benevolent Association, Milwaukee. 49158

Ladies' book of anecdotes and sketches of character. 82427

Ladies' Branch Bible Society of Baltimore. 106162

Ladies' Branch of the Union Benevolent Association, Philadelphia. see Union Benevolent Association, Philadelphia. Ladies' Branch.

Ladies' Centennial Committee, Salem, Mass. see Salem, Mass. Ladies Centennial Committee.

Ladies' Charitable Association of Christ Church Parish, New York. see New York (City) Christ Church Parish Ladies' Charitable Association.

Ladies' Chinese Association of Philadelphia. (61756)

Ladies' Christian Commission. Auxiliary to the U. S. Christian Commission. 38532

Ladies' Collegiate Institute, Boston. petitioners 90777

Ladies' companion. A monthly magazine. 38533, 84142, 85516

Ladies' companion and literary expositor. 38533

Ladies' Depository, Philadelphia. 61757

Ladies' Depository Philadelphia. Managers. 61757

Ladies depository . . . for supplying work. Nineteenth report. 38534

Ladies' Domestic Missionary Relief Association of the Protestant Episcopal Church. see Protestant Episcopal Church in the U. S. A. Ladies Domestic Missionary Relief Association.

Ladies' emporium. (52004)

Ladies' Fair for the Benefit of the New-England Asylum for the Blind, Salem, Mass., 1833. see Salem, Mass. Ladies' Fair for the Benefit of the New-England Asylum for the Blind, 1833.

Ladies' Friendly Society, Newburyport, Mass. Committee on Organization. (54918)

Ladies' Greek Association, New Haven, Conn. see New Haven Ladies' Greek Association, New Haven, Conn.

Ladies' Home for Sick and Wounded Soldiers, New York. (54327)

Ladies' Home Missionary Society, New York. see New-York Ladies Home Missionary Society.

Ladies' Hospital Relief Association, Rochester, N. Y. Christmas Bazaar. (72352)

Ladies Industrial Aid Association, of Union Hall. 38535

Ladies Industrial School Association, Detroit. see Detroit Ladies Industrial School Association.

Ladies' Liberia School Association. 40924

Ladies' literary cabinet. 38536

Ladies' literary gazette. 54819

Ladies' literary magazine. 45521

Ladies' literary portfolio. 61939

Ladies' Literary Union, Hillsdale College. see Hillsdale College, Hillsdale, Mich. Ladies' Literary Union.

Ladies' London Emancipation Society. 38537

Ladies' magazine (ca 1819) 38538

Ladies' magazine (ca 1841) 90002

Ladies' memorandum book. 38539

Ladies' Missionary Association of Christ Church, Philadelphia. see Philadelphia. Christ Church. Ladies' Missionary Association.

Ladies' monitor, a poem. 24220

Ladies Mount Vernon Association of the Union. 17968

Ladies' National Army Relief Association. 38540

Ladies' National League of St.Louis. 75352

Ladies' New-York City Anti-slavery Society. 54328

Ladies of Cambridge to their sisters of the fourth district. 10137

Ladies of the mission. pseud. Old brewery. 57115

Ladies of the White House. 32560

Ladies Philadelphia shopping guide & house-keeper's companion. 61759

Ladies' philosophy of love. 90855

Ladies' Protection and Relief Society, San Francisco. see San Francisco Ladies' Protection and Relief Society.

Ladies' Relief Association of the District of Columbia. 20310, (59046)

Ladies' Relief Association of the District of Columbia. Patent Office Fair, Washington, D. C., 1864. 20310, (59046)

Ladies' repository. 85144

Ladies' repository, and gatherings of the west. 38541

Ladies' Seamen's Friend Society of the Port of San Francisco. 76052

Ladies' Seminary, North Granville, N. Y. see North Granville Female Seminary, North Granville, N. Y.

Ladies Society, Established in New-York, for the Relief of Poor Widows with Small Children. see Ladies' Society for the Relief of Poor Widows with Small Children, New York.

Ladies' Society for Promoting the Education of the Children of Negroes in the British West Indies. 38543

Ladies' Society for the Promotion of Education at the West. 38542

Ladies' Society for the Relief of Poor Widows with Small Children, New York. 54329, 85971-85975

Ladies' Society for the Relief of Poor Widows With Small Children, New York. Charter. 85970

Ladies songster. 100653

Ladies' Southern Relief Association of Maryland, Baltimore. 45179

Ladies' Tract and City Missionary Society, New Bedford, Mass. 52460

Ladies Union Aid Society of St. Louis. 75353

Ladies' Union City Mission, Philadelphia. 61760

Ladies' Union Relief Association, Baltimore. 3016

Ladies' United Aid Society of the Methodist Episcopal Church, Philadelphia. (61761)

Ladies' wreath. 29670

Lador, J. A. 38544

Ladron de Guevara, Ant. see Guevara, Antonio Ladron de.

Ladron de Guevara, Baltasar. 38545

Ladron de Guevara, Diego. see Guevara, Diego Ladron de, Bp.

Ladron de Guevara, J. de Arroyo. 98347

Ladron de Gueuara, Ioan. see Gueuara, Ioan Ladron de.

Ladue, P. A. 38546

Ladvocat, C. 29395, 40913, 95072

Ladvocat, P. see Ladvocat, C.

Lady. pseud. ed. 102716

Lady. pseud. American women responsible for the existence of American slavery. see Foote, C. C.

Lady. pseud. Aningait & Ajutt. see Penny, Miss ---------.

Lady. pseud. Boston common. see Farren, Mrs. --------.

Lady. pseud. Christian's song. 101865

Lady. pseud. Collection of exotics from the island of Antigua. 1697

Lady. pseud. Flora's dictionary. see Wirt, Elizabeth Washington Gamble.

Lady. pseud. How to be happy. see Sigourney, Lydia (Huntley) 1791-1865.

Lady. pseud. Letter from a lady on nursing. 96146

Lady. pseud. Letters to young ladies. see Sigourney, Lydia (Huntley) 1791-1865.

Lady. pseud. Liberal American. 40918

Lady. pseud. My cave life in Vicksburg. 51617

Lady. pseud. Observations on Mr. Burke's bill. 56497

Lady. pseud. On the conservative elements of the American republic. see Douglas, Mrs. R.

Lady. pseud. Poems chiefly amatory. 63611

Lady. pseud. Poems on different subjects. 36320

Lady. pseud. Poetic reveries. see Robinson, Anne Steele.

Lady. pseud. Poetical picture of America. see Ritson, --------.

Lady. pseud. Quintessence of long speeches. see Pinckney, Maria.

Lady. pseud. Reflections on the conservatory elements of the American republic. see Douglas, Mrs. R.

Lady. pseud. Reflections on the tomb of Columbus. 14669

Lady. pseud. Reign of reform. 69103

Lady. pseud. Remarks on a poem, called, "the scourge of fashion." 69404

Lady. pseud. Resignation. 70064

Lady. pseud. Rural hours. see Cooper, Susan Fenimore.

Lady. pseud. Sermons to children. 79300

Lady. pseud. Six months in Kansas. see Ropes, H. A.

Lady. pseud. Slavery past and present. note after 92624

Lady. pseud. Snow drop. 85566

Lady. pseud. Step-mother. see Whitford, Helena (Wells)

Lady. pseud. Stranger of the valley. 92719

Lady. pseud. Two poems. 97577

Lady. pseud. Vicissitudes of human life. 99423

Lady. pseud. Visit to Nahant. 51726

Lady. pseud. tr. Voyages, adventures & situation of the French emigrants. see Mentelle, Madame --------. supposed author

Lady. pseud. Widow of the rock. see Blennerhassett, Margaret (Agnew)

Lady. pseud. Young lady's friend. see Farrar, Eliza Ware Rotch.

Lady Angeline. 55382

Lady and the dressmaker. 24056

Lady at Cape Francois. pseud. Secret history. see Hassall, Miss ---------.

Lady, Author of "Julia." pseud. Dorval. see Wood, Sally Sayward Barrell Keating.

Lady Hearer. pseud. tr. 38312

Lady Huntington and her friends. 38115

Lady in black. (55215)

Lady in Worcester. pseud. Observations on free masonry. 56495

Lady killer. 31720

Lady lieutenant. 50418

Lady, native of Virginia. pseud. Potomac muse. see Elwes, Mrs. Alfred W. supposed author

Lady of Boston. pseud. Memoir of Mrs. Chloe Spear. see Webb, Mary, d. 1861. supposed author

Lady of Boston. pseud. Ouabi. see Morton, Sarah Wentworth Apthorp.

Lady of Boston. pseud. Series of letters on free masonry. see Crocker, Hannah Mather.

Lady of Boston. pseud. Stories about General Warren. see Brown, Rebecca (Warren)

Lady of Boston. pseud. Tales of the Emerald Isle. see Weston, M. A.

Lady of Boston. pseud. Tales of the fireside. see Weston, M. A. supposed author

Lady of Charleston. pseud. Carolina house-wife. (87804)

Lady of Charleston, S. C. pseud. Miscellaneous poems. see Murden, Eliza.

Lady of Fredericksburg, Va. pseud. Refutation of the principles of abolition. 68796

Lady of Gettysburg. pseud. Diary. 19957, 27232

Lady of honour. pseud. Golden island. 79216

Lady of Lexington. pseud. Wreath. see Littleford, ----------.

Lady of Maine. Author of Julia, etc. pseud. Tales of the right. see Wood, Sally Sayward Barrell Keating.

Lady of Maryland. pseud. Extracts in prose and verse. 23537

Lady of Massachusetts. pseud. Amelia. see Wood, Sally Sayward Barrell Keating.

Lady of Massachusetts. pseud. Coquette; or, the history of Eliza Wharton. see Foster, Hannah.

Lady of Massachusetts. pseud. Coquette, or, the life and letters of Eliza Wharton. see Locke, Jane E.

Lady of Massachusetts. pseud. Fayette in prison. see Eliot, James.

Lady of Massachusetts. pseud. First settlers of New-England. see Child, Lydia Maria. and Sanders, Elizabeth (Elkins) incorrectly supposed author

Lady of Massachusetts. pseud. Julia. see Wood, Sally Sayward Barrell Keating.

Lady of Massachusetts. pseud. Memoirs of a grandmother. see Richards, Mrs. A. M.

Lady of Massachusetts. pseud. Poem, and other thoughts. see Wellman, Mary W.

Lady of Massachusetts; Author of Julia, The speculator, and Amelia. pseud. Ferdinand & Elmira. see Wood, Sally Sayward Barrell Keating.

Lady of New England. pseud. Poem. 63578

Lady of New-Hampshire. pseud. Genius of oblivion. see Hale, Sarah Josepha.

Lady of New Orleans. pseud. Tit for tat. see Southwood, Marion.

Lady of New-York. pseud. Patent key to Uncle Tom's cabin. note after 92624

Lady of Ohio. pseud. Three years in Chili. see Merwin, Mrs. C. B. supposed author

Lady of Pennsylvania. pseud. Kelroy. 37323

Lady of Philadelphia. pseud. World enlightened. 105487

Lady of Philadelphia, author of Adelaide. pseud. Viola or the heiress of St. Valverde. see Botsford, Margaret.

Lady of Richmond. pseud. Wreath. see Littleford, ---------.

Lady of South Carolina. pseud. British partizan. see Davis, Mary Elizabeth (Moragne) b. 1815.

Lady of the lake. 95594A

Lady of the principality. pseud. History of Wales. 102618

Lady of Virginia. pseud. Diary of a southern refugee. see McGuire, Mrs. John P.

Lady of Virginia. pseud. Ruth Churchill. 74450

Lady of Virginia. pseud. Tales and souvenirs of a residence in Europe. see Rives, Mrs. William Cabel.

Lady of the west. 2970

Lady Superior. pseud. Answer to Six months in a convent. see Mary Edmund St. George. Sister

Lady Superior. pseud. Reply to "Six months in a convent." see Mary Edmund St. George. Sister

Lady Superior. pseud. Review of the Lady Superior's reply. see Mary Edmund St. George. Sister

Lady, the translatress of four select tales from Marmontel. pseud. Several rational sermons. 79358

Lady Washington·left Mount Vernon in June 1778. 101883

Lady Washington's lamentation, American star, and Hurrah! for the bonnets of blue. 101830

Lady Washington's lamantation [sic] for the death of her husband. 101832

Lady Washignton's [sic] lamentation for the death of her husband. 101831

Lady who was confined thirty-three days. pseud. Trial. 96941

Lady who was taken prisoner by the Indians. pseud. Affecting narrative. 5676

Lady, who enjoyed the hospitalities of the government for a "season." pseud. Old capitol and its inmates. 57116

Lady, who for fifty years belonged to the Society of Friends. pseud. Quakerism. see Greer, Sarah D.

Lady's almanac, for the year 1854. 38548

Lady's and gentleman's diary. 93052

Lady's book. A magazine. (38549)

Lady's friend. 38550

Lady's life among the Mormons. 91222

Lady's magazine. 82974, 82976

Lady's magazine. see Southern lady's magazine.

Lady's magazine and repository of entertaining knowledge. 38551

Lady's monthly magazine. 6499

Lady's second journey round the world. (71342)

Lady's travels round the world. 61337

Lady's voyage round the world. 61338

Laemmert, Eduardo. 38552, 71457

La Encina, Louis Gonzaga de. (38553)

Laer, A J. F. van. see Van Laer, Arnold Johan Ferdinand van, 1869-

Laerdommens og pagtens bog for Jesu Christi Kirke af sidste dages hellige. 83215-83218

Laerdommens og pagtens bog for Jesu Kristi Kirk af sidste dages hellige. 83219

Laet, J. de. see Laet, Joannes de, 1593-1649.

Laet, Joannes de, 1593-1649. (4196), 5045, 7588, 9389, 29186, 33015, 38554-38562, 41288, 63028, (76810), 94352, note before 100436

Laet, Juan de. see Laet, Joannes de, 1593-1649.

Laetus, Pomponius. 72023

Lafaragua, J. M. 38612-38614

La Farelle, F. de. 38563

Lafargue, Etienne de. (38564)-(38565), (56137)

Lafasse, --------. 38566

La Faye Brehier, J. de. see Delafaye Brehier, Julie.

Lafayette, Marquis de. pseud. Epistle from the Marquis de Lafayette, to General Washington. see Bannerman, Anne. supposed author and Hamilton, George. supposed author

Lafayette, George Washington. ed. 38575

Lafayette, Marie Jean Paul Roche Yves Gilbert du Motier, Marquis de, 1757-1834. 8040, (13744), 27040, 33618, 38570, 38574-38578, 38581, 43082, 69716, 70350, 77163, 82974, 82976, 84904, 88969, 96990

Lafayette, Marie Jean Paul Roche Yves Gilbert du Motier, Marquis de, 1757-1834. supposed author 38572, 40370

Lafayette, Marie Jean Paul Roche Yves Gilbert du Motier, Marquis de, 1757-1834. defendant 38583, 98682

Lafayette, Fort, N. Y. (24163)

Lafayette, La. petitioners (38585)

Lafayette; a poem. (64774)

Lafayette and Louis Philippe. 77097

Lafayette Baptist Association. see Baptists. Wisconsin. Lafayette Baptist Association.

Lafayette Beneficial Society of Pennsylvania. 60188

Lafayette College, Easton, Pa. 38586, 68064

Lafayette College, Easton, Pa. petitioners 60189

La Fayette en Amerique. 38583

Lafayette en Amerique en 1824 et 1825. (40734)

Lafayette en Amerique et en France. (59570)

La Fayette et la revolution de 1830. (77096)

Lafayette Female Academy, Lexington, Ky. (40886)

Lafayette Female Academy, Lexington, Ky. Exercises in Honor of General Lafayette, 1825. 23583, 2d note after 100603

Lafayette in America in 1824 and 1825. 40735

La Fayette in Mount Vernon. 47381

Lafayette music. 38583

Lafayette, or disinterested benevolence. 51101

La Fayette, or the castle of Olmutz. 38583, 105186, 105195

Laferriere, E. 38588

Laffauris, -------. 38589

Laffond Ladebat, -------. (1534), (27337)

Lafitau, Joseph Francois. (32040), (38591)-38598, 47530, (77989)

Lafitau, Joseph Francois. petitioner 38595

Lafite (J.) & Co. firm. (38590)

Lafitte, or the Barratariah chief. 83784

Lafitte; or, the Greek slave. 38599, 72706

Lafitte, the pirate of the gulf. 34774, note after 83599

Lafleche, Louis. 38600-38601

Lafond de Lurcy, Gabriel. 38602-38606

Lafont, Charles. (38607)

Lafont, Jules. tr. 24626

La Fontaine, D. A. 20906-20907

La Fontaine, Jean de. 38608

La Fontaine, L. H. 38609, 39106

Laforest, citoyen de couleur. (38610)

Lafosse, J. F. 38611

Lafoy, J. B. M. D. pseud. Complete coiffeur. see Woodworth, Samuel.

Lafragua, Jose M. 38614, 47586, 71485 see also Mexico. Legacion. Spain.

Lafragua, Jose M. supposed author 38612, 48489, 64331, 76734

La Fruston, Fr. de, 1806-1864. 38615

La Fuente, Antonio Gutierrez de. (38616)

Lagarde, Ernest. ed. (71194)

Lagarde, N. Chauveau. see Chauveau-Lagarde, N.

Lagarde (Ernest) & Co. firm publishers (71194)

La Gasca, M. (38618)

Lager-beer system in other cities. 93745

Lago, Antonio Bernardino Pereira do. 38620-(38621)

Lago de asfalto en la isla de Trinidad. 72783

Lagos, Manoel Ferreira. tr. 67483

Lagrange, -------. 29181, 96355, 1st note after 93861, 106315

Lagrange de Checieux, G. A. F. Simon de. 38622

La Grange, Ga. Southern Female College. see La Grange College, La Grange, Ga.

La Grange College, La Grange, Ga. 38623, 88349

La Grange, Texas. Division No. 48, Sons of Temperance. see Sons of Temperance of North America. Texas. La Grange Division, No. 48.

Lagresse, Juan. defendant 70124

Lagrimas de Aganipe vertidas por la pluma. 94379

Lagrimas de los dos Americas. 74786

Lagrimas gustosas que en las exequias celebradas. (36788)

La Grue, Thomas. tr. 73318

Lagrymas de la paz. 38624, 96273

La Guaira, Venezuela. Junta de Fomento. 38625

Laguna, -------, Conde de Santiago de la. see Santiago de la Laguna, -------, Conde de.

Laguna, Francisco Gonzaelz. 38626

Laguna, Joseph de Rivera Bermudez, Conde de Santiago de la. see Rivera Bermudez. Joseph de, Conde de. Santiago de la Laguna.

Legunas, Juan Baptista de. 38627

Lagunas y Castilla, Pedor Joseph Bravo de. see Bravo de Lagunas y Castilla, Pedro Joseph.

La Harpe, Bernard de. 38631

La Harpe, Jean Francois de, 1739-1803. 8946, 22023, 25853, 38632

Lahetius, Joan. (63711)

La Hontan, N., Baron de. 29142, 38633-38648, 1st note after 38648, 62957, note after 98472

Laical observer. pseud. Impartial review. 93205

Laicus. pseud. Remarks on religious association. 38650

Laicus. pseud. Review of the Rev. William Croswell's letter. (17683)

Laicus. pseud. Sober reply to a mad answer. see Private brother. pseud.

Laicus. pseud. Trial tried. see Warren, Ira. supposed author

Laight, Edward W. 91462

Laing, David, 1793-1878. (38652), 73797, 91853

Laing, John. (38653)

Laird, D. reporter 65627

Laird, Macgregor. 38654

Laird Brothers. firm (5571), 16853

Laisne de Villeveque, ---------. 44062, 44391

Laity of Trinity Church, Boston. see Boston. Trinity Church. Laity.

Laity's directory. 48217, 97963

Laity's directory for the church service. 11521

Lajoie, Antonie Gerin. see Gerin-Lajoie, Antonie, 1824-1882.

Lake, Sir Byby. respondent (69482)

Lake, William. 38655

Lake and river guide. 22662

Lake Champlain and Connecticut River Rail Road . . . remarks. 38656

Lake Clark-Central Kuskokwim Region, Alaska. 83722

Lake commerce. 3848

Lake Erie and Mad-River Railroad Company. Charter. 38658 see also Mad River and Erie Railroad Company.

Lake Erie Female Seminary, Painsville, O. Trustees. 92232

Lake Forest Illinois. Academy. see Lake Forest Academy, Lake Forest, Ill.

Lake Forest Academy, Lake Forest, Ill. 38662

Lake George. 13791

Lake George and Lake Champlain. 38659

Lake George: its scenes and characteristics. 19193

Lake George, Lake Champlain, Montreal and Quebec. 95555

Lake Ontario and Hudson River Railroad.
(38666)
Lake Parima. 77787
Lake Shore; or the slave, the serf and the
apprentice. 38668
Lake Superior. 506
Lake Superior Copper Mining Company.
Trustees. 38674
Lake Superior. Early history, situation,
harbor, etc. 4048, 75246
Lake Superior Iron Company. 38671
Lake Superior Railroad. 20863
Lake View Water-Cure Institution, Rochester,
N. Y. see Rochester Lake View-Cure
Institution.
Lakey, James. 19333
Lakota [sic] A B C wowapi. (71337)
La Lande, J. J. de. 38677
La Leck, L. Th. Grave van Nassau. see
Theodorus, Lodewijk, Grave van Nassau
la Leck.
Lalemant, Charles. 80018
Lallemant, A. J. N. tr. 26742, 31183
Lallemant, Charles, 1587-1674. 13329,
(38679)-(38682), note after 69259, 84484
Lallemant, Friedrich Christian Benedict Ave-.
see Ave-Lallemant, Friedrich
Christian Benedict, 1809-1892.
Lallemant, Jerome, 1593-1673. 38683-38689,
(39956), 39958, (67491), (67495), 67498,
note after 69259, 84484
Lallemant, Robert Christian Berthold Ave-.
see Ave-Lallemant, Robert Christian
Berthold.
Lallement, Guillaume. 38691-38692
Lally-Tolendal, T. G. 38694, 40728
Lalor, John. 38695
LaLource, Jean Charlemagne, d. 1768.
(38696), 47528
La Luzerne, Cesar Henri, Comte de, 1737-
1799. 17168, 21062, 38697-38698,
42751-42753, 75059, 75060, 75081,
88969, note after 93793 see also
France. Legation. United States.
France. Ministre de la Marine.
Lam, Ian Dierckszoon. 38699, 1st note after
100931
La Madelene, Genry de. (38700)
Lamadrid, Gergorio Araoz de. 38701
Lamar, G. B. claimant 1480
Lamar, Lucius Quintus Cincinnatus, 1825-
1893. 38703
Lamar, Mirabeau Buonaparte, Pres. Texas,
1798-1859. 38704-38705, 94989, 95018-
95022, 95024-95027, 95057-95958,
95077, 97675 see also Texas
(Republic) President, 1838-1841 (Lamar)
Lamar y Cortozar, Jose de, 1776-1830.
93812, 99498
Lamarck, Jean Baptiste Pierre Antoine de
Monet de, 1744-1829. 67461
Lamar's address to the Texian troops.
95077
Lamartine, Alphonse Marie Louis de, 1790-
1869. (38706)-38710, 82796, 84915
La Martiniere, Pierre Martin de. 38711-
38716, note after 100855
Lamas, Andres. (20435), (20441), 38717-
38719, (70311)
Lamb, Dana. 38720
Lamb, Edward. 99232
Lamb, E. E. 38721
Lamb, F. 38722
Lamb, J. H. 57074
Lamb, John. (39521)
Lamb, R. 38723-38724

Lamb, Thomas. 62483
Lamb slain, worthy to be praised. 79425
Lambardo, F. M. 38725
Lambert, -------, fl. 1761. 94126
Lambert, Aylmer Bourke, 1761-1842. (38726)-
38728, 66728
Lambert, B. tr. (48704)
Lambert, Claude Francois. (32017), 38729-
38731
Lambert, Edward R. 38732
Lambert, Gillaume, 1818- 38733
Lambert, John. 35222, (38734)
Lambert, J. R. 83175
Lambert, M. (38735) see also France.
Comptroller General.
Lambert, Nathaniel. 38736
Lambert, Thomas R. 38737
Lambert, William. (38738)-38739
Lambertie, Charles de. 38741
Lambertini, Prospero, 1675-1758. see
Benedict XIV, Pope, 1675-1758.
Lambert Lilly. pseud. see Hawks, Francis
Lister.
Lambertius, -------. 76838
Lamberty, L. B. T. de (38742)
Lambly, John. (38744)
Lambrechtsen, N. C. 38745
Lamb's book. note after 101417
Lambton, John George. see Durham, John
George Lambton, 1st Earl of.
Lame, J. S. 38752
Lame Fleury, Jules Raymond, 1797-1878.
24753-24756
Lamego, Manuel Rodriguez. see Rodriguez
Lamego, Manuel.
Lament of Columbus. 34146
Lament of Quinton McKell. 43397
Lament of the Albany Brewers. 19369, note
after 94503
Lament of the Cherokee. 42704
Lamenta la ciudad de Mexico. 48510
Lamentable llanto de la muy noble muy leal
ciudad Mexicana. 67361
Lamentable state of New England. 24734
Lamentacion de puben. 38753
Lamentacion juridica, que la provincia de
Carmelitas Descalzos de Indias hace.
38754
Lamentacion juridica, que la provincia de
Carmelitas Descalzos de S. Alberto de
Indias hace. 75984
Lamentacion juridica, que la provincia de S.
Alberto de Carmelitas Descalzos de
la Nueva Espana hace. (74788)
Lamentation for Gen. Washington. 101773,
101823, 101833
Lamentation for New-England. 8372
Lamentation for the death of Washington.
101773, 101823, 101934
Lamentation of a bad market. 92709
Lamentation of Burgoyne. 63622
Lamentation of Miss *******. 5584
Lamentation of the poor African. 91213
Lamentation on the death of Abraham
Lincoln. (19527)
Lamentations of a sow. 38755
Lamentations of Charles. 68026
Lamentations of General Burgoyne. 9262
Lamentations of her surviving partner in a
poem. 61064, 94817
Lamentations of Jeremiah. 66431, (66433)-
(66436), (66440)-(66441)
Lamentos Americanos. 26511
Lamercier, N. Louis. 38756
Lamiral, Dominique Harcourt, d. 1795. 38762
Lamirande, Ernest Sureau. 38761

Lammens, --------. 34903, 38763, 75005
Lamon, Ward H. 38764
Lamoni gazette. 83302
La Monja Alferez, ---------. 16930
Lamont, Mrs. Eneas. 38765
Lamont, George D. 38766-38676
Lamont, James. (38768)
Lamothe, Guillaume. defendant 38769, 74983
Lampadarius. (46374)
Lampe, Barnet. 102039, 102920
Lampenwarter. 17936
Lampionajo romanzo. (17938)
Lamplighter. 17935
Lamport, William. 38770
Lampredi, --------. 38771
Lampsins, Adrian. 72324
Lampsins, Gelein. 72324
Lampsins, Jean. 72324
Lampter Square, Pa. Anti-masonic Meeting, 1839. see Anti-masonic Party. Pennsylvania. Lancaster County.
Lamson, Alvan. 38772-38776, 39441
Lamson, Alvin. supposed author 19221, 38776, note after 90752
Lamson, David R. (38777)
Lamson, William. (38778)-38780
Lamst, --------. pseud. tr. see Sedillot, L. P. E. A. tr.
Lamy, John Baptist, Abp., 1814-1888. 72968 see also Santa Fe (Archdiocese) Archbishop (Lamy)
Lamzweerde, St. a. 38781
La Nassy, D. de. see Nassy, David de Isaac Cohen.
Lancashire, England. Ministers and Office Bearers. pseud. see Ministers and Office Bearers in the County of Lancaster. pseud.
Lancashire artisan. pseud. Practical guide to emigrants. see Macleod, Malcolm.
Lancaster, Daniel. ed. (38783)-(38784), (55802)
Lancaster, J. 81521
Lancaster, James. 103883
Lancaster, Sir Adam. 66686
Lancaster, Joseph. 38785-38787, 59427
Lancaster, Mass. Church. 95259
Lancaster, Mass. Evangelical Church. 15454
Lancaster, Mass. Industrial School for Girls. see Massachusetts. Industrial School for Girls, Lancaster.
Lancaster, Mass. Library. 38791
Lancaster, Mass. Washington Benevolent Society. see Washington Benevolent Society. Massachusetts. Lancaster.
Lancaster, Ohio. Boys' Industrial School. see Ohio. Boys' Industrial School, Lancaster.
Lancaster, Ohio. Grand Encampment of Greemasons, 1843. see Freemasons. Ohio. Grand Encampment.
Lancaster, Ohio. Reform School. see Ohio. Boys' Industrial School, Lancaster.
Lancaster, Ohio. State Reform Farm. see Ohio. Boys' Industrial School, Lancaster.
Lancaster, Pa. Convention of the Medical Society of Pennsylvania, 1848. see Medical Society of Pennsylvania. Convention, Lancaster, 1848.
Lancaster, Pa. Court. 97700
Lancaster, Pa. Deutschern Hohen Schule. 38795

Lancaster, Pa. Evangelical Lutheran Church of the Holy Trinity. 77477
Lancaster, Pa. Franklin and Marshall College. see Franklin and Marshall College. Lancaster, Pa.
Lancaster, Pa. Indian Conference, 1757. see Pennsylvania (Colony) Indian Conference, Lancaster, 1757.
Lancaster, Pa. Indian Conference, 1762. see Pennsylvania (Colony) Indian Conference, Lancaster, 1762.
Lancaster, Pa. Patriot Daughters. see Patriot Daughters of Lancaster. pseud.
Lancaster, Pa. Presbyterian Church Council, 1764. see Presbyterian Church in the U. S. A. Council, Lancaster, 1764.
Lancaster, Pa. Second Annual Exhibition of the Pennsylvania State Agricultural Society, 1852. see Pennsylvania State Agricultural Society. Exhibition, 2d, Lancaster, 1852.
Lancaster, Pa. State Medical Convention, 1848. see Medical Society of Pennsylvania. Convention, Lancaster, 1848.
Lancaster, Pa. Strasburg Academy. see Strasburg Academy, Lancaster, Pa.
Lancaster, Pa. Temple of Honor, No. 48. see Sons of Temperance of North America. Pennsylvania. Lancaster Temple of Honor, No. 48.
Lancaster, Wisc. Lancaster Institute. see Lancaster Institute, Lancaster, Wisc.
Lancaster County, Pa. Collector of Excise. 38802 see also Graff, George. Hay, William. Turbett, Samuel.
Lancaster County, Pa. Committee of Inspection, Observation and Correspondence. 38793
Lancaster County, Pa. Court. (34042)
Lancaster County, Pa. Court of Common Pleas. 64251, 2d note after 96883
Lancaster County, Pa. Grand Jury. 105608
Lancaster County, Pa. Lieutenant. (37979), (38801) see also Elder, Joshua. Humbley, Adam. Kirkbride, Joseph. Ross, John, fl. 1785.
Lancaster County, Pa. Sheriff. (38798), note after 92058 see also Stone, Frederick.
Lancaster County, Pa. Sub Lieutenant. (37979), (38801) see also Orth, Adam. Smith, Samuel.
Lancaster almanack; for . . . 1776. 38792, 79779
Lancaster & Harrisburg Rail Road. Superintendent. (60190)
Lancaster and Schuylkill Bridge Company. Managers. 38800
Lancaster country business directory. 38797
Lancaster county, to wit: to the electors of the borough and county of Lancaster. (38798), note after 92058
Lancaster gazetteer and express. 76391
Lancaster, Harrisburg, Lebanon, and York directory. (38796)
Lancaster Institute, Lancaster, Wisc. 38804
Lancaster, May 30th, 1799. (59975)
Lancaster Memorial Hall, Boston. see Boston. Lancaster Memorial Hall.
Lancaster pocket almanack, for the year 1778. 79780
Lancaster School, Georgetown, D. C. see Georgetown, D. C. Lancaster School.

Lancaster Temple of Honor, No. 48. see
  Sons of Temperance of North America.
  Pennsylvania. Lancaster Temple of
  Honor, No. 48.
Lance, W., fl. 1857. (38807)
Lance, William. (38805)-38806, 92878
Lancet. 84276
Lanceta. (38808)
Lancey, James de. see De Lancey, James.
Lancey, S. Herbert. 38809
Lancey, William Heathcote de. see De
  Lancey, William Heathcote.
Lanciego, Manuel. ed. 94574
Lanciego y Eguilaz, Joseph de, Abp., d.
  1728. 38810 see also Mexico
  (Archdiocese) Archbishop (Lanciego y
  Eguilaz)
Lancival, Luce de. ed. 72303, 1st note after
  99746
Lanctot, Mederic. 38812
Lancy, James de. see De Lancy, James.
Land, T. 38813
Land and fresh water shells. 32243
Land and fresh-water shells of North
  America. 5502-(5503)
Land & Immigration Association of South
  Carolina. see South Carolina Land
  & Immigration Association.
Land and labor. (38816)
Land birds. 56349
Land certificates, reported as genuine and
  legal. 95045
Land-claim. 3638
Land claims, &c. under Choctaw treaty.
  38815
Land der Zwarten in Hayti. 67535
Land for sale. 102132
Land for the landless. 28995
Land grant investigation. 92948
Land grant of the Northern Pacific R. R.
  Company. 55822
Land in the moon. 98618
Lnad, lake, and river illustrations. 3784,
  note after 104504
Land laws of Pennsylvania. 79214
Land laws of Tennessee. note after 94774
Land laws of the United States. (38817)
Land log book. 32374
Land mourneth. 74739
Land of desolation. 31021
Land of gold. 31272
Land of Powhatan. 38823, 6th note after
  100577
Land of promise to free colored men. 40926
Land of the Aztecs; or, two years in Mexico.
  80162
"Land of the Aztecs," translated from the
  Mexican poet, Heredia. 1063
Land-office . . . communicating the annual
  report. 38818
Land Otuquis in Bolivia. 38319
Land owner. 38822
Land owner's manual. 29732
Land, plantations, stocks and city property.
  88302
Land preeminently blessed. 91153
Land titles in California. 93182
Land titles in San Francisco. 103174
Land travels of Davyd Ingram and others.
  103051
Land und Leute. 77640
Land und Leute, Arbeiter und Arbeiten.
  9321
Land und Leute in Amerika. 28807-28808
Land und Leute in der Alten und Neuen Welt.
  41828

Land und Leute in dern Union. 20669
Land-und Seereisen nach Nordamerika und
  Westindien. 8873
Land und Volk der Vereinigten Staaten. 8871
Land we live in. A delineation by pen and
  pencil. (62692)
Land we live in; or, travels, sketches, and
  adventures. 27872
Land we love. 38821
Landa, --------. 63563
Landa, Ambrosius Cerdan de. (38824)
Landa, Carlos de. 38825
Landa, Diego de, Bp., d. 1579. 7423, 7440
Landa, Esteban de Terralla y. see Terralla
  y Landa, Esteban de.
Landa, Francisco Joseph Diaz de Espada y.
  see Espada y Landa, Francisco Joseph
  Diaz de.
Landa, Juan Jose Diaz de Espada y. see
  Espada y Landa, Juan Jose Diaz de.
Landaff, N. H. Citizens. 52791, note after
  98998
Landais, Peter. 38827-38829
Landaluze, Victor Patricio de. ed. (36901)
Landbouw in de Kolonie Suriname. 94585
Lande, J. J. de la. see La Lande, J. J. de.
Landed credit system. 42947
Landed proprietor. pseud. Reflections on our
  present critical situation. 68695
Landenge Darien, Gujana, Peru, Paraguay und
  Tucuman. 106339
Lander, F. W. 38860, 69900, 69946
Lander, Mrs. F. W. 38831
Lander, M. M. 38832
Lander, S. 38833
Lander, Thomas. 38834
Lander am Uruguay. 37640
Landers, Anthony. 38835
Landfall of Columbus on his first voyage to
  America. 4218
Landholder. pseud. Address to the freemen
  of Rhode Island. see Potter, Elisha R.
Landholder. pseud. Address to the people
  of Rhode Island. see Updike, Wilkins.
  supposed author
Landholder. pseud. Plain statement. see
  Moore, Clement C.
Land-holder's assistant, and land-office guide.
  37745
Landin, S. M. defendant 37740
Landing at Cape Anne. 91853, 95638
Landing of our forefathers. 82808, 97196
Landing of the French Atlantic cable at
  Duxbury. 21493, 38836, 1st note after
  95377
Landis, Charles K. 71294
Landis, Robert W. 38837-(38838)
Landivar, Raphaele. 38839
Landkroom, Gust. 72237
Landman's and seaman's almanac. 90946
Landmark of freedom. 52200, 93663
Landnamabok. 74880
Landolphe, J. F. 38840
Landon, George. 38841
Landon, S. (38842)
Landon, William. defendant 59050, 64283
Landor, H. 38844
Landor, Henry. 38843
Landor, Walter Savage, 1775-1864. 38845,
  (40606)
Landowner. pseud. Demerara after fifteen
  years of freedom. 19469
Landre, Ch. (24937), 2d note after 93879
Landreis van't Prins van Wallis Fort.
  (31184)

Landreise nach den Kusten des Nordpolar-
meeres. 2618
Landres, J.-R. Frey de. see Frey de
Landres, J.-R.
Landreth, C. 38847
Landreth, David. (38846)-38847
Landreth's rural register and almanac 1868.
(38846)
Landrum, John. 50923, 102466
Lands in Illinois to soldiers of the late war.
103346
Lands of the slave and the free. 51497
Lands of the Southern Pacific Railroad
Company of California. 88426
Landscape book. (32740), (38848)
Landscape gardening. (82391)
Landscape painter. pseud. Letters. see
Lanman, Charles.
Landscape, sketches in New-Hampshire.
17353
Landscape views of New England. 50641
Landscapes and popular sketches. 77121
Landschaften. (73934)
Landschaftliche Bilder Brasiliens. 9346
Landschaftsbilder und Skizzen aus dem
Volksleben. (77120)
Landsdown Land Company. 61762
Landseer, John, 1769-1852. illus. 13420
Landsman's log. 83395
Landthom, A. F. tr. 92617
Landtschafft Fetu in Africa. 99534
Landverhuizers naar Texas. 29495
Landverhuizing naar de Vereenigde Staten
van Noord-Amerika. 38849
Landverhuizing, of aarom bevordering wij de
Volksverhuizing. 8746
Lane, --------. defendant 34727
Lane, David M. defendant (38089)
Lane, E. 38851
Lane, E. H. 38852
Lane, Ebenezer, 1793-1866. 84743
Lane, Edward. 38850
Lande, G. C. (38853)
Lane, George. defendant 48191, 84738,
note after 93976
Lane, Henrie. 66686
Lane, Henry Smith, 1811-1881. (38854)
Lane, J. F. W. 101460, note after 101476
Lane, James C. (38855)
Lane, James Henry, 1814-1866. 38856,
89215, 90412
Lane, James Henry, 1814-1866. petitioner
89926
Lane, Jeremiah. 38857
Lane, Joseph, 1801-1881. 38858, 91532
Lane, Lunsford. 38859
Lane, Michael. cartographer 16277, 35953-
35954, 35962, 35966-35968, (40141),
(55557)
Lane, Oliver W. 66444
Lane, Thomas. 95938-95940, 95945
Lane, William C. (38860)
Lane Theological Seminary, Cincinnati.
(13088), 39961
Lane Theological Seminary, Cincinnati.
Students. 38861, note after 90755
Lane Theological Seminary, Cincinnati.
Trustees. 38861
Lane Theological Seminary, its history,
condition, and claims. 38861
La Nevfville, Legeuen de. (38862)
La Neuville, N. J. 38863
Lang, Brigitte. tr. 86492
Lang, Carl. 38864
Lang, John. ed. and publisher (22678),
(32961), 105152

Lang, John Dunmore. 38865-38868, 3d note
after 94534
Lang, William Bailey. 38869
Langdon, Chauncy. 38870
Langdon, John, 1741-1819. (38871A), 52897,
52932 see also New Hampshire.
Governor, 1809-1811 (Langdon)
Langdon, John, fl. 1840. 38871
Langdon, Mary. pseud. Ida May. see Pike,
Mary H.
Langdon, Samuel, 1723-1797. 7244, 38872-
38875, 76339, 95642
Langdon, Timothy. 38876
Langdon (John) and Son. firm publishers
54459
Lange, ------ Godard. see Godard-Lange,
--------.
Lange, -------- Janet. see Janet-Lange,
--------.
Lange, Henry. cartographer 7394
Lange, Johan Martin Christian, 1818-1898.
71433-71435
Lange, Johann Elias. ed. 7707
Lange, Max. (38877)
Lange, Olao. tr. 22036
Lange syne or the wards of Mount Vernon.
83567
Langeac, N. de l'Espinasse, Chevalier de.
see Espinasse, N. de l', Chevalier de
Langeac.
Langen, J. G. 31365, (31367)
Langenes, Barent. (9839), 38880-38881, 95757,
note after 100632
Langevin, E. 38882
Langevin, Hector L. 38883
Langevin, Jean. 38884-38885
Langford, John. of Montreal 38887-(38888),
92940
Langford, John, fl. 1655. 38886, 92940
Langford, John Alfred. 38889
Langford, Jonas. (38890)
Langford, W. 38891
Langford & Chase. firm (30910), 38892,
72400
Langh-verwachten donder-slach. 39241, 97530
Langley, Henry G. 9980, 38893, 58079, 76092
Langley, John. 38894
Langley, Samuel Pierpont, 1834-1906. 84986,
84988, 84990, 85072, 85097
Langley Aerodynamical Laboratory. Advisory
Committee. see Smithsonian Institution.
Advisory Committee on the Langley
Aerodynamical Laboratory.
Langley memoir on mechanical flight. 85072
Langlois, Jean Thomas. 25674, (29042)
Langlois, Victor. 66508
Langman, Christopher. 19029, 3d note after
97085
Langren, -------. cartographer 41363
Langres, Bruno de. see De Langres, Bruno.
Langsdorff, Georg Heinrich von. (38895)-38898
Langstaff, Launcelot. pseud. Book of vagaries.
see Paulding, James Kirke, 1778-1860.
Langstedt, F. L. (38899)
Langston, Lawrence. pseud. Bastiles of the
North. see Sangston, Lawrence. and
Johnson, Reverdy, 1796-1876. incorrectly
supposed author
Langton, John, 1808-1894. 38901, (74581),
74583
Language of a soul taken in the nets of salva-
tion. 46429
Language of affliction. 64236
Language of divine providence in death. 72710
Language of the Dakota or Sioux Indians. 72586
Language of the Indians. 21383

Language of the Yncas of Peru. 44612
Languages of the American Indians. 2251
Langworth, Henry H. (72343) see also Rochester, N. Y. Health Officer.
Langworthy, Asahel. supposed author 36275
Langworthy, Edward. 38902-38903
Langworthy, Franklin. (38904)
Langworthy, Isaac P. 38905
Langworthy, J. P. 45890
Langworthy, Lucius H. 38906
Langworthy, William A. 94516
Lanier, J. F. D. 24345, (38907)
Lanigan, G. F. 38908
Lanini, -------. 50618
Lanjuinais, J. D., Comte. 7980, 38909-38911
Lanman, Charles. 6142, (38912)-38922, 38924-38926, 60930
Lanman, Charles. incorrectly supposed author 38923, note after 95662
Lanman, James. 38927
Lanman, James H. 38928-38929
Lann, Adolph. 38930
Lanoye, Ferdinand Tugnot de. see Tugnot de Lanoye, Ferdinand, 1810-1870.
Lanphear, Orpheus T. complainant 85212
Lans, W. H. (38932)-38934
Lans, W. H. supposed author 22396, 2d note after 93855
Lansberge, Henrique van. 38935
Lansdowne, Henry Petty-Fitzmaurice, 3d Marquis of, 1780-1863. 38936
Lansdowne, William Petty-Fitzmaurice, 1st Marquis of, 1737-1805. (15052), 50567, 56933, 80111
Lansegue, ------ de. see De Lansegue, ----------.
Lansing, -------. defendant 41637-41638
Lansing, -------. illus. 79099
Lansing, Abraham. 38937
Lansing, Dirck Cornelius, 1785-1857. 38938-38939
Lansing, John, 1754-1829. 41638, 78749, note after 106002 see also New York (State) Chancellor.
Lansing, R. R. 38940
Lansing, W. E. 38941
Lansing, Mich. Industrial School for Boys. see Michigan. Industrial School for Boys, Lansing.
Lansing, Mich. Michigan Female College. see Michigan Female College, Lansing, Mich.
Lansing, Mich. Michigan Female Seminary. see Michigan Female College, Lansing, Mich.
Lansing, Mich. State Library. see Michigan, State Library, Lansing.
Lansing, Mich. State Reform School. see Michigan. Industrial School for Boys, Lansing.
Lanson, --------. 38943
Lant (J. H.) & Co. firm publishers 22190, (54905)
Lantern. 38944
Lanterne magique of toverlantaern. 38945
Lanus, Anacarsis. 38946
Lanus, Corry O'. pseud. Corry O'Lanus: his views and experiences. see Stanton, John.
Lanusse, Armand. 38947
Lanuza, V. Blasco de. 38949
Lanz, -------. 38948
Lanz, J. B. 56747
Lanzerota, -------. 26875
Lanzi, Luiz. (38950)

Lanzol y Borja, Rodrigo. see Alexander VI, Pope, 1431?-1503.
Laon, Jean de, sieur d'Aigremont. 38951
Laosipas, Ulises. 38952
Laoureim, ------- Guinan. see Guinan-Laoureim, --------.
Lapa, Ludgero da Rocha Ferreira. 38953
La Paz, Juan Bautista Orendayn, Marques de see Orenday, Juan Bautista, Marques de la Paz.
La Paz, Mexico. 48298
La Paz, Mexico. Aduana Maritima. 48298
La Paz (Diocese) Bishop (Mata) (55248), 89107 see also Mata, Nicolas Vrbano, Bp.
La Paz (Diocese) Bishop (Rodriguez Delgado) 16070 see also Rodriguez Delgado, Augustin, Bp.
La Paz (Diocese) Bishop (Valencia) 16066, 98346 see also Valencia, Pedro de, Bp.
La Paz (Diocese) Bishop (Vega) 98742 see also Vega, Feliciano de la, Bp.
La Paz (Diocese) Synod, 1619. 16066, 98346
La Paz (Diocese) Synod, 1620. 16066, 98346
La Paz (Diocese) Synod, 1638. 98742
La Paz (Diocese) Synod, 1738. 16070, 72539
La Parra, Jacinto de. see Parra, Jacinto de la.
Lapelin, ------- de. 68380
La Pena, D. M. de. 38956
La Pena, F. Javier de. see Pena, Francisco Javier de la.
La Pena y Pena, Manuel de. see Pena y Pena, Manuel de la.
La Perouse, Jean Francois de Galaup, Comte de, 1743-1788. 21211-21215, 3118I, 38958-38969, 56064, (59572), 98444, note after 99740, 100855
Laperriere, -------. 39985, note after 94187
La Peyrere, Isaac de, 1594-1676. 4865, 4935-4936, 13015, 14374, 25997, 38970-38975, note after 69262, note after 100853, note after 100854, 100855
La Peyrouse: a comedy. 38280
Lapham, Increase A. 39876-38979, 85072
Lapham Institute, North Scituate, R. I. 38980, 85098
Lapi, Michel Angelo. 38981
Lapidary character. 60605, 78475, 104455
Lapie, Pierre. 38982
Lapis e monte excisus. (46531), note after 92154
Laplace, --------. tr. 4373
Laplace, Cyrille Pierre Theodore. 21211-21215, 38983-38985
Laplace, Pierre Simon, Marquis de, 1749-1827. 7000
Laplante, Eduardo. illus. 17782
La Plata (Archdiocese) Archbishop (Moxo) 51215-51217 see also Moxo, Bentio Maria de, Abp.
La Plata (Archdiocese) Archbishop (San Alberto) 669-670, 75971-75979 see also San Alberto, Joseph Antonio de, Abp.
La Plata, Brazil, and Paraguay, during the present war. 37390
La Plata, the Argentine Confederation, and Paraguay. 58161
La Poepe, Claude de. 39005-(39006)
La Poix de Freminville's voyage to the North Pole. 43396
La Poix Ferminville, M. J. de. 39007, 43396, 62509
La Popeliniere, Lancelot Voisin, Sieur de, 1541-1608. 39008, 47888

Laporte, Joseph de, 1713-1779. 19359-19361, (20544), 23580, (68417), 99403, 3d note after 100846

La Porte, Lucas de. see Porte, Lucas de la.

Laporte, Ind. Medical College. see Indiana. Medical College, Laporte.

Laporte city directory for 1867-8. 39009

La Potherie, ------ de Bacqueville de. see Bacqueville de la Potherie, -------- de.

Laprade, Victor de. 39010

Laprado, A. E. 39011

Lapsley, --------. plaintiff 5161

Lapsley, J. W. 39012

Lapsley vs. Brashear. 5161

Lapuente, Laurindo. 39013

La Pylaie, A. J. M. Bachelot de. see Bachelot de la Pylaie, A. J. M.

Lara, ------- Leon de. see Leon de Lara, -------.

Lara, Alon. Perez de. see Perez de Lara, Alon.

Lara, Francisca. defendant 96209

Lara, J. M. Beristain de Souza Fernandez de. see Beristain de Souza, Jose Mariano, 1756-1817.

Lara, Jacob, de. complainant. 47349

Lara, Jos. Fernandez de. defendant 34710, 1st note after 99650

Lara, Joseph M. de. 39015

Lara, Juan Jose Fernandez de. 39016

Lara, Mariano Aniceto de. 39017

Lara Fernandez, Antonio Ferreira de. see Fernandez, Antonio Ferreira de Lara.

Lara Galan, Joseph de. (39014)

Lara y Consortes, Jose Fernandez de. see Fernandez de Lara y Consortes, Jose.

Larchevesque-Thibaud, -------. 39018-39020

Larcom, Henry. 39021

Larcom, Lucy. ed. 52305, 57942, 76692

Lard, Rebecca (Hammond) 38521, 39022

Lardier, J. A. 38585, 100810-100811

Lardner, Dionysius, 1793-1859. 16367, 21287, 24087, 39023

Lardomens och forbundets bok. 83229

Larea, Bernardo de. 39024

La Reintrie, Henry Ray de. petitioner 39026

La Renaudiere, Philippe Francois de, 1781-1845. 10296, 10299, 36434, (39027)-39030, 100990 see also Societe de Geographie, Paris. Commission Speciale.

La Reynie de la Bruyere, J.-B.-M.-L. 68085

Large, Joseph-Adrien le, Abbe de Lignac. see Lignac, Joseph-Adrien le Large, Abbe de.

Large . . . account of him [i. e. Thomas Symmes.] 8506

Large additions to Common sense. 85212-(85214), 95718

Large appendix. 101063

Large collection of celebrated psalm and hymn tunes. 94015-94016

Large collection of psalm tunes. 94014

Large collection of songs, epilogues, &c. 25798, (45498), note after 45694

Large dictionary. (79616)

Large extract from a pamphlet. (4686), (4687)

Large family Bible. 95412

Large letter from the Rev. Mr. Jonathan Edwards. 104399

Large-paper edition. American statesmen. 84335

Large postscript, occasioned by the reading of these letters. 83439, note after 103623

Larger [and shorter] catechism. 39031

Larger catechism. 15445, 80715, 80720

[Larger] catechism, agreed upon the the Assembly of Divines. 39032

Larger catechism; as received by the Associate Reformed Church. 65170

Larger catechism formed by the Westchester Associated Presbytery. note after 65546

Largest liberty defined. 74534

Laribas, Juan. plaintiff 57674, 74858

Larimer, Sarah L. (39033)

Larimore, J. W. 39034

Larios, Hieronymo. 39035

Larivas, Juan. see Laribas, Juan.

La Rivas, Manuel Joseph de. 39036

Larke, Julian K. 39037-(39038)

Larkin, Samuel. 39040

Larkin (E. & S.) firm 39039

Larkin & Belden. firm publishers 76092

Larkins, William George. 2648

Larned, E. C. (39041)

Larned, Edward C. reporter (27983), (27985)

Larned, Edwin C. (39041)

Larned, Josephus Nelson, 1836-1913. 84701, 84861, 85151

Larned, Mrs. L. 39042

Larned, Sylvester. 29302

Larned, W. A. 105417

La Rocha, P. F. see Rocha, Pedro Francisco de la.

La Roche, -------. see Roche, ------- de.

La Roche, A. 39044

Laroche, A. J. M., 1797-1852. 13475, 16482, 16496, 16511, 39045, 44942-44943

Laroche, Pierre Marie Sebastien Catineau. see Catineau Laroche, Pierre Marie Sebastien.

La Roche, R. 39047-39048

La Roche, Sophie von. supposed author 10309, note after 100811

La Roche Gallichon, F. C. de. (39050)

Laroche-Heron, Henri de Courcy de. see Courcy de Laroche-Heron, Henri de.

La Rochefoucauld, Francois, duc de. see Rochefoucauld, Francois, Duc de la, 1613-1680.

La Rochefoucauld-Liancourt, Francois Alexandre Frederic, Duc de, 1737-1827. 25573, 39051-39058, 46984, 50576-50577, 56609, (62074), (81136), 85205, 85295, 90235, 102540, 102542

La Rochefoucauld-Liancourt, Francois Alexandre Frederic, Duc de, 1747-1827 supposed tr. 16118-16119, 100342

La Rocque, ------- de. see 39060, 73148

La Rocque, C. 39050

La Roque, ------- de. see La Rocque, ------ de.

La Roquette, Jean Baptiste Marie Alexandre Dezos de, 1784-1868. 26330, 33709, 39061-(39062), 52105, (73151)

La Rosa, Hipolito Buena de. 39063

La Rosa, Luis de. see Rosa, Luis de la.

La Rosa, Manuel de. see Rosa, Manuel de la.

La Rosa Toro, Agustin de. 39066-(39067)

Larpent, Sir George. 39068

Larra, Victor. pseud. Echos democraticos. see Souza Pinto, Antonio de, 1843-

Larrabee, Charles. 39069-(39070)

Larrabee, William C. 39071-39073

Larragoiti, J. N. 39074

Larrainzar, Federico. 39075

Larrainzar, Manuel. 20101, (39076)-(39080), 48436
Larranaga, B. J. de. (39084)
Larranaga, Bruno Francisco. 39082-(39083)
Larraz, Pedro Cortes y. see Cortes y Larraz, Pedro, Abp.
Larrazabal, Antonio. (39085)-(39086)
Larrazabal, Antonio de. (34838)
Larrazabal, Felipe. 6186, 14578, 39087-39090, note after 39187
Larrea del de Alcantara, Juan de. respondent 87160
Larreategui, Joseph Dionisio. 38678, 39091-39092
Larreategui, Mariano Colon de. 14658
Larrey, P. J. de. (39093)
Larreynaga, Miguel. 39094
Larrian, Jose Toribio. defendant 26208
Larrinaga, Jose Pastor. 39096, 58388
Larriva, Jose Loay de. 39097-39098
Larriva y Ruiz, J. J. 39099
Larroque, Luis. 39100
Larroque, Patrice. 39101
Larrosa, G. A. tr. 92419
Larroya, Pedro Sabau y. see Sabau y Larroya, Pedro.
Larry, the army dog robber. 29482
Larsen, Juan Mariano. (39102)
Lartigue, J. J. (39105)-39106
Lartigue, Joseph, 1791-1876. 26558, (39103)-39104
Larue, -------, Chevalier de, fl. 1821. (39107)
La Rue, F. A. H. 10455, (12573), 39108, (41510)
Lary, J. Lucie-. see Lucie-Lary, J.
Larzelere, Jacob. (39109)
Lasaga, Juan Lucas de. 98815
La Salle, A. de. 39111, 98298
La Salle, Adrien Nicolas. 39112, 4th note after 94174
La Salle, Antoine de. 39110
La Salle, Robert Cavelier, Sieur de, 1643-1687. 23726, 25853, 76838, (80023), 96172
La Salle de l'Estang, Simon Philibert de, d. 1765. supposed author 1st note after (74627), (77219)-77220
La Salle documents and other contemporaneous papers. (80023)
Lascallier, D. tr. 5909
Lascaris, Janus. 25088
Las Casas. pseud. Charleston courier and the slave trade. 81926
Las Casas, Balthazar de. see Casas, Bartholome de las, Bp. of Chiapa, 1474-1566.
Las Cases, Emmanuel Dieudonne Marie Joseph, Comte de. (39124)-39125, 40161
Lascaux, Paul de. 39126
Lascelles, Arthur R. W. 39127
Lasell Female Seminary, Auburndale, Mass. (39128)
Lash. 93999
Lash for petty tyrants. (39130)
Las Nieves Robledo, Maria de. see Robledo, Maria de las Nieves.
Laso, Alonso Carrillo y. see Carrillo y Laso, Alonso.
Laso, B. 39131
Laso de la Vega, Alonso Carrillo. see Carrillo Laso de la Vega, Alonso.
Laso de la Vega, Antonio de Cordova. plaintiff 16776, 39132

Lasor a Varea, Alphonso. 39133, 2d note after 98594
Las Plazas, Ramon Casaus Torres y. see Casaus Torres y Las Plazas, Ramon.
Lassaga, Juan Lucas de. petitioner 39135, 42724, note after 98814
Lasselle, Mrs. N. P. 39136
Lassepas, U. S. 39137
Lasserra, Inigo Abad y. see Abad y Lasserra, Inigo.
Lasso de la Vega, Antonio de Cordova. see Laso de la Vega, Antonio de Cordova.
Lasso de la Vega, Gabriel. 39138-39140
Lasso de la Vega, Luis. 39141, note after 98362
Last address of Winslow Russell. 74410
Last address, to his beloved countrymen. (43681)
Last agony of the great bore. 5537
Last appeal. 39142
Last appeal to the congregation of St. Mary's Church. (62214)
Last appeal to the "Market Street Presbyterian Church and congregation." 43005
Last appeal to the stockholders. 10889
Last campaign of the Twenty-Second Regiment. 39143
Last canto of Childe Harold's pilgramage. 84915
Last confederate cruiser. (33842)
Last confession and dying speech of Peter Porcupine. 14027
Last confession made by a young woman. 46588
Last days and happy death of Fannie Kenyon. 91936
Last day's debate on the tariff. 39144, 88065
Last days of Gordon. 27986
Last days of Lee and his paladins. 16318
Last days of the American republic. 34966
Last days of the Goth. 81204
Last days of the 69th in Virginia. 47248
Last discourse of the late Mr. Dickinson. 4095
Last East-Indian voyage. (39146)
Last editorial in the Knoxville whig. 8704
Last enemy destroyed. 47000
Last general court of the South-Sea Company. 88184
Last farewell to the world. 98056
Last joint debate. 20692
Last kick of anti-masonry. 93282
Last king of the Lenape. 31438, 94196
Last leaf from Sunny Side. (61373)
Last lecture. 104654
Last legacy, and useful family guide. 104250, 104252, 104254
Last legacy, or the useful family herb bill. 104251
Last legacy, or the useful family herbal. 104253
Last legacy to the people of the United States. 104249
Last letter. 88669
Last letter of Mr. Buchanan. 8862
Last Lexington speech. 13540
Last look at the United States. 57164
Last man. 83788
Last men of the revolution. 31871
Last message [of President Jackson.] 69479, 6th note after 88114
Last news from Philadelphia. 103386
Laste newes from Virginia. 100483

Last night an express arrived from
Philadelphia. 100012
Last night of Pompeii. 23695
Last night of the session of the Assembly.
10018
Last ninety days of the war. 89309
Last-novelties. 21983
Last of his race. 65253
Last of the aborigines. 102250
Last of the Arctic voyages. 4389
Last of the Aztecs. 46908
Last of the Dinsmores. 104176
Last of the Fillibusters. 91711
Last of the foresters. 16323
Last of the Lenape. 35762
Last of the Mohicans. 16430, 16452, 16460
Last of the Ramapaughs. 82506
Last of the Washingtons. (41399)
Last official address. 101533, 101543
Last official report of Sir J. P. Grant.
35605
Last political writings of Gen. Nathaniel
Lyon. 42864
Last rambles amongst the Indians. 11540
Last report of the English wars. 61195
Last report of the Trustees. 45648
Last respects of George Washington. 33134
Last sermon [by Joseph Smith.] 83254
Last sermon [by Nehemiah Walter.] 101171
Last sermon, delivered at the April Con-
ference, 1844. 83288
Last sermon in the Old Meetinghouse at
West Springfield. 39199
Last sermon preached by Mr. Lunt. (71772)
Last sermon preached in First Church,
Chauncy Street. 22325
Last sermon preached in the Ancient Meeting
House. 37752
Last sermon . . . to the First Congregational
Church. 82240
Last sermon written . . . by Mr. Sears.
71789
Last servant of Jesus Christ. pseud.
Summary, or general arguments of the
late manifesto. 93605
Last seven years of the life of Henry Clay.
14776
Last shepherd. 68185
Last signs. 26076
Last solemn scene! (51518)
Last spark of freedom. 91815
Last speech and confession of Henry Halbert.
29602
Last speech & dying words of William
Welch. 102526
Last speech and repentance of Lieutenant
Richard Smith. 83762
Last speech, confession and dying words of
John Smith. 82874-82876
Last speech on Congress. 101598
Last speech in Parliament. 63068
Last summons. 84626
Last three speeches on Kansas and freedom.
93664, 93684
Last times and the great consummation.
78940
Last tribute to the merits of a deceased
author. 98911
Last trumpet. 66774
Last vacation. 88486
Last wigwam of the Pawnees. 6307
Last will and testament, and obituary notice
of Edward E. Powers. 64786
Last will and testament and three codicils
of Henry Parish. 58610

Last will and testament of Captain John Smith.
19051, 82831
Last will and testament [of George Washington.]
36361, note after 101900
Last will and testament of Gen. George
Washington. 101754, 101762, 101899
Last will & testament, of General George
Washington. 101764
Last will and testament of General George
Washington. With a schedule of his
property directed to be sold. 101760
Last will and testament of John McDonogh.
43175
Last will and testament of Miss Sophia Smith.
84242
Last will and testament of Oliver Smith. 83687
Last will and testament [of Peter Porcupine.]
14007
Last will and testament of Springfield
Presbytery. (43605), 43606, (52324),
56493, 89893, 92031
Last will and testament, of the late Rever-
end and Renowned George Whitefield.
103552
Last will and testament of the late Rev.
George Whitefield. 103600
Last will and testament of the late Reverend
Mr. George Whitefield. 103523
Last will and testament of the late Robert
Richard Randall. 67798, 74977
Last will and testament of the Rev. Mr.
Whitefield. 103553
Last will and testament of William Turpin.
(39145), 97500
Last will [of Andrew Jackson.] 21445
Last words and dying confession of William
Gross. (28941)
Last words, and dying speech of Elisha
Thomas. 95388
Last words and dying speech of James Buchanan.
105350A
Last words and dying speech of Levi Ames.
1307
Last words and dying speech of Robert
Young. 106092, 106093
Last words and dying speech of Samuel Smith.
83985
Last words [of Ebenezer Mason.] 45432
Last words of grand father's chair. 30991
Last words of the purest patriot. 100668
Last words of William Huggins and John
Mansfield. 105354
Last writing: of Marion Ira Stout. 92358
Last year of the war. 63864
Lastarria, Jose Victorino. 39147-39151,
76857
Lasteirie, C. P. 39152
Lasteyrie, Ferdinand, Comte de. 39153
Lastra, Jose de la. 71638
Lastri, Marco. (24396), (39154)
Late acting president. (69707)
Late address of a faction there. 46756, 2d
note after 99797
Late address of Governor Hamilton. 66067,
88068
Late American statesman. pseud. Weakness
and inefficiency of the government. see
Mercer, Charles Fenton.
Late American war. 10935
Late and further manifestation of the progress
of the Gospel. 22162
Late and true relation of the calamities.
(42761), 96156

Late association for defence, encourag'd. 82872-82873, 94694

Late association for defence farther encouraged. 94695

Late association for defence, further encourag'd. 94696

Late attack upon the navy. 37451, 98425

Late authentic account of the death of Miss Jane M'Crea. 11304

Late author. pseud. Account of the conduct of the war in the Middle Colonies. see Galloway, Joseph, 1729?-1803. and Wesley, John, 1703-1791.

Late author. pseud. Account of the rise and Progress of the American war. see Wesley, John, 1703-1791.

Late celebrated author. pseud. Short extract. 100868

Late Charleston Union Presbytery. 85298, 85331

Late contemplated insurrection in Charleston, S. C. 12054, 82003

Late declaration and remonstrance. 60057, 64448

Late defamatory publication by the Rev. Wm. White. 96318

Late detestation shewn by the friends of liberty in this city. 95987

Late dialogue. 32955

Late discovery of a fourth island in Terra Australis, Incognita. 35255, 82181-82183

Late discovery of a fourth island near Terra Australis, Incognita. 82184

Late eminent writer. pseud. Discourse on the English constitution. 20243

Late famous protest. 7918

Late General Stephen Elliott. 96788

Late government there. 46731-46732, 58359, (65323), note after 70346, 92350

Late judge. pseud. Letter. see Yeates, Sir Joseph. supposed author

Late King of Spain's will. 39155

Late lieutenant. pseud. Glance at the reorganization. (52125)

Late Lord Mayor of London. pseud. Present for an apprentice. 65310

Late Maryland convention. 45180

Late member. pseud. Oaths, signs, ceremonies and objects. 38343

Late member of Congress. pseud. ed. Life and opinions of Julius Melbourn. see Hammond, Jabez D.

Late member of the Continental Congress. pseud. True merits of a late treatise. 97127

Late member of the craft. pseud. Revelations in masonry. 70161

Late member of the General Court. pseud. National arithmetick. see Swan, James.

Late member of the same. pseud. Address to the Baptist Church in Middletown, Vt. see White, Timothy.

Late member . . . who rejected the said constitution. pseud. Remarks on the constitution. 69449

Late memoir of Sebastian Cabot. 97657

Late memorable providences relating to witchcrafts and possessions. 46375

Late merchant. pseud. Perils of Pearl Street. see Greene, Asa.

Late message of the President of the United States. 66067, 88068

Late military revolution in Buenos Ayres. 50613

Late Moses Brown Ives. 35313

Late occurrences in North America. 39156

Late officer in the United States Army. pseud. Topographical description. see Cutler, Jervase.

Late official address of George Washington. 65343, 101873

Late pastoral letter of the Synod of Philadelphia. (62367), note after 99808

Late patriot prisoner in Canada. pseud. Loose leaves. see Sutherland, Thomas Jefferson.

Late persecution of the Church of Jesus Chirst. (64967)

Late pious author. pseud. Some serious and awful considerations. see Benezet, Anthony. supposed author

Late proceedings in St. Peter's Parish, Salem. 75667

Late proceedings of the Grand Lodge of South-Carolina. 87846

Late regulations respecting the British colonies. (20043)

Late religious commotions in New-England considered. 12316, (21935), 67786

Late resident. pseud. Canadas as they now are. 10390

Late resident. pseud. Sketch of the state of affairs in Newfoundland. (81637)

Late resident of that colony. pseud. Information to emigrants. 34706

Late retailer. pseud. Peep into Catharine Street. 59529

Late Samuel Flewwelling. 73977

Late Samuel Ward. 37785

Late sermon on the death fo Rev. Samuel Moodey. 50303

Late sermon on the death of the Reverend Mr. Joseph Emerson. (22444)

Late smiles of providence represented. 47138

Late staff officer. pseud. War in Florida. see Potter, Woodburn.

Late stipendiary magistrate in Jamaica. pseud. Introduction and concluding remarks. see. Bourne, Stephen.

Late surgeon. pseud. Essay on the bilious or yellow fever. see Blicke, Charles.

Late Theodore Parker. (3536)

Late treaty between the United States and Great Britain. (17531), 2d note after 99216

Late trials at Canandaigua. 50684

Late Under Secretary of State. pseud. Considerations on the present state of the nation. see Knox, William, 1732-1810.

Late Under Secretary of State. pseud. Extra official state papers. see Knox, William, 1732-1810.

Late voyage of Captain Sir John Ross. 33626

Late war between the United States and Great Britain. 33854-33855

Late war with Mexico. 11517

Late worthy old Lyon. 90141

Later facts about the famine. 88347

Later poems. 83601

Later years. 65544

Laternenmann. 17936

Laternenwarter. 17936

La Terriere, Pierre de Salles. 39157

Lates, Bonet de. see Bonet, de Lates, 16th cent.

Latest form of infidelity. 71518-71519, 71521

"Latest form of infidelity," examined. 71521
Latest news from three worlds. 92786
Latham, A. (39158), 90780
Latham, Allen. 100521
Latham, George Robert, 1832-1917. 39159
Latham, Henry, 1794-1866. 39160-39161
Latham, Marcus. (39162)
Latham, Milton Slocumb, 1827-1882. (39163)
Latham, Robert Gordon, 1812-1888. 39164-39167, (62550)
Latham, Wilfred. 39168
Latham prize poems. (65399)
Latham's Mission on Fort Hill, Boston. see Boston. Marcus Latham's Mission on Fort Hill.
Lathrop, A. C. 39169
Lathrop, Charles C. (39170)
Lathrop, D. W. 39171-39172
Lathrop, David. 39173
Lathrop, E. 39174
Lathrop, Edward. 90117
Lathrop, George. defendant (39175)
Lathrop, Horace. 34025, 39176
Lathrop, John, 1740-1816. 2632, 6517, 15043, 20238, 39177-39187, 89700, 93232, 101866, note after 102250, 103830, 104056
Lathrop, John, 1772-1820. (39188)-39190, 55304
Lathrop, John H. 34518, 39191-(39192) see also Indiana. University. President.
Lathrop, Joseph. 7655, 39193-39200
Lathrop, L. E. 39201
Lathrop, Noah. 39202
Lathrop, S. K. 39203
Lathrop, Samuel. 45832
Lathrop family tree. 39204
Latimer, Miss E. 21607, 39205
Latimer, George. 84621
Latimer, George. petitioner 39206
Latimer, L. D. 88914
Latimer, W. K. defendant at court of inquiry (36269), (39207)
Latin accidence. 12392
Latin elegy upon John Hull. 104086
Latin grammar. By John Read. 68159, 73398-73400
Latin grammar. [By Whittenhall.] 91385
Latin grammar for the use of the University and Academy of Pennsylvania. (39209)
Latin grammar, lately printed by Andrew Stewart. 22785
Latin preface. 46532
Latin school. 41487
Latine letter. (56742)
La Tombe, Joseph de. see Letombe, Joseph.
Lato-Monte, Ludovici de. 39210-(39211)
Latopoia. Chickasaw Indian Chief 96601
La Torre, Gonzalo Cayetano de. see Torre, Gonzalo Cayetano de la.
La Torre, Jose Maria de. see Torre, Jose Maria de la.
La Torre, Luis de. see Torre, Luis de la.
La Torre, Manual de. see Torre, Manuel de la.
La Torre, Miguel de. see Torre, Miguel de la.
La Torre, Pedro de. see Torre, Pedro de la.
La Torre, Pedro Jose Bermudez de. see Bermudez de la Torre, Pedro Jose.
La Torre Lloreda, Manuel de. see Torre Lloreda, Manuel de la.

La Torre Miranda, Antonio de. see Torre Miranda, Antonio de la.
Latouanne, -------, Vicomte de. 6874
Latour, Arsenio Lacarrier. (39214)-39215
La Tour, Bertrand de. 39216
Latour, L. A. Huguet. 39217, 50239
Latour Dufay, L. Pierre Dufay de. see Dufay de Latour Dufay, L. Pierre, Marquis.
La Tourette, James. 39218
Latrappe, ------. tr. 82264
Latreiche, Antoinette Francoise Anne Symon de. see Drohajowska, Antoinette Francoise Anne Symon de Latreiche, Comtesse.
Latreille, --------. 21210
La Trobe, Benjamin, 1725-1786. 17411, 88828, 93385, 1st note after 97862
Latrobe, Benjamin Henry, 1764-1820. 2992, 12494, (19418), 27463, 38118, 39219-(39220), 60046, 60451, 62116, 63126, 84647, 84648, 86005, 95648, 104587 see also Baltimore and Ohio Railroad Company. Chief Engineer. Pittsburgh and Connellsville Railraod Company. President. Washington, D. C. Surveyor of Public Buildings.
Latrobe, Charles Joseph, 1801-1875, (39221)-39222, 55362
Latrobe, Christian Ignatius, 1778-1836. (42110), 97849 see also United Brethren. Great Britain. Secretary.
Latrobe, John Hazlehurst Boneval, 1803-1891. 39223-39226, (45211A), 91673, 94472, 1st note after 95737
La Trobe, P. ed. 88932
Latson, John W. defendant (15879)
Latta, John E. 39227, 98979
Latta, S. A. 39228
Latter-day glory of the Church. 94666
Latter-day judgments. 89369
Latter day luminary. 39229
Latter Day Saints. see Church of Jesus Christ of the Latter Day Saints.
Latter day saints. 83289
Latter-day saints. A contemporary history. 47126, 83279, 85168
Latter day saints: a short history of this sect. 25907
Latter-day saints emigrants' guide. 13680
Ladder-day saints in Utah. 70913, 85563
Latter-day saints' messenger and advocate. 50743, 83289
Latter day saints' millennial star. 39230, 50744, 82989, 83163, 83245-83246, 83258, 83283, 83496, 83937
Latter-day saints. With memoirs of the life and death of Joseph Smith. 47126, 83279, 85168
Latter days' intelligence. 82972
Latter part of the charge. 61763
Latter sign discoursed of. 46696-(46697)
Lattre, Ph.-Albert de. (39231)
Lauanha, Jo. Bap. 38232
Laubyan y Vieyra, E. R. del Rio. (39233)
Laudatio fvnebris. Ad regias. 98122
Laudatio funebris Ferdinandi VI. 38624, 96273
Laudatio funebris Elisabethae Farnesiae. (64336)
Laudatio funebris, pro-regis. (39233)
Laudatory verses. 27752
Laudonniere, H. (8784)
Laudonniere, Rene Goulaine de. 24902, (25854), 39234-39236, note before 99284

Laudun, ------- Vallette de. see Vallette
 de Laudun, ----------.
Laugel, Auguste. 39237-39240
Laugh of a layman. 71135
Laugh with the ladies. (13435)
Laughable poem. (35894)
Laughan, ------. (39242)-39243, 41790
Laughlin, J. L. ed. 82304
Laughton, J. K. 101175
Laugier, --------. tr. 1639, 100803
Laujon, A. de. 39244
Laujon, A. P. M. 39245
L'Aulne, Anne Robert Jacques, Turgot, Baron
 de. see Turgot, Anne Robert Jacques,
 Baron de l'Aulne, 1727-1781.
Launay, Jules Henri Robert Belin de. see
 Belin de Launay, Jules Henri Robert,
 1814-1883.
L'Aunay, Mosneron de. 39247
Launay de Valery, Cordier de. 39246
Launcelot Langstaff. pseud. see Paulding,
 James K.
Laune, Thomas de. see De Laune, Thomas,
 d. 1685.
Laura. pseud. see Ferguson, Elizabeth
 (Graeme)
Laura, Miseno de. 39250
Laura A. W. Spear & Antoinette A. Spear,
 by W. G. Hunting. 89081
Lauraguais, -------, Comte de. 39251
Laure, Jules. (39252)
Laureau, --------. (39253)
Laurel: a gift for all seasons. 39254
Laurel de Apolo. 98771
Lavrel de Apolo, con otras primas. 98770
Laurel Hill Cemetery, Philadelphia. see
 Philadelphia. Laurel Hill Cemetery.
Laurel leaves. 91034
Laurence, Isaac. 39256
Laurens, Edward R. 39257
Laurens, Henry, 1724-1792. 9837, 35985,
 39258-39259, 50360, 53286, 66394,
 67499, 82975-82976, 87366, 88969,
 88005, 96569 see also U. S. Peace
 Commissioners, Paris, 1782.
Laurens, Henry, 1724-1792. supposed author
 23532, 39925-39926, 79322, 1st note
 after 87356, 87824-note after 87824,
 note after 96924
Laurens, J. Wayne. (39261)
Laurens, John. 39260, 81267, 88969
Laurens District, South Carolina. Citizens.
 petitioners 47664-(47665)
Laurent, J. L. M. 98298
Laurent, Paul Marie. 39262
Laurentii Gambarae Brixiani De navigatione
 Christophori Columbi. (26500)
Laurie, Thomas. (39263)-39264, 56164,
 56185, (62685), 66300
Laurin, le chansonnier Canadien. 39265
Laurnaga, Pablo de. 39266
Lausan, --------. engr. 27650, (36966),
 68421
Lausanne, ------. 100745
Laussat, Anthony. (39267)
Laut, J. H. 68213
Lautere Wahrheit. 25522, 25563, 88824
Lauters, --------. lithographer 4737
Lauts, G. 39268-(39270)
Lautveranderung Aztekischer Worter. (9527)
Lautveranderungen Aztekischer Worter.
 (9524)
Lauwer-strijt. 67130
Lauwerkrans voor Washington. 39273, 101835

Lauzun, Duc de. see Biron, Armand Louis
 de Gontaut, Duc de Lauzun, afterwards
 Duc de, 1747-1793.
Lava, Alvarez de. 39274
Lavagnino, ------. 39275
Laval, Antoine Jean de. 39276, 98393
Laval, Francois Pyrard de. see Pyrard,
 Francois, ca. 1570-1621.
Laval, J. Belin. 39277
Laval de Montmorency, Francois de. petitioner
 39278
Lavalette, Antoine de. see De Lavalette,
 Antoine.
Lavalle, Jose A. de. 29280, 58566
Lavallee, --------. tr. 22727
Lavallee, Joseph, Marquis de Bois-Robert,
 1747-1816. 39281-39292, 103139
Lavallee, Th. ed. 44159
Lavante. pseud. Poets and poetry of
 America. 63654
Lavastida y Davalos, A. de. see Labastida y
 Davalos, Pelagio Antonio de, Abp., 1816-
 1891.
Lavaux, Madame ------. 39286
Lavaux, C. 39285
Lavayasse, J. J. Dauxion. see Dauxion-
 Lavayasse, J. J.
Lavaysse, Francois Dauxion. 65419
Lavayssiere, ------. 39287-39288
Laveaux, Etienne. 39289
Lavedan, A. 39290
Lavega, Antonio de. 39291
La Vega, Bernardo de. 39292
La Vega, Garcilaso de. see Garcilaso de la
 Vega, called el Inca, 1539-1616.
La Vega, Gonzales de. 39293
La Vega, Manuel de. see Vega, Manuel de la.
La Vega, R. de. 39295
Laverdiere, Charles Honore, 1826-1873.
 20892, 39296, note after 69259
Lavicomterie, L. (39297)
La Ville, Jean Ignace de. see De la Ville,
 Jean Ignace.
Lavin, Manuel Garcia. 39298
Laviolette, Pierre. 34041, 69661
Lavison, Etienne Rufz de. see Rufz de
 Lavison, Etienne, 1806-1884.
Lavoisier, Antoine Laurent, 1743-1794.
 88905
Lavoisne, C. V. (1062), 15055, 39125
Lavolle, Charles Hubert. 39300
Lavollee, M. P. 39301
Law, Andrew. 39302
Law, Edmund, Bishop of Carlisle, 1703-1787.
 39303
Law, Edward. see Ellenborough, Edward
 Law, Baron, 1750-1818.
Law, George. 39304-39305
Law, James. 39306
Law, John, 1671-1729. 39307-39308, 39312-
 39315, 99323
Law, John, 1796-1873. 39316-39317, 57068
Law, Lyman. 33974, 101813
Law, N. 90943
Law, Stephen D. 39319-(39321)
Law, Thomas. 14866, (39322)-note after
 (39323), (63271)
Law, William, 1686-1761. (4673), 14373,
 (39324)-39326, 59699, 95711
Law, William, fl. 1815. 39327
Law, William, fl. 1866. appellant 24571
Law-abiding Christian. 43467
Law-abiding conscience. 89092
Law Academy of Philadelphia. (61765),
 97646

Law Academy of Philadelphia. Charter. (61765)

Law almanac for the year 1870. 39328

Law and government. 37882

Law and lawyers. 39329

Law and miscellaneous books. 92306

Law and practice of United States naval courts-martial. 39786

Law and prerogative. 90878

Law and temperance. A sermon. 89087, 89093

Law and the facts. (39330)

Law and the offence. 42367

Law and the testimony concerning slavery. 39331

Law Association, Philadelphia. 61766

Law Association, Philadelphia. Charter. 61766

Law Association, Philadelphia. Library. 61766

Law authorizing the incorporation of the Delaware, Lehigh, Schuylkill & Susquehanna Railroad Company. 60048

Law case. (39340)

Law-central, a monthly magazine. 84869, 84887

Law commission. 52538

Law concerning public schools in Nova Scotia. 56147

Law Department of the University of . . . New York. Annual announcement. 54708

Law dictionary. 6981

Law established by the Gospel. 104090

Law establishing and regulating common schools in the state of California. 10001

Law establishing the New-Bedford Fire Department. 52457

Law for preventing and estinguishing fires. 54330

Law for the due observance of the Lord's day. 53725

Law given at Sinai: a poem. 18921, 2d note after 106134

Law in all respects satisfied by Our Saviour. 82216

Law in Maryland concerning religion. 38886, 92940

Law in New-England, confirmed by the crown. 90609

Law Institute, New York. see New York Law Institute.

Law Institute, Philadelphia. (61767)

Law journal. 39332

Law Library Association of St. Louis. 75354

Law Library Association of St. Louis. Library. 75354

Law Library Company, Philadelphia. (61768)

Law made and pass'd . . . first Wednesday in May, 1732. 70511

Law . . . [made and passed] fourth Tuesday in January 1732 [i. e. 1733]. 70511

Law . . . [made and passed] Providence, on the last Wednesday of Octobre, [sic] 1730. 70511

Law . . . [made and passed] third Monday in June 1735. 70511

Law magazine. see American jurist, and law magazine.

Law of burial. 73956, 73977

Law of Christian rebuke. 9483

Law of colored seamen. 87856

Law of contraband of war. 64938

Law of deposit of the flood tide. 18806, 85072

Law of evidence. 60191

Law of evidence. 60191

Law of extradition. (22015)

Law of flats. 7004

Law of freedom and bondage in the United States. 33988

Law of God, against all irrelegious associations. (56356)

Law of God and the statutes of men. note after (58767)

Law of honor. 101387

Law of human progress. 93665

Law of insanity. 35804

Law of intellectual property. 89610

Law of libel. 95602

Law of libels. 39333

Law of liberty. 106388

Law of liberty, or, royal law. 79824

Law of love: a missionary sermon. 32429

Law of love: an address delivered in the Second Presbyterian Church. 97368

Law of Maine and the law of God. 39334

Law of marque. 17180

Law of Maryland concerning religion. 45181

Law of New Jersey for purchasing clothes for New Jersey regiments. 53142

Law of passive obedience. 79825, 93140

Law of railways. (68501)

Law of retribution. 79826, 93140

Law of separate schools in Upper Canada. (74563)

Law of slavery. 13861

Law of slavery in the United States. 9190, 39335

Law of slavery. Speech . . . in the Senate. 13266

Law of special reprisals. 80153

Law . . . [of the Maine Charity School.] 43967

Law of the state of New York, relating to the city of Schenectady. 77595

Law of the territories. 24505, 39336

Law of warrants. 58149

Law organizing the militia of the state of New-York. 91450

Law our school-master. 4493

Law papers & documents relating to the management of the old, or Fulton ferry. 8291, 39337

Law Reform Association. (39339)

Law reform tracts: compiled by a member of the Ohio bar. 39338

Law reform tracts. Published under the superintendence of the Law Reform Association. (39339)

Law register. 41625

Law register of the United States. 28832

Law relating to roads and highways in the state of Ohio. 67433

Law relating to subjects and aliens. 14088

Law relating to the rights of the Central Branch Union Pacific R. R. Co. (55196)

Law reporter. 17552, 19916, 65111, 70231, 71361, 82066, 92827

Law reports. 39208

Law School, St. Louis. see St. Louis Law School.

Law school at Worcester. 105360

Law school of Harvard College. (58703)

Law Society of Upper Canada. 98080

Law Society of Upper Canada. Benchers in Convocation. Committee. 98080

Law students and lawyers. 71260

Law the only sanction of liberty. 56406

Law to provide for the purchase of a lot of ground. 94299

Law to regulate public markets. 54331
Law to revise and amend the several acts. (8295)
Lawes, Henry, 1596-1662. 11166, 76465-(76466), 91718
Lawful and courageous use of the sword. 21138
Lawfulness, excellency, and advantage of instrumental musick in the publick worship of God. 39341
Lawfulness, excellency, and advantage of instrumental music in the public worship of God, but chiefly of organs. 38342, 78729
Lawfulness of a defensive war. 82872-82873, 94694
Lawfulness of defensive war. (40972)
Lawfulness of hearing the publick ministers. 56357
Lawfulness of war for Christians, examined. 51112
Lawne, ------. 72110
Lawrence, --------, fl. 1777. 39363
Lawrence, --------. defendant 54701
Lawrence, A. A. 35680
Lawrence, A. B. 95091, 95122
Lawrence, A. Gallatin. 39346
Lawrence, Abbott. 7256, (39344)
Lawrence, Amos. 39384
Lawrence, Amos A. 17109, 39345
Lawrence, Cornelius van Wyck, 1791-1861. (54394), 94262 see also New York (City) Mayor, 1834-1836 (Lawrence)
Lawrence, Cornelius W. defendant 39347
Lawrence, E. A. 39349
Lawrence, Edward Alexander, 1808-1883. (39348)
Lawrence, G. G. 39352-39353
Lawrence, Garrett. 106199-106200
Lawrence, George. (39350)
Lawrence, George Alfred. 39351
Lawrence, George N. 2809, 69946
Lawrence, Isaac. 39382, 51972
Lawrence, James. tr. 38283
Lawrence, James. USN 39355-39356
Lawrence, John. 39357
Lawrence, John. surveyor (53236), (80693)
Lawrence, Jonathan. 53473, 54042, 83604
Lawrence, Jonathan, 1807-1833. 39360
Lawrence, Levin. 39361
LAwrence, Margarette Woods. (39362)
Lawrence, Myron. 39364-39365
Lawrence, Richard. defendant 39366
Lawrence, Robert F. 39367
Lawrence, S. 63686
Lawrence, Samuel. 39368
Lawrence, Samuel A. petitioner 39369
Lawrence, Sidney. 39370
Lawrence, T. Bigelow. petitioner 39372
Lawrence, Thomas. 39371
Lawrence, W. S. 60720
Lawrence, William, 1722-1780. (39373)
Lawrence, William, 1783-1848. 39374
Lawrence, William, 1819-1899. (39375)-(39376)
Lawrence, William Beach, 1800-1881. 32187, 34801, 39377-39383, 70674
Lawrence, William Beach, 1800-1881. plaintiff 39377
Lawrence, William R. 39384-(39385)
Lawrence & Lemay. firm publishers (39386)
Lawrence, Mass. 39395, 39398
Lawrence, Mass. City Mission. 39399

Lawrence, Mass. Committee of Relief for Suffers of the Pemberton Mill. see Committee of Relief for Sufferers of the Pemberton Mill.
Lawrence, Mass. Essex Company. see Essex Company, Lawrence, Mass.
Lawrence, Mass. Franklin Library Association 39391
Lawrence, Mass. Pacific Mills Library. see Pacific Mills Library, Lawrence, Mass.
Lawrence, Mass. Public Schools. 39396
Lawrence, Mass. School Committee. 39396
Lawrence Academy, Groton, Mass. 39388-39389
Lawrence & Lemay's North Carolina almanack. (39386)
Lawrence directory for 1864. 39402
Lawrence Langston. pseud. see Sangston, Lawrence. and Johnson, Reverdy, 1796-1876. incorrectly supposed author
Lawrence Machine Shop. Committee. 39397
LAwrence Machine Shop. Treasurer. 39397
Lawrence Manufacturing Company. (39390)
Lawrence Manufacturing Company. Agent. 88678 see also Southworth, William S.
Lawrence Monroe. 88668
Lawrence Scientific School. see Harvard University. Lawrence Scientific School.
Lawrence University, Appleton, Wisc. 39400-(39401)
Lawrence University, Appleton, Wisc. Endowment Agent. (39401)
Lawrence University, Appleton, Wisc. Library. (39401)
Lawrence Water-Cure, Brattleboro, Vt. 7444
Lawrie, A. (39403)
Lawrie Todd. 26456, 95610
Lawrie's history of freemasonry. (39403)
Laws, S. S. 39404
Laws "agreed upon to be printed." 45788
Laws and abstracts of laws relating to army and navy pensions. 60807
Laws and acts of Barbadoes from 1643 to 1763. 3274
Laws & acts of the General Assembly for Their Majesties province of New-York. 53726
Laws and acts of the General Assembly of His Majestys province of Nova Caesarea or New Jersey. 53143
Laws and by-laws of the Danville and Pottsville Rail Road Company. 60034
Laws and by-laws relating to the Springfield, Mt. Vernon and Pittsburg Railroad Company. 89902
Laws and catalogue [of the Gardiner Lyceum.] 26634
Laws and catalogue of Troy Library. 97074
Laws and charters in Michigan, Indiana, and Illinois. 48761
Laws & constitution of the British colonies in the West Indies. 105104
Laws and constitution of the Scots Thistle Society. (62233)
Laws and decisions in relation to the Virginia military land titles. 58149
Laws and decrees of the state of Coahuila and Texas. 13810, 39405, 94948
Laws and general ordinances of . . . New-Orleans. 53333
Laws and information relating to claims. 12826, 39406
Laws and members of the Cambridge Humane Society. 10152
Laws and orders made at several General Courts. 45790

Laws and ordinances . . . A. D. 1833-1834. 54346

Laws and ordinances . . . during the mayoralties. 54343

Laws and ordinances . . . during the mayoralty of Jacob Radcliff. 54342

Laws and ordinances . . . 1827. (54345)

Laws and ordinances . . . 1823. 54344

Laws and ordinances of the New Netherlands, 1638-1674. 53727

Laws and ordinances of the city of Brooklyn. 8297

Laws and ordinances of the Common Council [of Albany.] 621

Laws and ordinances of the Common Council of the city of Albany. 622

Laws and ordinances of the Mayor, Recorder, Aldermen and Commonality of the city of Albany. 620

Laws and ordinances, ordained and established by the Mayor. 54336

Laws and ordinances, ordained and established . . . in the mayoralty. (54337)

Laws and ordinances . . . passed during the mayoralty of De Witt Clinton. (54341)

Laws and ordinances . . . . Passed . . . 1808. 54340

Laws and ordinances . . . . Passed . . . 1805. (54339)

Laws and ordinances . . . . Passed . . . 1803. 54338

Laws and ordinances relating to the B. and O. R. R. Co. 2992

Laws and ordinances relating to the Western Maryland Rail Road Co. 45396

Laws and ordinances relative to the . . . public law of . . . New York. (54347)

Laws and resolutions . . . from 1827 to 1861. 34516

Laws and resolutions. Instituted at Charleston. 87883

Laws and resolutions of a public nature. 55635

Laws and resolutions of the Medical Society of South-Carolina. 87882

Laws and resolutions passed by the General Assembly of . . . North Carolina. 55636

Laws and resolutions relating to the direct and excise taxes. 39407

Laws and policy of England. 103121

Laws and regulations . . . as revised and adopted. 55054

Laws and regulations for governing and disciplining the militia of the United States. 91437, 91452

Laws & regulations for the government of Union-College. 97783

Laws and regulations; for the militia of the state of South-Carolina. 87696, 91428

Laws and regulations of the American Philosophical Society. 1178

Laws and regulations of the Boston Episcopal Charitable Society. 6701

Laws and regulations of the College of William and Mary. 104153

Laws and regulations of the Female Department. (56415)

Laws and regulations of the Marine Society of Marblehead. 44472

Laws and regulations of the . . . [Massachusetts Historical] Society. 45856

Laws and regulations of the Massachusetts Society for Promoting Agriculture. (45896)

Laws and regulations of the Post Office Department. (64483)

Laws and regulations of the Royal Canadian Yacht Club. 73786

Laws and regulations of the Social Library, in Beverly. 85694

Laws and regulations of the Trenton Library Company. 96772

Laws and regulations of the Western and Atlantic Rail Road. 102963

Laws and regulations. May, 1797. 96773

Laws and the fees of officers. 99075

Laww and votes of the last session of the General Assembly. (53144)

Laws approved Oct. 25-Dec. 20, 1836. 94994

Laws, by-laws, and organization of the Reform School. 20307

Laws concerning the record, . . . of marriage. 48748

Lavves diuine, morall and martiall, &c. 99866

[Laws enacted] At the annual session of the President and Fellows. 105817

Laws enacted by the General Assembly, of the state of South-Carolina. 87632

Laws enacted in a General Assembly of the . . . commonwealth of Pennsylvania. 60194

Laws enacted since June 1815. (52845)

Laws establishing a common school system. 24876

Laws for forming and regulating the militia of the state of New-Hampshire. 91437, 91452

Laws for regulating and governing the militia. (45791)

Laws for regulating and governing the militia of the commonwealth of Massachusetts. 91456

Laws for the army and navy of the Confederate States. 15279

Laws for the government of the Advocate's Library, Montreal. 50253

Laws for the government of the College of Louisiana. 42225

Laws for the government of the Collegiate and Medical Departments. 60758

Laws for the government of the Collegiate Department. 60758

Laws for the government of the Massachusetts militia. (45792)

Laws for the protection of the canals of Ohio. 56946

Laws . . . from the first day of December. 60195

Laws . . . from the second day of October. 60195

Laws . . . from the seventh day of December. 60195

Laws in force and use in Her Majesty's plantations. 81, note after 100381

Laws in force on the 14th of March, 1842. (39408)

Laws in Indian and English. 39409, 96105

Laws . . . in relation to banking associations. 53742

Laws in relation to the village of Brooklyn. (8296)

Laws incorporating the Philadelphia, Wilmington and Baltimore Rail-Road Company. 62051

Laws, instructions and forms. 64484

Laws, joint resolutions, and memorials passed. (52193)

Laws, made and pass'd . . . at Newport, by adjournment. 70511

Laws, made and pass'd . . . at Newport, on the first Wednesday. 70511

Laws . . . [made and passed] first Monday in December 1733. 70511

Laws . . . [made and passed] first Monday in February 1733 [i. e. 1734]. 70511

Laws . . . [made and passed] last Wednesday in February 1736 [i. e. 1747.] 70511

Laws . . . [made and passed] last Wednesday in October 1735. 70511

Laws . . . [Made and passed] last Wednesday in October 1734. 70511

Laws . . . [made and passed] last Wednesday in October 1736. 70511

Laws . . . [made and passed] last Wednesday of October, 1732. 70511

Laws . . . [made and passed] Newport, by adjournment, on the second Monday of June, 1731. 70511

Laws . . . [made and passed] Newport, by adjournment, on the third Tuesday of February, 1730. 70511

Laws . . . [made and passed] second Monday in June 1736. 70511

Laws . . . [made and passed] second Monday in June 1732. 70511

Laws . . . [made and passed] second Monday of June 1733. 70511

Laws . . . [made and passed] third Monday in August 1735. 70511

Laws . . . [made and passed] third Monday in June 1734. 70511

Laws . . . [made and passed] third Tuesday in February 1734 [i. e. 1735.] 70511

Laws . . . [made and passed] Warwick. 70511

[Laws made] At a session of the General Assembly of Maryland. 45191

Laws made, manufactures set up, and trade carried on. 39410

Laws, memorials, and resolutions . . . passed at the sixth session. 50081

Laws, memorials and resolutions passed by the fourth Legislative Assembly. 34167

Laws, now in force, concerning roads. (75406)

Laws of a local nature. 34543

Laws of a public and general nature. 39411

Laws of Amherst College. (1324)

Laws of Antigua. By Anthony Brown. 8448

Laws of Antigua; consisting of the acts of the Leeward Islands. 85361

Laws of Barbadoes collected in one volume. 3275

LAws of Barbadoes. 1855. 3276

Laws of Bowdoin College. 7033

Laws of civilization. 32269

Laws of Congress in regard to taxes. 15278

Laws of Connecticut. An exact reprint. 15755

Laws of Connecticut from 1794 to 1800. 15766

Laws of Cumberland College. 17884

Laws of descent of the Iroquois. 50665

Laws [of Genesee College, Lima, N. Y.] 26920

Laws of Georgetwon College. 27006

Laws of Georgia. 27064

Laws of Grenada and the Grenadines, from the year 1766: in which those acts and parts of acts, only, are printed. 28756

Laws of Grenada, and the Grenadines; from the year 1766, to the year 1852. 85362

Laws of Grenada, from 1763 to 1805. 28755

Laws of Hamden Sidney [sic] College. (30134)

Laws of Harvard College. (30749)

Laws of Her Majesties colony of New-York, as they were enacted. 53728, 53729, (53731)

Laws of His Majesty's colony [of New York, 1719.] (53467)

Laws, of His Majesty's province of Upper Canada, in North America. 98061

Laws of His Majesty's province of Upper Canada, in North-America, enacted in the first session of the second Parliamen 98062

Laws of human progress and modern reforms. 19862

Laws of Indiana from Nov. 1816 to Jan. 22, 1820. 34542

Laws of Indiana Territory. (34540)

Laws of Jamaiaca: comprehending all the acts in force. 35625

Laws of Jamaica, passed by the Assembly, and confirmed by His Majesty in Council, April 17, 1684. 35623

Laws of Jamaica, passed by the Assembly, and confirmed by His Majesty in Council, February 23, 1683. 35622

Laws of Jamaica, pass'd by the Governours, Council and Assembly. (35624)

"Laws" of Kansas. 14343

Laws of Kemper College. 37342

Laws of Kentucky. 37537

Laws of Kenyon College. (37587)

Laws of Las Siete Partidas. 42244

Laws of Maine. 43959

Laws of Maryland. 45271

Laws of Maryland and Pennsylvania. (60280)

Laws of Maryland at large. 2684, 45186

Laws of Maryland, enacted at a session of Assembly. (45183)

Laws of Maryland, enacted at a session of Assembly, . . . held at . . . Annapolis. 45184

Laws of Maryland, enacted . . . at the city of Annapolis. 45185

Laws of Maryland, made and passed at a session of Assembly. 45188

Laws of Maryland, made and passed at a session of Assembly, held at Annapolis. 45187

Laws of Maryland, made since M, DCC, LXIII. (45189)

Laws of Maryland, . . . 1692 . . . to . . . 1799. 45190

Laws of Maryland . . . . Revised by Virgil Maxcy. 45192

Laws of Massachusetts relating to the duties. 27945

Laws of Michigan. (48746)

Laws . . . [of Middlebury College.] 48837

Laws of Mississippi. 84882

Laws of . . . Mississippi, embracing all acts of a public nature. (49515)

Laws of . . . Mississippi. Passed at a called session. (49515)

Laws of national growth. (17271)

Laws of nations. 20999

Laws of neutrality. 51020

Laws of New Bedford South School. (52483)

Laws of . . . New Jersey, compiled and published. 53148

Laws of New Jersey, regulating fisheries. 53145

Laws of . . . New Jersey. Revised. 53149

Laws of New-Jersey; revised and published. 53147

Laws of New-York, from the 11th November, 1752, to 22d May, 1762. 53732, 84576

Laws of New-York, from the year 1691, to 1751. (53730), 84576

Laws of New-York, from the year 1691, to 1773 inclusive. 53733

Laws of the province of the Massachusetts-Bay. 45700

Laws of the Quebec Medical Society. (67049)

Laws of the Redwood Library Company. 55054, 68533

Laws of the republic of Texas. 94998

Laws of the republic of Texas, in two volumes. 94994-94996

Laws of the republic of Texas, passed at the first session of the third Congress. 95000

Laws of the republic of Texas, passed the first session of third Congress. 94999

Laws of the several states relative to immigrants. 8226

Laws of the Sons of the African Society. 87107

Laws of the South-Carolina College. 87982

Laws of the South-Carolina College, adopted by the Board of Trustees. 87983

Laws of the South-Carolina College, enacted by the Trustees. 87980

Laws of the state of Alabama. 564

Laws of the state of Delaware. 19392

Laws of the state of Florida. 24881

Laws of the state of Louisiana. 42245

Laws of the state of Maine from the separation to 1833. 43957

Laws of the state of Maine, passed by the Legislature. 43954

Laws of the state of Maine relating to manufacturing corporations. 43959

Laws of the state of Maine; to which are prefixed the constitution of the U. States and of said state. (43955)

Laws of the state of Maine . . . with an appendix. 43957

Laws of the state of Maine; with the constitution. 43958

Laws of the state of Michigan. 48748

Laws of the state of Mississippi. 49513

Laws of the state of Missouri, . . . 1836-37 and 1838-39. (49605)

Laws of the state of Missouri; revised . . . by authority of the General Assembly. 49604

Laws of the state of Nebraska. 52194

Laws of the state of New-Hampshire, passed from December . . . 1805. 52844

Laws of the state of New Hampshire, together with the declaration of independence. 52843

Laws of the state of New Jersey. (5990)

Laws of the state of New-York. (53736)

Laws of the state of New-York, commencing with the first session. 53734

Laws of the state of New-York, comprising the constitution. 53735

Laws of the state of New-York, concerning infectious diseases. 49737

Laws of the state of New-York, . . . from the first to the fifteenth session. (53737)

Laws of the state of New-York, . . . from the first to the twentieth session. 53738

Laws of the state of New York, in relation to the Erie and Champlain Canals. 22745

Laws of the state of North-Carolina. (55637)

Laws of the state of Tennessee. 94776

Laws of the state of Tennessee, including those of North Carolina. 94777

Laws of the state of Vermont. 99126

Laws of the state . . . . Relating particularly to the city. (54348)

Laws of the state . . . . Revision of 1801. 53745

Laws of the Territory . . . Northwest of the Ohio. 39418

Laws of the Territory of Florida. 24877

Laws of the Territory of Iowa. 35017

Laws of the Territory of Kansas. (37064)

Laws of the Territory of Louisiana. 42246

Laws of the Territory of Michigan, condensed. (48747)

Laws of the Territory of Michigan . . . revised. (48747)

Laws of the Territory of Michigan; with marginal notes. (48747)

Laws . . . of the Territory of Nebraska. 52192

Laws of the Territory of Nevada. 52403

Laws of the Territory of New Mexico. 53281

Laws of the Territory of the United States, North-West of the Ohio. 56951

Laws of the Territory of the United States, Northwest of the Ohio River, passed . . 1799. 56953

Laws of the Territory of the United States Northwest of the Ohio River; with laws enacted. (39419)

Laws of the Territory of the United States, Northwest of the River Ohio. 56952

Laws of the Theological Institution in Andover. 1439

Laws of the United States, for the government of the militia. 20308

Laws of the United States, in relation to the Navy and Marine Corps. 32687

Laws of the United States of America. 15558, (39424), 94078

Laws of the United States of America, arranged and published under the authority of an act of Congress. 39425

Laws of the United States of America; comprising the acts. 39423

Laws of the United States of America, passed at a Congress. (39422)

Laws of the United States of America; . . . with a copious index. 39421

Laws of the United States relating to internal revenue. 34915, note after (39427)

Laws of the United States relating to patents. (17390)

Laws of the United States relating to patents and the patent Office. (39429)

Laws of the United States relating to the District of Columbia. (9198)

Laws of the United States relating to the military establishments. 39428

Laws of the United States relating to the Navy and Marine Corps. 10052

Laws of the United States relative to direct taxes and internal duties. (39426)

Laws of the United States relative to naturalization. (39427)

Laws of the United States relative to the Territory of Florida, passed by Congress prior to 1838. 24879

Laws of the United States relative to the Territory of Florida, passed prior to 1828. (24878)

Laws of the United States, resolutions of Congress under the confederation, treaties proclamations, and other documents. 39430

Laws of the United States, resolutions of Congress under the confederation, treaties proclamations, Spanish regulations, and other documents. (39431)

Laws of the United States, treaties, regulations and other documents. 39432

Laws of the University of Mississippi. 49549

Laws of the University [of Nashville.] 51880

Laws of the University of Vermont. 99212-99213

Laws of the Virginia Society for Promoting Agriculture. 100566

LAws of the Washington Literary, Scientific, & Military Gymnasium. 101970

Laws of trade in the United States. (50398)

Laws of Transylvania University. 96461

'Laws" of Vermont, 1824-34. 95486

Laws [of Vermont, 1797.] 95486, note after 99131

Laws of Virginia for 1680. 100232

Laws of Virginia now in force. 100380, 100459

Laws of wages, profits, and rent, investigated. 97301

Laws of war, and martial law. (29881), 39433

Laws of Washington College. 101999A-101999B

Laws of Waterville College, Maine. 102101

Laws of William and Mary College in Virginia. 104152A

Laws of William Penn. 59695

Laws of Williams College. 104420-104422

Laws of Williams College. 1829. 104423

Laws of Wisconsin. 29555

Laws of Yale College. 105824

Laws of Yale College, in New-Haven, Connecticut. 105825

Laws of Yale-College, in New-Haven, in Connecticut. 105813-105816, 105818, 105821-105823

Laws of Yale College passed since 1817. 105822

Laws, orders, and ordinances, established by the Mayor, Recorder, Aldermen, and Assistants of the City, convened in Common Council. 54333

Laws, orders, and ordinances of . . . New York. (54332)

Laws passed at the first session of the General Assembly [of Indiana.] 34541

Law passed at the first session of the Legislative Assembly of the Territory of Idaho. 34166

Laws passed at the 2d [i. e. adjourned] session of the 2d Congress of the republic of Texas. 94997

Laws passed by the [first] General Assembly of Illinois. 34284

Laws . . . passed by the Legislative Committee and Legislative Assembly. 57555

Laws, passed by the Legislature of the state of Coahuila and Texas. 94944

Laws passed by the Ohio Legislature. 56948

Laws passed from Nov., 1863, to March, 1864. 27064

Laws passed in the Territory of the United States, North-West of the Ohio River. 39418, 56950

Laws passed in the Territory of the United States North-West of the River Ohio. 56949, 94882

Laws regulating state and municipal elections. 56859

Laws regulating the militia in the state of New Jersey. 91435

Laws, regulations, rates of toll, and names. (53563)

Laws relating to burials. 84416

Laws . . . relating to common schools. (53741)

Laws relating to grammar and common schools. 10442

Laws relating to Indian affairs. 96594

Laws relating to pensions, military and naval bounty. 39438

Laws relating to public health, sanitary, medical, protective. 84416

Laws relating to public schools. 53150

Laws . . . relating to the assessment and collection of Taxes. 53739

Laws relating to the assessment and collection of taxes in the city of New York. 54014

Laws relating to the Boston Board of Health. 45797

Laws relating to the city and county of New York. (32400), 54351

Laws relating to the direct and excise taxes. 39436

Laws relating to the Illinois Industrial University. (34236)

Laws relating to the incorporation of villages. 14232

Laws relating to the Miami University. 48682

Laws relating to the Navy and Marine Corps. 39437

Laws relating to the public schools in . . . Maine. 43959

Laws relating to the relief and employment of the poor. 61769

Laws relating to the service of the Post Office Department. 64485

Laws . . . relative to highways and bridges. 48748

Laws relative to the Board of Wardens . . . of Philadelphia. 61770

Laws relative to the embargo. 22413, 39434

Laws relative to the quarantine and to the public health. 54352

Laws relative to quarantine in the port of New York. 54352

Laws relative to the Wabash and Erie Canal. 39435, 100879

Laws respecting intoxicating liquors. 60591

Laws . . . respecting navigable communication. 53740

Laws, rules and regulations of the Lodge of the Iron Crown. 86991

Laws, rules, and regulations of the Worcester North District Medical Association. 105436

Laws, statutes, ordinances and constitutions, ordained, made and established . . . . Published . . . 1748. 54334

Laws, statutes, ordinances and constitutions, ordained, made and established, by the Mayor, Aldermen, and Commonalty. 54335

Laws, such as were ordered to be printed. 45789

Laws to encourage immigration. 39439

Laws, treaties and other documents. (15559)

Laws which authorize the traffic in ardent spirit. 39440

Laws . . . with the constitutions of the state and the United States. 43956

Lawson, A. engr. 85105, 104597-104598

Lawson, Allen. see Lamson, Alvin.

Lawson, Deodat. (39442)-39444, 46687

Lawson, George. (39445)

Lawson, George C. 39446

Lawson, J. supposed author 99628

Lawson, James. 39447, 39449

Lawson, James supposed author 94244

Lawson, James. incorrectly supposed author 93448, 103694

Lawson, James. plaintiff 39450
Lawson, John. 39455
Lawson, John, d. 1712. 7800, 10957, 39451-
  39453, 91538
Lawson, John, fl. 1811. 39454
Lawson, Thomas. 2050-2051, 39456-(39458)
  see also U. S. Army. Surgeon
  General's Office.
Lawton, John. 39459, 59480
Lawton, Josiah. (39460)
Lawyer. pseud. Maritime capture. 44603
Lawyer, John O. 39461
Lawyer and citizen. pseud. Neutrality.
  52394
Lawyer of Illinois. pseud. Plea for impartial
  suffrage. 63383
Lawyer; or, man as he ought not to be.
  102163
Lawyers and legislaton. 39462, 55965
Lawyers' diary for . . . 1850. 39463
Lawyer's magazine. (39464)
Lawyer's test oath. 24571
Lawyer's unbought opinion. 35314
Laxe, Joao Baptista Cortines. see Cortines
  Laxe, Joao Baptista.
Lay, ------. 32863
Lay, Abigail. petitioner 83760
Lay, Benjamin. 39465, 79446, 82870
Lay, G. T. 71031
Lay, Henry Champlain. 39466
Lay, William. 39467, 51817
Lay co-operation in St. Mark's Church,
  Frankford. 62213
Lay Delegates of St. Peter's Church, Albany.
  see Albany. St. Peter's Church.
  Vestry. Lay Delegates to the Diocesan
  Convention, 1845.
Lay delegation in the Methodist Episcopal
  Church calmly considered. 64269
Lay-essayist. 104948
Lay member of the Diocesan Convention of
  New-Jersey. pseud. Letter addressed
  to Charles King. 40256
Lay member of the Protestant Episcopal
  Church of North Carolina. pseud.
  Examination of the doctrine. 35312
Lay of a scald. 75294
Lay of gratitude. 8786, 38583
Lay of the Apalachians. 55382
Lay of the Hudson. 32390
Lay of the last pilgrim. (39468), 57631
Lay of the last republican. 39469
Lay of the Scottish fiddle. 59202
Lay preacher. pseud. Essays. (19587),
  89498
Lay preacher. pseud. Political catechism.
  63754
Lay preacher. 19585-19586
Lay preacher's gazette. (19587), 89498
Laya, Alexandre. (39470)
Layfield, Eglambie. 66686
Laying of the cable. 51271
Laying of the corner-stone of the Church of
  the Covenant. 61536
Layman, Captain ------. (39471)
Layman. pseud. Address to the clergy of
  New-England. see Plumer, William.
Layman. pseud. Address to the members.
  see Donaldson, John I.
Layman. pseud. Bad effects of speculative
  theology. 2693
Layman. pseud. Bible view of slavery.
  5189
Layman. pseud. Church an engine of the
  state. (13001)

Layman. pseud. Claims of Thomas Jefferson
  to the presidency. see Brown, William,
  fl. 1799. supposed author
Layman. pseud. Common sense versus
  judicial legislation. see Sargent, John
  Osborne.
Layman. pseud. Dangers of church
  centralization. 18486
Layman. pseud. Exposition of the late
  controversy. see Jennings, Samuel K.
Layman. pseud. Laugh of a layman against
  a pamphlet. 71135
Layman. pseud. Layman's apology. see
  Southwick, Solomon.
Layman. pseud. Layman's inquiry into the
  right. (34816), 96412
Layman. pseud. Letter of a layman to any
  member of Congress. 95891
Layman. pseud. Letters to the Trinitarian
  Congregational Church. 101207
Layman. pseud. Moral miscellanies. see
  Smith, Nathaniel R.
Layman. pseud. Nineteenth century. 55347
Layman. pseud. Nutshell. 56344
Layman. pseud. Obstacles and objections.
  56605
Layman. pseud. Plagiarism. 63206
Layman. pseud. Puseyite developments.
  66744
Layman. pseud. Recent attempt to defeat
  the constitutional provisions. see
  Lowell, John.
Layman. pseud. Remarks and observations.
  69385
Layman. pseud. Remarks on the proceedings.
  see Bartlett, Bailey.
Layman. pseud. Review, by a layman.
  14912
Layman. pseud. Review of Dr. Dana's
  remonstrance. 18407
Layman. pseud. Rule in Minor's case again.
  see Sargent, John Osborne.
Layman. pseud. Sketch of the rise and
  progress of Grace Church. see Eames,
  Jane Anthony.
Layman. pseud. Spiritual food. 89513
Layman. pseud. Strictures on a pastoral
  letter. 32296
Layman. pseud. Strictures on the Rev. Mr.
  Thatcher's pamphlet. see Sullivan,
  James, 1744-1808.
Layman. pseud. Third chapter on the rule
  in Minot's case. see Sargent, John
  Osborne.
Layman. pseud. Thoughts on the proposed
  establishment. 95723
Layman. pseud. To any member of Congress.
  95890
Layman. pseud. To any member of Congress.
  Third edition. 95891
Layman. pseud. Two witnesses. see White,
  Josiah, of Northampton, Mass.
Layman. pseud. Vindication of the organiza-
  tion. 11436
Layman. pseud. What ought the diocese to do.
  see Meads, Orlando.
Layman. pseud. Word in season. see
  Irving, Washington, 1783-1859. supposed
  author
Layman; and member of the Church of
  England. pseud. True state of the
  establishment. 97156
Layman and platformist. pseud. Letter to a
  friend. 101125

Layman of Louisiana. pseud. Rights of
　laymen. 71370
Layman of St. Mary's Congregation. pseud.
　Address. (62214)
Layman of the Church of England. pseud.
　Observations upon the liturgy. see
　Knox, William, 1732-1810.
Layman of the Church of Scotland. pseud.
　Remarks on the constitution of the
　Canadas. see Blackwood, Thomas.
Layman of the congregation. pseud. Inquiry
　into the causes which led to the
　dissensions. (62214)
Layman of the Parish of Trinith Church.
　pseud. Brief statement. 77978, note
　after 96981
Layman of the Reformed Dutch Church.
　pseud. Remarks. 69416, 98496
Layman, of the Reformed Protestant
　Christian Church in the town of
　Trenton. pseud. Letter to the Rev.
　Nathaniel Smith. 83669
Layman's answer to Dr. Trapp. 39472
Layman's answer to 'Poor Trinity.' 32934
Layman's apology. 88643
Layman's inquiry into the right. (34816),
　96412
Layman's library. 7482
Layman's remarks on the eighteen Presby-
　terian ministers letter. 47276
Layman's remarks upon a letter to the
　Bishop of Massachusetts. (17683)
Laymen of the New School Presbyterian and
　Congregational Churches of New York
　and Brooklyn. pseud. Earnest plea.
　(54252)
Laymen of the Reform Episcopal Church.
　pseud. Appendix. 83522
Layne, Lewis. defendant 41180-41182, 41235
Laynez, Juan de Ayllon. 39473
Layres, Augustus. 39474
Lays and ballads. 68177
Lays and legends. 23695
Lays of an untaught minstrel. (41738)
Lays of ancient Virginia. (3790)
Lays of liberty. 39475
Lays of love and faith. 5085
Lays of Melpomene. 23695
Lays of the emigrants, as sung by the
　parties for Kansas. 37069
Lays of the emigrants, as sung by the
　second party for Kansas. 37069
Lays of the fatherland. 77237
Lays of the forest. 30987
Lays of the heart, and other poems. 80924
Lays of the Hudson, and other poems.
　32390
Lays of the palmetto. 81226
Lays of the pilgrim fathers. 78245
Lays of the western world. (44454)
Layseca, Francisco Martin de. plaintiff
　61136
Laza. firm see Iriarte y Laza. firm
Lazaga, Sebastian de Eslava y. see Eslava
　y Lazaga. Sebastian de.
Lazare, Carl. 84763
Lazaretto, Philadelphia. see Philadelphia.
　Lazaretto.
Lazarillo de ciegos caminantes desde Buenos-
　Ayres. 9566
Lazaro. Poema. 29351
Lazarus, Emma. 39477
Lazarus. 63613
Lazcano, Francisco Xavier, 1702-1762. 39478,
　(39480), 58003

Lazell, Warren. 105417
Lazerne, W. de. see La Luzerne, Cesar
　Henri, Comte de, 1737-1799.
Lazo, Alonso-Carrillo. 17176
Lazo, F. 39481
Lazo de la Vega, Alfonso Carrillo. see
　Carillo Laso de la Vega, Alonso.
Lazo Estrada, Francisco. see Estrada,
　Francisco Lazo.
Lazzari, V. tr. 33726
Lazzaro, Giuseppe. tr. 92590
Lea, Albert M. 39482, 39500
Lea, Henry Charles, 1825-1909. 5188, 39483-
　39485, 39487
Lea, Isaac. (39486)-(39496)
Lea, J. 10843, (15055)
Lea, John. 39497
Lea, Luke. 71476-71477 see also Rio Grande,
　Mexican, and Pacific Railroad Company.
　President.
Lea, M. Carey. ed. 39498
Lea, Pryor. (39499)-39501
Lea, Richard. 39502
Lea, Thomas F. 39503
Leach, ------. 29890, 91524
Leach, Edmund. (39504), (39510)
Leach, George. 39505
Leach, J. RA 39507
Leach, J. M. 39509
Leach, James Edward. 39506
Leach, John. 39508
Leach, W. T. 39511
Leach, William. (39504), (39510)
Leacock, John. 39512
Leacock, W. T. 58347
Lead mines. 39513
Leader (Baltimore) 88489
Leader (Toronto) 74582
"Leader and a judge among the pioneers."
　33099
Leader fallen. 38315
Leaders in thought and action. 84087
Leaders of the old bar of Philadelphia. 5478
Leading articles contributed to the New York
　tribune. (15463)
Leading oarsman. pseud. Life in a whale
　ship. 41013
Leading pursuits and leading men. (25730),
　(25733)
Leading republicans of Colorado. pseud.
　Statement. see Republican Party.
　Colorado.
Leaf for the people. 39514
Leaf in the political history of New York.
　18713, 64454
Leaflets of masonic biography. (50341)
Leaflets of memory. 39515
League. 25726
League for the union. 3129
Leage Island Navy-Yard. Speech . . . June
　7, 1866. 51634
League of states. 42135
League of the Ho-de-no-sau-nee or Iroquois.
　50666
League of United Southerners, Montgomery,
　Ala. (39520)
League of United Southerners of . . .
　Montgomery to the people of the
　southern states. (39520)
Leaguer of Boston. 16465
Leah and Rachel. 30102, 82976
Leah, the forsaken. 59083
Leake, Isaac Q. (39521)
Leake, John G. 102175
Leake, Stephen Martin. 39522

Leake and Watts Orphan House, New York.
see New York (City) Leake and Watts
Orphan House.
Leakin, S. C. (45050)
Leal, Antonio Carvalho Silva. see Silva
Leal, Antonio Carvalho.
Leal, Antonio Henriques. (19962), (41412)
Leal, F. J. Pereira. see Pereira Leal,
F. J.
Leal, Raimundus. 39524
Lealtad Peruana. 39525
Lealtad y patriotismo del M. I. V. Cabildo de
Valladolid. 98372
Leaman, John. 39526
Leaming, Aaron. ed. 39527, 89425
Leaming, James R. 39528
Leaming, Jeremiah. (15654), 39529-39531,
78555, 80391, 102571, 102574
Leander de Cosco. see Aliander de Cosco.
Leander of Sancto Martino. pseud. Otium
theologicum tripartitum. see Jones,
John, fl. 1621.
Leandro de Sacramento. Frei 75616
Leao, Bartholameu de. 5065
Leao, Jose da Rocha. 39532
Leap for freedom. 8592
Lear, Tobias. 22218, 39533, 64584, 101944
Lear, Tobias. petitioner 39533
Leardus, Johanes. 76838
Learned, Ebenezer. 15677
Learned, Edward. 39534
Learned, Erastus. 39535
Learned, J. C. 39536
Learned, Joseph D. (39538)
Learned, Joseph D. defendant at court
martial 39537
Learned, Robert C. 39539
Learned, William L. (39540)
Learned and ingenious gentleman in the
province of Pennsylvania. pseud. ed.
see Smith, William, 1737-1803.
Learned gentleman. pseud. Paper of verses.
see Milton, John, 1608-1674.
Learned gentleman of Boston. pseud. Letter.
see Mather, Cotton, 1663-1728.
Learned quackery exposed. 95603
Learned worke of Iulius Solinus Polyhistor.
(63961)
Learned world. 90648
Learner of law, and lover of liberty. pseud.
Narrative of a new and unusual American
imprisonment. 44079-44080, note before
51781
Leary, C. L. L. 39541
Lease, Luman. 68499
Lease and contract of the Catawissa Rail
Road. 59964
Leason, James van. see Decalves, Alonso
pseud.
Leatham, William Henry. 39542
Leather manufacture in the United States.
78006
Leather stocking and silk. 16317, (39543)
Leather-stocking tales. 16408, 16430, 16460,
16493
Leatherskin. 25105
Leaton, James. 39544
Leaumont, Laurent-Marie de. 39545
Leave old arm's. 98056
"Leave Pope to get out of his scrape."
43022
Leaven for doughfaces. 39546
Leavenworth, A. 4355
Leavenworth, Mark. (39547)
Leavenworth, Kansas. Public Schools. 84522

Leavenworth city directory. 93956
Leaves about the war. (39550)
Leaves from a Bible reader's diary. 66314
Leaves from a century plant. 61772, 61886
Leaves from a journal. 72484
Leaves from a minister's portfolio. 25679
Leaves from a physician's journal. 82432
Leaves from a sketch-book of a traveller.
10902
Leaves from a trooper's diary. (39551)
Leaves from an old church record book.
84234
Leaves from Margaret Smith's journal. 103807
Leaves from New York life. (41399)
Leaves from the American biographical sketch
book. 33900
Leaves from the backwoods. (39552)
Leaves from the battle-field of Gettysburg.
87262
Leaves from the diary of an army surgeon.
22331
Leaves from the diary of the Princess Salm-
Salm. (75808)
Leaves from the life of an old sailor. 61399
Leaves from the note-book of a New York
detective. 39553
Leaves from the past. 83563
Leaves from the sketch-book of a traveller.
10903
Leaves from the sketch book of experience.
50762
Leaves from the tree Igdrasyl. 74362
Leaves from the tree of life. 83582
Leaves from a pastor's journal. 12408,
(66632)
Leavitt, --------, fl. 1862. 85618
Leavitt, --------, fl. 1863. 39565
Leavitt, David. (39554)
Leavitt, Dudley. (39555)
Leavitt, Eli. 39556
Leavitt, Freegrace. 39557
Leavitt, H. H. 84743
Leavitt, I. K. (52546)
Leavitt, J. 39562
Leavitt, J. M. 80867
Leavitt, Jonathan. 39559-39560
Leavitt, Joshua, 1794-1863. 2675, 39561,
39563, 44324, 104273
Leavitt, Joshua, 1794-1863. petitioner 39564
Leavitt, O. S. 39566
Leavitt, T. H. (39567)
Leavitt, W. S. 39568-39570
Leavitt (George A.) & Co. firm 39571,
74679-74680, 74682
Leavitt, Strebeigh & Co. firm 39571, 89731
Leavitt & Wright. firm 85618
Leavitts genuine improved New-England
almanack. (39555)
Leavitt's improved New-England farmer's
almanack. (39555)
Le B., Sieur. 39572, 2d note after 100846
Lebanon, Conn. Baptist Convention, 1833.
see Baptists. Connecticut. Convention,
Lebanon, 1833.
Lebanon, Conn. Committee. see Committee
of the Towns of Bozrah, Lebanon and
Franklin in the State of Connecticut.
Lebanon, Conn. Indian Charity School. see
Indian Charity School, Lebanon, Conn.
Lebanon, Conn. Moor's Indian Charity School.
see Indian Charity School, Lebanon,
Conn.
Lebanon, Ill. McKendree College. see
McKendree College, Lebanon, Ill.

Lebanon, N. H. Centennial Celebration, 1867. 39573

Lebanon, N. H. Citizens. 52791, note after 98998

Lebanon, Ohio. Lebanon University. see Lebanon University, Lebanon, Ohio.

Lebanon, Ohio. National Normal School. see Lebanon University, Lebanon, Ohio.

Lebanon, Ohio. Southwestern Normal School and Business Institute. see Lebanon University, Lebanon, Ohio.

Lebanon, Ohio. Southwestern State Normal School. see Lebanon University, Lebanon, Ohio.

Lebanon, Lancaster County. 39574

Lebanon Springs Railroad Company. 39577

Lebanon Springs Railroad. Prospectus. 39577

Lebanon Valley Rail Road. 91121

Lebanon University, Lebanon, Ohio. 39575-39576, (57000), 88621

Le Barbier, -------. illus. 28193, 31900

Lebardin, --------. (39578)

Le Barnes, John W. petitioner 39579

Lebas, P. L. tr. 1368, 20366, 64391, 100835

Lebassu d'Helf, Josephine. 39580

Lebaudy, A. 39581

Lebby, Robert. 87534

Le Beau, C. 39582-39585

Leben Abraham Lincolns. 85148

Leben Ansons. 69135

Leben August Gottlieb Spangenbergs. 71550

Leben bei den Niedrigen. 92555

Leben Benjamin Franklins. (25540), 25556A, (25617), 38318

Leben der Lucretia Maria Davidson. 78779

Leben der Neger in den Sklavenstaaten Nordamerikas. 92564

Leben der Sklaven in Amerika. 92578

Leben des Amerikanischen Generals Friedrich Wilhelm von Steuben. 37097

Leben des Amerikanischen Generals Johann Kalb. 37096

Leben des Andreas Jackson. 35528

Leben des Benjamin Franklin. 25524

Leben des beruhmten Amerikanischen reise den John Ledyard. 88976

Leben des Capitans James Cook. (37956)

Leben des Fursten Johann Moritz von Nassau-Siegen. 20946

Leben des Georg Waschington. 102479

Leben des Herrn Nicholaus Ludwig Grafen und Herrn von Zinzendorf und Pottendorf. 88931

Leben des Herrn Penn. 21049

Leben des Indiaermissionars David Brainerd. 22711

Leben des Obersten. (25845)

Leben des Periquillo Sarmiento. 41663

Leben des Sebast. Joseph von Carvalho und Mello. 63914

Leben des Sir. Th. Fowell Buxton. 9684

Leben des Weltumseglers und Entdeckers James Cook. 16265

Leben des W. Wilberforce. 103949

Leben en Heldendaden van M. A. de Ruiter. 74510

Leben evang. Heidenboten. 6277

Leben General Scott's. 78413

Leben Gottes in der Seele des Menchen. 78448-78449, 84568C

Leben Horace Greeley's. 58955

Leben im Innern der Vereinigten Staaten. 21073

Leben in fernen Westen. 74503

Leben in Newyork. 91283

Leben Robert Pierots. 62752

Leben Tugenden uund Wunderwercke desz Apostels von Peru. 86229

Leben und Abentheuer Martin Chuzzlewit's. 20010

Leben und Abenteuer P. T. Barnum's. 3567

Leben und ausgewahlte Schriften. 25525

Leben und Bekenntniss des Georg Swearingen. 94030

Leben und Briefwechsel Georg Washingtons. 88977

Leben und die gantz ungemeine Begebenheiten. 72220

Leben und Meynungen des Dr. Benjamin Franklin. 25542

Leben und Schicksale des Martin Chuzzlewit. 20008

Leben und Schriften. Aus dem Englischen ubersetzt. 25521

Leben und Schriften, nach der von seinem Enkel W. T. Franklin. 25523

Leben und Seereisen. 20857

Leben und Sitte in Nordamerika. 97030

Leben und Sterben von Joh. Bunian. 62848

Leben und Tapffere Thaten der allerberuhmtesten See-Helden. 6441, 7407, note after 98470

Leben und Thaten der Admirale und anderer beruhmten Britanischen See-Leute. (10238)

Leben und Thaten des furtrefflichen See-Helden. 7408

Leben und Thaten Geo. Washington's. 101836

Leben und Wirken Abraham Lincoln's. (3618)

Leben und Wirken des Herzoglich Braunsch-weig'schen General-Lieutenants Friedrich Adolph Riedesel Freiherrn zu Eisenbach. (22002)

Leben und Wirken des Johann Friedrich Oberlin. 77724

Leben und Wirken des Johannes Wesley. 51896

Leben von Abraham Lincoln. 41194

Leben von David Brainerd. 7342

Leben Wilhelm Penns. 44821

Leben, Wirken und Reden von Abraham Lincoln. 41195

Lebende Bilder aus Amerika. 28809

Lebendiger Discours. 102893

Lebens- und Charakterbild. 38930

Lebens-beschreibung. 25582

Lebensbeschreibung Alexander Hamilton's. 85148

Lebensbeschreibung der vier Konige Georg von England. 85148

Lebensbeschreibung des Franz Dracke. 8548

Lebensbeschreibung des Georg Waschington. 102480

Lebensbeschreibung Menno Simonis. 69150

Lebensbeschreibung und merkwurdige Hand-lungen. 102481

Lebensbeschreibung von Gualtero Bodano. 39587

Lebensbeschreibungen sammtlicher Unter-zeichner. 4714, 39586

Lebensbild eines Ehrenmannes in Amerika. 56736, 56738

Lebensbild fur Jung und Alt. 77668-77669

Lebensbilder aus beiden Hemispharen. 64542

Lebens-Bilder aus dem Staat Uruguay. 86854

Lebensbilder aus der Westlichen Hemispare. 64541, 64543-64544

Lebensbilder und Reisen in Amerika. 5128

Lebensgang Georg Washingtons. 56737

Lebensgeschichte der ehrwurdigen Vaters
  Peter Claver. (24746)
Lebensgeschichte des Generals Harrison.
  35423
Lebensgeschichte des Volksmannes Abraham
  Lincoln. 41238
Lebensgeschichte eines Amerikanischen
  Quakers. 12720
Lebensgeschichte Georg Washington's. 35190
Lebens-Wandel, und Todtes-Bengebenheit.
  94331
Lebensweise, Sitten und Gebrauche der vers-
  chiedenen Volker der Erde. 69110
Lebercht de Wette, Wilhelm Martin. see
  Wette, Wilhelm Martin Leberecht de.
Le Bissonnais, -------. 39589
Le Blanc, -------. 39594-39595
Le Blanc, Jean Bernard. supposed author
  (59090), 97259
Leblanc, L. 9043, 93807 see also France.
  Marine. Rear-Admiral Commanding the
  French Naval Forces on Station of
  Brazil and of the South Seas.
Le Blanc, Vincent. 39590-39593
Leblanc de Marconnay, H. see Marconnay,
  H. Leblanc de.
Leblois, Leduard. 39597
Le Blond, F. F. 39599-39602
Le Blond, Frank C. 39598
Leblond, Jean Baptiste. 39603-39607
Lebon, Hubert. (39608)
Le Borgne, Jeanne Francois. 39609
Le Borgne, Jeanne Francois. petitioner
  39609
Leborgne de Boigne, Claude Pierre Joseph,
  1764-1832. (37642), 39610-39611, 62892
Le Bosquet, John. 39612
Leboucher, Emile. 39614
Le Boucher, Odet-Julien, 1744-1826. 6840,
  (39613)-39614
Le Boulanger, Joseph Ignatius. 80015
Le Boulanger, Joseph Ignatius. supposed
  author 80015
Le Brasseur, --------. (39615)
Lebreton, ---------. illus. 14940, 69017
Le Breton, Adrien. see Jarry de Mancy,
  Adrien (Le Breton)
Le Breton, Guillaume. see Guillaume,
  Le Breton.
Le Breton, Raymond. see Breton, Raymond,
  1609-1679.
Le Brigant, Jacques, 1720-1804. 36525
Lebrija, Elio Antonio de, 1441?-1522. (1549)-
  1551, (6034), 17843, 45010, 52204-
  52206, (66411), (66621), 94853, 106244
Lebrixa y Pruna, Manuel de. 98905 see also
  Gremio de Panaderes, Vera Cruz.
  Thesorero Veedor y Diputado.
Le Brocq, Philio. 39616
Lebroke, A. G. 39617
Lebrun, --------, Citoyen. 12166, 39618
Lebrun, Camile. pseud. Trois mios a la
  Louisiane. (39619)
Lebrun, Henri. (16952), (35210), (39620)-
  39623
Lebrun, Isidore Frederic Thomas. 10392,
  39624, 43857, 99772
Le Brun, Laur. 39625
Le Brun, N. 61888
Le Brun, P. 39626
Le Cadet, St. Denis. pseud. Lottery. see
  Denison, Edward.
Le Candele, P. 102922
Lecart, Eugene. 92542
Le Cat, C. N. (39627)

Leccion del Dr. Gustavo Minelli. (23068
Lecciones de agricultura practica nacional.
  19972
Lecciones de aritmetica para las escuelas
  primarias. 77131
Lecciones de derecho constitucional. 27801
Lecciones de derecho maritimo internacional.
  80882
Lecciones de geographia historia. 42061
Lecciones de historia universal y miscelanea.
  31481
Lecciones de la gramatica y la filosofia de la
  lengua Mexicana. 73162
Lecciones espirituales para las tandas de
  ejercicios de S. Ignacio. 34191, 39628
Lecciones orales sobre la historia de Cuba.
  (76805)
Le Challeux, Nicolas. 4795, 39630-(39635),
  1st note after 97102
La Chatel, Martin Fumee, Sieur de Marley-
  see Fumee, Martin, Sieur de Marley-
  le-Chatel, 16th cent.
Lechevalier, Jules. 29191, 39636-(39638),
  94850
Lechavalier, T. 39639
Lechford, Thomas. 39640-39642
Lechler, John. defendant 39643
Lechmere-Point Library Association, Cam-
  bridge, Mass. 10147
Leck, Lodewijk Theodorus, Grave van Nassau
  la. see Theodorus, Lodewijk Grave van
  Nassau la Leck.
Leckie, Gould Francis. 39645
Leclair, A. tr. 5675, 39646, note after
  (64532)
Lecler, M. D. Estrada y. see Estrade y
  Lecler, M. D.
Leclerc, --------. ed. 68082
Leclerc, Charles. 39647
Leclerc, Charles Victor Emmanuel, 1772-1802.
  6978, 17481
Leclerc, Ferderic. 39652
Le Clercq, Chrestien. 25853, 39648-39651,
  80002, (80023)
L'Ecluse, Charles de. see Ecluse, Charles
  de l'.
Lecointe-Puiraveau, --------. 39656
Lecompte, E. A. (39653)
Lecomte, Ferdinand. 39657-39661
Lecompton conspiracy. 5443
Lecompton constitution; a measure of African-
  ize the Territories. (11733)
Lecompton constitution, and the admission of
  Kansas. 27827
Lecompton constitution, 1859. 39654
Lecompton constitution founded neither in law
  nor the will of the people. 18918
Lecompton constitution in the House of Repre-
  sentatives. 39654, 91261
Lecompton constitution. Speech . . . February
  24, 1858. 27942
Lecompton constitution. Speech . . . in the
  House . . . March 20, 1858. 14344
Lecompton constitution. Speech . . . March
  17, 1858. (17556)
Lecompton constitution. Speech of Hon. James
  Buffinton. 9065
Lecompton constitution. Speech of Hon. James
  F. Simmons. 81168
Lecompton constitution. Speech of Hon. John
  Sherman. 80376
Lecompton constitution. Speech of Hon. S. G.
  Andrews. 1515
Lecompton crisis. 65722
Lecompton question. 39655

Lecomte, Francois-Hippolyte. 3549
Lecomte, John. 6155
Le Conte, John Lawrence, 1825-1883. 39662-
39666, 47469, 77371, 77374, 85072
Le Count & Strong. firm publishers 76092
Le Count & Strong's San Francisco city
directory. 76092
Lecraw, J. B. 39667
Lector benevole. 55888
Lecture against American slavery. (78055)
Lecture . . . Albany. (35699)
Lecture . . . April 10th, 1851. 47490
Lecture, . . . at Aylmer, L. C. (50648)
Lecture at Boston, on a special & mournful
occasion. (46565), 3d note after 97160
Lecture at Boston, on June 10th. 1694.
104082
Lecture . . . at Chelmsford. 35315
Lecture at Cincinnati. 39317
Lecture . . . at Frankfort, Ky. (41505)
Lecture at Maryland Institute. 17651
Lecture . . . at the Copper Union. 81050
Lecture . . . at the opening of the . . .
Pictou Academical Institute. 43131
Lecture before St. John Early Closing As-
sociation. (33315)
Lecture before the American Institute.
(70407)
Lecture before the American Institute, New
York. 79587
Lecture . . . before the American Institute
of Instruction . . . at Pittsfield, Ms.
58147
Lecture . . . before the American Institute
of Instruction, at Providence, R. I.
(82463)
Lecture . . . before the American Institute
of Instruction, . . . August 26, 1863.
55839
Lecture before the American Union Academy
of Literature, Science and Art. 58985
Lecture before the Boston Mercantile Library
Association. 93688
Lecture before the Boston Young Men's
Society. (27978)
Lecture before the Brockville Library As-
sociation and Mechanic's Institute.
40817
Lecture . . . before the Democratic Union
Association of East Boston. 42708
Lecture . . . before the Glasgow Young Men's
Christian Association. 59765
Lecture . . . before the Law School of Har-
vard University. 58912
Lecture . . . before the Law School, of the
University of the City of New York.
78824
Lecture before the Literary and Scientific
Institution of Smyrna. 30002
Lecture . . . before the Lowell Institute.
30895
Lecture . . . before the Lyceum in Attle-
borough. (56412)
Lecture . . . before the Mechanics' Institute,
Montreal. 11789
Lecture before the Mechanics' Institute of
Hamilton. 93542
Lecture before the Mercantile Library As-
sociation. 93268
Lecture . . . before the M. W. Grand Lodge
of Louisiana. 62815
Lecture before the New York Geographical
and Statistical Society. 10842
Lecture before the New-York Lyceum of
Natural History. 98541

Lecture . . . before the Newburyport Lyceum.
42708
Lecture before the North Brookfield Lyceum.
(72175)
Lecture . . . before the Philomathean Society
and Hamilton Lyceum. 82793
Lecture . . . before the Philomathean Society
of Indiana University. 79749
Lecture before the Portsmouth Lyceum. 59354
Lecture before the Protestant Alliance. 71956
Lecture before the Protestant Alliance of Nova
Scotia. (37780)
Lecture . . . before the Quincy Lyceum. 42714
Lecture . . . before the Society for the Promo-
tion of Useful Knowledge. 80122
Lecture . . . before the Soldiers' and Sailors'
National Union League. 41682
Lecture before the Springfield Lyceum. 4411
Lecture . . . before the Stamford Lyceum.
80758
Lecture . . . before the St. Louis Mercantile
Library Association. 64471
Lecture . . . before the State Board of Agri-
culture. 55205
Lecture before the Teachers' Institute of Yates
and Ontario Counties. 29615
Lecture . . . before the University of Oxford.
82679
Lecture, before the Warren Library Association.
21012
Lecture . . . before the Young Men's Associa-
tion . . . December 15, 1843. 2644
Lecture . . . before the Young Men's Associa-
tion for Mutual Improvement. 51729
Lecture . . . before the Young Men's Associa-
tion in Geneva, New-York. 29615
Lecture . . . before the Young Men's Christian
Association, of Angusta, Ga. 33243
Lecture before the Young Men's Christian As-
sociation of Gettysburg. 43631
Lecture . . . before the Young Men's Polemic
Association of Cleveland. 82431
Lecture, Boston. see Boston. Lecture.
Lecture . . . by a retired editor. 8391
Lecture [by Alden Partridge.] (59499)
Lecture. By Alexander Morris. (50796)
Lecture. By Benjamin Scott. 78244
Lecutre . . . by Caleb Reed, Esq. 68540
Lecture, by Daniel Foster. 25208
Lecture . . . by Ernest Jones, Esq. 36496
Lecture . . . [by F. W. Newman.] 55008
Lecture by Frederick Douglass. 20709
Lecture. By George H. Perry. 61032
Lecture. [By George Mooar.] (50293)
Lecture . . . by Goldwin Smith. 82678
Lecture . . . [by Henry A. Miles.] 48928
Lecture . . . [by Horace Mann.] 44324
Lecture by Horatio Seymour. 79650
Lecture. By J. Willis Menard. (47795)
Lecture . . . . [By James H. Means.] 47254
Lecture . . . by John Hay. 35846
Lecture. By John Miles. 48934
Lecture . . . [by John William Dawson.] 18955
Lecture. By L. U. Reavis. 68306
Lecture. By Leone Levi, Esq. 40754
Lecture . . . by Matthew H. Richey. 71115
Lecture by Michael Doheny. 20533
Lecture. By Newman Hall. (29833)
Lecture . . . by Ninian Pinckney. 62907
Lecture . . . [by Orville Dewey.] 19862
Lecture by Philip Carteret Hill. 31853
Lecture. . . . By Rev. G. G. Lawrence. 39353
Lecture . . . by Rev. George W. Hill. 31821
Lecture by Rev. James Keogh. (37592)
Lecture by Rev. Mr. Mitchell. 49730

Lecture. By Rev. Thomas Crisp. 17542

Lecture . . . . [By Robert Sedgewick.] 78768

Lecture by the late Hon. James McDowell. (43195)

Lecture. By the Rev. Dr. Dill. (20157)

Lecture by the Rev. Hugh Stowell Brown. 8486

Lecture. By the Rev. Joseph Fletcher. 24730

Lecture. By the Rev. Lord Wriothesley Russell. (74411)

Lecture . . . by the Rev. Marmaduke Miller. 49039

Lecture by the Rev. William Beven. 5106

Lecture, by the Rev. William Sommerville. 86860

Lecture . . . [by Thomas Wentworth Higginson.] 31755

Lecture by Wendell Phillips. 62528

Lecture . . . [by William Elder.] 22097

Lecture. By William Morris. (50882)

Lecture comprising the history of the Second Parish in Beverly. 92044

Lecture concluding the university course. (69092)

Lecture . . . December 3, 1849. 42888

Lecture . . . December 21st, 1848. 12150

Lecture, delivered April, 1834. 103048

Lecture, delivered April 17, 1843. 88864

Lecture delivered at Alleghany, Penn. 89920

Lecture, delivered at Astoria, N. Y. 20511

Lecture delivered at Bradford, Ms. 89568

Lecture . . . delivered at Brooklyn, N. Y. 62528

Lecture delivered at Ithica. (37804)

Lecture delivered at Jefferson Medical College. 70177

Lecture, delivered at Lee, Mass. 83738

Lecture, delivered at Lyceum Hall, Lynn. 79677

Lecture delivered at New Haven, Feb. 16, 1852. 80362

Lecture delivered at New Haven, Ct. 83754

Lecture delivered at North Chelsea. (11216)

Lecture delivered at Oxford, England. 21719

Lecture delivered at Petersburg. 97608

Lecture, delivered at Philadelphia. 97647

Lecture delivered at the Brooklyn Academy of Music. 9615

Lecture . . . delivered at the capitol. 27693

Lecture delivered at the Catholic Institute. 68551

Lecture delivered at the Cheshnut Literary Scientific Institution. 8182

Lecture delivered at the Congregational Orthodox Church. 77299

Lecture delivered at the Friend's Institute, London. 78246

Lecture delivered at the Lyceum in Stock-bridge. 78835

Lecture delivered at the opening of the Medical Department. 79469

Lecture delivered at the opening of the Medical Department of the Columbian College, Washington, D. C. 31328

Lecture delivered . . . at the request of the Columbian Teachers' Association. 18139

Lecture delivered at the Rush Medical College. 24764

Lecture delivered at the time of the Trent difficulty. 17591

Lecture delivered at Timstall. 64121

Lecture delivered . . . before Bell's Com-mercial College. 78485

Lecture delivered before the alumni of the Law Department. (68164)

Lecture delivered before the American Institute of Instruction, at Concord. 13418

Lecture delivered before the American Institute of Instruction, at . . . Lowell . . . 1838. 70872

Lecture delivered before the American Institute of Instruction, at Montpelier. 8340

Lecture delivered before the American Institute of Instruction, at their anniversary, in August, 1834, at Boston. 92307

Lecture delivered before the Catholic Institute of Baltimore. 78380

Lecture delivered before the Chicago Lyceum. 2928

Lecture delivered before the Detroit Lyceum in 1831. 77868

Lecture delivered before the Dublin Young Men's Christian Association. 9855

Lecture delivered before the Eagle Artillery. 37377

Lecture delivered before the Essex Institute. 103365

Lecture delivered before the Georgia Histori-cal Society. 11174

Lecture delivered before the Lancaster Literar Institute. 76391

Lecture delivered before the Law Academy of Philadelphia. 68004

Lecture delivered before the Litchfield County Bar. 78814

Lecture delivered before the Lyceum of the Lane Street Public School. 49551

Lecture delivered before the Maryland Institute for the Promotion of the Mechanic Arts. 97610

Lecture delivered before the Mercantile Association of Chicago. 10207

Lecture delivered before the Mercantile Library Association, Clinton Hall, December 29, 1835. 28101

Lecture delivered before the Mercantile Library Association, . . . January 5, 1856. 28145

Lecture delivered before the Mercantile Librar Association of San Francisco. 78398

Lecture, delivered before the Mercantile Library Company of Philadelphia. (79202

Lecture delivered before the New England Society. 37684

Lecture, delivered before the New York His-torical Society. 101338

Lecture delivered before the New York His-torical Society . . . 1st of June, 1853. 23249

Lecture delivered before the N. Y. Historical Society, in December, 1864. 82681

Lecture delivered before the Onondaga His-torical Society. 24567

Lecture delivered before the Smithsonian Insti-tution. 11390

Lecture delivered before the students of the Massachusetts Normal Art School. 84492

Lecture, delivered before the Young Men's Association of the city of Troy. 8975

Lecture delivered before the Young Men's Associations of . . . Buffalo and Lockport. 32933

Lecture delivered before the Young Men's Christian Association. 92348

Lecture delivered before the Young Men's Democratic Club of Philadelphia. 66543

Lecture delivered before the Young Men's Mercantile Library Association, of Cincinnati. (7150)

Lecture delivered before the Young Men's Mercantile Library Association of Cincinnati, December 3, 1846. 2729

Lecture delivered before the Young Men's Mutual Improvement Association. 10168

Lecture delivered by C. Stuart, Esq. 93139

Lecture, delivered by him [i. e. M. W. Philipps] before the Young Men's Christian Association. 62453

Lecture delivered by invitation in Petersburg, Va. (29860)

Lecture delivered by invitation of the "Hollywood Memorial Association." 51315

Lecture delivered by Ninian Pinkney. 62968

Lecture delivered by Prof. J. R. Buchanan. 8868

Lecture delivered by the Hon. F. P. Stanton. 90414

Lecture, delivered December 30th, 1852. 92160

Lecture, delivered in Baltimore. 20513

Lecture, delivered in Buglin and London. (72309)

Lecture delivered in N. Y., Jan. 11, 1863. 18790

Lecture, delivered in New-York, Washington, Boston, and other cities. (18793)

Lecture delivered in Philadelphia. 84494

Lecture delivered in . . . Portland. 31013

Lecture delivered in Rev. Mr. Vickers' Church. 90112

Lecture delivered in Smith & Nixon's Hall, Cincinnati. 90111

Lecture delivered in Texas, in 1860. 69544

Lecture . . . delivered in the Catholic Summer School extension course. 84516

Lecture delivered in the Corn Exchange Hall. 4020

Lecture, delivered in the course of scientific lectures. 99269

Lecture, delivered in the Friends' Institute . . . March 26th, 1866. 3634

Lecture delivered in the hall of All Souls' College. 4944

Lecture delivered in the Mechanics Institute of Hamilton and Rossville. 43140

Lecture delivered in the Music Hall. 95491

Lecture delivered in the University of Maryland. 32395

Lecture delivered Oct. 24, 1854. 8792

Lecture, delivered on Sunday evening, December 19, 1847. 74541

Lecture delivered on the 4th of August 1864. 89785

Lecture, delivered on the sixteenth of August. 22429

Lecture, delivered on the 10th December, 1862. 42026

Lecture, delivered through and by S. Judd Pardee. (58560)

Lecture delivered to the senior class of Andover Theological Seminary. 85224

Lecture . . . Dublin . . . October the 26th, 1864. 9857

Lecture . . . Feb. 9, 1869. (58695)

Lecture . . . February 7th, 1833. 29895

Lecture . . . Feb. 12, 1869. 29630

Lecture: . . . February 20th, 1866. 46177

Lecture, . . . 5th December, 1837. (64646)

Lecture first. 96187

Lecture for the times. (36934)

Lecture . . . given before the Young Men's Association. 2647

Lecture in aid of the Public Library, Newburyport. 42708

Lecture . . . in . . . Albany. 47181

Lecture in behalf of the Toledo University of Arts and Trades. 91013

Lecture in Boston. 30 d. 9 m. 1710. 46427

Lecture in Boston 20. d. 1. m. 1690. 46465

Lecture, . . . in Buffalo, N. Y. (56792)

Lecture, in conclusion of a series in relation to the Chinese people. 89253

Lecture . . . in continuation of the popular view of the American civil war. 32898

Lecture in defence of the Maine law. 30845

Lecture . . . in Lowell, Jan. 4, 1852. 26801

Lecture in opposition to the Temperance Society. 77014

Lecture . . . in . . . Pittsburgh, . . . April 3, 1852. 64617

Lecture . . . in Providence, R. I. 24182

Lecture . . . in review of "The catholic chapter in the history of the United States." 2875

Lecture in St. Anne's Church. (21878)

Lecture, in the audience of the General Assembly. 46463

Lecture; in the audience of the General Assembly at Boston. (46227)

Lecture in the Free Trade Hall, Manchester. (16217)

Lecture delivered in the New Jerusalem Temple. 93183

Lecture . . . in . . . Troy, December 10th, 1839. 4618

Lecture . . . in Washington, D. C. (31246)

Lecture, introductory to a course of law lectures. (14829)

Lecture introductory to a course of lectures. 69654

Lecture introductory to the course of lectures. (81049)

Lecture introductory to the eighty-third course. 83654

Lecture introductory to the second course. 7090

Lecture . . . January, 1845. 11902

Lecture . . . January 5, 1854. 42965

Lecture, . . . January 19, 1853. [By Robert M. Charlton.] 11250

Lecture. . . . January 19, 1853. By Samuel A. Eliot. (22174)

Lecture, . . . January 16, 1870. 65379

Lecture . . . January 26, 1853. (58346)

Lecture . . . January 31, 1850. 33593

Lecture . . . June 21, 1852. 38269

Lecture . . . March 8, 1852. 33589

Lecture . . . March 7, 1854. 25051

Lecture, . . . March 22d, 1854. 26347

Lecture . . . March 26, 1843. (43541)

Lecture . . . March 24th, and repeated . . . July 28, 1869. 32439

Lecture . . . Medical Department of the University of Nashville. 41313

Lecture . . . New York, before the Young Ladies' Society for Mutual Improvement. 105487

Lecture, . . . November 10th, 1860. (50861)

Lecture, . . . November 24th, 1862. 28163

Lecture, occasioned by the death of the Rev. E. W. Channing. 41387

Lecture of a course by members of the Massachusetts Historical Society, delivered before the Lowell Institute, Feb. 5, 1869. 71787

Lecture of a course by members of the
Massachusetts Historical Society,
delivered . . . Feb. 16, 1869. 22428
Lecture of Gen. Thomas L. Kane. 37010
Lecture of the Honourable Charles Sumner.
93641
Lecture on African civilization. 12953
Lecture on alleged violations of neutrality
by England. 4943
Lecture on British colonial slavery. (35434)
Lecture on British Columbia and Vancouver's
Island. 43149
Lecture on Christianity and the civil laws.
(42859)
Lecture on colonial slavery. 29892
Lecture on colonization and emigration.
32359
Lecture on drunkenness. 81670
Lecture on earthquakes. 104853
Lecture on education. [By Alden Partridge.]
58962
Lecture on education. By Horace Mann.
44320
Lecture on existing evils, and their remedy.
105593
Lecture on Exodus 18. 21. 7811
Lecture on Garrisonian politics. 31948
Lecture on "human progress." 93721
Lecture on infant baptism. (82540)
Lecture on . . . intoxicating drinks. 39334
Lecture on money and currency. 69093
Lecture on Mormonism. 91595
Lecture on mysterious knockings. 43686
Lecture on mysterious religious emotions.
97734
Lecture on national character. (56807)
Lecture on national character, . . . at the
Jamaica Lyceum. 56812
Lecture on national defence. (56499), (58963)
Lecture on natural history. 11729
Lecture on Negro slavery. 67305
Lecture on non-intervention. 90111
Lecture on oaths. 26797
Lecture on political morality. 79850
Lecture on popular education. 41315
Lecture on railroads. 35476
Lecture on Sable Island. 27460
Lecture on scientific education. 39887
Lecture on secession. 30833
Lecture on slavery, delivered in . . .
Salford. 95506
Lecture on slavery, delivered in the Wesleyan
Chapel. 95507
Lecture on slavery the cause of the civil war
in the United States. (21691), 82072
Lecture on some of the means of elevating
the character of the working classes.
49703
Lecture on some parts of the natural history
of New Jersey. 49744
Lecture on telegraphic language. 62638
Lecture on temperance, delivered in . . .
Charlestown. 22309
Lecture on Texas. 16775
Lecture on Texas, delivered by Mr. J. de
Cordova. (19190)
Lecture . . . [on] that system. (72622)
Lecture on the affair of the Trent. (29837)
Lecture on the alleged uncertainty of the law.
62638
Lecture on the anti-slavery enterprise.
93666
Lecture on the backward march of American
society. (32808)
Lecture on the city of Patterson. 20021

Lecture on the character and services of James
Madison. 3450
Lecture on the condition and true interests of
the laboring class. 89974
Lecture on the condition of the country.
(62500)
Lecture on the condition of the United States.
(9656)
Lecture on the . . . decline of political and
national morality. 31101
Lecture on the development of the intellectual
faculties. 11117
Lecture on the different races of men. 42764
Lecture on the discovery of America by the
Northmen. 18794
Lecture on the diversities of the human
character. 82921
Lecture on the duties of physicians. 105949
Lectures on the early closing movement.
39831
Lecture on the epidemic cholera. 78849
Lecture on the excellency of the Gospel of
Christ. 90203
Lecture on the expediency of establishing a
Medical College and Hospital. 44482
Lecture on the fifty-second Pslam. 3500
Lecture on the gulf stream. (2588)
Lecture on the Haytien revolutions. 82794
Lecture on the historical destiny of women.
42413
Lecture on the history and uses of Athenaeums.
40985
Lecture on the history of commercial enter-
prise. 89334
Lecture on the history of the state of New
Jersey. 37786
Lecture on the importance of a Christian
basis of political economy. 33593
Lecture . . . on the importance of the militia
system. (56499)
Lecture on the improvement of medical
education in the United States. 58193
Lecture on the late improvements in steam
navigation. 76978
Lecture on the life and military services of
General James Clinton. 10279
Lecture on the life of Dr. Franklin. 43599
Lecture on the literary opportunities of men
of business. (68546)
Lecture on the Maine law. 9409
Lecture on the mechanical industry. 36334
Lecture on the mercantile law of Lower
Canada. 50207
Lecture on the mineralogy of Nova Scotia.
38834
Lecture on the moral, social and political
condition of Utah Territory. 7949
Lecture on the nature, character, and value
of our civil institutions. 29855
Lecture on the north and the south. 24458,
51593
Lecture on the occult sciences. 54995
Lecture on the Oregon Territory. 8673
Lecture on the origin and development of the
first constituents of civilization. 40985
Lecture on the Ottawa River. 61032
Lecture on the past, the present, and the
future. 43579
Lecture on the pilgrim fathers; illustrative of
the government prize picture by Charles
Lucy. 32539
Lecture on the pilgrim fathers, illustrative of
the picture by C. Lucy. 67436
Lecture on the pleasures and vices of the city
(29753)

Lecture on the present relations of free labor to slave labor. 12954

Lecture on the prodigal son. 103554

Lecture on the rail road to the Pacific. 14777

Lecture on the recession of Niagara Falls. (39857), 74632

Lecture on the romance of American history. 68608

Lecture on the source of all civilization. 36982

Lecture on the subject of prohibitory laws. 42367

Lecture on the topography and history of New-York. 79651

Lecture on the trials and dangers of frontier life. 33195

Lecture on the use and abuse of emulation. 17626

Lecture on the used of history. 44376

Lecture on the usefulness of lyceums. (62519)

Lecture on the value of the American Union. 25020, 39671

Lecture on the Working Men's Party. 23271

Lecture on true mercantile character. 25009

Lecture on war, foreign and civil. 16778

Lecture on witchcraft. 94504

Lecture I. The Eldorado of the north. 83599

Lecture prononcee par Messire H. Rouxel. 73520

Lecture prononcee par Mr. Rameau. 67623

Lecture publique faite a l'Institut Canadien. 19766

Lecture read at a quarterly meeting. 33384

Lecture read at the City Hall in Roxbury, Mass. 66768

Lecture read before the Boston Fraternity. 82677

Lecture read before the Law Academy of Philadelphia. 79862

Lecture, read before the Worcester Lyceum. 101516

Lecture read December, 1865. 10842

Lecture read May 6, 1863. 5232

Lecture . . . September 8, 1863. (33598)

Lecture sermon, asserting God's right. 92098

Lecture sermon, delivered before the First Universalist Society. 83578

Lecture-sermon had at Boston, July 2. 1719. 91966

Lecture-sermon (June 25. 1701.) 50303

Lecture sermon on the spring season of the Gospel. 81595

Lecture sermon, preached at Hadley. 12335

Lecture sermon, preaching at New Milford. 9331

Lecture-sermon, preach'd at the North Society in Lyme. 22140

Lecture showing why females should be interested in Odd-Fellowship. (67178)

Lecture . . . Springfield, October 19th, 1867. 20455

Lecture sur l'education, devant l'Institut Canadien. 50704

Lecture . . . the 15th August 1864. 46841

Lecture, . . . the morning after the funeral of the Misses Haven. 43382

Lecture III. From the gold fields to the land of the midnight sun. 83599

Lecture to the Bridgeport Lyceum. 31636

Lecture to the normal classes of the Academy and Female Seminary. 92040

Lecture to working men. 29832

Lecture, . . . Troy, February 24, 1846. 4618

Lecture . . . 29th December, 1851. 37789

Lecture, twice delivered at Leeds. 103881

Lecture II. In the heart of the Alaskan gold fields. 83599

Lecture upon the controversy between Pennsylvania and Virginia. (17364)

Lecture, upon the moral and religious education of the people of California. 91996

Lecture upon the naturalization law of the United States. 8674

Lecture upon the recession of Niagara Falls. 74632

Lecture . . . Worcester, November 24, 1846. 58597

Lectures addressed not behind a curtain to one unfortunate man. 52330

Lectures, and annual reports, on education. 44321

Lectures and sermons. 1808

Lectures before the Huntington Library Association. 80150

Lectures before the Middlesex County Lyceum. 39669

Lectures, corrected and improved. 84108

Lectures delivered before the American Institute of Education. 77887

Lectures delivered before the American Institute of Instruction. 50219

Lectures delivered before the American Institute of Instruction, at Lowell, Massachusetts. 42484

Lectures delivered before the American Institute of Instruction, at New Bedford, August 17, 1842. (52489)

Lectures delivered before the American Institute of Instruction, at New Haven, Conn. 52983

Lectures delivered before the American Institute of Instruction, at Plymouth. 63478

Lectures delivered before the American Institute of Instruction, at Portland, August, 1844. 64348

Lectures delivered before the American Institute of Instruction, at Providence, R. I. 66275

Lectures delivered before the American Institute of Instruction, . . . 1831. (39668)

Lectures delivered before the Lowell Institute. 59354

Lectures delivered in a course before the Lowell Institute in Boston. 45854

Lectures . . . 1867-68, and '69. 58701

Lectures, etc. 29836

Lectures historical, expository, and practical 39670

Lectures, literary and biographical. 30778

Lectures of George Thompson. 95497

Lectures [of Giesecke.] 57576

Lectures of Lola Montez. 50129

Lectures [of the American Institute of Instruction.] 85202

Lectures [of the Philadelphia Catholic Summer School Extension.] 84516

Lectures of W. A. Smith. (64773)

Lectures on African colonization and kindred subjects. 12954

Lectures on American literature. 38075

Lectures on botany. (43383)

Lectures on British India. 95498

Lectures on chemistry. 105792

Lectures on city life and character. 13466

Lectures on colonial slavery. 96400

Lectures on colonization and colonies. 47973

Lectures on courtship, love and marriage. 84541

Lectures on elocution. 80347

Lectures on faith. 83160, 83163, 83223-83224, 83229

Lectures on geology. 42764

Lectures on geology; being outlines of the science. 98542

Lectures on great men. 51629

Lectures on gold. 36879

Lectures on history. 98304, 105938

Lectures on history and chronology. 10698

Lectures on history, and general policy. (65513)

Lectures on human governments. 46902

Lectures on mental philosophy and theology. (70947)

Lectures on modern history. (82680)

Lectures on modern history, from the irruption of the northern nations. 85343-85344

Lectures on mollusca. 11000

Lectures on moral philosophy. 104940, 104945, 104946

Lectures on occasion of the recent religious excitements. 96187

Lectures on philosophy. 98634

Lectures on poetry. 76381

Lectures on popular subjects. 25050, 39671

Lectures on revivals of religion. 89736-89737

Lectures on school-keeping. 29844

Lectures on slavery. (39672)

Lectures on slavery and its remedy. 61361

Lectures on slavery, delivered in the First Presbyterian Church. 70849

Lectures on slavery: delivered in the North Presbyterian Church. 70850

Lectures on temperance. 56036

Lectures on the apostolical succession. 85284, 85285, 82587, 85290, 85302, 85312, 85314, 85319

Lectures on the British and American constitutions. 535

Lectures on the discovery of America. 18531

Lectures . . . on the discovery, resources & progress of North America. 30773

Lectures on the elements of political economy. 16621

Lectures on the English language and on education. 102400

Lectures on the evidences of the Christian religion. 84109

Lectures on the philosophy and practice of slavery. 84742-84742A

Lectures on the prayer of faith. 70950

Lectures on the prelatical doctrine of apostolical succession. 85297

Lectures on the present crisis by the late Theodore Parker. 85750

Lectures on the progress of civilization and government. 42032

Lectures on the restrictive system. 19835

Lectures on the study of history. 82681

Lectures on the ventilation of buildings. 74491

Lectures on the "west." 76969

Lectures on the works and genius of Washington Allston. 101411

Lectures on theology. 97595, 97597-97598

Lectures on various subjects. 44324

Lectures on witchcraft. 98039

Lectures read at quarterly meetings. 66305

Lectures read to the seniors in Harvard College. 11896

Lectures to young ladies. 61355

Lectures to young men on their dangers. 82428

Lectures to youth. 84284

Lectures upon drawing. 84495

Lectures upon natural history. 24791

Lectures upon portions of history. 6791

Lectures upon the philosophy of history. 80076

Lecutt, A. pseud. Saturniad. see Baker, W. D.

Lecuy, -------. tr. 25583, 78109

Ledderhose, Carl Frederick. 39673

Leddra, William. 72199

Lede, Ch. van. 39674

Lederer, -------. 83287

Lederer, John. 39676

Lederstrumpg-Erzahlungen. (16461)

Ledesma, Antonio Colmenero de. see Colmenero de Ledesma, Antonio.

Ledesma, B. A. 39677

Ledesma, Clemente de. (39678)

Ledesma, Ph. Rod. de. 39680

Ledesma, Valentine. 39681

Ledesme, -------. (39682)

Lediard, Thomas. (39683)

Lednum, John. 39684

Ledo, Octaviano Munoz. see Munoz Ledo, Octaviano.

Ledo y Burguiza, P. Munoz. see Munoz Ledo y Burguiza, P.

Ledoux, L. P. 39686

Ledru, Andre-Pierre. 39687-39688

Leduard Lebois, au Calomniateur Therou. 39597

Leduc, ------- St. Germain. see Saint-Germain-Leduc, -------.

Le Duc, Eugene Emmanuel Viollet. see Viollet le Duc, Eugene Emmanuel, 1814-1879.

Le Duc, W. G. 39689

Ledyard, Isaac. 39690

Ledyard, John. 10973, 39691-(39692), 87896, 88976, 88991, 88993, 1st note after 96495

Lee, A. 70741

Lee, Alfred, Bp., 1807-1887. 39693-(39694), 83792

Lee, Andrew. 39695-39696

Lee, Ann, 1736-1784. 102602-102603

Lee, Arthur, 1740-1792. 5220, 20052, (35918), (39697)-(39706), 39785, 69549, 80040, 88969, 89179, 93611, 96598, 97159 see also U. S. Commissioners to the Six Nations of Indians.

Lee, Arthur, 1740-1792. supposed author 1258, 1783, (39697), 1st note after 100576

Lee, C. H. 39718

Lee, Charles. supposed author note just before 100452, 100583

Lee, Charles, 1731-1782. (3684), 9259, (11881), 16587-16588, (26320), 26867, 38902-38903, 39707-39714, 50380, 66807, 69549, 74870, 92830-92831, 92850, 101687

Lee, Charles, 1731-1782. defendant at court martial 39711-39713

Lee, Charles, 1758-1815. 27095, 69760 see also U. S. Department of Justice.

Lee, Charles, fl. 1863. 24002

Lee, Charles A. 31331, 39715-(39716)

Lee, Charles Carter. (39717), 39751

Lee, Chauncey. 39719-39720

Lee, Christopher. 100576

Lee, D. 39723

Lee, Daniel. 39721, (61169)

Lee, Daniel, 1806-1895. (39724)

Lee, Day Kellogg. 39722

Lee, Dumont. 3423

Lee, Edmund F. 39725

Lee, Elias. 39726
Lee, Elisha. (39727)-39728
Lee, Eliza Buckminster. 39729-(39731)
Lee, F. A. 39732
Lee, F. D. 39733
Lee, Fitzhugh, 1835-1905. 15364, (19568)
Lee, Frances. 27387, 39734
Lee, Gideon, 1778-1841. 54395 see also
  New York (City) Mayor, 1833-1834 (Lee)
Lee, H. T. 39758
Lee, Hannah F. 39737-39738, 4th note after
  94244, 94652, note after 96341
Lee, Henry, 1756-1818. (3684), 14162-14163,
  39739-39749, (49322), 78997, 100220-
  100224, 101803, note after 101813, 2d
  note after 101883, 2d note after 104027
  see also Virginia. Governor, 1791-
  1795 (Henry Lee)
Lee, Henry, 1756-1818. supposed author
  100423, 100428, 100508
Lee, Henry, 1782-1867. 10889, 23363, 23449,
  39753-39757, (39766), 1st note after
  69741, 70258, 92843
Lee, Henry, 1787-1837. (39742), (39750)-
  39751
Lee, Henry, 1787-1837. supposed author
  39752
Lee, Henry W., Bp. 39759-39761
Lee, J. A. (69154), 83665
Lee, J. K. 39766
Lee, James. 39762
Lee, Jerena. 39763
Lee, Jesse. (39764)-39765, 95758
Lee, John. 39767
Lee, John, fl. 1742. 97454
Lee, John Hancock. 39768, 39802
Lee, Jonathan, 1718-1788. 39769-39770
Lee, Jonathan, fl. 1837. 39771
Lee, Joseph, 1742-1819. 39772-39773, 92241
Lee, L. P. 32214, note after 89469
Lee, Leroy M. 39774
Lee, Luther. 39775-39776
Lee, Martin. (31868)
Lee, Mary Elizabeth. 39777
Lee, Mary Randolph (Custis) 1806-1873.
  (18157)
Lee, Nelson. 39778
Lee, Pamela. defendant 39779
Lee, Richard Bland. 39780-39781
Lee, Richard E. 39782
Lee, Richard Henry, 1732-1794. 383, 15596,
  30179, (39783)-39788, 40583, 79369,
  97533 see also U. S. Continental Con-
  gress, 1775. Committee to Prepare the
  Address.
Lee, Richard Henry. 1794-1865. 39789
Lee, Robert Edward, 1807-1870. 7467, 15403,
  (39790), 39793, (70984), 88422
Lee, Samuel, 1625-1691. 39793-39797, 44124
Lee, Samuel, 1803-1881. 39798-39799
Lee, Samuel J. 87942
Lee, Samuel Phillips, 1812-1897. 39800
Lee, Silas. 39801
Lee, Stephen D. (19568)
Lee, Thomas, 1690-1750. 99989 see also
  Virginia (Colony) Governor, 1749-1750
  (Thomas Lee)
Lee, Thomas Hancock. see Lee, John
  Hancock.
Lee, Thomas J. 45090 see also Maryland.
  Commissioner on the Survey of the
  Boundary Between Maryland and Virginia.
Lee, W. 39805
Lee, W. B. (39806)
Lee, William. 19276
Lee, William. reporter 18123

Lee, Sir William, 1688-1754. (15052)
Lee, William, 1739-1795. (39804), 65110,
  88969 see also U. S. Commissioner
  to the Netherlands.
Lee, William, 1772-1840. 39803
Lee, William Henry Fitzhugh, 1837-1891. 15364
Lee, William Phillips. petitioner note before
  51856
Lee, Z. Collins. (39807)-39808
Lee & Walker. firm publishers (39809)
Lee, Mass. Lee Academy. see Lee Academy,
  Lee, Mass.
Lee Academy, Lee, Mass. 39810
Lee and his generals. 85554
Lee, and his lieutenants. (63868)
Lee & Walker's musical almanac for 1869.
  (39809)
Leech, ---------. 29890, 91524
Leech, D. D. T. 39811, (64499), 64502
Leech, John. illus. 59176, 92465, 97035
Leech, Samuel. 39812
Leech. (39813)
Leechman, William. (39814)
Leeds, Daniel, 1652-1720. 28453, (37183),
  39815-39821, 66735-66736, 66740-66743,
  1st note after 94666
Leeds, Felix. 39822
Leeds, Francis Godolphin Osborne, 5th Duke of,
  1751-1799. 80625
Leeds, George. (39823)
Leeds, Joseph. 39824
Leeds, S. P. 39825
Leeds, Titan. (39826)-39827, (78760), 84552
Leeds (Henry H.) & Minor. firm 83842, 83852
Leeds, England. Anti-slavery Meeting, 1855.
  29236, (39828)
Leeds' almanac for 1724. 37125, 96482, note
  after 101268
Leeds Anti-slavery Association. (39828),
  91960
Leeds anti-slavery tracts. (39828)
Leeds Copper Mining . . . Company. 39829
Leeds mercury. 9689, (10621), 103118
Leemans, C. (39830)
Leeming, John. 39831
Leer-en grondbeginselen van burgerlijke vryheit
  en regeering enz. (27927)
Leerrede bij gelegenheid der gelukkige hereeni-
  ging van Curacao. 51288
Leerrede, uitgespoken te Taunton den 18. en
  25. Febr. 1776. 96330
Leerwijze der Engelsche taal. 67343
Lees, A. H. (39832)
Lees, Thomas J. 39833
Lee's anonymous strictures on a pamphlet.
  92850
Lee's last campaign. 26270, 28031
Leesboek voor de jeugd. (35191), 101840
Leese, Joseph P. 39834
Leeser, Isaac. 39835, 56633
Leete, -------. 39836
Leeven en daaden der doorluchtigste zee-helden.
  6440
Leeven en daden der doorluchtigste zee-helden
  en ont-deckers van landen. (6439), note
  after 98470
Leeven van de weleerwaarden en zeer geleerden
  Heer Jonathan Edwards. 21952
Leevensschets van den Generaal George Washing-
  ton. 5361, 101777
Leeward Islands, Bishop of the. see Coleridge,
  William Hart, Bishop of Barbados, 1789-
  1849.
Leeward Islands. Governor (Hamilton) 84563
  see also Hamilton, Walter.

Leeward Islands. Laws, statutes, etc. (1699), (10891), 12025, 39416, 85361
Leewis, Denis de. see Richel, Dionisio.
Le Febure, --------, fl. 1662. 93224
Lefebre de Cheverus, Jean Louis Anne Magdelene. see Cheverus, Jean Louis Anne Magdelene Lefebre de, Cardinal, 1768-1836.
Lefebvre, H. P. tr. 12240
Lefebvre, Rene. pseud. Paris en Amerique see Laboulaye, Édouard Rene Lefebvre de, 1811-1883.
Lefebvre, Rene. pseud. Paris in America. see Laboulaye, Édouard Rene Lefebvre de, 1811-1883.
Le Febvre de Villebrune, -------. tr. 36805, 2d note after 97686
Lefever, J. defendant 25807, note after 91560
Le Fevre, C. F. 37369, 39837
Lefevre, E. (39838)-39839, 47036
Le Fevre, Jacques, d'Etaples, d. 1537. 69130, 74801
Lefevre, P. F. A. (39841)
Lefevre, Pierre Paul. 37115
Leffingwell, Clark & Co. firm 39842
Lefort, ------. tr. 67692
Le Francois, Armand. tr. 69048
Lefroy, Sir John Henry, 1817-1890. 39843, 74710, 82862, 83631
Leftwich, W. M. (39844)
Legacies of Washington. 101711
Legacion de Buenos Aires en Montevideo. 9019, (39845)
Leacion de Chile en Bolivia. 87255
Legacy for children. 31826
Legacy of fun. 41196
Legacy of James Wilmer. 104574
Legacy [of Samuel Hartlib.] 30702
Legacy of the father of his country. 101553, 101586, 101592, 101686
Legacy to his friends. 35752
Legacy to Irish Americans. (56653)
Legacy to the people of America. 101899
Le Gal, Eugene. (39846), 77829-(77830)
Legal, G. 39847-39848
Legal and evangelical repentance distinguished. 20059
Legal and political hermeneutics. 40977
Legal argument before the Supreme Court. 91629
Legal bearings in the Louisiana case. 39849
Legal bibliography. 45032
Legal claim of the British sugar colonies. 39850, 3d note after 102842
Legal classic. 61381
Legal effect of the secession troubles. 39851, 42019
Legal forms for the acknowledgement of deeds. 1126
Legal guide for oil companies and stockholders. (79771)
Legal opinion of Richard W. Greene. 66276
Legal opinion of the Hon. William Hunter. 66276
Legal opinion to Baring, Brothers & Co. (36917), 102321
Legal opinions of Attorney Generals McKean & Dallas. 5679
Legal opinions of the Honorable Joseph M. White. 103427
Legal opinions on certain titles to land. 95095
Legal opinions on the title of Richard Hackley. 29479
Legal policy of the United States. 94491
Legal, political and business manual. 45238

Legal proceedings in Manshire against sin. 3485
Legal profession. 92185
Legal provision respecting the education and employment of children. 3469, 15725
Legal reform. 24274
Legal remedy. (77011)
Legal Representatives of the Late Francis Pelletreau. claimants 59584, 93383
Legal resistencia al despotismo. 31520
Legal restrictions upon the commerce in money. 61970
Legal restrictions upon the commerce in money. 61970
Legal review of the case of Dred Scott. 78260
Legal rights, liabilities, and duties of women. 44376
Legal tender act. 89033
Legal-tender acts. 89094
Legal tender notes. 89036
Legal title to property in slaves. 30386
Legal view of the "Alabama" case. 64102
Legal view of the seizure of Messrs. Mason and Slidell. 45451
Legal views of the Alabama case. 58731
L'Egalite, Messrs. pseud. Spectavle nouveaux. 89134
Legand, John D. 100418
Legare, Hugh Swinton, 1797?-1843. 39853-39855 see also U. S. Department of State
Legare, J. D. ed. 88273
Legare, J. M. 39856
Legare, Mary Swinton. see Bullen, Mary Swinton (Legare)
Legaspi, Michael Lopez de. see Lopez de Legaspi, Michael.
Legatio babilonica occeanea decas. Poemata. 1565, 45013
Legazpi, Garcia de. defendant 86404 see also Philippine Islands (Spanish Colony) Adelantado (Legazpi) defendant
Legeay, Urbain. 8407
Legend de Cachuati. 44249
Legend for Christmas. 82518
Legend of Baltimore. 20482
Legend of Boston. 57150
Legend of Captain Jones, relating to his adventure to sea. 41683
Legend of Captaine Jones, the two parts. 41684
Legend of frontier life. 10767
Legend of Gotham. 77346
Legend of Kentucky. 29786
Legend of Lookout Mountain. A poem. 51455
Legend of Mexico. 9234
Legend of Multnomah Falls. 84303
Legend of Northern Mexico. 69080
Legend of "Norwood." 18354
Legend of old Orange. 55013
Legend of Quetzalcoatl. 55012
Legend of Rockland Lake. 82511
Legend of Sleepy Hollow. 18582, 35186-35187
Legend of St. Domingo. 18537
Legend of St. Inigoe's. (37419), (37423)
Legend of the border. 97171
Legend of the early settlement of New England. 69552
Legend of the Katskill Mountains. 35194
Legend of the Katskills. 71486
Legend of the Manitou Rock. (39857), 74632
Legend of the Mohawk in 1778. 22297
Legend of the mound-builders. 46828, 46836, 46840
Legend of the Ohio. (4724)
Legend of the rocks, and other poems. 51699
Legend of the Santee. 81237-(81238)
Legend of the sleeping dew. (38371)

Legend of the Susquehanna. 65068
Legend of the White Sulphur. 103491
Legend, with historical and traditionary notes.
    51040
Legendary, consisting of original pieces.
    104508
Legendary, dramatic tale. 103992
Legendary lore of the lower St. Lawrence.
    (40004)
Legende Canadienne. 29257
Legende doree et poems sur l'esclavage.
    41915
Legende Latine de S. Brandaines. 39858
Legendes Canadiennes. 11330
Legendes Canadiennes. Recueilles par J.
    Huston. 34040
Legendes des treize republiques. 16462
Legendes Indiennes recueillies chez les peup-
    lades sauvages. 46834
Legends and poetry of the Hudson. 33517
Legends of a log-cabin. 39859, 1st note after
    95662, 2d note after 102991
Legends of Ireland. 103049
Legends of Mexico. (41399)
Legends of Montauk. 2524
Legends of New England. By Frances Lee.
    39734
Legends of New-England. . . . By John G.
    Whittier. 103808
Legends of New England. By Julia Gill and
    Frances Lee. 27387
Legens of New-York. 8846
Legends of the gulf. 29743
Legends of the pine-tree state. 34345
Legends of the revolution. 41393, (41399)
Legends of the Shawangunk. 83719
Legends of the south. 83664, note after 86785
Legends of the St. Lawrence. 42527
Legends of the sea. (12572)
Legends of the war of independence. 84406
Legends of the west. (29787)
Legends of the west: sketches illustrative of
    the habits. 29788
Legends of the White Mountains. 78482
Legends of Virginia. (23816)
Leger, B. Mercier Saint. see Saint-Leger, B.
    Mercier.
Leger and the lexicon. 4571
Leger-Felicite Sonthonax, Commissaire-Civil
    de la Republique. 87114
Legerdemain exposed. 98895
Legere refutation d'un Mexicain. (23047)
Leggat, -------. 25108
Leggatt, W. see Leggett, William.
Legge, Charles. 39860
Leggett, Abraham. 9538, 39861
Leggett, Samuel. 39862
Leggett, Samuel. petitioner 39939, 78738,
    103717
Leggett, William. 17548, 39863-39866, 63214,
    1st note after 94244, 94247
Legion. pseud. Letter from Legion to His
    Grace the Duke of Richmond. 40330
Legion. pseud. Letters on responsible govern-
    ment. see Sullivan, Robert Baldwin.
Legion. pseud. To the public. 95969
Legion. pseud. To the publick. New-York,
    October 27, 1774. 95992
Legion of liberty! and force of truth. 39867,
    (39868), 95068, 95096
Legion of liberty. Remonstrance of some free
    men, states, and presses. 39867-(39868),
    95069, 95097
Legionaires of Luxembourg. see Luxembourg
    Legionaires.

Legislacao Brasileira, ou colleccao chrono-
    logica. 51688
Legislacao Brazileira. 88730
Legislacao do Brasil. 7596
Legislacao sobre a Alfandega dos Estados-
    Unidos da America. 43215
Legislacion ultramarina. 72562
Legislateur de la Caroline. 38446
Legislation as an implement of moral reform.
    17371
Legislation commerciale. (48278)
Legislative acts in force in the state of Ten-
    nessee. 94773
Legislative and documentary history of the
    Bank of the United States. (13438)
Legislative and documentary history of the
    banks of the United States. 51134
Legislative Assembly. House of Representatives.
    101920-101921
Legislative authority of the British Parliament.
    42909
Legislative black-list of Upper Canada. 43435
Legislative directory. 85175-85176
Legislative documents and journals of the
    Senate and House of Representatives.
    (37541)
Legislative documents compiled by order of
    the General Assembly. 35021
Legislative documents of the Senate and As-
    sembly of . . . New York. (53747)
Legislative excursion, February, 1869. (48749)
Legislative guide for conducting business.
    (9325)
Legislative hand book. 85177
Legislative honors to the memory of President
    Lincoln. 53748
Legislative investigation into masonry. 29888,
    45506
Legislative manual of the state of Minnesota.
    49262
Legislative manual of the state of New York.
    68469
Legislative nomination of Daniel Webster.
    103272
Legislative, political and commercial view of
    our colonies. 14725
Legislative power is Christ's peculiar pre-
    rogative. (2219)
Legislative protection to the industry of the
    people. 70815
Legislative register of the state of Maine.
    90454
Legislative reports of the General Assembly.
    of Illinois. 34291
Legislative rights of the commonality vindicated.
    11156
Legislative roll, rules of the House of Repre-
    sentatives. 15742
Legislative sketches from a reporter's note
    book. 35992
Legislature at their last session. 104443
Legislature of North Carolina. (55644)
Legislature's reply to Kellogg's pronunciamento.
    42303
Legitime. 64555
Legitime und die Republikaner. 39869, 64541,
    64546-64547
Le Gobien, -------. ed. 40697
Le Gouve, -------. 94126
Legoyt, Alfred. 39870
Legrand, -------. 58165
Legrand, John C. 39872, (45097), 45137,
    45195
Le Grand, Jean-Baptiste-Bernard. 39871
Legrand, Louis. pseud. Life of Maj.-Gen. Geo.
    B. McClellan. see Victor, Orville James.

Legrand, Louis. pseud. Military hand-book.
see Victor, Orville James.
Legras, A. 4047, 6836, 39876, 46972, 46974
Legrete, Pecho Celestino. defendant 27755,
52253
Legubris virtutum planctus in tumulo. 80880
Le Guen, Louis. defendant 28147
Le Guen, Louis. plaintiff 39877
Le Guen vs. Gouveneur S. Kemble. 39877
Lehigh and Delaware Water Gap Railroad.
60199
Lehigh and Delaware Water Gap Railroad.
Charter. 60199
Lehigh and Susquehanna Coal Company. 39882
Lehigh Coal Company. Board of Managers.
(39881)
Lehigh Luzerne Railroad Company. Directors.
60200
Lehigh Luzerne Railroad Company. Engineer.
60200
Lehigh River Navigation Convention, Conyngham
Town, Pa., 1832. see Nescopeck Canal
Convention, Conyngham Town, Pa., 1832.
Lehigh University. 39884
Lehigh Valley Railroad Company. Charter.
60201
Lehigh Valley Railroad Company. Managers.
60201
Lehman, --------, fl. 1827. (60516)
Lehmann, G. W. ed. 2798
Lehmann-Nitsche, R. ed. 90039
Lehrbegriff der ganzen Christlichen Religion.
90027
Lehrbuch der Erdbeschreibung. 4857A
Lehrbuch der Geographie. 10687
Lehre, Thomas. defendant 39885
Lehre nach der Gottseligkeit. 69151
Lehre und Bundnisse der Kirche Jesu Christi
der Heiligen der Letzten Tage. 83225
Lehre und Zucht-Ordnung der Vereinigten
Bruder in Christo. 97865
Lehritter, H. F. tr. 64733
Lehrreiche und Anmuthige Begebenheit. 91786
Lehrreicher Wegweiser fur Deutsche Aus-
wanderer. (38200)
Lei de presupuestos de los gastos jenerales.
12778
Lei de I de Outobro de 1828. 16977
Lei N. 1507 de 26 de Setembro de 1867.
(56203)
Leib, Charles. (39886)
Leib, James R. 39887
Leib, Michael. 39888-39889
Leiba, Diego de. 39892
Leiba, Diego de. supposed author 24818,
29033, 39891
Leiber, F. (27494)
Leibgarde. 25835
Leibnitz, Gottfried Wilhelm. 39893-(39894)
Leicester, Mass. 39900
Leicester, Mass. Academy. see Leicester
Academy, Leicester, Mass.
Leicester, Mass. Christ Church. 39899
Leicester, Mass. Commemoration of the
Fiftieth Anniversary of the Settlement
of Rev. John Nelson, 1862. 52315
Leicester, Mass. Congregational Church.
(39897)
Leicester, Mass. School Committee. 39900
Leicester, Mass. Selectmen. 39896
Leicester Academy, Leicester, Mass. 39902
Leicester Academy, Leicester, Mass. Trustees.
39902
Leicester Auxiliary Anti-slavery Society.
81771

Leiden, voor 300 jaren en thans. 63419
Leidenfrost, C. Fl. tr. 30534, 42621
Leidens-und Todesgeschichte des Herren der
Herrlichkeit. 105633
Leidy, Joseph. 39903-39908, 85072, 85732
Leidy, Paul. (39909)
Leig, Ch. 39910
Leigh, Benjamin Watkins, 1781-1849. 39912-
(39916), 39929-(39930), 84705, 94091
Leigh, Benjamin Watkins, 1781-1849. supposed
author 40352, 6th note after 100483
Leigh, Benjamin Watkins, 1781-1849.
incorrectly supposed author (28281),
(39911), 80854
Leigh, Charles. 66686
Leigh, Charles C. 38157, 39917-39921
Leigh, Sir Egerton. 39923-39927, 1st note after
87356, 87790, note after 87810, note after
87824 see also South Carolina (Colony)
Court of Vice Admiralty, Charleston.
Leigh, Sir Edward. supposed author 17593,
26256, (56466), 87849, 87904
Leigh, Edwin. (39922)
Leigh, John Studdy. 29941
Leigh, Joseph. (39928)
Leigh, Watkins. see Leigh, Benjamin Watkins,
1781-1849.
Leigh, William, fl. 1771. (39931)
Leigh, William, fl. 1860. 39932
Leighton, Albert. 59307
Leighton, R. 76250
Leighton, Robert, Abp. of Glasgow, 1611-1684.
(78447)
Leighton, William B. 39933
Leighton children. 85370
Leininger, Barbara. 73752
Leinsula, Franciscus. 39934
Leipzig. Bibliothekar Reichard. see Biblio-
thekar Reichard, Leipzig.
Leipzig. Societas Naturae Curiosorum see
Societas Naturae Curiosorum, Leipzig.
Leipziger Zeitung. 85082
Leiris, --------. tr. 39935
Leisler, Jacob. pseud. Letter to the people
of Pennsylvania. see Bradford, Vincent L.
Leisler, Jacob, 1640?-1691. 40907, 53647
Leiste, Christian. 17830, 39937
Leisure hours. A monthly magazine. (39938)
Leisure hours at sea. 39864
Leisure hours or desultory pieces. 38380
Leisure hours; or poems, moral, religious,
& descriptive. 44715
Leisure hours peotically employed. (80536)
Leisure labors. 13846
Leisure moments of an American artist. 7197
Leisure moments of an artist. 7197
Leitao, Antonio Jose Osorio de Pina. 39939
Leitao, Francisco de Andrade. 39940
Leitao e Carvalhosa, Manuel Francisco de
Barros e Sousa de Mesquita de Macedo.
see Santarem, Manuel Francisco de
Barros e Sousa de Mesquita de Macedo
Leitao e Carvalhosa, Visconde de.
Leitch, William. (39941)
Leite Pacheo Malheiro e Mello, Antonio Manuel
see Malheiro e Mello, Antonio Manuel
Leite Pacheo.
Leitende Anweisungen fur Auswanderer. 6016
Leitfaden fur Auswanderer. 8206
Leith, --------. 39942
Leithold, Theodor von. 39943-(39944)
Leitte Azevedo, Leonardo de Souza. see Souza
Leitte Azevedo, Leonardo de.
Leiva, Pedro de Toledo y. see Toledo y
Leiva, Pedro de, Marques de Mancera,
1585-1654.

Lejarza, Juan Jose Martinez de. 38385, (39945)
Lejeune, Andre. ed. (44652)
Le Jeune, Paul. 39946-39958, (61004), note after 69259
Le Keux, --------. engr. 92814
Lekture zur belehrenden unterhaltung. 7924
Leland, Aaron W. 23467, 39959-39961
Leland, Charles Godfrey. 6356, 39962-39964
Leland, Charles Godfrey. supposed author 85375
Leland, Henry P. 39965-39966
Leland, John. 39967-39972, 100553
Leland, John. supposed author 55350, 105973
Leland, P. W. 39973
Leland, Sherman. 39974
Leland, T. C. reporter 33461, 37728
Leland, Thomas. (39975)
Leland magazine. 39974
Leland Seminary, Townshend, Vt. (39976)
Leland Stanford Junior University. see Stanford University.
Le Large, Joseph-Adrien de Lignac. see Lignac, Joseph-Adrien le Large de.
Lelewel, Joachim, 1786-1861. 39977-(39978), 77804
Lelievre, Simeon. 10495, 70360
Le Long, Isaac, b. 1683. (21940), 39979
Le Long, John. 39980-39984
Le M. de C. pseud. see C., Le M. de. pseud.
Le Mage, Gaspard. pseud. Pleiade rouge. see Chauveau, -------. supposed author and Tache, Joseph Charles. supposed author
Lemaire, Henri. (39986)
Le Maire, Jacob, 1585-1616. 14348, (14350)-(14351), 14353, 14957-14960, 31539-31543, 44057-44059, 57765, 66686, 68455, 77920, 77930, 77963, 89444-89448A, 89450-89451
Le Mascrier, J. B. (4932), (9605)
Lemaur, Francisco. (56729)
Lemay, Leon Pamphile. (39987), 41914, (66995)
Le Mayre, Jacobo. see Le Maire, Jacob, 1585-1616.
Lembeye, Juan. (39988)
Lembrancas e apontamentos de governo provizorio. 76902
Lembrancas e curiosidades do valle do Amazonas. 88721
Lemer, Julien. tr. 4567
Lemercier, Anatole, Comte. 39989
Le Mercier, Andrew. (39990)
Le Mercier, Andrew. supposed author 86696
Le Mercier, F. J. 39953-39954, 39957, note after 69259
Le Mercier, Francois. 6413, 16676, (19247), (39991)-(39998), 67012-67014, 67498, note after 69259
Lemercier, N. L. 39999
Lemerle, E. 40000
Lemesle, Charles. 40001
Le Meynard de Queilhe, L. see Meynard de Queilhe, L. le.
Le Mierre, Antoine Martin, 1723-1793. 90520
Le Mire, Aubert, 1573-1640. 40002, 49403-49405
Lemmon, J. 26131, 40003
Lemmon slave case and slavery. 8346
Lemnio, Simone. 20211
Lemoine, Henry. ed. 21755, 41587
Le Moine, J. M. (40004)-40008
Lemoine, Stephen P. 40009
Lemon Hill, in its connection with the efforts of our citizens. 37696

Le Monnier, Pierre Charles, 1715-1799. 40010, 46946
Lemonnier-Delafosse, J. B. 40011
Lemour, Francisco. 65928
Lemos, Pedro Fernandez de Castro Andrade y Portugal, Conde de. see Castro Andrade y Portugal, Pedro Fernandez de, Conde de Lemos, 1634-1672.
Lemos Faria e Castro, C. A. de. (40014)
Lemos y Andrada, ---------, Conde de. 40013
Le Moyne de Morgues, Jacob. (8784)
Lempriere, Charles. 40015-40016
Lempriere, John. 40017-40018
Lempriere, William. 40019
Lempriere's biographical dictionary. 40017
Lemus, Diego de. 40020, 74863
Lenapee spelling-book. 47377
Lenapi wawipoetakse ave apwatuk. 47377
Lenda mytho-religiosa Americana. 93587
Lendas da India. 11385
Lendas e romances por Bernardo Guimaraes. 29237
Lenderman. pseud. Lenderman's adventures. (40021)
Lenderman's adventures among the spiritualists and freelovers. (40021)
Lendrick, William E. 40022
Lendum, John. 32123, 40023-40024, 50937, 84115, 101779
Leney, ---------. illus. 67695
L'Enfant, Pierre Charles, 1754-1825. 87696, note before 91395, 91428
Leng, John, Bishop of Norwich, 1665-1727. 40025
Leng, William C. 40026
Lengerke, H. von. ed. (19796)
Lenglet Dufresnoy, Nicolas, 1674-1755. 3255A, (8784), 21149, 21550, (40027)-40029, 73435
Leni Leoti. (4724)
Lennard, C. E. Barrett. 40030
Lennep, J. H. van. (40035)
Lennep, Jacob van. (40033)-(40034)
Lennep Coster, G. van. (40031)-40032
Lennox, Arthur. (35584)
Lennox, Charles. see Richmond, Charles Lennox, 3d Duke of, 1735-1806.
Lennox, Mary. 40036
Lennoxville, Quebec. Bishop's College. see Bishops' College, Lennoxville, Quebec.
Lennoxville Mining Company. 40037
Lenoble, Eustache. tr. 10821, 26851
Lenoir, Alexandre, 1762-1839. 23795, 40038, 101364
Lenoir, J. M. B. B. tr. 77064-(77066)
Lenoir, Marie Alexandre. see Lenoir, Alexandre, 1762-1839.
Lenoir du Pare, ---------. 40039
Lenore. 63547
Lenormant, Francois, 1837-1883. 85791
Lenox, David. 9837
Lenox, James, 1800-1880. (8784), 14641, (40041), 41659, 82823, 94095, 94096, 101686
Lenox, Robert. defendant 100777
Lenox, Mass. Centennial Celebration, 1876. (72442)
Lenox Academy. 40042
Lenstrente Skizzen. 106328
Lent usages. 5086
Lenthall, John. 84957 see also U. S. Bureau of Construction. Chief.
Lenz, Ingen. Alfr. tr. 6783
Leo XIII, Pope, 1810-1903. 84201 see also Catholic Church. Pope, 1878-1903 (Leo XIII)

Leo, Andre. (40043)

Leo, John, a More. see Leo Africanus, Joannes, 16th cent.

Leo Africanus, Joannes, 16th cent. (40044)-40047, 66686, note after 99383C, 106294, 106330-106331

Leolin. pseud. Letter to Harrison Gray Otis. 40048, 70067

Leominster, Mass. School Committee. 40049

Leominster, Mass. Washington Benevolent Society. see Washington Benevolent Society. Massachusetts. Leominster.

Leompart, J. Mesa y. see Mesa y Leompart, J.

Leon, A. J. Rodriguez de. see Rodriguez de Leon, A. J.

Leon, Alonzo de Cueva Ponce de. see Ponce de Leon, Alonzo de Cueva.

Leon, Antonio de, Bp. 16069 see also Arequipa, Peru (Diocese) Bishop (Leon)

Leon, Antonio de, fl. 1834-1841. 40066-40067

Leon, Antonio Rodriguez de. see Rodriguez de Leon, Antonio.

Leon, Carlos Celedonio Velasquez de Cardenas y. see Velasquez de Cardenas y Leon, Carlos Celedonio.

Leon, Christoual Araque Ponze de. see Araque Ponze de Leon, Christoual.

Leon, Edwin de, 1828-1891. 40071, 95738

Leon, Francisco Ponce de. see Ponce de Leon, Francisco.

Leon, Francisco Ruiz de. see Ruiz de Leon, Francisco.

Leon, Gabriel de. 40072

Leon, J. A. (40073), 57281, 93456

Leon, Jean. see Leo Africanus, Joannes, 16th Cent.

Leon, Joaquin Velasquez de. see Velasquez de Leon, Joaquin.

Leon, Joaquim Velazquez de. see Velasquez de Leon, Joaquin.

Leon, Jose Socorro de, 1831-1869. 17766, 86191-86192

Leon, Joseph Antonio de. 40074

Leon, Joseph Antonio Eugenio Ponce de. see Ponce de Leon, Joseph Antonio Eugenio.

Leon, Joses Mariano Ponce de. see Ponce de Leon, Joses Mariano.

Leon, Juan Bautista Ponce de. see Ponce de Leon, Juan Bautista.

Leon, Juan Recio de. see Recio de Leon, Juan.

Leon, Juan Rodriguez. see Rodriguez Leon, Juan.

Leon, Lorenzo Vander Hammen y. see Hammen y Leon, Lorenzo Vander.

Leon, Luis de. 40079

Leon, Marie Jean. see Hervey de Saint-Denys, Marie Jean Leon, Marquis d', 1823-1892.

Leon, Martin de, fl. 1600. (40080)-40085, 44404

Leon, Martin de, fl. 1612. 69193

Leon, Moses Pereira de. see Pereira de Leon, Moses.

Leon, Nicolas Suarez Ponce de. see Suarez Ponce de Leon, Nicolas.

Leon, P. de. see Pereira de Leon, Moses.

Leon, Pedro de Cieza de. see Cieza de Leon, Pedro de.

Leon, Rodriguez de. 40089

Leon, Thomas de Gijon y. see Gijon y Leon, Thomas de.

Leon, Thomas Gisson y. see Gijon y Leon, Thomas de.

Leon de Lara, -------. 40068

Leon Pinelo, Antonio Rodriguez de, d. 1660. 18335, 40050-(40059), (62932)-62934

Leon Pinelo, Didacus de. see Leon Pinelo, Diego, fl. 1660.

Leon Pinelo, Diego, fl. 1660. 40069-40070, 86372

Leon Pinelo, Diego de. see Leon Pinelo, Diego, fl. 1660.

Leon y Gama, Antonio de. (26486), 40059-(40065)

Leon y Messia, Francisco Garabito de. see Garabito de Leon y Messia, Francisco.

Leon y White, Diaz de. ed. 69596

Leon, Mexico. Seminario de la Madre Santissima de la Luz. see Seminario de la Madre Santissima de la Luz, Leon, Mexico.

Leon, Mexico (Diocese) Bishop (Diez de Solano) 20138 see also Diez de Solano, Jose Maria, Bp., 1820-1881.

Leon, Spain. 87314

Leonard, Abiel. 40091-40092

Leonard, Alexander S. 40093

Leonard, Benjamin G. 40094, 100521

Leonard, C. H. (40096)

Leonard, Charles C. (40095)

Leonard, Daniel. 40097-40100

Leonard, Daniel. incorrectly supposed author 40101, 92828

Leonard, David. 40102

Leonard, David A. 40103

Leonard, Ellen. supposed author 54695, note after 95734

Leonard, Frederic. ed. 40104, 68452

Leonard, G. M. G. 72402

Leonard, George. 40106-40107

Leonard, George. petitioner (40105)

Leonard, Henry C. 40108

Leonard, James. defendant (15879)

Leonard, Jonathan W. 40109

Leonard, Joseph. (40110)

Leonard, Joshua. 40111

Leonard, Levi W. 40112-40114, 84013

Leonard, Nathaniel. (22007), 64274, 94921, note after 103633, 5th note after 103650 see also Number of Ministers Conven'd at Taunton, Mass., 1745.

Leonard, R. H. ed. 89500

Leonard, William. 79703

Leonard & Co. firm 77026, 86788-86789, 92320

Leonard Eugene Wales. A memoir. 84091

Leonardo da Vinci. cartographer 44070

Leonardus, Bartholomaeus, fl. 1682. 61109

Leone, Carli. 40115

Leone, Giovan. 67730, 67743

Leone, Ioanne, Arabe. see Leo Africanus, Joannes, 16th cent.

Leonhart, R. 40116

Leonidas. pseud. Reply to Lucius Junius Brutus' examination of the President's answer. (40117)

Leonis Africani, Ioannis. see Leo Africanus, Joannes, 16th cent.

Leonnie St. James. 91162

Leonora. pseud. [Letters.] 9214

Leontine and Matilda. (25888), 1st note after 97876

Leopold II, Emperor of Austria, 1747-1792. (69722) see also Austria. Sovereigns, etc., 1790-1792 (Leopold II)

Leopold I, King of the Belgians, 1790-1865. (36119)

Leopoldo, Jose Feliciano Fernandes Pinheiro, Visconde de S. see Fernandes Pinheiro, Jose Feliciano, Visconde de S. Leopoldo, 1774-1847.

Leotaud, Antoine. (40119)

Leovy, Henry J. 53333
Leoyd, Owen. 40120
Le Page, John. 40121
Le Page du Pratz, -------. 40122-40125, 42180, 42308, 42895, 2d note after 96185
Le Paon, -------. engr. 27650, (63966), 68421
Lepautre, -------. engr. 63700
Le Pays, ---------. 40126
Le Pelletier de Saint Fargeau, ----. 94126
    see also France. Avocat General.
Lepelletier de Saint-Remi, R. see Lepelletier de Saint-Remy, R.
Lepelletier de Saint-Remy, R. 40127-40129, 75485
Le Pelletier du Clary, ---------. 96071
    see also Martinique. Conseil Colonial. Commission Chargee de Reponder a la Report de M. de Tocqueville. President.
Leper, and other poems. 34139
Le Pers, Jean Baptiste. 12127
Le Petit, Mathurin, 1693-1739. 4936
Le Petit Martin, Angelique. see Martin, Angelique le Petit.
Le Picquier, -------. (40130)
Lepidopteres. 21210
Lepidopteres de la Californie. (6154)
Lepouze, Constant. 40131
Leprohon, Rosanna Eleanor, 40132
Lequerica, ------. 87221-87223
Le Ray de Chaumont, J. see Chaumont, J. le Ray de.
Le Raye, Charles. 18170, 3d note after 96185
Lerch, -------. 40133
Lercher, Laux. 40134
Lerdo, Ignacio Maria. (40136), 41665
Lerdo de Tejada, Miguel. 40138-40140 see also Mexico. Ministerio de Hacienda.
Lerdo de Tejada, Sebastian, 1824-1889. 86976 see also Mexico. President, 1872-1876 (Lerdo de Tejada)
Lerdo de Texada, J. 40137
Lerdo de Tejado, Fran. 40135
Lere nouvelle. 29261, (48595)
Lerio, Ioanne. see Lery, Jean de, 1534-1611.
Lerius, John. see Lery, Jean de, 1534-1611.
Le Rouge, --------, Sieur. 40142-40143, 68450
Leroux, Xavier. 100745
Lerow, George L. (40144)
Leroy, ---------. tr. 29719
Le Roy, David, 1624?-1803. 25573
Le Roy, Herman. appellant 102175
Le Roy, Maria. see Roy, Maria le.
Leroy, Marie Manert. see Manert-Leroy, Marie.
Le Roy, P. L. 40145-40146, 90063
Le Roy, Bayard & Co. firm defendants (57622)
Le Roy, N. Y. Convention of Delegates Opposed to Free Masonry, 1828. see Convention of Delegates Opposed to Free Masonry, Le Roy, N. Y., 1828.
Le Roy, N. Y. Convention of Seceding Masons, 1828. see Convention of Seceding Masons, Le Roy, N. Y., 1828.
Le Roy, N. Y. Ingham Collegiate Institute. see Ingham Collegiate Institute, Le Roy, N. Y.
Lery, Jean de, 1534-1611. (4793), (8784), 6118, 6120, 32041, 40148-40156, 66686, 79343, 94273
Lery, Joannis. see Lery, Jean de, 1534-1611.
Lesaga, Juan Lucas de. petitioner 98815

Le Sage, A. cartographer (1062), (15055), (39124)-39125, 40161
Le Sage, Alain Rene, 1668-1747. 4163, 40157-40160
Le Sage ten Broek, Joaquim George. see Broek, Joaquim George Le Sage ten, 1775-1847.
Le Saint, L. (40162)
Lescallier, --------. tr. 38678, 39092
Lescallier, Daniel. 40162-(40165), 68753, 91083
Lescarbot, Marc. 16212, 40166-40179, 57765, 66686, 91853, 99728
Leschenault de la Tour, -------. 40180
Les Cayes, Haiti. Corps du Commerce see Corps du Commerce, Les Cayes, Haiti.
Lesdernier, Emily P. 40182
Lesebuch fur die Jugend. 101904
Lesebuch fur Kinder. 72232
Lesebuch zur Selbstbelebrung. 4857A
Lesecabinet fur die Jugend. 92578
Leset und Gebt es euren Nachbarn! 85897, 91010
Lesguillon, J. 40183
Lesieur, Santiago. (40184)
Lesley, J. P., fl. 1849. 40185
Lesley, Joseph. 34529, 59964
Lesley, Joseph Peter, 1819-1903. (24233), 41086-(41089), 63124, 86814
Leslie, Miss ------. 40203, 99840
Leslie, Charles. 12365, 40190-40197, 80598, 85363-85365, 101194, 103655, 105650
Leslie, Charles Robert. (40198)
Leslie, Frank. 40199-40200, note after 89964
Leslie, George. (40210)
Leslie, Sir John. (40201)-40202, 51787
Leson, James van. see Vandeleur, John. pseud.
Lespade, A. 40204
Lesperut, A. 40205
L'Espinasse, N. de. see Espinasse, N. de l', Chevalier de Langeac.
L'Espine, H. de. tr. 92443
Lesquereux, Leo. 9959, 34253, 34529, (40206)-40207
Lesseps, Jean Baptiste Barthelemy, Baron de, 1766-1834. (38964)-38965, (40208)-40209, (59572)
Lesser, James. 31092, 42730
Lessing, Hofrath. ed. 17830
Lessius, L. (67586)
Lesslie, George. 95254-95256
Lessman, F. (40211)-(40212)
Lesson, A. 21210
Lesson, Rene Primevere, 1794-1849. 21353, 40214-40215, 78689
Lesson for the day. 6505, 9400, 9404
Lesson of St. Domingo. 105579
Lesson of '76 to the men of '56. 58660
Lesson of the hour. Justice as well as mercy. 12537
Lesson of the hour. Lecture . . . delivered at Brooklyn. 62528
Lesson on the mode of studying and profiting by the reflections. 104186
Lesson to John Bull. 105970, 106050
Lessons for mankind. 759
Lessons from biography. 40216
Lessons from the history of medical delusions. 32867
Lessons from our late rebellion. 59347
Lessons from the life of Theodore Parker. 11932
Lessons from the past. 21628
Lessons from the war. 34170
Lessons in elocution. 105790
Lessons in elocution: or a selection of pieces. (78388)

Letter addressed to Judge Yates. 94675
Letter addressed to Lord John Russell.
22508
Letter addressed to Martin Van Buren.
37451, 74141, 98425
Letter addressed to Mercator. 40257, 47892,
95356, 95358
Letter addressed to Messrs. Baring Brothers
and Co. 29371
Letter addressed to parents and heads of
families. 40258
Letter addressed to R. H. Bishop. 105672
Letter addressed to Randle Jackson. 102779
Letter, addressed to Rev. Francis Brown.
74430
Letter addressed to Robert H. Ives. 31112
Letter addressed to Sir F. B. Head. 8854
Letter addressed to that body by an English-
man. 101450
Letter addressed to the Abbe Raynal. 58222
Letter addressed to the Agricultural Society
of Jefferson County. 30101
Letter addressed to the anonymous author of
''England and America.'' (33076)
Letter addressed to the Anti-masonic Com-
mittee of York County. 74255
Letter address'd to the author. 86619
Letter addressed to the author by the Wardens
. . . of Christ Church. 57317
Letter, addressed to the author of ''The
question answered.'' (68558)
Letter addressed to the Chief Justice. 91625
''Letter'' addressed to the church by sundry
individuals. 12403, 54184
Letter addressed to the citizens of British
America. 56421
Letter addressed to the citizens of the United
States. 95693
Letter addressed to the Congregational Church
in Purchase Street. 71522
Letter addressed to the Congregational clergy
of Massachusetts. 45798
Letter addressed to the Earl of Liverpool.
103653
Letter addressed to the editor of the Christian
examiner. 47078
Letter addressed to the editor of the New-
York evening post. 93522
Letter addressed to the editor of Washington's
writings. 88978
Letter addressed to the editors of the Boston
daily atlas. 64775
Letter addressed to the Hon. Daniel Webster.
34635, 5th note after 100864, note after
100928
Letter addressed to the Hon. Harrison Gray
Otis. 97389
Letter addressed to the Hon. James Madison.
40259
Letter addressed to the Hon. Stephen Hopkins.
101332
Letter addressed to the Hon. John Davis.
(10747)
Letter addressed to the House Committee of
Ways and Means. 24342, 29929
Letter addressed to the inhabitants of Prince
George's County. (21481)
Letter addressed to the inhabitants of the
Niagara District. 48024
Letter, addressed to the legislators of the
several states. 40260
Letter addressed to the Liverpool Society for
Promoting the Abolition of Slavery.
17618
Letter addressed to the Liverpool Society for
the Abolition of Slavery. 76333

Letter addressed to the Marquis [de Chastellux.]
8017
Letter addressed to the Marquis of Chandos.
95674
Letter addressed to the members of the Legis-
lature of Pennsylvania. 40261
Letter addressed to the members of the Legis-
lature of South-Carolina. 87857
Letter addressed to the members of the Parish
of Christ Church. (50689)
Letter addressed to the Opera House Meeting,
Cincinnati. 1389A
Letter addressed to the people in power. 15942
Letter addressed to the people of Maryland.
96162
Letter addressed to the people of Piedmont.
3423
Letter addressed to the people of the United
States. 20998
Letter addressed to the planters. 29311
Letter addressed to the President of the United
States. 22934, 40262
Letter addressed to the Republicans of the city.
54353
Letter addressed to the Rev. Aaron Bancroft.
63992
Letter, addressed to the Rev. Doctor Beech.
36679
Letter, addressed to the Rev. Enoch Pond.
95350
Letter addressed to the Rev. James McGregor.
(73348)
Letter addressed to the Right Hon. Lord
Brougham and Vaux. 71924
Letter addressed to the Rt. Hon. Lord Hobart.
62681
Letter addressed to the Right Hon. Lord North.
16012
Letter addressed to the Secretary of State.
18204
Letter addressed to the . . . society for ef-
fecting such abolition. 25479
Letter addressed to the southern delegates.
55375
Letter addressed to Thomas Clarkson. 13499
Letter addressed to Thomas Jefferson. (54024)
Letter addressed to Thomas L. M'Kenney.
43412
Letter addressed to two great men. 1661,
20684, 26900, 29043, 40263, 40293,
40479, 60862, 68296, 69470, note after
96403
Letter addressed to William Wilberforce.
17619
Letter addressed to young persons. 89513
Letter, addressed, without permission, to the
Earl of Shrewsbury and Waterford. 86776
Letter and accompanying documents, addressed
to the Government Commissioners. 82561
Letter and accompanying documents from the
Hon. Richard Rush. 74256
Letter and authentic documentary evidence.
49047
Letter and documents, in relation to the dis-
solution of the engagement. 60750
Letter and documents in relation to the location
of the railroad bridge. (51873)
Letter and enclosures from the Governor of
North Carolina. 94745
Letter and mis-statements of the Hon. Cad-
wallader D. Colden. 93513-93514
Letter and proposals of the International Steam-
ship Company. 40264
Letter and resolutions from the Grand Lodge
of Georgia. 87846

Letter and report of the Secretary of the Navy. 97282

Letter and statement, in the case of Olmstead. 47236

Letter and two speeches. 5749

[Letter announcing the election of persons.] 76532, 76549, 76647

Letter as it came to our hands. 91318

Letter-bag of the Great Western. 29689-29690

Letter (being his second) to the people of Pennsylvania. 84642

Letter book of Governor [William] Bradford. 106053

Letter-book of Samuel Sewall. 79449

Letter book [of William Allen.] 84586

Letter by a clergyman not named. (14525)

Letter. By a gentleman to his friend. 93900

Letter by a Massachusetts man. 13776, 70563

Letter by Alexander Hamilton. 29957

Letter by an American citizen. (32394)

Letter by another hand. 104901

Letter by B. Franklin of Philadelphia. 31198, 34792

Letter . . . by Charles Phillips. 64014

[Letter by Dr. Dunlop to Mr. Hutchings.] 78247

Letter [by Dr. Huntington.] 71889

Letter, by Dr. J. S. Newberry. (76566), 76647

Letter . . . [by E. A. Brown.] (30089), note after 96853

Letter [by Gansevoort.] 92144

Letter by Geo. Ticknor Curtis. 23271

Letter [by George Whitefield.] 80680

Letter by Jas. Robb. 71726-(71727)

Letter [by John Cripps.] 56650

Letter. [By John Earl.] (21622)

Letter [by John Ravenel.] 67988

Letter [by Jonathan Mitchel.] 49655-49656

Letter by Langdon Cheves on state rights. 33572

Letter [by Miller.] 30381

Letter by Mrs. Sarah Gill. 65594

Letter [by Phocion.] 47872

Letter by Prof. Walter Smith. 84496

Letter [by R. C. Waterston.] 76992

Letter. . . . By Rev. G. F. W. Mortimer. 50987

Letter . . . by the Hon. Charles E. Clarke. 37885

Letter by the Marquis of Sligo. 9225

Letter [by the Trustees of the Corporation for the Relief of Presbyterian Ministers, their Widows and Children.] (42384), 66908

Letter [by William Pitt, on his resignation.] 69405

Letter carriers. pseud. "Letter carriers' address." see Rees, James.

"Letter carriers' address." 68641

Letter, censuring the United States Bank. 74258

Letter, commercial and political. 17997, 104646

Letter concerning an American bishop, &c. (11876)

Letter concerning family history. 8446

Letter concerning lanes for the steamers. 46974

Letter concerning libels. 2d note after 104010

Letter concerning the consequence of an incorporating union. 18559

Letter concerning the labors of Mr. John Augustus. 2385

Letter concerning the naval store bill. 40265

[Letter concerning the proposed union.] 87846

Letter concerning the privileges of the Assembly of Jamaica. 35630

Letter concerning the seasoning. 2224

Letter concerning the success of the Gospel. 46699

Letter concerning the Ten Pound Court in the city of New York. (12376)

Letter concerning the union. 40266

Letter containing a brief reply to the Rev. James R. Wilson's pamphlet. 55373

Letter containing a remarkable history of an imposter. 46587, note after 101451

Letter . . . containing reasons for refusing to sign. 26801

Letter containing remarks on the same work. 56487, 73061

Letter, containing reminiscences of Henry Clay. 71577

Letter, containing some candid observations. 40267

Letter containing some remarks on a late piece. 90149

Letter, containing the present state of Castile in Peru. 31510, 1st note after 97141

Letter concerning toleration. 41728

Letter, connected with a pamphlet. (41299)

Letter dated at Troy. 34037

Letter dated Boston, May 4, 1818. 21002, 56521, 93538

Letter dated Camp at Lake George. (36338)

Letter, dated Federal City. 58225

Letter, dated Philadelphia. 84590

Letter, dated "Rio Janeiro." 5672

Letter dated St. Louis University. (34468), 82261

Letter dated 10th August, 1729. (21200)

Letter, December 20th, 1837. 35535, note after 93439

Letter, declaring his [i.e. George Washington's] acceptance. 101717

Letter depicting the alarm and danger. 8005

[Letter] describing a visit to Massachusetts. 3540

Letter descriptive of the different settlements. (40268)

Letter directed, to Edmund, Lord Bishop of London. 97097

Letter directed to John Burril. 6709, 6711, 21088, (40332), 1st note after 99800

Letter . . . discovering and correcting the errors. 39767

Letter, discovering the cause of Gods continuing wrath. 72711

Letter VIII. The true and living God. 89369

Letter XI. Latter-day judgments. 89369

Letter . . . enclosing . . . the condition of the banks. 59905

Letter erom [sic] an English gentleman. 90277

Letter, &c. 5644, (7850)

Letter, etc. (to Mr. Courtenay), with appendix. 39629

Letter, &c. to the merchants, manufacturers, and others. (44306)

Letter extra, to Thomas Herttell. 88650

Letter V. From Elias Smith to the church in Woburn. 82483

Letter V. The gift of the Holy Ghost. 89369

Letter IV. From the church at Woburn, to Elias Smith. 82483

Letter IV. On water baptism. 89369

Letter from ********, in London. (40313)

Letter from a calm observer, to a noble lord. 1200, 36779

Letter from a chancellor out of office. 40269
Letter from a churchman in town. 72574
Letter from a churchman to his friend in New-Haven. (40270)
Letter from a citizen of Indiana. (40350)
Letter from a citizen of Port-Royal in Jamaica. 40271
Letter from a citizen to his friend in the country. 99813
Letter from a clergy-man in the country, to a clergy-man in the city. 66929
Letter, from a clergyman in town. 59269
Letter from a clergyman to his parishioners. 89473
Letter from a cobler to the people of England. 40272
Letter from a committee to the President of the Congress. 26443
Letter from a Congregationalist to a friend. 40273
Letter from a country gentleman at Boston. 6708, 40274
Letter from a country gentleman to his friend in town. 95722
Letter from a countryman to his friend. 60202
Letter, from a deformed gentleman to a young lady, who slighted him, &c. 103339
Letter, from a deformed gentleman to a young lady, who slighted him: with the rules of prudence. 103338
Letter from a Dutch farmer. 100873
Letter from a farmer in the county of Rockingham. 40275
Letter from a farmer to his friend. 40275
Letter from a foreign traveller in New-York. (23111)
Letter from a freeman of South Carolina. (40277)
Letter from a friend at J——— ———. 82761
Letter from a Friend in America, to Luke Howard. 78283, 78289
Letter from a friend in the country. 76339
Letter from a friend in the north to a friend in the south. (40278)
Letter from a friend in the north, with special reference to the effects of disunion upon slavery. 14916
Letter from a friend to a young gentleman of Maryland. 52064
Letter from a friend to some of his intimate friends. (40279)
Letter from a gentleman at Barbadoes. (4016)
Letter from a gentleman at Elizabeth Town. 22192, 40280, 68143
Letter from a gentleman at Halifax. 7889, 19249, 29702, 40281, 40457, 57868, 69455, 3d note after 99800
Letter from a gentleman at New-York, to his friend. (12491)
Letter from a gentleman at Rome. (69494)
Letter from a gentleman, containing some remarks. 40282
Letter from a gentleman in America. 16611, 16615, (22509), 2d note after 95677
Letter from a gentleman in Barbados. 2195
Letter from a gentleman in Boston to a merchant in London. 22649
Letter from a gentleman in Boston to a Unitarian clergyman. (70193)
Letter from a gentleman in Boston to his friend in Connecticut. 40283
Letter, from a gentleman in Boston to his friend in Philadelphia. 97397

Letter from a gentleman in Boston to Mr. George Wishart. 12317
Letter from a gentleman in Connecticut. 58632
Letter from a gentleman in Connecticut, relative to a paper currency. 40284
Letter from a gentleman in Connecticut to his friend in London. (23375), 38178
Letter from a gentleman in England. 40285, 61773
Letter from a gentleman in Guadaloupe to his friend in London. 16723
Letter from a gentleman in Halifax to his friend in Boston. 40286
Letter from a gentleman in London, to a merchant in the west of England. 21419
Letter from a gentleman in London, to his friend in America. (23375), 38178
Letter from a gentleman in London, to his friend in Pennsylvania. 40287, 66930, 84627
Letter from a gentleman in London to his friend in the country. (18761)
Letter from a gentleman in Maryland. 23506
Letter from a gentleman in Massachusetts. 22990, 104221
Letter from a gentleman in Mount Hope. 40288
Letter from a gentleman in New-England, to his friend in Glasgow. 69400, 90595-90597, 103594, 3d note after 103650
Letter, from a gentleman in New England, to his friend in Pennsylvania. (4094), 102569
Letter from a gentleman in New-York, to his friend in Brunswick. (40289), (69681), 86592, 96960, note after 96961
Letter from a gentleman in Newport to his friend in Boston. 43663, (55031), (65578), 96298
Letter from a gentleman in North-America. 84574
Letter from a gentleman in Nova-Scotia. 100866
Letter from a gentleman in one of the back-counties. 1663, (15209), 59268
Letter from a gentleman in Philadelphia, to a freeholder. (61775)
Letter from a gentleman in Philadelphia to his friend in Bucks. (61774)
Letter from a gentleman in Philadelphia to his friend in England. 16611, 16615, (22509), 2d note after 95677
Letter from a gentleman in Philadelphia to his friend in London. (20043)
Letter from a gentleman in Scotland. (40290), note after 103628
Letter from a gentleman in South-Carolina. 19817
Letter from a gentleman in the city. 59711
Letter from a gentleman in the country to a member of Parliament. 24089, 1st note after 96400
Letter from a gentleman in the country to a member of Parliament in town. 17610
Letter from a gentleman in the country to his friend in Boston. (28006)
Letter from a gentleman in the country, to his friend in Boston, respecting some late observations. 58897
Letter from a gentleman in the country, to his friend in Edinburgh. 103629
Letter from a gentleman in the country, to his friend in Philadelphia. 56485, (60284)
Letter from a gentleman in the country to his friend in town. 40263, 40293
Letter from a gentleman in the country to S—— W———. 40294

Letter from a gentleman in the east, entitled, The present state of the colony of Connecticut considered. 13213, 26353, note after 105924

Letter from a gentleman in the eastern part of said colony. 13213, (26353), 32309, note after 105924, 105927, 1st note after 105937, note after 106230

Letter, from a gentleman in the Massachusetts-Bay. 22990, 104221

Letter from a gentleman in the West Indies to a merchant in London. 47917

Letter from a gentleman in town to his friend (an old revolution whig of distinction), in the country. 34329

Letter from a gentleman in town to his friend in the country. 60605, 78475, 104455

Letter from a gentleman in Transilvania. 5219, 6th note after 96481

Letter from a gentleman in Virginia to a merchant in Philadelphia. (16724), (40219), 60716, 2d note after 95968, 3d note after 100449, 2d note after 100483

Letter from a gentleman in Virginia, to the merchants of Great Britain. 40292, 3d note after 100483

Letter from a gentleman in Weathersfield. 4102

Letter from a Gentleman of Barbadoes. (65328), (69514)

Letter from a gentleman of Baltimore. 80086, 89236

Letter from a gentleman of New-Brunswick. 52522

Letter from a gentleman of that country. 52757

Letter from a gentleman of the bar at Harrisburg. (60283)

Letter from a gentleman of the city of New-York. (40295)

Letter from a gentleman of the law. 86695

Letter from a gentleman of the said island [i. e. Barbadoes.] (3256)

Letter from a gentleman of undoubted credit. 99249

Letter from a gentleman of Long-Island. 96335

Letter from a gentleman resident there, to his friend in England. 22496, 71241

Letter from a gentleman residing there, to his friend in London. 28914

Letter from a gentleman to his friend. 81509, note after 105083

Letter from a gentleman to his friend. [By Abraham Panther.] 93892-93894, 93896, 93898-93899, 93901-93905

Letter from a gentleman to his friend. [By John Adams.] 251, 5th note after 95677

Letter from a gentleman to his friend in Dutchess-County. 78553

Letter from a gentleman to his friend, in England. 10504

Letter from a gentleman to his friend in New York. 40296

Letter from a gentleman to William Parks. 45295

Letter from a gentleman travelling through Bucks County. (40297), 61776

Letter from a gentleman who has resided many years in Pennsylvania. (17666), 84589-84593

Letter from a girl to her sweetheart in the army. 93040

Letter from a Grenanda planter to a merchant in London. 7865, 104904

Letter from a lady on nursing. 96146

Letter from a landed proprietor. 68695

Letter from a late judge. 40793

Letter from a Long-Island farmer. 40298

Letter from a meeting of the brethren called Quakers. (40299)

Letter from a member of Parliament in town. (40301)

Letter from a member of Parliament to a conconstituent. 68727

Letter from a member of Parliament, to a friend in the country. 104005

Letter from a member of Parliament to his friends in the country. 101146

Letter from a member of Parliament to His Grace the Duke of *****. 40300

Letter from a member of St. Paul's shewing the source of the present Wranglings. 12358, 40302, 59267, 62218

Letter from a member of the Boston Bar. 24959

Letter from a member of the last Parliament. 40303

Letter from a member of the Parliament of Scotland. 18560, 78220, 2d note after 98925

Letter from a member of the Society for Propagating the Gospel in Foreign Parts. 85939

Letter from a merchant at Jamaica. 40304

Letter from a merchant in Amsterdam. 40305

Letter from a merchant in Boston, in answer to one received. 27833

Letter from a merchant in Boston, to his friend in the country. 20725

Letter from a merchant in Halifax, to a merchant in Boston. 40306

Letter from a merchant in London, to his nephew in America. 97346

Letter from a merchant in London to his nephew in North America. 2548, 66648, 86724, 97352

Letter from a merchant in London trading to America. (68258)-(68260)

Letter from a merchant of the city of London. 40307

Letter from a merchant to a farmer and planter. 40308

Letter from a merchant who has left off trade. 40309

Letter from a merchant at Boston. 40502

Letter from a minister in Boston to his friend in New York. 103622

Letter from a minister in London, to his friend in Massachusetts. 59066

Letter from a minister of the Church of England to his dissenting parishioners, containing a brief answer to the most material objections. 78732, 86750

Letter from a minister of the Church of England to his dissenting parishioners, shewing the necessity of unity and peace. (40421), 103068

Letter from a minister, to one of his neighbors. 102425

Letter from a mother to her daughter. 73896

Letter from a mother to her son. 22664

Letter from a newly elected member. (34881)

Letter from a patriot in retirement. 40310

Letter from a person of eminency and worth in Caledonia. 78197

Letter from a post captain in the Navy. (16725)

Letter from a radical. 82007

Letter from a reputable farmer. 12483

Letter from a resident of Washington. (20326), 32355

Letter from a residing member. 40311
Letter from a Romish priest in Canada. 78904
Letter from a Russian sea officer. 35254, 40312, 40673
Letter from a son of candor. 28774, 4th note after 94663, 99813
Letter from a tradesman in Lancaster. 38209
Letter from a tradesman, recently arrived from America. 40315
Letter from a traveller. 19721
Letter from a traveller in the Caribbees. 3291, note before 93803
Letter from a traveller, to his friend in South Carolina. 13709, 2d note after 96480
Letter from a treasurer of a corporation. 11219, note after 96512
Letter from a veteran. 40316, (65256), note after 99390
Letter from a Virginian to a New Yorker. 27443
Letter from a Virginian, to the members of the Congress. 40317, 7th note after 100577
Letter from a volunteer of 1806 to the volunteers of 1860. 63369
Letter from A. W., farmer, intitled A view of the controversy. 29955
Letter from a weaver to the Rev. Mr. Sherman. 40318, 80391
Letter from a West-India merchant. 40319, 1st note after 102785
Letter from a West India merchant to a West India planter. 60985, 72255, 1st note after 102858
Letter from a western citizen to his friend in Pennsylvania. 95116
Letter from a young lady lately received by him into the church. 95231-95235, 95237, 95240
Letter from a young lady received by him into the church. 95252
Letter from a young man, a Quaker in Pennsylvania. (7990)
Letter from Albemarle Street to the Cocoa-Tree. 40320
Letter from Alexander Hamilton, concerning the public conduct and character of John Adams. 261, 9863, 13135, 23995, 29959-29961, 40446, 99802, 102361
Letter from Alex. Smyth to Francis Preston. 85185
Letter from an adopted citizen of the republic. 96795
Letter from an aged and retired citizen of Boston. (40322), 57860
Letter from an aged layman. 20063
Letter from an American, now resident in London. 5458-(5459), (40321)
Letter from an American traveller. 42894
Letter from an American woman to . . . Lord Palmerston. 18169
Letter from an assembly-man in Carolina. 40937, note after 87866
Letter from an elder in an Old School Presbyterian Church. 40323
Letter from an English gentleman in China, to the Earl of *****. 90272
Letter from an English gentleman, now residing in China, to the Earl of ****. 90251, 90253, 90257, 90259-90261, 90266, 90276
Letter from an English gentleman, now residing in China, to the Earl of *******. 90262

Letter from an English gentleman, now residing in Pekin in China. 90250
Letter, from an English gentleman residing in China, to his friend in England. 90263, 90285
Letter from an English gentleman, residing in China, to the Earl of ***. 90271
Letter from an English gentleman residing in China, to the Earl of ****. 90269
Letter from an English gentleman residing in China, to the Earl of ******. 90265
Letter from an English gentleman residing in China, to the Earl of *******. 90264, 90267, 90268, 90270, 92073, 90278, 90286
Letter from an English gentlemam [sic] residing in China, [to] the Earl of *******. 90274
Letter from an English gentleman residing in China, [to] the Earl of *******. 90281
Letter from an English gentleman residing in China, to the Earl of ***********. 90280
Letter from an English gentleman, residing in China, to the Earl of ************. 90282
Letter from an English gentleman residing in China, to the Earl of Chesterfield. 90283
Letter from an English officer at Canada. 48965
Letter from an inhabitant of His Majesty's island of Nevis. 80588
Letter from an inhabitant of one of His Majesty's Leeward Caribbee Islands. 3291, note before 93802
Letter from an Irish gentleman in London. 63764
Letter from an officer at New-York to his friend in London. 40324
Letter from an officer of marines to his friend in London. 21419
Letter from an officer of the 71st. Regiment. 87824
Letter from an officer on board the Burfotd. (36722), 1st note after 102842
Letter from an officer retired, to his son in Parliament. 40325
Letter from an officer, who arrived at Philadelphia. 101697
Letter from an old man of business. 41680
Letter from an old printer. 61579
Letter from an old whig in town. 10505
Letter from Anna Braithwaite to Elias Hicks. 7359
Letter from Aristocles to Authades. (20062)
Letter from B. C. Wilson. 12359
Letter from Bartholomew de Fonte. 20404
Letter, from Batista Angeloni. 80049-80050
Letter from Benjamin Bates. 47687
Letter from Benj. Bullivant. 9132
Letter from Benjamin Jones in Alexandria. 36457
Letter from Bishop Chase to Bishop McIlvaine. 37591
Letter from Bishop Hopkins. (44755)
Letter from Blake to the Commodore. 5792, 36395
Letter from Brev. Brig. Gen. Jos. G. Totten. 60203
Letter from Britannia to the King. 40326
Letter from C. S. Mattoon. 46904
Letter from C. T. Harvey. 75423
Letter from Candor to the public advertiser. 40327
Letter from Captain Duncan. 20363
Letter from Capt. J. S. Smith. 82760
Letter from Captain John Tosier. 96315
Letter from Carroll Spence. 89276

Letter from Cassius M. Clay. Slavery. 13536

Letter from Cassius M. Clay . . . with a review. 13536

Letter from Cephus to Bereas. 105252

Letter from Charles Read, Esq. 22192, 40280, 68142-68143

Letter from Charles-Town in Carolina. (87848A)

Letter from "Chenango." 103281

Letter from Chief Justice Jay. 101686

Letter from Cicero to Cataline the Second. 26433

Letter from Cicero to the Right Hon. Lord Viscount H—e. (26432)

Letter from citizens of Newburyport, Mass. 102320

Letter from Clements Burleigh. 47436

Letter from Cocoa Tree, to the country gentleman. 40328

Letter from Col. Benton to the people of Missouri. 4786

Letter from Col. H. Caldwell to Gen. Murray. 67022

Letter from Col. Hardie to the Secretary of War. 30313

Letter from Col. Jonathan Williams. 104296

Letter from Colonel Pickering. 62651, 64747

Letter from Commodore Preble. 65004

Letter from Common Honesty. (40329)

Letter from Connecticut to Elder Elias Lee. 84693

Letter from Cornelivs Bvrrovhs. 9461

Letter from Cornelius Van Sloetton [sic]. 82180

Letter from Daniel Bedinger. 4282

Letter from Daniel J. Morrell. 50779

Letter from Daniel Rathbun. 67949

Letter from Daniel Webster. 45686

Letter from David D. Porter to Hon. Gideon Welles. (64224)

Letter . . . from De Witt Clinton. (13710)

Letter from Delta to Senex. 19456

Letter from Dr. A. P. Dostie. 20666

Letter from Dr. Alison. 70716

Letter from Dr. Auchmuty. (35326)

Letter from Dr. Barton. 3810

[Letter from Dr. Bellows.] 76574, 76647

Letter from Dr. Benjamin Rush. 74221

Letter from Dr. Bray, directed to such as have contributed. 7478, 105651

Letter from Dr. Burton. 38184, 95751

Letter from Dr. Chalmers to an American clergyman. 89744

Letter from Doctor Edward Jenner. 98272

Letter from Dr. J. S. Newberry to Hon. W. P. Sprague. 54896, (76590), 76647

Letter from Dr. James Mann. 105991

Letter from Dr. John Lining. 12837, 41333

Letter from Dr. John Sibley. 80824

Letter from Dr. Scudder. 78523

Letter from Don Blas de Lezo. 99249

Letter from E. K. Collins. 14433

Letter from Earl Bathurst. 3956

Letter from Edmund Burke, Esq; one of the representatives in Parliament. 65, 9290-9291

Letter from Edmund Burke to the Committee of Correspondence. 9292

Letter from Edward King. 37799

Letter from Edward P. Livingston. 41619

Letter from Edward Stanly. 90325

Letter from Elizabeth Webb. 102212

Letter from Ex-President Houston. (33881)

Letter from Father Le Chaise. (38458)

Letter from Franklin Bache. 2590

Letter from freeman of South-Carolina. (25788), 87858

Letter from G. W. P. Curtis. (18153)

Letter from Gabriel Moore. (50376)

Letter from General Benjamin Lincoln. (43923)

Letter from Gen. Butler. 9615

Letter from Gen. C. F. Henningsen. (31378)

Letter from General Calvin Jones. 36460

Letter from Gen'l H. H. Heath. 31187

Letter from General Harper. 30429

Letter from General John P. Van Ness. 98527

Letter from General Lee, declining an interview. 39708

Letter from General Lee to General Gurgoyne. 39708

Letter from Gen'l Ripley. 71529

Letter from Gen. Rosecrans. (73256)

Letter from Gen. T. Seymour. 79671

Letter from General Turreau. 83824

Letter from General Washington, accepting his appointment. 101715

Letter from General Washington to Congress. 101697

Letter from General Washington to General Green. [sic] 101718

Letter from General Washington to the President. 101714

Letter from George Nicholas. (55167)

Letter from George Peabody. (59366)

Letter from George R. Russell. 74333

Letter from . . . George Whitefield. 103555

Letter from Gerrit Smith on the reciprocity treaty. 82642

Letter from Gerrit Smith to Auditor Benton. 82647

Letter from Gerrit Smith, to Edward C. Delava[(82640)

Letter from Gerrit Smith, to Hon. Henry Clay. (82643)

Letter from Gerrit Smith to Hon. Mr. Church-ill. 82641

Letter from Governor James L. Orr. 87560

Letter from Governor Jay. 30424

Letter from Governor Monroe. 100228

Letter from Governor Pownall. 64823, 82303

Letter from Governor R. K. Call. 10049

Letter from Governor Reeder. 68628

Letter from Governor St. Clair. 75019

Letter from Gov. Schley. 34867

Letter from Granville Sharp. 79827

Letter from H. Brackinridge. 38111

[Letter from H. W. Bellows to the Governor of New York.] 76672

Letter of H. W. Bellows to the Secretary of War. (76675)

Letter from Harriet Martineau. 49192

Letter from Harrison Gray Otis. (57858), note after 103304

Letter from Head to Lord Glenelg. 98067

Letter from Henry Darnell. 18601

Letter from Henry Laurens. 39259

Letter from His Excellency George Washington. 101706

Letter from His Excellency James L. Orr. 87561

Letter from His Excellency John Sevier. 94756

Letter from His Excellency Thomas Chittenden. 99002

Letter from His Grace the Archbishop of Canterbury. 70085, 85946

Letter from Hon. Edward Stanly. 90323

Letter from Hon. Horatio King. (37805)

Letter from Hon. J. K. Paulding. 64321

Letter from Hon. John Sherman. 80377

Letter from Hon. Joseph P. Bradley. 7283

Letter from Hon. Nathan Appleton. 80283

Letter from Hon. S. C. Pomeroy. 63939

Letter from Hon. William Jay. 35867

Letter from Horace Binney. (5479)

Letter from J. C. Lovejoy. 42367

[Letter from J. Foster Jenkins.] 76626

[Letter from J. Foster Jenkins to the editor of the Boston journal.] (76673)

Letter from J. Freeman. 25769

Letter from J. H. Douglass. 20718

Letter from J. J. Speed, Esq. of Baltimore, to a landholder of Baltimore County. 89237

Letter from J. J. Speed, Esq. of Baltimore, to a landholder of Maryland. 89238

Letter from J. J. Speed, Esq., of Baltimore, to the representatives. 89239

Letter from J. J. Speed, of Baltimore, to a landholder. 89240

Letter from J. J. Speed, of Baltimore, to his friend. 89241

Letter from J. L. [sic] Papineau and J. Neilson. (58490)

Letter from J. Washington Tyson. 97639

Letter from James J. Strang. 92685

Letter from James Moore. 50014

Letter from James Stuart, Esquire, to the Right Hon. Lord Goderich. 93171

Letter from James Stuart, Esq., to the Right Hon. Lord Viscount Goderich. 93173, 93177, 99597

Letter from James Whittaker. 97884

Letter from Jeremiah Hubbard. 14732, 32351

Letter from Jesse Chickering. 6614

Letter from Joe Strickland. 92809

Letter from John B. Colvin. 14903

Letter from John Bowden. 6987, 91745

Letter from John D. Sherwood. 17759

Letter from John H. Alexander. 45339

Letter from John I. Slingerland. 82149

Letter from John Leeds Kerr. 45370

Letter from John Ross, Principal Chief of the Cherokee Nation. 73391

Letter from John Ross, the Principal Chief of the Cherokee Nation. 73392

Letter . . . from John W. Garrett. 26697

Letter from Jonas Michaelius. 48688

Letter from Joseph Aspinall. 2214

Letter from Joseph John Gurney. 51789, 55959

Letter from Joseph John Gurney, with remarks thereon. 94129

Letter from Joseph Pease. (59467)

Letter from Judge Gayarre. (26794)

Letter from L. M. Sargent. 77012

Letter from Legion to His Grace the Duke of Richmond. 40330

Letter from Lemuel H. Arnold. 2075

Letter from Lemuel Shattuck. 79880

Letter from Lewis XV. to G——l M——t. (40776)

Letter from Lewis Thurenstein. 106354

Letter from Lexington, Kentucky. 37485

Letter from Lieut. Christopher Claxton. 13527

Letter from Lieut. Gen. Burgoyne to his constituents. 9251, 9263, 9266, 18348, 27144, 27188

Letter from Lieut. Gen. Sir Henry Clinton. 13750

Letter from Lieut. Hugh Mackay. 9830, (43362), 56845, 2d note after 87848

Letter from Lord Denman. 19579

Letter from Lord Macaulay. 42949

Letter from Lord Shelburne. 45933

Letter from Major Robert Carmichael-Smyth. 85259

Letter from Major Thomas Savage. 77246

Letter from Martha Washington. 82979

Letter from . . . Martin Van Buren, and . . . Joshua Leavitt. 44324

Letter from Martin Van Buren, in reply to the letter. 98414

Letter from Master Robert Evelin. 19724, 63310, 63312

Letter from Miss S————a to Mrs. R————. 74639

Letter from Mr. Bostick. 8984

Letter from Mr. Caleb Spurrier. 89939

Letter from Mr. Clay. 96362, 101069

Letter from Mr. Dalrymple. 18340

Letter from Mr. Davenport. 104369

Letter from Mr. Dickinson. (32311)

Letter from Mr. Erskine. 22797

Letter from Mr. Goad. 104336

Letter from Mr. Habersham. 29468

Letter from Mr. Hornblower. (33027)

Letter from Mr. James Boorman. (6378)

Letter from Mr. Jay. 35841

Letter from Mr. Jefferson to Mr. Dunbar. 85198

Letter from Mr. Jefferson to Mr. Hammond. 96579

Letter from Mr. John Clayton. (13575)

Letter from Mr. Joseph Adams. 329

Letter from Mr. Keene. 72044

Letter from Mr. Kirk. 26443

Letter from Mr. Knox. 38175

Letter from . . . Mr. Lodowick. 41768

Letter from Mr. Mann. 44324

Letter from Mr. Mather. 46723, 1st note after 65324

Letter from Mr. Monroe. 50013

Letter from Mr. Randolph. 1st note after 99797

Letter from Mr. Renwick. 69651

Letter from Mr. Richard Rush. 74253

Letter from Mr. Stanly. 90324

Letter from Mr. Sullivan. 93484

Letter from Mr William Cobbett. 13887

Letter from Mrs. Anne Dutton. 21466

Letter from Mrs. Cooper. 16624, (16626), 1st note after 102803

Letter from Montgomery E. Letcher. 40240

Letter from M. Birkbeck. 24911

Letter from M. Champagny, the French Minister. 11823

Letter from M. Lambert, Comptroller General of the French finances. (38735)

Letter of M. Turgot, late Comptroller-General of the Finances of France. 235, 65450, 97457

[Letter] from New England. (69679), 74624, 91382-91383

Letter from New-England, concerning the state of religion there. 57179

Letter from New England, concerning their customs, manners, and religion. 52641, note after 100866, 101286

Letter from New-England, to their dear countrymen of Lancashire. 46780

Letter from New Jersey in America. (40331), note before 94160, 95531

Letter from Noah Webster. (56489)

Letter, from one in Boston, to his friend in the country. 6709, 21088, (40332), 1st note after 99800

Letter from one in the country to his friend in Boston. 14536-14537, 103900

Letter from one in the country to his friend in the city; in relation to the distresses occasioned by inoculation. 34793, 40333

LETTER

Letter in answer to a criticism of the Edinburgh review. 46989

Letter in answer to an invitation. 9936

Letter in answer to inquiries. 1267

Letter . . . in answer to the Hon. J. M. Clayton. (33581)

Letter in answer to the Rev. Daniel Perry's short view. 28884

Letter in answer to the speech of the Rev. Dr. Mason. 86271

Letter in defence of Dr. Waterland's discourse on regeneration. (20062)

Letter in defence of Mr. Fox and others. 25339

Letter in defence of the clergy of the District of Columbia. 37338

Letter in defence of the Hartford Convention. 57860

[Letter in German.] 78012

Letter in regard to the tariff on iron and labor. 44376

Letter in relation to the failure of Culver, Penn, & Co. 17870

Letter . . . in relation to the lead mines of the United States. 39513

Letter in reply to his [i. e. Joshua Hill's] enemies. (31847)

Letter in reply to the attacks of the Hon. George Brown. 74556

Letter . . . in reply to the editor of the State Capitol reporter. 20693

Letter in reply [to the letter from a member of St. Paul's.] 12358, 40302, 59267, 62218

Letter in reply to the report of the Van Wyck Committee. (17913)

Letter in St. James's post. 35669, 1st note after 99808

Letter in the Gazetteer of October 22, 1768. 28751

Letter in the London Times on the war in America. 51103, 69420

Letter, in vindication of Mr. Whitefield's itineracy and conduct. 31302

Letter in which an attempt is made to prove that slavery is not immoral. 30854

Letter inferring publique communion in the parish assembles. 72102

Letter intercepted by them. 79781

Letter introductory from Messrs. Olmstead, Harris, Trowbridge and Richardson. 90788

Letter, lately addressed to the . . . Earl of Selkirk. 43146

Letter lately published on the subject. 85260

Letter list advertising in New York City. 4097

Letter; more respectfully addressed. 104014

Letter, New-York, Sept. 8, 1856. 91106

Letter IX. The priesthood. 89369

Letter no. 2. 9068

Letter occasioned by the death of Mrs. Abigail Conant. 15093

Letter, occasioned by the perusal of a paper. 60204

Letter of A. B. Sloanaker. 82165

Letter of a committee appointed at a public meeting. 98414

Letter of a farmer. 47276, 97107

Letter of a layman to any member of Congress. 95891

Letter of a Republican. (17630)

Letter of acceptance [of Gen. McClellan.] 19510, (43021)

Letter of acceptance [of Mr. J. G. Blaine.] 5731

Letter of acceptance of the Pittsburgh nomination. 63347

Letter of advice to a young American. 27674

Letter of advice to a young gentleman. 41326-41327

Letter of advice to the churches of the ninconformists. 46377

Letter of Aegles. 40351

Letter of Agassiz. 44505

Letter of Albert G. Brown. 8435

Letter of Alexander, addressed to De Witt Clinton. 13731

Letter of Americanus. 18239

Letter of Amerigo Vespucci. note before 99327, 99381

Letter of Andrew Jackson. (43589)

Letter of Appomatox to the people of Virginia. 40352, 6th note after 100483

Letter, of August 28, 1830. (67132)

Letter of Benjamin Bates. 47619, 86043, 100522

Letter of Bishop Kenrick. 14800

Letter of . . . Brown. 8453

Letter of Capt. Richard Delafield. 62051

Letter of Charles J. Ingersoll. 34735, 92851

Letter [of Christopher Columbus.] 1547, 32005, 74659

Letter of Col. John Spencer. 89343

Letter of Columbus to Luis de Santangel, 1493. 14641, (40041)

Letter of Commodore Stockton on the slavery question. 91896

Letter of condemnation sent to friends. 24082

Letter of congratuation from Britannia to the King. (40353)

Letter of courtship to his virtuous and amiable widow. (78690)-78691

Letter of Daniel R. Goodloe. 27862

Letter of Daniel Webster. 38269

Letter of David Hubbard. 33419

Letter of December 19, 1825. 82780

Letter of directions to his father's birthplace. 32608

Letter of Dr. F. A. Ross. 73354

Letter of Dr. Guthrie. (12406)

Letter of Dr. William Eustis. 23122

Letter of E. Allen. 792

Letter of E. Everett. (17762)

Letter of Edmund Burke. 62, 65-66, 5007, 11158, (11767)

Letter of Edward L. Pierce. (62709)

Letter of Edwin Gray. 68198

Letter of Elder Galusha. 92869

Letter of Elihu Burritt. 88296

Letter of Emanuel to Leo X. 34100-34107

Letter of Eugene Casserly. 11367

Letter of Ex-Governor Johnson. 31808

Letter of explanation. 51643

Letter of Ex-President Van Buren. 98425

Letter of F. P. Stanton. 90415

Letter of Father De Smedt. (34468), 82261

Letter of Father Silvestre Velez de Escalante. (80023)

Letter of G. W. Campbell. 10219

Letter of General A. J. Hamilton. 29995

Letter of Gen. Almanzon Huston. 34037

Letter [of General Burgoyne.] 18348

Letter of General Cox, of Ohio. 20098

Letter of General Dix, his opinion of the Chicago platform. 20341, 40611

Letter of General H. M. Naglee. 78735

Letter of Gen. Hensseir. 31435

Letter of Gen. Houston to Santa Anna. 95030-95031

Letter of General Joseph Dickson. (32506)

Letter of Gen. Mirabeau B. Lamar. 38704

Letter to a friend. [By T. Rankin.] 51829, (67887), 100437

Letter to a friend. By the Rev. Mr. Shirley. 80543

Letter to a friend. [By Thomas Foxcroft.] (25402), 103904

Letter to a friend. [By Valerius Corvinus.] 69475

Letter to a friend. By W. T. 95645

Letter to a friend, concerning the late proposals. 100604

Letter to a friend, concerning the proposals. 40381

Letter to a friend, containing a short vindication. (10681), 47130

Letter to a friend: containing remarks on a pamphlet. 78281, 102638

Letter to a friend, containing remarks on certain passages of a sermon. 12318-12319, 23318-23319, (34766), (41644), 2d note after 99800

Letter to a friend dated Philadelphia, November 26, 1838. 40385

Letter to a friend; giving a concise, but just, account. (12320), (40382), 97569, 8th note after 100869, 7th note after 100870, note after 101077

Letter to a friend, giving a concise, but just representation. 12321, 6th note after 100870

Letter to a friend in a slave state. 34726

Letter to a friend [in defence of George Whitefield.] 24391

Letter to a friend in Ireland. 40383

Letter to a friend in London. 46563, 2d note after 97085

Letter to a friend in New England in 1649. 49659

Letter to a friend in Paris. 65509

Letter to a friend, in reply to a recent pamphlet. 88572

Letter to a friend in the country. 60741, 2d note after 97014

Letter to a friend in the country, attempting a solution of the scruples. 46379, 104242

Letter to a friend in the country. By a minister in Boston. (16635)

Letter to a friend in the country. [By Benjamin Franklin.] (25496)

Letter to a friend in the country. [By Horace Walpole.] 59030, 101143

Letter to a friend in the country. By James Allen. 830

Letter to a friend in the country, containing the substance of a sermon. 25527, 31295-31296, 69518

Letter to a friend in the country, on the late expedition to Canada. 21199

Letter to a friend in the country, upon the news of the town. 40384

Letter to a friend in the United States. 81840

Letter to a friend, in vindication of the Directors. 88185

Letter to a friend; in which some account is given. (40386)

Letter to a friend, . . . [July 30th, 1850.] 58325

Letter to a friend, occasioned by the unhappy controversy. 101125

Letter to a friend on the conduct of the adherents to Mr. Burr. 12377

Letter to a friend, on the pretentions of the American colonies. 27926

Letter to a friend, on the subject of Rev. Mr. Noye's proposed examination. 56231

Letter to a friend. Recommended to the perusal. (78297)

Letter to a friend, relating to the differences. 75669

Letter to a friend, relative to the present state. (42383)

Letter to a friend, requesting the same. 72404

Letter to a friend. Taken from the Gospel magazine. 97269

Letter to a friend, together with a preface. 12316, (21935), 67768

Letter to a friend: wherein some free thoughts are offered. 105932

Letter to a friend. With a postscript. 96429

Letter to a friend. With an appendix. 105012

Letter to a friend. With observations and reflections. 95686

Letter to a friend. With proper attestations. (80666)-80667

Letter to a friend who had joined the Southern Independence Association. (55007)

Letter to a friend, written during the administration of John Adams. 98266

Letter to a general officer, acquitted by court martial. 6814, 56848

Letter to a general officer, remarkably acquitted by a c——t m——l. 27017

Letter to a gentleman at Portsmouth. 53297

Letter to a gentleman at Washington. 32215, note after 91888

Letter to a gentleman chosen to be a member. 45800

Letter to a gentleman, concerning the boundaries of the Province of Maryland. 4519

Letter to a gentleman; containing a plea for the rights. 40387

Letter to a gentleman, giving an account. (65604)

Letter to a gentleman, relating to the office. 40390, 69700, 86603

Letter to a gentleman in Albany. 31975, 43670

Letter to a gentleman in Boston. 100891

Letter to a gentleman in England. 90943

Letter to a gentleman in London. (40388), 7th note after 100483

Letter to a gentleman in Maryland. 79820

Letter . . . to a gentleman in New York. (36379)

Letter to a gentleman in the Massachusetts General Assembly. (45801)

Letter to a gentleman. In which is added, a postscript. 35588

Letter to a gentleman of Baltimore. 49051

Letter to a gentleman of Maryland. 40389

Letter to a great character. 17972

Letter to a great m————r. 40391, note after 98023

[Letter to] . . . A. J. Boreman. 19085

Letter to a lady in France. 11217, 40392

Letter to a landholder. 40393

Letter to a member, &c. 68279

Letter to a member of Congress. By a citizen of the United States. (17301), 56504

Letter to a member of Congress in relation to Indian civilization. 40394

Letter to a member of Congress, on the national currency. (40820)

Letter to a member of Congress, on the subject of a British war. (40395)

Letter to a member of Congress; respecting the alien and sedition laws. 97378

Letter to a member of Parliament. 10732, 15026, 16971, 16032, (23367), 26889, 40396, 64143, 68690, 69687, (78668), 86737, 90617

Letter to a member of Parliament. [By A. B.] 101150, note after 103106

Letter to a member of Parliament. By a West-India planter. 27607, 4th note after 102788

Letter to a member of Parliament. [By J. Way.] 102179

Letter to a member of Parliament. [By Peter Williamson?] 104486

Letter to a member of Parliament. [By Thomas Jefferys.] (35957)

Letter to a member of Parliament. [By William Bollan.] 6218

Letter to a member of Parliament, concerning the importance of our sugar colonies. 40397

Letter to a member of Parliament, concerning the naval store bill. 40398

Letter to a member of Parliament. Concerning the present state of affairs. 40399

Letter to a member of Parliament concerning trade. 102844

Letter to a member of Parliament, containing a statement of the method pursued. 86186, 1st note after 98076

Letter to a member of Parliament from a friend in the country. 42889

Letter to a member of Parliament from an inhabitant of New England. 6215, 10731

Letter to a member of Parliament. Fully answering a paper. 97146

Letter to a member of Parliament, occasion'd by the South-Sea Company's scheme. 40400

Letter to a member of Parliament, on the importance of the American colonies. 40401

Letter to a member of Parliament on the present unhappy dispute. 40402

Letter to a member of Parliament on the regulation. 2555, 40403

Letter to a member of Parliament, on the settling a trade. 40404, 88186

Letter to a member of Parliament, setting forth the value. 40405

Letter to a member of Parliament, wherein the power of the British legislature. 40406

Letter to a member of the Bahama Assembly. 85235

Letter to a member of the British House of Commons. (52213)

Letter to a member of the British Parliament. 40407

Letter to a member of the Congress of the United States. 40408

Letter to a member of the General Assembly of North Carolina. 40409

Letter to a member of the General Assembly of the colony of New-York. 67115

Letter to a member of the General Assembly of Virginia. 40410, 1st note after 97378, 100484

Letter to a member of the Honourable House of Commons. 40411

Letter to a member of the House of Commons. 34393, 34396, note after 73770, note after 102839

Letter to a member of the House of Representatives of the colony of Connecticut, in vindication of Yale College against the false aspersions. 28222, (40413), 105933

Letter to a member of the . . . House of Representatives, on the present state of the bills of credit. 40412

Letter to a member of the Lower House of Assembly of the colony of Connecticut. 26348, 26350, 28222, (40413), 105933-105934

Letter to a member of the present Parliament. 79227

Letter to a member of the Society of Friends. (3896)

Letter to a member of the Young Men's Christian Association. 13639

Letter to a merchant at Bristol. 40377, 40414

Letter to a merchant in Boston. 27833, 40415, 74420, 3d note after 97116

Letter to a minister. 69400, 103594

Letter to a minister of the Church of Scotland. 103606

Letter to a minister of the Gospel. 69306

Letter to a neighbouring minister. (62645)

Letter to a New-Hampshire land owner. 40417

Letter to a New-Jersey farmer. 40418

Letter to a noble duke. 63763

Letter to a noble lord. 15949, (21200) 21400, 57865

Letter to a noble lord. By a country gentleman. 15999

Letter to a noble lord concerning the late expedition. 10507

Letter to a noble lord, &c. 34087, note after 92858

Letter to a noble lord retired from power. 63758

Letter to a noble lord, wherein is demonstrated that all the great and mighty difficulties. 40419

Letter to a noble peer. 80606, 86616, 86668

Letter to a noble peer, relating to the bill. 40420

Letter to a nobleman. 40649

Letter to a nobleman, on the conduct of the war in the middle colonies. 26422-(26423), 26429, 26431, 26436, 26440, 26443

Letter to a nobleman, on the unfortunate capture. 58423

Letter to a parishioner, relative to the recent ordination. (29538)

Letter to a parishioner, which J. Mott pretended to answer. (40421), 103068

Letter to a person of quality. 9753, 46642, (78233)

Letter to a person of quality containing the author's apology. 18554

Letter to a physician in England. 43602

Letter to a pious friend in England. 80258

Letter, to a precious friend there. 80199

Letter to a radical member of Congress. (62957)

Letter to a representative. 32889, 103002

Letter to a Republican member. (40422)

Letter to a rev'nd gentleman. 98778

Letter to a reviewer. (70326)

Letter to a Right Honourable patriot. 28987

Letter to A. S., M. D. 34793, 46744

Letter to A. S., M. D. and F. R. S. (34791)

Letter to A——— S———, M. D. & F. R. S. 20720

Letter to a sick soldier. 14466

Letter to a student. (13424)

Letter to a victim of arbitrary arrests. 17605, 43877, note just before 63791

Letter to a Whig member. 82682

Letter to a Whig neighbor. 40423

Letter to a worthy member of the Honourable House of Commons. 102824

Letter to a young clergyman. 68202

Letter to a young friend. 90193

[Letter to Gabriel Jones.] 98977
Letter to General Andrew Jackson. 25457
Letter to General Burgoyne. (9261)
Letter to General Franklin Pierce. 57826
Letter to General Grant on the currency. 80805
Letter to General Hamilton. 23995, 29960, 102361
Letter to Gen. John H. Cocke. 19368
[Letter] to General Lafayette. 38583
Letter to General Washington. 21053
Letter to . . . George Canning. (42415)
Letter to Geo. Hammond. 96576
Letter to Geo. Whitefield. (22795)
Letter to George Washington, on . . . the late treaty. 58228, 101809
Letter to George Washington, President of the United States; containing strictures on his address. (20989), note after 96799, 96800, note before 101837
Letter to George Washington, President of the United States. . . . On affairs public and private. (15588), (37437), (58224), (58249), 90446, note after 101837
Letter to Gilman Marston, Esq. 76235
Letter to Governor King. 19369
Letter to Governor Lincoln. (28384)
Letter to Gov. Morgan of New York. 4575
Letter to Governor Seymour. 16594
Letter to Governor Wright. 40436
Letter to Granville Sharp. (79828)
Letter to Gulian C. Verplanck. 24274, note after 99270, 99274
Letter to Harrison Gray Otis. 40048, 70067
Letter to Henry Banning, Esq. 5710, 43404
Letter to Henry Clay. 11913
Letter to Henry Gregoire. (3421)
Letter to Henry J. Grew. 37369
Letter to Henry Williams. (11905)
Letter to her [i. e. Hannah Cook's] husband. 91662
Letter to Her Majesty the British Queen. 93965
Letter to Her Majesty's Under Secretary of State. 40437
Letter to Her R——l H——s. 40438
Letter to him [i. e. George Whitefield.] 13220 105826
Letter to his [i. e. John Thayer's] brother. 95239, 95244, 95252
Letter to his [i. e. Jonathan Mitchel's] brother. (49660)
Letter to his [i. e. John Vandike's] brother in Amsterdam. 98488
Letter . . . to his [i. e. John A. King's] constituents. 37816
Letter to his [i. e. Wilson Cary Nicholas' constituents. 55180
Letter to his [i. e. John Stanly's] constituents, May 1, 1802. 90340
Letter to his [i. e. John Stanly's] constituents, May 10, 1809. 90341
Letter to his [i. e. John Stanly's] constituents, May 10, 1810. 90342
Letter . . . to his [i. e. John P. Hale's] constituents on the proposed annexation of Texas. 29641
Letter . . . to his [i. e. John Pendleton Kennedy's] constituents. (37423)
Letter to his countrymen. By J. Fenimore Cooper. (16464), (18093)
Letter to his [i. e. William Wirt's] daughter. 104865
Letter . . . to His Excellency Benj. Stanton. 23331

Letter to His Excellency Gov. Harris. 18275
Letter to His Excellency Governor Manning on public instruction. 95649
Letter to His Excellency Governor Manning, on the boundary. 87376
Letter to His Excellency Governor Wright. 103562
[Letter] to His Excellency Henry J. Gardner. 30247
Letter to His Excellency Henry W. Edwards. 93526
Letter to His Excellency, John Henry Clifford. 15467
Letter to His Excellency Marcus Morton. (31792)
Letter to His Excellency Patrick Noble. 40985
Letter to His Excellency Sir George Arthur. (30721)
Letter to His Excellency T. Watkins Ligon. 90879
Letter to His Excellency the Prince of Tallyrand Perigord. 103954
Letter to His Excellency William C. C. Claiborne. 56303
Letter to His Excellency William H. Seward. (28415)
Letter to his friend. 99224
Letter to his [i. e. Andrew Jackson Downing's] friends. 20775
Letter to His Grace the D——of N——e. 40440, (80051)
Letter to His Grace the Duke of Buccleugh. 82303
Letter to His Grace the Duke of Grafton. 28773, 40439, 3d note after 94663
Letter to His Grace the Duke of N********. 40441
Letter to his kinsfolk. 25511
Letter to His Lordship [the Bishop of Llandaff.] 23319
Letter to His Lordship [the Earl of Mansfield.] 63401-63402, note after 104453
Letter to His Majesty's Justices of the Peace. 60208
Letter to His Majesty's Under Secretary of State. 93178
Letter to His Royal Highness the Duke of Gloucester. 95656
Letter to his uncle, at Philadelphia. 98468
Letter to Hon. —— member of Congress. 13644
Letter to Hon. A. P. Edgerton. 12196
Letter to Hon. Abraham Lincoln. 44253
Letter . . . to Hon. B. F. Butler. 12200
Letter . . . to Hon. C. Sumner. 62792
Letter to Hon. Charles Sumner, dated Jan. 1866. 59643
Letter to Hon. Charles Sumner, December 5, 1864. 82638
Letter to Hon. E. D. Morgan . . . on the amendment. 40985
Letter to Hon. E. D. Morgan, U. S. Senator from New York. 21868
Letter to Hon. Edward Everett. 815, 95705
Letter to Hon. H. C. Goodwin. 82673
Letter to Hon. H. S. Foote. 89964, 89975
Letter to Hon. Harrison Gray Otis. 14313
Letter to Henry Clay. 74355
[Letter to] Hon. Henry Watson. 19808
Letter to Hon. J. J. Crittenden. (6930)
Letter to Hon. James B. Doolittle. 26403
Letter to Hon. James Buchanan. 57654
Letter to Hon. James Doolittle. 52288
Letter to Hon. James Hamilton. 30016, 97984
Letter to Hon. John B. Dickey. 23893

Letter to Mr. Brown. 92785
Letter to Mr. Channing. 11924
Letter to Mr. Daniel Humphreys. 82487
Letter, to Mr. Daniel Webster. 8397
Letter to Mr. E. Turell. 17672, 85663
Letter to Mr. Endicot. 104333
Letter to Mr. Franklin. (25613)
Letter to Mr. French. 25859
Letter to Mr. G——r. 40448
Letter to Mr. Hitchings. 78247
Letter to Mr. Hobby. 23583, 32316
Letter to Mr. Israel Holly. 104716
Letter to Mr. James Moore. 90149
Letter to Mr. John R. Moreland. 92028
Letter to Mr. John Stancliff. 50399, 90149
Letter to Mr. John Wesley. 63764
Letter to Mr. Law. 39310
Letter to Mr. Nelson. 8190
Letter to Mr. Nicholas Chester. 93240
Letter to Mr. Penn. (59684), 59714
Letter to Mr. Powys. 40449
Letter, to Mr. Robert Gourlay. 98077
Letter to Mr. Robert Sandeman. (62832),
    76343
Letter to Mr. Robert B. Taney. 40450
Letter to Mr. Shedd. 104927
Letter to Mr. Tho. Edwards. 21992
Letter to Mr. Ticknor. 55865
Letter to Mr. Washington. 101739-101740
Letter to Mr. Whitefield. (62645)
Letter to Mr. Wilberforce. 14021
Letter to Mr. William Seward. 103506
Letter to Mrs. ——. (33333)
Letter to Mrs. E. Cady Stanton. 82616
Letter to Mrs. P——s. 40452
Letter to M. de Sartiges. 74368
Letter to M. Jean Baptiste Say. 32356,
    (32358)
Letter to M. Roume. 3807
Letter to Moses Taylor. 24347
Letter to Moses Williams. 27905
Letter. . . . To my neighbor. 5741
Letter to Napoleon Bonaparte in 1801. (7379)
Letter to Ohio Legislature, Feb. 3, 1863.
    note just before (73261)
Letter to one of the directors. 19251, (58160),
    96427
Letter to one of the members of the General
    Assembly. 40453, 98434
Letter to P. Randolph. (26230)
Letter to Parsons Cooke. 16337-16338
Letter to Peter Cooper. 37997
Letter to Piero Soderini. 99379
Letter to Philo Africanus. 40451, 62542,
    92694
Letter to "Plain fact." 63240, note after
    95739
Letter to "Plain Truth, Junior." 63240, note
    after 95739
Letter to President Fillmore's lady. 19322
Letter to President Grant . . . [on] the Na-
    tional Labor Union. (43859)
Letter to President Grant on the subject of
    the removal. 68308
Letter to President Johnson. 26730
Letter . . . to President Lincoln. (44466)
Letter to President Lincoln, by a citizen of
    Kentucky. 63264
Letter to President Lincoln, August 5, 1863.
    40454, 76572, 76647
Letter to . . . President of the African Insti-
    tution. 42954
Letter to Professor Stuart. 101311
Letter to Professor Stuart, in answer to his
    letters. 93205, 101203
Letter to R. D. Mussey. 92388

[Letter] to R. G. Payne. 33823
Letter to R. Hamilton. 104293
Letter to R. Toombs. 27891
Letter to Rev. Dr. Price. 56406
Letter to Rev. Dr. Stevens. 103172
Letter to Rev. E. E. Hale. 67266
Letter . . . to Rev. Enoch Pond. 56050
Letter to Rev. Frederick T. Gray. 28390,
    51592, 64993
Letter to Rev. George Strebeck. 93240
Letter to Rev. H. W. Bellows. 76624
Letter to Rev. Henry M. Dexter. 58691
Letter to Rev. Henry Ward Beecher. 68661
Letter to Rev. Howard Crosby. (44749)
Letter to Rev. J. Wesley. 14242
Letter to Rev. Joseph Buckminster. 25233
Letter to Rev. M. A. DeWolf Howe. 32930,
    33320
Letter to Rev. Nehemiah Adams. 82243
Letter to Rev. Parsons Cooke. 58679
Letter to Rev. Sam. Hopkins. (30648)
Letter to Rev. Samuel Spring. 105325
Letter to Rev. Thomas Foxcroft. 23582
Letter to Rev. William Hobby. (13597)
Letter to Reverdy Johnson. 39872
Letter to Richard Kent, Esq. (37480)
Letter to Richard Kent, Esq., one of His
    Majesty's Justices of the Peace. 1703,
    note after 97417
Letter to Rt. Hon. W. E. Gladstone. (33315)
Letter to Rt. Rev. Bishop Onderdonk. (63414)
Letter to Robert Hibbert. 16624, (16626),
    1st note after 102803
Letter to Robert Owen, of New Lanark.
    86871
Letter to Robert Schuyler. 67904
Letter to Robert Troup. 13712, 94188
Letter to Robert Wilmot Horton. 102845
Letter . . . to Roberts Vaux. (41617)
Letter to S. F. Wetmore. (1472)
Letter . . . to S. G. Perkins. 4575
Letter . . . to S. M. Hopkins. 82673
Letter to Samuel B. Ruggles. 3206
Letter to Samuel Bowles. 90868
Letter to Samuel J. Peters. 91193
Letter to Samuel Johnson. (36296)
Letter to Schuyler Colfax. 10842
Letter to Scripturista. (18419)
Letter to Secretary McCulloch. 15928
Letter to Senator Fessenden. (18048)
Letter to Senator Foot. (68500)
Letter . . . to Senator Johnson. 20817
Letter to Senator Sam Houston. 33882
Letter . . . to . . . Sir G. Calvert. 104786
Letter to Sir George Grey. 4883
Letter to Sir George Murray. (51495)
Letter to Sir George Saville. 56437, 80107,
    80112
Letter to Sir Henry Parnell. (5925)
Letter to Sir J. R. 69714, note after 100519
Letter to Sir John Keane. (25622)
Letter to Sir John M'Neil. 772
Letter to Sir Richard Steele. 88183
Letter to Sir Robert Peel, Bart. on . . .
    British colonial slavery. 10245
Letter to Sir Robert Peel. By Thomas
    M'Combie. (43083)
Letter to Sir Sam. Hood. (9885)
Letter to Sir William Hamilton. (74300)
Letter to Sir William Howe. 26443
Letter to Sir William Meredith. 47946
Letter to Sir William Poulteney. 18326
Letter to Stephen Chase. 31302
Letter . . . to Stephen Colwell. 43455
Letter to Stephen Gould. (3841)
Letter to Stephen R. Bradley. 28228

Letter to sundry disaffected individuals.
5277

Letter to T. Frelinghuysen. 16806

Letter to T. Paine. (15588)

Letter to Thacher. 96412

Letter to that gentleman |i. e. Lord Kenyon.|
69396

Letter to that gentleman [i. e. John Meares]
by George Dixon. 20361

Letter to the abolitionists. 11911

Letter to the addressers. (71242)

Letter to the alumni of Dartmouth College.
42043

Letter to the American Anti-slavery Society.
35849

Letter to the American Colonization Society.
47230

Letter to the American Peace Society. 27273

Letter to the Archbishop of Canterbury.
40455, 47276, 65149

Letter to the artisans. 35689

[Letter to the Assembly.] 100229

Letter to the Associate Presbyterian Congregation. 90514

Letter to the Associate Presbytery, of Cambridge. 90513

Letter to the Attorney General. 94104

Letter to the author [i. e. Sir Robert Walpole.]
(66641), 101148 ·

Letter to the author [i. e. Sir William Yonge.]
66643

Letter to the author [i. e. Stephen West.]
102752

Letter to the author. By a member of the
Synod. 20060, 69515

Letter to the author from Washington Irving.
78686

Letter to the author of A full vindication of
the measures of the Congress. 29955,
78580-78581, 2d note after 99553, 4th
note after 100862

Letter to the author of a late pamphlet.
102425

Letter to the author of Dispassionate thoughts.
20270, 26440, 97340

Letter to the author of Lucubrations during a
short recess. 40456

Letter to the author of The case stated.
86619

Letter to the author of "The clockmaker."
85258

Letter to the author of The faithful narrative,
&c. (30647), 96092

Letter to the author of The Halifax Letter.
19249, 40457

Letter to the author of The narrative. By
William Hart. (30647), 96092

Letter to the author of the pamphlet called,
An answeer [sic] to the Hampshire narrative. 7656, (30136)

Letter to the author on the same subject.
83796

Letter to the author to be communicated to
his attestators. 7789

Letter to the Bank-Directors of Portland.
52161

Letter to the Baptist Association at Philadelphia. 8368

Letter to the Belfast . . . Volunteers. 40458,
42768

Letter to the Bishop of London. 103565

Letter to the Bishop of Massachusetts. (17683)

Letter to the Bishop of North Carolina. 45481

Letter to the Bishop of the Diocese of Massachusetts. (17683)

Letter to the bishops and clergy. 26139

Letter to the . . . bishops of Tennessee.
63845

Letter to the Bishops of the P. E. Church.
20393

Letter . . . to the Bishops of the Reformed
Church in America. 93704

Letter to . . . the Board of Trustees of the
University of Mississippi. 3459

Letter to the Boston Association of Congregational Ministers. 58738, note after
(58767)

Letter to the Brethren of the First Church of
Christ. (65240)

Letter to the Canada Land Company. 79132,
94684

Letter to the candid. 103723

Letter to the Catholic clergy. 10425

Letter . . . to the Catholics of Worcester.
30955

Letter to the Chairman, &c., of the North
American Colonial Association. 26454

Letter . . . to the Chairman of the Committee
of the Legislature on the License Law.
45802

Letter to the Chairman of the Naval Committee. 33468

Letter to the Chairman . . . of the North
Atlantic Colonial Association. (26453)

Letter to the children of America. (16604)

Letter to the Christian laity. 40459

Letter to the citizens of Charleston. 23467,
39959

Letter, to the citizens of Lancaster County.
49201

Letter to the citizens of . . . Pennsylvania.
(61663)

Letter to the citizens of Pennsylvania on the
necessity of promoting agriculture.
41790

Letter to the citizens of the slave-holding
states. 44308

Letter to the clergy and congregations of the
Church of England. 91648

Letter . . . to the clergy and laity of his
[i. e. G. W. Doane's] diocese. 20391

Letter to the clergy and laity of the Protestant Episcopal Church. 32401

Letter to the clergy of the Church of England.
(72332)

Letter to the clergy of New York and New
Jersey. 29381

Letter to the clergy of the colony of Connecticut. 15817

Letter to the clergy there. 46722, 46731-
46732, 58359, (65323), note after 70346,
92350

Letter to the clergy of various denominations.
13489

Letter to the clergy of Virginia. 5861

Letter to the collector. 87724

Letter to the Commission of Bishops. 24244

Letter to the Commissioner of Indian Affairs.
12464

Letter to the committee chosen by the American Tract Society. 35867

Letter to the Committee of Elizabeth City,
County, Virginia. 98418

Letter to the Committee of Correspondence.
63240, note after 95739

Letter . . . to the Committee of the Mass
Meeting in Philadelphia. 20341

Letter to the Committee of the Third-District
Medical Society. (56954)

Letter to the Committee of Ways and Means.
40460, note after 42673

Letter to the Common Council of London. (40461)

Letter . . . to the Common Council . . . of New York. 26334

Letter to the Comte de Sartiges. 23254

Letter to the congregation of St. James' Church, York, U. Canada. 92645

Letter to the Congregational Church in London. 72110

Letter to the Congregational Deputation. 82243

Letter to the congregations of the eighteen Presbyterian (or New Light) ministers. 40462, 97107

Letter to the congregations of the said ministers. 47276, (78736), 97107

Letter to the consulting physicians of Boston. 68188

Letter to the Corporation and Overseers of Harvard College. 58321, note just before (30750)

Letter to the Corporation of Brown University. 8626

Letter to the corporation of Trinity Church. 26631

Letter to the correspondent. 94074, 94077, 102518

Letter to the Councillors [sic] of the University of . . . New-York. (54709)

Letter to the Countess of Lincoln. 106052

Letter to the Craftsman. 1335A, 86644

Letter to the dedicator of Mr. Emlyn's "Inquiry." 9422, 93820

Letter to the Delaware pilots. 19393

Letter to the Democratic Party on the issues of the day. 32920

Letter . . . to the Democratic State Central Committee. 36504

Letter to the Directors of the Bank of Philadelphia. (61780)

Letter to the Directors of the Lawrence Manufacturing Company. 88678

Letter to the Directors of the London Missionary Society. 93261

Letter to the Duke of Grafton. 48939-(48940)

Letter to . . . the Duke of Newcastle. 30028

Letter to the Duke of Portland. By a gentleman of the island [of Trinidad,] 63747, 2d note after 96979

Letter to the Duke of Portland on the subject of the black troops. 11769

Letter to the Duke of Wellington. 40463

Letter to the Earl of Aberdeen. 7822

Letter to the Earl of Aberdeen, by a gentleman resident in Monte Video. 73219

Letter to the Earl of Aberdeen. By Alfred Mallalieu. 44125

Letter to the Earl of Abingdon, discussing a position. 11158

Letter to the Earl of Abingdon, in which His Grace of York's notions of civil liberty are examined. 97572

Letter to the Earl of B---. 40465

Letter to the Earl of Bute. 40466

Letter to the Earl of Bute, on the preliminaries of peace. 40464

Letter to the Earl of Chatham, concerning his speech. 40467

Letter to the Earl of Chatham, on the Quebec bill. 40468, (47945)-47946

Letter . . . to the . . . Earl of Halifax. 29043

Letter to the Earl of Hillsborough. 1792A, 16138

Letter to the Earl of Hillsborough, dated at Port Praya. 36396

Letter to the Earl of Liverpool. 20698

Letter to the Earl of Nottingham. 74287

Letter to the Earl of Pembroke. 89151

Letter to the Earl of Shelburne, on his speech. 58229

Letter to the Earl of Shelburne on the peace. (40479)

Letter to the Earl Temple. 69530

Letter to the Edinburgh Reviewers. 105610

Letter to the editor of the Anti-slavery advocate. 25705

Letter to the editor of the Boston daily advertiser. 9615

Letter to the editor of the Charleston observer. 98040

Letter to the editor of the "Church." 71114

Letter to the editor of the New York daily sentinel. 10889

Letter to the editor of the "Palladium." 71718

Letter to the editor of the Quarterly review. 98925

Letter to the editor of the Spirit of the pilgrims. 97594

Letter to the editor of the Unitarian miscellany. (49064)

Letter to the editors of the American monthly review. 13886

Letter to the editors of the American Presbyterian. 52289

Letter to the editors of the Baltimore American. 65472

Letter to the editors of the Irish press. 43264

Letter to the editors of the Louisville journal. 40470

Letter to the editors of the National intelligencer. 3482

Letter to the Edwards Church. (55072)

Letter to the elders and brethren. 103942

Letter to the electors of President and Vice-President. (26931), 40471

Letter to the English nation. 40472

Letter to the Evangelical Congregational Church. 23902, 90998

Letter to the Examiner and chronicle. 15095

Letter to the Executive Committee of the Benevolent Fraternity of Churches. 97392

Letter to the farmers, and other inhabitants of North America in general. 78574-78575, 4th note after 100862

Letter to the farmers of Massachusetts. 14535

Letter . . . to the Finance Committee. 23331

Letter to the First Congregational Paedobaptist Church. 73140

Letter to the followers of Elias Hicks. (29314)

Letter to the free colored population. 81992

Letter to the freeholders and qualified voters. 6523, (40475)

Letter to the freeholders and other inhabitants of the Massachusetts-Bay. 13134, 40473, 67182

Letter to the freeholders and other inhabitants of this province. 40474

Letter to the freeholders of the town of Boston. 40476

Letter to the freemen and freeholders of the city of New York. 40477

Letter to the freemen and freeholders of the province of New-York. 96961

Letter to the freemen, etc., of the city of New York. (34613)

Letter to the friends and stockholders of the York and Cumberland Railroad. (82564)

Letter to the friends of Rev. F. T. Gray.
28390, 64993

Letter to the friends of temperance in Massachusetts. 21979

Letter to the friends of the Troy and Boston Rail Road. 95784

Letter . . . to the General Assembly of Virginia. (39916)

Letter to the General Convention of the Ministers. 42037, 92099

Letter to the gentleman of the Committee of London Merchants. 40478

Letter . . . to . . . the Governor. 57860

Letter . . . to the Governor, . . . December 30, 1858. 53821

Letter to the Governor of Massachusetts, on occasion of his late proclamation. 1475, 9801

Letter to the Governor of Massachusetts, upon his veto of a bill. (33333)

Letter to the Governor of Virginia on cultivating the silkworm. 31998, 35676, 99886

Letter to the governors, instructors and trustees. 102362

Letter to the governors of the College of New York. (35827)

Letter to the governors, legislatures, and proprietors of plantations. 64327

Letter to the Grand Master of the Grand Lodge of Massachusetts. (19901)

Letter to the great man. 40479

Letter to the Honorable A——r M——re. (40480)

Letter to the Hon. Abbott Lawrence. 13226

Letter to the Hon. Abraham Edwards. 105094

Letter to the Hon. Alexander H. H. Stuart. 3742

Letter to the Hon. Baron Ashburton. 3385

Letter to the Hon. Benjamin R. Curtis. 37996

Letter to the Honorable Brockholst Livingston. 97065

Letter to the Hon. Charles J. Ingersoll. 58340

Letter to the Hon. Charles Sumner. 14139

Letter to the Hon. Constantine John Phipps. 33056, 69478

Letter to the Hon. Daniel Webster, on the causes of the destruction of the steamer Lexington. 13659, 5th note after 96480, 102321

Letter to the Hon. Daniel Webster on the political affairs of the United States. (44480), 102321, note after 102362

Letter. To the Hon. E. D. Morgan. 30019

Letter to the Honourable Edward Vernon. 11518, 17794, 2d note after 99245

Letter to the Hon. Edwin D. Morgan. 35849

Letter to the Hon. Francis Hincks. 31932, (33315)

Letter to the Hon. George E. Badger. 37350

Letter to the Hon. George T. Davis. 90870

Letter to the Hon. Gideon Welles. 20018

Letter to the Hon. Harrison Gray Otis, a member of the Senate of Massachusetts. 282-283, 40482

Letter to the Hon. Harrison Gray Otis, Peleg Sprague, and Richard Fletcher. 7248

Letter to the Hon. Henry Clay, of Kentucky. 9370

Letter to the Hon. Henry Clay on the annexation of Texas to the United States. 11912-11913, 80853, 92829, 1st note after 95112, 4th note after 95112, 95141, note after 103316

Letter . . . to the Hon. Howell Cobb. 20162

Letter to the Hon. Horace Mann. (8044)

Letter to the Hon. Ira Harris. 18355

Letter to the Hon. Isaac Parker. 101476

Letter to the Hon. J. B. Floyd. 51003

Letter to the Hon. James Buchanan. 3695

Letter to the Hon. James Clark. (13351)

Letter to the Hon. James F. Simmons. 40481, 81171

Letter to the Hon. James H. Lane. 24450

Letter to the Hon. John C. Calhoun, on the annexation of Texas. 30095, 95098

Letter to the Honourable John C. Calhoun, Vice-President. 28857

Letter to the Hon. John H. Eaton. 14102

Letter to the Honorable John Pickering. 10236

Letter to the Hon. John Pickering, President of the Salem Mill Dam Corporation. 290

Letter to the Hon. John Quincey [sic] Adams, occasioned by his letter to Mr. Otis. 283, 40482

Letter to the Hon. John Quincy Adams, on the Oregon question. 2843

Letter to the Hon. John Randolph. 40483, 67849

Letter to the Hon. John Sherman. 13389

Letter to the Hon. Josiah Quincy, Judge of the Municipal Court. 67255

Letter to the Hon. Josiah Quincy, . . . on the law of libel. 57856

Letter to the Hon. Lewis Cass. 20863

Letter to the Hon. Luther Bradish. 18397

Letter to the Hon. Micah Sterling. 29549

Letter to the Hon. Millard Fillmore. (6384)

Letter to the Hon. Milton S. Latham. 1573, 51959

Letter to the Hon. Mr. Calhoun. 9951, 10889

Letter to Hon. Mr. Ch——s F——x. 25338

Letter to the Honorable Mr. Hawes. 40484, 102946

Letter to the Hon. R. Baldwin. 5075

Letter to the Hon. Reverdy Johnson. 45195

Letter to the Hon. Robert M'Clelland. 3848

Letter to the Hon. Robert Morris. 19064

Letter to the Hon. Rufus Choate, by a conservative Whig. 12859, (67211), 72651

Letter to the Hon. Rufus Choate, containing a brief exposure. (72075)-(72076)

Letter to the Hon. S. A. Eliot. 40485

Letter . . . to the Hon. Salmon P. Chase. 58024

Letter to the Hon. Samuel A. Eliot. 19890, (30195)

Letter to the Hon. Saml. L. Mitchell. 99271

Letter to the Hon. Samuel Shellabarger. 7171

Letter to the Hon. Samuel W. King. 17233

Letter to the Honorable Secretary of War. 335

Letter to the Hon. Stephen Allen and G. B. Throop, Esquires. 95783

Letter to the Hon. Stephen Allen, of New York. 73226

Letter to the Hon. Thomas C. Deye. 44897

Letter to the Hon. Thomas Corwin. (43135)

Letter to the Hon. W. Gwin. 78053

Letter to Hon W. Huskisson. 2285

Letter to the Hon. Whitemarsh B. Seabrook. 39257

Letter to the Hon. William C. Preston. 40985

Letter to the Hon. Wm. C. Rives. (1815)

Letter to the Hon. William H. Seward. 43534

Letter to the Hon. William H. Seward, Secretary of State. (19659)

Letter to the Hon. Wm. M. Gwin. 95463

Letter to the Honourable William Morris. 50881, 92650

Letter to the Independent reflector. 4713, 40486, (44576)

Letter to the infamous Tom Paine, in answer to a letter written by him to General Washington. 14005, 13888, 101837

Letter to the infamous Tom Paine, in answer to his brutal attack on the federal constitution. 14005, 13888, 101837

Letter to the inhabitants of Northumberland. 65509

Letter to the inhabitants of the British colonies. 39701

Letter to the inhabitants of the city and state of New York. 40488

Letter to the inhabitants of . . . the Massachusetts-Bay. 40487

Letter to the inhabitants of the province of Quebec. (40489)

Letter to the inhabitants of said grants. 56564, 2d note after 99000

Letter to the jurors of Great Britain. 40490

Letter to the King. [By Incognitus.] 95687

Letter to the King. [By Sincerus.] 63216

Letter to the King of *****. (40491)

Letter to the Knox Presbytery. 93184

Letter to the late General George Washington. 58227

Letter to the late Mr. John Ellicott. 33031

Letter to the legislative authority of Connecticut, in relation to debt and gaols. 15767

Letter to the legislative authority of Connecticut, on imprisonment for debt. 40493

Letter to the Legislature of Alabama. 565

Letter to the Legislature of Massachusetts. 40492

Letter to the Legislature of South Carolina. 13730

Letter to the Liverpool Society for the Abolition of Slavery. 40494

Letter to the London Times on the war in America. 51103, 69420

Letter to the Lord Bishop of London. (27313)

Letter to the Lord Chancellor. 91841A

Letter to the Lord Chancellor, on the abolition of slavery. 40495, 1st note after 102802

Letter to the Lord Glenelg. 34786

Letter to the . . . Lord Mayor. 31193

Letter to the Lord Mayor of London. 23530

Letter to the Lord Mayor of London, bank directors, &c. 69535

Letter to the Lords . . . assembled at Westminister. 104146

Letter to the Lords Commissioners of Trade and Plantations. 13809

Letter to the Lords of Trade and Plantations. 5861

Letter to the Lords Spiritual and Temporal assembled at Westminster, in this present Convention. 104144

Letter to the Lords Spiritual and Temporal assembled at Westminster in this present Convention, January 22. 1688. 104145

Letter . . . to the Loyal National League. 12200

Letter to the majority of the Joint Committee. 5922

Letter to the majority of the Trustees of the Dudley Observatory. 21099

Letter to the Marquess of Normanby, relative to the present state of Jamaica. (82148)

Letter to the Marquis of Chandos. 102846

Letter to the Marquis of Landsdowne. 71016

Letter to the . . . Marquis of Normanby, on the state of Newfoundland. 50859

Letter to the . . . Massachusetts Medical Society. 3756

[Letter] to the masters and mistresses of families in the English plantations abroad. 10894, 27312-(27313), 71968

Letter to the Mayor of Savannah. 77265

Letter to the mechanics of Boston. (45898)

Letter to the members and friends of the Methodist Episcopal Church. 101407

Letter to the members of Parliament, on the address. 11089

Letter to the members of Parliament who have presented petitions. 34788, 82004, 2d note after 102785

Letter to the members of the Associate Reformed Church, illustrating the acts of synod. 65172

Letter to the members of the Associate-Reformed Church, in North-America. (40496)

Letter to the members of the congregations and parish of Trinity Church. 77982

Letter to the members of the Genesee Consociation. (22449), 26921

Letter to the members of the imperial Parliament. 40497

Letter to the members of the Methodist Episcopal Church. 95225

Letter to the members of the Pennsylvania Legislature. (50598)

Letter to the members of the Presbyterian churches, . . . in the United States of America. 38865

Letter . . . to the members of the Presbyterian churches in the United States, on the present crisis. (49064)

Letter to the members of the Protestant Episcopal Church, in Nashville. 102562

Letter to the members of the Protestant Episcopal Church in the United States. 88580

Letter to the members of the Society for Propagating the Gospel. 11203, 95950

Letter to the members of the South Carolina Legislature. 20208

Letter to the merchant in London. 40499

Letter to the merchants of Great Britain. (40500)

Letter to the merchants of London. 15207

Letter to the merchants of New York. 56660

[Letter] to the missionaries there. 10894, 27312-(27313), 71968

Letter to the Moderator of the New Hampshire Association. 52946, 8th note after 95843, note after 105328

Letter to the Mohawk Association of Universalists. 56687

Letter to the Most Honorable the Marquis of Chandos. 40501, 3d note after 102788, 1st note after 102846

Letter to the Most Noble the Marquis of Chandos. 3653, 40502, 2d note after 102846

Letter to the National Convention of France. 3423, 3426

Letter to the Negroes lately converted . . . in America. And particularly to those . . . at Mr. Jonathan Bryan's in South Carolina. 40504

Letter to the Negroes lately converted in America and particularly those at the plantation of J. Bryan. 8798

Letter to the new Parliament. (40503)

Letter to the New-York Chamber of Commerce. 31411

Letter to the "New York Times." 11343

Letter to the noblemen, gentlemen, &c. 40505

Letter to the North American. 20038

Letter to the Rev. Dr. Cooper. 16589, 40514

Letter to the Reverend Dr. Durell. 103564

Letter to the Rev. Dr. Nott. 93209

Letter to the Rev. Dr. Price. By the author of the Defence of the American colonies. 56060

Letter to the Rev. Dr. Price, F. R. S. Wherein his Observations. 91680

Letter to the Rev. Dr. Richard Watson. 40515

Letter to the Rev. George Junkin. (38838)

Letter to the Rev. George Strebeck. 92759

Letter . . . to the Rev. H. D. Walker. 7960

Letter to the Rev. Henry Ward Beecher. (43198)

Letter to the Rev. James C. Richmond, Presbyter of Rhode Island. 40516, 88113

Letter to the Rev. James C. Richmond, principal agent. 57309

Letter to the Reverend James Davenport. 12331

Letter to the Rev. Jedediah Morse. 40517, 2d note after 97378, note after 104434

Letter to the Rev. John Bachman, D. C. (51024)

Letter to the Rev. John Kelly. 105036

Letter to the Rev. John Murray. 105296

Letter to the Rev. John Tucker of Newbury. 79747, 97319

Letter to the Reverend John Wesley. 102702

Letter to the Reverend Josiah Tucker. 23079, 97350

Letter to the Rev. Leonard Bacon, D. D., by J. Halsted Carroll. 11077

Letter to the Rev. Leonard Bacon, D. D. [By John Marsh.] (44749)

Letter to the Rev. Lyman Beecher. 26694

Letter to the Rev. Matthew Hale Smith. 83586

Letter to the Rev. Mr. Benjamin Lord. 2632

Letter to the Reverend Mr. Cummings. 4497

Letter to the Rev. Mr. Davenport. 62646

Letter to the Reverend Mr. Foxcroft. 25386

Letter to the Reverend Mr. George Whitefield. 65671

Letter to the Reverend Mr. George Whitefield, an itinerant preacher. 65238

Letter to the Reverend Mr. George Whitefield. By Canonicus. 103632

Letter to the Reverend Mr. George Whitefield, by way of a reply. 103566, 103901

Letter to the Reverend Mr. George Whitefield, publickly calling upon him. 25386, 103633

Letter to the Reverend Mr. George Whitefield, vindicating certain passages. 12322

Letter to the Rev. Mr. Hobby. 7664, 32317

Letter to the Rev. Mr. J. Wesley. 96354

Letter to the Rev. Mr. James Chandler. (11858), 97315

Letter to the Rev. Mr. John Wesley. 63771

Letter to the Rev. Mr. John Wesley, occasioned by his Calm address to the American colonies. 23138-(23139)

Letter to the Rev. Mr. John Wesley; on his 'Calm address.' 102647

Letter to the Reverend Mr. John Wesley, relating to his sermon. 103617

Letter to the Reverend Mr. Joseph Bellamy . . . by the Committee of the First Society in Danbury. 23697, 99820, 103374

Letter to the Rev. Mr. Joseph Bellamy of Bethlem. 18768

Letter to the Reverend Mr. Joshua Gee. 26831, 65237

Letter to the Rev. Mr. Macclanechan. (11877), 64328

Letter to the Reverend Mr. Nathaniel Eells. 23585, 26831, 65237

Letter to the Rev. Mr. Niles, of Braintree. 3888

Letter to the Rev. Mr. Noah Hobart. 104985

Letter to the Rev. Mr. Prince, author of the Christian history. 94688

Letter to the Rev. Mr. Prince of Boston. 5759

Letter to the Reverend Mr. Thomas Church. 103565

Letter to the Rev. Mr. Wesley. 102676

Letter to the Rev. Mr. Whitefield. 38813

Letter to the Reverend Mr. William Hobby, a pastor of a church at Reading. (13597), 32316, 97539

Letter to the Rev. Mr. William Hobby. By J. F. 23583, 32316

Letter to the Reverend Mr. William Hobby. . . . By Richard Pateshall. (59064)

Letter to the Reverend Mr. William Hobby, occasioned by sundry passages. 31302

Letter to the Rev. Moses Stuart. 82074, 93197

Letter to the Rev. Nathaniel Hall. (10747)

Letter to the Rev. Nathaniel Smith. 83669

Letter to the Rev. Nathaniel Thayer. 11117, 95259

Letter to the Reverend Nathaniel Whitaker. (30648)

Letter to the Rev. R. Johnson. 72144

Letter to the Rev. Samuel C. Aiken. 43419

Letter to the Rev. Samuel C. Thatcher. 11924, 105305

Letter to the Reverend Samuel Frink. 106389

Letter to the Rev. Samuel Hopkins. 42684

Letter to the Rev. Samuel Miller. (49063)

Letter to the Rev. Seth Payson. 105326

Letter to the Rev. T. Coke. 14252, 14338, 103663

Letter to the Reverend the clergy of that diocess. [sic] 103596

Letter to the Reverend the ministers of the Baptist congregations. 37929

Letter to the Rev. the President, and Professors. 30764, 103566

Letter to the Rev. Thomas Baldwin. 105313

Letter to the Rev. Thomas Chalmers. 92646

Letter to the Rev. Thomas Hinton. 40518

Letter to the Rev. William Berrian. 35867

Letter to the Rev. William E. Channing, on the subject of his letter. 105305

Letter to the Rev. William E. Channing, on the subject of unitarianism. 105312

Letter to the Rev. William Smith, D. D. 5883, 84692

Letter to Robert Wilmot Horton. 40358, 102845

Letter to the Right Honourable and Right Reverend Beilby. 82005

Letter to the Right Honourable author of a letter to a citizen. 40519

Letter to the Rt. Hon. Benjamin Disraeli. 373

Letter to the Rt. Hon. C. B. Adderley. (33315)

Letter to the Right Honourable Ch—— T ——nd. 40521

Letter to the Right Honourable Charles Jenkinson. (40520)

Letter to the Right Hon. E. G. Stanley. 95371

Letter to the Right Honourable Earl Grey. 40522, 85261

Letter to the Right Rev. L. Silliman Ives. 35859

Letter to the Right Reverend the Lord Bishop of London. 10894, (27313), 71968

Letter to the Rt. Rev. Wm. H. Delancey. (18715)

Letter to the Rt. Rev. William Henry Odenheimer, D. D. 83521

Letter to the Rt. Rev. William Henry Odenheimer, D. D., with explanatory notes. 83522

Letter to the Right Rev. William White, D. D. 40985

Letter to the Roman Catholics of Philadelphia. 40539

Letter to the Roman Catholics of the city of Worcester. 103095

Letter to the Roman Catholics of the city of Worcester, from the late chaplain of that society. 103092

Letter to the Roman Catholics of the city of Worcester in England. 103090

Letter to the said Bulkeley. 9095

Letter to the Second Church and congregation in Scituate. (22007), 94921, note after 103633

Letter to the secretary of a certain board; a supplement to the original papers. 40541, 99245

Letter to the secretary of a certain board, to which no answer has been returned. 40540-40541, 99243, 99245

Letter to the secretary of a certain board, with verses to Admiral V. 40540, 99245

Letter to . . . [the] Secretary of State for the Colonies. 16747

Letter to the Secretary of State for War. 36072

Letter to the Secretary of State, from London, 1796. (37835)

Letter to the Secretary of State of the United States. 23920

Letter to the Secretary of State on the construction of a ship canal. 55328

Letter to the Secretary of State, on the registration of births. 79881

Letter to the Secretary of State, recommending the ratification. 96564

[Letter to the Secretary of the Interior.] 90416

Letter to the Secretary of the Navy of the United States. (21744)

Letter to the Secretary of the Navy, with an analysis. 82571

Letter to the secretary of the same board. 99243

Letter to the Secretary of the Treasury, August 20, 1862. 13333

Letter to the Secretary of the Treasury. By W. B. Pierce. 62745

Letter to the Secretary of the Treasury. Dated Boston, January 16, 1869. 40542

Letter to the Secretary of the Treasury on importations of scrap iron. 52137

Letter to the Secretary of the Treasury, on taxation. 76439

Letter to the Secretary of the Treasury, on the commerce. 1977, 102364

Letter to the Secretary of the Treasury, on the history and causes of steamboat explosions. (68512)

Letter . . . to the . . . Secretary of the Treasury . . . on the subject of the New York financiers. 51978

Letter . . . to the Secretary of the Treasury . . . relative to the culture of the sugar cane. (36378)

Letter . . . to the Secretary of War. 31319

Letter to the Secretary of War, January 31, 1862. 64059

Letter to the Secretary of War on sickness and mortality. 29900

Letter to the Secretary of War, or, review of the controversy. 40543, 78714

Letter to the Senate and House of Assembly. 10828

Letter to the Senate and House of Representatives of the United States. 81178

Letter to the Senate and House of Representatives of the United States upon the expediency of a uniform system. 3195, 40544

Letter to the seven churches. 105234

Letter to the several churches invited on that occasion. 97311

Letter to the several colonies. 22624, note after 41286

Letter to the shareholders of the Grand Trunk Railway of Canada. 42982

Letter to the shareholders of the Vermont Central Railroad. 67264

Letter to the so-called "Boston churches." 81160

Letter to the Society from the Bishop of Montreal. 99582

Letter to the Society of Arts, Agriculture and Economy. (14971), 53620

Letter to the South Sea Proprietors. 16399

Letter to the . . . Speaker of the House of Representatives of the United States. 43309

Letter to the special agents and commissioners. 87402

Letter to the Special Commissioner of the Revenue. 71803

Letter . . . to the Standing Committee of the Proprietors. 11924

Letter to the stockholders, by the late agent. 88678

Letter to the stockholders of the Michigan Southern & Northern Indiana Railroad Company. 5923

Letter to the stockholders of the Pennsylvania Railroad Company. (60357)

Letter to the stockholders of the Philadelphia & Atlantic Steam Navigation Co. 61943

Letter to the stockholders of the Winnisimmet Company. 46893

Letter to the Surgeon General of the state of New York. 53994

Letter to the Tammany Society. (14160)

Letter to the Texas almanac. 67790

Letter to the Times on American affairs. 89281

Letter to the Tories. 40548-40549

Letter to the Treasurer of the Society. 55238

Letter to the Trinitarian Congregational Church. 101207

Letter to the Trustees of Columbia College. 104016

Letter to the Trustees of the Building Fund of the New York Historical Society. 35849, 54475

Letter to the Trustees of the South-Carolina College. 87985

Letter to the ungospellized plantations. (46380)

Letter to the union meeting. 40985

Letter . . . to the Unitarian Society of Cincinnati. 11932

Letter to the Universities of Oxford and Cambridge. 25828

Letter to the Vestry of Trinity Church. 32294

Letter to the Vicar of Grantham. 31653

Letter to the Virginia Legislature. 42413, 46962

Letter to the volunteers in the Federal army. 11212

Letter . . . to the war Democracy of Wisconsin. 20341

Letter to the Wardens and Vestry of Christ Church, Cincinnati. 40545

Letter to the Wednesday Evening Club. 91604

Letter to the Wesleyan societies in the island of Jamaica. 106095

Letter to the West India merchants. 40546, 3d note after 102846

Letter to the Whig Committee of the state of Maine. 59446

Letter . . . to the Whig State Central Committee. (18048)

Letter to the Whig State Committee of Maine. 67222

Letter to the Whigs. 40547

Letter to the Whigs. [By Willis Hall.] 29864

Letter to the Whigs, occasion'd by the letter to the Tories. 40548

Letter to the Whigs with some remarks. 40549

Letter to the women of England, on slavery. 40550, note after 94405

Letter to the women of the north-west. 4575, (76589), 76647

Letter to the wool growers of the United States. 92036

Letter to the young men of Maine. 18050

Letter . . . to their Unitarian brethren. 6654

Letter to Thomas Brand. 6236

Letter to Thomas Clarkson, by James Cropper. 8117, 93137, 93139

Letter Tho. Folwell Buxton, Esq. 9695

Letter to Thomas Fowell Buxton, in refutation of his allegations. 43172

Letter to Thos. Gillison. (32464)

Letter to Thomas Jefferson, Esq., Ex-President of the United States. 14190, 92649

Letter to Thomas Jefferson, President of the United States. 10065, 36926

Letter to Thomas Maule. 62420

Letter to Thomas Paine. (58249), note after 101837

Letter to Thomas Pinckney. 21142

Letter to Thomas Whittemore. 13352

Letter to those gentlemen. 104930

Letter to those ladies whose husbands possess a seat. 40551

Letter to those of his brethren in the ministry. 80797

Letter to Timothy Pickering, Esq. Secretary of State, from the Chevalier de Yrujo. 62655, 106215

Letter to Timothy Pickering, Secretary of State. 62983

Letter to Tom Paine. (13897)

Letter to Unitarians and reply to Dr. Warre. 101375, 105132

Letter to us, from one of ourselves. (40552)

Letter to Viscount Goderich. 99773

Letter to Viscount Melbourne. 38751

Letter to Viscount Melville. 8916

Letter to Viscount Palmerston. 25634

Letter to W. E. Channing, D. D. on the . . . abuse of the flag. 43695, note after 96999

Letter to W. E. Channing, . . . in reply to one addressed to him. 43695, note after 96999

Letter to W. Manning, Esq., M. P., on the causes of the rapid and progressive depreciation of West-India property. 6444, 40364, 40553, 102847

Letter to W. Manning, Esq. M. P. on the proposition. 102848

Letter to W. Manning, Esq. M. P. on the progressive depreciation of West India property. 6444, 40364, 40553, 102847

Letter to W. W. Whitmore. 42953

Letter to Walter S. Cox. 89391

Letter to Washington. 51661

Letter to . . . Whitemarsh B. Seabrook. (28426)

Letter to Wm. A. Atkinson. 51720

Letter to William B. Reed. 30366

Letter to William Bainbridge. 68137

Letter to Wm. E. Channing, D. D. . . . on the abuse of the flag of the United States. 40555

Letter to William E. Channing, D. D. on the subject of religious liberty. 93202

Letter to William Gibbes Hunt, Esq. 25172, 33905, 96466

Letter to William Gridley. 82483

Letter to William H. Crawford. 17447

Letter to William Meade Addison. (40554)

Letter to William Roscoe. 73227

Letter to William Staughton. 63238

Letter to William Wilberforce. [By Gilbert Wakefield.] 34108

Letter to Wm. Wilberforce, Esq. By Philo-Africanus. 62541

Letter to William Wilberforce, Esq. M. P. On the proposed abolition of the slave trade. 84699

Letter to Wm. Wilberforce, Esq. M. P. on the subject of impressment. 98144

Letter to William Wilberforce, Esq. M. P. Vice President of the African Institution. 42954, 95656, 95658-95659

Letter to William Wilberforce, on the justice and expediency of slavery and the slave trade. 31534, (40556)

Letter . . . transmitting a statement of the affairs. 59905

Letter . . . transmitting a treatise on the rearing of silkworms. 47270

Letter transmitting information in relation to steam-engines. 105102

Letter . . . transmitting reports. (3179)

Letter . . . transmitting tabular statements of the condition of the banks. 59905

Letter treating upon the subject and mode of baptism. 2632

Letter II. From Thomas Baldwin of Boston. 82483

Letter II. Immediate revelation. 89369

Letter II. On certain political measures. (3422)

Letter II. To the same, on the same subject. 103599

Letter XII. On the restitution of all things. 89369

Letter, under the signature of A. W. Farmer, 29956

Letter upon the connexion of the Methodist Episcopal Church with slavery. 19022

Letter . . . upon the general character and tendency of freemasonry. (14282)

Letter upon the subject of ordination. 92825

Letter wherein the demolition of Louisbourg is shewn to be absurd. 42176

Letter which came from one who hath been a magistrate. (73483), 78753

Letter (which I have seen) of John Leverat.
25355

Letter which I received the 3d instant.
101742, 101746

Letter which lately passed between His
Excellency Governor Tryon. 97291

Letter which was delivered to the King.
47156

Letter which was sent from one who was a
magistrate. (73483)

Letter, with a letter of Mr. Madison appended.
51002

Letter. With an address to each of those
gentlemen. 92930

Letter with enclosures of the Consul-General
of China. 79493

Letter writ by George Keith. 17584

Letter writer. 40557

Letter written by a learned gentleman of
Boston. 86588

Letter written by a pious lawyer. 51492

Letter written by Gen. Elijah Clark. 13276

Letter, written by him [i. e. J. S.] in Jamaica.
(74619)

Letter written by him [i. e. Thomas Paine]
to General Washington. 101837

Letter written by him [i. e. John Vandeleur]
to his uncle. 98469

Letter written by John Lowell. 98558

Letter, written by Joseph C. Dean. 105465

Letter, written by Mr. James Young. 100970

Letter written by Mr. Luis C. Vanuxem.
97000

Letter written by Mr. R. W. 72103

Letter written by Mr. Robert Rich. 70896

Letter written by Mr. Thomas Parker, a
learned and Godly minister. 58770

Letter written by Mr. Thomas Parker, pastor
of the Church of Newbury. 58769

Letter written by S. B. Ruggles. 53660

Letter written by the Rev. Charles T. Torrey.
(28349)

Letter written by the said Gouvernour to the
Bewinthebbers of the West-India Company. 102912A

Letter written by the same author. 72109

Letter written from Buffalo. 30820

Letter written from Jamestown. 51810, 2d
note after 100494

Letter written Gov. Fenton by Hon. John
Covode. 35849

Letter written in February, 1815. 95378

Letter written in reply to inquiries. 76644

Letter written to his brother. 95231-95235,
95237, 95240

Letter written to His Majesty from Naples.
104744

Letter written to my immediate representative
Gov. Smith. 59647

Letter written to the President of Congress.
39699, 39700

Letter written to the President of the United
States. 30820

Letter wrote by Mr. Samuel Pike. (62832),
76343

Letter wrote by Mr. Vale. 98339

Letter wrote in Spanish by Father James
Hernandez. 31518

Letter wrote to a member of the House of
Representatives. 26348

Lettera all' Avv. Cav. Cornelio Desimoni.
76522

Lettera allo Stampat. Sig. P. Allegrini. 10706

Lettera apologetica. 40560

Lettera: che a scritto Luigi Gonzales de Merchado. (63179)

Lettera che mando Arriano all' Imperadore
Adriano. 67736

Lettera da lui scritta al Re di Spagna. (58305)

Lettera d'Alberto Campense. 67736

Lettera d'Andrea Corsali Fiorentino. 67730

Lettera de la nobil citta nuouamente ritrouata.
40558

Lettera del Cavaliere Amadio Ronchini di
Parma. 73071

Lettera del Marchese Santa Croce. 76757

Lettera del medesimo avtore. 67736

Lettera del P. Giov. Gonzalez Ciaparro.
13038

Lettera dela nobil citta nuouamete ritrouata.
40559

Lettera dell' Avvocato Carlo Phillips. 64014

Lettera dell' Illustrissimo D. Fra Guiseppe de
Peralta. 19209

Lettera dellisole che ha trouato nuouamente
il re dispagna. (14635), 18657

Lettera di Amerigo Vespucci a Piero Soderini.
note before 99327, 99353, 99361, 99369,
99374, 99379

Lettera di Amerigo Vespucci delle isole nuo-
vamente trovate. 99379

Lettera di Amerigo Vespvcci Fiorentino.
67730

Lettera di M. Otto. 10915

Lettera di Sybilia venuta al Signor Don Lope.
41966, 63180

Lettera in lingua Spagnuola. 14640

Lettera . . . intorno ai viaggi e scoperte
settentrionali. 106410

Lettera mandata dal R. Padre Frate Francesco
da Bologna. 25435

Lettera rarissima di Christoforo Colombo.
14643, (50598)

Lettera scritta da un Gesuita. 71553

Lettera II. 67730

Lettera venuta da Genova. 16671

Lettere. 67740

Lettere annve d'Ethiopia, Malabar, Brasil e
Goa. 18538, 32008, 40561-40562

Lettere de V. Dandolo. 2246

Lettere del Capitano Francesco Vazquez di
Coronado. 67740

Lettere del Conte Carlo Vidua. 99504

Lettere del Prefetto della India la Nuoua
Spagna detta. (63177)

Lettere di Francesco Vazquez di Coronado.
67740

Lettere di Pietro Arias Capitano Generale.
1974

Lettere di principi, le quali o si scrivono
da principi. 40564

Lettere di principi libro primo. (40563)

Lettere d'un Peruviana. 28194, 40560

Lettere d'una Americana. 12616

Lettere edificanti scritte dalle Missioni
Straniere. 40706

Lettere mediche. 44399

Lettere scritte dal Illvstrissimo Signor Don
Antonio di Mendozza. 67740

Letterman, Jonathan. 40565

Letters about the Hudson River. 33849

[Letters] addressed by Mr. Lawrence. 7256

Letters addressed from Philadelphia, 1823.
(26897)

Letters addressed to a brother in the church.
95155

Letters addressed to a worthy minister of the
Gospel. 105268

Letters addressed to Caleb Strong. 103230

Letters addressed to Dorothy Ripley. 71499

Letters addressed to Francis O. J. Smith.
(28603)

Letters addressed to her by Major Andre.
79477-79479, 79485, (79488)
Letters, addressed to Joel Mann. 25319
Letters addressed to John Sergeant. (40566)
Letters addressed to Lord Liverpool and the
Parliament. 40567
Letters addressed to Lord Liverpool, on the
late American war. 14011
Letters addressed to Martin Van Buren.
98425
Letters, addressed to Miss Seward. 79480-
(79483)
Letters addressed to President Lincoln.
29927
Letters addressed to Rev. Moses Thacher.
24096, 95158
Letters addressed to some gentlemen of this
city. (74720), 97772A
Letters addressed to the army. 40569
Letters addressed to the Bishops, clergy and
laity. (32931)
Letters addressed to the Board of Health.
44301
Letters addressed to the citizens of the Uni-
ted States. (33643)
Letters, addressed to the Democratic members
of the Legislature. (11798)
Letters addressed to the editor of "A collec-
tion of essays." 14375, 40570
Letters addressed to the editors of the United
States gazette. 103458
Letters addressed to the electors of represen-
tatives. 105068
Letters addressed to the friends of freedom
and the union. 36072
Letters addressed to the greatest politician
in England. (79223)
[Letters] addressed to the Hon. H. Clay.
10889
Letters addressed to the Hon. John Quincy
Adams. 31091
Letters addressed to the members of the
eighteenth Congress. 78967
Letters, addressed to the people of Penn-
sylvania. 20997
Letters addressed to the people of the
Canadas. 40571, 102611
Letters addressed to the people of the United
States, by a native of Virginia. (40572)
Letters addressed to the people of the United
States of America. 62654
Letters addressed to the Rev. Allen Steele.
6222, 91104
Letters addressed to the Rev. Messrs. John
Cree. 40573
Letters addressed to the Rev. Samuel Miller.
(33224)
Letters addressed to the Right Honourable
Lord M———. 40574
Letters, addressed to the taxpayers of England.
13882
Letters addressed to the yeomanry of the
United States. By A. Hamilton. 29966
Letters addressed to the yeomanry of the
United States; shewing the necessity of
confining the public revenue. 39243,
41790
Letters, addressed to Thomas Jefferson, Esq.
23186, 94189
Letters addressed to Trinitarians and Cal-
vinists. 101379
Letters addressed to W. L. Stone. 40568,
89351
Letters, affidavits, and other documents.
37643

Letters against the immediate abolition of
slavery. 93545
Letters and addresses of George Thompson.
95499
Letters and certificates. 102568
Letters and conversations on the Cherokee
Mission. 12465, 97521
Letters and conversations on the Indian
Missions. 97522
Letters and correspondence of Mrs. Virginia
Myers. 51643
Letters and correspondence on the Halifax
and Quebec Railroad. 27654
Letters and dialogues. 4494
Letters and dissertations upon sundry subjects.
By J. C. Pickett. 62672
Letters and dissertations on various subjects,
by the author of the Letter analysis.
17704
Letter and documents, in relation to the dis-
solution of the engagement of Loammi
Baldwin. 60750, note after 97766
Letters and documents of distinguished citizens
of Tennessee. 40575, 94799
Letters and documents relative to the appli-
cation to connect League Island. 103089
Letters and essays. (25529)
Letters and essays on sugar farming in Jama
Jamaica. 103667
Letters and essays on the small-pox and
inoculation. 67169, 1st note after 102848
Letters and extracts of letters from settlers
in Upper Canada. 98081
Letters and hymns. 12523
Letters and journal of Daniel Wheeler. 103180-
103182
Letters and journals relating to the war of the
American revolution. (71302)
Letters and legends about our summer home.
28796, 83335
Letters and memoirs relating to the war of
American independence. 71301
Letters and memorials which have lately
passed. 40576
Letters and notes. 11536, (11538)
Letters and observations on agriculture, &c.
88040
Letters and observations relating to the
controversy. (23190)
Letters and other documents. (2211)
Letters and other papers relating to the pro-
ceedings. (10924)
Letters . . . and other papers relative to the
Chesapeake and Delaware Canal Com-
pany. (39220)
Letters and other pieces, written by
Margaret Jackson. (35446)
Letters and other writings of James Madison.
43710
Letters and papers of Cadwallader Colden.
84566
Letters and papers of Major-General John
Sullivan. 93510
Letters and papers of the late Hon. Joshua
Steele. 20095, 49755, note after 91132
Letters and papers on agriculture. 29703,
2d note after 95847
Letters and papers on philosophical subjects.
25506
Letters and papers relating chiefly to the
provincial history. 2871
Letters and papers relating to Cherokee
affairs. 6859
Letters and poems. 46881
Letters and political speculations. (47405)
Letters and recollections. 57791

Letters and remarks. 3105, 97296, 105243

Letters and sketches. 82262

Letters, and sketches of sermons. (51520)

Letters and speeches, by Horace Mann. 44323

Letters and speeches [of Lewis Cass.] 11356

Letters; being an answer to "Papal Rome." 77736

Letters, being an answer to "The Christmas holidays in Rome." 77737

Letters, being the whole of the correspondence between the Hon. John Jay. (35833)

Letters, between a friend and his correspondent. 62891

Letters between James Monroe. 50015

Letters between Monsieur Voltaire. (72882)

Letters between the Vice King of Santa Fee. 11132, 1st note after 99245

Letters between Theophilus and Eugenio. 25528, note after 95316

Letters. By a citizen of Pennsylvania. (26388)

Letters by a gentleman of South Carolina. 66803

Letters by a South-Carolinian. 40577, 88114

Letters by . . . Cyrus Prindle. 56583

Letters . . . by D. F. Drinkwater. 20952

Letters by Historicus. 30301

Letters [by J. A. Coles.] (14331)

Letters . . . by James Gallatin. 26401

Letters by James Robb. 71726

Letters, by John M'Donald. 43156

Letters [by Mr. Birkbeck.] 23956

Letters concerning Guiana. (67551)

Letters concerning the complaints. 40578

Letters concerning the constitution and order of the Christian ministry. (33224), 49052

Letters concerning the English nation. 100751

Letters concerning the general health. (32961), 73016

Letters concerning the lineal descent. 79823

Letters concerning the present state of England. 40579

Letters concerning the present state of Poland. 41284

Letters dedicated to A. H. 90794

Letters descriptive of a tour. 1488

Letters descriptive of personal appeals. 100969

Letters descriptive of the Virginia springs. 55236, 2d note after 100484

Letters developing the character and views of the Hartford Convention. 57857

Letters developing the conspiracy. 3392

Letters domestick and foreign. 97289

Letters entitled, the American commercial claims. 40580

Letters, essays, and other tracts. (44094)

Letters, etc. 40634

Letters, etc. [By John Macpherson.] (43637)

Letters, &c., by Robert Gourlay. (28140)

Letters, &c. from Washington. (50137), (55169), 100451

Letters &c. published by order of Congress. 87364

Letters exhibiting the most prominent doctrines. 89370

Letters explanatory of the difficulties existing. 75799

Letters, first published in the Boston daily advertiser. 93527

Letters for the people. 40581, note after 90548

Letters for the times. 70236

Letters forming part of a correspondence. 79132, 94684

Letters found in the state of Tennessee. 22622, 94793

Letters from a Chinese. 25304, 1st note after 101235

Letters from a country clergyman. 40582

Letters from a farmer in Pennsylvania. 20044

Letters from a father to his sons in College. (49064)

Letters from a Federal farmer. 40583

Letters from a general officer to his son. (40584)

Letters from a gentleman in Transilvania. 5219, 6th note after 96481

Letters from a gentleman, resident there, to his friend in England. 22496, 71241

Letters from a gentleman to his friend. 53643, 59284, 104441

Letters from a landscape painter. 38920

Letters from a Maryland mail bag. 40585

Letters from a Peruvian princess. 28196, 40560

Letters from a rambler in the west. (34260)

Letters from a resident in Jamaica. 56420, 4th note after 95756

Letters from a southerner to a northern friend. 63853, (63877)

Letters from a Spaniard in London to his friend in Madrid. 40586

Letters from abroad to kindred at home. (78780)-78781

Letters from Alabama, chiefly relating to natural history. 28062

Letters from Alabama on various subjects. (73820)

Letters from America. 27662

Letters from America, containing observations. 24780

Letters from America, historical and descriptive. 21801

Letters from America to a friend in England. 40588

Letters from an adopted citizen of the republic. 96795

Letters from an American farmer. 2527, 17496-17497, 1st note after 69470, 98479

Letters from an American loyalist. 35438

Letters from an early settler of Texas. (19842)

Letters, from an English resident in the United States. 73912

Letters from an Egyptian in New York. (40587)

Letters from an officer in one of those regiments. 7210, 1st note after 100462

Letters from and to Sir Dudley Carleton. 10901

Letters from Buenos Ayres and Chili. 18746

Letters from Canada. 32900

Letters from Canada, by Radcliff. 67403

Letters from Canada, with numerous illustrations. 40589

Letters from Canada, written during a residence there. (28393)

Letters from Canadian politicians. 10625

Letters from Chili. 36315

Letters from Cuba. (37766)-37767

Letters from David Henshaw. 103003

Letters from . . . Denis B. Viger. 99597

Letters from distinguished individuals. 52826, 92068

Letters from distinguished merchants and men of science. 3906

Letters from the commercial correspondent of an Association of Cotton Manufacturers. 40597

Letters from the distinguished clergymen. 28628, 104118

Letters from the Dorking emigrants. 3355, 98083

Letters from the east and from the west. 29772

Letters from the English Kings and Queens. 31963

Letters from the First Church in Glocester. 7268, 27584, 103399

Letters from the Forty-Fourth Regiment M. V. M. (29560)

Letters from the frontiers. 42970

Letters from the Havana. 29439

Letters from the Health Office. 2747, 4057

Letters from the Hon. Abbott Lawrence, on the tariff. (39344)

Letters from the Hon. Abbott Lawrence to the Hon. William C. Rives. (39344)

Letters from the Hon. J. G. Palfrey. 64099

Letters from the Hon. William C. Rives. 71666

Letters from the House of Representatives. (32551), 7th note after 97146, 97147

Letters from the Illinois. 24911

Letters from the island of Teneriffe, Brazil, the Cape of Good Hope. 37777

Letters from the Marquis de Montcalm. 50091

Letters from the mines. 6141

Letters from the Mountains. (28296)-28297

Letters from the Navy Department. 91900

Letters from the New-York tribune. 19862

Letters from the old world. 29541

Letters from the Pacific slope. 70832

Letters from the President of the Council of New-Hampshire. 66514

Letters from the prisons and prison-ships of the revolution. 40598, 91754

Letters from the Rev. Samuel Davies. (18761)

Letters from the San Francisco daily herald. 52436

Letters from the Secretary of State. 12486

Letters from the Secretary of the Navy. 43180

Letters from the Secretary of the Treasury. 17126

Letters from the slave states. 91845

Letters from the south. 40599, 59196, 59203

Letters from the south and west. 17544

Letters from the south and west. By Arthur Singleton. 38116

Letters from the south. By a northern man. 40599

Letters from the south on northern and southern views. 9752

Letters from the town of Boston to C. Lucas. 6736

Letters from the United States. 105064

Letters from the United States, Cuba and Canada. 51486

Letters from the United States of America. 40600

Letters from the Virgin Islands. 40601, 2d note after 99840

Letters from the west; containing sketches of scenery. 29789

Letters from the west, comprising a tour. (56806)

Letters from the West Indies, during a visit. 41699

Letters from the West Indies: relating especially to the Danish island of St. Croix. (33214)

Letters from the west; or, a caution to emigrants. 105612

Letters from the wife of an emigrant officer. 96441

Letters from Thomas Paine, to the citizens of America. 58231

Letters from Thomas Paine to the citizens of the United States. 58230

Letters from two captains of Turkish men of war. 24983, 4th note after 100818

Letters from under a bridge. 104509

Letters from Upper Canada. 4483

Letters from Van Dieman's Land. 100969

Letters from Virginia, translated from the French. 40595, (59204), note after 97301, 3d note after 100484

Letters from Washington. 102160, 102164

Letters from Yorick to Eliza. 91343-91344, 91355

Letters home from Spain, Algeria, and Brazil. 13292

Letters in answer to Dr. Price's two pamphlets. 91600

Letters in opposition to the new constitution of Virginia. (50137)

Letters in reply to Mr. Wickliffe. 12809

Letters in reply to the attacks of foreign ecclesiastics. 74555

Letters in reply to the Superintendent of Education for Lower Canada. 28232

Letters in vindication of the rights of the British West India colonies. 24739

Letters, including an account. 9917, 1st note after 96334, 4th note after 100532

Letters . . . inscribed to . . . Doctor Samuel Cooper. 40602

Letters laid before the Senate. 58977

Letters lately published in the Diary. 40603, 2d note after 99312

Letters lately received from the West Indies. (10676)

Letters, lately written by President Adams. 263

Letters, occasioned by the publication. 56816

Letters occasioned by three dialogues. 104706

Letters of a British spy. 104875

Letters of a farmer, containing his thoughts in the ninety-fourth year of his age. (63436)

Letters of a farmer to the people of Georgia. 27066

Letters of a gentleman uninterested. 9926

Letters of a man of the times. (37414)

Letters of a Nova Scotian. (40604)

Letters of a Peruvian princess. 28197, (40693)

Letters of a traveller. 8819

Letters of a traveller. Second series. 8820

Letters of a Westchester farmer. 2d note after 99553

Letters of a young lady of seventeen. 10982

Letters of Ada R. Parker. (58644)

Letters of Adelaide De Sancere. 76261

Letters of Aegles. 102120

Letters of Agricola. 40607, 106083

Letters of Albert Gallatin. (26389)

Letters of Algernon Sydney in defence of civil government. 39912

Letters of Algernon Sydney, in defence of civil liberty. 94091

Letters of Amerigo Vespucci and other documents illustrative of his carreer. (63505), note before 99327, 99363, 99375-99376

Letters of Amos Kendell. 37354

Letters of an American. (40606)

Letters of an English traveller to his friend in England. 19857

Letters of an eye witness. 13031

Letters of Ann Cook, late Mrs. Beauchamp, to her friend in England. 4161

Letters of Ann Cook, late Mrs. Beauchamp, to her friend in Maryland. 16231

Letters of Aza. 28197

Letters [of Bill Arp.] (82395)

Letters of Bishop Moore. 9430

Letters of Brutus to certain celebrated characters. 8778

Letters of Captain Thomas Young to Sir Francis Windebank. 103051

Letters of Charlotte to a female friend. 87172

Letters of Collonel Stanhope. 90292

Letters of Colonel Burr. 9214

Letters of Colonel Clarke. 100036

Letters of Col. G. Moody. (50308)

Letters of Col. J. R. Preston. (14331)

Letters of Columbus. 14898

Letters of Columbus and Cortes. 41659

Letters of Common Sense. 40608

Letters of Curtins. 28427

Letters of Curtius. Addressed to General Marshall. 95582

Letters of Curtius, written by the late John Thomson. 95583

Letters of Decius. 17184, (19148)

Letters of Decius, in answer to the criticism. (19149), note after 96978

Letters of Decius; or, a few observations. (19150)

Letters of Decius to the Legislature. 40609

Letters of Doctor Richard Hill and his children. 31858, 82987

Letters [of Dunton.] 22148

Letters of Elias Hicks. 31712-31713

Letters of Eliza Wilkinson. 104023

Letters of Fabius. 23595

Letters [of Flaminius.] 24663

Letters [of Franklin. (13895), (14009), 25640, 101838, note after 101847

Letters of Freeman, &c. (25788), (85788), 87858, 87865

Letters of Freemen to the deputies of North America. (20919)

Letters of friendship to those clergymen. 40610

Letters of Gen. Adair and Gen. Jackson. (35374)

Letters [of General Braddock.] 51661

Letters of General Wood & Logan. 40611

Letters of Gerrit Smith. 27850

Letters of Governor Clinton. 13738

Letters of Governor Hutchinson. 34072

Letters of . . . Governor Lincoln. 45832

Letters of gratitude. (34387)

Letters of Hermann. 31497

Letters of Hon. Rosewell Marsh. (44759)

Letters of Isaac Bobin. 6095

Letters of Isaac Penington, . . . minister of the Gospel. 59660

Letters of Isaac Penington, written to his relations. 59660

Letters of J. Downing. 18799, 84148, 84155, note after 84162-84174

Letters of James Robb to Robert C. Wickliffe. (71725)

Letters of James Stephen. 44704

Letters of John Adams. 246

Letters of John Andrews. 1502

Letters of John Lowell. 98562

Letters of John Minor Botts. 6830

Letters of John Randolph. 67828

Letters of John W. Brooks. 8358

Letters of Jonathan Oldstyle. 35188

Letters of Judge Joseph Hopkinson. 100581

Letters of Junius. 36914

Letters of Junius complete. 36909

Letters of Junius; exposing to the public. 36918, 61781

Letters of life. 80925

Letters of Lillian Ching. 95776

Letters of Lowndes. 42532

Letters of loyal soldiers. 40611

Letters of loyal soldiers upon McClellan and the Chicago platform. 40612

Letters of Major-General Lee. 39710, 101687

Letters of Major Jack Downing. 84179-84181

Letters of Marcus addressed to De Witt Clinton. 98531

Letters of Marcus and Philo-Cato. 18863, note after 98531

Letters of Marius. 18985

Letters of Martha Smith. 83527

Letters of Mr. Cushing. 18090

Letters of Mr. Ingersoll. 34735, 92851

Letters of Mr. Lawrence. 7256

Letters of Mr. Slade to Mr. Hallett. 81680

Letters of Mrs. Adams. 264

Letters of Morris N. B. Hull. (33640)

Letters of Mutius. 51603

Letters of Novanglus. 243

Letters of Pacificus and Helvidius. (23985), 23987-23988, 23990, 29968

Letters of Pacificus: written in justification. (29967), 29987, 101839

Letters of Papinian. 34764, 58491

Letters of Peter Cooper. 16595

Letters of Peter Ghent. 994

Letters of Phillis Wheatley. 19051, 103142

Letters [of Phocion, i. e. H. W. Desaussure.] 87733

Letters of Phocion [i. e. William Loughton Smith.] 29948, 84818

Letters of Phocion, by G. T. Curtis. 20256, 45711

Letters of President Lincoln. 41151

Letters [of Professor Stuart.] 93205

Letters of Professors Pierce and Agassiz. (81481)

Letters [of Rev. Mr. Garden.] 103645

Letters of Rev. Dr. Schmucker and Gerritt Smith. 77725

Letters of Roger Williams. 51773

Letters of Rush, Adams, and Wirt. 74262

Letters of S. D. Bradford. 7256

Letters of Sam Slick. 29690

Letters of Secretary of State. 95042

Letters of Shahcoolen. 38076, 79687

Letters of Sicilius. 27067

Letters of Silas Standfast. 20256, 45711

Letters [of Sir Walter Raleigh.] 67573, 67583, 67584, 67598

Letters of Sulpicius. 93572

Letters of teachers and superintendents. 23523, 52685

Letters of the British spy. 104876

Letters of the deaf and dumb. 53450

Letters [of the Duke of Wharton.] 103104

Letters of the Hon. C. F. Cleveland. 13653

Letters of the Hon. J. C. Calhoun. 9943, 57565

Letters of the Hon. Joseph Holt. 32655

Letters of the Hon. Marcus Morton. 13653

Letters of the Honorable William B. Giles. (56531), 100506

Letters of the Justices of the Supreme Judicial Court. (18411)

Letters of the late Bishop England. 22587

Letters of the late Earl of Chesterfield. note before 90223

Letters of the late Ignatius Sancho. 76310

Letters of the late Lord Lyttleton. 42892

Letters of the late Rev. John Bowden. 104638

Letters of the Marquis de la Paz and Col. Stanhope. 38955

Letters of the Marquis de la Paz Secretary of State. 59332, 90292

Letters of the Provincial Council. 66673

Letters of the Rev. Dr. Beecher. 4345

Letters of the southern spy. 63870, 1st note after 97701

Letters of the two commanders-in-chief. (26320), 101687

Letters of Themistocles. 50766

Letters of Thomas B. Gould. (32371)

Letters of Thomas Clarkson. 20095, note after 91132

Letters of Thomas Jefferson. 100209

Letters of Thomas Nelson and Benjamin Harrison. 100210

Letters . . . [of Thomas Paine.] 58248

Letters of three seuerall Kings. (39146)

Letters of trial and travel. 51617

Letters of Valens. 98349

Letters of Veritas. 10629

Letters of Veritas re-published from the Montreal herald. 98978

Letters of Verus. 106216

Letters of Vetus. 99395

Letters of William Kennedy. 95118

Letters of Wyoming. 105685

Letters on a national currency. 40613

Letters on agriculture. 101719-101720, 101722

Letters on American affairs. (40614)

Letters on American affairs. [By Matthew Fontaine Maury.] 46962

Letters on American debts. 84314-84315, 84317, 84320

Letters on American slavery, addressed to Mr. Thomas Rankin. (67882)

Letters on American slavery from Victor Hugo. 33618

Letters on banks and banking. 81002

Letters on battles and relief work in Maryland. 4575

Letters on Canadian independence. 73336

Letters on civil government. 78249

Letters on clerical manners and habits. (49064)

Letters on college government, 3459

Letters on colonization. 39226

Letters on confederation, botheration, and political transmogrification. 26717

Letters on demonology and witchcraft. 78382

Letters on . . . education. (49958)

Letters on emigration. 22502, 40615

Letters on Florida. 24882, 40616

Letters on freemasonry. 90897

Letters on geology. 12951

Letters on hydraulics. (12514)

Letters on impressment. 98145

Letters on interesting subjects. (40617)

Letters on international copyright. 10842

Letters on Irish emigration. 29632

Letters on liberty and slavery. 70472

Letters on masonry, addressed to William L. Stone. 92136

Letters on masonry and anti-masonry. 92136

Letters on medical education. 29716

Letters on national subjects. 38787

Letters on our national struggle. 47249

Letters on Paraguay. 71962-71964

Letters on political liberty. 104187

Letters on Portugal. 7929, 91304

Letters on public education in Canada. 28232

Letters on public schools. 85349

Letters on religious subjects. 40618

Letters on responsible government. 74561, 93543

Letters on "responsible government," and an union of the colonies. 106073

Letters on slavery; addressed to the Cumberland congregation. 59264

Letters on slavery, addressed to the pro-slavery men. 25773, (72642)

Letters on slavery, by William Dickson. 20094

Letters on South America. 71965

Letters on southern slavery. (30098)

Letters . . . on sub-marine navigation and attack. 26197

Letters on superior education. 78389

Letters on the abolition of slavery. 40257, 47892, 95356

Letters on the abolition of the slave trade. 40257, 47892, 95356, 95358

Letters . . . on the admission of Kansas. 43506

Letters on the affairs of Spain. 94088

Letters on the American rebellion. 27638

Letters on the American republic. 2978

Letters on the American troubles. 62990

Letters on the American war. Addressed to the Mayor and Corporation. 30689

Letters on the American war, . . . to which is added a glimpse. 13890

Letters on the boundary line. 40619, 1st note after 98925

Letters on the calamitous state of affairs. 26681

Letters on the Chickasaw and Osage Missions. 97523

Letters on the Chickasaw Mission. 12673

Letters on the cholera asphyxia. 58192

Letters on the climate. 9725

Letters on the College of Physicians and Surgeons. 44301

Letters on the colonies. 41872

Letters on the Colonization Society. 10870, 10889

Letters on the comparative merits. 40620

Letters on the condition of the African race. 40621, (77884)

Letters on the condition of the poor. 10889, 61782

Letters on the constitutionality and policy of duties. 43712

Letters on the constitutionality of the power in Congress. 43711

Letters on the crimes of George III. 23117

Letters on the crisis. 43034

Letters on the cultivation of the Otaheite cane. 9850

Letters on the culture and manufacture of cotton. 35680

Letters on the death penalty. 67903

Letters on the design and importance. 58109

Letters on the eastern states. (10850), 97407, 97410

Letters on the elder question. 43515

Letters on the elevation of the laboring portion. 11924

Letters on the English nation. (80053)

Letters on the equality of the sexes. (28856)

Letters on the eternal generation of the Son of God. 93204

Letters on the eternal sonship of Christ. 93204

Letters which appeared in the United States
Gazette. 70238, 2d note after 102863
Letters which "first appeared in a Toronto
newspaper." 37886
Letters which passed between Admiral Vernon
and General Wentworth. 2455, 11131,
1st note after 99245
Letters which passed between several of the
leading characters of the day. 35723
Letters written by a native of Algiers. 763,
44623
Letters, written by a lady of Cape Francois.
30807, note after 78746
Letters written by a Peruvian princess.
28195
Letters written by an American youth. 97621,
3d note after 105973
Letters: written by Englishmen. (38117)
Letters, written, by him [i. e. William Penn],
on love and friendship. 59747
Letters written by him [i. e. John Binns] to
Edward Lyon. 42850, 91768, 96897
Letters written by Samuel H. B. Smith.
84080
Letters written by several gentlemen. 59066
Letters written by several gentlemen of un-
questionable veracity. 7847, 27588
Letters written by the late Right Honourable
Philip Dormer Stanhope. 90223, 90227-
90228
Letters, written by the relations, friends, and
contemporaries of Washington. 101794
Letters written during a residence of three
years in Chili. 36385
Letters written during a tour through the
northern and eastern states. 20913
Letters written during a tour through the
United States. 33372
Letters, written during a visit to Austin's
colony. (32528)
Letters written during a late voyage. (40658)
Letters written during the President's tour.
84147
Letters written from Colombia. 14598
Letters written from New-England. 21343,
46244, 65646
Letters written in 1852-53. 44362
Letters written in London by an American
spy. 40659
Letters written in London, 1764-65. 1222
Letters written in the interior of Cuba. 14
Letters written while on a tour to Illinois and
Wisconsin. 37868
Letters wrote by Dr. Franklyn. 66648
Lettra del Maestro di Campo Martin Soarez.
85659
Lettra di Amerigo Vespucci. note before
99327, 99353
Lettre a l'auteur de la Reponse au Patriote
Hollandois. 40660
Lettre a l'auteur du Mercure politique. 40661
Lettre a l'Empereur Alexandre. 103955
Lettre a l'Honorable Abraham Edwards.
105095
Lettre a Lord Glenelg. 67926
Lettre a M. S. D. (44147)
Lettre a Madame ***. (38481)
Lettre a M. Agenor de Gasparon. 5652
Lettre a M. Bryan Edwards. 98838
Lettre a M. Chaboillez. 4268
Lettre a M. de la Roquette. 77217
Lettre a M. Granier. 5652
Lettre a M. Havin. 40742
Lettre a M. Laisne de Villeveque. 3245A
Lettre a M. le Comte Mole. 4185

Lettre a M. le Ministre de la Marine et des
Colonies. 5652
Lettre a M. le Ministre des Finances. 16487
Lettre a M. Michel Chevalier. 40764
Lettre a M. Ponteves-Gien. 64016
Lettre a M. V. Schoelcher. 5652
Lettre a MM. les electeurs du Premier
College Electoral. 5652
Lettre a Napoleon III. 40662, 51596
Lettre a Sa Majeste l'Empereur Napoleon III.
40663
Lettre a Son Excellence Monseigneur le Prince
de Talleyrand Perigord. 103956
Lettre a S. Exc. M. le Ministre du Commerce.
(37839)
Lettre a son frere. 95247
Lettre a un amis. 97471
Lettre a un homme marie. 49678
Lettre a William Pitt. 36429
Lettre adresse a l'auteur par un actionnaire
desillusionne. 19729
Lettre adresse [sic] a M. l'Abbe Raynal.
58223
Lettre adressee a M. D***. 22575
Lettre adressee a M. le President de l'
Assemble Nationale. (32700)
Lettre adresee [sic] a Mons. le Redacteur du
Courier de Deux Mondes. 23064
Lettre adressee a M. le Redacteur en Chef.
(19762)
Lettre adressee au Directeur-General. 84477
Lettre adresse [sic] au Times. 74179
Lettre addressee [sic] aux habitants de la
province of Quebec. 10509, 40664
Lettre addressee [sic] aux habitants opprimes
de la province de Quebec. 40665
Lettre au Congres de l'Amerique. 106251
Lettre au Corps Legislatif. 59504
Lettre . . . au clerge sur l'esclavage. 21346
Lettre au Courrier de Saint-Etienne. 88821
Lettre au Docteur Maty. 17316
Lettre au Ministre de la Marine et des
Colonies. 5650
Lettre au Pape Innocent X. 58296
Lettre a l'Assemblee Coloniale de la partie
Francaise de Saint-Domingue. 49420
Lettre au Reverend Charles B. Smith. 14937
Lettre autografe edite et inedite di Cristoforo
Colombo. 14646
Lettre aux Espagnols-Americains. 100594
Lettre aux philantropes. 28726, 40666
Lettre circulaire aux Societes d'Etat. 49398
Lettre circvlaire de la mort de la Reuerende
Mere Catherine de S. Augustin. 67011
Lettre circulaire du Congres des Etats-Unis
de l'Amerique. 35834
Lettre circulaire pour la mort du P. Chau-
monot. 2d note after 93480
Lettre, contenant un precis detaille. 98507
Lettre de Baltimore. 98105
Lettre de Christophe Colomb. (14634)
Lettre de Delisle touchant la Californie. 4935-
4936
Lettre de D. Antonio de Mendoza. 94852
Lettre de Don Ramon de la Sagra. (74927)
Lettre de fue Monsieur Turgot. 49393
Lettre de G.-T. Raynal. (68072)
Lettre de Guillaume-le-Disputeur. (29230)
Lettre de Hammond, etc. (36415)
Lettre [de J. de Haze.] 94576
Lettre de . . . [J. de Zarate] Eveque d'Ante-
quera. 94854
Lettre de J. P. Brissot. (8020)
Lettre de Jean Schoner. 77800, 77807
Lettre de . . . [L. de Bienvenida] a Philippe
II. 94854

Lettre ecrite du Palais Royal. 69721

Lettre ecrite le 14 Mars 1793. 95733

Lettre ecrite par M. Beauge. (4170)

Lettre envoyee de Nouvelle France ou Canada. (56083)

Lettre escripte par le R. P. Denys Iamet. note before 69259

Lettre escrite a messievrs les Estats Generavx. 100933

Lettre et declaration des Deputes de Saint-Domingue. 75152

Lettre et journal. 6181

Lettre inedite qu'on pourrait appeler testament politique. 96345

Lettre missive envoyee aux Gouverneurs. 24855

Lettre missive, tovchant la conversion et baptesme. (5025), (40682)

Lettre ou instructions de l'Assemblee Generale Coloniale. 95733

Lettre pastorale de l'Eveque de Londres. 27311

Lettre que le R. P. Clavde d'Abbeville. 13505

Lettre, qu'un gentilhomme Portugais. 94621

Lettre scrite a M. le Comte de Peynier. 75150

Lettre signee du General Washington. 49393

Lettre sur la decouverte d'un manuscrit Mexicain. 4604

Lettre sur l'Amerique du Nord. 12596

Lettre sur le Canada. 3705

[Lettre] sur le sort de astronomes. 38489

[Lettre] sur les Anglais. 16803

Lettre sur les malheurs de Saint-Domingue en general. (10755), 23540

Lettre sur les missions. 43888

Lettre sur les superstitions du Perou. 94853

Lettre sur l'esclavage dans les colonies Francaises. 21159

Lettre sur l'esclavage des Negres dans nos colonies. 16803

Lettre sur l'esprit et les dispositions du gouvernement Francais. 101165

Lettre sur l'introduction du tabac en France. 19472

Lettre tres-curieuse. 69538

Lettre venant de la Floride. 24854, note after 99605

Lettres a Malthus. (77358)

Lettres a M. Alfred Maury. 55954

Lettres a M. de Jean. 12578, 40683

Lettres a M. l'Abbe de Pradt. (40684)

Lettres a M. le Duc de Broglie. 61261

Lettres a Monsieur Necker. 97337-97338

Lettres a un Ameriquain. (9066), (41054)

Lettres a un gentilhomme. (33339), (33342)

Lettres addresses a Monsieur Necker. 97339

Lettres adressees au R. Pere Mvtio Viteleschi. 32007

Lettres Americaines. 10912

Lettres au Doctor Priestley, en Amerique. (16687), 23085, 59593, 62702, 65510, 92070-92071, 103848

Lettres, au Tres-Honorable Comte de 13797

Lettres Cherakeesiennes. 46910-46911

Lettres choisies . . . 2° serie. 82263

Lettres choisies du Reverend Pere Pierre-Jean de Smet. 82263

Lettres choisies . . . 4° serie. 82263

Lettres choisies . . . 3° serie. 82263

Lettres civique a M. de Pradt. 55495

Lettres critiques adressees a M. Michel Chevalier. 10842

Lettres critiques et politiques. 21032

Lettres curieuses sur l'Amerique Septentrionale. 40685

Lettres d'Affi a Zurac. (19329), (38502)

Lettres d'attache sur la patente d'union. 40686

Lettres d'Aza. 28193, 40693

Lettres de Don Juan de Zumarraga. 94852, 94856, 106401

Lettres de Folcon. 47292

Lettres de Francoys Pizarro. 63178

Lettres de Franklin. 25596

Lettres de la Societe . . . a M. Necker. 85804

Lettres de la Venerable Mere Marie de l' Incarnation. 44562

Lettres de Leurs Excellences Messieurs Jonathan Trumbull et William Livingston. 97254

Lettres de M***. a M***. 42896, (75520)-75521

Lettres de Monsieur le Marquis de Montcalm. 50091

Lettres de . . . [P. de Alvarado] a Fernand Cortes. 94854

Lettres de provision de la charge de Viceroy. 40691

Lettres de quelques missionaires. 40697

Lettres de Verus. 106217

Lettres de chaplains. 95854

Lettres des diverses societes des amis de la constitution. 40694

Lettres des Indes Occidentales. 106367

Lettres des membres de la Second Audience. 94852

Lettres des missionaires-Catholiques au Canada. 20673

Lettres des Peres de la Compagnie de Jesus. 10572, 69274

Lettres diverses. 94852

Lettres-du-charge tirees. 44826

Lettres dv Chevalier de Villegaignon. 99725

Lettres du General Murinais. (1534), (27737)

Lettres du Japon et du Bresil. 40695

Lettres d'un Americain sur les Negres. 38503

Lettres d'un bourgeois de New-Haven. 15194

Lettres d'un citoyen des Etats-Unis a un de ses amis. 40687

Lettres d'un citoyen des Etats-Unis a un Francais. 40688, 79151

Lettres d'un citoyen sur la permission de commercer. 75519

Lettres d'un cultivateur Americain. 17494, 24338

Lettres d'un cultivateur Americain addresses a W^m. S . . . 17495

Lettres d'un fermier de Pensylvanie. 20045

Lettres d'un fils a son pere. 40689, note after 93857

Lettres d'un Francois a un Hollandois. 50563

Lettres d'un membre du Congres Ameriquain. 99579

Lettres d'un philosophe sensible. (19329), (38502)

Lettres d'un voyageur. 104709

Lettres d'une Peruvienne. 28182, 28193, 40692

Lettres d'une Peruvienne augmentees et suivies. (40693)

Lettres ecrites a la Loge l'Amenite no. 73. 40696, note after 101839

Lettres ecrites au Ministre de la Marine. 87115

Lettres ecrites de Cayenne. 11619

Lettres ecrites de l'Amerique. 40207

Lettres ecrites de Londres sur les Anglois. 100751

Lettres ecrites des rives de l'Ohio. 40912
Lettres ecrites es annees 1620 jusques en
    1624. 18538, 32008, 40562
Lettres ecrites par des colons. 29395,
    95072
Lettres ecrites pendant un sejour de deux
    annees. 7714
Lettres edifiantes. 1578-(1579), 6901, 11620,
    19520, 34872, 40006, (40705), 40707-
    40708, 40710, (52376), 73492, 100838
Lettres edifiantes, ecrites des missions
    etrangeres. (40701)
Lettres edifiantes ecrites par quelques
    missionaires. 40703
Lettres edifiantes et curieuses. 21853,
    24135, 40698, 40699-(40700), 40703,
    40708-40710, (52376), 91981, 1st note
    after 96502
Lettres edifiantes et curieuses concernant l'
    Asie, l'Afrique et l'Amerique. 40702
Lettres edifiantes et curieuses, ecrites des
    missions etrangeres. 40697
Lettres envoiees de la Novvelle France.
    38683, note after 69259
Lettres envoyes au chapitre general. 44932
Lettres et documents inedits. 10792
Lettres et discours sur differents sujets.
    38503
Lettres et memoires pour servir a l'histoire
    naturelle. (62610)
Lettres et notes du voyage. 21489
Lettres Illinoises . . . par J. A. P. 61007
Lettres Illinoises, qui renferment quantite d'
    anecdotes. 22906
Lettres Indiennes. 68085
Lettres inserees dans le "Journal de Paris."
    8015
Lettres Iroquoises. 46911-46912
Lettres patentes de concession de l'isle de
    Saint-Jean. 40711
Lettres patentes du octroi sous le grand seau.
    78224
Lettres patentes d'octroy accordees par Sa.
    Majeste Imperiale. 40712, 68792,
    102422
Lettres patentes du Roi, concernant le vente
    des biens des Jesuites. 75153
Lettres patentes du Roi 14 Septembre, 1712.
    42212
Lettres patentes du Roy, portant authorisation
    des status. 40713
Lettres patentes du Roy, portant confirmation
    du contrat d'infeodation. 4512, 40714
Lettres patentes en forme d'edit, portant
    establissement d'un compagnie de com-
    merce. (40716)
Lettres patentes en forme d'edit, portant
    revocation de la Compagnie de Saint
    Domingue. 40718, 75154
Lettres patentes portant revocation de la
    Compagnie de Saint Domingue. 40718,
    75154
Lettres-patentes portant revocation de la con-
    cession qui avoit ete accorde. 75155
Lettres patentes pour Compagnie d'Occident.
    40717
Lettres patentes pour la confirmation de l'
    etablissement. 56090
Lettres patentes pour l'etablissement de la
    Compagnie Royale de Saint Domingue.
    40719
Lettres patentes sur arrest concernat le com-
    merce. 40720
Lettres-patents [sic] du Roi qui accordant a
    la ville de Dunkerque. (40715)
Lettres philosophiques. 100751

Lettres politiques. Par Prevost-Paradol.
    65417
Lettres politiques sur les colonies. 5652
Lettres pour servir d'introduction a l'histoire.
    7433
Lettres sur Etats-Unis d'Amerique. 24180
Lettres sur le liberte politique. 104187
Lettres sur la prise de la Martinique. 44978
Lettres sur la race noire et la race blanche.
    98106
Lettres sur la vie et les ouvrages. 68099
Lettres sur l'administration du Bresil. 5797
Lettres sur l'Amerique, Canada, Etats-Unis,
    Havane, Rio de la Plata. 44643
Lettres sur l'Amerique du Nord. (12585)
Lettres . . . sur le gouvernment des Etats-
    Unis. 23192
Lettres sur le Mexique. 58076
Lettres . . . sur les crimes du Roi George
    III. 23118
Lettres sur les Etats-Unis d'Amerique, ecrite
    en 1832 et 1833. 40721, 75508
Lettres sur les Etats-Unis d'Amerique. Par
    le Lieutenant-Colonel Ferri Pisani.
    24180, 63023
Lettres sur les Etats-Unis, par le Prince
    Achille Murat. 51416
Lettres sur les moeurs et les institutions.
    16487
Lettres sur les nouveaux etablissemens. 5568
Lettres sur les resultats de l'abolition. 29313
Lettres sur l'etat primitif de l'homme.
    (61319)
Lettres sur l'Oceanie. 51037
Letts, J. M. 9971, 40722-40723
Letts, Malcolm. ed. 90060
Lettsom, John Coakley. 11184, 40724-40725,
    61319, 3d note after 96502
Lettsom, William Lanson. 86890
Lettura annva dell'Isole Filippine. 96253
Letzte de Mohicans. 16456
Letzte der Abencerrages. 12251
Letzte der Seminolen. 29676
Letzte Privat-Erklarung fur Pennsylvania.
    106355
Letzte Reysz der gestrengen, edlen vnd vesten
    Frantzen Draeck. (8784)
Letzte verbesserte Auflage. (81476)
Leubel, Alfredo G. 40726
Leubelfing, J. von. 40727
Leuli, J. 40728
Leusden, Johannes. 66451-66454
Leuter, Pieter. tr. 6872
Leutze, Emanuel. illus. (8821), (19919),
    40729, 89339-89340
Levacher, Michel Gabriel. (40730)
Le Vaillant, Francois. 40731, 56064, 1st
    note after 98298
Levanto, Leonardo. (40732)-40733
Levasseur, A. (40734)-(40737)
Levasseur, Emile. 40738-40739
Levasseur, Guillaume. 76838
Le Vasseur, Leon. 40740
Levasseur, V. 40741
Le Vassor de la Touche, Louis Charles.
    44972 see also Martinique (Colony)
    Governor, 1761-1762 (Le Vassor de la
    Touche)
Levees of the Mississippi. 30485
Le Veillard, -------. tr. 25550
Level, Andreas E. 40743
Level, Fanny. 40742
Level of Europe and North America. 22057,
    40744
Levelei Ejszakamerikábol. 35273, 105712
Leven, -------. tr. (16566)

Lewis, John, 1746-1792. 92887
Lewis, John, d. 1750. defendant 40815
Lewis, John, d. 1760. defendant 73406
Lewis, John Travers, Bp. 40817
Lewis, John W. 7075, 40818
Lewis, Joseph C. (40819)
Lewis, Joseph J. (40820)
Lewis, Lawrence. 101764
Lewis, Leonard. petitioner 90020
Lewis, Lothrop. 66773
Lewis, Matthew Gregory, 1775-1818. 38283, 40821-(40822), 97466
Lewis, Meriwether, 1774-1809. 21247, (24507)-24508, 40823-40836, 84162, 94201, 2d note after 96498, 96499
Lewis, Morgan, 1754-1844. 40838-40840, 54960, 1st note after 98220, 101785
    see also New York (State) Governor, 1804-1807 (Lewis)
Lewis, Oliver. 40841
Lewis, Oscar. 99381
Lewis, Osceola. 40842
Lewis, R. tr. 32487
Lewis, Reuben A. (49778)
Lewis, Robert. illus. 84041
Lewis, Robert Benjamin. 40844-40845
Lewis, Robert W. 40846
Lewis, Roswell W. 40847
Lewis, S. J. (40850)
Lewis, Sabin. 40848
Lewis, Samuel. 92398
Lewis, Seth. 40849
Lewis, Tayler, 1802-1877. 515, (40851)-40854
Lewis, Taylor. 56036
Lewis, Thomas. plaintiff? 40855
Lewis, Thomas H. (7067)
Lewis, W. 1795, note after 53697, note after 83791
Lewis, W. S. 101041
Lewis, Wales. 40856
Lewis, William, 1714-1781. 40837, 40857
Lewis, William, fl. 1809. 60470, 82884
Lewis, William D. 40858
Lewis, William G. W. (40862)
Lewis, William H. 40859-40861
Lewis, Winslow. (40863)-40866
Lewis, Zechariah. 40867
Lewis County, N. Y. Board of Supervisors. 40869
Lewis county Democrat. 95825
Lewis County Medical Society. 40868
Lewisburg, Pa. Bucknell University. see Bucknell University, Lewisburg, Pa.
Lewisburg, Pa. University. see Bucknell University, Lewisburg, Pa.
Lewisburg, [W.] Va. Convention to Deliberate on . . . Internal Improvement in Virginia, 1831. see Convention on Internal Improvement in Virginia, Lewisburg, [W.] Va., 1831
Lewisburg, Centre and Spruce Creek Railroad. 60211
Lewisburg University, Lewisburg, Pa. see Bucknell University, Lewisburg, Pa.
Lewis's Family School for Young Ladies, Lexington, Mass. see Dr. Dio Lewis's Family School for Young Ladies, Lexington, Mass.
Lewiston, Me. 40874
Lewiston, Me. Manufacturers' and Mechanics' Library Association. see Manufacturers' and Mechanics' Library Association, Lewiston, Me.
Lewiston, Me. School Committee. (40872)
Lewiston, Me. Selectmen. (40873)

Lewiston, Me. Maine State Seminary. see Maine State Seminary, Lewiston, Me.
Lewiston and Auburn directory. 40875
Lewiston Committee of the Convention of Seceding Masons. see Convention of Seceding Masons, Le Roy, N. Y., 1828. Lewiston Committee.
Lewiston Falls, Me. Academy. see Lewiston Falls Academy, Me.
Lewiston Falls Academy, Me. 40876
Lewiston Falls directory, and Maine farmer's almanac. 72065
Le Wright, J. 40877, 1st note after 97578
Lewsiana. 84737
Lewy's Island Lodge, no. 138, Princeton, Me. see Freemasons. Maine. Lewy's Island Lodge, no. 138, Princeton.
Lex. pseud. Condition of the rebel states. 40878
Lex mercatoria Americana. (9852)
Lex mercatoria. Or, the just rules of commerce declared. (46381)
Lex parliamentaria Americana. 18115
Lex parliamentaria: or, a treatise on the law and custom. 58055
Lex talionis. 17180
Lexica et praecepta grammatica. 3875
Lexicon geographicvm. 40879
Lexicon, o vocabulario de la lengua general de Perv. 20565
Lexicon of freemasonry. 43446
Lexicon vniversale. 32414
Lexikon der jetzlebenden Schriftsteller. 70153
Lexikon pseydonym Schriften. 42171
Lexington, Ky. Asylum for Insane see Kentucky. Asylum for Insane, Lexington.
Lexington, Ky. Botanic Gardens. see Transylvania University, Lexington, Ky. Botanic Garden.
Lexington, Ky. Jardin Botanique de l'Universite Transylvane. see Transylvania University, Lexington, Ky. Botanic Garden.
Lexington, Ky. Lafayette Female Academy. see Lafayette Female Academy, Lexington, Ky.
Lexington, Ky. Lexington Library Company. see Lexington Library Company, Lexington, Ky.
Lexington, Ky. Mass Meeting, 1847. 13550
Lexington, Ky. Mechanics and Manufacturers. petitioners (40884)
Lexington, Ky. Pro-slavery Convention, 1855. see Pro-slavery Convention, Lexington, Ky., 1855.
Lexington, Ky. Theological Seminary of the Protestant Episcopal Church. see Theological Seminary of the Protestant Episcopal Church in Kentucky, Lexington.
Lexington, Ky. Transylvania University. see Transylvania University, Lexington, Ky.
Lexington, Mass. Auditor. 40887
Lexington, Mass. Centennial Committee. 88689
Lexington, Mass. Committee to Investigate the Ministerial Fund. 40890
Lexington, Mass. Dr. Dio Lewis's Family School for Young Ladies. see Dr. Dio Lewis's Family School for Young Ladies, Lexington, Mass.
Lexington, Mass. Manual Labor Seminary. see Lexington Manual Labor Seminary.
Lexington, Mass. School Committee. 40891
Lexington, Mass. Selectmen. 40892
Lexington, Va. Military Institute. see Virginia Military Institute, Lexington.

Lexington, Va. Washington and Lee University.
see Washington and Lee University,
Lexington, Va.
Lexington, Va. Washington College. see
Washington and Lee University, Lexing-
ton, Va.
Lexington and Ohio Railroad Company.
defendants (5162)
Lexington and Ohio Railroad Company. Pres-
ident. 40885
Lexington calamity. A sermon . . . in . . .
Bleecker-St. . . . Church. 39837
Lexington city directory for 1864-5. 40883
Lexington intelligencer. 40577, 88114
Lexington Library Company, Lexington, Ky.
40881
Lexington Manual Labor Seminary, Lexington,
Mass. 40889
Lexington, with other fugitive poems. 103071
Ley de 28 de Abril de 1851. 85763
Ley del fondo piadoso de Californias. (10027),
(40897)
Ley del presupuesto general de la nacion
Argentina. 1955
Ley fundamental de instruccion publica y
ejercicio. (40898)
Ley, justicia y verdad. 29290, 59319
Ley organica de la milicia nacional. (40899)
Ley regulamentaria de elecciones. 61134
Ley reglamentaria de la administracion de
justicia. 55153
Ley reglamentaria del elecciones de diputados.
61134
Ley sobre aranceles de importacion y expor-
tacion. 75156
Ley sobre derechos y obvenciones parroquia-
les. (48511)
Ley sobre el comercio maritimo. 75157
Ley sobre politica jeneral. 56279
Ley y reglamentos organicos. (14599)
Leyba, Diego de. 40900
Leyba, Pedro de Toledo y. see Toledo y
Leyba, Pedro de, Marques de Mancera,
1585-1654.
Leyde, --------, Marques de. (47531), 96521
see also Spain. Legacion. Great
Britain.
Leyden. Church. 79353
Leyden. Mattschappij der Nederlandsche
Letterkunde. see Mattschappij der
Nederlandsche Letterkunde, Leyden.
Leyden. Netherlands Historical Society. see
Netherlands Historical Society, Leyden.
Leyden. Netherlands Literary Society. see
Maatschappij der Nederlandsche Letter-
kunde, Leyden.
Leyden. Taal- en Dichtlievende Genootschap.
see Taal- en Dichtlievende Genootschap,
Leyden.
Leydt, Johannes. see Ritzema, Johannes.
Leyenda. 42107
Leyenda Americana. 11654
Leyenda antigua. (48993)
Leyenda Cubana. 74629
Leyenda historica. 24153
Leyenda mistica tradicional. 42107
Leyenda moral e historica. 87244
Leyendas Americanas. 29102
Leyendas Mexicanas, cuentos y baladas del
norte de Europa. 71703
Leyendecker, --------. 40901
Leyes de confiscacion de Colombia. 98872
Leyes de la recompilacion de Indias. (26482)
Leyes de la republica de Colombia. 56280
Leyes de los reynos de Indias. 40905

Leyes de recopilacion; y los autos acordados.
56288
Leyes . . . del primer [-tercer] Congreso de
la republica de Tejas. 94976
Leyes Dominicanos. 20576
Leyes generales aprobados en las sessiones.
14747
Leyes i decretos espedidos por el Congreso
Constitucional de la Nueva Granada.
56281
Leyes relativas a papel sellado y ultimas.
48512
Leyes, tratados y documentos justificativos.
59301
Leyes y decretos del estado de Coahuila y
Texas. 13810, 39405, 94948
Leyes y ordenancas nueuame[n]te hechas por
Su Magestad pa[ra] la gouernacio[n] de
las Indias. 40902
Leyes y ordenancas nueva-mente hechas por
Su Magestad, para la gouernacio[n] de
las Indias. 40904
Leyes, y ordenancas nuevas, hechas por Su
Magestad. 40903
Leyes y reglamento, para al arreglo de la
instruccion publica. (48513)
Leypoldt, Friedrich. ed. 6173, 40906, 66533,
90803
Leysler, Jacob. see Leisler, Jacob.
Leyva, Pedro de Toledo y. see Toledo y
Leyva, Pedro de, Marques de Mancera.
Lezama, Juan de. 40908
Lezamis, Jose de. 40909-40910
Lezay, Adrien. 40911
Lezay-Marnezia, Cl. Fr. Ad. de. 40912
Lezermes, --------. tr. 44777
Lezica, --------. respondent 81411
LH--------, L. F. pseud. see L'Hertier,
Louis Francois, 1789-1852.
LH . . . . ., L. F. (de l'Ain). pseud. see
L'Hertier, Louis Francois, 1789-1852.
Lherminier, --------. 94390
L'Hermite, Bernard. 95332
L'Hermite, Jacques. see Hermite, Jacques l'.
L'Hertier, Louis Francois, 1789-1852. 29395,
40913, 95072
Lhoyd, Humfrey. 40914
Lhuys, Edouard Drouyn de. see Drouyn de
Lhuys, Edouard, 1805-1881.
Liability of stockholders in manufacturing
corporations. 45803, 68272
Liability of the government of Great Britain.
37997
Liais, Emmanuel. 40915
Liancourt, Francois Alexandre Frederic, Duc
de la Rochefoucauld. see La Roche-
foucauld-Liancourt, Francois Alexandre
Frederic, Duc de, 1747-1827.
Libarona, Agostina. 16930
Libbey, H. W. 40916
Libby life. 11591
Libel. Against a catechism published by
Francis Makemie. (44077)
Libel refuted. 28605
Libel suit of Chief Justice Ames. 5786
Libel trial. Report of the trial, Timothy
Upham vs. Hill & Barton. 98052
Libell of Spanish lies. 77289
Libelles d'Inivres. 99727-99728
Libelli supplicis exhibuit. 4638, 76813
Libelli supplicis majestati sui oblati. 67355
Libellus. 71137
Libellvs Ioannis Sacrobosco de anni ratione.
32681
Libellus sive epistola supplicatoria. (8784)

Liberty, glory and union. 9235

Liberty in Louisiana; a comedy. 105482

Liberty in slavery. 86713

Liberty is the birthright of all. 40946

Liberty minstrel. 25717

Liberty minstrel. By George W. Clark. 13289

Liberty National Nominating Convention, Albany, N. Y., 1841. see Albany Liberty National Nominating Convention, 1841.

Liberty Normal Institute, Liberty, N. Y. 40945

Liberty of conscience. 103203A

Liberty of flesh and spirit distinguished. 14373

Liberty of speech and of the press. A charge to grand juries. 377

Liberty of speech and of the press. A thanksgiving sermon. 73121

Liberty of the Gospel explained. 31062

Liberty of the press vindicated. 103041

Liberty of the spirit and of the flesh distinguished. 74499

Liberty of death. A tract. 42414

Liberty or death, or the mother's sacrifice. 37147

Liberty, or slavery? Daniel O'Connell on American slavery. 12200

Liberty or slavery; the great national question. 95775

Liberty or slavery, the only question. 47078

Liberty overthrown. 4501, (36412)

Liberty papers. (40947)

Liberty preacher. 40948

Liberty, property, and no excise. 90139-90140

Liberty, property, and no stamps. 100800

Liberty regain'd. (74636)

Liberty restored. 55838

Liberty saved. 40949

Liberty Society, Savannah. 92833

Liberty song. 5220

Liberty standard. 85345

Liberty, the nation, the occasion. 25193

Liberty tract no. 2. 71360

Liberty tracts. 40950

Liberty tracts.—No. 1. 92452

Liberty Tree Division, No. 47, Boston. see Sons of Temperance of North America. Massachusetts. Liberty Tree Division, No. 47, Boston.

Liberty tree; with the last words of grand father's chair. 30991

Liberty triumphant. 39512

Liberty triumphant, etc. (73118)

Liberty when used as a cloke of malifiousness, the worst of evils. (51432)

Liberty's dream. 46924

Liberty's ideal. 5615

Liberty's triumph. (38838)

Liborius, Carolina Litchfield de. plaintiff 40951

Liborius de Olavarria, Carolina. plaintiff 40951

Libra astronomica. 80977

Libra astronomica y philosophica. 80976

Librairie De Bure. (8784)

Librarian's manual. (29223)

Librarian's series, no. 3. 96287

Libraries of Sam. Wharton, Esq, & Sam. Garrigues. 103106

Library, Brooklyn, N. Y. see Brooklyn Library.

Library, Burlington, N. J. see Burlington, N. J. Library.

Library, Plymouth, Mass. see Plymouth, Mass. Library.

Library, Quincy, Mass. see Quincy, Mass. Library.

Library, Troy, N. Y. see Troy, N. Y. Library.

Library. 88221

Library Association, Blackstone, R. I. see Blackstone Library Association, Blackstone, R. I.

Library Association, Bridgeport, Conn. see Bridgeport Library Association.

Library Association, Cleveland. see Cleveland Library Association.

Library Association, Hornell, N. Y. see Hornell Library Association.

Library Association, Lynn, Mass. see Lynn Library Association, Lynn, Mass.

Library Association, Madison, Ind. see Madison Library Association, Madison, Ind.

Library Association, Middlebury College, Vt. see Middlebury College, Middlebury, Vt. Library Association.

Library Association, Newark, N. J. see Newark, N. J. Library Association.

Library Association, Petersburg, Va. see Petersburg Library Association.

Library Association, St. Louis. see St. Louis Library Association.

Library Association, St. Paul, Minn. see St. Paul Library Association, St. Paul, Minn.

Library Association, Springfield, Ill. see Springfield Library Association, Springfield, Ill.

Library Association, Steilacoom, Washington. see Steilacoom Library Association, Steilacoom, Washington.

Library Association of New York City. see New York City Library Association.

Library Association of Skowhegan, Maine. see Skowhegan Library Association.

Library Association of the United Kingdom. (64035)

Library Company, Easton, Pa. see Easton, Pa. Library Company.

Library Company, New Castle, Del. see New Castle Library Company.

Library Company, Norwich, Conn. see Norwich Library Company.

Library Company, Providence, R. I. see Providence, R. I. Athenaeum. Library.

Library Company, Southwark, Pa. see Southwark Library Company, Southwark, Pa.

Library Company, Springfield, Mass. see Springfield Library Company, Springfield, Mass.

Library Company, Trenton, N. J. see Trenton Library Company, Trenton, N. J.

Library Company, Washington, D. C. see Washington Library Company, Washington, D. C.

Library Company of Philadelphia. see Philadelphia. Library Company.

Library Company of Wilmington, Wilmington, Del. 104582

Library Company of Wilmington, Wilmington, Del. Charter. 104581

Library edition. Campaign against Quebec. 31401

Library for travellers and the fireside (Nelson's) 92454

Library Hall Company, Pittsburgh. see Pittsburgh Library Association. Library Hall Company.

Library journal. 84980

Library of American biography. 7058, 9364, 11896, 23256, 25439, 26517, (28601), 41591, 42143, 43424, (49054), 65299, 68548, 74736, 78779, 88980, 88981, note after 88982, note after 88984, 88985, 88992, 89744, 98046, 101411, 103161, 103696

Library of American history, containing biographical sketches. 40953

Library of American history. Intended to give the reader a full view of American history. 4430, 12998, 28243, 40952, 91742

Library of American linguistics. 2116, 2118, 2124, 8779, 27299-27301, 28252, 43887, 47861, 58420, 80007, 80015, 81475, 84380-84381

Library of Cape Cod history & genealogy. 84759

Library of commerce: practical, theoretical, and historical. 33850, 43358

Library of Congress. December 3, 1832. 15571

Library of entertaining knowledge. 96441

Library of humorous American works (Cary & Hart's) 84237

Library of humorous American works (Peterson's) 84239-84240

Library of information. 71142

Library of instructive amusement. 104827

Library of New England history, no. II. (12976)

Library of New England history, no. III. 12977

Library of religious literature. 84901

Library of select literature. 38099

Library of select novels. 94247

Library of southern literature. 85374

Library of the Four Monthly Meetings of Friends of Philadelphia. see Philadelphia. Library of the Four Monthly Meetings of Friends.

Library of the late Reverend and Learned Mr. Samuel Lee. 39797

Library of the Three Monthly Meetings of Friends of Philadelphia. see Philadelphia. Library of the Three Monthly Meetings of Friends.

Library of the world's best books. 100482

Library of useful and entertaining knowledge. (78656)

Library of useful knowledge. 80285

Library of wit and humor. 84159

Library reporter and book-buyer's guide. 40954

Library Society, Warren, R. I. see Warren Library Society, Warren, R. I.

Library Society of Exeter, N. H. see Exeter Library Society, Exeter, N. H.

Libre di Odoardp Barbessa Portoghese. 67730

Libreria Hispano-Americana, Paris. (75863)

Libretto di tutta la nauigation de Re de Spagna. 1547, 40955

Libri, Guillaume, 1803-1869. 40956

Libri de situ orbis tres. 63956

Libri duo elogiorum quibus viri aliqui clarissimi Florentini & alii decorantur. 6102

Libro ante-primero. 99525

Libro de actos del Ayuntamiento de la cuidad de Santiago de Guatemala. 76860

Libro de el Visitador Obispo D. Juan de Palafax y Mendoza. (73620)

Libro de grandezas y cosas memorables de Espana. (47348)

Libro de justis belli causis. 79180

Libro de la cosmographia vniversal del mvndo. 79328

Libro de la lei. 76699

Libro de la miseria y breuedad de la vida del hombre. 36134

Libro de la vida del Ven. Padre Bernardino Alvarez. 40957

Libro de la vida de los frayles menores. 44419

Libro de la vida del P. Bern. Alvarez. 1898

Libro de la vida del proximo evangelico, el Vener. Padre Bernardino Alvarez. 199(

Libro de la vida y milagros de Nvestro Senor Iesu Christo. 5022, note after 99728

Libro de las cinco excelencias del Espanol. (59635)

Libro de las constituciones del R. Orden Terzero de Penitencia. 40958

Libro de las cosas qve se traen de nuestras Indias Occidentales. (49937)

Libro de las costvmbres de todas las gentes del mvndo. 94273

Libro de los codigos. 72548

Libro de Mormon. 83139-83141

Libro de Oro. 42107

Libro del muy esforcado y inuencible Caualle de la Fortuna. 57995

Libro dela cosmographia de Pedro Apiano. 1753

Libro di Benedetto Bordone. 6417

Libro di Mattheo di Micheovo. 67738

Libro di Messer Marco Polo. 67736

Libro di Mormon. 83134

Libro di Odoardo Barbessa. 67730

Libro en prosa. (72784)

Libro en q[ue] esta[n] compiladas algunas bullas. 40959, (64915)

Libro intitvlado Arte para criar sede. 11290(

Libro llamado Silua d'avaria. 48233

Libro llamado thesoro de virtudes vtil & copioso. note after 27585, 40960, note after 47850

Libro primero de las genealogias del Nvevo Reyno de Granada. 45524

Libro primo de la conqvista del Perv. 10572

Libro primo de la conqvista del Perv & Prouincia del Cuzco. 105721

Libro primo de provisiones cedvlas. 22550, note after 40960

Libro primero del vocabulatio . . . la lengua general del Peru. 27774

Libro primo della historia de l'Indie Occidentali. 1565, 45013

Libro IV. Secando viaggio. 99504

Libro que continen todo los interesante a uso 9570

Libro qve trata de la nieue. (49937)

Libro rojo. 58274

Libro secvndo de las genealogias del Nvevo Reyno de Granda. 45524

Libro decundo delle Indie Occidentali. 1565, 45013

Libro segundo de las memorias antiguas historiales del Peru. (50125)

Libro vltimo del svmmario delle Indie Occidentali. 1565, (61097)

Libro I [-VIII] de la II. parte de los comentarios reales. 98755

Libro XX. de la segunda parte de la General Historia de los Indias. (57991)

Librorum series post praefationem ascripta. (77903)

Liburnius, Nicolo. tr. 16951

Licana, Bernardo de. 40961

Liceaga, Jose Maria de. 40962

[Licenciado Christoual de Moscoso y Cordoua con Alonso de Carrion. 51043

Licenciado [Christoual de Moscoso y
Cordoua] con Don Juan de Amassa.
51043 '
Licenciado [Christoual de Moscoso y Cordoua]
con Don Martin Carrillo de Aldrete.
51043
[Licenciado Christoual de Moscoso y Cordoua]
con Dona Francisca Arce de Otalora.
51043
Licenciado [Christoual de Moscoso y Cordoua]
con el Consulado. 51043
[Licenciado Christoual de Moscoso y Cordoua]
con el Duque del Infantado. 51043
Lic. D. A. de Souza y Amador . . . opositor
a la Canogia Magistral. 88813
Lic^{do}. Don Antonio Domingo Thello, y Bar-
bero. 95298
Licenciado Don Christoual de Moscoso y
Cordoua. 51043
Licdo. D. Joseph Balthasar de Somonte, y
Velasco. 86862
Licenciado Don Mathias de Solis y Vlloa.
86495
Lic. D. Pedro Alexandro Texeda. 95140
Licenciado Don Pedro de Solis Calderon.
86432
Lic. D. Pedro de Teran Rubin. 94835
Licenciado Matabalanzas. pseud. Soplamocos
literario. see Solano, Vicente, 1791
or 2-1865.
Licencia. 96268
Licencia del Padre Prouincial. 96268
Licencie de la Macha. pseud. Grenade. see
Martinez, Hernando.
License law. 45804
License question. (40963)
"Licensed houses." 77015, 2d note after
98269
Licentiousness unmasked. 40965
Liceo Mexicano. 40966
Liceo Venezolano. 14116
Lichefield, Nicholas. tr. 11391
Lichfield and Coventry, Bishop of. see Corn-
wallis, Frederick, Archbishop of Canter-
bury, 1713-1783. Cornwallis, James
Cornwallis, 4th Earl, Bp. of Lichfield
and Coventry, 1742-1824. Egerton, John,
successively Bishop of Bangor, Lich-
field and Coventry, and Durham, 1721-
1787. Hough, John, successively Bishop
of Oxford, Lichfield and Coventry, and
Worcester, 1651-1743. Hurd, Richard,
successively Bishop of Lichfield and
Coventry, and Worcester, 1720-1808.
Smalbroke, Richard, successively Bishop
of St. Davids, and Lichfield and Coventry, 1672-1749.
Licht der zee-vaert. 35775
Lichtenstegern, Georgius. 11512, 11515,
22090
Lichlenstein, H. 40968
Licking County Pioneer Association. see
Licking County Pioneer Society.
Licking County Pioneer, Historical and Anti-
quarian Society. see Licking County
Pioneer Society.
Licking County pioneer pamphlets. 78333,
85133, 85137-85138, 85143
Licking County Pioneer Society. 13573,
40969-(40970), 78333, 85133, 85137-
85138, 85143
Licking County Pioneer Society. Celebration
of American Independence, Clay Lick,
Ohio, 1869. 13573, (40970), 85133
Licking County Pioneers. see Licking County
Pioneer Society.

Licking County Soldiers Monumental Associa-
tion. 85138
Licking County's gallant soldiers. 85138
Liddell, -------. 42982
Liddell, J. P. 34564 see also Indiana.
Draft Commissioner.
Liddesdale: or the border chief. 39447
Liddle, William F. 72339
Liddon, John. 40971
Lidenius, John Abr. (40972)
Lidman, Jonas. 94036
Lidstone, James Torrington Spencer. 40973
Lie direct!! 104647
Lie-ary on America. (44696)
Liebaux, --------. engr. 95332
Liebe, Carl. (26842)
Liebergen, Arnout van. petitioner/defendant
40988
Lieber, Francis. 1003* [sic] 1491, 14806,
22556, (27494), 40974-40985, 62635,
(70885), 85072, note after 96069, 103911
Lieber, Oscar Montgomery. (40986)-40987,
87719-87722, 88005 see also South
Carolina. Mineralogical, Geological and
Agricultural Surveyor. South Carolina.
State Geologist.
Lieberkuhn, Samuel. tr. (19376), (40989),
72232, note after 106301
Liebhaber der historien. pseud. tr. 33667
Liebmann, F. M. 40990-40991
Liebsch, W. tr. 3814
Lieden [sic] der Negersklaven in Amerika.
92579
Liefhebber. pseud. Beschryvinghe van Turck-
yen. 74849
Lief-hebber. pseud. Claar vertooch. 7547
Liefhebber. pseud. Journael ende historis
verhael. 8427, 33678
Lief-hebber. pseud. Iournael ofte kort dis-
cours. 7593
Liefhebber. pseud. Vrye politijke stellingen.
100859
Lief-hebber der historien in't licht gebracht.
pseud. Monarchia Hispanica. see Zeiller,
Martin.
Liefhebber der waarheid. pseud. Kort handlei-
ding. 38258
Liefhebber des vaderlandts. pseud. Discovrs
over den Nederlandtschen vrede-handel.
20236
Lief-hebber des vaderlandts. pseud. Korte
observatien. 7595
Lief-hebber des vaderlandts. pseud. Levendich.
discovrs. 40745, 4th note after 102894
Lief-hebber des vaderlandts. pseud. Tegen-
advys. 94591
Liefhebber des vaderlandts inghestelt. pseud.
Kort onderrichtinghe ende vermaeninghe.
see Usselinx, Willem.
Lief-hebber des vaderlandts vertoont. pseud.
Vertoogh. 7575-7576, 99308
Lief-hebber eenes oprechten ende bestandighen
vredes voorghestelt. pseud. Bedenckling-
hen over den staet. see Usselinx, Wil-
lem.
Liefhebber van alle der welbevoeghde borgeren
even gelijke vryheit. pseud. Vrye polit-
ijke stellingen. 100859
Lief-hebber van het vaderlandt. pseud. Pol-
iticq discours. see Usselinx, Willem.
Liefhebber van't vaderlandt. pseud. Gril-
gesicht voor de verblinde. 7545, (7981)
Liegel, T. A. 40992
Liekens wastoti. 42771, 79981
Lienau, J. F. von. 40993
Lierzang. 101893

Lies, Eugene. 40994, 86012
Lieutenant and commander. 29724
Lieut.-Col. ————. pseud. see ————,
    Lieut.-Col. pseud.
Lieutenant Colonel in the Continental Army.
    pseud. Battle of Bunker's Hill. (9174)
Lieutenant-Colonel of the U. S. Army. pseud.
    Pauline, the female spy. (59221)
Lieut. Francis Hall's travels. 84304-84306,
    84320-84321
Lieut. General Pemberton's report. 15336,
    (36376)
Lieut.-General Simcoe understanding that the
    translation. (81136)
Lieutenant General. Speech of Mr. Smith, of
    Alabama. 84889
Lieut.-General U. S. Grant, his services and
    characteristics. 71878
Lieutenant in the fleet. pseud. see M., J.
    pseud.
Lieutenant in the navy. pseud. see J., J.,
    Lieutenant in the navy. pseud.
Lieut. James Moody's narrative. (50309)-
    50310
Lieut. M. F. Maury. Speech. 4461
Lieut. Maury's investigations of the winds
    and currents of the sea. 46974
Lieutenant, of the left wing. pseud. Sketch
    of the Seminole war. see Cohen, M. M.
    supposed author
Lieutenant of the left wing. pseud. Sketches
    of the Seminole war. see Cohen, M. M.
    supposed author
Lieut. Pringle. pseud. see Hines, David
    Theodore.
Lieutenant Weaver's vindicatory address and
    appeal. 102207
Lievano, Poncet Indalecio. (40995)
Life a journey, and man a traveller. 26624
Life: a poem in three books. 7387
Life, adventures, and opinions of Col. George
    Hander. 30227
Life, adventures and opinions of David Theo.
    Hines. 31950
Life, adventures and pyracies of Captain
    Singleton. 19281
Life, adventures, and travels in California,
    and scenes in the Pacific Ocean. (23868)
Life, adventures, and travels in California.
    To which are added, the conquest of
    California. 23869
Life, adventures, and unparalleled sufferings
    of Andrew Oehler. 56732
Life after dark in New-York. 54189
Life among the Apaches. 17470
Life among the Araucanian Indians. 12800
Life among the Choctaw Indians. 4750
Life among the giants. 6910
Life among the Indians: being an interesting
    narrative. 92743
Life among the Indians; or, personal reminis-
    cences. 24380
Life among the lawless. 2108A, note after
    93619
Life among the lowly. 92457-92459, 92461,
    92465-92466, 92468, 92474, 92485,
    92501, 92513
Life among the Mormons. (40996)
Life among the poor. 29903
Life among the red Indians and fur traders.
    2501
Life among the Sioux. (39033)
Life amongst the Indians. 11541
Life, anecdotes, and heroic exploits of Israel
    Putnam. 66806

Life and achievements of Gen. Winfield Scott.
    78408
Life and actions of James Dalton. 18351
Life and acts of Don Alonzo Enriquez de
    Guzman. 29367
Life and administration of Abraham Lincoln.
    (2650)
Life and administration of Ex-President Fill-
    more. (24332)
Life and adventure in the South Pacific.
    36440
Life and adventure on the prairies. 70980
Life and adventures in California, and scenes
    in the Pacific Ocean. (23867), 23871
Life and adventures of a certain Quaker
    Presbyterian Indian colonel. 96975
Life and adventures of a country merchant.
    36528
Life and adventures of a lap-dog. 32149
Life and adventures of Alexander Selkirk.
    33350
Life and adventures of Ambrose Gwinett.
    29385
Life and adventures of an Arkansaw doctor.
    67961
Life and adventures of Arthur Clenning.
    24792
Life and adventures of Arthur Spring. 89766
Life and adventures of Black Hawk. 28449
Life and adventures of Black Hawk, the great
    Indian chief of the west. 5677
Life and adventures of Black Hawk; with
    sketches of Keokuk. 20810
Life and adventures of Captain Jacob D.
    Armstrong. 2022
Life and adventures of Captain John Smith,
    by W. C. Armstrong. 2041
Life and adventures of Capt. John Smith,
    founder of the Virginian colony. 82863
Life and adventures of Charles Anderson
    Chester. 12529
Life and adventures of Christopher Carson.
    9213
Life and adventures of Christopher Hawkins.
    30949
Life and adventures of Colonel Daniel Boon.
    (6370), 40997
Life and adventures of Colonel David Crockett.
    Embracing his career. (17569)
Life and adventures of Col. David Crockett,
    of West Tennessee. (17568)
Life and adventures of Daniel Boone. (24793)
Life and adventures of David Crockett.
    (25865)
Life and adventures of Doctor Updike Under-
    hill. 97615
Life and adventures of Don. Pedro Aquilo.
    99429, note after 100822
Life and adventures of Duncan Cameron.
    40998
Life and adventures of Gen. Israel Putnam.
    66805
Life and adventures of Henry Lanson. 38942
Life and adventures of Henry Smith. 14332,
    82698
Life and adventures of Henry Kynaston. 38373
Life and adventures of James R. Durand.
    21411
Life and adventures of James P. Beckwourth.
    4265
Life and adventures of James Ramble. 67615
Life and adventures of James W. Marshall.
    58882
Life and adventures of Jeff. Davis. 42939
Life and adventures of Joaquin Murieta.
    51446, (71281)

1488

Life and adventures of John A. Murrell.
51553

Life and adventures of John James Audubon.
(8869), 92341

Life and adventures of John Kelly. 37314

Life and adventures of John Nicol. 55241

Life and adventures of Jonathan Jefferson
Whitlaw. 97031-97032

Life and adventures of Joseph T. Hare.
30364, 33251

Life and adventures of Joshua Penny. 60792

Life and adventures of Kit Carson. 61190

Life and adventures of Lewis Wertzel. 30682

Life and adventures of Martin Chuzzlewit.
20006

Life and adventures of Matthew Bishop.
(5613)

Life and adventures of Monroe Edwards.
(21980)

Life and adventures of Obadiah Benjamin
Franklin Bloomfield. 5991

Life and adventures of Olaudah Equiano.
98662

Life and adventures of Paul Jones. 36549

Life and adventures of Peter Porcupine.
(13892)

Life and adventures of Peter Wheeler.
103198

Life and adventures of Peter Wilkins.
58394, 74631, note after 104017

Life and adventures of Peter Williamson, a
native of Aberdeen. 104477

Life and adventures of Peter Williamson,
who was kidnapped. (36555)

Life and adventures of Robert Bailey. 2748

Life and adventures of Robert Dexter Romaine.
72890

Life and adventures of Robert, the hermit of
Massachusetts. 71857, 97198

Life and adventures of Robert Voorhis.
97199, note after 100770

Life and adventures of Simon Seek. 13635

Life and adventures of Smith Maythe. 20519

Life and adventures of the accomplished
forger and swindler. 40999

Life and adventures of the famous Capt.
Singleton. 81423

Life and adventures of the reformed inebriate
D. G. Robinson. 72066

Life and adventures of Timothy Murphy.
51474, 80968

Life and adventures of William Filley. 24328

Life and adventures of Wm. Harvard Stinch-
field. 72133

Life and adventures, songs, services, and
speeches. 29919

Life and amours of Thomas S. Hamblin.
29934

Life and astonishing adventures of Peter
Williamson. 104478-104479

Life and battles of John Paul Jones. (36551),
note after 94476

Life and battles of Yankee Sullivan. 93507

Life and battles of Yankee Sullivan, embracing
full and accurate reports. 93508

Life and battles of Yankee Sullivan, from his
first appearance in the prize ring.
93507

Life and beauties of Fanny Fern. 58961

Life and campaigns of General Robert E. Lee.
42961

Life and campaigns of George B. McClellan.
31873

Life and campaigns of Lieut. Gen. Thomas
J. Jackson. 18255

Life and campaigns of Lieut.-Gen. U. S.
Grant. 31164

Life and career of Major-General Ormsby M.
Mitchel. 31169

Life and career of Major John Andre. 77043

Life and career of Tiburcio Vazquez. 77304

Life and character of a strange he-monster.
41000

Life and character of Abraham Lincoln. A
memorial oration. 49068

Life and character of Abraham Lincoln. A
memorial oration, delivered at Franklin,
N. Y. 25635

Life and character of Abraham. With some
lessons from his death. 9236

Life and character of Adoniram Judson.
29530

"Life and character of Admiral Collingwood."
62907

Life and character of Benedict Arnold. (1065)

Life and character of Calvin. 85299

Life and character of Capt. Moses Stone.
92063

Life and character of Capt. Wm. B. Allen.
73595

Life and character of Frederick Augustus
Rauch. 52422

Life and character of Hon. David Daggett.
18263

Life and character of Hon. Wm. Gaston.
92700

Life and character of John Brown. 28741

Life and character of John Paul Jones, a
captain in the United States Navy. 80336

Life and character of John Paul Jones during
the revolutionary war. (36550)

Life and character of Major-General Putnam.
28950

Life and character of Miss Susanna Anthony.
32951

Life and character of Miss Susanna Anthony,
who died, in Newport. 32951

Life and character of Oglethorpe. 33244

Life and character of Rev. D. Howe Allen.
(82702)

Life and character of Rev. Samuel H. Stearns.
90986

Life and character of Richard H. Menifee.
44811

Life and character of Stephen Decatur. 101007

Life & character of the author, by John
Rodgers. 104942

Life and character of the Chevalier John Paul
Jones. 80334

Life and character of the Hon. John C.
Calhoun. 9953

Life and character of the Hon. William
Parkinson Greene. 82465

Life and character of the late Prof. Edward
C. Ross. (37318)

Life and character of the late Reverend Mr.
Jonathan Edwards. 21948

Life and character of the Rev. Aaron Bancroft.
(31806)

Life and character of the Reverend Benjamin
Colman. 97450

Life and character of the Rev. Sylvester Judd.
29717

Life and character of Wm. Penn. 21048

Life and choice writings of George Lippard.
41394

Life and confession of Amasa E. Walmsley.
101131

Life and confession of Amos Miner. (49199),
96905

Life and heroic exploits of Israel Putnam. (33806)

Life and history of General Harrison. 36503

Life and history of Paul Jones. (36553)

Life and imprisonment of Jefferson Davis. (18840)

Life and introduction, by Edward W. Hooker. 32847

Life and its aims. 41007

Life and journal of David Brainerd Edwards [sic]. 21928

Life and journal of Peter Jones. 36591

Life and journal of Rev. Mr. Henry Alline. 924

Life and journal of the Rev'd Christian Newcomer. 54940

Life and journal of the Rev. David Brainerd. 21949, 59608

Life and labors of Rev. Daniel Baker. 2851

Life and labours of Rev. Samuel Worcester. 105315

Life and labors of the Rev. T. H. Gallaudet. (33792)

Life and legends of the Sioux around Fort Snelling. 21685

Life and letters of Catharine M. Sedgwick. (78782)

Life and letters of David Coit Scudder. 78521

Life and letters of Eliza Wharton. 25229

Life and letters of George Mortimer. 2026

Life and letters of James Abraham Garfield. 84339

Life and letters [of John Cotton.] 106052

Life and letters of Joseph Story. 92331

Life and letters of Leonidas L. Hamline. 58382

Life and letters of Miss Eliza Waite. 100970

Life and letters of Mrs. Emily C. Judson. 37373

Life and letters of Nathan Smith. 83654

Life and letters of Rev. James May. 80540

Life and letters of Stephen Olin. 57173

Life and letters of Thomas Kilby Smith. 84512

Life and letters of Washington Irving. 35118

Life and letters of Wilder Dwight. (21567)

Life and letters, together with poetical and miscellaneous pieces. 61066

Life and liberty in America. 43355

Life and love in the Ottawa country. 44802

Life and manners in the United States. 41008

Life, and martyrdom of Abraham Lincoln. 41197

Life and memoirs of Major General Charles Lee. 38903

Life and memorable actions of George Washington. 102470, 102472, 102482, 102486, 102488, 102491

Life and memorials of Daniel Webster. (42795)

Life and military achievements of Tousant Loverture. 42354

Life and military career of Major-General Philip Henry Sheridan. (31163)

Life and military career of Maj. Gen. Scott. 78415

Life and military career of Major-General William Tecumseh Sherman. 31165

Life and military career of "Stonewall" Jackson. (35466)

Life and military career of Stonewall Jackson, from authentic sources. (18840)

Life and military career of Thomas Jonathan Jackson. 374

Life and military services of the late Brigadier General Thomas A. Smyth. 46937

Life and ministry of the Rev. Joseph Morgan Smith. 83364

Life and narrative of William J. Anderson. 1425

Life and naval career of Vice-Admiral David Glascoe Farragut. 31166

Life and observations of Rev. E. F. Newell. 54950

Life and opinions of Benj'n Franklin Butler. (43437)

Life and opinions of Julius Melbourn. 30097, (47418)

Life and opinions of Tristram Shandy. 91355

Life and particular proceedings of the Rev. Mr. George Whitefield. 103634

Life and particular proceedings of the Rev. Mr. George Whitefield, from the time of his going to Crip School. 103634

Life and political opinions of Martin Van Buren. 32515

Life and political writings of John Wilkes. 104004

Life and principles of Abraham Lincoln. 14344

Life and public American speeches of Louis Kossuth. 38269

Life and public services of Abraham Lincoln. (41199)

Life and public services of Abraham Lincoln. 68049

Life and public services of Andrew Jackson. (77238)

Life and public services of Arthur St. Clair. 75022, 84791

Life and public services of Benjamin F. Butler. 63930

Life and public services of Charles W. Fairbanks. 84793

Life and public services of Dr. Lewis F. Lynn. 41335

Life and public services of Gen. Andrew Jackson. 36007

Life and public services of Gen. Lewis Cass. (11353)

Life and public services of Gen. U. S. Grant. 21578

Life and public services of General Ulysses S. Grant. 61369

Life and public services of George Luther Stearns. note after 90885

Life and public services of Henry Clay. By A. H. Carrier. 11049

Life and public services of Henry Clay. By Epes Sargent. 13559, (76955)-(76956)

Life and public services of Henry Clay. [By William G. Brownlow.] 8703

Life and public services of Henry Clay down to 1848. 76957

Life and public services of Hon. Abraham Lincoln, of Illinois. 41198

Life and public services of Hon. Abraham Lincoln. To which is added a biographical sketch of Hon. Hannibal Hamlin. 3724

Life and public services of Hon. Henry Wilson. (74375)

Life and public services of Hon. James Buchanan. 8864

Life and public services of Horatio Seymour. 42962

Life and public services of James Buchanan. 33077

Life and public services of John Quincy Adams, sixth President. 79533

Life and public services of John Quincy Adams. With a eulogy before the Legislature of New York. 316

Life and public services of Lewis Cass. (11354)

Life and public services of Major-General Butler. 9617

Life and public services of Major-General McClellan. 43023

Life and public services of Major-General Meade. 47231

Life and public services of Martin R. Delany. 72849

Life and public services of Millard Fillmore. 3590

Life and public services of Salmon Portland Chase. 77996

Life and public services of Samuel Adams. 95201

Life and public services of Schuyler Colfax. 44863

Life and public services of the Hon. James K. Polk. (63839)

Life and public services of the Hon. James Knox Polk. 31698, (63839)

Life and public services of Winfield Scott. 78416

Life and recollections of John Howland. 92045

Life and recollections of Yankee Hill. (55759)

Life and reflexions of Charles Observator. 74671

Life and reign of Catherine II. 85161, 85168

Life and religious experience of Jarena Lee. 39763

Life and remarkable adventures of Israel R. Potter. 97200

Life and remarkable career of Adah Isaacs Menken. 47865

Life and reminiscences, with early sketches. (28985)

Life and resources in America. (50697)

Life and sayings of Mrs. Partington. 80476

Life and select discourses, 1846. 90988

Life and select discourses of Rev. Samuel H. Stearns. 90987

Life and services as a soldier of Major-General Grant. 28313

Life and services of Captain Philip Beaver. 85347

Life and services of Commodore William Bainbridge. 30526

Life and services of Gen. Anthony Wayne. (50388)

Life and services of Gen. Geo. B. McClellan. note after 43024

Life and services of General Lord Harris. (42719)

Life and services of Gen. U. S. Grant. By H. Coppee. 16702

Life and services of Gen. U. S. Grant, conquerer of the rebellion. (28314)

Life and services of General Winfield Scott. 44368

Life and services of Joel R. Poinsett. 91785

Life and services of Joseph Warren. 26084

Life and services of Major-General John Thomas. 14164

Life and services of Major-General the Marquis de Lafayette. 38568

Life and services of Professor B. B. Edwards. 58625

Life and services of Rev. Lyman Beecher. 788

Life and speeches of Andrew Johnson. 36173

Life and speeches of Henry Clay. 13541

Life and speeches of Henry Clay. Collected and arranged by James Swain. 13542

Life and speeches of Henry Clay . . . delivered mainly in the Senate and House. 13540

Life and speeches of Hon. Charles Warren Fairbanks. 84795

Life and speeches of President Andrew Johnson. 2652, 36174

Life and speeches of the Hon. Henry Clay. 13543

Life and spiritual sufferings of that faithful servant of Christ, Jane Hoskens. 33093

Life and strange surprizing adventures of Robinson Crusoe. (19282), 19285

Life and studies of Benjamin West. 26457

Life and sufferings of Miss Emma Cole. 14285

Life and surprising adventures of Captain Talbot. 94236

Life and surprising adventures of Charles McGhie. 43266

Life and surprising adventures of James Wyatt. 105645

Life and surprising adventures of Mary Anne Talbot. 94233

Life and time. 61186

Life and time of William Brewster. 91107

Life and times of Aaron Burr. 58949

Life and times of Abraham Lincoln. 8158

Life and times of Alexander Hamilton. (77706) 85151-85153, 85155-85159, 85162, 85164

Life and times of Andrew Johnson. 36176

Life and times of Benjamin Franklin. 58950

Life and times of Bertrand du Guesclin. 35743

Life and times of Christopher Carson. (41009)

Life and times of Christopher Columbus. 14663

Life and times of Daniel Boone. Including an account of the early settlement of Kentucky. 6374

Life and times of Daniel Boone, the hunter of Kentucky. 41010

Life and times of Daniel Webster. (42795)

Life and times of David Zeisberger. 19691, 78101

Life and times of Duncan K. McRae. 76384

Life and times of Francis Asbury. 92823

Life and times of Gen. Francis Marion. (50389)

Life and times of Gen. James Robinson. 66769

Life and times of Gen. Sam. Dale. 13192

Life and times of General Washington. 21865

Life and times of George Washington. 77707, 85156, 85159

Life and times of Henry Clay. By Calvin Colton. 13551, 14778

Life and times of Henry Clay. By Samuel M. Smucker. 77708, 85157

Life and times of Hon. Elijah Stansbury. 90369

Life and times of Hon. William Jarvis. 18209

Life and times of John Carroll. 85257

Life and times of John Dickinson. 91785

Life and times of Joseph Warren. (26083)

Life and times of Lewis Cass. 84811

Life and times of Martin Van Buren. 43436

Life and times of N. Edwards. (21984)

Life and times of Nathan Bangs. note after 91480

Life and times of old Billy McConnel. 43088

Life and times of Philip Schuyler. 42120

Life and times of Red-Jacket. 92132, 92137

Life and times of Rev. Allen Wiley. 32540

Life and times of Rev. Elijah Hedding. 13271

Life and times of Rev. William Patton. 42937

Life and times of Robert Emmet. (43697)

Life in an insane asylum. 83501
Life in Brazil. (23313)
Life in California. (10031), 72048
Life in Canada. 50306, 2d note after 98090
Life in death. 58128
Life in earnest. 82359
Life in England and Canada. 90069, 1st note after 94147
Life in Kentucky. 32617
Life in London. 77402
Life in Mexico. 9888-9889
Life in New-England. 71133
Life in New-York. 51206
Life in New York. By the author of "The old white meeting house." 41014, 65536
Life in New York, in doors and out of doors. 41015
Life in prairie land. 23862
Life in rebeldom. 74319
Life in San Francisco and Monterey. 94440
Life in Santo Domingo. 75158
Life in Sing Sing State Prison. 42631
Life in Texas. 64548
Life in the army. 28718
Life in the Argentine republic. 77078
Life in the clearings versus the bush. 50305
Life in the eastern states. 36050
Life in the far west. 37986
Life in the far west. A narrative of adventure. (80730)
Life in the far west. By George Frederic Ruxton. 74502
Life in the far west; or, the comical, quizzical, and tragical adventures of a Hoosier. (30615)
Life in the forcastle. (31121)
Life in the forest. 16607
Life in the itinerancy. 18861, (41017)
Life in the llanos of Venezuela. 58140
Life in the Maine woods. 52161
Life in the mountains. 103053-103054
Life in the new world. 41018, 64545
Life in the northern poor house. 22244, 52755
Life in the old field. 78686
Life in the saddle. 36861
Life in the south. 35469, note after 92160
Life in the south, from the commencement of the war. (35329), note after 36606
Life in the triangle. 50872
Life in the Union army. 41019
Life in the west. Backwood leaves. 41020
Life in the west. . . . By George Rogers. 72648
Life in the west; or, stories of the Mississippi Valley. 47378
Life in the wigwam. 20875
Life in the wilds. 44938
Life in the woods; a narrative of the adventures of a settler's family in Canada. 26841, note after 90307
Life in the woods. By J. T. Headley. 31147
Life in the woods. By W. P. Strickland. 92824
Life in the woods; or, the adventures of Audubon. 59544
Life in town and country. 78783
Life in town, or the Boston spy. 41016
Life in Washington. By J. B. Jones. 36532
Life in Washington. By Mrs. N. P. Lasselle. 39136
Life insurance illustrated. 83581
Life, journals, letters, and addresses of the Rev. Hezekiah Smith. 82723
Life journey from New England congregationalism. 33975

Life, labors, and travels of Elder Charles Bowles. 7075, 40818
Life, last words and dying confession, of Rachel Wall. 101087
Life, last words, and dying speech of Levi Ames. 91810
Life, last words and dying speech of Stephen Smith. 84249
Life let us cherish. 95880
Life, letters and last conversation of John Caldwell Colt. 14761
Life, letters and speeches of Kah-ge-ga-gahbowh. 16717
Life, life work and influence of Zenas Crane. 83328
Life made happy. 77310
Life memories. 67751
Life north and south. 29667
Life of A. H. Conant. (14465)
Life of A. P. Dostie. 68541
Life of a backwoodsman. (41021)
Life of a book agent. 52304
Life of a Negro slave. 3460
Life of a planter. 41018, 64545
Life of a planter in Jamaica, comprehending characteristic sketches of society in the West Indies. (41022)
Life of a planter in Jamaica; with sketches of society and manners. 44640
Life of a political trickster. 41023, 66706
Life of a soldier. 40775
Life of Aaron Burr. 38077
Life of Abraham Lincoln. (41200)
Life of Abraham Lincoln, by Henry J. Raymond. 68048
Life of Abraham Lincoln. By J. G. Holland. 32512
Life of Abraham Lincoln. [By Samuel Mosheim Smucher.] 85153
Life of Abraham Lincoln; for the home circle and Sabbath school. (28414)
Life of Abraham Lincoln; presenting his early history. (3617)
Life of Abraham Lincoln, sixteenth President. 17632
Life of Abraham Lincoln; with a condensed view of his most important speeches. 3616
Life of Adams. 344
Life of Admiral Lord Nelson. 13420
Life of Admiral Sir John Leake. 39522
Life of Admiral Vernon. 99249
Life of Admiral Viscount Exmouth. (57797)
Life of adventure. 69066
Life of Alexander Alexander. 719
Life of Alexander Carson. 50378
Life of Alexander Hamilton. By his son, John C. Hamilton. 30022, 74432
Life of Alexander Hamilton, by John Williams. 104279
Life of Alexander Smith, captain of the island of Pitcairn. (82323)
Life of Ames. 1304
Life of an actress. 92409
Life of an American slave. 24309
Life of an American slave, by himself. 5163
Life of Andrew Jackson, by James Parton. 58951-58952
Life of Andrew Jackson, condensed. 58953
Life of Andrew Jackson, Major General in the service of the United States. 21731-21732, note after (69016)
Life of Andrew Jackson, President of the United States. 84177
Life of Andrew Jackson, President of the United States of America. (13891)

Life of Andrew Jackson, private, military, and civil. 37352

[Life] of Andrew Johnson. 68048

Life of Anthony Caslo. 11339

Life of Archbishop Hughes. (33592)

Life of Archbishop Secker. 64328

Life of Archibald Alexander. 738

Life of Archibald Secker. (11877)

Life of Armalle Nicholas. 62418

Life of Arthur Lee. 39785

Life of Arthur Tappan. note after 94370

Life of Asa G. Sheldon. 80118

Life of Augustus Viscount Keppel. 37597

Life of Bavia. (35607)

Life of Bayard. (81232)

Life of Benedict Joseph Labre. 95232

Life of Benjamin Franklin. . . . B. Franklin's autobiography. 88982

Life of Benjamin Franklin. By O.L. Holley. 32535

Life of Benjamin Franklin, containing the autobiography. (25538), 88984

Life of Benjamin Franklin &c. 88982

Life of Benjamin Franklin. Illustrated by tales, sketches and anecdotes. 25535, (25539), (27907), 41024, 1st note after 105132

Life of Benjamin Franklin, including a sketch of the rise and progress of the war of independence. 25535, 41024, 1st note after 105132

Life of Benjamin Franklin, LL. D. 25531

Life of Benjamin Franklin. Printed by Mr. Spark's [sic] permission. 88983

Life of Benjamin Franklin; with many choice anecdotes. 102488

Life of Benjamin Franklin; with selections from his miscellaneous works. 90312

Life of Benjamin Franklin, written by himself. 25536

Life of Benjamin Franklins. [sic] 25537

Life of Benjamin Silliman. 24465

Life of Bishop Bass, of Massachusetts. 55894

Life of Bishop Bowen, of South Carolina. 55895

Life of Bishop Claggett, of Maryland. 55896

Life of Bishop Freeman, of Arkansas. 55897

Life of Bishop Henshaw, of Rhode Island. 55898

Life of Bishop Provoost, of New York. 55899

Life of Bishop Stewart, of Quebec. 55900

Life of Bishop Wainwright. 55902

Life of Black Hawk. 96082

Life of Boone. (17569)

Life of Brant. 92154

Life of Brissot. (8016), 8030

Life of C. Columbus. 27923

Life of Captain David Perry. 61028

Life of Captain James Cook. 41025

Life of Captain James Cook. . . . By Andrew Kippis. 37954

Life of Captain James Cook. [By Henry Nelson Coleridge.] 14318, 3d note after 102866

Life of Captain John Smith. 81228

Life of Captain Lewis, by T. Jefferson. 856, (40831)

Life of Captain Nathan Hale. 93163

Life of Capt. Oliver Read. 104175

Life of Cardinal Cheverus. 33556

Life of Cardinal Mezzofanti. 74318

Life of Carlotta Du Pont. 2347

Life of Catherine McAuley. 42955

Life of Celestina. 78193

Life of Charles Brockden Brown. 65299

Life of Charles Brockden Brown: together with selections from the rarest of his printed works. (21304)

Life of Charles Follen. 24955

Life of Charles James Fox. (25340)

Life of Charles Lee. note after 88984

Life of Charles Sumner. 30609, 93648

Life of Chauncey Jerome. (36063)

Life of Christ. (34593)

Life of Christopher Columbus. 41026

Life of Christopher Columbus. By Alphonse Lamartine. 38707

Life of Christopher Columbus. By Horace Roscoe St. John. 75241

Life of Christopher Columbus. By John S. C. Abbott. 38

Life of Christopher Columbus. From authentic Spanish and Italian documents. (73273)

Life of Christopher Columbus in short words. 17601

Life of Christopher Columbus, the discoverer of America. 31277

Life of Christopher Ludwick. (62039)

Life of Collin Reynolds. 3443

Life of Col. David Crockett, written by himself. 17570

Life of Col. Ethan Allen. 12820, 88980, 88985

Life of Col. Fremont. (25845)

Life of Colonel James Smith, of Kentucky. 82767

Life of Col. John Charles Fremont. 25839, 77710, 85161

Life of Col. Seth Warner. 12819-12820

Life of Colonel Talbot. (22773)

Life of Columbus. 62957

Life of Columbus, by his son. 13015, (14676)

Life of Commodore Edward Preble. 38003, 65003

Life of Commodore Oliver Hazard Perry. 43422

Life of Commodore Tucker. 80323

Life of Cortes. 16939

Life of Cotton Mather. 46624

Life of Cotton Mather. Abridged. 46626

Life of Count Zinzendorf. 88927

Life of Daniel Boon. 6373

Life of Daniel Boone. 20820

Life of Daniel Webster. 18040

Life of David Brainard. 4671

Life of David Brainerd. Chiefly extracted from his diary. 21928

Life of David Brainerd, missionary to the Indians, with an abridgment of his diary and journal. 21928, 93291

Life of David Brainerd, missionary to the North American Indians. 7344

Life of Deborah Sampson. 44315

Life of Dewitt Clinton. 69654

Life of Dr. B. Franklin. 8410

Life of Dr. Benjamin Franklin, written by himself. 25532

Life of Dr. Benjamin Franklin, written by himself; with essays, humorous, moral, and literary. 25534, 102487

Life of Doctor Benjamin Franklin, written chiefly by himself. 25534, 102487

Life of . . . Dr. Cotton Mather. 36038

Life of Dr. Elisha Kent Kane. 77711, 85162-85163

Life of Don Pedro Aquillo. 99431, note after 100822

Life of Edmund Burke. 5648

Life of Edward John Eyre. 33777

Life of Edward Livingston. 33841

Life of Edward Preble. 74736
Life of Edwin Forrest. 13436A
Life of Edwin Forrest. With reminiscences and personal recollections. 68640
Life of Elbridge Gerry. 2411
Life of Elder Abel Thornton. 95628
Life of Elias Hasket Derby. (19660)
Life of Elisha Tyson. 97650
Life of Eliza Sowers. 88828
Life of Esther De Berdt. 68611
Life of Ezra Stiles. 32582
Life of faith, exemplified and recommended. 4395
Life of faith in death. 44124
Life of faith, on Gal. 2. 19, 20. (17087)
Life of Father De Ravignan. 63998
Life of Father Isaac Jogues. (80023)
Life of Francis Marion. 81229, (81232), 81272
Life of Francis P. Blair, Jr. 42962
Life of Franklin Pierce. 30992
Life of Franklin, written for children. 11647
Life of Frederick William von Steuben. 37098
Life of Fremont. (25845)
Life of General Andrew Jackson. 36008
Life of General Daniel Morgan. 28214
Life of Gen. Edwin Lacey. 50425
Life of Gen. Francis Marion, a celebrated partizan officer. 30044, (30046), 69560, 102472, 102489, note after 102493
Life of Gen. Francis Marion: also, lives of Generals Moultrie and Pickens. 30681
Life of Gen. Francis Marion. . . . By Brig. Gen. P. Horry. 33045
Life of Gen. Frank Pierce. (31511)
Life of Gen. Franklin Pierce. 3723
Life of General George Washington. 101851
Life of General George Washington, by John Kingston. 37899, 101842
Life of General George Washington, late President of the United States of America. (16915), 101842
Life of General Greene. 10872
Life of General Israel Putnam. (32536)
Life of Gen. Jacob Brown. 41027
Life of General James Wolfe. 58057, 104989
Life of General Lafayette. 38568
Life of General Lafayette. . . . By P. C. Headley. (31167)
Life of General Lafayette. . . . by William Cutter. 18200
Life of General Lewis Cass: comprising an account of his military services. 11355
Life of General Lewis Cass, with his letters and speeches. 11356, 31699
Life of General Marion, and anecdotes illustrative to his character. (44595)
Life of General M. D. Stanley. 90315
Life of Gen. Narciso Lopez. (41994)
Life of Gen. P. H. Sheridan. (39038)
Life of General Sam. Houston. 33192
Life of General Scott. 78417
Life of General Thomas Sumter. 30684
Life of General Tom Thumb. 92733
Life of Gen'l. U. S. Grant. 90378
Life of General Ulysses S. Grant. 57216
Life of General W. A. Bowles. 7083
Life of General Washington. By John N. Norton. 55903
Life of Gen. Washington, Commander in Chief of the American army. 101841
Life of General Washington late President of the United States. (13318)
Life of General William Henry Harrison. (30587)
Life of Gen. William T. Sherman. 18926

Life of General Winfield Scott. By Edward D. Mansfield. 44367, 78410
Life of General Winfield Scott, Commander of the United States Army. 78410
Life of General Winfield Scott, embracing his campaign in Mexico. 44368
Life of Gen. Zachary Taylor. 15896, 26099
Life of Gen. Zachary Taylor, Whig candidate for the Presidency. 64098
Life of George B. McClellan. 19450
Life of George Fox. (35761)
Life of George Frederick Cooke. 16307
Life of George Lord Anson. 3665, 101175
Life of George M. Troup. 30310
Life of George Mifflin Dallas. 18320
Life of George P. Barker. 8790
Life of George Peabody. 30160
Life of George Washington. 1166, 101778, note after 104564
Life of George Washington. By Edward Everett. 23255
Life of George Washington. By J. T. Headley. 31154
Life of George Washington. By Jared Sparks. 88986-88988, 101747, 101767
Life of George Washington. By Washington Irving. 35189
Life of George Washington, Commander-in-Chief of the American armies. 88989
Life of George Washington, Commander in Chief of the American army. 3097
Life of George Washington, Commander in Chief of the American forces. 44787-44788, note after 101528, 101546, 101546A, 101710, 101843
Life of George Washington, Commander in Chief of the armes. (16915), 101842
Life of George Washington, Commander in Chief of the armies of the United States of America. 67695
Life of George Washington, first President of the United States. 2081
Life of George Washington. First President of the United States, and Commander in Chief of the armies. 97202, 101779, note after 101843
Life of George Washington. Illustrated by tales, sketches and anecdotes. 101844
Life of George Washington in Latin prose. 27551
Life of George Washington, late President and Commander in Chief of the armies. 16912-16914
Life of George Washington, late President of the United States of America. 101842
Life of George Washington; with curious anecdotes. 102486
Life of George Washington, written for children. 11646
Life of George Washington. Written for the American Sunday-School Union. 27502, 1st note after 99504, 101840, 101845, 101888
Life of George Washington. Written for the use of schools. 44790
Life of . . . George Whitefield. 103635
Life of Gerard Hallock. 29911
Life of Gilbert Motier de La Layette, a Marquis of France. 43345
Life of Gilbert Motier Lafayette. 1146
Life of God in the soul of man. 78440, (78444)-(78447)
Life of Godfried Swan. 94001
Life of Gould, an ex-man-of-war's-man. 28124
[Life of Governor Eaton.] 1095
Life of Greeley. A series of wonderful facts and startling revelations. 73285

Life of Greeley. . . . written in 9½ minutes. 73284

Life of Greene. (39750)

Life of Gregory Lopez, a hermit in America. 23565, 42586

Life of Gregory Lopez: written originally in Spanish. 102682

Life of Gouverneur Morris. 88990

Life of Hannah Weston. 70343

Life of Harman Blennerhassett. 74878

Life of Harriet Beecher Stowe. 92457, 92471

Life . . . [of Harriet Newell.] 54962

Life of Henry Bidleman Bascom. 31342

Life of Henry Clay. [By Calvin Colton.] 14775

Life of Henry Clay. By N. Sargent. 77028

Life of Henry Clay, the statesman and patriot. (13558)

Life of Hernan Cortes. 97163-97164

Life of Hiokatoo, and Ebenezer Allen. 78680-78681

Life of his brother, the Rev. Mr. John Tennent. 94706

Life of His Excellency Sir William Phips. 46455

Life of his father [by H. A. S. Dearborn.] 19077

Life of Hon. Nathaniel Chipman. (12818)

Life of Hon. Neal Dow. 13793

Life of Horace Greeley. (58954)

Life of Horace Mann. (44334)

Life of Increase Mather. (9868)

Life of Irving. 35218

Life of Israel Adams. 217

Life of Israel Putnam. 24022, 94058

Life of Israel Putnam, Major-General in the army. 18199

Life of its hero. 41721, 2d note after 94082

Life of J. Myrick. 51649

Life of J. P. Brissot. 8022

Life of Jacob Gruber. 92820

Life of James Aitken, commonly called John the Painter. 31837

Life of James Aitken, commonly called John the Painter, an incendiary. 31836

Life of James Fisk, Jr., a full and accurate narrative of his career. 90078

Life of James Fisk, Jr., being a full and accurate narrative. 24525, 90077

Life of James Knox Polk. 36006

Life of James Mars. 44710

Life of James Otis. 97408

Life of James Sullivan. 1344

Life of James W. Grimes. 75849

Life of James W. Jackson. 35431

Life of James Williams. 65946

Life of Jedidiah Morse. 89738

Life of Jefferson Davis, from authentic sources. 18839, note after 88114

Life of Jefferson Davis, with a secret history of the Southern Confederacy. 63872

Life of Jehudi Ashmun. (29303)

Life of Jeroboam O. Beanchamp. 41028

Life of Jeremy Belknap. 4441

Life of John Adams. 183, 253

Life of John Arndt. (50843)

Life of John Brainerd, brother of David Brainerd. 7353

Life of John Bright. (43269)

Life of John C. Calhoun. 9954

Life of John Caldwell Calhoun. 36009

Life of John Carter. 49104

Life of John Collins Warren. 101460, note after 101476

Life of John Cotton. 41599, 43061

Life [of John Croker.] 9416

Life of John Eliot. 338, 41599

Life of John Eliot, the apostle to the Indians. By Convers Francis. 25439

Life of John Eliot, the apostle to the Indians; including notices of the principal attempts to propagate Christianity. (22167), 104657

Life of John H. W. Hawkins. 30960

Life of John Heckewelder. 73081

Life of John Howes. 31702

Life of John Jacob Astor. [By H. C. Goodwin.] 27942

Life of John Jacob Astor. To which is appended, a copy of his last will. 58956

Life of John Jay; with selections from his correspondence and miscellaneous papers. 35861

Life of John Ledyard. 88991

Life of John Locke. 37825

Life of John P. Crozer. 82797

Life of John Randolph of Roanoke. (26670)

Life of John Southack. 88222

Life of John Stark. 23256

Life of John Tyler. 30779

Life of John Warren. 101460

Life of John Wesley. 6915

Life of Joice Heth. 31620

Life of Jonathan Edwards. (49054)

Life of Jonathan Trumbull. 93164

Life of Joseph. 83541

Life of Joseph Brant—Thayendanegea. 92132, 92139-92144

Life of Joseph Priestley. 16918

Life of Joseph Reed. 68548

Life of Joseph Ritner. 71583, 103476A

Life of Joseph the Prophet. 83302

Life of Josiah Henson. 31432, note after 92624

Life of Josiah Quincy of Massachusetts. 67186

Life of Judge C————. 104176

Life of Lafayette. . . . for children. 11645

Life of Lafayette, including an account of the memorable revolution. 38573

Life of Las Casas. (31278), 31280

Life of Leonard Calvert. 9364

Life of Lewis Cass. 11356, 31699

Life of Lieut. Gen. T. J. Jackson. (35467)

Life of Lieut. Gen. Thomas J. Jackson. 18254

Life of Lieut.-Gen. Whitelocke. 103676

Life of Lincoln. 14344

Life of Lord Horatio Nelson. 52312

Life of Lord Timothy Dexter. 38079

Life of Lord Viscount Nelson. 13023

Life of Luther C. Ladd. (38518)

Life of Madame de la Peitrie. 59594, 98171

Life of Maj.-Gen. Geo. B. McClellan. 39874, 99434

Life of Maj.-Gen. Geo. B. McClellan. Including campaign in Mexico, etc. note after 43024

Life of Major General Henry Lee. 30684

Life of Major General James Jackson. 12152

Life of Major-Gen. John C. Fremont. 43842

Life of Major-General Peter Muhlenberg. (51250)

Life of Major General Robert C. Schenck. 77584

Life of Major-General William Henry Harrison, comprising a brief account. 30585

Life of Major General William Henry Harrison, ninth President of the United States of America. 50140

Life of Major General Zachary Taylor, by H. Montgomery. 50141

Life of Major-General Zachary Taylor, the Whig nominee. 93724

Life of Major General Zachary Taylor; with notices of the war in New-Mexico. 26042

Life of Major-General Zachary Taylor, with sketches of the lives and heroic acts of Maj. Ringgold. 64748

Life of Major J. G. Semple Lisle. 41421

Life of Major John Andre. 77044

Life of Ma-ka-tai-me-shi-kia-kaiak. 5675, 39646, note after (64532)

Life of man on earth. 97737

Life of Martin Van Buren, by Thomas M'Elhiney. 43220

Life of Martin Van Buren, heir-apparent to the "government." 17567

Life of Mary Jamison. 105555

Life of Mary Russell Mitford. 49753

Life of Maximilian I. 29775

Life of Michael Adrian de Ruyter. 74511

Life of Michael Martin. 44902-44903, 2d note after 101000

Life of Michael Powers. (64799)

Life of Millard Filmore. [sic] 62686

Life of Millard Fillmore, and Andrew Jackson Donelson. 24333

Life of Mr. David Brainerd. (7340), 85994

Life of Mr. R. Baxter. 4014

Life of Mr. Richard Savage. 36298

Life of Mr. Stearne. 91341

Life of Mr. Thomas Beard. 4127

Life of Mr. Thomas Dudley. 46385

Life of Mr. Thomas Hooker. 46460

Life of Mrs. Ann H. Judson. 38153

Life [of Mrs. Aphra Behn.] 4370

Life of Mrs. Eliza A. Seton. 103358

Life of Mrs. Ellen Stewart. 91677

Life of Mrs. Hannah Childs. 12732

Life of Mrs. M. K. Everts. 23296

Life of Mrs. Virginia Hale Hoffman. 17929

Life of Monroe Edwards. (21980)

Life of Nathanael Greene, Major-General in the army of the revolution. By George Washington Greene. 28599

Life of Nathanael Greene, Major-General in the army of the revolution. Edited by W. Gilmore Simms. 81230

Life of Nathaniel Bacon. 101411

Life of Nathaniel T. Otis. 30009

Life of Nicholas Lewis Count Zinzendorf. 88932

Life of Nicolaus I., King of Paraguay. 55245, 92200

Life of North American insects. 35526-35527

Life of Olaudah Equiano. 98663

Life of Oliver Hazard Perry. 55320

Life of Oliver P. Morton. 84793

Life of Orson C. Warner. 101442

Life of Otis. 5220

Life of P. T. Barnum. 3564

Life of Patrick Henry. By William Wirt. 104877, 104882

Life of Patrick Henry, of Virginia. 2082

Life of Paul Cuffee. 32151

Life of Paul Jones. By Alexander Slidell Mackenzie. 43423

Life of Paul Jones, from original documents. 36554, 80335

Life of Pauline Cushman. 77089

Life of Peter Hanly. 30229

Life of Philander Chase. 83479

Life [of Philip Henry Gosse.] 28064

Life of Philip, the Indian chief. 77245

Life of piety resolv'd upon. (46386)

Life of Pizarro. 31279

Life of Pontiac, the chief of the Ottawas. 64017

Life of Pontiac the conspirator. 22296

Life of President Edwards. 21526

Life of Prince Henry of Portugal. 44069

Life of Raleigh. 67550, 67599

Life of Rear-Admiral John Paul Jones. (36557)

Life of Rear-Admiral Paul Jones. By Edward Hamilton. 30007

Life of Red Jacket. 92154

Life of Rev. Charles W. Jacobs. 41406

Life of Rev. Charles Wesley. 35465

Life of Rev. Freeborn Garrettson. 3167

Life of Rev. George Whitefield. 54949

Life of Rev. Jeremiah Hallock. 105751

Life of Rev. John Clark. 29737

Life of Rev. Joseph Emerson. 22451

Life of Rev. Joseph Snelling. 85416

Life of Rev. Michael Schlatter. (30285)

Life of Rev. Samuel H. Stearns. 90988

Life of Rev. Thomas Coke. 20932

Life of Rev. Thomas Shepard. (675), 41599

Life of Rev. William Summers. 34820

Life of Richard, Earl Howe. By George Mason. 45440

Life of Richard, Earl Howe, K. G. 3666

Life of Right Reverend Patrick Phelan. (61352)

Life of Robert A. Roberts. 26093

Life of Robert Fulton, by his friend Cadwallader D. Colden. 14277-14278, 14281, 21112

Life of Robert Fulton, one of the most distinguished inventors. (69100)

Life of Robert Morris. [By James Mease.] 47270

Life of Robert Morris, the great financier. 50869

Life of Robert Morris. . . . With extracts from his speeches. 28100

Life of Robert Owen. [By Frederic Adolphus Packard.] 58110

Life of Robert Owen. Written by himself. 58015

Life of Robert Stephenson. 35873

Life of Roger Williams, founder of the state of Rhode Island. 26517

Life of Roger Williams, the earliest legislator and true champion for a full and absolute liberty. 22369

Life of Rutherford Birchard Hayes. 84789

Life of Saint Angela Merici, of Bresci. (80023)

Life of Sam Houston (of Texas). (33191)

Life of Samuel Adams. 102599A

Life of Samuel Comstock. 15078

Life of Samuel F. B. Morse. 65537

Life of Samuel Green. (28556)

Life of Samuel Johnson. 11879

Life of Samuel Kirkland. 42143

Life of Samuel Miller. 49065

Life of Samuel Tucker. (80311)

Life of Samuel Tully. 97442

Life of Schuyler Colfax. 50326

Life of Sebastian Rale. 25439

Life of Silas Wright. (36010)

Life of Simon Bolivar. 39090

Life of Sir F. Drake. 18773

Life of Sir Henry Vane. 98041, 98046

Life of Sir James Fitzjames Stephen. 1st note after 91235, 2d note after 102829

Life of Sir Thomas Bernard, Baronet. 2826

Life of Sir Walter Raleigh. Based on contemporary documents. 21919

Life of Sir Walter Raleigh. [By John Shirley.] 67560, 67568

Life of Sir Walter Raleigh. 1552-1618.
75244
Life of Sir Walter Raleigh: founded on au-
thentic and original documents. 97659
Life of Sir Walter Raleigh, from his birth
to his death. (67570)
Life of Sir Walter Raleigh, Knt. 11630
Life of Sir William Johnson. 92154
Life of Sir William Pepperrell. 58921
Life of Sir William Phips. 9926-9927
Life of Skunk Peter Porcupine. 64164
Life of slavery, or the life of the nation?
Mass meeting of the citizens of New
York. 41029
Life of slavery, or the life of the nation?
Speech of Hon. Carl Schurz. 78034
Life of Stephen A. Douglas. By James W.
Sheahan. 80032
Life of Stephen A. Douglas: to which are
added his speeches and reports. 24767
Life of Stephen A. Douglas, U. S. Senator
from Illinois. (20695)
Life of Stephen A. Douglas . . . with selec-
tions from his speeches and reports.
20694
Life of Stephen Branch. 7386
Life of Stephen Decatur. 43424
Life of Stonewall Jackson. 18492, 2d note
after 100578
Life of Sumner Lincoln Fairfield. 23693
Life of T. Dudley. 19051
Life of T. H. Bowden Lambirth. 38743
Life of Te-cum-seh, a memoir. 97449
Life of Tecumseh and his brother the prophet.
20811
Life of Tecumseh, the Shawnee chief. 22297
Life of the great circumnavigator Captain
Cook. (34887)
Life of the Archbishop of Cambray. 86489-
86490
Life of the author [i. e. James Meikle.] 47402
Life of the author [i. e. John Cleveland.]
13662
Life of the author [i. e. Laurence Stearne.]
91355
Life of the author [i. e. Timothy Dexter.]
19906
Life of the author [i. e. Timothy Dwight.]
21566
Life of the author [i. e. Daniel Neal] and
account of his writings. (52144)
Life of the author [i. e. Adam Smith], and
introductory discourse. 82304
Life of the author. By Benjamin Green.
28509
Life of the author [i. e. William Robertson]
by Bishop Gleig. 72006
Life of the author [i. e. M. LaBorde], by
J. L. Reynolds. 87979
Life of the author [i. e. Samuel Shaw], by
Joshua Quincy. 79959
Life of the author [i. e. Daniel Neal], by
Joshua Tolmin. 52145
Life of the author [i. e. Sir Walter Raleigh ,]
newly compil'd. 67560
Life of the author [i. e. George M. Horton],
written by himself. 33070
Life of the late Gen. William Eaton. 65083
Life of the Blessed Sebastian of Apparizio.
105727A
Life of the Boston bard. 14186
Life of the Botocudo chieftan. 11724
[Life] of the brave General Montgomery.
101841
Life of the celebrated Munroe Edwards.
95142

Life of the celebrated Sir Francis Drake.
20832
Life of the Chevalier Bayard. 81231
Life of the Earl of Chatham. 27676
Life of the ever-memorable Mr. John Hales.
(41726)
Life of the great Columbus. 35649
Life of the great philosopher, [i. e. Benjamin
Franklin] written by himself. 25568
Life of the Hon. Edward Macon. 17031
Life of the Hon. James Buchanan. 8864
Life of the Hon. Jeremiah Smith. 50711
Life of the Honourable William Tilghman.
27712, 95821, 95822
Life of the late Doctor Benjamin Franklin.
25533
Life of the late Earl of Chesterfield. 90224
Life of the late Lord Bishop of Peterborough.
(37449)
Life of the late Reverend and Learned Dr.
Cotton Mather. 36038, 46625
Life of the late Rev. John Wesley. 103664,
103665
Life of the late Reverend, learned and pious
Mr. Jonathan Edwards. 21948, 21950
Life of the late Rev. Mr. David Brainerd.
102653
Life of the Marquis De La Fayette. 101139
Life of the most noble, the Marquis Corn-
wallis. 16814
Life of the Most Reverend John Hughes.
(30810)
Life of the Most Rev. M. J. Spalding. 88885
Life of the pilgrim Joseph Thomas. 95428
Life of the prophet Daniel. 91182
Life of the renowned John Eliot. (46561)
Life of the renowned Mr. John Eliot. 47151-
47152
Life of the Reverend & excellent, Jonathan
Mitchel. 46297
Life of the Rev. Ashbel Green. 28503
Life of the Rev. David Brainerd. 21951
Life of the Rev. David Brainerd, missionary
to the North American Indians. 64945
Life of the Reverend Devereux Jarratt. 35789
Life of the Rev. Dr. Jarratt, &c. 14306
Life of the Rev. Elisha Macurdy. 22261
Life of the Rev. Gregory T. Bedell. 97625
Life of the Rev. George Whitefield. 30608
Life of the Rev. John Eliot. 46384
Life of the Rev. John Murray. 103803
Life of the Rev. John Wesley. 102149
Life of the Rev. John Wesley, A. M. 102150
Life of the Rev. John Wesley; . . . compre-
hending an account of the great revival
of religion. 50382
Life of the Rev. John Wesley, M. A. 14252,
14338, 103663
Life of the Rev. Joseph Grafton. 84049
Life of the Rev. Mr. John Wesley. 102683
Life of the Rev. Orange Scott. (46966)
Life of the Rev. Robert B. Roberts. 22256
Life of the Rev. Robert Baird. 2783
Life of the Rev. William Marsh. 44725
Life of the Rev. William Squire. 35998
Life of the Rev. William Tennent. 6854,
94719
Life of the Right Honourable Edmund Burke.
65695
Life of the Right Honourable Horatio Lord
Vis-count Nelson. 30563
Life of the Rt. Rev. William White. 55901
Life of the valiant & learned Sir Walter
Raleigh. 67560, (67567), 67569
Life of the Venerable Father Claver. 24747

Life of the very Reverend and learned Cotton Mather. 36039, 46625, 46799
Life of Thomas Eddy. 38080
Life of Thomas Hooker. (32814), 41599
Life of Thomas J. Jackson. 35468
Life of Thomas Jefferson, author of the Declaration of independence. 41350
Life of Thomas Jefferson. By Henry S. Randall. (67785)
Life of Thomas Jefferson. By Samuel M. Schmucker. 85160
Life of Thomas Jefferson, Esq., late ex-President of the United States. 42805
Life of Thomas Jefferson Fisher. 89360
Life of Thomas Jefferson, third President of the United States. 97302
Life of Thomas Jefferson. With a portrait, and a parallel. 35931
Life of Thomas Jefferson, with selections from the most valuable portions. (68117)
Life of Thomas Morris. 50799
Life of Thomas Pain [sic], the author of the Rights of man. 11763, 57168-57169
Life of Thomas Paine, author of "Common sense," "Rights of man," "Age of reason," etc., etc. 98336, 98338
Life of Thomas Paine, author of Common sense, Rights of man, Age of reason, Letter to the addressers, &c., &c. (71242)
Life of Thomas Paine, author of Common sense . . . with a dedication to George Clinton. 12379, (75956)
Life of Thomas Paine. By the author of The religion of science. 5819
Life of Thomas Paine, by the editor of the "National. 32665, 58250
Life of Thomas Paine, interspersed with remarks and reflections. 13894, 14003
Life of Thomas Paine, written purposely to bind with his writings. 10921
Life of Thomas Story abridged by J. Kendall. 92326
Life of Thomas Story, carefully abridged. 37367, 92325
Life of Timothy Dexter. 38078
Life of Timothy Dwight. 89744
Life of Timothy Pickering. 62642, 98046
Life of To-ho-ra-gwa-ne-gen. 104213
Life of Toussaint Louverture. 42353
Life of Toussaint Louverture, chief of the French rebels in St. Domingo. 21031
Life of Toussaint Louverture, the black prince. (21441)
Life of Toussaint l'Ouverture, the Negro patriot of Hayti. 4125
Life of travels and researches in North America and South Europe. 67455
Life of Ulysses S. Grant. By H. C. Deming. 19482
Life of Ulysses S. Grant, General in Chief, U. S. A. (31155)
Life of Ulysses S. Grant, General of the Armies of the United States. 18397
Life of Ulysses S. Grant: his boyhood, campaigns, and services. 17348
Life of Ulysses S. Grant, President of the United States. 81407
Life of Van Amburgh. 102172
Life of Venerable Sister Mary of Jesus. 105733
Life of Washington. 101846
Life of Washington, and history of the American revolution. 101846A

Life of Washington. By James K. Paulding. 59205
Life of Washington [by Thomas Lowndes Snead.] 85374
Life of Washington in Latin prose. 101879
Life of Washington, in the form of an autobiography. 98041, 3d note after 101723
[Life of Washington in the Polish language.] 55265
Life of Washington the great. 102485
Life of Wesley; and rise and progress of Methodism. 88560
Life of Wesley; and the rise and progress of Methodism. 88557-88559, 88561-88562
Life of Wilber Fisk. 32483
Life of William Alexander, Earl of Stirling. 21113
Life of William Cobbett. 13893
Life of William Ellery. 11896
Life of William Gutherie. 21305
Life of William Henry Harrison of Ohio. 30589, 31783
Life of William Henry Harrison, (of Ohio,) the people's candidate. 30586, 35422
Life of William H. Seward, including his most famous speeches. 79598
Life of William H. Seward; with selections from his works. 2823, 79597
Life of William late Earl of Mansfield. 29902
Life of William M. Richardson. 71097
Life of William Penn, abridged and adapted to the use of young persons. 33611
Life of William Penn, and other poems. 102454
Life of William Penn, compiled from the usual authorities. 33612
Life of William Penn, the founder of Pennsylvania. 59741
Life of William Penn, the settler of Pennsylvania. 102490
Life of William Penn, to which is added, his reflections and maxims. (20893)
Life of William Penn, with a sketch of the early history of Pennsylvania. 26040
Life of William Penn; with numerous illustrative anecdotes. 59750
Life of William Penn: with selections from his correspondence and autobiography. 35762
Life of William Pinkney. 62971
Life of William Pitt. 63098
Life of William Plumer. 63453
Life of William Poole. 64038
Life of William T. Porter. 7994
Life of William Scoresby. (35452), 78184
Life of William Vans, a native of Massachusetts. 98556
Life of William Vans, written by himself. 98557
Life of William Wilberforce by his sons. 103949-103950
Life of William Wilberforce by the Rev. W. Wilberforce. 103496
Life of William Woodbridge. 38922
Life of Winfield Scott. 31156
Life of Zachary Taylor. 62686
Life on a farm. 39722
Life on the border. 50132
Life on the lakes. 38923, 57814, note after 95662
Life on the ocean. (41513)
Life on the plains and among the diggings. 19348
Life on the plains of the Pacific. 31953
Life on the plains; or, scenes and adventures in an overland journey to California. (10032), 41030

Life on the prairie. 71730
Life on the Rappahannock. 59445, 64092
Life on the wave. 82121
Life pictures: a poem. 64751
Life-poem, and other poems. 37682
Life, remains and letters of David Branerd. 7346
Life-Saving Benevolent Association, New York. see New York Life-Saving Benevolent Association.
Life-saving signal book. 72676
Life scenes as they are. 46198
Life scenes from mission fields. 50349
Life scenes in New York illustrated. 72182
Life scenes in Utah. (6052), (50750)
Life, services, and character of Edward Everett. 22327
Life, services, and military career of the noble trio, Ellsworth, Lyon and Baker. 59106
Life sketches and characters of curious and odd characters. 41032
Life sketches of executive officers and members of the Legislature. 41031
Life sketches of the state officers, senators, and members of the Assembly of the state of New York, in 1868. (30397)
Life sketches of the state officers, senators, and members of the Assembly of the state of New York, in 1867. 30396
Life, speeches and memorials of Daniel Webster. 77712, 85154, 85164-85165
Life, speeches, and public services of Abraham Lincoln. (41200)
Life, speeches, and public services of John Bell. 4462
Life, speeches and services of Andrew Johnson. 36175
Life, strange voyages, and uncommon adventures of Ambrose Gwinett. (29384)
Life swiftly passing and quickly ending. (46387)
Life the sure reward of grace to the penitent. 72691
Life thoughts gathered from the extemporaneous discourses of Henry Ward Beecher. 4316
Life, times, and correspondence of James Manning. (29224)
Life travels and books of Alexander Von Humboldt. 91937
Life, travels and Gospel labors of Eld Joseph Thomas. 95428
Life, travels, and opinions of Benjamin Lundy. (42693)
Life, travels, exploits, frauds, and robberies of Charles Speckman. 89132
Life, travels, voyages, and daring engagements of Paul Jones. 36555-36556, 104464
Life, trial, and confession of Simeon L. Crockett. (17579), note after 100660
Life, trial, and confessions of Samuel H. Calhoun. 28536
Life, trial, and execution of Captain John Brown. 8519
Life, trial, condemnation, and dying address, of the three Thayers! 95267-95270
Life, trial, condemnation, and dying address of the three Thayers!! 95271
Life, trial, confession and execution of the pirate and murderer Albert W. Hicks. 31709
Life, voyages, and discoveries of Christopher Columbus. 14664, 41033
Life, voyages, and discoveries of Captain James Cook. (41034)

Life, voyages, and exploits of Admiral Sir Francis Drake. (3667)
Life, voyages, and sea battles of that celebrated pirate Commodore Paul Jones. 41035
Life, voyages and travels of Capt. John Myers. (51631)
Life, voyages, travels, and wonderful adventures of Captain Winterfield. 104835
Life-wake or the fine Arkansas gentleman who died before his time. (41036), 62816
Life with the Esquimaux. 29739
Life with the Forty-Ninth Massachusetts Volunteers. 36152
Life with the Union armies. (38177)
Life without and life within. 57816
Life, wonderful adventures, and miraculous escapes of Miss Eliza Allen. 5411
Life work. A farewell sermon. 63353
Life-work of Mary M. Maynard. 13280
Life work of the teacher. 90989
Life-work of Theodore Parker. 54993
Life, writings, and character of Edward Robinson. 82708
Life's perilous places. 90300
Life's revenge. 92409
Life's work finished. 82209
Ligan: a collection of tales and essays. 20996
Ligeiro escobo da viagem de inauguracao ao Rio San Francisco. 71479
Ligeras indicaciones sobre la usurpacion de Tejas. 95100
Ligeret, -------. 27511 see also France. Corps Legislatiff. Conseil des Anciens. Commission.
Ligero bosquejo de la actual situacion en Mejico. 48514
Ligero extracto de las causas que implieron. 22114
Liggins, Joseph. 41037
Light, George W. (41038)
Light, Johann. 41039
Light, William. 33626
Light against light in three ranks! 70921
Light and dark of the rebellion. 40225
Light and darkness. 41040
Light and liberty. 82973
Light and shades of missionary life. 63039
Light and the truth of slavery. Aaron's history. (82009)-82010
Light and truth, collected from the Holy Bible. 40845
Light and truth, discovering and detecting sophistry and deceit. 24278
Light and truth, from ancient and sacred history. 40844
Light and truth of slavery. 41041
Light and truth triumphant. 103657
Light appearing more and more towards the perfect day. note before 92797, 103688-103689
Light Artillery, Boston. see Massachusetts. Militia. Light Artillery, Boston.
Light Artillery Corps, Philadelphia. see Pennsylvania. Militia. Light Artillery Corps, Philadelphia.
Light for young America. 41042
Light from the spirit world. 30088
Light-house guide. 49112
Light-houses, beacons, and floating lights of the United States, for 1838. (41045)
Light houses, beacons, and floating lights of the United States, in operation. 63408
Light houses . . . in operation on the 1st of July, 1842. 63409

Lima. Consulado. see Lima. Tribunal del
Consulado, y Junta General de Comer-
cio.
Lima. Corte Superior de Justicia. 67634
Lima. Gremios de Abastos. 36824
Lima. Iglesia Metropolitana. 60856
Lima. Junta General de Comercio. see Lima.
Tribunal del Consulado, y Junta General
de Comercio.
Lima. Maestrescolia. (47931)
Lima. Monasterio de la Encarnacion. 41124
Lima. Monasterio de Santa Clara. 76749
Lima. Ninos Expositos. 41101
Lima. Prison Penitenciaria. 59331
Lima. Religiosas. petitioners see Lima
(Archdiocese) petitioners
Lima. Seminario de Santa Toribio. 76803
Lima. Sociedad Academica de Amantes. see
Sociedad Academica de Amantes de Lima.
Lima. Sociedad de Beneficencia Publica. see
Lima. Sociedad de Beneficencia Publica. see
Sociedad de Beneficencia Publica de
Lima.
Lima. Tribunal de Cruzada. 97671
Lima. Tribunal de Quentas. Contador. 86377
see also Robina, Juan Joseph. defen-
dant
Lima. Tribunal del Consulado, y Junta
General de Comercio. 41134, 57480,
66104, 73866, 86597, 98931 see also
Bocangel y Vnzueta, Gabriel. Cosio,
Pedro. Costa, Thomas de.
Lima. Tribunal del Consulado, y Junta Gen-
eral de Comercio. petitioners 41119,
61136
Lima. Universidad de San Marcos. 29145,
(35821), 41078-(41079), 41091, 41122,
44423, (58829), 60856, 61151, 76154-
(76155), 97015, 98335, 99659
Lima. Universidad de San Marcos. Acto
Literario. 41103
Lima. Universidad de San Marcos. Charter.
(41092)-(41093)
Lima. Universidad de San Marcos. Rector.
60854, 98335 see also Boza y Garzes,
Antonio. Olmedo y Sossa, Isidoro de.
Lima (Archdiocese) (29131), 30415, 50070
see also Lima (Ecclesiastical Province)
Lima (Archdiocese) petitioners (69983)
Lima (Archdiocese) Archbishop [ca. 1754]
16071
Lima (Archdiocese) Archbishop [ca. 1837]
41104
Lima (Archdiocese) Archbishop [ca. 1865]
41107
Lima (Archdiocese) Archbishop [ca. 1866]
41095
Lima (Archdiocese) Archbishop (Arrieta)
99499 see also Arrieta, Francisco
Sales de, Abp.
Lima (Archdiocese) Archbishop (Barroetta y
Angel) (41115) see also Barroetta y
Angel, Antonio de, Abp.
Lima (Archdiocese) Archbishop (Guerrero)
16065, 16071 see also Guerrero,
Bartholome Lobo, Abp.
Lima (Archdiocese) Archbishop (Linan y Cis-
neros) 56748 see also Linan y Cis-
neros, Melchor de, Abp.
Lima (Archdiocese) Archbishop (Maria de
Heras) 44541 see also Maria de Heras,
Bartolome, Abp.
Lima (Archdiocese) Archbishop (Mogroveius)
30415, 50070 see also Mogroveius,
Toribius Alphonsius, Saint, Abp.

Lima (Archdiocese) Archbishop (Ugarte)
16067, 16071 see also Ugarte, Fernando
Arias de, Abp.
Lima (Archdiocese) Archbishop (Villagomez)
99633-99637 see also Villagomez,
Pedro de.
Lima (Archdiocese) Synod. (14367), 30415
Lima (Archdiocese) Synod. 1613. 16065,
16071
Lima (Archdiocese) Synod, 1636. 16067, 16071
29131, note after 41711
Lima (Archdiocese) Synod, 1637. 16067, 16071
Lima (Archdiocese) Synod, 1754. (29131),
note after 41711
Lima (Ecclesiastical Provice) 61074 see
also Lima (Archdiocese)
Lima (Ecclesiastical Province) Council, 1567.
41088, 93584
Lima (Ecclesiastical Province) Council, 1583.
(14367), (15452), 20420, 30415, 41086-
41088, 57101, 67161, 67163, 68461,
93584
Lima (Ecclesiastical Province) Council, 1591.
(14367)
Lima (Ecclesiastical Province) Council, 1601.
(14367), 42669, 98324-98325
Lima (Ecclesiastical Province) Council, 1621.
61074
Lima (Ecclesiastical Province) Council, 1684.
41089
Lima (Ecclesiastical Province) Council,
1748. 61074
Lima (Ecclesiastical Province) Council, 1772.
61074
Lima (Ecclesiastical Province) Council, 1776.
61074
Lima, N. Y. Geneseee College. see Genesee
College, Lima, N. Y.
Lima, N. Y. Genesee Wesleyan Seminary.
see Genesee Wesleyan Seminary, Lima,
N. Y.
Lima: a visit to the capital and provinces of
modern Peru. 44613
Lima contra el espejo de mi tierra. (41116)
Lima, equisses historiques. 26117
Lima fundada. 60852, 63182
Lima inexpugnable. 60853
Lima limata conciliis. 30415
Lima por dentro y fuera. 2503-2504, 41117,
94860-94861
Lima. Sketches of the capital of Peru. 26118
Lima trivmphante. 60854
Limantour, --------, fl. 1863. 41136
Limantour, Jose Yves, 1854- claimant 104625
Limare, ---------- Camus de. see Camus
de Limare, ----------.
Lime, N. H. Citizens. 52791, note after
98998
Limerick, Thomas Dongan, Earl of, 1634-1715.
78969 see also New York (Colony)
Governor, 1682-1688 (Limerick)
Limitacion de internaciones. 99482
Limitations of human responsibility. 102188
Limites com a Guyana Francesza. 85648
Limits of civil obedience. (29830)
Limits of episcopal perrogative at a canonical
visitation. 26743
Limits of legislation as to doctrine and
ritual. 82947
Limner. 95565
Limon, J. G. 41137
Limonade, Julien Prevost, Comte de. 3885,
41138-41140, 65415
Limpkin, Wilson. (42678)
Limos, Luis Antonio Innocencio de Moura e.
see Moura e Limos, Luis Antonio Inno-
cencio de.

Lincoln's treatment of Gen. Grant. 41209
Lincoln's treatment of General McClellan.
41209
Lind, James. (41277)-41278
Lind, John, 1737-1781. 15589, 41280-41286,
69549, 1st note after 95742
Lind, John 1737-1781. supposed author.
2761, 18347, 22624, 27145, note after
41286, (62991), note after 71369
Lind, Jonathan. see Lind, John, 1737-1781.
Lind University, Chicago. Medical Depart-
ment. see Northwestern University
Evanston, Ill. Medical School, Chicago.
Linda, Lucas de, 1625-1660. 41288
Linda; or, the young pilot of the Belle Creole.
31436
Lindau, M. B. tr. 9700-9701, 9703, 26646,
(28714)-28715, 29286, 45478, 74503
Lindau, W. A. (2544), 12271, 17961, 33922
Lindemann, Charles. 4594
Lindemann, Johann Gottlieb. 41289
Linden, Joannes van der, 1756?-1835. tr.
26341, note after 94197, 98480
Linden Hall, Litiz, Pa. (41290)
Linden Rhymes. 36037
Lindenau, Gotzke. 25997, 28641, (38973)-
38974, 51334, note after 100853, note
after 100854
Lindenau, Karl Friedrich von, 1742-1817.
41301
Lindenberg, Fr. X. 2329
Lindley, George. 41291
Lindley, John. 41292-41293, 67461
Lindley, Thomas. 4858A, 41294-41297
Lindley's Reise nach Brasilien und Aufenthalt
daselbst. 41297
Lindman, Jonas. 94036
Lindo, A. A. (41299)
Lindo, Abraham. 41298
Lindoe, Robert. 41300
Lindsay, ---------, fl. 1864. 27640
Lindsay, Alexander. see Balcarres, Alexander
Lindsay, 6th Earl of, 1752-1825.
Lindsay, Hon. Colin, 1755-1795. 41301
Lindsay, David. 41302
Lindsay, E. G. 41303
Lindsay, John. 41304
Lindsay, W. S. 41306
Lindsay, William. 41305
Lindsey, Charles. 41307-41309
Lindsey, H. 41310
Lindsley, Aaron L. 41311
Lindsley, John Berrien, 1822-1897. 41312-
41313, 51880 see also Nashville. Uni-
versity. Chancellor.
Lindsley, Philip. 41314-41316
Lindsly, Harvey, 1804-1889. 41317, 94650
Lindsly, Philip. see Lindsley, Philip.
Lindstrom, Peter. 10202
Line and staff in our navy yards. 41318
"Line" and "staff" [of the navy.] (41319)
Line etchings. 89109
Line of the Union Pacific Railway. 16696
Line to the scoffers at religion. 18700,
50464, 69025
Linea divisoria de los estados de las coronas
de Espana. 96547
Lineage of the Lloyd and Carpenter family.
82402
Lineal arithmetic. (63375)
Lineal descendants of Abraham Peirce. 59547
Linen, James. 41320
Linen, William. 41321
Linen draper. pseud. Commercial conduct of
the province of New York considered.
(14971), 53620

Linen Manufactory, Philadelphia. 61482,
103256
Linen Manufactory Association, Philadelphia.
see Association for Carrying on the
Linen Manufactory, Philadelphia.
Lines adapted to the occasion. 80790
Lines addressed to the Rev. James Davenport.
50464
Lines composed by Miss Ann Saunders. 77170
Lines, composed on the death of four young
ladies. 105614
Lines composed on the death of General
Washington. 101847
Lines for a family of her acquaintance.
102525
Lines for October. 18927
Lines in pleasant places. 80477, 80482
Lines made after the great earthquake in 1755.
41323
Lines occasioned by the death of the Rev. Dr.
Henry J. Feltus. 24048
Lines of inclination and intensity. 74700
Lines of intensity between the Cape of Good
Hope and Australia. 74700
Lines of magnetic declination in the Atlantic.
74704
Lines on a serenade. 86828
Lines on my cottage. 97577
Lines on slaves killing their masters. (41324)
Lines on the crucifixion. 103335
Lines on the death of Rev. John Freeman.
84285
Lines on the . . . death of Rev. Thomas Coke.
44713
Lines on the death of the Indian Chief Occola.
94289
Lines sacred to the memory of the late
Major-General Joseph Warren. 101479
Lines suggested by the death of James Mc-
Clurge. 89744
Lines to a Democratic young lady. 17353
Lines to the memory of Miss Bethiah Burton.
(64261)
Lines to the recorder. 29874
Lines upon the death of John Alden, Esq.
(697)
Lines written on the preceding. 106197
Linforth, James. (41325)
Lingan, T. 102020
Lingard, R. 41326-41327
Lingard, William H. 41328
Lingham, Edward James. 34780, 41329
Linguet, S. N. H. 9267, 41332-note after
41332, 69717
Lington, Burr. pseud. see Humboldt, Gay.
pseud.
Linguistischer Theil. 51284
Linieres, Eduardo Enrique Teodoro de Turreau
de. see Turreau de Linieres, Eduardo
Enrique Teodoro de.
Linieres, Louis Marie Turreau de. see Tur-
reau de Linieres, Louis Marie, Baron,
1756-1816.
Liniers y Bermond. firm (41331)
Liniers y Bermond, Santiago. . . . Proclama.
(41331)
Lining, John. 11773, 12837, (22979), 41333
Link, Heinrich Friedrich, 1767-1851. (59572)
Linley, George, 1798-1865. 17936
Linn, ---------, fl. 1806. (14375), 40570
Linn, A. L. 41334
Linn, E. A. 41335
Linn, John Blair. 31105, 41335-41338, (49447),
note after 60301, 63651, 4th note after
106134
Linn, Lewis Fields, 1796-1843. 41339-(41341),
61017

List & Francke. firm 85669
List and abstract of documents relating to South-Carolina. 88005
List and abstract of papers in the State Paper Office. 88005
List and description of indigenous plants, etc. (15269)
List giving the taxable income for . . . 1863. 54321
List of accounts required from the collectors. (41428)
List of admirals. 91092
List of all academical honors conferred. (14860)
List of all bills paid by the auditor. (54212)
List of all officers elected by the General Assembly from 1800 to 1850. 83354
List of all officers elected by the General Assembly from the organization of the legislative government of the colony to 1800. 83353
List of all state and parish officers. 4446
List of all the academical honours conferred. 14830
List of all the cavalry regiments. 7195
List of all the chaplains to Congress. 26250
List of all the entries in the Virginia Military District. 41782
List of all the incorporations in the state of New York. 13238
List of all the names (who were skreen'd). 88187
List of all the officers of the army. 41429
List of all the post offices in the United States. 7055
List of American, French, Spanish, and Dutch ships. 91092
List of arrearages of taxes, due from the several towns in the state of Vermont, on the 15th day of September, A. D. 1795. 99045
List of arrearages of taxes, due from the several towns in the state of Vermont. On the 21st day of October, A. D. 1796. 99046
List of articles contained in the Anatomical Museum. 60328
List of balances due from the several counties for taxes. 100418
List of bankrupts in the United States Court for the Eastern District of Pennsylvania. (60212)
List of bankrupts in the United States Court for the Western District of Pennsylvania. (60213)
List of banks in the New England states and New Jersey. 13223
List of bills and resolutions passed during the session of 1878. 85174
List of books. 80637, (80638)
List of books and manuscripts. 70887
List of books and papers in the Office of the Secretary of State. (53751)
List of books in the Quincy Public Library. 67293
List of books, pamphlets, and more important contributions to periodicals. 74688
List of books printed between 1493-1700. 70887
List of books recommended and referred to. 85343
List of books sent to the new settlements. 15639
List of booksellers in the United States and the Canadas. 37098

List of British ships lost, taken, or destroyed. 91092
List of burials in the city . . . in 1798. 54357
List of Captain Francis Charloville's volunteers. 34301, 82960
List of cities and towns in the states. (17563)
List of citizens who have served or are serving in the army and navy. (52491)
List of churches, benevolent and religious societies, &c. 8554
List of claims for bounty land for revolutionary services. 82963
List of committees held in Philadelphia, June, 1864. 61791
List of committees of the House of Representatives of Connecticut. 15743
List of commodities, proper for a trade to the South-Sea. 40404, 88186
List of contributions . . . for ecclesiastical purposes. 54983
List of contributions received from various societies. (33333)
List of contributors to Putnam's monthly magazine. 66844
List of convicts discharged by expiration of sentence or pardon. 53752
List of copies of charters. (41430)
List of damages, actions and pretenses. 11492
List of delegates and officers to the convention. (60214)
List of described birds. 85035
List of diplomatic and consular officers of the United States. 41431
List of Dr. Kirkland's publications. 106054
List of Dr. Miller's publications. 89744
List of domestic institutions in correspondence. 85031
List of dredging stations in North American waters. 84125
List of duties payable upon every article imported. 41432
List of editions of the Bible. 17041
List of deditions of the Holy Scriptures. (56613)
List of establishments, discontinuances and changes. 15282
List of families and other persons residing in Baltimore. 3040
List of foreign correspondents. 85032
List of foreign institutions in correspondence. 85032
List of general and staff officers on the establishment in North-America. 41433
List of general officers, nominated in the United States Senate. 41434
List of government officers for 1822 and 1826. 43960
List of graduates, and those who have received degrees, at all the New England colleges. 23829
List of graduates, and those who have received degrees at the several colleges in the states of New York and New Jersey. 23830
List of graduates in the Philadelphia College of Medicine. 61982
List of grievances. (15528), 15544
List of infusorial objects. 14293
List of inn-keepers. 41435, 54358
List of institutions in the United States. 85031
List of interments. (49378), 61843
List of its [i.e. the First Baptist Church, Boston] members. 6643

List of its [i. e. the Widows' Society, Boston]
  members. 6786
List of jurors, in the city of New York.
  54359
List of Kentuckians in the battle of New
  Orleans. 84934
List of lands donated to the Mobile and Ohio
  Rail Road. 49783
List of lands to be sold in November, 1815.
  53753
List of light-houses. (41045)
List of light-houses, lighted beacons, and
  floating lights. 41046
List of literary publications. 23832
List of lots in Sheffield's, Wight's and
  Ellston's additions to Chicago. 12624
List of maps, charts and geographical works.
  94311
List of masonic lodges in America and
  Europe. 34137
List of medical graduates . . . April 7, 1826.
  60758
List of members and officers who served in
  the Pennsylvania Legislature. 60215
List of members, and rules of the Senate of
  Rhode-Island. 70593
List of members belonging to the Worcester
  Association of Mutual Aid in Detecting
  Thieves. 105380
List of members living. 104496
List of members of Bowdoin College. 7037
List of members . . . [of Bowdoin Street
  Church, Boston.] 6637
List of members, of Garden-Street Church.
  6646
List of members [of Park Street Church,
  Boston.] 6668
List of members of South Carolina Rangers.
  88032
List of members of the church for 1736-1843.
  93254
List of members [of the Columbian Peith-
  ologian Society.] 14825
List of members of the Constitutional Con-
  vention of Maryland, of 1867. 45196
List of members [of the First Baptist Church,
  Cambridge.] 10126
List of members of the First Baptist Church,
  in Providence. 66261
List of members of the . . . [Free School]
  Society, New York . 54285
List of members of the House of Representa-
  tives, 1809. 45805
List of members of the Massachusetts Society
  of the Cincinnati. 86107
List of members [of the Maverick Church,
  Boston.] 6657
List of members of the New York Club. 54451
List of members [of the Pine Street Church,
  Boston.] (6670)
List of members of the Rowe-Street Baptist
  Church. 6671
List of members of the Roxbury City Guard.
  73727
List of members [of the Society for the Propa-
  gation of the Gospel in Foreign Parts.]
  101276
List of members of the Society of St. George.
  62260
List of members of the Washington Street
  Baptist Church, Buffalo. 9063
List of members, with the rules and regula-
  tions and articles of faith, of the Pine
  Street Baptist Church, Providence, R. I.
  66289

List of merchant vessels of the United States.
  (41436)
[List of militia field officers.] 100412
List of mines and minerals belonging to the
  Maine Mining Company. 35401
List of ministers and consuls and other diplo-
  matic and commercial agents. 41437
List of names of persons burnt out, and of
  removals. 25201
List of national banks suspended and in
  liquidation. 20145
List of non commissioned officers and privates
  100521
List of non-commissioned officers and sea-
  men and marines. 82961
List of non-commissioned officers and soldiers
  of the Illinois Regiment. 34301, 82960
List of non-commissioned officers and soldiers
  of the Virginia Line. 82965
List of non-commissioned officers and soldiers
  of the Virginia State Line. 82964
List of non-commissioned officers and soldiers
  reported to the executive. 82962
List of North-American gasteropoda. 5501
List of numbers that came up prizes in Biles-
  Island Lottery. 5372
List of numbers that came up prizes in the
  second class. 41438
List of observatories. 85033
List of officers and associates of the U. S.
  Sanitary Commission in Philadelphia.
  62358
List of officers and managers of the Washing-
  ton National Monument Society. 102033
List of officers and members for 1868 [of the
  California Academy of Sciences.] 9960
List of officers and soldiers of the Virginia
  Continental Line. 82962
List of officers and soldiers, who have been
  allowed bounty land. 82962
List of officers confined at Columbia. (74745)
List of officers, etc., of the Chicago Histori-
  cal Society. 13621
List of officers, fellows, and members [of the
  American Statistical Association.] 1233
List of officers in commission in Massachu-
  setts since 1833. 45806
List of officers of marines, who have received
  lands. 82961
List of officers of the army and navy, who
  have received lands. 82958
List of officers of the continental army who
  served. 68021
List of officers of the Illinois Regiment, and
  of Crockett's Regiment. 34301, 82960
List of officers of the Illinois Regiment,
  who have not received lands for revo-
  lutionary services. 34301, 82960
List of officers of the navy and marine corps.
  41439
List of officers [of the New Bedford Young
  Men's Christian Association.] (52494)
List of officers of the state navy. 82961
List of officers of the Virginia continental
  and state lines. 82959
List of officers, together with a list of interic
  points. 88344
List of officers who marched with the army.
  41440
List of papers before the Senate Committee.
  43255
List of pastors, deacons and members of the
  1st Congregational Church in Concord.
  6962
List of pastors, officers, and members of Old
  South Church. 57145

List of patents for inventions and designs. (59039)

List of patents granted by the United States. (59038)

List of patents of lands, &c. 53754

List of pensioners for the year 1786. 100017

List of pensioners, provided for by Congress. 100018

List of periodicals and transactions of societies taken in. 2254

List of persons assessed a state, town and county tax. 12112

List of persons assessed in the city tax. 66277

List of persons assessed in the town tax. 66277

List of persons, born in Machias, who have removed therefrom. 43314, 84750

List of persons, copartnerships, and corporations. 6617

List of persons, corporations, and co-partnerships. 7123

List of persons, corporations, and companies, and estates. 84972

List of persons enrolled for the draft in the town of Gravesend. (28357)

List of persons enrolled in the town of Flatlands. 24676

List of persons enrolled in the town of New Lotts. (53267)

List of persons enrolled in the town of New Utrecht. 53418

List of persons in the city of Cambridge. (10151)

List of persons supposed to be worth one hundred thousand dollars. 6616

List of plants found in the District of Columbia. 20304

List of plants that have been discovered in the District of Columbia. (20305)

List of portraits in the hall of the . . . [Massachusetts Historical] Society. 45856

List of post-offices and postmasters in the United States. 20325

List of post-offices and postmasters in the United States. With the post-offices arranged by states and counties. (64499)

List of post-offices in the United States. (64499)

List of post offices in the United States of Canada. 41690

List of premiums. (33680)

List of premiums and regulations, for the fourteenth annual exhibition. 53811

List of premiums and regulations for the sixteenth annual exhibition. 67068

List of premiums awarded in . . . 1837. 60326

List of premiums to be given by the Baton Rouge Industrial Fair Association. 3958

List of prices for which the books, engravings, etc., belonging to Mr. William Menzies, were sold on Monday. 74682

List of prices of the journeymen house-carpenters. 41441

List of private armed vessels. 22519

List of private claims brought before the Senate. 41442

List of public libraries in the United States. 85034

List of public libraries, institutions, and societies in the United States and British provinces of North America. 70475, 70476

List of publications [of the Smithsonian Institution.] 85037

List of publications of the Smithsonian Institution, 1846-1903. 85037

List of real estate belonging to the corporation of the city of New York. 54360

List of rejections and expulsions. 100474

List of representatives in the Assembly of . . . New York. 53755

[List of representatives to the Grand Lodge of Massachusetts.] 87033

[List of returns of delinquents for Augusta County.] 100067

List of shareholders. 45807

List of slaves, remaining on Tangier Island. 20461

List of soldiers (of the invalid regiment.) 82962

List of soldiers (prisoners of war) belonging to the Pennsylvania regiments. (41444)

List of soldiers, (Virginians,) who were reported to the Senate. 82962

List of some of the benevolent institutions of . . . Philadelphia. 14438, (61792)

List of some of the descendants of Mr. Edward Woodman. 14177

List of stages from Cumberland, in Maryland, to Chillicothe, in Ohio. 100798

List of stamp duties. 20145

List of stockholders . . . in the Banks of Maine. (43912)

List of stockholders in the national banks of Boston. 6621

List of streets, roads, lanes, alleys, &c. (61793)

List of subscribers to Chauchard's maps published by Stockdale. 102541

List of subscribers to the Company of Scotland. (78225)

List of tax payers for 1859 [of Charleston, S. C.] (12055)

List of taxable polls and estates in the town of Quincy. 67290

List of taxes assessed in the town of Brookline. 8255

List of that portion of Armand's Corps. 82962

List of the agricultural, horticultural, and pomological societies. (41445)

List of the American navy. 41446

List of the attorneys and counselors of the Supreme Court. 30253

List of the birds hitherto observed in Greenland. 69116

List of the bishops, deans, &c. who have preached before the Society. 101276

List of the boot and shoe manufactures and dealers. 6382

List of the butterflies of New England. (78526)-78527

List of the cabinet, Jan. 20, 1783. 91092

List of the clergy of New York and Brooklyn. 8554

List of the Coleoptera of North America. 39665

List of the committees of the Great Central Fair. 61705

List of the courts in the New-England states and state of New-York. 5th note after 99205, 99236, 101230

List of the daily burials from the commencement to the conclusion of the Yellow Fever. 61672

List of the deceased soldiers and sailors. 66291-66292

List of the delegates who attended the Congress held at Philadelphia. 41447

List of the editions of the works of Louis Hennepin and Alonso [i. e. Antonio] de Gerrera. (74693)

List of the flag-officers of His Majesty's
fleet. 41448

List of the fortunate numbers drawn in the
Washington Hotel lottery. 41449

List of the fortunate numbers in the first
class of the United States lottery. 97971

List of the founders, the pastors, the ruling
elders and deacons, and the members
[of the Old South Church, Boston.]
(6663)

List of the general and field officers as they
rank in the army. 41450

List of the general and staff officers. 41451

List of the general and staff officers serving
in North America. 13755

List of the graduates [of Jefferson Medical
College.] (21278)

List of the grand officers and members of
the Supreme Council. 45507

List of the Indian and Dutch names in Long
Island. 19321

List of the institutions, libraries, colleges,
and other establishments in the United
States. 85031

List of the justices of the peace. (60216)

List of the Lieutenant-Governors, Presidents
and administrators of Upper Canada.
101212

List of the Lords, spiritual and temporal.
27068

List of the medicines recommended in the
treatment of diseases. 95446

List of the members of the assembly. 41452

List of the members [of the Society for the
Propagation of the Gospel in Foreign
Parts.] 100900

List of the members of the . . . New York
Society Library. 54545

List of the members [of the Philadelphia
Society for Promoting Agriculture.]
62036

List of the members of the Society of the
Sons of St. George. 86166

List of the members of the State Society of
the Cincinnati of Pennsylvania. 86127

List of the merchants, mechanics, traders,
and others. 6696

List of the ministers, churches and religious
assemblies. 91738

List of the minority in the House of Commons.
41453

List of the names of a part of the seamen of
the United States. 18204

List of the names of all the different Indian
Nations. 85254

List of the names of citizens of Watertown.
102096

List of the numbers that came out prizes.
(41454)

List of the numbers that came up prizes.
41455

List of the officers and members [of the
Brookline Baptist Church.] 8254

List of the officers and members [of the
Boston Episcopal Charitable Society.]
6700

List of the officers of the army serving in
North America. 41456

List of the officers of the city of Cambridge.
(10144)

List of the officers of the city of Charlestown.
(12120)

List of the officers [of the Connecticut Historical Society.] (15710)

List of the officers of the customs in the
several districts and ports. 91089

List of the officers of the town. 102096

List of the owners or keepers of dogs in . . .
Providence. 66278

List of the pastors, deacons and members of
the First Congregational Church in Concord, N. H. 23831

List of the post-offices in the United States;
their names, counties, and states. 91487

List of the post-offices in the United States;
with the counties in which they are
situated. (64499)

List of the post-offices in the United States;
. . . with the laws and regulations.
(64499)

List of the post offices in the United States
with the names of the postmasters on
the 1st of July, 1855. (64499)

List of the premiums of the [Pennsylvania
State Agricultural] Society. 60376

List of the presbyteries, ministers, proba-
tioners, and congregations. 41457

List of the presbyteries . . . of the synod.
65163

List of the present holders of the original
stock. 37493

List of the prices now in force in the town
of Wenham. 102629

List of the principal officers of Seneca County.
79102

List of the principal scientific and literary
institutions. 85036

List of the printed editions of the works of
Fray Bartolome de las Casas. (74694)

List of the printed maps of Boston. 80780

List of the prize numbers that came up prizes.
41458

List of the prizes & blanks drawn in the
Washington Hotel lottery. 102020

List of the prizes and fortunate numbers.
88126

List of the prizes drawn in the Delaware
lottery. 19394

List of the property of H. T. Litchfield.
41466

List of the public officers of the city of
Charleston. 101426

List of the reported dangers to navigation in
the Pacific Ocean. 41459

List of the resident members of St. Andrew's
Society. 62209

List of the shells of Cuba in the collection.
17786

List of the shells of South America in the
collection. 57459

List of the shipping belonging to the district.
64426

List of the Smithsonian publications. 85037

List of the society, instituted in 1787. 82011

List of the soldiers from Dublin. 21006

List of the stockholders of the Clinton Hall
Association. 54089

List of the sub-committees appointed by the
Committee for the City and Liberties
of Philadelphia. 61794

List of the subscribers to the Company of
Scotland. 78226

List of the succession of Scot's bishops.
(15654), 39529, 78555-78556

List of the taxable inhabitants, . . . of Pennsylvania. 60217

List of the taxable inhabitants, with the number of deaf, dumb and blind persons in
this commonwealth. note just before
60250

List of the Union soldiers buried at Andersonville. 1429

List of those that have been executed.
4889A, 41460
List of those Tories who took part with Great
Britain. 5679
List of town, county, and state taxes. 47302
List of two hundred Indian names. 19321
List of vacancies in the army. 41461
List of vessels of the South Atlantic Block-
ading Squadron. 18277
List of vessels taken from Great Britain
during the war. (32223), 74337
List of volunteers from Passaic and Bergen
Counties. (41462)
[List of voters in the several wards,] 1846
[Roxbury, Mass.] 73647
List of voters in the town of New Bedford.
52490
Lost of votes in Cambridge. 10150
List of wealthy persons in Boston in 1852.
6622
List of whale ships, belonging to the United
States. (52491)
List of words in the Iroquois, Mohegan, Shaw-
nee, and Esquimeaux tongues. 41878
List of works published by the Smithsonian
Institution. 85037
List of zoological works and memoirs, 1850-
1875. 78139
Lista alfabetica de los professores de medi-
cina y cirugia. (48516)
Lista alfabetica de los senores empleados e
individuos. 48517
Lista alfabetica y cronologia de los individuos
que forman. 48517
Lista de los generos frutos y efectos de pro-
cedencia extrangera. 48517
Lista de los individuos matriculados en el
ilustre y nacional Colegio de Abogados
de Mexico. 48517
Lista de los individuos que componen la muy
ilustre Archicofradia de Ciudadanos de
la Santa Veracruz. 76804
Lista de los individuos que forman el ilustre
Colegio de Abogados de Puebla. 66560
Lista de los Sres. que han contribuido en las
islas de Cuba y de Puerto-Rico. 41463
Liste, ------- de. 4935-4936
Liste chronologique des eveques et des pretes.
10510
Liste de membres . . . [de la Societe Bien-
veillante de Quebec.] 85784
Liste des actionnaires de la Compagnie du
Grand Tronc de Chemin de Fer. (28269)
Liste des eveques des autres possessions
Britannique de l'Amerique du Nord.
10510
Liste des fautes d'impression et de traduction
de l'edition Francaise de la description
du voyage. 47015-47016
Liste des Francois et Suisses. 87867
Liste generale des flottes et azogues. 94854
Listen to the voice of truth. (50745)
Listener. pseud. Infernal conference. (34693)
Liston, James K. 41464
Lists of distances. 41465
Lists of persons enrolled in the sixth, ninth,
twelfth and eighteenth wards, Brooklyn,
N. Y. 8298
Lists of persons . . . taxed on six thousand
dollars and upwards. (6618)
List of persons . . . who were taxed on ten
thousand dollars and upwards. 6619
List of persons . . . who were taxed on twenty
thousand dollars and upwards. 6620

Lists of the founders, the pastors, the ruling
elders and deacons, and the members
[of the Old South Church, Boston.] (6665)
Litch, Samuel. 93905
Litchfield, Harvy T. 41466
Litchfield, Paul. 41467
Litchfield de Liborius, Carolina. see Liborius,
Carolina Litchfield de.
Litchfield, Conn. (37736)
Litchfield, Conn. Agricultural Society. see
Litchfield Agricultural Society.
Litchfield, Conn. Associated Churches. see
Congregational Churches in Connecticut.
Litchfield Association.
Litchfield, Conn. Centennial Celebration of
Litchfield County, 1851. see Litchfield
County, Conn. Centennial Celebration,
Litchfield, 1851.
Litchfield, Conn. Convention of the North and
South Consociations of Litchfield, 1852.
see Congregational Churches in Connect-
icut. Convention of the North and South
Consociations of Litchfield, 1852.
Litchfield County, Conn. Centennial Celegration
Litchfield, 1851. 41470
Litchfield Agricultural Society. 41468
Litchfield County centennial celebration, held
at Litchfield, Conn. 41470
Litchfield County South Association. see Con-
gregational Churches in Connecticut.
Litchfield South Association.
Litchfield Festival. An address to the people
of Connecticut. 41474, 81493
Litchfield North Conscioation. see Congrega-
tional Churches in Connecticut. Litch-
field North Consociation.
Litchfield Sentinal. 50887
Litchfield South Association. see Congregational Churches in Connecticut. Litchfield South Association.
Litchfield South Consociation. see Congregational Churches in Connecticut. Litchfield South Consociation.
Literal report of the medical testimony.
(2482)
Literal reprint of the Bay Psalm Book.
(66429)
Literal translation of Dr. Cotton Mather's
famous Latin preface. 46532
Literar-historische Studie. (8756)
Literary Adelphi, of the Academical and Theo-
logical Institution, New-Hampton, N. H.
see Academical and Theological Institu-
tion, New-Hampton, N. H. Literary Adel-
phi.
Literary advertiser. 55867
Literary, agricultural and temperance monthly
magazine. 88491
Literary almanac for 1852. 55868
Literary and critical journal. 17547
Literary and cricial remarks, on sundry emi-
nent divines and philosophers. 41475
Literary and educational register for 1854.
55869
Literary and evangelical magazine. 41476
Literary & historical journal. 10640
Literary and historical miscellanies. (3131)
Literary and historical register. (51575)
Literary and historical Society of Quebec.
10620, 11141, 11143, 38901, 47556,
(55404), 67015, 67018-67025, 69256,
72307, 74074, 80872, 2d note after 85897,
85818, 93129, 1st note after 94271,
104014
Literary and Historical Society of Quebec.
Charter. 67015

Literary and Historical Society of Quebec. Council. (67017)

Literary and Historical Society of Quebec. Library. 67016, 85818

Literary and Historical Society of Quebec. Mineralogical Collection. 67018

Literary and miscellaneous gazette. 74177

Literary and miscellaneous journal. 105442

Literary and philosophical repertory. 41477

Literary and Philosophical Society, Manchester, Eng. 89284

Literary and Philosophical Society of New York. 54761-54762, (74699)

Literary and Philosophical Society of New York. Charter. 54761

Literary and Philosophical Society of South Carolina. 87868

Literary and Philosophical Society of South Carolina. Secretary. 87869

Literary and professional magazine. 43669

Literary and religious magazine. 43062

Literary and religious souvenir. 49473

Literary and Scientific Institution of Vermont. see Vermont Literary and Scientific Institution.

Literary and scientific journal of original and select articles. 49215

Literary and scientific museum. 58929

Literary and scientific periodical. 60760

Literary and scientific repository and critical review. 41478

Literary and Scientific Society of Nova Scotia. see Nova Scotia Literary and Scientific Society.

Literary and Theological Institution, Fairfax, Vt. 52951

Literary and Theological Institution, Granville, O. see Denison University, Granville, O.

Literary and Theological Institution of Maine. see Colby College, Waterville, Me.

Literary and theological review. 41479

Literary Brass Band, Louisville, Ky. see Louisville Literary Brass Band.

Literary cabinet. 41480, (59554), (62740), 86838, 105849

Literary companion. 41481

Literary compiler. 14884

Literary diary [of Ezra Stiles.] note after 91736, 91750

Literary emporium. 84162

Literary, entertaining and scientifc journal. 49215

Literary essays. 80077

Literary evening fireside. 74172

Literary expositor. 38533

Literary focus. (41482)

Literary fountains healed. (49064)

Literary fracas, a literary tale. 59508

Literary friend. pseud. ed. (23243)

Literary garland. (41483)

Literary garland, a montlhy magazine. 41484

Literary gazette. see Athenian and literary gazette.

Literary gazette and American anthenaeum. 41485

Literary gazette and publisher's circular. 55867

Literary gazette: or, journal of criticism, science, and the arts. 41486

Literary gentleman. pseud. ed. (67694)

Literary history of Pennsylvania. 84585

Literary Institute, Philadelphia. see Philadelphia Literary Institute.

Literary Institution, Nashua, N. H. see Nashua Literary Institution.

Literary Institution and Teacher's Seminary, Concord, N. H. see Concord Literary Institution and Teacher's Seminary.

Literary intelligencer. 55066

Literary journal. 85515

Literary journal. see American monthly review; or literary journal. Monthly journal: or, literary journal. Western monthly magazine, and literary journal.

Literary journal, and weekly register of science and the arts. 41489

Literary journal, or universal review of literature. 41488

Literary journal. Vol. I. Latin school. 41487

Literary labors of the laboring man. 29488

Literary letter. 21687, 29736, 55870

Literary life of James K. Paulding. 59206

Literary life of Thomas Pennant. 59758

Literary lounger. pseud. Scraps and sketches. see Willis, J. H.

Literary magazine, and American register. 8457, 41490

Literary magazine and British review for 1788. (41491)

Literary messenger. 35071

Literary miscellany. 41492

Literary miscellany containing elegant selections. 91311

Literary miscellany. No. I. 91311

Literary miscellany of the United States. 5019?

Literary miscellany; or, monthly review. 4149.

Literary monthly, devoted to the interests of the University [of Pennsylvania.] 60759

Literary museum or monthly magazine. 41494

Literary panorama. A review of books. 41495, 85250

Literary panorama and national register. 4149?

Literary paper. 92718

Literary picture gallery. 41496

Literary, political, & agricultural. 90493

Literary proposal. 95411

Literary prospects of Georgia. (24770)

Literary record and journal of the Linnaean Association of Pennsylvania College. (41497), 60313

Literary recorder. 16801

Literary register. see Christian review and literary register.

Literary register and bookbuyers alamanac. 55871

Literary register and monthly catalogue of old and new books. 74695

Literary register, May 25, 1865. 11079

Literary remains of J. Zimmerman Johnson. (36232)

Literary remains of John G. C. Brainard. 7332, 103819

Literary remains of Joseph Brown Ladd. 3851?

Literary remains of Martha Day. 18972

Literary remains of the late William B. O. Peabody. 59382

Literary remains of the late Willis Gaylord Clark. 13332

Literary remains of the Rev. Jonathan Maxcy. 47001

Literary repository. see New-York magazine; or, literary repository.

Literary review. see Register of the times, and literary review.

Literary, Scientific, & Military Gymnasium, Washington, D. C. see Washington Literary, Scientific, & Military Gymnasium, Washington, D. C.

Literary societies: their uses and abuses. (50157)

Lives and confessions of John Williams, Francis Frederick, John P. Rog, and Peter Peterson. (41584), 104281

Lives and deaths of the holy evangelists and apostles. 84553

Lives and exploits of bandetti and robbers. (43246)

Lives and exploits of the most noted highwaymen. 41585

Lives and portraits of curious and odd characters. 41586

Lives and portraits of remarkable characters. 21755, 41587

Lives and portraits of the Presidents of the United States. 21500

Lives and reminiscences of the pioneers of Rochester and western New York. 37325

Lives and services of Major General John Thomas. 14164

Lives and speeches of Abraham Lincoln and Hannibal Hamlin. 33354

Lives and trial of Gibbs & Wansley. 101243

Lives and voyages of Drake, Cavendish, and Dampier. 20833

Lives, characters, and anecdotes of the military and naval officers. (1188)

Lives, characters and sufferings of the fathers of New England. 41588

Lives, English and forein [sic]. (41589)

Lives of American merchants. By Freeman Hunt. 33851, (67216)

Lives of American merchants, eminent for integrity. 26043, 97511

Lives of benefactors. 27913

Lives of celebrated American Indians. (27908)

Lives of celebrated Americans. 32115, 42121

Lives of celebrated Spaniards. 67322

Lives of celebrated statesmen. (288)

Lives of celebrated travellers. 75245

Lives of Christopher Columbus, the discoverer of America, and Americus Vespucius the Florentine. 14665

Lives of the distinguished American naval officers. 16470

Lives of distinguished shoemakers. 41590

Lives of early Methodists. 35464

Lives of eminent American physicians and surgeons. 28938

Lives of eminent Christians of various deonominations. (26054)

Lives of eminent individuals, celebrated in American history. 41591, 88992

Lives of eminent men of modern times. 41592

Lives of eminent Methodist ministers. 28037

Lives of eminent missionaries. (10943)

Lives of eminent persons. 5791, 41593

Lives of eminent Philadelphians, now deceased. 81346

Lives of Father Joseph Anchieta, S. J. 1375

Lives of Franklin and Washington. 101848

Lives of Franklin & Washington. 101848

Lives of Fremont and Dayton. 70021

Lives of Gen. U. S. Grant and S. Colfax. 28318

Lives of General Zachary Taylor and General Winifield Scott. 93725

Lives of Gens. Halleck and Pope. 70943

Lives of Generals Moultrie and Pickens, and Governor Rutledge. 30681

Lives of George Washington and Thomas Jefferson. 81372

Lives of Hernando Cortes, the discoverer of Mexico, and Francisco Pizarro. 41594

Lives of Horatio Seymour and Frank P. Blair. (79661)

Lives of illustrious men. 41595

Lives of illustrious men of America. 3591

Lives of Increase Mather and Sir William Phipps. 41599, 63984

Lives of Isaac Heath, and John Bowles. 95639

Lives of James Madison. 289

Lives of Joaquin Murieta and Tiburcio Vasquez. (71281)

Lives of John Jay and Alexander Hamilton. 69650

Lives of John Smith, Boone, and Randolph. 1099

Lives of John Wilson, John Norton and John Davenport. 41599, 43062

Lives of judges infamous as tools of tyrants. 31770

Lives of men of letters and science. 8410

Lives of missionaries. North America. 41596

Lives of northern worthies. 14317

Lives of patriots and heroes. 36012

Lives of Phelps and Nash. 55904

Lives [of Plutarchus.] 95341

Lives of Rueben H. Walcot and Charles O' Conor. 39383

Lives of St. Thomas of Villanova. 17188

Lives of Sir Francis Drake, and Admiral Blake. 36298

Lives of Sir Walter Raleigh and Capt. John Smith. 67571

Lives of sixteen New York citizens. 4975

Lives of Southern heroes and patriots. 41596

Lives of state criminals who suffered for high treason. 41598

Lives of sundry eminent persons. 13446

Lives of the admirals and other eminent seamen. 10236

Lives of the author [i. e. Sir Walter Raleigh], by Oldys and Birch. 67599

Lives of the British admirals, from the earliest periods. (10237)

Lives of the brothers Humboldt. 38047

Lives of the chief fathers of New England. 338, (675), (32813)-(32814), 43061-43062, 63984

Lives of the departed heroes and statesmen of America. (16627)

Lives of the departed heroes, sages, and statesmen of America. 72737

Lives of the discoverers and pioneers of America. (41600)

Lives of the fallen braves and living heroes. 79992

Lives of the filibusters and pirates. (36196)

Lives of the four Georges, Kings of England. 85151-85153

Lives of the Governors of New Plymouth and Massachusetts Bay. (50393)

Lives of the Governors of the state of New York. 36011

Lives of the heroes of the American revolution. 41601

Lives of the illustrious. 41602

Lives of the Indians. 95217

Lives of the most eminent and evangelical ministers. 41603

Lives of the most eminent foreign statesmen. 35697

Lives of the most eminent naval commanders. (10237)

Lives of the necromancers. 27675

Lives of the Presidents of the United States, embracing a brief history. (42122)

Lives of the Presidents of the United States; with biographical notices. 41262

Lives of the Presidents of the United States, from Washington to Pierce. 26044

Lives of the Presidents, with the acts of their administrations. 42126

Livres curieux. 41659
Livres heroiques et historiques des Quiches.
　(7436)
Livro anteprimeyro prologomeno a toda a
　historia do futuro. 99524
Livro da viagem da nao "Bretos." 88727
Livro das obras de Garcia de Ressende.
　70062
Livro do povo. (72504)
Livro recreativo das familias. (51570)
Liuros quatro & quito da Historia do des-
　cobrimento & conquistada India pelos
　Portugueses. 11385
Lizana y Beaumont, Francisco Xavier de Abp.
　41660-41662, 48319, (48629) see also
　Mexico (Archdiocese) Archbishop (Lizana
　y Beaumont) Mexico (Viceroyalty) Virrey,
　1809-1810 (Lizana y Beaumont)
Lizardi, Jose Joaquin Fernandez de. see
　Fernandez de Lizardi, Jose Joaquin,
　1776-1827.
Lizarraga Vengoa, -------, Conde de.
　(22365), 55377
Lizarza, Facundo. 10653, 56248
Lizarzaburu, J. A. (41667)-41668
Llaguno Amirola, Eugenio de. ed. 41997
Llamamiento de la Isla de Cuba a la nacion
　Espanola. 17787, 43692
Llamas, Diego Osorio de Escobar y. see
　Escobar y Llamas, Diego Osorio de, Bp.
Llana, Francisco Murcia de la. see Murcia
　de la Llana, Francisco.
Llana, Manuel Gonzales. 22818
Llandaff, Bishop of. see Copleston, Edward,
　Bishop of Llandaff, 1776-1849. Cresset,
　Edward, Bishop of Llandaff, d. 1755.
　Ewer, John, successively Bishop of Llan-
　daff, and Bangor, d. 1774. Gilbert, John,
　Abp. of York, 1693-1761. Newcome,
　Richard, successively Bishop of Llandaff,
　and St. Asaph, d. 1769. Shipley,
　Jonathan, successively Bishop of Llan-
　daff, and St. Asaph, 1714-1788. Sumner,
　Charles Richard, successively Bishop of
　Llandaff, and Winchester, 1790-1874.
　Van Mildert, William, successively
　Bishop of Llandaff, and Durham, 1765-
　1836. Watson, Richard, Bishop of Llan-
　daff, 1737-1816.
Llano y Valdes, F. de. 41672
Llano y Zapata, Joseph Eusebio de. 41669-
　41671
Llanos de Apam, Mexico. Hacendados. see
　Hacendados de los Llanos de Apam,
　Mexico.
Llanto de Flora desatado. (71416)
Llanto de la religion. 99625
Llanto de las aguas en la muerte del mas
　caudaloso rio. 10317
Llanto de las pietras. (11032)
Llanto de los ojos de los Jesuitas de Gauthe-
　mala. (49886)
Llanto de Mexico. 13627
Llanto del occidente en el ocaso del mas claro
　sol de las Espanas. (77048)
Llanto sagrado de la America Meridional.
　(73032)
Llavallol, Jaime. 96247
Llave de la Cabana del tio Tom. 92419
Llave real del cielo. 75578
Llera, Mariano Escadon y. see Escadon y
　Llera, Mariano.
Lleras, Lorenzo M. 41673
Lleva anadido una doctrina de la lengua Nao-
　lingo. (6304)

Llibre de la congregacio y germandat de la
　Sanctissima Verge del Socorro. 19688
Llontisca, Antonio. 87233-87234
Lloreda, Manuel de la Torre. see Torre
　Lloreda, Manuel de la.
Llorente, --------. 41674-41675
Llorente, Juan Antonio, 1756-1823. 11235,
　11237, (11240), 11276, (65985)
Llosa, M. E. de la. 41676
Lloyd, Caroline. 19850, 41677
Lloyd, Charles. 41678, 41680-41681, 4th note
　after 97116
Lloyd, Charles. supposed author (15202)-
　(15203), 95750, 103123
Lloyd, Clinton. 41682
Lloyd, David, 1597-1663. 41683-41685
Lloyd, David, fl. 1724-1727. 22692, 61622,
　66608, (41792), 37241, 60773, note after
　99809
Lloyd, David, fl. 1845. 104886
Lloyd, G. C. ed. 83710, 95605
Lloyd, H. Evans. tr. 47017, 74646, 89551
Lloyd, H. H. 41686
Lloyd, James, 1769-1831. (41688)
Lloyd, James, fl. 1794. 41687
Lloyd, James T. 41689-41691
Lloyd, John Augustus. 41692-(41693)
Lloyd, John Uri, 1849-1936. 83710, 95605
Lloyd, Mary Clarke. 41694
Lloyd, Owen. see Leoyd, Owen.
Lloyd, Richard. ed. 40914
Lloyd, Samuel. 41695
Lloyd, Susette Harriet. 41696
Lloyd, T. S. 89754
Lloyd, Thomas. (381), 7970, 8956-8957,
　(12205), 15492, 15608, 32936, 37178,
　37205, (41697)-41698, 42867, 60040,
　60402, 79011-(79012), 84904, 96809,
　note before 96946, 102637, 104627,
　104631, 2d note after 105986
Lloyd, Thomas. defendant 21142
Lloyd, W. A. 41700-41701
Lloyd, W. F. 41702
Lloyd, William. 41699
Lloyd. firm publishers 97362
Lloyd (H. H.) & Company. firm publishers
　41686
Lloyd (Lodowick) firm publishers 41005,
　55881, 55885
Lloyd Library of Botany, Pharmacy, and
　Materia Medica, Cincinnati. 83710,
　95605
Lloyd's Association, New York. 41703
Lloyd's battle history of the great rebellion.
　41686
Lloyd's list of post offices in the United States
　and the Canadas. 41690
Lloyd's pocket companion and guide through
　New York City. 41698
Lloyd's southern railroad guide. 41700
Lloyd's steamboat and railroad guide. 41701
Lloyd's steamboat directory. 41691
Lloyd's universal American register of ship-
　ping. 41703
Llufriu, Jose J. 41704
Llyfr athrawiaeth a chyfammodau perthynol i
　Eglwys Iesu Grist. 83231
Llyfr Mormon. 83146
Lo, George St. see St. Lo, George.
Lo! here and lo! there, or the grave of the
　heart. 79713
Lo mas y lo menos. 49406
Lo maximo en lo minimo. 10897, 11056
Lo mucho que Dios le da. 76015

Lo que se sigue es un pedaco de una carta y relacion que escriuio cierto hombre. 11228, 11235, (11249), 11267, 11283, 11289

Lo referente a la isla de Puerto-Rico. 94352

Lo scoprimento dell'America. 98665

Lo subcedido a la armada de Su Magestad de que es Capitan General. 76761

Loa famosa. 99400

Loa o la aclamacion de nuestro Rey. 69194, 98383

Loa, y poetica exposicion del arco. 98163

Loaisa y Quinones, Pedro de. defendant 98314

Loaisaga, Manuel de. 41705

Loan bill and the currency. 42815

Loan bill. Speech . . . February 15, 1848. (55256)

Loan for the completion of the Chesapeake and Ohio Canal. 29655

Loan fund of the Church Extension Society. 48207

Loan of two hundred thousand pounds. 64840

Loan, revenue, and currency acts of 1863. (41706)

Loans! Fruits of commercial restrictions! 105397A

Lobe, Guillaume. 41710-41711

Lobesthone. 100755

Lob-lied dem in Gott geehrten Vatter Friedsam. 95458

Lobo, Manuel. 41712

Lobo, Ovidio da Gama. see Gama Lobo, Ovidio da.

Lobo da Silveira, Joaquim. see Silveira, Joaquim Lobo da.

Lobo Guerrero, Bartholome. see Guerrero Bartholome Lobo, Abp.

Lobos, Eleodoro. supposed author 86552

Lobrede auf diejenigen tapfern Manner. 7187

Lobs. Gedachtnuss der Patrum so die Societat. 47866

Lobschrifft zu ehren Johannes Lerio. (8784)

Lobspruch. 41714, 4th note after 103943, 2d note after 105675

Lobster's voyage to the Brazils. 7599

Loca. 63725

Loca aliquot. 63956, (63958)-63960

Loca aliqvot ex Pomponianis commentariis repetita. 63957

Local American history series. 5985

Local and business directory for 1869. 32676

Local and private acts. 10499

Local and private statutes of New Brunswick. 52540

Local Biblical researches in Palestine. 72067

Local drama. 54293

Local government of Jamaica and British Guiana. 35631

Local guide to British Guiana. 31780

Local history of Camden. (24558)

Local law in Massachusetts and Connecticut. 25326

Local laws and private acts of the state of Missouri. 49606

Local laws of the territory of Iowa. 35018

Local laws relating to the country of Philadelphia. (60059)

Local loiterings. 20344

Local nomenclature of the Makah. 94011

Local play. 20971

Local poem, historic and descriptive. 51025

Local preacher. pseud. God bless Abraham Lincoln! 41189

Local sketches. (62905)

Local Visiting Committee of Bellevue and Other Hospitals, New York. 86150

Localities, streets and their lengths. 51904

Locality one of its [i. e. consumption's] chief causes. 6991

Locarvm ac mirabilivm mvndi descriptio. (66478)

Lochington, Charles. see Lockington, Charles

Lochinvar. pseud. Encouragements for such as shall have intention. see Gordon, Sir Patrick, of Lochinvar, d. 1627?

Lock, David. 41716

Lock-Haven and Tyrone Railroad Company. Charter. 60221

Lock-Haven and Tyrone Railroad Company. Engineer. 60221

Lock-Haven and Tyrone Railroad Company. President. 60221

Locke. pseud. Exposition of the Virginia resolutions of 1798. see Upshur, Abel Parker, 1791-1844. supposed author

Locke, Calvin S. 41717

Locke, Charles H. reporter 50334

Locke, David Ross, 1833-1888. 41718-(41722) 84185-84187, 86183, 2d note after 94082

Locke, E. W. 41723

Locke, J. Adams. 28839

Locke, Jane Ermina (Starkweather) 1805-1859 25229, 41724-41725

Locke, John, 1632-1704. 11067, 13017, 13419 31630, 37825, (41726)-41728, 77887, 84584, 85072, 1st note after 87851, 97354, 97364

Locke, John Goodwin. 41729-41730

Locke, John L. 41731

Locke, Joseph. (41732)

Locke, N. C. 41733

Locke, Samuel. 41734

Locke, Una. 41735

Locke, William E. (41736)

Locke, William Henry. 41737

Locke and Co. firm see Ward, Lcoke and Co firm publishers

Locke Amsden, or the schoolmaster. 95481

Locke, legislateur de la Caroline. 38446

Lockerby, Elizabeth N. (41738)

Locket. 105195

Lockett, E. plaintiff 82144

Lockhart, Ephraim. 33826, 41739, (51820), 90773

Lockhart, Ephraim. supposed author 91841

Lockhart, James, 1806-1857. (41740)

Lockhart, John Ingram. tr. (19983)

Lockington, Charles. petitioner (2592), note after 95821

Lockman, --------. ed. 40708-40709, 1st note after 96502

Lockman, John, 1698-1771. 41741

Lockport, N. Y. Evangelical Lutheran Church 41745

Lockport, N. Y. Holland Purchase Convention 1827. see Holland Purchase Convention Lockport, N. Y., 1827.

Lockport, N. Y. Meeting, 1827. see Holland Purchase Convention, Lockport, N. Y., 1827.

Lockport, N. Y. Meeting of the Citizens of Rochester, Buffalo, Lockport and Palmyra 1839. see Western Canal Convention, 1839.

Lockport, N. Y. Meeting of the Citizens with Reference to the Improvement of the Erie Canal, 1839. see Western Canal Convention, Rochester, N. Y., 1839.

Lockport, N. Y. Union School. 41744

Loganian Library, Philadelphia. see Phila-
delphia. Library Company. Loganian
Library.
Logans' directory for 1867. 34582
Logan's Indianapolis directory for 1868. 34582
Logan's Indianapolis directory for . . . July 1,
1868. 8489, 34582
Logarithmick arithmetick. 83541
Loge l'Amenite, No. 73, Philadelphia. see
Freemasons. Pennsylvania. Friendship
Lodge, No. 73, Philadelphia.
Loggers; or, six months in the forests of
Maine. 41821
Loggin, Robert. 41822
Logia de los gatos. Numero 2. 99709
Logia de los gatos. Numero 4. 99698
Logia de los gatos. Numero 3. 99710
Logia revolucionaria de los gatos fracmasones.
99707, 99709-99710
Logic and law of Col. Johnson's report on
Sabbath mails. 36278, 41823
Logic of facts. (21143)
Logic primer. 22163
Logica Mexicana. (73860)
Logical, historical, tragical, magical, symp-
apthetic, and democratical account of the
late glorious revolution. 20654
Logical impossibility of any new compromise.
23317
Logocanon, ou regle proportionelle. 33563
λογοι περι της φυσεδξ. 4343
Logs of the first voyage made by the Great
western. 13528
Loguen, J. W. (41824)
Lohenschiold, Ottone Christiano de. (41825),
(52385)
Loher, Franz. 41826-41828
Lohman, Anna (Trow) 1812-1878. defendant
41829, 70101
Lohmann, H. J. ed. 35184
Lohmann, Van C. W. 41830
Lohner, H. W. tr. (58310)
Loi de commerce. 29570
Loi donnee a Paris le 13 Aout 1792. 75476
Loi du 18 Septembre 1850. 77749
Loi et ordinances relatives a la republique d'
Haiti. (29579)
Loi penale. 29570
Loi relative a la deliberation prise par la Com-
mune. 75476
Loi relative a l'envoi dans la colonie de Saint-
Domingue. 75159
"Loil" legislature of Alabama. (41831)
Loire (Department) Prefet. 84478
Lois Europeennes et Americaines. 84478
Lois municipales des republiques de la Suisse
et des Etats-Unis. 4217
Lois physiques a consulter. (9826)
Loiseau, ------. (68072)
Loisel, Francisco. 41832
Loisirs d'un aveugle. 40000
Loiterings amid the scenes of story and song.
43238
Loiterings of travel. 104510
Loix de la nomenclature et de la classification
de l'empire organique. 67465
Loix de police. (66983)
Loix et constitutions des colonies Francoises.
50573, 50578
Lok, M. 1563-1564, 45011, 2d note after
102836, 106330
Lok, Michael. cartographer 29592-29593
Lokman. pseud. 96123, 1st note after 105926
Lola Montez. 59492
Lolme, Jean Louis de, 1740-1806. (41645),
41646, note after 91540

Lola de Angel. 99691
Lomas, John. 41833, 54441, 101112
Lomas, John. reporter 96832, 96939, 104224
Lomax, John Taylor. 41834-41835
Lomax, Judith. 41836
Lombard, Alexander. 41837
Lombard, Ammi Cutter. 41838
Lombard, Israel. 41839
Lombard, J. K. ed. 86945
Lombard University, Galesburg, Ill. (41840)
Lombardo, Juan Pablos. (42063)
Lombardo, Natal. 41841-(41842)
Lomeni, ------. tr. 6263
Lomenie, Charles F. de. 10359, 14866,
41843-41844
Lomenie, Louis de. (41845)-41846
Lomond, Robert. 41847
Lonck, Heinrich Cornelis. 7567, (8784), 33674,
41848-(41850), note after 99260, 101421
Loncq, Heinrich Cornelius. see Lonck, Hein-
rich Cornelis.
Lond, Enoch. defendant 41268, note after
97069
London, Archibald. 42165, 101219
London, Daniel H. 41851
London, H. Berthoud. tr. 71447
London, John. 33149
London, Bishop of. see Blomfield, Charles
James, successively Bishop of Chester,
and London, 1786-1857. Gibson, Edmund,
successively Bishop of Lincoln, and Lon-
don, 1669-1748. Hayter, Thomas, suc-
cessively Bishop of Norwich, and Lon-
don, 1702-1762. King, John, Bishop of
London, 1559?-1621. Lowth, Robert,
successively Bishop of St. Davids, Oxford,
and London, 1710-1787. Monteigne,
George, Abp. of York, d. 1628. Osbaldis
tun, Richard, successively Bishop of
Carlisle, and London, 1690-1764.
Porteus, Beilby, successively Bishop of
Chester, and London, 1731-1808. Sher-
lock, Thomas, successively Bishop of
Salisbury, and London, 1678-1761. Ter-
rick, John, successively Bishop of Peter-
borough, and London, 1710-1777.
London. 99249
London. African Institution. see African
Institution, London.
London. American Association. see American
Association in London.
London. Anthropological Society. see Anthro
pological Society of London.
London. Baker Street Bazaar, 185-? 2852,
7764
London. Banquet Held in Honor of C. W.
Field, 1868. see Banquet Held in Honor
of C. W. Field, London, 1868.
London. Banquet to Thomas W. Kennard,
1865. 37379
London. Board of Customs. see Great
Britain. Customs Establishment.
London. British and Foreign Anti-slavery
Society. see British and Foreign Anti-
slavery Society, London.
London. British and Foreign Freed-men's
Aid Society. see British and Foreign
Freed-men's Aid Society, London.
London. Buckingham Palace. Bal Costume,
1842. 85203
London. City Council. 95918
London. Committee Appointed by the Adven-
turers to Prosecute the Discovery of the
Passage to the Western Ocean of Amer-
ica. see Committee Appointed by the
Adventurers to Prosecute the Discovery

of the Passage to the Western Ocean
of America, and Extend the Trade,
and Settle the Countires Beyond Hudson's Bay, London, 1749.

London. Committee for the Abolition of the
Slave Trade. see Committee for the
Abolition of the Slave Trade, London.

London. Committee of Mexican Bondholders.
see Committee of Mexican Bondholders,
London.

London. Committee of West India Planters
and Merchants. see West India Planters and Merchants, London.

London. Company for Propagation of the
Gospel in New England and Parts Ad-
jacent in America. see Company for
Propagation of the Gospel in New Eng-
land and Parts Adjacent in America,
London.

London. Constitutional Society. see Constitutional Society, London.

London. Corporation. Court of Common
Council. 451

London. Corporation for Promoting and
Propagating the Gospel of Jesus Christ
in New England. see Corporation for
Promoting and Propagating the Gospel
of Jesus Christ in New England, London.

London. Court of Common Council. see
London. Corporation. Court of Common Council.

London. Court of Old Bailey. see London.
Royal Courts of Justice.

London. Dinner Given by Mr. George Peabody to the Americans Connected with
the Great Exhibition, 1851.

London. Divers Churches, Owning Personal
Election and Final Perseverance. see
Divers Churches in London, Owning
Personal Election and Final Perseverance.

London. Ethnological Society. see Ethnological Society, London.

London. Exhibition of the Works of Industry
of All Nations, 1851. see London.
Great Exhibition of the Works of Industry of All Nations, 1851.

London. Factors. see Merchants or Factors
of London.

London. General Anti-slavery Convention,
1840. see General Anti-slavery Convention, London, 1840.

London. General Anti-slavery Convention,
1843. see General Anti-slavery Convention, London, 1843.

London. K. Geographischen Gesellschaft. see
Royal Geographical Society, London.

London. Geological Society. see Geological
Society, London.

London. Governor and Company for the Plantation of the Summer Islands. see Bermuda Company.

London. Great Exhibition of the Works of
Industry of All Nations, 1851. 28445

London. Great Exhibition of the Works of
Industry of all Nations, 1851. English
Guiana Section. 29164

London. Guildhall. 104543

London. Horticultural Society. see Royal
Horticultural Society, London.

London. International Exhibition, 1851. see
London. Great Exhibition of the Works
of Industry of All Nations, 1851.

London. International Exposition, 1862.
Brazilian Commission. President. 50585

London. International Exposition, 1862.
Canadian Department. 34927

London. International Exposition, 1862.
Nova Scotian Department. 34928, (56124)

London. International Statistical Congress,
1860. see International Statistical Congress, London, 1860.

London. Italian Merchants. see Portugal,
Italian, and Spanish Merchants, London.

London. Livery. petitioners 99816 see
also London. Lord Mayor and Livery.
petitioners

London. Lord Mayor, 1769. 451 see also
Beckford, William, 1709-1770.

London. Lord Mayor, 1776. 15583, 98439

London. Lord Mayor and Livery. 15583

London. Lord Mayor and Livery. petitioners
15146, 98439 see also London. Livery. petitioners

London. Meeting at the Mansion House of the
City of London, in Aid of the Columbia
Mission, 1857. see Meeting at the
Mansion House of the City of London,
in Aid of the Columbia Mission, 1857.

London. Meeting of the West-India Merchants
and Planters, 1784. see Meeting of the
West-India Merchants and Planters,
London. 1784.

London. Meeting on Behalf of the Preservation of the British West India Colonies,
1832. see Meeting on Behalf of the
Preservation of the British West India
Colonies, London, 1832.

London. Merchants. see also Merchants
or Factors of London.

London. Merchants. petitioners 14272-
14274, 69938

London. Merchants, and Others, Members
of the Bermuda Company. petitioners
see Bermuda Company. petitioners

London. Merchants and Traders. 28609

London. Merchants or Factors. see Merchants or Factors of London.

London. Merchants, Traders, and Others.
petitioners 95938-95940, 95945

London. Merchants Trading to Spain, East
Indies, and Newfoundland. petitioners
see Merchants Trading to Spain, East
Indies, and Newfoundland, London. petitioners

London. Ministers and Elders, Met Together
in a Provincial Assembly, 1649. see
Provincial Assembly of Presbyterian
Ministers, London, 1649.

London. Museum of Practical Geology. 36879

London. National Association for the Pro-
motion of Social Science. see National
Association for the Promotion of Social
Science, London.

London. New England Company. see Com-
pany for Propagation of the Gospel in
New England and the Parts Adjacent in
America, London.

London. Nonconformist Ministers. petitioners
see Nonconformist Ministers of London.
petitioners

London. Old Bailey. see London. Royal
Courts of Justice.

London. Peabody Fund. see Peabody Fund,
London.

London. Philological Society. see Philological Society, London.

London. Portugal, Italian and Spanish Merchants. petitioners see Portugal,
Italian, and Spanish Merchants, London.

London. Provincial Assembly of Presbyterian Ministers, 1649. see Provincial Assembly of Presbyterian Ministers, London, 1649.

London. Public Breakfast Held in Honour of William Lloyd Garrison, 1867. see Public Breakfast Held in Honour of William Lloyd Garrison, London, 1867.

London. Public Meeting to Commemorate the Fourth Anniversary of John Brown's Death, 1863. see Public Meeting to Commemorate the Fourth Anniversary of John Brown's Death, London, 1863.

London. Public Meeting of Persons Interested in the Preservation of the British West India Colonies, 1833. see Public Meeting of Persons Interested in the Preservation of the British West India Colonies, London, 1833.

London. Public Record Office. see Great Britain. Public Record Office, London.

London. Royal Academy. see Royal Academy, London.

London. Royal College of Physicians. see Royal College of Physicians, London.

London. Royal Courts of Justice. 90540, 97265, 102781

London. Royal Geographical Society. see Royal Geographical Society, London.

London. Royal Horticultural Society. see Royal Horticultural Society, London.

London. Royal Institution. see Royal Institution, of Great Britain, London.

London. Royal Society. see Royal Society, London.

London. Royal Society of Arts. see Royal Society of Arts, London.

London. St. Thomas in the East Branch Association of the Incorporated Society for the Convention and Religious Instruction and Education of Negro Slaves. see Society for the Conversion and Religious Instruction and Education of Negro Slaves. St. Thomas in the East Branch Association, London.

London. Sion College. see Sion College, London.

London. Society for Constitutional Information. see Society for Constitutional Information, London.

London. Society for Educating the Poor of Newfoundland. see Society for Educating the Poor of Newfoundland, London.

London. Society for Promoting Christian Knowledge, see Society for Promoting Christian Knowledge, London.

London. Society for the Civilization and Improvement of the North American Indians Within the British Boundary. see Society for the Civilization and Improvement of the North American Indians Within the British Boundary, London.

London. Society for the Conversion and Religious Instruction and Education of Negro Slaves. see Society for the Convention and Religious Instruction and Education of Negro Slaves, London.

London. Society for the Diffusion of Useful Knowledge. see Society for the Diffusion of Useful Knowledge, London.

London. Society for the Encouragement of Arts. see Royal Society of Arts, London.

London. Society for the Encouragement of Arts, Manufactures and Commerce. see Royal Society of Arts, London.

London. Society for the Extinction of the Slave Trade, and for the Civilization of Africa. see Society for the Extinction of the Slave Trade, and for the Civilization of Africa, London.

London. Society for the Mitigation and Gradual Abolition of Slavery. see Society for the Mitigation and Gradual Abolition of Slavery Throughout the British Dominions London.

London. Society for the Permanent Support of Orphan and Destitute Children. see Society for the Permanent Support of Orphan and Destitute Children, London.

London. Society for the Sale of Lands in America. see Society for the Sale of Lands in America, London.

London. Society for the Promotion of Permanent and Universal Peace. see Society for the Promotion of Permanent and Universal Peace, London.

London. Society for the Propagation of the Gospel in Foreign Parts. see Society for the Propagation of the Gospel in Foreign Parts, London.

London. Society for the Purpose of Effecting the Abolition of the Slave Trade. see Society for the Purpose of Effecting the Abolition of the Slave Trade, London.

London. Society Instituted for the Purpose of Effecting the Abolition of the Slave Trade. see Society for the Purpose of Effecting the Abolition of the Slave Trade, London.

London. Society of Noblemen and Gentlemen, for the Relief and Instruction of Poor Germans, and their Descendants, Settled in Pennsylvania, and the Adjacent British Colonies in America. see Society of Noblemen and Gentlemen, for the Relief and Instruction of Poor Germans, and their Descendants, Settled in Pennsylvania and the Adjacent British Colonies in America, London.

London. Southern Independence Association. see Southern Independence Association, London.

London. Spanish Merchants. petitioners see Portugal, Italian, and Spanish Merchants, London. petitioners

London. State Paper Office. see Great Britain. Public Record Office, London.

London. Sugar Refiners. petitioners see Sugar Refiners of London. petitioners

London Theatre-Royal, Covent Garden. 88533 88536, 88537, 88540-88541, 88543

London. The Times. see Times, London.

London. Tottenham-Court Chapel. 86583

London. Tottenham-Court Chapel. Centenary Commemoration, 1857. 71072

London. Unitarian Body. see Unitarian Body, London.

London. Wesleyan Missionary Society. see Wesleyan Missionary Society, London.

London. West India Body. see West India Body, London.

London. West India Planters and Merchants. see West India Planters and Merchants, London.

London. World's Fair, 1851. see London. Great Exhibition of the Industry of All Nations, 1851.

London. Worshipful Company of Haberdashers. see Worshipful Company of Haberdashers see London.

London. Zoological Society. see Zoological Society, London.

London (Diocese) Bishop and Clergy. peti-
tioners 9372, 81492
London, Ontario, Bishop of. see Pinsoneault,
-------, Bishop of London, Ontario.
London, Ontario. Wiberforce Colony. see
Wilberforce Colony, London, Ontario.
London and country brewer. 41861
London and New-York; their crime and police.
27119
London and Westminister review. (44939),
45014
London Anti-slavery Society. 37769, 66666,
69690, 81762, 90683, 90776, 95959
London Anti-slavery Society. Committee.
(81800)
London art journal. 27534, 40222
London Baptist Missionary Society. Com-
mittee. 3624
London calendar. 41855
London chronicle. 10732, 33340, 41856,
(42384), 59713, 66908
London Company of the Summer Islands.
see Bermuda Company.
London Company of Virginia. see Virginia
Company of London.
London cries. 105063
London daily advertiser. 84589, 103506
London daily news. 19759
London eclectic review. 81838
London Emancipation Society. Anti-slavery
Meeting, Spafield's Chapel, 1859. 41857
London evening post. 15523, (19253), 97572,
98349, 102786
London friend. pseud. Sober dialogue.
85662
London Friends' Institute. 83315
London Friends' Tract Association. see
Tract Association of the Society of
Friends, London.
London gazette. 14389, (23479), 41858,
(50044), 93962, 99249
London gazetteer. 94142
London journal. 86777
London magazine and monthly chronologer.
(41859), 52121, 88221, 91308
London magazine: or, gentleman's monthly
intelligencer. (41859), 52121, 88221,
91308
London Mathews. (46825)
London medical gazette. 4411
London mining journal. 90820, 90822
London Missionary Society. (59572), 82905-
82906
London Missionary Society. petitioners
82905
London Missionary Society. Directors.
23427, 82899, 82900, 82905, 82910
London Missionary Society. Directors.
Committee. (49480), (59572), note after
104633
London Missionary Society. Missionaries and
Catechists. 23463
London Missionary Society's report of the
proceedings. 82905
London morning chronicle. 2549, 39381-39382
London morning post. (46925), 92853
London morning post. Canada correspondent.
72306, 93469 see also Roche, Alfred R.
London National Loan Fund Life Assurance
Association. see National Loan Fund
Life Assurance Association of London.
London packet. 80040, 97565
London public advertiser. see Public
advertiser, London.
London quarterly review. 23351, 34481,
67599, note after 96593

London Religious Tract Society. see Religious
Tract Society, London.
London review. 96061
London review. see European magazine,
and London review.
London review of English and foreign literature.
41860
London Society for the Abolition of Slavery.
see Society for the Abolition of Slavery,
London.
London spy. 101285-101286
London stage. 88543
London tales on Uncle Tom's cabin. note
after 92624
London theatre. 88542
London times. see Times, London.
London Tract Association of the Society of
Friends. see Tract Association of the
Society of Friends, London.
London v. New York. 41862
London weekly history of the progress of the
Gospel. 25284, 83439, note after 103623
Londonderry, Charles William Vane Stewart,
3d Marquis of, 1758-1854. 91705
Londonderry, Robert Stewart, 2d Marquis of,
1769-1822. 1010, 1013, (16872), 91705
see also Great Britain. Foreign Office.
Londonderry, N. H. Old Nutfield Celebration,
1869. see Celebration of the One
Hundred and Fiftieth Anniversary of the
Settled Part of Old Nutfield, N. H.,
1869.
Londonderry celebration. 43347
Londonio, C. G. 41865
Londoy, Jorge. defendant 74860
Lone house; a peom. 23663
Lone star; or, the Texas bravo. 72127
Loney, Francis B. 41866
Long, ------, fl. 1789. supposed author
(5198)
Long, Alexander, 1816-1886. 41867
Long, Andrew K. defendant at court of
enquiry 41868
Long, Anthony. (31919)
Long, C. E. de. see De Long, C. E.
Long, Clement. 41869
Long, David. 41870
Long, Edward, 1734-1813. 41871-41872,
93365
Long, Edward M. 41873
Long, Enoch. defendant 27438, 42168
Long, George. 26984, 41874-41875, 97307
Long, H. M. supposed author 41877
Long, Henry C. 41876
Long, Isaac le. see Le Long, Isaac, b. 1863.
Long, John. Indian trader (64394), 41878-
41881
Long, John Dixon. (41882)
Long, John Le. see Le Long, John.
Long, Morris. 41883
Long, R. H. (41885)
Long, Robert Cary, d. 1849. (41884), 54476
Long, Samuel. 97060
Long, Stephen H. 35682-(35683), (37137),
41876, 41886-41888, 59955, (60572),
95746
Long, Zachariah. defendant 6326, 1st note
after 96956, 1st note after 97284
Long and short span railway bridges. 72575
Long Dock Company of New Jersey. Directors.
41889
Long expected tea ship arrived last night at
Sandy-Hook. 95982
Long Finne, a story of the New World. 59200
Long Island. 36626
Long-Island almanack, for . . . 1828. 89584

Long Island and New-York in olden times. 57315

Long-Island Bible Society, Jamaica, N. Y. 41893

Long Island College Hospital. (41896)

Long Island Congregational Convention. see Congregational Convention of Long Island.

Long-Island farmer. pseud. Letter. 40298

Long Island Historical Society. 18503, (24293), 41897, 84127

Long-Island journal of philosophy, and cabinet of variety. 41898

Long Island miscellanies. 74425

Long Island People. petitioners see Kings County, N. Y. petitioners New York (City) petitioners New York (County) petitioners Queens County, N. Y. petitioners Suffolk County, N. Y. petitioners

Long Island Railroad Company. Directors. 41899

Long Island tale, of the seventeenth century. 68513

Long-Island village. (33978)

Long Island Water Works Company. Charter. 8323

Long-Legged Joe. 90009

Long long time ago. 2560, 8870, (45211A)

Long lost Jackson boy, William Filley. 24328

Long memoire addresse par l'Empereur Maximilien. 34945, note after 48507

Long moss spring. 31436

Long-rifle hunter. 41902

Long-Run Association of Baptists. see Baptists. Kentucky. Long-Run Association.

Long talk at the first anniversary meeting [of the Alexandria Tammany Society.] 747

Long talk, delivered before the Tammany Society. 39889

Long talk, delivered before the Tammany Society or Columbian Order. 63050

Long vacation in the Argentine alps. 36216

Long Wharf, Newport, R. I. Trustees. School House. see Newport, R. I. School House Erected by the Trustees of the Long Wharf.

Longacre, J. B. illus. 75022, 84791

Longacre, James B. 31577, 2d note after 52014, 82987

Longchamp, ---------- de, fl. 1720. 41904

Longchamp, Marcelin. 4815, 69611-(69613), 69615

Longchamps, Pierre de, d. 1812. 38339, 41905

Longchamps, Walthere de Selys. see Selys-Longchamps, Walthere de.

Longer accidence. 99366

Longevidad de la tierra. 4914

Longevity. 32391

Longfellow, Henry Wadsworth, 1807-1882. 33390, 35221, (39987), (41906)-41910, (41912)-(41932), 44455, (46832), 55008, (63623), 68667, (70978), 79003, 84139-84141, 84143, 84146, 85536, 86890, note before 94463, note after 97969, 106207

Longfellow, Samuel, 1819-1892. 41933

Longfellow, Stephen L. 41934

Longley, Alcander. Ex. 85699

Longolius, Christophorus. 25088, 25994, 79345

Longperier, Adrien de. 41935

Long's first expedition. 35682

Long's second expedition. (37137)

Longstreet, Judge. see Longstreet, Augustus Baldwin, 1790-1870.

Longstreet, Augustus Baldwin, 1790-1870. (41936)-(41937)

Longview Hospital for the Insane. see Hamilton County, O. Longview Hospital Carthage.

Longworth, --------. 102461

Longworth, D. 41939-41940

Longworth, Thomas. 41939

Longworth's American almanack, . . . and city directory. 54459

Longworth's American alamanck, New York register and city directory. 41939

Longworth's [New York] . . . directory. 54459

Longworth's pocket almanack and New York and United States kalendar. 41940

Longworth. firm publishers 41940, 54459

Longworthy, A. supposed author 16084, 94946

Longworthy, Isaac P. 15479

Longyear, J. W. 41942

Lonsdale, M. 86902

Loocock, Aaron. 86670A

Loods. 16497

Look at some popular impositions. 33775

Look at the life of Theodore Parker. 13412

"Look before you leap." Addresses to the citizens of the southern states. 10889

Look before you leap. An address to the people of Massachusetts. 41944

Look before you leap; or a few hints to such artizans. (41943)

Look within for fact and fiction. (36836)

Looker-on. pseud. Eventful day in the Rhode Island rebellion. see Swaim, --------

Looker on. pseud. Jay's pamphlet reviewed. (35842)

Looker-on. pseud. Local loiterings. see Dix, John Ross.

Looker on. pseud. Sketch of Camden City, New Jersey. see Orr, Hector.

Looker on. pseud. Slavery. 82111

Looker on here in Verona. pseud. Sketches of United States' senators. see Holan, J. supposed author

Looker on in Vienna. pseud. Sights and notes. 80902

Looking glass: being a true report and narrative. (61240)

Looking glass for a Right Honourable mendicant 41945

Looking-glass for all merchants and planters. 104573

Looking-glass for changlings. 91757

Looking-glass for Elder Clarke and Elder Wightman. 13187

Looking-glass for high churchmen. (66176)

Looking-glass for impostors in philosophy, physic and government. 32236

Looking glass for overturning the ballance of power. 68690

Looking-glass for Presbyterians. 41946

Looking-glass, for Presbyterians. 60223

Looking-glass for the Americans. 68691

Looking-galss for the modern deists. 41948

Looking glass for the nullifiers. 10889

Looking-glass for the Presbyterians at New London. 72690

Looking glass for the times, etc. (24948)

Looking-glass for the worthies of the Buffalo Convention. 189

Looking-glass. Nos. I and II. 41947

Looking-glasse both for saints and sinners. 13477

Looking towards sun set. (12727)
Looking unto Jesus: a sermon, . . . Burling-
    ton, on the Sunday . . . after the decease
    of the Rev. Benjamin Winslow. 20391
Looking unto Jesus. [By Uriah Smith.]
    84473, 84476
Loomis, A. W. 41949
Loomis, C. A. (41950)
Loomis, D. W. 41952
Loomis, Dwight. 41951
Loomis, Elias, 1811-1889. 41953-41955,
    85072
Loomis, G. J. 601, 41956
Loomis, Harvey. 41957
Loomis, I. N. ed. 52047
Loomis, J. R. 41958
Loomis. firm publishers 41959
Loomis' calendar , or New-York and Vermont
    almanack. 41959
Loomis' Pittsburgh almanac, for the year 1841.
    41959
Loon, Geraard van. 41960
Loon, J. van. 100766
Loose leaves. 93966
Loose remarks on certain positions. 42945
Loose then from earth, and grasp of fond
    desire. 104949
Loosey, Charles F. 41961-41962
Loosjes, A. 41963-41965
Loosjes, P. tr. 71999
Lope del Rodo, Juan. see Rodo, Juan Lope
    del.
Loper, Richard F. 41967, 42571
Lopes, ------. 76848
Lopes de Mendonca, Antonio Pedro. see
    Mendonca, Antonio Pedro Lopes de.
Lopes de Moura, Caetano, 1780-1860. 12260,
    (16454), 16500, 49085
Lopes de Souza, Pedro. See Souza, Pedro
    Lopes de.
Lopes Ulhoa, Diogo. see Ulhoa, Diogo Lopes.
Lopesio, Gregorio. see Lopez, Gregorio.
Lopez, Abraham. (41969)
Lopez, Andres. petitioner (41971)
Lopez, Antonio Prudencio. 41972
Lopez, Antonio Xavier Perez y. see Perez
    y Lopez, Antonio Xavier.
Lopez, D. U. 41977
Lopez, Francisco. (61105)
Lopez, Francisco. supposed author 61149,
    note after 97695
Lopez, G. 41980
Lopez, Gernando. 86411
Lopez, Gregorio, 16th cent. 28739, 41978
Lopez, Gregorio, fl. 1674. 42578, 75605
Lopez, Hipolito Ruiz. see Ruiz Lopez,
    Hipolito, 1754-1815.
Lopez, John. defendant 6326, 1st note after
    96956, 1st note after 97284
Lopez, Jose Francisco. 41983-41984
Lopez, Juan Luis. 31987, 41987, 61103,
    61109, 61110, (61114), (61150)
Lopez, Lucio. 41988
Lopez, Manuel Antonio. (41990)-41991
Lopez, Mateo de Vesga. see Vesga Lopez,
    Mateo de.
Lopez, Matthias. 105192
Lopez, Patricio Antonio. (41996)
Lopez, Thomas. 41999
Lopez, Thome. 67730
Lopez, Vicente Fidel. 42000-42001, (70311)
Lopez a Mendizabala, Gregorius. 41979
Lopez Aguado, Juan. 41985
Lopez Aguado, Juan. supposed author (30382)
    (44529)

Lopez Arbizu, Miguel Romero. see Romero
    Lopez Arbizu, Miguel.
Lopez Cancelada, Juan. 10652-10655, 35299,
    41986, 56248, 94607, 94609, 99452-99455
Lopez Cogolludo, Diego. see Lopez de
    Cogolludo, Diego.
Lopez de Aragon, Manuel. (41989)
Lopez de Ayala, Pedro. 41997
Lopez de Bustamente, Jose. see Bustamente,
    Jose Lopez de.
Lopez de Castillo, Dom. 41975
Lopez de Cogolludo, Diego. 14210-14212,
    41973, 80883
Lopez de Couarruuias, Pedro. see Couarru-
    uias, Pedro Lopez de.
Lopez de Escobar, Diego. petitioner (41974),
    1st note after 96979
Lopez de Gomara, Francisco. see Gomara,
    Francisco Lopez de, 1510-1560?
Lopez de Guzman y Ayala, Sebastian. 44418
Lopez de Haro, Damian. see Haro, Damian
    Lopez de.
Lopez de Hinojoso, Alonso. 41970
Lopez de Hortigosa, Tomas. see Hortigosa,
    Tomas Lopez de.
Lopez de Legaspi, Michael. 66686
Lopez de Lisboa y Lyon, Diego. see Lisboa
    y Lyon, Diego Lopez de.
Lopez de Mendoza, Juan. see Mendoza, Juan
    Lopez de.
Lopez de Peralta y Pujadas, Maria Geronyma.
    defendant 94874
Lopez de Santa Anna, Antonio. see Santa
    Anna, Antonio Lopez de, Pres. Mexico,
    1795-1876.
Lopez de Solis, Francisco. see Solis,
    Francisco Lopez de, d. 1664.
Lopez de Sousa, J. P. see Sousa, J. P.
    Lopez de.
Lopez de Zubiria, Jose Antonio, Bp. 41982
    see also Durango (Diocese) Bishop
    (Lopez de Zubiria)
Lopez Gonzalo, Victoriano. see Gonzalo,
    Victoriano Lopez, Bp.
Lopez Matoso, Antonio Ygnacio. see Matoso,
    Antonio Ygnacio Lopez.
Lopez Mellado, Francisco. see Mellado,
    Francisco Lopez.
Lopez Moscoso, Andres. see Moscoso, Andres
    Lopez.
Lopez Negrede, Agustin. see Negrede,
    Agustin Lopez.
Lopez Pacheco y Bobadilla, Diego. (41976)
Lopez Portillo, Jesus. see Portillo, Jesus
    Lopez.
Lopez Rayon, Ignacio. see Rayon, Ignacio
    Lopez.
Lopez Ruiz, Santiago Jose. see Ruiz,
    Santiago Jose Lopez.
Lopez Ruiz, Sebastian Josef. see Ruiz,
    Sebastian Josef Lopez.
Lopez Salazar, Jose Antonio. see Salazar,
    Jose Antonio Lopez.
Lopez Uraga, Jose. 93578
Lopez Yepes, Joaquin. see Yepes, Joaquin
    Lopez.
Lopezio Portillo, Antonio. see Portillo,
    Antonio Lopezio.
Lorain, John. 42002
Lorain, P. (42003)
Loranger, T. J. J. 42004-(42005)
Lord, ------, fl. 1830. 52887
Lord, ------, fl. 1850. 42033
Lord, A. D. ed. (56986)
Lord, Benjamin, 1694-1784. 42007-42013,
    105855

Lord, C. E. 42017

Lord, Charles Eliphalet, 1817-1902. 42014-42016

Lord, Dan. defendant 96900

Lord, Daniel. 39851, 42019, 93647

Lord, Daniel. supposed author 42018, 57245, 64054

Lord, Elazer, 1788-1871. 40018, 42020-42024, 54448, 95715

Lord, G. A. 42025, 90578

Lord, Henry. (42026)

Lord, Henry C. petitioner 42039

Lord, Henry W. 42027

Lord, John. 42028

Lord, John Chase, 1805-1877. 8790, (42029)-42032, 81152, 89736

Lord, John Keast, 1818-1872. 42033-42035

Lord, John Perkins, 1786-1877. (42036)

Lord, Joseph. 3554, 21670, 42037-42038, 92095, 92099, 92101, 92104, 92105, 103617

Lord, Joseph L. petitioner 42039

Lord, Nathan, 1793-1870. (31378), 40354, 42040-42045

Lord, Nathaniel James. (42046)

Lord, Otis Phillips, 1812-1884. 42047

Lord, W., fl. 1820. (43992)

Lord, Rev. W., fl. 1841. 69673

Lord, William Blair. reporter 34982, 42048, 45124, 48728, 87508

Lord, William H. (42049)-42050

Lord, William Wilberforce, 1819-1907. (42051)-42052

Lord a stronghold in the day of trouble. (17372)

Lord Anson's voyage round the world. 1635

Lord Bacon and Sir Walter Raleigh. 67599

Lord Baltamore's [sic] case, uncased and answered. 100547

Lord Baltamore's [sic] printed case, uncased and answered. 100547

Lord Baltemore's case. 100546

Lord Bathurst's despatch of the 9th of July. 8005

Lord Brougham's speech on the maltreatment of the North American colonies. 8416

Lord Brougham's speech upon the Ashburton Treaty. (8411)

Lord Burley's ten precepts. 90233, 90236-90237, 90246

Lord Ch---am's prophecy, an ode. 63094

Lord Campbell and Professor Morse. 50963

Lord Chatham's speech in the British House of Lords. 63070

Lord Chesterfield's advice to his son. 90236-90237, 90246

Lord Chesterfield's advice to his son, on men and manners. 90230, 90233

Lord Chesterfield's letters to his son Philip Stanhope, Esquire. 90229

Lord Chesterfield's principles of politeness. 90238

Lord Chesterfifld's [sic] advice to his son. 90243

Lord Cornbury's commission and instructions. 39527

Lord Glenelg's despatches to Sir F. B. Head, Bart. (28301)

Lord Glenelg's reply thereto. 31138

Lord Grenville's reception of Citizen Gallatin. 14008

Lord Hail-Fair. pseud. Fame and fancy. see Cobb, Enos. supposed author

Lord-High-Admiral of all the seas, adored. 46390

Lord Howe's extraordinary gazette. 52069

Lord is on our side. 16398

Lord is to be praised for the triumphs of his power. 2480

Lord Jesus Christ the . . . supeream head of the church. 3471

Lord Jesus walking in the midst of the churches 46559, 96766

Lord Lyons in the Council with the Democracy. 62352

Lord Mansfield's speech. 51546

Lord N——th condemned. (55516)

Lord North's te deum for the victorious defeat at Boston. 105974

Lord of Talladega. (77836)

Lord our helper; a sermon in commemoration of the sixth anniversary. 18702

Lord our helper. A sermon, preached in St. James' Church. 93079

Lord our light. 103510

Lord our righteousness. 103567, 103573

Lord reigneth. (19605)

Lord shall rejoice in His works. (14497)

Lord Stanley's speech, in the House of Commons. 90303

Lord Viscount Howe. 50185, 82379

Lords Commissioners of Appeals in Prize Causes. see Great Britain. High Court of Appeals for Prizes.

Lords Commissioners of Prizes. The William Galley. 104157

Lord's day proved to be the Christian Sabbath. 4287

Lord's freeman. 26059

Lord's ministers are the people's helpers. 30166

Lord's prayer in one hundred languages. 28134

Lord's prayer: or, a new attempt to recover the right version. 46897

Lords protest against the convention-treaty. 42053

Lord's protest on the treaty of peace, union and friendship. 42054

Lord's songs. 88889

Lord's voice in the earthquake. 50793

Lord's voyage, crying to his people. 13204

Lorea, Antonio de. 42055-(42056)

Loreau, Henriette. tr. 17939, 69017, 59040, 69042, 69060

Lorente, Sebastian. 42057-42061

Lorento, ---------Penalver, Conde de Santa Maria de. see Penalver, ------, Conde de Santa Maria de Lorento.

Lorenz de Rada, Joseph. see Rada, Joseph Lorenz de.

Lorenzana y Buitron, Francisco Antonio, Cardinal. 16938-16939, (16953), 16958, 16964, 42062-42066, 47702, 48559, 55934, 69229, 72519, note after 90828, 94355 see also Mexico (Archdiocese) Archbishop (Lorenzana y Buitron) Michoacan (Archdiocese) Archbishop (Lorenzana y Buitron)

Lorenzana y Buitron, Francisco Antonio, Cardinal. petitioner 48559 see also Mexico. (Archdiocese) Archbishop (Lorenzana y Buitron) petitioner

Lorenzo de San Milian, Francisco. defendant 42067 see also Mexico (Viceroyalty) Contador de la Visita de las Caxas Reales. defendant

Lorenzo de Vidaurre y Encalada, Manuel. see Vidaurre y Encalada, Manuel Lorenzo de.

Lorenzo del S[anto] Sacramento. Fray 42068

Lorenzo and Oonalaska. 72284

Lorenzo's journal. (20753), 20757

Lorenzo's thoughts on various religious opinions. 20757

Loreto, --------, Conde de Sta. Maria de. see Sta. Maria de Lorento, --------, Conde de.

Lorette. History of Louise, daughter of a Canadian nun. 6919, (42069)

Lorgnette; or, studies of the town. 49674

Lorgues, Antonio Francois Felix, Comte Roselly de. see Roselly de Lorgues, Antoine Francois Felix, Comte, 1805-1898.

Loria, Jose de Soto. see Soto Loria, Jose de.

Lorillard, ----------. defendant 96923

Lorimer, George C. 84053

Lorimer, John. 26763, 42070

Lorimer, John Gordon. (42071), (78726), 85273, 104001

Lorimer, Mary. 42072

Lorimer, William. 104184

Lorin. Indian Chief 4391, 15429

Loring, --------. defendant 96847

Loring, Amasa. (42073)

Loring, Bailey. 42074

Loring, Charles Greely, 1794-1867. 6505, 9400, 9404, 16880, 42075-42078, 92068, 93270, 101056, 105613

Loring, Edward G. 42079

Loring, F. W. (42080)

Loring, George B. 42081-42083

Loring, Israel. 42084-42088, 94067

Loring, James Spear. 42089

Loring, Jerome. 42090

Loring, John G. 42092

Loring, Joseph. defendant at court martial 42093-(42096), (45728), 48976, 8th note after 96930A

Loring, Nathaniel Hall. 42097, 104063

Loring, Nathaniel Hall. petitioner 42098

Loring, Thomas. 42099

Loring, W. W. see Lorring, William Wing, 1818-1886.

Loris, Heinrich. see Glareanus, Henricus, 1488-1563.

Lorito, Antonio Ardoino, Marques de. see Ardoino, Antonio, Marques de Lorito.

Lormendi, ------. 69233

Lorne, John George Edward Henry Douglas Sutherland Campbell, Marquis of. see Argyll, John George Edward Henry Douglas Sutherland Campbell, 9th Duke of, 1845-1914.

Lorra Baquio, Francisco de. 42102

Lorner, M. 42101

Lorrain, Paul. tr. (51443)

Lorraine, E. 42103

Lorring, William Wing, 1818-1886. 15369, 42100

Lorry Luff. pseud. see Luff, Lorry. pseud.

Lort, Michael. (42105)

Loryea, Joseph. 42104

Los Hoyos, Juan de. see Hoyos, Juan de los.

Los Ovios, Alonso Vascallero de. see Vascallero de los Ovios, Alonso.

Los Rio, Epitacio J. de. see Rios, Epitacio J. de los.

Los Rios, J. P. de. see Rios, J. P. de los.

Los Rios, Jose Amador de. see De los Rios, Jose Amador.

Los Rios y Rosas, Antonio de. see Rios y Rosas, Antonio de los.

Losa, Francois de. see Loza, Francisco.

Losada, Basilio Sebastian Castellanos de. 2534, 2539

Losada, Juan Miguel de. 42107

Loschke, J. T. 1864

Loskiel, Georg Heinrich. 42109-42111

Loss of a wife. (67878)

Loss of Central America. 90831

Loss of the American brig Commerce. 71398

Loss of the Orion. (38474)

Loss of the San Francisco. A sermon at Newport, R. I. 7756

Loss of the San Francisco, by Rev. W. H. Cooper. 16646

Loss of the soul. 12335

Loss of the Sparrow-Hawk in 1626. 41560, (42112), note after 89026

Lossa, Francisco. see Loza, Francisco.

Lossada, Diego de Quiroga y. see Quiroga y Lossada, Diego de.

Lossada, Domingo. (42113)

Losses and gains of a church. 37848

Losses to literature and art by the great fire in Boston. 60937

Lossing, ---------. cartographer and engr. 83931

Lossing, Benson John, 1813-1891. 5220, 16352, (18157), 28312, 30449, 28901, (30969), (32981), 42114-42135, 42860, 43545, (58457), 77983, (80023), 89336, 89341, 92904, note after 96144, 97212

Lossing, P. J. ed. 104205

Lost amid the fogs. 43116

Lost among the floes. 90508

Lost and found; or life among the poor. 29903

Lost and won. 90564

Lost arm. 72600

Lost cause; a new southern history of the war. 63873

Lost cause regained. 63875

Lost chapter in American history. 83715, 83719

Lost flocke triumphant. 70889, note after 99857

Lost Greenland. (28652)

Lost in the forest. 42136

Lost pleiad and other poems. 12854

Lost prince. 30267, 104213

Lost principle. 78307-78308

Lost sailors. 16530

Lost sister of Wyoming. 52321, 96089

Lost steamer. 42137

Lost trappers. 17319

Lost treasure found. 9985, (11475)

Los Teques, Venezuela. Citizens. 94829

Lot van lichaam en ziel by's menchen dood. 98586

Lotbiniere, Joly de. ed. 94850

Lotgevallen der Protestanten in Engelandt en Schotlandt. 52146

Lotgevallen en ontmoetingen van een gezelschap. 27175

Lotgevallen en ontmoetingen van Kapitien Bonneville. 35128

Lotgevallen op eene zeereis naar de West-Kust van Amerika. 18450, note after 97587

Lotgevallen op zijne gedane zee-en landreizen van 1790-1818. 38344

Lotgevallen van Kapitein Alderick. 32787

Lothian, William Schomberg Robert Kerr, Marquis of. (37633)-37834

Lothian, William Henry Kerr, 4th Marquis of d. 1755. 94691

Lothrop, Amy. pseud. Dollars and cents. see Warner, Anna Bartlett.

Lothrop, S. H. 6652

Lothrop, Samuel Kirkland. 42139-42149

Lotsen. Sjoberattelse. 16501

Louisiana. Auditor of Public Accounts. see Louisiana. Auditor's Office.

Louisiana. Auditor's Office. 42194, (42274)

Louisiana. Board of Education for Freedmen. 42224

Louisiana. Board of Health. 42196

Louisiana. Board of Registration. (42198)

Louisiana. Board of Swamp Land Commissioners. 42199

Louisiana. Board of Works. 42197

Louisiana. Bureau of Immigration. 42200

Louisiana. Centenary, College. see Shreveport, La. Centenary College of Louisiana.

Louisiana. Charity Hospital, Shreveport. 42203

Louisiana. Circuit Courts. see Louisiana. Courts of Appeal.

Louisiana. Citizens. petitioners 42261, 42263, (42281), 61269

Louisiana. Commission of Levee Engineers. petitioners 42248

Louisiana. Commissioners to Revise the Statutes. 42213

Louisiana. Constitution. 1269, 1271, 2071, 5316, 6360, 16103, 16107, 16113, 16133, 25790, 27576, 33137, 42214-42215, 42227, 42265, (47188), 57627, 59771, 65866, (66397), 104198

Louisiana. Constitutional Convention, 1844-1845, New Orleans. 42240, 42242, 42278, 42287

Louisiana. Constitutional Convention, 1864. 42217, (42276)

Louisiana. Constitutional Convention, 1867-1868. (42277)

Louisiana. Convention, 1861. 42275, 65866

Louisiana. Courts of Appeal (1st Circuit) 27318, 96920

Louisiana. Criminal Court of the First Judicial Circuit. see Louisiana. Courts of Appeal (1st Circuit)

Louisiana. General Assembly. (42219)-42220, 422294, 42303, 42306, 105479

Louisiana. General Assembly. petitioners 42260

Louisiana. General Assembly. Comite de Proceder a une Enquete a l'Effet de Decouvrir la Cause des Mesures Militaires qui ont ete Exercees. 42286

Louisiana. General Assembly. Joint Committee of Finance. 42293, 63365

Louisiana. General Assembly. Joint Committee on the Affairs of the Citizens' Bank of Louisiana. 42195

Louisiana. General Assembly. Joint Committee on the Investigation of Banks, 1840. 42195

Louisiana. General Assembly. Standing Committee on Levees, Drainage, etc. 42295

Louisiana. General Assembly. House of Representatives. 42236, 42238, 42241, (42273)

Louisiana. General Assembly. Senate. 42221, 42237, 42239, (42243), (42279), (71971)

Louisiana. Geological Reconnoissance. 42230

Louisiana. Governor, 1812-1816 (Claiborne) 33150 see also Claiborne, William Charles Cole, 1775-1817.

Louisiana. Governor, 1820-1824 (Robertson) (71971) see also Robertson, Thomas Bolling, 1784-1828.

Louisiana. Governor, 1839-1843 (Roman) 72893 see also Roman, Andrew Bienvenu, 1795-1866.

Louisiana. Governor, 1853-1856 (Herbert) 42268 see also Hebert, Paul Octave, 1818-1880.

Louisiana. Governor, 1856-1860 (Wickliffe) 33150, 42269 see also Wickliffe, Robert Charles, 1820-1895.

Louisiana. Governor, 18620-1862 (Moore) 42234 see also Moore, Thomas Overton, 1805-1876.

Louisiana. Governor, 1864-1865 (Allen) 42271, 42307, 83921 see also Allen, Henry Watkins, 1820-1866.

Louisiana. Governor, 1864-1865 (Hahn) (42235), (42247), 42271 see also Hahn, Michael, 1830-1886.

Louisiana. Insane Asylum, Jackson. 42233

Louisiana. Laws, statutes, etc. 9119, 23765, 39414, 41614-(41615), 42181, 42184-42185, 42204-42210, 42213, 42221-42222, 42225, 42227, 42228, 42244-42245, 42251, (42299)-42302, 42310, 52051, 53300, 53314, (57512), 62890, 65866, 70820-70821, 72156, 82438, 88304, 88405, 88610, 89066, 97758, 98104, 102763

Louisiana. Militia. New Orleans Tigers. see Louisiana. Militia. Washington Artillery Battalion, New Orleans.

Louisiana. Militia. Washington Artillery Battalion, New Orleans. 53317

Louisiana. Penitentiary. 42254

Louisiana. Secretary of State. 42223

Louisiana. State Engineer. 42296

Louisiana. State Library, New Orleans. 42257

Louisiana. State Seminary of Learning. see Louisiana. State University and Agricultural and Mechanical College.

Louisiana. State Seminary of Learning and Military Academy. see Louisiana. State University and Agricultural and Mechanical College.

Louisiana. State Treasurer. see Louisiana. Treasurer's Office.

Louisiana. State University and Agricultural and Mechanical College. 42274

Louisiana. State University and Agricultural and Mechanical College. Board of Supervisors. 42258, 42310

Louisiana. Sundry Inhabitants. petitioners see Sundry Inhabitants of Louisiana. petitioners

Louisiana. Superintendent of Public Instruction. 42223-42224

Louisiana. Supreme Court. 28247, 42251, (51560), 82142-82144, 82145, 105479

Louisiana. Supreme Court (Eastern District) 96920

Louisiana. Treasurer's Office. 42297

Louisiana. Union Bank. see Union Bank of Louisiana.

Louisiana. University, New Orleans. see Tulane University of Louisiana.

Louisiana. 62506

Louisiana and Mississippi directory. 42249

Louisiana and the Floridas (Diocese) Bishop (Penalver y Cardenas) 72945, (80023) see also Penalver y Cardenas, Luis Ignatius, Bp.

Louisiana and the tariff. (42250)

Louisiana Bank, New Orleans. Committee of Stockholders. see Louisiana Bank, New Orleans. Stockholders. Committee.

Louisiana Bank, New Orleans. Stockholders. Committee. 42195

Louisiana College. see Tulane University of Louisiana.

Louisiana constitution. 18181

1529

Louisiana Convention of the Friends of
Universal Suffrage, 1865. see Convention of the Friends of Universal Suffrage
of Louisiana, 1865.
Louisiana delegation. 18181
Louisiana digest. 42251
Louisiana. Ein Taschenbuch. 8207
Louisiana English grammar. note before
83906, 83921
Louisiana; episode emprunta a la domination
Francaise en Amerique. 26690
Louisiana Free State Party. see Free State
Party. Louisiana.
Louisiana Homestead Aid Association. 42252
Louisiana; its colonial history and romance.
26795
Louisiana: its history as a French colony.
26796
Louisiana law journal. (42253)
Louisiana Mechanics and Agricultural Fair
Association. see Mechanics and Agricultural Fair Association of Louisiana.
Louisiana merchants' & planters' almanac.
89574
Louisiana Native American Association.
(42185) see also American Party.
Louisiana.
Louisiana preserved. 103417
Louisiana Relief Lodge, New Orleans. see
Freemasons. Louisiana. Louisiana
Relief Lodge, New Orleans.
Louisiana Rock-Salt Company. 42280
Louisiana State Colonization Society.
petitioners 42255
Louisiana State Colonization Society. Facts
in regard to African colonization.
42255
Louisiana state gazetteer and business man's
guide. 42256
Louisiana State Medical Society. Committee
on the Meteorology and Hygiene of the
State and its Vital Statistics. 81294
Louisiana swamp doctor. 94822
Louisianais. pseud. Apercu topographique
de la Louisiane. 42191
Louisiane. 101350
Louisianian. pseud. Biography of the Hon.
Solomon W. Downs. 20791
Louisville, Ky. (42313), 42332
Louisville, Ky. plaintiff (42317)
Louisville, Ky. American Indian Missionary
Association Meeting, 3d, 1845. see
American Indian Missionary Association.
Annual Meeting, 3d, Louisville, 1845.
Louisville, Ky. Auditor. (42314)
Louisville, Ky. Catholic Benevolent Society
see Catholic Benevolent Society,
Louisville, Ky.
Louisville, Ky. Chamber of Commerce.
42324
Louisville, Ky. Chancery Court. (5162)
Louisville, Ky. Charter. 42316, 42319
Louisville, Ky. Collegiate Institute. see
Collegiate Institute, Louisville, Ky.
Louisville, Ky. Commercial Convention, 1869.
see Commercial Convention, Louisville,
Ky., 1869.
Louisville, Ky. Commercial Convention, 1871.
see Southern Commercial Convention,
Louisville, Ky., 1871.
Louisville, Ky. Filson Society. see Filson
Society, Louisville, Ky.
Louisville, Ky. First Annual Meeting of the
Indian Missionary Association, 1843.
see Indian Mission Association. Annual
Meeting, 1st., Louisville, Ky., 1843.

Louisville, Ky. Friends of General Jackson,
1827. see Democratic Party. Kentucky.
Louisville.
Louisville, Ky. Kentucky Mechanics' Institute.
see Kentucky Mechanics' Institute,
Louisville, Ky.
Louisville, Ky. Mayor, 1866. (42313)
Louisville, Ky. Medical Institute. 42329, 4233
Louisville, Ky. Mercantile Library Association. 42337
Louisville, Ky. National Guard. 42338
Louisville, Ky. Ordinances, etc. 42311,
42316, (42320)
Louisville, Ky. Protestant Episcopal Orphan
Asylum. see Protestant Episcopal Orphan
Asylum of the City of Louisville, Ky.
Louisville, Ky. Schools. 42311
Louisville, Ky. Schools. Trustees. 42311,
42321
Louisville, Ky. Society for the Advancement
of Natural Sciences. see Society for the
Advancement of Natural Sciences,
Louisville, Ky.
Louisville, Ky. South-Western Railroad Bank.
see South-Western Railroad Bank,
Louisville, Ky.
Louisville, Ky. Stockholders Meeting of the
Southern Pacific Railroad Company,
1858. see Southern Pacific Railroad
Company (Texas) Stockholders Meeting,
Louisville, Ky., 1858.
Louisville, Ky. University. defendants
(42317)
Louisville, Ky. University. Medical Department. 42342
Louisville, Ky. Washington Fire-Engine
Company. see Washington Fire-Engine
Company, Louisville, Ky.
Louisville (Diocese) 26905, 72975
Louisville (Diocese) Bishop (McCloskey)
(72948) see also McCloskey, William,
Bp.
Louisville (Diocese) Bishop (Spalding) 72946-
72947 see also Spalding, Martin John,
Abp., 1810-1872.
Louisville (Diocese) Synod, 1850. 72946
Louisville (Diocese) Synod, 1862. 72947
Louisville (Diocese) Synod, 1874. (72948)
Louisville and Jefferson County Horticultural
Society. 42322
Lousiville and Nashville Railroad Company.
President. 83629 see also Smith,
Milton Hannibal, 1836-1921.
Louisville and Portland Canal Company.
42323
Louisville, Cincinnati, and Charleston Railroad
Company. 42325
Louisville, Cincinnati, and Charleston Railroad
Company. Meeting of Stockholders.
42325
Louisville, Cincinnati, and Charleston Railroad
Company. President. (31042), 42325
see also Hayne, Robert Young, 1791-1839.
Louisville Daily reporter. Editor. 104022
see also Browne, Thomas Edgerton.
Louisville democrat. 84403
Louisville directory for the year 1832. 42326
Louisville Gas and Water Company. 42328
Louisville gazette. 102473
Louisville, her commercial, manufacturing and
social advantages. 19236
Louisville Jockey Club. 42328
Louisville journal. 17654, 22978, (40629),
84403
Louisville journal. Editor. 65064 see also
Prentice, George D.

Louisville journal of medicine and surgery. 102992

Louisville Literary Brass Band. (37861)

Louisville Mechanics' Institute. see Kentucky Mechanics' Institute, Louisville, Ky.

Louisville municipal reports. 42332

Louisville Pilots' Benevolent Society. (42333)

Louisville Refugee Commission. 42334

Louisville Temperance Society. 42335

Lounsbery, Edward. 42344

Loureiro, Joao Bernardo da Rocha. 42345

Loureiro, Lorenco Trigo de. 42346

Loureiro, P. (42347)

Lourmel, Felix Esprit de. tr. 11554, 51419, 51422

Louth, Robert. see Lowth, Robert, successively Bishop of St. Davids, Oxford, and London, 1710-1787.

Louvain, Belgium. Society for the Propagation of the Faith. see Society for the Propagation of the Faith, Louvain.

Louveau, Jean. tr. 26668

Louverture, François Dominique Toussaint. see Toussaint Louverture, Francois Dominique, 1743-1803.

L'Ouverture, Isaac. 48211

Louverture, Pierre Dominique Toussaint. see Toussaint Louverture, Pierre Dominique.

Louvet de Couvray, Jean Baptiste. 42357-42358

Love, --------, fl. 1863. (42361)

Love, Alfred H. 42359

Love, Charles, fl. 1651. 101877

Love, Charles, fl. 1800. 42360

Love, Christopher, 1618-1651. 92713-92714

Love, Mrs. Christopher. 92714

Love, Horace T. (42362) see also Brown University. Agent.

Love, William. defendant 47194

Love, William Deloss. (42363)-42364

Love affair of Benedict Arnold. 93713

Love affairs in our village twenty years ago. 46873

Love afloat. 80291

Love and arsenic. 51208

Love and constancy of two savages in the desert. 12240

Love and friendship. 1692, 63577

Love and land. Founded on the invasion of Maximilian. 18271

Love and land: poems. (77445)

Love and liberty. 65115

Love and loyalty. 89303

Love and patriotism! 42357

Love and war in 1860-61. 23741

Love-Country, Justice. pseud. Dialogue. see Gooch, Sir William, Bart., 1681-1751.

Love, forest flowers and sea shells. 40783

Love in death. 79866-(79867)

Love in Mexico. 77454

Love in the wilderness. (69083)

Love life of Brig. Gen. Henry M. Naglee. 51717

Love-life of Dr. Kane. 25373

Love of country: a discourse, delivered . . . Thanksgiving Day. 81642

Love of country. A discourse preached in . . . New Haven. 13589

Love of country. A sermon . . . April 28, 1861. 3504

Love of God, benevolence, and self-love, considered together. 101504

Love of Jerusalem, the prosperity of a people. 33949

Love of money. A discourse. 89744

Love of no politics. 103291

Love of our country. A sermon. 34017

Love of our country recommended and enforced. 92275

Love of our country represented and urged. 104349

Love of pleasure. 37976

Love; or woman's destiny. 29670

Love-scrapes of a lifetime. (67620)

Love . . . sermon . . . ordination of the Reverend Mr. William Vinal. 24440

Love to Christ. 101865

Love to our neighbour explained and urged. (71509)

Love to our neighbour recommended. 50661

Love token for children. 78788-78789

Love towards enemies and the way to manifest it. 3613

Love triumphant. 46391

Love waxing cold. 85310

Love, wisdom, justice and power of God manifested. 91817

Lovechild, Nurse. pseud. Tommy Thumb's picture book. see Fenn, Eleanor (Frere) Lady, 1743-1813

Loved and the lost. 42365

Lovejoy, J. M. 55683

Lovejoy, Joseph Cammet, 1805-1871. 39334, 42366-42367, 85345, 96281

Lovejoy, Owen, 1811-1864. 42366, 42368-42369, 42371, 79524

Lovejoy's lecture on . . . intoxicating drinks. 39334

Lovelace, Francis, 1621-1675. 53729 see also New York (Colony) Governor, 1668-1673 (Lovelace)

Lovell, James, 1737-1814. (6737), 42372-42375

Lovell, John, 1710-1778. (25749), 30754, 42376-42378, 78670

Lovell, John Epy, 1795-1892. 42379-(42381)

Lovell, Joseph. 39456, 42382, 48172 see also U. S. Army. Surgeon General's Office.

Lovell, Langford. (42383)

Lovell, Laura H. 82049

Lovell, Mansfield, 1822-1884. 16873

Lovell, Solomon. 9925

Lovell (John W.) Company. firm publishers 85165

Lovell's fight. 94109

Lovell's library a daily publication of the best current and standard literature. 85165

Lovely sisters. 80967

Loven, Hermes van. 48175

Lover, Samuel. illus. 43846

Lover and friend of mankind. pseud. Affectionate address. 492

Lover of Africa. pseud. Anecdotes of Africans. 81849

Lover of astronomy. pseud. New England kalender. 52695, 62743

Lover of constitutional liberty. pseud. Appendix. 1792, note after 45640, 81891

Lover of Cudworth and truth. pseud. Cudworth defended. see Cheever, George Barrell.

Lover of good men, however vilified and abused. pseud. Vindication of the Reverend Mr. George Whitefield. 99827

Lover of his country. pseud. Address to the inhabitants. (45602)

Lover of his country. pseud. Brief account of the state of the province. 45657

Lover of his country. pseud. ed. Historical account of the expedition against the Ohio Indians. see Smith, William, 1727-1803.

Lover of his country. pseud. Modest enquiry. (49823)

Lover of his country. pseud. Money the sinews of trade. (49973)

Lover of his country. pseud. South-sea scheme detected. 88201

Lover of his country. pseud. Temporal interest of North America. see Morgan, Joseph.

Lover of his king and country. pseud. Christian's duty. (12930), note after 66918

Lover of his [i.e. William Penn's] memory. pseud. ed. see Rhodes, John.

Lover of his country. 1691, 14021

Lover of honesty. pseud. Some errors of the Quakers. see Plain man, and a lover of honesty. pseud.

Lover of improvement. pseud. English practice. 22620

Lover of improvement. pseud. Statement, showing some of the evils and absurdities. see Sedgwick, Henry Dwight, 1785-1831.

Lover of internal devotion. pseud. tr. and publisher 80622-80623

Lover of King George and of every real Christian. pseud. see J., W., a lover of King George and of every real Christian. pseud.

Lover of liberty, a poem in three books. (67609)

Lover of liberty; being a discourse. 33036

Lover of mankind. pseud. Mighty destroyer displayed. see Benezet, Anthony, 1713-1784.

Lover of mankind. pseud. Potent enemies of America laid open. see Benezet, Anthony, 1713-1784.

Lover of peace. pseud. Seasonable address. see Wesley, John, 1703-1791.

Lover of peace and good government. pseud. Letter to the Rev. Dr. Price. see Stewart, James, d. 1794?

Lover of peace and liberty. pseud. Rhaposdical execration on the slave trade. 102701

Lover of religion and learning. pseud. Letter to a member of the House of Representatives. see Graham, John.

Lover of righteousness. pseud. ed. see Pennyman, John.

Lover of the art military. pseud. New exercise of firelocks and bayonets. 52764

Lover of the fine arts. pseud. Judith, Esther, and other poems. see Brooks, Maria (Gowen) 1795-1845.

Lover of the mathematicks. pseud. Almanac. 62743

Lover of the present happy constitution. pseud. Gloria Britannorum. 27586

Lover of the truth. pseud. Mystery revealed. 51660

Lover of the truth. pseud. Short direction. 80619

Lover of the truth. pseud. Some farraginous remarks. see Haynes, J. supposed author

Lover of the truth. pseud. Trial. see Prentiss, Charles.

Lover of their precious souls. pseud. History of the Holy Jesus. 84553

Lover of true English liberty. pseud. Notemaker noted. 55945

Lover of true piety, in opposition to enthusiasm. pseud. Methodism anatomiz'd. (48178)

Lover of truth. pseud. Address to the Rev. Dr. Alison. (42384), 66908

Lover of truth. pseud. Disputation concerning church-members and their children. (20274)

Lover of truth. pseud. Late religious commotions. see Rand, William.

Lover of truth. pseud. To the public. 95981

Lover of truth, T. M. pseud. For the service of truth. see Maule, Thomas.

Lover of truth and decency. pseud. Vindication of the Bishop of Landaff's sermon. see Inglis, Charles, Bishop of Nova Scotia, 1734-1816. supposed author

Lover of truth, and his country. pseud. Letter to a member of the Lower House of Assembly. see Gale, Benjamin, 1715-1790.

Lover of truth and justice. pseud. Inquiry into the origin of modern anaesthesia. see Smith, Truman, 1791-1884.

Lover of truth and liberty. pseud. Essential rights and liberties of protestants. see Williams, Elisha. supposed author

Lover of truth and liberty. pseud. History of England. see Ralph, James.

Lover of truth and peace. pseud. tr. 55889

Lover of truth and peace. pseud. Late religious commotions. see Rand, William.

Lover of truth, and the British constitution. pseud. Letter to the Rev. Mr. John Wesley. 102647

Lover of truth, in America. pseud. Impartial view. 80543

Lover thereof. pseud. Serious and earnest address. 79251

Lovera, Francisco de Seixas y. see Seixas y Lovera, Francisco de.

Loveridge's School, Albany, N. Y. see Mrs. Loveridge's School, Albany, N. Y.

Lovering, Joseph. 42386

Lover's adventures in Louisiana. (69063)

Lover's gift. 82512

Lovers of peace. pseud. eds. 19160

Lovers of youth pseud. Juvenile guide. see Youngs, Isaac Newton.

Love's ambuscade. (19423)

Love's apprenticeship. 84868

Love's calendar. 32390

Loves of the oysters. 80148

Love's pedigree. 104091-2 [sic]

Lovetruth, Nathaniel. pseud.??? Two letters. 103560

Lovett, John. 42387-42388, 9th note after 96966, 1st note after 101887

Lovewell lamented. (37711), 94107, 94112

Lovewell's fight. 59655

Loving brothers NHDDMMS. pseud. Gospel music. see Holmes, NAthaniel, 1599-1678.

Loving epistle, &c. 22351

Loving invitation. 62920

Loving-kindness of God displayed. 82491

Loving sister, Bull-a. pseud. Beauties of Brother Bull-us. 4205

Lovinski, -----. see Louvet de Couvray, Jean Baptiste.

Lovy, H. 42390

Low, A. A. 42391

Low, Conrad. 42392

Low, David. 42393

Low, Edward Luther. 42394

Low, Frederick Ferdinand, 1820-1894. 42395
  see also California. Governor, 1864-
  1868 (Low)
Low, Henry R. 42396
Low, Henry R. petitioner 42397
Low, Henry R. plaintiff 42397
Low, Hermann. 42398
Low, Isaac. 96022, 96024, 98982
Low, James W. 42399, 54459
Low, John. 42400-42401
Low, Nathaniel. 42402, 62743
Low, Samuel, b. 1765. (18865), (42404)-
  42406, 104826
Low (Sampson) and Son, and Co. firm
  publishers (42403)
Low Dutch prisoner. 65489
Low Dutch Reformed Church. New Jersey.
  25755, 25974, 98572
Low Dutch Reformed Church, North Branch,
  N. J. see North Branch, N. J. Low
  Dutch Reformed Church.
Low Dutch Reformed Church, Raritan, N. J.
  see Raritan, N. J. Low Dutch Reformed
  Church.
Low Dutch Reformed Church, Three Mile Run,
  N. J. see Three Mile Run, N. J. Low
  Dutch Reformed Church.
Low value set upon human life. 6074
Low wages and hard work. 18305
Lowber, John C. 61596, 61903
Lowe, A. T. 42408
Lowe, Andr. F. 42407
Lowe, Anna C. 42420-42421
Lowe, Charles. 42409-(42410)
Lowe, Enoch Lewis, 1820-1892. 2995,
  (42411)-42413, 45340, 46962 see also
  Maryland. Governor, 1851-1853 (Lowe)
Lowe, F. C. engr. 84779-84780
Lowe, Frederick. 85346
Lowe, J. S. tr. 92556
Lowe, John. 42414-42416
Lowe, Joseph. 42417, 89293
Lowe, Martha Ann (Perry) 1829-1902. (42418)
Lowe, P. P. 42419
Lowe, R. engr. 101881
Lowe, Ralph Phillips, 1805-1883. 33150,
  35004 see also Iowa. Governor,
  1858-1860 (Lowe)
Lowell, Charles, 1782-1861. 6576, 42422-
  42429
Lowell, Charles, 1793-1858. plaintiff 96895,
  101476
Lowell, Francis C. 42432
Lowell, James Russell, 1819-1891. 2299,
  (42433)-42438, 55562, 63534, 63570-
  43571, 64034, 84185-84187
Lowell, John, 1704-1767. 42439-42441
Lowell, John, 1743-1802. 42442
Lowell, John, 1769-1840. 1068, (4338), 6649,
  9623, 12485, 12490, (23236), 23271,
  28965, 28976, 30756, 31760, (31970),
  42443-(42463), 70204, 92886, 1st note
  after 93806, 94678, 1st note after 95729,
  96412, 98558, 98562, 98678, 4th note
  after 98684, 1st note after 99829, 2d
  note after 101856, note after 105966
Lowell, John, 1769-1840. supposed author
  42445, 42459, 43375, (55475), (62502),
  95669
Lowell, John Amory, 1798-1881. 1824, 8344-
  (8345), 42464-42465
Lowell, Joshua A., 1801-1874. 42466
Lowell, Robert Trail Spence. 42467-(42468)
Lowell, Mass. (42471), 42474, 42498, (42500),
  (42502)-42503
Lowell, Mass. petitioners 19655

Lowell, Mass. American Institute of Instruction.
  see American Institute of Instruction,
  Lowell, Mass.
Lowell, Mass. Auditor. 42470
Lowell, Mass. Cemetery. Proprietors.
  42485
Lowell, Mass. Charter. 42472-42473
Lowell, Mass. City Council. 42498
Lowell, Mass. City Council. Joint Special
  Committee on a Supply of Water. 42499
Lowell, Mass. City Council. Joint Special
  Committee on the Effects of Lead Pipes
  Upon Well-Water in the City. 42499
Lowell, Mass. City Library. 42475
Lowell, Mass. City Library. Directors.
  42475
Lowell, Mass. City School Library. 42475
Lowell, Mass. Dispensary. see Lowell
  Dispensary, Lowell, Mass.
Lowell, Mass. Female Inhabitants. petitioners
  42494
Lowell, Mass. Females Actively Employed
  in the Mills. 42491, 49192-49193,
  (52711), 2d note after 95375
Lowell, Mass. Fire Department. 42487
Lowell, Mass. Fire Department. Chief
  Engineer. 42487
Lowell, Mass. Five Cent Savings Bank. see
  Lowell Five Cent Savings Bank, Lowell,
  Mass.
Lowell, Mass. Framingham Academy. see
  Framingham Academy, Lowell, Mass.
Lowell, Mass. Hospital Association. see
  Lowell Hospital Association, Lowell, Mass.
Lowell, Mass. Mayor, 1837. 42469
Lowell, Mass. Mayor, 1858 (Huntington)
  42478 see also Huntington, E.
Lowell, Mass. Mayor, 1864 (Hosford) 42483
  see also Hosford, Hocum.
Lowell, Mass. Mayor, 1867 (Richardson)
  71007 see also Richardson, George F.
Lowell, Mass. Middlesex Mechanic Association.
  see Middlesex Mechanic Association,
  Lowell, Mass.
Lowell, Mass. Minister at Large. see Lo-
  well, Mass. South Parish Missionary
  Society. Minister at Large.
Lowell, Mass. Ordinances, etc. 42472-42473,
  42498
Lowell, Mass. Public Schools. 42479-42480
Lowell, Mass. Sabbath School Union. see
  Lowell Sabbath School Union, Lowell,
  Mass.
Lowell, Mass. St. Anne's Church. Thirtieth
  Anniversary Commemoration, 1855.
  (21878)
Lowell, Mass. St. Anne's Church. Wardens
  and Vestry. plaintiffs (48013)
Lowell, Mass. School Committee. 42480
Lowell, Mass. South Parish Missionary
  Society. Minister at Large. 42497
Lowell, Mass. Superintendent of Public Schools.
  42480
Lowell, Mass. Supreme Court. (56380)
Lowell, Mass. Ter-centenary Celebration of
  the Birth of William Shakespeare, 1864.
  see Ter-centenary Celebration of the
  Birth of William Shakespeare, Lowell,
  Mass., 1864.
Lowell, Mass. Treasurer. 42470
Lowell, as it was, and as it is. 48928
Lowell Cemetery. see Lowell, Mass.
  Cemetery.
Lowell directory . . . by B. Floyd. (42476)
Lowell directory: containing the city record.
  42477

Lowell directory for 1855. 42477
Lowell directory for 1853. 42477
Lowell directory for 1864-65. By Samuel A. McPhetres. 42477
Lowell directory [for 1861] by Adams, Sampson & Co. 42477
Lowell directory for 1866. By Sampson, Davenport & Co. 42477
Lowell Dispensary, Lowell, Mass. 42486
Lowell Dispensary, Lowell, Mass. Charter. 42486
Lowell Five Cent Savings Bank, Lowell, Mass. 42488
Lowell Five Cent Savings Bank, Lowell, Mass. Charter. 42488
Lowell Five Cent Savings Bank. The officers, act of incorporation, by-laws, &c. 42488
Lowell Foundation lectures, 1839. (23257)
Lowell Hosiery Company. 42490
Lowell Hosiery Company. Charter. 42490
Lowell Hosiery Company. Act of incorporation and by-laws. 42490
Lowell hydraulic experiments. 25441
Lowell Hospital Association, Lowell, Mass. 42489
Lowell Institute, Boston. 27877, 28598, 30895, 45854, 58322, 59354, 71787
Lowell Institute lectures. 27877, 28598, 30895, 45854, 58322, 59354, 71787
Lowell Missionary Society. see Lowell, Mass. South Parish Missionary Society.
Lowell offering. 42491, 49192-49193, (52711), 2d note after 95375
Lowell patriot and advertiser. 31762
Lowell Putnam. (66842)
Lowell Railroad Corporation. Grantees. (6768)
Lowell Republican. 31762
Lowell Sabbath School Union, Lowell, Mass. (42492)
Lowell Shakespeare memorial. 42493
Lowencourt, F. de, Sieur de Vauchelles. tr. 20845
Lowenorn, P. de. 42504
Lowenstern, Isidore. 42505-42506
Lower Canada. see Quebec (Province)
Lower Canada Agricultural Association. see Agricultural Association of Lower Canada.
Lower Canada Agricultural Society. see Quebec Agricultural Society.
Lower Canada law almanac. (42520)
Lower Canada municipal & road act of 1855. 10496
Lower Canada register, for 1829. 50258
Lower Canada reports. 10495
Lower-Canada watchman. 12842, 42521, 100872
Lower St. Lawrence or Quebec to Halifax. 42527
Lowig, Gustav. 42529
Lowndes. pseud. Letters. 9952, 42532
Lowndes, John. 42530
Lowndes, William, 1782-1822. (42531)
Lownes, Caleb. 7265, (42533), 99868
Lowrey, Grosvenor Porter. 22614, 42534
Lowrie, John C. (42535)
Lowrie, John M. 42536-42538
Lowrie, Walter, 1784-1868. 1228, 42539
Lowrie, Walter Macon, 1819-1847. 42539
Lowry, John. defendant 96943
Lowry, Robert. 42541
Low's pocket almanack for the year M.DCC. XCI. 42394
Low's railway directory for 1858. 42399

Lowth, Robert, successively Bishop of St. Davids, Oxford, and London, 1710-1787. 11879, 42542, 65456
Lowville, N. Y. Rural Cemetery. 42543
Lowville, N. Y. Rural Cemetery. President. 42543 see also Hough, F. B.
Loyal address. 36919
Loyal address of the clergy of Virginia. 42545, 5th note after 101484
Loyal address of the Virginians. 14008
Loyal American. pseud. To the dis-united inhabitants. 95916
Loyal and Patriotic Society of Upper Canada. 92649
Loyal Associated Refugees Assembled at Newport, R. I. see His Majesty's Loyal Associated Refugees Assembled at Newport, R. I.
Loyal Cherokees. see Cherokee Nation (Loyal Cherokees)
Loyal citizen. pseud. Money question in 1813 and 1863. 49972
Loyal citizens of New Jersey. see New Jersey. Loyal Citizens.
Loyal heart. 42547
Loyal international bulletin. 27831, 42548
Loyal League of Union Citizens, New York. 14961, 28452, 28472, 41029, 42551, 54589, 54607
Loyal Leagues, Utica, N. Y. see Loyal National League of the State of New York.
Loyal Mass Meeting, Cooper Institute, New York, 1863. see Loyal League of Union Citizens, New York.
Loyal meeting of the people of New-York, to support the government. 42551
Loyal Meeting, to Support the Government, Prosecute the War, and Maintain the Union, Cooper Institute, New York, 1863. see Loyal League of Union Citizens, New York.
Loyal National League of the State of New York. 28461, 42549-42550, 42552, 42553-42555, 53485, 54663, 57404, note after 93725
Loyal National League. Opinions of prominent men. 42553
Loyal National Union journal. 42556
Loyal patriot. pseud. Political thoughts. 63813
Loyal patriot. pseud. Some observations of consequence, in three parts. 86680
Loyal Pennsylvanians at Washington, 1864. 59857
Loyal publication of the National Union Association of Ohio. No. 3. 8400, 42559, 52034
Loyal Publication Society. 744, 1003, 1003*, (1388), (1389), 2136, 9638, 11579, 12200, 16594, 17781, (21847), 22113, 24251, 25671, 26734, 30019, 30022, 33230, (33231), 33232, 38445, 40611, 40985, 41567, 42549, 42557, 42558, 47704, 53485, 54364, (55459), 55834, 57406, (66799), 68318, 67487, 80419, 82613, 86327, 91018, 93667, 94085, 95516, note after 95516, 95517, 95753, 97587, 98891
Loyal reprints. 42557, 98891
Loyal soldier. 90549
Loyal soldiers. pseud. Letters. 40611
Loyal soldiers. pseud. Letters of loyal soldiers upon McClellan and the Chicago platform. 40612
Loyal supremacy. 17355
Loyal verses of Joseph Stanbury and Doctor Jonathan Odell. 90375

Loyal voice from Louisiana. 20666
Loyal Women of the Republic. Meeting, New York (City), 1863. see Meeting of the Loyal Women of the Republic, New York (City), 1863.
Loyalist. pseud. Directions to the American loyalists. 20222
Loyalist history—John Grant. 84422
Loyalist; or, the channel scourge. 63004
Loyalist peotry of the revolution. (42560)
Loyalist refugee. pseud. American wanderer through various parts of Europe. see Lee, Arthur, 1740-1792. supposed author
Loyalists. pseud. Opinions. 57404
Loyalist's ammunition. 42564
Loyalists at Shelburne. 84422
Loyalists confined in Mason's Lodge, 1777. petitioners (59889)
Loyalists of America and their times. 74565
Loyalty. 104175
Loyalty a Christian obligation. 4836
Loyalty. A sermon preached in Northampton. 33210
Loyalty. A voice from the sanctuary concerning the civil war. 22354
Loyalty above party. (6381)
Loyalty and devotion of colored Americans. 42565
Loyalty and disloyalty. 42566
Loyalty and religion. 22177
Loyalty demanded by the present crisis. 16404
Loyalty for the times. 42567
Loyalty in the American republic, what is it? 33320
Loyalty of the Episcopal Church vindicated. (46767)
Loyalty on the frontier. 5599
Loyalty to country and its duties. 51514
Loyalty to government. (42694)
Loyalty to our government. (21443)
Loyalty to the government, and to God. 75267
Loyalty to the government. Speech of Hon. Peter Hitchcock. 32264
Loyalty vindicated. 42569
Loyalty. What is it? To whom or what due? 42568
Loyaute trahie. 29938
Loyd, Samuel. 95612
Loyd, Samuel Jones. see Overstone, Samuel Jones Loyd, Baron, 1796-1883.
Loyd, Thomas E. 42570
Loyer, R. F. see Loper, Richard F.
Loyola, Jacobo Ugarte y. see Ugarte y Loyola, Jacobo.
Loyola College, Baltimore. 42572
Loysel, Francisco. 42573-(42574)
Loza, Augustin Joseph Mariano del Rio de. see Rio de Loza, Augustin Joseph Mariano del.
Loza, Francisco. 23565, 42575-42587
Loza, Jose Manuel. supposed author 99448
Loza, L. Rio de la. 42588
Lozano, Abigail. 42589
Lozano, Antonio Ruiz. see Ruiz Lozano, Antonio.
Lozano, M. 49757
Lozano, Pedro. 19696, 24135-24138, (42590)-42599, 79138, 97102, 1st note after 98488
Lozano, Pedro. petitioner 56396, 79138
Lozano, Pedro. supposed tr. 12835, 24138, 1st note after 98488

Lozara, ------. 41671
Lozere, Privat Joseph Claramond, Comte Pelet de la. see Pelet de la Lorere, Private Joseph Claramond, Comte.
Lorier, John Hogarth. 42600
Lozieres, Louis Narcisse Baudry des. see Baudry des Lozieres, Louis Narcisse.
Luaces, Joaquin Lorenzo. ed. 17766, 86191-86192
Lubbock, Sir John. 42601-42602
Lubelfing, J. von. see Leubelfing, J. von.
Lubin, Augustin. (42603)
Lublink, J. 84110
Lublink, J. the Younger tr. 37335, note after 98475
Luc de la Porte, --------. tr. 27780
Lucae de Linda descriptio orbis. 41288
Lucas, ------, fl. 1930. 92531
Lucas, Ansil. 42604
Lucas, Carlos. 42607
Lucas, Charles. 42605-42607
Lucas, D. R. 42608
Lucas, Eliza. see Pinckney, Eliza (Lucas)
Lucas, F. 42610-(42611)
Lucas, G. W. (42612)
Lucas, H. 42613
Lucas, John B. C. 42614-(42615)
Lucas, Joseph. 98552
Lucas, Pierre Hippolyte, 1815?-1899. 74922
Lucas, Rachael. 42616
Lucas, Robert, 1781-1853. 57039, 57051 see also Ohio. Governor, 1832-1836 (Lucas)
Lucas, Samuel. 42617-42619
Lucas de Lassaga, Juan. see Lassaga, Juan de.
Lucas de Montiguy, Gabriel, b. 1782. 49399-(49400)
Lucas de Oliveira, Manoel. see Oliveira, Manoel Lucas de.
Luccock, John. 42620-42621
Luce, John. 42622
Luce, Stephen B. 42623, 58776
Lucerna y avisos de peligros en el puerto de la eternidad. 75992
Lucernariae and their allies. 85072
Lucero de Tacubaya. Periodico politico, cientifico y literario. 42624
Luceros y nebulosas. (71637)
Luces del cielo. (75768)
Lucia. Novela, sacada de la historia Argentina. (26563)
Lucie Hardinge. 16472
Lucie-Lary, J. ed. 86471
Luciennes, Victor. (42625)
Lucifer & Co. pseud. see Michael, Ludifer & Co. pseud.
Lucifer's decree. 42626, 60224
Lucinda, or the mountain mourner. 44435
Lucio, Melchior Rodrigues. 42627
Lucio de Azevedo, J. see Azevedo, J. Lucio de.
Lucius Catiline. pseud. 25339
Lucius Crassus. pseud. Examination of the President's message. see Hamilton, Alexander, 1755-1804.
Lucius Junius Brutus. pseud. Examination of the President's answer to the New Haven remonstrance. see Coleman, William, 1766-1829. supposed author and Cranch, William, 1769-1855. supposed author
Luck of the roaring camp. 20650
Luckenbach, Abraham. 42628-42629
Luckenbach, J. tr. (19375)

Luckenbach, W. H. 42630
Luckenbuch, A. ed. 19373, 106298
Luckey, John. 42631-42632
Luckey, Samuel. 42633
Luckock, Benjamin. (42634)
Lucubrati uncula de morbo Gallico. (77661)
Lucubrations during a short recess, by a
    member of Parliament. 40456, (42636)
Lucubrations during a short recess, containing
    a plan for a more equal representation
    of the people. (81398)
Lucubrations on ways and means. (4885)
Luculentissima quaeda terrae totius descriptio.
    77804
Lucy, Charles. illus. 32539, 67436
Lucy, Richard de. 42637
Lucy Harding. 16471
Lucy Hardinge. 16473
Lucy Hosmer. 95482
Lucy Howard's journal. (80930)
Lucy Lee. (26166)
Lucy Temple; or, the three orphans. 73611
Lud, Gualterus, 1448-1527. 28193-28194,
    40691, 69130, 99327
Ludd, Walter. 42638, note after 89151
Ludde, ------. 11038
Ludden, Patritio A., Bp. 72973 see also
    Syracuse (Diocese) Bishop (Ludden)
Ludecus, Eduard. 42639
Ludekenio, Th. see Muller, And.
Luden, Heinrich. ed. 4953
Luder, A. F. 42640
Luders, Ludwig. 42641
Ludewig, B. pseud. Wahrer Bericht. see
    Zinzendorf, Nicolaus Ludwig, Graf von,
    1700-1760.
Ludewig, Hermann Ernst, d. 1856. 1557,
    42643-42645
Ludewig's Wahrer Bericht de dato German-
    town. 42642
Ludington, C. V. R. (42646)
Ludlam, R. 42647
Ludlow, E. G. plaintiff 69824, 100796
Ludlow, Edward G. 42648
Ludlow, Fitz Hugh, 1836-1870. (42649)
Ludlow, H. G. 42650
Ludlow, J. L. 42652
Ludlow, James M. 42653
Ludlow, John. 42651
Ludlow, John Malcolm. 42654-(42656)
Ludlow, Peter. 42657
Ludlow, Mass. First Congregational Church.
    65848
Ludloff, H. 42659
Ludovici, a Thurenstein. pseud. Epistola ad
    bonos Pensilvaniae cives Christo non
    inimicos. see Zinzendorf, Nicolaus
    Ludwig, Graf von, 1700-1760.
Ludovici a Thurenstein in antiqvissima
    Fratrum Ecclesia ad taxin kai euschem-
    osynen diaconi constituti. 106356
Ludovico, A. (42660)
Ludvigh, Samuel. 42661
Ludwig, Carl. tr. (12261)
Ludwig, Johann Friedrich. (42662)
Ludwig, M. R. 42663
Ludwig genealogy. 42663
Luetke, Fedor Petrovich, Graf, 1797-1882.
    21211-21215, 42738-(42739)
Luetken, Christian Frederik, 1827-1901.
    42740, (69112)-69114, 71433, 71435
Luff, Lorry. pseud. Texas captain and the
    female smuggler. (42664)
Luffman, John. 42665-42666
Lugo, Bernardo de. 42667

Luiken, Jan. illus. 26367, 47474, 2d note
    after 102813
Luis I, King of Spain (48612) see also
    Spain. Sovereigns, etc., 1724 (Luis I)
Luis de Valdivia. see Valdivia, Luis de,
    1561-1642.
Lujan, Pedro Jimenez de Gongara y. see
    Almodovar del Rio, Pedro Jimenez de
    Gonara y Lujan, Duque de, d. 1794.
Luke Darrell, the Chicago newsboy. 42672
Lukens, John. 84678C
Lukins, Joseph. defendant 28120, 80736,
    96938
Lulio, Raymundo. 48993
Lullaby. 92173B-92174A
Lulli, --------. 42673
Lullus, Antonius. 25994, 79345
Lumajo romango Americano. 17937
Lumber manufacturers of the south. 84909
Lumiere. 42674
Lumieres naturelles. pseud. Americains.
    1033
Lumina, -------- Poullin de. see Poullin de
    Lumina, --------.
Lumley, ---------, Lord, fl. 1721. 65865,
    88192
Lummer, O. 85072
Lummus, C. F. 42837
Lumnius, J. F. 42675
Lumpkin, John Henry, 1799-1867. 42676
Lumpkin, John W. 27051
Lumpkin, Joseph H. (42677)
Lumsden, James. 42679
Luna, J. G. de. (42681)
Luna, Juan de Mendoza y. see Mendoza y
    Luna, Juan de, Marques de Montesclaros.
Luna, Juan de Prado Mayeza Portocarreno
    y. see Prado Mayeza Portocarrero y
    Lina, Juan de.
Luna, Lino de Monte Carmelo. 42680
Luna y Arellano, Miguel de. ed. 51042
Lunan, John. 42682-42683
Lunar hermit. pseud. Letter to the Rev.
    Samuel Hopkins. 42684
Lunar tidal wave in Lake Michigan, demon-
    strated. 28219
Lunar tidal wave in the North American lakes,
    demonstrated. 28219
Lunario de un siglo. 93296
Lunario de un siglo que comienza en Enero
    del ano de 1740. 93295
Lunatic Asylum, Blackwell's Island, New York.
    see New York (City) Lunatic Asylum,
    Blackwell's Island.
Lunatic Asylum, Columbus, Ohio. see Ohio.
    State Hospital, Columbus.
Lunatic Asylum, Utica, N. Y. see New York
    (State) State Hospital, Utica.
Lund, Anthon H. tr. 83219
Lund, J. J. 42685
Lund, Orlando. 42686, 87010, 87014
Lund, Peter Wilhelm, 1801-1880. 42687-
    42689
Lund, Theodore. 12730, 42690
Lundie, Mrs. J. C. 1017, 21262, 42691
Lundin Brown, Robert C. see Brown, Robert
    C. Lundin.
Lund's defence of the Order of the Sons of
    Temperance. 87010
Lund's Sons of Temperance. 87010
Lundt, -------. 35267
Lundt, J. H. 42692
Lundy, pseud. Annexation of Texas. 95068
Lundy, Benjamin. (11856), 26951, (42693),
    95069, 95096, 95134

Lycosthenis, Conradi. (66488)
Lycurgan Association, Yale University. see
Yale University. Lycurgan Association.
Lycurgus. pseud. Thoughts on the state of
the American Indians. see Wood,
Silas.
Lycurgus. pseud. War, or no war. 42755,
2d note after 101265
Lyde, Augustus Foster. 42756
Lydekker, Gerrit. 80901
Lydius, Balthasar. (34105)
Lydius, Jac. (42757)
Lyell, Sir Charles, Bart., 1797-1875. (36213),
(39857), 42759-42764, (54494), 74632
Lyell, Thomsa. 42765
Lyford, Stephen C. 42766
Lyford, William G. 2999, (42767), 100468
Lygon, William. see Beauchamp, William
Lygon, 1st Earl of.
Lyhykaisesti kerrottu ja haunulla kuvauksilla
valaistu. 92523
Lying ballad. 105016
Lying hero. 46847
Lying-In Charity and Nurse Society, Philadel-
phia. see Philadelphia Lying-In
Charity and Nurse Society.
Lying-in Hospital, New York. see Society
of the Lying-In Hospital, New York.
Lykens Valley Rail Raod and Coal Company.
60225
Lykens Valley Rail Road and Coal Company.
Charter. 60225
Lukfeest van Washington. 98245, note after
101848
Lykins, Johnston. 42769-42771, (79977),
79980-79981
Lyle, W. W. 42772
Lyles, James H. 42773
Lylva de Aguiar, Lucas da. ed. 94594
Lyman, Asa. (42774)
Lyman, Azel S. (42775)
Lyman, Benjamin Smith. 42776
Lyman, C. S. 42777
Lyman, Caleb. 6661, 42778, 78621-(78622),
95166, 2d note after 99813
Lyman, Elias. appellant 96896, 97879
Lyman, Eliphalet. 42779-(42780)
Lyman, G. T. 42782
Lyman, George. 90998
Lyman, George D. 103893
Lyman, Gershom C. 42781
Lyman, Henry. 42783, 95541
Lyman, Huntington. 42784
Lyman, Jonathan Huntington, 1783-1825. 42785
Lyman, Joseph, 1749-1828. 5592, 28628,
28903, 42787-42791, (76449), 92884,
104113, 104117-104118
Lyman, Joseph B. ed. 19629, 32821
Lyman, Joseph Dardwell, 1829-1872. 19629,
(42792)
Lyman, Justin. appellant 96896, 97879
Lyman, Payson Williston, 1842- 42793
Lyman, Samuel P., 1804-1869. (42795)
Lyman, T. P. H. 42805
Lyman, Theodore, 1792-1849. 6785, 9799,
26709, 42796-42802, (45736) see also
Boston. Mayor, 1834-1835 (Lyman)
Lyman, Theodore, 1792-1849. defendant
(42801), 102321, 1st note after 103741
Lyman, Theodore, 1833-1897. 26709, 42803-
42804
Lyman, William. 42806
Lyman (Nathan) firm 89122
Lyman & Rawdon. firm (74684), 84093

Lymburner, ---------. 42807, 67032 see
also Quebec (Province) petitioners
Agent.
Lymburner, Adam. 42807
Lynceus. pseud. Letters for the people.
see Starr, Frederick.
Lynch, Anne Charlotte. 42808, 70713
Lynch, Eugene H. 42809
Lynch, F. T. 42810
Lynch, Mrs. Henry. 42811
Lynch, James, fl. 1829. 42812
Lynch, James, fl. 1858. 86079
Lynch, Jasper. 42813
Lynch, John. 42814
Lynch, John, 1825- 42815
Lynch, Sir Thomas, d. 1684. 5966-5967,
35633, note after 41144 see also Jamaic
Governor, 1862-1864 (Lynch)
Lynch, Thomas H. 42816
Lynch, W. F. USN 42817-(42819)
Lynch, W. R (42820)
Lynch law. 97032
Lynchburg, Va. Fifteenth Annual Session of
the Virginia Grand Division of the Sons
of Temperance, 1859. see Sons of
Temperance of North America. Virginia.
Grand Division. Fifteenth Annual Session,
Lynchburg, 1859.
Lynchburg and Tennessee Railroad Company.
President. 42822
Lynchburg and Tennessee Rail Road. Letters
from T. S. Bocock. 42822
Lynd, S. W. 42823
Lynde, Benjamin. 32362, 37712, 96946, 96951
2d-3d notes after 102623
Lynde, Samuel. 6711, 9449, 21088, 42824,
1st note after 99800
Lyndes, T. 66686
Lyndon. pseud. Margaret. 42825
Lyndon, John W. ed. (64029)
Lyndon Academy, Lyndon Center, Vt.
(42826)
Lyndon Center, Vt. Lyndon Academy. see
Lyndon Academy, Lyndon Center, Vt.
Lyne, Charles. 42827
Lyne, James. 54639
Lyne, T. A. 42828
Lynfield, Mass. (42846)
Lynfield, Mass. School Committee. (42846)
Lynn, David. defendant (42829), 47985, note
after 96896
Lynn, Mass. 42832, 42835, 42838
Lynn, Mass. Board of Health. 42831
Lynn, Mass. Charter. 42834, (42843)
Lynn, Mass. Committee of Arrangements on
the Funeral Ceremonies for George
Washington, 1800. 95203
Lynn, Mass. Free Public Library. (42841)
Lynn, Mass. High School. 42840
Lynn, Mass. Library Association. see Lynn
Library Association, Lynn, Mass.
Lynn, Mass. Mayor, 1850. 42839
Lynn, Mass. North Randolph Church. 55728
Lynn, Mass. Ordinances, etc. 42834
Lynn, Mass. Pine Grove Cemetery. 62926
Lynn, Mass. Pine Grove Cemetery. Com-
missioners. 42845
Lynn, Mass. Public Schools. 42844
Lynn, Mass. School Committee. 37836,
42833, 42844
Lynn, Mass. Society of Young Men. see
Society of Young Men Belonging to Lynn,
Mass.
Lynn directory and town register for 1832.
42837

Lynn directory, . . . with an almanac for . . . 1854. 42837
Lynn Library Association, Lynn, Mass. (42841)
Lyon, -------. 75540 see also France. Corps Legislatif. Conseil des Cinq-Cents. Commission des Colonies.
Lyon, Caleb, 1821-1875. 34168-34169, 42847 see also Idaho (Territory) Governor, 1864-1866 (Lyon)
Lyon, Charles H. 42848
Lyon, D. S. 94392, 94394-94394A
Lyon, De Chateau. (42849)
Lyon, Diego Lopez de Lisboa y. see Lisboa y Lyon, Diego Lopez de.
Lyon, Edward. defendant 42850, 91768, 96897
Lyon, G. Parker. ed. 52884
Lyon, George. 94428
Lyon, George Francis. RN (42851)-(42854)
Lyon, I. S. (42855)
Lyon, James, 1735-1794. 42856
Lyon, James, fl. 1800. 42857-42858, 52002-52003
Lyon, James A. (42859)
Lyon, John. 50740
Lyon, Lemuel. 42860, (58457), note after 96144
Lyon, Lucius. 42861
Lyon, M. 42863
Lyon, Mary. 24521
Lyon, Matthew, 1746-1833. 42862
Lyon, Matthew, 1746-1833. supposed author 105048
Lyon, Nathaniel. 42864-42865
Lyon, Patrick. plaintiff 25374, 42866-42867
Lyon, Richard. 66431-(66441)
Lyon, Sidney S. 37513, 42868
Lyon, Sylvanus. 89888, note after 94615 see also Springfield, N. J. Centennial Celebration, July 4, 1876. Committee of Publication.
Lyon, Theodore C. (42869)
Lyon, Theophilus. 42870
Lyon, W. F. 42871
Lyon, William N. 42872
Lyon, France. Academie. 68076
Lyon, France. Academie des Sciences. 44239
Lyon, France. Commission d'Enquete du Chemin de Fer de Saint-Etienne. 84478
Lyon, France. Societe Royale d'Agriculture. see Societe d'Agriculture, Lyon.
Lyonne, Matrin. (67497)
Lyons, Israel. 42873, (78598), 79458
Lyons, J. 42874
Lyons, Joseph A. 42875
Lyons, M. E. 68214
Lyons, Richard Bickerton Pemell Lyons, 1st Earl, 1817-1887. (16869), 19753, (23505), 42876, 45451, 55527 see also Great Britain. Legation. United States.
Lyra, J. M. de. 65931
Lyra Americana. 71276
Lyra Urbanica. 50804
Lyre of my youth. 104658
Lyre of Tioga. 95465
Lyric gems. 84050
Lyric ode. 26878
Lyric poems, by William B. Tappan. 94371
Lyric poems, sonnets and miscellanies. 42708
Lyric works of Horace. 33005, 100545
Lyrica sacra. 63453
Lyrical and other peoms. (81233)

Lyrical ballads, with other poems. 105466
Lyrics and idyls. 91065
Lyrics. By William B. Tappan. 94372
Lyrics by the letter H. (29920), (42877)
Lyrics of freedom; and other poems. 42878
Lyrics, incidents, and sketches of the rebellion. (5373)
Lyrics of a day. 8684, (42879)
Lyrics of loyalty. 50359
Lyrics of the war. (42880)
Lyrisch-epische Dictung. 6825
Lysander. pseud. Annals of the corporation. see Cheetham, James.
Lysander. pseud. Correct statement of the late melancholy affair of honor. see Van Ness, William Peter. supposed author and Wills, Thomas. supposed author
Lyschander, Clauss Chrystopherson. 42882
Lysons, D. 42883
Lyst der scheepen. 42885
Lyste der bylagen, relatief tot het berigt. 93836
Lyste van 't ghene de Brasil. 7600
Lysten van de Hollandsche shceepen. 42886, 90015
Lyster Copper Company. (42887)
Lyteria: a dramatic poem. 67271-67272
Lyttleton, George Lyttleton, 1st Baron, 1709-1773. 19238, 42889-(42890), 62464, 64143
Lyttleton, George William Lyttleton, 4th Baron, 1817-1876. 42888
Lyttleton, Thomas Lyttleton, 2d Baron, 1744-1779. 40467, 42891-42894
Lyttleton, Thomas Lyttleton, 2d Baron, 1744-1779. incorrectly supposed author 40468, (47945)
Lyuro das obras de Garcia de Resende. 70061

M

M . . . pseud. Conquete du Mexique par Fernand Cortez. 15889
M. pseud. Decision. 103806
M. . . pseud. Discurso opinado. 16160
M-------. pseud. Political essay upon commerce. 63773
M. pseud. Souvenirs des Antilles. see Montlezun, -------, Baron de.
M. pseud. Vous entres prie. 100797
M . . . . pseud. tr. 31989
M., an Anabaptist. pseud. Dialogue. see Young, Samuel, fl. 1690-1700.
M . . ., einem Amerikaner. pseud. Historischer Abriss. see Buisson, Paul Ulrich du.
M***. pseud. tr. (9141), 94228, 94231
M***. pseud. tr. see Le Febvre de Villebrune, -------.
M***. pseud. Amusements geographiques et historiques. see Navarre, P.
M***. pseud. Lettres critiques et politiques. see Buisson, Paul Ulric du. and Dubuc, Jean Baptiste.
M.*** pseud. Memoires sur la Louisiane. see Le Page du Pratz, -------.
M***. pseud. Roman politique. see Saintard, P.
M***. pseud. Relations curieuses de differents pays nouvellement decouverts. see Du Fresne de Francheville, Joseph.
M***, Americain. pseud. Abrege de la revolution de l'Amerique Angloise. see Buisson, Paul Ulric du.

M***

M***, Ancien Capitaine de Vaisseau. pseud.
　Decouvertes des Francois. see
　Fleurieu, Charles Pierre Claret, Comte
　de.
M***, Ancien Officier de Dragons. pseud.
　tr. 35585
M***, Capitaine de Vaisseau du Roi. pseud.
　Journal. see Vallette de Laudun,
　-----------.
M***, Comte de. pseud. Memoire sur les
　colonies Occidentales de la France.
　42905
M***, einem Amerikaner. pseud. Histor-
　ischer Abriss. see Buisson, Paul
　Ulrich du.
M***, von. pseud. Der in dem wilden
　America. (42897)
M****. pseud. tr. 82306
M****. pseud. Lettre de M****. 40667
M****. pseud. Voyage au Kentouckey.
　42898, 1st note after 100806
M.****, Jullien. pseud. Voyage dans
　l'Amerique Meridionale. see Mellet,
　Jullien.
M********. pseud. Memoires de Billaud-
　Varennes. (42899)
M., A. pseud. Niagara. 42901
M., A. pseud. Reflections on the American
　contest. see Morris, Apollos.
M., A. pseud. State of religion in New-
　England. 69400, 90595-90597, 103594
M., A. B. pseud. Guia de la ciudad de
　Nueva York. 42902
M., A. W. pseud. Smuggler's son. see
　Mitchell, Agnes Woods.
M., Ant. pseud. Histoire vniverselle des
　Indes. see Magini, Giovanni Antonio.
M., C. pseud. engr. 98288
M., C. pseud. Baptistes. see Mather,
　Cotton, 1663-1728.
M., C. pseud. Del tolerancia. see Munguia,
　Clemente de Jesus, Bp.
M., C. A. L. T. de. pseud. Almanach
　Americain. 941
M., D. pseud. Essai sur les interets du
　commerce maritime. see O'Heguerty,
　Domingo, Comte de Magnieres, 1699-
　1790.
M., D. A. J. R. B. F. D. pseud. ed. Diario
　notable. 19954, 48427
M., D. G. J. V. D. G. Y. pseud. tr. see
　Guzman y Manrique, Joaquin de.
M., D. L. pseud. Voyage des pais septen-
　trionaux. see La Martiniere, Pierre
　Martin de.
M., E. pseud. Aenmerkenswaardige en
　zeldsame West-Indische zee- en land-
　reisen. see Melton, Edward.
M., E. pseud. Lettre a Napoleon III. see
　Musson, Eugene.
M., E. pseud. Stand up for Jesus! 91918
M., E., of Antwerp. pseud. Historiae
　Belgicae. 13033
M., E. C. M. J. D. pseud. Proyecto de una
　contribucion nacional. (42906)
M., F. pseud. Brief sketch of the republic
　of Costa Rica. see Molina, Felipe.
M., F. pseud. Coup d'oeil rapide sur la
　republique de Costa-Rica. see Molina,
　Felipe.
M., F. pseud. Neu-entdecktes norden.
　5905, 52359
M., F. pseud. Some proposals to benefit
　the province. 86716
M., F. L. pseud. Banished count. see
　Mortimer, F. L.

M., F. M. pseud. tr. 3092
M., F. M. pseud. Nouveau dictionnaire
　historique. 42914
M., G. F. V. pseud. tr. 72237
M., G. G. D. pseud. Vie de Phil. Emm. de
　Lorraine. see Montpleinchamp, J. Chr.
　B. de.
M., H. pseud. Remarks upon my book of
　immediate revelation. 103703
M., H. L. pseud. Florence Murray. see
　Murray, H. L.
M., H. V. Z. pseud. Voor-reden. 106291
M., I. pseud. Original rights of mankind.
　see Mather, Increase, 1639-1723.
M., I. pseud. To the reader. see Mather,
　Increase, 1639-1723.
M., J. pseud. Grammatica over de Creoolske
　sprog pä de Danske eilande i America.
　42910
M., J. pseud. Legislative authority of the
　British Parliament. 42909
M., J. pseud. Missionary's burial. 82907
M., J. pseud. Preface, to encourage and
　perpetuate the singing of psalms. 66446
M., J. pseud. Secession aux Etats-Unis et
　son origine. see Mortimer, J.
M., J. pseud. Verses. see Milton, John,
　1608-1674.
M., J., a Lieutenant in the Fleet. pseud.
　Maritime campaign of 1778. 44602
M . . . ., Jʰ. pseud. tr. see
　Mandrillon, Joseph H.
M., Jʰ. pseud. Precis sur l'Amerique
　Septentrionale. see Mandrillon, Joseph H.
M*********, Jʰ. pseud. Recherches
　philosophiques. see Mandrillon, Joseph
　H.
M*********, Jʰ. pseud. Spectateur Americain.
　see Mandrillon, Joseph H.
M., J. A. pseud. see Moerbeeck, Jan
　Andries.
M., J. B. pseud. Disertacion conta la
　tolerancia religionsa. see Morales, J. B.
M., J. B. pseud. Verdadera esplicacion de
　la voz independencia. 98937
M., J. B. de V. y. pseud. see V. y M., J.
　B. de. pseud. tr.
M., J. G. pseud. tr. 50047
M., J. F. M. pseud. tr. 96544
M., J. F. M. pseud. Relacao da embaixada
　que o poderoso Rei de Angome . . .
　mandou. see Mascarenhas, Jose Freire
　de Monteroyo.
M., J. L. pseud. Native bards. see Martin,
　J. L.
M., L. pseud. tr. see Lok, M. tr.
M., L. pseud. Solfeada y palo de ciego. see
　Montana, Luis. supposed author
M., L. B. de. pseud. Coup d'oeil sur l'etat
　actuel des Etats-Unis d'Amerique. 42913
M*****, M. pseud. tr. 75474
M., M. pseud. Additional postscript. see
　Mason, Martin. supposed author
M., M. L. L. pseud. ed. Memoires
　historiques. see Le Mascrier, J. B.
M . . ., M. V. pseud. tr. 64886
M., Matt. Robinson. see Montague, Matthew
　Robinson.
M., O. pseud. Plain reasons for removing a
　certain great man. 42915
M., O. pseud. St. Vincenz in Pennsylvanien.
　see Moosmuller, Oswald.
M., P. pseud. tr. (77892)-77893
M., P. pseud. Refutacion documentada.
　42916

M.

M., P. J. pseud. Aanmerkingen over den koophandel en het geldt. 39307

M., P. J. pseud. Kurtze remarqves. see Marperger, Paul Jakob, 1656-1730. supposed author

M., P. V. pseud. tr. 59678

M., R. pseud. General survey of that part of the island of St. Christopher's. (42917)

M., R. pseud. Letters. 70894

M., R. pseud. Nevves of Sr. Walter Rauleigh. 54971, 67574, 82979

M., R. pseud. Relation of Mr. R. M.'s voyage to Buenos Ayres. 42918

M., R. R. pseud. Two pieces descriptive of Cuban slavery. see Madden, R. R.

M . . ., Rokus. pseud. tr. 92584

M., S. W. pseud. Children's hour. 74609

M., T. pseud. Abstract of a letter to Cotton Mather. see Maule, Thomas.

M., T. pseud. Beginning, progress and conclusion of Bacon's rebellion. 4366

M., T. pseud. Remarks on several acts of Parliament. see Blumeau, Jonathan.

M., T. pseud. Viaggio di un Livornese al Canada. 99406

M., T. C. pseud. Priest's truf-cutting day. 42919

M., T. N. pseud. Southern primer. 88448

M., W. pseud. Account of the present state of Nova-Scotia. 56104

M., W. pseud. Controversy between "Erskine" and "W. M." 16192, 22799

M., W. pseud. Pettie's Island Land and Cash Lottery. see Masters, William.

M., W., a witness for the truth. pseud. Brief character of the antient Christian Quaker. see Mather, W.

M., W. T. pseud. Reminiscences of a trans-Atlantic traveller. 42920

M. de V., B. L. pseud. Mexico por dentro y fuera. see Villarroel, Hipolito. supposed author

M. del C., F. pseud. Reflexiones en contestacion al articulo. 68732

M. y E. pseud. Nuevo viajero universal, en America. 42921

M. ***. pseud. tr. see Le Febvre de Villebrune, --------. tr. and Raulin, Joseph. tr.

M. ***. pseud. see Wante, Charles Etienne Pierre.

M. ****. pseud. tr. see ****, M. pseud. tr.

M. A. Coccii Sabellici Opera omnia. 74666

M. A. de Ruiter. In X boeken. 41964

M. A. G. B. pseud. see Bellemare, M. A. G.

M. A. L. V. A. pseud. see A., M. A. L. V. pseud.

M. A. R. F. pseud. see F., M. A. R. pseud.

M. Antonii Coccii Sabellici Rapsodiae historiarvm ab orbe condito Enneadis primae. 74658

M. Antonii Magni oratio habita Neapoli in fvnere Ferdinandi Hispaniarvm Regis. 43829

M. Antonivs Sabellicvs: Avgvstino Barbadico Serenissimo Venetiano Principi et Senatvi felicitatem. 74658

M. B. pseud. see B., M. pseud.

M. B**. pseud. tr. see Bourrit, Marc Theodore. tr.

M. B. C. pseud. see C., M. B. pseud.

M. B. J. L. et E. pseud. see L. et E., M. B. J. pseud.

M. Blvndeville his exercises. 6024

M. C. pseud. see Carey, Mathew, 1760-1839.

M. C. S. y L. pseud. see S. y L., M. C. pseud.

M. Cabet a Julien jeun Icarien dispose. 9786

M. Chevalier on Central America. 12596

M. D. pseud. see Dumesnil, Marie.

M. D***. pseud. see Chevrier, Antoine.

M. D. B***. pseud. see Buisson, Paul Ulric du.

M. D. L. C. pseud. see La Condamine, Charles Marie de.

M. D. L. S. pseud. see Sauvage, -------- de la.

M. D. P. pseud. tr. see Pure, Michel de. tr.

M. D. S. pseud. see Rousselot de Surgy, Jacques Philibert.

M. de L. pseud. see Longchamps, Pierre de.

M. E. **. pseud. tr. see Eidous, Marc Antoine. tr.

M. E. A. pseud. see Acevedo, M. E.

M. E. B. pseud. see Blake, Mary E.

M. Fernandez de Navarrete. Viajes de Amerigo Vespucio. note before 99327, 99380

M. G. pseud. see G., M. pseud.

M. G. pseud. see Gobert, M.

M. G. pseud. see Godwyn, Morgan.

M. G. pseud. see Gordon, William.

M. G. C. pseud. see C., D. M. G. pseud. tr.

M. G. T. C. pseud. see Toral y Cabanas, Manuel German.

M. G. Z. pseud. see Zenouwitz, G.

M. Guzman acusado criminalmente por algunos indigenas del mismo pueblo. 10060

M. H. pseud. see H., M. pseud.

M. H. D1. pseud. see Hilliard D'Auberteuil, Michel Rene.

M. J. C. pseud. see C., M. J. pseud.

M. J. H. pseud. see H., Miss M. J. pseud.

M. J. J. pseud. see J., M. J. pseud. tr.

M. J. O. D. pseud. see Odolant-Desnos, Pierre Joseph. ed.

M. J. S. pseud. see Seizas, Manuel Justiniano de.

M. J. pseud. see K., M. pseud.

M. K. pseud. ed. see Kerney, Michael.

M. L. pseud. see Lok, M. pseud. tr.

M. L. L. M. pseud. see Le Mascrier, J. B.

M. L V. pseud. see Sargent, Lucius M.

M. le B. E. pseud. see Engel, Samuel.

M. Louise Greene, a student of five years at Kent's Hill, Me. 28605

M. M*****. pseud. see M*****, M. pseud. tr.

M. M. pseud. see Mason, Martin. supposed author

M. M. S. pseud. tr. see S., M. M. pseud. incorrectly supposed tr.

M. M. V. pseud. see Vargas, M. M.

M. N. pseud. see Nougaret, M.

M. N. O. pseud. see O., M. N. pseud.

M. O. T. des P. pseud. see P., M. O. T. des. pseud.

M——ch——ts of G——t B——n. pseud. petitioners (66110)

M. P. D. L. C. pseud. see Peyroux de la Coudreniere, ---------.

M. P de L. pseud. tr. see L., M. P. de. pseud.

1541

M. P. S. pseud. see S., M. P. pseud.
M. P. V. pseud. see Vissier, Paul.
M. Q. C. S. pseud. see Quiros Y Campo.
   Sagrado, Manuel de.
M. R******. pseud. see Riddell, Maria.
   supposed author
M. R. D. S. pseud. see Smith, Mary
   Rebecca Darby, 1814-1886.
M. R. de F. pseud. see F., M. R. de.
   pseud.
M. R. F. de la B. pseud. see B., M. R. F.
   de la. pseud.
M. R. G. pseud. see G., M. R. pseud.
M. Ringmannus Philesius. V. Jacobo Bronco
   suo Achati. s. p. d. 99333
M. S. pseud. see S., M. pseud.
M. S. pseud. see Goodwin, John. supposed
   author
M. S. pseud. see Menno Simons.
M. S. pseud. see Sparke, Michael.
M. S. pseud. see Stoddard, Mrs. M.
M. S. H. pseud. see H., M. S. pseud.
M. S. to A. S. With a plea for libertie of
   conscience. 74624, 91382-91383
M. T. pseud. see T., M. pseud.
M. T. pseud. see Maule, Thomas.
M. T. C. pseud. see C., M. T. pseud.
M. T. Cicero's Cato major, or his discourse
   on old-age. 13040
M. T. Cicero's Cato major, or discourse on
   old age. 13042
M. T. y C. pseud. see T. y C., M. pseud.
M. Tobias Wagners Abschieds-Rede. 100956
M. V. pseud. see Vidaurre y Encalada,
   Manuel Lorenzo de.
M. V. M . . . pseud. tr. see M . . ., M.
   V. pseud. tr.
M. Van Buren. 98425
M. Van Buren's last letter. 88669
M. W. C. pseud. see Chapman, Maria
   Weston.
M. Washburn, ex-ministre des Etats-Unis.
   58528
Ma bibliotheque Americaine. 6460
Ma justification des infamies devitees contre
   moi. 20736
Ma deportation a la Guyane, 1797-1801.
   8742
Maandelijksche Nederlandsche Mercurius.
   42922
Maanedligt flyveblad. 55486
Mabel Vaughan. 17939
Mabew otiwekiti. (79977)
Mably, Gabriel Bonnot de. 42923-(42926),
   47206, 53021
McAdam, Adam. 42927, 43146
McAdam, D. (42928)
McAdoo, Mary Faith (Floyd) 84942
McAdoo, Mrs. W. G., Sr. see McAdoo,
   Mary Faith (Floyd)
M'Afee, Robert B. 42929
McAll, Samuel. (42930)
McAllister, F. M. 42931
McAllister, James. defendant 97771
McAlpine, J. (42932)
McAlpine, William J. 8329, 42933-42936,
   52493, 104021
M'Anally, D. R. 42937
McAndrew, --------. 42938
Macao. 39300
McArone. pseud. Life and adventures of
   Jeff. Davis. 42939
MacArthur, C. L. 97072
MacArthur, Charles L. 42940
M'Arthur, John, 1755-1840. 13420, 42941
MacArthur, Robert Stuart, 1841-1923. 84277

MacArthur & Wilson. firm publishers 97972
MacArthur & Wilson's Troy city directory.
   97072
Macarthy, Harry. 42942
Macartney, George Macartney, Earl, 1737-1806.
   (57146), (59572), 90843, 99320, note after
   99776
Macarty, Capt. -------- supposed author
   1779, 5th note after 102788
Macaulay, Angus. 42943
Macaulay, Catharine (Sawbridge) see Graham,
   Catharine (Sawbridge) Macaulay, 1731-
   1791.
Macaulay, D. ed. 53356
Macaulay, George Henry. (11561), 42947-
   42948
Macaulay, John. supposed author 97708
Macaulay, Thomas Babington Macaulay, 1st
   Baron, 1800-1859. 13491, (20377), 23659,
   25146, (26766), 32491, 42949, 59743,
   58172-(58173)
Macaulay, W. 42950
Macaulay, Zachariah. see Macaulay, Zachary,
   1768-1838.
Macaulay, Zachary, 1768-1838. 14726, (21855),
   (42951)-42954, 81955, 95656, 95658,
   98836, 1st note after 102832
Macaulay, Zachary, 1768-1838. supposed
   author 94175
Macaulay charges. 20376
Macaulay on Democracy. 42949
Macaulay's portrait of the founder of Quakerism
   (26766)
Macauley, James. 42956
McAuley, Thomas. 51828
Macaya, Armand d'Avezac. see Avezac-
   Macaya, Armand d', 1800-1875.
McBlair, C. H. defendant at court martial
   (42957)
Macbride, Captain --------. 18336
McBride, James, 1788-1859. 42959
M'Bride, John Rogers, 1832-1904. 42958
McC, Wm. ed. 93185
McCabe, James Dabney, 1808-1875. 23374,
   42960, 3d note after 88547
McCabe, James Dabney, 1842-1883. 42961-
   42962
M'Cabe, John Collins. (42963)
MacCabe, Julius P. Bolivar. 40882, (49154)
McCabe, W. Gordon. 86161
M'Caffrey, John. 42965
McCaffrey, Michael J. A. 42964
McCagg & Fuller. firm see Scammon,
   McCagg & Fuller. firm
McCahn, James. (37068)
M'Caine, Alexander. 42966-42968
MacCaleb, Theodore H. 42969
McCall, George Archibald, 1802-1868. 40611,
   42970
McCall, H. S. 42972
M'Call, Hext. (42971)
M'Call, Hugh. (42973)
McCall, John. (42974)
M'Call, John C. 42975
M'Call, P. 42976
McCall, S. 42977
McCalla, Daniel. 42978
M'Calla, John M. 32337
McCalla, W. L. 42979
McCallum, D. C. 42980, 47313 see also
   U. S. Army. Military Railroads.
   Director and General Manager.
M'Callum, Pierre F. 42981
M'Callum, Pierre F. supposed author
   63747, 2d note after 96979
M'Callum, Pierre F. reporter 62683

McCord, T. (43095)
M'Cord's reports. 87455
M'Corkle, Samuel Eusebius. 43096-(43097)
M'Corkle, William. 22384, 91126
McCorkle, William A. 43098
M'Cormack, Samuel. 99581
M'Cormick, Charles. 43099
McCormick, Cyrus H. 84518
M'Cormick, Daniel. petitioner 97941
McCormick, J. C. 85041
McCormick, John D. 83982
M'Cormick, R. (43100)
McCormick, Richard C. 43101-(43102)
M'Cormick, Samuel. supposed author 15032,
  99581
M'Cormick, Samuel Jarvis. ed. 61210,
  64383
McCosh, James. (43103)
McCoskry, Samuel Allen, Bp. 43104-43105
M'Coun, William T. (43106), (53637) see
  also New York (State) Vice Chancellor.
McCoy, A. D. 43107
McCoy, Amasa. 43108, 56036
McCoy, C. F. 22085
M'Coy, Isaac 43109-43113, 60931
McCoy, William. supposed author 36728
McCrady, Edward, 1833-1903. (43144),
  70263, 87716, 88005
McCrady, Edward, 1833-1903. plaintiff
  83854
McCrady, John, 1831-1881. 43115, 87532,
  87738
McCrawsville, N. Y. New York Central
  College. see New York Central Col-
  lege, McGrawsville, N. Y.
McCrea, Robert Barlow. 43116
M'Cready, B. W. 43117
McCreary, R. G. 43118
McCreery, Thomas Clay, 1816-1890. 43119
M'Cron, John. 43120
McCrum, James. 17386
McCullagh, William Torrens. 43121
McCulloch, -------. 43122-43123, 2d note
  after 104889
McCulloch, Hugh, 1808-1895. 43124, 89214
M'Culloch, John. 15117-15118, (43125)
McCulloch, John Ramsay, 1789-1864. (31775),
  32695, 43126-43130, 71086, 78981-
  78982, 82304, (82311), 83926, 97330
M'Culloch, Thomas. 43131
McCulloch's literature of political economy.
  (31775)
Mc'Culloch's pocket almanack, for . . . 1805.
  (43125)
McCulloh, ---------. defendant 68042
M'Culloh, James H. (43142)-43134
M'Culloh, R. S. (6384), (43135)-(43137)
McCullough, Bruce Welker. 83785
McCullough, Hiram. 45207
M'Cullough, John W. 43138
McCully, Jonathan. 56161, (56188)
McCurdy, Charles. 72134
McDaniel, Samuel W. 43139
Mac-Dermott, A. tr. 4047, (24627)-(24628)
Macdill, D. 43140-43141
MacDonald, ---------, fl. 1805. (68946),
  85187
McDonald, ---------, fl. 1822. (54082)
McDonald, ---------, fl. 1850. (43169)
Macdonald, A. J. 43147
Macdonald, Alejandro, fl. 1842. (43143)
McDonald, Alexander, L. R. C. S. E. 43142
M'Donald, Alexander, fl. 1769-1779. 97094
Macdonald, Alexander, 1832-1903. 43144
Macdonald, Angus W. supposed author
  43148, 2d note after 100582

Macdonald, Archibald. 42927, 43145-43146
MacDonand, C. F. 84277
McDonald, Charles James, 1793-1860. 79511
  see also Georgia. Governor, 1839-1843
  (McDonald)
M'Donald, Donald. 84363
Macdonald, Duncan George Forbes. 43149
Macdonald, G. 43150, 104607
Macdonald, James Madison, 1812-1876.
  43151-43153
M'Donald, John. see M'Donald, Thomas.
M'Donald, John, of Glasgow. 43159
M'Donald, John, 1775-1853. 43160
M'Donald, John, d. 1821. (43154)-(43157)
Macdonald, Sir John Alexander, 1815-1891.
  43161-43162
Macdonald, John M. (43163)-43164
McDonald, Mrs. Mary Noel. 43165
Macdonald, Moses, 1815-1869. 43166
M'Donald, Philip. (43167)
M'Donald, Thomas. 43158
M'Donald, William K. (43168)
McDonald, William Naylor. supposed author
  43148, 2d note after 100582
M'Donalds. 59495
M'Donell, Alexander. 43170
Macdonell, Allen. (43171)
Mac-Donnel, Edward. tr. 41915
M'Donnell, Alexander. 43172-43173, 97578
M'Donnell, Matthew. see M'Connell, Mathew.
McDonnold, --------. 82783
M'Donnough, William. defendant 43174
McDonogh, John, 1779-1850. 43175, 43177,
  28247
Macdonogh, T. M. 43178
McDonogh Educational Fund and Institute,
  Baltimore. Trustees. 43176-43177,
  (69916) see also Mayer, Brantz, 1809-
  1879.
McDonogh Estate Agents and Commissioners.
  see McDonogh Eduaction Fund and
  Institute, Baltimore. Trustees.
McDonogh Estate Trustees. see McDonogh
  Educational Fund and Institute, Baltimore,
  Trustess.
Macdonough, Augustus R. 43179, 89496-89497
Macdonough, Augustus R. reporter 70181
Macdonough, Thomas, 1783-1825. 43180
MacDonough, William E. 54489, 87061
Macdouall, John. 43181
McDougall, Alexander. 86868
McDougall, Frances Harriet (Whipple) Greene.
  22102, 22677, 103302-103303
M'Dougall, George. petitioner (43182)
Macdougall, G. Gordon. tr. 28179
M'Dougall, George F. 23608, 43183
McDougall, James. 43184
McDougall, James Alexander, 1817-1867.
  43185-(43186)
MacDougall, Patrick Leonard, 1819-1894.
  43187
McDowall, John Robert. 43188-43191, note
  after 103223
McDowall, John Robert. defendant 43191
McDowall, John Robert. defendant before
  Presbytery 43191
McDowall's defence, nos. 1 and 2. (43189)
McDowall's journal. (43190)
McDowell, ---------. lithographer 84774
MacDowell, E. B. 43192
McDowell, Irwin. defendant before court of
  inquiry 43193
McDowell, James. (43194)-(43195)
McDowell, John, 1780-1863. 43196, 89736
McDowell, Joseph Jefferson, 1800-1877.
  43197

McDowell, Joseph N. (43198)
Macdowell, n. C. 43199
Macduff, J. 43200
McDuffie, George, 1790-1851. 10889, (27641),
  30003, 43202-43205, 46140, 48097,
  51919, 87421, 87422-87423, 87426,
  87428, 87478, 87545-87546, note after
  90638, 96073, 98425 see also South
  Carolina. Governor, 1834-1836
  (McDuffie)
Mace, -------. 66686
Mace, Fayette. 43206
Macedo, Antonio de. 43207
Macedo, Antonio de Souza de. see Souza de
  Macedo, Antonio de.
Macedo, Francisco a San Augustino. (43208)
Macedo, Ignacio Jose de. 43209-43211
Macedo, Joaquim Manoel de. 43212-43214
Macedo, Joaquim Teixeira de. 43215
Macedo, Jose Agostinho de. 43216
Macedo, M. 43217
Macedo, M. A. de. 43218
Macedo, M. de Souza de. see Souza de
  Macedo, M. de.
Macedo, Melchor de Castro. see Melchor
  de Castro Macedo. Fray
Macedo Leitao e Carvalhosa, Manuel
  Francisco de Barros e Sousa de
  Mesquita de. see Santarem, Manuel
  Francisco de Barros e Sousa de
  Mesquita de Macedo Meitao e Carval-
  hosa, Visconde de.
Macedon Academy. 43219
Macedon Convention, 1847. 27850
M'Elderry, Hugh. 3189
M'Elhiney, Thomas. 43220
McElhone, John J. reporter 90390
McElligott, James N. (43221)
McElrath, Thomas, 1807-1888. 37092, 93347
McElrath, Thomas, 1807-1888. defendant
  (16421)
Mac El'Rey, J. H. 43222
M'Elroy, A. 61606, 83733
McElroy, J. (43223)
M'Elroy, Joseph. (43224)-43225
McElroy, Sanuel. (43226)
McElroy, Thomas. (43227)
McElroy and Company. firm publishers
  61606
McElroy and Co.'s city business directory.
  61606
McElroy prize compositions. 43228
McElroy's wholesale business directory.
  61606
McElvain, John. 96660, 96666-96667 see also
  U. S. Commissioner to the Band of
  Delaware Indians, Upon the Sandusky
  River, in the State of Ohio. U. S.
  Commissioners to the Mixed Bands of the
  Senecas and Shawnee Indians. U. S.
  Commissioners to the Shawnee Indians.
M'Elwee, Thomas B. 92910
Macer, Jehan. 43229
McEvoy, H. ed. 57364
M'Evoy, James. petitioner 45257
McEvoy. firm see Sutherland & McEvoy.
  firm publishers
McEvoy (H. N.) firm publishers 49622,
  note after 93956
McEwen, Abel. 43230-43232
M'Ewen, John A. 43233
McEwen, M. H. 43234
M'Ewen, R. S. 43235
MacFadyen, James. (43236)
McFalls, T. B. 43237
McFarland, Mrs. --------. (43241)

MacFarland, Andrew. 43238
M'Farland, Asa. (34239)-43240, 95535
McFarland, Daniel, b. 1820. defendant (43241)
MacFarland, Joel B. 43242
MacFarland, W. H. 43244-(43245)
McFarland, William. 43243, 93229
MacFarlane, Charles, 1799-1858. 17374,
  (43246)-43247
MacFarlane, James. 43248
Macfarlane, Robert, 1734-1804. 26997-26998,
  (32210), 43249, 96997, 96998
MacFarlane, Robert, 1815-1883. 43250-43251
McFarlane, land agent see Synder and
  McFarlane. land agents
M'Farren, Samuel. (43252)
M'Ferrin, John Berry, 1807-1887. 88384
Macfie, Matthew. 43253
McFingal. 97239-97239B
M'Fingal, a modern epic poem. 97210-97215,
  97218-97231, 97234
M'Fingal, an epic poem. 97216-97217
McGarrahan, William. (43254)-43255
McGarrahan, William. claimant (79901)
McGarrahan, William. litigant (58984)-58985
McGarrahan memorial. (43254)
McGaughey, E. W. 43256
MacGavock, Randall W. 26775, 43257
McGaw, James F. (43258)
McGaw, Jacob, 1778-1867. 78997, 2d note
  after 101883
McGeachy, Edward. 43259
McGee, Thomas D'Arcy. 37116, 43260-43264,
  80015
McGeorge, Robert Jackson. (43265)
McGiffert, Joseph N. 43267-43268
McGilchrist, John. (43269)
McGill, A. T. 43270-43271
McGill, P. M. 43272
McGill College and its medals. 76411
McGill University, Montreal. 43273
McGill University, Montreal. Governors.
  43273
McGill University, Montreal. Medical Faculty.
  43273
McGillivray, M. illus. 84815
McGillivray, Simon. supposed author 20699,
  note after 51790
Macgillivray, W. ed. 33744-33745
McGinley, William A. 43274
McGinn, John. 43275
McGinnes, --------. 7052
M'Ginnes, James Y. 33579, 43276
McGinnes theory of the Schuylkill coal forma-
  tion. 7052
M'Glochlin, James. defendant 13697, 96849
Macgowan, Daniel J. 43277
McGowan, Edward. 43278
M'Gowan, James. defendant 96889
McGowan, John. supposed author 25882
Macgowan, John, 1726-1780. 65499, (79890),
  83541
McGowen, Charles. (56691)
McGrath, A. G. 87724 see also South
  Carolina. Secretary of State.
McGrawsville, N. Y. New York Central
  College. see New York Central College,
  McGrawsville, N. Y.
McGregor, Daniel. ed. 83151
M'Gregor, James. 43279
McGregor, John. (43280)-43289
Macgregor, John. (43290)
McGregor, John. P. 43291
McGregor western railway directory for 1867.
  43292
MacGregore, David. 55, 9907, 43293, 50462,
  58896

McGruder, J. W. 83857
McGuier, Henry. 43294
McGuire, Edward C. (43295)-(43296)
McGuire, J. C. ed. (43721)
M'Guire, J. G. ed. 43709
McGuire, Mrs. John P. (19959), 43297
Machabees Canadiens. 5152
Machado, Diogo Barbosa. 43298-43299
Machado, Ignacio Barbosa. 43300
Machado, Manuel Leite. 43301
Machado e Silva, Antonio Carlos Ribeiro de
    Andrada. see Ribeiro de Andrada
    Machado e Silva, Antonio Carlos.
Machado Guimaraes, Jose Joaquim. see
    Guimaraes, Jose Joaquim Machado.
Machault, Jacques de. 21408, 43302
M'Henry, George. 9857, 43303-43308
McHenry, James, 1785-1845. 1156, 43309-
    43311, 89148, 94294, 101159, 101164,
    1st note after 101905, 103986, 103987,
    103989
McHenry, James, 1785-1845. supposed author
    105691
McHenry, John H. 43312
M'Henry, William. 43313 see also Bucks
    County, Pa. Sub Lieutenant.
Machias, Me. Centennial Anniversary, 1863.
    43314, 84750
Machias, Me. Church. (65826)
Machias, Me. Citizens. petitioners 43314,
    84750
Machias, Me. Court. 96895, 101476
Machias, Me. Natives Resident Abroad. see
    Natives of Machias Resident Abroad.
    pseud.
Machias genealogies. 43314, 84750
Machiavelisme du cabinet Francais. 41138
Machie, William. plaintiff 96900
Machoni de Verdena, Antonio. 11697, (43315)
Machorie de Cerdena, Antonio. see Machoni
    de Cerdena, Antonio.
Machpelah. 43316
Machpelah Cemetery, Philadelphia. see
    Philadelphia. Machpelah Cemetery.
Machuca, Bernardo de Vargas. see Vargas
    Machuca, Bernardo de.
Machuca, Francisco de Vargas. see Vargas
    Machuca, Francisco de.
Machuca, Juan de Vargas. see Vargas
    Machuca, Juan de.
Machuca, Pedro de Vargas. see Vargas
    Machuca, Pedro de.
McHugh, James. defendant 43317
Maciel do Amaral, Delfim Augusto. see
    Amaral, Delfim Augusto Maciel do.
McIlrath, Charles. 88414 see also Southern
    Minnesota Railroad Company.
M'Ilvain, James. petitioner 43318
McIlvaine, Abraham Robinson, 1804-1863.
    43319
McIlvaine, Charles Pettit, Bp. 5574, 12170,
    19339, (20385), 20394, 20395, 34009,
    43320-43324, 47243, 88253, 89736
McIlvaine, J. H. 43335
M'Ilvaine, Joseph. (43326)
McIlvaine, William. (43327)
McIlvaine, William, Jr. 43328
McIlwaine, H. R. ed. 99908, 99927, 100037,
    100192, 100209-100210, 100212
McIntosh, ----------. USA 49073
Mac-Intosh, A. 43329
M'Intosh, Cynthia I. ed. 92752
M'Intosh, David. 71977
McIntosh, Duncan. 43330
M'Intosh, George. 43331
M'Intosh, George. defendant 43331

McIntosh, John. (43332)-43333
M'Intosh, L. 43334
M'Intosh, Lacklan. 96600 see also U. S.
    Commissioners to the Cherokee Indians.
M'Intosh, Maria J. 43335-43336
M'Intyre, Archibald, 1772-1858. 43337, 97777,
    97779-97781, 105998
M'Intyre, Archibald, 1772-1858. complainant
    97779-97781, 97785
McIntyre, James. complainant 97779-97781,
    97785
M'Jilton, John Nelson, 1805-1875. 3002, 41784
    (43338)-43340 see also Baltimore.
    Delegates to the Educational Conventions
    of Buffalo and Boston, 1860.
Mack, A. W. 43341
Mack, Alexander. 43342
Mack, D. 43343
Mack, Ebenezer. 43344-43345
Mack, J. Martin. 68992
Mack, Mrs. R. E. illus. 22215
Mack, Robert. 43346
Mack, Robert C. 43347
Mack, Solomon. 83496
Mack, W. G. 43348
Mack genealogy. 84243
Mac-kah-tah-mo-ah. Potawatomi Indian Chief
    96705
MAckall, Henry C. 45207
Mackall, Leonard L. 83978, 96573
Mackarthy, Dennis, d. 1718. defendant 32182,
    (32197)
Mackau, ----------, Baron de. (39638)
Mackay, Alexander. 37122, 43349-43353
Mackay, Charles, 1814-1889. 43354-43358,
    47126, (74336), 83279, 85168
Mackay, Charles, fl. 1847. (43359)
McKay, David. (28462), 43360
M'Kay, Daniel. 98503
McKay, Donald. 43360-43361, 70242
Mackay, Elizabeth. plaintiff 40855
Mackay, Hugh. 9830, (43362), 56845, 2d note
    after 87858
Mackay, J. 43363
Mackay, James. tr. 41018, 64545
M'Kay, Medad. defendant (43001), 96901
McKay, Neil. 43364
Mackay, R. supposed author 43365, (58021),
    note after (63501), note after 100508
Mackay, Robert W. Stuart. 10416, (43366),
    50261, 67045
Mackay, Samuel. RA 43367
Mackay, Samuel, fl. 1816. 43368
Mackay, Samuel, d. 1831. tr. 38499
M'Kay, Samuel M. 43369
Mackaye, James, 1805-1888. 43370-43372
McKayes, J. (58023)
MacKay's Quebec directory. 67045
McKean, Joseph, 1776-1818. 43373-43379,
    79285, 2d note after 98343, 101471
McKean, Joseph, 1776-1818. supposed author
    (18435), 42459, 43375-43376, 79285
McKean, Thomas, 1734-1817. 5679, 9936,
    19381, (43380), (59821), 60040, 60772,
    83554, 1st note after 92859, note after
    99586, 104627 see also Pennsylvania.
    Governor, 1799-1808 (McKean)
McKean and Elk Land and Improvement
    Company. (43381)
McKean and Elk Land and Improvement Com-
    pany. Directors. (43381)
McKee, R. 43382-(43383)
McKee, Samuel, 1774-1826. 43385
McKee, Samuel, 1833-1898. 43384
McKee, Thomas J. ed. 97617
McKee, W. H. 43386

McKeehan, J. B. (43387)
M'Keehan (David) firm publishers 26741
McKeen, Joseph. (43388)-(43391)
McKeen, Joseph. defendant 7036, 92313
McKeen, Silas, 1791-1877. 43392-(43394)
McKeever, Harriet B. 43395
M'Keevor, Thomas. 43396, 62509
McKell, Quinton. pseud. Lament. 43397
McKellar, Patrick. 43398
Mackellar, Thomas. 43399-43400
McKelvey, M. T. (76442)
Mackemie, Francis. 44081, 2d note after
    100507, 3d note after 102552
McKendree College, Lebanon, Ill. 43401
Mackenna, Benjamin Vicuna. see Vicuna
    Mackenna, Benjamin.
M'Kenney, Mordecai. 60063, 60066
McKenney, Thomas L. 1978, 2030, 34470,
    (43402)-(43411), 96652, 96654 see also
    U. S. Commissioners to the Chippewa,
    Menomonie and Winnebago Indians.
    U. S. Commissioners to the Creek
    Indians.
McKenny, Thomas L. supposed author 5710,
    43404
McKenny, Thomas L. see McKenney, Thomas
    L.
Mackentosh, John. 43413
Mackenzie, Sir Alexander, 1763-1820. 43414-
    43418, 83623
McKenzie, Alexander, 1830-1914. 43419
Mackenzie, Alexander Slidell. (43420), 43422-
    43425, 78542
Mackenzie, Alexander Slidell. defendant at
    court martial 16515, 43421, 43426
Mackenzie, Charles. 43427
Mackenzie, E. (43428)
Mackenzie, Henry. 43429, 94025
Mackenzie, Henry. supposed author 18347,
    27145, note after 71369
McKenzie, James A. 43430
Mackenzie, John. (25788), (87588), 87858,
    87865
Mackenzie, Quin. tr. 74898
Mackenzie, Robert. (43432)-(43434)
Mackenzie, Robert Sheldon, 1809-1880.
    26607, 50401
Mackenzie, Roderick. RA. 30226, 43431,
    94397
Mackenzie, William Lyon. 10577, 43435-
    43438
Mackenzie, William Lyon. defendant 43439,
    93964, 93966
Mackenzie, William Lyon. petitioner 43439
McKeon, J. 43442
McKeon, John, 1808-1883. 43440-43441
MacKercher, Daniel. 43443, 4th note after
    100486, 101487
McKerrell, R. 43444, note after 98924
Mackey, Albert G. (43445)-43448, 87833,
    87838, 87843, 88297
Mackey, E. W. M. 87522 see also South
    Carolina. Legislature. House of
    Representatives. Speaker.
Mackey, T. J. 43448
McKibbin, J. C. 43449
Mackie, Andrew. 43450
Mackie, George. 43451
Mackie, J. Milton. 43453
Mackie, John. 43452
McKillop, John. 72017
M'Kim, Isaac. (45067), 93938 see also
    Maryland. Susquehannah Commissioners.
M'Kim, J. Miller. 43455
McKim, John. (43454)

McKinley, William, Pres. U. S., 1843-1901.
    83366, 85097 see also U. S. President,
    1897-1901 (McKinley)
McKinley, the people's choice. 83366
M'Kinnen, Daniel. 21901, 43456-43457
Mac-Kinnen's Reise nach dem Brittischen
    Westindien. 43457
McKinney, Mordecai. 43458-43459
M'Kinnon, John D. (43460)
Mackinnon, L. B. (43461)-43463
Mackinnon, William Alexander. 43464-43465
McKinnon, William Charles. (43466)
McKinny, David. 43467
McKinstry, E. W. 43468
McKinstry, J. 43469
Mackintosh, Sir James. 43470
McKnight, George H. 43471
McKnight, James. 43472
M'Knight, John, 1754-1823. (41630), 43473-
    43474
M'Knight, John, Jr. 43475
McKnight, Robert. 43476
McKnight, Thomas. (43477)
M'Konochie, Alexander. 43478-43479
McKown, ---------, fl. 1840. 83019
McKoy, Isaac. see McCoy, Isaac.
Mackrill, Joseph. 43480
Mackworth, Sir Humphrey. 43481-43482
Macky, ----------. 478
McL., J. pseud. engr. 93075
M'Lachlan, Alexander. 43483
McLain, M. G. 34495
M'Lain, William, 1806-1873. (43484), 82952
McLain, A. tr. 99822, 99825
M'Lane, David, d. 1797. defendant 43485,
    96902
M'Lane, Louis. 43486-43487
McLane, R. 43488
McLane, Robert Milligan, 1815-1898. 12813,
    43489, 58083-58084 see also Pacific
    Mail Steamship Company. President.
    U. S. Legation. China.
McLane, Robert. 89203
Maclaren, Alexander. 83894-83895
McLaren, Archibald. 43490
McLaren, D. (43491)
Maclaren, James. 43492-43493, 56517
McLaren, W. E. 43494
M'Laughlin, Charles. illus. 28562
McLaughlin, D. D. T. 43496
McLaughlin, Daniel. 43495
McLaughlin, E. A. 43497
McLaughlin, H. C. 15390, 25018
McLaughlin, J. Fairfax. 9620, 43499
M'Laughlin, John. 43498
McLaughlin, John T. 43500
McLaughlin, S. 67045
Maclaurie, -------. (43501)
Maclaurin, J. 104485
Maclaurin, Jo. reporter 102434
Maclay, Archibald. 43502
Maclay, Edgar Stanton. 83960
Maclay, William B. 43503-43506
McLean, ----------, fl. 1829. 43518
M'Lean, Alexander, fl. 1828. 43507
McLean, Alexander, fl. 1861. 43508
Maclean, Allan, 1725-1784. (36740)
M'Lean, Allen. 43509
M'Lean, Archibald. ed. (22678), (32961),
    105152
M'Lean, C. G. 43511
M'Lean, Charles B. 43510
M'Lean, Francis. 9925
M'Lean, Hector. 43512
M'Lean, James. (43513)

M'Niel, John. 96659 see also U. S. Commissioners to the Winnebago Indians.

McNutt, Alexander Gallatin, 1802-1848. 2407, 43609, 49518 see also Mississippi. Governor, 1838-1842 (McNutt)

Macomb, Alexander, 1782-1841. 43613

Macomb, David B. (43612)

Macomb, Robert. 43614-43615, 49335, note after 103267

Macomb County, Mich. Citizens' Meeting, for the Improvement of the Linton River, Mt. Clemens, 1849. see Meeting of the Citizens of Macomb County, for the Improvement of Clinton River, Mt. Clemens, Mich., 1849.

Macome, Alexander. 43610-43611

Macon, Nathaniel. 40639, 43617-43618

Macon, Ga. Board of Trade. petitioners 43619

Macon, Ga. Georgia Female College. see Wesleyan College, Macon, Ga.

Macon, Ga. Mercer University. see Mercer University, Macon, Ga.

Macon, Ga. Wesleyan College. see Wesleyan College, Macon, Ga.

Macon & Brunswick Railroad Company. 43620

Macon and Western Railroad Company. 43621

Maconochie, Alexander. see M'Konochie, Alexander.

Macoy, Robert, 1815-1895. 43622, 45511

McPhail, G. Wilson. 43623

McPhail, Leonard. 43624

McPheeters, S. B. 75344

McPheeters, William M. ed. 75395

Macpherson, Charles. (43625)

Macpherson, David. 43626

McPherson, Edward. 43627-43631

Macpherson, James. 43632-43633

Macpherson, James, 1736-1796. 18348, (25912), (62991)

Macpherson, James, 1736-1796. supposed author 18347, 27145, 27283, note after 41286, 43633, (62991), 68743, note after 71369, 80708, 104592

Macpherson, John, ca. 1726-1792. 43635-43638, 51164

McPherson, John, fl. 1862. 43634

M'Pherson, L. T. plaintiff 96815

McPherson, Smith, 1848-1915. 84519

Macpherson. firm publishers (61601)

Macpherson, the great confederate philosopher and southren blower. 31907

Macpherson's directory for the city and suburbs of Philadelphia. (61601)

Macpherson's letters, etc. (43637)

McPhetres, Samuel A. 42477, (43639)

McQueen, Hugh. 43640

Mcqueen, James. 43641-(43643)

Macqueen, John Fraser. 43644

Macquire, Carney. 94039

Macquoid, T. R. illus. 92474

MacRae, Alexander. 43645

MacRae, Alexander. plaintiff 96904

MacRae, Archibald, 1820-1885. 27419

MacRae, D. K. (43647)

Macrae, David. 43646

McRae, Duncan G. defendant before military commission 43648

McRae, J. C. engr. 84141

McRae, J. J. 43649

Macreading, Charles S. 43650

Mcready, Mrs. -------. 43651

McReady, Benjamin W. ed. (54787)

Macready, William C. (43652), 69158

McRee, Griffith J. 43653-43654

Macret, --------. illus. (67696)

Macrobe, --------. 76838

M'Robert, Patrick. 43655

McRoberts, Samuel. 43656

McRoberts, Samuel. plaintiff 76831

Macrobius Aurelius. 43657

Macrobius Integer nitidus suoq decori a Joanne Riuio restitutus. 43657

McRuer, D. C. 90212

M'Shane, -------. 765-766, (80579), 80632

McShea, John. 33658

McSherry, James. 43659

McSherry, Richard. 43660-43661

McSherry, William, 1799-1839. (57311), 103352-103353

Macsimas de la guerra cuyo comentario es la historia. 11466

Macsparran, James. 1758-1759, 43662-43664, (52608), (55031), (65578), 82976, 96298, 98029

Macsparran, James. plaintiff 43663, (65578), 69298

Mactaggart, John. 43665

M'Tavish, Fraser and Co. firm petitioners 43666

McTyeire, H. M. 43667, note before 93267

McVean, Charles. 43668, 54723

McVey, W. G. D. 43669

McVey's literary and professional magazine. 43669

McVicar, P. ed. 37031

McVickar, Archibald, ed. 40833-40834

McVickar, John. (28816), 31975, 43670-43679, 69537, 70085, 85946, 92845

McVickar, M. 857

McVickar, W. A. 43680

Macwhorter, Alexander. (43681)

Macwhorter, Alexander C. 43682

McWilliam, James Ormiston. (43683)

McWillie, William, 1795-1869. 33150, (43684), 49506, 88083 see also Mississippi. Governor, 1856-1860 (McWillie)

McWright, A. 43685

Macy, Benjamin Franklin. 43686

Macy, Joseph. respondent 51752

Macy, Obed. 43687

Macy, Seth W. 70674

Macy, Silvanus J. 43688-43689

Mad poets. pseud. Elixier of moonshine. (13435)

Mad River and Erie Railroad Company. 43690 see also Lake Erie and Mad River Railroad Company.

Mad River Valley pioneer. (43691)

Mad Tom convicted to blackest ingratitude. (37437)

Mad world my masters. 54972

Madalena, Juan de la. see Estrada, Juan. tr.

Madam Willis's letters and her character. 104501

Madame de ***. pseud. see Villeneuve, Gabrielle Suzanne Barbot Gallon de.

Mme Marlet, de la commune Robert, Martinique. 5652

Madan, Cristobal. 17787, 43692

Madan, Martin, 1726-1790. 56487, 73061

Madariaga, Jose Cortes. 43693

Madden, Jerome. 88426 see also Southern Pacific Railroad Company. Land Agent.

Madden, R. R. 43694-(43697), 63605, note after 96999

Madden, Samuel. 43698
Madden. firm see Graham & Madden.
firm publishers
Maddox, Isaac, successively Bishop of St.
Asaph, and Worcester, 1697-1759.
(43699)-43700, 52147
Madelene, Henry de la. see La Madelene,
Henry de.
Madiana, J. B. Ricord. see Ricord Madiana,
J. B.
Madicanscutter, Peter. pseud. Siege of
Chepacket. see Dogherty, Roger.
Madiedo, Manuel Maria. 43702
Madinier, Henry. tr. (31792)
Madion, Thomas. 43703-43704
Madison. pseud. Read and judge for your-
self. 18832
Madison. pseud. Signs of the times. see
Citizen of Abbeville. pseud.
Madison, Dolley (Payne) 1768-1849. 82979
Madison, Henry. defendant 90576
Madison, James, Bp., 1749-1812. 35739,
43705-43706, 84139-84141
Madison, James, Bp., 1749-1812. supposed
author 40517, note after 97378, note
after 104434
Madison, James, Pres. U. S., 1751-1836.
(445)-448, 3299, 4549, 11005, 12486,
12489, (14151), 15945, 17448, (17885)
18934, 20450, 21533, 22233, (22237),
22412, 23453, 23502, (23979)-23993,
23996, 25876, 26399, 29968, (31832),
34398, 34400, (35886), 41427, 42265,
42456, 43707-(43721), 46031, 47622-
47623, 48065-(48074), 48148, 51002,
51133, (53773), 53975, (56498), 56959,
57627, 62521, 63811, 65359, 69816,
70237, 72475, 72847, 74353, (77416),
77419, 78647, 80405, 83809-83810,
83812-83817, 84823, 84835-84837,
84904, 89198, 90639, 93470, 96020,
97901, 99315, 100072, 100081, 100427,
2d note after 100462, 1st note after
100486, note after 100545A, note after
101547, 101270, note after 102768,
104204-104205, note after 106002
see also U. S. Department of State.
U. S. Legation. Great Britain. U. S.
President, 1809-1817 (Madison)
Madison, James, Pres. U. S., 1751-1836.
supposed author 11587, (17297),
43708, 105034
Madison, James, Pres. U. S., 1751-1836.
petitioner 47623, 2d note after 100486,
100528
Madison, James M. (43722)
Madison, Ind. Library Association. see
Madison Library Association, Madison,
Ind.
Madison, Wisc. 96860
Madison, Wisc. Board of Education. 43732,
43742
Madison, Wisc. First Congregational Church.
43746
Madison, Wisc. Madison Institute. see
Madison Institute, Madison, Wisc.
Madison, Wisc. Ordinances, etc. 43736
Madison, Wisc. Sacred Music Society. see
Sacred Music Society, Madison, Wisc.
Madison, Wisc. St. George's Society. see
St. George's Society, Madison, Wisc.
Madison County, N. Y. Board of Supervisors.
43727
Madison County, N. Y. Court of Oyer and
Terminer. 32232, 103945-103947

Madison County, N. Y. Number of Citizens.
pseud. see Number of Citizens of
Madison County, N. Y. pseud.
Madison County, Wisc. 43749
Madison Agonistes. 46917
Madison and Indianapolis Railroad Company.
(43747)
Madison and religion. 95300
Madison Baptist Association. see Baptists.
New York. Madison Baptist Association.
Madison city directory. 43740, 83028
Madison directory. 43741
Madison, Indianapolis, and Peru Railroad
Company. President. (43726)
Madison Institute, Madison, Wisc. 43744
Madison Institute, Madison, Wisc. Library.
43744
Madison Manufacturing Company. 43735
Madison Mutual Insurance Company. (43745)
Madison papers. 62521
Madison Square. 54366
Madison Square Church. 354
Madison Square Presbyterian Church, New Yo.
see New York (City) Madison Square
Presbyterian Church.
Madison Tenas, M. D. pseud. see Lewis,
Henry Clay.
Madison, the capital of Wisconsin: its growth,
progress, condition, wants and destiny.
20900
Madison; the capital of Wisconsin, its progres
capibilities and destiny. 43743
Madison University, Hamilton, N. Y. 43730-
43731
Madison's report. (22237), 23453, 2d note
after 100462, note after 100545A.
Madisson, James. see Madison, James, Pre
U. S., 1751-1836.
Madmen's chronicle. 43750
Madness of mankind. 24389
Madoc. 88556, 88563-88564
Madoc, a poem. 88563
Madou, ---------. lithographer 4737
Madox, Isaac. see Maddox, Isaac, successiv
Bishop of St. Asaph, and Worcester, 1697
1759.
Madoz, Paschal. 43751
Madoz e Ifanez, Pascual. tr. (50554)
Madraoz, D. P. de. ed. (70315)
Madras School, New Brunswick. 43752
Madre de Deos, Gaspar de. see Gaspar de
Madre de Deos, 1715-1800.
Madre de Deus, Manuel da. (43754)
Madre de Dios, Jose de la. see Jose de la
Madre de Dios.
Madre de Dios, Juan de la. see Juan de la
Madre de Dios.
Madre di Dio, Giuseppe della. see Jose de
la Madre de Dios.
Madregon, J. Andr. 43756
Madria y Ormaechea, G. tr. 32032
Madrid, Jose Fernandez de. see Fernandez
de Madrid, Jose.
Madrid, Manuel I. 44272
Madrid. Academia de la Historia. see
Academia de la Historia, Madrid.
Madrid. Academia Real de Sciencias. see
Academia Real de Sciencias, Madrid.
Madrid. Gaceta Oficial. see Spain.
Madrid. Musee Archeologique. 73301
Madrid. Sociedad Abolicionista Espanola. se
Sociedad Abolicionista Espanola, Madrid.
Madriga, Pedro de. 11607, 31504-31506,
31510, 43760

Madrignano, Archangelo. 50058, note after
99383C, 1st note after 106378
Madriz, F. T. (43761)
Madriz, Pedro Fernandez de la. see
Fernandez de la Madriz, Pedro.
Mae dos Homens, Francisco da. see
Homens, Francisco da Mae dos.
Maelen, Ph. van der. (43762)
Maerkvaerdigt brev om Mormonernes
skjaendigheder. 5427
Maersch, Adolpho. 81300
Maerschalckin, T. surveyor 79332
Maertyrer Geschichte. 74162
Maeso, Justo. 9044, 26211
Maesse de Campo Don Antonio Vrrutia de
Vergura dize 98160
Maesse de Campo Don Antonio Vrrutia de
Vergara, dize 98159
Maesse de Campo Don Antonio Vrrutia de
Vergara, dize: que auiendo acabado su
oficio de Virrey de la Nueua Espana.
98161
Maesse de Campo Iuan Recio de Leon,
dize 68356
Maesse de Campo Iuan Recio de Leon. Dize
que el principal efecto. 68360
Maesse de Campo Iuan Recio de Leon, dize,
que la riqueza que se ha sacado. 68357
Maesse de Campo Iuan Recio de Leon . . .
propose a V. M. 68359
Maestre de Campo D. Juan Fernandez de
Salinas y la Cerda. (75788)
Maestres-Scolia de la Santa Iglesia Catedral
de la Caracas. see Caracas, Venezuela.
Catedral. Maestres-Scolia.
Maestro, M. Rivera. see Rivera Maestro, M.
Maestro de Campo Iuan Recio de Leon
dize 68361
Maestro D. F. Payo de Ribera Obispo de
Goatemala, [sic] y Obispo de la Vera
Paz, representa al Real Acuerdo. (70802)
Maestro D. F. Payo de Rivera, Obispo de
Gvatemala y de la Vera Paz, representa
al Real Acuerdo destas Provincias de
Gvatemala. 59305
Maestro Fr. A. Bazquez Despinosa. 98725
Maestro Fray Bernardino de Solorcano.
86414
Maestro Fray Fra[n]cisco de Herrera. 96757
Maestro Fr. Martin de Canizares. 56282
Maet, Jan. 7534
Maffee, ---------. tr. 31382
Maffei, Giovanni Pietro, 1533-1603. 43769-
(43784)
Maffei, Joan. Petri. see Maffei, Giovanni
Pietro, 1533-1603.
Maffei, Raffaele, of Volterra, 1451-1522. 30483,
43763-43768, 74659
Maffit, John Newland. see Maffitt, John
Newland, 1794-1850.
Maffit against Goldsborough. 43785, 45197
Maffitt, John Newland, 1794-1805. (2588),
12081, 43786-43790, 54752, 87386,
99798
Maffitt, John Newland, 1794-1850. defendant
43790
Maffitt, John Newland, 1794-1850. plaintiff
8911, 96840
Maffitt's trial. 43790
Maga excursion papers. 43791
Maga social papers. 43791
Maga stories. 43791
Magalhaes, Fernando de, 1480-1521. (9208),
20518, 21211-21215, 26874, 26875,
33660, 57458-57459, 66686
Magalhaes-Strasse. 77800, (77802), 77804

Magalhanes, Domingos Jose Goncalves de. see
Goncalves de Magalhanes, Domingos Jose,
Vicsonde de Araguaya, 1811-1882.
Magalhanes de Gandavo, Pero de. 43794-(43795)
Magallanes, ------. (43796)
Magana, Juan Santos. see Santos Magana,
Juan.
Magapica, Magi. pseud. British and American
liturgy. 43797
Magarinos Cervantes, Alejandro, 1826- 11654,
11711-11714, (43798)
Magasin du Bas-Canada. 43799
Magasin encyclopedique. 12234
Magaw, Samuel. 43800-43804, (79281), 84641
Magazin. 34359
Magazin der ausl. Heilk. 4849
Magazin der merkwurdigen Reisebeschreibungen.
38969
Magazin der neuesten und besten auslanderischen
Reisebeschreibungen. (43805), 100689
Magazin fur die neueste Geschichte der
evangelischen Missions- und Bibelgesell-
schaften. (43807)
Magazin von merkwurdigen neuen Reisebeschrei-
bungen. 3872, 19645, 25139, 31185,
43808, 98444, 101242, 102536
Magazin von neuen Resiebeschreibungen. 1370
Magazine. (38549)
Magazine and industrial record. 24483
Magazine for literature, philosophy, and
religion. 19920
Magazine for the million. 43811
Magazine for the young manhood of America.
(57374)
Magazine miscellany. 18938, 83423
Magazine of agriculture, manufactures and
domestic economy. 88348A
Magazine of arts. 88392
Magazine of American history. (71909),
80022, 83462, 93185, 97069
Magazine of English and American abolitionism.
(81866)
Magazine of general literature. 55814
Magazine of history. 10615, 12982, 14775,
15043, (15716), (19522), 19933, 29982-
29983, 30662, 32709, 33005, 44258,
53495, (56818)-(56819), 59498, (79403),
81132, 85433, note after 90846, 91066,
91539, 91883, 91940, 92247, 92607,
93232, note after 93549, 93691, 94100,
94112, 94381, 94383, 95114, 3d note after
95765, 95325, 3d note after 96334, 96421,
96422, 97145, 97200, 97291, 97903, note
after 98049, note after 98091, 4th note
after 98269, 99021, note after 99300,
99433, note after 95065, 100545, 100995,
101480, note after 101593, note after
101993, 102008, 102060, 2d note after
102065, 103893, 104000, 104013, 105116,
note after 105690
Magazine of horticulture, botany, and all useful
discoveries and improvements. 1089,
33208, 43809
Magazine of knowledge and fun. 92363
Magazine of literature & science. 55850
Magazine of literature, civil and military
affairs. 55813
Magazine of literature, science and arts.
88382
Magazine of literature, science, and education.
41400
Magazine of miscellaneous selections. (57307)
Magazine of natural history. 78148, 84434-
84435
Magazine of remarkable characters. 37961

Magazine of science, literature and miscellany. 88616

Magazine of the Reformed Dutch Church. 43810

Magazine of travel in various countries both of the old world and new. 43812

Magazine of wit. 86180-86181

Magazine of wit, and American harmonist. (43813)

Magazine of wonders, addressed to the people of New-York. 13020

Magdalen Asylum, Philadelphia. Managers. 61800

Magdalen facts. No. 1. (54367)

Magdalen Female Benevolent Society, New York. see New York Magdalen Female Benevolent Society.

Magdalen Society, New York. see New York Magdalen Society.

Magdalen Society of Minnesota. see Minnesota Magdalen Society.

Magdalen Society of Philadelphia. (61801)

Magdalen Society of Philadelphia. Charter. (61801)

Magdalena, Augustin de la. 43814

Magdalena Santin y Valcarce, Joseph Bruno. 43815-43816

Mage, Gaspard le. pseud. Pleiade rouge. see Chauveau, --------. supposed author and Tache, Joseph Charles. supposed author

Magee, John. petitioner 43817

Magellan, Ferdinand. see Magalhaes, Fernando de, 1480-1521.

Magellan, Cook, Parke, Franklin, Livingstone. 51092

Magellan, oder die erste Reise am die Erde. (9208)

Magens, Jochum Melchior. tr. 51735

Magestuosa, real pyra, que en las funeral exequias del N. S. D. Luis Primero. 42668

Maghalhaes de Gandavo, historia do Brasil. (14363)

Mahometanism. 71852

Magi Magapica. pseud. see Magapica, Magi. pseud.

Magi maid. 83545

Magician's own book. 104233

Magick of Quakerism. 103657-103658

Magicon. 59230

Magie, David. 43819-(43820)

Magill, John. 43821

Magikon. 59229

Magin, Anthonie. see Magini, Giovanni Antonio, 1555-1617.

Magini Giovanni Antonio, 1555-1617. 43822, 66492-66493, 66495-66496, 66506, 66508, 105699, 105701

Maginnis, John S. 43823

Maginnis, Martin, 1841-1919. 91163

Magino, Jo. Antonio. see Magini, Giovanni Antonio.

Magistracy an institution of Christ upon the throne. 831

Magistrados Despojados por la Revolucion Judicial. petitioners 61093

Magistrat. pseud. ed. 68081

Magistrat du Japon. pseud. Lettre. 68455

Magistrates ministers of God to punish evil-doers. 39264

Maglathan, H. B. (43824)

Magna carta. (7056), 10819, (36317)

Magnae Britanniae notitia. 11787

Magnabal, J. G. ed. and tr. 86485

Magnaghi, Alberto. 99353, 99374, 99379, 99383A, 99383C-note after 99383C

Magnalia Christi Americana. 5631, 7299, 42037, 46235, 46280, (46371), 46392, 46393, 46540, 46693, (46749), 52140, 56392, 92099, 94022, note after 103702

Magnanimous Amazon. 95323

Magnenius, J. Chr. 43825

Magnetic and meteorological observations. 27419

Magnetic atlas. 13026

Magnetic observations made during the voyages. 74706

Magnetic survey of a considerable portion of the North American continent. 74703

Magnetic survey of the southern hemisphere between the meridians of 0° and 125° east. 74703

Magnetic telegraph. 50963

[Magnetical and meteorological observations] at Fort Confidence. 39843

Magnetical and meteorological observations at Lake Athabasca and Fort Simpson. 39843

Magnetical and meteorological observations made at Toronto, Canada. (74707)

Magnetical and meteorological observations made at Washington. 27418

Magnetical investigations. 78173-78174

Magnetical observations in the Arctic sea. 77906, 85073

Magnetical observations made at the Magnetical Observatory, Toronto. (37898)

Magnetical Observatory, Toronto, Canada. see Toronto, Canada. Magnetical Observatory.

Magnetique. 25916

Magnieres, Domingo O'Heguerty, Comte de. see O'Heguerty, Domingo, Comte de Magnieres, 1699-1790.

Magnifica parentacion, y funebre pompa. 50528

Magnificent argument. The union forever. 32653

Magnitude of the preacher's work. A sermon . . . March 15, 1815. 64230

Magnitude of the preacher's work. A sermon . . . October 27th, 1814. 64229

Magno de Castilho, Alex. see Castilho, Alex. Mango de.

Magnolia, Wisc. Magnolia Division No. 93. see Sons of Temperance of North America Wisconsin. Magnolia Division No. 93, Magnolia.

Magnolia. 43827, 85572

Magnolia, an American gift book. 43828

Magnolia Cemetery, Charleston, S. C. see Charleston, S. C. Magnolia Cemetery.

Magnolia Division No. 93, Sons of Temperance of North America. see Sons of Temperance of North America. Wisconsin. Magnolia Division No. 93, Magnolia.

Magnolia; or southern Apalachian. 88382

Magnolia; or southern monthly. 88382

Magnum, --------. 102287

Magnus, Antonius. 43829

Magnus, Olaus, Abp. of Upsula, 1490-1558. 28929, 43830-43835, 57106

Magnus' hand-book of travel, and tourst's guide. 43836

Magoffin, Beriah, 1815-1885. 23382, 37577, 69859 see also Kentucky. Governor, 1859-1862 (Magoffin)

Magoon, E. L. 32707, 43837-43841

Magoon, James. 43842

Magora, Juan. 69186

Magoun, George F. 34985, 43843-43844, 43884

Magrath, --------. illus. 96372

Magrath, A. G. 43845, 79189, 87467
Magrath, T. W. 43846
Magre, P. tr. 6028-6030, (43847)
Magri, Dominici. ed. 24163
Magruder, --------, fl. 1866. 89232
Magruder, Allan B. 43848
Magruder, Henry R. (43849)
Magruder, John Bankhead, 1810-1871. 43850
Magruder, J. H. T. 45137
Magruder, Patrick. (15563)
Magruder, W. H. N. 43852
Maguire, H. N. 43853
Maguire, James L. plaintiff 7690
Maguire, John Francis. 43854-43856, 51207
Maguire, Thomas. 10392, 43857-43858, 84701, 99772, 99776
Maguire's "Irish in America." 51207
Magusanische Europa. 20605
Magwire, John. (43859)
Maha Indians. Treaties, etc. 96650
Mahaffy, John P. (43860)
Mahan, --------. 28492
Mahan, Asa, 1800-1889. 43861, 56416
Mahan, Dennis Hart, 1802-1871. 43862-43863, 88405
Mahan, M. 43865-43868
Mahan, John B. defendant 43864, 98688
Mahican Indians. 36337, 49348
Mahican Indians. Treaties, etc. 39337, (39339), 60255, 65759
Mahickander Indians. see Mahican Indians.
Mahlerische Beschreibung der Insel Jamaica. 4250
Mahlmann, H. 43870-43872
Mahnung an die Nation. 2436
Mahogany tree, its botanical characters, qualities and uses. 43873
Mahogany tree, in the West and Central America. (11775)
Mahon, Philip Henry Stanhope, Lord. see Stanhope, Philip Henry Stanhope, 5th Earl of, 1805-1875.
Mahoney, Dorah. 43874
Mahoney, James W. 43875
Mahoney, William D. supposed author 10193, (21638), note before 94254, note after 98870
Mahony, D. A. 17605, (43876)-43878, note just before 63791
Mahony, Matthew. defendant 86587
Mahplya ekta oicimani ya. 71341
Mahy, Nicolas. (43879)-43880
Mahy de Cormere, J. F. 43881
Mahy y Romo, Nicolas. (34712) see also Cuba. Gobernador, 1821-1822 (Mahy y Romo)
Mai-Blomsten. 92438
Mai-Jour (translated May-Day,) General George Barnum McClellan. 43028
Maia, Joaquim Jose da Silva. 43882
Maia, Jose Antonio da Silva. 43883
Maiblumchen. 92434-92435
Maiblume. 92436
Maid of Canal Street. 43884
Maid of Hungary. 97465
Maid of Louisiana. 72133
Maid of the oaks, a comedy. 51508
Maid of Wyoming. 7061
Maid, wife & widow of a day. (22199)
Maid with seven lovers. 98340
Maid's and bachelor's friend. 102478
Maiestro Don Fray Payo de Ribera Obispo de Goatemala [sic] defiende lo vna vez propuesto en informa. 70803
Mail robbers. 47464
Mailhe, J. B. 43885

Maillardiere, Charles Francois, Viscomte de la. 43889
Maillard, H. 63434
Maillard, N. Doran. 43886
Maillard, Pierre. 43887-43888
Maillefer, P. D. Martin. see Martin-Maillefer, P. D.
Maillefert, --------. 35807
Maillefert, E. 48486
Maillet, B. de. 43891-43892, note after 94626
Maillet Duclairon, Antonie. 43890
Mailly, Edouard. 43893
Main, Thomas. 43894
Main intention of the letter. 7919, note just before 53081
Main intentions of religion. 46220
Main line of the Pennsylvania state improvements. 60227
Main pillar of Antichrist's kingdom shaken. 82479
Main point in question. 101126
Maine (District) Convention, Portland, 1795. 43901, 1st note after 106023
Maine. 16852, 20469, (24964), 43926, 43945, 43960, (44007), 44051, 50993, 55538, 70614, note after 96789, 101350, 103041
Maine. Adjutant General. 43998
Maine. Agent to Inquire Into and Report Upon Certain Facts Relaingt to Aggressions Upon the Rights of the State, and of Individual Citizens Thereof, by Inhabitants of the Province of New-Brunswick. (18682), 44013 see also Davies, Charles S.
Maine. Attorney General. 43910-43911, (44028)
Maine. Bank and Insurance Examiner. (43912) see also Maine. Bank Examiner.
Maine. Bank Commissioners. (43912)
Maine. Bank Examier. (43912) see also Maine. Bank and Insurance Examiner.
Maine. Board of Agriculture. (43939)
Maine. Board of Agriculture. Secretary. 43962
Maine. Board of Education. (43933)
Maine. Census, 1810. 103306, 103307
Maine. Census, 1811. 43907
Maine. Census, 1820. 84350
Maine. Census, 1831. 43919
Maine. Circuit Court. 7031
Maine. Circuit Courts Martial. 44031
Maine. Commission of Fisheries. 25257, 44032
Maine. Commissioner on the Defence of the State. 64059, 64067 see also Poor, John A.
Maine. Commissioners of Fisheries. see Maine. Commission of Fisheries.
Maine. Commissioners of Public Lands. 43946, 43949
Maine. Commissioners of the Hydrograhpic Survey. see Maine. Hydrographic Survey.
Maine. Commissioners on Equalization of the Municipal War Debts. 44017
Maine. Commissioners on Portland Harbor. 64058, 64376
Maine. Commissioners on the North Eastern Boundary. 44016
Main. Commissioners on the Settlement of the Public Lands. see Maine. Commissioners of Public Lands.
Maine. Commissioners to Examine into the Doings and Transactions of the . . . Banks of This State. (43912)

Maine. Commissioners to Settle the Line
Between New-Hampshire and Maine.
see Commission to Survey the Boundary
Between New Hampshire and Maine.
Maine. Constitution. 1269, 1271, 2071,
5316, 6360, 16103, 16107, 16113,
16133, 33137, 43917-(43920), 43954-
43958, 44039, (47188), 59771, (66397),
69450, 104198
Maine. Constitutional Convention, Portland,
1819-1820. (43920), 43945
Maine. Convention, Brunswick, 1816. 8776,
36735, 44045, 82577
Maine. Convention, Portland, 1819. 43905
Maine. Convention, Hallowell, 1834. 44004
Maine. Courts. 88569
Maine. Geological Survey. (35400), (43936)-
43940
Maine. Governor, 1820-1822 (King) 43995
see also King, William, 1768-1852.
Maine. Governor, 1827-1829 (Lincoln)
(43942) see also Lincoln, Enoch,
1788-1829.
Maine. Governor, 1829-1830 (Cutler)
(44028)-44029 see also Cutler, Nathan,
1775-1861.
Maine. Governor, 1831-1834 (Smith) 43941,
84038-84040 see also Smith, Samuel
Emerson, 1788-1860.
Maine. Governor, 1834-1838 (Dunlap) 43940
see also Dunlap, Robert Pinckney,
1794-1859.
Maine. Governor, 1838-1839 (Kent) 43996
see also Kent, Edward, 1802-1877.
Maine. Governor, 1857-1858 (Hamlin)
(43944) see also Hamlin, Hannibal,
1809-1891.
Maine. Governor, 1858-1860 (Morrill) 33150
see also Morrill, Lot Myrick, 1813-
1883.
Maine. Governor, 1861-1863 (Washburn)
43943 see also Washburn, Israel,
1813-1883.
Maine. Hydrographic Survey. 44015, (44052)
Maine. Hydrographic Survey. Secretary.
(44052)
Maine. Insane Hospital, Augusta. see Maine.
State. Hospital, Augusta.
Maine. Land Agent. 43952
Maine. Land Office. 43953
Maine. Laws, statutes, etc. 3154, 3156,
7019, 7031, 18117, 23109, 23765, 28722,
39414, 40871, 43897-(43899), 43932,
43954-43959, 43980, 43997, 44002,
44003, 44039, 52051, 60828, 63274,
(64344), (64345), 64363, 70820-70821,
72399, 74777, (80290), 82438, 88569,
89066
Maine. Legislature. 18906, 36842, (43899)-
43900, 43922, 43925, (43979), 44010,
44011, 44033-(44036), 63274, 84039
Maine. Legislature. Committee on Elections.
44020
Maine. Legislature. Committee on Fresh
Water Basin in Portland Harbor. 64371
Maine. Legislature. Committee on Kennebec
and Portland Railroad. 44021
Maine. Legislature. Committee on Road from
Kennebec River to the British Provinces
of Canada. 44022
Maine. Legislature. Committee on State
Lands. 43951
Maine. Legislature. Committee on the
Judiciary. 43898, (44028)
Maine. Legislature. Committee on the
Military. 43999

Maine. Legislature. Committee to Contract
for State Printing. 44018
Maine. Legislature. Democratic Members.
see Democratic Party. Maine.
Maine. Legislature. Joint Select Committee
on Defalcation of Benjamin J. Peck.
44026
Maine. Legislature. Joint Select Committee
on Infraction of the Treaty of Washington.
(44025)
Maine. Legislature. Joint Select Committee
on Northeastern Boundary. 44019, 44023-
44024, 84039
Maine. Legislature. Joint Select Committee
to Whom Was Referred "So Much of the
Governor's Message as Relates to the
Geological Survey." 43940
Maine. Legislature. Joint Standing Committee
on Claims. 44027
Maine. Legislature. Joint Standing Committee
on the Library. (43971)
Maine. Legislature. House of Representatives.
44008, 44041
Maine. Legislature. House of Representatives.
Committee on Federal Relations. 82568
Maine. Legislature. Senate. (44009), 64064,
84038
Maine. Medical School. see Bowdoin College,
Brunswick, Me. Medical School.
Maine. Militia. First Heavy Artillery.
Company C. 84941
Maine. Militia. Portland Light Infantry.
90504
Maine. Militia. Portland Rifle Company.
64366
Maine. Narraganset Township, No. 1. see
Buxton, Me.
Maine. Office of the Secretary of State.
43895-(43896) see also Maine. Secretary
of State.
Maine. Public Schools. 43931
Maine. Secretary of State. (43896), 43931,
(44037) see also Maine. Office of the
Secretary of State.
Maine. State Geologist. 35399-(35400),
(43937)-(43939) see also Hitchcock,
Charles Henry, 1836-1919. Holmes,
Ezekiel. Jackson, Charles Thomas, 1805-
1880.
Maine. State Hospital, Augusta. Directors.
43972
Maine. State Hospital, Augusta. Steward.
(43973)
Maine. State Hospital, Augusta. Superintendent.
(43973)
Maine. State Hospital, Augusta. Trustees.
(43973)
Maine. State Library. 43987
Maine. State Library. Librarian. 43987
Maine. State Normal and Training School,
Farmington. 44054
Maine. State Prison. Chaplain. (44028)
Maine. State Prison. Inspectors. (44028)
Maine. State Prison. Physician. (44028)
Maine. State Prison. Warden. (44028)
Maine. State Superintendent of Common
Schools. (43934)
Maine. Supreme Judicial Court. 3527, 13249,
16384, 44042, 89331
Maine. Supreme Judicial Court for the County
of Washington. see Washington County,
Me. Supreme Judicial Court.
Maine. Treasurer. 43895, 44048-44049
Maine. University. 84506
Maine. 31069
Maine Anti-slavery Society. 85345

Maine as a field for immigration. 64062
Maine Baptist Convention. see Baptists. Maine. Convention.
Maine business directory. (43964)
Maine Central Railroad Company. Directors. 43965
Maine Charitable Mechanic Association. Exhibition and Fair, 1st, Portland, 1838. 43966
Maine Charity School, Bangor, Me. see New Theological Seminary, Bangor, Me.
Maine Church Association (Unitarian) see Unitarian Church Association of Maine.
Maine collection of church music. 71805
Maine Colonization Society. Board of Managers. (43916)
Maine Convention of Universalists. see Universalist Church in the United States. Maine. Convention.
Maine Convention of Universalists. Proceedings. (43968)
Maine farmer's almanac. By Daniel Robinson. 43969
Maine farmers' almanac, for 1852. 72065
Maine farmers' almanac, for . . . 1828. 72065
Maine farmer's almanack, for the year of Our Lord, 1819. 89838
Maine Historical Society. 9243, 19195, 28020, 37711, 40751, (43970)-43971, 50221, 58096, 79441, 84343, 90611, 92664, 101005, 104525
Maine Historical Society. petitioners (43971)
Maine Historical Society collections. 9243, 19195, 28020, 33146, 37711, 40751, 50221, 58096
Maine journal of education. 43974
Maine law a failure. (13256)
Maine law: an address . . . in Sterling, April 13, 1853. (31806)
Maine law in New-York. 43975, 53843
Maine law in the balance. (43976), 59311
Maine law: its constitutionality . . . operation and . . . acceptance. (43977)
Maine law. Remarks . . . in the Assembly of . . . New York. 39917
Maine law. Speech of Hon. Myron H. Clark. 13339
Maine law. Speech of Lieutenant Governor Lawrence. 39383
Maine law triumphant. 88666
Maine law; with the opinions of Professor Stuart, of Andover. 93206
Maine legislative manual. (43979)
Maine liquor law. An act for the suppression of drinking-houses and tippling-shops. 43980
Maine liquor law debate. 43604
Maine liquor law. Documents relating to its principles, operation, etc. 43978
Maine liquor law; its origin, history, and results. 13793
Maine liquor law; with the opinions of Prof. Stuart and L. M. Sargent. 43980
Maine Literary and Theological Institution. see Colby College, Waterville, Me.
Maine Medical Association. 43981-43982
Maine Missionary Society. (5978), 82892, 92119
Maine Missionary Society. Treasurer. (5978)
Maine Missionary Society. Trustees. (5978), 43983, 101313, 43983
Maine, New Hampshire, and Vermont. (19369)

Maine Normal . . . . Volume I. 43984
Maine reform in temperate doses. 70129
Maine register. 43985
Maine register and national calendar. 43985
Maine register, and state reference book. 43985
Maine register, and United States' calendar. 43985
Maine state political manual. 43988
Maine State Seminary, Lewiston, Me. 43989
Maine State Temperance Convention, Augusta, 1852. see State Temperance Convention, Augusta, Me., 1852.
Maine teacher. 43986
Maine Union in Behalf of the Colored Race. Convention, 1835. 43990
Maine Unitarian Church Association. see Unitarian Churches. Maine. Church Association.
Maine Universalist Educational Society. (43968)
Maine Universalist Missionary Society. (43968)
Maine Universalist Tract Society. (43968)
Maine Wesleyan Seminary, Hallowell. 43991
Maine Wesleyan Seminary and Female College, Kent's Hill. Trustees. 28605
Maintain plighted faith. 12200
Maintenance and progression of the American union. 94384
Maintonomah, and other poems. 3623
Mainwaring, --------. petitioner (44055), 100439, 4th note after 102831
Maioli, Simonis. 44056
Maior India. 99365
Maipo. Sociedad del Canal. see Sociedad del Canal de Maipo.
Maire, Jacob le. see Le Maire, Jacob, 1585-1616.
Maire, Jacques le. see Le Maire, Jacob, 1585-1616.
Maires, P. de. 14349
Mairobert, Matthiew Francois Pidansat de. see Pidansat de Mairobert, Matthieu Francois.
Mais, Charles. (44060)
Maisch, John M. 44061
Maison, --------. 44063
Maison, Alonso de Bonne. see Buena-Maison, Alonso de.
Maison, Hypolite. see Mansion, Hypolite.
Maison Silvestre. firm booksellers 94845
Maison de Dieu. 99283
Maison d'Education ou Seminaire d'Enfans a la Savane des Jeufs, Paramaribo. 66079
Maison rustique, a l'usage des habitans de la partie de la France Equinoxiale. (65038)
Maison rustique de Cayenne. 1st note after (74627), (77219)-77220
Maissin, E. 5832, 79139
Maitin, Jose A. 44064
Maiz, Carman. 44065
Maize, or Indian corn. 3755
Majblomann. 92439
Majer Jack Downing. pseud. see Downing, Majer Jack. pseud.
Majer Jack Downing's letters. 84184
Majesty and mortality of created Gods. 97188
Majesty of the people asserted. 34448
Major, Eleazer. 44066
Major, J. R. 44068
Major, Johann Daniel, 1634-1693. 44067, 44076, 98357
Major, Richard Henry. 14629, 14633, (14635), 14670-14671, 27784, 44069-(44071), 92664

Malacca. 39300
Malachi. (46394)
Malady and the remedy. 21721
Malaeska. 91281, 91284
Malaga Batallon. see Cuba. Ejercito.
  Batallon de Malaga.
Malagueta. Redactor. pseud. 100793
Malan, Caesar Henri Abraham. 44088, 3d
  note after 94085
Maland, Sarah. defendant 96847
Malapart, -------- Sieur. (44089)
Malaspina, Alessandro, 1754-1809. 44090,
  (57257)
Malaspina, M. (44091)
Malavasic, F. ed. and tr. 92605
Malaver, A. E. ed. 70308
Malbone, -------. illus. 28897
Malbone: an Oldport romance. 31755
Malcolme, David. 44092-(44094)
Malcom, Howard. 44095-44096
Malcom, J. P. engr. 33005, 100545
Malden, Mass. 44097
Malden, Mass. Church. 44098
Malden, Mass. Edgeworth Association. see
  Edgeworth Association, Malden, Mass.
Malden, Mass. School Committee. 44102
Malden, Mass. Town Hall. 44101, 93538
Malden Bridge Corporation. (44100)
Malden bridge to the people. (44100)
Maldonado, -------, fl. 1683. 48608
Maldonado, Alonso. (44103)-44104
Maldonado, Eugenio Gonzalez. 67940
Maldonado, F. P. 44106
Maldonado, Fernando Nicolas. (44105)
Maldonado, Francisco Severo. see Severo
  Maldonado, Francisco.
Maldonado, Joao Vicente Pimentel. 44107
Maldonado, Lorenzo Ferrer. 3660, (44108)-
  44111
Maldonado, Theodoro de Sousa. 44112
Male and Female Collegiate Institute, Moores
  Hill, Indiana. see Moore's Hill Male
  and Female Collegiate Institute, Moores
  Hill, Indiana.
Malenfant, -------. 44114
Malerische Reise durch Nordamerika. 93991
Malerische Reise in Brasilien. (73934)
Malerische Reise in Sud- und Nord-Amerika.
  57456
Malerische Reise um die Welt. 21214
Males de la desunion. 96272
Malespine, A. 44115-(44116)
Malet, A. 44117
Malet, William Wyndham. 44118
Malet du Gravier, ---------, Comte de.
  74047
Malevolence defeated. (79484)
Malfactor's calendar. 44113
Malfatti, C. (11103)
Malham, John, 1747-1821. 30394, 44119-
  44120
Malheiro e Mello, Antonio Manuel Leite
  Pacheo. (43869)
Malheiros, Agostinho Perdigao. see Perdigao
  Malheiros, Agostinho, Marques, 1824-1881.
Malherbe, Alfred. (44121)
Malheurs des prejuges. (4959)
Malheurs d'un famille esclave. 92542
Malignant pustule in the United States. 4445
Malignity exposed. 12208, 12413
Malin, W. G. (44122), 60330, 60348, 86581
Malina Gray. 91280
Mall, Thomas. 44124
Mallaby, Francis. USN 101284
Mallalieu, Alfred. 44125-44126

Mallard, John B. (44127)-(44127A)
Mallarme, S. tr. 63546
Mallary, Rollin Carolas, 1784-1831. 9235,
  44128-44129
Mallen, Pedro Salva y. see Salva y Mallen,
  Pedro.
Mallery, Carel de, 1571-1635. engr. 92666-
  92667
Mallespine, Michael. 95299
Mallet, Allain Manesson. 44130
Mallet, David, 1705?-1765. 75240, 84678C
Mallet, F., fl. 1797. 44131
Mallet, John William. 44132
Mallet, Marie. 44133
Mallet, Philip. 44134
Mallett, Edward J. complainant 44135
Malleus, Trepidantium. pseud. see Young,
  Samuel, fl. 1690-1700.
Mallorca, Mexico (Diocese) Bishop [ca. 1820]
  44136
Mallory, ------. illus. 82251
Mallory, Daniel. ed. 13543
Mallory, R. C. 44137
Mallory, R. P. illus. 9181, 82251
Mallory, Rollin Carolas. see Mallray, Rollin
  Carolas, 1784-1831.
Mallory, Stephen Russell, 1813-1873. 15280,
  15312, 15314, 44138, (69898) see also
  Confederate States of America. Navy
  Department.
Mallory and Company. firm see Rickey,
  Mallory and Company. firm
Malmesbury, James Howard Harris, 3d Earl
  of, 1807-1889. 69708
Malmgren, Anders Johan. 44139
Malo, ---------, fl. 1767. (64336)
Malo, Charles, 1790-1871. 44140-44141
Malo, Charles, 1790-1871. supposed author
  3885, note just before 75128
Malo, Feliz Venancio. 38624, 96273
Malo, J. R. 44142
Malo de Luque, Eduardo. pseud. see
  Almodovar del Rio, Pedro Jimenez de
  Gongara y Lujan, Duque de, d. 1794.
Malo de Molina, Camillo Quintanilla y. see
  Quintanilla y Malo de Molina, Camillo.
Malo de Villavicencio, Johannes a. see
  Villavicencio, Johannes a Malo de.
Malombra, Giovanni. ed. 66505
Malone, T. 102008
Malome Sandstone Company. (44144)
Malouet, V. P. (44145)-(44152), 97026, 98671
  see also France. Ministere de la
  Marine.
Maltby, Erastus. (44153)
Maltby, Isaac. 44154
Maltby, J. 44155
Malte-Brun, Conrad, originally Malthe Conrad
  Bruun, 1775-1826. 3658, 7432, (7438),
  7441, 12272, 31802, 38982, (44156)-
  44166, (64949), 47870, (51196), 55954,
  56093, 56593, 76833, 76844, 85781,
  89976, 94843, 94847-94848, 94851,
  95146
Malte-Brun, Victor Adolphe, 1816-1889.
  (21479), 37256, 43044, 44159, 44167-
  44173
Malte-Brun's neuestes Gemalde von Amerika.
  44162
Maltes. pseud. Maltes al gistoriador de
  Buenos Ayres. 44174
Malthes al Historiador de Buenos Ayres.
  44174
Malthus, Thomas Robert, 1766-1834. 23233-
  (23234), 27676, (82311)

Malthus (Thomas) firm publishers defendant (23479)
Malvenda, T. 44175-44176
Malves, Gua de. ed. and tr. 1637-1639, 101186-4th note after 101186, 1st note after 101187
Mamby, Thomas. 44198
Mamiani, Luis Vicencio. 44178-44180
Mamiferos. 74921
Mammalia and ornithology. (59428)
Mammalia, by George R. Waterhouse. 18649
Mammalia. By J. E. Gray. 31945
Mammalia. By James E. De Kay. (53783)
Mammalia, by John Edward Gray. 28401, 71032
Mammalia, I. 28401, 71032
Mammals. 69946, 71033
Mammals. [By Henry Beaumont Small.] 82195
Mammals, by S. F. Baird. 27419
Mammals, by Spencer F. Baird. 69946
Mammals coll. on an explor. expedition from the Missouri to Utah Lake. 2805
Mammals of North America. 2805
Mammals of North America, coll. or observed on the different routes for the Pacific Railroad. 2805
Mammals of the boundary. 22538
Mammals of the United States and Mexican boundary. 2805
Mammiferes. 74922
Mammiferes, oisseaux, reptiles et poissons. 21354
Mammology and ornithology. 11370
Mammoth Vein Consolidated Coal Company. 44181
Mammoth Vein Consolidated Coal Company. Directors. 44181
Mammoth Vein Consolidated Coal Company. Trustees. 44181
Mamvsse wunneetupanatamwe up-Biblum God naneeswe kukkone testament kah wonk wusku testament. (22156)
Mamvsse wusku wunneetupanatamwe up-Biblum God naneeswe Kukkone testament kah wonk wusku testament. (22154)
Man, Albon P. 88406, 88410 see also Southern Minnesota Railroad Company. Trustee.
Man, George F. (44182)
Man, Jan Willem Engelbert de. 44183
Man, Thomas. 44184-44186
Man. 52161
Man a sojourner. 77226
Man and his destiny, men, politics, and morals. note after 42429
Man and his migrations. 39165
Man and his modern inventions. 47181
Man and his work. 84045
Man and the soldier. 66783
Man and the state. Social and political. 3454
Man as he is, and the world as it goes. 104567
Man as he ought ont to be. A tale. 102163
"Man behind the curtain." pseud. ed. Prompter's whistle. 65993
Man eaters and other odd people. (69053)
Man eating the food of angels. 46395
Man for the times. 61036
Man humbled by being compar'd to a worm. 16633
Man in earnest. (14465)
Man in the smoke, and a friend endeavouring to help him out. 82492

Man in the woods looking after liberty. pseud. Deformity of a hideous monster. see Ely, Samuel.
Man is the divinely constituted guardian of man. 64210
Man of abilities for the Earl of B---------e. (44187)
Man of bronze. (77859)
Man of business. pseud. Democratic party. 19509
Man of candor, who is totally divested of party prejudices. pseud. Letter to Mr. Powys 40449
Man of enterprise. 89407
Man of feeling. 27145
Man of God. (67783)
Man of God furnished. 46396
Man of God furnished with supplies from the tower of David. 46589
Man of God thoroughly furnished to every good work. (9717)
Man of his word. 46397
Man of mystery. 83671
Man of no party. pseud. Recovery of America. 68411
Man of real sensibility. 78356
Man of reason. 46398
Man of sixty. pseud. Five lessons for young men. see Southwick, Solomon.
Man of the mountain. 101428, 104447
Man of the people. 81241
Man of the times. pseud. Letters. see Kennedy, John Pendleton, 1795-1870.
Man of the world. 90224
Man of two lives. 94087
Man of Uz, and other poems. 80931
Man of war. 104093
Man-of-war life. 55461
Man-of-war's-man. pseud. Maritime scraps. 44606
"Man shall not live by bread alone." 31755
Man stealing and slavery denounced by the Presbyterian and Methodist churches. 6920
Man-stealing, legitimate servitude. 37882
Man that was used up. 63540
Man, the deed, the event. (29830)
Man: the hero: the Christian! (68253)
Man unmasked. 39927
Man upon the sea. 27885
Man who has been an actor in many scenes. pseud. Sketch of the origin and progress of the causes. 81530
Man who supposed himself to be Moses, no Moses at all. 36181
Man without a country. 29627
Management of Indian affairs. 9327
Management of lunatics, with illustrations of insanity. 58804
Management of the school-room. 58597
Manager of the . . .[Rosine] Association. pseud. Reports and realities. 62198
Manager's assistant. 85385
Managers of the Deleware Lottery for the College of New Jersey, &c. 19397
Managers of the Girard Trust. see Girard Trust. Managers.
Managers of the Marine and City Hospitals, Philadelphia. petitioners 84648
Managers on the part of New-York. 54368, 95935
Manahan, A. (44188)
Manalic, Jaime. supposed author 32020, 55245, 92200-92201
Mananas de la alameda de Mexico. (9578), 44189

Mananitas del molar. 87233-87234
Manasseh ben Joseph ben Israel, 1604-1657.
(44190)-44194, 95650
Manby, George William. 44195-44197
Mancera, Pedro de Toledo y Leiva, Marques
de. see Toledo y Leiva, Pedro de,
Marques de Mancera, 1585-1654
Manchester, Elias. 44200
Manchester, George Montagu, 4th Duke of,
1737-1788. 44199
Manchester, George Montagu, 4th Duke of,
1737-1788. petitioner 90590
Manchester, Eng. Anti-slavery Conference,
1854. see Anti-slavery Conference,
Manchester, Eng., 1854.
Manchester, Eng. Literary and Philosophical
Society. see Literary and Philosophical
Society, Manchester, Eng.
Manchester, Eng. Scientific Students' Associa-
tion. see Scientific Students' Associa-
tion, Manchester, Egn.
Manchester, Eng. Society for Printing,
Publishing & Circulating the Writings
of the Honourable Emanuel Swedenbourg.
see Society for Printing, Publishing &
Circulating the Writings of the Honourable
Emanuel Swedenbourg, Manchester.
Manchester, Eng. Southern Independence
Association. see Southern Independence
Association, Manchester, Eng.
Manchester, Mass. Orthodox Church. (44201)
Manchester, N. H. 85227
Manchester, N. H. Amoskeag Veterans. see
Amoskeag Veterans, of Manchester,
N. H.
Manchester, N. H. Athenaeum. 44212
Manchester, N. H. Centennial Celebration of
the Incorporation of Derryfield, 1851.
64620
Manchester, N. H. City Council. 44211,
82748, 85227
Manchester, N. H. Committee on Finance.
44205
Manchester, N. H. Convention of the Repre-
sentatives of the New-Hampshire
Settlers, 1775. see Vermont. Conven-
tion, 1775.
Manchester, N. H. House of Reformation for
Juvenile and Female Offenders. see
New Hampshire. Industrial School,
Manchester.
Manchester, N. H. Industrial School. see
New Hampshire. Industrial School,
Manchester.
Manchester, N. H. Librarian. 44213
Manchester, N. H. Library. 44213, 44216
Manchester, N. H. Library Treasurer.
44231
Manchester, N. H. Library. Trustees.
44213, 44216
Manchester, N. H. Mayor, 1852-1854 (Smyth)
44211, 85227 see also Smyth, Frederick,
1819-1899.
Manchester, N. H. Mayor, 1856. (44210)
Manchester, N. H. Mayor, 1864 (Smyth)
85227 see also Smyth, Frederick,
1819-1899.
Manchester, N. H. Mayor, 1868-1869 (Weston)
44222 see also Weston, -------.
Manchester, N. H. Mayor, 1869-1870 (Smith)
82748 see also Smith, Isaac William,
1825-
Manchester, N. H. Merrimack Normal
Institute. see Merrimack Normal
Institute, Manchester, N. H.

Manchester, N. H. New England Agricultural
Society Annual Exhibition, 7th, 1870.
see New England Agricultural Society.
Annual Exhibition, 7th, Manchester, N.
H., 1870.
Manchester, N. H. Old Nutfield Celebration,
1869. see Celebration of the One
Hundred and Fiftieth Anniversary of the
Settled Part of Old Nutfield, N. H.,
1869.
Manchester, N. H. Ordinances, etc. 44209,
(44217), (44220)
Manchester, N. H. Public Library. see
Manchester, N. H. Library.
Manchester, N. H. School Committee. 44206
Manchester, N. H. School District No. 2.
44218
Manchester, N. H. Selectmen. 44219
Manchester, N. H. State Reform School. see
New Hampshire. Industrial School,
Manchester.
Manchester, Vt. Burr Seminary. see Burr
Seminary, Manchester, Vt.
Manchester and its vicinity. 44224
Manchester and Lawrence Railroad Corporation.
Directors. 44225
Manchester and Lawrence Railroad Corporation.
Investigating Committee of the Stock-
holders. 44225
Manchester chronicle. 16612
Manchester Colonization Society. see Richmond
and Manchester Colonization Society.
Manchester democratic—extra. (44214)
Manchester directory, containing the city
record. (44215)
Manchester homicide. 90531
Manchester Library Association, South
Manchester, Conn. 88145
Manchester manufacturer. pseud. England,
Ireland, and America. see Cobden,
Richard, 1804-1865.
Mancilla, A. 44226
Mancius, George Wilhelmus. 44227
Manco-Capac, premier Inca du Perou, tragedie.
39595
Manco, the Peruvian chief. 37904
Mancur, John H. 44228
Mancy, Adrien (Le Breton) Jarry de. see
Jarry de Mancy, Adrien (Le Breton)
Mandamiento u ordenanza acerca del orden.
98797
Mandan Indians. Treaties, etc. 96645
Mandar, Theophile. 4933
Mandar-Argeant. anagram see Gaterau,
Armand.
Mandate of God for Israel's advancement.
36514
Mandauilla, Joanne de. 44229
Mandement contre l'insurrection partielle du
Bas Canada. (39105)
Mandement van d'Edele Hove van Hollant.
27122
Mander, Carel van, 1548-1606. 4804
Mander Schilder, Karel vander. see Schilder,
Karel vander Mander.
Manderson, James. 91090
Manderville, Payneta. 44235
Mandeville, --------- Marigni de. see Marigni
de Mandeville, -------.
Mandeville, G. Henry. 44230-44231
Mandeville, H. 44232-(44233)
Mandeville, H. D. 44234
Mandeville, Sir John. 66686
Mandingo slave in Georgia. pseud. Gospels
written in the Negro patois of English.
see Hodgson, W. B.

Mando que se imprimiesse este escrito.
61135

Mandrillon, Joseph. 13797, 1st note after
100846

Mandrillon, Joseph H. 13797, 44236-44240,
note after 89135, 1st note after 100846

Maneiro, Joannis Aloysius. (44241)-44243

Manent, Graviora. pseud. Letters on the
College of Physicians and Surgeons.
see Manley, James R.

Manera de rezar el rosario y los misterios
del. 72811

Manero, Jose Mariano de. 44244

Manert-Leroy, Marie. 98175

Manesse, -------, fl. 1791. (68072)

Manetense, Bernardo. 44245

Manford, Erasmus. (44246)

Manfredo, ------. 44247

Manfredus, Hieronymus. ed. 66471

Manganese Mining Company. 44248

Mangel du Mesnil, Emilio. see Mesnil,
Emilio Mangel du.

Mangeur de poudre. 4903A

Mangin, Arthur. 15428, 44249-44250

Mangino, R. tr. 25555

Mangino, Rafael. defendant 582, (65925)

Mangles, James. 44251, 58445

Mangold, F. ed. 76347

Mangora, King of the Timbusians. 50440

Mangum, Adolphus W. 44252

Manhattan. pseud. Marion. see Scoville,
Joseph A., 1811-1864.

Manhattan. pseud. What shall be done with
the confiscated Negroes? 44253

Manhattan, Kansas. State Agricultural College.
see Kansas. State Agricultural College,
Manhattan.

Manhattan College, New York. 44254, 54247

Manhattan College, New York. Charter.
54247

Manhattan Company. 44255

Manhattan Co-operative Relief Association.
44256

Manhattan Quartz Mining Company. 44257

Manhattan souvenir and New York sketch book
for 1850. (43169)

Manhattan souvenir, and New York sketch
book, for 1851. (30875)

Manhattaner in New-Orleans. 29713

Manheim, Frederic. 44258

Manheim tragedy. 72374

Manhood, or scenes from the past. 63453

Maniac. pseud. Poem; from the manuscript
of a maniac. 89469

Maniac harper. 3969, 52150

Maniac, with other poems. 39454

Maniacs; or, fantasia of Bos Bibens. 44259,
2d note after 102802

Maniac's confession, a fragment of a tale.
81177

Maniau, J. B. 44260

Maniere van procedeeren voor den Edele
Achtbarren Hove van Civile Justitie der
Colonie Surinamen. 93846

"Manifest destiny." (73256)

Manifest destiny of the American union.
(44262)

Manifest door d'Inwoonders van Pernambuco.
38256, 44263, 1st note after 102894,
102895

Manifest ende redenen van oorloge. 44264

Manifest ende remonstrantie. 38256, 44263,
1st note after 102894, 102895

Manifest of the charge preferred to the Navy
Department. 3828, 8458

Manifest, ofte reden van den oorlogh tuschen
Portugael. 44265

Manifest vnd Vertragbrieff, der Australiscehn
Company. 68983, 98188-98189, 98199

Manifest van George III., in een waar daglicht
gesteld door Cato Batavius de Jonge.
44266

Manifest van pardon van de Koninck van
Spaignen. 44267

Manifest van 't Koninghryck van Portugael.
44268

Manifestacion . . . a la nacion de su conducta
militar. 59255

Manifestacion al Gobierno Supremo del
Tribunal de Guerra y Marina. 44269

Manifestacion al publico de los actos
practicados por el en Junta Liquidataria
de la deuda Espanola. 57580

Manifestacion breve, radical, y fvndamental.
73849

Manifestacion communicada por el Emperador
de los Franceses. 51763

Manifestacion de C. Jose Maria Tornel.
96203

Manifestacion de la indemnidad del informe.
66561, (66573)

Manifestacion de los Arzobispos y Obispos de
la republica Mexicana. 26720

Manifestacion de los patriotas de Honduras.
32769, 44270

Manifestacion de los Sres. Arzobispados y
Obispos de la republica Mexicana.
(48414)

Manifestacion de los trabajos revolucionarios
de Sud-Chichas. 88840

Manifestacion de un hecho. 97717

Manifestacion del Ciudadano Manuel de Mier
y Teran al publico. 48886

Manifestacion del estado de la hacienda de la
republica del Peru. 50501

Manifestacion del Senador Tomas C. de
Mosquera a la nacion. (51075)

Manifestacion del Vice-Presidente de la
republica de Honduras. 68788

Manifestacion historica y politica de la
revolucion de la America. 44271

Manifestacion publica del ciudadano Marcial
Zebadua. 106286

Manifestacion que ha hecho al publico D.
Mariano Arizcorreta. 70094

Manifestacion que hace a este ilustrado
publico. 36962

Manifestacion que hace al Gefe Supremo de
la republica. (26521)

Manifestacion que hace al publico con motivo
de la conducta. 73222

Manifestacion que hace al publico el de
Santiago Bombalier. 44272

Manifestacion que hace al publico el Ex-
General A. Alvarez. 44273

Manifestacion que hace al publico para
vindicar su conducta. 47969

Manifestacion que hace como Rector de
Escuelas de este capital. 20138

Manifestacion que hace el Comandante en
Gefe de la Seccion Auxiliar de Chiapas.
44274

Manifestacion que hace el gobierno eclesiastico
de Guadalajara. 44275

Manifestacion que hace la Junta Directiva de
Estudios del Departamento de Jalisco.
35553

Manifestacion que hace un ciudadano Mexicano.
76735

Manifestacion que hacen la clero y fieles de sus diocesis. 48518

Manifestacion que hacen al venerable clero y fieles. 44276

Manifestacion que hacen Pluma y Aguilera por Cardenas. 63438

Manifestacion que Manuel de la Mota hace. (51099)

Manifestacion que saco a luz el defensor de los bienes. 98967

Manifestacion que se hace de orden del Tribunal del Consulado. 86507

Manifestacion sobre la conducta que ha observado. 41704

Manifestando el acto tan tiranico. 6305

Manifestation de la conducta que ha observado. 98323

Manifestation of Christ to his people. 83738

Manifestation of the causes mooving [sic] such as have lately undertaken. 17057, 103396

Manifestation of the hungring desires. (22152), note before 92797, note after 104794

Manifestation or state and case of the Quakers. 44277

Manifestations eclatantes de la grace divine. (65540)

Manifestations in Nova Scotia. 17506

Manifestations of the beneficence of divine providence towards America. note after 43706

Manifeste des motifs que legitiment la declaration de guerre. 44278, 44281

Manifeste d'Orlie-Antoine 1er. 57629

Manifeste du gouvernement Americain. 43715

Manifeste du Roi Christophe. 3885

Manifeste du Roi [d'Haiti.] 73830

Manifeste du Roi [Henri Christophe]. 29580

Manifeste faisant suite sur le proces dit de Calinas. 37692

Manifeste sur l'infamie. 39596

Manifesto a la nacion Espanola. 10679

Manifesto a la nacion y a la prensa Espanola. 85718

Manifesto a la republica Mejicana. 24322

Manifesto a los hombres de la justicia que llama justicia. (77091)

Manifesto a los pueblos de la republica Mejicana. 35065

Manifesto a sus compatriotas. 44279

Manifesto al mundo la justicia y la necesidad. 38399

Manifesto and declaration of the Free Associate Presbytery of Miami. 48683

Manifesto con otras documentos. 34190

Manifesto; containing a plain statement of facts relative to the acts and doings of the General Assembly. 60229

Manifesto, containing a plain statement of facts relative to the acts and doings of the General Assembly of the Presbyterian Church. 65173

Manifesto de Ayala y Medrano sobre la cuestion bonos. 44280

Manifesto de Dr. Jose Alvarez de Toledo. 16159

Manifesto de D. Anastasico Bustamente. 9565

Manifesto de la diputacion de Buenos Aires. 9020

Manifesto de la justicia de D. Abraham y Jacob Franco. 25481

Manifesto de las razones que legitiman de la declaracion de guerra. 44278, 44281, 73215

Manifesto de la riqueza de la negociacion de minas. 48519

Manifesto de los motivos en que se ha fundado la conducta. 44282

Manifesto del Congreso de los Pueblos. 44286

Manifesto del General J. C. Falcon. 27816

Manifesto del Ilustre de la Real y Pontifica Universidad de Mexico. 26577

Manifesto del Obispo Electo de Michoacan el Lic. Clemente Munguia. 51322

Manifesto del Fayo de Rosario a sus compatriotas. 99708

Manifesto del Sr. Quintana Roo. 73086

Manifesto dirige a sus compatriotas como General en Gefe del Ejercito. 8564

Manifesto documentado que el Supermo Gobierno. 44283

Manifesto dos factos que na crise actual suscitao a plena. 19225

Manifesto, &c. of the Court of Vresailles. 56505

Manifesto impreso en Palma de Mallocra en 1811. 98858

Manifesto in defence of the policy of General Comonfort. (48522)

Manifesto juridico por parte de D. N. Benitez. (70796)

Manifesto, justifying his conduct in relation to the late convention. 62443

Manifesto legal por D. Maximo Mendicta. 47811

Manifesto of Don Gerardo Varrios. 3636

Manifesto of General Washington to the inhabitants of Canada. (26320), 101687

Manifesto of His Catholic Majesty. (56589)

Manifesto of the Court of Versailles. 69499

Manifesto of the Lord Protector of the Commonwealth. 49142

Manifesto of the Minister of Foreign Affairs of Chile. 44284

Manifesto of the Trustees of the City Library. 54619

Manifesto, or a declaration of the doctrine and practice of the Church of Christ. 21309, 79717, 92025, note after 97880

Manifesto, or declaration of the doctrine and practice of the Church of Christ. 21310

Manifesto or declaration set forth by the undertakers. 6635

Manifesto or official declaration. 83283

Manifesto politico-legal, en que se procura persuadir justa. 56447

Manifesto politico y moral a mis bompatriotas [sic]. 99660

Manifesto. Proceedings at the semi-annual General Conference of the Church of Jesus Christ of Latter-Day Saints. 83283

Manifesto, published by the government of Colombia. (14600), 99485

Manifesto published in the newspapers. 19456

Manifesto que ao respeitavel publico faz o Conde de Villa Flor. 99617

Manifesto que el General Vicente Prieto hace de la importancia y ventajas que la Renta del Tabaco. 65518

Manifesto que el Real Convento de Religiosas de Jesus Maria de Mexico hace. 38545

Manifiesto en que se publica el resultado de los conferencias. (76204)

Manifiesto en que se vindica a la division restauradora. 16758

Manifiesto filosofico contra los cometas. 80977

Manifiesto historico de los procedimientos del Tribvnal del Santo Oficio. 87361

Manifiesto imparcial de los acontecimientos de la capital del Peru. 41118

Manifiesto juridico en defensa del R. P. Provincial. 87175

Manifiesto juridico, en que por parte de D. Nicolas Benitez Coronel. 24824

Manifiesto juridico, politico, y moral, en que se justifica la possession. 95210

Manifiesto legal, cosmografico y historico en defensa del derecho del Rey. 11698

Manifiesto legal por Don Josef Bernardo de Tagle y Portocarrero. 94211

Manifiesto legal por D. Maximo Mendicata. 47811

Manifiesto legal, que se escrivio para demonstrar la pureza. 86377

Manifiesto, o reconvencion juridica. 98884

Manifiesto o satisfaccion pundonorosa, a todos los buenos Espanoles Europeos. 978, note after 96117

Manifiesto, Oct. 5, 1821. 76747

Manifiesto por los oficiales del Batallon Ligero de Tarragona. 16167

Manifiesto primero que presenta al pueblo el ciudadano Manuel de Vidaurre del Atentado. 99486

Manifiesto publicado en Nueva-Orleans, el 17 de Marzo de 1831. 59514, 71417

Manifiesto publicado por el apostata y traidor Miguel Hildago Costilla. 105736

Manifiesto que a Su Magestad (que Dios guarde) y Senores de su Real, y Supremo Consejo de las Indias. 99650

Manifiesto que Clemente Munguia, Obispo de Michoacan, dirige. 51323

Manifiesto que da al publico en vindicacion de los cargos. 98027

Manifiesto que da en su despendida de Chile. 105222

Manifiesto que dan un Americano y un Europeo. 98879

Manifiesto que de sus operaciones en la campana de Tejas. (76739)

Manifiesto que di en Trujillo en 1824. (38616)

Manifiesto que dirige a la nacion el General Juan Alvarez. 48527

Manifiesto que dirige el General Manuel Rincon. (71418)

Manifiesto que dirige el Honorable Congreso del Estado de Puebla. 66563

Manifiesto que el Soberno Congreso Constituyente hizo a sus pueblos. 48527

Manifiesto que el Supremo Director del Estado de Nicaragua. (55154)

Manifiesto, que ha dado al publico la Compania Guipuzcoana de Caracas. 29251, 68237

Manifiesto que hace a la nacion de su conducta publica. 67349

Manifiesto que hace a las naciones el Congreso General Constituyente de las Provincias-Unidas del Rio de la Plata. 44292

Manifiesto que hace a los pueblos de Venezuela. 96220

Manifiesto que hace al publico. 76737

Manifiesto que hace al publico D. Angel Miguel de Quintanilla. 67331

Manifiesto que hace de la conducta que ha observado. 76736

Manifiesto que hace el General Manuel Valdes. 98316

Manifiesto que hace el Gobierno de Colombia. 14601, 99485

Manifiesto que hace Francisco Rodriguez de Toro. 96210

Manifiesto que hacen al publico el Alcalde, Regidores y Sindico. 66564

Manifiesto que hacen al publico los diez oficiales del Batallon de Tarragona. (44293)

Manifiesto que Jose Manuel Sucre. 93402

Manifiesto que Manuel Gomez Pedraza. 27770

Manifiesto que ofrece. 99611

Manifiesto que para satisfacer al mundo entero. 96221

Manifiesto que presenta al publico el Doctor Carlos Augusto Torally. 96216

Manifiesto que saca a luz el Defensor de los Bienes. 67402

Manifiesto respecto de la conducta. 76748

Manifiesto satisfactorio anunciado. (3706)

Manifiesto segundo del ciudadano Manuel de Vidaurre. 99487

Manifiesto sobre la conducta observada por Diego Moreno. 50604

Manifiesto sobre la infamia. 57589

Manifiesto sobre la inutilidad delos provinciales. 48883

Manifiesto sobre la nulidad de las elecciones. 44285, 99488

Manifiesto sobre las tropellas y bejaciones. (10054)

Manifiesto sobre los representantes que corresponden. (61137), 99489

Manifiesto tercero del Manuel de Vidaurre. 99487

Manifeisto tercero que hace a los habitantes de la isla de Cuba. 79184

Manifiesto y decretos expedidos por . . . Benito Juarez. 48518

Manifiesto y decretos publicados en Veracruz. 66113

Manifiesto y demas documentos relativos a la guerra. 44294

Manifiesto y esclamacion que haze la Universidad de Cargadores. 41134, 73866, 98931

Manifiestos de la correspondencia. 96221

Manifiestos de los Jenerales Orbegoso y Nieto. 57450

Manigault, -------. 84816

Manigault, Peter. 87354

Manignault, G. 44295

Manila, Philippines. plaintiffs 23516

Manille. 39300

Manitoba, and the north-west of the dominion. 89289-89290

Manitoba et le nord-ouest du Canada. 89291

Manitou, Colorado, U. S. A. 86504

Manitou. The Gitche spirit of the red man. 83485

Manitowoc and Mississippi Rail Road Company. President. 44296

Manitowompae pomantamoonk. (4076)

Manjarres, Franz. Cruz. 44297

Mankin, H. 44298, note after 95678

Mankind is highly concerned to support. 95842

Mankind the criminal. (31246)

Manley, J. P. ed. 47327

Manley, James R. (44299)-44301

Manley, John. 44302, 46936

Manliffe, Richard. 78661

Manlius; with notes and references. 28016
Manly, Basil. 44303
Manly, Charles M. 85072
Mnaly, J. G. 44304
Manly Christianity. 46399
Manly, independent thinker. 19460
Mann, A. Dudley. 44308-44309
Mann, Ab. (44306)
Mann, Abijah. (44305)
Mann, Ariel. 44307
Mann, Cameron. 44310
Mann, Cyrus. 44311-44312
Mann, Edwin John. 44313
Mann, Herman. 14858, 44314-44316, note
 after 75924
Mann, Horace, 1796-1859. (8044), 14997,
 (19223), 22429, 28612, (44317)-44324,
 44326, 46107, (66050), (80279), 83572,
 83586, 104950 see also Antioch
 College, Yellow Springs, Ohio. President.
 Massachusetts. Board of Education.
 Secretary.
Mann, Mrs. Horace. see Mann, Mary Tyler
 (Peabody) 1806-1887.
Mann, J. 44331
Mann, James. 44329
Mann, James, 1759-1832. 44329, 105991
 see also U. S. Surgeon-General's
 Office.
Mann. James A. 44333
Mann, Joel, 1789-1884. 25319, (44330),
 92847
Mann, John. plaintiff 53542
Mann, Julius. 44332
Mann, Karl. 92571
Mann, Mary Tyler (Peabody) 1806-1887. 44326,
 (44334), 77078
Mann, Mercy. plaintiff 53542
Mann, Samuel. 44335
Mann, Stafford. 84976 see also Smithfield,
 R. I. Town Clerk. Smithfield, R. I.
 Town Treasurer.
Mann, W. J. ed. 44338, 78014
Mann, W. W. 44339
Mann, William. 44336-(44337)
Manna gathered in the morning. 58893
Manne-Vilette, Dapres de. 44334
Mannequin, Th. 1665A, 15428, (44340)-
 44343
Manner how the first Sabbath was ordained.
 (66872)
Manner in which the rights of the subjects
 within the realm were communicated.
 1968
Manner of making of coffee. 11788
Manner of raising and dressing flax, and
 hemp. 78985
Manner of raising radishes. 78985
Manner of the children spending their time.
 103506
Manner of the giving and receiving of the
 covenant of grace. 17059, (17072),
 (70107)
Manners, Charles. see Rutland, Charles
 Manners, 4th Duke of, 1754-1787.
Manners, George. 44345, (51433)
Manners, Motley. pseud. Parnassus in
 pillory. see Duganne, Augustine J. H.
Manners, Nicholas. 44346-44347
Manners-Sutton, Charles, Archbishop of
 Canterbury, 1755-1828. 93973
Manners and customs in the West India
 islands. (50619)
Manners and customs in the West Indies.
 46847

Manners and customs in Washington recently.
 2159
Manners and customs of several Indian tribes.
 33920
Manners, customs, and antiquities of the
 Indians of North and South America.
 27909
Manners, lawes and customs of all nations.
 6120
Manners of the Americans. 14766, 80151,
 note after 97028
Manners of the times; a satire. 62414
Manners; or, happy homes and good society
 all the year round. 29670
Manni, M. 44348
Manning, Jacob Merrill, 1824-1882. (44349)-
 44350
Manning, James. 44351
Manning, James, 1738-1791. (29224)
Manning, Jethro W. 44352
Manning, John Lawrence, 1816-1889. 87501,
 87549 see also South Carolina.
 Governor, 1852-1854 (Manning)
Manning, Richard Irving, 1789-1836. (44355)
Manning, Robert. 35306, (44353)-(44354)
Mannling, M. J. C. (18524)
Mann's emigrant's complete guide to Canada.
 44336
Mann's emigrant's complete guide to the United
 States. (44337)
Mannucci, Teobaldo. see Manutius, Aldus,
 1450-1515.
Manoel I, King of Portugal. see Emanuel I,
 King of Portugal, 1469-1521.
Manoel da Costa, Claudio. 44356
Manoel da Conceicao, Jose. see Conceicao,
 Jose Manuel da, 1714-1767.
Manoel Beckman, drama original Brasileiro
 en 5 actos. 77162
Manoeuvres of horse artillery. 23390
Manoir, Philippe Francois Pinel du. see
 Dumanoir, Philippe Francois Pinel.
Manolia; or, the vale of Tallulah. (69545)
Manomin: a rhythmical romance of Minnesota.
 14682
Manomin. Rhythmical romance of Minnesota.
 44358
Manoncourt, Charles Nicolas Sigisbert Sonnini
 de. see Sonnini de Manoncourt, Charles
 Nicolas Sigisbert, 1751-1812.
Manor or Rensselaerwyck. (60837)
Manos destadas del mejor Abner. 76163
Manozca, Juan de. (44359), 98809 see also
 Catholic Church in Peru. Inquisidor
 Apostolico. Quito. Real Audiencia.
 Visitador.
Manozca, Juan Saenz de. see Saenz de
 Manozca, Juan.
Manrique, Joaquin de Guzman y. see Guzman
 y Manrique, Joaquin de.
Manrique, Jose Maria Vaca de Guzman y. see
 Vaca de Guzman y Manrique, Jose Maria.
Man's chief end to glorifie God. 2734
Man's dignity and duty as a reasonable creature.
 13350
Man's duty in magnifying God's work discovered
 (73545)
Man's duty, in relation to the Lord's work.
 92255
Man's eternal progression. 84026
Mans extremity, Gods opportunity. 96302
Man's hope destroyed by the death of the
 young. 88673
Man's liableness to be deceiv'd about religion.
 (74371)

Man's life considered under the similitude
of a vapour. (12323)
Man's nature and destiny. 84472
Man's present state compar'd with withering
grass and flowers. 100913
Man's projects and God's results. 29299
Man's record of his own existence. 62624
Man's victim God's chosen. 28053, 92943
Manse of Sunnyside. 61375, note after 93772
Mansel, Sir Robert. 66686
Mansergh, ----------. ta 87138
Mansfeldian motiues. 9758
Mansfeldt, Julius. 44360
Mansfield, Achilles. 44361
Mansfield, C. B. 44362
Mansfield, C. B. 44362
Mansfield, Charles Finney. 44383
Mansfield, Daniel. 44363
Mansfield, David Murray, 2d Earl of, 1727-
1796. 64572
Mansfield, Edward D. 9139, (20813), (44364),
44366-44376, 78410
Mansfield, Edward D. supposed author
15623, 44365
Mansfield, Isaac. 44377
Mansfield, J. B. (16369), (44379)
Mansfield, Jacob. 44378
Mansfield, James. supposed author 51544
Mansfield, Jared. 91361
Mansfield, John. defendant 105354
Mansfield, John L. 44380
Mansfield, Joseph. (44381)
Mansfield, Joseph K. F. (44382)
Mansfield, L. D. 44383
Mansfield, L. W. (30110), 44384
Mansfield, William Murray, Earl of, 1704-
1793. 34416, 40451, 40467, 40490,
51545-51546, 62542, 63401-63402,
92694, 96175-96176, note after 104453
Mansfield, Conn. Ecclesiastical Council,
1806. see Congregational Churches in
Connecticut. Ecclesiastical Council,
Mansfield, 1806.
Mansfield, Conn. First Church. (80370)-
80371, note after 100602, 102522
Mansfield, Mass. Anti-slavery Society. see
Mansfield Anti-slavery Society.
Mansfield, Mass. Society for Detecting Horse-
Thieves, and Recovering Stolen Horses.
see Society for Detecting Horse-Thieves,
and Recovering Stolen Horses, Wrentham,
Franklin, Medway, Medfield, Walpole,
Foxborough, Mansfield, adn Attleborough,
Mass.
Mansfield Academy, Brooklyn, N. Y. 77134
Mansfield Anti-slavery Society. 90890
Mansfield domestic silk-grower's manual.
72045
Mansfield's soliloquy 105354
Manship, Andrew. 44387-44388
Mansie, Alexander. 44389
Mansilla, Lucio V. 44390
Mansion, Hypolite. 44062, 44391
Manso de Contreras, Christobal. 16185,
44392
Manso de Noronha, Juana. 44395, 55499
Manso Pereira, Joao. see Pereira, Joao
Manso.
Manso de Velasco, Joseph Antonio, Conde de
Superunda. 44394, 61136, (61164),
79146 see also Peru (Viceroyalty)
Virrey, 1745-1761 (Manso de Velasco)
Manso de Velasco, Joseph Antonio, Conde de
Superunda. defendant 29459, 93778

Manso y Zuniga, Francisco, Abp. 44393,
86421 see also Mexico (Archdiocese)
Archbishop (Manso y Zuniga)
Mante, Thomas. 44396
Mantegazza, Carlo. 44397
Mantegazza, P. 44398-44399
Mantis. Synopt. New genera and species of
trees and shrubs. 67464
Mantissa. 46602
Mantovani, Paolo Luigi. 44400
Mantovano, Marco. 44401-44402
Mantua, Pa. Academie Classique et Militaire.
62099, 98402
Mantuanus, Baptiste. 44403
Manual and catalogue of the First Church of
Christ. 89863
Manual and catalogue of the officers and
members of the First Congregational
Church in Springfield. 89864
Manual and catalogue of the officers and
members of the Olivet Congregational
Church in Springfield, Mass. 89871
Manual . . . and catalogue of the United
Congregational Society. 52985
Manual and directory of the First Reformed
(Dutch) Church. 77593
Manual and evolutions of the cavalry. 91444
Manual and record of the Church of Paramus.
59543
Manual breve y forma de administrar los
santos sacramentos. 40081, 40082,
44404
Manual [by A. B. Johnson.] 16137
Manual, compiled . . . for the use of the
Assembly. 13239
Manual comprendio de el regio patronato
Indiano. (70785)
Manual containing information respecting the
growth. 13847
Manual, containing the rules of the Senate
and House of Representatives . . .
[of Michigan.] 48750
Manual das municoes e artificios da guerra.
88703
Manual de administrar los sanctos sacramentos
a los Espanoles. 16186
Manual de administrar los santos sacramentos
a los Espanoles y naturales de esta
provincia. 79310
Manual de administrar los santos sacramentos
. . . sacado de las manuales de los
padres. 99387
Manual de adultos. (44406)
Manual de biografia Mejicana. 2109
Manual de biografia Yucateca. 87181
Manual de deputados ou advertencia aos
senhores deputados. 88831, 88836
Manual de elecciones. 93298
Manual de exercicios. 87152-87153
Manual de forasteros en la la [sic] ciudad de
Matanzas. 46197
Manual de geografia y estadistica de la
republica Mejicana. 31512
Manual de geografia y estadistica del alto
Peru o Bolivia. 47846
Manual de historia universal. 27815
Manual de historia y cornologia de Chile.
(47847)
Manual de historia y cronologia de Mejico.
2110
Manual de la isla de Cuba. 17789
Manual de la isla de Cuba. Compendio de su
historia. 26570
Manual de la navigation dans le rio de la
Plata. 6836

Manual de los sanctos sacramentos. 58297

Manval de los santos sacramentos. 74863-
74864

Manual de los santos sacramentos, conforme
al ritual de Paulo Quinto. (59625)

Manual de los santos sacramentos en el
idioma de Michuacan. 44956

Manual de Neuva York. 38956

Manual de providencias economico-politicas
para uso de los habitantes. (72546)

Manual . . . del bibliofilo Hispano-Americano.
93319, 93325

Manual del cocinero Cubano. 17790

Manual del Cristiano. 74952

Manual del derecho parlamentario. 35889

Manual del ganadero Chileno. 60917

Manual del Sagrado Orden de Charidad de S.
Hypolito Martyr. 26372

Manual del viajero en Mejico. (2111)

Manual do Cacador. 7546

Manual do cidadao Brasileiro. 81094

Manual do empregado de fazenda. 14356

Manual do procurador dos feitos de fazenda
nacional. 60873

Manual en lengua Mixteca. 49772, 98716

Manual exercise. (Abridged for the accom-
modation of non-commissioned officers.)
91432

Manual exercise and evolutions of the cavalry.
91443

Manual exercise, and evolutions of the cavalry:
as practiced in the late American army.
(44405), 91434, 91445, 91454, 91458,
91461, 91462

Manual exercise & evolutions of the cavalry
as practiced in the late American army.
91424, 91451

Manual exercise, as ordered by His Majesty.
30771, 81142, 100010

Manual for councils. 51802

Manual for emigrants to America. 14779

Manual for the communicants of the Congregational Church in Yorktown. 106047

Manual for the communicants of the Edwards
Church. 77348

Manual for the communicants of the First
Presbyterian Church. 21431

Manual for the congregational Church in
South Norwalk, Conn. 88149

Manual for the Constitutional Convention.
53758

Manual for the directors and teachers of
common schools. 60231

Manual for the government of the Senate and
House of Representatives . . . of
Pennsylvania. 60232

Manual for the information of officers and
members of legislatures. 72217

Manual for the instruction of "rings." 58958

Manual for the members of the First Congregational Church. 98140

Manual for the patriotic volunteers on active
service in regular or irregular war.
25044

Manual for the treasurers and collectors of
the Anti-slavery Cent-a-Week Societies.
88239, 4th note after 103852

Manual for the use of notaries public. 72589

Manual for the use of teachers, employers,
trustees. 64617

Manual for the use of the Convention to
Revise the Consitution of . . . New-
York. (53756)

Manual for the use of the First Free
Presbyterian Church in . . . New York.
54586

Manual for the use of the General Court.
45808

Manual for the use of the Legislature of . . .
New York. 53757

Manual for the use of the members of the
Congregational Church in Danbury.
92111

Manual for the use of the members of the
Congregational Church, in Sturbridge,
January, 1843. 93254

Manual for the use of the members of the
Second Presbyterian Church. 85300

Manual for the use of visiters to the falls
of the Niagara. 34778

Manual for United States Consuls. (31430)

Manual for visiters. 55129

Manual guide des voyageurs aux-Etats-Unis
de l'Amerique du Nord. 24123

Manval instrvcion, y orden de recibir, y dar
habito, y vel a las monjas. 76749

Manual Labour Academy of Pennsylvania.
Trustees. 60230

Manual Labor High School, Worcester County,
Mass. see Worcester Academy,
Worcester, Mass.

Manual Labor Seminary, Lexington, Mass.
see Lexington Manual Labor Seminary,
Lexington, Mass.

Manval Mexicano de la administracion de los
santos sacramentos. 42102

Manual moral ordenado primariamente a los
senores parachos. 57101, 68461

Manual no. 3, of the First Church, in Stamford,
Conn. 90120

Manual of American geography. 44407

Manual of American literature. 73843

Manual of American principles. 105594

Manual of archaeology. (36124)

Manual of arms. 88405

Manual of botany for North America. 21708

Manual of botany for the northern and middle
states. 21707

Manual of botany for the northern states.
21706, 44408

Manual of business for Sons of Temperance.
87011

Manual of camp and garrison duty. 67277

Manual of Canadian literature. 50647

Manual of church discipline. 15486, 69921

Manual of coal and its topography. 40188

Manual of congregationalism. 63985

Manual of court forms. 61803

Manual of currency. 64638

Manual of decisions of the National Division of
the Sons of Temperance of North
America. 87012

Manual of devotion and hymns for the House
of Refuge. 85955

Manual of directions and plans for grading.
9469

Manual of English literature. 79961

Manual of exercise and evolutions of the
cavalry as practiced in the late American
army. 91428

Manual of flax culture and manufacture.
24683, 50344

Manual of geography. 49722

Manual of geography. Being a description of
all the empires. 74625

Manual of geology. 22518

Manual of geology . . . with special reference
to American geological history. 18420

Manual of gold and silver coins of all nations.
21787

Manual of good manners. 79712, 106199

Manual of horse-breeding. 44409
Manual of infantry and rifle tactics. 71095
Manual of instruction. 34241
Manual of instructions for capturing all kinds of fur-bearing animals. 55000
Manual of instructions to . . . deputy surveyors. 34871
Manual of internal rules and regulations for men-of-war. 40765
Manual of laws, regulations, instructions, froms, and official decisions. 67435
Manual of legislative practice and order of business in the Legislature of the state of New-Jersey. 81470
Manual of legislative practice and order of business of deliberative bodies. 93960
Manual of linear perspective. 83793
Manual of marine warfare. 31125
Manual of military surgery, for the use of surgeons in the Confederate Army. 12846
Manual of military surgery. Prepared for the use of the Confederate States Army. 44410
Manual of mineralogy. 18421
Manual of mineralogy and geology. 22518
Manual of missionary geography and history. 6018
Manual of missions. (42535)
Manual of outpost duties. 19567
Manual of parliamentary practice, for the use of the Senate of the United States. (9325), 16105-(16106), 16117, 35887, 93958, 93960
Manual of parliamentary practice: rules of proceedings and debate in deliberative assemblies. 18114
Manual of parliamentary practice, with an appendix. 98084
Manual of peace. 98051
Manual of pensions, bounty, and pay. 67434
Manual of plantership in British Guiana. 43645
Manual of political economy. By E. Peshine Smith. (82528)
Manual of political economy [by Thomas Cooper.] 16621
Manual of political economy, with particular reference to the institutions. 62530
Manual of political ethics. 40980
Manual of political intelligence. (32591)
Manual of practice and rules of order and debate. 83293, 84431
Manual of preliminary drill. (56149)
Manual of public libraries. 70476
Manual of religious information. 24862
Manual of religious liberty. 44411
Manual of rules for the government of both branches. 60233
Manual of rules of the General Assembly, and legislative directory. 60233
Manual of rules of the General Assembly of Pennsylvania. 85175
Manual of signals. 51626
Manual of south-eastern Kansas. 88381
Manual of southern sentiment on the subject of slavery. (27864)
Manual of spiritual exercises and instructions for Christians. 26602
Manual of the Albany Institute. 64933
Manual of the American Legal Association: compiled by John Livingston. 41629
Manual of the . . . [American Legal] Association: containing its plan. 1126

Manual of the Arch Street Presbyterian Church. 61477
Manual of the Baptist Church at North Haven. 55716
Manual of the Baptist Church, in Columbus, Mississippi. 44412
Manual of the Baptist Church, Roxborough, Pennsylvania. (73624)
Manual of the Baptist Church, Southington, Conn. 88586
Manual of the Board of Education. 54121
Manual of the Board of Trustees of the College . . . [of New York.] 54198
Manual of the botany of the northern United States. 28366
Manual of the Broad Street Baptist Church, Philadelphia. 61508
Manual of the Broadway Tabernacle Church. (54136)
Manual of the Brooklyn Common Council. 8300
Manual of the climate and diseases of tropical eountries [sic]. 12840
Manual of the Common Council of the city of Brooklyn. 5603
Manual of the Congregational Church at Rocky Hill. 72457
Manual of the Congregational Church in the First Ecclesiastical Society in Stamford, Conn. 90118
Manual of the Congregational Church in West Boylston, Mass. 24604
Manual of the Congregational Church of Richmond [Mass.] (71160)
Manual of the Congregational Church, Pittsfield, N. H. 63161
Manual of the Congregational Church, Plymouth, N. H. (63496)
Manual of the Congregational Church [Shrewsbury, Mass.] 80746
Manual of the Congregational Church, Stanwich. 90450
Manual of the Congregational Church, Stanwich, Conn. 90451
Manual of the Congregational Church, Stockbridge, Vt. 91875
Manual of the constitution of the United States. 23885
Manual of the corporation of the city of New York. 18941, 54369
Manual of the cultivation of the sugar-cane. (80166)
Manual of the culture of the grape. 77399
Manual of the direct and excise tax. 6975
Manual of the First Baptist Church, [Providence, R. I.] 66261
Manual of the First Church in New Haven. 52985
Manual of the First Church in Porthampton, Mass. 55766
Manual of the First Congregational Church in Rockport, Mass. 72408
Manual of the First Congregational Church in South Hadley Falls, Mass. 88128
Manual of the First Congregational Church, in Suffield, Conn. 93425
Manual of the First Congregational Church, Madison. 43746
Manual of the First Congregational Church [of Middleborough, Mass.] (48829)
Manual of the First Congregational Church, of Norwich, Conn. 55922
Manual of the First Congregational Church, Spencerport, N. Y. 89397

Manual of the First Congregational Church, Stamford, Ct. 90119

Manual of the First Evangelical Congregational Church in Cambridge-Port. 10131

Manual of the First Independent Church [of St. Louis.] 75348

Manual of the First Independent Presbyterian Church, [Oakland,] California. 56389

Manual of the First Lutheran Church in the city of Albany. 89754

Manual of the First Presbyterian Church of Hudson. (33504)

Manual of the First Presbyterian Church. With a history of its formation. 49159

Manual of the First Reformed Dutch Church, [Hudson, N. Y.] (33504)

Manual of the foreign missions of the Presbyterian Church. (42535)

Manual of the Fourth Congregational Church, Westminster Hall, Providence, R. I. 66262

Manual of the Free Evangelical Congregational Church, Providence, R. I. 66264

Manual of the Grand Army of the Republic, containing its principles and objectives. 17427

Manual of the Grand Army of the Republic, together with memorial day. 48751

Manual of the history of the political system of Europe. 31232

Manual of the history of the United States. 78253

Manual of the House of Hope Presbyterian Church, Saint Paul. (49263), (75455)

Manual of the House of Representatives for 1832-3. 34292

Manual of the House of Representatives of the United States. 44413

Manual of the Lancasterian system of teaching. 44414, 54285

Manual of the lance and lance exercise for the cavalry service. 44415

Manual of the laws of North Carolina. 31086, 55645

Manual of the Legislature . . . 1827. 53759

Manual of the . . . Litchfield South Consociation. 41471

Manual of the medical botany of the United States. 67456

Manual of the medical botany of the United States of North America. 67457

Manual of the Memorial Church, for 1866. 89867

Manual of the Mystic Church. 51662

Manual of the North Congregational Church. 89869

Manual of the North Presbyterian Church. 55726

Manual of the Olivet Baptist Church. 57219

Manual of the ornithology of the United States and Canada. 56349-56350

Manual of the Park Presbyterian Church of Brooklyn, N. Y. (8301)

Manual of the pension laws. (60808)

Manual of the pension laws of the United States of America, embracing all the laws. 30403

Manual of the pension laws of the United States of America, with the forms and instructions. 25037

Manual of the Providence Aid Society. 66297

Manual of the Plymouth Church, Brooklyn, L. I. 8299

Manual of the Plymouth Church of Rochester, N. Y. (72347)

Manual of . . . the primary . . . New York Public Schools. (79337)

Manual of the principles and practice of operative surgery. 84276

Manual of the principles, doctrines, & usages of congregational churches. 73748

Manual of the public schools of . . . Providence 66363

Manual of the railroads of the United States. 64056

Manual of the Reformed Church. 83526

Manual of the Reformed Protestant Dutch Church in North America. 16983

Manual of the Religious Society of Spring Valley. 89830

Manual of the Rensselaer County Medical Society. 69639

Manual of the revised statutes of . . . New York. 53760

[Manual of the Second Presbyterian] Church [of New York.] 54586

Manual of the Seventh Presbyterian Church . . . New York. 54586

Manual of the Seventh Regiment, National Guard, S. N. Y. 54370

Manual of the South Church. 89876

Manual of the Spring Street Congregational Church. 49159

Manual of the state of Pennsylvania. 85177

Manual of the Sunday-School Union. 48205

Manual of the system of discipline and instruction. 45371

Manual of the Tabernacle Church in Salem, Mass. 75754

Manual of the Templars of Honor and Temperance. 36140

Manual of the Third Presbyterian Church. 61885

[Manual of the] Third [Presbyterian] Church. 54586

Manual of the Third Presbyterian Church, Philadelphia. 7368

Manual of the U. S. bankruptcy act. 70820

Manual of the United Congregational Church. 55037

Manual of the Walnut Street Presbyterian Church. 62373

Manual of topographical drawings. 83793

Manual of United States history. (22172)

Manual of United States surveying. (30919)

Manual of useful studies. 102368

Manual on school-houses and cottages for the people. 12171

Manual on the cultivation of the sugar cane. 44416, 81038

Manual or digest of the statute law of the state of Florida. (24883), 2d note after 95517

Manual or prudential maxims for statesmen and courtiers. 67599

Manual para administrar a los Indios del idioma Cahita. 44418

Manual para administrar los sacramentos. (44417)

Manual para administrar los santos sacramentos de penitencia. 26560

Manval para catekizar. 5854, 74018

Manual Pereira. 201

Manual prepared for the use of the Brooklyn Common Council. 8300

Manual politico del Venezolano. 98867

Manual razonado del litigante Mexicano. 71706

Manual Romano Toledano. 74525

Manual serafica. 44419

Manual teorico practico sobre el beneficio. (43761)

Manval Toledano. 42102

Manual trilinque. 79310

Manual, with rules and orders. (70595)

Manual y correspondencia de Delitos y Penas. 86225

Manuale ad usum patrum Societatis Jesu. (58520)

Manuale formarum juramentorum ab his praestandorum. (44420)

Manvale Pervanvm. 57542

Manuale secundum. (44421)

Manualito otomitica para los principiantes. 60903

Manualito para administrar el viatico y extremanucion. 48528

Manuals of the Common Council. (69567)

Manvdiction for Mr. Robinson. 72103

Manuductio ad ministerium. 46400, 46532

Manuel I, King of Portugal. see Emanuel I, King of Portugal, 1469-1521.

Manuel de la Vega. see La Vega, Manuel de.

Manuel de Herla. 44423, (58829), 61151, (76155)

Manuel de la Sota, Juan. see Sota, Juan Manuel de la.

Manuel de Mello, Francisco. see Mello, Francisco Manuel de, 1608-1666.

Manuel y Rodrigues, Miguel de, fl. 1780. 103429

Manuel arreglado al ritual Romano. 24139

Manuel de administrar los santos sacramentos. 79311

Manuel de geologia extractado de la lethaea geognostica de Broon. 71444

Manuel de la istoria de Chile. 41991

Manuel de la navigation dans le mer des Antilles. 37622

Manuel d'economie politique. 82529

Manuel del abogado Americano. 56366

Manuel des braves. 96332

Manuel des consuls. 49139

Manuel des emigrants en Californie. 48894

Manuel des habitans de Saint Domingo. 21066

Manuel des langues mortes et vivantes. 70903

Manuel diplomatique. 27262

Manuel du collectionneur de timbres-poste. 49826

Manuel du droit parlementaire. 35888

Manuel du Pelerin de Notre Dame de Bon-secours a Montreal. 44867

Manuel du publiciste et de l'homme d'etat. 35240

Manuel historique du system politique des etats de l'Europe et de leurs colonies. 31233

Manuel Rodriguez de la Compania de Iesvs. 72525

Manuel Roret. (36678)

Manufactories of Buffalo. 9059

Manufacture of domestic wine. 62566

Manufacture of paper and printed books in Pennsylvania. 58439

Manufacture of pot-ash in the British North-American plantations. (45402)

Manufacture of sugar, in the colonies and at home. 78155

Manufacturers' and farmers' journal. 65667, 71157

Manufacturers' and Mechanics' Library Association of Lewiston. 40871

Manufacturers and Village Library, Somersworth, N. H. see Somersworth, N. H. Manufacturers and Village Library.

Manufacturers and Village Library at Great Falls, N. H. see Somersworth, N. H. Manufacturers and Village Library.

Manufacturers' Association of Detroit. see Detroit Manufacturers' Association.

Manufacturers' book of wages. (50654)

Manufacturers, Exporters of Goods, and Mechants, of the City of Glasgow. petitioners see Glasgow. Manufacturers, Exporters of Goods, and Merchants. petitioners

Manufacturers' magazine. 47914

Manufacturers, Mechanics, Merchants, Traders, and Others, of the City and County of Philadelphia. petitioners see Philadelphia. Citizens. petitioners and Philadelphia County, Pa. Citizens. petitioners

Manufacturers National Convention, Cleveland, 1867. see National Convention of Manufacturers, Cleveland, 1867.

Manufacturers of Hats, Philadelphia. petitioners 61822

Manufacturers of Naval Machinery for the United States. petitioners 47644

Manufacturers of Philadelphia. Census of 1860. 61804

Manufacturers of Salt, Kanawha County, [W.] Va. petitioners 36996-36997

Manufactures and statistics of the United States. 44429

Manufactures, &c., No. 3. 44430

Manufactures of the United States. 11675

Manufactures of the United States in 1860. 44428

Manufacturing Association, Pittsburgh, Pa. see Pittsburgh Manufacturing Association.

Manufacturing interests of the United States. 44431

Manumission Society of New York. see New York Manumission Society.

Manumission Society of Tennessee. 94800-94801

Manumission Society of the City of New York. see New York Manumission Society.

Manvmission to a manvdvction. 72102

Manuscript. 28840

Manuscript books and papers of the Commission of Enquiry. 85247

Manuscript collection of annals relative to Virginia. 100464

Manuscript, found hanging on a post at Gorham Corner. 91779, 97109

MS. journal of eighty voyages. (14196)-14197

Manuscript journal, relating to the operations before Quebec. 67022

Manuscript journal relating to the siege of Quebec in 1759. 25684

Manuscript of a maniac. 89469

Manuscript of Diedrick Knicherbocker, Jr. 35192, 2d note after 44432

Manuscripto coetaneo existente na Bibliotheca publica Portuense. 98649

Manuscripts and printed books in possession of Obadiah Rich. 70887

Manuscripts relating to the early history of Canada. The invasion of Canada in 1775. 36393

Manuscripts relating to the early history of Canada. Fourth Series. 67024

Manuscripts relating to the early history of Canada. Published under the auspices of the Literary and Historical Society of Quebec. 67022

Manuscrit de Paris. 67023

Manuscrit hieratique des anciens Indiens. 73301

Manuscrit pictographique Americain. 20550-(20551), 61309-61310
Manuscrit Troano. (44433), 49464, 76007
Manutio, P. 44434
Manutius, Aldus, 1450-1515. 25088, 67736
Manuzio, Teobaldo. see Manutius, Aldus, 1450-1515.
Manvill, Mrs. Elias F. 44435
Manwaring, ------. supposed author 96075
Manwaring, Christopher. 44436-44437
Many. pseud. 91747
Many. pseud. To the people. 95957
Many Citizens and Inventors. petitioners 69580
Many citizens being desirous of seeing the motion. 100787
Many Divines, and Others of the Classical Congregational, and Other Perswasions. petitioners 96029
Many entertaining and curious observations, not taken notice of by Sir John Narborough. 9108-9109
Many incidents in the life of this wonderful man. 9467
Many members of the Library Company of Philadelphia 61788
Many Ministers in Old England. pseud. Letter. 2171, (40355)
Many missions. 83392
Many mysteries unravelled. 62891
Many of the electors of the two, to the electors of the four. 97710
Many Persons in Bolton, Mass. pseud. see Bolton, Mass. Many Persons. pseud.
Many Respectable Freeholders and Inhabitants, Philadelphia. see Philadelphia. Freeholders and Inhabitants.
Many respectable freeholders and inhabitants of this city, justly alarmed at the resolutions. 62311, 95772
Manypenny, George W. (32746), 40341, (44438)-(44439) see also U. S. Commissioner of Indian Affairs. U. S. Office of Indian Affairs.
Manzanares, Ignacio Guerra. 40066
Manzaneda y Encinas, Diego Miguel Bringas de. see Bringas de Manzaneda y Encinas, Diego Miguel.
Manzaneda y Enzinas, Diego Bringas de. see Bringas de Manzaneda y Encinas, Diego Miguel.
Manzi, Pietro. 44441-44442
Manzini, Nicolas B. L. (44443)
Map and description of proposed metropolitan park for Boston. 17561
Map and description of Texas. (50353)
Map and description of the main battlefields. 83420
Map and guide to all the emigration colonies. 23158
Map and report of Lieut. Allen. (77847)
Map and street directory of San Francisco. 76053
Map by Bernard Ratzer. 53549
Map for sailing in those seas. 35712
Map of America . . . exhibiting the principal trading stations. (55736), 55982
Map of Boston harbour, 1689. 88221
Map of British and French dominions. 49695
Map of Bureau County, Illinois. 46876
Map of Cabotia. 66697
Map of Cairo city property and catalogue of lots. 9861
Map of Canada. (11601), 2d note after 105598-9 [sic]

Map [of Indiana.] 34577, note before 90593
Map of Kentucky. 84936
Map of Maryland. 44830
Map of Maryland, according to the bounds mentioned in the charter. 80586, 1st note after 100521
Map of New-England. (33445), 106052
Map of New-England, etc. 33446
Map of New-York [by David H. Burr.] 9439
Map of New York. [By Williams.] 90082, 1st note after 104412
Map of North America. (11601), 2d note after 105598-9 [sic]
Map of Philadelphia. 84983
Map of the battle field of Fredericksburg. 7467, 4444
Map of the battlefield of Chattanooga prepared to accompany report of Maj. Genl. U. S Grant. 84774
Map of the bounty lands in the Illinois and Missouri Territories. 34293
Map of the British empire in America. 64146
Map of the Christian world. 66683
Map of the city [of Brooklyn.] 8265
Map of the city of New-York and island of Manhattan. 7825
Map of the city of Quebec. 50185, 82379
Map of the coast of New England, from Staten Island to the island of Breton. 88221
Map of the country contiguous to the Savannah, Ogechee & Altamaha Canal. 105561
Map of the country, at large. 103769
Map of the District of Maine. 93499
Map of the English prairie and the adjacent country. 5567
Map of the gold regions of California. 10004, 105655
Map of the lands, islands, gulfs, seas, and fishing banks comprising the whole. (6208)
Map of the middle British colonies, &c. in North America. (64835)
Map of the middle British colonies in North-America. 64832
Map of the military bounty lands in the Illinoi and Missouri Territories. 34293
Map of the Mohawk country. (80023)
Map of the province of Upper Canada. 85205
Map of the seat of Civil War in America. 72994
Map of the southern part of Bergen Township, Hudson County, N. J. (44445)
Map of the state [of Pennsylvania.] 8470
Map of the Tennessee government. (82420), 3d note after 94805
Map of the United States and territories. 599
Map of the United States. [By Henry Schenck Tanner.] 94310
Map of the United States, published by J. Webster, New-York. 102324
Map of the United States, shewing Mr. Birkbec journey. 5567
Map of the United States, showing the boundary line proposed by the British Commissioners. 47434
Map of the U. S. Territory, from the Mississippi to the Pacific Ocean. 37150
Map of the U. S. traveller's directory, and statistical view. 104169
Map of the village of Worcester. 105444
Map of the whole world. 44446
Map of the world. 66683
Map of the world. [By S. A. Mitchell.] (4971
Map of those parts of the country most famous for being harassed by the Indians. 93499

Map of Virginia; also its constitution. 21988

Map of Virginia. VVith a description of the covntrey. 82823, 82832, 82855, note after 92664, 2d note after 101510

Map of Wayne and Pike Counties, Pennsylvania. 96282

Map, showing the boundary line proposed by each party. 9943, 57565

Map: showing the location of the Sterling Iron Estate. 44447

Mapa de las composiciones y nuevo descubrimiento. 44448

Mape of France. 66684

Mapes, James J. (1209), (25655), 44449

Mapimiha, Mexico. Alcalde. (44450)

Maple Grove Cemetery Association. see Albany, N. Y. Maple Grove Cemetery Association.

Maple knot. pseud. Life and adventures of Simon Seek. see Clemo, Ebenezer.

Maple leaves: a budget of legendary, historical, critical, and sporting intelligence. 40005

Maple leaves. By George Washington Johnson. 36215

Maple leaves from Canada. 9409, (44452), 55909

Mapleson, T. W. Gwilt. 44453-44455

Mapleton; or New York for the Maine law. 12991, 44456

Mapp and description of New-England. 740, 91853

Mapp of Virginia discovered to ye falls. 2d note after 100557, 104191

Mapp of ye improved part of Pensilvania in America. 60234

Mappa mondo di Fra Mauro Camaldolese. 106411

Mappa reduzido do threatro da guerra presente. 20944, 56000

Mappa terrae habitabilis flores historiarum. 76838

Mappas geraes do commercio de Portugal. (44457)

Mappe de Tepechpam, mappe Tlotzin and mappe Quinatzin. 48529

Mappe Quinztzin. 48529

Mappe Tlotzin. 48529

Mappemonde by Leonardo da Vinci. 44070

Mappemonde [of Sebastian Cabot.] 19050

Maps and list of real estate belonging to the corporation. (54212)

Maps and reports of the San Juan del Rio Ranche. 12479

Maps, manuscripts, engravings, coins, &c. 53828

Maps of the Racket River and its head waters. 48018

Maps. Stanbury's expedition. 90370

Maps. Stanbury's report. 90370

Mapukapa, Jakoba Fr. tr. 83133

Maquama. A Slave 82089

Maquas Castles (Indians) see Three Maquas Castles (Indians) Sachems.

Maqueen, Daniel. (44458)

Mara: or, a romance of the war. 74628

Maraccio, P. H. 44459

Maragarite of America. 41765, (41766)

Marah spoken to. 46401

Marana. pseud. Future of America. (44460)

Maranhao (Brazilian Province) Laws, statutes, etc. 26495

Maranhao (Brazilian Province) Presidente (Costa Barros) 24259 see also Costa Barros, Pedro Jose de.

Maranhao (City) Camara. 24259

Maranhao (City) Sociedade de Instruccao Elementar. see Sociedade de Instruccao Elementar, Maranhao, Brazil.

Maranhao (Diocese) Bishóp (Silveira) 81118 see also Silveria, Manuel Joaquim da, Bp.

Maranon, y Amazonas. 72524

Marat, Jean Paul. (44462)

Maraver, Juan de Santa Maria. see Santa Maria Maraver, Juan de.

Maraviglia Americana. 44463

Maravilla, O. (44464)

Maravilla Americana. 9814

Maravillas de Ntra. Sra. de la Salud de la ciudad de Pazcuaro. 77093

Maravillas del divino amor. 76114

Maravillosa aparicion de Santa Maria de Guadalupe. 74023

Maravillosa conversion de infieles. 105733

Marazzedo, ------- Salazar y. see Salazar Mazarredo, ---------.

Marban, Pedro. 44465

Marble, Manton. (44466)-44467, (68620)

Marble, Susan B. 44468

Marble worker's manual. 44469

Marblehead, Mass. 44470, (44473)

Marblehead, Mass. Marine Society, see Marine Society, Marblehead, Mass.

Marblehead, Mass. Ordinances, etc. 102629

Marblehead, Mass. School Committee. (44473)

Marblehead. 105979

Marblehead advertiser. see Salem gazette and Newbury and Marblehead advertiser.

Marblehead Union Moral Society. 44471

Marbles of Vermont. 29513

Marbois, Francois de Barbe. see Barbe-Marbois, Francois de, Marquis, 1745-1837.

Marbury, -------. (44475)

Marc dans son ile. 16427

Marcandier, ------- (44476)

Marcaria; or, altars of sacrifice. 23136

Marcay, ------- de. 44477

Marcel, J. J. ed. 57436

Marcellus. pseud. Essay on the liberty of the press. (44479)

Marcellus. pseud. Letter. see Ramsay, Allan.

Marcellus. pseud. Letter to the Hon. Daniel Webster. see Webster, Noah, 1758-1843.

Marcellus. pseud. To the Hon. Timothy Pickering. 95933

Marcellus. pseud. To the public. 95981

Marcellus; published in the Virginia gazette. 44478

Marcelo de S. Joseph. 84384

Marcenado, Alvaro de Navia Osorio, Marques de Santa Cruz de. see Santa Cruz de Marcenado, Alvaro de Navia Osorio, Marques de, 1684-1732.

Marcgraf, Georg, 1610-1644. 1371, 7588, 63028-(63029)

March, Major. pseud. Faca. see Willcox, Orlando Bolivar, 1823-1907.

March, A. 616

March, Alden, 1795-1869. 44481-44482

March, Angier. 34434, 44483, 86361, 105172

March, Charles W. 44484-44485

March, Daniel. 44486-44487

March, Edmund. 44488, 97311

March, Edward. 13350, 102425

March, Francis A. 44489

March, Walter. pseud. Shoepac recollections. see Willcox, Orlando Bolivar, 1823-1907.

March, Walter. pseud. Walter March; or, shoepac recollections. see Willcox, Orlando Bolivar, 1823-1907.
March y Labores, J. (44491)
Marcha, Jose Maria Solano y. see Solano y Marcha, Jose Maria.
Marcha dedicada a la Sra. Da. Ana Maria Guarte. 100627
Marcha patriotica por el ciudadano M. B. 98906
Marcha que en celebridad de comenzarse la grande obra. 98348
Marchand, Etienne. 24851, 44492
Marchant, -------. illus. 95405
Marchant, John. (5988), 44493
Marchant, William. (44494)
Marchants' humble petition and remonstrance. 2847
Marchants mapp. of commerce. 71906
Marche-Courmont, Ignatius Hungari de la. 28193, 28197, (40693)
Marche du Colonel Bosquet. 84647
Marches of Lord Cornwallis in the southern provinces. 94397
Marchese, Domenico Maria. (44495), 73190
Marchese, Maria. see Marchese, Domenico Maria.
Marchetti, P. Marie. tr. 57702
Marching and fighting of the Tenth Maine Regiment. (74303)
Marching through Georgia. 83677
Marchmont, Hugh Hume Campbell, 3d Earl of. supposed author 90630-90631
Marci Antonii Coccii Sabellici In rapsodiam historiarvm. 74658
Marci Antonii Coccii Sabellici Rapsodiae historiarvm. 74658
Marci Bnuetani Monachi Celestine co[n] gregationis mathematici. (66476)
Marci Pauli Veneti, Historici fidelissimi justa ac praestantissimi. 59231
Marci Velaseri, Matthaei F. Ant. N. Reip. Augustanae quodam duumviri. 102615
Marcilla, Pedro Garces de. supposed author 99454
Marcina. pseud. Dialogo. (19233)
Marckmann, J. W. 44496
Marco-Antonio. pseud. Saldos contra o paiz. 44497
Marco Polo Venetiano. 44498
Marcokv Esyvkiketv. 51589
Marconnay, H. Leblanc de. 44499
Marcou, Jane (Belknap) 4441
Marcou, Jules, 1824-1898. 5808, 44500-44505
Marcoy, Paul. pseud. Scenes et paysages dans les Andes. see Saint-Cricq, Laurent.
Marcoy, Paul. pseud. Voyage a travers l'Amerique du Sud. see Saint-Cricq, Laurent.
Marcoy, Paul. pseud. Travels in South America. see Saint-Cricq, Laurent.
Marcullus. pseud. Reflections on itinerary parliaments. see Kershaw, Philip G.
Marcus. pseud. 105142
Marcus. pseud. Examination of the expediency and constitutionality of prohibiting slavery in the state of Missouri. see Blunt, Joseph.
Marcus. pseud. Letters of Marcus addressed to De Witt Clinton. see Van Ness, William Peter.
Marcus. pseud. Letters of Marcus and Philo-Cato. see Van Ness, William Peter.

Marcus. pseud. Plot discovered. see Van Ness, William Peter. and Davis, Matthew L. incorrectly supposed author
Marcus. pseud. Reply. 44510
Marcus, Moses. 44509
Marcus Brutus. pseud. Serious facts. 35932, 79263
Marcus Latham's Mission on Fort Hill, Boston. see Boston. Marcus Latham's Mission on Fort Hill.
Marcus-Riff oder der Krater. 16429
Marcus Voss, aus Travemunde. 28653, 100785
Marcus Warland. 31436
Marcy, E. E. ed. 55547
Marcy, Marvin, Jr. defendant 12105, (12110), 96947, 96950, 4th note after 98168
Marcy, Randolph Barnes, 1812-1887. 36377, 44511-44516, 58775, 68476, 84774, 85356
Marcy, William Learned, 1786-1857. 44517-44518, 53687, 53922, (60810), 78366, 78368, 78405, 78407, 98409 New York (State) Governor, 1833-1839 (Marcy) see also U. S. Department of State. U. S. War Department.
Mardi Gras in New Orleans. 44519
Mardiros, Bp. of Arzendjan, 15th cent. 75417
Mardis, Samuel Wright, 1800-1836. 26346
Mare clausum. (78971)-78974
Mare, ex jure naturae seu genitum. (78971), 78982
Mare liberum. (78971)
Mare magnum. 29148
Mare undique apertum. 38781
Marechal de Bellefonds. 86861
Maregnier, -------. 44520
Mareou, John. 69946
Mares, Leon. 44521
Mareschal, Ambrose, 1764-1828. 44522 see also Baltimore (Archdiocese) Archbishop (Mareschal)
Marest, G. 37949, 40707, note after 96500
Marestier, M. 44523
Marett, Philip. 96929 see also Portugal. Consulado. Boston.
Maretzek, Max. 44524
Marforie, pseud. Pasquin and Marforie on the peace. 58994
Margallo, Pedro. 44525
Margaret: a story of life in a prairie home. 42825
Margaret. A tale of the real and ideal, blight and bloom. 36840
Margaret Moncrieffe. 9214
Margaret Percival in America. 44526
Margaret Smith. pseud. see Whittier, John Greenleaf, 1807-1892.
Margaretha Roberval op het eiland la Demo-iselle. 19557
Margarida Ignacia. Sor 34186
Margarita filosofica. 69132
Margarita philosophica. 69121-(69122), 69124), 69128, 69130-69131
Margarita philosophia cu[m] additionibus nouis. 69125, (69129)
Margarita philosophica noua cui annexa sunt sequentia. 69128
Margarita philosophica noua cui insunt sequen tia. 69127
Margarita philosophica noua cui insunt sequentia epigrammata. 69126
Margarita philosophica nova. 69126

Margarita Philosophica, rationalis, moralis philosophiae principa. 69130
Margarita philosophica toti9 philosophie ratio-[n]alis. 69125
Margarita philosophica totius phiae ratio[n]alis. 69124
Margarita phylosophica. (69123)
Margarot, Maurice. defendant (78988)
Margil, Antonio. 44527-(44529)
Margileida. (39083)
Marginal notes. (32953), note after 102754
Marginalia. 61070
Margini, Giovanni Antonio. see Magini, Giovanni Antonio, 1555-1617.
Margolle, Elie, 1816-1884. tr. 46971
Margonne, ---------, fl. 1642. 75014
Margraf, J. 44530
Margret Howth. 44531
Margry, Pierre, 1818-1894. 44532-(44534), 96172
Marguerite de Valois, Queen Consort of Henry IV, King of France, 1553-1615. 44535-44536
Maria del Occidente. pseud. Zophiel. see Brooks, Maria (Gowen)
Maria Francisca, Queen of Portugal, 1734-1816. 14378 see also Portugal. Sovereigns, etc., 1777-1816 (Maria I)
Maria Isabella Louisa, Queen of Spain, 1830-1904. see Isabel II, Queen of Spain, 1830-1904.
Maria Theresa, Empress of Austria, 1717-1780. 82915, 96543-96544 see also Austria. Sovereigns, etc., 1740-1780 (Maria Theresa)
Maria, --------- Santa. see Santa Maria, ----------.
Maria, Agostinho de Santa. see Santa Maria, Agostinho de.
Maria, Pedro Beltran de Santa Rosa. see Beltran de Santa Rosa Maria, Pedro.
Maria, Bernardo de Santa. see Bernardo de Santa Maria. Fray
Maria, Domingo Santa. see Santa Maria, Domingo.
Maria, Felix de Jesus. see Jesus Maria, Felix de.
Maria, Francis. pseud. Joseph Brown; or the young Tennessean. see Summers, Thomas Osmond.
Maria, Goncalo Garcia de Sancta. see Garcia de Sancta Maria, Goncalo.
Maria, Isidoro de. 44538
Maria, Juan de Santa. see Santa Maria, Juan de.
Maria, Miguel de Santa. see Santa Maria, Miguel de.
Maria, Miguel Santa. see Santa Maria, Miguel.
Maria, Nicolas de Jesus. see Nicolas de Jesus Maria.
Maria, Pedro de Santa. see Pedro de Santa Maria.
Maria de Alcala, Josef. (44539)
Maria de Heras, Bartolome, Abp. 31455, 44541, 71450 see also Lima (Arch-diocese) Archbishop (Maria de Heras)
Maria de Lorento, --------- Penalver, Conde de Santa. see Penalver, -------, Conde de Santa Maria de Lorento.
Maria Jaboatam, Antonio de Santa. see Jaboatam, Antonio de Sancta Maria.
Maria Jaboatam, Antonio de Sancta. see Jaboatam, Antonio de Sancta Maria.
Maria Maraver, Juan de Santa. see Santa Maria Maraver, Juan de.

Maria Rugama, Laeciado da Jose. see Da Jose Maria Rugama, Laenciado. petitioner
Maria y Sevilla, Manuel Santa. see Santa Maria y Sevilla, Manuel.
Maria Antoinette, Queen of France, who, from gambling, was brought to the guillotine. 102473
Maria Monk and her impositions. (49996)
Maria Monk and the nunnery of Hotel Dieu. 84021, 92145
Maria Monk's show-up. (49996)
Maria R******. pseud. see Randall, Maria.
Maria Santissima pintandose milagrosamente en bellissima imagen. 22061
Maria Ward's disclosures. note after 101315
Mariage aux Etats-Unis. (10918)
Mariages de Canada. 40158
Marian, Ala. Bell and Everett Club. see Bell and Everett Club, Marian, Ala.
Marian Rooke. 78846
Mariana. Sor 44557
Mariana, ---------, fl. 1625. 44556
Mariana, Juan de. 1536-1624. (44543)-44554, (49188), 77904
Mariana, Juan de, fl. 1768. (44555)
Marianae, Joannis. see Mariana, Juan de, 1536-1624.
Marianela, Juan de Meneses y Padilla, Marques de. see Meneses y Padilla, Juan de, Marques de Marianela.
Marianna Flora (Ship) in Admiralty 96929
Mariano de Jesus. 76222
Mariano, Jos. 44557A
Mariano de Abarca, Joseph. 24157, 44557B
Mariano de Manero, Jose. see Manero, Jose Mariano de.
Mariano Mozino, Jose. see Mozino, Jose Mariano.
Mariategui, F. J. 44559
Marie Charlotte Amelie Augustine Victorie Clementine Leopoldine, Empress of Mexico. see Carlota, Empress of Mexico, 1840-1927.
Marie de Berniere. 81234
Marie de L'Incarnation, Mere, 1599-1672. 44562-(44563), 44861, 70132, 5th note after 99504
Marie de Saint Bonaventure, Mere Superieure. 67011-67014, (67494) see also Hospi-talieres. Quebec. Mere Superieure.
Mare, --------- Poyen Sainte-. see Poyen Saint-Marie, ---------.
Marie, Jane. 44560
Marie, P. 44561, 3d note after 96964
Marie-Galante. 101350
Marie, ou les moeurs du jour. 16550
Marie, ou l'esclavage aux Etats-Unis. 4188
Marietta, Ohio. Citizens. 98639
Marietta, Ohio. College. see Marietta College, Marietta, Ohio.
Marietta, Ohio. English School. 44571
Marietta, Ohio. Ordinances, etc. (44564)
Marietta, Ohio. Public Schools. 44567
Marietta, Ohio. Semi-Annual Session of the Ohio Grand Division of the Sons of Temperance, 1851. see Sons of Tem-perance of North America. Ohio. Grand Division. Semi-Annual Session, Marietta, 1851.
Marietta & Cincinnati Railroad Company. 44565
Marietta and the oil and mineral region. 44566
Marietta College, Marietta, Ohio. (44569), (44572)

Marietta College, Marietta, Ohio. Library.
(44569)
Marietta College, Marietta, Ohio. Society of
Inquiry. 86074
Marietta College, Marietta, Ohio. Society of
Inquiry. Cabinet. 86074
Marietta College, Marietta, Ohio. Society of
Inquiry. Library. 86074
Marietta College, Marietta, Ohio. Trustees.
(44569), 44570
Marietta Collegiate Institute and Western
Teachers' Institute. see Marietta
College, Marietta, Ohio.
Marietta Female Seminary. see Marietta
College, Marietta, Ohio.
Marietta register. 84386
Marig, John. (44573)
Marigni de Mandeville, -------. (44574)
Marilia de Itamaraca. 81300
Marillier, P. G. engr. 27650, (63966),
68421
Marin, Buena Ventura. 44575
Marin, Gom. M. 44578
Marin, J. 44580
Marin, Jose, 1619-1699. 78217
Marin, Juan de Campos. defendant 53968
Marin, Manuel Gomez. (44579)
Marin, Miguel Angel. 44581
Marin, T. defendant 65926
Marin Ben Jesse, David. 4713, 14833, 40486,
(44576)-44577
Marin del Solar, Mercedes. see Solar,
Mercedes Marin del, 1804-1866.
Marine Bible Society, Boston. 36035
Marine Bible Society, Charleston, S. C. 12092
Marine Bible Society, New York. 54373
Marine Corps in Mexico. 19822
Marine Court of the city of New York. (42928)
Marine des Etats-Unis avant la guerre et la
marine actuelle. 43361
Marine disasters on the western lakes.
(29823)
Marine engines. 70816
Marine insurance. (80361)
Marine Insurance Companies of Baltimore.
petitioners 94531
Marine mammals of the north-western coast
of North America. (77441)
Marine practice of physic and surgery. 94063
Marine Quarantine Hospital, New York. see
New York (City) Marine Quarantine
Hospital.
Marine Seizures. 44582
Marine Society, Boston. 6734
Marine Society, Marblehead, Mass. 44472
Marine Society, Newburyport, Mass. 54919
Marine Society, Newport, R. I. 55038
Marine Society, New York. 54372
Marine Society, New York. Charter. 54372
Marine Society, Salem, Mass. (75670)-75671
Marine telegraphic list of merchant vessels.
72676
Marineide risate e la strigliate del S. Robusto
Pogommega. (51557)
Marineo, Lucio. 44583-44587
Mariner call'd upon. 46269
Mariners and Others of the Ship Bristol.
petitioners 35571
Mariner's chronicle, containing narratives of
the most remarkable disasters at sea.
44588
Mariner's chronicle; or authentic and complete
history of popular shipwrecks. 21252
Mariner's Church, Boston. see Boston.
Mariner's Church.

Mariner's Church, Philadelphia. see Phila-
delphia. Mariner's Church.
Mariners' Church, Portland, Me. see Port-
land, Me. Mariners' Church.
Mariner's Church, Philadelphia. 61805
Mariner's dictionary, or American seaman's
vocabulary. 44590, 50410
Mariner's Family Industrial Society of the Por
of New York. 54374
Mariner's library. 44591
Mariners' marvellous magazine. 44592, 93423
Mariners of England. 86885, 86896, 5th note
after 101885
Marinho, Jose Antonio. 44593
Marins Francais. 6892
Marin's trumpet air. 78217
Marion, Francis. 35723
Marion, M. (17716), 44594, 72371-(72372)
Marion, Robert. 33044-(33046), 102489
Marion, Mass. Selectmen. (44596)
Marion, N. Y. General Convention of the
Christian Church, 1850. see Christian
Church. General Convention, Marion,
N. Y., 1850.
Marion County, Ky. St. Mary's College. see
St. Mary's College, Marion County, Ky.
Marion. Beelden uit het leven te New-York.
78463
Marion. By Manhattan [pseud.]. 78462
Marion College, Mo. 44597
Marion Harland. pseud. see Terhune, Mary
Virginia Hawes.
Marion; or, the hero of Lake George. 55375
Marion Union School, Cleveland. see Cleve-
land. Marion Union School.
Mariposa Company. Committee of the Bond-
holders. 44599
Mariposa Company, . . . New York. 44599
Mariposa estate. 44600
Maris, --------. (44601)
Maris, George. 66737
Marital power exemplified in Mrs. Packard's
trial. 58105
Maritime and mercantile tables. 71154
Maritime campaign of 1778. 44602
Maritime canal of Suez. (56059)
Maritime capture. 44603
Maritime flags of all nations, together with a
geographical sketch. 44604
Maritime flags of all nations. With a geo-
graphical description of every empire.
24311
Maritime journal. 14692
Maritime law. (16890), 44605
Maritime Mission, Boston. see Boston Mari-
time Mission.
Maritime rights and obligations of belligerents
30234
Maritime sanitary service of the United States
84260
Maritime scraps. 44606
Marius. pseud. Letters of Marius. see Day
Thomas.
Mariz, Pedro de. 44608
Mariz Carneiro, Antonio de. 44607
Marjoribanks, Alexander. 44609
Marjoribanks, John. (44610), 82075
Mark and hasty. 82012
Mark H. Newman's almanac. (55015)
Mark of Zion's children. 50661
Mark Pencil. pseud. see Pencil, Mark.
pseud.
Mark Rowland; a tale of the sea. 82119
Marke, Desdemona. 44611
Marker, Henry M. 58675

Marrat, W. ed. 50202
Marratt, Joseph. 94680-94682
Marre, J. de. 100766
Marrero, Abraham. 44681
Marriage, Francis. 44682
Marriage act. (80053)
Marriage: an epic poem. 102439
Marriage and morals in Utah. (64968)
Marriage ceremonies as now used. 44683
Marriage customs and modes of courtship.
   50439
Marriage in the United States. (10919)
Marriage of Cana. 103570
Marriage of Pocahontas. 42135
Marriage process in the United States.
   84201-84202, 84212
Marriage rites, customs, and ceremonies.
   29999, 44684
Marriages from 1851-1870. (66238)
Married off. 4851
Married or single? 78790-78791
Marriot, Sir James, Bart., 1730?-1803. see
   Marriott, Sir James, Bart., 1730-1803.
Marriott, Charles. 32996, 44685
Marriott, G. 44686
Marriott, Sir James, Bart., 1730?-1803.
   27283, 44687-44691, (81429), 96892,
   100949 see also Great Britain. Judge
   Advocate General.
Marriott, John. (44692)
Marrocas, F. J. dos Sanctos. see Sanctos
   Marrocas, F. J. dos.
Marron, P. H. 44693
Marrons de la Jamaique. 69055
Marroquin, Francisco, Bp. 44694
Marrow of historie. 67599
Marrow of the Gospel. 46402
Marrow of the most modern divinity. 79272
Marryat, Frank. 44695
Marryat, Frederick, 1792-1848. 11217, 40392,
   (44696)-44702, 102148
Marryat, Frederick, 1792-1848. supposed
   author 18450
Marryat, Joseph. 39068, 42953, 44703-44709,
   95689, 102780
Marry-it, Captain, C. B., (Common Bloat).
   pseud. see Captain Marry-it, C. B.,
   (Common Bloat). pseud.
Marrying by lot. 50963
Mars, Emmanuel. 1717
Mars, Gabrielle Anne Cisterne de Courtiras,
   Vicomtesse de Saint. see Saint Mars,
   Gabrielle Anne Cisterne de Courtiras,
   Vicomtesse de, 1804-1872.
Mars, James. 44710
Mars, R. Weston. 85361
Marsden, J. 44713
Marsden, J. B. 44711-44712
Marsden, Joshua. 44713-44716
Marsden, Peter. 44717
Marsden, William. 44718-44719
Marseille, France. Academie. 98351
Marsellus, Nicholas J. (44720)
Marsenie, --------. 97472
Marsequunt. Indian Chief (15440)
Marsh, --------. M. D. 99217
Marsh, Abram. 44721
Marsh, Anne. 44722
Marsh, Anthony. 66686
Marsh, Miss C. 44725
Marsh, Miss C. incorrectly supposed author
   44724
Marsh, Carolina (Crane) 44723
Marsh, Charles, 1774?-1835. 44726
Marsh, Charles, 1774?-1835. incorrectly
   supposed author 99395

Marsh, Charles, fl. 1814. 44727
Marsh, Daniel. 44728, 102466
Marsh, Daniel. engineer 44729-44730,
   72369, 93145
Marsh, Ebenezer Grant. 44731-44732, 93804,
   105938 see also Yale University. Class
   of 1803. Tutor.
Marsh, Ephraim. 44733
Marsh, George Perkins, 1801-1882. 14828,
   21545, (44734)-44737
Marsh, Mrs. George Perkins. see Marsh,
   Caroline (Crane)
Marsh, Henry. 66020
Marsh, Herbert. (44738)
Marsh, J. W. 44740
Marsh, James. 44739
Marsh, John. reporter 52560
Marsh, John, 1743-1821. 4102, (44741)-44744
Marsh, John, 1788-1868. 1240, 44745-(44749)
Marsh, Jonathan. 44750-44752
Marsh, Jonathan B. defendant 96908
Marsh, Joseph, fl. 1878. 99001
Marsh, Joseph, fl. 1833. 44753
Marsh, Josiah. (44754)
Marsh, Lennard. (44755), (57296)
Marsh, Luther Rawson. 44756, 91632
Marsh, Othniel Charles, 1831-1899. 44757
Marsh, Robert. 102466
Marsh, Roswell. 44758-(44759), 91471
Marsh, Sidney H. 44760
Marsh, W. 44761
Marsh, William H. 44762
Marsh. firm publishers 44763
Marshal, R. 44764, 2d note after 95515
Marshal of France. 81174
Marshal of the District of Columbia. 38764
Marshall, --------. illus. 31471
Marshall, Mrs. --------. 44806
Marshall, --------, fl. 1849. 10015
Marshall, A. E. reporter 27036
Marshall, Alexander K. 44765
Marshall, B. petitioner 44766
Marshall, Christopher. 44767-44768
Marshall, Edward Chauncey. (44769)-44770
Marshall, Emily. ed. 73252
Marshall, Emma. 44771
Marshall, G. W. 34330
Marshall, George. 44772
Marshall, Henry. 97441
Marshall, Herbert. 44773
Marshall, Humphrey, 1756-1841. 44774-44775,
   (44778)-44780, (67442)
Marshall, Humphrey, 1812-1872. 44781-(44782)
   56422
Marshall, Humphry, 1722-1801. 44776-44777
Marshall, James, fl. 1825-1833. 44783-44784
Marshall, James, 1834-1896. 44785
Marshall, James V. 44786
Marshall, John. defendant 20630 see also
   Bank of Illinois. President. defendant
Marshall, John, 1755-1835. 2446, 8246, 9426,
   27081, 27293, 44787-44796, 82974, 8297
   100066, note after 101528, 101546-10154
   101710, 101843, 105321 see also Vir-
   ginia. General Assembly. Committee
   to Superintend an Edition of All Legisla-
   tive Acts Concerning Lands.
Marshall, John, 1784?-1837. 44797
Marshall, John A. 44798
Marshall, John G. 44802
Marshall, John George, 1786-1880. 44799-
   44801
Marshall, Joshua. 44803
Marshall, Josiah T. 44804-44805
Marshall, Mary M. (Dyer) fl. 1818. 11976,
   21593-(21598), 57844, note after

97893-97895, note after 104781, note
after 105575
Marshall, Orsamus H. 44807, 51806, (55421)
Marshall, S. V. (44808)
Marshall, Stephen. 80205
Marshall, T. A. reporter 82247-82248
Marshall, T. W. M. 44813
Marshall, Thomas. 44809, 70270, 2d note
after 100580
Marshall, Thomas F. 44810-44812, (70981)
Marshall, William. 96595, 96695 see also
U. S. Commissioner to the Miami
Indians. U. S. Commissioner to the
Potawatomi Indians.
Marshall, William, illus. 76456
Marshall, William, of Philadelphia. 44814
Marshall, William H. 10716
Marshall. firm 89541
Marshall, Mo. Marshall Academy. see
Marshall Academy, Marshall, Mo.
Marshall Academy, Marshall, Mo. 44815
Marshall College, Mercersburg, Pa. (44816)
Marshall College, Mercersburg, Pa. Goethean
Literary Society. (44816)
Marshall College, Mercersburg, Pa. Goethean
Literary Society. Library. (44816)
Marshall tragedy. Its cause. 84810
Marshalls, appointed by the Committee of the
Honorable Legislature. 101871
Marshalship in North Carolina. 27863
Marshfield, Mass. School Committee. 44817
Marshfield Agricultural and Horticultural
Society. (44818)
Marshpee Indians. see Mashpee Indians.
Marsh's masonic register. 44763
Marsillac, J. (44820)-44821
Marston, Edward. 44822
Marston, George. 44823
Marston, Morrill. defendant at court martial
34824
Marsupiale Americanum. 98637
Marsy, Francois Marie de. (44825)
Martel, M. 44826
Martelo o Otero, Jose Ramon. 44827
Martels, Heinrich von. 44828
Marten, Anthony. 44820
Marten, Ennalls. 44866
Marten, Frederick. (72185)-72187
Marten, Nathaniel. 66686
Martene, Edmond. 99363
Martenet, Simon J. 44830
Martens, Charles de. 44831-(44832), 44833
Martens, Friedrich. 4935-4936, 14374, 31593,
(38712), 44834-44838, note after 100855
Martens, Georg Griedirch von, 1756-1821.
44839-44849
Martens, M. 44850
Martensen, H. A. tr. 77690
Martenze, Claes. 44851
Martha. pseud. Some arguments against
wordly-mindedness. see Smith, Eunice.
Martha (Ship) in Admiralty 29308
Martha Preble Oxnard. 65009
Martha Washington. 42135
Martha Washington Society. 97813
Martha Washington Temperance Society, New
Haven, Conn. (53016)
Martha Washington Total Abstinence Society,
New Bedford, Mass. see New Bedford
Martha Washington Total Abstinence
Society.
Martha Washingtonianism. (36252)
Martha's Vineyard Agricultural Society. 44852
Martha's Vineyard Camp Meeting. Agent.
(14188)

Martial achievements of Great Britain and her
allies. 44853
Martial law. 55176
Martial law in the colonies. 44854
Martial law . . . report. 101918
Martial law: what is it?' and who can declare
it? 35463
Martial wisdom recommended. 104408
Martin de Nantes. Pere 44906, 51750
Martin de Valencia. 40960, 44930-44932, 2d
note after 98344
Martin Legionensis, Saint. 42066
Martin, of Megiddo, Saint. see Martin
Legionensis, Saint.
Martin, of Werden. printer 99335
Martin, ---------, fl. 1782. (15052)
Martin, ---------, fl. 1838. 25371
Martin, ----------, fl. 1840. 101435
Martin, ----------, fl. 1858. 87793
Martin, --------- San. see San Martin,
----------.
Martin, ---------- Saint. see Saint Martin,
----------.
Martin, Alexander, 1740-1807. supposed author
53397
Martin, Angelique le Petit. 44855
Martin, Antoine Jean Saint. see Saint Martin,
Antoine Jean.
Martin, Baillot de Saint. see Baillot de Saint
Martin, ------.
Martin, Barkley. (44856)
Martin, Sir Benjamin. 4936
Martin, Benjamin, 1704-1782. 26888, 44857
Martin, Benjamin Ellis, d. 1909. 44858
Martin, Bobert Montgomery. see Martin,
Robert Montgomery.
Martin, Charles. (44859)
Martin, Charles. illus. 37985
Martin, Clara Barnes. 44860, 51155
Martin, Claude. 44861, 70132, 5th note after
99504
Martin, D. illus. 50185, 82375-82376, 82379
Martin, Daniel, 1780-1831. 87479 see also
Maryland. Governor, 1828-1829 (Martin)
Maryland. Governor, 1830-1831 (Martin)
Martin, David. reporter 44862, note after
96881
Martin, Edward Winslow. 44863-44865
Martin, Felix, 1804-1886. (7735), 10522,
10573, 44867-44869, 56612, note after
69259, (80023)
Martin, Francois Xavier, 1762-1846. 42227,
44870-(44874), (55670)
Martin, Frederick, 1830-1883. 43127, 44875
Martin, Frederick S. 44876
Martin, G. 73434
Martin, Gabriel. (8784)
Martin, George. 88221
Martin, Gershom. 44878
Martin, Henri. 26734
Martin, Henry. 44879
Martin, Sir Henry William, Bart. 44880
Martin, Horace. 44881
Martin, Isaac. 44882
Martin, J. H. (44884)
Martin, J. L. 42912, 44885
Martin, J. Sella. 44887
Martin, James. reporter 29000
Martin, James, fl. 1796. (44883)
Martin, James, fl. 1836. 90512
Martin, James Ranald. (44886)
Martin, James Sullivan. supposed author
51794
Martin, John, 1741-1820. (44888)

Martin, John, fl. 1827. 44889
Martin, John, fl. 1827. defendant 44889
Martin, John Paul. pseud. Triumph of truth.
see Bishop, Abraham. supposed author
Martin, Jonas. 44891
Martin, Jose de San. see San Martin, Jose
de, 1778-1850.
Martin, Jose Maria San. see San Martin,
Jose Maria.
Martin, Joseph. ed. 44894
Martin, Joseph, 1740-1808. 96600-96601 see
also U. S. Commissioners to the
Cherokee Indians. U. S. Commis-
sioners to the Chickasaw Indians. U. S.
Commissioners to the Choctaw Indians.
Martin, Joseph G. 44895
Martin, Leopold C. 44896
Martin, Louis Aime. ed. 40702
Martin, Luther, 1748?-1826. 4771, 22233,
37155, 44897-44898, 78749, note after
106002
Martin, M. L. 104884
Martin, Maria. (44900)
Martin, Marie (Guyard) see Marie de
l'Incarnation, Mere, 1599-1672.
Martin, Michael, d. 1821. defendant (44901)-
44903, 2d note after 101000
Martin, Morgan L. 44904
Martin, Moses. 44905
Martin, P. tr. 37828
Martin, Robert Montgomery. 14693, 44907-
44918, note after 93457
Martin, Samuel. 44920
Martin, Theodor. 50542
Martin, Thomas. 44921
Martin, Thomas M. (44922)
Martin, William. USA 44925
Martin, William Charles Linnaeus. (44926)
Martin, William Frederick. (44927)
Martin, William T. 44928
Martin de Chaves, Joseph. 44893
Martin de la Guardia, Heraclio. see Guardia,
Heraclio Martin de la.
Martin de Moussy, V. 44426, 44923-44924,
(51202), 85781
Martin de Pueirredon, Juan. see Pueyrredon,
Juan Martin de.
Martin-Maillefer, P. D. 44919
Martin Tanco, Diego, see Tanco, Diego
Martin.
Martin y Guzman, Jose. 44892
Martin & Co. firm see Howell (J. F.),
Martin & Co. firm
Martin & Thayer. firm 75747
Martin Behaim. 50844
Martin Chuzzlewits liv og haendelser af Boz.
20013
Martin Chuzzlwits liv og levnetslob. 20011
Martin Doyle. pseud. see Hickey, William.
Martin Faber. 81216, 81245, 81278
Martin Faber: the story of a criminal. (81236)
Martin Hylacomylus Waltzemuller ses ouvrages
et ses collaborateurs. 2493
Martin Luther vs. Luther M. Borden and others.
29889
Martin Rattler. 2952
Martin Van Buren. [Address of the Committee
of Friends of Van Buren of Philadelphia.]
(62363)
Martin Van Buren als Staatsman und kunftiger
Prasident. (29008)
Martin Van Buren: lawyer, statesman and man.
9662
Martin Van Buren, President of the United
States of America. To all and singular

to whom these presents shall come,
greeting. 96736
Martindale, Henry C. (44933)
Martindale, Joseph C. (44934)-44935, 101219
Martineau, Harriet, 1802-1876. (14444),
44936-44944, 49192, 81240, 82091, 7th
note after 88114, 103819, 103993
Martineau, James. 44945
Martineau, Mathurin Eyquem, Sieur du. see
Eyquem, Mathurin, Sieur du Martineau.
Martinelli, Vincenzio. 44946
Martinena, Juan Martin de Juan. 44947, note
after 98949
Martines, Joan. cartographer 76838
Martinez, ---------, fl. 1722. 74033
Martinez, Antonio Joaquin Perez. 44948-
(44949), (60897)-60898
Martinez, Domingo. ed. 75987
Martinez, Henrico. 44952
Martinez, Hernando. 94853
Martinez, J. 44954
Martinez, J. G. de Campos y. see Campos
y Martinez, J. G. de.
Martinez, Juan. (44955)
Martinez, Juan Chrys. 44957
Martinez, Juan Gregoria de Campos. 44958
Martinez, M. 44959
Martinez, Maria Loretto. 44960
Martinez, Matthia. tr. 35791
Martinez, Miguel. 85666
Martinez, Miguel G. (44961)
Martinez, Pierre. 44962-44965, 89536-89538,
note after 98538
Martinez, S. F. 94945 see also Coahuila
and Texas (Mexican State) Governor
(Martinez)
Martinez de Araujo, Juan. 44956
Martinez de Chavero, Francisco. 57646
Martinez de la Puente, Jose, fl. 1681. 44953,
(76428)
Martinez de la Torre, Rafael. (44966), 47036,
58273
Martinez de la Vega, Dionisio. 86377 see
also Panama (Province) Audiencia
Presidente.
Martinez de Lejarza, Juan Jose. see Lejarza,
Juan Jose Martinez de.
Martinez de Pinillos, Claudio. 17749, 19968,
(23515), (44951), 62956
Martinez de Yrujo y Tacon, Carlos. see Casa
Yrujo, Carlos Martinez de Yrujo y Tacon
Marques de, 1763-1824.
Martinez Rubio, Nicholas Antonio Guerrero.
see Rubio, Nicholas Antonio Guerrero
Martinez.
Martingale, Hawser. pseud. see Sleeper,
John Sherburne, 1794-1878.
Martinho de Mesquita. (44967)
Martini, Francisco. 4935-4936, 44968
Martini Zeilleri. Itinerarium Hispaniae.
106296
Martiniano de Alencar, J. 44969
Martinico. Number II. 103349
Martiniere, Antoine Augustin Bruzen de la.
see Bruzen de la Martiniere, Antoine
Augustin, 1662-1746.
Martiniere, Pierre Martin de la. see La
Martiniere, Pierre Martin de.
Martinique. 44972, 44975
Martinique. Commissaires du Commerce.
56471
Martinique. Conseil Colonial. 33474
Martinique. Conseil Colonial. Commission
Chargee de Reponder a la Report de M.
de Tocqueville. President. 96071 see
also Le Pelletier du Clary, ----------.

Martinique. Conseil Souverain. 19735

Martinique. Conseil Superieur. 44980

Martinique. Constitution. 79096

Martinique. Governor, 1761-1762 (Le Vassor de la Touche) 44972 see also Le Vassor de la Touche, Louis Charles.

Martinique. Hommes de Couleur. petitioners see Hommes de Couleur de la Martinique. petitioners

Martinique. Laws, statutes, etc. 21412, 44973, 44974, 61263, 77751

Martinique. Principal Inhabitants and Proprietors. Agents. petitioners 95299, 102861 see also Thellusson, George Woodford.

Martinique. Regiments. petitioners 44979

Martinique. Societe de Agriculture et d'Economie Politique. see Societe d'Agriculture et d'Economie Politique a la Martinique.

Martinique. Trois Hommes de Couleur. petitioners see Trois Hommes de Couleur de la Martinique. petitioners

Martinique. 101350

Martinique. Description en vers. 7715

Martinique en 1819. 42637

Martinique en 1820. 42637

Martinique et Guadeloupe. 33474

Martinique et les iles de la Guadeloupe. 50555

Martinique. Observations sur le regime commerciale de cette colonie. 21175

Martinius, C. F. Ph. de. see Martius, Karl Friedrich Philipp von, 1794-1868.

Martins, Antonio de Souza. see Souza Martins, Antonio de.

Martins, Francisco de Souza. see Souza Martins, Francisco de.

Martins Pereira de Alencastre, Jose. see Pereira de Alencastre, Jose Martins.

Martinvs Iacomilvs. see Waldseemuller, Martin.

Martir, Peter. see Anghiera, Pietro Martire d', 1457-1526.

Martirologio de algunos de los primeros insurgentes. 9580

Martirologio de los primeros insurgentes. 48530

Martius, Galleottus. ed. 66471

Martius, Karl Friedrich Philipp von, 1794-1868. 22562, 31593, 38241, 44984-44999, 52240, 57195, (65038), 77220, 1st note after (74627), 77968, 89548-89551

Martling-man. 13717

Marton, Manuel M. 44899

Martyn, Benjamin. 45000-(45003), 83978, 86573, 86574

Martyn, Benjamin. supposed author (56847), 66723, 87900

Martyn, J. H. 45005

Martyn, Joannis. 45004

Martyn, Richard. 99860

Martyn, S. T. 45006-45007

Martyn, W. Carlos. 45008

Martyr, Bp. d'Arzendjan. see Mardiros, Bp. of Arzendjan, 15th cent.

Martyr, Peter. see Anghiera, Pietro Martire d', 1457-1526.

Martyr de Buenacasa, Pedro. see Buenacasa, Pedro Martyr de.

Martyr. (28510)

Martyr age in the United States. By Harriet Martineau. (44939)

Martyr age of the United States of America. 45014

Martyr of freedom. 92121

Martyr of Sumatra. 42783

Martyr of the nineteenth century. 41522

Martyr president. 41211

Martyr president. A discourse, delivered in in the First Presbyterian Church. 90550

Martyr president. [A poem.] (54959)

Martyr president. A sermon preached before the Baldwin Place Church. 21806

Martyr president. A sermon preached in Grace Church, Brooklyn Heights, N. Y. 32396

Martyr-president. A sermon preached in the Church of St. Paul, Leavenworth. 22017

Martyr president. An oration . . . before the colored citizens of Raleigh, N. C. 82500

Martyr president. Our grief and our duty. 9647

Martyr prince. 2877

"Martyr to liberty." 21811

Martyrdom in Missouri. (39844)

Martyrdom of Frederick. 33965-33966

Martyrdom of Jacques De Molay. 85516

Martyrdom of John Brown. 8523

Martyrdom of Joseph Smith and his brother Hyrum. 83153, 83160

Martyrdom of Lopez. (30325)

Martyrdom of the two prophets, Joseph and Hiram Smith. 71919

Martyre du Venerable P. Bernardin de Guistang. 9873

Martyred president: a sermon preached in the First Presbyterian Church. 72059

Martyred president. Grand funeral march. 64286

Martyria; or Andersonville prison. 30073

Martyris, Petri. see Anghiera, Pietro Martire d', 1457-1526.

Martyrologium magnum oder il cudesch grands dels martyrs. 45015

Martyrs and heroes of Illinois. 3533

Martyrs, and the fugitive. 63358

Martyr's monument. 40981

Martyrs' Monument Association, New York. 94461

Martyrs' Monument Association, New York. Finance Committee. 94461

Martyrs of Jesus, and sufferers for His sake, vindicated. 5631, note after 103702

Martyrs, or a history of persecution. (74429)

Martyrs to the revolution in the British prison-ships in the Wallabout Bay. 94461

Martyr's triumph. (47442)

Martyrs, who for our country, gave up their lives. 1430, (45016), 72820

Marure, Alejandro. 45017-45020

Marure, Alejandro. supposed author 45020, 50228, 69179

Marvel, Ik. pseud. Reveries of a bachelor. see Mitchell, Donald Grant.

Marvel of nations. 84472, 84475-84477

Marvell, Andrew. 45021-45022

Maruelle, Francisco Antonio. 46951

Marvellous things done by the right hand. (12324)

Marvellous works of creation and providence. 25975

Marvelous chronicle. 25676

Marvelous works of God. 89265

Marvels of prayer. 83582, 83587

Marvin, Abijah P. 45023-45026

Marvin, Dan. 45027

Marvin, Dudley. 45028

Marvin, Elihu P. 45029-45030

Marvin, Henry. (45031)

Maryland. Citizens. 23537

Maryland. Citizens. petitioners (45084), 45276

Maryland. Commission On the Survey of the Sounds Lying On the Eastern Shore of Virginia, Maryland and Delaware. see Commission for Survey of the Sounds on Eastern Shore of Virginia, Maryland and Delaware.

Maryland. Commissioner on the Survey of the Boundary Between Maryland and Virginia. 45090 see also Lee, Thomas J.

Maryland. Commissioners Appointed to Examine into the Practicability of a Canal from Baltimore to the Potomac. 3066, 45098

Maryland. Commissioners Appointed to Examine into the Practicability of a Canal from Baltimore to the Potomac. Engineer. 3066, 45098

Maryland. Commissioners Appointed to Revise the Rules of Practice, Pleadings, &c., in the Courts of the State. 65473

Maryland. Commissioners Appointed to Survey the River Potomac. see Commissioners of Maryland and Virginia Appointed to Survey the Potomac River.

Maryland. Commissioners For the Improvement of the Navigation of the River Susquehannah. see Maryland. Susquehannah Commissioners.

Maryland. Commissioners For the Survey of the Sounds Between Cape Charles and Henlopen. see Commission For Survey of the Sounds on Eastern Shore of Virginia, Maryland and Delaware.

Maryland. Commissioners on a Proposed Canal from Baltimore to Conewago. 3073, 45098

Maryland. Commissioners on the Boundary Lines of the States of Maryland, Pennsylvania & Delaware. see Joint Commissioners on the Boundary Lines of the States of Maryland, Pennsylvania & Delaware.

Maryland. Commissioners on the Potomac River. see Commissioners of Maryland and Virginia Appointed to Survey the Potomac River.

Maryland. Commissioners on the Western Boundary. 45090, 45986

Maryland. Commissioners to Adjust the Boundary Line of Virginia and Maryland. see Joint Commission for Marking the Boundary Line Between Maryland and Virginia.

Maryland. Commissioners to Build an Hospital for Insane Persons. 45323

Maryland. Commissioners to Run and Mark the Division Line Between Maryland and Virginia, on the Eastern Shore of Chesapeake Bay. see Joint Commission for Marking the Boundary Line Between Maryland and Virginia.

Maryland. Commissioners to Survey the Potomac River. see Commissioners of Maryland and Virginia Appointed to Survey the Potomac River.

Maryland. Commissioners to Wait on the President of the United States. 45322

Maryland. Committee Appointed by the Several Counties of the Province of Maryland, Annapolis, 1774. see Maryland (Colony) Convention, Annapolis, 1774.

Maryland. Committee on Public Instruction. 45134

Maryland. Constitution. 1269, 1271, 2071, 5316, 6360, 9672, 16086-16092, 16097, 16099-16103, 16107, 16113, 16118-16120, 16133, (19476), 25790, 33137, 45113-45117, 45123, 45124-45126, 45138, 45146, 45189, (47188), 59771, (66397), 85595, 100342, 104198

Maryland. Constitutional Convention, Annapolis, 1850-1851. 45237, (54123)

Maryland. Constitutional Convention, Annapolis, 1850-1851. Webster Dinner, 1951. 89202

Maryland. Constitutional Convention, Annapolis, 1850-1851. Committee on the Fugitive Slave Case. (45332)

Maryland. Constitutional Convention, Annapolis, 1864. 45124, 45356

Maryland. Constitutional Convention, 1867. (45294), 45356

Maryland. Convention. 1788. 22233, note after 106002

Maryland. County School Commissioners. 45135

Maryland. Court of Appeals. 8481, 39873, 45112, 68042

Maryland. Court of Chancery. 104870

Maryland. Declaration of Rights. 85595

Maryland. Electors, 1840. 45288

Maryland. Episcopal Ministers. petitioners see Protestant Episcopal Church in the U. S. A. Maryland (Diocese) Clergy. petitioners

Maryland. Evangelical Lutheran Synod. see Evangelical Lutheran Synod of Maryland and Virginia.

Maryland. General Assembly. 45061, 45136, 45161, 45278, 45292, 45297, 45352, 45362, 45809, 77448, 87538, 99771

Maryland. General Assembly. Committee on Agriculture. 45158, 45327

Maryland. General Assembly. Committee on Claims. 45324

Maryland. General Assembly. Committee on Education. 45137

Maryland. General Assembly. Committee on Message of the Governor. 45266

Maryland. General Assembly. Committee on Public Lands. 45360

Maryland. General Assembly. Committee on the University. Majority. (45389)

Maryland. General Assembly. Committee on the University. Minority. (45389)

Maryland. General Assembly. Committee on Ways and Means. 45326, (45335)

Maryland. General Assembly. Democratic Members. see Democratic Party. Maryland.

Maryland. General Assembly. Joint Committee on Federal Relations. (45336)

Maryland. General Assembly. Joint Committee on the Memorial of the Regents of the University. (45389)

Maryland. General Assembly. Joint Committee on the Penitentiary. 45233, 45257

Maryland. General Assembly. Joint Committee on the State Library. 45370, 77448

Maryland. General Assembly. Joint Committee Upon Reports and Memorials of the Police Commissioners and the Mayor and City Council of Baltimore. 3078

Maryland. General Assembly. Joint Committee to Adjust and Mark the Eastern Shore Boundary Between Maryland and Virginia. 45090

Maryland. General Assembly. Joint Committee to Investigate the Affairs of the Maryland

Maryland. Joint Commissioners on the Boundary Lines Between the States of Pennsylvania, Delaware and Maryland. see Joint Commissioners on the Boundary Lines between the States of Maryland, Pennsylvania & Delaware.

Maryland. Laws, statutes, etc. 2992, 3008, 3053-3054, 3061, (9198), 12501, (18789), 20298-(20299), 23765, 27004, 31596, 39414, 43177, 45048, 45081, 45107, 45112, 45126, 45132, (45138)-45139, 45150, 45162, 45166-45167, 45169, 45191, (45203), 45207, (45220), 45243, 45262, 45271, (45274), 45300-45301, 45355, 45367, 45396, 47113, 47915, 45809, 52051, 62051, (62080), 68712, 70820-70821, (76752), 82438, 87331, 88397, 89066, 91422, 93920, 93938, 99760, 100398, 101996, 105506

Maryland. Medical and Chirurgical Faculty. see Medical and Chirurgical Faculty of the State of Maryland.

Maryland. Meeting of the Deputies Appointed by the Several Counties of the Province of Maryland, at the City of Annapolis, 1774. see Maryland (Colony) Convention, Annapolis, 1774.

Maryland. Militia. 3025, 13158, 31704, 51599

Maryland. Militia. Courts Martial (Hanson) (30261)

Maryland. Militia. First Baltimore Battalion. 63283

Maryland. Militia. 39th Regiment. Officers. 45264

Maryland. Penitentiary. Board of Directors. 45233

Maryland. Penitentiary. Board of Directors. Committee. (45232)

Maryland. Quartermaster General. 45267

Maryland. School Commissioners. 45137

Maryland. School for the Blind, Baltimore. Directors. 45227

Maryland. Southern Rights Convention, Baltimore, 1861. see Southern Rights Convention, Baltimore, 1861.

Maryland. State Agricultural Chemist. 45157-45158 see also Higgins, James. Tyson, Philip T.

Maryland. State Board of Education. 45137

Maryland. State Convention on Internal Improvements, Baltimore, 1825. see Convention on Internal Improvements, Baltimore, 1825.

Maryland. State Convention to Frame a New Constitution, 1864. see Maryland. Constitutional Convention, Annapolis, 1864.

Maryland. State Convention to Frame a New Constitution, 1867. see Maryland. Constitutional Convention, 1867.

Maryland. State Librarian. 45370, (71282)-71283 see also Ridgely, David.

Maryland. State Library. 45369-45370, 71483

Maryland. State Normal School, Baltimore. (45371)

Maryland. State Normal School, Baltimore. Principal. 45135

Maryland. State Superintendent of Public Instruction. see Maryland. State Board of Education.

Maryland. State School for the Deaf, Frederick. (45226)

Maryland. State Vaccination Agent. 82780 see also Smith, James, 1771-1841.

Maryland. Superintendent of Public Instruction. see Maryland. State Board of Education.

Maryland. Supreme Court. Chief Justice. 93214

Maryland. Susquehannah Commissioners. 93938 see also Ellicott, Thomas. Howard, William. M'Kim, Isaac. Patterson, J. W. Winder, William H.

Maryland. Topographical Engineer. (45156), 45158 see also Alexander, John H.

Maryland. Treasurer. 45158, 45380

Maryland. Treasurer of the Western Shore. 45121, 45381

Maryland. Treasury Board. 49334

Maryland. Treasury Department. Comptroller. 45380

Maryland. Union Bank. see Union Bank of Maryland.

Maryland. University. (45199), (45386), (45389)

Maryland. University. Academic Department. (45389)

Maryland. University. Faculty of Physic. 45387

Maryland. University. Medical Department. 45388

Maryland. University. Medical Department. Professors. petitioners (45389)

Maryland. University. Regents. petitioners (45389)

Maryland. University. Register. (45199)

Maryland. University. Trustees. (45389)

Maryland. University. Trustees. petitioners (45389)

Maryland. Washington Society. see Washington Society of Maryland.

Maryland. Western Shore Treasury. 45080

Maryland Academy of Science and Literature. 45198

Maryland Administration Convention, Baltimore, 1827. 45291

Maryland ahiman rezon. 37138, 45200

Maryland almanack for . . . 1759. 45201

Maryland and Delaware Railroad Company. President and Directors. 45202

Maryland and Massachusetts. 45809

Maryland and the union. 89391

Maryland Anthracite Coal Company. (45203)

Maryland campaign of September, 1862. 19630

Maryland Central Railroad. 45205

Maryland Central Railroad. To the citizens of Baltimore and others interested. 45205

Maryland citizen's companion to the polls. (5866), 1st note after 100788, 2d note after 104412

Maryland Club, Baltimore. see Baltimore. Maryland Club.

Maryland code. 45207

Maryland colonization journal. 45208

Maryland Colonization Society. see Maryland State Colonization Society.

Maryland Committee of the United States Christian Commission. see United States Christian Commission. Committee of Maryland.

Maryland contested election case. 30834

Maryland Convention on Internal Improvements, Baltimore, 1825. see Convention on Internal Improvements, Baltimore, 1825.

Maryland educational journal. (45209)

Maryland, &c., versus Mary Harris, &c. 67065

Maryland Eye and Ear Infirmary, Baltimore.
see Maryland Eye and Ear Institute,
Baltimore.
Maryland Eye and Ear Institute, Baltimore.
45210
Maryland farmer and machinist. pseud.
Brief narrative. see Stabler, Edward.
Maryland farmer and mechanic. (45211)
Maryland gazette. 45076, 100233, 100317,
102399
Maryland historical magazine. 3886, 83828,
92940
Maryland Historical Society. 812, 9364,
(11068), (18821), 27378, 30480-(30481),
35563, 39225, 39840-(39481), 35563,
37409, 39225, (45211A), 45215-45217,
(47096), 47098, 47104-47105, 50844,
55504, 62972, (74106), 80327, 83018,
83976, 92793, 103352-103353, 105651
Maryland Historical Society. Library. 45213
Maryland Historical Society. Picture Gallery.
Annual Exhibition, 1st, 1848. 45214
Maryland Historical Society. President.
45212
Maryland Historical Society and the Peabody
Institute. (45211A), 45217, 47105
Maryland Hospital, Baltimore. see Baltimore.
Maryland Hospital.
Maryland Industrial School for Girls, Balti-
more. 45219
[Maryland] Inebriate Asylum, report of the
Committee. 45168
Maryland Institute for the Education of the
Deaf and Dumb. see Maryland. State
School for the Deaf, Frederick.
Maryland Institute for the Instruction of the
Blind. see Maryland. School for the
Blind, Baltimore.
Maryland Institute for the Promotion of the
Mechanic Arts, Baltimore. 45225,
97610
Maryland Institute for the Promotion of the
Mechanic Arts, Baltimore. Annual
Exhibition, 1827. 45225
Maryland Institute for the Promotion of the
Mechanic Arts, Baltimore. Annual
Exhibition, 1848. 45221, (45224)
Maryland Institute for the Promotion of the
Mechanic Arts, Baltimore. Annual
Exhibition, 1849. 45221
Maryland Institute for the Promotion of the
Mechanic Arts, Baltimore. Annual
Exhibition, 1850. 45221
Maryland Institute for the Promotion of the
Mechanic Arts, Baltimore. Annual
Exhibition, 1851. (45223)
Maryland Institute for the Promotion of the
Mechanic Arts, Baltimore. Annual
Exhibition, 1851. Judges. 45225
Maryland Institute for the Promotion of the
Mechanic Arts, Baltimore. Board of
Managers. 45222
Maryland Institute for the Promotion of the
Mechanic Arts, Baltimore. Library.
45225
Maryland Institute for the Promotion of the
Mechanic Arts, Baltimore. Library
Department. 45225
Maryland Institute for the Promotion of the
Mechanic Arts, Baltimore. Treasurer.
45222
Maryland Institute of Education. (45220)
Maryland Jockey Club. (45227)
Maryland jockey club [rules]. (45227)
Maryland journal. 22337, 99771

Maryland Ladies' Southern Relief Association.
see Ladies' Southern Relief Association
of Maryland, Baltimore.
Maryland line in the Confederate States Army.
(27717)
Maryland Marble Company, Baltimore. 45229
Maryland Medical and Chirurgical Faculty.
see Medical and Chirurgical Faculty of
the State of Maryland.
Maryland medical journal. 83664
Maryland Military Academy. 45230
Maryland muster roll. War of 1812. 45231
Maryland, my Maryland. 83677
Maryland not a Roman Catholic colony. 52286
Maryland pension roll. Doc. 514. 45234
Maryland pocket almanack, for . . . 1834.
(45235)
Maryland pocket annual. 45092
Maryland pocket magazine. 45236
Maryland politics and the election of speaker.
91683
Maryland Prayer Book and Homily Society.
see Protestant Episcopal Church in the
U. S. A. Maryland (Diocese) Prayer
Book and Homily Society.
Maryland Protestant Episcopal Theological
Seminary. see Protestant Episcopal
Theological Seminary of Maryland.
Maryland Reform Convention. see Maryland.
Constitutional Convention, Annapolis,
1850-1851.
Maryland register. 45238
Maryland Relief Association of the Penitentiary.
see Relief Association of the Maryland
Penitentiary.
Maryland report, . . . relative to school lands.
45136
Maryland resolutions. 47009
Maryland scheme of expatriation examined.
45239
Maryland school journal. (45240)
Maryland Scott Corresponding Club. see Scott
Corresponding Club of Maryland.
Maryland slavery and Maryland chivalry.
38752
Maryland Society for Promoting the Abolition
of Slavery. 45241
Maryland Society for Promoting the Abolition
of Slavery. petitioners 47745
Maryland Society for Promoting the Abolition
of Slavery, and the Relief of Free
Negroes, and Others, Unlawfully Held in
Bondage. see Maryland Society for
Promoting the Abolition of Slavery.
Maryland Soldiers' Relief Association. 45365
Maryland State Bible Society. Board of
Managers. 45242
Maryland state business directory. 45248
Maryland State Colonization Society. 45244
see also Friends of African Colonization.
Meeting, Baltimore, 1827.
Maryland State Colonization Society. Board of
Managers. 45246
Maryland State Colonization Society. Charter.
45243
Maryland State Colonization Society. President.
45331
Maryland State Fair, for the Christian and
Sanitary Commissions, Baltimore, 1864.
34427
Maryland State gazetteer and business directory
(45247)
Maryland State Temperance Society. 45249
Maryland toleration. 810
Maryland Tract Society. (45148)

Mason, Stephen N. petitioner (70673)

Mason, Stevens Thomson, 1811-1843. 48753-48754, 96572 see also Michigan (Territory) Governor, 1835-1836 (Mason)

Mason, Stevens Thomson, 1811-1843. defendant 96860

Mason, T. B. 7151

Mason, Theodorus Bailey Myers. see Myers-Mason, Theodorus Bailey.

Mason, Thomas. 45483

Mason, William. 45487

Mason, William. defendant 12105, (12110), 96947, 96950, 4th note after 98167

Mason, William, 1724-1797. 45485

Mason, William, 1764-1847. 45484

Mason, William, fl. 1776. 96353

Mason, William, fl. 1860. 45486

Mason, William Powell. 45488-45489, 1st note after 96930A, 1st note after 96936

Mason. firm publishers 45421

Mason, N. H. Centennial Celebration, 1868. 31846

Mason, N. H. School Committee. 45490

Mason, N. H. Selectmen. 45491

Mason County, Ky. Circuit Court. 43864, 98688

Mason and Dixon's line. 98736

Mason and Dixon's line: a history. 98734

Mason and Slidell: a yankee idyll. 42435

Masonic address and vindication of masonry delivered before the brethren. 84864

Masonic address at Grafton, Mass. 13454

Masonic address at laying the corner stone of St. John's Episcopal Church. 8920

Masonic address at Leicester, Mass. 3877

Masonic address at Lowell. (37747)

Masonic address at Princeton. 13454

Masonic address at Walpole. 19038

Masonic address . . . at Wiscasset. 58668

Masonic address [by James Tillary.] 95823

Masonic address [by John H. Spencer.] 89360

Masonic address, by John J. W. Payne. 59289

Masonic address, Dedham, 1816. 19038

Masonic address, delivered before Burns Lodge. 91494

Masonic address, delivered before the fraternity in Waco. 89267

Masonic address, delivered before the Grand Royal Arch Chapter. 96365

Masonic address, delivered before the Worshipful Master. 91924

Masonic address, delivered in St. John's Church, Portsmouth. 91925

Masonic address of James D. Westcott. 102959

Masonic address which was delivered by Rev. Mr. Starr. 90566

Masonic addresses. 31342

Masonic advertiser. 34551

Masonic almanac for 1828. 45509

Masonic & social address. 70922

Masonic and social address pronounced at laying the corner-stone. 64433

Masonic biography and dictionary. 73526

Masonic biography; or sketches of eminent freemasons. 50340

Masonick blasphemy. 70596

Masonic calendar. 52651

Masonic character and correspondence, of General Washington. (50333), 101849

Masonic charge at Boston, Dec. 27, 1780. 37233

Masonick charge: delivered at Greenfield, Massachusetts. 100782

Masonic chronicle. 45510

Masonic code; containing an historical synopsis of the Grand Lodge of Alabama. 77411

Masonic code for trials and punishments. 58975

Masonic constitutions, or illustrations of free masonry. 50400

Masonic Convention, Knoxville, Tenn., 1814. 94797

Masonic digest. (82292)

Masonic dirge. 101870

Masonic discourse at Amherst, N. H. (24539)

Masonic discourse at Danvers, Mass., Sept. 26, 1810. 3913

Masonic discourse at Newton. (71532)

Masonic discourse at Princeton, July 24, 1823. 30330

[Masonic] discourse at Providence, Jan. 1, 1784. (57213)

Masonic discourse at the consecration of Ancient Land Mark Lodge. 70926

Masonick discourse; delivered at Greenfield. 83728

Masonic discourse, delivered before the Mount Vernon Lodge in Washington. 81596

Masonic discourse, delivered before the Missouri Lodge. 64691

Masonic discourse, delivered December 27th, Anno Lucis 5800. 70929

Masonic discourse pronounced before . . . Tyrian Lodge. 70921

Masonic discourse, spoken at Greenfield. 3877

Masonic discourses. (11866)

Masonic discourses at Lexington, Mass., June 24, 1803. 4350

Masonic discourses, 1798 and 1803. 97602

Masonic eclectic. 45511

Masonic emblems explained. 30521

Masonic eulogy on . . . the late Thomas Smith Webb. 33906

Masonic eulogy, on the life of the Illustrious Brother George Washington. 5769

Masonick eulogy, pronounced 24th June, 1794. 30521

Masonic eulogy upon the death of Brother Seth Smith. 97477

Masonic family re-united. 87841

Masonic Festival, Dubuque, Iowa, 1867. see Freemasons. Iowa. Masonic Festival, Dubuque, 1867.

Masonic Fire Society, Gloucester, Mass. 27598

Masonic formalities of burying the dead. 91363

Masonic funeral discourse. (41805)

Masonic garland. (50333)

Masonic gavel. 45512

Masonic hymn. 70915, 70929

Masonic jewel. (45513)

Masonic journal. see Crystal and masonic journal.

Masonic journal; devoted to masonry, science, and literature. (45514)

Masonic lament, on the death of Washington. 101717, 101850

Masonic library. 34138

Masonic manual, or freemasonry illustrated. 84309

Masonic martyr. 50872

Masonic melodies. (64779)

Masonic messenger. 45515

Masonick minstrel. 99835
Masonic mirror (1863?-1868) 45516
Masonic mirror (1870-   ) 45517
Masonic mirror and American keystone.
    45518
Masonic mirror and mechanic's intelligencer.
    45519, 92847
Masonic mirror and mechanic's intelligencer.
    Editor. (50333), 101849 see also
    Moore, Charles W.
Masonic mirror and organ of the Grand Lodge
    of Kentucky. 45520
Masonic miscellany and ladies' literary
    magazine. 45521
Masonic monitor. 45522
Masonic monthly. (45523)
Masonic monthly journal, devoted to the
    interests of the craft. 37545
Masonic monthly journal. . . . Edited by
    George Frank Gouley. 25802
Masonic notice. The annual session of the
    Grand Lodge of the State of Vermont
    will be holden. 99185
Masonic oaths neither morally nor legally
    binding. 95156
Masonic oaths, with notes. 99145
Masonic obligations unlawful. (46628)
Masonic ode. 91925
Masonic oration. 91925
Masonic oration at Charleston, S. C., March
    21, 1803. (18299)
Masonic oration at Charleston, S. C., Sept.
    23, 1801. (18299)
Masonic oration at Nantucket, 1796. 40102
Masonic oration at Newburyport, June 24,
    1801. 11214
Masonic oration . . . by S. Hempstead, Esq.
    (31298)
Masonic oration, delivered by Jesse Bledsoe.
    (5895)
Masonic oration; delivered on the 24th June,
    1817. 101908
Masonic penalties. 91681, 99197
Masonic poem at Masnfield. (35746)
Masonic portrait of Washington. 31011
Masonic prayer. 71515
Masonic principia. A poem. 70921
Masonic record; a monthly magazine. 45524
Masonic register. see Marsh's masonic
    register.
Masonic register. see Vocal companion, and
    masonic register.
Masonic register and union. 45525
Masonic register for 5855. 50109
Masonic register for 5812. 30305
Masonic register, for the year of masonry,
    5843. 89382
Masonic review. 45526
Masonic review and keystone. 45527
Masonic Seminary of North Carolina. see
    Freemasons. North Carolina. Grand
    Lodge. Masonic Seminary. Trustees.
[Masonic] sermon at Boston. 8641
Masonic sermon at Groton. 30521
Masonic sermon at Haddam. 33129
Masonic sermon at Lancaster. 365
Masonic sermon at New Marlborough. 11545
Masonic sermon at Newburyport. (3887)
[Masonic] sermon at St. John's, N. B. (5640)
Masonic sermon at Walpole, Mass. 14224
Masonic sermon at Worcester. 3105
Masonic sermon on general benevolence.
    81409
Masonic sermon, preached at Greenfield,
    Massachusetts. 71510

Masonic signet and journal. 45528
Masonic sketches and reprints. 33576
Masonic song book. 45529
Masonic sun. 45530
Masonic tidings. 45531
Masonic token. 45532
Masonic trestle-board. (50333)
Masonic trowel. 45533
Masonic union. 45534
Masonic vocal manual. 43622
Masonick . . . see Masonic . . .
Masonry and anti-masonry. 17466
Masonry on Christian principles. (37664)
Masonry revived. 79255
Masonry the same all over the world. 45535
Mason's handbook to California. 45421
Mason's Inn at Mitchell Lighthouse. 96335
Maspeth poems. (26221)
Masque. 84678C
Masquerade and other poems. (77339)
Mass Meeting, Cooper Institute, New York,
    1862. see Loyal League of Union
    Citizens, New York.
Mass Meeting, Cooper Institution, New York,
    1863. see Loyal League of Union
    Citizens, New York.
Mass Meeting, Cooper Institute, New York,
    1869. see Republican Party. New
    York State.
Mass Meeting, Lexington, Ky., 1847. see
    Lexington, Ky. Mass Meeting, 1847.
Mass Meeting, New York, 1865. see National
    Celebration of Union Victories, New
    York, 1865.
Mass meeting at . . . [Philadelphia.] 62078
Mass Meeting by the Democratic Republican
    Citizens of New York, Opposed to the
    Wilmot Proviso, 1850. see Democratic
    Party. New York State. New York
    City.
Mass Meeting Held at Washington's Head
    Quarters, Newburgh, N. Y., 1852. see
    Democratic Party. New York State.
    Newburgh.
Mass meeting in Union Square, New York,
    March 6th, 1865. 51942
Mass meeting of the citizens of New York, at
    the Cooper Institute, March 6, 1862.
    41029
Mass meeting of Citizens of New York to
    Approve the Principles Announced in the
    Message of Andrew Johnson, New York,
    1866. see Republican Party. New
    York State. New York City.
Mass meeting of citizens of New York to
    approve the principles announced in the
    message of Andrew Johnson. 36181
Mass Meeting of Citizens of Pierce County,
    Washington Territory. see Pierce
    County, Washington (State) Mass Meeting.
Mass Meeting of Loyal Citizens, Union Square,
    New York, 1862. see Loyal League of
    Union Citizens, New York.
Mass Meeting on the North Pennsylvania Rail
    Road, Philadelphia, 1854. see Phila-
    delphia. Mass Meeting on the North
    Pennsylvania Rail Road, 1854.
Massa, Joao Alves. 45536
Massachusee psalter. 45537
Massachuset psalter. 45537
Massachusettensis. pseud. Origin of the
    American contest. see Leonard, Daniel.
Massachusettensis. pseud. Strictures and
    observations. 40101, 92828
Massachusettensis. 40097

Massachusettensis: or a series of letters.
40100

Massachusetts. pseud. Eleven reasons for
believing that Amherst College will be
in [sic] incorporated. 89138, 1st note
after 104432

Massachusetts. pseud. New states. 45538

Massachusetts. pseud. Treaty of Ghent, and
the fisheries. 277, 96755

Massachusetts, Junior. pseud. Plea for the
south. 45539

Massachusetts (Colony) (7962), (21090),
25791, 32968, 33698, 39706, 45622,
45661, 45965, 46722, 53388, 56966,
58359, 59034, 62743, 63488, (65323),
78431, 85217, 90611, 97158, 104846,
106052

Massachusetts (Colony) appellants 45665,
52803, 52847

Massachusetts (Colony) plaintiffs (45666)-
45667

Massachusetts (Colony) Agent. (25510)

Massachusetts (Colony) Charter. 1069,
(7962), 12162-12163, 19051, (41430),
45417, 45565, 45567, 45571, (45673),
45674, 45697, 45921-45922, 45939,
52140-52141, 59034, (63477), 91853,
95638, 98182, 1st note after 99889

Massachusetts (Colony) Citizens. petitioners
95946

Massachusetts (Colony) Commissioners on the
Boundary Between Massachusetts and
New York, 1767. 36738, 45689

Massachusetts (Colony) Commissioners to
the Six Nations of Indians, 1745. 34601

Massachusetts (Colony) Commissioners to
Treat with the Eastern and Penobscot
Indians, 1753. 15436, 36737 see also
Bowdoin, James, 1729-1790. Hubbard,
Thomas. Pepperell, Sir William, Bart.,
1696-1759. Wendell, Jacob. Winslow,
John.

Massachusetts (Colony) Commissioners to
Treat with the Eastern Indians, 1749.
34083 see also Choate, John, 1697-
1765. Hutchinson, Thomas, 1711-1780.
Otis, James. Williams, Israel.

Massachusetts (Colony) Commissioners to
Treat With the Eastern Indians, 1752.
(34857), 36736, 62579, 5th note after
102623 see also Hubbard, Thomas.
Russel, Chambers. Watts, Samuel.
Wendell, Jacob.

Massachusetts (Colony) Continental Navy
Board. (45945)

Massachusetts (Colony) Council. (4924),
6219-6220, (19157), 34084-34086, (45656),
45940, (45945), (45953), (46094), 46132,
80545, (80546), 80549, 88221, 102181,
104088 see also Massachusetts (Colony)
Governor and Council.

Massachusetts (Colony) Council. Agent.
6219-6220

Massachusetts (Colony) Council. Secretary.
78202 see also Addington, I.

Massachusetts (Colony) Court of Admiralty.
96954-96955, 96957

Massachusetts (Colony) Election sermon. see
Massachusetts. Election sermon.

Massachusetts (Colony) General Assembly.
see Massachusetts (Colony) General
Court.

Massachusetts (Colony) General Court. 5628,
9455, 9462, 10134, 16688, (19157),
25354, 34071-34072, (45653), (45680),

45790, (45945), (45953), 46099-46100,
(52609), (53384), (53385), 57493, 63488,
79373, 93334-93336, 96301, 97995,
98500, 101330, note after 103712,
104088, 104796

Massachusetts (Colony) General Court.
petitioners 9462, 33695-33696

Massachusetts (Colony) General Court.
Committee to Enquire Into the Cause
of the Failure of the Penobscot Expedition. (45945)

Massachusetts (Colony) General Court. Committee to Build the Light-House on the
Gurnet. 63476

Massachusetts (Colony) General Court.
Council. see Massachusetts (Colony)
Council.

Massachusetts (Colony) General Court. House
of Representatives. 2349, 4922, 23507,
25296, (32551), 34071, 34084-34086,
45633, (45680), 45695, 45730, 45782-
(45784), (45787), 46012, (46131), 46171,
80545-(80546), 80549, 88221, 2d note
after 89220, 7th note after 97146, 97147

Massachusetts (Colony) General Court. House
of Representatives. petitioners 45933

Massachusetts (Colony) General Court. House
of Representatives. Speaker. (32551)

Massachusetts (Colony) Governor. 82975-
82976 see also Massachusetts (Colony)
Governor and Company. Massachusetts
(Colony) Governor and Council. Massa-
chusetts (Colony) Governor, Council and
Convention.

Massachusetts (Colony) Governor, 1630-1634
(Winthrop) (21090), 33698, 78431-78433,
104846, 106052 see also Winthrop,
John, 1588-1649.

Massachusetts (Colony) Governor, 1637-1640
(Winthrop) (32842) see also Winthrop,
John, 1588-1649.

Massachusetts (Colony) Governor, 1649-1664
(Endicott) 33695-33696 see also
Endicott, John, 1558-1665.

Massachusetts (Colony) Governor, 1673-1679
(Leverett) (25355) see also Leverett,
Sir John, 1616-1679.

Massachusetts (Colony) Governor, 1679-1686
(Bradstreet) see also Bradstreet,
Simon, 1603-1697.

Massachusetts (Colony) Governor, 1687-1689
(Andros) (45953) see also Andros,
Sir Edmund, 1637-1713.

Massachusetts (Colony) Governor, 1689-1692
(Bradstreet) see also Bradstreet,
Simon, 6103-1697.

Massachusetts (Colony) Governor, 1697-1701
(Bellamont) 78202 see also Bellamont,
Richard Coote, 1st Earl of, 1636-1701.

Massachusetts (Colony) Governor, 1702-1715
(Dudley) (19157), 45633, 45705, 46127,
45822, 52601, 67086, 104088 see also
Dudley, Joseph, 1647-1720.

Massachusetts (Colony) Governor, 1716-1723
(Shute) (15436)-(15437), 34654, 80806,
80808 see also Shute, Samuel, 1653-
1742.

Massachusetts (Colony) Governor, 1716-1723
(Shute) petitioner (80807) see also
Shute, Samuel, 1653-1742. petitioner

Massachusetts (Colony) Governor, 1725-1729
(Burnet) 78904 see also Burnet,
William, 1688-1729.

Massachusetts (Colony) Governor, 1730-1741
(Belcher) 4391, 15429, (15440) see also
Blecher, Jonathan, 1682-1757.

Massachusetts (Colony) Governor, 1741-1749 (Shirley) 15435 see also Shirley, William, 1694-1771.

Massachusetts (Colony) Governor, 1749-1753 (Phips) (34857), 62579 see also Phips, Spencer.

Massachusetts (Colony) Governor, 1753-1756 (Shirley) 36730 see also Shirley, William, 1694-1771.

Massachusetts (Colony) Governor, 1760-1769 (Bernard) (15954), 16683, 30754, (32551), (46131), 2d note after 89220, 90611, 7th note after 97146, 97147 see also Bernard, Sir Francis, 1712-1779.

Massachusetts (Colony) Governor, 1769-1774 (Hutchinson) 34071-34072, 34084-34086, (46131)-46132, 2d note after 89220, 103136 see also Hutchinson, Thomas, 1711-1780.

Massachusetts (Colony) Governor and Company. 33698, 78431, 104796, 104846 see also Massachusetts (Colony) Governor.

Massachusetts (Colony) Governor and Company. petitioners 78431

Massachusetts (Colony) Governor and Council. (45656) see also Massachusetts (Colony) Council. Massachusetts (Colony) Governor.

Massachusetts (Colony) Governor, Council, and Convention. petitioners 97547

Massachusetts (Colony) Indian Conference, Arrowsick Island, 1717. (15437)

Massachusetts (Colony) Indian Conference, Concord, 1646. 80205

Massachusetts (Colony) Indian Conference, Deerfield, 1735. (15440)

Massachusetts (Colony) Indian Conference, Falmouth, 1726. 15441, note after (34632)

Massachusetts (Colony) Indian Conference, Falmouth, 1727. 15442, note after (34632)

Massachusetts (Colony) Indian Conference, Falmouth, 1732. 4391, 15429

Massachusetts (Colony) Indian Conference, Falmouth, 1749. 34083

Massachusetts (Colony) Indian Conference, Falmouth, 1754. 36730

Massachusetts (Colony) Indian Conference, George Town, 1717. (15436)-15437, 34654, 80806

Massachusetts (Colony) Indian Conference, St. Georges, 1742. 15435

Massachusetts (Colony) Indian Conference, St. Georges, 1753. 15436

Massachusetts (Colony) Laws, statutes, etc. 91, 6010, 6375, 17042, 22368, (23517), 23522, 25354, 27833, (28387), 39410, 39414, 45546, 45563-45569, 45571, 45652-(45653), 45664, (45673)-45674, 45700, 45733, 45741-45743, 45788-(45792), 46159, 46319, 52140-52141, 52595, 52601, (52603), (53384)-53386, 53388, 63488, (69482), (73483), 74086, 74420, 80205, 86684, 90609, 3d note after 97116, 97546, note after 100381

Massachusetts (Colony) Legislature. see Massachusetts (Colony) General Court.

Massachusetts (Colony) Lieutenant Governor, 1692-1701 (Stoughton) 92349 see also Stouchton, William, 1632-1701.

Massachusetts (Colony) Lieutenant Governor, 1732-1757 (Phips) 34083, (34857) see also Phips, Spencer, 1685-1757.

Massachusetts (Colony) Lieutenant Governor, 1771-1774 (Oliver) 34071-34072, (34085), 103136 see also Oliver, Andrew, 1706-1774.

Massachusetts (Colony) Magistrates. 104843, 104848-104849

Massachusetts (Colony) Militia. 45547, 45727, 45934, 1st note after 48978

Massachusetts (Colony) New Plymouth Patent. 19051, 53034, (63477)

Massachusetts (Colony) President and Council (New Plymouth) 52619, 66686

Massachusetts (Colony) Provincial Congress, Cambridge, 1774. 15529, 15597, 23533, 28391, 45731, 45785, 2d note after 97553

Massachusetts (Colony) Provincial Congress, Cambridge, 1775. 23533, 26318, 45731, 45785, 51804

Massachusetts (Colony) Provincial Congress, Watertown, 1775. (45767), 95952

Massachusetts (Colony) Provincial Congress, 1777. 46096, 70081

Massachusetts (Colony) Secretary. 6735, 45940 see also Oliver, Andrew, 1706-1774.

Massachusetts (Colony) Superior Court, Boston. see Boston. Superior Court.

Massachusetts (Colony) Treaties, etc. 34083, 34601, 85217

Massachusetts. 10734, 12119, 19583, 20468, 27092, (30759A), 44813, (45683), 45717, (45953), 45720, 46068, 55538, 58453, 70578, 83750, 90611, 92392, 96850, 96893, 101350, 103001

Massachusetts, claimants 46068

Massachusetts. defendants (31093), 45686, 46154, 70497, 70550, 70751

Massachusetts. plaintiffs 2599, 8911, 19583, 45682, 46149, (46151)-46154, 57856, (69415), 70646, 70752-70753, 82560, 85430, 96840, 96893, 102319, 4th note after 103741

Massachusetts. Adjutant General. 45620-45621, (45792), 45925, 45919, 45964, 46148, 91456, 92037-92039, 93720, 104842 see also Stone, Ebenezer Whitten. Sumner, William Hyslop.

Massachusetts. Agent for the Prosecution of the Claim Upon the United States for Militia Services During the Last War, 1841. 45993 see also Davis, John.

Massachusetts. Agent on the Claim Against the General Government. 45698, note before 93483, 93484 see also Sullivan, George, 1771-1838.

Massachusetts. Alms Houses. see Massachusetts. State Alms Houses.

Massachusetts. Ancient and Honourable Artillery Company. 74086, 82945, 93468, 90173, 103727 see also Artillery Election sermon.

Massachusetts. Ancient and Honourable Artillery Company. Charter. 74086

Massachusetts. Assayer. 92673

Massachusetts. Associated Mechanics and Manufacturers. see Associated Mechanics and Manufacturers of Massachusetts.

Massachusetts. Asylum for the Insane, Charlestown. see Charlestown, Mass. Asylum for the Insane.

Massachusetts. Attorney General. 5253, 13689, 38091, (45644)-(45645), 46070, (48013), 64269, 65469, 85430, 89627, 96843, 2d note after 101449 see also Adams, Charles. Austin, James

MASSACHUSETTS

Trecothick, 1784-1870. Bidwell,
Barnabas. Clifford, John Henry, 1809-
1876.
Massachusetts. Attorney General. defendant
85212 see also Waterman, Andrew J.
defendant
Massachusetts. Attorney for the Common-
wealth. see Massachusetts. Attorney
General.
Massachusetts. Auditor's Office. 45646
Massachusetts. Bank Commissioners. 45629,
(71091)
Massachusetts. Board of Agriculture. see
Massachusetts. State Board of Agri-
culture.
Massachusetts. Board of Commissioners
of Internal Improvement. see Massa-
chusetts. Board of Internal Improve-
ment.
Massachusetts. Board of Directors of Internal
Improvement. see Massachusetts.
Board of Internal Improvement.
Massachusetts. Board of Education. 44324,
(45649), 84499, 92305
Massachusetts. Board of Education.
Secretary. 22429, 28612, (44317),
44321-44322, 44324, (45649), 45894
see also Mann, Horace, 1796-1859.
Massachusetts. Board of Health. see Massa-
chusetts. State Board of Health.
Massachusetts. Board of Internal Improve-
ment. 5700, 6768, 45996-45998
Massachusetts. Board of Railroad Commis-
sioners. 45963, 90930
Massachusetts. Board of State Charities.
45651
Massachusetts. Board of State Charities.
Secretary. 46126, 76251 see also
Sanborn, Franklin Benjamin.
Massachusetts. Boundary Commissioners.
45999
Massachusetts. Bureau of Labor Statistics.
see Massachusetts. Bureau of Statistics
of Labor.
Massachusetts. Bureau of Statistics of Labor.
46000
Massachusetts. Census, 1840. 79886
Massachusetts. Census, 1845. (45545)
Massachusetts. Citizens. petitioners 27092,
45916, 69728, 97939
Massachusetts. Commissioner of Agriculture.
14535, (69758), 102319 see also Col-
man, Henry.
Massachusetts. Commissioner of Jails.
45681
Massachusetts. Commissioner on Questions
of Title to Land and Boundary Lines at
Gay Head. 59469 see also Pease,
Richard Luce.
Massachusetts. Commissioners for the
Enlargement of the State House for the
Library. (46008)
Massachusetts. Commissioners for the Survey
of a Railway from Boston to Albany.
46009
Massachusetts. Commissioners for the Estab-
lishment of a State Reform School for
Girls. 46007
Massachusetts. Commissioners in Relation to
the Flats in Boston Harbor. 6724, 46010
Massachusetts. Commissioners of Alien
Passengers and Foreign Paupers.
(46011)
Massachusetts. Commissioners of Fisheries
and Game. 46012

Massachusetts. Commissioners of Internal
Improvement. see Massachusetts.
Board of Internal Improvement.
Massachusetts. Commissioners of Sanitation.
see Massachusetts. Sanitation Com-
mission.
Massachusetts. Commissioners of the Fire
District of Pittsfield. see Pittsfield,
Mass. Fire District. Commissioners.
Massachusetts. Commissioners of the Revenue
69496
Massachusetts. Commissioners on an Agri-
cultural School. 45989
Massachusetts. Commissioners on Boston
Harbor. see Massachusetts. Commis-
sioners on Mystic River, Boston Harbor
and Dorchester Bay.
Massachusetts. Commissioners on Boston
Harbor and Back Bay. 6724
Massachusetts. Commissioners on Cape Cod
and East Harbors. 10734
Massachusetts. Commissioners on Criminal
Law. 45935
Massachusetts. Commissioners on Dorchester
Bay. see Massachusetts. Commis-
sioners on Mystic River, Boston Harbor
and Dorchester Bay.
Massachusetts. Commissioners on Inland
Fisheries. 24448
Massachusetts. Commissioners on Matrons
and Labor in Common Jails. (46014)
Massachusetts. Commissioners on Mystic
River, Boston Harbor and Dorchester
Bay. 46015, 51665
Massachusetts. Commissioners of Public
Lands. 43946
Massachusetts. Commissioners on the Boundary
Line Between Rhode Island and Massa-
chusetts, 1846. (46053)
Massachusetts. Commissioners on the Boundary
Line Between Rhode Island and Massa-
chusetts, 1847. (46001)
Massachusetts. Commissioners on the Boundary
Line Between Rhode Island and Massa-
chusetts, 1847. Minority. (46001)
Massachusetts. Commissioners on the Boundary
Line Between Rhode Island and Massa-
chusetts, 1851. 45923
Massachusetts. Commissioners on the Boundary
Line Between Rhode Island and Massa-
chusetts, 1867. 46002
Massachusetts. Commissioners on the Code.
46003
Massachusetts. Commissioners on the Condi-
tion of the Indians in Massachusetts.
(46017)
Massachusetts. Commissioners on the Geo-
logical Survey. see Massachusetts.
Geological Survey. Commissioners.
Massachusetts. Commissioners on the Hoosac
Tunnel. see Massachusetts. Commis-
sioners on the Troy and Greenfield Rail-
road and Hoosac Tunnel.
Massachusetts. Commissioners on the . . .
Pauper System. 46004
Massachusetts. Commissioners on the Revision
of the Statutes. (45627), (46006)
Massachusetts. Commissioners on the Routes
of Canals from Boston Harbour, to
Connecticut and Hudson Rivers. 46013
Massachusetts. Commissioners on the Troy
and Greenfield Railroad and Hoosac
Tunnel. 46016
Massachusetts. Commissioners on the Zoolo-
gical and Botanical Survey. see Massa-
chusetts. Zoological and Botanical Survey.

Massachusetts. General Court. Committee
for the Exercises in Honor of George
Washington, 1800. 101871

Massachusetts. General Court. Committee
of Claims. 46035

Massachusetts. General Court. Committee
of Investigation on Amherst College.
1330, 90716

Massachusetts. General Court. Committee
of Investigation on the Hoosac Tunnel
Loan. 30859

Massachusetts. General Court. Committee
on a System for the Management of the
Lands in the District of Maine. 43950

Massachusetts. General Court. Committee
on Agriculture. (46032)

Massachusetts. General Court. Committee
on as Much of the Governor's Address
as Relates to the Emigration of Young
Women to the West. (46033)

Massachusetts. General Court. Committee
on Banks and Banking. 83857

Massachusetts. General Court. Committee
on Cape Cod Harbor. (46034)

Massachusetts. General Court. Committee
on Certain Military Orders Issued by
Levi Lincoln. 45982

Massachusetts. General Court. Committee
on Education. 23237, 46036, (46077)

Massachusetts. General Court. Committee
on Elections. (23243), 27597, 46027,
68974

Massachusetts. General Court. Committee
on Foreign Relations. (46025)

Massachusetts. General Court. Committee
on Interdicting Slavery in the New
States. 46024

Massachusetts. General Court. Committee
on Labor. 83856

Massachusetts. General Court. Committee
on Memorial of the New England Coal
Mining Company. 69865

Massachusetts. General Court. Committee
on Mr. Browninshield's two Resolutions.
46037

Massachusetts. General Court. Committee
on Petition of Cornelius Coolidge.
(16370)-16371

Massachusetts. General Court. Committee
on Petition of the President and Fellows
of Harvard University. (30759A), (45991)

Massachusetts. General Court. Committee
on Petition of Tufts College. Wesleyan
Academy and Harvard University. 45990

Massachusetts. General Court. Committee
on Petitions of Amherst and Williams
Colleges. 1328

Massachusetts. General Court. Committee
on Pauperism and a House of Industry
in the Town of Boston. 69833

Massachusetts. General Court. Committee on
Public Lands. 45976, 69823

Massachusetts. General Court. Committee
on Railroads and Canals. 46038, 90774

Massachusetts. General Court. Committee
on Slavery. 45817

Massachusetts. General Court. Committee
on So Much of the Governor's Message,
as Relates to Capital Punishment. 45699

Massachusetts. General Court. Committee
on the Boston and Lowell Railroad. 6768

Massachusetts. General Court. Committee
on the Commonwealth Flats Near South
Boston. 46023

Massachusetts. General Court. Committee
on the Embargo. 46040

Massachusetts. General Court. Committee
on the Hollowell and Augusta Bank.
32563

Massachusetts. General Court. Committee
on the Hoosac Tunnel. see Massachusetts. General Court. Committee
on the Troy and Greenfield Railroad
and Hoosac Tunnel.

Massachusetts. General Court. Committee
on the Judicial Reform. (46039)

Massachusetts. General Court. Committee
on the Judiciary. (46019)

Massachusetts. General Court. Committee
on the Kennebeck Claims. (37384), note
before 90746

Massachusetts. General Court. Committee
on the Loan of Arms by the Adjutant
General, 1843. 45983

Massachusetts. General Court. Committee
on the Massachusetts Medical Society.
3756

Massachusetts. General Court. Committee
on the Purchase of the Hancock Estate.
(30181)

Massachusetts. General Court. Committee
on the Revised Statutes. 45786

Massachusetts. General Court. Committee
on the Southern Boundary of Massachusetts. 46042

Massachusetts. General Court. Committee
on the Troy and Greenfield Railroad
and Hoosac Tunnel. 46066

Massachusetts. General Court. Committee
on the War with England, and For
Selecting Delegates to Meet in Convention
46030

Massachusetts. General Court. Committee
of Valuation. see Massachusetts.
General Court. Valuation Committee.

Massachusetts. Committee to Examine and
Report Whether Monies Drawn From the
Treasury, Have Been Faithfully Applied.
(46020)

Massachusetts. General Court. Committee
to Inquire Into Facts Relating to the
Amherst Collegiate Institution. 1327

Massachusetts. General Court. Committee
to Inquire Into the Conduct of the
Proprietors of the Kennebeck Bridge.
37381

Massachusetts. General Court. Committee
to Investigate the Affairs of the Boston
and Providence Railroad Corporation.
6768

Massachusetts. General Court. Committee
to Investigate the Affairs of the Old
Colony Railroad Company. 57121

Massachusetts. General Court. Committee
to Investigate the System of the Public
Charitable Institutions. 45901

Massachusetts. General Court. Committee to
Investigate the Ursuline Convent, Charles
town. 12115, 29620, 68579, note after
93800, 2d note after 98168

Massachusetts. General Court. Committee
to Make a Valuation of the Polls and
Property of the Commonwealth. see
Massachusetts. General Court. Valuation Committee.

Massachusetts. General Court. Committee
to Meet the Exigency Resulting from the
Secession of Maine, 1820. 46026

Massachusetts. General Court. Committee
to Prevent the Admission of Texas as
a Slave State. 46041

Massachusetts. General Court. Committee to Report on a Charge Delivered to the Grand Jury, November Term, 1806, by Theophilus Parsons. 2396

Massachusetts. General Court. Committee to Whom was Referred the Memorial of the Boston Sanitary Association. 46043

Massachusetts. General Court. Committee to Whom was Referred the Message of the Governor. 70654

Massachusetts. General Court. Committee to Whom was Referred the Petition of William Vans. 98552

Massachusetts. General Court. Court of Impeachment. 62642, (65250)

Massachusetts. General Court. Democratic Members. see Democratic Party. Massachusetts.

Massachusetts. General Court. Federal Party Members. see Federal Party. Massachusetts.

Massachusetts. General Court. Joint Committee on a Licence Law. 46087

Massachusetts. General Court. Joint Committee on Education. 30765

Massachusetts. General Court. Joint Committee on Freemasonry. (45505), 45977

Massachusetts. General Court. Joint Committee on Insanity in the State. 46045
Massachusetts. General Court. Joint Committee on the State Prison. 46044

Massachusetts. General Court. Joint Committee Relative to Calling a Convention to Amend the Constitution. (46046)

Massachusetts. General Court. Joint Committee to Whom was Referred the Petition Praying the Removal from Office of Brigadier-General David Putnam. 66773

Massachusetts. General Court. Joint Committee Upon the Proposed Canal to Unite Barnstable and Buzzard's Bays, 1860. 46047

Massachusetts. General Court. Joint Select Committee to Which was Referred the Memorial of the Directors of the Western Rail-Road Corporation. 101519

Massachusetts. General Court. Joint Special Committee on Capital Punishment. 45987

Massachusetts. General Court. Joint Special Committee on Modifying the Laws Relating to the Registration of Births, Marriages, and Deaths. 46049

Massachusetts. General Court. Joint Special Committee on State Lunatic Paupers. 46048

Massachusetts. General Court. Joint Special Committee on the Boston Water Petition. 6785

Massachusetts. General Court. Joint Special Committee on the Boundary Question. 46051

Massachusetts. General Court. Joint Special Committee on the Burial of Massachusetts Dead at Gettysburg. (27248)

Massachusetts. General Court. Joint Special Committee on the Education of Deaf-Mutes. 46048

Massachusetts. General Court. Joint Special Committee on the Message of the Governor Transmitting Resolutions of South Carolina. 46058

Massachusetts. General Court. Joint Special Committee on the Petition of George

Latimer and More than Sixty-Five Thousand Citizens of Massachusetts. 39206

Massachusetts. General Court. Joint Special Committee on the Shire Town of Norfolk County. 73645

Massachusetts. General Court. Joint Special Committee on the Warren Bridge. 8363, 2d note after 101499

Massachusetts. General Court. Joint Special Committee to Consider the Powers of the Legislature, Under the Constitution, in Regard to the Government of Harvard University. (30759A)

Massachusetts. General Court. Joint Special Committee to Whom was Recommitted the Report and Bill Relating to the Suppression of the Evils of Intemperance. (45777)

Massachusetts. General Court. Joint Standing Committee on Federal Relations. 42079, 45883

Massachusetts. General Court. Select Committee Upon the Late Resolutions of the General Assembly of Georgia. 46056

Massachusetts. General Court. Special Committee on Legalizing the Study of Anatomy. 46055

Massachusetts. General Court. Special Committee on the State Liquor Agency. 45995

Massachusetts. General Court. Valuation Committee. 6627, (45716), 45778, (46022), 46028

Massachusetts. General Court. Council. see Massachusetts. Council.

Massachusetts. General Court. House of Representatives. 6408, 11117, 18118, 18119, 27838, 28010, (34074), (37678), 37934, 39206, 40964, 45586-45587, (45616), 45714, 45764, 45768, 45805, (45960), (45948), 45979, 45992, 46081, 46083, 46096, 46113, (46115), 46129, 70091, 88994-88995, 92885-92886, 96874, 97413, 102419

Massachusetts. General Court. House of Representatives. petitioners 45917

Massachusetts. General Court. House of Representatives. Clerk. 98564 see also Cushing, Luther Stearns, 1803-1856.

Massachusetts. General Court. House of Representatives. Committee of Conference. 46027

Massachusetts. General Court. House of Representatives. Committee on Claim of William Vans. 98564

Massachusetts. General Court. House of Representatives. Committee on Impressed Seamen. 46029

Massachusetts. General Court. House of Representatives. Committee on State Printing. 106131

Massachusetts. General Court. House of Representatives. Committee on the Judiciary. 3907

Massachusetts. General Court. House of Representatives. Committee to Consider the Expediency of Abolishing Capital Punishments. 45981, 67908

Massachusetts. General Court. House of Representatives. Committee to Improve the Ventilation in the Representatives' Hall. 46021

Massachusetts. General Court. House of Representatives. Minority. 45954

Massachusetts. General Court. House of
Representatives. Speaker, 1841. 45961

Massachusetts. General Court. Library.
45669

Massachusetts. General Court. Senate.
(1231), 1467-1468, 1479, (2600), 6724,
8363, 8907, 8908, 10734, 11117, 15488,
(19090), 23449, (34074), 45715, (45895),
(45948), (45960), 46010, 46031, (46116),
64653, 77528, 78854, 88215, 85412,
89697, 92885, note after 93362, 2d note
after 101499

Massachusetts. General Court. Senate.
Clerk. 98564 see also Calhoun,
Charles.

Massachusetts. General Court. Senate.
Committee on Amherst College. (1231),
note after 93362

Massachusetts. General Court. Senate. Committee on Claim of William Vans.
98556, 98564

Massachusetts. General Court. Senate.
Committee on Mercantile Affairs and
Insurance. 88215

Massachusetts. General Court. Senate.
Committee on Railways and Canals.
78854, 89697

Massachusetts. General Court. Senate.
Committee on the Kilby Bank. 37738

Massachusetts. General Court. Senate.
Committee on the Petition of the See-
konk Branch Railroad Company. see
Massachusetts. General Court. Senate.
Committee on Railways and Canals.

Massachusetts. General Court. Senate.
Committee on the Votes for Governor
for 1806. Majority. 45606

Massachusetts. General Court. Senate.
Committee on the Votes for Governor
for 1806. Minority. 45606

Massachusetts. General Court. Senate.
Minority. 45955

Massachusetts. General Court. Whig
Members. see Whig Party. Massachusetts.

Massachusetts. Geological Survey. (35400),
45750-45753, 45755

Massachusetts. Geological Survey. Commissioners. 45754

Massachusetts. Governor. 45699

Massachusetts. Governor, 1780-1785 (Hancock)
(45953), 64028, 99007 see also
Hancock, John, 1737-1793.

Massachusetts. Governor, 1785-1787 (Bowdoin)
(45953) see also Bowdoin, James,
1729-1790.

Massachusetts. Governor, 1788-1793 (Hancock)
85865 see also Hancock, John, 1737-
1793.

Massachusetts. Governor, 1800-1807 (Strong)
92885 see also Strong, Caleb, 1745-
1819.

Massachusetts. Governor, 1807-1808 (Sullivan)
42094, 45685, 93495, 93497 see also
Sullivan, James, 1744-1808.

Massachusetts. Governor, 1808-1809 (Lincoln)
45982 see also Lincoln, Levi, 1749-
1820.

Massachusetts. Governor, 1810-1812 (Gerry)
44154, 46128, 58609 see a lso Gerry,
Elbridge, 1744-1814.

Massachusetts. Governor, 1812-1816 (Strong)
(23236), 27838, 33150, 42448, (45960),
46129, 92886, 96874 see also Strong,
Caleb, 1745-1819.

Massachusetts. Governor, 1816-1822 (Brooks)
8357, 43945 see also Brooks, John,
1752-1825.

Massachusetts. Governor, 1823-1825 (Eustis)
97413, 93720 see also Eustis, William
1753-1825.

Massachusetts. Governor, 1825-1834 (Lincoln)
41258, 45698, 45832, 45919, 70654,
note before 93483, 102586, 104842 see
also Lincoln, Levi, 1782-1868.

Massachusetts. Governor, 1834-1835 (Davis)
23237, 72483 see also Davis, John,
1787-1854.

Massachusetts. Governor, 1835-1836 (Armstrong) 46036 see also Armstrong,
Samuel.

Massachusetts. Governor, 1836-1840 (Everett
45572, 45582 see also Everett, Edward
1794-1865.

Massachusetts. Governor, 1840-1841 (Morton)
31784, 37792, 45572 see also Morton,
Marcus, 1784-1864.

Massachusetts. Governor, 1841-1843 (Davis)
45572, 45920 see also Davis, John,
1787-1854.

Massachusetts. Governor, 1843-1844 (Morton)
(67260) see also Morton, Marcus,
1784-1864.

Massachusetts. Governor, 1844-1851 (Briggs)
7943, 45686, 45921-45922 see also
Briggs, George Nixon, 1796-1861.

Massachusetts. Governor, 1851-1853 (Boutwell
45923, 46148, 92038 see also Boutwell
George Sewall, 1818-1905.

Massachusetts. Governor, 1854-1855 (Washburn) 101520 see also Washburn,
Emory, 1800-1877.

Massachusetts. Governor, 1855-1858 (Gardner
64269, 89627 see also Gardner, Henry
James, 1819-1892.

Massachusetts. Governor, 1858-1861 (Banks)
33150 see also Banks, Nathaniel
Prentiss, 1816-1894.

Massachusetts. Governor, 1861-1866 (Andrew)
1470, 1475, 9801, (46033), 46125,
(49198), 70235 see also Andrew, John
Albion, 1818-1867.

Massachusetts. Governor, 1875-1876 (Gaston)
84961 see also Gaston, William, 1820-
1894.

Massachusetts. Harbor Commissioners.
45762

Massachusetts. Historical Agent. 45922,
64099 see also Poore, Benjamin Perley

Massachusetts. Industrial School for Girls,
Dorchester. Board of Managers. (20628

Massachusetts. Industrial School for Girls,
Lancaster. 38788, 46135, 72649

Massachusetts. Industrial School for Girls,
Lancaster. Trustees. 46135

Massachusetts. Industrial School for Girls,
Winchester. (45773)

Massachusetts. Insurance Commissioners.
45776, 45888, 79975

Massachusetts. Laws, statutes, etc. (139),
(611), (6174), 6397, 6540, 6556, 6576,
6593, 6612, 6630, (6692), (6731), 6768,
(6777), 6780, (7962), (10139)-(10140),
(10144), 11869, (12099), 12104, 16078,
17251, (17563), 18117, 18171, 20070,
20072, (21202), (21666), 23012, 23015,
23701, 23703, 23707, 23745, 23748,
23765, 25081, 27945, 28722, 28959,
28969, 30670, (30709), (30749), 30765,
32706, 34449, 39391, 39414, 35559,

40964, (42482), 42486, 42488, 42490,
(42830), 42834, (42482), 45542, (45558)-
45562, 45564, 45569-(45573), 45663,
(45672), (45679), 45687-(45688), 45701,
45744-45748, 45760, 45765, 45772,
(45777)-45778, (45791)-45797, (45799),
45804, 45815, 45827-45829, 45831,
45835, (45845)-45846, (45850), 45859,
45862, (45867), 45869, 45871, 45873-
45874, 45902, 45912, 45924-45925,
(45932), 45938, 45958, 45979, 46095-
46096, 46107, 46120, 46123, 46134,
46148, 46160, 48015, 48849, 48979-
48981, 49146, 52051, 52198, 52336,
52457-52458, 52470-52471, (52496),
52665, (52673), (52745), 52726, 52919-
52920, (55095), 55100, 57119, 57145,
57980, 63466, 67235, 67241, 67254,
(67297), 67722, 69481, (69610), 70081,
70129, 70820-70821, 71047, (71091),
72627, (73233), (73629), 73643, 73653,
73657, (73726), (73731), 74976, 75203,
75627-75629, 75635, 75638, 75641-
75642, 75644, 75645, 75656, 75671,
75674, 75694, 75701-75702, 75711-
75712, 75723, 75727, (75735), 75738,
75802, 77015, (79450), (81943), 82438,
85545, 85632, 85831, 85865, 86643,
88118, 88162, 88215, 88339, 89066,
89642, 90173, 90734, 90771, 91426-
91427, 91429, 91456, 92038-92039,
92166, 93437, 93829, 97812, 2d note
after 98269, 101413, 102758, 103001,
103087, 103484, 103718, 105342, 105410,
105420, 105447
Massachusetts. Lunatic Hospital, Northampton,
46138
Massachusetts. Lunatic Hospital, Taunton.
46138
Massachusetts. Lunatic Hospital, Taunton.
Trustees. 46138
Massachusetts. Lunatic Hospital, Worcester.
45988, 46138 see also Massachusetts.
Commissioners to Superintend the
Erection of a Lunatic Hospital at Wor-
cester.
Massachusetts. Lunatic Hospital, Worcester.
Trustees. 46138
Massachusetts. Meeting of Citizens from
Every Part of the State, Boston, 1815.
45599, 67205, 103783
Massachusetts. Meeting of Citizens for Every
Part of the State, Boston, 1815. Presi-
dent. 45599, 67205, 103783 see also
Whiton, Joseph.
Massachusetts. Meeting of Citizens from
Every Part of the State, Boston, 1815.
Secretary. 45599, 67205, 103783 see
also Greenleaf, Thomas.
Massachusetts. Merchants and Manufacturers.
(82573)
Massachusetts. Militia. 42860, (45728),
45806, (46117), 46148, 74080, 74082,
92037-92039, note after 96144
Massachusetts. Militia. Adjutant General.
see Massachusetts. Militia. Adjutant General.
Massachusetts. Militia. Boston Hussars.
75087
Massachusetts. Militia. Courts Martial
(Binney) 48976, 8th note after 96930A
Massachusetts. Militia. Courts Martial
(Brown) 8525
Massachusetts. Militia. Courts Martial
(Goodale) 27838, 96874
Massachusetts. Militia. Courts Martial (Howe)
48976, 8th note after 96930A

Massachusetts. Militia. Courts Martial
(Kent) 96952, 102153
Massachusetts. Militia. Courts Martial
(Livermore) 96952, 102153
Massachusetts. Militia. Courts Martial
(Loring) 42093-(42096), (45728), 48976,
8th note after 96930A
Massachusetts. Militia. Courts Martial
(Orcutt) 96931
Massachusetts. Militia. Courts Martial
(Prouty) 96952, 102153
Massachusetts. Militia. Courts Martial
(Watson) 96952, 102153
Massachusetts. Militia. Courts Martial
(Winthrop) 104842
Massachusetts. Militia. First Cavalry Regi-
ment. Prescott Light Guard, Company
A (1863-   ) (65301)
Massachusetts. Militia. First Division.
Independent Company of Cadets. 45770
Massachusetts. Militia. First Infantry Regi-
ment. Veteran Association. see First
Massachusetts. Infantry Veteran Associ-
ation.
Massachusetts. Militia. Fourteenth Division.
Officers. petitioners 69582
Massachusetts. Militia. Judge Advocate.
96952, 102153
Massachusetts. Militia. Light Artillery,
Boston. 57585
Massachusetts. Militia. Lincoln Guard, Boston.
41271
Massachusetts. Militia. Master of Ordnance.
45621
Massachusetts. Militia. New Bedford Home
and Coast Guard. Company C. 52506
Massachusetts. Militia. Quartermaster
General. see Massachusetts. Quarter
master General.
Massachusetts. Militia. Roxbury Artillery.
see Massachusetts. Militia. Roxbury
City Guard.
Massachusetts. Militia. Roxbury City Guard.
73727
Massachusetts. Militia. Roxbury Horse Guard.
73723
Massachusetts. Militia. Second Battalion of
Infantry. Company B. see New England
Guards.
Massachusetts. Militia. Surgeon General.
45621, 46155
Massachusetts. Militia. Volunteer Light
Infantry Company. 100758
Massachusetts. Militia. Washington Artillery,
Boston. 101976
Massachusetts. Militia. Winslow Blues,
Boston. 104815
Massachusetts. Mount Pleasant State Prison.
45926
Massachusetts. Overseers of the Poor.
45552
Massachusetts. Quartermaster General.
45621, 45925, 46104 see also Sumner,
William H.
Massachusetts. Railroad Commissioners. see
Massachusetts. Board of Railroad
Commissioners.
Massachusetts. Rainsford Island Hospital,
Boston. Inspectors. 67536
Massachusetts. Rainsford Island Hospital,
Boston. Superintendent. 67536
Massachusetts. Reform School, Westborough.
45903, 46141
Massachusetts. Reform School, Westborough.
Nautical Branch. Trustees. 46141

Massachusetts. Reform School, Westborough.
Superintendent. 90565 see also Starr,
William E.
Massachusetts. Reform School, Westborough.
Trustees. 46141
Massachusetts. Sanitary Survey. 8340, 79886
see also Massachusetts. Sanitation
Commission.
Massachusetts. Sanitation Commission.
39399, 45986, 79884-79885 see also
Massachusetts. Sanitary Survey.
Shattuck, Lemuel, 1793-1859.
Massachusetts. Sanitation Commission.
Chairman. 39399
Massachusetts. School for Idiotic and Feeble-
Minded Youth, Boston. see Massachu-
setts. Walter E. Fernald State School,
Waltham.
Massachusetts. Secretary of State. see
Massachusetts. Secretary of the
Commonwealth.
Massachusetts. Secretary of the Common-
wealth. 45541, 45543-45544, 45549-
45551, 45553-45555, 45712, 45807,
45919, 46076, 46105, 46108, (46146),
46157, 79886, 91456 see also Palfrey,
John Gorham. Warner, Oliver.
Massachusetts. Special Commission on the
Hours of Labor. 46057
Massachusetts. Special Commissioner on the
Appeal of Egbert C. Smyth from the
Visitors of the Theological Institution
in Phillips Academy in Andover. 85212
see also Robinson, George D.
Massachusetts. State Alms House, Bridge-
water. Inspectors. 46134
Massachusetts. State Alms House, Monson.
Inspectors. 46134
Massachusetts. State Alms House, Tewksbury.
Inspectors. 46134
Massachusetts. State Alms Houses. 45663,
46134
Massachusetts. State Archives. 84300
Massachusetts. State Board of Agriculture.
45623, 45824, (45949)
Massachusetts. State Board of Agriculture.
Committee. (24765)
Massachusetts. State Board of Agriculture.
Committees to Visit the County Societies.
45623
Massachusetts. State Board of Agriculture.
Exhibition, 1st, Boston, 1857. 45824
Massachusetts. State Board of Agriculture.
Secretary. (24754), 45623, 45900
Massachusetts. State Board of Agriculture.
State Cabinet. 45900
Massachusetts. State Board of Education. see
Massachusetts. Board of Education.
Massachusetts. State Board of Health. 45650
Massachusetts. State Commission on Cheap
Railway Transportation Between Boston
and Lake Ontario. 45978
Massachusetts. State Director of Art Edu-
cation. 84499 see also Smith, Walter,
1836-1886.
Massachusetts. State Exhibition of the Massa-
chusetts Board of Agriculture. 1st
Boston, 1857. see Massachusetts.
State Board of Agriculture. Exhibition,
1st, Boston, 1857.
Massachusetts. State Hospital, Boston. 12101
Massachusetts. State Library, Boston. 46136-
(46137) see also Massachusetts. State
Archives.
Massachusetts. State Librarian. (46137)

Massachusetts. State Lunatic Hospital,
Northampton. see Massachusetts.
Lunatic Hospital, Northampton.
Massachusetts. State Lunatic Hospital, Taunton.
see Massachusetts. Lunatic Hospital,
Taunton.
Massachusetts. State Lunatic Hospital, Wor-
cester. see Massachusetts. Lunatic
Hospital, Worcester.
Massachusetts. State Normal School, Bridge-
water. 46139
Massachusetts. State Normal School, Framing-
ham. 46139
Massachusetts. State Normal School, Salem.
75748-75749
Massachusetts. State Normal School, West
Newton. 46139
Massachusetts. State Normal School, West
Newton. Principal. 46139
Massachusetts. State Normal School, West-
field. 46139
Massachusetts. State Prison. 7247, 45719,
45902, 73228, note after 90640 see also
Massachusetts. Mount Pleasant State
Prison.
Massachusetts. State Prison. Board of
Visitors. 45902
Massachusetts. State Prison. Directors. 45902
Massachusetts. State Prison. Governor and
Council. 45902
Massachusetts. State Prison. Inspectors.
45902
Massachusetts. State Prison. Officers. 45902
Massachusetts. Street Railway Commissioners.
45725, 46147
Massachusetts. Sundry Citizens. petitioners
see Massachusetts. Citizens. petitioners
Massachusetts. Sundry Inhabitants. petitioners
see Massachusetts. Citizens. petitioners
Massachusetts. Superintendent of Alien
Passengers for the Port of Boston.
(45630)
Massachusetts. Superior Court for the
Counties of Plymouth, Barnstable, &c.
46875, 95436
Massachusetts. Supreme Court. see Massachusetts. Supreme Judicial Court.
Massachusetts. Supreme Court of Probate.
76505
Massachusetts. Supreme Judicial Court.
2490, 4111, 5292, 6148, 6703, 7127,
(8249), (9089), (10144), 12030, 12699,
13162, (13370), 13689, 16395, (18411),
18450, 20072, (21627), 23672, 27591,
30765, 38066, 38091, (42801), (45799),
47291, 58909, 62486, (64800), 65469-
65470, 65979, 66841, (71091), 74372-
74373, 75691, (76977), 76979-76980,
81910, 82578, 83881, 85212, 85430,
85486, 88163, note after 91015, 93506,
93642, 95603, 96808, 96828, 96844,
96848, note after 98561, note after 96852,
96859, 96862, 96893, 96919, note after
96920, 96947, 96950, 97622, 4th note
after 98168, 100902, 101521, 101522,
102319, 102321, 102329, 102586, 102600,
103183, 1st note after 103741, 105543
Massachusetts. Supreme Judicial Court.
Chief Justice. 62486, 79942, 79945,
96919 see also Shaw, Lemuel, 1781-
1861.
Massachusetts. Survey. 45718
Massachusetts. Treasurer. 45557, 45710,
45919, (46059), 46133, 46169
Massachusetts. Treasury. see Massachusetts.
Treasurer.

Massachusetts. University, Amherst. 45811

Massachusetts. Valuation Committee. see Massachusetts. General Court. Valuation Committee.

Massachusetts. Walter E. Fernald State School, Waltham. 45893

Massachusetts. Walter E. Fernald State School, Waltham. Trustees. 45893

Massachusetts. Zoological and Botanical Survey. 22429, 30523, 46069, 46082, (46085), 46086, 59383 see also Dewey, Chester. Gould, Augustus Addison, 1805-1866. Harris, Thaddeus William, 1795-1856. Peabody, William B. D. Storer, David Humphreys, 1804-1891.

Massachusetts. (21090)

Massachusetts a field for church missions. 33964

Massachusetts Abolition Society. 45810

Massachusetts. Agricultural College, Amherst. see Massachusetts. University, Amherst.

Massachusetts agricultural journal. (45812)

Massachusetts agricultural repository and journal. (45812)

Massachusetts Agricultural Society. see Agricultural Society of Massachusetts.

Massachusetts almanack for 1790. 45813

Massachusetts almanac, or the merchant's and farmer's calendar, for 1832. 45814

Massachusetts, and other poems. 21156

Massachusetts and rum. (17833)

Massachusetts and South Carolina. 87870

Massachusetts and the war tax. Speech. 9133

Massachusetts anti-liquor law. 45815

Massachusetts anti-liquor law no failure. (45732)

Massachusetts Anti-masonic state Convention, 1829. see Anti-masonic State Convention of Massachusetts, Boston, 1829.

Massachusetts Anti-masonic State Convention, 1830. see Anti-masonic State Convention of Massachusetts, Boston, 1830.

Massachusetts Anti-masonic State Convention, 1831. see Anti-masonic State Convention of Massachusetts, Boston, 1831.

Massachusetts Anti-slavery Society. 45816, 45817, 52655, 81731

Massachusetts Anti-slavery Society. Board of Managers. 52655

Massachusetts Anti-slavery Society. Committee on Slavery. 45817

Massachusetts Anti-slavery Society. Committee to Consider the Recent Case of Kidnapping from our Soil. 45817

Massachusetts Anti-slavery Society. Committee to Edit the Abolitionist. eds. 52655, 81731

Massachusetts. Anti-slavery Society. Executive Committee. 45810

Massachusetts Anti-slavery Society. Managers. 45817

Massachusetts Anti-slavery Society. Proceedings . . . at the annual meetings held . . . 1854, 1855, & 1856. 45816

Massachusetts archives. 90611

Massachusetts Army and Navy Union. 45819

Massachusetts Army Association. 45818

Massachusetts artillery election sermon. 27304, 28687, 101173 for a complete list of all Artillery Election Sermons, see Artillery election sermon.

Massachusetts Associated Banks for the Suppression of Counterfeiting. see

Associated Banks of Massachusetts for the Suppression of Counterfeiting.

Massachusetts Association of Citizens to Erect a Monument in Honor of Gen. George Washington. see Washington Monument Association, Boston.

Massachusetts Association of the New Jerusalem. see New Jerusalem Church.

Massachusetts Ministers.

Massachusetts Asylum for the Blind. see Perkins Institution and Massachusetts Asylum for the Blind.

Massachusetts Baptist Charitable Society. 45821

Massachusetts Baptist missionary magazine. 45822

Massachusetts Baptist Missionary Society. 45822-45823

Massachusetts Bay. 101002

Massachusetts Bay and New Hampshire. 52847

Massachusetts Bay Company. 106052

Massachusetts Bible Society. 45647

Massachusetts Bible Society. Executive Committee. 45647

Massachusetts business directory. 45825

Massachusetts calendar. 2d note after 95414

Massachusetts calendar & Thomas' New England almanac, 1772. 45826

Massachusetts centinel. 31748-(31749), note after 94676, 1st note after 105630

Massachusetts Charitable Eye and Ear Infirmary, Boston. 45827

Massachusetts Charitable Eye and Ear Infirmary, Boston. Committee. 45827

Massachusetts Charitable Eye and Ear Infirmary, Boston. Surgeons. 45827

Massachusetts Charitable Fire Society. 45828, 103830

Massachusetts Charitable Fire Society. 45828

Massachusetts Charitable Mechanic Association. 8904, 45829

Massachusetts Charitable Mechanic Association. Charter. 45829

Massachusetts Charitable Mechanic Association. Committee on the Annual Fair. 45829

Massachusetts Charitable Mechanic Association. Committee on the Relation of Apprentices to Their Employers. 45829

Massachusetts Charitable Mechanic Association. Exhibition and Fair, 1st, Boston, 1837. 45829

Massachusetts Charitable Mechanic Association. Exhibition of American Manufactures, 10th, 1865. Judges on New Inventions and Machines. 90809

Massachusetts Charitable Mechanic Association. Exhibition of American Manufactures, 11th, Boston, 1869. 45829

Massachusetts Charitable Mechanic Association. Triennial Festival, 16th, 1845. 45829

Massachusetts Charitable Mechanic Association. Triennial Festival, 19th, 181863. (13231)

Massachusetts Church Missionary Society. 45830

Massachusetts clergyman. pseud. Law of Maine and the law of God. 39334

Massachusetts Coal Company (Proposed) 105361

Massachusetts collection of martial music. (72049)

Massachusetts College of Pharmacy. 45831

Massachusetts College of Pharmacy. Charter. 45831

Massachusetts Colonial Society. see Colonial Society of Massachusetts.

Massachusetts Colonization Society. 45832, (81833), 81977, 90703

Massachusetts Colonization Society. Board of Managers. 45832

Massachusetts Committee of Those Opposed to the Licence Law, 1838. (69709)

Massachusetts compendium. 105033-105033A

Massachusetts compiler of sacred vocal music. 45834

Massachusetts Congregational Charitable Society. 45835

Massachusetts Congregational Charitable Society. Charter. 45835

Massachusetts Connecticut Association. see Connecticut Association, Massachusetts.

Massachusetts Constitutional Society. 45836

Massachusetts Convention of Congregational Ministers. see Congregational Churches in Massachusetts. Convention of Congregational Ministers.

Massachusetts defrauded in relation to the public lands. 103273

Massachusetts Dental Agency. 45838

Massachusetts directory. 31073

Massachusetts Division No. 71, Sons of Temperance of North America. see Sons of Temperance of North America. Massachusetts. Division No. 71.

Massachusetts Domestic Missionary Society. 45840

Massachusetts ecclesiastical law. 8882

Massachusetts election! . . . American nomination. 45841

Massachusetts election sermon, 1684. 29637

Massachusetts Emigrant Aid Company. see Emigrant Aid Company of Massachusetts.

Massachusetts Episcopal Missionary Society. (45842)

Massachusetts Episcopal Missionary Society. Board of Directors. (45842), 93081

Massachusetts Episcopal Missionary Society. Treasurer. 93081

Massachusetts Episcopal Society for the Religious Instruction of Freedmen. (45843)

Massachusetts Evangelical Missionary Society. see Evangelical Missionary Society of Massachusetts.

Massachusetts family almanac. 45844

Massachusetts farmer. pseud. Thoughts in a series of letters. see Lowell, John, 1769-1840. supposed author

Massachusetts Fire and Marine Insurance Company. Charter. (45845)

Massachusetts Freeman. pseud. Appeal to the people of Massachusetts. see Allen, George. supposed author

Massachusetts gazette. 1829, 28958, 40097, 51516, 94517, 103126, 104056

Massachusetts gazette and Boston news-letter. 86760

Massachusetts General Hospital, Boston. 56846

Massachusetts General Hospital, Boston. Charter. 45846

Massachusetts General Hospital, Boston. Committee on By-laws. 45846

Massachusetts General Hospital, Boston. Trustees. 45846, 93540

Massachusetts General Hospital. Acts, resolves, by-laws, and rules and regulations. 45846

Massachusetts Grand Consistory. see Grand Consistory of the State of Massachusetts, Valley of Boston.

Massachusetts great apologie examined. 103223

Massachusetts Health Insurance Company. 45847

Massachusetts historical collections. see Collections of the Massachusetts Historical Society.

Massachusetts Historical Society, Boston. 170, 290, 647, 1054, 1521-1522, 1809, 2357, 3762-3763, 6220, 7262-7263, 9260, 12331, (12705), 12985, 13307, 13471, 15747, 17042-17043, 17104, (18844), 18895, (19047), 19049, 19051, (19639), (20190), 20328, 20793, 21972, 22075, 22129, 22144, 22146-22147, (22152), 22162, 22166, 22305-22306, 22352, 23277, 23828, 23825, 23936, 25439, (25762), 25874, (26625), (27515), 27832, 27959-27960, 28017, 28020, (28387), 28557, (29773), (30506), 30521, 31739, note after 31743, (32581), 32583, 32968, 33443, 33925, (34074), (36204), (36286), (36672), 37424, (38004), 39641, 40751, 41565, 41570, (41650), 41779, 42638, (43923), (44931), 45455, 45652, (45850)-45853, 45856-45859, 46642, 46817, (47395), 47648, 50786, (51198), 51201, 51810, 52518-52519, 52619, 53249, 54946, (54965), 57498, (58100), 59494, 59619, (59707), 60918, 62560, 62575, (63477), 64974, 65296, 65585, 65936, 66039, 67189, 67217, 70889, (71779), 72102, (73288), (73981), 75957, 77234, 77246, 77610, 78431, 78438, 79391, 79466-(79447), 79449, (79835), 80205, 80207-80208, (80827), 82815, 82819, 82823, 82831, 82834, 84824, 85217, 86730, 86799, 86843, 88221, 88961, note after 89151, 89312, 90070, 90110, 90220, note after 91855, 91945, 92349, 92664, 92716, note before 92797, 92810, 93270, 93506, 93697, note after 94086, 95632, 95825, 96954, 3d note after 96963, 4th note after 96963, 5th note after 96963, 10th note after 96966, 97103, 97115, 97141, 97145, 97409, 97562, 97733, 98034, 98327, 98330-98332, 2d note after 98334, 98544-98545, 98691, 98908, 98938, note after 98944, 99249, 99259, 99328-99329, 99332, 99335-99339, 99341, 99345, 99347, 99352, 99353, 99363, 99366, 99747, 99766, 99808, 99844-99845, 99847-99851, 99857-note after 99857, 99861, note after 99867, 99873, 99884, 2d note after 99911, 100006, 100448, 1st note after 100449, 100458, 1st note after 100459, 1st note after 100478, 100486, 2d note after 100494, 100502, 1st note after 100507, 3d note after 100527A, 100546, 100572, 1st note after 100572, 100575, 100770, 100828, 100838, 100916, 101025, 101330, 101847, 102227, 102876, 2d-3d notes after 102903, 102904, 102921, 103142, 103223, 103397, 103558, 103689, 6th note after 103943, 104111, 104330-104331, 104339, note after 104653, note after 104794, 104795, 104797, 104844, 104847, 1st note after 105675, 3d note after 106221, 106401

Massachusetts Historical Society, Boston. petitioners 54856, (52687), 67252

Massachusetts Historical Society, Boston. Charter. (45850)

Massachusetts Historical Society, Boston. Committee on Exchanges of Prisoners During the American Revolutionary War. (45858)

Massachusetts Historical Society, Boston. Library. 45851, (45858)

Massachusetts Historical Society, Boston.
Library. Thomas Dowse Library.
45851
Massachusetts Historical Society, Boston.
Members. 71787
Massachusetts Historical Society collections.
see Collections of the Massachusetts
Historical Society.
Massachusetts Home Missionary Society.
45860
Massachusetts Home Missionary Society.
Executive Committee. 92255
Massachusetts Homoeopathic Medical Society.
45861
Massachusetts Homoeopathic Medical Society.
Committee. 45861
Massachusetts Homoeopathic Medical Society.
Publications.... for 1861-62. 45861
Massachusetts Horticultural Society. 45862,
101315, 103044
Massachusetts Horticultural Society. Annual
Exhibition, 20th, 1848. 45862
Massachusetts Horticultural Society. Com-
mittees. 45862
Massachusetts Horticultural Society. Flower
Committee. 45862
Massachusetts Horticultural Society. Library.
45862
Massachusetts Horticultural Society. Presi-
dent Elect, 1852. 45862
Massachusetts Horticultural Society. Retiring
President, 1852. 45862
Massachusetts Horticultural Society. Triennial
Festival, 3d, 1848. 45862
Massachusetts Hospital Life Insurance Com-
pany. (45863)
Massachusetts Humane Society. see Humane
Society of the Commonwealth of Massa-
chusetts.
Massachusetts in agony. (11679), 45641,
45864
Massachusetts in mourning. 31755
Massachusetts in the rebellion. (31168)
Massachusetts income tax. 84521
Massachusetts Infant Asylum, Boston. see
Massachusetts Infant Asylum, Jamaica
Plain.
Massachusetts Infant Asylum, Jamaica Plain.
45865
Massachusetts Infirmary for Diseases of the
Lungs. 45866
Massachusetts Institute of Technology. (45867)
Massachusetts Institute of Technology. Charter.
(45867)
Massachusetts Institute of Technology. School
of Industrial Science. (45867)
Massachusetts Institute of Technology.
Officers. Extract from act of incorpora-
tion. Objects and plan. (45867)
Massachusetts journal. (12697), (12703),
102313
Massachusetts Journeymen Shipwrights' Union.
45868
Massachusetts justice: a treatise upon the
powers and duties of justices of the
peace. 18854
Massachusetts justice: being a collection of
the laws of the commonwealth. 45869
Massachusetts lawyer. pseud. Review of a
treatise on expatriation by George Hay,
Esq. 30998
Massachusetts magazine. 45870, 95409, 95411,
2d note after 95414
Massachusetts man. pseud. Letters on the
comparative merits of the Pennsylvania

and New York systems of penitentiary
discipline. 40620
Massachusetts man, resident in Providence.
pseud. Close of the late rebellion, in
Rhode-Island. 13776, 70563
Massachusetts manual. 9215
Massachusetts Mechanical Assocaition. 45872
Massachusetts Medical Benevolent Society.
45875
Massachusetts Medical College. 7145, 30765,
45874
Massachusetts Medical Society. 6992, 45873-
45874, (61350)
Massachusetts Medical Society. defendants
3756
Massachusetts Medical Society. petitioners
45874
Massachusetts Medical Society. Charter.
45873-45874
Massachusetts Medical Society. Committee.
45861
Massachusetts Medical Society. Committee
on the Charter and By-laws. 45874
Massachusetts Medical Society. Counsellors.
45874
Massachusetts Medical Society. Norfolk
District Medical Society. 55471
Massachusetts Medical Society. Southern
District Medical Society. 88339
Massachusetts Medical Society. Southern
District Medical Society. Charter.
88339
Massachusetts Medical Society. Suffolk
District Medical Society. 93441
Massachusetts Medical Society. Suffolk
District Medical Society. Board of
Censors. 45874, 93442
Massachusetts Medical Society. Suffolk
District Medical Society. Board of
Censors. petitioners 45874, 93442
Massachusetts Medical Society. Worcester
District Medical Society. 105426
Massachusetts Medical Society. Worcester
District Medical Society. Library.
105426
Massachusetts Medical Society. Worcester
North District Medical Association.
105436
Massachusetts militia act. 91426, 91427,
91429
Massachusetts Mining Company. 45876
Massachusetts missionary magazine. 45877
Massachusetts missionary register. 45878
Massachusetts Missionary Society. 45879,
95888
Massachusetts Missionary Society. Secretary.
95888 see also Austin, Samuel.
Massachusetts Missionary Society. Trustees.
89802
Massachusetts monthly museum. (27559),
51531
Massachusetts National Democratic Convention,
and speeches of Gen. Cushing. (45880)
Massachusetts Navy Union. see Massachusetts
Army and Navy Union.
Massachusetts or the first planters of New-
England. (21090), 33698, 78431-78433,
104846, 106052
Massachusetts Peace Convention, Boston, 1838.
see Peace Convention, Boston, 1838.
Massachusetts Peace Society. 45881, 105316
Massachusetts personal liberty bill. 45883
Massachusetts Philo-Italian Society. 45884
Massachusetts Prison-Discipline Society. see
Prison-Discipline Society of Massachusetts.

Massachusetts quarterly review. 7007, (45885)

Massachusetts register. 87340 see also North-American almanack and Massachusetts register.

Massachusetts register: a state record for 1852. 45886

Massachusetts register and United States calendar. (24699), 45887

Massachusetts reports. 85212

Massachusetts reports on life insurance. 45888

Massachusetts Republican resolutions, 1855. 46089

Massachusetts resolutions. 300

Massachusetts Rifle Club. 45889

Massachusetts Sabbath School Society. 338, (675), 16205, (32211), (32813), 41599, 43061-43062, 45890, 63984, 97516, 97519

Massachusetts Sabbath School Society. Committee of Publication. 1901, 15481, (32211), 86279, 88668, 94022, 97007, 97517-97519, 97524, 99628, 102197

Massachusetts Sabbath School Teachers Convention. see Sabbath School Teachers of Massachusetts. Annual Convention.

Massachusetts Sabbath School Union. (45891), 62448, 99628

Massachusetts Sabbath School Union. Publishing Committee. 16205, 90461, 97515-97516, 97520-97523

Massachusetts school fund. Extract from the twenty-second annual report of the Secretary of the Board of Education. 45894

Massachusetts School of Agriculture. (45892)

Massachusetts school returns. Abstracts. (5312)

Massachusetts school returns for 1837. 44324

[Massachusetts] Senate, no. 58. Report of the Committee on the Kilby Bank. 37738

[Massachusetts] Senate, no. 34. Report relating to the Kilby Bank. 37738

Massachusetts Senate report on the petition of the Trustees of Amherst College, 1837. (45895)

Massachusetts Society for Encouraging Industry and Employing the Poor. see Society for Encouraging Industry and Employing the Poor, Massachusetts.

Massachusetts Society for Promoting Agriculture. (45896)

Massachusetts Society for Promoting Agriculture. Trustees. (45812), (45896)

Massachusetts Society for Promoting Christian Knowledge. 45897

Massachusetts Society for Promoting Christian Knowledge. Directors. 45897

Massachusetts Society for the Suppression of Intemperance. see Massachusetts Temperance Society.

Massachusetts Society of the Cincinnati. 86108

Massachusetts song of liberty. 5220

Massachusetts spy. 1792, 24549, note after 45640, 81891, 89930, 93890, 95413, 2d note after 95414

Massachusetts State Cabinet. see Massachusetts. State Board of Agriculture. State Cabinet.

Massachusetts state charities. Report of the . . . Committee. 45901

Massachusetts State Convention of Whig Young Men, Worcester, 1839. see Whig Party. Massachusetts. State Convention of Whig Young Men, Worcester, 1839.

Massachusetts State Disunion Convention, Worcester, 1857. (45950)

Massachusetts State Military Convention, Worcester, Mass., 1835. see Military Convention, Worcester, Mass., 1835.

Massachusetts state papers. (46131)

Massachusetts state record and year book of general information. (10747)

[Massachusetts state] record, New England register, and year book. (10747)

Massachusetts State Temperance Alliance. 46142

Massachusetts State Temperance Alliance. Committee. 70235

Massachusetts State Temperance Alliance. Secretary. 45904

Massachusetts State Temperance Committee. 46143

Massachusetts State Temperance Convention, Boston, 1840. (45905)

Massachusetts State Texas Committee. 33236, 95092

Massachusetts system of common schools. 44322

Massachusetts teacher. 45906

Massachusetts Teachers' Assocaition. 45907

Massachusetts Temperance Convention, Worcester, 1833. 45908, 94645

Massachusetts Temperance Convention, Worcester, 1852. 45815

Massachusetts Temperance Society. 11906, 36035, (45898), 45909, 101514

Massachusetts Temperance Society. Board of Counsel. (45898)

Massachusetts Temperance Society. Committee (45898)

Massachusetts Temperance Society. Council. (11905)-11906, 45909, 93435

Massachusetts Temperance Union. 45910

Massachusetts Tin-plate, Copper, and Sheet-Iron Workers' Association, Boston. 45911

Massachusetts Universalist Convention. see Universalist Church in the U. S. Massachusetts.

Massachusetts Universalist Convention. Minute of the first session of the council. 45912

Massachusetts vs. Benjamin Rider. 71274

Massachusetts vs. David Lee Child. (12703)

Massachusetts vs. J. T. Buckingham. 8911

Massachusetts vs. Moore and Sevey. (28610)

Massachusetts Washington Benevolent Society. see Washington Benevolent Society. Massachusetts.

Massachusetts Washington Total Abstinence Society. 45913

Massachusetts Whig Young Men's Convention, Worcester, 1839. see Whig Party. Massachusetts. Young Men's Convention, Worcester, 1839.

Massachusetts yeoman. 815, 95705

Massachusetts zoological and botanical survey. (19845)

Massacre at Fort Pillow. 25164

Massacre at Owego. (33869)

Massacre au Fort George. 40006

Massacre et destruction presque generale de l'armee et des colons. 19086, (75094)

Massacre of Cheyenne Indians. (23154)

Massacre of Miss Jane M'Crea, by the Indians 89552

Massacre of whites by Indians and Negroes in Florida. (27655)

Massasoit's daughter. 21155

Massasoyt. Indian Chief (51198)-51200, note after 104797

Masse, ---------, fl. 1865. tr. 57425

Masse, E. M. 46173

Masseras, E. 46174

Masses: saved, with the Sabbath-school. (47896)

Massett, Stephen C. 46175

Massey, Edmund. 46176

Massey, Thomas E. 46177

Massey, William. 46178

Massie, James William, 1799-1869. 46184-46186

Massie, Joseph, d. 1784. (46180)-46183, 95962

Massie, Nathaniel. 97255

Masson, E. 46187

Massow, F. van. 46188

Massuet, ---------. tr. 14541

Massus, Isaac. 67355

Mast, Thomas. illus. 79909-79911

Masta. see Wzokhilain, Peter Paul.

Mastai-Ferretti, Giovanni Maria. see Pius IX, Pope, 1792-1878.

Master, Sir Harcourt, fl. 1721. 65865, 88192

Master and pupil. (37359)

Master builder. 39722

Master mason. pseud. Free masonry. 45501, 96366

Master of Greenway Court. (16314)

Master of life. 46840

Master of the Steamship "Star of the West." petitioner 66109

Master taken up from the sons of the prophets. 14499, 95737, 100915

Master William Mitten. (41937)

Masterman, George Frederick. (46189)

Masterman, George Frederick. petitioner 57711

Masterpieces of the Centennial International Exhibition illustrated. 84493

Masters, Josiah, 1763-1822. 89207

Masters, Thomas. 46190

Masters, William. 46191-46192

Master's house. 41819, note before 95663

Masters of old age. 83673

Mastership and its fruits. 43371

Mastology. 27663

Masukkenukeeg Matcheseaenvog Wequetoog. 46701

Mata, Nicolas Vrbano, Bp. (55248), 89107 see also La Paz (Diocese) Bishop (Mata)

Matamoros, Joseph. 16969

Matamorus, Alfonsus Garsia. 77902

Matanzas (Cuban Province) Diputacion Provincial. 79185

Matanzas (Cuban Province) Milicia Nacional Local. 46196

Matappika Landbouwkundig Genootschap. 46193

Match for a widow. 2284

Match girl. 46198

Matchelder, J. M. 101507

Matchett, Richard J. 46199

Mat-chis-jaw. Potawatomi Indian Chief 96702

Mate to the temperance ox. 104456

Matelief, Cornelis, fl. 1605. 14957-14960, 68455

Matelot Parisien. pseud. Journal. (56063)

Matelot Provencal. pseud. Journal. (56063)

Mateo de Otero, Jose. 46200

Mateos, Juan A. 46201-46202

Mateos, Nicomedes Martin. (46203)

Materia medica. 90959

Materia medica Americana potissimvm regni vegetabilis. (77756)

Material bearing of the Tennessee campaign of 1862. 46204

Material condition of the people of Massachusetts. note after (58767)

Material creation. 44316

[Material for hospital clothing.] 76579, 76647

Materiales para la historia de Sonora. (46205)

Materiales para una cartografia Mexicana. (57642)

Materiales relativos a la historia de la Isla de Cuba. 17791, 85747

Materialism of the Mormons. 64949

Materialism's last assault. 76966

Materiality of the soul. 71919

Materials for a bibliography of America. 70887

Materials for a bibliography of the public archives. note before 87347

Materials for a catalogue of the masters and scholars. 6756, 46206

Materials for a monograph of the North American orthoptera. 78528

Materials for history printed from original manuscripts. 50360

Materials for the future history of Minnesota. (49264)

Materials towards a history of the Baptists in Pennsylvania. 21981

Materials towards a history of the Baptists in Jersey. 21981

Maternal Association, New York. see New York Maternal Association.

Maternal Association, West Boylston, Mass. see West Boylston, Mass. First Congregational Church. Maternal Association.

Maternal consolations. 46404

Matham, T. illus. 63319

Mathematical tracts. 101175

Mathematicians glory. 91832

Mathenet, Jean Claude. (34593), 36969, 46821

Mather, Azariah. 46207-(46210)

Mather, Cotton, 1663-1728. 828, 1786, 2625, 4009, 4010, 4398, 5196, 6531, 7143, 7208, 7299, 9097, 9926-9927, 11040, 12914, (13424), (17040), (18478), 18710, (19046), 19051, 20884, 22186, (22439), 22698, 27384, (27834), 28052, 28506, 31881, 35103, 35754, (36506), (36851), 37185, 37202, 37209, 37212, (37215), 37234, 37655, 39795, (40252)-(42053), 42037, (44077), 45733, (45410), (46211)-46583, 46585-46622, (46631), 46646, (46648), 46673, 46687, 46693, 46695, (46698), 46735, 46741, (46749), 46788, 46790, 46817, 47151-47152, 49657-(49658), 50296, 52140, 52611, 60643, 62757, (65613), 65689, (66440), (66441), 67164, 69355, 72689, 74095, 75736, 78442, 82975-82976, 84350, note after 85661, 86588, 89479, 89927, 90160, 91833, 91945, 92099, note after 92154, 92351, 93265, 3d note after 93916, 94022, 2d note after 94666, 2d note after 94857, note after 94885, 94916, note after 95317, note after 95360, note after 95669, note after 95738, 4th note after 96106, 1st note after 96107, note after 96368, note after 96508, note after 96762, 96766, 2d note after 97085, 97093, 5th note after 97146, 3d note after 97160, 4th note after 97284, 97495, 98039, note after 98241, note after 98363, 4th note after 98925, 5th note after 98925, note after 99319, 1st note after 99407, 3d note after 99448, 1st-2d notes after

99604, 2d note after 99797, note after
100591, 101016, 101195, note after
101451, 1st note after 103119, note after
103702, 1st note after 103852, 103920,
105855, note after 104098, 104243,
104260-104261, 105227, note after
105465, note after 105468, note after
105484, note after 106242 see also
Eight Ministers Who Carry On the
Thursday Lecture in Boston. Ministers
of the Gospel in Boston.

Mather, Cotton, 1663-1728. supposed author
22186, 39409, 46379, 49822, 52622,
62560, 86618, 96105

Mather, Cotton, 1663-1728. incorrectly
supposed author 46379, (46584), 2d
note after 100616, 104242

Mather, Eleazer. (46627)

Mather, Elihu. defendant (46628)

Mather, Increase, 1639-1723. (2112), (9371),
3972, 10740, 14477, 24678, 24928,
27384, 28052, 31881, 35490, (36851),
37207-37208, 37213, 37234, (39894),
(40253), (40337), 42088, (44077), 46241,
46261, 46263, 46274, 46280, 46355,
(46371), 46407, 46474, 46491, 46500,
46517, (46528), 46553, 46587, 46607,
(46627), 46629-46721, 46723-46730,
46733-46755, 46757-46760, 46787, 46817,
49656-(49658), 49979, 50296, 52445,
56383, 1st note after 65324, (56500),
(65613), 67164, 97190, 70445, 80621,
81492, 82975, 82976, 84350, 86359,
91941, 91945, 91950-91954, 92351,
94113, 95195, note after 95738, 96303,
99805, note after 101451, 102223, 103400,
103402, 104068, 104078, 104097-
104098, 104242, 104243, 104255-104256,
104257, note after 105090

Mather, Increase, 1639-1723. supposed author
9708, (36851), 46651, 46695, 52597

Mather, Increase, 1639-1723. incorrectly
supposed author 46318, 46722, 46731-
46732, 46756, (56323), note after 70346,
92350, 2d note after 99797

Mather, Increase, 1639-1723. petitioner
9372, 81492

Mather, J. (46761)

Mather, J. see Mather, Increase, 1639-1723.

Mather, J. C. defendant 64282

Mather, J. H. 46766

Mather, James. 46762

Mather, James M. ed. 46763

Mather, John. 46764

Mather, John C. defendant 46765

Mather, Moses, 1719-1806. (4486), 4495,
46767-46770

Mather, Moses, 1719-1806. supposed author
1276, 46770

Mather, Nathaniel, 1631-1697. 46771-46773,
(46786)

Mather, Nathaniel, b. 1670. 46774, 62843

Mather, Richard, 1596-1669. 18704, 31496,
46775-46784, 63331, (66428)-66430, note
before 96158, 1st note after 102552, 2d
note after 103846, 106052

Mather, Samuel, 1626-1671. (46785)-46787,
80252, 92113

Mather, Samuel, 1651-1728. 56788-(56789)

Mather, Samuel, 1674-1733. 46790

Mather, Samuel, 1706-1785. 25474, 34598,
36038, 46400, (46456), 46496, 46625,
46788, 46791-46807, 46817, 69400,
90595-90596, 103594, 3d note after
103650

Mather, Samuel, 1706-1785. supposed autho
95907

Mather, Thomas G. 46808

Mather, W. 46809

Mather, Warham. supposed author 46508

Mather, William C. 53790

Mather, William W. 46810-46816, 56920-
56921

Mather family. 63986

Mather papers. 46817

Mather papers. Cotton Mather and Salem
witchcraft. 64046

Mathero, Crescentio. see Mather, Increase
1639-1723.

Mathers, William. (46818)

Mathers weighted in the balances, and found
not wanting. (27631)

Matherus, Crescentius. see Mather, Increas
1639-1723.

Matheson, James. 14224, (68535)-(68536)

Mathetees Archaios. pseud. Serious letter
to the young people of Boston. 46819

Matheu y Sanz, Lorenco. tr. 86540

Mathevet, Jean Claude. 46820-46821

Mathew, George. 87856 see also Great
Britain. Consulate. Charleston, S. C.

Mathew, Thomas. illus. 90555

Mathews, Alfred E. 46822-46823

Mathews, Anne Jackson. 46824-46827

Mathews, C. ed. 1927

Mathews, Charles. 46824, 46826, 46827

Mathews, Cornelius. 11935, 46828-46840,
65992

Mathews, E. 25187

Mathews, Edward. 46841-46842

Mathews, J. M. (46843)-46845

Mathews, Joanna H. (46846)

Mathews, John. 31799

Mathews, Samuel Augustus. 46847

Mathews, Thomas. 100055

Mathews, W. 46848, (46900), 102024

Mathias, -------. 51037

Mathiasen, -------. tr. 83215-83218

Mathies, James. 46849

Mathiesen, J. 46850-46851

Mathieson, Alexander. of Milwaukee 46852

Mathieson, Alexander. of Montreal 46853

Mathiot, George. 46854

Mathison, Gilbert. 46855-46857, 95656

Mathison, Gilbert Farquhar. 46858

Matias, Pedro. 46859

Matias Campanillas y Roque Pechuga. 46860

Matilda. pseud. Poems. see Smiley, ------
--------.

Matilda Berkely. 46862

Matilda Montgomerie. 71039

Matilda; or, the Barbadoes girl. 32413

Matile, G.-A. 46863

Matilla, Pedro. (73032)

Matilla, Pedro. petitioner (73032)

Matlack, Lucius C. 5163, 46865-(46866)

Matlack, Robert C. (46867)

Matlack, Timothy, 1736-1829. 17308, 46868

Matlack, White. petitioner 60723

Matorras, Geronimo. 46869

Matoso, Antonio Ygnacio Lopez. defendant
(48475)

Matrat, J. B. 46870

Matraya y Ricci, Juan Jos. (46871)

Matrimonial brokerage in the metropolis.
46872

Matrimonial infelicities. (14184)

Matrimonio civil. (73163)

Matrimony. 46873

Matroos, Wolphus Johan Beeldsnijder. 93845
see also Dutch Guiana. Gouverneur
Generaal, 1783-1784 (Matroos)

Matsell, George W. defendant (15879)
Matson, Frances F. 46881
Matson, H. J. 46874
Matson, Nathaniel. plaintiff 46875, 95436
Matson, Nehemiah, 1816-1883. 46876
Matson, William A. 46877
Matson Meier-Smith. Memories of his life and work. 83571
Mattapan Literary Association, Boston. (46878)
Mattapan Literary Association, Boston. (46878)
Mattapoisett Academy. 46879
Matteawan, N. Y. Asylum for Insane Convicts. see New York (State) State Hospital, Matteawan.
Matteawan, N. Y. State Hospital. see New York (State) State Hospital, Matteawan.
Matter coming from New England since this book was printed. 55884
Matter for the times. 17257
Matter, manner, and spirit of preaching. 80078
Matter of fact, delineated after the life. 97206
Matter of fact versus Messrs. Huskinson and Peel. 10889
Matters and things in general. 7651
Matters objected against Sir Edmund Androsse, &c. 1522
Matters of fact relative to lake occurrences. 46880
Matters of Josiah Oakes, Sen'r. (56380)
Matteson, David Maydole. 84336
Matteson, Orsamus Benajah, 1805-1889. 46882
Matteson, T. H. illus. (63475)
Matthaeus, of Paris. see Paris, Matthew.
Matthaei, C. Chr. 46883
Matthew, George F. 2743
Matthew, Patrick. 46884
Matthew Grant's old church record. 28309, 91754
Matthewnim Taaiskt. 88874-88875
Matthews, ---------. defendant 49386, note after 101854
Matthews, ---------. engr. 77182
Matthews, ---------, fl. 1821. (43001), 96901
Matthews, Albert, 1860-   ed. 84816, 84819, 84824, 84827-84832, 84835, 84837, 87863
Matthews, Charles J. 46885
Matthews, Eliza Jane. 46886
Matthews, J. T. 46889
Matthews, James. ed. 65724
Matthews, James M. ed. 15416-15417, 15339, (15342)-15343, 15345-15346
Matthews, John. 46887-46888, 2d note after 102871
Matthews, Lyman. 46890-46891
Matthews, Mordecai. 46892
Matthews, Nathan. 46893
Matthews, O. see Matthews, V.
Matthews, V. 95961
Matthews, Washington. 80015
Matthews, William. 46894-46895
Matthias, the false prophet. alias defendant see Matthias, the prophet. alias defendant
Matthias, the prophet. alias (46897)
Matthias, the prophet. alias defendant 46896, 46898
Matthias, Benjamin. 46889
Matthias, T. 64014
Matthias and his impostures. 92146

Mattingly, ---------. plaintiff 20018
Mattingly, Ann. 46848, (46900), 102024
Mattingly vs. the Washington and Alexandria Steamboat Company. 20018
Mattioli, Pietro Andrea. tr. 66502
Mattison, H. 46901
Mattison, Israel. 46902
Mattison, Seth. 46903
Mattocks, Samuel. 99135 see also Vermont. Treasurer.
Mattoon, C. S. 46904
Mattos, Jose Ferreira de. 46905
Mattos, Raimundo Jose da Cunha. see Cunha Mattos, Raimundo Jose da.
Mattoso Camara, Eusebio de Queiroz Coitinho. 46906 see also Brazil. Ministerio da Justicia.
Mattschappij der Nederlandsche Letterkunde, Leyden. (41062)
Mattschappij van de Protestantsche Surinaamsche Mettry op Lustrijk. 93858
Matugene de Keralio, ---------. 46907
Matured, paid-up and single endowments in the . . . [New York Mutual Life Insurance] Company. 54826
Maturin, Edward. 46908
Maturin (Colombian Department) petitioners 100790
Maty, Matthew. ed. 90063
Maubert, ----------. tr. 13485
Maubert de Gouvest, J. H. 46910-46912
Mauch, ed. tr. 16485
Maude. pseud. White rose in Acadia. see Jennings, Clotilda.
Maude, John. 46913, 7th note after 100603
Mauduit, Israel, 1708-1787. 15208, 46914-46928, (80038), 80043, 92853-92854, 95722, 2d note after 95742, 4th note after 95742
Mauduit, Israel, 1708-1787. supposed author 9294, 15928, 26438, (28768)-(28769), (46918), 46928, 69436, 103123
Mauduit, Jasper. supposed author 80580-(80581)
Mauduit-Duplessis, ---------. tr. (46929)
Mauge, Augustin P. 46930
Maule, Joseph E. 46931
Maule, Thomas. 46932-46933, (46935), 62420
Maule, Thomas. defendant 46934
Maule, Thomas. supposed author (62421), 1st note after 96964
Mauley, John. see Manley, John.
Maull, D. W. 46937
Maulsby, --------. 45090
Maund. firm see Schaeffer and Maund. firm
Maumee Baptist Association. see Baptists. Ohio. Maumee Baptist Association.
Maund, G. C. (46939)
Maunder, Samuel, 1785-1849. 38069, 46940-46942
Mauny, --------, Comte de. (46944)
Maupertuis, Pierre Louis Moreau de. 46945-46946
Mauran, Edward C. 70541 see also Rhode Island. Adjutant General.
Mauran, J. (46947)
Maurault, J. A. 46948
Maure, Am. see Moure, Amedee.
Maurel et Consorts. firm petitioners 46950
Maurel et Consorts a MM. les Commissaires Nationaux Civils. 46950
Maurelle, Antonio. 38966, 984444
Maurelle, Francisco Antonio. 3628
Maurer, U. 46952
Maurer, Valentine. 91836

Maurice, Charles Saint. see Saint Maurice,
  Charles.
Maurice, F. D. 46953
Maurice Henry. 46954
Maurice, James. (46955), 75951, 2d note
  after 96891
Maurice, James. plaintiff (46955), 75951,
  2d note after 96891
Mauricio, Leonardo de Porto. see Porto
  Mauricio, Leonardo de.
Mauricius, Jan Jacob. see Mauritius, Johan
  Jacob.
Mavrile de S. Michel, ----------. 46987
Maurin, ---------. illus. 73935
Mauritiados libri VI. 46956
Mauritius Nassovus. 46956
Mauritius, Johan Jacob. 68458, 93844, 1st
  note after 93862 see also Dutch
  Guiana. Gouverneur Generaal, 1742-
  1751 (Mauritius)
Mauritius, Johan Jacob. defendant 68458
  see also Dutch Guiana. Gouverneur
  Generaal, 1742-1751 (Mauritius)
  defendant
Mavritivs Redvx . . . ex orbe Americano.
  3407
Maurits, Prince of Nassau, fl. 1648. 7588
Mauro Camaldolese. cartographer 106411
Mauro, F. 76838
Mauro, Lucio. tr. (27745)
Mauro, M. 32677, 74810
Mavrolycus, Franciscus. 46957-46958, 66670,
  96108
Maury, Abram P. 46959
Maury, Alfred. see Maury, Louis Ferdinand
  Alfred, 1817-1892.
Maury, Ann. ed. 24986-24987
Maury, D. H. 46960
Maury, Louis Ferdinand Alfred, 1817-1892.
  (46975), 56038, 85791
Maury, Matthew Fontaine, 1806-1873. 2258,
  (2588), 12081, 17240, 46961-46974,
  72507, 87396
Maury, Sarah Mytton. 46976-(46977)
Maury, Thomas W. 100539
Maury's wind and current charts. (46965)
Mausoleo levantado a memoria da excelsa
  rainha de Portugal. 88708
Maussion Cande, -------- de. 46978
Mauvillon, J. tr. 68095
Mauvillon, M. de. tr. 36812, 2d note after
  97689, 4th note after 97689
Maverick, Augustus. 7940, 46979
Maverick, P. R. engr. 5169, 44258, 105687-
  note after 105687, note after 105689,
  note after 105690
Maverick, Peter. cartographer 49746
Maverick Church, Boston. see Boston.
  Maverick Church.
Mavor, William. 5910, 22312, 35712, 43415,
  (46980)-(46985), (58171), 62572, 98444,
  102540
Mavor, William Fordyce. 46986
Mavor's travels in North America. 46984,
  102540
Maw, Henry Lister. 46988-46989
Mawe, John. 46990-48996
Mawson, Matthias, successively Bishop of
  Chichester, and Ely, 1683-1770. 46997
Mawuni nachgohumewoaganall enda auwegenk
  welsittangik Lenapewinink. 50518,
  106297
Maxcy, Jonathan. 46999-47005
Maxcy, Milton. 47006

Maxcy, Virgil. 45135, 45192, 47007-47010,
  89005
Maxim, Hudson. 84235
Maximas de buena educacion. 79171
Maximes de Washington; discours. 25173
Maximilian, Emperor of Mexico, 1832-1867.
  17157, 20548, 29354, 34839, 34945,
  (39838), (47027)-47028, 47036, note
  after 48507 see also Mexico.
  Sovereigns, etc., 1864-1867 (Maximilian)
Maximilian, Emperor of Mexico, 1832-1867.
  defendant 47036, 58273 see also
  Mexico. Sovereigns, etc., 1867-1867
  (Maximilian) defendant
Maxan. *** pseud. see ***, Maxan. pseud.
Maximilian Alexander Philipp, Prinz zu Wied.
  see Maximilianus, Transylvanus.
Maximilian I. Kaiser von Mexico. (31258)
Maximilian and the Mexican Empire. 47029
Maximilian Library. 47037
Maximiliani Transyluani Caesaris a secretis
  epistola. 47039-47040
Maximiliano y los ultimos sucesos del imperio
  en Queretaro y Mexico. 55490
Maximilianus, Transylvanus. 34100-34107,
  47011-47026, 47028-47042, 55455, 62509,
  62806, 67730, 77803, note after 90319,
  1st note after 99406
Maximilien, Empereur du Mexique. 47030
Maximilien et le Mexique. 31484
Maximilien et le monarchie au Mexique.
  47031
Maximilien, ode elegiaque. 4588
Maximo en lo minimo la portentosa imagen.
  10897
Maxims and common sayings. (25598)
Maxims and methods of piety. 22186, (46621),
  46302
Maxims and moral reflections by the Duke de
  la Rochefaucault. [sic] 72328
Maxims [by William Penn.] 50439
Maxims, counsels, and instructions on the art
  of war. 58562, 64874
Maxims for the promotion of the wealth of
  nations. (47043)
Maxims of state. 67572-67573, 67577-67584,
  67588, 67598-67599
Maxims of Washington, collected and arranged.
  77983
Maxims of Washington; political, social, moral,
  and religious. (77984)
Maximum occidentis sydus. 72534
Maximus, Q. Fabius. see Fabius Maximus.
Maxiscatzin Citlalpopoca, Nocolas Salazar.
  see Salazar Maxiscatzin Citlalpopoca,
  Nicolas.
Maxon, C. H. 53981 see also New York
  (State) Librarian.
Maxson, D. E. 47044
Maxson, Edwin. 47045
Maxson, William B. 47046
Maxwell, ---------. (59766)
Maxwell, A. M. 47047
Maxwell, Hugh. 47049, (72166), 84649
Maxwell, Hugh. defendant 99277
Maxwell, Hugh. reporter 3392, note after
  96820, note after 98992
Maxwell, James. 47051
Maxwell, John. 47050
Maxwell, Maria. 47052
Maxwell, S. H. 47056
Maxwell, Samuel. 47053, 62743
Maxwell, Sidney D. 47054-(47055), 84725-
  84727 see also Cincinnati. Chamber

of Commerce and Merchants' Exchange.
Superintendent.
Maxwell, William, 1784-1857. 47057-47058,
 94883
Maxwell, William, 1784-1857. supposed author
 40595, (52204), note after 97301, 3d
 note after 100484
Maxwell, William P. defendant at court
 martial 62977, 96942
Maxwell, Wright & Co. firm 47059
Maxwell's code. 94882
May, C. 13015
May, Caroline. (47061)
May, Charles. 47062
May, Charles S. 47063
May, Eleazer. 47064
May, George Ryan. defendant 47065
May, George T. (47066)
May, Henry, 16th cent. 66686
May, Henry, 1816-1863. 31188, (47067)
May, Hezekiah. 47068
May, James, alias see Porter, James.
 defendant
May, James, 1805-1863. (47069), 77572,
 80540
May, John, 1748-1812. 47070
May, John, fl. 1855. (47071)
May, John Frederick. 47072
May, John M. 30501
May, Joseph. 101871
May, Louis du. see Dumay, Louis, d. 1681.
May, Robert. 47074
May, Samuel. 26128
May, Samuel J. 47075-47078, 62614, 104757
May, Sophie. 47079
May, Thomas. 47080
May, Thomas Erskine. (47081)-47082
May, Thomas P. defendant 18181
May, Walter W. 47083
May, William. 47084
May, William. defendant at Court Martial
 47084
May, William H. 47085
May & Co. firm publishers see McLellan,
 May & Co. firm publishers
May (Ship) in admiralty 11307
May day annual. 89071
May day in New York. 18800, 84144, 84150,
 84158, note after 84162
May flower. 92451
May flower, and miscellaneous writings.
 92423
May gift, dedicated to the ladies who . . .
 aided the New England Institution for
 the Blind. 30290
May historical and biographical chart of the
 United States. 67683
May Martin. 95483, 95481, 95483
May Martin, and other tales of the Green
 Mountains. 95484
May morning. 101392
May of Maryland. 80586
May Queen Union, no. 2, Natick, R. I. see
 Daughters of Temperance. Rhode Island.
 May Queen Union, no. 2, Natick.
May 30, 1870. 80182
May 29. 1773. To the freemen, citizens of
 Philadelphia. 61807
Maya primer. 31305
Mayall, S. 47087
Maybee. 20050
Mayberry, David F. defendant 47088
Maycock, James Dottin. (47089)
Maydens of Londons brave adventures. 100486
Maye, John Cornelitz de. see De Maye, John
 Cornelitz.

Mayer, A. A. 47090
Mayer, Brantz, 1809-1879. (11068), 16234,
 22401, (45211A), 43176, 45217, (45316),
 (47091)-47105, 54177, 69292, (69916),
 note after 80002, 85072, 90483, 103353
 see also McDonogh Educational Fund
 and Institute, Baltimore. Trustees.
Mayer, Charles F. 3084, 43177, (45211A),
 (47106)
Mayer, Charles Joseph. 47107
Mayer, D. 47108
Mayer, F. 64709
Mayer, Johann. (47109)-(47110)
Mayer, Joseph. (47111)
Mayer, Lewis. 45207, (45211A), 45213,
 47112-47113
Mayer, Philip F. 47114
Mayer von Esslingen, -------. 47115
Mayerhoffer, V. P. 47116
Mayerne-Turquet, Louis de. 47117-47118
Mayes, Daniel. (47119)
Mayeza Portocarrero y Luna, Juan de Prado.
 see Prado Mayeza Portocarrero y Luna,
 Juan de.
Mayfield, Millie. pseud. Carrie Harrington.
 47120
Mayfield, Millie. pseud. Progression. 47120
Mayflower. 92421-92424, 92426-92428, 92448-
 92449, 92452, 92455
Mayflower descendant. 104795
Mayham, S. L. 47122
Mayhew, Experience, 1673-1758. 2869, 45337,
 47123-(47125)
Mayhew, Henry, 1812-1887. 47126-47127,
 77713, 83279, 85168
Mayhew, Ira, b. 1814. 47128-(47129), 48725,
 48801
Mayhew, Jonathan, 1720-1776. 1853, 1856,
 8641, (10681), 13593, (13597), 32955,
 47130-(47134), (47136)-47140, 47142-
 47150, 5th note after 69412, 78713-78714,
 78719, 95642, note after 99295
Mayhew, Jonathan, 1720-1776. supposed author
 12982, 25296, 86684, 3d note after 95765,
 2d note after 102065
Mayhew, Matthew. 47151-47152
Mayhew, Thomas. 3213, (22152), 22166,
 (47153), note before 92797, note after
 92800, 3d note after 103687, 103688,
 note after 104794
Maylem, John. 15886, (47154)-47155
Maylins, Robert. 47165
Maynadier, William. 47157-47159
Maynard, -------, fl. 1849. 64810
Maynard, -------, fl. 1863. 47167
Maynard, Aaron. 47160-(47161)
Maynard, C. J. 47162
Maynard, Felix. 47163
Maynard, George Henry. 36666
Maynard, Horace. 47164-(47166), (47190)
Maynard, Sampson. 47168
Maynard, Theophile. 47169
Maynard, William H. (47170)
Maynarde, Thomas. 47171
Mayne, F. 47173
Mayne, R. C. 47174
Maynwaringe, E. 97551
Mayo, ----------. cartographer/surveyor
 77785
Mayo, A. D. 47175-47183, (47195)
Mayo, C. 47184
Mayo, E. D. 58958
Mayo, H. B. 47185
Mayo, Robert. 47186-47193, 60811
Mayo, Robert. defendant 47186

Mayo, Robert. plaintiff 47186
Mayo, Samuel M. defendant 47194
Mayo, Sarah C. (Edgarton) (47195), 73249
Mayo, Warren. (47196)
Mayo, William Starbuck. 47197
Mayor, Geronimo de Monte. see Monte
    Mayor, Geronimo de.
Mayor. 61808
Mayor alma del mundo Aurelio Augustino.
    71474
Mayor and City Council of Baltimore vs. the
    B. and O. R. R. Co. 2992
Mayor excelencia de San Pedro. 94636
Mayor gloria y felicidad de Cantabria. 29063
Mayora, Jose Mariano de Aguira y. see
    Aguira y Mayora, Jose Mariano de.
Mayora, Juan. 47198, 69186
Mayordomo. 49916
Mayorga, Francisco Xavier Tello de. see
    Tello de Mayorga, Francisco Xavier.
Mayorga, Martin de. 47199, (58609), 69992
    see also Mexico (Viceroyalty) Virrey,
    1779-1783 (Mayorga)
Mayoria del pueblo Valenciano. 98022
Mayor's address and . . . annual report [of
    Biddeford, Me.] 5227
Mayor's address, and annual report of the
    receipts and expenditures. 20745
Mayor's address, and annual reports made to
    the City Council of Hallowell. 29915
Mayor's address and annual reports of the
    several departments, of the city govern-
    ment, for the financial year 1863-64
    [of Portland, Me.] 64351
Mayor's address and annual reports of the
    several departments of the city govern-
    ment [of Saco, Me.] 74778
Mayor's address and elective officers for
    1866 [of Chelsea, Mass.] 12417
Mayor's address, at the organization of the
    City Council [of Newburyport.] 54913
Mayor's address at the organization of the
    city government, April 20, 1846. 73649
Mayor's address at the organization of the
    city government [of Cambridge, Mass.]
    10142
Mayor's address . . . [Providence, R. I.]
    66249
Mayor's address to the officers of the Fire
    Department. 73650
Mayor's annual report, on city affairs, and
    operation of the liquor law. 64350
Mayor's inaugural address, and annual reports
    of the several departments of the city
    of Salem. 75672
Mayor's message, with accompanying report
    of the City Treasurer. 18721
Mayor's messages to the Common Council.
    49160
Mayor's report, January 1st, 1789. 101427
Mayor's report of the financial concerns of
    the city of Portland. 64349
Mayr, Johann. see Mayer, Johann.
Mayre, Iacobo de. see Le Maire, Jacob,
    1585-1616.
Maysville road. 47200
Maza, Manuel Vicente de. see De Maza,
    Manuel Vicente.
Maza Arredono, Fernando de la. see
    Arredono, Fernando de la Maza.
Mazama Mountain Climbing Society of Port-
    land, Ore. 84533
Mazariegos, Mariano Robles Dominguez de.
    see Robles Dominguez de de Mazariegos,
    Mariano.

Mazarredo, Eusebio de Salazar y. see Salazar
    y Mazarredo, Eusebio de.
Mazarredo, Josef Salazar de. see Salazar
    de Mazarredo, Josef.
Maze, H. 47201
Mazeline, --------. defendant 47527
Mazelli, and other poems. 76438
Mazenc, Adhemar. tr. 99383C
Mazeres, --------, fl. 1792-1816. 47202-
    47203, 98674, 98676
Mazero, Felipe. 47204
Mazet, Dominique. 64179
Mazois, E. 47205
Mazon. pseud. Carta. 56452
Mazyck, Alexander. 87486, 87489, 87530
Mazzei, Filippo, 1730-1816. 15194, 35933,
    47206-47207, note after 92859, 97457
Mazzinghi, Joseph, 1765-1844. 105527
Mazzini, Guiseppe, 1805-1872. 33618
Mazzoni, Baldassar. ed. and tr. 92587
Mazzuchelli, Samuele. 47208
Mdewakanton Indians. Treaties, etc. 96662,
    96715
Me, Phil Arcanos, Gent. Student of astrology.
    pseud. Grand arcanum detected. see
    Green, Joseph, 1706-1780.
Me, the hon. B. B. Esq. pseud. Entertainment
    for a winter's evening. see Green,
    Joseph, 1706-1780.
Meacham, A. G. (47211)-47212
Meacham, Henry H. 47213
Meacham, James. 47214, 85054, 85074
Meacham. Jeremiah. 13202
Meacham, John. supposed author 18608,
    79723-79727, note after 94924, note after
    97880, note after 106196
Meacham, Joseph. 97884
Mead, --------. petitioner 25781
Mead, --------. supposed author 101091-
    101092
Mead, Mrs. --------. 47225
Mead, Asa. 47215-(47216)
Mead, Charles. 47217-47218
Mead, Daniel M. 47219
Mead, Edward C. 47220
Mead, H. 47221
Mead, H. E. (47222)
Mead, H. H. 47223
Mead, Joseph. 47224
Mead, Matthew. 46293
Mead, Peter B. 47226
Mead, Samuel. 47227
Mead, W. defendant 90540, 97265
Mead, Whitman. (47229)
Mead, William, fl. 1670-1712. 66926
Mead, William, fl. 1670-1712. defendant 59723
Mead, William, fl. 1819. 47230
Meade, George Gordon, 1815-1872. 31164,
    47233, 51019
Meade, Richard K. 47234
Meade, Richard Worsam, 1807-1870. defendant
    at court martial 47236
Meade, Richard Worsam, 1807-1870. defendant
    at court of inquiry 47236
Meade, Richard Worsam, 1807-1870. petitioner
    47236
Meade, William, M. D. 47237
Meade, William, Bp., 1789-1862. 20394-20395,
    47238-47243, 57309, 58157, 81566, 88253,
    93816
Meader, J. W. 47244
Meadows, Kenny. illus. 68181
Meadows, Sir W. 103681
Meads, Orlando. (47245)
Meadville, Pa. Alleghany College. see
    Alleghany College, Meadville, Pa.

Meadville, Pa. Meadville Academy. see Meadville Academy, Meadville, Pa.

Meadville, Pa. Theological School. see Meadville Theological School, Meadville, Pa.

Meadville Academy, Meadville, Pa. 47246

Meadville Theological School, Meadville, Pa. 47247

Meadville Theological School, Meadville, Pa. Library. 47247

Meadville Theological School, Meadville, Pa. Treasurer. 47247

Meadville Theological School. A report to the Executive Committee of the American Unitarian Association. 91044

Meagher, Thomas Francis. 42871, 47248-47249

Meaner hand. pseud. Relation of some former and late proceedings. 20779

Meaning of the terms in the constitution. (47250)

Means, John Hugh, 1812- 47251-47254, 87548, 87701 see also South Carolina. Governor, 1850-1852 (Means)

Means, John O. 47255

Means and ends of universal education. 47128

Means and ends, or, self-training. 78792-(78793)

Means for the preservation of public liberty. 101437

Means of diffusing religious knowledge. 73882

Means of ministerial efficiency. 21663

Means of peace: a sermon. (71267)

Means of preserving health and preventing diseases. 71237

Means of promoting the intellectual improvement of the students and physicians of the valley of the Mississippi. 20825

Means of the perpetuity and prosperity of our republic. 104803

Means to suppress the practice of duelling. 78875

Meanwell, ---------. ed. 47256

Meanwell's town and country almanack for 1774. 47256

Meares, John. 20361-20363, (47257)-47265, 51818

Mears, -------. 52580, 64396

Mease, James. 47266-47270, 84365, 104694

Meason, C. F. H. 47271

Measure of a life. 84066

Measure proposed to secure to the people a safe treasury. 85584

Measure to Africanize the territories of the United States. (11733)

Measures adopted in Boston, Massachusetts. (47272)

Measures, not men. 9955, 47273

Measures of equality. 46457

Measures proposed for the prevention of Asiatic cholera. 66280

Meat out of the eater, and sweetness out of the strong. 22440

Meat out of the eater. Or, funeral-discourses, occasioned by the death of several relatives. (46405)

Meat out of the eater: or, meditations concerning the necessity, end, and usefulness of afflictions. 19034-19035, 103925-103928

Meath, Bishop of. see O'Beirne, Thomas Lewis, Bishop of Meath, 1748-1823.

Meaux, Jean Mocquet de. see Mocquet de Meaux, Jean.

Mebold, C. A. tr. 19542, 23770, 102622

Mecanique celeste. 7000

Mechanic. pseud. 83713

Mechanic. pseud. Address to the mechanics and laboring classes. 54065

Mechanic. pseud. Address to workingmen on the low prices of wages. 54068

Mechanic. pseud. Mechanic. America's offering. 47274

Mechanic. pseud. Mechanic. "Common sense" especially addressed to the most suffering portion of our fellow citizens. 47275

Mechanick. pseud. Mechanick's address to the farmer. 47276, 97107

Mechanic. pseud. To the tradesmen, mechanics, &c. of the province of Pennsylvania. 60728

Mechanic. America's offering. 47274

Mechanic and Agricultural Institution, South Reading, Mass. see South Reading Mechanic and Agricultural Institution.

Mechanic and Scientific Institution, New York. see New York Mechanic and Scientific Institution.

Mechanic arts favorable to liberty and social progress. 9133

Mechanic Association, Hampden, Mass. see Hampden Mechanic Association, Hampden, Mass.

Mechanic association, instituted February 5, 1824. 30126

Mechanic. "Common sense" especially addressed to the most suffering portion of our fellow-citizens. 47275

Mechanic Library, Salem, Mass. see Salem Mechanic Library, Salem, Mass.

Mechanic Library Society, New Haven, Conn. 52974

Mechanic of Charlestown. pseud. Patriot. 59080

Mechanical Association of Massachusetts. see Massachusetts Mechanical Association.

Mechanick. pseud. see Mechanic. pseud.

Mechanick's address to the farmer. 47276, 97107

Mechanics and Agricultural Fair Association of Louisiana. Grand State Fair, 4th, 1870. 47277

Mechanics & Agricultural Fair Association of Louisiana. Report of their fourth grand state fair. 47277

Mechanics' and Apprentices' Library, Providence, R. I. see Providence, R. I. Mechanics' and Apprentices' Library.

Mechanics and Arts Association of New Hampshire. see New Hampshire Mechanics and Arts Association.

Mechanics' and Farmers' magazine of useful knowledge. 47278

Mechanics' and Gardeners' Mutual Education, and Manual Labour Association, at Woodville, Long Island. 47279

Mechanics' and inventors' pocket almanac for 1861. 47280

Mechanics and Manufacturers of Lexington, Ky. petitioners see Lexington, Ky. Mechanics and Manufacturers. petitioners

Mechanics and Other Workingmen of New York. 54054

Mechanics and Other Workingmen of New York. General Executive Committee. 54054

Mechanics' and Tradesmen's General Society, New York. see New York Mechanics' and Tradesmen's General Society.

Mechanics' Association, New Bedford, Mass. see New Bedford Mechanics' Association.
Mechanics' Association, Newark, N. J. see Newark Mechanics' Association.
Mechanics' Association of New York State. see New York State Mechanics' Association.
Mechanics' Co-operative Association of Roxbury, Mass. 73651
Mechanics Employed in the Manufacture of Iron, Philadelphia. see Iron Workers of Philadelphia.
Mechanics' Festival, Providence, R. I., 1860. see Providence Association of Mechanics and Manufacturers. Mechanics' Festival, 71st, 1860.
Mechanics' Festival. An account of the seventy-first anniversary of the Providence Association of Mechanics and Manufacturers. 66305, 92046
Mechanics' Festival of the Providence Association of Mechanics and Manufacturers, 1860. see Providence Association of Mechanics and Manufacturers. Mechanics' Festival, 71st, 1860.
Mechanics' Institute, Louisville, see Louisville Mechanics' Institute.
Mechanics' Institute and Library Association of Nashville. First Exhibition, 1855. (51874)
Mechanics' Institute of Montreal. General Committee. 50254
Mechanics' Institute of Montreal. Library. 50254
Mechanics' Institute of Pittsburgh. see Pittsburgh Library Association.
Mechanics' Institute of San Francisco. Industrial Exhibition, 1st, 1857. 76054
Mechanics' Institute of San Francisco. Industrial Exhibition, 8th, 1871. 76054
Mechanics' Institute—past, present and future. (31396)
Mechanics' Institution, Boston. see Boston. Mechanics' Institution.
Mechanic's intelligencer. 45519
Mechanic's journal. 84176
Mechanics' Library Association, Newburgh, N. Y. 54901
Mechanics' magazine. (47281)
Mechanic's magazine and register of inventions and improvements. 47283
Mechanics mirror. (47284)
Mechanics' Mutual Benefit Association, Springfield, Mass. 89866
Mechanics' Mutual Protection of the U. S. A. Grand Convention, Buffalo, N. Y., 1847. 65856
Mechanics' Mutual Protections of New York. Annual Convention, 1847. 53761
Mechanics of Boston. see Boston. Mechanics.
Mechanics of this city are earnestly requested to meet. 95986
Mechlin, A. H. 47285
Meck, F. B. 47171, 85072
Mecklenburg County, N. C. Citizens. (19178), (47286)
Mecklenburg County, N. C. Declaration of Independence. (19178), (47286)-(47287)
Mecklenburg County, Va. Citizens. petitioners 47288
Mecklenburg Gold Mining Company. 47289
Mecklenburg Gold Mining Company. Charter. 47289

Mecklin, W. T. 68963
Mecom, B. 83980
Mecom, Benjamin, b. 1732. ed. and publisher (52697)
Mecorney, W. 47290
Mecure des Isles du Vent. 66078
Med, a slave. defendant 6703, 47291, 81910
Medaganesset. Indian Chief 4391, 15429
Medaille de la liberte. 47292
Medalla de Lopez. 96435
Medallas de las colonias. 24833
Medallic memorials of Washington. 85582
Medals, miniature and profile painting and shades. 105613A
Medary, Samuel, 1801-1864. 37035, 47293, 56877, 57063 see also Kansas (Territory) Governor, 1859-1860 (Medary
Medawah-Kanton Indians. see Medwakanton Indians.
Medbery, James K. 47294
Medbery, Rebecca B. 47295
Medbury, N. 64419
Medecin. pseud. Docteur Americain. see Revoil, Benedict Henry.
Medecin Americain. pseud. Souvenirs. 88696
Mededeelingen betreffende den Halveston Houston en Henderson spoorweg. 47296
Medeiros, F. L. d'Abreu. 47297
Medeiros Correa, Joao de. see Correa, Joao de Medeiros.
Medfield, Mass. 47298
Medfield, Mass. Baptist Church. 50920
Medfield, Mass. School Committee. 47298
Medfield, Mass. Society for Detecting Horse-Thieves, and Recovering Stolen Horses. see Society for Detecting Horse-Thieves, and Recovering Stolen Horses, Wrentham, Franklin, Medway, Medfield, Walpole, Foxborough, Mansfield, and Attleborough, Mass.
Medfield. 94247
Medfield Library, Dedham, Mass. 47299
Medford, Macall. 47301, 97135
Medford, Michael. 47300
Medford, Mass. 47302
Medford, Mass. Auditing Committee. 47302
Medford, Mass. Public Library. 47302
Medford, Mass. School Committee. 47302
Medford, Mass. Tornado Committee, 1851. 8339
Medford, Mass. Tufts College. see Tufts College, Medford, Mass.
Medford, Mass. Tufts Library. 47302
Mediation address to England. (36119)
Mediation in America. 36118
Mediation position of France in connection with a congress of nations. (36119)
Mediator. pseud. 22d of February. see Rush, Benjamin, 1811-1887.
Mediator between north and south. (47303)
Mediator's kingdom not of this world. 20495
Medical Academy, Castleton, Vt. see Vermont Medical Institution, Castleton, Vt.
Medical advertiser for 1844. 10990
Medical advice for the use of the army and navy. 73599
Medical advice to the inhabitants of warm climates. 95446
Medical adviser. (47304)
Medical and agricultural register, for the years 1806 and 1807. 191, 47305
Medical and Chirurgical Faculty of the State of Maryland. 45254, 83664
Medical and Chirurgical Faculty of the State of Maryland. Library. 45254

Medical and miscellaneous observations, relative to the West India islands. 104460

Medical and philosophical essays. (80068)

Medical and philosophical review and journal. 47306

Medical and physical journal. 85250

Medical & physical memoirs. 9899

Medical and physical researches. 30392

Medical and surgical history of the war of of the rebellion. 47307

Medical and surgical journal. 47308

Medical & surgical memoirs. 83653

Medical & surgical monographs B. 76536, 76647

Medical & surgical monographs C. 76540, 76647

Medical and surgical register. 47309

Medical and surgical reporter. 47310, 84449

Medical annals and Baltimore. 83664

Medical annals of Maryland. 83664

Medical apocalypse. (47311)

Medical application of electro-magnetism. 84027

Medical assistant. 18460

Medical Association for the Supply of Lint, Bandages, etc. to the United States Army, New York. see New York Medical Association for the Supply of Lint, Bandages, etc. to the United States Army.

Medical Association, Franklin, Mass. see Franklin Medical Association.

Medical Association, New Haven, Conn. see New Haven Medical Association, New Haven, Conn.

Medical Association of Franklin County, Mass. see Franklin Medical Association.

Medical Association of Kentucky. see State Medical Association of Kentucky.

Medical Association of Middlesex County, Mass. see Middlesex Medical Association.

Medical Association of South-Carolina. see South-Carolina Medical Association.

Medical Association of Southern Central New York. (47312), 54855

Medical Benevolent Society of Massachusetts. see Massachusetts Medical Benevolent Society.

Medical botany, containing a botanical, general, and medical history of medicinal plants. 3863

Medical botany of the state of South Carolina. 64157

Medical chronicle. 47313

Medical College, Memphis, Tenn. see Memphis Medical College.

Medical College, New York. see New York Medical College, New York.

Medical College for Women, New York. see New York Medical College for Women.

Medical College of Massachusetts. see Massachusetts Medical College.

Medical College of Ohio, Cincinnati. see Cincinnati. University. Medical College of Ohio.

Medical College of Philadelphia. see Philadelphia College of Medicine.

Medical College of South Carolina. see South Carolina. Medical College.

Medical College of South Carolina. 87875

Medical communication, with the proceedings of the sixty-ninth annual convention of the Connecticut Medical Society. 15783

Medical communications of the Mass. Med. Soc. 6992

Medical companion. 23314

Medical companion and temperance advocate. 47314

Medical Convention, Lancaster, Pa., 1848. see State Medical Convention, Lancaster, Pa., 1848.

Medical Convention of Ohio, Cincinnati, 1842. 57025

Medical Convention of Ohio. 3d, Cleveland, 1839. 56942

Medical Convention of South Carolina, Charleston, 1848. 87877

Medical counselor. 47315

Medical Department. Annual announcements of lectures. 54710

Medical Department . . . at Philadelphia. 60313

Medical Department of the University of Pennsylvania. 11371, 60758

Medical directions for the use of navigators and settlers in hot climates. 104834

Medical directions written for Governor Winthrop. 90070

Medical discourse, on several narcotic vegetable substances. 24474

Medical discourse, or an historical inquiry into the ancient and present state of medicine. 48866

Medical education in the United States. 91782

Medical essays and observations. 5638

Medical examiner (1838-   ) 47316

Medical examiner (1845-1856) (47317), 74193

Medical Faculty of Paris. see Paris. University. Medical Faculty.

Medical flora. 67457

Medical gazette. 47318

Medical heroes. 4457

Medical inquiries and observations. (74198), 74208, 74224, (74226)-74229

Medical inquiries and observations, upon the diseases of the mind. note after 74241

Medical Institute of Louisville. see Louisville, Ky. Medical Institute.

Medical institution at Bowdoin College. 7034

Medical institution at Geneva College. 26939

Medical Institution of Geneva College. see Geneva College, Geneva, N. Y. Medical Institution.

Medical Institution of Geneva College, plaintiff in error. 89386

Medical Institution of New Hampshire. see New Hampshire Medical Institution.

Medical institution of Yale College, Feb. 1835. 105918

Medical intelligencer. (47319)

Medical investigator. 47320

Medical jurisprudence. (13297)

Medical, literary, and social influence of the alumni. 82715

Medical magazine. 47321

Medical news. (47322)

Medical opinion in the Parish will case. 4473

Medical opinions upon the mental compentency of Mr. Parish. 58611

Medical plans [of Johns Hopkins Hospital.] 84276

Medical police. 30132

Medical profession and the duties of its members. 72634

Medical progressionist. 88301

Medical properties of the St. Catherines Mineral Waters. 75006

Medical recollections of the Army of the Potomac. 40565

Medical record. 47323, 84258, 84264, 84266, 84271-84273, 90888

Medical register of the city of New York and and vicinity. 47324

Medical register of the city of New York, for . . . 1866. 26223

Medical reporter. A quarterly journal. 47325

Medical reporter, a semi-monthly record. (47326)

Medical repository. 84411

Medical repository and review. 47327

Medical review, and analectic journal. 47328

Medical School, Albany, N. Y. see Albany Medical School.

Medical School, Rock Island, Ill. see Rock Island, Ill. Medical School.

Medical School of Maine. see Bowdoin College, Brunswick, Me. Medical School.

Medical School of Northwestern University, Chicago. see Northwestern University, Evanston, Ill. Medical School, Chicago.

Medical science and the medical profession. 41317

Medical sketch book. 62590

Medical sketches of the campaigns. 44328

Medical Society of Charleston, South-Carolina, to the inhabitants of South-Carolina. 87885

Medical Society of Chester County, Pa. see Chester County Medical Society.

Medical Society of Connecticut. see Connecticut Medical Society.

Medical Society of Delaware County, Pa. see Delaware County Medical Society.

Medical Society of Hampden District, Mass. see Hampden District Medical Society.

Medical Society of Harvard University. see Harvard University. Boylston Medical Society.

Medical Society of Illinois. see Illinois State Medical Society.

Medical Society of Indiana. see Indiana State Medical Society.

Medical Society of Kentucky. see Kentucky State Medical Society.

Medical Society of Lewis County, N. Y. see Lewis County Medical Society.

Medical Society of Louisiana. see Louisiana State Medical Society.

Medical Society of Massachusetts. see Massachusetts Medical Society.

Medical Society of Minnesota. see Minnesota State Medical Society.

Medical Society of Missouri, St. Louis. see St. Louis Medical Society of Missouri.

Medical Society of New Hampshire. see New Hampshire Medical Society.

Medical Society of New Haven County. see New Haven County Medical Society.

Medical Society of New Jersey. see New Jersey Medical Society.

Medical Society of New-Jersey. Transactions, 1864. 53152

Medical Society of New York. see Medical Society of the State of New York.

Medical Society of North Carolina. Annual meeting, 10th, 1859. 55646

Medical Society of Ohio. see Ohio State Medical Society.

Medical Society of Pennsylvania. (60430)

Medical Society of Pennsylvania. Convention, Lancaster, 1848. 60235

Medical Society of Philadelphia. see Philadelphia Medical Society.

Medical Society of Philadelphia County, Pa. see Philadelphia County Medical Society.

Medical Society of Rensselaer County, N. Y. see Rensselaer County Medical Society.

Medical Society of Rhode Island. see Rhode Island Medical Society.

Medical Society of Richmond County, N. Y. see Richmond County Medical Society.

Medical Society of Sacramento, Calif. see Sacramento Medical Society, Sacramento, Calif.

Medical Society of San Francisco. see San Francisco Medical Society.

Medical Society of South Carolina. 87878, 87880-87885, 87886, 87889

Medical Society of South Carolina. Committee on a Protest Signed by a Minority of the Members. 87888

Medical Society of South Carolina. Committee on the Most Efficient Means to Preserve the Health of the City of Charleston. 87879

Medical Society of South Carolina. Library. 87878, 87880, 87882-87883

Medical Society of South Carolina. Minority. 87888

Medical society of South-Carolina. 20093

Medical Society of Suffolk District, Mass. see Massachusetts Medical Society. Suffolk District Medical Society.

Medical Society of the County of New York. 53458, 53765, (53987), 54185

Medical Society of the County of New York. petitioners 54185, 54376

Medical Society of the County of New York. Committee on the Epidemic Fever of Bancker Street. 54376, note after 96392

Medical Society of the County of New York. Committee on the Epidemic Small Pox and Chicken Pox. 69929

Medical Society of the County of New York. Committee to Enquire into the Pestilentia Disease, in New York During the Summer and Autumn of 1798. 54376

Medical Society of the County of New York. Committee to Investigate the Subject of a Secret Medical Association. 54376

Medical Society of the County of New York. President. 54376 see also Romayne, Nicholas.

Medical Society of the State of California. see California Medical Society.

Medical Society of the State of Kentucky. see Kentucky State Medical Society.

Medical Society of the State of New York. 4225, 43762, 53764, 53765, 72477, 84276 85604, 90893, 3d note after 94138, 103419

Medical Society of the State of New York. Committee to Enquire Into the Symptoms, Origin, Cause, and Prevention of the Pestilential Disease. (53763)

Medical Society of the State of New York. Committee on Medical Education. 53765

Medical Society of the State of Tennessee. 94802

Medical Society of Vermont. see Vermont Medical Society.

Medical Society of Worcester District, Mass. see Worcester District Medical Society.

Medical statistics, consisting of estimates relating to the population of Philadelphia. 22432

Medical statistics; or a comparative view of the mortality in New-York. 55327

Medical theses. 84354, 93167, 96161

Medical topography of Brazil and Uruguay. (33035)

Medical topography of Newark. 13323

Medical topography of Upper Canada. 20686

Medical world. 47329, 82811

Medici, Giovanni Angelo. see Pius IV, Pope, 1499-1565.

Medici, Giulio de'. see Clement VII, Pope, 1478-1534.

Medicina Britannica. 80573, 80575

Medicina practica, en que se declara laconicamente los mas util de ella. 98841

Medicinal mineral waters, natural and artificial. 84072

Medicinal, poisonous, and dietetic properties of the cryptogamic plants. 64155

Medicinal waters of Saratoga. 47330, 76433

Medicinischen Chinarinden Neu-Granada's. 37106

Medico. pseud. Review of Jacksonian fanaticism and its influence. (70206)

Medico-botanical catalogue of the plants and ferns. 64157

Medico botanico criollo. 28942, 69601-69602

Medico-Chirurgical College, Philadelphia. (61811)

Medico do Povo. (47457)

Medico-legal record. 84246

Medicos discoursos, y practica de curar el sarampion. 98608

Medicus. pseud. Address to the guardians of the Washington Asylum. 101961

Medicus, Fried. Cas. 47331

Medill, William, 1801-1865. 47332-47333, 56922, 79107 see also Ohio. Governor, 1853-1856 (Medill)

Medina, Antonio de, fl. 1625. 47334

Medina, Antonio de, fl. 1710. petitioner 56396, 79138

Medina, Antonio de, fl. 1823. 47335

Medina, Balthasar de, d. 1697. 2987, 47336-47337

Medina, Bernardo de. 47338

Medina, Cristobal Gutierrez de. see Gutierrez de Medina, Cristobal.

Medina, Eduardo de. ed. 85683

Medina, Francisco de. (47339)

Medina, Francisco G. de. (47340)

Medina, Ivan Vazquez de. see Vazquez de Medina, Ivan.

Medina, Jose Toribio, 1852-1930. 10193, note after 94254, 96268, 98301, 98328-98329, 98334, note after 98770, 99469

Medina, Joseph Marinao. 47343

Medina, Juan Tello de Guzman y. see Tello de Guzman y Medina, Juan.

Medina, Pedro de. 47344-(47348)

Medina, Solomon de. complainant 47349

Medina de la Torres, Duque de. see Olivares, Gaspar de Guzman, Conde Duque de, 1587-1645.

Medina Rincon, Juan de. 47341, note after (71415)

Medina Rincon, Juan de. incorrectly supposed author 27360, 47342, note just before (71416)

Medina y Saravia, Joseph Diego de. defendant 26122 see also Mexico (Viceroyalty) Real Casa de Moneda. Tesorero Proprietario. defendant

Medina Academy. Burroughsian Lyceum. 47350

Medine, Pierre de. see Medina, Pedro de.

Medinilla, Maria de Estrada. see Medinilla, Maria Estrada de.

Medinilla, Maria Estrada de. 47351, 99400

Medios en servicio de Sv Magestad. 97673

Meditaciones de la vida oculta de Christo. 75812

Meditaciones del Santo Via-Crucis. (64399)

Maditaciones piadosas sobre la venida de los Santos Magos de Belen. 76864

Meditaciones sobre el desastre de Cumana. (58568)

Meditaciones sobre las postrimerias. 75817

Meditasjon arieba soefrimeentoe di noos Senjoor Hesoe Kriestoe. 66750

Meditation on coal. 13812

Meditations and experiences made public. 80459

Meditations and observations on the natural history and habits of bees. 66688

Meditations and observations, theologicall, and morall. 66688

Meditations and prayers. 72112

Meditations and spiritual exercises of Mr. Thomas Shepard. 80210, 80258

Meditations, awakened by the death of the Reverend Mr. Joshua Moodey. 46590

Meditations concerning the necessity, end, and usefulness of afflictions unto Gods children. 103925-103928

Meditations of Lamartine. 82796

Meditations on death. (46702)

Meditations on divine subjects. 41694

Meditations on the glory of the heavenly world. 46703

Meditations on the glory of the Lord Jesus Christ. 46704

Meditations on the incomprehensibility of God. 100869

Meditations on the sanctification of the Lord's Day. (46705)

Meditations on the uncertainty of mans life. 97494

Meditations on various subjects. 47402

Meditations upon the ark as a type of church. 46609

Meditations written during the prevalence of the yellow fever. 17484

Meditatus. pseud. Poems. 63610

Mediterranean and Oriental Steam Navigation Company. (47352)

Medium. pseud. Note of the author. 89511

Medizinische und chirurgische Bemerkungen uber das Klima. 47353, 72571

Medley, John, Bishop of Fredericton, 1804-1892. 25697, 47354

Madley: a monthly periodical conducted by an Association of Students of Yale College. 47355, 105851

Medley. By Catharine Weller. 102561

Medley. By Timo. Titterwell, Esq. 95871

Medley. By W. Gilmore Simms, Esq. 81210

Medley, humbly inscribed to Squire Lilliput, Professor of Scurrility. (61612)

Medley of incidents in the life of a poor root doctor. 95568

Medley of sketches and scraps. 86787

Medley; or Harlequin have at all. 39512

Medley, or monthly miscellany. 47356

Medrano, Balthasar Rodriguez. see Rodriguez Medrano, Balthasar.

Medrano, Miguel de Olabarrieta. see Olabarreita Medrano, Miguel de.

Medrano, Petro de. 47357

Medrano, Sebastian Fernandez de. 31374, 47358-47360

Medway, Ga. Church. 23589

Medway, Mass. 47361

Medway, Mass. Social Library. 47362

Medway, Mass. Society for Detecting Horse-
Thieves, and Recovering Stolen Horses.
see Society for Detecting Horse-
Thieves, and Recovering Stolen Horses,
Wrentham, Franklin, Medway, Medfield,
Walpole, Foxborough, Mansfield, and
Attleborough, Mass.

Mee Lochinvar. see Gordon, Sir Robert,
of Lochinvar, d. 1627?

Meech, Asa. 47363

Meech, L. W. 85072

Meehan, Charles H. W. (15576), 47364

Meehan, Thomas, 1826-1901. (47365)

Meehan, Thomas F. ed. 106398

Meek, A. B. 47366-47368

Meek, Fielding Bradford. 10008, 34253,
47369-(47371), 85072

Meeker, B. B. 47372

Meeker, E. 47373

Meeker, John. 47374

Meeker, Jotham. 47375-47377, 57883

Meeker, N. C. 47378

Meer oder Seehanen Buch. 42392

Meer Ontario. 16494

Mees, G. tr. 65279-65280

Meeting, St. Thomas' Parish, S. C., 1832.
see St. Thomas' Parish, S. C. Meeting,
1832.

Meeting, Washington, D. C., 1833. see
Washington, D. C. Meeting, 1833.

Meeting Against the Change of the Route of
the Erie Canal, Schenectady, N. Y.,
1836. see Schenectady, N. Y. Inhabitants' Meeting Against the Change of
the Route of the Erie Canal, 1836.

Meeting at Nomony, Va., 1802. see Nomony,
Va. Meeting, 1802.

Meeting at Tammany Hall . . . March 4th,
1858, to strengthen the President. 65722

Meeting at the Mansion House of the City of
London, in Aid of the Columbia Mission,
1857. 31908

Meeting at Upton's, in Dock Street, Philadelphia, 1831. (69574)

Meeting Convened at Martlings, New York,
1811. see New York (City) Meeting
Convened at Martlings, 1811.

Meeting du 29 Mars 1866 et rapport du Comite
Genevois. 79270

Meeting Expressing the Sense of the Citizens
on Improving the Navigation Around the
Falls of the Ohio River, Cincinnati, 1846.
57067

Meeting for Devising Means to Suppress
Gambling, Richmond, Va., 1833. Committee of Twenty-four. (71192)

Meeting for Devising Means to Suppress
Gambling, Richmond, Va., 1833. Committee of Twenty-four. Minority.
(71192)

Meeting for Promoting a Plan Proposed by
M. A. Vattemare, Albany, N. Y., 1847.
see Albany. Meeting for Promoting a
Plan Proposed by M. A. Vattemare, 1847.

Meeting for the Promotion of Temperance in
the United States, Washington, D. C.,
1832. 65758, 101947

Meeting for the Promotion of the Cause of
Temperance, in the United States, Washington, D. C., 1833. 65758, 101948

Meeting for the Purpose of Choosing Delegates
to the Anti-tariff Convention, Boston,
1831. see Boston. Meeting for the
Purpose of Choosing Delegates to the
Anti-tariff Convention, 1831.

Meeting Held at Lockport, N. Y., 1827. see
Holland Purchase Convention, Lockport,
N. Y., 1827.

Meeting held at Metropolitan Hall, Chicago,
1863. see Chicago. Meeting Held at
Metropolitan Hall, 1863.

Meeting Held at Princeton, N. J., 1824. to
Form a Society in New Jersey to Co-
operate with the American Colonization
Society. see New Jersey Colonization
Society.

Meeting Held by Deaf-Mutes, New York, 1853
see New York (City) Meeting Held by
Deaf-Mutes, 1853.

Meeting Held in Furtherance of the Establish-
ment of a Free Church for British
Emigrants at the Port of New York,
New York, 1845. (3354)

Meeting House, White Haven, Conn. see
White Haven, Conn. Meeting House.

Meeting houses considered. 19896

Meeting in Favor of Municipal Reform, New
York, 1844. see New York (City)
Meeting in Favor of Municipal Reform,
1844.

Meeting in Relation to St. Ann's Church for
Deaf-Mutes, New York, 1858. see New
York (City) Meeting in Relation to St.
Ann's Church for Deaf-Mutes, 1858.

Meeting in Relation to the Establishment of a
Large National Bank in this City, New
York, 1863. see New York (City)
Meeting in Relation to the Establishment
of a Large National Bank in this City,
1863.

Meeting in Relation to the Measures Taken to
Enforce the Observance of the Sabbath,
and the Attempt to Establish a Christian
Party in Politics, Auburn, N. Y., 1828.
2354

Meeting of a Large Number of Gentlemen
from Various Towns in the County of
Berkshire, for the Purpose of Expressing
the Views and Feelings of the County in
Relation to the Proposition to Remove
Williams College, Pittsfield, Mass., 1819
see Berkshire County, Mass. Meeting
on the Removal of Williams College,
Pittsfield, 1819.

Meeting of a Number of Citizens of Philadelphia, 1776. see Philadelphia. Meet
of a Number of Citizens, 1776.

Meeting of a Number of Sufferers at Wyoming
During the Revolutionary War, their
Descendants and Others, Wilkes-Barre,
Pa., 1837. see Wilkes-Barre, Pa.
Meeting of a Number of Sufferers at
Wyoming During the Revolutionary War,
their Descendants and Others, 1837.

Meeting of authors and publishers . . . April
9, 1868. 34925

Meeting of Bank Officers, New York, 1863.
see New York (City) Meeting of Bank
Officers, 1863.

Meeting of Certain Manufacturers of Philadelphia, and Others, 1828. see Philadelphia. Meeting of Certain Manufactur
and Others, 1828.

Meeting of Citizens, Boston, 1815. see Mas
chusetts. Meeting of Citizens from Ever
Part of the State, Boston, 1815.

Meeting of Citizens Favorable to the Construc
tion of a Canal from Rochester, on the
Erie Canal, to Olean, on the Allegany
River, New York, 1835. 65796

Meeting of Citizens Favorable to the Construction of a Canal from Rochester, on the Erie Canal, to Olean, on the Allegany River, New York, 1835. petitioners 65796

Meeting of Citizens, Favourable to the Entire Abolition of Lotteries, Philadelphia. 1833. see Philadelphia. Meeting of Citizens, Favourable to the Entire Abolition of Lotteries, 1833.

Meeting of Citizens from Every Part of the State of Massachusetts, Boston, 1815. see Massachusetts. Meeting of Citizens from Every Part of the State, Boston, 1815.

Meeting of Citizens in Cambridge, in Reference to the Assault on Senator Sumner, June 2, 1856. see Cambridge, Mass. Meeting of Citizens in Reference to the Assault on Senator Sumner, June 2, 1856.

Meeting of Citizens of Auburn, N. Y., 1838. see Auburn, N. Y. Meeting of Citizens, 1838.

Meeting of Citizens of Boston and Vicinity, Dec, 3, 1819, on Restraining the Further Extension of Slavery. see Boston. Citizens.

Meeting of Citizens of Nashua, N. H., 1842. see Nashua, N. H. Citizens.

Meeting of Citizens of New York and Others, Convened at the Request of the Board of Managers of the American Bible Society, 1816. see New York (City) Meeting of Citizens of New York and Others, Convened at the Request of the American Bible Society, 1816.

Meeting of citizens of Philadelphia, Favourable to the Entire Abolition of Lotteries, 1833. 97643

Meeting of Citizens on the Claim of Louisa Browning, Baltimore, 1825. see Baltimore. Meeting of Citizens on the Claim of Louisa Browning, 1825.

Meeting of Citizens on the Occasion of the Execution of John Brown, Providence, R. I., 1859. see Providence, R. I. Meeting of Citizens on the Occasion of the Execution of John Brown, 1859.

Meeting of Citizens Opposed to Secret Societies, Philadelphia, 1829. see Philadelphia. Meeting of Citizens Opposed to Secret Societies, 1829.

Meeting of Committees, from the Different Towns in the County of Washington, N. Y., 1808. see Washington County, N. Y. Meeting of Committees from the Different Towns, 1808.

Meeting of Delegates, Carlisle, Pa., 1816. see Carlisle, Pa. Meeting of Delegates, 1816.

Meeting of delegates at Carlisle. (47379)

Meeting of Delegates from Newburn, Washington, [etc.], Washington, N. C., 1827. see Washington, N. C. Meeting of Delegates from Newburn, Washington, [etc.], 1827.

Meeting of Delegates from the Southern Rights Association of South Carolina, Charleston, 1851. 87925

Meeting of Delegates of Every Town and District in the County of Suffolk, Mass., 1774. see Suffolk County, Mass. Convention, 1774.

Meeting of Delegates of Various Banks, from Different States in the Union, New York, 1838. see Bank Convention, New York, 1838.

Meeting of Episcopalians, New York, 1857. see New York (City) Meeting of Episcopalians, 1857.

Meeting of Episcopalians in the City of New York, 1812. (70071)

Meeting of Episcopalians in the City of New York, 1812. petitioners 54062

Meeting of Episcopalians in the City of New York, 1812. Committee. 54062

Meeting of Freeholders of Augusta County, Va., Staunton, 1775. see Augusta County, Va. Meeting of Freeholders, 1775.

Meeting of Friends of Rev. John Pierpont, Boston, 1839. see Boston. Hollis Street Church. Meeting of Friends of Rev. John Pierpont, 1839.

Meeting of Friends of the Administration, Washington, Pa., 1827. see National Republican Party. Pennsylvania. Washington, Pa.

Meeting of Irishmen, New York, 1825. see New York (City) Meeting of Irishmen, 1825.

Meeting of Irishmen in New York. To the people of Ireland. 47380

Meeting of Landholders, Dover, N. Y., 1838. 90807

Meeting of Mechanics and Other Workmen, New York, 1831. see New York (City) Meeting of Mechanics and Other Workmen, 1831.

Meeting of Merchants and Other Inhabitants, Wilmington, Del., 17th June, 1801. see Wilmington, Del. Meeting of Merchants and Other Inhabitants, 17th June, 1801.

Meeting of Merchants and Other Inhabitants, Wilmington, Dec., 20th July, 1801. see Wilmington, Del. Meeting of Merchants and Other Inhabitants, 20th July, 1801.

Meeting of Ministers of All Religious Denominations in the District of Columbia, Washington, D. C., 1865. (41226)

Meeting of our English nauie and the Spanish fleete. 77289

Meeting of Pennsylvania Freeholders, Philadelphia, 1817. 40261, (59860)

Meeting of Persons Interested in the Preservation of the British West India Colonies, London, 1833. see Public Meeting of Persons Interested in the Preservation of the British West India Colonies, London, 1833.

Meeting of Representatives of the Several Railroad Companies Between New York, Boston, Philadelphia and Baltimore, Chicago, Cincinnati, and the Ohio and Mississippi Rivers, Cleveland, 1854. 65798

Meeting of Salt Manufacturers, New Bedford, Mass., 1827. 65762

Meeting of Ship Masters and Ship Owners, New York, 1839. 97001

Meeting of Sundry Citizens of Harford County, Harve de Grace, Md., 1836. see Harford County, Md. Meeting of Sundry Citizens, Harve de Grace, 1836.

Meeting of the Association for the Improvement of Common Schools in Indiana. 34506

Meeting of the Chapin Family, Springfield, Mass., 1862. 11952

Meeting of the Chicago Historical Society. 12621

Meeting of the Citizens in Relation to the Great Pennsylvania Railroad, Philadelphia, 1846. see Philadelphia. Meeting of the Citizens in Relation to the Great Pennsylvania Railroad, 1846.

Meeting of the Citizens of Buffalo, N. Y., With Reference to the Improvement of the Erie Canal, 1839. see Western Canal Convention, Rochester, N. Y., 1839.

Meeting of the Citizens of Central Mississippi on the Slavery Question, 1850. 49533

Meeting of the Citizens of Detroit on the Southern Boundary of Michigan, 1836. see Detroit. Meeting of the Citizens on the Southern Boundary of Michigan, 1836.

Meeting of the Citizens of Hamilton and Rossville, Ohio, on the Subject of a Western National Armory, 1841. 69738

Meeting of the Citizens of Kershaw District, Camden, S. C., 1826. see Kershaw District, S. C. Tariff Meeting, Camden, 1826.

Meeting of the Citizens of Lockport, N. Y., With Reference to the Improvement of the Erie Canal, 1839. see Western Canal Convention, Rochester, N. Y., 1839.

Meeting of the citizens of Macomb County, at Mt. Clemens, Dec. 1, 1849, for the improvement of Clinton River. 43616

Meeting of the Citizens of Macomb County, for the Improvement of Clinton River, Mt. Clemens, Mich., 1849. 43616

Meeting of the Citizens of New York, to Express Sympathy and Respect for the Mexican Republican Exiles, New York, 1865. 54594

Meeting of the Citizens of New York, to Express Their Regret at the Death of Sir Walter, Scott, 1833. see New York (City) Meeting of the Citizens of New York, to Express Their Regret at the Death of Sir Walter Scott, 1833.

Meeting of the Citizens of Palmyra, N. Y., With Reference to the Improvement of the Erie Canal, 1839. see Western Canal Convention, Rochester, N. Y., 1839.

Meeting of the Citizens of Providence, Friendly to the Promotion of Temperance, Providence, R. I., 1828. Committee. 66345

Meeting of the Citizens of Rochester, N. Y., With Reference to the Improvement of the Erie Canal, 1839. see Western Canal Convention, Rochester, N. Y., 1839.

Meeting of the Citizens of the United States at Paris, 1843. see Paris. Meeting of the Citizens of the United States, 1843.

Meeting of the citizens of Washington. 101942A

Meeting of the Citizens of Windsor County, Vt., Woodstock, Vt., 1833. see Windsor County, Vt. Meeting, Woodstock, 1833.

Meeting of the class of 1813, on the 16th and 17th of August, 1843. 105880

Meeting of the Class of 1820 of Yale College, New Haven, Conn., 1840. see Yale University. Class of 1820.

Meeting of the class of 1820 was held by invitation. 105882

Meeting of the class of 1821, on the annual commencement of Yale College, Sept. 14, 1831. 105883

Meeting of the Class of 1822 of Yale College New Haven, Conn., 1835. see Yale University. Class of 1822.

Meeting of the Class Which Graduated at Yale College in 1810, New Haven, Conn, 1840 see Yale University. Class of 1810.

Meeting of the Clerical Association in the Church of the Holy Trinity, Friday, November 9th, 1866. 13642

Meeting of the Committee of Inspection, Observation and Correspondence. 38793

Meeting of the convention [of Baptists of Vermont.] 99151

Meeting of the Free Colored People of Baltimore, 1839. see Baltimore. Meeting of the Free Colored People, 1839.

Meeting of the Freeholders from the State, Philadelphia, 1817. see Meeting of Pennsylvania Freeholders, Philadelphia, 1817.

Meeting of the Freeholders of Chester County Pa., 1774. see Chester County, Pa. Meeting of the Freeholders, 1774.

Meeting of the Friends and Admirers of Lord Metcalf, Montreal, 1847. 48148

Meeting of the Friends of Africa, Baltimore, 1827. see Friends of African Colonization. Meeting, Baltimore, 1827.

Meeting of the Friends of Civil and Religious Liberty, Baltimore, 1837. see Great Meeting of the Friends of Civil and Religious Liberty, Baltimore, 1837.

Meeting of the Friends of Temperance, New Bedford, Mass., 1840. (52500)

Meeting of the Friends of the General Administration, Greensburgh, Pa., 1827. see National Republican Party. Pennsylvania Greensburgh. and National Republican Party. Pennsylvania. Westmoreland County.

Meeting of the Friends of the Present Administration, Winchester, Va., 1828. see National Republican Party. Virginia. Winchester.

Meeting of the Friends of the Union and the Constitution, Portland, Me., 1835. 65791

Meeting of the Friends of the Union, Baltimore. 1861. see Baltimore. Public Meeting of the Friends of the Union, 1861.

Meeting of the Friends to the Election of John Quincy Adams, Philadelphia, 1828. see National Republican Party. Pennsylvania Philadelphia.

Meeting of the General Committee Appointed by the World's Temperance Convention, 1st, Albany, 1854. see General Committee Appointed by the World's Temperance Convention, New York, 1853. Meeting, 1st, Albany, 1854.

Meeting of the Grand Lodge of the State of Vermont, Oct. 7, A. L. 5834. 99192

Meeting of the Inhabitants of Saratoga and Warren Counties, Cornish, N. Y., 1846. (76922)

Meeting of the Inhabitants of Schenectady, Opposed to the Change of the Route of the Erie Canal, 1836. see Schenectady N. Y. Meeting, 1836.

Meeting of the Inhabitants of the Town of Salem, Mass., 1831. see Salem, Mass Town Meeting, 1831.

Meeting of the Loyal Women of the Republic, New York, 1863. 65869, 90405

Meeting of the Massachusetts Episcopal Society for the Religious Instruction of Freedmen. (45843)

Meeting of the Merchants of Philadelphia, 1824. Committee. Delegates. 61564

Meeting of the National Republican Young Men, Worcester, Mass., 1812. see Democratic Party. Massachusetts. Worcester.

Meeting of the Officers of Colleges and Academies, Albany, N. Y., 1863. see New York (State) University.

Meeting of the people! 94297

Meeting of the people . . . On the Subject of the Pacific Rail Roads, and Oregon Rail Roads, Portland, Ore., 1867. see Portland, Ore. Meeting of the People . . . On the Subject of the Pacific Rail Roads, and Oregon Rail Roads, 1867.

Meeting of the Printers of the District of Columbia, Washington, D. C. 1834. 101967

Meeting of the Receivers and Exporters of American Leaf Tobacco, New York, 1865. see Receivers and Exporters of American Leaf Tobacco. Meeting, New York. 1865.

Meeting of the Signers of the Memorial to Congress, New York, 1834. 69918, note after 97799 see also Union Committee, New York, 1834.

Meeting of the Society of the Church of the Puritans, May 3, 1860. Argument of Benjamin K. Phelps, Esq., in support of the resolutions of Mr. Smith. (61367)

Meeting of the Tax Payers of the City of Milwaukee, 1858. see Milwaukee. Meeting of the Tax Payers of the City, 1858.

Meeting of the three friends. 103235

Meeting of the Towns of the County of Worcester, Mass., 1782. see Worcester, Mass. Convention, 1782.

Meeting of the Union and State Rights Party, Charleston, S. C., 1832. see Union and State Rights Party (South Carolina) Meeting, Charleston, 1832.

Meeting of the waters of Hudson & Erie. 105187

Meeting of the West-India Merchants, and Planters London, 1784. 834, 102789

Meeting of the West India Merchants and Planters, London, 1784. Secretary. 834, 102789 see also Allen, James.

Meeting of the Whig Young Men of New York City, 1834. see Whig Party. New York, New York City.

Meeting of the Young Men of Maryland, Baltimore, 1831. (45255)

Meeting [of those students of the South Carolina College in favor of forming a Southern Rights Association, March 6, 1851.] 87986

Meeting of Working-men and Other Persons Favorable to Political Principle, Albany, N. Y., 1830. 82355, 104222

Meeting of Working-men and Other Persons Favorable to Political Principle, Albany, N. Y., 1830. Assistant Chairman. 82355, 104222 see also Farnham, Henry.

Meeting of Working-men and Other Persons Favorable to Political Principle, Albany, N. Y., 1830. Chairman. 82355, 104222 see also Smith, Benjamin F.

Meeting of Working-men and Other Persons Favorable to Political Principle, Albany, N. Y., 1830. Secretary. 82355, 104222 see also Wilson, John.

Meeting of Workingmen and Others, Albany, N. Y., 1830. see Meeting of Working-men and Other Persons Favorable to Political Principle, Albany, N. Y., 1830.

Meeting of young men in Maryland, Dec. 20th, 1831. (45255)

Meeting on a Proposed College for Colored Youth, New Haven, Conn., 1831. see New Haven, Conn. Meeting on a Proposed College for Colored Youth, 1831.

Meeting of Behalf of the Preservation of the British West India Colonies, London, 1832. 65761

Meeting on Free Religion, Boston, 1867. 25715

Meeting on Occasion of the Arrival of the Tea Ship, Philadelphia, 1773. see Philadelphia. Public Meeting on Occasion of the Arrival of the Tea Ship, 1773.

Meeting on Texas, New York, 1836. see Great Meeting on Texas, New York, 1836.

Meeting on the Cause of Intemperance in the United States, Washington, D. C., 1833. see Meeting for the Promotion of the Cause of Temperance in the United States, Washington, D. C., 1833.

Meeting on the Clergy Reserved Lands and the King's College, Toronto, 1830. see Toronto. Meeting on the Clergy Reserved Lands and the King's College, 1830.

Meeting on the Practicability and Utility of Immediately Constructing a Central Railway, from Pottsville to Sunbury and Danville, Sunbury, Pa., 1830. see Sunbury, Pa. Meeting on the Practicability and Utility of Immediately Constructing a Central Railway, from Pottsville to Sunbury and Danville, 1830.

Meeting on the Religious Instruction of the Negroes, Charleston, S. C., 1845. see Charleston, S. C. Meeting on the Religious Instruction of the Negroes, 1845.

Meeting on the Rights of the Cherokee Indians, Boston, 1830. 71382, 71384, 104800

Meeting on the Rights of the Cherokee Indians, Boston, 1830. petitioners 71382, 71384, 104880

Meeting on the Subject of the Cases of Captain Abraham Wendell, Jr., and the Crew of the Ship William Engs, Boston, 1838-1839. 97002

Meeting . . . proceedings of the Commissioners of the Soldiers' National Cemetery Association. 27233

Meeting Respecting St. Ann's Church for Deaf-Mutes, New York, 1853. see New York (City) Public Meeting Respecting St. Ann's Church for Deaf-Mutes, 1853.

Meeting the sun. (81377)

Meeting to Commemorate the Landing of William Penn on the Shore of America, Philadelphia, 1824. 59745

Meeting to Consider the Propriety of Forming the Protestant Episcopal Historical Society, Hartford, Conn., 1850. see Protestant Episcopal Historical Society.

Meeting to Further the Enterprise of the Atlantic Telegraph, New York. 1863. 2302

Meeting to Further the Enterprise of the
Atlantic Telegraph, New York, 1863.
Secretary. 2302
Meeting to Promote the Election of Clinton
and Tallmadge, Albany, N. Y., 1824.
see Democratic Party. New York.
Albany.
Meeting to Take into Consideration the
Condition of the Freed People of the
South, Philadelphia, 1863. see Phila-
delphia. Meeting to Take into Consider-
ation the Condition of the Freed People
of the South, 1863.
Meetings and resolutions of the citizens of
Sacramento, Marysville and Stockton.
37808, 97098
Meetings on the Proposed Operatic and
Dramatic House, Philadelphia, 1839.
see Philadelphia. Meetings on the
Proposed Operatic and Dramatic House,
1839.
Meg, a pastoral. 106372
Megeath, J. G. 90739
Megerle, Therese von. 92574
Megia, Felix. 47381
Meginness, J. F. 47382
Megister, Hieron. 5905, 47383-47384
Mehlotist lska i nana ulhpisa puta. 48186
Mehrerer Gelehrten. pseud. ed. (27208)
Meier, Adolphus. 47385
Meier, Heinrich Ludewig. tr. 98746
Meier-Smith, Matson. see Smith, Matson
Meier, 1826-1887.
Meighan, Thaddeus W. 47386
Meigs, Charles D. 22514, (35460), 47387-
47388 see also Commission Appointed
to Visit Canada, for the Investigation of
the Epidemic Cholera, 1832.
Meigs, H. 47389
Meigs, James Aitken, 1829-1879. 47390-
(47391), 56038
Meigs, Josiah, 1757-1822. ed. 47392, 52992
Meigs, M. C. 47393 see also U. S. Quarter-
master's Department.
Meigs, Return Jonathan, 1764-1824. 9538,
(31792), 47394-47398, 64492-64497,
101319-101320 see also U. S. Post
Office Department.
Meigs, Return Jonathan, 1764-1824. petitioner
47399
Meigs, Return Jonathan, 1764-1824. incorrectly
supposed author 47394
Meijer, H. A. 47400
Meik, James Patrick. tr. 83146
Meikle, James. (47401)-47402
Meikle, W. (47403)
Meilleur, J. B. 47404
Mein, John. 6558, (47405)-47406, note after
90614
Mein, John. supposed author (1969), (3111),
38180, 56562, 2d note after 103122
Mein and Fleeming. firm publishers 47407-
47408, 62743
Mein and Fleeming's Massachusetts register.
47407
Mein and Fleeming's register for New England
and Nova Scotia. 47408
Mein Besuch Americans, in Sommer 1824.
51672
Mein Lieber Bruder oder Schwester 106357
Meine Aufenthalt und meine Reisen in den-
selben vom Jahre 1834 bis 1841. 8678
Meine Ausflucht nach Brasilien. 39943
Meine Auswanderung nach den Vereinigten
Staaten. 26379

Meine Auswaunderung nach Polen und Norda-
merika. 22769
Meine Reise nach Brasilien im Jhare 1826.
44360
Meine zweite Weltreise. 61341
Meinecke, C. 47409
Meinem insonders lieven Freunden. 66466
Meiners, Christoph. (47410)-47412
Meinicke, C. E. 47413
Mein's Circulating Library, Boston. 47406
Meio de nao perder nas loterias. 88709
Meios de fazer fortuna. 78118
Meisner, L. F. F. 47414
Meissner, J. P. 47415
Meissner, N. N. W. tr. 91296
Meissner, R. 47416
Meistens Auszung aus einem Tagebuche seines
Lebens und seiner Reisen. 105201
Meister. pseud. Gesprach zwischen einem
Jungling und Meister. 89430
Meisterschlussel zu den Geheimnissen des
hohern Ordens. 50680
Mejia, Pero. see Mexia, Pero.
Mejicano. pseud. see P., J. M. pseud.
Mejico . . . see also Mexico . . .
Mejico en 1842. 71640
Mejico en 1856 y 1857. 64332
Mejico intervencion y la monarquia. 48531
Mejico y el Archiduque Fernando Maximiliano.
29356
Mejico y sus revoluciones. 50483
Mejor, coleccion de materiales para hacerla
quien lo supiere mejor. (73899)
Mejor parte de la gloria de Maria. 76014
Mejorada, ---------- Marques de. 34177,
47147, 86398 see also Spain. Ministerio
de Estado.
Mejorda, --------, Marques de. see Mejorada
----------, Marques de.
Mel, Mary. pseud. Poems and tales. see
Blake, Mary E.
Mela, Pomponius, 1st cent. 63855-(63961),
76838, 86390
Melanchthon, Philipp, 1497-1560. 74803
Melancholy case of Mrs. Ackerman. 100873
Melancholy case of William Webb, alias Kelly.
102245
Melancholy fate of Sir John Franklin and his
party. 67427
Melancholy man. 92345
Melancholy narrative of the distressful voyage.
30551
Melange. 81193
Melange de litterature. 55304
Melanges. (69592)
Melanges de litterature, d'histoire, et de
philosophie. (1914)
Melanges de morale, d'economie et de politique
25544
Melanges de morale et de litterature. 77361
Melanges et correspondance d'economie
politique. 77360
Melanges hymenopterologiques. 77217
Melanges interessans et curieux. 73491-73492,
100838
Melanges litteraires. 12248, (12275)
Melanges orthopterologiques. 77217
Melanges politiques et philosophiques extraits
des memoires. 35890
Melanges religieux. 44867
Melanges scientifiques et litteraires. (5522)
Melania (Boughton) Smith. 82449
Melanie and other poems. 104511-104512
Melanospermeae. 30782

Melantseetoa Indians. Treaties, etc. 96644
Melastrome Brasiliane. 67407
Melbourn, Julius. 30097, (47418)
Melbourne, Australia. American Citizens. 47419
Melbourne, and the Chincha Islands. 59473
Melcher, Adam. 96004
Melcher, Israel. 96004
Melcher, John. 83400, 84553
Melchor de Castro Macedo. Fray 47420
Melcombe, George Bubb Dodington, Baron, 1691-1762. 20516
Melendez, Juan. (47422)-47423, 73182
Melgar, Esteban Sancho de. 47424
Melguizo, A. 47425
Melillanca y Guanalcoa, -------. 47426
Meline, James F. (47427)
Melish, John, 1771-1882. 5567, 19714, (19725), 39125, 47428-47437
Melisone, Androvinci. see Tassoni, Alessandro.
Mella, Nicolas Romero de. see Romero de Mella, Nicolas.
Mellado, Francisco Lopez. 86400
Mellen, George W. F. 47438
Mellen, Grenville. 6363, 38583, 47439, (47442)
Mellen, John. 47443-47447
Mellen, John. (47448)-47449
Mellen, Nicholas. 19029, 2d note after 97085
Mellen, William P. 47450
Meller, Henry James. 47451
Mellet, Jullien. 47452
Mellichampe. A legend of the Santee. 81205, 81237, (81238), 81245, (81279)
Mellini, Dominico. (47453)
Mellish, John H. (47454)
Mello, A. d'A. 47455
Mello, Antonio Dais Coelho e. see Coelho e Mello, Antonio Dias.
Mello, Antonio Jose das Neves e. see Neves e Mello, Antonio, Jose das.
Mello, Antonio Manuel Leite Pacheo Malheiro e. see Malheiro e Mello, Antonio Manuel Leite Pacheo.
Mello, Emilio Xavier Sobreira de. see Sobreira de Mello, Emilio Xavier de, d. 1885.
Mello, Felisardo de Souza e. see Souza e Mello, Felisardo de.
Mello, Francisco Freire de. 47460
Mello, Francisco Manoel de. 69287
Mello, Francisco Manuel de, 1608-1666. 44424-44425, 3d note after 96170
Mello, Joaquim Guennes da Silva. see Silva Mello, Joaquim Guennes da.
Mello, Jose Rodriguez de. see Rodrigues de Mello, Jose, 1704-1783.
Mello, Josephi Rodriguea de. see Rodrigues de Mello, Jose, 1704-1783.
Mello, Pedro Americo de Figueriedo e. see Figueiredo e Mello, Pedro Americo de.
Mello, Roberto Calheiros de. 69309 see also Alagoas (Brazilian Province) Vice Presidente (Mello)
Mello, Sebastiao Jose de Carvalho e. see Pombal, Sebastiao Jose de Carvalho e Mello, Marquis de.
Mello, Sebastiao Souze e. see Souza e Mello, Sebastiao.
Mello, Urbino Sabino Pessoa de. see Pessoa de Mello, Urbano Sabino.
Mello e Alvim, Miguel de Souza. see Souza Mello e Alvim, Miguel de.
Mello e Netto, Ladislau de Souza. see Souza Mello e Netto, Ladislau de.

Mello Freire, Paschoal Jose de. 42346
Mello Moraes, Alexandre Jose de, 1816-1882. 7529, 47456-47459
Mellon, Michael. defendant 47464
Melmoth, Cortney. pseud. Sublime and beautiful of scripture. see Pratt, Samuel Jackson.
Melmoth, Sydney. 47456
Melo, Matias Suarez de. see Suarez de Melo, Matias.
Melodias campestres. 62951
Melodies, duets, trios, songs, and ballads, pastoral, amatory, sentimental, patriotic, religious, and miscellaneous. 105188
Melodies for the craft, or songs for freemasons. 47466.
Melo-drama. 80869
Melodrama alegorico de D. J. M. V. C. 99679
Melodrama heroico en un acto. 57684
Melo drama, in three acts. Adapted to the New-York theatres. 101111
Melo-drama, in three acts, as performed at the New-York Park Theatre. 105195
Melo-drama, in three acts. [By W. H. Hver.] 73154
Melodrama in two acts. 86903
Melo drama, in two acts. As performed at the New-York Theatre. 91998
Melo-dramtico burlesco. (37861)
Melodrame a grand spectacle tire de l'ouvrage de M. de Chateaubriand. 12257
Melodrame en trois actes, a spectacle. 3978, 101895
Melodrame en trois actes, de M. Le Blanc. 39594
Melodrame historique en trois actes. 63174
Melo drame, in three acts. With marches, combats and chorusses. 97465
Melody, G. H. C. 47467
Melrose, Mass. Endeavour Engine Company. see Endeavour Engine Company, Melrose, Mass.
Melrose, Mass. School Committee. 47468
Melrose, Mass. Selectmen. 47468
Melrose memorial. 28056
Melsheimer, Frederick Ernst. 46469
Melsheimer, Frederick Val. 47470-47471
Melsheimer, Frederick Val. incorrectly supposed author 94200
Melton, Edward. pseud.? (484), 5046, 47472-47474, 2d note after 102813
Melvil, C. 47475
Melvill van Carnbee, Pieter, Baron, 1816-1856. ed. 47476, 49982, 80864
Melvill, Thomas. (47477)
Melville. pseud. Ethan Allen. 805, (47484)
Melville, David. 47478
Melville, Henry. 47479
Melville, Herman, 1918-1891. 47480-47482
Melville, J. alias see M'Clean, James Sylvanus. defendant
Melville, Lawrence. supposed author 47483, (52419)
Melville, P. ed. 47476, 49982
Melville letters. 43667, note before 93267
Melvin, James. note after 7269, 47485-(47486)
Me-mat-way. Potawatomi Indian Chief 96709
Member. pseud. reporter (63075)
Member. pseud. Address delivered before the New York African Society for Mutual Relief. 81751
Member. pseud. Address, delivered February 4, 1806. see Buel, William Samuel.

MEMBER

Member. pseud. Authentic historical memoir
of the Schuylkill Fishing Company. see
Milnor, William.
Member. pseud. Claims of benevolence
upon the young men of the community.
106161
Member. pseud. Heroic address. see
Joline, John K.
Member. pseud. How the south rejected
compromise in the Peace Conference
of 1861. see Chase, Salmon Portland,
1808-1873.
Member. pseud. Memoirs of a New England
village choir. see Gilman, Samuel.
Member. pseud. Notices of the First
Church and its ministers. 50715
Member. pseud. Oration delivered before
the Washington Association. 101979
Member. pseud. Oration, in memory of the
virtues of Gen. George Washington.
57442, 2d note after 101866
Member. pseud. Principal and objects of
the National Reform Association.
(65660)
Member. pseud. Serious address to the
candid members of the Methodist com-
munion. (79244)
Member. pseud. Terrible mysteries of the
Ku-Klux-Klan. 20360
Member. pseud. Vindication of the minority
of the Congregational Church in the
South Parish, Augusta. see Weston,
Daniel Cony.
Member appointed for that purpose. pseud.
Eulogium on the late General George
Washington. 101805
Member dissenting from the church. pseud.
Speech said to have been delivered.
89193
Member from 21st ward. pseud. Speech on
the "water question." 89192
Member of Assembly. pseud. Essay on the
present state of the province of Nova-
Scotia. 56125
Member of Congress. pseud. Dialogue be-
tween a one thousand-dollar clerk and
a member of Congress. 19932
Member of Congress. pseud. Rights of the
free states subverted. see Giddings,
Joshua R. supposed author
Member of Congress from South Carolina.
pseud. Massachusetts and South
Carolina. 87870
'Member of Convention.' pseud. Observations.
52933
Member of Dartmouth College. pseud. Cohos.
see Wheelock, John. supposed author
Member of it, who is not a minister. pseud.
History of the origin and design of the
. . . [Massachusetts Congregational
Charitable] Society. 95178
Member of Lincoln's Inn, F. R. S. pseud.
Three letters to Dr. Price. see
Fitzherbert, Sir William. supposed
author and Lind, John. supposed
author
Member of Parliament. pseud. Conduct of a
R. Hon. Gentleman. 63088
Member of Parliament. pseud. Detection of
the false reasons and facts. (19779)
Member of Parliament. pseud. Examination
into the conduct of the present adminis-
tration. 23346
Member of Parliament. pseud. Free and
impartial examination of the preliminary
articles of pacification. 25702

Member of Parliament. pseud. Letter from
a member of Parliament to His Grace
the Duke of *****. 40300
Member of Parliament. pseud. Letter from
a member of Parliament to his friends
in the country. see Walpole, Robert,
1st Earl of Orford, 1676-1745.
Member of Parliament. pseud. Letter to the
Belfast . . . Volunteers. 40458
Member of Parliament. pseud. Letter to the
Right Honourable Lord M*****. 40523
Member of Parliament. pseud. Letters to
the Earl of Liverpool. 40643
Member of Parliament. pseud. Lucubrations
during a short recess. see Sinclair,
Sir John, Bart., 1754-1835.
Member of Parliament. pseud. Observations
on a pamphlet. (56490)
Member of Parliament. pseud. Observations
on the papers relative to the rupture with
Spain. see Wilkes, John, 1727-1797.
Member of Parliament. pseud. Reflections
upon the present state of affairs. 68727
Member of Parliament. pseud. Some ob-
servations on the importance of the
navigation-laws. see Colchester, Charles
Abbott, 2d Baron.
Member of Parliament. pseud. Vindication
of Mr. Pitt. 99797
Member of Parliament in town. pseud. Letter.
(40301)
Member of said Council. pseud. Result of a
Council of Nine Churches at Northampton.
see Edwards, Jonathan, 1703-1758.
Member of St. Mary's Church. pseud. Answer
to an "Address by a Catholic layman,"
(62214)
Member of St. Paul's. pseud. Letter. 12358,
40302, 59267, 62218
Member of St. P[au]l's. pseud. True copy
of a letter. 97108
Member of that community. pseud. Dialogue.
see Positive. pseud.
Member of that institution. pseud. View of
the New York State Prison in the city of
New York. 54711
Member of that society. pseud. Letter
addressed to the Liverpool Society for
the Abolition of Slavery. see Sandars,
Joseph.
Member of the African Society in Boston,
pseud. Sons of Africans. 87108
Member of the Agricultural Society of the
State of New-York. pseud. Treatise on
silk worms. 96743
Member of the Albany bar. pseud. Opinion.
633
Member of the Assembly. pseud. Plea for
voluntary societies. 63400
Member of the Assembly. pseud. Preface.
see Franklin, Benjamin, 1706-1790.
Member of the Association. pseud. Philosophy
of the Temperance Society. 90563
Member of the Baltimore bar. pseud. Com-
pilation of the insolvent laws of Maryland.
45112
Member of the bar. pseud. Alphabetical index
to the laws of Texas. 95000-95001
Member of the bar. pseud. California diggings
see Kip, Leonard.
Member of the bar. pseud. Camp Charlotte.
10179
Member of the bar. pseud. Essay on industry.
84130, 1st note after 95758
Member of the bar. pseud. Opinion of the
court. 39885

1618

Member of the bar. pseud. Remarks on the judiciary system of Massachusetts. (45969)

Member of the bar. pseud. reporter Report of the arguments of counsel. (17391), 2d note after 96854

Member of the bar. pseud. Report of the opinions of the three judges. 60589

Member of the bar. pseud. reporter Report of the trial and conviction of John Haggerty. 29519

Member of the bar. pseud. reporter Report of the trials of Capt. Thomas Wells. see S., A. B. pseud. reporter

Member of the bar. pseud. Right of Universalists to testify in a court of justice vindicated. 71357

Member of the bar. pseud. reporter Trial of Isaac, Israel, Jr., and Nelson Thayer. 95272

Member of the bar. pseud. reporter Trial of Isaac Spencer. 89331

Member of the bar. pseud. reporter Trial of John Blaisdell. 96828

Member of the bar. pseud. Trial of Mrs. Hannah Kinney. 37932

Member of the bar. pseud. reporter Trial of Reuben Crandall. 96855

Member of the bar. pseud. Volcanic diggings. see Kip, Lemuel.

Member of the bar of Philadelphia. pseud. Report of the case of the Commonwealth of Pennsylvania, versus John Smith. 60470, 82884

Member of the bar of Richmond. pseud. Four essays on the right and propriety of secession. (25280)

Member of the Belfast Literary Society. pseud. Short account of the author [i. e. Thomas Romney Robinson.] 72197

Member of the "Bloody-First." pseud. Reminiscences of a campaign in Mexico. see Robertson, J. B.

Member of the Board. pseud. General Theological Seminary. 26911, (54291)

Member of the Board of Public Works, of the State of South Carolina. pseud. Observations suggested by the late occurrences in Charleston. 87906

Member of the Boston bar. pseud. Account of the origin of the Mississippi doctrine of Repudiation. see Austin, Iver James.

Member of the Boston bar. pseud. Affairs of Rhode Island. see Bolles, John Augustus.

Member of the Boston bar. pseud. Letter. see Folsom, Abby, H.

Member of the Boston bar. pseud. Review of the D'Hauteville case. see Chandler, Peleg Whitman.

Member of the Brazilian Association of Liverpool. pseud. Some remarks and explanatory observations. 86731

Member of the Brenthren's Church. pseud. History of the Moravian missions. 32185, 2d note after 97850

Member of the Chamber of Commerce. pseud. Review of the financial affairs in the United States. 24344, 70205

Member of the Chambersburg bar. pseud. Enquiry into the political grade. see Denny, John F.

Member of the Charleston bar. pseud. reporter Digest of the cases reported in the Constitutional Court of South-Carolina. 87455

Member of the church. pseud. Appendix, containing an account of the Church of Chirst in Plymouth. see Cotton, John, 1584-1652.

Member of the church. pseud. Case of the Right Rev. Henry U. Onderdonk. 57318

Member of the church. pseud. Memorial of the revival in Plymouth Church, Brooklyn. 8302

Member of the church. pseud. Review of Bishop Meade's Counter statement. 47238

Member of the Church of England. pseud. Dialogue between the pulpit and the reading-desk. see Green, William. supposed author and Perronet, Charles. supposed author

Member of the Cincinnati bar. pseud. Objects of the rebellion. (56426)

Member of the class of '67. pseud. Shakings. see Benjamin, Park.

Member of the club. pseud. Address. 89214

Member of the committee. pseud. Jail question. 35537

Member of the Committee of Peace in Paris. pseud. Letter to the American Peace Society. see Gibbes, George M.

Member of the community. pseud. Life of Madam de la Pletrie. see Mary St. Thomas. Mother

Member of the conference. pseud. Reply to the same "Address." 20657

Member of the congregation. pseud. Rev. John N. Campbell, D. D. 10256, 89744

Member of the Consociation and Association of New-Haven County. pseud. Defence of the doings of the Reverend Consociation. see Todd, Jonathan.

Member of the corporation. pseud. Letter to the President of Harvard College. see Eliot, Samuel Atkins.

Member of the Council. pseud. Result of an ecclesiastical council at Princeton. see Goffe, Joseph.

Member of the Council. pseud. Result of council at Princeton incapable of vindication. see Goffe, Joseph.

Member of the Court of Policy. pseud. Address to the colonists of British Guiana. 8102

Member of the Dakota Mission. pseud. English and Dakota vocabulary. see Riggs, Mary Ann. C.

Member of the Dominica Legislature. pseud. Appeal and caution to the British nation. 81869

Member of the Easton bar. pseud. reporter Trial of Charles Getter. 96870

Member of the Episcopal Church. pseud. Address to the ministers and congregations. see Seabury, Samuel, Bp., 1729-1796.

Member of the Executive Committee. pseud. Report. see Mott, Jordan L.

Member of the Georgia Conference. pseud. Mysterious messenger. 51658

Member of the Hickory Club. pseud. Reply to the sketches. (47188)-47189

Member of the House of Assembly of Newfoundland. pseud. Short reply to the speech of Earl Aberdeen. see Morris, Patrick.

Member of the House of Commons. pseud. False accusers accused. 23756

Member of the House of Commons. pseud. Some calculations relating to the proposals made. 86606

Member of the House of Commons. pseud.
West India agricultural distress. 102770

Member of the House of Representatives.
pseud. Address to the people of Maryland. see Dennis, L. P.

Member of the House of Representatives.
pseud. Notes on the finances of the
state of South-Carolina. see Desaussure, Henry William, 1713-1839.
supposed author and Johnson, William,
1771-1834. supposed author

Member of the Howard Association of New
Orleans. pseud. Diary of a Samaritan.
see Robinson, William L.

Member of the Humane Society. pseud.
Barnstable, Massachusetts. see Davis,
Wendell.

Member of the Humane Society. pseud.
Description of the eastern coast of the
county of Barnstable. see Freeman,
James.

Member of the Humane Society. pseud. Life
boat. A poem. see Davis, John.

Member of the Inner Temple. pseud.
Argument at a court of grand sessions.
1966, 10892

Member of the Inner Temple, London. pseud.
ed. 47901

Member of the institution. pseud. View of
the New-York State Prison. 54711,
99570

Member of the junior class. pseud. Address.
see Mitchell, John.

Member of the junior class. pseud. Home
in the west. see Upham, Thomas
Cogswell.

Member of the last Parliament. pseud.
Letter. 40303

Member of the late board. pseud. To the
people of the United States. see
Maclure, William.

Member of the late Board of Water Commissioners. pseud. Inquiry into the best
mode of supplying the city of Boston
with water. 6785

Member of the late Parliament. pseud.
Remarks on an address. (69410),
(69491), 93796, 102863

Member of the legal profession. pseud.
Statement of reasons. see Upton, F. S.
supposed author and Upton, F. V.
supposed author and Upton, Francis
Henry. supposed author

Member of the Legislative Assembly from
Upper Canada. pseud. Seigniorial
question. see Hincks, Francis.

Member of the Legislature. pseud. Concise
history of the Eastern Penitentiary of
Pennsylvania. 60078

Member of the Louisiana bar. pseud. Legal
bearings in the Louisiana case. 39849

Member of the Manumission Society. pseud.
Address. see Anderson, Isaac. supposed
author

Member of the Maryland Legislature. pseud.
Bastiles of the North. see Sangston,
Lawrence. and Johnson, Reverdy,
1796-1876. incorrectly supposed author

Member of the Massachusetts bar. pseud.
Mysteries of crime. (51654)

Member of the Massachusetts bar. pseud.
National rights and state rights. see
Pickering, John.

Member of the Mass. Board of Education.
pseud. Strictures on the sectarian

character of the Common school journal.
83572

Member of the Mississippi bar. pseud. Right
of the states. 71384, 104880

Member of the N. E. Hist. Gen. Society. pseu
Memoir of the Farrar family. see
Farrar, Timothy.

Member of the New England Historic-Genealogical Society. pseud. Pedigree of the
Dane Family. see Dean, John.

Member of the New Orleans bar. pseud.
Sketches of life and character in Louisiana. 42304

Member of the N[ew] O[rleans] Washington
Artillery. pseud. Clarimonde. 13237

Member of the New York bar. pseud. Liquor
law; its uses and abuses. 41408

Member of the New-York bar. pseud.
Presbyterianism. 65231

Member of the New York bar. pseud.
Reconstruction in America. see
Kingsley, Vine Wright.

Member of the Numismatic Society of Philadelphia. pseud. Historical sketch of the
paper money issued by Pennsylvania.
32085

Member of the Ohio bar. pseud. ed. Law
reform tracts. 39338

Member of the Ohio bar. pseud. Niagara.
55120

Member of the old Congress. pseud. Plea
for literature. 63384

Member of the old Congress. pseud. Sketche
of French and English politicks in
America. (81559)

Member of the order. pseud. Order of the
Sons of Temperance. see Lund, Orland

Member of the Order of Mercy. pseud. Life
of Catherine McAuley. 42955

Member of the Order of the Blue-String.
pseud. History of the garret, &c. &c.
see Bradford, John.

Member of the Parliament of Scotland. pseud
Letter. see Philonax Verax. pseud.

Member of the Philadelphia bar. pseud. ed.
American Chesterfield. 90221

Member of the Philadelphia bar. pseud.
American oratory. 1173

Member of the Philadelphia bar. pseud.
Celebrated trials of all countries.
11649-11650

Member of the Philadelphia bar. pseud.
Criticism of Mr. Wm. B. Reed's aspersions. see Johnson, John G.

Member of the Philadelphia bar. pseud. Few
remarks upon the subject of a railroad
to the Pacific. 24241

Member of the Philadelphia bar. pseud.
History of the trial of Castner Hanway
and others. 30274

Member of the Philadelphia bar. pseud.
Remarks on Mr. Binney's Treatise.
5485

Member of the Philadelphia bar. pseud.
Reply to Horce Binney. see Brown,
David Boyer.

Member of the Philadelphia bar. pseud.
Report of the case of the Commonwealth
see Member of the bar of Philadelphia
pseud.

Member of the Philadelphia bar. pseud.
Wealth and biography of the wealthy
citizens of Philadelphia. 62377

Member of the Political Economy Club. pseu
Budget. see Torrens, Robert,

Member of the Protestant Episcopal Association, in South-Carolina. pseud. Strictures on the love of power in the prelacy. see Purcell, Henry.

Member of the Protestant Episcopal Church in the Diocese of New-York. pseud. True issue sustained. see Smith, Hugh, 1795-1849.

Member of the recently organized Oregon Legislature. pseud. Journal of events. 103997

Member of the Red River Conference. pseud. Post-oak circuit. see Summers, Thomas Osmond. supposed author

Member of the Rev. Mr. Wesley's society. pseud. Rev. John Fletcher's arguments. 24727

Member of the Richmond bar. pseud. Shall the freedmen be admitted to the right of suffrage. 79735

Member of the Rock County bar. pseud. State rights and the appelate jurisdiction. see Bundy, J. M.

Member of the Royal-Academy of Berlin. pseud. History and philosophy of earthquakes. 32111

Member of the Royal Academy of Florence. pseud. tr. 27267

Member of the Royal Geographical Society. pseud. ed. Gazette of the world. 26812

Member of the said church and parish. pseud. Statement of the proceedings in the First Church and Parish in Dedham. see Haven, Samuel. supposed author and Lamson, Alvin. supposed author

Member of the said Council. pseud. Result of a Council of Nine Churches. see Edwards, Jonathan, 1703-1758.

Member of the said society. pseud. Bibliothecae Americanae primordia. see Kennett, White, Bishop of Peterborough, 1660-1728.

Member of the said Synod. pseud. Remarks upon a discourse. see Dickinson, Jonathan, 1688-1727.

Member of the same. pseud. Letter to the so-called "Boston churches." see Simmons, George Frederic, 1814-1855.

Member of the same society, at Boston. pseud. World alarm'd. see Mather, Cotton, 1663-1728.

Member of the Senate of the United States. pseud. Eulogium on the death of General George Washington. 101804

Member of the society. pseud. Address delivered before the Washington Benevolent Society, Brimfield. 101769

Member of the society. pseud. Appendix containing a short sketch. 105037

Member of the society. pseud. Brief remarks on the organization and action. 7890

Member of the Society for Propagating the Gospel in Foreign Parts. pseud. Letter. see Chamberlayne, John. supposed author

Member of the Society of Arts and Manufacturers of Philadelphia. pseud. Essay on the manufacturing interest. see Coxe, Tench.

Member of the Society of Friends. pseud. Modern geography. 49806

Member of the Society of Universal Good Will. pseud. Enquiry into the origin, progress, and present state of slavery. (22645)

Member of the Society of Universal Goodwill, in London and Norwich. pseud. Inquiry into the origin, progress & present state of slavery. 81998

Member of the Sodality of the B. V. Mary, Church of the Most Holy Redeemer, East Boston. pseud. Influence of the Catholic Christian doctrine. see Fitton, James.

Member of the Staunton Convention. pseud. Constitution of '76. (16122), 2d note after 100449, 100554

Member of the Stock Exchange, London, pseud. Foreign loans and their consequences considered. 41709

Member of the Suffolk bar. pseud. Letter to the Hon. Josiah Quincy. see Otis, Harrison Gray, 1765-1848.

Member of the Suffolk bar. pseud. Remarks upon an oration. see Ward, S. Dexter.

Member of the Suffolk bar. pseud. reporter Report of a case before William N. Green. 96936

Member of the Suffolk bar. pseud. Truth revealed. 23683

Member of the Suffolk Committee of 1829. pseud. Catalogue of books on the masonic institution. see Gassett, Henry.

Member of the Sumter County Medical Society. pseud. Essay on the summer and autumnal fevers of south Alabama. 93726

Member of the Synod. pseud. Synod of New-York and Philadelphia vindicated. see Blair, John, 1720-1771.

Member of the twenty-seventh Congress. pseud. Defence of the Whigs. see Kennedy, John Pendleton, 1795-1870. and Colton, Calvin, 1789-1857. supposed author

Member of the University of Cambridge. pseud. Suggestions on the abolition of slavery in the British colonies. 93468

Member of the Vermont bar. pseud. Adventures of Timothy Peacock. see Thompson, Daniel Pierce.

Member of the Washington bar. pseud. Slavery code of the District of Columbia. 82086

Member of the Washington Society. pseud. Address to the electors of . . . New York. 53498

Member of the West India Body. pseud. Remarks on Lord Viscount Goderich's dispatch. 69417

Member of the western bar. pseud. Life of Stephen A. Douglas. 20694

Members elected on the claim of successors. 86109

Members of Congress who Opposed the Passage of the Bill to Organize the Territories of Nebraska and Kansas. pseud. Address to the people of the United States. 37015

Members of the said church. 101206

Members of the Assembly of Jamaica. (72262)

Members of the Association. pseud. Account of the true nature and object of the late Protestant Episcopal Clerical Association of . . . New-York. see Turner, Samuel Hulbeart.

Members of the bar of the Supreme Court of the District of Columbia and the United States Court of Claims. pseud. Eulogies. 90394

Members of the bar [Practicing Before the U. S. Circuit Court of Maine District.] pseud. Resolutions on the late decease of Hon. Joseph Story. 92320

Members of the Bowdoin-Street Church, Feb. 1, 1841. 6637

Members of the . . . church, January 1, 1863. 57145

Members of the Church of Malden. see Malden, Mass. Church.

Members of the City Council of Baltimore, their clerks, and officers of the corporation. 47487

Members of the Common Council of . . . Philadelphia, 1704 to 1776. 61812

Members of the congregation of St. Peter's Church. 635

Members of the Essex South Conference. see Congregational Churches in Massachusetts. Essex South Conference.

Members of the Faculty of Yale College. see Yale University. Faculty.

Members of the House of Representatives of the Congress of the United States. see Sullivan, George, 1771-1838. and U. S. Congress. House of Representatives.

Members of the Late Convention, 1869. see Texas. Convention, 1869.

Members of the Legislature of Massachusetts. see Massachusetts. Legislature.

Members of the medical profession of Philadelphia. 51032

Members of the Medical Society of South-Carolina, resident in Charleston. 87886

Members of the Mendon Association. see Congregational Churches in Massachusetts. Mendon Association.

Members of the National Academy of Design. illus. see National Academy of Design. Members. illus.

Members of the New York press. pseud. Brief popular account. 7887

Members of the New York press. pseud. Night-side of New York. (55297)

Members of the Philermenian Society of Brown University. 8609, 8634

Members of the Protestant Episcopal Church. pseud. eds. Quarterly theological magazine. (66970)

Members of the Society of Friends. pseud. eds. Quaker. 66931

Members of the South-Carolina Institute. 30101, 88006

Members who now belong to the Massachusetts State Society of the Cincinnati. 86110

Membre, Zenobe, 1645?-1687? 25853, 80002

Membre adoptif de la Nation Oneida. pseud. Voyage dans la Haute Pensylvania. see Crevecoeur, J. Hector St. John, 1735-1813.

Membre de la Chambre d'Assemblee. pseud. Appel au Gouvernement Imperial. see Blanchet, Francois.

Membre de la Chambre d'Assemblee. pseud. Appel au Parlement Imperial. 10354

Membro della Societa Leopoldina. pseud. Della chiesa Cattolica negli Stati Uniti d'America. 19440

Memento mori. A plain discourse to a plain people. 50793

Memento of friendship. 50639

Memento of the donnors and founders of the Theological Seminary. 37589

Mementoes of the Swett family. 95640

Memet, Chaggi. 66686

Memin, -------- St. see St. Memin, -----------.

Memin, M. de St.-. see St.-Memin, M. de.

Memmi, Giovanni Battista. tr. 24136

Memmi, Juan Bapt. 47488

Memminger, Christopher Gustavus, 1803-1888. 6357, 15246, 15275, (15276), 15281, (34851), 47489-47490, 49462, 56313, 87434-87435, note after 87802, note after 87896, note after 89146 see also Confederate States of America. Treasury Department. South Carolina. Commissioner to Virginia.

Memoir. 37836, 52424, (54999), (63551), 84572

Memoir addressed to persons of the Jewish religion in Europe. 72201

Memoir addressed to the General, Constituent and Legislative Assembly. 1446

Memoir and annotations by Robert Ashton. 72110

Memoir and character of Sarah. (47491)

Memoir and journals of Rev. Paul Coffin, D. D. 14183

Memoir and list of his [i. e. Thomas Paine's] publications. 65582

Memoir and official correspondence of Gen. John Stark. 90518

Memoir and poems of Phillis Wheatley. 56712, 103133

Memoir and portrait of Edwin Forrest, Esq. 85169

Memoir and preface by Josiah Quincy. 28245

Memoir and select remains of Rev. W. Nevins. 104813

Memoir and select remains of the late Rev. John R. M'Dowall. 43191

Memoir and select writings of William Reed Prince. (65625)

Memoir and services of Rev. Wm. J. Armstrong. 68153

Memoir and writings of James Handasyd Perkins. 60956

Memoir. Appended, a sketch of slavery in the United States. 41169

Memoir au Soutien de l'appel de la fabrique de N. D. de Montreal. (4170)

Memoir, biographical and genealogical, of Sir John Leverett, Knt. 40747

Memoir, by a Mississippian. 78750

Memoir by Ab. Moise. 30294

Memoir [by C. F. Hudson.] 90567

Memoir. [By Ezra Shaw Goodwin.] (27938)

Memoir by F. W. P. Greenwood. 95190-95191

Memoir, by G. Truman. 50430

Memoir [by George S. Hillard.] (13660)

Memoir, by her [i. e. Sarah C. Edgarton Mayo's] husband. (47195)

Memoir. By his brother, F. S. Daniel. (18493)

Memoir by his [i. e. John K. Lord's] father. 42033

Memoir, by his oldest son, Sylvanus Cobb, Jr. (13857)

Memoir, by his sister, C. Hanson. 30268

Memoir, [By J. M. Le Moine.] 40008

Memoir by John H. Ingram. 63534

Memoir by John Keese. 32873

Memoir by Joseph Browne. 54602

Memoir by Mary Howitt. 9452

Memoir, by one of his [i. e. Edmund Randolph's] descendants. 67819

Memoir by Rufus Wilmot Griswold. 63571

Memoir by S. E. Dwight. 21974

Memoir . . . by Samuel J. Spalding. 88922

Memoir by Samuel M. Smucker. 77710, 85161

Memoir. By Samuel Rodmond Smith. 84091

Memoir by Samuel V. N. Smucker. 25839

Memoir by the Rev. E. A. Park. 21892

Memoir. By the Rev. T. B. Murray. 51542

Memoir by the Rev. W. B. Sprague. 66415

Memoir, by Thomas M. Hanckel, Esq. 22283

Memoir. By Tunstall Smith. 84467

Memoir by Wm. Gilmore Simms. 39260

Memoir concerning an animal of the class of reptilia or amphibia which is known in the United States by the name of Alligator. 3812

Memoir concerning New Britain and the north coast of New Guianea. 18344

Memoir concerning the commercial relations of the United States with England. 47492-94259

Memoir concerning the disease of goitre. 3813

Memoir concerning the fascinating faculty which has been ascribed to the rattlesnake. 3816

Memoir concerning the fascinating faculty which has been ascribed to various species of serpents. 3817

Memoir, correspondence, and miscellanies. 35891

Memoir, descriptive and explanatory, to accompany the charts of the northern Atlantic Ocean. 66700

Memoir descriptive and explanatory to accompany the general chart of the northern ocean. (66699)

Memoir, descriptive and explanatory, to accompany the new chart of the Atlantic Ocean. 66698

Memoir descriptive of the march of a division. (33581)

Memoir. . . . Edited by George Allen. 28242

Memoir. Edited by Tunstall Smith. 84468

Memoir explanatory of the transunion and Tehuantepec route. (9514)

Memoir, historical and political. 28633, 95370

Memoir. John H. Sheppard—Register of Probate, 1817-1834. 80313

Memoir justificatory of the government of Venezuela. (7798)

Memoir, letters and journal of Mrs. Elizabeth Seton. 79336

Memoir, letters, and remains of Alexis de Tocqueville. note after 96072

Memoir of a remarkable man. 83463

Memoir of Abijah Hutchinson. 34066

Memoir of Abner Kingman Nott. 56028

Memoir of Abraham Lincoln. 41212

Memoir of Addison Pinneo. (62974)

Memoir of Adjt. M. W. Smith. 83502

Memoir of Albert Newsam. 66859

Memoir of Alexander Anderson. 42135

Memoir of Alexander Macomb. 70940

Memoir of Alexander McLeod. 105669

Memoir of Alexander Viets Griswold. 92078

Memoir of Alexander Wilson. 104604

Memoir of Alfred Bennett. 30776

Memoir of Alvan Stone. 105571

Memoir of Amos Twitchell. 6993

Memoir of an eventful expedition in Central America. 98812

Memoir of Andrew Meneely. 28743

Memoir of Angelica Irene Hawes. 30915

Memoir of Ann Eliza Starr. 90543

Memoir of Ann Maria Slade. (64660)

Memoir of Anzonetta R. Peters. 13313

Memoir of Asahel Grant. 39169

Memoir, of August 1817. 17300

Memoir of Barbara Ewing. 23323

Memoir of Barnum himself. 90803

Memoir of Bartholomew Brown, Esquire. (695)

Memoir of Benjamin Banneker. 39225, (45211A)

Memoir of Benjamin Hanover Punchard. 26178, 66656

Memoir of Benjamin Lay. 12722

Memoir [of Bishop White.] 84678C

Memoir of Blennerhasset. 5906, 74878

Memoir of C. A. Luzenberg. 41806

Memoir of Cambridgeport. 32588

Memoir. of Captain M. M. Hammond. 30105

Memoir of Captain Nathan Hale. (2573), 29647

Memoir of Captain Paul Cuffee. 17850, 104325

Memoir of Catherine Seely. 78860

Memoir of Catherine Brown. (1420)

Memoir of Charles Frost. 58921

Memoir of Charles Greely Loring. 58912

Memoir of Charles Lathrop Winslow. 104793

Memoir of Col. Ethan Allen. 50390

Memoir of Colonel Havilland Le Mesurier, &c. &c. &c. 97449

Memoir of Colonel John Allen. 47493

Memoir of Col. Joshua Fry. 81708

Memoir of Colonel Seth Warner. 12820, 88985

Memoir of Commodore David Porter. 64225

Memoir of Commodore O. H. Perry. 21574

Memoir of Cornelius Conway Felton. 3467, (24040)

Memoir of Cousin Alice B. Haven. (30871)

Memoir of Cyrus Peirce. 47078

Memoir of Daniel Appleton White. 7947

Memoir of Daniel Safford. 74872

Memoir of David Hoover. 32894

Memoir of . . . David Marks, minister. 44625

Memoir of De-Witt Clinton. (33088)

Memoir of Dr. Amos Binney. 28089

Memoir of Dr. Brainerd. 72192

Memoir of Dr. Godman. 79470

Memoir of Dr. J. E. Holbrook. 87887

Memoir of Dr. John D. Godman. 79471

Memoir of Dr. Luther V. Bell. 4474

Memoir of Dr. Robbins. (71802)

Memoir of Doctor [Thomas Buckingham] Smith. 9771, 84383

Memoir of Dr. Thomas Henderson. 82557

Memoir [of Dr. William Smith.] 84622

Memoir of Edmund Dwight. (7057)

Memoir of Edward Augustus Holyoke. 59560

Memoir of Edward J. Young. 84012

Memoir of Edward Rawson. 68019

Memoir of Edward Dorr Griffin. 51845

Memoir of Elder Abner Jones. 36441

Memoir of Elder Brewster. 106053

Memoir of Elder Elijah Shaw. 79906

Memoir of Eli Bickford. 9539

Memoir of Eli Whitney, Esq. (57238)

Memoir of Elihu W. Baldwin. 30843

Memoir of Elizabeth Ann Moulton. 51127

Memoir of Elizabeth Anne Taylor. 94534

Memoir of Elizabeth Jones. 36493

Memoir of Elizabeth T. King. 37802

Memoir of Ellen May Woodward. (48923)

Memoir, of February 1817. 17300

Memoir of Frances Racillia Hackley. 80960

Memoir of Frances Wright. 27347

Memoir of Francis West. 41504

Memoir of G. R. T. Hewes. 6778, 70137

Memoir of Gen. Christopher Gadsden. 88005

Memoir of Gen David Blackshear. 49073

Memoir of General Graham. 28237

Memoir of General Louis Bell. 6946

Memoir of . . . George Canning. 26045, 26901

Memoir of George Dana Boardman. 37779

Memoir of George Jehoshaphat Mountain. 51185

Memoir of George Livermore. 19049

Memoir of George McClellan. 18606

Memoir of George N. Briggs. 70974

Memoir of George P. Cammann. 39528

Memoir of George R. T. Hewes. 6778, 70137

Memoir of George Ticknor. 30622

Memoir of George Whitefield. 66917, note after 103655, 103656

Memoir of . . . George Whitefield. 103614

Memoir of Ginevra Guerrabella. (47495)

Memoir of Granville Sharp. 93140

Memoir of Hannah Hobbie. 2038

Memoir of Harlan Page. 29909

Memoir of Harriet Dow. 92370

Memoir of Harriet Eliza Snow. 41952

Memoir of Henry Augustus Ingalls. 9363

Memoir of Henry Lyman. 42783

Memoir of her [i. e. Mrs. Sarah E. Hall's] life. 29845

Memoir of her [i. e. Elizabeth M. Chandler's] life and character. (11856)

Memoir of Herbert Marshall. 44773

Memoir of Hernando de Escalante Fontaneda. 87205

Memoir of Hezehiah Packard. (58119)

Memoir of his [i. e. Carlos Wilcox's] life. 103968

Memoir of his [i. e. Charles Henry Wharton's] life. 103094

Memoir of his [i. e. Edward D. Griffin's] life. 28818

Memoir of his [i. e. James Marsh's] life. 44739

Memoir of his [i. e. John Henry Hobart's] life. 32297

Memoir of his [i. e. Jonathan Maxcy's] life. 46999, 47001

Memoir of his [i. e. Maynard Davis Richardson's] life. 71075

Memoir of his [i. e. Nathaniel Emmons'] life. 22526

Memoir of his [i. e. Rufus Choate's] life. 12860

Memoir of his [i. e. William Craft's] life. 17325

Memoir of his [i. e. William Miller's] life. 49076

Memoir of his [i. e. Jesse Appleton's] life and character. 1808

Memoir of his [i. e. Jonathan Edwards'] life and character. (21975)

Memoir of his [i. e. Joseph Bellamy's] life and character. 4497

Memoir of his [i. e. Joseph Stevens Buckminster's] life and character. 8735

Memoir of his [i. e. Thomas Shepard's] life and character. 80262

Memoir of his [i. e. William Howard Seward's] life and selections from his letters from 1831 to 1846. (79507)

Memoir of his [i. e. John Henry Hobart's] life and writings. 32302, 77986

Memoir of his [i. e. John M. Daniel's] life, by his brother. (18493), 71205

Memoir of his [i. e. Worthington Smith's] life, by Rev. Joseph Torrey. 84929

Memoir of his [i. e. Sereno Edwards Dwight's] life, by William T. Dwight. 21527

Memoir of his [i. e. Nathaniel Appleton Haven's] life, by George Ticknor. 30890

Memoir of his [i. e. Thomas B. Gould's] life. By William Hodgson. 28125, (32371)

Memoir of his [i. e. Thomas Shepard's] own life. 80198, 106052

Memoir of his [i. e. R. Lamb's] own life. 38723

Memoir of Hon. Abbot Lawrence. (45855)

Memoir of Hon. John Davis. 25440

Memoir of Hon. John Pickering. 65296

Memoir of Hon. Reuel Williams. (64065)

Memoir of Hon. Robert Hooper. 80312

Memoir of Hon. Stephen Minot Weld. 50956

Memoir of Hon. William Appleton. (71779)

Memoir of Hon. William Tudor. 97409

Memoir of Horace Binney, Jr. 91785

Memoir of Hugh Lawson White. 78343

Memoir of Increase Sumner. 93714

Memoir of Indian wars and other occurrences. 93185

Memoir of Isaac. H. Julian. (36887)

Memoir of Isaac Parrish. 35459

Memoir of J. C. Fremont. 25844

Memoir of J. D. Paxton. 59265

Memoir of J. K. Gibbons. 8980

Memoir of J. Miller. (7250)

Memoir of J. R. Gilpin. 27462

Memoir of James Brainerd Taylor. 70844

Memoir of James Brown. 31874

Memoir of James C. Crane. (9474)

Memoir of . . . James Currie. 18004

Memoir of James de Veaux. (27278)

Memoir of James Grahame. 67217

Memoir of James Jackson, Jr., M. D. with extracts from his letters. 35426

Memoir of James Jackson, Jr., M. D. written by his father. 35427

Memoir of James Logan. 2004

Memoir of James Monroe, Esq. 50017

Memoir of Jared Sparks, LL. D. . . . By Brantz Mayer. (45211A), 47098

Memoir of Jared Sparks, LL. D. By George E. Ellis. 22305

Memoir of John A. Swett. 43117

Memoir of John Arch. 1901

Memoir [of John Brazer.] 7495

Memoir of John Bromfield. (67216)

Memoir of John Brooks. 8340

Memoir of John Conolly. 13302

Memoir of John Cotton. 55886

Memoir of John D. Alexander. (45211A), 62972

Memoir of John D. Lockwood. 41751

Memoir of John Endicott. 22561

Memoir of John Fanning Watson. 20637

Memoir of John Gallison. (26418)

Memoir of John Griscom. 28877

Memoir of John H. Alexander. (45211A), 62972

Memoir of John H. Sheppard. 80313

Memoir of John Macon Peck. 2574, 59487

Memoir of John Slafter. 81695

Memoir of John Taylor. 94479

Memoir of John the Painter. 41587

Memoir of John Treadwell. (57238), 96511

Memoir of . . . John Watts, M. D. 50437

Memoir of John White Brown. (8636)

Memoir of John Whitman and his descendants. 103734

Memoir of John Woolman. 33264, 105204

Memoir of Jonathan Leavitt. 39560

Memoir of Joseph Curtis. 18057, 78794

Memoir of Joseph Grinnell. 28870

Memoir of Joseph Stone. 92084

Memoir of Joseph Story. 31875

Memoir of Joseph Wistar. 27407

Memoir of Josiah White. 71923

Memoir of Lieut. Col. John T. Greble. (42124)

Memoir of Lieut. E. L. Mitchell. 49682

Memoir of Louis Wright. 65706

Memoir of Lucy Maria Bigelow. 5285

Memoir [of Luis de Onis.] 99313

Memoir of Luther Severance. 5732

Memoir of Luther V. Bell. 22306

Memoir of Major-General Shirley. 20880

Memoir of Major Samuel Ringgold. (45211A)

Memoir of Malvina Forman Smith. 83504

Memoir of Maria Elizabeth Clapp. 71785

Memoir of Marshall P. Wilder. 80314

Memoir of Martha C. Thomas. 95434

Memoir of Martha Thompson Sharp. 31260

Memoir of Martin Van Buren. 98425

Memoir of Mary Anne Hooker. (32824)

Memoir of Mary L. Ware. (29753)

Memoir of Mary Lothrop. 44096

Memoir of Matthew Edwards. 9092

Memoir of Mead Holmes, Jr. 32618

Memoir of Miss Hannah Adams. 213

Memoir of Miss Margaret Mercer. (50802)

Memoir of Miss Nancy M. Clark. 97007

Memoir of Mr. and Mrs. Wood. 105052

Memoir of Mr. James Clap. 103201

Memoir of Mr. John Lowell. (23257)

Memoir of Mrs. Ann H. Judson. 38153

Memoir of Mrs. Catherine M. Dimmick. 20191

Memoir of Mrs. Chloe Spear. 89073, note after 102224

Memoir of Mrs. Deborah H. Porter. 20951

Memoir of Mrs. Eliza Aston Rumpff. 2789

Memoir of Mrs. Elizabeth B. Dwight. 21518

Memoir of Mrs. H. W. Winslow. 104808

Memoir of Mrs. Harriet L. Winslow. 104809

Memoir of Mrs. Harriet Newell Cook. 80932

Memoir of Mrs. Harriet Wadsworth Windslow. 104807

Memoir of Mrs. Henrietta Shuck. 36093

Memoir of Mrs. Jane Greenleaf. 47494

Memoir of Mrs. John V. L. Pruyn. 66415, 89739

Memoir of Mrs. Julia H. Scott. 77303

Memoir of Mrs. Louisa A. Lowne. 23675

Memoir of Mrs. Louisa Adams Leavitt. 82337

Memoir of Mrs. M. P. Cote. 18219

Memoir of Mrs. Macready. 43651

Memoir of Mrs. Mary Barr. 3581

Memoir of Mrs. Mary E. Van Lennep. 30926

Memoir of Mrs. Myra W. Allen. 44312

Memoir of Mrs. Sarah Emily York. 47295

Memoir of Mrs. Sarah L. Huntington Smith. 32815, note after 84134

Memoir of Mrs. Sarah Louisa Taylor. 36584

Memoir of Mrs. Sarah Tappan. 94369

Memoir of Mrs. Susanna Rowson. 51885

Memoir of Mrs. Thomazin Johnson. 36253

Memoir of Moreton Stille. (32548)

Memoir of Nathan Hunt. (33884)

Memoir of Nathanael Emmons. (58621)

Memoir of Nathaniel B. Smithers. 84969

Memoir of Nathaniel Bowditch. 7001

Memoir of Nathaniel Bowditch, by his son. 7000

Memoir of Nathaniel Curtis, Esq. 18060

Memoir of Nathaniel Ingersoll Bowditch. 42144

Memoir of Nathaniel Langdon Frothingham, D. D. 31218

Memoir of Nathaniel Macon. 21887

Memoir of Nicholas Hill. (31851)

Memoir of Nicholas Tillinghast. 21989

Memoir of Normand Smith. 30922

Memoir of Otis Brown. 18585

Memoir of Patrick Tracy Jackson. 42464

Memoir of Paul Cuffe. 2005

Memoir of Penn, by James Brown of Virginia. 59725

Memoir of Phebe Bartlett. 54933

Memoir of Phebe Hammond. 80967

Memoir of Philip and Rachel Price. 65429

Memoir of Phillis Wheatley. 95218

Memoir of Pierre Toussaint. 39737, note after 96341

Memoir of Rev. Abiel Brown. 8462

Memoir of Rev. Albert W. Duy. (13367)

Memoir of Rev. Alexander Gordon. 49007

Memoir of Rev. Alvan Hyde. 34115

Memoir of Rev. Asahel Nettleton. 97598

Memoir of Rev. Bela Jacobs. 35496

Memoir of Rev. Charles Mason. 59348

Memoir of . . . Rev. Charles Nisbet. 49055

Memoir of Rev. Ebenezer Fitch. 21422

Memoir of Rev. Elisha Mitchel. 49685

Memoir of Rev. Gordon Hall. 3373

Memoir of Rev. Gustavuus F. Davis. 18788

Memoir of Rev. H. B. Soule. 87265

Memoir of Rev. Henry Bacon. 2642

Memoir of Rev. James C. Bryant. 77248

Memoir of Rev. James M. Cook. 2653

Memoir of Rev. Jeremiah Hallock of Connecticut. 29908

Memoir of Rev. John Allyn. 25440

Memoir of Rev. John Prince. 98042

Memoir of Rev. John Smith. 82880, 84302

Memoir of Rev. Jonathan Parsons. (28662)

Memoir of Rev. Joseph Badger. By E. G. Holland. 32502

Memoir of Rev. Joseph Badger; containing an autobiography. 47496

Memoir of Rev. Jotham Sewall, of Chesterville, Maine. 79435

Memoir of Rev. Lemuel Covell. 8464

Memoir of Rev. Levi Parsons. 50995

Memoir of Rev. Luther Rice. 94474

Memoir of Rev. Nathan Parker. 17136

Memoir of Rev. Nathan W. Fiske. 33793

Memoir of Rev. Nathaniel Colver. 83464

Memoir of Rev. Patrick Copland. 52288

Memoir of Rev. Philip F. Mayer. 91986

Memoir of Rev. S. Bacon. (2683)

Memoir of Rev. S. Davies. (18771)

Memoir of Rev. S. Osgood Wright. 95219

Memoir of Rev. Stephen R. Smith. 77326, 84281, 84284

Memoir of Rev. Thaddeus Mason Harris. 26066

Memoir of Rev. Thomas Baldwin. 12523, 12525

Memoir of Rev. Thomas Sumner Winn. 104785

Memoir of Richard and Joseph Merrick. 13426

Memoir of Richard Williams. 30017

Memoir of Rip Van Dam. 19625

Memoir of Robert Swain. 50712, 2d note after 93998

Memoir of Robert Troup Paine. 58193

Memoir of Robert Vaux. 61306

Memoir of Robinson. 72110
Memoir of Roger Williams. (38154)
Memoir of S. S. Prentiss. 65093
Memoir of Samuel Breck. 24477
Memoir of Samuel Budgett. 8965
Memoir of Samuel G. Drake. 80315
Memoir of Samuel George Morton. 47388
Memoir of Samuel John Mills. 89772
Memoir of Samuel Slater. 103385
Memoir of Sarah Ann Bliss. (5934)
Memoir of schools and schoolmasters. 10899
Memoir of Sebastian Cabot. 5248
Memoir of Seth Burroughs. 51847
Memoir of Sir Brenton Halliburton. (31820)
Memoir of Stephen Hopkins. 32968, 1st note
    after 97146
Memoir of Susan Allibone. (39694)
Memoir of Susan B. Marble. 44468
Memoir of Susannah Elizabeth Bingham.
    58885
Memoir of Thaddeus William Harris. 31753
Memoir of the antiquities of the western parts.
    (13718)
Memoir of the author [i. e. Edward L.
    Parker.] 58663
Memoir of the author [i. e. Francis Baily.]
    2770
Memoir of the author [i. e. George P.
    Morris.] 50823
Memoir of the author [i. e. Henry Bond.]
    (6283)
Memoir of the author [i. e. J. B. Pitkin.]
    63040
Memoir of the author [i. e. John Callender.]
    (10076), 70719
Memoir of the author [i. e. John Trumbull.]
    note after 97204, 97210, 97234
Memoir of the author [i. e. Robert Ray.]
    (54483)
Memoir of the author [i. e. Susannah Rowson.]
    73608
Memoir of the author [i. e. Washington
    Irving.] (35214)
Memoir of the author [i. e. William Leete
    Stone.] 92138
Memoir of the author [i. e. William Wells
    Brown.] 8586, (8596)
Memoir of the author, [i. e. Thomas Prince]
    an attempt towards a perfect catalogue
    of his writings. (65586)
Memoir of the author [i. e. Benjamin
    Hawkins] and a history of the Creek
    Confederacy. 30947
Memoir of the author [i. e. Nathanael Howe
    and explanatory notes.] 33322
Memoir of the author [i. e. John Callender];
    biographical notices of some of his
    distinguished contemporaries. (11076)
Memoir of the author [i. e. Josiah Quincy],
    by Edmund Quincy. (67213)
Memoir of the author [i. e. Lewis Mayer];
    by Elias Heiner. 47112
Memoir of the author [i. e. Thomas Say]
    by George Ord. 77371, 77374
Memoir of the author [i. e. James Nack] by
    George P. Morris. 51700
Memoir of the author [i. e. Andrew Jackson
    Downing], by George W. Curtis. 20775
Memoir of the author [i. e. John W. Francis],
    by Henry T. Tuckerman. 25447
Memoir of the author [i. e. Nathan Parker]
    by Henry Ware. 58718
Memoir of the author [i. e. Elizabeth Erma
    Holmes], by her sister. 32597
Memoir of the author [i. e. G. W. Park
    Custis], by his daughter. (18157)

Memoir of the author [i. e. Francis Ward],
    by his surviving consort. 101293
Memoir of the author [i. e. Isaac Jogues],
    by John Gilmary Shea. (36142)
Memoir of the author [i. e. James Nack] by
    P. M. Wetmore. (51698)
Memoir of the author [i. e. Obadiah Jennings],
    by Rev. M. Brown. 36044
Memoir of the author [i. e. George Whitefield]
    by S. Drew. 103588
Memoir of the author [i. e. Xavier Donald
    Macleod], by the Most Rev. John B.
    Purcell. 43546
Memoir of the author [i. e. John Stanford],
    by the Rev. George Upfold. 90182
Memoir of the author [i. e. John M. Lowrie].
    By the Rev. William D. Howard. 42538
Memoir of the author [i. e. William B. Reed],
    edited by Manton Marble. (68612)
Memoir of the author [i. e. William Robertson
    from that by Dugald Stewart. 71988
Memoir of the authoress [i. e. Harriet
    Beecher Stowe.] 92486
Memoir of the author's [i. e. Joseph Lathrop's
    life, written by himself. 39200
Memoir of the Baron De Kalb. (45211A),
    83018
Memoir of the British doctrine of neutral
    trade. 47497
Memoir of the Church at Medway, Ga. 32589
Memoir of the Committee of the Free Trade
    Convention. (47498)
Memoir of the construction, cost, and
    capacity of the Croton Aqueduct. 37787
Memoir of the discovery of the Mississippi.
    25853
Memoir of the embarkation of the sick and
    wounded. (33118)
Memoir of the family of Barton. 91057
Memoir of the Farrar family. 23886
Memoir of the Federal Street Church and
    Society. 11919
Memoir of the first poet in New Netherland.
    51460, 51464, 91169
Memoir of the fossil genus Basilosaurus.
    27279
Memoir of the French and Indian expedition
    against New York. 54476
Memoir of the French protestants. 32583
Memoir of the geological survey of the state
    of Delaware. 6385
Memoir of the Gloucester Fox Hunting Club.
    49133
Memoir of the history of the celebrated
    treaty. 21385
Memoir of the Honorable Abbott Lawrence,
    LL. D. 86793
Memoir of the Hon. Abbott Lawrence, prepared
    for the Massachusetts Historical Society.
    (1816)
Memoir of the Hon. Abbott Lawrence. Pre-
    pared for the National Portrait Gallery.
    65297
Memoir of the Hon. Benjamin Robbins Curtis.
    71780
Memoir of the Hon. Caleb Strong. 92886
Memoir of the Hon. James Duane. 36606
Memoir of the Hon. Joshua Atherton. 2271
Memoir of the Hon. Josiah Bartlett. 3764
Memoir of the Hon. Samuel Howe. 22327
Memoir of the Hon. William Sturgis. 42076,
    93270
Memoir of the Indian prophecy. 101828
Memoir of the language and inhabitants of
    Lord North's Island. 62638

Memoir of the last year of the war for independence. (21631)

Memoir of the late Captain Peter Heywood. 94199

Memoir of the late Enoch Hall. 11901

Memoir of the late H. H. Post. 64456

Memoir of the late Hon. Christopher Gore. (71532)

Memoir of the late Hon. Daniel P. Cook. 8581

Memoir of the late Isaac Collins. 14439

Memoir of the late James Stephen. 91234

Memoir of the late John Murray. 21816

Memoir of the late Joseph Peabody. (59372)

Memoir of the late Lewis David von Schweinitz. 36333

Memoir of the late Martha Hazeltine Smith. 83529

Memoir of the late Mr. Leach. 39506

Memoir of the late Rev. John Freeman. 84285

Memoir of the late Rev. John Pierce. 30715

Memoir of the late Rev. Savillion W. Fuller. 50327

Memoir of the late Rev. William Black. 71113

Memoir of the late Rev. Wm. Croswell. 17679

Memoir of the late Samuel Breck. 34747

Memoir of the life and character of Ebenezer Porter. 46891

Memoir of the life and character of George Chevne Shattuck. 35805

Memoir of the life and character of James B. Rogers. 11087

Memoir of the life and character of Mrs. Mary Anna Boardman. 77985

Memoir of the life and character of Prof. Valentine Mott. 25452

Memoir of the life and character of Rev. Joseph Vaill. 58884

Memoir of the life and character of Rev. Lewis Warner Green. 29922

Memoir of the life and character of Rev. Samuel Hopkins. (24097)

Memoir of the life and character of Samuel Hopkins. (58622)

Memoir of the life and character of the late Hon. Theo. Frelinghuysen. 11803

Memoir of the life and character of the late Joseph Parrish. 105030

Memoir of the life and character of the Rev. Samuel Bacon. (2206)

Memoir of the life and character of the Right Hon. Edmund Burke. 65694

Memoir of the life and labors of the Rev. Thomas G. Stewart. 91708

Memoir of the life and public services of John Charles Fremont. 5306

Memoir of the life and religious experience of Ray Potter. 64664

Memoir of the life and scientific labors of Samuel George Morton. 59135

Memoir of the life and services of Admiral Sir William Hargood. 848

Memoir of the life and times of General John Lamb. (39521)

Memoir of the life and times of Henry Melchior Muhlenberg. 91985

Memoir of the life and times of the Rev. Isaac Backus. (33203)

Memoir of the life and writings of Rev. Jonathan Mayhew. 7225

Memoir of the life and writings of the Hon. Teunis G. Bergen. 66721

Memoir of the life and writings of the Rev. Thomas Prince. 20876

Memoir of the life and writings of Thomas Cartwright. (8236)

Memoir of the life, character, and principles of Calvin. 85266

Memoir of the life, character, and writings of John Adams. (17390)

Memoir of the life, character, and writings of Thomas Jefferson. 84076

Memoir of the life of Captain Nathaniel Fanning. 23782

Memoir of the life of Daniel Webster. 38081

Memoir of the life of Edward Stabler. 90023

Memoir of the life of Eliza S. M. Quincy. (67190)

Memoir of the life of Harriet Prebel. (39786)

Memoir of the life of Henry Ware, Jr. 101396, 101400, 101403

Memoir of the life of James Gore King. 37788

Memoir of the life of James Milnor. 92076

Memoir of the life of Job Scott. (78291)

Memoir of the life of John Quincy Adams. (67218)

Memoir of the life of Josiah Quincy, Jun., of Massachusetts. (67192), (67219)

Memoir of the life of Josiah Quincy, Junior, of Massachusetts: 1744-1775. 67220

Memoir of the life of La Salle. (14762)

Memoir of the life of Nathaniel Stacy. 90033

Memoir of the life of Richard Henry Lee. 39787

Memoir of the life of the author [i. e. Timothy Dwight.] (21558)

Memoir of the life . . . of the late Hon. Henry Wm. De Saussure. 30445

Memoir of the life of the Rev. Amos Pettengil. 30638

Memoir of the life of the Rev. Jacob Bailey. 3720, 66194

Memoir of the life of the Right Honourable Charles Lord Sydenham. (78507)-78508

Memoir of the life of the Rt. Rev. Alexander Viets Griswold. 92077

Memoir of the life of the Rt. Rev. Richard Channing Moore. 31427

Memoir of the life of the Right Reverend William White. 104608

Memoir of the life of William Livingston. 78841, 84576

Memoir of the life of Z. Macaulay. 92004

Memoir of the life, travels and Gospel labour of George Fox. 25361

Memoir of the life, travels, and religious experiences, of Martha Routh. 73504

Memoir of the megatherium. 32373

Memoir of the Mosquito Territory. 105609

Memoir of the naval life and services of Admiral Durham. 47499

Memoir of the new perpetual calendar. (43327)

Memoir of the Niagara Falls and international suspension bridge. 58448, (72576)

Memoir of the north-eastern boundary. 26390

Memoir of the northern Kingdom. 36033

Memoir of the Onondaga Salt Springs. (19871)

Memoir of the Pawtucket tribe of Indians. 883

Memoir of the Penacook Indians. 23818, 50392

Memoir of the pilgrimage to Virginia. 47500

Memoir of the Plummer family. 63467

Memoir of the political life of the Right Honourable Edmund Burke. 17598

Memoir of the proposed territory of Arizona. 51212

Memoir of the public and private life of
Fanny Elssler. 47501

Memoir of the public services of William
Henry Harrison, of Ohio. (29790)

Memoir of the Rev. Austin Dickinson. 20028

Memoir of the Rev. Bernard Whitman.
103741

Memoir of the Rev. C. Colden Hoffman.
25366

Memoir of the Rev. Charles T. Torrey.
42367, 96281

Memoir of the Rev. Convers Francis. (54965)

Memoir of the Rev. Daniel Mahar Chandler.
65681

Memoir of the Rev. Daniel Holbrook Gillette.
27410

Memoir of the Rev. David Brainerd: missionary to the Indians. 21953

Memoir of the Rev. David Brainerd, missionary to the North American Indians.
64945

Memoir of the Rev. Ebenezer Hill. 31845

Memoir of the Rev. Edward D. Griffin.
89740

Memoir of the Rev. Edward Payson, D. D.
. . . by Asa Cummings. (17918)

Memoir of the Rev. Edward Payson, D. D.
late pastor of the Second Church in
Portland. 59310

Memoir of the Rev. Elijah P. Lovejoy. 42366

Memoir of the Rev. Francis Higginson.
24035

Memoir of the Rev. Gregory T. Bedwell.
97627

Memoir of the Rev. J. E. Emerson. 13365

Memoir of the Rev. Jacob J[ones] Janeway.
(35756)

Memoir of the Rev. James Chisholm. 15891

Memoir of the Rev. James H. Linsley.
41377

Memoir of the Rev. James McGregor. (59134)

Memoir of the Rev. James Manning. 27648

Memoir of the Rev. Jesse Lee. 95758

Memoir of the Rev. John H. Rice. 47057

Memoir of the Rev. John Stanford. 86856

Memoir of the Rev. Joseph Sanford. (76492)

Memoir of the Rev. Joseph Stibbs Christmas.
42021

Memoir of the Rev. Joseph W. Barr. 94064

Memoir of the Rev. Louis Dwight. 36034

Memoir of the Reverend Mr. Samuel Hidden.
14214

Memoir of the Rev. Nathan Parker, D. D. By
Henry Ware, Jr. 101388

Memoir of the Rev. Nathan Parker, D. D.,
late pastor of the South Church and
Parish in Portsmouth, N. H. 101389

Memoir of the Rev. Nathaniel Ward. 19033

Memoir of the Rev. Pliny Fisk. (6275)

Memoir of the Rev. Samuel Barrett. 64994

Memoir of the Rev. Samuel Green. 92256

Memoir of the Rev. Samuel Willard. 104059

Memoir of the Rev. Walter Gunn. 41384

Memoir of the Rev. William Adams. (11574)

Memoir of the Rev. William Metcalfe. 48169

Memoir of the Rev. William Smith. 91785

Memoir of the Rev. William Staughton. 42823

Memoir of the Rev. William Tennent. 6855,
94619

Memoir of the Rev. William Robinson. 72067

Memoir of the salubrity of the Isle of Pines.
(31523)

Memoir of the services of William Henry
Harrison. 30576

Memoir of the Stebbins family. 91005

Memoir of the surities of Thompson J. Skinner.
81651

Memoir of the survey. 6768, 45996

Memoir of the Trent affair. 17023

Memoir of the Trenton Delaware Falls
Company. 96774

Memoir of the U. S. Artillery. 55979

Memoir of the voyage of d'Entrecasteuaux.
9390

Memoir of Theodore Lyman. 42799

Memoir of Theophilus Parsons. 58910

Memoir of Thomas Addis Emmet. (43697)

Memoir of Thomas Addis Emmet; by Charles
Glidden Haines. (29550)

Memoir of Thomas B. Wilson. 22629

Memoir of Thomas Brand-Hollis, Esq. 20268

Memoir of Thomas Burchell. 9204

Memoir of Thomas C. James. 97649

Memoir of Thomas Chalkley. 33265

Memoir of Thomas Chittenden. (12821)

Memoir of Thomas Handasyd Perkins. 11218

Memoir of Thomas Jefferson. 85162

Memoir of Timothy Dwight. 21566

Memoir of Timothy Gilbert. 26194

Memoir of transactions that took place in
St. Domingo. 67533

Memoir of Tristram Burges. 7060

Memoir of Usher Parsons. 58877

Memoir of Valentine Mott. 28939

Memoir of W. C. Walton. 18472

Memoir of W. Carey. (10826)

Memoir of W. H. (Sedley) Smith. 84786

Memoir of Warren Colburn. (21878)

Memoir of William A. Jackson. 35479

Memoir of William A. Smith. 84992

Memoir of William Benjamin Smith. 84752

Memoir of William Burke. 9316

Memoir of William Ellery Channing. 11932

Memoir of William G. Crocker. 47295

Memoir of William H. Klapp. 15175

Memoir of William H. Prescott. 30622

Memoir of William Henry Harrison. 447

Memoir of William Knibb. 31967

Memoir of William Maclure. (51024)

Memoir of William Madison Peyton. 61322

Memoir of William Parsons Lunt. 26067

Memoir of William Penn. 59742

Memoir of William R. Fales. 23729

Memoir of William R. Grant. 2317

Memoir of William Randall Saxton. 96281

Memoir of William Rawle. 103110

Memoir of William Taggart. 94202

Memoir of William Wilberforce. 65456

Memoir of Zerah Colburn. 14257

Memoir on a mappemonde by Leonardo da
Vinci. 44070

Memoir on American fortification. 51004

Memoir on contagion. 64657

Memoir on Boston harbor. 18807

Memoir [on] maize, or Indian corn. 3420

Memoir on mechanical flight. 85072

Memoir on mososaurus. (27280), 85072

Memoir on slavery. 30418

Memoir on the antiquities of the western part
of the state of New York. 47502

Memoir of the birds of Greenland. 74708

Memoir on the boundary question pending
between the republic of Costa Rica and
the state of Nicaragua. 49885

Memoir on the constitution of matter. 71255

Memoir on the controversy between W. Penn
and Lord Baltimore. 21316

Memoir on the cultivation of the vine in
America. (56725)

Memoir on the dangers and defences of New
York City. 51004

Memoir on the different species of Quinquina. 38728
Memoir on the discovery of America. (13179)
Memoir on the European colonization of America. 106326
Memoir on the expediency and practicability of improving or creating home markets. 95782, 95785
Memoir on the explosiveness of nitre. 85072
Memoir on the extinct sloth tribe of North America. 39908, 85072
Memoir on the extinct species of American ox. 39907, 85072
Memoir on the extraneous fossils. 97482
Memoir on the geography and natural and civil history of Florida. 18532
Memoir on the geography of the North-Eastern part of Asia. 9389
Memoir on the geological position of a fossil tree. 77860
Memoir on the history, culture, manufactures, uses, &c. of the tobacco plant. 102165
Memoir on the internal improvement contemplated by the state. (55647)
Memoir on the island of Navassa, W. I. 26767
Memoir on the last sickness of General Washington. 35428
Memoir on the life and character of Philip Syng Physick. 67825
Memoir on the locality of the great treaty between William Penn and the Indian natives in 1682. 98702
Memoir on the Megatherium. 58012
Memoir on the navigation of South-America, to accompany a chart of that station. 47503
Memoir on the . . . orbits of the eight principal planets. 85072
Memoir on the organization of the army of the United States. 47594
Memoir on the origin, cultivation and uses of cotton. 78551
Memoir on the physical and political geography of New Grenada. 51070
Memoir on the present state . . . of Siberia. 58340
Memoir on the present state of the English language in the United States. 62637
Memoir on the progress of military discipline. 97919
Memoir on the public libraries of the antients [sic]. (33033)
Memoir on the recent surveys. 94318
Memoir on the rise, progress, and present state of the Chesapeake and Delaware Canal. 27461
Memoir on the scientific character and researches of James Smithson. 84985
Memoir on the scientific character and researches of the late James Smithson, Esq. 84989
Memoir on the secular variations of the elements of the orbits. 91921
Memoir on the subject of a general Bible society. 47505
Memoir on the subject of slavery. 88058
Memoir on the subject of the wheat and flour in the state of New York. 47506
Memoir on the subject of wheat and flour in the state of New-York. (14326)
Memoir on the tariff laws. 39564
Memoir on the topography, weather, and diseases of the Bahama Islands. 96392

Memoir on the U. S. Artillery. 69712
Memoir on the use of the thermometer in navigation. 104297
Memoir, or defence of Hugh Peters. 24034
Memoir, prepared at the request of a Committee of the Common Council of the city of New York. (14279), 92149
Memoir presented to the American Convention for Promoting the Abolition of Slavery and Improving the Condition of the African Race. 76389
Memoir read before the Ashmolean Society. (18661)
Memoir, read before the Historical Society of the State of New-York. 4743-4744, 4755
Memoir sent in 1693. 96172
Memoir showing how to bring the lead. (17379)
Memoir to accompany a military map of the peninsula of Florida. 35307
Memoir to accompany the map of the territory of the United States from the Mississippi River to the Pacific Ocean. 69946
Memoir to Their High Mightinesses the States General. 247
Memoir towards a character of Rev. John Eliot. 43373
Memoir upon Stephenson's silver mine. 89685
Memoir upon the extinct species of fossil ox. (39907)
Memoir upon the fossil footprints and other impressions. 19054
Memoir upon the geological action of the tidal and other currents of the ocean. 18807
Memoir upon the late war in North America. 64708
Memoir upon the negociations between Spain and the United States, which led to the treaty of 1819. 24884, 47507
Memoir upon the negotiations between Spain and the United States of America. 47356
Memoir upon the northern inter-oceanic route. 17380
Memoir vanden 30 December 1664. 20786, note after 98953
Memoir, with sermons, of Rev. Josiah Peet. 59537, 80289
Memoir written in the year 1804. 49853
Memoire a consulter, et consultation, &c. contre la Nouvelle Compagnie des Indes. 47508
Memoire a consulter et consultation pour les Jesuites de France. 94390
Memoire a consulter pour les colons de la Guyane Francaise. 29177
Memoire a l'Assembleee Nationale de France. 96080
Memoire a l'effet de determiner le caractere grammaticale. 21382
Memoire a Leurs Hautes-Puissances les Seigneurs Etats-Generaux. 248
Memoire a plaider devant la Cour Supreme de la Louisiane. 28247
Memoire a Sa Majeste l'Empereur Napoleon III. 38495
Memoire aan den Koing. 67412
Memoire accompagnant la requete. 10512
Memoire addresse a la Chambre des Deputes. 12353
Memoire addresse a S. M. Napoleon III. 23083, (27480)
Memoire adresse a L'Assemblee Nationale. 73468
Memoire, adresse a LL. HH. PP. par John Adams. 98505

Memoire adresse aux souverains de l'Europe. 35987, 64827, 64829, 2d note after 96457

Memoire adresse par les ministres du Roi. 75160

Memoire analytique. 39060, 73148

Memoire apologetique. (20731)

Memoire au Ministre de la Marine et des Colonies. 5652

Memoire au Ministre Plenipotentiare des Etats-Unis. 44236

Memoire aux Chambers par un citoyen des Stats-Unis. 27303, 96445

Memoire compose de la plaidoirie de T. J. J. Loranger. 42004

Memoire concernant le fue Sr. de Rochemore. 47509, 72330

Memoire concernant les greves du Sault-au-Matelot. 67060

Memoire concernant les prises faites. (47510), 69720

Memoire contenant le precis de faits, avec leurs pieces justificatives. 15205, (41650), (47511)-47512, 51661, 68283-68284, note after 80055, note after 91855, 101710

Memoire contenant un apercu statistique de l'Etat de Guatemala. 56419

Memoire couronne le 25 Aout 1784. 58826

Memoire de l'Abbe Morellet. 50595, (52216)

Memoire dans l'affaire de Canada. 11722

Memoire dans l'affaire du Canada. 6156, 47525

Memoire de Barbe Marbois, &c. (1534), (27337)

Memoire de Denis Benjamin Viger. 99598

Memoire de Jean Woolman. 105205

Memoire de la Chambre de Commerce d'Aunis. 47513

Memoire de la defence d'un plan d'acte. (45416)

Memoire de M. de Blanchelande. 5843

Memoire de M. de Vergennes. 97457

Memoire de M. Kerlerec. 72330

Memoire de M. l'Abbe Morellet. 50595, (52216)

Memoire de Mr. l'Ambassadeur Yorke. 106043

Memoire de M. le Docteur Catel. (12481)

Memoire de M. Loranger contenant sa replique. (42005)

Memoire de M. Roume, Commissaire et Ordonnateur de l'Ile de Tabago, charge par le Ministre de la Marine de repondre aux reclamations des hypothecaires Anglais: qui refute des representations faites par les creanciers Anglais de colons de Tabago. 73469

Memoire de M. Roume, Commissaire et Ordonnateur de l'Isle de Tabago, charge par le Ministre de la Marine de repondre aux Reclamations des hypothecaires Angalis, qui, refute un memoire adresse a l'Assemblee Nationale. 73468

Memoire de Montcalm Vengee. 40006

Memoire de Ramel. (67631)

Memoire de Sa Majeste au Pape Clement XIII. 47823

Memoire de Sam. F. B. Morse. 50963

Memoire des dits creanciers. 73469, 96048

Memoire des habitans des colonies Francaises. 47514

Memoire des habitans & negocians de la Louysiane. (47515)

Memoire des officiers, bas-officiers, &c. du regiment de la Martinique. 44979

Memoire des officiers municipaux de la ville de Sainte-Pierre ile Martinique. 5848

Memoire des services rendus. 94854

Memoire door den Heer Ridder Yorke. 106045

Memoire du Chev. Yorke. 67155

Memoire du Compte de Grasse. 28333

Memoire du Corps du Commerce des Cayes. 75101

Memoire du General de Brigade Andre Rigaud. 71317

Memoire du Ministre de la France. 14054

Memoire, du 4 Octob. 1751. 69671, note after 96403

Memoire du Sieur de Ramezay. 67021

Memoire du Sieur Jean Balfour. 2930

Memoire du Sieur Joly de St. Valier. 36430

Memoire du Sieur Rossignol Desdunes. 21220

Memoire dv voiage en Rvssie. (38494), 77218

Memoire en faveur des gens de couleur, ou sang-meles de St. Domingue. (28730)

Memoire en faveur des gens de couleur, ou sang-meles, de Saint Domingue. (17167), (28732)-(28733)

Memoire en forme de discours. (52384)

Memoire en replique a la justification publiee. 17168

Memoire en reponse a MM. les soi-disant philantropes. 82013

Memoire et observations du Sieur Barbe de Marbois. 3310

Memoir et prospectus. 67128

Memoire historique des dernieres revolutions. 75161

Memoire historique et politique . . . . Par le Colonel Malenfant. 44114

Memoire historique et politique pour la ville de la Basse-Terre. (3890)

Memoire historique et politique sur la Louisiane. 98971

Memoire historique sur la decadence et la ruine des missions des Jesuites. 44924

Memoire historique sur la negociation de la France & de l'Angleterre. 3898, (10513), 47516, 69530

Memoire historique sur les Indes braves et les forvans Francois. (47518)

Memoire historique sur Toussaint-Louverture. 68812

Memoire imprime pour M. le Comte de Malet du Gravier. 75057

Memoire instructif, adresse aux notables. 47519

Memoire instructiff des droits et des justes motifs. 47520

Memoire instructiv [sic] des droits et des justes motifs. 48532

Memoire juridique ou l'on examine. 42748

Memoire justificat de la conduite de la Grande Bretagne. 27283

Memoire justificatif, avec des observations sur Saint-Domingue. 72498

Memoire justificatif de Joseph-Paul-Augustin Cambefort. 10103, (75171), 96341

Memoire justificatif de la conduite de la Grande Bretagne. (44689)

Memoire justificatif de la Cour de Londres. 27283, 56580

Memoire justificatif des hommes de couleur de la Martinique. 5652

Memoire justificatif des hommes de couleur de la Martinique, condamnes par arret de la Cour Royale de cette colonie. (47521)

Memoire justificatif du citoyen Larchevesque-Thibaud. 39018

Memoire justificatif pour servir a reponse a l'expose, &c. de la Cour de France. 27282, 27283, 44282

Memoire justificatif que M. de la Luzerne. 42752

Memoire justificatif qu'il a publie en Juin 1790. 42753, note after 93793

Memoire laisse par M. Barbe de Marbois. 3311

Memoire lu a la Societe d'Ethnologie le 22 Fevrier 1850. (64697)

Memoire lue par M. d'Avezac. 30604

Memoire ou coup-d'oeil rapide sur mes differens voyages. 48949

Memoire ou journal de l'Adjutant-General Ramel. 67628

Memoire, ou precis historique sur la neutralite armee et son origin. 27685

Memoire ou replique a la justification de W. de Lazerne. 17258

Memoire par Fontanedo. 24894, note after 94854, 94856

Memoire par Lopez de Mendoz. 24894, note after 94854, 94856

Memoire partiel de l'etat des missions Indiennes. 6297

(Memoire, por le Marquis de Vaudreuil.) 98684

Memoire pour Alexander M'Clure. 43057

Memoire pour Daniel de Joncaire-Chabert. (47522)

Memoire pour des negocians de l'Orient. 47524

Memoire pour Eloy Imbert. (34352)

Memoire pour Frederick Williams. 104223

Memoire pour Fulwar Skipwith. 81656

Memoire pour James C. Mountflorence. 81657

Memoire pour le Chef de Brigade Magloire Pelage. 25674, (29042), 59568

Memoire [pour le Sr. Cazotte et la Dlle. Fouque] sur les demandes formees. 94390

Memoire pour le Sieur de Boishebert. 6156, 47525

Memoire pour le Sieur de Naoilles. 75162

Memoire pour le Sieur Duverger de Saint Blin. 75004

Memoire pour le Sr. Jean-Francois Willart. 104125

Memoire pour le Sieur Peter Walsh. 101152

Memoire pour le Sieur Ralph J. Reed. 68576

Memoire pour le Sieur Thomas Walpole. 101149

Memoire pour les citoyens Verneuil, Baillio jeune, Fournier et Gervais. (2765), 75163, 99242

Memoire pour les colonies Francaises. 47526

Memoire pour les Etats-Unis d'Amerique demandeurs. 47527

Memoire pour l'establissement du commerce au Japon. 4935-4936

Memoire pour MM. Garesche Freres negocians a la Rochelle. 26662

Memoire pour Messire Francois Bigot. (38696), 47528

Memoire pour Michel-Jean-Hughes Pean. Chevalier. 59429

Memoire pour Michel-Jean-Hugues Pean. 2352

Memoire pour Mr Charles de Saint Estienne. (47523)

Memoire pour Pierre Monroux. 50034

Memoire pour Rodolphe Tillier. 95824

Memoire pour servir a l'histoire de la revolution. 64709

Memoire pour servir a l'histoire de l'eglise de l'Amerique du Nord. (47529)

Memoire pour servir a l'histoire du Tapir. 73467

Memoire pour servir d'addition & d'eclaircissement a la relation abregee, &c. 63908

Memoire presente a la Chambre des Deputes. 59110

Memoire presente a la Cour de Cassation. 81659

Memoire presente a la nation par le citoyen Verneuil. 99241

Memoire presente a Sa Gr. Mylord Duc de Newcastle. 66725

Memoire presente a Son Altesse Royale M. le Duc d'Orleans. 38595, 47530

Memoire presente a Son Excellence. 104017

Memoire presente au gouvernement. 75536

Memoire presente au Protecteur d'Angleterre. (47531), 96521

Memoire presente aux Etats de Hollande. 106044

Memoire presente aux Etats-General par l'Ambassadeur d'Angleterre. 65049

Memoire presente par les Commissaires de Sa Majeste. 69671, note after 96403

Memoire presente par M. le Chevalier Yorke. 106045

Memoire publie au nom de plusieurs anciens colons-proprietaires. 93824

Memoire publie contre lui par M. le Vicomte de Turpin. (19762)

Memoire que etablit. 5030

Memoire, que les Etats-Generaux auroient pu faire presente. 106042

Memoire qu'il avoit appris qu'on se proposoit de presenter. 8834

Memoire reconditte di Vittorio Siri. 81445

Memoire; ridige par John le Long. 39984

Memoire redigee par M. Richard de Lucy. 42637

Memoire relatif a l'abolition de la traite Africaine. (47902)

Memoire relatif a l'administration de la partie Francois de St. Domingue. 101245

Memoire, statuts et prospectus. (67129)

Memoire supplementaire de Fulwar Skipwith. 81658

Memoire sur cette question. 47532

Memoire sur des materiaux pour servir a l'histoire. (19335)

Memoire sur divers crustaces nouveaux du Mexique et des Antilles. 77210-77211

Memoire sur la canalisation projetee de l'ismus de Nicaragua. 2506

Memoire sur la collection des grandes et petits voyages. (8784)

Memoire sur collection des grands et petits voyages. 10328

Memoire sur la colonie de la Guiane Francaise et sur les avantages politiques et commerciaux de sa possession. 27499, 29178, 99458

Memoire sur la Compagnie des Indes. 39251

Memoire sur la condition de la classe servile au Mexique. 5521

Memoire sur la conduite de la France. 47533

Memoire sur la culture du cotonnier dans les Terres Basses. 39605

Memoire sur la culture du poivrier. 4941

Memoire sur la decouverte de l'Amerique au dixieme siecle. (67481)-(67482)

Memoire sur la decouverte du nouvel emploi de l'ether sulfurique. 51031

Memoire sur la fievre jaune. (27350)
Memoire sur la fievre jaune d'Amerique. 73513
Memoire sur la frequence des chutes de greles a l'ile de Cuba. (63662)
Memoire sur la geographie de la Perse. 68443
Memoire sur la Guadeloupe. (74627)
Memoire sur la Guiane Francaise. 35513
Memoire sur la Guiane Francaise. Par M. Nayer. (56211)
Memoire sur la Guyane Francaise. (29179)
Memoire sur la Guyane Francaise. Par J. Itier. 35281
Memoire sur la longitude de Buenos-Ayres. (11723)
Memoire sur la Louisiane. 35514
Memoire sur la Louisiane, ou le Mississippi. (68417)
Memoire sur la naturalisation des arbres forestiers. 48698
Memoire sur la nature. 29240
Memoire sur la navigation dans la Mer du Nord. 22572
Memoire sur la navigation de France aux Indes. 44344
Memoire sur la non-contagion de la fievre jaune. 18578
Memoire sur la numeration dans la langue et dans l'ecriture sacree. 73308
Memoire sur la partie de la Guyane. 70401
Memoire sur la partie meridionale de l'Asie Central. 68443
Memoire sur la peinture didactique et l'ecriture figurative. (7419)
Memoire sur la position des Isles de la Mer du Sud. (62948)
Memoire sur la pretendu decouverte. (38427)
Memoire sur la priorite de la decouverte de la cote occidentale d'Afrique. 76835, 76838
Memoire sur la question de savoir a quelle epoque l'Amerique Meridionale a cesse d'entre representee dans les cartes geographiques. 76841
Memoire sur la serie lineaire des plantes polypetales. 75235
Memoire sur la situation actuelle de la Compagnie des Indes. 50595-50596
Memoire sur la situation commerciale de la France. 94303
Memoire sur la situation de Saint-Domingue a l'epoque du mois de Janvier 1792. 16790
Memoire sur la situation des colonies Francaises. 21359
Memoire sur la succession de Madame de Castaing. (11374)
Memoire sur la terrain tertiaire. 16743
Memoire sur la vie de M. de Laval. 39216
Memoire sur l'acclimatement des races en Amerique. 10920
Memoire sur le Bresil. 38897
Memoire sur le Canada. 10515
Memoire sur le Canada [par M. Hocquart?] 67020
Memoire sur le choix et l'etat des lieux. (62948)
Memoire sur le coca du Perou. 26120
Memoire sur le commerce de la France et de ses colonies. 96126
Memoire sur le commerce etranger avec les colonies Francaises de l'Amerique. 14715, (47534)
Memoire sur les Incas et sur les langues colonial. 47535

Memoire sur le commerce maritime et les colonies. 47205
Memoire sur le cypres de la Louisiane. 17822
Memoire sur le decouverte de l'Amerique au dixieme siecle. 67471, 67480
Memoire sur le effets desastreux pour les colonies Francaises. 5402
Memoire sur le genevrier rouge de Virginia. (17823)
Memoire sur le genre Tozzia. 75235
Memoire sur le Guatemala. (47536)
Memoire sur le moyen de reparer les torts faits. 105642-105643
Memoire sur le passage par le Nord. 17714-17715
Memoire sur le pays de l'Asie et de l'Amerique 71874, note after 98694
Memoire sur le system d'agriculture adopte par les Brasiliens. 75221
Memoire sur le system grammatical des langues. 21383
Memoire sur le systeme a suivre dans une guerre purement maritime avec l'Angleterre. (6437)
Memoire (sur les affaires de St. Domingue.) 42751
Memoire sur les avantages qu'il y auroit a changer la nourriture des gens de mer. 19754, (63713)
Memoire sur les bateaux a vapeur. 44523
Memoire sur les bois d'Amerique. 101347
Memoire sur les causes de la fievre jaune. (48689)
Memoire sur les causes des troubles et des desastres. (67518)
Memoire sur les causes du peu de produit des terres de Cayenne. (27500)
Memoire sur les colonies Americaines. 97456
Memoire sur les colonies occidentales de la France. 42905
Memoire sur les demandes formees contre le Generale. 94390
Memoire sur les differentes idees. (8833)
Memoire sur les establissements d'un Conseil de Marine. (6437)
Memoire sur les fongeres du Mexique. 44850
Memoire sur les fossiles secondaires re-cueillis dans le Chili. 20560
Memoir sur les Incas et sur les langues Aymara-Quichua. 69655
Memoire sur les institutions politique. 76842
Memoire sur les limites veritables de la Guiane Francaise. 81291
Memoire sur les maladies les plus communes a Saint Domingue. 6897, note after 100841
Memoire sur les moeurs, coutumes et rellLgion [sic] des sauvages. 61022
Memoire sur les moyens d'appliquer le travail des Europeens. 4940
Memoire sur les moyens de soumettre les rebelles de Saint-Domingue. 14463
Memoire sur les Negres pour servir de materiaux aux cahiers des colonies. (47537)
Memoire sur les noirs de l'Amerique Septen-trionale. (8023)
Memoire sur les operations hydrographiques et geodesiques executives. 50001
Memoire sur les pays de l'Asie et de l'Ameriq l'Amerique. 8831
Memoire sur les principes et les lois de la neutralite maritime. 47438
Memoire sur les races humaines repandues dans l'oceanie, la malaisie. 40215

Memoire sur les relations commerciales des Etats-Unis avec l'Angleterre. 94260

Memoire sur les voyages executes dans l'ocean glacial Arctique. 38982

Memoire sur l'esclavage colonial. 20179

Memoire sur l'esclavage des Negres. (20381)

Memoire sur l'esclavage et sur la traite des Negres. 9748

Memoire sur l'etat actuel de l'Amerique. 10089

Memoire sur l'etat de Guatemala. 66853

Memoire sur l'etat present du Canada. 67020, lst note after 94271

Memoire sur l'exploitation des bois de la Guyane Francaise. 29180

Memoire sur l'ile d'Haiti. 59592

Memoire sur l'importance, pour la colonie de St. Domingue. 75164

Memoire sur l'inamobibilite des cures en Canada. 39106

Memoire sur l'origine Japonaise. (58551)

Memoire sur Saint-Domingue. 99532

Memoire sur in insecte. 29111

Memoire sur un nouveau passage de la Mer du Nord. 38408

Memoire sur un nouvel equipage de chaudieres. 47439

Memoire sur une espece du coton. 50574

Memoire sur une nouvelle famille des vochislees. 75235

Memoire sur une question de geographie-pratique. 71875

Memoire touchant la Californie. 4935, 4936

Memoire touchant le commerce du Japon. 68455

Memoire touchant l'etablissement des P. P. Jesuites. 25924

Memoire touchant l'etablissement des Peres Jesuites. 47540

Memoire vande Heere Gorge [sic] Downing. 20782

Memoire voor Jean Joly, cum suis. (36423)

Memoiren aus meinem Tagebuche. 2165

Memoiren, oder Beitrage zur Lebensgeschichte des Generals Lafayette. 68928

Memoires authentiques. (12277)

Memoires autographiques de Don Augustin Iturbide. 35292

Memoires biographiques litteraires et politiques de Mirabeau. 49399

Memoires chronologiques. 44668, 47541

Memoires complets, oeuvres morales et litteraires. 25551

Memoires concernant diverses questions d'astronomie. 40010

Memoires concernant l'histoire des Chinois. 68352

Memoires, consultation, pieces justificatives, &c. (44970)

Memoires, contenant des details sur les deportes. 25823

Memoires contenant la verite sur divers evenements. (39107)

Memoires, correspondance et mansucrits du General La Fayette. 38575

Memoires de Barbe Marbois. (1534), (27337)

Memoires de Barnum. 3565

Memoires de Beauchene. 40158

Memoires de Billaud-Varennes, ex-conventionnel. (42899)

Memoires de Bravet. 7458

Memoires de D. Ulloa. 10912

Memoires de fue M. de Maillet. 43891

Memoires de Florincourt. 99412

Memoires [de George Anne Bellamy.] 4484

Memoires de Jean Ker. 37601

Memoires de John Tanner. (35686), 94329

Memoires de la Compange des Decouvertes dans les meres de l'Inde. 28763

Memoires de la Societe d'Agriculture du Department de la Seine. 47543

Memoires de la Societe d'Anthropologie. 28058

Memoires de la Societe de Geographie de Geneve. 77203

Memoires de la Societe des Antiquaires de l'Amerique du Nord. 69656

Memoires de la Societe des Ingenieurs Civils. 24638

Memoires de la Societe d'Ethnographie. 70371, 70373, 70376-70377, 73303, 73310

Memoires de la Societe du Department de la Seine. 48698

Memoires de la Societe Ethnologique. 22076, 47544

Memoires de la Societe Historique de Montreal. 50292, note after 98976, 99601

Memoires de la Societe Imp. de Lille. 12880

Memoires de la Societe Royale des Antiquaires du Nord, Copenhagen. 47545, (67472), 67480, 77841

Memoires de la vie privee de Benj. Franklin. 25549

Memoires de l'Academie des Sciences. 8831, (11723)

Memoires de l'Academie des Sciences de l'Institut Royal. 101364-101365

Memoires de l'Amerique Septentrionale. 38636, (38642)

Memoires de l'Institut National. 8831, (47542)

Memoires de l'Institut National des Sciences et Arts. 94260

Memoires de M***. 52091

Memoires de Madame Newell. 105133

Memoires de M. Bigot. 7650

Memoires de M. de Floricourt. 99412

Memoires de Monsieur du Guay-Trouin. 29098

Memoires de M. Dumont. (9605)

Memoires . . . de M. Marigin de Mandeville. (44574)

Memoires de Mgr. J. Brumauld de Beauregard. 8742

Memoires de morale et de politique. 28723

Memoires de Paul Jones. 36559

Memoires de Sebastien-Joseph de Cavalho et Melo. 63913

Memoires de 1755. 6877

Memoires de Thomas Chalkley. 11752

Memoires des Commissaires de deux puissances. (774), 16023, (47546)-(47547), note after (47740)-47742, note after 96403

Memoires des Commissaires de Sa Majeste Tres-Chretienne et de ceux de Sa Majeste Britannique. (774), (47546), note after (47740), note after 96403

Memoires des Commissaires du Roi et de ceux de sa Majeste Britannique. (47547), 47741, (56129), 69463, note after 96403

Memoires des principaux officiers que ont commande en ces pays. 13768

Memoires du Baron Pierre-Barthelemy d'Albaredes Portal. 64190

Memoires du Capitaine Landolphe. 38840

Memoires du Capitaine Peron. (61001)

Memoires du Cercle des Philadelphes. 47548

Memoirs and anecdotes of Philip Thicknesse. 95343

Memoirs and autobiography of some of the wealthy citizens of Philadelphia, with a fair estimate of their estates. 47561

Memoirs and auto-biography of some of the wealthy citizens of Philadelphia . . . . With an appendix. 61813

Memoirs and character of Sarah. 76911

Memoirs and confessions of Capt. Ashe. 2178

Memoirs and considerations concerning the trade and revenues. 2192-2194

Memoirs and correspondence of Admiral Lord de Saumarez. 73373

Memoirs and correspondence of George, Lord Lyttleton. 62464

Memoirs and correspondence of Mrs. Grant. 28297

Memoirs and correspondence of Viscount Castlereagh. 91705

Memoirs and letters, and journals of Major-General Riedesel. 22003

Memoirs and letters of . . . Colonel Armine S. H. Mountain. 51184

Memoirs and letters of Mrs. Mary Dexter. 96306

Memoirs and maps of California. (71425)

Memoirs and recollections of Count Segur. 78917

Memoirs and remains of John Oliphant. 57182

Memoirs and remains of Rev. Willard Judd. 36848

Memoirs and remains of Stephen Beekman Bangs. 43852

Memoirs and select papers of Horace B. Morse. 9459

Memoirs and select thoughts, of the late Rev. Edward Payson. 59310

Memoirs and services of Lieut. Gen. Leith in the West Indies. 39942

Memoirs and sketches. 49072

Memoirs and writings of Mrs. Hannah Maynard Pickard. 57843

Memoirs by distinguished biographers. 26414

Memoirs correspondence and manuscripts of General Lafayette. 38576

Memoirs, correspondence, and private papers of Thomas Jefferson. 35892

Memoirs, &c. &c. of General Moreau. 62449

Memoirs, &c., of S. Fothergill. 25273

Memoirs for the curious. 50187

Memoirs in illustration of the progress of British commerce. 6922

Memoirs, journal, and correspondence of Thomas Moore. 50447

Memoirs, journal and letters of Seth Coleman. (14309)

Memoirs, life, and character of the great Mr. Law. 39311

Memoirs of a British officer. 26508

Memoirs of a captivity among the Indians of North America. (33921)

Memoirs of a Church of England missionary. 30

Memoirs of a French refugee famliy. 24986

Memoirs, of a fugitive. (31786)

Memoirs of a fugitive, a new picture of American slave life. (31787)

Memoirs of a fugitive. By Richard Hildreth. 31791

Memoirs of a grandmother. 47562, 70909

Memoirs of a Huguenot family. 24987

Memoirs of a late eminent bookseller. 954

Memoirs of a late officer. 47563

Memoirs of a life. 28418-28419

Memoirs of a New England village choir. (27436), 47564

Memoirs of a nullifier. 47565

Memoirs of a provincial. 51109

Memoirs of a staff-officer. 16320

Memoirs of a water drinker. (21308), 95362

Memoirs of a West-India planter published from an original MS. 69243

Memoirs of a West India planter. Re-published from an original manuscript. 71389-71390

Memoirs of Aaron Burr. (9424), 18864

Memoirs of Aaron Haynes Hurd. 32484

Memoirs [of Abigail Abbot Bailey.] 2722

Memoirs of . . . Abraham Luckenbach. 42628

Memoirs of Admiral Sir George Cockburn, G. C. B. 23144, note after 101938

Memoirs of Alexander Campbell. 71083

Memoirs of America. 1908

Memoirs of American governors. 50394

Memoirs of American missionaries. 41954

Memoirs of an America. (47566)

Memoirs of an American lady. (28296)

Memoirs of an American loyalist. 47467

Memoirs of an American officer. (8891)

Memoirs of an American young lady. 44314, note after 75924

Memoirs of an unfortunate young nobleman. 1600

Memoirs of an unfortunate young nobleman, return'd from a thirteen years slavery in America. 1599

Memoirs of an English missionary. 95529

Memoirs of an Irishman now in America. 31688

Memoirs of an officer in the army of Wolfe. 36519

Memoirs of an old disciple and his descendants. 37943

Memoirs of Andrew Jackson, late Major-General and Commander in Chief of the southern division of the army. 82809

Memoirs of Andrew Jackson, Major-General in the army of the United States. 101008-101009

Memoirs of Andrew Sheburne. 80330-80331

Memoirs of Anthony J. Pearson. 6133

Memoirs of Archy Moore. 31789-(31790), 82065

Memoirs of Augustin de Iturbide. 35291, (35296)

Memoirs of Benjamin Franklin, written by himself and continued by his grandson. 25546

Memoirs of Benjamin Franklin; written by himself. With his most interesting essays. 25547

Memoirs of Capt. Henry Gardiner. 26616

Memoirs of Captain James Wilson. 28820, note after 104633

Memoirs of Capt. Lemuel Roberts. 71905

Memoirs of Capt. Roger Clap. (13206)-13209

Memoirs of Captain Roger Clap. 106052

Memoirs of Catharine Seely and Deborah S. Roberts. 78861

Memoirs of celebrated characters. 38709

Memoirs of celebrated naval commanders. (41757)

Memoirs [of Champegny]. 25853

Memoirs of Charles Denis Rusoe d'Eres. (22731)

Memoirs of Charles Mathews, comedian.
46826-46827
Memoirs of Chateaubriand. 12256
Memoirs of Christian missionaries. 26617
Memoirs of Col. Ariel Bragg. 7321
Memoirs of Colonel Edward Marcus Despard.
3209
Memoirs of commercial delusions. 43358
Memoirs of Cowper, Bishop Heber, and
Howard the philanthropist. 94541
Memoirs [of Daniel Drake.] (20821)
Memoirs of Darien. 6328
Memoirs of David Brainard. 7345
Memoirs of David Nasmith. 10246
Memoirs of deceased alumni of St. John's
College. 66222
Memoirs of distinguished Americans. 47568
Memoirs of Dr. Joseph Priestly. 65511
Memoirs of Dr. Samuel Powell Griffiths.
22431
Memoirs of Dolly E. Hoyt. (33400)
Memoirs of Don Manuel de Godoy. 27668
Memoirs of Don Pedro, ex-Emperor of Brazil.
26523
Memoirs of Dona Maria Loretto Martinez.
44960
Memoirs of Elder John Peak. (59415)
Memoirs of Eleanor Eldridge. 22102, 103303
Memoirs of Elizabeth Collins. 14434
Memoirs of Elkanah Watson. 102133
Memoirs of eminent Christians. 26617A
Memoirs of eminent female writers. 25856
Memoirs of eminent Pennsylvanians. 59916
Memoirs of eminent Pennsylvanias. By John
R. Goodman. (27865)
Memoirs of eminent persons, with portraits
and facsimiles. 29813
Memoirs of eminent physicians who have
flourished in America. 95147
Memoirs of eminently pious women. 18405
Memoirs of Enoch Crosby. (3559)-3562
Memoirs of extraordinary popular delusions.
43356-43357
Memoirs of extraordinary popular delusions
and the madness of crowds. 43358
Memoirs of Fanny Newell. 54952
Memoirs of Field-Marshal the Duke de
Saldanha. 82917
Memoirs of four brothers engaged in the
service of their country. (47569)
Memoirs of Francis Barnett the Lefevre of
"No fiction." 3534, (39840)
Memoirs of Frederic Charlton. 102807
Memoirs of General Andrew Jackson. 35375
Memoirs of General Andrew Jackson, seventh
President of the United States. 35377
Memoirs of Gen. Andrew Jackson, together
with the letter of Mr. Secretary Adams.
35376
Memoirs of Gen. George Washington. 97202,
101779, note after 101843, 101851
Memoirs of General La Fayette, and of the
French revolution of 1830. (77098)
Memoirs of Gen. Lafayette; with an account
of his tour through the United States.
38579
Memoirs of General Lafayette. With an
account of his visit to America. 38083
Memoirs of General Ramel. 67629
Memoirs of General Wilkinson. 104028
Memoirs of General [William] Miller. 49028
Memoirs of General William T. Sherman.
80416
Memoirs of George Berkeley. 4882, 91872
Memoirs of George Frederick Cooke. 95362

Memoirs of George Washington. 101710
Memoirs of George Whitefield. 12913, (66917)
note after 103655
Memoirs of Gilbert Motier La Fayette. 32643
Memoirs of Granville Sharp. 32288
Memoirs of Great Britain and Ireland. 18348
Memoirs of great commanders. 35697
Memoirs of Gregor M'Gregor. 67488
Memoirs of Governor William Smith, of
Virginia. 84724
Memoirs of Hans Hendrik. 71440
Memoirs of Henry More Smith. 3947
Memoirs of Henry Obookiah. (56429)
Memoirs of her [i. e. Hannah Logan Smiths']
husband, and other Quakers. 41791
Memoirs of her [i. e. Harriet Newell's] life.
105141
Memoirs of her [i. e. Jane Colman Turell's]
life and death. (14513), 97451
Memoirs of his daughter, Mrs. Conklin, and
his son, Samuel Buell. 8983
Memoirs of his [i. e. Joseph Stebens Buck-
minster's] life. 8936
Memoirs of his [i. e. Samuel Buell's sons']
life. 8985
Memoirs of his [i. e. Matson Meier-Smith's]
life and work. 83571
Memoirs of his [i. e. John Wilkes'] life, by
John Almon. 104003
Memoirs of his [i. e. James Houstoun's] own
life-time. 33198
Memoirs of his [i. e. Mathieu Dumas's] own
time, including the revolution. 21191
Memoirs of his [i. e. Alexander Graydon's]
own time. With reminiscences of the
men and events of the revolution. 28420
Memoirs of Hon. Thomas Jefferson. 19161
Memoirs of illustrious and celebrated women.
31061
Memoirs of . . . illustrious seamen. 10230
Memoirs of individuals who have been
distinguished by their writings. 101409
Memoirs of Isonnonthouan. 35265
Memoirs of [of J. Burchett.] 41072
Memoirs of James Gordon Bennett and his
times. 4729, 84988
Memoirs of Jas. McClurg. 43000
Memoirs of James Wilmer. 104568
Memoirs of Jemima Wilkinson. 33485, 104033
Memoirs of John Amiralle. 88630
Memoirs of John Brown. 76249
Memoirs of John Fothergill. 40725
Memoirs of John Horne Tooke. 28230
Memoirs of John Howard Paine. 59288
Memoirs of John Ker. 37600
Memoirs of John Law of Lauriston. 39312
Memoirs of John Mooney Mead. 47215
Memoirs of Joseph John Gurney. 7361
Memoirs of Joseph Sturge. 70902
Memoirs of Josias Rogers. 27467
Memoirs of Lafitte. 47570
Memoirs of libraries. 21919
Memoirs of Lieutenant Colonel Sir Thomas
Picton. 72081
Memoirs of Lieut.-General Scott. 78418
Memoirs of Lieut. Henry Timberlake. 95836
Memoirs of Lieutenant Joseph Rene Bellot.
4566
Memoirs of Lord North's island. 32473
Memoirs of Lorenzo da Ponte. 64005
Memoirs of Major-General Heath. 31192
Memoirs of Maj.-Gen. J. McRee. 43654
Memoirs of Major-General Lee. 66807
Memoirs of Major Robert Stobo. 91869
Memoirs of mammouth and various other
extraordinary and stupendous bones. 2179

Memoirs of many of the most eminent persons. 37900

Memoirs of Margaret Fuller Ossoli. 57816

Memoirs of Matthias the Prophet. (46897)

Memoirs of Mirabeau. (49400)

Memoirs of Miss Caroline E. Smelt. 100883

Memoirs of Miss Lucy Richards, written by herself. (70956)

Memoirs of Miss Susanna Anthony. 32951

Memoirs of Mr. John Tobin. 96057

Memoirs of Mr. Wesley's missionaries to America. 76409

Memoirs of Mrs. Abigail Bailey. 2722, 82534

Memoirs of Mrs. Coghlan. 14208-14209

Memoirs of Mrs. Eleanor Emerson. 105306

Memoirs of [Mrs.] E[liza] M. S[aunders.] 59012

Memoirs of Mrs. Elizabeth Hamilton. 96057

Memoirs of Mrs. Elizabeth Wilson. 104695

Memoirs of Mrs. Emily Egerton. 56352

Memoirs of Mrs. Gale and . . . Mrs. Esther Peak. (59415)

Memoirs of Mrs. Harriet Newell. 105134

Memoirs of Mrs. Harriet Newell, wife of the Rev. S. Newell. 54956

Memoirs of Mrs. Joanna Bethune. (5080)

Memoirs of Mrs. Mary Ann Bise. 40226, 103198

Memoirs of Mrs. Ruth Patten. 59123

Memoirs of Mrs S*****. 79335

Memoirs of Mrs. Susan Huntington. 104912

Memoirs of Mrs. Susan Huntington, of Boston, Mass. 104911

Memoirs of Molly Ward. 101318

Memoirs of my life work. 16310

Memoirs of my own times. (71302), (104028A)

Memoirs of Niambanna. 80885-80886, 93373, 93375, 93377

Memoirs of Nicholas Ferrar. 43178

Memoirs of North-Britain. 47571, 78227

Memoirs of odd adventures, strange deliverances, etc., in the captivity of John Giles, esq. 27370

Memoirs of odd adventures, strange deliverances, etc., in the captivity of John Gyles, esq. 29386

Memoirs of Peter Henry Bruce. 8726

Memoirs of Philip Thicknesse. 95343

Memoirs of pious females. 15447

Memoirs of Rear-Admiral Paul Jones. 36558

Memoirs of Rear-Admiral Sir W. Edward Perry. 58856

Memoirs of remarkable characters. 21754

Memoirs of remarkables in the life and death of the ever-memorable Dr. Increase Mather. (46447)

Memoirs of Rev. Benjamin C. Cutler. 28392

Memoirs of Rev. David Rice. 5618

Memoirs of Rev. Joseph Buckminster. 39729

Memoirs of Rev. Michael Wigglesworth. (19035)

Memoirs of Rev. Philetus B. Peck. 59490

Memoirs of Rev. Thos. Cleland. 33787

Memoirs of . . . Rev. William Marshall. 44814

Memoirs of Rhode Island officers. 3744

Memoirs of Samuel Smith. 9538, 83998

Memoirs, select thoughts and sermons. 59310

Memoirs of service afloat. 79081

Memoirs of Simeon J. Milliken. 62962

Memoirs of Simeon Wilhelm. 105923

Memoirs of Simon Bolivar. (21069), (32644)

Memoirs of Sir Philip Francis. 58778

Memoirs of Sir Thomas Fowell Buxton. (692)

Memoirs of Sir Walter Raleigh. 95303

Memoirs of six deceased members of a single Sabbath school. 102097

Memoirs of Stephen B. Stedman. 91070

Memoirs of Stephen Burroughs. (9466)

Memoirs of Sylvester Daggerwood. 58422

Memoirs of T. L. Winthrop. 24967

Memoirs of Tarleton Brown, a captain in the revolutionary army. 8564, 9538

Memoirs of teachers, educators, and promoters and benefactors of education. 3465

Memoirs of that truly eccentric character. (19908), 86840

Memoirs of the administration of the colonial government of Lower Canada, by Sir Henry Craig and Sir Geo. Prevost. 12938

Memoirs of the administration of the government of Lower Canada by the Right Honorable the Earl of Dalhousie. 10516

Memoirs of the administrations of the colonial government of Lower Canada, &c., by Sir Gordon Drummond. 12935

Memoirs of the administrations of Washington and John Adams. 104984

Memoirs of the American Academy of Arts and Sciences. 1034, 6288, 7017, 18428, 18807, 18845, 32241, 35402, 42442, 47572, 62631, 62637-62638, 67942, 82939, 104351

Memoirs of the American revolution; from its commencement to the year 1776, inclusive. 20914

Memoirs of the American revolution, so far as it related to the states of North and South Carolina, and Georgia. 51142

Memoirs of the Anthropological Society of London. (6207)

Memoirs of the author's [i. e. Sir William Petty's] life. (61308)

Memoirs of the battle, at Piggwackett. 94107

Memoirs of the Bloomsgrove family. 32255

Memoirs of the Board of Agriculture of . . . New York. 53544

Memoirs of the Boston Athenaeum. 6593

Memoirs of the campaign of the North Western Army. (33643)

Memoirs of the celebrated and beautiful Mrs. Ann Carson. 13436A

Memoirs of the civil war. 23690

Memoirs of the Confederate war for independence. 6401

Memoirs [of the Congress of Americanists, 1865.] 73308

Memoirs of the Connecticut Academy of Arts and Sciences. 15703

Memoirs of the conquistador Bernal Diaz del Castillo. (19983)

Memoirs of the court and reign of Catherine the Second. 85170

Memoirs of the dead. 47573

Memoirs of the Duke de Lauzun. (39272)

Memoirs of the Duke de Ripperda. 71536

Memoirs of the Duke of Ripperda. 71537

Memoirs of the Dutch trade in all the states. 47574

Memoirs of the first settlement of the island of Barbadoes. 3278

Memoirs of the Geological Survey. (35584)

Memoirs of the Gloucester Fox Hunting Club near Philadelphia. 27600

Memoirs of the Graysons. 31439, 97306

Memoirs of the great and good of all nations and all times. 77224

Memoirs of the Historical Society of Pennsylvania. see Memoirs of the Pennsylvania Historical Society.

Memoirs of the Hon. Thomas Jefferson. 11004

Memoirs of the illustrious citizen and patriot, Andrew Jackson. 101009

Memoirs of the illustrious Lord Nelson. 41583

Memoirs of the late Charles Lee, Esq. 38902-38903

Memoirs of the late Dr. Benjamin Franklin. 25615, 1st note after 104563

Memoirs of the late Hannah L. Murray. 89777

Memoirs of the late Mrs. Susan Huntington. 104909-104910

Memoirs of the late Rev. Alexander Proudfit. 25152

Memoirs of the late Rev. John Wesley, A. M. (30147)

Memoirs of the late Reverend Theophilus Lindsey. 4598

Memoirs of the late Wm. Cobbett. 33627

Memoirs of the leadings of divine providence. 104633

Memoirs of the life, adventures, and military exploits of Israel Putnam. 66807

Memoirs of the life and a view of the character of the late Dr. John Fothergill. 95514

Memoirs of the life and achievements of Lord Viscount Nelson. 52312

Memoirs of the life and administration of the Right Honourable William Cecil, Lord Burghley. 51770

Memoirs of the life and adventures of Tsonnonthouan. 97293

Memoirs of the life and campaigns of Hon. Nathaniel Greene. 9897

Memoirs of the life and character of Rev. John Eliot. 50421

Memoirs of the life and character of the late Rev. George Atwell. 94892

Memoirs of the life and character of the Rev. Matthias Bruen. 8737

Memoirs of the life and death of Joseph Smith. 47126, 85168

Memoirs of the life and death of the pious and ingenious Mrs. Jane Turell. (14513), 97451

Memoirs of the life and gallant exploits of the old highlander. 95606

Memoirs of the life and gallant services of Admiral Lord Nelson. 52312

Memoirs of the life and Gospel labors of Stephen Grellet. 28748

Memoirs of the life and Gospel labours of the late Daniel Wheeler. 103182

Memoirs of the life and ministry of the Rev. John Summerfield. 32507

Memoirs of the life and reign of King George the Third. 36075

Memoirs of the life and religious labors of Thomas Scattergood. (77452)

Memoirs of the life and services of Admiral Sir P. C. H. C. Durham. 51485

Memoirs of the life and services of Daniel Drake. 44369

Memoirs of the life and services of John Sanders. 51006

Memoirs of the life, and travels, in the service of the Gospel. 91324

Memoirs of the life and travels of B. Hibbard. 31677

Memoirs of the life and travels of James Houstoun. (33197)

Memoirs of the life and travels of John Ledyard. 88993

Memoirs of the life and travels of the late Charles Macpherson. (43625)

Memoirs of the life and works of George Romney. (73064)

Memoirs of the life and works of the late Rt. Hon. Sir John Sinclair. 81402

Memoirs of the life and worth: lamentations for the death, and loss of the every way admirable Mr. Vrian Oakes. 46462

Memoirs of the life and writings of Benjamin Franklin. 25545, 25569, 25571

Memoirs of the life and writings of Lindley Murray. 51534

Memoirs of the life and writings of Luis de Camoens. 367

Memoirs of the life and writings of the late John Coakley Lettsom. 61299

Memoirs of the life and writings of the Rev. William Richards. 23170

Memoirs of the life, conversion, and happy death, of Mrs. Eleanor Emerson. 105307

Memoirs of the life of a modern saint. (47575), 103571

Memoirs of the life of Anthony Benezet. 4694, 98704

Memoirs of the life of Benejamin Franklin. 25548

Memoirs of the life of Catherine Phillips. 62474

Memoirs of the life of David Ferris. 24189

Memoirs of the life of David Rittenhouse. 3855

Memoirs of the life of George Fox. 97433

Memoirs of the life of George Frederick Cooke 21306

Memoirs of the life of John Law of Lauriston. 105050

Memoirs of the life of Martha Laurens Ramsay 67699

Memoirs of the life of Miss Caroline Elizabeth Smelt. 100882

Memoirs of the life of Mr. Nicholas Ferrar. 59497

Memoirs of the life of Mrs. Abigail Waters. 33976

Memoirs of the life of Mrs. Sarah Osborn. 32952

Memoirs of the life of Samuel E. Foote. 25023

Memoirs of the life of Samuel Smith. 83997

Memoirs of the life of Sir Samuel Romilly. (73063)

Memoirs of the life of Sir Walter Ralegh [sic]. 95591

Memoirs of the life of the author [i. e. John Burgoyne]. 9250

Memoirs of the life of the late Charles Lee, Esq. 38903

Memoirs of the life of the late Major-General Andrew Burn. 9353

Memoirs of the life of the late Reverend Increase Mather. 46406, (46447)

Memoirs of the life of the Reverend George Whitefield. 27415, 103611

Memoirs of the life of the Rev. Richard Price. 50674

Memoirs of the life of the Rev. William Tennent. 94719

Memoirs of the life of Thomas Paine. (80428)

Memoirs of the life of Vice-Admiral Lord Viscount Nelson. (61300)

Memoirs of the life of William Pitt. 13615
Memoirs of the life of William Wirt. 37415
Memoirs of the lives and persecutions of the primitive Quakers. 37328
Memoirs of the lives of Benjamin Lay and Ralph Sandiford. 98705
Memoirs of the Long Island Historical Society. (24293)
Memoirs of the maritime affairs of Great-Britain. 66627
Memoirs of the Marquis de la Fayette. 9635
Memoirs of the Marquis of Pombal. 82915
Memoirs of the Marshal Count de Rochambeau. 72304, 2d note after 99746
Memoirs of the Mexican revolution. (72202)-72203
Memoirs of the military career of the Marquis de la Fayette. 38579
Memoirs of the most eminent American mechanics. 33302
Memoirs of the most eminent persons, who have flourished in Great Britain. 27115
Memoirs of the mother and wife of Washington. (15627)
Memoirs of the Museum of Comparative Zoology, at Harvard College. (51572)
Memoirs of the National Academy of Sciences. 51914
Memoirs of the naval worthies. 3668
Memoirs of the northern courts. 18487
Memoirs of the notorious Stephen Burroughs. 9476
Memoirs of the Pennsylvania Agricultural Society. 60297
Memoirs of the Peabody Academy of Science. 59386
Memoirs of the Pennsylvania Historical Society. 7211, 16190, 19596, 24477, 60143, 68399, 77035, (77042), 82985, 84610, 84678C, 91785, 97649, 98637, 98699, 98702, 103110, 105029
Memoirs of the Philadelphia Society for Promoting Agriculture. 62036
Memoirs of the Prilgrims at Leyden. 93697
Memoirs of the pillory. 47576
Memoirs of the principal persons who sat in judgment of King Charles the First. 11569
Memoirs of the principal transactions of the late war. 80550-80551
Memoirs of the private and public life of William Penn. 25146, 100979
Memoirs of the Protestant Episcopal Church in the United States of America. 6350, 103463
Memoirs of the public life of John Horne Tooke, Esq. (69096)
Memoirs of the rebellion in 1745 and 1746. (36394)
Memoirs of the reign of Bossa Ahadee. 55507
Memoirs of the reign of Charles the First. 23690
Memoirs of the reign of George III. 4600
Memoirs of the Rev. Ammi Rogers. 72608
Memoirs of the Rev. C. H. O. Cote. 18219
Memoirs of the Rev. Eleazar Wheelock, D. D. (43066), 103208, 1st note after 103214
Memoirs of the Rev. G. T. Bedell. 97628
Memoirs of the Rev. J. S. Buckminster. 95191
Memoirs of the Rev. John H. Livingston. 29280
Memoirs of the Rev. John McDowell. 89741
Memoirs of the Rev. John Rodgers. (49056)

Memoirs of the Rev. Jonathan Edwards. 32950
Memoirs of the Rev. Joseph Eastburn. (28504)
Memoirs of the Rev. Nicholas Murray. 65538
Memoirs of the Rev. Noah Worcester. 101400
Memoirs of the Rev. Richard Whatcoat. 62582, note after 103120
Memoirs of the Rev. Robert Finley, D. D. 8492
Memoirs of the Rev. Robert Finley, of Georgia. (24385)
Memoirs of the Rev. Samuel J. Mills. 89771
Memoirs of the Rev. Samuel Munson. 95541
Memoirs . . . of the Reverend Theophilus Lindsay. 4596
Memoirs of the Rev. Thomas S. Winn. 71525
Memoirs of the Rev. Walter M. Lowrie. 42539
Memoirs of the Rev. Wm. Tennent. 94719
Memoirs of the Rhode-Island bar. 98030
Memoirs of the Right Honourable Edmund Burke. 43099
Memoirs of the Right Hon. Sir John Sinclair, Bart. 81393
Memoirs of the Right Rev. Simon Wm. Gabriel Brute. (4052)
Memoirs of the services of . . . flag-officers. 44797
Memoirs of the Seymour family. 83513
Memoirs of the siege of Quebec. 26630
Memoirs of the "Society of Virginia for Promoting Agriculture." 86177, 1st note after 100527A
Memoirs of the society to Congress. (22964)
Memoirs of the southern states. (14435)
Memoirs of the state officers, judiciary and members of the twentieth Legislature of Minnesota. 49265
Memoirs of the twentieth century. 43698
Memoirs of the war in the southern department. (39741)-39743
Memoirs of the wars of the Cevennes. 96037
Memoirs of the Wesley family. 6915
Memoirs of the yellow fever. 18001
Memoirs of the young prince of Annamaboe. 73755
Memoirs of the young prince of Annamaboe, his slavery in Barbadoes. 47577
Memoirs of Thomas Chalkley. 11754
Memoirs of Thomas Hollis. 5690
Memoirs of Thomas Scattergood. 77453
Memoirs of Thomas Ward. 101340
Memoirs of three thousand contemporary public characters. 58432
Memoirs of transactions at sea. 9206
Memoirs of transactions with the Indians of Louisiana. 25853
Memoirs of Washington. 37990
Memoirs of West African celebrities. 98661
Memoirs of West Indian fever. 104656
Memoirs of William A. Porter. 64319
Memoirs of William and Nathan Hunt. 33903
Memoirs of William Forster. (78847)
Memoirs of William Miller. 5937
Memoirs of William Sampson. 75952
Memoirs of William Sampson, an Irish exile. 75953
Memoirs of youthful days of Mr. Mathews. 46827
Memoirs, official and personal. 43403, 43408
Memoirs, of the military resources of the valley of the Ohio. 76387, (76388)
Memoirs, or a variety of adventures in England and America. 21366
Memoirs presented to the California Academy of Sciences. 9959
Memoirs read before the Anthropological Society of London. 47578

Memoirs read before the Boston Society of
Natural History. 47579
Memoirs, relating to the lives. (46371)
Memoirs, speeches and writings of R. Rantoul,
Jr. 67905
Memorabilia [by Nauclerus.] 93881
Memorabilia in the life of Jedidiah Morse.
50968
Memorabilia mundi. 66894
Memorabilia mundi; or, choice memoirs of
the history and description of the world.
34033
Memorabilia; or, recollections, historical,
biographical, and antiquarian. 77235
Memorabilem provinciae Brasiliae historiam.
(8784)
Memorabilium opus cum emendatione et scholiis
P. Castalii. 48033
Memorable accidents and remarkable trans-
actions. 47581
Memorable accidents and unheard-of trans-
actions. 9502
Memorable accidents, and unheard of trans-
actions, containing an account of several
strange events. (47580)
Memorable days in America. 23933
Memorable events in the life of Andreas
Bernardus Smolnikar. 85107, 85129
Memorable historia del Sr. B. Carranza.
75998
Memorable letter from the venerable Gran-
ville Sharp. (79829)
Memorable men and memorable events. 17826
Memorable providences, relating to witchcrafts and possessions. 37212, 46375,
46407-46408
Memorable repository. Containing, a curious
and most astonishing account of the
revivication of young J. Taylor. 94521
Memorable repository, containing, a curious
and most astonishing account of the
revivication of young J*. Taylor. 94518
Memorable scenes in French history. 85145-
85146, 85155, 85162, 85164, 85170
Memorable women of the puritan times.
1403
Memorable women: the story of their lives.
17647
Memorable works of a son of thunder and
consolation. 9462
Memoralia. 12854
Memoranda and official correspondence rela-
ting to the republic of Texas. 36455
Memoranda and prospectus of the North-West
Transportation and Land Company.
(55735)
Memoranda concerning Baltimore city and sur-
roundings. 3041, 1st note after 47581
Memoranda de hacienda y credito publico.
48535
Memoranda, historical, chronological, &c.
19895
Memoranda of a residence at the court of
London. 74264-74265
Memorandana of a settler in Canada. 22476
Memoranda of a settler in Lower Canada. 29
Memoranda of a visit to the site of Mathraval
Castle. 82402
Memoranda of four claims against Mexico.
48533
Memoranda of my life. 86685
Memoranda of past fires. (4442)
Memoranda of persons, places, and events.
18791
Memoranda of Philo S. Shelton. 80154

Memoranda of some of the descendants of
Richard Dana. 18430
Memoranda of some of the proceedings of the
Friends of Baltimore Yearly Meeting.
(47582)
Memoranda of the . . . decennial meeting at
Hanover. 71233
Memoranda of the descendants of Amos Morris
50797, note after 92778
Memoranda of the experience, labors, and
travels of a Universalist preacher.
72644
Memoranda of the pestilence which raged in
that city. 15891
Memoranda of the Preston family. By Orlando
Brown. 8542
Memoranda of the Preston family. Compiled
by John Mason Brown. note after 65389
Memoranda on railways. 69900, 69946
Memoranda relating to the present crisis.
3171
Memoranda respecting King's College at
Windsor. 34770
Memoranda respecting the families of Quincy
and Adams. 28185, 47584
Memoranda respecting the French slave trade
in 1820. 47583
Memorandum. 61928, 70961
Memorandum and articles of association of
"The South Brazilian Railway" Company
Limited. 87342
Memorandum [by George Bancroft.] 67221
Memorandum by the Hon. J. Cauchon. 33551
Memorandum concerning the Charlestown
Post-Office. 2394
Memorandum de associacao e estatutos da
Companhia "The South Brazilian Railway"
Company, Limited. 87342
Memorandum de negociations pendantes entre
le Mexique et l'Espagne. 47585, 48534
Memorandum de los negocios pendientes entre
Mexico y Espana. 38614, 47586, 71485
Memorandum del gobierno de la provincia de
Buenos Aires. 9021
Memorandum del Senor D. Eusebio de Salazar
y Mazarredo. (59323)
Memorandum, for a report. 102045, 1st note
after 103846
Memorandum in regard to a fire-proof build-
ing. 85038
Memorandum in relation to a joint resolution.
85000
Memorandum in relation to the gold mines of
the Chaudiere. 18961
Memorandum of a late visit to the Auburn
Penitentiary. (58111)
Memorandum of points submitted by the sitting
member. 56980
Memorandum of the steps. 32349
Memorandum on the necessity of a Secretary
of State. 85261
Memorandum on the relative importance of the
West and East Indies to Great Britain.
(47587)
Memorandum sobre el proceso del Archiduque
Fernando Maximiliano de Austria.
47036, 58273
Memorandum Society, Mount Holyoke Female
Seminary, South Hadley, Mass. see
Mount Holyoke Female Seminary, South
Hadley, Mass. Memorandum Society.
Memorandum, with two patents granted to
Augustine Herman. 45118
Memorandums addressed by the Commission.
85234

Memorandums, for a report. 102045
Memorandums of a tour made by Josiah
  Espy. (22918)
Memorandums of Jane Bettle. 5092
Memoria. 47863
Memoria acerca de los medios que se
  estiman justos. 47588
Memoria acerca de los terrenos de Met-
  labtoyuca. 47589
Memoria acerca del estado de la ensenanza
  en la Universidad de la Habana. 29440
Memoria acompanado un proyecto de ley.
  32912
Memoria afectuosa de los empleos honorificos.
  99689
Memoria apologetica do Arcebispo de Bahia.
  47590
Memoria constitucional e politica. 49415
Memoria Cristiano-politica sobre lo mucho
  que debe temer. 76220
Memoria curiosa de los sangrientos sucesos.
  99664
Memoria da origem. 43883
Memoria de Don Francisco Antonio Zea.
  74014
Memoria de D. Jose de Azanza y D. Gomz.
  o-Farill. (2529)
Memoria de estatuto. 67350
Memoria de hacienda durante el tiempo en
  que F. M. Lambardo. 38725
Memoria de hacienda presentada al Exmo.
  Sr. Presidente de la republica. 59298
Memoria de incorporacion en la Sociedad
  de Farmacia. 86436
Memoria de la conducta publica y adminis-
  tratica de Manuel Jose Arce. 1899
Memoria de la conservacion de los montes.
  56746
Memoria de la corporacion municipal que
  funciono el ano de 1851. 48539
Memoria de la Direccion de Colonizacion e
  Industria. 48540
Memoria de la Direccion General de la
  Industria Nacional. 48540
Memoria de la Hacienda Nacional de la
  republica Mexicana. 48541
Memoria de la Junta Inspectora de Instruccion
  Primaria del estado de San Luis Potosi.
  76148
Memoria de la municipalidad de la ciudad de
  Buenos Aires . . . continene ademas
  todas las ordinanzas. 9021
Memoria de la municipalidad de la ciudad de
  Buenos Aires correspondiente a los anos
  1856 y 1857, 1858, 1859. 9021
Memoria de la municipalidad de la ciudad de
  Buenos Aires . . . 1860. (47591)
Memoria de la Primera Secretaria de Estado
  y del Despacho de Relaciones Interiores
  y Esteriores de los Estados-Unidos
  Mexicanos. (38613)
Memoria de la regencia de estudios del
  Seminario de Santa Toribio. 76803
Memoria de la republica di Tlaxcalla. 9581
Memoria de la Secretaria de Estado y del
  Despacho de Fomento. 81005
Memoria de la Secretaria Jeneral de Estado
  del Supremo Gobierno de Guatemala.
  (75563)
Memoria de la Secretario de Estado y del
  Despacho de Fomento. 48543
Memoria de la Secretario de Estado y del
  Despacho de Relaciones Interiores y
  Esteriores de la republica Mexicana.
  48542

Memoria de la Secretario de Estado y
  Relaciones Esteriores. 14602
Memoria de la Sociedad de Beneficencia Publica.
  85725
Memoria de las operaciones que han tenido
  lugar. (47592)
Memoria de las quinas de Santa Fe. 74005
Memoria de las virtudes y usos de la raiz
  de la planta llamada yallhoy. 73998
Memoria de los abonos. 10778
Memoria de los acontecimientos ocurridos en
  el Pueblo. (75775)
Memoria de los acontecimientos tristes y
  lamentables. 41671
Memoria de los ramos del Ministerio de
  Relaciones Interiores y Esteriores.
  48544
Memoria de los ramons municipales formada
  por el Exnio Ayuntamiento en 1846.
  (48545)
Memoria de los trabajos de la Sociedad
  Economica de Amigos de Guatemala.
  29088, 87213
Memoria de los trabajos ejecutados por la
  Comision Cientifica de Pachuca. 945
Memoria de Marina. 48536
Memoria de nacionalizacion. (48537)
Memoria de ramo de la Hacienda Federal da
  los Estados Unidos Mexicanos. (48547)
Memoria de relaciones exteriores. 47593
Memoria de relaciones interiores y esteriores
  della republica, 1826. 48538
Memoria dedicada al consulado de comercio
  de Guatemala. (73424)
Memoria del Capitan Don Carlos Vazquez de
  Coronado. 98720
Memoria del D. Jos. Ant. E. de Otiro y
  Baldillo. (57839)
Memoria del despacho de Guerra y Marina.
  61138
Memoria del Ejecutivo de Oaxaca. 56402
Memoria del estado actual de la Parroquia
  de S. Martin Xilotepeque. (52115)
Memoria del estado de Jalisco. 35554
Memoria del estado de la Parroquia de
  Concepcion de Villa Nueva. (52116)
Memoria del estado que guarda la adminis-
  tracion publica de Yucaton. 69159
Memoria del Gobernador de Panama. 58407
Memoria del Gobernador de Pasto. (59007)
Memoria del Gobernador de Popyan. 64102
Memoria del hecho. 14659
Memoria del Ministerio de Fomento de 1857.
  57646
Memoria del Ministerio de Gobierno y Rela-
  ciones Exteriores. 71455
Memoria del Ministerio de Guerra y Marina.
  87207
Memoria del Ministerio de Justicia y Negocios
  Ecclesiasticos. 48546
Memoria del Ministerio de Relaciones [de
  Mexico.] (73028)
Memoria del Ministerio de Relaciones, en la
  parte relative a Tejas. 95111
Memoria del Ministerio de Relaciones
  Exteriores. 38988
Memoria del Ministerio del Interior de la
  Republica Arjentina. 70011
Memoria del Ministro de Estado en el Despacho
  de la Guerra. 6198
Memoria del Ministro de Hacienda D. Monifacio
  Gutierrez. 48454
Memoria del Ministro de Hacienda J. M. de
  Pando. 61144

Memoria del Ministro de Interior y Relaciones Esteriores. (47595)

Memoria del Ministro de Justicia e Instruccion Publica. 48546

Memoria del Ministro de Relaciones Exteriores y Gobernacion. 48546

Memoria del Ministro de Relaciones y Gobernacion de Costa-Rica. 47594

Memoria del Ministro del Interior de la Republica Argentina. 9021

Memoria del Mr. Otto sobre el verdado descubridor de America. (13179)

Memoria del pleyto entre D. Francisco Pizarro. 63181

Memoria del Prof. Baldassare Poli. 63735

Memoria del Ramo de Hacienda Federal de los Estados-Unidos Mexicanos. (48547)

Memoria del relaciones exteriores. 61139

Memoria del Secretario de Estado al Congreso de la Union. 48549

Memoria del Secretario de Estado de la Nacion Mexicana. 48549

Memoria del Secretario de Estado y del Despacho de Justicia e Instruccion Publica. 48548

Memoria del Secretario de Estado y del Despacho de la Guerra. 14603

Memoria del Secretario de Estado y del Despacho de la Guerra, pres a las Camaras, Enero, 1846. 48549

Memoria del Secretario de Hacienda i Fomento de la Union Colombiana. 14607

Memoria del Secretario del Despacho de Hacienda. (48550)

Memoria del Secretario del Estado y del Despancho de Marina. 14606

Memoria del Secretario del Tesoro y Credito Nacional. 47596

Memoria del Sr. Iturbide. 99708

Memoria descriptiva sobre Tucuman. 652

Memoria di Annibale Ranuzzi. 67909

Memoria dirigida a la representacion del Peru. 71606

Memoria dirigida al Sr. Marquez de Loreto. 99517

Memoria dirigida por el Ministerio de Estado a la Assemblea Constitugente. 32773

Memoria dirijida desde Amberes al Congreso del Peru. 71604

Memoria dirijida por el Ministerio de Estado a la Asemblea Constitugente. (55137)

Memoria dirijida por el Ministerio de Estado a la Asamblea Constitugente . . . en Diciembre de 1847. (55137)

Memoria documentada offerecida a nacao Brazileira. (7601)

Memoria documentada que al Illmo Sr. Arzobispo Coadjutor de esta Santa Iglesia. (39085)

Memoria dos remedios exquisitos. 79073

Memoria economica de la municipalidad de Mexico. 26514

Memoria en que el Ministero de la Confederacion Argentina en las cortes de Inglaterra, Francia y Espana da cuenta. 1956

Memoria en que se trata del insecto grano o cochinella. 991

Memoria enviada al Instituto Historico de Francia. (77079)

Memoria escrita en Alemania por D. F. Sarmiento. (77074)

Memoria escrita por D. Fernando de Alva Ixtlilxuchitl. (9576), 35318

Memoria escrita y presentada a la Sociedad Mexicana de Geografia y Estadistica. (39076)

Memoria estadistica da Provincia do Ceara. 63953, 88744

Memoria estadistica da Provincia de Goyaz. 81105

Memoria estadistica de Oaxaca y descripcion del valle de misme nombre. 51444

Memoria estadistica del estado de Occidente. 71309

Memoria general del Despacho de Relaciones Exteriores. 61139

Memoria geografica de los viajes practicados. 58047

Memoria geologica sobre os terranos do Carral Alto. 9807

Memoria historica das causas e acontecimentos 88758

Memoria historica de la provincia de Chiapa. 72254

Memoria historica de la villa de Santa Clara. 27820

Memoria hist. do . . . Imperador e Rei . . . D. Joao VI. 15100

Memoria historica do Museo Nacional. 88784

Memoria historica e biographica do Clero Pernambucano. 42680

Memoria historica e documentada das aldeias dos Indios. 88806

Memoria historica, geografica y estadistica de Cienfuegos y su jurisdiccion. 57210

Memoria historica sobre el Canal de Nicaragua 45019

Memoria historica sobre las operaciones e incidencias. 1930

Memoria historica sobre los derechos de soberania. 1540

Memoria historica sobre los sucesos ocurridos desde la caida de D. Bernardo O'Higgins. (76786)

Memoria hydrographia, contendo reflexoes sobre as viagens dos mais celebres navegedores. 24979

Memoria instructiva de los derechos y justas causas. (26547)

Memoria instructiva sobre el comercio general. 68806

Memoria instructiva sobre el maguey o agave Mexicano. 106325

Memoria justa del heroismo. 44106

Memoria justificativa de la carta geo-coro-topografia. 62605

Memoria justificativa em que se explicao estado dos colonos establecidos no Mucury. (57900)

Memoria justificativa sobre a conducta do Marechal de Campo Luis do Rego Barreto. 68930

Memoria leida a la Facultad de Humanidades el 17 de Octubre de 1843. 77080

Memoria leida a las Cortes por el Encargado del Despacho de Governacion. 47597

Memoria leida el 11 de Octubre de 1858. 77076

Memoria leida en el Callao a la Convencion Nacional. 99616

Memoria leida en la Junta General. 58276

Memoria leida en las Camaras de 1851. 48551

Memoria leida por su Presidente en la Junta General de Accionistas. (15021)

Memoria letta alla Societa Ligure di Storia Patria. 76522

Memoria o dissertazione sopra la Nueva China. 2246

Memoria ofrecida a la consideracion. 47598

Memoria para el plano de medico. 57643

Memoria para la carta hidrografica. (57644)

Memoria para servir a la carta general de la republica Mexicana. 26556

Memoria politica sobre a Capitania de Santa Catherina. 8135

Memoria politica sobre si conviene en Chile la libertad de cultos. 47599, 103421

Memoria politico e historica de revolucao da Provincia da Bahia. 7391

Memoria politico-instructiva. 72277

Memoria presentada a la Sociedad Amigos del Pais. 85720

Memoria presentada a las dos Cameros del Congreso General. 48552

Memoria presentada a S. E. el Jefe Supremo Provisorio. (61140)

Memoria presentada a S. M. el Emperador por el Ministro de Fomento. 47036, 48552, 61333

Memoria presentada al Congreso Nacional en 1841. 12780

Memoria presentada al Congreso Nacional por el Ministre de Estado. 12781

Memoria presentada al Congreso Primero Constitucional. 66565

Memoria presentada al Consejo Universitario de Chile. 77073

Memoria presentada al Exmo. Sr. Presidente Sustituto de la republica. 40140

Memoria presentada al Saherano Cuerpo Lejislativo. 32770

Memoria presentada al Soberano Congreso Mexicano. 48552

Memoria presentada por Don Jose Portugues. 9021, 64440

Memoria presentada por Don Miguel Cabrera Nevares. 42673

Memoria presentada por el Ministro de Estado en el Departamento de Guerra y Marina al Congreso Nacional de 1865. 9021

Memoria presentada por el Ministro de Estado en el Departamento de Hacienda. 9021

Memoria presentada por el Ministro de Estado en el Departamento de Justicia, Culto e Instruccion Publica. 9021

Memoria presentada por el Senor Ministro Jeneral Laenciado Da Jose Maria Rugama. 32771

Memoria presentado por el Ministro de Relaciones y de los Interio. 47600

Memoria que dirige a la Legislatura Nacional de 1865. 47602

Memoria que dirija a la Legislatura Nacional de 1865 el Ministro de Credito Publico. 47602

Memoria que dirije a la Asamblea Legislativa de Guayana. 47601

Memoria que dirije Don Emilio Mangel du Mesnil. (48043)

Memoria que el Administrador Principal de Rentas Municipales. 10779

Memoria, que el Doctor D. Miguel Ramos de Arispe. 67670

Memoria que el Ex-Secretario de Estado en el Despacho de Hacienda y Comercio presenta al Jefe Supremo Provisorio. (58569)

Memoria que el Ministro de Estado en el Departamento de Gobieron, Obras Publicas y Policia presenta. (61142)

Memoria que el Ministro de Estado en el Departamento de Hacienda presenta. 12785

Memoria que el Ministro de Estado en el Departamento de Justicia, Culto e Instruccion Publica presenta. 12783

Memoria que el Ministro de Estado en el Departamento de Marina presenta al Congreso Nacional de 1868. 47603

Memoria que el Ministro de Estadó en el Departamento del Interior presenta al Congreso Nacional de 1844. 12786

Memoria que el Ministro de Estado en los Departamentos de Guerra y Marina presenta al Congreso Nacional. 12784

Memoria que el Ministro de Estado en los Departamentos de Guerra y Marina presenta al Congreso Nacional ano de 1835. 12782

Memoria que el Ministro de Gobierno, Policia y Obras Publicas presenta. 61141

Memoria que el Ministro de Hacienda y Comercio presenta. (61142)

Memoria que el Ministro de Justicia, Instruccion Publica y Beneficencia presenta al Congreso Extraordinario reunido en 1858. (61142)

Memoria que el Ministro de Relaciones Exteriores presenta. (61142)

Memoria que el Ministro Estado en el Departamento de Relaciones Exteriores presenta al Congreso Nacional de 1836. (12787)

Memoria que el Secretario de Estado en el Despacho de Relaciones Exteriores presenta. (61142)

Memoria que el Secretario de Estado y del Despacho de Hacienda. 48553

Memoria que el Secretario de Estado y del Despacho de Hacienda presento al Congreso de Colombia. 14604

Memoria que el Secretario de Estado y del Despacho de Justicia e Instruccion Publica presenta al Congreso de la Union. 48553

Memoria que el Secretario de Estado y del Despacho de Relaciones Esteriores e Interiores. 48553

Memoria que el Secretario de Estado y del Despacho del Interior, presento. 14605

Memoria que el Senor Don Francisco Solano Astaburaga presenta. 86244

Memoria que en cumplimiento del articulo 120. 48554

Memoria que en la abertura de las sesiones del Real Consulado. 97173

Memoria que escribio en Liorna a 27 de Setiembre 1823. 35293

Memoria que la Direccion de Colonizacion e Industria presento. 48554

Memoria que para informar sobre el origen y estado actuel. 50482

Memoria que por orden del Supremo Gobierno Constitucional de la republica. 59301

Memoria que presenta a la H. Disputation Provincial de Caracas. 47604

Memoria que presenta a la Sociedad de Beneficencia. 67914

Memoria que presenta al Ministro del Interior. 86245

Memoria que presenta al segundo Congreso de Oaxaca. 9864

Memoria que presenta el Gobernador de Guanajuato al Congreso Constituyente. 48555

Memoria que presenta el Ministro de Estado en el Departamento de Gobierno, Policia y Obras Publicas. (61142)

Memoria que presenta el Ministro de Estado en el Departamento de Justicia, Instruccion Publica, Beneficencia y Culto. (61142)

Memoria que presenta el Ministro de Hacienda al Congreso del Ecuador. 21799

Memoria que presenta el Ministro de Hacienda de Peru. (61142)

Memoria que presenta el Ministro de la Guerra a las Cameras Legislativas. 6201

Memoria que presenta el Ministro de la Guerra a las Cameras Lejislativas en el ano de 1810. 6200

Memoria que presenta el Ministro de Relaciones Esteriores de la republica de Bolivia. (6199)

Memoria que presenta el Secretario del Interior al Congreso. 47605

Memoria que presenta el Secretario del Interior de los negocios. 47605

Memoria que presentan a todas las comunidades. 42066

Memoria que presento a la Sociedad Economica en el junta general. 85751

Memoria que presento al Congreso Federal de Centro-America. 47606

Memoria que presento en 16 de Enero de 1776. 70089

Memoria que sobre el estado de la hacienda nacional. 48556

Memoria relativa a los ramos de la administracion. 12692

Memoria segunda escrita por el Oidor Honorario Don Jose Ildefonso Suarez. 93302

Memoria sobre a absoluta necessidade. 26491

Memoria sobre a bronchocele ou papo America Septentrional. 3815

Memoria sobre a cultura do tabaco nos Estados Unidos. 97920

Memoria sobre a fundacao e costeio de uma fazenda. 59170

Memoria sobre a immigracao pelo Director A. C. Tavares Bastos. 85775

[Memoria sobre a immigracao] pelo Director German Haupt. 85775

Memoria sobre a necessidade de abolir a introduccao dos escravos Africanos no Brasil. (17005)

Memoria sobre a nobreza no Brasil. 26493, 47608

Memoria sobre a plantacao dos algodoes. 5091

Memoria sobre a prioridade dos descobrimentos Portuguezes na costa de Africa Occidental. 76843

Memoria sobre a salubridade publica. 78946

Memoria sobre as ilhas de S. Thome e Principe, etc. 24980

Memoria sobre as Minas de Carvao de Pedra do Brazil. (58591)

Memoria sobre as Quinas. 52416

Memoria sobre as salitreiras naturaes de Monte Robrigo. 17205

Memoria sobre caminos, en la isla de Cuba. 74770

Memoria sobre conspiracao de 1817. 47607

Memoria sobre diversos ramos. 93286

Memoria sobre el ante-proyecto del ferrocarril. 85715

Memoria sobre el canal proyectado en el istmo de Nicaragua. 2505

Memoria sobre el comercio, cultivo y elaboration del tabaco da esta isla. (24144)

Memoria sobre el cultivo del cafe en Escuintla. 58277

Memoria sobre el cultivo del maiz en Mexico. 73173

Memoria sobre el estado actual de las Americas. 9819

Memoria sobre el estado de la agricultura e industria de la republica. 48556

Memoria sobre el estado de la hacienda de ? republica Boliviana. 39015

Memoria sobre el estado presente de Chile. 12788

Memoria sobre el estado y situacion politica en que se hallaba el reyno de Nueva-Espana en Agosto de 1823. 65113

Memoria sobre el fuego de los volcanes. 39094

Memoria sobre el influjo de la mineria en la agricultura. 22118

Memoria sobre el magrey Mexicano. 5876

Memoria sobre el maguey Mexicano y sus diversos productos. (59299)

Memoria sobre el mineral de Pachuca. 716?

Memoria sobre el uso del termometro en la navegacion. 104297

Memoria sobre immigracion y linea de front eras. 35068

Memoria sobre la administracion de Puerto-Rico. 16769, 2d note after 96138

Memoria sobre la conservacion del puerto de la Habana. 14680

Memoria sobre la conservation del puerto de la Habana. 47609

Memoria sobre la Convencion Espanola. (59296)

Memoria sobre la cria de abejas y cultivo d la Cera. 63377

Memoria sobre la cria de ganado mular y caballar y mejora de sus castas. 5674

Memoria sobre la decadencia de las misione Jesuiticas. 44426

Memoria sobre la deuda esterior de la republ Mexicana. 51476

Memoria sobre la escuela militar. 66601

Memoria sobre la evacuacion militar. 58850

Memoria sobre la geografia. (51069)

Memoria sobre la introduccion y progresos c la vacuna. 73011

Memoria sobre la legitima calaguala y otras dos raices. (73999)

Memoria sobre la libertad de imprenta. 948

Memoria sobre la ordenanza de matriculas y reglamento de montes. 98729

Memoria sobre la poblacion del reino de Neu Espana. 52111

Memoria sobre la primera Escuadra Naciona (70395)

Memoria sobre la propriedad eclesiastica. 29403, 48556

Memoria sobre la renta del tabaco. 98028

Memoria sobre la revolucion de Diciembre d 1857. 59300

Memoria sobre la seda silvestre. 79327

Memoria sobre la utilidad e influjo de la mineria. 22058, 47610

Memoria sobre las apariciones y el culto de Nuestra Senora de Guadalupe. 51347

Memoria sobre las Casas de Moneda de la republica. 48557

Memoria sobre las causas que han originado la situacion actuel. 62880

Memoria sobre las enfermedades epidemicas. 98312

Memoria sobre las immensas ventajas que resultarian de introducir y generalizar en esta isla el uso de los camellos. 47611

Memoria sobre las minas de la jurisdiccion Puerto-Principe. 66590

Memoria sobre las negociaciones entre Espar y los Estados-Unidos de America. 251 57355

Memoria sobre las observaciones astronomicas. 681, (69221)

Memoria sobre las primeras campanas en la guerra. 4634

Memoria sobre las principaes causas. 26266

Memoria sobre las virtudes y usos de la planta llamada en el Peru, Bejuco de la estrella. 74000

Memoria sobre las virtudes y usos de la raiz de purhampuy. 74001

Memoria sobre les cuestiones de limites que se versan. 49884

Memoria sobre los huracanes en la isla de Cuba. (31563)

Memoria sobre los medios de desterrar la embriaguez. 57686

Memoria sobre los medios de destruir la medicidad. 29089

Memoria sobre los medios que podran adoptarse para fomentar las haciendas en orden al ganado vacuno y mular. 50589

Memoria sobre los principios politicos que segui en la administracion del Peru. 61143

Memoria sobre los trabajos de la caja de ahorros. 2610

Memoria sobre meies de promover a colonisacao. 73

Memoria sobre o credito em geral. 96263

Memoria sobre o descobrimento da America no seculo decimo. 67483

Memoria sobre o establecimiento de uma companhia de colonisaca. 21362

Memoria sobre o estado actual da fabricacao do assucar no Bresil. (20943)

Memoria sobre o melhoramente da provincia de S. Paulo. 98829

Memoria sobre o methodo economico de transportar para Portugal. 60880

Memoria sobre os meios de promover a colonisacao. 21363

Memoria sobre os trabalhos de Commissao Mixta Brasileira e Portugueza. 47612

Memoria sobre peticion con dus proyectos. 29456

Memoria sobre proporcionar arbitrios para la construccion de caminos. 35823

Memoria sobre reformas del arancel mercantil. 48558

Memoria sobre un sistema de defensa para la costas y fronteras. 23645

Memoria sopra alcune piante esculenti del Prazile. 67406

Memoria sulla canonizzazione di C. Colombo. 76522

Memoria sulla scoptera dell' America nel secolo decimo. 67484

Memoria tercera del Oidor Honorario Don Jose Ildefonso Suarez. 93303

Memoria Wilsoniana. 46409

Memoria y cuenta general. 85756

Memoria y plano de las majoras propuestas para el puerto ejecutados. 14207

Memoriael gepresenteert aenden Coningh van Spaengien. 33489, 67355

Memorirael van de Heere Ulloa Eerste Minister van Sijne Koncklijcke Majesteyt van Portugael. 97677

Memorial. 31686, 47613, 57427, 72344, 76236, 79446

Memorial abrege de ce qui s'est dit ou fait. (35771)

Memorial address at laying the corner-stone of the South Hall of Livet College. 50895

Memorial address . . . at the funeral of Captain Samuel S. Hayden. 57982

Memorial address by C. M. Ellis, Esq. 75274

Memorial address . . . by Hon. Leonard Myers. (51633)

Memorial address. By Rev. T. M. Eddy. 21817

Memorial address delivered before the John Albion Andrew Monument Association. 76974

Memorial address, delivered in Library Hall. 91045

Memorial address delivered in the Peoples Church. 84066

Memorial address on Abraham Lincoln. 22292

Memorial address on the life and character of Abraham Lincoln, delivered at Concord, New-Hampshire. (59138)

Memorial address on the life and character of Abraham Lincoln, delivered, at the request of both Houses of the Congress of America. (3132)

Memorial address, Prof. David S. Conant. 17627

Memorial addressed to the Legislature of the state of Georgia. 102110

Memorial addressed to the Lords Commissioners of the Board of Trade. 104017

Memorial addressed to the sovereigns of America. 64824, 64834, 2d note after 96457

Memorial addressed to the sovereigns of Europe and the Atlantic. 64825, 64834, 2d note after 96457

Memorial addressed to the Trustees of the Massachusetts General Hospital. 42039

Memorial addresses on the life and character of Henry H. Starkweather. 90535

Memorial addresses on W. P. Fessenden. 24223

Memorial adjustado contra los officiales de Casa de Monedo. 47614

Memorial adopted by the Board of Regents. 84395

Memorial adresse au Roy. 63968

Memorial against holding an election in Texas. 74668

Memorial against it. 78206, 78211-78213

Memorial against Mr. Asa Whitney's railroad scheme. 63443

Memorial against the division of the city of Roxbury. (73652)

Memorial . . . against the tariff law of 1828. 47706

Memorial ajustado de D. Josef Antequera. 10803

Memorial ajustado de la vida y virtudes de la Madre Sor Antonio de S. Joaquin. 72551

Memorial ajustado de los diversos espedientes seguidos. (47615)

Memorial ajustado, hecho de orden del Real y Supremo Consejo de Indias. 14658

Memorial ajustado, que de orden del Consejo. 98150

Memorial ajustado, que de orden del Consejo Supremo de Indias. 98359

Memorial ajustado que de orden del Consejo Supremo de Indias . . . sobre visitar, y exercer los actos de la jurisdiccion diocesana. 47616

Memorial al Papa Urbano VIII. 12972

Memorial al Rei Felipe IV. 75891

Memorial al Rey Nuestro Senor. 36086

Memorial al Rey piadiendo remedio. (47844)

Memorial and affidavits showing outrages. 47617

Memorial and claim of Amelie Eugenie Caron de Beaumarchais, 4180, 96342

Memorial, and documents concerning the first Texian loan. 95101

Memorial and evidence. 89323

Memorial, and observations concerning the islands of St. Lucia, Dominico, St. Vincent, and Tabago. 102814

Memorial and observations of the Trustees of the New York Free School. 54115, 69689

Memorial and other documents relating to the present condition. 8106

Memorial and papers concerning the expedition to the Ohio. 47512

Memorial and petition of John Barney. 3539

Memorial and petition of John G. Cunow. 17977, 86170

Memorial and petition of the Cherokee Delegates to the Senate. 12437

Memorial and petition of the Council and Assembly of Jamaica. 35632

Memorial & petition of the people of Rupert's Land. 47618

Memorial and petition of the proprietors of the New York and Havre Mail Steamers. (54734)

Memorial and petition of the religious society of Friends, (commonly called Quakers) 100527A

Memorial and petition of the religious society of Friends, (commonly called Quakers,) respectfully sheweth— 100525

Memorial and petition of the Society of Friends, to the Legislature of Virginia. 86043, 100522

Memorial and petition of the Society of Friends, . . . to the Legislature of Virginia, on the subject of militia fines. 47619

Memorial and petition of the Society of the New York Hospital. 86155

Memorial and proceedings of the City Council of Charleston. 12056

Memorial and protest of the union men of Kentucky. (37546)

Memorial and remonstrance. 100528

Memorial and remonstrance . . . by His Excellency James Madison. (43719)

Memorial and remonstrance of Isaac Howell and White Matlack. 60723

Memorial and remonstrance of the Committees Appointed by the Yearly Meetings of Friends, of Genesee, New York, Philadelphia, and Baltimore. 47620

Memorial and remonstrance of the Commonwealth of Virginia. 100427

Memorial and remonstrance of the Corporation of Trinity Church. 86744

Memorial and remonstrance of the Legislature of Massachusetts. (45914)

Memorial and remonstrance of the Legislature of the state of Georgia. 69839

Memorial and remonstrance of the public creditors. (47621), 60704

Memorial and remonstrance, on the religious rights of man. (43721), 1st note after 100486

Memorial and remonstrance, presented to the General Assembly of . . . Virginia. 47623, 2d note after 100486

Memorial and remonstrance to Congress. 42260

Memorial and remonstrance to the General Assembly of Virginia. 47622, 100427, 3d note after 100486

Memorial and report of the citizens of Boston (56590)

Memorial and representation of Doctor John Morgan. 50652

Memorial and representation, of . . . merchants 47624

Memorial and resolutions adopted at the Antitariff Meeting. (47625)

Memorial and resolutions of citizens of Philadelphia. (61814)

Memorial and resolutions [of the Rockingham Convention, 1812.] 72390, 93487, 102319

Memorial and statement of the Philadelphia bar 61815

Memorial and statement of the President and Fellows of Yale College. 105797

Memorial and tear of lamentation. 38857

Memorial aos habitantes da Europa. (47626)

Memorial apologetico, historico, juridico y politico. 64596

Memorial . . . April 1, 1840. 34657

Memorial breve. 10058

Memorial . . . by citizens of Boston and vicinity. 47707

Memorial [by Hotchkins.] 57749

Memorial, by John Wayland. (79795)

Memorial. By Joseph Sewall. 74871, 79446

Memorial [by Logan.] 60207

Memorial . . . by natives of Ireland. (47708)

Memorial by Professor D. S. Talcott. 80180

Memorial, by Richard Hill. 31856

Memorial celebration comprising the address delivered on the occasion by Rev. S. Granby Spees. 89264

Memorial ceremonies at the graves of our soldiers. 50361

Memorial ceremonies at the National Cemetery, Arlington, Virginia. 82558

Memorial Church, Springfield, Mass. see Springfield, Mass. Memorial Church.

Memorial Church of the Rev. Henry Anthon. 54377

Memorial circulated by the Agents of the Fore Improvement Company. 60455

Memorial. Claims against Venezuela. 24666

Memorial compiled by a member of the congregation. 10256, 89744

Memorial concerning a canal navigation, &c. 13719, 53766

Memorial concerning a summary of facts. 152 (41650), (47511)-47512, 51651

Memorial concerning several ministers and others. 37636

Memorial concerning several ministers, deceased. 47627

Memorial concerning the furr-trade of New-York. 14272

Memorial concerning the political disabilities of southern union men. 74669

Memorial concerning the recent history and the constitutional rights and privileges of Harvard College; presented by the President and Fellows to the Legislature. (30750), 88996

Memorial concerning the recent history and the constitutional rights and privileges of Harvard College; presented by the President and Fellows to the Legislature, January 17, 1851. 88995

Memorial: containing a brief sketch of the history of St. Peter's Parish. 89021

Memorial containing a summary of facts, with the vouchers. 15205

Memorial containing a summary view of facts, with their authorities. 17365, (41650), (47511)-47512, 51205, 51661, 101710

Memorial containing, in substance, the address delivered in Princeton, New Jersey. 43164

Memorial, dated 30th April 1790. 47259

Memorial day. A sermon . . . Jan. 1, 1860. (37879)

Memorial day. May 30, 1870. 80182

Memorial de Gouverneur Morris, homme d'etat Americain. 88997

Memorial de justas quejas. 99789

Memorial de la calidad, y servicios de Don Cristoval Alfonso de Solis i Enriquez. (59589), 86394

Memorial de la jornada y pacificacion que tengo hechos a V. M. antes della. 68365

Memorial de las historias del nuevo mundo del Piru. 75784

Memorial de las historias del nuevo mondo del Peru y excellencias de la ciudad de Lima. 75593

Memorial de l'education du Bas-Canada. 47404

Memorial de lo qve continen los papeles presentados. 98809

Memorial de lo svcedido en la ciudad de Mexico. 47628

Memorial de los religiosos de la Compania del nombre de Iesus. 56265, (77142)

Memorial de los seruicios del Doctor Do[n] Matias Suarez de Melo. 93323

Memorial de ocho padres de la Compania de Jesus. 24319

Memorial, de sus partes, meritos, y seruicios, para que se le haga merced. 99640

Memorial de tachas puestas por parte del fisco. 98810

Memorial del Gobernador del Socorro. 86189

Memorial del Ilustrisimo y Reverendisimo Senor Manuel Jose Mosquera. (51066)

Memorial del Maestro Fr. Fernando de Carvajal y Ribera. 11177

Memorial del Padre Julian de Pedraca. 76026

Memorial del peligrosos estado espiritual. 87184

Memorial del Peru. (58131)

Memorial del pleyto que Don Alonso Suarez de Solis. 93329

Memorial del pleyto sobre denunciacion de la Mina de Demasias. (34719)

Memorial del que succedio entre el Obispo de Cartagena y la Audiencia Real. 47629

Memorial del R. P. M. Pedro Calderon de la Comp. de Jesus. (9886)

Memorial delivered before the Century Club. (17322)

Memorial delivered to His Excellency the Commander in Chief. 104017

Memorial delivered to His Majesty. 98511

Memorial dirigido al Supremo Consejo de las Indias. 80834

Memorial discourse; by Rev. Henry Highland Garnet. 26677

Memorial discourse, delivered in the Bureau Baptist Church. 16407

Memorial discourse, occasioned by the death of Colonel Charles Townsend. 89917

Memorial discourse, occasioned by the death of Lieut. Col. J. M. Green. (72060)

Memorial discourse on occasion of the fiftieth anniversary of the Concord Female Charitable Society. 6963

Memorial discourse on the character and career of Abraham Lincoln. 30882

Memorial discourse on the character of Abraham Lincoln. 18975

Memorial discourse on the life and character of Rev. Joel Smith Bacon. 75962

Memorial discourse on the life and character of Rev. O. W. Burnham. 64785

Memorial discourse on the life, character and services of General Jeremiah Johnson. 36321

Memorial discourse. The beneficient ministries of an early Christian death. 58706

Memorial discvrsivo sobre el oficio de Protector General. 74599

Memorial e informacion en derecho del Licenciado Don Thomas Svarez de Giles. 93322

Memorial edition. Poems and essays by Edgar Allan Poe. 63534

Memorial en la causa del Real Collegio de S. Fernand de Quito. 67118

Memorial, &c. [of Dr. Bray.] 105652

Memorial, &c. [of Nathaniel Sackett.] 74756

Memorial, &c. of the Virginia Yazoo Company. 100571, 2d note after 106003

Memorial, &c. relative to the missionaries. 25265

Memorial, &c. To the Legislature of Virginia. 100525

Memorial for a grant of land in Florida. 61017

Memorial for a national rail-road. 104000

Memorial for a private charter, asked for by Dr. Hartwell Carver. 11182

Memorial for an act to render Masonic and extrajudicial oaths penal. 45915

Memorial for erecting Wisconsin Territory, 1832. (48752)

Memorial for remuneration as discoverer of the pain-subducing properties of sulphuric-ether. 51032

Memorial for the established or parochial schoolmasters in Scotland. 84628

Memorial for the establishment of a homoeopathic military hospital. 47630

[Memorial] for the establishment of a separate territorial government for Wisconsin. (48752)

Memorial for volunteers and militia. 27379

Memorial from a portion of stockholders, of the city of Philadelphia. 94811

Memorial from California on the ship-building interests of the United States. 47631

Memorial from certain shipowners at Liverpool. 55533

Memorial from churches and citizens. 12073

Memorial from Francis Lieber. 40985

Memorial from His Catholick Majesty. 88181

Memorial from James Stuart, Esquire. 93174

Memorial from Mr. [James] Stuart. 27567

Memorial from some 3050 clergymen of . . . New England. 71351

Memorial from the auctioneers, of . . . New-York. 54106

Memorial from the auctioneers of Philadelphia. (60509)

Memorial . . . from the Canal Convention at Chicago. 47709

Memorial . . . from the Chamber of Commerce of New York. 47710

Memorial from the citizens of Columbus. 14895

Memorial from the citizens of Maine. 7807

Memorial from the citizens of Milwaukee. 49161

Memorial from the Kentucky Historical Society. 37512

Memorial from the Legislative Assembly of the Territory of Kansas. (68629)

Memorial from the . . . Levee Commissioners of . . . Louisiana. 42248

Memorial from the representatives of the Society of Friends in New England. 93676

Memorial from the Rhode-Island Regiment of drafted militia. 70597

Memorial . . . from the Union League of Philadelphia. 47711

Memorial from the United Society of Believers,
or Shakers. 47632

Memorial from Williams College. 89138, 1st
note after 104432

Memorial given in against their [i. e. the
Darien Company's] taking subscriptions
at Hamburgh. 18563

Memorial Hall, Dedham, Mass. see Dedham,
Mass. Memorial Hall.

Memorial, historical and political. 28633

Memorial historico Espanol. 47633

Memorial history [of Augusta, Georgia.] 85357

Memorial history of Boston. 82823, 82855,
93430

Memorial hymn by Mrs. Sarah Helen Whitman.
66292

Memorial humbly shewing the past and present
state of the land. 47624

Memorial i discvrso de las razones que se
ofrecen. 86530

Memorial i informacion por las iglesias metro-
politanas. 47635

Memorial. Impeachment of James Buchanan.
8863

Memorial in behalf of adapting the canals.
73957

Memorial in behalf of . . . New York. (53767)

Memorial in behalf of the architect of our
federal constitution. 102402

Memorial in behalf of the European and North
American Railway Co. 64062

Memorial, in behalf of the Southern Central
Rail-Road. 88318

Memorial . . . in favor of the increase of duty
on woollen goods. (47659)

Memorial . . . in relation to his claims on
Mexico. 40763

Memorial . . . in relation to the Delaware
Avenue. 61817

Memorial in the case of the ship Hunter. 33939

Memorial in the French language. 47641,
102192

Memorial informativo del Consulado de la ciudad
de Los Reyes. 687

Memorial informatoria al Rey en su Real
Conseio de las Indias. 20133

Memorial informatorio al Rey Nvestro Senor.
10057

Memorial informatorio, etc. 10057

Memorial, informe, y manifiesto del P. F.
Bvenaventura de Salinas y Cordova. 75785

Memorial juridico. 23338, 96309

Memorial juridico-politico de la S. Iglesia Catedral de la Puebla de los Angeles. (9884)

Memorial jvridico, y legal. 12974

Memorial Lincoln biography. 41214

Memorial meeting, February 13, 1918. 84508

Memorial most humbly addressed to the Sovereigns of Europe. 35987, 54826-64827,
64829, 64834, 2d note after 99457

Memorial now before the Legislature. 25032

Memorial o discvrso informativo ivridico, historico, politico. 86533

Memorial of a citizens of the United States.
27274

Memorial of a committee in behalf of cotton
manufacturers. 66282

Memorial of a committee of the Chespeake and
Ohio Canal Company. 12503

Memorial of a convention of citizens of the
commonwealth. 97770

Memorial of a convention of delegates representing the merchants and other interested
in commerce. 47636

Memorial of a delegation from the Cherokee
Indians. (12466)

Memorial of a delegation to the Cherokee
Tribe of Indians. 47637

Memorial of A. Fitch. 24561

Memorial of A. Fitch in behalf of Fitch Brothers & Co. 24560

Memorial of a ministry of 25 years. 80267

Memorial of a soldier. 85521

Memorial of Aaron Ogden. (56797)

Memorial of Abraham Lincoln, . . . delivered
in Flemington, N. J. 41187

Memorial of Abraham Lincoln, late President
of the United States. 41213

Memorial of Abraham Pierson, first Rector of
Yale University. 26796

Memorial of Albert Drake. 696

Memorial of Albert J. Myer. 51626

Memorial of Alexander Murray. (51484)

Memorial of Alfred B. Soule. 12845, note just
before 87264

Memorial of Alfred G. Benson. 4740

Memorial of Ambrose Spencer. 89350, 89744

Memorial of Amos Pilsbury. 26867

Memorial of Ann Parker Green Hough. 28512

Memorial of Augustu V. Van Horne. 98516

Memorial of B. Marshall. 44766

Memorial of Benjamin Rodman. 72483

Memorial of Benjamin Silliman. 81048

Memorial of Bishop Hobart. 11882, 32302,
77986

Memorial [of Bishop Sherlock.] 11878

Memorial of bondholders of the Indiana State
Bank. 34526

Memorial of Brevet Brigadier General Lewis
Benedict. 4662

Memorial of Capt. Cyprian Southack. 88221

Memorial of Capt. Geo. Henry Preble. 65010

Memorial of Capt. Geo. Henry Preble, U. S. N
to the forty-third Congress. 65011

Memorial [of Captain Isaac Coffin.] 49343

Memorial of Captain Joseph Smoot. 85130

Memorial of Capt. Louis C. Sartori. (77111)

Memorial of Captain Obadiah Conger. 12407

Memorial of Captain Richard C. Derby. 30162

Memorial of Capt. Thornton Posey. 64446

Memorial of certain . . . tailors of Boston.
(47638)

Memorial of Chancellor Bland. 5862, (45103)

Memorial of Charles Finney Masnfield. 44383

Memorial of Charles H. Marshall. (9663)

Memorial of Chas. Howard, Wm. H. Gatchell,
John W. Davis. 3042

Memorial of Charles Thomas Wells. 84445-
84446

Memorial of citizens of Chesterfield. 47639

Memorial of . . . citizens of Milwaukee. 4916

Memorial of . . . citizens of Philadelphia.
61818

Memorial of citizens to the Legislature. 3699

Memorial of claimants under Georgia. 27069

Memorial of Clark B. Cochrane. 14075

Memorial of Clark Stevens. 91491

Memorial of closing scenes in the life of Rev.
George B. Little. (41515)

Memorial of Colonel John A. Bross. 8384

Memorial of Commander James McMcIntosh.
43558

Memorial of common-sense. 47640

Memorial of Count Zinznedorf. 63987

Memorial of Cyrus Buckland. (8915)

Memorial of Dana Pond Colburn. 14255

Memorial of Daniel Webster, from the city of
Boston. 31875

Memorial of David Hatch. 33253

Memorial of David Jones. 36485

Memorial of David Magie. 62789
Memorial of Deac. Isaac Newton Beach. 39264
Memorial of Dr. David L. Dodge. 47645
Memorial of Dr. Franklyn. 69499
Memorial of Dr. Henry Perrine. 61016
Memorial of Dr. James Smith. 82780
Memorial of Dr. John Bell. 35459
Memorial of Dr. Packard. 85209
Memorial of Duncan, Sherman & Co. (21265)
Memorial of E. K. Collins & his associates. 14433
Memorial of Easter, 1865. 77434
Memorial of Edmund Pendleton Gaines. (26333)
Memorial of Edward Everett: a discourse . . . Dorchester . . . Jan. 22, 1865. (29830)
Memorial of Edward Everett, from the city of Boston. (9069), (23273)
Memorial of Edwin A. Stevens. 91493
Memorial of Edwin M. Snow. 85498
Memorial of . . . 1866, to the Legislature of Massachusetts. 30859
Memorial of Elias Durand. 65943
Memorial of Eliphas Spencer, of Texas. 89313
Memorial of Elisha Lord Cleaveland. 13590
Memorial of Elizabeth Cady Stanton. 90404
Memorial of Elliot Beecher Preston. 65367
Memorial of Evan Thomas, and others. 95389
Memorial of farmers, mechanics, and others. 1596
Memorial of Federal Street Meeting House. 6642
Memorial of Fernando Fairfax. (23686)
Memorial of fifty years by J. E. A. Smith. 83334
Memorial of First Lieutenant James W. Schaumburg. 77521
Memorial of Francis L. Hawks, D. D. (21501)
Memorial of Frederick Knight. 38114, 1st note after 95623
Memorial of French citizens of Wayne County. 47641, 102192
Memorial of . . . Friends to the Legislature of Virginia. 9322, 100522
Memorial of Fulwar Skipwith. 81655
Memorial of G. A. Simmons. 81158
Memorial of Gen. J. K. F. Mansfield. (44381)
Memorial of Gen. W. S. Rosecrans. 73257
Memorial of Gen. William Barton. 90727
Memorial of George Minto. 49319
Memorial of George Wilkes. 83832
Memorial of Gerard Hallock. 11078
Memorial of Giles F. Ward, Jr. 8966
Memorial of God's goodness. 30175
Memorial of Governor John Endicott. 75798
Memorial of Harrison G. Otis and others. 89698
Memorial of Harrison Gray Otis and others from the repeal of the law. 34959
Memorial of Harrison H. Cocke. (14101)
Memorial of Harvard, Williams, and Amherst Colleges. 23271, 30765
Memorial of Henry D. Gilpin. 27459
Memorial of Henry D. Gilpin, John T. Sullivan, and Peter Wagner. 3189
Memorial of Henry Fry. (26097)
Memorial of Henry G. Comingo. 14949
Memorial of Henry Messonier. 48161
Memorial of Henry O'Rielly. 57590
Memorial of Henry Theodore Tuckerman. 21502
Memorial of Henry Ware Hall. (25376)
Memorial of . . . her beloved husband, who died . . . August 15, 1869. (38010)

Memorial of Herman Ten Eyck Foster. 15472
Memorial of Hiram F. Mills. 49106
Memorial of Hon. Francis Parsons. 72635
Memorial of inhabitants of . . . Albany and County of Sullivan. 47642
Memorial of inhabitants of . . . Albany . . . praying further protection. 47642
Memorial of inhabitants of Dutchess County. 47642
Memorial of inhabitants of Mecklenburg County. 47288
Memorial of inhabitants of Michigan. 88314
Memorial of inhabitants of Newberry District. 47642
Memorial of inhabitants of Otsego County. 47642
Memorial of inhabitants of Philadelphia, praying that the Baltimore and Ohio Rail Road Company may not be permitted to import. 61816
Memorial of inhabitants of . . . Philadelphia to Congress. 47643
Memorial of inhabitants of South Carolina. 87890
Memorial of Isaac Hayes. 55910
Memorial of J. T. Soutter. 88679
Memorial of James B. Moore and Company. 50404
Memorial of James Chapman. 11987
Memorial of James Fenimore Cooper. (16573)
Memorial of James H. Lane. 89926
Memorial of James Hall. 29809
Memorial of James Hamilton. 30016
Memorial of James M'Ilvain. 43318
Memorial of James Smith. 82779
Memorial of Jan. 21, 1839. 93920-93921
Memorial of Joel S. Polack. (63724)
Memorial of John A. Poor. 64064
Memorial of John Allan. (21503)
Memorial of John Augustus Smull. 85177
Memorial of John B. Morris. 50841
Memorial of John C. Dalton. 28545
Memorial of John Chandler. 45256
Memorial of John, Earl of Egmont. 60862
Memorial of John Ferdinand Dalziel Smyth. 85247
Memorial of John Foot. (25004)
Memorial of John H. Smith. 82969-82971
Memorial of John Magee. 43817
Memorial of John Parker, of Boston. 58708
Memorial of John R. and Robert J. Livingston. 41631
Memorial of John Reeves, late naval architect. 68676
Memorial of John Reeves, naval architect to the Sultan. 68676
Memorial of John Ross. 73390
Memorial [of John Smith.] 82873
Memorial of John Townsend. 89744
Memorial of John W. Foster. (25244), 59349
Memorial [of Jonas P. Levy.] 40763
Memorial of Joseph Henry. 85039
Memorial of Joseph Smoot. 86130
Memorial of Joseph Tuckerman. 97388
Memorial of Joseph W. Brackett and Samuel Leggett. 78737, 103717
Memorial of Joshua Bates. 3942
Memorial of Newis and Susan Benedict. 29817
Memorial of Levi Lincoln. 41259
Memorial of Lexington battle. 59313
Memorial of Lieut. Colonel J. M. Gamble. (26507)
Memorial of Lt. Daniel Perkins Dewey. 19850, 41677
Memorial of Lieut. Franklin Butler Crosby. 17634

Memorial of Lieut. John W. Groat. 18165

Memorial of Lieut. Joseph P. Burrage. (9838)

Memorial of Lieut. Robert B. Riell. (71304)

Memorial of . . . Machias. 84941

Memorial of Mad. Susanne Kossuth Meszlenyi. (48163)

Memorial of Major Edward Granville Park. 58629

Memorial of manufacturers of naval machinery for the United States. 47644

Memorial of March 11, 1839. 93920, 93922

[Memorial of Maria L. Saunders, of Paducah, Kentucky.] 77185

Memorial of Marvin Wait. 21727

Memorial of Mary C. Rand. 42494

Memorial of Mary E. Smalley. 77060

Memorial of Mary Elizabeth Stirling. 91850

Memorial of Mary White Wicker. 2418

Memorial of . . . members of the Roman Catholic . . . Church of St. Mary's. (62214)

Memorial of merchants and traders of New York. 54378

Memorial of merchants of Boston. 6525

Memorial of Messrs. M'Tavish, Fraser and Co. 43666

Memorial of Miss Susanna Anthony. 63988

Memorial of Mrs. Carolina M. Severance. 79378

[Memorial of] Mrs. Elizabeth Sargent. 52314

Memorial of Mrs. Louisa C. McAllister. 42931

Memorial of Mrs. Lydia Willis. 104502

Memorial of Mrs. Mary F. Dexter North. 55521

Memorial of Mrs. Susan Charlotte Farley Maxwell. (57928)

Memorial of Moody Kent. (9460)

Memorial of Myron Holley to the Legislature of New York. 32531

Memorial of Nahum Capen. (10747)

Memorial of Nathan B. Crocker. 20983

Memorial [of Nathaniel Bowditch.] 6944

Memorial of Nathaniel Greene Cleary. 13586

Memorial of Nathaniel Hall Loring. 42098

Memorial of Nathaniel James Lord. (42046)

Memorial [of Nathaniel Morton.] 80910

Memorial of Nathaniel W. Taylor. 2675

Memorial of Negro emancipation. 95844

Memorial of Noah Porter. 64295

Memorial of officers of the army of the United States. 47646

Memorial of officers of the United States Navy, for an increase of pay. 47647

Memorial of officers of the U. S. Navy to Congress. (53592)

Memorial of our daughter, for her child. 65430

Memorial of owners of ground lying in the inland side. 98580

Memorial of Patience Corlies. 16788

Memorial of Peter Livius. 41656, note after 102630

Memorial of Peter Williamson. 104485

Memorial of Porter C. Bliss. 57711

Memorial of Prof. Charles Hooker. 76494

Memorial of Prof. [Thomas S.] Ridgway. 71292

Memorial of Return Jonathan Meigs, Junior. 47399

Memorial of Reuben M. Whitney. 103778

Memorial of Reverdy Johnson to the Legislature of Maryland. 36265

Memorial of Rev. Abraham Polhemus. 63734

Memorial of Rev. E. B. Hall. (29754)

Memorial of Rev. Ephraim Peabody, D. D. 50713

Memorial of Rev. Joseph Tuckerman. 97399

Memorial of Rev. Pitt Clarke. (13441)

Memorial of Rev. Thomas Smith. 84299

Memorial of Richard A. Gilpin. 61819

Memorial of Richard W. Meade. 47236

Memorial of Robert Fulton and E. P. Livingston 26203

Memorial of Rodolphe Tillier's justification. 95825

Memorial of S. W. Newland. 55002

Memorial of . . . St. Louis. 75356

Memorial of Samuel Appleton, of Ipswich, Massachusetts. 36113

Memorial of Samuel C. Crafts and others. 17337

Memorial of Samuel F. B. Morse. 50963

Memorial of Samuel Henry Cook. 89744

Memorial of Samuel Norriss. 96696

Memorial of Samuel Rodman. 72487

Memorial of Samuel T. Hopkins. 55055

Memorial of Sarah Ball. 71568

Memorial of Sa-sa-na, the Mohawk maiden. 41785

Memorial of Senators and Representatives from Massachusetts. (82573)

Memorial of Senators and Representatives in Congress from Massachusetts. 82575

Memorial of Sir James Jay. (35829)

Memorial of some of the part-owners and proprietors of the patents. 47628

Memorial of some remarkable occurrences in N. E. 52646, note after 62743

Memorial of Stephen Sayre. (77416), 77419

Memorial of sugar refiners. 47649

Memorial of sundry banks of . . . Philadelphia. 60647

Memorial of sundry citizens of Alleghany County 47650

Memorial of sundry citizens of Northumberland County. (55845)

Memorial of sundry citizens of Orangeburgh District. 57431

Memorial of sundry citizens of . . . Philadelphia 61820

Memorial of sundry citizens of Philadelphia, praying to be protected. 61821

Memorial of sundry farmers of . . . Pennsylvania. 60237

Memorial of sundry inhabitants of the counties of Randolph and St. Clair. (47651)

Memorial of sundry inhabitants of Massachusetts 45916

Memorial of sundry inhabitants of the upper counties. 87891

Memorial of sundry manufacturers of hats. 61822

Memorial of sundry masters of American vessels. 12057

Memorial of sundry merchants and traders . . . of Philadelphia. (62186)

Memorial of sundry merchants of Newburyport. 20249

Memorial of sundry presbyters of the Protestant Episcopal Church. 23458, 51232, 66177

Memorial of sundry proprietors . . . of American steam vessels. (47652)

Memorial of sundry tallow chandlers. 3043

Memorial of sundry umbrella-makers of Philadelphia. (61823)

Memorial of T. D. Shaw. 79964

Memorial of that society [i. e. Society of Arts and Manufacturers of Philadelphia] to Congress. 17296, (22964)

Memorial of the agents in behalf of the principal inhabitants. 95299

Memorial of the agents of the New England Mississippi Land Company. 52708, 2d note after 99829

Memorial of the alluvions, or obstructions. (26931)

Memorial of the American Colonization Society. 14732

Memorial of the American Philosophical Society, and of the Historical Society of Philadelphia. 47653, 61824

Memorial of the American Society for the Diffusion of Useful Knowledge. 47654

Memorial of the American Society for the Encouragement of Domestic Manufactures. 47655

Memorial of the anti-slavery and abolition societies of the United Kingdom. 96026

Memorial of the artists and manufacturers of Philadelphia. 44431

Memorial of the auctioneers of New York to Congress. 54106

Memorial of the auctioneers of Philadelphia. 61825

Memorial of the author [i. e. Elizabeth Stuart Phelps] by Austin Phelps. (61373)

Memorial [of the Baltimore millers.] 96991

Memorial of the Board of Commissioners of Health. 54118

Memorial of the Board of Controllers of Public Schools. 61501

Memorial of the Board of Direction of the [Northern Pacific Railroad] Company. 55819

Memorial of the Board of Managers [of the Pennsylvania Society for the Encouragement of Manufactures and the Useful Arts.] 60367

Memorial of the Board of Manufactures [of the Pennsylvania Society for the Encouragement of Manufactures and the Useful Arts.] 60367

Memorial of the Board of Trade and Common Council. (3483)

Memorial of the Board of Trade of Macon, Georgia. 43619

Memorial of the Boston Sanitary Association. 35803, 46043, 47656

Memorial of the Burlington Island Association. 9342, 51925

Memorial of the Canal Board & Canal Commissioners. 53768, 73977

Memorial of the case of the German emigrants. 25554

Memorial of the centennial anniversary of the settlement of Machias. 43314, 84750

Memorial of the Chamber of Commerce, in the city of Cincinnati. 13070

Memorial of the Chamber of Commerce of . . . New-York. 53587

Memorial of the Chamber of Commerce [of Philadelphia.] (61975)

Memorial of the Chamber of Commerce of St. Paul. 69884

Memorial of the Chamber of Commerce of San Francisco. 76039

Memorial of the Chamber of Commerce of Sheffield. 26454

Memorial of the Chamber of Commerce of the citizens of Charleston. 12058

Memorial of the Chamber of Commerce of the city of New York. 54161

Memorial of the . . . Chamber of Commerce . . . relative to the Bank of the United States. (61975)

Memorial of the Charles and Elizabeth Ludlow Professor of Ecclesiastical Polity and Law. 90659

Memorial of the Cherokee Indians. 47657

Memorial of the Choctaw citizens of the state of Mississippi. 34658

Memorial of the Cincinnati Chamber of Commerce. 13071

Memorial of the citizens of Abbeville District, S. C. 47658

Memorial of the citizens of Baltimore. 2992

Memorial of the citizens of Boston. (47659)

Memorial of the citizens of Buffalo. (22746)

Memorial of the citizens of Cairo and vicinity. 47660

Memorial of the citizens of Charleston, praying the establishment of a uniform system of bankrupsy. (12059)

Memorial of the citizens of Charleston to the Senate and House of Representatives of the state of South-Carolina. 87892

Memorial of the citizens of Chester District. 47661

Memorial of the citizens of Cincinnati to the Congress of the United States. 13095, 47662

Memorial of the citizens of Edgefield. 47663

Memorial of the citizens of Georgetown, South Carolina. 47663

Memorial of the citizens of Kershaw District, South Carolina, adverse to the proposed tariff on woollens. 37639

Memorial of the citizens of Kershaw District, South Carolina, to the honorable the Senate and House of Representatives of the United States. 37639, 88076, note after 94393

Memorial of the citizens of Laurens District, South Carolina, adverse to the present tariff. 47664

Memorial of the citizens of Laurens District, South Carolina, against any increase of the tariff, &c. (47665)

Memorial of . . . the citizens of northern Pennsylvania. 55823

Memorial of the citizens of Philadelphia to Congress. 10889

Memorial of the citizens of Plymouth and Kingston, Mass. 63479

Memorial of the citizens of St. Louis, Missouri. (75355)

Memorial of the citizens of Sandusky, for the establishment of a naval depot, &c. 16304

Memorial of the citizens of the counties of St. Lawrence, Franklin and Clinton. (47666)

Memorial of the citizens . . . of the Indiana Territory. (34555)

Memorial of the citizens of Union District. 47667

Memorial of the citizens to Congress. 91623, 2d note after 101924

Memorial of the City Council for an extension of Faneuil Hall Market. (67238)

Memorial of the City Council . . . to the Legislature. 54158

Memorial of the city of Lafayette, Louisiana. (38585)

Memorial of the city of Utica. 98227

Memorial of the class graduated at Dartmouth College, July, 1849. 90299

Memorial of the clerks in the executive departments. 47668, 47712

Memorial . . . of the clerks . . . of the executive departments. 47668, 47712

Memorial of the coal-owners and iron-masters of Richmond. 71184

Memorial of the college life of the class of 1827. 17625

Memorial of the College of Physicians & Surgeons to the University. (54000)

Memorial of the colonial agents to Earl Bathurst. 3956

Memorial of the commemoration by the Church of the Disciples. 13413

Memorial of the Commissioners of . . . Philadelphia to the Legislature. 61826

Memorial of the committee appointed by the "Free Trade Convention." (26399), 47669

Memorial of the Committee of the . . . Trustees. (60097)

Memorial of the Comptroller General of S. Carolina. 87410

Memorial of the congregational ministers and churches of the Illinois Association. 11125

Memorial of the Corporation . . . March 26, 1853. 54379

Memorial of the Corporation, of Harvard College, on the . . . Theological School. (30759A)

Memorial of the Corporation of South Hanover College, Indiana, praying for a donation of a township of land. 88135

Memorial of the Corporation of South Hanover College, Indiana, praying the donation of a tract of land. 88136

Memorial of the Council of Proprietors of the Eastern Division of New Jersey. 53153

Memorial of the Count de Guines. 29240

Memorial of the Creek Nation of Indians. 47670

Memorial of the deceases at Union-Village, Ohio. 97882

Memorial of the dedication of monuments erected. 47671, (68991)

Memorial of the delegates appointed by various sections of the District of Columbia. 20314

Memorial of the Delegates of the Cherokee Nation. 12467

Memorial of the Delegation of the Cherokee Nation. 47672

Memorial of the Delaware & Hudson Canal Co. 19409

Memorial of the Democratic members of the Legislature of Rhode Island. 64635, 70725

Memorial of the "Democratic members" of the Legislature of Vermont. 82367

Memorial of the Democratic members of the Rhode Island Legislature. (70598), 70728

Memorial of the difficulties. 4731

Memorial of the Directors . . . [of the Iron Mountain Railroad Company.] (35096)

Memorial of the Directors of the . . . [New England Mississippi Land] Company. (52708)

Memorial of the . . . Directors . . . [of the Philadelphia House of Refuge.] 61729

Memorial of the Directors of the Western Rail-Road Corporation. 101519

Memorial of the Eliot Sabbath School. 73641, note after 95465

Memorial of the family of Thomas and Dorothy Burgess. 9240

Memorial of the farmers . . . of the county of Kent. 37474

Memorial of the Federal-Street Meeting-House. (26529)

Memorial of the fire of 1835. 54380

Memorial of the First Great South-Western Turnpike Road Company. 47673

Memorial of the Florida Telegraph Company. 69676, 84773

Memorial of the free citizens of color in Pittsburg and vicinity. 60238

Memorial of the French Benevolent Society of the City of New York. 85815

Memorial of the General Assembly of Illinois. (34203)

Memorial of the golden wedding of Leonard and Jenette Hodgman. 32354

Memorial of the golden wedding of Nicholas and Susan Longworth. 41941

Memorial of the goodness of God. 47674, 62534

Memorial of the Great Sanitary Fair held in the city of Albany. 634

Memorial of the head men and warriors of the Creek Nation of Indians. 47675

Memorial of the . . . Historical Society to the . . . Legislature. 54475

Memorial of the holders and owners of the floating debt. 76055

Memorial of the Honorable George Leonard. (40105)

Memorial of the Honourable Thomas Walpole. 101150

Memorial of the Hon. William Jay. (58964)

Memorial of the House of Representatives of the Commonwealth of Massachusetts. 45917

Memorial of the House of Representatives of the Mississippi Territory. 69830

Memorial of the House of Representatives of the Territory of Orleans. 57626

Memorial of the Ilinois [sic] and Ouabache Land Companies. 34295, 84578, 4th note after 97876

Memorial of the Illinois and Wabash Land Company. 34294, 84577-84578, 2d-3d notes after 97876

Memorial of the Illinois Association. 34297

Memorial of the inauguration of the statue of Franklin. 80781

Memorial of the inhabitants of Dutchess County 47676

Memorial of the inhabitants of Machias. 43314 84750

Memorial of the . . . inhabitants of New Orlean (53334)

Memorial of the inhabitants of Pennsylvania. 60239

Memorial of the inhabitants of Richland District 71118

Memorial of the inhabitants of Rochester. 7236

Memorial of the inhabitants of the town of Salem. 85673, 92309

Memorial of the inhabitants of Waterford. 102054

Memorial of the inhabitants . . . on the Niagar frontier. (47677)

Memorial of the iron manufacturers of New England. 31026

Memorial of the Keystone Publishing and Manufacturing Company. 37699

Memorial of the late Honorable David S. Jones. 36627

Memorial of the late James L. Petigru. 61249

Memorial of the late Rev. Baron Stow. 52169

Memorial of the late Walter Joy. 91136

Memorial of the Legislative Council and House of Representatives of the Mississippi Territory. 69735

Memorial of the Legislative Council of the Territory of Michigan. (48752)

Memorial of the Legislature of Illinois to Congress. 34206

Memorial of the Legislature of the free state of Arkansas. (1992)

Memorial of the Legislature of the state of Georgia. (27071)

Memorial of the Legislature of the state of South Carolina. 87484

Memorial of the lessees. 57015

Memorial of the life and character of J. W. Francis. 25444

Memorial of the life and services of the late Rev. Henry A. Rowland. 73567

Memorial of the life of J. Johnston Pettigrew. 96788

Memorial of the life of the Right Rev. William Meade. (36157)

Memorial of the Louisville and Cincinnati Commercial Conventions. 88325

Memorial of the Maine Grand Lodge. (43992)

Memorial of the Maine Historical Society. (43971)

Memorial of the . . . Managers of the . . . [Pennsylvania State Temperance] Society. 60383

Memorial of the manufacturers of salt in Kanawha County. 36997

Memorial of the manufacturers of salt, in the county of Kanawha. 36996

Memorial of the manufacturers of salt, of Barnstable, Mass. 3552

Memorial of the marine insurance companies of Baltimore. 94531

Memorial of the Marshpee Indians. 44819

Memorial of the martyred Lovejoy. 73122

Memorial of the masonic festival. 47678

Memorial of the Massachusetts Historical Society. (52687)

Memorial of the [Massachusetts Historical] Society to the Legislature . . . February, 1858. 45856

Memorial of the Mayor and City Council of Baltimore. 3044

Memorial of the Mechanics and Manufacturers of Lexington. (40884)

Memorial of the medical faculty of Jefferson College. 61746

Memorial of the Medical Society of the City . . . of New York. 54376

Memorial of the Memphis, El Paso and Pacific Railroad Company. 47679

Memorial of the merchants and traders of . . . Philadelphia. 61828

Memorial of the merchants and traders of the city of Baltimore. 3045

Memorial of the merchants and traders of the city of Philadelphia. 95951

Memorial of the merchants, . . . in Salem. 47680, 1st note after 92309

Memorial of the merchants of Baltimore. 3046, 62969

Memorial of the merchants of . . . Boston, in . . . Massachusetts. 47682

Memorial of the merchants of . . . Boston Jan. 20. 1806. 6524

Memorial of the merchants of Boston praying the repeal. 47681

Memorial of the merchants of New Haven. 52986

Memorial of the merchants of . . . New-York. 54382

Memorial of the merchants of New York, Jan. 6, 1806. 54383

Memorial of the merchants of Philadelphia. 62167

Memorial of the merchants of the city of New-York. 54381

Memorial of the merchants of the town of Boston. 6526

Memorial of the Milwaukee and Rock River Canal Company. (49169)

Memorial of the Mine Hill and Schuylkill Haven Rail Road Company. 60252

Memorial of the Missionary Society [of the Reformed Dutch Church in North America.] 68773

Memorial of the Mississippi River Improvement and Manufacturing Company. 49552

Memorial of the Morses. 50911

Memorial of the New England clergymen. 20693, 33195

Memorial of the New England Coal Mining Company. 69865

Memorial of the New Idria Mining Co. of California. 53022

Memorial of the New-York and Erie Rail-Road Company. (54729)

Memorial of the New York Commissioners [on Quarentine.] 53231

Memorial of the New-York Convention . . . of the Friends of Domestic Industry. 53769

Memorial of the New York Convention of the Friends of Domestic Industry, to the Congress of the United States. 53770

Memorial of the New York Mail Steamship Company. (54800)

Memorial of the North American Coal and Mining Company. 55545

Memorial of the Northampton Slate Quarry Company. 55775

Memorial of the officers and soldiers of the Rhode Island Bridgade. 9235, 70599

Memorial of the officers of Harvard College. (42447)

Memorial of the officers of the United States Navy to Congress. 75342

Memorial of the Ohio Anti-slavery Society to the General Assembly. (56969)

Memorial of the Ohio Teachers' Association. 57013

Memorial of the owners and underwriters of the American ship, New Jersey. 23361, 47683

Memorial of the owners of real estate in the vicinity of the Washington Military Parade Ground. 47684

Memorial of the owners of the steamship Meteor. 69767

Memorial of the owners of water of the Genesee River. 26925

Memorial of the owners . . . of wharf property on the river Delaware. 61829

Memorial of the Panama Railroad Company. (58410), 73977

Memorial of the paper manufacturers. 47685

Memorial of the patriotic martyrs of the city and county of Albany. (13361)

Memorial of the Pennsylvania Society for the Promotion of American Manufactures. 60369

Memorial of the people of Louisiana. 42262

Memorial of the people of the district of Spartanburgh, S. C. 89028

Memorial of the People's Pacific Railroad Company. 60828

Memorial of the pewholders and worshippers of St. Paul's Chapel. 75463

Memorial of the . . . [Philadelphia] Board of Trade. 61970

Memorial of the Philadelphia Society for the Promotion of American Manufactures. 62324

Memorial of the Pier and Warehouse Company. (54384)

Memorial of the pilgrim fathers. 8913

Memorial of the present deplorable state of New-England. 49822, 62560

Memorial of the President . . . and Company for Erecting a Permanent Bridge over the River Schuylkill at . . . Philadelphia. 62231

Memorial of the President and Directors [of the Baltimore and Susquehannah Railroad Company.] 2993

Memorial of the President and Directors of the Bank of Kentucky. 37493

Memorial of the President and Directors of the First Great South-western Turn-Pike Road Company. 22355

Memorial of the President and Directors [of the Philadelphia, Easton and Water-Gap Railroad Company] to the Councils. (61993)

Memorial of the President and Directors of the South Carolina Canal and Rail Road Company. 87961

Memorial [of the President and Fellows of Harvard College.] 30751, 45918

Memorial of the President, Directors, and Company of the Bank [of Pennsylvania.] 59910

Memorial of the President . . . of the Danville and Pottsville Rail Road Company. 60034

Memorial of the President of the United States. 26399

Memorial of the Prison Association to the Governor of . . . New York. 53891

Memorial of the Professors and Tutors of Harvard University. 30751

Memorial of the Professors of the Medical School. (45389)

Memorial of the Proprietors of the New South Meeting-House in Dorchester. 10743, 20621, (20626)

Memorial of the Proprietors of the New York and Liverpool Line of American steamers. 14433, 93819

Memorial of the publick creditors, citizens of . . . New-Jersey. 53154

Memorial . . . of the public creditors who are citizens of the commonwealth of Pennsylvania. (47621), 60704

Memorial of the quarter-centennial celebration of the establishment of normal schools in America. (47686)

Memorial of the railroad companies on the exemption law. 15287

Memorial of the religious society of Friends. 56957

Memorial of the religious society of Friends to the Legislature of Virginia. 47687

Memorial of the representatives of the people south of the Ohio. note after 94720

Memorial of the representatives of the religious society of Friends in Pennsylvania, New Jersey and Delaware. 77451

Memorial of the representatives of Wade Hampton. 30152

Memorial of the resident instructors. (30759A)

Memorial of the Rev. Bird Wilson. 8234

Memorial of the Rev. Ezekiel Rich. 79871

Memorial of the Reverend George Putnam. (66794)

Memorial of the Rev. Henry William Duchalet. 23317

Memorial of the Rev. John Chester. 37972

Memorial of the Rev. John Knox. (38166)

Memorial of the Rev. John N. Campbell. 10256, 89744

Memorial of the Rev. John Snelling Popkin. (24040)

Memorial of the Rev. Lewis P. Bayard. 4032

Memorial of the Rev. Royal Robbins. 89814

Memorial of the Rev. Samuel Davies. 63989

Memorial of the Rev. Thomas Mather Smith. 61056, 84408

Memorial of the Rev. William C. Brownlee. 8700

Memorial of the Rev. William Honeywood Ripley. 77431

Memorial of the Rev. Wm. J. Hoge. 32433

Memorial of the revival in Plymouth Church, Brooklyn. 8302

Memorial of the Rio Grande, Mexican, and Pacific Railroad Company. 71477

Memorial of the St. Augustine Catholic Church. (75001)

Memorial of the St. Louis Chamber of Commerce. 75340

Memorial of the San Diego Chamber of Commerce. 88507

Memorial of the . . . Schuylkill and Susquehanna Navigation, and the Delaware and Schuylkill Canal Navigation. 60725, 78072

Memorial of the semi-centennial anniversary of the American Colonization Society. 47688

Memorial of the semi-centennial celebration of the founding of Hamilton College. 30062

Memorial of the semi-centennial celebration of the founding of the Theological Seminary at Andover. 1440, note after 94507

Memorial of the semi-centennial of the American Colonization Society. 14732

Memorial of the Senators and Representatives, and the constitution of the state of Kansas. 37038, 37070

Memorial of the Seneca Indians. (79113)

Memorial of the 7th day of May, 1790. 90605

Memorial of the several incorporated insurance companies of the state. 60239

Memorial of the Shakers of Watervliet. 11988

Memorial of the Society of Friends in Dinwiddie County, Va. 20205

Memorial of the Society of Friends in regard to the Indians. 47689

Memorial of the Society of Friends . . . praying for the abolition of slavery in the District of Columbia. 37818

Memorial of the Society of New-Lebanon. 9789

Memorial . . . of the Society of Paper Makers. (47713)

Memorial of the society of people of Canterbury . . . and Enfield. (79714), note after 97880, note after 103334

Memorial of the society of people of New Lebanon. 97890

Memorial of the South Pacific Railroad Co. 88153

Memorial of the special services held at St. Philip's Church. 87931

Memorial of the Sprague family. 87288

Memorial of the state of Missouri. 49608

Memorial of the subscribers, citizens of —— in Massachusetts. 97939

Memorial of the subscribers, citizens of the city and county of Philadelphia. 97942

Memorial of the subscribers, merchants and traders of ———. 97940

Memorial of the subscribers, owners, and insurers of the ship New Jersey. 53155

Memorial of the subscribers . . . Philadelphia. 61830

Memorial of the Sunday schools. (8318), 24445, note after 93743

Memorial of the Tax-Payers' Convention. 87942, 88078, 1st note after 94434

Memorial of the Texian Loan contractors. 95102

Memorial [of the Town Meeting of Philadelphia.] 62078

Memorial of the town of Deerfield, &c. 47691

Memorial of the Trustees of the Mariners' Church. 43994

Memorial of the Trustees . . . [of the New York College of Physicians and Surgeons] in reply to the "Professors of Rutgers' Medical Faculty." (54000)

Memorial of the Trustees of the Peabody Education Fund. 59387

Memorial of the Trustees of the Southern Female Institute. 88350

Memorial of the Trustees of the University of Maryland. (45389)

Memorial of the Trustees of the University of Pennsylvania. 61746

Memorial of the Trustees of Williams College. 104424-104425

Memorial of the twelfth General Assembly of Iowa. 35023

Memorial of the twenty-fifth anniversary of the North Avenue Sabbath School. 76511

Memorial of the undersigned, citizens of Washington. 101953

Memorial of the undersigned Committee of the Board of Managers of the Susquehanna and Tide Water Canal Companies. 93922

Memorial of the undersigned, sureties of T. J. Skinner. 46164

Memorial of the underwriters and merchants of the city of Baltimore. 3047

Memorial of the United Illinois and Wabash Land Companies, to the Senate and House of Representatives of the United States. 97877

Memorial of the United Illinois and Wabash Land Companies to the Senate and House . . . of the United States. 34296, 5th note after 97876

Memorial of the United States Bank for a renewal of their charter. 26399

Memorial of the United States Naval Engineers. (47692)

Memorial of the West India Dock Company. 102782

Memorial of the Western Railroad Corporation. 32889, 103002

Memorial of the William Penn Parlor, in the Great Central Fair. 47693

Memorial of the wool growers and manufacturers. 47694

Memorial of the workers in iron of Philadelphia. 47695

Memorial of 30,000 disfranchised citizens of Philadelphia. 61831

Memorial of Thomas Lowndes Snead. 85374

Memorial of Thomas Pinckney. 62908

Memorial of Thomas R. Hazard. 31112

Memorial of Thomas Storm. 12386

Memorial of 3,000 clergymen. (23267)

Memorial of Tobias Lear. 39533

Memorial of unassuming piety. 88674

Memorial of various pew-holders and worshippers in St. Paul's Chapel. 96980

Memorial of virtue. 3794

Memorial of Washington Irving. 21499

Memorial of what God hath wrought. 105244

Memorial of Wm. Hayard & Co. 4042

Memorial of William Kirkland Bacon. 2689

Memorial of William Spooner. 89625

Memorial of William Ware. 4575

Memorial of Williams College. 89138

Memorial on behalf of the citizens resident and concerned in the city of Washington. 101943

Memorial on behalf of the Pittsburgh Manufacturing Association. 63136

Memorial on behalf of the Royal African Company. 73771

Memorial on behalf of the surviving officers of the revolutionary army. (35474), 47696

Memorial . . . [on ocean steam navigation.] 53589

Memorial on personal representation. 47697

Memorial on slavery in America. 47698

Memorial . . . on steamboat navigation in the west. 47714

Memorial on the civil and military government of the Tennessee country. 94415

Memorial on the free sale of books. 4480

Memorial . . . on the impolicy . . . of certain enactments. (68512)

Memorial on the life and character of the Rev. Prince Demetrius A. de Gallitzin. 31649

Memorial on the national, political, and civil state of the province of Cohahuila. 14226

Memorial on the natural, political, and civil state of the province of Cohauila. (67671)

Memorial on the necessity of inviting foreign emigration to West Virginia. 19085

Memorial on the need of a national advisory committee for aeronautics. 85042

Memorial on the obstructions at the head of navigation of Hudson River. 53771

Memorial on the practicability of growing vineyards in the state of South-Carolina. 87740

Memorial on the question of liberal education in Upper Canada. 74584

Memorial on the sixteenth census. (47699)

Memorial on the state of medical education in South Carolina. 88042

Memorial . . . on the subject of a geographical survey of the state. 53616

Memorial on the subject of a revision of the patent laws. 63942

Memorial on the subject of the alien and sedition laws. 56837

Memorial on the subject of the claim of Caron Beaumarchais. (4181)

Memorial on the subject of the late tariff. 27070

Memorial, on the war of St. Domingo. 42188

Memorial; or a short account of the Bahama-Islands. (28348)

Memorial oration by S. F. Miller. 49068

Memorial oration, delivered at Franklin, N. Y. 25635

Memorial papers. 47700, 70086

Memorial para la conversion de Indios. 79038

Memorial passed at a meeting of certain manufacturers of Philadelphia. (61832)

Memorial por el Licenciado D. Alonso de Castillo de Herrera. 31537

Memorial por el Tribunal del Consulado de Lima. 41119

Memorial por los reinos del Peru. 11716

Memorial . . . praying a grant of land for the relief and support of the indigent curable and incurable insane. (20336A)

Memorial . . . praying a repeal of the existing duty on books imported. 47653

Memorial . . . praying for a donation of land. 37263

Memorial praying for the enactment of measures to preserve the constitution and union of the states. 2810

Memorial, praying for the impeachment of Alfred Conkling. 7305

Memorial . . . praying that a national discovery and exploring expedition be sent out to the South Seas. 23781

Memorial prepared for the New-England historical and genealogical register. 65015

Memorial presentada al Congreso sobre el estado de la hacienda publica. 58418

Memorial presente au Roi d'Espagne. 25089

Memorial presente au Roy d'Espagne. 10806

Memorial presente par les PP. Jesuites a N. S. P. le Pape Clement XIII. (68740)

Memorial presented by General Cass. 89926

Memorial presented by the inhabitants of Louisiana. 42261

Memorial presented by the Secretary of the Treasury. (48276)

Memorial presented to His Grace My Lord the Duke of Newcastle. 66726

Memorial presented to His Grace the Duke of Newcastle. 87893

Memorial presented to Ld. Shelburne in Sept. 1783. 85252

Memorial . . . presented to the Board of Common Councilmen. 6785

Memorial presented to the Governors of the East-India Company of Holland. 66727

Memorial presented to the Legislature of . . . New-York. 47701

Memorial presented to the Legislature . . . relative to the "Sunday question." 60241

Memorial, presented to the Senate of the United States. 35349

Memorial Proceedings in Honor of Abraham Lincoln, Ann Arbor, Mich., 1865. see Ann Arbor, Mich. Memorial Proceedings in Honor of Abraham Lincoln, 1865.

Memorial proceedings in honor of . . . Abraham Lincoln, held in Ann Arbor, Michigan. 41215

Memorial, proposing a plan, for the conquest and emancipation of Spanish America. 105483

Memorial provisional presentada al Soberano Congreso. 48552

Memorial que dio el Padre Luys de Valdivia. 98329

Memorial, que el P. Diego Lvys de Sanvitores. 76901

Memorial qve el Padre Predicador Fray Lvis Flores. 24822

Memorial que eleva al Soberano Congreso Chileno. 51407

Memorial qve Fray Ivan de Santander. 4636, (76810)

Memorial qve ofrece el Licenciado Don Juan de Aguilar del Rio. 71453

Memorial que presentan a todas las comunidades. 47702

Memorial que presentan a todos estados los ninos expositos. 42066, 48559

Memorial, que presente a Su Magestad el Licenciado Juan Ortiz de Cervantes. 57718

Memorial que various ciudadanos de los Estados-Unidos de America. 95103

Memorial record. In memory of Hon. Increase Sumner. 78510

Memorial record of the nation's tribute to Abraham Lincoln. 50800

Memorial record of the New York Branch of the United States Christian Commission. 54385

Memorial record of the soldiers who enlisted from Greensboro. 72854

Memorial relating to the Kennebeck Indians. 79441

Memorial relating to the tobacco-trade. 43443, 4th note after 100486, 100487

Memorial relative to the American flag. 52390

Memorial relative to the Union Canal Company in Pennsylvania. 43337

Memorial relativo de el hecho en derecho. 11291

Memorial, remonstrating against a certain act. 97892

Memorial reported to have been laid before the "General Council" of the Bishops, Clergy and Laity. 47703

Memorial, representing the present state of religion. 7479

Memorial, resolutions and proceedings had at a convention. 70037

Memorial . . . respecting a new route to the Pacific Ocean. 49118

Memorial sermon and address on the death of President Lincoln. 63118, 85462

Memorial sermon, by Rev. Rufus Babcock. 88856

Memorial sermon by Rev. W. Sparrow. (36157)

Memorial sermon, delivered at the anniversary, May 11, 1871. (82702)

Memorial sermon delivered by Thomas Brindley Fogg. 24950

Memorial sermon, occasioned by the death of Rev. Pierpont E. Bishop. (77396)

Memorial sermon of . . . Nicholas Hamner Cobbs. 18126

Memorial sermon of Rev. Job Borden Boomer. 3228

Memorial sermon on Bishop Andrew. 84992

Memorial sermon on the death of Theron J. Dale. 69014

Memorial sermon preached in the House of Worship of Chapel Street. 61395

Memorial sermon. Preached on the national funeral day of Abraham Lincoln. 13242

Memorial sermon . . . the death of Rev. Pierpont E. Bishop. 30486

Memorial sermons: being two discourses preached in Tremont Temple. 36985

Memorial service for the late Hon. James Ritchie. 71570

Memorial Service for Three Hundred Thousand Union Soldiers, New York, 1866. see New York (City) Memorial Service for Three Hundred Thousand Union Soldiers, 1866.

Memorial service for three hundred thousand union soldiers. 47704, note after 95516.

Memorial, setting forth the rights and just reasons which the government of the United States of Mexico has. (26548), note after 47704, (48560)

Memorial sketch of George N. and Bushrod W. Harris. 21824

Memorial sketch of the author by Rev. Charles C. Sewall. 79452

Memorial sobre las cosas de la Nueva Espana. (4635)

Memorial; sobre las oposiciones del Padre Provincial del Piru. (44359)

[Memorial] sobre los injustos, grandes, y excessiuos agrauios. 76299

Memorial sobre quitar las doctrinas y curatos. 61145

Memorial soliciting a state hospital for the insane, submitted to the Legislature of New Jersey. (20336A)

Memorial soliciting a state hospital for the insane, submitted to the Legislature of Pennsylvania. (20336A), 60242

Memorial soliciting a state hospital for the protection and cure of the insane. (20336A)

Memorial soliciting adequate appropriations for the construction of a state hospital for the insane, in the state of Mississippi. (20336A)

Memorial soliciting aid in rebuilding Lawrence Academy. 39389

Memorial soliciting an appropriation for the State Hospital for the Insane, at Lexington. (20336A)

Memorial soliciting enlarged and improved accomodations for the insane of the state of Tennessee. (20336A)

Memorial . . . submitted by various canal conventions. 47715

Memorial . . . submitted to the Legislature. 54185

Memorial submitted to the Secretary by sundry line officers of the navy. 71589

Memorial, submitting a new plan of roadway. 49118

Memorial. The case of the schooner Reward. 92308

Memorial. The memorial of the citizens of Kershaw District. 88076, note after 94393

Memorial . . . to aid construction of railroad and telegraph lines. 88427

Memorial . . . to churchmen. 85886

Memorial to Congress. 62707

Memorial . . . to . . . Congress. 63392

Memorial to Congress against an increase on duties on importations. 47705

Memorial to Congress, asking aid in completion of their [i. e. the Pittsburgh and Connellsville Railroad Company's] road. 63126

Memorial to Congress, asking for the return of the government deposites. 62089

Memorial to Congress. [By I. D. Marks.] 44628, (48569)

Memorial. To . . . Congress [by citizens of Pennsylvania.] 60236

Memorial to Congress. [By the Boston Meeting on the Rights of the Cherokee Indians, 1830.] 71382, 71384, 104880

Memorial to Congress [by the Colored People's Convention of the State of South Carolina.] 87808

Memorial to Congress [by the Massachusetts Legislature.] 45609

Memorial to Congress [by the Mormon American exiles.] 85534

Memorial to Congress [by the Union Committee, New York, 1834.] 26399, 54653, 69918, note after 97799

Memorial to Congress, concerning work on the dome of the capitol. (35747)

Memorial to Congress. Dated Feb. 14 [1863]. 19013

Memorial . . . to Congress, Feb. 1820. 14732

Memorial to Congress for the establishment of a national foundry and gun-boat yard at Ironton, Ohio. 35101

Memorial to Congress for the purchase of Catlin's collection. (29303)

Memorial to Congress from a Committee of the Reorganized Church of Jesus Christ of Latter Day Saints. (50746), 83294

Memorial to Congress from Archibald C. Crary. 17422

Memorial to Congress from some Virginian agricultural societies. 102201

Memorial to Congress from the citizens of San Francisco. 76056

Memorial to Congress from the Convention at Dubuque, Iowa. 55855

Memorial to Congress, in favor of erection of the Territory of Wisconsin. (48752)

Memorial to Congress, New York, Feb. 11, 1834. 26399

Memorial to Congress of the Agents of the New England Mississippi Land Company. 69389, 1st note after 100571

Memorial to Congress of the National Commercial Convention. 51950

Memorial to Congress of the Pennsylvania Society for the Encouragement of American Manufactures. 10889

Memorial . . . to Congress [of the Philadelphia Chamber of Commerce.] (61975)

Memorial [to Congress on a] financial system of the nation. (19831)

Memorial to Congress [on taxation.] (53592)

Memorial to . . . Congress on the contract. 47718

Memorial to Congress, on the . . . northern boundary of Missouri. 49609

Memorial . . . [to Congress] on the subject of "floating mercantile schools." 25051

Memorial to Congress, on the subject of seamen and marine disasters. 6583

Memorial to Congress on the Texas election frauds. 29996

Memorial to Congress on utilizing rail road capital. 80446

Memorial to Congress . . . praying for the gradual abolition of slavery. 20314, (81761)

Memorial to . . . Congress . . . regarding the abolition of the Presidency. 47720

Memorial to Congress, respecting the illegal conduct of General Wilkinson. (53321†), 104030

Memorial to Congress "setting forth the evils of the existing tariff." 39753, 92843

Memorial to Congress upon the subject of a national armory. 968

Memorial to Governor Clinton. 98472

Memorial, to justify Peter Landai's conduct during the late war. 38827-38828

Memorial to . . . Lord John Russell. (4420), (35060)

Memorial to Peter Smith Byers. 26176

Memorial . . . to show the present rate of duties. (53588)

Memorial to Sir Robert Peel. 37716

Memorial . . . to the citizens of Louisiana. 42255

Memorial to the Commercial Convention of Detroit. 8850

Memorial to the Commissioners of the Albany Basin. 47717

Memorial . . . to the Congress . . . complaining of the action of the Board of Naval Officers. (40766)

Memorial to the Congress . . . concerning several great inventions. 5035

Memorial to the Congress of the United States, adopted by a meeting of the citizens of Windsor County, Vt. 104769

Memorial to the Congress of the United States for a general bankrupt law. 47719

Memorial to the Congress of the United States of the Executive Committee of the Convention held at Chicago, July 5, 1847. 12632

Memorial to the Congress of the United States, on behalf of the sufferers from the bombardment and destruction of Grey-Town. 28799

Memorial to the Congress of the United States, on the subject of restraining the increase of slavery in new states. (6527), 82014, 102319

Memorial to the Congress of the United States, relative to revolutionary events. 3196, 97921

Memorial to the Congress of the U. States, with the documents accompanying the same. 9147

Memorial to the Congress . . . praying repeal or modification of the act 30th January, 1779. (28519)

Memorial . . . to the Councils of . . . Philadelphia. 60278

Memorial to the Councils of the city of Philadelphia. 55724

Memorial to the fifteenth General Assembly of Missouri. 49592

Memorial to the General Assembly of Maryland, by James M'Evoy. 45257

Memorial to the General Assembly of Maryland. [By Theodric Bland.] 5862, (45103)

Memorial to the General Assembly of Maryland on behalf of the Baltimore and Susquehanna Rail Road. (45258)

Memorial to the General Assembly of Rhode Island. (52642)

Memorial to the General Assembly, to be holden in East Grenwich. 70600

Memorial to the General Convention of the Protestant Episcopal Church. (52272)

Memorial to the government of the United States, from the citizens of Chicago, Ill. 12658, (47721)

Memorial to the government of the United States from the citizens of Pittsburgh. 63119

Memorial to the Governor and Legislature of New-York. 15683, 47722

[Memorial] to the Honorable Cotton Supply Association. (21478)

Memorial to the Hon. Secretary of War. (20512)

Memorial . . . to the Honourable Senate and House of Representatives of the United States, January 1, 1809. (12487)

Memorial. To the Honorable the Congress of the United States of America. 97921

Memorial . . . to the Honorable the General Assembly in behalf of the insane of Maryland. (20336A)

Memorial. To the Honourable the House of Representatives of the commonwealth of Massachusetts. 88994

Memorial to the Honorable the Legislature of the State of New-York. (20336A)

Memorial. To the Honorable the Legislature of the State of New York, in Senate and Assembly convened. 102952

Memorial to the Honorable the Senate and House of Representatives in Congress assembled. 35806

Memorial to the Honorable the Senate and House of Representatives of the Commonwealth of Massachusetts. 85412

Memorial to the Honorable the Senate and House of Representatives of the United States, in Congress assembled. 95464

Memorial. To the Honorable the Senate and House of Representatives of the United States, in Congress Assembled. 86325

Memorial to the inhabitants of the British American colonies. (15528), 15544

Memorial to the King. 72524

Memorial to the Legislature. 65796

Memorial . . . to the Legislature . . . against . . . an act. 8303

Memorial . . . to the Legislature and the school authorities. 54688, 1st note after 94139

Memorial . . . to the Legislature [by Resselaer Polytechnic Institute.] 69641

Memorial to the . . . Legislature . . . for founding a state woman's hospital. 53978

Memorial to the Legislature . . . from citizens of New York. 54386

Memorial to the Legislature, Jan. 1, 1858. 85956

Memorial . . . to the Legislature, March 6th, 1841. 54723

Memorial to the Legislature of Alabama. 87328

Memorial to the Legislature of Kentucky. 90646

Memorial to the Legislature of Maryland. 50841

Memorial to the Legislature of Massachusetts. 18516

Memorial to the Legislature of Massachusetts, by citizens of Boston and vicinity. 23449, 39754

Memorial to the Legislature of Massachusetts. [By Dorothea Dix.] (20336A)

Memorial to the [Legislature] of Massachusetts [By Hermann Haupt.] 30859

Memorial. To the Legislature of Massachusett [relative to a charge delivered to the Grand Jury.] 2396

Memorial to the Legislature of Massachusetts, . . . reprinted from Barnard's American journal of education. 11117

Memorial to the Legislature of Massachusetts, Sept. 13, 1859. (58703)

Memorial, to the Legislature of New York. [By the Herkimer Manufacturing and Hydraulic Company.] (31493)

Memorial to the Legislature of New York. [By the International Bridge Company.] 34922

Memorial to the Legislature of New York, on the adjustment of the demands of the state. 59576

Memorial to the Legislature of . . . Pennsylvania, against the navy yard. 61833

Memorial [to the Legislature of Pennsylvania for a geological survey of the state.] 8675

Memorial to the Legislature of Pennsylvania, for the incorporation of La Fayette College, at Easton. 60189

Memorial to the Legislature of Rhode-Island. 47726

Memorial to the Legislature of the state of Alabama. 94813

Memorial to the Legislature of the state of New-York, by the Society for the Reformation of Juvenile Delinquents. 85957

Memorial to the Legislature of the state of New York, concerning the ferries between New York and Long Island. 8291

Memorial to the Legislature of the state of New York upon the effects of the passage of the trade of the western states. 47724

Memorial to the Legislature of the state of New York upon the present state of the canals. (47725)

Memorial to the Legislature of Vermont, for the repeal of acts. 99197

Memorial to the Legislature respecting a canal on the west side of the Schuylkill. 60243

Memorial to the Massachusetts Constitutional Convention. 39579

Memorial to the Massachusetts Legislature. 3907

Memorial . . . to the Mayor, Aldermen and Commonality. (54732)

Memorial to the Mayor and Commonalty of . . . New York. 54387

Memorial to the . . . New York & Erie Railroad Company. (54729)

Memorial to the President and Congress of the United States. 12635

Memorial, . . . to the President, Senate, and House of Representatives. (49541)

Memorial to the Queen. 47727

Memorial to the Right Honourable the Board of Trade. 5926, 102854

Memorial. To the Senate and House of Representatives of . . . Pennsylvania. 61834

Memorial to the . . . Senate and House of Representatives of the United States . . . . By a company of Swiss settlers. 47723

Memorial to the Senate and House of Representatives of the United States of America, 1852. 2318

Memorial to the Senate and House of Representatives, or the history of the Stafford projectiles. 90080

Memorial to the Senate . . . from the Tobacco Cutter's Association. 47728

Memorial to the Senate of Georgia relative to the Cherokee-Indians. 10265

Memorial to the sovereigns of Europe. (35987)

Memorial . . . to the Supervisors. 51610

Memorial . . . to the Trustees . . . [of the University of Pennsylvania.] 60758

Memorial to the twenty-seventh Congress. 55767

Memorial to the United States' Congress. 5036

Memorial to the United States Senate. [sic] and House of Representatives. 47729

Memorial to the Very Reverend the Synod of the Presbyterian Church of Nova Scotia. 26826

Memorial to . . . William Wyndham Grenville. 47258

Memorial tribute, by Rev. Lyman Whiting. 18098, 85409

Memorial. Twenty-fifth anniversary of the Mt. Holyoke Female Seminary. 51159

Memorial ultramarino e maritimo. 47730

Memorial upon the free admission of foreign copper ores. 47731, 85541

Memorial . . . upon the subject of the land acquired by treaty. 49517

Memorial verses, by William Ellery Channing. 76249

Memorial volume. 1837-1871. 65204

Memorial volume of sermons. (54840)

Memorial volume of the Evang. Luthern Church of the Holy Trinity. 77477

Memorial volume of the first fifty years of the A. B. C. F. M. 47732

Memorial volume of the Popham Celebration. 2953, 64061

Memorial volume to commemorate the twenty-fifth anniversary of the installation of Nehemiah Adams. 6641

Memorial, vouchers and statement. 99134

Memorial; with circular and questions of the Episcopal Commission. 47700, 70086

Memorial with the resolutions adopted at the Anti-tariff Meeting. (47733)

Memorial: written by friends of the late Mrs. Osgood. 31643, 91035

Memorial written on several occasions. 47747

Memorial y carta del Padre Magino Sola de la Compania de Iesus. 85223

Memorial y carta en que el Padre Alonso de Valle. (57971)-57974, 98376

Memorial y defensoria por Don. Fr. Bernardino de Cardenas. 10805

Memorial y defensorio al Rey Nvestro Senor. 76026

Memorial y defensorio al Rey N. S. por el credito, &c. 10803

Memorial, y noticias sacras del imperio de las Indias Occidentales. 20134

Memorial, y noticias sacras, y reales del imperio de las Indias Occidentales. 10058

Memorial y ordenanzas de D. Francisco de Toledo. 69239

Memorial y relacion verdadera para el Rey N. S. 10807

Memorial, y resvmen breve de noticias de las Indias Occidentales. 10059

Memoriale di Diego Colombo. 65990

Memoriale, presentado dal Generale dei Gesuiti. 63905

Memoriales de P. Julian de Pedraca. 76026

Memoriales del P. Julian de Pedraza. 10803

Memoriales informativos. 81095

Memoriales presentados a la Magestad Catholica. 87235

Memorialis libellus Serenissimo Hispaniarum Regi oblatus. 68346

Memorialists reply. 47734

Memorialls of Margaret de Valoys. 44536

Memorials and documents in the case of Col. Hugh Hughes. 33585

Memorials and petitions of . . . citizens. (45082)

Memorials and petitions of the Board of Trustees of Jefferson College. 69844

Memorials and petitions of the President and Directors of the Chespeake and Delaware Canal Company. 12495

Memorials and resolutions adopted by the Chamber [of Commerce of San Francisco.] 76037

Memorials and resolutions of sundry merchants. 47735

Memorials: being a genealogical, biographical and historical account. 51230

Memorials. By Rev. Samuel Kissam. 38016

Memorials concerning Anna M. Thorne and Sarah M. Upton. 95624

Memorials concerning deceased Friends. (53667)

Memorials concerning deceased Friends: being a selection from the records of the Yearly Meeting for Pennsylvania, &c. 47736

Memorials concerning deceased Friends, members of the Yearly Meeting of Philadelphia. (47737)

Memorials concerning St. Lucia. (774), note after (47740), note after 96403

Memorials concerning several Friends, and others, deceased. 86062

Memorials concerning several ministers, and others, deceased. 47738

Memorials, &c., to the Commander-in-Chief. (35978)

Memorials from the city of New York. 53956

Memorials from the county of Allegany. 53979, note after 90676

Memorials of a birthday breakfast. 19638

Memorials of a century. 36041

Memorials of a number of citizens of . . . Pennsylvania. 60029

Memorials of Benjamin P. Johnson and Herman Ten Eyck John Foster. 36185

Memorials of Captain Charles Stewart and other officers. 44138

Memorials of Captain Obadiah Conger. 15461

Memorials of Christ Church, Philadelphia. 20638

Memorials of citizens of Massachusetts, purchasers under the Georgia Company, &c. 27092, 69728

Memorials of Col. J. Howard Kitching. 50549

Memorials of Columbus; or a collection of authentic documents. 14666

Memorials of Columbus, read to the Maryland Historical Society. 20511, (45211A)

Memorials of deceased Friends, of New-England Yearly Meeting. 47739, 52754

Memorials of early piety. 46410

Memorials of Elder John White. 37277

Memorials of Franklin Whitall Smith. 82696

Memorials of George Fisher. 24460

Memorials of George Washington and Benjamin Franklin. 86264

Memorials of John B. Morris, . . . and others. 45079

Memorials of John Bartram and Humphrey Marshall. 18597, (20167), 4th note after 96966

Memorials of John Bowen. 7062

Memorials of John Pitkin Norton. 55906

Memorials of Margaret Elizabeth. (47740)

Memorials of Methodism. 91479

Memorials of Mrs. Henrietta A. L. Hamlin. (39362)

Memorials of Mrs. John V. L. Pruyn. 66415, 89739

Memorials of Morgan L. Smith. 83636

Memorials of North Carolina. (36580)

Memorials of Peter Smith. 83712

Memorials of prison life. 24381

Memorials of Rebecca Jones. 36597

[Memorials of] T. Bigelow Lawrence. 39382

Memorials of the Association of Jamaica Proprietors. (35621)

Memorials of the Chaunceys. (25327)

Memorials of the citizens of Boston to the Legislature. 6528

Memorials of the citizens of Louisiana. 42263

Memorials of the citizens of the state of New York. 22747

Memorials of the dead in Boston. 7839

Memorials of the descendants of William Shattuck. 79882

Memorials of the discovery and early settlement of the Bermudas. 83631

Memorials of the early progress of Methodism in the eastern states. 91478

Memorials of the English affairs. 59715, note after 103670

Memorials of the English and French Commissaries concerning St. Lucia. (47547), 47741, note after 96403

Memorials of the English and French Commissaries concerning the limits of Nova Scotia or Acadia. (47547), 47742, note after 96403

Memorials of the English Commissaries. (47547), (56129), note after 96403

Memorials of the families of Mr. James Thompson and of Dea. Augustus Thompson (32816), note after 95556

Memorials of the First Church in Dorcester. 30516

Memorials of the Friends of African Colonization. 37404

Memorials of the graduates at Harvard University. (23833)

Memorials of the graduates of Harvard University. 30751

Memorials of the introduction of Methodism into the eastern states. 91478-91479

Memorials of the late civil service rifle-corps 81349

Memorials of the Moravian Church. 50523, 68992

Memorials of the professional life and times of Sir William Penn. 59671

Memorials of the proprietors of the Upper Locks and Canal on Connecticut River. 15869

Memorials of the public life and character of the Right Hon. James Oswald. 57829

Memorials of the Quebec Conference. 40232

Memorials of the Rev. Joseph Sumner. 93708

Memorials of the sea. 78175-78178

Memorials of the Seneca Indians and others. (46067)

Memorials of the Society of the Cincinnati of Massachusetts. 86111

Memorials of the United Illinois and Ouabache Land Companies. 84577-84578, 2d-3d notes after 97876

Memorials of [Wesleyan] missionary life in Nova Scotia. 13013

Memorials of William Smith Shaw. (24036)

Memorials on several occasions. 47743

Memorials on the death of George Washington. 33154

Memorials praying a repeal of suspension of the law. 10864, 1st note after (60039)

Memorials presented by the Deputies of the Council of Trade. 47744

Memorials presented to the Congress of the United States of America. 47745

Memorials, presented to the Legislature. 47746, 54388

Memorials relating to the Lane, Reyner and Whippe families. 38851

Memorials relative to the navigation of the Ohio River. 57066

Memorials to Congress . . . 1861-2. 49162

Memorials to Congress, &c. 12443

Memorials to the Governor and Legislature of New York. 15683

Memorials to the King, the Lords of the Treasury, &c. 85243

Memorials to the Lords of the Treasury. (4923)

Memorias agustas al Rey Fernando el Catholico. 75892

Memorias antiguas historiales del Peru. (50125)

Memorias con documentos justificativos. (22843)

Memorias contemporaneas. 39089

Memorias criticas sobre los principales sucesos. 20662

Memorias da Academia Real das Sciencias de Lisboa. 47748

Memorias de campanha do Senor D. Pedro d'Alcantara. 17956

Memorias da viagem de Suas Magestades Imperiaes a provincia da Bahia. 88710

Memorias da viagem de Suas Magestades Imperiaes a provincia de Penrambuco. 88711

Memorias de Don M. Godoy. 27667

Memorias de el siervo de Dios Gregorio Lopez. 86430

Memorias de la Academia de la Historia, Madrid. (10814)

Memorias de la clase de derecho patrio del Real y Conciliar Colegio Seminario de la Habana. 29441

Memorias de la colonia Francesa de Santo Domingo. 26339

Memorias de la institucion agronoma de la Habana. 74928

(Memorias de la intervencion.) 46202

Memorias de la Junta Inspectora de Instruccion Primaria. 47749

Memorias de la portentosa imagen de Ntra. Sra. de Xuquila. 74049

Memorias de la portentosa imagen de Nuestra Senora de Xuquila. 74050

Memorias de la Primera Secretaria de Estado y del Despacho. 48561

Memorias de la Real Academia de la Historia. 47750

Memorias de la Real Academia Medica de Madrid. 73992

Memorias de la Real Sociedad Economica de la Habana. 29442-29443, 85746

Memorias de la Real Sociedad Patriotica de la Habana. 29443, 85746

Memorias de la Real Sociedad Patriotica de la Habana, 1793. Escritas por el Dr. D. Felix Veranes. 98921

Memorias de la revolucion de Megico. (72204)

Memorias de la Seccion de Historia de la Real Sociedad Patriotica de la Habana. 85747

Memorias de la Sociedad Economica de Amantes de Guatemala. 85752

Memorias de la Sociedad Economica de Amigos del Pais. 85741

Memorias de la Sociedad Patriotica desde 1835-1855. 17750

Memorias de las operaciones que han tenido la Oficina de Desamortizacion del Distrito de Mexico. (48562)

Memorias de litteratura Portugueza. (47751)

Memorias de lo acontecido en Cordova. 35241

Memorias de Lord Cochrane. 61117

Memorias de Lord Cochrane, Conde de Dundonald. 14079

Memorias de los diversos departamentos de la administracion. (47752)

Memorias de los Vireyes que han gobernado el Peru. 26119

Memorias de Puerto-Rico. 98367

Memorias de Sor Mariana fundadora y abasida del Monasterio de Guadalupe. 44557

Memorias de um sargento de milicias. 47753

Memorias de un guerillero. 46201

Memorias de un loco. 24153

Memoriasde un matancero. (752)

Memorias de un oficial de la Legion Britanica. 10193, note before 94254, note after 98870

Memorias de un oficial de marina Ingles al servicio de Chile. note after 98870

Memorias de un viajero. (34684)

Memorias de Urquinaona. (69223), 98148

Memorias del fisico aeronauta. 95306

Memorias del General Miller. 49029

Memorias del Ministerio de Relaciones Exteriores del Brasil. 39523, note after 93820

Memorias diarias de la gverra del Brasil. 14153

Memorias diarias de la guerra del Brazil. 676

Memorias do Instituto da Ordem dos Advogados Brasileiros. 47754

Memorias do Instituto Historico e Geographico Brasileiro. 7602, 47755

Memorias do Marquez de Sancta-Cruz. 78953

Memorias edificantes sobre la vida religiosa del P. Carlos Odescalchi. 56719

Memorias funebres, o exequias de el Illust. Senor Dr. D. Manuel Antonio Roxo, Rio, y Vieyra. 72809, 73740

Memorias funebres y exequias del Illmo. Sr. D. Manuel Rojo. 72809, 73740

Memorias historicas da Capitania do Rio de Janeiro. 63186

Memorias historicas da provincia de Pernambuco. 26489

Memorias historica de la Congregacion de el Oratorio de la Ciudad de Mexico. 18778

Memorias historicas dc la Congregacion de el Oratorio fundada en Mexico. 48563

Memorias historicas de la ultima guerra. 13837

Memorias historicas do Rio de Janeiro. 2546

Memorias historicas e politicas da provincia da Bahia. 89, (11707)

Memorias historicas sobre la legislacion y gobierno del comercio delos Espanoles. 1724, 47756

Memorias historico-physicas critico-apologeticas de la America-Meridional. 41670

Memorias historico-politicas. 29349

Memorias historico-politicas de Don Vicente Pazos. 59342

Memorias historico-politicas de Jeneral Joaquin Posada Gutierrez. 64443

Memorias honorificas funebres. 36091

Memorias, negociaciones y documentos. (67644)

Memorias o apuntaciones sobre el origen de la poblacion de America. 87194

Memorias offerecidas a nacao Brasileira. 81081

Memorias para a historia da Capitania de S. Vicente. 26724, 43753, (47757)

Memorias para a historia do reino do Brasil. (76328)

Memorias para la historia de la campania Nacional. (60906)

Memorias para la historia de la guerra de Tejas. 24324

Memorias para la historia de la Nueva Grenada. 63378

Memorias para la historia de la revolucion de Centro-America. 45020, 50228, 59179

Memorias para la historia de la revolucion de Nicaragua. (60906)

Memorias para la historia del antiguo reyno de Guatemala. 59567

Memorias para la historia Megicana. (48564)

Memorias para servir a la historia de la literatura de Neuva Espana. 86383

Memory of the just: a sermon delivered on the occasion of the death of John Nitchie. 103388

Memory of the late James Grahame. 67221

Memory of Washington. 102032

Memory of Washington. A sermon preached in the First Congregational Church, Litchfield, Conn. 70935

Memory of Washington: an oration, by the Rev. Noah Hunt Schenck. 77570

Memory of Washington. An address before the members of St. John's Lodge. 14333

Memory of Washington: comprising a sketch of his life and character. 101841, 101852

Memory of Washington; with biographical sketches of his mother and wife. 31608

Memory's milestones. 83702

Memory's tribute to the life, character, and work of the Rev. T. H. Stockton. 13243

Memphis, Tenn. 47786-47787

Memphis, Tenn. Chamber of Commerce. 47771, (47773), 47784

Memphis, Tenn. Chamber of Commerce. Secretary. (47773) see also Toof, Jonathan S.

Memphis, Tenn. Chamber of Commerce and Merchants' Exchange. see Memphis, Tenn. Chamber of Commerce.

Memphis, Tenn. City Schools. (47772)

Memphis, Tenn. Commerical Convention, 1869. see Commercial Convention, Memphis, Tenn., 1869.

Memphis, Tenn. Convention in Relation to the Pacific Railroad, 1849. see Convention in Relation to the Pacific Railroad, Memphis, Tenn., 1849.

Memphis, Tenn. Southern and Western Commercial Convention, 1853. see Southern and Western Commercial Convention, Memphis, Tenn., 1853.

Memphis, Tenn. Southern Pacific Railroad Company Stockholders Convention, 1858. see Southern Pacific Railroad Company (Texas) Stockholders Convention, Memphis, Tenn., 1858.

Memphis, Tenn. Southwestern Convention, 1845. see Southwestern Convention, Memphis, Tenn., 1845.

Memphis almanac for 1856. 47776

Memphis and Charleston Railroad Company. Directors. 47777

Memphis and Ohio Railroad Company. (47778)

Memphis directory, for 1865. 47774

Memphis, El Paso and Pacific Railroad Company. petitioners 47679

Memphis, El Paso and Pacific Railroad. 85447

Memphis, Helena and St. Louis Levee Railroad. 47779

Memphis; her great men. 8335

Memphis Medical College. 47780-(47781)

Memphis medical recorder. (47781)

Memphis memorial. 28566

Memphis riots. 47782

Men and events, at home and abroad. 30018

Men and events. By "Sentinel." 6129

Men and government, the laws and customs of Cuba. 17816, 62423

Men and manners, from 1774 to 1809. 104569

Men and manners in America. 30034-30035, 55863

Men and mysteries of Wall Street. 47294

Men and things I have seen. (27919), 85431

Men and things in America. 4447, 95454

Men and things; or short essays on various subjects. 2830

Men and times of the revolution. 102133

Men and women medical students. 60244

Men and subject to errors. 94093

Men furnished and public funds expended. 54389

Men of color to arms! 47788

Men of history. 47789

Men of Manhattan. 89496

Men of mark. 83608

Men of old. 47790

Men of our day. 8159

Men of the age. 17542

Men of the olden time. 82389

Men of the time: being biographies. (47792), 99434

Men of the time: being biographies of Generals Halleck, [and others.] (47792), 99434

Men of the time: biographies of Generals Butler [and others.] (47792), 99434

Men of the time: biographies of Generals Hooker [and others.] (47792), 99434

Men of the time in 1852. (47791)

Men of Vermont. 83679

Men offering violence to their knowledge. (18468)

Men to make a state. 20391

Men who advertise. (47793), 73591

Men who have risen. 47794

Men who made Texas free. 85231

Mena, Pedro de. ed. 86229

Mena, Pedro Nolasco. 97672

Menachem. 46411

Menamin, R. S. ed. (65690)

Menana. 37319

Menard, J. Willis. (47795)

Menard, Pierre. 96657-96658 see also U. S. Commissioners to the Potawatomi Indians. U. S. Commissioners to the Winnebago Indians. U. S. Commissioners to the Winnebago Tribe and the United Tribes of Potawatomi, Chippewa, and Ottowa Indians.

Menard, Theophile. 47796

Menasseh Ben Israel. see Manasseh ben Joseph ben Israel, 1604-1657.

Mencke, J. B. 47797

Mendana, Alvarez de. (72372)

Mendell, Miss -------. 47798, 55958

Mendelssohn Musical Institute, Pittsfield, Mass. (63151)

Mendenhall, Edward. 47800

Mendenhall, Thomas. 47799

Mendenhall, William. 47800

Mendes, Luis Antonio de Oliveira. 47802

Mendes, Ramon Ignacio. see Mendez, Ramon Ignacio, Abp., d. 1839.

Mendez, ------ de la Cruz. see De la Cruz Mendez, --------.

Mendez, Andres. 47805

Mendez, Jose Antonio. (48665), 98823, 1st note after 99783

Mendez, Juan Francisco. 47806

Mendez, Juan de Dios. (47807)

Mendez, L. 47808

Mendez, Ramon Ignacio, Abp., d. 1839. 40704, 47803, 67662, 98869, 2d note after 98873, 98874, 98881 see also Caracas (Archdiocese) Archbishop (Mendez)

Mendez de Almeida, Candido. 47801

Mendez Pinto, Fernan. see Pinto, Fernan Mendez.

Mendez y Labarta, Ramon Ignacio. see Mendez, Ramon Ignacio, Abp., d. 1839.

MENDEZ

Mendez y Lachica, Tomas de. (47809)
Mendibil, Pablo de. 47810
Mendicta, Maximo. plaintiff 47811
Mendieta, Alphonsum von. see Mendieta, Alphonso de.
Mendieta, Alphonso de. 86229
Mendieta, Geronomi de. 47812
Mendinilla, ------- Somano y. see Somano y Mendilla, -------.
Mendive y Daumy, Rafael Maria, 1821-1886. ed. 47813, 70306-70307
Mendivelzua, Juan de Dios. defendant 93402 see also Caracas. Administracion General de Tabaco. Interventor.
Mendivil, Jose Maria Tornel y. see Tornel y Mendivel, Jose Maria.
Mendizabal, Gregorius Lopez a. see Lopez a Mendizabal, Gregorius.
Mendizabal, Horacio. 47814
Mendizabal, L. de. 47815, 86368, 98715
Mendizabal, Pedro Josef de. (47816)
Mendizbal, L. de. see Mendizabal, L. de.
Mendo, Andres. 47817
Mendo, Herbert. (47818)
Mendoca, Juan Goncalez de. see Gonzalez de Mendoza, Juan, Abp., 1571-1639.
Mendoca, Vicente de Zaldivar y. see Zaldivar y Mendoca, Vicente de.
Mendoca Catano y Aragon, Luis de. (47831)
Mendoca Corte Real, Diogo de, 1658-1736. 47824-47825, 102441, 102889A see also Portugal. Legation. Netherlands.
Mendoca Corte Real, Diogo de, 1658-1736. petitioner 102441, 102889A see also Portugal. Legation. Netherlands. petitioner
Mendoca Furtado, Tristao de. 23509, 96517-96519, 102891 see also Portugal. Legation. Netherlands.
Mendoca, Lorenco de. (47830)
Mendon, Dan. pseud. Lo! here and lo! there. 79713
Mendon, Mass. Fraternal Communion. see Fraternal Communion, Mendon, Mass.
Mendon, Mass. Society for Detecting Horse Thieves. see Society for Detecting Horse Thieves in the Towns of Mendon, Bellingham and Milford.
Mendon, Mass. Two Hundredth Anniversary Commemoration, 1868. 47819, note after 90463
Mendoca, Antonio Pedro Lopes de. 47822
Mendonca, Francisco Maria de Souza Furtado de. see Souza Furtado de Mendonca, Francisco Maria de.
Mendonca, Hypolito Jose de Costa Pereira Furtado de. see Costa Pereira Furtado de Mendonca, Hypolito Jose da.
Mendonca, Joao Jacyntho de. (76903) see also Sao Paulo (Brazilian Province) Presidente (Mendonca)
Mendonza, Al. de. 47823
Mendosa Jardis, Tristan de. 47832
Mendosse Jardis, Tristan de. see Mendosa Jardis, Tristan de.
Mendoz, Lopez de. 24894, note after 94854, 94856
Mendoza, ------, Bp., fl. 1847. 47845 see also Cuzco (Diocese) Bishop (Mendoza)
Mendoza, Antonio de, Conde de Tendilla. 47833, 67740, 84379, 94852, 94854 see also Mexico (Viceroyalty) Virrey, 1535-1550 (Mendoza)
Mendoza, Balthazar de Zuniga Guzman Sotomayor y. see Zuniga Guzman Soto-

mayor y Mendoza, Baltazar de, Marques de Valero.
Mendoza, Daniel Perez. 47834
Mendoza, Diego de. 47835
Mendoza, Domingo Joseph de Arquellada. tr. 49889
Mendoza, Eufemico. 47836
Mendoza, Fadrique de Toledo Osorio y. see Toledo Osorio y Mendoza, Fadrique de.
Mendoza, Garcia Hurtado de. 47837
Mendoza, Javier de. 47838
Mendoza, Joannis de Palafox y. see Palafox y Mendoza, Juan de, Abp., 1600-1659.
Mendoza, Juan de. defendant 44289, 74862
Mendoza, Juan de, Abp. 75884 see also Mexico (Archdiocese) Archbishop (Mendoza)
Mendoza, Juan de, fl. 1672-1684. (47839)-47840
Mendoza, Juan de, fl. 1776. 47841
Mendoza, Juan de Palafox y. see Palafox y Mendoza, Juan de, Abp., 1600-1659.
Mendoza, Juan Gonzalez de. see Gonzalez de Mendoza, Juan Abp., 1571-1639.
Mendoza, Juan Lopez de. petitioner 93317
Mendoza, Juan Palafox y. see Palafox y Mendoza, Juan de, Abp. 1600-1659.
Mendoza, Juan Suarez de. see Suarez de Mendoza, Juan.
Mendoza, Lorenco Hurtado de. (47844)
Mendoza, Luis Torres de. see Torres de Mendoza, Luis.
Mendoza, Manuel Ignacio de Soria y. see Soria y Mendoza, Manuel Ignacio de.
Mendoza, Pedro Salazar de. see Salazar de Mendoza, Pedro.
Mendoza Ayala, Juan de. (47842)-47843
Mendoza Capellan, Lorenzo de. see Capellan, Lorenzo de Mendoza.
Mendoza y Luna, Juan de, Marques de Montesclaros. (41092), 98332 see also Peru (Viceroyalty) Virrey, 1607-1615 (Mendoza y Luna)
Mendozza, Antonio di. see Mendoza, Antonio de.
Mendozza, Giouanni Gonzalez di. see Gonzalez de Mendoza, Juan, Abp., 1571-1639.
Mendrano, ------- Ayala i. see Ayala i Mendrano, -------.
Menendez, Baldomero. 47846-(47847)
Menendez de San Pedro, Diego Antonio. 47847-47849
Meneses, Duart de. 66686
Meneses, F. de. note after 27585, 40960, note after 47850
Meneses, Francisco Tello de. see Tello de Meneses, Francisco.
Meneses, Francisco Xavier de, Conde de la Erizeira. (64154)
Meneses Bracamonte, Bernardino de. 4951, 47850
Meneses y Padilla, Juan de, Marques de Marianela. defendant 51043 see also Venezuela (Spanish Colony) Gobernador, 1624-1630 (Meneses y Padilla) defendant
Menesis y Arce, Gonzales Andres. (1897), 73183
Menesses, Joanne. ed. 61074
Menet, Albert. 33494
Meneville, F. E. Guerin. see Guerin-Meneville F. E.
Menezes, ------- Paula. see Paula Menezes, -------.
Menezes, Antonio Telles da Silva Caminha e. see Telles da Silva Caminha e Menezes, Antonio, Marques de Resende, 1790-1875.

1664

Mercado, -------. 29276
Mercador de Feiras. (36942)
Mercantile advertiser. 84241
Mercantile agency and United States business directory. 47879
Mercantile agency manual for 1871. 21225
Mercantile Association of Chicago. see Chicago Mercantile Association.
Mercantile Club, Philadelphia. 61835
Mercantile Division, No. 131. see Sons of Temperance of North America. Pennsylvania. Mercantile Division, No. 131.
Mercantile exchange tables, and pocket book companion. (42767)
Mercantile honor and moral honesty. 19897
Mercantile influence weighed. 13879, 95799
Mercantile journal (Boston) 40646
Mercantile journal (New York) see New York mercantile journal.
Mercantile law of Great Britain. 40753
Mercantile laws of the state of New York. 53772
Mercantile Library, Boston. see Boston Mercantile Library.
Mercantile Library, Louisville. see Louisville Mercantile Library.
Mercantile Library, Portsmouth, N. H. see Portsmouth Mercantile Library.
Mercantile Library . . . accession list. 54391
Mercantile Library Association, Boston. see Boston. Mercantile Library Association.
Mercantile Library Association, Brooklyn. see Brooklyn Library.
Mercantile Library Association, Louisville, Ky. see Louisville, Ky. Mercantile Library Association.
Mercantile Library Association, New York. see New York (City) Mercantile Library Association.
Mercantile Library Association, St. Louis. see St. Louis Mercantile Library Association.
Mercantile Library Association, St. Paul, Minn. see St. Paul Mercantile Library Association, St. Paul, Minn.
Mercantile Library Association of Baltimore. 3024
Mercantile Library Association of Baltimore. Board of Directors. (3048)
Mercantile Library Association of Baltimore. Charter. 3024
Mercantile Library Association of Montreal. 50240
Mercantile Library Association of New Orleans. 53335
Mercantile Library Association of San Francisco. 76058, (76095)
Mercantile Library Association of San Francisco. Committee to Consider and Report a Plan for the Erection of an Edifice for the Uses of This Association. 76060
Mercantile Library Association of San Francisco, Library. 76057, (76095)
Mercantile Library Association of San Francisco. President. 76059
Mercantile Library Association of the city of Brooklyn. The first annual report of the Board of Directors. (8304)
Mercantile Library Association. Report of the Committee Appointed to Consider and Report a Plan. 76060
Mercantile Library Company of Philadelphia. see Philadelphia. Mercantile Library Company.

Mercantile Library Hall Company, St. Louis. see St. Louis Mercantile Library Association.
Mercantile Library of San Francisco. see Mercantile Library Association of San Francisco. Library.
Mercantile library reporter. (47880)
Mercantile man. pseud. American memoranda see Lumsden, James.
Mercantile memorials. 10889
Mercantile record of Chicago. (12633)
Mercantile register, containing a list. 63120
Mercantile register, or business man's guide. 61837
Mercata[n]te. pseud. Discorso. 67736
Mercator. pseud. see Smith, Samuel, 1836-1906.
Mercator. pseud. Communication of "Mercator." 20697
Mercator. pseud. Communications. 47890
Mercator. pseud. Financial problem. 47891
Mercator. pseud. Letters on the abolition of slavery. 47892, 95356
Mercator. pseud. Letters on the abolition of the slave trade. 40257
Mercator. pseud. Several new, pressing and weighty considerations. 47893
Mercator. pseud. Third letter on the abolition of the slave-trade. 95356
Mercator, Gerardus, 1512-1594. 5714, 25964-25956, 32750, 35773, (47881)-47889, 66490-66491, 66494, 66497-66498, 67432, 82816, 82823, 82829
Mercator, Rumoldus. cartographer 66492-66493
Mercator's atlas. 32750, 47885, 82823, 82829
Merced, Orden de la. see Mercedarians.
Mercedarians. 62601, 74799, 98897-98898
Mercedarians. Mexico. 47894
Mercedes de Castile. 16480
Mercedes of Castile. 16424, 16476
Mercedes of Castille; or, the voyage to Cathay. 16477
Mercedes; or, the days of Columbus. 16478
Mercedes: or, the outlaw's child. 47895
Mercein, T. F. Randolph. (47896)
Mercein, Thomas R. 47897, 54093
Mercein. firm publishers 54459
Mercein's directory for 1820-21. 54459
Mercer. pseud. Letter concerning the Ten Pound Court. see Cheetham, James.
Mercer, A. S. 47899
Mercer, Alexander G. (47898)
Mercer, Charles Fenton, 1778-1858. 45423, 47900-(47902), 47905
Mercer, John. 100386-100387, 100390
Mercer, John, 1772-1817. 47903
Mercer, John Francis. 47904, 92841
Mercer, Nathan. 47906
Mercer, Silas. 47907
Mercer University, Macon, Ga. 47908
Mercersburg, Pa. Marshall College. see Marshall College, Mercersburg, Pa.
Mercersburgh review. 47909
Merchado, Luigi Gonzales de. see Gonzales de Merchado, Luigi.
Merchandise of a people holiness to the Lord. (14500)
Merchant, Charles. alias see White, John Ducan. defendant
Merchant. pseud. Attempt to strip Negro emancipation. 2324, 81897
Merchant. pseud. Consolatory thoughts on American independence. see Tod, Thomas.

Merchant. pseud. Dialogue between a merchant and a planter. 19925
Merchant. pseud. Evil effects of a high tariff. 23308
Merchant. pseud. Free and impartial remarks. 25703
Merchant. pseud. Free trade and the American system. 25724, 87830
Merchant. pseud. Interesting additions. 26827, note after 96426
Merchant. pseud. Letter from a merchant. 40308
Merchant. pseud. Letter to certain bank directors. 40432, 61778
Merchant. pseud. Observations on the crisis. 56515
Merchant. pseud. Observations on the pending question. see Koster, T.
Merchant. pseud. Remarks upon the Bank of the United States. see Henshaw, David.
Merchant. pseud. Some considerations upon financial policy. 86629
Merchant. pseud. Times. 95842
Merchant. pseud. Two letters to the Marquis of Londonderry. 97571
Merchant. pseud. View of the relative position. see Bird, H. M.
Merchant. 74334
Merchant and citizen of London. pseud. Britain's mistakes in the commencement and conduct of the present war. (8065)
Merchant and citizen of London. pseud. Supplement to Britain's mistakes. 93798-93799
Merchant at Jamaica. pseud. Letter. 40304
Merchant enterprise. 26265
Merchant in Amsterdam. pseud. Letter. 40305
Merchant in Boston. pseud. Good of the community impartially considered. see True friend to liberty. pseud.
Merchant in Boston. pseud. Some observations on the scheme projected. see Douglass, William.
Merchant in Halifax. pseud. Letter. 40306
Merchant in London. pseud. Letter from a merchant in London to his nephew in North America. see Tucker, Josiah, 1712-1799.
Merchant in London trading to America. pseud. Reasons for a war against Spain. (68260)
Merchant long resident at Tahiti. pseud. Rovings in the Pacific. 73525
Merchant of America. pseud. Common sense. 14998
Merchant of Amsterdam. pseud. Vindication of the Dutch Westindia trade. 99806
Merchant of Boston. pseud. Currency or money. see Hooper, Samuel.
Merchant of Boston. pseud. Present state of New-England. see S., N. pseud.
Merchant of Boston. pseud. Short inquiry. see Homer, James Lloyd.
Merchant of Bristol. pseud. Dissertation on the present conjuncture. 20283
Merchant of London. pseud. State of the trade. 90634
Merchant of London. pseud. True interest of Great Britain. see Bacon, Anthony. supposed author
Merchant of London trading to America. pseud. Reasons for a war against Spain. (68258)-68259
Merchant of many years' residence in the West Indies. pseud. West-India trade and islands. 14980, 102800

Merchant of Philadelphia. pseud. End of the irrepressible conflict. 22557
Merchant of Philadelphia. pseud. Ides of March. 34180
Merchant of Philadelphia. pseud. Memoirs and auto-biography of some of the wealthy citizens of Philadelphia. 47561, 61813
Merchant of Philadelphia. pseud. Spanish America and the United States. 88941
Merchant of the City of London. pseud. Letter. 40307
Merchant of the old school. pseud. Crisis of the dispute with the United States. (17529), 101267
Merchant of the old school. A tribute to the memory of James Johnson. 41566
Merchant retir'd. pseud. Address to the merchants of Great Britain. 423
Merchant retir'd. pseud. Review of the conduct of the administration. 423
Merchant retired from business. pseud. French encroachments exposed. see Payne, J.
Merchant vessel. 55463
Merchant who has left off trade. pseud. Letter. 40309
Merchants: a . . . lecture. 31755
Merchant's and banker's almanac for 1852. (32698), 47910
Merchant's and banker's register for 1859. (32698), 47911
Merchants' and Clerks' Library Association, New York. 54392
Merchants' and Clerks' Library Association, New York. Charter. 54392
Merchants' & farmers' almanack. 47912
Merchants & farmers calendar . . . 1833. 45844
Merchant's and farmer's calendar, for 1832. 45814
Merchants and Farmers' directory for Maryland. 90587
Merchants' and manufacturers' business register. 47913
Merchants' and manufacturers' magazine. 47914
Merchants and Manufacturers of Boston. Committee. see Boston. Committee of Merchants and Manufacturers.
Merchants and Manufacturers of Massachusetts. see Massachusetts. Merchants and Manufacturers.
Merchants' and Mechanics' Mutual Life Insurance Company, of . . . New-York. (54393)
Merchants' and Miners' Transportation Company, of Baltimore, Norfolk, and Boston. 47915
Merchants, and Others of London, Members of the Bermuda Company. petitioners see Bermuda Company. petitioners
Merchants and Planters Trading To, and Interested In the Plantations of Virginia and Maryland. petitioners 100477
Merchants, and Planters, Trading To, and Residing In, Virginia, and Maryland. plaintiffs 11312, 100440
Merchants and Ship Owners of Liverpool. petitioners see Liverpool. Merchants and Ship Owners. petitioners
Merchants and Shop Owners of St. John, New Brunswick. petitioners see St. John, New Brunswick. Merchants and Shop Owners. petitioners
Merchant's and trader's guide. (30188)
Merchants and Traders of London. see London. Merchants and Traders.

Merchants and Traders of New York. petitioners see New York (City) Merchants
and Traders. petitioners

Merchants and Traders of Philadelphia. see
Philadelphia. Merchants and Traders.

Merchants and Traders of the City of Baltimore. petitioners see Baltimore.
Merchants and Traders. petitioners

Merchants and Traders of the City of Philadelphia. petitioners see Philadelphia.
Merchants and Traders. petitioners

Merchants' and travellers' directory. 47916

Merchants' avizo. 8503

Merchants' Bank of St. Louis. Board of
Directors. 75360

Merchant's complaint against Spain. 47917

Merchants Concerned in the West India Trade,
and the Owners of Ships and Vessels
Belonging or Trading to the Port of
London. petitioners 102791

Merchants' day-book. 90010

Merchants' directory, 1868-69. 54459

Merchants' directory for 1865 and 1866.
30371

Merchants' directory, for 1869 and 1870.
54459

Merchants' directory for 1866 and 1867.
30371, 54459

Merchants' Exchange, Cincinnati. see Cincinnati. Chamber of Commerce and
Merchants' Exchange.

Merchants' Exchange, New Haven, Conn. see
New Haven, Conn. Merchants' Exchange.

Merchants' Exchange and Reading Room, St.
Louis. see St. Louis. Chamber of
Commerce. Merchants' Exchange and
Reading Room.

Merchants' Exchange Association of San Francisco. 76061

Merchants, Factors and Agents, Residing at
Kingston, Jamaica. complainants see
Kingston, Jamaica. Merchants, Factors
and Agents. complainants

Merchants, factors and agents, residing at
Kingston, in . . . [Jamaica,] complainants,
against the inhabitants of Spanish-Town.
47918, note before 98976

Merchants Fund, Philadelphia. 91580

Merchants Fund, Philadelphia. Board of Managers. 91580

Merchants Great Democratic Meeting, New
York, 1856. see Democratic Party.
New York. New York City. Merchants
Great Democratic Meeting, 1856.

Merchants, . . . in Salem, Mass. petitioners
see Salem, Mass. Merchants. petitioners

Merchants Insurance Company. defendants
42985, (82143)-82144

Merchants' magazine, and commercial review
(2781), (5291), 17109, 11218-11219,
15624, 24483, 24648, (33852), 34907,
35806, 39345, 39564, 47919-47920,
(64500), 93270

Merchants' magazine, and commercial review,
(Indexes) 33853, 47920

Merchants' magazine extra. 15624

Merchants map of commerce. (71907)-(71909)

Merchants mappe of commerce. 71906

Merchants, mechanics, and travellers' atlas
and geography combined. note before
83906, 83957

Merchant's memorandum book, and pocket
almanac. 47921

Merchants of Baltimore. petitioners see
Baltimore. Merchants. petitioners

Merchants of Boston. see Boston. Merchants

Merchants of Charles-Town, S. C. see
Charleston, S. C. Merchants.

Merchants of London. petitioners see London. Merchants. petitioners and London. Merchants, Traders, and Others.
petitioners

Merchants of London their petition to the King
1775. 95940

Merchants of New Haven. petitioners see
New Haven, Conn. Merchants. petitioner

Merchants of Philadelphia. petitioners see
Philadelphia. Merchants. petitioners

Merchants of Philadelphia. Meeting, 1824.
see Meeting of the Merchants of Philadelphia, 1824.

Merchants of Philadelphia, as Subscribed to
the Non-Importation Resolutions, October
25, 1765. see Non-importation Association, Philadelphia, 1765.

Merchants of the City of New York. petitioners
see New York (City) Merchants. petitioners

Merchants of the City of Norfolk. see Norfolk, Va. Merchants.

Merchants of this city are earnestly requested
. . . . 61838

Merchants of this city are . . . requested to
meet. (47922)

Merchants or Factors of London. 69714, note
after 100519

Merchants' Protective Union, Organized . . .
for the Promotion and Protection of
Trade, Throughout the United States and
British Provinces, New York. 50173

Merchants' second edition of Mr. Cambreleng's
report. (10111)

Merchants' sketch book and guide to New York
City. 27489

Merchants, Traders, and Others, of the City
of London. petitioners see London.
Merchants, Traders, and Others. petitioners

Merchants Trading to Spain, East Indies, and
Newfoundland, London. petitioners (69584)

Merchants Trading to the Islands of Nevis and
St. Christophers. petitioners see St.
Christophers. petitioners and Nevis.
petitioners

Merchants Underwriters of New York. 93474

Merchants Union Law Company. 47923

Mercier, Alfred. 47924-47925

Mercier, Andrew le. see Le Mercier, Andrew

Mercier, F. J. le. see Le Mercier, F. J.

Mercier, Francois le. see Le Mercier,
Francois.

Mercier, Louis Sebastien. supposed author
35487, 1st note after 100816

Mercier de Lacombe, H. (38472)-(38473),
(47926)

Mercier Saint-Leger, B. see Saint-Leger, B.
Mercier.

Mercies remembered. (67858)

Merciful rebukes. 38315

Merckwurdige Lebens- und Reise-Beschreibung.
38339

Merckwurdige Missionen— und Reise—Beschreibung. 106394

Merckwurdige Reisen nach der Erd-enge Darien
100947

Merckwurdige Reisen und Begebenheiten. (4001)

Merckwurdige und neue Reise. 39583

Merckwurdiger Discurss von dem Orsprung der
Thier. (48983)

Mercur, Ulysses. 47927

Mercure. 12269

Mercure Ameriquain. 47928, (46094)
Mercure de France. 50090, 69254, 69266, (69271), 69280
Mercure de la Nouvelle France. 47929
Mercure depuis 1640-1655. 81448
Mercure des Isles du Vent ou essaix philosophiques. 47930
Mercvre Francois. (47931), note after 69259
Mercure Hollandois. 47932
Mercvre Indien. 40242, 73297-73298
Mercure politique. 40661
Mercurio. 99646
Mercurio Britannico. pseud. Mundus alter et idem. see Hall, Joseph.
Mercurio Chileno. 47933
Mercurio de Nueva-York. see New York mercury.
Mercurio de Valparaiso. 35080, 72505
Mercurio geografico overo guia geografica in tutte le parti del mondo. 73418
Mercurio Italico. 47934
Mercurio, ovvero historia de' tempi correnti. (81447)
Mercurio Peruano. (38824), 41100, 47936-47937, 61089, 61153, 81615, 85681, 94564, 97711
Mercurio Peruano de historia, literatura, y noticias publicas. (47935)
Mercurio Peruano del dia 17 de Marzo de 1793. 47937
Mercurio religioso. 80880
Mercurio volante con la noticia de la recuperacion de las provincias. 80978
Mercurio volante, con las noticias de la restauracion del Nuevo Mexico. 80978
Mercurius Americanus. 103223
Mercurius anti-mechanicus. 101321
Mercurius politicus. 47939
Mercurius ponticus. (47940)
Mercury (Philadelphia) 60450, (69370)
Mercury. 60450
Mercy and judgment of God. 64255
Mercy Disborough. 92147
Mercy exemplified. 15217
Mercy magnified on a penitent prodigal. 104094
Mercy of God. 104385
Mercy remembered in wrath. A sermon . . . on the 19th of February, 1795. 45463
Mercy remembered in wrath. A sermon preached by the Rev. Dr. Fuller. 26168 (12369)
Mercy with God for the chief of sinners. (12369)
Mercy's dream. 66795
Merda, Rafael D. 47941
Mere, Charles. 100745
Mere de Washington. (11041)
Meredia, Jose Maria. 55122
Meredith, Edmund A. (47942)
Meredith, Jonathan. 45264
Meredith, Thomas. 47943
Meredith, William. 47947
Meredith, Sir William, Bart., d. 1790. (47944)-47946
Meredith, Sir William, Bart., d. 1790. supposed author 40468
Meredith, William Morris, 1799-1873. 5235, 7255, 47948-47949, 61892, 62369
    see also U. S. Treasury Department.
Meredith Baptist Association. see Baptists. New Hampshire. Meredith Baptist Association.
Meredith; or, the mystery of the Mischianza. 47950
Mereno, Juan Joseph. see Moreno, Juan Joseph.

Merewether, Henry Alworth. 47953
Merfart. 99363
Meriam, E. ed. 54517, 54720
Meriam, Jonas. (47954)
Meriam, Matthew. 47955
Merian, --------, Baron de. 47956
Merian, Mariam Sibyllam. (47957)-47961
Merian, Marie Sibille. see Merian, Mariam Sibyllam.
Merian, Matheo. (8784)
Merida, Rafael D. 47962
Merida, Venezuela (Departement) Gobernador (Paulo Toro) (11176) see also Paulo Toro, Francisco de.
Merida, Venezuela (Diocese) Bishop (ca 1839) 47964
Merida, Venezuela (Diocese) Synod, 1839. 47964
Meriden, Conn. 47966
Meriden, Conn. Anti-slavery Society. see Meriden Anti-slavery Society.
Meriden, Conn. Ordination Council, 1769. see Congregational Churches in Connecticut. Ordination Council, Meriden, 1769.
Meriden Anti-slavery Society. 47965
Meriden Institute, Meriden, Conn. 47967
Meriden Village, N. H. Kimball Union Academy. see Kimball Union Academy, Meriden Village, N. H.
Merilhou, Francois Xavier. 47968
Merimee, E. 86471
Merino, Antonio. 47969
Merino, Fernando A. de. 47970
Merino, Ignacio. 41117, 94861
Merit, Joseph. defendant 92736
Merit of doing good. 47447
Merit roll of the New York Free Academy. 54284
Meriton, George. 47971
Meritorious price of man's redemption. (66867), 66868, 66871
Meritorious price of our redemption, justification, &c. 55882, 66868, (66870)
Meritos contraidos a la iglesia Cuzquena. 75556
Meritos del Doctor D. Francisco de Samaniego. 75893
Meritos que ha justificado y probado el Ldo. D. Antonio de Sossa. 11224
Meritos, y excelencias de la ciudad de Lima. 75784
Meritos y servicios con que el Sr. D. Claudio Martinez de Pinillos. 62956
Meritos, y servicios de D. Diego Miguel Bravo de Rivero. 7464, (71648)
Merits of the Bartholomew books presented. 84501
Merits of the Dred Scott Decision. 44380
Merits of the new administration duly stated. 47972
Merits of Thomas W. Dorr. 18041
Merivale, Herman, 1806-1874. 47973, 58778
Meriwether, David. 47974
Meriwether, J. A. (47975)
Meriwether, James. 96636 see also U. S. Commissioners to the Creek Indians.
Merkantilischgeschichtliche Barstellung. 96170
Merkwaardig verhaal van Reinier Hylkes. 34130
Merkwaardige en beknopte historie. 74512
Merkwaardige lotgevallen van vermaarde reiziges en zeelieden. 5833
Merkwaardigheden uit alle bekende landen van Amerika. 94467

Mervellous and faythefull expounder of nughte visiones. 83735
Mervine, William M. ed. 83983
Merwin, Mrs. C. B. supposed author 12808, 1st note after 95756
Merwin, Samuel. 48036
Merwin (H.) firm publishers 48035, (49232), 74997
Merwin & Co. firm see Bangs, Merwin & Co. firm
Merwin-Clayton Sales Company. firm 84735
Merwin's Connecticut River business directory. 48035
Merwin's directory of . . . Minneapolis. (49232)
Merwin's directory of . . . Saint Anthony. 74997
Mery, Joseph. 48037
Mery, Mederic Louis Elie Moreau de Saint-. see Moreau de Saint-Mery, Mederic Louis Elie, 1750-1819.
Mes de Maria en la Parroquia de Sasaima. Ano de 1866. 48038
Mes itineraires dans les provinces du Rio de la Plata. 64700-64701
Mes premieres reflexions sur Haiti. 98695
Mes voyages en Amerique. 31609
Mesa, Francisco Antonio Cabello y. see Cabello y Mesa, Francisco Antonio.
Mesa, Francisco de Paula. 48039
Mesa y Leompart, J. 48040
Mesanza, Andres. ed. 106245
Meschacebeennes. 73481
Mescua, Antonio Mira de. see Mira de Mescua, Antonio.
Meseguer, Francisco. (48041)
Meserve, Arthur L. 48042
Meses y dias liquidos dirigidos a ajustar las cuentes a los operarios. 47849
Mesle, Jean Baptiste Torchet de Bois. see Bois-Mesle, Jean Baptiste Torchet de.
Mesmin, E. Menu de Saint. see Menu de Saint-Mesmin, E.
Mesnard, Thomas. 95995
Mesnil, Emilio Mangel du. illus. 56026
Mesnil Emilio Mangel du. petitioner (48043)
Mes-quaw-buck. Potawatomi Indian Chief 96699
Mes-quaw-buck Band of Potawatomi Indians. see Potawatomi Indians (Mesquaw-buck Band)
Mesquita, J. J. de. 48044
Mesquita, Martinho de. see Martinho de Mesquita.
Message 64585
Message . . . accompanied by a report of the Canal Commissioners. note just before 60250
Message . . . accompanying a copy of the treaty . . . 8th March, 1796. 96586
Message . . . accompanying a copy of the treaty . . . 29th March 1796. 96589
Message . . . accompanying a statement of expenditures from January 1, 1797. 48059
Message . . . accompanying an official statement of the expenditure to . . . 1795. 48049
Message . . . accompanying copies of treaties concluded with the Delaware and Piankeshaw Indians. (48062)
Message . . . accompanying sundry papers relative to the affairs . . . with the French republic, 18th January, 1799. 48054

Message . . . accompanying sundry papers relative to the affairs . . . with the French republic, 22d January, 1799. 48054
Message . . . accompanying report of the Massachusetts Commissioners on the Boundary Line. 45923
Message and correspondence with the Commissioners from Virginia. 87554
Message . . . and documents from which the injunction of secrecy has been removed. 48115
Message and documents on the negotiations for peace with England. 42267
Message and inaugural address to the Senate and House of Representatives. (8707)
Message annuel . . . a l'Assemblee Generale. 42270
Message . . . April 3, 1798; with despatches from the envoys to the French republic. 48054
Message . . . calling for correspondence. 48126
Message . . . communicating a copy of the treaty with the Mexican republic. 48115
Message . . . communicating cessation of intercourse. 48128
Message . . . communicating copies of correspondence with . . . Mexico. 48109
Message . . . communicating documents in the case of the Black Warrior. 48124
Message . . . communicating . . . information in regard to the occupation by American citizens of the island of Navasca. 48131
Message . . . communicating, . . . information in relation to the massacre at Mountain Meadows. 48135
Message . . . communicating, . . . information in relation to the states of the union lately in rebellion. (48141)
Message . . . communicating . . . letters . . . between the Secretary of State and the envoy . . . of Great Britain. (48069)
Message . . . communicating, . . . the correspondence of Lieutenant General Scott. 48132
Message . . . communjcating the instructions to, and dispatches from, the . . . ministers in China. 48134
Message . . . communicating the proceedings of the Commissioners for the Adjustment of Claims. 48127
Message . . . communicating the report of the Commissioners Appointed to Survey the River Potomac. 48083
Message concerning Texas and New Mexico. 91562
Message . . . containing observations on some of the documents. 48050
Message de M. Buchanan. 6130, 40330, 40663
Message . . . December 2, 1834. 48099
Message . . . December 7, 1847. 48113
Message . . . December 7, 1842. (48107)
Message . . . December 3, 1818. 48076
Message . . . December 3, 1866. 48143
Message . . . delivered January 11, 1867. (34556)
Message, delivered to the Iowa General Assembly. (34974)
Message du Directoire concernant les prises faites. 99663
Message du gouvernement de Buenos Ayres. 9022, 73217
Message du President Jefferson Davis au Senat. 15301

lately made between the United States and sundry tribes of Indians. 96592

Message from the President of the United States, transmitting copies of treaties, which have lately been entered into. 96591

Message from the President of the United States, transmitting correspondence: 1st. On the subject of the attack on the Chesapeake. 12488

Message from the President of the United States, transmitting information in relation to the execution of the act. 24892, 103434

Message from the President of the United States transmitting information touching an illegal combination of private individuals. 9428

Message from the President of the United States, transmitting report of the Indian Peace Commissioners. (69754)

Message from the President of the United States, transmitting sundry documents. 27073

Message from the President of the United States, transmitting the amended treaty with the New York Indians. 54781

Message from the President of the United States, transmitting the annual report of the Inspectors of the Penitentiary. 20314

Message from the President of the United States, transmitting the information required by a resolution. 15489

Message from the President of the United States, . . . with the documents. (35378)

Message from the President . . . relating to the treaty with Spain. 24888

Message from the President, relative to Indian affairs. 95015

Message from the President . . . relative to the cession of Louisiana. 42264

Message from the President . . . relative to the proceedings of the Commissioner for Running the Boundary Line. 24886

Message from the President . . . report of Theodric Bland. 5864

Message from the President . . . returning to the House . . . the . . . bill. 47200

Message from the President . . . transmitting a copy of the report. (55711)

Message from the President . . . transmitting a report from the Governor. 48755

Message from the President, transmitting a report of the Secretary of State. (17885)

Message from the President . . . transmitting a report of William Lambert. 38739

Message from the President . . . transmitting copies of the laws of the Mississippi Territory. (49519)

Message from the President, . . . transmitting sundry papers. 24887

Message from the President . . . transmitting the constitution of Louisiana. 42265

Message from the President . . . transmitting the information required. 14990

Message from the President . . . transmitting the laws of the Indiana Territory. 34544

Message from the President, upon which they were founded. 22412

Message from the Senate by Mr. Seldon. 100084

Message . . . in complaince with a resolution. (16864)

Message . . . in reference to the imprisonment of Mr. Greely. 48105

Message . . . in relation to a military appointment. 48138

Message . . . in relation to a postal arrangement. 48116

Message . . . in relation to . . . a road from Little Rock to Cantonment Gibson. 48090

Message . . . in relation to our affairs with Spain. 48077

Message . . . in relation to the boundary line between Ohio and Michigan Territory. 48100

Message . . . in relation to the construction of floating dry docks. 48112

Message . . . in relation to the consular establishment. (48098)

Message . . . [in relation to the defence of New York.] (53774)

Message . . . in relation to the difficulties between the British authorities and San Salvador. (48119)

Message . . . in relation to the . . . Exploring Expedition. 48104

Message . . . in relation to the formation of a new government. 48093

Message . . . in relation to the Indian barbarities in Minnesota. 48139

Message . . . in relation to the Inter-Oceanic Canal. 48121

Message . . . inclosing a report. 48055

Message . . . inclosing a treaty and conventions. (48060)

Message . . . Indian hostilities in Florida. 48103

Message . . . January, 1866. 70602

Message . . . January 9, 1865. 70602

Message . . . July 31, 1854. (48123)

Message . . . June session, 1866. 85228

Message . . . March 20, 1866. (48142)

Message . . . November 8th, 1808. 48065

Message . . . November 5th, 1811. 48066

Message . . . November 26, 1844. 30101

Message, number I. [of Gov. George McDuffie.] 87545

Message, no. I. [of Gov. Henry Middleton.] 87543

Message no. I. [of Gov. J. H. Adams.] 87508

Message no. I of His Excellency, F. W. Pickens. 87557

Message no. I, of His Excellency Governor Manning. 87549

Message no. I of His Excellency M. L. Bonham. 87558

Message no. 3. Referred to the Committee on Federal Relations. 87548

Message no. II. from His Excellency the Governor. 87539

Message no. 2, with the papers accompanying the same. 87538

Message . . . October 8, 1862. (15296)

Message . . . October 2, 1862. (15296)

Message of Acting Governor Arny to the Legislative Assembly. 53276

Message of Acting Governor Stevens T. Mason. 48754

Message of Andrew G. Curtin, . . . relative to miltary arrests. 60249

Message of Andrew G. Curtin, . . . to the Legislature, January, 1862. 60249

[Message of Andrew G. Curtin, . . . to the Legislature,] January 7, 1863. 60249

Message of August 6, 1850, concerning Texas and New Mexico. 78765, 91278

Message of Gen. Bradford. 7237

Message of Governor A. B. Roman. 72893

Message of Governor A. J. Faulk. 18297

Message of Governor A. J. Faulk, to the Legislative Assembly. 18297

Message of Governor Abram A. Hammond.
35024

Message of Governor Andrew G. Curtin,
relative to the Reserve Corps. 60249

Message of Gov. Bernard to the Minisink
Indians. (49225)

Message of Governor Bigler, in relation to the
Franklin Canal Company. (25648), note
just before 60250

Message [of Governor Bigler of California.]
76077

Message of Governor Bigler returning bill no.
590. note just before 62050

Message of Governor Buckingham, accompanying
the report of Col. H. H. Osgood, giving
the number of drafted men in the state,
December 10, 1862. 15785

Message of Governor Buckingham, accompanying
the report of Col. H. H. Osgood, giving
the number of drafted men in the state,
to the General Assembly, December 10th,
1862. 15744

Message of Governor Cannon. 19389

Message of Governor Cummings to the Legislative Assembly, Territory of Colorado,
January, 1866. 14740

Message [of Governor Cummings . . . to the
Legislature of Colorado Territory,]
December 13, 1866. 14740

Message of Governor Gamble. 49610

Message of Governor Henry Watkins Allen.
42271

Message of Governor Houston, of Texas, on
secession. 33195

Message of Governor I. I. Stevens. 101918

Message of Gov. James H. Adams. 87524

Message of Governor James Iredell. 55648

Message of Governor James M. Smith, to the
General Assembly of Georgia, 1875. 82795

Message of Governor James M. Smith, to the
General Assembly of Georgia, 1874. 82795

Message of Governor James M. Smith, to the
General Assembly of Georgia, 1877. 82795

Message of Governor James M. Smith, to the
General Assembly of Georgia, 1876. 82795

Message of Governor James M. Smith, to the
General Assembly of Georgia, 1872. 82795

Message of Governor James M. Smith, to the
General Assembly of Georgia, January 8,
1873. 82795

Message of Gov. Kent. 43996

Message of Governor Letcher to the Legislature
of Kentucky. 40239

Message of Gov. Levi Lincoln. 45919

Message of Governor Lyon, of Idaho. 34169

Message of Governor Lyon, of Idaho. Delivered
November 16, A. D. 1864. 34168

Message of Governor McDuffie. 87546

Message of Governor Medary. 56877

Message of Governor Morgan. 53776

Message [of Governor Morton of Massachusetts.]
31784

Message of . . . Governor of Nebraska. 52195

Message of Governor of Pennsylvania. 28219

Message of Governor Paul O. Herbert. 42268

Message of Governor Rencher. 69605

Message of Gov. Sam Houston, on the South
Carolina resolutions. 33195

Message [of Governor Seymour.] 30901

Message of Governor Seymour, of New York.
79660

Message of . . . Governor . . . special session.
(34556)

Message of . . . Governor Sprague. 70601

Message of Governor Stevens T. Mason. 48753

Message of Governor Tompkins. 69776

Message of Governor Troup. 27074

Message of . . . Governor Van Buren. (53775)

Message of Gov. W. S. Holden. (55612)

Message of Governor Wolcott, of Connecticut.
10889, 22987

Message of His Excellency Frederick Smyth.
85228

Message of His Excellency Governor Clinton.
(53775)

Message of His Excellency Governor Griswold.
15744

Message of His Excellency Gov. Harrison
Reed. 68544

Message of His Excellency, James Y. Smith.
(70602)

Message of His Excellency Joseph E. Brown.
(27075)

Message, . . . of His Excellency, . . . November 28, 1843. 30101

Message of His Excellency the Governor, to
the Legislature of Massachusetts. 8357

Message of His Excellency the Governor, to
the Legislature of Massachusetts, enclosing the Adjutant General's return.
93720

Message of His Excellency the Governor, to
the Senate. 102586

Message of His Excellency, the President, in
reply to a resolution of the Senate.
95022

Message of His Excellency the President of
the Confederate States to Congress.
(15299)

Message of His Excellency to the General
Assembly of Connecticut. 28889

Message of His Excellency William A. Buckingham, Governor of Connecticut to the
Legislature of the state, May session,
1862. 15744

Message of His Excellency William A. Buck-
ingham, Governor of Connecticut, to the
Legislature of the state, special session
November, 1863. 15744

Message [of James Madison.] (56498)

Message of January 28th, 1808. (43380), 607?

Message of Jefferson Davis to the Confederate
Congress. 46962

Message of Jefferson Davis to the Congress of
the Confederate States. 58700

Message of John Ross. 12473

Message of Mirabeau B. Lamar. 95026

Message of Moses Bigelow. (54875)

Message of November 7th, 1907, to the Legislature. 83629

Message of President Polk. 43091

Message of Robert C. Wickliffe. 42269

Message of Robert K. Scott. (78353)

Message of Robert T. Conrad. 61839

Message of Seth Padelford. (70603)

Message of the Acting Governor. 37547

Message of the Executive, to the Legislature
of Maryland. 45068

Message of the 1st of June. 46031

Message of the government of Buenos Ayres.
9023

Message of the Governor . . . Andrew G. Cur
. . . January 7, 1864. 59885

[Message of the Governor . . . Andrew G.
Curtin, . . .] January 30, 1865. 59885

Message of the Governor in relation to dis-
arming the state militia. (45263), 4526?

Message of the Governor in relation to the
report . . . of the Committee on the
Public Lands. 45260

Message of the Governor . . . January 2,
1850. 59884

1674

Message of the Governor . . . January 6, 1857. 53528

Message of the Governor . . . October 7, 1864. 42271

Message of the Governor of Florida to the General Assembly. 24885

Message of the Governor of Illinois. 34298

Message [of the Governor of Indiana] . . . Jan. 6, 1865. (34556)

Message of the Governor of Indiana, to the General Assembly. (34556)

Message of the Governor of Kentucky. 87423

Message of the Governor [of Maine.] (44028)

Message of the Governor of Maine, to both branches of the Legislature. 84040

Message of the Governor of Maryland. (45261)

Message of the Governor [of Massachusetts.] 1470

Message of the Governor of Minnesota. 49267

Message of the Governor of Montana. (50081)

Message of . . . the Governor of New Jersey. 53157

Message of the Governor [of North Carolina] in relation to the University of North Carolina. (55644)

Message of the Governor of Ohio. 56958

Message of the Governor [of Pennsylvania, ca. 1832.] 60503, 60508

Message of the Governor [of Pennsylvania, ca. 1835.] 60528

Message of the Governor of Pennsylvania, . . . with . . . documents. (59883)

Message of the Governor of the state . . . June 2, 1820. 43995

Message of the Governor of the Territory of Washington, delivered December 7th, 1858. 101923

Message of the Governor of the Territory of Washington; delivered in joint session of the Council and House of Representatives. 101910

Message of the Governor of Washington Territory. 101911

Message of the Governor to the General Assembly of Georgia. 27076

Message of the Governor to the Legislature . . . 1856. 57556

Message of the Governor to the Legislature of . . . Mississippi. 49518

Message of the Governor to the Legislature returning the bill. 54725

Message of the Governor . . . transmitting resolutions of South Carolina. 46058

Message of the Governor, . . . with documents. 47236

Message of . . . the Governor . . . with the report. 53156

Message of the Lieutenant and Acting Governor of Kentucky. 37549

Message of the Lieutenant Governor to the Legislative Council. 56150

Message of the Mayor of Baltimore, of January 15th, 1866. 26697

Message of . . . [the] Mayor of . . . New Orleans. (53336)

Message of the Mayor, transmitting seals and documents. 6588

Message of the President [i. e. James Madison.] 72847

Message of the President [i. e. Jefferson Davis.] 15289, (15291), 15314, (15318)

Message of the President . . . [i. e. John Adams.] 34865

Message of the President and documents on a demand of the Spanish government. 42267

Message of the President, and report of Albert Pike. 15292

Message of the President, April 18, 1862. (15296)

Message of the President. April 10, 1862. (15295)

Message of the President at the opening of the 2d session of the 24th Congress. 34607

Message of the President, communicating correspondence. 37071

Message of the President . . . communicating documents respecting Louisiana. 42266

Message of the President [December 20, 1864.] 15310

Message . . . of the President, February 14, 1837. 33120

Message of the President [February 3, 1865.] 15312-15313

Message of the President, February 12, 1864. 48146

Message of the President [February 20, 1865.] 15315-15316

Message of the President in relation to the boundaries. 90419

Message of the President in relation to the survey of a route. 4946

Message of the President inclosing a letter. 48052, note after 87538

Message of the President [January 4, 1865.] 15311

Message of the President [January 10, 1864.] 15302

Message of the President [January 13, 1864.] 15303

Message of the President. January 12, 1863. (15297)-(15298)

Message of the President [January 25, 1864.] 15304

Message of the President. March 11, 1862. (15294)

Message of the President [March 13, 1865.] 15317

Message of the President . . . March 23, 1808. 2025, 50013, 58478

Message of the President, May 21, 1865. 51086

Message of the President [November 11, 1864.] 15309

Message of the President [November 7, 1864.] (15308)

Message of the President of the Confederate States. January 11th, 1864. 65358

Message of the President of the republic of Liberia. (40928)

Message of the President of the United States . . . accompanied by a report of Carl Schurz. 78035

Message of the President of the United States, and the report of the Secretary of the Treasury. 66067

Message of the President of the United States, at the opening of the second session of the eleventh Congress. 34398, 83812

Message of the President of the United States communicating the discoveries made in exploring the Missouri, Red River, and Washita. 40824

Message of the President of the United States, Dec. 20, 1858. 12813

Message of the President of the United States, in relation to a military appointment of the Hon. Francis P. Blair. 5741

Message of the President of the United States, June 6, 1846. 49207

Message of the President of the United States . . . . May 11, 1846. (48493)

MESSAGE

Message of the President of the United States, of the 19th January, 1799. 25886

Message of the President of the United States, of the 17th of December last [i. e. 1836.] 85070

Message of the President of the United States relative to the affair of William Blount. 5001

Message of the President of the United States to Congress, December 7, 1847. 48574

Message of the President of the United States, to Congress, November 29, 1809. 83817

Message of the President of the United States to Congress relative to France and Great-Britain. 48045

Message of the President of the United States, to the two houses of Congress. 83809-83810

Message of the President of the United States. Transmitting a letter. 101715

Message of the President of the United States, transmitting a treaty. 96613

Message of the President of the United States, transmitting treaties. 54781

Message of the President of the United States, with copies of the charges. 48922

Message of the President . . . [on] making a road from Cumberland. 56959

Message of the President . . . on our relations with France. 25429

Message of the President, on the subject of our Mexican relations. 95023

Message of the President . . . on transmitting a letter from Commodore Preble. 65004

Message of the President relative to the Seminole War. 79069

Message of the President. Richmond, November 18, 1861. 15293

Message of the President, submitted to both houses. 95019

Message of the President . . . to both houses of Congress, April 3d. 1798. 59593, 62702, 103848

Message of the President, to both houses of Congress. Delivered, Nov. 21, 1837. 95007

Message of the President to both houses of Congress. Received September 28, 1837. 95006

Message of the President, to the Congress of the Confederate States of America. (15290)

Message of the President, to the fifth Congress of the republic. 95024

Message of the President to the first session thirty-ninth Congress. 58468

Message of the President to the second session, fortieth Congress. (58469)

Message of the President . . . transmitting . . . constitution of Kansas. 37023

Message of the President, transmitting information. 17448

Message of the President, 28th Congress, 2d session, Doc. II. 31769

Message of the Principal Chief, and correspondence between the Cherokee Delegation and the Hon. W. Wilkins. 73393

Message of the Principal Chief of the Cherokee Nation. 12468

Message of . . . W. F. Packer, to the Legislature. 60248

Message of William B. Smith, Mayor of Philadelphia. 84748

Message . . . on a military expedition. 48065

Message . . . [on] admitting Michigan into the union. 48798

Message . . . on our relations with France. 48102

Message . . . [on] the act of Congress . . . 1806. 48064

Message [on the Hampton Roads Conference.] 65358

Message . . . on the seizure and confiscation of the barque Georgianna. 48120

Message . . . on the state of affairs between Maine and New Brunsiwkc. 48106

Message . . . on the subject of the Mexican war. 48114

Message . . . on the subject of the northern boundary. (57039)

Message on the 29th of November 1809. 838

Message . . . providing for the settlement an confirmation of private land claims in Florida. (48091)

Message relating to slavery. 53151

Message . . . relative to arms loaned to Rho Island. 45920

Message . . . [relative to Central America] December 31, 1853. 48122

Message . . . [relative to Central America] January 21, 1853. 48122

Message . . . relative to France and Great Britain. 48047

Message . . . relative to neutral rights. 481

Message . . . relative to rank, &c. 48118

Message . . . relative to the affairs of the United States on the Mississippi. (4805

Message . . . relative to the condition of the Treasury. note just before 60250

Message . . . relative to the employment of United States troops. 48110

Message . . . relative to the finances . . . a the accounting departments of the gover ment. note just before 60250

Message . . . relative to the finances . . . a recommending a temporary loan. note just before 60250

Message . . . relative to the free navigation the River St. Lawrence. (48092)

Message . . . relative to the French republic 48050

Message . . . relative to the invasion of the western frontier of this state. (53774)

Message . . . relative to the military establishment. 48053

Message . . . relative to the Orders in Counc 48067

Message . . . relative to the seizure . . . in Peru. 48130

Message . . . returning the bank bill. 48096

Message . . . returning with his objections, th apportionment bill. note just before 602

Message, sent by the Upper to the Lower Hou of Assembly of Maryland. 45069, 4531{

Message . . . September 4, 1862. (15296)

Message . . . September 30, 1862. (15296)

[Message] September 12, 1862. (15296)

Message . . . September 24, 1862. (15296)

Message . . . showing the progress of the negotiations for peace. 48072

Message. Speech of Hon. Emory B. Pottle. 64675

Message . . . suppression of hostilities in Florida. 48108

Message to Congress, Nov. 29, 1809. 83814, 83816

Message to Congress, of December 7, 1830. 29932

Message to explain the causes of the failure of the arms. 48071

Message to the fourth moot congress of the Law Department. 48804

[Meteorological register for twelve years,]
from 1843 to 1854. (39457)
Meteorological register for twelve years,
from 1831 to 1842 inclusive. (39457)
Meteorological report of Prof. James P. Espy.
22917
Meteorological sketches. By an observer.
48174, (68512)
Meteorological stations and observers of the
Smithsonian Institution. 85040
Meteorological tables. 87534
Meteorological tables for 1825-27. (53996)
Meteorologie. (21011)
Meteorologique. 25916
Meteorology. 25122
Meteranus novus. 48177
Meteran, Emanuel van. 48175-48177
Meteron, ------- van. tr. (11708)
Method and influence of theological studies.
(80079)
Method and plain process for making pot-ash.
91308
Method for determining the best climate of
the earth. 66727
Method humbly proposed. 102210
Method of discharging the national debt. 39534
Method of introducing religion into common-
schools. 74415
Method of nature. 22460
Method of practice in the small-pox. 104317
Method of salvation. A sermon. 18770
Method proposed, which will effectually reduce
France and Spain. 86656
Method to prevent dangerous fires. 94404
Methode de former des etablissemens sur la
frontiere. 84676, 1st note after 101814
Methode pour etudier la geographie. (8784),
21149, (40027), 73435
Methode pour etudier l'histoire. 40028
Methodism anatomiz'd. (48178), 49871
Methodism and slavery. 3878, 59472
Methodism exposed. 92859
Methodism in America. (20369)
Methodism in Charleston, S. C. (50294)
Methodism in the maritime provinces. 84422
Methodism in the state of New York. 48180
Methodism inspected. 48179
Methodism vindicated. 95207
Methodist almanac. 48189
Methodist Book Concern. defendants 84738
Methodist chapel property case. 48190, 74566
Methodist Church (Canada) 48207
Methodist Church (Canada) plaintiffs 48190,
74566
Methodist Church (England) Conferences.
102707
Methodist Church (England) Gloucester. plain-
tiffs 103500
Methodist Church (England) Missions. see
Wesleyan Missionary Society, London.
Methodist Church (United States) 102695-102697
see also Methodist Protestant Church.
Methodist church property case. Arguments
of Messrs. Adam N. Riddle, Judge Lane,
and Thomas Ewing. 84743
Methodist church property case. Report of the
suit of Henry B. Bascom and others vs.
George Lane and others. 48191, note
after 93976
Methodist Episcopal Church. 12891, 20757,
48182, 48184-48186, 48200, 48207,
63939, 72118, 84358-84362, 84365 see
also Joint Centenary Committee of the
Methodist Episcopal Church and the
Methodist Episcopal Church, South.

Methodist Episcopal Church. Bishops. 79291
Methodist Episcopal Church. Board of Man-
agers. Resident Members. (1235)
Methodist Episcopal Church. Centenary Com-
mittee. see Joint Centenary Committee
of the Methodist Episcopal Church and
the Methodist Episcopal Church, South.
Methodist Episcopal Church. Church Extension
Society. 48207
Methodist Episcopal Church. Committee on
Slavery, 1860. Majority. 44074
Methodist Episcopal Church. Committee on
Slavery, 1860. Minority. 44074
Methodist Episcopal Church. Conferences.
48182, 48188, 48200-48204, 48207,
84753
Methodist Episcopal Church. Conferences.
Alabama. 49357
Methodist Episcopal Church. Conferences.
Cincinnati. (13096), 89894 see also
Methodist Episcopal Church. Conferences.
Ohio.
Methodist Episcopal Church. Conferences.
East Maine. (49368) see also Methodist
Episcopal Church. Conferences. Maine.
Methodist Episcopal Church. Conferences.
Genesee. 93248 see also Methodist
Episcopal Church. Conferences. New
York.
Methodist Episcopal Church. Conferences.
Genesee. Nazarite Union. 52138
Methodist Episcopal Church. Conferences.
Illinois. 34215, (49372) see also Meth-
odist Episcopal Church. Conferences.
Rock River.
Methodist Episcopal Church. Conferences.
Indiana. 82925
Methodist Episcopal Church. Conferences.
Iowa. 34980
Methodist Episcopal Church. Conferences.
Kansas and Nebraska. 49373
Methodist Episcopal Church. Conferences.
Maine. 43961, 49374 see also Meth-
odist Episcopal Church. Conferences.
East Maine.
Methodist Episcopal Church. Conferences.
Michigan. 48758
Methodist Episcopal Church. Conferences.
Minnesota. 49295
Methodist Episcopal Church. Conferences.
Missouri. 49612
Methodist Episcopal Church. Conferences.
Natchez. 49524
Methodist Episcopal Church. Conferences.
Nebraska. see Methodist Episcopal
Church. Conferences. Kansas and
Nebraska.
Methodist Episcopal Church. Conferences.
New England. 52644
Methodist Episcopal Church. Conferences.
New England. Committee on the Case
of Rev. Ephraim K. Avery. 2484
Methodist Episcopal Church. Conferences.
New Hampshire. 52853
Methodist Episcopal Church. Conferences.
New Jersey. 53173
Methodist Episcopal Church. Conferences.
New York. 33398, (43002) see also
Methodist Episcopal Church. Conferences.
Genesee. Methodist Episcopal Church.
Conferences. Oneida. Methodist Epis-
copal Church. Conferences. Troy.
Methodist Episcopal Church. Conferences.
New York. Missionary to Civilize and
Convert to Christianity the Natives of
Rio de Janeiro. 76322

Methodist Episcopal Church. Conferences.
New York. Seminary. see New York
Conference Seminary, Charlottesville,
N. Y.

Methodist Episcopal Church. Conferences.
New York East. (54766)

Methodist Episcopal Church. Conferences.
Northern Ohio. 79291 see also Meth-
odist Episcopal Church. Conferences.
Ohio.

Methodist Episcopal Church. Conferences.
Ohio. 79291, 82776 see also Meth-
odist Church. Conferences. Cincinnati.
Methodist Episcopal Church. Conferences.
Northern Ohio.

Methodist Episcopal Church. Conferences.
Ohio. Wyandotte Mission, Upper Sandusky. 105644

Methodist Episcopal Church. Conferences.
Oneida. 93248 see also Methodist
Episcopal Church. Conferences. New
York.

Methodist Episcopal Church. Conferences.
Philadelphia. Ladies' United Aid Society. see Ladies' United Aid Society
of the Methodist Episcopal Church in
. . . Philadelphia.

Methodist Episcopal Church. Conferences.
Philadelphia. Union Female Missionary
Society. see Union Female Missionary
Society, Philadelphia.

Methodist Episcopal Church. Conferences.
Providence. 66283

Methodist Episcopal Church. Conferences.
Rock River. 34216 see also Methodist
Episcopal Church. Conferences. Illinois.

Methodist Episcopal Church. Conferences.
South Carolina. 87894-87895

Methodist Episcopal Church. Conferences.
South Carolina. Committee on the
Schism in Charleston. 12079, 87895

Methodist Episcopal Church. Conferences.
South Carolina. Missionary Society.
87894

Methodist Episcopal Church. Conferences.
Troy. 58809, note after 97074 see also
Methodist Episcopal Church. Conferences.
New York.

Methodist Episcopal Church. Conferences.
Wisconsin. 83755

Methodist Episcopal Church. Convention of
Laymen, New York, 1852. 65755

Methodist Episcopal Church. Council of Ministers. 43790, 99798

Methodist Episcopal Church. General Conference. 48181, 72124

Methodist Episcopal Church. General Conference. Majority. 3878, 59472

Methodist Episcopal Church. General Conference. Minority. 3878, 59472

Methodist Episcopal Church. Historical Club.
102700

Methodist Episcopal Church. Missionary Society. see Methodist Missionary Society.

Methodist Episcopal Church. National Associ-
ation of Local Preachers. see National
Association of Local Preachers of the
Methodist Episcopal Church.

Methodist Episcopal Church. New England
Centenary Convention, Boston, 1866. see
New England Methodist Centenary Con-
vention, Boston, 1866.

Methodist Episcopal Church. New York Conference Seminary. see New York Conference Seminary, Charlottesville, N. Y.

Methodist Episcopal Church. Sunday School
Union. 48205

Methodist Episcopal Church. Tract Society.
see Methodist Tract Society.

Methodist Episcopal Church. Young Men's
Central Home Mission, Philadelphia.
see Young Men's Central Home Mission, Philadelphia.

Methodist Episcopal Church, South. 48183,
48187, 66968, 84740, 84742A, 88384,
88473, note before 93632 see also Joint
Centenary Committee of the Methodist
Episcopal Church and the Methodist Episcopal Church, South.

Methodist Episcopal Church, South. complainal
84738

Methodist Episcopal Church, South. Conferences. Virginia. 84743

Methodist Episcopal Church, South. Conferences. Virginia. Soldiers' Tract Society. 86294

Methodist Episcopal Church, South. Soldiers'
Tract Association. see Soldiers' Tract
Association, Methodist Episcopal Church,
South.

Methodist Episcopal Church, Barre, Vt. see
Barre, Vt. Methodist Episcopal Church.

Methodist Episcopal Church, Cherry Valley,
Mass. see Cherry Valley, Mass. Methodist Episcopal Church.

Methodist Episcopal Church, Newark, N. J.
see Newark, N. J. Methodist Episcopal
Church.

Methodist Episcopal Church and slavery. 1982

Methodist Episcopal Church in Canada. see
Methodist Church (Canada)

Methodist Episcopal Church in the United
States. 48193

Methodist Episcopal Church Meeting, Baltimore,
1828. (3062)

Methodist Episcopal Church . . . vs. new
organization. 48194

Methodist Episcopal Society, Newark, N. J.
see Newark, N. J. Methodist Episcopal
Church.

Methodist error. 102705

Methodist General Biblical Institute, Boston.
48195

Methodist in search of the church. 43571

Methodist magazine (London) 48196

Methodist magazine (New York) see Methodist
review.

Methodist magazine and quarterly review. see
Methodist review.

Methodist ministry defended. 80744

Methodist Missionary Society. 48198, 48207

Methodist new connexion magazine. 85443

Methodist of the Church of England. pseud.
Strictures on the substance of a sermon.
see Wesley, Charles, 1707-1788. supposed author

Methodist; or, incidents and characters from
life. 24732

Methodist protestant. 85443

Methodist Protestant Church. 48206 see also
Methodist Church (United States)

Methodist Protestant Church. General Convention, Boston, 1839. 48206

Methodist Protestant Church in British North
America. see Methodist Church (Canada)

Methodist pulpit south. 84993-84994

Methodist quarterly review. see Methodist
review.

Methodist review. (14944), (48197)

Methodist Soldiers' Tract Association. see Soldiers' Tract Association, Methodist Episcopal Church, South.
Methodist Tract Society. (48199)
Methodistes et baptistes Americains. (5814)
Methodists and enthusiasm. 103636
Methodists in trouble. 85538
Methodo de cultivar o tabaco na Virginia. 86248
Methodo facil de remediar algunas enferme-dades. 98608
Methods and motives for a society to suppress disorders. 46413
Methods for improving the manufacture of Carolina indigo. 10973, 87896
Methods for improving the manufacture of indigo. 10973, 87896
Methods of improving the homes of the laboring and tenement house classes. 84261
Methodus figurarum. 17855
Methold, William. 66682
Methuen, Mass. 48208
Methuen, Mass. School Committee. 48208
Methuen transcript. 83395
Metis de la Savane. (11044)
Metlahkatlah. 21264, 47174
Metlar, George M. (48209)
Metodo curativo de las viruelas formado. 48210
Metodo de curar tabardillos. 99647
Metodo de hacer una buena confecion. 76002
Metoposcopia et ophthalmoscopia. 26106
Metral, Antoine. 48211-48212
Metric system explained and adapted. 18751
Metrica panegyrica descripcio de las fiestas. (48213)
Metrical description of a fancy ball. 48214
Metrical gossamer thoughts. 50640
Metrical romance. 92768
Metrical romance, in seven cantos. 84153
Metrical romance. In three cantos. 100562
Metrical tale, in four cantos. 101062
Metrologie ou trate de mesures. 59172
Metrology universalized. 48215
Metropolitan. pseud. Puritania. 66711
Metropolitan. 48216
Metropolitan Academy and Gymnasium, New York. 54396
Metropolitan Art Museum, New York. see New York (City) Metropolitan Museum of Art.
Metropolitan Art Museum in . . . New York. Proceedings of a meeting. 54397
Metropolitan Bank, New York. respondents 64285
Metropolitan board of health. (54188)
Metropolitan catholic almanac. 11521
Metropolitan catholic almanac, and laity's directory. 48217, 97963
Metropolitan Club. 48218
Metropolitan Fair, New York, 1864. see New York (City) Metropolitan Fair, 1864.
Metropolitan Fair, In Aid of the United States Sanitary Commission, New York, 1864. see New York (City) Metropolitan Fair, 1864.
Metropolitan Fair in aid of the United States Sanitary Commission. 54401, (76656)
Metropolitan guide. 54402
Metropolitan influence. 39174
Metropolitan Mechanics' Institute, Washington, D. C. First Exhibition, 1835. (48219)
Metropolitan Medical College, New York. 54403
Metropolitan merchants' and manufacturers' business directory, for 1867 and '68. 54459

Metropolitan merchants' and manufacturers' business directory, for 1866 and '67. 48220
Metropolitan police. 3513
Metropolitan Railroad Company. 73653
Metropolitan Railroad Company. Charter. 73653
Metropolitan Railroad Company. Directors. 48221
Metropolitan record. 48222
Metropolitan sketches. (5546)
Metz, Gauthier de. 76838
Metzger, ------. 92574
Meulen, M. E. van der. 48223
Meunier, Victor. 48224-48225
Meunrios, Francisco Xaviero de, Comte de Barcelona. pseud. Description historique. see Louis XVIII, King of France, 1755-1824.
Meurer, Theodore. (69296)
Meuron, Abraham. 66724
Meursinge, A. 48227
Meurte politica de la republica Mexicana. 51244
Meusel, Joanne Georg. ed. 93112
Meusnier de Querion, Anne Gabriel, 1720-1780. 65402, (68417)
Mevil, Charles. 48228
Mew, W. M. 48229
Me-won-t-toc. 48230, 72183
Mexia, Diego. (48231)
Mexia, Jose Maria Zenon y. see Zenon y Mexia, Jose Maria.
Mexia, Luis. 75567-75568
Mexia, Pedro, 1496?-1552? 48233-48249
Mexia y Ocon, Juan Roxo. 48232
Mexicaansche geschiedenis. 69078
Mexicain. pseud. Mexique. see Guiteras, Pedro J.
Mexicain. pseud. Simples observations. see Rus de Cea, Genaro.
Mexicain. pseud. Trois lettres adressee par un Mexicain. see Gorostiza, --------.
Mexicaines, poesies. 5139
Mexican. 79887
Mexican affairs. (17271)
Mexican and United States Claim Commission. see United States and Mexican Claims Commission, 1869-1876.
Mexican antiquities. 74950
Mexican author. pseud. Historie of the Mexican nation, described in pictures. 66686
Mexican Company of Mines. Chief Director. 98183 see also Uslar, Justus Ludwig von.
Mexican Company of Mines. Secretary. tr. 98183
Mexican empire and the American union. (58667)
Mexican empire and the American war. (58667)
Mexican extraordinary. 48568
Mexican illustration, founded upon facts. 4169
Mexican indemnity payments. (48569)
Mexican letter. (7170)
Mexican letters, containing humourous and satirical observations. 48570
Mexican merchant. pseud. Texas and Mexico. 95119
Mexican Ocean Mail and Inland Company. 48571
Mexican Ocean Mail and Inland Company. . . . Report 48571
Mexican: or love and land. 18271
Mexican Pacific Coal and Iron Mining and Land Company. (48572)

Mexican Pacific Coal and Iron Mining and Land Company. Exploring Expedition. (48572)

Mexican Pacific Company. Engineer. (64035) see also Poole, Henry Ward.

Mexican papers, containing the history of the rise and decline of commercial slavery in America. 21231

Mexican papers. The Mexican question. 21230

Mexican patriot. 24787

Mexican prophecy. 78300-78301

Mexican question. 21230

Mexican seeds. 44639

Mexican tale; and other poems. 96163

Mexican tale of land and water. (42664)

Mexican treacheries and cruelties. (48573)

Mexican treaty: speech . . . June 20, 1854. 4078

Mexican treaty. Speech of Hon. G. S. Houston. 33182

Mexican war. A discourse delivered on the annual fast, 1847. 7369

Mexican war. A discourse . . . in Fair Haven. 30620

Mexican war: a history of its origin. 44370

Mexican war and its heroes. 48575

Mexican war and its warriors. (26045)

Mexican war. Review of the annual message of the President. 48574

Mexican war; speech . . . December 24, 1846. 27993

Mexican war. Speech . . . in the Senate. 11349

Mexican war. Speech of Hon. L. P. Stanton. 90417

Mexicana. 39140

Mexicana, del siervo de Dios Gregorio Lopez. 98787

Mexicana praecedentiae. Stantibus &c. 96234

Mexicanische Zustande aus den Jahren 1830-1832. 38238

Mexicanische Zustande in den Jahren 1830 bis 1832. 48576

Mexicano. pseud. Desengago a los Indios. see V., A., el Mexicano. pseud.

Mexicano. pseud. Observaciones criticas. 99656

Mexicano. pseud. Ocios de un Mexicano. 56649

Mexicano. pseud. Se nos ha entregado en Tejas. 95112

Mexicano. pseud. Sencillas observaciones. see Rus de Cea, Genaro.

Mexicano libre potosinense. 93790

Mexicanos pintados por si mismos. 48577

Mexicanos ¿ quereis mas ? 98115

Mexicanos y su pas. (48578)

Mexico. 15082-15083, 19268, (20272), 26577, 36791, 44291, 47585, 48109, 48115, (48254), (48380), (48382), 48397, 48202, 48408, 48410, 48423, 48434, 48439, 48478, 48485, 48623, 48637, 48638, 48644, 48661, 51475, 52248, 56764, 58076, 59297, 59301, 59302, 63692-(63693), 67104, (67644), 67845, 67910, 68680, 68834, 70057, 61628, (72279), 75781, 76728, 79032, 93783, 93785, 93788, 93791, 94603, 95074, 96205, 106240

Mexico. defendants 48340

Mexico. Administracion General de Correos. 48644, 48498

Mexico. Alcalde 3 Constitucional. 57840 see also Otero, Mariano, 1817-1850.

Mexico. Alcaldes Constituciones. 23575

Mexico. Archivo General de la Nacion. (46205), 70163

Mexico. Cancillaria. 71628

Mexico. Citizens. petitioners 48415, 48473, 67083, 69975

Mexico. Clero. petitioners see Catholic Church in Mexico. petitioners

Mexico. Colegio de Abogados. see Colegio de Abogados de Mexico.

Mexico. Colegio de Espiritu Santo. see Colegio de Espiritu Santo de Mexico.

Mexico. Colegio de S. Ildefonso. see Colegio de S. Ildefonso de Mexico.

Mexico. Colegio Mayor de S. Maria de Todos Santos. see Colegio Mayor de S. Maria de Todos-Santos de Mexico.

Mexico. Colegio Militar. 48644

Mexico. Colegio Nacional de Mineria. 48273

Mexico. Colegio Nacional de Mineria. Antiguo Profesores. 48273

Mexico. Comercio. petitioners 76311

Mexico. Comision de Estadistica Militar. see Sociedad Mexicana de Geografia y Estadistica.

Mexico. Comision de Limites. 12892, (48885)

Mexico. Comision de Relaciones. 48498, 68678

Mexico. Comision Eclesiastica. 48434, 50096 68678

Mexico. Comision Especial de Mineria. 4847.

Mexico. Comision Formar un Plan de Colonizacion en el Ysmo de Hoazacoalco o Tehuantepec. 48302, 94592

Mexico. Comision Nombrada Para la Reforma del Arancel, de las Aduanas Maritimas y Fronterizas. 23432

Mexico. Comision que Firmaron el Tratado de Paz con los Estados-Unidos. 22914

Mexico. Comision Mixta de Reclamaciones Mexicanas y Americanas. see United States and Mexican Claims Commission, 1869-1876.

Mexico. Comisionado del Ramo de Coches de Providencia. 39926 see also Suarez de Peredo, Agustin.

Mexico. Comisiones de Hacienda y Comercio Unidas. 20120

Mexico. Comisiones de Justicia. Mayoria. (78909)

Mexico. Comisiones Unidas de Industria y Primera de Hacienda. 20112

Mexico. Comisiones Unidas de Relaciones y Guerra. 20113

Mexico. Commissioner in the Joint Claims Commission. 48342 see also United States and Mexican Claims Commission, 1869-1876.

Mexico. Commissioner to the Conference with the Commissioner of the United States, Queretaro, Mexico, 1847. 23433

Mexico. Conferencias entre el Ministro de Relaciones Exteriores Plenipotenciario y el Contra Almirante Plenipotenciario de Francia Sobre el Arreglo de las Diferencias entre Ambas Naciones, Jalapa, Mexico, 1838. 35539-35540

Mexico. Congreso. (48254), 48525, 48630, 48631, 48644, 69576

Mexico. Congreso. Comision de Negocios Eclesiasticos. (20105)

Mexico. Congreso. Comision Nombrada Form un Proyecto de Bases de Organizacion. 48631

Mexico. Congreso. Comision Especial Forma un Proyecto de Constitucion. 48631

Mexico. Congreso. Camara de Diputados.
48524, 48650, 48658, (48665), 68681
Mexico. Congreso. Camara de Diputados.
Comision de Credito Publico. 20102,
48431-48432
Mexico. Congreso. Camara de Diputados.
Comision de Hacienda. 20103, 20110,
49394, 98621
Mexico. Congreso. Camara de Diputados.
Comision de Puntos Constitucionales.
20106
Mexico. Congreso. Camara de Diputados.
Comision Encargada de Formacion de
Proyecto de Arancel de Aduenas Mari-
timas. 48631
Mexico. Congreso. Camara de Diputados.
Comision Especial Sobre el Privilegio
Concedido a D. Jose Garay. 26550
Mexico. Congreso. Camara de Diputados.
Comision Para Arreglar los Aranceles
Para las Aduanas Maritimas. 48433
Mexico. Congreso. Camara de Diputados.
Comisiones Eclesiastica y de Relaciones.
20109, 98952
Mexico. Congreso. Camara de Diputados.
Gran Jurado. 582, 35066, (65925)
Mexico. Congreso. Camara de Diputados.
Gran Jurado. Sesiones Unidos. 76747
Mexico. Congreso. Camara de Senadores.
56451, 98823
Mexico. Congreso. Camara de Senadores.
Comision de Guerra. 20111, 106224
Mexico. Congreso. Camara de Senadores.
Comision de Puntos Constitucionales.
106224
Mexico. Congreso. Camara de Senadores.
Comision de Relaciones. 66567
Mexico. Congreso. Camara de Senadores.
Comision Eclesiastica. 66567
Mexico. Congreso. Camara de Senadores.
Comision Especial de Tehuantepec Encar-
gada de Escaminar las Varias Resolu-
iones Dictadas con Motivo de Privilegio
Concedido a D. Jose Garay. 26550
Mexico. Congreso. Camara de Senadores.
Comision Sobre la Aprobacion del Traito
con los Estados Unidos. 20104
Mexico. Congreso. Camara de Senadores.
Comisiones Reunidas. 48604
Mexico. Congreso. Camara de Senadores.
Comisiones Unidas de Puntos Consti-
tucionales y Guerra. 34413, 98624,
106224
Mexico. Congreso. Camara de Senadores.
Gran Jurado. 67845
Mexico. Congreso Constituyente, 1822. (48656)
Mexico. Congreso Constituyente, 1823. Com-
ision. 48252
Mexico. Congreso Constituyente, 1824. 48527,
66051
Mexico. Congreso Constituyente, 1824-1830.
48351, 48412
Mexico. Congreso Constituyente, 1842. Com-
ision Especial Formar un Proyecto de
Constitucion. Mayoria. 48631
Mexico. Congreso Constituyente, 1842. Com-
ision Especial Formar un Proyecto de
Constitucion. Minoria. 48631
Mexico. Congreso de Panama, 1826. see
Congreso de Panama, 1826.
Mexico. Consejo. 48644, 68862
Mexico. Consejo Administrativo. 48406
Mexico. Consejo de Estado. (20115)
Mexico. Consejo de Guerra. 67340, 71419
Mexico. Conservadores de los Provincias.
23444, 48452

Mexico. Constitution. 16084, 39283, 40352,
48253, 48300-48301, 48303, 48349,
48379, 48389, 48527, (48626), (51321),
57349, 76062, 94939, 94942-94943,
94946
Mexico. Contrador Jeneral de las Réntas
Nacionales de Tabaco y Polvora. 98027
see also Unzueta, Juan Antonio de.
Mexico. Contrador Mayor, Gefe de la Oficina
de Rezagos. 98028 see also Unzueta,
Juan Antonio de.
Mexico. Corte del Ramo Criminal. 11403
Mexico. Corte Suprema de Justicia. see
Mexico. Suprema Corte de Justicia.
Mexico. Cortes. 34831
Mexico. Diputacion Encargada a Ofrecer la
Corona de Mejico al Archiduque Maxi-
miliano. Presidente. 29354
Mexico. Direccion de Colonizacion e Industria.
48540, 48554
Mexico. Direccion de las Fabricas. 69982
Mexico. Direccion General de Adunas. 34833
Mexico. Direccion General de Agricultura e
Industria. 48556
Mexico. Direccion General de Industria
Nacional. 48540
Mexico. Ejercito. (48352), 48458, 48605,
(48611), 48627, 48644, 67661, 68859,
68870
Mexico. Ejercito. Caballera. (48352)
Mexico. Ejercito. Corte Marcial (Celis)
67340
Mexico. Ejercito. Corte Marcial (Rangel)
67845
Mexico. Ejercito. Comandante en Gefe de la
Division de Operaciones Sobre Guada-
lajara. see Robles Pezuela, Manuel.
Mexico. Ejercito. Cuerpo Medico Militar.
48631
Mexico. Ejercito. Cuerpo Permanente de
Artilleria. 48290
Mexico. Ejercito. Cuerpo Permanente de
Ingenieros. 48290
Mexico. Ejercito. Gefe del Estado Mayor
General. 68870
Mexico. Ejercito. Guarnicion de Veracruz.
57661
Mexico. Ejercito. Seccion Auxiliar de Chiapas.
Comandante en Gefe. 44274
Mexico. Ejercito. Suprema Corte Marcial.
70052
Mexico. Fabricas Nacionales de Hilados y
Tegidos de Algodon. Empresarios.
petitioners see Empresarios, de Fab-
ricas Nacionales de Hilados y Tegidos
de Algodon. petitioners
Mexico. Fiesta Nacional, Sept. 16, 1866.
47036, 66549
Mexico. Fiscal. 105953 see also Alvarado,
Antonio. Castro, Tomas de.
Mexico. Fiscal. plaintiff 73864
Mexico. Gremio de Panaderos. see Gremio
de Panaderos de Mexico.
Mexico. Hacendados de los Llanos de Apam.
petitioners see Hacendados de los
Llanos de Apam. petitioners
Mexico. Instituto Literario. see Instituto
Literario de Mexico.
Mexico. Instituto Nacional de Geografia y
Estadistica. see Sociedad Mexicana de
Geografia y Estadistica.
Mexico. Joint Claims Commission. see
United States and Mexican Claims Com-
mission, 1869-1876.
Mexico. Junta Civica. Comision. 52332,
68791

Mexico. Sociedad de Geografia y Estadistica. see Sociedad Mexicana de Geografia y Estadistica.

Mexico. Sociedad Economica. see Sociedad Economica de Mexico.

Mexico. Sociedad Patriotica Promovedora de la Defensa Nacional. see Sociedad Patriotica Promovedora de la Defensa Nacional de Mexico.

Mexico. Sociedad Promovedora de Mejores Materiales y Morales. see Sociedad Mexicana Promovedora de Mejores Materiales y Morales.

Mexico. Suprema Corte de Justicia. 23446, 29290, 34714, 44269, 44288, 48282, 59319, 64444, (69976), 99653, 100791

Mexico. Suprema Corte de Justicia. Presidente. 48441

Mexico. Suprema Corte de Justicia. Primera Sala. defendants (48665), 98823, 1st note after 99783

Mexico. Suprema Corte de Justicia. Tercera Sala. 11295, (17846)

Mexico. Supremo Poder Conservador. 96205, 96207

Mexico. Supremo Tribunal de Guerra y Marina. see Mexico. Suprema Corte de Justicia.

Mexico. Tesoreria General. 48644

Mexico. Treaties, etc. 48115, 48365, 48369, 48398, 59301, 66114, (73030), 76747, 94966, 95035

Mexico. Tribunal de Guerra y Marina. see Mexico. Suprema Corte de Justicia.

Mexico. Tribunal de Revision de Cuentas. 48644

Mexico. Tribunales. 47808, 48364, 79055

Mexico. United States and Mexican Boundary Survey. see U. S. United States and Mexican Boundary Survey.

Mexico. Varios Ciudadanos. petitioners see Mexico. Citizens. petitioners

Mexico. Varios Individuos. petitioners see Mexico. Citizens. petitioners

Mexico. Varias Personas. petitioners see Mexico. Citizens. petitioners

Mexico (Archdiocese) 14298, 34836, 42066, 42985, 48360, 48369, 48387, (56245), 68840, 73867, 97707, 98919

Mexico (Archdiocese) petitioners 84518

Mexico (Archdiocese) plaintiffs 67333

Mexico (Archdiocese) Archbishop (ca 1650) defendant 98773

Mexico (Archdiocese) Archbishop (ca 1703) 74517

Mexico (Archdiocese) Archbishop (ca 1864) 47034

Mexico (Archdiocese) Archbishop (Fonte) 24995, 48651 see also Fonte, Pedro Jose, Abp.

Mexico (Archdiocese) Archbishop (Garza y Ballesteros) 26719, 26721, (38617), 39476, 44276, 48320, (48395), 48396 see also Garza y Ballesteros, Lazaro de la, Abp., 1785-1862.

Mexico (Archdiocese) Archbishop (Hara y Peralta) 16064, 30411 see also Hara y Peralta, Alonso Nunez de, Abp.

Mexico (Archdiocese) Archbishop (Iturrigary) 65930 see also Iturrigary, Jose de, Abp. Mexico (Viceroyalty) Virrey, 1803-1808 (Iturrigary)

Mexico (Archdiocese) Archbishop (Labastida y Davalos) 39283-39284 see also Labastida y Davalos, Pelagio Antonio de, Abp., 1816-1891.

Mexico (Archdiocese) Archbishop (Lizana y Beaumont) 41661-41662, 48319, (48629) see also Lizana y Beaumont, Francisco Xavier de, Abp. Mexico (Viceroyalty) Virrey, 1809-1810 (Lizana y Beaumont)

Mexico (Archdiocese) Archbishop (Lanciego y Egualiz) 38810 see also Lanciego y Eguilaz, Joseph de, Abp., d. 1728.

Mexico (Archdiocese) Archbishop (Lorenzana y Buitron) 42062-42066, 47702, 55934, 69229, 72519, note after 90828, 94355 see also Lorenzana y Buitron, Francisco Antonio, Cardinal.

Mexico (Archdiocese) Archbishop (Lorenzana y Buitron) petitioner 48559 see also Lorenzana y Buitron, Francisco Antonio, Cardinal. petitioner

Mexico (Archdiocese) Archbishop (Manso y Zuniga) 44393, 86421 see also Manso y Zuniga, Francisco, Abp.

Mexico (Archdiocese) Archbishop (Mendoza) 75884 see also Mendoza, Juan de, Abp.

Mexico (Archdiocese) Archbishop (Montufar) (42063) see also Montufar, Alonso de, Abp.

Mexico (Archdiocese) Archbishop (Moya de Contreras) (36795), 42064, 42066, 48373-(48374), 76223, 76332, note after 90828 see also Moya de Contreras, Pedro, Abp.

Mexico (Archdiocese) Archbishop (Nunez de Haro y Peralta) 16064, 30411 see also Nunez de Haro y Peralta, Alonzo, Abp., 1729-1800.

Mexico (Archdiocese) Archbishop (Palafox y Mendoza) 74863 see also Mexico (Viceroyalty) Virrey, 1642 (Palafox y Mendoza) Palafox y Mendoza, Juan, Abp.

Mexico (Archdiocese) Archbishop (Ribera) 70804 see also Guatemala (Diocese) Bishop (Ribera) Mexico (Viceroyalty) Virrey, 1673-1680 (Ribera) Ribera, Payo Henriquez de, Abp. Vera Paz (Diocese) Bishop (Ribera)

Mexico (Archdiocese) Archbishop (Rubio y Salinas) (48448), 48469, 73867-73872, 94171 see also Rubio y Salinas, Manuel Joseph, Abp.

Mexico (Archdiocese) Archbishop (Serna) (48440), 76332, note after 90828 see also Serna, Juan de la, Abp.

Mexico (Archdiocese) Archbishop (Vega) 98741 see also Vega, Feliciano de la.

Mexico (Archdiocese) Archbishop (Vizarron y Eguiarreta) 100637 see also Mexico (Viceroyalty) Virrey, 1734-1740 (Vizarron y Eguiarreta) Vizarron y Eguiarreta, Juan Antonio de, Abp.

Mexico (Archdiocese) Bishop (Zumarraga) 994, 27168, 71100-71101, 94852, 94856, 106398-106401 see also Zumarraga, Juan de, Bp.

Mexico (Archdiocese) Cabildo. 48434, 48451, 48604, 50096, 78948

Mexico (Archdiocese) Canoniga Magistral. 77054

Mexico (Archdiocese) Canoniga Magistral. petitioners 58391

Mexico (Archdiocese) Colegio Seminario. 78948

Mexico (Archdiocese) Convocatoria. Comision Especial. 20108

Mexico (Archdiocese) Gobernador de la Sagrada Mitra. 35546, (48338) see also Sainz de Alfaro y Beaumont, Isidro.

Mexico (Archdiocese) Jueces di Diezmos. 19259

Mexico (Archdiocese) Presbitero. pseud.
see Presbitero de Este Arzobispado
[i. e. Mexico]. pseud.
Mexico (Archdiocese) Vicario Capitular.
93348
Mexico (City) 24157, 34348, 40078, 47032,
(48457), (48516), 48587, 48603, 48644,
note before 98814
Mexico (City) Academia de Derecho Espanol.
see Academia de Derecho Espanol,
Mexico (City)
Mexico (City) Academia de Jurisprudencia.
see Academia de Jurisprudencia,
Mexico (City)
Mexico (City) Academia de San Felipe Neri.
see Academia de San Felipe Neri,
Mexico (City)
Mexico (City) Academia Medico-Quirurgica.
see Academia Medico-Quirurgica,
Mexico (City)
Mexico (City) Academia Nacional de San
Carlos de Mexico. 48324
Mexico (City) Archicofradia de Arcangel San
Miguel. see San Miguel (Parroquia),
Mexico (City) Archicofradia de San
Miguel.
Mexico (City) Archicofradio de Ciudadanos
de Santa Verracruz. see Santa Verra-
cruz (Parroquia), Mexico (City) Archi-
cofradia de Ciudadanos.
Mexico (City) Archicofradia de San Miguel.
see San Miguel (Parroquia), Mexico
(City) Archicofradia de San Miguel.
Mexico (City) Ayuntamiento. 48299, 48353,
48523, 48598, (58590), (68464), 73867,
96228, 99595
Mexico (City) Ayuntamiento. petitioners
69988
Mexico (City) Ayuntamiento. Ramos Muni-
cipales. (48545)
Mexico (City) Casa de Ninos Expositos. see
Mexico (City) Casa del Senor S. Joseph
de Ninos Expositos.
Mexico (City) Casa del Senor S. Joseph de
Ninos Expositos. 16064
Mexico (City) Casa del Senor S. Joseph de
Ninos Expositos. Junta de Senoras
Encargada de la Direccion. 23442
Mexico (City) Catedral. 34347
Mexico (City) Catedral. plaintiffs 75584
Mexico (City) Catedral. Dean y Cabildo.
23337, 51342
Mexico (City) Catedral. Dean y Cabildo.
defendants (72561), 99464
Mexico (City) Catedral. Dean y Cabildo.
plaintiffs 12958, 93331-93332
Mexico (City) Catedral. Maestro de Ceremonias.
98786
Mexico (City) Charter. 47199, (48509)
Mexico (City) Cofradia de Santiago. see
Cofradia de Santiago, Mexico (City)
Mexico (City) Colegio de la Paz. 48388
Mexico (City) Colegio de San Gregorio. 67111
Mexico (City) Colegio de San Ignacio de
Loyola. see Mexico (City) Colegio de
la Paz.
Mexico (City) Colegio de San Ildephonso de
Mexico. 13058, 48336, 48391, (57722),
76115-76116
Mexico (City) Colegio del Espiritu Santo.
(16057)
Mexico (City) Colegio Mayor de Santa Maria
de Todos Santos. plaintiffs 48262
Mexico (City) Colegio Mayor de Santa Maria
de Todos Santos. petitioners 68333-
68334

Mexico (City) Comisionados del Desague.
48500
Mexico (City) Congregacion de Nuestra Senora
de Aranzazu. see Congregacion de
Nuestra Senora de Aranzazu, Mexico
(City)
Mexico (City) Congregacion de Nuestro Padre
San Pedro. see Congregacion de Nuestro
Padre San Pedro, Mexico (City)
Mexico (City) Congregacion del Alumbrado y
Vela Continua al Santissimo Sacramento.
see San Sebastian (Parroquia), Mexico
(City) Congregacion del Alumbrado y
Vela Continua al Santissimo Sacramento.
Mexico (City) Congregacion del Esclavos
Cocheros del Santiss. Sacramento. see
Salta de Agua (Parroquia), Mexico (City)
Congregacion del Esclavos Cocheros del
Santiss. Sacramento.
Mexico (City) Congregacion del Esclavos del
Divinisimo Senor Sacramentado. see
San Jose (Parroquia), Mexico (City)
Congregacion del Esclavos del Divinisimo
Senor Sacramentado.
Mexico (City) Consistorio. 66052
Mexico (City) Congregacion de el Oratorio.
see Congregacion de el Oratorio, Mexico
(City)
Mexico (City) Convento de Corpus Christi.
11459
Mexico (City) Convento de Nuestra Senora de
Bethlem y San Francisco Xavier (Beth-
lemite) 86550
Mexico (City) Convento de Religiosas de Jesus
Maria. 38545, 56325
Mexico (City) Convento de San Diego. Prelado
48416
Mexico (City) Convento de Santa Clara.
defendants 86408
Mexico (City) Convento de Senor San Felipe
de Jesus (Capuchin) 94171
Mexico (City) Convento Real de Jesus Maria.
see Mexico (City) Convento de Reli-
giosas de Jesus Maria.
Mexico (City) Corporacion Municipal. peti-
tioners 48539
Mexico (City) Esclavitud de la Santissimo
Sacremento. see Esclavos Confrades
de la Esclavitud de la Santissimo Sacra-
mento, Mexico (City)
Mexico (City) Esclavos Cocheros del Santiss.
Sacramento. see Salta de Agua (Par-
roquia), Mexico (City) Congregacion del
Esclavos Cocheros del Santiss. Sacra-
mento.
Mexico (City) Esclavos Confrades de la Escla-
vitud de la Santissimo Sacramento. see
Esclavos Confrades de la Esclavitud de la
Santissimo Sacramento Mexico (City)
Mexico (City) Escuela de la Inmaculada Con-
cepcion de la Parroquia de Vera Cruz.
see Vera Cruz (Parroquia), Mexico
(City) Escuela de la Inmaculada Con-
cepcion.
Mexico (City) Exposicion del Flores, Arbustos
Frutas, la., 1849. 48442
Mexico (City) Exposicion General de Industria,
1853. see Exposicion General de In-
dustria, Mexico (City), 1853.
Mexico (City) Fiscal. 9813, 98932
see also Soles, Martin de.
Mexico (City) Hospicio de Pobres. 48616
Mexico (City) Hospital Real y General de los
Indios. 56249-56250
Mexico (City) Iglesia Catedral. see Mexico
(City) Catedral.

Mexico (City) Iglesia de la SS. Trinidad. Congregacion de Nuestro Padre San Pedro. see Congregacion de San Pedro.

Mexico (City) Iglesia Metropolitana. see Mexico (City) Catedral.

Mexico (City) Iglesia Parrochial de la Santa Vera-Cruz. 93581

Mexico (City) Illustre Archicofradia de San Miguel. see San Miguel (Parroquia), Mexico (City) Archicofradia de San Miguel.

Mexico (City) Jueces de Letras. 23446

Mexico (City) Juez Primero de lo Criminal. 76747

Mexico (City) Junta de Policia. 48652

Mexico (City) Jurado de Sentencia. (23061)

Mexico (City) Juzgado Ecclesiastico. 74517

Mexico (City) Milicia. 48644

Mexico (City) Museo Nacional. (34151), 99641

Mexico (City) Museo Nacional. Conservador. 67642 see also Ramirez, Jose Fernando.

Mexico (City) Museo Nacional de Antiguedades. see Mexico (City) Museo Nacional.

Mexico (City) Ninos Expositos. petitioners see Ninos Expositos de la Imperial Ciudad de Mexico. petitioners

Mexico (City) Oficina de Desamortizacion. (4562)

Mexico (City) Ordinances, etc. (26476), 47199, (48322), (48509), 48608, (48612), 48616, 48617, 48618, 48644, (48663), 68888, 73867

Mexico (City) Parian. 48353, (58590)

Mexico (City) Parroquia de Salto de Agua. see Salto de Agua (Parroquia) Mexico, (City)

Mexico (City) Parroquia de San Jose. see San Jose (Parroquia), Mexico (City)

Mexico (City) Parroquia de San Miguel. see San Miguel (Parroquia), Mexico (City)

Mexico (City) Parroquia de San Sebastian. see San Sebastian (Parroquia), Mexico (City)

Mexico (City) Piadosa Compania de Cocheros y Lacayos. see Piadosa Compania de Cocheros y Lacayos, Mexico (City)

Mexico (City) Real Jardin. 63314

Mexico (City) Rector de Escuelas. 20138 see also Diez de Solano, Jose Maria.

Mexico (City) Reunion de los Gobiernadores de los Estados Para Proveer a las Exigencias del Erario Federal, 1851. (48443)

Mexico (City) Reverendos Padres Bethlemitas del Convento de Nuestra Senora de Bethlem, y San Francisco Xavier. see Mexico (City) Convento de Nuestra Senora de Bethlem y San Francisco Xavier (Bethlemite)

Mexico (City) Sala del Crimen. (48475), 87161

Mexico (City) Santa Iglesia Catedral. see Mexico (City) Catedral.

Mexico (City) Santa Verracruz (Parroquia) see Santa Verracruz (Parroquia), Mexico (City)

Mexico (City) Siervos de Maria Santisima de los Dolores. see Tercer Orden de los Siervos de Maria Santisima de los Dolores, Mexico (City)

Mexico (City) Sociedad. see Sociedad, Mexico (City)

Mexico (City) Sociedad de Subcritores del Teatro de la Ciudad. see Sociedad de Subscritores del Teatro de la Ciudad de Mexico.

Mexico (City) Tercer Orden de los Siervos de Maria Santisima de los Dolores. see Tercer Orden de los Siervos de Maria Santisima de los Dolores, Mexico (City)

Mexico (City) Tribunal de Jurados. 99703

Mexico (City) Universidad. 26577, 48494, (48501), 48662, 52090, (57264), 58292, 72532, 86444

Mexico (City Universidad. defendants 48262

Mexico (City) Universidad. Claustro Pleno. (48501), 86550

Mexico (City) Universidad de Mercaderes. see Universidad de Mercaderes de Mexico.

Mexico (Departamento) see Mexico (State)

Mexico (Diocese) see Mexico (Archdiocese)

Mexico (Ecclesiastical Province) Council, 3d, 1585. 42066, 76223, 86332, note after 90828

Mexico (Empire, 1822-1823) 48258

Mexico (Empire, 1822-1823) Ejercito. Primer Gefe. 65551

Mexico (Empire, 1822-1823) Imperial Orden de Guadalupe. see Orden de Guadalupe (Mexico)

Mexico (Empire, 1822-1823) Junta Nacional. (49422)

Mexico (Empire, 1822-1823) Soberano Congreso. Comision Encargada de Formar el Ceremonial que Para la Inauguracion Consagracion y Coronacion de Su Majestad el Emperador Augustin Primero. 35294, 66405

Mexico (Empire, 1822-1823) Sovereigns, etc., 1822-1823 (Iturbide) 49385 see also Iturbide, Augustin de, Emperor of Mexico, 1783-1824.

Mexico (Empire, 1864-1867) 17157, (37607)-(37609), 47036, (48446), (48456), 48459, 70163

Mexico (Empire, 1864-1867) Cabinete Civil. 48645

Mexico (Empire, 1864-1867) Cabinete Militar. 48645

Mexico (Empire, 1864-1867) Comision scientifica. 48286

Mexico (Empire, 1864-1867) Comisionados en los Estados-Unidos. see Mexico (Empire, 1864-1867) Legation. United States.

Mexico (Empire, 1864-1867) Consejo de Guerra. (57673)

Mexico (Empire, 1864-1867) Ejercito. 44671

Mexico (Empire, 1864-1867) Laws, statutes, etc. 47036, (48278), 48306, 48345, 48645

Mexico (Empire, 1864-1867) Legation. United States. 73025

Mexico (Empire, 1864-1867) Ministerio de Fomento. 47036, 48552, 61333 see also Pezuela, Luis Robles.

Mexico (Empire, 1864-1867) Ministerio de Gobernacion. Seccion de Fomento. (48499)

Mexico (Empire, 1864-1867) Ministerio de Instruccion Publica. 48286

Mexico (Empire, 1864-1867) Ministerio de Relaciones Interiores y Esteriores. 26547-26548, 47520

Mexico (Empire, 1864-1867) Secretaria de Fomento. (48278)

Mexico (Empire, 1864-1867) Sovereigns, etc., 1864-1867 (Maximilian) 1867, (39838), 47033, 47036, 58292, 86444 see also Maximilian, Emperor of Mexico, 1836-1867.

Mexico (Empire, 1864-1867) Sovereigns, etc., 1864-1867 (Maximilian) defendant 47036, 58273 see also Maximilian, Emperor of Mexico, 1836-1867. defendant

Mexico (Federal District) Alcaldes de Cuartel. 23575

Mexico (Federal District) Asamblea Municipal. Presidente. defendant 35066 see also Suarez Iriarte, Francisco. defendant

Mexico (Federal District) Capoteros. petitioners see Capoteros, Mexico (Federal District) petitioners

Mexico (Federal District) Gefes de Manzana. 23575

Mexico (Federal District) Gobernador (Trigueros) (23061) see also Trigueros, Ignacio.

Mexico (Federal District) Oficina Especial de Desamortizacion. (47592)

Mexico (State) 48282, 76147, 99595

Mexico (State) Administracion de Rentas. 48660

Mexico (State) Comision. 48498

Mexico (State) Gobernador (Arizcorreta) 70094 see also Arizcorreta, Mariano.

Mexico (State) Laws, statutes, etc. 48411, 48438

Mexico (State) Legislatura. 48438, 63687

Mexico (State) Legislatura. complainants (48665), 98823, 1st note after 99783

Mexico (Viceroyalty) (9891), 27823, (44420), 44947, 48339, (48380), 48408, 48481, 56252-56253, (56263), (72561), 93775, note after 96350

Mexico (Viceroyalty) Academia de San Carlos. see Academia de San Carlos de Nueva-Espana.

Mexico (Viceroyalty) Audiencia. see Mexico (Viceroyalty) Real Audiencia.

Mexico (Viceroyalty) Chancilleria. 50110, 93586

Mexico (Viceroyalty) Citizens. 94854

Mexico (Viceroyalty) Consejos de Guerra. 93775

Mexico (Viceroyalty) Constitution. 48330

Mexico (Viceroyalty) Consulado. 86415

Mexico (Viceroyalty) Consulado. defendants 98018

Mexico (Viceroyalty) Contador de la Visita de las Caxas Reales. defendant 42067 see also Lorenzo de San Milian, Francisco. defendant

Mexico (Viceroyalty) Contador Jeneral de las Rentas Nacionales de Tabaco y Polvora. 98027-98028 see also Unzueta, Juan Antonio de.

Mexico (Viceroyalty) Correo Maritimo. 98490

Mexico (Viceroyalty) Cuerpo de Invalidos. 68861

Mexico (Viceroyalty) Cuerpo de la Mineria. 56260

Mexico (Viceroyalty) Cuerpo de Patriotas Distinguidos de Fernando Septimo. 98856

Mexico (Viceroyalty) Ejercito. 68881

Mexico (Viceroyalty) Ejercito. Presidio de Nuestra Senora del Carmen de la Isla de Tris. Guarnicion. 68885

Mexico (Viceroyalty) Ejercito. Presidio de San Felipe de Bacalar, Yucatan. Guarnicion. 68878

Mexico (Viceroyalty) Ejercito. Presidio del Carmen. Guarnicion. 34830

Mexico (Viceroyalty) Ejercito. Presidio del Carmen. Guarnicion. Hospital. 34837

Mexico (Viceroyalty) Ejercito. Real Cuerpo de Artilleria. 98861

Mexico (Viceroyalty) Fiscal. 9813, 98932 see also Soles, Martin de.

Mexico (Viceroyalty) Fiscal. defendant 73042

Mexico (Viceroyalty) Fiscal. plaintiff 87161 see also Zepeda y Castro, Gaspar de. plaintiff

Mexico (Viceroyalty) Hospital de los Indios. see Mexico (City) Hospital de los Indios

Mexico (Viceroyalty) Junta de Censura. 93789

Mexico (Viceroyalty) Junta Jeneral. 99688

Mexico (Viceroyalty) Junta Superior de Real Hacienda. 70285

Mexico (Viceroyalty) Junta Suprema. 48508

Mexico (Viceroyalty) Juzgado. 57478

Mexico (Viceroyalty) Juzgado de Bienes de Difuntos. (9891), note after 96350, 99629

Mexico (Viceroyalty) Laws, statutes, etc. 4419, (9891), 34830, 36899, 47199, 47833, 48334, 48358, 48413, 48504-48506 (48509), 48615, (48637), 48644, 52109, 56242, 56247, 56249-56250, 56254, 56255, 56256-56257, 56261, 56262, 56403, (57470)-57471, 57478-57479, 57486, 57516, 57518, 58417, 65996, 66407, 66605, 68386-68390, 68860-68861, 68872-68873, 68878, 68881, 68885, 68888, 70285-(70287), 72430, (72549), (75600), 76861, (77671), 86411, 93586, 99447, note after 95563, note after 96350, 96475, 98794, 98797, 98856-98857, 99408

Mexico (Viceroyalty) Orden de Carlos III. see Orden de Carlos III. Mexico.

Mexico (Viceroyalty) Pobres Mendigos. petitioners see Pobres Mendigos de Mexico. petitioners

Mexico (Viceroyalty) Real Aduana. 68888

Mexico (Viceroyalty) Real Audiencia. 4419, (9891), 48812, 50110, (72561), 87160, 93586, 94852, 98967, 99619, note after 96350

Mexico (Viceroyalty) Real Casa de Moneda. 48615

Mexico (Viceroyalty) Real Casa de Moneda. Tesorero Proprietario. defendant 26122 see also Medina y Saravia, Joseph Diego de. defendant

Mexico (Viceroyalty) Real Faxa. (9891), note after 96350

Mexico (Viceroyalty) Real Colegio de Escribanos. see Real Colegio de Escribanos de Mexico.

Mexico (Viceroyalty) Real Fabrica y Estampa de Naypes. 56246

Mexico (Viceroyalty) Real Hacienda. 99685

Mexico (Viceroyalty) Real Renta de la Polvora 56256

Mexico (Viceroyalty) Real Renta de los Naype (56255)

Mexico (Viceroyalty) Real Renta del Tabaco. 56257

Mexico (Viceroyalty) Real Tribunal de Mineria 69992

Mexico (Viceroyalty) Real Tribunal de Protomedicato. 24156, 96251

Mexico (Viceroyalty) Real Tribunal General. 56260

Mexico (Viceroyalty) Reales Tributos. 56264

Mexico (Viceroyalty) Resgardo Unido de Rentas Reales. 48505

Mexico (Viceroyalty) Sala del Crimen. 4419, (9891), note after 96350
Mexico (Viceroyalty) Senado. 62444, 68334
Mexico (Viceroyalty) Treaties, etc. 98794
Mexico (Viceroyalty) Universidad de Mercaderes. see Universidad de Mercaderes de la Nueva-Espana.
Mexico (Viceroyalty) Virrey. 34839, 93586
Mexico (Viceroyalty) Virrey, 1521-1526 (Cortes) 6420, 48287, 93580 see also Cortes, Hernando, 1485-1547.
Mexico (Viceroyalty) Virrey, 1535-1550 (Mendoza) 47833, 67740, 94852, 94854 see also Mendoza, Antonio de, Conde de Tendilla.
Mexico (Viceroyalty) Virrey, 1590-1595 (Velasco) 98794-98797 see also Velasco, Luis de, Marques de Salinas, 1534-1617.
Mexico (Viceroyalty) Virrey, 1595-1603 (Zuniga y Acevedo) 98794 see also Zuniga y Acevedo, Gaspar de, Conde de Monterey.
Mexico (Viceroyalty) Virrey, 1624-1635 (Osorio) (48440), 56247, 66052 see also Osorio, Rodrigo Pacheco, Marques de Cerralvo.
Mexico (Viceroyalty) Virrey, 1642 (Palafox y Mendoza) 99456 see also Palafox y Mendoza, Juan de, Abp., 1600-1659.
Mexico (Viceroyalty) Virrey, 1673-1680 (Ribera) 50110, 70804, 93586 see also Guatemala (Diocese) Bishop (Ribera) Mexico (Archdiocese) Archbishop (Ribera) Ribera, Payo Henriquez de, Abp. Vera Paz (Diocese) Bishop (Ribera)
Mexico (Viceroyalty) Virrey, 1696-1701 (Valladares) (48501), 98783 see also Valladares, Jose Sarmiento, Conde de Montezuma.
Mexico (Viceroyalty) Virrey, 1711-1716 (Alencastro Marona y Silva) 57479 see also Alencastro Marona y Silva, Fernando de, Marques de Valdafuentes.
Mexico (Viceroyalty) Virrey, 1716-1722 (Zuniga Guzman Sotomayor y Mendoza) 69185 see also Zuniga Guzman Sotomayor y Mendoza, Baltazar de, Marques de Valero.
Mexico (Viceroyalty) Virrey, 1722-1734 (Acuna) 11224 see also Acuna, Juan de, Marques de Casafuerte.
Mexico (Viceroyalty) Virrey, 1722-1734 (Acuna) complainant 26122 see also Acuna, Juan de, Marques de Casafuerte. complainant
Mexico (Viceroyalty) Virrey, 1734-1740 (Vizarron y Eguiarreta) 100637-100639 see also Mexico (Archdiocese) Archbishop (Vizarron y Eguiarreta) Vizarron y Eguiarreta, Juan Antonio de, Abp.
Mexico (Viceroyalty) Virrey, 1746-1755 (Guemes y Horcasitas) 29104 see also Guemes y Horcasitas, Juan Francisco de.
Mexico (Viceroyalty) Virrey, 1771-1779 (Bucareli y Ursua) 8836, 68861, 98490 see also Bucareli y Ursua, Antonio Maria, 1717-1779.
Mexico (Viceroyalty) Virrey, 1779-1783 (Mayorga) 47199, 69992 see also Mayorga, Martin de.
Mexico (Viceroyalty) Virrey, 1787 (Nunez de Haro y Peralta) 30411 see also Nunez de Haro y Peralta, Alonso, Abp., 1729-1800.

Mexico (Viceroyalty) Virrey, 1789-1794 (Guemes Pacheo de Podilla) 70288 see also Guemes Pacheo de Podilla, Juan Vicente de, Conde de Revillagigedo.
Mexico (Viceroyalty) Virrey, 1794-1798 (Grua Talamanca) 76861 see also Grua Talamanca, Miguel de la, Marques de Branciforte.
Mexico (Viceroyalty) Virrey, 1803-1808 (Iturrigary) 35299, 65930 see also Iturrigary, Jose de, Abp. Mexico (Archdiocese) Archbishop (Iturrigary)
Mexico (Viceroyalty) Virrey, 1809-1810 (Lizana y Beaumont) (48629) see also Lizana y Beaumont, Francisco Javier, Abp. Mexico (Archdiocese) Archbishop (Lizana y Beaumont)
Mexico (Viceroyalty) Virre, 1810-1816 (Venegas de Saavedra) 98550-98557, 98559-98861 see also Venegas de Saavedra, Francisco Javier.
Mexico (Viceroyalty) Visitador. 98783 see also Contreras, Pedro.
Mexico (Viceroyalty) Visitador General. (48499) see also Galvez, Jose de, Marques de Sonora.
Mexico . . . see also Mejico . . .
Mexico. 73258
Mexico als Ziel fur Deutsche Auswanderung. 77119
Mexico and Guatemala. 49816
Mexico and her financial questions with England, Spain, and France. 59302
Mexico and her military chieftains. (72071)
Mexico and Mr. Poinsett. 48580
Mexico and the Nunroe [sic] doctrine. (48581)
Mexico, and the solidarity of nations. 13799
Mexico, ancient and modern. 12592
Mexico as it is. 46177
Mexico as it was and as it is. 47099, 47103, 90483
Mexico aus d. Span. Ubers. (27208)
Mexico; Aztec, Spanish and republican. 47100, 47103
Mexico: before and after the conquest. (12591)
Mexico before the French invasion. 80163
Mexico. By H. G. Ward, Esq. 101303
Mexico como nacion independiente. 48582, 96434
Mexico conquestada. 22839
Mexico considerado como nacion independiente y libre. 57724
Mexico delivered. 92908
Mexico dividida en quarteles. (48583)
Mexico el imperio y la intervencion. (48584)
Mexico en 1554. 75566
Mexico en 1840 y en 1847. 29262, (29355)
Mexico en 1847. 48585
Mexico en 1863. 14358
Mexico Gulf Railway Company. Chief Engineer. 48686
Mexico illustrated. 62498
Mexico im Jahre 1827. 101304
Mexico in ancient and modern times. 29917
Mexico in den ereignissvollen Jahren 1832 und 1833. 4220
Mexico in 1842. (24968)
Mexico in 1861 and 1862. 40016
Mexico in 1827. 101302
Mexico in 1823. (9142)
Mexico in miniature. 81601
Mexico: its geography. 23870
Mexico. Its revolutions. 12987
Mexico. Landscapes and popular sketches by C. Sartorius. 77121

Mexico. Landschaftsbilder und Skizzen aus dem Volksleben. (77120)
Mexico libre. 57684
Mexico necesita sus ferrocarriles. note just before (73261)
Mexico. Par Emile de la Bedolliere. 38418
Mexico plausibile con la triumphal demonstracion. 48587
Mexico por dentro y fuera. 9582, 2d note after 98255, note after 99675
Mexico. Speeches of Hon. Z. Chandler. 11888
Mexico. Statistical and financial items. 48579
Mexico: the country, history, and people. 48588
Mexico under Maximilian. 24768
Mexico versus Texas. 95143
Mexico y el Sr. Embajador D. Joaquin Francisco Pacheco. 59304
Mexico y la intervencion. 48589
Mexico y sus alrededores. (48590)
Mexico y sus cuestiones financieras. 59301
Mexicos bregner, en system. 40990
Mexicos halvgraes. 40991
Mexicos og Centralamerikas acanthaceer. (56735)
Mexicus exterior. (75565)-75566
Mexikanische Bilder. 45478
Mexikanische Kriegsbilder. 4528
Mexikanische National Gott Huitzilopochtli. (51291)
Mexikanischen Frage beleuchtet. 71226
Mexiko im Jahre 1812. 64541, 64560-64561, 1st note after 99840
Mexiko. Reisebilder von Madame Giovanni. 21184
Mexiko und die Mexikaner. 95763
Mexiko und die Mexikaner von demselben Verfasser. 95765
Mexio, Pedro. see Mexia, Pedro, 1496?-1552?
Mexique. 12596
Mexique ancien et moderne. (12588)
Mexique avant la conquete. 101350
Mexique. Conquete du Mexique par Fernand Cortez. 51408
Mexique conquis. 6124, 86479
Mexique considere au point du vue medicochururgical. (14235)
Mexique contemporain. 4084
Mexique devant les Chambres. 35824
Mexique d'hier et le Mexique de demain. 5140
Mexique. Discours de M. Corta. 16927
Mexique en 1823. (9141)
Mexique (en vers) 73486
Mexique et Guatemala. 39030
Mexique et l'Amerique tropicale. 36683
Mexique et l'Archiduc Fernand Maximilien d'Autriche. 29357
Mexique et les Etats-Unis. (38472), (47926)
Mexique et l'expedition Francaise. 77212
Mexique et l'intervention. 48591
Mexique et l'intervention Europeenne. 39839
Mexique et Maximilien. 23063
Mexique et Texas. 48593
Mexique illustre. 44161
Mexique. L'empire et l'intervention. 48592
Mexique, ou les Francais a Mexique. 21009
Mexique ou Nouvelle-Espagne. 101350
Mexique. Par J. C. Beltrami. 4607, 74948
Mexique. Par Mathieu de Fossey. 25191
Mexique. Par M. Michel Chevalier. 12590
Mexique. Resume geographique, statistique, industriel, historique et social. (3381)

Mexique, ses ressources et son avenir. 48594
Mexique sous la maison de Habsbourg. 30913
Mexique. Souvenirs d'un voyageur. 42506
Mexique, souvenirs et impressions de voyage. (12154)
Mexique tel qu'il est. (20552)
Mexique. Un mot sur l'expose. 29261, (48595
Mexitli; or, the conquest of Mexico. 67382
Meyen, Franz Julius Ferdinand. 48666-48667
Meyen, Johann Jacob. 48668
Meyer, Albertus. 34948, 48669-48670
Meyer, Carl. ed. (52376), 91981
Meyer, E. 48671
Meyer, Edward. 84672
Meyer, Georg Friedrich Wilhelm. 48673
Meyer, H. J. 8204, 48674
Meyer, M. 48676
Meyer, Lewis H. plaintiff 72589
Meyer, Ph. A. G. von. tr. 35180
Meyers, Leon. (48677)
Meyer's universum. 8204, 84674
Meynard de Queilhe, L. le. 48678
Meynardie, E. J. 48679
Mezenzio tragedia originale. 64014
Meziere, --------. 85791
Mi carta al Puebla. 97047
Mi opinion sobre los jueces de letras. 62937
Mi P: rector. Pax Christi. &c. 87246
Miall, Charles. 48680
Miall, James G. 48681
Miami, Ohio. Free Associate Presbytery. see Free Associate Presbytery of Miam
Miami Association of Regular Baptists. see Baptists (Regular Baptists) Ohio., Miami Association.
Miami Indians. Treaties, etc. 96605, 96620, 96695, 96731, 96737
Miami Indians (Thorntown Party) see Eel River Indians.
Miami University, Oxford, Ohio. 48682
Miami University, Oxford, Ohio. Charter. 56948
Miami University, Oxford, Ohio. Erodelphian Society. (41482), 48682
Miami University, Oxford, Ohio. Union Litera Society. (41482)
Miami University and Cincinnati. 58033
Mich, --------. see Migt, ---------.
Michael, John. 86700
Michael, Lucifer & Co. pseud. eds. 105854
Michael Bonham. 81239
Michaeler, K. 48686
Michaelis, Christian Friedrich. tr. 16467, 44196-44197
Michaelis, D. S. F. tr. 88976
Michaelis, G. (48687)
Michaelis, Johannes. 99333
Michaelius, Jonas. 48688
Michaus, J. M. 48336
Michaux, --------, fl. 1793. 48708
Michaux, Andre, 1746-1802. (8754), (48690)-48692
Michaux, Andre, fl. 1852. (48689)
Michaux, Francois Andre, 1770-1855. 776, 48693-48707, 56351, 62506, 67461, (70888), 89287
Michauxs Reise in das Innere der Nordamerikansichen Freistaaten. 48707
Michel, -------- de. ed. 36760
Michel, -------- Fernand. see Fernand-Mich ---------.
Michel, -------- Mavrile de S. see Mavrile de S. Michel, ---------.
Michel, Middleton. 82998, 83003

Michel (E. A.) & Co. firm publishers
53344, 53346
Michelant, H. 11141-11142
Michelbacher, M. J. (48709)
Michelena y Rojas, F. (48710)
Michelin, --------. illus. (54578)
Michels, Ivan C. 4355
Michelson, Albert A. 85072
Michener, Ezra. 48711
Micheovo, Mattheo di. 67738
Michiel, Nicolo di. 67736
Michiels, Alfred. tr. 92532
Michielsen, Michel. 49410
Michigan (Territory) Commissioners to
Revise the Territorial Laws. (48747)
Michigan (Territroy) Conseil Legislatif. see
Michigan (Territory) Legislative Council.
Michigan (Territory) Convention, Ann Arbor,
1836. 48723, (48743)
Michigan (Territory) Governor, 1805-1812
(Hull) 48755, 48780 see also Hull,
William, 1753-1825.
Michigan (Territory) Governor, 1835-1836
(Mason) 48753-48754 see also Mason,
Stevens Thomson, 1811-1843.
Michigan (Territory) Laws, statutes, etc.
48712-(48715), (48746)-(48747), 48774,
48797
Michigan (Territory) Legislative Council.
48713, (48744)
Michigan (Territory) Legislative Council.
petitioners (48752)
Michigan (Territory) Legislature. Senate.
48729, (48731), 48745
Michigan (Territory) Presiding Judge.
(48755), 48780
Michigan. 27249, 48784, 48791, 92392
Michigan. plaintiff 24559
Michigan. Acting Superintendent of Indian
Affairs. see U. S. Office of Indian
Affairs.
Michigan. Asylum for the Insane, Kalamazoo.
Trustees. 48759
Michigan. Adjutant and Quartermaster Gen-
eral. 48719, 48785
Michigan. Attorney General. 48720, (48776)
see also Howard, Jacob Merritt, 1805-
1871.
Michigan. Auditor General. 48720
Michigan. Board of Internal Improvement.
48720
Michigan. Census, 1854. 48724
Michigan. Census, 1860. 48800
Michigan. Citizens. petitioners 88314
Michigan. Commissioner of the Land Office.
see Michigan. Land Office. Com-
missioner.
Michigan. Commissioner on the Soldiers'
National Monument, at Gettysburg, 1864.
27249, 48791
Michigan. Constitution. 1269, 5316, 9672,
16113, 29731, 33137, (47188), (48727),
(48793), 48804, 59771, (66397)
Michigan. Constitutional Convention, 1867.
48728
Michigan. Geological and Mineralogical Survey.
(48737)
Michigan. Geological Survey. 48734-48735,
48736
Michgian. Governor, 1846-1847 (Felch) 48739
see also Felch, Alpheus, 1806-
Michigan. Governor, 1847-1848 (Greenly)
48799 see also Greenly, William L.,
1813-

Michigan. Governor, 1805-1852 (Barry) 33150
see also Barry, John Stewart, 1802-1870.
Michigan. Governor, 1855-1859 (Bingham)
48740 see also Bingham, Kinsley Scott,
1808-1861.
Michigan. Governor, 1861-1865 (Blair) 27249,
48740, 48791 see also Blair, Austin,
1818-1894.
Michigan. Industrial School for Boys, Lansing.
(48772)
Michigan. Inhabitants. petitioners see
Michigan. Citizens. petitioners
Michigan. Land Office. Commissioner. 48721
Michigan. Laws, statutes, etc. 19782, 23765,
28559, 29731, 39556, 48726, 48748,
48761, 48768, 48794-48795, 48801-48802,
52051, 70820-70821, 75423, 82438, 89066
Michigan. Legislative Excursion, 1869. (48749)
Michigan. Legislature. (48730), 48741, 48750
Michigan. Legislature. Committee of Ways
and Means. 48781
Michigan. Legislature. Committee on Agri-
culture. 48717
Michigan. Legislature. Committee to Survey
and Level the Huron River Between
Ypsilanti and Flat Rock. 69801
Michigan. Legislature. Finance Committee.
(48783)
Michigan. Legislature. Joint Committee on
the Geological Survey. 48738
Michigan. Legislature. Special Committee to
Inquire into the Military Expenditures of
the State. 48786
Michigan. Legislature. Special Committee to
Investigate the Proceedings, &c., of the
Boards of Internal Improvement. 48787
Michigan. Legislature. House of Represent-
atives. (24527), (48730), (48742)
Michigan. Legislature. House of Represent-
atives. Committee on Internal Improve-
ments. (48782)
Michigan. Legislature. Senate. 41547, 48729
Michigan. Quartermaster General. see
Michigan. Adjutant and Quartermaster
General.
Michigan. Secretary of State. 48724, (48796)
Michigan. State Agent for Emigration. 48803
Michigan. State Agricultural College, East
Lansing. see Michigan. State Univer-
sity, East Lansing.
Michigan. State Board of Agriculture. Secre-
tary. 48717
Michigan. State Geologist. 48733, 48738
Michigan. State Librarian. 48788
Michigan. State Library, Lansing. 48771
Michigan. State Normal School. (48772)
Michigan. State Reform School, Lansing. see
Michigan. Industrial School for Boys,
Lansing.
Michigan. State Teachers' Institute. (48772)
Michigan. State Treasurer. (48796)
Michigan. State University, East Lansing.
(48716)
Michigan. State University, East Lansing.
President. (48716)
Michigan. Superintendent of Indian Affairs
(Acting) see United States. Office of
Indian Affairs.
Michigan. Superintendent of Public Instruction.
48722, 48725, 48789, 80036, 84814 see
also Sherman, Francis W.
Michigan. University. 11962, 48804
Michigan. University. Board of Regents.
48804

Michigan. University. Chancellor. 48804
Michigan. University. Department of Arts and Sciences. 48804
Michigan. University. Library. 48804
Michigan. University. President. 48804
Michigan (Diocese) see Sault St. Marie (Diocese)
Michigan advertiser. see Detroit journal and Michigan advertiser.
Michigan almanac . . . 1870. 48757
Michigan and Ouisconsin territories. 23834
Michigan Baptist Convention. see Baptists. Michigan. Convention.
Michigan Central College, Spring Arbor. see Hillsdale College, Hillsdale, Mich.
Michigan Central Railroad Company. 48761
Michigan Central Railroad Company. Charter. 48761
Michigan Central Railroad Company. Directors. 48761
Michigan Central Railroad Company. Treasurer. 48761
Michigan. Eine geographisch-statisch-topographische Skizze. 8208
Michigan farmer. 48762
Michigan Female College, Lansing. 48763
Michigan Female Seminary, Lansing. see Michigan Female College, Lansing.
Michigan first regiment. (48764)
Michigan freemason; a monthly magazine. (48765)
Michigan general shippers' guide. 33602
Michigan Historical Society. 84082
Michigan Indians. Treaties, etc. 96647 see also Chippewa Indians. Treaties, etc. Fox Indians. Treaties, etc. Iowa Indians. Treaties, etc. Menominee Indians. Treaties, etc. Ottowa Indians. Treaties, etc. Potawatomi Indians. Treaties, etc. Sauk Indians. Treaties, etc. Sioux Indians. Treaties, etc. Winnebago Indians. Treaties, etc.
Michigan journal of education and teachers' magazine. 48766
Michigan, seine Vorzuge und Hulfsquellen. 48756
Michigan Southern and Northern Indiana Railroad Company. 48768
Michigan Southern and Northern Indiana Railroad Company. Charter. 48768
Michigan Southern and Northern Indiana Railroad Company. Directors. 48768
Michigan Southern and Northern Indiana Railroad Company. President. 5923
Michigan Southern and Northern Indiana Railroad business gazetteer. 48768
Michigan Southern Railroad. (48767)
Michigan State Agricultural Society. 48717
Michigan state gazetteer and business directory for 1863-4. 48769
Michigan state gazetteer, shippers' guide, and business directory. 48770
Michigan Synod. see Presbyterian Church in the U. S. A. Synod of Michigan.
Michigan teacher. 48773
Michigan Teachers' Association. (48772)
Michigan Teachers' Institute. (48772)
Michigan Tobacco Cutter's Association. see Tobacco Cutter's Association of Michigan.
Michigan Young Men's State Temperance Convention, Ann Arbor, 1836. see Young Men's State Temperance Convention, Ann Arbor, Mich., 1836.
Michler, N. (48806)
Michler, N. H. 36377, 84774
Michoacan (State) 48814, 48816, (57235)

Michoacan (State) Comision de Justicia. see Michoacan (State) Congreso. Comision de Justicia.
Michoacan (State) Congreso. Comision de Justicia. 48810
Michoacan (State) Congreso Constituyente, 1824-1825. 48808, 48809
Michoacan (State) Congreso Constituyente, 1827-1829. 48809
Michoacan (State) Constitution. 48808
Michoacan (State) Gobernador (Caballero) 48816 see also Caballero, Joaquim.
Michoacan (State) Laws, statutes, etc. 48809, (51321), 51322
Michoacan (Archdiocese) 34836, 51322
Michoacan (Archdiocese) petitioners 48518
Michoacan (Archdiocese) Archbishop (ca 1859) 44276
Michoacan (Archdiocese) Archbishop (ca 1864) 47034
Michoacan (Archdiocese) Archbishop (Lorenzana y Buitron) 69229 see also Lorenzana y Buitron, Francisco Antonio, Abp.
Michoacan (Archdiocese) Archbishop (Munguia) (36092), 51320-51325 see also Munguia, Clemente de Jesus, Abp.
Michoacan (Archdiocese) Bishop (Morina y Zafrilla) 50698, 86370 see also Moriana y Zafrilla, Marcos, Bp.
Michoacan (Archdiocese) Bishop (Portugal) (11628), 59633 see also Portugal, Juan Cayetano, Bp., 1783-1850.
Michocana (Archdiocese) Bishop (Queipo) (67080), 99500 see also Queipo, Manual Abad, Bp.
Michoacan (Archdiocese) Bishop (Quiroga) 50611 see also Quiroga, Vasco de, Bp., ca. 1470-1565.
Michoacan (Archdiocese) Bishop (Truxillo y Guerro) 97279 see also Truxillo y Guerro, Felipe Ignacio de, Bp.
Michoacan (Archdiocese) Cabildo. 48807
Michoacan (Archdiocese) Comisionados para el funeral y Exequias del Antonio de San Miguel. 34185, (48815), (76183) see also Barcena y Arce, Manuel de la. Escadon y Llera, Mariano. Sierragorda, -----, Conde de.
Michoacan (Diocese) see Michoacan (Archdiocese)
Michoacan (Ecclesiastical Province) defendants 48812
Michoacanos. pseud. De el Sr. Cevallos. 48817
Mickle, Isaac. (48818)
Mickle, Samuel. 85589
Mickley, J. M. 25181, note after 48819
Mickley, Jos. J. 48819
Micmac Indians. Treaties, etc. 33004
Micmac Missionary Society. (48820)
Mico, Francisco Vidal y. see Vidal y Mico, Francisco.
Mico, John. 28052, 28506, 65689
Mico, Tuckahatchee. petitioner 44766
Micoud d'Umons, Charles E. 48821, note after 93822
Microcosmvs, or the historie of man. 66677
Microcosmus Philadelphicus. 56311
Microscope, edited by a fraternity of gentlemen. 105852
Microscopic structure of some Canadian limestones. 18955
Microscopical examination made by the U. S. Coast Survey. 2739, 85072
Microscopical observations made off the Atlantic coast. 2740, 85072

Middelburch, Andries Jassz van. 67980

Middelburg, Netherlands. Zeeuwsch Genootschap der Wetenschappen. see Zeeuwsch
Genootschap der Wetenschappen, Middelburg.

Middelen en motiven om het kopen en verkopen.
15935, 51613, 1st note after 102888,
102896, 102911

Middelgeest, Simon van. supposed author
39241, 55449, 57379, 97530, 98216,
99316

Middelhoven, M. W. D. tr. 7804

Middle age. 82582

Middle District Association. see Baptists.
Virginia. Middle District Association.

Middle District Association met at Cedar-
Creek Meeting-House. 48822

Middle line. 48823, 1st note after 102599

Middleboro, Mass. Church. 48826

Middleboro, Mass. Ecclesiastical Council,
1822. see Congregational Churches
in Massachusetts. Ecclesiastical Council,
Middleboro, 1822.

Middleboro, Mass. First Church. 48827

Middleboro, Mass. First Church of Christ.
48824

Middleboro, Mass. First Congregational
Church. (48829)

Middleboro, Mass. School Committee. (48829)

Middleboro, Mass. Two Hundredth Anniversary
Celebration, 1869. 48225

Middlebrook, Elijah. (48830), 93025

Middlebrook, Grace. 48831

Middlebrook's astronomical diary. (48830)

Middlebury, Vt. Convention of Freemasons,
1819. see Freemasons. Vermont.
Convention, Middlebury, 1819.

Middlebury, Vt. General Convention of Congregational and Presbyterian Ministers
of Vermont, 1807. see General Convention of Congregational and Presbyterian
Ministers of Vermont, Middlebury, 1807.

Middlebury, Vt. Middlebury College. see
Middlebury College.

Middlebury College. 48834-48835, 48837-
48839, 104042

Middlebury College. Charitable Society.
48836

Middlebury College. Library. 48833

Middlebury College. Literary Association.
62554

Middlebury College. Philological Society.
Library. 48833

Middlebury College. School of Medicine,
Woodstock, Vt. see Vermont Medical
College, Woodstock, Vt.

Middlebury College. Semi-centennial Celebration, 1850. 48832

Middlebury College. Vermont Academy of
Medicine. see Vermont Medical Institution, Castleton, Vt.

Middlebury College and Vermont Academy of
Medicine. 48838

Middlesex County, Jamaica. 70080

Middlesex County, Mass. 48847, 86703

Middlesex County, Mass. Bible Society. see
Middlesex County Bible Society.

Middlesex County, Mass. Convention for
Suppressing Violations of the Lord's
Day, Andover, 1814. 48845

Middlesex County, Mass. Grand Jury. 93069

Middlesex County, Mass. Medical Association.
see Middlesex Medical Association.

Middlesex County, Mass. South Conference of
Churches. see Congregational Churches

in Massachusetts. South Middlesex Conference of Churches.

Middlesex County, Mass. Whig Party Convention, 1838. see Whig Party Massachusetts. Middlesex County. Convention, Concord, 1838.

Middlesex Agricultural Society. (48840)

Middlesex almanack, or lady's and gentleman's
diary. 93052

Middlesex Auxiliary Society for the Education
of Pious Youth. 48844

Middlesex Auxiliary Society for the Education
of Pious Youth. Directors. 48844

Middlesex Canal Corporation. Agent. 41804,
(48841) see also Eddy, Caleb.

Middlesex Canal Corporation. Board of Directors. (48841)

Middlesex Canal Corporation. Board of Directors. Committee. (48841)

Middlesex Canal Corporation. Committee.
(48841)

Middlesex collection of church music. (48842)

Middlesex County Bible Society. 48846

Middlesex County directory. 48848

Middlesex County Whig Convention, Concord,
Mass., 1838. see Whig Party. Massa-
chusetts. Middlesex County. Convention,
Concord, 1838.

Middlesex gazette. note after 92979, 93891

Middlesex gazette, or foederal advertiser.
84553

Middlesex harmony. (48842)

Middlesex Mechanic Association, Lowell, Mass.
42496, 48848

Middlesex Mechanic Association, Lowell, Mass.
Exhibition, 1st, 1851. 42496

Middlesex Mechanic Association, Lowell, Mass.
Exhibition, 2nd, 1859. 42496

Middlesex Mechanic Association, Lowell, Mass.
Library. (42495)

Middlesex Medical Association. 102065

Middlesex North Sabbath School Union. see
Worcester and Middlesex North Sabbath
School Union.

Middlesex Society of Husbandmen and Manufacturers. see Society of Husbandmen
and Manufacturers of Middlesex, Mass.

Middlesex Sunday School Society. 48850

Middlesex standard. 103817

Middleton, Major. pseud. see Hines, David
Theodore.

Middleton, A. 48853

Middleton, Arthur. pseud. Excursions in
North America. see Wakefield, Priscilla (Bell)

Middleton, Charles. defendant 28120, 80736,
96938

Middleton, Charles Theodore. 48854

Middleton, Christopher. 3664, 13833, (19715),
20404, 20407, 48855-48858

Middleton, David. 66686

Middleton, Erasmus. 48859

Middleton, Sir Henry, d. 1613. 66686

Middleton, Henry, 1717-1784. 10509, 13584,
15516, 40664, 48860 see also U. S.
Continental Congress, 1774. President.

Middleton, Henry, 1770-1846. 87543 see also
South Carolina. Governor, 1810-1812
(Middleton)

Middleton, Henry, 1797-1876. 21794, (48861)-
(48863), 1st note after 88112

Middleton, Henry A. defendant 35314

Middleton, J. C. (48865)

Middleton, John. 48864

Middleton, N. R. 87738

Middleton, Peter. 48866

Middleton, Robert T. 48867
Middleton, William Henry. (32143), 48868
Middleton, Mass. School Committee. (48869)
Middletoun Payne, A. R. see Payne, A. R. Middletoun.
Middletown, Conn. American Literary, Scientifick, and Military Academy. see American Literary, Scientifick, and Military Academy, Middletonw, Conn.
Middletown, Conn. Democratic State Convention, 1828. see Democratic Party. Connecticut. Convention, Middletown, 1828.
Middletown, Conn. Democratic State Convention, 1835. see Democratic Party. Connecticut. Convention, Middletown, 1835.
Middletown, Conn. Indian Hill Cemetery. 48870
Middletown, Conn. Special Superior Court. 94079
Middletown, Conn. Wesleyan University. see Wesleyan University, Middletown, Conn.
Midgley, R. L. (48874)
Midnight, and other poems. (48875)
Midnight cry. 48876
Midnight cry. An essay for our awakening. 46414
Mid-night-cry from the temple of God. 72687
Midnight Mission, New York. 54405
Midnight queen. (41399)
Midshipman. 42818
Midshipman of the United States Navy. pseud. Leisure hours at sea. see Leggett, William.
Midshipman of Board the Centurion. pseud. History of Commodore Anson's voyage. see Walter, Richard.
Midwinter's day dream. By Aliquis. (48878)
Midsummer's day-dream: Libellus; or, a little book. 71137
Midsummer's fete at Woodland Hall. 48877
Midsummer's ride on the Great Lakes. 80995
Miechow, Matthew. 34100-34107
Mielziner, M. 48879
Mientras mas hay comiciones &c. 94380
Mientras no hay inquisicion. 48880
Mier, ------- de. ed. (11236), 39116
Mier, Manuel de. incorrectly supposed author 11094, 48884, 78907, 103421
Mier Cazo y Estrada, Francisco de. 48881
Mier Noriega y Guerra, Jose Servando Teresa de, 1765-1827. 49888, 55489
Mier Noriega y Guerra, Jose Servando Teresa de, 1765-1827. supposed author 11094, 48884, 78907, 103421
Mier Quatemoczin, Juan Rosillo de. 48883
Mier y Guerra Servando, Jose de. 48882
Mier y Teran, Manuel de. 12892, (48885)-48886
Mierre, Antoine Martin le. see Le Mierre, Antoine Martin, 1723-1793.
Miers, Edward J. 28401, 71032
Miers, John. 48889
Miertsching, Johann August. 48892-48893
Miette de Villars, ---------. 48894
Mifflin, Elizabeth. ed. 27314
Mifflin, Thomas, 1744-1800. 18862, 48895, 60155, 61499, 84621, 100219 see also Pennsylvania. Governor, 1788-1799 (Mifflin)
Mifflin, Thomas, 1744-1800. supposed author (60695)
Mifflin, Warner, 1745-1798. 48897, 79262
Miger, P. M. A. supposed tr. 11626, note after 98779

Miggrode, Jacoben de. see Miggrode, Jacques de.
Miggrode, Jacques de. tr. 11235, 11267-11269, 11272, 11277, 1st note after 39118
Might and right. 48898
Might, not right. 48899
Mighty destroyer displayed. (4674)
Mignard, Jacques. 48900-(49901)
Mignet, F. A. M. 48902-(48904)
Mignot, L. R. illus. 73425
Migt, --------. 48905, 79236
Miguel, King of Portugal, 1802-1866. 7556, 7611 see also Portugal. Sovereigns, etc., 1828-1833 (Miguel)
Miguel Maria Evaristo de Braganza. see Miguel I, King of Portugal, 1802-1866.
Miguel, Andres de San. see San Miguel, Andres de.
Miguel, Jose Peregrino San. see Sanmiguel, Joseph Peregrino.
Miguel, Juan de San, fl. 1685. see Juan de San Miguel, fl. 1685.
Miguel, Juan de San, fl. 1691-1709. see Juan de San Miguel, fl. 1691-1709.
Miguel, Juan Rodriguez de San. see Rodriguez de San Miguel, Juan.
Miguel, Juan San. see San Miguel, Juan.
Miguel, Matias Sanz de San. see San Miguel, Matias Sanz de.
Miguel, N. A. Diez de San. see Diez de San Miguel, N. A.
Miguel, P. A. G. 48907
Miguel, Phelipe Sico de San. see Sico de San Miguel, Phelipe, Bp.
Miguel, Vicente Tofino de San. see Tofino de San Miguel, Vicente.
Miguel, Ysidro de San. see San Miguel, Ysidro de.
Mijangos, Ioan de. (48908)-48909
Mijia, --------. 20548
Mijn uitstap naar Brazilie. (39944)
Mijnssen, H. J. G. tr. 24018
Mijst, Gerardus de la. 27120, (48910), note after 98990
Mikan, Johann Christian, 1769-(1844). 7607, 48911-(48912), (77973)
Mike Fink. (4724)
Mikell, J. Jenkins. 87738
Mikpókosmos. 31656
Mila, G. tr. 19703
Mila, or the last wigwam of the Pawnees. 6307
Mila, ou la dernier wigwam des Pawnies. 6306
Milagro de la pintura. 78931
Milagros de la cruz. 57985
Milagrosa invencion de un tesoro escondido en un campo. 24813
Milagrosa invencion de un thesoro escondido en un campo. 24814
Milagroso hallazgo del tesoro escondido. 24819
Milam. pseud. Texas. see Thompson, Henry. supposed author
Milanes, Jose J. 48914
Milberg, J. H. 48915
Milbert, Jacques Gerard. illus. 48916
Milburn, William Henry. 48917-48919
Milburn, Mrs. William H. 48920
Milcent, C. L. M. 48921
Mildenhall, John. 66686
Mildert, William van. see Van Mildert, William successively Bishop of Llandaff, and Durham, 1765-1836.
Mildmay, William. (774), 16023, (47546)-(47548), note after (47740)-47742, (56129), 62694, note after 96403, 103121 see also

Great Britain. Commissioners on the
Limits of St. Lucia and Nova Scotia.
Mile-stones in our life-journey. 57791
Miles, ---------. (16860), note after 87402,
87436, 87438 see also South Carolina.
Commission to Negotiate with the Gov-
ernment of the United States, 1860-1861.
Miles, Dixon H. defendant before court of
inquiry 48922
Miles, G. I. 48925
Miles, George D. (48923)
Miles, George H. 48924
Miles, Henry A. 48926-48928
Miles, Henry H. 48929
Miles, James B. 48930-(48931)
Miles, James W. 48932-48933
Miles, John, fl. 1830. 61587
Miles, John, fl. 1851. 48934
Miles, Nelson A. 32479
Miles, Pliny. 48935-48937
Miles, S. D. defendant before court of inquiry
(36270)
Miles, Thomas Jefferson. 48938
Miles, W. Porcher. (48942)
Miles, William Augustus. 48939-48941
Miles Christianus. 68014
Miles Standish, Jr. pseud. see Standish,
Miles, Jr. pseud.
Miles Wallingford. 16471, 16475
Milet, Peter. (80023)
Milet, Pierre. 48944
Milet-Mureau, M. L. A. ed. (38960)-(38964)
Milford, Mass. 48945
Milford, Mass. Montgomery Lodge. see
Freemasons. Massachusetts. Montgomery
Lodge, Milford.
Milford, Mass. School Committee. (48948)
Milford, Mass. Society for Detecting Horse
Thieves. see Society for Detecting
Horse Thieves, in the Towns of Mendon,
Bellinghan and Milford.
Milford Baptist Association. see Baptists.
Massachusetts. Milford Baptist Associ-
ation.
Milford directory. (48948)
Milfort, -------, General, d. 1817. 48949
Milian, Francisco Lorenzo de San. see
Lorenzo de San Milian, Francisco.
Milicia nacional local de Matanzas. 46196
Milicia y descripcion de las Indias. 98604
Miliken, James. 3129
Milione di Marco Polo. 99383B
Militao, Gabriel. 48950
Militar. pseud. Podra tener una mismo
regencia y generalisimo? see T.,
A. M. R. pseud.
Militares Patrioticos del Real Cuerpo de
Artilleria. see Mexico (Viceroyalty)
Ejercito. Real Cuerpo de Artilleria.
Military Academy at West Point. 48951
Military Academy at West Point, unmasked.
48952, note after 102946
Military adventures of a shoemaker. 103263
Military adventures of Charles O'Neil. 57343
Military adventures of Enoch Crosby. 103263
Military and civil history of Connecticut.
17585
Military and financial policy of the national
government. (14120)
Military and naval magazine of the United
States. 48953, 93715
Military and naval operations in the Canadas.
12938-12939
Military and naval situation. 48954
Military and political hints. 38499

Military and topographical atlas of the United
States. 47432
Military anecdotes. 8557
Military appointment of Francis P. Blair.
5741
Military assistant. 74326, 91464
Military Association, Clinton County, N. Y.
see Clinton County Military Association.
Military Association of the State of New York.
65911
Military bill. 48955
Military bridges. 30859
Military brochure. 8851
Military career of King David. 37650
Military catechism. 71095
Military code of . . . New York. 53777
Military collections and remarks. 20598
Military College, Wilmington, Del. (48956)
Military College. Catalogue of officers and
students. (48956)
Military Commission. Proceedings in the case
of the United States. 43648
Military Commission to Europe, in 1855 and
1856. 50532
Military companion. 91460
Military control, or command and government
of the army. (26650)
Military Convention, Harrisburg, Pa., 1832.
60420
Military Convention, Worcester, Mass., 1835.
45951
Military defences of Canada. 48957
Military despotism! Arbitrary arrest of a
judge!! 48958
Military despotism! or observations on the
law. 48959
Military despotism! Suspension of the habeas
corpus! 48960
Military dictionary. 20994
Military discipline. 6375, 22368, (66440)
Military discipline for the regulation of the
troops of the United States. 91441-91442
Military discourse, delivered in Carlisle.
41346
Military discourse, whether it is better for
England to give an invader present
battle, or to temperize and defer the
same. 67599
Military districts. 48961
Military documents. 47433
Military duties, recommended to an artillery
company. (46415)
Military duty. 77436
Military education. (79672)
Military essay, containing reflections on the
raising. 18345, 81142
Military execution of American citizens. 48962
Military exercise for the government of the
troops. 91436
Military expedition of General Charles Scott.
85142
Military expeditions of the North West Terri-
tory. 85142
Military gazette. (48963)
Military gentleman. pseud. New military
dictionary. 53286
Military glory. A sermon preached at . . .
Brooklyn, N. Y. (23813)
Military glory of Great Britain. 48964
Military governor among abolitionists. 90325
Military guide. 84642
Military guide for young officers. 81142
Military hand-book, and soldier's manual of
information. 39875, 99434
Military heroes of the revolution. 61235

Military heroes of the war of 1812. 61236
Military heroes of the war with Mexico.
61237
Military history of Europe, &c. 5336, 7956
Military history of Great Britain, for 1756.
48965
Military history of the state of New Hampshire.
64621
Military history of Wisconsin. 67301
Military historian & economist. 83471
Military incapacity. 22206
Military institutes. 26902
Military instructions for officers detached in
the field. 33403, 91607
Military instructor. 94784-94785
Military interference in elections. 77165
Military interference in the elections. 64756
Military interference with elections. 33253
Military journal. A history of the operations
of a partisan corps. 81135
Military journal during the American revo-
lutionary war. 95152
Military journal, kept by Major E. Denny.
68399
Military journal of Major Ebenezer Denny.
19596
Military journals of two private soldiers,
1758-1775. 42860, (58457), note after
96144
Military laws, and rules and regulations for
the armies of the United States. 48966
Military laws of . . . Pennsylvania. 60250
Military laws of the Confederate States.
(15319)
Military laws of the province of Massachusetts
Bay. 6375, 22368
Military laws of the state of Connecticut.
15768
Military laws of the United States, relating to
the army, volunteers, militia, and to
bounty lands and pensions. 10050
Military laws of the United States, including
those relating to the army, marine corps,
volunteers, and to bounty lands and
pensions. 31621
Military laws of the United States; including
those relating to the marine corps.
(17664)-(17665), 48967
Military lessons taught by the war. (82176)
Military maxims of Napoleon I. 88405
Military medical and surgical essays prepared
for the United States Sanitary Commission.
30113, 76540, 76647, 76657, 76676,
76695, 84268
Military memoirs of four brothers. (48968)
Military memoirs of Great Britain. 67680
Military monitor and American register.
48969
Military monitor; or, advice to the officers
and soldiers of the American army.
48970
Military occupation of Chicago. 79919
Military operations around Chattanooga. 84770
Military operations in Eastern Maine and
Nova Scotia. 37715
Military operations on the Delaware. 48971
Military opinions of General Sir John Burgoyne.
9252
Military Order of the Loyal Legion of the
United States. 48972
Military Order of the Loyal Legion of the
United States. Massachusetts Command-
ery. (45833)
Military Order of the Loyal Legion of the
United States. Ohio Commandery. 84035

Military Order of the Loyal Legion of the
United States. Pennsylvania Commandery.
84508
Military papers, containing reflections. 72726-
72727, 84618
Military policy of the administration set forth
and vindicated. (43027)
Military Post Library Association, New York.
48973, 86297
Military power a blessing. 61396
Military preparations. 48974
Military profession in the United States. 9609
Military pyrotechny. 48975
Military record of civilian appointments. 31393
Military reflections. 46998
Military reporter. 48976, 8th note after 96930.
Military review of the campaign in Virginia &
Maryland. 61225
Military roster. 95209
Military route to Richmond. 44878
Military sermon at the request of Capt. John
Sumner. 74382
Military sketch of the present war in America.
49004
Military sketches. (20937)
Military small arms. 84035
Military souvenir. 73460
Military souvenir; a portrait gallery of our
military and naval heroes. 7371
Military system, for the New-Jersey cavalry.
103354
Military system of South-Carolina. 87698
Military system of the republic of Switzerland.
(48977)
Military tactics or the soldier's companion.
104819
Military treatise by R. J. Rombauer. 73017
Military treatise on the appointments of the
army. 102230
Military view of recent campaigns in Virginia
and Maryland. 12520
Military view of the United States. 101854
Militia act: being a law, to organize the
militia. 53778
Militia act of Massachusetts. 91427
Militia act of Pennsylvania. 71541
Militia act passed by the Great and General
Court or Assembly. 45925
Militia act; together with the rules and regu-
lations. 45924
Militia acts of 1781-6. 45925
Militia and patrol laws of South-Carolina.
December, 1844. 87700
Militia and patrol laws of South Carolina,
December, 1841. 87699
Militia and patrol laws of South Carolina, to
December, 1859. 87702
Militia and patrol laws of South Carolina: to
December, 1851. 87701
Militia & staff laws. 87703
Militia discipline. 7743
Militia: its place in our government system.
74145
Militia law. 53778
Militia law. An act to amend an act entitled
"An act to amend and reduce to one act,
the several acts." 100379
Militia law of Massachusetts, 1866. 45925
Militia law of Ohio. 56960
Militia law of . . . Rhode Island. 70604
Militia law of South Carolina. 91428
Militia law of the state of New-York. 91454
Militia law of the state of Tennessee. 94779
Militia law of the United States, and that of
the state of New York. 91458

Militia law of the United States and the
militia law of South Carolina. 91428
Militia law of the United States, and the
militia law of the state of New-York.
91454
Militia law, passed at the first session of the
fifth General Assembly. 94778
Militia law. State of New-Hampshire. 52849
Militia laws of the state of Connecticut.
15769
Militia laws of the Territory of Michigan.
48774
Militia laws of the United States, and . . .
Massachusetts. 48979-48980
Militia laws of the United States, and of the
commonwealth of Massachusetts. 91456
Militia-man. pseud. Dialogue between a
colonel of the militia, and a militia-man.
35364
Militia-man. pseud. Seasonable address.
78662
Militia of the United States. 93715, note after
97921
Militia of the United States. What it has been.
39757
Militia report of William H. Sumner. 45925
Militia reporter. 48976
Militia soldier's pocket companion. 48981,
91459
Militia system of South-Carolina. 87704
Milius, Abraham. 48982-(48983)
Milk for babes. 22161, (34471)
Milk trade in New York and vicinity. 51272
Mill, James. 48984
Mill, John Stuart, 1806-1873. (20097), (48985)-
48988, 56424, (82311)
Mill, Nicholas. 48989
Mill Corporation, Boston. see Boston Mill
Corporation.
Mill Creek and Mine Hill Navigation and
Railroad Company. President. 60251
Mill Creek Cannel Coal and Oil Company.
(48990)
Mill-girls. (48991)
Mill Pond Wharf Corporation. (48992)
Milla, Jose. (48993), 85751 see also Socie-
dad Economica de Amantes de la Patria
de Guatemala. Secretario.
Millan, Jose Maria Quiros y. see Quiros y
Millan, Jose Maria.
Millan de Poblete, Juan. 48993
Millar, Andrew, 1707-1768. (78330)
Millar, Robert. 48995
Millard, --------. 30706
Millard, D. 79906
Millard, J. ed. 70455
Millard, Nelson. 48996
Millault, --------. tr. 71996
Millbury, Mass. 48997
Millbury, Mass. School Committee. 48997
Mille, C. W. 49014
Mille et deuxieme nuit. 63523
Milledgeville, Ga. Anti-tariff Convention, 1832.
see Anti-tariff Convention, Milledgeville,
Ga., 1832.
Milledgeville, Ga. Convention, 1850. see
Georgia. Convention, Milledgeville, 1850.
Milledgeville, Ga. Convention, 1861. see
Georgia. Convention, Milledgeville and
Savannah, 1861.
Milledgeville, Ga. Convention, 1861. see
Georgia. Convention, Milledgeville, 1865.
Milledoler, Philip, 1775-1852. 48998, 81522,
89736, 103231
Millenarianism. 76243
Millennial Church. see Shakers.

Millennial harbinger. 10206, 48999, 91762,
91764
Millennial institutions. 49000, 49003
Millennial praises. 79719, 97893
Millennial state no. 2. 84425
Millennium. 21983
Millennium, and other poems. 64969
Millennium; or, the age to come. (49001)
Millennium; or, the American consummation of
equality. 49002
Millennium; or, the thousand years of pros-
perity. 4497
Millennium: the good time coming. 49003
Miller, ----------, fl. 1832. (60574)
Miller, ----------, fl. 1862. 49004
Miller, A. (60519)
Miller, A. E. 1902, 49009-49010, 87903
Miller, A. H. 49012
Miller, Adam. 49005
Miller, Alexander. (49006)
Miller, Amanda. 49007
Miller, Andrew. 49008, 62237
Miller, Andrew. petitioner 60540
Miller, Andrew G. 49011
Miller, Anson S. 49013
Miller, C. S. 61596
Miller, Carl. 38398
Miller, Daniel T. tr. 83144
Miller, E. Spencer. 79192
Miller, Edward. 62078, 78086, 93731 see
also North Pennsylvania Railroad Com-
pany. Chief Engineer. Schuylkill Navi-
gation Company. Chief Engineer. Sun-
bury & Erie Rail Road Company. Chief
Engineer.
Miller, Edward, 1760-1812. 49016
Miller, Emily. 49016
Miller, George. 83154
Miller, George. supposed author 96490, 1st
note after 102871, note after 106194
Miller, George B. 49017
Miller, George F. (49018)
Miller, George W. 49019, 53993, 54826 see
also New York (State) Insurance Depart-
ment. Superintendent.
Miller, Heinrich. see Miller, John Henry,
1702-1782.
Miller, Henry. 106033 see also York County,
Pa. Collector of Excise.
Miller, Henry, 1800-1874. 49021
Miller, Herman. tr. 83146
Miller, J. R. 49034
Miller, Jacob W. 49022
Miller, James. 104701
Miller, James M. 49023
Miller, James P. 49024
Miller, James William, d. 1829. 49025, 103296,
105956
Miller, John, 1666-1724. 49026, (70023), 72464
Miller, John, fl. 1786. 49027
Miller, John, fl. 1828. 49028-49029
Miller, John B. ed. 87685
Miller, John B., fl. 1847. 49030
Miller, John G. reporter 56930
Miller, John Gaines, 1812-1856. 49031
Miller, John Henry, 1702-1782. 62393, 1st note
after 94085
Miller, Jonathan. (49032)
Miller, Josiah. (49033)
Miller, K. 83493
Miller, L. Merrill. 49036
Miller, Leo. (49035)
Miller, Linus W. 49037
Miller, Maria. 49038
Miller, Marmaduke. 49039
Miller, Morris S. 49040

Miller, Moses. 49041
Miller, O. D. 49043
Miller, Oliver. (49042)
Miller, Peter. ed. 59972
Miller, Philip. 26256, (56466), 87849, 87904
Miller, R. 49044
Miller, Rodney A. 49045
Miller, Rutgers B. 30381, 49046-49047, 2d
    note after 96986
Miller, Samuel, 1769-1850. 9918, (33224),
    49048-(49064), 89736, 93204, 102562,
    104944
Miller, Samuel, 1799-1852. reporter 19915,
    49067, 65221
Miller, Samuel, 1816-1883. 49065-49066
Miller, Samuel F. 49068-(49069)
Miller, Silvanus. ed. 81135
Miller, Silvanus. plaintiff 49074, 55375
Miller, Stephen B. (49070)
Miller, Stephen D. 49071
Miller, Stephen F. 49072-49073
Miller, Thomas C. supposed author 60545
Miller, W. E. ed. 58975
Miller, W. P. 88107
Miller, William. defendant 103765
Miller, William. reporter (49077)
Miller, William, 1770-1825. 33150 see also
    North Carolina. Governor, 1814-1817
    (Miller)
Miller, William, 1796-1861. 49020, 49028-
    49029, 72482
Miller, William, fl. 1838-1841. 48876,
    (49075)-49076, 81629
Miller, William A. 49078
Miller, William Starr, 1793-1854. 49079
Miller, William W. (49080)
Miller (A. E.) firm publishers 87785-87789
Miller (James) firm publishers (54406)-
    54407, 70965-70966
Miller (Mark) firm publishers 90804
Miller overthrown. 96147
Millern, Alexander von. (49081)
Miller's guide to Central Park and mercantile
    directory. (54406)
Miller's guide to Saratoga Springs and vicinity.
    70965
Miller's new guide to the Hudson River.
    70966
Miller's New York as it is. 54407
Millers of Baltimore. petitioners see Balti-
    more Millers. petitioners
Miller's planter's and merchant's almanac
    for . . . 1824. 49009
Miller's planters' and merchants' almanacs.
    87785
Miller's planters' & merchants' state rights
    almanac, for the year of Our Lord 1865.
    87789
Miller's planters' & merchants' state rights
    almanac, for the year of Our Lord 1864.
    87788
Miller's planters' & merchants' state rights
    almanac, for the year of Our Lord 1861.
    87785
Miller's planters' & merchants' state rights
    almanac, for the year of Our Lord 1863.
    87787
Miller's planters' & merchants' state rights
    almanac, for the year of Our Lord 1862.
    87786
Miller's works. 49076
Millet, ------- Thomas. see Thomas-Millet,
    ----------.
Millet, F. A. 13510, 40930 see also Santo
    Domingo (French Colony) Commissaires
    des Colons a la Convention Nationale.

Millet, James. alias see Mullet, James.
    defendant
Millet, Joshua. 49082
Millet, Pierre. (18247), 39998, note after
    69259
Millet, Thomas. see Millet, F. A.
Millett, D. C. 49084
Millicent Halford. 69552
Millie Mayfield. pseud. see Mayfield, Millie
    pseud.
Milliet de Saint-Adolphe, J. C. R. 49085
Milligan, Dr. pseud. Short description of the
    province of South Carolina. see Johnstc
    Georges Milligen. supposed author
Milligan, Jacob. (12039)
Milligan, Lambdin P. 49087
Milligan, Lambdin P. petitioner 9612
Milligan, R. 23353, 49088
Milligen, George. pseud. Short description of
    the province of South Carolina. see
    Johnston, Georges Milligan. supposed
    author
Milliken, E. P. 88012
Milliken, James. 49089
Millikin, Thomas. 49090
Million of facts connected with the studies.
    62508
Millions for Texas! 95078
Millions of dollars tendered gratis. 49091
Milliroux, Felix. 49092-49093
Milliroux, J.-F. 49094-49095
Million de Caracas. 10780
Millot, ---------, fl. 1815. 3978, 101895
Mills, ---------, fl. 1771. (50807)
Mills, Alfred. 49097
Mills, Arthur. 49098
Mills, B. 102565
Mills, B. F. 88216
Mills, C. L. 83712
Mills, Caleb. 49099
Mills, Edmund. 49100
Mills, Edward. 49101
Mills, Elijah H. 49102
Mills, F. J. 49104
Mills, Henry. defendant 49105
Mills, Hiram F. petitioner 49106
Mills, J. A. 88216
Mills, J. B. 49107
Mills, J. H. 49108
Mills, John. 100600-100601
Mills, John B. 105562
Mills, John Henry. (49109)
Mills, Joseph L. 49110
Mills, Lewis Este. 49111
Mills, Robert, 1781-1855. 49112-49118, 75835
    95746
Mills, Robert, 1781-1855. petitioner 49118
Mills, Robert C. 49119
Mills, Samuel John. 15008, 49120-49122,
    77609
Mills, Thomas. tr. 48247
Mills, William H. 49123
Mills, Zechariah. 56937
Mills. firm publishers see Mills and Hicks
    firm publishers and Robertson, Mills
    and Hicks. firm publishers
Mills (Henry James) firm publishers 96979
Mills and Hicks. firm publishers 49096
    see also Robertson, Mills and Hicks.
    firm publishers
Mills & Starke. firm publishers (71174)
Mills . . . and furnaces, coppers, &c. 2120A
Mills and Hicks' British and American registe
    49096
Mills' Trinidad almanac and pocket register.
    96979

Millson, John Singleton, 1808-1873. (49124)-
49125
Millspaugh, Andrew J. plaintiff (13756)
Millward, John. 66686
Milne, A. D. 49126
Milner, John T. 87330 see also South and
North Alabama Railroad Company. Chief
Engineer.
Milner, T. 49127
Milner, T. H. 49128
Milner, Vincent L. (49129)
Milnor, James, 1773-1845. 49130-49132
Milnor, William. 27600, 49133
Milns, W. 14868
Milo. pseud. Letters to a friend at Pittsburgh.
13732, 49134
Milord Alle'ar. pseud. see Milord All' Ear.
pseud.
Milord All' Ear. pseud. Espion Anglais.
62695-62697
Milord All' Eye. pseud. Espion Anglais.
62695-62696
Milrose. 72128
Milroy, Samuel. 96737 see also U. S. Com-
missioners to the Miami Indians.
Milroy, Samuel. petitioner 70725
Miltenberg, R. J. (49135)
Miltimore, James. (49136)-(49137)
Miltimore, William. 49138
Miltitz, Alex. de. 49139
Milton, Charles William. (49140)
Milton, John, 1608-1674. (19552), 49141-49143,
67591, 67599, 77887, 80993, 82979, note
after 93549, note after 98499, 101046
Milton, William. claimant 49145
Milton, William Fitzwilliam, Viscount, 1839-
1877. 24630-24631, 49144
Milton, Ind. Convention to Organize a State
Anti-slavery Society, 1838. see Indiana
Convention to Organize a State Anti-
slavery Society, Milton, 1838.
Milton, Mass. Auditor. 49146
Milton, Mass. First Congregational Church.
1568
Milton, Mass. Selectmen. 17251, 45701,
49146
Milton, Wisc. Milton College. see Milton
College, Milton, Wisc.
Milton College, Milton, Wisc. 49147
Milton Hill; a poem. 41419
Milwaukee. 91181
Milwaukee. petitioners 49161-49162
Milwaukee. Board of Trade. Committee.
(49148)
Milwaukee. Board of Trustees. 69740
Milwaukee. Board of Trustees. Committee.
69740
Milwaukee. Chamber of Commerce. 49153,
83898
Milwaukee. Charter. 49151
Milwaukee. Church of the Redeemer. Pastor.
90465 see also Staples, Carlton Albert.
Milwaukee. Citizens. petitioners 49162
Milwaukee. Commissioners of the Public Debt.
49152
Milwaukee. Comptroller. 49160
Millwaukee. Convention of Delegates from the
Several Baptist Churches of Central Wis-
consin, 1838. see Baptists. Wisconsin.
First Baptist Association of Central Wis-
consin.
Milwaukee. First Presbyterian Church. 49159
Milwaukee. Joint Committee of Citizens and
Common Council. 49179
Milwaukee. Mayor, 1848. 49155
Milwaukee. Mayor, 1863. 49160

Milwaukee. Mayor, 1868. 49181
Milwaukee. Meeting of the Tax Payers of the
City, 1858. Committee. (69787)
Milwaukee. Playmouth Church. Twenty-Fifth
Anniversary, 1866. (49178)
Milwaukee. Republican Party Convention, 1894.
see Republican Party. Wisconsin. Con-
vention, Milwaukee, 1894.
Milwaukee. School Commissioners. 49149
Milwaukee. Spring Street Congregational Church.
49159
Milwaukee. Young Men's Association. see
Young Men's Association of the City of
Milwaukee.
Milwaukee Academy. 49164
Milwaukee and Beliot Rail Road Company.
President. (49165)
Milwaukee and Horicon Railroad Company.
49166
Milwaukee and Mississippi Rail Road Company.
Directors. 49167
Milwaukee and Mississippi Rail Road Company.
Engineer. 49167
Milwaukee and Mississippi Rail Road Company.
Secretary. 49167
Milwaukee and Mississippi Rail Road Company.
Superintendent. 49167
Milwaukee and Mississippi Rail Road Company.
Treasurer. 49167
Milwaukee and Prairie du Chien Rail Road
Company. (49168)
Milwaukee and Rock River Canal Company.
(49169)
Milwaukee and Rock River Canal Company.
petitioners (49169)
Milwaukee and St. Paul Railway Company.
49170
Milwaukee & Superior Rail Road Company.
49171
Milwaukee business directory, city guide, and
almanac. (49154)
Milwaukee city directory, and business adver-
tiser. (49154)
Milwaukee city directory for 1857 and 1858.
(49154)
Milwaukee city directory for 1863. (49154)
Milwaukee Female College. 49172
Milwaukee Ladies' Association, for the Aid of
Military Hospitals. see Ladies' Asso-
ciation, for the Aid of Military Hospitals,
Milwaukee.
Milwaukee Ladies' Bible and Benevolent Asso-
ciation. see Ladies' Bible and Benevo-
lent Association, Milwaukee.
Milwaukee Musical Society. 49174
Milwaukee Orphan Association. 49175
Milwaukee Teachers' Association. 77824
Milwaukee, Waukesha, and Miss. R. R. Co.
Directors. 49177
Milwaukie & Superior Rail Road Company. see
Milwaukee & Superior Rail Road Company.
Milwaukie: report on its commerce. 49163
Mimic life; or, before and behind the curtain.
51206, 71561
Mimoses et autres plantes legumineuses. 33764
Min reise fra Lubeck til Rio di Janeiro. 67087
Mina, General. see Espoz y Mina, Francisco,
1781-1836.
Mina, Carolino Estrados de. defendant 49184
Mina, Francisco Espoz y. see Espoz y Mina,
Francisco, 1781-1836.
Mina, Francisco Xavier de. 49187
Mina, Lino Amalia Espos y. see Espos y
Mina, Lino Amalia.
Mina, Lucretia Espos y. see Chapman,
Lucretia. defendant

Mina de la Luz, Guanajuato, Mex. firm
73864
Mina de S. Nicolas. 49186
Minana, Jose Manuel. (49188)
Minas Geraes (Brazilian State) 88707, 88712
Minas Geraes (Brazilian State) Revolutionary
Government, 1842. 88707, 88712
Minas del Rincon del mineral de Temascaltepec.
49189
Minaya, Francisco Velasquez. see Velasquez
Minaya, Francisco.
Minchinhampton, England. defendants 103500
Mind amongst the spindles. A miscellany.
49192
Mind amongst the spindles: a selection. 49193
Mind in ruins. 89744
Minde of the front. 67560
Minde of the frontispiece. 76457
Minderbroeders. see Franciscans.
Mindetale over Washington. 49323
Minding the gap and other poems. 50428
Mine Hill and Schuylkill Haven Rail Road
Company. 60252
Mine Hill and Schuylkill Haven Rail Road
Company. petitioners 60252
Mine Hill and Schuylkill Haven Rail Road
Company. Charter. 60252
Mine Hill and Schuylkill Haven Rail Road
Company. Managers. (49194)
Minelli, Gustavo. (23068)
Miner, Alonzo A. 49195-(49198), 89627
Miner, Amos. defendant (49199), 88670,
96905
Miner, Charles, 1780-1865. 49200-49201,
64080
Miner, M. (77813)
Miner, T. B. (49205)
Miner, Thomas, 1777-1841. 49202-49204,
1st-2d notes after 97444
Miner. firm see Leeds (Henry H.) & Miner.
firm
Mineral and other resources of the Argentine
Republic. 71230
Mineral and thermal springs of the United
States and Canada. (4456)
Mineral and timber lands of California.
(76942)
Mineral lands and mine operators. 84529
Mineral lands of the Ohio Great Vein Mining
Company. 49206
Mineral lands of the United States. 49207
Mineral Point, Wisc. Common Council. 49208
Mineral Point, Wisc. Guards. 49209
Mineral Point, Wisc. Ordinances, etc. 49208
Mineral Point Industrial Art Union. Annual
Fair, 3d, 1860. 49209
Mineral Point Mining Company. 11727, (49210)
Mineral Point Mining Company reports. 11727
Mineral-Regionen der obern Halbinsel Mich-
igan's. 38203
Mineral resources of Canada. 82200
Mineral resources of northern Mexico. 12817
Mineral resources of the Philippine Islands.
84530
Mineral resources of the states and territories
west of the Rocky Mountains, by Rossiter
W. Raymond. (68065)
Mineral resources of the states and territories
west of the Rocky Mountains. Letter
from the Secretary of the Treasury.
8659
Mineral resources west of the Rocky Mountains.
68067
Mineral spring of Bellevue de la Cataracte.
49211

Mineral springs of western Virginia, with
remarks on their use. (9317), 50469-
50470
Mineral springs of western Virginia, with
remarks on their use, and the diseases
to which they are applicable. 9318
Mineral-wass'rige Centralpark- und Charakter-
Studie. 47409
Mineral waters of Avon, N. Y. 2499
Mineral waters of the United States and Canada.
(50467)
Mineralogia. 39066
Mineralogical notes. 18210
Mineralogical report on the coal region in the
environs of Blossburg. 60569, 94529
Mineralogie et geologie. 21216
Mineralogische Beschreibung der Bergwerks-
Reviere von Mexico. 86966
Mineralogy and chemistry: original researches.
82995, 82992
Mineralogy of New York. 4233, 53789
Mineralogy of Nova Scotia. (33218)
Minerals. 27419
Miners & business men's directory. 97445
Miners and travelers' guide to Oregon. (51274)
Miner's companion and guide. 81128
Miner's hand-book and guide to Pike's Peak.
49212
Miner's journal. 90821
Miners' journal coal statistical register. (49213)
Miners of California. Convention, 1866. 10038
Miner's progress. 49214
Minerva (Ship) 59584, 93383
Minerva. 49215, 84819, 96580, 102401,
106080
Minerva, a repository of national and foreign
literature. 75303
Minerva Brasiliense. Bibliotheca Brasilica.
(7603)
Minerva Brasiliense. Jornal de sciencias,
lettras e artes. 7604
Minerva. Ensayo politico sobre el reyno de
Nueva-Espana. 33714
Minerva, or literary and scientific journal of
original and select articles. see Minerva
Minerva; or literary, entertaining and scientific
journal. see Minerva.
Minerva; or, weekly literary, entertaining, and
scientific journal. see Minerva.
Minerve. 60609
Mines, Flavel S. (49216)
Mines, John. 82952
Mines and minerals. (56151)
Mines and mining. 49218
Mines and mining of the Rocky Mountains.
68067
Mines de Californie et d'Australie. 40738
Mines de la Californie. 86388-86389
Mines d'or de la Californie. 19427
Mines d'or et d'argent du Mexique. 49219
Mines et les mineurs. 81317
Mines, mills and furnaces of the Pacific states
and territories. 68067
Mines of Colorado. 32557
Mines of Copiapo. 41692
Mines of the west. (68066)
Mines. . . . 10th February, 1863. 56172
Mineur de Californie. 81312
Ming, Alexander. 26331, (45827), 49221,
50441
Mingatushka. Choctaw Indian Chief 96601
Mingohoopoie. Choctaw Indian Chief 96601
Ming's almanac. 26331
Ming's Hutchin's improved almanac. 49221
Ming's United States register. 26331, 49221,
50441

Minian, J. E. see Miniana, Joseph Manuel.
Miniana, Joseph Manuel. 44544, 44549
Miniature almanack, for . . . 1820. 49222
Miniature monthly magazine of choice literature. 85515
Miniature of Dansville Village. 13306
Miniaturgemalde. 19539
Minieres, E. Bellot des. see Bellot des Minieres, Ernest.
Mining and agriculture of Mexico. 80163
Mining and manufacturing laws of Pennsylvania. 52355
Mining and milling the Reese River region. 5886
Mining in the Pacific states of North America. 32271
Mining industry, by James D. Hague. 29523
Mining industry, free trade, &c. 22085
Mining industry in the Territory of Alaska. 84296
Mining industry in the Territory of Alaska during the calendar year 1916. 84297
Mining industry of the states and territories of the Rocky Mountains. 68067
Mining journey across the great Andes. 71231
Mining laws of Spain and Mexico. 22452
Mining magazine. 49223
Mining rights in Pennsylvania. (50861)
Mining scenes and sketches. (9966)
Mining statistics. 10008
Mining Stock Board, New York. see Consolidated Stock and Petroleum Exchange of New York.
Miniscalchi-Erizzo, F. (49224)
Minisick Indians. see Minisink Indians.
Minisinger, Seb. engr. 2313, 38348
Minisink Indians. (49225), 49348
Minisink Indians. Treaties, etc. 60255
Minister. pseud. Address of a minister to a church under his care. 52605
Minister. pseud. Caveat against unreasonable and unscriptural separations. 11594
Minister. pseud. Conference between a minister and the prisoner. 46559, 96766
Minister. pseud. Conversion of Juvenis. see Stanford, John.
Minister. pseud. Display of God's special grace. see Dickinson, Jonathan, 1688-1747.
Minister. pseud. Familiar dialogue between a minister and a gentleman. 20057
Minister. pseud. Mr. Turell's dialogue. see Turell, Ebenezer.
Minister. pseud. Plain and earnest address. 63209
Minister. pseud. Reflections. 105945
Minister. pseud. Second dialogue. see Bellamy, Joseph. and Taylor, Nathaniel. supposed author
Minister. A sermon, offer'd unto the Anniversary Convention of Ministers. (46416)
Minister and the age. 91046
Minister and three of his neighbours. pseud. Winter evening's conversation. see Webster, Samuel, 1719-1796.
Minister at Boston. pseud. [Letter.] 55240
Minister at Boston. pseud. Reply to the objections. 14502
Minister at Large, Boston. see American Unitarian Association, Boston. Minister at Large.
Minister at Large, Lowell, Mass. see Lowell, Mass. South Parish Missionary Society. Minister at Large.
Minister at Large, Portland, Me. 64352

Minister in Boston. pseud. Extract of a letter. 103622
Minister in Boston. pseud. Letter to a friend in the country. see Cooper, William, 1694-1743. supposed author and Mather, Cotton, 1663-1728. supposed author
Minister in Boston. pseud. Letter to Mr. Robert Sandeman. 76342
Minister in Boston. pseud. Narrative of the method. see Colman, Benjamin.
Minister in Boston. pseud. Reply to the objections. see Cooper, William, 1694-1743.
Minister in London. pseud. Letter. 59066
Minister in London. pseud. Very interesting letter. 7847, 27588
Minister in New-England. pseud. Some account of Mr. Shepard. see Prince, Thomas, 1687-1758.
Minister in the country. pseud. Tristitiae ecclesiarum. see Niles, Samuel.
Minister in Virginia. pseud. Address. 100420
Minister of Boston. pseud. Letter to a friend in the country. see Cooper, William, 1694-1743.
Minister of God approved. 95539, 104112
Minister of that church. pseud. Veil withdrawn. see Bell, R.
Minister of that place. pseud. Truest and largest account of the late earthquake. 35559, 35665, 97172
Minister of the Church of England. pseud. Letter from a minister of the Church of England, to his dissenting parishioners. Shewing, how far the book is from answering the title. see Johnson, Samuel, 1696-1772.
Minister of the Church of England. pseud. Letter from a minister of the Church of England to his dissenting parishioners, shewing the necessity of unity and peace. see Wetmore, James.
Minister of the Church of England. pseud. Second letter. see Johnson, Samuel, 1696-1772.
Minister of the Church of England. pseud. Serious address to the clergy. see Philanthropos. pseud.
Minister of the Church of England. pseud. Third letter. see Johnson, Samuel, 1696-1772.
Minister of the Church of Jesus Christ of Latter-Day Saints. pseud. Address. 50726
Minister of the country. pseud. Biographical sketch of the Rev. Thomas Davis. 18888
Minister of the Gospel. pseud. Incidents of personal experience. see Snow, Herman, 1812-1905.
Minister of the Gospel. pseud. Poor orphans legacy. 64073
Minister of the Gospel. pseud. Reasonableness of, regular singing. see Symmes, Thomas.
Minister of the Gospel. pseud. Serious reflections on the times. (79267)
Minister of the Gospel. pseud. Zebulon advised. see Parkman, Ebenezer.
Minister of the Gospel in Massachusetts. pseud. Slavery in its relation to God. 42030
Minister of the Gospel, making his just and sad complaint. (46221)
Minister of the Gospell. pseud. see D., I., Minister of the Gospell. pseud.
Minister of the Presbyterian Church. pseud. Eutaxia. 23124
Minister of the Presbyterian Church. pseud. Politics and the pulpit. 63827

Minister preaching his own funeral sermon. 95838

Minister who remained in the city during the pestilence of 1798. pseud. Pastoral letter. 59015

Ministere de la Marine et des Colonies. Commission . . . pour l'examen des questions. 14717

Ministerial almanach addressed to the Rt. Hon. Lord Thurlow. 68410

Ministerial catechise. 49226

Ministerial courtesy. 14137

Ministerial crisis and Mr. Viger. 49227

Ministerial duties and immunities. 70936

Ministerial faithfulness considered and described. 73979

Ministerial fidelity. A discourse . . . at Canton. 62733

Ministerial fidelity exemplified. (28592)

Ministerial fidelity illustrated and urged. 90969

Ministerial fidelity. Sermon . . . at the ordination of . . . Daniel Fitz. 18405

Ministerial firmness. 18405

Ministerial labour and support. 66227

Ministerial necessity. (73560)

Ministerial perils. 19345

Ministerial perplexities and solaces. 48672

Ministerial prejudices in favour of the convention. 49228

Ministerial support. 63964

Ministerial union. 91915

Ministerio de Hacienda del Peru ene sus relaciones. 61148

Ministerio de 31 de Agosto. 49229

Ministers . . . A sermon. 17108

Ministers and Elders, Met Together in a Provincial Assembly, London, 1649. see Provincial Assembly of Presbyterian Ministers, London, 1649.

Ministers and Office Bearers in the County of Lancaster, England. petitioners 47698

Ministers, and other Christians exhorted to be fellow-helpers to the truth. 96387

Ministers and people under special obligations. 14501

Minister's appeal to his hearers. 97312

Ministers . . . at earthen vessels. 56043

Ministers are men of like passions with others. 26785

Ministers are to separate [sic] men to the . . . ministry. 59375

Ministers are to "testify the Gospel . . . ." 12389

Minister's care about his life and doctrine. 58900

Ministers cautioned against the occasions of contempt. 12331

Ministers considered as fellow-workers. 97316

Minister's duty to preach the pure word of God. 67769

Ministers, elders and messengers. 98011

Ministers exhorted . . . . A sermon preached before . . . the . . . Annual Convention. 12331

Ministers exhorted and encouraged. 67770

Minister's farewell. 85471

Minister's final charge. 104814

Ministers from Divers Parts of Massachusetts, Assembled at Boston, 1697. see Convention of Congregational Ministers of Massachusetts, Boston, 1697.

Ministers in Barnstable County, Mass. see Congregational Churches in Massachusetts. Barnstable County Ministers.

Ministers in Old England. pseud. Letter. (40355)

Ministers insufficient of themselves. 42085

Ministers must certainly and shortly die. 42086, 94067

Ministers must preach Christ Lord. (67771)

Ministers of Barnstable County, Mass. see Congregational Churches in Massachusetts. Barnstable County Ministers.

Ministers of Christ are to enrich those they minister unto. 67772

Ministers of Christ at Boston in New England. pseud. Arrow against profane and promiscuous dancing. (2112), 46632

Ministers of Christ freed from blood-guiltiness. 73561

Ministers of Christ should be careful. 21244

Ministers of Christ should be speedy and earnest. (17096)

Ministers of God's word must approve themselves unto God. (22007)

Ministers of Hampshire County, Mass. see Congregational Churches in Massachusetts Hampshire County Association.

Ministers of New-England. pseud. Letter. 55889

Ministers of Scotland. see Church of Scotland

Ministers of the Associate Church in America. see Associate Church in America. Ministers.

Ministers of the County of Hampshire, Mass. see Congregational Churches in Massachusetts. Hampshire County Association.

Ministers of the county of Windham, to the people of their charge. 104761

Ministers of the Gospel, as ambassadors for Christ. (22007)

Ministers of the Gospel, as spiritual guides to their people. 97317

Ministers of the Gospel characterized. 92241

Ministers of the Gospel considered as fellow-labourers. (32311)

Ministers of the Gospel in Boston. pseud. Principles of the protestant religion maintained. 828, (46466), note after 104098 see also Allen, James, 1632-1710. Mather, Cotton, 1663-1728. Moode Joshua, 1633-1697. Willard, Samuel, 1640-1707.

Ministers of the Gospel in or Near London. 94708

Ministers of the Gospel should speak. (17097)

Ministers of the Gospel should take heed. 85409

Ministers should carefully avoid giving offence in any thing. 97452

Ministers should have a sincere and ardent love. (67773)

Ministers should live of the Gospel. 64692

Ministers spiritual builders of God's house. 93705

Ministers, spiritual parents, or fathers in the church of God. 25398

Ministers Who Presented the Petition to the Parliament, Feb. 11, 1652. petitioners 104336

Minister's wife. pseud. From dawn to daylight. see Beecher, Eunice White (Bullard) 1813-1897.

Minister's wooing. 92440-92442

Ministrant church. 64471

Ministro ben informato dell' istessa. pseud. Deduzzione abbreviata. 63904

Ministro de estado. pseud. A missao Paranhos. see Souza Ferreira, Joao Carlos de, 1831-

Council and Treaty of Jonathan Carver, May 1, 1767, 1867. 11192
Minnesota history. 94934
Minnesota Horticultural Society. 49276
Minnesota in seinen Hauptverhaltnissen. (59595)
Minnesota in zijne hulpbronnen, ontwikkeling. 38056
Minnesota; its advantages to settlers. (31639)
Minnesota; its place among the states. (49279)
Minnesota: its progress and capabilities. 49280
Minnesota: its resources and progress. (49281)
Minnesota Magdalen Society. President. 49282
Minnesota messenger. 49283
Minnesota Mining Company. Directors. 49220
Minnesota: or, "a bundle of facts." 104820
Minnesota State Agricultural Society. Annual Fair, 9th, 1867. 49284
Minnesota State Bible Society. (49285)
Minnesota state business directory. 49286
Minnesota state gazetteer and business directory. 49287
Minnesota State Library. Annual report. 49288
Minnesota State Medical Society. (49289)
Minnesota State Sabbath School Association. Annual Convention, 10th, Faribault, 1868. (49292)
Minnesota teacher and journal of education. (49293)
Minnesota territory. Its present condition and prospects. (80822)
Minnesota tourist's and traveller's guide. (49294)
Minnesota year book for 1851. 39689
Minnetaree Indians. see Belantse-etoa Indians.
Minnie Myrtle. pseud. see Johnson, Anna C.
Minnigerode, Charles. 49313
Minns, Thomas, d. 1835. 106058
Minor, Benjamin Blake, 1818-1905. 49651, 82848, 88393, 95066, 100230, 3d note after 100533, 106131
Minor, D. K. 47283, 54771, 100685
Minor, John D. plaintiff 49314
Minor, Lucian. 49315
Minor, Peter. 49316
Minor. firm see Leeds (Henry H.) & Minor. firm
Minor American atlas. (10857)
Minor encyclopedia. 95466
Minor encyclopedia; or, cabinet of general knowledge. 30521
Minor poems. (63518)
Minor prophets. 22871
Minority of the Select Committee on the contested seat. 71742
Minority report by James Boyd. 46072, 67908
Minority report from the Committee on Banks. (74453)
Minority report, in favor of extending the right of suffrage. 19297
Minority report, of a Committee of the General Association of Connecticut, on the sin of slavery. (49317), 60952
Minority report of a Select Committee. (61840)
Minority report of Mr. Stevens. 29890, 91524
Minority report of the Commission appointed under resolution of the Legislature. (43114), 87716
Minority report of the Committee, in the case of the contested seat of Holton vs. Maclin. 32660

Minority report of the Committee of the Judiciary. (49317)
Minority report of the Committee of Visitation. 67244
Minority report of the Committee of Ways and Means. 15320
Minority report of the Committee on Banks. 60253
Minority report of the Committee on Corporatio 70605
Minority report of the Committee on Education, of the General Assembly of the State of Rhode Island. 70606
Minority report of the Committee on Education, . . . upon the petition of Isaac Rice and others. 70607
Minority report of the Committee on Elections. (36246)
Minority report of the Committee on Federal Relations. 87516
Minority report of the Committee on Federal Relations, respecting certain resolutions relating to the importation of slaves. 87527
Minority report of the Committee on Internal Improvements. (45097)
Minority report of the Committee on Public Printing. 37830
Minority report [of the Committee on the contested election case of Ridgely vs. Grason (71284)
Minority report of the Committee on the Judiciary. (49317)
Minority report on the currency. (49317)
Minority report, on the navy yard question. 70242
Minority report on the reduction of letter, periodical, and pamphlet postage. 21433
Minority report [on the true boundary line.] (46001)
Minority report touching the propriety of "recalling our commissioners to foreign powers." (49317)
Minority report [of the Committee on the memorial of] W. T. G. Morton. 51032
Minority report of the Committee on the Proposed Amendment. 37557
Minority report of the Committee on the remonstance of Wm. R. Huston. (73655)
Minority report of the Examining Committee. 52850
Minority report of the Finance Committee. 61841
Minority report of the Hon. Z. Kidwell. (3379
Minority report of the Joint Special Committee 70608
Minority report of the Select Committee, on . . . the consolidation of . . . Philadelph 60254, 61842
Minority report of the Select Committee . . . on the New Orleans riots. 53337
Minority report of the Senate Committee on Territories. 14360
Minority report [of the Special Committee of House of Representatives, of South Carolina.] 87521
Minority report of the Treasury Investigating Committee. 2840, 29386
Minority report of William Butler. 70609
Minot, George, 1817-1858. 49318, 49320, 61208
Minot, George, 1817-1858. petitioner 49319
Minot, George Richards, 1758-1802. 39749, 49321-(49325), 78997, 101803, 101868, 2d note after 101883

Minot, George Richards, 1758-1802. incorrectly supposed author 35441, 93506, 3d note after 95720

Minot, Me. School Committee. 49326

Minot's case. (76977), 76979, 97680

Minshall, Francis. petitioner 54977

Minshull, John. 49328

Minstrel and other poems. 21712

Minstrel boy. 51700

Minstrel girl. 103811

Minstrel maiden of Mobile. pseud. Wild shurbs of Alabama. see Harriss, Julia Mildred.

Minstrel pilgrim. 24295

Minstrelsey of Edmund the Wanderer. 89287

Mint at Philadelphia. 95585

Mint at Philadelphia. . . . December, 1861. 49333

Minthorne, Mangle. 49335

Minto, Walter. 49336

Minturn, Robert B. 49337

Minty. firm publishers see Carter & Minty. firm publishers

Minuajimouin au St. Mathiu. 57083

Minuajimouin gainajoinot au St. Luke. 57084

Minuta historico-apologetica da conducta do Bacharel Manuel Antonio Leitao Bandeira. 11457, 88776

Minute account of the naval conflict on Lake Erie. 8557

Minute account of the various military and naval operations. 7163

Minute description of . . . every object of interest. 62051

Inute description of the Philadelphia, Wilmington and Baltimore Rail Road. 49338

Minute expressing sympathy and brotherly love. 49339

Minute gun. 49340

Minute of the vestry adopted August 14, 1902. 84507

Minute on a subscription for the Negro fund. 49341

Minute on African slave trade and slavery. 49341

Minute on immigration slave trade. 49341

Minute, on the distribution of "the address to sovereigns, &c." 49341

Minute on the presentation of the address on slavery. 49341

Minute on the slave trade and slavery. 49341

Minute recommending subscription for the abolition of slave trade and slavery. 49341

Minute recommending subscription for the education of the Negroes. 49341

Minutes and address of the State Convention of the Colored Citizens of Ohio. 56961

Minutes, and circular letter. 102969

Minutes and papers of the Transylvania Presbytery. 96458

Minutes and phonographic report. 65201

Minutes and proceedings of a division court martial. 42095

Minutes and proceedings of a general court martial. (42096)

Minutes and proceedings of the Assembly of New Jersey. 53107

Minutes and proceedings of the division court martial. 8525

Minutes and proceedings of the first Annual Convention of the People of Colour. 49342

Minutes and proceedings of the General Convention, for the Improvement of the Colored Inhabitants of Canada. 1334

Minutes and proceedings of the Genesee Branch of the Western Association of Universalists. 102968

Minutes and proceedings of the joint meeting of the Council and General Assembly of . . . New Jersey. 53158

Minutes and proceedings of the Memphis Convention. (47783)

Minutes and proceedings of the National Quarantine and Sanitary Convention. (52017)

Minutes and votes of the House of Assembly. 53108

Minutes . . . at an occasional meeting held at New-York. 97975

Minutes . . . at an occasional meeting held at Washington. 97975

Minutes at Media, Dane County, Wisc. 18463

Minutes des deliberations du Comite sur l'Election de Lotbiniere. (42138)

Minutes du Conseil. 10352

Minutes . . . 1871, . . . held in Bethel A. M. E. Church. 87736

Minutes, 1821 [of the Holland Purchase Baptist Association.] 32517

Minutes for 1815 [of the Franklin Baptist Association.] 25646

Minutes from the record of the proceedings of a court martial. 96872

Minutes, June 14, 1820 [of the Black Water Baptist Association.] 5682

Minutes of a conference of general officers. 15321

Minutes of a conspiracy against the liberties of America. 49387

Minutes of a convention of delegates from the several Baptist churches. 104887

Minutes of a court martial . . . for the trial of Capt. Sir Home Popham. 64132

Minutes of a court martial held on board His Majesty's Ship Dodo. 49343

Minutes of a court of inquiry upon the case of Major John Andre. 1457

Minutes of a General Convention of the Christian Church. 49344

Minutes of a meeting of the . . . Trustees of the University of Mississippi. 49549

Minutes of a treaty held at Easton, in Pennsylvania. 60255

Minutes of an address. 76255

Minutes of an adjourned session [of the American Convention for Promoting the Abolition of Slavery.] 49358

Minutes of anniversaries of the Miami Association of Regular Baptists. 48684

Minutes of conferences, held at Easton, in August, 1761. 49349

Minutes of conferences, held at Easton, in October, 1758. 49348

Minutes of conferences held at Fort-Pitt. 17589

Minutes of conferences, held at Lancaster. 49350

Minutes of conferences, held with the Indians, at Easton, in the months of July, and August, 1757. 49347, 102508

Minutes of conferences, held with the Indians, at Easton, in the months of July and November, 1756. 49345

Minutes of conferences, held with the Indians at Harris's Ferry, and at Lancaster. (49346)

Minutes of Council, containing His Majesty's late regulations. 23503

Minutes of Council, of the 20th of September, 1798. 23503

Minutes of Council relating to the records of Canada. 10351

Minutes of Daniel Cushing of Hingham. 18099

Minutes of debates in council on the banks of the Ottowa River. (49351)

Minutes of evidence and proceedings of the Select Committees. 49369

Minutes of evidence, etc. (29165)

Minutes of evidence in the matter of the Demerara and Berbice manumission. 19467

Minutes of evidence on Ceylon and British Guiana. 49352

Minutes of evidence on the trial of John Smith. 82899

Minutes of evidence taken at the bar of the House of Lords. 49353

Minutes of evidence taken before the Committee on Manufactures. (49354)

Minutes of evidence taken before the House of Commons. 49353

Minutes of evidence taken on Committee of the House of Commons. (49370)

Minutes of meeting at Bridgewater. 7830

Minutes of meetings . . . held in 1859 [of the La Crosse Valley Baptist Association.] (38509)

Minutes of New-London Baptist Association, held at Lebanon. (53258)

Minutes of our yearly meeting, . . . in Baltimore. (45364)

Minutes of proceedings of the Board of Supervisors of the county of Oswego. (57836)

Minutes of proceedings of the Court of Enquiry. (33636)

Minutes of proceedings of the courts of inquiry and court martial. 64221

Minutes of proceedings of the Institution of Civil Engineers. (41693)

Minutes of proceedings of the Requited Labor Convention. (49355)

Minutes of proceedings of the Supreme Grand Council. (49356), 55811

Minutes of session of 1855 [of the Marquette Baptist Association.] 44667

Minutes of several conversations. 48200

Minutes of the acts and proceedings of the Associate-Reformed Synod. 65160

Minutes of the adjourned session of the twentieth biennial American Convention for Promoting the Abolition of Slavery. 49358, 82015

Minutes of the Alabama Conference. 49357

Minutes of the anniversary of the Baptist General Association of Illinois. 34212

Minutes of the annual conferences of the Methodist Episcopal Church for the years 1773-1828. (48202)

Minutes of the annual conferences of the Methodist Episcopal Church. Spring conferences of 1886. 84753

Minutes of the annual conferences of the Wesleyan-Methodist Church in Canada. 102706

Minutes of the annual meeting, 1841, of the Associate Alumni. (54291)

Minutes of the annual meeting of the Evangelical Consociation of Rhode Island. 50781

Minutes of the annual meeting of the Long-Run Association of Baptists. (49103)

Minutes of the annual meeting of the Pennsylvania Baptist State Convention for Missionary Purposes. 60303

Minutes of the annual meeting of the Rhode Island Congregational Conference. (70717)

Minutes of the annual meetings of the South-Western Conference of Congregational Churches and Ministers. 88611

Minutes of the . . . annual session of the Hartwick Synod. 30718

Minutes of the . . . annual session of the Iowa Annual Conference. 34980

Minutes of the Associate Synod of North America. 98181

Minutes of the Associate Synod of North America at their annual meeting. (65174)

Minutes of the Associate Synod of North America, at their meeting at Pittsburgh. 65162

Minutes of the Baltimore Baptist Convention. 3049

Minutes of the . . . Bank Convention. (54107)

Minutes of the Baptist Association held at New-York. (54111)

Minutes of the Baptist Association held at Philadelphia. 61497

Minutes of the Baptist Association [of Philadelphia.] 61497

Minutes of the Baptist Committee held at Nuckols's Meeting-House. 49360

Minutes of the Baptist Convention met at Mount Pleasant. 51166

Minutes of the Baptist General Association of Virginia. 100432

Minutes of the Baptist General Committee held at Waller's Meeting-House. 97845

Minutes of the Baptist General Committee, holden at Muddy-Creek Meeting-House. 49359

Minutes of the Baptist General Meeting, of Correspondence. 100433

Minutes of the . . . [Baptist State Convention] of South-Carolina. 87797

Minutes of the Baptist Yearly Meeting of the Ancient Order of Six Principles of the Doctrine of Christ. 49360

Minutes of the Barnstable Baptist Association. 3553

Minutes of the Bethel Association. 5072

Minutes of the Board of Admiralty. 49343

Minutes of the Board of Directors of the Press Association. (65362)

Minutes of the Board of Foreign Ministers of the Presbyterian Church. (65142)

Minutes of the Board of Supervisors of the county of Kings. 37874

Minutes [of the Canadian Anti-slavery Baptist Association.] 10404

Minutes of the Cayuga Baptist Association. 11637

Minutes of the centennial celebration. 85183

Minutes of the Charleston Association. 49361

Minutes of the Charleston Baptist Association . . . 1802. 49361

Minutes of the Charleston [Baptist] Association held at the Welch Neck. 87795

Minutes [of the Chenango Baptist Association.] 12424

Minutes of the Christian Anti-slavery Convention. . . . 1850. 49362

Minutes of the Christian Anti-slavery Convention. . . . 1851. 49362

Minutes of the Christian Convention, held at Aurora, Illinois. 49363

Minutes of the Cincinnati Annual Conference. (13096)

Minutes of the Coetus [of the Reformed Church in America.] 68775

Minutes of the Commission of the Synod. (31294)

Minutes of the Committee of the Whole of the Convention of the state of Pennsylvania. (60256)

Minutes of the Common Council . . . [of Philadelphia] for 1835-6. 61553

Minutes of the Common Council of . . . Philadelphia. 1704 to 1776. 61553

Minutes of the conference held in Vassalborough. 37383

Minutes of the Congregational Association of Oregon. (57557)

Minutes of the Congress at Fort Stanwix, in October and November, 1768. 25595, 34579-34580, 99584, note just before 103108

Minutes of the convention assembled at East Windsor. 23528

Minutes of the Convention of Banks, of the City of Charleston. 12060

Minutes of the Convention of Delegates from the Synod of New-York and Philadelphia. 15819, 49364

Minutes of the Convention of Delegates Met to Consult on Missions. 49365

Minutes of the Convention of Freedmen's Commissions. 25745

Minutes of the Convention of . . . New-Jersey. 53159

Minutes of the Convention of the commonwealth of Pennsylvania, which commenced at Philadelphia, . . . the twentieth day of November. 60257

Minutes of the Convention of the commonwealth . . . [of Pennsylvania,] which commenced at Philadelphia, . . . the twenty-fourth . . . [day of] November. 60258

Minutes of the Convention of the Delaware State. (19396)

Minutes of the convention that formed the constitution of Pennsylvania. 60435, 80768

Minutes of the Council and General Court. 99908

Minutes of the Council of the province of New-York. 53665, 84566

[Minutes of the Cumberland Association] held in . . . Jay (Maine). 17880

Minutes of the Cumberland Association, Paris, Me. 17880

Minutes of the Cumberland Conference of Churches. 17886

Minutes of the Danbury Baptist Association. (18458)

Minutes of the debate in the Legislature of Pennsylvania. 60260

Minutes of the discussion at a meeting of the Board of Council for Trade and Foreign Plantations. 49366

Minutes of the Dover Baptist Association. (49367)

Minutes of the East Maine Conference of the Methodist Episcopal Church. (49368)

Minutes of the Eastern New-Brunswick Baptist Association. 52541

Minutes of the eighteenth session of the American Convention for Promoting the Abolition Slavery. 49358

Minutes of the eight annual Stone's River Association. 92158

Minutes of the eighth session of the Baptist Convention of Nova Scotia. 3239

Minutes of the eighth session of the Missouri Annual Conference. 49612

Minutes of the Essex Baptist Association. 23018

Minutes of the Evangelical Consociation, Rhode Island. 82057

Minutes of the evidence taken at the bar of the House of Lords. (49370)

Minutes of the evidence, taken before a Committee of the Whole House, to whom it was referred to consider of the slave-trade, 1790. Number III. 81737

Minutes of the evidence, taken before a Committee of the Whole House, to whom it was referred to consider of the slave-trade, 1790. Number II. 81736

Minutes of the evidence, taken before a Committee of the Whole House, to whom it was referred to consider of the slave trade, 1791. Number IV. 81738

Minutes [of the Federal Convention.] 22233

Minutes of the fifth annual meeting, 1852 . . . [of the New York Central College Association.] 54754

Minutes of the fifth annual meeting of the General Conference of Congregational Churches. 49296

Minutes of the 51st anniversary, Belleville, 1859 [of the Black River Baptist Association.] 5682

Minutes of the first anniversary of the First Baptist Association of Central Wisconsin. 104888

Minutes of the first anniversary of the Milford Baptist Association. 48947

Minutes of the first anniversary of the Providence Baptist Association. (66313)

Minutes of the first anniversary of the Salem Baptist Association. 75713

Minutes of the first annual meeting of the General Association of Baptists in Kentucky. 37558

Minutes of the first annual meeting of the Narragansett Association. 51772

Minutes of the first annual meeting of the North Western Freedmen's Aid Commission. 55743

Minutes of the first annual session. Indianapolis, Dec. 25, 1854. 34513

Minutes of the first fifteen annual meetings of the General Convention of Ministers in the state of Vermont. 99169

Minutes of the first Kansas Baptist Convention. (37073)

Minutes of the first meeting of the Sabbath School Convention. 75715

Minutes of the first meeting of the Trustees [of the Illinois Industrial University.] (34236)

Minutes of the first session of the Council [of the Massachusetts Universalist Convention.] 45912

Minutes of the first session, of the sixth General Assembly. 60261

Minutes of the first session of the Western Baptist Association. 56152

Minutes of the formation of the Grand Board of Pennsylvania. 60127

Minutes of the forty-fifth session of the Maine Annual Conference. 43961

Minutes of the forty-second anniversary of the Rensselaerville Baptist Association. 69642

Minutes of the fourteenth anniversary of the Rhode Island Baptist Sunday School Convention. 70712

Minutes of the Freedmen's Convention, held in the city of Raleigh. 67600

Minutes [of the Free-Will Baptist Connection in North America.] (25728)

Minutes of the general and annual conferences of the African Methodist Episcopal Church. 48181

MINUTES

Minutes of the General Assembly of the
Presbyterian Church in the United States
of America, 1821-1835. 65176
Minutes of the General Assembly of the
Presbyterian Church in the United States
of America, from A. D. 1789 to A. D.
1802. 65163
Minutes of the General Assembly of the
Presbyterian Church, in the United States
of America [New School.] (65178)
Minutes of the General Assembly of the
Presbyterian Church in the United States
of America, 1789-1820. 65175
Minutes of the General Assembly of the
Presbyterian Church in the United States
of America: with an appendix. A. D.
1822. 65177
Minutes of the General Assembly of the
Presbyterian Church in the United States
of America: with an appendix. New
series. 65179
Minutes of the General Association, June,
1855. 34978
[Minutes of the General Association,] June,
1856. 34978
Minutes of the General Association of Baptists
in Kentucky. 37558
Minutes of the General Association of Baptists
in Kentucky, of the Kentucky and Foreign
Bible Society, and of the Roberts' Fund
and China Mission Society. 37558
Minutes of the General Association of Congregational Ministers & Churches in
Kansas. 37072
Minutes of the General Association of Con-
gregational Ministers in Massachusetts.
45739
Minutes of the General Association of Con-
necticut. 15816
Minutes of the General Association of Con-
necticut at their meeting in Danby.
15820
Minutes of the General Association of Illinois.
(34213)
Minutes of the General Association of Massa-
chusetts Proper. 45738
Minutes of the General Association of Michigan.
48775
Minutes of the General Association of New
Hampshire. 52823-52824
Minutes of the General Association of New
Hampshire, at their meeting, at Keene.
52851
Minutes of the General Association of New
York, . . . August 26th, 1841. (53679)
Minutes of the General Committee in Virginia.
100434
Minutes of the General Committee . . . [of
the Charleston Baptist Association.]
87795
Minutes of the General Conference at their
annual meeting. 44000
Minutes of the General Conference of the
Congregational Churches in Maine. 44001
Minutes of the General Conference of the
Congregational Churches in Massachusetts,
at their first annual session. 45740
Minutes [of the General Conference of the
Congregational Churches in Massachusetts,
1865.] 85218
Minutes of the General Convention of Congre-
gational and Presbyterian Ministers in
Vermont. 99169
Minutes of the General Convention of Congre-
gational Ministers and Churches in Ver-
mont. 99224

Minutes of the General Convention of the
Independent Order of the Sons of Malta.
60161
Minutes of the General Convention of Univer-
salists in the United States. (49371)
Minutes of the General Synod of the Reformed
Presbyterian Church. 65180
Minutes of the Georgia Association. . . . [At]
Clark's Station, October, 1788. 27077
Minutes of the Georgia Association. At Kiok
MDCCCIV. 27077
Minutes of the Georgia Association. At New-
ford, . . . October, 1804. 27077
Minutes of the Georgia Association. At Powe
Creek, . . . October [1794.] 27077
Minutes of the Georgia Association. At What
ley's Mill, October, 1803. 27077
Minutes of the . . . Georgia Convention. 270
Minutes of the Grand Committee of the Whole
Convention. 60259
Minutes of the Grand Committee of the Whole
Convention of the Delaware State. 1939
Minutes of the Grand Consistory [of New Yor
53691
Minutes of the Grand Division of the Sons of
Temperance, of the State of Virginia.
87094
Minutes of the Grand Division, Sons of Tem-
perance, State of Minnesota. 87053
Minutes of the hearing before the Mayor of
the city of New York. 84774
Minutes of the High-School Synod. 17270,
90007, note before 96989
Minutes of the Illinois Baptist Pastoral Union
34211
Minutes of the Illinois Converence of the
Methodist Episcopal Church, 1854. 342
Minutes of the Illinois Conference of the Met
odist Episcopal Church, for . . . 1862.
(49372)
Minutes of the Indiana Annual Conference, of
the Methodist Episcopal Church. 82925
Minutes of the Indiana Yearly Meeting, held
at White-Water. 34498
Minutes of the Iowa Baptist State Convention.
34979
Minutes of the jubilee anniversary of the
Oneida Baptist Association. 57338
Minutes of the Kehukee Baptist Association,
held at Whitfield's Meeting House. 371
97839
Minutes of the Kehukee Baptist Association,
holden at Parker's Meeting-House. 978
Minutes of the Kennebec Conference of Churc
37383
Minutes of the Kentucky Baptist anniversaries
(37559)
Minutes of the Madison Baptist Association.
43729
Minutes of the Maine Baptist Convention.
43963
Minutes of the Maine Conference of the Meth
odist Episcopal Church. 49374
Minutes of the . . . Maryland Baptist Union
Association. 45204
Minutes of the Massachusetts Baptist Con-
vention. 45821
Minutes of the Maumee Baptist Association.
46938
Minutes of the meeting at Nomony, Westmorl
County, Virginia. 55417
Minutes of the Meeting for Sufferings of New
York. 53779
Minutes of the meeting of the Baptist Asso-
ciation. (38587)

Minutes of the meeting of the Ohio State Sunday School Convention. (57011)

Minutes of the meetings of creditors and bondholders. (34316)

Minutes of the Methodist conferences. 48201

Minutes of the Military Commission at the meeting in Greenville, S. C. 87717

Minutes of the Mississippi Annual Conference. 49524

Minutes of the Minnesota Annual Conference. 49295

Minutes of the Minnesota Baptist Association. 49270

Minutes of the Morgan County Sabbath School Convention. 50691

Minutes of the National Christian Convention. 51944

Minutes of the New England Annual Conference of the African Methodist Episcopal Church. 52643

Minutes of the New England Annual Conference of the Methodist Episcopal Church. 52644

Minutes of the New-England Yearly Meeting of Friends. 52754

Minutes of the New England Yearly Meeting of Women Friends. 52636

Minutes of the New Hampshire Association. (52852)

Minutes of the New Hampshire Annual Conference. 52853

Minutes of the New Hampshire Baptist Convention. (52858)

Minutes of the New York Baptist Association. (54748)

Minutes of the New York East Conference. (54766)

Minutes of the New York State Christian Convention. 53815

Minutes of the New-York Yearly Meeting of Friends. (54559)

Minutes of the nineteenth annual meeting of the General Association of the Baptists of Missoui. 49613

Minutes of the nineteenth annual session of the Michigan Annual Conference of the Methodist-Episcopal Church. 48758

Minutes of the Nova Scotia and New Brunswick Baptist Association. 56153

Minutes of the one hundred and seventy-fifth session of the Orange Presbytery. 65181

Minutes of the 100th annual meeting of the German Evangelical Lutheran Ministerium of Pennsylvania. 60120

Minutes of the Oneida Baptist Association. 57338

Minutes of the Onondaga Baptist Association. 57359

Minutes of the Ontario Baptist Association. (57369)

Minutes of the organization and proceedings of the New England Soldiers' Relief Association. 52747

Minutes of the original Particular Synod. 68775

Minutes of the Otsego Baptist Association. (57876)

Minutes of the Particular Synod of Albany; convened at Schenectady, May, 1837. (49375)

Minutes of the Particular Synod of Albany, convened in regular session. 68781

Minutes of the Particular Synod of New-York. 53854

Minutes of the Philadelphia Baptist Association, from 1707 to 1807. 27407

Minutes of the Philadelphia Baptist Association, . . . Oct. 6, 1789. (61962)

Minutes of the . . . [Philadelphia] Society [for Promoting Agriculture.] 62036

Minutes of the Philadelphian Association in MDCCLXIX. (62412)

Minutes of the Piankashaw Council, held at Post St. Vincent's, April 15, 1784. 24336, 34355

Minutes of the Piankashaw Council, 1784. (34358)

Minutes of the Portsmouth Baptist Association. 64437, 100435

Minutes of the Presbyterian and Congregational Convention. 12659

Minutes of the Presbytery of Philadelphia. (65209)

Minutes of the proceedings at the trial of Admiral Knowles. (38151), note after 96893

Minutes of the proceedings of a brigade court martial. 96931

Minutes of the proceedings of a Convention, Holden at Warren, Ohio. 60299, 101491

Minutes of the proceedings of a Convention of Baptist Churches at New York. 49376

Minutes of the proceedings of a court martial assembled and held on board His Majesty's Ship Belleisle. 104651

Minutes of the proceedings of a court-martial held on George Crookshanks. 17612

Minutes of the proceedings of a special meeting of the fifteenth American Convention for Promoting the Abolition of Slavery. 49358, 82019

Minutes of the proceedings of the Bank Convention. 49377

Minutes of the proceedings of the Board [of the General Protestant Episcopal Sunday School Union.] 66152

Minutes of the proceedings of the Committee. (49378), 61843

Minutes of the proceedings of the Congregational Church and Society of Winsted. 63916

Minutes of the proceedings of the Congress, held at Cambridge. 23533, 45731

Minutes of the proceedings of the Convention of Delegates from the Abolition Societies. (49379)

Minutes of the proceedings of the court martial held at Portsmouth. 5913, 49380

Minutes of the proceedings of the first General Synod of the Associate-Reformed Church in North-America. 65161

Minutes of the proceedings [of the General Association of New Hampshire.] 52824

Minutes of the proceedings of the Grand Encampment of Pennsylvania of the Independent Order of Odd Fellows. 60160

Minutes of the proceedings of the Institution of Civil Engineers. (41693)

Minutes of the proceedings of the joint meeting of the Council and General Assembly. 53160

Minutes of the proceedings of the joint meeting of the Senate and General Assembly. 53137

Minutes of the proceedings of the Legislative Assembly of the district of San Francisco. 76062

Minutes of the proceedings of the Legislative Council of New-Jersey. 53161

Minutes of the proceedings of the Medical Convention of South-Carolina. 87877

Minutes of the proceedings of the National Medical Convention, held in New-York, . . . May, 1846. 52007, 54414

Minutes of the proceedings of the Pittsburgh Convention. 63121

Minutes of the proceedings of the Quarantine Convention. 49381

Minutes of the proceedings of the second Convention of Delegates from the Abolition Societies Established in Different Parts of the United States. 82016

Minutes of the proceedings of the South-Carolina Medical Association, at its annual meetings, February, 1849-50. 88017

Minutes of the proceedings of the South Carolina Medical Association, at the meeting convened in Charleston. 88018

Minutes of the proceedings of the Teachers' Society of the state of Georgia. 94561

Minutes of the proceedings of the third American Convention for Promoting the Abolition of Slavery. 82017

Minutes of the proceedings of the thirteenth American Convention for Promoting the Abolition of Slavery. 82018

Minutes of the proceedings of the twenty-first American Convention for Promoting the Abolition of Slavery. 82019

Minutes of the proceedings of the Western Association of Universalists. 102966

Minutes of the Providence Annual Conference. 66284

Minutes of the Provincial Council of Pennsylvania. 31104

Minutes of the Regents of the University [of the State of New York.] (54000)

Minutes of the Rhode Island Baptist State Convention. 70711

Minutes of the Rock-River Conference of the Methodist-Episcopal Church. 34216

Minutes of the . . . [Rockingham] Conference . . . at Portsmouth. 72388

Minutes of the Rockingham Conference, at the annual meeting in Chester. 72388

Minutes of the Sab. School Teachers Convention of the Worcester Baptist Association. 105385

Minutes of the San Francisco Baptist Association. 76089

Minutes of the Sanitary Commission. 76658

Minutes of the Saratoga Baptist Association. 76923

Minutes of the Savannah Baptist Association, held at Black Swamp, in the state of South Carolina. 77267, 87947

Minutes . . . [of the Savannah Baptist Association, held] Savannah, from Jan. 14th to 17th, 1804. (77267)

Minutes of the Savannah Baptist Association, held in the city of Savannah, state of Georgia, 1803. (77267)

Minutes of the second convention. 60258

Minutes of the secret committee. 74496

Minutes of the session of the Evangelical-Lutheran Synod of Maryland and Virginia. 49382

Minutes of the session of the Racine Baptist Association held in 1849. 67393

Minutes of the Seventh-Day Baptist General Conference. 79363

Minutes of the Shaftsbury Association at their annual convention. 49383

Minutes of the sixth anniversary of the Salem Baptist Association. 75714

Minutes of the sixth session of the Sabbath School Convention. 75715

Minutes of the South-Carolina Conference. 87894

Minutes of the South Kentucky District Association. 88142

Minutes of the Southern and South-Western Presbyterian Convention. 65182

Minutes of the State Convention of Colored Citizens, held at Albany. 53780

Minutes of the State Convention of Coloured Citizens of Pennsylvania. 60262

Minutes of the State Education Convention, Columbus, O. 56962

Minutes of the Stonington Association. 92164

Minutes of the Stonington Baptist Association. 62164

Minutes of the Strawberry District Association. 92748

Minutes of the Sturbridge Association, at Wilbraham. 93255

Minutes of the Sturbridge Association, holden at Thompson. 93256

Minutes of the Synod of New-York and New-Jersey. 53666

Minutes of the Synod of New York, from A. D. 1745 to 1758. (65209)

Minutes of the Synod of Philadelphia and New York. (65209)

Minutes of the Synod of Philadelphia, from A. D. 1717 to 1758. (65209)

Minutes of the Synod of South Carolina and Georgia, at their sessions in Augusta, Dec. 1830. 87915A

Minutes of the Synod of South Carolina and Georgia; Columbia, S. C., December, 1833. (49384)

Minutes of the . . . Synod of the Evangelical Lutheran Ministerium . . . of New York 53658

Minutes of the . . . Synod of the Evangelical Lutheran Ministerium of the State of New York, and Adjacent Parts. 49385

Minutes of the Taunton Baptist Association. 94420

Minutes, of the Tennessee Association of Baptists. 94788

Minutes of the tenth annual meeting of the Medical Society of . . . North Carolina. 55646

Minutes of the testimony taken before J. Q. Wilson. (15793)

Minutes of the third anniversary of the Pennsylvania Baptist Convention. 60303

Minutes of the third anniversary of the Sabbath School Convention. 75715

Minutes of the third session of the Hartwick Synod and Ministerium. 53658

Minutes of the third session of the Kansas and Nebraska Annual Conference. 4937

Minutes of the thirteenth anniversary of the Damariscotta Baptist Association. (1834

Minutes of the thirty-eighth anniversary of the Strait-Creek Baptist Association. 92672

Minutes of the thirty-third anniversary of the Monroe Baptist Association. 50029

Minutes of the thirty-third annual meeting of the South District Baptist Association. 49614, 88122

Minutes of the trial and examination of certain persons. 49386, note after 101854

Minutes of the triennial meeting, 1841, of the Associate Alumni. (54291)

Minutes of the twelfth anniversary of the Cattaraugus Baptist Association. 11555

Minutes of the twelfth annual meeting of the Edwardsville Baptist Association. 22000

Minutes of the twentieth session of the Primitive Methodist Western Annual Conference. 65557

Minutes of the twenty-eighth anniversary of the St. Lawrence Baptist Association. 75313

Minutes of the twenty-first anniversary of the New Jersey Baptist State Convention. 53168

Minutes of the twenty-first annual meeting of the Rock River Baptist Association. 72414

Minutes of the twenty-ninth anniversary of the Sunbury Baptist Association. 93736

Minutes of the United Baptist Association, formerly called the Kehukee Association, holden at Davis's Meeting-House. 97841

Minutes of the United Baptist Association, formerly called the Kehukee Association, holden at Flat-Swamp Meeting-House. 97842

Minutes of the United Baptist Association, formerly called the Kehukee Association, holden at Reedy-Creek Meeting-House. 97840

Minutes of the United Baptist Association, formerly called the Kehuky Association, held at Whitefield's Meeting-House. 37166, 97839

Minutes of the United States Military Philosophical Society. 97975

Minutes of the Upper Canada Baptist Association. 10525

Minutes of the Vermont Association at their annual convention, holden at Orwel, Vermont. 99153

Minutes of the Vermont Association: at their annual convention, holden at Pittsfield. 99154

Minutes of the Vermont Association, at their annual convention: holden at Wallingford. 99152

Minutes of the Vermont Association at their annual meeting, holden at Wallingford. 99156

Minutes of the Vermont Association, met at Salem, New-York. 99155

Minutes of the Vermont Baptist Association, held at the Baptist Meeting-House, in Granville, N. Y. 99158

Minutes of the Vermont Baptist Association. Holden at Salem, N. Y. 99157

Minutes of the Virginia Portsmouth Baptist Association. 100435

Minutes of the votes and proceedings of the sixty-fifth General Assembly of . . . New Jersey. 53162

Minutes of the Warren Association, held at Sutton. 49388, note after 101497

Minutes of the Warren Association, held at the South Baptist Meeting-House in Middleborough. 3240

Minutes of the Warren Association, held in Boston. 82483

Minutes of the Warwick Association. 101510

Minutes of the Wendell Baptist Association. 102626

Minutes of the Western-Shore Association. 103017

Minutes of the Westfield Baptist Association. 103029

Minutes of the Woodstock Association. 105145

Minutes of the Worcester Baptist Association [for 1840.] 105375

Minutes of the Worcester Baptist Association, held at the Baptist Meeting-House, in Shrewsbury. 105384

Minutes of the Yearly Meeting of Friends, held in New York. (53667)

Minutes of the Yearly Meeting of Friends, held in Philadelphia. 61645

Minutes of the Yearly Meeting of Women Friends. 86059

Minutes of the York Baptist Association. 106021

Minutes of three trials . . . at Roseau. 61188

Minutes taken at the several annual conferences. 48204

Minutes taken at the several conferences of the Methodist Episcopal Church in America. 48203

Minutoli, J. H. von. tr. 71445

Miocene. 47369

Miquel, F. A. G. 49389-(49390)

Miqueorena, A. de. 49391

Mira, Jose Joaquin de. tr. 13520

Mira de Mescua, Antonio. (4587)

Mirabeau, Honore Gabriel Riquetti, Comte de, 1749-1791. 2496, 13118, 17165, 56776, (49392)-49402, 65449, (65451), 67693, 75145

Mirabeau, Jean Antoine Joseph Charles Elzaer Riquetti, 1717-1794. 49399-(49400)

Mirabeau, Victor Riquetti, Marquis de, 1715-1789. 49399

Mirabilia Dei. An essay on the very seasonable & remarkable interpositions of the divine providence. 46417

Mirabilia Dei inter Indicos. (7340), 85994

Mirabilia Romae. 72884

Mirabilia Rome opusculum de mirabilibus noue et ueteris urbis Rome. 667

Mirabilis vita et mirabiliora acta. 31561

Miracles of art and nature. 9502

Miraculous cure of Sister Beatrix Myers. 51628

Miraculous preservation of fifteen English His Majesties subjects. 96315

Miraculous revelation of the nature and cause of the present war and rebellion. 19819, 21430

Mirada hacia el porvenir de la hacienda nacional de Venezuela. 7403

Mirada retrospectiva sobre la hacienda de Venezuela. 7404

Miraeus, Aubertus. see Le Mire, Aubert, 1573-1640.

Miraflores, Peru. 26112, 44291, 76158

Miralla, Jose Antonio. 49406-49407

Miramichi, New Brunswick. Citizens. (51433)

Miramon, Miguel. 20548, (49408)

Miran de Butron, Jacinto. see Moran de Butron, Jacinto, 1668-1749.

Miranda, ----------, fl. 1860. 49409

Miranda, A. de la Torre. see Torre Miranda, A. de la.

Miranda, F. X. 49413

Miranda, Fr. J. 49412

Miranda, Francisco de. 49411

Miranda, Henrique de Souza de Tavares da Silva, Conde de. see Souza de Tavares da Silva, Henrique da, Conde de Miranda.

Miranda, Joao Antonio de. 49414, 49415

Miranda, Rafael. 49416-49417

Miranda, Roque. 49418

Mirandula, Ioannes Franciscus Picus. tr. (66478)

Miravalle, Jose Joaquin Trebuesto y Casasola, Conde de Miravalle.

Miravalle, Pedro Alonso Davalos Bracamonte y Espinosa, Conde de. see Davalos Bracamonte y Espinosa, Pedro Alonso, Conde de Miravalle.

Miravalles, Pedro Alonso de Avalos y Bracamont, Conde de. see Avalos y Bracamont, Pedro Alonso de, Conde de Miravalles.

Miraville, Maria Catharina Davalos Bracamont
y Orozco, <u>Condesa</u> de. <u>see</u> Davalos
Bracamont y Orozco, Maria Catharina,
<u>Condesa</u> de Miraville.
Mirbeck, Frederic Ignace de. 49419-49420
Mire, Aubert le. <u>see</u> Le Mire, Aubert,
1573-1640.
Miriam Coffin. 49421
Mirick, B. L. 49422, 103819
Mirmont, Alexandre Jean Joseph Delaville de.
<u>see</u> Delaville de Mirmont, Alexandre
Jean Joseph.
Mirnstill, J. <u>ed.</u> 66958
Miro, Estaban. 5906, 74878
Miroir de la cruelle, & horrible tyrannie.
11270, 2d note after 39116
Miroir de la tyrannie Espagnole. 11270, 2d
note after 39116
Miroir du monde, ou, exposicion des parties
de la terre. 24933, 58546
Miroir du monde, reduict premierement en
rithme brabanconne. 31666
Miroir Oost & West-Indical. 89451
Miron and Florilla. 49423
Mirror. 49424
Mirror and casket of the davghters of indvstry.
49425
Mirror and repository of amusement. (66077)
Mirror for several articles. 105465
Mirror for the female sex. 62852
"Mirror for the pretended democracy." 49426
Mirror in America. 50046
Mirror library. 62965, 104504, 104509
Mirror of Calvinist, fanatical revivals. 92787
Mirror of Calvinistic fanaticism. 92788
Mirror of fortune. 12609
Mirror of merit and beauty. 82774
Mirror of misery. 49427, 82020
Mirror of modern democracy. 36630
Mirror of New York. (8667)
Mirror of olden time border life. 65720
Mirror of Parliament. (49428)
Mirror of taste, and dramatic censor. 49429
Mirror of the Patent Office in the United States.
(1116), 81602
Mirror of the Philomathean Society. (49430)
Mirror; or, a delineation of different classes
of Christians. 36094
Mirrovr or looking-glasse both for saints and
sinners. 13447-13448
Mirror, reflecting the light of truth. 70822
Mirrour . . . <u>see</u> Mirror . . .
Mirth and song. 91499
Mirval, C. H. de. (49431)
Mis ausencias. 7799
Mis deberes para con la sociedad. 49454
Mis en valeur des terres pauvres. 5166
Mis Mac Rea, roman historique. 31904
Mis memorias sobre Queretaro y Maximiliano.
75807
Misanthrope of the mountain. 49432
Miscegenation or amalgamation. (17271)
Miscegenation: the theory of the blending of
the race. 49433
Miscelane de ciencias, literatura, artes, e
industria. 9876
Miscelanea. 50476
Miscelanea Americana. 25123
Miscelanea Austral. 2469
Miscelanea cientifica, artistica, y literaria.
70305
Miscelanea de ciencias, literatura, artes e
industria. 79051
Miscelanea de comercio, artes y literatura.
93780

Miscelanea de economica, politica, y moral.
25555
Miscelanea de literatura, ciencia e historia.
(72784)
Miscelanea de literatura viajes y novelas.
(56643)
Miscelanea Hispano-Americana de ciencias,
literatura i artes. (49434)
Miscelanea instructiva de variedades y cos-
tumbres de ambos mundos. 26281
Miscelanea instructiva y amena consagrada
a la religion. (69669)
Miscelanea militar Mejicana. 49435
Miscelanea, o coleccion de macsimas y pensa-
mientos critico-politico-morales. (47340)
Miscelanea pintoresca de amenidades curiosas
e instructivas. 51566
Miscelanea poetica. 62606
Miscelanea politica, estractada y redactada de
las mejores fuentes. 23773
Miscelanea politica y literaria. (49436)
Miscelanea util y curiosa. (67959)
Miscelaneas del Duque de Villahumbrosa.
94275
Miscelaneo espiritual en el idioma Zapoteca.
522, 106254
Miscellanea austral. (18676)
Miscellanea: comprising reviews, lectures,
and essays. 88908, 88910
Miscellanea curiosa. Being a collection of
some of the principal phaenomena in
nature. 49437
Miscellanea curiosa. Containing a collection
of curious travels. 49437
Miscellanea curiosa. Containing a collection
of some of the principal phaenomena in
nature. (13575), 49438
Miscellanea e trouas. 70062
Miscellanea economica, politica, etc. 49439
Miscellanea historica, curiosa e instructiva.
81108
Miscellanea poetica. 49440
Miscellanees historiques, scientifiques, et
litteraires. 5206
Miscellaneo espiritual en idioma Zapoteca.
522, 106254
Miscellaneous and fugitive pieces. [By Samuel
Johnson.] 36299
Miscellaneous and fugitive pieces. [By T.
Davies.] 18773
Miscellaneous and patriotic poems. 27288
Miscellaneous anecdotes, illustrating a variety
of topice. 84757, 84757A
Miscellaneous collection, consisting of an
original letter from the pen of Columbus.
14642, 29396, 49441
Miscellaneous collection of original pieces.
(74338)
Miscellaneous collections of the Smithsonian
Institute. 27301
Miscellaneous collections relating to vaccinatie
98271
Miscellaneous compositions, in poetry and pro
91813
Miscellaneous correspondence. (49442)
Miscellaneous correspondence, . . . relative t
natural and civil history. 44847
Miscellaneous discourses and reviews. 33794
Miscellaneous documents of the Senate of the
United States. 49443
Miscellaneous documents of the United States
Sanitary Commission. 76659
Miscellaneous documents read in the Legis-
lature. 60263
Miscellaneous English books. 70887

Miscellaneous essay, concerning the courses pursued by Great Britain. 43123
Miscellaneous essay on the political parties of the country. 3673
Miscellaneous essays and discourses. (32941)
Miscellaneous essays and occasion writings of Francis Hospkinson, Esq. (32979), 84606, 84608, 84678C
Miscellaneous essays [by Mathew Carey.] 10871
Miscellaneous journal. 55562
Miscellaneous letters on every subject from a prince to a peasant. 90446
Miscellaneous observations, concerning penal and sanguinary laws. 106082
Miscellaneous observations made during a tour in . . . 1835. 31796
Miscellaneous observation relating to the United States of America. 96328
Miscellanous observations respecting the United States. (19708), 96327
Miscellaneous ode. 40936
Miscellaneous odes, &c. 93082
Miscellaneous pamphlets, chiefly on American affairs. (5459)
Miscellaneous paper, devoted to the belles lettres. 94184
Miscellaneous papers. [By Timothy Claxton.] 13530
Miscellaneous papers, on political and commercial subjects. 102369
Miscellaneous papers relating to anthropology. 85041
Miscellaneous poems. By a lady of Charleston, S. C. 51430
Miscellaneous poems, by Cassius C. Cullen. 17859
Miscellaneous poems. By Chapman Whitcomb. 103339-103340
Miscellaneous poems. By Charles Leland Porter. 64206
Miscellansous poems. By E. A. McLaughlin. 43497
Miscellaneous poems. [By Jane Ermina Locke.] 41725
Miscellaneous poems. By John H. Hewitt. 31641
Miscellaneous poems. [By Joseph Story??] (49444), note before 92310
Miscellaneous poems. By Peter Markoe. 44621
Miscellaneous poems. By Susanna Rowson. (73612)
Miscellaneous poems. [By William Augustus Weaver.] 102206
Miscellaneous poems compos'd at Newfoundland. 38513
Miscellaneous poems, composed between the years 1814 and 1830. 7418
Miscellansous poems, &c. By Charles R. Smith. 82401
Miscellaneous poems. Intended for the amusement if not the instruction of those who may read. 62922
Miscellaneous poems, moral and divine. 49922
Miscellaneous poems of the Boston bard. 14187
Miscellaneous poems, on divers occasions. 7209, 95819
Miscellaneous poems, on moral and religious subjects. 57739
Miscellaneous poems selected from the United States literary gazette. 49445, note after 97969
Miscellaneous poems, with several specimens. 79399, (79402)

Miscellaneous poetry. 103360
Miscellaneous production. (27559), 51531
Miscellaneous productions in poetry and prose. (24292)
Miscellaneous propositions and queries. 72112
Miscellaneous remarks on the police of Boston. 6529, 102418
Miscellaneous remarks, on the proceedings of the state of New-York. 817, 99000
Miscellaneous remarks upon subjects relating to the West India question. 56593, 102853
Miscellaneous remarks, vindicating the rights of the people to form a state. 818, 98999
Miscellaneous repertory. see American law journal and miscellaneous repertory.
Miscellaneous repository. see New-York weekly magazine; or, miscellaneous repositiory.
Miscellaneous repository; a periodical publication. 3931, 24455
Miscellaneous repository of instruction and amusement. 51571
Miscellaneous review of the politics of the United States. 24221
Miscellaneous selections and original pieces. (12173)
Miscellaneous selections of passages from eminent authors. (1532)
Miscellaneous sketches in prose and verse. 67606
Miscellaneous sketches of incidents during the late American war. 14943
Miscellaneous sketches, or hints for essays. 8641
Miscellaneous statistics for 1866. 10521
Miscellaneous statistics of Canada for 1866. 10402
Miscellaneous thoughts. 49446
Miscellaneous thoughts, in prose and verse. 51312
Miscellaneous thoughts on men, manners, and things. 32395
Miscellaneous thoughts, on several subjects of divinity. 82783
Miscellaneous thoughts on the present posture both of our foreign and domestic affairs. 31607
Miscellaneous tracts, essays, satires, &c. 31695
Miscellaneous tracts [of Sir Thomas Browne.] 8677
Miscellaneous trifles in prose. 10872
Miscellaneous verses. 5349
Miscellaneous views of the coins. 85423
Miscellaneous works. By Eliphalet Nott. 56035-56036
Miscellaneous works [by William Marsden.] 44719
Miscellaneous works, consisting of essays, political and moral. 62454
Miscellaneous works of Colonel Humphreys. 33808
Miscellaneous works of David Humphreys. (33809)
Miscellaneous works of Henry C. Carye. 10833
Miscellaneous works of Hugh Boyd. 7109
Miscellaneous works of J. T. Headley. 31158
Miscellaneous works of James Meikle. (47401)
Miscellaneous works of Mr. Philip Freneau. 25896
Miscellaneous works of the late Richard Penn Smith. 83786
Miscellaneous works of the Rev. John Witherspoon. 104940

Miscellaneous works, prose and poetical.
(41337), (49447), 4th note after 106134
Miscellaneous writings: addresses, lectures,
and reviews. 33410
Miscellaneous writings, literary, critical,
juridical, and political. 92310
Miscellaneous writings of Beriah Green. 28511
Miscellaneous writings of F. W. P. Greenwood.
28685
Miscellaneous writings of George W. Burnap.
9364
Miscellaneous writings [of John Evelyn.] 23208
Miscellaneous writings of Joseph Story. 92311
Miscellaneous writings of Miles P. Squier.
90004
Miscellaneous writings of Redemptio. 24925,
83790
Miscellansous writings of the late Samuel J.
Smith. 84081
Miscellaneous writings of William Sharswood.
79868
Miscellaneous writings on slavery. 35862
Miscellaneous writings, on the same subject.
(13889)
Miscellania. (70063)
Miscellanies. 94258, note after 99271, note
after 99276
Miscellanies, and a biographical sketch. 36848
Miscellanies, by an officer. (19622)
Miscellanies. [By Catharine Maria Sedgwick.]
78807
Miscellanies. [By Cornelius Mathews.] 46840
Miscellanies. [By Harriet Martineau.] 44944
Miscellanies. By J. T. Headley. 31158
Miscellanies. [By Mathew Carey.] 10841
Miscellanies. [By Philip Wharton.] 103104
Miscellanies. By Stephen Collins. 14451
Miscellanies. By the author of "Letters on the
eastern states." 97410
Miscellanies by the Honourable Daines Barrington.
3628
Miscellanies. By the Rev. James Martineau.
44945
Miscellanies. [By Thomas Pennant.] (59756)
Miscellanies consisting of I. Letter to Dr.
Channing on the Trinity. 93207
Miscellanies for sentimentalists. 90225, 96502,
104939
Miscellanies, historical, literary and political.
13846
Miscellanies in prose and verse. 50876
Miscellanies in verse. 102610
Miscellanies, moral and instructive. (49448)
Miscellanies [of Barrington.] 46951
Miscellanies [of Voltaire.] 100748
Miscellanies old and new. 82944
Miscellanies selected from the public journals.
8095
Miscellanies, viz. I. The time-piece. (49449)
Miscellany. 27660
Miscellany. [By Adam Waldie.] 100998
Miscellany. [By Colman.] 84162
Miscellany. By Isaac F. Shepard. 80185
Miscellany. [By Thomas Stephens.] 91311
Miscellany: consisting of essays, biographical
sketches, and notes of travel. (50878)
Miscellany conta-ning choice specimens in
poetry and prose. 49450
Miscellany, containing several tracts on various
subjects. 4877
Miscellany, entertaining and useful. (49451)
Miscellany for travellers and the fireside. 50777
Miscellany for young persons. 95216
Miscellany in prose and verse. (12038)
Miscellany in prose and verse, by Isaac Clark.
(13299)

Miscellany, in verse and prose. (65439)
Miscellany [of Charles Kingsley.] 67599
Miscellany [of Constable.] 16045
Miscellany of instructive & entertaining tracts.
(35272)
Miscellany of knowledge. (49452)
Miscellany of literature. 22415
Miscellany of poems, odes, and songs. 14289
Miscellany wholly composed by the factory
girls. 49192
Miscellany wholly composed by the factory
girls of an American city. 49193
Mischianza. 82974, 82976
Mischiefs of legislative caucuses. 97175
Misconduct of the present city councils. 62369
2d note after 102052
Miscowaulik Mining Company. Directors.
49453
Miser. pseud. Dialogue between a miser and
a spendthrift. see Wills, Archibald.
Miserable case of the British sugar planters.
49455
Miserable creature, who stood condemned for
murdering her infant befotten in whoredom
pseud. Solemn words. 104087
Miserable sinner. pseud. On the vanity of
human actions. see Smith, Michael,
Minister of the Gospel.
Miserables. (33619)
Miseria y brevedad de la vida del hombre.
3996
Miseries of civil war. 22515, (64975)
Miseries of dissention and civil war. 97996
Miser's heir. 51638
Misery and duty of an oppress'd and enslav'd
people. 102421
Misery of invasive warre. 67561, 67587
Misfortunes of Mary Roesly. 72600
Misfortunes of the great. 22133, 23952,
38583, 51101
Mishaps of an Indian agent. (19652)
Misiatrus, Philander. pseud. see Philander
Misiatrus. pseud.
Misioneros de la herejía. 28928
Misiones de la antigua y neuva California.
49457
Misiones del Paraguay. 49456
Mislukte reis naar Noord-Amerika. 34432
Misma geringa con distinto palo. 93789
Misrekening, zijnde een tweede vervolg. 77514
Misrepresentation and falshood, detected and
exposed. 25232, 73562, 102947
Misrepresentation detected. (80370), 102522
Misrepresentations corrected, and truth vin-
dicated. 21954
Misrepresentations corrected: review of Dr.
Cleaveland's anniversary sermon. 64304
Misrepresentations exposed. 90667
Misrepresentations of James Hall. 9652
Misrepresentations of "A member of the
Hickory Club." 47189
Miss Coleson's narrative. 14335
Miss Debby Smith's juvenile spirit. 36147,
84145
Miss Fanny Braddock. 102473
Miss Gilbert's career. 32512
Miss in her teens. 88605
Miss Martha Brownlow. 70448-(70449)
Miss Martineau on America, reviewed. 44941
Miss Ravenel's conversion from secession to
loyalty. 19292
Miss Seward's monody on Major Andre. (7948
Miss Slimmens' window, and other papers.
59373, 99432
Missa Gothica seu Mozarabica. 49459

Missal with psalms, hymns, and Gregorian chants. 21436

Missale Romanum. 49460

Missao especial do Visconde de Abrantes de Outubro. 21364, 49461

Missien van den Oregon. 82264

Missing deed. 80457

Missing Jo. 31324

Missing links to Darwin's origin of speeches [sic]. 49654

Missio Canadensis. note after 69259

Mission, Philadelphia. see Philadelphia City Mission.

Mission, an original poem. 44716

Mission and authority of Christ. 13856

Mission and Tract Society of New York City. see New York Mission and Tract Society.

Mission au Canada de 1751 a 1769. 39288

Mission catholique de la Riviere Columbie. 2878

Mission chez les Iroquois. 27630

Mission de Cayenne. 11620, 19520

Mission de la Colombie. 6181

Mission de l'Oregon. 36876

Mission de M. Ouseley et du Baron Deffaudis. (57944)

Mission del Jeneral Castelli a Bogota. 11408

Mission del Rio Mayo en Cinaloa. 70789

Mission der Evangelischen Bruder in Gronland. 42111

Mission der Kirchlichen Missionsgesellschaft in England. 86874

Mission du Canada. 10522, 44869

Mission du P. Dubuisson de la Compagnie de Jesus. 21039

Mission geographique dans les archives d' Espagne. 19474

Mission House of the Protestant Episcopal Church, Philadelphia. see Philadelphia. Mission House of the Protestant Episcopal Church.

Mission in den Polarlandern. (49485)

Mission in the island of Trinidad. 164

Mission of Abraham Lincoln. (35952)

Mission of America. 30880

Mission of Children. 85522

Mission of intellect. 21156

Mission of nations. 8551

Mission of peace from Virginia. (39163)

Mission of South Carolina to Virginia. 47490, 49462, note after 87896

Mission of the children of the church. 15911

Mission of the church; or systematic beneficence. (39348)

Mission of the educated man. 90409

Mission of the North American people. 27469

Mission of the Protestant Episcopal Church in Boston. 9630

Mission of William Cornell Jewett to Europe. (36119)

Mission schools. Shall they be abolished or sustained? 49463

Mission scientifique au Mexique et dans l' Amerique Centrale. 77213

Mission scientifique au Mexique et dans l' Amerique Centrale, linguistique. (44433), 49464

Mission Society, New York. see New York City Mission Society.

Mission to England. (29303)

Mission to Gelele, King of Dahome. 9498

Mission to the Indians, from the Indian Committee. 32917

Mission to the Indians of Orialla, in South America. 5980

Mission to the Indians of Orialla, South America. 5979

Mission to the westward of the Allegany Mountains. 21928

Mission unter den Freien Buschnegeren in Surinam. 39673

Missionaire Francois. pseud. Telliamed. see Maillet, B. de.

Missionaire Russe en Amerique. (26375)

Missionaires de Pe-Kin. see Jesuits.

Missionare der Gesellschaft Jesu. pseud. Nachrichten. 51481

Missionaries and Catechists of the London Missionary Society. see London Missionary Society. Missionaries and Catechists.

Missionaries and the state of Georgia. 61844

Missionaries at Constantinople. see American Board of Commissioners for Foreign Missions. Missionaries at Constantinople.

Missionaries at Dwight, Ga. see Presbyterian Church in the U. S. Synod of South Carolina. Missionaries at Dwight, Ga.

Missionaries at the Sandwich Islands. pseud. Duty of the Present generation. 21477, 76451

Missionaries from the Venerable Society for the Propagation of the Gospel in Foreign Parts, to the Mohawk Indians. pseud. trs. see Andrews, William tr. Barclay, Henry, tr. Oglivie, John. tr.

Missionaries in the Chahta Nation. pseud. Spelling book. see Byington, Cyrus. and Wright, Alfred.

Missionaries in the Cherokee Nation. see Presbyterian Church in the U. S. Synod of South Carolina. Missionaries in the Cherokee Nation.

Missionaries of Nova Scotia and its dependencies. 56154

Missionaries of the American Baptist Board of Foreign Missions. see American Baptist Board of Foreign Missions. Missionaries.

Missionaries of the A. B. C. F. M. see American Board of Commissioners for Foreign Missions. Missionaries.

Missionaries of the Unitas Fratrum, or United Brethren. trs. see Austen, C. A. tr. and Latrobe, C. J. tr.

Missionaries of the Wesleyan Church in Jamaica. see Wesleyan Methodist Church. Jamaica. Missionaries.

Missionarium de Propaganda Fide. see Society for the Propagation of the Faith.

Missionary. pseud. Chahta ikhananchi. see Williams, L. S. and Wright, Alfred.

Missionary. pseud. Telliamed. see Maillet, B. de.

Missionary; a poem. 7085

Missionary abominations unmasked. 84433

Missionary address from the Trustees. 15812

Missionary adventures in Texas and Mexico. (20553)

Missionary anecdotes. 49465

Missionary argument. 20391

Missionary at work. 55235

Missionary biography. 93215

Missionary catechism, for the use of children. 105924

Missionary chronicle. 82910

Missionary chronicle; containing the proceedings of the Board of Foreign and Domestic Missions. 49466

Missionary chronicle of the Presbyterian Church. 49467

Missionary-encouragement. 90840

Missionary enterprise: a collection of discourses on Christian missions. 92369, 92371

Missionary enterprise a true development of the life of the church. 15183

Missionary enterprise. By Rev. Chandler Robbins. 71781

Missionary enterprises in many lands. 9403

Missionary from the Honourable Society for Propagating the Gospel, &c. pseud. Letter from a minister of the Church of England. see Wetmore, James.

Missionary Fund, Roxbury, Mass. see Roxbury Missionary Fund, Roxbury, Mass.

Missionary gazetteer, and a general history of missions. 11960

Missionary gazetteer; comprising a geographical and statistical account of the various stations of the American and foreign protestant missionary societies. 21891

Missionary gazetteer; comprising a geographical and statistical account of the various stations of the Church, London, Moravian, Wesleyan, Baptist, and American, missionary societies. 104179

Missionary geography. 49468

Missionary herald. 58424

Missionary herald for the year 1821. (49469)

Missionary in Jamaica. 83507

Missionary intelligence. 65183

Missionary intelligencer, and religious miscellany. see United Brethren's missionary intelligencer, and religious miscellany.

Missionary jubilee. An account of the fiftieth anniversary of the American Baptist Missionary Union. (49470), 84062

Missionary labours in British Guiana. 4952

Missionary labors of Mr. and Mrs. Charles Spear. 89069

Missionary lately employed. pseud. Short trip to Rome. 103645

Missionary leaflets. 83599

Missionary link. 49471

Missionary magazine. see General Assembly's Missionary magazine. Panoplist and missionary magazine.

Missionary magazine. Published by the American Baptist Missionary Union. (49472), 84062

Missionary manual and directory of the Unitas Fratrum. 86171

Missionary memorial: a gift book for all seasons. 50136

Missionary memorial: a literary and religious souvenir. 49473

Missionary of the Andes. 7085

Missionary of the latter society. pseud. Address delivered to the First Baptist Church. 66237

Missionary; or the church in the wilderness. 12478

Missionary paper by the Bishop Seabury Mission. 78591

Missionary paper. Number six. By the Associate Mission for Minnesota. 49474

Missionary paper, no. III [of the Southern Board of Foreign Missions.] 85327, 88313

Missionary paper, no. 12. Missionary biography. 93215

Missionary paper no. II [of the Charleston Juvenile Missionary Society.] 85341

Missionary paper of the Domestic and Foreign Missionary Society. 66178

Missionary pioneer. (49704), note after 101083

Missionary record, detailing the proceedings of the Church Missionary Society. 49475

Missionary record of the Domestic and Foreig Missionary Society. 49476, 89482

Missionary records. 49477

Missionary remains. 17270, 49478, 89783

Missionary reminiscences. 16800

Missionary report. 91663

Missionary researches in America. 82471

Missionary rule. 85478

Missionary scapegoat employed by brutal convert-hunting nimrods. 81362

Missionary scapegoat, employed by convert hunting nimrods. 49479

Missionary series. 97515, 97517-97519, 97523

Missionary sermon, delivered at Hartford. 42806

Missionary sermon delivered in Chillicothe. 32429

Missionary sermon, delivered in Hartford. (8165)

Missionary sermon, . . . in Hartford, . . . May 17, 1814. 48036

Missionary sermon . . . Philadelphia. 28818

Missionary sermons and addresses. 82470

Missionary sketches. 84051-84052, 84059

Missionary Smith. 82906

Missionary Society, Hampden, Mass. 30127

Missionary Society, London. see Missionary Society.

Missionary Society, Lowell, Mass. see Lowe Mass. South Parish Missionary Society.

Missionary Society, New York. see New Yor Missionary Society.

Missionary Society, Yale College. see Yale University Missionary Society.

Missionary Society Connected With the South Parish, Lowell, Mass. see Lowell, Ma South Parish Missionary Society.

Missionary Society for Seamen, New York. se Protestant Episcopal Church Missionary Society for Seamen, New York.

Missionary Society of Connecticut. 15633, 15639, 15805-15806, 15810, 15812

Missionary Society of Connecticut. Charter. 15806

Missionary Society of Connecticut. Trustees. 15639, 15806, 15811-15812, 96511

Missionary Society of Connecticut. Act of incorporation. With address of trustees. 15806

Missionary Society of East Tennessee. see East Tennessee Missionary Society.

Missionary Society of London. see London Missionary Society.

Missionary Society of Maine. see Maine Missionary Society.

Missionary Society of Massachusetts. see Massachusetts Missionary Society.

Missionary Society of New Hampshire. see New Hampshire Missionary Society.

Missionary Society of New-Jersey. 53163

Missionary Society of New York. see New-York Missionary Society.

Missionary Society of Portsmouth, N. H. see City Missionary Society of Portsmouth, N. H.

Missionary Society of the Methodist Church, Within the Bounds of the Philadelphia Conference. Union Female Auxiliary. see Union Female Missionary Society, Philadelphia.

Missionary Society of the Methodist Episcopal Church. see Methodist Missionary Society.

Missionary Society of the Methodist Episcopal Church in South Carolina. see Methodist Episcopal Church. Conferences. South Carolina. Missionary Society.

Missionary Society of the North West Territory. 70470

Missionary Society of the Protestant Episcopal Church in Pennsylvania. see Protestant Episcopal Missionary Society of Pennsylvania.

Missionary Society of the Reformed Church in America. see Reformed Church in America. Missionary Society.

Missionary Society of the Reformed Dutch Church in North America. see Reformed Church in America. Missionary Society.

Missionary Society of Vermont. see Vermont Domestic Missionary Society.

Missionary spirit. 20391

Missionary stories. 97853

Missionary to the Negroes in Liberty County, Georgia. (40944)

Missionary tour in the territory of the Hon. Hudson's Bay Company. 74586

Missionary tract, addressed to the members. 105335

Missionary tract, no. 2. 105336

Missionary voyage to the south Pacific Ocean. (59572)

Missionary voyage to the southern Pacific Ocean. (49480), note after 104633

Missionary's appeal to the religious public. 164

Missionary's burial. 82907

Missionary's farewell sermon. 165

Missionary's reward. 65714

Missionbilder. (49485)

Missionen der Evangelischen Bruder in Gronland und Labrador. 97854

Missionerio. pseud. Copia de dos cartas escritas. 16666, 47172

Missionnaire. pseud. Esclavage dans les Etats Confederes. 22832

Missionnaire. pseud. Histoire de l'eau-de-vie en Canada. 67020

Missionnaire en Californie. 39288

Missionnaire Russe en Amerique. (26375)

Missionnaires du Paraguay. 5004

Missions: a poem. 94373

Missions and missionaries. 37897

Missions d'Amerique, d'Oceanie et d'Afrique. 50222

Missions de l'Amerique. 50213

Missions de l'Oregon et voyages aux Montagnes Rocheuses. 82265

Missions de l'Oregon et voyages dans les Montagnes Rocheuses. 82266

Missions de MM. Deffaudis et Walewski. 19270

Missions-Histoire om de Evangeliske Broeders Mission. (57151)

Missions of the Moravians. 49483

Missions-Reise nach Suriname und Barbice. 71305

Missions—the church's work. 67784

Missions to the heathen, no. 45. 90108

Missions to the North American Indians. 49484

Missisquoi Spring water and its wonderful cures. 49486

Missisquoi Springs and their wonderful cures. 49486

Mississippi (Territory) (37434), 58452

Mississippi (Territory) Citizens. petitioners 49531

Mississippi (Territory) General Assembly. (49541)

Mississippi (Territory) General Assembly. petitioners (49541)

Mississippi (Territory) General Assembly. House of Representatives. 18819

Mississippi (Territory) General Assembly. House of Representatives. petitioners 59830, 69735

Mississippi (Territory) General Assembly. Legislative Council. petitioners 69735

Mississippi (Territory) Governor, 1798-1801 (Sargent) 58452 see also Sargent, Winthrop, 1752-1820.

Mississippi (Territory) Inhabitants. see Mississippi (Territory) Citizens.

Mississippi (Territory) Laws, statutes, etc. (49487), 49493, 49499, 49512, (49519), (49547), 96328

Mississippi. plaintiffs 49545

Mississippi. Agricultural Survey. see Mississippi. Geological and Agricultural Survey.

Mississippi. Auditor of Public Accounts. 49535

Mississippi. Bank Commissioners. (49536)

Mississippi. Chancellor. 82247 see also Bucknor, Robert H.

Mississippi. Constitution. 1269, 1271, 2071, 5316, 6360, 16103, 16107, 16113, 16133, 33137, 33282, (47188), (49493)-(49496), 59771, (66397), 104198

Mississippi. Constitutional Convention, 1865. (49508), 49510

Mississippi. Constitutional Convention, 1868. Select Committee. 49538

Mississippi. Convention, 1850. 49533

Mississippi. Convention, 1861. (49511)

Mississippi. Geological and Agricultural Survey. 30421

Mississippi. Governor, 1838-1842 (McNutt) 49518 see also McNutt, Alexander Gallatin, 1802-1848.

Mississippi. Governor, 1856-1860 (McWillie) 33150, 49506 see also McWillie, William, 1795-1869.

Mississippi. Governor, 1865-1868 (Humphreys) 49538 see also Humphreys, Benjamin Grubb, 1808-1882.

Mississippi. High Court of Errors and Appeals. 82244, 82248

Mississippi. Institution for the Deaf and Dumb, Jackson. see Mississippi. School for the Deaf, Jackson.

Mississippi. Laws, statutes, etc. 23765, 33282, 39414, (35941), 49488, 49491-(49493), (49496), 49498, (49511), 49513-49515, 49532, 49542-49543, 49548, 52051, 63686, 64995, 70820-70821, 82438, 84882, 88405, 89066, 102763

Mississippi. Legislature. Committee on State and Federal Relations. Majority. 49516

Mississippi. Legislature. Committee on State and Federal Relations. Minority. 49516

Mississippi. Legislature. Committee on the Collection of the Revenue. 49538

Mississippi. Legislature. Select Committee on Banks and Currency. 49538

Mississippi. Legislature. Select Committee on State Bonds. 49538

Mississippi. Legislature. Select Committee on the Tariff. 49538

Mississippi. Legislature. House of Representatives. 49507

Mississippi. Legislature. Senate. 49509-49510

Mississippi. Meeting of the Citizens of Central Mississippi on the Slavery Question, 1850. see Meeting of the Citizens of Central Mississippi on the Slavery Question, 1850.

Mississippi. Penitentiary. 49529

Mississippi. School for the Deaf, Jackson. 49527

Mississippi. State Geologist. (49503)-49504, 49540

Mississippi. State Library, Jackson. (49490)

Mississippi. State University. see Mississippi. University.

Mississippi. Superior Court of Chancery. 82244, 82247

Mississippi. Treasurer. 49539

Mississippi. University. Commissioners. 49546

Mississippi. University. Trustees. 49549

Mississippi and Atlantic Railroad. 49521

Mississippi and Lake Borgne Grand Junction Canal Company. 91702

Mississippi and Lake Borgne Grand Junction Canal Company. Articles of association [etc.]. 91702

Mississippi & Mexican Gulf Ship Canal. (56222)

Mississippi and Missouri River Air-Line R. R. Co. (49522)

Mississippi and Ohio Rivers. 19018, 22207

Mississippi and Pacific Railroad. 49523

Mississippi-Bilder, Licht- und Schaltenseiten. 27185

Mississippi bridge cities, Davenport, Rock Island and Moline. 68648

Mississippi College, Clinton, Miss. (49526)

Mississippi et Indiana. 21173

Mississippi etension of the Watertown & Madison R. R. 3526

Mississippi free trader. 101071

Mississippi Historical Society. (49544), 88430

Miss. Hist. Soc. Publs. 88430

Mississippi navigator. (49528)

Mississippi. Nederlands tegenwoordige financiele nood. 49520

Mississippi Presbytery. see Presbyterian Church in the U. S. Presbytery of Mississippi.

Mississippi question fairly stated. 10172, 21000

Mississippi Railroad Company. 49525

Mississippi River Improvement and Manufacturing Company. 49552

Mississippi River Improvement Convention, Dubuque, Iowa, 1866. 49552

Mississippi River, its geological character, overflows, &c. 19018

Mississippi scenes. 13848

Mississippi State Colored Convention, Vicksburg, 1865. 49530

Mississippi state gazetteer and shippers' guide. 80325

Mississippi State Historical Society. see Mississippi Historical Society.

Mississippi Synod. see Presbyterian Church in the U. S. Synod of Mississippi.

Mississippi-Thal. 57256

Mississippi valley business directory. 49553

Mississippi Valley Convention, Chicago, 1847. see Chicago. Mississippi Valley Convention, 1847.

Mississippi valley: its physical geography. 25245

Mississippi valley memorial. 71619

Mississippi Valley Railroad Convention, St. Louis, 1852. 49554

Mississippian. pseud. Secret of success. 78750

Mississippian scenery. 47218

Missive aan . . . R. M. van Goens. 35064

Missive aen den Koninck van Groot-Brittangien van den Staten-Generael. 49556, 1st note after 102896

Missive by den voornoemden Directeur. 102912

Missive, daer in kortelijck ende grondich vertoont wort. 19670, 3d note after 102890

Missive. Daer in kortelijck ende grondigh werdt vertoont. 49557, 2d note after 102896

Missive daer in kortlijck ende grondigh wert verthoont. 49558, 3d note after 102896

Missive den geheelen staet van de Vereenichde Oost-Indische Compagnie. 19671, 4th note after 102890

Missive en memoire door Zyne Hoogheid den Heere Prince van Orange en Nassau. 106234

Missive, gheschreven by den Generael Weerdenburch. 16678, 100935, 102497

Missive gheschreven by een vry man, in Brasil. 7562, 16679

Missive gheschreven van Fernambock. 50231

Missive . . . houdende elucidatien raakende de memorien. 69607

Missive van Bewindhebberen der Westindische Compagnie, met een deductie door den Commandeur van St. Eustatius, J. de Graaf. 49560, 102897

Missive van Bewindhebberen der West-Indische Compagnie, met een deductie door J. de Graff. 49560

Missive ban Bewinthebberen der West Indische Compagnie ter Kamer Amsterdam. 49561

Missive van de Bewint-Hebberen der West-Indische Compagnie ter Camere van Amsterdam. 49559, 2d note after 102897

Missive van de Hoofd Participantien der Geoctroyeerde West-Indische Compagnie. 22994

Missive van de Staeten Generael der Vereenigec Nederlanden. 96454

Missive van de Staten Generael aen de Koninck van Groot-Brittannien. (49663)

Missive van de Staten van Hollandt. (49562)

Missive van den Commandeur Binckes. 5426

Missive van den Commandeur J. Binckes. (49564)

Missive van den Directeur Generael Johan van Vlackenburgh. 102912

Missive van den Secretaris F. Valckenier. 49565

Missive van den Secretaris Frederiko Valckenier. 98303

Missive van Directeuren van de Societeit van Suriname. 93840

Missive van een Amsterdamsch burger. (49566)

Missive van een burger te Amsterdam. 49567

Missive van G. Fagel. (39804)

Missive van G. Fagel 1684. 49568

Missive van Hare Ho: Mo: de Heeren Staten Generael. 102912

Missive van Raaden van Politie te Suriname. 93841

Missive van twee Indiaansche coninghen. 49569

Missive . . . van Vice-Admirael Reynst. 70460
Missive van William Penn. 59712, 59716-59717
Missive van Zyn Hoogheid met een reglement. (39093)
Missive van Z. Hoogheid omtrent de 2 Engelsche pryscheepen. 36562
Missive vande President ende Raden. 7578
Missive waarby in 't breede verslag wordt gedaan van zekere memoire. 98508
Missive, awerinne voorghistelt werde de ghelegentheyt van de Oost Indische Compagnie. 16736
Misson, ---------. defendant 32182, (32197)
Missouri (Territory) Laws, statutes, etc. 1990, 39411, 49575, (49588)
Missouri. (27613), 49640, 50734, 75407
Missouri. petitioners 49608
Missouri. plaintiffs 75407
Missouri. Adjutant General. 49578
Missouri. Auditor of Public Accounts. 49632
Missouri. Bank. see Bank of Missouri.
Missouri. Board of Immigration. 49582
Missouri. Board of Public Works and State Engineer. 49583
Missouri. Colored People. 81750
Missouri. Commissioner of Statistics. 49579
Missouri. Commissioner to Revise the Statutes. 49642–(49643)
Missouri. Constitution. 1269, 1271, 2071, 5316, 6360, 6972, 16107, 16113, 33137, (47188), (49585), 49626, 49641, 59771, (66397), 75345, 75378, 104198
Missouri. Constitutional Convention, 1845. 49598
Missouri. Convention, St. Louis, 1861-1863. 49599
Missouri. Convention, St. Louis, 1865. (49603)
Missouri. Courts (Fifth Judicial Circuit) 50734, 83238-83239
Missouri. General Assembly. 50734, 83238
Missouri. General Assembly. Committee on the Financial Affairs of the State. (49634)
Missouri. General Assembly. Committee to Investigate the Conduct and Management of the Militia. Majority. 49635
Missouri. General Assembly. Committee to Investigate the Conduct and Management of the Militia. Minority. 49635
Missouri. General Assembly. Joint Committee on State Credit. (49571)
Missouri. General Assembly. House of Representatives. (49600), 96084
Missouri. General Assembly. Senate. 49601, 96084
Missouri. General Assembly. Senate (Confederate) 49602
Missouri. Geological Survey. 49593
Missouri. Governor, 1857-1861 (Stewart) 33150 see also Stewart, Robert Marcellus, 1815-1871.
Missouri. Governor, 1861-1864 (Gamble) 49610 see also Gamble, Hamilton Rowan, 1798-1864.
Missouri. Governor, 1865-1869 (Fletcher) 24741-(24742), (49584), 64113 see also Fletcher, Thomas Clement, 1827-1899.
Missouri. Institution for the Deaf and Dumb, Fulton. see Missouri School for the Deaf, Fulton, Mo.

Missouri. Insurance Department. Superintendent. see Missouri. Superintendent of the Insurance Department.
Missouri. Laws, statutes, etc. 23765, 39411, 39414, (49571)-49574, 49604-49606, 49618-49619, 49621, 49641-(49643), 52051, 50820-50821, 75329, 75338-75339, 75345, 75345, 75347, 75371, 75378-(75379), 75384, 75387, 75384, (75392), 75404-(75406), 82438, 88374, 89066, 90448
Missouri. Lieutenant Governor (Reynolds) 70446 see also Reynolds, Thomas C.
Missouri. Militia. 49627
Missouri. Paymaster General. 49636
Missouri. Quartermaster General. (49637)
Missouri. State Board of Agriculture. 49645
Missouri. State Engineer. see Missouri. Board of Public Works and State Engineer.
Missouri. State Entomologist. 49645, 71391 see also Riley, Charles V.
Missouri. State Hospital, Fulton. 49624
Missouri. State Lunatic Asylum, Fulton. see Missouri. State Hospital, Fulton.
Missouri. State Treasurer. (49646)
Missouri. State University. see Missouri. University.
Missouri. Superintendent of Common Schools. 49638
Missouri. Superintendent of Public Instruction. 49639
Missouri. Superintendent of the Insurance Department. 49580
Missouri. Superintendent to Revise the Statutes of Missouri. 49641
Missouri. University. 49649, 49651, 68147
Missouri. University. Curators. 49647
Missouri. University. Medical Department. 49649
Missouri Agricultural and Mechanical Association. Fiar, 2d, 1857. (49611)
Missouri and Illinois farmer's almanac. 49615
Missouri and iron mountain cities. 49618
Missouri Anti-Jackson Convention. see National Republican Party. Missouri. Convention, 1828.
Missouri as it is in 1867. 58724
Missouri Committee, 1863. see Radical Union Party. Missouri.
Missouri compromise act of 1820. 16112
Missouri compromise: an address delivered before the citizens of Pittsfield. 33794
Missouri compromise; or, the extension of the slave power. 1801
Missouri compromise. Sketch of the remarks. 66817
Missouri Emancipation Convention, 1862. see Emancipation Convention, Jefferson City, Mo., 1862.
Missouri General Emancipation Society. see General Emancipation Society of Missouri.
Missouri hand-book. 58725
Missouri Historical and Philosophical Society. 49616, 104905
Missouri home guards. Speech of Hon. Joseph W. McClurg. 43079
Missouri Indians. see also Oto and Missouri Indians.
Missouri Indians. Treaties, etc. 96648, 96662, 96691, 96714
Missouri Infantry. 49627
Missouri Iron Company. 49618
Missouri Juvenile Reform School. Charter. 49619
Missouri medical and surgical journal. 49620

MISSOURI

Missouri Medical College, St. Louis. 37339,
37341
Missouri Medical Society. St. Louis Branch.
see St. Louis Medical Society of
Missouri.
Missouri or a voice from the South. 42942
Missouri Petroleum and Mining Company.
49621
Missouri question. A freedom policy and
reconstruction. 6005
Missouri question. By D. Raymond, Esq.
(68041)
Missouri republican. 878, 20815, 32420,
75330-75333, 75374, 1st note after
95666
Missouri Sacs. see Sauk Indians.
Missouri School for the Deaf, Fulton, Mo.
49617
Missouri should be included in the proclama-
tion. 8453
Missouri state convention, and its ordinance
of emancipation. 20817
Missouri state gazetteer and business direc-
tory. 49622, note after 93956
Missouri state gazetteer, shipper's guide,
and business directory. 49623
Missouri State Sunday-School Convention.
1st, St. Louis, 1866. 49631
Missouri Synod. see Presbyterian Church
in the U. S. Synod of Missouri.
Missouri test oath. Argument in the Supreme
Court of the United States. 31317
Missouri test oath. Argument of Samuel T.
Glover. 27614
Missouri und Illinois. 49625
Missouri vs. Samuel T. Glover. (27613)
Missouri voters' oath. 20817
Missourian. pseud. Douglas' doctrine of
popular sovereignty. (20696)
Missourian lays, and other western ditties.
97704
Missouri's jubilee. (24742)
Missy, Jean Rousset de. see Rousset de
Missy, Jean.
Mist, -------- van Uitenhage de. see Hoven,
Madame ------- (van Uitenhage de
Mist) de.
Mistakes: a poem. 93749
Mistakes and corrections. 102370
Mistakes and failures of the temperance
reformation. 56628
Mistakes in the Hebrew lexicon of Gesenius.
102370
Mistakes of the past. 36885
Misteca theologia. 49653
Mr. Abiel Foster's motion for an amendment.
25194
Mr. Adams, from the Select Committee on the
message of the President. 85070
Mr. Addison's opinion of our trade and com-
merce. 92802
Mr. Aislabie's two speeches and case con-
sidered. 548, 80329, 88168
Mr. Alexander Baring's speech in the House
of Commons. (3386)
Mr. Ambrose's letters on the rebellion.
37416
Mr. Amos Sheffield, Saybrook, Conn. 80094
Mr. & Mrs. Solomon. 86510
Mr. Armstrong's plan of the country. 6516
Mr. Arnold's first semi-annual report. 2066
Mr. Arthur Spencer. 89301
Mr. Ashbee's occasional fac-simile reprints.
67599
Mr. Balch's reply to the articles of error.
7268, 27584

Mr. Bancroft and his Boston critics. 3135
Mr. Bancroft's letter on the exchange of
prisoners. 3130, 3134
Mr. Baxter baptiz'd in bloud. 4003
Mr. Bayard's speech. (4027)
Mr. Baylies, . . . made the following report.
55848
Mr. Beecher's reasons for lecturing in the
"Fraternity course." 4315, 26706
Mr. Bell's suppressed report. 4459
Mr. Bigelow's farewell address. (5276)
Mr. Bigelow's letter to sundry disaffected
individuals. 5277
Mr. Birkbeck's opinions upon this subject.
87307
Mr. Birney's letter to the churches. (5578)
Mr. Birney's second letter. 5579
Mr. Blaine's letter of acceptance. 5731
Mr. Bradish's remarks in Assembly. (7270)
Mr. Breck's confession of faith. 16640
Mr. Brockway's apology to the Rev. Nathan
S. S. Beman. 8166
Mr. Bromley's second address. 8195, 8198
Mr. Brown's reply to that letter. 92785
Mr. Bryant's address on his life and genius.
35221
Mr. Buchanan's administration on the eve of
the rebellion. 8861
Mr. Buchanan's reply. 35348
Mr. Buckingham's address to the people of the
United States. 8898
Mr. Buckingham's travels in the eastern and
western world. 8893
Mr. Burchett's justification. 9207
Mr. Burlingame against this. 9333
Mr. Burlingame's sentiments. 9333
Mr. Burwell's motion. 9512
Mr. Burwell's motion [in the House of Repre-
sentatives.] 9511
Mr. Butler's letters to Harmanus Bleecker.
9611
Mr. Butler's statement. 9657
Mr. Calhoun's defence of the tariff and internal
improvement. 97751
Mr. Calhoun's reply to Col. Benton. 9936
Mr. Calhoun's sentiments. 9936
Mr. Carroll . . . . Chairman. 45113
Mr. Chandler's statement. 55827
Mr. Chase's financial scheme. 12201
Mr. Chatfield's report to the Senate. 69418
Mr. Cheever convicted of ignorence and mis-
representation. 98033
Mr. Child's report. (46077)
Mr. Chilton's letters. 12809
Mr. Clark's replys. (13256)
Mr. Clay and Gen. Jackson. 13552
Mr. Clay's moral character. 13560
Mr. Clay's reply. 35348
Mr. Clay's speech at the Lexington dinner.
35348
Mr. Clay's speech upon the Tariff. 27375
Mr. Clayton submitted the following report.
74138
Mr. Clompton's motion. 13771
Mr. Cook's just and seasonable vindication.
16305
Mr. Cooley's remarks in the Senate. 16362
Mr. Cooper's confession of faith. 16630
Mr. Cossham on America. 17000
Mr. Cotton's letter examined and answered.
51773
Mr. Cotton's letter lately printed. 17069,
17082, 104341
Mr. Crosswell's reply to a book lately published
17675, 20056, 95316

Mr. Jenkinson's porter. pseud. Answer to Vamp Overreach's letter. 36027

Mr. Jeremiah Wilson, from the Select Committee. 85492

Mr. John A. Rockwell . . . made the following report. 72432

Mr. John Bright's speech at Rochdale. 7965

Mr. John Dunn Hunter defended. 55485

Mr. Iohn Goodwin whipt with his own rod. 50773

Mr. John Quincy Adams, from the Select Committee. 85069

Mr. John Randolph's motion. 67829

Mr. Johnson from the Committee to Frame an Address, reported. 100497

Mr. Johnson's report on the transportation of the mail on Sunday. 36278

Mr. Joutel's journal of his voyage to Mexico. 36763

Mr. Justice Vallieres de St. Real explained the grounds of his judgement [sic] as follows. 98304

Mr. Justice Wilson. An address. 84520

Mr. Keith's captivity among the Indians. 84129, note after 93109, 1st note after 95758

Mr. Kendall's address to the people of the United States. 37348

Mr. L., an Episcoparian [sic]. pseud. Dialogue. see Young Samuel, fl. 1690-1700.

Mr. Lacock . . . reported. 39471, note before 92843

Mr. Laurens' true state of the case. 35985, 39258

Mr. Laurie's report as to the extension of the railway. 56164

Mr. Leach's oration. 39506

Mr. Leach's protest against the exclusion of their delegates. 29890, 91524

"Mr. Lee's plan—March 29, 1777." 50380

Mr. Legare . . . made the . . . report. 39853

Mr. Lincoln; aribtrary arrests. 41216

Mr. Lincoln—the presidency—action of legislatures. (55108)

Mr. Linn submitted the following report. 41339

Mr. Linn submitted the following report on Henry Perrine's memorial. 61017

Mr. Livermore's speech. (41562)

Mr. Lloyd's speech . . . Dec. 9, on the bill. (41688)

Mr. Lloyd's speech . . . on the bill. (41688)

Mr. Lloyd's speeches . . . on Mr. Hillhouse's resolution. (41688)

Mr. Lyon's speech, in favor of peace. 42862

Mr. M., an anabaptist. pseud. Dialogue. see Young, Samuel, fl. 1690-1700.

Mr. McDuffie's speech. 43205

Mr. McDuffie's speeches against the prohibitory system. 43205

Mr. McLean . . . made the following report. 43518

Mr. Madison thought it wrong to admit in the constitution the idea of property in man. 93643, 93645

Mr. Madison's instructions to the American plenipotentiaries. 53975, 90639

Mr. Madison's letter. 47622, 100427, 3d note after 100486

Mr. Madison's motion for commercial restrictions. (43721)

Mr. Madison's war. (42452)

Mr. Mallory, from the committee . . . made the following report. 44129

Mr. Mann's letter, &c. (44306)

Mr. Mason made the following report. 45449

Mr. Mason's and Mr. Ames' orations on George Washington. 45459

Mr. Maulsby. . . . report . . . on the bill. 45090

Mr. Meares' memorial. 47259

Mr. Mercer considers Mr. Ross's publication against him. 92841

Mr. Merryman's monthly. (51226)

Mr. Miner K. Kellogg to his friends. 37297

Mr. Minot's address. 49320

Mr. Mitchel's letter to his brother. (49660)

Mr. Monroe's letter on the rejected treaty. 50018

Mr. Murphy, . . . made the following report. 51462

Mr. Murray unmask'd. 17675

Mr. Murray's opinion relating to the courts of justice. 84556

Mr. Nicholson's motion. 55231

Mr. Niles' plan for the construction of a ship canal. 55328

Mr. Niles' resolution. 55323

Mr. Nondescript. pseud. ed. The ———. 95279

Mr. Nonius. pesud. ed. The ———. 95279

Mr. Northrop's reply, October 7, 1864. 55840

Mr. Northrop's reply. Sept. 29, 1864. 55840

Mr. Noxon's observations, &c. 93809

Mr. Noyes' address. 56236

Mr. O'Leary's plea for liberty of conscience. 57171

Mr. Osgood's address to the United Whig Club. 57785

Mr. Otis's speech. . . on the sedition law. 57860

Mr. Otis's speech to the citizen [sic] of Boston. 57860

Mr. P——. pseud. Speech. see Pitt, William, 1st Earl of Chatham, 1707-1778.

Mr. Parker, a bill was sent up. 84575

Mr. Parker and his views. 2290, 58757

Mr. Patrick Kennedy's journal up the Illinois River, &c. (34358)

Mr. Patten's sermon. 59126

Mr. Pattison's reply to certain oral and written criticism. 27323, 59151

Mr. Peabody's gift to the poor of London. 86791

Mr. Peel's speech in the British Parliament. 43091

Mr. Peters last report of the English wars. 61195

Mr. Peyton's experiments. 29666

Mr. Phelps's appeal to the people of Vermont. (61393)

Mr. Phelps's rejoinder to Mr. Slade's "reply." 61394

Mr. Pickering's letter to a neighbouring minister (62645)

Mr. Pickering's letter to Mr. Whitefield. (62645)

Mr. Pickering's speech, in the Senate. 62659

Mr. Pickering's speech . . . on the resolution. 62659

Mr. Pickering's speech . . . 26th and . . . 28th of February. 62659

Mr. Pierce and the anti-slavery movement. (82021)

Mr. Williams's sermon after the earthquake. 104214

Mr. Williams's sermon before he Maine Missionary Society. 104388

Mr. Wlson's [sic] oration. (61411), 104632

Mr. Zenger; I received two days ago a letter. 103224

Misterios de Buenos Aires. 59573

Misterios de la inquisicion. 93348

Mistica Diana. 76892

Mistica teologia. 76005

Mistica theologia. 76003-76004

Mistick Krew of Comus. 49654

Mrs. Abigal Bayley. 50995

Mrs. Barney's letter to President Jackson. (3543)

Mrs. Brown in America. 73242

Mrs. Brown on the Alabama Claims. 73243

Mrs. Carson's last adventures. 96847

Mrs. Clack's Christmas gift. 13177

Mrs. Elizabeth Sargent. 52314

Mrs. Gurney's apology. 29316

Mrs. H. B. Stowe on Dr. Monod and the American Tract Society. 92447

Mistress Hutchinson. 13447

Mrs. Judith Hull, of Boston. 79442

Mrs. Kemble's journal. 28430

Mrs. Loveridge's School, Albany. 42385

Mrs. Luch Wilder Stearns. 90920

Mrs. Marianne Fitch Stranahan. 89091

Mrs. Mead's School, Richmond. 47225

Mrs. Nemo. pseud. see Nemo, Mrs. pseud.

Mrs. Olsen's narrative. 57254

Mrs. Packard's reproof to Dr. McFarland. 58105

Mrs. Partington's carpet-bag of fun. 80482

Mrs. Partington's knitting work. (80478)

Mrs. Rivardi's Seminary, Philadelphia. Trustees. 90835

Mrs. Royall's Pennsylvania. 73821

Mrs. Royall's southern tour. 73822

Mrs. Skagg's husbands. 30650

Mrs. Stephens' illustrated new monthly. 91286

Mrs. Stowe in England. note after 92624

Mrs. Teachem. pseud. see Teachem, Mrs. pseud.

Mrs. Tucker's delight. 88494

Mrs. Washington's reception day. 70027

Mrs. Willard reviewed. 104049

Mrs. Willard's appeal. 104043

Mitbringende einen Sitten-Calender. 60067

Mitchel, John. 103920

Mitchel, Jonathan, 1624-1668. (18703)-18704, (46683), (46778), 49655-49662, 66059, 80212-(80213), 80252, 80253, 92351

Mitchel, Martin. 49663-(49664)

Mitchel Ormsby McKnight. (49665)

Mitchell, --------, fl. 1846. 17653

Mitchell, Agnes Woods, 42903, 85171

Mitchell, Anne M. 49666

Mitchell, B. Gibbs. 49667

Mitchell, B. Rush. 49668, 100645

Mitchell, D. W. 49671

Mitchell, David J. (82602)

Mitchell, David M. 49670

Mitchell, Donald Grant. 49672-49680

Mitchell, Edward. 49681

Mitchell, Elisha, 1793-1857. 49683-59684

Mitchell, G. R. 58082

Mitchell, Hector. 49686

Mitchell, Henry. 49687

Mitchell, I. 49688

Mitchell, J. C. 49692

Mitchell, J. W. S. 49705

Mitchell, James, fl. 1851-1862. 49689, 49701

Mitchell, James, fl. 1851-1862. defendant (45332)

Mitchell, James, fl. 1867. 49690

Mitchell, James Coffield, 1786-1843. 49691

Mitchell, John, d. 1768. (41354), 49693-(49696)

Mitchell, John, 1794-1870. 49697-(49699), 70210, 105907

Mitchell, John, fl. 1829. plaintiff 85190

Mitchell, John, fl. 1861. (49700)

Mitchell, John, fl. 1862. see Mitchell, James, fl. 1851-1862.

Mitchell, John K., d. 1858. 49702-49703

Mitchell, Jonathan. see Mitchel, Jonathan, 1624-1668

Mitchell, Joseph. (49704), note after 101083

Mitchell, Mary. 49706

Mitchell, Nahum, 1769-1853. (11202), 49707

Mitchell, Nelson. 49708

Mitchell, Ormsby MacKnight, 1809-1862. 49709, 59099, (80852)

Mitchell, O. P. (49710)

Mitchell, R. Charlton. 49711

Mitchell, S. 49712

Mitchell, S. S. 49723

Mitchell, S. T. 49724

Mitchell, S. Weir. 85072

Mitchell, Samuel Augustus, 1792-1868. 8215, (11601), 19716, 26918, (49713)-49722, 2d note after 105598-9 [sic]

Mitchell, Samuel Augustus, 1792-1868. supposed author (34260), 34325

Mitchell, Samuel Latham. see Mitchill, Samuel Latham, 1764-1831.

Mitchell, Singleton. 67071

Mitchell, Thomas Duche, 1791-1865. 17653, 49725, 90779

Mitchell, Thomas Rothmaler, 1783-1837. (49726)

Mitchell, W. H. 49731-49734

Mitchell, Walter. (49727)

Mitchell, William, 1791-1868. 49728

Mitchell, William, fl. 1849-1857, 49729-49730

Mitchell, William M. 49735

Mitchell, Ames and White. firm publishers 77380

Mitchell Family Festival, South Britain, Conn., 1858. 49736

Mitchell's goegraphical question book. 49722

Mitchell's geographical reader. 49722

Mitchell's intermediate or secondary geography. 49722

Mitchell's map of North America. (11601)

Mitchell's map of the world. (49713)

Mitchell's new map of Texas, Oregon, and California. 49714

Mitchell's new traveller's guide. (49718)

Mitchell's primary geography. 49722

Mitchell's reference and distance map. (49715)

Mitchell's school and family geography. 49722

Mitchell's school atlas. 49722

Mitchell's school geography. 49722

Mitchell's series of geographies. 49722

Mitchell's series of outline maps. 49722

Mitchell's traveller's guide through the United States. 49717

Mitchil, Jonathan. see Mitchel, Jonathan, 1624-1668.

Mitchill, Smauel Latham, 1764-1831. 1154, 10530, 18210, 44518, 47327, 49737-49749, 54362, 55613, 59758, 65322, 77380, 79748, 86702, 102346 see also North Carolina. Geologist.

Mitchill, Samuel Latham, 1764-1831. supposed author 9917, 1st note after 96334, 4th note after 100532

Mite cast into the treasury. 4694, 49750
Mite into the treasury. 29747
Mite of praise. 101855
Mitford, Mary Russell. (49751)-49753
Mitgetheilt fur Auswanderer. 8744
Mithridate, Hippocrate, Apoth. pseud. Some serious thoughts. (49754)
Mithridates oder allgemeine Sprachenkunde. 453, 5269, 11042, 31600
Mitigation of slavery. 20095, 49755, note after 91132
Mitleidens voll Antworth auf das Bitt-Schreiben. 4886
Mitologia sacra. 77049
Mitos volcanicos en ambos nundos. 72785
Mitre, Bartolome. (34436), 49756-49759
Mitre and crown. (49760)
Mitsgarders een tweede reys in't selve jaar 1603. (10690)
Mitteilungen. 99362
Mittelberger, -------. 36991, 73490
Mittelberger, Gottlieb. 49761
Mittelmaier, C. J. A. (49763)-49764
Mitten, Wilhelm. 49762
Mitternachtige Schiffarth. 73294
Mittheilungen aus der Geographie und Geschichte. 9984
Mittheilungen aus Justus Perthes' geographischer Anstalt. 49765
Mittheilungen aus Nordamerika. 7454
Mittheilungen betreffen die Deutsche Kolonie Dona Francisca. 33623
Mittheilungen des Berliner Vereins. 32525
Mittheilungen fur Auswanderungslustige. 52062
Mittheilungen uber die handschriftlichen Werke. (77618)
Mittleren Staaten der Union. 77696
Mix, Ebenezer. ed. 78680-78681
Mix, G. A. 21042
Mix, James B. 49766
Mix, L. C. 49767
Mix, Silas. (49768)
Mix, Stephen. 49769
Mixed Bands of Seneca and Shawnee Indians. see Seneca Indians. and Shawnee Indians.
Mixed Commission on British and American Claims Under Article XII of the Treaty of Washington, 1871. 88829
Mixed Commission on Private Claims Established Under the Convention Between Great Britain and the United States, 1853. 33030
Mixed dish from Mexico. 43660
Mizaldi de mundi sphaera seu cosmographia libri tres. 49773
Mizner, L. B. (49774)
Mizpah. pseud. Bible view of polygamy. see Lea, Henry C.
Mnemonika; or, chronological tablets. 49775
Mnemonika; or the tablet of memory. 18535
Moat, Thomas. plaintiff 96908
Mob, under pretense of law. 92230
Moberly, W. 49776
Mobile, Ala. Board of School Commissioners. (49784)
Mobile, Ala. Charter. (49778)
Mobile, Ala. Committee to Investigate the Late Mortality. (49786)
Mobile, Ala. Coroner's Jury. 57253
Mobile, Ala. Order of Working Brothers. see Order of Working Brothers, Mobile, Ala.
Mobile, Ala. Ordinances, etc. (49778)

Mobile, Ala. Planters and Merchants Bank. see Planters and Merchants Bank of Mobile.
Mobile, Ala. Public Schools. (49784)
Mobile, Ala. St. Joseph's College. see Spring Hill College, Mobile, Ala.
Mobile, Ala. Spring Hill College. see Spring Hill College, Mobile, Ala.
Mobile (Diocese) Synod, 1861. 72949
Mobile & Montgomery Railroad Company. Charter. 87327
Mobile and Ohio Railroad Company. 49793
Mobile and Ohio Railroad Company. Stocholders Meeting. 49783
Mobile Branch of the Bank of the State of Alabama. see Bank of the State of Alabama. Mobile Branch.
Mobile directory, or strangers' guide for 1839. (49780)
Mobs. 26536
Mocion hecha al Ayuntamiento. 67328
Mocion que hace el Regido que suscribe al Excmo. Ayuntamiento. 67329
Mock auction. 49787
Mock bird and the red bird. 84624
Mock heroic poem. 49787
Mock-heroic poem. By Henry Hedgehog. 64158
Mock heroic poem. Supported with copious extracts. 43344
Mock marriage. 74177
Mocking bird. 49788
Mocquet de Meaux, Jean. 49790-49794
Moctesuma, Joseph. defendant 98156
Mode of baptizing. 101216
Mode of baptism. 85389
Mode of infusing aristocracy into the policy of the United States. 94491
Mode of making partition of the western reserve. 103013
Mode of partition, of the western reserve. 103012
Mode of protecting domestic industry. (73103)
Mode of sumptuously providing for a large and expensive family. 22521
Model administration. 68613
Model architect. (82164)
Model character George Washington. (33598)
Model first reader. 71340
Model for erecting a bank of credit. (49795)
Model for the maintaining of students. 21882
Model man. 18057, 78794
Model merchant. 8965
Model of an advertisement for a Canadian furrier. 7121
Model of church and civil power. 104331
Model of the government of the province of East-New-Jersey. 78186
Model physician exemplified in an address. (65257)
Model plan. (9077), 25638
Model village. 89674
Modelo de los Cristianos. 24148, 49796, (63962), 76221
Modelo para llevar las cuentas de la Tesoreria General. 49797
Modena, Angelo Vincenzo. 49799, 64175
Modena (Duchy) Treaties, etc. 96543
Modera, J. 49800
Moderados y el estado de Mexico. (49801)
Moderate and safe expediente. (49802)
Moderate breeze. 63582, 100804
Moderate houses for moderate means. A letter to Rev. E. E. Hale. 67266

Moderate houses for moderate means. An argument for cheap trains. 67265
Moderate whig. pseud. Observations and remarks upon the state of our controversy. 56463
Moderate whig. pseud. Some seasonable observations and remarks. 86760-86761
Modern acting drama. 83787-83788
Modern age. 49803
Modern agitators. 3725
Modern American cookery. 83731
Modern American spiritualism. 30342
Modern and ancient geography. 83927
Modern atlas. 50938
Modern author's instructor. (62429)
Modern babes in the wood. 82695
Modern battle of the keys. 49804
Modern benevolence. 61371
Modern British essayists. 84320
Modern cavalry. (19568)
Modern characters for 1778. 79728
Modern chivalry. 7191, 97972
Modern crusades. 72419
Modern democracy. 50791
Modern eloquence. 97499
Modern emigrant. 33036
Modern epic poem. 97210-97215, 97218-97231, 97234
Modern expediency considered. 73123
Modern gazetteer. 75823-(75826)
Modern geography. 5727
Modern geographical dictionary. (78330)
Modern geography. A description of the empires. 3827, 62959
Modern geography. . . . Abridged. 62959
Modern geography, and a compendious general gazetteer. 49805
Modern geography, for the use of schools, academies, etc. 83775
Modern geography, . . . with brief notices of European discovery. 49806
Modern Gilpin. 49807
Modern government, and its true mission. 49808
Modern gratitude, in five numbers. 37155, 44898
Modern history of universalism. 103799
Modern history, or the present state of all nations. (49809), 49906, (56847), 87900
Modern honor. A tragedy in five acts. 103414
Modern infidelity. 64269
Modern inquiries. 5300
Modern inquisition. 29305
Modern methodism. 82582
Modern moralist. pseud. Letter to Lord Melbourne on the executions in Canada. 40445
Modern mysteries explained and exposed. 43861
Modern patriotism exemplified. 49810
Modern philosopher. 24213
Modern poem. 105496
Modern Presbyterianism unmasked. 24607
Modern priest. 69341, 103342-103344
Modern problems. 84067
Modern prophecy. 103442
Modern protestant church courts unmasked. 49811, 1st note after 98684
Modern Quaker. (49812)
Modern quixotism. 94237
Modern reform examined. 91763
Modern saint. pseud. Memoirs. (47575)
Modern slavery and the slave trade. 8182
Modern slavery destitute of a divine warrant. (43252)

Modern songster. 49813
Modern spiritualism. 10765
Modern standard drama (French's) (16551), 84241, note after 102637
Modern standard drama (Taylor's) 84783-84784
Modern things as they are practiced in the present day. 82475-82476
Modern thinker. (49814)
Modern toleration. 49815
Modern tragedy. 22133, 23952, 38583, 51101
Modern traveller. 14613, 15167, 15169, 29080, 49816
Modern traveller: being a collection of useful and entertaining travels. 49817
Modern traveller: popular description of Colombia. 14613
Modern women and what is said of them. 49818
Modern view of the thirteen United States of America. 49819
Moderne Geschichtschreiber. 3125
Modest account concerning the salutations and kissings in ancient times. 72404-72405
Modest account from Pennsylvania. 66739
Modest account of the principal differences in doctrine. 37201
Modest account of the principal difficulties betwixt George Keith. (37180)
Modest address . . . occasioned by the ill success. 49820
Modest & brotherly ansvver to Mr. Charles Herle his book. 46781-46782, note before 96158
Modest and brotherly dispute of the government of the Church of Scotland. 74458
Modest and cleare answer to Mr. Ball's discourse. 17070
Modest and impartial narrative of several grievances. 40907
Modest answer to a malicious libel against His Excellency Francis Nicholson, Esq; &c. 55222
Modest apology for my own conduct. 49821
Modest apology for the former, so far as they materially differ. 6011
Modest enquiry into the grounds and occasions of a late pamphlet. 49822
Modest enquiry into the nature and necessity of a paper currency. (25556)
Modest enquiry into the nature of witchcraft. 29637
Modest enquiry into the present state of foreign affairs. (49823)
Modest examination of lay-mens preaching. 105475
Modest inquiry into the state of the dead. 4095
Modest paper, &c. 86632
Modest proof of the order and government settled by Christ. (7850), 12362, 12364, 20055, (20061), (25402), 25407, 99800, 101194, 103904
Modest proposal to the present convention. 9372, 81492
Modest reply to a letter from a gentleman to his friend. 78553
Modest reply to the speech of Isaac Norris, Esq. (60625), 61845
Modest vindication of the late New-Jersey Assembly. 49824
Modo de administrar el baptismo a los Indios adultos. 74863
Modo de administrar el baptismo, a los Indios infantes. 74863

Modo de ensenar la doctrina Christiana a los Indios. 40083

Modo facil de beneficiar las malvas. 97276

Modolo de los Cristianos presentado a los insurgentes. 76221

Modtibolt. pseud. Republic of North America. 49825

Modulacoes poeticas. 88807

Moens, J. B. 49826

Moens, Petronella. 49827

Moerbeeck, Jan Andries. 49828, (68495), 98961-98962

Moerenhout, J. A. 49829

Moesta, Carlos. 49830, 70301

Moesta, Carlos Guillermo. (49831)

Moeurs, coutumes, caracteres des peuples Argentins. 77070

Moeurs des sauvages Americains. (38594A), (77989)

Moeurs des sauvages Ameriquains comparees aux moeurs des premiers temps. 38596-38597

Moeurs domestiques des Americains. 97033

Moeurs du jour. 16550

Moeurs et coutumes des habitans. 94853

Moeurs et coutumes des peuples. 49832

Moeurs et usages des Indiens. 73935

Moeurs et usages des Ostiackes. 4936

Moffat, James C. (49833)

Moffatt, Mary Anne Ursula. see Mary Edmond St. George. Sister

Moffette, Joseph F. (49834)

Mofras, Eugene Duflot de. see Duflot de Mofras, Eugene, 1810-1884.

Mogg Megone, a poem. 103809

Mogridge, George. 49835

Mogroveius, Torobius Alphonsius, Saint, Abp. 30415, 49836, 50070 see also Lima (Archdiocese) Archbishop (Mogroveius)

Mohaque Indians. see Mohawk Indians.

Mohawk. 6176, note after 92721

Mohawk and Hudson Rail Road. (49852)

Mohawk and Hudson Railroad Company. (49852)-49853)

Mohawk and St. Lawrence Rail Road and Navigation Company. 49854

Mohawk chief. 49856

Mohawk Indians. 49348, 66061 see also Five Nations of Indians.

Mohawk Indians. Treaties, etc. 36337, 60255

Mohawk Valley Railroad Company. 49855

Mohawks; a satirical poem with notes. 49857

Moheagan Indians against the Governor and Company of Connecticut. 15751-15752

Moheconic Indians. see Stockbridge Indians.

Mohegan Indians. 36351, 49348-49349

Mohegan Indians. appellants 15748-15752

Mohegan Indians. plaintiffs 45455

Mohegan Indians. Guardian. appellants 15748-15752 see also Mason, John. appellant Mason, Samuel. appellant

Mohegan maiden. 7061

Mohiconick Indians. see Stockbridge Indians.

Mohickon Indians. see Mahican Indians. and Mohegan Indians.

Mohikander Indians. see Mahican Indians.

Mohl, Robert von. (49860)-49861

Mohnike, Gottlieb. Tr. 67479

Mohocks; a tragi-comical farce. 26788

Mohun; or, the last days of Lee and his paladins. 16318

Moine, J. M. le. see Le Moine, J. M.

Moise, Ab. 30294

Moise, F. Tr. 98793

Moivre, Abraham. 3206A

Moke, J. H. 49862

Molard, -------- Durand. see Durand-Molard, --------.

Molas, Mariano Antonio. 49863

Molde de operarios. 106378

Molesworth, Sir William, Bart. 49864-49865, 101300

Moletius, Josephus, ed. (66489), 66503-66505

Moleto, Gioseppe. see Moletius, Josephus.

Molguin, Diego de Goncalez. see Gonzales Holguin, Diego, d. 1552.

Moliere, Jean Baptiste Poquelin, 1622-1673. 84241

Molina, Alonso de, d. 1585. (49866)-(49878), (73309)

Molina, Antonio de. 57458, 57459

Molina, Camillo Quintanilla y Malo de. see Quintanilla y Malo de Molina, Camillo.

Molina, Felipe. 42907-(42908), 49879-49885

Molina, Francisco Javier. (49886)

Molina, Giovanni Ignazio. see Molina, Juan Ignazio.

Molina, J. Ignatius. see Molina, Juan Ignacio.

Molina, Juan Ignacio. 12756, 38366, (49887)-49895, note after 99468-99469

Molina, Luis de. 49896

Molina, Luis de Neve y. see Neve y Molina, Luis de.

Molina, Marcos. (49897)

Molina, Tirso de. pseud. Gloria de loz Pizarros. see Tellex, Gabriel, 1571?-1648

Moline, Ill. Citizens. petitioners 51925

Molineaux, -------. 90612

Molino Torres, Julian del. see Torres, Julian del Molino.

Molkenboer, Julian Hendrik, 1816-1854. 20802

Moll, G. 49901

Moll, Herman, d. 1732. (2308), (33801), 38644, (42744), (49809), (49902)-49906, (56847), (57156), 68451, 87900, 91537, 99553

Moll, Herman, d. 1732. incorrectly supposed author (49907)

Moll Carey. 86891

Moll Pitcher, a poem. 49900, 103810

Moll Pitcher, and the minstrel girl. Poems. 103811

Molleda, Gregorio de, Bp. (55263) see also Isauria (Diocese) Bishop (Molleda)

Molleda y Clerque, Gregorio de. (49908)

Moller, Marthold. 99334

Mollhausen, Balduin. 33735, (49909)-49916

Mollien, G. 49917-49921

Mollineau, M. Emmerie. cartographer (29594)

Mollineaux, Mary. 49922

Molling, Peter August. 49923

Molloy, Charles. 49924

Mollusca and shells. 29089

Mollusca. [By Augustus Addison Gould.] 28087

Mollusca, by Edgar A. Smith. 28401, 71032

Mollusca. [By John Matthew Jones.] 36544

Mollusca, by R. B. Hinds. 31945

Mollusques. 21353

Mollusques. Par Alcide d'Orbigny. 74922

Molony, Patrick. defendant 83725

Moltke, L. ed. 65299

Molucco nutts. 44639

Moluscos. 74921

Molyneaux, Thomas More. 49925

Mombert, J. Isidor. 49926-49927

Momentous epistle. 85114

Momus, formerly of Mount Plympus. 49928

Mon, Alejandro, 1801-1882. 67141

Mon droit. pseud. Criticism[s] on the declaration of independence as a literary document. see Seldan, R. E.

Mon second voyage aotour du monde. 61343

Mon voyage au Mexique. 12157

Monachesi, ‑‑‑‑‑‑‑‑‑. illus. 89552

Monachesi, Herbert D. ed. 90803

Monacho, R. see Robertus Monachus.

Monagas, Jose Ruperto. 49930 see also
Venezuela. President, 1868-1870 (J. R.
Monagas)

Monagas and Paez. 104391

Monahan, Deane. pseud. Sons of the border.
see Steele, James William.

Monarchia Hispanica ofte een reysbesvhryvinge.
106296

Monarchia Hispanica vervaatende een korte
reysbeschryvinge. 106296

Monarchical projects. 9024, note after 101223

Monarchist; an historical novel. 36530

Monarchs of ocean. 49935

Monarchy and republicanism analyzed. 34863

Monarchy v. republic. 7606

Monard, Nicolas. see Monardes, Nicoloso
de.

Monardes, Nicoloso de. 14355, 31801, 49936-
49948, 57667, 57668-57670, 104966

Monardis, Nicolao. see Monardes, Nicoloso
de.

Monarque, J. B. defendant 96924

Monarquia constitucional. 86376

Monarquia de Espana. 75588

Monarquia dischosa. 26413

Monasterio de Santa Clara, Lima. see Lima.
Monasterio de Santa Clara.

Monastery of the Visitation, Georgetown, D. C.
see Georgetown, D. C. Monastery of
the Visitation.

Monastica theologia. 64859

Monatsbericht der Kon. Preussischen Akademie
der Wissenschaften. 49949

Monatsberichte der Berliner Akademia.
(9527)

Monatschrift ersten und launigen Inhalts.
(68216)

Monatsschrift fur Erinnerungen. 19799

Monbars l'exterminateur. 62677

Monbrion, ‑‑‑‑‑‑‑‑. ed. 43128

Moncada, Antonio. 49950

Moncada, Balthasar de. 19697, (49951)

Moncada, Tecla. pseud. Continuacion y con-
clucion del dialogo. see Valencia, P. F.

Moncada, Tecla. pseud. Dialogo. see
Valencia, P. F.

Moncayo, Pedro. (21797), 58054

Monchy, Solomon de. 49952

Monck, John. see Munk, Jens.

Monckton, Robert. 44972, (49953)-49954

Monckton, Robert. defendant at court martial
49954

Moncon, Luis Cerdeno y. see Cerdeno y
Moncon, Luis.

Moncrief, ‑‑‑‑‑‑‑‑. RA. 49955

Moncure, R. C. L. (49956)

Monday morning, December 27. 1773. (49957)

Monde. 4562

Monde Americain. 81308, 81313

Monde illustre. 100745

Monde, ou la description des ses quatre
parties. 18911-18912

Monde primitif. (17174)

Mondelet, Charles. (49958)

Mondelet, Dominique. 49959, 2d note after
96445

Mondelt, D. 69780 see also Quebec
(Province) Commissioners to Visit the
United States' Penitentiaries.

Monderie, Thiebault de. 49960

Mondes nouveaux. 55134

Mondo e sve partie. 73195

Mondo elementare et celeste. 73196

Mondo nvovo. 6803

Mondo nvovo del Cavalier Tomaso Stigliani.
91729

Mondo nvovo del Sig. Siovanni Giorgini da
Iesi. 27473, note after 36086

Mondot, Armand. 49962

Mondragon, Alonso de. 76007

Mondragon, Benito de Penalosa y. see
Penalosa y Mondragon, Benito de.

Mondragon, Carlos Ximenez de. see Ximenez
de Mondragon, Carlos.

Mone, Franz Joseph, 1796-1871. 2225, 50537

Mone, Frederick. (49963), 50372

Monedero. 63184

Monell, John J. 49964

Monet de Lamarck, Jean Baptiste Pierre
Antoine de. see Lamarck, Jean Baptiste
Pierre Antoine de Monet de, 1744-1829.

Monetary difficulties of America. 74837

Monetary policy of England and America.
49965, 94503

Monette, John W. 49966-(49967)

Money, C. F. S. (49968)

Money: a lecture before the New York
Geographical and Statistical Society.
10842

Money and banking. (49969)

Money and paper. 29294

Money and trade considered. 39313

Money. By Charles Moran. 50507

Money by steam. 49970

Money differs. 95478, 95483

Money, its history, evils and remedy. 19015

Money; its nature, history, uses, and responsibilities. (49971)

Money-king and other poems. 77340

"Money-maker." 41620

Money, panics and specie payment. 63468

Money question in 1813 and 1863. 49972

Money the sinues of trade. (49973)

Money toss'd in a bag. 105488

Money versus the higher law. (58350)

Moneypenny, George W. 49974

Monneypenny, or, the heart of the world.
46840

Monfart, ‑‑‑‑‑. 66686

Monge, M. 49975

Monglave, Eugene de. 49976, 59516

Mongrelites. 49977

Mongrolle, ‑‑‑‑‑‑‑‑‑‑. 49978

Monica Americana. (46418)

Monicion caritativa de un religiosa. (69334)

Moniface, Joseph Xavier. 75542-75543

Monikins. 16482-16483

Monino, Antonio R. Rodriguez. see Rodriquez
Monino, Antonio R.

Monis, Judah. 14477, 49979

Monita secreta. Instruccoes secretas que
devem, guardar todos os religiosos da
Companhia. 49980

Monita secreta Societatis Jesu. (49981)

Moniteur. 5392, 5652, 35933, 49983, 75111,
note after 92859

Moniteur colonial. 75165

Moniteur des Indes-Orientales et Occidentales.
47476, 49982, 80864

Moniteur general de la partie Francaise de
Saint-Domingue. 75166

Moniteur industrial. 18667

Moniteur universel. 5393, 40956, 50065,
50228

Moniteur universel. Gerant. defendant 40956

Monitor. pseud. Letter to the inhabitants of the British colonies. see Lee, Arthur, 1740-1972.

Monitor. pseud. Rights and privileges of the Passaick and Hackinsack Bridge Company examined. 58999

Monitor, Elias. pseud. Stranger's apology for the general associations. see Worcester, Noah, 1758-1837. supposed author

Monitor (Boston) 49985

Monitor (Tuscaloosa) see Tuscaloosa monitor.

Monitor de los masones libres. 102243

Monitor for communicants. 46419

Monitor for delaying sinners. 94113

Monitor for Gospel ministers. 8939

"Monitor" iron clads. 49986

Monitor o guia de los frac-mazones utilisimo. 102244

Monitor of freemasonry. 71008

Monitor; or, an address to the people of Great Britain. (4151)

Monitor: or British freeholder. 32775, 49987, 66909

Monitor; or, jottings of a New York merchant. 32408

Monitor republicano. 68736

Monitorial instruction. 28878

Monitorial School, Boston. see Boston. Monitorial School.

Monitor's letter to the inhabitants of the British colonies. 39701

Monitory, and hortatory letter. 46430

Monitory hints to the ministers. 49988

Monitory letter about the maintenance of an able and faithful ministry. (46484), 72689

Monitory letter to them who needlessly and frequently absent themselves. 46421

Monitum ad lectorem. 79180

Moniz, Nuno Alvares Pereira Pato. 49990

Moniz, Patricio. 49991

Moniz Barreto, Domingos Alves Branco. see Barreto, Domingos Alves Branco Moniz.

Moniz Barretto, Francisco. 49989

Monja Alferez, ----- la. see La Monja Alferez, -----------.

Monja Alferez. (50073)

Monk, Sir James, fl. 1776-1820. supposed author 90622

Monk, Sir James, fl. 1776-1820. defendant at impeachment 42518, 96926-96927

Monk, Maria, d. ca. 1850. (49992)-49993, (49996)-(49997), 84021, 92145 see also Slocum, J. J. supposed author

Monk and Washington. 29265

Monk of Wissahikon. (41399)

Monkey of Porto Bello. 79756

Monmonier, Charles de. tr. (66858)

Monmonier, J. F. 49998

Monmouth and Buccleuch, James, Duke of, 1649-1685. 49999

Monmouth, Ill. Monmouth College. see Monmouth College, Monmouth, Ill.

Monmouth. 82108

Monmouth College, Monmouth, Ill. 50000

Monnick, Joan. see Munk, Jens.

Monnier, P. 50001-50002

Monnier, Pierre Charles le. see Le Monnier, Pierre Charles, 1715-1799.

Mono-dramatico poem. 79852

Monod, Frederic. tr. (65540)

Monody . . . by Rev. James A. Neal. 8930

Monody in honor of the chiefs who have fallen. 50003

Monody inscribed to Benjamin Church. 67183

Monody on certain members of the "Press Club." 61238

Monody on His late Royal Highness the Duke of Cumberland. 106040

Monody on Major Andre. 51562, 79477-79487

Monody, on the death of Brigadier General Zebulon Montgomery Pike. 105620

Monody on the death of General Washington. 101866

Monody on the death of John Syng Dorsey. 56637

Monody on the death of Major Andre. 83421-83422

Monody on the death of Major Gen[l]. James Wolfe. 104989

Monody on the death of the Honourable Thomas Russell. 101470

Monody on the victims and sufferers by the late conflagration. (27436)

Monody, sacred to the memory of the Rev. John Lovejoy Abbott. (39188)

Monody to the memory of the Rev. Dr. Charles Nisbet. 55351

Monogram on our national song. 51886

Monograph A of "Military medical and surgical essays." 76657, 76676

Monograph A[-T of "Military medical and surgical essays."] 76536, 76555, 76647, 76657, 76676

Monograph B [of "Military medical and surgical essays."] 76536, 76555, 76647, 76657, 7667

Monograph D [of "Military medical and surgical essays."] 76555, 76657

Monograph IV of the U.S. Catholic Historical Society. note after 99383C

Monograph of American Corbiculadae. 65541

Monograph of authors who have written on the languages of Central America. 89959, 89977

Monograph of North American insects. (77387)

Monograph of the bats of North America. 816

Monograph of the birds forming the tanagrine genus Calliste. 78140

Monograph of the family Unionidae of Naiades of Lamarck. 15903

Monograph of the fulviatile bivalve shells of the river Ohio. 50004, 67460

Monograph of the fossil Squalidae of the United States. (27281)

Monograph of the freshwater univalve mollusca. 29610

Monograph of the genus Anculotus of Say. 15904

Monograph of the great rebellion. 59499

Monograph of the Limniades. (29609)

Monograph of the Odontophorinae. 28109

Monograph of the Pittidae. 22228

Monograph of the Ramphastidae. (28110)

Monograph of the species of Sphaerium of North and South America. 65541

Monograph of the Tetraoninae, or family of the grouse. 22229

Monograph of the Trilobites of North America. 28527

Monograph of the Trochilidae, or humming-birds. (28112)

Monograph of the Trogonidae, or family of Trogons. 29111

Monograph of the ancient monuments of the state of Kentucky. 89978

Monograph on the family Osteodesmacea. 17196

Monograph on the silver dollar, good and bad. 71254

Monograph upon the moral sense. 82921
Monographie de l'erythroxylon coca. 28059
Monographie de Turbinolies fossiles du
  Kentuki. 67462
Monographie der Scydmaeniden Central und
  Sudamerika's. (77518)
Monographie des Coquilles bivalves et
  fluviatiles de la Riviere Ohio. 67458
Monographie des Coquilles bivalves fluviatiles
  de la Riviere Ohio. 12430, 67459
Monographie des Eumeniens. 77208
Monographie des genres Sauvagesia et
  Lavradia. 75235
Monographie des Guepes Sociales, ou de la
  tribu de Vespiens. 77208
Monographie des Guepes Solitaires, ou de la
  tribu de Eumeniens. 77208
Monographie des Masariens. 77208
Monographie des Melastomacees, comprenant
  toutes les plantes. 33762
Monographie de Melastomacees . . . . Rhexies.
  (33763)
Monographie des picides. (44121)
Monographie des rosiers de l'Amerique
  Septentrionale. 67462
Monographie du gentre Anculotus de Say.
  15905
Monographie du Trigonocephale des Antilles.
  50557
Monographie historique et medicale de la
  fievre jaune. 50556
Monographs of the Diptera of North America.
  41775, 57823
Monographs of the United States Catholic
  Historical Society. 99357, note after
  99383C, 101017, 106398
Monongahela Navigation Company. 60264
Monongahela of old. 98735
Monongahela of old; or, historical sketches of
  south-western Pennsylvania to the year
  1800. 98734, 98736
Monongahela of old; or, history of Fayette
  County, Pennsylvania. 98735A
Monopolie. (72107)-(72108)
Monoxe, Edward. 66686
Monrio, Antonio. 80979
Monro, Alexander. 50006-50008
Monro, Robert. pseud. Description of the
  Genesee Country. see Williamson,
  Charles. supposed author
Monroe, A. F. (50010)
Monroe, James, Pres. U. S., 1758-1831.
  (445)-448, 1898, 4549, 12496, 12489,
  (14151), 14849, 14981, (15594), 18005,
  24859, 24887, 25876, 27073, 29982-29983,
  35345, (35378), 35883, 37456, 38739,
  (40345), 43707, 46068, 48075-48086,
  48148, 50011-50020, 50023, (59090),
  63811, 65359, 69421-69422, 78647,
  (79068)-79069, 89198, 83270, 96421-
  96422, 96563-96564, 96593, 96632-96635,
  100229-100230, 101011, 101270, 104204-
  104205 see also U. S. Department of
  State. U. S. Legation. Great Britain.
  U. S. President, 1817-1825 (Monroe)
  Virginia. Governor, 1799-1802 (Monroe)
Monroe, James, Pres. U. S., 1758-1831.
  claimant 98363
Monroe, John. 50026
Monroe, John Albert, 1836-1891. 50027
Monroe, Michael. defendant 50028
Monroe, Peter J. 12386
Monroe, Victor. 103424
Monroe, Michigan. Common Council. 104778

Monroe, Michigan. Horticultural Association.
  see Horticultural Association of Monroe,
  Michigan.
Monroe County, N. Y. Agricultural Society.
  see Monroe County Agricultural Society.
Monroe County, N. Y. Board of Supervisors.
  (50031)
Monroe County, N. Y. Insane Asylum. 50030
Monroe County, N. Y. Junior Pioneer Associa-
  tion. see Junior Pioneer Association of
  the City of Rochester and Monroe County,
  N. Y.
Monroe County, N. Y. Teachers' Institute of
  the Third Assembly District. see
  Teachers' Institute of the Third Assembly
  District of Monroe County, N. Y.
Monroe County, N. Y. Workhouse. 50030
Monroe County, N. Y. Workhouse. 50030
Monroe and Pinkney's treaty, 1806. 96563
Monroe Baptist Association. see Baptists.
  New York. Monroe Baptist Association.
Monroe Cole and Iron Company. (50033)
Monroe County Agricultural Society. 50030
"Monroe doctrine," and our relations with
  Mexico. (73256)
Monroe doctrine. By Edward Everett. 23258
Monroe doctrine. By Joshua Leavitt. 39564
Monroe doctrine. Speech of Hon. D. C.
  Jarnette. 35788
Monroe's embassy. 50022
Monroux, Pierre. 50034
Monroy, Antonius de. 98122
Monroy, Jos. 50036
Monsalve, Miguel de. 50037
Monseigneur Flaget, Eveque de Bardstown et
  Louisville. 19733
Monsieur de la Crocheterie. 50511
Monseiur De Pointi's expedition of Carthagena.
  63703
Monseiur de Raousset et Sonore. 16709
M. Lamiral, refute par lui-meme. 38762
Monsieur Thomas. note after 88547
Monsieur traducteur. pseud. tr. see Clopper,
  Jonas.
Monsieur Violette. 44699
Monsigny, Mary. 50038
Monson, Alfred S. 50039
Monson, Sir William. 13015
Monson, Mass. Selectmen. 50040
Monson, Mass. State Alms House. see
  Massachusetts. State Alms House, Monson.
Monson Academy, Springfield, Mass.
  Semicentennial anniversary, 1854. 50041,
  92272
Monster North American circus. 88865
Monster of monsters. 12982, 25296, 86684,
  3d note after 95765, 2d note after 102065
Monstrum horrendum! pseud. see Patriot.
  Monstrum horrendum! pseud.
Monstruo de dos cabezas. 34414
Monstruo de Santidad S. Bernardo panegirico.
  22062
Mont, J. du. ed. 56062
Mont-Serrat, E. de. 20542
Montacute, or the new home. (37991)
Montagnac, --------. 72219
Montagne, J. de la. tr. 7733
Montagne, Jean Francois Camille, 1784-1866.
  21216, 50042-50043, 74921-74922
Montagu, Charles. see Halifax, Charles
  Montagu, 1st Earl, 1661-1715.
Montagu, Lord Charles-Grenville, 1741-1784.
  87358 see also South Carolina (Colony)
  Governor, 1768-1769 (Montagu)
Montagu, Edward. see Sandwich, Edward
  Montagu, 1st Earl of, 1625-1672.

Montagu, George. see Manchester, George
   Montagu, 4th Duke of, 1737-1788.
Montagu, John. see Sandwich, John Montagu,
   4th Earl of, 1718-1792.
Montagu, Matthew Robinson. 1794, 50045,
   72149-72155
Montagu, Montagu, 1787-1863. (50044)
Montagu, Lord Robert, 1825-1902. 50046
Montague, E. J. (50048)
Montague, Elijah. 94890
Montague, Emily. 50047
Montague, Erastus. defendant 96906
Montague, Frederick. (15052)
Montague, William L. (50049), (71174)
Montague, Mass. Baptist Church. see
   Leverett, Mass. Baptist Church.
Montague's Illinois and Missouri state
   directory. (50049)
Montague's Richmond directory and business
   advertiser. (71174)
Montaigne, Michel Eyquem de, 1533-1592.
   99866
Montalboddo, Antonio Fracanzano da. see
   Fracanzano da Montalboddo.
Montalboddo, Fracanzano da. see Fracanzano
   da Montalboddo.
Montalboddo Fracan. al suo amicissimo
   Ioanimaria Anzolello Vicentino S. 50050
Montalembert, Charles Forbes, Comte de.
   50065-50068
Montalvan, Perez de. (50073)
Montalvao, Jorge Mascarenhas, Marquez de.
   see Mascarenhas, Jorge, Marquez de
   Montalvao.
Montalvo, Francisco Antonio de. 50069-50072
Montalvo, Juan Ordonez. (50075)
Montalvo, Luis Berrio de. (4987), 50076
Montalvo, P. 50077
Montana, Jos. Isidro. 50078
Montana, Luis. supposed author 86383
Montana (Territory) Auditor. 50083
Montana (Territory) Governor, 1866-1869
   (Smith) (50082) see also Smith, Green
   Clay, 1832-1895.
Montana (Territory) Laws, statutes, etc.
   (50079)-50081
Montana (Territory) Legislative Assembly.
   petitioners 50081
Montana (Territory) Superintendent of Public
   Instruction. 50083
Montana (Territory) Treasurer. 50083
Montana Historical Society. (50080)
Montanas, or under the stars. 30190
Montanez, J. de Ortega. (67658)
Montanini poetry. 57755
Montano, Benito Arias. (50084), 69173
Montano, J. 50085
Montanus, Arnoldus. 24081, 47472, 50086-
   (50089), 1st note after 97721
Montanus, Petrus. see Dalthenus, Petrus,
   d. 1590.
Montanya, --------. 58089
Montauban, --------, Sieur de. (11274), note
   after 39117, (67986)
Montayo, Ignacio Joseph de Urruha. see
   Urrutia y Montoya, Ignacio Jose de.
Montbeillard, -------- de. tr. 78771
Montcalm Saint-Veran, Louis Joseph, Marquis
   de, 1712-1759. supposed author 50091
Montcalm Saint-Veran, Louis Joseph, Marquis
   de, 1712-1759. spirit author 19937,
   67022
Montcalm's expedition to Fort George. 37949
Montchal, Charles A. Louis Barentin de. see
   Barentin de Montchal, Charles Paul
   Nicolas, Vicomte, 1737-1824.

Montchal, Charles Paul Nicolas, Vicomte
   Barentin de, 1737-1824. see Barentin
   de Montchal, Charles Paul Nicolas,
   Vicomte, 1737-1824.
Montchal, Louis Barentin de. see Barentin
   de Montchal, Charles Paul Nicolas,
   Vicomte, 1737-1824.
Montclair, J. W. 50092
Monte, Ludovici de Lato. see Lato-Monte,
   Ludovici de.
Monte Carmelo Luna, Lino de. see Luna,
   Lino de Monte Carmelo.
Monte Mayor, Geronimo de. 50112
Monte Rodrigues de Araujo, Manuel do, Bp.,
   1798-1863. 47590, 72500-72503 see also
   Rio de Janeiro (Diocese) Bishop (Monte
   Rodrigues de Araujo)
Monte y Tejada, Antonio del. see Delmonte
   y Tejada, Antonio, 1783-1861.
Monte-Christo. 50098
Monte de turba ardiente. 72765
Monte Pio de Oficias de esta Nueva-Espana,
   etc. 65996
Monte Pio de Viudas, Huerfanos y Madres de
   Oficiales Militares, Reglamento de.
   68860, 68872-68873
Monte Pio de Viudas y Huerfanos, Reglamento
   de. 68860, 68872-68873
Monte Pio, de Viudas y Pupilos, Reglamento
   del. 68860, 68872-68873
Monte Pio Militar, Reglamento del. 68238
Monte sancto di Dio. 66470
Monteagudo, Bernardo. 50094-50095, (51348),
   61122, 61170 see also Peru. Ministerio
   de Relaciones Esteriores.
Monteagudo, Matias. 50096
Monteath, Walter. 50097
Montecuma, Emperador de Mexico. 11590
Montefiore, Joshua. (50099)-50100
Montego Bay, Jamaica. Court. 69913
Monteigne, George, Abp. of York, d. 1628.
   103330-103331
Monteiro, -------. 85772
Monteiro, Joze Maria de Souza. see Souza
   Monteiro, Joze Maria de.
Monteiro, Manuel. 50103
Monteiro, Paulo Pereira. see Pereira Mon-
   teiro, Paulo.
Monteiro Baena, Antonio Ladislau. 50101-
   50102
Monteiro da Vide, Sebastiao. 50104
Monteith, James. 50105
Montelle, ---------. (29173), 47870
Montellier, ------- du. see Du Montellier,
   --------, Sieur.
Montemaior de Cuenca, Juan Francisco de.
   see Montemayor Cordova de Cuenca,
   Juan Francisco de, 1620-1685.
Montemayor y Belena, -------- de. 58417,
   (72549)
Montemayor y Cordova de Cuenca, Juan Fran-
   cisco de, 1620-1685. 11424, 50010, 50106-
   50111, 58417, 93586, note after 96260 see
   also Santo Domingo (Spanish Colony)
   Gobernador, 1653-1655 (Montemayor y
   Cordova de Cuenca)
Montemont, Albert. 4349, 6865, 9140, 14095,
   16275, (21145), 23780, 50113-50116, 97033,
   98442
Montenegro, A. C. de. 80880
Montenegro, Alonso de la Pena. see Pena
   Montenegro, Alonso de la, Bp.
Montenegro, Antonio Casimiro. 50117
Montenegro, J. G. 50118
Montenegro, Juan. defendant 27309, (51797),
   69915, 93808, 96948

Montenegro Colon, Feliciano. see Colon,
Feliciano Montenegro.
Montengon, P. 50119
Monterey, Gaspar de Zuniga y Acevedo,
Conde de. see Zuniga y Acevedo,
Gaspar de, Conde de Monterey.
Monterey, Calif. Library Association. 50120
Monterey; and other poems. 17633
Montero, Felipe. 99711
Montero, Vitorino. supposed author 61124
Montero Prieto de Bonilla, A. A. defendant
48418
Monteros, Ignacio Espinosa de los. see
Espinosa de los Monteros, Ignacio.
Monteroyo Mascarenhas, Jose Freire de. see
Mascarenhas, Jose Freire de Monteroyo.
Montes, Ezequiel. 48396 see also Mexico.
Ministerio de Justicia.
Montes, Jose Varela de. see Varela de
Montes, Jose.
Montes de Oca, ---------. illus. (76029)
Montes de Oca, Ignacio. 50121, 56608
Montes de Oca, J. J. ed. 70308
Montes de Oca, Juan Evanhelista. pseud.
Carta de un particular. see Valdes,
Rafael.
Montesano, R. R. 50122
Montesclaros, Juan de Mendoza y Luna,
Marques de. see Mendoza y Luna,
Juan de, Marques de Montesclaros.
Monteseguro, Antonio Arteta de. see Arteta
de Monteseguro, Antonio.
Monteserin, Nicolas Pastrama y. see
Pastrama y Monteserin, Nicolas.
Montesinos, Fernando de. (50124)-50127
Montesquieu, Charles de Secondat, Baron de
la Brede et de, 1689-1755. 96413
Montessori system, in theory and practice.
84333
Montesuma, ou Fernand Cortes. 20980
Montevideo. Legacion de Buenos Aires. see
Buenos Aires (Province) Legation.
Montevideo.
Montez, Diego. 14670
Montez, Lola. 50129, 58492
Montezinus, Antony. 44193
Montezon, F. de. see Demontezon, Fortune.
Montezuma, Francisco Gomes Brandao. see
Brandao Montezuma, Francisco Gomes.
Montezuma, Jose Sarmiento Valladares, Conde
de. see Valladares, Jose Sarmiento,
Conde de Montezuma.
Montezuma, a ballad of Mexico. 39542
Montezuma. Historisches Schauspiel in funk
Akten. 77728
Montezuma; the last of the Aztecs. 46908
Montfaucon, Bernard de. 66508
Montford, Robert. 96008
Montgaillard, Juan Gabriel Maurice Roques de.
50130
Montgolfier, ---------. incorrectly supposed
author 50131, 4th note after 99504
Montgolfier, Adelaide de. tr. 92526
Montgomerie, John, d. 1731. 54168, (54170)
see also New York (Colony) Governor,
1728-1731 (Montgomerie)
Montgomery, Cora. 50132-50134
Montgomery, Corinne. pseud. Texas and her
presidents. see Cazneau, Mrs. William
Leslie. supposed author
Montgomery, Cuthbert. ed. 50136
Montgomery, Elizabeth. 50138
Montgomery, G. W. 50139
Montgomery, Henry. 50140-50142

Montgomery, Hugh. defendant 32362, 96946,
96951, 2d note after 102623, 3d note after
102623
Montgomery, James, 1771-1854. 32507, 50142-
50147, 104910
Montgomery, James, fl. 1789. supposed author
(50137), (55169), 100451
Montgomery, James, fl. 1822. 50148
Montgomery, James, fl. 1840. 50149-50150,
note after 92844
Montgomery, James Eglinton. 50151
Montgomery, John T. 5487, 50152
Montgomery, Joseph. 50153
Montgomery, M. W. 50154
Montgomery, Richard, 1736-1775. (22673),
50155-50156, 75901
Montgomery, Richard, 1736-1775. spirit author
19947, note after 96403
Montgomery, Sir Robert, Bart., 1680-1731.
(19719)
Montgomery, Thomas, d. 1828. 43385
Montgomery, Thomas, fl. 1852. (50157)
Montgomery, Thomas Harrison, 1830-1905.
(50158), 84585, 84597, 84608, 84611,
84622, 84641, 84643, 84678C, 84845
Montgomery, W. 90338
Montgomery, William. 50159
Montgomery, William, 1789-1844. 50160
Montgomery, William B. 57737, note after
101510
Montgomery, Ala. Constitutional Convention,
1867. see Alabama. Constitutional Con-
vention, Montgomery, 1867.
Montgomery, Ala. Convention, 1861. see
Alabama. Convention, Montgomery, 1861.
Montgomery, Ala. Convention of the Com-
missioners of Appraisement, 1864. see
Convention of the Commissioners of
Appraisement, Montgomery, Ala., 1864.
Montgomery, Ala. League of United Southerners.
see League of United Southerners, Mont-
gomery, Ala.
Montgomery, Ala. Southern Rights Convention,
1852. see Southern Rights Convention,
Montgomery, Ala., 1852.
Montgomery, N. Y. Academy. see Montgomery
Academy, Montgomery, N. Y.
Montgomery, N. Y. Classis. see Reformed
Dutch Church. Classis of Montgomery.
Montgomery County, N. Y. Auxiliary Bible
Society. see Auxiliary Bible Society of
the Counties of Montgomery, Fulton and
Hamilton, N. Y.
Montgomery County, N. Y. Board of Super-
visors. 50163
Montgomery County, N. Y. Fort-Plain Seminary
and Female Institute. see Fort-Plain
Seminary and Female Institute, Montgomery
County, N. Y.
Montgomery County, N. Y. Washington Bene-
volent Society. see Washington Benevolent
Society. New York. Montgomery County.
Montgomery County, Pa. Collector of Excise.
50164
Montgomery County, Pa. Democratic Young
Men's Meeting, 1838. see Democratic
Party. Pennsylvania. Montgomery County.
Young Men's Meeting, 1838.
Montgomery County, Pa. Harvest Home Meet-
ing, Valley Forge, 1828. see Harvest
Home Meeting of Chester and Montgomery
Counties at Valley Forge, July 28, 1828.
Montgomery Academy, Montgomery, N. Y.
50162

Montgomery & Eufaula Railroad Company.
Charter. 87327
Montgomery Classis. see Reformed Church
in America. Classis of Montgomery.
Montgomery county almanac. 73066
Montgomery County Auxiliary Bible Society.
see Auxiliary Bible Society of the
Counties of Montgomery, Fulton and
Hamilton, N. Y.
Montgomery Lodge, Milford, Mass. see
Freemasons. Massachusetts.
Montgomery Lodge, Milford.
Montgomery; or, the falls of Montmorency.
24392
Montgomery, or the West Indian adventurer.
50616
Montgomery White Sulphur Springs, Va.
Southern Historical Convention, 1873.
see Southern Historical Convention,
Montgomery White Sulphur Springs, Va.,
1873.
Montgomery's Tippecanoe almanac. 50142
Month of freedom. 50165, 101341
Month with the blue noses. 17321
Monthly advertiser. 53181
Monthly agricultural, industrial and educational
magazine. 88117
Monthly American journal of geology and
natural science. 23964, 50166
Montly anthology, and Boston review. 1441,
21247, (40825), 70224, 95190, 97410
Monthly assembly. A farce. (50168)
Monthly bibliographical journal. 62544
Monthly bulletin of the operations of the
Cincinnati Branch of the United States
Sanitary Commission. 13097, 76660
Monthly chronicle. 86917
Monthly chronicle for the British colonies.
50169 see also American magazine
and monthly chronicle for the British
colonies.
Monthly chronicle, for the years 1728-31.
50170
Monthly chronicle, of events, discoveries,
improvements and opinions. 50171
Monthly chronicle of original literature.
50172
Monthly chronicle of the Merchants' Protective
Union. 50173
Monthly chronologer. (41859)
Monthly church magazine. 23291
Monthly circular of the National Anti-monopoly
Cheap Freight Railway League. 51921
Monthly circulars. 84005
Monthly commercial record and business
directory of San Francisco. 50174
Monthly concert lectures. 63991
Monthly, devoted to the institutions and family
literature of the south. 88338
Monthly eclectic magazine of general literature
and science. 11524
Monthly financial record. 52692
Monthly freemason. 50175
Monthly illustrated journal of the industrial
arts. (59044)
Monthly Indiana freemason. 50175
Monthly intelligencer. (26954)
Monthly journal devoted to agriculture,
horticulture, etc. (17869)
Monthly journal, devoted to agriculture,
horticulture, rural & domestic economy.
86214
Monthly journal, devoted to southern education.
79009
Monthly journal devoted to the history and
genealogy of the Davis family. 18907

Monthly journal, devoted to the principles of
1776 and 1787. (57133)
Monthly journal for teachers, parents, and
children. 77811
Monthly journal for the farm and garden, etc.
(17869)
Monthly journal of agriculture. 50176 see also
Farmer's library and monthly journal of
agriculture.
Monthly journal of choice reading. 84982
Monthly journal of education. 50177
Monthly journal, of literature, art and science.
88385
Monthly journal of medical literature. 50178
Monthly journal of medicine. 50178
Monthly journal of sacred symbols and prophecy
31732
Monthly journal [of the American Unitarian
Association.] 1255
Monthly journal of the National Freedmen's
Relief Association. 51981
Monthly journal of the United Brethren in
America. 50524
Monthly jubilee. 50179
Monthly law magazine. (41626), 50180
Monthly law reporter. 50180
Monthly legal examiner. 50180
Monthly letter to a friend in Holland. 53808
Monthly literary journal. 98050
Monthly literary journal. Editors. 98050
Monthly magazine. see American museum
of science, literature, and the arts. A
monthly magazine. Anti-masonic review
and monthly magazine. Belles-lettres
repository; an monthly magazine. Freemason; a monthly magazine. Ladies'
companion. A monthly magazine. Leisure
hours. A monthly magazine. Literary
museum or monthly magazine. Masonic
record; a monthly magazine. Michigan
freemason; a monthly magazine. Rhode-
Island literary repository, a monthly
magazine. Smith & Barrow's monthly
magazine. Southern literary journal, and
monthly magazine.
Monthly magazine (1806-   ) (50181),
102166
Monthly magazine and American review.
1213, 50182
Monthly magazine, consisting of original performances. (63893)
Monthly magazine devoted mainly to a discussion
of African slavery. 88337
Monthly magazine devoted to agriculture,
horticulture, manufactures, and mechanic
arts. 88359
Monthly magazine, devoted to criminal reform.
65712, 89068, 89070
Monthly magazine, devoted to freemasonry and
its literature. 51666
Monthly magazine, devoted to historical tales.
88682
Monthly magazine, devoted to religion. 67419
Monthly magazine, devoted to the advancement
of general literature. 41484
Monthly magazine, devoted to the dissemination
of political information. 70005
Monthly magazine, devoted to the interests of
the freed colored people. 25736
Monthly magazine devoted to the interests of
the legal profession. 84887
Monthly magazine devoted to the interests of
the Sunday school. 93744
Monthly magazine. Edited by W. M. Reynolds.
50183

Monthly magazine for literature, philosophy, and religion. 19921

Monthly magazine of agriculture, horticulture, home improvement, and family literature. 55741

Monthly magazine of American literature, politics, and art. 70004

Monthly magazine of American literature, science, and art. (66843)

Monthly magazine of choice literature. 66520

Monthly magazine of horticulture, agriculture, botany, agricultural chemistry, entomology, &c. 24906

Monthly magazine of literature, science, and art. 57618

Monthly magazine of select literature. 88395

Monthly magazine of tales, sketches, poetry, music, engravings. 41484

Monthly medical news. 89453

Monthly mercury. 97458

Monthly military repository. 50185, 82375, 82379

Monthly mirror. 95331

Monthly miscellany. 12911 see also Colonial magazine, or monthly miscellany. Huntingdon literary museum, and monthly miscellany. Medley, or monthly miscellany.

Monthly miscellany containing a view of the history. 14869, note after 97998

Monthly miscellany of religion and letters. 50186

Monthly miscellany, or memoirs for the curious. 50187

Monthly miscellany or Vermont magazine. 50188, 1st note after 99197

Monthly museum. see Massachusetts monthly museum.

Monthly museum of knowledge and rational entertainment. 45870, 95409, 95411, 2d note after 95414

Monthly museum of southern literature. 84870

Monthly nautical magazine. (50189)

Monthly observations and predictions for the present year, 1692. 62743

Monthly observations and predictions for this present year. 58966

Monthly offering. 50190

Monthly paper. 14996

Monthly periodical conducted by an association of students. 47355, 105851

Monthly periodical, containing chiefly selections from the best catholic reviews. (69337)

Monthly periodical, devoted to agriculture, horticulture, and the household arts. 88445

Monthly periodical devoted to literature and religion. see Ladies' repository, and gatherings of the west. Southern lady's companion, a monthly periodical.

Monthly periodical devoted to odd fellowship and general literature. 26773

Monthly periodical, devoted to the investigation of every variety of rituals in religion. 83830

Monthly periodical. Edited and published by the Erodeephian [sic] and Union Literary Societies of Miami University. (41482)

Monthly phonographic magazine. 50191

Monthly planet reader. 8426

Monthly publication. 26970

Monthly publication.—April. (74151)

Monthly publication designed to improve the soil and the mind. (17869)

Monthly publication devoted to agriculture, commerce, manufactures, and the arts. 1105, (36716)

Monthly publication of sermons by living ministers. 40919

Monthly reader for school and home instruction of youth. 77888

Monthly record. 85475

Monthly record of church missions. 50192

Monthly record of geography. 73792

Monthly record of surgical science. 10381

Monthly record . . . [of the Five Points House of Industry.] 54280

Monthly recorder. 50193

Monthly register and review of the United States. 50194

Monthly register of new publications. (6366)

Monthly religious magazine (1844-   ) 28688, (50195), 71786 see also Lutheran pulpit, and monthly religious magazine.

Monthly religious magazine and independent journal. (71769), 71778

Monthly report . . . see Report . . .

Monthly repository. 10570 see also New Church herald, and monthly repository. Philadelphia magazine and review, or monthly repository.

Monthly review. see Literary miscellany; or, monthly review. South western literary journal and monthly review. Southern literary journal and monthly review. Southern magazine and monthly review. Western literary journal, and monthly review.

Monthly review and literary miscellany of the United States. 50199

Monthly review: devoted to the civil government of Canada. 50200

Monthly review of medical and surgical science. 9063

Monthly review of the most interesting political occurrences. 14001

Monthly review of the political occurrences. 14002

Monthly reivew; or, literary journal. 26429, 50198, 84589, note after 102651

Monthly review. Samuel Harrison Smith, submits to the patronage. 84077

Monthly rose. 50201

Monthly scientific journal. 50202

Monthly table of daily means of meteorological elements. 76337

Monthly traveller. (50203)

Monthly Tuesday Lecture, Pembrook, Mass. see Pembrook, Mass. Monthly Tuesday Lecture.

Monthly view of the political state of the British colonies. 1139

Monthly visitor. (50259)

Monticello Academy, Sullivan County, N. Y. 50205

Monticello Female Seminary, Ill. (50204)

Montigny, ----- de. see Buisson, Jean Francois.

Montiguy, ------ Dumont de. see Dumont de Montiguy, -------, Lieutenant.

Montiguy, Gabirle Lucas de. see Lucas de Montiguy, Gabriel, b. 1782.

Montirat, -------- de. tr. 100944

Montizambert, Edward L. 50207

Montlezun, ---------, Baron de. 50208-50210, note after 100813

Montlinot, C. (50211)

Montlong, Wilhelm van. (50212)

Montluc, A. de. 74762

Montmignon, Jean Baptiste. 50213

Montmorency, Francois de Laval de. see
Laval de Montmorency, Francois de.

Montoro, Reinaldo Carlos. 50214

Montoto, Genaro. 50215

Montour County. Pa. Reception to Henry C.
Carey, 1859. 10841, note after 94911

Montour Falls, N. Y. People's College.
30867-(30868), 60820

Montoya, Antonio Ruiz de. see Ruiz de
Montoya, Antonio.

Montoya, Ignacio Jose de Urrutia y. see
Urrutia y Montoya, Ignacio Jose de.

Montoya, Ignacio Joseph de Urruha. 50216

Montoya, Isidro Sicilia y. see Sicilia y
Montoya, Isidro.

Montoya, Josef Gonzalez y. see Gonzalez
Montoya, Josef.

Montoya, Juan de, fl. 1602. 69210

Montpalau, Antonio. 50217

Montpelier, Vt. Anti-masonic State Convention
1829. see Antimasonic State Convention
of Vermont, Montpelier, 1829.

Montpelier, Vt. Anti-masonic State Convention,
1830. see Antimasonic State Convention
of Vermont, Montpelier, 1830.

Montpelier, Vt. Anti-masonic State Convention,
1831. see Antimasonic State Convention
of Vermont, Montpelier, 1831.

Montpelier, Vt. Anti-masonic State Convention,
1833. see Antimasonic State Convention
of Vermont, Montpelier, 1833.

Montpelier, Vt. Democratic Party Convention,
1828. see Democratic Party. Vermont.
Convention, Montpelier, 1828.

Montpelier, Vt. Green Mount Cemetery. 50219

Montpelier, Vt. Republican Convention Friendly
to the Election of Andrew Jackson to the
Next Presidency of the United States,
1828. see Democratic Party. Vermont.
Convention, Montpelier, 1828.

Montpelier, Vt. Washington County Grammar
School. see Washington County Grammar School, Montpelier, Vt.

Montpelier Congregational Association. see
Congregational Churches in Vermont.
Montpelier Congregational Association.

Montpleinchamp, Jean Chrysostome Brusle
de. see Brusle de Montpleinchamp,
Jean Chrysostome.

Montreal, Bishop of. see Fulford, Francis,
Bishop of Montreal, 1803-1868.
Mountain, George Jehosaphat, successively
Bishop of Montreal, and Quebec, 1789-
1863.

Montreal. 50155, 50281, 59148

Montreal. Advocate's Library. see Advocate's
Library, Montreal.

Montreal. Association a la Propagation de
la Foi. see Association de la Propagation de la Foi, Montreal.

Montreal. Board of Works. 50277

Montreal. Cabinet de Lecture. 73520

Montreal. Canada Education and Home
Missionary Society. see Canada Educa-
tion and Home Missionary Society,
Montreal.

Montreal. Census. 50284

Montreal. Central Auxiliary Society for promoting Education and Industry Among
the Indians and Destitute Settlers in
Canada. see Central Auxiliary Society
for Promoting Education and Industry
Among the Indians and Destitute Settlers
in Canada, Montreal.

Montreal. Charter. 50246

Montreal. Chief of Police. see Montreal.
Police. Chief.

Montreal. City Council. 74983

Montreal. City Council. Police Committee.
38769, 74983

Montreal. City Surveyor. (50278)

Montreal. Convention Anti-seigneurial, 1854.
see Convention Anti-seigneurial, Montreal
1854.

Montreal. Cour du Banc du Roi. see
Montreal. Court of King's Bench.

Montreal. Court of King's Bench. 84409,
99598

Montreal. Ecole de Medecine. see Ecole de
Medecine, Montreal.

Montreal. Harbor Commissioners. 75471

Montreal. Inspector of Buildings. 50240

Montreal. Inspector of Roads. 50274

Montreal. Ladies' Benevolent Society. see
Ladies' Benevolent Society, Montreal.

Montreal. Library. (50265)

Montreal. Magill University. see Magill
University, Montreal.

Montreal. Mayor, 1849. 50251

Montreal. Mechanics' Institute. see
Mechanics' Institute of Montreal.

Montreal. Meeting of the Friends and Admirer
of Lord Metcalf, 1847. see Meeting of
the Friends and Admirers of Lord
Metcalf, Montreal, 1847.

Montreal. Mercantile Library Association.
see Mercantile Library Association of
Montreal.

Montreal. Natural History Society. see
Natural History Society of Montreal.

Montreal. New-England Society. see New-
England Society of Montreal.

Montreal. Ordinances, etc. 50244, 50246, (50248

Montreal. Police. Chief. 50240

Montreal. Societe Bienveillante de Notre Dame
de Bonsecours. see Societe Bienveillante
de Notre Dame de Bonsecours, Montreal.

Montreal. Societe de Construction Metropolitai
see Societe de Construction Metropoli-
taine, Montreal.

Montreal. Societe de Nostre Dame de Montrea
Pour la Conuersion des Sauuages de la
Nouuelle France. see Societe de Nostre
Dame de Montreal Pour la Conuersion des
Sauuages de la Nouuelle France.

Montreal. Societe du Feu. see Societe du
Feu, Montreal.

Montreal. Societe Historique. see Societe
Historique de Montreal.

Montreal. Societe Permanente de Construction
Jacques Cartier. see Societe Permanente
de Construction Jacques Cartier, Montreal.

Montreal. Societe for Religious Liberty and
Equality. see Society for Religious
Liberty and Equality, Montreal.

Montreal. Society for the Propagation of the
Faith. see Society for the Propagation
of the Faith, Montreal.

Montreal. Special Sanitary Committee upon
Cholera and Emigration, 1834. 50279

Montreal. Supreme Court of Judicature.
96858

Montreal. Treasurer. 50242

Montreal. Trinity House. 96987

Montreal. University Lying-In Hospital.
50244

Montreal. Water Committee. 50280

Montreal. Superintendent of the Water Works.
(50241)

Montreal (Comte) Assemblee des Electeurs, St. Laurent, 1837. 65748
Montreal (Comte) Comite Central et Permanent. 65748
Montreal (Diocese) Association Diocesaine de Ville-Marie. Conseil Central. 50239
Montreal (District) petitioners (56545)
Montreal (District) Societe de Construction. see Societe de Construction du District de Montreal.
Montreal almanack. 50258
Montreal and Kingston Railway Company. 50257
"Montreal" and "the Ottawa:" two lectures. 37146
Montreal Auxiliary Bible Society. 50240
Montreal city advertiser and monthly visitor. (50259)
Montreal city directory. 50261
Montreal daily advertiser. 98073
Montreal directory. (50260)
Montreal et ses principaux monuments. 50262
Montreal gazette. 96495
Montreal herald. 10600, 20697, 42927, 43146, 95369, 95373, 98978
Montreal Historical Society. see Societe Historique de Montreal.
Montreal Horticultural Society. 50263
Montreal in 1856. 50264
Montreal Mining Company. 50266
Montreal monthly journal of medicine & surgery. 47313
Montreal museum. 50267
Montreal pilot. 50268
Montreal pocket almanack. 52069, note after 90523
Montreal Protestant Orphan Asylum. 50240
Montreal River Mining Company of Lake Superior. 50270
Montreal Sanitary Association. 50240
Montreal story. 74452
Montreal transcript. 7121
Montresor, J. 50221, 91057
Montrol, F. de. 85816
Montrond, Maxime de. 50222
Monts, --------, Sieur de. 40175-40176, 50223, 57765
Montserrat, Guillaume de. 11238
Montserrat. Assembly. 26102
Montserrat. Laws, statutes, etc. (50224)-(50226)
Montserrat. President of the Council. 26102 see also Frye, George.
Montserrat code of laws. (50226)
Montucla, --------. tr. 11188
Montufar, Alonso de, Abp. (42063) see also Mexico (Archdiocese) Archbishop (Montufar)
Montufar, Lorenco de. 56617 see also Guatemala (Colony) Secretario de Camara.
Montufar, Manuel. incorrectly supposed author 45020, 50228, 59179
Montule, Edouard de. (50229)-50230, 62509
Montuval, -----------, Marques de. 50231
Monumens de tous les peuples. 7738
Monument. 50232
Monument a Christophe Colomb. 36435
Monument Association of New Jersey. see New Jersey Monument Association.
Monument Cemetery, Philadelphia. see Philadelphia. Monument Cemetery.
Monument Cemetery. By-laws of the . . . managers. 61846
Monument Cemetery of Philadelphia. (Late Pere la Chaise.) 61846

Monument of a beneficent mission from Boston to St. Johns. 50233
Monument of infamy to Dr. Leib. 39889
Monument of parential affection to a dear and only son. 27462
Monument of patriotism, being a collection of biographical sketches. 73840
Monument of patriotism. Biographical sketches. 72699
Monument of thankfulness. 26818
Monument placed before the Senate by Charles Gould. 24561
Monument to Bishop White. 61758
Monument to the memory of General Andrew Jackson. 21445
Monument to the memory of Henry Clay. 11050
Monument to the praise of the Lord's goodness. 17962
Monument to the victims of prison ships. 51465
Monumenta politico-ecclesiastica. 91723
Monumenta saecularia. 38347
Monumental engraving. 101856
Monumental gratitude attempted. 50235, 105936
Monumental inscription, Latin and English. 58057, 104989
Monumental inscriptions to the seven mutineers. 50236
Monumental memorial of marine mercy. 91184
Monumental memorials of the Appleton family. (1810), 50237
Monumental remains of Georgia. 36479
Monumenti relativi al giudizo pronunziato. 10707
Monumentos de Mejico tomados del natural y lithographiados. 29048
Monumentos historicos del Nuevo Mundo Peruano. 75784
Monumentos literarios del Peru. 71450
Monumentos pertenecientes a las controversias de los regulares. 10803
Monuments anciens du Mexique. 7345
Monuments anciens du Mexique. Palenque, Ococingo et autres ruins. 7434
Monuments de la geographie. 36432, 77804
Monuments, grave stones, burying grounds, cemeteries, temples, etc. 43147
Monuments of a beneficent mission from Boston to St. John's. 105269
Monuments of New Spain. (37800)
Monuments of patriotism. 101748
Monuments of the Cathedral Church and Parish of St. Catherine. 72263
Monuments of Washington's patriotism. 101724
Monuments to the memory of General Andrew Jackson. 94403
Mooar, George. (50293)
Mood, F. A. (50294)
Moodey, Joshua, 1633-1697. 727, (2112), 33442, 37209, (46466), 46632, 50295-50299, note after 104098 see also Ministers of the Gospel in Boston.
Moodey, Samuel. (50300)-50303
Moodie, Susanna (Strickland) 1803-1885. 50304-50306
Moodie, Susanna (Strickland) 1803-1885. incorrectly supposed author 10607, 2d note after 98090
Moody, --------. plaintiff 104413
Moody, Charles C. P. 50307
Moody, G. USA (50308)
Moody, James, 1744?-1809. 9538, (50309)-50311
Moody, Loring. 50314-50318, 53232

Moody, Ruel B. (50319)
Moody, Samuel. (50312)
Moody, Silas. 50320
Moody, Thomas. 50321
Moody. firm see Dakin & Moody. firm
Moon, Charles W. (50322)
Moon, Henry Frederic. alias see Smith,
   Henry More.
Moon story. 28839
Mooney, Thomas. 50323
Mooney. firm lithographers see Hall &
   Mooney. firm lithographers
Moor, ---------. RN (19715)
Moor, C. R. 50324
Moor, Richard. 36679
Moore, ---------. defendant (28610), 50334
Moore, ----------, fl. 1820. 11958
Moore, Major. pseud. see Hines, David
   Theodore.
Moore, A. Y. 50326
Moore, Alpheus. 50325
Moore, Andrew Barry, 1807-1873. 33150
   see also Alabama. Governor, 1857-
   1861 (Moore)
Moore, Archy. pseud. Slave. see Hildreth,
   Richard.
Moore, Asher. 50327
Moore, Augusta. ed. 4318, 50328
Moore, Bartholomew Figures, 1801-1878.
   50330, (55688)
Moore, Benjamin, Bp., 1748-1816. 9430,
   41348, (50329), 84680, 104326
Moore, Benjamin F. 66298
Moore, Charles B. 50331
Moore, Charles W. (25809), 45760, 50332-
   (50333), 101849 see also Masonic
   mirror and mechanics' intelligencer.
   Editor.
Moore, Charles W. defendant 50334
Moore, Clement Clarke, 1779-1863. (28481),
   35908, 50335-50339, 54580, 72717
Moore, Cornelius. 50340-(50341)
Moore, D. 50343
Moore, D. D. T. 24683, 50344
Moore, Daniel. (35710), 94137
Moore, David. 101936
Moore, Dugald. 50345
Moore, E. D. 50349
Moore, Edward. 50346
Moore, Edwin W. defendant 95005
Moore, Ely, 1798-1861. 50347-(50348)
Moore, F. see Mone, Frederick.
Moore, F. A. 50374
Moore, Francis, Jr. (50353), 95126
Moore, Francis, fl. 1744. 50352
Moore, Frank, 1828-1904. 3562, 7965, 7967,
   36170-36173, 39749, 40590, 41029,
   (43011), 43370, 50354-50371, 59088,
   note after 68327, 74401, 89506, 89687-
   89688, 92297, 92299, 94431, 104873
Moore, Franklin. (50373)
Moore, Gabriel. (50375)-(50376)
Moore, George. 50377
Moore, George A. 102920
Moore, George C. 50378
Moore, George H. (50379)-50381, 74871,
   79446
Moore, H. Judge. 50386
Moore, Mrs. H. Judge. 50387
Moore, H. N. (50388)-(50389)
Moore, Henry, 1751-1844. 14252, 14338,
   50382, 103661, 103663
Moore, Henry, fl. 1860. 50383
Moore, Henry D. (50384)-(50385)
Moore, Hugh. 50390
Moore, Humphrey. (50391)

Moore, Mrs. J. T. 94750
Moore, Jacob Bailey, 1797-1853. 7222, 18055,
   23837-23839, 36327, 50392-(50398),
   52884, 65234, 73592, 94112, note after
   99796, 100759, note after 105101
Moore, Jacob Bailey, 1797-1853. supposed
   author 269, (50398), note after 99796,
   note after 105101
Moore, Jacob Bailey, 1797-1853. incorrectly
   supposed author 16181, 30577
Moore, James, of Pennsylvania. 50399, 90149
Moore, James, Surgeon, 9th Pennsylvania
   Cavalry. 37744, 50401-50403
Moore, James, fl. 1796. 96458
Moore, James, fl. 1808. 50400
Moore, James Lovell. 50405
Moore, John, M. D. 50408
Moore, John, successively Bishop of Norwich,
   and Ely, 1646-1714. 50406
Moore, John, Archbishop of Canterbury, 1730-
   1805. 50407
Moore, Sir John, 1761-1809. 98839
Moore, John, fl. 1794-1829. defendant 96943
Moore, John C. 77530
Moore, John F. 66298
Moore, John G. 50409
Moore, John Hamilton, d. 1807. 44590, 50410-
   50413, 55448, 90270
Moore, John S. 37339
Moore, John Weeks, 1807-1889. 50414
Moore, John Wilson, 1789-1865. 50430
Moore, Sir Jonas. 50415
Moore, Josiah. 50416, 103045 see also Dux-
   bury, Mass. First Parish. Committee.
Moore, Lindley Murray. (50417)
Moore, M. A. 50425
Moore, M. B. 50426-50427
Moore, Madeline. 50418
Moore, Mark. (50419)
Moore, Martin. 50420-(50424)
Moore, Mollie E. 50428
Moore, N. F. 50429
Moore, Nathaniel Schuyler. 105937
Moore, R. 50433
Moore, Rachel Wilson. 50430
Moore, Richard. 50431
Moore, Richard, fl. 1762. 50432
Moore, Richard Channing, Bp. 31427
Moore, Roger. 50434
Moore, S. S. 50436
Moore, Samuel. 3280
Moore, Samuel McDowell, 1796-1875. 50435
Moore, Samuel W., 1786-1854. 50437
Moore, Sydenham, 1817-1862. 50438
Moore, T. V. 50449-(50450)
Moore, Theophilus. 50439
Moore, Thomas, pseud. 26331, 49221, 50441-
   50442, (54837)
Moore, Thomas, of Maryland. 50444
Moore, Sir Thomas. see More, Sir Thomas,
   Saint, 1458-1535.
Moore, Sir Thomas, d. 1735. 50440
Moore, Thomas, fl. 1746. 50443
Moore, Thomas, 1779-1852. 50445-50447,
   100663
Moore, Thomas L. 50448
Moore, Thomas Overton, 1805-1876. 42234
   see also Louisiana. Governor, 1860-1862
   (Moore)
Moore, Thompson. 50451
Moore, W. 50452
Moore, W. W. 50457
Moore, William Thomas, 1832- 50453-50454
Moore, William V. pseud. Indian wars of the
   United States. see Frost, John.
Moore, William W. 50456, 97950

Moore, Zephaniah Swift, 1770-1823. 50458-
(50459), 89138, 1st note after 104432
Moore. firm publishers see Damrell &
Moore and George Coolidge. firm
publishers Hill and Moore. firm
publishers
Moore (D. T.) firm publishers 24683
Moore (J. W.) firm publishers 82987
Moore (James B.) and Company. petitioners
50404
Moore's American country almanack. 50443
Moore's hand-book of Montreal, Quebec, and
Ottawa. 50460
Moores Hill, Indiana. Male and Female Col-
legiate Institute. see Moore's Hill Male
and Female Collegiate Institute, Moores
Hill, Indiana.
Moore's Hill Male and Female Collegiate
Institute, Moores Hill, Indiana. 50461
Moore's rural manuals, no. 1. 24683, 50344
Moore's rural New-Yorker. 50344
Moore's select library. 82987
Moorfields, Eng. Public Meeting Held at Fins-
bury Chapel, to Receive Frederick
Douglass, 1846. see Public Meeting
Held at Finsbury Chapel, to Receive
Frederick Douglass, Moorfields, Eng.,
1846.
Moorhead, James Kennedy, 1866-1884. 8382,
37274, 50463
Moorhead, John. 55, 50462, 58896, 95745
Moorhead, Sarah (Parsons) 18700, 50464,
96025
Moorhead, Thomas. 50465
Moorman, John J. 50466-50470
Moorman, T. T. 9318
Moormann, John J. see Moorman, John J.
Moors, John F. (50471)
Moor's Indian Charity School, Lebanon, Conn.
see Indian Charity-School, Lebanon, Conn.
Moorsom, W. 50472
Moose-hunter. 52161
Moosmuller, Oswald. 50473
Moosthal, Erwin von. tr. 16485
Mooy, Maarten. 50474
Mopso al tatita. 76222
Mor de Fuentes, Jos. see Fuentes, Jos. Mor
de.
Mora, Agustin. supposed author 76168
Mora, Andres Sanchez. see Sanchez Mora,
Andres.
Mora, Antonia. 50475
Mora, Geronimo. 50477
Mora, J. A. de. 50478-50480
Mora, Jose Joaquin de, 1793-1864. 50481,
(70315), (72204)
Mora, Jose Maria. 50482
Mora, Jose Maria Luis. 50483-(50484)
Mora, Juan Gomez de. see Gomez de Mora,
Juan.
Mora, Miguel Diez de la. see Diez de la
Mora, Miguel.
Moraes, Alexandre Jose de Mello. see Mello
Moraes, Alexandre Jose de, 1816-1882.
Moraes, Eduardo Jose de. 50485
Moraes, Emanuel de. 7588, 63028
Moraes da Silva, A. de. tr. 32035
Moraes Navarra, Jose Gregorio de. 50486
Moraes y Vasconcelos, Francisco Botello de.
see Botello de Moraes y Vasconcelos,
Francisco.
Moragne, Miss. see Davis, Mary Elizabeth
(Moragne) b. 1815.
Moragne, W. C. (50488)
Morais, S. 50489-(50490)

Moral y Castillo, Jose Antonio de. 50491
Moral almanac, for . . . 1852. (50492)
Moral and entertaining letters. 73541
Moral and intellectual influence of libraries.
19626
Moral and physical thermometer. note after
74241
Moral and political condition of the republic.
48913, 95117, 1st note after 95515.
Moral and political sketch of the United States.
51417
Moral and political theory in trade, and taxes.
97341
Moral and political truth. 31618
Moral and political work. (30222)
Moral and religious aspect of the future
America. 38865
Moral and religious influences of autumn.
46853
Moral and religious quotations from the poets.
70863
Moral and religious sketches and collections.
11062
Moral and religious tale. 17615
Moral and religious uses of mechanical exhi-
bitions. 103758
Moral and scientific dialogues. 89368
Moral and social benefits of cheap postage.
39564
Moral and theological review. 12921
Moral aspect and destitution of the city of New-
York. 3210
Moral aspect of California. (23810)
Moral aspect of our country. 55324
Moral aspects of city life. 11947
Moral aspects of the national capital. 4572
Moral causes of the welfare of nations. 220
Moral character of civil government. 43569
Moral character of the American government.
50493
Moral dignity of the missionary enterprise.
102189
Moral disquisitions. 89894, 89797, 94368
Moral distichs, and Lily's paedogigical admoni-
tions. 91846
Moral distichs. Englished in couplets. 11548,
13040
Moral domestic drama in five acts. 84782-
84784, 84786
Moral domestic drama of American life. 84785
Moral education. A lecture, delivered on the
sixteenth of August. 22429
Moral education. An address . . . before the
teachers and pupils. 42714
Moral education. By a disciple of the Old
School philosophy. (50494)
Moral heroism. 14417
Moral influence of manufacturing towns. 19896
Moral influence of the American government.
30455
Moral instructor, and guide to virtue and
happiness. 96288-96294
Moral law the essential element of American
liberty. 31636
Moral machinery simplified. 16329
Moral mas bien enxerto. 36091
Moral maxims and reflections. 90235
Moral meaning of our present commercial
difficulties. 4755
Moral miscellanies. 83667
Moral monitor. 24549
Moral ode for the year 1771. 103637
Moral of history. (26054)
Moral pieces in prose and verse. 90833, 90843
Moral reflection, on the sudden death. 94156

Moral Reform Society, Salem, Mass. 102588
Moral responsibility of the citizen and nation.
  80130
Moral resurrection. 62772
Moral review of the revolutionary war.
  36841
Moral revolution. 103380
Moral rule of political action. 62772
Moral significance of the contrasts between
  slavery and freedom. 29657, 29828
Moral significance of the Crystal Palace.
  4575
Moral significance of war. 2752
Moral Society, Yale University. see Yale
  University. Moral Society.
Moral state of nations. (50495), 91693
Moral story, for youth. 86825
Moral suasion without law. 77023
Moral tale. 83511
Moral tale, founded on facts. 105693
Moral views of commerce, society and politics.
  19858
Moralejo, J. M. tr. 12274, 16557
Morales, Ambrosio de, 1513-1591. (54096),
  75568
Morales, Antonio Bachiller y. see Bachiller
  y Morales, Antonio.
Morales, C. D. C. Anastaf de. pseud. Vida
  de Hernan-Cortes. see San Rafael,
  Tomas de.
Mrales, Carlos Ruiz. see Ruiz Morales,
  Carlos.
Morales, Christoval Ruiz Guerra y. see Ruiz
  Guerra y Morales, Christoval.
Morales, Felix Varela y. see Varela y
  Morales, Felix, 1788-1853.
Morales, Francisco Jose de. 100630
Morales, J. Antonio Davila. 50497
Morales, J. B. 50498
Morales, Juan Bautista, 1788-1856. 42911,
  50499
Morales, L. (50502)
Morales, Rodrigo de Torres y. see Torres
  y Morales, Rodrigo de.
Morales, V. 50504
Morales Chofre, Mateo. see Chofre, Mateo
  Morales.
Morales Pastrana, Antonio. see Pastrana,
  Antonio Morales.
Morales Sigala, Geronimo. see Sigala, Gero-
  nimo Morales.
Morales Valverde, Juan de. (72290)
Morales y Ugalde, Jose de. 50500-50501
  see also Peru. Ministerio de Hacienda.
Morales Lemus y la revolucion de Cuba.
  62942
Moralista filalethico Americano. (46971)
Moraliste Americain. (61510)
Moralite treselegante composee par le susdit
  Ian Parmentier. 58825
Morality and the state. 51851
Morality not to be relied on for life. 104095
Morality of a citizen. 50505
Morality of public men. 99256
Morality of public men. A second letter.
  99256
Morality of the Nebraska bill. 50506
Morality of the riot. 26077
Morality, religion, & salvation. 92790
Morals of freedom. 11869
Morals of manners. 78770, 78795
Morals of pleasure. 78829, 106134
Morals of slavery. 81240, 82091, 7th note
  after 88114
Moran, Charles. 50507
Moran, Thomas. illus. 84041

Moran, Trinidad. 57450
Moran, William. ed. 48568
Moran de Butron, Jacinto, 1668-1749. 9665,
  50508-50509
Moran y Crivelli, Tomas. 50510
Morancy, Alexandre. 50511
Moranda, Antonio de la Torre. see Torre
  Miranda, Antonio de la.
Morande, Theveneau de. 17165
Morandiere, ------- Turmeau de la. see
  Turmeau de la Morandiere, -------.
Morange, William D. 50512
Morato, Francisco Manuel Tirgoso de Aragua.
  50513
Moravian and antinomian justification consider
  20059
Moravian Brethren. see Moravians. and
  United Brethren.
Moravian church miscellany. 50524
Moravian College, Bethlehem, Pa. see Mora
  vian Seminary and College for Women,
  Bethlehem, Pa.
Moravian heresy. 72311
Moravian Historical Society, Nazareth, Pa.
  47671, 50526, 68988, (68991), 68993
Moravian Indian boy. 50525
Moravian manual. 78102
Moravian mission among the Germans. (2950
Moravian Seminary and College for Women,
  Bethlehem, Pa. 50516-50517, 68989-
  68990
Moravian Seminary for Young Ladies, Bethleh
  Pa. see Moravian Seminary and Colle
  for Women, Bethlehem, Pa.
Moravian Young Ladies' Seminary, Bethlehem
  Pa. see Moravian Seminary and Colle
  for Women, Bethlehem, Pa.
Moravians. 4223, 58940, 80611, 97858 see
  also Bohemian Brethren. and United
  Brethren.
Moravians. Directors of the Missionary Con-
  cerns. see United Brethren. Director
  of the Missionary Concerns.
Moravians. Missionaries to Greenland. 3489
Moravians in Dutchess County. 18883
Moravians in Greenland. 97855
Moravians in Labrador. 97856
Moravians in North Carolina. 68986
Morazan, F. 50527
Morceaux choisis de la conquete du Mexique.
  86485
Morceaux choisis des lettres edifiantes et
  curieuses. 9847
Morceaux inedits de morale et de litterature.
  12269
Morch, Otto Andreas Lowson, 1828-1878.
  71433-71435
Morcillo Rubio de Aunon, Alfonso Carrio y.
  see Carrio y Morcillo Rubio de Aunon,
  Alfonso.
Mordacque, L. H. tr. (50530), (75878)
Mordecai, Alfred. 8582, 50531-50532
Mordecai, Samuel. 50533-50534
Mordecai Servertus. pseud. Mystic's plea.
  see Winchester, Elhanan.
Morden, Robert, d. 1703. (9920), 18556, 505
  78218
More, C. pseud. Series of letters. see
  Smith, Seymour R.
More, Caleb. (50536), 101454
More, Franz Joseph. see Mone, Franz Jose
  1796-1871.
More, George H. 79446
More, H., fl. 1663. 101877
More, Hannah, 1745-1833. 50538
More, John J. 50540

More, Juan de. 50539
More, Roger, pseud. 54082-54083
More, Thomas, pseud. 64089-64091, 87756-87759
More, Sir Thomas, Saint, 1478-1535. 50542
More divisions amongst the Quakers. 37185, 37202
More exact, plain, and easie introduction. 13692
More excellent observations of the estate and affaires of Holland. 20233, 49557-49558, 102989, 3d note after 102896
More humorsome and interesting "traveller's guide to the west." 104013
More impartial and comprehensive view of the dispute. 29955
More important incidents in the life of William Delany Patton. 59165
More just vindication of the Honourable Sir William Keith. 37243
More laborers needed for the Gospel harvest. 17327
More last words to these churches. 50996
More light on masonry. 50548
More news from Robinson Crusoes island. (68724)
More nevvs from Virginia. 100448
More particular . . . account of Quebec. 10330
More particular history of the two great revulsions. 7887
More private conference of a minister with them. 46271
More than conqueror. 50549
More than one hundred reasons why William Henry Harrison should and will have the support of the Democracy. (50550), 105470
More thoughts, occasioned by two publications. 44705
More thoughts still on the state of the West-India colonies. 44706
More wonders of the invisible world. 9926-9927, (19046), 20884, 75736, 89927
More work for George Keith. 59718
More work for the Maine law. 12991, 44456
More Yankee drolleries. 79913
Moreau, --------. 50563
Moreau, C. 50561
Moreau, Cesar, 1791-1829. 50562
Moreau, Henry. petitioner 50564-(50565)
Moreau, Joseph N. 50567
Moreau, Pierre. 50724, (50579)-(50580)
Moreau, Rene. tr. 14544
Moreau de Dammartin, --------. 50566
Moreau de Jonnes, Alexandre. 50551-50560
Moreau de Maupertuis, Pierre Louis. see Maupertuis, Pierre Louis Moreau de.
Moreau de Saint-Mery, Mederic Louis Elie, 1750-1819. 2537, (50568)-50576, 50578, 67522
Moreau de Saint-Mery, Mederic Louis Elie, 1750-1819. incorrectly supposed author 39053-(39054), 50576-50577
Morehead, Charles Slaughter, 1802-1868. 33150, 37535, 50581 see also Kentucky. Governor, 1855-1859 (Morehead)
Morehead, D. C. (50582)
Morehead, James Turner, 1797-1854. 37519, 50583
Morehead's family almanac for . . . 1859. (50582)
Morehouse, Abraham. 50696, 105629
Morehouse, George R. 85072
Morehouse, H. L. (50584)
Moreira, Carvalho. 50585

Moreira, J. de C. 50586
Moreira, Jacinto Calero y. see Calero y Moreira, Jacinto.
Moreira, Nicolao Joaquim. 50587-50588
Moreiras, Francisco Javier. 96238-96239, 99790 see also Colchagua (Chilean Province) Intendente.
Morejon, Juan Antonio. 50589
Morejon, Pedro. 7926, 1st note after 100872, note after 105625
Morel de Santa Cruz, Pedro Agustin, Bp. (50590) see also Cuba (Diocese) Bishop (Morel de Santa Cruz)
Moreland, John R. 92028
Morelet, Arthur. 50591-50594
Morelia, Mexico. 69986
Morelia, Mexico. Ciudadanos. 75774
Morellet, Andre. (35895), 50595-50597, (52216), 71991, 71993-71995, 72013, 2d note after 100506
Morellet, C. tr. 98441
Morelli, Ab. see Morelli, Jacobo.
Morelli, Cyrianci. pseud. Fasti novi orbis. see Muriel, Domingo.
Morelli, Jacobo. 1547, 14643, (50598)
Morenas, --------. (49434)
Morenas, J. 50600
Moreno, --------. illus. 35325
Moreno, A. M. 50602
Moreno, Celso Cesare. (50603)
Moreno, Diego. 50604
Moreno, Francisco Javier. 98879
Moreno, Gabriel. 61076
Moreno, Geronymo. (50605)
Moreno, J. Demetrio. 50606
Moreno, Jose Ignacio. 50607-50608
Moreno, Jose Maria. 50609, 70308
Moreno, Juan Becerra. 50610
Moreno, Juan Joseph. 47952, 50611
Moreno, M. 50615
Moreno, Manuel, 1782-1857. 39886, 49757, 50613-50614 see also Argentine Republic. Legation. Great Britain.
Moreno, Manuel Antonio. (40063)-40064, 50617
Moreno, Martim Soares. see Soares Moreno, Martim, 1586?-
Moreno, Martin de San Antonio. see San Antonio Moreno, Martin de.
Moreno de Texada, J. Prudencio. 50612
Moreno Porcel, Francisco. see Porcel, Francisco Moreno.
Moreno Solano, Fernando C. see Solano, Fernando C. Moreno.
Moreno y Castro, Alonso Francisco. 50601
Moreno y Castro, Juan, Marques de Valle-Ameno. (50075)
Moreno y Jove, Manuel. 50616
More's almanack for 1773. 87759
More's almanack, for the year of Christian account, 1770. 87756
More's almanack, for the year of Christian account, 1771. 87757
More's almanack, for the year of Christian account, 1772. 87758
More's country almanack for the year of Christian account, 1765. 64090
Mores, leges, et ritvs omnivm gentivm. 6118, 94273
Moreto, --------. 50618
Moreton, J. B. 46847, (50619)-(50621)
Moreton, Julian. 50622
Moretus, Balthasarus. ed. 66494
Morewood, Samuel. 50623-50624
Morey, Charles. 89523
Morey, George. (50626)
Moreyra, Mariano. 50625

Morfi, J. A. (50627)
Morford, Henry. (50628)-50630
Morford, Henry. supposed author 89924
Morga, Antonio de. 50631-50632
Morgan. pseud. Morganiana. see Baron
　Munchausen, Jr. pseud.
Morgan, --------, fl. 1796. 98574
Morgan, ---------, fl. 1867. 60147
Morgan, Abel. 24391, 50633-50634, 86739
Morgan, Sir Charles Gould, Bart., 1726-1806.
　96932 see also Great Britain. Army.
　Judge Advocate General.
Morgan, Christopher, 1808-1877. (22754),
　24582, 51355, 53647, (56665), 61280,
　69741, (73448), 74124, 74126, 74129,
　90330, 1st note after 98997, 2d note
　after 98997, 99573, 102983, 104441,
　104442
Morgan, Daniel. 28214
Morgan, Daniel, Jr. 65760, 94516
Morgan, Edward Delmar. 82862
Morgan, Edwin Barber, 1806-1881. 50635
Morgan, Edwin Dennison, 1811-1883. 34923,
　50636, 53616, 53776, 53932, 54400
　see also New York (State) Governor,
　1859-1863 (Morgan)
Morgan, Frederick. (50637)
Morgan, G. Campbell. 83895
Morgan, George. 31799
Morgan, George C. 50641
Morgan, George G. W. 50639-50640
Morgan, George H. 75335 see also St. Louis.
　Union Merchants' Exchange. Secretary.
Morgan, George Hallenbrooke, 1828-　50642
Morgan, George Washington, 1820-1893. 50643
Morgan, Gilbert. 50644, 60157
Morgan, Sir Henry, 1635?-1688. 79781
Morgan, Sir Henry, 1635?-1688. plaintiff
　(23479)
Morgan, Henry, 1825-1884. 50646
Morgan, Henry James, 1842-1913. 657, 8852,
　50647-(50648), 1st note after 96333
Morgan, J., fl. 1732. (67586), 78377
Morgan, Jacob. 50649 see also Berks
　County, Pa. Lieutenant.
Morgan, James. 102682
Morgan, James. defendant 46735
Morgan, John, Resident of Brazil. 50656
Morgan, John, 1735-1789. 25279, 50650-50653,
　84611-84612
Morgan, John, fl. 1825. (50654)
Morgan, John, fl. 1856. 50655, 1st note after
　96986
Morgan, John B. 50657
Morgan, Joseph, 1674-1740. 50658-50661,
　94671
Morgan, Joseph C. 50662
Morgan, Lewis Henry, 1818-1881. 45576,
　50663-50668, 85072
Morgan, Morris. 50669, (63275)
Morgan, Nathaniel H. (50670)-50671
Morgan, P. B. 50672
Morgan, Richard Price, 1828-1910. 26363,
　50673
Morgan, Thomas Gibbes. 42206
Morgan, William, 1750-1833. 50674-(50675)
Morgan, William, 1774-ca. 1826. 36660,
　(50676)-50680, 90894
Morgan, William Ferdinand, 1817-1888. 30972,
　50686-50690, 5th note after 96966
Morgan, Willoughby. 96662 see also U. S.
　Commissioners to the Confederated
　Tribes of Sauks and Foxes; the Medwa-
　kanton, Wahpekute, Wahpeton and Sisseton
　Bands or Tribes of Sioux; the Omahas,
　Iowas, Otos, and Missori Indians.

Morgan (A. W.) & Co. firm publishers
　76092
Morgan and his captors. (79144)
Morgan County Sabbath School Convention,
　Jacksonville, Ill., 1866. 50691
Morgan genealogy. (50670)
Morgan horses: a premium essay. 41375
Morgan Lewis. (29393)
Morgan revived, with an appendix. 50548
Morgan, the buccaneer. 79354, 105692
Morganiana, or the wonderful life and terrible
　death of Morgan. 50692
Morgota, Antonio Augustin. defendant 64176,
　99624
Morgridge, Charles. 25878, 50693
Morgues, Jacob le Moyne de. see Le Moyne
　de Morgues, Jacob.
Morhard, --------. 50694-50695
Morhardt, --------. lithographer 84774
Morhouse, A. defendant 96907
Morhouse, Abraham. 50696
Mori, Arinori. (50697)
Mori-Ortiz, Manuel E. 50708
Moriana y Zafrilla, Marcos, Bp. 50698,
　86370 see also Michoacan (Archdioces
　Bishop (Moriana y Zafrilla)
Moriarty, --------. 50699
Moriarty, E. A. tr. 19998, 20010
Morilla, Jose Maria. (50700)
Morillas, Pedro. (50701)
Morillo, Apolinar. defendant (50702)
Morillo, Pablo, Conde de Cartegena. see
　Cartegena, Pablo Morillo, Conde de.
Morillo, Pablo Morillo y. see Morillo y
　Morillo, Pablo, Marques de la Puerta,
　1778-1837.
Morillo y Morillo, Pablo, Marques de la Puer
　1778-1837. 96221
Morin, Augustin Norbert. 20906-20907, 50704
　99598 see also Quebec (Province)
　Legislature. Legislative Assembly.
　Agent.
Morineau, A. de. 50706
Moriniere, Simon Barthelemi Joseph Noel de
　la. see Noel de la Moriniere, Simon
　Barthelemi Joseph.
Moring, H. E. 50707
Morino, Antonio. illus. 17848
Moris, Gedeon. 50709
Morison, James. plaintiff 96908
Morison, John Hopkins. 50710-50716, 2d note
　after 93998
Morison, William. (50718)-50721
Morisot, Claudius Bartholomaeus. (50579),
　(50722)-50724
Moritz, Johann. tr. 3411, 7531
Morke, John. 34329
Morlaix, Bernard Barrere de. see Barrere
　de Morlaix, Bernard.
Morleigh. pseud. Life in the west. 41020
Morley, Edward W. 85072
Morley, John. 50725
Morley: ancient and modern. 84731
Mormon delusions and monstrosities. 39122
Mormon expositor. (50747)
Mormon fanaticism exposed. 58915
Mormon imposture. 50748
Mormon prophet. pseud. Law case. (39340)
Mormon question. 50749
Mormon rebellion and the bill to raise volun-
　teers. (18064)
Mormon trip. (6052), (50750)
Mormon wife. note after 101315
Mormonen-Ansiedlungen. 90373
Mormonen. Een overzigt van het ontstaan.
　9519

Mormonen, ihr Prophet, ihr Staat, und ihr Glabue. 9508

Mormonen in Thale der grossen Salzsees. 29286

Mormonenmadchen. 49912

Mormonerne, eblu de fidste dages hellige. 50752

Mormoniad. 50753

Mormonism. 11180

Mormonism. A lecture . . . January 26, 1853. (58346)

Mormonism: an exposure of the impositions. 2188

Mormonism and the Mormons. 37706

Mormonism. [By W. J. Conybeare.] 50754

Mormonism: embracing the origin, rise and progress of the sect. 50755

Mormonism explained. 80134

Mormonism exposed! A epistle of Demetrius, Junior. 50756

Mormonism exposed and refuted. 93758

Mormonism exposed, being a journal of a residence in Missouri. 94026

Mormonism exposed: in which is shown the monstrous imposture. 93759

Mormonism exposed, internally and externally. (2598)

Mormonism: its leaders and designs. 34124

Mormonism: its rise, progress, and present condition. 28554, 83553-83554

Mormonism or the Bible? 50757

Mormonism triumphant. 24674

Mormonism unmasked. (49968)

Mormonism unvailed. [sic] (33290)

Mormonism unveiled. 66011

Mormonism unveiled; or, a history of Mormonism. 50758

Mormonism unveiled: Zion's watchman unmasked. 93758

Mormonismen och Swedenborgianismen. 50759

Mormonismen wederlagd of den Heliga Skrifts. 50760

Mormonismens hemmelighder. 34723

Mormonismens historie tilligemed en kort oversigt. 6824

Mormonites. By Charles H. Smith. 82390

Mormonites, or Latter Day Saints. 25907

Mormons. see Church of Jesus Christ of Latter Day Saints. Reformed Church of Jesus Christ of Latter Day Saints.

Mormons. A discourse delivered before the Historical Society of Pennsylvania. 37011

Mormons at home. 24186

Mormons bog. 83115-83119

Mormons bok. 83142-83143

Mormons; or knavery exposed. 50761

Mormons, or Latter-Day-Saints. 47126, 83279, 85168

Mormons, or, Latter-Day Saints, in the valley of the Great Salt Lake. (29285)

Mormons; or, life at Salt Lake City. 22605

Mormons: or the Lattery-Day Saints. 47126, 83279, 85168

Mormons. Par Amedee Pichot. 62612

Mormons. Par Paul Duplessis. 21372

Mormons. Par preface par Pierre Vincard. 23096

Mormons (Saints des Derniers-Jours) et leurs ennemis. 91222

Mormons, suite du Batteur d'Estrade. 21373

Mormons. The dream and the reality. 50762

Mornand, Felix. (31792), 50763

Mornay, Edward de. 50764

Morne-au-diable. 93415, 93417

Morning and evening gazette. 101579

Morning and evening prayer. The litany, and church catechism. 13181, (50765)

Morning and evening prayer, the litany, church catechism, family prayers. 13180

Morning and evening prayer, translated . . . with . . . hymns. 57882

Morning and evening's meditation. 40241

Morning chronicle. 84314, 95533

Morning courier and New York enquirer. 92813

Morning health no security. 65605

Morning herald. 17117

Morning post (London) see London morning post.

Morning post and evening star (New York) see New York morning post and evening star.

Morning prayer for the University. 60758

Morning prayer. Oe keuh maukhkenun pohtummouwaus. 79195

Morning star (New York) 85530-85540

Morning star (Newburyport, Mass.) see Newburyport morning star.

Morning star. 46681, 46686

Morning stars of the New World. 58672

Mornington, Richard Colley Wellesley, Earl of. see Wellesley, Richard Colley, Marquis Wellesley, 1769-1842.

Moro, Cayetano. see Moro, Gaetano.

Moro, Gaetano. 26546, 26549, 26550, 60767-60771, note after 93913, note after 94591, 7th-8th notes after 94592

Moro, Gerardo. 50772

Moro, J. P. Eguia y. see Eguia y Moro, J. P.

Moro-mastix. 50773

Moro trasportaro nell' inclita citta di Venetia. (10909), 2d note after 62591

Morocco. Treaties, etc. 15493

Moron, Fermin Gonzalo. ed. 70303

Moron, a tale of the Alhambra. 103392

Moroni, C. G. tr. 34749

Morote, Luis. 50774

Morpeth, Lord ---------, fl. 1721. 65865, 88192

Morpeth, George William Frederick Howard, Viscount. see Carlisle, George William Frederick Howard, 7th Earl of, 1802-1864.

Morpheus Stupor. pseud. see Sturop, Morpheus. pseud.

Morphy, Paul. 65394

Morphy's match games. 90298

Morrell, Abbe Jane. 50776

Morrell, Arthur. 50777

Morrell, Benjamin. 50778

Morrell, Benjamin, Jr. 21211-21215

Morrell, Calvin. 97881

Morrell, Daniel Johnson, 1821-1885. 50779-50780

Morrell, L. A. 50781

Morrell, Thomas. 50782

Morrell, Thomas H. (50783)-50785

Morrell, William. 50786

Morrell's miscellany for travellers and the fireside. 50777

Morrill, David L. 50787

Morrill, Isaac. (50788)-50789, 71828

Morrill, Justin Smith, 1810-1898. 50790-50791, 65336

Morrill, Loy Myrick, 1813-1883. 33150, 50792 see also Maine. Governor, 1858-1860 (Morrill)

Morrill, Nathaniel. 50793

Morrin, Joseph. 50794, 67050

Morris, Captain. see Morris, Charles.

Morris, ---------. cartographer 35969

Morris, ---------, fl. 1810. 1011, note after 102574

Morris, Alexander. (50795)-(50796)

Morris, Anthony. 66737

Morris, Anthony Saunders. 50797, note after 92778

Morris, Apollos. 42900

Morris, B. F. 50798-50800

Morris, B. W. 50801

Morris, Buckner S. defendant before military commission 9381

Morris, Casper, 1805-1884. (50802), 103950

Morris, Charles. 50803-50805

Morris, Corbyn. (50807)

Morris, Daniel, 1812-1889. (50808)

Morris, Drake. 50809-50810

Morris, Eastin. 50811

Morris, Edmund. 50812-50815, note after 94673

Morris, Edward Dafydd, 1825-1915. 50816, 59006

Morris, Edward Joy, 1815-1881. 50817

Morris, Edward S. 50818

Morris, Ellwood. 50819, 71937

Morris, F. 53438 see also New York (Colony) Secretary.

Morris, George Pope, 1802-1864. 50820-50825, 51700, (53288), 54819, (70978), note before 94463

Morris, Gouverneur. 11005, 12220, 22740, 22755, 50826-50833, 73360, 81394, 88990, 88997, 101270, 101803 see also New York (State) Commissioners in Internal Navigation.

Morris, Gouverneur. supposed author 8126-8127

Morris, Harrison S. 84509

Morris, Henry Gage. defendant 96888

Morris, Isaac. RN 1639, (50834)

Morris, Isaac Newton, 1812-1879. 50835-50836

Morris, J. B. 45078

Morris, Jacob. 50837

Morris, James, 1752-1820. 50838-50839, 2d note after 90803

Morris, James, 1755-1844. 50837, 102136

Morris, James M. 50892

Morris, James P. 50840

Morris, John. (55502), note after 87925

Morris, John, Jr. 60153 see also Pennsylvania (Colony) Provincial Conference, 1776. Secretary.

Morris, John B. petitioner 45079, 50841

Morris, John G. (45211A), 50842-50845, (59393)

Morris, John H. 50846

Morris, John M. 15713, 17585

Morris, Lewis, 1671-1746. 41762, 44082, 50849-(50851), 53108, 63318, 81390, 83376, 84557, 98436 see also New Jersey (Colony) Governor, 1738-1746 (Morris) New York (Colony) Supreme Court of Judicature. Chief Justice.

Morris, Lewis, 1671-1746. supposed author 19341, 84557

Morris, Lewis, 1671-1746. defendant 50847

Morris, Margaret. (50852)

Morris, Maria. defendant 96888

Morris, Maurice O'Connor. 50853

Morris, Morris. 50854, 60671, 94633

Morris, Myron N. (50855)

Morris, O. W. 50856

Morris, P. Pemberton. (50861)

Morris, Patrick. 50857-50859

Morris, Pete. 50860

Morris, Richard V. defendant at court of inquiry 50862

Morris, Robert. pseud. Organization of the public debt. see Gibbons, James S.

Morris, Robert, 1734-1806. 28100, 50866-50869, 70072, 82979, 84577-84578, note before 90715, 2d-3d notes after 97876 see also United Illinois and Wabash Land Companies. Agents. United Illinois and Wabash Land Companies. Council. petitioners United States. Superintendent of Finance.

Morris, Robert, 1734-1806. petitioner 34294, 84577 see also United Illinois and Wabash Land Companies. Council. petitioners

Morris, Robert, 1734-1806. incorrectly supposed author 50865, 84620-84621

Morris, Robert, fl. 1782. 50863

Morris, Robert, fl. 1789. 50864

Morris, Robert, 1818-1888. 37544, 50871-50872

Morris, Robert, fl. 1822. claimant 90725

Morris, Robert H. plaintiff 54320 see also New York (City) Mayor, 1841-1844 (Morris) plaintiff

Morris, Robert Hunter, 1700-1764. 50874, 59943, 60025 see also Pennsylvania (Colony) Governor, 1754-1756 (Morris)

Morris, Robert T. 50873

Morris, Roderick N. 50896

Morris, T. B. (36574)

Morris, Thomas. 50876

Morris, Thomas Asbury, Bp., 1794-1874. 4750, 29737, 50877-(50878)

Morris, Valentine. 50879 see also St. Vincent. Governor (Morris)

Morris, Walker. (50880)

Morris, William, fl. 1838. 50881, 92650

Morris, William, fl. 1862-1865. (50882)-(50883)

Morris, William E. (60561)

Morris, William Gouverneur. (50884)-50885

Morris, William M. (50898)

Morris, William S., fl. 1858. (50886)

Morris, William S., fl. 1862. 88503 see also Southern Telegraph Companies. President

Morris, William Walton. 16005, 95075

Morris. firm see Braislford & Morris. firm

Morris County, N. J. Associated Presbytery. see Presbyterian Church in the U. S. A. Associate Presbytery of Morris County.

Morris County Associate Presbytery. see Presbyterian Church in the U. S. A. Associate Presbytery of Morris County.

Morris, Arnold, and Battersby. 50863

Morris Canal and Banking Company. (50888), 50890

Morris Graeme. 34776

Morris Morris's reasons for his conduct in the present Assembly. 50854

Morrison, ----------. claimant 96909

Morrison, Charles Robert, 1819-1893. 52822, 52881

Morrison, E. 50891, 87070 see also Sons of Temperance of North America. Nova Scotia. Howard Division, No. 26, Halifax. Worthy Patriarch.

Morrison, J. H. 50893

Morrison, James. defendant 37561

Morrison, John. 94296

Morrison, Marion. (50894)

Morrison, N. J. 50895

Morrison, W. R. 50899

Morrison, William. (50897)

Morrison, William. defendant 6326, 1st note after 96956, 1st note after 97284

Morrison, William M. (50898)

Morrison's stranger's guide to the city of Washington. (50898)

Morrissey, John. defendant 64038-64039
Morristown, N. J. Baptist Church. (50900)
Morristown, N. J. Presbyterian Church.
(50900)
Morristown ghost. 72720-72721, 106070
Morrone, Joseph. 1183
Morow, Jeremiah, 1770-1852. 56929, 101500
see also Ohio. Governor, 1822-1826
(Morrow)
Morrow, John. 50901
Morrs, M. 84435
Morse, Abner, 50902-50911
Morse, Charles E. 89199
Morse, Charles W. cartographer (50912)
Morse, Ebenezer. (50913)
Morse, Ebenezer Belknap. 50914
Morse, Edward, S. 50915
Morse, F. B. (17630)-17631
Morse, F. H. (50916) see also U. S.
Consulate. London.
Morse, F. W. 50917
Morse, Horace Bassett. 9459, 50918
Morse, Horace J. 15785 see also Connecti-
cut. Adjutant General.
Morse, Isaac Edwards, 1809-1866. 50919
Morse, James. 50920
Morse, Jason. 50921
Morse, Jedediah, 1761-1826. 214, 1592,
4596, 5338, 5361, 12114, 12121, 25764,
31751, 32123, (34816), 40024, 40517,
42461, 50922-(50953), 50971, 57181,
(62679), 70204, 71515, (78330), 84162,
91812, 96412, 97086, 2d note after
97378, 101594, 101634, 101651, 101777,
101841, 101852, 101874, 2d note after
101887, 101899, note after 104434
Morse, Jedediah, 1761-1826. supposed author
(21555), (50944)
Morse, John. (59624)
Morse, John T. 50954, 84335
Morse, Oliver A. 50955
Morse, Pitt. ed. 84281
Morse, Porter. ed. 88489
Morse, Richard C. (50941), 89738
Morse, Robert M. 50956
Morse, Samuel Finley Breese, 1791-1872.
8777, 18734, 50957-50963, 83653, 85024
Morse, Samuel Finley Breese, 1791-1872.
appellant 30334
Morse, Samuel Finley Breese, 1791-1872.
claimant 28097
Morse, Samuel Finley Breese, 1791-1872.
petitioner 50963
Morse, Samuel Finley Breese, 1791-1872.
respondent 82559
Morse, Sidney Edwards. 50936, (50940),
50964-50971
Morse, Sidney H. ed. 67419
Morse, Thomas. 50972
Morse, Verranus. 50973
Morse, William, fl. 1829. 50974
Morse, William, fl. 1837. 70103
Morse, William S. 86324
Morse (C. and M.) firm publishers 72340
Morse (M.) firm publishers see Morse
(C. and M.) firm publishers
Morsell, Joshua. 50975
Morsels. By William H. Weller. 102566
Morsels of information. 33783
Morse's general atlas of the world. (50912)
Morse's new map of the state. 14259
Morse's North American atlas. 50969
Morse's patent. 37353

Morse's telegraph and the O'Reilly contract.
37353
Morshead, -------. 59031
Morsman, Oliver. 50976
Morss, James, 1779-1842. 50577-(50979)
Morss, James, fl. 1852. (50980)
Mort de Lincoln. Poeme dramatique. 41217
Mort de Maximilien. 3977
Mort du President Lincoln. Par E. Prarond.
64926
Mort du President Lincoln; par J. Poisle
Desgranges. 63710
Mort du President Lincoln, poeme. 21226
Mort glorieuse du Pere Christophe de Mendoza.
20945
Mortality statistics of the seventh census.
11672, 19119
Mortero principeno. 50981
Mortes illustres et gesta eorum de Societate
Jesu. 713
Mortage . . . to Montcure Robinson. 62051
Mortgat, Guillermo. 50982
Mortier (P.) firm publishers 25062
Mortimer, C. B. 50983
Mortimer, F. L. 88927
Mortimer, Favell Lee (Bevan) 1802-1878.
50984
Mortimer, G. F. W. 50987
Mortimer, George, RN (17258), 50985-50986,
(64394)
Mortimer, George, of Toronto. 2026
Mortimer, J., fl. 1824. 50988
Mortimer, J., fl. 1861. 50989, (78703)
Mortimer, John. reporter 47464
Mortimer, Thomas. (50990)-50991
Morton, A. C. 50993, (75309)
Morton, Andrew. 50992
Morton, Charles, 1627-1698. (46631), 50994,
52611
Morton, Charles, 1627-1698. supposed author
46756, 2d note after 99797
Morton, Charles S. ed. (55830)
Morton, Daniel Oliver, 1788-1852. 50995,
89896
Morton, Ebenezer. 50996
Morton, Ellis W. (50997)
Morton, George, d. 1624. see Mourt, G.
Morton, George W. (54347)
Morton, Henry J. 50998
Morton, J. C. 51006
Morton, J. W. 51007
Morton, Jackson, 1794-1874. supposed author
(51005)
Morton, Jacob. 50999, (54206)
Morton, James. 51000, 77812
Morton, James St. C. 51003-51004
Morton, Jeremiah, 1799-1878. 51001-51002
Morton, Jeremiah, 1799-1878. supposed author
(51005)
Morton, John. (72095), 72110
Morton, Lloyd. 51008, 70686 see also Rhode
Island. Commissioner on the Physical
Condition of the Rhode Island Regiments,
now in the Field. 1863.
Morton, Marcus, 1784-1864. 13653, 20256,
31784, 37792, 45572, 45711, 51009-(51011),
(67260), 63063 see also Massachusetts.
Governor, 1841-1841 (Morton) Massa-
chusetts. Governor, 1843-1844 (Morton)
Morton, Nathaniel, 1613-1685. (28046), 32480,
37208, 51012-51017, (53384), 80910
Morton, Oliver Hazard Perry Throck, 1823-
1877. 22498, (34556), 51018-51020, 66624,
84808, 87310 see also Indiana. Governor,
1861-1867 (Morton)

Morton, Perez. (6737), 51020

Morton, Samuel George, 1799-1851. 51022-
(51024), 56040, 98579

Morton, Sarah Wentworth Apthorp. 2654,
51025-51027, (82501), note after 100593

Morton, Thomas. defendant 96904

Morton, Thomas, 1575-1646. 51028

Morton, Thomas, 1764?-1838. 51029-51030

Morton, W. 103191

Morton, William Thomas Green. 51031

Morton, William Thomas Green. petitioner
51032

Morton Montague. 50983

Morton oder die grosze Tour. 64541, (91549)-
91550

Morton of Morton's Hope. 51109

Morton Price. pseud. see Rhys, Horton.

Morton's Hope. 51109

Mortuary record of the city of Troy, N. Y.
7997

Mortuary tables of San Francisco. 77300

Morus, Gerardus. (51033)

Morvan de Bellegarde, Jean Baptiste. see
Bellegarde, Jean Baptiste Morvan de.

Morveau, Louis Bernard, Baron Guyton de.
see Buyton de Morveau, Louis Bernard,
Baron, 1737-1816.

Moryson, Francis. 4889, (50717), 100380,
100390, 100459 see also Virginia
(Colony) Governor, 1661-1662 (Moryson)

Mo-sack, Chief of the Pottawattamie Indians.
96710

Mosaic book of the American Adoptive Rite.
(51034)

Mosaic Templars of America, Europe, Asia
and Africa. American Adoptive Rite.
(51034)

Mosaico Mexicano y coleccion de amendidades
curiosos e instructivos. (51035)

Mosaico poetico. 24318

Mosaics. 77176-77177

Mosaique. (51036)

Mosblech, Boniface. 51037

Mosby, Charles L. 51038

Mosby, M. M. (Webster) 51040, note after
102330

Mosby and his men. 17440

Moscardon, Gachupin. 93445

Moscoso, Andres Lopez. plaintiff 93314

Moscoso y Cordoua, Christoual de. 51041-
51044 see also Spain. Consejo Real.
Fiscal.

Moscoso y Cordoua, Christoual de. plaintiff
51043

Moscoso y Peralta, Juan Manuel de, Bp.
51045, 68838 see also Cuzco, Peru
(Diocese) Bishop (Moscoso y Peralta)

Moscoviti nella California. 96311

Moscozo, Flore Celestine Therese Henriette
Tristan y. see Tristan y Moscozo,
Flore Celestine Therese Henriette.

Moseley, Benjamin. 51047-51050

Moseley, Ebenezer. 51051

Moseley, Edward. defendant 105702

Moseley, Elisha. 51052

Moseley, Humphrey. 67561

Moseley, Jonathan Ogden. 51053

Moseley, Joseph. 51054

Moser, Johann Jacob. 51055

Moses, F. J. 51056

Moses, Julian. 51057

Moses, Montros Jonas, 1787-1934. ed.
92513

Moses, Myer. 51058-51060

Moses a witness to our Lord and Saviour Jesus
Christ. (14525)

Moses and Aaron. 56218

Moses and Joshua. 67879

Moses B. Mendel. 51061

Moses Ben Saam. pseud. Speech. see
Robertson, Robert.

Moses en Washington vergeleeken. 5361, 101777

Mose's letters. 51046

Moses on Nebo. 89773

Moses; or, the man who supposes himself to be
Moses. 36181

Moses Turn-Spit. pseud. see Turn-Spit, Moses.
pseud.

Mosheim, --------. 99822, 99825

Mosher, ------. 45264

Mosier, Hugh A. 51062

Mosloy, Louis Guillaume Otto, Comte de.
see Otto, Louis Guillaume, Comte de
Mosloy, 1754-1817.

Mosqueador. 75769

Mosquera, J. de. see Mosquera, Manuel Jose,
Abp.

Mosquera, Manuel Jose, Abp. 51065-51067
see also Bogota (Archdiocese) Archbishop
(Mosquera)

Mosquera, Tomas Cipriano de, 1798-1878.
31536, 51068-51072, 51074-51075, 52778

Mosquera, Tomas Cipriano de, 1798-1878.
defendant 51073, 51075

Mosquera de Figueroa, Christoual. 51063

Mosquera y Figueroa, Manuel. 51064

Mosquito Indian and his Golden River. 13015

Mosquito-Kuste und Texas. 51087

Mosquito, Nicaragua, and Costa Rica. 51086,
90614

Mosquito Shore (British Colony) see British
Honduras.

Moss, Charles, successively Bishop of St.
Davids, and Bath and Wells, 1711-1802.
51088, 79279

Moss, J. J. 83831

Moss, Joseph. 51089-51090

Moss, Lemuel, 1829-1905. 51091, 83465,
83495

Moss rose. 85572

Mosses & liverworts. 69946

Mosses and liverworts by W. S. Sullivant.
28366

Mosses from an old manse. 30994

Mossman, Samuel. 51092

Most authentic account yet published. 31028

Most bloody and cruel murder. 105024

Most celebrated works of the best American
humorists. 84185-84187

Most certain means of promoting the wealth.
10866

Most compleat compendium of geography.
21760

Most Considerable Proprietors of the Island
of Barbados. see Barbados. Proprietors

Most eminent orators and statesmen of ancient
and modern times. 30610

Most exact and accurate map of the whole
world. 51093

Most feasible plan yet offered. 60923

Most friendly farewell given by a wel-willer.
51094

Most grave, and modest confutation. 67948

Most happie fortune of that braue gentillman
William Graftone. 57926, 71894

Most humble proposal to the Lords Regents,
&c., of Great Britain. 51095, 62559

Most humble proposal to . . . the Lords
Regents of Great Britain. 51095, 62559

Most humble supplication. 104331

Most important convention of reformers of every description. 85128

Most important extra. 51096, 85121

Most important part of Kent's commentaries. 37926

Most Loyal Associated Refugees, Newport, R. I. see His Majesty's Loyal Associated Refugees Assembled at Newport, R. I.

Most Noble and Right Honourable the Lords Commissioners of Appeals in Prize Causes. see Great Britain. High Court of Appeals for Prizes.

Most of the institutions in our country. 105360

Most plain and easie directions. 82841-82842

Most plain and easy directions. 82843

Most plain harmonious sense of scripture the test of opinions. 105329

Most remarkable prophecy, concerning wars and political events. 51097

Most startling expose of doings of this extensive secret band. 38342

Most strange and prodigious birth. 54970

Most tragical series of remarkable judgments. 102683

Most useful experiments for improving land. 17237

Most friendly farewell. (71893)

Mosto, Alvise Ca da. see Ca da Mosto, Alvise, 1432?-1480?

Mosto, Alvise de Ca de. see Ca da Mosto, Alvise, 1432?-1480?

Mot a l'oreille. 15444

Mot de verite sur les malheurs de Saint-Domingue. 2766

Mot sur l'emancipation de l'esclavage. 38604

Mot sur les colonies Francaises. 2349, 19084

Mot sur l'expose des principes. 29261, (48595)

Mota. Potawatomi Indian Chief 96595

Mota, J. J. de la. 19338, 51098

Mota, Manuel de la. (51099)

Mota Padilla, Matias de la. 51100

Mota Band of Potawatomi Indians. see Potawatomi Indians (Mota Band)

Motezuma, tragedia en cinco actos. 98119

Mothe-Fenelon, Francois de Salignac de la. see Fenelon, Francois de Salignac de la Mothe-, Abp., 1641-1715.

Mothe le Vayer, ------ de la. pseud. Nauwkeurige beschrijving. see La Peyrere, Isaac de.

Mother. pseud. Letter from a mother to her son. 22664

Mother. pseud. Rudiments of taste. 73896

Mother. pseud. Short stories from the lives of remarkable women. 80695

Mother Goose. 86901

Mother Goose's melodies. 86901

Mother Goose's melodies for children. 86917

Mother Goose's melody. 86917

Mother Goose's quarto. 86917

Mother Goose's tales. 86917

Mother in the spirit sphere. pseud. Spirit communications. see Hall, Mrs. A. B.

Mother of Henry Clay. 84935

Mother of Mary Lundie Duncan. pseud. America as I found it. see Lundie, Mrs. J. C.

Mother of Washington, and other tales. 88698

Mother perishing in a snow-storm. 84156

Mother's fireside book of first lessons. 88383

Mother's journal during the last illness of her daughter. 103828

Mother's law. 71782

Mother's peace offering to American houses. 41522

Mother's primer. 18293, (71344)

Mother's sacrifice. 37147

Mother's tale, a fragment. 103392

Mother's tribute to a beloved daughter. 83504

Motier, Gilbert de. 51101

Motier, Marie Jean Paul Roche Yves Gilbert du. see Lafayette, Marie Jean Paul Roche Yves Gilbert du Motier, Marquis de, 1757-1834.

Motifs des guerres et des traites de paix de la France. 1620

Motifs qui doivent determiner les ministres plenipotentiaires, Francais et Americains, etc. 15915

Motins politicos. 67540

Motion, April 11, 1808. 63684

Motion . . . by Mr. Henry Remsen. 100787

Motion de M. de Cocherel Depute de Saint Domingue, a la seance de 29 Aout 1789. 14052

Motion de M. de Cocherel Depute de Saint-Domingue, a la seance du Samedi 29 Aout 1789. 14051

Motion de M. de Curt, Depute de la Guadeloupe. 50575

Motion de M. de Curt, Depute de la Guadeloupe, au nom des colonies reunies. 18017

Motion de M. le Comte de Reynaud. 70400

Motion, December 24, 1811. 63686

Motion, December 23d. 1811. 63046

Motion d'ordre fait par Du Fay. 21122

Motion d'ordre fait par P. Thomany. 95374

Motion d'ordre prononcee au Conseil des Cinq-Cents par Sonthonax. 87121, 87126

Motion d'ordre sur l'etat actuel de nos rapports. (59027)

Motion faite le 27 Novembre 1789. 93815

Motion. February 7, 1806. 67829

Motion, Feb. 10, 1806 [by Jacob Crowninshield.] 17710

Motion, Feb. 10, 1806 [by Joseph H. Nicholson.] 55231

Motion February 24, 1808. 82287

Motion for an abolition of the slave trade. 81932

Motion for an amendment to the constitution. 25194

Motion for an inquiry into the conduct of H. Innes. (73528)

Motion ofr authorizing the President immediately to employ the public armed vessels. 9512

Motion for commercial restrictions. (43721)

Motion for the mitigation and gradual abolition of slavery. (81949)

Motion [in the House of Representatives.] 9511

Motion . . . increasing the number of delegates. 28118

Motion, January 24, 1806. 28382

Motion, Jan. 22, 1805. 23121

Motion. March 3d, 1812. 83989

Motion. November 13th, 1811. 83988

Motion of Charles Ellis, Esq. concerning the slave trade. 89209

Motion of Henry Brougham, Esq. 82906

Motion [of James Sloan.] 82153

Motion [of John Rhea.] 70467

Mount Gilead, Ohio. Presbyterian Church. (65852)

Mount Holly, N. J. Convention of the Friends of Education, 1847. see Convention of the Friends of Education, Mount Holly, N. J., 1847.

Mount Holly, N. J. Washington Benevolent Society. see Washington Benevolent Society. New Jersey. Mount Holly.

Mount Holyoke Female Seminary, South Hadley, Mass. 51156

Mount Holyoke Female Seminary, South Hadley, Mass. Memorandum Society. 51156

Mt. Holyoke hand-book, and tourist's guide for Northampton. 21825

Mount Hope. 42704

Mount Hope, an evening excursion. 71156

Mount Hope Cemetery, Dorchester, Mass. see Dorchester, Mass. Mount Hope Cemetery.

Mount Hope Cemetery in Dorchester and West Roxbury. (51160)

Mount Hope Cemetery, West Roxbury, Mass. see Dorchester, Mass. Mount Hope Cemetery.

Mount Hope Institution, Baltimore. 51161, 92013

Mount Hope; or, Philip, King of the Wampanoags. 32553

Mount Lebanon Cemetery Company, Philadelphia. see Philadelphia. Mount Lebanon Cemetery Company.

Mount Moriah cemetery. 51162, 61848

Mount Moriah Cemetery Association, Philadelphia. see Philadelphia. Mount Moriah Cemetery Association.

Mount Morris, Ill. Rock River Seminary. see Rock River Seminary, Mount Morris, Ill.

Mount Olivet Cemetery, Baltimore. see Baltimore. Mount Olivet Cemetery.

Mount Pleasant, Iowa. Wesleyan University. see Iowa Wesleyan University, Mount Pleasant, Iowa.

Mount Pleasant, N. Y. Baptist Convention, 1791. see Baptists. New York. Convention, Mount Pleasant, 1791.

Mount Pleasant, N. Y. Farmer's Association. see Farmer's Association, Mount Pleasant, N. Y.

Mount Pleasant, N. Y. Prison. see New York (State) State Prison, Mount Pleasant.

Mount Pleasant, Ohio. Meeting of the Associated Executive Committee of Friends on Indian Affairs. 1st, 1870. see Friends, Society of. Associated Executive Committee on Indian Affairs. Meeting, 1st, Mt. Pleasant, Ohio, 1870.

Mount Pleasant Academy, Sing Sing, N. Y. 51167

Mount Pleasant Boarding School for Boys, Amherst, Mass. see Mount Pleasant Institute, Amherst, Mass.

Mount Pleasant Classical Institution, Amherst, Mass. see Mount Pleasant Institute, Amherst, Mass.

Mount Pleasant Institute, Amherst, Mass. 1333, 51168-51169

Mount Pleasant, May 5, 1766. 51164

Mount Pleasant Prison, N. Y. see New York (State) Prison, Mount Pleasant.

Mount Pleasant Prison, Massachusetts. see Massachusetts. Mount Pleasant State Prison.

Mount Saint Mary's College, Emmitsburg, Md. (51170)

Mount Saint Mary's College, Emmitsburg, Md. President. 36823

Mount St. Vincent's Hospital, Baltimore. see Baltimore. Mount St. Vincent's Hospital.

Mount Sinai Hospital, New York (City) see New York (City) Mount Sinai Hospital.

Mount Union, Ohio. College and Normal Seminary. (51174)

Mount Vernon. 64583

Mount Vernon: a letter to the children of America. (16604)

Mount Vernon, a poem. 78658, note after 101799

Mount Vernon and its associations. 42117, 42125

Mount Vernon, and other poems. 70833

Mount Vernon Association of the Union. see Mount Vernon Ladies' Association of the Union.

Mount Vernon Cemetery Company, Philadelphia. see Philadelphia. Mount Vernon Cemetery Company.

Mount Vernon Classical School, Boston. see Boston. Mount Vernon Classical School.

Mount Vernon Congregational Church, Boston. see Boston. New Congregational Church.

Mount Vernon, July 15, 1773. 51175

Mount Vernon Ladies' Association of the Union. 34337, 51177

Mount Vernon Ladies' Association of the Union. Lady Managers. 34337

Mount Vernon Ladies' Association of the Union. Secretary. 34337

Mount Vernon Ladies' Association of the Union. Vice Regents. 34337

Mount Vernon Lodge, Boston. see Freemasons. Massachusetts. Mount Vernon Lodge, Boston.

Mount Vernon paper. 23259

Mount Vernon record. (51176)

Mount Washington Collegiate Institute, New York. 51182

Mount Washington in winter. (51183)

Mount Zion Tabernacle, No. 3, Philadelphia. see Philadelphia. Mount Zion Tabernacle, No. 3.

Mountain, Armine S. H. 51184

Mountain, Mrs. Armine S. H. ed. 51184

Mountain, Armine Wale, 1823-1885. 51185

Mountain, George Jehosaphat, successively Bishop of Montreal, and Quebec, 1789-1863. 13005-13006, 51186-51187, 66981

Mountain, George Jehosaphat, successively Bishop of Montreal, and Quebec, 1789-1863. incorrectly supposed author 91663, 99582

Mountain, Jacob, bishop of Quebec. (51188)

Mountain. (35453)

Mountain cottager. 89439

Mountain Max. 72129

Mountain missionary. (7400)

Mountain mourner. 44435

Mountain muse. 8787

Mountain of Gold, or the priestess of the sun. 72130

Mountain of the Lord's House. 51190

Mountain scenery. 14792

"Mountain society." 33406

Mountain top track. 22209

Mountain top tracks in the state of Virginia. 58448, (72576)

Mountain wild flower. 40226, 103198

Mountaineer. pseud. Appeal for rectitude in primary politics. see Wright, Charles.

Mountaineer. pseud. Our political practice. see Wright, Charles.

Mountaineer. pseud. Prospect. 105567

Mountaineer. 89160-89162

Mountains and molehills. 44695

Mounteney, Barclay. 51191

Mountflorence, James Cole. 81656-81657, 81659, 81661-81662

Mountford, William. 51192

Mountford, Bioren & Co. firm publishers 79729

Mountgomery, Sir Robert. 51193-51194

Mouqueron, Arsene. 59326, 59335

Moura, Antonio Bonifacio de. pseud. Algumas Vergalhadas. see Souza, Bernardo Xavier Pinto de.

Moura, Caetano Lopes de. see Lopes de Moura, Caetano, 1780-1860.

Moura e Limos, Luis Antonio Innocencio de. 51195

Moure, Amedee. (46948), (51196)-51197

Mourner admonished. (81637)

Mourners cordial against excessive sorrovv. 104096

Mourner's friend. 32729

Mourner's hope. 101453

Mournful Easter. 29741

Mournful elegy of Mr. Jonathan Frye. 37711, 94112

Mournful elegy, on the death of Martin Willcocks. 104126

Mournful lamentation for the sad and deplorable death of Mr. Old Tenor. (28549)

Mournful song upon the battles of America 29th of April, 17 of June. 95736

Mournful word to the merry-hearted in Zion. 98098

Mourning days. 26074

Mourning for an only son. 64647

Mourning for the righteous. 90363

Mourning piece. 19830

Mo[u]rning Virginia. 100489

Mourt, G. 7263, (51198)-51201, note after 104797, 106053

Mourt's relation. 7263, 51200

Mouse-trap, or the battle of the Cambrians and mice. 32487

Mouse-trap, or the battle of the Welsh and the mice. 65527

Mousseaux, Henry Roger Gougenot de. see Gougenot de Mousseaux, Henry Roger.

Moussy, V. Martin de. see Martin de Moussy, V.

Mouttet, Etienne. 51203

Mouzon, Henry. 35953-35954, 35962, (40141)

Movement de la population de la Havane. (74930)

Movement for a university in California. 10001

Movila, F. de la. (51204), 69185

Movilla, Gregorio de. 51025

Movimento dos seculos. 88749

Movimento general de la Aduana de Buenos Aires. 9025

Movimiento de poblacion de la republica. (12742)

Moving mirror of the lakes. 9444

Moving power. (26240)

Mowatt, Anna Cora. see Ritchie, Anna Cora (Mowatt)

Mowatt, J. A. 51207

Mowrey, James D. 51208

Mowris, J. A. 51209

Mowry, Ahaz. 48971

Mowry, Sylvester. 51210-51212

Moxo, Benito Maria de, Abp. 51213-51215, 51217 see also La Plata (Archdiocese) Archbishop (Moxo)

Moxo y de Francoli, Benito Maria de. 51216

Moxon, Joseph. 51219, 105574

Moya, Juan de. 51220

Moya de Contreras, Pedro, Abp. (36795), 42064, 42066, 48373-(48374), 76223, 76332, note after 90828 see also Mexico (Archdiocese) Archbishop (Moya de Contreras)

Moyamensing (District), Philadelphia. Charter. (59823)

Moyamensing (District), Philadelphia. Children Home. see Moyamensing Union School, and Children's Home, Moyamensing, Pa.

Moyamensing (District), Philadelphia. Commissioners. (59823)

Moyamensing (District), Philadelphia. Ordinances, etc. (59823), 61591, (51906)

Moyamensing (District), Philadelphia. Union School, and Children's Home. see Moyamensing Union School, and Children's Home, Moyamensing, Pa.

Moyamensing, Pa. see Moyamensing (District) Philadelphia.

Moyamensing Union School, and Children's Home, Moyamensing, Pa. 61851

Moyen facile de payer les impots. 25596, 78109-(78112), 78114-78115

Moyen facile de payer les impots, dans les possessions de l'Amerique Angloise. 25583

Moyen pour prevenir los inondations de la ville et la vallee de Mexico. 51221

Moyens de rendre les colonies a la France. (48901)

Moyens de restituer graduellement aux homme leur etat politique. 6318

Moyers, ------. 51222

Moyes, Robert. 51223

Moyne de Morgues, Jacob le. see Le Moyne de Morgues, Jacob.

Moyses Lusitano. 26411

Mozarabic missal. 42066

Mozin, --------. 12237

Mozino, Jose Mariano. 51224

Mozis Addums. pseud. Mozis Addum's new letters. see Bagby, George William.

Mozis Addums' new letters. (51225)

Muceus, Peter. tr. 83119

Much admired ballad of the willow. 92174B

Much admired song, translated from the German. 85372

Much in little: a history of the characters, government, etc. 24717

Much in little; or three brief essays. 46422

Much useful information on the coasting naviga tion of Cape Horn. 102431

Mucius. pseud. To the freemen of America. 51227, 95924

Mucius to the freemen of America. 51227, 95924

Muck-Rose. Potawatomi Indian Chief 96595

Mudd, Samuel A. defendant 41180-41182, 41235

Muddy-Creek Meeting-House, Powhatan County Va. General Committee of Baptists. see Baptists. Virginia. General Committee, 1793.

Mudford, William. tr. 28197

Mudge, Alfred. 51230

Mudge, B. F. 37032 see also Kansas. Stat Geologist.

Mudge, E. R. (51235)-51236 see also U. S. Commission to the Paris Exposition, 1867

Mudge, Enoch. 51233-51234

Mudge, Z. A. 51237-51240

Mudge family. 51231

Mudie, Robert. 51241
Mu^ehlen, Mu^ehl Pla^etze und Plantaschen. 106249
Mueller. see also Muller.
Mueller, Ferdinand, Freiherr von, 1825-1896. 85072, 86970
Mueller, Johann Bernhard. 4936
Mueller, Johannes, Regiomontanus, 1436-1476. 1757, 66479, (66482)
Muenscher, Joseph. (51242)
Muenster, Sebastian. see Munster, Sebastian, 1489-1552.
Mueran Santa-Anna y pedraza fusilados en la plaza. 94147
Muerte de la republica Mexicana. 79349
Mverte de Pie de Palo. (51243), 69235, 2d note after 78907
Muerte del primer Gobernador Constitucional del estado de Jalisco. 71699
Muerte del Sr. Poncha. 76747
Muerte politicia de la republica Mexicana. 34149, 93910, note after 99718
Muestra del poder de Dios. 86443
Muffled drum. 88047A
Muger edificativa panegyrico funebre. 22066
Muggleton, Lodowick. 59720
Muhlbach, L. 51245-51246
Muhle, Carl Adolf. 51247
Muhlenberg, Frederick Augustus Conrad, 1759-1801. 17308, 77477
Muhlenberg, Gotthilf Henry Ernest. see Muhlenberg, Henry, 1753-1815.
Muhlenberg, Heinrich Melchior, 1711-1787. supposed author 98023
Muhlenberg, Henry, 1753-1815. 51248-51249, 67461, 82788
Muhlenberg, Henry Augustus, 1752-1844. (51250)-51251
Muhlenberg, William Augustus, 1796-1877. 23458, 51252-51256, 66167, 75279-75280, 84139-841 41; 84143, 84146 see also Protestant Episcopal Church in the U. S. A. Sundry Presbyters. petitioners
Muhlenberg College, Allentown, Pa. 51257
Muhlenpfordt, Eduard. 51258
Muilkerk, W. E. J. Berg van Dussen. see Berg van Dussen Muilkerk, W. E. J.
Muir, James. 51259-51261
Muir, Robert. 97124
Mulcaster, George Frederick. 87364
Mulchahey, James. 51262
Mulchinock, William Pembroke. 51263
Mulder, J. engr. 26367, 62704
Mulford, E. (51264)
Mulford, Isaac S. 51265-51266
Mulgrave, Constantine John Phipps, 2d Baron, 1744-1792. (30938), 31389, (54897), 62572-62576
Mulhall, E. T. 51268-51269
Mulhall, Michael G. 51267-51269
Mulkins, Hannibal. 51270
Mullaly, John. 1426, 51271-51273
Mullan, John, 1830-1909. (51274)-51275, 69946
Mullane, A. J. (51276)
Mullen, -------. illus. 29919, 46175
Mullen, John. defendant 96943
Mullen, William J. 42359
Muller. see also Mueller.
Muller, -------. illus. 80369, note after 96778
Muller, Dr. --------. 24013, 51076
Muller, A. F. 60328
Muller, A. P. 51278
Muller, Albert A. 51277
Muller, Albert A. defendant 51277

Muller, Andreas. 57448, 59231
Muller, Franz. defendant 51279
Muller, Ferdinand, Freiherr von. see Mueller, Ferdinand, Freiherr von, 1825-1896.
Muller, Friedrich, 1834-1898. (34101), 51283-51284
Muller, Gerhard Friedrich. 29865, 51285-(51286)
Muller, Heinrich. see Miller, John Henry, 1702-1782.
Muller, J., fl. 1816. 51288
Muller, J., fl. 1819. 51287
Muller, J. G. 51290-(51291)
Muller, Johann Jacob, fl. 1740. 2463, 51292-51293, 60766, 4th note after 97845
Muller, Johannes. 77780
Muller, John. 51289
Muller, Joseph. 72236
Muller, K. L. M. tr. 61014, 72040
Muller, N. G. P. see Muller, Gerhard Friedrich.
Muller, Niclas. tr. 51294, 63549
Muller, P. N. 51296
Muller, Peter. 51295
Muller, S. see Muller, Gerhard Friedrich.
Muller, W. J. 89554A, 99534
Muller (Frederik) & Co. firm publishers 51280-51282
Mullet, James. defendant 6326, 1st note after 96956, 1st note after 97284
Mulligan, John, b. 1793. 54705, 94095-94096, note after 99392
Mullin, John. 2998
Mullin, Joseph, 1811-1882. (51297)
Muloch, Miss. pseud. Silas Marner. see Eliot, George. pseud.
Mullock, John Thomas, Bp. 51299
Mulock Craik, Mrs. D. M. see Craik, Mrs. D. M. Mulock.
Mulon. alias see Suarez, Jose Ildefonso.
Mulready, W. supposed author 7599
Multivallis, Joannes. 23114
Multum in parvo. 85122
Mulvany, D. H. 8239, 62120
Mumford, Gurdon Saltonstall, 1764-1831. 89207
Mumford, John I. 51300
Mumford, Paul M. 51301
Mumford, Sarah. plaintiff 89104
Mumford, T. H. engr. 102140
Mun, Thomas, 1571-1641. 66686, (71909)
Munatones, Lorenzo Salazar. see Salazar Munatones, Lorenzo.
Muncaster, John Pennington, 1st Baron, 1737-1813. 51302
Munch, Ernst. (38278), 51303-51304
Munch, Friedrich. 51305-(51307)
Munchausen, Baron, Jr. pseud. see Baron Munchausen, Jr. pseud.
Munchausen, Capt. pseud. Munchausen at the pole. (51308)
Munchausen at the pole. (51308)
Munchen. see Munich.
Munck, Johann. see Munk, Jens, 1579-1628.
Muncken, Joan. see Munk, Jens, 1579-1628.
Munday, Eugene H. 51309, 65999
Munday, William. 51310
Munde, Charles. 51311
Mundell, Marque B. 51312
Mundi, Amicus. pseud. see Amicus Mundi. pseud.
Mundsmag vaa Mormonismen i Utah. 51313
Mundungus. pseud. Friendly debate. see Walter, Thomas, 1696-1725.
Mundungus. nick-name. see Williams, John, fl. 1721-1722.

Mundus alter et idem siue terra australis.
(29819)
Mundus mirabilis tripartitus. 30278
Mundus novus. 99327-99330, 99332-99333,
99338-99339, 99345, 99361, 99363,
99366, 99367-99369, 99379, note after
99383C
Mundus nouus Albericus Vesputius Laurentio
Petri de Medicis salutem plurimam
dicit. 99334, 99378
Mu[n]dus nouus. Albericus Vesputius Laurentio
Petri de Medici salutem plurimam
dicit. note before 99327, 99335
Mundus nouus de natura & moribus [et]
ceteris id generis gentis. note before
99327, 99339
Mundus nouus. De natura et moribus [et]
ceteris id g[e]n[er]is ge[n]t[is] que
i[n] nouo mundo opera. note before
99327, 99336
Mundus nouus. De natura et moribus et
ceteris id generis gentisque in nuuo
mu[ndo] opera. note before 99327, note
after 99383C
Mundus nouus de natura et morib[u]s et
ceteris id generis ge[n]tis q[ue] in nouo
mu[n]do op[er]a. note before 99327,
99338
Mundus novus. Ein Bericht Amerigo
Vespucci's. note before 99327, 99378
Mundus subterraneus. 37967
Mundy, Geofrey Basil. 51314
Munford, George Wythe. 51315
Munford, William. 51316
Mungen, William. 51317
Munger, T. T. 51318
Mungnier, S. A. 51319
Munguia, Clemente de Jesus, Abp. (36092),
42904, 51320-51325 see also Michoacan
(Archdiocese) Archbishop (Munguia)
Munguia, Jose Maria. ed. 87245
Munibe, Jose Maria de. (51326)
Munich. Akademie der Wissenschaften. see
Akademie der Wissenschaften, Munich.
Munich. K. Hof- und Staats-Bibliothek.
2313, 38348
Munick. K. Universitat. 2313, 38348
Municipal government examined by its own
records. 51327
Municipal history of the town and city of
Boston. (67228)
Municipal officer's assistant. (80161)
Municipal ordinances for the government and
regulation of the city and port of Grey-
Town. 51328
Municipal police, or day and night watch.
54584
Municipal register, containing the city charter
and ordinances [of Concord, N. H.]
(15148)
Municipal register containing the city charter
and ordinances, . . . of . . . Newburyport.
54920
Municipal register, containing the city charter . . . [of Lynn, Mass.] (42842)
Municipal register containing the city charter,
ordinances, regulations, and rules of
order, of the city councils. 75674
Municipal register, containing the city charter,
with rules and orders of the City Council;
also, the ordinances and a list of the
officers of the city of Fall River.
23758
Municipal register, containing the city charter,
with rules and orders of the City Council,

and a list of the officers of the city of
Roxbury. 73657
Municipal register, containing rules and orders
of the City council, since 1851. 42498
Municipal register for 1857. (10144)
Municipal register for 1860. 42834
Municipal register, for the year 1849-50.
10123
Municipal register. Members of the Common
Council. 8305
Municipal register of the city of Charlestown.
12113
Municipal register of the city of Concord.
15147
Municipal register: . . . of the city of
Lawrence. 39395
Municipal register, rules and orders of City
Council. 6749
Municipal returns. 10402, 10521
Municipal returns for Upper and Lower Canada.
10526
Municipal situation in Ohio. 83963
Municipal subscriptions made by the city.
61852
Municipalida y vecindario de la ciudad leal de
Cojutepequa. 51329
Municipalist. 34908
Municipalist. In two parts. 51330, note after
71222
Municipalite de Brest. see Brest, France.
Municipalite.
Munition des Loyalisten. 42564, (51331)
Muniz, Pedro. (51332)
Munk, Jens, 1579-1628. 13015, 28641, 33679,
(38973), 51333-51336
Munk, Johann. see Munk, Jens, 1579-1628.
Munk, John. see Munk, Jens, 1579-1628.
Munn, Lewis C. 51337-51338
Munn (Orson D.) & Co. firm 51339-51340
Munnich, P. tr. 92522
Munon, Sancho Sanchez de. see Sanchez de
Munon, Sancho.
Munon Chimalpain, Juan Bautista de San Anton.
see Chimalpain, Juan Bautista de San
Anton Munon.
Munoz, Bernardo. 51341
Munoz, D. J. ed. 94853
Munoz, Jose Fernando. (51342)
Munoz, Juan Bautista. 9567, 27768, 35298,
(44579), (51342)-51347, 70884, 74945,
87205, 94352
Munoz, Juan Martin. petitioner 86379
Munoz, Juan R. (51348)
Munoz, Louis. 42577
Munoz, Miguel. 51349
Munoz, P. 51353
Munoz Casimire Ortega, J. B. 31517
Munoz de Castro, Pedro. 23337, 51352
Munoz de Velasco, Joaquin de la Pezula y
Sanchez. see Pezula y Sanchez Munoz de
Velasco, Joaquin de la, 1. Marques de
Viluma, 1761-1830.
Munoz Ledo, Octaviano. 39685, 51350
Munoz Ledo y Burguiza, P. 51351
Munoz Sanabria, Marcos. see Sanabria,
Marcos Munoz.
Munoz y Romero, Tomas. 51354
Munoz, visitador de Mejico, drama en tres
journadas y en verso. 72512
Munro, Robert. pseud. Description of the
Genesee Country. see Williamson,
Charles. supposed author
Munro (George) firm publishers 95611
Munroe genealogy. 41730
Munro's ten cent novels. 85611

Munsee Indians. Treaties, etc. 96618, 96736
Munsell, Charles. 51356
Munsell, Joel. 596, 601, 1311, 5985, 7301, (9253), 11597, 19788, 21694, 33138, (33148), (33510), 47105, (51357)-(51376), 51887, 57496, 57498, (71302), (72725), 74496, (80003), 86941, 89120, 90375, 95406, 105498
Munsell, William Augustus. 51377
Munsell's Albany directory and city register. 51368
Munsell's guide to the Hudson River. (33510), 51369
Munsell's historical series. 1311, 7301, (9253), 11597, 19788, 21694, 33138, (33148), 51370, 57496, (72725), 74496, (80003), 90375
Munsell's series of local American history. 5985, 47105, 51371, 51887, (71302)
Munson, --------. 102346
Munson, Merritt. (51378)
Munson, Reuben. 2879, 72619, 101441
Munson, S. B. engr. 83653
Munson, Samuel. 95541
Munster, Sebastian, 1489-1552. 16961, (21826), (27689), 34100-34107, 51379-51406, 66484, 66486-(66488), (66502), (66890)-66891, 76838, note after 99383C
Munster. Anabaptists. see Anabaptists. Munster.
Munstersaal aller Teutschen Mundarten. (67425)
Muoarra, Emmanuele. ed. 61074
Mur, Juan Francisco. 51407
Mur, Juan Francisco. petitioner 51407
Mur, Pedro de. 19951, 22877
Mura, Pierre de. see Gand, Pierre de.
Muraour, E. 51408
Murat, Achille. 51409-51417
Muratori, Lodovico Antonio, 1672-1750. 11554, 18335, 51418-51428, (58517), 75904
Muratori, Lodovico Antonio, 1672-1750. incorrectly supposed author (51427), (58535), (63900)
Murch, Abel B. 8803
Murcia de la Llana, Francisco. 51429
Murcia Saldana, Antonio. see Saldana, Antonio Murcia.
Murdaugh, --------. defendant 104022
Murden, Eliza. 51430
Murder a great and crying sin. (12369)
Murder & mystery. 91055
Muder in Cedar Bluff. 91725A
Murder most foul. (72166)
Murder of Batchelder. 6505, 9400
Murder of Dr. George Parkman. 17486
Murder of James J. Strang. 92687
Murder of the Christian Indians in North-America. 51431
Murder trials and executions in New Hampshire. 65235
Murder will out; being a short, but true, account. 97262
Murder will out. The first step in crime leads to the gallows. (19107)
Murderer. Discourse occasioned by the trial and execution. (37973)
Murderers, thieves, and blacklegs. 9401
Murderous assault. 92687
Murder's cave. 100929
Murders in Bussey's Wood. 7718
Murders in the Rue Morge. 83540
Murders. Report of the trial of James Johnson. (75954), note after 96890

Murdin, Cornelius. (51432)
Murdoch, ------. (78694)
Murdoch, Beamish. (51433), 74592
Murdoch, David. 51434-51435
Murdok, Elipahlet. 88652
Murdock, James, 1776-1856. 51436, 18991
Murdock, James E. 51437
Murdock, John. 97014
Murdock, John N. 51438-51439
Murdock, K. B. 104653, 104655
Murdock, William D. C. 51440-51441
Mureau, M. L. A. Milet. see Milet-Mureau, M. L. A.
Murel, J. A. see Murrell, John A., d. 1835.
Muret, Pierre. 51442-(51443)
Murgira y Galardi, Jose. 51444
Murguia, M. (65550)
Murguiendo, ---------. petitioner 59149
Murhard, Frederic. 44845
Muriedas y Compania. firm 88728
Muriel, Domingo. 51445
Muriel, Dominique. tr. 12131, 1st note after 98488
Murillo, --------. (19966)
Murillo Velarde, Pedro. 51448-51449
Murillo y Gordillo, Antonio. 51447
Murinais, --------. (1534), (27337)
Murk van Fhelgum, ---------. 51450
Muro, Antonio de San Jose. 51451, 76125
Muros y Salazar, Salvador Jose de. see Someruelos, Salvador Jose de Muros y Salazar, Marques de, 1754-1813.
Murphey, Archibald De Bow, 1777-1832. 51452
Murphy, Arthur, 1727-1805. 36302, (51453), 75949, 2d note after 96930A, 98519-98520
Murphy, B. P. 51454
Murphy, Dave. 51455
Murphy, Dennis F. reporter 10995, 51456-51457, 69942, 84728, 88394, 89212
Murphy, George Mollett. 51458, note after 92624
Murphy, Henry. 51459
Murphy, Henry Cruse, 1810-1882. 8287, 9771, 18503, 20596, 26272, 48688, 50629, 51460-51466, 69997, 84383, 91167-91169, note after 98474, note after 99310, 100853
Murphy, James J. reporter 69942, 88394, 90212 see also U. S. Congress. Senate. Reporter.
Murphy, John McLeod. 51468-51470
Murphy, Joseph W. 51472
Murphy, Murdoch. 104785
Murphy, P. P. 51473
Murphy, Th. 51475
Murphy, Timothy. 80968
Murphy, Tomas. 51476
Murphy, William D. 51477
Murphy (J. Arthurs) and Co. firm 51467
Murphy (John S.) firm publishers 51471
Murr, Christoph Gottlieb von, 1738-1811. 4043, (13179), 51478-(51482), 98777
Murr, M. de. 62805
Murray, Lieut. pseud. Red Rupert. see Ballou, Maturin Murray, 1820-1895.
Murray, Lieut. pseud. Scarlet flag. see Ballou, Maturin Murray, 1820-1895.
Murray, A. 51485
Murray, Alexander. petitioner (51484)
Murray, Alexander. plaintiff (51484)
Murray, Sir Alexander. (51483)
Murray, Alexander, 1811-1885. 10460, 54988
Murray, Amelia M. 51486
Murray, Andrew. 51487
Murray, Benjamin B. 51488
Murray, Charles Augustus. (51489)-(51491)
Murray, Daniel. 51492

Murray, David. 51493-51494
Murray, David, 1727-1796. see Mansfield,
David Murray, 2d Earl of, 1727-1796.
Murray, G. engr. 104597-104598
Murray, George W. 51496
Murray, H. L. (51498)
Murray, Henry A. 51497
Murray, Hugh, 1779-1846. 31939, (40201)-
40202, (51499)-51503, 51787
Murray, James, 1725?-1794. 38164, 67023
see also Canada. Governor General,
1760-1768 (Murray)
Murray, James, 1732-1782. 51504-51511,
79288, 94558, 96502, 104939
Murray, James, 1732-1782. supposed author
102647
Murray, James, fl. 1816. 101542
Murray, James B. 1529
Murray, James O. (51513)-51514
Murray, John. civil engineer 51528
Murray, John, Jr. 97938
Murray, John, Jr. incorrectly supposed author
21816, 54026, 54481
Murray, Mrs. John. see Murray, Judith
(Sargent)
Murray, John. of Montreal 51525
Murray, John, 1732-1809. see Dunmore,
John Murray, 4th Earl of, 1732-1809.
Murray, John, 1741-1815. (51520)-51524,
103803
Murray, John, 1742-1793. 3955, 51516-51519,
note after 104356, 105296
Murray, John, fl. 1825. defendant 73459
Murray, John, fl. 1832. 51526
Murray, John, fl. 1867. 51515
Murray, John B. 43599
Murray, John W. B. (51529)
Murray, Joseph. 51530, 84556, 84558
Murray, Judith (Sargent) (27558), 51524,
51531
Murray, Lindley, 1745-1826. 51533-51534
Murray, Lindley, fl. 1833. complainant
104500 see also Friends, Society of.
New York Monthly Meeting. Trustees.
complainants
Murray, M. 51535
Murray, Nicholas. 33593, 51536-51539
Murray, Orson S. 51540
Murray, Thomas Boyles. 32713, 51541-
51543
Murray, W., fl. 1739. 99894
Murray, W. W. (51551)
Murray, William. 55846 see also
Northumberland County, Pa. Sub
Lieutenant.
Murray, William, 1704-1793. see Mansfield,
William Murray, Earl of, 1704-1793.
Murray, William, fl. 1754. (51547)
Murray, William, fl. 1836. 31939
Murray, William Henry Harrison, 1840-1904.
51548-51549
Murray, William Vans. 257, (51550), 84832,
2d note after 104983
Murray (John) firm publishers (41319),
(18647), 35160, 51527, 78382
Murray's colonial library. (14319)
Murray's family library. 35160, 78382
Murray's home and colonial library. (18647)
Murray's official handbook of church and
state. 51527
Murray's railroad reading. (9692)
Murray's tourist's guide to the city of
Montreal. 38887
Murrell, John A., d. 1835. defendant 33250
Murrell, William Meacham. (51554)

Murrell's associates. defendants 33250, note
before 91708
Murry, Jo. Andrew. tr. 36987
Murs, O. des. see Des Murs, O.
Mursinna, Friedrich Samuel. 27210, 51555
Mursinna, Friedrich Samuel. supposed author
101819
Murto, A. L. 51556
Murtola, G. (51557)
Murton, John. (72095)
Murton, John. supposed author 104331
Musa, Antonius, fl. 23 B. C. 106294, 106330-
106331
Musa Americana. Poema. 51558
Musa Americana, seu de Deo carmina. (51559)
Musacus. pseud. Argument. 95280
Musaico poetico. 88808
Musci Alleghanienses. 28367
Musci Americani. 20975
Musci Austro-Americani. 49762
Muscipula: the mouse-trap. 32487
Muscipula sive Cambromyomachia. 65527
Muscogee Indians. see Creek Indians.
Muscogee or Creek Nation of Indians versus
the United States. 51583
Muscovie. 34100-34107
Muse, J. H. (51560)
Muse, James. 86700
Muse, Joseph E. 51561
Muse, Philip. 86700
Muse of Hesperia. (62740)
Musee Archeologique, Madrid. see Madrid.
Musee Archeologique.
Musee literaire du siecle. 92536
Musei Petiveriani. 61288
Musenalmanach. 86371
Museo Americano. 51563
Museo de ambas Americas. 51564
Museo de cuadros de costumbres. (51565)
Museo de Limenades. (72804)
Museo Mejicano. Antiguos Redactores. see
Antiguos Redactores del Museo Mejicano.
eds.
Museo Mexicano. 72267
Museo Mexicano, o miscelanea pintoresca.
51566
Museo Nacional de Antiguedades Mexicana,
Mexico (City) see Mexico (City) Museo
Nacional.
Museo Nacional de Mexico, Mexico (City) see
Mexico (City) Museo Nacional.
Museo pintoresco Mejicano. (51567)
Museo Publico de Buenos Aires. see Buenos
Aires. Museo Publico.
Museo Venezolana. (51568)
Museo Yucateco, periodics cientifico y literario
51569
Muses de la Nouvelle-France. (40169),
40172, 40174
Muse's pocket companion. 51562
Museu Imperial e Nacional, Rio de Janeiro.
see Rio de Janeiro. Museu
Nacional.
Museu Nacional, Rio de Janeiro. see Rio de
Janiero. Museu Nacional.
Museu Pittoresco. (51570)
Museum, Philadelphia. see Philadelphia
Museum.
Museum, Providence, R. I. see Providence,
R. I. Free Public Library, Art-Gallery,
and Museum.
Museum; a miscellaneous repository of instruc-
tion and amusement. 51571
Museum Americanum. 33631

Museum and Curiosity Shop, New York. see New York (City) Museum and Curiousity Shop.

Museum Company, Philadelphia. see Philadelphia Museum Company.

Museum d'Histoire Naturelle, Paris. see Paris. Museum d'Histoire Naturelle.

Museum museorum. 98357

Museum of Comparative Zoology, Harvard University. see Harvard University. Museum of Comparative Zoolohy.

Museum of Delaware. 102474

Museum of history. 51573

Museum of John R. Rhinelander. 70492

Museum of natural history.

Museum of Practical Geology, London. see London. Museum of Practical Geology.

Museum of remarkable and interesting events. 51574

Museum of the American Indian, Heye Foundation, New York. see New York (City) Museum of the American Indian, Heye Foundation.

Museum: or, the literary and historical register. (51575)

Museum Royal d'Histoire Naturelle, Paris. see Paris. Museum d'Histoire Naturelle.

Musgrave, G. W. 51576-51577

Music and odes of the Order of Sons of Temperance of the United States. 87013

Music . . . by Carl Lazare. 84763

Music Hall, Boston. see Boston. Music Hall.

Music Hall discourses, miscellaneous sketches, ministerial notes. 50646

Music-Hall sermons. 51549

Music in commemoration of the death of George Washington. 32475, 51578, note after 74795, note after 101879, 104278

Music in miniture. 5416

Music mad. 52164

Music of the spheres. 50630

Music performed at Newburyport, Mass. 54921, 1st note after 101856

Musical advertiser and masonic journal. 51579

Musical almanac for 1868. 22321

Musical biography. 58711

Musical bouquet. 94131

Musical companion. 95292

Musical Congress, New York, 1854. see New York Musical Congress, 1854.

Musical drama . . . . By Thomas Morton. 51030

Musical drama, in one act. 86928

Musical entertainment. 86902

Musical Fund, New York. see New York Musical Fund.

Musical Fund Society of Philadelphia. 61853

Musical Fund Society of Philadelphia. Charter. 61853

Musical Fund Society of Philadelphia. Joint Board of Officers. 61853

Musical grammar. 104115

Musical Institute, New York. 54408

Musical interlude, in one act. 21309, 105957

Musical magazine. 101811

Musical reporter. 51580

Musical review. see Theatrical censor and musical review.

Musical review, and record of musical science, literature and intelligence. 51581

Musical Society, Milwaukee. see Milwaukee Musical Society.

Musignano, Charles Jules Laurent Lucian Bonaparte, Prince de. see Bonaparte, Charles Jules Laurent Lucien, Prince de Canino, 1803-1857.

Musing of Carol. 39833

Musings of a recluse. (19667)

Muskingum legends. 64805

Muskingum Oil Spring Petroleum Company. 50266

Muskogee hymn book. 51584

Muskogee hymns. 51589

Muskogee Indians. see Creek Indians.

Mvskoke mopunvkv, nakchokv setempohetv. 51586

Mvskoke nakcokv eskerretv esvhokkolat. 72018

Muskokee (Creek) assistant. 51588

Muskokee hymns. 51585

Muskokee Indians. see Creek Indians.

Muskokee or Creek first reader. (51587), 72019-72020

Muskoki imvnaitsv. 51588

Mussani, C. (51590)

Musselman, Henry Kobler. defendant 51591, note after 104533

Musset, Georges. ed. 100828, 100830, 100832-100834

Mussey, Benjamin B. 51592, 64993

Mussey, Osgood. 51595

Mussey, R. D. 51594-51595

Musson, Eugene. 40662, 51596

Musson, John P. 51597

Must colored men be members of the congregation? 75473

Must the war go on? 24671

Mustang Gray. 13620

Mustee. 65115

Muster. 88048

Muster-roll, and other sketches. 48973

Muster roll of Captain ————. (51598)

Muster-roll of citizen soldiers at North Point. 51599

Muster rolls of Pembroke Massachusetts. 84300

Muster roll of the Union Army. 73342

Muster rolls of the New York State Volunteers. 53781

Mustered in and out of service. 95863

Mustered into service. 88048A

Mustered out. 37974

Musters, George Chaworth. (51600)

Mutability of created things. 92258

Mutability of the world. 105087

Mutations of the earth. 82921

Muter, George. (44778)

Mute's almanac, for . . . 1840. 51601

Muths, J. Ch. F. Guts. see Guts Muths, J. Ch. F.

Mutiny and murder. 27295, 101243

Mutiny on board the Lady Shore. 51602

Mutius. pseud. Letters of Mutius. 51603

Mutter, Thomas D. (51604)

Mutual Alliance Division, No. 130, New York. see Sons of Temperance of North America. New York. Mutual Alliance Division, No. 130.

Mutual Assistance Bag Company. 54409

Mutual Assurance Company, Philadelphia. (61854)

Mutual Assurance Society, Richmond. 100490-100493

Mutual Assurance Society, Richmond. Charter. 100492-100493

Mutual Assurance Society against fire on buildings. 100493

Mutual Assurance Society, Against Fire on Buildings in the State of Virginia. see Mutual Assurance Society, Richmond.

"Mutual Assurance Society, Against Fire on Buildings in the State of Virginia." Authorized to be established. 100492

Mutual Assurance Company, for Insuring Houses from Loss by Fire, New York. (51605)

Mutual banking. 51606

Mutual benefit building and loan associations. 51608

Mutual Benefit Life Insurance Company. 51607

Mutual Benefit Life Insurance Company. President. 51607

Mutual care the members of Christ's body owe to each other. 103322

Mutual Fire Society, Worcester, Mass. 105362

Mutual Insurance Association of Nassau, Schodack and Chatham, N. Y. 51609

Mutual interest of Great Britain and the American colonies considered. 6218

Mutual Life Insurance Company of New York. see New York Mutual Life Insurance Company.

Mutual Marine Insurance Company. 51611

Mutual obligation upon ministers, to speak. 19830

Mutual Relief Society, New York. 54411

Mutual rights. 85442

Mutual rights & Christian intelligencer. 85442

Mutual rights of the ministers and members. 51612

Muy noble, y leal ciudad de Santiago de Chile. 98301

Muyden, G. van. ed. 4540, 5135

Muys van Holy, D. see Muys van Holy, Nicolaes.

Muys van Holy, Nicolaes. 15935, 51613, 1st note after 102888, 102896, 102911

Muzafir. pseud. Yankeeland in her trouble. see Stocqueler, Joachim Haywood.

Muzzey, ARtemas B. 51614

Muzzey, Henry W. 51615

Muzzy, Harriet. 51616, 95226

My address to all those who may disbelieve. 92003

My adopted country. 72648

My adventures afloat. 79082

My adventures in Italy. 47047

My adventures in Texas. 75255

My ancestors in America. (62744)

My bondage and my freedom. 20714

My campaigns in America. 19801

My cave life in Vicksburg. 51617

My concise opinion of published arguments in the penalty of death. 71131

My connection with the Atlas newspaper. (31792)

My conscience! (9633)

My consulship. 40227

My country: a discourse delivered in the Protestant Reformed Dutch Church. 44231

My country; an illustrated and illuminated version of the American national anthem. 84054

My country, 'tis of thee. 83677, 84042, 84045, 84062

"My country, 'tis of thee," and the latest poems. 84053

My days and nights on the battlefield. 14168

My dear Pulteney. 82303

My design is, to shew you. 103262

My diary in America. 75546

My diary in Mexico in 1867. (75808)

My diary, north and south. 74398-74399, 74402

My diary; or, three weeks on the wing. (7337)

My egotistigoraphy. 30332

My experience. 82552

My farm of Edgewood. 49675

My father. 78178

My first campaign. 51618

My first seven years in America. 14330

My first visit to Europe. 20026

My friends and countrymen. 96182

My grandmother. 92170, 92175, 92176A

My imprisonment. 28634

My kind benefactors a new year commences. 103147

My last cruise. (29466)

My late engagements of a public nature. (68570)

My life-work. 84008

"My Lord. However . . . 60267

My Lords, ... 95397

My married life at Hillside. (14184)

My mind and its thoughts. 51027

My mother. (49699)

My mother's gold ring. (77011), 77016

My name was Captain Kidd, as I sail'd. (37705)

My native land. A poem. (51619), 89169

My native land, and other poems. 89170

My native land. [By Frederick J. Keyes.] 37682

My new home. (51620)

My own biography. 91813

My own book. 18293, (71344)

My own experience. 51621

My own memoir. 59165

My own times. Embracing also, the history of my life. 70420

My own times, or 'tis fifty years since. 11902

My progress in error and recovery of truth. 83583

My record in rebeldom. 76395

My ride to the barbecue. 51622

My satchel and I. 91006

My southern friends. 27450, 51623

My thirty years out of the Senate. 84142, 84145, 84151, 84162

My Uncle Hobson and I. 36588

My uncle's family 83506

My uncle's wedding. 83788

My vineyard at Lakeview. 51624

Mycall, John. (51625)

Mycall. firm publishers 95255

Myer, Albert J. 51626

Myer, Albert J. petitioner 51626

Myer, Paul. see Gonneville, Jean Binot Paulmyer de.

Myerle, David. 90720

Myers, -------. RA. 51630

Myers, Albert C. 82873, 83984

Myers, Amos, 1824-1893. 51627

Myers, Beatrix. Sister 51628

Myers, Frederic. 51629

Myers, H. Melville. ed. 87715

Myers, Harvey. ed. 37532, (37536), 85376

Myers, John. (51631)

Myers, John C. 51632

Myers, Leonard. (51633)-51634

Myers, P. Hamilton. (51635)-51638, 59197

Myers, Sarah Ann. 51639

Myers, Theodorus Bailey. (51640), 54105, 82774

Myers, Thomas. (51642)
Myers, Virginia. 51643
Myers-Mason, Theodora Bailey. 51641
Myers (P. M.) & Co. firm 88410
Mygatt, Frederick T. 51644
Myle, Arnold van der. see Mylius, Arnold, 1540-1604.
Myles, William. 51645
Myles Standish. 90169, 90171
Mylius, Abraham. see Milius, Abraham.
Mylius, Arnold, 1540-1604. 27691 27646, 66491
Mylius, Arnold van der. see Mylius, Arnold, 1540-1604.
Mylius, C. 51647
Mynde, -------. cartographer 84566
Myra: the child of adoption. 91287
Myrand, Dominique Prosper. 51648
Myrick, J. defendant 51649
Myritius, Ioannem. 51650
Myron. pseud. [Poems.] see Holmes, Abiel.
Myrrhen Berg. 106364
Myrsineae Centro-Americanae et Mexicanae. (56735)
Myrtaceae Centroamericanae. 4842A
Myrthe, A. T. pseud. Ambrosio de Letinez. see Ganihl, Anthony.
Myrtilla: a fairy extravaganza. 70830
Myrtis; with other etchings and sketches. 80934
Myrtle, Frank. pseud. Poems. see Spencer, Caleb Lynn.
Myrtle, Minnie. pseud. Iroquois. see Johnson, Anna C.
Myrtle leaves. 44252
Myself. pseud. Handle for the battle axe. see Waterous, Timothy, Sr. Waterous, Timothy, Jr. Waterous, Zachariah.
Myself: a romance of New England life. 51652
Myst, Gerardus de. see Mijst, Gerardus de la.
Mystagogus Candidus. pseud. Two letters. 97572
Mysteres de l'esclavage aux Etats-Unis. 92528
Mysteres de l'Inquisition. 93348
Mysteres de Montreal. (12573)
Mysteries and miseries of New-York. 36862
Mysteries and miseries of Philadelphia. (41399), 51653
Mysteries and miseries of the great metropolis. 59598
Mysteries, fallacies, and absurdities of spirit-rapping. 67919
Mysteries less mysterious. 84963
Mysteries, miseries, and rascalities of the Ohio Penitentiary. 43235
Mysteries of astrology and the wonders of magic. (71720)
Mysteries of bee-keeping explained. (67180)
Mysteries of California. (10035)
Mysteries of city life. 68642
Mysteries of crime. (51654)
Mysteries of free masonry. (50679)
Mysteries of government. 87897, note after 89935
Mysteries of Greene Street. (51655)
Mysteries of neutralization. 8513
Mysteries of New York. 51656
Mysteries of Providence. 9192
Mysteries of shopping. 59529
Mysteries of the backwoods. 95663
Mysteries of the castle. 103415
Mysteries of the scout service. 18131
Mysteries of the three cities. 21156

Mysteries of the trapper's cave. 79851
Mysteries of Washington City. (51657)
Mysteries of Worcester. 89558
Mysteries; or glimpses of the supernatural. 22258
Mysteries revealed. 72853
Mysterious being of the cave. 36582
Mysterious bridal, and other tales. 92147-92148
Mysterious chief. 105179
Mysterious messenger. 51658
Mysterious miner. 27946
Mysterious nothing. (74635)
Mysterious stranger. 3947
Mystery, a sermon. 85479
Mystery. [By Arthur Cleveland Coxe.] (77160)
Mystery. [By Henry Wadsworth Longfellow.] (41932)
Mystery developed. 31054, 96830, 101012
Mystery finished. 51659
Mystery hid from ages and generations. 12331
Mystery of a Christ within, explained. (46584), 2d note after 100616
Mysterh of animal magnetism revealed to the world. 90965
Mystery of Camp White. 31324
Mystery of Christ opened and applyed. 46706
Mystery of Edwin Drood. 54960
Mystery of Foxcraft. 66743
Mystery of God finished. 103435
Mystery of iniquity. 76415
Mystery of Israel's salvation. 46707
Mystery of Night Island. 77335
Mystery of Providence. 2015
Mystery of the Gospel. 3471
Mystery of the mischianza. 47950
Mystery of the Perrys. (64195)
Mystery of the seven stars in Christ's right hand. 26785
Mystery of the Trinity. 46249
Mystery of the two Adams, explained. (46483)
Mystery of the Westeroefts. 19292
Mystery revealed; or, the way of peace. 51660
Mystery reveal'd; or truth brought to light. 15205, (41650), (47511)-47512, 51661, 101710
Mystery solved; a Canadian tale. (13634)
Mystic Church. 51662
Mystic-Hall Seminary, West Medford, Mass. 51663
Mystic mount, and the voice. (26945)
Mystic River Railroad (Proposed) 51664
Mystic River Works. 51665
Mystic star. 51666
Mystic temple. 51667
Mystic tie. (51668)
Mystical craft. (51669)
Mystical marriage. 46423
Mysticism and its results. 19334
Mystico fenix que renace y se eterniza en su muerte. 86423
Mystic's plea for universal redemption. 104725
Myth of Hiawatha, and other oral legends. 77835, (77861)
Mythen und Sagen der Indianer America's. 51670
Mythische Vorstellungen vom Ursprungen der Volker und Sprachen. (64599)
Mythology. 50038
Myths of the New World. 7998

N

"N." pseud. Political remarks. see
Northrop, Claudian Bird, 1812-1865.
N***. pseud. Voyages aux cotes de Guinee.
51677, note after 100827
N——b——H——n. pseud. Address to the
public. see Thurston, Benjamin.
N., C. pseud. ed. 57476
N., D. pseud. Proposals for traffick and
commerce. 66039
N., D. pseud. Writings. 26906
N., E. D. pseud. Maryland not a Roman
Catholic colony. see Neill, Edward
Duffield.
N., F. J. pseud. Barnum's baby show.
51671
N., G. A. y. pseud. see A. y N., G.
pseud.
N., J. pseud. Indice de las materias.
51673
N., J. pseud. Letter on the present state of
the Spanish West Indies. 19726, (40369)
N----, J----. pseud. Liberty and property
of British subjects asserted. 40937,
note after 87866
N., J. pseud. Observations upon Mr.
Fauquier's essay. (51674)
N., J. pseud. Revolutionary claims.
(51674A)
N., J. C. pseud. Naauwkeringe beschryving
van Noord-America. 51675
N., J. H. pseud. Suriname in losse tafereelen.
see Nagel, J. H.
N., J. St. pseud. History of baptism. see
St. Nicholas, John.
N——, Katty. pseud. History of Miss Katty
N——. (51676)
N., L. M. pseud. tr. see Lenoble,
Eustache. tr.
N., M. pseud. Voyages interessans. see
Nougaert, M.
N., N. pseud. America. see Peake, Thomas.
N., N. pseud. Brief van NN. aan zijnen
vriend A. 51679
N., N. pseud. Cort verhael. 45404, 51680
N., N. pseud. Che la platina Americana era
un metallo conosciuto dagli antichi.
51681
N., N. pseud. Examiner examin'd. see
Brown, John, 1724-1791.
N., N. pseud. Some reflections on the law
of bankruptcy. 51682
N., N. pseud. Verses. 33442
N., N. pseud. Vie du Venerable Dom Jean de
Palafox. see Dinouart, Chanoine de S.
Benoit. and Champion, P.
N., N. de. pseud. Suplemento. 93789
N., R. pseud. tr. 10158
N., R. pseud. New attractive. see Norman,
Robert.
N., S. pseud. engr. (25283)
N., S. pseud. Abraham in arms. see
Nowel, Samuel.
N., S. von. pseud. Mein Besuch Americas.
51672
N., T. pseud. tr. see Nicholas, Thomas.
N., W., of the Middle-Temple. pseud. Large
additions. 10819
N. A., J. P. F. pseud. Dialogo constitucional
Brasileiro. see Nabuco de Araujo, Jose
Paulo de Figueiroa.
N. A. pseud. see A., N. pseud.
"N. A. R." (33333)
N. B. pseud. see B., N. pseud.

N. B. pseud. see Barre, Nicolas.
N. B. C. pseud. see Craig, Neville B.
N. B. E. Society. see Northern Baptist
Education Society.
N. B. S. pseud. see Shurtleff, Nathaniel
Bradstreet, 1810-1874.
N. C. pseud. see Collins, Nathaniel.
supposed author
N de N. pseud. see N., N. de. pseud.
N. E. pseud. see E., N. pseud.
N. E. C. pseud. see C., N. E. pseud.
N. G. pseud. see Geelkerchken, Nic. van.
supposed author
N. G. C. pseud. see Clark, N. G.
N. G. W. pseud. tr. see Wolf, N. G. tr.
N. H. pseud. see Harris, Nicholas.
N. H. pseud. see Hobart, Nehemiah.
NHDDMMS, Loving Brothers. pseud. see
Holmes, Nathaniel, 1599-1678.
N. L., Gentleman. pseud. see Lichefield,
Nicholas. tr.
N. L. B. pseud. see Napoleon III, Emperor
of the French, 1808-1873.
N. L. S. pseud. see Smith, Nina L.
N. M. T. pseud. see T., N. M. pseud.
N. N. pseud. see N., N. pseud.
N. N. pseud. see Champion, P.
N. N. pseud. see Dinouart, Chanoine de S.
Benoit.
N. N. pseud. see Peake, Thomas. supposed
author
N. O. pseud. see Cuoo, A.
N. R. pseud. see Mather, Cotton, 1663-1728.
N. S. pseud. see S., N. pseud.
N. S. pseud. see Strong, Nehemiah.
N. S. Presbyter. pseud. see S., N.,
Presbyter. pseud.
N. T. Pharmacopola. pseud. see Mainwaring,
Mr. ---------. supposed author
N. V. G. pseud. see Geelkercken, Nic. van.
N. W. pseud. see Whittemore, N.
Na berita a me na kauoha o ka ekalesia o Iesu
Kristo. 83227
Na na none do wau gau ne u wen noo da.
79117
Naamrol der predikanten in de gemeenten.
51683
Naar, D. ed. 53174
Naarder reglement of het subject. 51684
Naaukeurige landkaarten van den Heere N.
Sanson. (38504)
Naaukeurige versameling der gedenk-waardigste
zee en land-reysen. 3, 3960, 4806-4807,
5905, (6035), (10690), 77683, 82817,
82822, 82838, 82853, 86427, 90056-90057,
99281, 1st note after 103943
Naauwkeurig verkal van de zeer schrikkelyke
aardbeving. (35559), 51685, 97172
Naauwakeurige beschryving van Noord-America.
51675
Naauwkeurige beschryving van Noord-America,
zynde thans het toneel des oorlogs. 55430
Naauwkeurige Hollandsche almanach. 51686
Naauwkeurige naamlyst der plantagien en
gronden. 93859
Nabby (Schooner) in Admiralty 97747
Nabuco, -------. 85773
Nabuco de Araujo, Jose Paulo de Figueiroa.
51687-51688

Nach Amerika! 27182

Nach den gegenwartigen Zustanden des Landes
und Volkes. 11682
Nach den neuesten Materielien. 1464
Nach den Reisebriefen der Verfassers frei
bearbeitet von Robett Schweichel. 7078

Nach dreissing Jahren! 91198
Nach Venedig uberbrachte Mohr. (10910)
Nachgelassene schriften und correspondenz. 25556A
Nachgelassenen Papieren. 24008
Nachklang zum Gesang der einsamen Turtel Taube. 51689
Nachlasse Herman Billroth's. 5421
Nacho, -------. pseud. Dialogo entre D. Chepe y D. Nacho. 76197
Nachricht seiner von Gott geschehenen volligen Herausfuhrung aus Babel. 72590
Nachricht von Californien. 98844
Nachricht von d. Franzosische Guiana. 11623
Nachricht v. d. gagenwartig. Zustand d. Englisch. Colonien. 96191
Nachricht von dem Sprachen der Volker am Orinokofulsse. 98777
Nachricht von dem zu Gettysburg in Pennsylvanien. 97538
Nachricht von den Durch das Blut. 38040
Nachricht von den neuesten Endeckungen der Englander. 16243
Nachricht von den Sprachen der Volker am Orinokoflusse. 51480, (51482), 98777
Nachricht von den vielen Lastern. 35794
Nachricht von denen Granzstreitigkeiten. 57162
Nachricht von der Bekehrung des Herrn Johann Thayer. 95250
Nachricht von der Geschichte. (31208)
Nachricht von der Provincz Virginien. 51690, 100494
Nachricht von einer Hochteutschen Evangelischen Colonie zu Germantown. 27160, 101420
Nachricht von Sumatra. 38398
Nachricht von Surinam und seiner Einwohner. 51691
Nachricht von Suriname und seinen Einwohnern. 66941
Nachricht wegen der Landschaft Pennsylvania in America. 59710, (59719), 59733
Nachrichten. 23094, 4th note after 97845, note after 106352
Nachrichten aus der Bruder-Gemeinde. 51692
Nachrichten aus der Heidenwelt. 75767
Nachrichten aus Portugal. 22827
Nachrichten uber Chile und die Halbinsel Patagonien. 106338
Nachrichten uber den Gronlandischen Wallfischfangst. 64449
Nachrichten uber die fruheren Einwahner von Nord-Amerika. 57819
Nachrichten uber die fruheren Einwohner von Nord Amerika und ihre Denkmaler. 2225, 50537
Nachrichten uber die Witterung und Krankheiten in Sudcarolina. 11773
Nachrichten und Erfahrungen uber die Vereinigten Staaten. 97922
Nachrichten und Erinnerungen an Verschiedene Deutsche Volker. 51693
Nachrichten vom Lande Guiana. 27381
Nachrichten von d. General Hauptmannschaft Caracas. 19646
Nachrichten von dem Westlichen Lande. 34359
Nachrichten von den Englischen Colonisten Georgiens. (38041)
Nachrichten von den Kaiserl. Osterreichischen Naturforschen in Brazilien. 7607, (77973)
Nachrichten von den Sitten und Gebrauchen der Tarahumaren. 91187

Nachrichten von den Vereinigten Deutschen Evangelisch-Lutherischen Gemeinen in Noord-America. 51694, 78013-78014
Nachrichten von den Westlichen bisjetzt noch unbekannten Theilen von America. (19130)
Nachrichten von der Amerikanischen Halbinsel Californien. (4363), note after 51694
Nachrichten von der Landschaft Guiana. 12835
Nachrichten von der Pest in London. 10888
Nachrichten von diesem Lande. 21432
Nachrichten von Gronland. 22040
Nachrichten von Island, Gronland und der Strasse Davis. 1405
Nachrichten von Kentucky. 85251
Nachrichten von Pensylvanien. 12557
Nachrichten von seinen Reisen. 8727
Nachricthen von Surinam und von seiner Expedition. 91080
Nachrichten von Suriname, dem letzten Aufruhr. 91079
Nachrichten von verschiedenen Landern. 4043, 51481
Nachrichten zur Geschichte von Cayenne und dem Franzosischen Guiana. 2813
Nachrichtung vor alle die jenihe welch. 102899
Nachtrag zu dem Berichte meiner Reise. 86848
Nachtrag zu der Schrift: Frankreichs verfahren. 99303
Nachtrag zu meiner Schrift: "Nordamerikas Stellung." 4842
Nachtrage, Berichtigungen und Zusatze sur der Beschreibung meiner Reise im Ostlichen Brasilien. 47013
Nachweisung aller Volker der Erdbodens. (4858)
Nacimiento de la mejor aurora. 76780
Nacimiento i benedicion de Cain. 76700
Nacimientos del Susquehanna. 16506
Nacion. 51695
Nacion Argentina. 38946
Nacion. Periodico politico, cientifico y literario. 51696
Nacional Colegio de Abogados de Mexico. (48455), (48465), 48517
Nacional y Mas Antiguo Colegio de S. Ildefonso de Mexico. see Colegio de San Ildefonso de Mexico.
Naciones no pueden despojar a la iglesia de su bienes. 51697
Nack, James. (51698)-51700
Nack, Johann Bernhard. tr. 39584
Nacoochee Hydraulic Mining Company. 51701
Naccochee; or, the beautiful star. 12854
Nactividade e Silva, Galdino Augusto. 69316 see also Alagoas (Brazilian Province) Presidente (Nactividade e Silva)
Nada contrapuesta en los balanzas de Dios. 22063
Nada mas gloriosa. 76187
Nadaillac, Jean Francois Albert du Pouget, Marquis de, 1818-1904. 21392
Nadal, Bernard H. (51702)-51703
Nadal de Saintrac, Louis. 51704
Nadasus, Joannes. 713
Nader aanteekening van Dordrecht, Rotterdam en Schiedam. 36563
Nader informatie en bericht voor de gene die genegen zijn. (59707), 102227
Nader ordre, ende reglement, vande Hooghe Moghende Heeren Staten Generael der Vereenighde Nederlanden, gearresteert by advijs. 51705, 1st note after 102899

Brookline, Cambridge, and Worcester Massachusetts. 72834

Names of soldiers who died in defence of the American Union, interred in New Hampshire. (72826)

Names of soldiers who died in defence of the American Union, interred in New York, Illinois, Virginia, West Virginia, Missouri. 72830

Names of soldiers who died in defence of the American Union, interred in New York, New Jersey, Pennsylvania, Maryland, Virginia. 72829

Names of soldiers who died in defence of the American Union, interred in the eastern district of Texas. 72823

Names of soldiers who died in defence of the American Union, interred in the national and public cemeteries in Kentucky. (72835)

Names of soldiers who died in defence of the American Union, interred in the national cemeteries at Antietam, (Maryland.) (72833), (72844)

Names of soldiers who died in defence of the American Union, interred in the national cemeteries, at Baltimore, Maryland, Petersbury, Virginia. 72837, (72844)

Names of soldiers who died in defence of the American Union, interred in the national cemeteries at Chattanooga, Stone's River, and Knoxville, Tenn. 72828, 72844

Names of soldiers who died in defence of the American Union, interred in the national cemeteries at Corinth, Mississippi. (72838), (72845)

Names of soldiers who died in defence of the American Union, interred in the national cemeteries at Fort Harrison, Va. (72836), (72844)

Names of soldiers who died in defence of the American Union, interred in the national cemeteries at Fortress Monroe and Hampton, Va. (72822)

Names of soldiers who died in defence of the American Union, interred in the national cemeteries at Marietta, Ga. 72828, 72841

Names of soldiers who died in defence of the American Union, interred in the national cemeteries at Memphis, Tennessee. 72839

Names of soldiers who died in defence of the American Union, interred in the national cemeteries at Washington, D. C. 72818

Names of soldiers who died in defence of the American Union, interred in the national cemetery at Nashville, Tennessee. 51875, 72840

Names of soldiers who died in defence of the American Union, interred in Wisconsin, New York, Pennsylvania, Iowa. 72827

Names of soldiers who died in defence of the Union, interred in the national cemeteries at Beaufort. (72838), (72842), (72845)

Names of soldiers who died in defence of the Union, interred in the national cemeteries at Mound City, Illinois. (72833), (72836)- 72837, 72843-(72844)

Names of soldiers who died in defence of the Union, interred in the national cemeteries at Vicksburg, Miss. (72842), (72845)

Names of soldiers who died in defence of the Union, interred in the national cemeteries

in Fredericksburg, Virginia. 72843- (72844)

Names of soldiers who, in defence of the American Union, suffered martyrdom in the prison pens throughout the south. 72832

Names of subscribers to the Bunker Hill Monument. (9179)

Names of the aduenturers, with the sums paid to Sir Edwin Sandys. 99877

Names of the aduenturers, with their seuerall sums aduentured. 99877

Names of the foundation members. 10147

Names of the members of the First or North Church of Christ. 64423

Names of the officers and members of the Union League of Philadelphia. 51745

Names of the officers and privates who fell in the battle of Gettysburg. 27238

Names of the owners or occupants of buildings. (66285)

Names of the proprietors of the unclaimed dividends. (51746)

Names of the pupils of the Round Hill School. 55772

Names of the streets, lanes, and alleys in the town of Boston. 6531

Names of the streets, lanes, and alleys within the town of Boston. 6530

Names of the subscribers for the establishment. 100493

Names of the tax payers. 8255

Names of voters in Fayette Co., Ky. 51744

Names should succeed ideas. 83916

Nancey Dawson. 104455

Nancrede, Joseph G. 51747

Nancrede (J.) firm 88555

Nancy, France. International Congress of Americanists, 1st, 1875. see International Congress of Americanists, 1st, Nancy, France, 1875.

Nancy, France (Diocese) Bishop (Janson) (35771) see also Janson, Forbin, Bp.

Nancy Blake letters to a western cousin. 7590, 51748

Nancy Dawson. 96322

Nancy van Hann [sic] vs. Silas E. Burrows. 9478, 96842

Nantes, Bernardo de. 51749

Nantes, Martin de. see Martin de Nantes. Pere

Nantes, France. Plusieurs Anciens Colons- Proprietaries. petitioners see Plusieurs Anciens Colons-Proprietaires Residant a Nantes. petitioners

Nantes, France. Societe d'Agriculture, des Artes & du Commerce. see Societe d'Agriculture, des Artes & du Commerce de Nantes.

Nanticoke Indians. 45343, 49348-49349

Nanticoke Indians. Treaties, etc. 36337, (36339), 60255, 65759

Nantucket, Mass. Public Schools. 51753

Nantucket, Mass. School Committee. 51753

Nantucket, Mass. School Committee. Committee of Teachers. 51733

Nantucket Agricultural Society. 51755

Nantucket Athenaeum. 51751

Nantucket in the revolution. 90505

Naomi, a Cherokee woman. 93215

Naomi; or, Boston two hundred years ago. 39730

Naphegyi, Gabor. (51756)

Napier, ----------, fl. 1740. (19715)

Napier, Charles James. (51757)

Narrative, &c. The following late transactions. 87898

Narrative founded on facts. 99423

Narrative, founded on recent and interesting facts. (68537)-(68538)

Narrative journal of travels, from Detroit northwest through the great chain of American lakes. (77862), 77878

Narrative journal of travels through the northwestern regions of the United States. (77862), 77878

Narrative, interspersed with remarks, and an appendix. 58790, 58792

Narrative of a boat expedition up the Wellington channel. (43100)

Narrative of a captivity among the Mohawk Indians. (36142), (80023)

Narrative of a commuted pensioner. 104461

Narrative, of a five years' expedition. 12723, 91057, 91075, 91076, 95606

Narrative of a great deliverance at sea. 36336

Narrative of a journey. 74730

Narrative of a journey across the cordillera of the Andes. 65951

Narrative of a journey across the Rockey Mountains. 96381-96382

Narrative of a journey, by Mr. Ellis. 22299

Narrative of a journey, . . . &c. 25626

Narrative of a journey from Lima to Para. 85346

Narrative of a journey from Santiago de Chile to Buenos Ayres. 31681

Narrative of a journey in the Prairie. 62815

Narrative of a journey of five thousand miles through the eastern and western states of America. 23956

Narrative of a journey round the world. Comprising a winter passage across the Andes to Chili. 27183

Narrative of a journey round the world, during the years 1841 and 1842. (81343)

Narrative of a journey through the eastern and western states of America in 1817. 84304-84306, 84320-84321

Narrative of a journey to Guatemala. 50139

Narrative of a journey to the shores of the Arctic Ocean. (37831)

Narrative of a journey to the shores of the Polar Sea. (25624)-(25625), 25627

Narrative of a late expedition against the Indians. 38109

Narrative of a mission to Nova Scotia. 44716

Narrative of a missionary tour. 17210

Narrative of a most extraordinary work of religion. 29784

Narrative of a new and unusual American imprisonment of two Presbyterian ministers. 44079-44080, note before 51781

Narrative of a nine months' residence in New Zealand. 21624

Narrative of a passage from the island of Cape Breton. 42622

Narrative of a patriot exile. (79359)

Narrative of a person who was present when he died. 94539-94540

Narrative of a private soldier in the 92d Regiment. 51781

Narrative of a recent visit to Brazil. 9244, 10675

Narrative of a residence at the court of London. 74266

Narrative of a residence in a Brazilian valley. 59278

Narrative of a residence of six years on the western side. 17267

Narrative of a revival of religion, in Springfield, Vermont. 89896

Narrative of a revival of religion, in the Third Presbyterian Church. 101229

Narrative of a second expedition to the shores of the Polar Sea. 25628-25629

Narrative of a second voyage in search of a north-west passage. 73370, 73381, 73384

Narrative of a second voyage in the Victory. 7360

Narrative of a shipwreck on the island of Cape Breton. 65079

Narrative of a tour in North America. 97401

[Narrative of a tour in the northwest in 1817.] 92227

Narrative of a tour of observation. 50023

Narrative of a tour through the island. 30780

Narrative of a tour through the state of Indiana. 104304

Narrative of a tour to, & one year's residence. 104013

Narrative of a very tragical accident. 46313

Narrative of a visit to Brazil, Chile, Peru, and the Sandwich Islands. 46858

Narrative of a visit to the Right Rev. Philander Chase. 2749

Narrative of a voyage around the world. 4390

Narrative of a voyage from Dublin to Quebec. 104640

Narrative of a voyage from Dumfries to Saint John. 41305

Narrative of a voyage in the East India Squadron under Com. George C. Read. 2095, (31430)

Narrative of a voyage of discovery, performed in H. M. Vessel the Lady Nelson. 28306

Narrative of a voyage of discovery towards the North Pole. (31020)

Narrative of a voyage round the world during the years 1835, 36, and 37. 74186

Narrative of a voyage, taken by Capt. James Vanleason. note before 98445, 98468

Narrative of a voyage taken by James Van Leason. 98462

Narrative of a voyage to, and travels in Upper Canada. 94471

Narrative of a voyage to Brasil. 41294

Narrative of a voyage to Hudson's Bay. (12005)

Narrative of a voyage to Maryland. 103353

Narrative of a voyage to Patagonia. 43181

Narrative of a voyage to Quebec. 43159

Narrative of a voyage to Spitzbergen. 89542

Narrative of a voyage to Surinam. (74750)

Narrative of a voyage to the Ethiopic and South Atlantic Ocean. 50776

Narrative of a voyage to the north west coast of America. 25432

Narrative of a voyage to the Pacific. 4347

Narrative of a voyage to the south seas. 27929

Narrative of a voyage to the southern Atlantic Ocean. 102429

Narrative of a voyage to the Spanish Main. 51782

Narrative of a voyage to the West Indies and Mexico. 11842

Narrative of a voyage, with a party of emigrants. (8830)

Narrative of a whaling voyage round the globe. 4726

Narrative of adventure. (80730)

Narrative of adventures in the Oregon and Rocky Mountains. 73327

Narrative of adventures in the western wilderness, forty years ago. (36535), (80732), note after 89943

Narrative of adventures in the wilderness. 36533

Narrative of affairs lately received from His Majesties island of Jamaica. 35633

Narrative [of Alexander Campbell.] (50834)

Narrative of Alvar Nunez Cabeca de Vaca. Translated by Buckingham Smith. 9771, 84383

Narrative of Alvar Nunez Cabeza de Vaca. 16951

Narrative of Amos Dresser. 20924

Narrative of an African prince. 51783

Narrative of an attack upon a party of travellers. 20100

Narrative of an attempt to reach the North Pole. 51784, 58868

Narrative of an English farmer. 34795, 62640

Narrative of an expedition against the revolted Negroes of Surinam. 91075

Narrative of an expedition in H. Majesty's Ship Terror. 2617

Narrative of an expedition into the land of Canaan. 37405, 93092

Narrative of an expedition of five Americans. (51785)

Narrative of an expedition through the upper Mississippi. 77863, 77878

Narrative of an expedition to, and the storming of, Buenos Ayres. 9026, 51805

Narrative of an expedition to the east coast of Greenland. 28179

Narrative of an expedition to the Polar Seas. 105518

Narrative of an expedition to the shores of the Arctic Sea. (67428)

Narrative of an expedition to the source of St. Peter's River. (37137)

Narrative of an extraordinary escape out of the hands of the Indians. 82278

Narrative of an official visit to Guatemala from Mexico. 95511

Narrative of Andersonville. 89300

Narrative of Arctic discovery. 80488

Narrative of Arctic discovery and adventure. (38135)

Narrative of Arctic experience in search of survivors. 29739

Narrative of Arthur Gordon Pym. 63524-63525

Narrative of Asa-Asa. 65569

Narrative of calamitous and increasing shipwrecks, &c. 51840

Narrative of Capt. Cranebrook. 17408

Narrative of Captain Samuel Mackay. 43367

Narrative of certain events connected with the late disturbances in Jamaica. 35634

Narrative of certain facts, related by Mr. Lawrence. 39363

Narrative of certain matters relative to Trinity Church in Newport, R. I. 6935, (77412)

Narrative of certain occurrences at the late special convention of the Diocese of New-York. 51786, note after 89350, 1st note after 94541

Narrative of Colonel David Fanning. 23778-23779

Narrative of Col. Ethan Allen's captivity. 793-796, 798

Narrative of conversion to the faith. 90536

Narrative of criminal trials in Scotland. 9495

Narrative of Dimmock Charlton. 12146

Narrative of discovery and adventure. 55792

Narrative of discovery and adventure in the North Pacific. (64029)

Narrative of discovery and adventure in the Polar Seas and regions. (40201), 51787

Narrative of Dr. M. Lorner. 42101

Narrative of Dorah Mahoney. 43874

Narrative of early travels in California. 104616

Narrative of Ebenezer Fletcher. 9538, 24719

Narrative of Edward McGowan. 43278

Narrative of Eleazer Sherman. (80357)

Narrative of eleven months' residence in Bogota. 91389

Narrative of events, as they occurred from time to time. 103420

Narrative of events and difficulties in the colonization of Oregon. 37263

Narrative of events at Harper's Ferry. 1414

Narrative of events at Lake George. 19194

Narrative of events connected with the acceptance. 35813

[Narrative of events connected with the rise and progress of the Protestant Episcopal Church] in Maryland from 1632 to 1838. 30963, 1st note after 100494

Narrative of events connected with the rise and progress of the Protestant Episcopal Church in Virginia, with appendix of the journals. 30963, 30967, 1st note after 100494, 100513

Narrative of events in the life of William Green. 28565

Narrative of events in the south of France. (16324)

Narrative of events since the first of August, 1834. 104237-104238

Narrative of events since the 1st of August, 1834. 104239

Narrative of events which occurred in Baltimore town. 51788, 66731

Narrative of every-day life in the Arctic Seas. 85560

Narrative of excursions, voyages, and travels. 67911

Narrative of explorations and adventures, in Kansas. 25839, 77710, 85161

Narrative of facts. 28648, 34462, 51431

Narrative of facts . . . a protest against the consecration of the Rev. Dr. Hawks. 66972

Narrative of facts and circumstances that have tended to produce a secession from the Society of Friends. 51789, 55959, 2d note after 92833

Narrative of facts and incidents. 5888

Narrative of facts. By her mother, H. L. M[urray.] (51498)

Narrative of facts. By James Cook Richmond. 71140-(71141)

Narrative of facts connected with the change in the political condition. (59343)

Narrative of facts relative to the conduct of some of the members of the Legislature of Pennsylvania. 51801, 60268

Narrative of five youth from the Sandwich Islands. 51790, (76453)

Narrative of four voyages, to the South Sea. 50778

Narrative of Francisco Ulloa. 16951

Narrative of General Ramel. 67633

Narrative of God's love to William Thoresby. 95613

Narrative of the claim and title of Samuel Allen to New Hampshire. 51800

Narrative of the conduct and adventures of Henry Frederic Moon. 3948

Narrative of the conduct and conversion [of John B. Gough.] 28083

Narrative of the conduct of members of the Legislature of Pennsylvania. 51801, 60268

Narrative of the consecration of the Rev. Henry U. Onderdonk. 57318

Narrative of the contest in 1860. 17827

Narrative of the controversy between the Rev. Jedediah Morse. 214

Narrative of the corruptions in the state courts. 41321

Narrative of the cruel treatment of James Williams. 104240

Narrative of the cruise of the Alabama. 577

Narrative of the cultivating of clove trees in Dominica. 51802

Narrative of the dangers and distresses. (50834)

Narrative of the dealing of the Third Baptist Church. 95435

Narrative of the death of Captain James Cook. 75970

Narrative of the deportation to Cayenne, and shipwreck on the coast of Scotland. 545

Narrative of the deportation of Cayenne, of Barthelemy. 11621, (67630)

Narrative of the deputation from the Baptist Union in England. (17256)

Narrative of the destruction of the "Amazon." 5979

Narrative of the difficulties in the First Presbyterian Church of Brooklyn. 8306

Narrative of the discoveries of the north coast of America. 81374

Narrative of the discovery of America. 38949

Narrative of the discovery of the fate of Sir John Franklin. 43043

Narrative of the disputation held at Portsmouth. 50661

Narrative of the dispute between John Taylor. 94480

Narrative of the dissolution of the Medical Faculty of Transylvania University. 105950

Narrative . . . of the division among the members of the Associate Body. 51803

Narrative of the division in the Reformed Presbyterian Church. 78252

Narrative of the doings during the siege of Quebec. (80871)

Narrative of the early days and reminiscences of Oceola Nikkanochee. (56642), 1st note after 102515

Narrative of the early history of a . . . Moravian . . . clergyman. 50983

Narrative of the early life, travels, and Gospel labours of Jesse Kersey. 37635

Narrative of the embarrassment and decline of Hamilton College. 18825

Narrative of the entire massacre of the white population. 12356

Narrative of the establishment of the said Academy. 62102

Narrative of the events attending the massacre. 89389

Narrative of the events connected with the rise and progress of the Protestant Episcopal Church in Virginia. 30963

Narrative of the events preceding and following the seizure of the Chincha Islands. 11710

Narrative of the excursion and ravages of the King's troops. 26318, 51804

Narrative of the excursion to the west. 61970

Narrative of the exertions and sufferings of Lieut. James Moody. 9537-9538, (50309)-50311

Narrative of the expedition into the Mipmuch country. 52872

Narrative of the expedition of an American squadron to the China Seas and Japan. (30968)

Narrative of the expedition of H. M. S. Assistance. 4389

Narrative of the expedition of Luis Hernandez de Biedma. 24858

Narrative of the expedition of the Marquis de Nonville. 51806, (55421)

Narrative of the expedition to, and the storming of Buenos Ayres. 9026, 51805

Narrative of the expedition to South America. (8455)

Narrative of the expedition to the Polar Sea. (22578)

Narrative of the expedition to the Rivers Orinoco and Paure. (31988)

Narrative of the expedition which sailed from England in 1817. 29476

Narrative of the Exploring Expedition to the Rocky Mountains. 25836, (25841)

Narrative of the extraordinary adventures of four Russian sailors. 29383, 89543

Narrative of the extraordinary hardships suffered by the adventures in this voyage. 62458

Narrative of the extraordinary life of Amos Wilson. 104605

Narrative of the extraordinary life of John Conrad Shafford. 79686

Narrative of the extraordinary sufferings of Mr. Robert Forbes. 7288

Narrative of the facts connected with the change affected. 25433

Narrative of the facts . . . relating to the kidnapping and presumed murder of William Morgan. 50684

Narrative of the facts relative to the conduct of Vice-Admiral Gambier. 26504

Narrative of the facts relative to the trial of Joe Denny. 19598

Narrative of the failure of an attempt to establish a great national institution. 38462

Narrative of the fall & winter campaign. 43037

Narrative of the Fenian invasion, of Canada. 86822

Narrative of the festivities observed in honor of the completion. 92149

Narrative of the founding and settling the new-gathered congregational church in Boston. (17673)

Narrative of the first voyage to Maryland by the Rev. Father Andrew White. 103353

Narrative of the general course of history. 51807

Narrative of the gracious dealings of God in the conversion of W. Mooney Fitzgerald and John Clark. (49140)

Narrative of the grand civic and military demonstration. 50024

Narrative of the great success God has been pleased to give His Highness forces in Jamaica. (51808)

NARRATIVE

Narrative of the Gywnedd cut-off of the
North Pennsylvania Rail Road. 60278
Narrative of the Honourable John Byron.
9730
Narrative of the horrid massacre. 51809,
note before 94472
Narrative of the horrid murder & piracy.
103227
Narrative of the imprisonment and escape of
Capt. Chas. H. Brown. 8459, 93422
Narrative of the incidents attending the
capture, detention, and ransom of
Charles Johnston. (36355)
Narrative of the Indian and civil wars in
Virginia. 51810, 2d note after 100494
Narrative of the Indian Charity School, begun
in Lebanon. 19372, 103209-103212
Narrative of the Indian Charity-School, in
Lebanon. 103208
Narrative, of the Indian-massacre. (15209),
59268
Narrative of the Indian wars in New-England,
from the first planting thereof in the
year 1607. 33447-33451
Narrative of the Indian wars in New-England,
from the first planting thereof in the
year 1607, to the year 1677. 33452
Narrative of the insurrection and rebellion
in the island of Grenada. 95627
Narrative of the insurrection in the island
of Grenada. (30999)
Narrative of the last cruise of the U. S.
Steam Frigate Missouri. 6250
Narrative of the last Grinnell Arctic Exploring
Expedition. 27659, 43043
Narrative of the last moments of the life of
Don Augustin de Iturbide. 4666
Narrative of the late awful and calamitous
earthquake. 51811
Narrative of the late expedition against the
Indians. 38109
Narrative of the late fires at Miramichi.
(51433)
Narrative of the late massacres, in Lancaster
County. 25557, note after 38799
Narrative of the late revivals. 51812
Narrative of the late riotous proceedings.
13098
Narrative of the late troubles and transactions
in the church in Bolton. 360, 11967-
11968, 3d note after 96741
Narrative of the late work of God, at and near
Northampton. (21956), 102684
Narrative of the late work of work [sic] at
and near Northampton. (21956)
Narrative of the life, adventures, travels and
sufferings of Henry Tufts. 97416
Narrative of the life and actions of John
Ibeby. 47333
Narrative of the life and adventures of Charles
Ball. 2934
Narrative of the life and adventures of Henry
Bibb. (46966)
Narrative of the life and adventures of Levi
Hanford. 9538, 9541
Narrative of the life and adventures of
Matthew Bunn. 9186
Narrative of the life and adventures of Venture,
a native of Africa. 84480
Narrative of the life & adventures of Venture,
a native of Africa. 84481
Narrative of the life and adventures of Venture,
a native of Africa, but resident above
sixty years in the United States. 84482
Narrative of the life and confession . . . of
John Lewis. 73406

Narrative of the life and conversion of
Alexander White. 103350
Narrative of the life and labors of Rev. G. W.
Offley. 56789
Narrative of the life and medical discoveries
of Samuel Thomson. 95604
Narrative of the life and singular adventures
of Josephine Amelia Perkins. 60962
Narrative of the life and sufferings of Mrs.
Jane Johns. 36154, 2d note after 102515
Narrative of the life and sufferings of the Rev.
William Beebey Lighton. 41052
Narrative of the life and sufferings of William
B. Leighton. 39933
Narrative of the life and travels of John
Robert Shaw. 79932
Narrative of the life and travels of Mrs.
Nancy Prince. 65570
Narrative of the life and travels, preaching &
suffering. 65443
Narrative of the life, last dying speech & con-
fession of John Young. 106080
Narrative of the life, occurrences, vicissitudes
and present situation, of K. White.
103438
Narrative of the life of David Crockett. 17571
Narrative of the life of Francis Uss. 98185
Narrative of the life of Frederick Douglass.
20711
Narrative of the life of General Leslie Combs.
(14929)
Narrative of the life of George Melvin Kelsey.
39202
Narrative of the life of Israel Adams. 217
Narrative of the life of J. D. Green. 28530
Narrative of the life of James Allen. 835
Narrative of the life of James Pearse.
59438
Narrative of the life of John Lewis. 40815
Narrative of the life of John Marrant. 44678
Narrative of the life of Mary Jemison.
78680-78681
Narrative of the life of Miss Lucy Cole.
62963
Narrative of the life of Mrs. Hamilton.
30029
Narrative of the life of Mrs. Mary Jemison.
105548-105554
Narrative of the life of Mrs. Mary Jemison,
her father and mother killed. 105555
Narrative of the life of Mrs. Mary Jemison,
who was taken by the Indians. 78678-
78679
Narrative of the life of Moses Grandy.
28277, note after 95499
Narrative of the life of Rev. Noah Davis.
18870
Narrative [sic] of the life of Solomon Mack.
83496
Narrative of the life of the Reverend Mr.
George Whitefield. 71860
Narrative of the life of Thomas Cooper.
32995
Narrative of the life of W. Beadle. 4102
Narrative of the life of William Beadle. 4102
Narrative of the life, sufferings, adventures,
and surprising escape from slavery, of
John Brown. 8516
Narrative of the life, travels and sufferings
of Thomas W. Smith. 84420
Narrative of the Lord's wonderful dealings
with John Marrant. 44679
Narrative of the loss of His Majesty's Packet,
the Lady Hobart. 24019
Narrative of the loss of the brig Charles.
20761

Narrative of the loss of the Esk and Lively. 78179

Narrative of the loss of the ship Hercules. 51813, 92354

Narrative of the loss of the schooner Clio. (59070)

Narrative of the loss of the steam-packet Home. 51814, 103355

Narrative of the loss of the Wager. 51815

Narrative of the manner in which the campaign against the Indians, in the year one thousand seven hundred and ninety-one, was conducted. (75020)

Narrative of the martyrdom at Boston in 1659. (6532)

Narrative of the massacre at Chicago. 12660, 37940

Narrative of the massacre, by the savages, of the wife & children of Thomas Baldwin. 2922

Narrative of the massacre of counterfeiters. 47271

Narrative of the material facts in relation to the building of the two Greek frigates. 16173

Narrative of the measures pursued at the anniversary election. (8945)

Narrative of the method and success of inoculating the small pox. 14502, (16635)

Narrative of the Mexican Empire, 1861-7. (37609)

Narrative of the military actions of Colonel Marinus Willett. 104138

Narrative of the military operations of Major-General George B. McClellan. 16279

Narrative of the miseries of New-England. (9371)-9372, (46708)-46709, 81492

Narrative of the mission of the United Brethren. (31205)

Narrative of the missions of the new settlements. 15789-15790, (15807)-15810

Narrative of the modes and measures pursued at the anniversary election. 51716

Narrative of the most extraordinary and distressing shipwreck. 12189

Narrative of the most memorable passages of his life and times. 4013

Narrative of the most remarkable particulars in the life of James Albert Ukawsaw Gronnoiosaw. 28922

Narrative of the mutiny, on board His Britanic Majesty's Ship Bounty. 4908A

Narrative of the mutiny on board the schooner Plattsburgh. 57354

Narrative of the mutiny on board the ship Globe. 39467, 51817

Narrative of the mysterious cave. 21453

Narrative of the nativity, experience, travels, and ministerial labors of Rev. C. Giles. (27366)

Narrative of the negotiations occasioned by the dispute between England and France. 51818

Narrative of the New England Anabaptists. 46638

Narrative of the official conduct of Anthony Stokes. 91993

Narrative of the official conduct of Valentine Morris. 50879

Narrative of the Onondaga tradition. (13330)

Narrative of the operations for the recovery of the public stores. 20076

Narrative of the operations of a small British force. 51819

Narrative of the oppressive law proceedings. 33826, (51820), 91841A

Narrative of the origin and progress of the Church of the United Brethren. 51821

Narrative of the origin and progress of the Congregational Church in Homer, N. Y. 37162

Narrative of the origin and progress of the difficulties in the vicinity of Dartmouth College. (18621)

Narrative of the origin and progress of the First Free Congregational Church, in Buffalo. 45005

Narrative of the Pennsylvania frontier. 98428, 2d note after 105691

Narrative of the perilous adventures, miraculous escapes and sufferings of James W. Parker. 58685

Narrative of the persecution of Hippolytas Joseph da Costa Pereira Futado de Mendonca. 18256

Narrative of the pious death of the penitent Herny Mills. 49105

Narrative of the piracy and plunder of the ship Friendship. 22561

Narrative of the planting of the Massachusetts colony anno 1628. 78434

Narrative of the present controversy. 26969, 101256

Narrative of the presentation to sovereigns and those in authority. 51822

Narrative of the principal circumstances relative to the Rev. Mr. Wesley's late conference. 80543

Narrative of the principal events of the siege. 19788, 33138

Narrative of the principal incidents in the life and adventures of Capt. Jacob Sheburne. 80333

Narrative of the proceedings against Thomas Cooper, Esquire. (16622)

Narrative of the proceedings . . . concerning the lands. 51825-51826, 90629

Narrative of the proceedings . . .. from . . . March 1835. 50286

Narrative of the proceedings in America. 3463, 25264

Narrative of the proceedings in the Bank Street Ch. 28781

Narrative of the proceedings in the North Parish in Hingham. 95223

Narrative of the proceedings in Venezuela. (12550)

Narrative of the proceedings of a meeting of the inhabitants of Buckram. 51823

Narrative of the proceedings of H. M. S. Resolute. 1918, (43072)

Narrative of the proceedings of Pedrarias Davila. 18783

Narrative of the proceedings of Sir Edmond Androsse and his accomplices. 46731-46732, note after 70346, 92350

Narrative of the proceedings of the Associate Presbytery of Albany. 90512, 90514

Narrative of the proceedings of the Baptist Church in Medfield. 50920

Narrative of the proceedings of the black people. 36442

Narrative of the proceedings of the Board of Engineers. 41887

Narrative of the proceedings of the Board of Trustees of Dickinson College. 20081, 99393

Narrative of the proceedings of the Committee Appointed by the Adventurers. (51824)

Narrative, relating to his [i. e. John Dean's] suffering. 104686
Narrative, respecting the conduct of the British. 104570
Narrative respecting the destruction of the Earl of Selkirk's settlement upon Red River. 43145
Narrative, 1776-1782. 28379
Narrative, shewing the entrance of the Shakers into the western country. 105124
Narrative shewing the promises made to the officers of the . . . Continental Army. (31848)
Narrative, shewing why the Rev. John Phillips is not in connexion. 52495
Narrative, showing the origin and progress of the difficulties. (68973), 95524
Narrative, showing the progress of British enterprise. 81151
Narrative of the Wesleyan Mission to Jamaica. 21263
Narrative written by himself [i. e. James Boarden.] 94087
Narratives of adventure. 16540
Narratives of adventure and shipwreck. 78538
Narratives of an old traveller. 38092
Narratives of early Maryland. 38886, 92940, 100547, 103353
Narratives of early Virginia. 82832
Narratives of fugitive slaves in Canada. (20931)
Narative of Gen. Hall [and others.] 34461
Narratives of John Pritchard. 65715
Narratives of massacres and depredations on the frontiers. 34659
Narratives of remarkable conversions and revival incidents. 15096
Narratives of shipwreck and Indian captivity. 80018
Narratives of shipwrecks and adventures at sea. 18488
Narratives of South America. (22548)
Narratives of the captivity and extreme sufferings of Mrs. Clarissa Plummer. 63462
Narratives of the career of Hernando de Soto. 87206
Narratives of the discoveries of America, no. 3. 99374
Narratives of the insurrections. 46731-46732, note after 70346, 92350
Narratives of the lives and deeds of the most prominent women. 58944
Narratives of the lives of pious Indian children. (47125)
Narratives of the most remarkable wrecks. 80538
Narratives of the perils and sufferings of Dr. Knight and John Slover. 38111
Narratives of the Trans-Mississippi frontier series. 101405
Narratives of the voyages, missions, and travels among the Indians. 25853
Naratives of wonderful adventures. 51573
Narrator. pseud. As the public have had much writing. 94662
Narraway, J. R. 51842
Narrazione dei quatro viaggi intrapresi da Cristofo Colombo. 52103
Narrazione storica trographica. 59171
Narre du voyage faict pour la mission des Abnaquiois. 20928
Narrow way. 80087
Narrowness of the call for the Baltimore Convention. 35849

Narsh, William. 23524
Narte, Sejo Amira de. pseud. Clamores de la America. see Teran, Jose Maria.
Narvaez, Francisco. 51843
Nasaassunik univkat. 22848
Nasby, Petroleum V. pseud. see Locke, David Ross, 1833-1888.
Nasby papers. (41720), 84185-84187
Nascentes d'Azambuja, Jose Bonifacio. 51844 see also Espirito Santo (Brazilian Province) Presidente (Nascentes d'Azambuja)
Nascentes de Azambuja, Joaquim Maria. see Azambuja, Joaquim Maria Nascentes de.
Nascimento Castro a Silva, Manoel de. see Castro a Silva, Manoel de Nascimento.
Nascimento Silva, Josino do. see Silva, Josino do Nascimento.
Nash, Ansell. 51845
Nash, Daniel. 51846
Nash, Frederick. 45689
Nash, J. A. 51847
Nash, Jonathan. (51848)
Nash, Melaliah. (51849)
Nash, Nathaniel C. (51850)
Nash, P. W. ed. 88324
Nash, Simeon. 51851
Nash, Solomon. 9538, (51852)
Nash, Sylvester. 51853-(51854)
Nash family. (51854)
Nash family, in part, traced down from Thom Nash. 51853
Nashauanittue meninnunk wutch mekkiesog. 17071
Nashe, Thomas. 94165
Nashotah Mission. 51855
Nashotah Theological Seminary. 51856
Nashpe mukkiesog woh tauog wunnammuhkutte 22161
Nashua, N. H. 51858
Nashua, N. H. Citizens. 51864
Nashua, N. H. First Unitarian Congregational Society. (51865)
Nashua, N. H. First Unitarian Congregational Society. Pastors. (51865)
Nashua, N. H. Meeting of Citizens, 1842. see Nashua, N. H. Citizens.
Nashua, N. H. Ordinances, etc. (51863)
Nashua, N. H. School Committee. 51858, (51865), 68944
Nashua, N. H. Schools. 51857, 68944
Nashua, N. H. Selectmen. 51858
Nashua, N. H. Second Annual Convention of the Young Men's Christian Association, 1869. see Young Men's Christian Association, New Hampshire. State Convention, 2d, Nashua, 1869.
Nashua, N. H. Young Men's Christian Association. see Young Men's Christian Association, Nashua, N. H.
Nashua and Lowell Railroad Corporation. 51859
Nashua and Lowell Railroad Corporation. Committee of Investigation. 51859
Nashua and Lowell Railroad Corporation. Directors. 51859
Nashua and Lowell Railroad Corporation. Engineer. 51859
Nashua and Lowell Railroad Corporation. Grantees. 51859
Nashua directory. (51860)
Nashua Literary Institution, Nashua, N. H. (51861)
Nashville, Tenn. Board of Education. 51867
Nashville, Tenn. Charter. 51870

Nashville, Tenn. Christian Church. Dissentient Members. 24094
Nashville, Tenn. City Council. Committee. 51877
Nashville, Tenn. Cumberland College. see Cumberland College, Nashville, Tenn.
Nashville, Tenn. Fire Department. 51866
Nashville, Tenn. Jackson Committee. see Jackson Committee of Nashville.
Nashville, Tenn. Mayor, 1859. 51869
Nashville, Tenn. Mechanics' Institute and Library Association. see Mechanics' Institute and Library Association, Nashville, Tenn.
Nashville, Tenn. Ordinances, etc. 51870
Nashville, Tenn. Public Schools. 51867 see also Nashville, Tenn. School Department.
Nashville, Tenn. Recorder. 51866
Nashville, Tenn. Republican Party Convention, 1870. see Republican Party. Tennessee. Convention, Nashville, 1870.
Nashville, Tenn. School Department. 51866 see also Nashville, Tenn. Public Schools.
Nashville, Tenn. Soule Female College. see Soule Female College, Nashville, Tenn.
Nashville, Tenn. Southern Convention, 1850. see Southern Convention, Nashville, Tenn., 1850.
Nashville, Tenn. Superintendent of Public Schools. 51867
Nashville, Tenn. Superintendent of Water-Works. 51866
Nashville, Tenn. University. 51880
Nashville, Tenn. University. Chancellor. 51880 see also Lindsley, John Berrien, 1822-1897.
Nashville, Tenn. University. Law Department. 51880
Nashville, Tenn. University. Literary Department. 51880
Nashville, Tenn. University. Medical Department. 51880
Nashville, Tenn. University. Society of the Alumni. 4458, 29922
Nashville, Tenn. Western Military Institute. see Western Military Institute, Nashville, Tenn.
Nashville and Chattanooga Rail Road. Commissioners. 51876
Nashville and her trade for 1870. (71859)
Nashville clarion. 94730
Nashville directory, for 1867. 51872
Nashville journal of medicine and surgery. (51878)
Nashville republican. (14929), 39752
Nashville, state of Tennessee, and general commercial directory. 10257, (51879)
Nashville whig. 94760
Naso, Publius Vergilius. see Vergilius Naso, Publius.
Nason, Daniel. 51881
Nason, Elias. 33322, 41208, 51882-51888, (74375)
Nason, Reuben. 51889
Nassau la Leck, Lodewijk Theodorus, Grave van. see Theodorus, Lodewijk, Grave van Nassau la Leck.
Nassau, N. Y. Mutual Insurance Association. see Mutual Insurance Association of Nassau, Schodack and Chatham, N. Y.
Nassau Hall Grammar School, Princeton, N. J. see Princeton University. Grammar School.

Nassau Hall of Princeton, N. J. see Princeton University.
Nassau Presbytery. see Presbyterian Church in the U. S. A. Presbytery of Nassau.
Nassau rake. 51892
Nassau Water Company. Charter. 8233
Nassau Water Department, Brooklyn. see Brooklyn. Nassau Water Department.
Nassy, D. 10883-10884, 51893
Nassy, D. de la. see Nassy, David de Isaac Cohen.
Nassy, David de Isaac Cohen. (27218), (40086)-40088, (51894), 3d, 6th-7th notes after 93855
Nast, Thomas, 1840-1902. illus. 21497, 30453, 41719, (41722), 89340, 2d note after 94082
Nast, Wilhelm. 51895-51896
Natches [sic]. 82808, 97196
Natchez (Diocese) Bishop (Elder) 51898, 72950, (72952) see also Elder, William Henry, Bp.
Natchez (Diocese) Synod, 1859. 72950
Natchez (Diocese) Synod, 1862. (72951)
Natchez (Diocese) Synod, 1874. (72952)
Natchez. 12248, 12251, 12258, (12261)-12263
Natchez; an Indian tale. 12259
Natchez courier. 81570, 95093
Natchez courier. Editor. 95093
Natchez daily courier. 1790
Natchez: historia Americana pelo Viscomte de Chateaubriand. 12260
Natchez Institute. 51897
Natchez, novella Americana. (12261)
Natchez, ou la tribu serpent. 12257
Natchez, roman Indien. 12257
Nathan. pseud. Nathan to Lord North. 51899
Nathan, John. 51900
Nathan Ben Saddi. pseud. Chronicle of the kings of England. see Chesterfield, Philip Dormer Stanhope, 4th Earl of, 1694-1773. and Dodsley, Robert, 1703-1764. supposed author
Nathan Ben Saddi. pseud. Chronicles of the kings of England. see Chesterfield, Philip Dormer Stanhope, 4th Earl of, 1694-1773. and Dodsley, Robert, 1703-1764. supposed author
Nathan Ben Saddi. pseud. Fragments of the chronicles. see Dodsley, Robert, 1703-1764. supposed author
Nathan der Quaker. 5556
Nathan, der Squatter-Regulator. 64544, 95104
Nathan Hale, a poem. (43580)
Nathan Nobody. pseud. see Nobody, Nathan. pseud.
Nathan Read. 68148
Nathan to Lord North. 51899
Nathanael's character display'd. 12325
Nathaniel Greene. 28600
Nathaniel Very's renunciation of free masonry. 99319
Naticoke Indians. Treaties, etc. 65759
Natick, Mass. 51901, (51907)
Natick, Mass. Celebration of the Two Hundredth Anniversary of the Settlement of the Town, 1851. 51905
Natick, Mass. Selectmen. 51902
Natick, Mass. South Congregational Church. 106051
Natick, Mass. Town Clerk. 51902
Natick, Mass. Town Library. 51903
Natick, Mass. Young Men's Christian Association. see Young Men's Christian Association, Natick, Mass.

National banking act of . . . 1864. 59854
National bankrupt law. (51937)
National bankruptcy register. 51937
National banks. Speech of Hon. Carl Schurz. 78026
National banks. The system unmasked, greenbacks forever. 51938
National banner. 93797
National Baptist Education Convention, New York, 1870. 51939
National "barley cake." 2404
National behest. 86178
National bereavements. 71084
National bimetallism. 83886
National blessings of Christians. 28944
National blessings; sources of national obligations. 52310
National Board of Fire Underwriters. Annual Meeting, 1st, New York, 1867. 51940
National Board of Fire Underwriters. Executive Committee. 51940
National Board of Health. 84276
National Board of Trade. Meeting, Cincinnati, 1868. 51941
National Board of Trade. Meeting, Philadelphia, 1868. 51941
National Board of Trade. Meeting, Richmond, 1869. 71193
National board of trade. 25419
National book. 57913, 61356
National business directory. 64984
National calamities, a sermon on the death of President Lincoln. 27406
National calamities founded in national dissension and dissipation. (33932)
National calamities procured by national sins. 104615
National calamities the effect of divine displeasure. 91225
National calendar. see Maine register and national calendar.
National calendar, and annals of the United States. 25056
National Canal Convention, Chicago, 1863. see National Ship-Canal Convention, Chicago, 1863.
National capital is moveable. (68307)
National capital movable. 68308
National capitol, the national archives, and the national government saved. 81345
National cause: its sanctity and grandeur. 60838
National Celebration of Union Victories, New York, 1856. 51942
National celebration of union victories. . . . Mass meeting in Union Square, New York. 51942
National Cemetery, Gettysburg, Pa. see Soldiers' National Cemetery Association.
National centennial 1776.—1876. 85586
National change in morals. 51943
National character. 9485
National characteristics: an address delivered before the literary societies of Hamilton College. 25026
National characteristics. By Charles Sealsfield. 64537
National Cheap Freight Railway League. President. 66046
National Christian Convention, Opposed to Secret Societies, Pittsburgh, 1868. 51944
National circular. 51945
National Clay melodist. 51946

National club on the reconstruction of the union. 27684, 51947
National colors of the United States and of Great Britain fully explained. 51948
National comedy, founded on the opening of the revolution. 36829, 94241
National comic almanac, 1852. (51949)
National Commercial Convention, Boston, 1868. petitioners 51950
National Commercial Convention, Boston, 1868. Committee on Foreign and Domestic Commerce. 51950
National commercial convention. A discourse . . . in Boston. 26536
National Committee of British Freed-men's Aid Societies. (8101)
National Compensation Emancipation Society. 51951
National Conference of Charities and Corrections. 84255
National Conference of Charities and Corrections. 32d, Portland, Ore., 1905. 84069
National Conference of Charities and Corrections. Committee. 84265B
National Conference of Commissioners on Uniform State Laws. 84516
National Conference of Commissioners on Uniform State Laws. President. 84516
see also Smith, Walter George, 1854-1926.
National Conference of Unitarian and Other Christian Churches. 3d, New York, 1868. (51952) see also Unitarian Churches. U. S.
National Congregational Council, Boston, 1865. see National Council of Congregational Churches, Boston, 1865.
National Congress on Penitentiary and Reformitory Discipline, Cincinnati, 1870. 51953
National congress on penitentiary and reformitory discipline, . . . held in Cincinnati, Ohio, October . . . 1870. 51953
National Congress on Uniform Divorce Laws, Philadelphia, 1906. 84513
National considerations upon importing iron in bars from America. 51954
National convention. Call of a convention of inventors. 34952
National convention. Circular of the national committee of the Pittsburgh convention. 51955, 63113
National Convention for the Promotion of Education in the United States, Washington, D. C., 1840. (65875)
National Convention for the Protection of American Interests, New York, 1841. 65876
National Convention of Artists. 1st, Washington, D. C., 1858. 65877
National Convention of Artists. 2d, Washington, D. C., 1859. 65877
National Convention of Artists. 3d, Washington, D. C., 1860. 65877
National Convention of Business Men, Philadelphia, 1837. 61856
National Convention of Business Men, Philadelphia, 1837. Philadelphia Delegates. 62079
National Convention of Cotton Manufacturers and Planters. (51931)
National Convention of Farmers, Gardeners and Silk Culturists, New York, 1846. 64878

National Convention of Fire Underwriters, New York, 1866. (69895)

National Convention of Fruit Growers, New York, 1848. (65879)

National Convention of Journeymen Printers of the United States, New York, 1850. 65880

National Convention of Manufacturers, Cleveland, 1867. 65881

National Convention of Silk Growers and Silk Manufacturers, New York, 1843. 65882, 81014

National Convention of the Colored Men, Syracuse, N. Y., 1864. 65883

National Convention of the Colored Men, Washington, 1869. 65883

National Convention of the Friends of Common School Instruction, 1849. Baltimore Delegation. see Baltimore. Commissioners of Public Schools. Delegation of the National Convention of the Friends of Common School Instruction, 1849.

National Convention of the Friends of Education, Philadelphia, 1849. (51956)

National Convention of the Soldiers of the War of 1812. 1st, Philadelphia, 1854. 61857, 65884

National Convention of the Soldiers of the War of 1812. 2d, Washington, D. C., 1855. 65885

National Convention of Those Interested in the Manufacture, Refining, and Sale of Spirits, Washington, D. C., 1867. 20296

National Council of Congregational Churches, in the United States.

National covenant. 80715

National crisis. A sermon . . . in Philadelphia. (44922)

National crisis. A sermon preached at Columbia, Pa. 28850

National crisis. A letter to the Hon. Milton S. Latham. 1573, 51959

National crisis; . . . an address . . . Dartmouth College, N. H. 65093

National crisis. An address delivered before the Young Men's Christian Association of San Francisco. (1423)

National crisis. . . . May 15, 1860. (51958)

National currency. (51960)

National currency. A review of the national banking law. 42024

National currency. An act . . . 1863. (51964)

National currency. An act proposed by a New York state banker. 51962

National currency and banking association bill. 51966

National currency and government credit. 51967

National currency and the banking system. 21515

National currency. By Sidney George Fisher. 24504

National currency instead of national bank notes. 66624

National currency. July 15, 1862. (51963)

National currency law. (59003)

National currency. New York, March 28, 1864. 51961

National currency. Speech of Hon. John B. Steele. 91129

National currency. Speech of the Hon. J. M. Broomall. 8377

National currency. Speech of William Sprague. 89724-89725

National currency. What is needed. 51968

"National custom" plea examined. 93745

National dangers, and means of escape. 51969

National deaf mute gazette. (51970)

National debt and finances. (79039)

National debt and the "Monroe doctrine." (9667), 81634

National debt, taxation, currency, and banking system. (26402)

National defence. 103727

National defences. (19569)

National democrat. pseud. New York hards and softs. 45780

National Democratic Executive Committee, 1860. see Democratic Party. National Executive Committee, 1860.

National democratic quarterly review. 51972

National Democratic Union Club, Harrisburg, Pa. see Harrisburg National Democratic Union Club.

National Democratic Volunteers, New York. see New York (State) National Democratic Volunteers.

National department of education. Official circulars. 21885

National destiny and our country. 71945

National destruction threatens us. (25316)

National development. 67970

National directory, containing an account of th roads. 31633

National disappointment. 5437

National discourse, delivered before the Troy Conference. 87267

National divergence and return. 79534

National divorce congress. 84513

National drama, in five acts. As performed at the Charleston theatre. 103417

National drama, in five acts. By Dr. Emmons 22530

National drama, in five acts. By William Ioor. 34969

National drama, in two acts. 101828

National education. By J. Orville Taylor. 94512

National education associations—1866. 51974

National Emigration Convention of Colored People, Cleveland, 1854. (65887)

National entail. 31218

National era. (82021), 92457

National eulogy of the illustrious George Washington. 39748

National exchange. 51975

National exhaltation. 54993

National Exhibition of Horses, 1st, Springfield Mass., 1853. 89880

National Exhibition of Horses, 2d, Springfield, Mass, 1855. 89880

National Exhibition of Horses, 3d, Springfiled, Mass., 1857. 89880

National Exhibition of Horses, 4th, Springfield Mass., 1860. 89858, 89880

National Exhibition of Horses, 4th, Springfield Mass., 1860. Committees. 89858

National Exhibition of Horses, 5th, Springfield Mass., 1867. 89880

National expenditures . . . speech . . . Februar 25, 1868. (39376)

National farm and fireside and pure food magazine. 88348

National fast. A discourse delivered on the day appointed. 68141

National fast. A fast day sermon, delivered in the city of Flint. 82233

National fast. A sermon, preached at Coldwater, Mich. 33210

National fast day and the war. 85459

National fast-day sermon, delivered at the Baptist Church, Lima, N. Y. 91112

National fast day sermon, delivered in the Baptist Church, Springfield. 91110

National-fast sermon, May 9, 1798. (28505)

National fast. Why it should be kept, and how. (35997)

National faults. 24465

National finances: a letter. 51978

National finances and a national bank. 51976

National finances and a resumption of specie payments. 42815

National finances and the public faith. 51979

National finances. By W. 101119

National finances. Confiscation and emancipation. 89035

National finances, currency, banking, &c. 26403

National finances. Letter to Congress. 51977

National finances. National bank—state banks. 89036

National finances. Speech . . . March 10, 1870. 50780

National finances. Speech of Hon. Milton I. Southard. 88235

National finances. Speech . . . on the loan bill. 32877

National foundry—Deep River, N. C. 51980

National foundry for the west. 13389

National Free Soil Convention, Buffalo, N. Y., 1848. see Free Soil Party. National Convention, Buffalo, N. Y., 1848.

National Freedman's Relief Association, New York. see American Freedmans' Union Commission. New York Branch.

National Freedman's Relief Association of the District of Columbia. 51983

National Freedmen's-Aid Union of Great Britain and Ireland. 51982

National freemason. 51984

National Gallery, New York. see New York (City) National Gallery.

National gazette. 14899, 56533, (57604), 95108, 1st note after 100506

National gazette and literary register. 65043

National geography for schools. 27922

National government journal. 25057

National guard. Camp Pennsylvania, Baltimore, Md. 51986

National handbook of facts and figures. 51987

National happiness. 39199

National history of the United States. 42126

National humiliation: a sermon . . . in Hollis Street Church. 62772

National humiliation and repentence recommended. 16589, 40514

National hymns, original and selected. (38090)

National illustrated rural . . . newspaper. 50344

National Industrial League. 91008

National ingratitude lamented. 23164

National inquirer. 85198

National Institute, Washington, D. C. 33910, 51988, note after 64141

National Institute, Washington, D. C. Recording Secretary. 51988

National Institute of Letters, Arts and Sciences, New York. 51989

National Institution for Promoting Industry in the United States. 51991

National Institution for the Promotion of Industry. 433

National Institution for the Promotion of Science, Washington, D. C. 51990

National Institution for the Promotion of Science, Washington, D. C. Committee. 51990

National intelligencer. 311, (15534), 18070, (18156), 20292, 23200, (28283), 30578, 34400, 35345, (68715), 70236, 78967, 80856, 83513, 83816, 83826, 83828, 84075, 84151, 85075, 92110, 94488, 97282, 97915, 97946, 99577, 99810, 105149

National intelligencer and Washington advertiser. 84079

National interests and domestic manufactures. 51992, 62040

National jewels. 44387

National Johnson Club. 51993 see also Republican Party.

National journal. (70770)

National Labor Congress, Detroit, 1869. 24287

National Labor Union. Convention, 2d, New York, 1868. 65889

National law. 51994

National legal directory. 33459

National lessons from the life and death of President Lincoln. 2773

National Liberty Convention, Buffalo, N. Y., 1848. 65890

National library. 88421

National library building—the proposed plan. 84980

National Life and Travellers' Insurance Company of New York. 51997

National life: containing biographical sketches. 51995

National Life Insurance Company of the United States. 51996

National life, its characteristics and perils. 18436

National Lincoln memorial. 19663

National Lincoln Monument, Springfield, Ill. see Springfield, Ill. National Lincoln Monument.

National loan; embracing the appeal in its behalf. 12200

National Loan Fund Life Assurance Association of London. 90554

National Lord's Day Convention, Baltimore, 1844. 51998

National magazine. see Great republic monthly. A national magazine.

National magazine and industrial record. (51999)

National magazine and republican review. 52000

National magazine: devoted to literature, art, and religion. (52001)

National magazine: or a political, biographical, historical and literary repository. 42857, 52002

National magazine, or cabinet of the United States. 52003

National magazine, or ladies' emporium. (52004)

National man. pseud. Life and times of Andrew Johnson. 36176

National medical almanac for 1848. 52005

National Medical College, Washington, D. C. see George Washington University, Washington, D. C. School of Medicine.

National Medical Convention, New York, 1846. 52007, 54414, (65892)

National Medical Convention, Philadelphia, 1847. (65892)

National medical journal. 52008
National melodist. 52009
National memorial: containing, Washington's farewell address. 101725
National memorial day. 23644
National men and national measures. 11065
National merchant. 4732
National military asylums. 23873
National military drama. 3214A
National Mining Company. Directors. (69856)
National Mining Company. Treasurer. (69856)
National Minute Men, New York. 54415
National money. 52010
National Museum, Washington, D. C. see U. S. National Museum, Washington, D. C.
National Musical Convention, Boston, 1841. 52011
National Musical Convention, Boston, 1845. 52011
National nest-stirring. 7698
National normal. 52012
National Normal School, Lebanon, Ohio. see Lebanon University, Lebanon, Ohio.
National observatory. 46966
National observatory. The isthmus line to the Pacific. 46967
National observer. 88646, 88653
National ode. 88852
National oration, by J. Hyatt Smith. 82973
National organizations. 52710
National paper, published at the seat of government. 26811
National party histories. 83748
National party platforms. 65351
National party platforms, by Walter W. Spooner. 83748
National patriotic poem. (23149)
National patriotic songs, written to popular airs. 68578
National Peace Jubilee and Musical Festical, Boston, 1869. see Great National Peace Jubilee and Musical Festical, Boston, 1869.
National perils. (12183)
National Pharmaceutical Convention, Philadelphia, 1852. 65893
National plan for an Atlantic and Pacific Rail Road. 52013
National plan of an Atlantic and Pacific Railroad, and remarks. 62815
National poem. 9121
National poem: in six cantos. 82461-(82462)
National poems. 87262
National policy. 52014
National politics. Speech . . . at Warren, O. 26664
National politics. . . . Speech . . . August 15, 1866. (39376)
"National politics. Speech of Abraham Lincoln." 41160
National politics, Speech of Hon. Henry M. Fuller. (26160)
National politics. Speech of Hon. S. P. Brooks. 8367
National portrait gallery of distinguished Americans. 6981, 31577, 2d note after 52014, 82987, 98046
National portrait gallery of eminent Americans. 21504
National portrait of Washington. 56706, note after 101863
National postulata on patriot evolutions. 96438

National preacher. 6393, 85409, 89103, 92835
National prejudice opposed to national interest. (52015)
National problem. An oration delivered at Delphi. 24566
National problem solved! 48670
National prosperity perpetuated. (24568)
National protestant. (52016)
National Quarantine and Sanitary Association of the United States. (52017), (66944)
National Quarantine and Sanitary Association. Report . . . on external hygiene. (66944)
National Quarantine and Sanitary Convention, 1st, Philadelphia, 1857. (52017)
National Quarantine and Sanitary Convention, 3d, New York, 1859. 65756
National Quarantine and Sanitary Convention, 4th, Boston, 1860. 85501
National quarterly review. 39382, 52018
National reconstruction. 51703
National record of education. (52019)
National recorder. (52020), 62027, 77145
National reformer. 85560
National regeneration. 64471
National register. see Literary panorama and national register. Niles' national register.
National register (London) 103673
National register (New York) 52022
National register (Washington, D. C.) 52021
National register for 1869. 10175
National register for the year 1850. 20325
National Republican Central Committee of Baltimore. see National Republican Party. Maryland. Baltimore Central Committee.
National Republican Convention of Young Men, Washington, D. C., 1832. (65896), note after 101943
National Republican Party. 28493
National Republican Party. Convention, Baltimore, 1831. 36729
National Republican Party. Convention, Baltimore, 1831. Vermont Delegation. see National Republican Party. Vermont.
National Republican Party. Convention, Baltimore, 1832. 93603
National Republican Party. Convention, Baltimore, 1832. Maryland Delegation. see National Republican Party. Maryland.
National Republican Party. Convention of Young Men, Washington, D. C., 1832. see National Republican Convention of Young Men, Washington, D. C., 1832.
National Republican Party. Connecticut. Convention of Young Men, Hartford, 1832. 15794
National Republican Party. Kentucky. Convention, Frankfort, 1830. 65895
National Republican Party. Kentucky. Fayette County. Corresponding Committee. 93806
National Republican Party. Maryland. 45063
National Republican Party. Maryland. Convention, Baltimore, 1830. (45050)
National Republican Party. Maryland. Young Men of the Fifth Congressional District. 45056
National Republican Party. Maryland. Baltimore Central Committee. 45102, 95810
National Republican Party. Massachusetts. Central Committee. 314, (45583)
National Republican Party. Massachusetts. Convention, Worcester, 1832. 36741, 102282

National Republican Party. Massachusetts.
Worcester. Young Men's Meeting,
1832. 105363
National Republican Party. Missouri. Con-
vention, 1828. 49628
National Republican Party. New Hampshire.
Convention, Concord, 1828. 52790,
65753
National Republican Party. New Hampshire.
Convention, Concord, 1828. President.
52790 see also Badger, William,
1779-1852.
National Republican Party. New York. 53491,
82598, 93603
National Republican Party. New York. Con-
vention, Albany, 1828. 53491, 69910,
82598
National Republican Party. New York.
Albany. Meeting, 1824. 627
National Republican Party. New York. New
York City. 54038
National Republican Party. Pennsylvania.
Convention, 1832. 60421
National Republican Party. Pennsylvania.
Franklin County. 60400
National Republican Party. Pennsylvania.
Greensburgh. 28675
National Republican Party. Pennsylvania.
Philadelphia. (40566) see also
Philadelphia. Great Meeting of Irishmen,
to Prevent the Re-election of Andrew
Jackson, 1832.
National Republican Party. Pennsylvania.
Washington. 100661, 102013
National Republican Party. Pennsylvania.
Westmoreland County. 28675
National Republican Party. Rhode Island.
Committee to Examine Certain Charges
Against Lemuel H. Arnold, 1821.
(1665), 2077
National Republican Party. Vermont. 91198
National Republican Party. Virginia. 100496-
100500
National Republican Party. Virginia. Conven-
tion, Richmond, 1827-1828. 71188,
100496
National Republican Party. Virginia.
Winchester. 100495
National Republican Young Men's Meeting,
Worcester, Mass., 1832. see National
Republican Party. Massachusetts.
Worcester. Young Men's Meeting, 1832.
National responsibility. 92384
National revolutions. 42618
National righteousness and national sin.
41311
National righteousness national security.
102078
National rights and state rights. 62634
National road to California. 11527
National Sabbath Convention, Saratoga, N. Y.,
1863. 77492
National safety. 43005
National Sailors' Home, Quincy, Mass.
(67297)
National self-government in Europe and
America. 65747
National sermons. (30881)
National Ship-Canal Convention, Chicago,
1863. 12637-12638
National Ship-Canal Convention, Chicago,
1863. petitioners 12635
National Ship-Canal Convention, Chicago,
1863. Chicago Committee on Statistics.
12637, 52211

National sin and retribution. 27605
National sin must be expiated by national
calamity. (67312)
National sins: a call to repentance. 84544
National sins. A sermon delivered in
Dorchester. 14132
National slavery and national responsibility.
27409
National Society for Promoting Industry in the
United States. 52024
National Soldier's Historical Association,
Cincinnati. 63290
National song-book. 104642
National songs, ballads, and other patriotic
poetry. 42996
National songs of America. 84042
National songster. To which is prefixed a
sketch. (41503)
National songster; to which is prefixed a
sketch of the life. 13555
National souvenir. 101164
National souvenir, illustrated with portrait.
35372
National standard. 90154
National state rights. 43204
National sufferings the result of national sins.
(58372)
National Sunday School Convention, 5th,
Indianapolis, 1872. 52025
National Sunday School Society. see Unitarian
Sunday School Society, Boston.
National Sunday school teacher. 93744
National symptoms. 61397
National system of finance. 52026, 73938
National tale. 104170
National tax law, as amended. 29762, 52028
National tax-law, (complete.) 52027
National Teachers' Association. 51974, 52029
National Telegraphic Union, New York. 54417
National temperance advocate. 52030
National temperance almanac. 52031
National Temperance Convention, 4th, Saratoga
Springs, N. Y., 1851. 1240, 65897
National temperance offering. (11210)
National Temperance Society. 52031
National Temperance Society and Publication
House. 52030
National Temple of Honor of the United States.
see Templars. United States. National
Temple of Honor.
National thanksgiving. A discourse delivered
in Zanesville. 68572
National thanksgiving discourse, by the Rev.
J. Glentworth Butler. 9646
National thanksgiving sermon, delivered at the
Methodist E. Church, Lima. 91111
National thanksgiving sermon. "Thy prayer
is heard." 30006
National thanksgiving services held December
7, 1865. 52032
National Theological Institute and University,
Boston. 65899
National tract. 74656
National tragedy. 64669
National tribute, commemorative of the great
civil victory. 101164
National Typographical Union. 2d Session,
1853. 65900
National union. (52033)
National union. A sermon . . . in . . .
Bainbridge. 33599
National Union Association of Ohio. 8400,
42559, 52034
National Union Club, Philadelphia. 52035,
61858

National Union Club, Washington, D. C.
17221, 89214

National Union Club documents. 17221,
89214

National Union Convention, Baltimore, 1864.
see Republican Party. National Convention, Baltimore, 1864.

National Union Democracy. see Democratic
Party.

National Union Democratic Party. see
Democratic Party.

National Union Executive Committee, New
York, 1860. 53487

National Union Party. Convention, Chicago,
1868. 12662

National Union Party. Ohio. Convention,
1862. 57028

National Union Party. Pennsylvania. Philadelphia. 61859

National Union Republican Party. see National Union Party.

National union, the test of American loyalty.
(21135)

National union upheld and preserved. 91636

National Unitarian Convention, New York,
1865. 65768

National unity. 29866

National vanity. A sermon. 12148

National wagon road guide. 100930

National War Committee of the Citizens of
New York City. 54418

National warning, a sermon preached . . . as
an improvement of calamity. 4995

National warning: a sermon, preached on the
Sabbath. 89329

National weakness. (31216)

National whig. 85447

National Women's Rights Convention, Cleveland, 1853. 65901

National-Zeitung. 71473

National Zoological Park, Washington, D. C.
see Washington, D. C. National
Zoological Park.

Nationale Charakteristiken. 64534-64535

Nationalen Sonntags-Convention zu Saratoga,
New York, 1863. see National Sabbath
Convention, Saratoga, N. Y., 1863.

Nationalism. A fragment of political science.
50985

Nationalities. 27850

Nationality of a people. (21569)

Nationality; or, the law relating to subjects
and aliens. 14088

Nationality versus sectionalism. 24095

Nationernas under. 84475

Nation's ballot and its decision. 22309

Nation's bereavement. 63118, 85462

Nation's blessing in trial. 89095

Nations catholiques et les nations protestantes.
(73488)

Nation's changes. 44785

Nation's crime and danger. (20065)

Nation's crisis and the Christian's duty.
6392

Nation's danger and the nation's duty. 83523

Nation's discipline. 18743

Nation's duty. 36219

Nation's Ebenezer. 20524

Nation's first pledge of emancipation. 36348

Nation's gratitude. A discourse . . . at the
United States General Hospital. 44785

Nation's gratitude and hope. 59266

Nation's great crisis. 92356

Nation's grief: a funeral discourse. 20391

Nation's grief. Death of Abraham Lincoln.
44785

Nation's grief for its fallen chief. 26817

Nation's hope in the Democracy. (17271)

Nation's hour. 3794

Nation's inquiry. 44785

Nation's joy and jeopardy. 78165

Nation's last hope. 28850

Nation's loss. A discourse upon the life,
services, and death of Abraham Lincoln.
17718

Nation's loss. A poem on the life and death
of the Hon. Abraham Lincoln. 70760

Nation's loss. A sermon upon the death of
Abraham Lincoln. 81700

Nation's loss. [By E. S. Atwood.] 2342

Nation's manhood. 52036

Nation's peril. Oration of Rev. Luther Lee.
39775

Nation's prospects of peace. 44785

Nation's sacrifice. 47177

Nation's sin and punishment. 32355, 52037

Nation's sorrow. 92939

Nation's success and gratitude. 7681

Nation's trial: a discourse delivered in the
Universalist Church. (75268)

Nation's trial: the proclamation. 9113

Nation's trust in the present struggle. (17724)

Nation's wail. 21136

Native. pseud. Annals of pioneer settlers on
the Whitewater. 71159

Native. pseud. Reflections on the present
state government of Virginia. 100518

Native. pseud. To Aaron Clark. 95881

Native. pseud. View of the political and civil
situation of Louisiana. 99571

Native African. pseud. Thoughts and sentiments
on the evil of slavery. see Cugoano,
Quobna Ottobouh.

Native American. pseud. Men and manners,
from 1774 to 1809. see Wilmer, James
Jones.

Native American. pseud. Native-Americanism
detected and exposed. see Hildreth,
Richard.

Native American. pseud. Reflections on the
character and public services of Andrew
Jackson. 35387

Native American. pseud. To the friends of
freedom and public faith. 95928

Native American. pseud. "Young Sam" or
native American's own book! see
Hutchinson, E.

Native American. a gift for the people.
52038

Native American Association of Louisiana.
see Louisian Native American Association.

Native American Association of the Unincorporated Northern Liberties, Philadelphia.
(61860) see also American Party.
Pennsylvania. Philadelphia.

Native American Hall Company of Cedar Ward
Philadelphia. see American Party.
Pennsylvania. Philadelphia. Native
American Hall Company of Cedar Ward.

Native American newspaper, New Orleans.
(7871)

Native American Party. see American Party

Native American party. 61862

Native American review. 52039

Native-Americanism detected and exposed.
31781

Native Americans of Philadelphia. see
American Party. Pennsylvania. Philadelphia.

Native American's own book! (34062)

Native and half-caste Indians. pseud. Statement. (33542)

Native and inhabitant of the place. pseud. History and present state of Virginia. see Beverley, Robert.

Native and inhabitant of the place. pseud. History of Virginia. see Beverley, Robert.

Native, and member of the House of Burgesses. pseud. Summary view of the rights of British America. see Jefferson, Thomas, Pres. U. S., 1743-1826.

Native bards; a satirical effusion. 42912, 44885

Native born citizen of the United States. pseud. Exposition of part of the patent law. see Evans, Oliver.

Native born Virginian. pseud. Several letters. 79371, 88478

Native born Virginian. pseud. Southern rights and northern wrongs. 79371, 88479

Native Canadian. pseud. Canada: is she prepared for war? see Denison, George T.

Native citizen. pseud. Brief outline for a national bank. (7885)

Native citizen and servant of the state. pseud. Political scheems and calculations. see Hanson, Alexander Nontee.

Native eloquence. 89187

Native Georgian. pseud. Georgia scenes. see Longstreet, Augustus B.

Native Indians. 5112-5113, 1st, 3d notes after 100480

Native of a Republican state. pseud. True merits of a late treatise. 97127

Native of Algiers. pseud. Algerine spy in Pennsylvania. see Markoe, Peter.

Native of America. pseud. Calm address to Americanus. 102647

Native of America. pseud. tr. see Parke, John.

Native of Barbados. pseud. Candid observations on two pamphlets. 3262

Native of Boston. pseud. Boston Ebenezer. see Mather, Cotton, 1663-1728.

Native of Boston. pseud. Brief review of "Considerations respectfully submitted." 7894

Native of Boston. pseud. Review of "Considerations." 67210

Native of Boston. pseud. Thoughts upon the political situation of the United States. see Jackson, Jonathan. and Minot, George R. incorrectly supposed author and Sullivan, James, 1744-1808. incorrectly supposed author

Native of Charleston. pseud. Letter. see Smith, William Loughton, 1758-1812. supposed author

Native of Donehall. pseud. tr. 59270

Native of Jamaica. pseud. Present ruinous situation. 65313

Native of Louisiana. pseud. Louisiana and the tariff. (42250)

Native of Maryland. pseud. Documentary history of slavery in the United States. 81959

Native of Maryland. pseud. Observations on the political character. 56547

Native of Maryland. pseud. To the citizens of the United States. 97935

Native of New-England. pseud. Address to the people of New-England. see Aplin, John.

Native of New England. pseud. New-England diary. see Bowen, Nathan.

Native of New-England. pseud. Origin of the American contest with Great-Britain. see Leonard, Daniel.

Native of New-England. pseud. Present political state of the province of Massachusetts-Bay. see Leonard, Daniel.

Native of New England. pseud. MDCCXXL. The New-England diary. see Bowen Nathan.

Native of Newark. pseud. Aspect of the times. 2212

Native of Pennsylvania. pseud. Essays upon French spoliations. see Fitzsimmons. pseud.

Native of Pennsylvania. pseud. Plea of the colonies. see Williamson, Hugh. supposed author

Native of Pennsylvania. pseud. Serious address to such of the people called Quakers. see Grey, Isaac.

Native of Pennsylvania, 1861. pseud. Why Pennsylvania should become one of the Confederate States of America. see McHenry, George.

Native of Philadelphia. pseud. System of education for the Girard College of Orphans. see McClure, David.

Native of Scotland. pseud. Poems, chiefly in the Scottish dialect. see Bruce, David, d. 1830.

Native of South-Carolina. pseud. Tocsin. 96074

Native of Spanish America. pseud. Letter addressed to the Right Honourable Lord M——. 40574

Native of that colony. pseud. Address to the Convention of the colony and ancient dominion of Virginia. see Braxton, Carter.

Native of the British West-Indies. pseud. To the people of North-America. 102870

Native of the island. pseud. Letter to the North American. 20038

Native of the place. pseud. True copy of eight pages. see Beverley, Robert.

Native of the province. pseud. Sermon preached at Litchfield in Connecticut. see Andrews, Samuel.

Native of the south. pseud. Memoirs of a nullifier. 47565

Native of the south-west. pseud. Family and slavery. 81973

Native of the southwest. pseud. Family and slavery; showing the influence of slavery. 81974

Native of the United States. pseud. American sketches. 1215

Native of this state. pseud. Treatise on gardening. see Randolph, John, Jr.

Native of the West Indies. pseud. Poems. 63624

Native of Virginia. pseud. Letter addressed to the poeple of the United States. (40572)

Native of Virginia. pseud. Public defaulters brought to light. see Giles, William Branch.

Native of Virginia. pseud. Rebellion in Tennessee. see McLeod, Daniel.

Native of Virginia. pseud. Rejected stone. see Conway, Moncure Daniel.

Native poets of Maine. 38809

Native, resident in the island. pseud. Defence of the conduct of Barbadoes. (3264)

Native tribes of North America. 21322
Natives of Greenland. pseud. eds. 22854
Natives of Ireland. (35061)
Natives of Ireland. petitioners (47708)
Natives of Ireland, Residing Within the United States of America. petitioners 95928
Natives of Machias Resident Abroad. see Machias, Me. Citizens.
Natives of Ohio's Celebration of the Forty-Fifth Anniversary of the First Settlement of Cincinnati and the Miami Country, 1833. see Cincinnati. Celebration of the Forty-Fifth Anniversary of the First Settlement of Cincinnati and the Miami Country, by Natives of Ohio, 1833.
Natives of Virginia. 103394
Natividad Saldanha, Jose de la. see Saldanha, Jose de la Natividad.
Natividade Silva, Galdino Augusto da. 60888 see also Alagoas (Brazilian Province) Vice-Presidente (Natividade Silva)
Nativisim. (52040)
Natstock, Joshua. 36731
Natterer, Johann, 1787-1843. 7607, 59597, (77973)
Nattie of the Lake Shore. 72133
Natuerlyke historie van de Couchenille. 74500
Natur und das Leben in den Vereinigten Staaten von Nordamerika. 95764
Natur- und Sittengemalde der Tropen-Lander. 100686
Natur- und Sittenschilderungen. 36974
Natur und Vortrefflichkeit der Christlichen Religion. 78449
Natural and aboriginal history of Tennessee. 31085
Natural and artificial methods in education. 13418
Natural and civil history of California. 98845
Natural and civil history of the French dominions in North and South America. 35964
Natural and civil history of Vermont. 104350
Natural and moral government and agency of God. 65606
Natural and moral historie of the East and West Indies. 131
Natural and physical history of the Windward and Leeward colonies. 29899
Natural and political history of the state of Vermont. (819)
Natural and statistical view. 20822
Natural de la philosophia deste mundo visible. 98502
Natural equality. 96419
Natural history and objects of general interest. 860
Natural history of America. (22979)
Natural history of Barbados. 33582
Natural history of birds inhabiting the United States. 6264, 104598
Natural history of Carolina. 11508-11509, 22090
Natural history of chocolate. 12861
Natural history of coffie. 52041
Natural history [of Louisiana.] (9605)
Natural history of man. (65475), 65480
Natural history of Nevis. 84563
Natural history of New York. 4233, 53575, (53783), 53789, (53997)
Natural history of New York. Part 3. 4233, 53789
Natural history of North Carolina. 7800

Natural history of Nova Scotia. 84435
Natural history of quadrupeds. 15075
Natural history of secession. 27955
Natural history [of sugar.] 2120A
Natural history of the American aborigines. 25122
Natural history of the birds of the United States. 6264, 104597-104598
Natural history of the fishes inhabiting the river Ohio. 67453
Natural history of the fishes of Guiana. 77788
Natural history of the fishes of Massachusetts. 82810
Natural history of the human races. (35975)
Natural history of the human species. (82393)-82394
Natural history of the insects of North America. 37963, 71029
Natural history of the Negro race. 29108
Natural history of the order Catacea. (19866)
Natural history of the ordinary Cetacea or whales. (52042)
Natural history of the quadrupeds of Paraguay and the River La Plata. 2540
Natural history of the rarer Lepidopterous insects of Georgia. 25, 82789
Natural history of the Red River of Louisiana. 68476
Natural history of the sperm whale. 4108
Natural history of the state of New York. 53782
Natural history of the varieties of man. 39166
Natural history of those parts. 100940
Natural history of Vermont. 95555
Natural history of volcanoes. 57506
Natural History Society, Harvard University. see Harvard University. Natural History Society.
Natural History Society of Hartford, Conn. 30675
Natural History Society of Illinois. see Illinois Natural History Society.
Natural History Society of Montreal. 10637, 43093, 50271
Natural History Society of Montreal. Library. 50271
Natural History Society of Montreal. Museum. 50271
Natural History Society of New Brunswick. 52528
Natural hystoria de las Indias. 57987-57988
Natural principles of liberty. 52043
Natural principles of rectitude. (28933)
Natural productions and conveniences of the country. 5112-5113, 1st, 3 notes after 100480
Natural religion aided by revelation. 32258
Natural religion, . . . Dudleian-Lecture. (26783)
Natural resources and their development. 49106
Natural resources of Arkansas. (52044)
Natural road of specie payments. 14149
Natural spirit of Federalism exposed. 23974
Natural, statistical and civil history of the state of New York. 42956
Natural system of volcanic rocks. 9959
Natural wealth of California. 17608
Natvrale et generale historia dell' Indie Occidentali. 67740
Naturaleza. 52045
Naturaleza y civilizacion de la grandiosa de Cuba. (72553)

Naturalist. pseud. Journal. see Cooper, Susan Fenimore.
Naturalist. 52046
Naturalist and journal of natural history. 52047
Naturalist in Bermuda. 36544
Naturalist in Vancouver Island and British Columbia. 42035
Naturalist on the River Amazons. 3932A
Naturaliste Canadien. 52049
Naturalist's directory. (52048)
Naturalist's guide in collecting and preserving objects. 47162
Naturalist's library. 77788
Naturalist's sojourn in Jamaica. 28063
Naturalization. 18357
Naturalization and immigration. 22101
Naturalization in the American colonies. (52050)
Naturalization, Ireland, Fenianism, right of expatriation, protection of citizens, &c. 72207
Naturalization law of the General Congress. 13810
Naturalization laws of the United States. 52051
Naturalization of aliens. 78269
Nature; addresses and lectures. 22460
Nature and art. 92332
Nature and character of the true church of Christ. 21310
Nature and claims of Young Men's Christian Associations. 85303
Nature and constitution of the law. 76473
Nature and danger of heresy. 34116
Nature and design of the evangelical ministry considered. 92896
Nature and duties of the office of ruling elder. 83340
Nature and duty of rejoicing in the Lord. 104682
Nature and effects of drunkenness. 2704
Nature and effects of justifying faith. 81337
Nature, and evil, of seleishness [sic] considered and elustrated [sic]. 92125
Nature and evil of selfishness, considered and illustrated. 92126
Nature and excellency of the Christian religion. (78444)-(78445), (78447)
Nature and extent of Christ's redemption. 91863
Nature and extent of parliamentary power considered. 52052
Nature and extent of the apostolical commission. 81605-81607
Nature and fruits of political antimasonry. (14308), 52053
Nature and human nature. 29691
Nature and importance of a natural rhetoric. (80080)
Nature and importance of being always ready for our Lord's coming. 102422
Nature and importance of rightly divining the truth. 89798
Nature and influence of the historic spirit. 80081
Nature and influence of war. 59354
Nature and necessity of a growth in grace. 14413
Nature and necessity of conversion. (9717)
Nature and necessity of our union to Christ. 20059
Nature and necessity of regeneration. A discourse. 82399

Nature and necessity of regeneration. Handled in a discourse. 46568
Nature and necessity of regeneration. Sermon . . . preached at Newark. (20062)
Nature and necessity of repentance. 72694
Nature & necessity of spiritual conversion. (72695)
Nature and principles of congregationalism. 93275
Nature and properties of the sugar cane. 64252
Nature and treatment, of gun-shot wounds. 94063
Nature and worth of Christian liberty. 3099
Nature and worth of the science of church history. 82709
Nature, design and general rules of the Methodist Society. (52054)
Nature display'd, a new work. 98634-98635
Nature explored, &c. 100845
Nature, extent and history of the jurisdiction. 18358
Nature, extent, and importance of the duty of allegience. 10217
Nature, folly, and evil of rash and uncharitable judging. 9906
Nature, manner, and evidences of the work. 81337
Nature of a conversion to real and vital piety. 46271
Nature of a foederal union. 97439
Nature of adoption. 94705
Nature of assurance, witness of the spirit, and a call to the ministry. 85304
Nature of contracts consider'd. 96429
Nature of early piety. (14525)
Nature of regeneration opened. 94705
Nature of religious fasting opened. 9802
Nature of religious thanksgiving opened. 9803
Nature of riches. 94671
Nature of saving conversion. 91955
Nature of that faith. 106390
Nature of the four elements. 53023
Nature of the French tongue. 86696
Nature of the government in its relation to theology. 52055
Nature of true virtue. 21967, (30648), 32955
Nature: on freedom of mind: and other poems. 52056
Nature, pleasure, and advantages of church musick. 366
Nature the base of a true theology. 82673
Nature will be nature still. 96324
Naturel-historie. 22022
Naturell, die Krankheiten, das Arzthum und die Heilmittle der Urbewohner Brasiliens. 44994
Naturell-Historie und Beschreibung der Situation. 22024
Naturforscher am Amazonenstrom. 3934
Naturgeschichte der Saeugethiere von Paraguay. 69614
Naturgeschichte des Menschengeschlechts. 65479
Naturgeschichte von Guiana in Sud-Amerika. 3107
Naturhist. Beschreibung von Carolina. (11510)
Naturhistorische Reise nach der Westindischen Insel Hayti. 71595
Naturhistoriske bidrag til en beskrivelse af Gronland. 71435
Naturkrafte im Dienste des Menchen. (24692)

Naval dry docks of the United States. 93147-93148

Naval duties and discipline with the policy and principles of naval organization. 72573

Naval engagement at Port Royal. (38518)

Naval. Examination of "A reply to 'Hints on the re-organization of the navy.'" 74187

Naval gazetteer. 44119

Naval general court-martial. 82572

Naval history of Britain. 4888

Naval history of England. (39683)

Naval history of Great Britain, and origin and progress of the British power at sea. 31604

Naval history of Great Britain, from the declaration of war by France, in February, 1793. 35720

Naval history of Great Britain, from the declaration of war by France in 1793. 35721

Naval history of Great Britain, from the year MDCCLXXXIII. 7726

Naval history of Great Britain with the lives. 52078

Naval history of the United States. 13378

Naval journal. see Nautical magazine and naval journal. Sailor's magazine and naval journal.

Naval life. 42818

Naval light artillery tactics, &c. 51641

Naval magazine (1836-1837) 52079, 97982

Naval monitor. (52080)

Naval monument. 7045

Naval officer. pseud. Letter to the Right Hon. Lord Rodney. 40525

Naval officer. pseud. Pirate doctor. 63013

Naval officers. pseud. Letters. 40591

Naval patriotic song. 97284

Naval percussion locks and primers. 18277

Naval rank. 52081

Naval reform board. 82138

Naval register. (52082)

Naval register of the United States. 7045

Naval regulations issued by command of the President of the United States. 52083

Naval remembrancer. 91093

Naval remembrancer: or, the gentleman's naval chronology. 91092

Naval researches. 103458-103459

Naval retiring board. Speech . . . in the Senate. 33195

Naval retiring laws and Rear Admiral Goldsborough. 83605

Naval scenes in the last war. 83641

Naval sketch book. 27547, 52084

Naval sketches. 80337

Naval songster, being a collection of naval victories. (52085)

Naval songster. Songs of the sea. 52086

Naval staff officer. pseud. Naval staff rank. 52087

Naval staff rank. 52087

Naval stories. 39865

Naval temple. 1165, 2696

Naval tracts, in six books. 13015

Naval triumph. 52088

Navara, J. I. Maria de. 52089

Navares, M. Cabrera de. see Cabrera de Navares, M.

Navarijo, Ignacio Rodriguez. ed. 52090

Navarin, Ch. tr. 36794

Navarra, Jose Gregorio de Moraes. see Moraes Navarra, Jose Gregorio de.

Navarra y Rocaful, Melchor de, Duque de la Palata. 56748, 58311, (61115), (61164)
see also Peru (Viceroyalty) Virrey, 1681-1691 (Navarra y Rocaful)

Navarre, P. 52091-52092, note after 100836

Navarre, Pedro. 1998

Navarrete, A. 52093

Navarrete, Eustaquio Fernandez de. see Fernandez de Navarrete, Eustaquio, 1820-1866.

Navarrete, Domingo Fernandez. see Fernandez Navarrete, Domingo, Abp., d. 1689.

Navarrete, Juan Gomez. (52096)

Navarrete, Martin Fernandez de, 1765-1844. 974, 52097-52105, 70884, note before 99327, 99375, 99380, note after 99383C

Navarrete, Pedro. (52106)-52107

Navarete, Pedro Fernandez. see Fernandez Navarrete, Pedro.

Navarrette, Fernandez. see Fernandez Navarrete, Domingo, Abp., d. 1689.

Navarro, Diego. 52109

Navarro, Joannis. 52112

Navarro, Joaquin. tr. 65267

Navarro, Jose Maria. 52114-(52116)

Navarro, Juan Suarez. see Suarez y Navarro, Juan.

Navarro, Juan Suarez y. see Suarez y Navarro, Juan.

Navarro, Louis Diez. 52118

Navarro e Ibarra, Joaquin. (52113)

Navarro-Viola, Miguel, 1830-1890. 9021, 9040, 63329, 64440

Navarro y Noriega, Fernando. 52110-52111, 56245

Navassa Phosphate Company. 52119

Navegacao feita da cida de do Gram Para. 24982

Navegacao interior do Brasil. 50485

Navegacion especulativa y practica. 27797

Naves de Cortes destruidas. 293735, note after 98270

Navesink, N. J. All Saints' Memorial Church. Rector. 71402 see also Riley, T. M.

Navia Osorio, Alvaro de. see Santa Cruz de Marcenado, Alvaro de Navia Osorio, Marques de, 1684-1732.

Navies of England, France, America, and Russia. (7150)

Navies of the world. 9557

Navigacion especulativa, y practica. (9816)

Navigantium atque itinerantium bibliotheca. 5057, (11608), 16771-16772, 30482-30483, 55448, 77962, 89452

Navigateurs. 19550

Navigateurs modernes. 2500

Navigatio. (34105)

Navigatio ac itinerarivm Iohannis Hvgonis Linscotani. 41366, (41367)

Nauigatio ad Indos Occiduos inchoatur. 77904

Navigatio in Brasiliam Americae. (8784)

Navigatio Salomonis ophiritica. 41390

Navigatio Septentrionalis det er relation eller beskrivelse. 51336

Navigatio Septentrionalis paa Dansk. 51335

Navigation and advantages of the River Schuylkill. 60269, 78063

Navigation and commerce. 23208

Navigation australe de Jacques le Marie. 68455

Navigation aux cotes du Bresil. (73497)

Navigation da Lisboa all' isola di San Thome. 67730

Nauigation del Capitan Pietro di Sintra. 67730

Navigation del Capitano Pedro Alvares.
67730
Navigation du Capitaine Martin Frobisher,
Anglois. 52120. 79343
Navigation du Captaine Frosiher ez regions
d Est et Nord-Oest. 5652
Navigation du vaillant capitaine de mer
Jacques le Maire. 31543
Navigation et geographie. 25917
Navigation et hydrographie. 25916
Navigation of the lakes. 36206
Navigation of the Pacific Ocean. 4219
Navigation of the three oceans. 73415
Navigation, poeme en 6 chants. 22880
Navigation spiritualized. (24680)
Navigation sur les deux oceans. 74988, note
after 100812
Navigation verso le Indie Orientali. 67730
Navigatione del grandissimo fiume Maragnon.
67740
Nauigatione del Mar Rosso & sino Persico.
67730
Navigatione del Mar Rosso fino alle Indie
Orientali. 67730
Navigatione di Hannon. 67730
Navigatione di Hannone Carthaginese. 67730
Navigatione di Iambolo mercatante. 67730
Navigatione di Nearcho capitano di Alessandro
Magno. 67730
Navigatione di Sebastiano Cabots. 67738
Navigatione di Vasco di Caman. 67730
Nauigatione oceani ad nouu orbem. (5518)
Navigationes primae in Americam. (34105),
note after 99383C
Navigationi et viaggi nel qvale si contengono
la nauigationi al Mondo Nuouo. 67740-
67742, 99281, 105724
Navigationi et viaggi nel qvale si contengono
l'historia delle cose de Tartari. 67736
Navigationi et viaggi raccolto gia da M. Gio.
Battista Ramvsio. (67737)-67738,
67741
Nauigationi fatte dipoi alle dette Indie. 67740-
67742
Navigations de Frobisher. 68419
Navigations Francaises et la revolution mari-
time. 44532
Navigator. 17384-17386
Navigator, or the theory and practic principles
of the art. 75852
Navigator, shewing and explaining all the
chiefe principles. 75851
Navigator's kalendar. 90946
Navillus. pseud. Plenty of money. 63416
Navolging van een Engelsch gedigt. 52121
Navorscher. 36564
Navy a quarter of a century behind the army.
52126
Navy and Marine Corps laws. 10051
Navy Department, December 31, 1864. 51743
Navy. Hints on the re-organization of the
navy. 31978, 69696, 74187, 74189
Navy in Congress. 52127
Navy Library and Institute, Charlestown,
Mass. 12100
Navy of the United States. An exposure of its
condition. 20018
Navy of the United States, from 1775 to 1853.
(52128)
Navy of the United States, from the commence-
ment. 22519
Navy royal and sea service. 67587
Navy royalle and sea-service. 67561, 67587
Navy Union of Massachusetts. see Massa-
chusetts. Army and Navy Union.

Navy yard at Patuxent River. (2588)
Navy Yard Committee, New London, Conn.
see New London Navy Yard Committee,
New London, Conn.
Navy yard exposition and navy yard abuses.
62473
Navy's friend. (52129)
Naxera, Emmanuel. see Naxera, Manuel
Crisostomo.
Naxera, M. de. 52133
Naxera, Manuel Crisostomo. 52130-52132
Nayler, James. 70894
Naylor, Benjamin. 52135
Naylor, Charles. 52136
Naylor & Company. firm 52137
Naylor's system of teaching geography.
52135
Nazarene. 84284
Nazarene; or, the last of the Washingtons.
(41399)
Nazareno. pseud. Cosas de los Estados
Unidos. 16987
Nazareth, Pa. Moravian Historical Society.
see Moravian Historical Society,
Nazareth, Pa.
Nazareth, Pa. Nazareth Hall. see Nazareth
Hall, Nazareth, Pa.
Nazareth Hall, Nazareth, Pa. Reunion Society.
68987
Nazarite documents. 52138
Nazarite Union, of the Genesee Conference of
the Methodist Episcopal Church. see
Methodist Episcopal Church. Conferences.
Genesee. Nazarite Union.
Nazarite's vow. 104792
Nazianzensus, Gregorius. see Gregorius
Nazianzensus, Saint, Patriarch of
Constantinople.
Ne sutor ultra crepidam. 104097
Neagle, J. B. engr. 12891, 84143, 84146,
84358-84362, 84365
Neal, Alice Bradley. (53139)
Neal, Daniel, 1678-1743. 14502, 28792, 43700,
52140-52147, 96331
Neal, James A. 8930
Neal, John, 1793-1876. 854, 3069, 8390,
52148-52157, (52159)-52161, note after
102121, 105956
Neal, John, 1793-1876. supposed author
36145, 43045
Neal, John, 1793-1876. incorrectly supposed
author 52158, 59212, 81508
Neal, Joseph C. 52162-52165
Neal, Theodore Augustus. 52166
Neal record. 52166
Neale, --------. plaintiff 97700
Neale, Adam. tr. 2224
Neale, J. 55485
Neale, John. 96771
Neale, Mary Peisley. 52167, 52172
Neale, Rollin Heber. 52168-52170
Neale, Samuel. (52171)-52172
Neal's charcoal sketches. 52164
Neal's history of the puritans. 52145
Neander, August. 2795
Neander, Johann. (52173)
Neander, M. 52174-52175
Near connection. pseud. Sketch of the life of
Lieut. Mathew Hughes. 33600
Near home. A poem. 52176
Near Newark, Ohio. Mound builder's works.
85140
Near relation of Old Mother Hubbard. pseud.
Whimsical incidents. 103295
Nearcho. 67730

7586, 7608, 7636-7637, 7648, 7696,
(15186), 15713, 15930-15932, 16732-
(16734), 16738, 19227, 20594, (22992),
23344, 29505, 38028-38029, 38259,
38260, 41848-(41850), 47764, 47766-
47767, 47824-47825, 55280-55281,
(55386), (56663)-56679, 68493, (68495),
68899, 69589, 89149, 93834, 93842,
93843, 95749, 97527, 98248, note after
98474, 98988, note after 99260, note
after 99310, 101421, 102027, 102441,
102875-102878, 102880-102883, 102885-
102888, 102889A, 3d note after 102889A,
102890, 2d note after 102890, 7th note
after 102890, 102891, 1st note after
102891, 102892, 3d note after 102893,
102894, 2d note after 102894, 1st note
after 102895, 102899, 102900, 1st note
after 102910, 4th note after 102913,
5th note after 102913, 102914-102922,
note after 102926. 102927-102936, note
after 102936
Nederlandsche West Indische Compagnie.
petitioners (16680), 38259, (57320),
69588, 1st note after 102889A
Nederlandsche West Indische Compagnie.
Administratie. 98248
Nederlandsche West Indische Compagnie.
Beheerderen. 16738, 102890
Nederlandsche West Indische Compagnie.
Bewinthebberen. 7552, 7636-7637,
15705-15706, 15712, 16731, (19226),
(22992)-22993, 47765-47766, 49559-
49562, 51705-51706, 56018, (56666),
56672-56674, 57537, 66524, 68792,
695543, note after 89149, 93854,
95749, 102296, 102442, note after 102886,
2d note after 102888, 2d note after
102889A, 1st note after 102890, 5th note
after 102895, 102897, 2d note after 102897,
2d note after 102897, 1st-2d notes after
102899, 102901, 2d note after 102905A,
1st note after 102911, 5th note after
102911, 102913, 102920-102921, 102924,
102926
Nederlandsche West Indische Compagnie.
Bewinthebberen. petitioners 15930-
15932, 47766, 51712, 69585, 69586,
69587, 69589, 95749, 102888, 102889A,
3d note after 102895, 4th note after
102899, 2d-3d note after 102911, 2d
note after 102913
Nederlandsche West Indische Compagnie.
Bewinthebberen. Gecommitteerde.
93834
Nederlandsche West Indische Compagnie.
Bewinthebberen. Gedeputeerde. 69586
Nederlandsche West Indische Compagnie.
Charter. 7648, 51707, (56665)-56679,
57498, 57532-57537, 63192, 63194-63202,
(66523), 69540, 102884, 3d note after
102899, 102901-102902, 2d note after
102903, 3d note after 102903, 102904-
102905, 102905A-102908, 102909-102910,
102920-102921, 102923-102924, 102929
see also Surinam. Charter.
Nederlandsche West Indische Compagnie.
Commissioners and Deputies. see
Nederlandsche West Indische Compagnie.
Bewinthebberen.
Nederlandsche West Indische Compagnie.
Directeur-Generael. 102912-102192A
see also Valckenburgh, Johan van.
Nederlandsche West Indische Compagnie.
Directeurs. 27260, 51712, 102925

Nederlandsche West Indische Compagnie.
Hooft Participanten. 22994, (56666),
56672, 56674, 69588, 4th note after 102911
Nederlandsche West Indische Compagnie.
Hooft Participanten. Gecommitteerde.
16731, 22994, 2d note after 102889A
Nederlandsche West Indische Compagnie.
Representant. (22992)
Nederlandsche West-Indische Eilanden in
derzelver tegenwoordigen toestand. 94586
Nederlandsche West Indische Ontginning- en
Handel-Maatschappij. (57372)
Nederlandsche zeereizen in het laatst der XVI,
XVII en in het begin der XVIII eeuw.
4715, 52229, 3d note after 103943
Nederlandschen uitgeever. pseud. tr. 7936,
22991
Nederlandtschen bye-korf. 98191-98192,
98195, 98200-98201, 98206, 98209, 98212,
98216
Nedermeyer van Rosenthal, J. Th. H. 52230,
(73283)
Nedham, Marchamont. tr. (79873)
Nedy, William. alias see Eddy, William.
defendant
Nee de la Rochelle, Jean Francois, 1751-
1838. 19621
Nee-boash. Potawatomi Indian Chief 96702
Needful capital for rebuilding a burnt district.
89612
Needful caution against a sin that easily besets
us. 46711
Needful caution in a critical day. (58894)
Needful word, to temper the tract. 13350,
102425
Needham, Daniel. (52231)
Needham, John Rainsford. 52232
Needham, Mass. First Parish Church.
Sabbath School Library. 52234
Needham, Mass. School Committee. 52234
Needham, Mass. Temperance Society. see
Needham Temperance Society, Needham,
Mass.
Needham Temperance Society, Needham,
Mass. 52233
Needle Pickets, Quincy, Ill. see Illinois.
Militia. Needle Pickets, Quincy.
Needles, Edward. 52235-52236, (61730),
62304
Needles, Samuel H. tr. 81308
Neele, -------. cartographer (35895)
Neely, Phil. P. 49357, (52237)
Neerinckx, Carolus. (52238)-(52239)
Neerlands heldendaaden ter see. 95777
Neerlandsch West-Indie in zijne belangen.
4585
Nees von Esenbeck, C. G. 44999, 52240
Neef, David. tr. 83144
Neff, Jacob K. 52241-52242, 2d note after
95758
Neff Petroleum Company. 52243
Neffens aanmerkungen over den oorspring en
voortgang. 4385
Negbauer, -------. (52244)
Negbauer's comic almanac. (52244)
Néger élet a rabszolgatartó Amerikai államokban.
92583
Neger-Engelsch woordenboek. 24936
Neger hut. 92522
Negeraufstand in Jamaica. 5889
Negergeschichte. 92554
Negerhut. 92398
Negerhut. (Uncle Tom's cabin.) 92521
Negerhut van Oom Tom. (21177)
Negerkonig Zamba. 3702

Negerleben in den Nordamerikan Sklavenstaaten. 92561

Negerleben in den sklavenstaaten Amerikas. 92548-92549, 92551, 92557-92560, 92562-92563

Negerleben in den sklavenstaaten des freien Nordamerika. 92568

Negerleben in Nord-Amerika. 92573

Negerleven in den Sklavenstaaten von Nordamerika. 92562

Negerlifvet i Amerika. 92617

Negerlifvet i Amerikanska slafstaterna. 92616

Negerliv i de Amerikanske slavestater. 92518

Negerlivet i Amerikas slavestater. 92517

Negerlivet i de Amerikanske slavestater. 92594

Negeropstanden paa St. Domingo. (33615)

Negers. 35269

Negersclave. 2935

Negerslaven in de kolonie Suriname en de uitbreiding van het Christendom. 94587

Negerslavereit i Vestindien. 26135

Negerstaat van Hayti of Sint Domingo. 52245, 98678

Neglect of Christ the killing sin. 103510

Neglect of supporting and maintaining the pure worship of God. 826

Negley, James S. (52246)

Negociacion pena. 52247

Negociacion Yancy. 17841

Negociaciones diplomaticas entre el Brasil, la republica Argentina y el Paraguay. 87189

Negociaciones entre la republica oriental del Uruguay. 38719

Negocians de Bordeaux. pseud. see Bordeaux. Negocians. pseud.

Negocians de l'Orient, Interesses au Commerce des Etats-Unis. petitioners 47524

Negocians du Bresil. see Brazil. Negocians. petitioners

Negociant. pseud. Lettre. 40672

Negociant experimente. pseud. Voyageur Americain. see Cluny, Alexander.

Negociations pendantes entre le Mexique et l'Espagne. 52248

Negociations du Sieur Lange a la Chine. 4936

Negociator's magazine. 31028

Negocios do Rio Grande. 88768

Negocios eclesiasticos en el negocio relativo al breve de Su Santidad el Sr. Pio IX. (78909)

Negotiant du pays. pseud. Description historique. see Louis XVIII, King of France, 1755-1824.

Negotiation for Cherokee lands. 52249, 69778

Negotiations. (12253)

Negre comme il y a peu de blancs. 39281

Negrede, Agustin Lopez. (52250)

Negreiros, Andrea Vidal de. see Vidal de Negreiros, Andrea.

Negreiros, Antonio Thomas de. see Thomaz de Negreiros, Antonio.

Negres. pseud. Poesises. 92533

Negres de la Louisiane. (22470)

Negres Marrons de la Jamaique. 69055

Negresse, ou la pouvoir de la reconnaissance. 67417

Negrete, --------, fl. 1828. 93791

Negrete, Modesto Cacho. 52252

Negrete, Pedro Celestino. 52253, 56441

Negrete, Pedro Romulo. 76195, 89963

Negrete, R. defendant 11295

Negreyros y Seria, Jose Ignacio. 93775

Negri, G. 52254

Negrin, J. J. 25812, 52255, 87840

Negro. pseud. Address to the Negroes in . . . New York. 53506

Negro. pseud. No rum, no sugar. 55368

Negro, Alonso. 50050-50064, 1st-5th notes after 106378

Negro—a distinct species. 14325

Negro a man, but not a brother. 82022

Negro and Aborigines Fund. see Friends, Society of. London Yearly Meeting. Committee on the Negro and Aborigines Fund.

Negro and Aborigines Fund. Report of the Meeting for Sufferings. 52258

Negro and Jamaica. (62873)

Negro apprenticeship in the British colonies. 52259

Negro apprenticeship in the colonies. 52260

Negro at home. 89784

Negro boy's tale, a poem. 57397

Negro Christianized. 46426

Negro conspiracy in the city of New York. 33061

Negro emancipation: a dialogue between Mr. Ebenezer Eastlove and Giles Homespun. 52261

Negro emancipation and West Indian independence 94501

Negro emancipation made easy. 52262

Negro equality. 5668

Negro equality—the right of one man to hold property in another. 90381

Negro equalled by few Europeans. 39292, 103139

Negro farce. 83022

Negro foreget me not songster. (52263)

Negro girl seventeen years of age. pseud. Ode of verses. see Peters, Phillis (Wheatley) 1753?-1784.

Negro has a soul. 51659

Negro in the American rebellion. 8595

Negro is not a citizen of the state. 51659

Negro labor question. (52264)

Negro law of South Carolina. 57332, 3d note after 87898

Negro life in the slave states of America. [By Harriet Beecher Stowe.] 92467, 92471-92472, 92490-92492

Negro life in the slave states of America. [By Richard Hildreth.] 31788

Negro-mania. 10248

Negro melodies. (52263)

Negro pew. 52265

Negro plot. (30013)

Negro problem solved. 68154

Negro question. 58847

Negro race. 56039

Negro Religious Instruction Fund, for Assisting in the Erection of Additional Places of Worship and School-Houses. 85940, 102849

Negro servant. 52266

Negro School of the Society of Friends, Philadelphia. see Philadelphia. Negro School of the Society of Friends.

Negro singer's own book. (52263)

Negro slave. A tale. 51730

Negro slavery. 5218, 52267

Negro slavery. [By Henry Broughman.] 8419

Negro slavery. [By John Vaughan.] 98687

Negro-slavery defended by the word of God. 70472

Negro slavery described by a Negro. 101433A

Negro slavery in the United States of America. 16625

Negro-slavery, no evil. (27864), 92866-92867

Negro slavery not unjust. 13291, 56660, 84084

Negro slavery. Observations. 52268, (56479)

Negro slavery, or, a view of some of the more prominent features. 52269, 94526

Negro slavery unjustifiable. 43528

Negro slaves; a dramatic historical piece. 38280

Negro slaves; or, the black man and the black bird. 43490

Negro soldiers. 72859

"Negro suffrage." 9857

Negro suffrage in the south. 84856

Negro. The ancient story of the Negro race. 52256

Negro turn'd Christian. (31807)

Negro: what is his ethnological status? 52270, (78545), 81894, 89152

Negro woman's lamentation. 87173

Negroes advocate. 70325

Negroes and Africans as freedmen and soldiers. 52271

Negroes and religion. (52272)

Negroes and the Anglo-Africans. 25833

Negroes at Port Royal. 62711

Negroes in Negroland. 31273

Negroes in Ohio. (77327)

Negroes' jubilee. 95844

Negroleum, formerly known as petroleum. 52276

Negron, Francisco Tamayo y. see Tamayo y Negron, Francisco.

Negrophile, comedie en une acte et en verse. 11589

Negrophobia "on the brain" in white men. 31027

Negro's and Indians advocate. 27677-27678, 3d note after 93806

Negros en America. 92607

Negro's flight from American slavery to British freedom. 52273

Negro's friend; consisting of anecdotes. 10763, 51733, 52274, 98663A

Negros' friend; containing the entertaining and affecting history of Gustavus Vassa. 10763, 52274, 98663A

Negro's friend, no. 7. 63234

Negro's friend, no. 3. 10763, 52274, 68663A

Negro's memorial. 52275

Negro's place in nature. 9498

Negro's place in nature. A paper read. (33868)

Negro's revenge. 93418

Nehemiah. A brief essay on divine consolations. 46427

Nehemiah on the wall in troublesom [sic] times. (49661)

Nehemiah, or the struggle for liberty nevery in vain. (51518)

Nehiro. 19378

Neidhard, Charles. 52277

Neidhard, Karl. 1288

Neighbor. pseud. Result of an ecclesiastical council at Bolton. see Chaplin, Ebenezer.

Neighbour. pseud. Second treatise on church-government. see Chaplin, Ebenezer.

Neighbour. pseud. Treatise on church-government. see Chaplin, Ebenezer.

Neighbor Parley. pseud. Five letters. see Goodrich, Samuel Griswold, 1793-1860.

Neighbor Smith. pseud. Cracked jug. see Williams, Moses.

Neighbors and allies. 91015

Neighbour's tears. 96154

Neil, Thomas. 85307

Neil, William C. (6765), note after 97006

Neill, A. 52279

Neill, Edward Duffield, 1823-1893. 41888, (52280)-52288

Neill, Henry, fl. 1850. 63156

Neill, Henry, fl. 1858. 52289

Neill, James. 52290

Neill, P. 52291

Neill, William, 1778?-1860. 2799-(2800), 52292-52293, 89736

Neilson, Charles. 52294

Neilson, John. (58490), 69780 see also Quebec (Province) Commissioners to Visit the United States' Penitentiaries.

Neilson, John, of Jamaica. (52295)

Neilson, Joseph. 52296

Neilson, Peter. 52297

Neilson, William. 97094

Neimeyer Bellegrade, Henrique Luis de. 52299

Neisser, Georg. ed. 106351

Neiuwe in-teyckeninge ende verkooginge der capitalen. (55286), 102900

Nek nechenenawackgissitschik bambilak naga geschiechauchsitpanna Johanessa elekhangup. 19377

Nekossa Lumbering Company. (52300)

Nelegapta Jesuib Kristusib. 22862

Nell, William Cooper, 1816-1874. (6765), (52301)-(52303)

Nelles, Abraham. 6352

Nelles, Annie. see Dumond, Annie (Hamilton) Nelles, 1837-

Nelly's hospital. 52305, 57942, 76692

Nelse Seymour's big-shoe songster. 79667

Nelson, ———. defendant (14087)

Nelson, Charles A. ed. 67420

Nelson, D. supposed author 34960

Nelson, David, 1793-1844. 52306, 104668

Nelson, E. 52307

Nelson, Henry. 52308

Nelson, Henry A. 52309-52310

Nelson, Horace. ed. 52311, 55804

Nelson, Horatio Nelson, Viscount, 1758-1805. 13420

Nelson, John. 52313-52315

Nelson, Joseph. 52316

Nelson, Levi. (52317)

Nelson, Mayron Andrews. 93475

Nelson, Robert. 52318-52319

Nelson, Samuel. 84738, 103765

Nelson, T. S. reporter (18605)

Nelson, Thomas, 1738-1789. 100210 see also Virginia. Governor, 1781 (Thomas Nelson)

Nelson, Thomas A. R. 52323

Nelson (Thomas) & Sons. firm publishers 33527, 52320-52322, 55116, 57940, 92454

Nelson Copper Mining Company. 69956

Nelson's British library. 52321

Nelson's guide to Lake George and Lake Champlain. 52322

Nelson's guide to the city of New York. 52322

Nelson's illustrated guide to the Hudson. 52322

Nelson's library for travellers and the fireside. 92454

Nelson's northern lancet. 52311, 55804

Nemar, R. M. see M'Nemar, Richard.

Nembhard, J. F. (52325)

Nemnich, --------. tr. 73379

Nemo. pseud. Few thoughts on the confiscation act. 52326

Nemo. pseud. Remarks on the policy of recognizing the independence of the southern states. 52327, 69485

Nemo. pseud. Sketch of the history of Framingham. see Ballard, William.

Nemo. pseud. Straws. see Coffin, Roland F. supposed author and Vans, Miss ----------, of Boston. supposed author

Nemo, Mrs. pseud. Series of appeals. see, Roberts, Mary E.

Nemo, of Louisiana. pseud. Reveries in rhyme. 52328

Nemo Nobody, Esquire. pseud. Something. see Fennell, James.

Nemours, Pierre Samuel du Pont de. see Du Pont de Nemours, Pierre Samuel.

Nene karighwiyoston tsinihorighhoten ne Saint John. 49846, 95145

NeomiAnism Unmaskt. 12334

Neonomianism unmask'd. 12333, 104184

Neoshoo valley. 30698

Nepenthes evangelicum. 46428

Nephew, Carolina Clifford. (40886)

Nephite records. 83071

Nepomuceno Almonte, Juan. (956), 20548, 52332

Nepomuceno Rosains, Juan. 52333, 73199, 79032

Nepomuceno Troncoso, Juan. see Troncoso, Juan Nepomuceno.

Neponset Bridge. Proprietors. see Proprietors of Neponset Bridge.

Neptune. pseud. Ship Archer and the caulkers' strike. 80499

Neptune Americo-Septentrional. 52337

Neptune Division, No. 64. see Sons of Temperance of North America. Pennsylvania. Neptune Division, No. 64.

Neptune Fire Engine Company, No. 5, Utica, N. Y. 98229

Neptune occidental. 35965

Neptune's car. 2327

Nereis Australis. 30781

Nereis boreali-Americana. 30782, 85072

Nereus. pseud. Letters on the subject of the naval war with America. see Croker, John Wilson, 1780-1857.

Neri, Philip, Saint. see Philip Neri, Saint, 1515-1595.

Neri, Oratory of St. Philip. see Oratorians.

Neriah. 16297

Nerreter, D. ed. 73324

Nerses Klaietsi, Saint, d. 1173. 65020-65021

Nersetis Clajensis. Saint see Nerses Klaietsi, Saint, d. 1173.

Nervi, Giuseppe. 4565

Nesbit, J. C. 52338

Nesbitt, C. R. (7111)

Nescopeck Canal Convention, Conyngham Town, Pa., 1832. 65781

Neshobe. 99097

Nesi, Lorenzo. tr. 46994

Nesmith, James Willis, 1820-1885. 52341

Nesmith, John. (52339)-(52340), note after 95697

Nesquehoning Valley Railroad Company. 60270

Ness, Christopher. 52342

Ness, Cornelius Peter van. see Van Ness, Cornelius Peter.

Ness, John Peter van. see Van Ness, John Peter.

Ness, William Peter van. see Van Ness, William Peter.

Ness, William W. van. see Van Ness, William W.

Nest of corruption! 90579

Nest of love disturbed. (52343)

Nestor. pseud. Nestor's address to the Pennsylvania militia. 52344

Nestor. pseud. To the militia of Pennsylvania. (60709)

Nestor's address to the Pennsylvania militia. 52344

Nests at Washington. (62595)

Net for a night-raven. 100502

Net in the bay. (52345), 74147

Netherclift, Frederick G. 52346

Netherland disturbances. 11256

Netherland-historian. (52347)

Netherlands. 2155A, 7501, 7520, 13686, 15201, 16903, 41963, 44264-44265, (56516), 69459, 75200, 93853, 102449

Netherlands. Constitution. 11701, 32012

Netherlands. Department van Kolonien. 38326

Netherlands. Estats-General. see Netherlands. Staten Generael.

Netherlands. Laws, statutes, etc. 2154A, 16674, 22996-22998, 26815, 27126, 28930, 51705-51707, (56665)-56679, (56682), 57105-57107, 57498, 57532-57537, 63190-63202, (66395), (66523), (68750), 68899, 68912, 68922, 69540, 72766, 93834, 93836, 93842-93843, 100936-100939, 102880, 102884, 1st-3d notes after 102899, 102901-102921, 102923-102924, 102931

Netherlands. Legatie. Great Britain. 93427, 98511, 98926 see also Beverningk, H. van. Jongestal, A. P. Nieupoort, W. Perre, J. van de. Van Gogh, M. Welderen, ---------, Graaf van.

Netherlands. Legatie. Portugal. 66057

Netherlands. Menigte. 68800

Netherlands. Ministre des Affaires Etrangeres. 104130 see also Verstolk de Soelen, Johan Gijsbert, d. 1845.

Netherlands. Raedt van Staten. see Netherlands. Staatsraad.

Netherlands. Richteren. 77999

Netherlands. Sovereigns, etc., 1815-1840 (Willem I) 44033, 44046, 65017, 102931, 104030 see also Willem I, King of the Netherlands, 1772-1844.

Netherlands. Sovereigns, etc., 1815-1840 (Willem I) defendant 105162 see also Willem I, King of the Netherlands, 1772-1844. defendant

Netherlands. Staatsraad. 484

Netherlands. Stadholder, 1751-1795 (Willem V) 36562, 106234 see also Willem V, Prince of Orange, 1748-1806.

Netherlands. Staten Generael. 228, 247-248, 486, 1652, 2154A, 4814, 7516, 7552, 7636-7637, 7648, 7696, (15184)-(15186), 15705-15707, 15712, 15930-15932, 16664, 16674, 19186, 20594, 21542, 23513, 26815, 29170, 36563, (36569), 36570, 47764, 44556, (49563), 51705-51706, 51710, 52225, 55280-55281, 55286, (56663)-56680, (56682), 56769, 57498, 57532-57537, 63190-63202, 63286, 66523, 68458, (68750), 68899, 69540, 70070, 72766, 75200, note after 89149, 93834, 93836, 93842-93843, 1st note after 93862, 95454, 96569, note after 98474, 99310-note after 99310,

100936-100939, 102027, 102875, 102877, 102880-102881, 102884, note after 102886, 102887-102889A, 2d note after 102891, 102892, 1st note after 102895, 1st note after 102896, 1st-2d notes after 102899, 102900-102910, 102915-102912A, 102920-102921, 102923-102924, note after 102926, 102927, note after 102936

Netherlands. Staten Generael. Commissarisen. 23509, 102891

Netherlands. Staten Generael. Gecommitteerden. 69543, 1st note after 102911

Netherlands. Staten Generael. Gedeputeerden. 20786, note after 98953

Netherlands. Staten Generael. Secretaris. 20597, note after 98474, note after 99310 see also Tienhoven, -------- van.

Netherlands. Staten Generael van Hollandt. see Netherlands. Staten General.

Netherlands. States General. see Netherlands. Staten Generael.

Netherlands. Treaties, etc. 2146-2147, 2150, 2154, 2154B-2154C, 2155-2158, (6361), 14378, 15493, 15930-15932, (16088)-16090, 16119, 17198, 19274, 19186, 23509, 26872-26873, 37723, 38259, 39155, 41849, 47770, 51710, 52223-52224, 56475, 63286, 65045, 65110, 68457, 68934, 69589, 78000, 86742, 91092-91093, 92762, 94070, 95655, 95749, 96517-96520, 96522-96525, 96540, 96543-96545, 96569, 98926, 98987-98988, note after 99260, 99307, 102875, 102888, 102891, 2d note after 102894

Netherlands. Ziekenhuisen. 68800

Netherlands Literary Society, Leyden. see Maatschappij der nederlandsche Letterkunde, Leyden.

Nets of salvation. 46429

Netscher, A. D. van der Gon. 52348

Netscher, P. M. 52349-52350, 5th note after 93855

Nettle, Richard. 52351

Nettles, Joshua. defendant 11005

Nettleton, Asahel. 4345, (52353)-52354

Nettleton, Charles. 52355

Nettleship, Henry. 52352

Netto, A. da Silva. see Silva Netto, A. da.

Netto, Ladislau de Souza Mello e. see Souza Mello e Netto, Ladislau de.

Netum ewh oomahzenahegun owh Moses. 36593

Neu-auffgerichtetes Rust- und Zeughauss der Natur. 98357

Neu Aufgerichteter Americanischer Mayerhof. 47108

Neu daflen lythyrennol o'r prif eiriau yn y Bibl sanctaidd. 50634

Neu-Englander oder Skizzen von Charakteren und Sitten. 101086

Neu-Entdecktes Norden. 5905, 52359

Neu-Eroffnetes Amphitheatrvm. 52360

Neu-Eroffnetes Raritaten-Cabinet. 37746, 52361

Neu-gefundenes Eden. 52362

Neu Jahrs Geschenk aus Jamaica. 35635

Neu-polirter Geschichte- Kunst- und Sittenspiegel. 25462

Neu-vermehrt- und vollstandiges Gesang-Buch. 52363, 60271

Neu-vermehrte Reiss-Beschreibung. 79165

Neudeutschland in Westamerika. 7453

Neue . . . Abhandlung von Tabacksbau. 2620

Neue Americanische Landwirthschafts Calender. 52364

Neue Americanische Landwirthschafts-Calender auf das Jahr . . . 1814. 68215

Neue Anweisung zur Gesundheit. 95605

Neue Beitrage zur Volker- und Landerkunde. 89763

Neue Beschreibung der Insel Jamaica in America. 1339

Neue Bibliothek der wichtigsten Reisebeschreibungen. 1645, 18672, 22828, 40835, 42621, 91612, 94201, 98613, 101304

Neue Entdeckung des vierten Eylandes in dem unbekannten Suder-Land. 35256, 82187

Neue Entdeckung vieler sehr grossen Landschaften in America. (31367)

Neue Entdeckungen vieler sehr grossen Landschaften in America. 31365

Neue Erdbeschreibung von ganz Amerika. 52365, (77659)

Neue Hoch Deutsche Americanische Calendar. 52366

Neue Hoch Deutsche Americanische Calender, auf . . . 1798. 44258, 105687

Neue Jegund- und Hausbibliothek. 2694, (69072)

Neue Land- und Seebilder. 64539

Neue Land- und Seebilder fur die Jugend. 20124

Neue merckwurdige Reise-Beschreibung nach Neu Spanien. 26309

Neue Nachricht alter und neuer Merckwurdigkeiten. 10974, 87899

Neue Nachrichten von den Missionen der Jesuiten in Paraguay. 51425

Neue Nachrichten von denen neuentdecken Insuln in der See zwischen Asien und Amerika. (52367), 78015

Neue Nordische Beytrage. 91218

Neue Pennsylvanische Stadt und Land Calender. 52368

Neue Pflanzen Species. note after 77796

Neue Readinger Calender. 68215

Neue Reise Beschreibung durch viele Lander. (31366)

Neue Reise Beschreibung nach America. (31368)

Neue Reise durch die Nord-Amerikanischen Freistaaten. 8033

Neue Reise durch die Vereinigten Staaten. 8032

Neue Reise durch Nordamerika. 72037

Neue Reise in die Nordischen Landschafften. 38715

Neue Reise nach Cayenne. 11622-11623

Neue Reise um die Welt in den Jahren 1823, 24, 25 und 26. 38286

Neue Reise um die Welt worinnin umstandlich Beschreiben wird. 18389

Neue Reisen durch die Vereinigten Staaten. 27184

Neue Reisen nach Guiana. 3605

Neue Reisen aach Guiana, Peru und durch das Sudliche America. (52369)

Neue Reisen nach West-Indien darinnen Nachrichten. 6468, 25133

Neue Reisen nach Westindien. 6469

Neue Sammlung der merkwurdigen Reisegeschichten. 52370

Neue Sammlung geistlicher Lieder. 61589

New and complete system of universal geography. 59284, 104442

New and complete tax-payer's manual. (52444)

New and comprehensive gazetteer of Virginia. 44894

New and comprehensive system of modern geography. (51642)

New and concise system of arithmetick. 91486

New and correct map of the countries. 11509

New and exact account of Jamaica. 40190

New and experimentall discoverie of New England. 97733

New and familiar system of arithmetic. 90538

New and further discovery of the Isle of Pines. 82180

New and further narrative of the state of New-England. 52445, 65324

New and impartial collection of interesting letters. (52446)

New and impartial universal history. 2064

New and important region! 55723

New and improved edition. The New England primer, improved. 52719

New and interesting view of slavery. 33682

New and most exact account of the fertile and famous colony of Carolina. 17334

New and most exact map of America. (71907)

New and old. (52447)

New and original musical extravaganza. 89421

New and popular description of the United States. 78650

New and popular pictorial description of the United States. 78651

New and popular songs. 52448

Newe and strange newes from St. Christophers of a tempestous spirit. 54942, 75017

New and the old. (58365)

New and universal gazetteer. (78330)

New and universal history of the United States. 52449

New and useful plan to establish free labor. 1185

New annual register. (52450)

New-Ark Land and cash lottery. (52451)

New arithmetic. note before 83906, 83911-83912, 83958

New arithmetic or third book. 83911

New army list of the United States. (52452)

New arrangement of the courts of justice. 45268

New Association for the Abolition of Slavery, Glasgow. see Glasgow New Association for the Abolition of Slavery.

New atlas; containing a geographical and historical account. 52453

New atlas; or, travels and voyages in Europe. 52454

New atmosphere. 20506

New attempt to recover the right version. 46897

New attractive. 55496

New authentic and complete collection of voyages round the world, including Captain Cook's three voyages. 52455

New, authentic, and complete collection of voyages round the world: undertaken and performed by royal authority. 32438

New ballad on the taking of Porto-Bello. 52456, 99249

New banking system. 89612

New Bedford, Mass. 52479, 52490, 52492, 52502, (52508)

New Bedford, Mass. Alms House. 52499

New Bedford, Mass. American Institute of Instruction. see American Institute of Instruction.

New Bedford, Mass. Board of Firewards. 52457

New Bedford, Mass. Board of Overseers. 52501

New Bedford, Mass. Celebration of the Two Hundredth Anniversary of the Incorporation of the Town of Dartmouth, 1865. 18600

New Bedford, Mass. Charter. 52471, (52496)

New Bedford, Mass. City Council. 52471, (52496), 71130

New Bedford, Mass. City Library. see New Bedford, Mass. Free Public Library.

New Bedford, Mass. City Solicitor. (52483)

New Bedford, Mass. Committee of the Citizens to Draft a City Charter. 52482

New Bedford, Mass. Committee on Elections. 52502

New Bedford, Mass. Committee on Finance. 52502

New Bedford, Mass. Committee on the Introduction of Fresh Water. 52493

New Bedford, Mass. Congregational Church. 52473

New Bedford, Mass. Convention and Conference of Ministers and Delegates of Christian Churches, 1834. see Convention and Conference of Ministers and Delegates of Christian Churches, New Bedford, Mass., 1834.

New Bedford, Mass. Ecclesiastical Council, 1850. see Congregational Churches in Massachusetts. Ecclesiastical Council, New Bedford, 1850.

New Bedford, Mass. First Baptist Church. 52462, 52507

New Bedford, Mass. First Congregational Church. Library. 52467

New Bedford, Mass. First Congregational Society. 26241, 52509

New Bedford, Mass. First Universalist Society. Library. 52467

New Bedford, Mass. Fourth Street School. Library. 52467

New Bedford, Mass. Free Public Library. 52466-52467

New Bedford, Mass. Free Public Library. Trustees. 52467

New Bedford, Mass. Friends' Academy. see Friends' Academy, New Bedford, Mass.

New Bedford, Mass. Good Will Division, No. 17. see Sons of Temperance of North America. Massachusetts. Good Will Division, No. 17, New Bedford.

New Bedford, Mass. Home and Coast Guard. Company C. see Massachusetts. Militia. New Bedford Home and Coast Guard. Company C.

New Bedford, Mass. Ladies' Tract and City Missionary Society. see Ladies' Tract and City Missionary Society, New Bedford, Mass.

New Bedford, Mass. Mayor, 1847. 52472

New Bedford, Mass. Mayor, 1870 (Richmond) 71130 see also Richmond, George B.

New Bedford, Mass. Meeting of Salt Manufacturers, 1827. see Meeting of Salt Manufacturers, New Bedford, Mass., 1827.

New Bedford, Mass. Meeting of the Friends of Temperance, 1840. see Meeting of the Friends of Temperance, New Bedford, Mass., 1840.

New Bedford, Mass. North Congregational Church. Library. 52467

New Bedford, Mass. Old Dartmouth Centennial Celebration, 1864. see Old Dartmouth Centennial Celebration, New Bedford, Mass., 1864.

New Bedford, Mass. Ordinances, etc. 52459, 52464, 52471, (52491), (52496)

New Bedford, Mass. Orphans' Home. 52486

New Bedford, Mass. Orphans' Home. Managers. 52486

New Bedford, Mass. Overseers of the Poor. 52503, (52510)

New Bedford, Mass. Protecting Society. see Protecting Society, of New Bedford, Mass.

New Bedford, Mass. Public Schools. (52483)

New Bedford, Mass. School Committee. (52483)

New Bedford, Mass. Selectmen. (15465), 52504

New Bedford, Mass. Social Library. 52467

New Bedford, Mass. Social School. (52498)

New Bedford, Mass. South Christian Church. Library. 52467

New Bedford, Mass. South School. (52483)

New Bedford, Mass. Town Temperance Committee. see Town Temperance Committee, New Bedford, Mass.

New Bedford, Mass. Two Hundredth Anniversary Celebration of the Incorporation of the Town of Dartmouth, 1864. see Dartmouth, Mass. Two Hundredth Anniversary Celebration, New Bedford, Mass., 1864.

New Bedford, Mass. United Trade Society of Journeymen Sailmakers. see United Trade Society of Journeymen Sailmakers, of the City of New Bedford, Mass.

New Bedford, Mass. Wachusett Nurseries. see Wachusett Nurseries, New Bedford, Mass.

New Bedford, Mass. Washington Total Abstinence Society. see Washington Total Abstinence Society, New Bedford, Mass.

New Bedford, Mass. Water Works. 52493

New Bedford, Mass. Young Men's Christian Association. see Young Men's Christian Association, New Bedford, Mass.

New Bedford, Mass. Young Men's Institute. see Young Men's Institute, New Bedford, Mass.

New Bedford, Mass. Young Men's Temperance Society. see Young Men's Temperance Society, New Bedford, Mass.

New Bedford and California Joint Stock Mining and Trading Company. 52461

New Bedford Art Exhibition, 1858. 52468

New Bedford Athenaeum. (52465)

New Bedford Auxiliary Society, for the Suppression of Intemperance. 52475

New Bedford directory. (52491)

New Bedford harbor signal book. 41310

New Bedford Horticultural Society. 52470

New Bedford Lyceum. 52474

New Bedford Martha Washington Total Abstinence Society. 52475

New Bedford, Massachusetts. 15471

New Bedford Mechanics' Association. 52476

New Bedford money matters. 15469

New Bedford Port Society for the Moral Improvement of Seamen. 85545

New Bedford Port Society for the Moral Improvement of Seamen. Board of Managers. 52485, 85545

New Bedford Port Society for the Moral Improvement of Seamen. Charter. 85545

New Bedford Reform and Relief Association. 52463

New Bedford rural cemetery. (52477)

New Bedford town accounts. 52492

New Bedford traders in rhyme. 37265

New Bedford water works. 52493

New Bedford water-works. Contract and specifications. 52493

New Bedford Women's Reform and Relief Association. 52484

New bond of love. 52511

New book of a thousand. 52512

New book of directions. 72996

New book of knowledge. 52513

New book of nonsense. 52514

New book of poems. 104726

New book of the sufferings of the faithful. 25381

New books printed for J. Stockdale. 90093

New Braintree, Mass. Ecclesiastical Council, 1799. see Congregational Churches in Massachusetts. Ecclesiastical Council, New Braintree, 1799.

New Brighton, N. Y. Charter. (52515)

New Brighton, N. Y. Christ Church. Churchwardens and Vestrymen. 52516

New Brighton, N. Y. Ordinances, etc. (52515)

New Brighton, N. Y. Protestant Episcopal Church. 14439, 52519

New Brighton, N. Y. Trustees. (52515)

New Brighton, Pa. Christ Church. 22225

New Brighton Association. see Baptists. New York. New Brighton Association.

New Britain. 22299

New Britain directory for 1870. 52517

New British novelist. 94246

New British theatre. 14526, 86903, note after 105986

New Brunswick. 16862, 20469, 43926, 52530

New Brunswick. Auditor General's Office. 52531

New Brunswick. Board of Agriculture. 52529, 52551

New Brunswick. Census, 1851. 52549

New Brunswick. Chamber of Commerce, St. John. 7112

New Brunswick. Chief Commissioner of Public Works. 52552

New Brunswick. Commissioner of Agriculture. 52553

New Brunswick. Commissioners to Inquire into the Judicial Institutions of the Province. (52533)

New Brunswick. Geological Survey. (31935)

New Brunswick. Laws, statutes, etc. 52526-52527, 52539-52540, 52561

New Brunswick. Legislature. 31137, 98067

New Brunswick. Legislature. Joint Committee on a Penitentiary. 52554

New Brunswick. Legislature. Council. 52535, 52538

New Brunswick. Legislature. House of Assembly. 52537, 52560

New Brunswick. Lieutenant Governor, 1844. 55789

New Brunswick. Militia. Courts Martial (Burns) 96841

New Brunswick. Parish Schools. 52559

New Brunswick. Post Office Department. (52546), 52550

New Brunswick. Provincial Lunatic Asylum, St. John. Medical Superintendent. 52555

New Brunswick. Railway Commissioners.
52558

New Brunswick. Secretary. (30205)

New Brunswick. University, Fredericton.
52532

New Brunswick (Archdeaconry) Church
Society. see Church of England in
Canada. Church Society of the Arch-
deaconry of New Brunswick.

New Brunswick, N. J. Convention, 1776.
see New Jersey (Colony) Convention,
New Brunswick, 1776.

New Brunwick, N. J. Provincial Congress,
1776. see New Jersey (Colony)
Provincial Congress, New Brunswick,
1776.

New Brunswick, N. J. Queen's College. see
Rutgers University, New Brunswick,
N. J.

New Brunswick, N. J. Rutgers University.
see Rutgers University, New Brunswick,
N. J.

New Brunswick, N. J. Theological Seminary
of the Reformed Church in America.
see Reformed Church in America.
Theological Seminary, New Brunswick,
N. J.

New Brunswick, N. J. Theological Seminary
of the Reformed Dutch Church. see
Reformed Church in America. Theological Seminary, New Brunswick, N. J.

New Brunswick, N. J. Union Benevolent and
Trade Society. see Union Benevolent
and Trade Society, New Brunswick,
N. J.

New-Brunswick. 50007

New Brunswick almanac, and register.
52542

New Brunswick and Nova Scotia. 52543

New Brunswick & Nova Scotia Land-Company.
52544, 81551

New Brunswick, as a home for emigrants.
[By J. V. Ellis.] 22324

New Brunswick, as a home for emigrants.
[By James Brown.] 8500

New Brunswick, as a home for emigrants.
[By W. R. M. Burtis.] 9488

New-Brunswick Auxiliary Bible Society.
(52556)

New Brunswick Baptist Association (Eastern)
see Baptists. New Brunswick. Eastern
Association.

New Brunswick Baptist Convention. see
Baptists. New Brunswick. Convention.

New Brunswick directory for 1867-8. 52534

New Brunswick. Early reminiscences: a
poem. 78335

New Brunswick for the emigrant, Australia
a mistake. 52545

New Brunswick Natural History Society. see
Natural History Society of New Brunswick.

New Brunswick post office directory. (52546)

New Brunswick Presbytery. see Presbyterian
Church in the U. S. A. Presbytery of
New Brunswick.

New-Brunswick review. 52523

New Brunswick Society for the Encouragement
of Agriculture, Home Manufactures and
Commerce. (52536), 52557

New Brunswick Society for the Encouragement
of Agriculture, Home Manufactures and
Commerce. Provincial Ehxibition,
1852. 52547

New Brunswick. With note for emigrants.
27223, 52548

New Building for National Museum. 85043

New business guide. 52148

New business in Wall Street. 83886-83887

New Canaan. 51028

New Canadian dominion. 74567

New Castle, Del. Library Company. see
New Castle Library Company.

New Castle, Mass. petitioners (61266)

New Castle, Pa. Publishing Bureau of the
I. W. W. see International Workers of
the World. Publishing Bureau, New
Castle, Pa.

New Castle and Frenchtown Turnpike and
Rail-Road Company. 52566

New-Castle. February 6. 1772. 52571

New-Castle, June 15, 1771. 52570

New Castle Library Company. (52565)

New-Castle Lottery, instituted by the friends
of the American china manufactory.
(12927)

New Castle Presbytery. see Presbyterian
Church in the U. S. A. Presbytery of
New Castle.

New catalogue of books, with the prices.
106130

New catalogue of Harvard College Library.
18193

New chain of plain argument. 105330

New chapter in his life. 59071

New chapter in the early life of Washington.
62616

New chapter on freemasonry. 90898

New chapters of ethnological inquiry. 56038

New charitable monthly. 24634, 54419

New chart of the Atlantic. 6026

New chart of the Atlantic Ocean. 66698

New chart of the British empire in North
America. 88221

New charter of the city of Brooklyn. 8286

New chorographical description. 5222

New Church. see New Jerusalem Church.

New Church, Boston. see Boston. New
Church.

New Church herald, and monthly repository.
52572

New Church in the United States. see New
Jerusalem Church.

New Church magazine for children. 52573

New Church messenger. 52574

New Church monthly periodical. 70164

New Church repository and monthly review.
52575

New Church Tract Society. 52575

New churchman. 52575

New citizens' hand-book. 84911

New city buildings. 61552

New code of laws for the government of the
Negro slaves. 35627

New collection of fashionable, modern songs.
100652

New collection of laws. 103429

New collection of patriotic, national, naval,
martial, professional, convivial, humorous,
pathetic, sentimental, old, and new songs.
88515

New collection of the most approved songs.
100647

New collection of verses applied to the first
of November. 52576

New collection of voyages and travels. 91537

New collection of voyages and travels, into
all parts of the world. (13056), 39452,
91537

New collection of voyages and travels, into
several parts of the world. 91538

New collection of voyages and travels, never before published in English. 52577

New collection of voyages, discoveries and travels. 38163, 84617-84618

New comic almanack. 52578

New comic songs. 79908

New commission of the Governor of Quebec. 52579

New common school geography. 83771, 83775

New compass for sea-men. (24680)

New compend of Geography. 82897

New, complete, and universal collection of authentic and entertaining voyages and travels. 52580, 64396

New, complete, and universal collection of authentic voyages and travels. 54397

New conductor generalis. 52581

New Confederacy of the Iroquois. see Iroquois Indians.

New Congregational Church, Boston. see Boston. New Congregational Church.

New constitution and the Christian church. 52582

New constitution . . . adopted March 24, 1862. 34220

New constitution and its relation to railroads. 45269

New constitution of Kentucky, 1850. 37501

New constitution of Louisiana. 27576

New constitution . . . [of Missouri], as revised. 49626

New constitution of New-York, and the fifty dollar act. 95470

New constitution [of Ohio.] 47293

New constitution of the state of New York. (71223)

New constitution of the state of New York, examined. (57279)

New constitution of the state of South Carolina. 87715

New constitution: with a description of the road to liberty. 90963

New converts exhorted to cleave to the Lord. 11857, 11894

New cordial, alexiterial, and restorative electuary. 30785

New covenant; or . . . manner of the giving and receiving of the covenant of Grace to the elect. 17059, (17072), (70107)

New covenant, or the saints' portion. 65369

New creation brought forth in the holy order of life. 84552

New creature describ'd. 12331

New Creek Company. 60272

New crime against humanity. note after (58767)

New crisis. By an old whig. 12382, 52583

New crisis, or grand appeal to the nation. 60925

New crisis of American independence. 52584

New critical pronouncing dictionary of the English language. 52585

New crusade. 83701

New customs house. 6533, 52586

New dangers to freedom. 44324

New Darien artifice laid open. 18562

New Democratic doctrine. 52587

New description of that fertile and pleasant province of Carolina. 1902, 49010, 87903

New description of the world. 13449

New description of the world. . . including America, &c. (18009)

New Dido. 52588

New digest of the statute laws. 9119

New Diggins and Shullsburg Mining Company, Wisconsin. (52589)

New Diogenes, a cynical poem. 15894

New directions for sailing along the coast of North America and into its several harbours. 101047

New directions for sailing along the coast of North America, from Halifax to Florida. 52590

New directory of the town of Boston. 6696

New discourse of trade. 12708

New discoveries concerning the world. 52591

New discovery of a vast country in America. 31370-(31372), 95332

New discovery of Terra Incognita Asutralis. (74823)

New discovery of the great river of the Amazons. 44614

Nevv discoveryes. 95650

New dispensation. 55347

New display of the United States. 97923

New division of wards. (52592)

New doctrine of clerical privilege. 23684

New doctrine of intervention. 6075, 42979

New dogma of the south. 18918

New dominion; a poem. 9488

New dominion as a home for Englishmen. 71687

New dominion monthly. (52593)

New drunkard's looking-glass. 102471

New eclectic; a monthly magazine of select literature. 88395

New eclectic magazine. (52594), 88395

New edition, containing one letter of Marcus. 18863, note after 98531

New edition, enlarged, of the second part of the North American pilot. 35968

New edition of Captain Ross's voyage to the North Pole. (73383)

New edition of the demand of William Vans. 98558

New El Dorado. 16819

New elements of geometry. 84152

New emancipation cause. (9508), note after 103490

New embargo law. 27376

New England. President and Council. see Massachusetts (Colony) President and Council.

New England (United Colonies) see United Colonies of New England.

New-England a degenerate plant. (73483)

New England: a poem. 93288

New England academies and classical schools. 30092

New England Agricultural Society. 52645

New England Agricultural Society. Annual Exhibition, 1st, Springfield, Mass., 1864. 52645

New England Agricultural Society. Annual Exhibition, 7th, Manchester, N. H., 1870. 52645

New England Agricultural Society. Fair, Brattleborough, Vt., 1866. see Fair of the New England and Vermont State Agricultural Societies, Brattleborough, Vt., 1866.

New England almanac and masonic calendar. 52651

New-England almanack. By E. Freebetter. 52649

New England almanac. [By Elijah Fenton.] 70733

New England almanack for . . . 1825. 55101

New-England almanack, for . . . 1785. 93052

New England almanack for 1781. (52650)

New-England almanack, for . . . 1781.
92987

New-England almanack for the year of Our
Lord. 1686. 52646, note after 62743

New-England almanack, for the year 1700.
52647

New-England almanack; or, the Massachusetts
calendar. 2d note after 95414

New England almanac, 1772. 45826

New England almanack, 1772, by Benjamin
Wirt, M. A. 52648

New-England almanack, 1703. (13777)

New-England almanack shewing the day of
the month. (79028)

New-England Anabaptists. see Anabaptists.
New England.

New England and her institutions. 33

New England and Michigan Mining Company.
52653

New-England and New-York law-register.
31076

New England, and other poems. 94374, 94378

New England and the west. (30805)

New England anti-masonic almanac, for . . .
1829. (52654)

New-England anti-slavery almanac. 52655

New England Anti-slavery Convention, Boston,
1834. (81796)

New England Anti-slavery Convention, Boston,
1834. Committee. 52635

New England Anti-slavery Convention, Boston,
1843. 52655

New England Anti-slavery Convention, Boston,
1860. 58768, 12th note after 96966

New England Anti-slavery Society. see
Massachusetts Anti-slavery Society.

New-England Anti-slavery Tract Association.
1801, 13489, 27850, 40366, 52656,
102549

New England Art Union, Boston. 52657

New England Art Union . . . . Catalogue of
paintings. 52657

New England Asylum for the Blind. see
Perkins Institution and Massachusetts
Asylum for the Blind.

New-England Asylum for the Blind, instituted
in February, 1829. 52658

New England Bible Association of Friends.
65750

New England botanic medical and surgical
journal. 52659

New England boys. 91825, 91828

New England Branch of the American Tract
Society. see New England Tract
Society.

New England business directory. 52661

New England. [By Hermann Bokum.] 6176,
note after 92721

New England. [By William Ellery Channing.]
11929

New-England calendar. (19217)

New England calendar and ephemeris, 1800.
(52663)

New England calendar, for . . . 1812. 20207

New England callendar, for 1795. 52662

New-England chronology. (7226)

New England cities business directory.
(52663)

New England Clergymen. petitioners 20693,
33195, 71351

New England Coal Mining Company. 52665

New England Coal Mining Company. petitioners
69865

New England Coal Mining Company. Directors.
52664

New England coasting pilot. 88221

New England Company, London. see Company
for Propagation of the Gospel in New
England and the Parts Adjacent in
America, London.

New England Company, for the Civilization and
Conversion of the Indians, Blacks, and
Pagans, in the British Colonies in America
and the West Indies. see Company for
the Propagation of the Gospel in New
England and the Parts Adjacent in America
London.

New England Company of 1649 and John Eliot.
note before 85867

New-England confederacy of MDCXLII. 290

New England Conservatory of Music, Boston.
(52666)

New England Copper Company. 52667

New England coquette, a tragic drama.
(52668), 103731

New England Cotton Manufacturers' Association
52669

N. E. Cotton Manufacturers' Association.
Proceedings of the semi-annual meeting.
52669

New England courant. (41003), 94107, 100759,
104243

New-England diary, or almanack, for the year
1725. 7063, 52670

New-England directory. 31073

New England directory, for 1860. 52671

New-England distinguished. 94815

New-England Education Society. 52672

New England Educational Commission for
Freedmen. see New England Freedmen'
Aid Society.

New England Emigrant Aid Company. Boston.
(27864), 32188, (49648), (52673), 92867

New England family circle. 52674

New England farm advertiser. 52675

New-England farmer. pseud. Essay on
hereditary titles. 22941

New-England farmer. pseud. Mr. Madison's
war. see Lowell, John, 1769-1840.

New-England farmer. pseud. Perpetual war.
see Lowell, John, 1769-1840.

New-England farmer. 83824

New England farmer; a semi-monthly journal.
52677

New-England farmer and gardener's journal.
52676

New England farmer. Containing essays,
original and selected. 52676

New England farmer. Devoted to agriculture.
52678

New-England farmer; or, geographical dictionary.
19056

New England farmer's almanack. 52679

New-England farmer's almanack, for 1828.
24220

New-England farmer's almanack, for the year
of Our Lord Christ, 1794. 90958

New-England farmers' and mechanics' journal.
52680

New-England farmer's diary and almanac.
52681

New-England farrier. 36116

New England Female Medical College. 24049,
52682, (52683)

New England Female Medical College. Chemical
Department. (52683)

New England Female Medical College.
Directors. (52683)

New England Female Medical College. Circular
to the members. 52682

New England Female Moral Reform Society.
52684

New-England-fire-brand quenched. 25363-
(25364)

New England Freedmen's Aid Society. 23523,
25739, 40357, 52685

New England Freedmen's Aid Society.
Teachers and Superintendents. 23523,
25739, 52685

New England freedom. 65084

New-England freemen warned and warmed.
58029

New England fruit book. 35306, (44354)

New England galaxy. 52161, 85425, 85430,
95483, 105956

New-England galaxy and masonic magazine.
63894

New England gazetteer. 31074-31075

New England genealogical register. see
New England historical and genealogical
register.

New England Guards. (52686)

New England harmony. 94018

New England Historic Genealogical Society,
Boston. (6977), 7309, 12704, 16919,
17604, 19032, 19034, 19036, 20869,
20882, 20884, 23278-23279, 23823,
24272, 24401, 25229, 38851, 50909,
(51883), (52687)-52688, 52886, 60946,
72613, 74291, 75790, 76253, (78338),
80242, 80305, 80306, 80312, 80314,
80323, 81693, 82852, 83742-83743,
83582, 84293, 84300, 84925, 85586,
86793, 86794, 86917, 91005, 91030,
93713-93714, 93716-93718, 93720,
94112, 95636, 95640, 12th note after
96964, 103754-103755

New England Historic Genealogical Society,
Boston. petitioners (52687), 67252

New England Historic Genealogical Society,
Boston. Committee on the Date of
Sudbury Fight. 52688

New England Historic Genealogical Society,
Boston. President. 1465 see also
Andrew, John Albion, 1818-1867.

New England Historic Genealogical Society,
Boston. Tercentenary Celebration of
the Birth of Shakespeare, 1864. 80322

New England Historic-Genealogical Society to
the members of the General Court of
Massachusetts. (52687)

New England historical and genealogical
register. (6977), 7309, 12704, 16919,
17604, 19032, 19034, 19036, 19051,
20869, 20882, 20884, 23279, 23823,
24272, 24401, 25229, 38851, 50909,
52688, 52886, 60946, 72613, 74291,
75790, 76253, (78338), 80262, 80305,
80306, 80312, 80314, 80323, 82852,
83742-83743, 83852, 84293, 84300,
84925, 85586, 86793, 86794, 86917,
91005, 93713-93714, 93716-93718,
93720, 94112, 95636, 95640, 103754-
103755

New England history. 22260

New-England Hospital for Women and Children,
Boston. see Boston. New-England
Hospital for Women and Children.

New-England hymn. 103526

New England illustrated almanac. 52690

New England Institution for the Education of
the Blind. see Perkins Institution and
Massachusetts Asylum for the Blind.

New England insurance gazette. 52692

New England Inventors' and Mechanics'
Association. Industrial Exhibition,
Boston, 1855. Investigating Committee.
52693

New-England journal. 49204, 2d note after
97444

New England journal of medicine and surgery,
and collateral branches. 5031, 52694

New England journalist. pseud. Ramrod
broken. (67674)

New England judged: being certain writings.
5629, 91318

New-England judged, by the spirit of the Lord.
5631

New England judged, not by man's but by the
spirit of the Lord. 5628, (70000), (73483)

New England judged. The second part.
5630

New England kalendar, for 1703. 52695

New England Land Company. Agents.
petitioners 27092, 69728

New-England legends. 89557

New England life in a village. 12432

New England Loyal Publication Society.
52696, 67255, 80289

New England Loyal Publication Society.
Executive Committee. 52696

New-England loyal publication society. 32820

New-England loyal publication society. Senator
Sherman's fallacies. 80389

New England magazine (1831-1835)
(52698), 85433, 95153, note after 103816

New England magazine; an illustrated monthly.
83687, 84041, 93430

New-England magazine of industry and trade.
(52699)

New England magazine of knowledge and
pleasure. (52697)

New England man. pseud. Advantages of
League Island for a naval station. 39517,
69684

New-England man. pseud. Attempt to demon-
strate the practicability. 52700, 81896

New-England-man. pseud. Letter on the
maintainance of the clergy. see Franklin,
Benjamin, 1706-1790.

New-England-man. pseud. Letter to the freeholders and qualified voters. 6523,
(40475)

New-England man. pseud. Letter to the
inhabitants of . . . the Massachusetts-Bay.
40487

New England man. pseud. Sketch of old
England. see Paulding, James K. and
Neal, John, 1793-1876. incorrectly sup-
posed author

New England Manufacturers' Convention,
Worcester, Mass., 1868. 65902

New England medical gazette. 52701

New England medical review and journal.
52702

New England memorandum book. (52703)

New-England mercantile union business directory.
(52704)

New England meridian. (52705)

New England Methodist Centenary Convention,
Boston, 1866. (62586)

New England Methodist Historical Society.
14198

New England Mining and Quarrying Company.
52706

New England Mining and Quarrying Company.
Charter. 52706

New England minister. pseud. Letters on the
origin and progress of the New Haven
theology. see Tyler, Bennet.

New England minister. pseud. Margaret
Percival in America. see Hale, Edward
Everett, 1822-1909.

New England missionary intelligencer and general repository. 52707

New England Mississippi Land Company. claimants 92376

New England Mississippi Land Company. Agents. petitioners (52708), 69389, 2d note after 99829, 1st note after 100571

New England Mississippi Land Company. Directors. (52708)

New England Mississippi Land Company. Directors. claimants (52708)

New England Mississippi Land Company. Directors. petitioners (52708)

New England mountain in labor. 31892

New England Mutual Life Insurance Company of Boston. 52709

New England Mutual Life Insurance Company of Boston. Directors. 52709

New England Non-resistance Society. 52710

New England offering. 42491, (52711), 2d note after 95375

New-England. Or a briefe enarration of the ayre. 50786

New-England pastor. pseud. Platform of ecclesiastical government established. see Emmons, Nathaniel.

New England patriot. 42453, 2d note after 101856

New England persecutors mauld with their own weapons. 46934

New England pilgrim's festival. 8808

New-England pleaded with. 56382

New England pocket songster. 52712

New England poem. 1365, 71321, 97204

New England primer. 52715, 52722-52725, 52731, 52733, note after 65546

New England primer containing the Assembly's catechism. note after 65546

New England primer, enlarged. note after 52712, (52713), note after 65546

New-England primer, enlarged and improved. 52718, note after 65546

New England primer, improved. 52719-52721, 52726-52728, (52734), note after 65546

New England primer improved for the more easy attaining the true reading of English. 52714, 52716, 52730, note after 65546

New England primer, much improved. 52717

New-England primer, or an easy and pleasant guide to the art of reading. note after 65546

New-England primer, or, the first step to the art of reading. note after 65546

New-England primer, restored. 52732

New England Protective Union. Central Division. 66956

New England Protective Union. Division No. 181, South Boston, Mass. 87336

New England psalm book. 52735, 52736, (66427)-66430, (66442)

New-England psalm-singer. 5417, (5419)

New-England psalter. (66441)

New England psalter, or, psalms of David. 52737

New-England psalter: or, psalms of David: with the proverbs of Solomon. (66463)

New England quarterly journal of medicine and surgery. (62738)

New England quarterly magazine. 52739

New England railroad guide. 32446

New England Railroad Transportation Company. Argument of Daniel S. Richardson. 70996

New England register. (10747)

New-England religious astronomical diary. 12901

New England romance. 89148

New England Sabbath school minstrel. 52740

New England Sabbath School Union. 52741

New England Sabbath School Union. Committee of Publication. eds. 102097

New England scenery, from nature. 52742

New England scenes. 52743

New England selection. (68158)

New England sheriff. (30709)

New England sketch. 92448, 92455

New England sketch book, for 1851. (30875)

New England Social Reform Society. 85698

New England Society, Charleston, S. C. 12086

New-England Society for the Improvement of Domestic Poultry. (52744)

New England Society for the Promotion of Manufactures and the Mechanic Arts. (52745)

New England Society, in the City of New York. (52746)

New England Society of Cincinnati. 13063

New England Society of Columbus, Ohio. 14896

New England Society of Montreal. Dinner, 1856. 16764

New England Society of Orange County, N. Y. 57429

New England Society of Quincy, Ill. (67279)

New England Soldiers' Relief Association, New York. 52747

New England Soldiers' Relief Association, New York. Superintendent. 52747

New England Spiritualists' Association. (52748)

New England states. 28702

New England story . . . founded on facts. 71111

New England tale, and miscellanies. 78797

New England tale; or sketches of New England character and manners. 78796, 78800, 78807

New-England tale (unfinished). 88565

New-England telegraph. 95205

New-England telegraph, and eclectic review. 52749

New England Temperance Convention, 1st, Boston, 1866. 65951

New England theocracy. 42619

New England theology. 58623

New England tour of His Royal Highness the Prince of Wales. 52751

New England town and country almanac. 52752

New England Tract Society. (52660), 52750, 64084, 99138, 102468

New England Tract Society. District Secretary. 72455 see also Rockwood, L. B.

New England tragedies. 41917

New England Unitarian Book Society. 52753

New England Unitarian Book Society. Library. 52753

New-England vindicated from the unjust aspersions. 46712, 80621

New England volunteer. 65487

New-England Women's Auxiliary Association, Boston. see United States Sanitary Commission. New-England Women's Auxiliary Association, Boston.

New England Yearly Meeting. see Friends, Society of. New England Yearly Meeting.

New England Yearly Meeting Boarding School, Providence, R. I. see Friends' School, Providence, R. I.

New Englander. 2670, 3676, 9542, (23888), 50506, 52762, 59164, 64304, 64307, (66050), 69402, (70326), 73144, 73146, 80281, (81592), 89535, 93279, 97203, 105215

New Englander over-sea. pseud. Authorship, a tale. see Neal, John, 1793-1876.

New Englanders. 8390, 52151

New-Englandism not the religion of the Bible. 8691, 52763

New-Englands advice to Old-England. 39641

New England's chattels. 22244, 52755

New-Englands choicest blessing. 827

New Englands crisis. 96155

New-Englands duty and interest. 56229

New England's ensigne. 52756

New-England's faction discovered. 18229, 52757, 55060

Nevv Englands first fruits. 52758-52759, note before 92797

New-Englands Jonas cast up at London. (12705)-12706, 45664, 1st note after 98664, 104797

New England's lamentations [sic]. 103400

Nevv Englands lamentation for Old Englands present errours. 80211

New-England's lamentations for the decay of Godliness. 103401

New England's lamentations under these three heads. 68261, (75668), 99805, 103400, 104901

New England's memorial. (28046), 32480, 51013-51017

New-England's memoriall. 51012

New-England's misery. 52760

New-Englands plantation. 31739-31740, 106052

New-England's present sufferings. 103100

Nevv Englands prospect. 65646, 82823, 82974, 82976, 105074-105077, 106052

New-Englands rarities discovered. (36674)-36675

New-Englands salamander. 1st note after 98664, 104797

New-Englands sence, of old-England and Irelands sorrowes. (32809)

New-England's spirit of persecution transmitted to Pennsylvania. 37203, (37226), 1st note after 96931, 2d note after 96956, 2d note after 97284

New England teares, for old England's feares. 32810-32811

New England's tears for her present miseries. (52761), 96156

New Englands trials. 66686, 82812, 82823, 82833-82837, 82855

New-England's true interest, further declared. (49658), 92351

New-Englands true interest; not to lie. 49657-(49658), 65607, 92351

New-England's vindication. 26604

New English Canaan. 65646

New English Canaan or New Canaan. 51028

New English captives. pseud. Poems. 104261

New-English congregational churches are, and always have been, consociated churches. 104985

New English grammar. 83921

New English reader. 79385

New English theatre. 88533

New English verson of the Psalms of David. 52765

New epitaph. 16194

New Era Division, No. 175, Boston. see Sons of Temperance of North America. Massachusetts. New Era Division, No. 175, Boston.

New era extra. 98418

New essay. (By the Pennsylvanian farmer.) (20046)-20047, 84678C

New essay on the constitutional power of the Parliament. 64820

Nevv essayes or observations divine and morall. 72104

New-Europa oder die Alte in der Neuen Welt. 106316

New "examen." (58173)

New exercise of firelocks and bayonets. 52764

New experiments and observations on electricity. 25505, 25559

New farmer's almanac for 1849. 47160

New federal calculator. (82286)

New federal songs. 101857

New financial project. 52766

New flora and botany of North America. 67461

New fortune teller. 85410

New found vvorlde, or Antarctike. 95339

New France. 84701

New France. Armee. 21036

New France. Conseil Superieur de Quebec. 10476, 10486, 17851, 17852, (66984)

New France. Governor General. 17851-17855

New France. Governor General. 17852, 40691, (66984) see also Dampuille, --------, Duc de.

New France. Habitants. petitioners 39278

New France. Intendant. 10356, 10476, 10482, 10486, note after (10603), 10851-10855, (66984)

New France. Laws, statutes, etc. 10486, 10356, 17851-17855, 20676, (66983), (66984), (66985), (67031), 67061, 67720, 68441, 73741, 100763

New Fremont song. 3906

New French and English grammar. 45039

New fresh water shells from California. (39496)

New fresh-water shells of the United States. 15904

New fugitive slave law. (39041)

New game of cards. 52767

New gazetteer. 18694

New gazetteer of the United States of America. (18536)

New genera of Michaux and others. (70888), 1st note after 94129

New genera of trees and shrubs. 67464

New general atlas. [By A. Arrowsmith.] 2113

New general atlas, containing a geographical and historical account. 52769, 79124

New . . . general atlas, containing maps of each of the United States. 42610

New general atlas, containing maps of the various countries of the world. 49719

New . . . general atlas. Comprising all the new discoveries to the present time. 50939

New general atlas, exhibiting the five great divisions of the globe. 44163

New general atlas of the West India islands. (42611)

New general atlas of the world. 82381

New general collection of voyages and travels. 28539, 65402, 65406, 84559-84560, 84562, 85380

New Genesee farmer. 26922

New Genesee farmer and gardener. 52770

New genus of fossil. (39486)

New geographical and historical grammar. (75827)-75828

New geographical dictionary. (18534)

New geographical, history and commercial grammar. (29327)

New geographical, historical, and commercial history of Canada. 52771

New geographical tables [of] Europe . . . and America. 64745

New geography containing map questions. note before 83906, 83956

16097, 16099-16103, 16107, 16113,
1 6118-16120, 16133, (19476), 25790,
33137, (47188), (52799), 52810, 52814,
52816-52817, 52843, 52931, 59771,
(66397), 95570, 100342, 101982
New Hampshire. Constitutional Convention,
1777. 52788
New Hampshire. Constitutional Convention,
1781. 52787
New Hampshire. Constitutional Convention,
1782. 52788, 2d note after 52940
New Hampshire. Constitutional Convention,
1783. (52789), 52813
New Hampshire. Constitutional Convention,
1792. 52802
New Hampshire. Constitutional Convention,
1796. 52815
New Hampshire. Constitutional Convention,
1850. Committee on the Judicial
Department. 52818
New Hampshire. Convention, 1788. 22233
New Hampshire. Council. President. 66514,
1st note after 99003
New Hampshire. Election sermon. 895, 12989,
16342, 17640, 18405 20067, 25875,
28404, 30892, 33306, 38875, 42045,
43050, 43240, 47994, (49136), (50291),
(50718), (56817), 58673, 58717, (59317),
(59377), 64288, (73574)-73575, 80791-
80792, 97596, 104321, 105019, 105113,
105250
New Hampshire. Fish and Game Commissioners. 52909
New Hampshire. General Court. 6965, 18620,
21674, 37486, (38871A), 52896, 52897,
52928-52929, 52932, 69858, 79711, 91437,
101595, 105250
New Hampshire. General Court. Committee
on an Agricultural College. (52915)
New Hampshire. General Court. Committee
on Banks. 52916
New Hampshire. General Court. Committee
on Claims. 52917
New Hampshire. General Court. Committee
on the Petition of Elijah Gould, and
Others. 28103
New Hampshire. General Court. Committee
to Secure a Survey of the Canal Route
from the Piscataqua River by Alton Bay
to Pemigewasset River near Plymouth.
52914
New Hampshire. General Court. Examining
Committee on the New Hampshire State
Prison. Minority. 52850
New Hampshire. General Court. Select
Committee on Fisheries. 52909
New Hampshire. General Court. House of
Representatives. 52838-52839, 52893,
52896, 52931, 52949
New Hampshire. General Court. House of
Representatives. Select Committee on
Building an Insane Hospital. 52920
New Hampshire. General Court. Senate.
52840-52841, 52893, 52986, 52931
New Hampshire. Geological Survey. 52830-
52833
New Hampshire. Governor, 1809-1811
(Langdon) (38871A), 52932 see also
Langdon, John, 1741-1819.
New Hampshire. Governor, 1812-1813
(Plumer) 52949, 63450 see also
Plumer, William, 1759-1850.
New Hampshire. Governor, 1813-1816
(Gilman) 33150, 52896 see also
Gilman, John Taylor, 1753-1828.

New Hampshire. Governor, 1816-1819 (Plumer)
52848 see also Plumer, William, 1759-
1850.
New Hampshire. Governor, 1819-1823 (Bell)
52809 see also Bell, Samuel, 1770-1850.
New Hampshire. Governor, 1844-1845 (Steele)
52786 see also Steele, John Hardy,
1789-1865.
New Hampshire. Governor, 1857-1859 (Haile)
33150 see also Haile, William, 1807-
1876.
New Hampshire. Governor, 1861-1863 (Berry)
52808 see also Berry, Nathaniel
Springer, 1796-1894.
New Hampshire. Governor, 1863-1865
(Gilmore) 82332 see also Gilmore,
Joseph Albree, 1811-1867.
New Hampshire. Governor, 1865-1867 (Smyth)
(52938), 85228-85229 see also Smyth,
Frederick, 1819-1899.
New Hampshire. Governor, 1869-1871 (Stearns)
90930 see also Stearns, Onslow, 1810-
1878.
New Hampshire. Governor, 1881-1883 (Bell)
84704 see also Bell, Charles Henry,
1823-1893.
New Hampshire. House of Reformation for
Juvenile and Female Offenders, Manchester.
see New Hampshire. Industrial School,
Manchester.
New Hampshire. Industrial School, Manchester.
see also New Hampshire. Commissioners
for Locating and Building a House of
Reformation for Juvenile and Female
Offenders Against the Laws.
New Hampshire. Industrial School, Manchester.
Commissioners. (52906)
New Hampshire. Industrial School, Manchester.
Trustees. (52905), 52923
New Hampshire. Insurance Commissioners.
(52918)
New Hampshire. Laws, statutes, etc. (12178),
13184, (15148), 18117, 23765, 28446, 28722,
39414, 44204, 44208-44209, 52051, 51859,
(52780), 52783-52785, 52810; (52812),
52822, 52828, 52843-(52845), 52849, 52872-
(52873), 52878, 52892, 52898, (52915),
(52929)-52930, 52935, 1st note after 52940,
(55825), 64413, 66418, 66426, 66529, 70820-
70821, 82438, 89066, 91429, 91437, 91452,
93510, 93562, 97750, 97875, 104787
New Hampshire. Legislature. see New
Hampshire. General Court.
New Hampshire. Militia. 93510
New Hampshire. President and Council. 66514,
1st note after 99003
New Hampshire. Provincial Congress, 1780.
52783-52784, 1st note after 52940
New Hampshire. Quartermaster General.
(52919)
New Hampshire. Railroad Commissioners.
52926
New Hampshire. State Geologist. 52833
New Hampshire. State Hospital, Concord.
52857
New Hampshire. State Hospital, Concord.
Board of Visitors. 52857
New Hampshire. State Hospital, Concord.
Superintendent. 52857
New Hampshire. State Hospital, Concord.
Trustees. 52857
New Hampshire. State Librarian. 52921
New Hampshire. State Library. (52804)
New Hampshire. State Library. Trustees.
52921

New Hampshire. State Prison. Warden.
(52924), 52939

New Hampshire. State Reform School, Manchester. see New Hampshire. Industrial School, Manchester.

New Hampshire. State Treasurer. 50395, (52922)

New Hampshire. Superintendent of Public Instruction. (52906)

New Hampshire. Superior Court of Judicature. 13184, 18623, 52809, 52891

New Hampshire. Supreme Court. 11886, 18110, 21006, 23887

New Hampshire. Treasurer. see New Hampshire. State Treasurer.

New-Hampshire agricultural repository. 52855

New Hampshire Agricultural Society. (52888), 76240

New Hampshire and Nebraska. 63783

Newhampshire [sic] and Vermont almanack. 74325

New Hampshire annual register, and United States calendar. 52884

New Hampshire Anti-slavery Convention, Concord, 1834. (15149), 52856

New Hampshire Anti-slavery Society. 52856

New Hampshire Anti-slavery Society. President. 105032 see also Root, David.

New Hampshire as it is. 12147

New Hampshire authors. pseud. Gems for you. 50374

New Hampshire Baptist Convention. see Baptists. New Hampshire. Convention.

New Hampshire Baptist Domestick Mission Society. (52859)

New Hampshire Bible Society. (52860)

New Hampshire book. 52861

New Hampshire Branch of the American Education Society. see American Education Society. New Hampshire Branch.

New Hampshire business directory. (52863)

New-Hampshire calendar. 52864

New Hampshire Centennial Celebration of the Introduction of the Art of Printing, Portsmouth, 1856. see Centennial Celebration of the Introduction of the Art of Printing into New Hampshire, Portsmouth, N. H., 1856.

New Hampshire churches. 39367

New Hampshire Colonization Society. 52858

New Hampshire Colonization Society. Board of Managers. 52867

New Hampshire collections. see Collections of the New Hampshire Historical Society.

New Hampshire Conference Seminary. see Tilton Seminary, Tilton, N. H.

New Hampshire confession revised. 52869

New-Hampshire diary. (52870)

New Hampshire election sermon. 18405

New Hampshire Female Cent Institution and Home Missionary Union. 52875, (52879)

New Hampshire gazette. 52871, (82477), 83400, 84553, 87147

New Hampshire gazetteer. 83398-83399

New Hampshire Grantees. see Proprietors of the New Hampshire Grants.

New Hampshire Grants. 61280, 1st-2d notes after 98997 see also Proprietors of the New Hampshire Grants. and Vermont.

New Hampshire grants being transcripts of the charters. 1st note after 98997

New Hampshire Grants Convention, 1765-1777. see Vermont. Conventions, 1765-1777.

New Hampshire Grants Convention, 1777. see Vermont. Convention, 1777.

New Hampshire Grants Convention, Cornish, N. H., 1778. see Vermont. Convention, 1778.

New Hampshire Grants Convention, Cornish, N. H., 1779. see Vermont. Convention, 1779.

New Hampshire Grants General Convention, 1777. see Vermont. Convention, 1777.

New Hampshire historical collections. see Collections of the New Hampshire Historical Society.

New Hampshire Historical Society, Concord. 458-460, 9260, 9481, 16579, (20190), 23818, 23828, 41883, 46723, 50392, 52872, 59077, 1st note after 65324, 78431, 82801, 93510, 101038, 103200

New Hampshire Iron Factory Company. (52870)

New Hampshire journal. (31832)

New Hampshire journal of education. (52874)

New-Hampshire journal of medicine. 52875

Newhampshire [sic] Latin grammar. 82880

New-Hampshire, Massachusetts, and Vermont almanack. 23858

New Hampshire Mechanics and Art Association Exhibition, 1st, Concord, 1868. 52876

New Hampshire Mechanics and Art Association First exhibition at Concord, N. H. October 6, 1868. 52876

New-Hampshire Medical Institution. 52877

New-Hampshire Medical Society. 52878, 52948, 83654, 84907

New-Hampshire Medical Society. Center District. 52878

New-Hampshire Medical Society. Charter. 52878, 52948

New-Hampshire Medical Society. Eastern District. 52878

New Hampshire Missionary Society. (52879), 69358, 95229

New Hampshire Missionary Society. Trustees. (52879)

New Hampshire, New Jerusalem, and primitive religious intelligencer. 52880

New Hampshire patriot. (50398), 77530, 98052, 98053, note after 99796, note after 105101

New Hampshire probate directory. . . . By Charles R. Morrison. 52881

New-Hampshire probate directory: containing all the statute laws. (12178)

New Hampshire provincial and state papers. 52791, 66514, note after 98998, 1st note after 99003

New Hampshire Publishers, Editors and Printers' Association. 52882

New Hampshire Publishers, Editors and Printers Association. Convention, Wolfeborough, 1868. see Convention of New Hampshire Publishers, Editors, and Printers, Wolfeborough, 1868.

New Hampshire rambles. (52883)

New-Hampshire register. 52884, 97988

New-Hampshire register, and United States calendar. 52885

New-Hampshire Religious Tract Society. 99138

New-Hampshire repository. 14222, 52886

New Hampshire Republican State Convention of Delegates Friendly to the Election of Andrew Jackson, Concord, 1828. see Democratic Party. New Hampshire. Convention, Concord, 1828.

New-Hampshire sentinel. 92785

New-Hampshire Settlers Convention, Manchester N. H., 1775. see Vermont. Convention, 1775.

New-Hampshire Society for the Promotion of Temperance. 52887

New Hampshire State Agricultural Society. see New Hampshire Agricultural Society.

New Hampshire state papers. 101077

New Hampshire statistical almanac. (52889)

New Hampshire Temperance Society. Executive Committee. 94647

New Hampshire. The (late) House of Representatives there complainants. 52854

New-Hampshire town officer. 71098

New-Hampshire Unitarian Association. see Unitarian Churches. New Hampshire. Association.

New Hampshire vs. Samuel Small. (52925)

New Hampshire Young Men's Christian Association. see Young Men's Christian Association, New Hampshire.

New Hampton, N. H. Academical and Theological Institution. 52951

New Hampton, N. H. Academical and Theological Institution. Literary Adelphi. 52951

New Hampton, N. H. Academical and Theological Institution. Social Fraternity. 85690

New Hampton, N. H. Academical and Theological Institution. Social Fraternity. Library. 85689

New Hampton, N. H. Female Seminary. see New Hampton Female Seminary, New Hampton, N. H.

New Hampton Female Seminary, New Hampton, N. H. Young Ladies Association For the Promotion of Literature and Missions. 52951, 106136

New Hanover County, N. C. Committee on the Improvement of the Cape Fear Bar. (52952)

New Harmony disseminator of useful knowledge. 77385

New-Harmony gazette. (25708), 52953

New Harmony of Zion. 4050, 94333-94334

New Haven (Colony) 53004-53005 see also United Colonies of New England.

New Haven (Colony) Laws, statutes, etc. 53017-53018

New Haven, Conn. (53002), 53006

New Haven, Conn. defendants 31669

New Haven, Conn. petitioners 52980, 52997

New Haven, Conn. American Institute of Instruction. see American Institute of Instruction.

New Haven, Conn. Anti-Nebraska Meetings, 1854. see Anti-Nebraska Meetings, New Haven, Conn., 1854.

New Haven, Conn. Board of Education. 52960

New Haven, Conn. Charter. 52968

New Haven, Conn. Christ Church. (7783)

New Haven, Conn. Christ Church. Rector. (7883) see also Brewster, Lyman D.

New Haven, Conn. Citizens. 53001

New Haven, Conn. City Auditor. 52957

New Haven, Conn. City Council. Committee on Supplying the City With Water. 53010

New Haven, Conn. City Council. Committee on the Sinking Fund. 52957

New Haven, Conn. City Council. Committee to Inquire into the Condition of the New Haven Burying Ground. 53008

New Haven, Conn. Collegiate and Commercial Institute. see Collegiate and Commercial Institute, New Haven, Conn.

New Haven, Conn. Committee to Aid in Furnishing Supplies to the Sick and Wounded Soldiers. 53009

New Haven, Conn. Congress of the Commissaries of the Colonies of New York and Massachusetts Bay, 1767. see Congress of the Commissaries of the Colonies of New York and Massachusetts Bay, on the Establishment of a Partition Line of Jurisdiction Between the Two Provinces, New Haven, Conn., 1767.

New Haven, Conn. Convention, 1811. see New Haven Convention, 1811.

New Haven, Conn. Ecclesiastical Council, 1785. see Congregational Churches in Connecticut. Ecclesiastical Council, New Haven, 1785.

New Haven. Female Education Society. see Female Education Society of New Haven.

New Haven, Conn. Finance Committee. 52957

New Haven, Conn. First Church. (18711), 52959, 52959, 52964, 52985

New Haven, Conn. First Ecclesiastical Society. 2660

New Haven, Conn. First Ecclesiastical Society. Committee. 53007

New Haven, Conn. First School Society. see First School Society, New Haven, Conn.

New Haven, Conn. Franklin Institute. see Franklin Institute, New Haven, Conn.

New Haven, Conn. General Hospital Society. see General Hospital Society of Connecticut, New Haven.

New Haven, Conn. Gymnasium. see New Haven Gymnasium, New Haven, Conn.

New Haven, Conn. Harmony Division, No. 5. see Sons of Temperance of North America. Connecticut. Harmony Division, No. 5, New Haven.

New Haven, Conn. Home for the Friendless. see Home for the Friendless, New Haven, Conn.

New Haven, Conn. Hopkins Grammar School. 52993

New Haven, Conn. Horticultural Fair, 1838. see Horticultural Fair, New Haven, Conn., 1838.

New Haven, Conn. Ladies' Greek Association. see New Haven Ladies' Greek Association, New Haven, Conn.

New Haven, Conn. Martha Washington Temperance Society. see Martha Washington Temperance Society, New Haven, Conn.

New Haven, Conn. Mayor, 1863-1864. 52957

New Haven, Conn. Mechanic Library Society. see Mechanic Library Society, New Haven, Conn.

New Haven, Conn. Medical Association. see New Haven Medical Association, New Haven, Conn.

New Haven, Conn. Meeting on a Proposed College for Colored Youth, 1831. (52970)

New Haven, Conn. Meeting of the Class of 1820 of Yale College, 1840. see Yale University. Class of 1820.

New Haven, Conn. Meeting of the Class of 1822 of Yale College, 1835. see Yale University. Class of 1822.

New Haven, Conn. Meeting of the Class Which Graduated at Yale College in 1810, 1840. see Yale University. Class of 1810.

New Haven, Conn. Merchants. petitioners 52986

New Haven, Conn. Merchants' Exchange. 52967

New Haven, Conn. Ordinances, etc. 52961, 52968, 53005

New Haven, Conn. Republican Committee of Publications. see Democratic Party.

Connecticut. New Haven. Committee of Publications.

New Haven, Conn. St. Paul's Missionary Society. see St. Paul's Missionary Society, New Haven, Conn.

New Haven, Conn. Social Library. see New Haven Social Library, New Haven, Conn.

New Haven, Conn. Social Library Company. see New Haven Society Library Company, New Haven, Conn.

New Haven, Conn. Soldiers' Aid Society. see Soldiers' Aid Society, New Haven, Conn.

New Haven, Conn. Special Committee Concerning the City Bank of New Haven. 53013

New Haven, Conn. Third Congregational Church. (52973)

New Haven, Conn. Treasurer. 52957

New Haven, Conn. Union Meeting, 1850. 53003

New Haven, Conn. United Congregational Society. (52973), 52985

New Haven, Conn. United Society. 52964

New Haven, Conn. Washington Temperance Society. see Martha Washington Temperance Society, New Haven, Conn.

New Haven, Conn. Young Ladies' Institute. see New Haven Young Ladies' Institute, New Haven, Conn.

New Haven, Conn. Young Men's Institute. see New Haven Young Men's Institute, New Haven, Conn.

New Haven, Conn. Young Men's Temperance Society. see Young Men's Temperance Society, New Haven, Conn.

New-Haven, a poem. 105189

New Haven as it is. 52987

New Haven catechism. 52959

New Haven Center, Conn. Associated Pastors. see Congregational Churches in Connecticut. New Haven Center Association.

New Haven Colony Historical Society. 8231, 52988, 75790

New Haven City Meeting on a Proposed College for Colored Youth, 1831. see New Haven, Conn. Meeting on a Proposed College for Colored Youth, 1831.

New Haven Convention, 1811. (15753), 52982

New Haven County Agricultural Society. 52994

New Haven County Association. see Congregational Churches in Connecticut. New Haven County Association.

New Haven County Association of the Western District. see Congregational Churches in Connecticut. New Haven County Western Association.

New-Haven County Bible Society. 52989

New Haven County Consociation. see Congregational Churches in Connecticut. New Haven County Consociation.

New Haven County Horticultural Society. 52990

New Haven County Medical Society. 52962, 52996

New Haven directory. 52991

New Haven East Consociation. see Congregational Churches in Connecticut. New Haven East Consociation.

New-Haven, 18 Sir, there is due from to the President and Fellows of Yale-College. 105859

New Haven Female Benevolence Society. see Female Benevolence Society, New Haven, Conn.

New Haven gazette, and the Connecticut magazine. 52992, 80405, 97204

New Haven Horticultural Society. 52994

New Haven, June 1835. Dear Sir. 105883

New Haven Ladies' Greek Association, New Haven, Conn. 52995

New Haven Medical Association, New Haven, Conn. 52996

New-Haven memorial to the President. 52997

New Haven remonstrance. 14312, (23365), (40117), 97440

New Haven Social Library, New Haven, Conn. 52963

New Haven Social Library Company, New Haven, Conn. 52963

New Haven theology, alias Taylorism, alias neology. 20746

New Haven Water Company. Charter. 52998

New Haven Water Company. Directors. 52998

New Haven Young Ladies' Institute, New Haven Conn. 52999

New Haven Young Men's Institute, New Haven, Conn. 53000

New Haven Young Men's Institute, New Haven, Conn. Library. 53000

New Haven Young Men's Temperance Society. see Young Men's Temperance Society, New Haven, Conn.

New Haven's settling in New-England. 53017-53018

New hieroglyphical Bible. 53019

New history of England. 67599

New history of Jamaica. 35585, (35636), 82167

New history of Oregon and California. 30825

New history of Texas. 91726, note after 95104

New history of the Bible. 90028

New home who'll follow? (37991)

New homes and a strange people. 7765

New homes in the west. 91650

New Hope, Pa. Delaware Division, No. 22. see Sons of Temperance of North America. Pennsylvania. Delaware Division, No. 22, New Hope.

New Hope, Pa. Public Meeting in Favor of an Out-Let Lock at Well's Falls, 1846. 6040

New hope, or, the rescue. 53020

New hymn book, designed for Universalist societies. 92792

New icon. 53021

New ideas on population. 23233

New idolatry. 26074

New Idria Mining Company of California. petitioners 53022

New Idria Mining Company of California. Counsel. 70261 see also Botts, C. T.

New illustrated family atlas. 36182

New illustrations of . . . Shakespeare. 9759

New index to the civil and military lists of Rhode Island. 83355

New Indian sketches. (82267)

New instructor. 70494

New interlude and a mery of the nature of the iiij. elements. 53023

New internal revenue guide, etc. 22424

New internal revenue law, approved June 20, 1866. 20925

New internal revenue law of June 30, 1864. (53024)

New introduction to the knowledge and use of maps. 53025

New Ipswich, N. H. Appleton Academy. see Appleton Academy, New Ipswich, N. H.

New ipswich, N. H. Centennial Celebration, 1850. 28090

New Ipswich, N. H. School Committee. 53028

New Ipswich, N. H. Selectmen. 53026

New Ipswich Academy. see Appleton Academy, New Ipswich, N. H.

New Ireland. Constitution. 16073, 53029
New islands. 34100-34107
New Jamaica almanack, and register. 35637
New Jamaica magazine from Jan. 1798 to May 1799. 35638
New Jersey (Colony) (1791), (7884), 32968, 39527, 53058, 83979
New Jersey (Colony) Agents for Settling the Boundary Line With New York. 63210, 95936
New Jersey (Colony) Board of Proprietors of the Eastern Division. see Board of Proprietors of the Eastern Division of New Jersey.
New Jersey (Colony) Chancery Court. see New Jersey (Colony) High Court of Chancery.
New Jersey (Colony) Charter. 39527, 89425
New Jersey (Colony) Citizens. 53031
New Jersey (Colony) Convention, 1776. (53140)
New Jersey (Colony) Council. (50851)
New Jersey (Colony) Council of Proprietors of the Western Division. see Council of Proprietors of the Western Division of New Jersey.
New Jersey (Colony) Court of Vice Admiralty. (8961)
New Jersey (Colony) General Assembly. 39527, (50851), 53107-53108, 53135, 53238, 53244-53245, 79369, 89425
New Jersey (Colony) General Assembly. Committee upon the New York Line. Chairman. 53053 see also Ogden, David.
New Jersey (Colony) General Assembly. Speaker. 53108 see also Johnston, Andrew.
New Jersey (Colony) Governor, 1720-1725 (Burnet) 53199 see also Burnet, William, 1688-1729.
New Jersey (Colony) Governor, 1738-1746 (Morris) 50850-(50851), 53108 see also Morris, Lewis, 1671-1746.
New Jersey (Colony) Governor, 1746-1757 (Belcher) 53200 see also Belcher, Jonathan, 1681-1757.
New Jersey (Colony) Governor, 1758-1760 (Bernard) (49225) see also Bernard, Sir Francis, 1712-1779.
New Jersey (Colony) Governor, 1763-1776 (Franklin) 25636 see also Franklin, William, 1729-1813.
New Jersey (Colony) High Court of Chancery. 5378-5379, 33874, (53066), 53074, 53200, 83979, 83982, 91855
New Jersey (Colony) Indian Conference, Burlington, 1758. (49225)
New Jersey (Colony) Laws, statutes, etc. 5379, 39410, 39414, 39527, 53034, 53040-53041, 53043-53046, 53059-53061, 53069, 53072, 53076, 53106, 53143-(53144), 53146, 53199-53201, 53238, 83979, 89425
New Jersey (Colony) Proprietors. see Board of Proprietors of the Eastern Division of New Jersey. Council of Proprietors of the Western Division of New Jersey.
New Jersey (Colony) Provincial Congress, Trenton, 1775. 53106, 53206
New Jersey (Colony) Provincial Congress, New Brunswick, 1776. 53139
New Jersey (Colony) Public Creditors. petitioners 53154
New Jersey (Colony) Scots Proprietors. see Board of Proprietors of the Eastern Division of New Jersey. Scots Proprietors.

New Jersey (Colony) Supreme Court, Burlington. 91939
New Jersey (Colony) Treasurer. plaintiff 83979 see also Smith, Samuel plaintiff
New Jersey (Colony) Treaties, etc. 53242, 60255
New Jersey. 15841, 53111, 83982
New Jersey. defendants 60817
New Jersey. Adjutant General. 53212
New Jersey. Anti-monopoly Convention, 1868. see Anti-monopoly Convention, Trenton, N. J., 1868.
New Jersey. Bar. Dinner Given to Thomas H. Dudley, 1868. 21091
New Jersey. Board of Education. see New Jersey. State Board of Education.
New Jersey. Board of Commissioners on Provision for Disabled Soldiers. 53073
New Jersey. Boards der Commissare fur Versorgung Invalider New Jersey Soldaten. see New Jersey. Board of Commissioners on Provision for Disabled Soldiers.
New Jersey. Canal Commissioners. 19414
New Jersey. Census. 1850. (53030)
New Jersey. Citizens. 35439
New Jersey. Commission for the Purpose of Ascertaining the Practicability and Expediency of a Canal, to Unite the Delaware and Raritan Rivers. (53223) see also New Jersey. Commission on the Delaware and Raritan Canal.
New Jersey. Commission to Investigate the Wreck off the Monmouth Coast. (53217)
New Jersey. Commission on the Delaware and Passaic Canal. (53213)
New Jersey. Commission on the Delaware and Passaic Canal. (53213)
New Jersey. Commission on the Delaware and Raritan Canal. 19413, (53227) see also New Jersey. Commission for the Prupose of Ascertaining the Practicability and Expediency of a Canal, to Unite the Delaware and Raritan Rivers.
New Jersey. Commission on the Delaware and Raritan Canal and Camden and Amboy Railroad. 10828, 19417, 53216
New Jersey. Commissioners on the Delaware River. 53211
New Jersey. Commissioners on the Eastern Boundary. 53125, 53234
New Jersey. Commissioners to Ascertain the Number of Lunatics and Idiots in the State. (53215)
New Jersey. Commissioners to Codify the School Law. 53218
New Jersey. Commissioners to Investigate Charges Made Against the Directors of the Delaware and Raritan Canal and Campden and Amboy Railroad and Transportation Companies, 1850. see New Jersey. Commission on Delaware and Raritan Canal and Camden and Amboy Railroad.
New Jersey. Commissioners to Meet Commissioners of Virginia and Other States, at Washington, 1861. (53214)
New Jersey. Commissioners to Settle the Question of Territory in Dispute with the State of New York, 1828. 53156
New Jersey. Committee of Safety. 53106, 53139
New Jersey. Constitution. 1269, 1271, 2071, 5316, 6360, 16086-16092, 16097, 16099-16013, 16107, 16113, 16118-16120, (19476), 23325, 25790, 33137, (47188), 53048, 53092, 53094, 53131, (53140), 59771, (66397), 93558, 100342, 104198
New Jersey. Constitutional Convention, 1844. (53136)

New Jersey. Militia. Union Brigade. 2403, 97766, note after 101874
New Jersey. Railroad Commission. 10828
New Jersey. School Fund. Trustees. see New Jersey. Trustees of the School Fund.
New Jersey. Secretary of State. 53228
New Jersey. Society for Establishing Useful Manufactures. see Society for Establishing Useful Manufactures, New Jersey.
New Jersey. Society of the Cincinnati. see Society of the Cincinnati. New Jersey.
New Jersey. Soldiers' Children's Home. see Soldiers' Children's Home of New Jersey.
New Jersey. State Board of Education. (53192), 53202
New Jersey. State Geologist. 16238-16239, 53118-53120, 53122-(53124), 72656 see also Cooke, George Mammell, 1818-1889. Rogers, Henry D.
New Jersey. State Hospital, Trenton. Managers. (53194)
New Jersey. State Hospital, Trenton. Officers. (53194)
New Jersey. State Library. 53085
New Jersey. State Lunatic Asylum, Trenton. see New Jersey. State Hospital, Trenton.
New Jersey. State Prison. 53063, 53196
New Jersey. State Prison. Inspectors. 53222
New Jersey. State Prison. Physician. 53222
New Jersey. State Superintendent of Public Instruction. see New Jersey. Department of Public Instruction.
New Jersey. State Teachers College and Normal School, Trenton. 53195
New Jersey. State Teachers College and Normal School, Trenton. Farnum Preparatory School. 53195
New Jersey. State Teachers College and Normal School, Trenton. Model School. 53195
New Jersey. State Teachers College and Normal School, Trenton. Trustees. 53195
New Jersey. Superintendent of Public Schools. see New Jersey. Department of Public Instruction.
New Jersey. Superior Court. (53102)
New Jersey. Supreme Court. 53084, 91629
New Jersey. Treasurer. (53223), (53241)
New Jersey. Trustees of the School Fund. 53064
New Jersey (Ship) 47683 see also Owners and Underwriters of the American Ship the New Jersey. petitioners Subscribers, Owners, and Insurers of the Ship New Jersey, And Her Cargo. petitioners
New Jersey Abolition Society. 53093
New Jersey Agricultural Society. see Agricultural Society of New Jersey.
New-Jersey almanack. 53165
New Jersey and New York almanack for 1800. 53166
New Jersey and Pennsylvania almanack for . . . 1800. 53167
New Jersey almanack. By William Ball. 53164
New Jersey and the rebellion. 25251
New-Jersey annual register and general calendar. 41695
New Jersey Bank Officers Committee. see Committee of New Jersey Bank Officers.
New Jersey Baptist Education Society. 53168

New Jersey Baptist State Convention. see Baptists. New Jersey. State Convention.
New Jersey Bible Society. Managers. 53169
New Jersey business directory. . . . Collected . . . by Stacy B. Kirkbride, Jr. 53141
New Jersey business directory, with commercial register. 53170
New Jersey Classical and Scientific Institute, Hightstown, N. J. 53171
New Jersey Classis. see Reformed Church in America. Classis of New Jersey.
New Jersey College. see Princeton University.
New Jersey Colonization Society. 53172
New Jersey Conference memorial. 53173
New Jersey contested election. 8431
New Jersey election. Speech of Mr. Smith. 84451
New-Jersey farmer. pseud. Columbiad. see Snowden, Richard, d. 1825?
New Jersey farmer (1855-1861) 53174
New Jersey for enfranchisement. 78458
New Jersey for the union. 78453, 78458
New Jersey for the war. 78454, 78458
New Jersey Franklinite Company. (53175)
New Jersey Franklinite Company. Charter. (53175)
New Jersey Historical Society. 1000, 21113, 24291, 25063, 37786, 50850, 53058, 53176-(53177), 53235, 54882, note after 66024, 82980, note before 91508, 95396
New Jersey Historical Society. Executive Committee. 53176
New Jersey Howard Association. 53178
New Jersey Indians. see Cranberry Indians. Croswick Indians. Pompton Indians. South Jersey Indians.
New-Jersey journal. 85207
New Jersey Lyceum. Executive Committee. 53179
New Jersey Lyceum. Paper no. 1. Circular of the Executive Committee. 53179
New Jersey magazine. (53180), 55814
New Jersey magazine and monthly advertiser. 53181
New Jersey medical reporter. 53182
New Jersey Medical Society. 74089
New Jersey Mining Company. 53184
New Jersey Missionary Society. see Missionary Society of New Jersey.
New Jersey monthly magazine. (53183)
New Jersey Monument Association. Officers. 53051
New Jersey Monument Association. Standing Committee. 53051
N. J. patent right oppression exposed. 22182, 59045
New-Jersey preacher. 84123
New Jersey Presbytery. see Presbyterian Church in the U. S. A. Presbytery of New Jersey.
New Jersey Prison Reform Association. 53186
New Jersey Prison Reform Association. Annual Meeting, 1st, Trenton, 1850. 53186
New Jersey Railroad and Transportation Company. (53185)
New-Jersey register . . . for . . . 1811. 53187
New Jersey register for 1837. 64682
New Jersey Riparian Association. 53109, 53188
New Jersey senatorial election. 53189
New Jersey senatorial question. 53189
New-Jersey, September 5. 1765. 103204
New Jersey Society for the Abolition of Slavery. 53190

New Jersey Society for the Establishment of Useful Manufactures. see Society for the Establishment of Useful Manufactures in New Jersey.

New Jersey Society for the Suppression of Vice and Immorality. 53191

New Jersey State Bank Officers. Committee. see Committee of New Jersey Bank Officers.

New Jersey state business directory for 1866. 53193

New Jersey. The Burlington almanack for . . . 1776. 53165

New Jersey Union Brigade. see New Jersey. Militia. Union Brigade.

New Jersey vs. Orrin Van Derhoven. 79985

New Jersey Volunteers. see U. S. Army. New Jersey Volunteers.

New Jersey Washington Benevolent Society. see Washington Benevolent Society. New Jersey.

New Jersey Zinc Company. (53197)

New Jersey's missing governor. 83982

New Jerusalem. 64957

New Jerusalem Church. 52575

New Jerusalem Church. General Convention, 8th-52d, New York, 1826-1870. 53248

New Jerusalem Church. General Convention, 36th, New York, 1854. 52575

New Jerusalem Church. General Convention, 45th, New York. 1863. 53248

New Jerusalem Church. Boston Society. 6659, 52575

New Jerusalem Church. Cincinnati First Society. 53248

New Jerusalem Church. Indiana. Union County Convention. (22096)

New Jerusalem Church. Massachusetts Ministers. 66883

New Jerusalem Church. Principle of the New Church. 53248

New Jerusalem magazine. 53247

New juvenile library. 100942

New law of grace examined and disproved. 20059

New Lebanon, N. Y. Shakers. see Shakers. New Lebanon, N. Y.

New Lebanon, N. Y. United Society. see Shakers. New Lebanon, N. Y.

New lecture on heads. 91501

New lessons for the day. note after (58767)

New letters. (51225)

New liberty song. 86866

New library of useful knowledge. 10385

New life of Virginia. (36286), 53249, note after 99867

New light on the prophecies! 89670

New lights of the west. 82430

New lights on Jacobinism. 92070

New London, Conn. 53255

New London, Conn. Committee on the Washington Funeral Ceremonies, 1800. 33974, 101813

New London, Conn. Court of Vice Admiralty. see Connecticut (Colony) Court of Vice Admiralty, New London.

New London, Conn. Ecclesiastical Council, 1736. see Congregational Churches in Connecticut. Ecclesiastical Council, New London, 1736.

New London, Conn. Ecclesiastical Council, 1737. see Congregational Churches in Connecticut. Ecclesiastical Council, New London, 1737.

New London, Conn. First Church. (9718), 106229

New London, Conn. Funeral Observances in Honor of Abraham Lincoln, 1865. 53255

New London, Conn. Harvard-Columbia Freshman Boat Race, 1895. see Harvard-Columbia Freshman Boat Race, New London, Conn., 1895.

New London, Conn. Monthly Meeting. see Friends, Society of. New London Monthly Meeting.

New London, Conn. Navy Yard Committee. see Committee Appointed by the Secretary of the Navy and the Legislature of Connecticut, on the Navy Yard at New London.

New London, Conn. North Parish. Ecclesiastical Council, 1737. see Congregational Churches in Connecticut. Ecclesiastical Council, New London, 1737.

New London, Conn. Second Congregational Church. (53263)

New London, Conn. Second Congregational Church. Sabbath School. (53264)

New London, Conn. School Visitors. 53250

New London, Conn. Some Baptist People, Called Quakers. see Friends, Society of New London Monthly Meeting.

New London, Conn. Yale-Harvard Boat Race, 1895. see Yale-Harvard Boat Race, New London, Conn., 1895.

New London, Conn. Yale University. see Yale University.

New London, Pa. New London Academy. see New London Academy, New London, Pa.

New London Academy, New London. Pa. 53265

New London almanack for . . . 1769. 53257

New London almanack for 1773. 53257

New-London as a naval station. 90707

New London Baptist Association. see Baptists. Connecticut. New-London Baptist Association.

New London city directory. 53259

New-London directory, for 1853-4. (53259)

New London gazette. 104265

New London Navy Yard Committee. see Committee Appointed by the Secretary of the Navy and the Legislature of Connecticut, on the Navy Yard at New London.

New London weekly oracle. 101574

New London, Willimantic and Palmer Railroad Company. 53261

New London, Willimantic and Springfield Railroad Company. Engineer. 53262

New Looking-glass. 62914

New Lotts, N. Y. (53267)

New Louisiana. 53268

New maid of the oaks. 51508

New man for the new times. 4575

New manual, and platoon exercise. 53269

New manual exercise. 53271

New manual exercise to be observed by His Majesty's troops. 53270

New map and hand-book of Kansas. 29282

New map of Texas, Oregon, and California. 49714

New map of the state [of Illinois.] 14259

New map of the United States. 94318

New map of ye isthmus of Darien in America. (9920), 18556, 78218

New maritime law. 74368

New Market, Ohio. Straight-Creek Baptist Association Meeting, 1852. see Baptists. Ohio. Strait-Creek Baptist Association.

New Marlborough, Mass. Committee on Accounts. (53272)

New masonic trestle-board. (50333)

New matrimonial tat-too. 102477

New matrimonial Yankee Doodle for the bachelors. 102495

New Meetinghouse, Hallowell, Me. see Hallowell, Me. New Meetinghouse.

New meeting house (so called) in Waldoboro. 101014

New memorandum, addressed to all real lovers of liberty. 53273

New memorandum book. 53274

New merry book of all fives. 104194

New method of inoculating for the small pox. 74208, (74226), (74230)

New method of ordering horses & sheep. 97285

New method of studying history. 40029

New method of studying history, geography, and chronology. 21150

New method of teaching sacred harmony. 84698

New Mexico (Territory) Governor, 1855-1861 (Davis) 18905 see also Davis, William Watts Hart, 1820-1910.

New Mexico (Territory) Governor, 1857-1861 (Rencher) 69605 see also Rencher, Abraham, 1798-1883.

New Mexico (Territory) Governor, 1857-1866 (Arny) 53276-53277 see also Arny, William Frederick Milton, 1813-1881.

New Mexico (Territory) Laws, statutes, etc. 53281, 53284, 72430

New Mexico (Territory) Legislative Assembly, Council. (53278), 53280

New Mexico (Territory) Legislative Assembly. House of Representatives. 53279

New Mexico (Territory) Supreme Court. Chief Justice. 53284 see also Davenport, James J.

New Mexico. 28786

New Mexico and California. Speech . . . in the House . . . February 10, 1849. 8437

New Mexico and California. Speech of Hon. F. P. Stanton. 90419

New Mexico and California. The ancient monuments. 89979

New Mexico and her people. 18900

New Mexico, Arizona and Colorado Missionary Association. 53282

New Mexico: her resources. 13683

New-Mexico, otherwise the voyage of Antonio de Espejo. 53283

New military dictionary. 53286

New military guide. 23835

New military, historical, and explanatory dictionary. 81142

New militia act. 53778

New militia force. 86823

New-milk cheese. 77018, note after 98576

New-milk cheese, no. 2. 30765

New ministry. 53287

New mirror for travellers. 53289, 59192, 59208

New mirror of literature. (53288)

New missionary field. (54274), 90079

New mode of government. 23210

New mode of petitioning. 23211

New monetary system. 37286

New monthly, devoted to the investigation . . . of the scriptures. 78620

New monthly gazette of the union and literary review. 52390

New monthly magazine. 30447, 93912

New monthly magazine of literature, fashion and the fine arts. (53291), 76963

New moral system of natural history. 71393-(71394)

New Munchausen. 59198

New mystery in physick discovered. 53292

New nation. (53293)

New nation to the public. 13799

New national banks. 8348

New national song book. 53294

New national tax law as approved. 53295

New naval history. (22669)

New naval station at League Island. 53296

New Netherlands (Colony) see New York (New Netherlands)

New news from Robinson Crusoe's island. 53297, 55065

New nomenclature of chemistry. 88905

New North-American pilot. (31194)

New North American spelling book. 53298

New North Church, Boston. see Boston. New North Church.

New offer to the lovers of religion and learning. 46430

New official manual for United States Consuls. (53299)

New olive branch. A solemn warning on the banks of the Rubicon. 30053

New olive branch: addressed to the citizens of South Carolina. 10874

New olive branch; or, an attempt to establish an identity of interest. 10873

New Orleans. 53377 see also New Orleans (Second Municipality)

New Orleans. appellants 87287

New Orleans. defendants (21256), (28363)

New Orleans. plaintiffs 28247

New Orleans. Association for the Relief of Jewish Widows and Orphans. see Association for the Relief of Jewish Widows and Orphans of New Orleans.

New Orleans. Board of Health. 53308

New Orleans. Celebration of the Anniversary of the National Independence, 1864. 53315

New Orleans. Chamber of Commerce. 49550

New Orleans. Chamber of Commerce. Committee on Ocean Steamers. 53343

New Orleans. Charity Hospital. Board of Administrators. 53363

New Orleans. Charter. 53314

New Orleans. Citizens. petitioners (53334)

New Orleans. Citizens, Creditors of the Late Republic of Texas. petitioners (61272)

New Orleans. City Council. 3837, 53366

New Orleans. City Council. Common Council. Special Committee. 53370

New Orleans. City Council. General Council. 88593

New Orleans. City Council. General Council. Secretary. 88593 see also Southmayd, F. R.

New Orleans. Commercial Bank. see Commercial Bank of New Orleans.

New Orleans. Common Council. see New Orleans. City Council. Common Council.

New Orleans. Comptroller. 53316

New Orleans. Constitutional Convention, 1844-1845. see Louisiana. Constitutional Convention, New Orleans, 1844-1845.

New Orleans, Convention of Delegations from the Diocese of Mississippi and Alabama, and the Clergy and Churches of Louisiana, 1835. see Protestant Episcopal Church in the U. S. A. Convention of Delegations from the Diocese of Mississippi and Alabama, and the Clergy and Churches of Louisiana, New Orleans, 1835.

New Orleans. Convention of the Republican Party of Louisiana, 1865. see Republican Party. Louisiana. Convention, New Orleans, 1865.

New Orleans. Directors of the Public Schools. see New Orleans. Public Schools. Directors.

New Orleans. Financial Commission, 1864. see U. S. Army. Department of the Gulf. Financial Commission of New Orleans, 1864.

New Orleans. First District Lyceum and Library Society. see Lyceum and Library Society, New Orleans (First District)

New Orleans. Free Library. 53353

New Orleans. Funeral Ceremonies in Honor of Calhoun, Clay and Webster, Dec. 9, 1852. (53327)

New Orleans. General Council. see New Orleans. City Council. General Council.

New Orleans. Grand Celebration in Honor of the Passage of the Ordinance of Emancipation, by the Free State Convention, 1864. 28256

New Orleans. Grand Jury on the Great Riot, July 30th, 1866. 53326

New Orleans. Home for Jewish Widows and Orphans. see Home for Jewish Widows and Orphans of New Orleans.

New Orleans. House of Refuge. Commissioners and Officers. 53310

New Orleans. Howard Association. see Howard Association of New Orleans.

New Orleans. John Brown Pioneer Radical Republican Club. see John Brown Pioneer Radical Republican Club, New Orleans.

New Orleans. Louisiana Bank. see Louisiana Bank, New Orleans.

New Orleans. Louisiana Relief Lodge. see Freemasons. Louisiana. Louisiana Relief Lodge, New Orleans.

New Orleans. Mayor, 1858. (53336)

New Orleans. Mayor, 1862. 53320

New Orleans. Mercantile Library Association. see Mercantile Library Association of New Orleans.

New Orleans. Native American Newspaper. see Native American Newspaper, New Orleans.

New Orleans. Ordinances, etc. 53324, 53333, 88593

New Orleans. Physico-Medical Society. see Physico-Medical Society of New-Orleans.

New Orleans. Public Schools. Directors. 53309

New Orleans. St. Anna's Asylum for the Relief of Destitute Females and their Children. see St. Anna's Asylum for the Relief of Destitute Females and their Children, New Orleans.

New Orleans. Sanitary Commission. 3835, 3837, 53366

New Orleans. Societe du Magnetisme. see Societe du Magnetisme de la Nouvelle-Orleans.

New Orleans. Society for the Relief of Destitute Females and their Helpless Children. see Society for the Relief of Destitute Females and their Helpless Children, New Orleans.

New Orleans. Southern and Western Railroad Convention, 1851. see Southern and

Western Railroad Convention, New Orleans, 1851.

New Orleans. Southern Bank. see Southern Bank, New Orleans.

New Orleans. Southern Commercial Convention, 1855. see Southern Commercial Convention, New Orleans, 1855.

New Orleans. Southwestern Bible Society. see Southwestern Bible Society of New Orleans.

New Orleans. Southwestern Exposition Association. see Southwestern Exposition Association of New Orleans.

New Orleans. State Library. see Louisiana. State Library, New Orleans.

New Orleans. Stockholders Meeting of the Southern Pacific Railroad Company, 1848. see Southern Pacific Railroad Company (Texas) Stockholders Meeting, New Orleans 1858.

New Orleans. Stockholders Meeting of the Southern Pacific Railroad Company, 1859. see Southern Pacific Railroad Company (Texas) Stockholders Meeting, New Orleans 1859.

New Orleans. Transportation Convention, 1869. 71619

New Orleans. Transportation Convention, 1869 petitioners 71619

New Orleans. University. see Tulane University of Louisiana.

New Orleans. Washington Artillery Battalion. see Louisiana. Militia. Washington Artillery Battalion, New Orleans.

New Orleans (Diocese) Synod, 1844. 72946

New Orleans (Ecclesiastical Province) Council, 1856. 72914

New Orleans (Ecclesiastical Province) Council, 3d, 1873. 72915

New Orleans (Second Municipality) 53323, 88593 see also New Orleans.

New Orleans (Second Municipality) plaintiffs 87280

New Orleans (Second Municipality) Council. 53309

New Orleans (Second Municipality) Ordinances etc. 53323, 88593

New Orleans (Second Municipality) Public School. Library. 53313

New Orleans Academy of Sciences. 53338

New Orleans Academy of Sciences. Special Committee on a Geological and Scientific Survey of the State of Louisiana. 53338

New Orleans and environs. (53360), (55494)

New Orleans and Nashville Railroad Company. 53339

New Orleans annual directory and commercial register. 53346

New Orleans as I found it. 53340

New Orleans as it is. (53341)

New Orleans bee and bulletin. 103114

New-Orleans book. 3573

New Orleans business directory. 53349

New Orleans Canal and Banking Company. 53342

New Orleans Canal Company. 53342

New Orleans Chamber of Commerce. 1856. Report of the Committee. 53343

New Orleans Commercial Bank. see Commercial Bank of New-Orleans.

New Orleans crescent. 27287

New Orleans daily crescent. 88327

New Orleans delta. 89748

New Orleans directory and register. (53306)

New Orleans directory, for . . . 1859. 53350

New-Orleans directory, for 1841. 53344

New-Orleans directory for 1842. 53345

New Orleans directory, including Jefferson City. (53347)

New Orleans era. Editor. see Hills, Alfred C.

New Orleans Insurance Company. defendants 82142

New Orleans, January 14, 1830. 3392

New Orleans Ladies' Benevolent Society. see Ladies' Benevolent Society, New Orleans.

New Orleans, La., Nov. 10, 1868. 42186

New Orleans medical and surgical journal. 53354, 92033

New Orleans medical journal. 53354

New Orleans medical news and hospital gazetter. A semi-monthly journal. (53355)

New Orleans miscellany. 53356

New Orleans picayune. (16754), (23525), 62673, 84237

New Orleans Presbytery. see Presbyterian Church in the U. S. Presbytery of New Orleans.

New Orleans Property Holders' Union. see Property Holders' Union of New Orleans.

New Orleans riot. Its official history. 53357

New Orleans School of Medicine. (53358)

New-Orleans sketch book. 53359, 103101

New Orleans Temperance Society. (53304)

New Orleans Tigers. see Louisiana. Militia. Washington Artillery Battalion, New Orleans.

New Orleans Unitarian Home Mission. see Unitarian Home Mission, New Orleans.

New Orphan Asylum, Cincinnati. see Cincinnati Orphan Asylum.

New pantheon. 53379

New Park Theatre, New York. see New York (City) New Park Theatre.

New pastoral. 68178

New path. 53380

New patriotic song. 101890

New penal code for Pennsylvania. 60273

New phase in ecclesiastical law and Presbyterian church government. 53381

New phase of the subject of slavery and free labor. 82023

New phases of the revolution. (80845)

New phenomenon in politics. pseud. Tragi-comic memoirs. 96438

New Philadelphia Coal Mining Company. 53382

New philosophical journal. see Edinburgh new philosophical journal.

New pictorial and illustrated family magazine. 53383

New picture of American slave life. (31787)

New picture of Philadelphia. 71864, 94325

New pictures and old panels. 20616

New pictures of the city. 62409

New pilgrim's progress. 100991-100992

New, plain and comprehensive English grammar. 95407

New plan of a perpetual civil calendar. (43327)

New plan of Philadelphia and adjoining districts. 61738

New plan to resume specie payments. (31631)

New play-thing for little boys and girls. 96134

New plottings in aid of the rebel doctrine of state sovereignty. 35844

New plottings to aid the rebellion. (35845)

New pocket almanac for the year 1789. 24972

New pocket atlas of the United States. 94326

New pocket biographical dictionary. 37901

New poem, in five parts. (46801)

New poems. 28105

New postage law of 1845. 1123

New post-office directory. 53389

New practical navigator. 50412

New practical system of human reason. 91694

New preface in reply to the accusations of Mr. Macaulay. (20377)

New priest in Conception Bay. 42467

New principle of tactics. 81321

New procedure in criminal and disciplinary causes of ecclesiastics. 84188-84191, 84201-84202, 84213-84214

New proclamation! By Thomas Gage. 97232

New project for reforming the English alphabet and orthography. 70871

New prospect before us. 20314, 94403

New psalm and a new funeral sermon. 63465

New purchase; or, early years in the far west. 29729

New purchase: or, seven and a half years in the far west. 29728

New quarterly review; and British colonial register. 53390

New quarterly review, and digest of current literature. 53391

New railway outlet from Chicago to the sea-board. 3146

New ready reckoner. 23977

New reasons for abolishing the slave trade. 91240

New rebellion. 63940

New recopilacion of the laws of Spain. 103429, 103434

New reformation in Europe and America. 769

New regime. see Norfolk new regime.

New "reign of terror" in the slaveholding states. 53392

New republic. 68309

New revolution. 31755

New Richmond theatre. A discourse. 9475

New river guide. 15123, (53393)

New Robinson Crusoe. 72232

New Rome. 63631

New route to California. 53394

New route to the east. 67430

New "sator resartus." 37771, 2d note after 94129

New sailing directions for the Caribbee or West-India islands. 66701

New sailing directions for the east coast of North America. 55487

New sailing directory for the Ethiopic or southern Atlantic Ocean; including the coasts of Brasil, &c. 66703

New sailing directory for the Ethiopic, or southern Atlantic Ocean, to the Rio de la Plata. 66702

New Salem, Mass. Academy. see New Salem Academy, New Salem, Mass.

New Salem, Mass. School Committee. 53396

New Salem Academy, New Salem, Mass. 53395

New scene interesting to the citizens. 53397

New scheme is clearly declared. 12305

New scheme, or essay for discharging the debts. 8070

New sea atlas. 79027

New sectional map of Illinois. 59486

New selection of arithmetical tables. 88501

New selection of sacred music. 85616

New selection of the most approved songs. 86950

New selection of the most popular songs. 86956

New self-supporting system of general education. 70872

Nw, slf-suportng systm of jnrl & librl education. (70874)

New sepulchure. 89774

New series of the Evangelical intelligencer. 53398, 65185

New series of the Harbinger of peace. 10081

New sermon for the fast day. 79891-(79894)

New set of copies. 95626

New sett of maps. (49903)

New settlement of Manamuskin. (14283)

New, sharp threshing instrument, having teeth. 53399

New slave laws of Jamaica and St. Christopher's examined. (35639)

New Society for the Benefit of the Indians, Washington, D. C. see Society for the Benefit of Indians, Washington, D. C.

New society, for the benefit of Indians, organized at the city of Washington, February, 1822. 34597, (53400)

New song, address'd to the Sons of Liberty. 86867

New song; or, the marvelous works of God. 89265

New song, on the repeal of the stamp-act. 90141

New song. To the tune of Nancy Dawson. 96322

New song. To the tune of the British grenadier. 101859

New song. To the tune of the British grenadiers. 101858

New song. Upon the flourishing of the settlement of Cohos. 103217

New songster. 12955

New south. 53401

New South American pilot. 55487

New South Church, Boston. see Boston. New South Church.

New South Church and Society. Sunday, July 28, 1816. 95191

New South Meeting-House, Dorchester, Mass. see Dorchester, Mass. New South Meeting-House.

New southern discovery. (67358)

New southern history of the war of the Confederates. 63873

New southerne discoverie. 67357

New Spain and the Anglo-American west. 105053

New Spain, or love in Mexico. 77454

New species of North American Coleoptera. 39666

New states. 45538

New states and territories. 49008

New story of an old monster. 12982, 17745, 3d note after 95765, 2d note after 102065

New supplies of gold. 55024

New survey of the West-India's. (26299)

New svrvey of the VVest-India's. (26298)

New survey of the West-Indies. 26300-26301

New Sweden, or the Swedish settlements on the Delaware. (133)

New sword exercise for cavalry. 96747

New system of education. 90230, 90233, 90236-90237, 90243, 90246

New system of fortification. 53404

New . . . system of geography. 48854

New system of geography, ancient and modern. (50940)

New system of husbandry. 98634, 98636

New system of military discipline. 53405

New system of modern geography, . . . by William Guthrie, Esq. 10858, (29327)

New system of modern geography; . . . . Compiled by Elijah Parish. (58603)

New system of modern geography, or a view of the present state of the world. 50970

New system of national military education. (82338)

New system of paper currency. 89613, 89615

New system of paper money. (53406)

New system of philosophy. 53407

New system of politics. 53408

New system of towing on canals and inland waters. 90852

New systeme of the mathematicks. 50415

New tables for determining the values of the coefficients. 85072

New tariff act. 104207

New tariff. Articles on which duties will be levied. (53409)

New tariff, of 1846. 31700

New tax bill. 65675

New tertiary fossil shells. (39486)

New Testament. 53411, (53414), 57090-57091

New Testament. . . . Appointed to be read by children. (53413)

New Testament dictionary. (82499)

New Testament in the Chippewa language. 12833

New Testament, in the Dakota language. 71332

New Testament interpretation of the Old. 2632

New Testament, in the Cree language. 17453

New Testament, in verse. 84553

New Testament of Our Lord and Saviour Jesus Christ; newly translated out of the original Greek. 53410

New Testament of Our Lord and Saviour Jesus Christ: translated into the Indian language. 22155

New Testament stories and reading book. 57086

New-Testament stories, in the Ojibua language. 26409

New Testament translated into the Choctaw language. 12875

New Testament. Translated into the Greenland language. 22875

New Testament . . . translated into the Ottawa. 57883

New test-i-ment. 91815

New Theatre, Philadelphia. see Philadelphia. New Theatre.

New themes for the protestant clergy. (14911), 14912

New Theological Seminary, Bangor, Me. 43967, (53415)

New theory of animal magnetism. 92135

New theory of political economy. 81373

New theory of terestial magnetism. 48166

New theory of the diurnal rotation of the earth. 105046

New theory of the earth. (80068)

New theory of the harmonious regularity. 93066

New theory of the two hemispheres. 95512

New theory on the causes of the motions of the planetary bodies. 71034

New thoughts on a serious subject. 15672, 102339

New thoughts on education. (63412)

New threepenny play thing for little giants. 96135

New times. 70251, 82898

New topographical war map of the southern states. 5611, 61015

New trade directory, for Philadelphia. 61606

New trade laid open. 53416

New traveller's guide through the United States. (49718)

New travels. 98464

New travels among the Indians of North America. 24509
New travels in the United States of America. 8028, 8031, 25139
New travels in the United States of America, including the commerce of America with Europe. 8026
New travels in the United States of America. Performed in 1788. (8025)
New travels in the United States of America, performed in M.DCC.LXXXVIII. (8016), 8027, 8029
New travels through North-America. (72036)
New travels to the westward. 19129, note before 98445-98445, 98447, 98451-98453, 98455, 98456, 98461, 98463, 98465
New treatise on large noses. 61873
New tribute to the memory of James Brainerd Taylor. 94475
New Union Free School and Academy, Newark, N. Y. 54885
New union song book. 59008
New unities. 84067
New universal atlas, exhibiting all the empires. 38022
New universal atlas, . . . with a special map. 49720
New universal biographical dictionary. 30322
New universal collection of authentic and entertaining voyages and travels. 20826
New universal collection of voyages and travels. 53417
New universal gazetteer. (50941)
New . . . universal geography. 37304
New universal history of the religious rites. 33993
New universal library. 82852
New universal traveller. (11183)
New Utrecht, N. Y. 53418
New vade mecum; or a pocket companion. 66529
New vade mecum; or, young clerk's magazine. 89384
New varieties of gold and silver coins. 21788
New version of the Psalms of David. By the Rev. Thomas Cradock. 17333
New version of the Psalms of David. By Thomas Cradock. 53419
New version of the Psalms of David, fitted to the tunes used in churches. 3471, 7315, 64998-(64999), (66441), 66449
New vicar of Bray. 3757
New view of society. 101368
New views of the causes, prevention, and cure of yellow fever. 68504
New views of the constitution of the United States. 94493
New views of the origin of the tribes and nations of America. 3819
New Virginia justice. 31340
New Virginia tobacco law. 100317
New voyage and description of the isthmus of America. 100940
New voyage into the northern countries. 38713
New voyage round the world. 18373-18374, 100940
New voyage round the world, by a course never sailed before. 19291
New voyage round the world in the years 1823, 24, 25, and 26. 38288
New voyage round the world in the years 1768, 1769, 1770, and 1771. 30936
New voyage to Carolina. 39451
New voyage to Georgia. 27079, 3d note after 106134

New voyage to Guinea. 84559, 94560
New voyage to the north. (38714)
New voyages and travels. 10616, 16772, 24453, 38292, 52158, 59212, 62509, 65696, 73150, 76707, 77858, 81508, 98614, 4th note after 100814, 101114
New voyages through North-America. 72035
New voyages to North-America. 29142, 38644-(38646), 62957
New way to carry a presidential election. (53420)
New way to get a husband. note after 88547
New Welt. note after 99383C
New Welt, das ist: Volkommen Beschreibung von Natur. 129
New Welt, der Landschaften vnnd Insulen. 24106, note after 99383C
New windmill. (10688)
New witnesses proved old hereticks. 59720
New work. 98634-98635
New work for the Maine law. 12991
New work on odd fellowship. 72853
New world (New York) 4349
New world (Philadelphia) note after 84079
New world. A poem. 83841
New world. [By Harriette Fanning Read.] 68150
New world. [Edited by Park Benjamin.] 84162
New world in 1859. 53421
New world: or, the morning and evening gazette. 101579
New world planted. 17682
New world series. 82523
New world the old. (31196)
New Yankee Doodle. 53422, note before 97297
New year. 103813
New-year, Christmas, and birth-day present. 106206
New-year verses of the printers lads. 53423
New-year well-begun. 46431
New-year's address delivered before the Boston Young Men's Christian Association. 44350
New year's address, delivered to the citizens of Centerville. 85449
New year's address of the carrier of the Albany morning express. 42972
New year's address to the patrons of the Pennsylvania freeman. 103813
New-years-day. 53424
New year's day. (53426)
New-years-day, for 1820. 53425
New year's discourse, . . . before the Literary Institution in Greenville. 58656
New-year's discourse, delivered in Angelica, N. Y. 68059
New year's discourse of St. Christopher. 38162
New year's discourse, preached at Brookline. 31218
New-year's-gift. Being a sermon at Philadelphia. 21982
New-years-gift for fainting souls. 90161-90162
New year's gift for scribblers. (59189), 85431, 2d note after 97259
New year's gift, from a daughter of liberty and lover of truth. 103643
New year's gift; on the subject of peace and union. 24444
New year's gift; presented especially to the young people. 37925
New-year's gift to the Democrats. (13896), 67817-67818, 1st note after 99797
New year's gifts of the spirit. 26078
New-year's hymn. 98295
New-year's-lay. 105497
New-year's ode. 103146

New-year's present to the people of South
Carolina. 87897, note after 89935
New-year's reflections. 53427
New year's sermon: delivered at Duxborough,
Jan. 1, 1806. 935
New-year's sermon; delivered at Providence.
(32257)
New year's sermon. Delivered in the Con-
gregational Church, Jewett City. 80529
New year's sermon, January 6, 1861. 28013
New year's sermon, preached at Lee, Jan.
1st, 1804. 34117
New year's sermon preached in Concord.
6953
New-year's sermon, preached . . . January
4th, 1824. 26624
New year's sermon, preached on the last day
of the old year. 89783
New years' sermons preached in . . . Bulfinch
Street Church. 28390
New year's verses, addressed to the kind
customers. (53428)
New-year's verses of those who deliver the
Pennsylvania ledger. 53429
New year's wish. "My kind benefactors a
new year commences." 103147
New year's wish. "Now fair aurora paints
the east." 103148
New year's wish of an affectionate minister
for the people of his charge. 30521
New year's wish. The author being absent by
reason of the small-pox. 103149
New-yeeres gift to Virginea. 17425, note after
99858, 2d note after 100502
New York (Archdiocese) 70079 see also New
York (Ecclesiastical Province) Roman
Catholics of New York City.
New York (Archdiocese) Archbishop (Hughes)
(30810) see also Hughes, John Joseph,
Abp., 1797-1864.
New York (Archdiocese) Archbishop (McCloskey)
72958-72959 see also McCloskey, John,
Cardinal, 1810-1885.
New York (Archdiocese) Synod, 1842. 72927
New York (Archdiocese) Synod, 1868. 72958
New York (Archdiocese) Synod, 1882. 72959
New York (City) 18588, 53515, 54022, 54069,
(54072), 54086, 54165, (54206), 54222,
(54226), 54357, 54359, 54369, (54522),
54601-54602, 54613, (54664), (54717),
(54732), 90290 see also Brooklyn.
New York (City) claimants 73956, 73961
New York (City) defendants 74603, (79837)
New York (City) petitioners 53956, 54379,
95462
New York (City) respondents 102175
New York (City) Abbot Collegiate Institution
for Young Ladies. see Abbot Collegiate
Institution for Young Ladies, New York.
New York (City) Academy of Arts. (54016)
New York (City) Adjourned Meeting of Delegates
of Various Banks, from Different States
in the Union, 1838. see Bank Con-
vention, New York, 1838.
New York (City) African Education and Civili-
zation Society. see African Education
and Civilization Society, New York.
New York (City) Agent to Attend the Exhibition
of the Industry of All Nations, 1851.
(36184) see also Johnson, Benjamin P.
New York (City) Agents Appointed to Establish
a School for Heathen Youth. see Agents
Appointed to Establish a School for
Heathen Youth, New York.
New York (City) All Saints' Church. Wardens
and Vestrymen. 90706

New York (City) Almshouse, Blackwell's Island.
54073 see also New York (City) Hospital
and Almshouse.
New York (City) Almshouse, Blackwell's Island.
Board of Governors. President. 54073
New York (City) Almshouse, Blackwell's Island.
Board of Governors. Select Committee.
54073
New York (City) Almshouse, Blackwell's Island.
Board of Governors. Select Committee.
Majority. 54073
New York (City) Almshouse, Blackwell's Island.
Commissioners. 54073
New York (City) Almshouse, Blackwell's Island.
Commissioners. plaintiffs 103312
New York (City) Almshouse and Penitentiary,
Bellevue. Chaplain. 90209 see also
Stanford, John.
New York (City) American Academy of the Fine
Arts. see American Academy of the Fine
Arts, New York.
New York (City) American Chess Congress,
1857. see American Chess Congress,
New York, 1857.
New York (City) American Female Guardian
Society. see American Female Guardian
Society, New York.
New York (City) American Geographical and
Statistical Society. see American Geo-
graphical Society of New York.
New York (City) American Geographical Society
see American Geographical Society of New
York.
New York (City) American Health Convention,
2d, 1839. see American Health Convention,
2d, New York, 1839.
New York (City) American Home Missionary
Society. see Congregational Home
Missionary Society.
New York (City) American Institute. see
American Institute of the City of New York
New York (City) American Musical Convention,
1845. see American Musical Convention,
New York, 1845.
New York (City) American Temperance Union.
see American Temperance Union, New
York.
New York (City) American Tract Society.
see American Tract Society. New York.
New York (City) Andiron Club. see Andiron
Club, New York.
New York (City) Annual Dinner of the Hide and
Leather Trade, 1859. see Annual Dinner
of the Hide and Leather Trade of the City
of New York, 1859.
New York (City) Anti-duelling Association.
see Anti-duelling Association of New
York.
New York (City) Anti-Lecompton Meeting,
1858. see Democratic Party. New York
New York City.
New York (City) Anti-slavery Convention of
American Women, 1837. see Anti-slavery
Convention of American Women, New York,
1837.
New York (City) Apprentices' Library. see
Apprentices' Library, New York.
New York (City) Arbeiterbund. see Arbeiter-
bund, New York.
New York (City) Ascension Association. see
New York (City) Church of the Ascension.
Association.
New York (City) Assessor. 7123
New York (City) Associated Banks. see
Associated Banks of New York City.

New York (City) Association for Improving the Condition of the Poor. see Association for Improving the Condition of the Poor, New York.

New York (City) Association for the Exhibition of the Industry of All Nations. see Association for the Exhibition of the Industry of All Nations, New York.

New York (City) Association for the Relief of the Industrious Poor. see Association for the Relief of the Industrious Poor, New York.

New York (City) Association of the Girls' Industrial School. see Association of the Girls' Industrial School, New York.

New York (City) Astor Library. see New York (City) Public Library. Astor Library.

New York (City) Athenaeum. see New York Athenaeum.

New York (City) Athenaeum Association. see Athenaeum Association, New York.

New York (City) Athenaeum Club. see Athenaeum Club, New York.

New York (City) Auctioneers. petitioners 54106

New York (City) Auditor. (54212)

New York (City) Auxiliary Bible and Common Prayer Book Society. see New York Auxiliary Bible and Common Prayer Book Society.

New York (City) Bank Convention, 1837. see Bank Convention, New York, 1837.

New York (City) Bank Convention, 1838. see Bank Convention, New York, 1838.

New York (City) Bank of America. see Bank of America, New York.

New York (City) Bank of Commerce. see Bank of Commerce, New York.

New York (City) Bank of Savings. see Bank of Savings, New York.

New York (City) Banks. see Banks of New York City.

New York (City) Banks. Delegates to the Bank Convention, 1837. see Bank Convention, New York, 1837. Delegates of the Banks of New York City.

New York (City) Banquet Given to Mr. Cyrus W. Field, 1866. see New York (State) Chamber of Commerce of the State of New York. Banquet Given to Mr. Cyrus W. Field, 1866.

New York (City) Banquet to Senor Matias Romero, 1867. see New York (City) Dinner to Senor Matias Romero, 1867.

New York (City) Baptist Association. see Baptists. New York. New York Baptist Association.

New York (City) Baptist Education Society. see Society of Correspondence in New York, with the Baptist Education Society in Philadelphia.

New York (City) Baptist General Convention for Missionary Purposes. 5th Triennial Meeting, 1826. see Baptists. New York. General Convention for Missionary Purposes. 5th Triennial Meeting, 1826.

New York (City) Baptist Theological Seminary. Board of Trustees. 90204

New York (City) Bar. 37476

New York (City) Bar. Committee. (31851)

New York (City) Barclay Street Gallery. see American Academy of the Fine Arts, New York. Barclay Street Gallery.

New York (City) Bellevue Hospital. 54412

New York (City) Bellevue Hospital. Board of Ten Governors. Select Committee. 54412

New York (City) Bellevue Hospital. Local Visiting Committee. see Local Visiting Committee of Bellevue and Other Hospitals, New York.

New York (City) Bellevue Hospital Medical College. see Bellevue Hospital Medical College, New York.

New York (City) Bethel Baptist Church. 69689

New York (City) Bethel Baptist Church. Trustees. 47746, 54388

New Uork (City) Bethel Free School. 54115

New York (City) Bethel Free School. petitioners 69589

New York (City) Bible and Common Prayer Book Society. see Bible and Common Prayer Book Society, New York.

New York (City) Bible Society. see New York Bible Society.

New York (City) Bloomingdale Asylum for the Insane. see Bloomingdale Asylum, White Plains, N. Y.

New York (City) Board for the Emigration, Preservation, and Improvement of the Aborigines of America. 20457

New York (City) Board of Aldermen. (54234), (54248), 54597 see also New York (City) Joint Meetings of the Board of Aldermen And Assistant Aldermen.

New York (City) Board of Aldermen. defendants 89349

New York (City) Board of Assistant Aldermen. (54248), 54597-(54598) see also New York (City) Joint Meetings of the Board of Aldermen And Assistant Aldermen.

New York (City) Board of Commissioners of Health. see New York (City) Board of Health.

New York (City) Board of Commissioners of Public Charities and Correction. 54419

New York (City) Board of Commissioners of the Central Park. 54156-54158

New York (City) Board of Commissioners of the Central Park. Special Committee. 54158

New York (City) Board of Commissioners of the Central Park. Engineer-in-Chief. 54158 see also Viele, Egbert Ludovickus, 1825-1902.

New York (City) Board of Commissioners of the Department of Public Parks. see New York (City) Department of Parks. Board of Commissioners.

New York (City) Board of Commissioners of the Metropolitan Fire Department. (54278)

New York (City) Board of Councilmen. see New York (City) Common Council.

New York (City) Board of Education. 24919, (54120)-54121, 54194, 54354, (79337)

New York (City) Board of Education. Board of Officers of the Seventh Ward. 54127

New York (City) Board of Education. Clerk. 54614, 66516 see also Boese, Thomas.

New York (City) Board of Education. Committee on the Annual Apportionment. 54121

New York (City) Board of Education. Committee on the Use of the Bible in the Public Schools. 54121

New York (City) Board of Education. Executive Committee on Normal Schools. 54121

New York (City) Board of Education. Grand Reception Extended by the Pupils of the Public Grammar Schools . . . to Peter Cooper, 1858. see Grand Reception Extended by the Pupils of the Public

Grammar Schools . . . to Peter Cooper, New York, 1858.

New York (City) Board of Education. School Inspector. 31202 see also Hacker, John.

New York (City) Board of Education. Select Committee on Establishing a Free Academy for Females. 54121

New York (City) Board of Education. Select Committee to Which was Referred a Communication from the Trustees of the Fourth Ward. 54121

New York (City) Board of Education. Special Committee on the Claims of the Public School Society. 54121

New York (City) Board of Education. Trustees of the Fourth Ward. 54121

New York (City) Board of Excise. see New York (City) Department of Excise.

New York (City) Board of Fire Underwriters. see Board of Fire Underwriters, New York.

New York (City) Board of Health. 53598, 54118, 54124, 54349, 54399-54400, (69947), see also Smith, Stephen, 1823-1922.

New York (City) Board of Health. Charter. 53457, 54399

New York (City) Board of Health. Sanitary Committee. 54124

New York (City) Board of Health. Sanitary Superintendent. 18439

New York (City) Board of Health. Select Committee on the Sources from Which Cows' Milk is Derived. Majority. 54124

New York (City) Board of Health. Select Committee on the Sources from Which Cows' Milk is Derived. Minority. 54124

New York (City) Board of Underwriters. see Board of Underwriters, New York.

New York (City) Bowery Savings Bank. see Bowery Savings Bank, New York.

New York (City) Boz Ball, 1842. see Boz Ball, New York, 1842.

New York (City) Branch of the United States Sanitary Commission. see United States Sanitary Commission. New York City Branch.

New York (City) Brick Presbyterian Church. 32435, 89767, note after 89770

New York (City) Brick Presbyterian Church. claimant 73956, 73961

New York (City) Broadway Railway Association. see Broadway Railway Association, New York.

New York (City) Broadway Tabernacle Church. (54136), (79299), (92272)

New York (City) Broadway Tabernacle Church. Session. (54136), 94370

New York (City) Broadway Tabernacle Anti-slavery Society. see Broadway Tabernacle Anti-slavery Society, New York.

New York (City) Bryant Festival, 1864. see Bryant Festival, New York, 1864.

New York (City) Burns Club. see Burns Club, New York.

New York (City) Cabinet of Natural History. see New York Academy of Sciences. New York State Museum.

New York (City) Cedar Street Presbyterian Church. Female Society for the Support of Theological Students.

New York (City) Celebration of the Centennial Anniversary of the Birth of Washington, 1832. 40838, 54149, 101785

New York (City) Celebration of the 85th Anniversary of the Birth day of Thomas Paine, Tammany Hall, 1832. see Celebration of the 85th Anniversary of the Birthday of Thomas Paine, Tammany Hall, New York, 1832.

New York (City) Celebration of the French Revolution, 1830. see Celebration of the French Revolution, New York, 1830.

New York (City) Celebration of the Settlement at Jamestown, 1860. see Old Dominion Society in the City of New York. Celebration of the Anniversary of the Settlement at Jamestown, Va., 1607, 1st, 1860.

New York (City) Celebration of Washington's Birthday, 1851. 54149

New York (City) Cemetery of the Evergreens. (23293)

New York (City) Census, 1807. 54150

New York (City) Census, 1865. 33154

New York (City) Central Fremont and Dayton Glee Club. see Central Fremont and Dayton Glee Club of the City of New York.

New York (City) Central Homoeopathic Dispensary. see New York Central Homoeopathi Dispensary.

New York (City) Central Park. Commissioners. see New York (City) Board of Commissioners of the Central Park.

New York (City) Century Association. see Century Association, New York.

New York (City) Century Club. see Century Association, New York.

New York (City) Chamber of Commerce. see New York (State) Chamber of Commerce of the State of New York.

New York (City) Charter. 6389, (32400), 54028, 54032, (54074), 54164-(54176), (54337), 54351, 74603

New York (City) Chatham-Street Chapel. Female Anti-slavery Society. 54270

New York (City) Children's Aid Society. see Children's Aid Society, New York.

New York (City) Children's Asylum. 54178

New York (City) Christ Church. 54180

New York (City) Christ Church. Vestry. 54180

New York (City) Chirst Church. Vestry. Committee. 54180

New York (City) Christ Church Parish Ladies' Charitable Association. 54179

New York (City) Christ Church Parish School Association. 54179

New York (City) Christian Union. see Christian Union of New York and Brooklyn.

New York (City) Church and Hospital for British Emigrants Arriving at New York (Proposed) 54088

New York (City) Church of Christ. 21923

New York (City) Church of Christ in Fair-Street. see New York (City) Fair-Street Church of Christ.

New York (City) Church of the Ascension. 4271-(4272), 56024

New York (City) Church of the Ascension. Association. President. 82943 see also Smith, John Cotton, 1826-1882.

New York (City) Church of the Ascension. Rector. 4271-(4272), 56024 see also Bedell, Gregory Thurston. Smith, John Cotton, 1826-1882.

New York (City) Church of the Ascension. St. Luke's Hospital Association. 75416

New York (City) Church of the Epiphany. Vestry. 84507

New York (City) Church of the Holy Communion Junior Association of St. Luke's Hospital. 75415

New York (City) Church of the Messiah. (54214

New York (City) Church of the Messiah. Charter. (54214)

New York (City) Church of the Puritans. 12403, 54184, (61367)

New York (City) Church of the Puritans. Deacons. 12403, 54184

New York (City) Citizens. 42551, 54588, 54589, 54596, 54607, 95993

New York (City) Citizens. petitioners, 54386, 54573, 69579, 84556

New York (City) Citizens' Banquet to Senor Matias Romero, 1867. see New York (City) Dinner to Senor Matias Romero, 1867.

New York (City) Citizens Committee on Obsequies of Abraham Lincoln in Union Square, April 25, 1865. (56438)

New York (City) Citizens' Committee on Public Honors to Lieutenant-General Grant, 1865. 28317

New York (City) Citizens' Committee on the Boz Ball, 1842. see New York (City) Committee of Citizens on the Boz Ball, 1842.

New York (City) Citizens' Dinner to Senor Matias Romero, 1864. see New York (City) Dinner to Senor Matias Romero, 1864.

New York (City) Citizens' Mass Meeting, 1866. see Republican Party. New York. New York City.

New York (City) Citizens' Meeting, 1773. see New York (City) Citizens.

New York (City) Citizens' Meeting, Convened at the Request of the Board of Managers of the American Bible Society, 1816. see New York (City) Meeting of Citizens of New York and Others, Convened at the Request of the Board of Managers of the American Bible Society, 1816.

New York (City) Citizens' National War Committee. see National War Committee of the Citizens of New York City.

New York (City) Citizens' Reception to the Survivors of the Officers and Crews of the United States Frigates Cumberland and Congress, 1862. see New York (City) Reception By Citizens of New York to the Survivors of the Officers and Crews of the United States Frigates Cumberland and Congress, 1862.

New York (City) City College. 54121, 54284

New York (City) City College. Class of 1868. 86935

New York (City) City College. Executive Committee. 54121

New York (City) City College. Library. 54284

New York (City) Clinton Hall. 54197

New York (City) Clinton Hall Association. see Clinton Hall Association, New York.

New York (City) Club National de Langue Francaise. see Club National de Langue Francaise, New York.

New York (City) College of New York. see Columbia University.

New York (City) College of Physicians and Surgeons. see Columbia University. Medical College.

New York (City) College of the City of New York. see New York (City) City College.

New York (City) Collegiate Church. 31237, (31250), 54616, 66448

New York (City) Collegiate Church. Consistory. 8700, 66448

New York (City) Collegiate Institution for the Education of Young Ladies. see Abbot Collegiate Institution for Young Ladies, New York.

New York (City) Collegiate Reformed Protestant Dutch Church. see New York (City) Collegiate Church.

New York (City) Colored Home. see New York (City) Lincoln's Hospital and Home.

New York (City) Colored Home and Hospital. see New York (City) Lincoln's Hospital and Home.

New York (City) Columbian Order. see Tammany Society, New Yotk.

New York (City) Commemoration of the Triumph of Liberty in France, 1830. 54210

New York (City) Commercial Academy. see Commercial Academy, New York.

New York (City) Commissioner of Docks and Ferries. 83847, 83849 see also Smith, Robert A. C., 1857-

New York (City) Commissioners of Common Schools. 54629 see also New York (City) Board of Education.

New York (City) Commissioners of Health. 54203 see also New York (City) Board of Health. New York (City) Department of Health.

New York (City) Commissioners of Public Charities and Correction. 54204

New York (City) Commissioners of the Almshouse. see New York (City) Almhouse, Blackwell's Island. Commissioners.

New York (City) Commissioners of the Central Park. see New York (City) Board of Commissioners of the Central Park.

New York (City) Commissioners of the Sinking Fund. (54212)

New York (City) Commissioners to Secure the Establishment, Government, &c. &c., of Common Schools. see New York (State) Commissioners to Secure the Establishment, &c. &c., of Common Schools in the City of New York.

New York (City) Committee Appointed at Mrs. Vanderwater's, 1784. 53473, 54042, 83604

New York (City) Committee Duely Appointed by a Meeting of Officers, Held on the 13th March, A. D. 1833. see New York (City) Committee of Officers of the War of 1812.

New York (City) Committee for the Relief of Portland. see Committee for the Relief of Portland, New York.

New York (City) Committee of Arrangement for the Funeral Ceremonies in Honor of the Late General Washington, 1800. 101814, 101880

New York (City) Committee of Citizens on the Boz Ball, 1842. 54715

New York (City) Committee of Correspondence, Duly Appointed by a Meeting of Officers, Held on the 15th September, A. D. 1826. see New York (City) Committee of Officers of the War of 1812.

New York (City) Committee of Mechanics. (53505), 54054

New York (City) Committee of Merchants and Bankers. see Committee of Merchants and Bankers of the City of New York.

New York (City) Committee of Merchants for the Relief of Colored People Suffering from the Late Riots. see Committee of Merchants for the Relief of Colored People Suffering from the Late Riots in . . . New York.

New York (City) Committee of Merchants, Opposed to the Auction System. see Committee of New York Merchants, Opposed to the Auction System.

New York (City) Committee of Non-Episcopalian Denominations. see Committee of Non-Episcopalian Denominations in New York.

New York (City) Committee of Officers of the War of 1812. 95953-95954

New York (City) Committee of Officers of the War of 1812. Agent. (38814), 95954 see also Watson, Joseph, fl. 1826.

New York (City) Committee of Safety. see New York (Colony) Committee of Safety, 1775-1776.

New York (City) Committee of the Greek Fund. see Committee of the Greek Fund, New York.

New York (City) Committee of the Sons of Liberty. see Sons of Liberty, New York. Committee.

New York (City) Committee of the Ward Schools. 83940, 83946, 83948

New York (City) Committee of Vigilance. see New York Committee of Vigilance.

New York (City) Committee on Fortifying the Harbor. (54636)

New York (City) Committee on Laws. 54637

New York (City) Committee on Salvages. (69824)

New York (City) Committee on the Festivities Observed in Honor of the Completion of the Grand Erie Canal, 1825. 92149

New York (City) Committee on the Fire in New Street. 54642

New York (City) Committee to Ascertain, By Direct Question, Whether Sundry Persons, Were Purchasing and Shipping Goods for the Troops at Boston, 1774. 95984, 95990

New York (City) Committee to Conduct the Order of Receiving Their Excellencies Governor Clinton and General Washington, 1783. 101860

New York (City) Committee to Consider the Expediency of Entering Into Measures to Encourage Industry and Frugality, and Employ the Poor. 54631

New York (City) Committee to Examine Public Accounts. 54641

New York (City) Committee to Prevent the Messrs. Murrays Involving Others in a Breach of the Association, 1775. 95999

New York (City) Committee to Promote the Passage of a Metropolitan Health Bill. see Committee to Promote the Passage of a Metropolitan Health Bill, New York, 1865.

New York (City) Committee Who Presented the Report on Ambulance and Camp-Hospital Corps to the Authorities in Washington, 1862. 54640 see also United States Sanitary Commission. New York City.

New York (City) Common Council. 18941, 30591, 54173, 54195, (54212), (54232), (54249), 54369, 54438, (54599), 54621, note after 54729, 56439, 65796, 86124, 105560

New York (City) Common Council. defendants 89349

New York (City) Common Council. petitioners 54158

New York (City) Common Council. Clerk. 56439 see also Valentine, David Thomas, 1801-1869.

New York (City) Common Council. Committee for Devising Measures to Suppress Gaming and Drunkenness. 54622

New York (City) Common Council. Committee for the Funeral Obsequies in Memory of William Henry Harrison. (30593)

New York (City) Common Council. Committee of Arrangements For the Funeral Ceremonies in Commemoration of the Death of Gen. Andrew Jackson. 54632

New York (City) Common Council. Committee of Arrangements of the Obsequies in Memory of Hon. Henry Clay. 13565

New York (City) Common Council. Committee on Fuel. Chairman. 54581, note after 97065 see also Troup, Robert.

New York (City) Common Council. Committee on New Streets. 54635

New York (City) Common Council. Committee on Pauperism. 54623

New York (City) Common Council. Committee on Public Schools. 54634

New York (City) Common Council. Committee on Wharves. 54639

New York (City) Common Council. Croton Aqueduct Committee. (54232)

New York (City) Common Council. Joint Special Committee for the Purpose of Making Arrangements for the Reception of Major-General Scott on His Return from Mexico. 78424

New York (City) Common Council. Select Committee on Erecting a Monument to the Memory of John Paulding. 59218

New York (City) Common Council. Select Committee to Inquire into the Application of that Part of the Literature Fund, Which is Apportioned by the Regents of the University. 54646

New York (City) Common Council. Special Committee to Make Arrangements for the Reception of Governor Louis Kossuth. 38267

New York (City) Common Council. Special Committee on Laying Out a New Park. 54652

New York (City) Common Council. Special Committee on Railroads. 54651

New York (City) Common Council. Special Committee on the Ordinance Creating the Aqueduct Department. Minority. (54232)

New York (City) Common Council. Special Committee on the Reorganization of the Police Department. 54584

New York (City) Common Council. Special Committee on the Route of the New York and Erie Railroad. (54729), 105560

New York (City) Common Council. Special Committee on the Use of Castle Garden as an Emigrant Depot. 54649

New York (City) Common Council. Special Committee on Widening West Street. Majority. (54659)

New York (City) Common Council. Special Committee on Widening West Street. Minority. (54659)

New York (City) Common Council. Special Committee Relative to the Catastrophe in Hague Street, 1850. 54648

New York (City) Common Council. Special Committee to Whom Was Referred the Communication from the Water Commissioners. (54232)

New York (City) Comptroller's Office. (54212), 54230, 54360

New York (city) Consolidated Stock and Petroleum Exchange. see Consolidated Stock and Petroleum Exchange of New York.

New York (City) Continental Club. see Continental Club, New York.

New York (City) Convention, 1836. 54174

New York (City) Convention, 1846. 54250, 54326

New York (City) Convention for Organizing the National Convention of Cotton Manufacturers and Planters, 1868. see National Convention of Cotton Manufacturers and Planters.

New York (City) Convention of Baptist Churches for Forming the New York Association, 1791. see Baptists. New York. Convention for Forming the New York Association, New York, 1791.

New York (City) Convention of Delegates, Appointed by Persons Interested in the Growth and Manufacture of Wool, 1831. see Wool Growers and Manufacturers Convention, New York, 1831.

New York (City) Convention of Delegates for the Formation of a Domestic Missionary Society, 1822. see Convention of Delegates for the Formation of a Domestic Missionary Society, New York, 1822.

New York (City) Convention of Delegates from Different Classes and Interests, 1864. see Fiscal Convention, New York, 1864.

New York (City) Convention of Delegates From the Anolition Society, 1794. see American Convention for Promoting the Abolition of Slavery, and Improving the Condition of the African Race.

New York (City) Convention of Insurance Companies, 1849. see Convention of Insurance Companies, New York, 1849.

New York (City) Convention of Laymen of the Methodist Episcopal Church, 1852. see Methodist Episcopal Church. Convention of Laymen, New York, 1852.

New York (City) Convention of Literary and Scientific Gentlemen, 1830. see Convention of Literary and Scientific Gentlemen, New York, 1830.

New York (City) Convention of Managers and Superintendents of Houses of Refuge and Schools of Reform in the United States, 1st, 1857. see Convention of Managers and Superintendents of Houses of Refuge and Schools of Reform in the United States. 1st, New York, 1857.

New York (City) Convention of Managers and Superintendents of Houses of Refuge and Schools of Reform in the United States, 2d, 1859. see Convention of Managers and Superintendents of Houses of Refuge and Schools of Reform in the United States. 2d, New York, 1859.

New York (City) Convention of the American Lyceum, 1831. see American Lyceum, or Society for the Improvement of Schools, and Diffusion of Useful Knowledge. Convention, New York, 1831.

New York (City) Convention of the Friends of Domestic Industry, 1831. see Friends of Domestic Industry.

New York (City) Convention of the Friends of Domestic Industry, 1832. see Friends of Domestic Industry.

New York (City) Convention of the Friends of National Industry, 1819. see Convention of the Friends of National Industry, New York, 1819.

New York (City) Convention of the Mutual Benefit Societies or Brotherhoods of the Protestant Episcopal Church in the United States, 1853. see Convention of the Mutual Benefit Societies or Brotherhoods of the Protestant Episcopal Church in the United States, New York, 1853.

New York (City) Convention of the Tobacco Trade, 1865. see Convention of Tobacconists, New York, 1865.

New York (City) Convention of Tobacconists, 1865. see Convention of Tobacconists, New York, 1865.

New York (City) Convention on the Location of the Post Office, 1836. see Convention on the Location of the Post Office in New York, New York, 1835.

New York (City) Cooper Institute Loyal Mass Meeting, 1863. see Loyal League of Union Citizens, New Yotk.

New York (City) Cooper Institute Loyal Meeting, to Support the Government, Prosecute the War, and Maintain the Union, 1863. see Loyal League of Union Citizens, New York.

New York (City) Cooper Union for the Advancement of Science and Art. see Cooper Union for the Advancement of Science and Art, New York.

New York (City) Coroner. 103190

New York (City) Coroner's Inquest on the Boiler Explosion on Board the U. S. "Double-Ender" Chenango, 1864. 6150, 12422

New York (City) Coroner's Jury. 40645

New York (City) Corporation of Trinity Church. see New York (City) Trinity Church.

New York (City) Council of Congregational Churches. see Congregational Churches in New York. Ecclesiastical Council, New York, 1589.

New York (City) Council of Hygiene. 84254

New York (City) Court of Common Pleas. 75948, 2d note after 96909

New York (City) Court of Oyer and Terminer. see New York (State) Court of Oyer and Terminer (New York County)

New York (City) Court of Sittings. (75958), 96875

New York (City) Court of Special Sessions. 8140

New York (City) Courts. 72617

New York (City) Croton Aqueduct. 37787

New York (City) Croton Aqueduct Board. (54232)

New York (City) Croton Aqueduct Department. (54232)

New York (City) Croton Aqueduct Department. petitioners (54232)

New York (City) Crystal Palace Exhibition, 1853. see New York (City) Crystal Palace Exposition, 1853.

New York (City) Crystal Palace Exposition, 1853. note after 56762, 70972

New York (City) Crystal Palace Exposition, 1853. Juries. note after 56762

New York (City) Crystal Palace Exposition, 1853. Jury on Musical Instruments. 54644

New York (City) Demilt Dispensary. see Demilt Dispensary, New York.

New York (City) Democratic Anti-abolition State Rights Association. see Democratic Anti-abolition State Rights Association, New York.

New York (City) Democratic Convention, 1840. see Democratic Party. New York. New York City. Convention, 1840.

New York (City) Democratic State Convention, 1840. see Democratic Party. New York. Convention, New York, 1840.

New York (City) Democratic State Convention, 1862. see Democratic Party. New York. Convention, New York, 1862.

New York (City) Democratic League. see Democratic League, New York.

New York (City) Democratic Republican Association. see Democratic Republican Association, New York.

New York (City) Democratic Society. see Democratic Society, New York.

New York (City) Democratic Young Men's General Committee. see Democratic Party. New York. New York City. Young Men's General Committee.

New York (City) Department of Excise. 54122, 54349, 54398

New York (City) Department of Health. 2747, 4057, 18862, 54689, 84262-84263 see also New York (City) Board of Health. New York (City) Commissioners of Health.

New York (City) Department of Health. Board of Health. see New York (City) Board of Health.

New York (City) Department of Parks. Board of Commissioners. 8313, 54241

New York (City) Deputies of Their High Mightinesses. pseud. see Deputies of Their High Mightinesses for the City of New York. pseud.

New York (City) Deutsche Gesellschaft. see Deutsche Gesellschaft der Stadt New York.

New York (City) Deutschen Gesellschaft. see Deutsche Gesellschaft der Stadt New York.

New York (City) Dinner to Senor Matias Romero, 1864. 73024, 73026

New York (City) Dinner to Senor Matias Romero, 1867. 73023

New York (City) Dispensaries. 54690 see also Demilt Dispensary, New York. Eastern Dispensary, New York. New York (City) North Western Dispensary. New York (City) Northern Dispensary. New York Dispensary, New York.

New York (City) Dispensary. see New York Dispensary, New York.

New York (City) Eagle Fire Company. see Eagle Fire Company, New York.

New York (City) East River Industrial School for Girls. see East River Industrial School for Girls, New York.

New York (City) Eastern Dispensary. see Eastern Dispensary, New York.

New York (City) Ecclesiastical Council, 1859. see Congregational Churches in New York, 1859.

New York (City) Eclectic Medical College. (54256)

New York (City) Economical School. see Economical School, New York.

New York (City) Eglise Protestante Francaise du Saint Spirit. see New York (City) French Church Du Saint Spirit.

New York (City) Eighteenth Ward Republican Festival, 1860. see Eighteenth Ward Republican Festival, New York, 1860.

New York (City) English Evangelical Lutheran Church. see English Evangelical Lutheran Church in New York.

New York (City) Episcopal Mission to Seamen. see Protestant Episcopal Mission to Seamen, New York.

New York (City) Episcopal Sunday School Society. see Protestant Episcopal Sunday School Society, New York.

New York (City) Episcopal Sunday School Union. see General Protestant Episcopal Sunday School Union, New York.

New York (City) Evangelical Union Anti-slavery Society. see Evangelical Union Anti-slavery Society, New York.

New York (City) Everett Club. see Everett Club, New York.

New York (City) Everett Literary Union. see Everett Literary Union, New York.

New York (City) Executive Committee of Citizens and Taxpayers for Financial Reform. see Executive Committee of Citizens and Taxpayers for Financial Reform of the City of New York.

New York (City) Executive Committee on Auction Regulations. see Executive Committee on Auction Regulations, New York.

New York (City) Exhibition of the Industry of All Nations, 1853-1854. 23398-23399, 81066 see also Association for the Exhibition of the Industry of All Nations, New York.

New York (City) Fair-Street Church of Christ. 54183

New York (City) Farewell Meeting for Dr. Massie, of London, 1863. see New York State Anti-slavery Society. Farewell Meeting for Dr. Massie, of London, New York, 1863.

New York (City) Farmers . . . and Other Working Men. see Farmers, . . . and Other Working Men, of the City and County of New York.

New York (City) Female Anti-slavery Society of Chatham-Street Chapel. see New York (City) Chatham-Street Chapel. Female Anti-slavery Society.

New York (City) Female Association. see Female Association, New York.

New York (City) Female Auxiliary Bible Society. see New York Female Auxiliary Bible Society.

New York (City) Female Benevolent Society. see Female Benevolent Society of New York.

New York (City) Female High School. 54273

New York (City) Female Society. see Female Society, New York.

New York (City) Female Society of the Presbyterian Congregation in Cedar Street for the Support of Theological Students. see New York (City) Cedar Street Presbyterian Church. Female Society for the Support of Theological Students.

New York (City) Festival Given to the National Unitarian Convention, 1865. see National Unitarian Convention, New York, 1865.

New York (City) Fire Department. Board of Commissioners. see New York (City) Board of Commissioners of the Metropolitan Fire Department.

New York (City) Fire Department. Chief Engineer. (54278)

New York (City) First Annual Meeting of the National Board of Fire Underwriters. see

National Board of Fire Underwriters.
Annual Meeting, 1st, New York, 1867.

New York (City) First Baptist Church. (58796),
90676

New York (City) First Baptist Church. Corporation. Majority. 90676

New York (City) First Congregational Church.
(54213)

New York (City) First Congregational Church.
Book and Tract Society. 2066

New York (City) First Free Presbyterian
Church. 54586

New York (City) First Presbyterian Church.
Pastor. 47674, 62534 see also Phillips,
William Wirt.

New York (City) Fiscal Convention, 1864. see
Fiscal Convention, New York, 1864.

New York (City) Five Points House of Industry.
24634, 54280, 54419

New York (City) Five Points House of Industry.
Board of Managers. 54280

New York (City) Five Points House of Industry.
Charter. 54280

New York (City) Five Points House of Industry.
Superintendent. 54280

New York (City) Five Points House of Industry.
Trustees. 54280

New York (City) Flushing Institute. see Saint
Paul's College, Flushing, N. Y.

New York (City) Foreign Missionary Society.
see Foreign Missionary Society of New
York and Brooklyn.

New York (City) Fourth Ward Industrial School
for Girls. 54281

New York (City) Free Academy. see New
York (City) City College.

New York (City) Free School. Trustees.
petitioners 54115, 69689

New York (City) Free School Society. see
Free School Society, New York.

New York (City) Fremont & Dayton Central
Club. see Fremont & Dayton Central
Club of the City of New York.

New York (City) French Benevolent Society.
see Societe Francaise de Bienfaisance,
New York.

New York (City) French Church du Saint
Spirit. petitioners 53665

New York (City) French Church du Saint
Spirit. Consistory. (73448)-73449, 2d
note after 97148, 99283

New York (City) French Protestant Church.
see New York (City) French Church du
Saint Spirit.

New York (City) French Reformed Protestant
Church. see New York (City) French
Church du Saint Spirit.

New York (City) Friends of Judge Yates.
Special Committee. see Special Com-
mittee Appointed by the Friends of Judge
Yates in the City of New York.

New York (City) Friends of Liberty. see
Friends of Liberty, New York.

New York (City) Funeral Services for Those
Slain in the Riots of July, September 20,
1863. 54700

New York (City) Gallery of the Fine Arts.
see New York Gallery of the Fine Arts,
New York.

New York (City) General Committee of Repub-
lican Young Men. see Democratic
Party. New York. New York City.
General Committee of Young Men.

New York (City) General Committee of Whig
Young Men. see Whig Party. New

York. New York City. General Committee of Whig Young Men.

New York (City) General Protestant Episcopal
Sunday School Union. see General
Protestant Episcopal Sunday School Union,
New York.

New York (City) General Republican Committee.
see Democratic Party. New York. New
York City. General Committee.

New York (City) General Society of Mechanics
and Tradesmen. see General Society of
Mechanics and Tradesmen of the City of
New York.

New York (City) General Theological Seminary
of the Protestant Episcopal Church in the
U. S. 26910, (54291), 54551, (66153)

New York (City) General Theological Seminary
of the Protestant Episcopal Church in the
U. S. Associate Alumni. (54291), 89107,
89342

New York (City) General Theological Seminary
of the Protestant Episcopal Church in the
U. S. Board of Trustees. 26910, 26911,
(66153)

New York (City) General Theological Seminary
of the Protestant Episcopal Church in the
U. S. Charles and Elizabeth Ludlow
Professor of Ecclesiastical Polity and Law.
petitioner 90659

New York (City) General Theological Seminary
of the Protestant Episcopal Church in the
U. S. Charter. (66153)

New York (City) General Theological Seminary
of the Protestant Episcopal Church in the
U. S. Directors. 29610

New York (City) General Theological Seminary
of the Protestant Episcopal Church in the
U. S. Dean. 72491 see also Johnson,
Samuel Roosevelt.

New York (City) General Theological Seminary
of the Protestant Episcopal Church in the
U. S. Library. (66153)

New York (City) General Theological Seminary
of the Protestant Episcopal Church in the
U. S. Special Committee on Amendments
to the Constitution. (66153)

New York (City) General Theological Seminary
of the Protestant Episcopal Church in the
U. S. Special Committee on the Memorial
of the Charles and Elizabeth Ludlow
Professor of Ecclesiastical Polity and Law.
90659

New York (City) General Theological Seminary
of the Protestant Episcopal Church in the
U. S. Society of Inquiry Respecting the
Advancement of Christianity. Committee
of Correspondence. (66153)

New York (City) General Theological Seminary
of the Protestant Episcopal Church in the
U. S. Trustees. (54291)

New York (City) General Theological Seminary
of the Protestant Episcopal Church in the
U. S. Visitors. (66153)

New York (City) German-American Citizens.
petitioners 54688, 1st note after 94139

New York (City) German Democratic Central
Club. see German Democratic Central
Club, New York.

New York (City) German Society. see German
Society of the City of New York.

New York (City) Girls' Industrial School
Association. see Association of the Girls'
Industrial School, New York.

New York (City) Grace Church Charity School.
54295

New York (City) Grace Church Education Society. 54295

New York (City) Grace Parish. 54295

New York (City) Graduated Tax Association. see Graduated Tax Association, New York.

New York (City) Grand Democratic Meeting, 1838. see Democratic Party. New York. New York City.

new York (City) Grand Miscellaneous Concert, for the Benefit of the Orphan Asylum, 1844. 54296

New York (City) Grand National Republican Meeting, 1830. see National Republican Party. New York. New York City.

New York (City) Grand Reception Extended by the Pupils of the Public Grammar Schools . . . to Peter Cooper, 1858. see Grand Reception Extended by the Pupils of the Public Grammar Schools. . . . to Peter Cooper, New York, 1858.

New York (City) Great Inaugural Mass Meeting of the Loyal National League, 1863. see Loyal National League of the State of New York.

New York (City) Great Meeting on Texas, 1836. see Great Meeting on Texas, New York, 1836.

New York (City) Great Peace Convention, 1863. see Great Peace Convention, New York, 1863.

New York (City) Great Public Meeting at the Tabernacle, 1854. (69349)

New York (City) Great Sanitary Fair, 1864. see New York (City) Metropolitan Fair, 1864.

New York (City) Great Union Meeting, 1859. see New York (City) Union Meeting, Dec. 19, 1859.

New York (City) Great Union War Ratification Meeting, 1862. see Loyal League of Union Citizens, New York.

New York (City) Greek Committee. see New York Greek Committee.

New York (City) Greene Street Synagogue. 57492

New York (City) Greenwich Reformed Dutch Church. Consistory. 73534

New York (City) Greenwood Cemetery. 28694, 28697-28700

New York (City) Half Orphan Asylum Society. see Society for the Relief of Half Orphan and Destitute Children in the City of New York.

New York (City) Harbor Commissioners. 54655

New York (City) Headquarters of the Fenian Brotherhood. see Fenian Brotherhood. New York. Headquarters, New York.

New York (City) Health Department. see New York (City) Department of Health.

New York (City) Heart-in-Hand Fire Company. see Heart-in-Hand Fire Company, New York.

New York (City) Home for the Friendless. see American Female Guardian Society, New York. Home for the Friendless.

New York (City) Hospital. see New York Hospital.

New York (City) Hospital and Almshouse. State Preacher. (22383)-22384 see also Ely, Ezra Stiles.

New York (City) House and School of Industry. see New York House and School of Industry.

New York (City) House of Mercy. see New York House of Mercy.

New York (City) House of Refuge. see Society for the Reformation of Juvenile Delinquents. New York. House of Refuge.

New York (City) Hubard Gallery. see Hubard Gallery, New York.

New York (City) Humane Society. see Humane Society of the State of New York.

New York (City) Industrial Exhibition, 1854. see New York Industrial Exhibition, New York, 1854.

New York (City) Infant Asylum. see New York Infant Asylum.

New York (City) Inhabitants. see New York (City) Citizens.

New York (City) Inspector of Firewood. 54192, (54278)

New York (City) Inspector of Health. 54618

New York (City) Inspector of Interments. 54193, 54689

New York (City) Inspector of Mortality. 54689, note after 94172

New York (City) Institution. see New York Institution, New York.

New York (City) Insurance Commissioner. 54323

New York (City) Italian School. see Children's Aid Society, New York. Italian School

New York (City) John-Street Church. (54151)

New York (City) Joint Meetings of the Board of Aldermen and Assistant Aldermen. 54606 see also New York (City) Board of Aldermen. New York (City) Board of Assistant Aldermen.

New York (City) Journeymen Cordwainers. see Journeymen Cordwainers of the City of New York.

New York (City) Journeymen House Carpenters. see Journeymen House Carpenters of the City of New York.

New York (City) Jury of Inquest on the Loss of the Steamboat Lexington, 1840. (26146), 103190

New York (City) Juvenile Asylum. see New York Juvenile Asylum.

New York (City) King's College. see Columbia University.

New York (City) Ladies' Anti-slavery Society. see Ladies' New York Anti-slavery Society Society.

New York (City) Ladies' Home for Sick and Wounded Soldiers. see Ladies' Home for Sick and Wounded Souldiers, New York.

New York (City) Ladies Society, for the Relief of Poor Widows With Small Children. see Ladies' Society for the Relief of Poor Widows With Small Children, New York.

New York (City) Law Institute. see New York Law institute.

New York (City) Leake and Watts Orphan House. Trustees. plaintiffs 54701

New York (City) Library. see New York (City) Public Library.

New York (City) Lincoln's Hospital and Home. 85981-85983

New York (City) Lincoln's Hospital and Home. Charter. 85981-85982

new York (City) Lincoln's Hospital and Home. Resident Physician. 54200

New York (City) Liquor Dealers and Brewers of the Metropolitan Police District. see Liquor Dealers and Brewers of the Metropolitan Police District, New York.

New York (City) Literary and Philosophical Society. see Literary and Philosophical Society of New York.

New York (City) Literary Society. see Literary Society, New York.

New York (City) Lloyd's Association. see Lloyd's Association, New York.

New York (City) Local Visiting Committee of Bellevue and Other Hospitals. see Local Visiting Committee of Bellevue and Other Hospitals, New York.

New York (City) Loyal League of Union Citizens. see Loyal League of Union Citizens, New York.

New York (City) Loyal Mass Meeting, Cooper Institute, 1863. see Loyal League of Union Citizens, New York.

New York (City) Loyal Meeting, to Support the Government, Prosecute the War, and Maintain the Union, Cooper Institute, 1863. see Loyal League of Union Citizens, New York.

New York (City) Lunatic Asylum, Blackwell's Island. Resident Physician. (54662)

New York (City) Lyceum. see New York Lyceum.

New York (City) Lyceum Building. Gallery. 54147

New York (City) Lyceum of Natural History. see New York Academy of Sciences.

New York (City) Lying-In Hospital. see Society of the Lying-In Hospital, New York.

New York (City) McClellan Legion. see McClellan Legion, New York.

New York (City) Madison Square Presbyterian Church. Session. 53381

New York (City) Madison Square Presbyterian Church. Young Men's Association. 54366

New York (City) Magdalen Society. see Magdalen Society of New York.

New York (City) Manhattan College. see Manhattan College, New York.

New York (City) Manumission Society. see New York Manumission Society.

New York (City) Marine Bible Society. see Marine Bible Society, New York.

New York (City) Marine Quarantine Hospital. Physician-in-Chief. (66944)

New York (City) Marine Society. see Marine Society, New York.

New York (City) Martyrs' Monument Association. see Martyrs' Monument Association, New York.

New York (City) Mass Meeting by the Democratic Republican Citizens of New York, Opposed to the Wilmot Proviso, 1850. see Democratic Party. New York. New York City.

New York (City) Mass Meeting, Cooper Institute, 1862. see Loyal League of Union Citizens, New York.

New York (City) Mass Meeting, Cooper Institute, 1863. see Loyal League of Union Citizens, New York.

New York (City) Mass Meeting, Cooper Institute, 1869. see Republican Party. New York. New York City.

New York (City) Mass Meeting of Citizens of New York to Approve the Principles Announced in the Message of Andrew Johnson, 1866. see Republican Party. New York. New York City.

New York (City) Mass Meeting of Loyal Citizens, Union Square, 1862. see Loyal League of Union Citizens, New York.

New York (City) Mass Meeting, Union Square, 1865. see National Celebration of Union Victories, New York, 1865.

New York (City) Maternal Association. see New York Maternal Association.

New York (City) Mayor, 1766-1776 (Hicks) 53620, 97291 see also Hicks, Whitehead, 1728-1780.

New York (City) Mayor, 1776-1777 (Duane) 54168 see also Duane, James, 1733-1797.

New York (City) Mayor, 1781-1782 (Cruger) 17721 see also Cruger, John, 1710-1792.

New York (City) Mayor, 1784-1789 (Duane) 54168 see also Duane, James, 1733-1797.

New York (City) Mayor, 1811-1815 (Clinton) 75949, 2d note after 96930A see also Clinton, De Witt, 1769-1828.

New York (City) Mayor, 1818-1821 (Colden) 2879, 72619, 96876, 101441 see also Colden, Cadwallader David, 1769-1834.

New York (City) Mayor, 1823-1826 (Paulding) 69957 see also Paulding, William, 1769-1854.

New York (City) Mayor, 1827-1828. 59218

New York (City) Mayor, 1833-1834 (Lee) 54395 see also Lee, Gideon, 1778-1841.

New York (City) Mayor, 1834-1836 (Lawrence) (54394), 94262 see also Lawrence, Cornelius Van Wyck, 1791-1861.

New York (City) Mayor, 1839-1841 (Varian) (54205) see also Varian, Isaac L.

New York (City) Mayor, 1841-1844 (Morris) plaintiff 54320 see also Morris, Robert H. plaintiff

New York (City) Mayor, 1844-1845 (Harper) 54584 see also Harper, James 1797-1875.

New York (City) Mayor, 1853-1854 (Westervelt) 54158 see also Westervelt, Jacob A.

New York (City) Mayor, 1857-1859 (Tiemann) 54056 see also Tiemann, Daniel F.

New York (City) Mayor, 1862-1864 (Opdyke) 57389 see also Opdyke, George.

New York (City) Mayor, 1879-1889 (Cooper) 84774 see also Cooper, Edward, 1824

New York (City) Mayor, Aldermen and Commonalty. defendants see New York (City) defendants

New York (City) Mayor, Recorder, Aldermen and Commonalty. see New York (City)

New York (City) Mayor's Court. 2879, 21923, 46955, 74432-74433, 75951, 75959, 96819, 96827, 2d note after 96891, 101441, 102461, 103185, 103188, 103312

New York (City) Mayor's Court. Reporter. see Clerk of the Court. pseud. reporter

New York (City) Mechanic and Scientific Institution. see Mechanic and Scientific Institution, New York.

New York (City) Mechanics and Other Workingmen. see Mechanics and Other Workingmen of New York.

New York (City) Medical College. see New York Medical College, New York.

New York (City) Medical College and Hospital for Women. see New York Medical College and Hospital for Women, New York.

New York (City) Medical Society. see Medical Society of the County of New York.

New York (City) Meeting, 1834. see Union Committee, New York, 1834.

New York (City) Meeting Convened at Martlings, 1811. 43615, note after 103267

New York (City) Meeting Held by Deaf-Mutes, 1853. 74996, note before 90783

New York (City) Meeting Held in Furtherance of the Establishment of a Free Church for British Emigrants at the Port of New York, 1845. see Meeting Held in Furtherance of the Establishment of a Free Church for British Emigrants at the Port of New York, New York, 1845.

New York (City) Meeting in Favor of Municipal Reform, 1844. 54592

New York (City) Meeting in Relation to St. Ann's Church for Deaf-Mutes, 1858. 65795 see also New York (City) Public Meeting Respecting St. Ann's Church for Deaf-Mutes, 1853. New York (City) St. Ann's Church for Deaf-Mutes.

New York (City) Meeting in Relation to the Establishment of a Large National Bank in This City, 1863. 54608

New York (City) Meeting of Bank Officers, 1863. Committee. 69934

New York (City) Meeting of Citizens Favorable to the Construction of a Canal from Rochester, on the Erie Canal, to Olean, on the Allegany River, 1835. see Meeting of Citizens Favorable to the Construction of a Canal from Rochester, on the Erie Canal, to Olean, on the Allegany River, New York, 1835.

New York (City) Meeting of Citizens of New York and Others, Convened at the Request of the Board of Managers of the American Bible Society, 1816. 54593

New York (City) Meeting of Delegates of Various Banks, from Different States in the Union, 1838. see Bank Convention, New York, 1838.

New York (City) Meeting of Episcopalians, 1812. see Meeting of Episcopalians in the City of New York, 1812.

New York (City) Meeting of Episcopalians, 1857. Committee. 90661

New York (City) Meeting of Irishmen, 1825. 47380

New York (City) Meeting of Mechanics and Other Workmen, 1831. 65867

New York (City) Meeting of Ship Masters and Ship Owners, 1839. see Meeting of Ship Masters and Ship Owners, New York, 1839.

New York (City) Meeting of the Citizens of New York, to Express Sympathy and Respect for the Mexican Republican Exiles, 1865. see Meeting of the Citizens of New York, to Express Sympathy and Respect for the Mexican Republic Exiles, New York, 1865.

New York (City) Meeting of the Citizens of New York, to Express their Regret at the Death of Sir Walter Scott, 1833. 43679

New York (City) Meeting of the Loyal Women of the Republic, 1863. see Meeting of the Loyal Women of the Republic, New York, 1863.

New York (City) Meeting of the Receivers and Exporters of American Leaf Tobacco, 1865. see Receivers and Exporters of American Leaf Tobacco. Meeting, New York, 1865.

New York (City) Meeting of the Signers of the Memorial to Congress, 1834. see Meeting of the Signers of the Memorial to Congress, New York, 1834.

New York (City) Meeting of the Whig Young Men, 1834. see Whig Party. New York. New York City.

New York (City) Meeting to Further the Enterprise of the Atlantic Telegraph, 1863. see Meeting to Further the Enterprise of the Atlantic Telegraph, New York, 1863.

New York (City) Memorial Service for Three Hundred Thousand Union Soldiers, 1866. 47704, note after 95516

New York (City) Mercantile Library Association. (8174), 54391, 54439, 54089

New York (City) Mercantile Library Association. Board of Directors. 54390-54391

New York (City) Mercantile Library Association. Charter. 54391

New York (City) Mercantile Library Association. Ex-Officers Union. 54391

New York (City) Mercantile Library Association. Library. 54391

New York (City) Merchants. petitioners 47624, 54381-54383

New York (City) Merchants and Traders. petitioners 54378

New York (City) Merchants Great Democratic Meeting, 1856. see Democratic Party. New York. New York City. Merchants Great Democratic Meeting, 1856.

New York (City) Merchants' Protective Union, Organized . . . for the Promotion and Protection of Trade, Throughout the United States and British Provinces. see Merchants' Protective Union, Organized . . . for the Promotion and Protection of Trade, Throughout the United States and British Provinces, New York.

New York (City) Merchants Underwriters. see Merchants Underwriters of New York

New York (City) Metropolitan Academy and Gymnasium. see Metropolitan Academy and Gymnasium, New York.

New York (City) Metropolitan Bank. see Metropolitan Bank, New York.

New York (City) Metropolitan Board of Excise. see New York (City) Department of Excise

New York (City) Metropolitan Board of Health. see New York (City) Board of Health.

New York (City) Metropolitan Board of Police. see New York (City) Police Department.

New York (City) Metropolitan Fair, 1864. (6932), 54143, 54401, (68402), 71717, (76656), 76665

New York (City) Metropolitan Fair, 1864. Art Exhibition. 54144

New York (City) Metropolitan Fair, 1864. Department of Arms and Trophies. 19617, (54145), (76645)

New York (City) Metropolitan Fair, 1864. Editorial Committee. 89496-89497

New York (City) Metropolitan Fair, 1864. Museum of Flags, Trophies and Relics. (54145)

New York (City) Metropolitan Fair, 1864. Treasurer. 54401, 89497

New York (City) Metropolitan Medical College. see Metropolitan Medical College, New York.

New York (City) Metropolitan Museum of Art. 54397

New York (City) Metropolitan Museum of Art. Committee. (54404)

New York (City) Metropolitan Museum of Art. Officers. (54404)

New York (City) Metropolitan Police. see New York (City) Police Department.

New York (City) Metropolitan Sanitary District. Charter. 53457, 54399

New York (City) Mining Stock Board. see Consolidated Stock and Petroleum Exchange Board of New York.

New York (City) Mission and Tract Society.
see New York Mission and Tract
Society.

New York (City) Mount Sinai Hospital. 51173

New York (City) Mount Sinai Hospital.
Directors. 51173

New York (City) Mount Washington Collegiate
Institute. see Mount Washington
Collegiate Institute, New York.

New York (City) Municipal Police. see New
York (City) Police Department.

New York (City) Museum and Curiosity Shop.
(54142)

New York (City) Museum of the American
Indian, Heye Foundation. 96268, 99362

New York (City) Musical Congress. see New
York Musical Congress, New York.

New York (City) Musical Fund. see New
York Musical Fund.

New york (City) National Academy of Design.
see National Academy of Design, New
York.

New York (City) National Anti-slavery Convention, 1841. see National Anti-
slavery Convention, New York, 1841.

New York (City) National Bank Convention,
1864. see National Bank Convention,
New York, 1864.

New York (City) National Bank Convention,
1869. see National Bank Convention,
New York, 1869.

New York (City) National Bank of Commerce.
see National Bank of Commerce, New
York.

New York (City) National Baptist Educational
Convention, 1870. see National Baptist
Educational Convention, New York, 1870.

New York (City) National Celebration of Union
Victories, 1865. see National Celebration of Union Victories, New York,
1865.

New York (City) National Conference of
Unitarian and Other Christian Churches,
3d, 1868. see National Conference of
Unitarian and Other Christian Churches.
3d, New York, 1868.

New York (City) National Convention for the
Protection of American Interests, 1841.
see National Convention for the Protection of American Interests, New York,
1841.

New York (City) National Convention of
Farmers, Gardeners and Silk Culturists,
1846. see National Convention of
Farmers, Gardeners and Silk Culturists,
New York, 1846.

New York (City) National Convention of Fire
Underwriters, 1866. see National Convention of Fire Underwriters, New York,
1866.

New York (City) National Convention of Fruit
Growers, 1848. see National Convention of Fruit Growers, New York, 1848.

New York (City) National Convention of
Journeymen Printers of the United
States, 1850. see National Convention
of Journeymen Printers of the United
States, New York, 1850.

New York (City) National Convention of Silk
Growers and Silk Manufacturers, 1843.
see National Convention of Silk
Growers and Silk Manufacturers, New
York, 1843.

New York (City) National Freedman's Relief
Association. see American Freedman's
Union Commission. New York Branch.

New York (City) National Gallery. 51985

New York (City) National Institute of Letters,
Arts and Sciences. see National Institute
of Letters, Arts and Sciences, New York.

New York (City) National Labor Union Convention, 1868. see National Labor Union.
Convention, 2d, New York, 1868.

New York (City) National Medical Convention,
1846. see National Medical Convention,
New York, 1846.

New York (City) National Minute Men. see
National Minute Men, New York.

New York (City) National Quarantine and
Sanitary Convention, 3d, 1859. see
National Quarantine and Sanitary Conven-
tion, 3d, New York, 1859.

New York (City) National Telegraphic Union.
see National Telegraphic Union, New
York.

New York (City) National Union Executive
Committee, 1860. see National Union
Executive Committee, New York, 1860.

New York (City) National War Committee. see
National War Committee of the Citizens of
New York City.

New York (City) New England Society. see
New England Society in the City of New
York.

New York (City) New England Soldiers' Relief
Association. see New England Soldiers'
Relief Association, New York.

New York (City) New Jerusalem Church General
Convention, 8th-52d, 1826-1870. see New
Jerusalem Church. General Convention,
8th-52d, New York, 1826-1870.

New York (City) New Jerusalem Church General
Church Convention, 36th, 1854. see New
Jerusalem Church. General Convention,
36th, New York, 1854.

New York (City) New Jerusalem Church General
Convention, 45th, 1863. see New Jerusa-
lem Church. General Convention, 45th,
New York, 1863.

New York (City) New Park Theatre. (69154),
83665

New York (City) New York Club. see New
York Club, New York.

New York (City) New York Friars Tontine.
see New York Friars Tontine, New Yotk.

New York (City) New York Gallery of the Fine
Arts. see New York Gallery of the Fine
Arts, New York.

New York (City) New York Infirmary for
Women and Children. see New York
Infirmary for Women and Children, New
York.

New York (City) New York Medical College and
Hospital for Women. see New York
Medical College and Hospital for Women,
New York.

New York (City) New York Whig Club. see
New York Whig Club, New York.

New York (City) Non-Importation Association,
1770. see Non-Importation Association,
New York, 1770.

New York (City) North Dutch Church. 55706

New York (City) North Presbyterian Church.
55726

New York (City) North Western Dispensary.
55740

New York (City) Northern Dispensary. (55793)

New York (City) Nursery for the Children of
Poor Women. see Nursery for the
Children of Poor Women in New York.

New York (City) O'Connell Club. see
O'Connell Club, New York.

New York (City) Old Dominion Society. see Old Dominion Society of the City of New York.

New York (City) Opthalmic Hospital. see New York Opthalmic Hospital.

New York (City) Ordinances, etc. (4442), 5259, (32400), 43168, 53664, (54036), 54139, 54158, (54242), 54246, 54268, (54278), 54307-54308, 54330-(54347), 54351, 54399, 54400, 54567-(54569), 54584, (54666)

New York (City) Orphan Asylum. (54571)

New York (City) Orphan Asylum Society. see Orphan Asylum Society, New York.

New York (City) Orphan's Home of the Protestant Episcopal Church in New York. 54572

New York (City) Park Theatre. (69154), 83665

New York (City) Patriot Orphan Home. see Patriot Orphan Home, New York.

New York (City) Pearl Street Merchants. 13734

New York (City) Penitentiary, Bellevue. see New York (City) Almshouse and Peniten- tiary, Bellevue.

New York (City) Police Commissioners. 84774 see also Erhardt, Joel B. Nichols, Sidney P. Smith, William Farrar, 1824-1903.

New York (City) Police Court (First District) 74759

New York (City) Police Department. 54400, 54584

New York (City) Police Department. Chief. (30527)

New York (City) Police Department. Deputy Superintendent. 54400

New York (City) Police Department. General Superintendent. 54400

New York (City) Port Society. see Society for Promoting the Gospel Among the Seamen in the Port of New York.

New York (City) Postal Reform Committee. see Postal Reform Committee, New York.

New York (City) Practitioners of Physic and Surgery. see Medical Society of the County of New York.

New York (City) Presbyterian Church. 83423

New York (City) Presbyterian Hospital. 54587

New York (City) Printers' Banquet, 1850. see New York Typographical Society. Printers' Banquet, New York, 1850.

New York (City) Prison. Inspector. pseud. see One of the Inspectors of the Prison. pseud.

New York (City) Prison Association. see Prison Association of New York.

New York (City) Protestant Episcopal Church Association. see Protestant Episcopal Church Association of . . . New York.

New York (City) Protestant Episcopal Clerical Association. see Protestant Episcopal Clerical Association of the City of New York.

New York (City) Protestant Episcopal Mission to Seamen. see Protestant Episcopal Mission to Seamen, New York.

New York (City) Protestant Episcopal Orphan's Home. see New York (City) Orphan's Home of the Protestant Episcopal Church in New York.

New York (City) Protestant Episcopal Press. see New York Protestant Episcopal. Press.

New York (City) Protestant Episcopal Public School. see New York (City) Trinity School.

New York (City) Protestant Episcopal Society for the Promotion of Evangelical Knowl- edge. see Protestant Episcopal Society for the Promotion of Evangelical Knowl- edge, New York.

New York (City) Protestant Episcopal Sunday School Society. see New York Protestant Episcopal Sunday School Society.

New York (City) Protestant Episcopal Sunday School Union. see General Protestant Episcopal Sunday School Union, New York

New York (City) Protestant Half Orphan Asylum Society. see Society for the Relief of Half Orphan and Destitute Children in the City of New York.

New York (City) Provident Society. see Provident Society of New York.

New York (City) Public Deliberative Meeting of the American Tract Society, 1842. see American Tract Society, New York. Public Deliberative Meeting, 1842.

New York (City) Public Deliberative Meeting of the American Tract Society, 1848. see American Tract Society, New York. Public Deliberative Meeting, 1842.

New York (City) Public Demonstration of Sympathy with Pius IX, 1847. (63171)

New York (City) Public Library. 37335, note after 98475, 99362

New York (City) Public Library. Astor Libra 2551-2554, 14218, 54679, 72586

New York (City) Public Library. Astor Libra Charter. 2249

New York (City) Public Library. Astor Libra Trustees. 2249, 2255

New York (City) Public Library. Trustees. 54619

New York (City) Public Meeting on Postal Reform, 1856. see Public Meeting on Postal Reform, New York, 1856.

New York (City) Public Meeting Respecting St. Ann's Church for Deaf-Mutes, 1853. 74996, note before 90783 see also New York (City) Meeting in Relation to St. Ann's Church for Deaf-Mutes, 1858. New York (City) Saint Ann's Church for Deaf- Mutes.

New York (City) Public School, No. 15. 85846

New York (City) Public School Society. see Public School Society, New York.

New York (City) Public Schools. see New York (City) Board of Education.

New York (City) Reception by Citizens of New York to the Survivors of the Officers and Crews of the United States Frigates Cumberland and Congress, 1862. 54025

New York (City) Recorder. (33058), 75949, 2d note after 96930A, 96939, 98520 see also Hoffman, Josiah Ogden. Horsman- den, Daniel.

New York (City) Recorder's Court. 94930

New York (City) Rector and Inhabitants. defendants see New York (City) Trinity Church. defendants

New York (City) Reformed Dutch Church. see New York (City) Collegiate Church.

New York (City) Reformed Protestant Dutch Church. see New York (City) Collegiate Church.

New York (City) Regiment of Artillery. see New York (State) Militia. Regiment of Artillery of the City and County of New York.

New York (City) Register's Office. 78969

New York (City) Religious Tract Society. see New York Religious Tract Society.

New York (City) Republican General Committee of Young Men Friendly to the Election of General Jackson. see Democratic Party. New York. New York City. General Committee of Young Men.

New York (City) Republican Union Festival, 1862. see Republican Union Festival, New York, 1862.

New York (City) Roman Catholic Orphan Asylum Ladies' Association. (72977)

New York (City) Roman Catholics. see New York (Archdiocese) and Roman Catholics of New York City.

New York (City) Roosevelt Hospital. 73117

New York (City) Rutgers Female College. see Rutgers Female College, New York.

New York (City) Rutgers Female Institute. see Rutgers Female College, New York.

New York (City) Rutgers Medical College. see Geneva College, Geneva, N. Y. Rutgers Medical College, New York.

New York (City) Sabbath Committee. see New York Sabbath Committee.

New York (City) Sailors' Snug Harbor. see Sailors' Snug Harbor, New York.

New York (City) Saint Ann's Church for Deaf-Mutes. 74996 see also New York (City) Meeting in Relation to St. Ann's Church for Deaf-Mutes, 1858. New York (City) Public Meeting Respecting St. Ann's Church for Deaf-Mutes, 1853.

New York (City) St. Francis Xavier's College. see St. Francis Xavier's College, New York.

New York (City) St. George's Church. Committee of the Congregation. 75209-(75211)

New York (City) St. George's Church. Vestry. 75212

New York (City) St. George's Church. Vestry. Committee. 75209, 75213

New York (City) St. George's Church. Vestry. Delegates to the Diocesan Convention. 75212

New York (City) St. George's Society. see St. George's Society of New York.

New York (City) St. John's College. see St. John's College, Fordham, N. Y.

New York (City) St. Jude's Protestant Episcopal Free Church. (54132)

New York (City) St. Luke's Home for Indigent Christian Females. see St. Luke's Home for Indigent Christian Females, New York.

New York (City) St. Luke's Hospital. 75413

New York (City) St. Luke's Hospital. Board of Managers. 75413-75414

New York (City) St. Luke's Hospital. Charter. 75413

New York (City) St. Mark's of the Bowery Church. 1673, 54377

New York (City) St. Matthew's Church (English Lutheran) 90693

New York (City) St. Nicholas Society. see St. Nicholas Society of the City of New York.

New York (City) St. Paul's Chapel. see New York (City) St. Paul's Church (Protestant Episcopal)

New York (City) St. Paul's Church (Lutheran) 86374

New York (City) St. Paul's Church (Methodist Episcopal) 94756-94756A

New York (City) St. Paul's Church (Protestant Episcopal) 20349, 101880

New York (City) St. Paul's Church (Protestant Episcopal) petitioners' 96980

New York (City) St. Paul's Church (Protestant Episcopal) Committee. 74363

New York (City) St. Paul's Church (Protestant Episcopal) Emmet Monument. 74363

New York (City) St. Paul's Church (Protestant Episcopal) Pewholders and Worshippers. petitioners 75463

New York (City) St. Paul's Church (Protestant Episcopal) Sunday School. Board of Directors. (72462)

New York (City) St. Paul's Church (Protestant Episcopal) Vestry. 75473

New York (City) St. Philips Church. Special Committee. 75473

New York (City) St. Thomas' Church. Wardens and Vestry. (75496)

New York (City) St. Thomas' Church. Wardens and Vestry. Committee of Investigation. (75497)

New York (City) Samuel R. Smith Infirmary. see New York (City) Staten Island Hospital.

New York (City) Sanitary Association. see Sanitary Association of New York.

New York (City) Sanitary Superintendent of the Metropolitan Board of Health. see New York (City) Board of Health. Sanitary Superintendent.

New York (City) School Inspector. see New York (City) Board of Education. School Inspector.

New York (City) Seaman's Retreat. see Seaman's Retreat, New York.

New York (City) Second Congregational Unitarian Church. see New York (City) Church of the Messiah.

New York (City) Second Presbyterian Church. 54586

New York (City) Seventh Presbyterian Church. 54586

New York (City) Shamrock Society. see Shamrock Society, New York.

New York (City) Sheltering Arms. see Sheltering Arms, New York.

New York (City) Sheriff. defendant at impeachment (36456) see also Orser, John. defendant at impeachment

New York (City) Sherman Institute for the Encouragement of Industry and Education. see Sherman Institute for the Encouragement of Industry and Education, New York.

New York (City) Skating Club. see New York Skating Club, New York.

New York (City) Social Party. see Social Party for the City of New York and Vicinity.

New York (City) Sociedad Democratica de los Amigos de America. see Sociedad Democratica de los Amigos de America, New York.

New York (City) Societa di Unione e Fratellanza Italiana. see Societa di Unione e Fratellanza Italiana, New York.

New York (City) Societa Italiana. see Societa Italiana in Nuova York.

New York (City) Societa Italiana di Unione e Benevolenza. see Societa Italiana di Unione e Benevolenza, New York.

New York (City) Societe Francaise de Bienfaisance. see Societe Francaise de Bienfaisance, New York.

New York (City) Societe for Establishing Useful Manufactures. see Society for Establishing Useful Manufactures, New Jersey.

New York (City) Society for Mental and Moral
Improvement. see Society for Mental
and Moral Improvement, New York.

New York (City) Society for Promoting Manual
Labor in Literary Institutions. see
Society for Promoting Manual Labor in
Literary Institutions, New York.

New York (City) Society for Promoting the
Gospel Among the Seamen in the Port
of New York. see Society for Promoting the Gospel Among the Seamen in
the Port of New York.

New York (City) Society for the Advancement
of Political and Social Science. see
Society for the Advancement of Political
and Social Science, New York.

New York (City) Society for the Diffusion of
Political Knowledge. see Society for
the Diffusion of Political Knowledge,
New York.

New York (City) Society for the Elevation of
Liberal Government. see Society for
the Elevation of Liberal Government,
New York.

New York (City) Society for the Employment
and Relief of Poor Women. see Society
for the Employment and Relief of Poor
Women, New York.

New York (City) Society for the Employment
and Relief of the Poor. see Society
for the Employment and Relief of Poor
Women, New York.

New York (City) Society for the Encouragement of Faithful Domestic Servants. see
Society for the Encouragement of Faithful Domestic Servants, New York.

New York (City) Society for the Prevention of
Pauperism. see Society for the Pre-
vention of Pauperism in the City of New
York.

New York (City) Society for the Promotion of
Industry. see Society for the Promotion
of Industry, New York.

New York (City) Society for the Reformation
of Juvenile Delinquents. see Society
for the Reformation of Juvenile Delinquents, New York.

New York (City) Society for the Relief of Half
Orphan and Destitute Children. see
Society for the Relief of Half Orphan
and Destitute Children in the City of
New York.

New York (City) Society for the Relief of Poor
Widows. see Society for the Relief of
Poor Widows, New York.

New York (City) Society for the Relief of
Poor Widows with Small Children. see
Ladies' Society for the Relief of Poor
Widows with Small Children, New York.

New York (City) Society for the Relief of the
Destitute Blind of New York and Its
Vicinity. see Society for the Relief of
the Destitute Blind of New York and its
Vicinity.

New York (City) Society for the Support of the
Gospel Among the Poor. see Society
for the Support of the Gospel Among the
Poor in the City of New York.

New York (City) Society of Associates of the
Cooper Union for the Advancement of
Science and Art. see Society of Associates of the Cooper Union for the Advancement of Science and Art, New York.

New York (City) Society for Commercial
Travellers. see Society of Commercial
Travellers, New York.

New York (City) Society of Correspondence
with the Baptist Education Society in
Philadelphia. see Society of Correspondence in New York, With the Baptist
Education Society in Philadelphia.

New York (City) Society of Gentlemen. pseud.
Universal receipt book. see Alsop,
Richard. supposed author

New York (City) Society of Mechanics and
Tradesmen. see General Society of
Mechanics and Tradesmen of the City of
New York.

New York (City) Society of St. George. see
Society of St. George, New York.

New York (City) Society of St. Tammany. see
Tammany Society, New York.

New York (City) Society of Teachers. see
Society of Teachers of the City and County
of New York.

New York (City) Society of the Friendly Sons
of Saint Patrick. see Society of the
Friendly Sons of St. Patrick, New York.

New York (City) Society of the New York
Hospital. see Society of the New York
Hospital, New York.

New York (City) Soldiers' and Sailors' Union.
see Soldiers' and Sailors' Union, No. 1,
of New York City.

New York (City) Soldiers' Depot. see New
York (State) Board of Managers of the
Soldiers' Depot.

New York (City) Sons of Liberty. see Sons of
Liberty. New York City.

New York (City) Southern Aid Society. see
Southern Aid Society, New York.

New York (City) Special Committee Appointed
by the Friends of Judge Yates. see
Special Committee Appointed by the
Friends of Judge Yates in the City of New
York.

New York (City) Special Committee to Make
Suitable Arrangements for Bringing on
From Mexico the Bodies of the Officers
of the New York Regiment of Volunteers,
and to Prepare and Present Medals to the
New York Regiment of Volunteers. 54660

New York (City) Special Sessions of the
Eastern New York Grand Division of the
Sons of Temperance, 1851. see Sons of
Temperance of North America. Eastern
New York. Grand Division. Special
Sessions, New York, 1851.

New York (City) Springler Institute. see
Springler Institute, New York.

New York (City) Stamp Act Congress, 1765.
see Stamp Act Congress, New York, 1765

New York (City) Stanton Street Baptist Church.
90449, note after 92355

New York (City) State Emigrant Hospital. see
New York (State) State Emigrant Hospital,
New York.

New York (City) Staten Island Hospital. 84093

New York (City) Statistischen Gesellschaft.
see Statistischen Gesellschaft zu New-
York.

New York (City) Stock Exchange. (54546)

New York (City) Stock Exchange. Society of
Members for Mutual Relief. see Society
of Members of the New York Stock
Exchange for Mutual Relief.

New York (City) Street Commissioner. see
New York (City) Street Department.

New York (City) Street Department. 54684

New York (City) Stuyvesant Institute. see
Stuyvesant Institute, New York.

New York (City) Stuyvesant Square Home Guard. see New York (State) Militia. Stuyvesant Square Home Guard, New York.

New York (City) Subscribers to the Non-Importation Agreement, 1770. see Non-Importation Association, New York, 1770.

New York (City) Subscribers to the Tontine Coffee House. see Tontine Association, New York.

New York (City) Suffolk Bank. see Suffolk Bank of the City of New York.

New York (City) Superintendent of Buildings. 54687

New York (City) Superintendent of Schools. see New York (City) Board of Education.

New York (City) Superior Court. 9478, 96842

New York (City) Tammany Society. see Tammany Society, New York.

New York (City) Temperance Beneficial Association. see Temperance Beneficial Association, New York.

New York (City) Theatre. 97242

New York (City) Theological Seminary. see New York (City) Union Theological Seminary.

New York (City) Third Presbyterian Church. 54586

New York (City) Thistle Society. see Thistle Society of the City of New York.

New York (City) Tontine Association. see Tontine Association, New York.

New York (City) Tontine Coffee House. see Tontine Association, New York.

New York (City) Tract Association of Friends. see Tract Association of Friends, New York.

New York (City) Tradesmen. 103224

New York (City) Treasurer. 54230

New York (City) Trinity Church. 18867, 36462, (54132), 96710, 4th note after 96984, 96985-96986

New York (City) Trinity Church. defendants 37724, 49046, 50655, 1st note after 96986

New York (City) Trinity Church. petitioners (7272), 86744, 3d note after 96984

New York (City) Trinity Church. Charter. 32293, 96982-96984

New York (City) Trinity Church. Greene Foundation. 69533

New York (City) Trinity Church. Special Committee on the Memorial of Various Pew-Holders and Worshippers in St. Paul's Chapel. 96980

New York (City) Trinity Church. Vestry. 85857, 88978, note after 96981

New York (City) Trinity Church. Vestry. Committee. 75463

New York (City) Trinity Church. Vestry. Committee on the Finances. 32934

New York (City) Trinity School. 54529, 73997

New York (City) Twenty-ninth Annual Session of the Grand Division of Eastern New York of the Sons of Temperance, 1873. see Sons of Temperance of North America. Eastern New York. Grand Division. 29th Annual Session, New York, 1873.

New York (City) Unconditional Union Central Committee. see Unconditional Union Central Committee, New York.

New York (City) Union Committee, 1834. see Union Committee, New York, 1834.

New York (City) Union Defence Committee. (54658), 54702

New York (City) Union League Club. see Union League Club of New York.

New York (City) Union Library Society. see Union Library Society, New York.

New York (City) Union Meeting, 1850. 54610

New York (City) Union Meeting, Dec. 19, 1859. 54564, (54626)

New York (City) Union Meeting, Dec. 15, 1860. 54596

New York (City) Union Theological Seminary. 54551, (82712), 97819

New York (City) United German Lutheran Churches. see Vereinigte Deutsche Gesellschaften der Stadt New York.

New York (City) United Sons of Liberty. see United Sons of Liberty, New York.

New York (City) United Whig Club. see United Whig Club, New York.

New York (City) Universalists General Convention, 1861. see Universalists. U. S. General Convention, New York, 1861.

New York (City) University. see New York University.

New York (City) Veterans of the National Guard. see Veterans of the National Guard, New York.

New York (City) Wallabout Committee. see Tammany Society, New York. Wallabout Committee.

New York (City) Washington Bank. see Washington Bank in the City of New York.

New York (City) Washington Benevolent Society. see Washington Benevolent Society. New York. New York City.

New York (City) Washington Centennial Celebration, 1832. 101785

New York (City) Washington Circulating Library. see Washington Circulating Library, New York.

New York (City) Water Commissioners. (54232), 54630, 54714

New York (City) Wesleyan Anti-slavery Society. see Wesleyan Anti-slavery Society, New York.

New York (City) West End Association. see West End Association, New York.

New York (City) William H. Seward Statute. (79599)

New York (City) Women's Central Association of Relief. see United States Sanitary Commission. Women's Central Association of Relief, New York.

New York (City) Wool Growers and Manufacturers Convention, 1831. see Wool Growers and Manufacturers Convention, New York, 1831.

New York (City) Wool Growers Convention, 1831. see Wool Growers and Manufacturers Convention, New York, 1831.

New York (City) World's Temperance Convention, 1853. see World's Temperance Convention, New York, 1853.

New York (City) Young Men's Anti-slavery Society. see New York Young Men's Anti-slavery Society.

New York (City) Young Men's Auxiliary Education Society of the City of New York.

New York (City) Young Men's Bible Society. see New York Bible Society.

New York (City) Young Men's Christian Association. see Young Men's Christian Association, New York.

New York (City) Young Men's Colonization Society. see Young Men's Colonization Society, New York.

New York (City) Young Men's Education Society. see Young Men's Education Society of New York City. and Young Men's Education Society of the Cities of New York and Brooklyn.

New York (City) Young Men's Missionary Society. see Young Men's Missionary Society of New York.

New York (City) Young Men's Republican Union. see Young Men's Republican Union, New York.

New York (City) Young Men's Society. see New York Young Men's Society.

New York (City) Young Men's Society for the Promotion of Temperance. see Young Men's Society for the Promotion of Temperance, New York.

New York (City) Zoological Institute and Reading Room. 106370

New York (Colony) 1967, 20597, (22754), 24582, 32968, 34052, 51355, 53647, (53570), (53599), 53653, 53681-53682, (56665), 61280, 53210, 65486, 69741, (73448), 74124, 74126, 74129, 79642, note after 98474, 1st-2d notes after 98997, 99573, 102983, 104441, 104442

New York (Colony) Agents on the Boundary Line Between New York and New Jersey, 1769. (7884), 54368, 63210, 95935 see also Bayard, William. Cruger, John, 1710-1792. Holland, Henry. Kisam, Benjamin. Scott, John Morris.

New York (Colony) Attorney General. 98429, 98431

New York (Colony) Commissaries on the Boundary Between New York and Massachusetts, 1767. (15431), 36738, 54689

New York (Colony) Committee of Safety, 1775-1776. 15146, 15583, 22988, 43615, 49335, 53479, 53615, 53723, 53947, 69335, 1st note after 96762, 98439, note after 103267

New York (Colony) Committee of Safety, 1775-1776. Chairman. 15583, 98439 see also Van Cortlandt, Pierre.

New York (Colony) Council. 14818, 16653, (24714), 26145, (53571), (53693), (53715), 53848, (53850), 53974, 54198, (73448), 84556, 84558, 84566, 84575, 98435

New York (Colony) Council. Committee on the French Church du Saint Spirit. (73448)

New York (Colony) Council. Committee on the Line Between New York and New Jersey. (53909), 97479

New York (Colony) Council. Committee on the Petition of the Merchants of London. 14272-14274

New York (Colony) Council. Committee to Whom it Was Referred to Examine and Make Inquiry Touching a Letter Found in the House of Mr. Alexander. 730-731, 30378, 30380, 84558

New York (Colony) Council. President. 98436 see also Clarke, George.

New York (Colony) Council. Secretary. 78201 see also Cosens, B.

New York (Colony) Court of Chancery. 47349, 58366

New York (Colony) Court of the Exchequer. 98429

New York (Colony) French Protestant Refugees. petitioners see French Protestant Refugees Inhabiting the Province of New York Generally. petitioners

New York (Colony) General Assembly. 792, 20987, 23508, 40289, 51825-51826, (53570) (53717)-53721, 53732, 53759, 53974, 54003-54008, 54381, (69681), 84556, 84558, 84566, 86960, note after 90602, 90629, 96960, 4th-5th notes after 98997, 98998

New York (Colony) General Assembly. Committee of Grievances. 98432

New York (Colony) General Assembly. House of Representatives. 86720

New York (Colony) Governor, 1664-1668 (Nicolls) 78969 see also Nicolls, Sir Richard, 1624-1672.

New York (Colony) Governor, 1668-1673 (Lovelace) 53729 see also Lovelace, Francis, 1621-1675.

New York (Colony) Governor, 1682-1688 (Limerick) 78969 see also Limerick, Thomas Dongan, Earl of, 1634-1715.

New York (Colony) Governor, 1691-1692 (Ingoldsby) 53729, 53848 see also Ingoldsby, Richard.

New York (Colony) Governor, 1692-1697 (Fletcher) 4035, 24712-(24714), 53435, (53571), 53671-53672 see also Fletcher, Benjamin. Delaware (Colony) Governor, 1693-1694 (Fletcher) Pennsylvania (Colon Governor, 1693-1694 (Fletcher)

New York (Colony) Governor, 1697-1701 (Bellamont) 16653-16654, 18563, 18574, 78201, 78202, 78238 see also Bellamont, Richard Coote, 1st Earl of, 1636-1701.

New York (Colony) Governor, 1702-1708 (Clarendon) 4033, 26145, 53436, 53729, 53849 see also Clarendon, Edward Hyde, 3d Earl of, 1661-1723.

New York (Colony) Governor, 1710-1719 (Hunte (53850) see also Hunter, Robert, d. 173

New York (Colony) Governor, 1728-1731 (Montgomerie) 54168, (54170) see also Montgomerie, John, d. 1731.

New York (Colony) Governor, 1731-1736 (Cosby 53438, (53693A), 53872, 94092, 98429, 98431 see also Cosby, William, 1695?-1736.

New York (Colony) Governor, 1731-1736 (Cosby defendant (53693), 98435 see also Cosby, William, 1695?-1736. defendant

New York (Colony) Governor, 1743-1753 (Clinton) 13740, 34601, 53759 see also Clinton, George, 1686?-1761.

New York (Colony) Governor, 1761-1765 (Colden) 54166 see also Colden, Cadwallader, 1688-1776.

New York (Colony) Governor, 1770 (Dunmore) 54162, 86153 see also Dunmore, John Murray, 4th Earl of, 1732-1809.

New York (Colony) Governor, 1771-1778 (Tryon 53630, 97291 see also Tryon, William, 1729-1788.

New York (Colony) Indian Conference, Johnson-Hall, 1765. 25595, 34579-34580, 99584, note just before 103108

New York (Colony) Indian Congress, Fort Stanwix, 1768. 25595, 34579-34580, 99584, note just before 103108

New York (Colony) Laws, statutes, etc. 81, 5378, 6010, 14272-14274, 14818, 23508, 32293, 39410, 39414, 53441-53444, 53466-53468, 53525-(53527), 53584, (53663),

53707, (53722), 53726, 53728-53733,
53848-(53851), 54162, 54164-54168,
54198, 54335, 54372, 64479, 84566,
84575-84576, 86153, 95975,
96982-96983, 98998, note after 100381
New York (Colony) Lieutenant Governor,
1753-1755 (De Lancey) 14818, 54198,
97479 see also De Lancey, James,
1703-1760.
New York (Colony) Provincial Congress,
1775-1776. 53723, 53948, 70078
New York (Colony) Secretary. 51740,
53438 see also Morris, F.
New York (Colony) Supreme Court of
Judicature. 731, 25124, 30380, 84558,
86889, 96305, 98429, 106304-106314
New York (Colony) Supreme Court of
Judicature. Chief Justice. 12024,
19340-19342, 50849, 84557, 98436
see also De Lancey, James, 1702-
1760. Morris, Lewis, 1671-1746.
New York (Colony) Treaties, etc. 13740,
24712, 34601, 36337, (36339), 65759
New York (County) 54086, (54226)
New York (County) petitioners 95462
New York (County) Board of Supervisors.
18358, 54128, 54315, (54600)
New York (County) Board of Supervisors.
Committee on Substitutes and Relief,
54128, 54638
New York (County) Board of Supervisors.
Special Committee on County Volunteers.
54650
New York (County) Board of Supervisors.
Special Committee on Volunteering.
see New York (County) Special Com-
mittee on Volunteering.
New York (County) Census, 1807. 54150
New York (County) Census, 1865. 33154
New York (County) Comptroller. 54211-
(54212)
New York (County) Court of General
Sessions. 8466, (16580), 27951,
(28231), 41829, 70101, 71953, 75949,
76831, 94098, 96877-96878, 2d note
after 96930A, 96939, 96943, 97250,
98520, 100985, 103189, 104224
New York (County) Court of Oyer and
Terminer. see New York (State) Court
of Oyer and Terminer (New York
County)
New York (County) Court of Probates. 104643
New York (County) Farmers, . . . and Other
Working Men. see Farmers, . . . and
Other Working Men, of the City and
County of New York.
New York (County) Grand Jury. 19340,
84557
New York (County) Inspector of Firewood.
see New York (City) Inspector of Fire-
wood.
New York (County) Medical Society. see
Medical Society of the County of New
York.
New York (County) Practitioners of Physic
and Surgery. see Medical society of
the County of New York.
New York (County) Regiment of Artillery.
see New York (State) Militia. Regiment
of Artillery of the City and County of
New York.
New York (County) Society of Teachers. see
Society of Teachers of the City and
County of New York.
New York (County) Surrogate. 58611,
104643 see also Bradford, Alexander

Warfield, 1815-1867.
New York (County) Surrogate's Court. 12955,
58611
New York (County) Supreme Court. 72589
New York (County) Special Committee on
Volunteering. (52628), 54627
New York (Ecclesiastical Province) Council,
1854. 59018, 72916
New York (Ecclesiastical Province) Council,
1861. 72917
New York (New Netherlands) (15186), 20594-
20597, (53570), 55280-55281, 69996,
note after 98474, note after 99310,
102887
New York (New Netherlands) petitioners
20595-20597, 69996, note after 98474
New York (New Netherlands) Charter.
102920-102921
New York (New Netherlands) Director and
Councilors. (55282)
New York (New Netherlands) Laws, statutes,
etc. 53727, 56614
New York (State) 13735, (22754), 24582,
29713, 34052, 51355, (53599), 53647,
53681, (53782)-53797, 53896, note after
54729, (56665), 61280, 69741, 71349,
(73448), 74124, 74126, 74129, note
before 91820, 92392, 1st note after
98997, 2d note after 98997, 99573,
102983, 104200, 104441-104442, 105569
New York (State) defendants 20341, 37724,
54320, 66969, 102625, 103382-103383,
103686
New York (State) petitioners (53767)
New York (State) plaintiffs 17677, 49046,
60817, 69824, 89304, note after 98533,
98616, 100796, 102037
New York (State) Adjutant General. 20341,
53516, (53699), 57401
New York (State) Agent of the New State
Prison. see New York (State) State
Prison, Auburn. Agent
New York (State) Agent to Procure and Trans-
cribe Documents in Europe, Relative to
the Colonial History of the State. 8176,
53653, 53669 see also Broadhead, John
Romeyn.
New York (State) Agent to Take the Census
or Enumeration of the Indians, 1846.
77874 see also Schoolcraft, Henry
Rowe, 1793-1864.
New York (State) Agricultural College, Albany.
53810
New York (State) Agricultural College, Albany,
Charter. 53810
New York (State) Agricultural College, Ovid.
89117
New York (State) Agricultural Rooms, Albany.
see New York (State) Agricultural
College, Albany.
New York (State) Albany Medical School. see
Albany Medical School.
New York (State) Appeals Court. see New
York (State) Court of Appeals.
New York (State) Arbitrators in the Case of
Orlandos et al vs. Le Roy, Bayard &
Co. et al. (57622)
New York (State) Assessors. 53962
New York (State) Association of Clergymen.
see Asosciation of Clergymen in New
York.
New York (State) Asylum for Idiots, Syracuse.
see New York (State) Institution for
Feeble Minded Children, Syracuse.

New York (State) Asylum for Insane Convicts, Matteawan. see New York (State) State Hospital, Matteawan.

New York (State) Attorney General. 14677, 17677, 50875, 53536, 53616, note after 98533, 98616, 102037 see also Bronson, Greene Carrier, 1789-1863. Cochrane, John. Hall, Willis.

New York (State) Auburn Prison. see New York (State) State Prison, Auburn.

New York (State) Auditor. 53615

New York (State) Bank Commissioners. 53538-53539

New York (State) Banking Department. Deputy Superintendent. 37681 see also Keyes, Emerson W.

New York (State) Banking Department. Superintendent. 37680, 53911, 53992

New York (State) Banking Department. Superintendent. respondent 64285 see also Van Dyck, Henry.

New York (State) Bar. (20032)

New York (State) Bar. Committee on the Judiciary System, Proposed by the New Constitution of the State, 1846. 53910

New York (State) Board of Agriculture. 53544, 63428, 88654, 90594

New York (State) Board of Agriculture. General Committee. (53543), 53918

New York (State) Board of Charities. see New York (State) Board of Social Welfare.

New York (State) Board of Commissioners for Improving the Navigation of the Hudson River. see New York (State) Hudson River Commission.

New York (State) Board of Education. see New York (State) University.

New York (State) Board of Examiners on the Affairs of the Mutual Life Insurance Company of New York. 51610

New York (State) Board of Managers of the Soldiers' Depot. 14919, 53841

New York (State) Board of Railroad Commissioners. 53887, 77603

New York (State) Board of Social Welfare. 84269

New York (State) Board of Social Welfare. Commissioners. 53546, 53963, 84269, 85958 see also Smith, Stephen, 1823-1922.

New York (State) Board of State Commissioners of Public Charities. see New York (State) Board of Social Welfare. Commissioners.

New York (State) Bureau of Military Record. see New York (State) Bureau of Military Statistics.

New York (State) Bureau of Military Statistics. 21153, 53552-53553, 53644, (76646) see also Doty, L. L.

New York (State) Cabinet of Natural History. see New York State Museum, Albany.

New York (State) Canal Appraisers. 53558, 64285

New York (State) Canal Board. (53564), 73955, 73977

New York (State) Canal Board. petitioners 53768, 73977

New York (State) Canal Commissioners. 22745, 22749, 22759-22761, (53559), (53563)-53566, 53907, 53921, 70189, 73977, 99779

New York (State) Canal Commissioners. petitioners 53768, 73977

New York (State) Canal Department. (53563)-(53564)

New York (State) Canal Department. Auditor. 53557, 53560, (53564)

New York (State) Canal Department. Engineers. (53563)

New York (State) Canal Fund Commissioners. see New York (State) Commissioners of the Canal Fund.

New York (State) Canals. 53561-(53563)

New York (State) Census, 1800. (53576)

New York (State) Census, 1821. 512

New York (State) Census, 1822. (53576)

New York (State) Census, 1825. (53576)

New York (State) Census, 1830. (53576)

New York (State) Census, 1835. 53577

New York (State) Census, 1840. 20325, 53809

New York (State) Census, 1845. 53577

New York (State) Census, 1855. 33137, 53577, 53703, 53859

New York (State) Census, 1865. 33154, 53577, 53703

New York (State) Census, 1875. 53577

New York (State) Central Asylum for the Instruction of the Deaf and Dumb, Canojoharie. 10647

New York (State) Central Asylum for the Instruction of the Deaf and Dumb, Canojoharie. Directors. 53578

New York (State) Chamber of Commerce of the State of New York. 7591, 8723, 17130, 37784, 53579, 53580, 53584-53585, (53592), (53594)-53595, 53806, 65903, 90585, 2d note after 96963 see also Joint Special Committee of the New York Chamber of Commerce and American Geographical and Statistical Society on the Decimal System.

New York (State) Chamber of Commerce of the State of New York. petitioners 47710, 53587-53589, 54161

New York (State) Chamber of Commerce of the State of New York. Charter. 37784, 53584

New York (State) Chamber of Commerce of the State of New York. Board of Underwriters. 21100

New York (State) Chamber of Commerce of the State of New York. Centennial Celebration, 1868. (53582)

New York (State) Chamber of Commerce of the State of New York. Committee on a Time and Weather Observatory. 54565

New York (State) Chamber of Commerce of the State of New York. Committee on Canal Navigation by Steam. (53591)

New York (State) Chamber of Commerce of the State of New York. Committee on the Charges at Quarantine for Lighterage, etc. (53592)

New York (State) Chamber of Commerce of the State of New York. Committee on the Expediency and Practicability of a Time and Weather Observatory. see New York (State) Chamber of Commerce of the State of New York. Committee on a Time and Weather Observatory.

New York (State) Chamber of Commerce of the State of New York. Committee to Consider the Condition of the Lighthouses of the United States. 53583

New York (State) Chamber of Commerce of the State of New York. Committee to Prepare a Memorial to Congress on Taxation. (53592)

New York (State) Chamber of Commerce of
the State of New York. Delegate to
the International Congress, York,
England, 1864. see International Congress, York, England, 1864. Delegate
of the New York Chamber of Commerce.
and Marvin, William.
New York (State) Chamber of Commerce of
the State of New York. Executive
Committee. (53592)
New York (State) Chamber of Commerce of
the State of New York. Library.
(53581)
New York (State) Chamber of Commerce of
the State of New York. Reception for
De Azambuja and Sarmiento, 1866.
53590
New York (State) Chamber of Commerce of
the State of New York. Reception to
His Excellency Senhor D'Azambuja, 1865.
7591, 53586
New York (State) Chamber of Commerce of
the State of New York. Select Committee on a Return to Specie Payments.
(53592)
New York (State) Chamber of Commerce of
the State of New York. Select Committee on Emigration. 22506
New York (State) Chamber of Commerce of
the State of New York. Select Committee on Quarantine. 53583
New York (State) Chamber of Commerce of
the State of New York. Select Committee on the Reciprocity Treaty.
(53592)
New York (State) Chamber of Commerce of
the State of New York. Special Committee on Maritime Intercourse in the
Time of War. (53592)
New York (State) Chamber of Commerce of
the State of New York. Special Committee on Testimonials to Captain,
Officers, and Crew of the United States
Sloop of War, "Kearsage." 37132
New York (State) Chamber of Commerce of
the State of New York. Special Committee on the Confiscation of Cotton in
the Southern States. 17130, 53940
New York (State) Chamber of Commerce of
the State of New York. Special Committee on the Decline of American
Commerce. (53592)
New York (State) Chamber of Commerce of
the State of New York. Special Committee on the Memorial of Officers of
the U. S. Navy to Congress for an
Increase of Pay. (53592)
New York (State) Chancellor. 41638, 54115,
61206, 69689, 76498, 95779, 98439,
102207 see also Kent, James, 1763-
1847. Lansing, John. Sanford, Nathan.
New York (State) Chief Engineer. see New
York (State) State Engineer and Surveyor.
New York (State) Circuit Court (Special), Lock-
port. see Niagara County, N. Y. Court.
New York (State) Circuit Courts. 59451,
98621
New York (State) Citizens. petitioners 22747,
70073
New York (State) Clinton State Prison. Agent.
see New York (State) State Prison
Clinton. Agent.
New York (State) College of Physicians and
Surgeons of the Western District, Fair-
field. see Albany Medical School.
New York (State) Commissary General. 53608

New York (State) Commission to Determine and
Ascertain the Qhota of this State, Under
the Different Calls for Troops. 53616
New York (State) Commission to Investigate
Port Conditions and Pier Extensions in
New York Harbor. Chairman. 83847-
83848 see also Smith, Robert A. C.,
1857-
New York (State) Commissioner on Lunacy.
84253 see also Smith, Stephen, 1823-
1922.
New York (State) Commissioner on the Enlarge-
ment of the Canals for National Purposes.
53895 see also Ruggles, Samuel B.
New York (State) Commissioner to Inquire
into the Expediency of a Total Abolition
of Capital Punishment. 53896 see also
Stilwell, A. M.
New York (State) Commissioner to the Paris
Exposition of 1867. 53817
New York (State) Commissioners for Internal
Improvements. 22757, 53904
New York (State) Commissioners for Settling
the Titles to Land in the County of
Onondaga. 23362, 57362, note after
102973, 106002 see also Yates, Robert.
New York (State) Commissioners of Emigration.
(39192), 53610 see also Van Heenrick,
Gustav.
New York (State) Commissioners of Fisheries.
(53611), 73107 see also Green, Seth.
Roosevelt, Robert Barnwell.
New York (State) Commissioners of Fortifica-
tions. 53616, (53774)
New York (State) Commissioners of Indian
Affairs. (33148)
New York (State) Commissioners of Public
Charities. see New York (State) Board
of Social Welfare. Commissioners.
New York (State) Commissioners of Quarantine.
53231, (53885), 54352
New York (State) Commissioners of the Canal
Fund. 53560, (53564), 53566
New York (State) Commissioners of the Code.
53857
New York (State) Commissioners of the Land
Office. 53906
New York (State) Commissioners on a Common
School Code. 53898
New York (State) Commissioners on a Rail-Road
from Boston to the Hudson River. 53901
New York (State) Commissioners on Internal
Navigation. 22755-22756, 50833, (53900),
53905 see also Clinton, De Witt.
Morris, Gouvernour. North W. Van
Rensselaer, Stephen, 1765-1839.
New York (State) Commissioners on New York
Harbor. see New York (State) Harbor
Commission.
New York (State) Commissioners on Practice
and Pleadings. 53908
New York (State) Commissioners on the Canals
from Lake Erie to the Hudson River and
from Lake Champlain to the Same. see
New York (State) Canal Commissioners.
New York (State) Commissioners on the
Eastern Boundary of New Jersey. 69776
New York (State) Commissioners on the Eastern
Boundary of New York. (53774)
New York (State) Commissioners on the Military
Grants. see New York (State) Com-
missioners for Settling the Titles to Land
in the County of Onondaga.
New York (State) Commissioners on the New
York and Connecticut Boundary. 15687,
53902

New York (State) Commissioners on the
Niagara Ship Canal. 55131

New York (State) Commissioners on the
Onondaga Salt Springs. 57362

New York (State) Commissioners on Washington Park, Brooklyn. 8317

New York (State) Commissioners Relative to
the Removal of the Quarantine Station.
(53885)

New York (State) Commissioners to Explore
the Route of an Inland Navigation, from
Hudson's River to Lake Ontario and
Lake Erie. see New York (State)
Commissioners on Internal Navigation.

New York (State) Commissioners to Investigate the Pecuniary Affairs of the Several
State Prisons. 53903

New York (State) Commissioners to Locate
the Hudson River Asylum for the Insane.
53616

New York (State) Commissioners to Prepare
the Revised Statutes. (53942)

New York (State) Commissioners to Revise
the Statute Laws. 53892, (53899)

New York (State) Commissioners to Revise
the Laws of Assessment and Collection
of Taxes. (53632)

New York (State) Commissioners to Secure
the Establishment, Government, &c. &c.,
of Common Schools in the City of New
York. 53616

New York (State) Commissioners to the
Oneida Indians. 96608

New York (State) Commissioners to the Seneca
Indians. 96610-96611 see also Phelps,
Oliver.

New York (State) Commissioners to Visit the
State Prisons. (53977), 69497, (73230)

New York (State) Committee to Explore the
Western Waters. (22754), 69741, 102983

New York (State) Common Schools. see New
York (State) Department of Public
Instruction. New York (State) University.

New York (State) Common Schools Department.
see New York (State) Department of
Public Instruction.

New York (State) Comptroller of Banks. see
New York (State) Comptroller's Office.

New York (State) Comptroller's Office.
(53563), 53618, (72141) see also Robinson, Lucius.

New York (State) Constitution. 1269, 1271,
2071, 5316, 6360, 9672, 16086-16092,
16097, 16099-16103, 16107, (16109),
16113, 16118-16120, 16133, 19174,
(19476), 25790, 29731, 29732, 33137,
36677, (40144), (47188), 51471, 53521,
53626, 53628, 53735, 53852, 53969-
(53970), (57279), 59771, (66397), 68469,
(71223), 93558, 95470, 100342, 101650,
101983-101984A, 101986, 101987, 101989,
101990, 104198, 105990

New York (State) Constitutional Convention,
1777. see New York (State) Convention
of the Representatives, 1776-1777.

New York (State) Constitutional Convention,
Albany, 1821. (53482), 53628, 53711,
53753, 53915, 53945, note after 92151,
98425

New York (State) Constitutional Convention,
Utica. 1837. 53471

New York (State) Constitutional Convention,
Albany, 1846. 53626, 53635, (53650),
(53712), (53756), 53916

New York (State) Constitutional Convention,
Albany, 1846. Members. (54043)

New York (State) Constitutional Convention,
Albany, 1867-1868. (53651), (53713),
53863, 53953

New York (State) Contractor. claimant
53600 see also Anderson, Elbert.
claimant

New York (State) Convention, Poughkeepsie,
1788. 22233, 51471, 53634, 53701,
100031, note after 106002

New York (State) Convention, Albany, 1801.
53710

New York (State) Convention, 1824. (29552),
1st note after 97583

New York (State) Convention of the Representatives, 1776-1777. 818, 53480, 53698,
53852, 53948, 70078, 98999, 106412

New York (State) Convention of the Representa
tives, 1776-1777. Secret Committee.
74496

New York (State) Convention of Young Men,
Utica, 1828. see Convention of Young
Men of the State of New York, Utica,
1828.

New York (State) Council of Appointment.
1795, (34385), 53451, note after 53697,
note after 83791

New York (State) County Superintendents of
the Poor. (53935), 53956

New York (State) County Superintendents of the
Poor. petitioners (53935)

New York (State) Court for the Trial of
Impeachments and the Correction of
Errors. (17391)-17392, 28147, 31299,
41637, 46765, 54320, 54701, 55717,
83019, 83493, 89298, 89386, 91365,
94263, 96762, 2d note after 96854,
96865, 96868-96869, 96881, 96885-
96887, 96870, 96896, 96900, 96903,
96932, 97822, 97879, 98438, 98616,
100777, 100996-100997, 101435-101436,
102175, 102624, 102625, 103153, 103383,
103686, 104412

New York (State) Court of Appeals. 15617,
18753, 21543, 26131, (31300), 39852,
40003, 48611, 59502, 64285, 70230,
89349

New York (State) Court of Appeals. reporter
pseud. see Reporter of the New York
Court of Appeals. pseud.

New York (State) Court of Chancery. 3344A,
53542, 54793, 76498, 91610, 93607,
96853, 96896, 97779-97781, 97879,
100997, 101112, 104500

New York (State) Court of Equity. 74104

New York (State) Court of Errors. see New
York (State) Court for the Trial of
Impeachments and the Correction of
Errors.

New York (State) Court of Oyer and Terminer
(New York County) (69914), (70423),
86863, 95142, 96945, 102461

New York (State) Courts. 20634, (78979),
79104, 79125, 80359, (80361)

New York (State) Department of Public Instruction. 20341, (53613), 53612, 53638,
53645, 53704, (53741), 53986, 53990,
67800-67801, 94501 see also Dix, John
Adams, 1798-1879. Randall, Samuel S.
New York (State) University.

New York (State) District Attorney (New York
City) 29713 see also Hall, Abraham
Oakey, 1826-1898.

New York (State) Deutsche Gesellschaft. see
Deutsche Gesellschaft der Stadt New
York.

New York (State) Legislature. Select Committee on . . . Intemperance and the Sale of Intoxicating Drinks. Majority. 53944

New York (State) Legislature. Select Committee on . . . Intemperance and the Sale of Intoxicating Drinks. Minority. 53944

New York (State) Legislature. Select Committee to Examine into Frauds Upon Emigrants. (53926)

New York (State) Legislature. Select Committee on the Abduction of William Morgan. (50685)

New York (State) Legislature. Select Committee on the Conduct of Elam Lynds. 8229

New York (State) Legislature. Select Committee to Investigate Matters Connected with the Publication of the State Work on Natural History. 22518

New York (State) Legislature. Select Committee on the Report of Trinity Church. 69710, 4th note after 96984, 96985

New York (State) Legislature. Assembly. 13239, 35783, (53564), 53602, 53649, 53700, 53708, 53755, 53835, 53954, 53981, 54009-54010, 84484, 85815, 86352, 89355

New York (State) Legislature. Assembly. Clerk. 53602

New York (State) Legislature. Assembly. Committee of Ways and Means. 586

New York (State) Legislature. Assembly. Committee on the Long Island Canal Company. 41895

New York (State) Legislature. Assembly. Committee to Examine the Claim of W. W. Niles. (24431)

New York (State) Legislature. Assembly. Select Committee on the Library. (2723)

New York (State) Legislature. Assembly. Select Committee on the Memorial of the French Benevolent Society of the City of New York. 85815

New York (State) Legislature. Assembly. Select Committee to Examine the State Prisons. (53977)

New York (State) Legislature. Senate. (2588), 8176, 19638, 20031, 28118, 33528, (40755), 53530, 53652, 53669, 53701, (53715), 53716, 53969, (53970), 54001, 69857, 73956, 73977, 77874, 78315, 82591, 95242, 89352, 91820, 96985, 102964

New York (State) Legislature. Senate. Committee of Privileges and Elections. 42397

New York (State) Legislature. Senate. Committee on Banks and Insurance Companies. 53911

New York (State) Legislature. Senate. Committee on Commerce and Navigation. 55130

New York (State) Legislature. Senate. Committee on Finance. 21107, 99821

New York (State) Legislature. Senate. Committee on the Accounts of Daniel D. Tompkins with this State. 53891

New York (State) Legislature. Senate. Committee on the Albany Bridge. 33528, 80841

New York (State) Legislature. Senate. Committee on the Albany Bridge. Minority. 33528

New York (State) Legislature. Senate. Committee on the Communication of the Hon. Jaspar Ward, 1826. (53929)

New York (State) Legislature. Senate. Committee on the Electoral Law. 53933

New York (State) Legislature. Senate. Committee on the Long Island Canal Company. 41895

New York (State) Legislature. Senate. Committee on the Watervliet Turnpike. 102108

New York (State) Legislature. Senate. Committee to Investigate Certain Pecuniary Affairs of Union College. 89345

New York (State) Legislature. Senate. President. 53750

New York (State) Legislature. Senate. Select Committee on the Affairs of Trinity Church. 96985

New York (State) Legislature. Senate. Select Committee on the Canal Bank Frauds. 630

New York (State) Legislature. Senate. Select Committee on the Completion of the Natural History of the State. 53798

New York (State) Legislature. Senate. Select Committee on the Publication of the Natural History of the State. 53798

New York (State) Legislature. Senate. Select Committee to Examine the State Prisons at Mount Pleasant and Auburn. (53607)

New York (State) Legislature. Senate. Select Committee to Investigate the Management of the Canals. (53568)

New York (State) Legislature. Senate. Select Committee to Investigate the Various Departments of the Government of the City of New York. 65805

New York (State) Legislature. Senate. Special Committee on the Application of the Northern Rail Road Company for Relief. 55828

New York (State) Legislature. Senate. Special Committee on the Present Quarantine Laws. (53885)

New York (State) Legislature. Senate. Special Committee to Investigate the Health Department of the City of New York. 54647

New York (State) Legislature. Whig Members. see Whig Party. New York.

New York (State) Librarian. 53830, 53981 see also Homes, Henry Augustus, 1812-1887. Mexon, C. H.

New York (State) Library. 32734, 53572, 53825-53828, 53830, 84558, 99054

New York (State) Library. Law Library. 53830

New York (State) Library. Trustees. (53824), 101353

New York (State) Lieutenant Governor, 1843-1844. (54729)

New York (State) Lunatic Asylum, Utica. see New York (State) State Hospital, Utica.

New York (State) Militia. 26890, 53685, 53777-53778, 53781, 53847, 53888, 53890, 54461, note just before 68399, 68959, 98518

New York (State) Militia. Adjutant General. see New York (State) Adjutant General.

New York (State) Militia. Board of State Officers. 53968

New York (State) Militia. Courts Martial (Corcoran) 16755

New York (State) Militia. Courts Martial (Dillon) (20178), 96857

New York (State) Militia. Courts Martial
(Spencer) 89304
New York (State) Militia. Fifth Cavalry.
6292, 6861
New York (State) Militia. Fifth Regiment.
Jefferson Guard. 53529
New York (State) Militia. Fiftieth Regiment.
Company A (De Witt Guards) 19881
New York (State) Militia. First Ira Harris
Guards. see New York (State) Militia.
Fifth Cavalry.
New York (State) Militia. Inspector General.
(53699), 53702
New York (State) Militia. Judge Advocate
General. 53724
New York (State) Militia. New York City.
54461
New York (State) Militia. One Hundred Six-
teenth Regiment Volunteers. (13444)
New York (State) Militia. Regiment of
Artillery of the City and County of New
York. Officers. 90669
New York (State) Militia. Regiment of Vol-
unteers. 69894
New York (State) Militia. Second Regiment of
Artillery. 53812
New York (State) Militia. Seventh Regiment.
54370
New York (State) Militia. Stuyvesant Square
Home Guard, New York City. 54685,
note after 93290
New York (State) Militia. Surgeon General.
53994
New York (State) Militia. Twenty Third
Regiment. Company A. 53623
New York (State) Mount Pleasant Prison. see
New York (State) State Prison, Mount
Pleasant.
New York (State) Museum. see New York
State Museum, Albany.
New York (State) National Democratic Vol-
unteers. 53486 see also Democratic
Party. New York.
New York (State) National Guard. see New
York (State) Militia.
New York (State) New York Harbor Commis-
sioners. see New York (State) Harbor
Commission.
New York (State) Normal and Training School,
Cortland. see New York (State) State
Normal School, Cortland.
New York (State) Normal and Training School,
Oswego. see New York (State) State
Normal School, Oswego.
New York (State) Normal and Training School,
Potsdam. see New York (State) State
Normal School, Potsdam.
New York (State) Normal School, Albany. see
New York (State) State College for
Teachers, Albany.
New Yotk (State) Office of the Adjutant Gen-
eral. see New York (State) Adjutant
General.
New York (State) Office of the Chief Engineer.
see New York (State) State Engineer
and Surveyor.
New York (State) Office of the Secretary of
State. see New York (State) Secretary
of State.
New York (State) Onondaga Commissioners.
see New York (State) Commissioners
for Settling the Titles to Land in the
County of Onondaga.
New York (State) Onondaga Salt Springs. see
New York (State) Superintendent of
Onondaga Salt Springs.

New York (State) Paymaster General. 53856
New York (State) Prison, Auburn. see New
York (State) State Prison, Auburn.
New York (State) Prison, Clinton. see New
York (State) State Prison, Auburn.
New York (State) Prison, Mount Pleasant. see
New York (State) State Prison, Mount
Pleasant.
New York (State) Provincial Congress, 1775.
see New York (Colony) Committee of
Safety, 1775-1776.
New York (State) Provincial Congress, 1776-
1777. see New York (State) Convention
of the Representatives, 1776-1777.
New York (State) Quartermaster General's
Department. 53886
New York (State) Railroad Commissioners.
see New York (State) Board of Railroad
Commissioners.
New York (State) Referee on Compensation to
Owners of Vaults in Cemeteries, and to
Relatives of Individuals Buried in Graves
Disturbed by Legal Proceedings. 73956,
73961 see also Ruggles, Samuel B.
New York (State) School Commissioners and
Supervisors. see New York (State)
University.
New York (State) Secretary of State. 20341,
21694, 33137, 33149, 51740, 53430-53431,
53554-53556, 53572, (53576), 53653,
(53678), 53689, 53727, (53751)-53755,
53956, 77874, 94430 see also Dix, John
Adams, 1798-1879. Tillotson, Thomas.
New York (State) Soldiers' Depot. see New
York (State) Board of Managers of the
Soldiers' Depot.
New York (State) Special Attorney to Prosecute
the Abductors of William Morgan. 89352
see also Spencer, John Canfield.
New York (State) Special Counsel on the
Abduction of William Morgan. 89352
see also Throop, Enos Thompson, 1784-
1894.
New York (State) Superintendent of Banks.
see New York (State) Banking Depart-
ment. Superintendent.
New York (State) State College for Teachers,
Albany. 53966
New York (State) State College for Teachers,
Albany. Executive Committee. 53967
New York (State) State Emigrant Hospital,
New York. 53964
New York (State) State Engineer and Surveyor.
53572, 53615, 53657, 53965 see also
New York (State) Surveyor General.
New York (State) State Hospital, Binghampton.
53821
New York (State) State Hospital, Binghampton.
Charter. 53821
New York (State) State Hospital, Binghampton.
Corresponding Secretary. 53821
New York (State) State Hospital, Matteawan.
53535
New York (State) State Hospital, Utica. 1118,
53831
New York (State) State Hospital, Utica.
Managers. (20336A), 53831
New York (State) State Hospital, Utica.
Patients. eds. (57385)
New York (State) State Hospital, Utica.
Physician. 53831
New York (State) State Hospital, Utica.
Trustees. 53831
New York (State) State Industrial School,
Rochester. 54012, 72366

New York (State) State Industrial School, Rochester. Charter. 72366

New York (State) State Industrial School, Rochester. Managers. (54013)

New York (State) State Normal School, Cortland. 53967

New York (State) State Normal School, Oswego. 53967, 57831, (57836)

New York (State) State Normal School, Potsdam. 53967

New York (State) State Prison, Auburn. 65711, 73228

New York (State) State Prison, Auburn. Agent. 37799, 53897, (53976), 64788 see also Powers, Gershom.

New York (State) State Prison, Auburn. Inspectors. (53977)

New York (State) State Prison, Auburn. Officers. defendants 64788

New York (State) State Prison, Clinton. Agent. 53603

New York (State) State Prison, Mount Pleasant. Board of Inspectors. 53545

New York (State) State School for the Blind, Batavia. 53822

New York (State) State Survey. Palaeontological Department. 15906

New York (State) Superintendent of Common Schools. see New York (State) Department of Public Instruction.

New York (State) Superintendent of Fisheries. see New York (State) Commissioners of Fisheries.

New York (State) Superintendent of Onondaga Salt Springs. 53989, 57362, 84484, 89390 see also Smith, Vivus Wood, 1804-1881. Spencer, Thomas.

New York (State) Superintendent of Public Instruction. see New York (State) Department of Public Instruction.

New York (State) Superintendent of the Banking Department. see New York (State) Banking Department. Superintendent.

New York (State) Superior Court. 614, 74603, 96908

New York (State) Supreme Court. 12397, (17391), 17641, 18034, 19145, 25124, 37724, 39852, 39877, 41548, 41637, 43529, 53536, 54158, 69305, 69451, (79837), 80738, 88290, 89384, 94044-94047, 94049, 94052-94053, 96832, 96842, 96875, 2d note after 97117, 102624, 103382, 105025, 105055

New York (State) Supreme Court. Chief Justice. 35831, 94044-94047, 94049, 94052-94053, 97787 see also Jay, John, 1745-1829.

New York (State) Surgeon General. see New York (State) Militia. Surgeon General.

New York (State) Surveyor General. 53615, 53657, 57342 see also New York (State) State Engineer and Surveyor.

New York (State) Surveyor of Railroad Statistics. see New York (State) State Engineer and Surveyor.

New York (State) Treasurer's Office. 53995, 90743

New York (State) Union Safety Committee. see Union Safety Committee.

New York (State) United German Lutheran Churches. see Vereinigten Deutschen Gesellschaften der Stadt New York.

New York (State) University. College of Physicians and Surgeons. see Columbia University. College of Physicians and Surgeons.

New York State) University. Medico-Chirurgical Society. see New York (State) University. Medical and Surgical Society.

New York (State) University Medical and Surgical Society. (54000)

New York (State) University. Regents. 30981, 53434, (53996)-(54000), 84395, 97787

New York (State) University. Regents. petitioners 84395

New York (State) University. Regents. Committee on the Education of Common School Teachers. (54000)

New York (State) University. Regents. Committee to Visit the College of Physicians and Surgeons. (54000)

New York (State) University Convention. see University Convention of the State of New York.

New York (State) Vice-Chancellor. (53637) see also M'Coun, William T.

New York (State) Vice-Chancellor (First District) 104500

New York (State) Water Commissioners. (43227)

New York (State) Western House of Refuge for Juvenile Delinquents. see New York (State) State Industrial School, Rochester.

New York (State) Woman's Hospital of the State of New York. 53978

New York. 89496

New York: a historical sketch. 54422

New York above-ground and under-ground. 25222

New York Academy of Medicine. 54423

New York Academy of Medicine. Committee on Military Surgery. 54423

New York Academy of Medicine. Standing Committee on Public Health and Legal Medicine. 54423

New York Academy of Sacred Music. 54424

New York Academy of Sciences. 5870, 6267, 19325, 49738, 53574-53575, 54146, (54365), 84126-84127, 85436, 89984

New York Academy of Sciences. Charter. (54365)

New York Academy of Sciences. Library. (54365)

New York African Society for Mutual Relief. 54718

New York Agricultural Society. see New York State Agricultural Society.

New York albion. 85162

New York almanac. 84948

New York almanac and yearly record. 54720

New York almanac and weather book for . . . 1857. 54720

New-York almanac for 1850. 54298

New-York almanac, for . . . 1833. (54719)

New York almanac for 1870. (54721)

New-York almanack, for . . . 1828. 89583

New York almanack for 1767. 53674

New York American. 8291, 17471, 35856, note after 101440

New York American Home Missionary Society. see American Home Missionary Society, New York.

New York American republican. 84162

New York American Widows Relief Association. see American Widows Relief Association, New York.

New York Anacreontic Society. see Anacreontic Society, New York.

New York Ancient Briton's Benefit Society.
see Ancient Briton's Benefit Society,
New York.
New York and African Exchange Company.
54722
New York and Albany Railroad. petitioners
54723
New York and Albany Railroad. Chief
Engineer. 54723
New York and Albany Railroad. President.
54723
New York and Albany Rail-Road. 54723
New York and Boston Oil Company. 54724
New York and Boston Railroad. 54725
New York and Boston Railroad. Engineer.
54725
New York and Boston Steam-Boat Company.
9167
New York and Boston Steam-Boat Company.
Charter. 54726
New York and Boston Steam-Boat Company.
Stockholders. 54726
New York and Brooklyn Auxiliary Society.
54727
New York and Brooklyn Coal Company.
54728
New York and Brooklyn Homoeopathic Direc-
tory. 82718
New York and Erie Railroad Company.
72157, 94430, 103072
New York and Erie Railroad Company.
petitioners (54729)
New York and Erie Railroad Company. Board
of Directors. (54729), 90668
New York and Erie Railroad Company. Presi-
dent. 64466
New York and Erie Railroad Company.
Trustees. 90668 see also Brown,
James.
New York and Erie Rail-Road guide book.
43545
New-York and farmer's almanack, for . . .
1830. 54730
New York and Galway Steam Ship Company.
54731
New York and Harlem Railroad Company.
(54732), 69683
New York and Harlem Railroad Company.
petitioners (54732)
New York and Hartford Railroad. Engineer.
54733
New York and Hartford Railroad. Executive
Committee. 54733
New York and Havre Mail Steamers. Pro-
prietors. petitioners (54732)
New York and its institutions, 1609-1872.
71142
New-York and Lake Superior Mining Company.
53735
New-York and Lake Superior Mining Company.
Trustees. 54735
New York and Liverpool Line of American
Steamers. Proprietors. petitioners
14433, 93819
New York and Michigan Company. 54736
New-York and Michigan Mining Company.
Trustees. 54737
New York and New-Haven Railroad Company.
Directors. (54738)
New-York and New-Jersey almanac. 82291
New-York and New-Jersey almanac, for . . .
1828. 54739
New-York, & New-Jersey almanac, for the
year of Our Lord, 1808. 84948
New York and Nicaragua Colonization Associa-
tion. 54740

New York and Stonington Rail Road. Charter.
65839
New York and Taconic systems. (54742)
New York and Texas Land and Emigration
Association. 54743
New York and the city travel. 4654
New York and the five cotton states. 54844
New York and the White mountains. 28129,
29227
New York and United States kalendar. 41940
New-York and Vermont almanack. 41959
New-York & Vermont almanack. 25667
New York and Vermont almanack: [by] A.
Beers. 23846
New-York annual register for the year of Our
Lord 1830. 53799, 104200
New-York Anti-secret Society Convention,
Syracuse, 1870. (53800)
New York Anti-slavery Society. see New
York State Anti-slavery Society.
New York Anti-tobacco Society. 54426
New York aristocracy. 36664
New-York—as it is; being the counter-part of
the metropolis of America. 4409
New-York as it is, in 1835. 54459, note after
104200
New-York as it is, in 1834. 54459, note after
104200
New-York as it is, in 1839. 54459, note after
104200
New-York as it is, in 1837. 54459, note after
104200
New-York as it is, in 1833. 54459, note after
104200
New York as it is, or stranger's guide book.
54407
New York as it was during the latter part of
the last century. (21114)
New York as it was in the days of the Dutch
governors. (18795), 54316
New York Associate Reformed Presbyterian
Synod. see Associate Reformed
Presbyterian Church.
New York Associate Reformed Synod. see
Associate Reformed Presbyterian Church
New York Associated Body of House Carpen-
ters. see Associated Body of House
Carpenters, New York.
New York Association for Colored Volunteers.
Secretary. 54427
New York Association for Restoration of
American Shipping Interests. 54428
New York Association for Restoration of
American Shipping Interests. petitioners
47631
New York Association for the Advancement of
Science and Art. (54745)
New York Association for the Benefit of
Colored Orphans. see Association for
the Benefit of Colored Orphans, New
York.
New York Association for the Improved Instruc-
tion of Deaf Mutes. see Association
for the Improved Instruction of Deaf
Mutes, New York.
New-York Association for the Improvement of
the Breed of Horses. 54846
New-York Association for the Improvement of
the Condition of the Poor. 54429
New York Association for the Relief of
Respectable Indigent Aged Females. see
Association for the Relief of Respectable
Indigent Aged Females, New York.
New York Association for the Relief of the
Industrious Poor. see Association for
the Relief of the Industrious Poor, New
York.

New York Association for the Suppression of
Gambling. 54430
New York Association of Friends for the
Relief of Those Held in Slavery.
32996, 44685 see also Friends, Society
of. New York Yearly Meeting.
New York Asylum for Lying-in Women.
Managers. 54431
New York Athenaeum. 54432
New York Athenaeum. Association. see
Athenaeum Association, New York.
New York Athenaeum. Charter. 54432
New York Athenaeum. Committee. 54432
New York Athenaeum. Committee to Amend
the Charter. 54432
New York Athenaeum. Committee to Amend
the Constitution. 54432
New York atlas. 64409
New-York, Aug. 29, 1775. 105223
New York Auxiliary Bible and Common Prayer
Book Society. (54116), 54433
New York bank note list. 12028
New York Bank Officers Meeting, 1863. see
New York (City) Meeting of Bank Offi-
cers, 1863.
New York Baptist annual for 1870. 54747
New York Baptist Association. see Baptists.
New York. New York Baptist Association.
New York Baptist Education Society. see
Baptist Education Society of New York.
New York Baptist Missionary Convention. 53540
New York Baptist Theological Seminary, New
York. see New York (City) Baptist
Theological Seminary.
New York Baptist Union for Ministerial Edu-
cation. see Rochester Theological
Seminary, Rochester, N. Y.
New York Benevolent Christian Society. see
Benevolent Christian Society, New York.
New York Benevolent Society. see Benevolent
Society, New York.
New York Bible Society. 5185, 49837, 49841,
54433, 94851, 106181
New York Board of Fire Underwriters. (54123)
New York Board of Fire Underwriters. Com-
mittee on Gas Machines, Carburators.
54750
New York Board of Trade and Transportation.
54266
New York Board of Underwriters. Committee
on Insurance Taxes. 90751
New York Board of Underwriters. Committee
to Investigate the Causes of the Loss of
the Steamer Central America. 54750
New-York book of poetry. 54751
New York Book Society. (54434)
New York Book Society. Constitution, by-laws,
etc. (54434)
New York Branch of the American Freedman's
Union Commission. see American
Freedman's Union Commission. New
York Branch.
New York Branch of the Linnaean Society of
Paris. see Societe Linneenne de Paris.
New-York business directory, for 1840 and
1841. 54459
New-York business directory, for 1844-1845.
54459
New-York business directory, for 1841 and
1842. 54459
New-York business directory, for 1846 and
1847. 54459
New-York business-man's companion. 19247
New York by gas light. 25226
New York by night and day. (41392)
New York cabinet. 54752
New York Catholic register for 1863. (54753)

New-York Central College, McGrawsville,
N. Y. (53804), 54754
New York Central College Association.
54754
New York Central Dispensary. see Central
Dispensary, New York.
New York Central Homoeopathic Dispensary.
54435
New York Central Railroad company. 53517,
53676, (54755)
New York Central Railroad Company. Board
of Directors. Committee. (54755)
New York central road. The Buffalo Con-
vention, and the St. Nicholas compact.
11343
New York Chamber of Commerce, and sugges-
tions for an enlarged sphere of action.
48937
New York Cheap Postage Association.
Directors. 54756
New York Chenango Baptist Association. see
Baptists. New York. Chenango Baptist
Association.
New York Children's Aid Society. see
Children's Aid Society, New York.
New York Children's Aid Society. Hudson
River Industrial School Association.
see Hudson River Industrial School
Association.
New York chronicle. 54757
New York church year book for 1859-60.
33580
New-York churchman. pseud. Obsequies and
obituary noticies. 57310
New York Crystal Palace. Illustrated descrip-
tion of the buildings. 11090
New York Circus. see Vilalliave Circus.
New York citizen and American republican.
84162
New York citizen and round table. 73473
New York Citizens' Association. see Citizens'
Association of New York.
New-York city and co-partnership directory,
for 1843 & 1844. 54459
New-York City Anti-slavery Society. 54436
New York city as a mission field. 2955
New York City Children's Aid Society. see
Children's Aid Society, New York.
New York City Christian Alliance. see
Christian Alliance, New York.
New York Clearing House Association. Tax
Committee. 3188
New York city directory . . . by G. Danielson
Carroll. 54459
New York city directory, 1860-1861. 84074
New York city directory for 1850-51. 54459
New York city directory for 1851-52. 54459
New York city directory, for 1852-3. 54459
New York city directory, for 1842. 54459
New York city during the American revolution.
54439
New York city Evangelical Union Anti-slavery
Society. see Evangelical Union Anti-
slavery Society of New York.
New York City Free School Society. see Free
School Society, New York.
New York City German Society. see German
Society of the City of New York.
New York city guide . . . for strangers and
citizens to the . . . objects of interest.
(54574)
New York city hall recorder. 54440, 72617
New York city hall reporter. 54441
New York City Ladies' Society for the Relief
of Poor Widows With Small Children.
see Ladies' Society for the Relief of

Poor Widows With Small Children, New York.

New York City Library Association. 54442

New York City Mariner's Family Industrial Society. see Mariner's Family Industrial Society of the Port of New York.

New York City Medical Society. see Medical Society of the County of New York.

New York City Mission and Tract Society. see New York Mission and Tract Society.

New York City Mission Society. 54445 see also New York Protestant Episcopal City Mission Society.

New York City partnership directory for 1849 and 1850. 54459

New York City Philological Society. see Philological Society in New York.

New York City Police Court. First District. Hon. M. Connolly, Justice. 74759

New York city railroad directory. 18678

New York city railroads. 39349

New York city street directory for 1851. 54459

New York city tax book, being a list of persons. 7123

New-York City Temperance Society. 54448, 95801

New York City Temperance Society. Board of Managers. 54550

New York City Temperance Society. Board of Managers. Executive Committee. 54448

New York City Young Men's Christian Association. see Young Men's Christian Association, New York.

New-York City Young Men's Moral Reform Society. 54450, 106180

New York civil list. 33143

New-York class-book. 74390

New York Classis. see Reformed Church in America. Classis of New York.

New York clerks and country merchant. 20971

New York Club, New York. 54451

New-York Coal Company. 54581, note after 97065

New York College of Dental Surgery, Syracuse, N. Y. (54758)

New York colonial documents. 69998

New York colonial records. 1521

New York Colonization Society. 53816, 54437

New York Colonization Society. General Agent and Corresponding Secretary. 106169 see also Proudfit, Alexander Moncrief, 1770-1843.

New-York Columbian. 13717, 33237

New York comic almanac. 93075

New York comic almanack for 1847. 54759

New-York commercial advertiser. 38076, 79687, 100885-100886, 100888, 100997

New York Committee for Relief to East Tennessee. 21654

New York Committee of Vigilance. 54046, 54452

New York Committee to Recruit the Ninth Army Corps. (69751)

New York Committee to Recruit the Ninth Army Corps. Secretary. (69751)

New York Company of Paris. see Company of New York.

New York Conference Seminary, Charlottesville, N. Y. 12145, (54760)

New-York, Connecticut, & New-Jersey almanack. 28671

New York Consolidated Stock and Petroleum Exchange. see Consolidated Stock and Petroleum Exchange of New York.

New-York conspiracy. (33060)

New York Conspiracy trials. (54761)

New York convention manual. 53805

New York Convention of the Friends of Domestic Industry, New York, 1831. see Friends of Domestic Industry.

New York Convention of the Friends of Domestic Industry, New York, 1832. see Friends of Domestic Industry.

New York Convention on the Great State Road, Newburgh, 1826. see Convention on the Great State Road, Newburgh, N. Y., 1826.

New York convention. Report on the production and manufacture of cotton. 17127, 35449

New York Corporation for the Relief of Widows and Children of Clergymen of the Protestant Episcopal Church. see Corporation for the Relief of Widows and Children of Clergymen of the Protestant Episcopal Church in . . . New York.

New York Corresponding Association for the Promotion of Internal Improvements. 22742, 29547, 29551, 53661

New York County Medical Society. see Medical Society of the County of New York.

New York courier and enquirer. (12729), 28494, 40650, 70431, 90794

New York Court of Appeals. Report of the Lemmon slave case. 40003

New-York cries in rhyme. 54453, 105063

New York Cuban Junta. 23612

New York daily advertiser. 10663, 63245, 84148, 84150, 84155, 84162, 84163, 84166, 84175-84176, 84819

New York daily bulletin. 89111

New York daily bulletin and auction record 89111

New-York daily express. 84162, 103304

New York daily news. 85374

New York daily times. 55568

New York daily transcript. 54454

New York daily transcript extra, containing the names. 54454

New-York daily tribune. 70243, 90001

New York day-book. 78259

New York, Dec. 1, 1862. 8447

New York Democratic Anti-abolition State Right Association. see Democratic Anti-abolition State Right Association of New York.

New York Democratic Anti-Lecompton Meeting. . . . February, 17, 1858. 54455

New York Democratic Association of Washington. 54762

New York Democratic Committee. see Democratic Party. New York. Committee.

New York Democratic difficulties. 84717

New York Democratic Vigilent Association. (30451)

New York dental journal. 54763

New York Dental Protective Association. (54764)

New York dental recorder. (54765)

New York detective. pseud. see B., J. pseud.

New York . . . directory. 54459

New-York directory and register, for . . .
1789. 54457
New-York directory, containing, a valuable
and well calculated almanack. 54456
New-York . . . directory, for 1853-43.
54459
New York . . . directory for 1854-66.
54459
New-York directory . . . for 1796. 54459
New-York directory . . . for . . . 1792.
54458
New-York Dispensary, New York. 54460
New-York Dispensary, New York. Board of
Trustees. 54460
New-York Dispensary, New York. Charter.
54460
New-York Dry Dock Company. President.
90672 see also Weeks, Ezra.
New York during the last half century.
(25445)
New York East Conference. see Methodist
Episcopal Church. Conferences. New
York East.
New York Eclectic Medical Society. see
Eclectic Medical Society of New York.
New York Ecclesiological Society. 54769
New York ecclesiologist. 54768
New York editor. pseud. Russian ball. see
Stedman, Charles J.
New York Education and Missionary Society
of the Protestant Episcopal Church.
see Education and Missionary Society
of the Protestant Episcopal Church in
the State of New York.
New York election and the state of the
country. 35849
New York election frauds. . . . Mr. W.
Lawrence, of Ohio. (39375)
New York enquirer. see Morning courier
and New York enquirer.
New York enrollment lists. 54461
New York Evangelical Lutheran Ministerium.
see Evangelical Lutheran Ministerium
of the State of New York and Adjacent
States and Counties.
New York Evangelical Lutheran Sunday School
Society. see Evangelical Lutheran
Sunday School Society, New York.
New-York Evangelical Missionary Society for
Young Men. 87968
New York evangelist. 17270, 80493, 90007,
note before 96989, 104273
New York evening post. 5307, 9344, 9611,
9639, 12201, (20309), 20861, 24274,
29953, 34456, 36072, 53660, (73952),
78405, 78843-78844, 83876, 84824,
89203, 89205, 93522, 93659, note
before 95127, note after 95722, 97362,
note after 99394, 102550, 105044
New York evening post. Extra. 53660
New York evening star. 13773
New York exhibition. 81066
New York Eye Infirmary. 54462
New York farmer and American gardener's
magazine. 54771
New-York farmer, and horticultural repository.
54772
New York farmer and mechanic. 54773
New York farmer's almanac. 54774
New-York farmer's almanack. 89586
New-York fauna. (53783)
New-York, February 15, 1773. (54420)
New York Female Association. see Female
Association, New York.
New York Female Auxiliary Bible Society.
54463

New York Female Benevolent Society. 54272
New York Female Benevolent Society. Audit-
ing Committee. Chairman. 43188, note
after 103223 see also Wheelwright,
John.
New York Female Bethel Union. 54464
New York Female Missionary Society of the
Western District. see Female
Missionary Society of the Western Dis-
trict of New York.
New York Female Society. see Female
Society, New York.
New York Female Union Society. (54465)
New-York Firemen Insurance Company.
plaintiffs 100996
New York fraud. 54775
New York Free Academy. see New York
(City) City College.
New York Free Produce Association of
Friends. Managers. 69882
New York Free School. see New York (City)
Free School.
New York Free School Society. see Free
School Society, New York.
New York Freedman's Savings and Trust Com-
pany. see Freedman's Savings and
Trust Company, New York.
New-York freeholder. (582A)
New York freeman's journal. (79994), 79996
New York Friars Tontine, New York. 54221
New York Gallery of Fine Arts, New York.
54467
New-York gardener. 54476
New-York Gas Regulator Company. 54777
New York gazette (Bradford's) 84566
New York gazette (Gaine's) see New York
gazette: and the weekly mercury.
New York gazette (Parker's) 84576, 84624,
84665, 84678C, 100788, 106080
New York gazette (Rivington's) see Riving-
ton's New York gazette.
New York gazette and general advertiser.
(22678), (32961), 105152
New York gazette: and the weekly mercury.
(14394)-14395, 84632, 84678C, 85249,
100867
New York gazette and weekly post boy.
103129
New York gazette, revived in the weekly post
boy. (14394)-14395, 84555, 84672
New York gazette and universal advertiser.
71690
New York gazetteer (1783-   ) 78581
New York gazetteer (Rivington's) see
Rivington's New York gazetteer.
New York genealogical and biographical record.
54778, 66717, (66718)-(66719), 83423,
84845
New York Genealogical and Biographical
Society. 54778-(54779), 66717-(66719),
83423, 84845
New York General Society of Mechanics and
Tradesmen. see General Society of
Mechanics and Tradesmen of the City of
New York.
New York General law magazine. 54441
New York Genesee Missionary Society. see
Genesee Missionary Society of the State
of New York.
New York Geographical and Statistical Society.
33746
New York globe. 85374
New-York Greek Committee. 100660
New York guardian. 84576
New-York hand book and merchant's guide.
(27622)

New York hards and softs. 54780

New York Hebrew Benevolent Society. see Hebrew Benevolent Society, New York.

New York Hebrew Young Men's Literary Association. see Hebrew Young Men's Literary Association, New York.

New York herald. 3570, (13744), 24985, 28892, 38269, (55574), 70350, 83423, 84886, 101938

New York Hibernian Provident Society. see Hibernian Provident Society, New York.

New York Hibernian Provident Society; or, the Danish inquisition under nine directors. 54468

New York High School Society. see High School Society, New York.

New York Historical and Philosophical Society. see Historical and Philosophical Society of New York.

New York Historical Association. see New York State Historical Association.

New York historical collections. see Collections of the New York Historical Society.

New York historical magazine. 29781

New York Historical Society. (133), 628, 3134, 3136, 3747, 4744, note after 7263, (7271), 8174, 10203, 13714, 20594, 20928, (21501)-21502, 21504, 26390, 26399, (33084), (37472), 38562, 40419, 49049, 50381, (53606), 53671-53672, (54471)-54476, (66038), 66062, 69996, (75021), (77850), 77875, 78059, 79353, 82845, 84566, 84570, 84571, 86744, 88844, 89993, 92154, 92830, note after 95562, 96171, 97975, note after 98474, 1st note after 98997, 99265, 99281, 99325, 2d note before 99889, 100852, 100853, 102920, 103152

New York Historiacl Society. petitioners 54475

New York Historical Society. Charter. (54471)

New York Historical Society. Committee of Publication. 84571

New York Historical Society. Committee to Prepare a Map. 77875

New York Historical Society. Fortieth Anniversary Dinner, 1844. 8174

New York Historical Society. Library. 54470-(54471)

New York Historical Society. Museum and Gallery of Art. (54471)

New York Historical Society. Semi-Centennial Celebration. 54477

New York Historical Society. Mr. Bancroft's letter on the exchange of prisoners. 3130, 3134

New-York Homoeopathic Dispensary Association. Trustees. (54478)

New York Homoeopathic Medical Society. see Homoeopathic Medical Society of the State of New York.

New York Horticultural Society. 53819, 54479, 54772

New York Horticultural Society. Charter. 54479

New York Hospital. 61349 see also Society of the New York Hospital, New York.

New York House and School of Industry. 54487

New York House of Mercy. 54485

New York House of Refuge. see Society for the Reformation of Juvenile Delinquents, New York. House of Refuge.

New York House of Refuge and its times. 59544

New York Howard Mission and Home for Little Wanderers. see Howard Mission and Home for Little Wanderers, New York.

New York Humane Society. see Humane Society of the State of New York.

New York Hydropathic and Physiological School. 54488

New York illustrated. By the Grand Division of Eastern New York. 87061

New York illustrated magazine. 84154

New York illustrated. With a map of the city. 54489

New York in a nutshell. 54490, 77178

New York in an uproar with a Greenwich horse race. 54110

New York in 1845. 54298, 54492

New York in 1828. 54491

New York, in favor of the Whig cause. 104593

New York in September, 1873. 78004

New York in slices. 25227

New York in the nineteenth century. (57789)

New York independent. (4313), 92447

New York independent press. 95506

New York Indians. claimants 54781

New York Indians. Treaties, etc. 54781, 96726

New York Industrial Exhibition, New York, 1854. 54493

New York Industrial Exhibition. General report of the British Commissioners. (54494)

New York Industrial Exhibition; its plans, purposes and prospects. 54493

New York Industrial Exhibition. Special report of Mr. Dilke. 20156

New York Industrial Exhibition. Special report of Professor Wilson. (54494)

New York Industrial Exhibition. Special report of Sir Charles Lyell. 42760

New York Industrial Home Association. 54495

New York Infant Asylum. (54496)

New York Infant School Society. see Infant School Society, New York.

New York Infantry. see New York (State) Militia.

New York Infirmary for Women and Children, New York. 54497

New York Institution, New York. 54498, 78522

New York Institution. Companion to American museum. 54498

New York Institution for the Education of the Blind. 54499

New York Institution for the Education of the Blind. Managers. 54499

New York Institution for the Instruction of the Deaf and Dumb. 54500, 93620

New York Institution for the Instruction of the Deaf and Dumb. Charter. 54500

New York Institution for the Instruction of the Deaf and Dumb. Directors. 54500

New York Insurance Company. (54782)

New York Irish Emigrant Association. 54501

New York Irish Relief Committee. see Irish Relief Committee of New York.

New York; its upper ten and lower million. (41395)

New York journal, and weekly register. 83604

New York journal. . . . an illustrated literary periodical. (54783)

New York journal of commerce. 54231, (70273)

New York journal of medicine. 1145, 24973, 54784, 84276

New York journal of medicine and surgery. 54785

New York journal of medicine, and the collateral sciences. (54786), 91787

New York Journal of Pharmacy. (54787)

New York journal: or the general advertiser. (25955), 77413, 86868, 95888, 100788, 102046, 102047, 102048

New York journalist. pseud. Memoirs of James Gordon Bennett and his times. see Pray, Isaac C.

New York Journeymen Shipwrights' Society. (54502)

New-York jubilee. Report, (the only one extant.) 102290

New York judicial repository. 54788

New-York, July 7, 1769. 97900

New York Juvenile Asylum. 54503

New York Juvenile Asylum. Charter. 54503

New-York Ladies' Home Missionary Society. 54504

New York lancet. 54790

New-York Law Institute. Library. 54505

New-York law magazine. 96832

New York ledger. 4313, 23258-23259

New-York legal observer. 37977, 54791

New-York legal register. 53807

N. Y. Legislature, 1859. In senate. (78268)

New-York Life Insurance and Trust Company. 54793

New-York Life Insurance and Trust Company. plaintiffs 54793

New-York Life Insurance Company. 54792

New York Life-Saving Benevolent Association. 54506

New York Linnaean Society. see Linnaean Society of New York. and Societe Linneenne de Paris.

New-York liquor law. 53808

New York Literary and Philosophical Society. see Literary and Philosophical Society of New York.

New-York literary and scientific repository. 54794

New York literary gazette, and Phi Beta Kappa repository. 54795

New York literary journal, and belles lettres repository. 54796

New York loyal gazette. 71690, 101739

New York Loyal National League. see Loyal National League of the State of New York.

New York Loyal Publication Society. see Loyal Publication Society, New York.

New York Lyceum. (54507)

New York Lyceum of Natural History. see New York Academy of Sciences.

New-York Lying-In Hospital. see Society of the Lying-In Hospital, New York.

New-York magazine. 21912

New York magazine: a Rochester new monthly. 54797

New York magazine and general repository of useful knowledge. 54798

New-York magazine, or literary repository. 39533, 54799, 64584, 84845, 101944

New-York Magdalen Female Benevolent Society. (54509)

New York Magdalen Society. (54367)

New York Magdalen Society. Executive Committee. (54510)

New York Mail Steamship Company. petitioners (54800)

New York Manumission Society. 94267

New York Manumission Society. Charter. 82024

New York Manumission Society. Committee. 94267

New-York, March 24, 1734-6. 54421

New Yorm Marine Bible Society. see Marine Bible Society, New York.

New York marine register. 54801

New York Marine Society. see Marine Society, New York.

New York Mariner's Family Industrial Society. see Mariner's Family Industrial Society. of the Port of New York.

New York Maternal Association. 54443, 54511

New-York. May 17, 1770. Advertisement. 93357

New-York Mechanic and Scientific Institution. (54375), 54512

New-York Mechanic and Scientific Institution. Charter. 54512

New York Mechanics' and Tradesmen's General Society. 54513

New York Mechanics' and Tradesmen's General Society. Charter. 54513

New York Mechanics' Association. see New York State Mechanics' Association.

New York Mechanics' Mutual Protesctions. see Mechanics' Mutual Protections of New York.

New-York medical and philosophical journal and review. 54802

New-York medical and physical journal. 4227, 54803, 82918

New-York medical and surgical reporter. (54804)

New York Medical Association for the Supply of Lint, Bandages, Etc. to the United States Army. 54805

New York Medical College, New. York. 54514

New York Medical College and Hospital for Women, New York. (54806)

New York Medical College . . . . Catalogue . . . and announcement. 54514

New York medical gazette. (54807)

New York medical gazette, and journal of health. 54808

New York medical independent, and pharmaceutical reporter. 54809

New York medical journal. 54810

New York medical magazine. 54811

New-York medical press. (54812)

New York medical repository. 4341, 4368

New York medical Society. see Medical Society of the State of new York.

New York medical times. 54813

New-York medico-chirurgical bulletin. 54814

New York Meeting of Friends. see Friends, Society of. New York Yearly Meeting.

New York Member of the Advisory Committee of the American Public Health Association. see Smith, Stephen, 1823-1922.

New York . . . mercantile . . . business directory. 54459

New York mercantile journal. 20254

New York Mercantile Library Association. see New York (City) Mercantile Library Association.

New York mercantile register. 54459
New-York mercantile union business direc-
tory. 54459
New-York merchant. pseud. Exposition of
some of the evils arising from the
auction system. 23450, 68302
New-York merchant. pseud. Negro labor
question. (52264)
New-York merchant. pseud. Plan looking
to an early resumption of specie pay-
ments. 63280
New-York merchant. pseud. Remarks upon
the usury laws. 69537
New York merchants' . . . advertising . . .
directory. 54459
New York Merchants' and Clerks' Library
Association. see Merchants' and
Clerks' Library Association, New York.
New York mercury. 12758, 16156, 23176,
36686, (36723), 46923, 54815, 67022,
67024, 84576, 89193, 92713, 95559
New York mercury extraordinary. April 9,
1783. 54815
New York messenger. (54816)
New York Midnight Mission. see Midnight
Mission, New York.
New-York military magazine. 54817
New York Military Post Library Association.
see Military Post Library Association,
New York.
New York minerva. 10663, 84819
New York Mining Stock Board. see Con-
solidated Stock and Petroleum Exchange
of New York.
New York Ministerium. see Evangelical
Lutheran Ministerium of the State of
New York and Adjacent States and
Counties.
New York mirror. 38536, 54818, 54819,
64013, 84145, 84162, 84903
New-York mirror, and ladies' literary
gazette. see New York mirror.
New York Mission and Tract Society. 7345,
35445, 54190, (54444), 54449
New-York missionary magazine, and reposi-
tory of religious intelligence. (54820)
New York Missionary Society. 54516
New York Missionary Society. Directors.
49059, 54516, 104280
New York monthly. (54821)
New York monthly, and working women's
advocate. 54822
New York monthly magazine. see Knicker-
bocker: or, New York monthly magazine.
Port folio, and New York monthly
magazine.
New York monthly register and United States
complete bankrupt's gazette. 54823
New-York morning chronicle. 16785, 84698,
84903
New York morning herald. 10889, 22989,
66530, 95360
New York morning post, and daily advertiser.
78581
New-York morning post, and daily advertiser.
Carrier. pseud. see Carrier of the
New York morning post, and daily
advertiser. pseud.
New York morning post, and daily advertiser.
News-carrier. pseud. see News-
carrier of the Daily advertiser. pseud.
New-York morning post and morning star.
Editor. 21577, (51799)
New York municipal gazette. 54517
New York Musical Congress, 1854. 66076

New York Musical Congress, New York.
54518, 66076
New York Musical Fund. 54518
New York Musical Institute. see Musical
Institute, New York.
New York musical pioneer. (54824)
New York musical world. 54825
New York Mutual Life Insurance Company.
51610, 53993, 54826, 83581, 83590
New York Mutual Life Insurance Company.
defendants 83881
New York Mutual Life Insurance Company.
petitioners 51610
New York Mutual Life Insurance Company.
Boston Committee of Policy-Holders.
56056
New York naked. 25227
New York National Freedman's Relief Associa-
tion. see American Freedman's Union
Commission. New York Branch.
New York National Union Executive Com-
mittee. see National Union Executive
Committee. New York.
New York Navigation and Colonization Company.
Olancho. An account of the resources
of the state of Honduras. 54828
New York needlewoman. 54829
New York, Newfoundland, and London Tele-
graph Company. 54830
New-York news-letter. 54831
New-York Northern Missionary Society. see
Northern Missionary Society of the State
of New York.
New-York, Nov. 24, 1783. 101860
New York observer. 8777, 50961, 54832,
82034, 85341, 96822, 96825
New York observer year book. 54832
New York 170 years ago. 51131
New York Opthalmic and Aural Institute.
54519
New York Opthalmic Hospital. 54520
New York Opthalmic Hospital. Surgeons.
54520
New York organ pictorial temperance almanac
for 1852. (54833)
New-York packet. 83980, 84840, 86744,
104939
New York Particular Synod. see Reformed
Church in America. Particular Synod
of New York.
New York: past, present, and future. 4410
New York pathfinder. 54834
New York Peace Society. see American Peace
Society.
New York pension roll. (54522)
New-York; Pensylvanie; Maryland. 101350
New York People's College. see Montour
Falls, N. Y. People's College.
New York Philharmonic Society. see New
York Philharmonic-Symothony Orchestra.
New York Philharmonic-Symphony Orchestra.
54523, 101880
New York Philological Society. see Philologi-
cal Society, New York.
New-York phonographical journal. 54836
New York Physico-Medical Society. see
Physico-Medical Society of New-York.
New York pictorial directory. 54459
New York pictorial directory. By Jones,
Newman, and J. S. Ewbank. (54524)
New York Pier and Warehouse Company. see
Pier and Warehouse Company, New York.
New York pocket almanack. 53674
New York pocket almanack. By Richard Moore.
50432

New York pocket almanac for 1805. 26331, 49221, 50441

New York pocket almanack for . . . 1802. 50442

New-York pocket almanack for . . . 1760. 26331, 49231, 50441, (54837)

New York pocket almanac for . . . 1761. 26331, 49221, 50441, (54837)

New-York pocket almanac, for the year of Our Lord, 1811. 84949

New-York pocket-book. 88848

New-York police reports. (81589)

New York political manual. 20325, 53809

New York Presbytery. see Presbyterian Church in the U. S. A. Presbytery of New York.

New-York price current. 54838

New York Prison Association. see Prison Association of New York.

New York Protestant Church Missionary Society for Seamen. see Protestant Episcopal Church Missionary Society for Seamen, New York.

New-York Protestant Episcopal Church Missionary Society for Seamen. see Protestant Episcopal Church Missionary Society for Seamen, New York.

New-York Protestant Episcopal City-Mission Society. 54526 see also New York City Mission Society.

New-York Protestant Episcopal City-Mission Society. Managers. 54526

New-York Protestant Episcopal Missionary Society. 54527

New-York Protestant Episcopal Press. Board of Trustees. 54528

New-York Protestant Episcopal Public School Corporation. see Corporation of the New-York Protestant Episcopal Public School.

New York Protestant Episcopal Society for Promoting Christian Knowledge in the Western District. see Protestant Episcopal Society for Promoting Christian Knowledge in the Western District of the State of New York.

New York Protestant Episcopal Society for Promoting Religion and Learning. see Protestant Episcopal Society for Promoting Religion and Learning in the State of New York.

New York Protestant Episcopal Sunday-School Society. (54261), 54530

New York Protestant Episcopal Sunday-School Society. Board of Managers. 54530

New-York Protestant Episcopal Tract Society. 54531

New York, Providence and Boston Railroad Company. 54839

New York, Providence and Boston Railroad Company. Directors. 54839

New York Public School Society. see Public School Society, New York.

New York pulpit in the revival of 1858. (54840)

New York quarterly. 54841

New-York quarterly magazine. 54842

New York railroads in 1858. 54843

New-York recorder and Baptist register. 23376

New York register and antimasonic review. 54844, 101298

New York register and city directory. 41939

New-York register, for 1804. 32648

New-York register of medicine and pharmacy. (54845)

New York registry law of 1859. 78270

New York Relief Society. see Relief Society of New York.

New York Religious Tract Society. 54532

New York republican. pseud. Sketches of the public services of Adams, Clay, and Crawford. 260, 81578

New York review. 23357, 23187, 35927, 39380, 39855, 54846, 65704, 69486, note after 97298, 2d note after 100577

New-York review and athenaeum magazine. 54847

New York review and quarterly church journal. 54848

New-York review; or, critical journal. (54849)

New York Robin-Hood Society. see Robin-Hood Society, New York.

New York royal gazette. 89637

New York royal sheet almanack. 53674

New York Sabbath Committee. 54279, 54533, 63397, (74654), 66492, 77493, 86277, 93740, 93745, 93746

New York Sacred Harmonic Society. 54534

New York Saint Andrew's Society. see Saint Andrew's Society of the State of New York.

New York Sanitary and Chemical Compost Manufacturing Company. 54850

New York Scotch Presbyterians. petitioners see Scotch Presbyterians of New York. petitioners

New-York semi-weekly tribune. 106326

New York, Sept. 4, 1850. 89975

New York, September 13, 1860. 65672

New York Seventh-Day Baptist General Convention. see Seventh-Day Baptist General Conference. New York.

New-York sheet almanac, for the year 1810. 84950

New York Ship-Owners' Association. see Ship-Owners' Association of the State of New York.

New York shipping and commercial list and price current. 54852

New York Skating Club, New York. Meteorologist. 54535

New-York sketch book and merchants' guide. 27621

New York sketch book for 1850. (43169)

New York Social Reform Society. see Social Reform Society of New York.

New York social science review. 54853

New York Society for Promoting Christian Knowledge and Piety. (54536)

New York Society for Promoting the Manumission of Slaves. 19939, (32948), (54851), (81945), 81956

New York Society for Promoting the Manumission of Slaves. petitioners 47745

New York Society for Promoting the Manumission of Slaves. Charter. (54851)

New York Society for the Diffusion of Christian Knowledge. see Society for the Diffusion of Christian Knowledge.

New York Society for the Diffusion of Political Knowledge. see Society for the Diffusion of Political Knowledge, New York.

New York Society for the Diffusion of Spiritual Knowledge. see Society for the Diffusion of Spiritual Knowledge, New York.

New York Society for the Education and Advancement of Young Seamen. see Society for the Education and Advancement of Young Seamen, New York.

New York Society for the Education and
Maintenance of Young Deaf Mutes. see
Society for the Education and Mainte-
nance of Young Deaf Mutes, New York.
New York Society for the Elevation of Liberal
Government. see Society for the
Elevation of Liberal Government, New
York.
New York Society for the Employment and
Relief of the Poor. see Society for
the Employment and Relief of Poor
Women, New York.
New York Society for the Encouragement of
Faithful Domestic Servants. 54537,
85898
New York Society for the Information and
Assistance of Persons Emigrating from
Foreign Countries. 54538
New York Society for the Prevention of
Pauperism. see Society for the Pre-
vention of Pauperism, New York.
New York Society for the Promotion of Agri-
culture, Arts and Manufactures. see
Society Instituted in the State of New
York, for the Promotion of Agriculture,
Arts and Manufactures.
New York Society for the Promotion of Knowl-
edge and Industry. (54539)
New York Society for the Promotion of Use-
ful Arts. see Society for the Promotion
of Useful Arts, New York.
New York Society for the Reformation of
Juvenile Delinquents. see Society for
the Reformation of Juvenile Delinquents,
New York.
New York Society for the Relief of Destitute
Children of Seamen. see Society for
the Relief of Destitute Children of Sea-
men, New York.
New York Society for the Relief of the
Destitute. see Society for the Relief
of the Destitute in the City of New York.
New York Society for the Relief of the
Ruptured and Crippled. 54540
New York Society for the Relief of the Widows
and Orphans of Medical Men. 54541
New York Society for the Relief of Worthy
Aged and Indigent Colored Persons. see
New York (City) Lincoln's Hospital and
Home.
New York Society for the Support of the
Colored Home. see New York (City)
Lincoln's Hospital and Home.
New York Society Library. 54543, 54545
New York Society Library. Charter. 54543,
54545
New York Society Library. Trustees. 54542,
54544
New York Society of Mechanics and Trades-
men. see General Society of Mechanics
and Tradesmen of the City of New York.
New York Society of Regulars. see Society
of Regulars, New York.
New York Society of St. Vincent de Paul. see
Society of St. Vincent de Paul, New York.
New York Society of Teachers. see Society
of Teachers of the City and County of
New York.
New York Society of the Cincinnati. see
Society of the Cincinnati. New York.
New York Society of the Friendly Sons of St.
Patrick. see Society of the Friendly
Sons of St. Patrick, New York.
New York Society of the Iron Man. see
Society of the Iron Man, New York.

New York Society of the Lying-In Hospital. see
Society of the Lying-In Hospital, New York.
New York Society of United Christian Friends.
see United Christian Friends, New York.
New York Soldiers' and Sailors' Union see
Soldiers' and Sailors Union of the State
of New York.
New York Soldiers' & Sailors' Convention,
Albany, 1866. see Soldiers' & Sailors'
State Convention, Albany, 1866.
New York Soldiers' Relief Association. see
Soldiers' Relief Association, New York.
New York songster. 54854
New York Southern Central Medical Association.
see Medical Association of Southern
Central New York.
New York Southern Sunday School Union. 54856
New-York spirit of the times. 89508, 92751
New-York sporting magazine, and annals of the
American . . . turf. 54857
New York standard—extra. 100676
New-York State Agricultural College. Charter,
ordinances, and regulations. 53810
New York State Agricultural Convention, Albany,
1832. 53810
New York State Agricultural Society. (19594),
24562, 53810-53811, 75792-75793
New York State Agricultural Society. Annual
Exhibition, 14th, 1854. 53811
New York State Agricultural Society. Charter.
53811
New York state agricultural transactions. see
Transactions of the New York State Agri-
cultural Society.
New York State and National Law School,
Ballston Spa. N. Y. see State and Na-
tional Law School, Ballston Spa, N. Y.
New York State Anti-slavery Society. 25641,
53801, (54425)
New York State Anti-slavery Society. Executive
Committee. 14400
New York State Anti-slavery Society. Farewell
Meeting for Dr. Massie, of London, New
York, 1863. 46186
New York State Auxiliary Clay Monument
Association. 53813
New York state banker. pseud. National
currency. 51962
New York state business directory. 53814
New York State Christian Convention, Newark,
N. Y., 1866. 53815
New York State Colonization Society. see New
York Colonization Society.
New York State Convention for Rescuing the
Canals from the Ruin With Which They
are Threatened, Rochester, 1859. 65903
New York State Convention for Rescuing the
Canals from the Ruin With Which They
are Threatened, Utica, 1859. 65903
New York State Convention of Colored Citizens,
Albany, 1840. 53780
New York State Convention of Colored People,
Albany, 1851. (53870)
New York State Convention of Delegates from
the Several Moral Societies, Albany, 1820.
see Convention of Delegates of the Several
Moral Societies in the State of New York,
Albany, 1820.
New York State Convention of Delegates of the
Several Moral Societies, Albany, 1821.
see Convention of Delegates of the
Several Moral Societies in the State of
New York, Albany, 1821.
New York State Convention of Mechanics, Utica,
1834. see State Convention of Mechanics,
Utica, 1834.

New York State Convention of Teachers and Friends of Education, Utica, 1831. 53492

New York State Convention of the Soldiers of the War of 1812, Syracuse, 1854. see Convention of the Soldiers of the War of 1812, Syracuse, 1854.

New York State Education and Missionary Society of the Protestant Episcopal Church. see Education and Missionary Society of the Protestant Episcopal Church in the State of New York.

New-York state guide. 20325, 53818

New York State Historical Association. 94200

New York State Horticultural Society. see New York Horticultural Society.

New York state illustrated. 53820

New-York State Institution of Civil Engineers. 53823

New York state journal of medicine. 84276

New York State Loyal National League. see Loyal National League of the State of New York.

New York State Lyceum. Annual Meeting, 1st, Utica, 1831. 53832

New York state mechanic. (53833), 90002

New York State Mechanics' Association. 53834

New York State Medical Society. see Medical Society of the State of New York.

New York State Military Convention, Syracuse, N. Y., 1853. see State Military Convention, Syracuse, N. Y., 1853.

New York State Museum, Albany. (53997), 54146

New York State Northern Missionary Society. see Northern Missionary Society in the State of New York.

New York State People's College, Montour Falls. see Montour Falls, N. Y. People's College.

New York State Protective War Claim Association. see Protective War Claim Association of the State of New-York.

New-York state register, for 1843. (32537), (53837)

New-York state register, for . . . 1830. 53836

New-York State Sabbath Convention, Saratoga Springs, 1844. (53838)

New York State School Convention, 1831. 69634

New York State Ship-Owners' Association. see Ship-Owners' Association of the State of New York.

New York State Society for the Promotion of Agriculture, Arts and Manufactures. see Society for the Promotion of Useful Arts, New York.

New-York State Society for the Promotion of Temperance. see New York State Temperance Society.

New York State Society of the Cincinnati. 86121

New York State Sunday School Teachers' Association. Annual Convention, 17th, Norwich, 1872. 54862

New-York State Teachers' Association. 54858

New York State Temperance Convention, 1853. Committee to Draft A Bill for the Suppression of the Traffic in Intoxicating Liquors. 53843

New York State Temperance Society. (34840), 53843, 54550, (65978)

New York State Temperance Society. Executive Committee. 43975, 53843, 94651

New York State Temperance Society. Managers. 54448

New York state tourist. (53844)

New York State Woman's Rights Committee. 90399

New York State Woman's Rights Convention, Albany, 1854. 90398

New York Stock and Exchange Board. see New York (City) Stock Exchange.

New York Stock Exchange. see New York (City) Stock Exchange.

New York Stock Exchange directory for 1866-7. (54546)

New York Stock Exchange manual. 30119

New York street views. 54691

New York sun. (64224), 93727

New York Sunday dispatch. 102249

New York Sunday mercury. 20760

New York Sunday-School Institute. 54547

New York Sunday School Union Society. 54548

New York Sunday times. 3971

New York Synod. see Presbyterian Church in the U. S. A. Synod of New York and Philadelphia.

New York Synod of Hartwick. see Hartwick Synod of the Evangelical Lutheran Church in the State of New York.

New York Tammanial Tontine Association. 63295, 1st note after 94296

New York Tammany Society. see Tammany Society, New York.

New York tax book. 18588, (54549)

New York . . . taxes. 54446

New-York teacher. 54858

New York teachers, and American educational monthly. (54859)

New York Temperance Alliance. 54447

New York Temperance Society. see New York State Temperance Society.

New York Texas Committee. 95114

New-York theatrical magazine. 67618

New York theological magazine. 54860, 95312

New-York Theological Seminary. see New York (City) General Theological Seminary of the Protestant Episcopal Church in the U. S. New York (City) Union Theological Seminary.

New York (State) Third Assembly District Teachers' Institute. see Teachers' Institute of the Third Assembly District of Monroe County, N. Y.

New York Third Presbytery. see Presbyterian Church in the U. S. A. Presbytery of New York.

New York Thursday's journal. (14394)-14395

New York times. 13822, (13824), (36895), (42795), 54861, 70431, 84254, 84786, 89034

New York times. Correspondent. 55402

New York Tract Association of Friends. see Tract Association of Friends in New York.

New York tract magazine and Christian miscellany. 54862

New York Tract Society, Auxiliary to the American Tract Society. see New York Mission and Tract Society.

New York Tract Society of Friends. see Tract Society of Friends, New York.

New York Trade Sale Association. 6368

New-York traveller. 89508

New York traveller . . . through the state. 54863

New York tribune. 9615, 10842, (15463), 19862, 25227, (28484), 29494, 30101, 35849, 37092, 37331, 55573, 69443, 71523, 79033, 81050, 81987, 82605, 84787, 85954, 86804, 91066, 93347, 93641, 95593, note after 97063, 103172

New York tribune extra, no. 63. 71523

New York tribune lecture series. Vol. I. 81050

New York tribune war tracts, no. 2. 9615

New York Typographical Association. see Typographical Association of New York.

New York Typographical Society. 54552

New York Typographical Society. Printers' Banquet, 1850. 25619, 54590

New-York under the Dutch. 56610

New York Union Safety Committee. see Union Safety Committee.

New York Unitarian book Society. 54553

New York United Christian Friends. see United Christian Friends, New York.

New York United Domestic Missionary Society. see United Domestic Missionary Society, New York.

New York United German Lutheran Churches. see Vereinigte Deutsche Gesellschaften der Stadt New York.

New York University. 14827, (54704)

New York University. Council. 54705

New York University. Faculty of Science and Letters. 14827, 54706, (54709), 1st note after 94368

New York University. Law Department. 54708

New York University. Law School. 54707

New York University. Medical Department. 20899, 54710

New York University. Medical Faculty. petitioners. 54710

New York University. Psi Upsilon Fraternity. (54704)

New-York, Vermont, Massachusetts and Connecticut almanack. 34049

New York vs. Elisha B. Fero. 64203

New York vs. Harry Croswell. 17677

New York vs. John H. Cooper. (16580)

New York vs. Taylor and Brennan. 6021

New York Veterans of the War of 1812. see Veterans of the War of 1812. New York.

New York visiter [sic] and parlor companion. 54864

New York Washing and Bathing Association. 54554

New-York Washington Military Society. (54555)

New-York Washington Mutual Assurance Company. 54865, 102028

New York Washington Mutual Assurance Company. Charter. 54865, 102027-102028

New-York watchman. 89309

New-York weekly caucasian. 84179

New-York weekly day-book. 84179

New York weekly journal. 53872, 86889, 89515, 98433, 98434, 103530, 103608

New-York weekly magazine. 54866

New York weekly museum. 54867

New-York Wesleyan Methodist Relief Society. 54556

New York Western Domestic Missionary Society. see Western Domestic Missionary Society of the State of New York.

New York Western Education Society. see Western Education Society of the State of New York.

New York Whig Club, New York. 54557

New York Whig Club, New York. Corresponding Committee. 54557

New York Williams Alumni Association. see Williams College, Williamstown, Mass. Alumni Association. New York.

New York world. 91061

New York Yacht Club. (54558)

New-York Young Men's Anti-slavery Society. 54560, note after 106153

New York Young Men's Christian Association. see Young Men's Christian Association, New York.

New York Young Men's City Bible Society. see Young Men's City Bible Society of New York.

New York Young Men's Missionary Society. see Young Men's Missionary Society of New York.

New York Young Men's Society. 54562

New York Young Men's Society for the Promotion of Temperance. see Young Men's Society for the Promotion of Temperance, New York.

New York Young Men's State Convention, Utica, 1838. (54868)

New Yorker. pseud. Annals of the Empire City. 54085

New Yorker. pseud. Hints on baking. see McVickar, John.

New-Yorker. pseud. New-York. 54422

New Yorker. pseud. Tale of a New Yorker. see Known Author. pseud.

New-Yorker. pseud. Winter in the west. see Hoffman, Charles Fenno.

New-Yorker. 84162

New-Yorker Volks-Kalender, 1850. (54869)

New-York's historia fran berldens begynnelse intill Hollandska valdets slut. (35168)

New Zealand and Australia (as emigration fields). 34015

New Zealand to New York. 57226

Newark, Del. Academy. see Delaware College, Newark, Del. Newark Academy.

Newark, Del. Delaware College. see Delaware College, Newark, Del.

Newark, N. J. 54883

Newark, N. J. Academy. see Newark Academy, Newark, N. J.

Newark, N. J. Bible Society. see Newark Bible Society.

Newark, N. J. Fire Association. see Newark Fire Association.

Newark, N. J. Library Association. 54880

Newark, N. J. Mechanics' Association. see Newark Mechanics Association.

Newark, N. J. Methodist Episcopal Church. 96141

Newark, N. J. Methodist Episcopal Church. Ministers. 96141

Newark, N. J. Methodist Episcopal Church. Stewards. 96141

Newark, N. J. Methodist Episcopal Church. Trustees. 96141

Newark, N. J. Methodist Episcopal Society. see Newark, N. J. Methodist Episcopal Church.

Newark, N. J. North Reformed Dutch Church. 54884

Newark, N. J. Ordinances, etc. 54871

Newark, N. J. Two Hundredth Anniversary Commemoration, 1866. 54882

Newark, N. Y. Mayor, 1857 (Bigelow) (54875) see also Bigelow, --------, fl. 1857.

Newark, N. Y. New Union Free School and Academy. see New Union Free School and Academy, Newark, N. Y.

Newark, N. Y. New York State Christian Convention, 1866. see New York State Christian Convention, Newark, N. Y., 1866.

Newark (Diocese) Bishop (Bayley) (4052)-4053, 72953-72954 see also Bayley, James Roosevelt, Bp.

Newark (Diocese) Bishop (Corrigan) 72954 see also Corrigan, Michael Augustine, Bp.

Newark (Diocese) Bishop (Wigger) 72955 see also Wigger, Michael Venantio, Bp.

Newark (Diocese) Synod, 1853. 72954
Newark (Diocese) Synod, 1856. 72953
Newark (Diocese) Synod, 1868. 72954
Newark (Diocese) Synod, 1878. 72954
Newark (Diocese) Synod, 1886. 72955

Newark Academy, Newark, Del. see Delaware College, Newark, Del. Newark Academy.

Newark Academy, Newark, N. J. 54876
Newark Academy, Newark, N. J. Young Ladies' Department. 54876

Newark Bible Society. (49080), 54878

Newark business directory, . . . with an appendix. (54874)

Newark city directory, for . . . 1872. (54874)

Newark city directory for 1865-6. (54874)
Newark city directory, for . . . 1869. (54874)
Newark city directory, for 1867-8. (54874)
Newark city directory for 1863-4. (54874)

Newark College, Newark, Del. see Delaware College, Newark, Del.

Newark Female Society for the Relief of Poor and Distressed Persons. see Female Society for the Relief of Poor and Distressed Persons in Newark, N. J.

Newark Fire Association. 54879

Newark Land and Cash Lottery, Christiana-Bridge, Del., 1771. 41438

Newark Land and Cash Lottery, Newcastle County, Del., 1773. Third Class. 41455

Newark Library Association, Newark, N. J. see Newark, N. J. Library Association.

Newark Mechanics' Association. 54881

Newbern, N. C. Board of Trade. 54887

Newbern, N. C. Newbern Guards. see North Carolina. Militia. Newbern Guards.

Newbern Guards. see North Carolina. Militia. Newbern Guards.

New Bern [sic] mercantile and manufacturers' business directory. 54888

Newbern, October 6th, 1794. 104167

Newberry, Elizabeth. 100587

Newberry, James Strong, 1822-1892. 31004, 34253, (34463), 35308, 52243, 54889-54896, (54925), 56926, 69946, 76551, 76560, (76566), (76590), 76601, 76610, 76623, 76647 see also Ohio. Geologist. United States Sanitary Commission. Western Department. Secretary.

Newberry District, South Carolina. Citizens. petitioners 47642

Newberry, John. 66686

Newberry, John, 1713-1767. 41540, 54898, 93453

Newberry (F.) publisher 16303, 31389, (54897)

Newbold, E. L. 54899

Newburgh, N. Y. Bank. see Bank of Newburgh, Newburgh, N. Y.

Newburgh, N. Y. Commissioners of the Alms House. 54903

Newburgh, N. Y. Committee on a Poor Law. 54903

Newburgh, N. Y. Convention on the Great State Road, 1826. see Convention on the Great State Road, Newburgh, N. Y., 1826.

Newburgh, N. Y. First Presbyterian Church. Library. 54901

Newburgh, N. Y. Glebe Lands. Charter. (54904)

Newburgh, N. Y. High-School Synod. see High-School Synod, Newburgh, N. Y.

Newburgh, N. Y. Mass Meeting Held at Washington's Head Quarters, 1852. see Democratic Party. New York. Newburgh.

Newburgh, N. Y. Mechanics' Library Association. see Mechanics' Library Association, Newburgh, N. Y.

Newburgh, N. Y. Theological Seminary of the Associate Reformed Synod of New York. see Associate Reformed Presbyterian Church. Theological Seminary, Newburgh, N. Y.

Newburgh, N. Y. Washington's Headquarters. 54900

Newburgh, N. Y. Water Commissioners. 54906

Newburgh city directory. (54905)
Newburgh directory for 1856-'57. (54905)
Newburgh directory, for 1860-61. (54905)
Newburgh directory for 1864-65. (54905)
Newburgh general and business directory, for 1868. (54905)

Newburgh letters. 2025, 14379, 15508

Newburgh poor system. 54903

Newbury, Mass. (54907), 54908
Newbury, Mass. First Church. 97311
Newbury, Mass. School Committee. 54909
Newbury, Mass. Schools. 54908

Newbury, Vt. Newbury Seminary. see Newbury Seminary, Newbury, Vt.

Newbury and Marblehead advertiser. see Salem gazette and Newbury and Marblehead advertiser.

Newbury Seminary, Newbury, Vt. 54910

Newburyport, Mass. 54924

Newburyport, Mass. Centennial Commemoration of the Death of George Whitefield, 1870. (54912), 90904

Newburyport, Mass. Charter. 54920

Newburyport, Mass. Citizens. 102320

Newburyport, Mass. Female High School. 54921

Newburyport, Mass. First Presbyterian Church. (54912), 90904

Newburyport, Mass. First Presbyterian Church. Session. 24607

Newburyport, Mass. First Religious Society. Sunday School Association. 54917

Newburyport, Mass. Ladies' Friendly Society. see Ladies' Friendly Society, Newburyport, Mass.

Newburyport, Mass. Marine Society. see Marine Society, Newburyport, Mass.

Newburyport, Mass. Mayor, 1863. 54913

Newburyport, Mass. Old South Church. see Newburyport, Mass. First Presbyterian Church.

Newburyport, Mass. Ordinances, etc. 54920
Newburyport, Mass. Public Library. 54922

Newburyport, Mass. Putnam Free School. see Putnam Free School, Newburyport, Mass.

Newburyport, Mass. Reception of the Sons of Newburyport Resident Abroad, 1854. (7320)

Newburyport, Mass. Relief Fire Society.
see Relief Fire Society, Newburyport,
Mass.
Newburyport, Mass. School Committee.
(54927)
Newburyport, Mass. Sundry Merchants. see
Sundry Merchants of Newburyport.
Newburyport, Mass. Town Hall. 54911
Newburyport, Mass. Treasurer. 54913,
54914
Newburyport, Mass. Union Society. see
Union Society, Newburyport, Mass.
Newburyport, Mass. Washington Benevolent
Society. see Washington Benevolent
Society. Massachusetts. Newburyport.
Newburyport, Mass. Washington Funeral
Commemoration, 1800. 54921
Newburyport. 89557
Newburyport morning star. 86510
Newburyport morning star. Printer. 95980
Newburyport Presbytery. see Presbyterian
Church in the U. S. A. Presbytery
of Newburyport.
Newburyport Railroad Company. 54923
Newburyport resolutions. 54924
Newburyport, Sept. 3, 1790. 95841
Newcastle Under Lyme, Henry Pelham Fiennes
Pelham Clinton, 5th Duke of, 1811-1864.
93459
Newcastle Under Lyme, Thomas Pelham-Holles,
1st Duke of, 1693-1768. 57614, 99249
Newcastle, Del. Convention, 1776. see Dela-
ware. Convention, Newcastle, 1776.
Newcastle, Me. Lincoln Academy. see
Lincoln Academy, Newcastle, Me.
Newcastle Co., Del. Newark Land and Cash
Lottery, 1773. see Newark Land and
Cash Lottery, Newcastle County, Del.,
1773.
Newcastle and Frenchtown Rail Road. 62051
Newcastle County Agricultural Society and
Institute, Wilmington, Del. 54929-
54930
Newcastle District Committee of the SPCK.
see Society for Promoting Christian
Knowledge. Newcastle District Com-
mittee.
Newcastle District Traveling Missionary So-
ciety. see Society for Promoting Chris-
tian Knowledge. Newcastle District
Traveling Missionary Society.
Newcastle Presbytery. see Presbyterian
Church in the U. S. A. Presbytery of
Newcastle.
Newcastle-Upon-Tyne, Eng. Society of Anti-
quaries. see Society of Antiquaries,
Newcastle-Upon-Tyne, Eng.
Newcomb, Ebenezer. 93080
Newcomb, Harvey, 1803-1863. (54931)-54933
Newcomb, Harvey, 1803-1863. supposed author
102197
Newcomb, Henry. supposed author 102197
Newcomb, John B. 54934
Newcomb, Richard, Bishop of Landaff. see
Newcome, Richard, Successively Bishop
of Llandaff, and St. Asaph, d. 1769.
Newcomb, Richard E. (54935)
Newcomb, Simon, 1835-1909. (54936)-54937,
85072
Newcomb firm publishers 89856
Newcomb's Springfield directory. 89856
Newcome, Ebenezer. 85544
Newcome, Richard, successively Bishop of
Llandaff, and St. Asaph, d. 1769. 54938,
84646
Newcome, Thomas. 54939

Newcomer, Christian, Bp. 54940
Newdegate, C. N. 54941
Newe . . . see New . . .
Newe Americanische Landwirthschafts-
Calender. 68215
Newe auszguhrliche Entdeckung und Beschrei-
bung der gantzen Welt. 57461
Newe Nortwelt. 5905
Newe Nort-Welt, das ist: Huundliche vnd
warhaffte Beschreiung. 47383
Newe Nort-West. 47383
Newe Schwarmgeister-Bruit. 54944
Newe-Sjalom te Serinam, Paramaribo. see
Paramaribo. Newe-Sjalom te Serinam.
Newe summarische Welt-Historia. 23605
Newe vnbekanthe Landte und ein newe Weldte.
50056, note after 99383C, 2d note after
106378
Newe vnd warhaffte Relation. 55242
Newe Welt. (51395)
Newe Welt vnd Americanische Historien. 50,
16961, 19952
Newe Welt, warhafftige Anzeigung. 11277
Newe zceyt von des Turcken Halben. 54946
Newe zeittung vo Pruszla vo Kay. Ma: Hofe
18 Martze. 1522. 54946, 3d note after
106221
Newe Zeittung. von dem Lande. 54946, 3d
note after 106221
Newe Zeytung aus Hispanien und Italien.
54945, (63177)
Newell, --------, fl. 1812. 36857
Newell, Abel. (54947)
Newell, Andrew. supposed author 18580
Newell, Chester. 32204, 54948, note after
95091
Newell, D. 54949
Newell, Ebenezer F. 54950
Newell, Fanny. 54951-54952
Newell, Frederick R. 54953
Newell, Frederick S. 54954
Newell, Harriet. 54955-54956, 2d note after
105132
Newell, Jonathan. 54957-54958
Newell, Robert Hasell. (54959)-54960, 84186
Newell, S. 54962
Newell, Samuel. 36857, 54961
Newell, Thomas M. defendant at court martial
54963
Newell, William. 54964-54967
Newell, William Augustus, 1817- 33150,
53151, 53207, 54968 see also New
Jersey. Governor, 1857-1860 (Newell)
Newell, William W. 54969
Newell's notes on Abraham Lincoln. 54954
Newell's notes on tar and feathers. 54954
Newell's notes on the licentious treatment of
the American female slaves. 54954
Newen Australischen oder Suder-Compagnie
durch Schweden. see Soder Compagniet.
Newen Weldt vnd Indianischen Konigreichs.
4797
Newenn Weldt vnd Indianischen Nidergangischen
Konigreichs. 4798
Newengland coquette. 103731
Newes . . . see News . . .
Newest keep-sake for eighteen hundred thirty-
nine. 54973
Newest sensation. 89633
Newfoundland, Bishop of. see Field, Edward,
Bishop of Newfoundland, 1801-1876.
Spencer, Aubrey George, successively
Bishop of Newfoundland, and Jamaica,
1795-1872.
Newfoundland. Charter. 66686

Newfoundland. Citizens. petitioners 11089, 54976, 94549

Newfoundland. Constitution. 54980

Newfoundland. General Assembly. 54982

Newfoundland. Geological Survey. 36878, 54988

Newfoundland. Governor, 1709-1712 (Collins) petitioner 54976, 94549 see also Collins, John. petitioner

Newfoundland. Governor, 1764-1769 (Palliser) 54986 see also Palliser, Sir Hugh.

Newfoundland. Governor, 1807-1809. (Holloway) 1646, 54991 see also Holloway. John.

Newfoundland. Inhabitants. see Newfoundland. Citizens.

Newfoundland. Laws, statutes, etc. 1646, 54975, 54991

Newfoundland. Supreme Court. (54990)

Newfoundland almanack, for . . . 1845. 54984

Newfoundland and Quebec. 54985

Newfoundland fishermen. 96164

Newfoundland in 1842. 6332

Newfoundland. List of contributions . . . for ecclesiastical purposes. 54983

Newfoundland missionary. pseud. Six months of a Newfoundland missionary's journal. see Wix, Edward.

Newfoundland School Society. 54974

Newgate of Connecticut: a history of the prison. 61389

Newgate of Connecticut; its origin and early history. 61391

Newhall, Ebenezer. 54992

Newhall, Fales Henry. 54993

Newhall, Frederic C. supposed author 90068

Newhall, J. B. 54996-54998

Newhall, James Robinson, 1809-1893. 40782, 54994-54995

Newhall, Joseph M. 87031

Newhouse, S. 55000

Newinachke & Guttasche Pipinasiki Gischekhaseiki Elekpanni Wedenastki Untschi Mechoweki Machgundowo agni Bambi. 42629

Newland, Jeremiah. 55001

Newland, S. W. 55002

Newlanders cure. 98694

Newlands, John. 55003

Newlight Church. 44764, 2d note after 95515

Newlin, W. H. (55004)

Newly discovered gold fields of British Columbia Described. (10896)

Newly elected member. pseud. Interest of Great Britain in the approaching Congress considered. (34881)

Newman, --------, fl. 1851. 54459

Newman, Alfred. 55005

Newman, Burkitt J. 55006

Newman, Francis W. 38268, 41929, (55007)-55008

Newman, Henry. note after 52702, 55009-(55010), 62743

Newman, J. P. 64953

Newman, John. (55011)

Newman, John B. 55012-55013, 84140-84141

Newman, Louis C. 55014

Newman, Louis C. supposed author (5190)

Newman, Mark H. (55015)

Newman, Samuel P. (55021)

Newman, Sylvanus Chace. 55016-55020, (66173)

Newman, Thomas Fox. 55022

Newman, Thomas W. 85345

Newman, Ursula. (55023)

Newman, William. alias see Smith, Henry More.

Newman Hall in America. 29836

Newman's interpreter. 21761

Newmarch, William. 55024

Newmarsh, John. 23391, 70106 see also Congregational Churches in New Hampshire. Ecclesiastical Council, Exeter, 1743. Moderator.

Newnham, Nathaniel. 95918

Newport, R. I. Artillery Company. 55034

Newport, R. I. Athenaeum. see Newport, R. I. Redwood Library Company.

Newport, R. I. Charter. 55033

Newport, R. I. Church of Christ. 80613-80614

Newport, R. I. City Council. Committee on Finance. 55028

Newport, R. I. City Council. Overseers of the Poor. 55028

Newport, R. I. Court of Common Pleas. Grand Jury. 90477

Newport, R. I. Firewards. 55028

Newport, R. I. Free Library. Directors. 55046

Newport, R. I. His Majesty's Loyal Associated Refugees. see His Majesty's Loyal Associated Refugees Assembled at Newport, R. I.

Newport, R. I. Home for Friendless Children, see Home for Friendless Children, Newport, R. I.

Newport, R. I. Inhabitants, Distillers of Rum and Importers of Molasses. petitioners see Inhabitants of Newport, Rhode Island, Distillers of Rum and Importers of Molasses. petitioners

Newport, R. I. James Hammond's Circulating Library. see James Hammond's Circulating Library, Newport, R. I.

Newport, R. I. Loyal Associated Refugees. see His Majesty's Loyal Associated Refugees Assembled at Newport, R. I.

Newport, R. I. Marine Society. see Marine Society, Newport, R. I.

Newport, R. I. Mayor, 1853-1854 (Calvert) 55028 see also Calvert, George Henry, 1803-1889.

Newport, R. I. Ordinances, etc. 55033, 55050

Newport, R. I. Overseers of the Poor. see Newport, R. I. City Council. Overseers of the Poor.

Newport, R. I. People's Library. -55032

Newport, R. I. Reading Room. 55047

Newport, R. I. Redwood Library. see Newport, R. I. Redwood Library Company.

Newport, R. I. Redwood Library and Athenaeum. see Newport, R. I. Redwood Library Company.

Newport, R. I. Redwood Library Company. 55053-55054, 68532-68534

Newport, R. I. Redwood Library Company. Charter. 55053, 68534

Newport, R. I. Redwood Library Company. Directors. (55052)

Newport, R. I. Re-union of the Sons and Daughters of Newport, 1859. General Committee of Arrangements. 45444

Newport, R. I. Saint Aloysius Juvenile Society. see Saint Aloysius Juvenile Society, Newport, R. I.

Newport, R. I. School Committee. 55028, (55030)

Newport, R. I. School House Erected by the Trustees of the Long Wharf. 55055B

Newport, R. I. Spring Street Church. Sabbath School. Library. 55032

Newton, Mass. Newton Theological Institution. see Newton Theological Institution, Newton, Mass.
Newton, Mass. Sabbath School Union. see Newton Sabbath School Union, Newton, Mass.
Newton, Mass. School Committee. (55098)
Newton, Mass. Second Congregational Church. 55090
Newton, Mass. Second Unitarian Society. Sunday School. Library. 55086
Newton, Mass. Soldiers' Monument. (55089)
Newton, Mass. Union League. see Newton Union League, Newton, Mass.
Newton, Mass. Young Men's Christian Association. see Young Men's Christian Association, Newton, Mass.
Newton Centre, Mass. Ecclesiastical Council, 1866. see Congregational Churches in Massachusetts. Ecclesiastical Council, Newton Centre, 1866.
Newton Centre, Mass. Ex-parte Ecclesiastical Council, 1866. see Congregational Churches in Massachusetts. Ecclesiastical Council, Newton Centre, 1866.
Newton Corner, Mass. Eliot Orthodox Congregational Church. 55086
Newton directory. (55092)
Newton Free Library, Newton, Mass. see Newton, Mass. Free Library.
Newton Mining Company, Canada East, organized under the general statutes of Massachusetts. 55100
Newton Sabbath School Union, Newton, Mass. 55094
Newton Theological Institution, Newton, Mass. (55095)
Newton Theological Institution, Newton, Mass. Board of Trustees. Committee. (55095)
Newton Theological Institution, Newton, Mass. Professors. (55095)
Newton Theological Institution: a sketch of its history. (55095)
Newton Union League, Newton, Mass. 55096
Newton Young Men's Christian Association. see Young Men's Christian Association, Newton, Mass.
Newtonian hypothesis examined. 53407
Newtonian reflector. 55101
Newtonville, Mass. Central Congregational Church. Sunday School. Library. 55102
Newtown, N.H. Baptist Church of Christ. 55103
Newzeit wie Vnnsers allergnadigistn Hern des Romanischn vnd Hyspaenischn Konigs leut ain costliche newe Laandschafft. 55105
Next presidency, the Chicago Convention. (55107), 79736
Next presidential election. 6376
Next presidential election. Mr. Lincoln-the presidency. (55108)
Neyn, P. de. 55109
Nez Perce Indians. Laws, statutes, etc. 103378
Nez Perces. 102564
Nez-Perces' first book. (55110), 88876
Nez-Perces spelling book. 88877
Ni o' i oh' dvs yuh' dah no twais' hiyu ne gah' ni go ah' geh. 105556A
Niagara (District), Ontario. Citizens. petitioners 28141, (47677), 98086
Niagara County, N.Y. Court. 103765
Niagara: a poem. By A.M. 42901

Niagara; a poem. By a member of the Ohio Bar. 55120
Niagara. A poem. By Rev. C.H.A. Bulkley. 9101
Niagara and Detroit Rivers Railroad. 55121
Niagara and other poems. (32503)
Niagara. [By Henry Howard Brownell.] (8687)
Niagara. [By Joseph H. Clinch.] 13703
Niagara. [By William Ellery Channing.] 11929
Niagara church case. 70414
Niagara Division, No. 14, Sons of Temperance. see Sons of Temperance of North America. Pennsylvania. Niagara Division, No. 14.
Niagara Falls: a poem. 41464
Niagara Falls companion, and fashionable miscellany. 55122
Niagara Falls guide. 55123
Niagara Falls Hydraulic Company. 55124
Niagara Falls port folio. 91138-91139
Niagara Falls suspension bridge &c. 58448, (72576)
Niagara Falls the great manufacturing village of the west. 55124
Niagara Falls, their physical changes and the geology and topography of the surrounding country. 29807
Niagara Frontier (District) Citizens. see Niagara (District), Ontario. Citizens.
Niagara frontier: embracing sketches of its early history. 44807
Niagara guide book. 91140
Niagara Manufacturing Company. claimants 73955
Niagara mineral spring at Monteagle House. 16289
Niagara quinze ans apres. 44505
"Niagara ship canal:" and "Reciprocity:" papers. 31022
Niagara ship canal: its military and commercial necessity. 55126
Niagara ship canal. Letter from Gerrit Smith to Auditor Benton. 82647
Niagara ship-canal. Speech of Hon. John C. Churchill. 13019
Niagara steamer, chartered for the Banks expedition in 1862. 55127
Niagara suspension railway bridge. 3439, 58448, (72576)
Niblack, William E. 55133
Niblo, William. (21501)
Niboyet, P. 55134
Nic. Josephi Jacquin Selectarum stirpium Americanarum historia. (35523)
Nica, Marco di. 66686
Nicaise, A. 55135
Nican y Cuiliuhtica ynin Xitlapoualcatea Mexica. (55136)
Nicaragua (Colony) see Guatemala (Colony)
Nicaragua. 1059, 34942, 32759, 55142, 55152, 55158, (55162), (65998)
Nicaragua. Constitution. 55140-55141
Nicaragua. Director Supremo del Estado. see Nicaragua. Supremo Director.
Nicaragua. Gobierno Provisorio. see Nicaragua.
Nicaragua. Laws, statutes, etc. 1059, 55139 55153, 55161, 72291-72292
Nicaragua. Legation. Great Britain. 55148
Nicaragua. Ministerio de Estado. 32773, (55137), 55150, 55156
Nicaragua. Ministerio de Relaciones Exteriores. 55148, 55151 see also Castellon, Francisco.

Nicaragua. Ministerio de Relaciones Interiores. see Nicaragua. Ministerio de Estado.

Nicaragua. Supremo Director, 1847-1849 (Guerrero) (55154), 55159 see also Guerrero, Jose.

Nicaragua. Supremo Director, 1853-1854. 55155

Nicaragua. Treaties, etc. 16201, (21123), 51709, (55149), 89975

Nicaragua y Costa Rica (Diocese) 34836

Nicaragua y Costa Rica (Diocese) Bishop (Garret y Arlovi) 72531 see also Garret y Arlovi, Benito, Bp.

Nicaragua. [By Marmaduke B. Sampson.] (75943)

Nicaracua canal contract, etc. (55157)

Nicaragua; its people, scenery, monuments. 89980

Nicaragua, legendes et notes. 40764

Nicaragua. Nach eigener Anschauung im Jahre 1852. 68979

Nicaragua: past, present and future. 92359

Niccolls, Samuel Jack, 1838- 55163, 77731

Nicely, W. S. 55164

Nicely, Wilson. (55165)

Nichol, James. 51503

Nicholas III, Pope, 1216?-1280. 68841 see also Catholic Church. Pope, 1277-1280 (Nicholas III)

Nicholas, George. 55166-(55167)

Nicholas, Sir Harris. 85344

Nicholas, John, b. 1759? (50137), (55169), 100451

Nicholas, John, fl. 1819. (55168), (57369)

Nicholas, John St. see St. Nicholas, John.

Nicholas, Robert Carter, 1728-1780. 31346, 55170-55171, 100449

Nicholas, Samuel Smith, 1796-1869. 37538, (40629), (55172)-(55179), 88002, 102321

Nicholas, Thomas. tr. 16964, (26298), 27751-27752, 106272

Nicholas, Wilson Cary, 1757-1820. 33150, 55180 see also Virginia. Governor, 1814-1816 (Nicholas)

Nicholas (Ship) 55181

Nicholas I. 85145-85146

Nicholas I. of Russia. 85161, 85168

Nicholas of the flue. 77468

Nicholas Rusticus. pseud. see Rusticus, Nicholas. pseud.

Nicholay, Nich. 66686

Nicholds, ---------. plaintiff 55182

Nicholl, John. (55183)

Nicholl, T. S. 55184

Nicholls, J. F. 55185

Nicholls, John. 55186

Nicholls, Robert Boucher. 25479

Nichols, Andrew. 18513, (55188)-(55190), 97258

Nichols, Beach. 4355, 55191

Nichols, Benjamin Ropes, 1786-1848. 55192, 88119 see also South Cove Corporation, Boston. President.

Nichols, Mrs. C. I. H. 55194

Nichols, Effingham H. 55195-(55196)

Nichols, George. ed. 9304, 85344

Nichols, George Ward, 1837-1885. (55197)-(55199)

Nichols, George Ward, 1837-1885. supposed author 12845, note just before 87264

Nichols, George Warner. 55200

Nichols, Ichabod, 1784-1859. 1802, 55201-55202

Nichols, J. C. ed. (26181)

Nichols, J. Horatius. 55187, 103731

Nichols, J. Howard. (52668), 103731

Nichols, James. 55203

Nichols, James R. 55204-55206

Nichols, John, 1745-1826. ed. (21345), 94069-94070

Nichols, John, fl. 1860. 55206

Nichols, John H. (55207)

Nichols, John M. 55208

Nichols, John T. Gilman. 55209

Nichols, Mary Grove. (55210)

Nicols, Philip. (18236), 20830, (20838)-20840, 20843, 20855-20856

Nichols, Rebecca S. (55211)

Nichols, Sidney P. 84774

Nichols, Thomas. defendant 6326, 1st note after 97284

Nichols, Thomas. tr. see Nicholas, Thomas. tr.

Nichols, Thomas L. 55212-(55215)

Nichols, W. T. 55217

Nichols, William. (55216)

Nichols (C. B. & F. B.) firm publishers (55193)

Nichols (F. B.) firm publishers see Nichols (C. B. & F. B.) firm publishers

Nichols & Gorman. firm publishers (55218)

Nichols' illustrated New York. (55193)

Nicholson, Alfred Osborn Pope, 1808-1876. 11171, 55219

Nicholson, E. G. (55220)

Nicholson, Sir Francis, 1660-1728. 55221-55222

Nicholson, J. J. 55229

Nicholson, J. S. 82304

Nicholson, James William Augustus, 1821-1887. 55224

Nicholson, John, of Herkimer Co., N. Y. 55227

Nicholson, John, d. 1800. 59772, 60768, 84577-84578, 2d-3d notes after 97876 see also United Illinois and Wabash Land Companies. Agents.

Nicholson, John, d. 1800. defendant 32418, 55225-55226, 60179, 1st note after 96883, 1st note after 96909

Nicholson, John, d. 1800. petitioner 34294, 84577 see also United Illinois and Wabash Land Companies. Council. petitioners

Nicholson, John, d. 1800. supposed author 99578

Nicholson, John Anthony, 1827-1906. 55228

Nicholson, Joseph. (55230)

Nicholson, Joseph Hopper, 1770-1817. 2658, 55231, note after 89216

Nicholson, T. 55234

Nicholson, T. H. illus. 92482

Nicholson, Thomas, fl. 1800. (55232)

Nicholson, Thomas, fl. 1853. 55233

Nicholson, William, 1753-1815. 77380

Nicholson, William R. 55235

Nicht wi' Burns, and other poems. 17026

Nick Hallabout. pseud. see Hallabout, Nick. pseud.

Nick of the woods. 5554

Nick Whiffles. A drama. 72133

Nick Whiffles on the border. 72129

Nickalls, James. 10499

Nickerson, Freeman. 58915

Nicklin, Philip Houlbrooke. 55236-55237, 2d note after 100484

Nickolls, John. tr. 63439

Nickolls, Robert Boucher. 55238

Niclutsch, Francisco. 55239

Nicodemus. 30899

Nicol, John, fl. 1600. 66686

Nicol, John, fl. 1740. 55240

Nicol, John, 1755-1825. 55241

Nieuwe reystogt rondom de werreld. 18385, 100943

Nieuwe tijdinge uyt Oost-Indien van den 1 February, 1673. 55289

Nieuwe verbeterde chirurgyns scheeps-kist. 6341, 32884, (57377), 98930

Nieuwe vermeerde Groenlandse walvisch-vangst. (55290)

Nieuwe volmaeckte beschryvinghe der vervaer-lijcker strate Magellani. (57952)

Nieuwe volmaeckte beschryvinghe der vervaer-lyker strate Magellani. 22584

Nieuvve vveerlt der landtschappen ende eylanden. 34107, note after 99383C

Nieuwe wereld. (Homes of the new world.) 7712

Nieuwe wereld. Verhalen uit de geschiedenis van Amerika. 20125

Nieuwe werelt, anders ghenaempt West-Indien. 14348, 31542, note after 102849

Nieuwe werelt der landschappen ende eylande. 16961

Nieuwe wereldt ofte beschrijvinghe van West-Indien. 38554

Nieuwe werken van het zeeuwsch Genootschap der Wetenschappen. 72767

Nieuwenhoff, E. (20593), note after 98474, note after 99310

Nieto, Juan. 20661

Nieves, J. M. 55292

Nieves Robledo, Maria de las. see Robeldo, Maria de las Nieves.

Niewindt, Johann. 55291

Nifo, Manuel Deogracias. 55293

Niger. pseud. Short statement of facts. 55294

Niger-expedition und ihre Bestimmung. (9688)

Nigger melodist. 55295

Nigger question. 10935

Nigger sale. (28485)

Nigger woman who took in work from Mrs. Lincoln and Mrs. Davis. pseud. Behind the scenes. 81903

Night in Buenos Ayres. 55296

Night in Charleston. 91232

Night of death. 85473

Night of freedom. 31197

Night side of New York. (55297)

Night watch. (55298)

Nightingale, Crawford. 55299

Nightingale, J. 55301

Nightingale, Joseph, 1775-1824. (55302)

Nightingale, Thomas. 55303

Nightingale. A collection of . . . popular, ancient, and modern songs. 39040

Nightingale. An essay on songs among thorns. 46432

Nightingale, or melange de litterature. 55304

Nights of solitude on sea and land. 82127

Nightshade. 72133

Nigon de Berty, L. 55305

Nigrinus or Schwartz, Franz. (55306)

Nihima Ayamie-Mazinahigan. 55307

Niina aiamie kak8edjindi8inimasinaigan ate gaie kekinoamagemagak. (11501), (34626)

Nijenhuis, Jan Tiberius Bodel. 48686, 55308

Nijhoff, Martinus. 55309

Nikimoani. (79977)

Nikimowani Siwinwike ealitowawice wastowice paptesewe mkitawkolieake. 79978

Nikkanochee, Oceola. see Oceola Nikkanochee. Indian Chief

Nil admirari. pseud. Trollopiad. see Shelton, Frederick William, 1814-1881.

Niles, --------, fl. 1813. 55323

Niles, Elisha. 84480

Niles, Henry Edward, 1823-1900. 55310

Niles, Hezehiah, 1777-1839. 55311-(55316), n after 95351

Niles, John B. 55317

Niles, John Milton, 1787-1856. 55318-55322, 59466, 71738, 91637, 99547

Niles, M. A. H. 55324

Niles, N. 55328

Niles, Nathaniel. 11304, (55325)-55326

Niles, Nathaniel, Junior. 55327

Niles, Peter. 55329

Niles, Samuel, 1674-1762. 55330-55332, 7992

Niles, Samuel, 1743-1814. 55333-55335

Niles, W. W. petitioner (24431)

Niles, William A. (55336)

Niles, William H. 55337

Niles, William Ogden. ed. 269, (55313)-(55316), (55338), 62027, 85184, 85199, 88343, note after 95855

Niles' national register. see Niles' weekly register.

Niles' register. see Niles' weekly register.

Niles' weekly register. 269, (55313)-(55316), (55338), 62027, 85184, 85199, 88343, note after 95855

Nimble-Chops, Aquiline, Democrat. pseud. Democracy. see Livingston, Brockhols 1757-1823.

Nimini, Notus. pseud. Letter to Hull Barton. see Ogden, George W.

Nimmo, Joseph. 55340

Nimni, Notus. pseud. Letter to Hull Barton. see Ogden, George W.

Nimrod, Harry. pseud. Fudge family in Washington. (26107), 55341

Nimrod of the west. 17574

Nina Canadienne. 44499

Nina Gordon. 92397

Ninas pintadas por ellas mismas. 74969

Ninde, W. W. 55342

Nine days' devotion in honor of St. Vincent of Paul. 89520

IX. Edinburgh cabinet library. Northern coasts of America. 97657

Nine extras issued by the iron platform. 214?

Nine grants in fee simple. 55343

Nine letters descriptive of the agricultural state. 36401

Nine letters, from Mr. Vander Neck. 9245, note after 98483

Nine letters on the subject of Aaron Burr's political defection. (12381)

Nine letters, particularly addressed to the people of the revolting Spanish provinces of the Caracas. 103298

Nine letters to Adam Seybert. 10875

Nine months in the Quartermaster's Departmen (39886)

Nine months in the United States during the crisis. 24416

Nine plain questions to the people of Connect-icut. 32482

Nine sermons on Psal. xcic. 96. 3471

Nine sermons upon the following subjects. 103573

Nine years a sailor. 55463

Nine years among the convicts of New Hamp-shire. 82466

Nine years in America. 50323

Nine years of Democratic rule in Mississippi. (55344)

Nine years' residence. (21077)

Nineteen months a prisoner of war. (74743)-74744

Nineteen numbers of the radical reformer. 8397

Nineteenth anniversary oration. 32270

Nineteenth century. 83876, 84419, 84445

XIX century. (55346)

Nineteenth century. A quarterly magazine. 55345

Nineteenth century; or, glances at home and abroad. 33181

Nineteenth century; or the new dispensation. 55347

Nineteenth report . . . see Report . . .

Ninetieth birthday gathering of Rev. Charles Cleveland. 13649, 59463

Ninety-four years. 58985

Nineveh threatened. 343

Nineveh's repentence and deliverance. 79424

Ningre-Gemeente, Paramaribo. see Paramaribo. Ningre-Gemeente.

Nino, Alonzo. 34100-34107

Nino Jesus, Pablo Antonio del. see Pablo Antonio del Nino Jesus.

Ninos Expositos de la Imperial Ciudad de Mexico. petitioners 48559

Ninth annual catalogue . . . see Catalogue . . .

Ninth annual circular . . . see Circular . . .

Ninth annual meeting of the convention [of Baptists of Vermont.] 99151

Ninth annual meeting of the Illinois State Medical Society. 34265

Ninth annual report . . . see Report . . .

Ninth census. Speech . . . December 16, 1869. 26664

[Ninth letter to the Rev. Samuel Miller.] (49063)

Ninth report . . . see Report . . .

Nipho y Cagigal, Francisco Mariano. (55349)

Nips, Jack. pseud. Yankee spy. see Leland, John. supposed author

Nis hr nea nent. ho yot duh. do shoo wa. 103453

Nisbet, Charles. 55351, 73361

Nisbet, James. 87268

Nisbet, Joseph Henry. (55352)

Nisbet, Richard. 55353-55354

Nisbet, Richard. supposed author 55354, 74206-74207, (82106), note after 99798, 2d note after 102803

Nisi Dominus frustra. 77593

Nispen, A. van. 55355

Nissen, Johan Peter. 55356

Nissen, M. tr. 20000

Nitsche, R. Lehmann. see Lehmann-Nitsche, R.

Nituk hollo nituk a isht anumpa hoke. 104307

Niveau de l'Europe et de l'Amerique Septentrionalle. 23568, 55357, 93480

Niven, Archibald Campbell, 1803-1882. 55358

Niven, Archibald Campbell, 1803-1882. defendant 42397

Niven, George W. defendant 75948, 2d note after 96909

Nixon, Barnaby. 55359-55360

Nixon, H. G. 37639, 88076, note after 94393 see also Kershaw District, S. C. Tariff Meeting, Camden, 1826. Committee to Draft a Memorial and Resolutions to Congress. Chairman.

Nixon, John. 60635 see also Pennsylvania (Colony) Committee of Safety, 1775-1776. Treasurer.

Nixon, John F. 55361

Nixon, John Thompson, 1820-1889. (53101), (53240)

Nixon, William. defendant 88828

Nix's mate. 18920

Nizza, Marco da. 16951, 67740

Njoe va wi masra en helpiman Jesus Christus. 55362

No abolition of slavery. 55363

No abolition; or, an attempt to prove. 55364

No bel-esprit. pseud. Gov. Strong's calumniator reproved. see Lowell, John, 1769-1840.

No cause nor need of pain in heaven. 104314

No church without a bishop. 64613

No church without a bishop; or, the controversy between the Rev. Drs. Potts and Wainwright. 64678

No colonies no funds. 55365, 3d note after 102802

No common laws, no Canada. (28143)

No compensation for slaves. (55366)

No compromise with slavery. 26712

No compromise with treason. (77579)

No cross, no crown. A discourse shewing the nature and discipline. 59722

No cross, no crown: or several sober reasons against hat-honour. 59721

No failure for the north. 55367

No fiction. 3534, (39840)

No fiction: a narrative. (68537)

No fiction: or, the test of friendship. (68538)

No fiction. The traditionary history of a narrow and providential escape. 34480

No government bounty to polygamy. 42837

No king, but Christ, in his church. 103203A

No military power to return any slave. 12700

No mistake. 30045

No more his fears alarming. 92174C

No more punishment for the south! 82648

No more, the senior's farewell, a poem. 29489

No new thing to be slander'd. 83445

No north no south. An address. 39383

No party—no creed. (48895)

No party now, but all for our country. 40985

No persons whatsoever is to presume to remove any merchandise. 61866

No placemen. 102953

No power in Congress to emancipate their slaves. 11065

No property in man. 93667

No rebuznaron en balde el uno y el otro alcalde. 97042

No refuge for American slavery in the New Testament. (12283)

No rum, no sugar. 55368

No se condenaran indultos ni asilos. 99482

No slave-hunting in the Old Bay State. An appeal to the people and legislature of Massachusetts. 9330, 55369

No slave-hunting in the Old Bay State. Speech of Wendell Phillips. 62523

No slavery in Nebraska. 82649

No slavery in the nation. 82649

No slur, else-slur. 71139

No song no supper. 55370, 92175B

No standing army in the British colonies. 55371

No terms with traitors. 82650

No thoroughfare. 55372

No treason in civil war. 82651

No treason. No. I. 89614

No treaty stipulations against the slave trade. 4703, 81812

No trust in dying man. 85396

No union of church and state. 55373

No union with Rome. 35816

No war with America. (29837)

Noah, Mordecai Manuel, 1785-1851. 55374-55375

Noah, Mordecai Manuel, 1785-1851. defendant 49074, 55375

Noah Webster's attack on Porcupine's answer. 14007, 102401

Noah's flood. 98295

Noailles, --------, Sieur de. plaintiff 75162

Noamira, Jose Ramo Zeschan. see Zeschan Noamira, Jose Ramo.

Noaquett, -------. 81140

Nobbe, C. F. A. (55376)

Nobiliaire universel de France. 34061

Nobiliario de la valle de Valdorba. (22365), 55377

Noble, B. G. ed. 78573

Noble, Daniel. 104433

Noble, David Addison, 1802-1876. (55385)

Noble, Frederic A. 55378

Noble, Herman S. 51853

Noble, John. 55379

Noble, Laz. 34562 see also Indiana. Adjutant General.

Noble, Louis L. 55380-55382

Noble, Mason. (55383)-55384

Noble, N. (34524) see also Indiana. Fund Commissioner.

Noble, Oliver. (55386)-55387

Noble, Patrick, 1787-1840. 87669, 87970 see also South Carolina. Governor, 1388-1840 (Noble)

Noble, Robert. 55296

Noble, Seth. (28126), 55388, 104528

Noble, Warren P. (55389)

Noble army of martyrs. 82908

Noble deeds of American women. 13630

Noble life. John N. Stearns. 90903

Noble lord. pseud. Dialogue between a noble lord and a poor woodman. 19930

"Noble pile." 67172

Nobleborough, Mass. petitioners (61266)

Nobleman. pseud. Reply to the pamphlet. see Malmesbury, James Howard Harris, 3d Earl of, 1807-1889.

Nobles, William H. 55390

Nobles de Guatemala. (55391)

Noble's instructions to emigrants. 55379

Noblest freedom. 2790

Noblet, --------. tr. 4266

Nobleza y piedad de los Montaneses. (50627)

Noblom, Jules. tr. 63874

Noboa, Pedro Vasquez de. see Vasquez de Noboa, Pedro.

Nobody. pseud. No slur, else-slur. see Richmond, James Cook.

Nobody, Nathan. pseud. "Simon Snapping Turtle," Esq. 55392

Nobody, Nemo, Esquire. pseud. Something. see Fennell, James.

Nobody knows who. pseud. To those born on the soil. 38144, note before 96041

Nobrega, -------. (16672), 55393

Noch einer andern relation davon. 32377, 98990

Nociones de cronologia universal. 47836

Noclauf, -------. 16741

Nocnopil Joseph de Yturrigaray Tecpilli Monetolti itechpa in Tlatecpantli Santiago. 106220A

Nocoes geographicas e administrativas da Provincia de Minas Geraes. 27121

Nocoes preliminares. 70790

Nocolosius, Giovanni Battista. 55258

Nocte cogitata. 79459

Noctes gymnasii. 101971

Nodal, Bartolome Garcia de. 55394-(55395)

Nodal, Goncalo de. 55394-(55395)

Nodal, Jose Fernandez. 55397-55398

Nodier, --------. 10754

Noel, --------. tr. 1369

Noel, Baptist Wriothesley. 55399-55401

Noel, Baptiste. 73489

Noel, Ernest. 55402

Noel, Garrat. 55403

Noel, J. illus. 14940

Noel, Jacques. (55404)

Noel, R. R. tr. (38216)

Noel, William, 1695-1762. 34416

Noel de la Moriniere, Simon Barthelemi Joseph. 55405-55406

Noel (Garrat) & Co. firm 55403

Noel Hill Mining and Smelting Company. 554●

Noell, John William, 1816-1863. 55408

Noell, William, 1695-1762. see Noel, Willi● 1695-1762.

Noetica: or the first principles of human knowledge. (36292)

Noetica, or things relating to the mind. 3629●

Nog copia, van een brief. (35768)

Nogales, Miguel Roman de. see Roman de Nogales, Miguel.

Noggerath, Johann Jakob, 1788-1877. tr. 4860, 9275

Nogit, Fran. 98907

Nogle bemaerkninger angaaende Gronlands oysterbygde. 32073

Nogle bemaerkninger om den indflydelse. 69116

Nogle ord fra praedikestolen i Amerika og Norge., 20131

Nogueira, Baptista Caetano de Almeida. see Almeida Nogueira, Baptista Caetano de.

Noir, Louis. (55409)

Noir marron. 19533

Noirot, A. ed. 70367

Noirot, A. M. A. ed. 87308

Noirs en Amerique. 92536

Noirs et blancs. 92545

Noirs et les petits blancs. 27451

Noisy member, and a silent monitor. 84963-84964

Noites Jozephinas de Mirtilo sobre a infausta morte. 88837

Nojoque. 31274

Nolasco Mena, Pedro. see Mena, Pedro Nolasco.

Noll, Henry R. 55410

Nollekens and his times. 83021

Nolte, Vincent. 55411-55412

Nomades of the west. (34113)

Nomenclator. 105074

Nomenclator avium neotropicalium. 78141

Nomenclator Ptolemaicvs. 66494

Nomenclatura brevis Anglo-Latino in usum scholarum. 55413

Nomenclature generale de tous les timbres adoptes. 49826

Nomenclature of human hybrids. 8676

Nomina Senatus Academici. 97775

Nomination of candidates. 55414

Nomination of Gen. Houston, Oct. 11. 52821

Nomination of President & Vice President of the United States. (55415)

Nomination of U. S. Grant. 55416

Nominees that ought to be elected in 1861. 10249

Nomony, Va. Meeting, 1802. 55417

Noms svrnoms et qualitez des Associez en la Compagnie de la Nouuelle France. 105● 55418

Nomsz, Johannis. (55419)

Non cessant anni, quamvis cessant homines. 62743

Non da hyu e gi gaz nah. 105557

Nonantum and Natick. 35505

Nonay, ---------. supposed author 93353

Non-committal. A comedy in five acts. 77816

Nonconformist Ministers of London. petitioners 8372, 81492

Noncomformist's [sic] memorial. (9868)

Nonconformist's plea for uniformity. 55420

Non-conformity to the world, in moral character. 47449

Nondescript, Mr. pseud. see Mr. Nondescript. pseud.

None but believers saved. 82216

None but Christ. 46208

None but the brave deserve the fair. 89497

Noneniotehaga nahononwentsioten, ne ratitsihenstatsi. 104213

Non-essentialism and the American church. 50457

Non-essentialism and the war. 50457

Non-extension of slavery. 58702

Non-fellowship with slaveholders the duty of Christians. 24004

Non-importation Association, Philadelphia, 1765. 61646

Non-importation Association, Philadelphia, 1770. 62311, 93356-93357, 95771-95772, 97563

Non-importation Association, New York, 1770. 93357

Non-importation Association, Worcester County, Mass., 1775. 105395-105396

Non-importation Association of Virginia, 1769. 99925, 100504

Non-importation Association of Virginia, 1770. 100503

Non-importation Association of Virginia, 1774. 100007

Noninius, Petrus. see Nunes, Pedro, fl. 1537.

Non-intercourse laws. 22412

Non-interference by Congress with slavery in the territories. 20693

Non-interference with insurrectionary districts. 82450

Non-intervention . . . April 24, 1852. 23329

Non-intervention—popular sovereignty. 20693

Nonius, Mr. pseud. see Mr. Nonius. pseud.

Nonius, Petrus. see Nunes, Pedro, fl. 1537.

Nonpareil quadrat. pseud. "Happy new year!" see Holden, J. G. P.

Non-resistance. 33481

Non-resistance Society of New England. see New England Non-resistance Society.

Nonsense. pseud. see Parson All-sense, alias Smallsense, alias, Nonsense. pseud.

Nonsense. 63931

Nonville, --------, Marquis de. see Denonville, Jacques Rene de Brisay, Marquis de, d. 1710.

Noodig berigt aan het publiek. 93861

Noodle, --------. 55422

Noodlot van Amerika. 11702, 55423

Nooley, B. 55424

Noon, Darby. supposed author 23634, 55425, 71500

Noon prayer meeting of the North Dutch Church. 11804

Noonan, --------. 55425

Noord-Amerik. Unie, hare wording, geschiedenis, geldmiddelen en toekomst. (30869)

Noord-Amerika. 106334

Noord-Amerikaansche oorlog van 1861-1865. 56430

Noord-Amerikaansche Staat Minnesota beschreven. (77628)

Noord-Pool. 106334

Noordsche Weereld. (38712), note after 100855

Noort, Juan de. engr. (16770), 75780

Noort, Olivier van, 1568-1611. (8784), 9387, 14349, 14957-14960, 33660, 55432-55448, 66686, 68455, 2d note after 105014

Nooteboom, Engelbert. tr. 21952

Nootwendich discovrs ofte vertooch aan de Hooch-Mogende Heeren Staten Generaal van de Participanten der Oost-Indische Compagnie tegens Bewinthebbers. 55449, (57379), 63196-63197, 99316

Nootwendigh discours, ofte vertoogh aende Hog: Mog: Heeren Staten Generael. 55449, (63197), 102908

Nor Peru (State) Laws, statutes, etc. 55450, 68868, 76766-76769

Norberto, F. see Parisot, Pierre.

Norberto de Sousa Silva, Joaquim. see Sousa Silva, Joaquim Norberto de.

Norcot, John. 22141

Nord-Amerika historisch und geographisch beschreiben. 55454

Nord-Amerika, in allen Beziehungen geschildert. 8204

Nord-Amerika in Bildern. 55455

Nord-Amerika in seinen verschiedenen Beziehingen. 2431

Nord-Amerika in . . . Umrissen. 1461

Nord-Amerika nach den Friedensschlussen vom Jahr 1783. 51055

Nord-Amerika oder neuestes Gemalde der Nord-Amerikanischen Freistaaten. (55456)

Nord de la Siberie. 26376

Nord du Globe. (59659)

Nord et le Sud. 15460

Nord et le Sud. L'espion noir. 12577

Nord et le Sud. Par Ernest Poulain. 64717

Nord-Polarlanden. 55457

Nord und Sud. Erzahlungen und Schilderungen aus dem westlichen Schneeflocken. 49916

Nord und Sud im Krieg und Frieden oder Scenen aus der jungsten Rebellion. 40116

Nord- und Sudamerika. 30080

Nordamericanischen Freistaaten. 44309

Nordamericanska fristaterna och deras invanare. 106340

Nordamerika—Ohio. 22581

Nordamerika, sein Volksthum und seine Institutionen. 52061

Nordamerika. . . . Von Pet. Schultze. 2431

Nordamerika. [Von Traugolt Bromme.] 8213

Nordamerika vorzuglich Texas im Jahre 1849. 91208

Nordamerika, Wisconsin, Calumet. 29409

Nordamerika. Wisconsin. Zwei Abetheilungen. 29410

Nordamerikaner. 16488

Nordamerikanische Bilder und Zustande. Deutsch von Spazier. 4189, 2d note after 96068

Nordamerikanische Bilder und Zustande. [Von J. G. Buttner.] 9675

Nordamerikanische Bundesstaatsrecht verglichen mit den politischen Einrichtungen der Schweiz. 74498

Nordamerikanische Freistaat Texas. 73357
Nordamerikanische Freistaat Wisconsin. 71221
Nordamerikanische Landwirth. 24696
Nordamerikanische Rathgeber. 27138
Nordamerikanische Revolution und das Recht der Volker. 73293
Nordamerikanische Revolution und ihre Folgen. 103884
Nord-amerikanische Sclaverei. 33472
Nordamerikanische Unabhangigkeits-Kreig. 61346
Nordamerikanische Zeitschrift fur Deutschland. 103032
Nord-amerikanischen Briefe. 21074
Nordamerikanischen Democratie und das von Tocqueville'sche Werke daruber. 21074
Nordamerikanischer Krieger, eine Selbstbiographie. 9674
Nordamerikanischer Roman. 5556
Nordamerikanischer Staats-Kalender. 95835
Nordamerikansk Roman af James Paulding. 59187
Nordamerika's Bewohner, Schonheiten, und Naturschatze in Allgemeinen. 8212
Nordamerikas sittliche Zustande. 36891
Nordamerikas Stellung zum Quintupel-Tractat. (4839), 4842
Norden, oder zu Wasser und Lande im Eise und Snee. 10736
Nordenflycht, Timothy, Baron. 55458
Nordenskiold, Nils Adolf Erik, Friherre, 1832-1901. 91866
Nordhoff, Charles. (55459)-55463
K. Nordske Oldskrift-selskab, Copenhagen. 23717, (28650), 29211, 47545, 55464, (67467), (67469)-(67472), 67480-(67482), (67486), 69656, 76838, 77841, 85824-85859
Nordstern, F. C. tr. 92569
Nordwestkuste von Amerika und der dortige Pelzhandel. 25129
Nordwestliche Bilder. 57894
Nordwestlichen Provinzen und die Cordilleren. 9347
Nores, Giasone di. 19603, 55465-55466
Norfolk, N. Y. 73842
Norfolk, Va. Charter. 55479
Norfolk, Va. Citizens. (55480)
Norfolk, Va. Colored Citizens. 55476
Norfolk, Va. Committee of Physicians. 55484
Norfolk, Va. Jamestown Tercentennial Exposition, 1907. see Jamestown Tercentennial Exposition, Norfolk, Va., 1907.
Norfolk, Va. Merchants. 55477
Norfolk, Va. Ordinances, etc. 55479
Norfolk County, Mass. (55472), 55481
Norfolk County, Mass. Anti-slavery Convention, Dedham, 1838. see Norfolk County Anti-slavery Convention, Dedham, Mass., 1838.
Norfolk County, Mass. Bar. (55474)
Norfolk County, Mass. Bible Society. see Norfolk County Bible Society.
Norfolk County, Mass. Sunday School Association. see Norfolk County Sunday School Association.
Norfolk Agricultural Society. (55467)
Norfolk Auxiliary Education Society. 2744 see also American Education Society of Norfolk County, Mass.
Norfolk city and business directory for 1866. 55478

Norfolk city directory for 1869. 55478
Norfolk city directory for 1870. 55478
Norfolk Convention . . . [of] Republican delegates from the County of Norfolk assembled at . . . Dedham. 55468
Norfolk County American Education Society. see American Education Society of Norfolk County, Mass.
Norfolk County Anti-slavery Convention, Dedha Mass., 1838. 55473
Norfolk County Bible Society. 55469, 55479
Norfolk county journal. 5538, (40235)
Norfolk County Sunday School Association. Directors. 55470
Norfolk democrat. 9154
Norfolk directory. 55478
Norfolk directory for 1851-1852. 55478
Norfolk District Medical Society. see Massachusetts Medical Society. Norfolk District Medical Society.
Norfolk Law Library, Dedham, Mass. see Dedham, Mass. Norfolk Law Library.
Norfolk new regime. 59558
Norgate, E. 55485
Norge og Amerika. 55486
Norges riiges historie indeholdende riigets aeldste historie. 77810
Norie, John William. 55487-(55488)
Noriega, --------, fl. 1741. 40733
Noriega, Fernando Navarro y. see Navarro y Noriega, Fernando.
Noriega, Jose Maria Diaz. see Diaz Noriega Jose Maria.
Noriega, Manuel. 55490
Noriega y Guerra, Jose Servando Teresa de Mier. see Mier Noriega y Guerra, Jose Servando Teresa de, 1765-1827.
Norie's New South American pilot. 55487
Norlin, Benedictus. 98390
Normal, Ill. State Normal University. see Illinois. State Normal University, Norma
Normal and Training School, Cortland, N. Y. see New York (State) State Normal School, Cortland.
Normal and Training School, Oswego, N. Y. see New York (State) State Normal School, Oswego.
Normal and Training School, Potsdam, N. Y. see New York (State) State Normal School, Potsdam.
Normal School, Albany. see New York (State) State College for Teachers, Albany.
Normal School, Halifax, N. S. see Nova Scotia. Normal School, Halifax.
Normal School, Philadelphia. see Philadelphia. Normal School.
Normal School, St. Louis. see St. Louis. Norma School.
Normal school advocate. 55491
Normal School for Colored Girls, Washington, D. C. 55492
Normal schools, and other institutions. 3469
Normal schools and teachers' seminaries. 92387
Normal schools: their relations to . . . institutions of learning. 61400
Norman, --------. engr. 7184-7185
Norman, Benjamin Moore, 1809-1860. 4608, 55360, 55493-(55494)
Norman, Lucia. 55495
Norman, Robert. 55496
Norman, William. (55497)
Norman Leslie. (23949)
Norman Maurice. 81241
Normand. 40040

Normandie, James de. see De Normandie, James.

Normandie (Departement) Chambre de Commerce. Syndics. 56473

Norman's New Orleans and environs. 53360, (55494)

Norona, Antonio Souza y. see Souza y Norona, Antonio.

Noronha, Juana Manso de. see Manso de Noronha, Juana.

Noronha Freire, Joao de. see Santa Teresa, Giovanni Gioseppe di.

Norri, Gabriel Pantaleon de Escoyti y. see Pantaleon de Escoyti y Norri, Gabriel.

Norridywalk Indians. see Norridgewock Indians.

Norridgewock Indians. 5391, 15429, 15435-(15437), 15441-15442, 34083, note after (34632), 34654, 36730, 80205

Norriega y Guerra, J. S. see Mier Noriega y Guerra, Jose Servando Santa Theresa de, 1765-1827.

Norris, -------, fl. 1823. 35867

Norris, --------, fl. 1849. plaintiff 82581

Norris, ---------, fl. 1851. plaintiff 55510

Norris, ----------, fl. 1864. 6150, 12422

Norris, Edwin. ed. (65475)

Norris, H. H. 77767

Norris, Isaac, 1701-1766. 22692, 55500-55501, 60006, (60625), 60645, 61203, 61622, 61845, note after 89175, 93253 see also Pennsylvania (Colony) Commissioners to the Ohio Indians.

Norris, J. P. 55501

Norris, J. Wellington. (12639)-(12640)

Norris, John, of Charleston, S. C., fl. 1712. 10962, (55502), 87745

Norris, John Saurin, 1813-1882. (45211A), 55503-(55505), note after 97651

Norris, Moses, 1799-1855. 55506

Norris, Robert. 55507

Norris, Thad. 55508

Norris, William Herbert. 55509

Norriss, Samuel. petitioner 96696

Norristown and Bridgeport directory for 1867-68. 55511

Norristown and Freemansburg Rail Road Company. Charter. 60274

Norristown free press. 8239, 62120

Norristown register. 89472

Norrmann, Gerhard Philipp Heinrich. supposed author 102834

Nort, Olivier du. see Noort, Olivier van, 1568-1611.

Norte de la contratacion de las Indias Occidentales. 98780

Nortes, Josephinas de Mirtilo. (55512)

Nortes Josephinas de Mirtilo sobre a infausta morte. (55512)

North, Lord. see Guilford, Frederick North, Earl of, 1732-1792.

North, -------. tr. 95341

North, -------, fl. 179-? 92175A

North, C. C. 84755

North, Edward. 55513

North, Elisha. (55514)

North, Frederick. see Guilford, Frederick North, Earl of, 1732-1792.

North, James W. 55520

North, M. L. 55522-55523

North, Nathaniel G. ed. 88615

North, Simon. 55524

North, W. 22755 see also New York (State) Commissioners on Internal Navigation.

North, W. of Charleston, S. C. 87781, 87783

North America; a descriptive poem. 20591, 55526

North America and the West Indies. 49465, (52048)

North America, Central America. 24104

North America. Correspondence relating to the steamers "Nashville" and "Tuscarora" at Southampton. 16887, 55534

North America. Correspondence respecting the negotiations with the United States' government on the question of the "Alabama." 55535

North America. Correspondence respecting the withdrawal by the government of the United States. 9159, 16887

North America its agriculture and climate. 74370

North America. Its people and the resources. 83377

North America. No. 8. Papers relating to the blockade. 5943, 55532

North America. No. 5. Correspondence respecting the seizure of Messrs. Mason, Slidell, McFarland, and Eustis. 45451, (55530)

North America. (No. 4.) 1864. 15003, 55529

North America. No. 6. 1863. 16887, (55531)

North America. No. 7. Correspondence respecting the enlistment of British seamen. 16886, (37131)

North America No. 7. Papers relating to the imprisonment of Mr. Shaver. 79888

North America. No. 10. Memorial of certain shipowners at Liverpool. 55533

North America. No. 3. Correspondence respecting international maritime law. 16886, (55528)

North America. No. 2. Extract of a dispatch. 19753, (23505), 55527

North America. Papers relating to the blockade of the ports. 5943, 55532

North America, the Cape, Australia, and New Zealand. 46844

North America viewed. 34701

North American. pseud. Address to General Lafayette. 38583

North American. pseud. Address to the Committee of Correspondence in Barbadoes. see Dickinson, John, 1732-1808.

North-American. pseud. American querist. see Cooper, Myles.

North American. pseud. Northern grievances. 55797

North American. pseud. To General Lafayette. 38583

North American (Philadelphia) 7772, (29009), 40656, 70202, 79122

North-American almanack. 90948-90952, 90955-90956

Northamerican [sic] almanack. 90953-90954

North-American almanack, and gentleman's and lady's diary. 90944

North American almanac and Massachusetts register. 55536

North-American almanack and Massachusetts register for 1770. 21833

North American and surgical journal. 22431

North American and the West-Indian gazetteer. 55537

North American atlas. 50969

North American atlas, selected from the most authentic maps. 23643

North and south, reason why Coleman Yellott. 55571

North and the south. A statistical view. 12179

North and the south! Letter from J. C. Lovejoy, Esq. 42367

North and the south misrepresented and misjudged. 55575

North and the south; or, slavery and its contrasts. 74246

North and the south. Reprinted from the New York tribune. 10842, 55573

North and the south. The crisis before us, for reading and reflecting men. 55572

North and the south: the crisis before us. From the N. Y. herald. (55574)

North and the south. The effects of Negro-slavery. 92866

North Association in the County of Hartford, Conn. see Congregational Churches in Connecticut. Hartford County North Association.

North Atlantic Telegraph Company (Great Britain) 55576

North Atlantic telegraph via the Faeroe Islands, Iceland, and Greenland. 55576

North-Attleborough, Mass. Baptist Church. 55577

North Branch. pseud. Review of the question. 5684, 60590, 70253

North Branch, N. J. Low Dutch Reformed Church. 25755, 25974, 98572

North Branch Canal Committee. 60275

North Branch Canal Company. Charter. 60275

North Branch Canal Company. Engineer. 55578, 60276 see also Foster, William B.

North Branch Canal Company. Superintendent. 55578, 60276

North Branch Canal Company; its prospects, and its laws of incorporation. 60275

North Branch Canal Convention, Tunkhannock, Pa., 1840. see Convention of Delegates from Luzerne, Susquehanna and Bradford Counties, Tunkhannock, Pa., 1840.

North Branch Canal Corresponding Committee. 60275

North Branch extension. 60276

North-Britain extraordinary. (36397)

North British review. 67599

North Briton. pseud. Notes. (57416)

North Brookfield, Mass. 55579-55580

North Brookfield, Mass. Congregational Church. 85400

North Brookfield, Mass. School Committee. 55581

North Carolina (Colony) 32968, 55624, 87359

North Carolina (Colony) Charter. 2169, 55641

North Carolina (Colony) General Assembly. 16688

North Carolina (Colony) General Assembly. House of Burgesses. 55649, 83613, 97092

North Carolina (Colony) Governor, 1754-1765 (Dobbs) (27056), 36718 see also Dobbs, Arthur, 1689-1765.

North Carolina (Colony) Laws, statutes, etc.
39410, 39414, 55582, 55585, 55601-55603, (55637), 55641, (55670), note after 94720, 94774-94775, 94777, 94780-94782

North Carolina (Colony) Lords Proprietors. 55641

North Carolina (Colony) Provincial Congress, Halifax, 1776. 55631-55632

North Carolina. 55675, 92392, note after 94720

North Carolina. Administration Convention, Raleigh, 1827. see Administration Convention, Raleigh, N. C., 1827.

North Carolina. Bill of Rights. 55641

North Carolina. Board of Public Charities. 55598

North Carolina. Board of Public Improvements. 55593

North Carolina. Citizens. petitioners (55610), 79519

North Carolina. Comptroller's Department. 55671, 55677, 55693

North Carolina. Constitution. 1269, 1271, 2071, 5316, 6360, 16086-16092, 16097, 16099-16103, 16107, 16113, 16118-16120, 16133, (19476), 25790, 33137, (47188), (55604)-55607, 55632, 55641, 55663, 59771, (66397), 94777, 100342, 104198

North Carolina. Constitutional Convention, Halifax, 1779. (55604)

North Carolina. Constitutional Convention, Raeigh, 1835. 55663

North Carolina. Constitutional Convention, Raleigh, 1868. (55606), 55627, 55698

North Carolina. Convention, Hillsborough, 1788. 22233, 55662, note after 106002

North Carolina. Convention, Raleigh, 1861-1862. 55628, (55657)-55658

North Carolina. Convention, Raleigh, 1865-1866. (55629), 55658

North Carolina. Convention of Freedmen, Raleigh, 1865. see Convention of Freedmen of North Carolina, Raleigh, 1865.

North Carolina. Declaration of Rights. 55632

North Carolina. Evangelical Lutheran Synod. see Evangelical Lutheran Synod of North Carolina and Bordering States.

North Carolina. General Assembly. 55609, 55665, 55685, (55690)

North Carolina. General Assembly. Joint Select Committee to Inquire Into the Causes Why Soldiers Were Paid in Confederate Treasury Notes. (55678)

North Carolina. General Assembly. Joint Special Committee on Federal Relations. (55680)

North Carolina. General Assembly. Joint Special Committee on the Alteration of the Tariff. 55679

North Carolina. General Assembly. House. 55594, (55634), 55686, (55690), 66530

North Carolina. General Assembly. Senate. 55633-(55634), (55690)

North Carolina. Geological and Agricultural Survey. 55615

North Carolina. Geological and Natural History Survey. 18059, 55620

North Carolina. Geological Survey. 55592, 55613-55621

North Carolina. Geologist. 55613-55621 see also Curtis, M. A. Emmons,

Ebenezer, 1799-1863. Kerr, W. C.

Mitchill, Samuel Latham, 1764-1831. Olmsted, Denison, 1791-1859.

North Carolina. Governor, 1795-1798 (Ashe) 14745 see also Ashe, Samuel, 1725-1813.

North Carolina. Governor, 1798-1799 (Davie) (18748) see also Davie, William Richardson, 1759-1820.

North Carolina. Governor, 1814-1817 (Miller) 33150 see also Miller, William, 1770-1825.

North Carolina. Governor, 1827-1828 (Iredell) 55648 see also Iredell, James, 1788-1853.

North Carolina. Governor, 1837-1841 (Dudley) (55644) see also Dudley, Edward Bishop, 1787-1855.

North Carolina. Governor, 1845-1849 (Graham) 28141 see also Graham, William Alexander, 1804-1875.

North Carolina. Governor, 1855-1859 (Bragg) 33150 see also Bragg, Thomas, 1810-1872.

North Carolina. Governor, 1862-1865 (Vance) 55692 see also Vance, Zebulon Baird, 1830-1894.

North Carolina. Governor, 1868-1871 (Holden) (55612), 55668 see also Holden, William Woods, 1818-1892.

North Carolina. Governor, 1868-1871 (Holden) defendant at impeachment 55594 see also Holden, William Woods, 1818-1892. defendant at impeachment

North Carolina. Historical Commission. 97092

North Carolina. Inhabitants. see North Carolina. Citizens.

North Carolina. Institution for the Deaf and Dumb and the Blind, Raleigh. see North Carolina. School for the Deaf and Dumb, Raleigh. North Carolina. School for the Blind, Raleigh.

North Carolina. Insane Asylum, Goldsboro. see North Carolina. State Hospital, Goldsboro.

North Carolina. Laws, statutes, etc. 19231, 23765, 31086, 39414, 44870, 47289, 51870, 52051, 55583-55586, 55597, (55602), 55605-(55606), 55632, 55635-55643, 55645, 55651, (55657)-55661, 55663, (55670)-(55674), (55687)-55689, (55691), 55700, 70820-60821, 82438, 89066, 94509, note after 94720, 94774-94775, 94777, 94780-94782, 100974

North Carolina. Legislature. see North Carolina. General Assembly.

North Carolina. Medical Society. see Medical Society of North Carolina.

North Carolina. Military Governor, 1862-1863 (Stanly) 90323 see also Stanly, Edward, 1810-1872.

North Carolina. Militia. Newbern Guards. 54886

North Carolina. Public Treasurer. see North Carolina. Treasury Department.

North Carolina. School for the Blind, Raleigh. Directors. (55626)

North Carolina. School for the Blind, Raleigh. Principal. (55626)

North Carolina. School for the Deaf and Dumb, Raleigh. Directors. (55626)

North Carolina. School for the Deaf and Dumb, Raleigh. Principal. (55626)

North Carolina. State Hospital, Goldsboro. Directors. 55625

North Carolina. Superintendent of Negro Affairs. 35701 see also James, Horace.

North Carolina. Superior Court (Carteret County) 95849

North Carolina. Superior Courts. 44873, 94509

North Carolina. Superintendent of Common Schools. 55694

North Carolina. Supreme Court. 10965, 94509

North Carolina. Supreme Court. Chief Justice 55668 see also Pearson, Richmond Mumford, 1805-1878.

North Carolina. Treasury Department. 55681 55686, 55699

North Carolina. University. 55701

North Carolina. University. Dialectic Society. 55701

North Carolina. University. Historical Society. see North Carolina Historical Society.

North Carolina. University. Philanthropic Society. 55701

North Carolina. University. Senior Class, 1844. Committee. eds. 55656

North Carolina. University. Trustees. 55700

North Carolina. 78314

North Carolina advocate. 83774

North Carolina Bible Society. 55596

North Carolina Branch of the Southern Historical Society. see Southern Historical Society. North Carolina Branch.

North Carolina business directory, for 1867-8 55599

North Carolina Christian advocate. Editor. 88518

North Carolina Copper Company. 35401

North Carolina gazetteer. 55650

North-Carolina geological . . . survey. Part II., agriculture. 55619

North Carolina Gold-Mine Company. 95644

North Carolina Gold-Mining Company 55651

North Carolina historical review. 97092

North Carolina Historical Society. 55701, 97092

North Carolina Indians. see Cherokee Nation

North-Carolina journal. 91431

North Carolina journal of education. 55652

North Carolina Land Company. (55653)

North Carolina law repository. (55654)

North-Carolina minerva, and Fayetteville advertiser. 101564

North Carolina school. (55655)

North Carolina University magazine. 55655

North Carolinian. pseud. Southern slavery considered on general principles. 88488

North Chelsea, Mass. School Committee. 55703

North Church, Hartford, Conn. see Hartford, Conn. North Church.

North Church, Salem, Mass. see Salem, Mass. North Church.

North Church of Christ, Portsmouth, N. H. see Portsmouth, N. H. First Church of Christ.

North Clear Creek Gold and Silver Mining Company. (55704)

North Congregational Church, New Bedford, Mass. see New Bedford, Mass. North Congregational Church.

North Congregational Church, Springfield, Mass. see Springfield, Mass. North Congregational Church.

North Coventry, Conn. Church. 55705

North Dutch Church, Albany. see Albany. North Dutch Church.

North Dutch Church, New York. see New
York (City) North Dutch Church.
North-Eastern Agricultural Society. 55707
North-eastern boundary of the United States.
18681, 29649, 55713, note after 97923,
note after 100780
North Georgia gazette and winter chronicle.
(55714), 58864
North Granville, N. Y. Female Seminary.
see North Granville Female Seminary,
North Granville, N. Y.
North Granville, N. Y. Ladies' Seminary.
see North Granville Female Seminary,
North Granville, N. Y.
North Granville Female Seminary, North
Granville, N. Y. (55715)
North Granville Ladies' Seminary, North
Granville, N. Y. see North Granville
Female Seminary, North Granville, N. Y.
North Haven, Conn. Baptist Church. 55716
North Haven, Conn. Twentieth Century Com-
mittee. 97180
North Haven in the nineteenth century. 97180
North Hempstead, N. Y. appellants (31300),
55717
North Hudson River Baptist Association. see
Baptists. New York. Hudson River
Baptist Association North.
North Illinois University, Henry, Ill. Academic
Department. 55718
North Illinois University, Henry, Ill. Board
of Trustees. 34246, 55718
North-Martinsburg Lead-Mining Company.
(55719)
North Middlesex Circulating Library, Groton
Centre, Mass. 55720
North-Middlesex Sunday-School Society. 55721

North Missouri and eastern Kansas businss

directory. (55722)
North Missouri Railroad Company. 32739
North Missouri Railroad Company. Directors.
55723
North Missouri Railroad Convention, St.
Charles, Mo., 1852. 49554
North must yield all—the south nothing!
(27453), 68322
North Pacific Exploring Expedition, 1853-
1856. 29914
North Pacific Surveying and Exploring
Expedition. (29466)
North Parish, Wrentham, Mass. see Wrent-
ham, Mass. North Parish.
North Parish Church, Wrentham, Mass. see
Wrentham, Mass. North Parish Church.
North Pennsylvania railroad. 60278
North Pennsylvania Railroad Company. 60278,
62157
North Pennsylvania Railroad Company.
defendants 60278
North Pennsylvania Railroad Company.
petitioners 55724
North Pennsylvania Railroad Company. Charter.
60277
North Pennsylvania Railroad Company. Chief
Engineer. 60278 see also Miller,
Edward.
North Pennsylvania Railroad Company. Com-
mittee Having in Charge the Fund Sub-
scribed for the Relief of the Sufferers
by the Collision . . . at Camp Hill,
1856. 60278
North Pennsylvania Railroad Company.
Directors. 62078

North Pennsylvania Railroad Company.
President. 62078
North Pennsylvania Railroad Company. Road
Committee. 62078
North Pennsylvania Railroad Company. Stock-
holders. 62078
North Pennsylvania railroad. . . . Mass
meeting at . . . [Philadelphia,] January
31, 1854. 60278
North Pennsylvania railroad, to connect
Philadelphia with north Pennsylvania.
62054
North Philadelphia Plank Road Company.
Charter. 61868
North Presbyterian Church, New York. see
New York (City) North Presbyterian
Church.
North Providence centennial. (55727)
North Randolph Church, Lynn, Mass. see
Lynn, Mass. North Randolph Church.
North Reading, Mass. 55729
North Reading, Mass. School Committee.
55729
North Reformed Dutch Church, Newark, N. J.
see Newark, N. J. North Reformed
Dutch Church.
North Scituate, R. I. Lapham Institute. see
Lapham Institute, North Scituate, R. I.
North Scituate, R. I. Smithville Seminary.
see Lapham Institute, North Scituate,
R. I.
North-side view of slavery. A sermon on the
crime against freedom. 25212
North side view of slavery.—The refugee.
(20931)
North star: the poetry of freedom. 55730,
note after 103813
North Street Union Mission, Boston. see
Boston. North Street Union Mission.
North Sutton Mining & Smelting Company.
(55732)
North—the south—and slavery. 91896
North west . . . see also Northwest . . .
North-west coast: a lecture . . . in Washington.
26665
North west coast of America. 4067
North-West Company (Canada) defendants
(20701), 79016, note after 96860, 2d
note after 106023
North-vvest Fox. 25410
North-West Mining Company. 55733
North-West Mining Company. Agent. 55733
North-West Mining Company. Directors.
55733
North-West Mining Company. Stockholders.
55733
North-West Mining Company of Michigan.
55733
North-West Mining Company. Report . . . of
a visit to the locations. 55733
North-west passage. 43074
North-west passage and the plans for the
search. 8517
North-West Territory, Canada. Citizens.
petitioners see People of Rupert's
Land and North-West Territory, British
America. petitioners
North West Territory. Reports of progress.
(31937)
North-West Transportation and Land Company.
(55735)
North-western . . . see also Northwestern
. . .
North-western American boundary. (55736),
55982

North-Western Branch of the American Society
for Educating Pious Youth for the Gospel
Ministry. see American Society for
Educating Pious Youth for the Gospel
Ministry. North-Western Branch.
North-Western Christian magazine. (55738)
North-Western Christian University, Indian-
apolis. (55739)
North Western Consociation of Vermont. see
Congregational Churches in Vermont.
North Western Consociation.
North Western Dispensary, New York. see
New York (City) North Western Dis-
pensary.
North western farmer. 55741
North Western Female College, Evanston,
Ill. (55742)
North-Western Fruit Growers Association.
Annual Meeting, 2d, Dixon, Ill., 1852.
55744
North-western journal of education, science,
and . . . literature. 55745
North-Western journal of homoeopathia.
55746
North-Western Medical Society. 55747
North-western medical and surgical journal.
55748
North Western Mining Company. 55749
North-Western Pennsylvania Oil and Coal
Company. (55750), 80027
North Western Railroad Company. (62079)
North Western Railroad Company. Charter.
(62079)
North Western Railroad Company. Chief
Engineer. 55751, (62079)
North Western Railroad Company. President
and Directors. 55751
North-Western Theological Seminary, 1857.
70857
North-Western Union Missionary Society.
55752
North Wood's Walton Club. (55755)
North Wrentham, Mass. Church. (68256),
105524
North Wrentham, Mass. Church. petitioners
(68256), 105524 see also Thacher,
Moses, 1795-1878. petitioner
North Wrentham, Mass. Church. Pastor.
petitioner (68256), 105524 see also
Thacher, Moses, 1795-1878. petitioner
North Wrentham, Mass. Ecclesiastical
Council, 1830. see Congregational
Churches in Massachusetts. Ecclesiasti-
cal Council, North Wrentham, 1830.
North Yarmouth, Me. Academy. see North
Yarmouth Academy, North Yarmouth,
Me.
North Yarmouth, Me. Cumberland Conference
of Churches. see Congregational
Churches in Maine. Cumberland As-
sociation.
North Yarmouth, Me. Ecclesiastical Council,
1822. see Congregational Churches in
Maine. Ecclesiastical Council, North
Yarmouth, 1822.
North Yarmouth, Me. First Church. (55757)
North Yarmouth Academy, North Yarmouth,
Me. 55756
Northall, William Knight. 55758-(55759)
Northamericanische Indianer. (49485)
Northampton. pseud. To George Bancroft.
55760
Northampton, Henry Howard, Earl of, 1540-
1614. 67545
Northampton, Mass. (55768)

Northampton, Mass. Agricultural Library.
55763
Northampton, Mass. American Institute of
Instruction. see American Institute of
Instruction.
Northampton, Mass. Book Club. see North-
ampton Book Club, Northampton, Mass.
Northampton, Mass. Citizens. petitioners
55767
Northampton, Mass. Clarke Institution for
Deaf Mutes. see Clarke Institution for
Deaf Mutes, Northampton, Mass.
Northampton, Mass. Congregational Church.
Committee. 90685
Northampton, Mass. Convention of Delegates
from the Counties of Hampshire, Frankl
and Hampden, 1812. see Convention of
Delegates from the counties of Hampshir
Franklin, and Hampden, Northampton,
Mass., 1812.
Northampton, Mass. Convention of Medical
Delegates, 1827. see Convention of
Medical Delegates, Northampton, Mass.,
1827.
Northampton, Mass. Council of Nine Churche
1750. see Congregational Churches in
Massachusetts. Ecclesiastical Council,
Northampton, 1750.
Northampton, Mass. Court of Common Pleas.
Grand Jury. 104287
Northampton, Mass. Ecclesiastical Council,
1750. see Congregational Churches in
Massachusetts. Ecclesiastical Council,
Northampton, 1750.
Northampton, Mass. Ecclesiastical Council,
1751. see Congregational Churches in
Massachusetts. Ecclesiastical Council,
Northampton, 1751.
Northampton, Mass. First Church. 55764,
55766
Northampton, Mass. First Congregational
Church. 89744
Northampton, Mass. Inhabitants. petitioners
see Northampton, Mass. Citizens.
petitioners
Northampton, Mass. Lunatic Hospital. see
Massachusetts. Lunatic Hospital,
Northampton.
Northampton, Mass. Public Library. 55763
Northampton, Mass. Round Hill School. 5577
Northampton, Mass. School Committee.
55770
Northampton, Mass. Selectmen. (55761)
Northampton, Mass. Smith College. see
Smith College, Northampton, Mass.
Northampton, Mass. Young Men's Institute.
see Young Men's Institute, Northampton
Mass.
Northampton, N. Y. Church. 90685, 97370
Northampton, N. Y. Church. Committee.
90685, 97370
Northampton, N. Y. Society. see North-
ampton, N. Y. Church.
Northampton County, Pa. Citizens. petitione
55773
Northampton County, Pa. Collector of Excise
55774 see also Graff, George. Jones,
Jesse.
Northampton County, Pa. Court of Oyer and
Terminer, and General Gaol Delivery.
96870
Northampton County, Pa. Inhabitants. see
Northampton County, Pa. Citizens.
Northampton County, Pa. Lieutenant. 55774
Northampton County, Pa. Sub-Lieutenant.
55774

Northampton Book Club, Northampton, Mass.
  Library. 55762
Northampton business directory and general
  advertiser. 55768
Northampton gazette. 12702, note after
  94937, note just before 95113
Northampton mercury. 19234, 19580, note
  after 92624
Northampton Slate Quarry Company. petitioners
  55775
Northborough, Mass. 55779
Northborough, Mass. Centennial Celebration,
  1866. (55778)
Northborough, Mass. Free Schools. 55777
Northborough, Mass. School Committee.
  55777
Northborough, Mass. Selectmen. 55776
Northbridge, Mass. Congregational Church.
  see Northbridge Centre, Mass. Con-
  gregational Church.
Northbridge, Mass. School Committee.
  55781
Northbridge Centre, Mass. Congregational
  Church. (55780)
Northcote, Sir Stafford. 86685
Northcote, William. 94063
Northend, Charles. 55782-55783
Northend, William D. 55784
Northern Academy of Arts and Sciences.
  55785
Northern almanac. 23848
Northern and eastern states and Canada.
  1094, 31113
Northern and southern friends. (18392)
Northern and western traveler. (55786)
Northern archives for history, statistics, etc.
  55787
Northern Association in the County of
  Hampshire. see Congregational Churches
  in Massachusetts. Hampshire County
  Northern Association.
Northern Association in the County of Hart-
  ford. see Congregational Churches in
  Connecticut. Hartford County North
  Association.
Northern Baptist Education Society. 55788
Northern Baptist Education Society. Vermont
  Branch. 99151
Northern Baptist Society. 3236 see also
  Baptists. U. S.
Northern boundary between New Brunswick
  and Canada. 55789
Northern boundary of Ohio. (55790)
Northern California. (48209)
Northern Central Railway Company. (62080)
Northern Central Railway Company. Charter.
  (62080)
Northern Central Railway Company. President.
  (62080)
Northern Central Railway Company. President
  and Directors. 55791
Northern coasts of America. 97657
Northern coasts of America, and the Hudson's
  Bay Territory. 55792
Northern counties gazetteer and directory.
  29760
Northern Democrats. What traitors say.
  (55793)
Northern Dispensary, New York. see New
  York (City) Northern Dispensary.
Northern Dispensary for the . . . Poor,
  Philadelphia. 61869
Northern Dispensary for the . . . Poor,
  Philadelphia. Charter. 61869
Northern Educational Union. 23874

Northern farmer and practical horticulturist.
  55795
Northern farmers' almanac for 1851. 55796
Northern friend. pseud. New phase of the
  subject of slavery and free labor. see
  Gifford, A. supposed author
Northern fruit culture. 27878
Northern grievances, set forth in a letter to
  James Madison. 55797
Northern guide. 95555
Northern hearts embrace southern homes.
  18300
Northern Home for Friendless Children,
  Philadelphia. 55798, (61870)
Northern Illinois Horticultural Society. (55799)
Northern Indiana Railroad Company. 34571,
  (55801)
Northern indicator. (55802)
Northern Inland Lock Navigation Company.
  Committee to Examine Hudson's River.
  33523
Northern Inland Lock Navigation Company.
  Directors. 69857, 102964
Northern invasion of October 1780. 33144
Northern Iowa. 35029
Northern Iowa Sanitary Fair, Dubuque, 1864.
  see Dubuque, Iowa. Northern Iowa
  Sanitary Fair, 1864.
Northern Iowa Sanitary Fair, held in Dubuque,
  June, 1864. 55803
Northern islander. 48805, 92674, 92677,
  92687
Northern lakes a summer residence for the
  invalids of the south. 20823
Northern lancet, and American journal of
  medical jurisprudence. 52311
Northern lancet and gazette of legal medicine.
  55804
Northern Lead Company of New-York. 55805,
  (69558)
Northern Liberties (District), Philadelphia.
  61852, 62060
Northern Liberties (District), Philadelphia.
  Charter. (59791)
Northern Liberties (District), Philadelphia.
  Citizens' Committee to Attend to and
  Alleviate the Sufferings of the Afflicted
  With the Malignant Fever, 1793. see
  Committee, Appointed on the 14th
  September, 1793, by the Citizens of
  Philadelphia, the Northern Liberties and
  the District of Southwark, to Attend to
  and Alleviate the Sufferings of the Afflicted
  With the Malignant Fever, Prevalent
  in the City and Its Vicinity.
Northern Liberties (District), Philadelphia.
  Infant School Society. see Infant School
  Society of the Northern Liberties and
  Kensington, Pa.
Northern Liberties (District), Philadelphia.
  Ordinances, etc. 61587, 61907
Northern Liberties (District), Philadelphia.
  Society for the Institution and Support
  of First-Day or Sunday Schools. see
  Society for the Institution and Support
  of First-Day or Sunday Schools in . . .
  Philadelphia, and the Districts of South-
  wark and the Northern Liberties.
Northern Liberties (District), Philadelphia.
  Watering Committee. 62371 see also
  Joint Watering Committee of Northern
  Liberties & Spring Garden Water Works.
Northern Liberties Gas Works, Philadelphia.
  61907
Northern Liberties Gas Works, Philadelphia.
  Charter. 59793

Northern light, devoted to free discussion.
55806
Northern lights. (55807)
Northern man. pseud. Abolition and sedition.
55809, 81713
Northern man. pseud. Curiosity visits to
southern plantations. 81945
Northern man, pseud. Diplomatic year. see
Ingersoll, Charles. incorrectly supposed
author and Reed, William B.
Northern man. pseud. Letters from the
south. see Paulding, James K.
Northern man. pseud. Planter. (63321)
Northern man. pseud. Review of Mr.
Seward's diplomacy. see Reed,
William B.
Northern man with southern principles.
55810
Northern Medical Association of Philadelphia.
61871
Northern Missionary Society in the State of
New York. 55812
Northern Missionary Society in the State of
New York. Directors. 55812
Northern Missionary Society in the State of
New York. Treasurer. 55812
Northern Missouri. 55723
Northern monthly. A magazine of general
literature. (53180), 55814, 85466
Northern monthly: a magazine of literature,
civil and military affairs. 55813
Northern monthly advertiser for January,
1865. 55815
Northern New York Railroad. see Northern
Rail Road of New York.
Northern no! 55816
Northern (Ogdensburgh) Railroad. Mr.
Chandler's statement. 55827
Northern Ohio Lunatic Asylum, Cleveland.
see Ohio. State Hospital, Cleveland.
Northern Pacific Railroad Company. 55818,
55821-55822
Northern Pacific Railroad Company. peti-
tioners 55820
Northern Pacific Railroad Company. Board
of Direction. petitioners 55819
Northern Pacific Railroad Company. Charter.
55821
Northern Pacific Railroad Company. Presi-
dent. 82957 see also Smith, John
Gregory, 1818-1891.
Northern Pacific Railroad Company, charter,
organization, and proceedings. 55821
Northern Pacific Railroad. Explanation of
the bill now before Congress. 55818
Northern Pacific Railroad. Memorial of the
Board of Direction. 55819
Northern Pennsylvania Railroad Corporation.
55824
Northern plea for peace. 68614
Northern plea for the right of secession.
3893A
Northern Presbyter. pseud. Letter of
inquiry to ministers of the Gospel. see
Lord, Nathan.
Northern Presbyter. pseud. Second letter to
ministers of the Gospel. see Lord,
Nathan.
Northern Presbyter's second letter to minis-
ters of the Gospel. (42044)
Northern priest. pseud. A——a to the
A——ts. 66232
Northern Rail Road Company. (55825)-55826
Northern Rail Road Company. Directors.
55826

Northern Rail Road Company. Engineer.
55826
Northern Rail Road Company. Stockholders.
Committee of Investigation. 55826
Northern Railroad in New York. With remarks
on the western trade. 55828
Northern Rail Road of New York. Directors.
55828
Northern Rail Road of New York. Examining
Committee. 55828
Northern Rail Road of New York. Sub-com-
mittee on Consolidation of Bonds and
Stocks. 55828
Northern Rail Road of New York. Trustees
of the Second Mortgage Bond Holders.
55828
Northern Rail Road of New York, Ogdenburg
to Rouse's Point. 55828
Northern regions. 55829, 3d note after 97726
Northern robbery. 87901
Northern spectator. 83541
Northern star and freemen's advocate. (55830)
Northern sugar plant. (31222)
Northern sympathiser. pseud. Letter on the
American war. 40363
Northern tour: being a guide to Saratoga.
27457, 55831
Northern traveller, and northern tour. (55833)
Northern traveller; containing the Hudson River
guide. 20325, note after 55831
Northern traveller; containing the routes to
Niagara. 55832
Northern traveller; containing the routes to
the springs. 21538, 21540
Northern tour. Northern states, and British
provinces. 29755
Northern true men and southern traitors.
55834
Northern University of Pennsylvania. see
University of Northern Pennsylvania.
Northern voice for the dissolution of the union.
55835
Northern whale fishery. 78180
Northerner. pseud. Thoughts on American
slavery. 95671
Northfield, N. H. New Hampshire Conference
Seminary. see Tilton Seminary, Tilton,
N. H.
Northfield Institute, Fitchburg, Mass. 55836
Northfield Slate-Quarry Company. 55837
Northmen in Iceland. 85824
Northmen in Maine. 19195
Northmen in New England. 83424
Northmore, Thomas. 55838
Northport Observer. see Observer, Northport
Ala.
Northrop, Birdsey Grant. 55839
Northrop, Claudian Bird, 1812-1865. 55842-
55843, note after 88421
Northrop, George. 37271, 55840
Northrop, Nira B., 1791-1878. 55841
Northrup, C. B. see Northrop, Claudian Bird,
1812-1865.
Northrup, G. W. 55844
Northup, George Tyler. tr. 99379
Northup, Solomon. 55847
Northup, William. ed. 83405-83406, 83416,
83419
North's guide for invalids. 55522
Northumberland, Hugh Percy, 2d Duke of,
1742-1817. 93710, 101687
Northumberland, Robert Dudley, Duke of.
see Dudley, Sir Robert, styled Duke
of Northumberland and Earl of Warwick,
1574-1649.

Northumberland County, Pa. Citizens.
petitioners (55845)
Northumberland County, Pa. Collector of
Excise. 55846 see also Wilson,
William.
Northumberland County, Pa. Lieutenant.
55846 see also Hunter, Samuel.
Northumberland County, Pa. Sub-Lieutenant.
55846 see also Clarke, Walter.
Murray, William.
Northumberland gazette. (16614)
Northwest . . . see also North west . . .
Northwest America. 91521
Northwest boundary. 76131
Northwest Company, carrying on trade from
Montreal. 43666
Northwest fur trade. 93270
Northwest ordinance. 28421
Northwest passage. A history of the most
remarkable voyages. 33628
Northwest passage by land. 24631
Northwest Territories, Canada. Citizens.
petitioners see People of Rupert's
Land and North-West Territory, British
America. petitioners
Northwest Territory, U. S. 58149
Northwest Territory, U. S. Charter. note
after 94720
Northwest Territory, U. S. Convention,
Chillicothe, Ohio, 1802. 94880
Northwest Territory, U. S. General Assembly.
House of Representatives. (56940),
94881
Northwest Territory, U. S. Governor, 1787-
1802 (St. Clair) 56953, 75019, 84791,
98639 see also St. Clair, Arthur,
1736-1818.
Northwest Territory, U. S. Laws, statutes,
etc. 12199, 16101, 39418-39420,
56949-56953, 57583, 94882-94883
Northwest Territory, U. S. Secretary's
Office. 94883
Northwestern . . . see also North western
. . .
Northwestern Branch of the American Edu-
cation Society. see American Education
Society. Northwestern Branch.
Northwestern centennial celebration, in La
Crosse, Wisconsin. 79639
Northwestern Dairymen's Association. Anni-
versary Meeting, 5th, 1871. 55849
Northwestern educator and magazine of
literature and science. 55850
Northwestern Freedmen's Aid Commission.
55743
Northwestern Freedmen's Aid Commission.
Annual Meeting, 1st, Chicago, 1864.
55743
Northwestern manual and traveler's directory.
(22252)
Northwestern medical and surgical journal.
55851
Northwestern miller. 83900
Northwestern quarterly magazine. 55852
Northwestern review, and commercial and
real estate reporter. 4418, 55853
Northwestern Sanitary Commission. 55854
see also United States Sanitary Com-
mission.
Northwestern Sanitary Commission. Treasurer.
(31431)
Northwestern Sanitary Fair, Chicago, 1865.
see Chicago. Northwestern Sanitary
Fair, 1865.

Northwestern Sanitary Fair. 1865. Catalogue
of the Department of Arms and Trophies.
55854
Northwestern Ship Canal Convention, Dubuque,
Iowa, 1864. petitioners 55855
Northwestern Ship Canal Convention. Memorial
to Congress. 55855
Northwestern University, Evanston, Ill. 55753
Northwestern University, Evanston, Ill. Medical
School, Chicago. (41287)
Northwestern University, Watertown, Wisc. see
Watertown, Wisc. Northwestern Uni-
versity.
Northwestern Virginia Railroad Company.
Directors. 55856
Northwestern Virginia Railroad Company.
President. 55856
Northwood Cemetery Company, Philadelphia.
61872
Northwood Cemetery Company, Philadelphia.
Charter. 61872
Northwood; or, life north and south. 29667
Nortmann, Robert Comtaeus. see Comtaeus,
Robert.
Norton, Mrs. ---------. 6667
Norton, A. 30757, 2d note after 69405
Norton, A. S. 55859
Norton, Albert B., 1823- 55857
Norton, Alfred. 55860
Norton, Andrews, 1786-1853. (25978), (55861)-
55865, 71518-71519, 71521, 88964,
90713
Norton, Andrews, 1786-1853. supposed author
93205
Norton, Anthony Banning. 55858
Norton, Bonham. tr. (67592)
Norton, Charles Benjamin, 1825-1891. 21687,
29736, (55866)-55872, 82823 see also
U. S. Commission to the Paris Exposition,
1867.
Norton, Charles Bowyer Adderley, 1st Baron,
1814-1905. 373
Norton, Charles Davis, 1820-1887. 9056,
(55873), note after 95451
Norton, Charles Eliot, 1827-1908. 55562,
55874-55875, 97289
Norton, E. tr. (77216)
Norton, E. H. 55876
Norton, Eugene L. 55877, 84955 see also
U. S. Navy Department. Agent.
Norton, Frank Henry, 1836-1921. ed. 24375,
54763
Norton, Herman. 55878
Norton, Humphry. supposed author 52756
Norton, Jacob, 1764-1858. 17681, 55879,
(78666), 78669, 95378
Norton, Jacob, 1764-1858. supposed author
(80597)
Norton, Jesse O. 55880
Norton, John, fl. 1606. tr. 57708
Norton, John, 1606-1663. 4013, 22359,
24037, 33360, (33362), 41005, 55881-
55889, 59659, (66867), (66870)-66871,
78431-78434
Norton, John, 1651-1716. 55890
Norton, John, 1716-1778. 55891-55892
Norton, John, fl. 1805. tr. 49846, 49849,
95145
Norton, John F. 55893
Norton, John L. defendant 96865
Norton, John N. 55894-55904
Norton, John Pitkin. (55905)-55906
Norton, Joseph. 55907
Norton, Lemuel. 55908
Norton, Robert. (44452), 55909
Norton, S. H. 55910

Norton, S. Sheldon. (55911)
Norton, Samuel. 37207
Norton, Thomas. defendant 95557
Norton, Thomas, Jr. (55655)
Norton, William. 55912
Norton (Charles B.) firm publishers 55867, 66532
Norton, Mass. School Committee. (55913)
Norton, Mass. Selectmen. (55913)
Norton, Mass. Treasurer. (55913)
Norton, Mass. Wheaton College. see Wheaton College, Norton, Mass.
Norton, Mass. Wheaton Female Seminary. see Wheaton College, Norton, Mass.
Norton: or, the lights and shades of a factory village. 1971
Norton's improved calendar. 55907
Norton's literary advertiser. 55867
Norton's literary almanac for 1852. 55868
Norton's literary and educational register for 1854. 55869
Norton's literary gazette and publisher's circular. 55867, 82823
Norton's literary letter. 21687, 29736, 55870
Norton's literary register. 55871
Norton's literary register and bookbuyer's alamac. see Norton's literary register.
Norval, James. 55914
Norvel, John. 23759
Norvell, John, 1789-1850. 55915
Norvell, Joseph. 94760
Norvell, L. C. (55916)
Norvell, Moses. 94760
Norwegian American Historical Association. 94934
Norwich, Abraham. 148, (55932)
Norwich, Bishop of. see Bagot, Lewis, successively Bishop of Bristol, Norwich, and St. Asaph, 1740-1802. Bathurst, Henry, Bishop of Norwich, 1744-1837. Gooch, Sir Thomas, Bart., successively Bishop of Bristol, Norwich, and Ely, d. 1754. Green, Thomas, successively Bishop of Norwich, and Ely, 1658-1738. Harsnet, Samuel, Abp. of York, 1561-1631. Hayter, Thomas, successively Bishop of Norwich, and London, 1702-1762. Leng, John, Bishop of Norwich, 1665-1727. Lisle, Samuel, successively Bishop of Norwich, and St. Asaph, 1683-1749. Manners-Sutton, Charles, Abp. of Canterbury, 1755-1828. Moore, John, successively Bishop of Norwich, and Ely, 1646-1714. Stanley, Edward, Bishop of Norwich, 1779-1849. Trumnell, Charles, successively Bishop of Norwich, and Winchester, 1663-1723. Yonge, Philip, successively Bishop of Bristol and Norwich, d. 1783.
Norwich, Conn. Celebration of the Two Hundredth Anniversary of the Settlement of the Town, 1859. 55926, note after 91084
Norwich, Conn. Charter. 55920
Norwich, Conn. Court of Common Council. 55921
Norwich, Conn. First Congregational Church. 55922
Norwich, Conn. Justice's Court. 2635
Norwich, Conn. Library Company. see Norwich Library Company.
Norwich, Conn. Ordinances, etc. 55918
Norwich, Conn. Otis Library. (55919)
Norwich, Conn. University. see Norwich University, Norwich, Conn.

Norwich, N. Y. New York State Sunday School Teachers' Association Annual Convention, 17th, 1872. see New York State Sunday School Teachers' Association. Annual Convention, 17th, Norwich, 1872.
Norwich, Vt. American Literary, Scientific, and Military Academy. see American Literary, Scientific, and Military Academy, Norwich, Vt.
Norwich, Vt. Charter. 55930
Norwich almanac, directory, and business advertiser. (55923)
Norwich and Boston Rail Road. 105447
Norwich and Worcester rail road. 105449
Norwich and Worcester Rail Road Company. 55924, 105449, 105452 see also Worcester and Norwich Rail Road Company.
Norwich and Worcester Rail Road Company. Directors. 105450-105451
Norwich and Worcester Rail Road Company. Stockholders. Committee. 55924
Norwich and Worcester Rail-Road. General statements by the directors. 105451
Norwich, August 26. 88944
Norwich city directory. 55925
Norwich jubilee. 55926, note after 91084
Norwich Library Company. (55919)
Norwich mine. (55929)
Norwich Mining Company. (55929)
Norwich Mining Company. Treasurer. (55929)
Norwich packet. 88944
Norwich University, Norwich, Conn. 55927
Norwich Water Power Company. 55928
Norwood, ---------, fl. 1646. 103441
Norwood, Abraham. supposed author. 148, (55932)
Norwood, E. defendant at court martial (65814)
Norwood, Henry, fl. 1649. 13015, 55933, 82823
Norwood, J. G. 34252
Norwood, Richard. 66686
Norwood: or, village life in New England. 4317, 12432
Nos, Sophie des. tr. 92431
Nos D. Francisco Antonio Lorenzana. 55934
Nos el Dr. D. Alonso Nunez de Haro, y Peralta. 56323
Nos los inquisidores contra la heretica pravedad. 34817, note after 55934
Nos va dando cierto olor a segundo emperador 99709
Nosegay, for the young men from 16 to 24 years of age. 64163
Nostak-Kobuk Region, Alaska. 83723
Nostradamus, Michel. 55935-(55937)
Nosum mosorum. 61873
Not 'a fool's errand.' 34776, 93773
Not careful but prayerful. 55938
Not impossible. 55939
Not "this or that" but "this and that." 6076
Nota ad inveniendum igitur regiones. (66472)
Nota analitica de los datos necesarios y convenientes. 95876
Nota, que puso el Maestro de Ceremonias de esta santa iglesia cathedral. 98786
Notable and memorable story of the cruel war 67599
Notable historie containing foure voyages made by certayne French captaynes. 29236
Notable men; a series of comprehensive biographies. (50361)
Notable men in "the House." 68485

Notable men of Pittsburgh and vicinity.
83703
Notable men of the time. (50358)
Notable women of olden time. (55940)
Notae ad dissertationem Hvgonis Grotii.
38561
Notario de la familia. pseud. Testamento
del ano de 1839. see Pacheco, Jose
Ramon.
Notaris, J. de. 55941
Notas a las tres partes de la mystica ciudad
de Dios. 105733
Notas, adiciones y correcciones al tesoro de
medicina. 75605
Notas al manifesto publicado en Nueva
Orleans. 59514
Notas conjeadas entre el gobierno de la
Confederacion Argentina. 9009
Notas criticas e historicas. 10299
Notas del enviado de la Republica Mexicana
en Washington. 17840, 57104, 1st note
after 94592
Notas diplomaticas, ultimas cambiadas entre
Ministerio de Relaciones Esteriores.
55942
Notas estadisticas del Departamento de
Queretaro. (55943)
Notas estadisticas sobre a produccao
agricola. 85629
Notas historicas de plan del Excmo. Sr. D.
Nicolas Mahy. (43879)
Notas historicas del plan del Excmo. Sr. D.
Luis Lacy. 38516
Notas historicas y criticas . . . por J. Sabau
y Blanco. (44550)
Notas historicas y una introduccion de D.
Manuel de Cuendias. 93348
Notas insertas en el redactor, no. 2. 68685
Notas muy circunstanciadas sobre el origin.
10655
Notas puestas. 51224
Notas se que citan en el cuaderno que dio a
luz el General Vic. Filisola. 24325
Notas sobre el Chaco. (77074)
Notas sobre la conquista de Mexico. 9567
Notas y esclarecimientos . . . por Jose F.
Ramirez. 65267
Notations sur la culture des Terres Basses.
(40165)
No-Taw-Kah. Potawatomi Indian chief
96705
Note a MM. les Membres du Conseil d'Etat.
(19762)
Note and argument of John Howard for
appellants. 33256-33257
Note-book of Morleigh in search of an estate.
41020
Note collective. (57944)
Note de M. V. Schoelcher. 5652
Note d'un viaggio nella America Meridionale.
(57768)
Note explicative sur l'emprunt de trente sept
millions de francs. (38590)
Note for the second Baltimore edition. 11919
Note from Anthony Benezet's account of the
people called Quakers. 93601
Note from Rev. R. Sherwood. (80452)
Note from the secret history of the
emancipation. 4862
Note, in addition to that of 1845, on the
Jesuits' estates. 55944
Note-maker noted, and the observer observed
upon. 55945, 55952
Note of authorities quoted on the part of
Joseph Knight. 102436
Note of the Pequod Indians. (1733)

Note of the shipping, men, and prouisions sent
and prouided for Virginia, by the Right
Honorable Henry Earle of Southampton.
99888
Note of the shipping, men, and provisions, sent
and prouided for Virginia, by the Right
Honorable, the Earle of Sovthampton,
55947, 2d note after 99883
Note of the shipping, men, and provisions, sent
to Virginia, by the Treasurer and Com-
pany, in the yeere 1619. 55946, 99877,
99879, 99882
Note officielle du Consul charge par interim
du Consulat General de France a Buenos-
Aires. 9027
Note on Negro slavery. 51417
Note on the winds. (69094)
Note pour servir a la canalization du Lac
Nicaragua. 2769
Note remis au Comite Colonial. 95731
Note storische ed una dissertazione intorno la
vera patria di lui. 14667
Note sur la Compagnie Belge de Colonisation.
55948
Note sur la condition des esclaves au Mexique.
5521
Note sur la fabrication du fer. 84411
Note sur la fondation d'une nouvelle colonie.
29191, 39637
Note sur la marine des Etats-Unis. 21261
Note sur la publication de l'atlas compose de
mappe-mondes. 76844
Note sur la systeme penitentiaire et sur la
mission confiee. 96069
Note sur l'argent jode du Chili. 18371
Note sur la wapite. 9127
Note sur les biens que les Jesuites possedaient.
55949
Note sur les Botecudos. 36433
Note sur un ancien manuscript Americain.
60907
Note sur une nouvelle espece d'ors de
l'Amerique du Nord. 9127
Note, this almanack us'd to contain but 24
pages. 25567
Note to the people called Quakers. 86739
Note to the reader. [By Frederick Starr, Jr.]
40581, note after 90548
Note to the reader. [By George Keith.]
79256
Note touching the Dutch. 66683
Notecia verdadeira da guerra de America.
38660
Notelijke consideratien die alle goede
liefhebbers. 55950
Notes, Nicholas. (46258)
Notes a M. le Baron de V. P. Malouet.
98571
Notes added by Prof. I. Daniel Rupp. 74200
Notes adressees par le Citoyen Adet. 455
Notes, and a biographical sketch of the author.
67695
Notes and a genealogy by D. Williams
Patterson. 32608
Notes and a memoir, by Epes Sargent.
25587, 76966
Notes and a preliminary essay. 33721
Notes & additions by Benjamin Gerhard.
18313
Notes and additions by H. Lee. (39742)
Notes and additions by Lewis F. Allen.
(82391)
Notes and additions, by R. G. Pardee. 52291
Notes & additions by Thomas I. Wharton.
18313

Notes explicatives, par Gragnon-Lacoste. 75127

Notes for a history of the Library Company of Philadelphia. 61788, 82983

Notes for American farmers. (55905)

Notes for an address to the farmers of Ontario County. 19334

Notes for an essay on some of the effects and abuses of the constitution of Maryland. 45270

Notes for emigrants. 27223, 52548

Notes for morning prayer. 62555

Notes for the history of the war between Mexico and the United States. 57845, (67723)

Notes for the history, on the conspiracy of Paez. 104391

Notes fournies au Comite de Salut Public. 58164

Notes from Citizen Adet. 456

Notes from Plymouth pulpit. 4318, 50328

Notes from the diary of a special agent of the Post Office Department. 32447

Notes from the diary of her [i. e. Rachel Wilson Moore's] husband. 50430

Notes, geographical and historical. 26220

Notes, historical and biographical. 51538

Notes historical and explanatory, by William R. Staples. 65849, 70617, 90478

Notes historiques et un precis de l'insurrection Americain. 5390

Notes historiques sur le colonie Canadienne de Detroit. 67623

Notes historiques, topographiques et critiques. 25823

Notes . . . illustrating the geological structure of the country. (31007)

Notes in defence of the colonies. 102803

Notes made during a journey in 1821. 59447

Notes made during a second visit to Canada. 24102

Notes made during an excursion to the highlands of New Hampshire. 29650, note after 104786

Notes of a five years' journey across the world. 66652

Notes of a journey through Canada. 41798

Notes of a journey to British Guiana. 35990

Notes of a military reconnoissance. 22536, 25837

Notes of a preliminary survey of the forces of the United States. 76647, 76650

Notes of a sermon taken in short hand. 7813

Notes of a short American tour. 84730

Notes of a short northern tour. 30311

Notes of a soujourn on the island of Zanzibar. 8658

Notes of a tour among the Indian tribes of southern Chili. 82443

Notes of a tour in America. 18886

Notes of a tour in the United States and Canada. 9404

Notes of a tour to the White Hills. 88628

Notes of a traveller in the tropics. 2972

Notes of a traveller through some of the middle and northern states. 21541, 95332

Notes of a traveller through the middle and northern states of America. 55955, 95352, 1st note after 96481

Notes of a trip from St. Paul to Pembina and Selkirk Settlement. 6284

Notes of a twenty-five years' service. 43514

Notes of a visit to some part of Haiti. 30232

Notes of American land shells. No. 4. 5504

Notes of an American lyre. 41836

Notes of an Army chaplain during Sherman's famous "march to the sea." (7279)

Notes of an excursion to the isthmus of Tehuantepec. (18301)

Notes of an exile to Van Dieman's Land. 49037

Notes of Canada West. 79678

Notes of conversations with a volunteer officer. 55956

Notes of decisions in the Court of King's Bench. 79623

Notes of . . . decisions in the Superior Courts of . . . North Carolina. 44873

Notes of eight years' travels and residence in Europe. 11533

Notes of eight years' travels and residence in Europe with his North American Indian collection, by Geo. Catlin. 11529

Notes of Florida and the campaigns. (14231)

Notes of hospital life. 55957

Notes of mourning-piety. 46608, note after 105465

Notes of proceedings at the meeting of the De Rochemont family. 19676

Notes of reference to certain Maryland statutes. 45271

Notes of reference to the constitution and laws. (5696)

Notes of testimony taken upon the examination of witnesses. 95471

Notes of the early history of Union Township. 58636

Notes of the flood at the Red River, in 1852. 1393, (74148)

Notes of the true church. (37204)

Notes of the United States of America. (62786)

Notes of the voyage, in '93. 95825

Notes of things seen in Europe and America. 8819

Notes of travel and life. 47798, 55958

Notes of travel in California. 25846

Notes of travel in Cuba and Mexico. 55493

Notes of travel in various parts of the U. S. 3538

Notes of travel through the peninsula. (55494)

Notes on a journey in America. 5569, 23956

Notes on a review of "The pre-Columbian discovery of America by the Northmen." 19197

Notes on a work entitled "A narrative of facts." 51789, 55959

Notes on Abraham Lincoln. 54954

Notes on American gardening and fruit. 25154

Notes on American geology. (15904A)

Notes on artillery. 8582

Notes on Brazilian questions. 12941

Notes on California and the placers. 10036

Notes on Central America. 89981

Notes on Colombia. 2593

Notes on colored troops and military colonies. 14753, 55961

Notes on clairvoyant revealments. (14201)

Notes on Colorado Territory. (55960), 72864

Notes on colored troops and military colonies. 55961

Notes on Columbus. 4565, 4918, 30603

Notes on Cuba. 76993, 105638

Notes on duels and duelling. 74735

Notes on fallacies peculiar to American protectionists. 40982

Notes on farming. 55962, note after 95562

Notes on federal governments. 43264

Notes on Haiti. 43427

Notes on Iowa, with a new map. 76971

Notes on the two reports from the Committee of the Honourable House of Assembly of Jamaica. 35640, 35666-35667, 2d note after 97578
Notes on the United States. (25198)
Notes on the United States of America. 50829
Notes on the United States of America, during a phrenological visit. 14924
Notes on the upper Rio Grande. 95817
Notes on the valleys of Piura and Chira. 89921
Notes on the Vice Royalty of La Plata. 38999, 2d note after 98174
Notes [on the vocabulary of the Cochinchinese language.] 1183
Notes on the West Indies, including observations relative to the Creoles and slaves. (62894)
Notes on the West Indies: written during the expedition. 62983, 102819
Notes on the western states. 29791
Notes on the Wisconsin Territory. 39482
Notes on Uncle Tom's cabin. 90880
Notes on Walt Whitman as poet and person. 9464
Notes on Wisconsin Territory. 39482
Notes original and selected. 4146
Notes philologiques avec un vocabulaire comprenant les sources principales du Quiche. 7427
Notes philologiques et d'un commentaire sur la mythologie. (7436)
Notes pour servir a l'histoire. 30604
Notes pour servir a une description geologique. 44505
Notes puisees dans les ouvrages de mm. de Humboldt. 71995
Notes recueillies en visitant les prisons de la Suisse. (17963)
Notes relating to Rawlins, or Rollins. 72865
Notes, relating to some particulars in the army. 4455
Notes repecting certain Indian mounds and earthworks. 94528
Notes respecting the family of Waldo. 36586
Notes respecting the Indians of Lancaster County, Pennsylvania. 25277
Notes respecting the United States of North America. 55974
Notes, shewing the accomplishment of their prophecies. 5631
Notes statistiques et commerciales. 4514
Notes statistiques, physiques et politiques sur l'Amerique Espagnole. 33732
Notes statistiques sur la Guayne Francaise. 35282
Notes sur John Brown. 12576
Notes sur la coutume de Paris. 67220
Notes sur le Chili. 12790, 55986
Notes sur le fleuve du Darien. 24638
Notes sur le projet de loi. 5652
Notes sur les Archives de Notre Dame de Beauport. 38885
Notes sur les colonies de Surinam et de Demerary. 29181, 86155, 1st note after 93861, 106315
Notes sur les cultures et la production de la Martinique. 39301
Notes sur les etats de Honduras et de San-Salvador. 89982
Notes sur les Guyanes Francaise, Hollandaise, Anglaise, et sur les Antilles Francaises. 86355
Notes sur les Indiens des Etats-Unis. 81310

Notes sur les plantes recueillies en 1858. 24109
Notes sur les produits Espagnols. 74931
Notes sur les registres de Notre Dame de Quebec. 24108
Notes sur les troubles de Saint-Domingue. 39020
Notes sur quelques passages de memoire de Ramel. (67631)
Notes sur quelques plantes caracteristiques. (75231)
Notes taken during the expedition commanded by Capt. R. B. Marcy. 44513, 58775
Notes, tending to show that the yellow fever of the West Indies and of Andalusia of Spain, was a disease well known to the ancients. 19810
Notes to accompany Keeler's map of the U. S. territory. 37150
Notes to illustrate the civil and ecclesiastical concerns. 104845
Notes to the second edition of a sermon. 99589
Notes to the Secretary of State. 13884
Notes to the senators and representatives from the state of Virginia. 3343
Notes upon a collection of orchids. 41293
Notes upon Californian trees. 51487
Notes upon Canada and the United States. From 1832 to 1840. 96086
Notes upon Canada and the United States of America. 96085
Notes upon copper and copper ores. 55975
Notes upon its [i. e. Kennebec County's] history and natural history. 6089
Notes upon Mr. de Liancourt's travels in Upper Canada. 85205
Notes upon the ancestry of William Hutchinson and Anna Marbury. 12540
Notes upon the geology of the western states. 29808
Notes upon the penal law of the Protestant Episcopal Church. 32402
Notes upon the south west boundary line. 55976
Notes upon the south western boundary line. 93127
Notes upon the western country. 33097
Notes upon his [i. e. Samuel Swett's] sketch of Bunker-Hill battle. 94059-94061
Noth- und Hilsruf an die Behorden und Menschenfreunde. 18677
Nothige Beantwortung der sogenannten getreuen Warnung gegan die Lockvogel. (60221)
Nothing but the truth. 14477, 49979
Nothing to do. 55977
Nothing to say. 95595
Nothing to wear. (9663A), 95595
Nothing's been done. 19483
Notice. 84571-84572
Notice au point de vue du droit international. 6904
Notice biographique [de Boyer-Peyreleau.] 7134
Notice biographique de Mgr. Lartique. 39059
Notice biographique & bibliographique par M. Gustave Brunet. 64529
Notice biographique et de considerations sur les ecrits de Raynal. 68082
Notice biographique et historique sur Michel Sarrasin. 77099
Notice biographique par M. Blanqui. (82311)
Notice biographique . . . Paris, 1818. 38568
Notice biographique sur Humboldt. 33730
Notice biographique sur [J. H.] Campe. 10296

Notice of T. S. Gholson's last pamphlet.
14419

Notice of the Academy [of Natural Sciences
of Philadelphia.] 61405

Notice of the Fauquier White Sulphur Springs.
9318

Notice of the important inventions. 5606

Notice of the late John Revere. 70178

Notice of the life and character of Mr.
Andrews Norton. 54967

Notice of the life and professional services
of William R. Grand. 59135

Notice of the life and writings of Boturini.
6834

Notice of the . . . metric system in the
United States. (58595)

Notice of the mineral waters of Saratoga.
22518

Notice of the natural history collections of
McGill University. 43273

Notice of the origin, progress, and present
condition of the Academy of Natural
Sciences of Philadelphia. 74191

Notice of the pamphlet by a citizen of Boston.
(47297)

Notice of the proceedings at the celebration.
11865

Notice of the proceedings of the society.
97644

Notice of the Rev. John B. Adger's article
on the slave trade. 82027

Notice on the sale of New Metz. 2092

Notice of the silver mines of Fresnillo.
(25911), (59980)

Notice of the tertiary fossils. 55981

Notice of the "types of mankind." 2612

Notice of the war cabinets of mineralogy and
geology. 72368

Notice of their habits and ranges. 18649

Notice of . . . three soldiers belonging to
the same company. 37880

Notice of Victor Hugo's views of slavery.
39226

Notice of villages. (7048)

Notice of William Thaddeus Harris, Esq.
12704, 20884

Notice on the life and character of Hon. John
Davis. 37935

Notice par J. A. C. Buchon. 72014

Notice relative to the geology of the coast of
Labrador. 91210

Notice respecting the boundary between His
Majesty's possessions in North America
and the United States. (55736), 55982

Notice sanitaire et geographique sur la ville
et le port de Panama. 56358

Notice scientifique sur l'or et son exploitation.
8805

Notice statistique. 26330

Notice statistique et commerciale sur la
republique orientale de l'Uruguay.
55983

Notice statistique sur la Guyane Francaise.
94850

Notice statistique sur le Chili. (55984)

Notice statistique sur le Chili et catalogue
des mineraux. 12791

Notice statistique sur l'isle Bourbon et
Guyane Francaise. 29182

Notice sur Alpina. 55985

Notice sur Bougainville. 6868

Notice sur Christophe Colomb. 38910

Notice sur Dona Francisca. (21460)

Notice sur F. Gabriel Theodat et son oeuvre.
74886

Notice sur Haiti. 38378

Notice sur la Canada. 98964

Notice sur la carte generale des pachaliks de
Hhaleb, Orfa et Bagdad. 68443

Notice sur la colonie de la Nouvelle Suede.
94851

Notice sur la culture des dunes de Cap-Breton.
6165

Notice sur la geographie du Texas. 82344

Notice sur la Guiane Francaise. 11526

Notice sur la guatt-pecha de Surinam. 5901

Notice sur la mission des Pottowatomies.
3578

Notice sur la position financiere actuelle.
41837

Notice sur la province de Texas. 101361

Notice sur la republique orientale de l'Uruguay.
Documents de statistique. 38719

Notice sur la republique orientale de l'Uruguay
suivie d'un recueil de pieces officielles.
98175

Notice sur la traite des noirs. 16751

Notice sur la transportation a la Guyane
Francaise. 29183

Notice sur la vie de l'auteur, et deux des ses
discours. 63719

Notice sur la vie et la morte de M. Michel
Prevost. (65416)

Notice sur la vie et les ecrits de Joel Barlow.
3423

Notice sur la vie et les ecrits de M. Joel
Barlow. 21390

Notice sur la vie et les travaux de M. da
Cunha Barbosa. 76845

Notice sur la vie et les travaux de M. le
Baron A. de Humboldt. (39062)

Notice sur la ville du Port-au-Prince. 64180

Notice sur le Chevalier Martin Behaim. 62805

Notice sur le Chili. 12790, 55986

Notice sur le golfe dans l'etat de Costa-Rica.
38606

Notice sur le golfe de Honduras. 46978

Notice sur le golfe du Mexique. 27652

Notice sur le gulf-stream. 6028

Notice sur le Lac Superieur Etats-Unis
d'Amerique. (71694)

Notice sur le navigation transatlantique.
37249

Notice sur le Palmier Carnuaba. 43218

Notice sur le port de Cobija ou Lamar.
14042

Notice sur le royaume de Mexico. 39029

Notice sur le territoire et sur la mission de
l'Oregon. 55988

Notice sur l'eglise de Saint Joseph de
Philadelphie. 21039

Notice sur les anciens voyages en Tartarie.
68443

Notice sur les bons effets du solanum. 98353

Notice sur les chemins de fer de l'etat de
New-York. 55989

Notice sur les colonies Francaises en 1858.
73742

Notice sur les etablissemens de charite et de
bienfaisance des les Etats-Unis d'Amerique. 98351

Notice sur les gisements des lentilles
trilobitiferes taconiques. 44505

Notice sur les hospitaux militaires aux Etats-
Unis. 23191

Notice sur les Indiens de l'Amerique du Nord.
98293

Notice sur les Indiens Ioways. 47467

Notice sur les isles Bermudas. 48699

Notice sur les missions du Diocese de Quebec.
67027

Notice sur les moeurs et coutumes des Indiens Esquimaux. (22863)

Notice sur les nouveaux etablissements agricole fondes au Venezuela. (55990)

Notice sur les plantes de familles de vacciniees et d'ericacees. 44850

Notice sur les plantes de Michaux. (8754)

Notice sur les sauvages de l'Amerique Septentrionale. 102093

Notice sur les travaux apostoliques de Mgr. Demers. 36876

Notice sur les travaux de la Societe Smithsonienne de Washington. 85044

Notice sur les troubles survenus dans la Province des Para. 13198

Notice sur l'etat actuel de la mission de la Louisiane. 55987

Notice sur l'etat actuel de la publication de l'atlas. 76846

Notice sur l'etat present des sciences physiques et naturelles. 98350

Notice sur l'expedition des Francais dans le Texas. 95105

Notice sur l'ideographie des Peaux-Rouges. 20550-(20551), 61130

Notice sur l'ile Sainte-Lucie. 2550

Notice sur Madame Elizabeth Galitzin. 26377

Notice sur [Madame George Anne Bellamy.] 4484

Notice sur M. Jean-Baptiste Bruyere. 8780

Notice sur Rene Goupil. (36143)

Notice sur un ancien manuscript Mexicain. 12022

Notice. To be sold, by public venue. 55978

Notice to emigrants. 104284

Notice to mariners. 46974

Notice to the members of the New York State Society of the Cincinnati. 86122

Notices and journals. (45307)

Notices biographiques de Messire C. Guavreau, V. G. 55991

Notices concerning Cincinnati. 20825

Notices et des reflexions historiques. 8407

Notices geographiques, ethnographiques, statistiques, climatologiques et economiques des differentes localities du Mexique. 64854

Notices of Big Bone Lick. 16644

Notices of Brazil in 1828 and 1829. 101153

Notices of Commodore Elliot's conduct in that engagement. 9232

Notices of his [i. e. Fisher Ames'] life and character. 1303

Notices of East Florida. (24889)

Notices of men and events. 96425

Notices of other matters. By Ignatius Loyola Robertson. 38084

Notices of Parkersburg, Virginia. (55992), note after 58777

Notices of Peter Penet and of his operations among the Oneida Indians. 33145

Notices of public libraries in the United States of America. 36107

Notices of St. Mary's Hall. (55993), (75437)

Notices of some antique earthen vessels found in the low tumuli of Florida. 77866

Notices of Sullivan's campaign. (57591), note after 93510

Notices of the celebrated Indian chief Tecumseh. (8152)

Notices of the character of the late Mrs. Adams. 48534

Notices of the early history of South Carolina. 1902, 49010, 87903

Notices of the First Church and its ministers. 50715

Notices of the hail storm which passed over New York City. 41955

Notices of the harbor at the mouth of the Columbia River. 14850

Notices of the histories of Boston. 77019

Notices of the history and institution of Methodism in America. 20370

Notices of the House of Representatives of . . Ohio. 56964

Notices of the internal improvements in each state. 1498

Notices of the late Rev. Peter Whitney. 10743

Notices of the life and character of Roger Girard Van Polanen. 63729

Notices of the life of Major General Benjamin Lincoln. 38004

Notices of the military services rendered by the militia. 33385

Notices of the New York ecclesiologists. 66744

Notices of the original, and successive efforts. 98706

Notices of the press concerning the Kentucky Coal Mining Company. (37518)

Notices of the principal writers . . . referred to. 17922

Notices of the projected inter-oceanic communications. (11775)

Notices of the rasberry, . . . and grape. 58558

Notices of the Rideau Canal. 55994

Notices of the Sears family. 78640

Notices of the silver mines of Fresnillo. (25911)

Notices of the slave trade in reference to the present state of the British isles. 30556

Notices of the triennial and annual catalogues of Harvard University. (80827)

Notices of the war of 1812. 2024, 98548

Notices of tumuli in Florida. 54476

Notices of western botany and conchology. (80563)

Notices on the claims of the Hudson's Bay Company. 33545

Notices respecting Jamaica. 46856

Notices respecting the history, settlement and geography of Rhode Island. 9843

Notices statistiques sur les colonies Francaises. 14720, 94786, 94850

Notices sur la vie et les ouvrages des Negres. 28727

Notices sur le matelot Selkirk et sur Saint-Hyacinth. 19554

Notices sur les colonies Francaises. 14718

Notices sur les progres des sciences physiques et naturelles. 98352

Noticia annalica y estado. 55995

Noticia biografia del Doctor y General Gonzalo Cardenas. 26583

Noticia biografia del Senor D. Manuel Francisco Pavon. 59257

Noticia biografia del Senor General Francisco de Paula Santander. 76808

Noticia biographia del distinguido literarto D. Miguel Larreynaga. 39095

Noticia biographia por Antonio Henriques Leal. (41412)

Noticia breve de la expedicion militar de Sonora y Cinaloa. (55996)

Noticia breve de la solemne, deseada, ultima dedicacion. 48596, 77050

Noticia da sua [i. e. Antonio Goncalves Dias] vida y obras. 19963

Noticia das conversao dos indomitos orizes procazes. 45407

Noticia de la California. 98848
Noticia de la causa seguida al Senador Diego Jose Benevente. 55997
Noticia de la Compania Formado en la Provincia de Guipuzcoa. 55998
Noticia de la lengua Huasteca. 94355
Noticia de la milagrosa imagen de S. Francisco Javier. 76117
Noticia de la victoria de Junin. (49434)
Noticia de la vida religiosa. 10102
Noticia de la vida y preciosa muerte del P. Nicolas de Tamaral. 2983
Noticia de las cosas notables succedidas a los Olandeses. 41121
Notica de las fincas pertenecientes a corporaciones civiles y eclesiasticas. (48597)
Noticia de las leyes y ordenes de policia. 23967
Noticia de los caudales, frutos, y efectos. 55293
Noticia de los descubrimientos hechos en las islas. 40138
Noticia de los premios aplicados a las mejores hilanderas. (29090)
Noticia de los puertos de Espana. 71632
Noticia de su vida y juicio critico de sus escritos por Don Vicente de la Fuente. (70780)
Noticia de un manuscrito muy interesante. 32031
Noticia de un Mejicano al corresponsal Veracruzano. 98887
Noticia de una nueva copia de original manuscrito. 14637
Noticia de varias producciones del Peru. (74002)
Noticia de vientos, mares, corrientes, paxaros, pescados y anfibios. 97684
Noticia del editor sobre el establecimiento del Oficio de Escribano. 55999
Noticia del establecimiento y poblacion de las colonias Inglesas. 975
Noticia del estado de las carceles de Filadelfia. 72329
Noticia del mondo antiguo y nuevo. 19360, 23580, 99343, 99403
Noticia descriptiva da provincia do Rio-Grande de S. Pedro do Sul. 20944, 56000
Noticia do archipelago dos Acores. 67667
Noticia do Brazil. 85635
Noticia do palacio da Academia Imperial das Bellas Artes. 71465
Noticia dos projectos apresentados para a junccao. 50485
Noticia, e justificacam do titulo. 56001 ,
Noticia en verso Castellano. 72252
Noticia estadisticas de Sonora y Sinaloa. 22844
Noticia explicativa por J. Lucio de Azevedo. 99524
Noticia funesta, "Temblores en San Salvador." 76205
Noticia historica de la conjuracion del Marques de Valle. 57645
Noticia historica de los Cuerpos de Infanteria Permanente y Actica. 56002
Noticia historica de Soconusco. (39079)
Noticia historico-biografica de su vida y escritos por Ramon Francisco Valdes. 73012
Noticia individual, de las poblaciones nuevamente fundadas. 96229
Noticia individual de los derechos. 56003
Noticia que se da ao publico. 56004
Noticia sobre el pejuco del Guaco. 74932

Noticia sobre el terreno carbonifero de Coronel i Lota. 3635
Noticia sobre la geografia politica de Colombia. 14614
Noticia sobre la persona y escritos del Sr. D. Avelino Diaz. 29344
Noticia sobre os selvagens do Mucury. (57900)
Noticia sobre su hacienda publica bajo el gobierno Espanol. 48598
Noticia sobre su vida y escritos. 106281
Noticia sobre suas principaes e mais esmeradas colleccoes. 88784
Noticia verdaderia da guerra da America. 38660
Noticia verdadera de los tres dias de ministerio. 56005
Noticia y juicio de los mas principales historiadores de Espana. (34148)
Noticia y justificacion del titulo y buena fe conque se fundo la nueva colonia. 38998
Noticia, y razon de los litigios que se han motiuado por la dignidad episcopal. 73849
Noticias Americanas. (36806), 97687
Noticias antecedentes, curiosas, e necessarias, das covsas do Brasil. 98651
Noticias biograficas del Exmo. Senor Don Lucas Alaman. 56006
Noticias biograficas y juicio critico de sus obras. 9583
Noticias biograficas de Francisco Homen de Magalhaes Pizarro. 11178
Noticias cvriosas, e necessarias das covsas do Brasil. 98653
Noticias curiosas e necessarias sobre o Brasil. 98654
Noticias curiosas sobre o Bresil. (7609)
Noticias de D. Bartholome Colon. (52094)
Noticias de la ciudad de Mexico. 48599
Noticias de la Nueva California. (34155)
Noticias de la provincia de Californias. 38381, 56007, (75765)
Noticias de la vida y escritos de Fray Toribio de Benavente. (34156), 56008
Noticias de los poblados de que se componen el Nuevo Reyno de Leon. (29144)
Noticias de los ramos que le estan consignados. 44827
Noticias del sur. 66149, note after 97695
Noticias del sur continuadas desde 6. de Nouiembre de 1685. 61149, note after 97695
Noticias del sur. Despacho y felices succesos de la armada en los reynos del Peru, Tierra Firme y Chile. (12792)
Noticias estadisticas de la Huasteca. 56009
Noticias estadisticas de Sonora y Sinaloa. 22844
Noticias estadisticas del estado de Chihuahua. 22844
Noticias estadisticas del estado de Durango. 22844
Noticias estadisticas sobre el departamento de Tuspan. 23647
Noticias fidelignas de lo occuradio el dia 4 de la ciudad de Mexico. 99711
Noticias geograf.-polit. del territorio de Colima. (30295)
Noticias geograficas y estadisticas de la republica Mexicana. 26556
Noticias geograficas y estadisticas del departemento de Zalisco. (56010)

Noticias historiales de las conquistas de
tierra firme en el Nuevo Reyno de
Granda. 81286
Noticias historiales de las conquistas de
tierra firme en las Indias Occidentales.
81285-81287
Noticias historiales practicas de los sucessos.
(10782), 15020, 68237
Noticias historicas de la republica Argentina.
56334
Noticias historicas, politicas, y estadisticas.
(56333)
Noticias historicas sobre las misiones en la
republica de Bolivia. (51590)
Noticias historicas sobre el orijen y desar-
rollo de la Ensenanza Publica Superior
en Buenos Aires. (29345)
Noticias historicas y descriptivas sobre el
gran pais del Chaco y Rio Bermejo.
1931
Noticias historicas y estadisticas de Durango.
67645
Noticias historicas y estadisticas de la
antigua provincia del Nuevo-Mexico.
62980
Noticias historicas y estadisticas de Nueva-
Mexico. 22844
Noticias importantes. 10058
Noticias muy importantes y recientes de los
Estados-Unidos del Norte. 56011
Noticias para formar la estadistica del
Obispado de Michoacan. 73034-73035
Noticias para la historia de Nuestra Senora
de los Remedios desde el ano de 1800.
(19974)
Noticias para la historia de Nuestra Senora
de los Remedios, desde el ano de 1808.
56012
Noticias para la vida de D. Hernando Colon.
(52094)
Noticias que tuvieron los Europas de la
America. (2607)
Noticias relativas a el primer plan de
independencia. 56013
Noticias sagradas de Sant. Madre del Rosario.
(980)
Noticias sagradas que a major honra y gloria
Dios y de Su. S. M. Maria S^ra. Nuestra
Retorna la Ciudad de la Puebla de los
Angeles. 56014
Noticias secretas de America. 36807, 1st
note after 97687
Noticias sobre algunas interesantes ruinas y
sobre los viages en America. (39102)
Noticias sobre el temporal de Octubre.
56015
Noticias sobre los dos sitios de la colonia
del Sacramento. 56016
Noticio de sus limites. 41673
Noticioso de ambos mundos. 56017
Noticioso de Chihuahua. 12692
Noticioso general nom. 741. 94158
Notificatie. De Bewinthebberen van de
Generale Geoctrooyeerde West-Indische
Compagnie deser landen maken bekent.
56018, 102296
Notificatie. De Hove van Politie en Crimineele
Justitie der Colonie Suriname, op den
30ste December 1795. 93847
Notification of town meeting. 6535
Notification to persons desiring to leave the
town. 6534
Notifications, orders, and instructions.
(56019)
Notings and reminiscences of a two years'
volunteer. 41019

Notions of anti-masonry. 23237
Notions of Mr. Locke and his followers.
97364
Notions of Mr. Locke, and his followers, that
all civil governments whatever. 97354
Notions of the Americans. (16486)
Notions on political economy. 36146
Notions on religion and politics. 66710
Notions sur la culture des Terres Basses.
91083
Notis Anglicis illustratae. 8362
Notitia Conciliorvm Hispaniae. 74856
Notitia de los premios aplicados a las mejores
hilanderas al torno. 56020
Notitia digitatum et administrationum omnium
tam civilium quam militarium in partibus
orientis et occidentis. (56021)
Notitia episcopatuum orbis Christiani. 49404
Notitia of New-Brunswick. 56022
Notitia orbis antiqui, sive geographia Plenior.
(11655)
Notitia orbis e variis peregrinationibus ab
illustribus viris susceptis deprompta.
94141
Notitia vtraqve orientis tvm occidentis vltra
Arcadii honoriiqve Caesarvm tempora.
56023
Notitiae of New Brunswick. 102432
Notitiae parochiales. 4271-(4272), 56024
Notitie van de schepen gedestineert uit dese
landen naar Groen-Land. 78978
Notitser til Gronlands ornithologi. [sic]
69116
Notitser til Gronlands ornithologie. 69116
Notizen uber die Einfuhrung und erste
Ausbreitung der Buchdruckerkunst in
Amerika. 23600
Notizia sulla moltiplicazione dell' Uccello
Americano Paroaria Cucullata. (59000)
Notizie d'atti esistenti nel publico archivio de'
notaj di Savona. 4565
Notizie e lettere pubblicate per cura del
Municipio di Bergamo. 73166
Notizie storiche e bibliografiche di Christoforo
Colombo. 10656
Notizie varie sullo stato presente della
republica degli Stati Uniti dell' America
Settentrionale. (28336)
Notman, W. illus. (56025), 76411, 89636
Notorias escandalosas injusticias del Tribunal
Mercantil de la Habana. (29444)
Notoriedades del Plata. 56026
Notorious and wicked design upon the river
of Thames. 28459
Notre cable transatlantique (France aux Etats-
Unis.) 56027
Notre Dame University, South Bend, Ind.
34522
Notre proces en escroquiere. (9784)
Nott, Abner Kingman, 1834-1859. 56028
Nott, Abraham. 92878
Nott, Benjamin. 56029
Nott, Charles B. 56030-(56032)
Nott, Charles G. supposed author (37994),
56030
Nott, Eliphalet. 56033-56036, 89695, 3d note
after 96966
Nott, Eliphalet. defendant 97779-97781,
89345
Nott, Henry Junius. ed. 56037, 81430
Nott, Henry Junius. reporter 87453, 87455,
87460, 87461
Nott, J. C. 56038-56040
Nott, Richard Means, 1831-1880. 56028
Nott, Sally. 56036
Nott, Samuel. civil engineer 56051, (66328)

Nott, Samuel, 1754-1852. 56041-56043

Nott, Samuel, 1788-1869. 40217, (56044)-56050

Nott & McCord's reports. 87455, 87461

Nottoway County, Va. Court. 102604

Nott's testimony in favour of Judson. 56050

Notulen der resolutien, genomen by den Edelen Achtbarren Hove van Civile Justitie. 93846

Notus Ninimi. pseud. Letter to Hull Barton. see Ogden, George W.

Notus Nimni. pseud. Letter to Hull Barton. see Ogden, George W.

Notus Nulli. pseud. see Nulli, Notus. pseud

Notwendige Nachricht von der newen Seefahrt vnd Kauffhandlung. 98187

Nouette-Delorme, Emile. (56053)-(56054)

Nougaret, Pierre-Jean-Baptiste, 1742-1823. 56055, 68098

Nourse, ------, fl. 1776. 15523, (56060)

Nourse, B. F. 51236, 56056 see also U. S. Commission to the Paris Exposition, 1867.

Nourse, J. D. 56058

Nourse, James. 56057

Nourse, Joseph E. (56059)

Nourse, Michael. 101546-101546A

Nous Leger-Felicite Sonthonax. 87123

Nouveau bibliotheque des voyages anciens et modernes. 56064

Nouveau dictionnaire complet geographique. 7787

Nouveau dictionnaire historique. 27789

Nouveau dictionnaire historique des sieges et batailles memorables. 42914

Nouveau et grand illuminant flambeau de la mer. 100767

Nouveau gres rouge en Europe. 44505

Nouveau magazin pittoresque. (51036)

Nouveau manuel complet du fabricant et de l'ameteur de tabacs. (36678)

Nouveau Mexique. 101350

Nouveau Mississippi. 35512, 73511

Nouveau-Monde, coutumes, moeurs et scenes de la vie Americaine. 14938

Nouueau Monde & uauigacitions [sic] de Almeric de Vespuce. 50064

Nouueau Monde et nauigations faites p̄ Emeric de Vespuce. 50062, note after 106378, 3d, 5th note after 106378

Novveau-Monde ov l'Ameriqve Chrestienne. 12294

Noveau Monde. Poeme. Par M. Le Suire. (40233)

Nouveau moyen de prevenir les inondations de la ville et la vallee de Mexico. 64726

Nouveau Nabuchodonosor. 56061, (68086)

Nouveau Nabuchodonosor ou Raynal parmi les quadrupedes. 56061, (68086)

Nouveau paysan du Danube. 47202

Nouveau prospectus de la Compagnie du Scioto. 78125

Nouveau recueil de chansons. 39265

Nouveau recueil de plaidoyers Francais. 40039

Nouveau recueil de traites. 44844

Nouveau recueil general de traites. 44847

Nouveau recueil traitez, d'alliance, de treve, de paix, et de commerce. 56062

Nouveau Robinson. 72219

Nouveau Robinson; traduit de l'Anglais par Charles Brandon. 44702

Nouveau systeme de compatabilitie agricole. 57810

Nouveau systeme de la colonisation pour St. Domingue. 39611

Nouveau systeme geographique. 71874, note after 98694

Nouveau theatre du monde. 6940

Nouveau voyage a la mer du Sud. (17716), 44594, 72371

Nouveau voyage autour du monde, en Asie, en Amerique, et en Afrique. 58167

Nouveau voyage autour de monde en 1838, 1839 et 1840. (56063)

Nouveau voyage autour du monde, ou l'on decrit en particulier. (18381)-18383, 100944

Nouveau voyage autour du monde. Par M. le Gentil. 38397

Nouveau voyage aux isles de l'Amerique. 38409-38412

Nouveau voyage dans les Etats-Unis de l'Amerique Septentrionale. 8035

Nouveau voyage en Guinee. 84561

Nouveau voyage fait au Peru. 17176

Nouveau voyage vers le Septentrion. 38716

Nouveaux memoires des deportes a la Guiane. (1534), (27337), 29157, 67625

Nouveaux principes d'economie politique. 81457

Nouveaux spectacle donne par le citoyen San Cuilot. 89134

Nouveaux supplemens au recueil de traites. 44845

Nouveaux voyages aux cotes de Guinee et en Amerique. 51677, note after 100827

Nouveaux voyages aux Indes Occidentales. 6465

Nouveaux voyages dans l'Amerique Septentrionale. 6470

Nouveaux voyages de Mr. le Baron de Lahontan. 38635, (38638)-(38640)

Nouveaux voyages du R. P. Louis Hennepin et de Sieur Dela Borde. 31353

Nouveaux voyages en diverses parties de l'Amerique. 99428

Nouvel abrege de tous les voyages autour du monde. 26683

Nouvel abrege des voyages dans l'Amerique. 71252

Nouvel abrege du voyageur Francais. 5948

Nouvel atlas portatif. 71867-71869

Nouvel avis aux colons de Saint-Domingue. 75168

Nouvel examen du rapport de M. Barnave. 49083

Nouvelle alliance a proposer entre les republiques Francaise et Americaine. 21058

Nouvelle Americaine. (11658)

Nouvelle Amerique. 20374

Nouvelle bibliotheque universelle des romans. 99413

Nouvelle carte de l'Amerique Septentrionale et Meridionale. 8735

Nouvelle collection de toutes les relations de voyages. 65402-65404

Nouvelle constitution de New-York. 36677

Nouvelle de Saint Domingue du 9 au 14 Mars 1790. 56065

Nouvelle decouverte au Mexique. 98928

Nouvelle decovverte de l'isle Pines. (56066)

Nouvelle decouverte des Indes Meridionales. 16781

Nouvelle decouverte d'un pays plus grand. 98752

Nouvelle decouverte d'un tres-grand pais, dans l'Amerique. 31352, 31355

Nova Francia: or the description of that part of New France. 40175-40176, 57765

Nova genera et species plantarum quas in itinere per Brasiliam. 44993

Nova genera et species plantarum quas in peregrinatione ad plagam aequinoctialem Orbis Novi colligerunt. 33761, 33766

Nova genera et species plantarum quas in regno Chilensi Peruviano. 63628

Nova Italiae Hodiernae descriptio. 32751

Nova Lusitania. 8130

Noua orbis descriptio ac noua oceani nauigatio. (66476)

Nova plantarum Americanarum genera. (63457)

Nova plantarum genera. 49694

Nova reperta. 92666-92667

Nova reperta sive rerum memorabilium recens inventarum. 58413

Nova Scotia, Bishop of. see Inglis, Charles, Bishop of Nova Scotia, 1734-1816. Inglis, John, Bishop of Nova Scotia, 1777-1850.

Nova Scotia. 56117-56119, (56126), (56130), (56140), 56163, 56165, 56167, 56171, 56190, 56195, (67517), 84435

Nova Scotia. Academic Schools. see Nova Scotia. Schools.

Nova Scotia. Agricultural Exhibition, Halifax, 1853. (56111)

Nova Scotia. Board of Statistics. Secretary. 56182

Nova Scotia. Board of Works. (56115)

Nova Scotia. Board of Works. Chairman. 56175

Nova Scotia. Census, 1861. 56182

Nova Scotia. Charter. 741, 3207, 16684, 73797, 91853

Nova Scotia. Chief Commissioner of Mines. see Nova Scotia. Commissioner of Mines.

Nova Scotia. Chief Gold Commissioner. see Nova Scotia. Gold Commissioner.

Nova Scotia. Commissioner for the International Exposition, 1864. 56173

Nova Scotia. Commissioner of Indian Affairs. 56178

Nova Scotia. Commissioner of Mines. 56176

Nova Scotia. Commissioner of Public Records. (56184) see also Akins, Thomas B. Nova Scotia. Record Commission.

Nova Scotia. Commissioners to Collect the Private and Local Laws. 56161

Nova Scotia. Commissioners to Revise the Statutes. (56188)-56189

Nova Scotia. Common Schools. see Nova Scotia. Schools.

Nova Scotia. Council of Public Instruction. 56147

Nova Scotia. Court of Vice Admiralty, Halifax. 91682, 97797

Nova Scotia. Crown Land Office. 56114, 56178

Nova Scotia. Delegation to Washington, D. C. (56122)

Nova Scotia. Department of Mines. (56180)

Nova Scotia. General Assembly. 31137, (56143), 98067

Nova Scotia. General Assembly. petitioners 56110

Nova Scotia. General Assembly. Committee on Strait of Canso. 56170

Nova Scotia. General Assembly. House. 56120, 56142, 56144, 56146

Nova Scotia. General Assembly. House. petitioners (56128), (56139)

Nova Scotia. General Assembly. House. Committee for Investigating the Official Conduct of the Judges of the Supreme Court. 91357, note after 94546

Nova Scotia. General Assembly. Legislative Council. 56121, 56145, 56191, 94546

Nova Scotia. General Assembly. Legislative Council. Delegates to England, 1835. 56179

Nova Scotia. Gold Commissioner. (14686), 56177, 81061

Nova Scotia. Governor, 1752-1756 (Hopson) 33004 see also Hopson, Peregrine Thomas, d. 1759.

Nova Scotia. Governor, 1764-1766 (Wilmot) 84583 see also Wilmot, Montague, d. 1766

Nova Scotia. Inspector of Mines. 56172

Nova Scotia. International Show Committee, 1863. see International Show Committee of Nova Scotia, 1863.

Nova Scotia. Laws, statutes, etc. 4392, 29701, 37873, (51433), (56101), 56107-56108, 56147-56148, 56160-56161, 56168, (56188)-56189, 56192-56194

Nova Scotia. Lieutenant Governor, 1792-1808 (Wentworth) 41656-41657, 102630 see also Wentworth, Sir John, 1737-1820.

Nova Scotia. Lieutenant Governor, 1792-1808 (Wentworth) defendant 41657, note after 102630 see also Wentworth, Sir John, 1737-1820. defendant

Nova Scotia. Lieutenant Governor, 1834-1840 (Campbell) 56150 see also Campbell, Sir John, 1776-1847.

Nova Scotia. Militia. (56149)

Nova Scotia. Model Schools. see Nova Scotia. Schools.

Nova Scotia. Normal School, Halifax. Principal. (56169)

Nova Scotia. Normal Schools. see Nova Scotia. Schools.

Nova Scotia. Post Office Department. (56186)

Nova Scotia. Postmaster General. 56174

Nova Scotia. Provincial Agricultural and Industrial Exhibition, 1868. 56162

Nova Scotia. Record Commission. 56166 see also Nova Scotia. Commissioner of Public Records.

Nova Scotia. Representatives of the Freeholders. petitioners see Nova Scotia. General Assembly. petitioners

Nova Scotia. Schools. (56113)

Nova Scotia. Secretary's Office. 56123

Nova Scotia. Superintendent of Education. (56169), 56183

Nova Scotia. Superior Schools. see Nova Scotia. Schools.

Nova Scotia. Supreme Court. 91357, note after 94546

Nova Scotia. Treaties, etc. 33004

Nova Scotia (Diocese) see Church of England in Canada. Nova Scotia (Diocese)

Nova Scotia. 66686

Nova-Scotia almanac for 1858. 17957

Nova Scotia and her resources. 38128

Nova Scotia and Nova-Scotians. 31821

Nova Scotia Baptist Convention. see Baptists. Nova Scotia. Convention.

Nova-Scotia calendar, or an almanack, for . . . 1783. 56155

Nova-Scotia considered as a field for emigration. 30027

Nova Scotia Delegation. Despatches laid before the Legislature. (67517)

Nova Scotia gold fields. 56156

Nova Scotia Historical Society. 84422
Nova Scotia, its condition and resources.
 57966
Nova-Scotia Literary and Scientific Society.
 56157
Nova-Scotia magazine and comprehensive
 review. 56158
Nova Scotia minstrel. 17222
Nova-Scotia people's almanac for . . . 1856.
 56305
Nova Scotia Railway. Chief Engineer. 56185
 see also Laurie, James.
Nova Scotia: report on the gold fields.
 (33316)
Nova Scotia Western Baptist Association. see
 Baptists. Nova Scotia. Western
 Baptist Association.
Nova Scotian. pseud. Descriptive sketches
 of Nova Scotia. see Frame, Eliza.
Nova Scotian. pseud. Letters. (40604)
Nova Scotian. pseud. Remarks upon the
 proposed federation of the provinces.
 (56197), 69534
Nova Scotian Institute of Natural Sciences,
 Halifax. 56159
Nova terrae descriptio secvndvm neotericorum
 obseruantium. 69130
Nova totius terrarum orbis geographica.
 14549
Nova typis transacta navigatio. 63367,
 82979
Nova Zemla. 77559
Novae novi orbis historiae. 4792, 4794,
 4796, 4799
Novae orbis liber secundus. (8784)
Novae stirpes Brasilienses. 11225
Novae symbolae mycologicae. 25959
Novanglus. pseud. Novanglus and Massa-
 chusettensis. see Adams, John, Pres.
 U. S., 1735-1826.
Novanglus. pseud. Review of a sermon.
 4345
Novanglus and Massachusettensis. 263
Noue, Pierre de la. tr. 58414
Noue, de la isole & terra ferma nouamente
 trouate in India. 16950, 56052
Novel. 30114, 32616, 35696, 37323, 40918,
 47120, 57752, 71046, 72579, 73618,
 74317, 76954, (78466), 78790-78791,
 (80053), 83788, 84392, 86301, 86785,
 89915, 90293, 92224, 95392, 95865,
 97034, 97373, 99422, 101049, 101457,
 102161, 102592, 103731, note after
 103973, 105059
Novel; founded on fact. 25229, 103731
Novel founded on facts. 73825
Novel, founded on recent facts. 105057
Novel newspaper—no. 460. 85411
Novel of American coast life. 50630
Novel of New York and the army, in 1862.
 50630
Novel of society and the field in 1863.
 (50628)
Novel of the great rebellion in 1861. 50630
Novel original. 99692
Novela. 92609, 92611-92612, 92614, 92615
Novela Americana. 9746
Novela Cubana. Original de D. Guillermo
 Mortgat. 50982
Novela Cubana. Tomo primero. 99691
Novela de costumbres. 13836
Novela de costumbres Cubanas. 99691
Novela de costumbres Mejicanas original.
 71484
Novela escrita en Ingles. 92613-92614,
 92615

Novela escrita en Ingles por el Capitan Mayne
 Reid. 69073
Novela historica. 27755
Novela historica Mexicana. (19975)
Novela historica original. 58068
Novela historica orijinal. 74608
Novela historica por Juan A. Mateos. 46201-
 46202
Novela historica por la Senorita Gomez de
 Avellaneda. 27756
Novela historica y de costumbres Mejicanas.
 63184
Novela historica y religiosa, escrita en France
 por E. Riviere. 71685
Novela historico, original. 22842
Novela original de costumbres contemporaneas.
 75555
Novela original de Jose Rivera y Rio. (71635)
Novela original escrita en Frances por
 Felisberto Pelissot. 59573
Novela, sacada de la historia Argentina.
 (26563)
Novelas Americanas. 98118
Novelists' library. 36391
Novelist's magazine. 29143, 100749
Novella Americana. (12261)
Novelle Americaine. 92437
Novelle aus dem Deutsch-Amerikanischen
 Leben. 86384
Novelle maritima. 16500
Novellen-Sammlung. 4527-4528
Novellen von Edgar Allan Poe. 63566
Novellettes of a traveller. 56037, 81430
Novellista Brasileiro. 56198
Novelties of the New World. 3229
Novelties which disturb our peace. (32931)
November, 1866. First monthly report of the
 Merchants' Union Law Company. 47923
Nov. 19, 1861. The war for the union.
 (26540)
November 3d, 1753. To the Honourable Robert
 Dinwiddie, Esq; His Majesty's Lieutenant-
 Governor, and Commander in Chief of
 the Colony and Dominion of Virginia.
 The humble address of the Council.
 99902
November 3d, 1753. To the Honourable Robert
 Dinwiddie, Esq; His Majesty's Lieutenant-
 Governor, and Commander in Chief, of
 the Colony and Dominion of Virginia,
 the humble address of the House of
 Burgesses. 99922
Novena de la milagrosa imagen de Nuestra
 Senora del Pueblito. 99615
Novena de la soberana Emperatriz de Cielo y
 Terra. 76799
Novena [Junta Publica de la Real Sociedad
 Economica de Guatemala.] 29085
Novenario del transito de Sr. S. Jose. 77117
Novendialia manium nobilissimae Helenae a
 Vega Samaniego. 75894
Novenas a la Santisima Virgen Maria. 56199
Novi avisi di piv lo che de l'India et massime
 de Brasil. (56200)
Novi freti. 77967
Novi orbis descriptio. 57687
Novi orbis Indiae Occidentalis admondvm
 Reverendissimorum PP. ac FF.
 Reverendissimi ac Illustrissimi Domini.
 63367
Novi orbis nova descriptio. 86424
Novi orbis pars dvodecima. (8784)
Novia del hereje o la inquisicion de Lima.
 42000
Novice. 38967
Noviomago, Gerardo. (63019)

Noviomagus, Joannes. see Bronchorst, Johann.
Novion, Citoyen de. pseud. Altar of Baal thrown down. see Sullivan, James, 1744-1808
Novisima recopilacion de las Indias. 72430
Novissima guia para eleitores e votantes. 81094
Novissima recopilacion de las leyes de Espana. 56201
Novissima sinica historiam nostri temporis illustratura. (39894)
Nouissime historiaru[m] omniu[m] repercussio[n]es. 25084
Nouissime hystoriaru[m] omniu[m] repercussiones. 25083
Nouo mondo. 50050-(50052), (50054)
Novo orbe serafico Brasilico. 35334
Novoe Snstetatneskoe Opnsanie Mineralbnago Kavineta Imperatorskago. 56202
Novorum generum plantarum Peruvianarum. 73994
Novos impostos. (56203)
Novum Belgium. 51130
Novum Belgium: an account of New Netherland in 1643-4. 36144, (80023)
Novum Belgium, description de Nieuw Netherland. (36143)
Novum lexicon geographicum. 24163
Novum testamentum, juxta exemplar Joannis Millii accuratissime impressum. 56204
Novvs atlas, das ist, Weltbeschreibung. 5719
Novus atlas, sive theatrum orbis terrarum. 35773
Novus orbis. 99358-99359
Novus orbis. Id est, navigationes primae in Americam. (34105), note after 99383C
Novus orbis regionum ac insularum veteribus incognitarum. (3596), 16949, note after 16965, 30482-30483, 34100-(34104), 40960, 62803, 63960, note after 99383C
Novvs orbis seu descriptionis Indiae Occidentalis libri XVIII. 38557, (76810)
Novvs orbis, sive descriptio Indiae Occidentalis. 5014, 14348, 31540, 44057
Novvs orbis, tabvlis Aeneis Secvndum rationes geographicas delineatvs. 48170
Now and then. (71277)
Now fair Aurora paints the east. 103148
Now fitting for a privateer. 101527
Now in the press, and next week will be published, &c. 56205, 103944
Now in the press, and speedily will be published. 90227
Now in the press, and will be speedily published. 96975
Now is the time to settle it. 8046
Now or never! 47788
Now or never is the time for men to make sure of their eternal salvation. 46713
Now ready for the press. 98392
Nowel, Samuel. 56206
Nowell, Alexander. 56207
Nowell, Thomas. (59572)
Noxon, James. 56209, 96985
Noxon, Thomas. 93809, 97097
Noyer, J. A. Alexandre, b. 1776? 29174, 56210-(56211)
Noyes, --------, fl. 1757. 56231
Noyes, --------, fl. 1840. defendant 101435
Noyes, Abigail. 103789
Noyes, Belcher. 95965
Noyes, Daniel J. 56212
Noyes, David. 56213
Noyes, George F. 56214

Noyes, George R. 56215
Noyes, J. H. ed. 55000, 60920, 89522
Noyes, Jacob. (56216)
Noyes, James, 1608-1656. 24401, 56218-45220, 58769
Noyes, James, 1778-1799. 56217
Noyes, James Oscar, 1829-1872. 56221-56223
Noyes, John. (56224)-(56225)
Noyes, John Humphrey. 56226
Noyes, Moses, 1643-1729. (56232)
Noyes, Nathaniel, 1735-1810. 56227
Noyes, Nathaniel, fl. 1854. 56228
Noyes, Nicholas, 1647-1717. 56229-56230, 72691
Noyes, Oliver, 1675-1721. supposed author 40282
Noyes, Thomas. (56233)-56236
Noyes, William Curtis. 28472, 56237-56238
Noyes and Snow. firm publishers 85596
Noyes' illustrated national guide. 56223
Noyes' illustrated national railway and steam navigation guide. 56223
Noyesism unveiled. 21677
Noyle, Isaac. 45239
Nozze di Figaro, dramma eroicomico. 64014
Nozze di Figaro, il Don Giovanni, e l'Assur Re d'Armus; tre drammi. 64014
Nu geweezen zee-officier. pseud. Tweede briefe. see Vlag, M. M. van der. pseud.
Nua semana bien empleada por un currutacio de Lima. 94863
Nubian geography. 66686
Nuckols's Meeting-House, Goochland County, Va. Baptist Committee, 1791. see Baptists. Virginia. Committee, 1791.
Nuda, L. illus. (48590)
Nuestra Senora de las Angvstias (Navio) 94285
Nuestra Senora del Rosario del Indios. 73208
Nuetzliche Anweisung oder Beyhulffe vor Deutsche und Englische zu lernen. 88826
Nuetzliche oder Beyhulfe vor die Teutschen um Englisch zu lernen. 77197
Nueva aljaba apostolica. 47671
Nueva coleccion de documentos para la historia de Mexico. 106405
Nueva coleccion de leyes y decretos Mexicanos. 71628
Nueva coleccion de todas las relaciones de los que se han hecho por mar. 65407
Nueva contestacion al periodico titulado l'Estafette. 72547
Nueva descripcion del orbe de la tierra. (57230)
Nueva discuscion entre el ajiente de S. M. B. y el Gobierno Supremo de Nicaragua. 55158
Nueva division de la isla de Cuba. 56241
Nueva Espana. see Mexico (Viceroyalty)
Nueva Espana bajo la proteccion de Maria Santisima de Guadalupe. 72517
Nueva-Espana, Nueva-Galicia y Nueva-Mexico, 1537. 84379
Nueva forma de gobierno en Mexico. 48600
Nueva Galicia (Diocese) 34836
Nueva Granada (Viceroyalty) Laws, statutes, etc. 56269, 68872
Nueva Granada (Viceroyalty) Virrey, 1590-1597 (Gonzales) 70098 see also Gonzales, Antonio.
Nueva Granada (Viceroyalty) Virrey, 1740-1748 (Eslava y Lazaga) 11131-11132, 11134, 19951, 22877, 1st note after 99245 see also Eslava y Lazaga, Sebastian de.

NUEVA

Nueva Granada (Republic of New Granada, 1832-1858) Comisiones del Ecuador y Nueva Granada en la Cuestion Sobre Limites de Ambos Estados. see Comisiones del Ecuador y Nueva Granada en la Cuestion Sobre Limites de Ambos Estados.
Nueva Granada (Republic of New Granada, 1832-1858) Congreso. Senado. Comision Sobre el Tratado de Amistad i Limites de esta Republica con el Imperio del Brasil. 68786
Nueva Granada (Republic of New Granada, 1832-1858) Laws, statutes, etc. 56269
Nueva Granada (Republic of New Granada, 1832-1858) Treaties, etc. 21800, (66220), 68786
Nueva Granada al empezar el ano de 1836. 56283
Nueva Granada i los Estados-Unidos de America. 56284
Nueva Guatemala. Escuela. (29090), 56020
Nueva Mexico (Province) Gobernador, 1598-1609 (Onate y Salazar) 69210, 98794 see also Onate y Salazar, Juan de.
Nueva obseruacion astronomica del periodo tragico. 3600
Nueva recopilacion de las leyes de las Indias. 29360, 73852
Nueva recopilacion. Las leyes de recopilacion. 56288
Nueva relacion que contiene los viages. 26312
Nueva Ruth de la Gracia. 31725
Nueva Segovia (Diocese) Bishop (Aduarte) 76772 see also Aduarte, Diego, Bp.
Nueva teorica y practica de los metales de oro y plata. 26715
Nueva Vizcaya (Diocese) petitioners 99442
Nueva Vizcaya (Diocese) Bishop (Hevia y Valdes) plaintiff 99442 see also Hevia y Valdes, Diego de, Bp. plaintiff
Nueva Vizcaya (Diocese) Bishop (Suarez de Escobar) 93310 see also Suarez de Escobar, Pedro, Bp.
Nueva Vizcaya (Province) Gobernador, 1620-1626 (Lesga Lopez) 99326 see also Vesga Lopez, Mateo de.
Nueva-Vizgaya (documents, etc.) (34155)
Nueva y curiosa guia para dentro y fuera de este corte de Mexico. 48601
Nueva, y grande relumbrante antorcha de la mar. 100767
Nuevas cartas. (75870)
Nuevas ciertas y didedignas de la citoria que ha alcancado. 96109
Nuevas empressas del peregrino Americano Septentrional Atlante. 44528
Nuevas impresas del peregrino Americano Septentrional Atlante. 22898
Nuevas observaciones sobre el opusculo. 22903
Nuevas ordenenzas de minas para e reino de Chile. 31942
Nuevas reflexiones sobre la cuestion Franco-Mexicana. 56289
Nuevas utilidades de la quina. (962)
Nueve sermones en lengua de Chile. 98334
Nuevitas, Cuba. Ayuntamiento. (17751)
Nuevitas, Cuba. Charter. (17751)
Nuevitas, Cuba. Comision del Camino. 34711, 56290, 66589
Nvevo apostol de Galicia. 27809, (67345)
Nuevo arancel de capturas aprobado por S. M. (56292)

Nuevo arbitrio para dar un grande aumento a la hacienda federal. 104840
Nuevo assiento. 56293
Nuevo atlas. 35774
Nuevo Bernal Diaz del Castillo. 9584
Nuevo descubrimiento del gran rio de las Amazonas. 150, 52380, 72524
Nuevo donativo. 56294
Nuevo escribano instruido. 56295
Nuevo estado. 87211
Nuevo Febrero Mexicano. 56296
Nuevo heroe de la farma. 98335
Nuevo Leon (State) Constitution. 56297
Nuevo Mundo descubrieto por Cristobal Colon. 98767
Nuevo Mundo pintoresco. 56299
Nuevo Mundo; poemma heroyco. (6797)-6798
Nuevo reglamento. 56300
Nuevo Reino de Granada. see Nueva Granada (Viceroyalty)
Nuevo Robinson. 10298, 72232
Nuevo Robinson Crusoe. 72230
Nuevo sacerdote y pontifice onias. 78903
Nuevo sistema de gobierno economico, para la America. 10314, 36661
Nuevo Ulisses. (11445)
Nuevo viajero universal, en America. 42921
Nuevo viajero universal. Enciclopedia de viajes modernos. 24141
Nuevo vocabulario filosofico democratico. 56301
Nuevo y facilisimo metodo de calumniar a cualquiera inventado. 93301
Nuevos documentos relativos a la cuestion de Mexico. 48602
Nugae. By Albert Pike. 62814
Nugae. By Nugator. 56302
Nugae Georgicae. 36341
Nugamenta: a book of verses. 70830
Nugator. pseud. Nugae. see Carter, St. L. L.
Nugent, H. P. (39214), 56303
Nugent, H. P. defendant 56303
Nugent, Maria. (56304)
Nugent's Nova-Scotia people's almanac for . 1856. 56305
Nugumouinum genunugumouat igiu anishinabeg anumiajig. 56306
Nuisances about dwelling houses. 85499
Nuisances about dwelling houses, continued. 85500
Nuits Peruviennes. 56307
Nuix, Giovanni. see Nuix, Juan, 1740-1783.
Nuix, Josef de. see Nuix, Juan, 1740-1783.
Nuix, Juan, 1740-1783. 56308-56310
Nuix y de Perpina, Josef de. see Nuix, Juan 1740-1783.
Nulli, Notus. pseud. Microcosmus Philadelphicus. 56311
Nullification. 56315, 96073
Nullification considered and defended. 5707
Nullification ordinance. 87668
Nullification unmasked. (17536), 59642
Nullifier. pseud. Memoirs. 47565
Nullus liber homo. 19867
Numa. pseud. Letter to the Honorable John Randolph. 40483, 67849
No. ——— Be it known. 85841
No. 8. An astronomical diary, or almanack. 89576
No. VIII. of Drucke und Holzschnitte des V. und XVI. Jahrhunderts. 99363
No. 18. Royal Mail Steam Packet Company. 73800
No. 11. Branch of Sanitary Commission. 76661
No. 59. British Guiana. 1835. 83487

(No. 5.) A list of officers of the state navy. 82961

No 5. An astronomical diary, or almanack. 89576

No V. Mundus Novus. 99379

Number V. Poor Richard's new farmer's almanac. 64079

(No. 4.) A list of officers of the Illinois Regiment. 34301, 82960

Number four. A sectarian thing. 77024

No. IV. Amerigo Vespucci. 99379

No. 4. An astronomical diary, or almanack. 89576

No. IV. An astronomical diary, or almanack for . . . 1820. 89582

No. 4. of some series of tracts. 82031

No. 14. Papers from the Society for the Diffusion of Political Knowledge. 33898

No. 41. 101816

Number of citizens. pseud. Central basin. 101927

Number of citizens. pseud. To the public. 95995

Number of citizens. pseud. To the publick. 95994

Number of citizens of Madison County, N. Y. pseud. To the electors. (43728)

Number of citizens of . . . Pennsylvania. petitioners see Pennsylvania. Citizens. petitioners

Number of Citizens of Pennsylvania, Appointed to Investigate the Evils of Freemasonry. see Pennsylvania. Legislature. Committe to Investigate the Evils of Freemasonry.

Number of depositions of witnesses. 48052, note after 87538

Number of Dry Goods Importers, Philadelphia. see Philadelphia. Dry Goods Importers.

Number of gentlemen. pseud. Christian scholar's and farmer's magazine. (12924)

Number of Gentlemen Whose Confidence in the Integrity and Patriotism of Governor Tompkins in Undiminished. Committee. 96150

Number of gentlemen whose confidence in the integrity and patriotism of Governor Tompkins in undiminished have requested a committee to examine the official documents. 96150

Number of his [i. e. Fisher Ames'] friends. pseud. comps. 273, 1303

Number [of] hymns composed on the death of several of his relations. 83496

Number of laymen. pseud. Testimony and advice. 94917

Number of letters to the Rev. William Rogers, &c. 104725

Number of Ministers Conven'd at Taunton, Mass., 1745. (22007), 94921, note after 103633, 5th note after 103650 see also Leonard, Nathaniel.

Number of ministers, elders, and deacons. pseud. / Reasons assigned. see Brokaw, Abraham.

Number of Ministers in Boston and Charlestown. see Congregational Churches in Massachusetts. Boston Association.

Number of Ministers in the County of Bristol, Mass. see Congregational Churches in Massachusetts. Bristol County Ministers.

Number of ministers, in the northern states of America. pseud. Sermons on some of the distinguishing doctrines. 79294

Number of Murell's Associates. defendants 33250, note before 91708

Number of New England Ministers Met at Boston, Sept. 25, 1745. see Convention of Congregational Ministers of New England, Boston, 1745.

Number of orations delivered by the young ladies. 62398, 2d note after 106135

Number of original pieces of poetry and select songs. 80197

Number of original poems. 33005, 100545

Number of patriotic and humorous songs. 86180

Number of sermons preached. 104275

Number of stories, mostly taken from the history of America. 102367, note after 102396

Number of the Associated Pastors of Boston and Charlestown. see Congregational Churches in Massachusetts. Boston Association.

Number of the beast found out by spiritual arithmetic. 70869

Number of the inhabitants of this city. 61876

Number of the late church and congregation. pseud. Brief account of the origin and progress of the divisions. 97073

Number one. 96411

No. I. 48943, 90167, note after 95840

(No. 1) A list of officers of the army and navy. 82958

No. I. Authentic anecdotes of American slavery. (81899)

No. I. Clergyman's looking-glass. 82476

No. I, containing two dissertations. 31078

No. 1, 1838. The Wesleyan anti-slavery review. 78345

No. 1, from 1797 to 1827. (13561)

No. 1. Hambletonian. 57924

No. 1. Hear both sides. (31176)

No. I. Historical collections of the Junior Pioneer Association of the City of Rochester and Monroe County, N. Y. 101291

No. 1. Indian bulletin for 1867. 36587

No. 1. Maine Farmer's almanack. 89838

No. I. Massachusetts Bay. 101002

Number one. Murder trials and executions in New Hampshire. 65235

No. I. of the new-milk cheese. 77018, note after 98576

No. I. Philadelphia, June 10th, 1773. 45021

No. I. Poetry of animated nature illustrated. 83844

No. I. Price 6 cents. 89974

Numb. I. Publick occurrences both foreign and domestick. 66526

No. I. Statement of the treasurer of Harvard College. 30765

Numb. 1. The Pennsylvania ledger. 60343

Numb. I. The universal instructor in all arts and sciences. 60754

No. 1. The weekly advertiser. 60779

No. I. To the committee of the Senate & House of Representatives. 84577-84578, 2d-3d notes after 97876

No. I. To the committees of the Senate & House of Representatives. 34294, 84577

No. I. Vol. I. Sargent's school monthly. (76964)

Num. 155. 101905

No. [1, 2] of a series of views. 102850

Number one [-six.] 100681

No. 7. An astronomical diary, or almanack. 89576

Nuova sfera pure in ottava rima. 90088

Nuove lirichi d'illustri Italiani. 14660

Nuovi avisi dell' Indie di Portogallo.
56340

Nuovo itinerario delle poste per tutto il
mondo. 14142, 17030

Nvper svp Castiliae ac Portvgaliae regibus.
77800, 77807

Nuptial dialogues. 101286

Nuremberg Chronicle. 77523-77527

Nuremburg, and other poems. 41910

Nurse and spy in the Union Army. (21869)

Nurse Charity, Philadelphia. 61879

Nurse Lovechild, _pseud._ Tommy Thumb's
song book. _see_ Fenn, Eleanor (Frere)
Lady, 1743-1813.

Nursery, Providence, R. I. _see_ Providence
Nursery, Providence, R. I.

Nursery for the Children of Poor Women
in New York. 56341

Nursery of William Kenrick, . . . annual
catalogue. 37463

Nursia, Benedictus de. _see_ Benedict,
Saint, Abbot of Monte Casino.

Nusdorfers, Bernhard. 56342

Nut for lawyers. 84896

Nutak, eller de Mye Testamente. 56343

Nute, Benjamin H. 32473

Nutfield Celebration, 1869. _see_ Celebration
of the One Hundred and Fiftieth Anniversary of the Settled Part of Old
Nutfield, N. H., 1869.

Nuts for future historians to crack. 9836,
82725

Nutshell. 56344

Nutt, Cyrus. (56346)

Nuttall, Thomas, 1786-1859. (56347)-56351,
67461

Nutting, Rufus. 56352

Nuture: together with the catalogue and
prospectus of St. Mary's Hall. (75438)

Nutzliche Anweisung. 56353, 77179, 88825,
88827

Nutzlicher Bericht des Licenciaten Dr. Diego
Garcia de Palacio. 58271

Nuw Welt. 51397, 51403

Nya Sverige i Sodra America. 8103

Nyack, N. Y. Rockland County Female Institute. _see_ Rockland County Female
Institute, Nyack, N. Y.

Nyckeln till Onkel Toms stuga. 92420

Nye, G. 56354, 86608

Nye, James Warren, 1814-1876. 11888,
51020, 52127, 56355, 86348

Nye, Jonathan. (56356), 99189

Nye, Philip, 1596?-1672. 3213, 17067,
21991, 27952-27954, 32828, 32832,
51773, 55888, (69679), 74624, 80205,
91383, note before 92797, note after
92800, 3d note after 103687, 104343
see also Church of Scotland. General
Assembly. Commission.

Nye, Philip, fl. 1683. 56357

Nye, W. F. 56358

Nye (S.) & Company. _firm publishers_
89485

Nye Archiv for Sovaesenet. 18274

Nye Testamente. 22041

Nye unbekande lande. 50057, note after
99383C, 2d note after 106378

Nyel, --------. 40708

Nyenborgh, Johan van. 56359-56360

Nylant, P. 56361

Nys, Ernest. _ed._ 100721

Nystrom, J. W. 56363

Nystrom, Juan Guillermo. 56362

Nywe Testament van ons Herr Jesus Christus.
56364

O

O. _pseud._ Observations on the mineral
waters. _see_ Horner, W. E.

O., A. _pseud._ Americanische Seerauber.
see Exquemelin, Alexandre Olivier.

O., B. Ey. _pseud._ Observations d'un
citoyen de la Plata. (56469)

O., B. V. _pseud._ Greto de alarma. 56365

O., D. J. E. _pseud._ Manuel del abogado
Americano. 56366

O., F. _pseud._ Government is an effect.
(56367)

O., J. _pseud._ New-England freemen warned
and warmed. _see_ Oxenbridge, John.

O., J. _pseud._ _ed._ Washington's monuments
of patriotism. _see_ Ormrod, John.

O., J. J. _pseud._ Oda al Jeneral Flores.
56686

O., J. R. _pseud._ Pamphlet. (40270)

O., M. N. _pseud._ Canadian crisis. 38751,
56368

O., N. _pseud._ Etudes philologiques. _see_
Cuoq, A.

O., N. _pseud._ Jugement errone de M.
Ernest Renan. _see_ Cuoq, A.

O., P. M. de. _pseud._ Minerva. _see_ Olive,
Pedro Maria de.

O., S. _pseud._ Adioynder of svndry other
particvlar wicket plots. _see_ Scott,
Thomas. of Utrecht

O***, T. _pseud._ De la necessite de differer
l'expedition. 56369

O. D., J. _pseud._ Souvenirs d'un jeune
voyageur. _see_ Odolant-Desnos, Pierre
Joseph.

O. B. _pseud._ _see_ Goodrich, Samuel
Griswold, 1793-1860.

O. Barrao do Castello de Paiva, A. Herculano
e. _see_ Paiva, A. Herculano e O Barrao
do Castello de.

O. C. _pseud._ see C., O. _pseud._

O. D. _pseud._ see Dapper, O.

O—— E —— a young student. _pseud._ _see_
Seccombe, Joseph, 1706-1760.

O. H. _pseud._ see H., O. _pseud._

O. J. V. _pseud._ _see_ Victor, Orville James.

O. K. _pseud._ _see_ Keye, Otto.

O. L. H. _pseud._ _see_ Heubner, O. L.

O. M. _pseud._ _see_ M., O. _pseud._

O. M. _pseud._ _see_ Moosmuller, Oswald.

O. P. Q. _pseud._ _see_ Worth, Gorham A.

O. U. A. _see_ Order of United Americans.

¡O Hay dos horas de deguello! 97053

O! Justitia. A complete trial. 60282

O le tala na tusia i le Lima o Mamona i
Papatusi. 83138

O le tusi a Mamona. 83138

O mores! 78384-78387

O rozszerzeniu wiary S. Chrzescianskiey
Katholickiey w Americe. 96258

O se cambia de ministros o perece la nacion.
99710

O se hace la guerra de Tejas. 56374, 95106

O shame! Where is thy blush? 12978

O soo moi! Fraai curieus! 38945

O tempora. 56375

O tempora! O mores! A poem delivered
at . . . Kimball Union Academy. 20681

O tempora! O mores! Or, the best new-
year's gift for a prime minister.
78384-78387

O

O Thou, whose presence went before. 103805
Oajaca (State) see Oaxaca (State)
Oak. 86825
Oak Dale Cemetery, Urbana, Ohio. see
 Urbana, Ohio. Oak Dale Cemetery.
Oak Hall. 56378
Oak Hall pictorial. 56378
Oak openings, or the bee-hunter. 16489
Oakbridge: an old-time story. 83337
Oakes, Abner. 43987
Oakes, Josiah. plaintiff (56380)
Oakes, Urian. 18476, 46462, (46670),
 56381-56385, 62743
Oakes, William. 56386-56387, 57099,
 89679
Oakesmith, Elizabeth. see Smith, Elizabeth
 (Oakes) 1806-
Oakey, P. D. (56388)
Oakey. firm publishers see Partridge &
 Oakey. firm publishers
Oakland, Calif. College of California. see
 California. University.
Oakland, Calif. First Independent Presbyterian
 Church. 56389
Oakland Coal and Iron Company. 56391
Oakland College, Claiborne County, Miss.
 56392
Oakland College, Claiborne County, Miss.
 Board of Trustees. 90437
Oakland Female Seminary, Hillsborough, Ohio.
 56393
Oakley, Charles. 34207, 56394
Oakley, Thomas Jackson, 1783-1857. 9478,
 96842
Oaks. From the French of Michaux. 48701
Oaks of the United States and Canada. 48700
Oakwood, Oliver. pseud. Village tales. see
 Potts, Stanley G.
Oasis. 12723, 91076
Oath a divine ordinance. 36929
Oath of allegiance to the United States.
 58344
Oath of allegiance to the United States dis-
 cussed. 58345
Oath of Marion. 61239
Oath to be administered to all such persons
 as enter. 56395
Oaths forbidden under the Gospel. 66926
Oaths or obligations of free masonry. 99145
Oaths, signs, ceremonies and objects of the
 Ku-Klux-Klan. 38343
Oaths that are appointed by act of Parliament.
 97112
Oatman, Lorenzo D. 92742-92743
Oatman, Olive A. 92742-92743
Oaxaca (City) Cabildo. 87227
Oaxaca (City) Cathedral. Dean y Cabildo.
 56396
Oaxaca (City) Cathedral. Dean y Cabildo.
 petitioners 79138
Oaxaca (City) Cathedral. Dean y Cabildo.
 plaintiffs 56396, 79138
Oaxaca (City) Santa Yglesia Cathedral. see
 Oaxaca (City) Cathedral.
Oaxaca (City) Seminario Conciliar. plaintiffs
 75561
Oaxaca (Diocese) defendants 75561
Oaxaca (Diocese) Bishop (ca 1826-1827)
 56399, 56401
Oaxaca (Diocese) Bishop (ca 1843) 56398
Oaxaca (Diocese) Cabildo. 56399, 56401
Oaxaca (Diocese) Junta Tridentina. 56398
Oaxaca (State) Constitution. 56398
Oaxaca (State) Gobernador, 1847-1853 (Juarez)
 36816, 56400 see also Juarez, Benito
 Pablo, Pres. Mexico, 1806-1872.

Oaxaca (State) Gobernador, 1868-1869. 5640
Oaxaca (State) Laws, statutes, etc. 56397
Obadiah Brown's Benevolent Fund. Trustees
 see Trustees of Obadiah Brown's
 Benevolent Fund, Providence, R. I.
Obadiah Palmer and others, complainants.
 58366
Obaldini, Petruccio. 97661
Obando, Jose Maria. 51068, 56404-56405
Obando, Manuel A. Solis de. see Solis de
 Obando, Manuel A.
Obbedienza data al Santissimo Papa Clemente
 VII. 67730
Obedience, a discourse preached in the city
 of Washington. 19862
Obedience a duty. 90440
Obedience in death. 55524
Obedience the best charter. 56406
Obedience the life of missions. 85305
Obedience to civil authority. 89103
Obedience to human law. A discourse delive
 on the day of public thanksgiving. 823?
Obedience to human law considered in the
 light of divine truth. 71048
Obedience to law. A sermon. 41518
Obedience to magistrates inculcated. (79789)
Obedience to rulers. (42363)
Obedience to the divine law, urged on all
 orders of men. 105088
Obedience to the law of God. (28505)
Obediencia que Mexico cabeca de la Nueva
 Espana dio. 99646
Obediencia que Mexico dio. 48603
Obedient sufferer. 46435
Obedientia Potestissimi Emanuelis Lusitaniae
 Regis. 56407
O'Beirne, Thomas Lewis, Bishop of Meath,
 1748-1823. 56408-56409, (80639)
Obelisco que en la ciudad de la Puebla de lc
 Angeles, celebrando. 56410, 66566
Obelitz, ------. (56411)
Ober, Benjamin. (56412)
Ober, Frederick Albion, 1849-1913. 99383A
 99383C-note after 99383C
Ober-Ammergau passion play. 85462
Oberbauer, Julius C. 56413
Oberea, Queen of Otaheite. pseud. Epistle
 . . . to Joseph Banks, Esq. (3204)
Oberea, Queen of Otaheite. pseud. Second
 epistle . . . to Joseph Banks, Esq.
 3205
Oberholtzer, Ellis Paxson, 1868-1936. 8458
Oberlin, Jacob. 56414
Oberlin, Johann Friedrich. 77724
Oberlin, Ohio. Public Meeting of the Colore
 Citizens. see Public Meeting of the
 Colored Citizens of Oberlin, Ohio.
Oberlin College. (56415)
Oberlin College. Female Department.
 (56415)
Oberlin Collegiate Institute. see Oberlin
 College.
Oberlin evangelist. 23679
Oberlin: its origin, progress and results.
 23678
Oberlin quarterly review. 56416
Oberlin students' monthly. 56417
Oberlin unmasked. 82430
Obert, L. H. C. 56419
Oberzigt van het ontstaan, de inrigting en
 geloofsleer deser sekte. 9519
Obes, -------- Pacheco y. see Pacheco y
 Obes, --------.
Obi; or, the history of Threefingered Jack.
 56420, 4th note after 95756
Obispo, casada y rey. 24153

Obiter dictum. pseud. Union of the British
  North American provinces considered.
  56421
Obituary. . . . 33625
Obituary address delivered on the occasion
  of the death of the Hon. John C. Calhoun.
  9956
Obituary address on the . . . death of General
  James Hamilton. 30016
Obituary address on . . . the death of Hon-
  Alexander H. Buell. 8978
Obituary addresses delivered on the occasion
  of the death of the Hon. Daniel Putnam
  King. 37793
Obituary addresses; namely, address of Col.
  Crittendon. 56422
Obituary addresses of Messrs. Pomeroy,
  Dixon, and Foster. 42865
Obituray addresses on the . . . death of Hon.
  James M. Clayton. 13577
Obituary addresses on the death of Hon. John
  C. Legrand. 39873
Obituary addresses on the . . . death of the
  Hon. Daniel Webster. 91903
Obituary addresses on the death of the Hon.
  Orlando Kellogg. 37299
Obituary addresses on the . . . death of the
  Hon. Robert H. Morris. 50875
Obituary addresses on . . . the death of the
  Hon. William R. King. (37858)
Obituary addresses on the occasion of the
  death of the Hon. Henry Clay. 13562
Obituary addresses on the occasions of the
  death of the Hon. John A. Quitman, . . .
  and of the Hon. Thomas L. Harris.
  67366
Obituary by Rev. Joshua Leavitt. 2675
Obituary discourse on the occasion of the
  death of Noah Henry Ferry. 16401
Obituary: (from the Journal of Christian
  education.) (59533)
Obituary. Horace Binney Wallace. 5480
Obituary memoir of Robert F. Mott. 8476
Obituary notice. Died, in New Orleans,
  August 23d, Charles Henry Bruce.
  8721
Obituary notice of Dr. William Darlington.
  35713
Obituary notice of . . . George L. Duyckinck,
  Esq. 50690
Obituary notice of Henry D. Gilpin. 34750
Obituary notice of Hon. R. S. Baldwin. 30558
Obituary notice of Joel Jones. 79865
Obituary notice of Mrs. Anna E. Horton.
  33079
Obituary notice of Professor Peck. 59494
Obituary notice of Rev. Francis Anthony
  Matignon. (46861)
Obituary notice of Rev. John Bradford. 28410
Obituary notice of Washington Irving. 16702
Obituary notice of . . . William Parsons.
  68540
Obituary notices and funeral services of James
  Humphrey. 33795
Obituary notices, and other testimonials of
  respect. 104180
Obituary notices and testimonials of respect.
  25012
Obituary notices of Aledander Bryan Johnson.
  36163
Obituary notices of Mrs. Abigail H. Flagg.
  24646
Obituary notices of the late Chief Justice
  Shaw and Judge White. 42077
Obituary notices [of the late . . . Nicholas H.
  Cobbs.] 14034

Obituary notices of the Rev. John Chester,
  D. D. 12535
Obituary notices of Thomas Poynton Ives.
  27649
Obituary of C. P. Frost, M. D. 84908
Obituary of Madame Eliza B. Jumel. (36895)
Obituary of Major N. Baden. (2695)
Obituary of Mrs. Mary P. Clark. 13338
Obituary of the late Maj. Gen. S. G. Hathaway.
  67786
Obituary of the members of the Society of
  Friends in America. 1045, 86029
Obituary record of graduates of Amherst
  College. 1325
Obituary sermon. 41755
Obituary sketch [of Henry Clay.] 13551
Objecciones del Senor Doctor Julian Viso.
  56450
Objeciones satisfactorias del mundo imparcial
  al folleto. 96118
Object and principles of civil government.
  37582
Object of obtaining a war governor. 105402
Object of the ministry. 59362
Object of the southern rebellion and its
  northern allies. 88336
Object, subjects, and methods of the ministry
  at large. 26536
Objections against the Gospel refuted. 18405
Objections against the internal evidences
  answered. 20059
Objections [by Sepulveda.] 11234, 39115
Objections of certain Cherokee Delegates to
  the proposition. (34632)
Objections of Rufus Easton. 21695
Objections raised in the report of the Com-
  mittee of Revolutionary Claims.
  103439
Objections to African colonization stated and
  answered. 32913
Objections to an act to quiet land titles.
  (56423)
Objections to exemption of old fire companies.
  15322
Objections to Mr. Ashley's sermon. 2197
Objections to re-organization of the Department
  of Arts. 60758
Objections to the abolition of the slave trade.
  (67717)
Objections to the act of Congress. (20644)
Objections to the approval by the City Councils.
  61880
Objections to the ballot. 56424
Objections to the bank bill. 60452
Objections to the Bank of Credit lately pro-
  jected at Boston. 21088
Objections to the President's emancipation
  proclamation considered. 2723
Objections to the Rev. Mr. Ashley's sermon.
  (23584)
Objections to the scheme of African coloni-
  zation. 82028
Objections to the taxation of the colonies by
  the Legislature of Great Britain, briefly
  considered. 6218, 25835, 36053, 57865,
  68744
Objections to the treaty. 96754
Objections to the whirlwind theory of storms.
  (68512)
Objections to Unitarian Christianity considered.
  63928
Objections to yielding to northerners the
  control. 2992
Objects a considerer sur un memoire. 8834
Objects and plan of an institute of technology.
  (45867)

Obras, publicadas con notas por Fr. Ramiro de Valenzuela. 86545

Obras q[ue] Francisco Ceruantes de Salazar a hecho, glosado, y, traduzido. 75567

Obras que Francisco Cervantes de Salazar ha hecho, glosado y traducido. 75568

Obras q[ue] Francisco Ceruantes de Salazar ha hecho, glossado, y traduzido. 75567

Obras sueltas de Jose Maria Luis Mora. (50484)

Obras varias posthumas del Doctor Don Juan de Solorzano Pereyra. 86545

Obras varias. Recopilacion de diversos tratados. 86543

Obras varias y posthumas. 86545

Obras y relaciones de Ant. Perez. 60896

Obreen, J. A. 56430

Obregon, Ignacio. ed. 29276

O'Brien, --------, fl. 1844. 61606

O'Brien, Frank P. ed. 91281, 91284

O'Brien, Godfrey S. 56431

O'Brien, J. W. 56433

O'Brien, John. 56432

O'Brien, John G. 61606

O'Brien, Matthew. (80023)

O'Brien, R. B. 42955

O'Brien, Richard. 56434 see also U. S. Consulate. Algiers.

O'Brien, Thomas M. (26892), 56435

O'Brien's Philadelphia wholesale business directory. 61606

O'Brien's Philadelphia wholesale business merchants and manufacturers' directory. 61606

O'Brien's wholesale business intelligencer. 61606

O'Brien's United States advertising circular. 61606

Obrita curiosa. 96118

O'Bryan, Biany. 94039

O'Bryan, William. 56436

O'Bryen, Denis. 49988, 56437, 69535, 80107, (80109)-80110, 90102

O'Bryen, Denis. supposed author 80701, 99585

Obscure individual. pseud. Observations on a late pamphlet. (9280), 56486

Obsequies and obituary notices of the late Right Rev. Benj. Tredwell Onderdonk, D. D. 57310

Obsequies in honor of Andrew Jackson. 18320

Obsequies of Abraham Lincoln, in Newark, N. J. 25828

Obsequies of Abraham Lincoln, in the city of New York. 56439

Obsequies of Abraham Lincoln in Union Square, New York. (56438)

Obsequio que dedica un vecino de esta ciudad. (56440)

Observable things. 46280

Observacion critico-legal que servira de contestacion. (12848)

Observacion sagrada, cronologica e historica. (75771)

Observaciones a la carta que en 25 del ultimo Julio dirigio. 56441

Observaciones a un parrafo de la esposicion que hizo. 56442

Observaciones acerca de la intervencion Europa en Mejico. 74178

Observaciones acerca de la virtud de las aguas de Madruga. 105729

Observaciones al dictamen. 56443

Observaciones astronomicas hechas en el Observatorio Nacional. (49831)

Observaciones astronomicas y fisicas y operaciones trigonometricas. 73450

Observaciones astronomicas, y phisicas hechas de orden de S. Mag. 36808-36809, 36812, note before 97683, 2d and 4th notes after 97689

Observaciones criticas sobre la obra. 99656

Observaciones critico-apologeticas sobre la respuesta satisfactoria. (40063)-40064

Observaciones de los del Hon. Congreso de Zacatecas. (29023)

Observaciones de Regon contra los tratados de paz. 56444, 68932

Observaciones del Cabildo Metropolitano de Mexico. 48604

Observaciones del diputado saliente Manuel Crecencio Rejon. 69161

Observaciones del lic. Juan Ne-Promuoceno Rodrigues de San Miguel. 72548

Observaciones del M. C. Regon. 56444, 68932

Observaciones del Obispo y Cabildo de la Puebla de los Angeles. (56445)

Observaciones del Pensador Mexicano. (40136)

Observaciones, descripciones y demas trabajos cientificos. (26589)

Observaciones generales sobre el estableci-miento de caminos de hierro. 56446

Observaciones generales sobre la emigracion. 14698

Observaciones hechas al documento n° 4 de la memoria, 67646

Observaciones hechas por varios Yucatecos. 106224

Observaciones historico-canonicas. 56447

Observaciones magneticas y meteorologicas. 29445

Observaciones meteorologicas correspondientes al ano de 1862. (41667)

Observaciones. Pensamientos de antiguos labradores Venezolanos. 98880

Observaciones politicas por D. Jose Antonio Miralla. 49407

Observaciones politico-legales. 56448

Observaciones por un oficial del egercito Norte-Americano. 56449

Observaciones que a la humilde porcion del pueblo dirige. 98806

Observaciones que acera de algunas medidas encamin. 40901

Observaciones que el Arzobispo de Caracas hace. 98881

Observaciones que el Arzobispo de Caracas hace el Ejecutivo Nacional. 56450

Observaciones que el Obispo y Cabildo de la Santa Iglesia Catedral. 66567

Observaciones que el Pensador Mexicano hace. 41665

Observaciones que en 19 del ultimo Octubre hizo un Yucateco. 34413, 98624

Observaciones que hace el ejercutivo al proyecto de arancel. 48605

Observaciones que hace la Iglesia Catedral del Estado de Chiapa. 12615

Observaciones que hace la Iglesia Catedral del Estado de Chiapis acerca del dictamen. 56451

Observaciones que hace un patriota a la carta de un Mazon. 56452

Observaciones que hizo un Yucatano. 56453

Observaciones que sobre el proyecto de bases organicas hacen. 56454

Observaciones relativas a la pacificacion de Yucatan. 34413, 98624, 106224

Observaciones sobre el acuerdo de la Camara de Senadores. 98823

Observaciones sobre el clima de Lima. 97719

Observaciones sobre el comercio de la Nueva Granada. (56455)

Observaciones sobre el concordato de Venezuela. (81131)

Observaciones sobre el estanco de tabaco. 106223

Observaciones sobre la carta inserta en el registro oficial. (72279)

Observaciones sobre la convocatoria para el nombramiento de electores. (72258)

Observaciones sobre la defensa de la provincia de Buenos-Aires. 983

Observaciones sobre la esclavitud en la isla de Cuba. (57189)

Observaciones sobre la memoria del Senor Onis. 25149

Observaciones sobre la minera de la Nueva Granada. 56456

Observaciones sobre las inciativas que han dirigido. 106223

Observaciones sobre las instrucciones que dio el Presidente. 56524, 63695, 63697, 88939, 97913, 97925

Observaciones sobre las memorias postumas. 38701

Observaciones sobre las proclamas. 100849

Observaciones sobre las reformas politicas de Colombia. 75575

Observaciones sobre los apuntes para la Honorable Comision de Hacienda. 87256

Observaciones sobre reforma eclesiastica. 11719

Observaciones sobre un informe que dio. 67326, 73086

Observaciones sobre varios puntos concern-iento a la administracion publica. 73174

Observaciones y commentarios a la carta. 59294

Observacoes acerca de epidemia da febre amarella. 38690

Observacoes acerca de uma passagem da oracao funebre. 81103

Observacoes medicas. 79073

Observacoes sobre a carta constitucional. 7611

Observacoes sobre a carta que os membros de Junta do Porto dirigiram. 57196

Observacoes sobre o commercio Franco no Brasil. 41414

Observador. pseud. Impugnacion a la requesta dada al mensage del gobierno. 9016

Observador. pseud. Inquisicion se quito. see V., J. pseud.

Observador. pseud. Padre nuestro consti-tucional. see V., J. pseud.

Observador. pseud.. Publico no es juguete. see V., J. pseud.

Observador catolico. 56457

Observador de la republica Megicana. 98899

Observador de la republica Mexicana, periodico semanario. 56458

Observador ecclesiastico en Chile. 56459

Observador en Londres. pseud. 94864

Observador judicial y de legislacion. 48606

Observador judicial ye de legislacion. Editores. (22043)

Observador Portuguez historico e politico de Lisboa. 56460

Observanda. 46436

Observant citizen of the District of Columbia. pseud. Republican crisis. 70028

Observateur. pseud. Rougisme en Canada. see Huot, L. H.

Observateur Anglais ou correspondence secret 62695

Observateur, ci-devant la bibliotheque Canadienne. 5207

Observateur de bon sens, amie de la justice et de la verite, temoin de tous les evenemens. pseud. Veritables causes. 98976

Observatuer des colonies. 10754

Observateur philosophe. pseud. Question du droit de gens. see Billaud-Varennes, Jacques Nicolas.

Observateur resident sur les leiux. pseud. Vue de la colonie Espagnole du Mississipi. see Berquin-Duvallon, -----.

Observatio historica de Frisonum navigatione. 11366

Observation. 60450

Observation de l'eclipse de soleil. 97688

Observation on the air, soil, and waters. 11508

Observation on the tariff. 8801

Observationes super morbis Surinamensium. 77768

Observations a la Convention Nationale. 10103, (75171)

Observations about the fair at Meadville. 89271

Observations afloat and on shore. 42818

Observations and advices for the improvemen 31736

Observations and annotations upon the Apological narration. 56461

Observations and answers to those letters. 98562

Observations and closer remarks on Commod Johnstone's letter. 36396

Observations and conjectures on the earthqua of New-England. 104351

Observations and correspondence relative to various ornaments. (22548)

Observations and discoveries in the north of America. 82821

Observations, and discoueries, of Captain Iohn Smith. 82819-82820

Observations and documents relative to a calumny. 29765

Observations and reflections, on an act. 56462, note after 63734

Observations and reflections on the penitentia system. 2590

Observations and reflections upon what would probably be the consequences of an abolition of the slave trade. 4248

Observations and remarks, intended for the consideration of Friends. 5245

Observations and remarks made during the voyage. 50985

Observations and remarks on the putrid malignant sore throat. 35412

Observations and remarks upon the state of our controversy with Great Britain. 56463, 86760-86761

Observations arising from an enquiry into the nature of the vases. (64828)

Observations arising from the declaration of war against Spain. 56464, (69686)

Observations as to the importance of the River St. Lawrence. 8859

Observations as well historical as theological.
46603

Observations astronomical. 49749

Observations astronomiques et physiques.
71110

Observations at Springfield, Massachusetts.
89868

Observations at the magnetic and meteorological observatory. (56465)

Observations at the Ohio White Sulphyr, in
1858. 50468

Observations between Kergulen Island and
Van Dieman Island. (74701)

Observations by Jonathan Edwards when a
boy. 85210

Observations chronometriques et theorie
nouvelle. 21216

Observations communicated to the English
Royal Society. 79124

Observations concerning indigo and cochineal.
(56466), 87904

Observations concerning the canal bridge.
6601

Observations concerning the causes of the
magnificency and opulency of cities.
67577-67584, 67598

Observations concerning the funding system
of Pennsylvania. (56467)

Observations concerning the increase of
mankind. 13470-13471, (35450)

Observations concerning the royal navy and
sea-service. 67598

Observations concerning the scriptural
oeconomy. 85222

Observations critiques et politiques. 56468

Observations critiques sur le chapitre XIII.
51734

Observations critiques sur le poem de M.
Joel Barlow. 28734

Observations critiques sur l'ecrit intitule
Christophe Colombe. 7980

Observations critiques sur les nouvelles
decouvertes. 71876

Observations curieuses du philosophe La
Douceur. 1292

Observations curieuses sur les moeurs et
les coutumes. (24111)

Observations de la Societe Correspondante
des Colons Francais. 85789

Observations de l'Hon. D. B. Viger. 93177,
99598

Observations de M. de Cocherel, depute de
Saint Domingue. 14053

Observations de M. de Cocherel . . . sur le
memoire. 14054

Observations de M^{rs} de l'Academie Royale
des Sciences. 38483

Observations des Commissaires du Commerce
de la Martinique. 56471

Observations des negocians de Bordeaux.
56472

Observations des syndics de la Chambre de
Commerce de Normandie. 56473

Observations divine and morall. 72096-72097,
72104-(72105)

Observations du pendule. 25916

Observations d'un Americian des isles
neutres. 43890

Observations d'un Americain sur les ouvrages
de M. de Pradt. (64903)

Observations d'un catholique sur l'histoire du
Canada. 43858, 84701, 99776

Observations d'un citoyen de la Plata.
(56469)

Observations d'un habitant des colonies.
(17167), (28732)-(28733)

Observations d'un homme impartial. 56095,
56470, (62991)

Observations d'un membre des Etats Unis de
l'Amerique. 1288A, note before
99759

Observations en amelioration des lois des
chemins. 99599

Observations envoyees par les Ministers [sic]
d'Angleterre. (41650), (46511), 68283-
68284, note after 80055, 101710

Observations & additions du traducteur.
10912

Observations et des notes par Z. Macaulay.
81955

Observations et details sur la collection des
grandes & des petits voyages. (8784),
73435

Observations et impressions recueillies
pendant deux ans et demi. 77268

Observations et notions curieuses propres a
interesser toutes les personnes.
(11020)

Observations faites pendant le second voyage
du Capitaine Cook. (25141)

Observations faites sur ce detret par
l'Assemblee Provinciale du Nord.
75096

Observations faites sur les lieux. 73522

Observations for the improvement of the road
laws in force. 99600

Observations, . . . for the peculiar benefit
. . . of all British African and West-
India merchants. (64566)

Observations from a gentleman in town.
56474

Observations from Amsterdam. 78187

Observations from the law of nature and
nations. 56475

Observations generales et impartiales. 56476

Observations generales sur le commerce.
(26416)

Observations generales sur les maladies des
climats chauds. 56477

Observations geographiques sur le present
voyage. 66882

Observations, historical and practical.
(25399)

Observations, historical, geographical and
descriptive. (32528)

Observations, historical, geographical, . . . on
Texas. 57348

Observations historiques sur les voyages.
75417

Observations impartiales d'un vrai Hollandois.
(56478), 2d note after 93480

Observations impartiales sur les troubles de
Saint-Domingue. 5815

Observations in a letter from a gentleman of
the bar. (60283)

Observations, in answer to an "Address to the
clergy of the established church."
52268, (56479)

Observations in hospitals in Shenandoah Valley.
(30472)

Observations in opposition to the project. 869

Observations in relation to a communication.
50770

Observations in the north. 63876

Observations in Virginia. 49438

Observations introductory to reading the
declaration of independence. 62659

Observations leading to a fair examination of
the system of government. (39783)-
39784

Observations made at the Magnetic Observatories of Toronto. 74709

Observations made at the Magnetical and Meteorological Observatory at Hobarton. 74711

Observations made at the Magnetical and Meteorological Observatory at Toronto. 74710

Observations made by the Judges of the Court of Common Pleas. 66990, 67007

Observations made during a voyage round the world. 25140

Observations made in England in the year 1836. (78837)

Observations made in Greenland. (72186)

Observations made in the late voyage. 69478

Observations made on a tour from Bengal to Persia. (59572), 62957

Observations made on board Her Majesty's Ships Erebus and Terror. 74702

Observations made upon the Virginian nutts. 56480, 86678, 2d note after 100527A

Observations magnetiques. 98298

Observations meteorologiques. 98298

Observations moral and religious. 65076

Observations nautiques, meteorologiques, hydrographiques et de physique. 21210

Observations occasion'd by reading a pamphlet. 20721, 56481, 84538

Observations, occasioned by the attempts made in England. 25479

Observations occasioned by the stamp act. 56482

Observations occasioned by writings against alterations. 56483

Observations of a 'Member of convention.' 52933

Observations of a person of eminence and worth in Caledonia. 59137

Observations of a Tuscarora-chief. 89175

Observations of an American upon the works of M. de Pradt. 64904, note after 88938

Observations [oc Colonel Vallancey.] (42105)

Observations of Denys Rolle. 92223

Observations of Fernan Mendez Pinto. 66686

Observations of Governor T. B. Robertson on a pamphlet. (71971)

Observations of Lieut. Gen. Sir William Howe, on a pamphlet. 23499, 26429, 26443, note after 102651

Observations of life and manners. (4788)

Observations of M. Garran-Coulon. 75135

Observations [of Mr. Coust.] 91842

Observations of Mr. Dickerson, of New Jersey. 20019

Observations [of Samuel Hemphill.] 31293, 31297, (36017)

Observations of Senator Douglas on popular sovereignty. (81907)

Observations of Sir Richard Havvkins Knight. 30957

Observations of Sir Richard Hawkins K^{nt}. 30958

Observations of the author by the way. 6861, 6292

Observations [of the Bishop of Strasbourg.] 92645

Observations of the currents. 11030

Observations of the dispensing power of the Legislature. 12699

Observations of the merchants at Boston, in New-England. 6536

Observations of the physical geography and geology. 5810

Observations of the separate traders. 73757

Observations of the several members of the court. 64131

Observations [of Thomas Noxon.] 93809

Observations of two respectable writers. 96582

Observations on a "Bill for uniting the Legislative Councils." 92651

Observations on . . . "A dialogue on the actual state of Parliament." 56508

Observations on a direct exportation of sugar 56484

Observations on a Guinea voyage. 90175

Observations on a late epitaph, in a letter. 56485, (60284)

Observations on a late pamphlet, entituled, 'Considerations upon the Society or Order of the Cincinnati." 9279-(9280), 56486

Observations on a late pamphlet, entituled, The quaker unmask'd. (66993)

Observations on a late pamphlet, intituled, Considerations on the American trace. 97095

Observations on a late publication, entitled "The present state of the nation." 9294

Observations on a late publication, intituled, Thoughts on executive justice. 56487, 73061

Observations on a late scandalous paper. 90621

Observations, on a letter from George Nicholas. (55167)

Observations on a letter from James Stuart. 99597

Observations on a letter from Noah Webster. (56489)

Observations on a libel which has been tracte to a foreign ambassador. 23088

Observations on the living and effectual testimony against slavery. 35082

Observations on a new pamphlet, intituled A brief view. 33694

Observations on a pamphlet, entitled, A short history of opposition. (56490)

Observations on a pamphlet, entitled A state of the present form of government. 56491

Observations on a pamphlet, entitled, "A vindication of Mr. Randolph's resignation." (13896), 67817-67818, 1st note after 99797

Observations on a pamphlet, entitled, "Brief examination of scripture testimony." 40799

Observations on a pamphlet, entitled "Considerations on the Order of Cincinnati." (9280), (78988)

Observations on a pamphlet, entitled "Remark on Dr. Gale's Letter to J. W." 21587, 26351-26352

Observations on a pamphlet, entitled "Remark on the seventh annual report of the Hon. Horace Mann." 22429, 44324

Observations on a pamphlet, entitled "Slavery not forbidden by scripture." 74206

Observations on a pamphlet, entitled, "The political progress of Britain." 13875

Observations on a pamphlet, entitled, Thoughts on the cause of the present discontents. 9303, 42946, 95692

Observations on the diseases which appeared in the army of St. Lucia. 72869

Observations on the diseases which prevailed on board a part of His Majesty's Squadron. 27395

Observations on the dispatch written the 16th. January 1797. 94304

Observations on the dispute between the United States and France, addressed by Robert Goodloe Harper, Esq. one of the delegates of South Carolina. (30432), 30443, 50020

Observations on the dispute between the United States and France, addressed by Robert Goodloe Harper, Esq. one of the representatives in Congress. 30433-30436, 30443, 50020

Observations on the dispute between the United States and France, addressed by Robert Goodloe Harper, of South Carolina. (30431), 30443, 50020

Observations on the distinguishing views and practices. (29314)

Observations on the disturbances in Canada. 28018

Observations on the doctrines, and uncharitableness, &c. of the Rev. Mr. Jonathan Parsons. 97318

Observations on the doctrines, and uncharitableness of Rev. Jonathan Parsons. 58892

Observations on the Dutch manifesto. (56516)

Observations on the duties of a physician. 74208, (74226)

Observations on the dysentery of the West Indies. 51047

Observations on the effect of Californian and Australian gold. 43492, 56517

Observations on the effect of high duties. (57113), note after 104805

Observations on the emigration of Dr. Joseph Priestley. 13899, (65512)

Observations on the epidemic now prevailing in the city of New-York. 105993

Observations on the epidemic of 1819. (68658)

Observations on the epidemic yellow fever of Natchez. (49967)

Observations on the establishment of the College of Physicians and Surgeons. 33089

Observations on the evidence adduced against the bill. 4166

Observations on the evidence given before the Committee of the Privy Council. 67744

Observations on the excise bill. (56518)

Observations on the existing differences between the government of Spain and the United States. (56519), 99314

Observations on the existing difficulties between Spain and the United States. (56519), 99314

Observations on the fift [sic] article of the treaty with America. 26437

Observations on the finances of Massachusetts. 45927

Observations on the finances of the commonwealth of Massachusetts. 94008

Observations on the financial position and credit. 97058

Observations on the floating ice. 3632

Observations on the Florida Kays, reef, and gulf. 26764

Observations on the fourth and fifth articles of the preliminaries. 83609

Observations on the genus Salamandra. (30393)

Observations on the genus Unio. 39489-39490

Observations on the geography and archaeology of Peru. 89985

Observations on the geology and organic remains. 98579

Observations on the geology, mineralogy, &c. of the Perkiomen Lead Mine. 103061

Observations on the geology of North America. 18210

Observations on the geology of southern New Brunswick. 2743

Observations on the geology of the United States of America. (43552)

Observations on the geology of the West India islands. 43553

Observations on the government and laws of the United States of America. 42924

Observations on the government of the Indians. 40830

Observations on the government, trade, fisheries, and agriculture of Newfoundland. 56520

Observations on the herb 'Cassing.' 44639

Observations on the history of Virginia. 33928

Observations on the hurricanes and storms of the West Indies. (68512)

Observations on the importance of improving the navigation of the River Schuylkill. 21002, 56521, 93538

Observations on the importance of the American revolution. 49393-49394, 49402, 65449-65450, 97457

Observations on the importance of the British North American colonies. 2262

Observations on the importance of the northern colonies. 37393

Observations on the importance of the present life. 51261

Observations on the impressment of American seamen. 56522

Observations on the improvement of seminaries of learning. 36334

Observations on the improvements of the city of New York. 33835

Observations on the increase of mankind. 56523

Observations on the inflammatory endemic. 20064

Observations on the inhabitants. 3868

Observations on the inslaving, importing and purchasing of Negroes. 4676

Observations on the inslaving of Negroes. 8192

Observations on the insolent and seditious notes. 14004

Observations on the Institution for Blind Persons. 25821

Observations on the instruction of blind persons. 60339

Observations on the instructions given by the President of the United States of America. 48580, 56524, 63694, 88939, 97925

Observations on the intended application of the North-American Coal & Mining Company. (14280), 55545

Observations on the intended establishment of a naval arsenal. 56525

Observations on the isthmus of Panama. 56526

Observations on the isthmus of Panama, and on the hospitals of Havana. (33035)

Observations on the justificative memorial of the Court of London. 27282-27283, 68124

Observations on the kingdom of peace. 56527

Observations on the lake fevers and other diseases. 42648

Observations on the trial of William Parkonson. 58795

Observations on the tussac grass of the Falkland Islands. 32866

Observations on "the two sons of oil." (24361), 105669

Observations on the union of the Canadas. (10533)

Observations on the uses of the mounds of the west. 89986

Observations on the voyage of William Dunbar and Dr. Hunter. 40827

Observations on the war. (45471)

Observations on the West India Company bill. 56572, note after 102774

Observations on the West India Dock charter. 44707, 102780

Observations on the West India Dock salaries. 102779

Observations on the West Indian fever. 24374

Observations on the western trade. (28321)

Observations on the whale-fishery. 56573

Observations on the Wisconsin Territory. 84865

Observations on the writings of Thomas Jefferson. 39751

Observations on their natural state. 11509

Observations on their proceedings against the Rev. Mr. Hemphill. 31297, 2d note after 99826

Observations on trade. (5459)

Observations on two campaigns against the Cherokee Indians. 12469

Observations on waters surrounding the city of New York. (29540)

Observations on yellow fever. 101528

Observations par le corsaire l'Esperance. (56574)

Observations [par Adolphe Jollivet.] 96071

Observations, par M. Sully Brunet. 93570

Observations personnelles a l'intendant de Saint Domingue. 3311A

Observations, presentees a l'Assemblee de M.M. les electeurs de la partie du nord de Saint Domingue. 83461

Observations, presentees a l'Assemblee de M.M. les electeurs de la partie du nord de Saint-Dominique. 2691

Observations qu'il a publiees contre les lettres a un gentilhomme. (33339)

Observations, reasons and facts, disproving importation. (72886)

Observations relating to the foreign mining associations. 64812

Observations relative to the execution of Major John Andre. 95153

Observations relative to Negro slaves in the British West India Islands. 2345A

Observations relative to the establishment of the West India Agricultural Company. 102769

Observations relative to the manufacture of paper. 60286, 61925

Observations relative to the North-West Company of Montreal. 20702

Observations relatives au plan de l'establissement d'une colonie. 56575

Observations respecting the Chesapeake and Delaware Canal. 12496

Observations respecting the propriety of facing a central and inland situation. 50697, 56576

Observations sent by the English ministry to the courts of Europe. 15205, 17365, 47512, 101710, 105205

Observations, showing the great esteem had for the Royal African Company. 56577

Observations sommaires et preuves sur le navire le New-Jersey. 56578

Observations sommaires sur le "pour et le contre." 21034, 56579

Observations suggested by the late occurrence in Charleston. 87906

Observations sur la carte de l'Isle de Saint-Domingue. 75172

Observations sur la conduite du Ministre de Portugal. 63915

Observations sur la constitution du Bas-Canad (38449)

Observations sur la depeche ecrite le 16 Janvier 1797. 94305

Observations sur la famille des Rutacess. 75235

Observations sur la fievre jaune. 39605

Observations sur la memoire presente aux Etats-General. 65049

Observations sur la multiplication des bestiaux (29184)

Observations sur la nature de la liberte civile (65453)

Observations sur la prise du navire Americain la Juliana. (40130)

Observations sur la refraction. 39276

Observations sur la reponse de Mathieu, Lord Aylmer. (10535)

Observations sur la situation actuelle de l'ile de la Trinite. 9399

Observations sur la situation politique de Saint-Domingue. 63999

Observations sur la societe, les moeurs, en 1818-1820. 18642, note after 105597

Observations sur la structure primitive du corps animal. 24988

Observations sur la synonymie des coquilles bivalves. 24201

Observations sur la Virginie. (35895), 2d note after 100506

Observations sur l'acte de la 31e annee du regne de George III. 31337

Observations sur l'acte de navigation et de pieces justificatives. (75532)

Observations sur l'administration et le commerce des colonies Francaises. (18150)

Observations sur la brochure de M.M. les Abbes Laverdiere et Casgrain. 20892

Observations sur le commerce des Etats-Unis d'Amerique. 32638, 67693

Observations sur le deuxieme memoire du Sieur Roume. 2931

Observations sur le genre appele Dufoures par M.M. Willdenow et Bory de Saint-Vincent 75235

Observations sur le gouvernement et les loix des Etats-Unis. 42923, 47206

Observations sur le Memoire justificatif de la Cour de Londres. 4182, 27282-27283, 56580, 68123-68124

Observations sur le plan d'acte de Parlement. 10534

Observations sur le principe qui a produit les revolutions. 35261

Observations sur le projet de loi concernant l'etat des personnes libres. (38472)

Observations sur le projet du changement des tenures dans cette province. 4269

Observations sur le rapport du citoyen Dornie 58164

Observations sur le rapport et projet de decret. 75173

Observations upon the cause of the malignant bilious, or yellow fever. 74231

Observations upon the conduct and behavior of a certain sect. 103498

Observations upon the conduct of S—r W——m H————e. 26438, (46918)

Observations upon the congregational plan of church government. 56586

Observations upon the cranial forms of the American aborigines. (47391)

Observations upon the dispensing power of the legislature. 12699, note after 98561

Observations upon the doctrine, lately advanced. (56587)

Observations upon the downfall of the papal power. 17434

Observations upon the duties and emoluments of certain public offices. 56588

Observations upon the effects of certain late political suggestions. 101211

Observations upon the fall of Anti-Christ. 17434

Observations upon the Floridas. 99607-99608

Observations upon the government and laws of Connecticut. (73132)

Observations upon the government and resources of the republic of Mexico. 4169

Observations upon the government of the United States of America. 22639, 2d note after 88111, 93501

Observations upon the importance of the North American colonies. 29897

Observations upon the late proceedings of the House of Assembly. 1976

Observations upon the liturgy. 38183

Observationsupon the manifesto of His Catholic Majesty. (56589)

Observations upon the memorial and report of the citizens of Boston. (56590)

Observations upon the mines and mining associations. 57516

Observations upon the nature and cure of the gout. 74228

Observations upon the nature, and number, and the operations of the devisl. (46604)

Observations upon the oligarch. 56591

Observations upon the present government of Pennsylvania. 56592, (74232)-74233

Observations upon the present state of the clergy. 95171, 95173

Observations upon the report made by the Board of Trade. 28760

Observations upon the revolution in France. 17434

Observations upon the state of Negro slavery. 56593, 102853

Observations upon the state of the clergy of New-England. 93506, 95173

Observations upon the treaty between the crowns of Great-Britain, France, and Spain. 80700, 101147, 101167

Observations upon the treaty of Washington. 23962

Observations within the Antarctic Circle in the summer of 1840, 1841. (74701)

Observations within the Antarctic Circle, made on board Her Majesty's Ships Erebus and Terror. (74701)

Observator. pseud. Observator's trip to America. 56596, 67997

Observator. pseud. Thoughts on the increasing wealth. see Blodget, Samuel.

Observator, Charles. pseud. Life and reflections. see Sabin, Elijah R.

Observator observed. 56595

Observatorio fisico-meteorico de la Habana. 29445

Observator's trip to America. 56596, 67997

Observazione sur ragionamiento del primo scopritore. 51760

Observer. pseud. see Wilkes, John, 1727-1797.

Observer. pseud. Case of Dr. Bullions fairly stated. see Stark, Andrew.

Observer. pseud. Constitution amended. (53622)

Observer. pseud. Enquiry into the present system. see McNaughton, J.

Observer. pseud. Few thoughts on the hard times. 24245

Observer. pseud. Greenbacks. (56598)

Observer. pseud. Inquiry into the necessity and general principles. 56599

Observer. pseud. Letter to the Associate Presbytery, of Cambridge. see Stark, Andrew.

Observer. pseud. Meteorological sketches. see Redfield, W. C.

Observer. pseud. Observations on canal navigation. 22748, (56600)

Observer. pseud. Our Schuylkill County coal interests. 78075

Observer. pseud. Plain statement. (63233)

Observer. pseud. Remarks on the moral and religious character. (56601)

Observer. pseud. Review of address in respect to a late ordination. (56602)

Observer. pseud. Review of the trade and commerce of New York. 70274

Observer. pseud. Sketches of domestic life. 81557

Observer. pseud. True and faithful history. see Stark, Andrew.

Observer. pseud. Twelve letters to young men. see Young, W. supposed author

Observer. pseud. Two concluding articles of an observer. see Whitney, Reuben M. supposed author

Observer, Northport, Ala. Carrier. pseud. Carrier's address. see Smith, William Russell, 1815-1896.

Observer, Tuscalossa, Ala. see Tuscalossa Observer.

Observer and repository of original and select essays. (56604)

Observer observed. 56595

Observer of the dispute. pseud. Rules of trial. 74113

Observer trying the great reformation in this state. 95382

Observer's guide. 22057, 40744

Obstacles and encouragements. 90911

Obstacles and objections to the cause of permanent and universal peace. 56605

Obstacles to the greater success of common schools. 55782

Obstacles to the truth. 76988

Obstructions to the navigation of Hudson's River. 74496

Obstsorten Brasiliens. 9345

O'Byrne, John. 56606

Obyrne, William R. 56607

Oca, -------- Montes de. see Montes de Oca, -------.

Oca, Ignacio Montes de. see Montes de Oca, Ignacio.

Oca, J. J. Montes de. see Montes de Oca, J. J.

Oca, J. Montes de. see Montes de Oca, J.

Oca, Juan Evanjelista Montes de. pseud. Carta de un particular. see Valdes, Rafael.

O'Callaghan, Edmund Bailey, 1797-1880. 6095,
7856, (9253), 20597, (22754), 24582,
36748, 36764, 36766, 38679-38682,
51355, 53554, 53647, 53653, (53682),
53727, 54476, 55280, 56609-56615,
(56665), 61280, 69245, note after 69259,
69268-69269, 69741, (73448), 74124,
74126, 74129, note after 98476, 1st-2d
notes after 98997, note after 99310,
99573, 102920, 102983, 104441, 104442,
104994
O'Callaghan, Jeremiah. 56616
Ocampo, Andres Sanchez de. see Sanchez
de Ocampo, Andres.
Ocampo, Diego Gomez de. (50496)
Ocampo, Diego Gomez de. petitioner 56617
Ocampo, Florian de, 1499?-1555? (50496),
56618-56621
Ocane, Francis. (56622)
Ocangra aramee wa wa ka ka ra. (56623)
Ocangra prayer-book. (56623)
Ocariz, Jose Volante de. see Volante de
Ocariz, Jose.
Ocariz, Juan Florez de. see Florez de
Ocariz, Juan.
O'Cataract, Jehu. pseud. Battle of Niagara.
see Neal, John, 1793-1876.
Occasion of the publication. 46646
Occasional. 56625
Occasional bill in miniature. 19288, 87911
Occasional discourse . . . before the New
Hampshire Convention of Universalists.
49043
Occasional discourse, delivered soon after
the ordination. 30892
Occasional discourse, . . . in . . . York.
45485
Occasional discourse on the nigger question.
10934
Occasional discourses, including several never
before published. 102185, 102187,
102189-102190
Occasional discourses preached in Boston.
(13424)
Occasional essays. By Samuel Smith. 84009
Occasional essays on various subjects. 45417
Occasional essays on the yellow fever.
(62411)
Occasional letters on taxation. 56626
Occasional meditation on I. Sam. xxiii. 11, 12
(21087)
Occasional notes and observations. 36813,
6th note after 97689
Occasional notes, &c. 96490
Occasional ode, for February, 1800. 101861
Occasional offices of the Protestant Episcopal
Church in the United States. 56627
Occasional pamphlet. 56628
Occasional paper. By Democritus. 7192, note
after 90154
Occasional paper [of the Anglo-American
Church Emigrants' Aid Society.] 1571
Occasional paper [of the British Columbia
Mission.] 8093
Occasional paper [on the instruction and
relief of the freedmen of the south.]
66192
Occasional papers [of the New York Sabbath
Committee.] 93746
Occasional papers on the assiento, and the
affairs of Jamaica. 2229, 35668, 1st
note after 97148, 105079, 105081
Occasional papers. "Two lessons from the
future." 51641
Occasional pieces by Tracy Robinson. 72198
Occasional poem. [By Thomas Paine.] 58200

Occasional poem, written by appointment of
the Society of ΦBK. 31145
Occasional poems. By Thomas Mackellar.
43399
Occasional poems. [By William Shervington.]
83980
Occasional productions, political, diplomatic,
and miscellaneous. 74267
Occasional reflections addressed to the
citizens of the state of New-York.
54002, 92865, note after 99543
Occasional reflections on the importance of the
war in America. 104486
Occasional resolves. (15528), 15544
Occasional reverberator. 56629, 84576
Occasional reviews. 12600, 56630
Occasional sermon, delivered before the
United States General Convention. 11947
Occasional sermons and speeches. 58755
Occasional thoughts, in verse. 22466
Occasional thoughts of a free Briton. 56631
Occasional thoughts on the present German
war. 56632
Occasional writer, numb IV. 86687
Occeana (Brigantine) in Admiralty 47811
Occident, and American Jewish advocate.
56633
Occidentalis res Americae. 33013
Occidentis notitia breui commentario
illustrata. 105697-105698
Occidentis notitia breui commentario illustrata
studio et opera. 105696
Occom, Samson, 1723?-1792. 21971, 56634-
56636, 83414-83415, 83419, 103207
Occultations of the planets and stars by the
moon. 85072
Occultations visible in the United States during
the year 1851. 85072
Occultations visible in the United States during
the year 1852. 85072
Ockum, Samson. see Occom, Samson, 1723?-
1792.
Ocean. 28064
Ocean-born. 27666
Ocean carrier. 83378
Ocean freight rates. 83379
Ocean harp. 65537
Ocean mail service. 14433
Ocean mail steamers. The Sloo contract.
(50980)
Ocean monopoly and commercial suicide.
(3544)
Ocean plague. 56638
Ocean scenes, or, the perils and beauties of
the deep. 56639, (57949)
Ocean steam navigation and the ocean post.
67529
Ocean telegraph. 51271
Ocean telegraph cable, its construction. 73555
Ocean to ocean. 56640
Ocean waifs. 69056
Ocean waves in lyric strains. 77469
Oceanic ichthyology. 85072
Oceanic icthyology. Atlas. 85072
Oceanic Oil and Guano Company. 56641
Oceanic sketches. 55303
Oceanisch-Amerikanische Untersuchungen und
Aufklarungen. 8478
Oceanus (Steamship) Passengers. Committee.
see Cary, Edward. and French,
Justus Clement.
Oceola Nikkanochee. Indian Chief (56642), 1st
note after 102515
Ocoela, ou le grand chef des Seminoles.
69057

Ocho articulas distribuidos en igual numero de cartas. 97043

820 laminas sacadas de los tres reinos de la naturaleza. (51567)

Ocho dias a Dios. (38386)

Ocho los memoriales que a V. M. he presentado. 67353

Ochoa, Antonio Terreros. see Terreros Ochoa, Antonio.

Ochoa, D. Durama de. see Durama de Ochoa, D.

Ochoa, Eugene de. see Ochoa y Ronna, Eugenio de, 1815-1872.

Ochoa, J. 56645

Ochoa, Juan Ingacio de. 56646

Ochoa y Ronna, Eugenio de, 1815-1872. (56643)-56644

Ochs, Johann Rudolff. 56647

Ocios de Espanoles emigrados. 56648

Ocios de un Mexicano. 56649

Ockamickon. an Indian see Ockanickon. an Indian

Ockanickon. an Indian 8952, 17510, 56650, 105218

Ockside, Knight Russ. pseud. History and records of the Elephant Club. see Thomson, Mortimer, 1832-1875. and Underhill, Edward Fitch, 1830-1898.

Ocoee Mining Company. (56651)

Ocon, Juan Roxo Mexia y. see Mexia y Ocon, Juan Roxo.

O'Connell, Daniel, 1775-1847. 12200, 28747, 56652-(56653), 70902, 89204

O'Connell Club, New York. (56654)

O'Connor, --------, fl. 1749. 56657

O'Connor, Condorcet. 15194

O'Connor, Florence J. 56655

O'Connor, J. ed. see O'Connor, Thomas, 1770-1855.

O'Connor, J. D. 56656

O'Connor, Patrick. 94039

O'Connor, Thomas, 1770-1855. (27582), 56658

O'Connor, William Douglas. 56659

O'Conor, Charles, 1804-1884. 13291, 19536, 21782, 33610, 40639, 43617, 56660, 63005, (69090), 70244, 84084

Oconto County, Wisc. Board of Supervisors. 70083

Oct. B. pseud. see D'Exauvillez, Octave Boistel.

Octava carta pastoral que dirige a sus diocesanos. 39284

Octava [junta publica de la Real Sociedad Economica de Guatemala.] 29085

Octava maravilla del nuevo mundo. 24149, 66568

Octave marvilla y sin segundo milagro de Mexico. 11450, 56661

Octavas a la canonizacion de S. Juan de Dios. 86440

Octavas reales en loor del patriarca. 76893

Octavius Brooks Frothingham and the new faith. 91062

Octavo libro [do descobrime[n]to & conquista da India pelos Portugueses.] 11385

October 1, 1847. A catalogue of books. 70887

Oct. 20, 1740. My Lords, ... 95397

Octogenarian. pseud. Origin and end of the irrepressible conflict. 56662

Octogenarian. pseud. Reflections on passing events. see Halliburton, Sir Brenton.

Octogenarian, Ultra. pseud. Opuscula. see Robertson, John

Octogenarian lady of Charleston, S. C. pseud. Olden times in Carolina. see Poyas, Mrs. E. A.

Octogenarian of Philadelphia. pseud. Querist. see Carey, Mathew, 1760-1839.

Octogenarian's birth-day memorial. 92091

Octogenary. pseud. Memories, counsels, and reflections. see Huntington, Daniel.

Octroi of fondamenteele condition. (56663), 93843

Octrooy of condition. 56664

Octroy, by de Hoog Mogende Heeren Staten Generael. (56678), 102902

Octroy, by de Hooge Mog: Heeren Staten Generael. 56674, 102901

Octroy, by de Hooge Moghende Heeren Staten Generael. 56673, 102901

Octroy, by de Hoogh-Mog: Heeren Staten Generael. 56677, 102902

Octroy, by de Hoogh Mog: Heeren Staten Generael, verleent aen de West-Indische Compagnie, in date den twintighsten September. 56676, 102902, 102910

Octroy, by de Hooghe Mogende Heeren Staten Generael. (56665)-56668, 56672-56673, 102901, 102905

Octroy, by de Hooghe Moghende Heeren Staten Generael. 56669-(56671), 102901

Octroy, by de . . . Staten General. 56679, 102902

Octroy convede. 56675

Octroy der Staten Generael der Vereenigde Nederlanden. 56680

Octroy doer de Hoogh Mog Heeren Staten Generael. 16674

Octroy door d'Ed: Geoctr: Societeit van Suriname. 56681, note after 93841

Octroy eller privilegium som then stormechtigste hogborne Furst och Heere. 98202

Octroy for det Kgi. Danske West-Indiske og Guineiske Compagnie. 102934

Octroy oder privilegium, so der allerdurchleuchtigste, grossmechtigste Furst vnd Heer. 98203

Octroy ofte fondamentele condition. 102903

Octroy ofte fondamentele condition, onder de welcke haer Hoogh Mog. ten besten en voordele van de ingezetene deser landen. (56663), 93842

Octroy vnd privilegivm, so der allerdurchleuchtigste, grossmachtigste Furst vnd Herr. 98205

Octroy, van de Hoog: Moog: Heeren Staten Generael. 27126, (56682)

Octroy. 1682. 93834

Kongelige Octroyerde Danske West-Indiske og Guineiske Skibe. see West-Indiske og Guineiske Compagnie.

Oculaire, Temoin. pseud. Origine et progres. see Badin, S. T.

Oculus. psued. Home of the badgers. (56683)

Oculus, Ichabod. pseud. Picolilly. 56684

Ocupacion de San Juan. 76130

Ocursos de los acreedores al ramo de peages del camino de Vera-Cruz. 98901

Ocursos hechos por los acreedores al peage de Veracruz. 98900

Oda [al Iturbide.] 56685

Oda al Jeneral Flores. 56686

Oda de la desventurada cumana. 29058

Oda del Sr. D. Florencio Varela. 98595

Oda en la instalacion de la diputacion provincial de Mejico. 86383

Oda heroica. 97020
Oda patriotica dedicada a los soldados
urbanos. 63975
Oda que en el feliz cumple anos del Exmo.
Senor Virey. 98861
Odagurasse. Indian Chief 628, 66062 see
also Three Maquas Castles (Indians)
Sachems.
O'Daniels, D. C. 56697
Odd-Fellows' casket & review. 56693
Odd Fellows' Cemetery Company, Philadelphia.
see Philadelphia. Odd Fellows' Ceme-
tery Company.
Odd Fellows' Guide, to all encampments.
68827
Odd Fellows, Independent Order of. California.
Library Association of the City of San
Francisco. (76063)
Odd Fellows, Independent Order of. Connecti-
cut. Grand Lodge. 65858
Odd Fellows, Independent Order of. Illinois.
34307
Odd Fellows, Independent Order of. Illinois.
Grand Lodge. 34307
Odd Fellows, Independent Order of. Indiana.
New-Albany Lodge, no. I. (52433)
Odd Fellows, Independent Order of. Maryland.
Baltimore. (56696)
Odd Fellows, Independent Order of. Massa-
chusetts. Grand Lodge. 56692
Odd Fellows, Independent Order of. Massa-
chusetts. Boston. 61289
Odd Fellows, Independent Order of. Massa-
chusetts. Groton Lodge, no. 71. 45771
Odd Fellows, Independent Order of. Massa-
chusetts. Quinohequin Lodge, Jamaica
Plain. 67176
Odd Fellows, Independent Order of. Massa-
chusetts. Siloam Lodge, no. 2, Boston.
(81071)
Odd Fellows, Independent Order of. Massa-
chusetts. Suffolk Lodge, no. 8. 93433
Odd Fellows, Independent Order of. Minnesota.
Grand Lodge. (49255)
Odd Fellows, Independent Order of. New
England. 68827
Odd Fellows, Independent Order of. New
Hampshire. Grand Lodge. 52835
Odd Fellows, Independent Order of. New York.
(53692), 56688
Odd Fellows, Independent Order of. New York.
Grand Encampment of Patriarchs.
(53625)
Odd Fellows, Independent Order of. New
York. Grand Encampment of Patriarchs
of Northern New York, no. 1. 54770
Odd Fellows, Independent Order of. New
York. Grand Encampment of Patriarchs
of Southern New York. 65906
Odd Fellows, Independent Order of. New
York. Grand Lodge. 33861
Odd Fellows, Independent Order of. New
York. Richmondville Lodge no. 446.
71217
Odd Fellows, Independent Order of. Pennsyl-
vania. 60159
Odd Fellows, Independent Order of. Pennsyl-
vania. Grand Encampment. 60160
Odd Fellows, Independent Order of. Pennsyl-
vania. Grand Lodge. 60160
Odd Fellows, Independent Order of. South
Carolina. Grand Lodge. 87907-87909
Odd Fellows, Independent Order of. U. S.
56690, (56696), 87907
Odd Fellows, Independent Order of. U. S.
Grand Encampment. (53692)

Odd Fellows, Independent Order of. U. S.
Grand Lodge. 46689, (56691), (56696),
87907
Odd Fellows, Independent Order of. Wisconsin.
Southport Lodge, no. VII. 88597
Odd Fellows, Independent Order of. Wisconsin.
Union Lodge no. 71, Plymouth. 63497
Odd Fellows' Library Association of the City
of San Francisco. see Odd Fellows,
Independent Order of. California.
Library Association of the City of San
Francisco.
Odd-Fellows' literary magazine. 56694
Odd-fellows' offering. (56695)
Odd-fellowship—what is it? (56696)
Odd Ladies, United Order of Independent. see
United Order of Independent Odd Ladies.
Odd leaves from the life of a Louisiana
"Swamp doctor." 94821-94822
Odd man. pseud. True history of the wild
Methodist. see Abrams, Isaac. supposed
author
Odd man. pseud. Truths come out at last.
see Abrams, Isaac. supposed author
Odd man's experience. 97118, 97273
Odd man's tract. 91815
Odd people. (69053), 69058
Odd volume of facts. 9775
Oddi, Longaro degli. 1374, 56697, 100610
Odds and ends from the knapsack. 56037,
81430
Odds and ends; original and translated. 94040
Ode, H. (43762)
Ode. 41356, 101868
Ode. A copy of verses on Mr. Oglethorpe's
second voyage to Georgia. 27047, note
after 102702
Ode ad Joh. Kinkerum. 38051
Ode; addressed to Lieutenant General G-ge.
63094
Ode; and other poems. 14180
Ode: by Edmond Pillet. 36363
Ode. [By Henry Ware.] 101399
Ode [by Joseph Bartlett.] 3757
Ode by Robert Treat Paine, Jun.. 96374
Ode . . . by Samuel Low. (18865)
Ode [by Thomas Paine.] 47356
Ode, composed for the occasion, at the request
of the [Tammany] Society. 84845
Ode (composed for the occasion, by P.
Freneau.) 101437
Ode contenant vne briefve description du
voyage. 99725
Ode, entitled, The battle of Tippecanoe.
(5895)
Ode for independence, 1793. 104313
Ode for the canal celebration. 105190-1
Ode for the celebration of the battle of Bunker-
Hill. 47440
Ode for the celebration of the Philhermenian
Society. 28582
Ode for the dinner, given, at Boston, March
2, 1813. 77020
Ode for the Federal procession. 56698
Ode for the fourth of July, 1803. 96402
Ode for the new year, 1776. (56699)
Ode, for the thanksgiving day. 56700
Ode for the 23d of October, 1792. 93502
Ode, humbly inscribed to the Rt. Hon. the
Earl of M——F——D. 102041
Ode in celebration of the emancipation of the
blacks. 71243
Ode in commemoration of the first settlement.
56701
Ode, in honor of the champion of our consti-
tutional rights. 84996

Ode, in honour of the Pennsylvania militia, and a small band of regular continental troops. 7185, (56702), note after 101861

Ode in honor of the Pennsylvania militia, and a small band of regular troops. 7185, (56702), note after 101861

Ode, in two parts. 63095

Ode. Inscribed to Bryan Edwards. 94565

Ode made on the welcome news of the safe arrival. 78228

Ode of verses. 103134

Ode on General Washington's birthday. 97086, 101841, 2d note after 101886

Ode on Gen. Wolfe. 60346

Ode on His Majesty's coronation. 27586

Ode on painting. 106371

Ode on peace. 23388, 61547

Ode, on printing. 97631

Ode on science and liberty. 34091

Ode on the accession of His present gracious Majesty. 23376, 61547

Ode on the anniversary of the fifth half century. 92333

Ode on the birth-day of the President of the United States. 101862

Ode on the bones of the im-mortal Thomas Paine. 44803

Ode on the completion of the Erie Canal. 27365

Ode on the death of Abraham Lincoln. 4712

Ode, on the incarnation. 13765, 104301

Ode on the late glorious successes of His Majesty's arms. (23178)

Ode on the new-year, 1753. 84629

Ode on the peace. By the author of Edwin and Elturde. 104227

Ode on the peace: set to musick. 72881-(72882)

Ode on the proclamation of President Jackson. 51770

Ode on the prospect of peace. (56703)

Ode, on the reduction of Louisbourg. 65528, 97745

Ode, on the surrender at York-Town. 56704

Ode; par M. Ch. Roblot. 72256

Ode performed at the First Church of Universalists in Boston. 101863

Ode, performed by the choir of the Boston Academy of Music. 102215

Ode pindarica aos faustissimos recentes successos de Portugal. 88780

Ode. Por Joao Vicente Pimentel Maldonado. 44107

Ode: pronounced before the inhabitants of Boston. 89659

Ode recited at the commemoration of the living and dead soldiers. 42438

Ode saphica. 11456

Ode sapphica em Latin e vulgar. 81301

Ode set to music, oconsecrated to the memory. 56705, 103639

Ode, set to music, sacred to the memory of Dr. Franklin. 84610

Ode suggested by Rembrandt Peale's national portrait of Washington. 56706, note after 101863

Ode, suggested to the author by a late present. 102042

Ode sugn at the celebration of the American independence. 97755

Ode. Sung at the dinner given in Boston. 86955

Ode, sung at the lecture of the Congregational Charitable Society. 93503, 95178

Ode, sung at the thirty-first anniversary of the independence. 95187

Ode sur la conquete de l'Amerique. 40040

Ode sur l'independance d'Haiti. 12882

Ode-symphonie en quatre parties. 48037

Ode to a friend, on our leaving, together, South Carolina. (56707), 1st note after 87909

Ode to be sung at the thirty-first anniversary of the independence. 56710

Ode to Bogle. 5241

Ode to Britannia. 985

Ode to liberty. 4734

Ode to madness. (63893)

Ode to peace. 91608

Ode to peace, occasioned by the present crisis of the British empire. 56708

Ode to science read before the Western Museum Society. (56708)

Ode to the memory of the late Captain James Cook. 24613

Ode to the President of the United States. 101864

Ode to the sun. (79474)-79475

Ode to Thomas Jefferson. 24925, 83790

Ode to war. 42154, 75034

Ode. To which is added, The death of Hilda. 89476

Ode to wisdom. 100663

Ode, written for the celebrarion [sic] of the Republican Young Men. 105620A

Ode written for the twentieth anniversary. 103830

Ode written in the year 1780. 28593

Odell, James. 56711

Odell, Jonathan, 1738-1818. 84602, 90375

Odell, Jonathan, 1738-1818. supposed author 1244, 56713, note after 67117

Odell, Margaretta Matilda. (56712), 103133

Odell's Dayton directory and business adverti-ser. 56711

O'Democrat, Blarney. pseud. Irish-office-hunder-oniad. 35084

Odenheimer, W. H. 56714

Odent, Paul. 92288-92290

Oderahi. 56715

Oderay, usos, trages, ritos, costumbres y leyes. 56716, note after 106282

Odes, and fugitive poetry. 26524

Odes, &c. 28381

Odes of Horace in Cincinnati. (59554), (62740)

Odes, naval songs, and other occasional poems. (32499)

Odes set to music. 32675

Odes, songs, &c. 70917

Odes, suivies d'une lettre sur l'esclavage des Negres. 16803

Odes sung . . . February 22d, 1800. 70915

Odes, to be performed at the commencement of Union College. 56717

Odes to be sung at the Juvenile Patriotic Festival. 56718

Odes to Lord Howe. 100757

Odes: written by Re. Thomas C. Upham. 98050

Odescalchi, Benedetto. see Innocent XI, Pope, 1611-1689.

Odescalchi, Carlos. 56719

Odet-Pellion, -------. (56720)

Odiorne, James C. petitioner 89644

Odiorne, Thomas. 56722

Odizhijigeuiniua igui Gaanoninjig. 56723

Odlin, John, 1681-1754. 56724, 72616

Odlin, Woodbridge. 72616

Odlum, John. (56725)

Odofrieded, the outcast. 36828

O'Doherty, Sir Morgan. pseud. Reply to the libel. 56726

Odolant-Desnos, Pierre Joseph, ed. 88695

O'Donnel, Kane. 56727
O'Donnell, ---------, fl. 1866. 56728
O'Donoju, Juan. (56729)-56730
Odorico da Pordenone, 1286-1331. (67737)
Odorico da Udine. Beato see Odorico da
    Pordenone, 1286-1331.
Odriozola, Manuel de. (56731), 60804, note
    after 97719, 100850
Odwin, ---------. plaintiff 31398
Odwin vs. Forbes. 31398
Oe keuh maukhkenun pohtum-mouwaus. 79195
Oe taupaunnumeauk pohtum-mauwaus. 79196
Oeconomico Xenophontis. (43766)
Oeconomicum Xenophontis, ab eodem Latio
    donatus. 43768
Oeconomicus Xenophontis, ab eodem Latio
    donatus. 43765, 43767
Oeconomy of human life. 90250-90281,
    90283, 90286, 91846
Oedmann, S. ed. 2d note after 100947
Oedvkanohedv maduuwowelanvhi. 12460
Oehler, Andrew. 56732
Oeil-de-faucon. (16433)
Oeil-de-feu. 4903B
Oelen, A. Janszoon van. 56733
Oelsner-Monmerque. 56734
Oen floor ki J. J. Putnam ta boeta. 66751
Oersted, Anders Sandoe. (56735)
Oertel, Philipp Friedrich. 56736-56738
Oettinger, Edouard Marie. (56739)
Oeuvre des bons livres. (5153)
Oeuvre d'un grand peuple. 58060
Oeuvre posthume de D. D. Mateo Paz Soldan.
    59335
Oeuvres choises . . . comprenant Atala, Rene.
    12262
Oeuvres choisies de M. Eugene Sue. 93411
Oeuvres choisies du Prince Castriotta d'Albanie.
    106251
Oeuvres completes de Chamfort. 11816
Oeuvres completes [de Chateaubriand.] 12257
Oeuvres completes [de Dominique Francois
    Jean Arago.] 1862
Oeuvres completes [de James F. Cooper.]
    16561
Oeuvres completes [de Jouy.] (36769)
Oeuvres completes de Poivre. 63722
Oeuvres completes de William Robertson.
    72013-72014
Oeuvres [de Antoine de Bertin.] 4010
Oeuvres de C. F. Volney. 100692
Oeuvres [de Chamfort.] 11816
Oeuvres . . . de Chateaubriand. (12261)
Oeuvres de Condorcet. 15194
Oeuvres de Don Barthelemi de Las Casas.
    11237, 11276
Oeuvres [de Francois Arago.] 1865
Oeuvres de Humboldt. 33749
Oeuvres de J. F. Cooper. 16560
Oeuvres de J. Law. (39314)
Oeuvres. De l'esclavage. 11916
Oeuvres de M. Franklin. 25607
Oeuvres [de Maupertuis.] 46946
Oeuvres [de Richard Cumberland.] 17876
Oeuvres de Rulhiere. 74116
Oeuvres de Voltaire. 96332
Oeuvres diverses, contenant: catechisme
    d'economie politique. 77361
Oeuvres illustrees d'Eugene Sue. 93409,
    93413, 93417
Oeuvres inedites. 12272
Oeuvres litteraires et economiques d'Aramand
    Carrel. (11041)
Oeuvres melees. (38565)
Oeuvres morales, politiques et litteraires.
    25543

Oeuvres philosophiques. 59240
Oeuvres romantiques de M. le Vicomte de
    Chateaubriand. 12248
Oeuvres sociales de W. E. Channing. 11915
Oexmelin, Alexandre Olivier. see Exquemelin,
    Alexandre Olivier.
Of a war with Spain. 67589
Of a warning to the inhabitants of the said
    province. 60591, 70292
Of America, whether it was then peopled.
    66686
Of Andrew Johnson. 68048
Of being. 85213
Of civil government. (62421), 1st note after
    96964
Of coins. 65678, 103121
Of democracy, mixed monarchy. 8413
Of ecclesiastical power. 67589
Of errors and defects in class-books. 102342
Of errors and obscurities in the common
    version. 102342
Of imposition of hands. 61497
Of mirth and grief. 79385
Of monarchy and hereditary succession.
    58211
Of Negro slavery as it exists in our West
    India colonies. 56740
"Of persecution in New England." 11870
Of plighted faith so truly kept. 92174D
Of population. 27676
Of religious commvnion private, & publique.
    72106, 72110
Of sacred poetry and music. 1857
Of schism. 24401
Of Sturbridge, Bury, and the most famous fairs
    in Europe and America. 23710
Of taking heed to, and fulfilling the ministry.
    40773
Of the advantages which Europe has derived
    from the discovery of America. 82303
Of the alterations in the constitution. 101106
Of the birth and death of nations. (56741)
Of the cause of the yellow fever. 58232
Of the cetaceous animals. 28401, 71032
Of the circumfernace of the earth. 5195,
    61246
Of the circumference of the earth; or, a
    treatise of the northeast passage.
    33389
Of the cleare sun-shine. (56742), (80815)
Of the conversion of five thousand and nine
    hundred East Indians, in the isle
    Formose. (56742), (80815)
Of the conversion of 5900 East-Indians. With
    a post-script. 36923
Of the dominion, or, ownership of the sea.
    (78973)
Of the evidences of religion. 90856
Of the faith of the harmless Christians in
    the Netherlands. 12906
Of the first invention of shipping. (67543),
    67544
Of the glorious progresse of the Gospel
    breaking forth. (80815)
Of the Gospel, as the power of God unto
    salvation. 103464
Of the holiness of church-members. 17073
Of the laws of the United States relating to
    slavery. 93097
Of the making of sugar. 97289
Of the motives for establishing new colonies.
    82303
Of the nature and effects of Negro slavery.
    56743
Of the newe landes. 99365

Of the new la[n]des and of ye people founde
by the messengers of the Kynge of
Portygale named Emanuel. 22406
Of the newe landes and of ye people founde
by the messengers of the Kynge of
Portyngale named Emanuel. note before
99327, 99366
Of the origin and design of government in
general. 58211
Of the original, and fundamental cause of
natural, arbitrary, and civil war. 67589
Of the pastoral care. (46800)
Of the Patagonians. 23735
Of the present ability of America. 58211
Of the progresse of learning, in the Colledge
at Cambridge in Massachusetts Bay.
52758-52759, note before 92757
Of the Quakers of New-England. 97736
Of the taking of the castle of Chagre. 79781
Of the ten tribes of Israel. 56744
Of the truth & excellency of the Gospel.
50406
Of the unpardonable sin against the Holy-Ghost.
74292
Of the various stages of political society.
101106
Of the voyage for Guiana. 67555
Of the vvood called Gvaiacvm. (34096)-
(34097)
O'Fallon, Benjamin. 96639-96646, 96648-
96650 see also U. S. Commissioners
to the Belantse-etoa or Minnetaree
Indians. U. S. Commissioners to the
Crow Indians. U. S. Commissioners to
the Hunkpapa Indians. U. S. Commis-
sioners to the Maha Indians. U. S.
Commissioners to the Mandan Indians.
U. S. Commissioners to the Oto and
Missouri Indians. U. S. Commissioners
to the Pawnee Indians. U. S. Commis-
sioners to the Ponca Indians. U. S.
Commissioners to the Ricawa Indians.
U. S. Commissioners to the Siouan and
Ogalala Indians. U. S. Commissioners
to the Teton, Yancton, and Yanctonie
Indians.
O'Fallon, John. (81524)
O'Fallon Polytechnic Institute, St. Louis.
56745
O'Fallon Polytechnic Institute; its objects and
present condition. 56745
O'Farill, Joseph Ricardo. 56746-56747
O'Farrill, Gonz. (2529)
Ofensa, y defensa de la libertad eclesiastica.
56748
Off for Mexico. 84849
Off-hand sketches. 8225, 56749
Off-hand takings. (9162)
Offenbarung aller Geheimnisse, Seremonien,
Eides-formeln, Hangriffe und Sinnbilder
der dry ersten Grade. 36660
Offener Brief an die Redactionen der Deutschen
Tagespresse. 25425
Offentliche Bauwerke in den Vereinigten-Staaten
von Amerika. 64733
Offer of considerations for the tribe of Zebulun.
(46494)
Offer of disputation on fourteen proposalls.
104337
Offerendas pastoris. 98709
Offering and tribute of thanksgiving. 66664
Offering at the altar of truth. 7306
Offering for all seasons. 23289
Offering, for 1829. 56750
Offering of memorial. 22441

Offering to the owls. 66898
Offering to the Republican Democracy. 37229
Office and authority of a justice of the peace.
102214
Office and authority of a justice of the
peace . . . &c. according to the laws
of . . . North-Carolina. (44874)
Office and authority of a justice of the peace
explained and digested. 90521
Office and duty of sheriffs, under-sheriffs,
and coroners. 56751
Office and duty of the church of God. 83524
Office and function of deacons. 85306
Office and operation of the Holy Spirit
vindicated. 103574
Office and work of a minister of Christ.
82738
Office, duty, and authority of justices of the
peace, high sheriffs, under sheriffs,
coroners, constables, gaolers, jurymen,
and overseers of the poor. 58682
Office, duty and authority of justices of the
peace, high-sheriffs, under-sheriffs,
goalers, coroners, constables, jury-men,
over seers of the poor, and also the
office of clerks of assize. 15215
Office hunter under a religious cloak. (52040)
Office of a bishop. 20391
Office of Discount and Deposit, Baltimore.
see Baltimore. Office of Discount and
Deposit.
Office of Gospel ministers. 72713
Office of induction, adopted by the Bishop and
Clergy of the Diocese of Connecticut.
84693
Office of institution of ministers into parish
churches. 84694-84695
Office of institution of ministers into parishes
or churches. 56752, 66179, 84695
Office of institution of the Rev. Samuel Farma
Jarvis. 35816
Office of Superintendent of Public Schools,
Washington, May 24, 1870. 70977
Office of the Auditor of S. C., Columbia,
December 23, 1864. 87681
Office of the Christian ministry. 34173
Office of the Commissioner of Immigration
for West Virginia. 19085
Office of the ministers of Christ. 92933
Office of the New York and Harlem Rail Road
Company. New York, June 19th, 1840.
(54732)
Office of the Supervising Architect. 56753
Office of the Western Kansas Immigration
Society. (37074)
Office Southern Telegraph Companies. 88503
Officer. pseud. Annals of the Army of the
Cumberland. see Fitch, John.
Officer. pseud. Authentic journal of the
siege of the Havana. 2450
Officer. pseud. Brief observations on the
militia. 53548
Officer. pseud. Impartial sketch. (34384)
Officer. pseud. Journal of an officer during
the siege of Fort Detroit. 36704
Officer. pseud. Journal of the principal
occurrences. 80734
Officer. pseud. Miscellanies. see Depeyster
Arent Schuyler.
Officer. pseud. Narrative of an expedition
to, and the storming of Buenos Ayres.
9026, 51805
Officer. pseud. Naval monitor. (52080)
Officer. pseud. Our cruise in the Con-
federate States War Steamer Alabama.
57916

Officer. pseud. Refutation of the latter to
an Honble Brigadier-General. see
Thurlow, ------------. supposed
author

Officer. pseud. Short account of the naval
actions of the last war. 80589

Officer. pseud. Six plans of the different
dispositions of the English army. 7212

Officer. pseud. Sketch of the 126th Regiment
Pennsylvania Volunteers. see Rowe,
D. Watson.

Officer. pseud. Travels through the interior
parts of America. see Anburey,
Thomas.

Officer at Fort Frontenac. pseud. Letter to
the Right Honourable William Pitt, Esq.
40533

Officer at New Orleans. pseud. Present
state of the country and inhabitants.
42283

Officer at New-York. pseud. Letter. 40324

Officer attached to the expedition. pseud.
Concise narrative of the Seminole
campaign. 70966

Officer, employed on the expedition. pseud.
Belleisle. Impartial narrative of the
reduction of Belle-Isle. 4511, 34378

Officer in one of those regiments. pseud.
Expedition of Major General Braddock
to Virginia. 7210, 1st note after
100462

Officer in the army. pseud. History of the
civil war in America. see Hall,
--------. RA

Officer in the army. pseud. Speculative
ideas. 89151

Officer in the army of Wolfe. pseud. Haverhill. see Jones, James Athearn.

Officer in the British Army. pseud. Letter
to a young officer. see Drewe, Edward.

Officer in the field. pseud. Coming contraband. see Nott, Charles C.

Officer in the late army. pseud. Complete
history of the Marquis de La Fayette.
38569

Officer in the militia of this province. pseud.
104750

Officer in the Royal Navy. pseud. Twenty-
one plans. see Matthews, John.

Officer in the same service. pseud. Memoirs
of a late officer. 47563

Officer in the service of Walker. pseud.
Destiny of Nicaragua. 55146

Officer in the United States Army. pseud.
Notes on Colombia. see Bache,
Richard.

Officer in the U. S. Army. pseud. Soldier's
guide. 86289

Officer in the United States Navy. pseud.
Around the world. see Henshaw,
J. Sidney.

Officer late in the Colombian service. pseud.
Present state of Colombia. (14616)

Officer on Gen. Smith's staff. pseud. Narrative of the battle of Bladensburg. see
McKenney, Thomas L. supposed author
and Parker, Thomas, 1753-1820.
supposed author

Officer of rank. pseud. Plan for the systematic colonization of Canada. 10544

Officer of rank in the Continental Army.
pseud. American invincible. 1024

Officer of Marines. pseud. Letter. 21419

Officer of the Alexander. pseud. Journal of
a voyage of discovery. (36696)

Officer of the army. pseud. Regulations for
the field exercise. see Smyth,
Alexander, 1765-1830.

Officer of the army. pseud. Texas. see
Phillips, Edwin D.

Officer of the Brigade of New York. pseud.
Observations of the militia. 56532

Officer of the Colombian navy. pseud. Recollections of a service of three years.
14582, 14618, 2d note after 98882

Officer of the Commission. pseud. Kansas
in 1856. 37056

Officer of the Confederate States Army.
pseud. Experience of a Confederate
States prisoner. (23408)

Officer of the Corporation. pseud. Notes on
Mount Auburn Cemetery. 51151

Officer of the expedition. pseud. Authentic
narrative of the proceedings. see
Whitelocke, John. supposed author

Officer of the expedition. pseud. Letters
written during the late voyage of discovery. (40658)

Officer of the First Regiment of Ohio
Volunteers. pseud. Sketches of the
campaign. see Giddings, L.

Officer of the "Guard." pseud. Baltimore,
A. D. 1862. 2989

Officer of the line. pseud. Military control.
see Gardner, John L.

Officer of the militia. pseud. Instructions
for the cavalry. see Van Horne,
David.

Officer of the militia. pseud. ed. Soldier's
monitor. 86300, 91465

Officer of the militia of this province. pseud.
104753

Officer of the navy. pseud. Reply to Mr.
Urquhart's letters on impressment.
98145

Officer of the Ninth Army Corps. pseud.
Colored troops and military colonies on
southern soil. 14753

Officer of the 9th Army Corps. pseud. Notes
on colored troops and military colonies.
55961

Officer of the Ohio Volunteers. pseud.
Campaign in Northern Mexico. 10189

Officer of the 71st Regiment. pseud. Extaact
[sic] of a letter. 87824

Officer, of the United States Army. pseud.
Cadet life at West Point. see Strong,
George Crockett.

Officer of the U. S. Army. pseud. Delirium
of my childhood. 19435

Officer of the United States Army. pseud.
Life among the Mormons. (40996)

Officer of the United States' Army. pseud.
Researches on America. see M'Culloh,
James H.

Officer of the U. S. Artillerists. pseud.
Exercise for garrison and field ordnance.
23390

Officer of the U. S. Navy. pseud. Observations on the navy pension laws.
56537

Officer of the United States Navy. pseud.
Three years in the Pacific. see
Ruschenberger, W. S. W.

Officer of this establishment at Charlestown.
pseud. State prisons. see Bradford,
Gamaliel, 1795-1839.

Officer on board the Burford. pseud.
Journal of the expedition. (36722), 1st
note after 102842

Officer on board the Discovery. pseud.
Authentic narrative of a voyage to the
Pacific Ocean. 16244

Officer on board the said ship. pseud.
Voyage round the world. 9732-9734,
97668 see also Ufiziale della detta
nave. pseud.

Officer present at the expedition to Carthagena.
pseud. Conduct of Admiral Vernon
examin'd and vindicated. 99249

Officer retired. pseud. Letter from an officer
retired. 40325

Officer returned from that service. pseud.
Letter to the English nation. 40472

Officer serving as Quarter-Master General
with the forces engaged. pseud. Facts
relating to the capture of Washington.
see Evans, De Lacy.

Officer then serving in the fleet. pseud.
Candid and impartial narrative. 10658

Officer under Captain Cooke. pseud. Voyages,
distresses, and wonderful adventures of
Captain Winterfield. 104836

Officer under that General. pseud. History
of Don Francisco de Miranda's attempt.
see Bullard, Henry Adams.

Officer, who arrived at Philadelphia, from the
Army in Jersey. pseud. Extract of a
letter. 101697

Officer who has served upwards of twenty years
in the West-Indies. pseud. West-India
pilot. see Speer, Joseph Smith.

Officer who served in the expedition. pseud.
Narrative of the campaign of the British
Army. see Gleig, George Robert.

Officer who served in the expedition. pseud.
Narrative of the campaigns of the British
Army. see Gleig, George Robert.

Officer who served in the last war in America.
pseud. Reflections on the most proper
means of reducing the rebels. 68704

Officer who was present. pseud. reporter
31344

Officers, act of incorporation, by-laws, &c. [of
the Lowell Five Cent Savings Bank.]
42488

Officers and directors of the Southern Bible
Society and Pilgrims' Depository. 88312

Officers and members of the Union League.
62352

Officers and regents of the Smithsonian Institution. 85045

Officers and seamen of the expedition. pseud.
Arctic miscellanies. (1924)

Officers and Soldiers of the Rhode Island
Brigade. petitioners see Rhode Island
Brigade. petitioners

Officers, charter, constitution and life members
of the . . . [Pennsylvania State Agri-
cultural] Society. 60376

Officers, etc. [of the Horticultural Society of
the Valley of Genesee.] 33065

Officers killed in battle or who died in the
service. 68021

Officers' manual. 56754

Officers of Berks County, for one year, from
1752 to 1860. 93111

Officers of Harvard College. petitioners see
Harvard University. petitioners

Officers of our Union army and navy. 21080,
56755

Officers of the Army of the United States.
petitioners see U. S. Army. Officers.
petitioners

Officers of the Grand Division of the Sons of
Temperance, believing the letter of
Mr. Phillips to be a just and true ex-
pression. 87034

Officers of the Navy Who Were Transferred
From the Volunteer Naval Service.
petitioners see U. S. Navy. Officers
petitioners

Officers of the navy who were transferred
from the volunteer naval service by
authority of the act of July 25, 1866,
respectfully submit. 90657

Officers of the New York State Lunatic Asylum
Utica. 1118

Officers of the Ordnance Department, U. S.
Army. see U. S. Army. Ordnance
Department.

Officers of the United States Navy. petitioner
see U. S. Navy. Officers. petitioners

Officers, statutes and charter of the College
of William and Mary. 104154

Officia propria foederatis provinciis Americae
Septentrionalis concessa. 56756

Official account of his great march. 80414

Official account of naval victories. (56757)

Official account of the late defeat of the
Indians. 97196

Official account of the trial and execution of
Arbuthnot & Ambrister. 56758

Official accounts of the cruelties inflicted upon
Union prisoners. 68316

Official and full detail of the great battle of
New Orleans. 18876

Official and illustrated catalogue. 28445

Official and other accounts of all the battles.
7045

Official and other papers of the late Major-
General Alexander Hamilton. 29971

Official and private correspodence of Major
General J. S. Eustace. 23119

Official apologies of the American Tract
Society. 70243

Official army list of the western states.
56759

Official army register. 961, 2053, 56760

Official army register of the volunteer force.
56761

Official arrangements for the funeral solemnities. 56762

Official awards of juries. 2241

Official awards of the juries. note after
56762

Official book of records. 83492

Official catalogue and journal of the eleventh
exhibition of American manufactures.
45829

Official catalogue [of the New York Crystal
Palace Exhibition.] 70972

Official catalogue of the New-York Exhibition
of the Industry of All Nations. 2239

Official catalogue of the pictures contributed.
23398

Official catalogue of the pictures . . . in
the . . . gallery of the Crystal Palace.
note after 56762

Official catalogue of the products of the United
States of America. 56763

Official census of Maryland. (45273)

Official character of Rev. Nathanael Emmons.
104386

Official circular. 88366-88367

Official circulars. 21885

Official communication to the Speaker of the
House of Representatives. 101913

Official communications between the Prime
Minister at Washington. 37860
Official communications from General Pope.
64114
Official copy of orders from Governor Palliser.
45986
Official correspondence between Don Louis de
Onis. 57356
Official correspondence between the Agents
of Exchange. 15323
Official correspondence between the United
States and Mexico. 56764
Official correspondence of Brig. Gen. W. S.
Harney. 30409
Official correspondence of Fayette McMullin.
101913
Official correspondence on the claims of the
United States. 56765, 74344
Official correspondence on the fisheries.
(56766)
Official correspondence with the Department
of War. (35321)
Official correspondence with General Washington
and General Gates. 71301
Official corruption and hypocrisy unmasked.
43435
Official declaration of President Wilford
Woodruff. 83193
Official declaration of President Woodruff.
83208, 83220
Official declaration of President Woodruff, of
Sept. 24, 1890. 83207
Official defence of its cost, abuses and power.
(13824)
Official depositions of Wm. Tecumseh Sherman.
80420
Official despatches, correspondence and reports.
3745
Official directory and law register for the
United States. 41627
Official dispatches concerning the gold dis-
tricts. 10002
Official digest of the general, division and
special orders. 53516
Official documents, addresses, etc., of George
Opdyke. 47389
Official documents, containing a message of
the state of Georgia. 27080
Official documents of the Presbytery of Albany.
(12536), 17909, 97370
Official documents relating to a chaplain's
campaign (not) with General Butler.
18714
Official documents relating to a " Chaplain's
campaign (not) with General Butler,"
but in New York. 9618
Official documents relating to the operations
of the British Army. 56767
Official draft of instructions. 56768
Official expose of the causes. (54755)
Official extracts from the resolutions of the
States General. 56769
Official handbook of church and state. 51527
Official journal of the Conference Convention.
15433
Official journal of the Constitutional Convention.
56770
Official journal of the House of Representatives
of the state of Louisiana. (42273)
Official journal of the proceedings of the con-
vention, for framing a constitution for
the state of Louisiana. (42277)
Official journal of the proceedings of the convention for the revision and amendment
of the constitution of . . . Louisiana.
(42276)

Official journals of the proceedings of the
convention of the state of Louisiana.
42275
Official letter from the Commissioners of
Correspondence. (2719)
Official letter relating to the action. (50044)
Official letters of the Governors of the state
of Virginia. 100192, 100209-100210,
100212
Offical letters of the military and naval
officers of the United States. 7411
Official letters to Congress, 1796. 101742
Official letters to the Honorable American
Congress. 101726-101733
Official list of officers who marched with
the army. 56771, 83867
Official message of His Excellency Gov. A. H.
Reader. 68627
Official monthly bulletin [of the Grand National
Peace Jubilee.] 28263
Official monthly bulletin of the Great National
Peace Jubilee and Musical Festival.
56772
Official. New Orleans, La., Nov. 10, 1868.
42186
Official note from the Consul charged ad
interim of the General Consulate of
France in Buenos Ayres. 9028
Official notes from the Minister of the French
Republic. (56773)
Official opinions of the Attorneys-General of
the United States. 56774
Official papers; consisting of the Governour's
speech. 99199
Official papers, containing the speeches of
respective Governors of Vermont.
99199
Official papers printed for the Common
Council. 6537
Official papers [referring to S. Holmes and
the North Congregational Church in New
Bedford.] 32626
Official papers relating to the conduct of the
Legation of the United States at Paris
with regard to the Commissioners for
the International Exposition of 1867.
(42161), 56775, (58595)
Official papers relative to the dispute between
the courts of Great Britain and Spain.
56776
Official proceedings of a town meeting. 61883
Official proceedings of the Democratic National
Convention, held in 1860. 56777
Official proceedings of the Democratic State
Convention, held at Rome. (53846)
Official proceedings of the Mississippi State
Colored Convention. 49530
Official proceedings of the Mississippi Valley
Railroad Convention. 49554
Official proceedings of the National Democratic
Convention held in Cincinnati, June,
1856. 13803
Official proceedings of the National Democratic
Convention, held in Cincinnati, June 2-6,
1856. 13100
Official proceedings of the Republican Con-
vention convened in . . . Pittsburgh,
Pennsylvania. 70029
Official programme of the order of exercises.
89850
Official. Public expenditure from 1824 to
1838. 103265
Official railroad manual of the railroads of
North America. 42773
Official record from the War Department.
56778

Official record of Rhode Island. 56779,
70541, 70611

Official record of the corporators, April 30,
1868. (63456)

Official record of the National Congregational
Council. 15484

Official records of Robert Dinwiddie. 99994

Official register and business directory, for
the year 1862. (30200), 38131

Official register and year-book of facts.
38131

Official register of Missouri troops for 1862.
49627

Official register . . . of officers and agents
in the service of the United States.
56780

Official register of Rhode Island Officers
and soldiers. 56779, 70541, 70611

Official register of the army for 1867.
56781

Official register of the deaths which occurred
among the white population. 74335,
(77259)

Official register of the officers and cadets,
1867. 42310

Official register of the officers and cadets
of the State Seminary. 42274

Official register of the officers of the Illinois
Volunteers. 34302

Official register of the United States Naval
Academy. 56782

Official reply of the Board of Missions of
the General Assembly. 61186

Official report by Gustave de Beaumont.
96070

Official report by W. B. Lord. 48728

Official report, by William Sprague, Jr.
89720, 2d note after 97484

Official report from Capt. Leslie Combs to
General Green Clay. 14928

Official report made by the commanding officer.
21036

Official report of a visit to the Luray Caverns.
85009

Official report of Col. L. C. Baker. 2840,
29386

Official report of debates in the Louisiana
Convention. 42278

Official report of Gen. Casey. 51718

Official report of Gen. John O'Neill. 57347

Official report of Generals Johnston and
Beauregard. 56783

Official report of J. Ross Browne. 44600

Official report of Lieut.-Gen. Ulysses S. Grant.
28315

Official report of Major General John Pope.
64112

Official report of Missouri troops, for 1862.
49627

Official report of the battle of Bethel. 5070

Official report of the battle of Chickamauga.
12674, 15324

Official report of the battle of Chippeway.
96514

Official report of the California State Agricultural Society's third annual agricultural fair. 9993

Official report of the debates and proceedings
in the Constitutional Convention of . . .
Nevada. 52404

Official report of the debates and proceedings
in the state convention. 45928

Official report of the debates and proceedings
of the Southern Commercial Convention.
(56784), note after 88326

Official report of the Great Union Meeting.
54564

Official report of the Investigating Committee.
24059

Official report of the trial of Hon. Albert
Jackson. 35341

Official report of the trial of Mary Harris.
(30490)

Official report of the trials of sundry Negroes
37436

Official report of the United States' Expedition.
(42819)

Official report of the American Congress.
90851

Official report to the Board of Alms-House
Governors. (76512)

Official report to the Board of Education. By
Thomas Boese. 54616, 66516

Official report to the United States Engineer
Department. 27424

Official reported debates. 4783

Official reports. 62710

Official reports from the executive department
56785

Official reports of battles. (15325), 15327-
(15329)

Official reports of battles, as published by
order of the Confederate Congress at
Richmond. 15411

Official reports of battles; containing Colonel
Wm. J. Jackson's report of expedition
to Beverly. 15330

Official reports of battles, embracing the
defence of Vicksburg. (15326)

Official reports of battles. Published by order
of the Congress at Richmond. 56786

Official reports of Col. Fremont and Major
Emory. 25846

Official reports of engagements on the
Mississippi River. 56787

Official reports of General Kearney and General
Birney. 37129

Official reports of Genls. Persifer [sic]
F. Smith and B. Riley. 97652

Official reports . . . of the battle of Bethel.
56788

Official reports of the battle of Stone River.
5223

Official reports of the battles of Mechanicsville
Gaines' Mills, ... 42970

Official reports of the Canal Commissioners
of the state of New York. 22749,
(53564)

Official reports of the Senate of . . .
Louisiana. (42279)

Official reports on public credit. (29972)

Official reports on the inefficiency of the
U. S. S. Wampanoag. (35249)

Official reports, relating to the militia of the
state. 53847

Official responsibility affirmed and enforced.
5883

Official returns of election on constitutional
amendments. (13808)

Official review of the reports. 69946

Official souvenir program of the Yale-Harvard
Boat Race. 83492

Official state calendar of public officers and
institutions. 7278

Official statement of the Governor, and the
depositions. (16986), 58408

Official statements of President Joseph Smith.
83302

Officielle und eigenhandige Briefe und Berichte
101708

Officiellen Berichten des Nord-Amerikanischen
  Obersten Mason. 10015
Officier a bord de l'Alexandre. pseud.
  Journal. 23923, 73377
Officier am Board der Letztern. pseud.
  Kapitaine Portlock und Dixon's Reise.
  64393
Officier Americain. pseud. Lettres. see
  Eustace, Jean-Skey.
Officier bij deszelfs zeemagt. pseud.
  Erinneringen uit eene driejaringe dienst.
  14582, 14618
Officier de l'Armee de M. de Nouaille.
  pseud. Journal de la guerre du
  Micissippi contre les Chicachas.
  (36688)
Officier de l'armee navale. pseud. Journal.
  28331
Officier de l'armee navale en Amerique.
  pseud. Journal. see Estaing, Charles
  Hector, Comte d'.
Officier de l'armee royale. pseud. Voyages
  dans les parties interieures de l'Ameri-
  que. see Anburey, Thomas.
Officier de la marine de l'escadre de M. le
  Comte d'Estaing. pseud. Journal.
  23033
Officier de la marine Russienne. pseud.
  Lettre. 40673 see also Russian Sea
  Officer. pseud.
Officier de l'etat majeur de l'armee. pseud.
  Details sur quelques uns des evenemens.
  (19776)
Officier de marine. pseud. Relation de la
  Louisiane ou Mississipi. 4936, 69299
Officier du 1er regiment de lanciers
  Venezueliens. pseud. Campagnes et
  croisieres. see Vowell, Richard
  Longeville. supposed author
Officier Francais, detenu par Dessalines.
  pseud. Notice historique. (75167)
Officier general de la marine. pseud.
  Memoires. see Bory, Gabriel de.
Officier qui s'est trouve dans l'occasion.
  pseud. Relation de ce qui s'est passe
  au siege de Canada. (69258)
Officier unter des Herrn Obersten Specht
  Regimente. pseud. Tagebuch. 94200
Offizielle correspondenz. (57560)
Offne Thur zu dem verborgenen Heydenthum.
  72603
Offor, George. (46728)
Offrandes a Bonaparte. 101165
Offset to Mr. Adams's letter!! 92884
Oficial de causes. 25103
Oficial de la Legion Britanica. pseud.
  Memorias. see Mahoney, William D.
  supposed author and Vowell, Richard
  Longeville. supposed author
Oficial de marina Ingles al servicio de Chile.
  pseud. Memoria. see Vowell, Richard
  Longeville. supposed author
Oficial del egercito Norte-Americano. pseud.
  Observaciones. 56449
Oficial mayor, novela de costumbres Mejicanas
  original. 71484
Oficio circular de XXIV. de Marzo. 29096
Oficio de difuntos para sufragio. 56790
Oficio del Consul encargado interinamente del
  . Consulado General de Francia. 9027
Oficio que los gefes de egercito nacional
  pasaron. 61331
Oficios del Consulado de Veracruz. 56791
O'Flaherty, Thomas. (56792)

O'Flanaghan, J. (56793)
Ofrecimiento de los Senadores Eclesiasticos.
  66569
Ofrenda a muchachas calaberas. 56794
Ofrenda al Bazar de la Real Casa de
  Beneficencia. 56795
Ofrenda al Excelentisimo Senor Jose T.
  Monagas. 49932
Ofver Europeiska c olonial-valdets grundlag-
  gning. 26840
O'Gallagher, ---------. 103090
Ogallala Indians. see Oglala Indians.
Ogden, --------, fl. 1827. 21108
Ogden, Aaron, 1751-1839. 1795, 56796, note
  after 53797, (56798), note after 83791,
  90722
Ogden, Aaron, 1751-1839. petitioner (56797)-
  (56798)
Ogden, Aaron, 1751-1839. respondent 27293,
  103153
Ogden, Abraham. 1795, note after 53697,
  note after 83791
Ogden, Charles Richard. petitioner 56799
Ogden, D. A. 611
Ogden, D. B. 54723
Ogden, David. 53053, 56800-56801 see also
  New Jersey (Colony) General Assembly.
  Committee on the New York Line.
  Chairman.
Ogden, David. plaintiff (56802)
Ogden, David B. 56803
Ogden, David L. 56804
Ogden, George W. 55339, 56805-(56806)
Ogden, Gouverneur M. (56807)
Ogden, James. 56808
Ogden, James De Peyster. 56809-56812
Ogden, James Cosens. 10615, 25850, 38875,
  56813-(56819), 3d note after 96334, note
  after 98091, 99551, 99569, 105930
Ogden, James Cosens. supposed author
  97176, 105925
Ogden, Lewis M. 56820
Ogden, O. N. 56821
Ogden, Samuel S. defendant 84904
Ogden, Uzal. 56822-56825
Ogdensburgh, N. Y. Gouverneur Wesleyan
  Seminary. see Gouverneur Wesleyan
  Seminary, Ogdensburgh, N. Y.
Ogdensburgh, N. Y. Ordinances, etc. 56826
Ogdensburgh, N. Y. Schools. 56826
Ogdensburgh and Lake Champlain Railroad.
  56829
Ogdensburgh, Clayton and Rome Railroad
  Company. 56930
Ogdensburgh, Clayton and Rome Railroad
  Company. Chief Engineer. 56830
Ogdensburgh, Clayton and Rome Railroad
  Company. President and Directors.
  56830
Ogdensburgh directory for 1867-68. 56831
Ogdensburgh Rail Road. 56832
Ogdensburgh sentinel. Carrier. pseud.
  Address. 56827
Oge, Mort d'. see D'Oge, Mort.
Ogee, Quirk. pseud. Extracts from humbug-
  giana. 56833
Oghquagoe Indians. Treaties, etc. 36337
Ogier, T. L. 87887
Ogilby, Frederick, 1813-1878. 56834
Ogilby, Frederick, 1813-1878. supposed author
  69710, 4th note after 96984
Ogilby, John, 1600-1676. 1427, 24081,
  50088-(50089)
Ogilby, John D. 56835-56836

Ogilvie, -------. 96891
Ogilbie, James. 56837
Ogilvie, James G. 56838-56839
Ogilvie, John. (56840)
Oglala Indians. Treaties, etc. 96641
Ogle, Andrew Jackson, 1822-1852. 56841
Ogle, Alexander. 97274
Ogle, Sir Chaloner, 1681?-1750. defendant 56842-56843
Ogle, Charles, 1798-1841. 56844
Ogle, Samuel, d. 1780. 45108, 45366 see also Maryland (Colony) Governor, 1731-1732 (Ogle) Maryland (Colony) Governor, 1735-1742 (Ogle)
Ogle, Samuel, d. 1780. defendant (59685) see also Maryland (Colony) Governor, 1735-1742 (Ogle) defendant
Oglesby, Richard, 1824-1899. 34271 see also Illinois. Governor, 1865-1869 (Oglesby)
Oglethorpe. pseud. Doctrine of nullification examined. 20423, 56849
Oglethorpe, James Edward, 1696-1785. 9830, (45003), 56845-56846, 56848, 2d note after 87848, 87853
Oglethorpe, James Edward, 1696-1785. supposed author (56847), 66723, 87900
Oglethorpe University, Atlanta, Ga. 56850-56851
Oglethorpe University magazine. 56851
Ogletorpe, Elenore. defendant 104125
Oglivie, John. tr. 57488-57489
O'Gorman, ---------, fl. 1824. (70079)
O'Gorman, D. 56852
O'Gorman, Edith, see Teresa de Chantal. Sister
O'Gorman, Richard. 56854
Ogramić Olavčić, Nilola, Bp., 1630-1700. 55243, (63455)
Oguedagoa. Indian Chief 628, 66062 see also Three Maquas Castles (Indians) Sachems.
O'Halloran, -------. 56855
O'Hara, Theodore, 1820-1867. 56422
O'Heguerty, Domingo, Comte de Magnieres, 1699-1790. 31236, (56856), 69541
Ohiem Tom's hutte. 92555
Ohio (Territory) Constitutional Convention, 1802. 105505
Ohio (Territory) Laws, statutes, etc. 56937, 105505
Ohio. 36388, 37731, (57029), (66515) see also Northwest Territory, U. S.
Ohio. Adjutant General. (56874)
Ohio. Asylum for Idiotic and Imbecile Youth, Columbus. see Ohio. State Hospital, Columbus.
Ohio. Attorney General. 56880
Ohio. Auditor of State. (13140), 47026, 56881, 57062
Ohio. Auditor of State. defendant 30090, note after 90601
Ohio. Bank. see Bank of Ohio.
Ohio. Bank Commissioners. 56882
Ohio. Board of Agriculture. see Ohio. State Board of Agriculture.
Ohio. Board of Equalization. (56860), 56881, 57026
Ohio. Board of Public Works. 56886
Ohio. Board of State Charities. 56887
Ohio. Boys' Industrial School, Lancaster. 57053
Ohio. Boys' Industrial School, Lancaster. Commissioners. 56996
Ohio. Canal Commissioners. 56888
Ohio. Canal Engineer. 56929

Ohio. Census, 1840. 36021
Ohio. Citizens. 15877, 56871
Ohio. Commercial Hospital and Lunatic Asylum, Cincinnati. see Cincinnati General Hospital.
Ohio. Commissary General. 56892
Ohio. Commission to Enquire into the Causes of the Defalcation in the State Treasury, 1858. 57036
Ohio. Commissioner of Railroads and Telegraphs. 56893
Ohio. Commissioner of Statistics. 56894
Ohio. Commissioners of Morgan Raid Claims. (57034)
Ohio. Commissioners of the Canal Fund. (56896)
Ohio. Commissioners of the Sinking Fund. 56897
Ohio. Comptroller of the Treasury. 56900
Ohio. Constitution. 1269, 1271, 2011, 5316, 6360, 9672, 12199, 16102-16103, 16107, 16113, 16133, 25790, 29731, 33137, (47188), 56904-56905, 59771, (66397), 104198, 105505
Ohio. Constitutional Convention, 1850-1851. 57035
Ohio. Convention, Canton, 1830. see Ohio. State Convention, Canton, 1830.
Ohio. Convention of the Colored Citizens, Columbus, 1849. see State Convention of the Colored Citizens of Ohio, Columbus 1849.
Ohio. Courts. 79125
Ohio. Deaf and Dumb Asylum, Columbus. see Ohio State School for the Deaf, Columbus.
Ohio. Fund Commissioners. (56915)
Ohio. General Assembly. 14204, 37577, 56910, (56938), 56987, 57044, 57046, 57054, 57058, 64808, 69859, 75022, 84791
Ohio. General Assembly. Committee on Report of the Commissioners of Common Schools. 56895
Ohio. General Assembly. Committee on the Tariff. 57045
Ohio. General Assembly. Joint Committee on Finance. 57037
Ohio. General Assembly. Joint Committee on Public Institutions and Buildings. (57038)
Ohio. General Assembly. Joint Committee on the Communication of the Auditor of State. 3189
Ohio. General Assembly. Joint Select Committee on the Northern Boundary. (57039)
Ohio. General Assembly. Railroad Committee. 43690
Ohio. General Assembly. Select Committee on a Ship Canal Around the Falls of Niagara. 55131
Ohio. General Assembly. Select Committee on the Geological Survey. 56922
Ohio. General Assembly. Special Committee on the Geological Survey. 56918
Ohio. General Assembly. Standing Committee on the Currency. 57041
Ohio. General Assembly. Union Members. see Union Party. Ohio.
Ohio. General Assembly. House of Representatives. 14204, (56940), 56964, 85144
Ohio. General Assembly. Senate. 14204, 37004, 56881, 56943-56944
Ohio. General Assembly. Senate. Court of Impeachments. 48702, 56944

Ohio. General Assembly. Senate. Select Committee on Giving the Right of Suffrage to Females. (57040)

Ohio. Geological Survey. 56920-56921, (56924)-56928, 84797

Ohio. Geologist. (56925), 56926 see also Newberry, James Strong, 1822-1892.

Ohio. Girls' Industrial Home, Rathbone. 57032

Ohio. Governor, 1814-1819 (Worthington) 33150 see also Worthington, Thomas, 1769-1827.

Ohio. Governor, 1819-1822 (Brown) 56958 see also Brown, Ethan Allen, 1766-1852.

Ohio. Governor, 1822-1826 (Morrow) 56929 see also Morrow, Jeremiah, 1770-1852.

Ohio. Governor, 1832-1836 (Lucas) 57039, 57051 see also Lucas, Robert, 1781-1853.

Ohio. Governor, 1836-1838 (Vance) 57044 see also Vance, Joseph, 1786-1852.

Ohio. Governor, 1853-1856 (Medill) 56922 see also Medill, William, 1801-1865.

Ohio. Governor, 1856-1860 (Chase) 12200, 33150, 37577, 69859 see also Chase, Salmon Portland, 1808-1873.

Ohio. Governor, 1864-1866 (Brough) 8402 see also Brough, John, 1811-1865.

Ohio. Governor, 1866-1868 (Cox) 17259, 56936 see also Cox, Jacob Dolson, 1828-1900.

Ohio. Laws, statutes, etc. 9373, 12199, 13061, 13076, 13676, 14204, 23765, 29731, 38658, 39414, 39566, (44564), 48682, 48768, 52051, 56859, 56863-56869, 56917, 56937, 56945-56948, 56960, (56989), 56997, (57030), (57047)-57048, (57057), (57060), (62079), 67433, 70820-70821, 79125, 82438, 89066, 89823-89824, 89889, 94012, 97255, 97881, 98584, 104224

Ohio. Longview Asylum for the Insane. see Hamilton County, Ohio. Longview Hospital, Carthage.

Ohio. Lunatic Asylum, Columbus. see Ohio. State Hospital, Columbus.

Ohio. Medical College, Cincinnati. see Cincinnati. University. Medical College of Ohio.

Ohio. Medical Convention, Cincinnati, 1842. see Medical Convention of Ohio, Cincinnati, 1842.

Ohio. Medical Convention, Cleveland, 1839. see Medical Convention of Ohio, Cleveland, 1839.

Ohio. Militia. 56879, 56917, 56960

Ohio. Militia. Cincinnati Black Brigade. 13353

Ohio. Militia. First Regiment Volunteers. Officer. pseud. Sketches of the campaign. see Giddings, L.

Ohio. National Union Association. see National Union Association of Ohio.

Ohio. Northern Ohio Lunatic Asylum. see Ohio. State Hospital, Cleveland.

Ohio. Penitentiary. 56991

Ohio. Quartermaster General. 57031

Ohio. Reform School. see Ohio. Boys' Industrial School, Lancaster.

Ohio. Reform School for Girls, Rathbone. see Ohio. Girls' Industrial Home, Rathbone.

Ohio. Refugee Relief Commission. see Refugee Relief Commission of Ohio.

Ohio. School Commissioner. see Ohio. State Commissioner of Common Schools.

Ohio. Secretary of State. 57048-57050, 57055, 85134, 85136, 85141-85142, 85144, 94880

Ohio. Sinking Fund Commissioners. see Ohio. Commissioners of the Sinking Fund.

Ohio. Southwestern State Normal School, Lebanon. see Lebanon University, Lebanon, Ohio.

Ohio. Special Commissioner on the Treasury. 57062

Ohio. State Board of Agriculture. 56884

Ohio. State Board of Agriculture. Annual Fair, 2d, 1851. 56884

Ohio. State Commissioner of Common Schools. 56895, 56997, 57052, 57058, 85202 see also Smyth, Anson, d. 1886.

Ohio. State Convention, Canton, 1830. 57027

Ohio. State Education Convention, Columbus, 1837. see Ohio State Education Convention, Columbus, 1837.

Ohio. State Hospital, Cleveland. 56963

Ohio. State Hospital, Cleveland. Trustees. 55817

Ohio. State Hospital, Columbus. 56970

Ohio. State Hospital, Columbus. Directors. (56945)

Ohio. State Independent Free Territory Convention, Cincinnati, 1848. see State Independent Free Territory Convention of the People of Ohio, Cincinnati, 1848.

Ohio. State Library, Columbus. 57007, 75002

Ohio. State Library, Columbus. Commissioners. 57007

Ohio. State Reform Farm, Lancaster. see Ohio. Boys' Industrial School, Lancaster.

Ohio. Superintendent of the Common Schools. see Ohio. State Commissioner of Common School.

Ohio. Supreme Court. 89832, 91045

Ohio. Surgeon General. 57059

Ohio. Treasury Department. 30090, 56909, 57061, note after 90601

Ohio. University, Athens. 57015, 104682

Ohio. University, Athens. President. 57015, 104682 see also Wilson, Robert G.

Ohio. Volunteers. see Ohio. Militia.

Ohio County, Va. Committee of Vigilance. (35382)

Ohio: a sketch of industrial progress. (80567)

Ohio almanac, for . . . 1814-1815. 93231

Ohio almanac, for . . . 1806. 93231

Ohio almanac for . . . 1810. 56965

Ohio American Protestant Association. see American Protestant Association of Ohio.

Ohio and Indiana Railroad Company. 56956

Ohio and Mississippi navigator. (56967)

Ohio and Mississippi pilot. 27389

Ohio & Mississippi Railroad Company. 56968

Ohio & Pennsylvania Rail Road Company. 60358

Ohio annual register. 8796

Ohio Anti-slavery Convention, Putnam, 1835. 57043

Ohio Anti-slavery Society. (56969)

Ohio Anti-slavery Society. petitioners (56969)

Ohio archaeological and historical publications. 85144

Ohio archaeological and historical quarterly. 84791, note after 106203

Ohio Archaeological and Historical Society.
see Ohio State Archaeological and
Historical Society.
Ohio Archaeological Society. see Ohio State
Archaeological and Historical Society .
Ohio Baptist Book and Tract Society. 56971
Ohio Baptist Education Society. Trustees.
28328
Ohio Bible Society. Committee. 56972
Ohio boys in Dixie. (56973)
Ohio [by Rufus King.] 84342
Ohio canal. (56974), 100666
Ohio Colonization Society. see Ohio State
Colonization Society.
Ohio common school director. 56975
Ohio Company. (18173), 31799, 56976-
56977, 99584, 101150 see also Wharton,
Samuel.
Ohio Company. Agent. (18173) see also
Sargent, Winthrop, 1753-1820.
Ohio Company. Directors and Agents.
56978-56979, 98639
Ohio Company. Secretary. 98639 see also
Sargent, Winthrop, 1753-1820.
Ohio confederate. 56930
Ohio contested election. 56980
Ohio Editorial Association. 56981
Ohio educational monthly. see Ohio journal
of education.
Ohio Female College, College Hill, Ohio.
56982
Ohio Female College . . . with the plan.
56982
Ohio Free Sugar Advocates. 93460
Ohio gazetteer, and traveler's guide. 36021
Ohio gazetteer: or topographical dictionary.
37730
Ohio Grand Division of the Sons of Temperance.
see Sons of Temperance of North
America. Ohio. Grand Division.
Ohio Historical and Philosophical Society. see
Historical and Philosophical Society of
Ohio.
Ohio Historical Society. see Ohio State
Archaeological and Historical Society.
Ohio hunter. 56983
Ohio in the war: her statesmen, her generals,
and soldiers. (69092)
Ohio, Indiana, Illinois, Michigan, North-Western,
Missouri, Louisiana, Mississippi and
Alabama. 49008
Ohio Indians. Treaties, etc. (60738), 61203
Ohio Institution for the Education of the Deaf
and Dumb. see Ohio State School for
the Deaf, Columbus.
Ohio Institution for the Instruction of the
Blind. see Ohio State School for the
Blind, Columbus.
Ohio journal of education. (56986), 85202
Ohio justice and township officers' assistant.
98584
Ohio, Kentucky, and Indiana state register.
37759
Ohio layman. pseud. Review of the protest
and appeal of Bishop Doane. 20395
Ohio Legislature. Biographical notices of the
members. 56987
Ohio Lodge, no. I. of the American Protestant
Association of Ohio. see American
Protestant Association of Ohio. Ohio
Lodge, no. I.
Ohio Mechanics' Institute. 37261, (56989)
Ohio Mechanics' Institute. Annual Fair, 1st,
1838. (56989)
Ohio Mechanics' Institute. Board of Directors.
(56989)

Ohio Mechanics' Institute. Library and
Reading Room. (56989)
Ohio medical and surgical journal. 56990,
84074
Ohio National Union Association. see
National Union Association of Ohio.
Ohio Petroleum Company. (56992)
Ohio Philosophical Society. see Historical
and Philosophical Society of Ohio.
Ohio pioneer history. Cresap and Logan.
85141
Ohio pioneer history. The military expedition
of the North West Territory. 85142
Ohio prosperity, social and material. 14204
Ohio railway gazetteer. (56995)
Ohio railroad guide. 56993
Ohio railroad guide illustrated. 56994
Ohio register. 101320
Ohio. Reise nach Nordamerika. 22581
Ohio River and its obstructions. 19018
Ohio River Improvement Company. 57069
Ohio River Land and Marble Company.
57070
Ohio school laws. 56997
Ohio School Library, Cincinnati. see Cin-
cinnati. Public Library.
Ohio school library. 13094
Ohio school library. Catalogue. 56998
Ohio section. 30283
Ohio soldiers. pseud. Address. 57046
Ohio southern boundary line. (56999)
Ohio State and Union Law College, Cleveland.
57001
Ohio State Archaeological and Historical
Society. 30571, 84791, 85144, note
after 106203 see also Historical and
Philosophical Society of Ohio.
Ohio state business directory. 57002
Ohio State Christian Anti-slavery Convention,
Columbus, 1859. (57003)
Ohio State Colonization Society. Board of
Managers. 85875
Ohio state directory and shippers' guide.
57004
Ohio State Education Convention, Columbus,
1837. 56962
Ohio state gazetteer and business directory.
57005
Ohio State Horticultural Society. 57006
Ohio State Medical Society. 57008
Ohio State Phonetic Association. (57009)
Ohio state register and business mirror.
57010
Ohio State School for the Blind, Columbus.
11961, 56985
Ohio State School for the Deaf, Columbus.
56906, 56984
Ohio State Sovereignty Society. see State
Sovereignty Society of Ohio.
Ohio State Sunday School Convention, Delaware
1865. (57011)
Ohio Synod. see Presbyterian Church in
the U. S. A. Synod of Ohio.
Ohio teacher. (57012), note before 83906
Ohio Teachers' Association. petitioners
57013
Ohio Theological Seminary, Gambier, Ohio.
see Kenyon College, Gambier, Ohio.
Ohio valley historical series. (22918),
(57016), 82766, 84619
Ohio volunteer. pseud. Capitulation. see
Foster, James.
Ohio Wesleyan Female College, Delaware,
Ohio. see Ohio Wesleyan University,
Delaware, Ohio.

Ohio Welseyan University, Delaware, Ohio. 57017-57018

Ohio White Sulphur Springs. 50468

Ohio Women's Rights Convention, Akron, 1851. (57019)

Ohio Wool Growers' Association. Convention, Columbus, 1864. 67790

Ohio Yearly Meeting. see Friends, Society of. Ohio Yearly Meeting.

Ohsson, -------- d'. (57072)

Oidor. Drama historico en cinco actos. 62935

Oiga el gobierno verdades aunque la parezcan duras. 89416

Oil Creek and Allegany Oil Company. (57073)

Oil Creek business directory for 1865. 57074

Oil-Dorado of West Virginia. 57075

Oil on the waters. (57076), (71364)

Oil regions of Pennsylvania. 27390

Oil without vinegar. 47301, 97135

Oiseaux d'Amerique. 2370

Oiseaux de l'ile de la Trinidad. (40119)

Oiseaux du Bresil. 19692

Oiseaux nouvelles ou rares. 19749

Ojeada al Congreso de 1830. 98882

Ojeada al proyecto de constitucion. 29369

Ojeada ha publicado en Cumana el Sr. Antonio Jose Sotillo. 98389

Ojeada historica sobre el Paraguay. 57077

Ojeada retrospectiva sobre el movimiento intelectual. 21772

Ojeada sobre la campana que hizo el General Santa-Anna. 57078, 57522

Ojeada sobre la cuestion Espanola, 1864. 57079

Ojeada sobre las tendencias de la epoca actual. 26765

Ojebway spelling book, translated. 36592

Ojibue nagumouinun. (57086)

O-jib-ue spelling book. (57087)

Ojibwa hymns. 57088

Ojibwa nugumoshang. 57088

Ojibwa spelling-book. 5429

Ojibway-Eroberung. (36972)

O-kah-mause. Potawatomi Indian Chief 96702

Okalloutit Sabbatinne akkudleesiksaet Evangeliumit. 38295

Okalluhtualiaet, nuktersimarsut. (7409)

Okalluktuaet Bibelimit pisimasut Kirstumiudlo Apostelit. 91172

Okalluktuaet opernartut tersauko Bibelimit Testamentitokamidlo. 22864

Okalluktuautit sajmaubingmik annekbingmiglo Jesuse-Kristusikut. 38296

O'Keefe, John, 1747-1833. (64087), 86905, 86936, 94132

O-Kee-Pa. 11543

O'Kelley's rejoinder. 85439

O'Kelly, James. 57097, 85439

Okes, Thomas Verney. (57098)

Okes, W. see Oakes, William.

Okie, A. Howard. 57100

Okikinoadi-mezinaigan. 12834

Oklahoma. see also Indian Territory.

Okmulgee, Oklahoma. General Council, 1871. see Indian Territory. General Council, Okmulgee, 1871.

Olabarrieta Medrano, Miguel de. 57101, 68461

Olaguibel, M. de. 57102

Olancho. 54828

Olaneta, J. A. de. 94193

O'Lanus, Corry. pseud. Corry O'Lanus: his views and experiences. see Stanton, John.

Olarte, Antonio. defendant 55274, 57103, 1st note after 100684

Olarte, D. d'. 95854

Olarte, Ignacio de Salazar y. see Salazar y Olarte, Ignacio de.

Olarte, Ramon. 17840, 57104, 1st note after 94592

Olasagarre, M. (48502), 57105 see also Mexico. Ministerio de Hacienda.

Olasso, Jose Manuel Velez de Ulibarri y. see Velez de Ulibarri y Olasso, Jose Manuel.

Olathe, Kansas. Asylum for the Deaf and Dumb. see Kansas. Asylum for the Deaf and Dumb, Olathe.

Olaudah Equiano's oder Gustav Wasa's, des Afrikaners merkwurdige Lebensgeschichte vom ihm selbst geschreiben. 98664

O'Laughlin, Michael. defendant 41180-41182, 41235

Olavarria, Carolina Liborius de. see Liborius de Olavarria, Carolina.

Olavarria. firm defendants see Chartier y Chartier. firm defendants

Olave, A. S. de. note after 27585, 40960, note after 47850

Olavide, Pablo de. 39280

Olcott, Alexander. 1529

Olcott, Bulkley. 57107

Olcott, Henry S. 57108

Olcott, T. W. 21100

Olcott, Theodore. defendant 53931

Old, R. O. 57110

Old Abe, the miller. 41218, 57111

Old Abe's jokes. 41218

Old acquaintance. pseud. Familiar epistle to Robert J. Walker. see McHenry, George.

Old age. 59354

Old and experienced trader. pseud. American traveller. see Cluny, Alexander.

Old and experienced trader. pseud. British merchant. see Cluny, Alexander.

Old and new. 12912, 57112

Old and New Subjects, Inhabitants of the Province of Quebec. petitioners see Quebec (Province) Citizens. petitioners

Old and new tariffs compared. (57113), note after 104805

Old and New-Testament dissected. 93034

Old and new Unitarian Church. 57114

Old and the new; a sermon containing the history of the First Unitarian Church. 16220

Old and the new church. 89767, 89775

Old and the new. Speech . . . on the battle ground of Brandywine. 31703

Old bachelor. 104878

Old ballads. 78597

Old banner. 93264

Old brewery, and the new mission house at the Five Points. 57115

Old Cambridge Division, No. 26. see Sons of Temperance of North America. Massachusetts. Old Cambridge Division, No. 26.

Old Canaan during the revolution. 83486

Old capitol and its inmates. 57116

'Old Central School" re-union. 57117

Old Church, Worcester, Mass. see Worcester, Mass. First Church.

Old church recotd. 28309, 91754

Old churches, ministers and families of Virginia. (47240)

Old citizen. pseud. Comparative view and exhibition of reasons. 53617

Old citizen. pseud. Murder will out. see
De Beck, William L.
Old citizen. pseud. Pittsburgh Sanitary Fair.
63142
Old citizen. pseud. Richmond in by-gone
days. see Mordecai, Samuel.
Old citizen. pseud. Thoughts on the last
election. (50289)
Old citizen of New York. pseud. Verdict of
condemnation. 284, 98954
Old city, and its highways and by-ways.
57118
Old Clay whig. pseud. Reflections and sug-
gestions. 68688
Old clergyman. pseud. Clergyman's hymn
book. see Whitcomb, Chapman.
Old Colony and Fall River Railroad Company.
57119
Old Colony and Fall River Railroad Company.
plaintiffs 57119
Old Colony and Fall River Rail Road Company
vs. the Broadway Rail Road Company.
57119
Old Colony and Newport Railway Company.
Directors. (57120), 90930
Old Colony and Newport Railway Company.
President. 90930 see also Stearns,
Onslow, 1810-1878.
Old Colony Railroad Corporation. 57121
Old Colony Railroad Corporation. Investigating
Committee. 19662
Old Colony Railroad Corporation. President.
19662
Old Colony railroad: its connections. 83584
Old conservative. pseud. Letter to a whig
neighbor. 40423
Old constitution. 91055
Old continental, and the new greenback dollar.
57122
Old continental; or, the price of liberty.
(59209)
Old covenanting, and true Presbyterian layman.
pseud. Bridle for the ass. 47276,
(78736), 97107
Old Dartmouth Centennial Celebration, New
Bedford, Mass., 1864. 57123
Old days in Chapel Hill. 89309
Old dyas in the Old Dominion. 16321
Old days of the Second Church. 57124
Old Deerfield series, v. I. 83556
Old democrat. pseud. Contrast. see Hildreth,
Richard, 1807-1865. supposed author
Moore, Jacob Bailey, 1797-1853.
incorrectly supposed author
Old democrat. pseud. Life of James Buchanan.
8864
Old disciple. 24543
Old Dominion. A novel. 35696
Old Dominion battle-grounds. 35089
Old Dominion, illustrated. 5125
Old Dominion; or, the Southampton massacre.
35696
Old Dominion Society of the City of New York.
35738, 57125, 93623
Old Dominion Society of the City of New York.
Celebration of the Anniversary of the
Settlement at Jamestown, Va., 1607, 1st,
1860. 35738, 57125
Old England and America, against France and
all Europe. 74294
Old England and New England. (9184)
Old England for ever. 30525, 57126
Old England's triumph. 86082
Old English merchant, and a friend to the
King. pseud. Two chapters of the lost
book of Chronicles. 97553

Old English literature. (72208)
Old English valour. 67575
Old Etonian. pseud. Emigrant: a contrast.
22473
Old farm and the new farm. (32981)
Old farmer. pseud. Road to peace, commer
wealth and happiness. see Lowell,
John, 1769-1840.
Old farmer's almanack. 23844, 95447
Old-fashioned 'lection and the cake. 57127
Old fashioned Jackson democrat. pseud.
Dialogue between an old fashioned
Jackson democrat and a Copperhead.
19931, 42555
Old Father Janus. pseud. Life and death
of Old Father Janus. (41003)
Old Father Richard. pseud. Poor Richard
revived. (64074)
"Old Federalism" & "modern Democracy."
17871
Old ferry at Black Rock. 9056, (55873),
note after 95451
Old flag. 57128
Old flag. Fac-simile of a paper in militatio
of print. 47085
Old flag, first published by union prisoners
at Camp Ford. (57129)
Old Fort Duquesne. 57130
Old fox tarr'd and feather'd. 96184
Old Franklin almanac . . . for 1861. 57131
Old friend and schoolmate. pseud. Brief
sketch of the character. see Lewis,
H. P. and White, William.
Old friends. 57132
Old general. pseud. Hints to young generals
see Armstrong, John, 1758-1843.
Old gray horse. pseud. Horse story. see
Jones, Arthur T.
Old Grimes. 28582
Old guard, a monthly journal. (57133)
Old Haun, the pawnbroker. 57134
Old Hepsy. (19574)
Old Hicks the guide. 102248-102249
Old homestead. 91281, 91288
Old house by the river. 65544, 65545
Old houses of Salem. 75677
Old Humphrey. pseud. Indians of North
America. see Mogridge, George.
Old Humphrey. pseud. North American
Indians. see Mogridge, George.
Old hunter. pseud. Grizzly Jake. 28912
Old hunter. pseud. Old Nick of the swamp.
57139
Old Indian chronicle. 20878-20879, 52445,
(52623), 52638, 65324, 97085, 101454
Old inhabitant. pseud. Reminiscences of
Quebec. (69564)
Old inhabitant of British North America.
Observations upon the importance. see
Halliburton, Sir Brenton.
Old Ireland a new state? 22597
Old issues in regard to slavery are dead.
(72610)
"Old Jack" and his foot-cavalry. (57135)
Old Jersey captive. 1527
Old Jesuit unmasked. 9110
Old John Uncas. Indian Chief see Uncas,
Old John. Mohegan Indian Chief
Old John Uncas and the great part of the
tribe of Moheagan Indians. 15749
Old judge. 29692
Old Kentuckian. pseud. Liberty saved.
40949
Old line Webster whig. pseud. Political
conservative circular. 63757

Old line whig. pseud. States vs. territories. see Rockwell, John A.
Old line whigs for Buchanan and Breckinridge. 59432
Old log school-house. 13244
Old looking-glass for the laity and clergy. 49143
Old Mackinaw. 92821
Old man. pseud. Old man's story of old times. (57136)
Old man. pseud. Presidency. see White, Joseph M. supposed author
Old man. pseud. Return of an old man to his native place. see Swett, Samuel, 1782-1866.
Old man. pseud. Sketches of the history of the town of Hubbardton, Vt. see Church-ill, Amos. supposed author
Old man of business. pseud. Examination of the principles. see Lloyd, Charles.
Old man on the new side. pseud. [Essays] see Snethen, Nicholas, 1769-1845.
Old man's calendar. 26784
Old Man's Home, Philadelphia. Managers. 61884
Old man's honour. 46437
Old man's story. 105056
Old man's story of a young man's adventures. 31021
Old man's story of old times. (57136)
Old member of Parliament. pseud. Appeal to the Justice and interests of the people of Great Britain. see Lee, Arthur, 1740-1792.
Old member of Parliament. pseud. Con-siderations on the Attorney-General's propositions. 15966
Old member of Parliament. pseud. Doubts on the abolition of the slave trade. (20675)
Old member of Parliament. pseud. Looking glass for a Right Honourable Mendicant. 41945
Old member of the Society. pseud. Appeal and remonstrance to the people called Methodists. 14338
Old men's tears for their own declensions. 57137, 78434-78438
Old merchant. pseud. Thoughts on the cur-rency. see Nesmith, John.
Old merchants of New York City. 78464-78465
Old morality. pseud. Song of the sexton. 639, 57138
Old mountaineer. pseud. Laconia. see Scribner, J. P.
Old Narquois, the Negro driver. 28053, 92943
Old naval officer, who served under Lord Rodney, etc. pseud. Breaking the line. see C., G. pseud.
Old New York frontier. 83761
Old New York: or, democracy in 1689. 82514
Old New York; or, reminiscences of the past sixty years. (25446)-25447
Old Nick. pseud. tr. see Forgues, Paul Emile Daurand.
Old Nick of the swamy. 57139
Old North Church, Boston. see Boston. Second Church.
Old Nutfield Celebration, 1869. see Celebration of the One Hundred and Fiftieth Anniversary of the Settled Part of Old Nutfield, N. H., 1869.

Old oaken bucket. 105195
Old patriotic Quaker. pseud. Letters to the King. 17705, (40648)
Old path. 57140
Old paths. 89897
Old paths restored. 46438
Old Pike, the Indian trader. 25105
Old Pine Street Church, Philadelphia. see Philadelphia. Third Presbyterian Church.
Old Pine Street Church. 7348
Old Pine Street Church. Manual of the Third Presbyterian Church. 61885
Old pioneer. pseud. Father Clark. see Peck, John Mason.
Old plantation. (33833)
Old planter. pseud. Essay on plantership, &c. 22946
Old planter. pseud. Letters to a young planter. see Turnbull, Gordon.
Old planter. 88486
Old planters, the authors of the Old mens tears. pseud. Narrative of the planting of the Massachusetts Colony anno 1628. see Scottow, Joshua.
Old play in a new garb. 70830
Old play. The Bohemian. 6140, 12945
Old Pocahontas. sobriquet see Hillhouse, William.
Old principles of New-England. 46439
Old printer. pseud. Descriptive sketch of Philadelphia. 61579
Old probabilities. 79910
Old Quarter Master. pseud. Thirty-six years of a seafaring life. see Bechervaise, John. supposed author
Old redstone. 83304-83305
Old regime in Canada. 58802
Old resident. pseud. Aristocracy of New York. 54095
Old resident. pseud. Burke's guide. see Burke, Andrew.
Old resident. pseud. Immigrant's guide to Minnesota in 1856. 34366, 49253
Old resident. pseud. Pine lands and lumber trade of Michigan. (62927)
Old revolutionary soldier. 699
Old roll of fame. (57141)
Old rough and ready almanac. 57142
Old sailor. pseud. Chapter of American history. 12013
Old sanctuary. (70054)
Old scene painter. pseud. Emigrant's guide. (22479)
Old school and the new school. 71143
Old servant. pseud. Letter to the . . . Lord Mayor. see Heathcote, George.
Old settler. pseud. Garden of the world. see Dana, C. W.
Old settler: devoted to the early history. (57143)
Old Settlers' Association, Sauk County, Wisc. 77159
Old Settler's Festival, Buffalo, N. Y., 1867. 57144
Old Settler's Festival . . . in Buffalo . . . 1867. 57144
Old Settlers Homecoming Association, Smith County, Kansas. see Smith County Old Settlers Homecoing Association, Smith Centre, Kansas.
Old Settlers' Society, Springfield, Ill. (64772)
Old sly boots. pseud. Fugitive political essays. 26123
Old-south. pseud. Constitutional republican-ism. see Austin, Benjamin.

Old South Chapel Prayer Meeting, Boston. see Boston. Old South Church.

Old South Chapel Prayer Meeting; its origin and history. 6666

Old South Church, Boston. see Boston. Old South Church.

Old South Church, Newburyport, Mass. see Newburyport, Mass. First Presbyterian Church.

Old South Church, Worcester, Mass. see Worcester, Mass. First Church (Old South)

Old South Church and Society, Boston. see Boston. Old South Church.

Old South Church, in Boston, Mass. 57145

Old South leaflets. 22146-22147, 80207-80208, 82819, 93270, 98499, 99373, 99376, 101330, 101710, 102336, 102348, 102399, 102402, 103200, 103205, 103397, note after 104653, 104846

Old South Society, Boston. see Boston. Old South Church.

Old statesman. pseud. Lessons to a young prince. see Williams, David, 1738-1816.

Old stone farm house. 57146

Old story of the New World. 71611

Old Sudbury Inn. 11929

Old Testament Bible stories . . . in O-jib-ue. 57089

Old Testament, translated into Greenlandish. 22865

Old thing made new. 64165

Old-time story. 83337

Old times. (58986)

Old times and new. 77730

Old times in the New World. 59201

Old Toney and his master. 82029

Old trapper's pride. (36608)

Old traveler. pseud. Gay life in New-York! 54287

Old traveller. pseud. Short stories and reminiscences. 80694

Old trusty. pseud. To the Tories. see Donaldson, Arthur. supposed author

Old truths and established facts. (57147), 99320, note after 99776

Old 'un. pseud. Stray subjects. see Durivage, Francis A.

Old union wagon. 42600

Old vanishing into the new. 83341

Old Virginia Georgics. 94257

Old Virginian. pseud. To the members of both houses. 100530

Old whig. pseud. New crisis. see Cheetham, James.

Old whig in town. pseud. Letter. 10505

Old white meeting house. 41014, 65536, 65539

Old woman who lived in a shoe. 36065

Old woman's loyalty. 57148

Old world and the new. An address deliverec by George Wm. Brown. (8482)

Old world and the new; or, a journal of reflections and observations. (19859)

Old Yorkshire. 84731

Old Zeke. (57149)

Oldbuck, Anthony. pseud. Legend of Boston. 57150

Oldbug, John, Esq. pseud. Puritan. see Withington, Leonard.

Olden time. (17364)-17365, 47512, 78471, 84618, 84647, 101710

Olden time in Carolina. 64641

Olden time in New-York. 19293, 2d note after 95665

Older time of Carolina. 64841, 2d note after 87909

Olden times in Carolina. 10976

Oldenburgh, Henry. 52638

Oldendorp, Christian Georg Andreas. (57151) (57152)

Older one who has been through. pseud. Letter to a young man who has just entered college. 40424

Oldest and the newest empire. 89258

Oldest inhabitant. pseud. Sketches and recollections of Lynchburg. see Cabell, Julia Mayo.

Oldest known illustration of South American Indians. 99362

Oldfield, J. 57154, 96317

Oldfield, John, 1789-1863. (57153)

Oldham, W. S. (57155)

Oldham chronicle. 88316

Oldmixon, John. 57163-57164

Oldmixon, John, 1673-1742. (49907), 52140, (57156)-57157, 57159-57162, 1st-3d note after 103078

Oldmixon, John, 1673-1742. supposed author 8136, 41877, 47571, 78227

Oldmixon, John, 1673-1742. incorrectly supposed author (28941), 57158

Oldpath, Obadiah. pseud. Lin: or, jewels of the third plantation. see Newhall, James R.

Oldport romance. 31755

Olds, C. V. (76442)

Olds, Edson B. (57165)

Olds, Gamaliel S. (57166)-57167

Oldschool, Oliver. pseud. Brief outline of the life of Henry Clay. see Sargent, Nathan.

Oldschool, Oliver. pseud. Poetry of the Po? folio. see Dennie, Joseph, 1786-1812.

Oldstyle, Jonathan. pseud. Letters. see Irving, Washington, 1783-1859.

Oldys, Francis. pseud.? 11763, 57168, 57169

Oldys, William, 1696-1761. 17971, 30394, 67560, (67570), 67599, 71899

Olea, Nicolao de. 57170

O'Leary, Arthur, 1729-1802. 11072, 57171

Oleo. 36391

Olesia. 16552

Olin, Stephen. 57172-57174

Olinda, ghelegen int Landt van Brasil. (2712

Olio; being a collection of poems. (27411), 57175

Olio; collected by a literary traveller. 5717

Olio; or satirical poetic-hodge-podge. 57177

Oliphant, --------. 57178, 81890

Oliphant, Andrew. 57179

Oliphant, David. 57180

Oliphant, Edward. 57181

Oliphant, John. 57182

Oliphant, Laurence. 57183-(57184)

Oliphant, Margaret O. Wilson. 57185

Oliva, Anello. (57186)

Oliva, Fernan Perez de. see Perez de Oliva, Fernan, 1495?-1533.

Oliva, Manuel Perez de. see Perez de Oliva, Manuel.

Olivan, Alejandro. 57187-(57188), 98176

Olivan, Juan de. 99619

Olivares, Gabriel de. 57421

Olivares, Gaspar de Guzman, Conde Duque de, 1587-1645. (51243), 69235, 2d note after 78907

Olivares, Ignacio Gonzalez. (57189)

Olive, Pedro Maria de. 33714

Olive and the pine. (42418)
Olive branch. . . . By O. P. Mitchell. (49710)
Olive branch from America. 83876
Olive branch. No. IV. (10878)
Olive branch. No. III. (10878), 10889
Olive branch; or faults on both sides, Federal and Democratic. (10850)-10851, (10877)-10879, 10889
Olive branch: or, herald of peace and truth to all saints. 57190
Olive branch; or, the evil and the remedy. 49201
Olive-branch; or, White Oak Farm. 57191
Olive buds. 80935
Olive grove poems. 16297
Olive-leaf. 57192
Olive leaves. 80936
Oliveira, Antonio Rodrigues Velloso de. see Velloso de Oliveira, Antonio Rodrigues.
Oliveira, Candido Baptista de. (7628), 57193
Oliveira, Francisco Manuel de. 57194
Oliveira, H. V. d'. 57195
Oliveira, Joao Alfredo Correa de. see Correa de Oliveira, Joao Alfredo.
Oliveira, Jose Alvares de. 57197
Oliveira, Manoel Lucas de. 85623
Oliveira, Saturnino de Souza e. see Souza e Oliveira, Saturnino de, 1803-1848.
Oliveira, Saturnino de Souza e. see Souza e Oliveira, Saturnino de, 1824-
Oliveira Bastos, Manuel Jose de. 57198
Oliveira e Castro, Luis Joaquin de. tr. 88551
Oliveira e Daun, Joao Carlos de Caldanha de. see Saldanha, Joao Carlos de Saldanha Oliveira e Daun, l. Duque de, 1790-1876.
Oliviera Mendes, Luis Antonio de. see Mendes, Luis Antonio de Oliveira.
Oliveira Pinto, Basilio Jose de. see Pinto, Basilio Jose de Oliveira.
Oliveira Goncalves & Correa. firm 71460
Oliver, Andrew, 1706-1774. 6735, 34071-34072, (34085), 45940, 103136 see also Massachusetts (Colony) Lieutenant Governor, 1771-1774 (Oliver) Massachusetts (Colony) Secretary.
Oliver, Andrew, 1731-1799. 57199, 104858
Oliver, Benjamin L. 57200
Oliver, Daniel. 29615, 57201-57202
Oliver, Ebenezer. claimant (57208) see also New England Mississippi Land Company. Directors. claimants
Oliver, George, 1782-1867. 30514, 57203
Oliver, Henry K. 57204
Oliver, Isabella. 57205
Oliver, James McCarty. (57206)
Oliver, Jerusha (Mather) 46410
Oliver, John. 57207
Oliver, M. 57209
Oliver, Peter, 1713-1791. 57211, 79367, note after 104061
Oliver, Peter, 1822-1855. 32362, 37712, 57212, 96946, 96951, 2d-3d notes after 102623
Oliver, Thomas F. (57213)
Oliver, V. L. 84539
Oliver, William. 57214
Oliver y Bravo, Pedro. 57210
Oliver Dyer's phonographic report of the National Free Soil Convention. 21599
Oliver Evans to his counsel. 23181
Oliver Fairplay. pseud. see Jefferson, Thomas, Pres. U. S., 1743-1826.

Oliver Newman: a New-England tale (unfinished.) 88565
Oliver Oakwood. pseud. see Potts, Stanley G.
Oliver Oldschool. pseud. see Dennie, Joseph, 1786-1812. and Sargent, Nathan.
Oliver Optic. pseud. see Adams, William Taylor, 1822-1897.
Oliver Wendell Holmes in Berkshire. 83330
Olivers, Thomas. (57218)
Oliver's magazine. 57217
Olivet, Mich. Olivet Institute. see Olivet Institute, Olivet, Mich.
Olivet Baptist Church, Philadelphia. see Philadelphia. Olivet Baptist Church.
Olivet Congregational Church, Springfield, Mass. see Springfield, Mass. Olivet Congregational Church.
Olivet Institute, Olivet, Mich. 57220
Oliveyra, Francisca Xavier d'. 57221
Olivier, -------. 11820-11822
Olivier, J. tr. 29723, 94467
Olivier de Corancez, Louis Alexandre. 57222
Olivier-Schilperoort, T. tr. (77691)
Olivier de la Paix. 73831
Olivos, Alonso Vascallero de los. see Vascallero de los Olivos, Alonso.
Olla podrida, condimentada en Mexico. 46187
Ollanta. An ancient Ynca drama. 57224
Ollanta. Ein alt Peruanisches Drama. 57224
Ollanta, o sea la severidad de un padre. 57223
Ollantai. 57224
Ollapodiana papers. 13332
Olliffe, Charles. 57225
Ollivant, J. E. (38229), 57226
Olmedilla, Juan de la Cruz Cano y. see Cano y Olmedilla, Juan de la Cruz.
Olmedo, J. J. de. 56686, 57228-(57229)
Olmedo y Sossa, Isidoro de. 60854 see also Lima. Universidad de San Marcos. Rector.
Olmedo y Torre, Antonio de. 24312, 57227
Olmo, Jose Vicente del. (57230)
Olmos, Andres de, ca. 1491-1571. 57231-57233, 74951
Olmos, Didac. de. 57234
Olmos, Juan Manuel. 48814, (57235)
Olmoz, Andres de. see Olmos, Andres de, ca. 1491-1571.
Olmstead, Gideon. (30039), note after 57236, note before 96910
Olmstead, Gideon. claimant 57236, 93766
Olmstead, Gideon. plaintiff 7970, 57236
Olmstead, J. W. 57237
Olmsted, Denison, 1791-1859. 45433, 55613, (57238), 85072, 85386, 96511 see also North Carolina. Geologist.
Olmsted, Francis Allyn. (57239)
Olmsted, Frederick Law, 1822-1903. 27528, 76539, 76548-76549, 76639, 76647, 76670, 84268, 90788
Olmsted, Frederick Law, 1822-1903. supposed author 42018, 57245, 64054
Olmsted, W. N. 57247
Olmsted, Vaux & Co. firm 57246
Olney, Jeremiah. 57248
Olney, Jesse. 57249
Olney, Lafeyette W. 57250
Olney, William T. (57251)
Olneyville, R. I. Division No. 10, Sons of Temperance. see Sons of Temperance of North America. Rhode Island. Olneyville Division, No. 10.

Olofsson, Gudmund. 85484
Olographic will of John McDonogh. 43177
Olovčić, Nilola Ogramić. see Ogramić
    Olovčić, Nilola, Bp., 1630-1700.
Olsen, Mrs. --------. 57254
Olsen, Sophia B. 87130
Olshausen, Theodor. 57255-57256
Oltmanns, Jabbo. 33747, (33757), (57257)
Olympia Pythia, Nemea, Isthmia, Graece et
    Latine. 62917
Olympic Theatre, Philadelphia. see
    Philadelphia. Olympic Theatre.
Olympic Theatre. Proceedings. 61908
Olympus pump. 52164
Olyphant, John. 57258
Om Amerika samt om Emigrant-Foreningen i
    Stockholm. 57259
Om bodssystemet i de forende stater. 4193
Om Capitain-Lieutenant og Ridder W. A.
    Graah's undersogelsesreize. 62945
Om de udvandrede Nordmaende i Nordamerika.
    87942
Om den geographisk beskaffenhed af de Danske
    Handelsdistrikter i Nordgronland. 71436
Om emancipationen af faeroerne og Gronland.
    51247
Om evangelii forsta grundsattser eller herrans
    vag till att fralsa meniskorna. 85513
Om Gronland, dets indbyggere, productor og
    handel. 46851
Om huler i kalksteen i. d. indre af Brasilien.
    42689
Om monopolhanden paa Gronland. 71437
Om Mormonerne. 50751
Om Negerslavereit i Vestindien. 26135
Om unvandringen til Amerika. 86853
Omaha, Neb. Charter. 57260
Omaha, Neb. Ordinances, etc. 57260
Omaha daily bee. 87143
Omaha directory, June, 1866. 57261
Omaha Indians. Treaties, etc. 96662,
    96714
Omai, ------. 57263
Omana y Sotomayor, Gregorio. (57264)
Omar. pseud. Friend of peace. see Wor-
    cester, Noah, 1758-1837.
Omar. pseud. Six letters. see Worcester,
    Noah, 1758-1837.
Omar. pseud. Solitary reflections. see
    Worcester, Noah, 1758-1837.
Omar's solitary reflections. 105251, 105253,
    105257, 105260, 105263
O'Meagher, W. ed. (54812)
O'Meara, Frederick A. (57028), 57093-
    57095, 57265-57266, 79688-79690
Omega. pseud. Popery, a craft. 57267
Omicron. pseud. Plan of reform in
    Transylvania University. 96465
Omicron. pseud. Statement of the case of
    Bishop Provoost. 90719
Omissions and commissions of the adminis-
    tration. 61046
Ommelanden (Dutch Province) Laws, statutes,
    etc. 93834
Ommelanden (Dutch Province) Staten Generael.
    78000-(78001)
Omnibus. 48421
Omnibus and railroad. 4654
Omnium, Jacob. pseud. Is cheap sugar a
    triumph of free trade? 57268
Omnium, Jacob. pseud. Second letter to Lord
    John Russell. (35493)
Omnium gatherum, for November, 1809.
    (57269)
Omnivm gentivm mores, leges, et ritvs.
    6117, 106330

Omnium pene Europae, Asiae, Africae et
    Americae gentium habitus. 8739
Omrod, John. 35473, 101748-101749
Omstandig journaal van de reize naar Groen-
    land. 50474
Omstandigh verhael van de Fransche rodomo-
    ade voor het Fort Curassau. 57270
Omstoendelig og udforling relation. 22021
On a death-bed repentance. 84123
On a fossil Saurian of the new red sandstone
    formation. (39496)
On a metropolitan police. 62528
On a motion made, ordered, that the follow-
    ing . . . statement. 100093
On a new genus of the crustacea. 77389
On a reform of spelling. 102367, note after
    102396
On a soul pleading with God under a sense of
    its necessities. 97576
On Abiel Wood Sheppard. 80309
On American morals and manners. 19853
On American prisons. 2220
On American taxation. 9297
On Andrew and Butler. 79137
On asymmetry in the appendages of hexapod
    insects. 78531
On banking in the United States. 95956
On baths and mineral waters. 4455A
On behalf of an abused general. 89115
On beneficence, or univeral charity. 30239
On birds collected by Mr. George M. Whitely.
    78142
On birds from Duke of York Island. (71843)
On Bull Run. 74401
On certain political measures. (3422)
On certain storms in Europe and America.
    85072
On Champlain's astrolabe. 74299
On church government and discipline. 73408
On colonial intercourse. 5926, 102854
On comparative humanity. 25002
On comparative slavery. 25002
On conciliation with America. 9297
On constitutional liberty. 18037
On contributions for the sick and wounded.
    (73255)
On coral reefs and islands. 18427
On cotton. 2281
On councils. 360, 11967, 3d note after
    96741
On credit, currency and banking. (42022)
On crystallization. 84411
On cultivating a spirit of universal peace.
    72679
On currency, prices and wages. 95818
On death, the resurrection of the dead, a
    future judgment, &c. 84678C
On decision of the Supreme Court. (31825)
On democracy. (58969)
On diluvial deposits. 46811
On Dr. Monod and the American Tract Socie-
    92447
On doing good. 70862
On education, and the duties of civil life.
    51112
On emigration. 10889
On emigration and settlement on wild land.
    28139
On extraordinary fishes from California. 50
On faith. 89369
On field-husbandry. 22140
On fluctuations of level in the North America
    lakes. 85072, 103823
On foreign subsidies, etc. 80062
On freedom of mind. 52056

On Friday evening the 27th inst. 105806
On Friday next, the first day of May. 57274
On Friday next, the tenth day of April. 57274
On Friday next, the twenty-fourth day of April. 57274
On gathering. 89369
On government. 105648
On happiness. 98295
On his [i. e. John Caldwell Calhoun's] resolutions and in reply to Mr. Webster. 9936
On his [i. e. John Caldwell Calhoun's] resolutions in reference to the case of the Enterprise. 9936
On history and political economy. 40985
On human depravity. 79392
On indigenous intermittent fever. 32621
On inland navigation of the Merrimack. 93533
On international copyright. 40985
On irrigation in the West Indies. 43259
On labor, an address. 14535
On Leaia Leidyi-Cypricardia Leidyi. (39496)
On liberty. 48987
On liberty and self-government. 40974
On liberty, taxes, and the application of public money. 80062
On list of boards of trade. (31825)
On Louisiana legislation relating to freedmen. 29533
On love of country. (43647)
On McClellan's nomination and acceptance. 82612-82613
On medical colleges. 41313
On military commissions for the trial of citizens. 35707
On Mr. Belcher's return from his travels. 104108
On Mr. Thomas Hooker. 32860
On Monday morning of this week. 105942
On Monday next, the thirteenth day of April. 57274
On Monday, the ninth day of March. 57273
On Monday, the second day of March. 57272
On Monday, the sixteenth day of March. 57274
On Monday, the sixteenth instant. 57271
On Monday, the twenty-sixth instant. 61887
On monies, coins, weights, and measures. 57275, 93803
On moral unity, and the way of its attainment. 71116
On . . . Mount Auburn Cemetery. 5300
On natural theology as a study in schools. 48928
On new genera of plants from Brazil and Chile. 48891
On new sources of trade. (6415)
On new terrestrial mollusks and shells. 5870
On North-American Helicidae and on the geographical distribution of West-India land-shells. 5869
On north western American emigration. 38037
On objections to the disuse of West Indian slave produce. 102855
On paper money. (31190)
On patriotism. 19860
On perfect harmony in Music. (64035)
On Peruvian guano. 52338
On picket duty. 691
On planting the sciences in America. 84580
On political economy. 57276
On presidential arrests. 5264
On protection to West India sugar. 39068
On provision for the insane poor of . . . New York. (39716)

On raising Indian-corn. 98633
On receiving donations from holders of slaves. 57277
On recent occurrences at Litchfield. 57278
On recent proceedings of the Legislature of Barbados. 3279
On recommendation for a department of commerce. (31825)
On regeneration [by Duffield.] 69536
On regeneration. . . . [By John Blair.] 5746
On republican education. 94384
On retrocession. 94089
On rightly divining the word of truth. 90204
On Saturday evening about 9 o'clock. 93795
On Saturday, the 31st of July. 105944
On school rates in England and America. 81403
On self-government. (57279), (71223)
On Sherman's track. (37380)
On slavery. 57280, 82030
On slavery, and its remedy. 59468
On social welfare and human progress. (31388)
On some new fossil molluscs. (39496)
On some points in the history and prospects. 18955
On some preparations of the American revolt. 42619
On stamping freight receipts. (31825)
On sugar cultivation in Louisiana. (40073), 57281, 93456
On suspending our diplomatic relations with Austria. 11349
On synostitic crania among Aboriginal race of man. 18855
On taking an affectionate farewell from my kind benefactors in Boston. 103150
On the abolition of colonial slavery. (11774)
On the abolition of slavery. 19836
On the abolition of the slave trade. 57282
On the abolition petitions. 9936
On the aborigines of America. 27286
On the absorption and emission of air. 85072
On the abuse of the pardoning power. 95808
On the admission of Kansas. 80376
On the advantages of opening the river St. Lawrence. (79621)
On the affairs of the West Indies. 3653, 40502
On the African slave trade. 25002
On the agencies which affect the stability of the union. 21673
On the agricultural state of Canada. 24102
On the alligator of North America. 31437
On the amendment to admit Alabama. 15881
On the American prime meridian. 42386
On the analogy which exists between the marl of New Jersey. (51024)
On the applicability of the pacific principles. 21606
On the application of interference methods to spectroscopic measurements. 85072
On the arrest of C. L. Vallandigham. 41152
On the avoidance of the violent portions of cyclones. 72476
On the bailing of Jefferson Davis. 82614
On the Baltimore rail-road carriage. 93519
On the bankrupt bill. 9936
On the Barlingtonia Californica. 85072
On the beach at Long Branch song book. 41328
On the beauties, harmonies, and sublimities of nature. 8887

On the Beroid-Medusae of the shores of Massachusetts. 504
On the best means of bringing water. 38186
On the best ration for the soldier. 83367
On the bill for the admission of Michigan. 9936
On the bill for the occupation of the Oregon Territory. 9936
On the bill to distribute the proceeds of the public lands. 9936
On the bill to establish the Nebraska and Kansas Territories. 4461
On the bill to prevent the interference of certain federal officers in elections. 9936
On the bill to prohibit deputy postmasters from receiving. 9936
On the bill to refund the fine imposed on General Jackson. 3454
On the bill to repeal the force act. 9936
On the birth of George Washington. 101771
On the birth of Washington. 105016
On the border. 27452
On the British African Colonization Society. 14732, 32351
On the captivity of Benjamin Gilbert & family. 101219
On the carcinological collections of the Cabinet of Natural History. 27275
On the case of M'Leod. 9936
On the causes, nature, and cure of consumptions. 50408
On the causes of the success of the English and American revolutions. (29266)
On the character and fossils of the different coal seams. (64031)
On the Chicago surrender. 80419
On the Chinese sugar cane. (70736)
On the circumnavigation of Africa by the ancients. (4431)
On the citizens making a temporary submission to the British arms. 9278, note just before 87733
On the classification and geographical distribution of crustacea. 18422
On the climatic conditions of the summer of 1853. 5953
On the colour of the native Americans. (4431)
On the commencement of a new year. 18418
On the commencement of the year 1769. 102449
On the commerce of Southern America. (35109)
On the commercial intercourse between the United States and Germany. 77649
On the common school system of the United States. 81404
On the completion of the eighteenth century. 18418
On the compromise resolutions of Mr. Bell. 4787
On the condution of Negroes in the West-Indies. 25002
On the conditions of the deposition of coal. 18954
On the conduct of Gen. Putnam. 39723
On the conduct of the Society for Propagating the Gospel. 342
On the conservative elements of the American republic. (20689)
On the constitution. 13290
On the constitution of the United States. 16620
On the constitution of the water of the gulf stream. 19597

On the construction of a silvered glass telescope. 85072
On the construction of a silvered mirror telescope. 85072
On the construction, organization and general arrangements. 37981
On the contents of a bone cave in the island of Anguilla. 85072
On the continental money. 57283
On the conversion and apostleship of St. Pau 19238
On the course of college education. 57284
On the course of hurricanes. (68512)
On the cryptogamous origin of malarious and epidemic fevers. 49703
On the culture and commerce of cotton in India, and elsewhere. 73841
On the currency. 27975
On the cyclones or typhoons of the North Pacific Ocean. (68512)
On the Cynipidae of the North American oak and their galls. (57824)
On the danger of emancipation of the Negroe 8403
On the dangerous tendency to innovations and extremes in education. 104804
On the Darlingtonia California. 96296
On the death of Abraham Lincoln. (31445)
On the death of Beulah Worfield. 105467
On the death of Channing. 14345
On the death of Eaton. (21744)
On the death of General Washington. 101773 101823, 101865
On the death of his [i. e. John Stevens'] father. 91541
On the death of John Wagstaffe. 101416
On the death of Miss Polly Child. 104806
On the death of the Queen. 9712
On the death of the Reverend Benjamin Colr (14525), 21608, 78697
On the death of Uriah Brown. 104806
On the debt of the nation, compared with its revenues. 47285
On the departure of an infamous B-r---t. 96140
On the deplorable state of the Indians. 819 8198
On the densities of oxygen and hydrogen. 85072
On the discovery of the Mississippi. 23726 96172
On the discussion of the following question. 84843, note after 94295
On the dismemberment of Canada. 85252
On the distribution bill. 9936
On the distribution of the forests and trees of North America. 16574
On the disturbances in South America. 57286, 85674, 87317
On the duties of an ambassador of Christ. 11958
On the duty of females to promote the cause of peace. (38527)
On the effects of high temperature upon the public health. 84262
On the electrotyping operations of the U. S. Coast Survey. 46854
On the elevation of the poor. 97399
On the emancipation of the colonies. 69464
On the emery mine of Chester, Hampden Co Mass. 82996
On the establishment of a line of main streamers. 25048
On the establishment of a new bank in the District. 20314

On the establishment of an universal system
of meteorological observations. 46968
On the establishment of public schools in the
city of New York. 47287
On the evil of slander. 84121-84123
On the evils of a weak government. 82217
On the expediency and practicability of a time
and weather observatory. 54565
On the exploration of the north polar region.
57288, 57760
On the facilities for a ship canal communi-
cation. (41693)
On the finances of the island of Antigua.
65467
On the first hurricane of September 1853.
(68512)
On the first settlement of this country. 94104
On the fisheries. 94009
On the formal recognition of Chile and Peru.
(12793)
On the Fort Pillow and Plymouth massacre.
82615
On the forthcoming union of the two Canadas.
94464
On the fossil foot-marks in the red sandstone
of Pottsville. (39496)
On the foundation of civil government. 16620
On the foundation of the American colonies.
69464, 82681
On the 14th of June, 1723. 103422
On the freedom of the press. 84642
On the fresh-water glacial drift of the north-
western states. 85072, 103824
On the frontier, or scenes in the west.
57289, 59440
On the fruits of agriculture. (6415)
On the gales and hurricanes of the western
Atlantic. (68512)
On the general integrals of planetary motion.
85072
On the genus Acostaea of D'Orbigny. (39496)
On the geographical distribution of testaceous
mollusca. 42938
On the geological age of the White Mountains.
72671
On the geological and physical geography of
North America. (72667)
On the geological character of the beds on
which Philadelphia stands. 8676
On the geology of lower Louisiana. 85072
On the geology of North-America. 72658
On the glory of both soul and body in the
heaven of heavens. 46703
On the glory of the bodies of God's children.
46703
On the government of the territory of Columbia.
105152
On the great advantages likely to be derived.
81399
On the Greenland eight-whale. 22824
On the Greenland or polar ice. 78181
On the growth and trade of timber, in America.
57290
On the guilt and folly of being ashamed of
religion. 84121-84123
On the happiness of the souls of believers.
46703
On the dealth and management of European
soldiers. 80564
On the height of the Pacific Ocean at Panama.
(41693)
On the historical argument for slaveholding.
20255
On the illustrious life and character [of George
Washington.] 12, 101686

On the immediate abolition of slavery.
82431
On the importance of a knowledge of . . .
physiology. (70407)
On the importance of assisting young men.
4334
On the importance of establishing a colony in
Louisiana. (25854)
On the importance of studying and preserving
the languages. 32351
On the importance of the study of anatomy.
84417
On the impropriety of using and selling
spiritous liquors. 105464
On the improvement and present condition of
the tenement house population. 84263
On the improvement of the Ohio River. 50819
On the inconsistency of man. (57291)
On the increase and decrease of the slave
population. 102803
On the increasing importance of the British
West-Indian possessions. 102856
On the infusoria of the family Bacillaria.
2741
On the inhumanity of the slave trade. 59124
On the injurious tendency of the modifying of
our navigation laws. (41299)
On the internal structure of the earth. 85072
On the issues of the war. 9598
On the joys of heaven. 101370
On the junction of the Atlantic and Pacific
Oceans. 37257
On the Klondike. 84981
On the knowledge of the Lord. (78292)
On the latitude and longitude of Milwaukee.
28219
On the latitude and longitude of the U. S.
Naval Observatory. 54937
On the Laurentian limestones of North America.
33894
On the liability of the abolitionists to criminal
punishment. 99782
On the life and services of William Henry
Harrison. 43624
On the lightly sportive wing. 92175
On the longitude of Washington. 27419
On the love of praise. 84111
On the Maine law. [By Samuel Thayer Spear.]
89087, 89093
On the Maine-law. [By the Earl of Harrington.]
39895
On the Maine law. Extract from an address.
89087, 89093
On the Maine liquor law. (3496)
On the malignant fever. 384
On the maritime rights of Great Britain.
99777
On the means adopted in the British colonial
magnetic observatories. 74714
On . . . the means of grace. 5746
On the means of safety in steam boats.
93529
On the Melchizedek priesthood. 71919
On the memory of Mr. Robert Rich. 60893
On the meteorology of the Albion Mines, Nova
Scotia. 64032
On the military statistics of the United States
of America. 22262
On the minerals of the Wheatley Mine, in
Pennsylvania. 82997, 82999
On the mischief of usury laws. 57292
On the mode of constituting presidential electors.
(20339)
On the modern-reflecting telescope. 85072
On the mollusca of Peconic and Gardiner's
Bays. 84126

On the serpents of New York. 2806
On the slave trade. 28737
On the slavery of the Old World. (26100)
On the sources and benefits of professional
earnestness. 42647
On the sources of malaria and autumnal
diseases in Virginia. 100507
On the special action of the Department of
Justice, and Police. 87472
On the species of Orca inhabiting the northern
seas. 22824
On the statistics and geography of the produc-
tion of iron. 31638
On the stone implements of the Indians of
North America. 59420
On the subject of the embargo and other
public concerns. 93497
On the sub-treasury bill, in reply to Mr.
Webster. 9936
On the supposed increase of insanity. 35805
On the system of policy hitherto pursued.
3422
On the ten tribes of Israel. 57298
On the tendency of our system of intercourse.
10889
On the terribleness, and the moral cause of
earthquakes. (72696)
On the ties of the Atlantic and Pacific coasts
of the United States. (2588)
On the tracks of large birds. 3587
On the treasury note bill. 9936
On the 20th. of November, the following
address. 86730, 2d note after 99911
On the unconstitutional continuance of foreign
laws. 36052
On the Urari, or arrow poison of the Indians
of Guiana. (77790)
On the use of plaster of Paris splints, etc.
30113, 76657
On the utility of public loan offices and savings
banks. 47270
On the vanity of human actions. 83627
On the vanity of prayer and fasting. (72696)
On the vanity of this life. 79358
On the victory of P. Heyn in 1628. 32382
On the vital statistics of Montreal. 11001
On the vocal sounds of Laura Bridgman.
85072
On the war. 81073
On the war of 1812 '15. 98417
On the war-time ways of a modern statesman.
105566
On the winds of the northern hemisphere.
14174
On the works and character of James Smithson.
84985
On thorough drainage in Canada. 8669
On three several hurricanes of the Atlantic.
68510
On three several hurricanes of the American
seas. (68512)
On Thursday, December 16, sentence of death.
95666
On Thursday last, . . . Mr. Cornelius Bradford.
(57299)
On time. 57216
On Tuesday, at 12 o'clock, His Excellency
Governor McDuffie communicated.
87545
On two attempts to ascend the Chimborazo.
33701
On two new species of Laurineae from Guiana.
note after 77796
On Vallandigham and "arbitrary arrest."
41158

On war and its inconsistence with the Gospel.
4680, 79260
On water baptism. 89369
On Wednesday evening, 1st January, will be
presented. 101866
On Wednesday next, the sixth day of May,
1778. 57274
On Wednesday, the twenty-fifth day of March.
57274
On wheels and how I came there. 84749
On William Penn's treaty with the Indians.
47270
Ona, Pedro de. 57300-57304, 57629, 98772
Onate, Alonso de. 57305
Onate y Salazar, Juan de 69210, 98794,
99638-99639 see also Nueva Mexico
(Province) Gobernador, 1598-1609 (Onate
y Salazar)
Onbedriegh'lijcke leyd-sterre. 89746
Onbekende volkplanting in Zuid-Amerika.
49827
Onbezwekene gehechtheid en trouw. 57306
Once a month. (57307)
Once a month. . . . 1869. (57307)
Once well begun is half done. 93226
Oncle d'Amerique; scenes. 19538
Oncle Tom. 92537, 92544, 92546-92547
Oncle Tom racontre aux enfans par Mlle. de
Constant. 92547
Onder de Yankee's. 74165
Onderdaen ende Lieff-hebber van deselve.
pseud. Verthooninge. 99304
Onderdanig dank-adres. 100874
Onderdonk, Benjamin Treadwell, Bp., 1791-
1861. 4032, (35842), 47239, 57308,
71138
Onderdonk, Benjamin Treadwell, Bp., 1791-
1861. defendant at church court
57309, 71138, 100681
Onderdonk, Henry, 1804-1886. 57312-57315,
67068
Onderdonk, Henry, d. 1895. (57311)
Onderdonk, Henry M. 57316
Onderdonk, Henry U., Bp. 43324, 54811,
57317-57318
Onderdonk, John. 57319
Onderdonk, William H. ed. 23291
Ondersoeck der Amsterdamsche requesten tot
verdedigingh der onschuldighe. 16680,
(57320), 1st note after 102889A
Ondersoecker der waerheydt. pseud. Examen
over het vertoogh. 7575-7576
Onderwijs der Negerslaven in Suriname.
57321
Onderzoek naar den toestand der landverhuizers.
92726
Onderzoek ten gevolge der circulaire van Otto
Tank. 57322
Onderzoek van Groot-Britannjes gedrag.
(57323)
Onderzoek van het voordeel dat immer de
Engleschen of de Americanen. 97333
Onderzoekt en oordeelt. 91220, note after
93865
One acquainted with southern institutions.
pseud. Comments on the Nebraska bill.
14964
One among them. pseud. Address to young
people. see Wheeler, Mercy.
"One baptism;" its mode, subjects, pre-
requisites and design. 84426-84427
"One body;" or, the church of Christ under
the apostleship. 84428-84429
One chosen of God and called to the work of
the ministry. (14503)

One of his parishioners. pseud. Review of Mr. Mitchell's sermon preached at the last fast. 70210

One of its loyal citizens. pseud. Farcical tragedy. 23793

One of its readers. pseud. To the author of a letter to Doctor Mather. see Mather, Samuel, 1706-1785. supposed author

One of its trustees. pseud. Duty of Columbia College to the community. see Ruggles, Samuel B.

One of our chaplains. pseud. Camp and the field. 10178

One of ourselves. pseud. Letter to us. (40574)

One of Sister Rhody's collections of historical facts. 12694

One of the Aldermen of . . . Philadelphia. pseud. Exposition of the law. (60094)

One of the American people. pseud. Political intolerance. see Sargent, Winthrop, 1753-1820.

One of the assets of the American money enterprise. 83888

One of the attestators. pseud. see Cotton, John, 1584-1652.

One of the bachelors: a youth of eighteen. pseud. Valedictory oration. 98343

One of the best accounts of Braddock's defeat. 82767

One of the board of managers. pseud. History of the Boston Dispensary. see Lawrence, William R.

One of the commissioners. pseud. Remarks on the proceedings as to Canada. see Grey, Sir Charles Edward.

One of the commissioners under the said sixth article. pseud. Brief statement of opinions. 7904, (14989), 84842

One of the committee of the American Academy. pseud. Short reply to a pamphlet. see Bigelow, Jacob.

One of the company. pseud. Description of a great sea-storm. 19706

One of the company. pseud. Within Fort Sumter. 25168

One of the convention. pseud. Letter developing the character and views of the Hartford Convention. see Otis, Harrison Gray, 1765-1848.

One of the counsel for the petitioners. pseud. Substance of an argument. see White, Joseph M.

One of the craft. pseud. Masonic biography. see Moore, Cornelius.

One of the crew. pseud. Account of the loss of the ship Omartal. see Bolton, John.

One of the delegates in Congress from Pennsylvania. pseud. What think ye of Congress now? see Galloway, Joseph, 1729-1803.

One of the Democratic people of Jackson's day. pseud. Next presidency. (55107), 79736

One of the descendants of the first settlers of the town. pseud. Brief sketch of the first settlement of Deerfield, Mass. 19234

One of the directors. pseud. Address to the stockholders of the Winnisimmet Company. see Matthews, Nathan.

One of the disfranchesed. pseud. Sheep without a shepherd. 80088, 1st note after 96985

One of the editors. pseud. Examination of Mr. Barnes reply. see Ridgely, Greenburg William.

One of the executors. pseud. Will of Samuel Appleton. see Bowditch, Nathaniel Ingersoll.

One of the family. pseud. ed. Miscellaneous writings of the late Samuel J. Smith. 84081

One of the fraternity. pseud. Illustrations of masonry. see Morgan, William, 1774?-1826.

One of the fraternity. pseud. More light on masonry. 50548

One of the graduates. pseud. Poem, on liberty. see Van Vechten, Teunis A. supposed author

One of the hearers. pseud. reporter 46629

One of the inspectors of the prison. pseud. Account of the state prison or penitentiary house. see Eddy, Thomas. and Murray, John. incorrectly supposed author

One of the jury. pseud. reporter see Stansbury, Arthur Joseph.

One of the majority. pseud. Candid examination. 10662, 59956

One of the members. pseud. Condition of labor. 15187

One of the members. pseud. Labor Reform League of New England. (38425)

One of the memorialists. pseud. Exposition of the memorial. see Muhlenberg, William Augustus, 1796-1877.

One of the ministers in Boston. pseud. Sober sentiments. see Mather, Cotton, 1663-1728.

One of the ministers in Boston. pseud. Voice of God in a tempest. see Mather, Cotton, 1663-1728.

One of the ministers in the north-part of Boston. pseud. Soul upon the wing. see Mather, Cotton, 1663-1728.

One of the ministers of Boston. pseud. Marah spoken to. see Mather, Cotton, 1663-1728.

One of the missionaries to the Shawanoe Indians. pseud. Original and select hymns. 79979

One of the officers who accompanied Capt. Cook on his voyages. pseud. Extracts from the private MS. (78598)

One of the oldest settlers of Texas. pseud. Opinion of the four hundred leagues' grant of Texas Lands. see Burnet, David Gouverneur, 1788-1870. supposed author

One of the party. pseud. Ella V———. see Taylor, F.

One of the party. pseud. Souvenir of the trans-continental excursion. 88692

One of the people. pseud. Address to the legislature of Indiana. 34506, 57327

"One of the people." pseud. Annexation to the United States. 56112

One of the people. pseud. Enquiry into the propriety of granting charters. 87819

One of the people. pseud. Examination of the new tariff. see Cambreleng, Churchill C.

One of the people. pseud. Letter on currency matters. (40361)

One of the people. pseud. National and state rights considered. see McDuffie, George, 1790?-1851.

One of the people. pseud. [Note.] 94562

One of the people. pseud. Patriot or people's companion. 59085

One of the people. pseud. Plain statement addressed to all honest Democrats. see Moody, Loring.

One of the people. pseud. Reasons why the Hon. Elisha R. Potter should not be a Senator. see Burges, Tristam.

One of the people. pseud. Remarks on the policy of prohibiting the exportation of cotton. 69484

One of the people. pseud. Republic or the oligarchy? see Cheever, George B.

One of the people. pseud. Society without veil. 86178

One of the people. pseud. Things as they have been, are, and ought to be. 60668

One of the people. pseud. Thoughts on the constitution of the state of South-Carolina. 88079

One of the people. pseud. To the friends of Israel Israel. 95929

One of the people. pseud. To the Hon. W. J. Grayson. 88081

One of the people. pseud. To the public. 96013

One of the people. pseud. True policy of the state of Pennsylvania. 60745

One of the publick. pseud. Proposals for a plan. 66026

One of the rejected "Latham prize poems." (65399)

One of the removed. pseud. Statement of facts. see Tuxbury, George W.

One of the reports of the Joint Committee. (45389)

One of the reverend members. pseud. Great difficulty. (28443)

One of the reverend members. pseud. Necessity of brotherly love. (28443)

One of the Rhode-Island people. pseud. Reply to the letter of the Hon. Marcus Morton. see Pitman, John.

One of the secretaries. pseud. Address. 54041

One of the secretaries of the American Tract Society. pseud. Home evangelization. 32708

One of the secretaries of the Inquisition. pseud. Account of the cruelties. 53402

One of the Seventeenth. pseud. Soldiering in North Carolina. see Kirwan, Thomas.

One of the sixth generation. pseud. Thomas and Margaret Minshall. 49327, 2d note after 95449

One of the Smiths—W. W. pseud. Grand Canyon of Arizona. see Smith, W. W.

One of the Society of Friends. pseud. Letter. 40335

One of the surviving officers. pseud. Authentic narrative of the loss of the Doddington Indiaman. 2452, (20487)

One of the typos. pseud. Very brief and very comprehensive life of Ben. Franklin. see Shillaber, Benjamin Penhallow, 1814-1890.

One of the Vixen's crew. pseud. Narrative of the capture of the United States' Brig Vixen. 100636, 105178

One of the witnesses. pseud. Sugar question. 93457

One of their colleagues. pseud. Considerati in favor of the appointment of Rufus King. see Van Buren, Martin, Pres. U. S., 1782-1862.

One of their constituents. pseud. Letter on the use and abuse of incorporations. (40373)

One of their constituents. pseud. Thoughts concerning the Bank of North America. see Coxe, Tench.

One of their constituents. pseud. Thoughts concerning the bank, with some facts. see Coxe, Tench.

One of their fellow citizens. pseud. Addres to the inhabitants of the District of Maine. (43903)

One of their number. pseud. As you were! 2161

One of their number. pseud. Minister. see Mather, Cotton, 1663-1728.

One of their number. pseud. Rensselaer County Board of Supervisors' defence. see Tallmadge, S. W.

One of their number. pseud. Vindication of an association. see Parker, Benjamin supposed author

One of them. pseud. Bake-pan for the dough faces. (2816)

One of them. pseud. Hairbreadth escapes. see Fanning, Thomas W.

One of themselves. pseud. Enquiry whether the absolute independence of America is not to be preferred. 22651

One of themselves. pseud. Few words in behalf of the loyal women of the United States. 24251

One path. 16222

One poor girl. 80995

One progressive principle. 31161

One proposition sustained against the New School. 104673

One recently returned from the enemy's country. pseud. Letter on the state of the war. see Pollard, Edward A.

One shall be taken and another left. (16634)

One soweth and another reapeth. 33000

One test of character. 82652

One that desired information therein, by an inhabtant there. pseud. Narrative of the practices of the churches of New England. (51775)

One that desires to be faithfull to his country pseud. Religious retreat. see Ward, Nathaniel.

One that has had experience of them. pseud. Nightingale. see Mather, Cotton, 1663 1728.

One that has perused the Summer morning's conversation. pseud. Opinion. see Chauncy, Charles, 1705-1787.

One that hath formerly been conversant with the author in his life time. pseud. ed Tales and jests of Mr. Hugh Peters. 61196

One that hath lived there. pseud. New-Englands advice to Old-England. see Lechford, Thomas.

One that heartily desires the order, peace, and purity of these churches. pseud. ed. Explanation of the Say-Brook platform. 77394

One that heartily wishes the peace and prosperity of these churches. pseud. Some brief remarks. 69700, 86603

One that humbly desires the order, peace, and purity of these churches. pseud. Explanation of the Say-Brook platform. 15814, 23414, 32307

One that never borrowed, or let, an hundred pounds upon interest. pseud. Second part of South-Sea stock. 78738

One that was an eye and eare-witnesse of the carriage of matters there. pseud. Short story of the rise. see Winthrop, John, 1588-1649.

One that was once a scholar to him. pseud. Corderius Americanus. see Mather, Cotton, 1663-1728.

One that wisheth well to all mankind. pseud. Treatise shewing the need we have. 60732, 2d note after 96752

One thing needful. 44088, 85123, 3d note after 94085

One thousand and one home amusements. 104233

One thousand-dollar clerk. pseud. Dialogue. 19932

One union; one constitution; one destiny. (72860)

One week at Amer. 57328

One well acquainted with that affair. pseud. Historical account of the doings of the Christian Indians. see Gookin, Daniel.

One who, as a son with a father, served with him in the Gospel. pseud. Father departing. see Mather, Cotton, 1663-1728.

One who cordially imbraces whatsoever there is of tru [sic] religion in al [sic] professions. pseud. Som[e] free re-flections. see Penn, William, 1644-1718. supposed author

One who had free access to, and frequent conversation with him. pseud. Account of the behaviour of the unhappy sufferer. 94044, 94049, 94052-94053

One who has been there. pseud. Notes on California and the placers. 10036

One who has been there. pseud. State prison life. see Banka, J. Harrie.

One who has considered both sides of the question. pseud. Union. 97763

One who has examined public documents. pseud. Coast survey. 13822

One who has recently crossed. pseud. Passage of the isthmus. see Carrington, P. W.

One who has seen the elephant. pseud. Camp life of a volunteer. see Scribner, B. F.

One who has seen the elephant. pseud. Campaign in Mexico. see Scribner, B. F.

One who has seen the elephant. pseud. Mysteries of California. (10035)

One who has seen them. pseud. Peep at the Aztecs. see Payne, A. R. Middletoun.

One who has suffered. pseud. Brief narrative of incidents in the war in Missouri. 7881

One who has whistled at the plough. pseud. Canada, a battle ground. see Somerville, Alexander, 1811-1885.

One who has whistled at the plough. pseud. John, the traitor. (36148)

One who hates imposture. pseud. 51057

One who hath been a magistrate among them. pseud. Copy of a letter. see Cudworth, James.

One who is not a sailer, tho' of long service in the navy. pseud. Observations on a late scandalous paper. 90621

One who is personally a warm friend of the Irish. pseud. Arguments. 1970

One who knew him from his boyhood. pseud. History of Edwin Forest. (25107)

One who knew him well. pseud. Tribute to the life and character of Jonas Chickering. see Parker, Richard Green.

One who knows. pseud. Spider and the fly. see Herbert, H. W.

One who knows. pseud. Hingham and Quincy Bridges. 67289

One who knows. pseud. Inside out. see Coffey, W. A.

One who knows and who honors them. pseud. Few words to loyal Democrats. 24254

One who knows him. pseud. Letter concerning the labors of Mr. John Augustus. 2385

One who knows him well. pseud. Justice to buck. 8864

One who knows them. pseud. Aristocracy of Boston. see Wilson, Thomas L. V. supposed author

One who knows them. pseud. Easy Nat. 21700

One who knows they are not saints. pseud. Plain questions for Mormonites. 63226

One who listened to . . . the public hearing before the Council. pseud. Review of the result of an Ecclesiastical Council. 70110

One who served in the late war with Mexico. pseud. Guadaloupe. see Small, William F.

One who served in the campaign of 1846-47. pseud. Guadaloupe. see Small, William F.

One who visited among the unfortunate women. pseud. Tidal wave. see Smith, Maria L.

One who was a magistrate in New-England. pseud. True copy of a letter. see Cudworth, James.

One who was born in the colony of the Massa-chusetts-Bay. pseud. Free and calm consideration. see Prescott, Benjamin.

One who was many years a resident of Alta California. pseud. tr. see Robinson, Alfred.

One, who was not inspired with the spirit of Apollo. pseud. View of the Democratick Republican celebration. 99554

One who was present. pseud. Some account of the proceedings. 86583

One who was "sold." pseud. Sons of Malta exposed. 86998

One who went to it. pseud. District school as it was. see Burton, Warren.

One who wishes well to all mankind. pseud. Salvation for all men. see Chauncy, Charles, 1705-1787. and Clarke, John, 1755-1798. incorrectly supposed author

One wife, or many. 83295

One wife too many. 32994

One world: one Washington. 20388

One year in Savannah a poem, in five parts. 106071

One year in Scandinavia. 85510

One year of my life. 48831

O'Neal, Henry. 57329

O'Neall, John Belton. 57330-57332, 3d note after 87898

Oneby, John. defendant 57333

Oneida County, N. Y. Agricultural Society.
see Oneida County Agricultural Society.
Oneida County, N. Y. Board of Supervisors.
(57335)
Oneida County, N. Y. Washington Benevolent
Society. see Washington Benevolent
Society. New York. Oneida County.
Oneida and Genesee Conference Seminary,
Cazenovia, N. Y. see Oneida Con-
ference Seminary, Cazenovia, N. Y.
Oneida and Genesee Conference Seminary,
Cazenovia, 1828-29. 47336
Oneida and Oberlin. 93141
Oneida Association. see Oneida Community.
Oneida Association, Oneida Castle, N. Y. see
Oneida Community.
Oneida Bible Society, Utica, N. Y. 98230
Oneida Bible Society, Utica, N. Y. Directors.
98230
Oneida Baptist Association. see Baptists.
New York. Oneida Baptist Association.
Oneida Castle, N. Y. Oneida Association. see
Oneida Community.
Oneida circular. 89516
Oneida Community. (16356), (30208), (57337),
57339, 2d note after 93596
Oneida Community. New York and New Jersey
Convention, 1842. 60921
Oneida Conference. see Methodist Episcopal
Church. Conferences. Oneida Con-
ference.
Oneida Conference Seminary, Cazenovia, N. Y.
57336, (57340)
Oneida County Agricultural Society. Annual
Fair, Utica, 1853. 57341
Oneida Female Missionary Society. see
Female Oneida Missionary Society.
Oneida Indians. 49348-49349, 66061, 91588
see also Five Nations of Indians.
Oneida Indians. Treaties, etc. 36337, 60255,
96608
Oneida Indians (First Christian Party) Treaties,
etc. 96729
Oneida Indians (Orchard Party) Treaties, etc.
96729
Oneida Institute, Whitesboro, N. Y. Trustees.
57341
Oneida Institute, Whitesboro, N. Y. Antislavery
Society. see Whitestown and Oneida
Institute Anti-slavery Socities.
Oneida Institute of Science and Industry. see
Oneida Institute, Whitesboro, N. Y.
Oneida Medical Society. 57341
Oneida Presbytery. see Presbyterian Church
in the U. S. A. Presbytery of Oneida.
Oneida reserve. (25706)
Oneidoe Indians. see Oneida Indians.
O'Neil, -------, fl. 1810. 57346
O'Neil, Charles. 57343
O'Neil, Sieur de Beaulieu Hues. see Baillet,
Adrien, 1649-1706.
O'Neil, Elizabeth. supposed author. 57344,
95797
O'Neil, J. T. 39213, (57345), 88947
O'Neill, H. 57347
O'Neill, J. A. illus. 80005
O'Neill, J, W. 20866
O'Neill, John. 57348
O'Neill, Neal John. 57349
Oneota, or characteristics of the red race of
America. 77867
Oneota, or the red race of America. 77867
Onesimus. pseud. Doctrine of the new birth.
57350
Onesimus Secundus. pseud. True interpretation
of the American civil war. 57351

Oneyde Indians. see Oneida Indians.
Onffroy de Thoron, Enrique, Vicomte.
57352-(57353)
Onge, L. N. St. see St. Onge, L. N.
Ongeluckige voyagie van het schip Batavia.
74841
Ongelukkige schipbreuk en yslyke reystogt.
20017
On-hi, Hart. pseud.? Trodden dovvn streng
20864
Oni tahoghsonderoh St. Mark raorighwadogeas
6351
Onion, Stephen B. 57354
Onis, Luis de, 1769-1830. 25149, (56519),
57355-57356, 99313-99315, note after
102768 see also Spain. Legation.
U. S.
Onkel Thomas. 92517
Onkel Tom. 92556, 92561, 92574
Onkel Tom's Hutte. 92403, 92416, 92548-
92554, 92557-92560, 92562-92565,
92567-92579
Onkel Tom's Hutte, fur Kinder. 92577
Onkel Toms hytte. 92518, 92594
Onkel Tom's Schiksale. 92580
Onkel Toms stuga. 92407, 92420, 92439,
92446, 92616-92619
Only authentic life of Abraham Lincoln.
41218
Only authentic life of George Brinton
McClellan. 43030
Only copy of the life, and the testimony that
convicted Michael Monroe. 50028
Only compulsion proper to be made use of.
12331
Only correct account of the life, trial, and
confession of John Banks. 57357
Only effectual remedy against mortal errors.
50661
Only means of man's salvation. 105216
Only method to promote the happiness of a
people. 7657
Only safe expedient. 89815
Only seventeen working days in the United
States Senate. (25845)
Only son. 106141
Only sure way to prevent threatned calamity.
104073
Only way for a people to engage the presenc
of God with their armies. 104259
Only way to be saved. 85527, 85529-85530
[Only way to be saved. In Italian.] 85528
Onnei8t Indians. see Iroquois Indians.
Onnondage Indians. see Onondaga Indians.
Onnotague Indians. see Iroquois Indians.
Onomasia. 73361
Onondaga County, N. Y. Agricultural Society
see Onondaga County Agricultural
Society.
Onondaga County, N. Y. Board of Supervisor
(57358)
Onondaga County, N. Y. Commissioners for
Settling the Titles to Land. see New
York (State) Commissioners for Settling
the Titles to Land in the County of
Onondaga.
Onondaga County, N. Y. Superintendent and
Inspector of Salt. see New York
(State) Superintendent of Onondaga Salt
Springs.
Onondaga County, N. Y. Washington
Benevolent Society. see Washington
Benevolent Society, New York.
Onondaga County.

Onondaga County, N. Y. Whig Convention, Syracuse, 1834. see Whig Party. New York. Onondaga County. Convention, Syracuse, Syracuse, 1834.

Onondaga Baptist Association. see Baptists. New York. Onondaga Baptist Association.

Onondaga County Agricultural Society. 57361

Onondaga Indians. 49348-49349, 66061 see also Five Nations of Indians.

Onondaga Indians. Treaties, etc. 36337, 60255

Onondaga; or reminiscences of earlier and later times. 13329, 84484

Onondaga register. 88861

Onondaga Salt Springs. Superintendent. see New York (State) Superintendent of Onondaga Salt Springs.

Onondaga Teachers' Institute. 57362

Onondagoe Indians. see Onondaga Indians.

Onpartijdige raadgevinge tot eensgezindheid en moderatie. 31629

Onpartydich discours opte handelinghe vande Indien. 98206

Onpartydige beschrijvinge van Surinam. 101463

Onpartydige staat van het verschil tusschen de republiek en Groot-Britannien. 100875

Onpartydigh Coopman uyt Zeelant. pseud. Antwoort-Brief. 52222

Ons verdrag met Amerika. 37723

Onslow. pseud. Onslow in reply to Patrick Henry. see Calhoun, John Caldwell, 1782-1850.

Onslow, Arthur, 1691-1768. 57614, 99249

Onslow in reply to Patrick Henry. 57363

Ontario. 10420, 10436, 10526, 10581, 98066, 98085

Ontario. Administrator, 1796-1799 (Russell) 98058A-98058B see also Russell, Peter.

Ontario. Attorney General. 89178 see also Robinson, Sir John Beverley, Bart.

Ontario. Board of Agriculture. (10343)

Ontario. Census, 1850. (10403)

Ontario. Chief Superintendent of Schools. 10419-10420, 10428, 74545-74546, 74552-74554, 74557, (74563), 74568-(74569), 74571-74572, 74577-(74579), 90823 see also Ryerson, Adolphus Egerton, 1803-1882.

Ontario. Church University Board. see Church University Board of Upper Canada.

Ontario. Citizens' Central Committee. see Central Committee of the Inhabitants of Upper Canada.

Ontario. Commissioner of Public Works. 57364

Ontario. Commissioners of Agriculture and Arts. 10347

Ontario. Court of Assizes. 79016

Ontario. Court of Chancery. 85421

Ontario. Council. see Ontario. Parliament. Legislative Council.

Ontario. Crown Land Agent. 25879 see also French, T. P.

Ontario. Department of Agriculture. 10347

Ontario. Executive Council. 98059A-98059G

Ontario. Executive Council. Acting Clerk. 98059A see also Littlehales, E. B.

Ontario. Executive Council. Clerk. 98058A-98058B, 98059B-98059G, 98065E see also Small, John.

Ontario. House of Assembly. see Ontario. Parliament. House of Assembly.

Ontario. Inhabitants. Central Committee. see Central Committee of the Inhabitants of Upper Canada.

Ontario. Laws, statutes, etc. 10421, 10424, 10480, 10484-10485, (10489), 10499, 10501, 10518, 30189, 41690, 47873, 57365, 67722, 81674-81675, note before 93160, 98061-98063, 98079

Ontario. Lieutenant Governor, 1791-1796 (Simcoe) 81138, note after 81138, 98064-98065E, 100896 see also Simcoe, John Graves, 1752-1806.

Ontario. Lieutenant Governor, 1806-1817 (Gore) 85205 see also Gore, Francis, 1769-1852.

Ontario. Lieutenant Governor, 1836-1838 (Head) 31137-31142, 71718, 98067 see also Head, Sir Francis Bond, Bart., 1793-1875.

Ontario. Lieutenant Governor, 1836-1838 (Head) defendant 72871 see also Head, Sir Francis Bond, Bart., 1793-1875. defendant

Ontario. Midland District Assizes. 96883

Ontario. Militia. Courts Martial (Sutherland) 93965, 93967

Ontario. Parliament. 31137, 98064-98065, 98067, 98088

Ontario. Parliament. House of Assembly. 10420, 10470, 10492, 10501, 10590, 33551, 72871, 74552, (74563), 74568, (74569) 74571, 74572, 74577-(74581), 79757, 81138, 98060, 98064, 98084

Ontario. Parliament. House of Assembly. Committee on Grievances. see Ontario Parliament. House of Assembly. Select Committee on Grievances.

Ontario. Parliament. House of Assembly. Committee on the Welland Canal. 98088

Ontario. Parliament. House of Assembly. Select Committee on Grievances. 10577, 43439

Ontario. Parliament. House of Assembly. Select Committee on the Causes of Emigration from Canada to the United States and Elsewhere. 10440

Ontario. Parliament. Legislative Council. 10333, 10470, 10502, 81138, 98059A-98059G, 98064, 98084

Ontario. Parliament. Legislative Council. Select Committee on the Report of the Earl of Durham. 38751

Ontario. Parliament. Legislative Council. Select Committee on the State of the Province. 10578

Ontario. Post Office Department. 41690

Ontario. Secretary. 98065B see also Jarvis, William.

Ontario. Solicitor General. 72872 see also Hagerman, Christopher A.

Ontario. Surveyor General. 85205, 98058A see also Smyth, David William, 1764-1837.

Ontario. York Assizes. (20701)

Ontario. 16491

Ontario Agricultural Association. Annual Exhibition, 11th, Kingston, 1856. 66389

Ontario and St. Lawrence Steamboat Company. (57368)

Ontario and St. Lawrence Steamboat Company's hand-book. (57368)

Ontario Baptist Association. see Baptists. New York. Ontario Baptist Association.

Ontario Female Seminary, Canandaigua, N. Y. (57369)

Ontario Teachers' Association. see Teachers' Association of Ontario.

Ontedeckinge van 't eyland van Pines. 35257, 57370, 82188

Ontdeckinghe van rijcke mijnen in Brasil. 7612

Ontdekking van America. 10294

Ontdekking van Louisiana. (31357)

Ontdekking van 't geheel. (37772)

Ontdekkingen in de Zuidzee. 38969

Ontdekkings-reis naar het groote zuidland. (24758)

Ontdekkingsreis in de Zuid-Zee en naar de Berings-Straat. (38285)

Ontiveros, Felipe de Zuniga y. see Zuniga y Ontiveros, Felipe de.

Ontiveros, Felix Caballero y. see Caballero y Ontiveros, Felix.

Ontiveros, Mariano de Zuniga y. see Zuniga y Ontiveros, Mariano de.

Ontmoetingen op eene reise naar het eiland Pitcairn. 80485

Ontonagon Copper Company. (57371)

Ontwa, the son of the forest. 39448, 103694

Ontwerp eener Nederlandsche West-Indische ontginning- en Handel-Maatschappij. (47372)

Ontwerp ter verbetering van den financielen toestand der kolonie Suriname. 48044

Ontworp, en voorstel tot remedie. 57373, 1st note after 102903

Onward. (57374)

Onward age. 68179

Onze Indiens O-jib-be-was. 57375

Onzdige brief van een Voornaam Koopman te London. 97355

Oo meyo achimoowin St. Mark. 17454

Ooest-Indische Compagnie. see Nederlandsch Oest-Indische Compagnie.

Ooghen-slave tot verlichtighe. 55449, (57376), 99316, 2d note after 102903

Oonder-hoofden, or the undercliff. 104514

Oor in het kabinet. 55517

Oorzaken van den burgeroorlog in Amerika. 51104

Oorzaken van verval en middelen tot herstel der Surinaamsche plantaadjen. 38933

Oost-en West Indische Post. 102857

Oost- en West-Indische voyagie, door de Strate Magellanes naer de Moluques. 77933, 89448

Oost- en West-Indische voyagien. 30680, 55442, 77933, 89448, 98739

Oost- en West-Indische warande. Vervattende aldaar de leef-en genees-konst. 6341, 32884, (57377), 98930

Oost- en Westindische warande, vervattende de leeswys en geneeskonst daar gebruikt. 6336

Oost ende West-Indische spiegel der nieuvve navigatien. 89444

Oost ende West-Indische spiegel der 2. leste navigatien. 89445

Oost-Indianische Send-schreiben vor allerhand raren gewochsen baumen jubelen. 98357

Oost-Indische Compagnie. see Nederlandsche Oost-Indische Compagnie.

Oost-Indische ende VVest-Indische voyagien. 14349, 57901, 67597

Oost-Indische voyagien door dien begin en voortgangh. 30680, 31505, 55442

Ooste ende West-Indische spieghel waer in Beschreven Werden de twee laetste Navigatien. 98446

Oosten van Staveren, G. L. van. tr. 16457

Ootmoedighe beklagh-redenen aan de Hoogh-Mogende Heeren. 57379

Oowa wowapi. 57380

Op de memoire van den Ridder . . . Ambassadeur. 106045

Op de onafhankelykheid van Noord-America. 47381

Op de verschrikkelyke aardbevinge. (57382)

Op dem roemruchtigen zeeslag tegen de Engelschen. 91731

Op het inneemen van St. Eustatius. 57383

Op het ontset van Pier Heyns buyt. 100761

Op het tweede ontset. 100762

Op het tytel-bladt. (72762)

Opal: . . . . Edited by Mrs. Sarah J. Hale. (57384)

Opal: published by the patients in the State Lunatic Asylum, Utica. (47385)

Opdagelsen af Nordvestpassagen. 43075

Opdam, -------- van Wassenaer, Baron van. see Wassenaer, ------, van, Baron van Opdam.

Opdyke, George. 17993, 57389-57390 see also New York (City) Mayor, 1862-1864 (Opdyke)

Opdyke, George. plaintiff (57388), 57390

Opdyke libel suit. 47390

Open air grape culture. 62566

Open church. 57391

Open convents or nunneries and popish seminaries dangerous. 21539

Open door: a sermon preached in St. Andrew Church. 91576

Open door; or, light and liberty. 82973

Open letter to Joseph Smith and others. 83296

Open letter to the Historical Society of Wisconsin. 81696

Open letter to the Rev. A. A. Lipscomb. 55463

Open letter. To the Right Rev. William Bacon Stevens. 83525

Open polar sea. (31020)

Open traitor of the south. 97587

Opene brieven of octroy onder 't groot zegel van Schotland. 57392

Opening address at the sixth annual session of the Western Literary Institute. 62663

Opening address before the N. Y. State Teachers' Association. 36599

Opening address, by James Brewster, Esq. 52967

Opening address delivered at the inauguration. 104232

Opening address delivered before the Concord Young Men's Christian Association. 24668

Opening address of Mrs. L. F. Fowler. 54488

Opening and concluding addresses delivered before the Maryland Institute. 45221

Opening argument for complainant. 35314

Opening argument of Mr. Butler. 9615

Opening celebration of the Southern Minnesota Railway. 88408

Opening ode delivered at the inauguration of the equestrian statute of Washington. 33927, 3d note after 95515

Opening of George Northrop. 55840

Opening of St. James' Hall, Hagerstown, Md., 1842. 29515

Opening of the Adirondacks. 461

Opening the the Atlantic and Pacific Railroad. 57393

Opening of the fift [sic] and sixt [sic] verses of the 20th chap. of the Revelation. 17054

Opening of the Mississippi. 57394

Opening of the short route from Bridgeport to Chattanooga. 84774

Opening of Walker Hall. 90991

Opening poem, by E. Pollock. 104232

Opening sermon before the Synod of Alta California. 7933

Opening speech of John Graham. 28227

Opening speech of John W. Ashmead. 2202

Openlegging van het singulier en contrasteerend gedrag. 4809, 38250

Opera bouffe en trois actes. 100745

Opera [by George Colman.] 14526, note after 105986

Opera. By J. St. John. 75243

Opera comique. 47060

Opera [Conradi Lycosthenis.] (66488)

Opera, cum edita, tum inedita. 31517

Opera, cum edita, tum inedita, accurante regia historiae academa. 79180

Operia di D. Benedetto Stella. 91215

Opera en dous actos, imitacao do Francez. 43214

Opera en trois actes. (36768), 89596

Opera goer. pseud. Lorgnette. see Mitchell, Donald Grant.

Opera historiam naturalem spectatia. 61288

Opera historica et philologica, sacra et profana. 102615

Opera House, Philadelphia. see Philadelphia. Opera House.

Opera, in three acts, as performed at the Theatre-Royal, Drury-Lane. 86907

Opera in three acts. As performed at the Theatre Royal Drury Lane, with music composed by Stephen Storace. 92172

Opera in three acts; as performed at the Theatre-Royal in the Hay-Market. 77454

Opera, in three acts. [By Elihu Hubbard Smith.] 82503

Opera, in two acts. 55370, 92175B

Opera, in two acts, as it was performed in New York. 5944

Opera. Legatio babilonica occeanes decas. 1565, 45013

Opera lyrica em tres actos. 88803

Opera M. A. Coccii Sabellici. 74665

Opera Marc. Ant. Sabellici. 74664

Opera mathematica. 77805-(77806)

Opera nella quale si tratta del governo delle antiche republiche ec. 75531

Opera noua Baptistae Mantuani Carmelitae. 44403

Opera omnia . . . cum supplemento. 74666

Opera omnia Diui Eusebii Hieronymi Stridonensis. 99365

Opera omnia, in unum collecta. 25411

Opera omnia Latine scripta. (43784)

Opera omnia tam edita quam inedita. (78975)

Opera patrum Toletanorum. 42066

Opera, quae reperiri potuerunt omnia. 79179

Opera S. Martini Legionensis. 42066

Opera, scilicet legationis babylonicae libri tres. (1549)

Opera seria. 60835

Opera subcisiva. 24942

Operaciones ocurridas en la defensa de la capital de la republica. 48607

Operacoes do passo fundo. 88768

Operation of the apprenticeship system. 5105

Operations and results. 76627

Operations hydrographiques. 21210

Operations of God shewn to the operations of wisdom. 27291

Operations of the "Army of occupation" for one month. 10905

Operations of the Commission before Charleston. (12061)

Operations of the French fleet under the Count de Grasse. 28332, (80023)

Operations of the Indiana Legion and Minute Men. 34558

Operations of the U. S. Sanitary Commission at Beaufort and Morris Island. 76697

Operations of the war for the first twelve months. 57395, 101145

Operative. pseud. Factory tracts. No. 1. 23611

Operative and speculative masonry. 70923

Operatives' reply to Hon. Jere. Clemens. 23814

Opere [di Cardinal Bembo.] 4619

Opere [di Gabriello Chiabrera.] 12614

Operetti di Jacopo Morelli. (50598)

Opgaaf van het gebeurde omtrent dit onderwerp. 10887

Ophaevelse inden en vis kort tid af slaveriet. 18724

Ophir Mining Company. 57396

Ophiuridae and Astrophytidae. 42803

Opie, Amelia. 57397

Opimus. pseud. Controversy between Caius Gracchus and Opimius. (16191)

Opiner. pseud. [Essays.] see Snethen, Nicholas, 1769-1845.

Opinion. 57398

Opinion . . . against the right of the City Councils. 68169

Opinion . . . against the right of the Legislature of New Jersey. 68169

Opinion and argument of the Chief Justice of the Province of New York. 50849, 84557, 98436

Opinion by Hon. James B. Bradwell. 7311

"Opinion" by J. L. Petigru. 87856

Opinion . . . concerning the judicial authority. 18095

Opinion concerning the rights of the city of Cambridge. 35500

Opinion contained in the report of the Onondaga Commissioners. 23362, note after 102973

Opinion de divers auteurs, etc. (11681), 14724, 76882

Opinion de la presse du Canada. (57399)

Opinion de la presse Francaise. (11681), 14724, 76882

Opinion de M. Bertier. 5009

Opinion de M. de la Rochefoucault-Liancourt. (39052)

Opinion de M. le Marquis de Gouy d'Arsy. 28154

Opinion de M. Moreau de St.-Mery. 50575

Opinion de M. Roussillon. (75174)

Opinion de un Granadino sobre la division de la dueda Columbiana. 14559

Opinion de Vienot-Vaublanc. 98681

Opinion de Villaret-Joyeuse. 99662

Opinion del estado del Salvador. 76206

Opinion emise par Jomard. 58554

Opinion emitada . . . en el asunto de la testamentaria. 99687

Opinion generale sur l'origine et de la nature des races humaines. 74903

Opinion humbly offered to the General Assembly. 84556

Opinion in case of Jos. Hollman vs. H. Fulton. 32558

OPINION

Opthalmic and Aural Institute, New York.
see New York Opthalmic and Aural
Institute.

Opthalmic Hospital, New York. see New
York Opthalmic Hospital.

Optic, Oliver, pseud. see Adams, William
Taylor, 1822-1897.

Optician. pseud. Speculum for looking into
the pamphlet. 89152

Opus ad sanitatis coservationem. 66471

Opus de rebus Hispaniae memorabilibus modo
castigatum. (44585)

Opus elaboratum ingenti cura. 98915

Opus epistolarum Petri Martyris Anglerii
Mediolanensis. 1555-1556

Opuscoli pubblicati nell memorie dell' Ac-
cademia Imperiale. 51760

Opuscolo sobre la hacienda publica de Chile.
57417

Opuscula Academica. 26762, 31665

Opuscula. Essays chiefly philological and
ethnographical. 39167

Opuscula [naturalem historiam spectantia.]
(68517)

Opuscula nonnulla. 24942

Opuscula. Seria ac jocosa. (71959)

Opuscule sur le present et l'avenir du Canada.
38498

Opuscules. (5153)

Opuscules philosophiques et litteraires.
93292

Opusculo de la verdad y de la razon. 96780

Opusculo del Senor Espinosa contra el retrato
de la Virgen. 22903

Opusculo do D. Man. do Monte Rodrigues di
Araujo. 47590

Opusculo en defensa del clero de la iglesia
Mejicana. 57418

Opusculo en que se refutan las memorias
redactadas. 55490

Opusculo escrito por el Illmo. Sr. Obispo de
Michoacan. 51325

Opusculo politico. 65344

Opusculo publicado en Paris. 48589

Opusculo sobre a questao que tivera. 72503

Opusculo sobre ascensos militares. 57521

Opusculo sobre el huano. 3641

Opusculo sobre la estincion de las comandancias
generales. 57522

Opusculo sobre la republica de Centro-America.
19464, 21179

Opusculo sobre la situacion actual. (17844)

Opusculo sobre los catorce casos reservados.
(48374)

Opusculos acerca do Sebastianismo. (57419)

Opusculum de insulis nuper inventus. 94096

Opusculum de qualitate et natura chocolatae.
12861

Opusculum de mirabilibus novae et veteris
urbis Romae. 663-664, 666, 668

Opusculum geographicum. 76838

Opvscvlvm geographicvm ex diversorvm libris.
77801-(77802)

Opvscvlvm geographicvm rarvm, titivs eivs
negotii rationem. 51650

Opusculum globi astriferi nuper ab eode editu.
77798-(77799)

Opusculum vitae, virtutum et miraculorum.
55243, (63445)

Opwekking tot landverhuizing naar de republiek
der Vereenigde Staten. 56430

Opyt zhyvopisnavo puteshestviya po severnoi
Amerike. 93992

Oquendo, Francisco Xavier Conde y. see
Conde y Oquendo, Francisco Xavier.

Or et l'argent. 81314

Orab and Phoebe. 3495

Oracao academica gratulatoria. (17199)

Oracao aos annos do Serenissimo Principe D.
Jose. 64439

Oracao consolatoria na morte d' el Re
Catholico. 64439

Oracao de accao de gracias recitada. 17943

Oracao de Serenissimo Sr D. Jose. 6796

Oracao funebre de S. M. o Imperador do
Brasil. 81103

Oracao funebre do Muito Alto e Muito Poderoso
Sr. D. Pedro de Alcantara. 65395

Oracao funebre na exequias do Muito Alto e
Muito Poderoso Senhor D. Joao VI.
43210

Oracao funebre nas exequias da Serenissima
Princeza do Brasil. 81075

Oracao funebre, panegyrica e historica.
45406

Oracao funebre, pregada na igrejada miseri-
cordia. 88788

Oracao fuenbre, recitada nas exequias. 78954

Oracao funebre, recitada nas exequias que se
celebraram. 76314

Oracao funebres do Arcobispo da Bahia.
16829

Oracao na accao de gracas. 76313

Oracao panegyrica, que no felicissimo casa-
mento do Sr. D. Jose. 64439

Oracao, que na Real Capella d'Esta Corte.
32717

Oracao reditada na abertura das aulas do
Seminario Episcopal. 81119

Oracio qve se dixo en la solemno y magnifica
translacion. (50529)

Oracion a D. Philippo V. 68334

Oracion a Nuestro S. D. Philippo V. 62444

Oracion al Rey N. S. 68333

Oracion alos reyes en Latin y en Romance.
57714

Oracion civica pronunciada en la capital de
Mexico. 93344

Oracion civica pronunciada en la plaza.
81003

Oracion cominatoria. 57676

Oracion continua funebre. 22894

Oracion del funeral que hizo la muy noble y
leal ciudad de la Havana. 29446

Oracion Dominical en Mexicano. 73155

Oracion en alabanza. (23593)

Oracion espiritual a Sor Maria Francisca
Novicia. 98762

Oracion eucaristica por la fundacion del
Monasterio de Santa Monica. 72468

Oracion eucaristica que pronuncio el Dr. D.
Sicilia y Montoya. (29081), 80838

Oracion evangelica del sacro triunfo de
Jerusalem. 72570

Oracion familiar gratulatoria. 106302

Oracion funebras. 35286

Oracion funebre. 106283

Oracion funebre a expensas de los Dr D. Jose
de Herrera, y D. Antonio Cubero Diaz.
62995

Oracion funebre al ciudadano Jorge Washington.
12290, 1st note after 101866

Oracion funebre con que expresso el senti-
miento. 106220

Oracion funebre con que la Iglesia de las
Charcas. 94868

Oracion funebre de la exequias que se hicieron.
57420

Oracion fuenbre de los militares Espanoles
difuntos. 18786

Oracion funebre de Sen. Don. Ignac. Paz.
44260

Oracion funebre del D. A. M. Bucareli.
26578

Oracion funebre del D. S. Biempica y
Sotomayor. 60898

Oracion funebre del E. S. Don Augustin de
Jturbide. 19454

Oracion funebre del Excelent. Senor Conde de
la Union. 4912

Oracion funebre del Exmo. Senor D. Alonso
Nunez de Haro y Peralta. (11297)

Oracion funebre del Excelentisimo Senor Don
Luis de las Casas y Aragorri. 27810,
73008, 85742

Oracion funebre del F. Pedro Juan de Molina.
36079

Oracion funebre del Senor D. Alonso Nunez
de Haro y Peralta. 56324

Oracion funebre del Sr. D. Augustin de Iturbide.
50616

Oracion funebre del Senor Don Vincente
Morales Duarez. 4913

Oracion fuenbre del St. General D. Luis G. de
Osollo. 10320

Oracion funebre, dedicada la a memoria del
D. Matias de Galvez. 28173

Oracion ufnebre [sic] del . . . D. Diego de
Parada. 40074

Oracion funebre el Sr. Doct. Don Joseh Manuel
Velez de Ulibarri y Olasso. 98826

Oracion funebre en honras de los difuntos
militares. 77102

Oracion funebre en honras de P. Francisco
Montion Pacheco. 76819

Oracion funebre en honras del J. M. Santiago.
(57630)

Oracion funebre en las exequias del M. R. P.
Fr. Antonio Reboleno. 76301

Oracion funebre en las exequias del M. R. P.
Fr. Miguel Burguete. 74851

Oracion funebre en las exequias que el Exmo.
Sr. Marques de Cruillas. (72520)

Oracion funebre en las exequias que el
Religiosisimo Conventio de Corpus
Christi de Mexico. 29147

Oracion funebre en las exequias que la Provincia
de Zacatecas hizo. (72249)

Oracion funebre en las honras de la . . .
Maria de San Joseph. 76818

Oracion funebre en las sol. exequias par
animas. 31479

Oracion funebre panegyrica con que la gratitud.
(11442)

Oracion funebre panegyrica en las reales
exequias. 73430

Oracion funebre par M. C. LaRocque. 39059

Oracion funebre por los militares Espanoles
difuntos. 52133

Oracion funebre por R. J. Argote y Gorostiza.
64573

Oracion funebre predicado en el Convento
Imperial. 73622

Oracion funebre . . . pronunciada en la Iglesia
del Convento de San Agustin. 57421

Oracion funebre pronunciada en las solemnes
exequias. 14615

Oracion funebre pronunciada por el Sr.
Prebendado Lic. D. Miguel G. Martinez.
(44961)

Oracion funebre. Que a la justa memoria.
57808

Oracion funebre, que a la memoria del
Fidelissimo Senor D. Juan V. 26411

Oracion funebre que con motivo de las solemnes
exequias. 56329

Oracion funebre que dixo el Fr. Jos. de
Sierra. 80880

Oracion funebre, que en esta Santa Iglesia
Catedral de Mexico. 27470

Oracion funebre. Qve en honras del immortal
valor de los soldados. 57421

Oracion funebre que en las anniversarias
honras de los difuntos militares.
(57264)

Oracion funebre, que en las exequias celebrado
en esta S. Iglesia Cathedral. 41975

Oracion funebre que en las exequias de la
Reyna Madre Senora Dona Isabel
Farnesio. 57657

Oracion funebre, que en las exequias de
Nuestro Catolico Monarca el S^r. D.
Carlos III. 93334

Oracion funebre que en las exequias del
General J. T. Monagas pronuncio.
64004

Oracion funebre que en las exequias del P.
Juan Fogueras. 35284

Oracion funebre que en las exequias hechas
por el clero. 25177

Oracion funebre, que en las exequias que
celebradas los Senores D. J. M. Castonas

Oracion funebre, que en las honras anniversarias de los militares difuntos. 22840

Oracion funebre . . . que en las honras
celebradas el dia 24 de Octubre de
1799. 86369

Oracion funebre que en las magnificas, y
sumptuosas exequias. 44892

Oracion funebre que en las solemnes excequias
de Carlos III. 75980

Oracion funebre que en las solemnas ecsequias
[sic] el Jeneral de Division y Presidente de la republica Peruana. 57421

Oracion funebre que en las solemnes exequias
celebradas. 56329

Oracion funebre que en las solemnes exequias
celebradas en esta Santa Iglesia Catedral
de Puebla. 50606

Oracion funebre que en la solemnes exequias
de la R. M. Maria Antonio de San
Joseph. 9874

Oracion funebre que en las solemnes exequias
del Rey Nuestro Senor. 73902

Oracion funebre, que en las solemnes exequias
del Senor Presbitero Beneficiado Dr.
D. J. Desiderio de la Quadro. (75586)

Oracion funebre que en las solemnes exequias
en la Iglesia del Espiritu Santo de la
Puebla. 44948, 60898

Oracion funebre que en las solemnes exequias
que el Venerable Clero de la Villa de
Santa Maria de Puerto-Principe. 98892

Oracion funebre en las sol. exequias que hizo
la S. Iglesia Catedr. de Valladolid de
Michoacan. 26580

Oracion funebre que en la solemnes honras
celebradas en la magestuosa parroquia
de la ciudad de Santa Re Real. 67866

Oracion funebre que en las solemnes honras
de los militares. 106318

Oracion funebre que en las solemnes honras
del Presbiterio D. Jose Manuel Sartorio.
86371, 96275

Oracion funebre que en solemne anniversario
dotado. 51447

Oracion funebre que en su exequias del
D. Nicolas Carlos Gomez. 10799

Oracion funebre, que hizo F. Ponze de Leon.
(63970)

Oracion funebre . . . 28 de Setiembre de
1859. 55348

Oracion funebris quam in exequijs Emmanueli Antonio Roxo de Rio. 73740
Oracion gratulatoria que en la primera funcion. 67336
Oracion gratulatoria que en la solemne funcion. 63973
Oracion gratulatoria que en la solemne funcion dispuesta. (50502)
Oracion gratulatoria que en la solemne funcion dispuesta por el Clero de Oaxaca. 96477
Oracion inaugural a la catedra de mineralogia. 74933
Oracion inaugural para la apertura Nuevo Estudio de Botanica. 79327
Oracion inaugural que para la abertura y estrena del Anfiteatro Anatomixo. 97712
Oracion laudatoria de las virtudes y admirable gobierno. 75895
Oracion laudatoria sagradamente anunciada y pronosticada. 79087
Oracion moral deprecativa a la milagrosa imagen de Jesus Nazareno. 15163
Oracion panegirici en la titular de la S. Veracruz. 29018
Oracion panegirica, con que la Real Universidad de San Marcos. 98335
Oracion panegirica del Gran Principe de los Apostoles San Pedro. 50606
Oracion panegirica del Principe de los Apostoles, S. Pedro. 76120
Oracion panegirica en celebridad de la ereccion en Metropolitana de la Iglesia de Guatemala. 75580
Oracion panegirica que a glorias del Principe de los Apostoles. 20137
Oracion panegirica que a la felix llegada del D. A. de Gorrichategui. 57422
Oracion panegirica que dixo en nombre de la Real Universidad de S. Marcos. 58578
Pracion panegirica, que el dia 26. de Mayo del ano de 1794. 68807
Oracion panegirica, que el dia 27 de Febrero de 1791. 67337
Oracion panegirica, que en el dia deseado de la dedicacion. 39266
Oracion panegirica, que en la solemne accion de gracias. 58077
Oracion panegirica y proclamatoria de la Magestuosa Asuncion. 74866
Oracion panegirico-eucaristica. 4873
Oracion panegyrica a las honras del Capitan Martin de Eraso. 111
Oracion panegyrica dixo Octubre 18, 1761. 72516
Oracion panegyrica en la funcion de S. Fel. Neri de Mexico. 44578
Oracion panegyrica en la muerte de Fr. Mechior Lopez de Jesu. 38477
Oracion panegyrica en la solemnidad fiesta de glorioso Senor Vicentio Ferrer. (41989)
Oracion panegyrica en la solemnidad plausible. 74047
Oracion panegyrica funebre por el Sr. Dr. Miguel Joseph Cortes de Arredondo. 16970, 72809, 73740
Oracion panegyrica gratulatoria al D. Luis Enriques de Guzman. (24827)
Oracion panegyrica . . . por Fr. Jos. Manuel Rodriguez. 72517
Oracion panegyrica, que el 31. de Julio de 1727. 106378
Oracion panegyrica, que, en accion de gracias. 71246

Oracion panegyrica, que en la . . . fiesta . . . del celestial cingulo. (26412)
Oracion panegyrica, que en la fiesta que anualmente celebra. 72518
Oracion panegyrica que en la Santa Iglesia Cathedral de Mexico. 26413
Oracion panegyrica, que en la solemnidad de M. Patrona Santa Rosa. 41672
Oracion panegyrico-funebre. 16790
Oracion panegyrico polemica que en la Fiesta de la SS. Trinidad. 29129
Oracion panegyrico-funebre por el Sr. Dr. D. Miguel Joseph Cortes de Arredondo. 72809, 73740
Oracion pronunciada por el Coronel J. M. Tornel. 96206
Oracion que a glorias del Principe de los Apostoles M. P. S. Pedro. 19969
Oracion qve dixo . . . en accion de gracias. 60856
Oracion que dixo . . . en que fue reeligido [sic]. 60856
Oracion que el Illmo. Senor D. Manuel de Alday y Aspee. 57423
Oracion que en la fiesta de la instalacion de la Junta Suprema. 77115
Oracion que pronuncio civica en la Alameda de la Ciudad Federal. (11380)
Oracion sacropolitica panegyrico. 29129
Oraciones funebres que en las exequias. 67317
Oraciones funebres que se dijeron en ellas. (69199)
Oraciones funerales en exequias del Dr. Fr. Jos. de Lanciego y Eguilaz. 38811
Oraciones panegyricas funebres, en las exequias. 50035, note after 99684
Oraciones panegyricas que en el solemne recibimiento. 41122
Oraciones piadosas. (75866)
Oracle of liberty. 31500, 72493
Oracles of God. A sermon . . . at Boston. (59309)
Oracles of God, committed to the church for universal diffusion. 79934
Oracles of reason. 57424, 79287
Oracles vivants. 89744
Oraison Dominicale et autres prieres. 57425
Oraison funebre. 12288, 40696
Oraison funebre de Washington. 12291
Oral and written testimony. 66990, 67007
Oramaika. 57426
Oram, James. 54838, 84948
Oram's New-York almanac. 84948
Orange, Prince of. see Willem V, Prince of Orange, 1748-1806. William III, King of Great Britain, 1650-1702.
Orange, N. J. First Church. 57427
Orange, N. J. Library Association. see Orange Library Association, Orange, N. J.
Orange County, N. Y. Benevolent Society. see Benevolent Society of the County of Orange, N. Y.
Orange County, N. Y. Board of Supervisors. 57430
Orange County, N. Y. New England Society. see New England Society of Orange County, N. Y.
Orange County, N. Y. S. S. Seward Institute. see S. S. Seward Institute, Florida, N. Y.
Orange County, Vt. Court. 59416
Orange County, Va. 100071

Orange Bible and Tract Society. 90359
Orange Library Association, Orange, N. J.
57428
Orange Presbytery. see Presbyterian
Church in the U. S. Presbytery of
Orange.
Orangeburgh District, S. C. Citizens.
petitioners 57431
Orangeburgh District, S. C. Grand Jury.
87450
Orangeburgh Township, S. C. Charter.
87627
Orangeburgh Female College, S. C. 57432
Orangeism exposed. 97722
Orantes, Segundico. 57433
Oratio. 52112, 106358
Oratio ad Sixtum V. 62602
Oratio apologetica. 10323
Oratio de America et Americanarum gentium
origine. 63418
Oratio de navigationibus ac commerciis
Foederatum Belgarum. (82133)
Oratio de sapientum laude et dignitate.
11447
Oratio Dominica . . . editore Johanne
Chamberlaynio. 57435
Oratio Dominica CL linguis versa. 57436
Oratio Dominica in CCL. linguas versa.
57438
Oratio Dominica in CLV. linguas versas.
57437
Oratio Dominica . . . nimirum plus centum
linguis. (57434)
Oratio Dominica polyglotta, DCCCXVI. linguis
et dialectis. 57438
Oratio en honras de D. P. Alvarez de Abreu.
(56335)
Oratio funebris. 97143
Oratio funebris Caroli III. Hispaniarum et
Indiarum regis. 27767
Oratio fvnebris habita a Magistro Damiano
Goncalez de Cveto. 27772
Oratio funebris, in obitum Edvardi Wigglesworth.
1829, 94517, 104056
Oratio funebris in obitum Reverendi Domini
Benjaminis Wadsworth. 24929, 103899
Oratio funebris, in obitum Viri Reverendi
pariter atque honorandi D. Edvardi
Holyoke. 79469
Oratio funebris pro exequiis celebrandis viri
perillustris Jonathan Law Armigeri.
91743
Oratio funebris quam in exequijs Manilae
celebratis defuncto suo Archiepiscopo.
72809, 73740
Oratio funebris tristissimo in funere Exmi. ac
Reverendissimi Patris Magistri F.
Antonii Bremond. 80880
Oratio habita in capitolio Gulielmopolitano.
17021
Oratio habita in Ecclesia Cathedrali Limensi.
2495
Oratio habita in Metropolitano Templo
Guatemalensi. 10709
Oratio habita in Senatu Apostolico vi. calen.
Iulii. 94623
Oratio habita Neapoli in fvnere Ferdinandi
Hispaniarvm Regis. 43829
Oratio in funere . . . Henrici Flyntij, Arm.
(42373)
Oratio in funere Illmo. D. D. Emmanuelis
Rubio et Salinas. 72534
Oratio in fvnere Regis Catholici. 43829
Oratio in funere S. P. ac D. N. Clementis
XIV. 29130

Oratio in obitum Philippi II. 10721
Oratio inauguralis, a Samuele Stanhope Smith.
84112, 84115
Oratio inauguralis, de institutione Juventutis.
82923
Oratio inauguralis habita in Sacello Collegii
Yalensis. 91744
Oratio inauguralis, quam in Academica
Harvardiana. 102062
Oratio pro Carlo IV. Hispaniarum et Indiarum
potentissimo rege. 59628
Oratio pro conversione infidelium. 44418
Oratio, quam comitijs Cantabrigiensibus
Americanus peroravit. 103706
Oratio salutatoria Suffr. Ampliss. Facult.
Philos. Praesidae viro celeber. Domino
Gulielmo Smith. 84630
Oratio super praestanda solemni obedientia
Sanctissimo D. N. Alexandro Papae VI.
11175
Oratio y sermone funebre en las honras del
J. A. de Flores y Ribera. 24824
Oration addressed to the citizens of the town
of Quincy. 292
Oration, addressed to the fraternity of Free-
masons. 44328
Oration . . . Albany, N. Y., July 4, 1846.
30455
Oration and addresses . . . on that occasion.
57117
Oration and poem before the Society of
California Pioneers. 37662
Oration and poem, delivered at Brown Uni-
versity. (80037)
Oration and poem, delivered at the commence-
ment. (9996)
Oration and poem, delivered before the
Cincinnati Literary Club. 35679
Oration and poem delivered before the con-
vention of the Delta Kappa Epsilon.
57439, 3d note after 95515
Oration and poem delivered July 4, 1826.
22533
Oration and poem. Departure of Senior Class.
30765
Oration . . . anniversary . . . battles of
Champlain and Plattsburgh. 75934
Oration . . . anniversary of the Literary and
Philosophical Society of South Carolina.
22588
Oration . . . Apponaug, R. I. 37848
Oration . . . April 11, 1796. 9448
Oration at Abingdon, July 4, 1805. 32291
Oration at Amherst, N. H. 5327
Oration . . . at Arlington, Va. 26664
Oration . . . at Augusta, (Maine) on the fourth
of July, 1807. 18130
Oration . . . at Barre . . . July 4, 1808.
9911
Oration . . . at Barre, Massachusetts.
36016
Oration at Beaver Dam, July 4, 1865.
30827
Oration at Belford, Feb. 22, 1800. 57651
Oration at Biddeford, Me. July 4, 1805.
3759
Oration . . . at Billerica. (41732)
Oration . . . at Bolton, Mass. 42083
Oration . . . at Boston before the Colonization
Society of Massachusetts. 18095
Oration . . . at Boston, . . . July 4, 1806.
27565
Oration . . . at Boston, on the fourth day of
July, 1811. 19077
Oration, . . . at Bridgewater, October 1, 1801.
(57653)

Oration at Brixton, July 4, 1808. 8449
Oration . . . at Brookfield . . . fourth of July, 1807. (41257)
Oration at Brookfield, Mass., on the capture of Lord Cornwallis. 24479
Oration at Burlington College. 20391
Oration at Burlington, Vt. July 4, 1828. 2724
Oration, . . . at Byfield, February 22d, 1800. (58604)
Oration . . . at Byfield, July 4, 1799. 58609
Oration . . . [at] Chapel Hill. 51452
Oration at Charlestown, at the dedication of Warren Hall. 3769
Oration at Charlestown, June 17, 1794. 3768
Oration . . . at Charlestown, Massachusetts. 58714
Oration at Charlestown, Mass., July 5, 1809. (27564)
Oration at Charleston, S. C. (37397)
Oration . . . at Charlton, . . . anniversary of American independence. 38107
Oration at Charlton, Mass. July 4, 1811. 7498
Oration at Concord, July 4, 1794. 36620
Oration . . . at Connecticut Farms. 37128
Oration at Conway, July 4, 1798. (24204)
Oration . . . at Conway, on the fourth of July, 1804. 27635
Oration, . . . at Dedham, July 4th, 1810. (48167)
Oration . . . at Dedham, July 4th, 1823. 44324
Oration . . . at Dedham, July 24, A. D. 1820. 38084
Oration . . . at . . . Detroit, to Zion Lodge. 31701
Oration at Dighton, July 4, 1803. 40103
Oration . . . at Dorchester, on the 24th of June, A. L. 5807. 41420
Oration . . . at Douglass, July 5th, 1802. 24554
Oration at Elizabeth Town, before the Society of Cincinnati. 6857
Oration . . . at Elizabethtown, (N. J.) . . . July 4, 1912. 37128
Oration at Fitchburg. 190
Oration at Fitchburg, July 4, 1803. 17974
Oration at Flatbush, on the fourth of July, 1802. 42150
Oration at Flemington, July 4, 1799. 28320
Oration . . . at Germantown, Pennsylvania, on the 20th July, 1826. 36334
Oration . . . at Gill, before the Republican and Harmony Lodges. 61362
Oration at Goshen, July 4, 1805. 27636
Oration . . . at Great Barrington, July 4, 1849. 40229
Oration at Greenfield, Mass., July 4, 1799. (54935)
Oration . . . at Groton . . . Massachusetts. (18453)
Oration . . . at Halifax, Vt. (63442)
Oration at Hampden, Me. 50992
Oration, . . . at Hanover. 21283
Oration, . . . at Hardwick. (25221)
Oration . . . at Hingham, July 4, 1815. 42090
Oration at Hudson, N. Y. 26631
Oration . . . at Indian Rock. (48165)
Oration . . . at . . . Iowa College. 43844
Oration at Jamaica, Long Island. (44883)
Oration at Keene, N. H. (29709)
Oration at Kennebunk, fourth of July, 1798. 22462

Oration . . . at Kennebunk, on the fourth day of July, 1799. 24471
Oration . . . at King's-Chapel in Boston. 51020
Oration . . . at Kittery, the fourth of July, 1808. 28588
Oration . . . at Leicester, July 5, 1824. 52315
Oration . . . at Lexington . . . fourth of July, A. D. 1814. 26188
Oration at Lexington, June 24, 1816. 21681
Oration at Libertyville, N. Y., July 4, 1838. 33460
Oration at Litchfield, Con., July 4, 1842. 32553
Oration at Litchfield, N. H., July 4, 1803. 13182
Oration at Litchfield, on the anniversary of the independence of the United States of America. 28107
Oration . . . at Little Falls, N. Y., July 4th, 1856. 33998
Oration . . . at Littleton, July 4, 1806. 25216
Oration . . . at Manchester, N. H. (9913)
Oration . . . at Marshall, Wisconsin. 82586
Oration . . . at Middleborough. 4070
Oration, at Middlebury, before the alumni of the college. (26054)
Oration . . . at Millbury. 29890
Oration . . . at Natick. 2735
Oration . . . at New Haven, before the Connecticut Alpha of the Phi Beta Kappa. (57238)
Oration . . . at New-Haven, before the Society of Phi Beta Kappa. 31886
Oration . . . at New London. 44437
Oration . . . at New Salem. 24234
Oration at Newark. 56803
Oration . . . at Newburyport, July 4, 1808. 51051
Oration . . . at Newburyport, July 4, 1866. 42083
Oration at Newburyport . . . [July 4, 1809.] 3172
Oration . . . at Newburyport, . . . July 4, 1822. 17663
Oration . . . at Newburyport, June 24, 1811. 38084
Oration at Newburyport, Mass., July 4, 1814. 18405
Oration . . . at Newburyport, on the fourth of July 1810. 38084
Oration . . . at Newport, R. I., July 4th, 1861. 35698
Oration at North East, N. Y. (33307)
Oration . . . at Northampton, at the request of the Washington Benevolent Society. 49102
Oration . . . at Northampton, on the anniversary of American independence, 1811. 28764, (28869)
Oration at Norwich, Connecticut, 4th July, 1798. 38927
Oration . . . at . . . Norwich, Conn., on the anniversary of American independence. 60939
Oration at Nottingham, N. H. 3733
Oration at Ogdensburgh, July 4, 1827. 98472
Oration . . . at Old York. 48155
Oration, . . . at Orrington. 51234
Oration . . . at Paterson, July 4, 1825. 80461
Oration at Pembroke, Mass. 21237
Oration at Petersburg, March 4, 1803. 9274
Oration at Petersham, Mass., July 4, 1806. 868

Oration at Philadelphia, July 4, 1818.
35459
Oration at Pittsfield, July 4, 1826. 33425
Oration at Pittsfield, Mass., July 4, 1803.
875
Oration . . . at Plymouth. (41266)
Oration . . . at Portsmouth, N. H. July 5, 1813.
7284
Oration . . . at Portsmouth, N. H. on the
fourth day of July, 1812. 13189
Oration . . . at Poultney, July 4, 1808.
38870
Oration . . . at Poultney, July 4th, 1804.
38870
Oration . . . at Providence, . . . fourth of
July, 1803. 48151
Oration . . . [at] Providence, on the eighty-
fourth anniversary of American
independence. 13382
Oration . . . at Providence, September 6,
1825. 44324
Oration at raising the old flag over Fort
Sumter. (4320)
Oration at Rochester, July 4, 1801. 32590
Oration . . . at Rutland fourth July, 1826.
44128
Oration at St. Mary's College. 48924
Oration . . . at Salem, . . . fourth of July,
1812. (59540)
Oration at Saugus, Mass., July 4, 1815.
29826
Oration at Savannah Ga., July 4, 1812. 62747
Oration at Savannah, July 3, 1802. 12152
Oration at Saybrook, February 22, 1800.
(33127)
Oration, . . . at Schenectady, N. Y., on the
25th July, 1865. 7680
Oration at Schenectady on the fourth of July,
1822. 41334
Oration at Scituate, July 4, 1800. 57849
Oration at Sheffield, Mass. July 4, 1805.
5255
Oration . . . at Springfield . . . July 4, 1836.
39365
Oration, at Stonington-Borough, July 5, 1802.
25240
Oration, . . . at Tammany-Hall, on the twelfth
May, 1831. 51060
Oration, . . . at Temple, (N. H.) . . . July 4,
1809. 41579
Oration . . . at the anniversary celebration of
the Independent Order of Odd Fellows.
34002
Oration, . . . at the anti-masonic celebration,
at Syracuse. (79536)
Oration at the burial, by Bishop Simpson.
41219
Oration . . . at the capitol, July 5, 1858.
82699
Oration, at the celebration of American
independence. 5254
Oration at the celebration of the national
independence. 56214
Oration . . . at the Columbian College. 38155
Oration . . . at the . . . commemoration of the
landing of the pilgrims of Maryland.
39808
Oration . . . at the commemoration of the
landing of the pilgrims of Maryland,
celebrated May 16, 1842. 42965
Oration at the consecration of the National
Cemetery, Gettysburg. (23264)
Oration . . . at the consecration of Oriental
Lodge, Brigton. 32921
Oration . . . at the dedication of a monument
to John Hart. 58707

Oration . . . at the dedication of the Soldiers'
Monument in North Weymouth. 42083
Oration . . . at the firemen's celebration in
Greenfield. 28909
Oration . . . at the inauguration of Lyon
Monument Association. 8453
Oration at the inauguration of the Welsford
and Parker Monument. 31821
Oration at the interment of Mrs. Lydia, wife
of Stephen Northrop. 39971
Oration . . . at the interment of the Rev.
Moses Parsons. (25981)
Oration at the laying of the corner stone of
the State Arsenal. 71552
Oration, . . . at the natural celebration, at
New-Haven, Con. (49768)
Oration . . . at the Orphan-House of Charles-
ton. 32549
Oration at the raising of "the old flag," at
Sumter. 4319
Oration . . . at the request of the City Guards
of . . . Albany. 43004
Oration . . . at the request of the Washington
Light Infantry Company. 18095
Oration at the River House, July 4, 1867.
(13407)
Oration at the twenty-fifth anniversary of
the Society of California Pioneers.
43468
Oration . . . at the Washington Garden,
Boston. 22533
Oration at Topsham, Me., July 4, 1806.
22323
Oration at Walpole, N. H., July 4, 1799.
33434
Oration at Wareham, Mass. July 4, 1804.
43452
Oration . . . at Washington, Mo., . . . fourth
of July, 1862. 20817
Oration at Washington on 4th July, 1855.
10926
Oration at West Cambridge, July 4, 1808.
(55216)
Oration . . . at West Granville, . . . N. Y.,
July 5, 1830. (44933)
Oration, . . . at West-Springfield, July fourth.
22274
Oration, . . . at Westborough. 50914
Oration, . . . at Western. 44378
Oration, . . . at Westford, . . . July 4, 1804.
25216
Oration at Westminster, Vt. 7287
Oration, . . . at Westmoreland. 50325
Oration . . . at Wilbraham, Mass. 37740
Oration, . . . at Wilbraham on the 4th of July
1810. 60836
Oration . . . [at] Williams College July 11,
1810. 52315
Oration, . . . at Windham Centre. 35480
Oration at Windsor, Vt., Feb. 22, 1814.
21283
Oration . . . at Wiscasset . . . on the fourth
of July, 1799. 39801
Oration at Whitehall, N. Y., July 4, 1817.
44137
Oration . . . at Woodstock, July 4, 1809.
34091
Oration . . . at Worcester, . . . July 5,
1802. 50458
Oration, . . . at Worcester, . . . July 4th,
1805. 41245
Oration . . . at Worcester, July 4, 1800.
3162
Oration, . . . at Worcester, July 4, 1817.
47987

Oration at Worcester, July 4, 1803. (9909)

Oration at Worcester, July 4, 1795. 845

Oration at Worcester, Mass., July 4, 1811. 33437

Oration at Worcester, Mass. July 4th, 1816. 41267

Oration, . . . at Worcester, Mass. . . . July 4th, 1810. 31673

Oration, . . . at Worcester, Mass. . . . July 4th, 1810. 31673

Oration, . . . at Worcester, Mass. On the fourth of July, 1814. 55081

Oration at Wrentham, Mass. July 4, 1801. 44328

Oration at Yale College, Conn. 5256

Oration . . . August 23, 1832. (37470)

Oration . . . Bangor, on the fourth of July, 1838. 31218

Oration before Euphemian and Philomathian Society of Erskine College. 30047

Oration . . . before Mount Vernon Lodge. 32642

Oration before Saco Lodge. (22463)

Oration before St. John's Lodge. 14429

Oration before St. Paul's and Union Lodges, Montreal. (27564)

Oration . . . before . . . St. Peter's Lodge. 32879

Oration . . . before . . . St. Peter's Lodge, . . . Newburyport. (32334)

Oration . . . before . . . South-Carolina College. 48933

Oration, . . . before the Adelphic Union Society of Williams College. 52315

Oration . . . before the Alabama Alpha of the . . . Phi Beta Kappa. 3457

Oration before the Alumni Association of the college. 74435

Oration . . . before the alumni of Gilmanton Academy. 76246

Oration before the . . . alumni of Hamilton College. 49013

Oration before the alumni of Harvard University. 57791

Oration before the alumni of Jefferson College. 98733

Oration before the alumni of Middlebury College. 4618

Oration . . . before the . . . alumni of Middlebury College, at the . . . commencement . . . 15th August, 1827. 31429

Oration before the alumni of the University of Vermont. 21715

Oration before the alumni of Williams College. (24520)

Oration . . . before the American Republican Society of Philadelphia. 9899

Oration . . . before the Anti-slavery Society of New York. 8466

Oration . . . before "The Associated Disciples of Washington." 38084

Oration . . . before the authorities of . . . Boston. 44324

Oration . . . before the Boyer Lodge, 25th of June, 1827. 33578

Oration before the Bristol Lodge, Norton. (27564)

Oration . . . before the Calhoun Monument Association. 64321

Oration before the Cape Cod Association, at their first anniversary celebration. 78516

Oration . . . before the Chamberlain Philosophical and Literary Society. 17654

Oration . . . before the Charleston Library Society. (61248)

Oration before the Cincinnati Society of New Jersey. 31413

Oration before the citizens of Burlington. 20401

Oration, . . . before the citizens of . . . Kent. (44182)

Oration before the citizens of Middletown. (79670)

Oration . . . before the citizens of . . . Quincy. (41266)

Oration . . . before the citizens of Salem, . . . July 4th, 1862. 55784

Oration . . . before the citizens of Warren, R. I. 29543

Oration . . . before the city authorities of Boston, . . . fifth of July, 1869. (50997)

Oration before the city authorities of Boston, on the fourth of July, 1870. 23287

Oration before the city authorities of Boston, on the fourth of July, 1871. 76974

Oration before the city authorities of Boston, on the fourth of July, 1868. 22171

Oration . . . before the city authorities of Boston, on the fourth of July, 1865. (44349)

Oration before the Colchester Educational Association. 80172

Oration . . . before the colored citizens of Raleigh, N. C. 82500

Oration, . . . before the Connecticut Alpha of the Phi, Beta, Kappa, at New Haven. 55524

Oration . . . before the Connecticut Alpha of the Phi Beta Kappa at Yale College. 82345

Oration . . . before the Connecticut Alpha of the Phi Beta Kappa Society. 28862

Oration before the Connecticut Beta of the Phi Beta Kappa Fraternity. 28097

Oration . . . before the Connecticut Beta of the Phi Beta Kappa Society. 33320

Oration before the Delta Kappa Epsilon Fraternity. 64939

Oration before the Democracy of Worcester and vicinity. 8716

Oration . . . before the Erosophic Society of the University of Alabama. (81260)

Oration . . . before the Euphradian and Clariosophic Societies. 62621

Oration . . . before the Euphradian Society of the College of Charleston. 28862

Oration . . . before the Federal Delphi Society. 63054

Oration before the First Troop of City Cavalry. 8466

Oration . . . before the fraternity of Masons. 34034

Oration . . . before the Grand Lodge of . . . Masons of California. 37848

Oration before the Grand Lodge of the state of New Hampshire. 2969

Oration . . . before the Hermean Society. 18652

Oration . . . before the I. O. O. F. and citizens, of Lafayette, Ind. 43242

Oration . . . before the Independent Order of Odd Fellows, of South Carolina. 64321

Oration . . . before the inhabitants of Charleston. 25675

Oration, . . . before . . . the inhabitants of Charleston, South-Carolina. 15218

Oration . . . before the inhabitants of South Reading. 67908

Oration . . . before the . . . Leicester Academy. 3105

Oration before the Literary Association.
43506

Oration . . . before the Literary Societies of
Amherst College. 18095

Oration before the Literary Societies of
Dickinson College. 5079

Oration, before the Literary Societies of
Marshall College. 11848

Oration . . . before the Literary Societies of
the University of Georgia. 62904

Oration . . . before the Literary Societies of
the University of Virginia. (31890)

Oration . . . before the Literary Societies of
the Western Reserve College. (61025)

Oration before the Literary Societies of
Washington College. 43841

Oration, . . . before . . . the . . . Masons,
at Bangor. 47068

Oration . . . before the . . . Masons, of . . .
New-Hampshire. 41562

Oration . . . before the Mass Convention of
the R. I. Suffrage Association. 2874

Oration before the Medical and Surgical Society
of Baltimore. 91205

Oration . . . before the Medical Society of
South-Carolina. 27603

Oration . . . before the Medical Society of
South Carolina . . . Dec. 24th, 1807.
(36245)

Oration before the members of Murray's Lodge.
28589

Oration . . . before the Merrimack Humane
Society. 38084

Oration . . . before the Midway and Newport
Literary Society. (44127A)

Oration before the municipal authorities and
citizens of Providence. 21427

Oration . . . before the municipal authorities
of the city of Boston. 58660

Oration . . . before the New England Society,
in . . . New York. 32621

Oration before the New England Society of the
City of New York. (23202)

Oration before the New England Society of
New York. (9545)

Oration before the New York Typographical
Society. 11851

Oration, . . . before the Newport Moral and
Literary Association. 59549

Oration . . . before the Norwich Lyceum and
Mechanics' Institute. 32867

Oration . . . before the Onondaga Teachers'
Institute. note after (58767)

Oration . . . before the Order of United
Americans. (47166)

Oration, . . . before the Peucinian Society,
Bowdoin College. 31213

Oration . . . before the Phi Beta Kappa at
Yale College. (29484)

Oration . . . before the Φ B K Society, . . .
in New Haven. 44731

Oration . . . before the Phi Beta Kappa Society
of Brown University. 59354

Oration before the Phi Beta Kappa Society of
Brown University, Providence, R. I.
(28387)

Oration before the Phi Beta Kappa Society of
Dartmouth College, August 25, 1825.
(29484)

Oration before the Phi Beta Kappa Society of
Dartmouth College, July 30, 1845. 2675

Oration before the Phi Beta Kappa Society of
Harvard University. 5076

Oration before the Phi Beta Kappa Society of
Union College. 93665

Oration . . . before the Φ B K Society,
September 10th, 1822. 60869

Oration . . . before the Phi Kappa and
Demosthenian Societies. (61248)

Oration . . . before the Philadelphia Medical
Society . . . at the opening of its session
of 1844-5. (15173)

Oration before the Philadelphia Medical
Society . . . February 8, 1826. 27665

Oration . . . before the Philadelphia Medical
Society, February 19, 1831. 30526

Oration . . . before the Philadelphia Medical
Society . . . February 3, 1827. 39048

Oration . . . before the Philadelphia Medical
Society . . . . February 23, 1825.
49703

Oration, . . . before the . . . Philanthropic
Lodge of Free and Accepted Masons.
28508

Oration . . . before the Providence Association
of Mechanicks and Manufacturers, April
13, 1818. 33385

Oration . . . before the Providence Association
of Mechanics and Manufacturrs, at their
annual election. 48151

Oration before the Republican citizens of
Charlestown. (27564)

Oration . . . before the Republican citizens
of . . . Hingham. (27564)

Oration . . . before the Republican citizens
of Newburyport. 14219

Oration before the Re-union Society of Vermont
Officers. (28980)

Oration before the Rhode Island Alpha of the
Phi Beta Kappa Society. 74334

Oration . . . before the '76 Association . . .
4th July, 1841. 43845

Oration . . . before the Social Union Society
of Amherst College. (37290)

Oration . . . before the . . . Societies of the
College of New Jersey. 29730

Oration before the Society of Alumni of the
College of Charleston. 27495

Oration before the Society of Black Friars,
New York. 49749

Oration before the Society of California
Pioneers. (49774)

Oration . . . before the Society of California
Pioneers, at . . . the fifth anniversary
of the admission of . . . California.
36363

Oration before the Society of California
Pioneers, at their celebration of the
anniversary of the admission of the
state of California. 98588

Oration, . . . before the Society of Phi Beta
Kappa, at Dartmouth College. 38084

Oration . . . before the Society of the Phi
Beta Kappa . . . at Hanover. 43240

Oration . . . before the Society of United
Brothers, of Brown University. 37935

Oration before the soldiers of Scott County.
64797

Oration . . . before the State Rights and Free
Trade Party. 62904

Oration . . . before the students of Brown
University. 58184

Oration before the Tammany Society. 36244

Oration, before the Tammany Society, in
Poughkeepsie. 40848

Oration, before the Tammany Society . . . on
the fourth of July, 1821. 37842

Oration before the Tammany Society, 12th
May, 1798. (21612)

Oration before the Theta Delta Chi Fraternity.
32526

Oration before the two societies of South
Carolina College. 30101

Oration before the Union League of Philadelphia.
27286

Oration . . . before the Washington Association. (12303)

Oration before the Washington Benevolent
Society, and the Hamilton Society.
(1678)

Oration . . . before the Washington Benevolent
Society at Cambridge. 18450

Oration before the Washington Benevolent
Society at Fitchburgh. 30797

Oration . . . before the Washington Benevolent
Society . . . New York. 78827

Oration before the Washington Benevolent
Society of Maryland. 30262

Oration before the Washington Benevolent
Society of Pennsylvania, delivered . . .
on the 22nd of February, 1827. 21570

Oration before the Washington Benevolent
Society of Pennsylvania . . . on the
22nd of February, 1828. 8958

Oration . . . before the Washington Light
Infantry. 64320

Oration . . . before the Washington Society of
Maryland, on the fourth of July, 1810.
30444

Oration . . . before the Washington Society of
Maryland, on the twenty-second February,
1812. 31191

Oration . . . before the Washington Society,
in Charleston . . . 4th of July, 1839.
(33838)

Oration . . . before the Washington Society,
the fourth July, 1834. (61248)

Oration . . . before the Whigs of Philadelphia,
on the fourth of July, 1834. 47949

Oration . . . before the Whigs of Portsmouth.
18194

Oration . . . before the "young men of Boston."
57873-57874

Oration before the Young Men's Association.
(24977)

Oration . . . before the Zelosophic Society of
the University of Pennsylvania. 42976

Oration before the Zelosophic Society of the
University of Pennsylvania; May 18,
1848. 68547

Oration, before various societies in the city
of New York. 13742

Oration . . . Blandford, Mass. 6149

Oration . . . Bloomfield. (58651)

Oration . . . Boston, July 4, 1855. 49196

Oration . . . Boston, July 4, 1849. 28674

Oration . . . Boston, July 4, 1867. 31446

Oration . . . Boston, on the fourth of July,
1863. 32621

Oration by B. F. Hallett. (59557)

Oration by Beamish Murdoch. (51433)

Oration [by Capt. Samuel White.] 97766

Oration. By C. S. Henry. 31387

Oration by Chas. Gibbons. 27286

Oration by Charles P. James. 35679

Oration by Dr. George B. Loring. 42081

Oration . . . by E. C. Larned. (39041)

Oration: by Edmund B. Fairfield. 23691

Oration . . . by Edward D. Connery. 15880

Oration. By Edward Everett. 23253

Oration by Eugene Lies. 86012

Oration, by Francis E. Hoppin. 32997

Oration by Frederick T. Frelinghuysen.
25828

Oration by Gen. George B. McClellan. 43015

Oration by Gen. I. F. Shepard. 80182

Oration by General Wade Hampton. 88111

Oration by George Bancroft. 3137

Oration by Hon. George Bancroft. 41219

Oration . . . by Hon. Henry W. Hilliard.
2381

Oration by Hon. James O. Putnam. (66815)

Oration by Hon. James W. Patterson. 20744

Oration by Hon. Robert C. Winthrop. 63485

Oration . . . by Hon. Robert M. Palmer.
58373

Oration by Hon. S. S. Harding. 30336

Oration, by Isaac S. Demund. (19537)

Oration [by James D. Green.] 43060

Oration. [By James Edward Leach.] 39506

Oration [by James Wilson.] (61411)

Oration . . . [by John H. B. Latrobe.] 39226

Oration by John Romeyn Brodhead. (53606)

Oration, by Lyman Law, Esquire. 33974,
101813

Oration [by Manton Eastburn.] 14802

Oration by Mr. Custis. 18154

Oration by Nathan G. Babbitt. 99554

Oration: by Oliver Wendell Holmes. (52746)

Oration by Prof. Brainerd Kellogg. 37278

Oration. [By R. M. T. Hunter.] 33927

Oration by Rev. Alonzo H. Quint. 67313

Oration. By Rev. George W. Pepper. 60838

Oration by Rev. H. W. Teller. 89888, note
after 94615

Oration by Rev. President Stearns. 90989

Oration by Richard Henry Lee. 39788

Oration by Samuel F. Harris. 30501

Oration by Silas P. Holbrook. (19667)

Oration by Stephen A. Douglas. (35369)

Oration, by Sydney George Fisher. 27155

Oration by the Hon. J. A. J. Cresswell.
18830

Oration by the Hon. Joseph Hopkinson.
60778, 101992

Oration by the Hon. Theodore Frelinghuysen.
(30593)

Oration by the Rev. Augustus Woodbury.
66292

Oration, by the Rev. Noah Hunt Schenck.
77570

Oration . . . by the Rev. Robert J. Breckenridge. (13564)

Oration by Thomas Chase. 12213

Oration by W. P. Miller. 88107

Oration by Willard B. Farwell. 86010

Oration, by William A. Stokes. 92007

Oration. [By William Gilmore Simms.]
(81279)

Oration [by William H. Clark.] 9976

Oration, by William H. Seward. (79539)

Oration by William Howland. 16224

Oration, by William Maxwell Evarts. 23205

Oration, Cambridge, Mass., July 4, 1826.
(27564)

Oration . . . Charleston . . . 4th of July,
1814. (31042)

Oration, . . . Charleston, July 4th, 1849.
(48942)

Oration . . . Charleston, S. C., July 4th,
1837. 24536

Oration, . . . Charlestown . . . July 4, 1805.
(27564)

Oration, commemorative of American independence, . . . at Utica. 36162

Oration commenorative of American independence, delivered . . . at New Bedford, July 4, 1810. (57758)

Oration, commemorative of American independence, delivered on the fourth of
July, 1810. 103455

Oration commemorative of American independence; . . . July 6, 1824. 17910

Oration, commemorative of American independence. Pronounced at Hallowell, July fourth, 1809. 22533

Oration, commemorative of American independence, . . . Savannah. (24011)

Oration commemorative of laying the cornerstone of the College of the Louisville Medical Institute. (5162)

Oration, commemoriatve of the abolition of the slave trade. 80859

Oration, commemorative of the birth of Washington. 21454

Oration commemorative of the character and administration of Washington. 9898

Oration, commemoriatve of the declaration of American independence. 57440, 102958

Oration, commemorative of the declaration of independence. 22533

Oration commemorative of the illustrious General Washington. 35247

Oration commemorative of the late General Lafayette. 89742

Oration, commemorative of the late illustrious General Washington. 43049

Oration, commemorative of the late Major-General Alexander Hamilton. 45460, 86123

Oration commemorative of the life and death of General George Washington. 13603

Oration, commemorative of the nineteenth anniversary of American independence. 95826

Oration commemorative of the restoration of the union. (21443)

Oration commemorative of the Rev. John Holt Rice. 47058

Oration commemorative of the surrender of Lieut. Gen'l. Earl Cornwallis. 22533

Oration commemorative of the virtues and greatness of General Washington. (43803)

Oration commemorative of the virtues and services of General George Washington. 7330

Oration, commemorative of Washington. 17910

Oration, composed and delivered at the request of the Republican Society of Baltimore. 8841

Oration, composed and delivered by John P. Van Ness. 98528

Oration, composed at the request of the Selectmen. 28679

Oration concerning the origin of states. 21235

Oration delivered April 2d, 1771. 42374

Oration delivered at a meeting of the Democratic Association. 82154

Oration delivered at a national council. 17462

Oration delivered at Barnstable. 17658

Oration delivered at Boston, July 4, 1815. 79444

Oration delivered at . . . Boston, on the anniversary of American independence. 42800

Oration delivered at Bozrah. 102084

Oration, delivered at Bristol College. (37668)

Oration, delivered at Brookfield, July 5, 1813. 65085, 85397

Oration, delivered at Buckston. 88952

Oration delivered at Buffalo, July 4th, 1862. 13469

Oration delivered at Cambridge, before the Phi Beta Kappa Society. 66784

Oration, delivered at Cambridge, before the Society of Phi Beta Kappa. 19862

Oration delivered at Canterbury. 74430

Oration delivered at Charlestown, Massachusetts. 22307

Oration delivered at Charlestown, on the seventy-fifth anniversary. 23271

Oration delivered at Cherry Valley. 30111

Oration delivered at Cheshire. 39971

Oration delivered at Columbia College. (12183)

Oration, delivered . . . [at] Columbia, S. C. 9719

Oration, delivered at commencement, Harvard University, Cambridge, July 17th, 1799. 105127

Oration, delivered at commencement, Harvard University, Cambridge, July 20th, 1796. 105129

Oration delivered at Concord, April the nineteenth, 1825. 23262

Oration, delivered . . . at Concord, July 4th, 1801. 23945

Oration delivered at Concord, on the celebratic of the seventy-fifth anniversary of the events of April 19, 1775. 67906

Oration delivered at Conway. 94208

Oration delivered at Delphi, New York. 24566

Oration delivered at Douglass. 17401

Oration delivered at Dover, N. H. 2289

Oration, delivered at East-Greenwich. 97486

Oration, delivered at East-Haddam. 5812

Oration, delivered at Faneuil Hall. (26186)

Oration, delivered at Fayetteville. 5600

Oration, delivered at Flemington. 88248

Oration delivered at Flushing. 2027

Oration delivered at Freeport, Me. (3550)

Oration delivered at Geneva. 2523

Oration delivered at Georgetown. 43529

Oration, delivered at Gloucester. 91325

Oration delivered at Granville. 16360

Oration, delivered at Greenfield. (80273)

Oration, delivered at Greenville. (70473)

Oration, delivered at Groton. 11115

Oration, delivered at Hackinsack. 23163

Oration, delivered at Hanover, N. H. August 27th, 1812. 105100

Oration, delivered at Hanover, Newhampshire, at the request of the brethren. 105168

Oration delivered at Hartford. (81039)

Oration, delivered at . . . Hinesdale. 23691

Oration, delivered at Hingham. 41420

Oration, delivered at Holden. 2588

Oration, delivered at Huntington, L. I. 9599

Oration, delivered at Ipswich. (25981)

Oration delivered at . . . Iowa College. 64471

Oration delivered at Jamaica, Long Island. (43102)

Oration delivered at Jericho, July 4, 1809. 98523

Oration, delivered at Keene, N. H., before the Washington Benevolent Society. 16342

Oration delivered at Keene, N. H., February 22, 1832. 29665

Oration delivered at Key West, Florida. 7152

Oration delivered at Kingston, R. I. (64652)

Oration delivered at Lancaster, February 21, 1826. 27944

Oration delivered at Lancaster, Mass. in celebration of American independence, July, 1825. 104060

Oration delivered at Lenox, the 4th July 1793. (39727)

Oration delivered at Lexington, on the fourth of July, 1825. 91373

Oration delivered at Lexington, the 22d
February, 1800. 27579

Oration: delivered at Lockport. 66817

Oration delivered at Lowville, N. Y. (2029)

Oration, delivered at Manchester, on the 17th
day of August, 1795. 96097

Oration delivered at Machias, Me. (16578)

Oration delivered at Malden on the two
hundredth anniversary. 28528

Oration delivered at Marietta, April 7, 1789.
20966

Oration, delivered at Marietta, July 4, 1788.
98639

Oration, delivered at Mendon. 80829

Oration delivered at Middlebury. 104053

Oration delivered at Middletown. 33959

Oration delivered at Monmouth, Me. (11863)

Oration, delivered at Mont [sic] Vernon, New-
Hampshire. 83897

Oration delivered at Mount Aaron. (8810)

Oration delivered at Mount Pleasant, New-
York. 105987

Oration delivered at New-Castle, Del. 98497

Oration . . . delivered at New-Gloucester.
103734

Oration delivered at New Haven, before the
Phi Beta Kappa Society. 20093

Oration delivered at New Haven, July 4, 1861.
37646

Oration, delivered at New-Haven on the 7th.
of July, A. D. 1801. 21532

Oration, delivered at New-Salem. 101102

Oration, delivered at Newburgh. (57758)

Oration delivered at Newburyport, Mass.
18095

Oration, delivered . . . at Newport. 51301

Oration delivered at Ogdensburgh, January 4,
1861. 49036

Oration, delivered at Ogdensburgh, New-York.
98514

Oration, delivered at Oxford. 3843

Oration delivered at Philadelphia by William B.
Reed. 68615

Oration, delivered at Philadelphia Vauxhall
Gardens. 3394

Oration, delivered at Pittsfield, before the
Washington Benevolent Society. (35818)

Oration delivered at Pittsfield, July 4, 1807.
2645

Oration delivered at Pleasant Valley, Ohio.
30567

Oration, delivered at Plymouth, December 22d,
1864. 23261

Oration delivered at Plymouth, Dec. 22, 1802.
293

Oration, delivered at Plymouth, in New-Hampshire. 25297

Oration, delivered at Portchester, in the town
of Rye. 7235

Oration delivered at Portland, July 5, 1824.
24290

Oration, delivered at . . . Portland, July 4th,
1808. (25783)

Oration, delivered at Portland, July 4th, 1796.
18809

Oration delivered at Portsmouth, N. H., 4th
July, 1805. 23183

Oration, delivered at Portsmouth, New-Hampshire, on the fourth July, 1804. 102631

Oration delivered at Portsmouth, New-Hampshire, on the fourth of July, 1788. 79400

Oration, delivered at Potter's Field. 103654

Oration, delivered at Pownalborough. 103977

Oration, delivered at Providence, in the First
Congregational Meeting-House. 104635

Oration, delivered at Princeton, New Jersey.
24290

Oration delivered at Queens, L. I. 2028

Oration delivered at Quincy, Mass. 206

Oration delivered at Rochester. 13319

Oration, delivered at Roxbury. 4350

Oration, delivered . . . [at] St. Paul's College.
77988

Oration, delivered at Salem, on Monday, July
4, 1819. 21293

Oration delivered at Salem on the fourth of
July, 1806. 19077

Oration, delivered at Salem, on the fourth of
July, 1810. 89691

Oration, delivered at Salisbury, New-Hampshire,
July 4th, 1807. 102323

Oration, delivered at Salisbury, on the anniversary of American independence.
105331

Oration delivered at Sambridge on the fiftieth
anniversary of the declaration of the
independence. 23271

Oration delivered at St. Johnsbury, Vy. 76247

Oration delivered at Stoughton, Mass. 101036

Oration, delivered at Taunton, (Massachusetts)
before the King David's Lodge. 103719

Oration delivered at Taunton, . . . on the 4th
of July, 1799. (20529)

Oration delivered at the Baptist Church in the
city of Savannah. 4979

Oration delivered at the Baptist Church in the
city of Troy. 106228

Oration delivered at the celebration of American
independence, at Sheffield. 103709

Oration, delivered at the celebration of the
anniversary of American independence,
at Aurora. 93974

Oration delivered at the celebration of the
anniversary of our national independence.
91050

Oration, delivered at the celebration of the
first centennial anniversary of the South-
Carolina Society. 80036, note after
96180

Oration delivered at the centennial celebration
in Brookline, N. H. 77298

Oration delivered at the centennial celebration
of the evacuation of Fort Duquesne.
41949

Oration: delivered at the chapel in Boston.
28017

Oration. Delivered at the Charleston Orphan-
Asylum. 26226

Oration, delivered at the City-Hall, New-York.
73013

Oration; delivered, at the college chapel,
Hanover. 105308

Oration, delivered at the Columbian College.
92372

Oration delivered at the commencement of
Rhode Island College. 7831

Oration delivered at the dedication of the
Free Masons Hall. 88955

Oration delivered at the Democratic Republican
celebration of the sixty-fourth anniversary
of the independence. 106111

Oration delivered at the Democratic Republican
celebration of the sixty-second anniversary
of the independence. 25108

Oration delivered at the Encaenia in King's
College, Fredericton, June 28, 1849.
71723

Oration delivered at the Encaenia in King's
College, Fredericton, June 27, 1839.
71722

Oration, delivered at the first commemoration of the landing of the pilgrims of Maryland. 68192

Oration delivered at the fourth commemoration of the landing of the pilgrims of Maryland. 11864-11865

Oration delivered at the laying of the corner stone of a monument. (11866)

Oration . . . delivered at the laying of the corner stone of the new city hall. 72678

Oration, delivered at the Medical College. 86133

Oration; delivered at the Meeting House, Colchester. 100999

Oration delivered at the Meeting-House in Bennington. 48002

Oration delivered at the new meeting house, in Marietta. 73939

Oration, delivered at the North Church in Hartford. (3424)

Oration delivered at the North Meeting House, in Tiverton. 7953

Oration delivered at the Orphan-House of Charleston. 9084

Oration, delivered at the Presbyterian Church. 91814

Oration, delivered at the request of the assembled cavalry and infantry. 50721

Oration delivered at the request of the city government. 23237

Oration, delivered at the request of the Committee of Arrangements. 92908

Oration, delivered at the request of the Committee of Associated Mechanicks. 84278

Oration, delivered at the request of the Jefferson Society. (79085)

Oration, delivered at the request of the officers of the Brigade. (21613)

Oration, delivered at the request of the Republicans of Boston. 21293

Oration, delivered, at the request of the Society Φ B K. 38005

Oration, delivered at the request of the Washington Light Infantry Company. (25376)

Oration, delivered at the request of the Washington Society. 21293

Oration delivered at the request of the Young Men of Salem. (62519)

Oration, delivered at the Rev. Mr. Olcott's Church. 91751

Oration delivered at the second commemoration of the pilgrims of Maryland. 68193

Oration delivered at the South Parish in Woodstock, Vermont. 34091

Oration delivered at the State House in Philadelphia. 344

Oration, delivered at the tomb of the patriots. 54021, 94298

Oration, delivered at the town of Sunbury. 82374

Oration delivered at the Union Celebration. 7691

Oration delivered at the Union Meeting House. (30811)

Oration delivered at the United Celebration at Shepherdstown. 95425

Oration delivered at the United States Consulate in Aspinwall. 72198

Oration delivered at the Whig Celebration. 81591

Oration delivered at the Young Men's Celebration. 85523

Oration, delivered at Thomaston, July 4th, 1797. 103978

Oration delivered at Tolland, Conn. 29811

Oration, delivered at Topsham—District of Maine. 104116

Oration delivered at Trenton Falls. (8890)

Oration delivered at Utica, N. Y. 49030

Oration delivered at Vallejo. 24041

Oration, delivered at Wallingford, April 4, 1814. 90308

Oration, delivered at Wallingford, August 8th. 1805. 90309

Oration delivered at Waltham. (64776)

Oration delivered at Warwick, Mass. (64779)

Oration, delivered at Washington-Hall. 10144

Oration delivered at Washington, July fourth, 1809. 3425

Oration delivered at Watertown, March 5, 1776. (6737), 95172

Oration, delivered at Wethersfield, February 22, 1800. 44732

Oration delivered at Williamsoun. 2646

Oration delivered at Willston. 98524

Oration, delivered at Woodbridge, New-Jersey 93115

Oration delivered at Worcester, Massachusett July 4, 1818. 19595

Oration delivered at Worcester, . . . fourth o July, 1791. 3161

Oration delivered at Worcester, on the thirtie of April. 9414

Oration: delivered before a lodge of Free and Accepted Masons. 98640

Oration delivered before Capt. J. H. Byrd's Company of Volunteers. (17614)

Oration, delivered before Harmony Lodge no. 22. 93187

Oration, delivered before Montgomery Lodge. 90468

Oration, delivered before . . . St. Peter's Lodge. 35395

Oration delivered before the Agricultural and Mechanics' Association of Louisiana. 73428

Oration delivered before the Alumni Association. 5885

Oration, delivered before the American Philosophical Society, held in Philadelpl on the 27th of February, 1786. (74235) 74236

Oration delivered before the American Philosophical Society, . . . 18th October, 1823. 34730

Oration delivered before the American Philosophical Society, . . . 6th of June, 1821 21379

Oration, . . . delivered before the American Republican Society. 9899

Oration delivered before the American Whig and Cliosophic Societies. 77566

Oration delivered before the Artillery Compar of Wilmington. 43487

Oration delivered before the Augusta Washing tonian Temperance Society. 84854

Oration delivered before the authorities and citizens of Newport. 19592

Oration delivered before the authorities of the city of Boston . . . fifth of July, 1841. (18048)

Oration delivered before the authorities of the city of Boston, . . . July 5, 1847. 1121

Oration delivered before the authorities of the city of Boston, July 4, 1845. 93652, 93683

Oration, delivered before the authorities of the city of Boston, U. S. 93653

Oration delivered before the Beaufort Volunteer
  Artillery. 96786
Oration delivered before the Biennial Con-
  vention of the Alpha Delti Society.
  22008
Oration delivered before the Chemical Society
  of Philadelphia. 84411
Oration delivered before the Cincinnati and
  the '75 Association. 67710
Oration delivered before the Cincinnati
  Astronomical Society. 291
Oration delivered before the citizens of Boston,
  . . . July 4, 1837. 11991
Oration: delivered before the citizens of
  Boston, on the fifty eighth anniversary
  of American independence. By Edward
  G. Prescott. 65243
Oration. Delivered before the citizens of
  Boston on the fifty-eighty anniversary
  of American independence. [By Richard
  S. Fay.] 23942
Oration delivered . . . before the citizens of
  Boston, on the sixty fourth anniversary
  of American independence, July 4, 1840.
  64777
Oration delivered before the citizens of
  Buffalo, July 5th, 1852. 80126
Oration, delivered before the citizens of
  Burlington, N. J. 66613
Oration delivered before the citizens of
  Charlestown, on the fifty-second anni-
  versary of the declaration of Independence.
  23271
Oration delivered before the citizens of Hingham.
  (41266)
Oration delivered before the citizens of Ply-
  mouth. 79930
Oration, delivered before the citizens of Portland, and the Supreme Judicial Court of
  the commonwealth of Massachusetts.
  91926
Oration, delivered before the citizens of Portland, and the Supreme Judicial Court of
  Massachusetts. 94120
Oration, delivered before the citizens of the
  county of Hillsdale. 101015
Oration, delivered before the city authorities
  and citizens of Providence. July 4th,
  1867. 73937
Oration delivered before the city authorities
  and citizens of Providence, July 4, 1866.
  20188
Oration delivered before the city authorities
  of Boston, . . . July 4, 1848. 27369
Oration delivered before the city authorities
  of Boston, on the fourth of July, 1860.
  23271
Oration delivered before the city authorities
  of Boston, on the fourth of July, 1864.
  74376
Oration delivered before the City Council and
  citizens of Boston, July 4, 1843. 184
Oration delivered before the City Council and
  citizens of Boston, on the one hundred
  and fourth anniversary of the declaration
  of independence. 83859
Oration delivered before the corporation and
  faculty of Williams' College. 92883
Oration delivered before the . . . corporation
  and the military and civil societies of
  . . . Albany. 3451
Oration delivered before the Democratic citizens
  of the county of Worcester. 67908
Oration delivered before the Democratic Republicans of Portland. 1812

Oration delivered before the Democracy of
  Springfield. 3141
Oration delivered before the Democracy . . .
  Philadelphia. 20677
Oration delivered before the Democrats and
  Anti-Masons. 67908
Oration, delivered before the different Re-
  publican societies. 103158
Oration delivered before the Euphradian and
  Clariosophic Societies. 84545
Oration, delivered before the firemen of
  Charleston. 21169
Oration delivered before the Fourth of July
  Association. 49708
Oration, delivered before the Franklin Debating
  Society. 12429
Oration, delivered before the General Society
  of Mechanics and Tradesmen. 101437
Oration, delivered before the Gloucester
  Mechanic Association. 67903
Oration, delivered . . . before the inhabitants
  of Charleston. 65687
Oration delivered before the inhabitants of
  South Boston. 82811
Oration delivered before the inhabitants of
  the town of Boston. 95187
Oration delivered before the inhabitants of
  the town of Newburyport. 294
Oration, delivered before the inhabitants of
  Winchester, Mass. 6229
Oration . . . delivered before the Jackson
  Republican citizens. 104020
Oration, delivered before the Kentish Artillery
  and citizens of Apponaug. 37843
Oration delivered before the Legislature of
  Massachusetts. (28385)
Oration delivered before the Legislature of
  N. J. 18733
Oration, delivered before the literary societies
  of Dartmouth College. 22460
Oration delivered before the literary societies
  of Lafayette College. 7775
Oration delivered before the literary societies
  of Oglethorpe University. (81256)
Oration delivered before the literary societies
  of the New-York Free Academy. 31161
Oration delivered before the Masonic Society.
  20491
Oration delivered before the Mechanic Ap-
  prentices' Library Association.
  (78677)
Oration, delivered before the members of the
  Law Institute. 75935
Oration delivered before the military of the
  city of Albany. 51469
Oration delivered before the Mosheimian
  Society. 80791
Oration, delivered before the Most Ancient
  and Honorable Society of Free and
  Accepted Masons. 93696
Oration delivered before the municipal
  authorities and citizens [of Providence,
  R. I.] 66293
Oration delivered before the municipal
  authorities of . . . Boston. 74312
Oration delivered before the municipal
  authorities of the city of Boston, at the
  celebration of the seventy-eighth anniversary. 92018
Oration delivered before the municipal
  authorities of the city of Boston, July 4,
  1859. 93699, 93700
Oration delivered before the municipal
  authorities of the city of Boston, July 4,
  1853. (5326)

Oration, delivered before the Union Society, of Savannah. 81577

Oration, delivered before the Uranian Society. 93217

Oration, delivered before the various lodges . . . of . . . Odd Fellows. 24740

Oration delivered before the Washington Association, at a stated meeting. 101979

Oration delivered before the Washington Association of Philadelphia. 17307

Oration delivered before the Washington Benevolent Society, at Cambridge, July 4, 1814. 18440

Oration, delivered before the Washington Benevolent Society in Cambridge, July 4, 1815. 5278

Oration delivered before the Washington Benevolent Society, in the city of New-York, . . . on the twenty-second of February, 1809. (32061)

Oration delivered before the Washington Benevolent Society, in the city of New-York, on the twenty-second of February, 1810. (35853)

Oration delivered before the Washington Benevolent Society in Newbury, Vermont. 101103

Oration delivered before the Washington Benevolent Society, July 5, 1813. 34750

Oration, delivered before the Washington Benevolent Society, . . . New-York. (40847)

Oration delivered before the Washington Benevolent Society of Massachusetts, on the thirtieth day of April, 1813. 67229

Oration delivered before the Washington Benevolent Society of Massachusetts on the thirtiety day of April, 1812. 93556

Oration delivered before the Washington Benevolent Society of Pennsylvania. At their first anniversary meeting, February 22d, 1813. (30361)

Oration delivered before the Washington Benevolent Society of Pennsylvania; at their third anniversary meeting, February 22, 1815. 78319

Oration, delivered before the Washington Benevolent Society of the County of Columbia, at the Court-House in the city of Hudson, February 22d, 1811. 92918

Oration, delivered before the Washington Benevolent Society of the County of Columbia, at the Court-House in the city of Hudson, February 22, 1814. 101438

Oration delivered before the Washington Benevolent Society, of the County of Cortland in Home. 4645

Oration, delivered before the Washington Benevolent Society, of the County of Herkimer, on the 22d February, 1817. 79149

Oration delivered before the Washington Society of Alexandria, Va. 33259

Oration, delivered before the Washington Society, in Boston. 101374

Oration delivered before the Whig Association and the State Society of Cincinnati. (21290)

Oration, delivered before the Whig citizens of Philadelphia. 68613

Oration delivered before the Whigs of Bristol County. 11991

Oration delivered before the Young Men's Association of Brooklyn, N. Y. 35690

Oration delivered before the Young Men's Association of the city of Albany. 33460

Oration delivered before Wayne Lodge no. 25. 95859

Oration delivered by Anson Burlingam. 9333

Oration, delivered, by appointment before the Albany and Troy City Guards. 88629

Oration, delivered by appointment before the Union & State Rights Party. 82792

Oration: delivered by appointment of the committees of the corporation. 88664

Oration: delivered, by appointment, on the fourth day of July, A. D. 1828. 88645

Oration delivered by Asa Child. 86753, note after 100786

Oration delivered by Augustus D. Splivalo. 89554

Oration delivered by Charles Sumner. (66786)

Oration delivered by Dr. Joseph Warren. 30178, 101477

Oration delivered by Elihu Palmer. 63790

Oration delivered by F. G. Brown. 8472

Oration delivered by George D. Lamont. 38766

Oration delivered by Hon. O. H. Browning. 8694

Oration delivered by Hon. William D. Kelley. (37268)

Oration delivered by Horatio Stebbins. 91023

Oration: delivered by invitation. 88646

Oration delivered by John Hancock. 30178

Oration, delivered by Major-General Lee. 101758

Oration, delivered by Nathaniel Smith, Esq. 83666

Oration delivered by request of the city authorities, before the citizens of Boston. 2410

Oration, delivered by request of the municipal authorities, of the city of Boston. 104803

Oration delivered by Rev. Byron Sunderland. 93751

Oration, delivered by Richard Bland Lee. 39780

Oration delivered by Richard Rush. 74268

Oration delivered by Richard T. Merrick. 47988

Oration, delivered by Stephen W. Dana. 18455

Oration delivered by the Hon. David A. Bokee. 6168

Oration, delivered by William H. C. Ellis. 22336

Oration delivered . . . 1858, by James Louis Petigru. 88005

Oration delivered . . . 1859, by W. H. Trescott. 88005

Oration delivered . . . 1856, by J. Barrett Cohen. 88005

Oration, delivered February 4, 1774. 74237

Oration, delivered February 24, 1775. (71588)

Oration, delivered February 22d, 1815. 90310

Oration, delivered February 22, 1800. 3881

Oration delivered February 22d, 1813. 22385

Oration delivered February 22d, 1812. 51300

Oration . . . . Delivered, . . . February 22d. 1820. 57746

Oration delivered 4th July, 1827. 21915

Oration delivered . . . fourth of July, 1810. 12602

Oration delivered Friday, July 4, 1828. 93638

Oration, delivered in . . . at Rochester, July 5, 1852. 20716

Oration delivered in Brattleborough, July 4, 1811. (56225)

Oration delivered in . . . Charleston . . . July 4, 1831. 20917

Oration delivered in . . . Charleston on the fourth of July, 1809. 28858

Oration, delivered in . . . Charleston, South-Carolina; on . . . the fourth of July, 1817. 22253

Oration, delivered in . . . Charleston, South-Carolina, on the fourth of July, 1812. 17346

Oration delivered in Charlestown, in Virginia. 23687

Oration, delivered in Charlestown (Mass.) (23201)

Oration delivered in commemoration of the forty-seventh anniversary of the declaration of American independence. 28582

[Oration, delivered in Fairhaven.] 3949

Oration delivered in Faneuil Hall. 71289

Oration: delivered in Free Masons-Hall. 95408

Oration delivered in Greenburg, Pennsylvania. 104675

Oration delivered in Haverhill, Mass. 31122

Oration, delivered in . . . Hudson. (28952)

Oration delivered in Independence Square, in Philadelphia. 76975

Oration delivered in Independence Square, in the city of Philadelphia. (79204)

Oration, delivered in Leominster, July, 4th, 1809. 104051

Oration [delivered in New Bedford, July 4, 1833.] (30460)

Oration, delivered . . . in New-York. (22379)

Oration delivered in Newark, N. J. 17910

Oration delivered in Newbern, North Carolina. 35702

Oration delivered in Newburyport on the fifty-fourth anniversary of the declaration of American independence. 908

Oration delivered in Newburyport on the fourth of July, 1851. 26085

Oration delivered in Newport. 5588

Oration delivered in Portland. 19057

Oration delivered . . . in Providence, at the celebration, February 23, A. D., 1824. 20967

Oration delivered in . . . Providence, July 4, A. D. 1795. 47002

Oration delivered . . . in Providence, on the fourth of July, A. D. 1798. 7832

Oration, delivered in . . . Providence, on the fourth of July, 1801. 9235

Oration: delivered in public. 97174

Oration delivered in Richmond. 104881

Oration, delivered in St. Michael's Church, before the inhabitants of Charleston, South-Carolina, on Monday, the fifth of July, 1802. 84415

Oration, delivered in St. Michael's Church, before . . . the inhabitants of Charleston, South-Carolina; on the fourth of July, 1818. 62903

Oration, delivered in St. Michael's Church, before the inhabitants of Charleston, South-Carolina, on the 4th of July, 1795. 97384

Oration, delivered in St. Michaels Church, Charleston, South-Carolina. 96181

Oration delivered in St. Michael's Church . . . Charleston, South-Carolina, on the fourth of July, 1803. 20801

Oration, delivered in St. Michael's Church, in the city of Charleston. 101429

Oration delivered in St. Paul's Church. (18865)

Oration, delivered in St. Philip's Church, before the inhabitants of Charleston, South-Carolina, on Saturday, the fourth of July, 1807. 86134

Oration, delivered in St. Philip's Church, before the inhabitants of Charleston, South-Carolina, on the fourth of July, 1796. 84826-84827

Oration delivered in St. Philip's Church, Charleston, South-Carolina. 22285

Oration delivered in St. Phillip's Church. 74485

Oration delivered in Salem, July 4, 1826. 14530

Oration, delivered in Salem, on the fifth of July, 1813. 89692

Oration, delivered in Sheffield. 39728

Oration, delivered in South-Farms, in Litchfield. 50838

Oration delivered in Tammany Hall. 94296

Oration delivered in Tewksbury. 71059

Oration delivered in the African Zion Church 30038

Oration, delivered in the Baptist Meeting-House in Colebrook. 5928

Oration, delivered in the Baptist Meeting Hou in Thomaston. 103712

Oration, delivered in the Benevolent Congregational Meeting-House. 86129

Oration, delivered in the capitol in the city c Washington. (20025)

Oration, delivered in the Chapel of the U. S. Military Academy. 30348

Oration delivered in the city of Charleston. 97467

Oration delivered in the city of Nashville. 5366

Oration delivered in the city of Raleigh. 32477

Oration: delivered in the college-hall, at Providence. (58637)

Oration, delivered in the Dutch Church. 90553

Oration delivered in the First Congregational Church. (11865)

Oration delivered in the German Reformed Church. 12890

Oration, delivered in the Independent, or Con gregational Church, Charleston, before the State Rights & Free Trade Party. 86135

Oration, delivered in the Independent or Congregational Church, Charleston, before the State Rights & Free Trade Society. 31040

Oration, delivered in the Meeting House of t First Parish in Portland, January 24th 5796. 94121

Oration, delivered in the Meeting House of the First Parish in Portland, Monday, June 24th, 5799. 91927

Oration delivered in the Middle Dutch Churcl 40838, 101785

Oration, delivered in the new city hall. (21569)

Oration delivered in the New Dutch Church. 101437

Oration . . . delivered in the New York Academy of Music. 23271

Oration delivered in the Presbyterian Church at Morristown. 25064

Oration, delivered in the Presbyterian Meetir House. 95426

Oration delivered in the Senate Chamber of
Maryland. 39872
Oration, delivered in the South Parish, in
Weymouth. (71060)
Oration, delivered in the Third Episcopal
Church. 103416
Oration delivered in the Wesley Chapel.
92822
Oration; delivered in Trinity-Church, in New-
port. 33934
Oration delivered in Wallingford. 5595
Oration, delivered January 8, 1800. 27400
Oration, delivered, January 22 1773. 84631
Oration, delivered . . . July 5, 1824.
(23283A)
Oration, delivered July 5, 1790. At . . .
Boston. 28381
Oration, delivered July 4th, A. D. 1796.
22201
Oration delivered July 4, 1811. 77236
Oration . . . delivered July 4th, 1848. 43841
Oration delivered July 4th, 1846. 29890
Oration delivered July 4th, 1809. 99272
Oration delivered July 4, 1819. 19891
Oration delivered July 4, 1817. 11896
Oration delivered July 4th, 1865. 80127
Oration delivered July fourth, 1810. 7200
Oration, delivered July 4, 1839. 97629
Oration, delivered July 4, 1832. (67267)
Oration, delivered July 4, 1829. 9958
Oration, delivered July 4, 1826. 19683
Oration, delivered July 4th, 1783. 101471
Oration: delivered July 4, 1788, at . . .
Providence. 32256
Oration delivered July 4, 1788. At the request
of the inhabitants. 57859
Oration, delivered July 4, 1785. (26619)
Oration, delivered July 4, 1789, at the
Presbyterian Church. 72741
Oration, delivered July 4th, 1789, at the re-
quest of the inhabitants. 91797
Oration, delivered July 4, 1787. 18922
Oration, delivered July 4, 1786. 2416
Oration delivered July 4th, 1798. 79939
Oration, delivered July 4th, 1795. 105309
Oration, . . . delivered July 17th, 1799.
58200
Oration delivered July the fourth, 1810.
96375
Oration delivered July the fourth, 1813.
41562
Oration delivered March fifteenth 1775.
6249
Oration, delivered March 5th, 1781. 18923
Oration, delivered March 5th, 1783. 102617
Oration, delivered March 5, 1778. 2417
Oration, delivered March 5, 1774. 30177
Oration, delivered March 5th, 1779. (6737),
97404
Oration, delivered March 5th, 1777. 31689
Oration delivered March 5th, 1772. 833,
(6737), 6138, 30178, 101477
Oration delivered March fifth, 1733 [i. e.
1773.] 12983
Oration delivered Mar. 2, 1781. 5244
Oration, delivered March 6, 1780. 45468
Oration; delivered March sixth, 1775. (6737),
8546, 101478
Oration delivered May viii, M.DCC.LXXIX.
79461
Oration delivered . . . May 22d, 1796. 70471
Oration delivered . . . near the ground on
which Major Andre was taken. 42848
Oration, delivered November 10, 1791. 102111

Oration, delivered . . . on board the Nassau
Prison Ship. (57441)
Oration, delivered on commencement at Brown
University. 68559
Oration delivered on . . . July 5, 1858.
27976
Oration, delivered on Monday, fourth of July,
1825. 89660
Oration, delivered on Monday XXVIIth.
December. 98474
Oration, delivered on Mount Independence.
92795
Oration delivered on Rinehart's Island. 58638
Oration delivered on the anniversary of
American independence. (67701)
Oration, delivered on the anniversary of inde-
pendence, at Deerfield. 94497
Oration delivered on the anniversary of the
New-England Society. 103785
Oration delivered on the battlefield of Gettys-
burg. 23263, (27248), 46064
Oration, delivered on the centennial anniversary
of the birth of Washington. 63051
Oration delivered on the centennial anniversary
of the initiation of General George
Washington, among the Ancient and
Honorable Fraternity of Freemasons.
91698
Oration delivered on the dedication of Webster's
statue. 23271
Oration, delivered on the 11th of March, 1814.
98476
Oration delivered on the 11th of October,
1880. 77511
Oration delivered on the fifth anniversary of
the South Carolina Historical Society.
30164
Oration, delivered on the fifth of July, 1847.
(7150)
Oration, delivered on . . . the fifth of July,
1824. (3892)
Oration delivered on the fiftieth anniversary
of our national independence. 42419
Oration, delivered on the forty-eighth anni-
versary of the Orphan House. 85307
Oration, delivered on the 43d anniversary of
American independence. 13708
Oration delivered on the fourth day of July,
1835. 23271
Oration delivered on the fourth July, 1843.
7773
Oration: delivered on the fourth of July,
A. D., 1846. 93237
Oration delivered . . . on the fourth of July,
A. D. 1797. 9448
Oration delivered on the fourth of July, 1855.
(20618)
Oration, delivered on the fourth of July . . .
1841. 24740
Oration delivered on the fourth of July, 1804.
62638
Oration delivered on the fourth of July, 1862.
18043
Oration delivered on the fourth of July, 1820.
16621
Oration, delivered on the fourth of July, 1829.
2413
Oration delivered on the fourth of July, 1821.
93216
Oration, delivered on the fourth of July, 1827.
71744
Oration, delivered on the fourth of July, 1827
in the park. 103654
Oration, delivered on the fourth of July, 1827,
in the State House. 103111

Oration delivered on the fourth of July, 1826. (3140)

Oration delivered on the fourth of July, 1823. 18029

Oration, delivered on the fourth of July, 1812. 104052

Oration, delivered on the fourth of July, 1798. 102595

Oration delivered on the fourth of July 1796. 104357

Oration delivered on the fourth of March, 1813. 83030

Oration delivered on the late public commence-ment at Rhode-Island College. 5468

Oration delivered on the occasion of the decoration of the graves. 90104

Oration delivered on the occasion of the inauguration of the bust. 23320

Oration delivered on the occasion of the reinterment of the remains. 68616

Oration delivered on the 2d of March, 1839. 95515

Oration, delivered on the 2d of October, 1843. 15880

Oration, delivered on the 17th of March, 1819. 40009

Oration, delivered on the 22nd February, 1830. 103879

Oration, delivered on the 22nd of February, 1800. 39690

Oration, delivered on the 22d of February, 1813. 68043

Oration, delivered on Tuesday, August 5, 1856. 18049

Oration, delivered on Tuesday, the fourth of July, 1826. 67230

Oration delivered the fourth of July, 1808. 65246

Oration, delivered the preceding evening at the interment of the bodies. 90836

Oration, delivered . . . the twenty-ninth of November, 1796. 36540

Oration, delivered the twenty-second of February MDCCC. 29923

Oration, delivered to the citizens of Burlington. 28832

Oration, delivered to the Horanian Literary Society. 105647

Oration, delivered to the Society of Black Friars. 103165

Oration delivered to the Society of the Cin-cinnati in the commonwealth of Massa-chusetts, July 4, 1789. 103836

Oration delivered to the Society of the Cin-cinnati in the commonwealth of Massa-chusetts, July 4th 1787. 8357

Oration delivered to the Society of the Cin-cinnati in . . . Massachusetts, July 4, 1788. 33646

Oration, describing the influence of commerce. 71012

Oration . . . Dorchester . . . fourth of July, 1822. 82703

Oration eulogistic of O. N. Ogden. 56821

Oration . . . Fairfield, Herkimer County, New York. 82590

Oration, . . . February 22d, 1811. 47049

Oration, . . . February 22d, 1815. (59057)

Oration, Feb. 22, 1852. 10281

Oration, . . . fifth of July, 1813. 55192

Oration . . . fifth of July, 1824. 48853

Oration . . . for Jewish widows & orphans, January 12, 1862. 34328

Oration for the fourth of July, 1798. 21283

Oration, fourth anniversary of the College of California. 24042

Oration, 4th July, 1808. 5414

Oration . . . 4th July, 1803, at Newark. 56820

Oration, 4 July 1821, at the request of the Republicans of the town of Boston. (23671)

Oration (4th July, 1802), at Lenox, Mass. 27579

Oration . . . 4th July, 1802, at Stephentown, New York. (43608)

Oration, 4th July, 1794, Newark, New Jersey. 43682

Oration . . . fourth of July, 1856. 47078

Oration, . . . fourth of July, 1831. 59649

Oration, . . . fourth of July, 1821. 30015

Oration . . . fourth of July, 1823. 39855

Oration, . . . fourth of July, 1822. (51138)

Oration . . . 4th of July, 1792. 47903

Oration funebre en las exequias generales. (11297)

Oration . . . Gouverneur Wesleyan Seminary. 55342

Oration, . . . Grand Royal Arch Chapter. (22779)

Oration . . . Herkimer, July 4, 1859. 82590

Oration . . . Holliston, Mass. 23237

Oration . . . in Acton, Mass. (6977)

Oration . . . in Castleton, Vt. 38870

Oration, in celebration of American inde-pendence, July 4th, 1797. 20075

Oration in celebration of the 2d declaration of independence. (26670)

Oration, . . . in . . . Charleston, South-Carolina, on the fourth of July, 1810. (42971)

Oration . . . in . . . Charleston, South-Carolina; . . . the fourth of July, 1815. 28590

Oration in City Hall, Burlington. 20388

Oration in commemoration of American inde-pendence . . . at Brewster. 81332

Oration in commemoration of American inde-pendence, . . . July 4, 1804. 64279

Oration, in commemoration of the anniversar of American independence. Delivered Boston, July 4th, 1809. 103479

Oration, in commemoration of the birth of our illustrious Washington. 21283

Oration, in commemoration of the dissolution of the political union. 41562

Oration in commemoration of the founders o William and Mary College, delivered o the anniversary of its foundation. note after 43706

Oration in commemoration of the founders o William and Mary College, delivered o the anniversary of its foundation, Aug. 15, 1771. By Edmund Randolph. 6781

Oration in commemoration of the founders o William and Mary College, delivered o the anniversary of its foundation, August 15, 1771. By William Leigh, student. (39931)

Oration, in commemoration of the founders o William and Mary College, delivered o the anniversary of its foundation, August 15, 1772. 93159

Oration, in commemoration of the independe of the United States of America. (32257)

Oration in commemoration of the independe of the United States of North-America. 10221

Oration, in consequence of the death of Gene George Washington. 98537

Oration in Dover, 4th July, 1827. 33570

Oration . . . in Dryden, Tompkins County, N. Y. 47078

Oration . . . in Hancock, July 4th, 1803. 58177

Oration in honor of Gen. Lafayette. (33907)

Oration, in honor of the election of President Jefferson. 5596

Oration in honor of the late Charles Carroll. 63027

Oration in honor of the memory of George Clinton. 50832

Oration in honor of universal emancipation in the British empire. (12703)

Oration, in honour to the memory of General George Washington. 97414

Oration, . . . in Kennebunk, Maine. (22463)

Oration in memory of Gen. Montgomery, and of the officers and soldiers who fell with him. 84632

Oration in memory of General Montgomery, and the officers and soldiers, who fell with him. 84633-84639

Oration, in memory of the virtues of Gen. George Washington. 57442, 2d note after 101866

Oration . . . in . . . Middletown. 40841

Oration . . . in New-Haven. (19262)

Oration . . . in . . . New-York on the fourth of July . . . . By Elihu Price. 58351

Oration . . . in New York, on the fourth of July, 1856. 29907

Oration, . . . in Newburyport, . . . July 4, 1821. 18095

Oration . . . in Newburyport, on the fifty-seventh anniversary of American independence. 42708

Oration . . . in Newport. 33934

Oration . . . in Portland. 103734

Oration, . . . in Providence, on the fourth of July, 1799. 47005

Oration . . . in San Francisco. 37848

Oration . . . in . . . Savannah. 12152

Oration, . . . in Schenectady. 47006

Oration . . . in Stratham, N. H. (49136)

Oration, . . . in Sutton. 49100

Oration, in the capitol of the United States. 37666

Oration . . . in the New York Crystal Palace. 11944

Oration, . . . in Transylvania University. 71286

Oration, in vindication of free masonry. (23243)

Oration . . . in Winchester on the fortieth anniversary of American independence. (27439)

Oration . . . in Worcester (Massachusetts). 33289

Oration . . . in Wrentham, February 22, 1800. 27563

Oration intended to have been delivered at Springfield, Mass. 6048

Oration . . . July 5, 1819. 39781

Oration, . . . July 5th, 1813. 50832

Oration . . . July 5, 1802. 22465

Oration . . . July 5, 1784. 31690

Oration . . . July 4, 1851. (74601)

Oration, . . . July 5, 1856. (25017)

Oration, . . . July 4th, 1805. 47363

Oration . . . July 4th, 1804. 41934

Oration, . . . July 4, 1869. 37739

Oration . . . July 4, 1864. 19041

Oration, . . . July 4, 1863. 16980

Oration, July 4, 1803. 20

Oration, July 4, 1838. 5661

Oration, . . . July 4th, 1838, at Middleborough. 29890

Oration . . . July 4, 1812. 34735

Oration, July 4, 1828. 16207

Oration . . . July 4, 1829. 37293

Oration . . . July 4, 1827. 45489

Oration, July 4, 1789. (28505)

Oration, . . . July 4, 1794. (26496)

Oration, . . . July 4, 1799. 42454

Oration, . . . July 4, 1796. 39190

Oration, July 24, 1849. 21721

Oration . . . July 26, 1853. 4571

Oration: . . . June twenty fifth. 21228

Oration, . . . June 29, 1814. 50832

Oration . . . Lexington, Ky. (24449)

Oration . . . Lowell, July 4, 1848. 3729

Oration . . . Marblehead. (38112)

Oration, . . . March 5th, 1782. (49325)

Oration . . . March 16, 1870. 46868

Oration . . . Mathetican Society. 31589

Oration, May, 1832. 43790

Oration . . . May, 1822. 74755

Oration . . . Nantucket, July 4, 1829. 50974

Oration . . . Newburgh, July 4, 1855. (39540)

Oration . . . Newburyport, on the fifty-sixth anniversary of American independence. 18095

Oration, occasioned by the death of General George Washington. 71848

Oration occasioned by the death of Gen. George Washington. Pronounced . . . in the city of New York. 40103

Oration [occasioned by the death of General Washington], delivered at East-Haddam. 51053

Oration occasioned by the death of John Warren, M. D. 3770

Oration, occasioned by the death of Lieutenant General George Washington. 103075

Oration . . . occasioned by the death of Robert Kelly. 40093

Oration, Oct. 29, 1852. 20817

Oration of Charles D. Drake. 20815

Oration of Charles Sprague. 89661

Oration of Edward Everett. (27248)

Oration of General J. B. Hood. 88075

Oration of Hon. George W. Curtis. 78826

Oration of Hon. Geo. Wm. Curtis. 83332

Oration of Hon. O. P. Morton. 51019

Oration of Hon. Rufus B. Spalding. 88917

Oration of James Speed. 89227

Oration of Major General O. O. Howard. 27239

Oration of Ogden Hoffman. 32407

Oration [of R. M. T. Hunter.] 33927, 3d note after 95515

Oration of Rev. Luther Lee. 39775

Oration of Robert Strange. 92702

Oration [of Samuel White.] 2403, 97766, note after 101874

Oration of the Hon. H. C. Murphy. 50629

Oration of the Hon. R. B. Rhett. 9950

Oration of the Hon. R. B. Rhett, before the Legislature. 87480

Oration of the Hon. William D. Porter. 88103

Oration of the Ohio Medical Lyceum. 49725

Oration of the Rev. Edward N. Kirk. 37975

Oration on American education. 28862

Oration, on American independence; . . . at Taunton. (51011)

Oration on American independence, delivered at Akron. 88918

Oration on American independence, July 5, 1790. 26786

Oration, on the death of Mr. John Russell. (7120)

Oration on the death of Mr. Levi Hoppin. 22533

Oration on the death of Mr. Robert Grant. 103756

Oration on the death of Mr. William Heyliger. (18262)

Oration on the death of Thomas Illman. 21688

Oration on the defects in the present system of medical instruction. 13832

Oration on the discovery of America. 104727-104728

Oration on the duties and requirements of an American officer. 30106

[Oration] on the eclipse of the sun. 221

Oration on the extent and power of political delusion. 5590-5591, 5598, 15875, 95742, 102396, 105939

Oration . . . on the fiftieth anniversary of American independence, at Newport, R. I. (59118)

Oration on the fiftieth anniversary of American independence, July 4, 1826. (14133)

Oration on the fourteenth anniversary of the American Institute. 12890

Oration . . . on the fourth day of July, 1839. 57791

Oration . . . on the 4th July, 1811. 44620

Oration . . . on the fourth of July, 1851. 49022

Oration, . . . on the fourth of July, 1805. 55202

Oration on the fourth of July, 1800. 31905

Oration . . . on the 4th July, 1809. . . . By B. A. Markley. 44620

Oration . . . on the 4th of July, 1809, before the Tammany Society. 35117

Oration . . . on the fourth of July, 1861. 58912

Oration . . . on the fourth of July, 1866. 42149

Oration . . . on the fourth of July, 1862. 92001

Oration, on the fourth of July, 1810. 17910

Oration . . . on the fourth of July, 1820. 38806

Oration . . . on the 4th of July, 1829, in Southbridge, Mass. 58645

Oration, on the fourth of July, 1821. 17910

Oration, . . . on the fourth of July, 1798. (58780)

Oration on the illustrious George Washington. 80790

Oration on the importance of science and religion. 19887

Oration on the importance of scientific knowledge. (39460)

Oration, on the improvement of medicine. 20197

Oration . . . on the inauguration of the Jackson statue. 20693

Oration on the independence of the United States. (70924)

Oration on the influence of moral causes on national character. 17343

Oration on the influence of social institution upon human morals and happiness. 105512

Oration, on the intemperance of cities, &c. 20825

Oration on the landing of the pilgrims of Maryland. 39872

Oration on the late treaty with France. 36186

Oration on the life and character of Andrew Jackson. 63697

Oration on the life and character of Benjamin Franklin. 97614

Oration on the life and character of Gilbert Motier de Lafayette. 295

Oration on the life and character of Henry Winter Davis. (17487)

Oration on the life and character of John Quincy Adams. 28616

Oration on the life and character of Stephen A. Douglas. 68147

Oration on the life and services of Daniel Webster. (23322)

Oration on the life and services of Gen. David Wooster. 19483

Oration on the life, character, and public services of General Nathaniel Woodhull. 44756

Oration on the life, character and public services of the Hon. Felix Grundy. 7968

Oration on the life, character, and services of John Caldwell Calhoun. 30100

Oration on the life, character and services of Tristam Thomas. 17253

Oration, on the material growth and territorial progress. 18091

Oration, on the means of perpetuating independence. (58099)

Oration on the moral and political evil of slavery. (64041)

Oration on the moral grandeur of George Washington. (9460)

Oration on the national independence. 36500

Oration on the nature and effects of the art of printing. (9216)

Oration, on the nature and perpetuity of American independence. 78645

Oration on the necessity of political union at the present day. (858)

Oration . . . on the 19th of May, 1809. 79630

Oration, on the occasion of celebrating the fortieth anniversary of the battle of Lake Erie. 10085

Oration, on the occasion of laying the corner stone of the Lunatic Asylum. 17346

Oration . . . on the occasion of the inauguration of Andrew Jackson. 35709

Oration on the occasion of the national fast. 37976

Oration, on the power and value of national liberty. 104602

Oration on the practicability and expediency of reducing the whole body of the law to a code. 28862

Oration on the principal duties of Americans. 28860

Oration on the principles of liberty and independence. 71013

Oration . . . on the prospects of the young men of America. (23283A)

Oration, on the present measures of the American government. 105501

Oration . . . on the relationship between masonry and Christianity. 23317

Oration on the Republican celebration. (24652)

Oration on the revocation of the British orders in Council. 30097

Oration on the rise and progress of physic in America. 64649

Oration on the rise and progress of the United States of America. 279

Oration, on the second anniversary of the death of Abraham Lincoln. 21156

Oration on the sixty-ninth anniversary of American independence. 81261

Oration on the state of the country. New York, March 24, 1863. 51000, 77812

Oration on the sublime virtues of General George Washington. 1300, 101749

Oration on the sublime virtues of General George Washington . . . . Pronounced before the inhabitants of Portland. 58680

Oration on the temperance reform. 93955

Oration . . . on the third anniversary of the South Carolina Historical Society. (61248)

Oration on the thirteenth anniversary of the American Institute. (45429)

Oration on the three hundred and eighteenth anniversary of the discovery of America. 44517

Oration . . . on the 29th of May, 1795. 37288

Oration . . . on the twenty-second of February, 1806. (47902)

Oration on the union. 26134

Oration on the utility of literary establishments. 8052

Oration on the virtues and death of General George Washington. 38870

Oration on union. 36241

Oration . . . Oxford . . . July 5, 1841. 29890

Oration, poem, and chronicles. (57443)

Oration, poem, and speeches. (9996)

Oration, poem, speeches, &c. 44101, 93538

Oration . . . Portland . . . July 4th, 1800. 29623

Oration: . . . Portland, July 4, 1838. 52161

Oration . . . Portland, Oregon, July 4th, 1865. 23146

Oration prepared at the request of the Committee of Arrangement. 98582

Oration prepared for delivery at West Point, N. Y. 47157

Oration, prepared for delivery before the inhabitants of Charleston. 87910

Oration prepared for delivery on . . . laying the corner stone. 61247

Oration prepared for the American Revolution Society. 19683

Oration, prepared to be delivered at Nottinghamwest, N. H. (50391)

Oration. Project for the civilization of the Indians. (13240)

Oration, pronounced at Alfred. 32609

Oration, pronounced at Amherst. (23243)

Oration, pronounced at Bath. 1296

Oration, pronounced at Bennington, August 16, 1819. 106116

Oration, pronounced at Bennington, Vermont. 97620

Oration pronounced at Bethel. 45474

Oration, pronounced at Boston, 4th July, 1820. 57636

Oration, pronounced at Boston, on the fourth day of July, 1810. (41246)

Oration, pronounced at Brattleborough, Vermont. 22243

Oration, pronounced at Bridgewater, July 4, 1804. (57653)

Oration, pronounced at Bridgewater, October 4, 1798. 103742

Oration, pronounced at Brookfield, July 5, 1813. 85397

Oration, pronounced at Cambridge before the Φ. B. K. . . . July 21, 1796. (5328)

Oration pronounced at Cambridge, before the Society of Phi Beta Kappa. 23260

Oration, pronounced at Campton. (72698)

Oration, pronounced at Charlestown, at the request of the Artillery Company. (2428)

Oration, pronounced at Charlestown, July 4, 1797. 74349

Oration, pronounced at Charlestown, on the 4th of July, 1821. 104063

Oration, pronounced at Dover, New Hampshire (32325)

Oration, pronounced at East-Windsor. 101010

Oration, pronounced at Exeter. 93485

Oration pronounced at Franklin on the fourth of July, 1803. 15088

Oration, pronounced at Groton, July 4, 1801. 71099

Oration pronounced at Hallowell. 71501

Oration, pronounced at Hamstead, New-Hampshire. 89565

Oration, pronounced at Hanover, August 27, 1805. 100779

Oration, pronounced at Hanover, Massachusetts 103720

Oration, pronounced at Hanover, N. H. July 4, 1804. 23815

Oration, pronounced at Hanover, New-Hampshi the 4th day of July, 1800. 102254

Oration, pronounced at Hanover, Newhampshire January 9, 1800. (57444), 105169

Oration, pronounced at Hartford. 83462

Oration, pronounced at Hubbartston, before the Republicans of the north district of the county of Worcester, July 4, 1810. 103481

Oration, pronounced at Hubbardston, July 4, 1810. 103480

Oration pronounced at Johnson, July 4, 1826. 83685

Oration, pronounced at Lancaster, July 4, 1806. 7499

Oration, pronounced at Lexingtron, July 4, 1809. 28589

Oration pronounced at Lexington, Mass. . . . 4th July, 1815. 2412

Oration, pronounced at Londonderry. 100780

Oration pronounced at Ludlow Factory Village. 43507

Oration, pronounced at Middlebury. 28512

Oration . . . pronounced at Mr. Thaddeus Broad's. 82131

Oration pronounced at Nassau Hall. 5756

Oration, pronounced at New Bedford [Fairhaven], July 4, 1806. 75960

Oration pronounced at New-Bedford, Mass., February 22, 1823. 103315

Oration pronounced at New Haven. 31886

Oration, pronounced at Newipswich. [sic] 105310

Oration, pronounced at Newport, . . . Rhode-Island, . . . fourth of July, 1797. (44494)

Oration, pronounced at Newport, Rhode-Island, July 4, 1822. 2424

Oration pronounced at Northampton, July 4, 1805. 3935

Oration, pronounced at Northampton, July 4, 1810. 78851

Oration, pronounced at Northampton, on the sixth of March, 1810. 78850

Oration pronounced at Orleans. 102079

Oration pronounced at Paris. 33323

Oration pronounced at Peacham. 105245

Oration, pronounced at Plainfield. 65096

Oration pronounced at Plympton. Feb. 23, 1809. 19053

Oration, pronounced at Portland, July 4, 1795. 37288

Oration, pronounced at Portsmouth, N. H. 25774

Oration, pronounced at Salem. 92315

Oration, pronounced at Sharon. 82938

Oration pronounced at Springfield, Mass. 3163

Oration pronounced at Suffield. 26786

Oration, pronounced at Sutton, Massachusetts. 3164

Oration, pronounced at Templeton. (5320)

Oration pronounced at the Baptist Meeting-House, in Providence. 9447

Oration pronounced at the First Congregational Meeting-House, in Providence. 95829

Oration pronounced at the Working Men's Celebration. 84222

Oration pronounced at Tiverton. 19052

Oration, pronounced at Warren, O. 92112

Oration pronounced at Watertown. 26187

Oration pronounced at Waterville. 18130

Oration pronounced at Wiscasset. (7227)

Oration, pronounced at Worcester, July 4, 1815. 89705

Oration, pronounced at Worcester, . . . July 4th, 1812. (41247)

Oration, pronounced at Worcester, . . . July 4. 1797. 24554

Oration, pronounced at Worcester, (Mass.) . . . July 4, 1812. 5767

Oration, pronounced at Worcester, on the anniversary of American independence; July 4, 1796. 5768

Oration, pronounced at Worcester, on the fourth of July, 1798. 2423

Oration, pronounced at Wrentham, July 4, 1803. 9070

Oration pronounced before a public assembly in New-Haven. 47392

Oration pronounced before the citizens of Boston. 58325

Oration pronounced before the citizens of New-Haven, July 4th, 1788. 2911

Oration, pronounced before the citizens of New Haven, on the anniversary of the declaration of independence; July, 1802. 102372

Oration pronounced before the citizens of New-Haven on the anniversary of the independence of the United States. 102373

Oration, pronounced before the citizens of Pawtuxet. 95830

Oration pronounced before the citizens of Providence, on the fourth of July, 1831. 9235

Oration pronounced before the citizens of Providence, on the fourth of July, 1826. 33933

Oration pronounced before the Connecticut Alpha of Phi Beta Kappa Society. 28106

Oration pronounced before the Greene Association. (17234)

Oration, pronounced before the Handel Society. 24962

Oration pronounced before the Hibernian Providence Society. (72210)

Oration pronounced before the inhabitants of Boston, July the fourth, 1835. 31875

Oration, pronounced before the inhabitants of Boston, July the fourth, 1836. 37937

Oration: pronounced before the inhabitants of Boston, July the fourth, 1825. 89662

Oration pronounced before the inhabitants of Portland, July 4th, 1805. 32921

Oration, pronounced before the inhabitants of Portland, July 4th, 1803. (31895)

Oration, pronounced before the Knox and Warren Branches. 102374

Oration, pronounced before the people of Providence. 9235

Oration pronounced before the Phi Beta Kappa Society. 89744

Oration pronounced before the Republican inhabitants of Portland. 25857

Oration pronounced before the Republicans of Boston. (12703)

Oration, pronounced before the Society of Artists of the United States. (39220), 86005

Oration, pronounced before the Society of the Phi Beta Kappa. 102428

Oration pronounced before the students of Brown University. 784

Oration pronounced before the Washington Benevolent Society of the county of Hampshire. 3936

Oration, pronounced before the Washington benevolent Society of the county of Washington. 97481

Oration pronounced by Samuel H. Smith. 84078

Oration pronounced by William George Read. 68191

Oration, pronounced, February 22, 1797. 62674

Oration; pronounced in Princeton, Massachusetts. 74360

Oration pronounced in the Baptist Meeting-Hall, in Province. 74356

Oration pronounced in the Brick Meeting House, New Haven. 7669

Oration, pronounced in the Chapel, Dartmouth College. 7198

Oration, pronounced in the First Parish at Amherst, N. H. 2272

Oration, pronounced in the Meeting-House, at Rutland. 103482

Oration, pronounced in the Methodist Episcopal Church, Hempstead. 65624

Oration pronounced in the New Meeting House at Plymouth. (75961)

Oration pronounced . . . in the town of Northfield. (25221)

Oration pronounced in the Universalist Chapel. 18482

Oration, pronounced, in the White Meeting-House. 5590, 95742, 105939

Oration, pronounced July 5, 1819. 102601

Oration, pronounced July 4, 1808. 25240

Oration, pronounced July 4, 1808, at the request of the Selectmen of the town of Boston. 71557

Oration, pronounced July 4, 1808, before the citizens of the town of Roxbury. 83668

Oration, pronounced July 4th, 1808, before the inhabitants of New-Bedford. 4734

Oration, pronounced July 4, 1818. (28387)

Oration, pronounced July 4, 1805, at the request of the Federal Republicans of . . . Charlestown. 66755

Oration, pronounced July 4, 1805, at the request of the inhabitants of the town of Boston. 21472

Oration, pronounced July 4th, 1805, before the Young Democratic Republicans, of the town of Boston. 25857

Oration pronounced July 4, 1814. 103834

Ordenanza real para el establecimiento e
instruccion de Intendentes de Exercito.
26483
Ordenanzas de Comisariões de Barrio de esta
ciudad. 29447
Ordenanzas de la fiel executoria. (48612)
Ordenanzas de la Junta de Guerra de Indias.
57474
Ordenanzas de la Legislatura Provincial del
Socorro. 86190
Ordenanzas de la Real Renta de la Polvora.
56256
Ordenanzas de la Real Renta de los Naypes.
(56255)
Ordenanzas de la Real Renta del Tabaco.
56257
Ordenanzas de marina. 57475
Ordenanzas de mineria. 57476
Ordenanzas de tierras y aguas. 26466
Ordenanzas del Consejo Real de las Indias.
(57477)
Ordenanzas del Consulado de la Universidad
de los Mercadores. 56258
Ordenanzas del Consulado de Mexico Universidad
de Mercaderes. (48613), 98019
Ordenanzas del Juzgado General. 57478
Ordenanzas del Noblissimo Arte de la
Plateria. 57479
Ordenanzas del Peru. 2962, 61163
Ordenanzas del Tribunal del Consulado de esta
ciudad. 57480
Ordenanzas municipales para los ayuntamientos
constitucionales. 48614
Ordenanzaz para el Archivo General de Indias.
(57481)
Ordenanzas para el gobierno de la Casa de
Beneficencia. 29448
Ordenanzas para el gobierno de la labor de
monedas. 48614
Ordenanzas para el gobierno del Hospicio de
Pobres. 48616
Ordenanzas para el nuevo establecimiento de
alcaldes. 66570
Ordenanzas para el regimen, disciplina, sub-
ordinacion y servicio de la Guarda
Colombiana. (14616)
Ordenanzas para el regimen y gobierno de los
tenderos y tiendras de pulperia. 48617
Ordenanzas para el rejimen de las aduanas de
la republica Argentina. 70012
Ordenanzas que mando hacer D. Garcia Huertado
de Mendoza. 47837
Ordenanzas, que se han de observar, y guardar
en la muy nobilissima, y leal ciudad de
Mexico. 48618
Ordenanzas reales del Consejo de las Indias.
57483
Ordenanzas reales para el gobierno de los
Tribunales. (57484)
Ordenanzas reales para le Casa de la Con-
tratacion de Sevilla. 57485
Ordenanzas, resoluciones y acuerdas de la
H. Diputacion Provincial de Caracas.
10781
Ordenanzas rurales de la isla de Cuba.
17793
Ordenanzas sobre alcabalas. 57486
Ordenes y circulares espedidas por el
Supremo Gobierno. (48619)
Ordenzas provisionales de Excmo. Cabildo
Justicia y Regimiento. 9029
Order and harmony in the churches of Christ.
71889, 104315
Order and report. May, 1843. 54793

Order book of Capt. Leonard Bleeker. 5899
Order establishing salaries. 73658
Order for a second evening service in the
churches. 53198
Order for daily morning and evening prayer.
(57487)
Order for evening worship. 85215
Order for funeral services. 85308
Order for morning and evening prayer. 6351
Order for morning and evening prayer, and
administration of the sacraments.
57488-57489
Order for morning and evening prayer, as
used in York Academy. 106041
Order for the administration of the Holy
Eucharist. (15009), 75861
Order for the levy of 5000 blankets. 57490
Order for the observance of the Sabbath.
86277
Order in Council. 53451
Order in Council for improving the condition
of slaves in Trinidad. 10693
Order made last General Court at Boston.
80205
Order of American Knights. (57491)
Order of ceremonies and discourse. 106019-2(
Order of commencement exercises. 7035
Order of consecration of Christ Church at
Leicester. 39899
Order of Council for issuing a quo warranto.
45929
Order of divine service in the North Dutch
Church. 101867
Order of exercises. 105893, 106051
Order of exercises and theses for commence-
ment. 8628
Order of exercises at commencement, Yale
College. 105783
Order of exercises at the anniversary of the
Theological Department in Yale College.
105890
Order of exercises at the celebration of the
completion of two centuries. 73659
Order of exercises at the celebration of the
two hundredth anniversary of the settle-
ment of the town of Natick. 51905
Order of exercises at the consecration of
Forest-Hills Cemetery. 25079
Order of exercises at the dedication of the
First Congregational Church in the town
of Hillsborough. 31913
Order of exercises at the dedication of the
Meeting-House. (20628)
Order of exercises at the dedication of the
New Meeting-House in Hallowell. 29916
Order of exercises, at the dedication of the
Newton Free Library. (55093)
Order of exercises at the dedication of the
State Street Presbyterian Church.
90652
Order of exercises at the exhibition of the
Junior Class. 105893
Order of exercises at the exhibition of the
Junior Class in Yale College. 105893
Order of exercises at the Festival of the
Pilgrims. 6539
Order of exercises at the Junior Exhibition.
105893
Order of the exercises at the Junior Exhibition
in Yale College. 105893
Order of exercises at the Junior Exhibition,
Yale College. 105893
Order of exercises at the Old South Church,
commemorative of . . . James Monroe.
50025

Order of exercises, commencement, 1813. 30765

Order of exercises, for commencement: Yale College. 105783

Order of exercises for exhibition, Aug. 22, 1820. 62535

Order of exercises for 1795. 8627

Order of exercises, for the exhibition of the Junior Class, Yale College. 105893

Order of exercises in commemoration of the birthday of Washington. 89872

Order of exercises in the chapel of Transylvania University. 38583, 96464

Order of exercises of the Linonian Exhibition. 105900

Order of exercises seventy-seventh anniversary of American independence. 624

Order of Major-General Sickles. 87394

Order of masonic ceremonies. 27420

Order of Parliament for a day of publike thanksgiving. 76754

Order of Parliament for a day of thanksgiving. 5793

Order of performances at the anniversary, June 11, 1811. 33681

Order of performances. Instrumental dirge. 101868

Order of procession for the funeral of the late Governor Sumner. 93703

Order of procession, to be observed on the arrival of the President of the United States. 101869

Order of reference to the Commissioner. 85212

Order of San Francisco. see Franciscans.

Order of service at the consecration of the new synagoge, Greene Street. 57492

Order of service at the consecration of the Synagogue Roudafe Sholum. 61894

Order of services at Indiana-Place Chapel. 13415

Order of services at the Evergreen Cemetery, Brighton. 23292

Order of services at the installation of a pastor. 14535

Order of services at the installation of Rev. Joseph Angier. 1568

Order of services at the recognition of the Rev. Cortland W. Anable. 1356

Order of services at the twenty-fifth anniversary of the Eliot Sabbath School, Roxbury. 73641

Order of services of St. Peter's Church, Salem. 75707

Order of services to be performed at the consecration of the Synagogue Beth Israel. 61893

Order of services, 22d of December, MDCCCXIII. 45856

Order of solemnities. 101870

Order of the churches in N. England vindicated. 46714

Order of the churches in New-England. Vindicated. 46441

Order of the day & procession of the funeral of Washington in Salem. 101887

Order of the day, for Saturday, Feb. 8, 1800. 101871

Order of the Friendly Brothers of St. Patrick, Boston. see Ancient and Most Benevolent Order of the Friendly Brothers of St. Patrick, Boston.

Order of the General Court of April 29, 1668. 57493

Order of the Gospel, professed and practiced by the churches of Christ in New-England. 28052, 46714, 91945, 99805, note after 105090

Order of the Gospel revived. 46263

Order of the Grand Masonic Funeral Procession. 101872

Order of the House of Delegates. 62051

Order of the House [of Delegates of Maryland] . . . 9th February, 1839. 45098

Order of the King in Council. 57494

Order of the Knights of St. Crispin. Massachusetts. Lodge. (45848), 45859

Order of the Knights of St. Crispin. Massachusetts. Lodge. Charter. 45859

Order . . . of the Legislature. 41270

Order of the procession of "the Invincibles." 52495

Order of the Sons of Temperance; its origin— its history. 42686, 87014

Order of the Sovereigns of Industry. see Sovereigns of Industry.

Order of the Virginia Council. 100904

Order of United Americans. 57495

Order of United Americans. Arch-chancery. (56376), 57495

Order of United Americans. Massachusetts. 57495

Order of United Americans. New York. Chancery. (56376)

Order of United Americans. New York. Star-Spangled Banner Chapter, No. 96, Albany. 57495

Order of W. B. see Order of Working Brothers, Mobile, Ala.

Order of Working Brothers, Mobile, Ala. 19424

Order or anarchy. (22390)

Ordere, aen de Gouverneurs in Nieuw-Engelandt. 19319

Ordered, that the application of John Smith, Esq. 82882

Ordered that the public printer be directed to strike off. 100103

Orderly book of Lieut. Gen. John Burgoyne. (9253)

Orderly book of that portion of the American Army. (9722), 40785

Orderly book of the northern army. 57496

Orderly book of the siege of Yorktown. 57497

Orderly sergeant. pseud. Journal of incidents. 36711

Orders and artucles granted by the High and Mightie Lords the States Generales of the Vnited Provinces. 47598, 2d note after 102903

Orders and constitvtions, partly collected out of His Majesties letters patents; and partly by authority. (57499), 3d note after 99888

Orders and constitvtions, partly collected out of His Maiesties letters patents, and partly ordained vpon mature deliberation. 99878-99879

Orders and regulations of the faculty of Harvard University. 30753

Orders and rules of practice in the Court of King's Bench. 67028

Orders for governing His Majesty's forces in America. 57500

Orders from Governor Palliser. 54986

Orders in Council and instructions for blockade, &c. 57501

Ordinance to dissolve the union between the
state of South Carolina and other states.
87433, 87439, 87444

Ordinance to divide the city . . . into con-
venient election districts. 54568

Ordinance to enable the Commissioners of the
Treasury to borrow. 87627

Ordinance, to incorporate the subscribers to
the Bank of North America. 15967,
69398, 104628

Ordinance to prevent the operation of the
limitation-act. 87627

Ordinance to regulate and suppress houses of
ill fame. 75361

Ordinance to regulate the proceedings of the
Commissioners. (75678)

Ordinance to repeal part of an ordinance of
the General Assembly. 87615

Ordinances adopted by the Constitutional Convention of 1868. 87708

Ordinances adopted by the Convention of West-
Florida. 24903, 102765

Ordinances, and annual report of the officers
and committees. (9339)

Ordinances and by-laws of . . . Cincinnati.
57513

Ordinances and by-laws of the Western House
of Refuge for Juvenile Delinquents. 54012

Ordinances and constitution of Alabama.
(57514)

Ordinances and constitution of the state of
South Carolina. 87440

Ordinances and decrees of the consultation.
note after 94951, 94959

Ordinances and joint resolutions of the city of
San Francisco. 76065

Ordinances and joint resolutions of the . . .
Councils. 51898

Ordinances and parts of ordinances now in
force. 71186

Ordinances and resolutions passed by the North
Carolina State Convention. 55658

Ordinances and resolutions passed by the State
Convention of North Carolina. (55657)

Ordinances, &c. of the Grand Lodge of Vermont.
99186

Ordinances for regulating the militia. 53106

Ordinances for regulation of firemen. (54278)

Ordinances for the government and regulation
of the Central Park. 54158

Ordinances for the government of the city.
8287

Ordinances for the regulation . . . of Southwark.
61899

Ordinances made and passed by the Governor
and Legislative Council of . . . Quebec.
67030

Ordinances made and passed by the Governor
and Legislative Council of the province of
Quebec. 67030

Ordinances, made for the province of Quebec.
67029

Ordinances of Jersey City. 36070

Ordinances of . . . Moyamensing. (61906)

Ordinances of the borough of Norfolk. 55479

Ordinances of the City Council of Charleston.
12062

Ordinances of the City Council of Charleston,
S. C. 57515

Ordinances of the City Councils. 10160

Ordinances of the city in relation to fires.
(4442)

Ordinances of the city of Boston. 6540

Ordinances of the city of Brooklyn. 8309

Ordinances of the city of Cambridge. (10144)

Ordinances of the city of Charleston. 33049

Ordinances of the city of Chicago. 12650

Ordinances of the city of Hartford. 30657

Ordinances of the city of Nashua. (51863)

Ordinances of the city of New Bedford. (52496)

Ordinances of the city of Newport, revised.
55050

Ordinances of the city of Rochester. 72345

Ordinances of the city . . . . To which are
prefixed, the act of incorporation.
(61900)

Ordinances of the College. 53605

Ordinances of the Common Council of the
borough of Princeton. 65651

Ordinances of the Common Council of the city
and parish of Kingston. 37915

Ordinances of the Convention of the People of
the State of South Carolina. 87445

Ordinances of the corporation of Georgetown.
27004

Ordinances of the corporation . . . of Philadelphia. 61903

Ordinances of the corporation of . . . Southwark.
61905

Ordinances of the corporation of the Borough
of Frankford. 61904

Ordinances of the corporation of the city of
Baltimore. (3052)

Ordinances of the corporation of the city of
Baltimore, with the act of incorporation
and supplement. 3053

Ordinances of the corporation . . . to which
are prefixed the act of incorporation.
(61902)

Ordinances of the . . . Councils. 62000

Ordinances of the Governor, Judges, and acts
of the Territorial Assembly. 94777

Ordinances of the Mayor, Aldermen and
Commonalty of . . . New York. (54569)

Ordinances of the Mayor and City Council of
Baltimore. 3054

Ordinances of the mines of New Spain. 57516,
note after 95563

Ordinances of the Select & Common Councils
of . . . Pittsburgh. (63122)

Ordinances of the State Conventions. 55658

Ordinances of the village of Brooklyn. 8308

Ordinances passed at a convention held at . . .
Richmond. 100013

Ordinances passed at a convention held in . . .
Williamsburg. 100015

Ordinances passed at a general convention of
delegates. 100026

Ordinances. Passed by the General Assembly
of the state of Deseret. 98221

Ordinances passed by the Governor and Special
Council of Lower Canada. 42522

Ordinances passed by the Legislative Council
of Great Salt Lake City. 98221

Ordinances passed by the Town Council of the
Town of Smithfield. 84973

Ordinances . . . passed in 1846 & 1847.
(44217)

Ordinances . . . passed since the nineteenth
day of July. 61901

Ordinances relative to the interment of the
dead. 54268

Ordinances relative to the Northern Liberties
Gas Works. 61907

Ordinances, rules, and by-laws for the Alms-
House. 61455

Ordinarium Sacri Ordinis Heremitaru[m] Sancti
Augustini. 57517, (68936), note after
98913

Ordinary receipts and expenditures of Yale
College. 105857

Oregon. Board of Statistics, Immigration and Labor Exchange, Portland. see Portland, Ore. Board of Statistics, Immigration and Labor Exchange.

Oregon. Constitution. 1269, 16113, 33137, 57548, (66397)

Oregon. Laws, statutes, etc. 19012, 57545-57548, 57567, 79820-79821, 82438

Oregon. Legislature. House of Representatives. 57554

Oregon. Legislature. Senate. 57554

Oregon. Penitentiary. Superintendent. 57570

Oregon. State Agricultural Society. see State Agricultural Society of Oregon.

Oregon. University. 84528, 84532-84533

Oregon (Ecclesiastical Province) Council, 1st, 1848. 72918, (80023)

Oregon. 21144

Oregon archives. 28989, 57558

Oregon and California in 1848. 95630

Oregon and California. The exploring expedition to the Rocky Mountains. 25842

Oregon and Eldorado. 9093

Oregon and her resources. 82202

Oregon and its institutions. (31951)

Oregon. Claim of the United States to Oregon. 9943, 57565

Oregon Congregational Association. see Congregational Churches in Oregon. Congregational Association.

Oregon controversy reviewed. 57559

Oregon et les cotes de l'Ocean Pacifique du Nord. 24000

Oregon-Gebiet. (57560)

Oregon: its history, condition, and prospects. 31953

Oregon, its resources, soil, climate and productions. 57561, 64385

Oregon land law. (57550)

Oregon medical and surgical reporter. 57562

Oregon missions and travels over the Rocky Mountains. 82266, 82268, 82277

Oregon missions as shown in the Walker letters. 101101

Oregon; or a short history of a long journey from the Atlantic Ocean to the region of the Pacific. 105649

Oregon, our right and title. 72021

Oregon out of doors. 84533

Oregon. Par le R. Pere P. J. de Smet. 82276

Oregon question. 79133

Oregon question. A glance at the respective claims. 75944

Oregon question. By Albert Gallatin. 26391

Oregon question. Comparative chronological statement of events. 57563

Oregon question determined by the rules of international law. 101101

Oregon question examined. 97544

Oregon question; or, a statement of the British claims. 23728

Oregon question. Substance of a lecture. 93268

Oregon. Report of . . . an examination in . . . 1846. 33368

"Oregon Territory." 85433

Oregon Territory: a geographical and physical account. 55251

Oregon Territory and British North-American fur trade. 21322

Oregon Territory. Claims thereto of England and American considered. 81339

Oregon Territory, its history and discovery. 97545

Oregon Territory. Report of Committee. 57564

Oregon. The claims of the United States to Oregon. 9943, 57565

Oregon. The cost and the consequences. 57566

Oregon und Californien und Allgemeines uber das Mississippi- und Missouri-Thal. 77695

Oregonian and Indian's advocate. 57575

Oregonian; or, history of the Oregon Territory. 77349

Oreide, poeme de la Comte. 39601

Oreilly, --------, Comte de. (16154)

O'Reilly, Bernard, 1823-1907. 42032, 57576

O'Reilly, Henry. see O'Rielly, Henry, 1806-1886.

O'Reilly, Miles. pseud. Baked meats of the funeral. see Halpine, Charles Grahame.

O'Reilly, Miles. pseud. Life and adventures. see Halpine, Charles Grahame.

Orellana, Antonio de, 1653-1712. 57577, 98107

Orellana, Estevan de. 57578

Orellana, Fernando Pizarro y. see Pizarro y Orellana, Fernando.

Orellana, Francisco Jose. 57579

Orellana, Francisco Pizarro de. see Pizarro de Porellana, Francisco.

Orellana, Manuel. 57580

Orendayn, Juan Bautista, Marques de la Paz. 38955, 59332, 90292 see also Spain. Ministerio de Estado.

Orford, Edward Russell, Earl of, 1653-1727. 74287

Orford, Horace Walpole, 4th Earl of. see Walpole, Horace, 4th Earl of Orford, 1717-1797.

Orford, Robert Walpole, 1st Earl of. see Walpole, Robert, 1st Earl of Orford, 1676-1745.

Orford, N. H. Centennial Celebration, 1865. (57582)

Organ and church music. 22309

Organ der Freien Arbeiter. 85704

Organ des socialistischen Turnerbundes. 85707

Organ fur die gemeinsamen Interessen der Amerikanischen Deutschen Kirchen. 77496

Organ of ancient craft masonry. 37544

Organ of the Grand Lodge of Kentucky. 45520

Organ of the Mount Vernon Ladies' Association of the Union. 34337

Organ of the National Temperance Society and Publication House. 52030

Organ of the State Teachers' Association. 37031

Organ of the State Teachers Institute. 34244

Organe de l'Eglise de Jesus-Christ des Saints-des-Derniers-Jours. 68683

Organe des sections francaises. 85706

Organe politique des deux mondes. 70367

Organic act of the Territory of Utah. (28464)

Organic and general laws of Oregon. (19012)

Organic and other laws of Oregon, . . . 1845-1864. 57567

Organic and other laws of Oregon, . . . 1843-1872. 57567

Organic Christianity. 77317

Organic laws of Illinois. 57583

Organic laws of Oregon Territory. 58358

Organic sins. (81839)

Organisacao dos poderes constitucionaes nas monarchias. (57584)

Organisation judiciare et sur la police des tribunaux sur Hayti. 29581

Organizacion de la Confederacion Argentina. 654

Organizacion politico y economico de la Confederacion Argentina. 653

Organization and by-laws of the Roxbury Athenaeum. 73725

Organization and by-laws of the State Board of Education. 53202

Organization and charter of the Southern Railway Security Company. 88464

Organization and constitution of the Boston Light Artillery. 57585

Organization and proceedings of the first annual festival of the Sons of Penn. (57586)

Organization, constitution and by-laws of the Douglas Monument Association. (20696)

Organization for conducting the business and keeping the accounts of the Canal Department. 60358

Organization for conducting the business of the [Pennsylvania Rail] Road. 60358

Organization, objects, and plan of operations of the Emigrant Aid Company. (22474), 37054

Organization of a new Indian Territory. 16719

Organization of ocean commerce. 83380

Organization of Oregon Territory. 52200, 84463, 93663

Organization of the Board of Mobile School Commissioners. (49784)

Organization of the Dowse Institute. 20793

Organization of the educational forces in society. 77761

Organization of the empire. (33315), 31932

Organization of the free state government in Kansas. 37075

Organization of the House of Clerical and Lay Deputies. 66180

Organization of the House. Speech . . . Dec. 18, 1855. 27329

Organization of the House. Speech of Hon. Elijah Babbitt. 2569

Organization of the House. Speech of Hon. James A. Stewart. 91684

Organization of the military peace establishment of the United States. 57587

Organization of the militia. 19634

Organization of the municipal government, June 3, 1862. (66317)

Organization of the municipal government of... . . . Providence. 66287

Organization of the Protestant Episcopal Church of the Confederate States. 83770

Organization of the public debt and a plan for the relief of the treasury. 50870

Organization of the School Committee of . . . Providence. 66363

Organization of the service of the Baltimore and Ohio Rail Road. 57588

Organization of the "Society of Associates of the Cooper Union." 86007

Organization of the State Society of Pennsylvania. 86126

Organization of the United Companies. 62051

Organization of the Veterans of the War of 1812. see Veterans of the War of 1812.

Organization with schedule and statement. (73261)

Organizations dangerous to free institutions. 20391

Orhoengene neoni Yogaraskagh Yondereanayendaghkwa. 13181, (50765)

Oribe, Manuel. 39596, 57589

O'Reilly, Henry, 1806-1886. 29996, (53670), 57590-57594, 65903, 72355, 80445, 93510

Orient. pseud. Popham Colony. see Kidder, Frederic.

Oriental antiquities. (57072)

Oriental fragments. 50346

Oriental harp. 14187

Oriental philanthropist. 80332

Oriental planeta evangelico. 80979

Oriental pearls at random strung. 83564

Orientalisch- und occidentalischer Sprachmeist 25986, 78007

Orientalische Indien. (8784)

Orientalisches und occidentalisches A. B. C. Buch. 78008

Oriente conquistado a Jesu Christo. 88720

Origanus, D. (28931)

Origen. pseud. Word for the people. 57596

Origen de la guerra del Paraguay. 57597

Origen de los Indios de Nuevo Mundo. (26566 26567

Origen, verdadero, caracter, causas, resortes, fines y progressos. 57598

Origen y causa de los repartimientos de Indio (11055)

Origen y estado de la causa formada. 44422, (57599)

Origen, y institvto de la Compania de Jesus. 57720

Origin and causes of democracy in America. 9364, (45111A)

Origin and character of the old parties. (69411)

Origin and characteristics. 57600

Origin and compilation of the prayer book. 56714

Origin and consequences of our political dissensions. (17531), 2d note after 99216

Origin, and constitution of the Pennsylvania Baptist Missionary Society. 60303

Origin and development of the English languag 70829

Origin and end of the irrepressible conflict. 56662

Origin and ends of civil government. 39696

Origin and formation of the Baptist Church. 29704

Origin and foundation of the Franklin Street Church. 6645

Origin and genealogy of the American Hildreth 31782

Origin and growth of civil liberty in Maryland 8480

Origin and growth of the principal mechanic arts and manufactures. 5606

Origin and history of institutions for the promotion of the useful arts. 18358

Origin and history of missions. 84359-84362, 84365

Origin and history of " The century," 1856. 28145

Origin and history of the measures. 26824

Origin and nature of the representative and federative institutions. 39383

Origin and object of civil government. 86063

Origin and objects of ancient freemasonry. 19354

Origin and objects of the slaveholders' conspiracy. 29996, 57592

Origin and objects of the Society for the Propagation of the Gospel in Foreign Parts. 85941

Origin and operations of the United States Naval Astronomical Expedition. 27419

Origin and organization of the Department of Health. 84264

Origin and outline of the penitentiary system. 96070

Origin and present condition of freemasonry in Melrose. (28117)

Original astronomical observations, made in the course of a voyage towards the South Pole. 101030

Original charter of Columbia College, in the city of New-York. 14830

Original charter of Columbia College, . . . October 31st, 1754. 14831

Original comic songs. 79908

Original communications made to the Agricultural Society of South-Carolina. 87741

Original, compiled and corrected account of Burgoyne's campaign. 52294

Original compositions, in prose and verse. 24075

Original Congregational Church of Christ, Wrentham, Mass. see Wrentham, Mass. Original Congregational Church of Christ.

Original constitution, order and faith of the New-England churches. 57611, 63342

Original contracts for the survey of the coast. 57612

Original contributions to the American pioneer. 31798

Original de la co[n]cordia. 98502

Original definitive treaty of peace. 15493

Original Democrat and Whig. pseud. Whigs and the conservatives. 103292

Original desultory tales. 94234

Original documents of the important grants. 7907

Original domestic drama, in three acts. 42962

Original essay by John Sherman. 80369, note after 96778

Original essays, selected from the four first numbers. 100563

Original farce, in one act. 91843

Original gigantic moving panorama of the Mississippi River. 83010

Original grant of land on the White River. 16686

Original-Handschrift des Capitain Don Antonio del Rio. 71445

Original history of ancient America. (36501)

Original history of the late war. 2774

Original history of the Morristown ghost. 72721, 106070

Original history of the religious denominations at present existing in the United States. 74157

Original hymns, for public and private use. 89911

Original hymns for the fiftieth anniversary of the ordination. 42430

Original hymns in the Iowa language. (35040)

Original instutition of the General Society of Cincinnati. 86137

Original institution of the General Society of the Cincinnati, as formed by the officers of the army of the United States, at the conclusion of the Revolutionary War, which gave independence to America, together with the rules and by-laws of the state society of South Carolina. 13129

Original institution of the General Society of the Cincinnati as formed by the officers of the army of the United States at the conclusion of the Revolutionary War, which gave independence to America, with the rules and by-laws of the state society of South Carolina. 86136

Original journal and minutes kept by Mr. Phelps. 30829

Original letter from Major-General Sullivan to President Ware. 52827

Original letter from Moses Kirkland to Col. Laurens. 87364

Original letter from the pen of Columbus. 14642, 29396, 49441

Original letter of the author. 66627

Original letter on the slavery of the Negroes. 18983-18984, 18987

Original letters from Canada and the United States. (17145)

Original letters . . . of Abijah Mann. (44305)

Original letters of Ferdinand and Elizabeth. 57613

Original letters [of General John Burgoyne.] 9260

Original letters recently written by persons in Paris. (16687), note after 65502, 92070

Original letters to an honest sailor. 57614, 99249

Original letters, to the Methodist bishops. 20757

Original letters, with other curious papers. 97661

Original-Lustspiel in I Aufzuge. 2581, 104839

Original manuscript report of Captain Don Antonio del Rio. 71446

Original memoir by R. H. Stoddard. (63533)

Original memoir on the Floridas. (24891)

Original memoirs in medicine. 30392

Original moral essays. 83667

Original narratives of early American history. 38886, 46731-46732, note after 70346, 82823, 82832, 82850, 92940, 93950, 100547, 103353, 104845

Original novel, founded in truth. 101458

Original ode by Albert G. Reene. 8620

Original panorama of the Mississippi River. 17185

Original panoramic views of the scenes in the life of an American slave. 8591

Original papers and letters, relating to the Scots Company trading to Africa and the Indies. 18563, 18574, 78201-78202, 78238

Original papers; containing the secret history of Great Britain. 43632

Original papers on literature, science, art, and national interests. 66844

Original papers relating to Samuel Haines. 29545

Original papers relating to the expedition to Carthagena. 11134, 1st note after 99245

Original papers relating to the expedition to Panama. 99246

Original papers relating to the expedition to the island of Cuba. 11518, 17794, 2d note after 99245

Original patriotic songs and marching choruses 90574

Original plan, progress, and present state of the South-Sea-Company. 66628

Original poem. By a young gentleman of Philadelphia. 99449

Original poem, in five cantos. 99838

Original poem. In two books. 30072

Original poem, never before published. 100671

Original poem, with copious notes. 44716

Original poem, written and dedicated to Post 15. 57615

Original poems. 30417, note after 97486

Original poems, by a citizen of Baltimore. 57616, 96393

Original poems. By a layman. 83667

Original poems by Alfred B. Street. 33391, 92775

Original poems. By John Wharton, M. D. 103102

Original poems. By Thomas Green Fessenden. 24214

Original poems: consisting of sonnets and
odes. 101205
Original poems, on various subjects. By Mrs.
Williams. 104173
Original poems on various subjects. In three
parts. 104440
Original preface by Dr. Watts. 46624
Original preface by Grant Throburn. 26456
Original remarks, with various extracts from
historians. 5272
Original Republican. pseud. Remarks on the
existing rebellion. see Grover, S. T.
supposed author
Original researches. By Prof. J. Lawrence
Smith, of Louisville. 82995
Original researches in moneralogy and
chemistry. 82998
Original rights of mankind freely to subdue and
improve the earth. 46715
Original romance to which is annexed a variety
of original poetical pieces. 99838
Original shareholder. pseud. Brief account
of the Lake Superior Copper Company.
38669
Original state epigrams and minor odes.
54939
Original steam-boat supported. 3521, 24582,
74126
Original tale. 45042
Original tale of the American revolution.
84129-84130, note after 93109, 1st note
after 95758
Original titles of record in the General Land
Office. 94980
Original treatise on agriculture. 62964
Original voyage down the Mississippi! 83010
Original work. 98024
Original work, containing a great many good
things. 65087, 95366
Original works[[of William King.] 98182
Originalberichte des Herrn Mortiz Bach.
38319
Originallustspiel in einem Aufzug. 104839
Origination and constitution of the Society for
Worcester County and Vicinity. 105391
Origination of appropriation bills. 93684
Origine Asiatique d'un peuple de l'Amerique
du Sud. 58553
Origine et fondation des Etats-Unis d'Amerique.
(42003)
Origine et progres de la Mission du Kentucky.
2710, 37562
Origine et progres des eglises evangeliques
des Etats-Unis. 2793
Origine, formazione, meccanismo, ed armonia
degli' Idioni. 31600
Origine gentium Americanarum Israelitica a
Menasse Ben Israel. 89546
Origine, utilite et progres des institutions
Catoliques de Montreal. 39217
Origines Guelphicae. (33629)
Origines transatlantiques. 44533
Origins and religions. 10400
Origins de la civilisation et des religions de
l'antiquite. (7437)
Origins, purposes and principles of the American
Party. 18832
Orihuela, A. A. tr. 92606, 92608, 92609,
92615
Orihuela, E. Jose Calixto de. 57417
Orijenes del arte de imprimir en al America
Espanola. 29339
Orinoco (Colombian Department) petitioners
100790
Orinoco entre la cascada de Guaharivos i la
embocadura del Guaviare. (49434)

Orinoco illustrado, historia, natural, civile y
geographia. 29274
Orinoco ilustrado, y defendido. (29275)
Orion. 57618
Orizava, Mexico. 47032
Orizava, Mexico. petitioners (69989)
Orizava, Mexico. Ayuntamiento. petitioners
57621, 69981
Orizava, Mexico. Clero Secular y Regular.
petitioners 57621, 69981
Orizes conquistados. 45407
Orlando: or parental persecution, a tragedy.
103483
Orlandos, Johannis. plaintiff (57622)
Orleans, Francois Ferdinand Philippe Louis
Marie d'. see Joinville, Francois
Ferdinand Philippe Louis Marie d'Orleans,
Prince de, 1818-1900.
Orleans, William. 57623
Orleans de Rothelin, -------- d'. see
Rothelin, ---------.
Orleans, France (Diocese) Bishop (Brumauld
de Beauregard) 8742 see also
Brumauld de Beauregard, Jean, Bp.
Orleans, France (Diocese) Bishop (Dupanloup)
12346, 57624 see also Dupanloup, Felix
Antoine Philibert, Bp.
Orleans (Territory) see Louisiana (Territory)
Orleans County, N. Y. Board of Supervisors.
(57625)
Orleans County, N. Y. Court. (46628)
Orleans County, N. Y. Society of Natural
Sciences. see Orleans County Society
of Natural Sciences.
Orleans County, Vt. Historical Society. see
Orleans County Historical Society.
Orleans County Historical Society. 93709
Orleans County Society of Natural Sciences.
(57625)
Orleans gazette. 105477
Orleans Navigation Company. defendants
105479
Orlendius, F. 57628
Orllie-Antoine 1er Roi d'Araucanie et de
Patagonie. 57629
Ormaechea, G. Madria y. see Madria y
Ormaechea, G.
Ormaechea, J. B. (57630)
Ormildo Emeressio. pseud. see Alvise
Querini.
Ormond. pseud. Lay of the last pilgrim.
see Riley, William. supposed author
Ormond, J. J. 57632
Ormond. 8457
Ormrod, John. 35473, 101748-101749
Ormsby, R. McKinley. (57633)
Ormsby, W. L. engr. 12891, 84358-84362,
84365
Ormsby, Waterman Lilly, 1809-1883. 57634
Ormstone, George. 99252
Ormstone, Joseph. petitioner 53221, 57494
Ormuzd and Ahriman in the 19th century.
18829, 18833
Ornament of great price. (77571)
Ornamental and useful plants of Maine. 78478
Ornaments for the daughters of Zion. 46442
Orne, Caroline F. 57635
Orne, Henry. 14898, 28608, 57636-(57637)
Ornitholog. Bidrag til den Gronlandske fauna.
32441
Ornithological biography. 2366
Ornithologie Bresilienne ou histoire des
oiseaux du Bresil. 19692
Ornithologie du Canada. 40007
Ornithologie, par Alcide d'Orbigny. 74922

Ornithologische und klimatologische Notizen uber Gronland. 32443

Ornithologischer Beitrag zur Fauna Gronlands. (32442)

Ornithology and oology of New England. (75969)

Ornithology of North America. 6267

Ornithology of the United States. 96383

Oro, Joseph Francisco de Ozaeta y. see Ozaeta y Oro, Joseph Francisco de.

Orographie de l'Europe. 68443

Orondalee. A tale by Byron Whippoorwill. 57638, 103311

Orondalie: a tale of the crusades. 57638, 103311

Orono, Nicasio. (57639)

Oronoco, William. pseud. Dialogue. see Gooch, Sir William, Bart., 1681-1751.

Oronokesen. 78011

Oronoko, ou le royale esclave. 4373

Oronsoro, Pedro de. 44419

Oroonoko. 88547

Oroonoko, a tragedy. 88519-88524, 88526-88527, 88531-88533, 88535, 88539, 88542, 88545

Oroonoko. A tragedy. Altered from the original play of that name. 88529

Oroonoko, a tragedy and other plays. 88525

Oroonoko, a tragedy. Bell's edition. 88534

Oroonoko. A tragedy by J. Hawkesworth. 88528

Oroonoko. A tragedy, by Thomas Southern. Adapted for theatrical representation. 88537

Oroonoko: a tragedy, in five acts; by Thomas Southern. 88544

Oroonoko; a tragedy, in five acts; by Thomas Southern. As performed at the Theatre Royal, Covent Garden. 88540-88541

Oroonoko: a tragedy, in five acts, by Thomas Southern. Printed from the acting copy. 88546

Oroonoko. A tragedy. Written by Thomas Southern. 88536

Oroonoko, or the royal slave. A tragedy. 88538

Oroonoko; or, the royal slave. A true history. (4371)

Oroonoko; or, the royal slave. Altered from Southern. 88530

Oropeza, Bolivia. Gremio de Mineros Administradores de la Real Mina. see Gremio de Mineros Administradores de la Real Mina, Oropeza, Bolivia.

Orosco, ------- Borda y. see Borda y Orosco, ---------.

Orosius, Paulus. 26870

Orozco, J. M. 57640

Orozco, Maria Catharina Davalos Bracamont y. see Davalos Bracamont y Orozco, Maria Catharina, Condesa de Miraville.

Orozco, Seb. de Cobarruvias. 57647

Orozco y Berra, Manuel. 579, 57641-57646, 62878, 71630, 85760 see also Sociedad Mexicana de Geografia y Estadistica. Comision Nombrada Para Examinar la Obra de D. Francisco Pimentel.

Orpen, Jean. petitioner 69970

Orphan. 63204

Orphan Association, Milwaukee, Wisc. see Milwaukee Orphan Association.

Orphan Asylum, Buffalo, N. Y. see Buffalo Orphan Asylum.

Orphan Asylum, Cincinnati. see Cincinnati Orphan Asylum.

Orphan Asylum, New York. see New York (City) Orphan Asylum.

Orphan Asylum Society, New York. 54570-(54571)

Orphan Asylum Society, Washington, D. C. see Washington Orphan Asylum Society.

Orphan House, Charleston, S. C. see Charleston, S. C. Orphan House.

Orphan House, Savannah, Ga. see Savannah. Bethesda Orphan House.

Orphan House Academy, Savannah, Ga. see Savannah. Bethesda Orphan House.

Orphan-House in [Georgia. Dr. Orp]han House in Georgia, Cr. 103575

Orphan-letters. 103640

Orphan of Boston. 72465

Orphan Society, Philadelphia. see Philadelphia Orphan Society.

Orphanotrophium. 46443

Orphan's best legacy. 79425

Orphans' Farm School, Zelienople, Pa. 57648

Orphan's Home, New Bedford, Mass. see New Bedford, Mass. Orphan's Home.

Orphan's Home, Pittsburgh, Pa. see Pittsburgh, Pa. Orphan's Home.

Orphans' Home of Industry, Iowa City, Iowa. 35030, 57648

Orphans' Home of Industry, near Iowa City. 35030

Orphan's Home of the Protestant Episcopal Church in New York, New York. see New York (City) Orphan's Home of the Protestant Episcopal Church in New York.

Orphan's hymn. 85307

Orphan's legacy. 57134

Orphans well-provided for. 46443

Orpheliee Americaine. 5873

Orpheline de la Pennsylvanie. 3978, 101895

Orpheus C. Kerr. pseud. see Newell, Robert Henry, 1836-1901.

Orpheus C. Kerr papers. 54960, 84186

Orpheus Iunior. pseud. Golden fleece diuided into three parts. see Vaughan, William

Orpheus, priest of nature, and prophet of infidelity. 57649

Orquesta. 57650

Orr, Benjamin. 57651, 78997, 2d note after 101883

Orr, Benjamin G. 94572

Orr, Charles. 97733, 99766

Orr, George. 57652

Orr, Hector. 81505

Orr, Hector. comp. and pub. 52038

Orr, Hector, 1770-1855. (57653)-57654

Orr, Isaac. supposed author 10889, (39756), 92843

Orr, J. W. illus. 55129, 75242

Orr, James Lawrence, 1822-1873. 57655-57656, 87559-87561 see also South Carolina. Governor, 1866-1868 (Orr)

Orr, N. engr. 80369, 84158, 91825, 91828, note after 96778

Orrantia, Tomas de. 57657

Orrio, Francisco Xavier Alexo de. see Alexo de Orrio, Francisco Xavier.

Orruno, J. M. 57658

Orruno Irasusta y Uranga, Jose Maria. see Irasusta y Uranga, Jose Maria Orruno.

Orser, John. defendant at impeachment (36456) see also New York (City) Sheriff. defendant at impeachment

Orsini, Giovanni Gaetano. see Nicolas III, Pope, 1216?-1280.

Orsini, Pietro Francesco. see Benedict XIII, Pope, 1649-1730.

Orson Phelps. 61387
Orsted, A. (4764), 4842A
Orsted, A. S. 57659
Orsuna, Bravo de. (57660)
Orta, Fr. de P. 57661
Orta, Garcia de, 16th cent. 115, 13801, 14355, 49940, 57662-57670
Orta-Undis, and other poems. 39856
Orteaga, Jos. Joachin de. 57671
Ortega, Alonso de Jesus y. see Jesus y Ortega, Alonso de.
Ortega, Amado. defendant 100791
Ortega, Antonio de Saldana y. see Saldana y Ortega, Antonio de.
Ortega, C. F. ed. 99397
Ortega, Casimiro de. 9733, 57672
Ortega, Eulalio Maria. 47036, (57673), 58273
Ortega, Fernando de. plaintiff 57674, 74858
Ortega, Francisco, 1793-1849. 57675
Ortega, Francisco Luis. 57684
Ortega, J. B. Munoz Casimire. see Munoz Casimire Ortega, J. B.
Ortega, J. de San Antonio. 57683
Ortega, Jesus Gonzales. 57677-57679, 81474
Ortega, Jose de. 57680-57682
Ortega, Joseph de. 1768, 38234, 57680
Ortega, Juan Gualberto de. see Gualberto de Ortega, Juan.
Ortega, Jaun Pablo. defendant 75571
Ortega, Manuel. 57685
Ortega, T. F. 57686
Ortega de Arguello, Maria de la Soledad. see Soledad Ortega de Arguello, Maria de la.
Ortega Montanez, J. de. see Montanez, J. de Ortega.
Ortega y Pimentel, Isidro Joseph. 57676
Ortel, Abraham. see Ortelius, Abraham.
Ortelii Theatrum orbis terrarum. 57698
Ortelii Theatrum orbis terrarum denuo recognitum. 57696
Ortelii Theatrum orbis terrarum, opus nunc denuo ab auctore recognitum. 57699
Ortelii Theatrum orbis terrarum, opus nunc tertio ab ipso recognitum. 57697
Ortelius, Abraham. 27775, 32005, 57687-(57709), 66494, 66497, (66890)-66891, 77901
Orth, Adam. (38801) see also Lancaster County, Pa. Sub Lieutenant.
Orth, Godlove S. 57710-57711
Orthodox Christian. 62517
Orthodox Church, Manchester, Mass. see Manchester, Mass. Orthodox Church.
Orthodox clergyman. pseud. (80597)
Orthodox clergyman of Massachusetts. pseud. Seasonable and candid thoughts. see Norton, Jacob, 1764-1858.
Orthodox Congregational Church, Walpole, Mass. see Walpole, Mass. Orthodox Congregational Church.
Orthodox evangelist. 55887
Orthodox plea for the sanctuary of God. 963
Orthodoxy unmasked. 93210
Orthodoxy versus spiritualism and liberalism. 24446
Orthographical hobgoblin. 64049
Orthoptera nova Americana. 77215
Orthopteres de l'Amerique moyenne. 77211
Orthos. pseud. Chimasia. see Reeves, Henry.
Ortigosa, J. 57712
Ortigosa, Valentin. 68732
Ortigosa, Vicente. (57713)
Ortis de Zevallos, D. I. 68789, 94833
Ortiz, Alonso. 57714
Ortiz, J. 57719

Ortiz, Jose Santos. (67348)
Ortiz, Josef Alonso. tr. 82312-(82313)
Ortiz, Lorenzo. 57720
Ortiz, Luis G. 57721
Ortiz, Manuel E. Mori. see Mori-Ortiz, Manuel E.
Ortiz, Servo. 57723
Ortiz, Tadeo. 57724
Ortiz de Ayala, T. 57725
Ortiz de Casqueta, Antonio Joseph. see Casqueta, Antonio Joseph Ortiz de, Marquez de Altamira.
Ortiz de Casqueta, Bartholome Antonio Joseph. see Casqueta, Bartholome Antonio Joseph Ortiz de, Marquez de Altamira.
Ortiz de Castro, Geronomo. plaintiff 87229
Ortiz de Castro, Juan. defendant 87229
Ortiz de Castro, Juan. respondent 87229
Ortiz de Cervantes, Juan. see Cervantes, Juan Ortiz de.
Ortiz de Hinojosa, --------. (76300)
Ortiz de la Torre, Manuel. (47722)
Ortiz de Zuniga, Diego. 57716-57717
Ortiz Sepulveda, Diego. see Sepulveda, Diego Ortiz.
Orto, Garcia ab. see Orta, Garcia de, 16th cent.
Ortografia Castellana. 715
Orton, Edward. 56926
Orton, Harlow S. 57726
Orton, J. R. (57728)
Orton, James. 57727
Orton, Job. 91086
Orton, William. 57729
Ortuno, Francisco de Torija. see Torija Ortuno, Francisco de.
Orville, Andre Guillaume Contant d'. 57730-57731
O'Ryan, Michael. 57733
Os, P. van. tr. 92398
Osage first book. 57737, note after 101510
Osage Indian lands. 73350
Osage Indians. 95315
Osage Indians. Treaties, etc. 48145, 57738, 96637, 96697, 96733
Osage treaty. 57738
Osander. pseud. Miscellaneous poems. see Allen, Benjamin.
Osaldistun, Richard, successively Bishop of Carlisle, and London, 1690-1764. 57740
Osbon, Abiathar M. 57741
Osbon, Bradley Sillick, 1827-1912. 32662, 57742
Osbon, Bradley Sillick, 1827-1912. defendant 6230
Osborn, -----------. defendant 3189
Osborn, A. 57743
Osborn, A. O. ed. 94055
Osborn, Benjamin. (57744)
Osborn, Charles. 57745
Osborn, David. 57746
Osborn, Elbert. (57747)-57748
Osborn, G. (46590)
Osborn, H. S. 57750
Osborn, John. (57751)
Osborn, Joseph H. (49664)
Osborn, Laughton. 2466, 57752-57755, 81494, 3d note after 100601
Osborn, Samuel. 57756
Osborn, Samuel. defendant 69824, 100796
Osborn, Sarah. 57757
Osborn, Selleck. (57758)
Osborn, Sherard. ed. (43073), 43075, 57288, 57729-57760
Osborne, Cyrus Pearl. 57761

Osborne, Francis Godolphin. see Leeds, Francis Godolphin Osborne, 5th Duke of, 1751-1799.
Osborne, George Gerry. 52884, 57762
Osborne, John. (57763)
Osborne, M. engr. 84154
Osborne, Peter. (57764)
Osborne, Richard B. 60226
Osborne, S. ed. 23608
Osborne, Thomas. (18774), 26469, 40175, 54979, 57765, 101462, 1st note after 103122
Osborne, Thomas Burr, 1798-1869. 57766
Osborne's New-Hampshire register. 52884
Osbourne, -------. 2466
Oscar and other poems. 74527
Osceola. 80337
Osceola; or, fact and fiction. (81242)
Osceola the Seminole. 69059
Osculati, Gaetano. (57767)-(57768)
Oses, G. R. 57769
Osgood, Daniel. 57770
Osgood, David, 1747-1822. 57771-57778, 93492-93493
Osgood, Frances Sargent. (57779)-57781
Osgood, Gayton Pickman, 1797-1861. 57784
Osgood, George. 57782
Osgood, H. H. 15744, 15785
Osgood, H. L. 4th note after 99888
Osgood, Joseph. (57783)
Osgood, Joseph B. F. 75645
Osgood, Mussey. 24458, 51593
Osgood, S. ed. 52861
Osgood, Samuel, 1748-1813. 57785
Osgood, Samuel, 1812-1880. 57787-57791, 69336, 82479
Osgood, Samuel, fl. 1849. 57786
Osgood, Samuel Stillman. (57792)
Osgood, Samuel Stillman. illus. 57780
Osgood & Co. firm publishers 84500, 84502-84503
Osgood, the damon refugee. 29482
Osgood's circular. 84503
O'Shiell, B. B. 57793
Oshkosh, Wisc. Board of Education. 57795
Oshkosh journal. 73365
Osinga, S. 57796
Osler, Edward. (57797)-57798
Osler, Lemuel. (57799)
Osma, J. I. de. 57800
Osma (Diocese) Bishop (Palafox y Mendoza) see also Palafox y Mendoza, Juan de, Abp., 1600-1659.
Osma & di Xara & Zegio, Pietro di. 57669
Osorio, Alvaro de Navia. see Santa Cruz de Marcenado, Alvaro de Navia Osorio, Marques de, 1684-1732.
Osorio, Diego de Santisteuan. (57801)-57803
Osorio, Francisco de Solis. see Solis Osorio, Francisco de.
Osorio, Hieronymo. 57804-(57807)
Osorio, Juan Prudencio de. 11455
Osorio, Rodrigo Pacheco, Marques de Cerralvo. (48440), 56247, 66052 see also Mexico (Viceroyalty) Virrey, 1624-1635 (Osorio)
Osorio de Cepeda, Juan Suarez. see Suarez Osorio de Cepeda, Juan.
Osorio de Escobar y Llamas, Diego. see Escobar y Llamas, Diego Osorio de, Bp.
Osorio de Pina Leitao, Antonio Jose. see Leitao, Antonio Jose Osorio de Pina.
Osorio y Balcon, Juan Prudencio de. 57808
Osorio y Mendoza, Fadrique de Toledo. see Toledo Osorio y Mendoza, Fadrique de.
Ospina, Mariano. (51075)
Ospina, Pastor. 57809

Ossa Josephi. Or, the bones of Joseph. 14504
Ossav y Tovar, Joseph Pellicer de. see Pellicer de Ossav y Tovar, Joseph.
Ossawatomie sold, a mock heroic poem. 49787
Ossaye, M. F. 57810
Ossera y Estella, Joseph Miguel de. 57811
[Osservatione] sopra il mal Francese et donde fu traportato in Italia. 18508
Osservatione sopra la navigatione de gli Spagnuoli. 18508
[Osservatione] sopro gl' Indiani delle Mondo Nuevo. 18508
Osservazione a chiunque desideri passare in America. 25560
Osservazione sul ragionamiento del primo scopritore. 51760
Osservazioni ad un articolo della civilta Cattolica. 76522
Osservationi diverse historie de d'altri particulari degni de memoria. 18408
Osservazioni di un Toscano. 14661
Osservazioni storiche e fisiologische sopra gli Americani. 24997
Osservazioni sill' esame critico del primo viaggio. (57712)
Ossian. 18347, 27145
Ossoli, Sarah Margaret (Fuller) Marchesa d', 1810-1850. 19920, 57813, 57815-57816
Ossoli, Sarah Margaret (Fuller) Marchesa d', 1810-1850. incorrectly supposed author 57814, note after 95662
Ossorio, Diego. 57818
Ossorio,de Valdes, Garcia. see Valdes, Garcia Ossorio de.
Ossorio y Peralta, Didaco. 57817
Osswald, August. 57819
Osswald, H. Fr. (57820), 92725
Ost, N. C. 57821
Ost und West. 20124
Ost- und West-Indischer so wie auch sinesischer Lust- und Stats-Garten. 25463
Osten-Sacken, R. 41775, (57822)-(57824)
Osteology of the same. 77249
Ostermayer, H. 57825
K. Osterreichischen Naturforschen in Brazilien see Austria. K. Naturforschen in Brazilien.
Ostrea; or, the loves of the oysters. 80148
O'Sullivan, John L. 57826, 59408
Osunkhirhine, P. P. see Wzokhilain, Peter Paul.
Osunkhirkine, Pierre Paul. see Wzokhilain, Peter Paul.
Oswald, Eleazer. defendant 57272, 57828 see also Independent gazetteer. Editor. defendant
Oswald, H. Fr. see Osswald, H. Fr.
Oswald, James. 57829
Oswald, Richard, 1705-1784. 66384 see also Great Britain. Peace Commissioners, Paris, 1782-1783.
Oswald. 24125
Oswegatchie Lead and Smelting Company. 57830
Oswego. pseud. Strike but hear me. (22741), (22766), 92863
Oswego, N. Y. 57831
Oswego, N. Y. Board of Education. 57831
Oswego, N. Y. Board of Trade. 57832, 57834
Oswego, N. Y. City Library. 57837

Oswego, N. Y. Education Convention to Examine Into a System of Primary Instruction, 1862. see Education Convention to Examine Into a System of Primary Instruction, Oswego, N. Y., 1862.

Oswego, N. Y. Normal and Training School. see New York (State) State Normal School, Oswego.

Oswego, N. Y. State Normal School. see New York (State) State Normal School, Oswego.

Oswego, N. Y. Training School for Primary Teachers. see New York (State) State Normal School, Oswego.

Oswego County, N. Y. Board of Supervisors. (57836)

Oswego and Fulton directory and history for 1862-3. 57835

Oswego and Utica Rail Road Company. Chief Engineer. 57833

Oswego and Utica Rail Road Company. Report of Joseph D. Allen, Esq. 57833

Oswego Board of Trade. Reciprocity with British North America vindicated. 57834

Oswego directory for 1852-3. 57835

Oswego directory for 1864-and 1865. 57835

Oswego Normal and Training School, Oswego, N. Y. see New York (State) State Normal School, Oswego.

Otages de Durazno. 64702

Otakahe ekta wahantanka taku owasin kage. 18288, 69646

Otalora, Francisca Arce de. defendant 51043

Otawa anamie-misinaigan. (57884)-57885

Otchipwe anamie masinaigan. 3247B

Otechestvennyya zapiski. 93992

Oteiza, Juan Jose de. 99305

Oteiza y Vertiz, Joaquin Maria de. 57838

Oterio y Baldillo, Jos. Ant. E. de. (57839)

Otero, Jose Mateo de. see Mateo de Otero, Jose.

Otero, Jose Ramon Martelo y. see Martelo y Otero, Jose Ramon.

Otero, Juan de. tr. 72230

Otero, Manuel Ovilo y. see Ovilo y Otero, Manuel.

Otero, Mariano, 1817-1850. 57840, 58076 see also Mexico. Alcalde 3 Constitucional.

Otero, Miguel A. 57841

Otey, James Hervey, Bp. 43534, 49685, 57309, 57842, 65790

Othello. pseud. Strictures on the slave trade. 92857

Otheman, Edward. 57843

Other acts providing for the revenue. 10001

Other awful cases of young gamblers. 102473

Other commemorative pieces. 8341

Other congress convened. 97010

Other metrical compositions. 9087

Other original poems. 57658, 103311

Other side. 57845, (67723)

Other side of "facts for the people." 83690

Other side of Ohio. see 'Tother side of Ohio.

Other side of the question. In three parts. 57844, note after 97893, note after 105575

Other side of the question; or, a defense of the liberties of North-America. 16588, (41634)

Othoa, Jose Gabriel. 57847

Othoengene neoni yogaraskhagh yondereanayen-daghkwa. (50765)

Othonis Casmanni Marianrum quaestionum tractatio philosophica bipartita. 11340

Otia conchologia. (28085)

Otis, Amos, 1801-1875. 57848

Otis, Amos, d. 1834. defendant 36663, 57871

Otis, Belle. pseud. Diary of a milliner. see Woods, Caroline H.

Otis, C. N. 57850

Otis, Cushing. 57849

Otis, Eliza Henderson (Bordman) 1796-1873. 57861

Otis, F. N. 57851

Otis, George. 57852

Otis, George A. 30116, 57853, 69954

Otis, George Alexander. tr. 6820-6821

Otis, H. supposed author (6600), note after 97401

Otis, Harrison Gray, 1765-1848. 284, 6742, (40322), 57854-67860, 67255, (70271), 89659, 98954, note after 103304 see also Boston. Mayor, 1828-1831 (Otis)

Otis, Harrison Gray, 1765-1848. petitioner 34959, 89698

Otis, Harrison Gray, 1765-1848. incorrectly supposed author 37753, 57856

Otis, Mrs. Harrison Gray. see Otis, Eliza Henderson (Bordman) 1796-1873.

Otis, Horatio Nelson. 57862-57864

Otis, James. 34083, 40281, 57869, 3d note after 99800 see also Massachusetts (Colony) Commissioners to Treat With the Eastern Indians, 1749.

Otis, James. supposed author 15949, (21200), 57865, 105074-105077

Otis, James F. 57870

Otis, Oran G. 57872

Otis, Richard W. 42326

Otis, Samuel A. 15517

Otis, William F. 57873-57874

Otis. 4922

Otis' letters in defence of the Hartford Convention. 57860

Otis Library, Norwich, Conn. see Norwich, Conn. Otis Library.

Otium theologicum tripartitum. 97005

Oto Indians. Treaties, etc. 96648, 96662, 96691, 96714

Otoe hymn book. 57875

Otokahe ekta wahantanka taku Owasin kage cin qu IX Genesis eciyapi qa. 69646

Otokahe kin. 71326

Otra alegacion por los Religiosos Dominicos de Oaxaca. 86418

Otra cedula del mismo. 29104

Otro dia sere mas largo. 98255

Otro Padre de la misma Sagrada Relidion de la Provincia de Mexico. pseud. ed. 98849

Otro Religioso de la misma Compania. pseud. ed. see Restivo, Paulo.

Otroctvi ve svobodne Americe. 92515

Otsego County, N. Y. Board of Supervisors. (57877)

Otsego County, N. Y. Citizens. petitioners 57642

Otsego County, N. Y. Committee of Canvassers. Majority. (34385), note after 53697, note after 83791

Otsego County, N. Y. Committee of Canvassers. Minority. (34385), note after 53697, note after 83791

Otsego County, N. Y. Court of Oyer and Terminer and General Gaol Delivery. 96816-96817

Otsego County, N. Y. Inhabitants. see Otsego County, N. Y. Citizens.

Otsego Baptist Association. see Baptists. New York. Otsego Baptist Association.

Otsego herald. 59477

Ott, James Cramer. 57878

Ott genealogy. 57879
Ottarson, F. J. 57880
Ottawa. 37146
Ottawa Indians. Laws, statutes, etc. 47377
Ottawa Indians. Treaties, etc. 96599, 96605,
    96618, 96630, 96631, 96647, 96657,
    96668, 96687, 96692, 96605 see also
    Michigan Indians. Treaties, etc. United
    Tribes of Potawatomi, Chippewa, and
    Ottawa Indians. Treaties, etc.
Ottawa first book. (47376)-47377
Ottawa Mining Co. Lands situated in . . .
    Canada East. 57886
Ottawa past and present. 72605
Ottawa River Indian Council, 1791. see Indian
    Council, Ottawa River, 1791.
Ottawa scenery. 33937
Ottawah, the last chief of the Red Indians of
    Newfoundland. 57888
Ottaway Indians. see Ottawa Indians.
Otte, E. C. tr. (33708), 33729
Ottens, Josua. cartographer (57889), 69599
Ottens, Reinier. cartographer (57889), 69599
Otter, William. 57890
Otterloo, A. van. 24945
Ottman, S. 57891
Otto, Carolus. 57892
Otto, Ed. 57893
Otto, Everardus. 86521
Otto, F. 57894
Otto, Louis Guillaume, Comte de Mosloy,
    1754-1817. 10915, (13179)
Otto Keyens Kurtzer Entwurff von Neu-
    Niederland. 37675
Ottoe Indians. see Oto Idnians.
Ottolenghe, Joseph. 57895
Ottoni, H. B. 57899
Ottoni, J. E. 57897
Ottoni, Theophilo Benedicto. 51229, (57898)-
    (57900)
Ottono, C. B. 57896
Ottsen, Hendrick. 31228, 57901
Otway. pseud. Theater defended. 85330
Otzinachson. 47382
Ouabache Land Company. see United Illinois
    and Wabash Land Companies.
Ouabi: or the virtues of nature. 2654, 51026
Oude en nieuwe constitutie der Vereenigde
    Staaten van Amerika. (21193)
Oude en nieuwe tijds wondertoneel. 100856
Oude nieuws der ontdeckte weereld. 6442,
    note after 98470
Oudenarde, Hendrick. 57903
Oudenarde, Nicholas Aegidius. pseud. Book
    of Saint Nicholas. see Paulding, James
    Kirke, 1788-1860.
Oudiette, Jean. 57904, 70119
Ought American slavery to be perpetuated?
    (8708)
Ought Christians to bear arms? 50672
Ought politics to be discussed in the pulpit.
    4244
Ought private vessels to be exempt from
    capture. 47905
Ought-to-be governor of Wisconsin. pseud.
    Special message. 89110
Ought women to learn the alphabet? 31755
Oulbath, H. d', Vicomte. 57906
Ould, Robert, 1820-1882. 15323 see also
    Confederate States of America. Bureau
    of Exchange.
Oulton, N. C. ed. 79473
Oultreman, Pierre d'. 57907
Our acre and its harvest. 76663, 86316
Our admiral's flag abroad. 50151
Our alma mater. 58096

Our alma mater fifty years ago. 5885
Our American institutions. (26240)
Our ancestors. 58257
Our antient testimony renewed. 57908
Our architecture, and its defects. 48979
Our army at Monterey. 95664
Our army on the Rio Grande. 96665
Our artist in Cuba. 10902
Our artist in Peru. 10903
Our banners set up. 63441
Our battalion organization. 8851
Our battery. 18198
Our benevolent institutions. (26240)
Our book. A call from Salem's watch towers.
    13654, 57909
Our boys. (31803)
Our branch and its tributaries. (31431)
Our brothers and cousins. (43290)
Our camp journal. (57910)
Our campaign around Gettysburg. (27241)
Our campaign; or, thoughts on the career of
    life. 70408
Our cause in harmony with the purposes of
    God. 22279
Our cause, our confidence, and our consequent
    duty. 58128
Our children. 4088
Our chronicle of '26. 47441
Our city clubs. 57911
Our civil war, as seen from the pulpit. 760
Our civil war: its causes and issues. 51438
Our civil war. The principles involved. 4617
Our colonial blue laws. 88910
Our colonies: an address, Mechanic's Institute,
    Chester. (27530)
"Our colonies." By Arthur Wellington Hart.
    30618
Our colonies. By J. Hamilton Fyfe. 26264
Our commercial and political relations with
    China. (57912)
Our common schools. 50893
Our "constitutional rights" vindicated. 11301
Our country. (7046)
Our country . . . a discourse. (50384)
Our country. A sermon, . . . at Utica. 4423
Our country: a sermon . . . on thanksgiving
    day. 24935
Our country. An address . . . before the
    alumni of Waterville College. 52161
Our country and her claims. 73059
Our country and its cause. 89096
Our country, and its claims upon us. 266
Our country, and our country's constitution
    and laws. 82455
Our country, and our duty to it. 11789
Our country and our Washington. 9629
Our country and slavery. 26134
Our country and the church. 70851
Our country before party. 5773
Our country; by Mary H. Cutter and Mary T.
    Reed. 43228
Our country. By Sabin Smith. 83973
Our country. By William H. Ryder. 74539
Our country for the sake of the world. 71267
Our country, in its relations to the past,
    present, and future. 57913, 61356
Our country; its capabilities; its perils, and
    its hopes. 57914
Our country: its danger and duty. 41407
Our country: its dangers and destiny. 24536
Our country; its dangers and its destiny. 9328
Our country, its past, present, and future, and
    what the scriptures say of it. By L. A.
    Smith. 83481

Our country: its past, present, and future, and what the scriptures say of it. By Uriah Smith. 84472
Our country; its peace, prosperity and perpetuity. 39461
Our country: its peril and its deliverance. 7682
Our country—its perils—its deliverance. 7679
Our country, its position, obligation, and power. 24503
Our country: its trials and its triumphs. 59472
Our country must be saved. 58370
Our country not forsaken of God. 85216
Our country. Past and present. 17591
Our country safe from Romanism. 7349
Our country, the herald of a new era. (7150)
Our country, the marvel of nations. 84473, 84475-84477
Our country, to the rescue!! 36000
Our country versus party spirit. 17631
Our country vindicated. A thanksgiving discourse. 27605
Our country vindicated, and democracy sustained. 64688
Our countrymen in chains! 103814
Our countrymen; or brief memoirs of eminent Americans. 42127
Our country's achievements, military, naval, political and civil. (80021)
Our country's evils and their remedy. 2510
Our country's future. A sermon preached in the First Reformed Church. 91159
Our country's future. The United States in the light of prophecy. 84469, 84471
Our country's greatest danger and true deliverance. (57915)
Our country's martyr. 31003
Our country's mission in history. 905
Our country's peril and hope. (55336)
Our country's sin. 60963
Our cousins in Ohio. 33373
Our cruise in the Confederate States War Steamer Alabama. 57916
Our currency. (57917)
Our daily fare. (57918), 61910
Our danger and duty. A discourse, . . . December 6th, 1850. 64194
Our danger and duty. A sermon preached by Rev. John C. Rankin. 67883
Our danger and duty. Two sermons . . . November, 1808. 66228
Our danger and our duty. 88049, note after 95649
Our decisive battle. 19483
Our degeneracy lamented. 69548
Our democratic republic. 35993
Our departed president. 89918
Our doings with our neighbours. 21641, note after 90311
Our duties at this crisis. 17371
Our duty and destiny. 57710
Our duty, as Christian citizens, to the sailor. 33964
Our duty as conservatives. (26240)
Our duty in perilous times. 37976
Our duty in regard to the rebellion. 13589
Our duty in relation to southern slavery. 7491
Our duty in the crisis. 81165
Our duty in the present crisis. 79142
Our duty to our country in the present crisis. 43268
Our duty to the African race. 26169
Our duty to the freedmen. 35849
Our dying Saviour's legacy of peace. (31745)
Our early times. 78333

Our emblem. 87015
Our epoch: its significance and history. 16805
Our family genealogy. 50671
Our farrago. (71959)
Our father. 81475
"Our fathers." A historical discourse. 89315
Our fathers' altar. 33165
Our father's care. 79625
Our father's God, the hope of posterity. 19899
Our federal relations. 2943
Our federal union a cause for gratitude to God. (21137)
Our first men. 6623
Our first year of army life. 101040
Our five years' review. 13280
Our flag. (57919)
Our flag. Origin and progress of the flag of the United States. 65012
Our forefathers; their homes and their churches. 57921, (64842), 87812, note after 87910
Our form of government and the problems of the future. 38320
Our free trade policy examined. 57922
Our future relations with the Pacific islands and Mexico. 57934
Our garrisons in the west. 21254
Our globe. A universal picturesque album. 57923
Our good land, and its good institutions. 22309
Our governments: a view of the government of the United States. 43458
Our grammar schools. 30455
Our great American horses. 57924
Our great captains. 8160, 57925, 85153
Our great country foretold in holy scriptures. 63104
Our great king to be served with our best. 8506
Our great national reproach. 74363
Our great peace festival. 64838
Our grief and our duty. 9647
Our hardy grapes. 38159
Our help is in God. 26536
Our heroic dead. 85138
Our heroic themes. 6170
Our home and foreign policy. (75451)
Our houses are our castles. 29620
Our indebtedness to the fathers. 59115
Our intimation of our Saviour. 46257
Our knowledge of California. 32733
Ovr Ladys retorne to England. 57926, 71894
Our land policy. 36885
Our liberties in danger. 18163
Our liberty. 57927
Our living and our dead. 88368
Our living representative men. (77238)-77239
Our martyr President, Abraham Lincoln. 41219, 95516
Our martyr President. By John F. Baker. 2835
Our martyred President. A discourse on the death of President Lincoln. 36350
Our martyred President. By Mrs. P. A. Hanaford. 30161
Our mechanical industry. 89615
Our mercies of re-occupation. 8365
Our military experience, and what it suggests. 30809
Our modern Athens. 13388, 90648
Our monetary condition. 36162
Our monetary distresses—their legislative cause and cure. 8847
Our Mose. pseud. Mose's letters. 51046
Our mother. (57928)
Our nation. A discourse . . . at Pittsfield, Mass. 33794

Our triumph and our duties. 35849
Our true title to Oregon. 51441
Our twelve months' cruise. 2824
Our union and its defenders. 66613
Our union—God's gift. 9630
Our unity as a nation. 76896
Our village in war time. 45007
Our war and our religion. 3678
Our West Indian colonies. 23156
Our West Indian islands. 89142
Our world; or, the Democrat's rule. (36945)
Our world: or, the slaveholder's daughter. 57941
"Our writers." pseud. Appendix to a late essay. 1793, 2d note after 98175
Our young folks. 52305, 57942, 76692
Our youthful Gideons. 89259
Ours, Hans. 35876
Ourselves; our principles; our present controversy. 17367
Ouseley, Sir William Gore. 11346, 23369, 29486, 57943-57947, (69691), 71353
Out-door papers. (31754)
Out-lines, or sketch of a scheme. 22973
Out of prison. 57948
Out of the deep. 56639, (57949)
Out of the streets. 26799
Out on picket! 48973
Out-pouring of the Holy Ghost. 12331
Out west. (6433)
Outalissi, a tale of Dutch Guiana. 57950
Outcast; a dramatic poem. 36828
Outcast, a gentleman of South Carolina. pseud. Southern odes. see Northrop, Claudian Bird, 1812-1865.
Outcast. A romance of the Blue Ridge. 88662
Outcasts comforted. 104729
Outcroppings. (57951)
Outghersz, Jan. (57952)
Outhier, Reginald. 46946, 57953
Outhier, Renauld. see Outhier, Reginald.
Outinian lecturer. pseud. General address. 26864
Outlaw, David. (57954)
Outlaw, and other poems. 36468
Outlaw brothers. 44802
Outlaw. [By John Richardson.] 71046
Outlaw. [By William Gilmore Simms.] 81217
Outlaw. How to deal with it. 82094
Outlaw of the Bermudas. 34776
Outlawry of a race. 1682
Outlaw's bride. (35304)
Outlaw's child. 47895
Outline for immediate emancipation. 93144
Outline history of an expedition to California. 57955
Outline history of Orange County. 21614
Outline history of the fine arts. 42135
Outline map of New England. 5936
Outline maps. 52135
Outline narrative of the series of engagements. 79355
Outline of a consular establishment for the United States. 57956
Outline of a plan for a national bank. 19302
Outline of a plan for a national bank, with incidental remarks. 57957
Outline of a plan for classifying the archives. 58847
Outline of a plan for establishing a Baptist literary and theological institution. 27703, 105376
Outline of a plan for the total . . . abolition of slavery. 62503
Outline of a plan of an institution for the education of teachers. 11117

Outline of a plan to unite the Baltimore Library Company. 3055
Outline of a system of legislation. (51124)
Outline of a work of grace. 36578
Outline of an institution for the education of teachers. 11117
Outline of brief of appellant. 85212
Outline of Philippine government. 85429
Outline of plan of emigration to Upper Canada. 10437
Outline of studies. (45867)
Outline of the American debit or banking system. 13684
Outline of the American school system. 14425
Outline of the constitutional history and existing government. 49098
Outline of the constitutional history of New-York. 9610
Outline of the controversy of the New Hampshire Grants. 33160
Outline of the course of geological lectures given in Yale College. 81040
Outline of the course of improvement in agriculture. 71724
Outline of the doctrines in natural history. 49749
Outline of the flora of Jamaica. (35584)
Outline of the Franklin Institution of New-Haven. 52978
Outline of the future religion of the world. 83776
Outline of the geology of the globe. 32246
Outline of the history and cure of fever. 35454
Outline of the history of California. (67821)
Outline of the history of printing. 51372
Outline of the history of the British Church. 6984
Outline of the history of the church in Kentucky. 5618, 70826
Outline of the mineral deposits of the state. 8918
Outline of the natural history of Michigan. 77868
Outline of the Oliverian spirit of usurpation, examin'd. 101127
Outline of the order of business. 93968
Outline of the paradigma of a Chippeway vocabulary. 35687
Outline of the plan of education. 28626
Outline of the previous course of the American civil war. 10697
Outline of the revolution in Spanish America. 58265
Outline of the soldier's hymn book. 85309
Outline of the system of education. 55772
Outline of the terms on which peace may be restored. (22959)
Outline of the United States. 57958
Outline of the various acts passed. 8332
Outline of Virginia internal improvements. 17717
Outlines illustrative of the journal of F**** A*** K*****. (36357)
Outlines of a constitution for united North and South Carolina. 57959, note after 95644
Outlines of a national history. 67441
Outlines of a plan for a free city hospital. (13297)
Outlines of a plan for establishing a state society of agriculture. 57960
Outlines of a plan for establishing in New-York. 96364
Outlines of a plan for providing a settlement in South America. 57961

Outlines of a plan for reinstating the British empire. 68411

Outlines of a plan for the administration of the Girard Trust. 68169

Outlines of a plan for the general pacification. (1400)

Outlines of American history. 57962

Outlines of American political economy. 41427

Outlines of an address before the Naumkeag Mutual Trading and Mining Company. 105322

Outlines of an address . . . before the Wisconsin State Agricultural Society. (69001)

Outlines of ancient and modern history. 71934

Outlines of ancient history. 71834

Outlines of argument of District Attorney Hall. 29713

Outlines of character and manners. 40203

Outlines of chronology. 27922

Outlines of English literature. 79961

Outlines of general history. (58727)

Outlines of inquiry. 76664

Outlines of lectures on materia medica and botany. 3861

Outlines of mineralogy and geology of Boston. 18428

Outlines of modern geography on a new plan. 27874

Outlines of modern history, on a new plan. 71834

Outlines of nature. 83686

Outlines of natural philosophy. 69654

Outlines of political economy. (43677)

Outlines of the constitutional jurisprudence of the United States. 21115

Outlines of the geography of Peru. 39681

Outlines of the geography of plants. 48666

Outlines of the geological structure of Lake Superior mining region. 22083, 45735

Outlines of the life and character of Gen. Lewis Cass. (77869)

Outlines of the life and public services, civil and military, of William Henry Harrison. 18092, 30588

Outlines of the life of General Lafayette. 38580

Outlines of the life of Theodore Newell. 59427

Outlines of the life, travels and researches of C. S. Rafinesque. 67455

Outlines of the mineralogy and geology of Boston. 18412

Outlines of the natural history of vegetables. 3806

Outlines of the physical and political divisions of South America. 2114

Outlines of the principal events in the life of General Lafayette. 57963, note after 95803-95804

Outlines of a system of civil and criminal laws. 84401-84402

Outlines of United States history. 83514

Outlook in America in 1875. 88358

Outlook of freedom. 26195

Outrage in the Senate upon Charles Sumner. 57964, 93647

Outrage upon southern rights. 5580

Outrages in Kansas. 93674

Outrages of the Ku Klux Klan. (77307)

Outram, Joseph. 57965-57966

Outre mer. 48678

Outre mer, ou les interets coloniaux envisages dans leur rapport. 38589

Outreman, J. d'. see D'Outreman, J.

Outro padre. pseud. tr. 74029

Outsider. pseud. Early days at Racine, Wisconsin. see H. pseud.

Outward bound; or, hints to emigrant families 57967

Outward bound; or, young America afloat. 57216

Ouverture, Isaac l'. see L'Ouverture, Isaac.

Ouverture de l'Amazone. 39005

Ouverture du canal de jonction. (65954)

Ouviere, Felix Pascalis. see Pascalis-Ouviere, Felix.

Ouvilly, Balthazar Gerbier, Baron d'. see Gerbier, Sir Balthazar, 1592?-1667.

Ouvrage dans lequel on recherche laquelle des deux nations. (63831)

Ouvrage dans lequel on recherche son origin. 98354

Ouvrage dans lequel on traite du gouvernemen des anciennes republiques. 75529-75530

Ouvrage de M. l'Eveque Gregoire. 17507

Ouvrage de M. Schoelcher. 5652

Ouvrage original des indigenes de Guatemala. (7436)

Ouvrage ou l'on expose clairement la nature de tous les etres. 85453

Ouvrage du l'on expose les causes de ces evenemens. 11108, 75130

Ouvrage politique et legislatif. 31897, 75062

Ouvrage posthume de Mr. B. I. D. P. E. 688

Ouvrage revu par M. Guizot. (42003)

Ouvrage sur la priorite de la decouverte de la cote occidentale d'Afrique. 76834, 76836, 76851

Ouvrages de linguistique et de litterature orientales. 55309

Ouvrages de M. le Baron de Humbolt [sic]. 94853

Ouvrages de St. Jerome. 76838

Ouvrages sur l'Amerique. 55309

Ouvrages sur l'Amerique: l'Asie et l'Afrique. 55309

Ouvrages sur l'Amerique. [Par M. de Pradt.] 64905

Ouvriers des deux mondes. (57969)

Ouwerkerk de Vries, J. van. 58070

Ovalle, Alonso de. see Valle, Alonso de.

Ovalle's historical relation of the kingdom of Chili. 10315, 57972

Oveja negreta en el sentido de la produccion de lana. 73282

Ovenus. see Owen, John, 1560?-1622.

Over de beschaving van Negers in Amerika. 33122

Over de geografische verspreiding der fichtenader onderzoek omtrent de soorten. (49390)

Over de gevangenhuizen van Philadelphia. 39055

Over de hervorming van het regerings-stelsel in Nederlandsch West-Indie. 4586

Over de oorzaken van den strijd tusschen Engeland. 66948, 82250

Over de voortplanting van het evangelie in de colonien van den staat. (32415)

Over de voortteeling en wonderbaerlyke veranderingen der Surinaemsche insecten. (47959)

Over de ziekten en derzelver behandeling. 95455

Over den slavenstaand. 62424

Over den toestand der arbeiders en over de handwerks-genootschappen in Engeland en Noord-Amerika. 24018

Over Surinamasche hourtsoorten. 80992

Over the Alleghanies and across the prairies. 61323

Over volksverhuizingen in het algemeen. (57975)

Overantwortung auf eine predigt. 89175

Overbvry, Sir Thomas. reporter 67545

Overcoming evil with good. 28907

Overflowing scourage! 85539

Overijssel (Dutch Province) Ridderschap.
93834

Overijseel (Dutch Province) Steden. 93834

Overland guide. (33021)

Overland journey from Fort Leavenworth.
25836

Overland journey from New York to San
Francisco. 28490

Overland journey round the world. 33595,
81344

Overland monthly. 57976, 90931

Overland route to the Pacific. (19661)

Overland Traction Engine Company. 57977

Overlooked pages of reaper history. 90021-
90022

Overman, Frederick. 57978-(57979)

Overreach, Vamp. pseud. Letter. 36027

Overseer's guide. 57980

Overseers of the Poor, of Salem, for the year
1817, submit the following statement.
75679

Oversigt ov. Gronlands echinodermata. 42740

Overstone, Samuel Jones Loyd, Baron, 1796-
1883. 71086, 78981, 97330

Overthrow of Romanism and monarchy. (2910)

Overthrow of the ballot. 37563

Overton, John, 1766-1833. reporter 94734-
94735

Overton, John, 1766-1833. supposed author
(57981), 99811

Overton, William. 33630

Overton (John) firm publishers 2d note after
100557, 104191

Overture for the government. 65155

Overture. Presented to the Reverend Synod
of Dissenting Ministers. 20060, 69515,
95581

Overzeldzame gevallen van Capit. Rob. Boyle.
55285, 1st note after 99428

Oviatt, George Alexander, 1811-1887. 18814,
30130, 57982 see also Committee of
Pastors in Hamden County, Mass.

Ovid. see Ovidius Naso, Publius.

Ovid, N. Y. Agricultural College. see New
York (State) Agricultural College, Ovid.

Ovid, N. Y. Seneca Collegiate Institute. see
Seneca Collegiate Institute, Ovid, N. Y.

Ovid defended. (76455)

Ovideo, Gonzalo Hernandes de. (40563)

Ovidii Nasonis, tam de Tristibus quam de ponto.
57983

Ovidius Naso, Publius. 13040, 47984, 57983,
57984, (76455)-76463

Ovid's Metamorphosis. 76456-76463

Ovid's Metamorphosis Englished. 57984, 76458

Ovid's selfe-censure. (76455)

Ovieda, Andrea. 66686

Oviedo, Antonio de. 57985

Oviedo, Consaluo Fernando de. 67740

Oviedo, Juan, 1821- (57998). 66737

Oviedo, Juan Antonio de, 1670-1757. 24812,
24819, 57999-58002, 98842

Oviedo y Banos, Diego Antonio de. plaintiff
57986

Oviedo y Banos, Joseph de. 57997

Oviedo y Herrera, Luis Antonio de. 58003

Oviedo y Valdes, Gonzalo Fernandez de, 1478-
1557. 1561-1562, 1564-1565, 3350, (16952),
16957, 30483, (40563)-40564, 57458-57459,
57987-57996, 66696, 67740, 1st-3d notes
after 93588, 94853, 105724

Oviedo y Valdes, Gonzalo Fernandez de,
1478-1557. incorrectly supposed author
32018

Oviedo y Valdez, Gonzalo Hernandez de. see
Oviedo y Valdes, Gonzalo Fernandez de,
1478-1557.

Oviedo (Diocese) Bishop (Aldrete) 51043 see
also Aldrete, Martin Carrillo de, Bp.

Ouiedo De la natural hystoria de las Indias.
57987-57988

Ovilo y Otero, Manuel. 58004

Owase opeaticemowa Ceses Kliest. (79977)

Owdl Rich, Gruelon. (41685)

Owego, N. Y. Congregational Society. Committee. 58005

Owen, Allen Ferdinand, 1816-1865. 58010

Owen, B. F. 68213

Owen, David Dale. 4389, 34528-34529, 37513,
43550, 58006-58009, 75789 see also
Kentucky. State Geologist.

Owen, G. (75841)

Owen, Griffith. 66737

Owen, John, 1560?-1622. (31036)-31037

Owen, John, 1616-1683. 24401, 46745, 78434,
note after 92797

Owen, Joseph. 62581

Owen, Joseph. tr. 77689

Owen, Marie (Bankhead) 1869- 83004

Owen, N. (58011)

Owen, Sir Richard, 1804-1892. 785, 6240,
18649, 28400, 34529, 58012, (58013),
71031

Owen, Richard E. 58014

Owen, Robert, 1771-1858. 58015-58016, 86871,
101368

Owen, Robert Dale, 1801-1877. (25708), 28491,
34565, 43365, 58017-58024, 85025, note
after 100508, 105583, 105598-9, 105747

Owen, Samuel. ed. 54791

Owen, Thomas J. V. 96692 see also U. S.
Commissioners to the United Nation of
Chippewa, Ottawa, and Potawatomi Indians.

Owen, Thomas McAdory, 1866-1920. 83004

Owen, Tom. pseud. Taylor anecdote book.
see Thorpe, Thomas Bangs.

Owen, William. defendant 106311

Owen Sound times. 84919

Owen Syllivan. alias see Syllavan, Owen.
alias defendant

Owens, George. (58026)-58027

Owens, J. S. 45137

Owen's directory of the city of Reading. 68213

Owl Creek letters, and other correspondence.
65544-65546

Owliam, Maria. pseud. see Wallwille, Maria
(Owliam) Grafin von. pseud.

Owls-glass. pseud. Rebel brag and British
bluster. see White, Richard Grant.
supposed author

Owners and Underwriters of the American ship
the New Jersey. petitioners 23361,
47683

Owners of ground lying in the inland side of
the upper part of the Albany Basin.
petitioners 47717, 98580

Owners of real estate in the county of Westchester. petitioners 102952

Owners of real estate in the vicinity of the
Washington Military Parade Ground.
petitioners 47684

Owners of the Brig Armstrong. plaintiffs
(69090)

Owners of the Brig Armstrong vs. the United
States. (69090)

P. J. M. pseud. see Marperger, Paul Jakob,
1656-1730. supposed author
P—— J——a's witchcraft explain'd. 68969
P. K. pseud. see K., P. pseud.
P. L. H. pseud. see H., P. L. pseud.
P. M. pseud. see M., P. pseud.
P. M. D. S. pseud. see Rousselot de Surgy,
Jacques Philibert.
P. M. de O. pseud. see Olive, Pedro Maria
de.
P. Martyris ab Angleira Mediolanensi. Opera.
1565, 45013
P. Martyris Angli Mediolanensis opera.
1548
(P. P.) pseud. see (P., P.) pseud.
P: P: v: S. pseud. see S., P: P: v: pseud.
P. Q. pseud. see Q., P. pseud.
P. S. pseud. see S., P. pseud.
P. S. pseud. see Smith, Preserved, 1789-
1881.
P. S. pseud. see Stehenson, P. incorrectly
supposed author
P. S. pseud. see Stojadirouicx, P.
P. S. de dato Philadelphia dem 5ten Martii.
42642, note after 106351, 106359
P. S. T. S. pseud. see S., P. S. T. pseud.
P. T. pseud. see Carey, John L.
P. V. pseud. see Vissier, Paul.
P. V. pseud. see Villavicencio, Pablo de.
P. V. M. pseud. see M., P. V. pseud. tr.
P. V. S. pseud. see S., P. V. pseud. engr.
P. Z. pseud. see Paaneah, Zaphnath.
P's and Q's. 58067
Paaneah, Zaphnath. 92930
Paarl van groote waarde. 83273
Pabisch, F. J. 84192
Pablo Antonio del Nino Jesus. 19454, 55348
Pablo de Avecilla. 58068
Pablo de Prado. see Prado, Pablo de.
Pablo, Miguel Godinez y San. see Godinez y
San Pablo, Miguel.
Pablos, Juan. (75565), 98913
Pabodie, B. Frank. 22560
Pabor, William E. 58070
Pacaud, J. J. tr. 29313
Pacecchus, Dieghus. 99333
Pachecho, Anjel. 58071
Pacheco, Hernando. 86411
Pacheco, Joaquin F. ed. 58072, 106405
Pacheco, Jose Praxedes Pereira. 58073
Pacheco, Jose Ramon. 57840, 58074-58076,
(70341), 94904-94906, 4th note after 99402
Pacheco, M. T. 61096
Pacheco, N. 58078
Pacheco, Nicolas. 58077
Pacheco, Rodrigo. complainant 47349
Pacheco, Wenceslo de Linares y. see Linares
y Pacheco, Wenceslo de.
Pacheco y Bobadilla, Diego Lopez. see Lopez
Pacheco y Bobadilla, Diego.
Pacheco y Obes, ------. 58639
Pacheco y Obes, ------. plaintiff 73220
Pacheo de Podilla, Juan Vicente de Guemes.
see Guemes Pacheo de Podilla, Juan
Vicente de, Conde de Rivillagigedo.
Pacheo Malheiro e Mello, Antonio Manuel Leite.
see Malheiro e Mello, Antonio Manuel
Leite Pacheo.
Pacichelli, Giovanni Battista. 73185
Pacific almanac, 1865. 58079
Pacific and Indian Oceans. 70432
Pacific coast almanac and year book of facts.
58079
Pacific coast business directory for 1867.
38893

Pacific Congregational Church, Providence,
R. I. see Providence, R. I. Pacific
Congregational Church.
Pacific Congregational Church, in Providence,
R. I. A candid statement. 58080
Pacific-Eisenbahn in Nord-Amerika. 77642
Pacific gleaner. 58081
Pacific Gold Company, of Colorado. 58082
Pacific innuendo, and Gov. Ford's letter.
83288
"Pacific mail." A review of the report of
the president. 58083
Pacific Mail Steamship Company. 58084
Pacific Mail Steamship Company. President.
58083-58084 see also McLane, Robert
Milligan, 1815-1898.
Pacific medical and surgical journal. (58085)
Pacific Methodist College, Vacaville, Calif.
(58086)
Pacific Mills Library, Lawrence, Mass.
39393, 58087
Pacific monthly. 58088
Pacific ocean commerce. 46904
Pacific rail road: a discourse, delivered in
the Second Presbyterian Church, of
Lafayette. 104667
Pacific railroad. A defence against its
enemies. 58089
Pacific railroad act of Congress. 10023
Pacific railroad. An essay on the Pacific
railway. 24572
Pacific railroad and adjoining territories.
56640
Pacific railroad. [By Cassius Marcellus
Clay.] 13536
Pacific railroad. [By Edgar Conkling.] 156
Pacific Railroad Convention, Lacon, Ill., 185?
(38476), 58089
Pacific railroad. How it may be built. 7694
Pacific railroad. Importance to the United
States government. 58089
Pacific railroad—northern route. 91526
Pacific railroad of Missouri. (58090)
Pacific railroad. Speech of Hon. Isaac I.
Stevens. 91525
Pacific railroad. Speech of Hon. J. H.
Campbell. 10252
Pacific railroad. Speech of Hon. M. A. Oter
57841
Pacific railroad. Speech of William H.
Seward. 79541
Pacific railroad—three routes. 91527
Pacific railway. Unanimous action of the
Legislature. 101916
Pacific railway, and the claims of Saint John
84418
Pacific railway on British territory. 63370
Pacific Steam Navigation Company. 43150,
104607
Pacific telegraph and railway. 42167
Pacification and reconciliation of all political
and ecclesiastical parties and sects.
85113
Pacification of the churches. 55889
Pacificator. pseud. Letter to the clergy.
see Hoffman, Murray.
Pacificator. pseud. Nail hit on the head.
58091
Pacifick paper. 12305, 12335
Pacificus. pseud. Address to the inhabitan
of the New-Hampshire Grants. see
Walker, Timothy, 1705-1782.
Pacificus. pseud. Appeal to American Chr
tians. (58093)
Pacificus. pseud. Letters. see Hamilton
Alexander, 1755-1804.

Pacificus. pseud. Religious harmonist.
69340
Pacificus. pseud. Serious expostulation with
the Society of Friends. 58094, 62564
Pacificus. pseud. To the public. [July 16,
1768.] 60715
Pacificus. pseud. To the public. [July 25,
1768.] 60716, 2d note after 95968
Pacificus. pseud. What will Congress do?
103120
Pacificus: the rights and privileges of the
several states. 58092
Pacifique de Provins, --------. see Provins,
Pacifique de.
Pack of cards changed into a perpetual al-
manack. 52767
Packard, Alpheus Spring, 1798-1884. 1808,
58096, 85345
Packard, Alpheus Spring, 1839-1905. 58097-
58098, 68394, 89989
Packard, Asa. (58099)-(58100)
Packard, Charles. 58101
Packard, Clarissa. pseud. Recollections of
a housekeeper. see Gilman, Carolina
(Howard) 1794-1888.
Packard, David Temple. (58103)
Packard, Earl L. 84532
Packard, Elizabeth Parsons Ware. (58104)-
58105
Packard, Frederic Adolphus. 1236, 18282,
(28387), 34797, 58106-(58114), 62034,
65705, 95696, note after 99830
Packard, Hannah James. (58115)
Packard, Hezekiah. 58116-(58119), 89050
Packard, Levi. 58120
Packard, Theophilus. 58121
Packard, Theophilus, 1802-1885. (58122),
70936
Packard (S. S.) firm publishers 58123
Packard & Van Benthuysen. firm publishers
601
Packard's monthly. 58123
Packenham, Richard, 1797-1868. 9943, (57560),
57565 see also Great Britain. Legation.
U. S.
Packer, Joseph-Bill. defendant 58124
Packer, William Fisher, 1807-1870. 33150,
60248 see also Pennsylvania. Governor,
1858-1861 (Packer)
Packer, William Fisher, 1807-1870. reporter
21630
Packer Collegiate Institute, Brooklyn. 58125
Packet of prose and verse. (37253)
Pacto de la Confederacion Centro-Americana.
58126
Pacto social. 23773
Paddenburg, G. G. van. 58127
Paddenburg, G. G. van. incorrectly supposed
author (17983), 31486
Paddock, Benjamin H. 58128
Paddock, I. A. 102625
Paddock, John A. 58129
Paddock, Wilbur F. 58130
Paddy's experience among the Red Skins. 90009
Paddy's trip to America. 94227
Padelford, Seth. (70603) see also Rhode
Island. Governor, 1869-1873 (Padelford)
Padilla, Augustin Davila. see Davila Padilla,
Augustin.
Padilla, Juan de. (58131)
Padilla, Juan de Meneses y. see Meneses y
Padilla, Juan de, Marques de Marianela.
Padilla, Lorenzo de, 1485-ca. 1540. tr. 974
Padilla, Mariano. 58132-58133
Padilla, Matias de la Mota. see Mota Padilla,
Matias de la.

Padre Antonio, Procurador General de la
Prouincia del Paraguay, dize. 74030
Padre de la Compania de Jesvs. pseud. Arte,
y vocabulario de la lengua Morocosi.
51218
Padre de la dicha orden. pseud. Breue tratado.
98898
Padre [de la] dicha orden. pseud. Breue
tratado. 98897
Padre de la misma religion. pseud. Apos-
tolicos afanes. see Ortega, Jose de.
Padre [del] dicha orden. pseud. Breue
tractado. 74799
Padre Francisco Diaz Tano de la Compania de
Jesus. 19989
Padre Luis de Valdiuia, de la Compania de
Jesus, dize. 98662
Padre Luys de Valdiuia Viceprouincial de la
Compania de Iesus. 98333
P. Maestro Fray Juan Martinez, Vocabulario.
(44955)
Padre nuestro constitutcional. 98262
Padre santo. pseud. Sermon. see Sufras de
Santa Clara. fray
Padre Sebastian Izquierdo. 35324
Padron, Antonio Josef Ruiz de. see Ruiz de
Padro, Antonio Josef.
Padvinder. 16569
Padvinder, of het meer Ontario. 16494
Pady. pseud. Reflections of a few friends of
the country. 68690-68691
Pae, David. 58134
Paedagogical admonitions. 91846
Paederick, Roger. see Pederick, Roger.
Paes de Andrada, -------. 58135
Paesi nouamente retrouati. & Nouo Mo[n]do
da Alberico Vesputio Flore[n]tino intitulato.
(50051), (50054), 99379, 4th note after
106378
Paesi nouamente retrovati & Novo Mondo da
Alberico Vesputio Florentino intitulato.
(50051)-(50052), 99379
Paesi nouamente retrouati. Et Nouo Mondo da
Alberico Vesputio Florentino intitulato.
50050, 99369, note after 99383C, 4th note
after 106378
Paesi nouamente ritrouati per la nauigatione di
Spagna in Calicut. 50055, note after 99383C
Paesi nouamente ritrouati per la nauigatione
di Spagna in Calicut. Et da Albertutio
Vesputio Fiorentino intitulato Mondo Nouo.
50053, 50055, 4th note after 106378
Paesi nouame[n]te retrouati. Y Nouo Mo[n]do
da Alberico Vesputio Florentino intitulato.
(50052), 4th note after 106378
Paetus Coecinna. 64990
Paez, Jose Antonio, Pres. Venezuela, 1790-
1873. 10713, 14621, (58136)-58139, 1st
note after 98873 see also Venezuela.
President, 1839-1843 (Paez)
Paez, Ramon. 58140
Pagan, Blaise Francois de. 58141-58142
Pagan, William. 58143
Paganism. 71852
Page, --------. cartographer 91057
Page, --------, fl. 1617. 58157
Page, --------, fl. 1795. 16043, 19807,
(58163)-58165, 65022, 75038, 75178,
(75185), 96447 see also Santo Domingo
(French Colony) Commissaires.
Page, Ann. 58144
Page, Charles A. 58145
Page, Charles G. (58146)
Page, David Cook. 58147
Page, Frederic Benjamin. supposed author
88599, 93969, note before 95109

Page, Harlan M. 58148
Page, Henry Folsam. 58149
Page, J. W. 58154
Page, James. (60357), 61883
Page, John, 1743-1808. (58150)
Page, John, 1744-1811. 100035 see also
  Virginia. Council of State. President.
Page, John E. 50742, 58151-(58153), 92685
Page, John le. see Le Page, John.
Page, Joseph R. 58155
Page, Karl G. 58156
Page, P. F. 58158
Page, Richard. 58159
Page, Samuel. (58160)
Page, Sherman. defendant at impeachment
  49261
Page, Stephen Benson. 102097 see also
  Waterville, Me. Sabbath School. Superin-
  tendent.
Page, Thomas J. 58161
Page, William. 99006
Page, William P. 8887, 58162
Page du Pratz, ------- le. see Le Page du
  Pratz, --------.
Page, Commissaire de Saint-Domingue, a Paul
  Alliot. (58163)
Page from the colonial history of Philadelphia.
  5685
Pagean, Mathieu. see Sagean, Mathieu.
Pages, Alphonse. 12968
Pages, J. C. tr. 64890, (69612)
Pages, Pierre Marie Francois. 37618, 58167-
  (58171)
Pages and pictures from the writings of James
  Fenimore Cooper. 16492
Page's Darstellung der burgerlichen Verhalt-
  nisse. 58156
Pages from the ecclesiastical history of New
  England. 9242
Pages from the note-book of a state agent.
  61321
Paget, Sir James. 84445
Paget, John, fl. 1672. 18708
Paget, John, 1811-1898. 58172-(58173)
Pagina de derecho internacional. (10092)
Pagina de historia. 49229
Pagina memoravel de historia do reinado do
  Senhor Dom Pedro II. 17732
Pagina para la historia de la epoca actual.
  74937
Pagnini, G. M. tr. 100724
Paguenaud, E. 39125
Paia est le temps de regler & d'agrandir le
  commerce. 14967
Paid fire department. Letters to the judges.
  61912
Paid fire departments. To the intependent voters
  of . . . Philadelphia. 61911
Paige, Alonzo C. 58175
Paige, Lucius R. (58176)
Paige, Reed. 58177-(58178)
Paige, Rhoda Ann. (58179)
Paike, Florian. (59173)
Pain, Lewis. 68180, 66627
Paine, ---------, fl. 1809. 72084
Paine, Byron. 58181
Paine, Charles. 58182
Paine, Ebenezer. 31173
Paine, Elijah, 1757-1842. 95535, 106058
Paine, Emerson. 58184-58185
Paine, H. D. (58187)
Paine, Halbert E. 58186
Paine, Henry W. 18906
Paine, Horatio. tr. 66093
Paine, John, fl. 1690. 83760
Paine, John Alsop, 1840-1912. 58188

Paine, Levi L. (58189)
Paine, Lewis W. 58190
Paine, Martyn. (58191)-58193
Paine, Nathaniel, 1832-1917. (58194), 95406
Paine, Robert. 58195
Paine, Robert Traet, 1773-1811. 6502, 6758,
  58199-58201, 78997, 86891, 88852,
  89665, 96374, 97466, 2d note after 101⬛
  103478, 103484
Paine, Robert Treat, 1835-1910. 58196
Paine, Seth. (58198)
Paine, Thomas, 1695-1757. 24687, 58202-
  58205, 62743
Paine, Thomas, 1737-1809. 251, (2120), 106
  13888, 15526, (15588), 19243, 30372,
  34891, 34960, (37437), 43429, 47356,
  (46925), 57168, (58206)-(58249), 59081,
  59718, 60346, note after 63244, (71242)
  79187, (80429), 84642, 84678C, 84827,
  84842, 90446, 91818, 92853-92854,
  92856, 93776, 93777, 94025, 95315, 2d
  note after 95677, 95718, 95879, 95996,
  96130, 96910-96918, 97119, 97127, 974(
  97656, 98338, 1st note after 100516,
  100977, 101342, 101803, 101809, 10183
  note after 101837, 102114, 102144, 104⬛
Paine, Thomas, 1737-1809. supposed author
  40269, (57146)-57147, 96910-96918,
  99320, note after 99776
Paine, Thomas, 1737-1809. incorrectly sup-
  posed author 36914
Paine, Thomas, 1737-1809. defendant 96003
Paine, Thomas, 1773-1811. see Paine, Robe
  Treat, 1773-1811.
Paine, Thomas, fl. 1841. 58253
Paine, Timothy. 105368
Paine, Timothy O. 58254
Paine, William. (58255)
Paine, William P. 58256
Paine (George T.) firm publishers 104336
Paine family register. (58187)
Paine Festival, Cincinnati, 1840. 97738
Paine Festival, Cincinnati, 1856. 58251
Paine Festival. Celebration of the 119th anni
  versary of the birth-day of Thomas
  Paine. 58251
Paine's second part of the Age of reason
  answered. 97656
Painesville, Ohio. Lake Erie Female Semina⬛
  see Lake Erie Female Seminary, Pain⬛
  ville, Ohio.
Painful ministry the peculiar gift of the Lord
  104402
Painfully interesting narrative. 6911
Pains of memory. A poem. 48025
Painter, John the. alias see Aitken, James
  1752-1777. defendant
Painter, E. 58257
Painter, H. 58257
Painter, H. M. 58258-58259
Pairpoint, Alfred. 58260
Pais afortunado. 72517
Paisano. pseud. see T., A. M. R. pseud.
Paisano del autor. pseud. ed. (74771)
Paisano suyo. pseud. publisher 106323
Paisley, Scotland. Emancipation Society. se⬛
  Paisley Emancipation Society, Paisley,
  Scotland.
Paisley, Scotland. Soiree in Honour of Georg
  Thompson, Esq., 1837. see Soiree in
  Honour of George Thompson, Esq.,
  Paisley, Scotland, 1837.
Paisley Emancipation Society, Paisley, Scotla⬛
  95503
Paiva, A. Herculano e o Barrao do Castello
  de (58261)

Paiva, Antonio da Costa. see Costa Paiva, Antonio da.
Paiva, Octaviano Jose de. 58496
Paix a l'Amerique. 77738
Paix de 1782. (58262)
Paix en Amerique. 69372
Paix en apparence. 91247
Paix en Europe par l'alliance Anglo-Francaise. 5856
Pajaro Negro. Leyenda. 42107
Pajarotada. 94837, 97694
Pajeken, C. A. 58263
Pakachoag Division, No. 27, Worcester, Mass. see Sons of Temperance of North America. Massachusetts. Pakachoag Division, No. 27, Worcester.
Palabras del Pueblo. 59320
Palace beautiful, and other poems. 54960
Palaces of America. (78265)
Palacha, Augustus. defendant 97099
Palacin, Joseph Felix. (58264)
Palacio, Diego Garcia de. see Garcia de Palacio, Diego, fl. 1576-1587.
Palacio, F. G. 48342, (58272)
Palacio, Isidoro. 106013B
Palacio, Manuel de Pereda. see Pereda Palacio, Manuel de.
Palacio, Mariano Riva. 47036, 58273
Palacio, Vicente Rivas. 58274
Palacio Fajardo, Manuel. 5390, 58265-58267, 70352, note after 98597
Palacios, Enrique. 58276-58277
Palacios, Jose Felix Ribas y. see Ribas y Palacios, Jose Felix.
Palacios, Jose Gregorio de Torres. see Torres Palacios, Jose Gregorio de.
Palacios, Juan Garcia de. see Garcia de Palacios, Juan, Bp.
Palacios y Verdeja, Felipe Jose de Tres. see Tres-Palacios y Verdeja, Felipe Jose de, Bp.
Palaeontologische Monographie. 72592
Palaeontology, by Dr. B. F. Shumard. 68476
Palaeontology; by F. B. Meek and A. H. Worthen. 34253
Palaeontology; by J. S. Newberry, A. W. Worthen and L. Lesquereux. 34253
Paleontology; by O. St. John, A. H. Worthen, and F. B. Meek. 34253
Palaeontology. Description of vertebrates. 34253
Palaeontology [of Iowa.] (35000)
Palaeontology of New York. (53795)
Palaeontology [of Ohio.] 56928
Palaeontology of the upper Missouri. (47371), 85072
Palaeontology. Volume I. Carboniferous and jurassic fossils. 10008
Palaeontology. Volume III. Containing descriptions and figures. 53796
Palaeontology. Volume II. Cretaceous and tertiary fossils. 10008
Palaeontology. Volume II. Section I. Part I. Tertiary invertebrate fossils. 10008
Paleozoic fossils. 5410
Palafox, Giovanni di. see Palafox y Mendoza, Juan de, Abp., 1600-1659.
Palafox y Mendoza, Juan de, Abp., 1600-1659. (36797), 56265, 57520, 57540, 58279-(58284), 58287, 58290-58292, 58294-58300, 58302-58307, 72777, 73280, (73620), 74863, (77142), 86444, 94275, 99456, 98805, 99441, 2d note after 100585, 105987A see also Mexico (Archdiocese) Archbishop (Palafox y Mendoza) Mexico

(Viceroyalty) Virrey, 1642 (Palafox y Mendoza) Osma (Diocese) Bishop (Palafox y Mendoza) Puebla, Mex. (Archdiocese) Bishop (Palafox y Mendoza)
Palafox y Mendoza, Juan de, Abp., 1600-1659. plaintiff 98804 see also Puebla, Mexico (Archdiocese) Bishop (Palafox y Mendoza) plaintiff
Palafox y Mendoza, Juan de, Abp., 1600-1659. supposed author 93917
Palairet, J. (58308)-(58310)
Palaorama. Oceanisch-Amerikanische Untersuchungen und Aufklarungen. 8478
Palata, Melchor de Navarra y Rocaful, Duque de la. see Navarra y Rocaful, Melchor de, Duque de la Palata.
Paleen, M. de la. 1183
Pale-face hunter. 42547
Palenque tablet. 85072
Paleontologie. 74922
Paleske, Charles G. 58312, 60750, note after 97766
Palestine Missionary Society. 92259
Palestra historial de virtudes, y exemplares apostolicos. 9248
Palestra Scientifica, Rio de Janeiro. 71458
Palfray, Warwick. 5123, 58313
Palfrey, Francis Winthrop. (34418), 58314-(58315), (65323), 105074
Palfrey, John Gorham. 1825, (12012), 20256, note just before (30750), 37683, 45541, 45711, (46146), 46157, 55562, 58316-58325, 64099, (65323), 89004, 90290, 105074, see also Massachusetts. Secretary of the Commonwealth.
Palfrey, Sarah Hammond. 58326
Palingenessia. 71278
Palingenesy. 64471
Palinodia de J. F. L. 87219
Palinodia en respuesta al Padre Soto. 87216
Palisot de Beauvois, Ambroise Marie Francois Joseph, Baron. 4211, (58327), 59419
Palladium. 99548
Palladium of conscience. 5697
Palladium of knowledge, and Charleston pilot. 87782
Palladium of knowledge: or, the Carolina and Georgia almanac, for . . . 1800. 87777
Palladium of knowledge; or, the Carolina and Georgia Almanac, for . . . 1799. 87775
Palladium of knowledge: or, the Carolina and Georgia almanac, for the year of Our Lord, 1804. 87781
Palladium of knowledge: or, the Carolina and Georgia almanac, for the year of Our Lord, 1801. 87779
Palladium of knowledge: or, the Carolina and Georgia almanac, for the year of Our Lord, 1807. 87782A
Palladium of knowledge : or the Carolina and Georgia almanac for the year of Our Lord, 1803. 87780
Palladium of knowledge: or, the Carolina and Georgia almanac, for the year of Our Lord 1813. 87783
Palladium of knowledge: or, the Carolina and Georgia almanac, for the year of Our Lord, 1798. 87773
Palladium of knowledge: or, the Carolina and Georgia almanac, for the year of Our Lord, 1797. 87771
Palladium of knowledge: or, the Carolina and Georgia almanac, for the year of Our Lord, 1796. 87769

Palladium of knowledge; or, the Carolinian and
  Georgian almanac, for the year of Our
  Lord, 1788. 58328, 87765
Palladium of our liberties. 97751
Pallas, Peter Simon, 1741-1811. 29865,
  (37727), (58329), 91218
Pallen, M. M. 58330
Palliative and prejudiced judgments condemned.
  9476
Palliser, Sir Hugh. 54986, (58333) see also
  Newfoundland. Governor, 1764-1769
  (Palliser)
Palliser, John. 58331-(58333)
Pallmer, C. N. 58334
Palloto, Joao Baptista. 45403
Palluau et de Frontenac, Louis de Baude,
  Comte de. see Baude, Louis de, Comte
  de Palluau et de Frontenac, 1620-1698.
Palm-bearers. (46444)
Palma, Jose Gabriel. supposed author 85736
Palma, Manuel R. 58336
Palma, R. 94863
Palma, Ramon de. ed. 63320
Palma, Ricardo. (58337)-58338
Palma Faxardo, Francisco. 58335
Palmblatter und Schneeflocker. 49916
Palmer, --------, fl. 1820. (1964)
Palmer, Dr. --------, fl. 1826. supposed author
  99610, note after 105324
Palmer, --------, fl. 1833. 96939
Palmer, A. G. 58339
Palmer, A. L. 90683
Palmer, Aaron Haight. 58340
Palmer, Alonzo Benjamin. 90756
Palmer, Andrew. 58341
Palmer, Arabella. 92541
Palmer, Arabelle. 92596
Palmer, B. Frank. 58342
Palmer, Benjamin Morgan. 58343-58347
Palmer, Charles Ray. (1442) see also
  Andover Theological Seminary. Class of
  1859. Secretary.
Palmer, David. (58348)
Palmer, Don Mc. N. 58349
Palmer, E. C. (49249)
Palmer, E. F. 78724
Palmer, Edward. (58350)
Palmer, Edward Henry, 1840-1882. 84062
Palmer, Elihu, 1764-1806. 58351, 63790,
  66071
Palmer, Harvey. (58352)
Palmer, Henry. 58353
Palmer, Henry G. (58354)
Palmer, Henry Spencer. 58355
Palmer, J. C. R. (58363)
Palmer, J. N., fl. 1835. 52652
Palmer, J. N., fl. 1841. 58357
Palmer, James Croxall. 58356
Palmer, Joel. 58358
Palmer, John, of Lynn, Eng. 58360-58362,
  84304-84306, 84320-84321
Palmer, John, ca. 1650-1700. 46731-46732,
  58358, (65323), note after 70346, 92350
Palmer, John Williamson, 1825-1906. 67072
Palmer, Joseph. 58364
Palmer, Joseph W. (58365)
Palmer, N. B. 34491
Palmer, Obadiah. complainant. 58366
Palmer, Peter S. 58367
Palmer, Ray. 640, (58368)-(58372), 73970,
  73977, 92771
Palmer, Robert M. 58373
Palmer, Sir Roundell. 58374
Palmer, S. incorrectly supposed author 58375,
  (58730)
Palmer, Samuel. ed. (9868)

Palmer, Sarah L. 58376
Palmer, Stephen. 56236, 58377-58378
Palmer, Thomas H. 32076, 58379-58380
Palmer, Walter C. 58382
Palmer, William J. 37058, 58383
Palmer, V. B. 58381
Palmer's business men's almanac. 58381
Palmerston, Henry John Temple, Viscount,
  1784-1865. (58384)-58385
Palmetto. pseud. Address to the people of
  Barnwell District. 87937, 96177
Palmetto dictionary. 58386
Palmetto pictures. 58387
Palmieri, Matteo, 1405-1475. 23114
Palmieri, Mattia, 1423-1483. 23114
Palmiers. 57457
Palmskiold. Archivo. 91723
Palmyer de Courtonne, Jean. see Paulmier
  Jean, d. ca. 1669.
Palmyra, N. Y. Meeting of the Citizens of
  Rochester, Buffalo, Lockport and Palmy
  N. Y., 1839. see Western Canal Con-
  vention, Rochester, N. Y., 1839.
Palmyra, N. Y. Meeting of the Citizens with
  Reference to the Improvement of the E
  Canal, 1839. see Western Canala Con
  vention, Rochester, N. Y., 1839.
Paloeontology. 69946
Paloma penitente. 75608
Palomino, Bartolome Ivrado. tr. 4500
Palomino, Pichon. 39096, 58388
Palomo, Jose Garcia. 58389, (63889)
Palos, J. F. de. 58390-58391
Palos de nueva invencion. 27807
Palos wowapi kage ciqon. 71336
Palou, Francisco. (34115), (48440), (58392)
Paltock, Robert. 58394, 74631
Paltock, Samuel. supposed author 58394,
  74631, note after 104017
Paltsits, Victor Hugo. ed. 84576, ntoe after
  101547
Palvdanus, Bernard. ed. 41368-(41370)
Paludanus, Francois. tr. 4637, 76811
Pama, Pieter. 58395-58396
Pama, Pieter. petitioner 4813, 58396
Pambrun, Pierre Chrysologue. 65715
Pamfili, Giovanni Battista. see Innocent X,
  Pope, 1574-1655.
Pampero. 50613
Pamphile, Francois Joseph. see Lacroix,
  Francois Joseph Pamphile, Vicomte de
  1774-1842.
Pamphlet addressed to Lord Hobart. 26154
Pamphlet addressed to Martin Van Buren.
  37451
Pamphlet, addressed to Mr. Monroe. 95895
Pamphlet [addressed to the members of the
  congregation.] 635
Pamphlet addressed to the Republicans of th
  county of Saratoga. (70188)
Pamphlet against Riggs & Nourse. 91391
Pamphlet against the immoral conduct of ma
  of the Quakers. 58398
Pamphlet by H. May. 31188
Pamphlet, by Lt. Gov. Taylor and others.
  13786
Pamphlet [by the Sectional Dock Company.]
  70268
Pamphlet [by Thomas Smyth.] 85332
Pamphlet circulated by the Reading Rail Roa
  Company. 78080
Pamphlet containing a description of Reming
  ton's wonderful bridge. 69556
Pamphlet, containing a series of letters. 94
Pamphlet de MM Lacharriere et Foignet.
  5652

Pamphlet descriptive of north-western Iowa. 83318

Pamphlet entitled 'Considerations on the embargo laws.' 96013

Pamphlet, entitled, "Taxation no tyranny." 36306, 58399

Pamphlet for the people. By Thomas A. Devyr. (19832)

Pamphlet for the people: containing facts and arguments. (68310)

Pamphlet for the times. 15243, 37838

Pamphlet. From the Norfolk, Va., New regime. 59558

Pamphlet having a few days ago made its appearance. 63791, 105988

Pamphlet in relation to the state debt. 60290

Pamphlet issued by the Assistant Secretary of the Navy. (69688)

Pamphlet lately published by Messrs. Charles Barrell. 36778, 1st note after 97160

Pamphlet, lately published in London. (4686)- (4687)

Pamphlet, n°. 8. (70901)

Pamphlet no. 17 [of the Loyal Publication Society.] 1389, 11579

Pamphlet of James Gallatin, Esq. 9639

Pamphlet of the Commissioner of Indian Affairs. 12471

Pamphlet on a trust deed of the Hanover Street Church. 6650

Pamphlet on equal rights and privileges. To the people of the United States. Andrews County, Missouri. 58400

Pamphlet on equal rights and privileges, to the people of the United States, by Samuel B. Green. 28558

Pamphlet on highland emigration. 20704, (22080)

Pamphlet on Negro emancipation and American colonization. 92837

Pamphlet on specie reserves. 42465

Pamphlet, on the commerce of the American states. 5458-(5459), (40321)

[Pamphlet on the difficulties in the church of Maryland.] 94101

Pamphlet on "the privilege of the writ of habeas corpus." 9131

Pamphlet on the right of search. (11354)

Pamphlet on the slave power. 1825

Pamphlet on the subject of "assimilated rank." 71589

Pamphlet on the Washington miracle. 46848, (46900), 102024

Pamphlet printed by the professors and tutors of Harvard University. 23271, 30756, (42458)

Pamphlet publie par le gouvernement at [sic] sujet de Manitoba. 79770

Pamphlet published by a committee of the citizens of Berkshire. 69401, 2d note after 104432

Pamphlet published by a minority of the Eastern Subordinate Synod. 27320

Pamphlet published by Dr. T. T. Moorman. 9318

Pamphlet recently circulated by Mr. Edward Brooks. 42465

Pamphlet relating to the claim of Senor Don Jose Y. Limantour. 104625

Pamphlet said to be offered to the churches. 360, 11968, 3d note after 96741

Pamphlet showing how easily the wand of a magician may be broken. 58401

Pamphlet, written by George Wotherspoon. 22225

Pamphleteer. 1687, 2262, (2265), 7167, 1772, 14569, 15110, 15973, 16893, 17444, 24898, (35296), 38292, 42354, 42416, 57963, (58402), 64911, 67960, (68265), 70254, 71347, (81914), 81978, 90616, 90764, 91239, 91242, 94259, 95512, 95655, note after 95803, 95804, 98144, 98146, 98672, 3d note after 103852, 103954

Pampleto politico. 88733

Pamphlets and books printed in Buffalo. 103453

Pamphlets and extras, containing the articles of Unitarian. 98046

Pamphlets issued by the Loyal Publication Society. 54364

Pamphlets of Mountaineer. 105566

Pamphlets of Mountaineer—No. 7. 105566

Pamphlets of the Loyal Publication Society. 744, 1003, (1388), (1389), 2136, 9638, 11579, 12200, 16594, 21781, (21847), 22113, 24251, 25671, 26734, 30019, 30022, 33230, (33231), 33232, 38445, 40985, 41567, 42549, 42557, 53485, 54364, (55459), 55834, 57406, (66799), 68318, 67487, 80419, 82613, 86327, 91018, 93667, 94085, 95516, note after 95516, 95517, 95753, 95787, 98891

Pamphlets on "punishment of death," no. 4. 94515

Pamphlets on the constitution of the United States. 67681, 83604, 2d note after 87733, note after 101485, 102352, 102417, 104632

Pamphlets on the war. 85368

Pamphlets originally published in England. 102729

Panacea; or the universal medicine. 23216

Panama (Spanish Province) Audiencia. Presidente. 86377 see also Martinez de la Vega, Dionisio.

Panama (Spanish Province) Gobernador, 1669-1671 (Guzman y Gonzaga) 79781 see also Guzman y Gonzaga, Juan Perez de.

Panama (Province) Congreso, 1826. see Congreso de Panama, 1826.

Panama (Province) Gobernador, 1843 (Pindea) 58407 see also Pineda, Anselmo.

Panama (Province) Gobernador, 1856 (Fabrega) (16986), 58408 see also Fabrega, Jose.

Panama (Province) Sociedad de Amigos del Pais. see Sociedad de Amigos del Pais, Panama.

Panama (Diocese) 58406

Panama in 1855. 36508

Panama massacre. (16986), 58408

Panama, Nicaragua, and Tehuantepec. (22251), (41389)

Panama-Pacific International Exposition, San Francisco, 1915. 85023

Panama Rail Road Company. 52775, (58410)

Panama Rail Road Company. petitioners (58410), 73977

Panama Rail Road Company. Chief Engineer. 58409

Panama Rail Road Company. Directors. 58409

Pancirollus Guidus. 58411-58415

Pancoast, Joseph. (58416)

Pandectas Hispano-Mejicanas. 58417, (72549)

Pando, J. M. de. 61144, 67349 see also Peru. Ministerio de Hacienda.

Pando, Jose Maria de. 58418-58419

Pandolfi, Ubaldus de. tr. 105733

Pandosy, Marie Charles. 58420

Panegirei artifical. 29063

Panegirica dedicacion del templo. 76894

ΠΑΝΣΕΒΕΙΑ.   73313, 73314, 73316
Παυσε/βεια.   73315
Pansey, Henrion de.   58429
Pantaleon de Escoyti y Norri, Gabriel.   58430
Pantheon Canadien.   (5154)
Pantheon literraire.   58431
Pantheon of the age.   58432
Pantheon populaire.   10th Series.   92432,
    92531
Pantheon real.   58433
Panther, Abraham.   pseud.??   59238, 93891-
    93893, 93896, 93899-93900, 93902
Pantiga, Angel Alonso y.   see   Alonso y
    Pantiga, Angel.
Pantographia.   26094
Pantoja, Thomas Ximenez.   see   Ximenez
    Pantoja, Thomas.
Pantological system of history.   (33847)
Pantom, en deux actes.   100745
Pantomime entertainment, called Gil Blas.
    101866
Pantomime of Zero.   73784
Panzer, G. W.   tr.   11516
Pnazerschiffe Merrimac und Monitor und das
    Seegefecht.   58434
Paolo Iovio da Como delle cose della Moscovia.
    67736
Paon, ----- le. see Le Paon, ---------.
Papacy: a conspiracy against civil and religious
    liberty.   (37780)
Papal conspiracy exposed.   4303
Papal hierarchy.   77726
Papal Rome.   77736
Papel anonymo contra el libro de la vida
    interior.   (36797)
Papel de Da Carmen Maiz publicado hoy.
    44065
Papel de el Padre Lector de Theologia Fr.
    Bartolome de Letona.   86416
Papel del coyote.   99703
Papel del Escmo. Senor D. Dr. de Arango.
    1872, 3612
Papel escrito por el ciudadano M. L. Viduarre.
    99475
Papel Mexicano.   95074
Papel periodico de la ciudad de Santa Fe de
    Bogota.   72527
Papel politico.   13161
Papel Sellado.   58435
Papel sobre el verdadero y unico modo de
    beneficiar.   58436
Papeles curiosos de Guatemala.   (29091)
Papeles escritos contra mi.   99474
Papeles Peruanos.   58437
Paper addressed to the commissioner of the
    naval code.   82571
Paper addressed to the Mayor, Aldermen and
    Commonalty of the city of New-York.
    731, 30380, 84558
Paper and resolutions in advocacy.   38463
Paper book of the city of Philadelphia.   61914
Paper book: Sharpless John Hebler, and others
    vs. the city of Philadelphia.   58441
Paper by Thomas Jefferson.   65340, note before
    95775
Paper by Wm. Sooy Smith.   84898
Paper containing a statement and vindication
    of certain political opinions.   68617
Paper containing a statement of facts relating
    to the approaching cotton crisis.   43306
Paper containing exceptions against some things.
    58442
Paper containing . . . views on internal improve-
    ments.   48081
Paper directed to all true patriots.   (60625),
    note after 89175

Paper, headed, "In the days of Tiberius
    Caesar, ..."   30553
Paper left behind him.   98339
Paper manufacturers.   petitioners   47685
Paper money, and the rights and advantages
    of the public.   (24350)
Paper of art and literature.   21520
Paper of condemnation against George Keith
    and the rest of his friends.   8956-8957
Paper of tobacco.   58443
Paper of verses composed by a learned gentle-
    man.   80993, note after 98499
Paper on a general society for the study of
    American antiquities.   46863
Paper on building-stones.   64203
Paper on gold mining in Nova Scotia.   31936
Paper on New-England architecture.   (11783)
Paper on the cotton crop of the United States.
    1498
Paper on the Gneisses of Nova Scotia.   31936
Paper on the growth, trade and manufacture
    of cotton.   21083
Paper on the Gulf Stream and currents of the
    sea.   46974
Paper on the history and prospects of inter-
    oceanic communication.   92670
Paper on the influence of climate in the
    equatorial regions.   20320
Paper on the judicial and legal condition of
    the territory of Wisconsin.   49011
Paper on the Kuro-Siwo, or Japan stream.
    4757
Paper on the lost polar expedition.   85555
Paper on the militia.   93715
Paper on the motions of the deaf and dumb
    before instruction.   59536
Paper on the pioneer women of the west.
    85143
Paper on the removal of the Indians of Wis-
    consin.   38979
Paper, prepared at the request of a meeting.
    69357
Paper, presented by Maior Butler.   104336
Paper presented to the College of Physicians
    of Philadelphia.   68520
Paper question.   10842
Paper read at a family meeting of some of
    the descendants.   34000
Paper read at the annual meeting of the
    National Civil-Service Reform League.
    83963
Paper read at the bar of the House of Com-
    mons.   42807, 67032
Paper read at the Essex County Teachers'
    Association meeting.   84498
Paper read at . . . the Franklin Institute.
    33393
Paper read at the officers' reunion in Boston.
    (67276)
Paper read . . . at Washington, D. C.   37296
Paper read before the American Association
    for the Advancement of Education.   4655
Paper read before the American Geographical
    and Statistical Society, March 6, 1856.
    61044
Paper read before the American Geographical
    and Statistical Society, . . . New York,
    May 1, 1862.   24265
Paper read before the American Geographical
    and Statistical Society, . . . 21st Feb-
    ruary, A. D. 1856.   31638
Paper read before the American Geographical
    Society, February, 1870.   89985
Paper read before the . . . American Social
    Science Association, at Boston, January
    30, 1867.   (31825)

Paper read before the American Social Science Association, at New York, October 26, 1869. 89555

Paper read before the Buffalo Historical Society, December 28, 1863. (66091)

Paper read before the Buffalo Historical Society, February 1st, 1864. 5560

Paper read before the Buffalo Historical Society, February 6, 1863. 75791

Paper, read before the Court of Bishops. (20385), 88253

Paper read before the Historical Society Club. 91134

Paper read before the Juridical Society. 13259

Paper read before the Law School of Dickinson College. 84515

Paper read before the Literary and Historical Society of Quebec. 72307

Paper read before the Liverpool Philomathic Society, March 13, 1867. 84010

Paper read before the London Anthropological Society. (33868)

Paper read before the Maryland Historical Society. 812, (45211)

Paper read before the Massachusetts Historical Society, December 14, 1865. (58703)

Paper read before the National Sabbath Convention, Saratoga. 32943

Paper read before the New England Historic, Genealogical Society. 65013

Paper read before the New Jersey Historical Society, January 20th, 1853, 2019

Paper read before the New Jersey Historical Society, May 17, 1860. 82980

Paper read before the New-York Historical Society, June 25, 1861. 89687

Paper read before the New York Historical Society, May 3d, 1859. 18942

Paper read before the New York Historical Society, 3d March, 1857. (19631)

Paper read before "the Numismatic and Antiquarian Society of Philadelphia." (62491)

Paper read before the Ohio Commandery of the Military Order of the Loyal Legion of the United States. 84035

Paper read before the Pennsylvania State Bar Association. 84516

Paper read before the Rhode Island Historical Society. 92124

Paper read before the Rhode Island Historical Society, October 25th, 1860. (5764)

Paper read before the St. Louis Academy of Science. 84244

Paper read before the Society for the Reform and Codification of the Law of Nations. 84002

Paper read before the State Historical Society of Missouri. 85374

Paper read before the Temple Club of Congregational Ben Israel. 83966

Paper read before the Western Reserve Historical Society. 78336

Paper read by Commodore Thornton A. Jenkins. 36018

Paper read by him [i. e. J. de Cordova] before the New York Geographical Society. (19190)

Paper read by request before the Buffalo Historical Society. 91136

Paper read . . . in . . . New-York. 81248

Paper relating to the reconstruction of the monument. 8154

Paper supposed to have been written by Dr. Benjamin Franklin. (25561)

Paper to William Penn. 58444

Paper upon California. (30481), (45211A)

Paper upon the origin of the Japan Expedition. (18821), (45211A)

Paper which Judge-Advocate General Holt furnished to the President. 36262

Paper world. 83325

Paper, written by General Hamilton. 56035

Papers accompanying joint resolution. 25159

Papers accompanying Lieutenant Williams' application. 104235

Papers accompanying the annual report of the Canal Commissioners. (53564)

Papers, acts, and resolutions, of the Kentucky Legislature. (37564)

Papers and communications read to the Boston Society of Natural History. (6775)

Papers and despatches relating to the Arctic Searching Expedition of 1850-51. 58445

Papers, and despatches relating to the Arctic Searching Expeditions of 1850-1-2. 4425▮

Papers and documents relating to the Mohawk and St. Lawrence Rail Road and Navigation Company. 49854

Papers and further papers relative to British Colombia. 58446

Papers and letters on agriculture. 58447

Papers and letters on agriculture. 10347

Papers and personal reminiscences. 84035

Papers and practical illustrations of public works. 58448, (72576)

Papers and proceedings of the Aborigines Protection Society. 34649

Papers . . . by J. D. Hayes. 31022

Papers concerning the attack on Hatfield and Deerfield. 58449

Papers concerning the boundary between the states of New York and New Jersey. 18936

Papers concerning the capture and detention of Major Andre. 18936

Papers concerning the town and village of Yonkers. 18936

Papers containing minutes of the campaign and transactions to the northward. 8671◀

Papers containing several reasons why James Buchanan should receive the distinguishe◀ consideration of the people. 8864

Papers for the people. see Chamber's paper◀ for the people.

Papers for the people. . . . Issued weekly . . . under the patronage of the . . . Democratic delegation in Congress. 58450

Papers for the people.—No. IV. Issued by the Southern Independence Association. 88377

Papers for the people.—No. IX. Issued by the Southern Independence Association. 88377

Papers for the people.—[Nos. V-IX. Issued by the Southern Independence Association.] 88377

Papers from the experience of an American minister. 68406

Papers from the portfolio of an army chaplain. (17657)

Papers from the records of the New York . . . Mission and Tract Society. 54190

Papers from the Society for the Diffusion of Political Knowledge. 12995, (17630), 33898, 58451, 69699

Papers in explanation of measures adopted for◀ the amelioration of the condition of the slave population. 10693

Papers in relation to the case of Silas Deane◀ 19065, note after 79366

Papers in relation to the conduct of Winthrop Sargent. 77036

Papers in relation to the official conduct of Governor Sargent. 77037

Papers in relation to the official conduct of Winthrop Sargent. 58452

Papers issued by the Historical Club of the American church. 102700

Papers laid before the Royal Commission of Enquiry by Governor Eyre. 23562, (35643)

Papers, no. 4 [of the New York Society for Diffusion of Political Knowledge.] (17630)

Papers of a retired common councilman. 54182

Papers of Benjamin Franklin. 103107

Papers of Col. George Morgan. 31799

Papers [of George Washington.] 89013

Papers of James Madison. 43716

[Papers] of Judge Barker. 31799

Papers of Lewis Morris. 50850

Papers of Mirabeau Buonaparte Lamar. 97675

Papers [of Sir William Howe.] 16813

Papers of the American Historical Society. 84791

Papers [of the American Public Health Association.] 83367

Papers [of the American Society of Church History.] 84390

Papers of the Governor and Council of Vermont. 101077

Papers of the Historical Society of Delaware. 83864, 84091, 84969

Papers of the New Haven Colony Historical Society. 52988

Papers of the Society for the Diffusion of Political Knowledge, New York. 12995

Papers [of the Southern Historical Society.] 84724

Papers on agriculture. (45896)

Papers on emigration. 10625

Papers on fossils. (39496)

Papers on Spanish America. 80163

Papers on the boundary line between Massachusetts and the easterly line of Rhode Island. 58453

Papers on the British colonies in the West Indies. 58454

Papers on the colonial questions. (25681), 58455

Papers on the comparative merits of the cataptric and dioptric or catadioptric systems of light-house illumination. 41047

Papers on the contested election case from Baltimore. 45163

Papers on the defence of Boston and other places. 58456

Papers on the metallurgy of silver. 5803

Papers on the skirmishes at Lexington and Concord. 42860, (58457)

Papers on the slave power, first published in the "Boston whig." 58325

Papers on various subjects connected with the survey. 30818

Papers pertinent to the foregoing correspondence. 93647

Papers presented by His Majesty's command. (58458)

Papers presented pursuant to address. (58459)

Papers presented to Parliament in 1809. 58460

Papers presented to Parliament in 1813. 58461

Papers presented to the Committee Appointed to Enquire into the State and Condition of the Countries. 58462

Papers presented to the House of Commons relating to America. 58463

Papers, printed by order of the House of Commons. 102833

Papers printed for the use of students in the Massachusetts State Normal Art School. 84495, 84497

Papers put into the case of Rhode Island vs. Massachusetts. 70751

Papers relating chiefly to the Maryland line. 2872, note after 79366

Papers relating to a supposed libel. (32551), 7th note after 97146, 97147

Papers relating to America, presented to the House of Commons. (58464)

Papers relating to American loyalists. (58465)

Papers relating to an act of the Assembly of the Province of New-York. 14272

Papers relating to an affidavit made by His Reverence James Blair, Clerk. 55223

Papers relating to Boston in New England. (58466)

Papers relating to foreign affairs, accompanying the annual message of the President to the first session thirty-ninth Congress. 58468

Papers relating to foreign affairs, accompanying the annual message of the President to the second session, fortieth Congress. (58469)

Papers relating to foreign affairs accompanying the annual message of the President to the second session thirty-eighth Congress. 20214

Papers relating to foreign affairs, . . . communicated to Congress, December 1, 1862. 58467

Papers relating to foreign affairs, . . . communicated to Congress, December, 1864. 58467

Papers relating to foreign affairs, . . . communicated to Congress, December, 1863. 58467

Papers relating to free labour and the slave-trade. 58470

Papers relating to French affairs. 2025, 58478

Papers relating to Pemaquid and parts adjacent. 33146

Papers relating to the action between His Majesty's Sloop. 58471

Papers relating to the Arctic Relief Expedition. 25633

Papers relating to the blockade of the ports. 5943, 55532

Papers . . . relating to the British colonies in the West Indies. 36648

Papers relating to the canal frauds in New-York. 53853

Papers relaging to the coal mines of this state. 45764

Papers relating to the colonization experiment. 58472

Papers relating to the condemnation of the British barque "Springbok." 58473, note after 89831

Papers relating to the construction and first occupancy of Fort Dummer. 85217

Papers relating to the disturbances in Jamaica. 35645

Papers relating to the early history of Maryland. 92793

Papers relating to the Falkland Islands. 23733

Papers relating to the first settlement of New York by the Dutch. 102039

Papers relating to the Garrison mob. 26709, 42804

Papers relating to the great industrial exhibition. 73841

Para administrar el viatico. 96268-96269

Para cortar los peligros de nuestra actual division ¿Que haremos? 58504

Para e Amazonas pelo encarregado dos trabalhos ethnographicos. 88722

Para estos lances sirve la imprenta. 94597

Para eternizar su gloria. 98151

Para la historia. 27816

Para la historia de la America del Sur. 93399

Para la historia: efemerides sangrientas de la dictatura de J. Manuel Rosas. 73218

Para den de comer a los mvchachos los dvenos. 98800

Para qve el Corregidor de [blank] execvte enlas personas. 98800

Para qve el Corregidor y los demas donde sveren. 98800

Para qve en cada pueblo que uviere de duzientos Indios. 98798

Para que haca lista y padron de los pueblos. 98800

Para qve los Indios del distrito de [blank] qve tvvieren censos. 98799

Para qve los Indios no sean oprimidos ni detenidos. 98800

Para qve no de tengan los Indios los dvenos de Charcaras. 98800

Para qve no se repartan Indios para vinas ni Oliuares. 98800

Para qve se apremien. 98800

Para qve se gvarden. 98800

¿Para que sirven los Frayles en el mundo? Sermon panegirico que el dia 25 de Setiembre de 1814 dixo. 35050

Para que sirven los Frayles en el mundo? Sermon panegyrico con motivo de la celebracion. 57658

Parable of the merchant-man seeking goodly pearls. 42011

Parable of the ten virgins opened & applied. 80212-(80213)

Parable of the ten virgins, opened and applied. 80214-(80215)

Paracer sobre la observacia de el §. primero. 97707

Parada, Antonio. 58505

Parada, Vicente Gomez. see Gomez Parada, Vicente.

Parades, Jose Gregorio. ed. (41081), 41111

Parades, Robert, Comte de. (58506)

Paradigma apologetico arte. 94355

Paradine, A. Linstant. see Linstant-Paradine, A.

Paradis, Jean Michel de Venture de. see Venture de Paradis, Jean Michel de, 1739-1799.

Paradise lost. 49143

Paradise of fools. 55392

Paradise promised. (31895), 103350

Paradisisches Wunder-Spiel. (58507)

Paradol, L. A. Prevost. see Prevost-Paradol, L. A.

Paradox solved. (58508)

Paradys, Nicolai. 58509, 98992

Paraenetick or humble addresse to the Parliament and Assembly. 58510, 104342

Paraenetick to the five apologists. note before 17046, 17046, 2d note after 103852

Parafrasis del latigazo constitucional. 98615

Paragraphs on banks. 6237, 58511

Paragraphs on the subject of judicial reform in Maryland. 34422, 65471

Paraguai Jesuitique. 7458

Paraguay. 2533, 2539, 87189

Paraguay. Ministerio de Relaciones Esteriores. (58515)

Paraguay (Diocese) Bishop (Cardenas) 10803-10807, (21763) see also Cardenas, Bernardino de, Bp.

Paraguay (Province) Gobernador, 1721-1725 (Antequera Enriquez y Castro) 58393 see also Antequera Enriquez y Castro, Jose de.

Paraguay. A concise history of its rise, and progress. 58521

Paraguay and the alliance against the tyrant. 58522

Paraguay and the war in La Plata. 58523

Paraguay, Brazil, and the Plate. 44362

Paraguay et les republiques de la Plata. 58161

Paraguay, in zijnen vroegeren en tegenwoordigen Toestand. (58524)

Paraguay. La dynastie des Lopez avant et pendant la guerre actuelle. 39982

Paraguay moderne. 64703

Paraguay, par Ch. Quentin. 67093

Paraguay renversee. (51427), (58535), (63900)

Paraguay, son passe, son present et son avenir. 58525

Paraguayan question. (58526)

Paraguayo independiente. 58527

Parahyba (Brazilian Province) Laws, statutes, etc. 88778

Paralelo entre la isla de Cuba y algunas colonias Inglesas. 74772

Paralelo y proyecto de penitenciarias. 31724

Paralipomena Americae. (8784)

Parallel between intemperance and the slave trade. 33794

Parallel between the fiath and doctrine of the present Quakers. 58539

Parallel drawn between the administration in the four last years. 58540

Parallel history. 65574

Parallel of military errors. 67022

Parallela geographiae vetris et novae. (7934)

Parallele de ces monuments avec ceux de l'Egypte. 23795, 40038

Parallele des constitutions d'Angleterre, des Etats-Unis et de Geneve. 19758

Parallele entre les colonies Francaises et les colonies Angliases. (36419)

Paralleles historiques. 17207

Paramaribo, Dutch Guiana. Litterlievend Genootschap "Oefening Kweekt Kennis." see Litterlievend Genootschap "Oefening Kweekt Kennis," Paramaribo.

Paramaribo, Dutch Guiana. Maison d'Education ou Seminaire d'Enfants a la Savane des Juifs. see Maison d'Education ou Seminaire d'Enfans a la Savane des Juifs, Paramaribo.

Paramaribo, Dutch Guiana. Newe-Sjalom te Serinam. 93860

Paramaribo, Dutch Guiana. Ningre-Gemeente. 58542

Paramaribo, Dutch Guiana. Surinaamsche Koloniale Bibliotheek. (58541), 93871

Paramaribo, Dutch Guiana. Synagogue der Portugeesche Joodsche Gemeente. 93876

Paramaribo. 11519

Paramount claims of the Gospel. 64209

Paramus, N. J. Church. 58543

Parana, Argentina (Diocese) Bishop [ca. 1867] defendant 41983

Parana; with incidents of the Paraguayan War. 34090

Paranagua, Joao Lustosa da Cunha. see Cunha Paranagua, Joao Lustosa da.

Paranamartagh. pseud. Laactshures on various subjects. 38391

Paris. Bibliotheque Nationale. Department des Manuscrits. 56644
Paris. Bibliotheque Royale. see Paris. Bibliotheque Nationale.
Paris. Bibliotheque Saint-Genevieve. 56644
Paris. Bureau de Commerce. 20426
Paris. Comite Colonial de Saint Domingue, 1789. see Comite Colonial de Saint Domingue, Paris, 1789.
Paris. Commission de Geographie Commerciale. 85803
Paris. Commissioners Under the Convention of April 1803 with France. see U. S. Commissioners Under the Convention of April 1803 with France, Paris.
Paris. Committee of Peace. Member. pseud. Letter to the American Peace Society. see Gibbes, George M.
Paris. Compagnie de Colons de Saint Domingue. see Compagnie de Colons de Saint Domingue, Paris.
Paris, Compagnie de New York. see Company of New York.
Paris. Compagnie du Scioto. see Compagnie du Scioto, Paris.
Paris. Company of New York. see Company of New York.
Paris. Concours General des Lycees et Collages de Paris et de Versailles, 1854. see Concours General des Lycees et Colleges de Paris et de Versailles, 1854.
Paris. Congress, 1856. see Congress of Paris, 1856.
Paris. Council of Prizes. see France. Conseil des Prises, Paris.
Paris. Cour d'Assises. 73220
Paris. Dinner Given by the Americans in Paris, to Professor S. F. B. Morse, 1858. see Dinner Given by the Americans in Paris, to Professor S. F. B. Morse, Paris, 1858.
Paris. Exposition Universelle, 1855. Section Mexicaine. 48325
Paris. Exposition Universelle, 1867. (23466), 25890, 56763
Paris. Exposition Universelle, 1867. Argentina Division. 15427
Paris. Exposition Universelle, 1867. Comite des Poids et Measures et des Monnaies. (73953)
Paris. Exposition Universelle, 1867. Costa Rica Department. 17018
Paris. Exposition Universelle, 1867. Ecuador Division. 70049
Paris. Exposition Universelle, 1867. New York State Commissioner. see New York (State) Commissioner to the Paris Exposition of 1867.
Paris. Exposition Universelle, 1867. Nova Scotia Department. 56127
Paris. Exposition Universelle, 1867. Trinidad Division. 17170
Paris. Exposition Universelle, 1867. United States Commission. see U. S. Commission to the Paris Exposition, 1867.
Paris. Exposition Universelle, 1867. United States Division. see U. S. Commission to the Paris Exposition, 1867.
Paris. Institut des Archives Historiques. (39344)
Paris. Institut Historique. see Institut Historique, Paris.
Paris. Institut National des Sciences et Arts. 8831, (47542), 94260
Paris. Institut Royal. Academie des Sciences. see Academie des Sciences, Paris.

Paris. International Antislavery Conference, 1867. see International Antislavery Conference, Paris, 1867.
Prais. International Congress Called in 1879 to Examine the Plans for Constructing an Inter-oceanic Canal Between the Atlantic and Pacific. see Interoceanic Canal Convention, Paris, 1879.
Paris. Interoceanic Canal Convention, 1879. see Interoceanic Canal Convention, Paris, 1879.
Paris. Libreria Hispano-Americana. see Libreria Hispano-Americana, Paris.
Paris. Linnaean Society. see Societe Linneenne de Paris.
Paris. Medical Faculty. see Paris. Universite. Faculte de Medecine.
Paris. Meeting of the Citizens of the United States, 1843. 34931, 65799 see also American Citizens at Paris.
Paris. Museum d'Histoire Naturelle. 1583, 78689
Paris. New York Company. see Company of New York.
Paris. Parlement. see France. Parlement (Paris)
Paris. Proprietaires de Saint-Domingue. see Proprietaires de Saint-Domingue, Residans a Paris.
Paris. Quelques Ouvriers et Ouvrieres. petitioners 36420
Paris. Royal Academy. see Academie des Sciences, Paris.
Paris. Royal Academy of Medicine. see Academie of Medecine, Paris.
Paris. Seminaire des Missions Etrangeres. see Seminaire des Missions Etrangeres, Paris.
Paris. Societe Correspondante des Colons Francais. see Societe Correspondante des Colons Francais, Paris.
Paris. Societe d'Anthropologie. see Societe d'Anthropologie, Paris.
Paris. Societe de Geographie. see Societe de Geographie, Paris.
Paris. Societe de la Morale Chretienne. see Societe de la Morale Chretienne, Paris.
Paris. Societe de l'Amerique Meridionale. see Societe de l'Amerique Meridionale, Paris.
Paris. Societe de l'Histoire du Protestantisme Francais. see Societe de l'Histoire du Protestantisme Francais, Paris.
Paris. Societe des Americainistes. see Societe des Americainistes de Paris.
Paris. Societe des Amis des Noirs. see Societe des Amis des Noirs, Paris.
Paris. Societe d'Ethnographie. see Societe d'Ethnographie, Paris.
Paris. Societe d'Ethnographie Americaine et Orientale. see Societe d'Ethnographie Americaine et Orientale, Paris.
Paris. Societe Entolologique de France. see Societe Entomologique de France, Paris.
Paris. Societe Ethnologique. see Societe Ethnologique, Paris.
Paris. Societe Francaise pour l'Abolition de l'Esclavage. see Societe Francaise pour l'Abolition de l'Esclavage, Paris.
Paris. Societe Linneenne. see Societe Linneenne de Paris.
Paris. Societe Montyon et Franklin. see Societe Montyon et Franklin, Paris.
Paris. Societe Orientale. see Societe Orientale, Paris.

Paris. Societe Philologique. see Societe
Philologique, Paris.
Paris. Societe Philomatique. see Societe
Philomatique, Paris.
Paris. Societe pour la Propagation des Con-
naissances Scientifiques et Industrielles.
see Societe pour la Propagation des
Connaissances Scientifiques et Indus-
trielles, Paris.
Paris. Societe Royale de Geographie. see
Societe Royale de Geographie, Paris.
Paris. Societe Royale de Medecine. see
Academie de Medecine, Paris.
Paris. Tribunal de Commerce. 81662
Paris. Universal Exposition, 1855. see Paris.
Exposition Universelle, 1855.
Paris. Universal Exposition, 1867. see Paris.
Exposition Universelle, 1867.
Paris. Universite. Faculte de Medecine.
105993
Paris. Universite. Faculte de Theologie.
(68075), 68100
Paris. Washington Birthday Celebration, 1866.
(66815)
Paris (Archdiocese) Archbishop [ca. 1796]
11502
Paris en Amerique. 38439
Paris in America. 38440
Paris in Hayti. (17987)
Paris, la 10 Fructidor and 6 de la republique
Francaise. 6322
Paris, le 1ᵉʳ Thermidor, an 6. 87122
Paris papers. 19066
Paris, Personen in. pseud. see Personen
in Paris. pseud.
Paris, Personnes Residantes a. pseud. see
Personnes Residentes a Paris. pseud.
Paris, Persons in. pseud. see Persons in
Paris. pseud.
Paris Societe des Amis des Noirs. see
Societe des Amis des Noirs, Paris.
Paris Universal Exhibition of 1867. An address.
17229
Paris Universal Exhibition of 1867. Remarks.
17229
Paris Universal Exposition. 1867. Reports of
the United States Commissioners. 23534
Paris Universal Exposition, 1867. Reports of
the United States Commissioners. General
survey. (58595)
Paris Universal Exposition, 1867. Reports of
the United States Commissioners. Report
on cereals. 73959
Paris Universal Exposition, 1867. Reports of
the United States Commissioners. Report
on the fine arts. 40200
Paris Universal Exposition, 1867. Reports of
the United States Commissioners. . .
upon wool and manufactures of wool.
(51235)
Pariset, Nicholas. 58596
Parish, Ariel. 58597
Parish, Daniel. appellant 58611
Parish, Elijah. 18630, 18633, (43066), 50930-
50933, 58598-58609, 89805, note after
99814, 103208, 1st note after 103214,
note after 103219
Parish, Henry. 58610-58611
Parish, Sir Woodbine. 58612-58614
Parish and other pencellings. 51539
Parish annals. 1673
Parish directory of St. Paul's Church. 89851
Parish in affliction. 73884
Parish lectures on the prayer book. 85462
Parish memories of forty years. 13529

Parish of the Advent, Boston. see Boston.
Church of the Advent.
Parish orphan. (39731)
Parish sketch book. (80152)
Parish statistics of Christ Church, Elizabeth,
N. H. 22193, 32397`
Parish statistics [of Christ Church, New Haven
Conn.] (7783)
Parish statistics of the Church of the Ascension
New York. 4271-(4272), 56024
Parish statistics of the Protestant Episcopal
Mission Church of the Evangelists, South-
wark. 88603
Parish-the pulpit. 9058
Parish will case. 58611
Parish will case. Argument of John K. Porter.
58611
Parish will case before the Surrogate of the
City of New York. 58611
Parish will case, in the Court of Appeals.
Statement of facts. 58611
Parish will case, in the Court of Appeals. The
opinion of the court. 58611
Parish will case in the Court of Appeals. The
statement of facts. 58611
Parishioner. pseud. Half-way covenant. see
Bellamy, Joseph.
Parishioner. pseud. Second letter to J.
Bellamy. 78734
Parisian pastor's glance at America. 28276
Parisian sights and French principles. (35798)
Parismas, Thomas. 58615
Parisot, J. T. tr. 18642, 35292, note after
105597
Parisot, Pierre. (55451)
Park, Benjamin. 84162
Park, Edwards Amasa. 21982, 32955, (32730),
42045, 58616-58625, (79299, 92272, 93213)
Park, Harrison G. 58626
Park, John. 6506, 45593, 58627
Park, John Cochran. (58628)-(58630)
Park, John W. 58631
Park, Joseph. 58632
Park, Mungo, 1771-1806. (59572), 62957
Park, Roswell. (58633)-(58634)
Park, Samuel. 58635-58636
Park, T. W. 90320
Park, Thomas, 1759-1834. 30394, 71896, 1st
note after 97255
Park, Thomas, 1766-1844. (58637)
Park and its vicinity, in the city of New York.
18940
Park Brothers & Co. firm petitioners 91101
Park Presbyterian Church, Brooklyn. see
Brooklyn. Park Presbyterian Church.
Park Street Church, Boston. see Boston.
Park Street Church.
Park-Street pulpit; sermons. 51549
Park Theater, New York. see New York (City)
Park Theater.
Parke, Benjamin. 58638, 60065
Parke, John. supposed author 7184, 58640
Parke, John. USA 101739-101740
Parke, John, 1754-1789. 33005, 100545
Parke, John G. 58641, 69900, 69946
Parke, Jonathan G. see Parke, John G.
Parke, N. G. (58642)
Parke, R. tr. 27783
Parker, Maj. pseud. see Hines, David
Theodore.
Parker, Mr. supposed author 1968
Parker, ----------, fl. 1845. (58646)
Parker, ----------, fl. 1858. 12813 see also
U. S. Legation. China.
Parker, ----------, fl. 1863. 2670

Parker, A. A. 58643
Parker, A. X. 58648
Parker, Adaline Rise. (58644)
Parker, Addison. 58645
Parker, Alexander. 66926
Parker, Amasa J. 53952, (58647)
Parker, Benjamin. 58649
Parker, Benjamin. supposed author 2604, 99795
Parker, C. C. 58650
Parker, Charles H. 101660
Parker, Cortlandt. 25831, (58651)
Parker, D. G. 58658
Parker, Daniel, 1669?-1728. 58652
Parker, Daniel, 1782-1846. 58654-58646
Parker, Daniel, fl. 1847. (58653)
Parker, David. (58657)
Parker, Edward G. 58659-58660
Parker, Edward H. ed. 52875, 58661
Parker, Edward Latwycke. 58662-58663
Parker, Edward P. ed. 58663
Parker, Ely S. 58664
Parker, F. E. ed. 89699
Parker, Foxhall A. 58665
Parker, Francis. 58666
Parker, Francis J. (58667)
Parker, Freeman. 58668
Parker, G. engr. 85466, 89663
Parker, G. G. 58670
Parker, George. 58669
Parker, Helen F. 58671-58672
Parker, Henry. 103575
Parker, Henry E. 58673
Parker, Henry G. 58674
Parker, Henry M. 88255
Parker, Henry T. 88255
Parker, Henry W. 58676-58677
Parker, Isaac. (58678)-58681, 96820, 101803
Parker, J. M. 76092
Parker, Mrs. J. M. 58683
Parker, James, 1714?-1770. (7884), (14394)-
    14395, 15215, 58682, 83980, 84555,
    84576, 84624, 84665, 84672, 84676,
    84678C, 85936, 100788, 103129, 106080
Parker, James W., b. 1797. 58685
Parker, James W., fl. 1839. 58684
Parker, Jeroboam. 58686, 103771
Parker, Jesse. 58687
Parker, Joel, 1795-1875. (45748), 58688-
    (58703)
Parker, Joel, 1795-1875. petitioner (58703)
Parker, Joel, 1795-1875. reporter 16784,
    96854
Parker, Joel, 1799-1873. 58704-58706, 65203,
    (72214), 84414
Parker, Joel, 1816-1888. 58707
Parker, John. petitioner 58708
Parker, John A. (58709)
Parker, John L. 58710
Parker, John R. 58711
Parker, Joseph. 58713
Parker, Joseph. defendant (58712)
Parker, Leonard M. 58714
Parker, Mary Ann. 58715, 3d note after 100816
Parker, Moses. defendant 96945
Parker, Nathan. 58716-58718, 101388
Parker, Nathan H. 58719-58725
Parker, R. E. 104878
Parker, Richard Green. (58727)-58728, 4th
    note after 96964
Parker, S. D. 95602, 96850
Parker, S. H. 10011, 58733 see also Union
    League of America. California. Grand
    President.
Parker, S. P. 58734-58735
Parker, S. W. 58736

Parker, Samuel, Bp., 1744-1804. 58732
Parker, Samuel, 1779-1866. 58375, 58729-
    (58730)
Parker, Samuel, fl. 1863. 58731
Parker, Samuel D. 85430
Parker, Theodore. 2290, 6505, 9404, 23684,
    36924, 47115, 58737-58749, 58751-58761,
    58763, 58765-note after (58767), (70289)-
    70291, 76992, 87341, note before 90886,
    note after 97137
Parker, Theodore. supposed author 30833
Parker, Theodore. defendant (58767)
Parker, Theodore. mediumistic author 58750
Parker, Thomas. reporter 37436
Parker, Thomas, 1595-1677. 56218, 58769-
    (58771), (69679), 74624, 91382-91383
Parker, Thomas, 1753-1820. supposed author
    5710, 43404
Parker, Thomas, 1783-1860. 58772
Parker, Thomas H. 58773
Parker, Thomas J. 58774
Parker, W. B. 44513, 58775
Parker, Willard. 84441, 84445, 84446
Parker, William, d. 1618. 11030, 27799
Parker, William H. 58776-58777
Parkes, Joseph. 58778
Parkhurst, Henry M. reporter 1710, 87508
Parkhurst, J. L. ed. 94559
Parkhurst, Jabez. (58780)
Parkhurst, John G. ed. 56777
Parkhurst, Miles. 58782
Parkhurst, J. W. 58781
Parkins, Joseph Wilfred. defendant 58783,
    2d note after 97255
Parkinson, Richard. 58784-58786
Parkinson, Sydney. 31389, (58787)-58789
Parkinson, William. 58790-(58793), (58796)
Parkinson, William. defendant 58794-58796,
    105177
Parkman, Charles McDonogh. 58797, 1st note
    after 90684
Parkman, Ebenezer. 13205, 58798, 106289
Parkman, Francis, 1788-1852. 58799-58800
Parkman, Francis, 1823-1893. 50876, 58801-
    58803, 84617, 84619, 90002
Parkman, George. 58804
Parkman, John. 58805
Parkman, Samuel. ed. (52738)
Parks, Gorham, 1794-1877. (58806)
Parks, L. D. (58807), 87810
Parks, M. P. (58808)
Parks, Robert. 59174
Parks, Stephen. ed. 58809, note after 97074
Parks, William. ed. 103529, 103569
Parks and pleasure grounds. (82391)
Parks of Colorado. (14748)
Parlamentar. 56373
Parlement de Paris etabli au Scioto. 58810
Parley, Neighbor. pseud. Five letters. see
    Goodrich, Samuel Griswold, 1793-1860.
Parley, Peter. pseud. Five letters to my
    neighbor Smith. see Goodrich, Samuel
    Griswold, 1793-1850.
Parley, Peter. pseud. Life of C. Columbus.
    27923, 41026
Parley, Peter. pseud. Life of George Wash-
    ington. 101844
Parley, Peter. pseud. Lives of Franklin and
    Washington. 101848
Parley, Peter. pseud. Parley's cabinet
    library. see Goodrich, Samuel Griswold,
    1793-1850.
Parley, Peter. pseud. Peter Parley's book of
    the United States. see Goodrich, Samuel
    Griswold, 1793-1850.

Parley, Peter. pseud. Peter Parley's Canada. note after 61176

Parley, Peter. pseud. Peter Parley's common school history. see Goodrich, Samuel Griswold, 1793-1850.

Parley, Peter. pseud. Peter Parley's tales about America. see Goodrich, Samuel Griswold, 1793-1850.

Parley, Peter. pseud. Peter Parley's tales about animals. see Goodrich, Samuel Griswold, 1793-1850.

Parley, Peter. pseud. Peter Parley's tales about New York. see Goodrich, Samuel Griswold, 1793-1850.

Parlet, Peter. pseud. Peter Parley's tales. Lives of Franklin & Washington. 101848

Parley, Peter. pseud. Peter Parley's universal history. see Goodrich, Samuel Griswold, 1793-1850.

Parley, Peter. pseud. Popular biography. see Goodrich, Samuel Griswold, 1793-1850.

Parley, Peter. pseud. Tales about Canada. see Clark, Samuel, fl. 1839.

Parley, Peter. pseud. Tales about the United States of America. see Goodrich, Samuel Griswold, 1793-1850.

Parley, Peter. pseud. Tales of Peter Parley, about America. see Goodrich, Samuel Griswold, 1793-1850.

Parley's cabinet library for schools and families. 27913

Parley's magazine. 48028

Parley's Washington. 101844

Parliamentary accounts and papers. 82902-82905

Parliamentary chornicle. 79092

Parliamentary debates, from the year 1803. 30245, 30246

Parliamentary debates in England. 58811

Parliamentary debates on the subject of the confederation. 58812

Parliamentary debates relative to the conduct of Gen. Sir William Howe. (33343)

Parliamentary debates. Session, 1839. 9223

Parliamentary history. (11601), 2d note after 105598-9 [sic]

Parliamentary history of England, from the earliest period to the year 1803. 30245

Parliamentary history of England, from the Norman conquest in 1066. (58813)

Parliamentary or constitutional history of England. 58814

Parliamentary paper. 12796

Parliamentary papers; consisting of a complete collection. (58815)

Parliamentary papers for 1838. 97441

Parliamentary papers, N. America, no. 9. (12493)

Parliamentary papers no. 12, 1864. 16886, (37131)

Parliamentary papers relating to the West India Colonies. 58816

Parliamentary principles in their application. 85132

Parliamentary register. 32112, (58817)

Parliamentary report from the Select Committee on Sugar and Coffee Planting. 58818

Parliamentary reporter. 65635

Parliamentary reports of the correspondence. 58819

Parliamentary reports on the state of the colonies, for 1860. 58820

Parliamentary representation. 106079

Parliamentary representation acts. 10496

Parliamentary rules. 84472

Parliamentary sketches and water statistics. (11905)

Parliamente; holden to ye seniore menne yn Yale Schoole. 105937

Parlor companion. 54864

Parlour library, v. 84. 92496

Parlour song book. 58821

Parmelee, Ashbel. 58822

Parmelee Gold Company. see Smith & Parmelee Gold Company.

Parmenter, Frederick A. 58823

Parmenter, William, 1789-1866. 58824

Parmenter & Van Antwerp. firm publishers (33502)

Parmentier, Antoine Augustin, 1737-1813. 58826, 86653

Parmentier, Jan. 58825

Parmly, Eleazar. (58827)

Parnach, Elizaphan of. pseud. Liberty and property vindicated. see Church, Benjamin, 1734-1776.

Parnambuco. see Pernambuco (Brazilian State)

Parnaso Brasileiro, ou colleccao das melhores poesias dos poetas do Brasil. 58828, 99734

Parnaso Brasileiro, ou colleccao de poesias dos melhores poetas Brasileiros. 60883

Parnaso del Real Colegio de San Martin. 44423, (58829), 61151, (76155)

Parnaso del Real Collegio de S. Marcos. 44423, (58829), 61151, (76155)

Parnaso Maranhese. 58830

Parnaso Peruano. 58831

Parnassian pilgrim. 38655

Parnassian sprigs. 12285

Parnassian wild flowers. 79988

Parnassian shop. 92282

Parnassus. 41167, note before 94542

Parnassus in Philadelphia. 62915

Parnassus in pillory. 21156

Parnassus, the outlaw's bride [etc.], and other poems. (35304)

Parochial and township subdivisions of Lower Canada. 10638, 10611

Parochial congregations in England. 24401

Parochial Schoolmasters in Scotland. see Established or Parochial Schoolmasters in Scotland.

Parodie de la tragedia d'Alzire. 100727

Parody on some of the most striking passages. 67181, 79401

Paroisse du Fond-Des-Negres, Haiti. see Santo Domingo (French Colony) Assemble Provinciale, St. Marc.

Parola. 67909

Parole and documentary evidence delivered. 24362

Parole che usano gli habitatori dell' isola di Tidore. 67730

Parole de paix. (26729)

Parole del gigante. 67730

Parona, Cesare. 14675

Paroz, J. tr. 38240

Parquin, ------. 58832

Parr, John. (34763), 58833-(58834), 99410-99411, 2d note after 99795

Parra, Antonio. 58835-58836

Parra, Bartholome Phelipe Itta y. see Yta y Parra, Bartolome Felipe de.

Parra, Caracciolo. ed. 106245

Parra, Francisco de la. (58837)

Parra, Isaac de la. (40086)-40088, (51894), 3d, 6th-7th notes after 93855

Parra, Jacinto de. tr. 73179

Parra, Jacinto de la. 38954, 58838-58839

Particulars of the duel fought at Hoboken.
29990
Particulars of the emigrant's situation in
settling. (41021)
Particulars of the enquiry into Mr. Benjamin
Wolley's conduct. 58938, note after 105195
Particulars of the funeral honours to the
memory of General La Fayette. 38583
Particulars of the late duel. 9430
Particulars of the late horrid murder, of the
accomplished—but unfortunate Miss Maria
Pattan. 89626
Particulars of the late horrid murder of the
accomplished but unfortunate Miss Maria
Patten. (59119)
Particulars of the late melancholy and shocking
tragedy. (58939)
Particulars of the life of Thomas H. Daniels.
18499
Particulars of the progress made by the
Portuguese. 6209
Particulars of the tragical death of Mrs. Ann
Taylor. 80557
Particulars of the voyage of Sir Thomas Button.
5195, 61246
Particulars respecting the missions of the
United Brethren. 97857
Particulars respecting the schools for Negro
children, &c., under the direction of the
Moravian missionaries, in the West Indies.
No. V. 58940
Particulars respecting the schools for Negro
children, &c. under the direction of the
Moravian missionaries in the West Indies.
[No. VI.] 97858
Particulars respecting the schools for Negro
children . . . under the direction of the
Moravian missionaries in the West Indies.
102858
Particulas de la lengua Guarani. 74033
Partido conservador en Mexico. 58941
Partie 2^e. contenant la discussion et le detail.
(38696), 47528
Partie Francoise de Saint-Domingue. see
Santo Domingo (French Colony)
Partie historique. 57457, 60998
Partie linguistique par M. Gallatin. 69656
Partie Ire. contenant l'histoire de l'administra-
tion. (38696), 47528
Parties & partisans. 16362
Parties and politics. 51454
Parties and slavery, 1850-1859. 84340
Parties and their principles. (32591)
Parties in Massachusetts. (58942)
Parties Interested in the American vessels the
Hart, the Two-Friends, the Alpha and
Minerva. respondents 93383, 95984
Parties of the day. 79542
Parties Who Have Been Confined Therein.
pseud. Full sketches of other prisons.
(37300)
Parting address, as delivered in the Bowery
Theatre. 105588, 105595
Parting ode. By Albert Bigelow. 89672
Parting of the three Indians. 103235
Parting sermon . . . Winsted, Conn. (9100)
Parting word. (29837)
Parting words on the rejected militia bill.
42883
Partington, Ruth. pseud. Knitting-work. see
Shillaber, Benjamin Penhallow, 1814-1890.
Partingtonian patchwork. 80479
Partis Americae Septentrionalis. 96193
Partisan. 81245, (81279)
Partisan. A romance of the revolution. 81244
Partisan: a tale of the revolution. 81243

Partisan leader. 97374
Partisan leader; a tale of the future. 97374
Partisan life with Col. John S. Mosby. 78309
Partitio magnitvdinis vniversi orbis. 94185
Partnership. (27643), 2d note after 97091
Parton, James. 22513, 58943-58958
Parton, Sarah Payson Willis. 58959-58961
Partridge, Alden. 36701, (56499), 58962-note
after (58963)
Partridge, Alfred. (58964)
Partridge, Copernicus. 55542
Partridge, J. Arthur. 58967-(58969)
Partridge, John. 58965-58966
Partridge (Charles) firm publishers 89531
Partridge & Brittan. firm publishers 80106,
94608
Partridge & Oakey. firm publishers 92487
Partridge and Brittan's spiritual library.
94608
Partridge and Oakey's shilling edition. 92487
Party in power, and the new constitution.
58970
Party leaders. 2899
Party of Men, called Quakers at Philadelphia.
see Friends, Society of. Philadelphia
Monthly Meeting.
"Party of progress." (62857)
Party of the future. By A. J. H. 29996
" Party of the future," &c. &c. 96396
Party satire satirized, a poem. 58971
Party spirit. 105647
Party spirit exposed. 58972
Party-tyranny: or, an occaional bill in miniature.
19288, 87911
Parvin, R. J. 58973
Parvin, Theodore S. 34973, 58974-58975
Parvin, Theophilus. 58976
Parvum theatrum. 73000
Parvvm theatrvm vrbivm sive vrbivm praecip-
varvm totivs orbis. 73000
Parys in Amerika. 38441
Pas, C. de. illus. 78379
Pas, C. de. tr. 44268
Pasaeus, Simon. cartographer 82819
Pascal, Cesar. 58978-58979
Pascal Creuze, Michel. see Creuze, Michel
Pascal.
Pascalis-Ouviere, Felix. 47327, (57968),
58980-(58982), 90748
Pascentius. 46448
Paschal, ------- Creuze. see Creuze, Michel
Pascal.
Paschal, George W. (12457), (58984)-58985,
90114 see also U. S. Commissioners
to the Cherokee Indians.
Paschall, Edwin. (58986)
Paschall, Robert S. 50869
Paschall, Thomas. 8956-8957
Paschoud, -------. (58987)
Pascua, ------- Flores de. see Flores de
Pascua, --------.
Pascual, A. D. de. 58988
Pascual, Juan Vasco y. see Vasco y Pascual,
Juan.
Pascuas a un militar. 97048
Pascuas del Payo del Rosario. 99711
Paseo pintoresco por la Isla de Cuba. 17795
Pasevinius, Antonius. see Possevinus,
Antonius.
Pash, Mohammed. 58990
Pasha papers. 58990
Paskel, Thomas. see Paskell, Thomas.
Paskell, Thomas. 58991, 60445
Pasley, C. W. (58992)
Paso, Juan Jose. 44286, note after 95211
Pasqual. pseud. see V., A., el Mexicano.
pseud.

Pasqual, Antonio Raymundo. 58993

Pasquier, H. du. see Du Pasquier, H.

Pasquin. pseud. Pasquin and Marforie on
the peace. 58994

Pasquin, Anthony. pseud. Dirge. see
Williams, John, 1761-1818.

Pasquin, Anthony. pseud. Hamiltoniad. see
Williams, John, 1761-1818.

Pasquin and Marforie on the peace. 58994

Pasquin Shaveblock. pseud. see Shaveblock,
Pasquin. pseud.

Pasquino. pseud. American cyclops. see
McLaughlin, J. Fairfax.

Pass, Simon. illus. and engr. 67560, 82823-
82824, 82827-82828

Pass, William. engr. 82823-82828, 82830,
82857

Passa tiempo. (70786)

Passaeus, Crispiano. 58995-58996

Passage across the Cordillera of the Andes.
7388

Passage de la Cordillere des Andes. 58997

Passage de l'isthme de Panama. 74988, note
after 100812

Passage extracted from the Publick news
letter. 46723, 1st note after 65324

Passage in the opinion of Judge Daniel. 105215

Passage of the isthmus. 11060

Passage of the Pique across the Atlantic.
(2517)

Passage of the President's message. 99315,
note after 102768

Passages from Mr. Stoughton's election sermon.
65607, 92351

Passages from the American note-books.
30993

Passages from the diary of Christopher
Marshall. 44767

Passages from the English note-books of
Nathaniel Hawthorne. 30993

Passages from the history of the United States.
(40228)

Passages from the remembrance of Christopher
Marshall. 44768

Passages in an eventful life. 50304

Passages in the life and ministry of Elbert
Osborn. 57748

Passages in the life of Rev. John Hancock.
91997

Passages in the political history of the United
States. 25329

Passaic, a group of poems touching that river.
101342

Passavant, T. (49963), 50372

Passe de la Cumbre entre Mendoza et Santa-
Rosa. 58997

Passee et present. (69592)

Passenger from Lynn. pseud. Correct poetical
account. 42843, 70208

Passenger in the Hector. pseud. Life and
adventures of Peter Wilkins. see Paltock,
Samuel. supposed author

Passenger of the Waring and an eye witness
to the bloody scenes. pseud. Rebel
pirate's fatal prize. 68320

Passengers of the May Flower in 1620. 80782

Passeo, Guilh. engr. see Pass, William.
engr.

Passerini, Carol, 1793-1858. (59000)

Passi, Carlo. tr. 1559, 2d note after 45010

Passing bell. 59001

Passio gloriosi martyris beati partis fratris
Andree de Spoleto. (44931), 2d note after
98344

Passion and reality. 91291

Passion au Mexique. 5138

Passion flowers. 33318

Passion y trivmpho de Christo. 60856

Passive obedience considered. (28823)

Passy, -------. 33618

Past: a fragment. 4756

Past and future. 85460

Past and present—freedom national. 59002,
93657

Past and present of the United States. (3332)

Past and present, or a description of persons
and events. 11076, note before 89147

Past and present state of the tea trade. 44916

Past and the future. 103465

Past and the future of Nova Scotia. 29678

Past and the present. A discourse, delivered
before the Erosophic Society of the University of Alabama. 64202

Past and the present. A . . . sermon, . . .
before the Oneida and Wyoming Conferences. 59472

Past and the present of St. Andrew's. 91578

Past and the present. Semi-centennial address.
73960

Past dispensations of providence called to
mind. 7662, 104270

Past master. pseud. comp. Melodies for
the craft. 47466

Past mercies; present gratitude; future duty.
83644

Past meridian. 80937

Past of Ypsilanti. (25228)

Past, present and future of Atlantic Ocean
steam navigation. 84419

Past, present and future of Boston. 64653

Past, present and future of greenbacks. (59003)

Past, . . . present, and . . . future of the
medical profession. 49725

Past, present and future of the southern confederacy. 5366

Past, present, and future of the United States.
2009

Past, present, and future state of America.
104733

Past, the present and the future. By H. C.
Carey. (10834)

Past, the present, and the future. [By J.
Gales.] 26369

Past, the present and the future of our country.
6831, 59004

Past, the present and the future of the Pacific.
17399

Pasteur, J. D. 3873, 11190, (17258), 50986,
59005

Pastime, Peregrine. pseud. see Peregrine
Pastime. pseud.

Pastime. (59006), 97799

Pasto, Colombia (Province) Governor, 1843.
(59007)

Pastor. pseud. Annals of the church in
Brimfield. see Morse, Jason.

Pastor. pseud. Five years of ministerial
life. see Morris, Edward D.

Pastor. pseud. Serious questions for the
new year. see Sargent, John T.

Pastor, Antonio. 59008

Pastor, Tony. see Pastor, Antonio.

Pastor; a poem. 59010

Pastor and Church at West-Stafford. see
West Stafford, Conn. Second Church.

Pastor and Church, West Brookfield. see
West Brookfield, Mass. Church. and
West Brookfield, Mass. Church. Pastor.

Pastor and preacher. 52169

Pastor at large vindicated. 65531

Pastor bonus. 50108

Pastor de noche bvena. 58300

Pastor exhorted. 97418

Pastor in "the Congregational Church and Dartmouth College." pseud. Remarks made by the pastor. 18624

Pastor of the Old Stone Church. 57749

Pastor there. pseud. Quickening word for the hastening a sluggish soul. see Oxenbridge, John.

Pastoral. 106372

Pastoral a los curas y jueces eclesiasticos. 73872

Pastoral address. [By John Inglis.] 34771

Pastoral address, by the Right Reverend the Bishop of Honolulu. 90107

Pastoral address of the Rt. Rev. William Meade. (47241), 93816

Pastoral address, to the clergy and laity of the Diocese of Toronto. 92653

Pastoral address to the clergy and laity of the Protestant Episcopal Church in the United States of America. 59013, note after 103465

Pastoral address to the Old Colony Association. 7952

Pastoral address, to the parishioners of St. Mary's Church. 20391

Pastoral Aid Society of the Protestant Episcopal Church in the Diocese of New York. see Protestant Episcopal Church in the U. S. A. New York (Diocese) Pastoral Aid Society.

Pastoral assumption, and church forebearance. (67291)

Pastoral care. (18419)

Pastoral charge . . . . A sermon . . . at . . . Weymouth. 58205

Pastoral charge, delivered by the Right Reverend Henry. (62214)

Pastoral de Illmo. Sr. Obispo de Cuba. 59014

Pastoral del Illustrismo Senor Obispo. 29121

Pastoral desires. 46449

Pastoral do Arcebispo da Bahia. 86357

Pastoral drama, on the birth-day of an illustrious personage. 33005, 100545

Pastoral eclogue. 89940

Pastoral fidelity consistent with pastoral affection. 85310

Pastoral fidelity; or walking in the light. 77572

Pastoral, in two epistles. 101235

Pastoral letter. 32589

Pastoral letter, addressed to the clergy and laity of the Protestant-Episcopal Church in the Diocese of Pennsylvania. 64617

Pastoral letter, addressed to the clergy and laity of the Protestant Episcopal Church in the state of New York. (32301)

Pastoral letter addressed to the clergy of the diocese. 26139

Pastoral letter addressed to the members of St. John's Church. 7108

Pastoral letter addressed to the members of the Protestant Episcopal Church in the Diocese of Maryland. By James Kemp. 37337

Pastoral letter addressed to the members of the Protestant Episcopal Church in the Diocese of Maryland. By Thomas John Claggett. 13186

Pastoral letter addressed to the members of the Protestant Episcopal Church in the Eastern Diocese. (28881)

Pastoral letter, briefly declaring the duties incumbent on all persons. 46596, 1st note after 103852

Pastoral letter from the Apostolic Vice-Prefect. 6838, 64575

Pastoral letter from the Bishop of the said church. 45299

Pastoral letter from the Bishops of the Protestant Episcopal Church. 59016

Pastoral letter from the Lord Bishop of Toronto. 92637

Pastoral letter, from the Reverend Synod of New-York and Philadelphia. 59017

Pastoral letter from the Right Rev. Dr. John Carroll. 11075

Pastoral letter from the Synod of New-York and Philadelphia. 104941

Pastoral letter, of Mr. John Williams. 104261

Pastoral letter of the Archbishop and Bishops of the Province of New York. 59018

Pastoral letter of the . . . Archbishop of Baltimore, and the . . . prelates of the Roman Catholic Church. 59019

Pastoral letter of the Archbishop of Baltimore . . . on the consecration of the cathedral. 44522

Pastoral letter [of the Bishop of London.] (78594)

Pastoral letter, of the . . . Bishop of Natchez. 51898

Pastoral letter of the Bishop of North Carolina. 35815

Pastoral letter of the Bishops of the Protestant Episcopal Church. 43323

Pastoral letter of the First National Council of the United States. 59020

Pastoral letter of the First Provincial Council of Cincinnati. 59021

Pastoral letter of the House of Bishops, of the Protestant Episcopal Church, in the United States. 59022

Pastoral letter of the House of Bishops, to the clergy and laity. 59023

Pastoral letter of the House of Bishops, to the clergy and laity of the Protestant Episcopal Church in the United States. 66182

Pastoral letter of the ministers, bishops, &c. of the Presbytery of Baltimore. 75441

Pastoral letter of the Most Rev. M. J. Spalding, Archbishop. 88911

Pastoral letter of the Most Rev. Martin John Spalding. 88911

Pastoral letter of the Most Rev. the Archbishop of Baltimore. 88911

Pastoral letter, of the Presbytery of Baltimore. 87004

Pastoral letter of the Presbytery of Charleston. (12063), note after 87915A

Pastoral letter of the Presbytery of New Brunswick. (52524)

Pastoral letter [of the Rt. Rev. Benjamin Moore.] (50329)

Pastoral letter of the Right Rev. Bishop Hobart. (32005), 99815

Pastoral letter of the Rt. Rev. H. Potter, D. D. 64642, 92946

Pastoral letter of the Second Plenary Council. 88911

Pastoral letter of the Second Provincial Council. 13101

Pastoral letter of the Synod of Michigan. 48777

Pastoral letter of the Synod of Philadelphia. (62367), 2d note after 99808

Pastoral letter . . . on the regulation of the convention. 19345

Pastoral letter on the subject of the Bible and Common Prayer-Book Societies. 32296

Pastoral letter read to the congregation. 70860

Pastoral letter relating to measures for theological education. (32301)

Pastoral letter to clergy and laity of the Diocese of Toronto. 92654

Pastoral letter, to families visited with sickness. 46451

Pastoral letter to the churches under the care of the Harrisburg Presbytery. 30550

Pastoral letter to the clergy and laity of his diocese. 35311-35312

Pastoral letter to the clergy and laity of the Diocese of Quebec. 51187

Pastoral letter to the clergy and laity of the Diocese of New York. (64646)

Pastoral letter to the clergy and laity of the Diocess [sic] of Toronto. 92634

Pastoral letter to the clergy and the laity of the Protestant Episcopal Church. 59024

Pastoral letter to the members of the Protestant Episcopal Church in the United States. (59025)

Pastoral letter to the clergy of Maryland. 7477, 7483

Pastoral letter to the clergy of the Diocese of New York. 64643, 65117

Pastoral letter to the English captives, in Africa. 46450

Pastoral letter to the . . . friends of the Protestant Episcopal Church in the Diocese of Virginia. 47242

Pastoral letter to the laity . . . of New-York. 64644

Pastoral letter to the laity of the Protestant Episcopal Church in the state of New-York. 32296

Pastoral letter to the parishioners of Christ Church. 93227

Pastoral letter, to the parishioners of St. Peter's Church. 35396

Pastoral letter to the people of the Church of the Messiah. 57791

Pastoral letter to the reformed protestants in Barbados. 44082

Pastoral letter to the Sixth Presbyterian Church. 104739

Pastoral letter to the Sunday School children. 55083

Pastoral letter . . . with a sermon delivered. 17678

Pastoral letters from a minister to his flock. 59015

Pastoral letters from the House of Bishops. 66183

Pastoral letters of the Right Rev. Dr. Hughes. 33593

Pastoral memento. 85310

Pastoral memorial. 5279

Pastoral monitor. 80352

Pastoral offering from the Rector of St. Mark's. 30806

Pastoral office. 83757

Pastoral opera, in two acts. 105183

Pastoral para la ereccion de una Cofradia de la Doctrina Cristiana. 78948

Pastoral poem. 33005

Pastoral que.. . . D. Francisco Pablo Vazquez. 98716

Pastoral que el Illmo. Arzobispo D. Lazaro de la Garza dirige. 39476

Pastoral que el Ilustr. Senor D. D. Manuel Ignacio Goncalez del Campillo. 10312

Pastoral relation to the people of Harwich. 92096

Pastoral relation—what are its securities? 81608

Pastoral reminiscences. By the late Rev. Martin Moore. (50422)

Pastoral reminiscences . . . with an introduction by A. Alexander. (38228)

Pastoral report of Trinity Church, Pottsville. 64695

Pastoral report of the Rector of the Church of the Advent. (13367)

Pastoral romance. (79484)

Pastoral sacred to the memory of General Wolfe. 104989

Pastoral sketches. 59026

Pastoral sobre el Jubileo de 1847. 47845

Pastoral sobre las tristes noticias. 73869

Pastoral songs of P. Virgil Maro. 74350

Pastoral to the Salisbury Convention. 45481

Pastorale emanata del Sinodo della Chiensa. 66148

Pastorale internum ad D. Joannem de Palafox et Mendoza. 98166

Pastorate of 25 years. 89099

Pastoret, D'Emm. (59027)

Pastorius, Franciscus Daniel. 59028, 95394

Pastor's acknowledgement to his people. 76984

Pastors charge and cure. 103440

Pastor's farewell: containing a series of discourses. (18899)

Pastor's farewell to his flock. 104319

Pastor's jubilee. A discourse delivered in Ipswich. (37751)

Pastor's jubilee. A discourse delivered in the South Church, Salem, Mass. 22421

Pastor's jottings. 59011

Pastor's legacy. (45438)

Pastor's memorial. 5724

Pastor's new year's address to his parishioner 18976

Pastors of the Congregational churches in Boston. 11919

Pastor's office and business. 91548

Pastor's parting wish. 89106

Pastor's remembrances. 54966

Pastor's retrospect. (5280)

Pastor's report. 89870

Pastor's review. (34174)

Pastor's tribute to one of his flock. 89777

Pastor's twenty-fifth annual. 80267

Pastor's wife. 59012

Pastrana, Antonio Morales. 59029

Pastrana y Monteserin, Nicolas. 77141

Pat Mulloney's pilgrimage. (21916)

Patagone, Terre-du-Feu et Archipel des Malouines. (23767)

Patagonia y las Tierras Australes del continen Americano. 67125

Patagonian Missionary Society. Committee. 85556

Patagonian Missionary Society and some truths connected with it. 85556

Patagonische Robinson. 72231

Patapsco and other poems. 87135

Patavinus, Joannis Antonius Maginus. 59033, 66496

Patch, John, 1807-1887. 63656

Patchin, Freegift, d. 1831. 65495

Patchwork. 50846

Patent for New-Found-Land. 66686

Patent for Plymouth in New England. 59034

Patent for the Plantation of Virginia in 1606. 66686

Patent-Gesetz der Vereinigten Staaten. 51340

Patent granted by King William. 59035

Patent, granted . . . unto the West-India Company. 102906

Patent key to Uncle Tom's cabin. note after 92624

Patent laws. (59042)

Patent laws of the United States, together with information. 59040
Patent laws of the United States, with the decisions of the courts. 59041
Patent medicines in mob-town. 103341
Patent of the town of Southampton. 88231
Patent office and patent laws. 50409
Patent Office Fair, Washington, D. C., 1864. see Ladies' Relief Association of the District of Columbia. Patent Office Fair, Washington, D. C., 1864.
Patent Office. Report from the Commissioner of Patents. 59043
Patent om it Guineiske Compagnies oprettelse i kiobenhaffn. 102936
Patent right gazette. (59044)
Patent right oppression. 22182, 59045
Patent to Cabot. 29592
Patente d'union des missions des Freres Prescheurs. 40686
Patentee's manual. 22247
Patents of Canada. 10539, 1st note after 59045
Pater, Ezra. 59049
Pater, John K. see Porter, John K.
Pater, Theophilus Anti-. pseud. see Anti-Pater, Theophilus. pseud.
Pater Florian Paike's Reise in die Missionen. (59713)
Pater Lebats, aus dem Orden der Prediger-Monche. 38416
Pater Noster and Ave Maria in the Indian language. (79164)
Pater Noster et Ave Maria in lingva Para-qvariensi Hispanica et Latina. 79162
Pater Noster in Chuchon. 72811
Paternina, Estevan de. tr. (1373), 4828
Paterson, Daniel. 59051
Paterson, Neal. defendant 6326, 1st note after 96956, 1st note after 97284
Paterson, Paul. ed. 63371
Paterson, Thomas J. 59052
Paterson, William. supposed author 78197
Paterson, William, 1658-1719. 53147, 59054
Paterson, William, 1658-1719. claimant (18573), 78237, note after 90593
Paterson, William, 1658-1719. petitioner 18565, (18573), 59053, 59055, 78237
Paterson, William, 1745-1806. (59056)
Paterson, William B. (59057)
Paterson, N. J. Charter. 59058, 59063
Paterson, N. J. City Council. 59063
Paterson, N. J. Ordinances, etc. 59058, 59063
Paterson, N. J. Standing Committee to Fore-ward the Application for a Rail-Road from This Place to the Hudson River, Opposite New-York. 101061
Paterson and Hudson River Railroad Company. 59062
Paterson city directory. 59059
Pateshall, Richard. (5064)
Path of happiness for young people. 84292
Path of honour. 64692
Path of the just. 20391
Path of the pilgrim church. 59065
Path to riches. 93504-93505
Path way . . . see Pathway . . .
Pathetic history of the plague in London. 59066
Pathetical relation, of what occurr'd. (46485)
Patheticall discourse, presented to the King. 78372-(78373), 2d note after 100788
Pathfinder. 16460, 30617
Pathfinder; or, the inland sea. 16493
Pathfinder railway guide for the New England states. 59067

Pathology of drunkenness. 79471
Pathology of epidemic cholera. 80426
Pathway to erect a plantation. 82816
Path-way to experience. 82812-82813
Path-way to experience to erect a plantation. 82815
Pathway to health, peace, and competence. 82241
Patience. pseud. Black bondsman. 81906
Patience Welbeck. 33375
Patient continuance in well-doing. 30843
Patients in the State Lunatic Asylum, Utica, N. Y. see New York (State) State Hospital, Utica. Patients.
Patino, Andres. defendant 75584 see also Albaceta de S. Arzobispo de Mexico Ortega Montanes. defendant
Patino, Andres. plaintiff 59068
Patino, Pedro Pablo. (59069)
Pato Moriz, Nuno Alvares Pereira. see Moniz, Nuno Alvares Pereira Pato.
Paton, Alexander. (59070)
Paton, Allan Park. 59071
Paton, Bartholome Ximenez. see Ximenez Paton, Bartolome.
Paton, Catherine. 40618
Paton, Walter H. illus. 63539
Patot, Simon Tyssot de. see Tyssot de Patot, Simon.
Patouillet, Louis, 1699-1779. ed. 40697
Patria Chilena. (79351)
Patria en Cadenas. 59072
Patriae, Amicus. pseud. see Wise, John.
Patriae, Amor. pseud. see Amor Patriae. pseud.
Patriar, Americus. pseud. see Americus Patriar. pseud.
Patriarch. 59073
"Patriarch." Narrative of scenes and events. 13099, 38000
Patriarchal institutions. 12724
Patriarchial order, or plurality of wives. 89371-89372
Patrice, ou les pionniers de l'Amerique du Nord. 12349
Patricium, Philonem. pseud. Apologvs vanden Krijch der Gansen. (59074)
Patrick, J. 59075
Patrick, R. Shedden. 59076
Patrick, W. Cochran. 59076
Patrick, W. K. 90555
Patrick, William. 59077
Patrick Henry (C. S. A. Ship) see Confederate States of America. Navy. School-Ship Patrick Henry.
Patridge, John. 62743
Patridos. 57736
Patrie (Montreal) 67614
Patrie (Paris) (23047)
Patriganni, Giuseppe A. 59078
Patriot. pseud. Financial situation. 24352
Patriot. pseud. Future of the country. 26262
Patriot. pseud. Mystery reveal'd. 51661, 101710
Patriot. pseud. National finances. 51978
Patriot. pseud. Our national finances. see Townsend, Samuel P.
Patriot. pseud. Pangs of a patriot. 58423
Patriot. pseud. Political essay. 59082
Patriot. pseud. Second letter. 51978
Patriot. pseud. Spanish revolution in Cuba. 88946
Patriot. pseud. Three politicians. 95748
Patriot (Frankfort, Ky.) 10407, (71546)
Patriot (Toronto) 98088
Patriot (Toronto) Editor. 71718

Patriot. 59079
Patriot. A poem. 59080
Patriot. A sermon delivered at the annual fast. 27401
Patriot. Addressed to the electors of Great Britain. 36301-36302, note after 64980, 78302
Patriot. Addressed to the people. 59081
Patriot boy. 31169
Patriot boys and prison pictures. (27453)
Patriot chief. A tragedy. 44622
Patriot daughters of Lancaster. pseud. Hospital scenes after the battle of Gettysburg. 27237
Patriot dead. 85610
Patriot exile. pseud. Seven years of my life. (79359)
"Patriot" Harrisburg directory. 30541
Patriot highwayman. 59083
Patriot in retirement. pseud. Letter. 40310
Patriot known by comparison. 59084
Patriot. Monstrum Horrendum! pseud. Mystery reveal'd. 51661
Patriot muse. 65528, 97745
Patriot of '76 in captivity. 1103
Patriot of Texcuco. 100984
Patriot or people's companion. 59085
Patriot, or scourge of aristocracy. 59086
Patriot; or, union and freedom. 91504
Patriot Orphan Home, New York. 59087
Patriot preachers of the American revolution. 50363, 59088, 91803
Patriot song series. 84042
Patriot unmasked, or, a word to his defenders. 97055
Patriota. pseud. Observaciones. 56452
Patriota. pseud. Voz de la libertad. see Funes, Gregorio.
Patriota. 39087
Patriota Brasileiro. 7613
Patriota, jornal litterario, politico, mercantil. 59089
Patriota religioso. pseud. Soberania. 85665
Patriota Veracruzano. pseud. ed. Retrato de los R. R. P. P. Jesuitas. 70133
Patriotas de Honduras. petitioners 32769, 44270
Patriote Anglois. (59090), 97259
Patriote Hollandois. pseud. Sentiment. (23343), 40660, (79152)
Patriote voyageur. pseud. Nouveau Mississippi. see Roux, Sergeant Major.
Patriotes deportes de la Guadeloupe par les Anglois. 59091
Patriotic-address. 63797
Patriotic admonitions on the signs of the times. 1305, 29062
Patriotic and heroic eloquence. 59093
Patriotic Bank, Washington, D. C. 59094
Patriotic call to prepare in a season of peace. 44801
Patriotic drama. 105726
Patriotic effusions. 57175, 80561
Patriotic eloquence. 37992
Patriotic hymns. 25741
Patriotic mirror. (59095)
Patriotic perfidy; a satire. (59096)
Patriotic poem. 44775
Patriotic poems. [By Anna Marie Spaulding.] 89029
Patriotic poems. By Francis De Haes Janvier. 35777
Patriotic poems. [By George Burgess.] 9243
Patriotick proceedings of the Legislature of Massachusetts. 45931
Patriotic sketch. 90153

Patriotic song. 58200
Patriotic song book. 59097
Patriotic song, written by J. Hopkinson. 62019
Patriotic songs, for coming campaigns. (32623)
Patriotic songs of the freedom of the seas and Yankee tars. 21309
Patriotic songs, sonnets, &c. 99838
Patriotic songster. 59098
Patriotic speaker: consisting of specimens of modern eloquence. 68063
Patriotic speaker: extracts from the oratory of Judge Joseph Holt. 59099
Patriotic tragedy. 55187
Patriotic volunteer. 41717
Patriotica iniciativa que la Escma Asamblea Departamental de Jalisco eleva. 35555
Patrioticus. pseud. Old England and America see Russel, W. P.
Patrioticus. pseud. Solid reasons for continuance of war. see Russel, M. P.
Patriotischen Gesellschaft der Stadt und County Philadelphia. 61915
Patriotism. (22178)
Patriotism, a Christian virtue. 25671
Patriotism a moral duty. 24708
Patriotism. A sermon delivered before the Ancient and Honorable Artillery Company 82945
Patriotism aiding piety. 7350
Patriotism, and other papers. (37846)
Patriotism and piety. 92885
Patriotism and religion. 39187
Patriotism and the slaveholders' rebellion. 31387
Patriotism at home. 59100
Patriotism described and recommended. 10257
Patriotism, government nationality. (59101)
Patriotism in poetry and prose. 51437
Patriotism of Illinois. 21818
Patriotism . . . of the first settlers of Wyoming. 59012
Patriotism of the plough. (43102)
Patriotisme Americain. 59013
Patriosismo. De Nirgua y abuso de los reyes 59104
Patriotismo. Dialogo 2° entre Paulino y Rosa 98959
Patriots. 59092
Patriots and filibusters. (57184)
Patirots and guerillas of Tennessee and Kentucky. 7729
Patriots calendar. 59108
Patriot's friend. (35421)
Patriot's hope. 31197
Patriot's manual. 32922
Patriot's memorial. 59105
Patriot's monitor, for New-Hampshire. 95570
Patriot's monitor, for Vermont. 95571
Patriot's monitor: or, speeches and addresses of the late George Washington. 101734
Patriots of North-America: a sketch. 59109
Patriots of the revolution of 1776. (57141)
Patriot's offering. 59016
Patriot's plea for domestic missions. 22601
Patriot's referee. 59107
Patriot's song of victory. 13589
Patriot's vade-mecum. 59774
Patrocinio aplaudido y coronado. 77090
Patrol and quarantine laws. 87704
Patrol laws of South-Carolina. 87685
Patrol laws of this state. 87698
Patron, Felix. 59110-(59111)
Patronata en la nacion. (48621)
Patronato analizado contra el patronato embrollado. 59112
Patronato de Ntra. Sra. de Guadalupe. 75873

Patronato dialogo entre un cura y un abogado. 59113

Patronato nacional. 59114

Patrons of Husbandry. Southwestern Cooperative Association. 88613

Patroon van de Colonie van Rensselaers-wijck. pseud. Insinuatie, protestatie, ende presentatie. see Rensselaers, Kiliaen van.

Pattawatima Indians. see Potawatomi Indians.

Patten, David. 59115

Patten, E. 59116

Patten, George Washington, 1808-1882. 59117

Patten, J. Alexander. 58958

Patten, John F. van. see Van Patten, John F.

Patten, Joseph H. (59118)

Patten, Richard. defendant 96829

Patten, Robert. 59120, 75032

Patten, Ruth. 59123

Patten, William, 1738-1775. 59121

Patten, William, 1763-1839. 59122-59126

Patten, William, fl. 1851. (4279)

Patten, William Samuel, 1800-1873. 97091

Patten (James M.) firm publishers 52991

Patten (Nathaniel) firm publishers 44258, note after 105687

Patten's New Haven directory. 52991

Pattern for governours. 59127

Pattern in the mount. 29254

Pattern of mercy and holiness. 85311

Pattern of modesty. 6108, 92329

Patterson, --------. petitioner 59149

Patterson, --------, fl. 1847. 95817

Patterson, A. D. 1153, 59131

Patterson, A. W. 59132

Patterson, Adoniram J. (59128), 64412

Patterson, Albert Clarke. 59129

Patterson, Alexander. petitioner 59130

Patterson, David Williams, 1824-1892. 32608, 32804, 59133

Patterson, Elisabeth. plaintiff. (6268)

Patterson, George. (59134)

Patterson, George. petitioner 103768

Patterson, Henry Stuart. 59135

Patterson, J. 59137, 78197

Patterson, J. B. 5675, 39646, note after (64532)

Patterson, J. W. 93938 see also Maryland. Susquehannah Commissioners.

Patterson, James. 59136

Patterson, James Willis, 1823-1893. 20744, (59138)-59139

Patterson, Lawson B. 59140

Patterson, Oliver S. defendant 89386

Patterson, R. W. 44261

Patterson, Robert, 1792-1881. 59141

Patterson, Robert Maskell, 1787-1854. 1175, (59142)-59143

Patterson, Robert Mayne, 1832-1911. (59144)

Patterson, Samuel, b. 1785. 59145

Patterson, Stephen, 1812-1853. 59146

Patterson, William J. 50282, (50287), 59148

Pattie, James O. 33941, 59150

Pattison, E. W. (75379)

Pattison, Granville Sharp, 1791-1851. 1144, (27323), 59151-(59154)

Pattison, Margaret Amanda. 59155

Pattison, Robert Everett. 59156

Patton, Alfred S. (59157)

Patton, Benjamin. (59158)-59159

Patton, J. H. 59160

Patton, John M. 59161-(59162)

Patton, Robert M. 59163

Patton, William. 13269, 21937, 59164, 72067

Patton, William Delany. 59165

Patton, William W. (59166)-59168, 76562, 76647

Pattrich, F. illus. 59169

Patty (Brig) in Admiralty 60180, 60582, 94236

Paty do Alferes, Barao do. 59170

Pau, Augusto. 59171

Pauction, Alexis Jean Pierre, 1732-1898. 59172

Pauke, Florian. (59173)

Paul. pseud. 93721

Paul. pseud. Ultra-universalism. see Granger, Arthur. supposed author

Paul Wilhelm Friedrich, Herzog von Wurtemberg. 59182

Paul, Henry St. see St. Paul, Henry.

Paul, Hiland. 59174

Paul, Howard. 59175-59176

Paul, J. illus. 85105

Paul, James. ed. 35601

Paul, John. ed. 13623

Paul, Manuel. supposed author 45020, 50228, 59179

Paul, Marie Joseph Vincent de. see Vincent de Paul, Marie Joseph.

Paul, Nathaniel. 59180, 89204

Paul, P. de Saint-. see Saint-Paul, P. de.

Paul, Samuel B. 85374

Paul and Virginia. 105527

Paul and Virginia, and the Indian cottage. 78774

Paul and Virginia . . . translated by H. Hunter, D. D. 75474

Paul Ardenheim, the monk of Wissahikon. (41399)

Paul Erdmann Insert's, ehemal. konigl. Danisch. Oberarzte. 35243

Paul Jones. 36565

Paul Jones; a romance. 17960

Paul-Jones Corsaire, prophete & sorcier. pseud. Paul-Jones. (36567)

Paul Jones der kuhne Seemann und Grunder. (36568)

Paul Jones, ein Roman. 17961

Paul Jones, or the Fife coast garland. 36566

Paul Jones; or, the pilot of the German Ocean. 101111

Paul-Jones, ou propheties fur l'Amerique. (36567)

Paul Jones pine tree and rattle snake song book. 59178

Paul Jones, the son of the sea. 21183

Paul Marcoy. pseud. see Saint-Cricq, Laurent.

Paul Morphy's late secretary. pseud. Exploits and triumphs. (50775)

Paul Pry songster. 66705

Paul Redding: a tale of the Brandywine. 68180

Paul Spofford. Born, Georgetown, (Rowley,) Mass. 89569

Paul Venner. 59181

Paula Arias, Anselmo de. see Arias, Anselmo de Paula.

Paula Candido, Francisco de. (10669), 59183, 94836

Paula d'Almeida e Albuquerque, Francisco de. see Almeida e Albuquerque, Francisco de Paula d'.

Paula de Perez Galvez, Francisca de. see Galves, Francisca de Paula de Perez.

Paula de Sancta Gertrudes Magna, Francisco de. see Gertrudes Magna, Francisco de Sancta.

Paula del Villar, Francisco de. see Villar, Francisco de Paula del.

Paula Garcia Pelaez, Francisco de. see Pelaez, Francisco de Paula Garcia.

Paula Menezes, -------. 7610

Peaceable separation the true course. 68550, 78709

Peaceable temper and conduct divinely enjoined. (30458)

Peaceful end of a perfect and upright life. 14505

Peaceful end of the perfect man. 22392, 97205

Peaceful falling-asleep of God's beloved. (73887)

Peacemakers and peacemaking. 51439

Peach culture. 26193

Peacham, Vt. Caledonia-County Grammar School. see Caledonia County Grammar School, Peacham, Vt.

Peacham, Vt. Church of Christ. 105241

Peachey, James. illus. 65548

Peachey, John. supposed author 86674, 86678-86679

Peacock at home. 59413

Peacocke, James S. 59414

Peak, Esther. (59415)

Peak, John. (59415)

Peake, Rebecca. defendant 59416

Peake, Thomas. supposed author 51678, 102816

Peale, Charles Wilson. illus. (58327), 59417-59419, 75022, 84791

Peale, Franklin. 59420

Peale, Franklin. defendant (43137)

Peale, Harriet G. petitioner 59421

Peale, James. illus. 101686

Peale, Rembrandt. 13079, 56706, 59422-(59426), 101794, note after 101863, 6th note after 101872

Peale, Rubens. 59427

Peale, Titan R. (59428)

Peale's Museum, Philadelphia. (59327), 59419, (59423)

Pean, --------, Sieur. 7650

Pean, Michel Jean Hugues. defendant 2352, 59429

Pearce, --------, fl. 1830. 104196

Pearce, B. 601

Pearce, Dutee Jerauld, 1789-1849. (59430)

Pearce, James Alfred, 1805-1862. 59432-59433, 85059, 85074

Pearce, Stewart. 59434

Pearce, Zachary. (59435)-(59436)

Pearl (Ship) in Admiralty 5097, 61179

Pearl of great price. (59437), 83070, 83112, 83176, 83209, 83214, 83258-83270, 83282

Pearl of Orr's Island. (17828)

Pearl Street Merchants, New York. see New York (City) Pearl Street Merchants.

Pearls of American poetry. 44455

Pearse, James. 59438

Pearson, Anthony J. 6133

Pearson, C. H. 57289, 59439-59440

Pearson, Mrs. C. H. see Pearson, Emily Clemens.

Pearson, Ebenezer. defendant (27930)

Pearson, Edmund. ed. 97416

Pearson, Eliphalet. 25075, 59442-59444, (81980), note after 97552, 103723

Pearson, Emily Clemens. 59441, 59445, (63501)

Pearson, Henry B. 59446

Pearson, John, of Ewell, Surrey, Eng. 59447

Pearson, John, fl. 1767. 97311

Pearson, John James, 1800-1888. 30546, 60799

Pearson, Jonathan. (51365), 59448-(59450)

Pearson, Joseph. 59451

Pearson, Richmond Mumford, 1805-1878. 55668 see also North Carolina. Supreme Court. Chief Justice.

Pearson, Thomas Scott. 48834, 59452

Pearson, William. (59453), 70006

"Peasant bard." pseud. Harp and the plow. see Canning, Josiah D.

Peasant of Auburn; or the emigrant, etc. 16391

Peasant's fate: a rural poem. (32561)

Pease, A. G. 59454

Pease, Austin. 59458

Pease, Austin Spencer. 59455

Pease, Calvin. (59456)-59457

Pease, David. 59458

Pease, E. H. 59459

Pease, Frederick S. (59460)-59461

Pease, Giles. 3551, 13649, 59462-59464 see also Barnstable Conference of Evangelical Christian Churches. Committee.

Pease, J. I. engr. 31643, 84146, 84843, 91035

Pease, John. 59465

Pease, John, fl. 1851. (55655)

Pease, John C. 59466

Pease, Joseph. (59467)-59468

Pease, L. M. ed. 54280

Pease, L. T. 55319

Pease, Richard Luce. 59469 see also Massachusetts. Commissioner on Questions of Title to Land and Doundary Lines at Gay Head.

Peaslee, C. H. 59470

Peat-coal. 63885

Peath, Hormisdas. pseud. see Collin de Plancy, Jacques A. S.

Peaux noirs. 23553

Peaux rouges. 16526

Peaux-rouges. Par Paul Duplessis. 21374

Peaux rouges, scenes de la vie des Indiens. (23552)

Peaux rouges et peaux blanches. 12565

Pebble against the tide. (71784)

Pebblebrook, and the Harding family. 104816

Pebbles from Castalia. 80183

Pebbles from the Lake Shore. 64206

Pecador arrepentido de sus errores politicos. pseud. Triunfo de la libertad sobre el despotismo. (73223)-73224, note after 97019

Pecci, Gioacchimo Vincenzo. see Leo XIII, Pope, 1810-1903.

Peces, y reptiles. 74921

Pecha, Hernando. supposed author 56321

Pecheries du Canada. 40008

Peches dans l'Amerique du Nord. 70335

Pechey, John. supposed author 56480, 86678, 2d note after 100527A

Peck, --------, fl. 1839. 59489 see also Baltimore. Meeting of the Free Colored People, 1839. Delegates to Visit British Guiana, and the Island of Trinidad, for the Purpose of Ascertaining the Advantages to be Derived by Colored People Migrating to Those Places.

Peck, --------, fl. 1866. 33609-33610

Peck, C. S. 4355

Peck, George. (59471)-59472, 81544, 84368, 91480

Peck, George W. 59473

Peck, Henry E. 80503, 105885

Peck, Ira B. 59474

Peck, J. 59475

Peck, J. T. 63917

Peck, James H. defendant 59476, 1st note after 79364

Peck, Jedediah. 59477

Peck, Jesse T. 59478

Peck, John. defendant 24736

Peck, John, 1735?-1812. 59479
Peck, John, 1780-1849. 59480
Peck, John, 1780-1849. supposed author 66541, 89481
Peck, John J. 59481
Peck, John Mason. 2574, 59482-59487, 60955
Peck, L. B. 59488
Peck, Linus M. 59490
Peck, Lucius Benedict, 1802-1866. 59488
Peck, Nathaniel. 59489
Peck, Philetus B. 59490
Peck, Phinehas. 59491
Peck, Tracy. (59492)
Peck, W. D. 59493-59494
Peck, William Henry. 59495
Peck (Charles E.) firm publishers see Peck (William B. & Charles E.) firm publishers
Peck (William B. & Charles E.) firm publishers 55128
Peck defalcation. 44026
Peckard, P. 59496-59497
Peckham, Sir George. 59498, 97145
Peckham, James. 59499
Peckham, Robert. 59500
Peckham, Rufus Wheeler, 1809-1873. 59501
Peckham, Wheeler H. 59502
Peckolt, Th. 59503
Pecks' tourist's companion. 55128
Peckwell, Henry. 27548
Pecquet du Bellet, Paul. 59504-59505, 65413
Peculation and fraud by missionaries. 79982
Peculiar. A tale of the great transition. (76959)
Peculiar people. 85438
Peculiar presence of God with the good man. 92032
Peculiar treasure of the Almighty King opened. (17040), 46296
Peculiarities of the age. 9112
Peculiarities of the Shakers. 59506, 79716, note after 97880, 3d note after 100605
Peculio do Procurador de segunda instancia. 59507
Pedaco de una carta. 11239
Pedagogiad. 59508
Pedantry and power. 47181
Pedder, James. 59509
Peddler spy. 30044
Pederick Roger. 26245, 30710
Pederneiras, I. Velloso. 88811
Pedestrian sketches. 7053
Pedestrian tour of two thousand three hundred miles, in North America. 90376
Pedestrian tour of 2300 miles in North America. 59510
Pedestrian's adventures. 59511
Pedestrious tour. 23148
Pedigree of Appleton. 1811
Pedigree of Chase. 12188
Pedigree of Lawrence. 86793
Pedigree of Saltonstall. (62571)
Pedigree of the Dane family. 18461
Pedigree of the direct line of Gov. Sumner. 93722
Pedigree of the Odin family. 56721
Pedigree of Waldron. 86794
Pedimento de los Sres. de la Junta de Censura. (59512)
Pedimento de Sr. Fiscal suplente. 73864
Pedimento del Sr. Fiscal suplente, Mina de la Luz. 73864
Pedlar: a farce in three acts. 103065
Pedlar turn'd merchant. 9919
Pedley, Charles. 59513
Pedraca, Julien de. see Pedraza, Julien de.

Pedraza, Julien de. 10803, 10806
Pedraza, Julien de. petitioner 76026
Pedraza, Manuel Gomez. 27770, 59514-59515, 71417
Pedregal, C. tr. 9823
Pedreira do Coutto Ferraz, Luiz. see Ferra Luiz Pedreira do Coutto.
Pedreira Franca, Jose. see Franca, Jose Pedreira.
Pedro I, Emperor of Brazil, 1798-1834. 59516 see also Brazil. Sovereigns, etc., 1822 1831 (Pedro I)
Pedro III, King of Portugal, 1717-1786. 14378 see also Portugal. Sovereigns, etc., 1777-1816 (Maria I)
Pedro de Agurto. 59517
Pedro de Gante. 59518-59520
Pedro de la Concepcion. pseud. Soplos en defensa de la pura concepcion. see Alva y Astorga, Pedro de.
Pedro de San Cirilo. 86443
Pedro de Santa Maria. 86406, 86414 see als Augustinians. Provincial de Michoacan. Visitador.
Pedro de Tobar. (59521)
Pedro Quaerendo Reminisco. pseud. see Don Pedro Quaerendo Reminisco, a Private in the Ranks. pseud.
Pedro, Diego Antonio Menendez de San. see Menendez de San Pedro, Diego Antonio.
Pedro, Francisco de San. see San Pedro, Francisco de.
Pedro, Nicolas de San. see San Pedro, Nicolas de.
Pedro de Velasco de la Compania de Iesus. 98805
Pedro Moncayo y su nuevo folleto. (21797), 58054
Pedrosa, J. de la. supposed author 59523, 67647
Pedroso, Pedro Josef Rodriguez Saenz de. see Rodriguez Sanez de Pedroso, Pedro Josef.
Peebles, Cornelius Glen. 59524, 70191
Peel, Sir Robert, 1788-1850. 43091, 59525, 99832
Peel Park Museum, Salford, England. 89284
Peele, George, 1558?-1597? 59526, 78597
Peep across the threshold. 87264
Peep at caucus hall. 6486, 96472
Peep at China. 21324, 104773
Peep at fashionable folly. 24056
Peep at New-York society. 31249
Peep at number five. (61374)
Peep at the Aztecs. 59279
Peep at the creed-worshippers. 32488
Peep at the forum. 77815
Peep at the grand military ball. 85454
Peep at the great west. (7337)
Peep at the pilgrims in sixteen hundred and thirty-six. (12425), 59527
Peep at the trading inquisition of Curacao. 35111
Peep at the western world. 38390
Peep behind the curtain. By a supernumerary. 58527, note after 93777
"Peep behind the curtain" . . . Proceedings of the State Treasurer. 50395
Peep behind the family curtain. 2321
Peep into Catharine Street. 59529
Peep into my note book. 32395
Peep into the past by an ancient lady. 87912, 59530
Peep into the sanctuary. 59531
Peep into Uncle Tom's cabin. 59532, 92506, 92522

Peep of day. 88927
Peep of day into the language of the Ojibwa Indians. 57092
Peep of day. Vol. I. 61174
Peeps from a belfry. (80152)
Peers, Benjamin Orr. (59533)
Peet, Edward W. (59534)
Peet, Harvey Prindle. 59535-59536
Peet, Josiah. 59537, 80289
Peet, Stephen. 59538
Peih Sing-tseuen. ed. 79350
Peinado, Jose Maria. (34838)
Peinture des moeurs du siecles. 38503
Peirce, Augustus. 30755, 59539
Peirce, Benjamin, 1778-1831. (59540)
Peirce, Benjamin, 1809-1880. 30729-30730, 42706, 59541, 89533 see also Committee on Spiritualism, Boston, 1857.
Peirce, Benjamin Mills. (59542)
Peirce, Bradford K. (45703), 59543-59544
Peirce, Charles. 59545, 98021
Peirce, Cyrus. 59546
Peirce, Ebenezer Weaver. 59547
Peirce, I. 51771, 59548
Peirce, I. B. 59549
Peirce, J. D. 59551
Peirce, James. (59550)
Peirce, John. cartographer 103769
Peirce, Levi. 42213
Peirce, Nathaniel. 59552
Peirce, Proctor. 59553
Peirce, Thomas. see Pierce, Thomas.
Peirce, William. see Pierce, William.
Peirce, William Leigh. see Pierce, William Leigh.
Peirce Academy, Boston. see Boston. Peirce Academy.
Peirce family of the Old Colony. 59547
Peiresc, ------- de. ed. 39590
Peirpoint, Francis Harrison. see Pierpont, Francis Harrison, 1814-1899.
Peirpoint's pamphlet. 58558
Peirson, Abel Lawrence. 47321, 59559-59560
Peirson, Abraham. 22149, 59561
Peirson, Lydia Jane (Wheeler) 59562
Peissner, Elias. 59563
Peitho-Logian Society, Columbia University. see Columbia University. Peitho-Logian Society.
Peithologian Society, Wesleyan University. see Wesleyan University, Middletown, Conn. Peithologian Society.
Peixoto, Ribeiro dos Goimaraens. 59564
Peixoto de Lacerda Werneck, Luiz. see Lacerda Werneck, Luiz Peixoto de.
Peixotto, Daniel L. M. 59565
Pejepscot Company. (8764), 19252, 63498, (69482)
Pekin, Ill. Grand Division of the Sons of Temperance of the State of Illinois, 1863. see Sons of Temperance of North America. Illinois. Grand Division. Session, Pekin, 1863.
Pekin city directory for . . . 1870-71. (59566)
Pela Kesagunoodumumkawa tan tula uksakuma-menoo westowoolkw' sasoogoole Clistawit ootenink. 67760
Pelaez, Francisco de Paula Garcia. 58567
Pelage, Magloire. (29042), 25674
Pelage, Magloire. petitioner (29042), 59568
Pelayo: a story of the Goth. 81245
Pelayo: or, the cavern of Covadonga. 81245
Pelby, William. (59569)
Pelet de la Lozere, Privat Joseph Claramond, Comte. (59570)-59571

Pelham, Cavendish. (49480), (59572), 64390, 98444, 100819
Pelham, Edward. 14374
Pelham Clinton, Henry Pelham Fiennes. see Newcastle Under Lyme, Henry Pelham Fiennes Pelham Clinton, 5th Duke of, 1811-1864.
Pelham Fiennes Pelham Clinton, Henry. see Newcastle Under Lyme, Henry Pelham Fiennes Pelham Clinton, 5th Duke of, 1811-1864.
Pelham-Holles, Thomas. see Newcastle Under Lyme, Thomas Pelham-Holles, 1st Duke of, 1693-1768.
Pelham papers. 84791
Pelham's [sic] account of the preservation of eight men in Greenland. 13015
Pelican. 83788
Pelichet, C. L. tr. 67629
Pelissot, Felisberto. 59573
Pell, Alfred S. (59574)
Pell, Ferris. 59575-59576
Pell, Ferris. petitioner 59576
Pell, Joshua. appellant 96762
Pell, Robert Cruger. 59577
Pellegrini, Antonio Snider. see Snider-Pellegrini, Antonio, 1802?-
Pelleport-Jaunac, Jacques-Paul-Auguste. tr. 86483
Pelleprat, Pierre, 1606?-1667. 59578, (65038), (77219)-77220, 1st note after (74627)
Pellerin, ------. (59579)
Pellet, Elias P. 59580
Pelletan, Pierre Clement Eugene. 59581-59582
Pelletier, E. 59583
Pelletier, H. ed. 70356
Pelletier de Saint Fargeau, ------ Le. see Le Pelletier de Saint Fargeau, -------.
Pelleteir du Clary, -------- Le. see Le Pelletier du Clary, --------.
Pelletreau, Francis. claimant 59584, 93383
Pelletreau, William Smith. 59585, 88229-88230, 105071
Pellham, Edward. 13015, 59586
Pelli, Giuseppe Bencivenni. 99280
Pellicer de Ossau y Tovar, Joseph. (59587)-(59589)
Pellicer de Ossau y Tovar, Joseph. petitioner (59589), 86394
Pellicer y Saforcada, Juan Antonio. 59590
Pellion, ------ Odet. see Odet-Pellion, ----------.
Pelo restabelecimento da saude preciosa. 11456
Pels, E. 59591
Pelsaert, Francois. 74841
Pelt, Peter I. van. see Van Pelt, Peter I.
Pelterie, T. de. 59592
Peltier, -------. tr. 23085, 59593, 62702, (71399), 103848
Pelton, John C. (76073) see also San Francisco. Superintendent of Public Schools.
Pelton, O. engr. and cartographer 52135, 83928, 84143, 84146
Pelz, Eduard. 17936, (59595)
Pelz. firm see Smithmeyer and Pela. firm
Pelzel, Joseph Bernhard. 105986
Pelzeln, August von. 59596-59597
Pember, Arthur. 59598
Pemberton, Ebenezer, 1671-1717. (14525), (59599)-59603, (65613), (79411)
Pemberton, Ebenezer, 1704-1777. 21927, 41694, 59604-59609, 94708, 103131
Pemberton, Israel. 59610, 59612
Pemberton, Israel. petitioner (59611), 61671
Pemberton, J. C. 59617

Pemberton, J. Despard. (59618)
Pemberton, James. 59613, 86691 see also
Friends, Society of. Philadelphia Yearly
Meeting. Clerk.
Pemberton, John. 29615, 59614-59615, 62312,
note after 66909, 66922, 94925, note
after 95901-95902 see also Friends,
Society of. Philadelphia Yearly Meeting.
Clerk. Friends, Society of. Philadelphia
Yearly Meeting. Meeting for Sufferings.
Clerk.
Pemberton, John Clifford, 1814-1881. 15366,
(36376)
Pemberton, Samuel. 6739, 6741, 80668-80673,
101479 see also Boston. Committee to
prepare "A short narrative of the horrid
massacre in Boston," 1770.
Pemberton, Thomas. 45853, 59619
Pemberton Manufacturing Company. firm
90715, note after 92226
Pembroke, Mass. Congregational Churches.
59621
Pembroke, Mass. Militia. 84300
Pembroke, Mass. Monthly Tuesday Lecture.
(30171)
Pembroke, Mass. Presbyterian Churches.
59621
Pembroke, Mass. School Committee. 59620
Pen, Sylvan. pseud. Queen City. (13107)
Pen, William, Secundus. pseud. tr. see
Deken, Agatha. supposed author and
Wolff, Elizabeth Bekker. supposed author
Pen, William, Secundus. pseud. Hartmoerende
. . . bespiegeling. 106045
Pen-and-ink panorama of New-York city.
46837
Pen and ink portraits of the senators. 9163
Pen and ink sketches. 9619
" Pen and ink sketches." [By John Ross Dix.]
20343
Pen-and-ink sketches of American men and
manners and institutions. 43646
Pen and ink sketches of the mothers and
daughters of the church. 14328
Pen and ink sketches of Yale notables. 90006
Pen pictures and leaves of travel. 37171
Pen pictures from the battle field. 42772
Pen-pictures of distinguished American divines.
20345
Pen-pictures of the war. (5373)
Pen portraits of living American reformers.
3725
Pena, Andres Saenz de la. see Saenz de la
Pena, Andres.
Pena, Antonio de la. 59626
Pena, D. M. de la. see La Pena, D. M. de.
Pena, Francisco de la. 74860
Pena, Francisco Javier de la. 38957, 99620
Pena, Francisco Sains de la. see Sains de
la Pena, Francisco.
Pena, Gertrudis, de la. (67401)
Pena, Ignacio de la. 59627
Pena, J. de la. 59628
Pena, Josepho Antonio de la. 59629
Pena, Juan Nunez de la. see Nunez de la
Pena, Juan.
Pena, Manuel de la. 15080
Pena, Manuel de la Pena y. see Pena y
Pena, Manuel de la.
Pena, S. de Alvarado y de la. see Alvarado
y de la Pena, S.
Pena Montenegro, Alonso de la, Bp. 59632-
(59624) see also Quito (Diocese) Bishop
(Pena Montenegro)
Pena y Garcia, J. M. de la. 59630

Pena y Jauregui, Jose Maria Pena y. see
Pena y Pena y Jauregui, Jose Maria.
Pena y Pena, Manuel de la. (48665), (59631)-
59632, 96205, 1st note after 99783, 9882?
Pena y Pena y Jauregui, Jose Maria. 59633
Pena y Villar, Blas de la. 98884
Penal code of the state of Georgia. 27083
Penal enactment of the slave registry bill.
59634
Penal ordinances . . . of Rochester. (72346)
Penalosa y Mondragon, Benito de. (59635)
Penalties of greatness. 24098
Penalver, -------, Conde de Santa Maria de
Lorento. 21775, (59637)
Penalver, Fernando de. 59636
Penalver, Manuel de Echeverria y. see
Echeverria y Penalver, Manuel de.
Penalver, Nicolas. 21775, (59637)
Penalver y Cardenas, Luis Ignatius, Bp. 7294?
(80023) see also Louisiana and the
Floridas (Diocese) Bishop (Penalver y
Cardenas)
Penault, M. J. ed. (10342)
Pencil, Mark. pseud. White sulphur papers.
59638, note after 103490A
Pencil sketches. 40203
Pencilings along the way. 104514
Pencilings through Lehigh Valley. 84747
Penciller, Harry. pseud. Rural life in
America. 59639
Pencillings about Ephrata. 22681
Pencillings by the way. 104507
Pencillings by the way of its gold and gold
diggers! 43081
Pencillings in England and on the continent.
80337
Pencillings of scenes upon the Rio Grande.
852
Pendant zu dessen Beschreibung von Kamt-
schatka. 91218
Pender, Thomas. 59640
Pendleton, Edmund, 1721-1803. 15596, 30179,
(59641), 97533, 100023, 100040 see
also U. S. Continental Congress, 1775.
Committee to Prepare the Address.
Virginia. Convention, Williamsburg,
1776. President.
Pendleton, Edmund, fl. 1832. (17536), 59642
Pendleton, Edmund, fl. 1866. 59643
Pendleton, George H. 59645-59646
Pendleton, John. 100017-100018 see also
Virginia. Auditor's Office.
Pendleton, John. Jr. 103253
Pendleton, John S. 59647-59648, 1st note after
100532
Pendleton, Nathaniel G. 59649
Pendleton, Philip C. ed. 88382
Pendleton, William Kimbrough, 1817-1899.
10206, 48999, 91762, 91764
Pendleton, messenger. 30014, 30004
Pendleton's Lithography. firm Boston 95405
Pendock, ----------, fl. 1721. 65865, 88192
Penet, Peter. 33145
Peneveyre, H. 59650
Penfield, A. 59651-59652, 1st note after
94241
Penhallow, J. plaintiff (59653)
Penhallow, Samuel. (26625), 52872, 59654-
59655
Penhor mercantil. 59656
Penicault, Andre. (25854)
Penington, Edward. 59657
Penington, Isaac, 1616-1679. 59658-59662,
78295, 80035
Penington, John, 1655-1710. (37180), 59663-
59665

Pennsylvania. 512, (6107), 17303, 18313, 19915, 23184, 27464, (31103), 31105, 37740, (59925), (60028), (60216)-60217, note after 60301, (60577), (60658), 60762, 71541, 83762, 84605, 91869, 92392, note after 95562

Pennsylvania. claimants 60774

Pennsylvania. complainant 30333, 90390

Pennsylvania. defendants 61207, 65520

Pennsylvania. plaintiffs 15097, 17303, 18303, 19915, 49067, 57828, (60165), 60287-60288, 60470-60471, 65221, (69415), 74316, 82884, 90394, 1st note after 96854

Pennsylvania. respondents 57236, 93766

Pennsylvania. Adjutant General. 59865

Pennsylvania. Admiralty Court. see Pennsylvania. Court of Admiralty.

Pennsylvania. Agricultural Convention, Harrisburg, 1851. see Agricultural Convention, Harrisburg, Pa., 1851.

Pennsylvania. Asylum for the Insane Poor, Philadelphia. (60607)

Pennsylvania. Asylum for the Relief of Persons Deprived of the Use of Their Reason, Frankford. see Philadelphia. Friends' Asylum for the Insane.

Pennsylvania. Attorney General. 5679, 12421, (59902), 60470), 82884

Pennsylvania. Auditor General. 57236, (59903)-59905, (60609)

Pennsylvania. Bank. see Bank of Pennsylvania, Philadelphia.

Pennsylvania. Board of Canal Commissioners. 41888, 59952-59955, (59996), 60072, note before 60250, 60275, (60572) see also Pennsylvania. Commissioners to Examine the Claims Upon the Main Line of the Public Improvements.

Pennsylvania. Board of Canal Commissioners. Principal Engineer. 60608 see also Schlatter, Charles L.

Pennsylvania. Board of Commissioners to Settle the Estates of John Nicholson and Peter Baynton, 1840. 60103

Pennsylvania. Board of Military Claims. 59920

Pennsylvania. Board of Public Charities. 59919

Pennsylvania. Board of Revenue Commissioners. see Pennsylvania. Revenue Commission.

Pennsylvania. Canal Commissioners. see Pennsylvania. Board of Canal Commissioners.

Pennsylvania. Census, 1830. (59966)

Pennsylvania. Chief of Transportation and Telegraph Department. see Pennsylvania. Transportation and Telegraph Department. Chief.

Pennsylvania. Circuit Courts (15th Circuit) see Chester County, Pa. Court of Oyer and Terminer.

Pennsylvania. Circuit Courts (5th Circuit) 376, 380

Pennsylvania. Citizens. petitioners 60029, 60236-60239, 60388-60389, 60723, 69792

Pennsylvania. Citizens Association. see Citizens Association of Pennsylvania.

Pennsylvania. Citizens' Committee to Investigate the Evils of Freemasonry. see Pennsylvania. General Assembly. Committee to Investigate the Evils of Freemasonry.

Pennsylvania. Citizens of Northern Pennsylvania. petitioners see Citizens of Northern Pennsylvania. petitioners

Pennsylvania. Citizens Who are Public Creditors. petitioners see Public Creditors, Who are Citizens of the Commonwealth of Pennsylvania. petitioners

Pennsylvania. Cohocksink Beneficial Society. see Cohocksink Beneficial Society of Pennsylvania.

Pennsylvania. Coloured Citizens Convention, Harrisburg, 1848. see State Convention of Coloured Citizens of Pennsylvania, Harrisburg, 1848.

Pennsylvania. Commissary General. 59992

Pennsylvania. Commission to Investigate the Alleged Army Frauds. 60472

Pennsylvania. Commissioner on the Leins of the Commonwealth Upon the Lands of John Nicholson and Peter Baynton. 59827, 60562 see also Anthony, Joseph B.

Pennsylvania. Commissioner on the Soldiers' National Cemetery, Gettysburg. 60592

Pennsylvania. Commissioners Appointed to Examine All the Contemplated Routes for Collecting the Waters of Lake Erie and French Creek by Canal and Slack Water Navigation. 60473

Pennsylvania. Commissioners Appointed to Examine the Western Waters of the State. 33351, 60026

Pennsylvania. Commissioners Appointed to Explore the River Susquehanna. (60477)

Pennsylvania. Commissioners Appointed to Explore the Head-Waters of the Rivers Delaware, Lehigh, and Schuylkill, and the North-east Branch of the Susquehanna. 33351, 60026 see also Antes, Frederick. Dean, William. Howell, Reading.

Pennsylvania. Commissioners Appointed to Prepare a Revised Revenue Code. 60474, 60478

Pennsylvania. Commissioners Appointed to Revise the Civil Code. (60479)

Pennsylvania. Commissioners Appointed to Revise the Code. 60482

Pennsylvania. Commissioners Appointed to Revise the Penal Code, 1860. 60481

Pennsylvania. Commissioners Appointed to Superintend the Erection of the Eastern Penitentiary. 60206

Pennsylvania. Commissioners Appointed to View and Explore the Rivers Susquehanna and Juniata. 60576

Pennsylvania. Commissioners for Promoting the Internal Improvement of the State. 60459

Pennsylvania. Commissioners on Antietam National Cemetery, 1866. (60461)

Pennsylvania. Commissioners on National Cemeteries. (60485)

Pennsylvania. Commissioners on Practice of Equity in the Supreme Court of Pennsylvania. 60601

Pennsylvania. Commissioners on the Boundary Lines of the States of Maryland, Pennsylvania & Delaware. see Joint Commissioners on the Boundary Lines of the States of Maryland, Pennsylvania & Delaware.

Pennsylvania. Commissioners on the Internal Improvement Fund. (60483)

Pennsylvania. Commissioners on the Use of the Waters of the River Delaware. 60484

Pennsylvania. Commissioners to Examine the Claims Upon the Maine Line of the Public Improvements. 60476 see also Pennsylvania. Board of Canal Commissioners.

Pennsylvania. Commissioners to Investigate the Affairs of the Bank of Susquehanna County. 60468 see also Buckalew, Charles Rollin, 1821-1899. Wright, ----------.

Pennsylvania. Committee Appointed to Investigate the Evils of Lotteries. see Pennsylvania. General Assembly. Committee to Investigate the Evils of Lotteries.

Pennsylvania. Compacts, etc. 53145

Pennsylvania. Comptroller General's Office. 59927, 60768 see also Nicholson, John.

Pennsylvania. Constitution. 1269, 1271, 2071, 5316, 6360, 9672, 10662, 16086-16092, 16097, 16099-16103, 16107, 16110, 16113, 16118-16120, 16126, 16133, (19476), (19884), 20986, 25790, 33137, 36198, (36199), (47188), (59821), 59874, 59956, 60014-60018, 60020, 60063, 60195, 60233, 60435, 60447, (66397), 68804, 68811, 71541, 78114, 85175, 39558, 99008, 100342, 101542, 3d note after 102203, 104198

Pennsylvania. Constitutional Convention, 1776. 60014, 60435, 60447, 68804, 80768

Pennsylvania. Constitutional Convention, Philadelphia, 1789-1790. 60017, 60258, 60435, 80768

Pennsylvania. Constitutional Convention, Philadelphia, 1789-1790. Committee of the Whole. 60259

Pennsylvania. Constitutional Convention, Harrisburg, 1837-1838. 25371, 59771, 59874, 60032, (60170), (60214), 60401, 60660

Pennsylvania. Constitutional Convention, Harrisburg, 1837-1838. Committee of the Whole. (60256)

Pennsylvania. Convention, [n. d.] Minority. 59829

Pennsylvania. Convention, Philadelphia, 1787. 22233, 60257, 60040, 104627, note after 106002

Pennsylvania. Convention, 1827. 59835

Pennsylvania. Convention to Propose Amendments to the Constitution. see Pennsylvania. Constitutional Convention, Harrisburg, 1837-1838.

Pennsylvania. Council of Censors. 36720, 59836, 60015, 60171, 60435, (60661), 80768

Pennsylvania. Council of Censors. Minority. 10662, 59956, 60698

Pennsylvania. Council of Censors. Committee to Inquire Into the Conduct of the Legislature. 60698

Pennsylvania. Council of Censors. Committee to Enquire "Whether the Constitution Has Been Preserved Inviolate in Every Part." 60015, 69810-69811

Pennsylvania. Council of Censors. One of the Majority. pseud. see One of the Majority of the Council of Censors of Pennsylvania. pseud.

Pennsylvania. Council of Seafety. 31104

Pennsylvania. Court of Admiralty. 60180, 87456

Pennsylvania. Court of Common Pleas. 83707

Pennsylvania. Court of Common Pleas (Philadelphia County) 60597, (60625), 61803, 61845, (74111), note after 89175

Pennsylvania. Court of General Sessions (Philadelphia County) 19916, 37203, (37226), 70231, 1st note after 96931, 2d note after 96956, 2d note after 97284

Pennsylvania. Court of Oyer and Terminer (Philadelphia County) 13697, 61763, 83762, 83764, 88828, 96849

Pennsylvania. Court of Quarter Sessions. 83707

Pennsylvania. Court of Quarter Sessions (Philadelphia County) 61803

Pennsylvania. Court of Quarter Sessions (Philadelphia County) Grand Jury. 417

Pennsylvania. Courts. 17303, 18313, 60471, 83708, note after 96854, 103111

Pennsylvania. Department of Internal Affairs 59905

Pennsylvania. Department of Military Affair Executive Office. 59886

Pennsylvania. Department of Public Instruct 60004, 60044, 60565, 60604, (60609), 60648 see also Pennsylvania. Public Schools.

Pennsylvania. Deutsche Gesellschaft. see Deutsche Gesellschaft von Pennsylvanie Philadelphia.

Pennsylvania. Directors of Public Schools f the First Section of the First School District. Visiting Committees. see Philadelphia. Public Schools. Directors Visiting Committees.

Pennsylvania. District Court (Philadelphia) 61803, (74111), 96924

Pennsylvania. Divers Freemen. petitioners see Pennsylvania. Citizens. petitione

Pennsylvania. Eastern Penitentiary, Cherry Hill. (60079)

Pennsylvania. Eastern Penitentiary, Cherry Hill. Inspectors. 60080

Pennsylvania. Eclectic Medical College. se Eclectic Medical College of Pennsylvan

Pennsylvania. Electorial College, 1836. (60

Pennsylvania. Evangelical Lutheran Minister see Evangelical Lutheran Ministerum Pennsylvania and Adjoining States.

Pennsylvania. Evangelical Lutheran Synod. see Evangelical Lutheran Ministerium of Pennsylvania and Adjoining States.

Pennsylvania. Evangelischen Religionen Teutscher Nation. see Congregation o God in the Spirit. and United Brethre

Pennsylvania. Executive Council. see Penn sylvania. Supreme Executive Council.

Pennsylvania. Farmers' High School. see Pennsylvania State College.

Pennsylvania. First School District. see Philadelphia. Public Schools.

Pennsylvania. Franklin Institute. see Fran lin Institute of the State of Pennsylvani

Pennsylvania. Free Produce Society. see Free Produce Society of Pennsylvania.

Pennsylvania. General Assembly. 6030, 108 16807, (30039), 57236-note after 57236, 59820-(59821), 60033, 60038, 1st note after (60039), 60041-60042, 60154, 6016 60178, 60195-60197, 60232-60233, 6026 60261, 60263, 60281, 60402, 60419, 60563, 60583, 60586, 60595, 60611, 60623, 60820, 70074, 82978, 84499, 85175-85177, 85580, 89261, note before 96910

Pennsylvania. General Assembly. Committee of Conference. 60498

Pennsylvania. General Assembly. Committee of Inquiry in Regard to the Official Conduct of Thomas Sergeant, Secretary of the Commonwealth. 60500

Pennsylvania. General Assembly. Committee of Inquiry Relative to the Farmers and Mechanics' Bank. 60501

Pennsylvania. General Assembly. Committee of Privileges. 20994

Pennsylvania. General Assembly. Committee of Ways and Means. 60275

Pennsylvania. General Assembly. Committee on Claims. 60512

Pennsylvania. General Assembly. Committee on Domestic Manufactures. Chairman. 60469 see also Stevenson, ---------.

Pennsylvania. General Assembly. Committee on Education. 60513

Pennsylvania. General Assembly. Committee on Inland Navigation. 60460, (60516)

Pennsylvania. General Assembly. Committee on Inland Navigation and Internal Improvement. Minority. 101064

Pennsylvania. General Assembly. Committee on Internal Improvement. 60517

Pennsylvania. General Assembly. Committee on Revenue Bills. (60519)

Pennsylvania. General Assembly. Committee on Roads, Bridges and Inland Navigation. (60521)

Pennsylvania. General Assembly. Committee on the Coal Lands in the County of Elk, Pa. 13851

Pennsylvania. General Assembly. Committee on the Judiciary. 60522-60523, 64272

Pennsylvania. General Assembly. Committee on the Judiciary. Majority. 60523

Pennsylvania. General Assembly. Committee on the Judiciary. Minority. 60523

Pennsylvania. General Assembly. Committee on the Judiciary System. 60523

Pennsylvania. General Assembly. Committee on the Juniata and Conemaugh Canal. 60527

Pennsylvania. General Assembly. Committee on the Militia System. (60524)

Pennsylvania. General Assembly. Committee on the Normal School. 60541

Pennsylvania. General Assembly. Committee on Vice and Immorality. 60508, 60525

Pennsylvania. General Assembly. Committee to Enquire Concerning the Complaint of George Logan Against Samuel W. Fisher. 24499, 62134

Pennsylvania. General Assembly. Committee to Enquire Into the Disturbances at the Seat of Government, in December, 1838. 60488

Pennsylvania. General Assembly. Committee to Enquire Into the Expediency of Bringing in a Bill to Enable the People to Vote at the Next General Election, For or Against a Convention. 60489

Pennsylvania. General Assembly. Committee to Enquire Into the Official Conduct of the Governor. (60490)

Pennsylvania. General Assembly. Committee to Enquire Into the Operation of the Poor Laws. (60491)

Pennsylvania. General Assembly. Committee to Examine Into the State of the Bank of Pennsylvania and Philadelphia Bank. 60492

Pennsylvania. General Assembly. Committee to Examine the Pennsylvania Railroad Company. Majority. 60358

Pennsylvania. General Assembly. Committee to Examine the Pennsylvania Railroad Company. Minority. 60358

Pennsylvania. General Assembly. Committee to Inquire Into the Conduct of the Cashier and Directors of the Bank of Pennsylvania. 59910

Pennsylvania. General Assembly. Committee to Investigate the Cause of the Increased Number of Slaves Being Returned For that Commonwealth, By the Census of 1830. 60494

Pennsylvania. General Assembly. Committee to Investigate the Evils of Lotteries. 60462, 62123

Pennsylvania. General Assembly. Committee to Investigate the Evils of Freemasonry. 60005, 60495

Pennsylvania. General Assembly. Committee to Investigate the Official Conduct of the Canal Commissioners, 1832. 60496

Pennsylvania. General Assembly. Committee to Visit and Inquire Into the Condition of the Eastern Penitentiary and the House of Refuge, in Philadelphia, and the Moyamensing Prison. 60078, 60497

Pennsylvania. General Assembly. Committee to Visit the Western Penitentiary. 60781

Pennsylvania. General Assembly. Committee to Whom Was Referred Sundry Petitions, Praying That the Schuylkill Bridge Should Be Made a Free Bridge. 62151

Pennsylvania. General Assembly. Committee to Whom Was Referred the Memorials of a Number of Citizens of Pennsylvania, Praying That the Same Rates of Toll May be Charged on the Delaware Division of the Pennsylvania Canal. Minority. 60029

Pennsylvania. General Assembly. Committee to Whom was Referred the Message of the Governor, and Documents, Relative to the Delaware River. 60528

Pennsylvania. General Assembly. Democratic Members. see Democratic Party. Pennsylvania.

Pennsylvania. General Assembly. General Committee of Conference, For the Erection of a Monument to the Memory of Washington, 1833. 60109

Pennsylvania. General Assembly. Grand Committee to Investigate the Present System of Internal Improvement. 60530

Pennsylvania. General Assembly. Grand Committee to Investigate the Present System of Internal Improvement. Minority. 60530

Pennsylvania. General Assembly. Joint Committee on Frauds Upon Volunteers. 60536

Pennsylvania. General Assembly. Joint Committee on the Eastern State Penitentiary. 60532

Pennsylvania. General Assembly. Joint Committee on the Publication of the Geological Survey. 60533

Pennsylvania. General Assembly. Joint Committee on the System of General Education. 60535

Pennsylvania. General Assembly. Joint Committee to Examine Into the State of the Bank of Pennsylvania. 59773

Pennsylvania. General Assembly. Joint Committee to Investigate Whether Corrupt Means Had Been Used to Procure Legislation Favorable to the Banks. 60111, 60531

Pennsylvania. General Assembly. Joint Committee to Receive the Remains and Conduct the Obsequies of the Late Elisha Kent Kane, 1857. 37004

Pennsylvania. General Assembly. Joint Committee to Investigate Into Any Corrupt Means Which May Have Been Employed by the Banks, 1842. Majority. 60228

Pennsylvania. General Assembly. House of Representatives. Committee to Investigate the Affairs of the Philadelphia Savings Institution. 62136

Pennsylvania. General Assembly. House of Representatives. Committee to Investigate the Evils of Freemasonry. 60487, 60666

Pennsylvania. General Assembly. House of Representatives. Committee to Whom Was Referred the Petition of Andrew Miller and Others. Minority. 60540

Pennsylvania. General Assembly. House of Representatives. Committee to Whom Was Referred the Message of the Governor and Sundry Memorials Relating to the Abolition of Lotteries. 60503

Pennsylvania. General Assembly. House of Representatives. Select Committee on Election Frauds, 1865. (60570)

Pennsylvania. General Assembly. House of Representatives. Select Committee on the Alleged Frauds in the Election of United States Senator. 60553

Pennsylvania. General Assembly. House of Representatives. Select Committee on the Appointment Bill. note just before 60250

Pennsylvania. General Assembly. House of Representatives. Select Committee on the Estates of J. Nicholson. Majority. 60578

Pennsylvania. General Assembly. House of Representatives. Select Committee on the Estates of J. Nicholson. Minority. 60578

Pennsylvania. General Assembly. House of Representatives. Select Committee on the Exemption of Certain Persons from Military Duty. 60554

Pennsylvania. General Assembly. House of Representatives. Select Committee on the Public Records. 60550

Pennsylvania. General Assembly. House of Representatives. Select Committee on the Soldiers' National Cemetery. 27246

Pennsylvania. General Assembly. House of Representatives. Sixteen Members. see Sixteen Members of the Assembly of Pennsylvania. pseud.

Pennsylvania. General Assembly. Senate. (30039), (59864), 60038, 60174, 60176, (60444), 60568, 60584, 68577, 72663, 84648, 85465, 100666, 100670-100671, 100673, 100674, 100678, 100680, 100682-100683

Pennsylvania. General Assembly. Senate. Committee on Banks. Minority. 60253

Pennsylvania. General Assembly. Senate. Committee on Banks in Philadelphia. 60502

Pennsylvania. General Assembly. Senate. Committee on Finance. (60515)

Pennsylvania. General Assembly. Senate. Committee on Foreign Corporations. 60506

Pennsylvania. General Assembly. Committee on Imigration of Blacks and Mulattoes into the State. 60560

Pennsylvania. General Assembly. Senate. Committee on Revenue Bills. (60519)

Pennsylvania. General Assembly. Senate. Committee on Roads, Bridges, and Inland Navigation. 60071, 60564

Pennsylvania. General Assembly. Senate. Committee on the Call of a National Convention to Consider Amendments to the Constitution of the United States. (60559)

Pennsylvania. General Assembly. Senate. Committee on the Coal Trade. 60507

Pennsylvania. General Assembly. Senate. Committee on the Judiciary. 60522, 60538

Pennsylvania. General Assembly. Senate. Committee on the Judiciary System. 60504

Pennsylvania. General Assembly. Senate. Committee on the Memorial of Sundry Banks of Philadelphia. 60647

Pennsylvania. General Assembly. Senate. Committee on Vice and Immorality. 60508

Pennsylvania. General Assembly. Senate. Committee on Weights and Measures. (60463)

Pennsylvania. General Assembly. Senate. Committee to Inquire Into the Extent and Causes of the Present General Distress. 60505

Pennsylvania. General Assembly. Senate. Committee to Inquire Into the Organization of the Two Bodies Claiming to Be the House of Representatives. 60493

Pennsylvania. General Assembly. Senate. Court of Impeachment. 381, (30039), 60179, 64311, 96809, 1st note after 96927

Pennsylvania. General Assembly. Senate. Judiciary Committee. see Pennsylvania. General Assembly. Senate. Committee on the Judiciary.

Pennsylvania. General Assembly. Senate. Select Committee on the Admission of Kansas. 60552

Pennsylvania. General Assembly. Senate. Select Committee on the Bridge Across the Ohio River at Wheeling, Virginia. 60556

Pennsylvania. General Assembly. Senate. Select Committee on the Colonial Records. 60550

Pennsylvania. General Assembly. Senate. Select Committee on the Condition of the Several Institutions Receiving Aid from the Commonwealth. 60555

Pennsylvania. General Assembly. Senate. Select Committee on the Sale of the Public Works. 60575

Pennsylvania. General Assembly. Senate. Select Committee on the Tariff. Majority. 60539

Pennsylvania. General Assembly. Senate. Select Committee on the Tariff. Minority. 60539

Pennsylvania. General Assembly. Senate. Select Committee to Enquire Into the Authorship of a Speech, Purporting to Have Been Delivered [in the] Senate by Thomas C. Miller. 60545

Pennsylvania. General Assembly. Senate. Select Committee to Examine Into the Returns of James Hanna, As a Senator From the Second District, 1839. 60665

Pennsylvania. General Superintendent of Common Schools. see Pennsylvania. Department of Public Instruction.

Pennsylvania. Geological Society. see Geological Society of Pennsylvania.

Pennsylvania. Geological Survey. 60119, 72657, (72664)-(72666)

Pennsylvania. Governor, 1788-1799 (Mifflin) 18862, 48895, 60155, 61499, 84621, 100219 see also Mifflin, Thomas, 1744-1800.

Pennsylvania. Governor, 1799-1808 (McKean) (43380), 60772, 1st note after 92859, note after 99586 see also McKean, Thomas, 1734-1817.

Pennsylvania. Governor, 1808-1817 (Snyder) 33150, (43380), 57236, 60123, 60452, 60772 see also Snyder, Simon, 1759-1819.

Pennsylvania. Governor, 1823-1829 (Shulze) (59996), note just before 60250, (60509) see also Shulze, John Andrew, 1775-1852.

Pennsylvania. Governor, 1829-1835 (Wolf) 60503, 60508, 60513 see also Wolf, George, 1777-1840.

Pennsylvania. Governor, 1835-1839 (Ritner) (45141), (59996), note just before 60250, (60509), 60528, note after 104493 see also Ritner, Joseph, 1780-1869.

Pennsylvania. Governor, 1839-1845 (Porter) 59799, note just before 60250, (60519), 60534 see also Porter, David Rittenhouse, 1788-1867.

Pennsylvania. Governor, 1845-1848 (Shunk) (59883), 60156, 80768 see also Shunk, Francis Rawn, 1788-1848.

Pennsylvania. Governor, 1848-1852 (Johnston) (45089), 59884, 60246-60247, note just before 60250 see also Johnston, William Freane, 1808-1872.

Pennsylvania. Governor, 1852-1855 (Bigler) (25648), note just before 60250, 92909 see also Bigler, William, 1814-1880.

Pennsylvania. Governor, 1855-1858 (Pollock) note just before 60250 see also Pollock, James, 1810-1890.

Pennsylvania. Governor, 1858-1861 (Packer) 33150, 60248 see also Packer, William Fisher, 1807-1870

Pennsylvania. Governor, 1861-1866 (Curtin) 18019-18020, 27239, 59885, 60249 see also Curtin, Andrew Gregg, 1817-1894.

Pennsylvania. Governor, 1867-1873 (Geary) 26819 see also Geary, John White, 1819-1873.

Pennsylvania. High Court of Errors and Appeals. 60582, 94236

Pennsylvania. Historical Society. 7211, 10203, 16190, 19596, 19612, 21385, 24477, 27458, 36510, (59707), 60141, 60142, 60143, 60144, 60673, 68399, 77035, (77042), 79148, 82985, 84374, 84583, 84610, 84678C, 85249, 91785, 1st note after 95905, 97068, 97352, 97649, 98637, 98699, 98702, 102227, 102508, 103110, 105029

Pennsylvania. Historical Society. petitioners 61824

Pennsylvania. Historical Society. Building Committee. 85578 see also Jordan, John. Snowden, James Ross, 1809-1878.

Pennsylvania. Historical Society. Dinner in Celebration of the Landing of William Penn, 1852. 15895, (59744)

Pennsylvania. Historical Society. Committee Sent to New York For the Celebration of the 200th Birthday of William Bradford, 1863. 36510, 60144

Pennsylvania. Historical Society. Council. 105029

Pennsylvania. Historical Society. Librarian. 60140, 5th note after 94534 see also Taylor, Samuel Leiper.

Pennsylvania. Historical Society. Library. 60144

Pennsylvania. Historical Society. President. 60144 see also Ingersoll, Joseph Reed 1786-1868.

Pennsylvania. Homoeopathic Medical College see Homoeopathic Medical College of Pennsylvania.

Pennsylvania. Horticultural Society. see Horticultural Society of Pennsylvania.

Pennsylvania. Hospital for the Insane, Philadelphia. see Philadelphia. Pennsylvania Hospital for Insane.

Pennsylvania. House of Refuge for Western Pennsylvania, Pittsburgh. Officers. 60149

Pennsylvania. Independent Medical School. see Independent Medical School of Pennsylvania.

Pennsylvania. Industrial Home for Blind Women, Philadelphia. 60333

Pennsylvania. Inhabitants. petitioners see Pennsylvania. Citizens. petitioners

Pennsylvania. Inhabitants, Settled on Lands Claimed by Connecticut. petitioners see Pennsylvania. Citizens. petitioners

Pennsylvania. Inhabitants, Settled on the Lan Claimed Under Grants From the State Connecticut. petitioners see Pennsylvania. Citizens. petitioners

Pennsylvania. Inspector General. 60162

Pennsylvania. Institution for the Deaf and Dumb, Philadelphia. see Pennsylvania Institution for the Deaf and Dumb, Philadelphia.

Pennsylvania. Joint Commissioners on the Boundary Lines Between the States of Pennsylvania, Delaware, and Maryland. see Joint Commissioners on the Boundary Lines Between the States of Pennsylvania Delaware, and Maryland.

Pennsylvania. Kirche Gottes Aus Aller Evan gelischen Religionen. see Congregation of God in the Spirit. and United Bret ren.

Pennsylvania. Lafayette Beneficial Society. see Lafayette Beneficial Society of Pennsylvania.

Pennsylvania. Laws, statutes, etc. 1939, 8 10864, 12501, 13131, (15223), 15967, 20986, 22737, 23765, 25654, 27154, 27235, 27490, (27494), 28476, 30542, 30544, (30591), 30831, (35091), 38586, 39414, (43381), 50234, 50865, 51178, 51257, 52051, 52355, 55026, 55555, 57069, 59312, (59752), 59768-59769, 59772, 59775, 59778, 59782-(59794), 59799-(59802), 59804-59815, (59821)-59826, 59872, 59882, 59908, 59910, 59955, 59965, 59973, 59976, 59980, 59986, 59994, 59999-60004, 60011, 1st note after 60039, 60044, 60048, (60059 60062, (60064)-60068, 60075, 60077, 60082-60084, (60089), (60094), 60096, (60098), 60114-60116, 60134-60135, 60147, (60152), 60154, 60191, 60194-60199, 60201, 60215, (60218)-(60219), 60221, 60225, 60250, 60252, (60265), 60273-60275, 60277, (60279)-60281, 60293-60294, 60299, 60304, 60308, 60313, 60315-60316, 60322, 60326, 60338, 60339, 60345, 60349, 60356, 60358, 60364, (60368), 60376, 60380, 60385, 60442, 60454, 60498, 60510, 60537, 60604, 60612, 60634, 60640, 60648, 60650, 60652-60653, 60664,

(60669), (60749)-60750, 60758, 61405,
61435, 61457-61458, 61475, 61496,
61499-61500, 61505, 61518, 61534, 61548,
61561, 61569, 61584-61594, 61596, 61604,
61619, 61639, 61650, (61656), 61658,
61669, 61674-61675, 61697, 61700, 61703,
61717, 61720, 61726, 61728, (61765),
61766, 61770, 61785-(61786), 61788,
61790, 61798-61799, (61801), 61836,
61846, 61848-61849, 61853, 61868-61869,
61872, 61877, 61882, 61888, (61900)-
61905, 61943, 61946, 61948, 61953, 61967,
61970, (61981), 61984, 61986, (61988),
61992-(61993), 61998-(61999), 62001,
(62011)-62012, 62017, 62020, 62034,
62036, (62045)-62046, 62051, 62071,
62102, 62195, (62208), 62212, 62230,
(62235), 62261, (62266), 62300, 62351,
62354, 62357, (62359), 62369, 62374,
62378-62379, 62383-62384, 62386, 62394,
62398, 62407, 63116, (63122), 63129,
63149, 64587, 65129, 65391, 68214, 69398,
69433, 69622, 70820-70821, 71541, 71946,
72661, 74068, 74088, 74250, 78068,
78077-78078, 79192, 79214-79216, (79771),
82438, 84481, 84581, 84620, 84621, 84669-
84670, 85172, 85174, 85910, 85968-85969,
86092, 86174, 86811, 88155, 88509,
89066, 89817, 89821, 90815, 91312,
91418-91419, 91457, 93633-39634, 93730,
93737, 93918-93920, 93924, 93930, 93932,
94027, 97469-97471, 97505, 97646, note
after 97766, 97806, 97808-note after 97808,
note after 97815, 97862, 97965, 102021, 3d
note after 102203, 102414, 102527, 102760,
note after 102944, 104537, 104628, 105686,
106009, 2d note after 106135
Pennsylvania. Manual Labor Academy. see
Manual Labour Academy of Pennsylvania.
Pennsylvania. Medical Convention, Lancaster.
1848. see State Medical Convention,
Lancaster, Pa., 1848.
Pennsylvania. Medical Society. see Medical
Society of Pennsylvania.
Pennsylvania. Meeting of Freeholders, Phila-
delphia, 1817. see Meeting of the Free-
holders from Every Part of the State,
Philadelphia, 1817.
Pennsylvania. Military Association. 60598,
60096 see also Pennsylvania. Militia.
Pennsylvania. Military Department. see
Pennsylvania. Department of Military
Affairs.
Pennsylvania. Militia. 41444, 74068, 74078,
74080, 91396, 91418-91419 see also
Pennsylvania. Military Association.
Pennsylvania. Militia. Associated Independent
Troop of Volunteer Greens, Philadelphia.
61485
Pennsylvania. Militia. Col. Evans's Battalion.
92749
Pennsylvania. Militia. Courts Martial (Ancona)
(1378)
Pennsylvania. Militia. Courts Martial (Sharp)
79807
Pennsylvania. Militia. First Division. Second
Brigade. Philadelphia County Volunteers.
Second Battalion. 61989
Pennsylvania. Militia. First Division. Second
Brigade. Philadelphia County Volunteers.
Second Battalion. Companys A. B. and C.
Standing Committee. 61989
Pennsylvania. Militia. First Regiment. Company
A. ("Gray Reserve," Philadelphia) 61704
Pennsylvania. Militia. First Regiment of
Artillery. 60019

Pennsylvania. Militia. First Regiment of
Volunteer Artillery. 60019
Pennsylvania. Militia. Germantown Blues.
61698
Pennsylvania. Militia. Light Artillery Corps,
Philadelphia. (61789)
Pennsylvania. Militia. Pennsylvania Line,
1781. (59895)
Pennsylvania. Militia. Philadelphia. (61599)
Pennsylvania. Militia. Philadelphia City
Cavalry. First Troop. 61668, 84374
Pennsylvania. Militia. Philadelphia Grays.
9835
Pennsylvania. Militia. Philadelphia Home
Guard. 62002
Pennsylvania. Militia. Philadelphia Home
Guard. Commander. 63413 see also
Pleasonton, A. J.
Pennsylvania. Militia. Washington Blues,
Philadelphia. 101994
Pennsylvania. Navy. Officers. 60719
Pennsylvania. Northern University. see
University of Northern Pennsylvania.
Pennsylvania. Number of Citizens Appointed
To Investigate the Evils of Freemasonry.
see Pennsylvania. General Assembly.
Committee to Investigate the Evils of
Freemasonry.
Pennsylvania. Office of the Secretary of the
Commonwealth. see Pennsylvania.
Secretary of the Commonwealth.
Pennsylvania. Orphans' Court. 83707
Pennsylvania. Paymaster General. 60291
Pennsylvania. Polytechnic College, Philadelphia.
60351, 60396
Pennsylvania. President and Commissioners
Appointed To Superintend the Erection of
the Eastern Penitentiary. see Pennsyl-
vania. Commissioners Appointed to
Superintend the Erection of the Eastern
Penitentiary.
Pennsylvania. Proprietors of Lands. see
Subscribers, Proprietors of Lands in the
State of Pennsylvania.
Pennsylvania. Public Creditors. petitioners
(47621), (56467), 60704
Pennsylvania. Public Schools. 60231, 60449,
60565 see also Pennsylvania. Depart-
ment of Public Instruction.
Pennsylvania. Quartermaster General. (60441)
Pennsylvania. Railroad Commissioners. 93919
Pennsylvania. Register General's Office.
60448
Pennsylvania. Register's Court. 83707
Pennsylvania. Revenue Commission. (59922),
60588
Pennsylvania. Second Jefferson Benevolent
Institution. see Second Benevolent Insti-
tution, of Pennsylvania.
Pennsylvania. Secretary of Internal Affairs.
see Pennsylvania. Department of Internal
Affairs.
Pennsylvania. Secretary of State. see Penn-
sylvania. Secretary of the Commonwealth.
Pennsylvania. Secretary of the Commonwealth.
19163, (31103), 31105, 59770, note after
60301, (60587), (60609), 84605, 91869,
note after 95562
Pennsylvania. Society of the Cincinnati. see
Society of the Cincinnati. Pennsylvania.
Pennsylvania. Society of the War of 1812.
see Society of the War of 1812. Penn-
sylvania.
Pennsylvania. Soldiers' and Sailors' State
Central Committee. see Soldiers' and
Sailors' State Central Committee, Pennsylvania.

Pennsylvania. Soldiers' Convention, 1866.
see Soldiers' Convention in Pennsylvania.
1866.

Pennsylvania. State Agent, Washington, D. C.
60375

Pennsylvania. State Agent at the South West.
11791, 60375 see Chamberlain, James.

Pennsylvania. State Convention of Colored
Citizens, Harrisburg, 1848. see State
Convention of Colored Citizens of Penn-
sylvania, Harrisburg, 1848.

Pennsylvania. State Geologist. 60118, 72657,
72663 see also Rogers, Henry Darwin.

Pennsylvania. State Historian. 60630

Pennsylvania. State Hospital, Harrisburg.
60379, 60633

Pennsylvania. State Hospital, Harrisburg.
Superintendent. 60379

Pennsylvania. State Hospital, Harrisburg.
Trustees. 60633, 60379

Pennsylvania. State Hospital for Insane,
Danville. Commissioners. 60631

Pennsylvania. State Librarian. 60632

Pennsylvania. State Library. 60378

Pennsylvania. State Normal School, California.
88620

Pennsylvania. State Reporter. 84708 see also
Smith, Persifor Frazer, 1808-1882.

Pennsylvania. State Sabbath Convention, 1844.
see State Sabbath Convention, Harrisburg,
Pa., 1844.

Pennsylvania. Statistical Society. see Statistical Society of Pennsylvania.

Pennsylvania. Sundry Farmers. petitioners
see Pennsylvania. Citizens. petitioners

Pennsylvania. Sundry Inhabitants. petitioners
see Pennsylvania. Citizens. petitioners

Pennsylvania. Sundry Inhabitants, Settled on
the Lands Claimed Under Grants From
the State of Connecticut. petitioners see
Pennsylvania. Citizens. petitioners

Pennsylvania. Superintendent of Common
Schools. see Pennsylvania. Department
of Public Instruction.

Pennsylvania. Superintendent of Public Instruction. see Pennsylvania. Department of
Public Instruction.

Pennsylvania. Superintendent of Schools. see
Pennsylvania. Department of Public
Instruction.

Pennsylvania. Superintendent of Soldiers'
Orphans. 60649

Pennsylvania. Supreme Court. (5497), 9936,
14030, 15097, 17303, 18313, 27487, 39172,
42867, (51484) (57407), 58857, 59826,
60043, (60060), 60287-60288, 60470-60471,
60537, 60589, (60596)-(60597), 60601,
61803, 62037, 62267, 68162, 68165, 68169,
71916, (74111), 82884, 90700, note after
96854, 103111

Pennsylvania. Supreme Court. Chief Justice.
60470, 82884 see also Tilghman, William.

Pennsylvania. Supreme Executive Council.
(2062), 31104, 60433, (60436), (68570)

Pennsylvania. Supreme Executive Council.
President. (60436), (68570) see also
Franklin, Benjamin, 1707-1790. Reed
Joseph.

Pennsylvania. Supreme Executive Council.
Secretary. 61671

Pennsylvania. Surgeon General. 60654

Pennsylvania. Surveyor General. (60655)

Pennsylvania. Susquehanna Commissioners.
(60609)

Pennsylvania. Training School for Feeble-
Minded Children, Elwyn. see

Pennsylvania Training School for Feeble
Minded Children, Elwyn.

Pennsylvania. Transportation and Telegraph
Department. Chief. 60731

Pennsylvania. Treasury Department. 59927,
59777, 60167, 60443, 60637, (60639)

Pennsylvania. Treaties, etc. see Pennsylvania. Compacts, etc.

Pennsylvania. Union Canal Convention, Harri
burg, 1838. see Union Canal Conventi
Harrisburg, Pa., 1838.

Pennsylvania. University. (721), 23387-2338
60758, 60761, 61546-61547, (61582),
61642-61643, 62108, 63282, 83380,
84354, 84414, 84609-84610

Pennsylvania. University. petitioners 6075
Pennsylvania. University. Anatomical Muse
60756

Pennsylvania. University. Charity Schools.
60756

Pennsylvania. University. Charter. 60758,
(61416), 84581

Pennsylvania. University. Collegiate Depart
ment. 60758

Pennsylvania. University. Committee of Wa
and Means. 60758

Pennsylvania. University. Department of Ar
60758

Pennsylvania. University. Department of
Natural Sciences. 60758

Pennsylvania. University. Faculty of Arts.
60758

Pennsylvania. University. Grammar Schools
60756

Pennsylvania. University. Law Department.
Society of the Alumni. 86092

Pennsylvania. University. Law Department.
Society of the Alumni. Charter. 86092

Pennsylvania. University. Library. 60756

Pennsylvania. University. Medical Class.
60758

Pennsylvania. University. Medical Departme
60756, 60758, 105028

Pennsylvania. University. Philomathean
Society. 60390

Pennsylvania. University. Philomathean
Society. Committee. 60760

Pennsylvania. University. Philomathean
Society. Library. 60390

Pennsylvania. University. Provost. see als
Smith, William, 1727-1803.

Pennsylvania. University. Society of the
Alumni. 60758

Pennsylvania. University. Trustee. pseud.
Objections to re-organization. see
Trustee. pseud.

Pennsylvania. University. Trustees. 60758
84622

Pennsylvania. University. Trustees. petitic
ers 61746

Pennsylvania. University. Trustees. Comm
tee. 60758

Pennsylvania. University. Trustees. Preside
84622 see also Peters, Richard, 1704
1776.

Pennsylvania. University. Virginia Students
1812. 94568

Pennsylvania. University. Zelosophic Societ
60756

Pennsylvania. University. Zelosophic Societ
Committee. 60760

Pennsylvania. War Office. 71541

Pennsylvania. Washington Benevolent Society
see Washington Benevolent Society of
Pennsylvania.

Pennsylvania. Washington Monument Association of the First School District. see Washington Monument Association, Philadelphia.

Pennsylvania. Welsh Society. see Welsh Society of Pennsylvania.

Pennsylvania. Western Missionary Society. see Western Missionary Society of Pennsylvania.

Pennsylvania. Western Penitentiary. Inspectors. 60781

Pennsylvania. Western Pennsylvania Hospital, Harrisburg. see Dixmont, Pa. Western Pennsylvania Hospital.

Pennsylvania. Western University, Pittsburgh. see Pittsburgh. University.

Pennsylvania. Young Men's Colonization Society. see Young Men's Colonization Society of Pennsylvania.

Pennsylvania. A poem. 94470

Pennsylvania: a poem. By a student of the College of Philadelphia. 60292

Pennsylvania Academy of the Fine Arts, Philadelphia. 59990, 60293-60294

Pennsylvania Academy of the Fine Arts, Philadelphia. Board. 60294

Pennsylvania Academy of the Fine Arts, Philadelphia. Charter. 60293

Pennsylvania Academy of the Fine Arts, Philadelphia. Exhibition, 2d, 1812. 60616

Pennsylvania Academy of the Fine Arts, Philadelphia. Exhibition, 3d, 1813. 14881, 60616

Pennsylvania Academy of the Fine Arts, Philadelphia. Exhibition, 6th, 1817. 60294

Pennsylvania Academy of the Fine Arts, Philadelphia. Exhibition, 1838. 60294

Pennsylvania Academy of the Fine Arts, Philadelphia. Meeting of the Stockholders. 60294

Pennsylvania Agency of the American Tract Society, Philadelphia. see American Tract Society. Pennsylvania Agency, Philadelphia.

Pennsylvania Agricultural Society. 60297

Pennsylvania Agricultural Society. Directors. (31972), 60296

Pennsylvania Agricultural Society. Strictures upon Arator's attack. 60297

Pennsylvania almanac . . . for . . . 1803. (60298)

Pennsylvania almanac, for . . . 1796. (60298)

Pennsylvania almanack for 1733. 27656, (60298)

Pennsylvania and Ohio Canal Company. 60299

Pennsylvania and Ohio Canal Company. Charter. 60299

Pennsylvania and Ohio Canal Company's Charter. 60299

Pennsylvania and the federal constitution. 102415

Pennsylvania annual almanac, and reference, for . . . 1813. 60300

Pennsylvania anti-masonic almanac. 27332, 60301

Pennsylvania Anti-slavery Society. 60424 see also Pennsylvania Convention to Organize a State Anti-Slavery Society, Harrisburg. 1837.

Pennsylvania archives. 19163, (31103), 31105, note after 60301, 84605, 91869, note after 95562

Pennsylvania as a borrower. 60302

Pennsylvania Associate Presbytery. see Presbyterian Church in the U.S.A. Associate Presbytery of Pennsylvania.

Pennsylvania Association of the Defenders of the Country in the War of 1812. see Society of the War of 1812. Pennsylvania.

Pennsylvania Associators. see Pennsylvania. Military Association.

Pennsylvania Augustine Society, for the Education of People of Colour. 77186

Pennsylvania Baptist Convention. see Baptists. Pennsylvania. Convention.

Pennsylvania Baptist Education Society. 60303

Pennsylvania Baptist Missionary Society. 60303

Pennsylvania Baptist State Convention for Missionary Purposes. see Baptists. Pennsylvania. State Convention for Missionary Purposes.

Pennsylvania betrayed by the administration. 78096

Pennsylvania. Between Timothy Peaceable (on the demise of Dr. Fothergill and others, being the London Company) appellant. 92362

Pennsylvania Bible Society. 15008, 49121, 60304, 61967

Pennsylvania Bible Society. Charter. 60304, 61967

Pennsylvania Bible Society. Managers. 61966

Pennsylvania biography. (27865)

Pennsylvania Blackstone. 68564

Pennsylvania Branch of the General Union for Promoting the Observance of the Christian Sabbath. see General Union for Promoting the Observance of the Christian Sabbath. Pennsylvania Branch.

Pennsylvania Branch (Women's) U.S. Sanitary Commission. see United States Sanitary Commission. Women's Pennsylvania Branch.

Pennsylvania bubble. 6108, 92329

Pennsylvania business directory. 7125

Pennsylvania business directory . . . for 1854-5. 60306

Pennsylvania Canal and Railroad Company. Charter. 60498

Pennsylvania Canal Convention, Harrisburg, 1824. (60423)

Pennsylvania canal regulations and rates of toll. 59955

Pennsylvania canals. 60309

Pennsylvania chronicle. 12483, 84610, 98911

Pennsylvania chronicle and universal advertiser. (60310)

Pennsylvania College, Gettysburg. 60313

Pennsylvania College, Gettysburg. Charter. 60313

Pennsylvania College, Gettysburg. Club. 92750

Pennsylvania College, Gettysburg. Linnaean Association. Committee. (41497), 60313

Pennsylvania College, Gettysburg. Medical Department. 60313

Pennsylvania colonial records. 84604, 91869, 102508

Pennsylvania Colonial Society. see Colonial Society of Pennsylvania.

Pennsylvania Colonization Society. 60314

Pennsylvania Colonization Society. Managers. 60314

Pennsylvania Company for Insurances. 60315

Pennsylvania Company for Insurances. Charter. 60315

Pennsylvania Company for Insurances. President and Directors. 60315

Pennsylvania Constitutional Society. see Constitutional Society of Pennsylvania, Philadelphia.

Pennsylvania Convention to Organize a State Anti-slavery Society, Harrisburg, 1837. 60424 see also Pennsylvania Anti-slavery Society.

Pennsylvania Corporation for the Relief of Widows and Children of Clergymen, of the Protestant Episcopal Church. see Corporation for the Relief of Widows and Children of Clergymen, of the Protestant Episcopal Church, in Pennsylvania.

Pennsylvania, Delaware and Maryland Steam Navigation Company. Charter. 60316

Pennsylvania Domestic Missionary Society. 60317

Pennsylvania Eclectic Medical College. see Philadelphia University of Medicine and Surgery.

Pennsylvania Episcopal Society. see Episcopal Education Society of Pennsylvania.

Pennsylvania evening post. 60318

Pennsylvania evening post. Printer's Lads. (53428)

Pennsylvania farm journal. 60319

Pennsylvania farm journal. see National Agriculturist and Pennsylvania farm journal.

Pennsylvania Farmer. pseud. Letters. see Dickinson, John, 1732-1808.

Pennsylvania farmer, and scientific journal. (60320)

Pennsylvania farmer; being a selection from the most approved treatises. 71898

Pennsylvania Farmers' High School. see Pennsylvania State College.

Pennsylvania Female College, Harrisburg. 5341

Pennsylvania Fire Company. 60321

Pennsylvania Fire Insurance Company. 84374

Pennsylvania Fire Insurance Company. Charter. 60322

Pennsylvania First Constitution Club. see First Constitution Club of the State of Pennsylvania.

Pennsylvania Free Society of Traders. see Free Society of Traders in Pennsylvania.

Pennsylvania freedman's bulletin. 60323

Pennsylvania Freedmen's Relief Association. (60324)

Pennsylvania Freedmen's Relief Association. Meeting, 1863. (60324)

Pennsylvania Friendly Association for Preserving Peace With the Indians. see Friendly Association for Preserving Peace With the Indians in Pennsylvania.

Pennsylvania gazette. 7209, 14395, 23423, 37176, 39699-39700, 60181, 60325, 60754, 61643, 68026, 83980, 84610, 84624, 84642, 84643, 84678C, 85106, 85610, 86746, 94712, 94713, 95979, 97156, note after 97166, 97167, 98000, 106353

Pennsylvania gazette. Printer's Lad. pseud. Yearly verses. 106006

Pennsylvania gazette. Printers Lads. pseud. New-year verses. 53423

Pennsylvania gazette. Printers Lads. pseud. Verses, of the printers lads. 60765, 99295

Pennsylvania gazetee and weekly advertiser. 60754

Pennsylvania German Society. see Deutsche Gesellschaft von Pennsylvanien, Philadelphia.

Pennsylvania Hall. 103804

Pennsylvania herald. 104631

Pennsylvania hermit. 104605

Pennsylvania Historical Society. see Pennsylvania. Historical Society.

Pennsylvania Horticultural Society, Philadelphia 60148, 60326

Pennsylvania Horticultural Society, Philadelphia Committee for Visiting the Nurseries and Gardens in . . . Pennsylvania. 60148

Pennsylvania Horticultural Society, Philadelphia Exhibition, 10th, 1837. 60326

Pennsylvania Horticultural Society, Philadelphia Library. 60326

Pennsylvania Horticultural Society, . . . offers the Following premiums. 60326

Pennsylvania Hospital, Philadelphia. see Philadelphia. Pennsylvania Hospital.

Pennsylvania Hospital for Insane, Philadelphia. see Philadelphia. Pennsylvania Hospita for Insane.

Pennsylvania Hospital reports. Volume I. 60331

Pennsylvania in self-defence. 19841

Pennsylvania Indians. 60624

Pennsylvania Indians. Treaties, etc. 60740

Pennsylvania Infantry. see Pennsylvania. Militia.

Pennsylvania Infirmary, for Diseases of the Eye and Ear, Philadelphia. see Philadelphia. Pennsylvania Infirmary, for Diseases of the Eye and Ear.

Pennsylvania Infirmary, for diseases of the ey and ear established at Philadelphia. (60334)

Pennsylvania inquirer. 74244, 97949

Pennsylvania Institute of Design. (60335)-60336

Pennsylvania Institute of Design. Exhibition, 1st, Philadelphia, 1857. 60336

Pennsylvania Institution for the Deaf and Dum Philadelphia. 60337-60338, 102545

Pennsylvania Institution for the Deaf and Dum Philadelphia. Charter. 60338

Pennsylvania Institution for the Deaf and Dum Philadelphia. Directors. 60338

Pennsylvania Institution for the Instruction of the Blind, Philadelphia. 60339, 61487, 93247 see also Home for the Industric Blind, Philadelphia. and Association fo Establishing a School for the Education of the Blind in Philadelphia.

Pennsylvania Institution for the Instruction of the Blind, Philadelphia. Exhibition, 1st, 1833. 60339

Pennsylvania Institution for the Instruction of the Blind, Philadelphia. Managers. 60339, 85452

Pennsylvania Institution for the Instruction of the Blind, . . . in Philadelphia. Institut February 21, 1833. 60339

Pennsylvania Insurance Societies. petitioners see Several Incorporated Insurance Societies of the State of Pennsylvania. petitioners

Pennsylvania journal. (14394)-14395, 25576-25577, 60779, 61643, 82975-82976, 8343 84586, 84678C, 86867, 90028, 102050, 102246, note after 102623

Pennsylvania journal. Printer's Boy. pseud. see Printer's Boy that Carries About the Pennsylvania Journal. pseud.

Pennsylvania journal and weekly advertiser. 60779

Pennsylvania journal of medicine and the asso ciate sciences. 97050

Pennsylvania journal of prison discipline and philanthropy. 60340

Pennsylvania land. 71294

Pennsylvania Land Company. (60341)

Pennsylvania law journal. (60342)

Pennsylvania ledger. 60343, 91502

Pennsylvania ledger. Delivery Boys. 53429

Pennsylvania legislative hand-book. 85175

Pennsylvania Legislature. Names of the Senate and House. 60611

Pennsylvania Line. see Pennsylvania. Militia. Pennsylvania Line, 1781.

Pennsylvania Lyceum. 60344

Pennsylvania Lying-In and Foundling Hospital, Philadelphia. see Philadelphia. Pennsylvania Lying-In and Foundling Hospital.

Pennsylvania magazine of history and biography. (59707), 60673, 84583, 85249, 97352, 1st note after 95905, 98637, 102227

Pennsylvania magazine: or, American monthly museum. (2120), 60346, 84842, 103142, 104943

Pennsylvania manual. 85177

Pennsylvania-Maryland campaign of June-July, 1863. 19630

Pennsylvania masonic and civil almanac for . . . 1813. 60347

Pennsylvania Medical Society. see Medical Society of Pennsylvania.

Pennsylvania mercury, and universal advertiser. 92273

Pennsylvania minutes [of the Bridgewater Baptist Association.] 7841

Pennsylvania, New Jersey, Delaware, Maryland and Virginia almanac. 60348

Pennsylvania normal school laws. 60349

Pennsylvania, or travels continued in the United States. 73821

Pennsylvania packet (Dunlap's) see Dunlap's Pennsylvania packet.

Pennsylvania People's State Committee. see People's Party. Pennsylvania. State Committee.

Pennsylvania pocket almanac for . . . 1769. (60350)

Pennsylvania pocket remembrancer, for . . . 1814. 59917

Pennsylvania Pomological Society. 60352

Pennsylvania Poultry Society. Exhibition, 1st, 1852. 60353

Pennsylvania Poultry Society. Report of the first exhibition. 60353

Pennsylvania primer. 60354

Pennsylvania Property Company. 60355

Pennsylvania Protestant Episcopal Education Society. see Episcopal Education Society of Pennsylvania.

Pennsylvania Protestant Episcopal Missionary Society. see Protestant Episcopal Missionary Society of Pennsylvania.

Pennsylvania Protestant Episcopal Sunday-School Society. see Protestant Episcopal Sunday-School Society of Pennsylvania.

Pennsylvania Rail Road, its necessity and advantages to Philadelphia. 60358

Pennsylvania Railroad Company. 60072, 61033, 60358

Pennsylvania Railroad Company. plaintiffs 68169

Pennsylvania Railroad Company. Canal Department. 60358

Pennsylvania Railroad Company. Charter. 60356, 60358

Pennsylvania Railroad Company. Chief Engineer. 30859, 60358 see also Haupt, Hermann.

Pennsylvania Railroad Company. Directors. 60358

Pennsylvania Railroad Company. Investigating Committee. 60358

Pennsylvania Railroad Company. Meeting of the Stockholders, 1867. 60358

Pennsylvania Railroad: its origin, construction, condition, and connections. 81436

Pennsylvania railway gazetteer. 60359

Pennsylvania Relief Association for East Tennessee. Commission. 60360, 84391

Pennsylvania Relief Association for East Tennessee. Executive Committee. Commission Sent to Visit That Region. 60360

Pennsylvania. Reports of heads of departments, 1845. 85465

Pennsylvania reserves. 42970

Pennsylvania sailor. pseud. Letters. see Macpherson, John.

Pennsylvania sailor's letters. 43638

Pennsylvania school architecture. 9469

Pennsylvania school journal. 60361

Pennsylvania Seamen's Friend Society. 60362

Pennsylvania Seamen's Friend Society. Board of Managers. 60362

Pennsylvania Society for Discouraging the Use of Ardent Spirits. Committee. (60363)

Pennsylvania Society for Discouraging the Use of Ardent Spirits. Managers. (60363)

Pennsylvania Society for Promoting the Abolition of Slavery. 47745, 60364, 62293, 81753

Pennsylvania Society for Promoting the Abolition of Slavery. petitioners 47745

Pennsylvania Society for Promoting the Abolition of Slavery. Board of Education. 2639, 2682, 62293

Pennsylvania Society for Promoting the Abolition of Slavery. Charter. 60364

Pennsylvania Society for Promoting the Abolition of Slavery. Committee. 60397, 62072

Pennsylvania Society for Promoting the Abolition of Slavery. Ninetieth Anniversary Celebration, 1865. 60364

Pennsylvania Society for Promoting the Abolition of Slavery, and For the Relief of Free Negroes Unlawfully Held in Bondage. see Pennsylvania Society for Promoting the Abolition of Slavery.

Pennsylvania Society for Promoting the Culture of the Mulberry and the Raising of Silkworms. (60365)

Pennsylvania Society for the Advancement of Christianity. see Society for the Advancement of Christianity.

Pennsylvania Society for the Encouragement of Manufactures and the Useful Arts. 60367

Pennsylvania Society for the Encouragement of Manufactures and the Useful Arts. Board of Managers. petitioners 60367

Pennsylvania Society for the Encouragement of Manufactures and the Useful Arts. Board of Manufactures. petitioners 60367

Pennsylvania Society for the Encouragement of Manufactures and the Useful Arts. Dinner Given to Professor List, 1827. 41427

Pennsylvania Society for the Prevention of Cruelty to Animals. (60368)

Pennsylvania Society for the Prevention of Cruelty to Animals. Charter. (60368)

Pennsylvania Society for the Prevention of Cruelty to Animals. Committee. (60368)

Pennsylvania Society for the Promotion of American Manufactures. petitioners 60369

Pennsylvania Society for the Promotion of Internal Improvement. 10853, 60370, 95381

Pennsylvania Society for the Promotion of Internal Improvements in the Commonwealth. Acting Committee. 10889, 60370

Pennsylvanian. pseud. Extracts from the Crisis. see Carey, Mathew, 1760-1839.

Pennsylvanian. pseud. Extraordinary prosperity of Great Britain. see Carey, Mathew, 1760-1839. supposed author

Pennsylvanian. pseud. Facts and observations. see Carey, Mathew, 1760-1839.

Pennsylvanian. pseud. Fifty-one substantial reasons. see Carey, Mathew, 1760-1839.

Pennsylvanian. pseud. Looking-glass. 41947

Pennsylvanian. pseud. To the inhabitants of the city and county of Philadelphia. 62325

Pennsylvanian. pseud. Twenty-one golden rules to depress agriculture. see Carey, Mathew, 1760-1839.

Pennsylvanian. pseud. Warning voice to the cotton and tobacco planters. see Carey, Mathew, 1760-1839.

Pennsylvanian. 68214

Pennsylvanian cottage. 10269

Pennsylvanian farmer. pseud. New essay. see Dickinson, John, 1732-1808.

Pennsylvanian Society for the Suppression of Lotteries. see Pennsylvania Society for the Suppression of Lotteries.

Pennsylvanian system of prison discipline triumphant in France. (60384), 93701

Pennsylvanian tale. And other poems. 10268

Pennsylvanians, read, and assert your own dignity. (60699)

Pennsylvanisch Deitch. 67967

Pennsylvanische Nachrichten von dem Reichte Christi, Anno 1742. 42642, note after 106351, 106357, 106359

Pennsylvanischer Calender, auf das 1796ste Jahr Christi. 60791

Pennsylvanischer Staatbote, Oct. 20, 1775. 1st note after 94085

Penny, Miss --------, fl. 1771. 36295A, 60793

Penny, ---------, fl. 1867. 42948

Penny, Joshua. 60792

Penny, Virginia. 60794

Penny emigrant's guide to the United States. (25266)

Penny encyclopaedia. 27214

Pennyless, Peter. pseud. Sentimental lucubrations. 60795

Pennyman, John. 70896, 86701, 86706-86707

Pennypacker, Samuel Whitaker. 60746, 60796, 1st note after 97529

Penobscot Indians. 4391, 15429, 15435-(15437), 15441-15442, 34083, note after (34632), 34654, 36730, 80205

Penokie mineral range in Wisconsin. 60797

Penon Blanco, ------- Salinas de. see Salinas de Penon Blanco, ---------.

Penrhyn, Richard Pennant, Baron, 1737?-1808. 103959

Penrose, ---------, fl. 1800. 765-766, (80579), 80632

Penrose, -----------, fl. 1854. 61709

Penrose, Bernard. 60798

Penrose, Charles Bingham, 1798-1867. 30546, 60532, 60799

Penrose, John. 60800

Penrose, Llewellen. 60801

Penrose, Thomas. (60802)

Pensador. pseud. Tentativa del Pensador. see Fernandez de Lizardi, Jose Joaquin, 1776-1827.

Pensador. pseud. Pulgas y vomito prieto anuncian el dia del juicio. (66623)

Pensador. 41666

Pensador de las almas S. Miguel Arcangel. 76164

Pensador del Peru. pseud. A la nacion Espanola. 38782

Pensador del Peru. 60804, note after 97719

Pensador Mejicano. pseud. Algunas notas anidadas. see Fernandez de Lizardi, Jose Joaquin, 1776-1827.

Pensador Mexicano. pseud. Correo Seminario de Mexico. see Fernandez de Lizardi, Jose Joaquin, 1776-1827.

Pensador Mexicano. pseud. Ironico hablador. 98258

Pensador Mexicano. pseud. Observaciones. see Fernandez de Lizardi, Jose Joaquin, 1776-1827.

Pensador Mejicano. pseud. Observaciones politico-legales. see Fernandez de Lizardi, Jose Joaquin, 1776-1827.

Pensador Mexicano. pseud. Palinodia en respeusto al Padre Soto. see Fernandez de Lizardi, Jose Joaquin, 1776-1827.

Pensador Mexicano. pseud. Pensador Mexicano. see Fernandez de Lizardi, Jose Joaquin, 1776-1827.

Pensador Mexicano. pseud. Periquillo Sarmiento. see Fernandez de Lizardi, Jose Joaquin, 1776-1827.

Pensador Mexicano, por D. J. F. de L. 41666

Pensador Tapatio. pseud. see Tapatio, el Pensador. pseud. and Tapatio, un Pensador. pseud.

Pensador Tapatio a su censores. 94343

Pensamentos e maximas, por Frederico Jose Correia. 16841

Pensamiento nacional. 60805

Pensamientos de antiguos labradores Venezolanos. 98880

Pensamientos, maximas, sentencia, etc. 29346

Pensamientos sobre caminos. 35069

Pensamientos sobre moral, politica, literatura, religion y costumbres. 25586

Pensees sur la revolution de l'Amerique-Unie. 35987, 64829, 2d note after 96457

Pensees sur le systeme que les differentes puissances de l'Europe. 81395

Pensees sur les transactions touchant les isles de Falkland. 36311

Pensil Americano Florido en el rigor del invierno. 11057

Pensilvania bibble bubbled by the treasurer. 33095

Pension and bounty land laws. 60809

Pension, bounty, and prize money manual. 1508

Pension case of the late James T. Smith. 83969

Pension laws now in force. (60810)

Pension laws of the United States. 47187, 60811

Pensions required for the relief and support of disabled soldiers. 4575

Pensylvanie. 101350

Pentecost; or, the work of God in Philadelphia. 60812

Penuela, Ramon Pino y. see Pino y Penuela, Ramon.

Penuelas, -----. (60813)

Penuelas, P. A. 60814

Penzon, -------. 50050-50064, 1st-5th notes after 106378

Peoli, Gonzalo. 60815

Peon, A. M. (68805)

Peon, Jose Julian. 60816

Peon prince; a tale of Mexico. 21156

People. pseud. Whereas it has been reported. 102348

People called Quakers. pseud. Case of our
fellow creatures. see Benezet, Anthony.

People called Quakers cleared by Geo. Keith
from the false doctrines charged upon
them by G. Keith. 59665

People coming to power! 62528

People encouraging their pastor. 79791

People of Carroll County, Ky. see Carroll
County, Ky.

People of Colour. petitioners 14732

People of God invited to trust in him. 82888

People of Great Britain. petitioners see
Great Britain. Citizens. petitioners

People of Ireland. pseud. Address of the
people of Ireland to their countrymen and
countrywomen in America. (81754)

People of Ireland. pseud. Address of the
people of Ireland to the countrymen in
America. (56653)

People of Louisiana. petitioners see
Louisiana. petitioners

People of New-England put in mind of the
righteous acts of the Lord. 65607, 92351

People of New England reasoned with. 50299

People of Rupert's Land and North-West Territory, British America. petitioners 47618

People of Spotsylvania County, Va. petitioners
see Spotsylvania County, Va. Citizens.
petitioners

People of the state of New York, vs. Bird W.
Spencer. 89304

People of the District of Spartanburgh, S. C.
petitioners see Spartanburgh District,
S. C. Citizens. petitioners

People of the Northwest Ohio. see Ohio.
Citizens.

People of the state of Michigan, versus Abel
F. Fitch and others. 24559, 48784

People of the state of New York ads. the state
of New Jersey. 60817

People of the state of New York vs. John A.
Dix. 29713

People of the state of New York vs. the Rector,
&c. of Trinity Church. 49046

People ripe for the harvest. 105578

People, the sovereigns. 50019

People to the rescue. 57927

People vs. King Caucus. 13745

Peoples, John H. ed. 83867

Peoples, Barnard & Callahan. firm publishers
83867

People's almanac. 60818

People's ancient and just liberties asserted.
[sic] 59723

People's answer to the court pamphlet. 60819,
80686

People's book. An address to the citizens of
Boston. 82493

People's book of American history. 8686

People's book of ancient and modern history.
8685

People's book of biography. 58957

People's cabinet. 47999

People's Club of Philadelphia, in Favor of
General Simon Cameron for President.
10169, (61426) see also People's Party.
Pennsylvania.

People's College, Havana, N. Y. see Montour
Falls, N. Y. People's College.

People's College, Montour Falls, N. Y. see
Montour Falls, N. Y. People's College

People's College of the State of New York,
Montour Falls, N. Y. see Montour Falls,
N. Y. People's College.

People's Convention, Boston, 1862. 45942,
(72214)

People's Democratic guide. 60821

People's doctors. 60822

People's edition. 84320

People's edition. Journey beyond the Rocky
Mountains. 58375, (58730)

People's five cent novelettes, no. 1. 90522

People's friend. pseud. People's doctors.
see Drake, Daniel, 1785-1852. supposed
author

People's friend, the tyrant's foe. 89933

People's illustrated edition. 92471, 92487

People's interest in one article consider'd &
exhibited. 94116

People's keepsake. 78646

People's laureate. 84053

People's League of the Old and New World,
Wheeling, [W.] Va. 60823

People's Library, Newport, R. I. see Newport
R. I. People's Library.

People's library, no. 47. (79915)

People's magazine. 60824

People's military almanac for 1862. 60825

People's organ (Pittsburgh) 60826

People's organ (St. Louis) 84241

People's own book. 60827

People's Pacific Railroad Company. 60828

People's Pacific Railroad Company. petitioner
60828

People's Pacific Railroad Company. Charter.
60828

People's Party. Pennsylvania. 10169, (61426)
see also People's Club of Philadelphia,
in Favor of General Simon Cameron for
President.

People's Party. Pennsylvania. State Committee. (20696)

People's Perpetual Loan Association, Boston.
60829

People's plea for the exercise of prophecy.
72110, (74456)

People's plea for the exercise of prophesie,
against Mr. Iohn Yates his monopolie.
(72107)-(72108)

People's presidential candidate. 30589, 31783

People's privileges, &c. 14426

People's resolutions. 19511, 80444

People's right to election or alteration of
goverment [sic] in Connecticut. 9095

People's rights re-claimed. 31595, 60830

People's State Committee of Pennsylvania.
see People's Party. Pennsylvania.
State Committee.

People's ticket, in support of Andrew Jackson.
96771

People's Union Association of East Cambridge
Mass. see East Cambridge, Mass.
People's Union Association.

Peopling and planting the New World. 58061

Peor [sic] es lo roto que lo descosido. 97049

Peoria, Ill. Board of Trade. 60832

Peoria, Ill. Eye Infirmary and Orthopaedic
Institution. see Peoria Eya Infirmary
and Orthopaedia Institution.

Peoria and Oquawka Rail Road Company.
defendants 87299-87301

Peoria city directory for 1867-8. (60833)

Peoria directory for 1844. (60833)

Peoria Eye Infirmary and Orthopaedic Institution. 60834

Peoria Indians. 84577-84578, 2d-3d notes
after 97876

Peoria Indians. Treaties, etc. 96676

Pepe, a pirate. defendant 11223

Pepin de Degrouhette, --------. supposed
author 94177

Pepin-a-waw. Potawatomi Indian Chief 96705

Peregrine Prolox. pseud. Letters descriptive of the Virginia springs. see Nicklin, Philip Houlbrooke.

Peregrine Prolox. pseud. Pleasant peregrination. see Nicklin, Philip Houlbrooke.

Peregrino Sanmiguel, Jose. see Sanmiguel, Jose Peregrino.

Peregrino con guia, y medicina universal del alma. 76788

Peregrino in septentrional Atlante. 22898

Peregrino Indiano. 29380

Peregrino septentrional Atlante delineado. 44527

Peregrinus, A. S. 77900

Pereira, Albino Jose. defendant 97697

Pereira, Diego Sanchez. see Sanchez Pereira, Diego.

Pereira, Joao Manso. 60880, 98830

Pereira, Jose Saturnino da Costa. see Costa Pereira, Jose Saturnino da.

Pereira, Juan de Solorzano. see Solorzano Pereira, Juan de, 1575-1655.

Pereira, Nuno Marquez. 60891

Pereira Cabral, Fredrico Augusto de Vascancellos a. see Cabral, F. A. de Vasconcellos a Pereira.

Pereira Coelho, Jose Antonio. see Coelho, Jose Antonio Pereira.

Pereira Coruja, Antonio Alvares. 14364, 60879, 76904

Pereira Coutinho, Joaquim Forjaz. see Coutinho, Joaquim Forjaz Pereira.

Pereira da Silva, Jose Manuel, 1819-1898. 60881-60887, 99734

Pereira da Silva Portilho, Joao Anastacio de Souza. see Souza Pereira da Silva Portilho, Joao Anastacio de.

Pereira da Silva Ramos, Joaquim Jose, b. 1818. 67668, 81115

Pereira de Alencastre, Jose Martins. 60888

Pereira de Barros, Jose Mauricio Fernandes. 3649, 60890

Pereira de Berredo, Bernardo. see Berredo, Bernardo Pereira de.

Pereira de Castro, Eduardo de Sa. see Sa Pereira de Castro, Eduardo de.

Pereira de Costa, Constantino. see Costa, Constantino Pereira de.

Pereira de Leon, Moses. (27218), (40086)-40088, (51894), 3d, 6th, 7th notes after 93855

Pereira de Vasconceillos, J. M. 60889

Pereira do Lago, Antonio Bernardino. see Lago, Antonio Bernardino Pereira do.

Pereira Furtado de Mendonca, Hypolito Jose da Costa. see Costa Pereira Furtado de Mendonca, Hypolito Jose da.

Pereira Leal, F. J. 14299, 38994, 39523, note after 93820

Pereira Monteiro, Paulo. 85772

Pereira Pacheco, Jose Praxedes. see Pacheco, Jose Praxedes Pereira.

Pereira Pato Moniz, Nuno Alvares. see Moniz, Nuno Alvares Pereira Pato.

Pereira Pinto, Antonio. see Pinto, Antonio Pereira.

Pereira Reboucas, Antonio. see Reboucas, Antonio Pereira.

Pereira Rego, Jose. see Rego, Jose Pereira.

Pereira Viana, Miguel. see Viana, Miguel Pereira.

Pereira Gamba i Compania. firm publishers 60892

Pereire, E. 60893

Perera, Galeotta. 66686

Pretti, Anselmo Francisco. 69315 see also Recife (Brazilian Province) Presidente (Peretti)

Peretti, Felice. see Sixtus V, Pope, 1521-1590.

Pereyra, Diego Joseph Sanchez. see Sanchez Pereyra, Diego Joseph.

Pereyra, Juan de Solorzano. see Solorzano Pereira, Juan de, 1575-1655.

Perez, --------, fl. 1860. ed. 132

Perez, Antonio. 60896

Perez, Antonio Joaquin. see Martinez, Antonio Joaquin Perez.

Perez, Felipe. 60900

Perez, Francisco. 60903

Perez, Gio. 60904

Perez, Ignacio Carrillo y. see Carrillo y Perez, Ignacio.

Perez, Jeronimo. (60906)

Perez, Jose. 60907

Perez, Jose R. (60909)

Perez Josef. defendant 60908

Perez, Juan Pio. 60910

Perez, Manuel. 49876, 60911-60913

Perez, Martin. 66686

Perez, Trinidad Manuel. 60916

Peres de Anastaris, Ramon. 60915

Perez de Barreda, M. plaintiff 34720

Perez de Barreda, Pedro. 34720

Perez de Guzman y Gonzaga, Juan. see Guzman y Gonzaga, Juan Perez de.

Perez de la Serna, Juan. see Serna, Juan Perez de la.

Perez de Lara, Alonso. 60894

Perez de Oliva, Fernan, 1495?-1533. 75567-75568

Perez de Oliva, Manuel. 60914

Perez de Ribas, Andres. see Ribas, Andres-Perez de.

Perez de Ribas, Antonio. see Ribas, Antonio Perez de.

Perez de Santa Cruz, Miguel. see Santa Cruz, Miguel Perez de, Marques de Buenavista.

Perez de Torres, Simon. 3350

Perez de Villagra, Gaspar. see Villagra, Gaspar Perez de.

Perez Galvez, Francisca de Paula de. see Galves, Francisca de Paula de Perez.

Perez Gomar, Gregorio. 60905

Perez Martinez, Antonio Joaquin. see Martinez Antonio Joaquin Perez.

Perez Mendoza, Daniel. see Mendoza, Daniel Perez.

Perez Rosales, Vicente. see Rosales, Vicente Perez.

Perez Velasco, Antonio. 26577

Perez Ximeno, Fabian. see Ximeno, Fabian Perez.

Perez y Comoto, Florencio. (60901)-60902

Perez y Comoto, Florencio. supposed author 24146, 60902, 76217

Perez y Hernandez, Jose Maria. see Hernandez, Jose Maria Perez de.

Perez y Lopez, Antonio Xavier. (60899)

Perfect account of the religion. (77892)

Perfect and upright man characteriz'd and recommended. 72692, 2d note after 97559

Perfect and upright man: discourse preacherd . . . June 7, 1857. (16377)

Perfect description of an Indian sqva. (36674)-36675

Perfect description of Virginia. 60918, 1st note after 100507

Perfect house. (77573)

Perfect list of the several persons residenters in Scotland. 18564
Perfect man. 105665
Perfect recovery. 46452
Perfect through suffering. 49036
Perfecta religiosa, contiene tres libros. (40250)
Perfection. 79254
Perfection. A poetical epistle. 60919
Perfection of divine law. 82218
Perfectionist. 60920
Perfectionist and theocratic watchman. 60920
Perfectionists. see Oneida Community.
Perfidia de Napolean Bonaparte y sucesos de Espana. 76222
Perham, Josiah. 60922-60923
Perham, Sidney. 60924
Peri, ------. 2351
Periam, Joseph. 103506
Pericles. pseud. New crisis. 60925
Periegetes, Dionysius. see Dionysius Periegetes.
Pereir, ----- du. see Du Perier, ---------.
Perigord, Charles Maurice de Talleyrand. see Talleyrand-Perigord, Charles Maurice de, Prince de Benevent, 1754-1838.
Peril of our ship of state. 28013
Peril of the republic the fault of the people. 20677
Peril of the times displayed. 104098
Perilous adventure of Dr. B. L. Ball. 2933
Perilous incidents in the loves of sailors and travellers. 38093
Perilous trip across the great American desert to the Pacific. 11180
Perils and adventures on the deep. 60926
Perils and beauties of the deep. 59939, (57949)
Perils and beauties of the ocean. 56639, (57949)
Perils and captivity. 60927
Perils and safeguards of American liberty. 38156
Perils and the security of our country. 64237
Perils of a Peruvian family amid the wilds of the Amazon. 69044
Perils of a privateersman. 36517
Perils of Pearl Street. 28584
Perils of the ocean and wilderness. 80018
Perils of the period. 31592
Perils of the time. (8444)
Perils, pastimes, and pleasures of an emigrant. 60928
Perin, Rene. 60929, 96344
Perinchief, Octavius. 60930
Peringskild, Johann. tr. 85484
Periodical, account of Baptist missions within the Indian Territory. 43113, 60931
Periodical accounts relating to the missions of the United Brethren. 60932, note after 97858
Periodical conducted by the present and former members of the Albany Female Academy. 50201
Periodical devoted to religion, law, legislation, and public events. 66137, 69942, 88394
Periodical library. 10937
Periodical noticies of Rensselaer Institute. 69641
Periodical, no. 3 [of the Social Reform Society.] 70528
Periodial of the Social Reform Society—no. I. 96395
Periodical paper of the Domestic and Foreign Missionary Society. 66184
Periodical publication. 55304

Periodico aventurero. 68480
Periodico cientifico de la Sociedad Mexicana de Historia Natural. 52045
Periodico cientifico y literario. see Museo Yucateco, periodico cientifico y literario. Revista Mexicana. Periodico cientifico y literario.
Periodico critico, satirico, i de amena literatura. 71385
Periodico critico,y literario. 35072
Periodico cuotidiano politico y literario. 48259
Periodico da Sociedade Auxiliadora d [sic] Industria Nacional. 56370
Periodico de artes, ciencias naturales y literatura. 69665
Periodico de ciencias, literatura. 69662
Periodico de comercio, politica y literatura. 48566
Periodico de historia, literatura, lejislacion y economica politica. 58544
Periodico de la Sociedad Economica de Guatemala. 60933, 85753
Periodico de literatura, artes y bellas letras. 48261
Periodico de noticias religiosas, nacionales y extrangeras. (48405)
Periodico de politica general. 70297
Periodica de politica, literatura, y comercio. 81391
Periodico de politica, religion, literatura, teatros y avisos. 15921
Periodico de religion, variedades y anuncios. 48272
Periodico dedicado al pueblo. 76705
Periodico del estado libre de la Puebla de Los Angeles. 9832
Periodico en miniatura. 41977
Periodico general e independiente. 51695
Periodico imparcial. (16842)
Periodico independiente de politica, literatura, variedades y anuncios. (68132)
Periodico literario. 69596
Periodico literario, politico, aristico, industrial y de teatros. 26281
Periodico literario. Redactado por una Sociedad de Amigos. 68836
Periodico litterario. 88713
Periodico malicioso. 17607
Periodico mensal. 7613
Periodico mensal, destinado a promover a agricultura. 16047
Periodico mensual. 56648
Periodico mensual de historia Americana. 9040
Periodico mensual de historial y literatura de America. (70311)
Periodico mensual, dirigido por D. Francisco de P. Serrano. 29414
Periodico mensual por una Sociedad de Espanoles. 56648
Periodico Medicano. (48293)
Periodico noticioso, politico literario y mercantil. 24062
Periodico oficial del estado. 86563
Periodico oficial del gobierno de los Estados-Unidos Medicanos. (48382)
Periodico oficial del gobierno del Estado. 86979
Periodico oficial del supremo gobierno de los Estados-Unidos Mexicanos. 48623
Periodico Omniscio, de buen humor y con caricaturas. 57650
Periodico politico. see Sombra de Jarauta: periodico politico.

Periodico politico, cientifico y literario. see
Imparcial. Periodico politico, cientifico
y literario. Lucero de Tacubaya. Period-
ico politico, cientifico y literario. Nacion.
Periodico politico, cientifico y literario.
Progresista, periodico politico, cientifico
y literario.
Periodico politico, cientifico, literario e indus-
trial. 19265
Periodico politico, literario, economico y
mercantil. 50098
Periodico politico, literario y comercial. see
Democrata. Periodico politico, literario
y comercial. Heraldo, periodico politico,
literario y comercial. Regenerador.
Periodico politico, literario y comercial.
Periodico politico y literario. see Paz.
Periodico politico y literario. Razon de
Mexico. Periodico politico y literario.
Sabatina universal. Periodico politico y
literario. Sociedad. Periodico politico y
literario.
Periodico politico y noticioso. see Clave.
Periodico politico y noticioso. Revista
Yucateca. Periodico politico y noticioso.
Periodico poligloto. 16843
Periodico que contiene todas las leyes y
decretos. 48606
Periodico quincenal, bajo la direccion de
D. J. J. de Mora. (70315)
Periodico quincenal, de ciencias, literatura,
artes, modas, teatros, etc. 70306
Periodico quincenal de literatura. 35073
Periodico-quincenal, por Mendive y I. Q.
Garcia. 47813
Periodico religiosos, politoco-Cristiano,
cientifico y literario. 11549
Periodico religioso, politico, literario, artistico
y mercantil. 60805
Periodico religioso, social y literario. 56457
Periodico retozon, impolitico y de malas
costumbres. 16997
Periodico satirico-jocoso con abundanxia de
caricaturas. (36901)
Periodico satirico redactado por varios estu-
diantes de buen humor. 71385
Periodico semanario. 56458
Periodico semanario, de ciencias, artes,
historia y Americo literatura. 24831
Periodico semanario de la Puebla de los
Angeles. (23875)
Periodico seminario literario, cientifico, de
politica y comercio. (4271)
Periodico semioficial del Estado de Michoacan.
48816
Periodico y trata de todo. 48311
Periodista electrico. 87219
Periquillo Sarmiento por el Pensador Mexicano.
41664
Peritsol, Abraham. see Farrisol, Abraham.
Perjury case! Further developments. (13256)
Perjury exposed. 83969
Perjury prevalent. 64296
Perkins, --------. (49996)
Perkins, --------. reporter 66826
Perkins, --------, fl. 1864. 29219
Perkins, A. E. P. 60935
Perkins, Augustus Thorndike, 1827-1891. 60936-
60937
Perkins, Benjamin Douglas. (60842)
Perkins, Bishop. 60938
Perkins, Charles. 60939
Perkins, Charles C. (60940)
Perkins, Cyrus. 60941
Perkins, Elisha. (60942), 98686
Perkins, Elisha B. (60943)

Perkins, Ephraim. 60944
Perkins, Frederick Beecher. 22085, (22774),
54154, 57112, 60945-60947, 66801
Perkins, G. R. 22543
Perkins, G. W. (60950)-60952, 93197
Perkins, George A. 60948
Perkins, Mrs. George A. (60949)
Perkins, Granville. illus. 84041
Perkins, James. 28386, 60953 see also
Boston. Committee of Merchants and
Others, 1820.
Perkins, James Handasyd. 20395, 60954-
60956, 102993
Perkins, John, fl. 1770. 60957-60958, note after
95670, 97132, 8th note after 102552
Perkins, John, 1819-1885. 60959
Perkins, John Carroll. 84353
Perkins, Jonas. 60960
Perkins, Joseph. 60961
Perkins, Josephine Amelia. 60962
Perkins, Justin. 60963
Perkins, Lafayette. 60964
Perkins, Nathan, 1749-1838. (14309), 60965-
60969, 92962, 97593
Perkins, Oliver L. 23494
Perkins, S. K. B. 60974
Perkins, Samuel. 60970-60972
Perkins, Simeon. 60973
Perkins, Stephen H. 60975, 76593, 76647
Perkins, Thomas Handasyd. 11218, (33984),
60976, 105361
Perkins, Thomas Handasyd. defendant 96859
Perkins, W. S. 60977
Perkins, William. 62091-72094, 72110
Perkins family of Connecticut. 60946
Perkins Institution and Massachusetts Asylum
for the Blind. (60978)
Perkins Institution and Massachusetts Asylum
for the Blind. Trustees. 52691
Perkinmen Consolidated Mining Company.
Directors. (60979)
Perl o fawr bris. 83278
Perla de la America. 36882
Perle der Antillen. (81477)
Perleb, K. J. tr. 12263
Perley, Ira. 60980
Perley, Jeremiah. 60981
Perely, Jeremiah. reporter (43920)
Perley, Moses Henry, 1804-1862. 31939,
60982-60984
Perlite litteratoor. 8646
Permanence amid changes. 6964
Permanency of the pastoral relation. 12991
Permanent and effectual remedy suggested.
60985, 72255, 1st note after 102858
Permanent documents of the Society for the
Promotion of Collegiate and Theological
Education at the West. 85919
Permanent Exposition, New Orleans, La.
88614
Permanent identity of the human race. 82347
Permanent resolutions of the Board of Trustees
14842
Permanent temperance documents of the Ameri-
can Temperance Society. 1240, 60986
Permanent temperance documents [of the
American Temperance Union.] 1240
Permanent temperance documents, published
by direction of the state Temperance
Society. 88071
Permiso para fabricar extramuros. 29451
Pernambuco. Inhabitants. see Pernambuco.
Inwoonderen.
Pernambuco. Inwoonderen. 38256, 44263, 1st
note after 102894, 102895
Pernambuco. Inwoonderen. petitioners 44263

Pernambuco. Inwoonders Portugesen. petition-ers 60987

Pernambuco. Presidente (Boa Vista) (60992) see also Boa Vista, Barao da.

Pernambuco. Presidente (Cinha e Figueiredo) 60993 see also Cinha e Figueiredo, Jose Bento da.

Pernambuco. Presidente (Cunha Paranagua) 60991 see also Cunha Paranagua, Joao Lustosa da.

Pernambuco. Presidente (Gama) 60989 see also Gama, Antonio Pinto Chichorra da.

Pernambuco. Treaties, etc. 41849, note after 99260

Pernambuco libertado: drama em quatro actos. 9220

Pernetty, Dom. see Pernety, Antoine Joseph, 1716-1801.

Pernety, Antoine Joseph, 1716-1801. 6870, 59239, 59241-59244, 59246, 60997, 62957-62958

Pernety, Antoine Joseph, 1716-1801. supposed author 1292, 6327

Pernicious effects of intemperance in the use of ardent spirits. (65534)

Pernicious progress of bank speculation un-veiled. 6513, (11890)

Pero. El cumplimiento de la ley. 49895

Perodico [sic] sempre moral. 10789

Perogative [sic] of the Parliaments of England. 67599

Peron, Francois, 1775-1810. 60998-(61001), 62506-62507

Perou. (11741)

Perou avant la conquete Espagnole. 19740

Perou et Sainte Rose de Lima. 9560

Perou et ses derniers evenements. (61152)

Perou; Republique de Bolivar; le Chili. 101350

Perouse, Jean Francois de Galaup, Comte de la. see La Perouse, Jean Francois de Galaup, Comte de, 1741-1788.

Perpetual acts of the General Assemblies. 56160

Perpetual almanac of spiritual meditation. 61002

Perpetual calendar for old and new style. 80784

Perpetual calendar for old and new style; pre-paged for the use of those engaged in anti-quarian and historical investigations. 80783

Perpetual calendar, or economical almanack. (23241)

Perpetual laws of . . . New-Hampshire. 52892

Perpetual laws of the commonwealth of Massa-chusetts. (45932)

Perpetual war ending in anarchy or military despotism, etc. 19517

Perpetual war, the policy of Mr. Madison. 42456

Perpetuity of the Sabbath. 1808

Perpetuity of the union. 50463

Perpina, Josef de Nuix y de. see Nuix, Juan, 1740-1783.

Perpina, Juan de Nuix y de. see Nuix, Juan, 1740-1783.

Perrault, Charles Ovide. 61003

Perrault, Joseph Francois, 1753-1844. 61005

Perrault, Joseph Francois, fl. 1859-1864. 61006

Perrault, Julien, 1598-1647. 39950-39951, (61004), note after 69259

Perrault Proton, J. F. see Proton, J. F. Perrault.

Perre, J. van de. 98926 see also Netherlands. Legatie. Great Britain.

Perreau, J. A. 61007

Perrey, Alexis. 61008

Perrin, Edwin O. 61009

Perrin, Lavalette. 61010

Perrin, William. 61011

Perrin du Lac, F. M. 61012-61014, 62506

Perrine, Henry. petitioner 61016-61017

Perrine, Mathew la Rue. (61018)

Perrine (Co. O.) firm publishers 5611, 61015

Perrine's new topographical war map of the southern states. 5611, 61015

Perrinon, A. F. 61019

Perrodin, John C. 61020

Perronet, Charles. supposed author 85206-85207

Perronet Thompson, Thomas. see Thompson, Thomas Perronet.

Perrot, John, fl. 17th cent. 61021, 70894

Perrot, Nicolas. 61022

Perrott, John. see Perrot, John, fl. 17th cent.

Perrottet, George Samuel, 1793-1870. 61023

Perrottet, S. 29111

Perry, Aaron Fyfe, 1815-1893. 61024-(61025)

Perry, Albert James, 1841- 84247

Perry, Benjamin Franklin, 1805-1886. 61026-61027, 87445, 87520, 88080 see also South Carolina. Governor, 1865-1866 (Perry) South Carolina. Legislature. House of Representatives. Special Com-mittee on the Penitentiary System. Chair-man.

Perry, Daniel. 28884

Perry, Daniel. defendant 6326, 1st note after 96956, 1st note after 97284

Perry, David, b. 1741. 61028

Perry, David L. 61029

Perry, Ezra. (68973), 95524

Perry, Gardner B. 61030-61031

Perry, George H. 61032

Perry, Gideon B. 61034

Perry, Henry F. ed. 92752

Perry, James. 61035

Perry, James H. 61036

Perry, John B. 61037

Perry, John G. 70644 see also Rhode Island. Commissioner to the Universal Exposition at Paris, 1867.

Perry, John Jasiel, 1811-1897. 61038

Perry, John L. ed. 91095

Perry, Joseph. 61039-61041

Perry, Madison S. 33150 see also Florida. Governor, 1857-1861 (Perry)

Perry, Marshall S. 61042-(61043)

Perry, Matthew C. 61044

Perry, Matthew Galbraith. (30968)

Perry, Nehemiah, 1816-1881. 61045-61046

Perry, Oliver Hazard, 1785-1819. 22270, 61047

Perry, Oliver Hazard, 1785-1819. defendant at court martial 61047

Perry, Phil. Frank. 61048

Perry, T. S. ed. 55562

Perry, Thomas Johns, 1807-1871. 61049

Perry, William Stevens, Bp., 1832-1898. 30973, 61050-61060, 65947, (66172)-(66173), 84408 see also Protestant Episcopal Church in the U. S. A. Historiographer.

Perry County, Ohio. St. Joseph's College. see St. Joseph's College, Perry County, Ohio.

Perry Academy, Wyoming County, N. Y. 61061

Perry-Centre Institute, Perry-Centre, ?. 61062

Perry-Centre Institute at Perry-Centre. Cata-logue of officers and students. 61062

Perry-patetic songs and other jollification ditties. 18598

Perryman, L. C. tr. 61063

Perryman, S. W. tr. 61063

Perry's victory. 86955

Pers, Jean Baptiste le. see Le Pers, Jean Baptiste.

Persecucion contra el Obispo de San Luis Potosi. 76149

Persecution every Christian's lot. 103573

Persecution expos'd. 103701

Persecution in America! 61064, 94817

Persecution in New York. 61065

Persecution in the name of law. 95778

Persecution of the volunteer naval officers. (2065)

Perseverance. 96165

Persian patriot. (23243)

Persifer, ---------. USA 97652

Person, William. 61066

Person cast away on the place. pseud. Discovery of Fonseca. see S., I. pseud.

Person in the Jerseys. pseud. Letter. 86755

Person many years a resident there. pseud. Description of the island of St. John. 75278

Person of distinction. pseud. Proposal for humbling Spain. 8122, (66016)

Person of eminence and worth in Caledonia. pseud. Abstract of a letter. see Patterson, J.

Person of eminence and worth in Caledonia. pseud. Observations. see Patterson, J.

Person of honour. pseud. tr. 20585, 31381

Person of honour. pseud. ed. see Rowland, John. supposed ed.

Person of Honor. pseud. Jesuites policy. see Derby, Charles Stanley, 8th Earl of.

Person of honour. pseud. Spaniards cruelty and treachery. see Scott, Thomas. of Utrecht

Person of honour. pseud. Speech delivered in Parliament. 89176

Person of honour then present. pseud. Genuine speech of the truely honourable Adm-----l V-----n. 99244

Person of honor upon the spot. pseud. Massachusettensis. see Leonard, Daniel.

Person of quality. pseud. Full account of the actions of the late famous pyrate, Capt. Kidd. 37704

Person of quality. pseud. Full account of the proceedings in relation to Capt. Kidd. 37703

Person to whom it was communicated. pseud. Answer. see Burnett, William.

Person well acquainted with the sugar trade. pseud. Some considerations touching the sugar colonies. 86628

Person who has been an eye witness, for a considerable length of time. pseud. Just and true account of the prison. 61750

Person who lived there ten years. pseud. Historical and political view of the present and ancient state of the colony of Surinam. 24118

Person who renounced Deism. pseud. Some judicious remarks. see Guy, Francis.

Person who resided several years at Jamaica. pseud. Some observations on the assiento trade. 1653, 19251, 86683

Person who resided several years at Jamaica. pseud. State of the island of Jamaica. see B——, A.——. pseud.

Person who was an eye-witness to all the affair. pseud. Affecting narrative. 1634

Person who was an officer under Miranda. pseud. General account of Miranda's expedition. see Sherman, John H.

Person who was present when he died. pseud. Short account of the last sickness and death. see Ritchie, Elizabeth.

Person who was present when he died. pseud. Short account of the sickness and death. see Ritchie, Elizabeth.

Person zealously devoted. pseud. Publick good without private interests. see Gatford, Lionel.

Persona residente en la republica Mexicana. pseud. Exposicion. 23434

Personal. 71148

Personal adventures and travels of four years and a half. 18852

Personal adventures connected with twelve successful trips. 71877

Personal adventures in Upper and Lower California. 74532

Personal affliction and frequent reflection upon human life. 84641

Personal and historical recollections of the Baltimore and Ohio Railroad. 61067

Personal and military history of Philip Kearny 10635

Personal and political ballads. 50364

Personal census. 10401

Personal experiences. By Ubique. 27420

Personal experiences in the war of the great rebellion. 50917

Personal experiences of a soldier in the Army of the Potomac. (31803)

Personal forgiveness and public justice. 6393

Personal history of Ulysses S. Grant. (70984)

Personal humiliation demanded by the national dangers. 33964

Personal indexes prior to 1698 and index of 1698. 88595

Personal liberty and martial law. 34741

Personal liberty bill. 47181

Personal liberty laws. Remarks . . . before the Committee of the Legislature. 62712

Personal liberty laws, . . . and slavery in the territories. 58698

Personal memoir of Daniel Drayton. 20912

Personal memoir of my cruises and services in the "Sumter" and "Alabama." 79082

Personal memoirs and recollections of editorial life. 8906

Personal memoirs, anecdotes, and reminiscences. (8909)

Personal memoirs of a residence of thirty years with the Indian tribes. (11185), 77870

Personal narrative. By Elisha Kent Kane. (36998)

Personal narrative by Richard Henry Dana, Jr. 18449, note after 97587

Personal narrative of a tour through a part of the United States and Canada. 20370

Personal narrative of explorations and incidents in Texas. 3746

Personal narrative of James O. Pattie. 59150

Personal narrative of life at sea. 18448, note before 97587

Personal narrative of Mrs. Margaret Douglass. (20719)

Personal narrative of observation and adventure in Greenland. 31021

Personal narrative of proscription for being an abolitionist. (46866)

Personal narrative of that celebrated pirate. (67664)

Personal narrative of the discovery of the north west passage. 2017

Personal narrative of the first voyage of Columbus to America. (14668)

Personal narrative of the sufferings of J. Stephanini. 91230

Personal narrative of travels in the United States and Canada. 19677

Personal narrative of travels to the equinoctial regions. (33771)

Personal narrative of travels to the equinoctial regions of the new continent. 33770

Personal narrative of wanderings in Central America. 7136

Personal narratives of the author, during a tour through a part of the United States of America and Canada. (20369)

Personal narratives of many who escaped. 8803

Personal recollections of distinguished generals. 79755

Personal recollections of Minnesota and its people. 91543

Personal recollections of Sherman's campaigns. 60839

Personal recollections of the American revolution. 64460-64461, 97068

Personal recollections of the author first published. (12429)

Personal recollections of the far west one and twenty years ago. 61323

Personal record of a cruise. 91664

Personal reminiscences and historical incidents illustrative of Indian life and character. 24380

Personal reminiscences [of P. T. Barnum.] 3563

Personal reminiscences of the life and times of Gardiner Spring. 89778

Personal reminiscences of the Morgan abduction and murder. (28611)

Personal representation. 48987

Personal representation Society. petitioners 47697

Personal satire. 33785, 77885

Personal sketches of the members. (44379)

Personal slavery established. 61068

Personals; or, perils of the period. 31592

Personel, Francis Burdett. 61069

Personen in Paris. pseud. Briefe. (65501)

Personen, Land und Zustande in Nord-Amerika. 20670

Personne. pseud. Marginalia. 61070

Personnes residentes a Paris. pseud. Lettres au Dr. Priestley, en Amerique. (16687), 59593, 62702, 65510, 92070, 92071

Persons appointed, by the act of the last session. 100066

Persons held to service, fugitive slaves, &c. 102549

Persons in Paris. pseud. Copies of original letters. (16687), note after 65502, 92070

Persons who have emigrated. pseud. Letters. (41943)

Persons who have emigrated to Upper Canada. pseud. Canada. Letters from persons. 86184, note after 98068

Persoon, ---------. 67461

Perspective. pseud. Changery. 6513, (11890)

Perspective. 84553

Perspective des rapports politiques et commerciaux. 19640

Perspicuous compendium of invaluable advice for American emigrants. 55184

Persuasive to the instructing and baptizing of the Negro's and Indians. 27677

Perswasions from the terror of the Lord. 46453

Perswasive to make a publick confession of Christ. 58652

Pert, Sir Thomas. 66686

Perte de l'Amazone vaisseau a vapeur. (5981)

Perth Amboy, N. J. Charter. (61071)

Perth Amboy Manufacturing Company. 61072

Perth-Amboy, New-Jersey, 180[6]. Sir, it having been stated to me. 97280

Perthes, Justus. 49765

Pertinax Particular. pseud. Tales of the tripod. see Watkins, Tobias.

Pertinent observations on the present rebellion in America. 4761

Pertinente beschrijvinge, van de geheele Groenlandse-vaart. 74630, 78978

Pertiennte beschryvinge van Guiana. (3989), (4196), 29186

Peru. (59325)-59326, 59334-59335, 61112, (61119), 61122, 64879, 67135, 67142, 68833, 98311-98312

Peru. Administracion de las Rentas. 61107

Peru. American Citizens. petitioners 83711

Peru. Armada. Courts Martial (Cortes) 58565

Peru. Comision Constitucional. 99478

Peru. Comisionados. 26112, 44291, 76158

Peru. Congreso. Camara de Diputados. Comision de Instruccion. 61087

Peru. Congreso. Senado. Presidente (Telleria) 94618 see also Telleria, Manuel.

Peru. Consejo De Estado. (71311)

Peru. Constitution. 47599, 61098-61101, 99476, 99492, 103421

Peru. Convencion Nacional, 1833. Comision. 61156

Peru. Correos. (68852)

Peru. Direccion General de Contribuciones. (61140) see also Paz Soldan, Felipe.

Peru. Direccion General de Instruccion Publica. (61142)

Peru. Ejercito. Courts Martial (Egusquiza) 58565

Peru. Ex-Secretario de Estado en el Despacho de Hacienda y Comercio. pseud. Memoria. see Pardo, Manuel.

Peru. Gremio de Navieros. see Gremio de Navieros de Peru.

Peru. Gobierno Protectoria, 1837. 12779

Peru. Inspector Especial de Todos los Establecimientos Departamentales. 73175 see also Rosa, Manuel Toribio Gonzalez de la.

Peru. Labradores de los Valles Circunvecinos. see Labradores de los Valles Circunvecinos del Peru.

Peru. Laws, statutes, etc. 9882, (22892), 41107, 41113, 41114, 49895, 61079, 61090-61091, (61100)-61101, 61111, 61125, 61134, 61156-61160, 90775, 99477, 99482, 99493-99495, note after 103224

Peru. Legacion. Chile. Tesoro. 58564

Peru. Legacion. Colombia. 14576-14577, 16905, note after 99615 see also Villa, Jose.

Peru. Legacion. Ecuador. 61095 see also Quito, Ecuador. Conferencia Tenida Entre los Ministros Plenipotentiarios del Peru y del Ecuador Nombrados Para Transijir las Diferencias que Existen Entre Una y Otra Republica.

Peru. Legislatura. see Peru. Congreso.

Peru. Magistrados Despojados Por la Revolucion Judicial. petitioners see Magistrados Despojados Por la Revolucion Judicial. petitioners

Peru. Ministerio de Gobierno, Policia y Obras Publicas. see Peru. Ministerio de Gobierno y Policia.

Peru. Ministerio de Gobierno y Policia.
61141-(61142)

Peru. Ministerio de Gobierno y Relaciones
Esteriores. see Peru. Ministerio de
Relaciones Esteriores.

Peru. Ministerio de Guerra y Marina. 61138,
99616 see also Guarda, Manuel de la.
Villa, Jose.

Peru. Ministerio de Hacienda. 50501, (61142),
61144, 61148, 97716 see also Morales
y Ugalde, Jose de. Pando, J. M. de.
Unanue, Jose Hipolito.

Peru. Ministerio de Justicia y Culto. (61142)

Peru. Ministerio de Justicia, Instruccion
Publica, Beneficencia y Culto. see Peru.
Direccion General de Instruccion Publica.

Peru. Ministerio de Justicia, Instruccion
Publica y Beneficencia. see Peru.
Ministerio de Justicia y Culto.

Peru. Ministerio de Negocios Eclesiasticos.
50500

Peru. Ministerio de Relaciones Esteriores.
(14600)-14601, 41094, (50095), 61139,
(61142), 61170, 71455, 96223, 99482,
99485 see also Monteagudo, Bernardo.
Rio, Manuel del. Vidaurre y Encalada,
Manuel Lorenzo de. Torre, Pedro de la.

Peru. President, 1833-1835 (Orbegosa) 57421,
61123 see also Orbegosa, Luis Jose,
Pres. Peru.

Peru. President, 1836-1839 (Santa Cruz) 61146
see also Santa Cruz, Andres, Pres.
Bolivia, 1794-1865.

Peru. President, 1839-1841 (Gamarra) 61147
see also Gamarra, Agustin, Pres. Peru,
1785-1841.

Peru. President, 1865-1868 (Prado) 16904,
58514, 61077, 64879 see also Prado,
Mariano Ignacio, Pres. Peru, 1826-1901.

Peru. Provincia de los Doza Apostoles. see
Doze Apostoles del Peru (Ecclesiastical
Province)

Peru. Senores Encargados del Proyeto de
Constitucion. see Peru. Comision Constitucional.

Peru. Supremo Consejo de la Guerra. 58565

Peru. Treaties, etc. 61094

Peru (Viceroyalty) 8987, 25093, 44291, 61113,
61149, 76158

Peru (Viceroyalty) Agente Asesor. (41106)
see also Valle y Portillo, Manuel del.

Peru (Viceroyalty) Audiencia, Lima. 61110,
69239, 97671

Peru (Viceroyalty) Audiencia, Lima. Fiscales.
36952

Peru (Viceroyalty) Auditor General de la Gente
de Mar, y Guerra. 61103

Peru (Viceroyalty) Consejo. 85673, 98150

Peru (Viceroyalty) Ejercito. Gefes. 61331

Peru (Viceroyalty) Fiscal. defendant 63181,
94269

Peru (Viceroyalty) Fiscal. plaintiff 93318

Peru (Viceroyalty) Juzgado de Lanzas y Medias-
Anatas. 70462

Peru (Viceroyalty) Laws, statutes, etc. 2962,
36899, 38628, 44541, 47837, 61113-(61115),
61135, 61163-(61164), (68243), 69239,
70462, 96119, 98798-98801, 98872

Peru (Viceroyalty) Regni Collegio. 66896

Peru (Viceroyalty) Real Hacienda. 98358

Peru (Viceroyalty) Tribunal del Consulado,
Lima. see Lima, Peru. Tribunal del
Consulado, y Junta General de Comercio.

Peru (Viceroyalty) Virrey. 69239

Peru (Viceroyalty) Virrey, 1569-1581 (Toledo)
(41092), 69239, 98800 see also Toledo,
Francisco de, d. 1584.

Peru (Viceroyalty) Virrey, 1596-1604 (Velasco)
98798-98800 see also Velasco, Luis de,
Marques de Salinas, 1534-1617.

Peru (Viceroyalty) Virrey, 1607-1615 (Mendoza
y Luna) (41092), 98332 see also
Mendoza y Luna, Juan de, Marques de
Montesclaros.

Peru (Viceroyalty) Virrey, 1615-1621 (Borja y
Aragon) (41092) see also Borja y
Aragon, Francisco de, Principe de Es-
quilache, 1582-1658.

Peru (Viceroyalty) Virrey, 1622-1629 (Fernande
de Cordova) 98331 see also Fernandez
de Cordova, Diego, 1. Marques de Guadalcazar.

Peru (Viceroyalty) Virrey, 1639-1647 (Toledo
y Leiva) 2245, (35238), 96119 see also
Toledo y Leiva, Pedro de, Marques de
Mancera, 1585-1654.

Peru (Viceroyalty) Virrey, 1655-1661 (Henrique
de Guzman) 61135 see also Henriquez
de Guzman, Luis Conde de Alva de Aliste
y de Villaflor.

Peru (Viceroyalty) Virrey, 1666-1672 (Castro
Andrade y Portugal) 61165, (75986)
see also Castro Andrade y Portugal,
Pedro Fernandez de, Conde de Lemos,
1634-1672.

Peru (viceroyalty) Virrey, 1681-1691 (Navarra
y Rocaful) 56748, 58311 see also
Navarra y Rocaful, Melchor de, Duque d
la Palata.

Peru (Viceroyalty) Virrey, 1745-1761 (Manso
de Velasco) 61136, 79146, 93778 see
also Manso de Velasco, Jose Antonio,
Conde de Superunda.

Peru (Viceroyalty) Virrey, 1780-1784 (Jauregui)
68838 see also Jauregui, Agustin de, d.
1784.

Peru (Viceroyalty) Virrey, 1806-1816 (Abascal
y Sousa) 44541, (68243) see also
Abascal y Sousa, Jose Fernandez de.

Peru, a poem. In six cantos. 104228, 104230

Peru and Spain. 11710

Peru and the United States. 57800

Peru as it is. 82330

Peru-Bolivian. pseud. Expose of the existing
dissensions between Chili. 12772

Peru en 1860. 40726

Peru. Incidents of travel and exploration.
89987

Peru nach seinem gegenwartigen Zustande.
47936, 61153

Peru, Paraguay, etc. 106334

Peru y la Espana moderna. 44669

Peru y la influencia Europea. (61154)

Peruaen, Ignatius Inga. see Inga, Ignatius.

Peruanen. (55419)

Peruano. pseud. Carta de un Peruano. see
Heres, T. de.

Peruano. 61120

Peruano extraordinario. 98950

Peruano liberal. 61166

Perusal, or the book of nature unfolded. 10606

Peruvian; a comic opera. (61167)

Peruvian and Bolivian guano. 61168

Peruvian antiquities. 71645

Peruvian coast pilot. (26559)

Peruvian guano trade. (61169)

Peruvian hero; a tragedy. 38283

Peruvian Mining Company. Directors. 61075

Peruvian pamphlet. (50095), 61170

Peruvian tales, related, in one thousand and
one hours. 29143
Pervviana. (50722)
Peruvians. 39626
Peruviens: tragedie. 23859, 73846
Perversion of ye trewe and wonderrefulle
hystorie. 8421
Pesado, Jose Joaquin. 17840, 57104, 61171-
61172, 1st note after 94592
Pesame al Excmo. Sr. D. Nicolas Mahy. 43880
Pesames y parabienes por la muerte del D.
Bern. de Galuez. 27796
Peschel, Oscar. 61173
Pessoa de Mello, Urbano Sabino. 47463,
88800
Pestilence, a punishment for public sins. 93067
Pestilence . . . a sermon . . . August the third,
1849. (31414)
Pestilence—God's messenger and teacher.
17930
Pestilence, the judgment of God. 32381
Pestilential diseases, and the laws which govern
their propagation. (30472)
Petaubun. 57092, 61174
Petavius, Dionisius. 61175
Petavius, Pa. 76838
Pete Morris' American comic melodist. 50860
Peter, of Ghent. see Petrus a Gandavo, d.
1572.
Peter, Hugh. see Peters, Hugh, 1598-1660.
Peter, Robert, 1805-1894. 17653, 34529,
37513, 61176, (80563), 90779
Peter, William. ed. (73063)
Peter Atwell. pseud. see Waln, Robert,
1794-1825.
Peter Carl Zimmermanns Reise nach Ost- und
West-Indien. 106347
Peter Claver. 13514
Peter Dobbins. pseud. see Fessenden,
William.
Peter Faber's misfortunes. 52164
Peter Funks. 3563
Peter Gott, the Cape Ann fisherman. 70437
Peter Grievous. pseud. see Hopkinson,
Francis, 1737-1791.
Peter Loeflings Reise nach den Spanischen
Landern. 41773
Peter Madicanscutter. pseud. see Dogherty,
Roger.
Peter Oliver's " Puritan commonwealth" reviewed.
95641
Peter Pangloss. pseud. see Pangloss, Peter.
pseud.
Peter Parley. pseud. see Clark, Samuel, fl.
1839.
Peter Parley. pseud. see Goodrich, Samuel
Griswold, 1793-1860.
Peter Parley, pseud. see Parley, Peter.
pseud.
Peter Parley's annual. 83513
Peter Parley's book of the United States. 97927
Peter Parley's book of the United States, geo-
graphical, political and historical. 94243
Peter Parley's Canada. note after 61176
Peter Parley's common school history. (27914)
Peter Parley's tales about America. 27911,
27922, 94248
Peter Parley's tales of animals. 27912
Peter Parley's tales about Canada. 27924,
94242
Peter Parley's tales about New York. 27910
Peter Parley's tales about South America.
27911
Peter Parley's tales. Lives of Franklin &
Washington. 101848
Peter Parley's universal history. 27915

Peter Pennyless. pseud. see Pennyless, Peter.
pseud.
Peter Pepper Box, Poet and Physician. pseud.
see Fessenden, Thomas Green.
Peter Pilgrim: or a rambler's recollections.
(5558), 61177
Peter Pindar. pseud. see Pindar, Peter.
pseud.
Peter Pindar. pseud. see Wolcott, John.
Peter Pindar, Jr. pseud. see Pindar, Peter,
Jr. pseud.
Peter Ploddy and other oddities. 52165
Peter Ploddy's dream. 52164
Peter Ploughshare. pseud. see Beach, Samuel
B. supposed author
Peter Porcupine. pseud. see Cobbett, William,
1763-1835.
Peter Porcupine's descent into hell. 64158
Peter Porcupine's gazette. 14021
Peter Quince. pseud. see Story, Isaac,
1774-1803.
Peter Russell, esq; President, administering
the government of the province of Upper
Canada, &c. &c. 98058A
Peter Russell, esq. President, administering
the government of Upper Canada. 98058B
Peter Scriber. pseud. see Davis, Charles
Augustus.
Peter Scriber on protection. (61178)
Peter Squills. pseud. see Goodman, Charles
Holmes.
Peter the whaler. 37905
Peter Wilkins. 9245
Peter Williamson against W. Fordyce and
others. 104487
Peter Zig-Zag & Dolly Nig-Nag with two other
celebrated comic songs. 85454
Peterboro' and Auburn. 97549
Peterborough, Bishop of. see Hinchliffe, John,
Bishop of Peterborough, 1731-1794.
Kennett, White, Bishop of Peterborough,
1660-1728. Terrick, John, successively
Bishop of Peterborough, and London, 1710-
1777. Thomas, John, successively Bishop
of Peterborough, Salisbury, and Winchester,
1696-1781.
Peterborough, N. H. Altemont Lodge. see
Freemasons. New Hampshire. Altemont
Lodge, Peterborough.
Peterborough, N. H. Bethel Lodge. see Free-
masons. New Hampshire. Bethel Lodge,
Peterborough.
Peterborough, N. H. Charity Lodge. see Free-
masons. New Hampshire. Charity Lodge,
Peterborough.
Peterborough, N. H. Centennial Celebration, 1839.
82322
Peterhoff (Steamship) in Admiralty 5097,
61179-61180, 80499, 82452
Peterhoff. 82452
Peterkin, Joshua. 61181
Petermann, August Heinrich, 1822-1878. 49765,
61182-61183, 71228, 99362
Peters, Dr. --------, fl. 1864. 56832
Peters, Abaslom. 1113, 61184-61186, 104671
Peters, Bernhard Michael. 61187
Peters, C. 61188
Peters, C. H. F. 56832, 61189
Peters, De Witt Clinton. 61190
Peters, Hugh, 1598-1660. 24034, 46776, 61191-
61193, 61195-61196, 101130, note after
105462, 106018
Peters, J. defendant 96956
Peters, Jeremy. pseud. Chronicles of Turkey-
town. see Smith, Thomas Lacey, 1805-
1875.

Peters, Phillis (Wheatley) 1753?-1784. 19051,
  22714, 39282, 56712, 59606, (61199)-
  (61200), 98661, 103125-103142
Peters, Richard, 1704-1776. 61201-61203,
  84622, 84678C see also Pennsylvania
  (Colony) Commissioners to the Ohio
  Indians. Pennsylvania. University. Trus-
  tees. President.
Peters, Richard, 1704-1776. supposed author
  (61582), 84610
Peters, Richard, 1744-1828. 25961, 61204-
  (61205), 96866, 101719-101720, 101722
Peters, Richard, 1780-1848. (33241), 57236,
  61206-61208, 103160
Peters, Richard, 1780-1848. defendant 103160,
  103162
Peters, Samuel. supposed author 4015,
  (34763), note after 97633, 99410-99411
Peters, Samuel A. 1367, 61209-61213
Peters, Theodore C. 61214
Peter's portfolio. 62912
Petersburg, Va. Board of Education. 61215
Petersburg, Va. Citizens. 61221
Petersburg, Va. Inhabitants. see Petersburg,
  Va. Citizens.
Petersburg, Va. Library. 61216
Petersburg, Va. Library Association. see
  Petersburg Library Association.
Petersburg city directory for 1866. 61219
Petersburg intelligencer. see Virginia
  gazette & Petersburg intelligencer.
Petersburg Library Association. 61218
Petersburg Railroad Company. 61220
Peterson, B. von. 61222
Petersen, Carl. 61223-61224
Petersen, Frederick A. 61225
Petersen, Johan Christian Peter. 61226
Petersen, Magnus. tr. 11414
Petersen, N. M. 61227
Peterson, ------. 84565
Peterson, A. Everett. ed. 84564
Peterson, Charles J. 61228-61239, 73445
Peterson, Daniel H. (61240)
Peterson, Edward. (61241)-61242
Peterson, Henry. 61243-61244
Peterson, Mrs. Henry. see Peterson, Sarah
  (Webb) 1820-
Peterson, Nils, d. 1819. defendant 96944,
  note after 104281
Peterson, Peter, d. 1819. defendant (41584),
  104281
Peterson, R. supposed tr. 6812
Peterson, Sarah (Webb) 1820- ed. 38550
Peterson, T. B. 14344
Peterson (T. B.) firm publishers 61245
Peterson (T. B.) and Brothers. firm publishers
  94822
Peterson's complete coin-book. 61245
Peterson's illustrated uniform edition of humor-
  ous American works. 94822
Petheram, John. ed. 5195, 61246
Petherick, Thomas. 49458
Petherick, William. 8768
Peticion hecha al soberano Congreso. 48415
Peticion qve Iuan Velazquez de Salazar. 98817
Petigru, Charles. 61247
Petigru, James Louis. (61248), 87398, 87705,
  87856, 87991, 88005 see also South
  Carolina. Commission on the Code.
Petin de Villeneuve, Jerome. 61250
Petion et Haiti. 75483
Petit, Emilien. 14709, 20291, 61251-(61253)
Petit, Jacques. supposed author (61253)
Petit, Lizzie. 61254
Petit, Pablo. 61255
Petit, Pierre. 61256-61258

Petit de Baroncourt, ------. 61261-61262
Petit de Vievigne, -----. 61263
Petit Martin, Angelique le. see Martin,
  Angelique le Petit.
Petit-Radel, D. tr. 97471
Petit Thouars, Abel Aubert du. see Dupetit-
  Thouars, Abel Aubert, 1793-1864.
Petit Thouars, Aristide Aubert du. see
  Dupetit-Thouars, Aristide Aubert.
Petit almanach de nos grandes hommes. (716
Petit atlas. 71869
Petit atlas maritime recueil des cartes et pla
  4555
Petit blanc de Saint-Domingue. pseud. Anti-
  Brissot. see Baillio, -------.
Petit catechisme ov sommaire des trois
  premieres parties. (7742)
Petit Seminaire du Quebec. see Seminaire d
  Quebec.
Petit trappeur ou trois ans chez les Oricarea
  23922
Petit trate sur le gouvernement des esclaves.
  68977
Petitclair, Pierre. 34041, 69661
Petite bibliotheque des theatres. 98273
Petite bibliotheque Francaise. 92537
Petite epitre faute par l'auteur. 39633
Petite historie d'vn massacre. 4795
Petition. 51583
Petition a la Chambre des Deputes. Par C. A
  Bissette. 5652
Petition a la Chambre des Deputes, relative a
  l'amelioration du sort des esclaves aux
  Colonies. 5654
Petition a l'Assemblee Nationale, par les
  proprietaires de Saint-Domingue. 75176
Petition a MM. les membres de la Chambre
  des Deputes. (81718), 100617
Petition adressee a l'Assemblee Nationale.
  73470
Petition adressee a Messieurs les Pairs en
  faveur des residents Francais. 64704
Petition against the seigniorial tenure bill.
  93180
Petition against the union of Upper and Lower
  Canada. 98089
Petition (and accompanying correspondence)
  of Robert A. Parrish. (58849)
Petition and address from one hundred and
  four electors. 63945
Petition and address of John Gibson. 9372,
  81492
Petition and address, which was presented unt
  him by the General Court. 9455
Petition and memorial of citizens of the Unite
  States. 61265
Petition and memorial of David Quinn. 67306
Petition and memorial of the Assembly of
  Jamaica. 35646
Petition & memorial of the towns of Bristol,
  Nobleborough, New-Castle, Edgcomb, and
  Boothbay. (61266)
Petition and papers of Conrad W. Faber &
  Leopold Bierwirth. (23591)
Petition and protest of Richard S. Hackley.
  29480
Petition and remonstrance. (60702)
Petition and remonstrance of Jacob Sharp on
  behalf of the Broadway Railway Associa-
  tion. 54135, 79836
Petition and remonstrance of W. Wharton.
  103112
Petition and representation of certain member
  of the South Carolina Yazoo Company.
  88055

Petition and representation of the House of Representatives. 45933

Petition aux Membres de l'Assemblee Nationale. 26722

Petition by C. K. Halliday. 29901

Petition by Increase Mather. 9372

Petition de trois hommes de couleur. (47421)

Petition des citoyens de couleur de St. Domingue. 61267

Petition des citoyens de couleur des colonies. 61268

Petition des Commissaires de Guernesey. 104538

Petition des hommes de couleur de la Martinique. 5653

Petition des hommes de couleur libres de la Martinique. 5655

Petition et documens. 38987

Petition for a new corporation. 40255, (45634), 45970

Petition . . . for a rail-road from Boston to Woonsocket. 42078

Petition for a reconsideration of the case of Green vs. Biddle. (73530)

Petition for an act incorporating the College of the Holy Cross. 69481

Petition for an orphan asylum. 53893

Petition for incorporation [of the Essex Historical Society.] 23011

Petition for pardon. 27973, 36413

Petition for reformation. 97128

Petition for T. Breakenrig. 91649

Petition for the abolition of the slave-trade. 81745

Petition for the Bank of America, in . . . New York. 54109

Petition for the establishment of a College of Physicians. 45874

Petition for the extension of the Pennsylvania Canal from Columbia to the Maryland Line. (60307)

Petition . . . for the repeal of the licence law. 40646

Petition from certain inhabitants of the county of Westchester. 102957

Petition from inhabitants of Beaver County, Pa. 60387

Petition from James Stuart, to His Majesty. 93175

Petition from Lower Canada. 10386

Petition from the British inhabitants of the province of Quebeck. 67000

Petition from the General Congress at Philadelphia. 39705, 89179

Petition from the Governor and Company of the Sommer Islands. 100450, 104190, 104974

Petition from the people of Louisiana to Congress. 61269

Petition from the West India planters. 61270

Petition in behalf of stipulated arbitration. 1174

Petition, in behalf of W. Freeman. 10893

Petition in relation to the state debt. 70612

Petition nouvelle des citoyens de couleur. (61271)

Petition now before the . . . House of Commons. 40546, 3d note after 102846

Petition, now before the Massachusetts Legislature. 67274

Petition of a portion of the inhabitants of the Mississippi Territory. 49531

Petition of Abigail Lay. 83760

Petition of Albert Bowker and others. 78515

Petition of Alexander Scott of the state of South Carolina. (78241)

Petition of Amey Dardin. 18539

Petition of Andrew Miller and others. 60540

Petition of Anthony Buck. 8880

Petition of C. Stockbridge and others. (30658)

Petition of Caleb Foote and others. 75691

Petition of Cato West, and others. 102717

Petition of Charles Bean. (4118)

Petition of Charles Hyde. 82939

Petition of Charles Lochington. (2592), note after 95821

Petition of Charles Richard Ogden. 56799

Petition of Charles Stearns and others. 90873

Petition of Church Gray. 46092

Petition of citizens of New Orleans. (61272)

Petition of Col. Charles H. De Ahna. 19014

Petition of Commander John Calhoun. 9931

Petition of Congress to the King delivered by Mr. Penn. (16088)

Petition of Daniel Renner and Nathaniel H. Heath. 69618

Petition of David E. Evans and others. 53566

Petition of David T. Jackson to Congress. 35404

Petition of Edward Russell. 44027

Petition of Ferdinand Smyth Stuart. 85253

Petition of General Smyth. 85200

Petition of George Carew. 10823

Petition of George Howland, Jr. (52497)

Petition of George Latimer. 39206

Petition of George M'Dougall. (43182)

Petition of George M. Withington. (45948)

Petition of George R. M. Withington and others. 11117

Petition of Gilbert Tennent and Samuel Davies. 94708

Petition of Gov. Tevehaugh and others. 75019

Petition of Hartford and New Haven Railroad Company. 30671

Petition of Henry C. De Rham. 19673

Petition of Henry J. Duff and others. 21129, 80410

Petition of Hewing Wood. 33440

Petition of Horace P. Wakefield and others. (32988)

Petition of inhabitants of Newport, R. Island. 55051

Petition of inhabitants of Northampton County. 55773

Petition of Isaac P. Davis and others. 6748, 69912

Petition of Isaac Rice and others. 70607

Petition of Isaac T. Allard and others. 73706

Petition of Israel Stratton. 53226

Petition of J. Glasgow and others. 94745

Petition of James Jefferson and others. 70659

Petition of Jared Shattuck. 79875

Petition of John Gordon. 27987

Petition of John Hancock and another for a modification. 30185

Petition of John Jenkins and other bakers. 103404

Petition of John Pritchard. 65715

Petition of John R. and Robert J. Livingston. 41632

Petition of John White. 103404

Petition of Jonathan Jackson, &c. 35441

Petition of Jos. Boon and others. 87359, 87805

Petition of Joseph Ormstone. 99252

Petition of Joseph Segar, of Virginia. 78882

Petition of Levi Baker and others. (13254)

Petition of Lord and Lady Cardigan and Lord Montagu. 90590

Petition of Lot Wheelwright. 6604

Petition of Marinus Willett. 104137

Petition of Mr. Bollan. 6220

Petition of Mrs. C. M. Thompson. 53978

Petition of Moses M. Strong. 92948

Petition of Nathaniel Wood and others. 45470

Petition of Peter Sonmans, of New Jersey, and of Joseph Ormstone. 57494

Petition of Peter Sonmans, of New Jersey, and Jos. Ormstone, relating to shares of land. 53221

Petition of Peter Sonmans of New-Jersey in America. 99252

Petition of Richard B. Carmichael and others. 45275

Petition of Robert William Wetmore. 103076

Petition of S——— T——— Esq. for the exclusive trade of the River Senegal. 40377

Petition of S——— T———, Esq., to the King. 40414

Petition of S. W. Hall. 29849

Petition of Samuel A. Lawrence. 39369

Petition of Samuel C. Bishop. 5620

Petition of Samuel Hinkley and others. 13738, 31884

Petition of Samuel Milroy and sundry other citizens. 70725

Petition of Samuel Ward. 101336

Petition of several planters and other inhabitants. (80601)

Petition of Silas Hathway. 65098, 69392

[Petition of Smith to the] Comishionors of the United Colloneys. 83760

Petition of Stephen N. Mason, et al. (70673)

Petition of Stephen Sayre. 77417-77418

Petition of sundry British merchants and others. (69732)

Petition of sundry citizens of the county of Washington. 60499

Petition of sundry colored persons. 6760

Petition of sundry inhabitants of Louisiana. (42281)

Petition of sundry inhabitants of . . . Pennsylvania. 60388

Petition of sundry inhabitants of the counties of St. Clair & Randolph. 69829

Petition of sundry inhabitants of the state of Pennsylvania. 69792

Petition of the Adams Express Company. 37167

Petition of the Africans, living in Boston, &c. 1792, note after 45640, 81891

Petition of the Assembly of Massachusetts' Bay. 4925

Petition of the Board of Regents [of the University of Michigan.] 48804

Petition of the Boston and Worcester and Western Railroad Corporations. 90774

Petition of the Boylston Medical School. 7145

Petition of the Cherokee Delegates to the Senate. 12437

Petition of the city of Boston, for leave to introduce a supply of pure water. 6785

Petition of the city of Boston for power to bring into the city the water of Long Pond. 6785

Petition of the city of Charlestown for leave to take water from Mystic Pond. 18807

Petition of the corporation of Rhode Island 70716

Petition of the constitutionalists. 95372

Petition of the Continental Congress, to His Majesty. 15146, 15583, 98439

Petition of the Convention. 95372

Petition of the Council-General (of the Company of Scotland) (78229)

Petition of the Croton Aqueduct Department. (54232)

Petition of the Deputies of the United Moravian Churches. 69731, 1st note after 97845

Petition of the Directors of the Cambridge Water Works. 10155

Petition of the Earl of Stirling. note before 91856

Petition of the founders and proprietors. 1315

Petition of the General Court of Boston. 9462

Petition of the graduating class of 1835. 1021

Petition of the Grand American Continental Congress. 15581-15582

Petition of the Hartford-Bridge Company. 306?

Petition of the heirs of Caron de Beaumarchais 69804

Petition of the heirs of Gen. Thomas Nelson. 61273

Petition of the Honourable Thomas Walpole. 101150

Petition of the House of Assembly of Lower Canada. 10540

Petition of the inhabitants of Fall River. 2374

Petition of the inhabitants of New York. 5457?

Petition of the inhabitants of West Florida. 102768

Petition of the Ladies' Collegiate Institute. 90777

Petition of the Livery of the city of London. 99816

Petition of the Long Island people. 95462

Petition of the medical faculty of the University 54710

Petition of the members of the Legislature of South Carolina. 87485

Petition of the merchants and shop owners of Saint John, New Brunswick. 61274

Petition of the merchants of London. 69938

Petition of the merchants, traders, and others of the city of London. 95940

Petition of the New-England Historic Genealogical Society. 67252

Petition of the President and Fellows of Harvard College. (30759A), (45991)

Petition of the proprietors of plantations in the islands of St. Nevis and St. Christophers. (61275)

Petition of the public creditors to the House of Assembly. (56467)

Petition of the receivers and exporters of American leaf tobacco. (61276)

Petition of the securities of Robert McCallen. 53919

Petition of the Seekonk Branch Railroad Company. 78854, 89697

Petition of the Sierra Leone Company. 80887

Petition of the Sisters of the Visitation. 2700?

Petition of the Springfield Aqueduct Company. 89877, 90684

Petition of the stockholders of the Spot-Pond Aqueduct Company. 61277

Petition of the sufferers of Wyoming, Pennsylvania. (70351)

Petition of the Superior and Directors of the Seminary of Quebec. 67060

Petition of the town of East Hartford. (21648) 30672

Petition of the Troy and Greenfield Railroad. 61363

Petition of the Trustees of Amherst College. (46895)

Petition of thirty-six American citizens confined at Carthagena. 69841

Petition of Thomas George Clinton. 13757

Petition of Tristram Burges and others. (78855)

Petition of Trustees of Phillips Academy. 85212

Petition of W. C. 11397

Petition of W. Courten and others. 17180

Petition of W. E. Channing, and others. 67907

Petition of William Armstrong and others. 2040

Petition of Wm. Aspinwall and others. 8252, 68298

Petition of William Dixon and James Dixon. 20372

Petition of William Freeman. 25781

Petition of William L. Mackenzie. 43439

Petition of William Paterson, Esq. 18565

Petition of William Wright, and others. 88215

Petition on the sugar refineries of London. 4823, 95700

Petition . . . praying for a charter. 55820

Petition, praying for the establishment of " the Pennsylvania State Bank." 60377

Petition praying for the removal from office. 66773

Petition presented by Capt. Alexander Patterson. 59130

Petition presented by the West-India planters and merchants. 23302, (27606), 27607, (27610), 4th note after 102788

Petition, presented to the Assembly of Maryland. 22337, 99771

Petition, presented to the General Assembly of Maryland. 99771

Petition presented to the High Court of Parliament for redresse. 27713

Petition presented to the House of Assembly. 53067

Petition presented to the House of Commons, from the Directors of the London Missionary Society. 82899

Petition presented to the House of Commons, 19th August, 1836. 31138

Petition to the late General Assembly of Maryland. 22337, 99771

Petition relative a l'enquete ordonnee par le gouvernement Francais. 13645

Petition . . . relative to the claim of the officers. 16726

Petition, report and bill on the subject of a monument. 25880

Petition resolved upon at the late General Court. 75012

Petition respecting Patucket Falls. 61278

Petition. The following petition . . . was prepared. 93180

Petition to abolish capital punishment. 71131

Petition to Congress for a repeal of the internal revenue tax on books. 1848

Petition to Congress for claims of American citizens. 61279

Petition to Congress from the tobacco manufacturers. 13102

Petition to Congress of inhabitants of Pennsylvania. 60389

Petition to His Excellency the Governour, and the Honourable Council. 90962

Petition to His . . . Majesty from the General Assembly of Barbadoes. 4731

Petition to His Majesty King George the Third. 61280, 2d note after 98997

Petition to Parliament, from the merchants and ship owners of Liverpool. 86731

Petition to the Congress of the United States. 97928

Petition to the Congress of the United States. [By Henry Ray de la Reintrie.] 39026

Petition to the corporation, of the city of Philadelphia. 63163

Petition to the Duke of Bedford. 6220

Petition to the forty-first Congress. 80131

Petition to th[e] General Assembly of Maryland. 45276

Petition to the House of Assembly. 74568

Petition to the House of Commons. 82905

Petition to the House of Parliament. 61281

Petition to the Imperial Parliament. 98072, 98092

Petition to the King. 15544

Petition to the King in favour of the colonies. 40524

Petition to the King's Most Excellent Majesty in Council. 100904

Petition to the late General Assembly of Maryland. 22337

Petition to the Legislature. 87808

Petition to the Legislature for aid. 1315

Petition to the Legislature of . . . Connecticut against extra judicial oaths. 61283

Petition of the Legislature of the Catawba Navigation Company. 61282

Petition . . . to the Mayor and Aldermen of Charlestown. (9174)

Petition . . . to the Senate and House of Representatives. 46974

Petition to this present Parliament. 11398, 57765

Petition . . . to widen the draw of the New Bedford Bridge. 67908

Petition, which has been presented to His Majesty. 35586

Petitioner in behalf of the Seekonk Branch Company is informed. 89697

Petitioners case of certain inhabitants in the island of Cape Breton. 61284

Petitioners for the Abolition of the Slave Trade. petitioners 81898

Petitioners for Union of Upper and Lower Canada. Agent. see Stuart, Sir James, Bart., 1780-1853.

Petitions and memorials from various parties. 53665

Petitions and memorials of the Proprietors of West and East-Jersey, to the Legislature of New-Jersey. 83982

Petitions and memorials of the Proprietors of West and East Jersey, to the Legislature of New Jersey, together with a map. 53203

Petitions asking for a law. 62523

Petitions, &c. for the appointment of Joseph King, Jr. 37821

Petitions for and the remonstrances against a bridge. 33528

Petitions for leave to construct railroads, 1845. 6768

Petitions for the removal of Edward Greely Loring. (62520)

Petitions for tolls on railroads. 53567

Petitions from Pawtucket, Seekonk, Rehobeth, and Fall River. 46051

Petitions from Prince Edward Island. (61285), 65636, note after 93185

Petitions from the old and new subjects. 61286

Petitions from the province of Quebec. 67032

Petitions from various merchants of Rhode-Island. 56544

Petitions of Alexander Roxburgh. 73625

Petitions of citizens of Yuba and Nevada Counties. 97497

Petitions of grievance. (56545)

Petitions of John T. Hilton and others. 74313

Petitions of Mr. Bollan. 6219

Petitions of Obadiah Scott. 36485

Petitions of Robert Heysham. 56577

Petitions of Rufus Davenport. 18717

Petitions of sundry citizens of Rhode Island.
(20647), note after 96509
Petitions of the Boston, Hartford and Erie
Railroad Company. 70605, 70657
Petitions of the President and Directors of
the Chesapeake and Delaware Canal Com-
pany. 12495
Petitions of W. E. Channing. (11925), 67907
Petitions or addresses to His Late Majesty
King William. 53436
Petitions pour l'abolition complete et immediate
de l'esclavage. 81957
Petitions to, and resolutions of, the House of
Commons. 25313
Petitions to prevent slave hunting in . . . New
York. 53937
Petitions to the Legislature of the common-
wealth of Pennsylvania. (12497)
Petitpierre, Ferdinand Olivier, 1722-1790.
104735
Petits traites publies par l'Academie des
Sciences Morales et Politiques. 48903
Petitt, William V. (61307)
Petitval, J. B. 61287
Petiver, Jacobo. 61288
Peto, Sir Samuel Morton, Bart. 61289
Petra Pretiosior coeli, soli, et sali. 47357
Petrel, Eugenius. 64450
Petrarcha, Francesco, 1304-1374. 61290-61292
Petri, P. Aug. tr. 16535
Petri Apiani cosmographia. 1557
Petri Martyris ab Angleria Mediolanen. Oratoris
clarrismi. 1557
Petri Ribaldi Peruani Satyrar, liber I. 70787
Petrie, -----. 44124
Petrifactions recueillies en Amerique. 8839,
33733
Petrii di Horticosa Concilii Mexicani decreta.
33063
Petroleum: a history of the oil regions. 21740
Petroleum and petroleum wells. 6298
Petroleum, its history and properties. 51493
Petroleum, oil and railway guide of West
Virginia. (80147)
Petrolia. 15219
Petrology and economic geology of the Skykomish
Basin. 84534-84535
Petrus a Gandavo, d. 1572. 994
Petrus Albinus. (28957), 61293
Petrus Claver, sklave der negersklaven. 32685
Petrus Martyr, der Geschichtsschreiber des
Weltmeeres. 78017
Pettengill (S. M.) & Co. firm publishers
61295
Pettes, George W. 61295
Pettie's-Island Cash Lottery, Philadelphia, 1773.
see American Flint Glass Manufactory,
Pettie's-Island Cash Lotterie, Philadelphia,
1773.
Pettie's Island cash lottery. (61296)
Pettie's Island cash lottery, in three clases.
(61296)
Pettie's Island Land and Cash Lottery, &c.
46192
Pettie's Island land and cash lottery, for dis-
pensing of sundry houses and lots. (61296)
Pettie's Island land and cash lottery. . . .
William Masters. 46192
Pettigrew, J. Johnston. 61297, 87519
Pettigrew, Thomas Joseph. 61298-(61300)
Pettis, F. H. 61301
Pettis, Samuel. 61302
Pettis, Spencer. 61303
Pettit, D. ed. 53174
Pettit, John, 1807-1877. 61304

Pettit, Thomas M'Kean, 1797-1853. 61305-
61306, 96925
Pettrich, Ferdinand. illus. 59169, 64408
Petty, Sir William. (61308)
Petty-Fitzmaurice, Henry. see Lansdowne,
Henry Petty-Fitzmaurice, 3d Marquis
of, 1780-1863.
Petty-Fitzmaurice, William. see Lansdowne
William Petty-Fitzmaurice, 1st Marquis
of, 1737-1805.
Pettyplace, William. 82832
Petworth, Eng. Emigration Society. see Pe
worth Emigration Society, Petworth, Eng
Petworth Committee. see Petworth Emigrat
Society, Petworth, Eng. Emigration Co
mittee.
Petworth Emigration Society, Petworth, Eng.
(8830), 22500, 40594, 86184-86186, note
after 98068, note after 98069, 98070
Petworth Emigration Society, Petworth, Eng.
Emigration Committee. 86186, 1st note
after 98076
Petzeli, J. tr. 100723
Petzholdt, Julius. 61309-61310
Peucer, Kaspar, 1525-1602. 61311-(61312)
Peuchet, Jacques, 1758-1830. 29572, 38771,
(61313)
Peucinian Library, Bowdoin College. see
Bowdoin College, Brunswick, Me. Peuc
Library.
Peugh, Samuel A. 61314
Peuple de la republique d'Hayti, a Messieurs
Vastey et Limonade. 98667
Peuple de St.-Pierre. petitioners see St.-
Pierre. Citoyens. petitioners
Peuple Francais 61315
Peuple instruit. 68284, 80054
Peuple juge. 68284
Peuples du Bresil avant la decouverte de
l'Amerique. 3382
Peuples etranges. 69060
Peverelly, Charles A. 61316
Pew Holder. pseud. Pulpit sketches. 66633
Pewabic Mining Company. (62317)
Pewani ipi Potewatemi missinoikan. 61318
Pewholders and Worshippers of St. Paul's
Chapel, New York. petitioners see
New York (City) St. Paul's Church (Pr
testant Episcopal) Pewholders and Wor
shippers. petitioners
Pewter Smith. pseud. see Smith, Pewter.
pseud.
Peyere, Isaac de la. see La Peyrere, Isaac
de, 1594-1676.
Peyers, J. G. 72234
Peynier, --------, Sieur. 2386, 75187
Peyreleau, Eugene Edouard, Baron de Boyer c
see Boyer de Peyreleau, Eugene Edou
Baron de.
Peyrere, Isaac de la. see La Peyrere, Isaa
de.
Peyroux de la Coudreniere, ------. (61319)
Peysac, ------- de Vins, Marques de. see
Vins, -------- de, Marques de Peysac.
Peyster, Frederick de. see de Peyster,
Frederick.
Peyster, Johannes d'. see D'Peyster,
Johannes. petitioner
Peyster, John Watts de. see De Peyster,
John Watts.
Peyton, Jesse E. 51143
Peyton, John Lewis. 61320-61324
Peyton, Walter. 66686
Peyton, William M. (61326)
Peyton, William M. supposed author 78497
Peza, Ignacio de la. 55490

Pezuela, Jacobo de la. 61327-61330
Pezuela, Luis Robles. 47036, 48552, (61332)-
  61333 see also Mexico (French Empire)
  Ministro de Fomento.
Pezuela, Manuel Robles. see Robles Pezuela,
  Manuel.
Pezuela y Sanchez Munoz de Velasco, Joaquin
  de la, 1. Marques de Viluma, 1761-1830.
  61331 see also Peru (Viceroyalty)
  Virrey, 1816-1821 (Pezula y Sanchez
  Munoz de Velasco)
Pfefferkorn, Ignaz. 61334
Pfeiffer, George. 61335
Pfeiffer, Ida. 61336-61343
Pfeil, Adolph R. 61344-(61345)
Pfister, Ferdinand. 61346
Pflanzerleben. 64544
Pflichten der Adoptiv-Burger in der gegen-
  wartigen Krise. (61347)
Pflug, Webstuhl und Amboss. 10829
Phaedrus. see Inghirami, Tommaso, Fedra,
  1470-1516.
Phaenomena quaedam apocalyptica ad aspectum
  Novi Orbis configurata. 79443-79444,
  91940, 104083
Phaenomena, siue apparentia. 65940-65941
Phalanstere du Bresil. 2601
Phalansterian record. 85699
Phalanx. 85129
Phanerogamia. 28368
Phanerogamie. 21216
Phantom. 61348
Phantom barge and other poems. 95565
Phantom chief. A tale of the forest. 72046
Phantom of the forest. (4724)
Pharaou, F. 12576-12577
Phares de la mer des Antilles. 39876
Phares des cotes orientales de l'Amerique
  Anglaise. 39876
Phares du grand ocean. 39876
Pharisee and publican. 103573
Pharmaceutical reporter. 54809
Pharmacopoeia Nosocomii Neo-Eboracensis.
  61349
Pharmacopoeia of the Massachusetts Medical
  Society. (61350)
Pharmacopoeia of the New York Hospital.
  61349
Pharmacopoeia of the United States of America.
  61351
Pharmacopola, N. T. pseud. Good humour.
  see Manwaring, ---------. supposed
  author
Pharnambuco. see Pernambuco.
Pharo, O. ed. 53174
Phase in fashion. 97499
Phases et causes celebres du droit maritime
  des nations. 18143
Phases of "Crescent City" life. 29713
Phasmion, a poem. (43533)
Phazma. pseud. Anecdotes. see Field, M. C.
Phedrus, T. see Inghirami, Tommaso, Fedra,
  1470-1516.
Phelan, J. 34041, 69661
Phelipe, Pedro, Bp. 59522 see also Chile
  (Diocese) Bishop (Phelipe)
Phelipeau, --------. cartographer 50578
Phelps, --------, fl. 1769. 61401
Phelps, --------, fl. 1835. 69466
Phelps, A. R. 61366
Phelps, Almira (Hart) Lincoln, 1793-1884.
  41241, 57913, 61353-61358, 2d note after
  96966
Phelps, Alonzo. defendant 61359
Phelps, Amos A. (61360)-61361

Phelps, Ansel. 61362
Phelps, Ansel, Jr. 61363
Phelps, Anson G. 65093
Phelps, Anthony. 30829
Phelps, Austin. 61364-61365, (61373)
Phelps, Benjamin K. (61367)
Phelps, Charles. 61368, 99240
Phelps, Charles A. 61369
Phelps, Dudley. (61370)
Phelps, E. J. (61377)
Phelps, Edward E. cartographer 105444
Phelps, Egbert. 61371
Phelps, Eliakim. (63172)
Phelps, Elisha. 15776
Phelps, Elizabeth (Stuart) (61373)-61376, note
  after 93772
Phelps, H. (54574), 54575, 61378-(61379)
Phelps, James A. 61380, (80535)
Phelps, John. 61381, 99240
Phelps, John Smith, 1814-1886. 61382
Phelps, Mrs. Lincoln. see Phelps, Almira
  (Hart) Lincoln, 1793-1884.
Phelps, Matthew. 30829
Phelps, Nicholas. (73483)
Phelps, Noah A. (61384)-(61385)
Phelps, Oliver. 96610 see also New York
  (State) Commissioners to the Seneca
  Indians.
Phelps, Oliver Seymour. 61386-61387
Phelps, P. ed. 78620
Phelps, Phebe Harris. 61388
Phelps, Richard H. 61389-61391
Phelps, Samuel. 61392
Phelps, Samuel Shethar, 1793-1855. (61393)-
  61394, 81679
Phelps, Sylvanus Dryden. 61395-61398
Phelps, W. D. 61399
Phelps, W. W. 83147, 83242
Phelps, William F. 61400
Phelps, Fanning & Co. firm publishers
  (23786), (61379)
Phelps genealogy. 61387
Phelps' hundred cities and large towns of
  America. (61379)
Phelps' New York city guide. (54574)
Phelps' strangers and citizens guide to New
  York city. 54575
Phelps' traveller's guide through the United
  States. (61379)
Phenix, Thomas. 45287, 45368, (72166)
Phenix de la Africa Augustino, breve relacion
  de la invencion de S. Sag. cverpo. 76271
Phenix de la Africa Augustino, breve relacion
  de su sagrado cuerpo. 44957
Phenix de las becas. 73865
Phenix Mining Company. 61402
Phenix Society, Yale University. see Yale
  University. Phenix Society.
Phenomenes des Freres Davenport. 55213
Phettiplace, William. see Phettyplace,
  William.
Phettyplace, William. 82832, note after 92664,
  2d note after 100510
Phew Phelps phamily phacts phigures and
  phancies. 61403
Phi Beta Kappa. Connecticut Alpha, Yale
  University. (15727), 105908
Phi Beta Kappa. Maine Alpha, Bowdoin Col-
  lege. 7023
Phi Beta Kappa. Massachusetts Alpha, Harvard
  University. 30765, 41492, 45668
Phi Beta Kappa. New Hampshire Alpha,
  Dartmouth College. 52805
Phi Beta Kappa. New York Alpha, Union Col-
  lege. 54835, 97795-97796

Phi Beta Kappa. Rhode Island Alpha, Brown
University. 8608
Phi Beta Kappa repository. 54795
Phials of amber full of the tears of love.
12854
Phil Arcanos. pseud. Grand arcanum detected.
see Green, Joseph.
Phil Scot. pseud. Defence of the Scots abdicating Darien. see Ferguson, Robert,
d. 1814. and Harris, Walter, supposed
author and Hodges, James. supposed
author
Philadelphia. (61414), 61451, 61566, 61550,
61581, 61677-61678, 61733, 61852, 62060,
62087, 62095, (62226), (62269), 62283-
62284, 62286, 62288, 90717
Philadelphia. appellants 87287
Philadelphia. defendants 5472, 58441, 60043
Philadelphia. petitioners 10889
Philadelphia. Academy of Natural Sciences.
see Academy of Natural Sciences, Phila-
delphia.
Philadelphia. Academy of the Fine Arts. see
Pennsylvania Academy of the Fine Arts,
Philadelphia.
Philadelphia. Academy of the Protestant Epis-
copal Church. see Academy of the
Protestant Episcopal Church, Philadelphia.
Philadelphia. Adelphi School. see Philadelphia
Association of Friends for the Instruction
of Poor Children. Adelphi School.
Philadelphia. Agency of the American Tract
Society. see American Tract Society.
Pennsylvania Agency, Philadelphia.
Philadelphia. Albion Society. see Albion
Society, Philadelphia.
Philadelphia. Aldermen. (27494), (61543)
Philadelphia. Almshouse. 61455, 61503, 62060
Philadelphia. Almshouse. Medical Library.
61455
Philadelphia. Amenite Lodge, no. 73. see
Freemasons. Pensylvania. Amenite
Lodge, no. 73, Philadelphia.
Philadelphia. American Academy of Music.
see Philadelphia. Opera House.
Philadelphia. American Academy of Political
and Social Science. see American Academy
of Political and Social Science, Philadel-
phia.
Philadelphia. American Convention for Promot-
ing the Abolition of Slavery. see Ameri-
can Convention for Promoting the Abolition
of Slavery, and Improving the Condition
of the African Race.
Philadelphia. American Emigrants' Friend
Society. see American Emigrants' Friend
Society, Philadelphia.
Philadelphia. American Female Education
Society. see American Female Education
Society, Philadelphia.
Philadelphia. American Flint Glass Manufactory,
Pettie's-Island Cash Lottery, Philadelphia,
1773. see American Flint Glass Manu-
factory, Pettie's-Island Cash Lottery,
Philadelphia, 1773.
Philadelphia. American Hose Company. Charter.
61457
Philadelphia. American Sunday School Union.
see American Sunday School Union, Phila-
delphia.
Philadelphia. Americus Club. see Americus
Club, Philadelphia.
Philadelphia. Amicable Fire Company. 61463
Philadelphia. Anglo-American Beneficial Society.
see Anglo-American Beneficial Society,
Philadelphia.

Philadelphia. Anti-masonic Convention, 1830.
see Anti-masonic Convention, Phila-
delphia, 1830.
Philadelphia. Anti-slavery Church. (62094)
Philadelphia. Anti-slavery Convention, 1833.
see Anti-slavery Convention, Philadelp
1833.
Philadelphia. Anti-slavery Convention of
American Women, 1838. see Anti-
slavery Convention of American Women
Philadelphia, 1838.
Philadelphia. Apprentices' Library Company
see Apprentices' Library Company,
Philadelphia.
Philadelphia. Arch Street Presbyterian Chu
61477
Philadelphia. Arch Street Presbyterian Chur
Charter. 61477
Philadelphia. Arch Street Presbyterian Chur
Treasurer. 61477
Philadelphia. Associate Reformed Synod. se
Associate Reformed Presbyterian Chur
Philadelphia. Associated Independent Troop
Volunteer Greens. see Pennsylvania.
Militia. Associated Independent Troop
Volunteer Greens, Philadelphia.
Philadelphia. Association for the Care of
Colored Orphans. see Association for
Care of Colored Orphans, Philadelphia.
Philadelphia. Association of Friends at Phil
delphia and Vicinity, for the Relief of
Colored Freedmen. see Friends' Ass
ciation of Philadelphia for the Relief o
Colored Freedmen.
Philadelphia. Association of Friends for the
Relief of Colored Freedmen. see
Friends' Association of Philadelphia fo
the Relief of Colored Freemen.
Philadelphia. Asylum for the Insane Poor.
see Pennsylvania. Asylum for the Ins
Poor, Philadelphia.
Philadelphia. Auctioneers. petitioners (60
61825
Philadelphia. Auditor of Wills. 80813
Philadelphia. Bank of North America. see
Bank of North America, Philadelphia.
Philadelphia. Bank of Pennsylvania. see
Bank of Pennsylvania, Philadelphia.
Philadelphia. Bank Street Church. 28781
Philadelphia. Banks. petitioners 60647
Philadelphia. Baptist Convention for Missio
Purposes, 1814. see Baptists. Penn
vania. Convention for Missionary Pur
poses, Philadelphia, 1814.
Philadelphia. Baptist Education Society. se
Baptist Education Society, Philadelphia.
Philadelphia. Bar. 61486, 61598, 61965,
62081
Philadelphia. Bar. petitioners 61815
Philadelphia. Belmont Hospital. see Phila
delphia. Christ Church Hospital.
Philadelphia. Bible Association of Friends
America. see Bible Association of
Friends in America.
Philadelphia. Bishop White Prayer Book
Society. see Bishop White Prayer Bo
Society, Philadelphia.
Philadelphia. Board of Controller's of Publi
Schools. see Philadelphia. Board of
Public Education.
Philadelphia. Board of Guardians of the Po
Committee to Visit the Cities of Baltir
New York, Providence, Boston, and Sal
61503
Philadelphia. Board of Health. 18002, 4938
60061, 61504, 62291

Philadelphia. Board of Health. Sanitary Committee. 61504

Philadelphia. Board of Police. Marshal. see Philadelphia. Marshal of Police.

Philadelphia. Board of Public Education. 2588, (61529), 61561

Philadelphia. Board of Public Education. petitioners 61501

Philadelphia. Board of Public Education. Committee on Central High School. (61529)

Philadelphia. Board of Public Education. Committee on Revision of Studies. 61501

Philadelphia. Board of Public Education. Committee to Distribute the Appropriation for Night Schools. 61501

Philadelphia. Board of Public Education. Special Committee. 62173

Philadelphia. Board of Trade. 41306, 49330, 61912, 61970

Philadelphia. Board of Trade. petitioners 61970

Philadelphia. Board of Trade. Charter. 61970

Philadelphia. Board of Trade. Committee on Inland Transportation. 61970

Philadelphia. Board of Trade. Committee on the Existing Revenue Laws. 61970

Philadelphia. Board of Trade. Delegates to the Warren Convention, Warren, Ohio, 1833. 61970, 101491

Philadelphia. Board of Trade. Delegation to the Detroit Convention, 1865. 61970

Philadelphia. Board of Trade. Excursion Party, 1860. 61970

Philadelphia. Board of Trade. Secretary. 61970 see also Blodget, Lorin.

Philadelphia. Board of Trade. Special Committee on National Finances and Taxation. 61970

Philadelphia. Board of Trustees from the Old Thirteen States, 1860. see Board of Trustees from the Old Thirteen States, Philadelphia, 1860.

Philadelphia. Board of Wardens of the Port. 69822, 61770

Philadelphia. Board of Western Ladies for the Relief . . . of the Poor. see Board of Western Ladies of Philadelphia for the Relief . . . of the Poor.

Philadelphia. Book Trade Association. see Book Trade Association of the City of Philadelphia.

Philadelphia. Booksellers' Company. see Booksellers' Company of Philadelphia.

Philadelphia. Boot and Shoemakers. defendants see Boot and Shoemakers of Philadelphia. defendants

Philadelphia. Borough of West Philadelphia. see West Philadelphia.

Philadelphia. Bricklayers Corporation. see Bricklayers Corporation, Philadelphia.

Philadelphia. Broad Street Baptist Church. 61508

Philadelphia. Board Street Baptist Church. Trustees. 61508

Philadelphia. Brotherly Association for the Support of Widows. see Brotherly Association for the Support of Widows, Philadelphia.

Philadelphia. Bounty Fund Commissioners, 1863. 62129

Philadelphia. Burd Orphan Asylum. see Philadelphia. St. Stephen's Church. Vestry. Special Committee to Prepare a Plan for the Organization and Management of the Burd Prphan Asylum.

Philadelphia. Carpenters' Company. see Carpenters' Company of Philadelphia.

Philadelphia. Catholic Lay Citizens. see Catholic Lay Citizens of Philadelphia.

Philadelphia. Catholic Summer School Extension. Lectures. 84516

Philadelphia. Celebration of the Anniversary of the Glorious Battle of New Orleans, by the Personal and Political Friends of George Mifflin Dallas, 1846. see Celebration of the Anniversary of the Glorious Battle of New-Orleans, by the Personal and Political Friends of George Mifflin Dallas, Philadelphia, 1846.

Philadelphia. Celebration of the Seventy-Fourth Anniversary of the Signing of the Constitution, 1863. (61527)

Philadelphia. Centennial Celebration of Washington's Birthday, 1832. 62375

Philadelphia. Centennial Exposition, 1876. 77889

Philadelphia. Central Democratic Club. see Democratic Party. Philadelphia. Central Democratic Club.

Philadelphia. Central High School. (61529)

Philadelphia. Chamber of Commerce. 61974-(61975)

Philadelphia. Chamber of Commerce. petitioners (61975)

Philadelphia. Charter. 59805, 59806, 59820, 59972-59973, 60114, (61559), (61900), (61902)-61903, 66223

Philadelphia. Charity Hospital. 61531

Philadelphia. Christ Church. 13275, 61409, 61534, (66424), 66450

Philadelphia. Christ Church. Charter. 61534

Philadelphia. Christ Church. Ladies' Missionary Association. 61758

Philadelphia. Christ Church Hospital. 61435, 62093

Philadelphia. Christ Church Hospital. Charter. 61435

Philadelphia. Christ Church Parish. see Philadelphia. Christ Church.

Philadelphia. Church of Saint Andrew. (62395)

Philadelphia. Church of St. Matthias. 62215

Philadelphia. Church of the Advent. Rector. (13367)

Philadelphia. Church of the Covenant. 61536

Philadelphia. Church of the Epiphany. 61537

Philadelphia. Church of the Epiphany. Congregation. 97623

Philadelphia. Church of the Messiah. 61538

Philadelphia. Churches Believing in the Salvation of All Men. see Universalist Church in the U. S. Philadelphia.

Philadelphia. Citizens. 40513, 61422, 61432, 62082, 62087, 62311, 95772

Philadelphia. Citizens. petitioners 47643, (61814), 61816, 61818, 61820-61821, 61831, 62089, 62317, 97942

Philadelphia. Citizens' Committee on the Penn Square Improvement Bill. 59755

Philadelphia. Citizens' Meeting, Favorable To the Entire Abolition of Lotteries, 1833. see Philadelphia. Meeting of Citizens, Favorable To the Entire Abolition of Lotteries, 1833.

Philadelphia. Citizens' Meeting In Relation to the Great Pennsylvania Railroad, 1846. see Philadelphia. Meeting of the Citizens In Relation to the Great Pennsylvania Railroad, 1846.

Philadelphia. Convention, 1775. see Pennsylvania (Colony) Convention, Philadelphia, 1775.

Philadelphia. Convention, 1787. see Pennsylvania. Convention, Philadelphia, 1787.

Philadelphia. Convention and Supreme Grand Lodge of the Independent Order of the Sons of Malta, 1860. see Independent Order of the Sons of Malta. Pennsylvania. Convention and Supreme Grand Lodge, Philadelphia, 1860.

Philadelphia. Convention, Composed of Delegates From the Thirteen Original United States, 1852. see Convention of Delegates from the Thirteen Original States, Philadelphia, 1852.

Philadelphia. Convention of Delegates from the Abolition Societies Established in Different Parts of the United States. see American Convention for Promoting the Abolition of Slavery, and Improving the Condition of the African Race.

Philadelphia. Convention of Delegates From the Abolition Societies Established in the Different Parts of the United States. see American Convention for Promoting the Abolition of Slavery, and Improving the Condition of the African Race.

Philadelphia. Convention of Delegates From the Thirteen Original States, 1852. see Convention of Delegates From the Thirteen Original States, Philadelphia, 1852.

Philadelphia, Convention of Delegates Representing the Merchants and Other Interested in Commerce, 1820. see Convention of Delegates Representing the Merchants and Other Interested in Commerce, Philadelphia, 1820.

Philadelphia. Convention of Deputies From the Abolition Societies in the United States. see American Convention For Promoting the Abolition of Slavery, and Improving the Condition of the African Race.

Philadelphia. Convention of Iron Masters, 1849. see Ironmasters' Convention, Philadelphia, 1849.

Philadelphia. Convention of the People of Colour, 1st, 1831. see Convention of the People of Colour, 1st, Philadelphia, 1831.

Philadelphia. Cooper Shop Soldiers' Home. see Cooper Shop Soldiers' Home, Philadelphia.

Philadelphia. Cooper's Shop Volunteer Refreshment Saloon. see Cooper's Shop Volunteer Refreshment Saloon, Philadelphia.

Philadelphia. Council, May 17th, 1742. see Pennsylvania (Colony) Provincial Council.

Philadelphia. Councils. (43069), (49378), 61694, 61802, 61843, 61889, 61898, 62111, 62179, 62191

Philadelphia. Councils. Committee on a Water Supply. see Philadelphia. Watering Committee.

Philadelphia. Councils. Committee on City Property. 62237

Philadelphia. Councils. Committee on Fairmount Park Contribution. 61650

Philadelphia. Councils. Committee on Finance. 62141, 61841, 62285

Philadelphia. Councils. Committee on Highways. 62142

Philadelphia. Councils. Committee on Law. 62069

Philadelphia. Councils. Committee on Legacies and Trusts. (62143), 62268, 62391

Philadelphia. Councils. Committee on Plans. 61650

Philadelphia. Councils. Committee on Police (62126), 62144

Philadelphia. Councils. Committee on Police and Fire Alarm Telegraphs. 62145

Philadelphia. Councils. Committee on Public Highways. 62127

Philadelphia. Councils. Committee on Qualification of Teachers. 62146

Philadelphia. Councils. Committee on Railroads. 62147

Philadelphia. Councils. Committee on the Equalization of the Salaries of Teachers. 61555

Philadelphia. Councils. Committee on the Gas Works. 62000

Philadelphia. Councils. Committee on the Introduction of Wholesome Water Into Philadelphia. see Philadelphia. Watering Committee.

Philadelphia. Councils. Committee on the Navigation of the River Schuylkill. 62138

Philadelphia. Councils. Committee on the Schuylkill Bridge. (61468)

Philadelphia. Councils. Committee on the Sinking Fund. 62243

Philadelphia. Councils. Committee on the Water Works. see Philadelphia. Watering Committee.

Philadelphia. Councils. Committee to Inquire Into the Expediency of Making the Schuylkill Permanent Bridge a Free Bridge. 62229, 62231

Philadelphia. Councils. Committee to Whom Was Referred Sundry Memorials Against Lighting the City With Gas. 62150

Philadelphia. Councils. General Joint Special Committee. Sub-Committee To Visit Erie, Etc. on the Proposed Subscription By the Councils of Philadelphia To the Capital Stock of the Sunbury and Erie Rail Road Company. 62177

Philadelphia. Councils. Joint Committee on Bringing Water into the City. see Philadelphia. Watering Committee.

Philadelphia. Councils. Joint Committee on Steam Boats. (62153)

Philadelphia. Councils. Joint Committee on Superintending and Directing the Water Works. see Philadelphia, Watering Committee.

Philadelphia. Councils. Joint Committee on the City Debts and Expenditures. (62155)

Philadelphia. Councils. Joint Committee on the Erection of a House of Correction. 61727

Philadelphia. Councils. Joint Committee on the Extension of Fairmount Park. 61650

Philadelphia. Councils. Joint Committee on the Malignant or Pestilential Disease of Summer and Autumn of 1820. 62154

Philadelphia. Councils. Joint Committee on Watering the City. see Philadelphia. Watering Committee.

Philadelphia. Councils. Joint Special Committee on a Proposed Subscription to the Capital Stock of the Sunbury and Erie Rail Road Company. 62158

Philadelphia. Councils. Joint Special Committee on Removing the Railway on High, Third, and Dock Streets. (62159)

Philadelphia. Councils. Joint Special Committee on Steam Fire Engines. 62160

Philadelphia. Councils. Joint Special Committee on the Communication From the North Pennsylvania R. Road. 62157

Philadelphia. Councils. Joint Special Committee on the Pennsylvania Railroad. (62156)

Philadelphia. Councils. Joint Special Committee to Whom Was Referred Certain Queries From the American Medical Association. 62165

Philadelphia. Councils. Sanitary Committee. (62222)

Philadelphia. Councils. Sanitary Committee. Sanitary Commission to Visit Montreal and Quebec. 62131, 62221

Philadelphia. Councils. Select Committee to Examine the Accounts of the District of Kensuington. Minority. (61840)

Philadelphia. Councils. Special Committee on Communications from Messrs. Vodges & Gerard. 62173

Philadelphia. Councils. Special Committee on Fairmount Park. 61650

Philadelphia. Councils. Special Committee on Opening Eleventh Street. 62174

Philadelphia. Councils. Special Committee to Examine All Books, Papers, Vouchers, Warrants, &c. &c. of the City Treasurer's Office. 62170

Philadelphia. Councils. Special Committee to Investigate the Management of the Philadelphia Gas Works. 62175

Philadelphia. Councils. Special Committee to Report Upon the Western Canal. 62091

Philadelphia. Councils. Common Council. 61552-61553, 61555, 61614, 61748, 61812, 62164, 62200, 62205, 62323, 78064

Philadelphia. Councils. Common Council. petitioners 84648

Philadelphia. Councils. Common Council. Committee on a Paid Fire Department. 62140

Philadelphia. Councils. Common Council. Committee on the City Debts and Expenditures, and on City Credits and Resources. 61553

Philadelphia. Councils. Common Council. Committee to Investigate Certain Charges Against Hon. William B. Smith. 84748

Philadelphia. Councils. Common Council. Special Committee in Relation to the Sunbury and Erie Railroad. 62171

Philadelphia. Councils. Select Council. 61554, 61614, 61749, 62164, 62204-62205

Philadelphia. Councils. Select Council. petitioners 84648

Philadelphia. Councils. Select Council. Committee on Finances. 62124

Philadelphia. Councils. Select Council. Special Committee to Examine the Books, etc., of the Sunbury and Erie Railroad Company. 62169

Philadelphia. Counsel. 61889

Philadelphia. Court. 28120, 32936, 80736, 96938, 2d note after 105986

Philadelphia. Court of Chancery. (82175)

Philadelphia. Court of Chancery. Auditor. 50152 see also Sheppard, Furman.

Philadelphia. Degree Temple of Honor, no. 1. see Sons of Temperance of North America. Pennsylvania. Philadelphia Degree Temple of Honor, no. 1.

Philadelphia. Delegates to the National Convention of Business Men, 1837. see National Convention of Business Men, Philadelphia, 1837. Philadelphia Delegates.

Philadelphia. Democratic Association. see Democratic Association, Philadelphia.

Philadelphia. Democratic Rescue Association. see Democratic Rescue Association of Philadelphia.

Philadelphia. Democratic Society. see Democratic Society, Philadelphia.

Philadelphia. Deutsche Gesellschaft von Pennsylvanien. see Deutsche Gesellschaft von Pennsylvanien, Philadelphia.

Philadelphia. District Court. see Pennsylvania. District Court (Philadelphia)

Philadelphia. Divinity School of the Protestant Episcopal Church. see Protestant Episcopal Church in the U. S. A. Divinity School, Philadelphia.

Philadelphia. Dorcas Society. see Philadelphia. Tenth Presbyterian Church. Dorcas Society.

Philadelphia. Dry Goods Importers. 62311, 95772

Philadelphia. Emlen Institution for the Education of Children of African or Indian Descent. see Emlen Institution for the Education of Children of African or Indian Descent, Philadelphia.

Philadelphia. Entomological Society. see Entomological Society, Philadelphia.

Philadelphia. Evangelical Lutheran Church of St. John. Mission Tract Society. Managers. 61638

Philadelphia. Evangelical Lutheran Church of St. John. Sunday School. 61638

Philadelphia. Evangelical Reformed Congregation. 61639

Philadelphia. Evangelical Reformed Congregation. Charter. 61639

Philadelphia. Exhibition of Ingenuity and Design, 1st, 1857. see Pennsylvania Institute of Design. Exhibition, 1st, Philadelphia, 1857.

Philadelphia. Exhibition of Oil Paintings for the Benefit of the Soldiers' and Sailors' Home, 1865. see Exhibition of Oil Paintings for the Benefit of the Soldiers' and Sailors' Home, Philadelphia, 1865.

Philadelphia. Fair for the Soldiers' and Sailor Home, 1866. see Philadelphia. Soldiers Home. Fair, 1866.

Philadelphia. Fame Hose Company. see Fame Hose Company, Philadelphia.

Philadelphia. Farmer's and Mechanics Bank. 59809

Philadelphia. Federal Convention, 1787. see U. S. Constitutional Convention, 1787.

Philadelphia. Female Association for the Relief of Women. see Female Association of Philadelphia, for the Relief of Women.

Philadelphia. Female Medical College. see Female Medical College, Philadelphia.

Philadelphia. Female Seamen's Friend Society see Female Seamen's Friend Society, Philadelphia.

Philadelphia. Fenian Brotherhood National Convention, 7th, 1868. see Fenian Brotherhood. National Convention, 7th, Philadelphia, 1868.

Philadelphia. Fire Department. Chief Engineer (61659)

Philadelphia. Fire Marshal. 61660

Philadelphia. First Baptist Church. (32464), 90667

Philadelphia. First Congregational Society. 26241

Philadelphia. First Exhibition of the Pennsylvania Poultry Society, 1852. see Pennsylvania Poultry Society. Exhibition, 1st, 1852.

Philadelphia. First Free Church. (61662)

Philadelphia. First Moravian Church. (61664)

Philadelphia. Fifth Presbyterian Church. 61665, 62282

Philadelphia. First Society of Unitarian Christians. see Unitarians. Philadelphia. First Society.

Philadelphia. First Society of Unitarians. see Unitarians. Philadelphia. First Society.

Philadelphia. First Unitarian Society. 61667, 62261, 69449

Philadelphia. First Unitarian Society. Charter. 69449

Philadelphia. First Universalist Church. Charter. 61669

Philadelphia. Frankford (Borough) see Frankford, Pa.

Philadelphia. Frankford (District) see Frankford, Pa.

Philadelphia. Franklin Cemetery. 61673

Philadelphia. Franklin Fire Company. see Franklin Fire Company, Philadelphia.

Philadelphia. Franklin Institute. see Franklin Institute, Philadelphia.

Philadelphia. Free Trade Convention, 1831. see Free Trade Convention, Philadelphia, 1831

Philadelphia. Freeholders and Inhabitants. see Philadelphia. Citizens.

Philadelphia. Freeholders Meeting, 1817. see Meeting of the Freeholders From Every Part of the State, Philadelphia, 1817.

Philadelphia. French Consul. see France. Consulat. Philadelphia.

Philadelphia. Freyhalter und Einwohner. pseud. see Freyhalter und Einwohner der Stadt und County Philadelphia. pseud.

Philadelphia. Friendly Association for Regaining and Preserving Peace With the Indians by Pacific Measures. see Friendly Association for Regaining and Preserving Peace With the Indians by Pacific Measures, Philadelphia.

Philadelphia. Friends' Asylum for the Insane. (23142), 59900

Philadelphia. Friendship Division, no. 19. see Sons of Temperance of North America. Pennsylvania. Friendship Division, no. 19, Philadelphia.

Philadelphia. Friendship Fire Company. see Friendship Fire Company, Philadelphia.

Philadelphia. Friendship Lodge, no. 73. see Freemasons. Pennsylvania. Friendship Lodge, no. 73, Philadelphia.

Philadelphia. Funeral Solemnities in Honor of Gen. Washington, Dec. 26, 1799. 61479

Philadelphia. Gemeine Gottes im Geist Siebender Generals Synodus, 1742. see Congregation of God in the Spirit.

Philadelphia. General Executive Committee to Provide Means to Relieve the Sufferings in Ireland. see Philadelphia. Town Meeting, 1847. General Executive Committee to Provide Means to Relieve the Sufferings in Ireland.

Philadelphia. General Meeting of the Citizens of Philadelphia and Parts Adjacent, 1779. 61492

Philadelphia. General Meeting of the Merchants and Traders, 1765. 61918

Philadelphia. General Meeting of the Society of the Cincinnati, 1784. see Society of the Cincinnati. General Meeting, Philadelphia, 1784.

Philadelphia. General Town Meeting, 1779. see Philadelphia. Town Meeting, 1779.

Philadelphia. German Lutheran Church. 102774

Philadelphia. German Reformed Congregation. Charter. 61697

Philadelphia. Germantown Academy. see Germantown Academy, Philadelphia.

Philadelphia. Girard College. see Girard College for Orphans, Philadelphia.

Philadelphia. Girard College for Orphans. see Girard College for Orphans, Philadelphia.

Philadelphia. Glenwood Cemetery Comapny. see Glenwood Cemetery Company, Philadelphia.

Philadelphia. Grand Board of Pennsylvania, of the U. A. O. O. see U. A. O. O. Grand Board of Pennsylvania, Philadelphia.

Philadelphia. Grand Consistory of Columbia, Independent Order of the Sons of Malta, 1858. see Independent Order of the Sons of Malta. Grand Consistory of Columbia, Philadelphia, 1858.

Philadelphia. Grand Federal Procession, July 4, 1788. (61411), 104632

Philadelphia. Grand Jury. 61421, 62128

Philadelphia. Gray Reserve. see Pennsylvania. Militia. First Regiment. Company A (" Gray Reserve," Philadelphia)

Philadelphia. Grays. see Pennsylvania. Militia. Philadelphia Grays.

Philadelphia. Great Central Fair, 1864. 30911, (57918), 61705, 61910, 62223, (76637)

Philadelphia. Great Central Fair, 1864. Department of Arms and Trophies. 61577, 61705

Philadelphia. Great Central Fair, 1864. William Penn Parlor. 47693

Philadelphia. Great Central Fair for the Benefit of the United States Sanitary Commission, 1864. see Philadelphia. Great Central Fair, 1864.

Philadelphia. Great Meeting of Irishmen, to Prevent the Re-election of Andrew Jackson, 1832. 35391 see also National Republican Party. Pennsylvania. Philadelphia.

Philadelphia. Great Public Meeting on the Ship Pennsylvania and the Navy Yard, 1837. 61707

Philadelphia. Great Town Meeting, 1840. see Democratic Party. Pennsylvania. Philadelphia.

Philadelphia. Great Union Meeting, 1850. 62088

Philadelphia. Great Union Meeting, 1851. 61708

Philadelphia. Great Union Meeting, 1859. see Great Union Meeting, Philadelphia, December 7, 1859.

Philadelphia. Guardians for the Relief of the Poor. see Philadelphia. Board of Guardians of the Poor.

Philadelphia. Gurney Evening School. see Gurney Evening School, Philadelphia.

Philadelphia. Hahnemann Medical College. see Hahnemann Medical College, Philadelphia.

Philadelphia. Hand-in-Hand Fire Company. see Hand-in-Hand Fire Company, Philadelphia.

Philadelphia. Hannah More Academy. see Hannah More Academy, Philadelphia.

Philadelphia. Harmonia Sacred Music Society. see Harmonia Sacred Music Society, Philadelphia.

Philadelphia. Hebrew Charitable Fund. see Hebrew Charitable Fund, Philadelphia.

Philadelphia. Hibernia Fire Company. see Hibernia Fire Company, Philadelphia.

Philadelphia. Hibernian Society. see Society of the Friendly Sons of Saint Patrick, Philadelphia.

Philadelphia. Holmesburg Public School. 61723

Philadelphia. Home for Aged and Infirm Colored Persons. see Home for Aged and Infirm Colored Persons, Philadelphia.

Philadelphia. Home for Destitute Colored Children. see Home for Destitute Colored Children, Philadelphia.

Philadelphia. Home for Little Wanderers. see Home for Little Wanderers, Philadelphia.

Philadelphia. Home for the Industrious Blind. see Home for the Industrious Blind, Philadelphia.

Philadelphia. Home Guard. see Pennsylvania. Militia. Philadelphia Home Guard.

Philadelphia. Hospital. 61503

Philadelphia. Hospital of the Protestant Episcopal Church. 61726

Philadelphia. Hospital of the Protestant Episcopal Church. Charter. 61726

Philadelphia. House of Correction and Employment. Committee. 61727

Philadelphia. House of Employment. 61503

Philadelphia. House of Refuge. 61728, 61729

Philadelphia. House of Refuge. Charter. 61728

Philadelphia. House of Refuge. Directors. petitioners 61729

Philadelphia. House of Refuge. Managers. 61729, (62075)

Philadelphia. House of Refuge for Coloured Juvenile Delinquents. (61730)

Philadelphia. Howard Association. see Howard Association, Philadelphia.

Philadelphia. Howard Sunday School. Building Committee. 89744

Philadelphia. Hunt Female Beneficial Society. see Hunt Beneficial Society, Philadelphia.

Philadelphia. Independence Day Celebration, 1865. 27286

Philadelphia. Independence Hall. 61526

Philadelphia. Indian Conference, 1744. see Pennsylvania (Colony) Indian Conference, Philadelphia, 1744.

Philadelphia. Indian Conference, 1756. see Pennsylvania (Colony) Indian Conference, Philadelphia, 1756.

Philadelphia. Indigent Widows and Single Women's Society. see Indigent Widows and Single Women's Society, Philadelphia.

Philadelphia. Industrial Home for Girls. 61740

Philadelphia. Industrial Home for the Instruction of Girls in the Arts Of Housewifery. see Philadelphia. Industrial Home for Girls.

Philadelphia. Infirmary, for Diseases of the Eye and Ear. see Philadelphia. Pennsylvania Infirmary, for Diseases of the Eye and Ear.

Philadelphia. Inhabitants. petitioners see Philadelphia. Citizens. petitioners

Philadelphia. Institute for Colored Youth. see Institute for Colored Youth, Philadelphia.

Philadelphia. Iron Workers. petitioners see Iron Workers of Philadelphia. petitioners Workers in Iron of Philadelphia. petitioners

Philadelphia. Ironmasters' Convention, 1849. see Ironmasters' Convention, Philadelphia, 1849.

Philadelphia. Investigation of the Fire at Patterson's Bonded Warehouse, 1869. 61706

Philadelphia. Irving Library Institute. see Irving Library Institute, Philadelphia.

Philadelphia. Jefferson Medical College. see Jefferson Medical College, Philadelphia.

Philadelphia. Jewish Foster Home Society. see Jewish Foster Home Society, Philadelphia.

Philadelphia. Kensington District of the Northern Liberties. see Kensington, Pa.

Philadelphia. Ladies' Branch of the Union Benevolent Association. see Union Benevolent Association, Philadelphia. Ladies' Branch.

Philadelphia. Ladies' United Aid Society of the Methodist Episcopal Church. see Ladies' United Aid Society of the Methodist Episcopal Church in the City of Philadelphia.

Philadelphia. Ladies' Union City Mission. see Ladies' Union City Mission, Philadelphia

Philadelphia. Laurel Hill Cemetery. 39255, 61709, 61764, 82987

Philadelphia. Law Academy. see Law Academy of Philadelphia.

Philadelphia. Lazaretto. 61771

Philadelphia. Library Company. 61784-61785 61787-61788

Philadelphia. Library Company. Charter. 61785-(61786), 61788

Philadelphia. Library Company. Librarian. 82987, 83491 see also Smith, John Jay 1798-1881. Smith, Lloyd Pearsall, 1822 1886.

Philadelphia. Library Company. Loganian Library. 41797, 61797-61798

Philadelphia. Library Company. Loganian Library. Librarian. 82987 see also Smith, John Jay, 1798-1881.

Philadelphia. Library of the Four Monthly Meetings of Friends. 61524

Philadelphia. Library of the Presbyterian Historical Society. see Presbyterian Historical Society, Philadelphia. Library

Philadelphia. Library of the Three Monthly Meetings of Friends. 61524

Philadelphia. Light Artillery Corps. see Pennsylvania. Militia. Light Artillery Corps, Philadelphia.

Philadelphia. Lincoln Institution. see Lincoln Institution, Philadelphia.

Philadelphia. Linen Manufactory. see Linen Manufactory, Philadelphia.

Philadelphia. Logan Evening School for Young Men. Committee. (61796)

Philadelphia. Loganian Library. see Philadelphia. Library Company. Loganian Library.

Philadelphia. Loge l'Amenite no. 73. see Freemasons. Philadelphia. Friendship Lodge, no. 73, Philadelphia.

Philadelphia. Lying-In and Foundling Hospital see Philadelphia. Pennsylvania Lying-In and Foundling Hospital.

Philadelphia. Machpelah Cemetery. 61799

Philadelphia. Machpelah Cemetery. Charter 61799

Philadelphia. Maclurian Lyceum. see Maclurian Lyceum, Philadelphia.

Philadelphia. Magdalen Asylum. see Magdalen Asylum, Philadelphia.

Philadelphia. Magdalen Society. see Magdalen Society of Philadelphia.

Philadelphia. Major General George B. Mc-Clellan Club. see Major General George B. McClellan Club, Philadelphia.

Philadelphia. Managers of the Marine and City Hospitals. petitioners see Managers of the Marine and City Hospitals, Philadelphia. petitioners

Philadelphia. Manufacturers, Mechanics, Merchants, Traders, and Others. petitioners see Philadelphia. Citizens. petitioners

Philadelphia. Manufactuers of Hats. petitioners see Manufacturers of Hats, Philadelphia. petitioners

Philadelphia. Many Respectable Freeholders and Inhabitants. see Philadelphia. Citizens.

Philadelphia. Mariner's Church. 61805

Philadelphia. Marshal of Police. (61806)

Philadelphia. Mass Meeting on the North Pennsylvania Rail Road, 1854. 62078

Philadelphia. Mayor, 1726. 62323

Philadelphia. Mayor, 1765. (61543)

Philadelphia. Mayor, 1814 (Wharton) 103105 see also Wharton, Robert.

Philadelphia. Mayor, 1832. (27494)

Philadelphia. Mayor, 1854 (Conrad) 61839 see also Conrad, Robert Taylor, 1810-1858.

Philadelphia. Mayor, 1886 (Smith) 84748 see also Smith, William B.

Philadelphia. Mayor, 1886 (Smith) defendant 84748 see also Smith, William B. defendant

Philadelphia. Mayor's Court. 28121, 61803, 62181, 96940, note after 96948

Philadelphia. Mechanics Employed in the Manufacture of Iron. petitioners see Iron Workers of Philadelphia. petitioners

Philadelphia. Meeting at Upton's, in Dock Street, 1831. see Meeting at Upton's, in Dock Street, Philadelphia, 1831.

Philadelphia. Meeting of a Number of Citizens, 1776. 61493

Philadelphia. Meeting of Certain Manufacturers and Others, 1828. petitioners (61832)

Philadelphia. Meeting of Citizens, Favourable to the Entire Abolition of Lotteries, 1833. 7908, 42151, 97643

Philadelphia. Meeting of Citizens Opposed to Secret Societies, 1829. Committee. (61417)

Philadelphia. Meeting of Freeholders From Every Part of the State, 1817. see Meeting of Pennsylvania Freeholders, Philadelphia, 1817.

Philadelphia. Meeting of the Citizens in Relation to the Great Pennsylvania Railroad, 1846. 62090

Philadelphia. Meeting of the Citizens in Relation to the Great Pennsylvania Railroad, 1846. Committee. 62090

Philadelphia. Meeting of the Friends to the Election of John Quincy Adams, 1828. see National Republican Party. Pennsylvania. Philadelphia.

Philadelphia. Meeting of the Merchants, 1824. see Meeting of the Merchants of Philadelphia, 1824.

Philadelphia. Meeting of the National Board of Trade, 1868. see National Board of Trade. Meeting, Philadelphia, 1868.

Philadelphia. Meeting of the Pennsylvania Society for the Promotion of Manufactures and the Mechanic Arts, 1827. see Pennsylvania Society for the Promotion of Manufactures and the Mechanic Arts. Meeting, Philadelphia, 1827.

Philadelphia. Meeting on Occasion of the Arrival of the Tea Ship, 1773. see Philadelphia. Public Meeting on Occasion of the Arrival of the Tea Ship, 1773.

Philadelphia. Meeting to Commemorate the Landing of Willima Penn on the Shore of America, 1824. see Meeting to Commemorate the Landing of William Penn on the Shore of America, Philadelphia, 1824.

Philadelphia. Meeting to Take Into Consideration the Condition of the Freed People of the South, 1863. 62165

Philadelphia. Meetings on the Proposed Operatic and Dramatic House, 1839. (62080) see also Philadelphia. Committee of Twelve on the Proposed Operatic and Dramatic House.

Philadelphia. Members of the Medical Profession. see Members of the Medical Profession of Philadelphia.

Philadelphia. Mercantile Library Company. 61836

Philadelphia. Mercantile Library Company. Charter. 61836

Philadelphia. Mercantile Library Company. Library. 61836

Philadelphia. Merchants. petitioners 62167

Philadelphia. Merchants and Traders. 61688

Philadelphia. Merchants and Traders. petitioners 61828, (62186), 95951

Philadelphia. Merchants and Traders. General Meeting, 1765. see Philadelphia. General Meeting of the Merchants and Traders, 1765.

Philadelphia. Militia. see Pennsylvania. Militia. Philadelphia.

Philadelphia. Minne-ha-ha Lodge no. 1, Independent Order of the Sons of Malta. see Independent Order of the Sons of Malta. Pennsylvania. Minne-ha-ha Lodge no. 1, Philadelphia.

Philadelphia. Mission House of the Protestant Episcopal Church. (66206)

Philadelphia. Mrs. Rivardi's Seminary. see Mrs. Rivardi's Seminary, Philadelphia.

Philadelphia. Monument Cemetery. 50234, (61530), 61846

Philadelphia. Monument Cemetery. Charter. 50234, 61846

Philadelphia. Monument Cemetery. Lot Holders. 61846

Philadelphia. Monument Cemetery. Managers. 61846

Philadelphia. Mount Lebanon Cemetery Company. (61847)

Philadelphia. Mount Moriah Cemetery Association. 51162, 61848

Philadelphia. Mount Moriah Cemetery Association. Charter. 61848

Philadelphia. Mount Vernon Cemetery Company. 51178, 61849

Philadelphia. Mount Vernon Cemetery Company. Charter. 51178, 61849

Philadelphia. Mount Zion Tabernacle, No. 3. 61850

Philadelphia. Moyamensing (District) see Moyamensing (District), Philadelphia.

Philadelphia. Musical Fund Society. see Musical Fund Society of Philadelphia.

Philadelphia. National Anti-masonic Convention, 1830. see United States Anti-masonic Convention, Philadelphia, 1830.

Philadelphia. National Anti-slavery Convention, 1833. see National Anti-slavery Convention, Philadelphia, 1833.

Philadelphia. National Congress on Uniform Divorce Laws, 1906. see National Congress on Uniform Divorce Laws, Philadelphia, 1906.

Philadelphia. National Convention of Business Men, 1837. see National Convention of Business Men, Philadelphia, 1837.

Philadelphia. National Convention of the Friends of Public Education, 1849. see National Convention of the Friends of Public Education, Philadelphia, 1849.

Philadelphia. National Convention of the Soldiers of the War of 1812, 1st, 1854. see National Convention of the Soldiers of the War of 1812. 1st, Philadelphia, 1854.

Philadelphia. National Medical Convention, 1847. see National Medical Convention, Philadelphia, 1847.

Philadelphia. National Pharmaceutical Convention, 1852. see National Pharmaceutical Convention, Philadelphia, 1852.

Philadelphia. National Quarantine and Sanitary Convention, 1857. see National Quarantine and Sanitary Convention, Philadelphia, 1857.

Philadelphia. National Union Club. see National Union Club, Philadelphia.

Philadelphia. Native American Hall Co. of Cedar Ward. see American Party. Pennsylvania. Philadelphia. Native American Hall Co. of Cedar Ward.

Philadelphia. Native Americans. see American Party. Pennsylvania. Philadelphia.

Philadelphia. Negro School of the Society of Friends. Trustees. 61494

Philadelphia. New Theatre. Stockholders. 61691

Philadelphia. Non-importation Association, 1765. see Non-importation Association, Philadelphia, 1765.

Philadelphia. Non-importation Association, 1770. see Non-importation Association, Philadelphia, 1770.

Philadelphia. Normal School. Principal. 61867

Philadelphia. Northern Dispensary for the Poor. see Northern Dispensary for the Poor, Philadelphia.

Philadelphia. Northern Home for Friendless Children. see Northern Home for Friendless Children, Philadelphia.

Philadelphia. Northern Liberties (District) see Northern Liberties (District), Philadelphia.

Philadelphia. Northern Medical Association. see Northern Medical Association of Philadelphia.

Philadelphia. Northwood Cemetery Company. see Northwood Cemetery Company, Philadelphia.

Philadelphia. Numismatic and Antiquarian Society. see Numismatic and Antiquarian Society of Philadelphia.

Philadelphia. Odd Fellows' Cemetery Company. 61882

Philadelphia. Odd Fellows' Cemetery Company. Charter. 61882

Philadelphia. Office for Recording of Deeds. 94807

Philadelphia. Old Pine Street Church. see Philadelphia. Third Presbyterian Church.

Philadelphia. Olivet Baptist Church. 57219

Philadelphia. Olympic Theatre. 61908

Philadelphia. Opera House. 61458, 61888

Philadelphia. Opera House. Charter. 61458, 61888

Philadelphia. Ordinances, etc. 1939, (27494), 59822, 60198, 61544, (61559), 61583, 61596, 61769-61770, 61985, 61896-61903, 62000, 62369, 62297, note after 92782, 93732

Philadelphia. Orphan Society. see Orphan Society of Philadelphia.

Philadelphia. Orphans Court. (74111)

Philadelphia. Oxford Presbyterian Church. (58035)

Philadelphia. Patriotischen Gesellschaft der Stadt und Caunty Philadelphia. see Patriotischen Gesellschaft der Stadt und Caunty Philadelphia.

Philadelphia. Peale's Museum. see Peale's Museum, Philadelphia.

Philadelphia. Penitentiary. 73228

Philadelphia. Penn Medical University. see Penn Medical University, Philadelphia.

Philadelphia. Pennsylvania College. see Pennsylvania College, Gettysburg.

Philadelphia. Pennsylvania Horticultural Society. see Pennsylvania Horticultural Society, Philadelphia.

Philadelphia. Pennsylvania Hospital. 59890, 60330-60331

Philadelphia. Pennsylvania Hospital. Anatomical Museum. 60328

Philadelphia. Pennsylvania Hospital. Board of Managers. 60330

Philadelphia. Pennsylvania Hospital. Committee on Repairs and Alterations. 60330

Philadelphia. Pennsylvania Hospital. Medical Library. 60328

Philadelphia. Pennsylvania Hospital. Meeting 1867, 60330

Philadelphia. Pennsylvania Hospital for Insane. 60332, 87864

Philadelphia. Pennsylvania Industrial Home for Blind Women. see Pennsylvania. Industrial Home for Blind Women, Philadelphia.

Philadelphia. Pennsylvania Infirmary, for Diseases of the Eye and Ear. (60334)

Philadelphia. Pennsylvania Institution for the Deaf and Dumb. see Pennsylvania Institution for the Deaf and Dumb, Philadelphia.

Philadelphia. Pennsylvania Institution for the Instruction of the Blind. see Pennsylvania Institution for the Instruction of the Blind, Philadelphia.

Philadelphia. Pennsylvania Lying-In and Foundling Hospital. 60345

Philadelphia. Pennsylvania Lying-In and Foundling Hospital. Charter. 60345

Philadelphia. Pennsylvania Lying-In and Foundling Hospital. Managers. 60345

Philadelphia. People's Club in Favor of Gen. Simon Cameron for President. see People's Club of Philadelphia, in Favor of Gen. Simon Cameron for President.

Philadelphia. Pere la Chaise. see Philadelphia. Monument Cemetery.

Philadelphia. Pettie's-Island Cash Lottery, 1773. see American Flint Glass Manufactory, Pettie's-Island Cash Lottery, Philadelphia, 1773.

Philadelphia. Philadelphia Cemetery. 61973

Philadelphia. Subscribers to the Non-importation Agreement, 1770. see Non-importation Association, Philadelphia, 1770.

Philadelphia. Sundry Banks. petitioners see Philadelphia. Banks. petitioners

Philadelphia. Sundry Citizens. petitioners see Philadelphia. Citizens. petitioners

Philadelphia. Sundry Manufacturers of Hats. petitioners see Manufacturers of Hats, Philadelphia. petitioners

Philadelphia. Sundry Merchants and Traders. petitioners see Philadelphia. Merchants and Traders. petitioners

Philadelphia. Sundry Umbrella-Makers. petitioners see Umbrella-Makers of Philadelphia. petitioners

Philadelphia. Superintendent of Trusts. (62299)

Philadelphia. Supreme Grand Lodge of the Independent Order of the Sons of Malta, 1860. see Independent Order of the Sons of Malta. Pennsylvania. Supreme Grand Lodge, Philadelphia, 1860.

Philadelphia. Synagogue Beth Israel. 61893

Philadelphia. Synagogue Roudafe Sholum. 61894

Philadelphia. Synod of the United Evangelical Lutheran Church. see Evangelical Lutheran Ministerium of Pennsylvania and Adjoining States.

Philadelphia. Teachers' Institute. see Teachers' Institute, Philadelphia.

Philadelphia. Temporary Home Association. see Temporary Home Association, Philadelphia.

Philadelphia. Tenth Presbyterian Church. Dorcas Society. 61608

Philadelphia. Testimonial Dinner to Henry C. Carey, 1859. see Testimonial Dinner to Henry C. Carey, Philadelphia, 1859.

Philadelphia. Teutschen Gesellschaft. see Deutsche Gesellschaft von Pennsylvanien, Philadelphia.

Philadelphia. Theatre. 62224

Philadelphia. Third Presbyterian Church. 7348, 22384, 62310, 61886

Philadelphia. Third Presbyterian Church. Centennial Celebration, 1868. 61886, 61772

Philadelphia. 30,000 Disfranchised Citizens. petitioners see Philadelphia. Citizens. petitioners

Philadelphia. Theological Seminary of St. Charles Borromeo. see Theological Seminary of St. Charles Borromeo, Philadelphia.

Philadelphia. Topographical Commissioners. 62180

Philadelphia. Treasurer. 61407, 62343

Philadelphia. Town Major. 62272 see also Nicola, Lewis, 1717-1807.

Philadelphia. Town Meeting, 1779. 62086

Philadelphia. Town Meeting, 1827. Committee to Consider the . . . Pauper System of the City and Districts, and to Report Remedies for its Defects. see Philadelphia. Committee to Consider the . . . Pauper System of the City and Districts, and to Report Remedies for its Defects.

Philadelphia. Town Meeting, 1828. (62166)

Philadelphia. Town Meeting, 1847. General Executive Committee to Provide Means to Relieve the Sufferings in Ireland. 62152

Philadelphia. Town Meeting, 1852. Committee to Consider the Propriety of . . . a Paid Fire Department. see Philadelphia.

Committee to Consider the Propriety of . . . a Paid Fire Department.

Philadelphia. Town Meeting of the Citizens, Without Distinction of Party, to Hear the Report of Their Delegates to the National Convention of Business Men, 1837. 62079

Philadelphia. Town Meeting on the Establishment of a Dry Dock, and the Defences of the Delaware River. 61883

Philadelphia. Town Meeting to Memorialise Congress for an Appropriation for Constructing a Breakwater in the Delaware Bay, 1825. 62078

Philadelphia. Town Meeting to Take Into Consideration the Subject of Establishing "A Society for the Encouragement of Faithful Domestics." Committee. see Society for the Encouragement of Faithful Domestics, Philadelphia.

Philadelphia. Tract Society of Friends. see Tract Association of Friends, Philadelphia.

Philadelphia. Twenty-four Journeymen Tailors. defendants see Twenty-Four Journeymen Tailors, Philadelphia. defendants

Philadelphia. Two Meetings of Citizens Respecting Col. Clark's Plan for Ascending Rapids in Rivers, and Thereby Improving the Navigation of the River Delaware, Beyond Trenton, 1824. 62092

Philadelphia. Umbrella-Makers. petitioners see Umbrella-Makers of Philadelphia. petitioners

Philadelphia. Union Academy. see Union Academy, Philadelphia.

Philadelphia. Union Benevolent Association. see Union Benevolent Association, Philadelphia.

Philadelphia. Union Club. see Union Club of Philadelphia.

Philadelphia. Union Female Missionary Society. see Union Female Missionary Society, Philadelphia.

Philadelphia. Union League. see Union League of Philadelphia.

Philadelphia. Union Library Company. see Union Library Company of Philadelphia.

Philadelphia. Union School and Children's Home. see Southern Home for Destitute Children, Philadelphia.

Philadelphia. Union Temporary Home for Children. see Union Temporary Home for Children, Philadelphia.

Philadelphia. United States Anti-masonic Convention, 1830. see United States Anti-masonic Convention, Philadelphia, 1830.

Philadelphia. United States Beneficial Society. see United States Beneficial Society of Philadelphia.

Philadelphia. United States Fire Company. see United States Fire Company, Philadelphia.

Philadelphia. United States Sanitary Commission. Branch. see United States Sanitary Commission. Philadelphia Branch.

Philadelphia. Universal Lyceum. see Universal Lyceum, Philadelphia.

Philadelphia. University of Free Medicine & Popular Knowledge. see University of Free Medicine & Popular Knowledge, Philadelphia.

Philadelphia. Ury House School. 62362

Philadelphia. Vigilant Fire Company. see Vigilant Fire Company, Philadelphia.

Philadelphia. Wagner Free Institute of Science. see Wagner Free Institute of Science, Philadelphia.

Philadelphia. Walnut Street Presbyterian Church. 62373

Philadelphia. Washington Association. see Washington Association of Philadelphia.

Philadelphia. Washington Blues. see Pennsylvania. Militia. Washington Blues, Philadelphia.

Philadelphia. Washington Grays. see Pennsylvania. Militia. Light Artillery Corps, Philadelphia.

Philadelphia. Washington Monument Association. see Washington Monument Association, Philadelphia.

Philadelphia. Water Department. 62370

Philadelphia. Water Department. Chief Engineer. 62370

Philadelphia. Watering Committee. 60451, 62116, 62182, 62369, 62371, (78083), 78091, 81539, 84648

Philadelphia. Welch Society. see Welch Society, Philadelphia.

Philadelphia. West Philadelphia (Borough) see West Philadelphia, Pa.

Philadelphia. Western Association of Ladies for the Relief and Employment of the Poor, see Western Association of Ladies for the Relief and Employment of the Poor, Philadelphia.

Philadelphia. Whig Convention, 1848. see Whig Party. Convention, Philadelphia, 1848.

Philadelphia. William Penn Parkon, Great Central Fair, 1864. see Philadelphia. Great Central Fair, 1864. William Penn Parlor.

Philadelphia. Wills Hospital. 62390-62391

Philadelphia. Woodbury Library Company. see Woodbury Library Company, Philadelphia.

Philadelphia. Woodlands Cemetery. 62206

Philadelphia. Woodlands Cemetery Company. 62394

Philadelphia. Woodlands Cemetery Company. Charter. 62394

Philadelphia. Workers in Iron. petitioners see Iron Workers of Philadelphia. petitioners Workers in Iron of Philadelphia. petitioners

Philadelphia. Young Ladies Academy. 62398, 2d note after 106135

Philadelphia. Young Ladies Academy. Charter. 62398, 2d note after 106135

Philadelphia. Young Ladies Academy. Students. 62398, 2d note after 106135

Philadelphia. Young Ladies Academy. Trustees. 62398, 2d note after 106135

Philadelphia. Young Ladies' Institute. see Young Ladies' Institute, Philadelphia.

Philadelphia. Young Men. 61428

Philadelphia. Young Men's Association for the Suppression of Intemperance. see Young Men's Association for the Suppression of Intemperance, Philadelphia.

Philadelphia. Young Men's Central Home Mission. see Young Men's Central Home Mission, Philadelphia.

Philadelphia. Young Men's Christian Association. see Young Men's Christian Association, Philadelphia.

Philadelphia. Young Men's Home. 61865

Philadelphia. Young Men's Missionary Society of St. Andrew's Church. see Philadelphia. St. Andrew's Church. Young Men's Missionary Society.

Philadelphia. Young Men's Temperance Society. see Young Men's Temperance Society, Philadelphia.

Philadelphia. Youth's Missionary Society. see Youth's Missionary Society of Philadelphia

Philadelphia. Youth's Tract Society. see Youth's Tract Society of Philadelphia.

Philadelphia. Zane Street Girls' Grammar School. 62405

Philadelphia. County, Pa. defendants (7770)

Philadelphia. County, Pa. Board of Supervisor Committee on Estimates. 60514

Philadelphia. County, Pa. Board of Public Schools. Special Committee. 62172

Philadelphia County, Pa. Citizens. petitioners 62089

Philadelphia County, Pa. Collector of Excise. 3714-3716, 62273 see also Bartholomew Edward. Crispin, William.

Philadelphia County, Pa. Committee on Roads and Bridges. (62148)

Philadelphia County, Pa. Court of Common Pleas. see Pennsylvania. Court of Common Pleas (Philadelphia County)

Philadelphia County, Pa. Court of General Sessions. see Pennsylvania. Court of General Sessions (Philadelphia County)

Philadelphia County, Pa. Court of Oyer and Terminer. see Pennsylvania. Court of Oyer and Terminer (Philadelphia County)

Philadelphia County, Pa. Court of Quarter Sessions. see Pennsylvania. Court of Quarter Sessions (Philadelphia County)

Philadelphia County, Pa. District Court. see Pennsylvania. District Court (Philadelphia)

Philadelphia County, Pa. Jackson Club. see Jackson Club of the City and County of Philadelphia.

Philadelphia County, Pa. Lieutenant. 13834, (62280)-62281 see also Coats, William, fl. 1783. Henry, William.

Philadelphia County, Pa. Manufacturers, Mechanics, Merchants, Traders, and Others. petitioners see Philadelphia County, Pa. Citizens. petitioners

Philadelphia County, Pa. Patriotischen Gesell schaft. see Patriotischen Gesellschaft der Stadt und Caunty Philadelphia.

Philadelphia County, Pa. Prison. (61988)

Philadelphia County, Pa. Prison Committee of Investigation. (61988)

Philadelphia County, Pa. Prison. Inspectors. (61988)

Philadelphia County, Pa. Sub-Lieutenant. 62274-62279, 62281 see also Antes, William. Dewees, Samuel. Engle, Jacob Richards, Peter. Smith, George. Thompson, Archibald.

Philadelphia (Diocese) Bishop (Conwell) (6221 note after 97365 see also Conwell, Henry, Bp.

Philadelphia (Diocese) Bishop (Kenrick) (7296 see also Kenrick, Francis Patrick, Bp.

Philadelphia (Diocese) Synod, 1832. (72960)-72962

Philadelphia (Diocese) Synod, 1842. 72961-72962

Philadelphia (Diocese) Synod, 1847. 72962

Philadelphia (Diocese) Synod, 1853. 72962

Philadelphia (Diocese) Synod, 1855. 72962

Philadelphia (U. S. Frigate) 62408

Philadelphia, a satire. 15195

Philadelphia Academy of Medicine. see Academy of Medicine, Philadelphia.

Philadelphia Adult School Union. see Philadelphia Sunday and Adult School Union.

Philadelphia album. 61938

Philadelphia album and ladies' literary portfolio. 61939

Philadelphia almanac and general business directory for . . . 1848. (61942)

Philadelphia almanac for . . . 1776. 61940

Philadelphia almanack for the year 1778. 61941

Philadelphia American Literary Union. see American Literary Union, Philadelphia.

Philadelphia and Atlantic Steam Navigation Company. 61943

Philadelphia and Atlantic Steam Navigation Company. Charter. 61943

Philadelphia and Atlantic Steam Navigation Company. Directors. 61943

Philadelphia and Baltimore Central Railroad Company. President and Directors. 61944

Philadelphia and Columbia Railroad. Superintendent. (61945)

Philadelphia and Columbia Railroad. Superintendent's report for . . . 1853. (61945)

Philadelphia and Darby Rail Road Company. 61946

Philadelphia and Darby Rail Road Company. Charter. 61946

Philadelphia and Erie Rail Road Company. 61947

Philadelphia and Erie Rail Road Company. plaintiffs 68169

Philadelphia and Erie Rail Road Company. Stockholders. 61947

Philadelphia and her merchants. (71592)

Philadelphia and its manufactories and representative mercantile houses. 25732

Philadelphia and its manufactures. 25731

Philadelphia and Reading Rail Road. 61948

Philadelphia and Reading Rail Road Company. 61948, 67511

Philadelphia and Reading Rail Road Company. Charter. 61948

Philadelphia and Reading Rail Road Company. Committee of Investigation. 61948

Philadelphia and Reading Rail Road Company. Engineers. 61948

Philadelphia and Reading Rail Road Company. General Superintendent. 61948

Philadelphia and Reading Rail Road Company. President and Managers. 61948

Philadelphia and Sunbury Railroad. Directors. 61949

Philadelphia and the lakes. 61950

Philadelphia and the north-east valleys. (61951)

Philadelphia Anti-slavery Society. 61952

Philadelphia Anti-slavery Society. Managers. 61952

Philadelphia Arcade. Charter. 61953

Philadelphia Art Association. see Art Association of Philadelphia.

Philadelphia Art Union. see Art Union of Philadelphia.

Philadelphia Art Union reporter. 61954

Philadelphia Artists and Manufacturers. petitioners see Artists and Manufacturers of Philadelphia. petitioners

Philadelphia Artists' Fund Society. see Artists' Fund Society, Philadelphia.

Philadelphia as it is. (61955)

Philadelphia as it is, in 1852. 83733

Philadelphia Association for Carrying On the Linen Manufactory, Philadelphia. see Association for Carrying on the Linen Manufactory, Philadelphia.

Philadelphia Association for Establishing a School for the Education of the Blind. see Association for Establishing a School

for the Education of the Blind in Philadelphia.

Philadelphia Association for the Relief of Disabled Firemen. Trustees. 61956

Philadelphia Association in Aid of the Swiss Mission to Canada. 61957

Philadelphia Association Library Company. see Association Library Company of Philadelphia.

Philadelphia Association of Friends for the Education of Poor Children. 61958 see also Friends, Society of. Philadelphia Yearly Meeting.

Philadelphia Association of Friends for the Education of Poor Children. Adelphi School. 61446

Philadelphia Association of Friends for the Instruction of Poor Children. see Philadelphia Association of Friends for the Education of Poor Children.

Philadelphia Association of Friends for the Relief of Colored Freedmen. see Association of Friends at Philadelphia and Vicinity, for the Relief of Colored Freedmen.

Philadelphia Association of the Defenders of the County, in the War of 1812. see Society of the War of 1812. Pennsylvania.

Philadelphia Asylum for the Deaf and Dumb. (61960)

Philadelphia Athenaeum. 61496

Philadelphia Athenaeum. Architect. 61496

Philadelphia Athenaeum. Charter. 61496

Philadelphia Athenaeum. Directors. 61496

Philadelphia Athenaeum. President. 61496

Philadelphia Auctioneers. petitioners see Auctioneers of Philadelphia. petitioners

Philadelphia, August, 1793. 95342

Philadelphia Bank. see Bank of Philadelphia.

Philadelphia Banks Committee. see Committee of the Several Banks of Philadelphia.

Philadelphia Baptist Association. see Baptists. Pennsylvania. Philadelphia Baptist Association.

Philadelphia Baptist General Association. see Baptists. Pennsylvania. General Association of Philadelphia.

Philadelphia Baptist Institute. (61963)

Philadelphia Baptist Orphan Society. 61964

Philadelphia bar. A complete catalogue of members. 61965

Philadelphia Bible Society. see Pennsylvania Bible Society.

Philadelphia Bible Union. 61968

Philadelphia blue book. 61969, 84912

Philadelphia Board of Trade. see Philadelphia. Board of Trade.

Philadelphia book; or specimens of metropolitan literature. (61971)

Philadelphia Branch of the U. S. Sanitary Commission. see United States Sanitary Commission. Philadelphia Branch.

Philadelphia Branch, United States Sanitary Commission. see United States Sanitary Commission. Philadelphia Branch.

Philadelphia business directory, 1863-64. 61606

Philadelphia business directory . . . for . . . 1849. 61606

Philadelphia Carpenters' Company. see Carpenters' Company, Philadelphia.

Philadelphia Cemetery, Philadelphia. see Philadelphia. Philadelphia Cemetery.

Philadelphia Cemetery. Copy of deed trust. 61973

Philadelphia Chamber of Commerce. see
Philadelphia. Chamber of Commerce.
Philadelphia circulating business directory.
61606
Philadelphia Circulating Library. 61976
Philadelphia city and business directory.
61606
Philadelphia city guide. 61977
Philadelphia City Institute. 61978
Philadelphia City Institute. Managers. 61978
Philadelphia City Mission. (61979)
Philadelphia City Tract Society. 61980
Philadelphia Clearing House Association. 84374
Philadelphia Clearing House Association. Tax
Committee. 3188
Philadelphia clergy. 39789
Philadelphia Club. (61981)
Philadelphia Club. defendnats 23184
Philadelphia Club. Charter. (61981)
Philadelphia, College of. see Pennsylvania.
University.
Philadelphia College of Medicine. 61809,
61982
Philadelphia College of Music. 61983
Philadelphia College of Music. 1854. 61983
Philadelphia College of Pharmacy. 61984
Philadelphia College of Pharmacy. Charter.
61984
Philadelphia College of Physicians. see
College of Physicians, Philadelphia.
Philadelphia Commercial Exchange. see Phila-
delphia. Commercial Exchange.
Philadelphia Committee of Correspondence.
see Democratic Party. Pennsylvania.
Philadelphia. Committee of Correspond-
ence.
Philadelphia Committee of Friends of Van
Buren. see Democratic Party. Penn-
sylvania. Philadelphia.
Philadelphia Committee of Privates. pseud.
see Committee of Privates, Philadelphia.
psued.
Philadelphia Committee on Bridging the Dela-
ware. 69960
Philadelphia Committee on the Practicability
and Utility of Immediately Constructing a
Central Railway, From Pottsville to Sun-
bury and Danville. 60009
Philadelphia Committee on . . . Transatlantic
Steam Navigation. 62162
Philadelphia Company of Booksellers. 61985
Philadelphia Company of Printers and Book-
sellers. (61521), 89650
Philadelphia complete directory for 1857.
61606
Philadelphia Contributionship for the Insuring
of Houses for Loss by Fire. 61986
Philadelphia Contributionship for the Insuring
of Houses for loss by Fire. Charter.
61986
Philadelphia Corn Exchange Association. see
Philadelphia. Commercial Exchange.
Philadelphia County Medical Society. (36103)
Philadelphia County Volunteers. see Pennsyl-
vania. Militia. First Division. Second
Brigade. Philadelphia County Volunteers.
Philadelphia Daily advertiser. see Gazette of
the United States, and Philadelphia daily
advertiser.
Philadelphia, December 8, 1777. (61934)
Philadelphia Degree Temple of Honor, no. 1.
see Sons of Temperance of North America.
Pennsylvania. Philadelphia Degree Temple
of Honor, no. 1.

Philadelphia Democratic Committee. see
Democratic Party. Pennsylvania. Phila-
delphia. Committee.
Philadelphia Democratic Hickory Club. see
Democratic Hickory Club, Philadelphia.
Philadelphia described. 61990
Philadelphia directory and register. 30323
Philadelphia directory and register: . . . by
James Hardie. 61603
Philadelphia directory and register, for 1818.
61606
Philadelphia directory and register for 1813.
61606
Philadelphia directory and register for 1820.
61606
Philadelphia directory and stranger's guide,
for 1828. 61606
Philadelphia directory and stranger's guide,
for 1825. 61606, 104694
Philadelphia directory. By Clement Biddle.
61602
Philadelphia directory, by Francis White.
61600, note after 103383
Philadelphia directory, city and county register
for 1802. 61606
Philadelphia directory, 1852. 83733
Philadelphia directory for 1814. 61606
Philadelphia directory, for 1800. (61605), 2d
note after 90069
Philadelphia directory, for 1801. (61605), 2d
note after 90069
Philadelphia directory for 1817. 61606
Philadelphia directory for 1816. 61606
Philadelphia directory, for 1837. 61606
Philadelphia directory for 1824. 61606
Philadelphia directory, for 1798. (61605), 2d
note after 90069
Philadelphia directory, for 1799. (61605), 2d
note after 90069
Philadelphia directory, for 1797. (61605), 2d
note after 90069
Philadelphia directory, for 1796. 61604, 91312
Philadelphia Dispensary. 61991
Philadelphia, Dover and Norfolk Steam-Boat
and Transportation Company. Charter.
61992
Philadelphia, Easton and Water-Gap Railroad
Company. (61993)
Philadelphia, Easton and Water-Gap Railroad
Company. Charter. (61993)
Philadelphia, Easton and Water-Gap Railroad
Company. Committee. (61993)
Philadelphia, Easton and Water-Gap Railroad
Company. Chief Engineer. (61993)
Philadelphia, Easton and Water-Gap Railroad
Company. President and Directors.
petitioners (61993)
Philadelphia Education Society of the Presby-
terian Church. see Presbyterian Educa-
tion Society.
Philadelphia, 11th month, 18th, 1793. 61935
Philadelphia Emigrant Society. Committee to
Enquire Into the Nature and Operation
of the Emigration Laws in the State of
New York. 61994
Philadelphia Emigrant's Friend Society. see
Emigrant's Friend Society, Philadelphia.
Philadelphia Entomological Society. see Ento-
mological Society of Philadelphia.
Philadelphia Episcopal Missionary Society.
61620
Philadelphia evening journal. 1770
Philadelphia Exchange Company. firm 28171
Philadelphia, February 25. 103349
Philadelphia, Feb. 22, 1832. 56315, 96073

Philadelphia Female Anti-slavery Society. 61995

Philadelphia Female Bible Society. (61654)

Philadelphia Female Domestic Missionary Society. see Female Domestic Missionary Society of Philadelphia.

Philadelphia Female Hospital Society. see Female Hospital Society, Philadelphia.

Philadelphia Female Tract Society. 61996

Philadelphia Fire and Inland Navigation Insurance Company. Charter. 61998

Philadelphia Fire Association. see Fire Association of Philadelphia.

Philadelphia fire marshal almanac and underwriters' advertiser. (61999)

Philadelphia firemen's songster. 61661

Philadelphia, 4th. month, 10th, 1811. 99822, 99825

Philadelphia Franklin journal. see Franklin journal, and American mechanics' magazine.

Philadelphia Free Produce Association of Friends. 61997

Philadelphia Friendly Association for Mutual Interests. see Friendly Association for Mutual Interests, Philadelphia.

Philadelphia Friends Association for the Relief of Colored Freedmen. see Friends' Association of Philadelphia for the Relief of Colored Freedmen.

Philadelphia Fuel Savings Society. see Fuel Savings Society of the City and Liberties of Philadelphia.

Philadelphia Gas Works. Trustees. 62000

Philadelphia gazette. 13474, (46925), (62911), 92853, 96584, 97380

Philadelphia gaol, the 12th,of the 10th month, 1772. 62335

Philadelphia General Association of Baptists. see Baptists. Pennsylvania. General Association of Philadelphia.

Philadelphia, Germantown, and Norristown Railroad Company. 62001

Philadelphia, Germantown, and Norristown Railroad Company. Charter. 62001

Philadelphia, Germantown, and Norristown Railroad Company. President and Managers. 62001

Philadelphia Good Intent Beneficial Society. see Good Intent Beneficial Society, Philadelphia.

Philadelphia Grays. see Pennsylvania. Militia. Philadelphia Grays.

Philadelphia Gray's collection of official reports. 9835

Philadelphia harmony. 89423

Philadelphia Hibernian Provident Association. see Society of the Friendly Sons of St. Patrick, Philadelphia.

Philadelphia Hibernian Society. see Society of the Friendly Sons of St. Patrick, Philadelphia.

Philadelphia Hibernian Society, for the Relief of Emigrants from Ireland. see Society of the Friendly Sons of St. Patrick, Philadelphia.

Philadelphia Historical Society. petitioners 47653, 61824

Philadelphia Home Missionary Society. 62003

Philadelphia Hose Company. 62004

Philadelphia in 1868. A guide-book. 62007

Philadelphia in 1830-1. 62006

Philadelphia in 1824. 62005

Philadelphia index or directory for 1823. 61606

Philadelphia Institute. 62008

Philadelphia, January 15, 1772. 62334

Philadelphia. January 14, 1775. 92273

Philadelphia, January 17th, 1774. 61928

Philadelphia, January 16, 1776. 100004

Philada. Jan. 21, 1824. (62107)

" Philadelphia Jockey Club." (19494A), 13879, 13885, (78988), 95799

Philadelphia journal of homoeopathy. 62009

Philadelphia journal of the medical and physical sciences. 62010, 94094, 101133

Philadelphia, July 12, 1770. 71922

Philadelphia, June [24], 1773. 61926, 106049

Philadelphia Ladies' Aid Society. see Ladies' Aid Society of Philadelphia.

Philadelphia Ladies' Association, Auxiliary to the American Colonization Society. see Ladies' Association, Auxiliary to the American Colonization Society, Philadelphia.

Philadelphia Ladies' Association for Soldiers' Relief. see Ladies' Association for Soldiers' Relief, Philadelphia.

Philadelphia Ladies' Chinese Association. see Ladies' Chinese Association of Philadelphia.

Philadelphia Ladies' Depository. see Ladies' Depository, Philadelphia.

Philadelphia Law Academy. see Law Academy, Philadelphia.

Philadelphia Law Association. see Law Association, Philadelphia.

Philadelphia Law Institute. see Law Institute, Philadelphia.

Philadelphia Law Library Company. see Law Library Company, Philadelphia.

Philadelphia ledger. (29009)

Philadelphia liberalist. 88444A

Philadelphia Library Company. see Library Company of Philadelphia.

Philadelphia Literary Institute. (62011)

Philadelphia Literary Institute. Charter. (62011)

Philadelphia locksmith. 68637, 68644

Philadelphia Lying-In Charity and Nurse Society. 62012

Philadelphia Lying-In Charity and Nurse Society. Charter. 62012

Philadelphia Lying-In Charity and Nurse Society. Managers. 62012

Philadelphia magazine and review, or monthly repository. (62014)

Philadelphia magazine for 1788. 62013

Philadelphia malignants. 94400

Philadelphia. March 14, 1834. 85856

Philadelphia, May 19. 1766. 51164, (61916)

Philadelphia, May 22, 1770. 61921

Philadelphia medical and surgical journal. 3822, 62015-62016

Philadelphia Medical College. see Philadelphia College of Medicine.

Philadelphia medical museum. 17284

Philadelphia Medical Society. 62017

Philadelphia Medical Society. Charter. 62017

Philadelphia Medical Society. Committee on Epidemic Cholera. 61810

Philadelphia Medico-Chirurgical College. see Medico-Chirurgical College, Philadelphia.

Philadelphia Member of the Bar. pseud. see Member of the Bar of Philadelphia. pseud. reporter

Philadelphia Members of the Medical Profession. see Members of the Medical Profession of Philadelphia.

Philadelphia Mercantile Club. see Mercantile Club, Philadelphia.

Philadelphia merchants' & manufacturers' business directory. 61606

Philadelphia Merchants, As Subscribed to the Non-importation Resolutions, October 25, 1765. see Non-importation Association, Philadelphia, 1765.

Philadelphia Merchants Fund. see Merchants Fund, Philadelphia.

Philadelphia mischianza. 92853-92854

Philadelphia, Monday, May 25, 1840. 62018

Philadelphia monthly journal of medicine and surgery. 83664

Philadelphia monthly magazine. 62019, 85577, 101710, 101779

Philadelphia Museum. 61711, 61722

Philadelphia Museum Company. 62020

Philadelphia Museum Company. Charter. 62020

Philadelphia national gazette. 95108

Philadelphia Native American Association of the Unincorporated Northern Liberties. see Native American Association of the Unincorporated Northern Liberties.

Philadelphia newest almanac for 1775. 62021, note after 94610

Philadelphia Newsboys' Aid Society. see Philadelphia. Young Men's Home.

Philadelphia, 19th January, 1798. 106214

Philadelphia, 9th of December, 1773. 61927

Philadelphia Non-importation Association, 1765. see Non-importation Association, Philadelphia, 1765.

Philadelphia Non-importation Association, 1770. see Non-importation Association, Philadelphia, 1770.

Philadelphia, November 1, 1777. 13699

Philadelphia, November 14, 1829. 59909

Philadelphia, November 7, 1765. 61918

Philadelphia, November 21, 1769. 61920

Philadelphia, November 24, 1777. (61933)

Philadelphia Numismatic and Antiquarian Society. see Numismatic and Antiquarian Society of Philadelphia.

Philadelphia Nurse Charity. see Nurse Charity, Philadelphia.

Philadelphia Ocean Steamship Company. (62022)

Philadelphia, October 8, 1777. 16816

Philadelphia, October 1, 1777. (61929)

Philadelphia, October 10, 1777. 61930-(61931)

Philadelphia, October 31, 1777. (61932)

Philadelphia Old Man's Home. see Old Man's Home, Philadelphia.

Philadelphia; or glances at lawyers. (62023)

Philadelphia Orphan Society. 61909, 62024

Philadelphia Owners . . . of Wharf Property on the River Delaware. petitioners see Owners . . . of Wharf Property on the River Delaware, Philadelphia. petitioners

Philadelphia People's Club, in Favor of General Simon Cameron for President. see People's Club of Philadelphia, in Favor of General Simon Cameron for President.

Philadelphia Philanthropic Society. see Philanthropic Society, Philadelphia.

Philadelphia photographer. 62025

Philadelphia Prayer-Meeting Convention, 1860. 62026

Philadelphia Presbytery. see Presbyterian Church in the U. S. A. Presbytery of Philadelphia.

Philadelphia Prison Society. 62073

Philadelphia Progressive Gardner's [sic] Society. see Progressive Gardner's [sic] Society of Philadelphia.

Philadelphia Protestant Episcopal Book Society. see Protestant Episcopal Book Society, Philadelphia.

Philadelphia Provident Society for the Employment of the Poor. see Provident Society for the Employment of the Poor, Philadelphia.

Philadelphia pursuits of literature. 36922

Philadelphia register and city directory. 6160

Philadelphia register, and national recorder. (52020), 62027, 77145

Philadelphia Relief Committee to Collect Funds for the Sufferers by Yellow Fever, at Norfolk and Portsmouth, Va., 1855. 55482, (62163)

Philadelphia Repeal Association. 15897

Philadelphia repertory, devoted to literature and useful intelligence. (62028)

Philadelphia repository and weekly register. 62029

Philadelphia riots. 88910

Philadelphia Roman Catholic Society of St. Joseph. see Society of St. Joseph, Philadelphia.

Philadelphia Sabbath Association. 62030

Philadelphia Sabbath School Association. 62031

Philadelphia St. Patrick Benevolent Society. see St. Patrick Benevolent Society, Philadelphia.

Philadelphia Saving Fund Society. see Saving Fund Society, Philadelphia.

Philadelphia, Saturday, July 30, 1768. 61919

Philadelphia Saturday museum. 96382

Philadelphia School of Design. 62032, 62228

Philadelphia Seamen's Friend Society. 62033

Philadelphia Second Presbytery. see Presbyterian Church in the U. S. A. Presbytery of Philadelphia.

Philadelphia, September 29, 1775. 101688

Philadelphia, September 22, 1797. 94021

Philadelphia, September 23, 1771. (61924)

Philadelphia, September 23, 1773. (61296)

Philadelphia, 1794. Sir, a stranger in your country. 94306

Philadelphia Shakespeare Society. see Shakespeare Society of Philadelphia.

Philadelphia 6th of 12th mo. 1793. 61936

Philadelphia Soap-Boilers. see Soap-Boilers of Philadelphia.

Philadelphia Society for Bettering the Condition of the Poor. 62035

Philadelphia Society for Political Enquiries. see Society for Political Enquiries, Philadelphia.

Philadelphia Society for Promoting Agriculture 59850, 62036, 97051

Philadelphia Society for Promoting Agriculture Charter. 62036

Philadelphia Society for Promoting Agriculture Exhibition, 1851. 62036

Philadelphia Society for Promoting Agriculture Exhibition, 1855. 62036

Philadelphia Society for the Alleviation of the Miseries of Public Prisons. 23518, 58112, 60340, (60384), 60644, 62034, 78074, 85832, 90815

Philadelphia Society for the Alleviation of the Miseries of Public Prisons. Acting Committee. (60384), 62034, 93701

Philadelphia Society for the Alleviation of the Miseries of Public Prisons. Charter. 62034

Philadelphia Society for the Attainment of Useful Knowledge. see Society for the Attainment of Useful Knowledge, Philadelphia.

Philadelphia Society for the Defence of the
Catholic Religion from Calumny and
Abuse. see Society for the Defence of
the Catholic Religion from Calumny and
Abuse, Philadelphia.
Philadelphia Society for the Employment and
Instruction of the Poor. 62037
Philadelphia Society for the Employment and
Instruction of the Poor. petitioners
62037
Philadelphia Society for the Employment and
Instruction of the Poor. Committee . . .
on the Erection of a House of Industry.
62037
Philadelphia Society for the Encouragement of
Faithful Domestics. see Society for the
Encouragement of Faithful Domestics,
Philadelphia.
Philadelphia Society for the Encouragement of
Manufactures in Pennsylvania. see Penn-
sylvania Society for the Encouragement
of Manufactures, Philadelphia.
Philadelphia Society for the Establishment and
Support of Charity Schools. see Society
for the Establishment and Support of
Charity Schools, Philadelphia.
Philadelphia Society for the Improvement of
the City. see Society for the Improve-
ment of Philadelphia.
Philadelphia Society for the Promotion of
American Manufactures. petitioners
62324
Philadelphia Society for the Promotion of
Domestic Industry. 51992, 62040
Philadelphia Society for the Promotion of
National Industry. 10889, 22987, 62041
Philadelphia Society for the Relief of Free
Negroes, and Others, Unlawfully Held in
Bondage. see Society for the Relief of
Free Negroes, and Pthers, Unlawfully
Held in Bondage, Philadelphia.
Philadelphia Society of Constitutional Republicans.
see Society of Constitutional Republicans,
Philadelphia.
Philadelphia Society of St. Joseph. see Society
of St. Joseph, Philadelphia.
Philadelphia Society of the Sons of New England.
see Society of the Sons of New England
of the City and County of Philadelphia.
Philadelphia souvenir. 29814, 62042
Philadelphia stage from 1739 to 1821. 21413
Philadelphia statistics. 62043
Philadelphia Street Sweeping & Fertilizing Com-
pany. see Street Sweeping & Fertilizing
Company, Philadelphia.
Philadelphia Sunday and Adult School Union.
62044
Philadelphia Synod. see Presbyterian Church
in the U. S. A. Synod of New York and
Philadelphia. Presbyterian Church in the
U. S. A. Synod of Philadelphia.
Philadelphia Therapeutic Institute. see Thera-
peutic Institute of Philadelphia.
Philadelphia, Thursday, Sept. 27, 1770. 61923
Philadelphia Time Lock Company. Charter.
(62045)
Philadelphia Tract Association of Friends. see
Tract Association of Friends, Philadelphia.
Philadelphia True Republican Society. see
True Republican Society . . . of Philadel-
phia.
Philadelphia, 25th January, 1773. 60286, 61925
Philadelphia Typographical Society. 62046
Philadelphia Typographical Society. Charter.
62046

Philadelphia Union Benevolent Association. see
Union Benevolent Association, Philadel-
phia.
Philadelphia Union League. see Union League
of Philadelphia.
Philadelphia Unitary Building Association.
62047
Philadelphia Universalist magazine and Christian
messenger. 62048
Philadelphia Universty of Medicine and Surgery.
60081
Philadelphia Uranian Society for Promoting
the Knowledge of Vocal Music. see
Uranian Society for Promoting the Knowl-
edge of Vocal Music, Philadelphia.
Philadelphia Vaccine Society. see Vaccine
Society, Philadelphia.
Philadelphia vocabulary. 62049
Philadelphia vocabulary . . . a sketch of
mythology. 73361
Philadelphia vocabulary: English and Latin.
28690
Philadelphia, Wednesday, November 6, 1765.
61917
Philadelphia Welsh Society. see Welsh Society,
Philadelphia.
Philadelphia Western Clinical Infirmary. see
Western Clinical Infirmary, Philadelphia.
Philadelphia Western Library Association. see
Western Library Association of Phila-
delphia.
Philadelphia Whig. pseud. Appeal for the
union. 1770
Philadelphia wholesale business directory.
61606
Philadelphia wholesale business merchants and
manufacturers' directory. 61606
Philadelphia wholesale merchants' and artisans'
business directory. (12001), 61606
Philadelphia wholesale merchants' and artizans'
[sic] business directory, for 1853. 62050
Philadelphia, Wilmington and Baltimore Rail
Road Company. 62051
Philadelphia, Wilmington and Baltimore Rail
Road Company. defendants 62051
Philadelphia, Wilmington and Baltimore Rail
Road Company. President. 24046, 62051
see also Felton, Samuel Morse.
Philadelphia, Wilmington and Baltimore Rail
Road Company. Stockholders Meeting,
Wilmington, Del., 1855. 62051
Philadelphia, Wilmington and Baltimore railroad
guide. 18541, 62051
Philadelphia Yearly Meeting. see Friends,
Society of. Philadelphia Yearly Meeting.
Philadelphia Young Christians' Missionary
Association. see Young Christians'
Missionary Association, Philadelphia.
Philadelphia Young Man's Institute. see Young
Man's Institute, Philadelphia.
Philadelphia Young Men's Bible Society. 62052
Philadelphia Young Men's Christian Association.
see Young Men's Christian Association,
Philadelphia.
Philadelphia Young Men's Society. see Young
Men's Society, Philadelphia.
Philadelphia Young Men's Temperance Society.
see Young Men's Temperance Society,
Philadelphia.
Philadelphia Youth's Missionary Society. see
Youth's Missionary Society, Philadelphia.
Philadelphia Youths' Tract Society. see Youths'
Tract Society, Philadelphia.
Philadelphia Zoological Society. see Zoological
Society of Philadelphia.

Philadelphiad. 62409
Philadelphian. pseud. Address to the editor. 95799
Philadelphian. pseud. Age of error. 509
Philadelphian. pseud. Free remarks on the spirit of the federal constitution. see Walsh, Robert, 1784-1859. supposed author
Philadelphian. pseud. Hand-book for the stranger in Philadelphia. 30212, 61714
Philadelphian. pseud. Interesting essays. 62410
Philadelphian. pseud. May 29, 1773. 61807
Philadelphian. pseud. Philadelphia Jockey Club. see Tickler, Timothy. pseud.
Philadelphian. pseud. Occasional essays on the yellow fever. (62411)
Philadelphian. pseud. To the freemen, citizens of Philadelphia. [May 29, 1773.] 62321
Philadelphian. pseud. To the freemen, citizens of Philadelphia. [June 16, 1773.] 62322
Philadelphian Association. see Baptists. Philadelphia. Baptist Association.
Philadelphian magazine. 62413, 97087
Philadelphia's great north route. 62054
Philadelphiensis. pseud. Manners of the times. 62414
Philadelphiensis. pseud. Remarks on the Quaker unmask'd. 69495
Philadelphische Zeitung. 62415
Philadelphus. pseud. Friendly dialogue. see Towers, John.
Philadelphus. pseud. To the public. 60717, 62333
Philadelphus, Eusebius. pseud. see Eusebius Philadelphus. pseud.
Philadelphus, Theophilus. pseud. see Theophilus Philadelphus. pseud.
Philaeni. pseud. Strictures on the landed and commercial interest. 62416
Philaeus, Junius. pseud. see Junius Philaeus. pseud.
Philagathos. pseud. Poem, commemorative of Goffe. see Holmes, Abiel, 1763-1837. supposed author and Stiles, Ezra, 1727-1785. supposed author
Philalethe. pseud. publisher see Waring, E. supposed publisher
Philalethes. pseud. Christian piety. 62418
Philalethes. pseud. Essential rights and liberties of protestants. see Williams, Elisha. supposed author
Philalethes. pseud. Examiner. see Hancock, John, 1702-1744.
Philalethes. pseud. For the service of truth. see Maule, Thomas.
Philalethes. pseud. Friendly dialogue. see Spring, Samuel, 1746-1819.
Philalethes. pseud. Index to William Penn's works. see Portsmouth, Henry.
Philalethes. pseud. Letter of advice. see Mather, Cotton, 1663-1728.
Philalethes. pseud. Quaker vindicated. (66933)
Philalethes. pseud. Reviewer reviewed. see Sherwood, Reuben, 1789-1856.
Philalethes. pseud. To the public. see Montford, Robert.
Philalethes. pseud. Tribute to Caesar. see Maule, Thomas. supposed author
Philalethes. pseud. Two friendly letters. see Spring, Samuel, 1746-1819.
Philalethes, Demoticus. pseud. Yankee travels through the island of Cuba. 17816, 62423
Philalethes Eleutherus. pseud. Over den slavenstand. 62424

Philalethius, Ireneus. pseud. Tweede wachter. see Teelinck, Ewout.
Philan. pseud. Address. 101891
Philan. pseud. Rede, ueber den todt unseres unsterblichen Waschington's. 101542
Philanax, Calvin. pseud. Friendly epistle to Mr. George Keith. see Young, Samuel, fl, 1690-1700.
Philander. pseud. 19239
Philander Doesticks, Q. K. pseud. History and Records of the Eliphant Club. see Thompson, Mortimer, 1832-1875. and Underhill, Edward Fitch, 1830-1898.
Philander Misiatrus. pseud. Honour of the gout. 32791, 62425
Philandros. pseud. Truth stated and illustrated 97266
Philandros. pseud. Astonishing affair! 62426
Philanthrope Chretien. 94500
Philanthrope Europeen. pseud. Haitiade. 75127
Philanthropic results of the war. 8161, 62427, 85153
Philanthropic Society, Philadelphia. 62055
Philanthropic Society of the University of North Carolina. see North Carolina. University. Philanthropic Society.
Philanthropic tour through the United States. 62428
Philanthropische Resultate des Krieges. 85148
Philanthropist. pseud. Account of the beginnings, transactions, and discovery, of Ransford Rogers. see Kollock, Sheppard. supposed author and Rogers, Ransford. supposed author
Philanthropist. pseud. Guardian genius of the federal union. see Ames, Julius R.
Philanthropist. (81893), note after 102820
Philanthropist of Chester Country. pseud. [Pamphlet.] see Jones, Caleb.
Philanthropist; or, a good twenty-five cents worth of political love powder. 102492
Philanthropos. pseud. Address to the inhabitants of the state of Delaware. (81788)
Philanthropos. pseud. Appendix to the essays on capital punishments. 62432
Philanthropos. pseud. Brief illustration of the principles of war and peace. see Wells, Seth Youngs.
Philanthropos. pseud. Essays on capital punishments. 62431
Philanthropos. pseud. Letter to Aaron Burr. 8427
Philanthropos. pseud. Letters on liberty and slavery. see Rhees, Morgan J.
Philanthropos. pseud. Serious address to the clergy. 62430, 79245
Philanthropos. pseud. Solemn appeal to Christians of all denominations. see Ladd, William.
Philanthropos. pseud. Universal peace-maker. (62429)
Philanthropos. pseud. Valediction, for New Year's Day. 98342
Philastre, -----. 92539
Philatelist's album. 62434
Philbrick, E. S. 62435
Philbrick, Samuel. 62436
Phileleutheros. pseud. Address to the freeholders. 45597
Phileleutheros. pseud. Blow at the root of aristocracy. 62437
Phileluth. Bangor, V. E. B. pseud. Eusebius Ineramatus. see Foxcroft, Thomas.
Philemon. pseud. A opiniao e a coroa. see Souza Bocayuva, Quintino de.

Philemon Perch. pseud. Georgia sketches.
    see Johnston, Richard M.
Philemon Scank. pseud. Few chapters to
    Brother Jonathan. 62438
Philenia, a lady of Boston. pseud. Ouabi. see
    Morton, Sarah Wentworth Apthorp.
Philermenian Society, Brown University. see
    Brown University, Providence, R. I.
    Philermenian Society.
Philesius Vogesigena. see Ringmann, Matthias,
    1482?-1511.
Philesius, Martin Ringmann. see Ringmann,
    Matthias, 1482?-1511.
Philesius Vogesigena de laudibus & fructu
    Margarite philosophice. 69125-69126
Philetaeria, en ny slaegt af polemoniacurnes
    familie. 40991
Philethes. pseud. Reflections on the state-
    ments. 92439
Philharmonic Society, New York. see New
    York Philharmonic Symohony Orchestra.
Philiarcus. pseud. Letters to a friend. 62440
Philip. for Kings of Spain of this name, see
    Felipe.
Philip, Landgraff zu Hesse, fl. 1593. (8784)
Philip Neri, Saint, 1515-1595. 59523, 67647
Philip, Uncle. pseud. see Hawks, Francis
    Lister.
Philip, A. J. ed. 82852
Philip, A. P. Wilson. 83654
Philip, Robert. 62445
Philip Everhard; or a history of the Baptist
    Indian missions. 62446
Philip Kearny: soldier and patriot. (58651)
Philip, King of the Wampanoags. 32553
Philip Musgrave. 30
Philip Paxton. pseud. see Hammett, Samuel
    Adams.
Philip, or the aborigines, a drama. 62447
Philip Seymour. (43258)
Philip Thicknesse. pseud. see Adair, J. M.
Philipot, Thomas. (62448)
Philippart, John. 62449
Philippe, Adolphe. see Ennery, Adolphe
    Philippe, called d'.
Ph. Fermin's Historisch politische Uebersicht.
    24116
Philippi, A. R. ed. 70301
Philippi, Ferdinand. (62450)-(62451)
Philippi, Rudolph Amandus. 62452
" Philippiad." 6490
Philippine Islands (Province) Adelantado. defend-
    ant 86404 see also Legazpi, Garcia de.
    defendant
Philippine Islands. 50632, 84531
Philippine Islands. Department of Agriculture
    and Natural Resources. Bureau of Science.
    84529
Philippine Islands. Department of the Interior.
    Bureau of Science. 84530
Philippine Islands. Department of the Interior.
    Bureau of Science. Division of Geology
    and Mines. Chief. see also Smith,
    Warren De Pre, 1880-
Philippine Islands. Department of the Interior.
    Muning Bureau. 84527
Philippine Islands. Department of the Interior.
    Mining Bureau. Chief. 84527
Philippine Islands. Laws, statutes, etc. 84529
Philippine forests and timbers. 84529
Philippo, Jacobo. see Foresti, Jacobo Philippo.
Philipps, George. see Phillips, George.
Philipps, M. W. Louis. 62453
Philippvs Hispaniarvm et Indiarvm Rex. 66605
Philips, Erasmus. 62454-62455
Philips, George. 62456, 96497

Philips, Gillam. plaintiff 62457
Philips, Hannah. plaintiff 62457
Philips, John. 62458
Philips, John Arthur. 62459
Philips, Miles. 62460
Philips, Thomas. 13015
Philips, Wendell. 22713, note before 90885
Philips, William. 96498
Philips. firm publishers see Denio and
    Philips. firm publishers
Philips' Upper Patent Claimants. planitiffs
    see Claimants Under the Original
    Patentee of a Large Tract of Land, In
    Philips' Upper Patent. plaintiffs
Philipsburg and Juniata Rail Road Company.
    62462
Philipse, Adolph. defendant 58366
Philleo, Prudence (Crandall) 1803-1890.
    defendant (17391)-17392, 90705, 2d note
    after 96854
Phillimore, J. G. 62464-62465
Phillio, Calvin. 62466
Phillip, Arthur, 1738-1814. (59572)
Phillip, William. tr. 77962, 98738
Phillipiad. 62467
Phillippo, James M. 13312, 62468-62470
Phillipps, --------. 73398-73400, (73402)
Phillipps, Jamez Orchard Halliwell. see
    Halliwell-Phillipps, James Orchard.
Phillips, Samuel March, 1780-1862. ed. 67590
Phillips, Mrs. ---------, fl. 1749. 40452
Phillips, ----------, fl. 1838. 104413
Phillips, A. 62471
Phillips, A. E. (62472) see also U. S.
    Consulate, St. Jago de Cuba.
Phillips, B. 62473
Phillips, Catherine. 62474-62475
Phillips, Charles, 1787?-1859. 49685, (62476)-
    62477, 64014
Phillips, Daniel. (62478)
Phillips, Daniel W. 62479
Phillips, Ebenezer. (62480)
Phillips, Edwin D. 62481
Phillips, Ezra. plaintiff 62482
Phillips, George. 62483
Phillips, George. supposed author (21090),
    33698, 78431, 104846
Phillips, George Searle, 1815-1889. (62484)-
    62485
Phillips, Gillam. appellant 92694
Phillips, Henry. defendant 62486, 96919
Phillips, Henry, 1838-1895. 16163, 62487-
    (62491)
Phillips, Henry M., 1811-1884. 62492
Phillips, Isaac. (62493)
Phillips, J. M. (62500)
Phillips, J. V. 62501
Phillips, John, of Charleston, S. C. 62495
Phillips, John, 1631-1706. tr. 11235, (11286),
    note before 94570
Phillips, John, 1770-1823. (62496)
Phillips, John, fl. 1792. 62494
Phillips, John, 1800-1874. 62498
Phillips, John H. 52132 see also New Jersey.
    Department of Public Instruction.
Phillips, Jonas B. 62499
Phillips, Jonathan. (69709)
Phillips, Jonathan. supposed author 42445,
    (62502)
Phillips, Joseph. 62503
Phillips, Naphtali. 62504
Phillips, Nathaniel. 62505
Phillips, P. (69090)
Phillips, P. C. 101041
Phillips, Phebe. 104995
Phillips, Philip. (41607), 93744

Phillips, Philip Lee, 1857-1924. 84936
Phillips, Sir Richard, 1767-1840. 2180, 6182,
  10616, 16771-16773, 19644, 24453, 31489,
  (36696), 37230, 38292, 48706, 50230,
  52158, 59212, 60999, (61013), 62506-62507,
  62509, 65696, 73150, 76707, 77126, 77858,
  81047, (81136), 81508, 96496, 98614, 99551A,
  4th note after 100814, 101114
Phillips, S. defendant 84739
Phillips, Samuel, 1690-1771. 3475, (62510)-
  62517
Phillips, Samuel R., 1824-1880. supposed
  author 52196
Phillips, Stephen C. 62518-(62519)
Phillips, U. B. 42300
Phillips, W. 35406
Phillips, W. P. 75626 see also Salem, Mass.
  Water Commissioners. Chairman.
Phillips, W. S. 83146
Phillips, Wendell, 1811-1884. 3401, (6765),
  22713, 26712, 28782, 33204, (43721),
  (62520)-62528, 81919, 87034, 10th note
  after 96964, note after 97006, 98005
Phillips, Willard, 1784-1873. 46054, 46150,
  62529-62531
Phillips, William. 62532
Phillips, William Wirt. 47674, 62533-62534
  see also New York (City) First Presby-
  terian Church. Pastor.
Phillips & Sampson. firm auctioneers 62306
Phillips Academy, Andover, Mass. 1438,
  62535
Phillips Academy, Andover, Mass. Exhibition,
  1820. 62535
Phillips Academy, Andover, Mass. Philomathean
  Society. (49430)
Phillips Academy, Andover, Mass. Theological
  Institution. see Andover Theological
  Institution.
Phillips Academy, Andover, Mass. Trustees.
  89800
Phillips Academy, Andover, Mass. Trustees.
  petitioners 85212
Phillips Academy, Andover, Mass. Trustees.
  plaintiffs 85212
Phillips Church, South Boston, Mass. see
  South Boston, Mass. Phillips Church.
Phillips Church, South Boston. Alphabetical
  list of members, resident and non-resident,
  March, 1876. 87338
Phillips Exeter Academy, Essex, N. H. 23395,
  62536-62537
Phillips's United States diary, or an almanac.
  62505
Phillis. pseud. Phillis's poem. see Peters,
  Phillis (Wheatley) 1753?-1784.
Phillis, a servant girl of 17 years of age.
  pseud. Elegaic poem. see Peters,
  Phillis (Wheatley) 1753?-1784.
Phillis Wheatley. 103142
Phillis's poem on the death of Mr. Whitefield.
  103135
Philmont, N. Y. Philmont Lodge. see Phil-
  mont Lodge, Philmont, N. Y.
Philmont Lodge, Philmont, N. Y. 62538
Philmore, J. 62539, 1st note after 97555
Philo. pseud. [Essays.] 99610, note after
  105324
Philo. pseud. Ministry at large for the poor
  in cities. 49231, 97399
Philo. pseud. Philo's Essex almanack. 62540
Philo Africanus. pseud. Letter. 40451, 62542,
  92694
Philo-Africanus. pseud. Letter to Wm. Wilber-
  force. 62541

Philo-Americanus. pseud. American struggle.
  1234, 62543
Philo: an evangeliad. 36842
Philo-Bellum. sobriquet see Maylem, John.
Philo-Britain. pseud. Defence of the Scotts
  settlement at Darien, answered. 18550
Philo-Britain. pseud. Letter from Scots
  Sawney. see Scots Sawney. pseud.
Philo-Britannicus. pseud. Great question to
  be considered. see Penn, William, 1644-
  1718.
Philo-Caledon. pseud. Defence of the Scots
  settlement at Darien. see Fletcher,
  -------, of Saltoun. supposed author
  and Ridpath, George. supposed author
Philo-Cato. pseud. Celebrated letters. 62545
Philo-Cato. pseud. Letters of Marcus and
  Philo-Cato. see Davis, Matthew L.
Philo-Cor-rector. pseud. Notes on the sayings
  and doings. 38457
Philo Dramatis. pseud. Rights of the drama.
  62547
Philo Fidelitas. pseud. Slavery vindicated.
  82113
Philo-Freeman. pseud. Essex almanack.
  62540
Philo-Fulton. pseud. To the citizens of the
  United States. seee Carey, Mathew,
  1760-1839. supposed author
Philo-Hancock. pseud. Preface. (30196),
  103851
Philo-Italian Society of Massachusetts. see
  Massachusetts Philo-Italian Society.
Philo-Jackson. 62548
Philo-Mathemat. pseud. 1694. An almanack
  of the coelestiall motions. 62743
Philo Pacificus. pseud. Extracts from a
  pamphlet. see Worcester, Noah, 1758-
  1837.
Philo-Pacificus. pseud. Friend of peace. see
  Worcester, Noah, 1758-1837.
Philo Pacificus. pseud. Monument of a bene-
  ficent mission. see Worcester, Noah,
  1758-1837.
Philo Pacificus. pseud. Spirit of the south.
  see Wallcut, Robert Folger.
Philo Pacificus. pseud. Solemn review of the
  custom of war. see Worcester, Noah,
  1758-1837.
Philo Pacificus, author of "A solemn review
  of the custom of war." pseud. Friend
  of peace. see Worcester, Noah, 1758-
  1837.
Philo Pacificus, author of the "Friend of
  peace." pseud. Peace catechism. see
  Worcester, Noah, 1758-1837.
Philo Pat. Pat. Patria. pseud. (50137),
  (55169), 100451
Philo-Patriae. pseud. Religious harmonist.
  69340
Philo-Pax. pseud. Introductory note. 97093
Philo-Pennsylvania. pseud. Serious address
  to the freeholders and other inhabitants.
  60610
Philo Reflector. pseud. 84576
Philo-Reflector. pseud. Preface, exposing
  the artifices of our priests and craftsmen.
  (17350)
Philo Veritatis. pseud. To Pacificus in reply.
  62564
Philobiblia. pseud. Additional appendix.
  101891
Philobiblion. 62544
Philodemic Society, Georgetown University. see
  Georgetown University. Philodemic
  Society.

Philodemus. pseud. Conciliatory hints. see
Tucker, Thomas Tudor.

Philodicaios. pseud. Some reflections on the
disputes. see Young, Thomas, 1731-1777.

Philoerin, Sampflilus, Z. Y. X. W. &c. &c.
pseud. Beasts at law. see Woodworth,
Samuel.

Philoeunomos. pseud. Caveat against injustice.
see Sherman, Roger, 1721-1793.

Philolaos. pseud. Two letters. 10733, 97566

Philolethes. pseud. Short reply to Mr.
Stephen Hopkin's Vindication. 32968, 1st
note after 97146

Philolethus. pseud. ed. True and particular
history of earthquakes. 42592

Philolexian Society, Columbia University. see
Columbia University. Philolexian Society.

Philological proofs of the original unity and
recent origin of the human race. 36149

Philological Society, Middlebury College. see
Middlebury College, Middlebury, Vt. Philological Society.

Philological Society, London. 23112, (62549)-
(62550)

Philological Society, New York. 54576

Philologie. 21210

Philom. pseud. Philom's address. 62551

Philomathean Society, Albany, N.Y. 62552

Philomathean Society, Phillips Academy. see
Phillips Academy, Andover, Mass. Philomathean Society.

Philomathean Society, University of Pennsylvania. see Pennsylvania. University.
Philomathean Society.

Philomathes. pseud. Almanac for 1775.
62553

Philomathes. pseud. Some thoughts on education. see Smith, William, 1727-1803.

Philomathesian. 62554

Philomathesian Society, Kenyon College. see
Kenyon College, Gambier, Ohio. Philomathesian Society.

Philomathic Society, Liverpool, Eng. see
Liverpool Philomathic Society.

Philomela; with the notes for morning prayer.
62555

Philomela. With, the notes of morning-piety.
46608, note after 105465

Philometer. 62556

Philomithus est aliquo modo philosophis.
(78188)-78190

Philom's address to the people of New England.
62551

Philomythie or philomythologie. (78188)-78191

Philonax Verax. pseud. Letter from a member
of the Parliament of Scotland. 18560,
78220, 2d note after 98925

Philonem Patricium. pseud. see Patricium,
Philonem. pseud.

Philonus, Honorius. pseud. Nova typis transacta navigatio. see Plautius, Caspar.

Philopatria. pseud. Almanac for 1767. 62557,
62743

Philopatria. pseud. Discourse shewing. see
Paine, Thomas, 1737-1809.

Philopatriae. pseud. Essay on education.
84678C

Philopatriae. pseud. Letter to a member.
40412

Philopatris. pseud. Some observations.
62558

Philopatris. pseud. Answers to the objections.
73758

Philopatris. pseud. Dec. 5, 1723. A most
humble proposal. 51095, 62559

Philopatrius. pseud. Quaker unmask'd. see
Dove, David James.

Philopatrus, Andreas. pseud. Elizabethae
Angliae Regniae haeresim Calvinianam
propugnantis. see Parsons, Robert,
1546-1610.

Philopatrus, Andreas. pseud. Responsione.
see Parsons, Robert, 1546-1610.

Philopedos. pseud. Few remarks about sick
children in New York. see Stewart,
James, 1799-1864. supposed author

Philophron. pseud. Columbia and Britannia.
62561

Philopolites. pseud. Free and calm consideration. see Prescott, Benjamin.

Philopolites. pseud. Letter relating to a
medium of trade. 40375

Philopolites. pseud. Memorial of the present
deplorable state of New-England. see
Mather, Cotton, 1663-1728. supposed
author and Dudley, Joseph, 1648-1720.
incorrectly supposed author

Philoponus, Honorius. pseud. Nova typis
transacta navigatio. see Plautius,
Caspar.

ΦΙΛΟψΤΧΩΝ. pseud. Startling facts. see
Shimeall, Richard Cunningham, 1803-1874.

Philorthodoxo, Christian. pseud. Ungeheuchlte
theologische Unterredung. 97746

Philorthos. pseud. Orthographical hobgoblin.
see Poole, William Frederick, 1821-1894.

Philo's Essex almanack. 62540

Philos Harmoniae. pseud. Selection of hymns
and poems. see McNemar, Richard.
supposed author

Philosophe Anglais. 65408

Philosophe Anglois. 65409

Philosophe sensible. pseud. Lettres. see
Delacroix, Jacques Vincent, 1743-1832.

Philosopher's stone discover'd. 88164

Philospher's stone found out. (22183)

Philosophia ultima. 80465

Philosophic solitude. 41647-41648

Philosophical and miscellaneous papers. 25562

Philosophical and political history of the
British settlements. 68093-68094

Philosophical and political history of the establishments and commerce of the Europeans
in both the Indies. 68104

Philosophical and political history of the settlements and trade of the Europeans in the
East and West Indies. (68087)-(68092)

Philosophical and political history of the thirteen United States of America. 25620

Philosophical and practical essay on the gold
and silver mines of Mexico and Peru.
31518

Philosophical and practical grammar of the
English language. 102375

Philosophical and statistical history of the
inventions and customs of ancient and
modern nations. 50624

Philosophical contributions of the Royal Society,
London. 74704

Philosophical discourse, addressed to the
American Academy of Arts and Sciences:
. . . on the eighth of November. 7016

Philosophical discourse, addressed to the
American Academy of Arts and Sciences;
to which is added three memoirs. 7017

Philosophical discourse concerning the mutability
and changes of the material world.
28689

Philosophical emperor. 36161

Philosophical magazine. 48985

Philosophical meditation and address to the
Supreme Being. 84599-84600
Philosophical meditation, and religious address
to the Supreme Being. 84678C
Philosopichal register. (62562)
Philosophical Society of Ohio. see Historical
and Philosophical Society of Ohio.
Philosophical tendencies of the American mind.
9364
Philosophical theory of an "empiric." 95587
Philosophical transactions [of the Royal Society,
London.] 3868, 3892, 9389, 9889, (13575),
28689, 74700-74704, 84985, 104851
Philosophical treatise on the original and produc-
tion of things. 25467
Philosophical rudiments concerning government
and society. 42945
Philosophico-historico-hydrogeography of South
Carolina 103051
Philosphie ethnograpique. 75804
Philosophie, histoire, droit. 70356
Philosophie Indien. pseud. Telliamed. see
Maillet, B. de.
Philosophische Gemalde von West-Indien.
42169
Philosophische und politische Geschichte.
68095
Philosophische Untersuchungen uber die Ameri-
kaner. 59248
Philosophy of abolition. 42705, 58758, 67423
Philosophy of American slavery. 4476
Philosophy of animated existence. 28030
Philosophy of health. 84416
Philosophy of human nature, slavery, politics,
governments, &c. 7776
Philosophy of language illustrated. 80368
Philosophy of life as evolved by modern science.
69544
Philosophy of modern miracles. 62563
Philosophy of money. 78156
Philosophy of natural history. 82254-82255
Philosophy of political parties. 71260
Philosophy of reform. 82360
Philosophy of sectarianism. 5728
Philosophy of slavery. 79764
Philosophy of storms. 22917
Philosophy of strikes. 82083
Philosophy of the abolition movement. 62528
Philosophy of the human voice. 74251
Philosophy of the plays of Shakespeare. 4295
Philosophy of the temperance society. 90563
Philosophy of the world. 103389
Philosophy of trade. 91851
Philothea; a romance. (12727)
Philotheorus. pseud. Thoughts upon . . .
passages of scripture. see Sewall,
Stephen, 1734-1804. supposed author
Philotheos Physiologus. pseud. Country-man's
companion. see Tyron, Thomas.
Philotheos Physiologos. pseud. Friendly advcie
[sic] see Tyron, Thomas.
Philotheos Physiologos. pseud. Friendly advice.
see Tyron, Thomas.
Philp, James. (62565)
Philp's Washington described. (62565)
Phin, John. 62566
Phineas Stowe, and Bethel work. 84045
Phineas Stowe and his helpers. 84045
Phinney, Barnabas. defendant 80721
Phinney, Elias, 1780-1849. 33109, 62567-62568,
71508
Phinney, Henry F. 16444
Phinney. firm publishers see Ivison &
Phinney. firm publishers
Phinney (H. & E.) firm publishers 62569
Phinney's calendar. 62569

Phippen, A. R. ed. 77888
Phippen, George D. 62570-(62571)
Phipps, Constantine John. see Mulgrave,
Constantine John Phipps, 2d Baron, 1744-
1792.
Phipps, Harrison Gray Otis. 79394
Phipps, J. 68301, 97584
Phipps, Spencer, see Phips, Spencer, 1685-
1757.
Phipps, Sir William, 1651-1695. 36731, (69258)
Phipps, William, fl. 1842. 62577
Phipps Union Female Seminary, Albion, N. Y.
62578
Phips, Spencer, 1685-1757. 34083, (34857),
62579 see also Massachusetts (Colony)
Lieutenant Governor, 1732-1757 (Phips)
Phips, William, 1720-1798. 62580
Phiseldek, Conrad Friedrich von Schmidt. see
Schmidt-Phiseldek, Conrad Friedrich von.
Phisica, speculatio, aedita per R. P. F.
Alphonsum a Veracruce. 98914
Phisices compendium. 44525
Phiz. pseud. illus. see Browne, H. K.
illus.
Phlogobombos, Terentius. pseud. Buccaneers.
see Judah, Samuel B. H.
Phocion. pseud. American arguments for
British rights. see Smith, William
Loughton, 1758-1812.
Phocion. pseud. Essays. 97915
Phocion. pseud. Letter from Phocion to the
considerate citizens of New-York. see
Hamilton, Alexander, 1755-1804.
Phocion, pseud. Letters of Phocion. see
Curtis, G. T.
Phocion. pseud. Letters on the questions of
the justice and expediency. see Desaus-
sure, Henry William.
Phocion. pseud. Neutral rights. (52392)
Phocion. pseud. Observations respecting the
propriety. see Hartley, Thomas.
Phocion. pseud. Portrait of freemasonry.
see Spencer, John Canfield.
Phocion. pseud. Pretentions of Thomas
Jefferson to the presidency, examined.
23994, 84829
Phocion. pseud. Series of essays. 23994,
84832
Phocion's examination of the pretentions of
Thomas Jefferson. 84829
Phoebus, William. 62582, note after 103120
Phoenix, John. pseud. Phoenixiana. see
Derby, George Horatio, 1823-1861.
Phoenix, Jotham Phillips. defendant in error
98616
Phoenix, S. Whitneh. (62583)-(62584)
Phoenix and budget. 85466
Phoenix Britannius. (67586), 78377
Phoenix Fire Company, Washington, D. C.
101945
Phoenix Hose Company, Philadelphia. (62056)
Phoenix Insurance Company of Philadelphia.
62057
Phoenix Rifles, Charleston, S. C. see South
Carolina. Militia. Phoenix Rifles,
Charleston.
Phoenix Social Club, Philadelphia. 62585
Phoenixiana. (19665)
Phonetic Association of Ohio. see Ohio State
Phonetic Association.
Phonicisch-Cananaische und Carthagische
Pflanzstadt. 71447
Phonizier in der Innen-Landen der Europaisch
Westen. 20605
Phonographic report by Dr. James W. Stone.
51664

Phonographic report of the debates . . . of the New England Methodist Centenary Convention. (62586)

Phonographic report of the National Free Soil Convention at Buffalo, N. Y. 21599

Phosphate rocks of South Carolina. 32599

Photograph from the ruins of ancient Greece. 40854

Photographic and fine art journal. 85414-85415

Photographic art journal. 85411, 85415

Photographic mosaics. 39498

Photographic portraits of North American Indians. 85046

Photographic sketch of the war. (26635)

Photographic views, illustrative of the civil war. (62587)

Photographic views of Sherman's campaign. 3462

Photographs taken at Lord Selkirk's settlement. 31921

Photolithographische Afbeelding van een Platte-Grond. 63419

Photostat Americana Series of the Massachusetts Historical Society. see Americana Series of the Massachusetts Historical Society.

Phrases and religious lessons in the language of the Teu-au-Geh. 80704

Phrenological character of Reuben Dunbar. 21238, 3d note after 95517

Phrysius, Gemma. see Gemma, Reinerus, Frisius.

Phrisius, Laurentius. see Fries, Lorenz, of Colmar, ca. 1490-1531.

Phylanthus. pseud. Scourge of fashion. 69404, 78451

Physic and physicians. 62590

Physica speculatio ad modum. 98916

Physica specvlatio admodvm. 98915, 98917

Physical and medical topography. 68669

Physical and topographical sketch of the Mississippi Territory. 65056

Physical atlas of natural phenomena. (36354)

Physical enquiries. 94715

Physical geography and meteorology of the South Atlantic. 73417

Physical geography [of New Hampshire.] 52833

Physical geography of the sea. 46969

Physical geography of the state [of New York.] 19873

Physical history of the earth. 7049

Physical history of the Jewish race. 56040

Physical observations, and medical tracts and researches. 31628

Physical observations and medical tracts and researches. (33565)

Physical observations in the Arctic Seas. 31021, 77909, 85072

Physical, political, and statistical account of the world. 4453

Physical survey of Virginia. 46973

Physician. pseud. Address to the guardians of the Washington Asylum. 101961

Physician. pseud. Notes on Cuba. see Sargent, Joseph. supposed author and Wurdiman, F. supposed author

Physician. pseud. Two sermons. see Adair, James Makittrick. supposed author

Physician and surgeon. 84799

Physician, formerly resident in the south. pseud. Abolition exposed, corrected. 81729

Physician in the West Indies. pseud. Essay on the more common West-India diseases. see Grainger, James.

Physician of New Orleans. pseud. History of the yellow fever. 53328

Physician of Philadelphia. pseud. Observations on the mineral waters. see Horner, W. E.

Physician's almanac. 62591

Physick, Edmund. 19381

Physico-Medical Society of New-Orleans. (53361)

Physico-Medical Society of New-York. 54577

Physico-politico-theologico, lucubration. 18011, 101787

Physikalisch Undersuchung. 89836

Physikalische Beobachtungen. 105519

Physikalische und historische Nachrichten. 97689

Physikalischer Atlas. 4856

Physikalischer Schul-Atlas. 4857A

Physiognomie der tropischen Vegetation Sud-Amerika's. 4834

Physiognomy a poem. 3760

Physiognomy of Buffalo. 9056, (33100), note after 95451

Physiognomy of tropical vegatation. 4834

Physiographical sketch of that portion of the Rocky Mountain range. 58854

Physiography of the Skyomish Basin. 84534, 84536

Physiological essay on digestion. 83664

Physiologie des Negres dans leur pays. 63434

Physiologos, Philotheos. pseud. see Tyron, Thomas.

Physiology and philosophy opposed to materialism and atheism. 82921

Physiology of New England boarding-houses. 29283

Physionomie des Pflanzenreichs in Brasilien. 44995

Physique. Observations magnetiques. 98298

Physique. Observations meteorologiques. 98298

Physique, par Lottin. 26330

Physique. Par U. de Tessan. 21354

Physique, par Vincendon-Dumonlin et Coupvent-Desbois. 21216

Physitian in the contrery. pseud. Some observations made upon the Barbado seeds. 86673

Physitian in the contrery. pseud. Some observations made upon the Bermudas berries. 86675

Physitian in the contrery. pseud. Some observations made upon the Brasillian root. 86676

Pi Tau, Harvard University. see Harvard University. Pi Tau.

Pia disideria. 46454

Pia Mater 73871

Piacenca, D. Carli da. see Carli, Dionigio.

Piadosa Compania de Cocheros y Lacayos, Mexico (City) Constituciones. 16062

Piadoso bevocionario en honor del sagrado corazon de Jesu. 26506

Piaggio, -------, fl. 1812. 14662, 79309

Piang Pu. pseud. Revolution in Hell. (62592)

Piang pu. pseud. Revolution in Orcus. 62593

Piankashaw Council, Post St. Vincent, Indiana, 1784. 24336, 24338, 34355, (34358)

Piankashaw Indians. 24336, 24338, 34355, (34358), 84577-84578, 2d-4th notes after 97876

Piankeshaw Indians. Treaties, etc. (48062), 96591, 96605, 96615, 96626-96627, 96683, 99605

Piano dell' assedio de Luisburgo colla descrizione della isola reale. 62594

PIATT

Piatt, John James. (62595)-62598, 65063
Piatt, Sarah M. Bryan. (62595)
Piazza, histoire Mexicaine. 21392
Pic-nic, and other tales. 86712
Pic nic papers. 52162
Pica, Andrea Emeteria Volos. see Volos-
    Pica, Andrea Emeteria.
Picard, A. 62599
Picard, Bernard. 4921, 62600
Picard, H. 3211A
Picardie. 64927
Picardo y Tapia, Francisco. 62608
Picardus, Barnabas. ed. 66469
Picart, B. illus. (4932), 4934, 77218, 98752
Picart, Bernard, 1663-1733. 31581
Picayune (New Orleans) see New Orleans
    picayune.
Piccha, Gregorius. 62602
Piccini, O. tr. 105725
Picciola. 75543
Piccolomini, Enea Silbo Vicenzo, Conte. 52412
Piccolomini, Enea Silvio de. see Pius II,
    Pope, 1405-1464.
Pichardo, Esteban. 62603-62606
Pichardo, Jos. Ant. 62607
Piche, E. U. 62609
Pichegru, Charles, 1761-1804. 67626
Pichegru, Jean Charles. see Pichegru,
    Charles, 1761-1804.
Pichon, L. A. tr. 35888
Pichon, Thomas. (62610)-62611, 38164
Pichot, Amedee, 1796-1877. 62612, 65270,
    91222
Pick, Jan Corneliszoon. 62613
Pickard, Hannah (Maynard) 57843
Pickard, Kate E. R. 62614
Pickard, Samuel, 62615
Pickard & Co. firm publishers see Wilder,
    Pickard & Co. firm publishers
Pickaway County, Ohio. (13140)
Pickel, G. tr. 101017
Pickell, John. (62617)
Pickell, John, 1802?-1865. 62616
Pickell Mining Company. President. 62618
Picken, Andrew. (62619)-(62620)
Pickens, Andrew, 1739-1817. 96600-96601,
    96607 see also U. S. Commissioners
    to the Cherokee Indians. U. S. Com-
    missioners to the Chickasaw Indians. U. S.
    Commissioners to the Choctaw Indians.
Pickens, Francis Wilkinson, 1805-1869. 62621,
    87371, 87442, 87550-87557 see also
    South Carolina. Governor, 1860-1862
    (Pickens)
Pickens, Samuel. petitioner 94813
Pickens republican. 83670
Pickering, Colonel. see Pickering, Timothy,
    1745-1829.
Pickering, Charles. 62622-62624, 85072
Pickering, David. 62626-62626
Pickering, Edward Charles, 1846-1919. 85067
Pickering, Henry. 62627-62630
Pickering, John, 1777-1846. 219672, (22159),
    30828, 32473, 62631-62638, 67942, 102363
Pickering, John, 1777-1846. defendant 36744
Pickering, Joseph. 34795, 62639-62641
Pickering, Octavius. 62642-62643, 98046
Pickering, Theophilus, 1700-1747. (35046)-
    35047, 62644-62646
Pickering, Timothy, 1745-1829. 282, (11731),
    (41688), 62647-62659, 64747, 69698,
    (70219), 84906, 86732, 89207, 93421, note
    before 93501, 94304-94305, 101700,
    101742, 101746, 106215 see also U. S.
    Department of State.

Pickering, Timothy, 1745-1829. supposed author
    29982-29983
Pickering, William. 83826
Pickeroniad. 71548
Pickersgill, --------. RN (62660)
Pickersgill, F. R. illus. (63537)
Picket, Albert, senior. 62663
Picket, Albert, 1771-1850. 62661-62662
Picket, John W. 62661-62662, 102961
Picket-guard. 62664
Pickett, Aaron. 62665-(62666)
Pickett, Albert J. 62667-62669
Pickett, Charles Edward. 62670
Pickett, J. C. 62671-62672
Picketts' men. 30570
Pickings from the portfolio of the New Orleans
    " Picayune." 62673
Pickings from the portfolio of the reporter of
    the New Orleans " Picayune." (16754)
Pickle for the knowing ones. 19906-19907,
    38079
Pickman, Benjamin. 62674
Pickman, Pieter Janszoon. 67980
Picolilly. 56684
Picolo, F. M. 4935, 4936
Picolomini, Francisco. 62675
Picornell, J.-M. 95440
Picquenard, J. B. 62676-(62678), 106369
Picquet, Ch. 8735
Picquier, ----- le. see Le Picquier, -------
Pictet, C. tr. (50953), (62679)
Pictet, M. A. 62680
Picton, Sir Thomas, 1758-1815. (9885), 26154,
    26155, 62681, 72081
Picton, Sir Thomas, 1758-1815. defendant
    18324, 62682-62684
Pictorial advertiser and illustrated business
    directory. 75346
Pictorial and business directory of the city of
    New York. 8560
Pictorial and descriptive tour of the world.
    49127
Pictorial and descriptive tour through creation.
    49127
Pictorial and descriptive view of all religions.
    27875
Pictorial book of anecdotes and incidents of
    the war. (37999)
Pictorial book of the commodores. 26046
Pictorial business directory of Wall Street.
    (54578)
Pictorial description of Ohio. 42128
Pictorial description of the United States.
    78652
Pictorial directory of Boradway. 7124, 54459
Pictorial drawing room companion. 89640
Pictorial edition!! 23869
Pictorial family encyclopaedia of history.
    (26054)
Pictorial field-book of the revolution. 42129
Pictorial field-book of the war of 1812. 42130
Pictorial geography. 27922
Pictorial geography of the world. 27922
Pictorial guide to that far famed establishment
    (3571)
Pictorial guide to the falls of Niagara. 55129
Pictorial guide to the Mammoth Cave, Kentucky
    44881
Pictorial handbook of modern geography. 6143
Pictorial history of America. (27916)
Pictorial history of California. 26033
Pictorial history of England. 17374
Pictorial history of King Philip's war. 92881
Pictorial history of Mexico and the Mexican
    war. 26048

Pictorial history of remarkable events in
America. 62686
Pictorial history of the American civil war.
40199, note after 89964
Pictorial history of the American navy.
26047
Pictorial history of the American revolution.
78653
Pictorial history of the civil war in the United
States of America. 42131
Pictorial history of the great rebellion. 29113
Pictorial history of the state of New-York.
3328
Pictorial history of the United States. . . .
By Benson J. Lossing. 42132
Pictorial history of the United States. For
schools and families. 42133
Pictorial history of the United States of
America, from the discovery of the
Northmen in the tenth century to the
present time. (26049)
Pictorial history of the United States of
America, from the earliest discoveries,
by the Northmen. 95445
Pictorial history of the United States of
America, from the earliest period to the
close of President Taylor's administration.
(51502)
Pictorial history of the United States; with
notices of other portions of America.
27917
Pictorial history of the war for the union.
note before 91289
Pictorial life and adventures of David Crockett.
17572
Pictorial life of Andrew Jackson; containing
anecdotes. 35380
Pictorial life of Andrew Jackson. Embellished
with numerous engravings. (26054)
Pictorial life of General Lafayette. 38580
Pictorial life of General Lafayette; containing
anecdotes illustrative of his character.
51101
Pictorial life of General Washington. (26051)
Pictorial magazine. (78654)
Pictorial modern history. (26054)
Pictorial natural history. 27922
Pictorial New York and Brooklyn. 84954
Pictorial reader. 80938
Pictorial school history of the United States.
1410
Pictorial sketch-book of Pennsylvania. 7053
Pictorial view of California. 40723
Pictorial views of Massachusetts, for the young.
62687
Pictorial voyage, known as the seven mile
mirror to Canada. 60922
Picture and the men. 60947
Picture defining and reading-book. 26409
Picture exhibition. 62688
Picture Gallery of the Maryland Historical
Society. see Maryland Historical Society.
Picture Gallery.
Picture of a factory village. (44185)
Picture of a happy family. 89811
Picture of a republican magistrate of the new
school. 18512
Picture of America, exhibiting a view of the
United States. (22479)
Picture of Baltimore. 3056
Picture of Boston. 7043-7044
Picture of Christ healing the sick in the temple.
72116
Picture of Cincinnati. 13103
Picture of Cincinnati and the Miami country.
20822

Picture of colonial times. 79340
Picture of Nahant. 40783
Picture of Negro slavery drawn by the colonists
themselves. 82063
Picture of New-York, and stranger's guide.
(54579)
Picture of New-York in 1852. 73943
Picture of New-York in 1848. 73943
Picture of New-York in 1846. 73943
Picture of New York; or, the traveller's guide.
49746
Picture of Philadelphia. 47270
Picture of Philadelphia, giving an account of
its origin. 47268-47269
Picture of Philadelphia in 1811. 47268-47269,
104694
Picture of Philadelphia, for 1824. 47269,
104694
Picture of Philadelphia, or, a brief account of
the various institutions and public objects
in this metropolis. 62058
Picture of Quakerism drawn to life in 2 parts.
9072
Picture of Quebec. (6914), (67033)
Picture of Quebec and its vicinity. (67034)
Picture of Quebec; with historical recollections.
30946
Picture of Saratoga for 1843. 76914
Picture of slavery, drawn from the decisions
of the southern courts. 62689
Picture of slavery in the U. S. of America.
6921, 97929
Picture of slavery in the United States of
America. By Harriet Beecher Stowe.
92501
Picture of the baptism of Pocahontas. 63504
Picture of the battle of Gettysburg. 73439-
73440
Picture of the city of Washington. 101946
Picture of the great constitutional debate.
31172
Picture of the great metropolis after nightfall.
(55297)
Picture of the House of Representatives.
50963
Picture of the perfidy of corrupt administra-
tion. 55187
Picture of Washington and its vicinity, for
1845. 25061
Picture of Washington crossing the Delaware.
40729
Picture of Washington: giving a description
of all the public buildings, grounds, &c.
101965, 102166
Picture of Woonsocket, or the truth in its
nudity. 44186
Pictures and rhymes. 6356, 39962
Pictures and stories from Uncle Tom's cabin.
92507
Pictures and stories from Uncle Tom's Cabin.
(Designed to adapt Mrs Stowe's narrative
to the understandings of the youngest
readers.) 92508
Pictures from Italy. 19997
Pictures from life. 84440
Pictures from prison life. (31050)
Pictures of Canadian life. 12943
Pictures of Canadian places and people. 18978
Pictures of Cuba. 34003-(34004)
Pictures of Edgewood. 49676
Pictures of Kentucky slavery. 30387
Pictures of life in England and America. 21081
Pictures of life in Mexico. (45477)
Pictures of slavery and anti-slavery. 72123
Pictures of slavery in church and state.
(41882)

Pictures of slavery in the United States of
America. 92480

Pictures of the baptism of Pocahontas. 11992

Pictures of the conspiracy drawn in 1863.
37420

Pictures of southern life, social, political, and
military. 74403

Pictures of the gold region. 94440

Pictures of the olden time. (78641)-78642

Pictures of the "peculiar institution." 62690

Pictures of the times. 62691

Pictures of travel in the Canadas. 5360

Pictures of virtue and vice, drawn from real
life. 92804

Picturesque America. (62692)

Picturesque beauties of the Hudson River.
(33520)

Picturesque guide to Quebec and its environs.
14100

Picturesque illustrations of Buenos Ayres and
Monte Video. 99460

Picturesque pocket companion, and visitor's
guide. 51152

Picturesque souvenir. 8819

Picturesque tour of the island of Jamaica.
29591

Picturesque tourist; being a guide through the
northern and eastern states and Canada.
32538

Picturesque tourist; being a guide through the
state of New York. 62693

Picturesque views of American scenery, 1829.
(79936)

Picturesque views of American scenery, en-
graved by Hill. 79935

Pidansat de Mairobert, Matthiew Francois.
(47547), (56129), 62694-62697, note after
96403

Pidgeon, William. 62698

Pidgin, William, 1772-1848. (62699)

Pie, -------- Saint. see Saint-Pie, ---------.

Pie voleuse. 101895

Piece against Mr. Murray. 92709

Piece curieuse, et accompagnee de belles
recherches. 12010, 32022

Piece de vers. 88694

Piece qui a concouru pour le prix de l'Academie
Francois. 74811

Pieces a l'appui. 75177

Pieces deposees aux Archives de l'Assemblee
Generale. 75114

Pieces des agens du gouvernement Francais,
etc. 16685, 29576

Pieces du proces instruit contradictoirement
au Conseil Superieur. 44980

Pieces ecrites et recueillies pendant le voyage.
(39638)

Pieces first published in the Public advertiser.
62700

Pieces justificatives [c. 1761]. (10513)

Pieces justificatives [c. 1791]. 47559

(Pieces justificatives.) [c. 1791] 96080

Pieces justificatives [c. 1831]. 27393, 96445

Pieces justificatives des memoires concernant
les limites de l'Acadie. 62701

Pieces justificatives, et d'un notice biographique.
101122

Pieces justificatives qui constantent la conduite
de M. de Damas. 68366

Pieces justificatives, sans replique. 42743,
note after 93793

Pieces justificatives sur l'affaire de la Martinique. (18361)

Pieces officielles, messages, instructions,
depeches, &c. relatives a la negociation

que a eu lieu en 1797 & 1798. 23085,
59593, 62702, 103848

Pieces officielles, messages, instructions,
depeches, etc. relatives au differends
avec la France. 59593, 62702

Pieces officielles relatives aux negotiations
du gouvernement Francaise. (29582)

Pieces principales de la correspondance ex-
changee entre les ministres. 12798

Pieces relatives a la rupture avec l'Espagne.
62703

Pieces relatives a Saint Domingue et a
l'Amerique. 64905-64906

Pieces relatives aux dissensions entre la
primiere Audience de la Nouvelle-Espag
94852

Pieces, religious, moral, and miscellaneous.
742, 25318

Pieces sur le Mexique. Inedites. 94852,
94856, 106401

Piedad heroica de D. Fernando Cortes. 8098

Piedra de escandalo en el cielo. 94636

Piedra fundamental del sacrosanto cuerpo de
Jesucristo. 75580

Piedrahita, Lvcas Fernandez. 62704

Pieds fourchus. 4903C

Pieds noirs. 12566

Pieno discourso di M. Gioseppe Moleto Mate-
matico. 66503-66504

Pier and Warehouse Company, New York.
petitioners (54384)

Pier Francesco Giambvlari accademico Fior.
27265

Pierantoni, Augusto. 62705

Pierard, Aristide. 62706

Pieras, Miguel. 81475

Pierian Sodality, Harvard University. see
Harvard University. Pierian Sodality.

Pierce, --------, fl. 1854. (81481)

Pierce, Andrew. defendant (52925)

Pierce, Benjamin. 92979

Pierce, Charles. 62708

Pierce, Edward L. (62709)-62712 see also
U. S. Government Agent to the Negroe
at Port Royal, S. C.

Pierce, Franklin, Pres. U. S., 1804-1869. 47
11585, (17762), 20428, 37859, 48122-
48129, 49332, 62713-62715, (68967),
70277, (82658), 84015 see also U. S.
President, 1853-1857 (Pierce)

Pierce, George Foster, Bp., 1811-1884. 6271
62718, 84992, 88382

Pierce, H. N. 51245, 62720

Pierce, Henry M. 62719

Pierce, Isaac Bliss. 62721

Pierce, James. 62722

Pierce, John. (62723)-62733, 101686

Pierce, John D. 48722 see also Michigan.
Superintendent of Public Instruction.

Pierce, Jonas. alias see Allen, James.
defendant

Pierce, Josiah. 62734-62735

Pierce, L. 80104

Pierce, Lyman B. 62736

Pierce, M. B. 62737

Pierce, N. P. 62738

Pierce, S. L. 79931

Pierce, S. W. 62739

Pierce, Thomas. (59554), (62740)

Pierce, Thomas. supposed author (63645)

Pierce, Willard. 62741-62742

Pierce, William. 25791, 59555, 62743, (6642

Pierce, William Blake. (62744)-62745

Pierce, William Leigh. 21636, (59556), 6274
62747

Pierce County, Wash. (State) Mass Meeting, 1856. 101925
Piercy, -------. 27007, 86583
Piero Choralmi, Lorenzo di. see Choralmi, Lorenzo di Piero.
Pierola, F. A. de. 62750
Pierola, Nicolas Fern. de. 62751
Pierots, Robert. 62752
Pierpoint, Francis Harrison. see Pierpont, Francis Harrison, 1814-1899.
Pierpont, Francis Harrison, 1814-1899. 59558, (62753)-62756 see also Virginia (Anti-secession Government) Governor, 1861-1865 (Pierpont)
Pierpont, Jacob. 105856A
Pierpont, James, 1660-1714. 62757
Pierpont, James, 1660-1714. supposed author 15447-15448
Pierpont, John, Jr. 62780-62781
Pierpont, John, 1785-1866. 6651, 6653, (6977), (52746), 62758-62772, 62774-62776, 91372 see also Boston. Hollis Street Church. Pastor.
Pierpont, John, 1785-1866. defendant before Ecclesiastical Council 101515
Pierpont, John, 1785-1866. supposed author 79282, 84781
Pierre, ---------, Comte de S. see S. Pierre, --------, Comte de.
Pierre, ---------- Dralse de Grand. see Dralse de Grandpierre, ---------.
Pierre, J. H. Grand. see Grand-Pierre, J. H.
Pierre, Jacques Henri Bernardin de Saint. see Saint Pierre, Jacques Henri Bernardin de, 1737-1814.
Pierre, Louis de Saint. see Saint Pierre, Louis de.
Pierre Viaud. pseud. see Dubois-Fontanelle, Jean Gaspard.
Pierrepont, Edwards. 62783-62785, (67516)
Pierrie, T. H. G. (62786)
Pierron, Eduardo. (48499), 62787
Piers, Henri. (62788)
Pierson, Abraham. see Pierson, Abraham.
Pierson, B. T. (54874)
Pierson, D. H. 62789
Pierson, Emily Catharine. 62790
Pierson, Hamilton W. 62791-62792
Pierson, John. 62793-62795
Pierson, Jonathan. 97788
Pierson, Lydia Jane. 20092
Pierson, Usal. defendant 65098, 69392, 96810
Pierson, Uziel. defendant see Pierson, Usal. defendant
Pierson, William S. 62796
Pierson's directory of the city of Newark. (54874)
Pierson's Newark city directory for 1863-4. (54874)
Pierz, Franz. (62797)
Pieschal, Carl. 62798
Piet, ------. (77219)-77220, 1st note after (74627)
Pietas et gratulatio Colegii Cantabrigiensis apud Novanglos. 30754
Pietas in patriam. 5196, 9926-9927, (19046), 20884, 27384, 46455, 75736, 89927
Pietas Matutina. (46456)
Pieter. pseud. Amsterdamsche veerman op Middleburgh. 1354, note after 102878
Pieter. pseud. Discours van Pieter en Pauwels. 20230
Pieterszoon, Fredrik. 62799-62800
Piety and duty of rulers. (14506)
Piety and equity united. 46457
Piety and learning the great ornament. 31611

Piety & morality. 84414
Piety and patriotism. 1800
Piety encouraged. 18479
Piety of founding churches for the worship of God. 10683
Piety promoted, in a collection of dying sayings of many of the people called Quakers. 24279, 96142, 100959
Piety promoted; in brief biographical memorials. 25143
Piety promoted, in brief memorials of the virtuous lives, services, and dying sayings, of several of the people called Quakers. 100959
Piety secures the nation's prosperity. 62460
Piety which the present age demands. 82210
Piezas justificativas de la conducta politica de Yucatan. (62801)
Piezas justificativas de Mexico. (48624)
Piezas oficiales relativas a los acontecimientos de Cartajena. (3651), 11135, 62802
Pigafetta, Antonio. 1561, 38880, 47042, 62803-62807, 66686, 67730, note after 90319, 95757, 1st note after 99406, note after 100632
Pigafetta, Filippo. tr. 57703
Pigafetta's account of the voyage. 62806
Pigeard, Charles. tr. 6031
Piggot, A. Snowden. 62808
Piggott, Margaret. ed. 88385
Pighius, Albertvs. 62809-(62810)
Pigman, -------. 45090, 45370
Pigmatelli, Antonio. see Innocent XII, Pope, 1615-1706.
Pigmies and the priests. 62811
Pignoria, L. (11103)
Pigot, George, fl. 1722-1738. 62812
Pigott, Charles, d. 1794. 62813
Piguenard, J. B. 106369
Pigwacket Indians. see Pequawket Indians.
Pii II Pont. Max. Asiae Europaeque elegantis-sima descriptio. 63164
Pike, Albert, 1809-1891. 15292, 37060, 40652, (41036), 62814-62816
Pike, Frederick Augustus, 1817-1896. 52127, 62817
Pike, James, Corporal, 4th Regt., Ohio Cavalry. (62819)
Pike, James, 1703-1792. 62818
Pike, James Shepherd, 1811-1882. 62820
Pike, John. (62821)-62824
Pike, Joseph. 62825, 95752
Pike, Marshall S. 62826
Pike, Mary H. 62827-62829, note after 92320
Pike, Nicholas. 62830, 68217
Pike, Richard. 62831
Pike, Samuel. (62832)-62834, 76343-76344
Pike, Zebulon Montgomery, 1779-1813. 62836-62839
Pike County, Ill. Agricultural Society. see Pike County Agricultural Society.
Pike Beneficial Society of Philadelphia. (62059)
Pike County Agricultural Society. Exhibition, 10th, 1861. 62841
Pikin A. B. C. boekoe. 62843
Pilat, Ig. A. 68011
Pilate and Herod. 90311
Pilatte, Leon. tr. 92534, 92599
Pilaye, A. L. M. Bachelot de la. see Bachelot de la Pylaie, A. J. M.
Pilbrow. firm engrs. see Illman & Pilbrow. firm engrs.
Pilcher, Joshua. 96714, 96725 see also U. S. Commissioner to the Iowa Indians. U. S. Commissioners to the Oto, Missouri, Omaha, and Yankton and Santee Bands of Sioux.

Pilgervater oder Geschichte der Christlichen Ansiedler. 67976

Pilgrim. 80085

Pilgrim Celebration, Plymouth, Mass., 1853. see Plymouth, Mass. Pilgrim Celebration, 1853.

Pilgrim Conference of Churches. see Congregational Churches in Massachusetts. Pilgrim Conference.

Pilgrim-convert. 63027

Pilgrim fathers. A discourse in commemoration. (64470)

Pilgrim fathers: a lecture by the Rev. Hugh Stowell Brown. 8486

Pilgrim fathers; a poem. 13414

Pilgrim fathers' first meeting for public worship. 93192

Pilgrim fathers, neither puritans nor persecutors. 78246

Pilgrim fathers of New England. A history. 45008

Pilgrim fathers; or the founders of New England. 3789

Pilgrim fathers: or, the journal of the pilgrims at Plymouth. 51201

Pilgrim fathers, the defender of the congregational order. 5106

Pilgrim fathers. . . . Two memorial discourses. (27943)

Pilgrim John. pseud. Soldier's armor of strength. 62844

Pilgrim Jubilee, Providence, R. I., 1870. see Providence, R. I. Celebration of the Two Hundred and Fiftieth Anniversary of Congregationalism in this Country, 1870.

Pilgrim Jubilee. Celebration in Providence, R. I. 62845

Pilgrim memorials, and guide for visitors to Plymouth village. (74406)

Pilgrim memorials, and guide to Plymouth. 74407

Pilgrim of a hundred years. 88269

Pilgrim of ninety years. 50995

Pilgrim Society, Boston. Committee. 69930, 77236 see also Savage, James.

Pilgrim Society, Plymouth, Mass. 63471, 63480-63481

Pilgrim Society, Plymouth, Mass. Celebration of the Two Hundred and Fiftieth Anniversary of the Landing of the Pilgrims, Plymouth, 1870. 63480

Pilgrim Society, Plymouth, Mass. Festival, 1820. 63482

Pilgrim Spaniard. pseud. Treatise paraenetical. see Teixeira, Jose. supposed author

Pilgrim spirit. 92772

Pilgrim Sunday School, San Francisco. see San Francisco. Pilgrim Sunday School.

" Pilgrim temple-builders." 32613

Pilgrimage. 67578-(67579)

Pilgrimage in America. 4603

Pilgrimage in Europe and America. 4605-4606

Pilgrimage of Ormond. (39468), 57631

Pilgrimage of Thomas Paine. 30088

Pilgrimage over the prairies. 62846

Pilgrims. A sermon, preached in Wendell, Dec. 22, 1820. 103960

Pilgrims' address. (62850)

Pilgrims' anniversary, 1817. 32527

Pilgrims' first year in New England. 26360

Pilgrim's foot-prints. 91997

Pilgrim's hope; and other poems. (62924)

Pilgrim's hymn book. 95429

Pilgrim's legacy. 48843

Pilgrim's muse. By Joseph Thomas, minister of the Gospel. 63639, 95430

Pilgrims oder Christin Reise ausz dieser Welt nach der Zukuenfftigen. 62849

Pilgrims of Boston and their descendants. 7840

Pilgrims of hope. 13819, 62851, 89296

Pilgrims of Plymouth. 62779

" Pilgrims of the rock." (11866)

Pilgrims progress. 103682

Pilgrim's progress. [By Francis Bugg.] 9071

Pilgrim's progress, by John Bunyan. 71341

Pilgrim's progress from this world to that which is to come. 62847

Pilgrim's song. 22525

Pilgrim's song; or original hymns. 89911

Philhill, David. respondent 105082

Pilinski, Adam. 99344

Pilkerton vs. Popsquirt. (77011)

Pilkington, Mary Hopkins. 62852

Pill for Porcupine. 14018, 14029, note after 95866

Pill garlic and his friends. 85463

Pillar of gratitude. 46458

Pillars in the temple. 84755

Pillars of priestcraft shaken. 47131

Pillars of salt. (46458)

Pillet, Edmond. 36363

Pilling, John Constantine, 1846-1895. 39409, 96105

Pillori, Antonio. tr. (71997)

Pillow, Gideon J. defendant at court of enquir 62853-(62854)

Pillow case. 69858

Pills for the delegates. 28958

Pills, poetical, political, and philosophical. 62855

Pillsbury, G. C. tr. 83138

Pillsbury, Parker. 62856-62858

Pilmore, Joseph. 24334, 62859-62860

Pilon, Frederick. (62861), 86904

Pilot: a tale of the sea. 16495

Pilot for America. 35965

Pilot of the German ocean. 101111

Pilota. 16498

Pilota dell' Oceano Atlantico. 62862

Pilotage laws and regulations of Massachusetts 71047

Pilote, F. (62863), 74941

Pilote. 16496

Pilote Americain. 6028-6030, (43847)

Pilote Americaine septentrionale pour les cotes de Labrador. 35969

Pilote cotier des Etats-Unis. 6031

Pilote de la Terre Neuve. (62965)

Pilote de l'isle de Saint-Domingue. (62964)

Pilote de l'onde vive. 32560

Pilote du Bresil. 73498-73499

Pilote du golfe et de fleuve Saint-Laurent. 4047

Piloto. 16499

Piloto do Brasil. (73500)

Piloto, novelle maritima. 16500

Piloto Portoghese. pseud. Discorso sopra la navigatione. 67730, 67743

Pilots' Benevolent Society, Louisville. see Louisville Pilots' Benevolent Society.

Pilot's daughter. 34776

Pilots whom Washington plac'd at the helm. 86897

Pilsbury, Amos. 62867 see also Connecticu State Prison, Wethersfield.

Pilsbury, Timothy, 1789-1858. 62869

Pilsen, John. (62870)

Pim, Bedford Capperton Trevylian. 62871-(62873)

Pima Sprache. (6527)

Pima-Sprache und die Sprache der Koloschen. 9625

Pimenta, Nicholas. 66686

Pimenta Bueno, Jose Antonio. 8989

Pimental, D. M. 62874

Pimentel, Andres. 62875

Pimentel, D. 12972

Pimentel, Esperidiao Eloy de Barros. 62876 see also Alagoas (Brazilian Province) Presidente (Pimentel)

Pimentel, Francisco. 51716, 52878, 62877-62878, 71411, 72811, 85760

Pimentel, Isidro Joseph Ortega y. see Ortega y Pimentel, Isidro Joseph.

Pimentel, Manoel. 62882-62884

Pimentel Maldonado, Joao Vicente. see Maldonado, Joao Vicente Pimentel.

Pimentel y Sotomayor, Francisco. 62881 see also Caracas, Venezuela. Real Audiencia. Presidente.

Pimentel y Sotomayor, Francisco. plaintiff 62881 see also Caracas, Venezuela. Real Audiencia. Presidente. plaintiff

Pimienta, Francisco Diaz. 62885-(62886)

Pimienta, Francisco Diez. defendant 51042

Pimpeterre, E. 62887

Pin, L. Ellies du. see Du Pin, L. Ellies.

Pin e Almeida, Miguel Calmon du. 21362-21365, 49461, 62888 see also Brazil. Ministro da Fazenda.

Pin chitokaka ip okchalinchi Chisus Klaist. 12875

Pina, L. Alfaro y. see Alfaro y Pina, L.

Pina Leitao, Antonio Jose Osorio de. see Leitao, Antonio Jose Osorio de Pina.

Pina y Cuevas, M. defendant 62889

Pina y Cuevas, Manuel. 62889

Pinault, Pierre Olivier. tr. (51427), (58529), (58535), 63898, (63900), 68444, (68740)

Pinchback, P. B. S. 62890

Pinchbeck, William Frederick. 62891

Pinchinat, Pierre. 62892, 94901

Pinchion, W. see Pynchon, W.

Pinckard, George. 2224, 62893-(62894), 102819

Pinckney, Col. pseud. see Hines, David Theodore.

Pinckney, Charles, 1758-1824. 10663, 62895-62899, 84819, 87415, 87509, 87537, 87540 see also South Carolina. Governor, 1796-1798 (Pinckney) South Carolina. Governor, 1806-1808 (Pinckney)

Pinckney, Charles Cotesworth, 1812-1899. 2446, 62900-62901

Pinckney, Cotesworth. 62902

Pinckney, Eliza (Lucas) (42609)

Pinckney, Henry Laurens, 1794-1863. 12077, 62903-62904, 85334, 86135 see also Charleston, S. C. Mayor, 1838 (Pinckney)

Pinckney, James D. (62905)

Pinckney, Maria. 67341

Pinckney, Ninian. (62906)-62907

Pinckney, Thomas, 1750-1828. 62908-62909, 87419, 87742 see also U. S. Legation. Great Britain.

Pinckney, Thomas, 1750-1828. petitioner 62908

Pinckney, William. 89220

Pinda: a true tale. 11996

Pindar, Christopher Laoemedon. pseud.?? 62910

Pindar, Jonathan, Esq. pseud. Probationary odes. see Tucker, St. George. supposed author

Pindar, Peter. pseud. Pindariana. 62912

Pindar, Peter. 62913-62914

Pindar, Peter, Jr. pseud. Parnassus in Philadelphia. 62915

Pindar, Peter, Jr. pseud. Secession. 62916

Pindar, Roger. pseud. Remarkable speeches. 102394

Pindar Puff. pseud. State triumvirate. see Verplanck, Guilian Crommelin.

Pindar. No. 1. 62914

Pindari Olympia Pythia. 62917

Pindariac poem. (79347)

Pindariana. 62912

Pindaric ode. 40931

Pindaric ode. [By Charles Crawford.] 17434

Pindaric ode, not written by Mr. Gray. 73985

Pindaric ode. Occasion'd by the lamented fate. 65528, 97745

Pindarus. 62917

Pindemonte, Hyppolito. 81299

Pinder, Richard. 62918-62921

Pinder, W. 66686

Pindle, B. T. 62922

Pine, -------. illus. 28897

Pine, George. supposed author (56066)

Pine, George. incorrectly supposed author 35255, 82181-82184

Pine, George W. (62923)

Pine, J. engr. 86574

Pine, James Wallace. (62924)-62925

Pine, John Buckley. supposed author 86933

Pine and the palm. (68527)

Pine forests and hacmatack clearings. 82126

Pine Grove Cemetery, Lynn, Mass. see Lynn, Mass. Pine Grove Cemetery.

Pine lands and lumber trade of Michigan. (62927)

Pine Street Baptist Church, Providence, R. I. see Providence, R. I. Pine Street Baptist Church.

Pine Street Church, Boston. see Boston. Pine Street Church.

Pine Street Presbyterian Church, St. Louis. see St. Louis. Pine Street Presbyterian Church.

Pineda, ------. 62928

Pineda, Anselmo. 58407 see also Panama (Province) Gobernador, 1843 (Pineda)

Pineda, Emeterio. 62929

Pineda, Fr. Xav. Conde y. see Conde y Pineda, Fr. Xavi.

Pineda, J. A. y. (62930)

Pineda, Jose Laureano. 62931 see also Granada (Province) Director Supremo.

Pineda y Bascunan, Francisco Nunez de. 12754

Pinel, ------. 59051

Pinel, Philippe Francois. see Dumanoir, Philippe Francois Pinel, called, 1806-1865.

Pinelo, --------, fl. 1690. 80987

Pinelo, Antonio Rodriguez de Leon. see Leon Pinelo, Antonio Rodriguez de, d. 1660.

Pinelo, Didacus de Leon. see Leon Pinelo, Diego, fl. 1660.

Pinelo, Diego de Leon. see Leon Pinelo, Diego, fl. 1660.

Pinelo, Diego Leon. see Leon Pinelo, Diego, fl. 1660.

Pineres, Jerman G. de. 62935

Pineres, Tomas Gutierrez de. 1876, (57403), 62936-62937, 65400, 68790, 93304

Pineres, V*** G***. (62938)

Pinero, ------- Gonzalo. see Gonzalo Pinero, -------.

Pines, Joris. 57370

Pinet, Antoine du. 62940

Piney woods tavern. 30082

Pineyro, Enrique. 62941-62942
Pineyro, F. Ayuso. (62943)
Pineyro y Ulloa, Martin. 62944
Pingel, Christian. 28659, 62945
Pingeron, -------. tr. 58516
Pingeron, -------, fl. 1782. 62946
Pingortitsinermik. 62947
Pingre, Alexandre Guy, 1711-1796. (62948),
    98960
Pinheiro, Joaquim Caetano Fernandes. see
    Fernandes Pinheiro, Joaquim Caetano,
    1825-1876.
Pinheiro, Jose Feliciano Fernandes. see
    Fernandes Pinheiro, Jose Feliciano,
    Visconde de S. Leopoldo, 1774-1847.
Pinheiro Ferreira, Silvestre. see Ferreira,
    Silvestre Pinheiro.
Pinillos, Claudio Martinez de. see Martinez
    de Pinillos, Claudio.
Pinkerton, John, 1758-1826. 2180, 3605,
    3827, (5051), 5057, 6376, 6870, 9359,
    14095, 16275, 16984, 25999, 36813, 36496,
    (37617), (55278), 57953, 57972, 60999,
    62572, 62806, 62957-62959, 82830, 95349,
    6th note after 97689
Pinkerton Academy, Derry, N. H. 62961
Pinkerton Academy, Derry, N. H. Semi-
    centennial Anniversary, 1866. (62960)
Pinkham, Paul. 101047
Pinkham, Rebekah P. 62962-62963
Pinkham, T. J. 62964
Pinkney, Edward C. 62496, 62965-62966,
    72496
Pinkney, Ninian. 62967-62968
Pinkney, William, 1764-1822. 48065, 50016,
    (58464), 62970, 83809-83817, 96563,
    103161 see also U. S. Legation. Great
    Britain.
Pinkney, William, 1764-1822. petitioner 3046,
    62969
Pinkney, William, Bp., 1810-1883. (45211A),
    62971-62972
Pinneo, E. H. (62974)
Pinneo, O. (62974)
Pinney, George. 62975
Pinney, Norman. 62976
Pinniger, David. defendant at court martial
    62977, 96942
Pinnock, William. 58426, 62978
Pinnock's catechisms. 62978
Pinnwo, Bezeleel. 62973
Pino, Pedro Baptista. 62979-62980
Pino y Penuela, Ramon. 62981
Pinsger, Johannem. 62982
Pinsger, Johannem. tr. 30252, (73193)
Pinsoneault, -------, Bishop of London,
    Ontario. 74551, 74555
Pintado, Bernardo Vera y. see Vera y Pintado,
    Bernardo.
Pintard, -------, fl. 1696. 96790
Pintard, John Marsden. 62983
Pinto, A. de Souza. see Souza Pinto, Antonio
    de, 1843-
Pinto, Antonio Cerqueira. 62984
Pinto, Antonio de Souza. see Souza Pinto,
    Antonio de, 1843-
Pinto, Antonio Pereira. 62986
Pinto, Basilio Jose de Oliveira. 62987
Pinto, Bento Teixeira. 27754, 94595
Pinto, Fernan Mendez. 66686
Pinto, Isaac de, 1715-1787. 56095, 56470,
    62988-(62991)
Pinto, Isaac de, 1715-1787. tr. 62992
Pinto, J. de. see Pinto, Isaac de, 1715-1787.
Pinto, J. J. 62993

Pinto, Jose Maria Frederico de Souza. see
    Souza Pinto, Jose Maria Frederico de.
Pinto, Joseph Gonzalez del. see Gonzalez de
    Pinto, Joseph.
Pinto Chichorra da Gama, Antonio. see Gam
    Antonio Pinto Chichorra da.
Pinto de Serqueira, Thomas Jose. see
    Serqueira, Thomas Jose Pinto de.
Pinto de Sousa, Jose Carlos. 62994
Pinto de Souza, Bernardo Xavier. see Souza
    Bernardo Xavier Pinto de.
Pinto de Ulloa, Juana (Albares de Rosal) de
    Valverde. plaintiff 87160
Pinto Ribeiro, Joao. see Ribeiro, Joao Pinto
Pinto Ribeyro, Joao. see Ribeiro, Joao Pint
Pinto Soares Vaz Preto, D. Marcos. see
    Preto, D. Marcos Pinto Soares Vaz.
Pinto y Quesada, Alphonso. 62995
Pinzon, Cerbeleon. 62996, (64445)
Pinson, Manuel. 62997
Pinzon, Vincent. 34100-34107
Pinzon, Vicente Jaime. 86427-86428
Pio Perez, Juan. see Perez, Juan Pio.
Piomingo, a Headsman and Warrior of the
    Muscogulgee Nation. pseud. Savage. se
    Robinson, John.
Piomingo. Chickasaw Indian Chief 96601
Pioneer. pseud. Northern Iowa. 35029
Pioneer. pseud. Traveller's pocket dictionar
    96493
Pioneer: a narrative of the nativity, experien
    travels, and ministerial labors of Rev.
    C. Giles. (27366)
Pioneer. A poem. 79338
Pioneer and Democrat. 101914
Pioneer biography. 42959
Pioneer bishop. 92823
Pioneer boys. 42962
Pioneer church. 78057
Pioneer, consisting of essays, literary, moral
    and theological. 28203
Pioneer days from Ohio to Wisconsin 1846. 84
Pioneer directory and business advertiser.
    74901, note after 95419, 1st note after
    95449
Pioneer heroes of the New World. (62999)
Pioneer history: being an account of the first
    examinations of the Ohio valley. 31799
    84617
Pioneer history of Illinois. 70421
Pioneer history of Monroe County. 97489
Pioneer history of Ontario, Wayne, Livingsto
    Yates and Allegany. 97490
Pioneer history of the Champlain Valley. 27
Pioneer history of Medina County. 55841
Pioneer history of the Holland Purchase of
    Western New York. 97491
Pioneer history; or Cortland County and the
    border wars. 27942
Pioneer Lawmakers' Association of Iowa.
    83882
Pioneer life at North Bend. 30562
Pioneer life in Richland County, Ohio. (4325
Pioneer life in Kentucky. 20824
Pioneer life in the west. (24378)
Pioneer life in the west; comprising the ad-
    ventures of Boone. 63000
Pioneer Mills mine. 63001
Pioneer missionaries. 55904
Pioneer mothers of the west. 63002
Pioneer pamphlets [of the Licking County
    Pioneer Society.] 40969-(40970), 78333
    85133, 85137-85138, 85143
Pioneer paper-making in Berkshire. 83328
Pioneer preacher. 59482

Pioneer record and reminiscences of the early
settlers and settlement of Fayette County,
Ohio. 66838
Pioneer record and reminiscences of the early
settlers and settlement of Ross County,
Ohio. 66838
Pioneer of Kentucky. 6373
Pioneer of the wilderness. pseud. Canada in
1849. 12943
Pioneer of the wilderness. pseud. Emigrant
churchman in Canada. 12942
Pioneer, of California monthly magazine.
62998
Pioneer women of the west. 22211
Pioneering in the Pampas. 79668
Pioneers of France in the New World. 58802
Pioneers of Fuegia. 51639
Pioneers of Licking. 85143
Pioneers of New-York. 32390
Pioneers of old Ontario. 84815
Pioneers of Rochester. Festival, 1847. 72348
Pioneers of Rochester. Festival, 1848. 72348
Pioneers of the eastern townships. 18963
Pioneers of the west. 92824
Pioneers of western New York. 33115
Pioneers; or the sources of the Susquehanna.
16447, 16460, 16502
Pioneers, preachers and people of the Missis-
sippi valley. 48917
Pionniers. 16503
Pionniers Allemands en Amerique. 39288
Pionniers de l'Amerique du Nord. 12349
Pionniers de l'Oregon. 6882-(6883)
Pionniers et les peaux-rouges. (81309)
Pious cry to the Lord. (65608)
Pious dead blessed. 100922
Pious heart-elations. (59308)
Pious Indian convert. 100991
Pious Indian woman. 67765
Pious lawyer, late lieutenant in the American
navy. pseud. Extract from a letter. see
Murray, Daniel.
Pious memorials. (9395)
Pious men the nation's hope. 34171
Pious remains of a young gentleman lately
deceased. 63003
Piper, A. G. 63004
Piper, John. 21782, 63005
Piper, John J. 63006
Piper, R. U. 63007
Pipes, Jeems, of Pipesville. pseud. Biogra-
phical sketch. see Massett, Stephen C.
Pipino, Francesco. 67736
Pipon, J. (63009)
Piquero, Ignacio. 63010-63011
Piquet, -------. 63012
Piquete suavecito . . . al Americano vindicante.
99783
Piracy. Speech of Hon. William D. Kelley.
37272
Pirates de la America. 23471-23474
Pirate and the rigolets. 34776
Pirate [by Sir Walter Scott.] 16495
Pirate doctor. 63013
Pirate du Saint-Laurent. 12568
Pirate of the Gulf. 34774, note after 83599
Pirates, d. 1723. defendants. 55027
Pirates, d. 1796. defendants 41527
Pirates. 92171A, 92173B, 92174, 92174A,
92174C
Pirates. A tale for the amusement and instruc-
tion of youth. 102376
Pirate's almanac. 63014
Pirates de la Savane. (6895)
Pirates du Mississippi. 27194
Pirate's legacy. 77171

Pirates of the Mississippi. 27194
Pirates own book. 63015
Piratical barbarity. 58670
Pirckeymer, Bilibaldo. 63016-(63019)
Pires da Motta, Vicente. see Motta, Vicente
Pires da.
Pirkbeimer, Wilibald. see Pirckeymer,
Bilibaldo.
Piroleau, Thomas G. 87889
Piron, Alexis. 63020-63021
Pirscher, -------. 63022
Pirtle, Henry. (13287)
Pisani, M. V. P. C. Ferri. see Ferri-Pisani,
M. V. P. C.
Piscator evangelicus. 46460
Piscatoria, et nautica. 58926
Piscataqua evangelical magazine. 63024
Piscataqua Missionary Society. (63025)
Piscator, Fluviatilis. pseud. Business and
diversion inoffensive to God. see
Seccombe, Joseph, 1706-1760.
Pisciculture. 87738
Piscina Zacatecana. 76790
Piscium . . . Carolinensium descriptiones.
11516
Piscium, serpentum, insectorum, aliorumque
nonnullorm animalium necnon plantorum
quarundam imagines. 11515, 22090
Pise, Charles Constantine. 63026-63027
Piso, Guilielmo. 3409, 6341, 7588, 32884,
(57377), 63028-(63030), 98930
Pison y Vargas, Juan. 63031
Pissbury, Albert E. 83858
Pissis, A. ed. 70301
Piste de guerre. (69061)
Pistorius, Ioannis. ed. (77903)
Pistorius, Thomas. 63032
Pitcarin: the island, the people, and the pastor.
51543
Pitcairn's island, and the islanders, in 1850.
8181
Pitcher, Nathaniel. 87168
Pitchero threnodia. 63033
Pitchlyn, John. ed. 21168
Pitchlynn, P. P. 63034-(63037), 86386
Pitezel, John H. 63038-63039
Pithou, Nicolas. tr. 25994, 79343, 79345
Pitillas, Jorge. (66654)
Pitkin, J. B. 63040
Pitkin, J. R. G. 63041-63042
Pitkin, Timothy, 1727-1812. 63043-63044
Pitkin, Timothy, 1766-1847. (63045)-63046
Pitkin, William. supposed author (15860),
note after 95296
Pitman, Benn. ed. 41182
Pitman, Benn. reporter 96953
Pitman, Henry. 63047
Pitman, John. 63048-63054
Pitman, Joseph S. 8584-8585
Pitman, Joseph S. reporter 20650, 28621
Pitman, Robert Birks. (63055)
Pitman, Robert C. (49198), 63056
Pitman, Thomas G. defendant 66240
Piton, C. C. tr. 10289
Piton, E.-C. tr. 10288, 10292, 10296
Pitou, Louis-Ange. 63057-63061
Pitrat, John Claudius. 63062-63063
Pitt, Miss ----------. 95231-95235, 95237,
95240, 95247, 95249-95253
Pitt, Thomas. petitioner 101150
Pitt, William. pseud. Letters to the Hon.
James T. Morehead. see Wickliffe,
Robert, 1815?-1850.
Pitt, William, 1st Earl of Chatham, 1708-1778.
949, 7109, 25700, 40467, 52052, 63064-
63095, 63761, 69405, 2d note after 89187,
95918

Pittsburgh Female College. 63133

Pittsburgh, Fort Wayne and Chicago Railway Company. Board of Directors. 63129

Pittsburgh, Fort Wayne and Chicago Railway Company. Trustees. 63129

Pittsburgh, Fort Wayne and Chicago Railway, and its connections. 18816

Pittsburgh gazette. (63148)

Pittsburgh, her advantageous position and great resources. (28707), 63130

Pittsburgh Horticultural Society. 63134

Pittsburgh in 1826. 63131

Pittsburgh in the year eighteen hundred and twenty-six. 36603

Pittsburgh: its industry and commerce. 63132

Pittsburgh Landing. Battle of 1862. 63150

Pittsburgh Landing, (Shiloh,) and the investment of Corinth. 99434

Pittsburgh Manufacturing Association. petitioners 63136

Pittsburgh, Maysville and Cincinnati Railroad Company. 63137

Pittsburgh quarterly magazine. 63138

Pittsburgh quarterly trade circular. 63139

Pittsburgh recorder. 63140

Pittsburgh Sanitary Committee. 63141

Pittsburgh Sanitary Fair, June 1, 1864. 63142

Pittsburgh Synod of the Evangelical Lutheran Church. 63140

Pittsburgh town & county almanac. 63143

Pittsburgh, Washington and Baltimore Railroad Company. see Pittsburgh and Connellsville Railroad Company.

Pittsburgher. pseud. Review by a Pittsburgher. 70190

Pittsfield, Mass. 83326-83327

Pittsfield, Mass. Board of Education. Special Committee. 63158

Pittsfield, Mass. Committee for the Soldiers Monument. 83332

Pittsfield, Mass. Dedication of the Soldiers' Monument, 1872. 83332

Pittsfield, Mass. Fire District. Commissioners. 63159

Pittsfield, Mass. Gymnasium. 63154

Pittsfield, Mass. Library. 63155

Pittsfield, Mass. Meeting of a Large Number of Gentlemen from Various Towns in the County of Berkshire, for the Purpose of Expressing the Views and Feelings of the County in Relation to the Proposition to Remove Williams College, 1819. see Berkshire County, Mass. Meeting on the Removal of Williams College, Pittsfield, 1819.

Pittsfield, Mass. Meeting on the Removal of Williams College, 1819. see Berkshire County, Mass. Meeting on the Removal of Williams College, Pittsfield, 1819.

Pittsfield, Mass. Mendelssohn Musical Institute. see Mendelssohn Musical Institute, Pittsfield, Mass.

Pittsfield, Mass. Rural Cemetery. 63156

Pittsfield, Mass. School Committee. 83333

Pittsfield, Mass. Septuagenarian Dinner, 1870. 63160

Pittsfield, Mass. Washington Benevolent Society. see Washington Benevolent Society. Massachusetts. Pittsfield.

Pittsfield, N. H. Congregational Church. 63161

Pittsfield business directory. 83329

Pittsfield Commercial & Classical Boarding School. see Commercial & Classical Boarding School, Pittsfield, Mass.

Pittsfield directory for 1868. 63153

Pittsfield Fire District, Mass. see Pittsfield, Mass. Fire District.

Pittsfield Young Ladies' Institute, Pittsfield, Mass. see Young Ladies' Institute, Pittsfield, Mass.

Pitzinger, Eliza A. 63163, 86010

Pius II, Pope, 1405-1464. 63164, 77523 see also Catholic Church. Pope, 1458-1464 (Pius II)

Pius IV, Pope, 1499-1565. 63165 see also Catholic Church. Pope, 1559-1565 (Pius IV)

Pius V, Pope, Saint, 1504-1572. 9111, 63166-63167, 75884-75885, 94186 see also Catholic Church. Pope, 1566-1572 (Pius V)

Pius IV, Pope, 1717-1799. 11377, 63168 see also Catholic Church. Pope, 1775-1799 (Pius VI)

Pius IX, Pope,1792-1878. 26721, (38617), 39284, 39476, 41095, 44559, 48410, 63170-63173, (78909), 79289, (81131), 84193-84200, 84203-84211, 88911 see also Catholic Church. Pope, 1846-1878 (Pius IX)

Pius X, Pope, 1835-1914. (77142) see also Catholic Church. Pope, 1903-1914 (Pius X)

Pius, Antoninus. 66497

Pius VII. assists the cause of liberty in 1797. 63169

Pius VII. assists Ferdinand VII. against the patriots of South America and Mexico in 1816. 63169

Pixerecourt, R. C. Guilbert de. 63174

Pizarre, ou la conquete du Peru. 63175

Pizarro, Adolfo. supposed author 93395-93396

Pizarro, Fernando. 67740

Pizarro, Francisco, 1470?-1541. 16663, 20518, 41966, 50115, 56064, 61097, 63176-63180, 67740-67742

Pizarro, Francisco, fl. 1621. plaintiff 63181

Pizarro, Francisco, fl. 1732. 63182

Pizarro, Jose Antonio. 63183

Pizarro, Nicolas. 63184

Pizarro, R. 63185

Pizarro de Almeida Carvalhaes, Rodrigo Pinto. see Carvalhaes, Rodrigo Pinto Pizarro de Almeida.

Pizarro de Orellana, Francisco. 86546

Pizarro d Araujo, Jose de Sousa Azevedo. see Azevedo Pizarro e Araujo, Jose de Sousa.

Pizarro y Gardin, Jose de. (29438), (63187)

Pizarro y Orellana, Fernando. 20250, 63188-(63189)

Pizarro. 10302

Pizarro; a tragedy in five acts. 4791, 38281, 80340

Pizarro, or the conquest of Peru. (10304)

Pizarro; or the discovery and conquest of Peru. 17826

Pizarro, or the Spaniards in Peru. 80341-80342

Pizigani, ------. 76838

Pizing sarpent, sittin on a rail. 97989

Pizzuto, G. F. tr. 96115

Platts, -------- van der. supposed ed. 55284, 101231

Placaet. 63202

Placaet van de Doorluchtighe ende Hoogh-Mogende Heeren Staten Generael. 63201, 102908

Placaet van de Staten Generael. 63202

Placard des Etats-Generaux des Provinces-Unies. 63190

Placard donne par les Etats-Genereaux. (63191)

Placat om foringen. 102937

Placcaet. 63202

Placcaet by de Hooghmo: Heeren Staten Generael. 63192, 102908

Placcaet. De Staten Generael der Vereenighde Nederlanden. 102907

Placcaet de Staten Generael tot verbod van den handel op West-Indien. 63193, 102908

Placcaet ende ordonnantie vande Hoge ende Mog: Heeren Staten Generael der Vereenichde Nederlanden. 63195, 102908

Placcaet gevolght op de voorgaende eeerste requeste. (16680), (57320), 1st note after 102889A

Placcaet jeghens fameus libel. (63197), 102908

Placcaet tegen het: nootwendich discours oft vertooch aende Ho: Mo: Staten Generael. 63196

Placcaet teghens seecker fameus libel. (63197)

Placcaet. [Van] de Staten Generael der Vereenichde Nederlanden. 63194, 102908

Placcaet vande Doorluchtige ende Hoogh-Moghende Heeren Staten Generael. 63199, 102908

Placcaet vande Doorluchtige ende Hoogh-Moghende Heeren Staten Generael. 63198, 102908

Placcaet vande Doorluchtighe ende Hoogh Mogende Heeren Staten Generael. 63200, 102908

Placcius, Vincentius. 63203

Place, M. 63204

Place British Americans have won in history. (50648)

Place in thy memory. 19322

Place of the Ringgold Light Artillery of Reading. 31733

Placentia Bay Lead Company. (63205)

Placer County, Calif. Supervisors. 58089

Placide-Justin, -------. 36956-(36957)

Placido. pseud. Poesias. see Valdes, Gabriel de la Concepcion.

Placido, Dichter and Partyrer. (21404)

Plagi-Scurriliad: a hudibrastic poem. 10880

Plagiarism. 63206

Plague of wealth. 102351

Plaidoirie de Me Henry Moreau. 50564

Plaidoyer de l'Indien Hollandois. 98208, note after 101026

Plaidoyer de Me Blanchet. 5846

Plaidoyer pour Fulwar Skipwith. 81660

Plaidoyer pour le Syndic des Creanciers des Mr. Lioncey Freres. 63207, 94126

Plaidoyer pour les Sieurs Bissette, Fabien fils et Volney. 12346

Plain address to Episcopalians. 63208

Plain address to the Quakers. 73406

Plain and brief discourse to little children. 92094

Plain and brief rehearsal of the operations of Christ as God. 78698

Plain and candid statement of facts of the difficulty existing. 19039

Plain and comprehensive grammar of the English language. 102377

Plain and concise view of the system of education. 105092

Plain and earnest address from a minister. 63209

Plain and easy directions to navigators. 72992

Plain and easy introduction to Latin grammar. 73889

Plain and faithful narrative of the original design. 103205

Plain and faithful narrative, with other material. 103202

Plain and familiar Christian conference. 123?

Plain and friendly perswasive to the inhabitant 44081

Plain and full account of the Christian practic 62833, 76344

Plain and full state of the demands and preter tions of His Majesty's Colony of New-York. 63210

Plain and important facts for the consideratio of the electors of Newhampshire. [sic] (63211)

Plain and practical treatise on the epidemic cholera. 68659

Plain and seasonable address to the freeholde of Great-Britain. (63212)

Plain and serious hints of advice for the trader's conduct in business. 69362, 91149

Plain and serious hints of advice for the trade man's prudent and pious conduct. 91150

Plain and wel-grounded treatise concerning baptism. 13867

Plain answer to Mr. Brown's reply. 92785

Plain attempt to hold up to view the ancient Gospel. 33799

Plain concise practical remarks. 36524, 940€

Plain counsels for freedmen. 24516

Plain dealer. 59853, 104452-104453

Plain dealer: number II. (63213), 104453, 1st note after 106233

Plain dealer: or remarks on Quaker politics in Pennsylvania. 104453

Plain-dealer. Vol. I. 63214

Plain dealing: or, nevves from New-England. 39640

Plain dealing or news from New England. 39642

Plain dealing; or, the proud man fairly delt with. 23711

Plain-dealing with a traducing anabaptist. (59724)

Plain directions for settlers in Upper Canada. 10447, 10541, note after 98077

Plain directions how the duty of swearing, ma be safely managed. (46478)

Plain directions on domestic economy. (63215

Plain discourse. 62517

Plain discourse . . . at Byfield. 62517

Plain discourse delivered . . . at Boston. 62517

Plain discourse, occasioned by the late perpetration of that henious crime. 62514

Plain discourse, shewing who shall, & who shall not, enter into the kingdom of heav 46716

Plain discourse to a plain people. 50793

Plain discovery of many gross falshoods, &c. 24278

Plain discovery of the mighty and invincible power. (19437)

Plain doctrine of the justification of a sinner. 12307

Plain English. 63216

Plain evidences by which the nature and chara ter of the true Church of Christ may be known. 79717, note after 97880

Plain fact. pseud. Answer to a pamphlet. 63217

Plain facts addressed to the inhabitants of Boston. 6541

Plain facts and considerations. 8864

Plain facts: being an examination. 63221, 1st note after 103107

Plain facts. By the author of "Honesty the best policy." 63218

Plain facts for plain people. By Ezra M. Hunt.
33846

Plain facts for plain people; or, principle
against expediency. 63220

Plain facts, or a review of the conduct of the
late ministers. 17521

Plain facts, shewing the origin of the Spalding
story. 104719

Plain guide for emigrants and capitalists.
(55165)

Plain historical account of the tryal, between
the Honourable James Annesley, Esq.
63222

Plain historical statement of facts. 95567

Plain home-told facts for the young men and
working men of the United States. 63929

Plain investigation of that subject. 14725

Plain letter to the common people of England
and Wales. 97356

Plain man. pseud. Plain reasons of a plain
man. 35381

Plain man. pseud. Plain words to a plain
people. 63249

Plain man. pseud. Rod for the fool's back.
102396

Plain man, and a lover of honesty. pseud.
Some errors of the Quakers. 86636

Plain man, who signed the petition at Derby.
pseud. State of the question. 90626

Plain man, who signed the petition at Derby.
pseud. True state of the question.
97159

Plain narrative of the proceedings of the
Reverend Association and Consociation of
New-Haven County. 71829, 96091

Plain narrative of the proceedings which caused
the separation. (35046)-35047

Plain narrative of the uncommon sufferings
and remarkable deliverance of Thomas
Brown. 63223

Plain path to Christian perfection. 63224

Plain pathway to plantations. 21752

Plain political catechism. 104730

Plain politician. pseud. Honesty shewed to be
true policy. (32782), 63791, 105988

Plain practical man. pseud. Remarks upon
the auction system. 69527

Plain psalmodist. (68158)

Plain psalmody, or supplementary music.
32475

Plain question upon the present dispute with
our American colonies. 63225

Plain questions for Mormonites. 63226

Plain reasons for removing a certain great
man. 42915

Plain reasons for separating, &c. 78732

Plain reasons for the great Republican movement. (31388)

Plain reasons of a plain man. 35381

Plain reasons, I. For dissenting from the . . .
Church of England. 63227

Plain reasons why William Henry Harrison
should be elected President. 30590

Plain reasons why William Henry Harrison
should be elected President of the United
States, and why Martin Van Buren should
not. 16181, 30577, 31772, 98425

Plain refutation of Durant's exposition of animal
magnetism, &c. 64851

Plain sense. pseud. Right of suffrage. 71378

Plain sense, or national industry. 63228

Plain sense, or sketches of political frenzy
and federal fraud and folly. 63229

Plain, short, and useful manual. 46566, 4th
note after 97284

Plain short discourse. 24579

Plain state of the argument. 63230

Plain statement. 97061

Plain statement addressed to all honest Democrats. 50318, 63232

Plain statement, addressed to the proprietors
of real estate. 50337, 54580

Plain statement for the consideration of the
friends of the Protestant Episcopal
Church. (63233)

Plain statement of facts concerning the claims
of William Vans. 98559

Plain statement of facts . . . descriptive of
the present state of slavery in the West
Indies. 63234

Plain statement of facts, submitted to the consideration of the moderate of all parties.
90586

Plain statement of matters affecting the interests of St. Thomas' Church, Brooklyn.
(8310)

Plain statement of recent difficulties. (67291)

Plain statement of the advantages attending
emigration. 73875

Plain statement of the argument between Great
Britain and her colonies. 63231

Plain statement of the quarrel with Canada.
10542

Plain statement of the rights, &c. (63235)

Plain statement to the colored people of the
U. S. 2571

Plain statement to the common sense of the
people. 63236

Plain statement to the public. 42813

Plain story. (36148)

Plain tale. 63237, 104030

Plain talks on familiar subjects. 32512

Plain truth. pseud. Candid address to the
Episcopalians of Pennsylvania. 63217,
63239-63240

Plain truth. pseud. Letter to William Staughton.
63238

Plain truth. pseud. Three letters. 63240,
note after 95739

Plain truth. pseud. To the public. see Paine,
Thomas, 1737-1809.

Plain truth, Jr. pseud. Another candid
address. 63240-63241

Plain truth. [c. 1743] 25558, 83984

Plain truth. [c. 1764] 2464

Plain truth. [c. 1768] 60732, 2d note after
96752

Plain truth (1822-1823) (63242)

Plain truth, addressed to the independent élec-
tors of the state of New-Jersey. 63244

Plain truth; addressed to the inhabitants of
America. 10671, (11767), 15526, note
after 63244, (77423), 84594, 84642

Plain truth: addressed to the people of Virginia.
100508

Plain truth; containing, remarks on a late
pamphlet. 84642

Plain truth: containing remarks on various
subjects. 90896, 90899

Plain truth, . . . devoted to the defence of
primitive Christianity. 63243

Plain truth found to be plain falshood [sic].
69495

Plain truth: humbly address'd to the consideration of all the freemen of Pennsylvania.
66932-(66933)

Plain truth, in a series of numbers. 63245

Plain truth. . . . Jackson and Burr. (35382)

Plain truth on the affairs of Grace Church.
63246

Plain truth: or, a letter to the author of dispassionate thoughts. 20270, 26440, 97340

Plain truth: or, serious considerations on the present state of the city of Philadelphia. 25522, 25558, 25563, 88824, 2d note after 96428

Plain truths. 36847

Plain truths about stock speculation. 83647

Plain truths, addressed to the people of N. Hampshire. (63247)

Plain truths at parting. 93729

Plain truths in a homespun dress. 19906-19907

Plain truths of the Gospel. 16294

Plain word, concerning the late circular of the Rt. Rev. Manton Eastburn. 17684, (63248)

Plain words to plain people. 63249

Plaine and friendly perswasive to the inhabitants of Virginia and Maryland. 44081, 2d note after 100507, 3d note after 102552

Plaine and true relation of the going forth of a Holland fleet. 2553, 76215

Plaine and true relation, of the going forth of a Holland fleete. 2553, 76215

Plaine description of the Barmvdas, now called the Sommer Islands. 9759, note after 36681, 100460

Plainfield, N. H. Citizens. 52791, note after 98998

Plainfield, N. H. Inhabitants. see Plainfield, N. H. Citizens.

Plainfield, N. H. Union Academy. see Union Academy, Plainfield, N. H.

Plainfield, N. J. Greenland Family School. see Greenland Family School, Plainfield, N. J.

Plainness and innocent simplicity of the Christian religion. 4677

Plains of Abraham. 4146

Plainte de la Novvelle France dite Canada. 10543

Plainte de mandataires des hommes de coleur. 5653

Plainte portee contre la Cour Royale de la Guadeloupe. 63252

Plaintes et griefs presentes a Monsiegnevr de Colbert. 13767

Plaintiff's case. 34416

Plake, Kate. 63253

Plamondon, Louis. 63254, 99598

Plan de Carpin, Jean du. 68443

Plan, and address, adopted by the citizens of Columbia. 87806

Plan and charter of the Northwood Cemetery Company. 61872

Plan and charters of the Florence and Keyport Companies. (24804)

Plan and description proposing to re-model the city of New York. 79317

Plan and elevation of the present and intended buildings. 103562

Plan and extracts of deeds. (8764), 63498, (69482)

Plan and invention of Gaspar Richard. (70901)

Plan and powers of the provisional government of Texas. note after 94951

Plan and profile of the location of the [Boston and Worcester] Railroad. 6768

Plan and proposals for establishing a female seminary. (77295)

Plan and propositions for organization of joint stock companies. 61035

Plan, by Samuel Galloway, Esq. 11881, 16590-16591, 2d note after 103119

Plan combinado de educacion comun. (77083)

Plan de colonization. 36421

Plan de constitution pour la colonie de Saint-Domingue. (11720)

Plan de estudios para el estado libre y sobera de Puebla. 66572

Plan de hacienda para la republica Mexicana. 48625

Plan de independencia adoptada por la diputacion, 7 Nov. 1836. 63255

Plan de independencia Californiana, 1836. 63256

Plan de baie et du harve de Casco. 88221

Plan de la constitucion politica de la nacion Mexicana. (48626)

Plan de los establecimientos y estatutos generales. 97502

Plan de propios y arbitrios para fondos municipales, 1834. 63257

Plan de subsistencia para el ejercito. 63258

Plan de un taller publico de artes en Mexico. 94145

Plan de vente de 300 mille acres de terres. 60086

Plan del Peru. 99491

Plan del Senor Coronel D. Aug. Iturbide. (35296)

Plan d'une agence. 50694

Plan d'une colonie. 26769

Plan eener trapsgewijze emancipatie der slave 8781

Plan einer geregelten Deutschen Auswanderung 63259

Plan einer in Nord-Amerika zu grundern Deutschen Kolonie. 8214

Plan et portraict du fort que les Francois y ont faict. 24854, note after 99605

Plan exhibiting the situations of the capital towns and cities. 90946

Plan for a better defence of the British West Indies. (39471)

Plan for a change of the constitution. 56529, note after 90029

Plan for a general legislative union. 69403, 79623, 93181

Plan for a public park. (17562)

Plan for a funding bill. 33358

Plan for a great canal between Charleston and Columbia. 49117

Plan for a park for the city of Albany. 51494

Plan for a real national bank. 47799

Plan for a school and establishment similar to that of Ackworth. 5245

Plan for a system of public education. (45220

Plan for abolishing the American Anti-slavery Society. 81729

Plan for augmenting the army. 15929

Plan for civilizing the Indians of North Ameri 63260

Plan for colonizing the free Negroes. 7384

Plan for conciliating the jarring political interests. 63261

Plan for conducting Indian affairs. 19788, 33138

Plan for conducting the Inspector's Departmen 63262

Plan for conducting the Quartermaster Genera Department. 63263

Plan for conquering treason. 63264

Plan for correspondence and friendly intercourse. 63265

Plan for encouraging agriculture. 17305, 60391, 63266, 95667

Plan for establishing a chaplain of the Presbyterian denomination. 63267

Plan for establishing a General Marine Society 24073, 63268

Plan for establishing a national bank for the United States. 50866

Plan for establishing and disciplining a national militia. 63269

[Plan for establishing] the city school [at Memphis, Tenn.] (47991)

Plan for forming a Warehouse Company. 41838

Plan for improving female education. 104042

Plan . . . for insurance against fire for the city of New-Haven. 6092

Plan for laying out towns and townships on the new-acquired lands. 63270

Plan for liquidating certain debts. 60393

Plan for military education of Massachusetts. 21516

Plan for obtaining our presidents. (55178)

Plan for one uniform circulating medium. (63271)

Plan for phonetic printing with common type. 68439

Plan for promoting colonization in Upper Canada. 10531, 10545

Plan for promoting the fur trade and securing it to this country. 18341

Plan for reconciling the differences between Great Britain and her colonies. 82278

Plan for removing bars at the mouth of the Mississippi River. 66828

Plan for resuming specie payments without changing the volume of currency. 63272

Plan for returning to specie payments and free banking. 70994

Plan for returning to specie payments, without financial revulsion. 70993

Plan for securing to British North-America a larger share of emigration. 63273

Plan for seizing and carrying to New-York Coll. Wm. Goffe the regicide. 33149

Plan for settling Mexico harbour. 95135

Plan for settling the unhappy dispute between Great Britain and her colonies. 35986

Plan for shortening the time of passage. 23109, 63274

Plan for supplying the city . . . with fuel. 54581, note after 97065

Plan for terminating the war. 5828

Plan for the abolition of slavery in the West Indies. 50669, (63275)

Plan for the abolition of slavery consistent with the interests of all parties. 63276

Plan for the consolidation of charities. (61693)

Plan for the construction of a ship canal. 55328

Plan for tha drainage of said distirct. 63159

Plan for the establishment of public schools. 60393, (74238)

Plan for the extinction of slavery. 9398

Plan for the federal union of the British provinces. 79622

Plan for the formation of a society to assist the government. (24715)

Plan for the further support of the public credit. (29981)

Plan for the general arrangement of the militia of the United States. (38161)

Plan for the general establishment of schools. (16745), 27965, (28024), 28913

Plan for the government of some portion of our colonial possessions. 72583

Plan for the government of the Alms-House. 62060

Plan for the gradual manumission of slaves. 7888

Plan for the gradual resumption of specie payment. 17244

Plan for the immediate extinction of the slave trade. 899

[Plan] for the improvement and better management of the revenues. (29981)

Plan for the investigation of American ethnology. 77871

Plan for the maintenance of the ministers. 63277

Plan for the melioration and civilization of the British North American Indians. 8858

Plan for the organization of a law faculty. 9611

Plan for the payment of the national debt. 63278

Plan for the promotion of foreign trade at this port. 2827

Plan for the reconciliation of all interests. 30183

Plan for the settlement of 552,500 acres of land. 63279

Plan for the speedy construction of a Pacific Railroad. 47372

Plan for the systematic colonization of Canada. 10544

Plan generale de defense du royaume. 29583

Plan legitimo del Padre Arenas. 89417

Plan looking to an early resumption of specie payments. 63280

Plan for a code of laws for the province of Maryland. 45276

Plan of a code of laws for the province of Quebec. 44690

Plan of a currency agent. 63281

Plan of a general assembly of the freeholders. 95353

Plan of a loan of forty thousand dollars. 60129

Plan of a loan, proposed to be received by the Washington Benevolent Society of Pennsylvania. 60778, 101992

Plan of a military establishment. 8557

Plan of a performance of solemn musick, to be in the hall of the College of Philadelphia. 61547, 63282

Plan of a performance of solemn music, to be sung in the College of Philadelphia. 61547, 63282

Plan of a proposed literary institute. 97480

Plan of a proposed union between Great-Britain and the colonies. 11882, 16590-16591, 2d note after 103119

Plan of a review for the First Baltimore Battalion. 63283

Plan of a seminary for the education of instructors of youth. (26407)

Plan of a society for making provision for widows. 28008

Plan of a society for the sale of lands in America. 63284

Plan of a theological seminary adopted by the General Assembly. 63285, 65187

Plan of a treaty of commerce. 63286, 96569

Plan of an act of Parliament for the establishment and regulation of our trade with the American states. (11833)

Plan of an agreement among the powers in Europe and the United States of America. (81400)

Plan of an agricultural school. 64278

Plan of an American compact, with Great-Britain. 56558

Plan of an ancient fortification at Marietta, Ohio. (77039)

Plan of an improved system of the money concerns of the union. 6238

Plan of union, for admitting representatives from the American colonies. 63229

Plan of union of 1801. 63300

Plan of union; or, a history of the Presbyterian and Congregational Churches of the Western Reserve. (37446)

Plan of water works. 75835

Plan offered by the Earl of Chatham. (63071)

Plan og convention hvorefter det Kongel. Octroyerede Danske Westindiske og Guineiske Companies. 102938

Plan, or articles of perpetual union. 63301

Plan propuesto para la construccion de un camino de madera o de hierro. 63302

Plan pour l'approvisionnement des isles Francaises de l'Amerique. 21035

Plan submitted for colonizing Africa. 95661

Plan to ameliorate the circumstances of the Indians in North America. 33923, 68698

Plan to exclude the French from that trade. 104226

Plan to improve the present militia system of South Carolina. 87718

Plan to lessen and equalize the burthen of taxation. (62066)

Plan to place a Bourbon king on the throne of Buenos Ayres. 9024, note after 101223

Plan to reconcile Great Britain & her colonies. 63303

Plan to render our militia formidable. 22386

Plan to revive confidence, trade, and commerce. 10889

Plan to shorten the passage between Europe and America. (9596)

Plan to stop the present and prevent future wars. (4143)

Plan van accomodement. 22995, 65735

Plan, wherein the power of steam is fully shewn. 3521, 24582, 74126

Plan with proposals for forming a company to work mines. 31338

Plan . . . with works and encampments of His Majesty's forces. (62064)

Plana de Bolsillo. 17796, 36607

Plana mayor general del ejercicio escalanon general. 48627

Planas (Simon) y Compania. firm 63304

Plancarte, Joseph Antonio. 63305-63306

Planchard, P. ed. 8532, 79139

Planche, Augustin. tr. 10837, 91852

Planche, Gustave, 1808-1857. 85203

Planches de Seba. 78689

Planchette; or, the despair of science. 76960

Plancius, Petrus. cartographer 6023-6024, 41363

Plancy, Jacques A. S. Collin de. see Collin de Plancy, Jacques A. S.

Plane von Boston. 26980

Planen zu Constitutionen fur Freistaaten und einem Staaten-Bund. 71224

Planes etc. por C. de Berches. 9594

Planetarium. 92753

Planiglobium terrestre. 29470

Planisphere de Cecco d'Ascoli. 76838

Planitz, C. B. de. illus. 89133

Plano de las localidades. 83033

Planos de Bolsillo, de la isla de Cuba. 17796, 63307

Plans and objects of the . . . [Massachusetts Sabbath School] Society. 45890

Plans and operations of the Presbyterian Board of Publication. 65192

Plans and progress of internal improvement in South Carolina. 63308, 87388

Plans des forts faicts par le Regiment Carignan Salieres. (39994), 67012, note after 69259

Plans & journaux de M. Crozet. (17716), 44594, 72371

Plans for a national circulating medium. note after 39323

Plans for beautifying New York. 28142

Plans for the search for Sir John Franklin. 8517

Plans of systematic beneficence. (65189)

Plans [of the Boston and Providence Railroad Corporation.] 6768

Plans of the building [of Boston City Hospital.] (6692)

Plans of the Custom House. 21041

Plans of various lakes and rivers. 10546

Planta demonstrativa da posicao relativa das colonias. 88764

Planta general de los empleados. 63309

Plantada villa de Itaque. 88763

Plantadores de America. 16506

Plantae a D. Gulielmo Dampier in Brasilia. 68027

Plantae Brasilienses exsiccatae. 44990

Plantae Centroamericanae. (4764)

Plantae Fremontianae. 85072, 96297

Plantae lechlerianae Chilenses et Peruvianae. 77644

Plantae novae minusve cognitae. (21046)

Plantae rariores in regionibus Chilensibus. 14369

Plantae Surinamenses. 939

Plantae Wrightianae Texano-Neo-Mexicanae. Part I. 28373, 85072

Plantae Wrightianae Texano-Neo-Mexicanae. Part 2. 28374, 85072

Plantagenet, Beauchamp. 19724, 59667, 63310-63311

Plantarum Americanarum faciculus primus. 63459

Plantarum Americanarum faciculus primus-decimus. 9343

Plantarum animalium mineralium Mexicanorum historia. (31515)

Plantarum Brasiliae icones et descriptiones hactenus ineditae. 63679

Plantarum Brasiliensium decas 1 et 2. 5395

Plantarum Brasiliensium nova genera et species novae. 67407

Plantarum Guianae variorum icones et descriptiones. (73893)

Plantarum in America Meridionali. 33196

Plantarum Jamaicensium pugillus. 41353

Plantas en el Real Jarden de Mexico. 63314

Plantas Hartwegianas imprimis Mexicanas adjectis nonnullis Grahamianis enumerat. 4762

Plantation. (63315)

Plantation and farm instruction. 63316

Plantation justice. 63317

Plantation melodies. 12955, (76470)

Plantation of Musketequid. 105074

Plantation teacher. 88383

Plantation work the work of this generation. 41762, 63318

Plantations for slave labor the death of the yeomanry. 40985

Plante, Francisco. 63319

Plantel. 63320

Planter. pseud. Candid reflections upon the judgment. 10664

Planter. pseud. Dialogue between a merchant and a planter. 19925

Planter. pseud. Dialogue or conversation. 19945

Planter. pseud. Free trade and the American system. 25724, 87830

Platform of the American Party of Vermont. 99144
Platform of the Congregational Churches. 63346
Platform of the Free State Party. 42282
Platforms and candidates of 1856. 61038
"Platforms," containing the compromise Democratic. 63347
Platforms [of the Republican and Democratic Parties.] 63348
Platica. 94346
Platica Mexicana de P. Jesuita Ignacio Paredes en que explica quien es Dios. 73158
Platica Mexicana de P. Jesuita Ignacio Paredes sobre el misterio de la encarnacion del Berbo Divino. 73155
Platica Mexicana del Padre Jesuita Ignacio Paredes sobre la vida, pasion y muerte de Ntro. Sr. Jesu-Cristo. 73157
Platica Mexicana del Padre Jesuita Ignacio Paredes sobre el misterio de la Santisimi Trinidad. 73156
Platica que se predico a la Congregacion del Salvador. 93576
Platicas antiquas que en la excellentissima lengua Nahuatl. 3997
Platicas de Asmodeo sobre todas las cosas pasadas. 63349
Platicas de los principales mysterios de nuestra Sta. fee. 20568
Platicas morales de los Indios. 3243, 3998
Platicas sencillas. 105737
Platine, l'or blanc, le huitieme metal. (63350)
Plato, Ann. 63351
Platon, Lewis. tr. 101906
Plats of subdivisions of the city of Washington, D. C. 25157
Platt, Ebenezer Smith. defendant 63352
Platt, G. Lewis. 63353
Platt, Isaac L. 63354
Platt, James M. 83456
Platt, Jonas. 57622, 63355-63356, 78822, 96876
Platt, Mrs. Lorin L. (63357)
Platt, S. H. 63358
Platt, W. H. (63359)
Platte County Self-Defence Association. Committee. 92866
Plattes, Gabriel. 63360
Plattesville, Wisc. Plattesville Academy. see Wisconsin. State Teachers College, Plattesville.
Plattesville Academy, Plattesville, Wisc. see Wisconsin. State Teachers College, Plattesville.
Plattsburgh, N. Y. Celebration of the Anniversary of the Battle of Plattsburgh, 1843. (63363)
Plattsburgh, N. Y. Citizens. (63363)
Plattsburgh patriot. 104140
Plattsburgh republican,—extra. (63363)
Platzmann, Julius. 63364-63365, 74034-74038, 94346, 94424, 98324, 105954
Plausible gozo de la Nueva Espana. 63366
Plautius, Caspar. 63367, 82979
Plautus, Caspar. see Plautius, Caspar.
Play, Fair. pseud. see Fair Play. pseud.
Play. In five acts. By Henry Clay Preuss. 65397
Play, in five acts. [By John Tobin.] 96057
Play, in five acts. By Richard Penn Smith. 83779
Play in five acts. By Samuel M. Schmucker. 77714
Play, in five acts. By Samuel M. Smucker. 85169
Play in five acts, by "Sphinx." 89422
Play in five acts. By W. Sharswood. 79866

Play, in five acts. Dramatized (by special permission.) 92410
Play in five acts: interspersed with part of the Rocks. 104462
Play, in five acts; translated from the German. 38283
Play of destiny. 20770
Player-Frowd, H. G. 63368
Playdoyer sur l'incompentence du Conseil de Guerre Francais. (57673)
Playfair, A. W. 63369-63370
Playfair, Hugo. pseud. Brother Jonathan. 63371-63372
Playfair, Hugo. pseud. Playfair papers. 63371
Playfair, Lyon Playfair, 1st Baron, 1818-1898. 36879
Playfair, Robert. 63373
Playfair, William, 1759-1823. 14021, (20599), 63374-(63375), 82304-(82305)
Playfair papers. 63371
Playford, John, 1623-1686? 76467, 91718
Playhouse to let. 18689
Plays and poems [of George Henry Boker.] 6174
Plays and poems of William Shakespeare. 79729
Playter, George F. 63376
Plaza, Eugenio de la. 63377
Plaza, Jose Antonio de. 63378-63379
Plazarte, Antonio. 98884
Plazas, Ramon Casaus Torres y Las. see Casaus Torres y Las Plazas, Ramons.
Plea against duelling. 92939
Plea and answer of the Right Honourable William Ear of Stirling. 91855
Plea before the Ecclesiastical Council at Stockbridge. 24528, 33973, 63380
Plea before the Venerable Ecclesiastical Council at Stockbridge. 102755
Plea for a church hospital. (51253)
Plea for a Maine law. 8897
Plea for a miserable world. 1314, note after 102377
Plea for a national museum and botanic garden. 85094
"Plea for standing ministry." 43526
Plea for Africa. 25757
Plea for Africa. A sermon . . . in behalf of the American Colonization Society. 43790
Plea for Africa: a sermon, October 26, 1817. 28818
Plea for Africa; delivered in New Haven, July 4, 1825. 2675
Plea for amusements. 77311
Plea for authors and the rights of Literary property. 63381
Plea for Cuba. (61357)
Plea for discharged convicts. 89070
Plea for education, virtue and thrift. 16219
Plea for emigration. 79678
Plea for entire abstinence. 97369
Plea for equality in church maintenance. 105566
Plea for farming and farming corporations. 12693
Plea for friendship and patriotism. 43374
Plea for friendship and patriotism in two discourses. 43442
Plea for God. 104402
Plea for . . . Gospel institutions. 57914
Plea for greenbacks. 24286
Plea for Harvard. 67232
Plea for Hayti. 13253
Plea for home missions. 57914
Plea for hospitals. 63382

Plea for humanity. A sermon preached in . . . Cleveland, Ohio. 5659

Plea for humanity. By George W. Quinby. 67177

Plea for impartial suffrage. 63383

Plea for inebriate asylums. 6984

Plea for Jubilee College. 36821

Plea for libertie of conscience in a church way. 74624, 91382-91383

Plea for liberty in the church. 64642, 82946

Plea for liberty of conscience. 57171

Plea for liberty of conscience, and personal freedom. 103983

Plea for liberty of conscience for the apologists church way. (69679), 91383

Plea for libraries. 64305

Plea for literature. 63384

Plea for masonry. 80316

Plea for ministerial liberty. (21261)

Plea for New Mexico. (63385)

Plea for non-scribers. 22093

Plea for north-eastern Pennsylvania. (36934)

Plea for our foreign commerce. 31824

Plea for peace. A discourse delivered on fast day. 79792

Plea for peace. A sermon preached in Baltimore. 26134

Plea for peace and a platform for the times. 63386

Plea for practical heraldry in the New World. (63387)

Plea for Presbyterianism. 18745

Plea for pure water. (11905)

Plea for reason, religion and humanity against war. 22716

Plea for reform. 104714

Plea for religious liberty. (32882)

Plea for religious newspapers. 63388

Plea for sacramental communion on catholic principles. 92838

Plea for slave-holders. 9483

Plea for social and popular response. 3454

Plea for the American Bible Society. 17910

Plea for the American Colonization Society. 49131

Plea for the antient Gospel. 12335

Plea for the Bethesda Society. 92020

Plea for the Bible in the State Reform School. 78342

Plea for the Christian spirit. 51614

Plea for the church in Georgia. 82730

Plea for the confederation of the colonies. 71114

Plea for the copperheads. 63389

Plea for the cultivation of trees, shrubs, plants, vines, and grasses. 84275

Plea for the education of the people of Kentucky. 103880

Plea for the establishment of veterinary colleges. 8792

Plea for the evangelical press. 73047

Plea for the Farmer's College of Hamilton County. (63390), 70944

Plea for the freedom of the church in Missouri. 16075

Plea for the Gospel scheme for the abolition of slavery. 63391

Plea for the incorporation of co-operative loan and building associations. 67268

Plea for the Indians; with facts and features of the late war in Oregon. 4360-4361

Plea for the Indians . . . written as a memorial. 63392

Plea for the industrious poor and strangers, in sickness. 77987

Plea for the life of dying religion. 96303

Plea for the medical staff of the army. 63393

Plea for the ministers of New-England. 63394

Plea for the ministers of the Gospel. 46717

Plea for the militia system. 58325

Plea for the old foundations. (80442)

Plea for the orphan, delivered on the anniversary. 104354

Plea for the orphan; delivered . . . 20 October 1833. 43790

Plea for the poor. A sermon . . . December 20, 1842. 37976

Plea for the poor. An enquiry how far the charges against them of improvidence. 63395

Plea for the poor and distressed. 63396

Plea for the poor soldiers. 102412

Plea for the preaching of the Gospel to the poor. 85272

Plea, for the right of private judgment. 5468

Plea for the righteousness of God. (74290)

Plea for the Sabbath in war. 63397

Plea for the slave. 63398

Plea for the south. 63399

Plea for the south. [By Gerrit Smith.] 82624

Plea for the south. By Massachusetts Junior. 45539

Plea for the state canals. 61009

Plea for the supremacy of Christ. (28569)

Plea for the Swiss Mission in Canada. 4618

Plea for the Theological Seminary at Princeton, N. J. 41315

Plea for the union and the war. 30042

Plea for the west. By Lyman Beecher. 4335

Plea for the west. [By Philander Chase.] 12192

Plea for the west: sermon before the Missionary Society. 31415

Plea for unbroken fealty on the part of the loyal states. 4573

Plea for united Christian action. 104672

Plea for voluntary societies. 63400

Plea in arrest of judgment. 12365

Plea in behalf of western colleges. 3506

Plea in defence of the rights of private judgment. 21266

Plea in the cause of Lyman Beecher. 104676

Plea, in vindication of the Connecticut title. 97189

Plea in vindication of the rights of the First Church in Pepperell, Mass. 2566

Plea [of De Laune.] 78732

Plea of George A. Smith. 70913, 85563

Plea of humanity in behalf of medical education 91481

Plea of patriotism. 58118

Plea of the colonies, on the charges brought against them by Lord M------d, and others. 63401, note after 104453

Plea of the colonies on the charges brought against them by Lord Mansfield, and others. 63402, note after 104453

Plea of the innocent. 37178, 37205

Plea on the trial of Howard Egan. 82585

Plea to make the Smithsonian Institution a national institute of research. 85095

Plea with Christians for the cause of peace. 63403

Plea: written for the fair. 63404

Pleas, Elwood. 63406

Pleas and proceedings before the Hon. John Cadwalader. 63405

Pleas at the capitol in Williamsburg. 99975

Pleas of the Gospel-impenitents examin'd and refuted. 25400

Pleasant Grove Division, No. 386, Fulton Township, Pa. see Sons of Temperance of North America. Pennsylvania. Pleasant Grove Division, No. 386, Fulton Township.

Pleasant Hill, Ky. Shakers. see Shakers. Pleasant Hill, Ky.

Pleasant Hill, Ky. Society of Believers. see Shakers. Pleasant Hill, Ky.

Pleasant historie of the conquest of the West India. 16964, (26804), 27752

Pleasant memories of a happy day. 55083

Pleasant memories of pleasant lands. 80939-(80941)

Pleasant peregrination through the prettiest parts of Pennsylvania. 55237

Pleasant Valley Manufacturing Company. Charter. 63407

Pleasanton, Stephen. 63408-63409

Pleasantries about courts and lawyers of the state of New York. 21914

Pleasants, Julia. 63410-(63411)

Pleasants, Robert. plaintiff 100231

Pleasants, Samuel. petitioner (59611), 61671

Pleasants, W. H. supposed author (71211)

Please circulate. 84452, 100419

Please read this narrative. 98554

Please read this statement. 98555

Pleasing instructor. (63412)

Pleasonton, A. J. 63413 see also Pennsylvania. Militia. Philadelphia Home Guard. Commander.

Pleasure tour in the Canadas. 37907

Pleasures and advantages of friendly society. 76368

Pleasures and duties of wealth. 67465

Pleasures and pains of the student's life. (27436)

Pleasures of friendship. 43311

Pleasures of harmony. 31245

Pleasures of poverty. A poem. 52232

Pleasures of poverty. By Solomon Southwick. 88648

Pleasures of religion. 103932

Pleasures of religious worship. 90837

Pleasures of true piety. 46461

Pleasures of yachting. 5425

Plebian. pseud. Address to the people of . . . New York. see Smith, Melancthon. 1724-1798.

Plebian. pseud. Address to the people of the state of New-York. see Smith, Melancthon, 1724-1798.

Plebian. pseud. Reply to the manifesto of the Trustees of the City Library. 54619

Plebian of the western hemisphere. pseud. Little western against the great eastern. 82128

Plebs, Washington. (63414)

Pledges of history. 21015

Pleiade rouge. 39985, note after 94187

Pleijte, C. H. tr. 12575

Pleiocene fossils of South-Carolina. 87532

Pleissner, -------. 63415

Plenty of money. 63416

Plesant historie of the conquest of the West India. 27751

Plessis, Armand Jean du. see Richelieu, Armand Jean du Plessis, Cardinal, Duc de, 1585-1642.

Plessis, J. O. 63417

Plessis, Salomon du. 68458, 1st note after 93862 see also Dutch Guiana. Raad van Politie en Crimineele Justitie.

Pleuro-pneumonia. 24766

Plevier, J. 63418

Pleydenwurff, Wilhelm. engr. 77523

Pleyte, W. 63419

Pleyto de Hernan Cortez. 10686

Pliegos. 100635

Plik et Plok. 93409

Plimpton, John. 59726

Plinguet, J. A. (63420)

Plinio, -------. 67730

Plinius, Cayo. (63421)

Plinius Secundus. pseud. Curiae Canadenses. 10414, 17984

Plinius Secundus, C. 106294, 106330-106331

Plinius Fisk. 6277

Plinth, Octavius. 63422-63423

Pliny, Junior. pseud. Letters to the Earl of Hillsborough. 28758

Plitt, J. K. 63424

Plockhoy, Pieter Corneliszoon. 61169, 63425

Ploez, Juan Luis. (61115)

Plot. By way of a burlesk. 63426

Plot discovered. By Marcus [pseud.] 18866, 98532

Plot discovered. Containing an impartial account. 88188

Plough and the sickle. 9235, 93427

Plough boy. 63428

Plough-jogger. 59477

Plough, the loom, and the anvil. 10842, 63429

Ploughboy, a poem. 16297

Ploughboy and journal of the Board of Agriculture. 63428

Ploughboy's harrow. 16297

Ploughjoffer, Richard. pseud. Inquiry into the dissenting institution. (63430)

Ploughman. pseud. What a ploughman said about the "Hints to farmers." 103115

Ploughshare, Peter. pseud. Considerations. see Beach, Samuel B. supposed author

Plover, Hiram, Jr. pseud. Square egg. (63431)

Plow boy's almanac for 1845. 63432

Plowden,---------, Earl of Albion. see Albion, ------- Plowden, Earl of, fl. 1784.

Plowden, Charles. (2990), 63433

Plowman, Roger. pseud. Dialogue between Mr. Robert Rich, and Roger Plowman. (70897)

Plowman's complaint against a clergyman. 8368

Pluchonneau, -------. 63434

Plum, Nathaniel G. A. 63435

Plum, William. (63436)

Pluma, Joaquin de. 63437

Pluma y Aguilera, -------. 63438

Plumard de Dangeul, R. B. 63439-63440, 97691

Plumb, --------, fl. 1858. (48572)

Plumb, David. 63441

Plumb, Elijah W. (63442)

Plumb, Ralph. 80503

Plumb pudding for the humane. 10881

Plumbe, John. 63443-63444

Plumbensis, Nicolaus. see Ogramić Olovčić, Nilola, Bp., 1630-1700.

Plume, Porte. pseud. Trans-atlantic sketches. see Harding, W. M.

Plumer, William, 1759-1850. 52801, 52848, 52949, 63447-63450, note after 102255 see also New Hampshire. Governor, 1812-1813 (Plumer) New Hampshire. Governor, 1816-1819 (Plumer)

Plumer, William, 1759-1850. supposed author 13133, 28944

Plumer, William, 1789-1854. 63451-63453

Plumer, William, fl. 1807. (63446)

Plumer, William S. 63454

Plumier, Charles. 3603, 9343, 63455-63459, 93459

Plumley, G. S. 63460-(63461)

Plummer, Clarissa. 30466, 63462

Plummer, Frederick. (63463)

Plummer, George. 96033

Plummer, J. 63464

Plummer, Jonathan. 63465

Plummer, Rachel (Parker) 58685

Plummer Farm School, Salem, Mass. 63466

Plummer Farm School, Salem, Mass. Charter. 63466

Plummer Farm School. An appeal to the public. 63466

Plummer Hall, Salem, Mass. Dedication Ceremony, 1757. 63467

Plumptre, Anne. tr. 38280, 38282

Plunderer's grave. 77008-77009

Plunkett, Thomas F. 63468

Plu-ri-bus-tah. 95596

Plurality of the human race. 64706

Plurality of wives. 89371

Plurality of wives! 89372

Plus d'esclavage! 48156

Plus ultra. pseud. Remarks on the attack. see Allen, George.

Plus videre quam habere. (8784)

Plusieurs Anciens Colons-Proprietaires Residant a Nantes. petitioners 93824

Plusieurs chaps royaulx par ledit Ian Parmentier. 58825

Plusieurs Haitiens. pseud. eds. 29584

Plutarco Brasileiro. (60884)

Plutarco de los jovenes. 93299

Plutarchus. 95341

Pluto become a Brownist. 94477

Pluto: being the sad story and lamentable fate of the fair Minthe. 63469

Pluto Brasiliensis. 22830

Plymouth, Conn. Ecclesiastical Council, 1856. see Congregational Churches in Connecticut. Ecclesiastical Council, Plymouth, 1856.

Plymouth, Mass. 63472

Plymouth, Mass. Citizens. petitioners 63479

Plymouth, Mass. Commemoration of the Embarkation of the Plymouth Pilgrims from Southampton, England, 1855. see Plymouth, Mass. Cushman Celebration, 1855.

Plymouth, Mass. Cushman Celebration, 1855. (80785)

Plymouth, Mass. Cushman Monument. (18140)

Plymouth, Mass. Ecclesiastical Council, 1832. see Congregational Churches in Massachusetts. Ecclesiastical Council, Plymouth, 1832.

Plymouth, Mass. Library. 63484

Plymouth, Mass. Pilgrim Celebration, 1853. 63471

Plymouth, Mass. Pilgrim Society. see Pilgrim Society, Plymouth, Mass.

Plymouth, Mass. Superintendent of the Public Schools. 63486

Plymouth, Mass. Third Congregational Church. 63473

Plymouth, Mass. Water Commissioners. 63487

Plymouth, N. H. Congregational Church. (63496)

Plymouth, Wisc. Union Lodge, No. 71, Independent Order of Odd Fellows. see Odd Fellows, Independent Order of. Wisconsin. Union Lodge No. 71, Plymouth.

Plymouth County, Mass. Agricultural Society. see Plymouth County Agricultural Society.

Plymouth County, Mass. Association for the Improvement of Common Schools. see

Plymouth County Association for the Improvement of Common Schools.

Plymouth County, Mass. Superior Court. see Massachusetts. Superior Court for the Counties of Plymouth, Barnstable, etc.

Plymouth almanac, directory, and business advertiser. (63483)

Plymouth and the pilgrims. 3230

Plymouth Church, Brooklyn. see Brooklyn. Plymouth Church.

Plymouth Church, Milwaukee. see Milwaukee. Plymouth Church.

Plymouth Church, Rochester, N. Y. see Rochester, N. Y. Plymouth Church.

Plymouth colony. pseud. Papers on the boundary line. 58453

Plymouth Company, 1749-1816. (8764), 19252, 63498

Plymouth Company, 1749-1816. claimants (69482)

Plymouth County Agricultural Society. 63492-63493

Plymouth County Association for the Improvement of Common Schools. Educational Meeting, Hanover, Mass., 1838. 63494

Plymouth County Association for the Improvement of Common Schools, educational meeting, at Hanover, Sept. 3d. [1838.] 63494

Plymouth County directory. 63495

Plymouth County Railroad. 7955

Plymouth Library, Plymouth, Mass. see Plymouth, Mass. Library.

Plymouth Rock. 18139

Plymouth ss. Supreme Judicial Court. 88163

Pneumatic tower foundations. (72578)

Pneumatology! Signs of the times! A great debate. 85122, 85124

Pneumonia: its supposed connection, pathologica and etiological. 39047

Poakphuun, ----------. pseud. tr. 50887

Poblacion de Baldivia. 532

Poblanos a los habitantes de Mejico. (63499)

Poblete, Juan Millan de. see Millan de Poblete, Juan.

Pobre peregrino. 63500

Pobre que se canso de serlo. pseud. Testamento hecho. 94910

Pobre, que se canso de serlo. pseud. Testamento hecho. 94911

Pobre que ya se canso de serlo. pseud. Testamento codicilo. 94903

Pobres Mendigos de Mexico. petitioners 47702

Pocahontas. pseud. Cousin Franck's household. see Pearson, Mrs. C. H.

Pocahontas: a historical drama. 43365, (58021) note after 100508

Pocahontas; a legend, with historical and traditionary notes. 51040, note after 102330

Pocahontas; a proclamation: with plates. (31888), 63502, 100509

Pocahontas and her companions. 52287

Pocahontas . . . and her descendants. 82823

Pocahontas, and other poems. (80942)

Pocahontas, oder: Die Brundung von Virginien. 29746

Pocahontas; or the founding of Virginia. 31880

Pocahontas; or the settlers of Virginia. 18155

Poccianti, Michaele. (63505)

Pocket almanack, and general register. 50269, note after 90523

Pocket almanac and New-England calendar. (19217)

Poem, addressed to a young lady. 1692, 63577

Poem, addressed to the armies of the United States of America. 33810-33811

Poem, addressed to the First Lord of the Admiralty. 94567

Poem, addressed to the inhabitants of New-England. 48943, 90167, note after 95840

Poem addressed to the King. 1766

Poem after the manner of Mr. Pomfret. 12985, 1st note after 106134

Poem and address delivered on the first annual meeting. 86161

Poem and an ode to war. 42154

Poem, and other thoughts. 102581

Poem and valedictory oration . . . before the senior class in Yale College. (81017)

Poem and valedictory oration pronounced before the senior class in Yale College. 6147

Poem.. . . at Litchfield, July 4th, 1812. 38113, note before 93242, note after 97540

Poem . . . at Malden. 30883

Poem at the anniversary of the Brookfield Temperance Society. 33069

Poem at the celebration of the one hundredth anniversary of the incorporation of the town of Princeton, Mass. 23280

Poem [at the celebration of the two hundredth anniversary of the incorporation of the town of Bellerica, Mass.] 5403

Poem at the dedication of Mason Hall, Hudson, N. Y. 22780

Poem . . . at the dedication of the Dorchester High School. 32800

Poem . . . at the dedication of the Pittsfield Cemetery. 32621

Poem, . . . at the fifth anniversary of the Franklin Debating Society. 45446

Poem, at the laying of the corner stone of the Soldiers' National Monument. (29920)

Poem, . . . at the semi-centennial celebration of Bradford Academy. 55205

Poem. Auctore enginae societatis poeta. 30755, 59539

Poem, . . . before . . . Columbia College. (43580)

Poem . . . before the associate chapters of the Delta Phi. (82448)

Poem, before the Bridgewater Normal Association. 39506

Poem . . . before the Ciceronian Club. 47368

Poem . . . before the Connecticut Alpha. 60869

Poem before the Franklin Debating Society. 45446

Poem . . . before the literary societies in Amherst College. (47442)

Poem . . . before the Phi Beta Kappa Society, at Cambridge. (47442)

Poem . . . before the Phi Beta Kappa Society in Cambridge. (34004)

Poem . . . before the Phi Beta Kappa Society of Yale College. 32621

Poem before the Phi Beta Kappa Society of Yale College. . . . July 24, 1861. 5634

Poem . . . before the Philomathean Society of Pennsylvania College. 43341

Poem . . . before the Pickwick Club. 19497

Poem before the students of Hobart College. 32313

Poem . . . before the . . . University of . . . New-York. (43533)

Poem, . . . before the . . . University of Pennsylvania. 55085

Poem: being a serious address to the House of Representatives. 84672

Poem: by an American. (57415)

Poem, by a friend. 37660

Poeml by a lady of New England. 63578

Poem by Alfred B. Street. 90428

Poem; [by Alfred W. Arrington.] 93617

Poem by an American gentleman. 103885

Poem. By Atticus. 13388, 90648

Poem by Bayard Taylor. 51019

Poem. By Britannicus. 83841

Poem by Bro. Charles C. Van Zandt. 67780

Poem by C. A. L. Richards. 35679

Poem by C. G. Burgess. (59557)

Poem by Chas. E. Furman. 72342

Poem: by Charles Warren Stoddard. 9976

Poem by Edward C. Porter. 29492

Poem, by Francis Miles Finch. 23205

Poem, by Frank Johnston. (36362)

Poem, by G. H. Hollister. 32553

Poem, by Guy Bryan Schott. 77913

Poem by Harrison S. Morris. 84509

Poem by Harvey Rice. 16224

Poem, by Henry C. Whitaker. 32997

Poem, by Herbert Glesson. 89082

Poem, by Hon. Henry Chapin. 47819, note after 90463

Poem by Herman A. Dearborn. 31589

Poem by Isaac F. Shepard. 39902

Poem by J. G. Whittier. 12213

Poem by James Reed. 7827

Poem by John Addison Porter. 64278

Poem by John M. May. 30501

Poem: by John Pierpont. (52746)

Poem [by Joseph Bartlett.] 3757

Poem by Joseph Howe. (51433)

Poem by Levi Ward Smith. 83483

Poem [by Lilley Eaton.] (24776)

Poem, by Lovet Stimson. 64990

Poem, by Lucius Franklin Robinson. 72142

Poem, by Lyman D. Brewster. (7782)

Poem by Miss Eliza A. Pittsinger. 86010

Poem. By Miss M. P. S., of Sunnyside. 74628

Poem by Mr. Byles. 65597

Poem . . . by Mr. Smith, of Long-Island. 8464

Poem, by Mr. William S. Heywood. 103035

Poem by Mrs. J. C. R. Door. 37278

Poem by Mott: Dulany Ball. (2944)

Poem, by O. W. Holmes. 63156

Poem, by Peter Grievous, Junr. 10425

Poem, by Phillis. 103128

Poem by Rev. E. T. Winkler. 88111

Poem by Rev. Edward Hopper. 89264

Poem, by Rev. O. G. Wheeler. 99213

Poem by S. S. Osgood. (57792)

Poem by Samuel Mather. (47456)

Poem, by the Rev. Gurdon Huntington. (80908)

Poem, . . . by the Rev. Mr. Benjamin Colman. 59601

Poem. By Thomas P. Scovell. 78460

Poem by W. Gordon McCabe. 86161

Poem [by William Betts.] 14802

Poem . . . by William M. Rodman. 37757

Poem, by William W. Crapo. 89672

Poem, commemorative of Goffe, Whaley, & Dixwell. (61417), 91750

Poem compos'd on occasion of the sight seen on the great trees. 90139-90140

Poem; comprising a few thoughts suggested. 63579

Poem, containing a short abridgment of the foregoing testimony. 79725

Poem, containing two letters. 63580

Poem . . . Dartmouth College, Hanover, N. H. 15464

Poem dedicated to the American Association for the Advancement of Science. 92774

Poem. Dedicated to the honourable memory of the brave officers. 97744

Poem dedicated to the memory of the Reverend and Excellent Mr. Urian Oakes. 46462

Poem dedicated to the sons of H****d. 13633, 2d note after 97114

Poem delivered at Brookfield. 65085, 85397

Poem, delivered at Cambridge, before the Phi Beta Kappa Society, August 27, 1829. 89658

Poem, delivered at Cambridge, on the anniversary of the φ B K Society. 103833

Poem, delivered at Dartmouth College. (32709), note after 98049

Poem, delivered at Harvard College . . . April 21, 1780. 19902

Poem delivered at . . . Kimball Union Academy. 20681

Poem, delivered at Litchfield, Conn. 62770

Poem. Delivered at Suffield, Conn. (79989)

Poem, delivered at the anniversary of the Pittsfield Young Ladies' Institute. 92771

Poem, delivered at the anniversary of the Porter Rhetorical Society. 94373

Poem delivered at the celebration of the two hundredth anniversary of the incorporation of the town of Mendon. 11948

Poem delivered at the commencement of Rhode Island College. 20509

Poem, delivered at the first semi-centennial anniversary of the Philomathean Society. 92769

Poem delivered at the forty-sixth anniversary of the Philolexian Society. 75269

Poem, delivered at the Junior Exhibition of Trinity College. (71277)

Poem: delivered August 1st, 1862. 4467

Poem, delivered before the Alpha of Phi Beta Kappa Society. 92763

Poem delivered before the Alumni Association. 21628

Poem delivered before the alumni of Madison University. 70975

Poem: delivered before the . . . alumni of Washington College. (55207)

Poem, delivered before the Connecticut Alpha of the Phi Beta Kappa. 92772

Poem, delivered before the Erosinian and Philophrenian Societies. 93749

Poem delivered before the Eucleian and Philomathean Societies. 82451

Poem delivered before the Hermaean Society of Harvard University. 72140

Poem delivered before the House of Convocation of Trinity College. 37722

Poem, delivered before the Lyceum, Concord, Mass. (3614), 15130

Poem delivered before the Mechanic Apprentices' Library Association. 10271

Poem, delivered before the Mechanic Apprentices' Library Association, at their twenty-second anniversary. 93250

Poem delivered before the New-England Society. 62769

Poem, delivered before the Phi Beta Kappa Society, Alpha of Massachusetts. 13418

Poem, delivered before the Phi Beta Kappa Society, of Dartmouth College. 7299

Poem delivered before the Phi Beta Kappa Society of Harvard University: August 29, 1844. 92332

Poem, delivered before the φ B K Society of Harvard University, on their anniversary August 28, 1817. 101403

Poem delivered before the Pickwick Club. 19597

Poem delivered before the Porter Rhetorical Society. 18441

Poem delivered before the Society of United Brothers. 104513

Poem delivered before the thirteenth annual convention of the Delta Psi Fraternity of Columbia, S. C. 74286

Poem delivered before the United Brothers' Society, of Brown University. 104817

Poem delivered before the Washington Benevolent Society, in Brimfield. 65084

Poem delivered before the Washington Benevolent Society, of Newburyport. 62771

Poem delivered by Rev. S. F. Smith. 84055

Poem delivered in Boston, June 24, 1858. 80307

Poem, . . . delivered in Cambridge. 58200

Poem, delivered in Middleborough. 95379

Poem delivered in . . . Quincy. 17389

Poem, delivered in Saco. 22471, 87270

Poem, delivered in the Chapel of Harvard University. (44381)

Poem, delivered in the Chapel of Rhode Island College. 95520

Poem, delivered . . . in Yale College. 21472

Poem: delivered . . . January 17, 1831. 4112

Poem delivered on the anniversary of the Literary Fraternity. 100781

Poem delivered on the celebration of independence. 60964

Poem delivered on the 4th of July, 1863. 50629

Poem, delivered on the fourth of July. . . . The stranger. 92280

Poem delivered . . . on the opening of Tweddle Hall. 50512

Poem, descriptive of a pedestrian journey to the Falls of Niagara. 104600

Poem, descriptive of a pedestrian journey to the falls of Niagara, in the autumn of 1804. 104599, 105601

Poem descriptive of South America. 7084

Poem, descriptive of the interior of North-America. 47218

Poem, descriptive of the Nashville Convention. 30303, 84875

Poem, descriptive of the noted battle. 96325

Poem, descriptive of the terrible fire. 100864

Poem, descriptive, serious, and satirical. 105618

Poem, displaying the glorious campaigns. 15885

Poem dramatique de l'emancipation des esclaves. 38710

Poem en trois chants. (63707)

Poem, entitled Mr. W———d's soliloquy. 63581

Poem entitled The contrast. 106069

Poem entitled The day and the war. 4468

Poem epique en huit chants. 75127

Poem, etc. 70087

Poem, etc. [By David Hitchcock.] (32239)

Poem, first pronounced before the Western Newbury Lyceum. (81599)

Poem for natives and aliens. 38141

Poem for the hour. 18167

Poem for the times. 89654

Poem for the times, in six cantos. 13464

Poem, founded on a late fact. (70149)

Poem founded on the rebellion. 18271

Poem; from the manuscript of a maniac. 89469

Poem in blank verse. 85507

Poem in "commemoration of these poems." (37125), note after 101268

Poem, in five cantos. 91213

Poem, in five epistles. 101235

Poem, in five parts. [By Edward R. Young.] 106071

Poem, in five parts. By Hiram A. Reid. 69007

Poem, in four books. By J. Singleton. 81425

Poem, in four books. By Mr. Singleton. 81424

Poem, in four cantoes. 89923, note after 105176

Poem in four cantoes. By a student. 93239

Poem in four cantos. By George Webber. 102250

Poem, in four cantos. By Jonathan M. Scott. (78325)-(78326)

Poem in four cantos with notes. 94578

Poem, in four cantos. Written in 1774. 90855

Poem in four parts. 50143

Poem in honour of tobaco [sic]. 95621

Poem in honour of Washington. 98276

Poem. In imitation of the manner of Ossian. 41336

Poem in imitation of the VI. ode of the third book of Horace. 78204

Poem in Latin and English. 28818

Poem in memory of Admiral Vernon's action at Porto Bello. 99249

Poem in nine books. By James Ogden. 56808

Poem in nine books. By Joel Barlow, Esq. 3434, 100597

Poem in nine books. By N. M. Gordon. 27990

Poem, in retaliation for the "Philadelphia Jockey Club." (19494A), 13879, 13885, (78988), 95799

Poem in seven cantos. 33168

Poem in seven parts: containing, reflections upon a farewell. 63582, 100804

Poem. In six cantos. By Helen Maria Williams. 104228, 104230

Poem, in six cantos; with introductory notes. 5693

Poem. In ten books. By a female hand. 73542-73543

Poem, in ten books, by Thomas Northmore, Esq. 55838

Poem, in ten cantos. 72165

Poem, in ten epistles, containing some political hints. 84873

Poem in the style of Pope's Windsor Forest. 21547

Poem in three books. (67609)

Poem, in three cantoes. (59556), 62747

Poem in three cantos. 34161

Poem, in three cantos. 57649, 106332

Poem, in three cantos: and miscellaneous poems. 94535

Poem in three cantos, being hits at time on the wing. 71314

Poem, in three cantos. By an American youth. 63362, 105176

Poem in three cantos. By Burkitt J. Newman. 55006

Poem. In three cantos. By J. H. Powell. 64751

"Poem in three cantos, by J. Oldfield." 57154, 96317

Poem in three cantos; with other periodical works of an American. 104148

Poem, in three cantos, written at Chambery. 3420, note just before 30829

Poem, in three parts. 65971

Poem, in three parts. [By John Blair Linn.] (41337)

Poem, in three parts. By Samuel Webber. 102253

Poem, in three parts. [By William Kilty?] 100598

Poem, in three parts. Part I. Freedom's bower. 72648

Poem, in three parts. . . . The stranger. 92277

Poem, in three parts. Written in that island. 35592

Poem, in twelve books. 104731

Poem. In twenty-one cantos. 83610

Poem, in two books, written in the autumn of 1813. 31528, note after 105184

Poem, in two cantos. 25672

Poem: in two cantos. By the author of the "Bloody charter." 103713

Poem in two cantos to the memory of the Honourable Colonel John Maitland. 14902

Poem in two parts. And an ode to war. 75034

Poem, in two parts, by David Young. 106068

Poem in two parts, to which are added five other poems. 43311

Poem: in two parts. With notes. 92861

Poem in two parts: with other poems. 29670

Poem. Inscribed to General Conway. 97008

Poem inscribed to Satan. 97531

Poem. July 4, 1856. 72492

Poem, lately found in a bundle of papers. 40933

Poem . . . May 23, 1849. 43060

Poem not improperly conferr'd upon her. (36674)-36675

Poem, occasioned by hearing the late Reverend George Whitefield preach. 103641

Poem occasioned by the death of Jno. Alden. 17092, 98055

Poem, occasioned by the death of Master John Whitman. 103735

Poem occasioned by the death of the Hon. jonathan Law. 12984

Poem occasion'd by the late powerful and awakening preaching. 94709

Poem occasioned by the rise and fall of South Sea Stock. 2556

Poem, occasioned by the untimely death of Hugh Anderson. 63583

Poem, occasioned by the untimely death of Richard Wilson. 100952

Poem of Dr. O. W. Holmes. 23271

Poem of "Nothing to wear." 56223

Poem of Prof. Erastus Everett. 65648

Poem of the North American Indians. 71136

Poem of the days of seventy-six. (68186)

Poem of the south. 47366

Poem on a voyage of discovery. 63584

Poem on death, and on the resurrection. 59479

Poem on divine revelation. 7190

Poem on door-keeping. 63585, 104539

Poem on Elijah's translation. 14507

Poem on fame, and miscellanies. 56722

Poem on General Taylor. 59475

Poem on his design for Georgia. 103497

Poem on industry. (33813), (78988)

Poem on intemperance. 5349

Poem, on liberty. 63586, note after 98582

Poem, on liberty and equality. (72718)

Poem on New Amsterdam. 2466

Poem on reading President Washington's address. 32784, 1st note after 101872

Poem on reading the President's address. 63587, 1st note after 101872

Poem on religious ignorence. 103337

Poem, on religious ignorance, pride and avaric 103342-103344

Poem on some of the principal events of the American war. 65528, 97745

Poem, on the acquisition of Louisiana. 89435

Poem on the African slave trade. 5572

Poem on the American revolution. (65526)

Poem on the American war. 14856, 85590-85592

Poem on the apporaching peace. 66606

Poem on the awful catastrophy on board the United States Steam Frigate Princeton. 22310

Poem on the bill lately passed for regulating the slave trade. 104229

Poem on the capture of the American Frigate Chesapeake. (50044)

Poem on the capture of the silver-fleet by P. Heyn. 32382

Poem . . . [on] the completion of the granite monument. (6977)

Poem [on the death of Abraham Lincoln.] 17603

Poem on the death of Captain Biddle. 8120

Poem on the death of Capt. N. Biddle. 25891

[Poem on the death of Daniel Webster.] 58913

Poem, on the death of Deacon Willam [sic] Barns. 64650

Poem on the death of General George Washington. 42360

Poem on the death of Joseph Green. 56230

Poem on the death of His Late Majesty King George. 9713

Poem on the death of Mr. Whitefield. 103135

Poem on the death of the late Thomas Hollis. (73885)

Poem on the enemy's first coming to Boston. 63626

Poem on the execution of Levi Ames. 95296

Poem. On the execution of Samuel Frost. 105352

Poem on the execution of William Shaw. 79965

Poem, on the existence of God. 841

Poem, on the fourth of July, 1798. 74351

Poem on the glorious achievements of Admiral Vernon. 99249

Poem on the happiness of America. 33804, 33812

Poem; on the independence of America. (40932), 97379

Poem on the inhumanity of the slave-trade. 106007

Poem, on the joyful news of the Rev. Mr. Whitefield's visit to Boston. 103642

Poem on the late massacre in Virginia. 100510

Poem on the life and death of the Hon. Abraham Lincoln. 70760

Poem on the Lord's Day. 42870

Poem on the loss of the steamer President. 8789

Poem, on the mineral waters. (78649)

Poem on the peace. 65528, 97745

Poem, on the pleasures and advantages of true religion. 33950

Poem on the President's farewell address. 32785, 63588, 3d note after 101872

Poem on the prospects of America. 47003-47004

Poem, on the rise and progress of Moor's Indian Charity-School. 63590, 103208

Poem, on the rising glory of America. 7190, 25904

Poem, on the social state and its future progress. 63054

Poem on the taking of the Havannah. 57148

Poem on the war in the West Indies. 63592, 99249

Poem on visiting the Academy of Philadelphia. 84643

Poem . . . one hundredth anniversary of the incorporation of Westminster, Mass. (31090)

Poem or vision. 160212

Poem, partly founded on fact. 23663

Poem, personal and political. 52196

Poem presented to His Excellency William Burnet, Esq. 9378, (63593)

Poem pronounced at Cambridge, February 23, 1815. 101390

Poem, pronounced at the installation of the officers. 64778

Poem pronounced before the Phi Beta Kappa Society of Yale College. 68028

Poem pronounced at Geneva, N. Y. 33115

Poem pronounced at Roxbury, October VIII, MDCCCXXX. (28413)

Poem, pronounced before the Calliopean Society. 94589

Poem pronounced before the Phi Beta Kappa Society, at Cambridge. 8342

Poem pronounced before the Phi Beta Kappa Society of Yale College. (81015)

Poem pronounced before the Phi Beta Kappa Society, Yale College. 31262

Poem pronounced before the Senior Class of Yale College. 2690

Poem: pronounced by James Barron Hope. 32902

Poem, pronounced at the reunion of the Mt. Holyoke Class of 1864. 85524

Poem read before the Bangor Debating Club. 85516

Poem read before the Delta Kappa Sigma. (48865)

Poem read before the Phi Beta Kappa Society of Harvard University. 6170

Poem read before the Society of the Sons of New England, in Pennsylvania. 58342

Poem, read on the same occasion. (68253)

Poem recited at a meeting in Duxbury of the descendants. 87288

Poem, recited before the citizens of Edgartown. 18811

Poem, recited before the New Bedford Mechanics' Association. (72490)

Poem, recited before the Philermenian Society of Brown University. (64147)

Poem recited by St. George Tucker, Esq. 97607

Poem recited . . . on the Festival of the Pilgrims. 13414

Poem: sacred to the memory of George Washington. 964

Poem sacred to the memory of James Wolfe, Esq. 104989, 106117

Poem sacred to the memory of Mrs. Abigail Conant. 15087

Poem sacred to the memory of the Honorable Josiah Willard. 57211, note after 104061

Poem, satirical, allegorical, and moral, in three cantos. 105177

Poem, satirical and sentimental. 105189

Poem spoken at Cambridge, before the Phi Beta Kappa Society. (28387)

Poem spoken at the annual commencement of the Episcopal Academy. (65945)

Poem, spoken at the Exhibition of the Trinity College Parthenon. (71275)

Poem, spoken at the public commencement at Yale College. 3427, 105785A

Poem, spoken extempore, by a young lady. 63594, note after 106139

Poem spoken in the Chapel of Yale-College. 47398

Poem spoken on the summit of Wamang Mountain. 70443

Poem, suggested by scenes in the Brazils. 98242

Poem. Supposed to be sung at a love feast. 66541, 89481

Poem. To General Conway. 59410

Poem . . . to House of Convocation, 1856. 55382

Poem to James Oglethorpe, Esq. on his arrival from Georgia. 27079, 3d note after 106134

Poem. To Sir Thomas Robinson, Bart. 102451

Poem, to the memory of American heroes and statesmen. 93082

Poem to the memory of Aquila Rose. (6107), 73235

Poem, to the memory of John Eliot. 18470

Poem to the Rev. Messrs. Ramsay and Clarkson. 66540

Poem upon Admiral Vernon. 34967, 63595, 99249

Poem upon the death of Mrs. Martha Chandler. 63596

Poem, upon the great disaster, at Lawrence, Mass. (30224)

Poem, upon the much honoured and very exemplarily gracious Mrs. Maria Mather. 63597

Poem upon the undertaking of the Royal Company of Scotland. 73787

Poem which obtained the Chancellor's Medal. 100901

Poem which the Committee of the Town of Boston had voted unanamously to be published. 833, 6738

Poem.. . . with a prose introduction. 83611

Poem; with an allegory on life and futurity. (74635)

Poem. With an appendix. (41247), note after 99626

Poem with an illustration, from the London Punch. 41167, note before 94542

Poem; with appropriate notes. 103335

Poem; with explanatory notes. 39187

Poem, with historical and explanatory notes. 68635

Poem, with three portraits. 35875

Poem, without notes. 3969, 52150

Poem, written and published for the benefit of the sufferers. 44345

Poem written at sea. 94657

Poem written at sea, and in the West Indies. 57798

Poem written for his little son. 104261

Poem, written for the centennial celebration, June 16, 1852. 18513, (55190)

Poem, written the year 1775. 13165

Poem, wrote by a clergyman in Virginia, in a storm of wind and rain. 96323

Poema. 29351, 34437, 44356, 57303-57304, 63203, 63598, 64398, 96058, 106322, 106324

Poema a la solemne y magnifica funcion. 9765

Poema Americano. 19963

Poema (con notas y documentos) por Estevan Echeverria. (21773)

Poema de la comte. 39601

Poema de la proclamacion de Carlos III. (11445)

Poema del ciudadano Jose Maria Villasenor Cervantes. 99680

Poema di Ormildo Emeressio. 29112

Poema endecasilabo. 64192

Poema endecasylabo didactaco, en XIV cantos. (70786)

Poema epico. 50119

Poema epico de la vida de Santo Tomas de Aquino. 74852

Poema epico do descubrimiento da Bahia. 21416

Poema epico em XII cantos. 76331

Poema epico, la rendicion de Panzacola y conquista de la Florida Occidental. 26478, 72805

Poema eroico di Giovanni Villifranchi Volterran. 99744

Poema eroico mitologico. 94288

Poema eroico, publicado por la primera vez. 56240, note after 89754

Poema eroicomico d'Androvinci Melisone. 94402

Poema heroico a felicissima jornada d'el-Rei D. Joa V. 47855

Poema heroico en que se decanta. 60852, 63182

Poema heroyco. 74025

Poema heroyco, en celebridad de la colocacion de la estatua colosal. (39084)

Poema heroyco Hispano-Latino panegyrico. 98322

Poema heroyco. Por Don Jose de Escioquiz. 22839

Poema heroyco. [Por Luis Antonio de Oviedo y Herrera.] 58033

Poema historica. 50121, 56608

Poema historico. 50121, 56608

Poema historico descriptivo escrito en variedad de metros. 97004

Poema historico sagrado en quatro cantos. 14626

Poema joco-serioco. 46200

Poema libris duobus. 95622

Poema panegerico. 63306

Poema por D. J. G. de Magalhaes. 43793

Poema pronunciado en la instalacion de la Academia de Jurisprudencia. 80894

Poema, que en verso heroico Latino escribio. 51558

Poema sacro compuesto por el R. P. M. F. Fernando de Valuerde. 98404

Poema sacro de Nuestra Senora de Guadaloupe. 27787, 80983

Poema sacro e tragi-comico. 88719

Poema sacro-historico. 80973

Poemas. 48881

Poemas Brasilicos do Padre Christovao Valente. 19556

Poemas Castellanos. 98826

Poemas de Francisco Villela Barbosa natural de Rio de Janeiro. 99733

Poemas de la unica poetisa Americana, musa dezima. 17733, 17735, note after 34687, 36815

Poemas epicos. (2864)

Poemata [Mar. Ant. Sabellici.] 74664

Poemata [P. Martyris ab Angleria.] 45013

Poemata nunc primum impressa. 26503

Poemata omnia in vnum collecta. 26503

Poemata sacra in candidatorum Latinitatis gratiam elucubrata. 63599, 75999

Poeme. 27630, 38760, (41912), 73519, 75507, 95376

Poeme d'Ermengaud de Besiers. 76838

Poeme de Las-Casas. 73482

Poeme de six religievses Ursulines. 63600

Poeme didactique. 94164

Poeme dramatique. 41217

Poeme eclectique, en deux chants. 44919

Poeme en dix chants. 73482

Poeme en seize chants. 29250

Poeme en six chants. 39999

Poeme geographique de Goro Dati. 76838

Poeme geographique du XVe. siecle. 76838

Poeme Indo-Americain. (41928)

Poemes. 47925

Poemetti [di Gabriello Chiabrera.] 12614

Poemitas de Mariano de Jesus. 76222

Poemme; ye whykl bin spokenne bie Robberte. 105937

Poems and ballads. (82526)

Poems and compositions in prose. 51316

Poems and essays by Edgar Allan Poe. 63534

Poems and fugitive pieces. 18197

Poems and juvenile sketches. 102583

Poems and letter to Don Brown. 33774

Poems and plays, by William Richardson. (71089)

Poems and prose writings. By Richard H. Dana. 18441

Poems and prose writings [by Sumner Lincoln Fairfield.] 23695

Poems and sketches. [By Edgar Allan Poe.] 63571

Poems and sketches. By the late James William Miller. 49025

Poems and tales. 63601

Poems and tales in verse. 38765

Poems and translations. By Richard Dabney. 18250

Poems and translations, written between the ages of fourteen and seventeen. 39477

Poems both Latin and English. 104655

Poems. By a collegian. 81246

Poems by a Harvard student. 63602

Poems by a priest. 63603

Poems by a proser. 63604

Poems by a slave in the island of Cuba. 63605

Poems, by a South Carolinian. 63606, 3d note after 88114

Poems, by a young lady of Charleston. 63607

Poems, by a young nobleman. 42894

Poems [by Alexander H. Everett.] 23237

Poems. By Alexander M'Lachlan. 43483

Poems, by Alexander Wilson. 104603

Poems . . . [By Alonzo Lewis.] 40783

Poems. By Amanda T. Jones. 36453

Poems. By Amelia. 102515

Poems by an American. 62629

Poems. By Anne C. Lynch. 42808

Poems. By Astarte. 63608

Poems. By Augustus Julian Requier. 70055

Poems. By Caroline A. Briggs [Mason.] (45426)

Poems by Clement C. Moore. 50338

Poems. [By Charles G. Eastman.] (21672)

Poems by Col. David Humphreys. 33814

Poems . . . [by Cornelia J. M. Jordan.] 36642

Poems by Croaker, Croaker & Co., and Croaker, Jr. 20861

Poems, by Synthia Taggart. 94202

Poems. By D. Hardy, Jr. 30353

Poems. By David Hitchcock. 32237

Poems. By Dexter Smith, Jr. 82434

Poems. By Dr. J. Haynes. 31053

Poems. By Edgar A. Poe. 63531-(63532)

Poems by Edgar Allan Poe. (63533)

Poems, by Edward C. Pinkney. 62965

Poems. By Edward Stagg. 90087

Poems. By Edward S. Seward. 79492

Poems, by Eliza Allen Starr. 90547

Poems. [By Eliza Lee Follen.] 24955

Poems. By Ellolie. 48942

Poems. By Emma M. Blake. 69363

Poems by Eulalie. 79765

Poems, by Francis S. Osgood. (57779)

Poems by Frances Sargent Osgood. 57780

Poems. By Frederick Wing Cole. 14286

Poems. By Gay H. Naramore. 51766

Poems by George Bancroft. 3142

Poems. By George Lunt. 42704

Poems. By Gold-Pen. 63609

Poems. By Grace Greenwood. 41402

Poems by H. R. S. and H. W. 77876, 103695

Poems. By Hannah Flagg Gould. (28105)

Poems. By Helen M. Johnson. 36217

Poems, by Helen Maria Williams. 104230

Poems. By Henry Howard Brownell. (8687)

Poems. By Henry Wadsworth Longfellow. 41918

Poems. By Isaac C. Pray, Jr. 64989

Poems. [By Isaac Clark.] (13299)

Poems, by Jacob Porter. (64262)

Poems. By James G. Percival. 60967

Poems. By James Nack. 51700

Poems. By James Russell Lowell. (42436)

Poems, by James Sommarsall. 86844

Poems, by James T. Fields. 24301

Poems. [By Jedediah Vincent Huntington.] 33970

Poems. By John Cleveland. 13661

Poems. By John Edmund Harwood. (30788)

Poems. By John G. Saxe. 77341

Poems, by John G. Whittier. 103811, 103815

Poems, by John Marriott. (44692)

Poems by John Newland Maffitt. 43786

Poems . . . . [By John Savage.] 77237

Poems . . . [By McDonald Clarke.] (13435)

Poems. By Martha A. Smith. 83528

Poems. By Mary H. Pumpelly. 66651

Poems. By Matilda. 82283

Poems. By Meditatus. 63610

Poems by Michael Drayton. 20916

Poems, by Milton Ward. 101316

Poems. By Miss C. B. Sinclair. 81392

Poems by Miss Eliza A. Pitzinger, of San Francisco. 63163

Poems by Miss Seward. (79488)

Poems: by Mrs. Anna Marie Spaulding. 89029

Poems by Mrs. Elizabeth Hawes. 30917

Poems. By Mrs. Julia H. Scott. (78334)

Poems; by Mrs. L. H. Sigourney. 80944-(80945)

Poems, by Mrs. Mary Noel McDonald. 43165

Poems. By N. P. Willis. 104509

Poems. [By Oliver Wendell Holmes.] 32621

Poems. By Phil. Frank. Perry. 61048

Poems. By Ralph Waldo Emerson. 22458

Poems. By Rev. John N. M'Jilton. 43339

Poems by Richard B. Davis. 18880

Poems by Robert M. and Thomas J. Charlton. 12151

Poems by Robert Southey. 88556, 88566

Poems, by Rosa Vertuer Johnson. 36290

Poems. By Samuel Low. (42404)

Poems . . . by S. J. Coleridge. 14322

Poems, by S. Louisa P. Smith. 84135

Poems by St. John Honeywood. 32786

Poems. By Samuel Browning. 8696

Poems [by Sir Walter Raleigh.] 67598

Poems: by the author of "Moral pieces in prose and verse." 80943

Poems by the late Dr. John Shaw. 79924

Poems, by the late George Heartwell Spierin. 89435

Poems, by the late Hosias Lyndon Arnold. 2074

Poems. By the late John Augustus Shea. (79990)

Poems by the Rev. Cameron Mann. 44310

Poems. By the Rev. J. Hoyland. 33396

Poems; by the Rev. John H. Hanson. 30268

Poems by the Rev. Wheeler Case. 11304

Poems . . . [by Theophilus H. Hill.] 31863

Poems by Thomas Buchanan Read. 68181

Poems by Thomas Buchanan Read, George G. Boker, Francis de Haes Janvier, and other American authors. 51437

Poems . . . [by Thomas Kennedy.] 37439
Poems by Thomas Romney Robinson. 72197
Poems by Thomas William Parsons. 58913
Poems: by Una. 43584
Poems. [By Walter Mitchell.] (49727)
Poems, by William B. Tappan. 94375
Poems. By William B. Walter. 101202
Poems by William Cullen Bryant. (8821)-(8822)
Poems by William Ellery Channing. 11927-11928
Poems [by William Gilmore Simms.] 81258
Poems . . . [By William H. Holcombe.] 32469
Poems by William James Colgan. (14345)
Poems. By William James McClure. 43078
Poems by William Maxwell, Esq. 47058
Poems, by William W. Lord. 42052
Poems chiefly amatory. 63611
Poems chiefly imaginative. 81190
Poems, chiefly in the Scottish dialect. By Alexander Wilson. 104604
Poems, chiefly in the Scottish dialect. By Robert Burns. 9407
Poems, chiefly in the Scottish dialect, origin-ally written under the signature of the Scots-Irishman. 8730
Poems, chiefly occasional. (13694)
Poems, chiefly rural. 71088
Poems, collected and arranged by the author. 8823
Poems, comprising tales, fugitive pieces, and translations. 81323
Poems: comprising the Trial of Cain. 63612
Poems: containing the Indian, and Lazarus. 63613
Poems. Davies. 100579
Poems, descriptive and moral. 43634
Poems, descriptive, dramatic, legendary, and contemplative. 81247
Poems, dramatic and miscellaneous. 101486
Poems, edited by S. Russel. 74293
Poems. First, on the soul pleading with God. 63614
Poems fit for a bishop. (63615)
Poems for children. (80946)
Poems for the gay and merry. 62925
Poems for the hour. 4101
Poems for the old and young. 92805
Poems for the sea. 80947
Poems for the times. 38006
Poems: gleanings from spare hours of a busi-ness life. 39449
Poems, . . . Illustrated with . . . engravings on wood. 41919
Poems in Comitiis Collegii Columbiani pronun-tiatum. 28818
Poems in sunshine and firelight. (62597)
Poems, lyric and pastoral. 104195
Poems, lyrical and idyllic. 91063
Poems moral and divine. 63616
Poems, moral and religious. 82352
Poems, moral and sentimental. 51616, 95226
Poems, moral, descriptive, and political. 96185
Poems, moral, religious, & descriptive. 44715
Poems, national and patriotic. 18197
Poems. Now first collected. 28836
Poems occasioned by several circumstances. 11303, 63617
Poems occasioned by the recent visit of Lafayette. 8786
Poems, odes, songs, and other metrical effu-sions. 105192
Poems of Alfred B. Street. 92773
Poems [of Anna Bradstreet.] note after 94823
Poems of Arouet. 38518
Poems [of Du Bartas.] (30701)
Poems of G. C. Lane. (38853)

Poems of faith and affection. 48920
Poems of Frank Myrtle. 89305
Poems of George D. Prentice. 65063
Poems of George P. Morris. 50823
Poems of home and country. 84056
Poems of Ixtlilxochitl. 28255
Poems of J. O. T. 94894
Poems of John Godfrey Saxe. 77342-77343
Poems of John Howard Bryant. 8808
Poems of Leisure moments. 31080
Poems of Ossian. 79399
Poems of Philip Freneau. 25897
Poems of Robert Lowell. (42468)
Poems of Scott, and Logan. 78300
Poems [of Sir Henry Wotton.] 67599
Poems of Sir Walter Raleigh. 67599
Poems of the Boston Bard. 14187, (63618)
Poems of the Confederate States. (35421)
Poems of the late Francis S. Key. 37667
Poems of the Mohawk Valley. 10177
Poems of the prairies. 8533
Poems of the republic. (6932)
Poems of the Rt. Rev. George Burgess. 9243
Poems of the war. 6171
Poems of Thomas D'Arcy McGee. 43263
Poems [of Thomas Fitzgerald.] note after 102702
Poems of two friends. 62596
Poems of William B. Tappan. 94376
Poems of William B. Tappan, not contained in a former volume. 94377
Poems of William Cullen Bryant. (8824)
Poems of William Wye Smith. 84918
Poems on America. 63619
Poems on comic, serious, and moral subjects. 103137
Poems, on different subjects. 63620
Poems on divers subjects. 7784
Poems on man, in his various aspects. 46838, 46840
Poems on religion and society. 297
Poems, on religious and historical subjects. 102455
Poems on several occasions. . . . By a gentle-man of Virginia. 63621
Poems on several occasions, by Aquila Rose. 73235
Poems on several occasions. By John Swanwick 94025
Poems on several occasions. By the late Rev. Thomas Brown. 8566
Poems on several occasions, original and translated. 222
Poems on several occasions; to which are annexed; extracts from a journal. 29139
Poems on several occasions, with some other compositions. 23179, 84610, 84678C
Poems, on several occasions. Written in Pennsylvania. 84838-84841
Poems on several occurrences in the present grand struggle. 63622
Poems on several subjects. Written by Stephen Duck. 21064
Poems on several subjects; by the Rev. John Anketell. 105985
Poems on slavery. By Henry Wadsworth Longfellow. 41920
Poems on slavery, by Longfellow, Whittier, Southey, etc. (63623)
Poems on slavery: by Maria Falconar. 23720
Poems on slavery for Christmas, 1843. (81929)
Poems on slavery, grave, humorous, didactic, and satirical. 9309
Poems on some of the principal events of the late war. 65528, 97745

Poems, on subjects arising in England, and the West Indies. 63624

Poems on the abolition of the slave trade. 50145

Poems on the most solemn subjects. 95461

Poems on the several successes in America. 63625

Poems on various occasions. 65226

Poems on various subjects and different occasions. 78659

Poems on various subjects, but chiefly on the events and actors in the American war of independence. 25900

Poems on various subjects. By G. Walker. 101048

Poems on various subjects. . . . By Isabella Oliver. 57205

Poems on various subjects. [By J. C. Pickett.] 62672

Poems on various subjects. By Joseph Hazard. 31098

Poems on various subjects. By Judah Wright. 105615

Poems on various subjects, by Phillis Wheatley. 22714, 98661, 103139

Poems on various subjects, by Rev. Judge A. J. Cotton. 17038

Poems on various subjects, entertaining, elegaic and religious. 11593

Poems on various subjects, moral and entertaining. 39282, 103139

Poems on various subjects, religious and moral. 103138-103139

Poems on various subjects, religious, moral, sentimental and humorous. 68035

Poems, on various subjects, written by a youth. 106203

Poems on various subjects, viz. on the birth of Christ. 101370

Poems, or metrical gossamar thoughts. 50640

Poems, original and translated. 18251

Poems original, &c. 79322

Poems read at the opening of the Fraternity lectures. 76250

Poems relating to the American revolution. 25901

Poems, religious and elegiac. (80948)

Poems, religious, historical, and political. 85505-85506

Poems: sacred, passionate, and legendary. 91036

Poems, sentimental and descriptive. 74350

Poems sur des sujets pris de l'histoire de notre temps. 18222

Poems sur l'esclavage. 41915

Poems: the birth-day, a dramatic entertainment. 60793

Poems: the conflagration. 9714

Poems to the memory of C. H. 18327

Poems, . . . to which is added A descriptive account of a family tour. 30826

Poems upon several occasions. 63626

Poems, upon several sermons. 103643

Poems: with a sketch of the life and experiences of Annie R. Smity. 83749

Poems. With notes. By an Octogenarian. 29898, 69696

Poems written and published during the American revolutionary war. (25899)

Poems written between the years 1768 & 1794. 25898

Poems written chiefly in the West-Indies. By Byran Edwards. 21906

Poems, written chiefly in the West-Indies. [By Isaac Teale.] 94565

Poems written during the progress of the abolition question. 103816

Poems, written in Newfoundland. 65247

Poepe, Claude de la. see La Poepe, Claude de.

Poepoe, Josef M. tr. 83132, 83226

Poeppig, Eduard. 63627

Poesche, Theodore. 63631

Poesia a inauguracao da estatua equestre. 88809

Poesia inedita. 31482

Poesias. 72510

Poesias Americana. (29347)

Poesias Brazileiras. 88808

Poesias curiosas. 72563

Poesias de Basilio Jose de Oliveira Pinto. 62987

Poesias de D. Feliz M. Escalante. 22814

Poesias de D. Luis G. Ortiz. 57721

Poesias de Gonzalo Peoli. 60815

Poesias de Jose Marmol. 44649

Poesias de Jose Rivera Indarte. (34436)

Poesias de Juan Maria Gutierrez. 29348

Poesias de Manuel R. Plama. 58336

Poesias de Placido. 98308

Poesias de Ramon Velez Herrera. 31571, note after 98827

Poesias de un joven Americano. 63632

Poesias del ciudadano Dr. Jose Fernandez de Madrid. 43759

Poesias del ciudadano F. Ortega. 57675

Poesias del ciudadano Jose M. Heredia. 31482

Poesias del Coronel Don Manuel de Zequeira y Arango. 106323

Poesias del Sr. Doctor Don Manuel Carpio. (11019)

Poesias d'un Portuguez. 11217

Poesias en la vistosa porteria. 29336

Poesias liricas. 75913

Poesias Mexicanas por Jesus Echiaz. 21759

Poesias offerandos as Senhoras Brasileiras. 1869

Poesias originales y traducidas. 61172

Poesias que en obsequio de los primeros padres de la patria. 63633

Poesias liricas de D. J. M. Roa Barcena. 71704

Poesias que para el plausible dia en que la nobilisima ciudad de Mexico juro solumnemente la constitucion de la monarquia Espanola. 99683

Poesias tomadas de los antiguos cantares Mexicanos. 61171

Poesias varias a Ntra. Sra. de Guadalupe de Mexico. 76432

Poesias varias en loor de la independencia. 63634

Poesias varias sagradas y profanas. 76895

Poesias y oracion con que la Real Universidad de Cervera aplaudia. 51216

Poesie [di Gabriello Chiabrera.] 12614

Poesie et la philosophie d'un Turc a 81 queues. 106251

Poesie varie. 64014

Poesies Americaines. 73477

Poesies choises de Jean-Simon Chaudron. 12291

Poesies composees par des Negres. 92533

Poesies diverses. [Par Antoine-Leonard Thomas.] 95376

Poesies diverses, par Constant Lepouze. 40131

Poesies diverses. [Par Edouard Corbiere.] 16751

Poesies en langue Tupique. 73458

Poesies nouvelles par Dominique Roquette. (73480)

Poesies nouvelles. [Par Edouard Corbiere.] 16751
Poesies [par Chateaubriand.] 12248
Poesies. Par E. Lemerle. 40000
Poet. pseud. Three voices. see Read, T. B.
Poet. 89654
Poet among the hills. 83330, 83334
Poet and his sons. 63635
Poet laureate of the Know Nothings. pseud. Modern battle of the keys. 49804
Poet-soldier. 8980
Poeta e a inquisicao. 43792
Poetic art. 104817
Poetic miscellany. 30892
Poetic reader. (22449)
Poetic reverie. (62740)
Poetic reveries. 72051
Poetic tale. By a near relation of Old Mother Hubbard. 103295
Poetic tale of the western wilderness. 14192
Poetic tale. The scenery American. 49423
Poetic tributes. 76957
Poetic trifles. (49109)
Poetica idea del arco. 98162
Poetical account of the American campaigns of 1812 and 1813. 17223, 63636
Poetical address. 73617
Poetical address, delivered by Doctor Laurence Reynolds. 70439
Poetical address for the benefit of the Boston Bard. 8785
Poetical address to the nymphs of Saratoga Mineral Springs. 94661
Poetical and miscellaneous works of James Eliot. 22230
Poetical and prose illustrations of celebrated American painters. 63637
Poetical and prose writings of Charles Sprague. 89663-89664
Poetical and prose writings of Dr. John Lofland. 41784
Poetical and prose writings of James Linen. 41320
Poetical and prose writings of John Lofland. 41783
Poetical attempt. 33430, 105926
Poetical chronology of ancient and English history. 98395
Poetical chronology of English and American history. 63638
Poetical composition delivered in Yale College. 3428
Poetical descant on the primeval and present state of mankind. 63639, 95430
Poetical descant, or the pilgrim's muse. 63639
Poetical description of a Methodist camp-meeting. 63640
Poetical description of Lincoln's assassination. 41220
Poetical description of Texas. 37627
Poetical description of the existing controversy. 4664, note after 102109
Poetical description of the great and last judgment. 103917, 103918-103920, 103922-103923
Poetical description of the great and last judgment, abridged. 103921
Poetical dialogue between the envoys of America, X. Y. Z. and a lady. 13883
Poetical dialogues, calculated for the help of tumorous and tempted Christians. 70870
Poetical dictionary. (32239)
Poetical discription of the great and last judgment. 103918
Poetical dream, concerning stamped papers. 52576

Poetical effusions. 43789
Poetical epistle. 60919
Poetical epistle from the author in that island to a friend in England. 35592
Poetical epistle. Heroic and satirical. 58782
Poetical epistle, to a young friend. 97577
Poetical epistle to His Excellency George Washington. 94893, 103093
Poetical epistle to the enslaved Africans. 63642
Poetical epistle to the King of Hayti. 63643
Poetical epistle to the Rev. Dr. Robertson. 63644
Poetical epistle to the Right Honourable Lord N-----. 97634
Poetical essay, by a stander by. (65727)
Poetical essay. [By Beilby Porteus.] 64328
Poetical essay [by "Sympathes."] 1829, 94517, 104056
Poetical essay, delivered at Bennington. 3549?
Poetical essay, in imitation of Miltonic style. 59075
Poetical essay on the course of human action. 509
Poetical fate book. 85410
Poetical fragment, by a gentleman formerly of Boston. 6927
Poetical gift to the patrons of the Western spy. (63645)
Poetical history of the successive triumphs. 97012
Poetical illustrations of the Athenaeum Gallery. 6594, 63646
Poetical illustrations on each subject, by Andrew M'Makin. 61913, 103971
Poetical journal of a tour from British North America to England. 17224
Poetical legends: containing the American captive. 63648, note after 94220
Poetical meditations, being the improvement of some vacant hours. 104986
Poetical miscellany. 57762
Poetical nosegay. 100863
Poetical novel. 79476
Poetical oration by a southern nabob. 82113
Poetical paraphrase of Our Savior's Sermon on the mount. 17434
Poetical pen-pictures of the war. 31079
Poetical performance at the literary exhibition. 93691
Poetical petition against galvanizing trumpery. 24218, note after 94875
Poetical picture of America. (63648)
Poetical pieces written on several occasions. 19812
Poetical relation of the capture of the congregation. (75265)
Poetical remains of Lucretia Maria Davidson. 18734
Poetical remains fo Mary Elizabeth Lee. 39777
Poetical remains of the late Lucy Hooper. 32873
Poetical remains, with addenda. 42756
Poetical retrospect. 66797
Poetical rhapsody. 89475
Poetical rhapsody, addressed to her. 96500
Poetical rhapsody on the times. 14018, note after 95866
Poetical romance. 62826
Poetical scraps. 71244
Poetical selections, from the best English and American authors. (71234)
Poetical sinnings of William Rufus. (73926)
Poetical sketch of Fowler and Well's phrenological museum. 63649

Poetical tale of Patagonia. 34044
Poetical thought, or paraphrase. 101448
Poetical tract, describing the adventures. 70890
Poetical tributes to the memory of Abraham Lincoln. (41221)
Poetical vagaries of a Knight of the Folding-Stick. (32170), 63650
Poetical vision. 63647, note after 94220
Poetical wanderer. 63651
Poetical works . . . . Complete edition. 41924
Poetical works, . . . illustrated with upwards of one hundred designs. 41921
Poetical works, including his translations and notes. 41922
Poetical works of Anna Seward. 79489
Poetical works of Augustine J. H. Duganne. 21156
Poetical works of Charles G. Halpine. (29920)
Poetical works of David Hitchcock. (32238)
Poetical works of Edgar Allan Poe. (63537)- 63539
Poetical works of Edgar Allan Poe and Richard H. Dana. 63536
Poetical works of Edgar Allan Poe with a notice of his life and genius. 63535
Poetical works of Edmund Clarence Stedman. 90164
Poetical works of Elizabeth M. Chandler. (11856)
Poetical works of Fitz-Greene Halleck. 29875
Poetical works of George M. Horton. 33070
Poetical works of George Sandys. (76455), (76468)
Poetical works of Hector Macneill, Esq. 43603
Poetical works of Henry W. Longfellow. 41923
Poetical works of James Gates Percival. 60868
Poetical works of James R. Lowell. (42437)
Poetical works of John and Charles Wesley. 102643
Poetical works of John Scott. 78301
Poetical works of John Trumbull. note before 97204, 97207, 97210, 97234
Poetical works [of Joseph Williams.] 104301
Poetical works of Mrs. L. H. Sigourney. 80949
Poetical works of Samuel Woodworth. 105193
Poetical works of William H. C. Hosmer. 33115
Poetical writings of Elizabeth Oakes Smith. (82515)
Poetical writings, . . . with extracts from those of Joseph Rodman Drake. 29876
Poeticarvm institvtionvm liber cariis ethnicorvm, 63652, 73861
Poetische Erzahlung. 92746
Poetischer Zuruff an die Saltzburgischen Emigraten. 99391
Poetry. 98634
Poetry. A poem before the Franklin Debating Society. 45446
Poetry and history of Wyoming. 92132, 92150- 92151
Poetry, . . . by an Irish gentleman. (49452)
Poetry for children. 80967
Poetry for home and school. 42420
Poetry for schools. 71809
Poetry for seamen. 80950
Poetry of animated nature illustrated. 83844
Poetry of death. 12150
Poetry of feeling, and spiritual melodies. 80184
Poetry of freedom, by her friends. 55730, note after 103813
Poetry of locofocoism. 73236
Poetry of Nieuw-Neder-Landt. 51466

Poetry of Pope. 33248-33249
Poetry of the port folio. 57215
Poetry of travelling in the United States. 27429
Poetry on different subjects. 25269
Poetry original and select. 63653
Poets and poetry. 28491
Poets and poetry of America; a satire. 63654
Poets and poetry of America. With an historical illustration. (28895), 84156, 85433
Poets and poetry of the west. 14201
Poets and poetry of Vermont. 31283, 1st note after 99199
Poet's home. 38114, 1st note after 95623
Poet's leisure hours, no. 1. 63655
Poet's magazine. 90002
Poets of America. Illustrated by one of her painters. 37163
Poets of America, with occasional notes. 12395
Poets of Connecticut. (23219)
Poets of Great Britain. (28249)
Poets of Portsmouth. 59307
Poets of the west. 39072
Poet's offerings. 63656
Poet's song for the heart and the home. 61398
Poey, Andres. 29445, 63657-63667, 74935
Poey, Felipe, 63668-63673
Poey, Juan. (63674)-63676
Poey, Philip. see Poey, Felipe.
Poezias de Joao Candido. 10670
Poggi, A. C. de. (65028), 97249
Poggio-Bracciolini, 1380-1459. 67730
Pogommega, Rombusto. pseud. Marineide risate. see Borbazza, Andrea.
Pohl, Johann Emanuel. 63677-63680
Pohlman, H. N. (63681)
Poignet d'Acier, ou les Chippuouais. 12569
Poillon, ---------. tr. (23573)
Poincten van consideratie. 63682
Poincy, Lonvilliers de. 72316
Poincy, Lonvilliers de. incorrectly supposed author 72314
Poindexter, A. M. 36094
Poindexter, Geroge, 1779-1855. 9947, 49542, 63683-63686, 71742
Poindexter's Executor. defendant 33256
Poinsett, Joel Roberts, 1779-1851. 63687- 63697, 96721 see also U. S. Commissioner to the Sioux Indians. U. S. War Department.
Point-a-Pitre, ode. 72256
Point Breeze Park Association, Philadelphia. 63698
Point Breeze Park Association, Philadelphia. Charter. 63698
Point au Pelee Island. 84330
Point de la question sur les colonies. 41904
Point of honor. 71038
Pointer, John. (63699)
Pointi, ------ de. see Pointis, J. B. D. de.
Pointis, J. B. D. de. (10757), 31360, 63700- 73706, 2d note after (69261)
Points and authorities in support of the Price Charity. 18450, 65470
Points for consideration. 60358
Points in canon law. 84192, 84195
Points on claim to be the Grand Division of the New-York. 87059
Pointu, Jerome. 94614
Poirie de Saint-Aurele, De la Guadeloupe. (63707)-63708
Poirre, F. 63709, 70357
Poirson, J. B. cartographer (72039)
Poirson, M. cartographer 39603-39604
Poisle Desgranges, J. 63710
Poisson, Jo. Bapt. (63711)

Poissonnier, -------. (63712), 65984
Poissonnier-Desperrieres, -------. 19754, (63713)
Poissons. 74922
Poissons de l'ile de Cuba. 63673
Poissons ecrevisses et crabes. 69600
Poisy, ---------, Chevalier de. 63714
Poivre, Pierre. (63715)-63722, note after 100837
Poivre, Pierre. supposed author 1292
Poix Ferminville, M. J. de la. see La Poix Ferminville, M. J. de.
Pok. (22866)
Pok. Kalalek avalangnek. (22866), 63723
Polack, Joel S. petitioner (63724)
Polanco, Gabriel Roman i. 63725
Poland, Charles A. 14894, 56879
Poland, John S. ed. (63726)
Poland, Luke Potter, 1815-1887. (63727)-63728
Polar region. 57759
Polar regions. 71030
Polar regions of the western continent explored. 85426, 85428-85429
Polar exploring expedition. 1092
Polar seas and regions. 40202
Polar world. (30719)
Polarexpeditionen und die dabei gemachten wichtigern Entdeckungen. (24592)
Polarfahrt. 38242
Polari, Constant. 31487, 63730
Pole, Thomas. 96286
Pole, William. 35873
Pole nord. (21011)
Pole nord et l'equateur. (21011)
Pole nord, ou voyages et decouvertes dans les regions Arctiques. 39622
Polemical reflections. 29757
Polemical tale. 36919
Polemique sur les evenements de la Grand' Anse. 5652
Poles in the United States of America. 38297
Poletica, Pierre. 63731-63732, 93997
Poleur, Jean. tr. (57993)
Polhemus, Abraham. 63733-63734
Polhill, Charles. 56462, note after 63734
Polhill, David. respondent (11193)-11194
Poli, Baldassare. 63735
Police guard. 63736
Police manual. (62067)
Police record of the spies. 24585, (24587)
Police records and recollections. 77228
Polichinelle, Platon. 63737
Polichronicon de Ranulphus Hygeden. 76838
Policy and conduct of the American war. 99824
Policy, as well as honesty, forbids the use of secular force. 2632
Policy for the management of its [i. e. the Northern Pacific Railroad Company's] affairs. 55821
Policy for the present expansion of currency. 68582
Policy of appropriations being made. 63738
Policy of emancipation. 58022
Policy of England and France. 83470
Policy of England, Mexico, and Spain. 17765
Policy of England towards Spain. 69708
Policy of finance. A plan for returning to specie payments. 70994
Policy of finance. A plan for returning to specie payments, without financial revulsion. 70993
Policy of ministers. (81854)
Policy of the administration. 37272
Policy of the Democratic Party of the state of N. York. 63739

Policy of the nation, particularly as it respect a navy. 63740
Policy of the penal laws of Ireland. 63741
Policy of the President. (5444)
Polignac, Camille Armand Jules Marie de. 63742
Poliologia. 79635-79636
Polite philosopher. 90230, 90233, 90236-90237, 90246
Polite philosophfr [sic]. 90246
Polite repository of amusement and instruction 54867
Polite traveller. 63743
Politiae ecclesiasticae seu status religionis Christianae. 49405
Politiani, Angeli. see Poliziano, Angelo, 1454-1494.
Politica Brasilera en el Rio de la Plata. 7614 (63744)
Politica—comercio—estadistica—literatura—industria—agricultura. 40726
Politica de escriptvras. 106213
Politica de las grandezas y govierno del Svpremo y Real Consejo de las Indias. 40054
Politica de los Editores del Tiempo. 9585, 63745
Politica de los Estados-Unidos esplicada por los mismos. 63746
Politica del General Comonfort, durante su gobierno en Mejico. 15011
Politica del General Comonfort, y la situacion actual de Mexico. (15012)
Politica i comercio. 93404
Politica Indiana. 86534-86537, 86544-86545
Politica militar en avisos de generales. 44424
Political abolition. 14775
Political account of the island of Trinidad. 63747, 2d note after 96979
Political action of our church members and clergy. 63748
Political address. 101168
Political address as delivered in Masonic Hall. 105598-9 [sic]
Political advantages of Godliness. 40810
Political allegory. By Francis Hopkinson. (32981)
Political allegory. [By George T. Wilburn?] 103961
Political analysis of the war. 63749
Political and civil history of the United States of America. (63045)
Political and commercial changes to follow the war. 82179
Political and commercial importance of completing the line of railway. 52316
Political and commercial works of that celebrated writer Charles D'Avenant. 18687
Political and financial condition of the country. 88919-88920
Political and historical account of Lower Canad 39157
Political and historical register. 9125
Political and legal history of Trinity Church monopoly. 73104
Political and military essays. 38903
Political and miscellaneous works of Thomas Paine. 58233
Political and miscellaneous writings. 27649
Political and moral justice. 63750
Political and natural history of Portugal. 8171
Political and philosophical speculations. 9267, 41332
Political and public life of James K. Polk. 63841

Political and satyrical history of the years 1756-1759. 63751

Political annals of Lower Canada. (24701)

Political annals of South Carolina. (19120)

Political annals of the present United Colonies. 11765, 11766

Political anti-masonry, abolition, and amalgamation. 60394

Political arithmetic. 16621

Political aspect of Louisiana. 63041

Political atheism. 31127

Political balance, dedicated to those citizens. 63752

Poltical balance, in which the principles and conduct of the two parties are weighed. 63753

Political, biographical, historical and literary repository. 52002

Poltical biography of Polke, Dallas and Shunk. 63840

Political cabinet. 21247, (40825)

Political catechism, intended for the use of children. 63754

Political cause and consequences of the protestant "reformation." 43264

Political censor. 14001-14002

Political censor, for April, 1797. 14008

Political censor for December, 1796. 14005

Political censor for January, 1797. 10406

Political censor, for March, 1797. 14007

Political censor for November, 1796. 104004

Political censor for September 1796. 14003

Political censor for 1796. 14005

Political character of John Adams. 229, 14388

Political character of John Quincy Adams delineated. 317

Political character of the said John Adams. 241, (32634)

Political chart of Indiana. 82741

Political class book. 92293, 93558

Political class-book of the state of Pennsylvania. 26158

Political code . . . reported . . . by the Commissioners of the Code. 53857

Political, commercial and moral reflections. 43848

Political, commercial, and statistical sketches of the Spanish empire. (63755)

Political compendium for 1868. 19496

Political conduct of the Earl of Chatham. (63756)

Political conservative circular. 63757

Political conservatism. (66615)

Political considerations. 63758

Political constitution of Jamaica. (35647)

Political constitution of the free state of Coahuila & Texas. 94940

Political contest; containing, a series of letters. (36911)

Political controversy. 63759

Political craft. 63760

Political crisis. 40628, 91938

Political curiosities. 86077

Political debates. 63761

Political debates between Hon. Abraham Lincoln and Hon. Stephen A. Douglas. 41156

Political debates on His Majesty's speech. 100756

Political destiny of Canada. 82684-82685

Political detection. (39703)

Political dialogue. (37324), 3d note after 78761, note after 101786

Political dialogues. 63762

Political, diplomatic, and miscellaneous productions. 74269

Political disabilities. 78036

Political discourse, to the people of Alfred. 94033

Political discussions for 1808. 97271

Political dispatch. 23920

Political disquisitions; or an enquiry into public errors. 9246

Political disquisitions proper for public consideration. 63763

Political duenna. 63764

Political duplicity, the revilers of H. A. Muhlenberg. 51251

Political duties of Christian men and ministers. 82234

Political duties of Christians. 63765, note after 88147

Political duties of scholars. 68068

Political duties of the educated classes. 31875

Political, economical, and literary miscellanies. 36160

Political economists, from Jan. 24, to May 1, 1824. 10889

Political economy. [An examination of the Treasurer's report.] 10889

Political economy and industry. 48862

Political economy. By John McVickar. 43678

Political economy. Essay upon the principles of political economy. (63766)

Political economy for the people. 97307

Political economy: founded in justice and humanity. 95645

Political economy in a nutshell. 63767

Political economy: its objects, uses, and principles. 64614

Political economy—manufactures: being a review. 43091

Political economy of inland navigation. 94415

Political economy of prophecy. 80494

Political economy of slavery. 82031

Political economy of slavery; or, the institution considered. (73917)

Political economy. Read and ponder. 63768

Political education. (47166)

Political effects of the paper system considered. (19272), 94489

Political electricity. 63769

Political elements. 63770

Political empiricism. 63771

Political epistles. 63772

Political equilibrium. 30221

Political essay. 27673

Political essay on the commerce of Portugal. (17950)

Political essay on the kingdom of New Spain. 33715

Political essays. A series of letters addressed to the people of the United States. (62657)

Political essays. [By John M. Galt.] (26460), 63774

Political essays. By Thomas Cooper, Esq. (16614)

Political essay upon commerce written in French. 63773

Political essay upon the English and French colonies. 59082

Political essays. [By Vere Henry Hobart.] (32312)

Political essays concerning the present state of the British empire. 63775, note after 106063

Political essays on the nature and operation of money, public finances, and other subjects. 102402-102404, 102411-102412, 102415

Political essays, relative to the war of the French revolution. 105483

Political reasonings of Edmund Burke, Esq. 100754

Political reconciling-pamphlet. 63797

Political reconstruction, 1865-1885. 84342

Political record of . . . F. A. Sawyer. 43448

Political record of Hon. Michael Hahn. 29533

Political record of Stephen A. Douglas on the slavery question. (20696)

Political record of the Hon. John Bell. 49019

Political reflections on the late colonial governments. 26441, 63798

Political reformer. (63799)

Political register; and impartial review of new books. (63800)

Political register and U. S. farmer's almanac for . . . 1849. 89581

Political register; or, proceedings in the session of Congress. 10067

Political register, setting forth the principles of the Whig and Locofoco Parties. 8703

Political register. Vol. I. Containing debates in Congress. 63801, 102283

Political remarks by "N". 55842

Political remarks on some French works and newspapers. 98672

Political remarks upon certain French publications and journals. 98670

Political reminiscences, including a sketch. 19666

Political reveries. (63802)

Political revolutions in 1860 and 1861. 63803

Political right of secession a reserved power under the constitution. 63804

Political romance. 91355

Political rulers authoriz'd and influenc'd by God Our Saviour. 62512

Political running, or an account of a celebrated race. 60395

Political schemes and calculations. 30256

Political science quarterly. 83379, 84855, 84857

Political sermon. Addressed to the electors of Middlesex. 63805

Political sermon, preached in . . . Walsal. (18644)

Political sermons of the period of 1776. 95642

Political situation. 87310

Political situation . . . . [By George L. Prentiss.] 65093

Political situation at the south. 84808

Political situation in Texas. 29996

Political situation, resulting from the late state election. (63806)

Political sketch of America. (63807)

Political sketches inscribed to His Excellency John Adams. 257

Political sketches, inscribed to John Adams. (51550)

Political sketches of eight years in Washington. (47188)

Political sketches: twelve chapters on the struggles of the age. 70139

Political sophistry detected. 23140

Political state of Great Britain. (23504), 63808

Political state of the British empire. 466

Political statistics of nations. 43289

Political status of the Methodist Episcopal Church. 84991

Political status of the rebellious states. 63809

Political survey. 21130

Political survey of Britain. 10239

Political tables. 63810

Political tale. (19995), 99276

Political text book . . . a complete statement of the votes for . . . Harrison and . . . Van Buren. 63812

Political text book; containing the Declaration of independence. 18005, 63811

Political text-book for 1860. 28493

Political text-book, or encyclopedia. 13804

Political thoughts. No. I. Idea of a patriot president. (63814)

Political thoughts of a loyal patriot. 63813

Political touchstone, taken from Mount Pernassus. 78367

Political tract for the times. 7606

Political tract no. 4. November 1831. 94434

Political tract no. 7. March, 1832. 65912, 88067

Political tracts [by Edward Burnaby Greene.] 100754-100756

Political tracts. Containing, The false alarm, Falkland's Islands, The patriot; and Taxation no tyranny. 36302, 36310, note before 95709

Political tracts for the times. 63777, 63816

Political tracts, from November, 1779, to April, 1780. 28593

Political tracts, new series, no. 1, January 1, 1832. 87827

Political tracts, no. I. 105613

Political tracts, no. 1. August, 1831. 63815

Political transactions in and concerning Kentucky. 41506

Political transactions of the Rip Van Winkle Club. 63817

Political treason of . . . F. A. Sawyer. 43447

Political truth. A digest of political methods in vogue. 84391-84392

Political truth; or, an examination of a case. 1st note after 100510, 100584

Political truth: or animadversions on the past and present state of public affairs. 63818, 67815

Political union, formed by the enemies of both. 5592, 28903

Political view of Upper Canada. (10547)

Political wars of Otsego. 59477

Political wisdom. 33960

Political works of Thomas Paine. 58234

Political writings of Joel Barlow. 3426

Political writings of John Dickinson. 20048

Political writings of Richard Cobden. 14038

Political writings of Thomas Paine. 58235

Politician out-witted, a comedy. 42405

Politicians, a comedy. 46839-46840

Politician's manual containing returns of elections. 104202

Politician's manual: containing returns of elections in the United States, particularly the presidential election of 1832. 104201

Politician's manual, containing the Declaration of . . . independence. (40144)

Politician's manual: or, statistical tables. 63820, 104203

Politician's manual. The constitution of the United States. 63821

Politicians; or, a state of things. 63819

Politician's register; containing a brief sketch of the executive. 46899

Politician's register, containing the results of the elections which have taken place during the years 1844, 1845, 1846, 1847, 1848. 31705

Politician's register, containing the results of the elections which have taken place during the years 1836-1840. 63822

Politician's register, for 1838. 63823, 103264

Politician's register, for 1839. 63823, 103264

Politick systema van de Regeering van Amsterdam. 94140

Politick vertoog. 98506

Pombal, Sebastiao Jose de Carvalho e Mello, Marques de, 1699-1782. 11181, (51427), 58534-(58535), 63895-63903, 63907-63908, 82915-82916, 1st note after 98174

Pombal, Sebastiao Jose de Carvalho e Mello, Marques de, 1699-1782. supposed editor (81089)

Pombo, Lino de. ed. 56286

Pomerade's original panorama of the Mississippi River. 17285

Pomeroy, Benjamin. 63917-63918

Pomeroy, Brick. sobriquet see Pomeroy, Mark M.

Pomeroy, Charles, 1825-1891. 63919

Pomeroy, Charles C. 63920

Pomeroy, James M. 63921-63923

Pomeroy, John Norton. 63924-63925

Pomeroy, Jonathan L. 63926-63928

Pomeroy, Julian. 76119

Pomeroy, Mark M. 63929-63933

Pomeroy, S. C. see Pomeroy, S. L.

Pomeroy, S. L. 63941, 82896

Pomeroy, Samuel Clark, 1816-1891. 42865, 63934, 63937-63940

Pomeroy, Samuel Wyllys. petitioner 63942

Pomeroy, Theodore Medad, 1824-1905. 63943

Pomfret, Conn. First Church of Christ. One Hundred and Fiftieth Anniversary Celebration, 1865. 63944

Pomfret, Conn. One Hundred and Four Electors. petitioners 63945

Pomfret, Vt. Ecclesiastical Council, 1792. see Congregational Churches in Vermont. Ecclesiastical Council, Pomfret, 1792.

Pomme, ---------, fl. 1793. reporter 95731

Pomological manual. 65622

Pomp, R. 63947

Pompa, Geronimo. 63948-63949

Pompa fvnebre y exceqvias qve el Excel. S. D. Pedro de Toledo y Leyba Marques de Mancera. 2245, 35238

Pompa funeral en la muerte, y exequias del D. Joan de Salzedo. 27670

Pompa funeral en las exequias del Rey Fernando VI. 70799

Pompa qve huvo por la beatificacion de Santa Rosa de Lima. (47422), 73182

Pompeo de Souza Brazil, Thomaz. see Souza Brazil, Thomaz Pompeo de, 1852-

Pompey, N. Y. 63954

Pomponii Laeti De origine Maomethis. 72023

Pomponii Melae De orbis situ libri tres. 63957-63960

Pomponii Melae Hispani, Libri de situ orbis tres. 63956

Pomponius Laetus. see Laetus, Pomponius.

Pomponius Laetus De exortu Maomethis. 72023

Pomponius Mela. see Mela, Pomponius, 1st cent.

Pomponne, ------- Ruelle. see Ruelle-Pomponne, --------.

Pomposo Fernandez de San Salvador, Agustin. see San Salvador, Agustin Pomposo Fernandez de.

Pompton Indians. Treaties, etc. 53242

Pomroy, Swann Lyman. 63963-63964

Poncar Indians. Treaties, etc. 96639

Ponce, Alonso. 63965

Ponce, Jose de Varga y. see Varga y Ponce, Jose de.

Ponce, Nicolas. engr. 27650, 50578, (63966), 68421

Ponce de Leon, Alonzo de Cueva. plaintiff 63967-63968

Ponce de Leon, F. (63970)

Ponce de Leon, Francisco, 17th cent. 63969

Ponce de Leon, Joseph Antonio Eugenio. (63971)-(63972)

Ponce de Leon, Joses Mariano. 63973-63974

Ponce de Leon, Juan Bautista. 63975

Ponce de Leon, Nicolas Suarez. see Suarez Ponce de Leon, Nicolas.

Ponce de Leon, opera bouffon en trois actes. 5016

Ponceau, Peter Steven du. see Du Ponceau, Peter Steven, 1760-1844.

Ponceau, Pierre Etienne du. see Du Ponceau, Peter Steven, 1760-1844.

Poncelin de la Roche-Tillac, Jean Charles, 1746-1828. 941, (4932), 68423

Pond, Alvin. 63977

Pond, B. F. 63978

Pond, Benjamin. 28722

Pond, Enoch. 41599, 55886, (63979)-63992, 95350, 103728, 103730

Pond, Gideon H. (18286), 18290, 18292, 63995, 71326

Pond, Jerusha M. 95158

Pond, Preston. 63993

Pond, Preston. defendant 95157-95158

Pond, Samuel W. 18290, (63994)-63996

Pond, Thomas E. 63997

Ponlevoy, Armand de, 1812-1874. 63998

Pons, F. J. de. see Depons, F. J.

Pons, Fr. S. de. 9833

Pons, Francois Raymond Joseph de, 1751-1812. 4858A, 19640-19647, 62506-62507, 63999-(64000)

Pont, S. F. du. see Du Pont, S. F.

Pont de Nemours, Pierre Samuel du. see Du Pont de Nemours, Pierre Samuel.

Pont-Graue, -------- du. 40175-40176

Pontalba, ----------, Baronne de. claimant 103425

Pontanus, Johann Isacc. 3597, 14401, 64001-64003

Pontbriand, Henri Marie Dubreuil de, Bp., 1708-1760. 38164 see also Quebec (Archdiocese) Bishop (Pontbrinand)

Ponte, J. A. 64004

Ponte, Lorenzo da. see Da Ponte, Lorenzo.

Ponte Esteban. 64015

Ponteach: or the savages of America. (72729)

Pontes, Rodrigo de Souza da Silva. see Souza da Silva Pontes, Rodrigo de.

Ponthoz, A. van der Straten. see Straten-Ponthoz, A. van der.

Pontiac: or, the siege of Detroit. 43613

Pontifical y Real Universidad de Mexico. see Mexico. Universidad.

Pontille, Charles Guiot de. see Guiot, Charles.

Pontis, J. B. D. de. (10757), 63706

Pontius, --------, fl. 1562. 24902, 39236, note before 99284

Pontoia, Diego. 66686

Ponton, Mungo. 64018

Pontoosuc. pseud. Johnson protocol and international good neighborhood. see Kellogg, Ensign H.

Pontoosuc Lake. 83331

Pontoppidan, D. 64019

Pontos principaes a que se reduzem os abusos. 63905

Ponts, William de Deux. see Deux-Ponts, William de.

Pontus, Antonius. 64020

Ponze, J. M. V. 64021

Ponze de Leon, Christoual Araque. see Araque Ponze de Leon, Christoual.

Pool, ----------, 16th cent. 97495

Pool, David. 64022

Pool, J. T. (64025)

Pool, John, 1826-1884. 27863, (64023)-64024
Pool, Lot. 8525
Pool, S. D. ed. 88364
Poole, Alexis. 44628, 64026-64028, note after 90814
Poole, Charles H. 69946
Poole, Francis. (64029)
Poole, Henry. 56109, 64030-64033
Poole, Henry Ward. 64034-(64035)
Poole, Jonas. 66686
Poole, Richard. 64036
Poole, Thomas W. 64037
Poole, William. 64039-64039
Poole, William Frederick, 1821-1894. 6745, (34088), 36205, 45241, 46623, 60643, 64040-64049, 64133, 84980, 98039
Poole's annual register of the executive and legislative departments. 45628, 64028
Poole's statistical view of the executive and legislative departments. 45628, 64027
Pooley, Thomas. tr. 93408
Poor, Alfred. (32060), 64050-64052
Poor, Daniel W. 64053, 85386
Poor, Henry Varnum. 1203, 64055-(64057)
Poor, Henry Varnum. supposed author 42018, 57245, 64054
Poor, John A. 23109, 63274, 64058-(64068)
see also Maine. Commissioner on the Defence of the State.
Poor black boy. 92173
Poor boys who became great. 84057
Poor Caroline. 91829
Poor citizen. pseud. Appeal to the people of the city of New-York. see Sedgwick, Henry Dwight, 1785-1831.
Poor devoted town of Boston. 102045
Poor doubting Christian. . . . By Thomas Hooker. 32847
Poor doubting Christian drawn to Christ. 32846
Poore doubting Christian drawn to Christ. (32844)-32845
Poore dovting Christian drawne vnto Christ. 32843
Poor Job, 1755. 80282
Poor Job, 1752. (64069), 80282
Poor Job's country and townsman's almanack. 64070
Poor Joseph. 1759. 62743, 64071, 91618
Poor Joseph's almanack, for 1759. 62743, 64071, 91618
Poor-laws of . . . New York. (53858)
Poor laws of the state of New York. 67787
Poor lodger; a comedy. 103484
Poor man. pseud. Uncle Solomon and the Homan family. 97727
Poor man's advice to his poor neighbours. 64072
Poor man's advocate. 94558
Poor man's companion. 106082
Poor man's defence. 64665
Poor man's preservative against Popery. 92655
Poor man's son. pseud. Remarks on the militia system. 69474
Poor of Baltimore. 3057
Poor orphan's legacy. 64073
Poor peacemaker. pseud. Slavery quarrel. 82109
Poor persons who emigrated last year to Canada and the United States. pseud. Extracts from letters. (10444), 78506
Poor planter's physician. 24459, 23299, 94713
Poor-rich man. pseud. Our ruin. see Lindsley, John Berrien.
Poor rich man, and the rich poor man. 78798-78799

Poor Richard. pseud. Father Abraham's speech. see Franklin, Benjamin, 1707-1790.
Poor Richard. pseud. Massachusetts almanac 45813
"Poor Richard." 25568
Poor Richard, a famous Pennsylvania conjurer pseud. Father Abraham's speech. see Franklin, Benjamin, 1707-1790.
Poor Richard improved. 25596-25597, 102185
Poor Richard revived. Almanack for . . . 18 64076
Poor Richard revived; or, Baber & Southwick almanack. (64074)
Poor Richard revived: or, the Albany almanac 64075
Poor Richard, 1733. 25566
Poor Richard's almanack. 82974, 82976
Poor Richard's almanac for 1850. 25568
Poor Richard's almanack for . . . 1805. 6405
Poor Richard's almanack for . . . 1803. 6407
Poor Richard's almanack for the year 1760. 4206
Poor Richard's Franklin almanac, . . . for . . . 1808. 64078
Poor Richard's genuine New-England almanac 64077
Poor Richard's new farmer's almanac. 6407
Poor Robert, the scribe. pseud. Essays. se Miner, Charles.
Poor Robin. pseud. MDCCXXXV. The Rhod Island almanack. see Franklin (James publisher
Poor Robin. pseud. MDCCXXVIII. The Rho Island almanack. see Franklin (James publisher
Poor Robin's almanac, for the year of Our Lord, 1822. 79845
Poor Robin's almanack . . . 1742. 64081
Poor Roger, 1756. 64081
Poor Roger's almanack. 50434
Poor Roger's universal pocket almanack. 64083
Poor Sarah. (64086)
Poor Sarah, an Indian woman. 64084
Poor Sarah; or, the Indian woman. 64085, 97859
Poor Sarah, or the Indian woman, an Indian charactesr. [sic] 6860
Poor Sarah the Indian woman. (64086)
Poor soldier, opera. (64087), 86905
Poor soldier; an American tale. 64088, note after 90519
Poor Thomas improved. 64090
Poor Thomas's almanack for 1763. 64089
Poor Tom revived: being More's almanack for 1773. 87759
Poor Tom revived, being More's almanack, for the year of Christian account, 1770. 87756
Poor Tom revived: being More's almanack, for the year of Christian account, 1771. 87757
Poor Tom revived: being More's almanack, for the year of Christian account, 1772. 87758
Poor Tom's New York pocket almanack. 640
Poor Trinity. 32934
Poor white. 64092
Poor whites of the south. (68629)
Poor whites of the south. The injury done them by slavery. 64093
Poor Will's almanack, 1797. 96921
Poor Will's almanack for the year of Christi account, 1744. 64094

Poor Will's almanack, for the year of Our
Lord 1770. 64095
Poor Will's pocket almanack for 1771. 64095
Poor woodman. pseud. Dialogue between a
noble lord and a poor woodman. 19930
Poore, Benjamin Berley, 1820-1887. 15606,
41181, 45922, 64096-64097, 64098-64100,
66960, 83991, 85227-85229 see also
Massachusetts. Historical Agent.
Poorman, W. J. 86325
Pooshemastubie. Choctaw Indian Chief 96601
Pop, D. tr. 92600
Popayan (Diocese) Bishop (Jiminez) 86236
see also Jiminez, Salvador, Bp.
Popayan (Diocese) Eclesiastico. pseud. see
Eclesiastico de la Diocesis de Popayan.
pseud.
Popayan (State) Gobernador, 1843. 64102
Pope, Alexander, 1688-1744. 21547
Pope, Amos, 1771-1837. 64103
Pope, Augustus Russell. 1082, 64104-(64106)
Pope, Bolling A. 33488
Pope, C. C. 64107
Pope, Hambly. tr. 101189
Pope, J. J. 87516
Pope, James. 64108
Pope, John. 64109
Pope, John, 1770-1845. 64110-64111
Pope, John, 1822-1892. 64112-(64117), 64246,
64249, 69870, 69900, 69946
Pope, Leroy. (64119)
Pope, Leroy, Jr. 64120, 84705
Pope, Peter. 16691, 2d note after 99888
Pope, S. 90304
Pope, Samiel. 64121-64122
Pope, Thomas. (64123)
Pope, W. H. 64124-64125
Pope, William. 64126
Pope and the Presbyterians. 64127
Pope-day in America. 80019
Pope, or president? 64128
Pope Peter the First. 102725
Popeliniere, -------- de la. see La Pope-
liniere, -------, Sieur de, fl. 1630.
Popery, a craft, and popish priests, the chief
craftsmen. 57267
Popery adjudged. 93183
Popery, an enemy to civil and religious liberty.
8699
Popery and slavery display'd. 30525, 39120,
64130
Popery and the United States. 13365
Popery judged by its fruits. 1st note after
97687
Popery outdone. 29305
Popery truly display'd in its bloody colours.
11288
Pope's campaign in Virginia. (64118)
Pope's proclamation. 17324
Pope's startagem. 64129
Popham, George. (67551)
Popham, Sir John, 1531?-1607. 67545
Popham, Sir Home. defendant at court martial
64131-64132
Popham, W. 86121
Popham Celebration, 1862. Executive Commit-
tee. Secretary. 2953 see also Ballard,
Edward, 1804-1870.
Popham colony. 64133
Popish emissary instructed. 103990
Popish hierarchy suppressed. 7985
Popish idolatry. 47150
Popish inquisition. Newly erected in New
England. 33360, 33363, 52756
Popkin, John Snelling. 64134-64138

Poplicola. pseud. Monroe's embassy. see
Brown, Charles Brockden.
Poplicola. pseud. To the worthy inhabitants
of the city of New-York. 93244
Popol Vuh. Le libre sacre et les mythes de
l'antiquite Americaine. 7423, (7436)
Popple, Henry. cartographer 64140
Popular account of nature and man. (30719)
Popular account of the United States Coast
Survey. 64141
Popular amusements: a discourse . . . Win-
chester, Va. 38310
Popular arguments in favor of an elective
judiciary. 85167
Popular and authentic life of Ulysses S. Grant.
(44373)
Popular and authentic lives of Ulysses S. Grant.
and Schuyler Colfax. 44374
Popular and practical exposition of the minerals
and geology of Canada. 11977
Popular biography. 27918
Popular catalogue of the extraordinary curiosi-
ties. 33910, note after 64141
Popular deciduous and evergreen trees and
shrubs. (22265)
Popular delusions in relation to war. (64142)
Popular description, geographical, historical,
and topographical. 49816
Popular description of Colombia. 14613
Popular description of minerals and mineral
combustibles. 7049
Popular description of singular races of men.
(69053)
Popular dictionary of arts, sciences, literature.
22556, 62635, (70885), 84062, 103911
Popular dictionary of general knowledge. 52439
Popular education. An address delivered at the
annual commencement. 23024
Popular education: . . . By Ira Mayhew.
(47129)
Popular education in the United States. 19657
Popular education indispensable to the life of a
republic. 5939
Popular errors involved in the present war.
3895
Popular essay on subjects of penal law. 40985
Popular essay on the palaeophytic origin of
petroleum. (50883)
Popular essays on naval subjects. 43425
Popular excitements. 3316
Popular explanation of the system of circulating
medium. 93488, 93490
Popular geographical library. 91704
Popular government by divine right. 9549
Popular government successful in a great
emergency. 28
Popular history of America. 16402
Popular history of England. 38105
Popular history of palms. 58925
Popular history of the discovery of America.
(38216)
Popular history of the discovery, progress,
and present state of America. 48134
Popular history of the seven prevailing nar-
cotics of the world. (16325)
Popular history of the treatment of the natives.
33376
Popular history of the United States of America.
33374
Popular illustrated magazine of natural history.
58097
Popular industrial art education. 84497
Popular instruction and its relation to the
higher institutions of learning. 84928

Popular introduction to the history and re-
sources of that interesting and important
region. 1, 87318, 106195
Popular liberty and equal rights. 2874
Popular life of George Fox. (44754)
Popular memoir of William Penn. 64458
Popular monthly, devoted to religious and
useful literature. (33170)
Popular nomenclature of the American flora.
(78869)
Popular prejudices against the convention and
treaty with Spain. 64143, 69687, 86737
Popular science monthly. 64144, 84275, 85096
Popular scientific account of the natural history
of the animal and vegetable kingdoms.
30720
Popular sketch of the rise and progress of
Sunday-schools. 64145
Popular sketches of ship-building. 78542
Popular sovereignty in the territories. Judge
Douglas in reply to Judge Black. note
after 20693
Popular sovereignty in the territories. The
Democratic record. (64146)
Popular sovereignty the dividing line between
federal and local authority. 20693
Popular sovereignty—the will of the majority
against the rule of a minority. 31703
Popular sovereignty, theoretical and practical.
(17217)
Popular summary of the naval and military
forces of the union. 8642
Popular tales and legends. 22854
Popular terms illustrated in rhyme, etc.
(32239)
Popular tracts no. 3. 105583
Popular treatise on the teeth. 83602
Popular view of the American civil war.
32895, (32897)-32898
Popular voyages and travels throughout the
continents. 35742
Popular works of Captain Mayne Reid. 2108A,
note after 93619
Population and other statistics of the province
of New Brunswick. 52549
Population—immigration—colonies agricoles.
(70048)
Population of the United States in 1860. 11674,
37427
Populi, Tribunus. _pseud._ _see_ Tribunus
Populi. _pseud._
Populi, Vox. _pseud._ _see_ Vox Populi. _pseud._
Populous village, a poem, recited before the
Philermenian Society of Brown University.
(64147)
Populous village: a poem, recited before the
Philermenian Society of Providence, Sept.,
1826. 19062
Por amor y religion la paz de la Nueva Espana.
99684
Por condicion expresa del assiento ajustado.
99618
Por cumplir con la obligacion. 84384
Por disposicion del gufierno jeneral de Centro-
America. 32773
Por D. Antonio de Cordova Laso de la Vega.
16776, 39132
Por Don Carlos Vazquez Coronado. 16825,
note after 98301, note after 98720
Por Don Fernando Fernandez de Cordoba y
Sande. 96051
Por D. Francisco Lorenzo de San Milan. 42067
Por D. Franc Pimentel y Sotomayor. 62881
Por Don I. F. de Estrada. 99624
Por Don Ignacio Francisco de Estrada. 64176

Por Don J. A. Fernandez de Cordova y Sosa.
88723
Por Don Joseph Pardo de Figueroa. 89943
Por Don Juan Diego Gverrero de la Dueba.
98156
Por Don Ivan Leonel de Servantes Carabajal.
86419
Por D. Ivan Tapia de Bargas. 94351
Por Don Lvis de Benavides Cortes Marques
de Fromesta. 99436
Por Don Nicolas Romero de Mella. 73042
Por Don Rodrigo de Esquiuel y Carceres.
98314
Por Dona Maria Tello de Guzman. 94629
Por edicto svo contra laicos comis habitum
clericalem deturpantes. 99634
Por el Capitan Francisco de Torres. 96243
Por el Colegio Mayor de Santa Maria de Todo
Santos. 27341
Por el Coronel de Cavalleria Don Francisco
de Aguirre Gomendio. 98018
Por el Coronel D. Manuel de Rivas-Cacho.
71616
Por el Fiscal del Real Consejo de las Indias.
86541
Por el Ilvstrissimo Senor el Maestro D. F.
Diego de Hevia y Valdes. 99442
Por el Licenciado D. Diego Antonio de Oviedo
y Banos. 57986
Por el Maestro Martin Garcia [de Gastizabal.
26587
Por el Obispo de la Puebla de los Angeles.
(66574)
Por el Obispo de la Pvebla en defensa de la
jvrisdiccion ecclesiastica. 66573
Por Fray Geronimo Alonso de la Torre.
98600
Por informaciones, testimonios, titulos,
pareceras. 93338
Por Ivan de Zavala Fannarraga. 106281A
Por Ivan del Pverto, y Domingo del Pverto
su hermano. 75896
Por justas consideraciones al estado eclesias-
tico. 58389
Por la defensa de la juridiccion de Juzgado
General de Bienes de Disuntos. 99619
Por la pretension de los religiosos ministros
doctrineros. 98773
Por la Provincia de la Compania de Jesus de
la Nueua Espana. 72777, (73620)
Por la Provincia de Lima, del Orden de San
Agvstin. 97692
Por la Provincia de S. Hipolyto Martyr del
Sagrado de Predicadores. 56403
Por la Provincia de S. Juan Bautista de Pre-
dicadores. 87224
Por la Santa Yglesia Cathedral de la ciudad
de la Puebla. 86420
Por las religiones de S. Domingo. 86421
Por los interesados en la carga de frvtos.
94285
Por los Regidores de la ciudad de la Habana.
99437
Por los Regidores de la ciudad de la Hauana.
99438
Por Nicolas Vanresviqui. 98315
Por occasiao da muito sentido morte. 98710
Por parte del General D. Francisco de Torija
Ortuno. 87193
Por quando la experiencia ha manifestiado.
(70381)
Por quando las ciudades de Cadiz, y Sevilla.
70382
Por quanto en atencion a las repetidas instan-
cias. (76858)
Por quanto para la mejor forma. 96119

Por Sebastian Gomez Rendon. 86422
Porcacchi, Thomaso. 64148-64153
Porcel, Francisco Moreno. (64154)
Porcellian Club, Harvard University. see Harvard University. Porcellian Club.
Porcher, Dr. pseud. see Hines, David Theodore.
Porcher, F. A. 88005
Porcher, Francis Peyne. 64155-64157
Porcupine, Sir Christopher. pseud. ed. Frying pan for poor sinners. 97778
Porcupine, Peter. pseud. see Cobbett, William, 1763-1835.
Porcupine, Skunk. pseud. Petition to the corporation. 63163
Porcupine. 93572
Porcupine, a print. 14003
Porcupine alias the hedge-hog. 74623
Porcupine revived. 64165
Porcupine's answer. 14007, 102401
Porcupine's gazette. 14030, 84829, 84832
Porcupine's last will and testament. 14007, 102401
Porcupine's political censor, for April, 1797. 14008
Porcupine's political censor for December, 1796. 14005, 101837
Porcupine's political censor for January, 1797. 14006
Porcupine's political censor, for March, 1797. 14007, 102401
Porcupine's political censor for November, 1796. 14004
Porcupine's political censor, for September, 1796. 14003
Porcupine's remarks on the same. 14008
Porcupine's works. (13895), (14009), note after 101847
Porcupiniad; a hudibrastic poem. 10882
Porden, E. A. 64167
Pordenone, Odorico da. see Odorico da Pordenone, 1286-1331.
Pordilla, Pedro de la. (64168)
Poret, H. tr. 65277
Porfiado, Señor D. pseud. Ya volvio Santa-Anna. 76747
Porney, ---------. (30912)
Porque del recurso del Ayuntamiento de Guatemala. (75770)
Porras, J. D. 64169
Porras, Manuel. (64170)
Porreno, Baltasar. 64171-64172
Porres, Martini de. (64173)-64174
Porres Varnada, Diego. 64176
Porro, Girolamo. cartographer 64148-64153, 66492-66493, 66495-66496, 66506
Porro, Hieronymo. see Porro, Girolamo.
Port and Seamen's Aid Society, Boston. see Boston Port and Seamen's Aid Society.
Port-au-Prince, Haiti. Cercle des Philadelphes. see Cercle des Philadelphes, Port-au-Prince, Haiti.
Port-au-Prince, Haiti. Citoyens. Treaties, etc. see Santo Domingo (French Colony) Province du Sud. Treaties, etc.
Port-au-Prince, Haiti. Citoyens de Couleur. Treaties, etc. see Santo Domingo (French Colony) Province du Sud. Treaties, etc.
Port-au-Prince, Haiti. Guarde Nationale. 64177
Port-au-Prince, Haiti. Lycee National. 64181
Port-chaine. 16423
Port Deposite, Md. Citizens. Committee on the Proposed Canal from Columbia to Tide. 93925
Port folio (London) 10389

Port folio (1801-1827) 16964, 19071, 29813, (32499), (64182), 67377, 73248
Port folio, and companion to the select circulating library. 82983, 82987
Port folio, and New York monthly magazine. (64182)
Port folio enlarged. (64182)
Port folio of an editor. 64990
Port Huron and Lake Michigan Railroad Company—Chicago and Michigan Grand Trunk Railway Company. 3146
Port Huron and Lake Michigan Railroad. Report of J. Dutton Steele. 91120
Port Huron and Lake Michigan Railroad. Reports of J. Dutton Steele, Esq., civil engineer, and J. S. Gibbons. 91120
Port of Charles Town, in South Carolina, Nov. 1, 1736. 12064
Port-Plume. pseud. Trans-Atlantic sketches. see Harding, W. M.
Port regulations of St. Bartholomew. (75003)
Port Royal, Jamaica. Predikant. pseud. see Predikant van Port Royal. pseud.
Port Royal, S. C. U. S. Agent to the Negroes. see U. S. Government Agent to the Negroes at Port Royal, S. C.
Port Royal Mission. (25847)
Port Sheldon, Michigan. 64187
Port Society for Promoting the Gospel Among Seamen, Charleston, S. C. see Charleston Port Society for Promoting the Gospel Among Seamen, Charleston, S. C.
Port Society for the Moral Improvement of Seamen, New Bedford, Mass. see New Bedford Port Society for the Moral Improvement of Seamen.
Port Society of the City of Boston and its Vicinity. 6753
Port Society of New York. see Society for Promoting the Gospel Among the Seamen in the Port of New York.
Porta, Antonio. 64188
Portage Canal and Manufacturing Company. Charter. 64189
Portal, Pierre-Barthelemy d'Albaredes. 64190
Portales, Esteban. plaintiff (12764)
Portalis, A. Edouard. 64191
Portana, Antonio. defendant (51797), 69915, 96948
Portana, Juan Antonio. defendant 27309, 69915, 93808, 96948
Portau, Jos. 64573
Porte, -------. 75540 see also France. Corps Legislatif. Conseil des Cinq-Cents. Commission des Colonies.
Porte, Joseph de la. see Laporte, Joseph de, 1713-1779.
Porte, Lucas de la. tr. 27780, 32009, 47829
Porte Crayon. pseud. see Strother, David Hunter, 1816-1888.
Portegueda, Juan Bentura de. 64192
Portenti del divino amore. 73185
Portentosa imagen de Nuestra Senora de los Remedios. 10897, 11056
Porter, -----------, fl. 1834. 96304
Porter, -----------, fl. 1850. (60516)
Porter, ------------, fl. 1881. 87933
Porter, Lt. ---------. 64193
Porter, Mrs. ---------. 64193
Porter, A. A. 64194
Porter, A. N. (64200)
Porter, Albert Gallatin, 1824-1897. 64196
Porter, Alexander, 1785-1844. 64197-64198
Porter, Anna Emerson. see Porter, Lydia Maria (Emerson) 1816-1898.
Porter, Benjamin F. 64201-64202

Porter, Charles H. 64203
Porter, Charles Howell, 1833-1897. (64204)-
  (64205)
Porter, Charles Leland. 64206
Porter, Charles S. 64207-64210
Porter, Charles T. 64211
Porter, Clarkson N. 64622
Porter, David, 1761-1851. 64212-(64216)
Porter, David, 1780-1843. 24, 21211-21215,
  64217-64220, 64223, 96807, 1st note after
  101000
Porter, David, 1780-1843. defendant at court
  martial 64217, 64221-64222
Porter, David Dixon, 1813-1891. (64224)-
  64225
Porter, David H. 64226
Porter, David Rittenhouse, 1788-1867. 59799,
  note just before 60250, (60519), 60534
  see also Pennsylvania. Governor, 1839-
  1845 (Porter)
Porter, E. G. 88689
Porter, Ebenezer, 1772-1834. 64227-(64232),
  89736
Porter, Edward C. 29492, 64234, 86945
Porter, Edward Robert. 93598
Porter, Elbert S. 64235-(64239)
Porter, Eliphalet. 64240-64245, 101686
Porter, Fitz-John, 1822-1901. 64249
Porter, Fitz-John, 1822-1901. defendant
  at court martial 32653, (36267), 64246-
  64249
Porter, George B. 64251, 96681, 96687,
  96692, 2d note after 96883 see also
  U. S. Commissioner to the Menominee
  Indians. U. S. Commissioners to the
  Ottawa Indians. U. S. Commissioners to
  the United Nation of Chippewa, Ottawa,
  and Potawatomi Indians.
Porter, George Richardson, 1792-1852. 41874-
  41875, 64252-(64253), 97307
Porter, Gilchrist, 1817-1894. 64250
Porter, Henry H. 64254
Porter, Huntington. 64255-64260
Porter, J. A. (81056)
Porter, J. M. 38586
Porter, J. W. 64286
Porter, Jacob. (64261)-64264
Porter, James. of Pomfret, Conn. 64265-
  (64266)
Porter, James, 1808-1888. 64267-64269, 89627
Porter, James, fl. 1830. defendant 47464
Porter, James Madison, 1793-1862. 64270-
  64273
Porter, James Madison, 1793-1862. reporter
  64311
Porter, Jane. ed. 64323
Porter, John, 1716-1802. 7789, 64274-(64276)
Porter, John Addison. 64277-64278
Porter, John Ewing. 64279
Porter, John K. 58611, 59050, 64280-64285
Porter, Lydia Maria (Emerson) 1816-1898.
  (64195)
Porter, M. E. (64287)
Porter, Nathaniel, 1745?-1837. 64288-64290
Porter, Noah, 1781-1866. (64291)-(64297)
Porter, Noah, 1811-1892. (64298)-(64308),
  89875, 105886
Porter, Peter Buell, 1773-1844. 317, 4061,
  64309, 78405 see also U. S. War
  Department.
Porter, Robert, 1768-1848. (64310)
Porter, Robert, 1768-1848. defendant 64311
Porter, Rufus. 64312
Porter, Samuel, 1709-1857. 64313-(64314)
Porter, Samuel, 1760-1825. 64315
Porter, Sarah. 64316

Porter, T. O. 16923
Porter, William Augustus, 1821-1886. 64317-
  64319
Porter, William David, 1809-1864. 64322
Porter, William Dennison, 1810-1833. 64320-
  64321, 87489, 88103
Porter, William Ogilvie, 1774-1850. 64323
Porter, William Smith, 1799-1866. 22179,
  64324
Porter, William T., d. 1858. 1251, 30931,
  66953, 81613, 89508, 95662
Porter y Casanate, Pedro. 64325
Porter. firm see Badger & Porter. firm
  publishers
Porterfield, James. 86634
Porter's health almanac, for 1832. 64254
Porter's spirit of the times. 89508, note afte
  104000
Portes e Infantes, Tomas de, Abp. 81433
  see also Santo Domingo (Archdiocese)
  Archbishop (Portes e Infantes)
Porteus, Beilby, successively Bishop of Ches
  and London, 1731-1808. (11877), 64326-
  64328, (78715), 78718-78719
Portfolio of a traveller. (27561)
Portfolio of living American statesmen. 2405
Portichuelo de Ribadeneyra, Diego. 64330
Portico. 64329
Portilho, Joao Anastacio de Souza Pereira da
  Silva. see Souzca Pereira da Silva
  Portilho, Joao Anastacio de.
Portilla, Anselmo de la. 64332
Portilla, Anselmo de la. supposed author
  38612, 48489, 64331, 76734
Portilla, J. de la. 15010, 64333
Portilla, Pedro de la. 64335
Portillo, Antonio Lopezio. (64336)
Portillo, Jesus Lopez. (35550), (64334) see
  also Jalisco (Mexican State) Governor
  (Portillo)
Portion of the code of statute law of South
  Carolina. 87705
Portion of the evidence submitted to the Sena•
  3782
Portion of the friends of the high tariff exam
  ined. 48862
Portion of the Inhabitants of the Mississippi
  Territory. petitioners see Mississipp•
  (Territory) Citizens. petitioners
Portion of the Members [of the General Asse•
  bly of Georgia.] see Georgia. Genera•
  Assembly. Portion of the Members.
Portion of the secret history of the American
  revolution. 64337
Portion of the . . . address of the . . . Demo•
  cratic Committee of Virginia. (23627)
Portions of the Book of Common Prayer. 174
Portius. pseud. Letter to the Earl of Shel-
  burne on the peace. (40469)
Portland, Henry Bentinck, 1st Duke of, 1682-
  1726. 65865, 88192
Portland, William Cavendish-Bentinck, 3d Duk•
  of, 1738-1809. 98058A-98058B see als•
  Great Britain. Home Office.
Portland, Me. 64339
Portland, Me. Agent. (64362)
Portland, Me. American Institute of Instructio•
  see American Institute of Instruction.
Portland, Me. Association for the Relief of
  Aged, Indigent Women. see Associatio•
  for the Relief of Aged, Indigent Women,
  of Portland, Maine.
Portland, Me. Athenaeum. see Portland
  Athenaeum.
Portland, Me. Auditor. 64342, 64351

Portland, Me. Board of Aldermen. Committee to Investigate the Causes and Consequences of the Riot on the Evening of June 2, 1855. 64373, 71823

Portland, Me. Board of Trade. (64358)

Portland, Me. Charter. (64344)-(64345)

Portland, Me. Commissioners on Portland Harbor. see Maine. Commissioners on Portland Harbor.

Portland, Me. Committee of Public Safety. 82152

Portland, Me. Common Council. (64345)

Portland, Me. Constitutional Convention, 1819-1820. see Maine. Constitutional Convention, Portland, 1819-1820.

Portland, Me. Convention, 1795. see Maine (District) Convention, Portland, 1795.

Portland, Me. Convention, 1819. see Maine Convention, Portland, 1819.

Portland, Me. Convention of the Church Association of Maine, 1852. see Unitarian Churches. Maine. Church Association. Convention, Portland, 1852.

Portland, Me. Dispensary and Vaccine Institution. see Portland Dispensary and Vaccine Institution, Portland, Me.

Portland, Me. Ecclesiastical Council, 1812. see Congregational Churches in Maine. Ecclesiastical Council, Portland, 1812.

Portland, Me. Ecclesiastical Council, 1856. see Congregational Churches in Maine. Ecclesiastical Council, 1856.

Portland, Me. European and North American Railway Convention, 1850. see European and North American Railway Convention, Portland, Me., 1850.

Portland, Me. Exhibition and Fair of the Maine Charitable Mechanic Association, 1st, 1838. see Maine Charitable Mechanic Association. Exhibition and Fair, 1st, Portland, 1838.

Portland, Me. Fire Department. Chief Engineer. 64361

Portland, Me. Fire Department. Engineer. 64351

Portland, Me. First Church. Woman's Alliance. 84353

Portland, Me. First Parish. Committee. 64375

Portland, Me. Friends of the Union and the Constitution. Meeting, 1835. see Meeting of the Friends of the Union and the Constitution, Portland, Me., 1835.

Portland, Me. Institute and Public Library. 64363

Portland, Me. Institute and Public Library. Charter. 64363

Portland, Me. International Commercial Convention, 1868. see International Commercial Convention, Portland, Me., 1868.

Portland, Me. Irish American Relief Association. see Irish American Relief Association of Portland, Me.

Portland, Me. Light Infantry Company. see Maine. Militia. Portland Light Infantry.

Portland, Me. Mariner's Church. 64380

Portland, Me. Mariner's Church. Trustees. petitioners 43994

Portland, Me. Mayor, 1849. 64349

Portland, Me. Mayor, 1852. 64350

Portland, Me. Mayor, 1855 (Dow) 64373, 71823 see also Dow, ------------,

Portland, Me. Mayor, 1863-1864. 64351

Portland, Me. Mayor, 1864 (M'Lellan) 64351 see also M'Lellan, -----------.

Portland, Me. Mayor, 1866 (Stevens) (64340) see also Stevens, Augustus E.

Portland, Me. Mayor, 1868 (Jewett) 64346 see also Jewett, Jedediah, fl. 1858.

Portland, Me. Meeting of the Friends of the Union and the Constitution, Portland, Me., 1835. see Meeting of the Friends of the Union and the Constitution, Portland, Me., 1835.

Portland, Me. Minister at Large. see Minister at Large, Portland, Me.

Portland, Me. Ordinances, etc. 64343-(64345)

Portland, Me. Overseers of the Poor. 64351, (64353)

Portland, Me. Provident Association. see Provident Association of Portland, Me.

Portland, Me. Public Library. see Portland, Me. Institute and Public Library.

Portland, Me. Rifle Company. see Maine. Militia. Portland Rifle Company.

Portland, Me. St. Lawrence Street Church. (64377)

Portland, Me. School Committee. 64378

Portland, Me. Second Inquest on the Body of John Robbins, 1855. 71823

Portland, Me. Society for Suppressing Vice and Immorality. see Society for Suppressing Vice and Immorality, Portland, Me.

Portland, Me. Society of Natural History. see Portland Society of Natural History, Portland, Me.

Portland, Me. State Street Church. 64379

Portland, Me. Union Congregational Church. 64381

Portland, Me. Unitarian Church Association Convention, 1852. see Unitarian Church Association of Maine. Convention, Portland, 1852.

Portland, Ore. Board of Statistics, Immigration and Labor Exchange. 57561, 64385

Portland, Ore. 64383

Portland, Ore. Librarian. 64386 see also Gilliland, Lyle W.

Portland, Ore. Library. 64386

Portland, Ore. Mazama Mountain Climbing Society. see Mazama Mountain Climbing Society of Portland, Ore.

Portland, Ore. Meeting of the People.. . . on the Subject of the Pacific Rail Roads, and the Oregon Rail Roads, 1867. 64383

Portland, Ore. National Conference of Charities and Correction, 32d, 1905. see National Conference of Charities and Correction, 32d, Portland, Ore., 1905.

Portland, Ore. Portland Library Association. see Portland Library Association, Portland, Ore.

Portland, Ore. Relief Committee. see Relief Committee for the Relief of Sufferers by the Fire in Portland, Oregon.

Portland almanac & register: 1860. 64354

Portland and Lake Champlain Rail Road. 19082

Portland & Ogdensburg Rail Road. Directors. 64355

Portland & Ogdensburg Rail Road. President. 64355

Portland & Ogdensburg R. R. Reports of the President and Directors. 64355

Portland and Rutland Railroad Company. (64356)

Portland and Rutland Railroad Company. Across the continent. (64356)

Portland Athenaeum. 64357

Portland Athenaeum. Library. 64357

Portland Athenaeum. Annual report, October, 1852. 64357

Portland business directory. 64359

Portraitures of Yankee life. 84150, 84158-84159, 84161
Portrate und Trachten. (73934)
Ports Chinois. 39300
Ports Mexicaines occupes par les Americains. 20427
Portsmouth, Henry. 59706, (64411)
Portsmouth, N. H. 64412, (64416), 64427, 64429
Portsmouth, N. H. Athenaeum. 64425
Portsmouth, N. H. Centennial Celebration of the Introduction of the Art of Printing into New Hampshire, 1856. see Centennial Celebration of the Introduction of the Art of Printing into New Hampshire, Portsmouth, N. H., 1856.
Portsmouth, N. H. Charter. 64413, 64418, 64426
Portsmouth, N. H. City Council. (64420)
Portsmouth, N. H. City Missionary Society. see City Missionary Society of Portsmouth, N. H.
Portsmouth, N. H. Committee in Behalf of the Sufferers by the Fire, December, 1802. 64414
Portsmouth, N. H. Committee to Ascertain Statistics on Intemperance, 1845. 90818
Portsmouth, N. H. Court. 64621
Portsmouth, N. H. Ecclesiastical Council, 1834. see Congregational Churches in New Hampshire. Ecclesiastical Council, Portsmouth, 1834.
Portsmouth, N. H. First Church of Christ. 64423
Portsmouth, N. H. Friendly Botanic Society. see Friendly Botanic Society at Eastport, Mass., and Portsmouth, N. H.
Portsmouth, N. H. High School. 64427
Portsmouth, N. H. Humane Fire Society. see Humane Fire Society, Portsmouth, N. H.
Portsmouth, N. H. Mercantile Library. see Portsmouth Mercantile Library.
Portsmouth, N. H. North Church of Christ. see Portsmouth, N. H. First Church of Christ.
Portsmouth, N. H. Ordinances, etc. (64417)-64418, 64426
Portsmouth, N. H. Public Schools. 64432
Portsmouth, N. H. Rockingham Conference of Churches Annual Meeting, 1866. see Rockingham Conference of Churches. Annual Meeting, Portsmouth, N. H., 1866.
Portsmouth, N. H. St. John's Episcopal Church. 64433
Portsmouth, N. H. Selectmen. (66430), note after 96618
Portsmouth, N. H. Society for the Suppression of Vice. see Portsmouth Society for the Suppression of Vice.
Portsmouth, N. H. South Parish. Sunday School. Superintendents. 64434
Portsmouth, N. H. Superintending School Committee. (64415)
Portsmouth, Ohio. First Presbyterian Church. 64436
Portsmouth, Ohio. Portsmouth Company. see Portsmouth Company of Ohio.
Portsmouth, Va. Common Council. 51720
Portsmouth, Va. Mayor, 1863. 51720
Portsmouth, Va. Relief Association. see Portsmouth Relief Association, Portsmouth, Va.
Portsmouth. 89557
Portsmouth almanac, and Rockingham County handbook. 64424

Portsmouth Baptist Association. see Baptists. Virginia. Portsmouth Baptist Association.
Portsmouth city book and directory. 64426
Portsmouth Company of Ohio. 64435
Portsmouth directory: . . . . Also a street directory. 64426
Portsmouth directory . . . . By W. A. Greenhough, Jr. 64426
Portsmouth directory; containing city record. 64426
Portsmouth directory for 1869. 54426
Portsmouth disputation examined. 50661
Portsmouth: its advantages and needs. 38780
Portsmouth jubilee. 64427
Portsmouth Mercantile Library. 64422
Portsmouth register and directory. 64426
Portsmouth Relief Association, Portsmouth, Va. 64438
Portsmouth Society for the Suppression of Vice. Board of Council. 64428
Portugaelsen donder-slagh. 1708
Portugais. pseud. Considerations importantes. 81937
Portugais. pseud. Reflexions. see Pinault, P. O.
Portugais d'Amerique. 19330, 38567
Portugiesisch-Brasilianischer Dolmetscher. 6450
Portugal, Juan Cayetano, Bp., 1783-1850. (11628), 59633 see also Michoacan (Archdiocese) Bishop (Portugal)
Portugal, Pedro Fernandez de Castro Andrade y. see Castro Andrade y Portugal, Pedro Fernandez de, Conde de Lemos, 1634-1672.
Portugal e Castro, Francisco Paulo de. 64439
Portugal. 7516, 7547, 19154, 19225, 38256, 44263-44265, 44268, 75952, (76837), (76847), 101228, 1st note after 102894, 102895
Portugal. defendants 29177
Portugal. Academia Real das Sciencias, Lisboa. see Academia Real das Sciencias de Lisboa.
Portugal. Bibliotheca Publica. 98649
Portugal. Comissao Mixta Brasileira e Portugueza na Execucao dos Artigos 6.° e 7.° do Tractado de 29 de Agosto de 1825. see Comissao Mixta Brasileira e Portugueza na Execucao dos Artigos 6.° e 7.° do Tractado de 29 de Agosto de 1825.
Portugal. Consulado. Boston. 96929 see also Marett, Philip.
Portugal. Cortes. 7646, 101228
Portugal. Jueces Plenipotenciaros. 11698
Portugal. Laws, statutes, etc. 7619, 7590, 11576, 14365, 42346, 44461, (58529), 68809, 71316, 93811, 99324
Portugal. Legation. Netherlands. 7543, 17197-17198, 17452, 23509, 47824, 49410, 68494, 81096, 88954, 102441, 102889A, 102891 see also Mendoca Corte-Real, Diogo de. Mendoca Furtado, Tristao de. Sousa Coutinho, Francisco de, 1597?-1660. Souza de Tavares da Silva, Henrique de, Conde de Miranda. Telles de Faro, Fernando. Ulhoa, Diogo Lopes.
Portugal. Legation. Spain. 70089 see also Souza Coutinho, Francisco Inocencio de.
Portugal. Ministerio da Marinha e Ultramar. 47730
Portugal. Ministerio dos Estrangeiros. 11576
Portugal. Sovereigns, etc. 81117, 93811
Portugal. Sovereigns, etc., 1495-1521 (Emanuel I) 22405-22408, 34100-34107, 56407, 99335 see also Emanuel I, King of Portugal, 1469-1521.

Post, Jacob, 1822-1891. 64459
Post, Lydia (Minturn) 64460-64462, 97068
Post, Martin Mercillian, 1806-1876. 64463-64464
Post, Reuben. 64465
Post, S. S. 64466, 90696
Post, Truman M. 64467-64471, 58616
Post St. Vincent, Indiana. Piankashaw Council, 1784. see Piankashaw Council, Post St. Vincent, Indiana, 1784.
Post-Captain. 18850, 64472
Post Captain in the Navy of the United States. pseud. Copy of a letter. (16725)
Post-chaise companion. 86180-86181
Post-, Kanal- und Eisenbahnkarte der Vereinigten Staaten van Nord-Amerika. 8215
Post man. 80014
Post-oak circuit. 64473, 64921, 93631
Post office as it has been, is, and should be. (64500)
Post office calendar containing a list of all the post offices. 94507
Post Office Department, New Brunswick. The fourth annual report. 52550
Post Office Department. The postal laws and regulations. (64501)
Post-office directory. 64502
Post-office directory for 1863. 20325
Post-office directory of Ohio. (57020)
Post-office law, with instructions and forms. 64503
Post office laws, with instructions and forms. 64504
Post Office quarterly directory. 64505
Post-pliocene fossils of South Carolina. 32600
Post prandial rhyme. (21131)
Post-script of the Gospels good success also amongst the West-Indians. (56742), (80815)
Post-script, or a second part of Rober Earle of Essex his ghost. 78379
Post-script to the Boston gazette. 95963
Post-scriptum sobre la agregacion de los cuatro primeros distritos. 87211
Post wages. 99108
Postage stamp album. 64515
Postal and commercial statistical information. 30248
Postal convention between the United States and Bremen. 64516
Postal convention between the United States of America and the United Kingdom. 64517
Postal laws and regulations. (64501)
Postal laws, classified by subjects. 39811
Postal Reform committee, New York. (64518)
Postal reform: its urgent necessity and practicability. 48937
Postal Reform Meeting, New York, 1856. see Public Meeting on Postal Reform, New York, 1856.
Postal reform. Proceedings of a public meeting held March 24th, 1856. (64518)
Posted up. 64520
Postel, Gvlielmo. 64521-64531
Postels, Alexandre. illus. (42739)
Posterior pars eiusdem Rapsodiae M. Ant. Coccii Sabellici. 74661
Posterior pars ejustem Rapsodiae historiarum. 74662
Posteriores reflecsiones sobre la abolicion. (64532)
Posthumous and other writings. 25569
Posthumous influence. 536
Posthumous publication. 91541
Posthumous works of a late celebrated genius, deceased. 91342

Posthumous works of Anne Eliza Bleecker. 5896
Posthumous works of . . . John Henry Hobart. 32297
Posthumous works of the late George Menzies. 47876
Posthumous works of the late Mr. William Lake. 38655
Posthumous writing of Diedrich Knickerbocker. (35193)
Posthumous writings of Junius. 36912
Posthumous, R. tr. 28921, 39646
Postkarte der Vereinigten Staaten und 18 Nebenkartchen. 8203
Postl, Karl, 1793-1864. 22510, 39869, 41018, 64533-64560, 78599, 95104, 2d note after 96106, note after 97982, note after 98962, 1st note after 99840
Postlethwaite, --------. 95079, 95093
Postlethwaite, --------. defendant 97700
Postlethwayt, Malachy. 51918, 64562-64568, 77276-77277
Postman. 3285
Poston, Charles D. (64569)
Postprandial New-Year's day soliloquy. 90212
Posts at which the stores are. (62068)
Postscript addressed to the Earl of Stair. 90102
Postscript addressed to the Right Honorable John Earl of Stair. 56437, 80107
Postscript, addressed to the Right Honorable Lord Sheffield. 21910
Postscript, being remarks on the Pennsylvania instructions. 64820
Postscript by another hand. 2602
Postscript, by another hand, wherein those several texts generally reverted. 21657
Postscript by Daniel Leeds. (37183)
Postscript by Dr. Edmund Halley. (25926)
Postscript. [By Jesse Torrey.] 96286
Postscript. . . . [by John Valentine.] 98355
Postscript. [By Joseph Woods.] 105126
Postscript. [By Nathaniel White.] 103441
Postscript, by the editor, addressed to Sir W****** H***. 40506
Postscript by the editor, introducing Yariza, an Indian maid's letter. 34476, 84624
Postscript, [By William Hubbard.] (33445)-33446, 106052
Postscript. Character of Hugh Peters. 98043
Postscript, concerning the meeting at Salters-Hall. 96429
Postscript, containing a short refutation of the discourse. 99806
Postscript, containing an answer to the reasons given by a number of ministers conven'd at Taunton. (22007), 94921, note after 103633, 5th note after 103650
Postscript, in answer to a postscript addressed to the Earl of Stair. 90102
Postscript in 1732. 92101
Postscript, in vindication of the West-India merchants. 1335A, 86644
Postscript, in which the present war against the Americans is shewn. 23079, 97350
Postscript, of the benefits which may arise. 35588
Postscript of the judgments of God. 5631
Postscript on the debate and division in the House of Commons. (81854), note after 95491
Postscript, on the relations between the United Kingdom and the United States. 101269
Postscript, or the second part of Robert Earle of Essex his ghost. 78369

Postscript, relating to a book entitled, "The life of Sir William Phips." 9927

Postscript relating to a book intitled, The life of Sir William Phips. 9926

Postscript, relating to Mr. Mather's remarks. 104256

Postscript . . . to a preservative. (24469)

Postscript to abuses, &c., obviated. 64570

Postscript to all students in arts and sciences. 39820, 1st note after 94666

Postscript . . . to the Board of Commissioners. 93511

Postscript to the Pennsylvania gazette. 60325

Postscript to the reply "point by point." 95657, 95660

Postscript to the Rev. Mr. A--d--w C--w-ll. 18700, 50464, 96025

Postscript to the second edition of Mr. Robinson's proofs. (72244)

Postscript to the second series of letters. 101380

Postscript, wherein a short account of the country of Penobscot is given. 9925

Postscript, with some remarks on the Quaker-almanack. 39817

Postscript with some remarks on the Quakers almanach. 28453, 39817, 66735, 66743

Postscriptum au deux mots. 5652

Postscriptum dell'Abate Angelo Saguineti. 76522

Postumous. pseud. see Postumus. pseud.

Postumus. pseud. Observations on the South Carolina memorial. 64571, 87905

Pot aux roses. 64572

Potato pests. 71391

Potawatomi Indians. Treaties, etc. 64605, 64607, 96595, 96605, 96618, 96620, 96630, 96631, 96647, 96653, 96657-96658, 96692, 96702, 96705, 96709-96711, 96718, 99605 see also Michigan Indians. Treaties, etc. United Tribes of Potawatomi, Chippewa, and Ottawa Indians. Treaties, etc.

Potawatomi Indians (Aub-ba-nauba Band) Treaties, etc. 96701

Potawatomi Indians (Comoza Band) Treaties, etc. 96595

Potawatomi Indians (Mes-quaw-buck Band) Treaties, etc. 96699

Potawatomi Indians (Mota Band) Treaties, etc. 96595

Potawatomi Indians (Waw-ke-wa Band) Treaties, etc. 96700

Potawatomi Indians of Indiana. Treaties, etc. 96682

Potawatomi Indians of the Prairie. Treaties, etc. 96678

Potawatomi Indians of the Wabash. Treaties, etc. 96680

Potawatomie Indians. see Potawatomi Indians.

Potent enemies of America. (17541)

Potent enemies of America laid open. 4678, 102699

Poterat, --------, Marquis de. 64574

Poterie, Claud Florent Bouchard de la. see Bouchard de la Poterie, Claud Florent.

Potewateme missinoi-kan catechisme ipi neneonin etchitek Wayowat. 64577

Potewatemi nememiseniukin ipi nemenigamowinin. 26327

Potewatemi nememissinoikan. A. M. D. G. (64578)

Potewatemi nememissinoikan ewiyowat nemadjik Catholiques endjik. 64579

Potewatemi nemewinin ipi nemenigamowinin. 64580

Potgieter, Barent Janszoon. 64581-64582, 102500

Potgieter, E. J. 64583

Potherie, Claude Charles le Roy Bacqueville de la. see Bacqueville de la Potherie, Claude Charles le Roy, b. ca. 1668.

Pothier, Toussaint. respondent 99598

Potiere, Claude Florent Bouchard de la. see Bouchard de la Potiere, Claude Florent.

Potiphar papers. 18052

Potomac and Alleghany Coal and Iron Manufacturing Company. (64586)

Potomac and the Rapidan. 67314

Potomac Copper Company. 64587

Potomac Copper Company. Charter. 64587

Potomac Iron Company. (64588)

Potomac muse. 64589

Potosi, Mexico (Diocese) petitioners 84518

Potosi, Mexico (Diocese) Bishop [ca. 1859] 44276

Potosi, Peru. Gremio de los Azogveros. see Gremio de los Azogveros, Potosi, Peru.

Potosi, la Paz, and Peruvian Mining Association. 64594

Potrwatome nkumwinin, epe natotatewinin. 81140

Pots, Richard. 82832, note after 92664, 2d note after 100510

Potsandove. 16297

Potsdam, N. Y. Normal and Training School. see New York (State) State Normal School, Potsdam.

Potsdam, N. Y. St. Lawrence Academy. see St. Lawrence Academy, Potsdam, N. Y.

Potsdam, N. Y. State Normal School. see New York (State) State Normal School, Potsdam.

Potsdam & Watertown Railroad. Chief Engineer 64598 see also Brodhead, Edward H.

Pott, Augustus Friedrich. (64599)-64603

Pott, John Frederick. 64604

Potter, Alonzo, Bp., 1800-1865. 47700, (48924), (60438), 61535, 61611, 62093, 64608-64617, 70086

Potter, Arnold. 64618

Potter, Asa. (70634) see also Rhode Island Secretary of State.

Potter, Chandler Eastman, 1807-1868. (23856), (64619)-64621

Potter, Edward. 26105

Potter, Edward Tuckerman. 64623

Potter, Elam. 64624-64627

Potter, Elisha Reynolds, 1811-1882. 3468, (35451), 64628-(64637), 70743, 70565, (70661), (70667), 70683, 70684, 70691, (70695), 70718, 70719 see also Rhode Island. Office of Commissioner of Education.

Potter, George A. 64638

Potter, H. 55641

Potter, Heman B. 84221

Potter, Henry C. (64639)

Potter, Horatio, Bp., 1802-1887. 64640-(64646), 65117, 82946, 97630

Potter, Isaiah. 64647-64648

Potter, J. B. M. (64652)

Potter, J. J. complainant (70576)

Potter, J. S. 64653

Potter, James. 64649-64650

Potter, James. plaintiff 92068

Potter, John F. 64651

Potter, L. 65683

Potter, Lyman. (64654)

Potter, Nathaniel, d. 1768. 64655

Potter, Nathaniel, 1770-1843. 64656-64659

Potter, O. F. ed. (47326), 75397

Potter, O. W. (64660)
Potter, Paraclete. 36492, 64661
Potter, Ray. 64662-64666, (70742)
Potter, W. W. (64672)
Potter, William J. 64667-(64671), 1st note after 96966
Potter, Woodburn. 64673, 2d note after 101263
Potter, Zabdiel W. 64674
Potter Christ. pseud. see Potter, Arnold.
Potter Investigating Committee, 1862. 47159, 65398
Pottle, Emory Bemsley, 1815-1891. 64675
Potts, Abraham. defendant 96945
Potts, G. C. 64679
Potts, George. 64676-64678
Potts, J. C. 64683
Potts, John. 64680
Potts, Jonathan. (52280), 64691
Potts, Joseph C. 64682
Potts, Stacy G. 64684
Potts, Stanley G. 64685, 99631
Potts, William D. (64686)-64688
Potts, William S. 32435, 64689-64692, note after 89770
Pottsville, Pa. Mount Carbon House. 7052
Pottsville, Pa. Scientific Association. see Pottsville Scientific Association, Pottsville, Pa.
Pottsville, Pa. Trinity Church. 64695
Pottsville, Pa. Trinity Church. Rector. 64695
see also Washburn, D.
Pottsville Scientific Association, Pottsville, Pa. 64694
Poucel, Benjamin. 64696-64703
Poucel, Benjamin. petitioner 64704
Pouchet, Georges. 64705-64706
Pouchot, Pierre, 1712-1767. 64707-64708
Poudenx, H. 64709
Poueda, Bartholome Goncalez de. see Goncalez de Poueda, Bartholome.
Pougens, Charles. ed. and tr. 103406
Pouget, Jean Francois Albert du. see Nadaillac, Jean Francois Albert du Pouget, Marquis de, 1818-1904.
Poughkeepsie, N. Y. Collegiate School. 64713
Poughkeepsie, N. Y. Convention for the Purpose of Facilitating the Introduction of Colored Troops into the Service of the United States, 1863. see Convention for the Purpose of Facilitating the Introduction of Colored Troops into the Service of the United States, Poughkeepsie, N. Y., 1863.
Poughkeepsie, N. Y. Convention, 1788. see New York (State) Convention, Poughkeepsie, 1788.
Poughkeepsie, N. Y. Court of Oyer and Terminer. 105040
Poughkeepsie, N. Y. Dutchess County and Poughkeepsie Sanitary Fair, 1864. 21455
Poughkeepsie, N. Y. Eastman National Business College. see Eastman National Business College, Poughkeepsie, N. Y.
Poughkeepsie, N. Y. Female Bible Society. see Poughkeepsie Female Bible Society.
Poughkeepsie, N. Y. Rural Cemetery. 64715
Poughkeepsie, N. Y. Society of Dutchess County for the Promotion of Agriculture. see Society of Dutchess County for the Promotion of Agriculture, Poughkeepsie.
Poughkeepsie almanac, for the year of Our Lord 1848. 64712
Poughkeepsie and Fishkill Landing directory. 64710
Poughkeepsie barometer, 1805. 98531
Poughkeepsie Female Bible Society. (64714)
Poughkeepsie journal. 101581

Po[u]ghkeepsie, July 2d, 1788. 100031
Poughkeepsie Rural Cemetery, its by-laws, rules and regulations. 64715
Pougin, Ed. (64716)
Poulain, Ernest. 64717
Poulain, H. (64718)
Poulain de Bossay, P. A. 68443
Poulett Thomson, Charles Edward. see Sydenham, Charles Edward Poulett Thomson, 1st Baron, 1799-1841.
Poullin de Lumina, ------. 64720
Poulson, Charles A. tr. 50004, 67460
Poulson, Zachariah. 5520
Poulson (Zachariah, Jr.) firm publishers 10758, 62431, 64721, 95921
Poulson's daily advertiser. 10758, 62431
Poulson's town and country almanac, for . . . 1789. 64721
Poulson's town and country almanac for 1798. 95921
Poultney, Evan. (36271)-(36272), 45078-45079, 64722-64723
Poultney, Evan. defendant 45079, 64724
Poultney, Samuel. defendant 45079
Poultney, Ellicott & Co. firm 45078
Poultney, Ellicott & Co. firm defendants 45079
Poultney, Vt. Ripley Female College. see Ripley Female College, Poultney, Vt.
Poultney gazette. 83541
Poultry Society of Pennsylvania. see State Poultry Society of Pennsylvania.
Poumarede, J. A. 64726-64727
Pound, J. D. 64728
Pound, W. 64729
Pound Master. pseud. Village poet. see Winchell, J. F.
Pouppe-Desportes, J. B. R. 64730
Pour et le contre ou avis a ceux qui se proposent. 7802
Pour et le contre sur un objet de grande discorde. 21034-21035, 56579, 69719
Pour les appellans. 99598
Pour les Religieuses Hospitalieres de Kebec en Canada. 67035
Pouring out of the spirit. (17087)
Pourquoi le Canadien Francais quitte-il le Bas-Canada? 10646
Pourquoi de nord ne peut pas accepter le separation. 38436, 38442
Poursuites dirigees contre les citoyens Cabet et Krolikowski. (9784)
Pourtrait en vyzonderheeden aangaande den politiek-vertoog-schryver. (40761)
Pourtraiture of a good man. 46463
Poussielgue, E. 64731
Poussin, Guillaume Tell, 1794-1876. 4946, 64732-(64740)
Poutechestvie v ioujenoi okean. 38289
Poutechestvie vokroug sveta. 38290, 38327
Poutre, Felix. (64741)
Poutrincourt, ------ de. 40175-40176, 40178
Pouvoir de la priere. (65540)
Pouvoir de la reconnaissance. 67417
Pouzol, ------ Girot. see Girot-Pouzol, --------.
Poverty: its illegal causes and legal cure. 89616
Povey, Charles. 64743-(64744)
Povoleri, John. 64745
Pow-wow. 64838
Powel, D. tr. 64846
Powel, John Hare. 64747, 64751-(64752)
Powell, ------. illus. 89339-89340
Powell, C. Frank. 64848
Powell, David. ed. 40914

Powell, E. P. 64749
Powell, George May. 64750
Powell, H. W. 93161
Powell, Jer. 94663
Powell, John S. 14438, (61792)
Powell, John Wesley, 1834-1902. 64753-64754,
   note after 85023, 85048, 85062, 85086
Powell, Lazarus Whitehead, 1812-1867. (37488),
   56422, 64756-64759 see also Kentucky.
   Governor, 1851-1855 (Powell)
Powell, Mr. M. C. 64760
Powell, Mrs. M. C. 64760
Powell, Nathaniell. 82832, note after 92664,
   2d note after 100510
Powell, Richard. defendant at court martial
   96932
Powell, Samuel. 37658, (55964), 64761
Powell, Sarah. tr. 64537
Powell, T. S. 64763
Powell, Thomas, 1809-1887. 64762
Powell, Thomas, fl. 1843. 71114
Powell, William Byrd, 1799-1866? 63764
Powell, William Henry, 1835-1901. 64765-
   (64766)
Power, Alexander. petitioner 16726
Power, John, 1820-1872. 74674
Power, John Carroll, 1819-1894. 64767-
   (64772), note after 89851
Power, John Hamilton, 1798-1873. (64773),
   84782A
Power, Mrs. Sarah A. (Harris) 1824- (64772)
Power, Thomas. (64774)-(64779)
Power, Thomas A. tr. 34872
Power, Tyrone. 64780
Power: a sermon preached at St. Paul's Church,
   Richmond. 49313
Power and duty of Congress to enfranchise the
   nation. 63441
Power and duty of Congress to provide for the
   common defence. 5445
Power and duty of grand juries. 86799
Power and glory of faith. 88891
Power and grandeur of Great-Britain. (64781)
Power and efficacy of the prayers of the
   people of God. 104364
Power and policy of exclusion. 64782
Power, duty, and necessity of destroying slavery.
   2070
Power, duty, privileges of the constitutional
   voters. 5272
Power from on high. 84294
Power of a municipal corporation, &c. 85696
Power of amending the constitution. 59646
Power of Christ vindicated. 103658
Power of Christian benevolence. (32247)
Power of Christianity. A discourse preached
   at the dedication. 16378
Power of Christianity. By Mrs. Pogson Smith.
   84136
Power of congregational churches asserted and
   vindicated. 18708
Power of Congress in relation to the slaves.
   (40254)
Power of Congress over the District of Colum-
   bia. (20309), 102550
Power of Congress over the territories. Speech
   . . . March 13 and 14, 1850. 11349
Power of Congress over the territories. Speech
   of Hon. David Ritchie, of Penn. 71567
Power of Congress to equalize civil rights
   amongst citizens. (37630)
Power of conscience. 84130, 1st note after
   95758
Power of consuls to remove merchant captains.
   64783
Power of cotton. 81248

Power of divine truth. 89744
Power of faith exemplified in the extraordinary
   case. 39459
Power of faith exemplified in the life and
   writings of . . . Mrs. Isabella Graham
   of New York. 28210
Power of faith, exemplified in the life and
   writings of the late Mrs. Isabella Graham
   (28211)
Power of music, a poetic tale. 103295
Power of our Great Saviour over the invisible
   world. 46355
Power of prayer. (65540)
Power of religion. 78293
Power of religion on the mind. (9395)
Power of solitude. A poem. 92316
Power of sympathy. 64784
Power of the Commander-in-Chief to declare
   martial law. 18028, (22293)
Power of the directors. (71377)
Power of the Gospel: a narrative of facts.
   28648
Power of the Gospel, in the conversion of
   sinners. 37206
Power of the Legislature to suspend a law.
   98560
Power of the past. 47253
Power of the President to suspend the . . .
   habeas corpus. 59646
Power of the resurrection. 59351
Power of the "S. F." 22606
Power of truth and love. 70845
Power of virtuous and refined beauty. 8787
Power to make treasury notes a legal tender.
   59646
Power vnited. 78191
Powers, Dennis. 64785
Powers, Edward Epps. 64786
Powers, G. M. 99102
Powers, George W. (64787)
Powers, Gershom. (53976), 64788-(64789)
   see also New York (State) State Prison,
   Auburn. Agent.
Powers, Grant. 64790-64795
Powers, H. P. 64798
Powers, Hiram. 64796
Powers, Horatio N. 64797
Powers, Michael. defendant (64799)-(64800),
   note after 96920
Powers, P. O. 64803
Powers, Peter. 64801-64802, 89805, note
   before 99021
Powers, Stephen. 64804-64805
Powers, Thomas. defendant before military
   commission (31083)
Powers, Thomas E. 64806
Powers and duties of religious and school
   societies. 103710
Powers and duties of the several town officers
   103710
Powers and duties of towns. 103710
Powers, duties, and liabilities of town and
   parrish officers. 31575
Powers Institute, Bernardston, Mass. 64807
Powers of Congress. 10996
Powers of genius, a poem, in three parts.
   (41337)
Powers of the Executive Department of the
   government. 15619
Powers of the federal government to protect
   the colored people. 78601
Powers of the general governments. 64808
Powers of the government of the United States
   91685
Powers of the President of the United States
   in times of war. 64809

Powers of the vestry of a church. 64810
Powers' statue of the Greek slave. 64796
" Powers that be." A sermon, preached in
St. Paul's Church. 90881
" Powers that be," and "the fugitive slave
bill." (67859)
Powers vested in Congress. 97439
Poweshiek County, Iowa. A descriptive account.
(64811)
Powhatan; a metrical romance. 84153
Powiesc z nad bagien Amerykanskich. 92406
Powles, J. D. 64812-64813
Powles, Illingworth, i Compania. 56456
Powles Hook Company. see Associates of
the Jersey Company of Powles Hook.
Pownall, George. 995
Pownall, Thomas, 1722-1805. 30571, (35987),
64814-64837, 81486, 82303, note after
89189, 2d note after 96457, 2d note after
97583, 101047
Powow, being a complete and an exact des-
cription of an Indian banquet. 70765
Powring [sic] ovt of the seven vials. 17074
Powys, -----------, fl. 1791. supposed author
(10614), note after 95691
Poyais (Proposed Colony) Constitution. 64839
Poyais. An account of the British settlements.
21907
Poyas, Mrs. Elizabeth Anne. 10976, 57921,
59530, 64841-(64842), 2d note after 87909,
note after 87910, 87912
Poydras, Julien. 64843-(64847)
Poyen de Boisneuf, ------. see Payen de
Boisneuf, ------------.
Poyen St. Sauveur, Charles. 64851-(64852),
92135
Poyen Sainte-Marie. ----------. 64850
Poyer, John. 64853
Poyet, C. F. 64854
Poynton, T. (64855)
Poyntz, John. 64856-64858
Pozo, Antonio del. 64859
Pozobueno, -----------, Marques de. 90292
see also Spain. Legation. Great Britain.
Pozos Dulces, Francisco Frias y Jacott, Conde
de. see Frias y Jacott, Francisco, Conde
de Pozos Dulces, 1809-1877.
Pozzi, Gio. Benigno. tr. 67500
Practica de confessores de monjas. (6402)
Practica de la administracion y cobranza de
las rentas reales. 71493
Practica de la conuersion. 74017
Practica de la doctrina Christiana. 50497
Practica de la theologia mystica. 27661
Practica de los exercicios espirituales de
Nuestro Padre S. Ignacio. 35325
Practica y formulario de procedimientos en
materia civil y criminal. 76281
Practicability and importance of a ship canal.
64861
Practicability and importance of connecting
Halifax. (33315)
Practicability of conquering prejudice. 8117,
93137-93138
Practicability of peace. (64862)
Practicability of the abolition of slavery. 78835
Practicability of the different routes. 82994
Practicability of travelling pleasantly and safely
from New York to California. 64312
Practicability, safety and advantages of Negro
emancipation. 2945, 64863
Practicable route for the Pacific Railroad.
64864
Practical abridgment of American common law
cases. 103186

Practical account of what the author, and others
who visited that country for the same
objects, saw and did. 21319
Practical advice to British slave-holders.
104782
Practical advice to emigrants on all points.
22501
Practical American miner. 18257
Practical and instructive guide to all persons.
1647
Practical and mental arithmetic. note before
83906, 83909, 83922, 83928
Practical and mental arithmetic, designed
principally to accompany Daboll's system
of arithmetic. note before 83906-83906
Practical and mental arithmetic on a new plan.
83907-83908
Practical arguments against emigration. 31135
Practical arithmetic. 90295
Practical banker. pseud. Defence of the
currency of Massachusetts. see Congdon,
James B.
Practical banker. pseud. Letter to His Excel-
lency John Henry Clifford. see Congdon,
James B.
Practical banker. pseud. National currency.
51968
Practical business guide chiefly intended for
the use of retail stationers. 90803
Practical church member. 49697
Practical comparison of the cost of steam and
water power in America. 50150, note
after 92844
Practical considerations founded on the scrip-
tures. (82033), 4th note after 88114
Practical defeat of the abolition act. (64865)
Practical detail of the cotton manufacture.
50149-50150, note after 92844
Practical details for the information of emigrants of every class. 33366
Practical development of our own resources.
66095
Practical directions for the holding of elections,
and the canvassing of votes, under the
new . . . law. 54585
Practical directions for the holding of elections
. . . principally applicable to the city
of New York. 26932
Practical directory in the search for gold.
56136
Practical discourse against extortion. (25870)
Practical discourse concerning the choice bene-
fit of communion with God. 50298
Practical discourse of prayer. 13868
Practical discourse relating to the Gospel-
ministry. (25401)
Practical discourse, to sea-faring men. 84353
Practical discourses delivered on occasion of
the earthquakes. 47143
Practical discourses on the parable of the ten
virgins. 14509, 97450
Practical discourses on various texts. 59607
Practical discourses upon the parable of the
ten virgins. (14508)
Practical education. 84498
Practical emigration to the United States. 46870
Practical essay concerning the small-pox.
20724
Practical essay on a cement. 64866
Practical essays. 14868
Practical essays on medical education. 20825
Practical essay on typhous fever. 83654
Practical essays, political, legal, moral, and
miscellaneous. 22242, 22273
Practical experience. 50815, note after 94673

Practical farmer. pseud. Emigrant farmer. 22475

Practical farmer, and silk manual. 24220

Practical farmer: being a new and compendious system of husbandry. 89930

Practical farmer, by an association of practical farmers. 74164

Practical farmer, gardener, and house-wife. 32870

Practical farmer's guide. 102962

Practical gardener. pseud. American kitchen gardener. see Fessenden, Thomas Greene.

Practical Godliness the way to prosperity. 103747

Practical guide for British Shipmasters. 21986

Practical guide for emigrants to North America. 64867

Practical guide for the manufacture of paper and boards. 66093

Practical guide for tourists, miners, and investors. 31195

Practical guide to emigrants to the United States. 43542

Practical handbook for miners, metallurgists, and assayers. 81129

Practical hints on the culture of the mulberry tree. 72045

Practical hints to persons about to cross the isthmus of Panama. 11060

Practical history of a new epidemic eruptive military fever. 20724

Practical horticulturist. see Northern farmer and practical horticulturist.

Practical husbandry. 91830

Practical illustrations of the principles of school architecture. 3469

Practical influence of the Spanish colonial system. note after 97687

Practical information concerning the public debt. 71092

Practical information for emigrants. 64868

Practical information respecting New Brunswick. 64869

Practical information respecting New Brunswick, . . . soil, climate, productions, and agriculture. 52544

Practical instructions for military officers. 33403, 91607

Practical justice of the peace. 81376

Practical language interpreted. 82544

Practical liberty. 27369

Practical man. pseud. Examination of the reasons. 23370, 68302

Practical manipulator. 104129

Practical marine gunnery. 44772

Practical mineralogy, assaying and mining. 57978

Practical mode of studying the heart. 84799

Practical narrative of the autumnal epidemic fever. (79970)

Practical navigation. 79030

Practical navigator, and seaman's new daily assistant. 50412

Practical notes made during a tour in Canada. 24102

Practical observations on the British West India sugar trade. 64870, 2d note after 102858

Practical observations on the diseases of the army in Jamaica. 40019

Practical plan to secure the peace and prosperity of the Spanish-American states. (9667), 81634

Practical principles of rail-ways. 93512

Practical question piously resolved. 64871

Practical reflections in the Choctaw language. 12866

Practical reflections on the earthquakes. (80741)

Practical reflections on the late earthquakes. 80740

Practical religion exemplify'd. 70445

Practical remarks on the slave trade. 19578

Practical remarks on West-India diseases. 64872, 3d note after 102858

Practical route for the Pacific railroad. (3762?

Practical rules for the management and medica? treatment. (64873)

Practical shepherd. 67788

Practical stone-cutter. pseud. Some observations. 86690

Practical suggestions on mining rights and privileges. 30616

Practical summary of the principles and work. 89260

Practical system of book-keeping. 83907-83908

Practical system of book-keeping; for farmers and mechanics. 83911

Practical treatise on business. (25733)

Practical treatise on coal. 27224

Practical treatise on grasses and forage plants 24766

Practical treatise on prayer. 13868

Practical treatise on rail-roads. 105054

Practical treatise on the coniferae. 32871

Practical treatise on the cultivation of the sugar cane. 37632

Practical treatise on the culture of silk. 15071

Practical treatise on the diet, etc. of weakly subjects. (72125)

Practical treatise on the history, medical properties, and cultivation of tobacco. 36042

Practical treatise on the law of nations. 12852?

Practical treatise on the law of slavery. 103187

Practical treatise on the power to sell land. (5704)

Practical treatise on the powers and duties of justices of the peace. 29555

Practical treatise on the stamp act of July 1, 1862. 21914

Practical treatise on the trustee process. 18117

Practical treatise on the use of Preuvian and Ichaboe African guano. (80297)

Practical treatise on the water delivered by the Manhattan Company. (29540)

Practical treatise on vaccina or cowpock. 78164

Practical treatise upon several different and useful subjects. 94404

Practical treatise upon the bankrupt law. 24302

Practical treatise upon the law of railways. (68501)

Practical truth, plainly delivered. 46718

Practical truth's, tending to promote holiness. 46719

Practical turths tending to promote the power of Godliness. 46720

Practical value of physical science. 73088

Practical view of slavery. 81845

Practical view of the business of banking. 11219

Practical view of the common causes of inefficiency in the Christian ministry. 97930

Practical view of the present state of slavery. (3352)

Practical views of the proposed improvement of the Ohio River. 71937

Practical working of cheap postage. 39564

Practical commentary. (17076)

Practicas religiosas de Augusto Frederico de Castilho. 11415
Practice in the executive departments of the government. 79626
Practice of courts martial. 43610
Practice of fruit growing. 82204
Practice of justice our only security for the future. 37269
Practice of midwifery. (82252)-(82253)
Practice of naval summary courts-martial. 30786
Practice of piety. 4075-4076, 22165
Practice of the Court of Appeals from the Plantations. 13260
Practice of training new slaves. 50620
Practice of war. 58562, 64874
Practiicke van den Spaenschen aes-sack. (31660)-(31661)
Practischen Arzte. pseud. ed. Uber Brasilien. 7533
Practitioners of Physic and Surgery in the County and City of New York. see Medical Society of the County of New York.
Prada, Francisco de. 99437 see also Santo Domingo (Spanish Colony) Audiencia. Fiscal.
Prade, N. de. supposed author 2758, 64875
Pradelles, ------ van. see Van Pradelles, ---------.
Pradier-Fodere, P. 64876
Pradilla, Antonio M. 64877
Pradillo, Agustino. 55490
Prado, Agustin, Pres. Guatemala. 28973 see also Guatemala. Presidente, 1827 (Prado)
Prado, Joseph Garcia de. see Garcia de Prado, Joseph.
Prado, Juan de. 16670 see also Cuba. Gobernador (Prado)
Prado, Juan de. defendant at court of inquiry 29459
Prado, Marcos Ramirez de. see Ramirez de Prado, Marcos.
Prado, Mariano Ignacio, Pres. Peru, 1826-1901. 16904, 58514, 61077, 64879 see also Peru. President, 1865-1868 (Prado)
Prado, Pablo de. 58069, 64880
Prado, Pedro. 64881
Prado Mayeza Portocarrero y Luna, Juan de. 16670 see also Cuba. Gobernador, 1761-1762 (Prado Mayeza Portocarrero y Luna)
Pradt, Dominique Dufour de. see Pradt, Dominique Georges Frederic de Riom de Prolhiac de Fourt de, Abp., 1759-1837.
Pradt, Dominique Georges Frederic de Riom de Prolhiac de Fourt de, Abp., 1759-1837. 23915, (40684), 64882-64911, note after 88938, 99656
Praecipuae totius orbis imagines et statuae. 77606
Praeclara Ferdinandi. Cortesii de Noua Maris Oceani. 16947
Praedicatores. see Dominicans.
Praediumrusticum. 75949, 98519-98520, 2d note after 96930A
Praefatio ad benevolum lectorem. 77957
Praefatio ad lectorem benevolum. 77958
Praefatio Ae. Antonii Nebrissensis. 1551, 45010
Praefatio apologetica. 55888
Praefatio in fragmenta tabulae itinerariae antiquae. 66597
Praefatio inseqvens tabvlarvm Ptolemaei opva. 66494

Praelaticus. pseud. Dialogue. see Dickinson, Jonathan, 1866-1747.
Praelaticus triumphatus. 22115, 78493
Praematvrae solis apparitionis. 73295
Praemonitio ad lectorum. 93324
Praemonition to the intelligent reader. 78189
Praetorius, J. J. 64913
Praetorius, Johann Christophe. (58059), 64912, 96049
Prafatio ad lectorem. 41366
Pragmaticas del reyno. 64914
Praier [sic] duly said morning and euening. 99866
Prairie. 16460
Prairie; a tale. (16510)
Prairie. . . . Aus dem Englischen. 16512
Prairie bird, a lady of Massachusetts. pseud. Poem, and other thoughts. see Wellman, Mary W.
Prairie-bird. By the Hon. Charles Augustus Murray. (51489)
Prairie-breaking. 32450
Prairie chicken. 64916
Prairie Crusoe. 64917
Prairie du Chien. 8761
Prairie du Jacinto. 78599
Prairie farmer annual and agricultural and horticultural advertiser. 64918
Prairie farming in America. 9854
"Prairie flower." (4724)
Prairie flower, or adventures in the far west. (4724)
Prairie guide. 25105
Prairie guide; or the rose of the Rio Grande. (18061)
Prairie-Jake. 64919
Prairie missionary. 64920
Prairie mud circuit. 64921
Prairie scout. (64922)
Prairie. Traduction de la Bedolliere. 16511
Prairie. Traduction nouvelle. 16511
Prairie. Traduction nouvelle, par M. Benjamin Laroche. 16511
Prairie. Traduit par Defauconpret. 16511
Prairie trail. 22297
Prairie travel and scalp dances. 26687
"Prairie traveller." (44514)-(44515)
Prairiedom. 88599, 93969, note before 95109
Prairies of the western states. 41308
Praise due to God for all the dispensations. 94524
Praises bespoke for the God in heaven. 46602
Praises of American heroes. 62910
Praises of Lee and Jackson. 39791
Praktische Anleitung in Amerika Geld zu Erwerben. (25733)
Praktische Belehrungen und Rathsclage. 7454
Prall, John A. 64923-64924
Pramaticas del reyno. (64915)
Pranks of the modern puck. (70973)
Prarond, E. 64925-64927
Prasidenten Davis Botschaft. (64928)
Praslin, --------, Duc de Choiseul-. see Choiseul-Praslin, --------, Duc de.
Praslow, J. 64928A
Prat de Saba, Onuphrio. 64930
Prater, Horatio. 64929
Pratt, --------, fl. 1778. 79486
Pratt, ---------, fl. 1850. 64984
Pratt, ----------, fl. 1859. 64985
Pratt, Charles. see Camden, Charles Pratt, 1st Earl, 1714-1794.
Pratt, Daniel J. 64931-64933
Pratt, Dura D. 64934
Pratt, E. P. (64936)
Pratt, Enoch. (64937)

Preaching of Christ an expression of God's great love to sinners. 103213
Preaching of Jesus. (77574)
Preaching of the cross is to them that perish foolishness. 88933
Preaching of the word. 92079
Preaching peace by Jesus Christ. 62513
Preaching the Gospel. 85443
Preaching the Gospel the grand function of the minister. (79299), 92272
Preamble and constitution of the Dyottsville Apprentices' Library Company. 61609
Preamble and constitution of the Friendly Association for Mutual Interests. 61679
Preamble and constitution of the . . . [New York Young Men's Anti-slavery] Society. 54560
Preamble and constitution of the Rhode-Island Suffrage Association. 70739
" Preamble and resolution" of the town. 92787
Preamble and resolution offered by Mr. Logan. 41803
Preamble and resolutions adopted at the great anti-tariff meeting. 87914
Preamble and resolutions, adopted by a meeting held at the Exchange Coffee House. 65001
Preamble and resolutions adopted by the Common Council of the city of Alton. 968
Preamble and resolutions adopted by the Legislature. 94803
Preamble and resolutions adopted by the meeting of ship masters. 97001
Preamble and resolutions in regard to the objects of the present war. 45278
Preamble and resolutions of Dr. Sherwood. 82920
Preamble and resolutions of the Associates in Philadelphia. (76694)
Preamble and resolutions of the Decatur Bank. 19138
Preamble and resolutions of the Legislature. 37560
Preamble and resolutions . . . [of the Pennsylvania Seamen's Friend Society.] 60362
Preamble and resolutions passed at a meeting of the receivers and exporters of American leaf tobacco. 65002
Preamble, constitution, and by-laws of the O'Connell Club. (56654)
Preamble, constitution, &c. of the Society in Aid of Social Improvements. 85990
Preamble . . . of the Reformed Dutch Church, Hyde-Park. (80452)
Preamble, resolutions, and address. 37581
[Preamble, resolutions, rules of incorporation and list of members.] 46122, 85840
Preble, Edward. 65003-65004
Preble, George Henry, 1816-1885. 12217, 65004, 65006-65015, 83462
Preble, George Henry, 1816-1885. petitioner 65010-65011
Preble, Harriet. 16487, (39786)
Preble, Thomas M. 25695, 65016
Preble, William P. 19144, 43921, 55201, 65017-65018
Precationes et hymni Gronlandici. 95616
Precaution. 89934
Precaution. A novel. (16513)
Precaution, ou le choix de mari. (16514)
Precedents of American neutrality. 4626
Precedes de la Societe d'Agriculture du Bas-Canada. 10345
Preceding is a true copy of an act. 99104
Preceding is a true copy of an act passed by the Legislature of the State of Vermont, 29th October last. 99098

Precept upon precept. (69644)
Preceptos para le primera clase de Latinidad. 72536
Preces sancti Nersetis Clajensis. 65020
Preces sancti Nersetis Clajensis Armeniorum. 65021
Precidents bearing on the admission of members. 86112
Precious epistle of William Robinson. 28099
Precious in the sight of the Lord. (65609)
Precious morsels. (65019)
Precious treasure in earthen vessels. (79426)
Precis. 27650, (63966), 68421
Precis analytique des pieces fournies au Comite Colonial. 65022, 75178
Precis analytique des travaux de la Societe Medicale de la Nouvelle-Orleans. 94219
Precis de Blanchelande sur son accusation. 5845
Precis de cette guerre. 68421
Precis de deux lettres avec une reflexion generale. 75838
Precis de diverses ordonnances du Conseil special. 11737
Precis de faits. (47511), 68283-68284, note after 80055
Precis de la colonisation de la Mana. 21352
Precis de la geographie universelle. 44159
Precis de la justification de Joseph-Paul-Augustin Cambefort. (10104)
Precis de la mission qu'a remple aux Antilles Francais. (11407)
Precis de la reclamation du Sieur. 11643
Precis de la Revolution de Saint-Domingue. 65023
Precis de la vie de ce ministre. 98971
Precis de l'abolition de l'esclavage dans les colonies Anglaises. 12222, 65024
Precis de l'etat actuel des colonies Angloises dans l'Amerique Septentrionale. 5691, 65025, 96191
Precis de l'histoire de l'astronomie aux Etats-Unis d'Amerique. 43893
Precis de l'histoire des Etats-Unis d'Amerique. 59571
Precis de l'histoire des revolutions de l'Empire Bresilien. (75231)
Precis de l'histoire general de l'archipel des Canaries. 6438
Precis de l'histoire interessante des establissement des Europeens. 69098
Precis de l'histoire philosophique & politique des etablissements. 69097
Precis de l'insurrection Americaine. 5390
Precis des evenemens qui se sont passes a la Guadaloupe. 14459
Precis des evenements de la campagne du Mexique en 1862. (44859)
Precis des faits. 91869
Precis des gemessements des sangs-leles dans les colonies Francoises. 9745, 65026
Precis des gemissements des sang meles dans les colonies Francaises. 9745, 65026
Precis des regles suivies dans le Parlement d'Angleterre. 35888
Precis des victoires et conquetes des Francais. 6980
Precis des voyages entrepris pour se rendre par le nord dans les Indies. (9826)
Precis des voyages les plus interessans, par terre et par mer. 42989
Precis du droit des gens modernes de l'Europe. (44840)
Precis du traite de paix. 27650, (63966), 68421

Preface by a member of the Assembly. 26445, 104455

Preface by Anthony Benezet. 63224

Preface by Bishop Meade. 58157

Preface, by Bishop Meade. 81566

Preface by Cotton Mather. 39795

Preface by Dr. Increase Mather. 42088, 46491

Preface by Dr. Owen. 46745

Preface, by E. O. Haven. 43852

Preface by Francis Parkman. 84619

Preface by Garrison. 95498

Preface by George Combe. 33997

Preface, by Gilbert Brunet. (38445)

Preface by Henry Stevens. 63857

Preface by his executor, Rev. H. Byrd West. 20865

Preface by Hon. William Jay. 91011

Preface by Increase Mather. 14477, 46401, 49656, 49979

Preface by James Wellwood. 59715, note after 103670

Preface [by John Cotton.] 63331

Preface, by John Pye Smith. 93199

Preface [by John Quick.] 67164

Preface. [By Joseph Sewall and Thomas Prince.] 32736, 103932

Preface by Lorenzo Dow. 96361

Preface by Mr. Cooper. 25397

Preface by Mr. Foxcroft. (20062)

Preface, by Mr. Wood. 35660, 105080

Preface, by Mrs. C. M. Kirkland. 21685

Preface, by P. V. Daniel, Jr. 67818, 1st note after 99797

Preface—by Philo-Hancock. 103851

Preface by Rev. John Angel James. 21937

Preface by Richard Herne Shepherd. (63569)

Preface by Sundry ministers. 104400

Preface by T. Prince. 13208

Preface by T. Raylton. 24279

Preface by T. Wood. 69522

Preface by the Earl of Carlisle. 92494

Preface by the editor. 63294

Preface by the editor, in which some geographical, nautical, and commercial questions are discussed. 10053

Preface by the English editor. 29948, 84818

Preface . . . by the Presbytery of Newcastle. 58442

Preface by the publisher. 87818

Preface by the Rev. Charles Kingsley. 87346

Preface by the Rev. Charles Lee. 24002

Preface by the Reverend Dr. Colman and Mr. Cooper. 83428

Preface by the Reverend, Dr. Colman and Mr. Cooper, of Boston, New-England. 83430-83433, 103514, 103588, 103601

Preface by the Reverend Dr. Cotton Mather. (22439)

Preface by the Rd. Dr. Mather. 62757

Preface by the Reverend Dr. Sewall, Mr. Prince, and Mr. Foxcroft. 59604

Preface, by the Reverend Dr. Williams. 46477

Preface by the Reverend Edmund Calamy. 46406

Preface by the Reverend Mr. Benjamin Wadsworth. (25401)

Preface by the Reverend Mr. Buckley of Colchester. 104986

Preface by the Reverend Mr. Byles. 24679

Preface by the Reverend Mr. Cooper. 11894

Preface by the Rev. Mr. Danforth. 17098

Preface by the Reverend Mr. Fitch. 80794

Preface by the Rev. Mr. Gilbert Tennent. 103515

Preface by the Reverend Mr. Gilbert Tennent. 103593

Preface by the Reverend Mr. John Conder. 8791, 41605

Preface by the Reverend, Mr. John Higginson. (46599)

Preface by the Rev. Mr. Edwards. 4497

Preface by the Reverend Mr. Pemberton. (14525)

Preface by the Reverend Mr. Thomas Gibbons. 18757

Preface by the Reverend Mr. Wadsworth. 25408

Preface by the Rev. Pierce Conelly. 14773

Preface, by the Rev. T. Price, D. D. (65464), 73141

Preface by the Rev. W. Arthur. 24416

Preface by the Right Hon. the Earl of Carlisle. 92493, 92495

Preface by the Right Rev. George Burgess, D. D. 3720, 66194

Preface by the senior pastors of the town. 16632

Preface, by Theodore Sedgwick, Jr. 39863

Preface. [By Tho. Goodwin.] 32860

Preface by Thomas Goodwin and Philip Nye. 32832

Preface. [By Thomas Prince.] 104317

Preface by Walter George Smith. 84397

Preface by Will. Whiston. 46438

Preface by William Gilbert, Esq. 101555

Preface. [By William Hubbard.] 72691

Preface [by William Livingston.] 84576

Preface concerning the duty of singing psalms. 66432

Preface containing a further vindication of Sir Home Popham. 64131

Preface containing, amongst other things, the author's apology. 50650

Preface, containing an examination of the Rev. Mr. William Cooper's preface to Mr. Edwards's sermons. 12316, (21935), 67768

Preface, containing remarks on Dr. Roger's vindication. 11870

Preface, containing remarks upon the authorities. (11833)

Preface of Clement Duvernois. 34945, note after 48507

Preface de M. Charles de Remusat. 11907, 11924

Preface, des notes & des observations relatives a la culture de la cochenille. 95349

Preface d'Edward Wright. 27356

Preface et de notes nouvelles par Louis Lacour. 39271

Preface et d'une etude sur l'esclavage aux Etats-Unis. 11916

Preface et la biographie de Hepworth Dixon. 20374

Preface, exposing the artifices of our priests. (17350)

Preface, giving a short account of the Six Nations. 36337

Preface, giving some account of his life and character. 101171

Preface, giving some account of the fire. 100909

Preface, giving some account of the rise and progress of the scheme. 6163, 20220

Preface historique. 71864-71866, 71871

Preface in prose, in defence of Christianity. 17432

Preface in defence of the addressed. 100674

Preface in which the congregational discipline of the Churches in New-England is vindicated. (46754)

Preface in which there is a brief and true character. (46742)

Preface, notes, and addenda by his youngest
son. 34050
Preface of Dr. Increase Mather, and Dr.
Cotton Mather. 37234
Preface of foure poynts. 82824
Preface of Increase Mather, D. D. 94113,
103402
Preface of Mr. Caldwell's sermon on the trial
of the spirit. 43293
Preface of the Reverend Dr. Increase Mather.
46241
Preface of the Reverend Mr. John Allin.
(21090), 33698, 78431, 104846
Preface, offering some reasons for this publica-
tion. 94707
Preface, or an epistle containing some further
reasons to strengthen the overture. 95581
Preface par Aurelien Scholl. 26417
Preface par Charles Comte. 77354
Preface par Isaiah Townsend, Jr. (24993), note
after 96377, note after 101800
Preface par J. A. Llorente. (65985)
Preface par Mr. Arnout Vosmaer. 69600
Preface par Pierre Vincard. 23096
Preface recommendatory by the Rev. Mr.
Clarke. 106391
Preface to a speech of Mr. John Milton.
101046
Preface to, and report of, the trial of Edward
Lyon. 42850, 91768, 96897
Preface to both, giving some account of the
life and character of Mr. Willard. 104112
Preface, to encourage and perpetuate the sing-
ing of psalms. 66446
Preface [to John Dickinson's speech.] 20049,
104455
Preface to Mr. Edwards's sermons. 12316,
(21935), 67768
Preface to the Christian reader, 49662, 66059
Preface to the former account. 103496
Preface to the fourth edition of a letter to
William Wilberforce. 95658
Preface to the freeholders of Great Britain.
89127
Preface to the reader. 80202
Preface to the Rev. Mr. Tennent's five sermons
and appendix. 30172, 62419, 94687
Preface to the Reverend Mr. Whitefield's ac-
count. 103513
Preface to the third edition of a letter to
William Wilberforce. 95659
Preface upon the slavery of Negroes in the
British colonies. 44920
Preface de H. Settegart. 73282
Prefatory address by E Mayhew. 2869
'Prefatory address,' by the author. 99823
Prefatory address from the New York Com-
mittee of Safety. 15583, 98439
Prefatory address to Philip Doddridge, D. D.
94702
Prefatory address to Sir George Saville, Bart.
40472
Prefatory address to the citizens of the United
States. 2395
Prefatory address to the freemen of His
Majesty's English colony of Connecticut.
13213, (26354), note after 105924
Prefatory address to the gentlemen of America.
96358, note after 103042
Prefatory address to the Synods of New-York
& Philadelphia. 94693
Prefatory epistle by Mr. Matthew Mead. 46293
Prefatory epistle, to certain priests. (13870)
Prefatory epistle to the plenipotentiaries of the
late Congress. 97358
Prefatory epistle to the reader. (65600)

Prefatory inquiry respecting the real author.
36909
Prefatory letter by R[ichard] P[rice.] 100.
Prefatory letter by the Rev. John Hannah.
36137
Prefatory letter to the Right Hon. the Earl
Bathurst. (29586)
Prefatory note by Charles Deane. 82834
Prefatory note by George Brinley. 15755-
15765
Prefatory note by . . . J. G. Lorimer. 8527.
Prefatory note to the reader, by John B. Mur
43599
Prefatory notes and appendix. 45315
Prefatory notice by E. Ballard. 29474
Prefatory observations. 741, 16684, 91853
Prefatory observations and notes. 28737
Prefatory poem. (46258)
Prefatory remarks annexed to the constitution
(32305), 99815
Prefatory remarks by George Thompson, Esq
52273
Prefatory remarks, by J. J. E. Linton, Esq.
31377
Prefatory remarks by Joshua V. Himes. 102
Prefatory remarks on the subsequent abolition
of slavery. 13486
Prefatory reply, to the false and scurrillous
aspersions. 18571, (32340), note after
72819, 78234
Prefatory report and an appendix. 54988
Prefecto de Salas, Joseph. see Salas, Josep
Prefecto de.
Prefecto de Tlaxcala. pseud. Despojo a mar
armada. 19755-(19756)
Prefetto del la India. pseud. Copia delle le
6419-6421, 16669, 54945, (63177)
Prefontaine, --------, Chevalier de. (65038)
(77219)-77220, 1st note after (74627)
Pregeth ar helynt Bresennol America. 84645
Pregon en qve el Rey Nuestro Senor manda.
65039
Preguntas tocantes a la doctrina. 72811
Preguntas tocantes a la doctrina de como es
Christiano. (72812)
Preguntas tocantes a los mysterios de la mis
72811
Pre-historic and modern copper mines. 8408
Pre-historic copper implements. 81696
Prehistoric fishing in Europe and North Amer
85072
Prehistoric races and pre-territorial history
of Ohio. 85144
Pre-historic times, as illustrated by ancient
remains. 42602
Prehl, N. C. H. 65040
Preisen der Inland-passage. (9676)
Prejudice against colored people. 2511
Prejudice against the colored people. 65041
Prejudice vincible. 8117, 93137-93138
Prejudices rectified. 83450
Prelacy discussed. 93750
Prelados del Convento de S. Diego de Esta
Capital de Mexico. see Mexico (City)
Convento de S. Diego. Prelados.
Prelatical doctrine of apostolical succession
examined. 95312
Prelatical usurpation exposed. 65042, 99778
Preleccoes de diplomacia. 20973
Prelectio exponens vigessimam sextam dis-
tinctionem. (22064)
Prelections on some of the more important
subjects. 82921
Preliminar y cartas que preceden al tomo 1 .
41670
Preliminaries and definitive treaties of peace.
91091

Preliminaries and proceedings at Study Hill.
5702

Preliminary abstract of the views of Blumenbach.
82393

Preliminary account of the Indians. 32185,
2d note after 97850

Preliminary address. 65043

Preliminary articles of peace between Great
Britain and the United States of America.
65046

Preliminary articles of peace between His
Britannick Majesty and the States-General.
65045

Preliminary articles of peace, between His
Britannick Majesty, the Most Christian
King, and the Most Catholick King. 65044

Preliminary discourse. 97341

Preliminary economic studies of the war, no.
9. 83376

Preliminary essay on ancient and modern
aqueducts. 37787

Preliminary essay on medical jurisprudence.
(43241)

Preliminary essay on the laying out, planting
and managing of cemeteries. 82981

Preliminary field report of the United States
Geological Survey of Colorado and New
Mexico. 31005

Preliminary geological report, by William P.
Blake. 69900

Preliminary history of two discourses. 3094

Preliminary investigation of the alleged ancestry of George Washington. 12541

Preliminary lecture, delivered before the law-
students. 91000

Preliminary letter by Dr. Richard S. Stewart.
11201

Preliminary list of plants of Buffalo and its
vicinity. 13749

Preliminary notes to a report on the proposed
Hunduras Interoceanic Railway. 89988

Preliminary notice of new genera and species
of fossils. (35001)

Preliminary notice of the crustacea dredged.
84230

Preliminary notices of the celebration. 88036,
note after 96180

Preliminary observations by C. R. Nesbitt, Esq.
(7111)

Preliminary observations. [By William Wheelwright.] 90775, note after 103224

Preliminary prospectus of the Samana Bay
Company. 75882

Preliminary remarks. 94110

Preliminary remarks [by S. P. P. Fay.] 75208

Preliminary remarks, illustrative of the subject
in question. 9024

Preliminary remarks, the act of independence,
proclamation. 10775, (34898), note after
98877

Preliminary report. By E. G. Squier. 32767,
note after 89969

Preliminary report of a geological reconnoissance
of Louisiana. 42230

(Preliminary) report of Lieut. A. W. Whipple.
69946

Preliminary report [of the Buffalo, Warren,
and St. Louis Railroad.] 9063

Preliminary report of the census of . . . New-
York. 53859

Preliminary report of the Commissioners on
Criminal Law. 45935

Preliminary report of the geological survey
of Kansas. 37033

Preliminary report of the geology and agriculture of . . . Mississippi. 49502

Preliminary report of the geology and agriculture of the state of Mississippi. 30421

Preliminary report of the operations of the
Commission during the present campaign
in Northern Virginia. 76602, 76647

Preliminary report of the operations of the
Sanitary Commission in connection with
the engagement in the harbor at Charleston. 76596, 76647

Preliminary report of the operations of the
Sanitary Commission with the Army of the
Potomac. (76594), 76647

Preliminary report of the operations of the
U. S. Sanitary Commission in North
Carolina. 76613, 76647

Preliminary report of the physical geography.
58855

Preliminary report of the Texas Geological
Survey. 8918

Preliminary report of the United States Geological Survey of Wyoming. 31006

Preliminary report on the eighth census. 1860.
37428

Preliminary report on the geology of New
Brunswick. (31935)

Preliminary report on the mortality and sickness of the volunteer forces. 22262,
76571, 76647

Preliminary report on the plan of a penal code.
(41615)

Preliminary report on the projected North
West Railway. 24706

Preliminary report on the projected railway.
81348

Preliminary report on the treaty of reciprocity.
19662

Preliminary report on the water supply of the
city of Manchester. 77313

Preliminary report [to Councils] of the Committee on law. 62069

(Preliminary) report to the committee, May,
1863. 76605, 76647

Preliminary report to the President of the
United States. 85492

Preliminary report touching the condition and
management of emancipated refugees.
1087, 65047

Preliminary sketch for the formation of a
company. 86575

Preliminary sketch of Judaism, paganism, and
Mohammedanism. 4402

Preliminary sketch of the battle of the Alamance.
16352, (30969)

Preliminary sketch of the churches in the
Valley of Virginia. 18741

Preliminary sketch of the history of Ohio.
12199

Preliminary treatise concerning the origin of
springs. 3413

Preliminary treatise on the pre-emption laws.
(68526)

Prelude. 105466

Preludes. A collection of Poems. 40994

Prematica en que se Magestad manda. 65048

Premier apercu d'une nouveau mode de population. 39637

Premier et second rapports du Comite Special.
10564

Premier et second rapports du Comite Special
nomme pour s'enquerir. 10567

Premier etablissement de la foy dans la Nouvelle
France. 39650

Premier Inca du Perou. 39595

Premier Janvier 1858. 85825

Premier livre de l'histoire de l'Indie. 11387

Premier memoire de Sieur Tort. 29240

Premier memoire sur le Gynobase. 75235

Premier voiage de G. Spilberg. 68455

Premier voiage des Hollandois et des Zelandois. 68455

Premier voyage autour du monde. 62805

Premiere conferance entre le Commissaire Sonthonax et le General. (42350), 96343

Premiere denonciation solemnelle d'un ministre. 28152

Premiere et derniere lettre de Louis-Marthe Gouy. 8039

Premiere lettre a M. le Duc de Broglie. 61262

Premiere lettre de Mr. *****. 56095

Premiere lettre d'un citoyen de la Haye. 65049

Premiere mission des Jesuites au Canada. 10792

Premiere partie. Voyage a la Havane. (73274)

Premieres annees de la province de Massachusetts. 78778

Premieres oeuvres de Jacques de Vaulx. 76838

Premiers catalogues et circulaires. 96468

Premiers colons de la Pensylvanie. 2709

Premiers colons de Montreal. (73521)

Premiers rudiments de la constitution Britannique. (38449)

Premium, Barton. pseud. Eight years in British Guiana. 65050

Premium essay. 79160

Premium essay . . . . By N. Porter. 54299

Premium essay, by Rev. Hollis Read. 68151

Premium essay on agricultural education. 73918

Premium essay on the origin, history, and characteristics of this remarkable American breed of horses. 41375

Premium essay on the treatment and cultivation of the onion. 67068

Premium list and rules and regulations of the ninth annual fair. 49284

Premium list of the fair of the New England and Vt. State Agricultural Societies. 65051

Premium list of the N. E. Agricultural Society. 52645

Premium list of the second annual cattle show and fair. (15656)

Premium list of the South Carolina Institute. 88008

Premium list of the . . . [State Agricultural & Mechanic Society] . . . for the fourth annual fair. 88056

Premium questions on slavery. 82034

Premium questions on slavery, each admitting of a yes or no answer. 50971

Premium tract. By Enoch Pond. (63979)

Premium tract [of the Southern Board of Foreign Missions.] 85227, 88313

Premiums and gratuities awarded by the . . . [Massachusetts Horticultural] Society. 45862

Premiums and regulations, rules and instructions. 14887

Premiums awarded at the second annual fair. 56884

Premiums by the Society. 65052

Premiums for the advantage of the British colonies. 65053

Premiums offered by the Essex Agricultural Society. (23004)

Premiums offered for the advantage of the British American dominions. 65055

Premiums offered for the advantage of the British colonies. 65054

Premonition to princes. 67542-67544

Prendergast, Garrett Elliott. 65056

Prensa Espanola y los ultimos sucesos del Uruguay. 65058

Prensa libre. 98305

Prensa periodico Hispano-Mexicano. (65057)

Prentice, Archibald. (65059)

Prentice, Caleb. 65060

Prentice, Charles. (65061)

Prentice, George D. 65062-65065, 84403, 103819

Prentice, George Henry. (65066)-65068

Prentice, John. 65069-(65071), 94923

Prentice, Joseph. (65072)

Prentice, Josiah. 65073

Prentice, Thomas. 65074

Prentice, Thomas, 1702-1872. 65075-65078, 104112

Prenticeana. 65064, 65065

Prentices, John. 94067

Prenties, S. W. 65079-(65080)

Prentiss, Charles. 58201, (65081)-65088, 8539 93900, 95366, 96801

Prentiss, Charles. supposed author (29661), 65082, 93554, note before 97919

Prentiss, Charles D. 105363

Prentiss, George L. 65089-65093

Prentiss, John. 65094

Prentiss, Joseph. 65095

Prentiss, N. Smith. 89131

Prentiss, S. 65098

Prentiss, Samuel, 1782-1857. 65096, 65098-65099

Prentiss, Sergeant Smith, 1808-1850. 65100-65101, 101071

Prentiss, Thomas. 65102-(65108)

Prentiss, W. A. 49011

Prentiss, William O. 65109

Preparacion sacerdotal. 86393

Preparation for death. 102043

Preparation for death. [By Bolde.] 9463

Preparation of the heart. (32854)

Preparatoirlyk plan van een tractaat van commercie. 65110

Preparatory lessons for beginners. 105096

Prepost, Istvan. 35273, 105715

Prerogatiue of Parlaments in England. 67599

Prerogative of Parliaments in England. 67577 67584, 67598-67599

Prerogative rights and public law. 65111

Presas, Jose. (65112)-65114

Presbitero ciudadano J. Valera 98362

Presbitero de este Arzobispado. pseud. tr. 55262

Presbitero de este Arzobispado. pseud. Relacion de la funebre ceremonia y exequias. 30411

Presbitero de la misma ciudad. pseud. Relacion sencilla del funeral y exequias. 34185, (48815), (76183)

Presbitero secular do Gram Priorado do Crate pseud. Brazil. 7541

Presbury, B. F. 65115

Presbyter. pseud. Catholic work of the Protestant Episcopal Church in America. 11523

Presbyter. pseud. Hints on the general missions of the church. 65116

Presbyter. pseud. Letters on the missionary organization of the Protestant Episcopal Church. 40623

Presbyter. pseud. Reasons for organizing the American, Church-Missionary Society. see Stone, John Seely.

Presbyter. pseud. Review of "A pastoral lett to the clergy of the Diocese of New-York." 65117

Presbyter. pseud. Trinity Church case. see Morgan, John.

Presbyter, John. pseud. Some observations. 69488, 86671

Presbyter of Connecticut. pseud. Revivalism and the church. (70328)

Presbyter of Massachusetts. pseud. Millennium. (49001)

Presbyter of New Jersey. pseud. Homily for the times. see Sherman, Henry Beers.

Presbyter of New York. pseud. Thoughts on the division of dioceses. 95701, 103820

Presbyter of Old England. pseud. Answer to the plea of T. B. Chandler, D. D. see Fleming, Caleb.

Presbyter of said church. pseud. ed. 32806

Presbyter of the church. pseud. Lectures historical, expository, and practical. 39670

Presbyter of the church in Philadelphia. pseud. Review of Bishop Hopkins' Bible view of slavery. see Lundy, J. P.

Presbyter of the Church of England. pseud. Sermon, preacher in Rodnor Church. see Currie, William.

Presbyter of the Diocese of Massachusetts. pseud. Considerations on the Eastern Diocese. see Wainwright, Jonathan Mayhew. supposed author

Presbyter of the Diocese of New York. pseud. Letter to the wardens and vestry of Christ Church. 40545

Presbyter of the Diocese of Toronto. pseud. Sketches of Canadian life. see Darling, William Stewart.

Presbyter of the Protestant Episcopal Church in Western New York. pseud. Sketches of the Rev. Richard Cecil. 81579

Presbyter of the Reformed Episcopal Church. pseud. Comparison of prayer books. see Smith, Marshall B., 1832-1882.

Presbyter of Western New York. pseud. Sketches of Dingle Parish. 65119

Presbyterial critic. 45137

Presbyterian. pseud. Apology for congregational divines. 106097A

Presbyterian. pseud. Dialogue between an Episcopalian and a Presbyterian. 19927, 54245

Presbyterian. pseud. Lawfulness, excellency, and advantage of instrumental musick. 39341

Presbyterian. pseud. Letters addressed to the Rev. Messrs. John Cree. 40573

Presbyterian. pseud. Schools. see Blaikie, Alexander.

Presbyterian. 85475

Presbyterian almanac. 65191

Presbyterian and Congregational Convention, Chicago, 1847. 12659

Presbyterian and independent visible churches in New-England and else-where, brought to the test. 37207-37209

Presbyterian Church (Reformed) see Reformed Presbyterian Church in North America.

Presbyterian Church in Canada. Synod. (37334)

Presbyterian Church in Canada. Synod of Nova-Scotia. Committee to Prepare a Statement of Means for Promoting Religion in the Church. (65212)

Presbyterian Church in England. 53343

Presbyterian Church in the Confederate States of America. 396

Presbyterian Church in the Confederate States of America. General Assembly. 396, 65130

Presbyterian Church in the Confederate States of America. General Assembly. Council Appointed to Prepare an Address. 396, 65130

Presbyterian Church in the U. S. 65154, 65157

Presbyterian Church in the U. S. Charleston Union Presbytery. see Presbyterian Church in the U. S. Presbytery of Charleston (Union)

Presbyterian Church in the U. S. Committee of Publication. 86309

Presbyterian Church in the U. S. General Assembly. 39172, 65154, 65122, (65184), 65224, (65228), 85178, 2d note after 90734

Presbyterian Church in the U. S. Presbytery of Amite. 85180

Presbyterian Church in the U. S. Presbytery of Charleston. (12063), 66425, 87917, 87915, note after 87915A

Presbyterian Church in the U. S. Presbytery of Charleston (Union) (65211), (65228), 87916, 2d note after 90734

Presbyterian Church in the U. S. Presbytery of Mississippi. 13230, 85180

Presbyterian Church in the U. S. Presbytery of New Orleans. 85178

Presbyterian Church in the U. S. Presbytery of Orange. 65181

Presbyterian Church in the U. S. Southern and South-Western Convention, Cassville, Ga., 1840. see Southern and South-Western Presbyterian Convention, Cassville, Ga., 1840.

Presbyterian Church in the U. S. Synod of Kentucky. Convention, Versailles, Ky., 1840. 37565

Presbyterian Church in the U. S. Synod of Missouri. 64692

Presbyterian Church in the U. S. Synod of Virginia. (69432)

Presbyterian Church in the U. S. Synod of Virginia. General Assembly. see Presbyterian Church in the U. S. Synod of Virginia.

Presbyterian Church in the U. S. Union Theological Seminary. see Richmond, Va. Union Theological Seminary.

Presbyterian Church in the U. S. A. 22602, 49467, 51832, 63298, 65147, 65156, 65171, 65185, (65209)

Presbyterian Church in the U. S. A. Associate Presbytery of Albany. 90512, 90514

Presbyterian Church in the U. S. A. Associate Presbytery of Cambridge. 90516, note after 96840, 1st note after 97091

Presbyterian Church in the U. S. A. Associate Presbytery of Morris County. note after 65546, 99543

Presbyterian Church in the U. S. A. Associate Presbytery of Pennsylvania. 19164, 40574, 59898

Presbyterian Church in the U. S. A. Associate Presbytery of Westchester. note after 65546

Presbyterian Church in the U. S. A. Associate Reformed Synod of North America. see Reformed Presbyterian Church in North America. General Synod.

Presbyterian Church in the U. S. A. Associated Presbyteries. Convention. 7844, (65144)

Presbyterian Church in the U. S. A. Board of Church Extension. (65139), (65146)

Presbyterian Church in the U. S. A. Board of Domestic Missions. (65140)

Presbyterian Church in the U. S. A. Board of Education. 65141, 89260 see also Education Society of the Presbyterian Church in the United States. Presbyterian Education Society.

Presbyterian Church in the U. S. A. Board of Education. Semicentenary Celebration, 1869. 89260

Presbyterian Church in the U. S. A. Board of Foreign Missions. 20678, (65142)

Presbyterian Church in the U. S. A. Board of Home Missions. 65169

Presbyterian Church in the U. S. A. Board of Missions. 61186, 65143, 89783

Presbyterian Church in the U. S. A. Board of Publication. 65192, 65206, 85311, 86261, 86303, 94064 see also Presbyterian Church in the U. S. A. Publication Committee.

Presbyterian Church in the U. S. A. Church Erection Fund. Board. 65145

Presbyterian Church in the U. S. A. Church Extension Committee. see Presbyterian Church in the U. S. A. Board of Church Extension.

PResbyterian Church in the U. S. A. Committee of Home Missions. (65193)

Presbyterian Church in the U. S. A. Committee to Draught a Plan of Governmnet and Discipline. 65156, 104935

Presbyterian Church in the U. S. A. Committee to Draught a Plan of Government and Discipline. Chairman. 65156, 104935 see also Witherspoon, John.

Presbyterian Church in the U. S. A. Convention of Delegates from the Synod of New York and Philadelphia, and from the Associations of Connecticut, 1766-1775. 15819, 49364 see also Congregational Churches in Connecticut. Presbyterian Church in the U. S. A. Synod of New York and Philadelphia.

Presbyterian Church in the U. S. A. General Assembly. 40344, 53265, (54136), 63265, 63285, 63400, 65120, 65123, (65126)-65128, 65135, 65148, (65152), 65163, (65167), 65173, 65175-65177, 65179, 65185, 65187, (65190), 65208, 65217, 89783, 94370, 97874, 104741

Presbyterian Church in the U. S. A. General Assembly. Commission of Investigation on Home Missions. 65210

Presbyterian Church in the U. S. A. General Assembly. Committee for Revising the Form of Government, and the Forms of Process. 65215

Presbyterian Church in the U. S. A. General Assembly. Committee on Freedmen. 65166

Presbyterian Church in the U. S. A. General Assembly. Committee on Reunion. (65219)

Presbyterian Church in the U. S. A. General Assembly. Committee on the Plan of a Theological Seminary. 65214

Presbyterian Church in the U. S. A. General Assembly. Committee to Draught a Plan for Disciplining Baptized Children. 65218

Presbyterian Church in the U. S. A. General Assembly. Committee to Devise Ways and Means of Raising Funds for the Theological Seminary. 65217

Presbyterian Church in the U. S. A. General Assembly. Permanent Committee on Education for the Ministry. 65186

Presbyterian Church in the U. S. A. General Assembly. Special Committee on Systematic Beneficence. (65189)

Presbyterian Church in the U. S. A. General Assembly. Standing Committee on Missions. 65183

Presbyterian Church in the U. S. A. General Assembly. Trustees of the Fund for Disabled Ministers and Their Families. 65222

Presbyterian Church in the U. S. A. Presbytery of Albany. 623, (12536), 17909, 97370

Presbyterian Church in the U. S. A. Presbytery of Albany. Board of Domestic Missions. 65216

Presbyterian Church in the U. S. A. Presbytery of Baltimore. 75441, 87004

Presbyterian Church in the U. S. A. Presbytery of Boston. 55, 50462, 58896

Presbyterian Church in the U. S. A. Presbytery of Buffalo. Committee. 9063

Presbyterian Church in the U. S. A. Presbytery of Carlisle. Committee to Report the Work Entitled Duffield on Regeneration. 69536

Presbyterian Church in the U. S. A. Presbytery of Grafton. 69458

Presbyterian Church in the U. S. A. Presbytery of Chillicothe. 85179-85180, 97568

Presbyterian Church in the U. S. A. Presbytery of Cincinnati. 96825

Presbyterian Church in the U. S. A. Presbytery of Elizabethtown. 22189

Presbyterian Church in the U. S. A. Presbytery of Harrisburg. 30550

Presbyterian Church in the U. S. A. Presbytery of Indianapolis. 103215

Presbyterian Church in the U. S. A. Presbytery of Nassau. 30413

Presbyterian Church in the U. S. A. Presbytery of New-Brunswick. 37628, (52524), (53052), 79376, 94700

Presbyterian Church in the U. S. A. Presbytery of New Jersey. see Presbyterian Church in the U. S. A. Presbytery of New Brunswick.

Presbyterian Church in the U. S. A. Presbytery of New York. 43191, (45136), (53475), 94370

Presbyterian Church in the U. S. A. Presbytery of Newburyport. 24607

Presbyterian Church in the U. S. A. Presbytery of Newcastle. 52562, 58442, 84850, 101447

Presbyterian Church in the U. S. A. Presbytery of Newcastle. Moderator. 52562, 84850 see also Smith, William Richmond 1752-1820.

Presbyterian Church in the U. S. A. Presbytery of Oneida. 47334, 103683

Presbyterian Church in the U. S. A. Presbytery of Philadelphia. 3509, (36934), (62367), 65132, (65209), 65165, 86870, 96822, 2d note after 99808, 102637

Presbyterian Church in the U. S. A. Presbytery of Rochester. 72342

Presbyterian Church in the U. S.A . Presbytery of Salem. 13594, 103319, 103322

Presbyterian Church in the U. S. A. Presbytery of Springfield. (43605)-43606, (52324) 56493, 65137, 89893, 92031

Presbyterian Church in the U. S. A. Presbytery of Transylvania. 96458, 96459

Presbyterian Church in the U. S. A. Presbytery of Troy. 97093

Presbyterian Church in the U. S. A. Presbytery of West Lexington. 65437, 91765

Presbyterian Church in the U. S. A. Publication Committee. 65168, 65202 see also Presbyterian Church in the U. S. A. Board of Publication.

Presbyterian Church in the U. S. A. Reformed Presbytery of North America. see Reformed Presbyterian Church in North America. General Synod.

Presbyterian Church in the U. S. A. Second Presbytery of Philadelphia. see Presbyterian Church in the U. S. A. Presbytery of Philadelphia.

Presbyterian Church in the U. S. A. Supreme Judicatory. (2701), 65153

Presbyterian Church in the U. S. A. Synod of Cincinnati. 104676

Presbyterian Church in the U. S. A. Synod of Kentucky. (37496), (81767)

Presbyterian Church in the U. S. A. Synod of Kentucky. Committee. 37487, 81798

Presbyterian Church in the U. S. A. Synod of Michigan. 48777

Presbyterian Church in the U. S. A. Synod of Mississippi. 49500

Presbyterian Church in the U. S. A. Synod of New Jersey. see Presbyterian Church in the U. S. A. Synod of New York and New Jersey.

Presbyterian Church in the U. S. A. Synod of New York. (6789), (65209)

Presbyterian Church in the U. S. A. Synod of New York and New Jersey. 37628, 53666, 65164, 79376 see also Scotch Presbyterians of New York. petitioners

Presbyterian Church in the U. S. A. Synod of New York and New Jersey. African School. 65134

Presbyterian Church in the U. S. A. Synod of New York and New Jersey. Committee. (32166), (36833)

Presbyterian Church in the U. S. A. Synod of New York and Philadelphia. 41457, (54209), 59017, 63265, 65133, 65151-65153, 65157, 65163, 104936, 104941 see also Presbyterian Church in the U. S. A. Convention of Delegates from the Synod of New-York and Philadelphia, and from the Associations of Connecticut, 1766-1775. Presbyterian Church in the U. S. A. Synod of Philadelphia.

Presbyterian Church in the U. S. A. Synod of Ohio. 32429

Presbyterian Church in the U. S. A. Synod of Philadelphia. (5752), 17662, 27397, 31293-(31294), 31297, (36934), 58442, 62106, (62367), 65165, (65209), 94686, 94700, 96822, 2d note after 99826, 104741 see also Presbyterian Church in the U. S. A. Synod of New York and Philadelphia.

Presbyterian Church in the U. S. A. Synod of Philadelphia. Commission. (31294)

Presbyterian Church in the U. S. A. Synod of Philadelphia. Ministers. 61420

Presbyterian Church in the U. S. A. Synod of Philadelphia and New York. see Presbyterian Church in the U. S. A. Synod of New York and Philadelphia.

Presbyterian Church in the U. S. A. Synod of South Carolina. Missionaries at Dwight, Ga. 93215

Presbyterian Church in the U. S. A. Synod of South Carolina. Missionaries in the Cherokee Nation. 93215

Presbyterian Church in the U. S. A. Synod of South Carolina and Georgia. (49384), 87915A

Presbyterian Church in the U. S. A. Synod of South Carolina and Georgia. Committee on the Religious Instruction of the Colored Population. 65220

Presbyterian Church in the U. S. A. Synod of Virginia. 101563

Presbyterian Church in the U. S. A. Theological Seminary, Chicago. see Chicago. Presbyterian Theological Seminary.

Presbyterian Church in the U. S. A. Theological Seminary, Danville, Ky. see Danville, Ky. Theological Seminary of the Presbyterian Church in the U. S. A.

Presbyterian Church in the U. S. A. Theological Seminary, Princeton, N. J. see Princeton Theological Seminary, Princeton, N. J.

Presbyterian Church in the U. S. A. Third Presbytery of New York. see Presbyterian Church in the U. S. A. Presbytery of New York.

Presbyterian Church in the U. S. A. Vermont Convention of Ministers, 1807. see General Convention of Congregational and Presbyterian Ministers of Vermont, Middlebury, 1807.

Presbyterian Church in the U. S. A. Vermont General Convention of Congregational and Presbyterian Ministers. see Congregational Churches in Vermont. General Convention.

Presbyterian Church in the U. S. A. Western Theological Seminary, Alleghany City, Pa. see Western Theological Seminary of the Presbyterian Church, Alleghany City, Pa.

Presbyterian Church in the U. S. A. (New School) General Assembly. 65154, (65178), 72118

Presbyterian Church in the U. S. A. (New School) New York Theological Seminary. see New York (City) Union Theological Seminary.

Presbyterian Church in the U. S. A. (Old School) General Assembly. 65154, 65223

Presbyterian Church, Brooklyn, N. Y. see Brooklyn. Presbyterian Church.

Presbyterian Church, Cortland, N. Y. see Cortland, N. Y. Presbyterian Church.

Presbyterian Church, Cumberland, Pa. see Cumberland, Pa. Presbyterian Church.

Presbyterian Church, Kingston, Jamaica. see Kingston, Jamaica. Presbyterian Church.

Presbyterian Church, Morristown, N. J. see Morristown, N. J. Presbyterian Church.

Presbyterian Church, Mount Gilead, Ohio. see Mount Gilead, Ohio. Presbyterian Church.

Presbyterian Church, New York. see New York (City) Presbyterian Church.

Presbyterian Church, Southampton, N. Y. see Southampton, N. Y. Presbyterian Church.

Presbyterian Church, Steuebenville, Ohio. see Steubenville, Ohio. Presbyterian Church.

Presbyterian Church, Waterford, N. Y. see Waterford, N. Y. Presbyterian Church.

Presbyterian Church, Whitesboro, N. Y. see Whitesboro, N. Y. Presbyterian Church.

Presbyterian church government scriptural. 64692

Presbyterian Church in America. 25591

Presbyterian Church in Basking Ridge, N. J. 67884

Presbyterian Church in Blendon Township, Franklin County, Ohio. 71952

Presbyterian Church in Kentucky. Proceedings of the convention. 37565

Presbyterian Church of Harrisburg, April 19, 1865. 49723

Presbyterian church throughout the world. (63461)

Presbyterian clergyman looking for the church. (49216)

Presbyterian Churches, Pembroke, Mass. see Pembroke, Mass. Presbyterian Churches.

Presbyterian Committee of Publication, Richmond, Va. see Presbyterian Church in the U. S. Committee of Publication.

Presbyterian education repository. 32714

Presbyterian Education Society. (62070), 65194 see also Education Society of the Presbyterian Church in the United States. Presbyterian Church in the U. S. A. Board of Education.

Presbyterian Education Society. Board of Directors. 65194

Presbyterian Education Society. Indiana Branch. Directors. 34512

Presbyterian Education Society. Western Agency. 65194, note after 102961

Presbyterian family almanac. 65191, (65195)

Presbyterian government, not a hierarchy but a commonwealth. 7684

Presbyterian historical almanac and annual remembrancer. 65196

Presbyterian Historical Society. 84850, 104533

Presbyterian Historical Society. Executive Committee. 65197

Presbyterian Historical Society. Library. 64197

Presbyterian Hospital, New York. see New York (City) Presbyterian Hospital.

Presbyterian Hospital, Philadelphia. see Philadelphia. Presbyterian Hospital.

Presbyterian Hospital in Philadelphia. History, charter, and by-laws. 62071

Presbyterian liturgies. 23124

Presbyterian magazine. 12899A

Presbyterian magazine; a monthly publication. 65198

Presbyterian magazine. Edited by C. Rensselaer. 65199

Presbyterian minister. pseud. Bible, confession of faith, and common sense. see Smith, William D., d. 1848.

Presbyterian minister. pseud. What is Calvinism? see Smith, William D., d. 1848.

Presbyterian Ministers in Vermont. General Convention. see Congregational Churches in Vermont. General Convention.

Presbyterian Ministers. pseud. Letter. see Eighteen Presbyterian Ministers. pseud.

Presbyterian Ministers' Provincial Assembly, London, 1649. see Provincial Assembly of Presbyterian Ministers, London, 1649.

Presbyterian monthly. 65200

Presbyterian National Union Convention, Philadelphia, 1867. 65201

Presbyterian National Union Convention, held in . . . Philadelphia. 65201

Presbyterian of the west. 84762

Presbyterian of Virginia. pseud. Remarks on the act of the General Assembly of 1837. 65120

Presbyterian. Published daily as a reporter. (65190)

Presbyterian quarterly and Princeton review. see Princeton review.

Presbyterian quarterly review. 541, 3501, 56040, 65203

Presbyterian Reunion, Pittsburgh, 1869. (65207)

Presbyterian reunion: a memorial volume. 65204

Presbyterian Theological Seminary, Chicago. see Chicago. Presbyterian Theological Seminary.

Presbyterian Theological Seminary, Danville, Ky. see Danville, Ky. Theological Seminary of the Presbyterian Church in the U. S. A.

Presbyterian Theological Seminary of the North West, Chicago. see Chicago. Presbyterian Theological Seminary.

Presbyterian Tract and Sunday School Book Society. 65226

Presbyterian Western Foreign Missionary Society. see Western Foreign Missionary Society.

Presbyterian Board fur Veroffentlichung Religioster Schriften. see Presbyterian Church in the U. S. A. Board of Publication.

Presbyteriansm. A review of the leading measures. 65231

Presbyterianism: a sermon, delivered at the First Presbyterian Church. 83391

Presbyterianism in Cincinnati. 65232

Presbyterianism in her polity and practice. 90470

Presbyterianism, its true place and value in history. (18744)

Presbyterianism since the Reformation. 25152

Presbyterianism, the revolution, the declaration, and the constitution. 85313

Presbyterianism vindicated, and the character and intolerance of its enemies exposed. 98778

Presbyter's handbook of the church. 84414

Presbyter's letters on the West India question. (21257)

Presbytery and not prelacy the scriptural and primitive polity. 85284-85285, 85287, 85290, 85297, 85302, 85312, 85314, 85319

Presbytery of Springfield, Ky. see Presbyterian Church in the U. S. A. Presbytery of Springfield.

Presbytery reporter. 65233

Prescott, Abraham. defendant 65234-65235

Prescott, B. F. 90573

Prescott, Benjamin, 1687-1777. 8505, 23391, 26831, (65236)-(65240), 1st note after 69428, 70106, (75668), 75680 see also Congregational Churches in New Hampshire Ecclesiastical Council, Exeter, 1743. Scribe.

Prescott, D. F. L. (65241)

Prescott, Edward G. 6630, 65242-65244

Prescott, George B. 65245

Prescott, George Washington. 65246

Prescott, Guglielmo Hickling. see Prescott, William Hickling, 1796-1859.

Prescott, Guillermo H. see Prescott, William Hickling, 1796-1859.

Prescott, Henrietta. 65247

Prescott, Henry P. illus. 65248

Prescott, J. 90462

Prescott, James. defendant at impeachment 62643, (65249)-(65250)

Prescott, John F. 97072

Prescott, Luther. supposed author 92167

Prescott, Oliver S. defendant before church court 65252

Prescott, Robert, 1725-1816. 23503 see also Canada. Governor General, 1797-1808 (Prescott)

Prescott, S. C. 65253

Prescott, Thomas H. pseud. American encyclopedia of history. see Blake, William O.

Prescott, Thomas H. pseud. Volume of the world. see Blake, William O.

Prescott, William, 1726-1795. incorrectly supposed author 40316, (65256), note after 99390

Prescott, William, 1788-1875. (65256)-65258, 85838

Prescott, William Hickling, 1796-1859. 2002A, 4918, 9889, 13791, 16951, 35190, 35320, 64014, 65259-65297, 65299, 76381, 88910
Prescott-Innes, R. (73290)
Prescott & Wilson. firm publishers 97072
Prescott & Wilson's Troy city directory. 97072
Prescott Consolidated Mining Company. (65300)
Prescott Light Guard. see Massachusetts. Militia. First Regiment Cavalry. Prescott Light Guard, Company A.
Prescott memorial. 65298
Prescott memorial: or a genealogical memoir. 65258
Prescott's conquest of mexico. 88910
Presence and purpose of God in the war. 88870
Presence of Christ the glory of a church. (72474)
Presence of Christ the glory of His house. 6088
Presence of Christ, the glory of the temple. 39199
Presence of Christ with the ministers of the Gospel. 91957
Presence of God in His holy house. 91659
Presence of God with His people. 21245
Present. 65302
Present advantages and future prospects of the city of Freeport, Ill. 25819
Present advantages and future prospects of the city of Freeport, Ill., including a complete strangers' guide. (65303)
Present American revolution. 43264
Present and Former Members of the Albany Female Academy. eds. see Albany Female Academy, Albany, N. Y.
Present and future state of Jamaica considered. 49128
Present aspect of slavery in America. (58756)
Present aspects of our foreign relations. 82179
Present attempt to dissolve the American union. 50963
Present claims and complaints of America breifly and fairly considered. (65304)
Present condition and future prospects of the country. 41867
Present condition and hopes of our nation. 67894
Present condition and prospects of the university. 51880
Present condition of Boston. 6542
Present condition of Mexico. (65305)-(65306)
Present condition of the free colored people. 13418
Present condition of the Negro population. 93260
Present connection of the Methodist Episcopal Church with Slavery. 46901
Present crisis: a sermon . . . Thanksgiving day. 27634
Present crisis. A speech . . . by Dr. Geo. B. Loring. 42083
Present crisis, and its remedy. 65307
Present crisis of the colonies considered. (65308), 104246-104247
Present crisis, or the currency. 21467
Present crisis: with a reply and appeal to European advisers. 56048
Present crisis with respect to America, considered. 65309
Present distressed situation of our country. (64258), 64260
Present duty. An address. 2201
Present duty of American Christians. 19461

Present exigencies of the temperance cause. 11947
Present financial position of the United States. 74611
Present for an apprentice. 65310
Present for the whigs of '76 & '37. 36920, 1st note after 101601
Present for young ladies. 73619
Present General Assembly of this colony, in their first session. 95978
Present gratitude. 83644
Present hour. 65311
Present judiciary system of South Carolina. 87918
Present melancholy circumstances of the province consider'd. (65312)
Present of glorious and immence riches. 46564, 5th note after 97146
Present of summer-fruit. 46464
Present operations and future prospects of the Mexican Mine Associations analysed. 68020
Present pastor. pseud. Dedham pulpit. see Burgess, Ebenezer.
Present political state of the Massachusetts-Bay in general. (40099)
Present political state of the province of the Massachusetts-Bay in general, and the town of Boston, in particular. (40098)
Present position of the seceded states. 17626
Present Possessors of the French Lands in the Island of St. Christophers. petitioners 75012
Present prospect of the famous and fertile island of Tobago. 64857-64858
Present publisher. pseud. Introduction. see White, T. W.
Present ruinous situation of the West India islands. 65313
Present situation and future prospects of American railroads. 65314
Present situation and prospects of American railways. 10842
Present situation of affairs in North-America. 65315
Present situation of affairs in regard to the East and West India settlements. 65316
Present situation of other nations of the world. (50953)
Present state and condition of the free people of color. 60397, 62072
Present state of affairs in Carolina. 2168
Present state of affairs, with remarks upon certain transactions. 65317
Present state of Algiers. 5967, note after 41144
Present state of all nations. Describing their respective situations. (75826)
Present state of all nations, including a dissertation. (49809), 49906, (56847), 87900
Present state of America, with the mournful complaints. 65318
Present state of Carolina. 23586, 87919
Present state of Chili. 5865
Present state of Colombia. (14617)
Present state of Europe. 65319
Present state of Europe compared with ancient prophecies. (65513)
Present state of Europe compared with antient prophecies. (65513)
Present state of French America. 10330
Present state of Great Britain. 11787
Present state of Great Britain and North America. (49696)
Present state of Hayti, (Saint Domingo.) (25621)

Present state of Hayti, with remarks on its agriculture. 65320

Present state of His Majesties islands and territories in America. 5972

Present state of Hudson's Bay. 97702

Present state of Jamaica. 35649

Present state of learning in the College of New York. (49747)

Present state of liberty in Great Britain and her colonies. 65321

Present state of literature. A poem. 21472

Present state of Maryland. 45279

Present state of medical learning in the city of New York. 49749, 65322

Present state of New-England. Being a narrative of the troubles with the Indians in New-England. 33446

Present state of New-England. Considered in a discourse. 46455

Present state of New-England impartially considered. 46722, 58359, (65323)

Present state of New-England, with respect to the Indian War. 65324

Present state of New-English affaris. 46723, 1st note after 65324

Present state of North America. 9602, 30795, 34027, 2d note after 65324

Present state of Nova Scotia. 32545, 87291

Present state of Nova Scotia and Canada. 65325

Present state of our country considered. 99200

Present state of our national affairs. 298

Present state of Peru. 47936, 61153, 81615

Present state of Popery in England. 65326

Present state of religious controversy in America. 17921

Present state of the anti-slavery question in Tunis and Algiers. 13499

Present state of the British and French sugar colonies. 61011

Present state of the British and French trade to Africa and America. 65327

Present state of the British empire and description of its colonies. 22670

Present state of the British empire in Europe, Asia, Africa, and America. 27718

Present state of the British sugar colonies consider'd. 65328, (66041)

Present state of the Canadas. 10549

Present state of the Catholic mission 85257

Present state of the college. (13212)

Present state of the colony of Connecticut considered. 13213, 26353, 32309, note after 105924, 105927, 1st note after 105937, note after 106230

Present state of the controversy between the states of New-York and New-Hampshire. 801, 6th note after 99005

Present state of the country and inhabitants. 42283

Present state of the country, as to the polity of the government. 5112-5113, 1st note after 100480, 3d note after 100480

Present state of the European settlements on the Mississippi. 63103

Present state of the islands in the archipelago. 67811

Present state of the Morea. 67811

Present state of the nation. 9294, 15978, (28768)-(28769), 46928, 69436, 103123

Present state of the protestant religion in Maryland. 66036

Present state of the protestant religion in Maryland, under the government of Francis Nicholson Esqr. 7481

Present state of the question, in regard to the division of the Diocese of New-York. 65329

Present state of the revenues and forces. 65330

Present state of the slave trade, and the Negro's place in nature. 9498

Present state of the Spanish colonies. 101224

Present state of the sugar colonies consider'd. (65328), (69514)

Present state of the sugar plantations considered. 65331

Present state of the tobacco plantations in America. 65332

Present state of the universe. (49480), (5957) (59580), 64390, 98444, 100819

Present state of the West-Indies. 65333, 4th note after 102858

Present state of the whole world. 21486

Present state of Virginia. 36511-(36512)

Present state of Virginia, and the College. 30716, note after 104154

Present state, prospects, and responsibilities of the Methodist Episcopal Church. 316

Present status of workmen's compensation laws. 84514

Present teacher. pseud. Some account of Harvard Bible Class. see Brewer, William A.

Present time perilous. 17893

Present to be given to teeming women. 5720

Present to teachers and rulers of society. 10456

Present war and the stagnation of credit connected with it. 106079

Present war unexpected, unnecessary, and ruinous. 39185

Present way of the country in maintaining the Gospel ministry. 65334

Presentation addressed to, and historical discourse by, Rev. John M. McLeod. 4354

Presentation Meeting, Boston, 1855. see Boston. Presentation Meeting, 1855.

Presentation memorial to working men. 4319

Presentation of a portrait of the Rev. Profess Egbert Coffin Smyth. 85224

Presentation of an address to . . . Honorable Charles Francis Adams. 51982

Presentation of an address to . . . Honorable Reverdy Johnson. 51982

Presentation of causes tending to fix the position. (78276)

Presentation of flags of the New York volunte regiments. 53971

Presentation of regimental colors to the Legi lature. 53860

Presentation of vases to Governor Clinton. 13734

Presentation of the bar resolutions in regard to Mr. Lincoln's decease. 41186

Presentation of the Clinton vases. (65335)

Presentation of the statue of Alexander Hamil 29991

Presentation of the statue of Major General Greene. 65336

Presentation to Major-Gen. John A. Dix. 203

Presente amistoso dedicado a las senoritas Mejicanas. 59304

Presente amistoso dedicado a las senoritas Mexicanas. (65337)

Preservation and civilization of the Indians. 65338

Preservation of health in all hot climates. 36224

Preservation of life at sea. 51641

Preservation of the states united. 22308

Preservation of the union, a national economic necessity. (65339)

Preservation of the union. A treatise designed to promote peace and harmony. 65340, note before 95775

Preservation; or, the hovel of the rocks. 104462

Preservative against the doctrine of fate. 21930

Preservative against unsettled notions in religion. 102685

Preservative from damnable errors. (24469)-24470, 83436

Preservativo singularissimo contra los tremblores de tierra. 61121

Presidency. 35384, (65342), note after 103429

Presidency: a reply to the letter of Hon. Rufus Choate. 20353

Presidency—action of legislatures. (55108)

Presidency from Washington to the present time. 84913

Presidency. Letter. 20341

Presidency of Mexico. 57679

Presidency of the United States. 105153

Presidency; speech . . . House of R. 7671

Presidency. Speech of Lieut. E. F. Beale. 4105

Presidency. Winfield Scott, Franklin Pierce, their qualifications. 65341

President and Company for Erecting a Permanent Bridge over the Schuylkill at Philadelphia. see Schuylkill Bridge Company.

President and Congress. A hint to the south. 77631

President and Congress. Reconstruction and the executive power of pardon. 68321

President and Congress. Speech of Hon. Jacob H. Ela. 22092

President and Council of New England. see Massachusetts (Colony) President and Council.

President and Directors and Company of the Free Holders' Bank of Upper Canada. see Free Holders' Bank of Upper Canada.

President Andrew Johnson. 12888

President Burnet's argument. 95107

President, cabinet and Congress. 18181

President, Directors, and Company for Erecting a Permanent Bridge over the River Schuylkill. see Schuylkill Bridge Company.

President, Directors, and Company of the Bank of the United States. see Bank of the United States.

President, Directors & Company of the Westchester County Bank. see Westchester County Bank.

President, Directors and Company of the Worcester Bank. see Worcester Bank, Worcester, Mass.

President, Directors and Co. of Union Turnpike Road adms. Thomas Jenkins. 96890, 97822

President Dwight's decisions of questions. (21542)

President Haven's annual message. 48804

President: his assailants, and his policy. 36177 36177

President Holley—not the Transylvania University. 25172, 96466

President Houston's speech. 95008

President Johnson's views of the finances. 96396

President Joseph Reed of Pennsylvania. (68618)

President Lincoln, a faithful son. 29946

President Lincoln and General Grant on peace and war. 41157

President Lincoln and the American war. 20974

President Lincoln campaign songster. 41222

President Lincoln. From the Princeton review. 41223

President Lincoln: his figure in history. 43151

President Lincoln in history. 78623

President Lincoln on Vallandigham and "arbitrary arrest." 41158

President Lincoln's death. A discourse delivered in the Presbyterian Church in Caldwell, N. J. 89683

President Lincoln's death. Its voice to the people. 29777

President Lincoln's Erwiderung in Bezug auf die Verhaftung Vallendigham. 8402

President Lincoln's response relative to the arrest of Vallendigham. 8400, 52034

President Lincoln self-pourtrayed. [sic] 42654

President Lincoln's successor. (21847)

President Lincoln's views. The truth from an honest man. 41159

Prest. McLane's report reviewed. 58084

President Magoun's college statement. 43844

President of the United States. pseud. Friend of peace. see Worcester, Noah, 1758-1837.

President of the United States having been pleased to communicate to me. 100222

President Reed to Pennsylvania. 68619

President responsible for the Mexican War and its consequences. 20368

President Stiles's election sermon. MDCCLXXXIII. 91749

President, the people, and the war. 91024

President to General McClellan. 41159

President II. Being observations on the late official address of George Washington. 65343, 101873

President Ulysee Grant et son Vice-President. 12889

President Washington's resignation and address to the citizens of the United States, September 17, 1796. 101571, 101601

President Woodruff's manifesto. 83283

Presidente de la republica Mexicana a sus habitantes. 48407, 48628

Presidente de los Estados Unidos de Colombia. 31536

Presidente del Estado de Honduras a sus conciudadanos. 32772

Presidente del Salvador, a sus pueblos. 64345

Presidente e uma assemblea. 65344

Presidente lejitemo de la republica del Salvador a los Salvadorenos. 65346

Presidente y Cabildo de la Iglesia Catedral de la Puebla. see Puebla, Mexico (City) Basilica. Cabildo.

Presidente, y Oidores de la Audiencia Real de la ciudad de Mexico. 65347

Presidential base-ball match, Grant against Greeley. 65348

Presidential campaign of 1860. 50383

Presidential candidates: containing sketches. 3726

Presidential contest of 1856, in three letters. 43850

Presidential contest. To the thinking and reflecting supporters. 65349

Presidential design of the slavery agitation. (21334)

Presidential election. 95558

Presidential election, 1868. Proceedings of the National Union Republican Convention. 12662

Press Conference, Charleston, S. C., 1870.
70263
Press: its opportunities and responsibilities.
83768
Press. No. 1, . . . January 6, 1800. 65361
Press of Onondaga. 24567
Presse. 47978
Pressure and its causes examined. 95843
Prest, Jan Yves de Saint. see Saint-Prest,
Jean Yves de.
Prest-bref for kyrkoherden i vacacoa i maerica,
Jonas Lidman. 94036
Prestamo hecho a Colombia por D. Vicente
Rocafuerte. 72271
Prestamos, contribuciones y exacciones de la
Iglesia de Guadalajara. 65363
Preste Joam das Indias. 974
Prestien, Johann Augustus. 65364
Preston, pseud. Bell, Lincoln and Douglas.
65389
Preston, Ann. 65465
Preston, D. R. 65366
Preston, Elliot Beecher. petitioner 65367
Preston, Henry C. 35526, 65368
Preston, J. 79880
Preston, J. R. (14331)
Preston, John, 1587-1628. 65369
Preston, John, 1755- 941, (65370), note after
90810
Preston, John S. 1395, 11642, 65371-65372
Preston, Laura. 65373
Preston, Lyman. 65374
Preston, Margaret J. 65375
Preston, P. 65376
Preston, Paul. 101219
Preston, S. 65377
Preston, T. R. 65378
Preston, T. R. tr. 67322
Preston, Thomas S. 65379
Preston, Willard. 65380-65381, 104558
Preston, William, 1742-1818. 65383
Preston, William, fl. 1795. 65382
Preston, William, fl. 1865. 63118
Preston, William Ballard, 1805-1862. 8437,
(65384), (65395)-65396
Preston, William Campbell, 1794-1860. 65387,
80116
Preston, William P. 65388
Preston Coal and Improvement Company. 65390
Preston Retreat, Philadelphia. Charter. 65931
Preston Retreat, Philadelphia. Directors.
65391
Prestre, Jean de Verrier. 32016
Prestwich, J. 65392
Prestwich's Respublica. 65392
Presumer detected. 94706
Presumpscott Land and Water Power Company.
President. 89230 see also Speed,
John J.
Presumption of skeptical and careless contemners
of religion. (64233)
Presumptive evidence that the aborigines of the
western hemisphere are descended from
the ten missing tribes of Israel. 81282
Presumptuous sinner detected. 94705-94706
Presupuesto jeneral de los gastos de la republica
Boliviana. 6204
Pret of Le Pre aux Clercs. pseud. Book of the
drama. see Pray, Isaac C.
Prete du Diocese de Quebec. pseud. Questions
sur le gouvernement ecclesiastique. see
Chaboillez, ———.
Pretenciones de la villa imperial de Potosi.
76431
Pretendended antidote proved poyson. 37209

Pretended democracy of Martin Van Buren.
56841
Pretended plain narrative convicted of fraud
and partiality. (35046), 35047
Pretended prophet. pseud. Writings. 50696,
105629
Pretended riot explained. 1736, 85433
Pretended yearly meeting of the Quakers.
37210
Pretendentes. 43301
Pretendu citoyen d'Amsterdam. pseud.
Observations. 65049
Pretendue chute du serviteur de Dieu. 73270
Pretensiones de los Anglo-Americanos. 95109
Pretensions of New England to Commercial
pre-eminence examined. 65393
Pretensions of Thomas Jefferson to the presi-
dency examined. 23994, 84829, 84831-
84832, 2d note after 104983
Pretext of the rebels and their sympathizers.
80447
Preti, Jean. 65394
Preto, Marcos Pinto Soares Vaz. 65395
Pretres Francais emigres aux Etats-Unis.
50561
Prettie, Francis. 11605-(11606), note after
65395, 66686
Pretty, Francis. see Prettie, Francis.
Pretty new-year's gift. 65396, 85668
Pretty story. 32980
Pretyman, George. see Tomline, Sir George
Pretyman, Bart., successively Bishop of
Lincoln, and Winchester, 1750-1827.
Preuss, Henry Clay. 65397-(65399)
K. Preussischen Akademie der Wissenchaften,
Berlin. see Akademie der Wissenchaften,
Berlin.
Preuves donnees devant un Comite de la Cham-
bre des Communes. 81735
Prevailing wickedness. (30459)
Prevalence of religion and virtue in a state.
91559
Prevalence of the Gospel, and the abolition of
war. 84217
Prevencion contra los asesinos de la honra.
65400
Preventatives of the scurvy at sea. 94063
Prevention conveniente que habiendose hecho
a los Religiosos. 65401
Prevete, Louis. tr. 82262
Previa impugnacion a las reflexiones del
Contador D. Joseph de Villa-Senor y
Sanchez. 23606
Prevost, Antoine Francois, called Prevost
d'Exiles, 1697-1763. 3656, 13663, 16963,
28539, (38530), 48490, 52370, 65402-
65412, 84560, 85380, 92204
Prevost, Ferdinand. 65413
Prevost, Florent. 21354
Prevost, Julien, Comte de Limonade. see
Limonade, Julien Prevost, Comte de.
Prevost, Michel. (65416)
Prevost d'Exiles, Antoine Francois. see
Prevost, Antoine Francois, called Prevost
d'Exiles, 1697-1763.
Prevost-Paradol, L. A. 65417
Prey taken from the strong. 64973, 72688
Preyer, William. 65418
Prezeau, ----------, Chevalier. 65419-65420
Price, --------, fl. 1704. 79027
Price, --------, fl. 1821. (69154), 83665
Price, --------, fl. 1839. 59489 see also
Baltimore. Meeting of the Free Colored
People, 1839. Delegates to Visit British
Guiana, and the Island of Trinidad, for
the Purposes of Ascertaining the Advantages

to be Derived by Colored People Migrating
to Those Places.
Price, Abby H. 90031
Price, Daniel. 65421
Price, Ebenezer. 65422-(65424)
Price, Eli K. 61892, 62119, 65425-65434
Price, George. (65435)
Price, H. R. 65436
Price, J. C. see Rice, J. C.
Price, Jacob. 76054
Price, Jacob F. 65437, 91765
Price, James C. 65438, 3d note after 100577
Price, James H. (65439)
Price, James H. supposed author 65438, 3d
note after 100577
Price, John M. (37068)
Price, Joseph H. 65440
Price, Morton. pseud. Theatrical trip for a
wager! see Rhys, Horton.
Price, Nathaniel. defendant 65441-65442
Price, Philip M. defendant 97771
Price, Phinehas. 65443
Price, Richard, 1723-1791. 451, (4284), 18347,
20483, 23409, 24089-24090, (24724),
(25600), 27145, 27926-(27927), 32790,
40965, 41286, (44888), 49393-49394,
49402, (50675), 65444-65461, 1st note
after 69400, 69475, 69549, note after
71369, 84657, 91600, 91680-91681, 1st
note after 95742, 95743, 96174, 97457,
100343, 100755, 102487, 102694, 104706
Price, Rodman McCauley, 1816-1894. 53129-
53157 see also New Jersey. Governor,
1854-1857 (Price)
Price, Roger. 65462-65463
Price, Sterling, 1809-1867. 15330
Price, T. 73141, (65464)
Price, Thomas. defendant 6326, 1st note after
96956, 1st note after 97284
Price, Thomas, fl. 1699. supposed author
27615, 65465, 93889
Price, Thomas, fl. 1836-1837. 65466, 104237
Price, Thomas, fl. 1854. 65467
Price, Thomas L. 65468
Price, Thomas S. 59489
Price, William. cartographer 85489
Price, William, 1794?-1868. 34422, 45312,
65471-65473
Price, William, d. 1862? 65469, 65470
Price act. 102629
Price current. Charleston imports. 87920
Price current. Nantes, the I March. 1782.
104299
Price current, New-York. 101337
Price list of publications. 85037
Price of gold and the presidency. (65474)
Price of liberty. (59209)
Price of loyalty on the border. 32625
Prices current, Cape-Francois. 101090
Prices current for merchandises at Nantes.
102135
Prichard, Augustin. tr. 33728
Prichard, James Cowles, 1786-1848. 36149,
(65475)-65480, 82393
Prichard, William. 65481
Prickel-Vaersen. 63425, 91169
Prickeymherus, Bilibaldus. see Prickheymer,
Wilibald.
Prickheimer, Wilibald. see Prickheymer,
Wilibald.
Prickheymer, Wilibald. tr. (66482)-(66483),
66485-(66489), 66491
Pride and avarice, or the modern priest. 69341
Pride humbled. (59064)
Pride of America, the glory of the world.
47987

Pride of Britannia humbled. 14011
Pride of Lexington. 79339
Pride of Oak Lodge of the United Ancient
Order of Druids. see United Ancient
Order of Druids. Pennsylvania. Pride
of Oak Lodge.
Pride of the village. (81200)
Pride or a touch at the times. (74426)
Pride's looking glass. 102493
Pridgen, H. M. 65482
Prieres, L. J. C. 61003
Prieres, M. J. 61003
Prieres, cantiques, catechisme . . . en langue
Crise. 61003
Priest. pseud. Poem. see W., W. A. pse
Priest, Alexis de Guignard, Comte de Saint
see Saint Priest, Alexis de Guignard,
Comte de, 1805-1851.
Priest, J. A. 65483
Priest, Josiah, 1790?-1850? 65484-(65497),
note after 105014A
Priest, William. 65498
Priest of Cedar Grove called to order. 4051
88113
Priest, the puritan, and the preacher. 74594
Priestcraft defended. 65499, (79890)
Priestcraft exposed. 96036
Priester der Gesellschaft Jesu. pseud.
Nachrichten. see Begert, Jakob.
Priester der zelve Societeyt. pseud. tr.
94350
Priestess: a tragedy in five acts. 76961
Priestess of the sun. 72130
Priesthood. 89369
Priestley, Joseph, 1733-1804. 5697, 14012,
44945, 65500-65509, 65511, (65513),
74490, 92070, 93804, 102401, 103097,
105938
Priestley, Joseph, 1768-1833. 65511
Priestley, Timothy. (65514)
Priestley's remarks. 5697
Priestly, John. 84662
Priests prisons to be protected by law. 1765
Priest's turf-cutting day. 42919
Prieto, Alejandro. (65515)
Prieto, Guillermo. 65516-65517, 71636
Prieto, Joaquin, Pres, Chile, 1786-1854. 127
12789 see also Chile. President, 183
1841 (Prieto)
Prieto, Jose de Teron y. see Teron y Prie
Jose de.
Prieto, Vicente. 65518
Prieto de Bonilla, A. A. Montero. see Mont
Pireto de Bonilla, A. A.
Prieto de Bonilla, Joseph. plaintiff (70801)
Prieux, ----------. plaintiff 65519
Prigg, Edward, plaintiff 61207, 65520
Prim, Juan. (65521)-65522
Prim et le prince des Austuries. 65524
Prima e seconda lettera di Andrea Corsali
Fiorentino. 67730
Prima parte de la cronica del grandissimo
regno del Peru. 13047
Prima parte dell' historie del Perv. 13052
Prima parte dell' istorie del Perv. 13048-
13049
Prima relatione di Iacqves Cartier. 67740
Prima y segunda carta de un Americano a un
Espanol. 65525
Primo y segunda parte de la Araucana.
(22720)
Primary address to the Convention of the
Protestant Episcopal Church. 64617
Primary and quarto geography. 83927
Primary arithmetic, and federal calculator.
note before 83906, 83913

Primary charge to the clergy of the Diocese
of Rhode Island. 13385
Primary charge to the clergy of the Protestant
Episcopal Church . . . Iowa. 39761
Primary dictionary. 71809
Primary geography . . . . By M. B. Moore.
50427
Primary geography. [By S. Augustus Mitchell.]
49722
Primary grammar. 85352, 85355
Primary history of the United States. note
after 42135
Primary history of the United States: made
easy and interesting for beginners. 66888
Primary history of the United States of America.
29116
Primary school law with notes and forms.
48778
Primasa serafica na regiao da America. 1759B
Primavera Indiana. 80972-80973, 80982, 80987
Primavera Indiana, poema sacro de Nuestra
Senora de Guadaloupe. 27787, 80983
Primavera Indiana poema sacro-historico.
80973
Primazia serafica na regiam da America.
15099
Prime, Benjamin Young. (65526)-65527
Prime, Benjamin Young. supposed author
65528, 97745
Prime, Ebenezer, 1700-1779. 8986, (65529)-
65531
Prime, G. Wendell. 65532
Prime, Nathaniel S. (65533)-(65534)
Prime, Samuel Irenaeus. (21423), 41014,
65535-(65540), 85100
Prime, Temple, 1832-1903. 65541, 84127
Prime, W. C. 65542-65546
Prime nove del altro mondo. (65430)
Primeiras linhas sobre as letras de cambio e
da terra. 88797
Primeiras linhas sobre o processo civil
Brazileiro. 88798
Primeiro livro de leitura para uso da infancia
Brasileira. 6426
Primeiro liuro. . . . [do descobrime[n] to &
conquista da India.] 13383
Primeiros tracos da crise commercial. 85625
Primer almanaque. 65549
Primer apendice a los cuatro justisimos clamores.
(66591)
Primer calendario curioso dedicado a las
senoritas para el ano de 1851. (65550)
Primer for the use of the Mohawk children.
65547-65548
Primer for young children. 91295
Primer Gefe del Ejercito Imperial a los habitantes
de Mexico. 65551 Primer libro de actas
del Cabildo de Santiago. 12754
Primer libro de geografia de Smith. note before
83906, 83946-83950
Primer libro de geografia de Smith, o geografia
elemental. 72787
Primer libro de geografia de Venezuela segun
Codazi. 72786
Primer of freedom. 28051, 35090, 1st note after
95375
Primer subdito de la ley es el gobierno. 65552
Primer Synodo Diocesana, celebrola el Ilmo
D. Pedro Phelipe . . . en la Santa Iglesia
Cathedral. 59522
Primer Synodo Diocesana, celebrola el Illmo.
Sr. D. Pedro Phelipe de Azua e Yturgoyen,
Obispo desta Santa Iglesia de la Concepcion.
65553
Primer tome de la tourbe ardante. 72764

Primer voiage d'Et. van der Hagen aux Indes
Orientales. 68455
Primera amonestacion. 65554
Primera ascension al Pico de Naiguata. 89285
Primera carta del P. D. Manuel Echeverria y
Penalver. 21775
Primera epistola del Admirante Don Cristobal
Colon. 14637
Primera introduccion de Alpacas y Llamas.
(65555)
Primera parte de aravco domado. 57300
Primera parte de Cortes valeroso, y Mexicana.
39139
Primera parte de la araucana. 22724
Primera parte de la constitucion politica.
94942
Primera parte de la miscelanea austral.
2469
Primera parte, de la politica de escriptvras.
106213
Primera parte de las difere[n]cias de libros
q[ue] ay en [e]l vniuerso. 98502
Primera parte de las diferencias de libros
q[ue] ay en el vniuerso. 98501
Primera parte, de las elegias de varones
illustres de Indias. 11402
Primera parte, de las historias sagradas.
99670
Primera parte de las noticas historiales de
las conquistas. 81286-81287
Primera parte de los anales de Aragon. 1950
Primera parte de los comentarios, dificvltades,
y discvrsos lyterales, morales, y misticos;
sobre los evangelios de los Domingos
del Adviento. 99673
Primera parte de los commentarios, difficvltades,
i discvrsos literales, y misticos sobre
los evangelios de la Qvaresma. 99671
Primera parte de los comentarios relaes.
98743, 98747, 98751-98752, 98757,
98760
Primera parte del libro intitvlado Espeio de
vida Christiana. 93310
Primera parte del monte de la Turba Ardiente
alumbrando con la claridad de se fuego
toda la India-Occidental. 72765
Primera parte del monte de Turba Ardiente
allumbrando con la claridad de se fuego
todas las costas firmes. 72765
Primera parte del Parnaso antartico de obras
amatorias. (48231)
Primera parte del sermanario, dominical, y
sanctoral en lengua Mexicana. 49009
Primera parte del sermonario del tiempo de
todo el ano. 40084
Primera regla de Santa Clara de Assis. 11461
Primera[-segunda] parte de los comentarios
reales. 98758
Primera [segunda, tercera] parte de los veinte
i vn libros rituales i monarchia Indiana.
96212
Primera, segunda y tercera partes de la
araucana. (22722)
Primera, y breve relacion de las favorables
noticias. 106403
Primera y segvnda parte de la aravcana.
22721
Primera [y segunda] parte, de la historia de
Peru. 24133
Primera y segunda parte de la historia general
de las Indias. 27725
Primera y segunda parte dela historia general
de las Indias. 27724
Primera, y segvnda parte, y semana santa de
los comentarios. 99674-99675

Primera y segvnda y tercera partes de la
Historia medicinal. 49938
Primera y ultima festividad. 76229
Primeras lecciones de geografia fisica. 42061
Primeras lecciones de geografia para el
Colegio de Guadalupe. 42061
Primeros efectos de la ley de 22 de Marzo
de 1873. 85712
Primeros sucesos desagradables en la isla del
Puerto Rico. 66598
Primeros versos de Horacio Mendizabal.
47814
Primerva catechese dos Indios selvagens.
74029
Primeval monuments of Peru. 89989
Primivias de la cultura de Quito. (65556)
Primipilario, sv origen, significacion, ocvpacion,
y privilegios. 75896
Primitiae florae Essequeboensis. 48673
Primitiva Cecilia Caldes. 99691
Primitive Christianity revived. 59725
Primitive Methodist Church. Conferences.
Western Annual Conference, 20th, Shulls-
burg, Wisc., 1864. 65557
Primitive psalmody. 84696
Primitive Washingtonian. pseud. Resurrection
of the blue-laws. 70129
Primo da California. 43214
Primo (& secondo) libro di Mattheo di Micheovo.
67738
Primo viaggio intorno al globo terracqueo.
(62804)
Primo volume, & quarta editione. Delle naviga-
tioni et viaggi raccolto da M. Gio. Batt.
Ramvsio. (67733)
Primo volume, & seconda editione Delle naviga-
tioni et viaggi in molti lvoghi corretta.
67731
Primo volume, & terza editione Delle naviga-
tioni et viaggi. 67732
Primo volvme delle navigationi et viaggi.
67730, note after 99383C
Primoras lecciones de geografia e historia del
Peru. 42061
Primordaile certamen. 93774
Primrose, ---------, fl. 1649. 80255-(80256)
Prince, ---------. 67599
Prince, Deborah. 65590
Prince, Frederic. 65558
Prince, George. 73289
Prince, James. (65559)
Prince, John, 1751-1836. 65560-65562, 86749,
101882
Prince, John, 1820-1900. 65563
Prince, John, fl. 1848. 65565
Prince, Rev. John, fl. 1848. 65564
Prince, John T. 65566
Prince, Joseph H. 65567
Prince, L. Bradford. 65568
Prince, Mary. 65569
Prince, N. A. ed. (65525)
Prince, Nancy. 65570-(65571)
Prince, Nathan. 65572-65573
Prince, Oliver H. comp. 27038-27039
Prince, Philip Alexander. 65574
Prince, Sarah. see Gill, Sarah (Prince)
Prince, Thomas, 1687-1758. 13208, 17675,
20057, (20271), 20876, 20884, (21087),
21944, 21946, 28020, 32736, 32846,
43654, 45454-45455, 46274, 47124, 51017,
52736, (55031), 59604, 65575-(65588),
65590-65617, 65700, (66443), 79377,
79410, 80210, 80258, 80617, 82819,
86799, 92351, 94709, 84688, 96298,
97181, 97190, 98274, 101171, 103932,

104075, 104264, 104265-104271, 104317,
104854, 105085 see also Eight Minister
Who Carry On the Thursday Lecture in
Boston.
Prince, Thomas. 1786-1758. incorrectly
supposed author 65589, note after 10422,
104404
Prince, Thomas, 1722-1748. (65618), note after
103615
Prince, William, 1766-1841. (65619)-65623
Prince, William Reed, 1817-1845. (65625)
Prince, William Robert, 1795-1869. 65621-
65624
Prince (William) & Sons. firm 65621
Prince Castriotta d'Albanie. pseud. Oeuvres
choisies. see Zannovich, Stiepan, 1751-
1786.
Prince de Ligne. see Ligne, Charles Joseph,
Prince de, 1735-1814.
Prince Edward County, Va. Union Theological
Seminary. see Richmond, Va. Union
Theological Seminary.
Prince Edward Island. 65639
Prince Edward Island. petitioners (61285),
65636, note after 93185
Prince Edward Island. Census, 1841. 65626
Prince Edward Island. Census, 1855. 65626
Prince Edward Island. General Assembly.
31137, 65633, 65635, 98067
Prince Edward Island. Land Commissioners'
Court. 65627
Prince Edward Island. Laws, statutes, etc.
65628-(65630), (65638), 65642
Prince Edward Island. Legislative Council.
65632, 65634-65635
Prince Edward Island. Legislative Library,
Charlottetown. 65631
Prince Edward Island. Royal Agricultural
Society. see Royal Agricultural Society
of Prince Edward Island.
Prince Edward Island. Visitors of Schools for
the Western and Eastern Sections.
(65641)
Prince Edward Island: a brief but faithful
account of this fine colony. 40769
Prince Edward Island almanack; for 1868.
30784
Prince Edward Island Baptist Convention. see
Baptists. Prince Edward Island. Con-
vention.
Prince Edward Island calendar, for the year
1853. (65637)
Prince John. pseud. Prince John's epistles
to the barn-burners. see Van Buren,
John.
Prince John's epistles to the barnburners.
65645
Prince Library. A cataloque of the collection
of books and manuscripts. 65582
Prince Messiah's claims to dominion over all
governments. 104553
Prince of Angola, a tragedy. 88547
Prince of darkness. 88663
Prince of Gorigos. see Hethum, Prince of
Korghos, d. 1308.
Prince of Kashna; a west Indian story. 37767
Prince of Korghos. see Hethum, Prince of
Korghos, d. 1308.
Prince of Musignano. see Bonaparte, Charles
Jules Laurent Lucien, Prince de Canino,
1803-1857.
Prince of Orange. see William III, King of
Great Britain, 1650-1702.
Prince of Orange's speech to the Scots Lords
and gentlemen at St. James's. 9372,
81492

Prince of Panama. 82127
Prince of Parthia, a tragedy. (27658)
Prince of Wales in America. 16821
Prince, or maxims of state. 67599
Prince Paul: the freedman soldier. 59445
Prince Society. 6711, 9449, 9708, 14536,
 14538, 20725, (21088), 21343, 21611,
 22148, 35770, (34070), 34810, (40332),
 42824, 46244, (46637), 46642, 46689,
 46709, 46712, 46723-46725, 46731-46732,
 (46749), 46756, 52597, 52611, 52622,
 (65323), 1st note after 65324, 65646,
 note after 70346, 79377, 80621, 81697-
 81698, note before 85867, note before
 85932, 86618, 86630, 86716, 91853,
 92350, 96426, 98355, 98500, 4th-5th notes
 after 98549, 1st note after 99800, 101074,
 103223, 103755, 103900, 103902, note
 after 103907, 104068, 104848, 104899,
 104902, 105074, 105077, 105085, note
 after 105456, note after 105459
Prince's annual catalogue of fruit and ornamental
 trees. 65621
Prince's ball. A brochure. 91065
Prince's supplementary catalogue of the Linnaean
 Botanic Garden. 65621
Prince's visit: a discourse . . . October 21,
 1860. 26536
Prince's visit; a humorous description of the
 tour of His Royal Highness. 16778
Princesa Papantzin. 71703
Princess of Zanfara. 65647
Princeton, Me. Lewy's Island Lodge, no. 138.
 see Freemasons. Maine. Lewy's Island
 Lodge, no. 38, Princeton.
Princeton, Mass. Celebration of the One
 Hundredth Anniversary of the Incorpora-
 tion of the Town, 1859. 65648
Princeton, Mass. Convention for Organizing
 the Wachusett Baptist Association, 1842.
 see Baptists. Massachusetts. Convention
 for Organizing the Wachusett Baptist
 Association, Princeton, 1842.
Princeton, Mass. Ecclesiastical Council, 1847.
 see Congregational Churches in Massa-
 chusetts. Ecclesiastical Council, Princeton,
 1817.
Princeton, Mass. School Committee. 65649
Princeton, N. J. College of New Jersey. see
 Princeton University.
Princeton, N. J. Meeting to Form a Society
 in . . . New Jersey to Co-operate with
 the American Colonization Society, 1824.
 see New Jersey Colonization Society.
Princeton, N. J. Nassau Hall. see Princeton
 University.
Princeton, N. J. Nassau-Hall Grammar School.
 see Princeton University. Grammar
 School.
Princeton, N. J. Ordinances, etc. 65651
Princeton, N. J. Washington Benevolent Society.
 see Washington Benevolent Society. New
 Jersey. Princeton.
Princeton Biblical repertory. 65224
Princeton Latin grammar. (73399)
Princeton magazine. 65652
Princeton pulpit, a collection of sermons
 preached there. (21141)
Princeton pulpit. Edited by John T. Duffield.
 65653
Princeton review. 1164, 13320, 28427, (32329)-
 (32330), 41223, 58623-58625, 63400, 65208,
 65654, 69345, 70190, (82712), 85068,
 85341, 90441, 90604, 90610, 93196, 93200,
 99583
Princeton review (Indexes) 65654

Princeton semi-centennial jubilee, MDCCCLXII.
 89733
Princeton Theological Seminary, Princeton,
 N. J. 65655-(65657), 83759, 85483
Princeton Theological Seminary biographical
 catalogue. 83759
Princeton University. 53088
Princeton University. American Whig Society.
 53088
Princeton University. Centennial Anniversary,
 1847. 53088
Princeton University. Class of 1762. 48964
Princeton University. Class of 1763. 19942
Princeton University. Class of 1856. Secre-
 tary. 53088
Princeton University. Class of 1859. 53088
Princeton University. Class of 1860. 51892
Princeton University. Cliosophic Society.
 53088
Princeton University. Grammar School. 65650,
 (73399)
Princeton University. Library. 53088
Princeton University. Library. Cyrus H.
 McCormick Publication Fund. 99379
Princeton University. Senior Class, 1763.
 see Princeton University. Class of 1763.
Princeton University. Sophomore Class, 1858.
 see Princeton University. Class of 1860.
Princeton University. Trustees. 53032,
 (53087), 94690-94691
Princeton University. Trustees. petitioners
 94708
Princetown, N. Y. Princetown Academy. see
 Princetown Academy, Princetown, N. Y.
Princetown Academy, Princetown, N. Y. 65659
Principal actors in the siege and defence of
 Fort St. Phillip. 8107
Principal and objects of the National Reform
 Association. (65660)
Principal documents . . . October, 1834, to
 November, 1835. 30819
Principal documents relating to the survey of
 the coast. 30819
Principal documents relating to the survey of
 the coast of the United States since 1816.
 30819, 65661
Principal ecclesiastical movements in the reign
 of Queen Elizabeth. (8236)
Principal events in the life of that Indian chief
 [i. e. Joseph Brant.] 7413
Principal freeholder. pseud. Sentiments. see
 S., F. pseud.
Principal Inhabitants and Proprietors of the
 Island of Martinique. petitioners see
 Martinique. Principal Inhabitants and
 Proprietors. petitioners
Principal Inhabitants of the Mosquito-Shore.
 petitioners see British Honduras.
 Principal Inhabitants. petitioners
Principal legatees. 2701, note after 90697
Principal navigations, voiages, traffiqves and
 discoueries of the English nation. 29595
Principal navigations, voyages, traffiques and
 discoveries of the English nation. (24896),
 (29596), 31095, 37686, 53283, 59498,
 note after 65395, 67554, (67585), 69210,
 77289, 79342, 80349, 97145, 99281, 3d
 note after 99856, 1st note after 105510
Principal of universal salvation examined and
 tried. 80192
Principal points of the Mystic River Company.
 19662
Principal Subjects of the Mosquito-Shore. see
 British Honduras. Citizens.
Principales acontecimientos del Puerto Cabello.
 65662

Principales requetes du Procurer General.
10550

Principall navigations, voiages, and discoveries
of the English Nation. (29594)

Principe de la Paz. see Godoy Alvarez de
Faria Rios Sanchez y Zarzosa, Manuel
de, Principe de la Paz, 1767-1851.

Principe escondido. 75812

Principe qui a produit la revolutions de France.
65663

Principes de la langue des sauvages appeles
Sauteux. 4407

Principes de la revolution justifies dans un
sermon. 102144

Principes de la science sociale. 10837

Principes de l'etude comparative des langues.
47956

Principes de 1789 en Amerique. 65664

Principes d'economie politique appliques a la
legislation du commerce. 81451

Principes et interets. 26725

Principes fondamentaux de somiologie. 67465

Principia medicinae. 57817

Principia quaedam. 11234

Principia quaeda[m] ex quibus procendenum est.
11235

Principios de retorica y poetica. 76277

Principios elementares de chronologia. 63953

Principios fundamentales para servir de introduccion. 74934

Principio-perro de aguas. 38443

Principios politicos en la administracion del
Peru. 61155

Principios, y reglas de la lengva Cvmmanagota.
74017, 105954

Principle against expediency. 63220

Principle and passion in conflict. 71272

Principle events in the life of Brant. 20884

Principle, history, and use of air balloons.
(65665)

Principle of action in matter. 14268

Principle of reform. 91374

Principle of secrecy and secret societies.
85315

Principle of the New Church. 53248

Principle of truth in the heart of man. 99818

Principle, progress, tendency, obligations and
destiny of Democracy. 20533

Principle sources of civil prosperity. 20941

Principles and acts of Mr. Adams' administration vindicated. (50396)

Principles and acts of the revolution in America.
(55312)

Principles and articles agreed upon by the
members of the Constitutional Society.
60398

Principles and interests. 26726

Principles and maxims of the art of war.
65666

Principles and maxims on which the security
and happiness of a republic depend. 95199

Principles and measures of true democracy.
88296

Principles and men considered in reference to
the election of President. 35385

Principles and men: considered with reference
to the approaching election of President.
65667, 71157

Principles and mode of action of the American
Anti-slavery Society. 26712

Principles and objects of the American Party.
65668

Principles and objects of the Massachusetts
Medical Society. (61043)

Principles and observations applied to the
manufacture and inspection of pot and
pearl ashes. 96377

Principles and plan of the Mixed Communion
Church in Philadelphia. 65669

Principles and plans of the Board of Publication of the Presbyterian Church. 65206

Principles and policy of the conservatices.
65670

Principles and practice of embanking lands
from river-floods. (31647)

Principles and practice of operative surgery.
84276

Principles and practice of surgery. (82714)

Principles and practices of the Methodists.
65671

Principles and proceedings of the inhabitants
of the District of Niagara. 28141, 9808

Principles and prospects of the friends of
peace. (31388)

Principles and results of the Ministry at Larg
in Boston. 97385, 97396

Principles and rules, with the articles of fait
and covenant of the Trinitarian Church,
Fitchburg. 24601

Principles and suggestions for a remedial
code. 56050

Principles and tendencies of democracy.
59486

Principles, articles, and regulations. (61574)

Principles at issue. A speech . . . at New
York, Sept. 13, 1860. 66817

Principles at issue. New York, September 1
1860. 65672

Principles, &c. [By Noah Hobart.] 96094

Principles for which the American revolution
was fought. 83964

Principles illustrated by facts. 82425

Principles of a commercial system. 94794

Principles of a free government. 63750

Principles of a proposed national society.
65673

Principles of civil union and happiness considered and recommended. 27883

Principles of congregational churches relating
to the constitution. (32311)

Principles of congregationalism. 98044

Principles of currency and banking. 42024

Principles of democracy. 24803

Principles of duelling. 90446

Principles of early education. 103979

Principles of education as applied in the Mobi
Institute. 62976

Principles of free trade, illustrated in a seri
of short and familiar essays. 67504

Principles of geology. 42764

Principles of government: a treatise on free
institutions. 12824

Principles of government and commerce.
102367, note after 102396

Principles of government, monarchical goverm
ment. 8413

Principles of hospital construction. 84265A

Principles of hospital construction, being an
abstract of a report. 84265A

Principles of interpretation and construction
in law and politics. 40977

Principles of law and government. 65674

Principles of law and polity. 4925

Principles of legislation and law. (32611)

Principles of mathematical, physical, and
political geography. 44164

Principles of Mr. [J. Q.] Adams' administration. 318

Principles of morality. 90856

Principles of national development in their relation to statesmanship. 65969

Principles of national prosperity. 68999

Principles of naval staff rank. 13806, 74192, 2d note after 93829

Principles of politeness. 90235, 90238, 90239-90242, 90244-90245, 90247-90249

Principles of politeness, and of knowing the world. 90225, 90231-90232, 90234

Principles of political economy applied to the condition. 7058

Principles of political economy. By H. C. Carey, Esq. 10835

Principles of political economy. [By Henry Vethake.] 99393

Principles of polity, being the grounds and reasons of civil empire. 64830

Principles of religion and morality. 90856

Principles of representation in Congress. 30568

Principles of safe banking applied to trust companies. 83860

Principles of science applied to the domestic and mechanic arts. 64615

Principles of sin and holiness. 83799-83800

Principles of social science. 10836

Principles of statistical inquiry. 74301

Principles of Stephen A. Douglas illustrated in his speeches. (20696)

Principles of strict temperance. 78390

Principles of taxation: public finances—the new tax bill. 65675

Principles of taxation. Speech of Hon. H. J. Raymond. 68052

Principles of the American constitutions contrasted. 102399

Principles of the American government. 65676

Principles of the Christian religion, as taught in the Reformed Protestant Dutch Churches. 65677

Principles of the Christian religion . . . in the words of the Bible. 78496

Principles of the Christian religion. With scripture proofs. 80722

Principles of the congregational churches. (30648)

Principles of the consociated churches. 77394

Principles of the consociated churches of Connecticut. 15814, 23414, 32307

Principles of the government of the United States. 18873

Principles of the late charges impartially examined. 28774, 99813, 4th note after 94663

Principles of the Non-resistance Society. 52710

Principles of the policy of the United States. 94491

Principles of the present political parties examined. 63749

Principles of the protestant religion maintained. 828, (46466), note after 104098

Principles of the reformation. 98045

Principles of the revolution. 5858

Principles of the revolution: showing the perversion of them. 5829

Principles of the revolution vindicated. 102145

Principles of trade. 65678, 103121

"Principles that ought naturally to govern the conduct of neutrals and belligerents." 13259

Principles upon which the temperance reform is bases. 44200

Principles which enter into the inquiry of the Christian student. 88574

Prindle, --------, fl. 1863. 65679

Prindle, Charles. 65680

Prindle, Cyrus. 65681-54583

Pring, Martin. 66686

Pringe, Martin. 66686

Pringle, Lieut. pseud. see Hines, David Theodore.

Pringle, Edward J. (54584)-54585, note after 92624

Pringle, Hall. 35578, 65686

Pringle, Sir John. 58057, 104989

Pringle, John Henry. ed. 63067

Pringle, John J. 65687

Pringle, Norman. 93169

Pringle, Thomas. 65569

Pringle Smith, J. J. see Smith, J. J. Pringle.

Pringsheim, E. 85072

Prins, Jeurian. 65688

Prinsep, C. R. tr. 77363

Printed account of the conflagration of Richmond Theatre in Virginia. 71172

Printed but not published. 25328

Printed case of William Penn, Esq. 68710

Printed copy of an act made by Charles Gookin, Esq. 60399

Printed copy of the humble address of Her Majesty's Council. (52894)

Printed letter, of the 12th of February. 49684

Printed letter to the Rt. Hon. Sir George Murray. 9222

Printed minutes of the General Synod of the Reformed Dutch Church. 93074

Printed sermons, journals and letters. 103560, 103622

Printed speech of Edmund Burke, Esq. 80039

Printed speech, said to be spoken in the House of Commons. 97350, 97353

Printer. pseud. Few more words. see Bell, Robert, 1732?-1784.

Printer lads, who carry the Pennsylvania gazette to the customers. pseud. see Pennsylvania gazette. Printer Lads. pseud.

Printer not being able to publish Capt. Sweet's answer to Col. Wanton's address. 95980

Printer; read before the Franklin Society of the City of Chicago. 80033

Printer to the public: on the freedom of the press. 84642

Printer to the reader. (33445), (48248), 67599, 94165, 106052

Printer to the reader, and all worthy adventurers by sea. 82841

Printer to the readers. 36981, (60182)

Printers advertisement. Whereas there is prefixed unto a late pamphlet. 28052, 28506, 65689, 91945

Printers and printing in Providence, 1762-1907. 86772

Printer's Banquet, New York, 1850. see New York Typographical Society. Printers' Banquet, 1850.

Printer's Boy that carriers about the Pennsylvania journal. pseud. Verses. 99294

Printers' circular. (65690)

Printer's devil. pseud. Poetical gift to the patrons of the Western spy. see Pierce, Thomas. supposed author

Printer's devil. pseud. Verses for the year 1790. 99290

Printers' Festival, Boston, 1848. see Franklin Typographical Society, Boston. Printers' Festival, 1848.

Printers' Festival, Rochester, N. Y., 1847. (24956)

Printers' guide. 103373

Printer's lad, who carrieth about the Pennsylvania gazette. pseud. see Pennsylvania gazette. Printer's lad. pseud.

Printer's lads who carry about the Pennsylvania evening post. pseud. see Pennsylvania evening post. Printer's lads. pseud.

Printers lads, who carry the Pennsylvania Gazette to the customers. pseud. see Pennsylvania gazette. Printers lads. pseud.

Printers' Literary Union, Cambridge, Mass. 10147

Printers of the District of Columbia. Meeting, Washington, D. C., 1834. see Meeting of the Printers of the District of Columbia, Washington, D. C. 1834.

Printers' tracts. No. 1. 65691

Printz Hall. 65692

Prior, George. 65693

Prior, James, 1790?-1869. 62509, 65694-65696

Prior, Matthew, 1664-1721. 65697

Prior, Margaret. 65698

Prior, Samuel. 65699

Prior, Thomas. 65700

Prior, William, fl. 1838. 65701

Prior documents. 951, 955

Prior documents, 1777. 39706

Prior y Consules de la Universidad de los Mercaderes. 98020

Prior, y Consules de la Vniversidad de los Mercaderes de la Nueua-Espana: dizen. 79139

Priscianus, of Lydia. 76838

Priscien. see Priscianus, of Lydia.

Priscilla; or, trials for the truth. 3231

Prise & possession de l'isle Saint Christophe. 26770, note after 94151

Prise de la Dominique. 27650, (63966), 68421

Prise de l'isle de la Grenade. 27650, (63966), 68421

Prise de l'isle de Santo Paulo. 65702

Prise de M. de Damas. 65703

Prise de Pensacoal. 27650, (63966), 68421

Prise de Tabaco. 27650, (63966), 68421

Prise du Senegal. 27650, (63966), 68421

Prise d'vn Seigneur Ecossois et de ses gens. (44089)

Prision de un general gachupin. 86258

Prismatics. 31082

Prison Association of New York. 53861

Prison Association of New York. petitioners 53861

Prison Association of New York. Female Department. 54273

Prison books and their authors. 38889

Prison discipline. (58114), 65704-65705, note after 99830

Prison discipline in America. (28387)

Prison-Discipline Society, Boston. 65706

Prison Discipline Society, Boston. Board of Managers. 45936

Prison Discipline Society, St. Louis. see St. Louis Prison Discipline Society.

Prison-Discipline Society of Massachusetts. 45902

Prison life. By John M. Brewer. 7757

Prison life in the south. 27

Prison-life in the tobacco warehouse at Richmond. 30531

Prison life of Jefferson Davis. 17429

Prison Reform Association of New Jersey. see New Jersey Prison Reform Association.

Prison reminiscences. 82466

Prison ship. 65707

Prison-ship. 25891

Prison-ship, continued. 25891

Prison sketches. 42632

Prison Society of Philadelphia. see Philadelphia Prison Society.

Prisoner. pseud. Encarnacion prisoners. 22549, 65708

Prisoner. pseud. Two months in Fort Lafayette. (65709)

Prisoner in England. pseud. ed. Prisoners' memoirs. see Andrews, Charles.

Prisoner in Newgate. pseud. Scriptures and reasons. see Murton, John. supposed author

Prisoner of hope. 65711

Prisoner of state. 43878

Prisoner of the border. A tale of 1838. 51637

Prisoner of the mill. (31118)

Prisoner of war. 34421, 37168

Prisoner of war, and how treated. 71707

Prisoner of war, or five months among the Yankees. 37169

Prisoner; or, a collection of poetical pieces, &c. 65710

Prisoner released. 31055

Prisoner (that hath sitten in the prison-house of woful darkness.) 62919

Prisonero de la isla de Esteves. pseud. Espresiones. see S. y L., M. C. pseud.

Prisoneros Ingleses. 101905

Prisoner's diary. (67276)

Prisoner's friend. 65712, 89068, 89070

Prisoner's—Friend Association. 45937

Prisoners' hidden life. 58105

Prisoners in Mexico. 78306

Prisoner's magazine, no. 4. 101087

Prisoners' memoirs. (1484), 65713

Prisoners of Perote. 90483

Prisons de Philadelphie. 39053, (62074)

Prispevky ku poznani Americkeho petroleje. 25933

Pritchard, George. 65714

Pritchard, John. 65715

Pritchard, John. petitioner 65715

Pritchett, George James. 65717-65718

Pritts, Joseph. 65719-65721

Priuatus, Teucrius Annaeus. tr. (8784)

Privado del Virey. Drama. 72511

Private acts and resolutions [of the General Assembly of Connecticut.] 15777

Private acts and resolutions passed by the General Assembly. 15745

Private and confidential letters from Washington, Hamilton, Lafayette, and others. (13744)

Private and confidential on government matter 65722

Private and local acts of the General Assembly of Prince Edward Island. (65638)

Private and local laws of Nova-Scotia. 56161

Private and public life of Abraham Lincoln. 41224

Private and special acts of . . . Maine. 44000

Private and special statutes of the commonwealth of Massachusetts. 45938

Private brother. pseud. Letter to Mr. A. Croswell. 17672, 85663

Private brother. pseud. Sobre reply to a mad answer. 17672

Private case before the House of Lords, between Gillam Philips, Brother of Henr Philips deceased. 62457

Private case before the House of Lords, between James Lawson and Jno. Tait. 39450

Private case before the House of Lords relati to the affairs of James Dunlop. 21316

Private citizen. pseud. Attention! or, new thoughts on a serious subject. see Webster, Noah, 1758-1843.

Private citizen. pseud. Bird's eye sketch of the military concerns of the United States. 97909

Private citizen. pseud. Enquiries into the necessity or expediency of assuming exclusive legislation over the District of Columbia. 20302, 105152

Private citizen. pseud. New thoughts on a serious subject. see Webster, Noah, 1758-1843.

Private citizen. pseud. Private citizen's proposal. 65723

Private citizen. pseud. Three letters. see Publius, A private citizen. pseud.

Private citizen's proposal for the settlement. 65723

Private conference between Philalethes & Amatolos. 89794

Private confession of the murderer of Lincoln. 41225

Private correspondence between H. E. the Governor and Captain General of the Province of Buenos-Ayres. 9043, 93807

Private correspondence between the Governor and Capt. General of Buenos Ayres. 9043, 93807

Private correspondence of Benjamin Franklin. 25571

Private correspondence of Henry Clay. 13544

Private devotions, recommended to the Episcopal congregations. (15009)

Private diary. 80258

Private disinterested party independent and unconnected with any sect or party. pseud. Reasons for not signing the petition. 68268

Private history and confession of Pamela Lee. 39779

Private in gray. 84754

Private in the ranks. pseud. see Don Pedro Quaerendo Reminisco, a private in the ranks. pseud.

Private intirgues between the County of Gondamore. 95303

Private journal. Prepared from authentic domestic records. 64460

Private journal, kept by Mr. John Townsend. 96381

Private journal kept during a portion of the revolutionary war. (50852)

Private journal of a journey from Boston to New England. 38125

Private journal of a voyage from New York to Rio de Janeiro. (28116)

Private journal of a voyage to the Pacific Ocean. 91667

Private journal of Aaron Burr. (9424)

Private journal of an officer. 57916)

Private journal of G. F. Lyon. (42853)

Private journal of Harman Blennerhassett. 5906, 74878

Private journal of the Rev. C. S. Stewart. 91668

Private journal of W. H. B. Webster. 102429

Private journal [of Walter Brodie.] 8181

Private journal of William C. Holton. 32662, 57742

Private land claims.—Florida. 24892, 103434

Private laws. 61208

Private laws of . . . North-Carolina. (55659)

Private laws of the Confederate States of America. 15338, 15416

Private laws of the Confederate States of America . . . 1863-4. 15346

Private laws [of the Confederate States of America] . . . 1862-'63. 55660

Private laws of the Confederate States of America, passed at the first session of the first Congress, 1862. 65724

Private laws of the Confederate States of America, passed at the second session of the first Congress. 15339

Private [laws of the Confederate States of America, passed at the third session of the first Congress; 1863.] 15345

Private laws of the United States of America . . . 1845-6. 49318

Private laws of the United States of America, passed at the second session of the fortieth Congress, 1867-1868. 61208, 65725, 66517

Private laws passed by the General Assembly of . . . North Carolina. 55661

Private letter on the subject. 46500

Private letter to the . . . members of Congress. (39220)

Private letters from an American in England. (65726)

Private letters from London. 94142

Private letters of Lieut. General Scott. (78429)

Private libraries of New York. 9495

Private libraries of Providence. 72678

Private life of Daniel Webster. 38924

Private life of John C. Calhoun. 3945

Private life of the late Benjamin Franklin. 25573

Private life of Thomas Jefferson. 62792

Private meetings animated and regulated. 46467

Private-men no pulpit-men. 105475

Private Miles O'Reilly. pseud. see Halpine, Charles Grahame.

Private of Cape Antonio. 82120

Private or special laws of the state of Maine. 44002

Private papers [of Andrew Jackson.] 4787

Private person. pseud. Address to the people of England. 22599

PRivate record of J. B. 39553

Private report read to the Secretaries of His Majesty Ferdinand VI. note after 97687

Private Secretary to ———, etc. pseud. Fall of Fort Sumter. 23741

Private soldier. pseud. Narrative of the fall & winter campaign. see McClenthen, C. S.

Private soldier in the 92d Regiment. pseud. Narrative. 51781

Private thoughts on public affairs. (65727)

Private virtue and publick spirit displayed. 65728

Private voices to the public heart. (45426)

Private writings of Mr. Hirst on divers select and important heads. (14490)

Privateer of 1776. (13858)

Privateer system. 18894

Privateer's cruise. 11600

Privateers of the revolution. 91328

Privately printed. International copyright. 83878

Private's journal in the battles of Mexico. (30703)

Privatmittheilungen der HH. Sutter, Marshall, Brannan u. a. 10015

Privida y oficial correspondencia. 43815

Priviledges [sic] of the saints on earth. 32811

Privilege and dignity. 82035

Privilege du Roi. 26013

Privilege of communication. 99089

Privilege of Senators and Representatives of the United States. 18096

Privilege of the writ of habeas corpus under the constitution. 5481-5487, 9131, (28936), 65729

Privilege of the writ of habeas corpus under the constitution of the United States. 37445

Privileges and duties of an American citizen. A sermon . . . Utica. 20638

Privileges and duties of an American citizen. A discourse, . . . on thanksgiving day. 9364

Privileges and immunities of citizenship. 31735

Privileges and responsibilities of our country. 93237

Privileges of Jamaica vindicated. 57258

Privileges of members of Congress. 27329

Privileges of the island of Jamaica vindicated. 35650

Privilegi della ignoranza lettere d'una Americana. 12616

Privilegien vergunt aan de Ceur-Brandenburgse Americaense Compagnie. 65730

Privilegios y gracias singulares. 65731

Privy purse expenses of King Henry the Eighth. (55248)

Prix de la valeur. 18664

Prix d'adjudication des articles. 85669

Prix d'histoire obtenu au Concours General. 63709

Prize. 92173

Prize address, by Alvan Stuart, Esq. 91630

Prize address. [By W. B. Wood.] 69155

Prize address, For the New-York City Temperance Society. 91631

Prize address, no. III. 95801

Prize address, presented for the prize medal. (69154), 83665

Prize book no. IV of the Public Latin School of Boston. 94136

Prize book of the Public Latin School. 6757

Prize Committee on the Jenny Lind Song. 9661

Prize dissertation, which was honored with the Magellanic gold medal. 95646

Prize essay. An essay on the wages paid to females for their labour. 97397

Prize essay. [By H. D. Kitchel.] (38019)

Prize essay, by H. T. J. Macnamara. 43593

"Prize essay." [By Summer Stebbins.] 91053

Prize essay. By Thomas Frederick Knight. 38128

Prize essay, 1897. 38960

Prize essay. Fronteenac, Lennox & Addington. 16400

Prize essay. History and chemical investigation of maize or Indian corn. 75793

Prize essay, . . . illustrations of disease with a microscope. 64156

Prize essay [of the Boston Civil Service Reform Association.] 84505

Prize essay on civil service reform. 84505

Prize essay on fairs. (20494)

Prize essay on intemperance. 28868

Prize essay on medical and vital statistics. 33154

Prize essay, on the comparative economy of free and slave labour. (68058)

Prize essay on the history of New Brunswick. 9488

Prize essay on the history of the settlement of Halifax. 552

Prize essay on the preparation and application of manures. 70438

Prize essay, read in the Sheldonian Theatre. 42618

Prize essay. The canals of Canada. 37146

Prize essay. The necessity and means of improving the common schools. 64306

Prize essay. The teacher's manual. 58380

Prize essays on a congress of nations, for the adjustment of international disputes and for the promotion of universal peac 65732, 103738

Prize essays on a congress of nations for th adjustment of international disputes, wit out resort to arms. 38529

Prize essays on civil service reform. 8450Е

Prize essays on coal mining in England. 90

Prize essays on juvenile delinquency. (6207Е

Prize essays on mining bituminous coal. 90 90822

Prize essays published by the American Pea Society in 1840. 98051

Prize list and . . . proceedings of the Provi Agricultural and Industrial Exhibition о Nova Scotia. 1868. 56162

Prize list for 1858 [of the Agricultural Asso tion of Lower Canada.] 10347

Prize ode, recited by Mr. Finn. 2727

Prize ode, written by Charles Sprague. 650Е 6758, 89665

Prize poem, recited in the Theatre, Oxford. 14652

Prize Steamer "Cherokee," formerly the "Thistle." 25049

Prize story of the second American revolutic 27942

Prize tale. A New England sketch. 92448, 92455

Prize vessels. 65733

Pro bono publico. 65734

Pro Ivan Vazquez de Mendina. 98730

Pro memoria. [By Samuel Urlsperger.] 98

Pro memoria, dienende tot refutatie der con sideratien. 65735

Pro patria. pseud. Discourse, addressed tс the sons of liberty. 20237

Pro rata question. 8359

Pro y el contra de esta cuestion. 85666

Probabilities that the Americans are of that race. 95651

Probabilities, that those Indians are Judaical 95652

Probability of reaching the North Pole discussed. 3632, 93597

Probable effects of the dissolution of the cor nection. 104001

Probable origin of the American Indians. 37399

Probable origin of the American Indians wit particular reference to that of the Car 37400

Probasco, Henry. (65737)

Probasco, J. 65738

Probate Division. Appointment, &c. of attor 99106

Probate manual. 88569

Probationary odes of Jonathan Pindar, Esq. (62911), 97380

Probe, or one hundred and two essays on th nature of men and things. 36866

Probier -und Schmelzkunst. 3255C

Problem . . . freedom and slavery in the United States. 65739

Problem of American destiny, solved by scie and history. 65740

Problem of American nationality, and the ev which hinder its solution. 27367

Problem of free society. (65741)

Problem of freedom and slavery in the Unit States. 30002

Problem of government in the light of the p present and the future. 65742

Problem of the age. 65743

Problemi natvrali, e morali. 26668

Problems in the geography of foreign trade. 83381

Problems of rotary motion. 85072

Problems of the philosophy of history. 82710

Problems of the woman question. 89379

Probst, Antoine. defendant (65744)

Probst, Petro. ed. (52376), 91981

Probus. pseud. Adresse au Conseil Legislatif. 42189, (53303), 65745

Probus. pseud. Letter from Washington on the annexation of Texas. 12702

Probyn, J. W. 65746-65747

Procedes dans l'Assemblee du Bas-Canada. 96926

Procedes de l'Assemblee des Electeurs du Comte de Montreal. 65748

Procedes du Bureau d'Agriculture du Bas-Canada. 10346

Procedes du Comite General du Chemin de Fer du Nord. 65749

Proceedings, address and constitution of the New England Bible Association of Friends. 65750

Proceedings against Sir Walter Raleigh, Kt. 67545

Porceedings against the Rev. J. Smith. 82898

Proceedings against William Lloyd Garrison. 26710

Proceedings and address at the celebration of the one hundredth anniversary. 53088

[Proceedings and address of a Convention of the Friends of John Quincy Adams.] 96770

Proceedings & address of Democratic Republicans. 65751

Proceedings and address of the Anti-Jackson Convention of Missouri. 49628

Proceedings & address of the Committee of the anti-Jackson Men of Franklin County, Pennsylvania. 60400

Proceedings and address of the Convention of Delegates to the people of New Jersey. (53204)

Proceedings and address of the Convention of Young Men in Rockingham Councillor District. 65752

Proceedings and address of the . . . Democratic Convention, February 22, 1828. 53205

Proceedings and address, of the Democratic State Convention. 53862

Proceedings and address of the General Convention of Congregational and Presbyterian Ministers. 99234

Proceedings and address of the New Hampshire Republican State Convention. 65753

Proceedings and address of the Washingtonian Mass Convention. (65754)

Proceedings and addresses at the inauguration of Andrew Sloan Draper. 84895

Proceedings and addresses at the twenty-fifth anniversary of the founding of the Plymouth Church of Milwaukee. (49178)

Proceedings and addresses of the Vermont Republican Convention. 99173

Proceedings and addresses on the occasion of the death of Benjamin Franklin Butler, of New York. 9611

Proceedings and annual report of the Va. Baptist Educational Society. 100552

Proceedings and collections [of the Wyoming Historical and Geological Society, Wilkesbarre, Pa.] 93937

Proceedings and constitution of the Pennsylvania Branch of the General Union for Promoting the Observance of the Christian Sabbath. (60305)

Proceedings and constitution of the South-Carolina Anti-intemperance Society. 87952

Proceedings and constitution of the Universalist Sabbath School Association. 98015

Proceedings and correspondence relating to the pretensions of the state of Maine, Massachusetts and New Hampshire. 55538

Proceedings and debates at the convention of laymen. 65755

Proceedings and debates in the House of Representatives of . . . Delaware. 13579

Proceedings & debates in the House of Representatives of Massachusetts. 18118

Proceedings and debates of the Constitutional Convention. 53863

Proceedings and debates of the Convention of North-Carolina. 55663

Proceedings and debates of the Convention of North-Carolina, convened at Hillsborough. 55662

Proceedings and debates of the fourth National Quarantine and Sanitary Convention. 85501

Proceedings and debates of the General Assembly of Pennsylvania. 60402

Proceedings and debates of the proposed convention of the commonwealth of PEnnsylvania. 60401

Proceedings and debates of the third National Quarantine and Sanitary Convention. 65756

Proceedings and debates of the United States Senate . . . first session—thirtieth Congress. 15584, 33186

Proceedings and discussions in the French Chamber of Deputies. (65757)

Proceedings and documents relative to certain members. 104700

Proceedings and journal of the Geological Society of London. 18955

Proceedings and lectures of the National Teachers' Association. 51974

Proceedings [and] list of the members [of the Society for the Propagation of the Gospel in Foreign Parts.] 100900

Proceedings and meetings held in the capitol at Washington. 101947-101948

Proceedings and minutes [of the] New York and Boston Steam-boat Company. 9167

Proceedings and ordinances of the convention of 1st Dec. 1775. 100014

Proceedings and report at the opening of Clinton Hall. 54197

Proceedings and report of the Board of Civil Engineers. 75363

Proceedings and reports of the Commissioners for the University of Virginia. 100539

Proceedings and reports of the Massachusetts Board of Agriculture. 45824

Proceedings and reports of the Rhode-Island State Total Abstinence Society. 70738

Proceedings and resolutions of City Councils. 62076

Proceedings and resolutions of the Indiana soldiers. 34559

Proceedings and resolutions of the West India Body. 102792

Proceedings and second annual report [of the Commissioners of the Soldiers' National Cemetery at Gettysburg.] 27242

Proceedings at the festival given to the . . . National Unitarian Convention. 65768

Proceedings at the fiftieth anniversary of the New England Guards. (52686)

Proceedings at the first anniversary meeting of the Loyal Publication Society. 42558

Proceedings at the formation of the Worcester North Auxiliary Education Society. 105435

Proceedings at the General Courts of Proprietors. (65769)

Proceedings at the inauguration of Frederick A. P. Barnard. 3459, 14832

Proceedings at the inauguration of the monument. 88107

Proceedings at the laying of the corner-stone . . . of St. Stephen's College. 42658

Proceedings at the laying of the corner-stone of the Ludlow and Willink Hall of St. Stephen's College. 75493

Proceedings at the mass meeting of loyal citizens. 54589

Proceedings at the meeting of the Chapin family. 11952

Proceedings at the opening . . . at Suspension Bridge. 19806

Proceedings at the opening of the new buildings. 60385

Proceedings at the opening of the Patent Office Fair. 20310, (59046)

Proceedings at the opening of the Rhode Island Hospital. (70722)

Proceedings at the reorganization of the Loyal National League. 42554

Proceedings at the Printers' Banquet, at Niblo's, Broadway. 54590

Proceedings at the Printers' Banquet, held by the New York Typographical Society. 25619

Proceedings at the Printers' Festival, held by the Franklin Typographical Society. 65770

Proceedings at the public breakfast held in honor of William Lloyd Garrison. 26711

Proceedings at the quarter-century anniversary of the Society for the Promotion of Collegiate and Theological Education at the West. 85921

Proceedings at the reception and dinner in honor of George Peabody. 18517

[Proceedings at the second anniversary meeting of the Loyal Publication Society, Feb. 11, 1865.] 42558

Proceedings at the semi-centennial celebration of the Washington Light Infantry. (12065)

Proceedings at the two hundredth anniversary of the Second Church in Hartford. 65771

Proceedings at the two meetings dhring the session of 1823. 29705

Proceedings at the Universalist centennial held in Gloucester, Mass. 65772

Proceedings at the unveiling of the monument at Cooch's Bridge. 84969

Proceedings at their meetings, and biographical cataloupe of the members [of the class of 1831 of Amherst College.] 64977

Proceedings attending the inauguration of Hon. William A. Newell. 53207, 54968

Proceedings attending the presentation of regimental colors. 53971

Proceedings before a Joint Special Committee of the Massachusetts Legislature. 6785

Proceedings before Hon. D. P. Ingraham. (79837)

Proceedings before the Land Commissioners' Court. 65627

Proceedings before the Privy Council. 65773

Proceedings between Sir Guy Carleton. 10904

Proceedings, celebration of fourth of July, 1831. 88066

Proceedings commemorative of the death of Edward Everett. 21656, 33782

Proceedings commemorative of the settlement of Newark, New Jersey. 54882

Proceedings connected with the establishment of the Diocesan Missionary Society. 60068

Proceedings Dec. 16, 1863, in reference to emancipation. 45382

Proceedings, &c., 1805 [of the Humane Society of Massachusetts.] 33681

Proceedings, Feb. 1786-Feb. 1787 [of the Society for the Propagation of the Gospel in Foreign Parts.] 101468

Proceedings, Feb. 1721 [i. e. 1722]-Feb. 1722 [i. e. 1723 of the Society for the Propagation of the Gospel in Foreign Parts.] 102178

Proceedings for 1839 of the Grand Chapter of Freemasons of Vermont. 99179

Proceedings for 1828 of the Grand Chapter of Freemasons of Vermont. 99179

Proceedings for 1829 of the Grand Chapter of Freemasons of Vermont. 99179

Proceedings for 1827 of the Grand Chapter of Freemasons of Vermont. 99179

Proceedings for 1826 of the Grand Chapter of Freemasons of Vermont. 99179

Proceedings . . . for the year 1864 [of the Massachusetts Grand Encampment of Knights Templars.] 38133

Proceedings . . . for the year ending October, 1865 [of the Grand Encampment of Knights Templars of Massachusetts.] 38133

Proceedings in a public meeting composed of twenty-five clergymen of Chicago. 20693

Proceedings in behalf of the Morton testimonial. 51032

Proceedings in commemoration of the 89th anniversary American of independence. [sic] 27286

Proceedings in commemoration of the-fiftieth anniversary of the settlement of Tallmadge. 94271

Proceedings in Congress. (15607)

Proceedings in Congress attending the reception of the statue of Major-Gen'l Nathanael Greene. (28601), 70613

Proceedings in Congress. The Louisiana delegation. 18181

Proceedings in connection with the celebration at New Bedford. 18610

Proceedings in Massachusetts and New Hampshire. 45452

Proceedings in Pennsylvania for raising money and men. 102860

Proceedings . . . in reference to the death of . . . Edward Everett. 23274

Proceedings in reference to the death of Hon. John A. King. 37816

Proceedings in relation to Capt. Kidd's piracies, &c. 14390

Proceedings in relation to the building and dedication of the monument. 86347

Proceedings in relation to the presentation of the address. 65774

Proceedings in relation to the removal of Police Commissioners. 84774

Proceedings in the Assembly of Lower Canada. 42518, 96927

Proceedings in the case, Arthur Fenner vs. John Dorrance. 20652

Proceedings in the case of Francis Johnston, Esq. 8799, 36360

Proceedings in the case of John Merryman. (29463)

Proceedings in the case of Robert Fletcher. 24737

Proceedings in the case of the United States against Duncan G. McRae. 43648

Proceedings in the case of the United States versus William Christy. 12956

Proceedings in the cases of the impeachment of Charles Robinson. 72057

Proceedings in the city of Philadelphia. 62077

Proceedings . . . in the city of Portland, Me. 34924

Proceedings in the constitution of the Church of Christ in Fair-Street. 54183

Proceedings in the controversy between a part of the Proprietors and the pastor of the Hollis St. Church, Boston. 62775

Proceedings in the Court of King's Bench. 6912

Proceedings in the Criminal Court of St. Louis County. (27613), 75407

Proceedings in the First Baptist Church in the city of New York. (58796)

Proceedings in the House of Assembly of Lower-Canada. 96864

Proceedings in the House of Commons, on the slave trade. 25449

Proceedings in the House of Commons on Thursday, July 25, 1822. 93371

Proceedings in the House of Representatives of the United States of America. 65775

Proceedings in the House of Representatives of the United States, on the presentation of the sword of Washington. 65776

Proceedings in the House of Representatives of the United States, respecting the contested election. 27085

Proceedings in the Legislature of Massachusetts. 45809

[Proceedings in the Legislature of South Carolina.] (22284), 87514

Proceedings in the quo warranto case. 87378

Proceedings in the Rhode-Island Legislature. 70614

Proceedings in the Senate, and a summary of the debates in that house. 13579

Proceedings in the several assemblies. 16688

Proceedings in the Supreme Court of Rhode-Island. 89104

Proceedings in the trial of Andrew Johnson. 36178

Proceedings in the West Church on occasion of the decease of Charles Lowell. 42431

Proceedings . . . July 1 & 2, 1834. (106185A)

Proceedings . . . June 25th, 26th and 27th, 1850. (43968)

Proceedings . . . laying of the corner stone, . . . 1870. 51173

Proceedings . . . March 11, 1864. 53590

Proceedings . . . Oct. 20, 1864. 53590

Proceedings, . . . Oct. 26, 1847. (31494)

Proceedings of a board of general officers. 1454-1456

Proceedings of a board of rebel officers &c. 1455

Proceedings of a celebration of Huck's defeat. 87921

Proceedings of a collection of the "most respectable inhabitants !!! of W——— and L———." 105339

[Proceedings of a Committee of the Inhabitants of York.] 106034

Proceedings of a convention, held at Princeton Mass. 65777

Proceedings of a convention held in . . . Baltimore. 65778

Proceedings of a convention, held in . . . New York. (51931)

Proceedings of a convention of delegates, appointed by persons interested in the growth and manufacture of wool. (6577

Proceedings of a convention of delegates, chosen by the people of Massachusetts. 65780

Proceedings of a convention of delegates, elected by the citizens of the different districts interested in the connexion of the Susquehanna and Lehigh Rivers. 65781

Proceedings of a convention of delegates for the formation of a domestic missionary society. 97870

Proceedings of a convention of delegates from forty one towns. 105399

Proceedings of a convention of delegates from several of the New-England states. 65

Proceedings of a convention of delegates from the abolition societies in the United Sta (65782)

Proceedings of a convention of delegates from the citizens of Pennsylvania. (60403)

Proceedings of a convention of delegates from the counties of Hampshire, Franklin, an Hampden. 65783

Proceedings of a convention of delegates, from the different counties in the state of Ne York, opposed to Free-masonry. 65784

Proceedings of a convention of delegates, from the states of Massachusetts, Connecticut and Rhode-Island. 65785

Proceedings of a convention of delegates of the several moral societies in the state of New-York, Held . . . in . . . Alban January 12, 1820. 65786

Proceedings of a convention of delegates of the several moral societies in the state of New-York. Held . . . January 17, 1821. 65786

Proceedings of a convention of delegates oppo to Free masonry, . . . at Le Roy, Genesee Co., N. Y. (65787)

Proceedings of a convention of Democratic Young Men. 60404

Proceedings of a convention of Federal Repub cans. 105400

Proceedings of a convention of iron workers. 35099

Proceedings of a convention of lake under-writers. (38667)

Proceedings of a convention of medical delegates. 65788

Proceedings of a convention of ministers and delegates. 35864

Proceedings of a convention of Republican delegates. 100453

Proceedings of a convention of teachers. 87922

Proceedings of a convention of the Commissioners of Appraisement. 15335

Proceedings of a convention of the Friends o National Industry. 65789

Proceedings of a convention of the trustees o a proposed university. 65790

Proceedings of a convention of the various bi societies of South Carolina. 87800

Proceedings of a convention of young men. (65791), 102010

Proceedings of a convention on the location of the post office. 54591

Proceedings of a convention . . . on . . . the proposed annexation of Texas. 45939, note after 95109

Proceedings of a convention . . . Philadelphia, December, 1833. (81828)

Proceedings of a convention to form a Supreme Grand Lodge. (65792)

Proceedings of a Council of Congregational Churches. 54184

Proceedings of a county convention of delegates. 8060, 103278

Proceedings of a court-marshal. 9726

Proceedings of a court martial, for the trial of Colonel William King. 37854

Proceedings of a court-martial held at Cambridge. 31344

Proceedings of a court martial held at Quebec. 96826

Proceedings of a court martial held in Montreal in March, 1809. 96863

Proceedings of a court martial in the case of Capt. S. E. Ancona. (1378)

Proceedings of a court-martial on Commodore Thomas Ap Catesby Jones. 36613

Proceedings of a court martial on the trial of Col. Elisha Sheldon. 80120

Proceedings of a court of inquiry appointed to inquire into the intended mutiny on board the United States Brig of War Somers. 86804

Proceedings of a court of inquiry convened at Washington, D. C. 21581

Proceedings of a court of inquiry, convened by special order, no. 85. 24207

Proceedings of a court of inquiry, held at the Navy Yard, Brooklyn. 3643

Proceedings of a court of inquiry held at the request of Commodore John Rodgers. 72475

Proceedings of a court of inquiry, held at the special request of Bregadier-General [sic] Josiah Harmar. 30401

Proceedings of a court of inquiry, held on the U. S. Frigate Constitution. 19133

Proceedings of a division court-martial, constituted for the trial. 21689

Proceedings of a General Assembly at Cambridge. 10134

Proceedings of a general court martial for the trial of Lieut. Col. Louis Bache. (2591)

Proceedings of a general court martial for the trial of Major General Arnold. 2061

Proceedings of a general court-martial for the trial of Maj. Gen. Fitz John Porter, U. S. Vols. 64248

Proceedings of a general court-martial, . . . for the trial of Major-General Lee. 39713

Proceedings of a general court martial, held at Brunswick. 39711-39712

Proceedings of a general court-martial; held at Cambridge. (31343)

Proceedings of a general court martial, held at Chelsea Hospital. 103677

Proceedings of a general court-martial held at Fort Independence. 26639

Proceedings of a general court martial, held at Fort Royal. 96846

Proceedings of a general court martial, held at Major General Lincoln's quarters. 78059

Proceedings of a general court martial, held at Pensacola in West Florida, March 16-April 20, 1868. [sic] 24893

Proceedings of a general court martial held at Pensacola, in West Florida, March 16-April 20, 1769. [sic] 23840

Proceedings of a general court martial, held at Philadelphia. 33328

Proceedings of a general court martial, held at Sackett's Harbor. 96514

Proceedings of a general court martial held at the Horse-Guards. 96932

Proceedings of a general court martial, held at the Judge Advocate's Office. 49954

Proceedings of a general court martial, held at White Plains. (75021)

Proceedings of a general court martial, holden in Newport. 17409

Proceedings of a general court-martial, of the line. 2060

Proceedings of a general court martial [on John Smith.] 82902

Proceedings of a general court martial on Major Allen Cameron. 10163

Proceedings of a general court martial, whereof Maj. General Samuel Fessenden of the 5th Div. was President. 90457

Proceedings of a general court martial which convened at Fort Washitaw. 31426

Proceedings of a general meeting, held at Chester Court House. 87923

Proceedings of a great public meeting . . . at the Tabernacle. (69349)

Proceedings of a great Whig meeting of citizens of Boston. 6544, 103277

Proceedings of a Marine general court martial. 70426

Proceedings of a mass meeting of citizens of Pierce Co. W. T. 101925

Proceedings of a meeting and report of the committee of citizens. 65793

Proceedings of a meeting [at] Albany . . . November 27, 1847. 34931

Proceedings of a meeting . . . [at] Cincinnati. 57067

Proceedings of a meeting called to further the enterprise of the Atlantic telegraph. 2302

Proceedings of a meeting for sufferings, held in Providence, R. I. (52642)

Proceedings of a meeting held at Hibernian Hall. 88010

Proceedings of a meeting held at Lockport, on the 2d and 3d of January, 1827. 84221

Proceedings of a meeting held at Portland, Me. 65794

Proceedings of a meeting held at Princeton, N. J. 53172

Proceedings of a meeting held by deaf-mutes, . . . December 1st, 1853. 74996, note before 90783

Proceedings of a meeting held first month (January) 15th, 1867. 60330

Proceedings of a meeting held in Georgia, etc. 39144, 88065

Proceedings of a meeting held in Philadelphia. 85876

Proceedings of a meeting held . . . May 26th, 1845. (3354)

Proceedings of a meeting held . . . November 23, 1869. 54397

Proceedings of a meeting in favor of municipal reform. 54592

Proceedings of a meeting . . . in Philadelphia. 59745

Proceedings of a meeting in relation to St. Ann's Church for Deaf-Mutes. 65795

Proceedings of a meeting of citizens of central Mississippi. 49533

Proceedings of a meeting of citizens of Nashua. 51864

Proceedings of a meeting of citizens of New York and others. 54593

Proceedings of a meeting of citizens of New York, favorable to the construction of a canal. 65796

Proceedings of a meeting of citizens of New-York, to express sympathy and respect for the Mexican republican exiles. 54594

Proceedings of a meeting of freeholders of Augusta County, Va. (65797)

Proceedings of a . . . meeting of freinds of Rev. John Pierpont. 62776

Proceedings of a . . . meeting of ministers of all religious denominations. (41226)

Proceedings of a meeting of representatives of the several railroad companies. 65798

Proceedings of a meeting of the bar, 3d Judicial District. 101925

Proceedings of a meeting of the citizens of Detroit. 88314

Proceedings of a meeting of the citizens of the United States. 65799

Proceedings of a meeting of the . . . First Congregational Society. 26241

Proceedings of a meeting of the Friends of Africa. (65800)

Proceedings of a meeting of the Friends of African Colonization. 14732, 45245

Proceedings of a meeting of the Friends of the General Administration. 28675

Proceedings of a meeting of the people. 64383

Proceedings of a meeting of the stockholders of the Southern Pacific Rail Road Co. 88435

Proceedings of a meeting of the Whig young men. 54595

Proceedings of a meeting to form the [Broadway Tabernacle Anti-slavery] Society. 8147

Proceedings of a naval court martial, held at Norfolk, Va. 54963

Proceedings of a Pacific Railroad Convention, at Lacon, Illinois. (38476), 58089

Proceedings of a public deliberative meeting of the . . . American Tract Society. 65801, 73047

Proceedings of a public meeting held in London. 8523

Proceedings of a public meeting, held in the city of Buffalo. 93739

Proceedings of a public meeting, held in the Middle Dutch Church, 81832

Proceedings of a public meeting held March 24th, 1856. (64518)

Proceedings of a public meeting in behalf of the Society for the Promotion of Collegiate and Theological Education at the West. 85922

Proceedings of a public meeting in Buffalo. 65802

Proceedings of a public meeting . . . New Hope, February 14, 1846. 60405

Proceedings of a public meeting of citizens of Minnesota. (49297)

Proceedings of a public meeting of the citizens of Cincinnati. (13104)

Proceedings of a public meeting of the citizens of Providence. 57964, 93647

Proceedings of a public meeting of the citizens of Providence, . . . March 7, 1854. 65803

Proceedings of a public meeting of the Friends of the Union. (65804)

Proceedings of a Select Committee of the Senate of the state of New York. 65805

Proceedings of a Society for Promoting Gener Inoculation. 31031

Proceedings of a special communication of the Grand Lodge. 87842

Proceedings of a special meeting of the American Steamship Company. 65806

Proceedings of a special meeting [of the Socie of the Cincinnati.] 86102

Proceedings of a state convention of the Whig young men of Connecticut. 103270

Proceedings of a suit, as well in the Court of Chancery as in the Court for the Trial of Impeachments and Correction of Erro 5765

Proceedings of a town-meeting in Quincy. 67292

Proceedings of a town meeting of the citizens . . . of Philadelphia. 62079

Proceedings of a town meeting . . . Philadelphia, Dec. 28, 1825. 62078

Proceedings of a Whig county convention of delegates. 8060, 103278

Proceedings of an adjourned meeting of delegates of various banks. (65807)

Proceedings of an adjourned meeting of the second triennial convention. 10014

Proceedings of an adjourned meeting of the stockholders of the Southern Pacific Railroad of Texas. 88436

Proceedings of an anti-masonic meeting, held at Lampter Square. 65808

Proceedings of an Ecclesiastical Council, convened at Plymouth. 63470

Proceedings of an Ecclesiastical Council, in the case of the Proprietors of Hollis Street Meeting House. 6652

Proceedings of an Ecclesiastical Council, in the town of Berkley. 4889B

Proceedings of an improvement convention. 60406

Proceedings of an Indian Council, held at Cattaraugus, N. Y. 65809

Proceedings of an Indian Council, held at the Buffalo Creek Reservation. 65810

Proceedings of an inquiry and investigation instituted by Major-General Codd. 6581

Proceedings of an union meeting held in New York. 54596

Proceedings of Congress, in 1796. 65812

Proceedings of Congress relative to the national debt. 65813

Proceedings of convention and Supreme Grand Lodge of I. O. S. M. 60161

Proceedings of convention [of the Champlain Valley Horticultural Society.] 11845

Proceedings of Dr. Bray, Commissary for Maryland. 7470

Proceedings of encampments of the Grand Ar of the Republic. 49298

Proceedings of Grand Committee of the Legis lature of the state of Vermont. 99006

Proceedings of His Majesty's Council [of Nov Scotia.] 94546

Proceedings of His Majesty's Council of the province of Massachusetts-Bay. 45940

Proceedings of John A. Graham. 28230, 1st note after 99204

Proceedings of Joel Parker, Linus Child and Leverett Saltonstall. (72214)

Proceedings of Massachusetts State Council o the Order of Sovereigns of Industry. 88816

Proceedings of meetings of the citizens of Rochester, Buffalo, Lockport and Plamy 22752, 102972

Proceedings of meetings on the 9th November and 4th December. (62080)
Proceedings of Rip Van Dam, Esq. 98430
Proceedings of seven gentlemen. 104637
Proceedings of several courts-martial. (65814)
Proceedings of some members of Assembly. 60407
Proceedings of special meetings of stockholders & bondholders. 93928
Proceedings of sundry citizens of Baltimore. 3059
Proceedings of the Academy of Natural Sciences of Philadelphia. 61405
Proceedings of the adjourned Superior Court. 99074
Proceedings of the adjourned third annual meeting. 106192
Proceedings of the Agricultural Convention and of the . . . [State Agricultural Society] of South Carolina. 88058
Proceedings of the Agricultural Convention . . . at Harrisburg. 60408
Proceedings of the Albany Bar. 18585
Proceedings of the American Academy of Arts and Sciences. (1035), 72746
Proceedings of the American Antiquarian Society. 1053, 19050, 24961, (52625), 83980, 85211, 85214, 85222, 85224, 91853, 96481A
Proceedings of the American Antiquarian Society, . . . in reference to the death of . . . Edward Everett. 23274
Proceedings of the American Anti-slavery Society. (81828)
Proceedings of the American Association for the Advancement of Science. 1057, 82997, 83003, 85386
Proceedings [of the American Board of Commissioners for Foreign Missions.] (61360)
Proceedings of the American citizens at Paris. 30592
Proceedings of the American Continental Congress. 23530
Proceedings [of the American Education Society of Norfolk County, Mass.] 14224
Proceedings of the American Equal Rights Association. 65815
Proceedings [of the American Ethnological Society.] 106326
Proceedings of the American Geographical & Statistical Society of New York. 65816
Proceedings of the American Musical Congress. 65817
Proceedings of the American Philosophical Society. 1180
Proceedings [of the Ancient and Honorable Artillery Company.] 82945
Proceedings of the anniversary meeting. 14949
Proceedings of the annual conference of the Methodist Episcopal Church. (43002)
Proceedings of the annual convention of the Connecticut Medical Society. 15783
Proceedings of the annual convention of the South Carolina Agricultural & Mechanical Society. 88057
Proceedings of the annual convention of the University. 5626
Proceedings of the annual conventions of the National Art Association. 51926
Proceedings of the annual exhibition . . . held at Rising Sun Village. 62036
Proceedings of the annual meeting and annual report [of the Massachusetts Temperance Society.] 101514
Proceedings of the annual meeting, of School District Number Two. 44218

Proceedings of the annual meeting [of the Friends of Human Progress] held at Waterloo, N. Y., . . . 1857. (25954)
Proceedings [of the annual meeting of the Friends of Human Progress, held at] Waterloo, N. Y., 1857. (25954)
Proceedings of the annual meeting, [of the Law Association of Philadelphia.] 61766
Proceedings of the annual meeting of the Massachusetts Colonization Society. 45832
Proceedings of the annual meeting of the stockholders of the Bank of Charleston, S. C. 12066
Proceedings of the annual meeting of the stockholders . . . [of the Pennsylvania Academy of the Fine Arts.] 60294
Proceedings of the annual meeting of the stockholders of the Philadelphia and Erie Rail Road Company. 61947
Proceedings of the annual meeting of the stockholders of the South and North Alabama Railroad Co. 87329
Proceedings of the annual meeting of the stockholders of the Sunbury and Erie Railroad Company. 93733
Proceedings of the annual meeting of the Survivors' Association of the State of South Carolina. 88075
Proceedings of the annual meeting [of the Warren Street Chapel, Boston.] 6681
Proceedings of the annual meeting of the [Young Men's Temperance Society, of the City of Albany.] 106186
Proceedings of the Anti-Jackson Convention. 71188, 100496
Proceedings of the Anti Masonic Convention for . . . New York. 65819
Proceedings of the Anti-masonic Convention held January 16, 1835. 70615
Proceedings of the Anti-masonic Convention of the County of Cayuga. (65820)
Proceedings [of the Anti-masonic Republican State Convention.] 53531
Proceedings of the Antimasonic State Convention at their meeting in Providence, July 17, 1835. 70616
Proceedings of the Anti-masonick State Convention, holden at Montpelier. 99146
Proceedings of the Antimasonic State Convention, holden at Montpelier, June 15 and 16, 1831. 99148
Proceedings of the Anti-masonic State Convention holden at Montpelier, June 23, 24 & 25, 1830. 99147
Proceedings of the Anti-masonic State Convention, holden at Montpelier, Vt. June 26 and 27, 1833. 99149
Proceedings of the Anti-masonic State Convention, in Faneuil Hall, Boston. 45941
Proceedings of the Anti-masonic State Convention of Connecticut. 15795
Proceedings of the Anti-masonic State Convention of Massachusetts. 45548
Porceedings of the Antiquarian and Historical Society of Illinois. 34310
Proceedings of the Anti-Sabbath Convention. 58781
Proceedings of the Anti-slavery Convention, assembled at Philadelphia. 82036
Proceedings of the Anti-slavery Convention of American Women, held in Philadelphia. 82038
Proceedings of the Anti-slavery Convention of American Women, held in the city of New-York. 82037
Proceedings of the anti-slavery meeting held in Stacy Hall, Boston. 6500

Proceedings of the Anti-tariff Convention, held at Milledgeville. 27086

"Proceedings" of the Assembly of the state of California. 97497

Proceedings of the Association for Establishing a School for the Education of the Blind in Philadelphia and Pennsylvania. 60339, 61487

Proceedings of the Association of Citizens, to Erect a Monument in Honor of Gen. George Washington. 65821, 102026

Proceedings of the Bank Convention of the Confederate States. 65822

Proceedings of the Baptist Convention for Missionary Purposes. 51498

Proceedings of the Baptist Convention of Illinois. (34210)

Proceedings of the Baptist Convention of . . . Michigan. 48722

Proceedings of the Baptist Convention of . . . New-Hampshire. (52859)

Proceedings of the Baptist Convention of the state of Vermont. 99151

Proceedings of the . . . Baptist Missionary Convention. 53540

Proceedings of the Bar of Charleston, S. C. 61249

Proceedings of the Bar of Erie County. 8790

Proceedings of the Bar of Philadelphia, on the . . . increase in the number and compensation of the judges. 62081

Proceedings of the Bar of the city of New York. 37476

Proceedings of the . . . Bishops . . . as Visitors of the General Theological Seminary. (66153)

Proceedings of the Board of Assistances, . . . May 10, 1831, to May 8, 1832. (54598)

Proceedings of the Board of Commissioners in the case of the Right Reverend Charles Inglis. (34762), 84842

Proceedings of the Board of Commissioners of Public Works of Illinois. 34311

Proceedings of the Board of Councilmen, of . . . New York. (54599)

Proceedings of the Board of Directors of the Branch of the Merchants' Bank of St. Louis. 75360

Proceedings of the Board of Directors of the Protestant Episcopal Society. 66202

Proceedings of the Board of Health, in Philadelphia. 18002

Proceedings of the Board of Managers of the Western Methodist Historical Society. 102994

Proceedings of the Board of Marine Inspectors. 65823

Proceedings of the Board of Missions. (66141)

Proceedings of the Board of Overseers of Harvard University. 69399

Proceedings of the Board of Regents of the Smithsonian Institution. 85024

Proceedings of the Board of School Officers of the Seventh Ward. 54127

Proceedings of the Board of Supervisors of Montgomery County. 50163

Proceedings of the Board of Supervisors of Sheboygan County, Wis. 80063

Proceedings of the Board of Supervisors of the county of Cayuga. 11639

Proceedings of the Board of Supervisors of the county of Columbia. 65824

Proceedings of the Board of Supervisors, of the county of Cortland. (16979)

Proceedings of the Board of Supervisors of the county of Essex, for 1866. 23017

Proceedings of the Board of Supervisros of the county of Franklin. 25651

Proceedings of the Board of Supervisors of the county of Fulton. 26205

Proceedings of the Board of Supervisors of the county of Greene. (28623)

Proceedings of the Board of Supervisors of the county of Hamilton. 30066

Proceedings of the Board of Supervisors of the county of Herkimer. 31491

Proceedings of the Board of Supervisors of the county of Kings. 37875

Proceedings of the Board of Supervisors of the county of Lewis. 40869

Proceedings of the Board of Supervisors of the county of Livingston. (41654)

Proceedings of the Board of Supervisors of the county of Madison. 43727

Proceedings of the Board of Supervisors of the county of Monroe. (50031)

Proceedings of the Board of Supervisors of [the county of] . . . New York. 54128, (54600)

Proceedings of the Board of Supervisors of the county of Orange. 57430

Proceedings of the Board of Supervisors of the county of Orleans. (57625)

Proceedings of the Board of Supervisors of the county of Otsego. (57877)

Proceedings of the Board of Supervisors of the county of Putnam. 66846

Proceedings of the Board of Supervisors of the county of Queens. 67067

Proceedings of the Board of Supervisors of the county of Rensselaer. 69633

Proceedings of the Board of Supervisors of the county of Richmond. 71215

Proceedings of the Board of Supervisors of the county of St. Lawrence. (75314)

Proceedings of the Board of Supervisors of the county of Saratoga. 76928

Proceedings of the Board of Supervisors of the county of Schuyler. 78062

Proceedings of the Board of Supervisors of the county of Seneca. 79103

Proceedings of the Board of Trustees of Bowdoin College. 7036, 92313

Proceedings of the Board of Trustees of the General Theological Seminary. 26910, (66153)

Proceedings of the Boards of Aldermen and Assistant Aldermen. 54597

Proceedings of the Boston Society of Natural History. 6776, 78527, 78529-78530

Proceedings of the Bostonian Society. 88221

Proceedings of the Brunswick Convention on the separation of this district. 44045

Proceedings of the Buckeye Celebration. 3007

Proceedings of the [Bunker Hill Monument] Association. (9174)

Proceedings of . . . [the Bunker Hill Monument] Association] at the annual meeting, June 17, 1865. (9174)

Proceedings of [the Bunker Hill Monument Association] at the annual meeting, June 17, 1867. (9174)

Proceedings [of the Bunker Hill Monument Association] . . . June 17, 1862. (9174)

Proceedings of [the Bunker Hill Monument Association] . . . on the occasion of their fortieth anniversary. (9174)

Proceedings of [the Bunker Hill Monument Association] . . . on the occasion of their forty-first anniversary. (9174)

Proceedings of the California Academy of Natural Sciences. 9961

Proceedings of the California State Teachers' Institute and Educational Convention. 10001

Proceedings of the California State Teachers' Institute, in session at the city of San Francisco. 10001

Proceedings of the Canada Education and Home Missionary Society. 10433

Proceedings of the Canadian Institute. 39843

Proceedings of the Canal Board, held at . . . Albany. (53564)

Proceedings of the Cayuga County Convention of Delegates. 11638

Proceedings of the celebration of the 4th July, 1831. 12068

Proceedings of the centennial celebration, September 11, 1850. 28090

Proceedings of the centennial celebration, September 3, 1839. 3555

Proceedings of the Century Association in honor of the memory of Gulian C. Verplanck. 54159

Proceedings of the Century Association in honor of the memory of Brig.-Gen. James S. Wadsworth and Colonel Peter A. Porter. 11690, 54159

Proceedings of the Chamber of Commerce . . . at the opening of their new rooms. 53590

Proceedings of the Chamber of Commerce of . . . Memphis. 47784

Proceedings of the Chamber of Commerce of . . . New York for . . . 1862. 53590

Proceedings of the Chamber of Commerce of the State of New York. 578

Proceedings of the Cherokee Nation in General Council. 12438

Proceedings of the Chesapeake and Ohio Canal Convention. 12505

Proceedings of the Christian Convention, held at Indianapolis. 34585

Proceedings of the church and congregation at Machias. (65826)

Proceedings of the Church Society of the Archdeaconry of New-Brunswick. 52525

Proceedings of the church University Board. 92637

Proceedings of the Cincinnati Angling Club. 65827

Proceedings of the Cincinnati Astronomical Society. 13084

Proceedings of the Cincinnati, by their delegates in general-meeting. 86103

Proceedings of the Cincinnati, by their delegates in general meeting convened at Philadelphia. 86104

Proceedings of the Cincinnati Colonization Association. 13105

Proceedings of the citizens & City Council of Charleston. 12069

Proceedings of the citizens of Boston favorable to a revision of the laws. 85929

Proceedings of the citizens of Charleston on the incendiary machinations. 12067

Proceedings of the citizens of East Greenwich and vicinity. 65828

Proceedings of the citizens of Fayette County, Illinois. (23953)

Proceedings of the citizens of New Haven. 53001

Proceedings of the citizens . . . of Norfolk. (55480)

Proceedings of the citizens of Philadelphia relative to a rail road to Erie. 62082

Proceedings of the City Council of Baltimore in relation to the death of Abraham Lincoln. 41227

Proceedings of the City Council of Boston, April 17, 1865. 41228

Proceedings of the City Council [of Boston] in relation to the death of Joshua Bates, Esq. (3943)

Proceedings of the City Council of Providence on the death of Abraham Lincoln. 66293

Proceedings of the City Council [of Roxbury] on the death of John Quincy Adams. 319

Proceedings of the City Council [of Salem] on the death of the President. 7946

Proceedings of the City Council on the occasion of the death of Hon. Josiah Quincy. 67233

Proceedings of the city government upon the subject of international exchanges. 6759

Proceedings of the city of New-Haven. (53002)

Proceedings of the class of 1846 of Harvard College. 71516

Proceedings of the class of 1836, at the first general meeting. 105887

Proceedings of the class of 1821, at their meeting Aug. 1, 1831. 105883

Proceedings of the class of 1821, at their meeting August 17, 1836. 105883

Proceedings of the College . . . [of Physicians of Philadelphia.] 61548

Proceedings of the Colonization Society of . . . New York. 54437

Proceedings of the Colonization Society of Virginia. 100445

Proceedings of the Colonization Society of Virginia, and report of the Managers. 100446

Proceedings of the Colored National Convention. 65829

Proceedings of the Colored People's Convention of the State of South Carolina. 87808

Proceedings of the Colored People's Educational Convention. (49629)

Proceedings of the Commercial Convention at Memphis. 47785

Proceedings of the Commercial Convention, held in Detroit. 14972, (19790)

Proceedings of the Commissioners Appointed to Lay Out the Cumberland Road. 17887

Proceedings of the Commissioners for the Adjustment of Claims. 48127

Proceedings of the Commissioners of Indian Affairs. (33148)

Proceedings of the Commissioners of Indian Affairs . . . in the State of New York. 84484

Proceedings of the Commissioners of the Soldiers' National Cemetery Association. 27233, 65830

Proceedings of the Commissioners of the Soldiers National Cemetery at Gettysburg. 27242

Proceedings of the Committee Appointed for Relieving the Poor Germans. 87924

Proceedings of the Committee, Appointed to Inquire Into the Official Conduct of William W. Van Ness. 98534

Proceedings of the Committee of Observation for the Elizabethtown (now Hagerstown) District. 45144

Proceedings of the Committee of the Whole Council. 67002

Proceedings of the Common Council of New York. 30591

Proceedings of the Common Council of . . . Providence. (66294)

Proceedings of the conventions of the province of Maryland, held at . . . Annapolis in 1774, 1775 & 1776. 45285

Proceedings of the conventions of the province of Maryland, held at . . . Annapolis, . . . June, 1774. (45284)

Proceedings of the Convocational Congress, held in Christ Church. 65838

Proceedings of the Coroner, in the case of the Steamer Lexington. 103190

Proceedings of the corporation and of the alum alumni of BrownUniversity. 8629

Proceedings of the Corporation for the Relief of the Widows and Children of the Clergy of the Protestant Episcopal Church in Maryland. (45298)

Proceedings of the corporation . . . in regard to cemeteries in the city. 54601

Proceedings of the corporation of New-York, on supplying the city with pure . . . water. 54602

Proceedings of the corporation [of the Butler Hospital for the Insane.] 66243

Proceedings of the Council, and of the House of Representatives. 34084

Proceedings of the Council at ordination of Abiel Holmes. 32589

Proceedings of the Council of Censors, of the state of Vermont. 99016

Proceedings of the Council of Censors, of the state of Vermont, at their sessions holden at Rutland, in the year 1792. 99017

Proceedings of the Council of the "Loyal Cherokees." 12473

Proceedings of the Counsellors of the . . . [Massachusetts Medical] Society. 45874

Proceedings of the Court . . . December 16, 1844, for the trial of the Right Rev. Benjamin T. Onderdonk, D. D. 57309

Proceedings of the court-martial at Fort Brown, Texas. 20886

Proceedings of the court-martial for the trial of Major W. Gates. 26759

Proceedings of the court martial, held on the officers and crew of His Majesty's late ship of Java. 96933

Proceedings of the court-martial held upon Ensign Cullen and Assistant-Surgeon Morris. 35652

[Proceedings of the court martial, in the case of William Hull.] 33644

Proceedings of the court-martial in the trial of General Ftiz John Porter. 64247

Proceedings of the court-martial on the trial of Admiral Byng. (65839)

Proceedings of the court martial ordered . . . for Captain Oliver H. Perry. 61047

Proceedings of the court of inquiry into the case of Major General Scott. 78420

Proceedings of the court of inquiry, relative to the fall of New Orleans. 15337

Proceedings of the court of the Vice Admiralty in Charles-Town, South-Carolina; in the cause, George Roupell, Esq; v. the ship Ann and goods. 23532, note after 96924

Proceedings of the Court of Vice-Admiralty in Charles-Town, South-Carolina; in the cause, George Roupell, Esq; v. the ship Ann and Good. 39925, 1st note after 97356, note after 87824

Proceedings of the Cumberland Association. (19178), (47286)

Proceedings of the day. (5585)

Proceedings of the decennial meeting of the class of 1849. 87988

Proceedings of the Democratic and Free Democratic Conventions. 53867

Proceedings of the Democratic Antimasonic State Convention. (60411)

PRoceedings of the Democratic Association of Gloucester County. 27599

Proceedings of the Democratic Convention, . . . at Harrisburg, January 4, 1828. 60412

Proceedings of the Democratic Convention, . . . at Harrisburg, March 5, 1832. 60412

Proceedings of the Democratic Convention, held at the capitol. (53866)

Proceedings of the Democratic Convention of Pennsylvania. 60413

Proceedings of the Democratic Legislative Convention. 94388

Proceedings of the Democratic Meeting held at the Chinese Museum. 92007

Proceedings of the Democratic Meeting, held July 20, 1840. 100457

Proceedings of the Democratic National Convention, held at Baltimore. 65840

Proceedings of the Democratic National Convention, held in 1860 at Charleston and Baltimore. 65840

Proceedings of the Democratic Republican . . . Committee of the City of New York. 37444, 54603

Proceedings of the Democratic Republican Convention of the State of Indiana. 98425

Proceedings of the Democratic Republican Convention of Young Men of . . . Pennsylvania. 60414

Proceedings of the Democratic Republican General Committee of . . . New York relative fo the death of Colonel William D. Kennedy. 37444, 54603

Proceedings of the Democratic State Convention, . . . Albany, . . . 1861. 53868

Proceedings of the Democratic State Convention, . . . at Columbus, Ohio. 57021

Proceedings of the Democratic State Convention, composed of delegates from the several districts. 87813

Proceedings of the Democratic State Convention, . . . Harrisburg, Pa. (60415)

Proceedings of the Democratic State Convention, held at Charlottesville, Va. 100454

Proceedings of the Democratic State Convention held at Columbia, S. C., 5th and 7th of May, 1856. 87814

Proceedings of the Democratic State Convention of South Carolina held at Columbia, S. C. 87815

Proceedings of the Democratic Whig National Convention, which assembled at Harrisburg, Pennsylvania. 30545, 60416, 65841, note after 103268

Proceedings of the Democratic Whig State Convention. Held in Cahmbersburg, Pa. 103284

Proceedings of the Democratic Whig State Convention, March, 1840. 1993

Proceedings of the Directors, etc. [of the Albany and Harlem Railroad Company.] 590

Proceedings of the Directors of the South-Sea Company. 88189

Proceedings of the Domestic and Foreign Missionary Society of the Protestant Episcopal Church in the United States from its formation, to May, 1823. (66141)

Proceedings of the Domestic and Foreign Missionary Society of the Protestant Episcopal Church in the United States, May, 1813, to November, 1826. (66141)

Proceedings of the Eastern Association of Universalists. 98008

Proceedings of the Ecclesiastical Council [at Belchertown, Mass.] 64842

Proceedings of the Educational Convention, held at Oswego, N. Y. (65843)

Proceedings of the 88th and 89th general meetings [of the Society for Propagating the Gospel Among the Heathen.] 86172

Proceedings of the eighty-seventh general meeting of the Society for Propagating the Gospel Among the Heathen. 86172

Proceedings of the Electorial College of . . . Pennsylvania. (60417)

Proceedings of the electors of President, 1840. 45288

Proceedings of the Elliott Society of Natural History. 12052

Proceedings of the Elliott Society of Natural History, of Charleston, South-Carolina, November 1st, 1853. 22288

Proceedings of the Emancipation Convention held at Jefferson City. 49630

Proceedings of the engagement between Moritz Furst and the United States Consul at Leghorn. (26241)

Proceedings of the English colonie of Virginia since their first beginning from England. 82832, note after 92664, 2d note after 100510

Proceedings of the Entomological Society of Philadelphia. (57824), 61619

Proceedings of the Episcopal Conventions for forming an American constitution. 3721

Proceedings [of the Erie County Board of Supervisors.] 22733

Proceedings of the Essex Institute. 23016, (71882), (78526), 92784

Proceedings of the Ethnological Society. 78532

Proceedings of the Evangelical Consociation and Home Missionary Society of the Congregational Churches in Rhode Island. 70581

Proceedings of the [Evangelical Knowledge Society] . . . in South-Carolina. 87823

Proceedings of the Executive Committee [of the National Board of Fire Underwriters.] 51940

Proceedings of the Executive Committee of the State Agricultural Society of South Carolina. 88060

Proceedings of the Executive of the United States, respecting the insurgents. 1794. 60418, 65844

Proceedings of the foederal convention, held at Philadelphia. 62085

Proceedings of the fifth convention of the American Instructors of the Deaf and Dumb. 65845

Proceedings of the fifth triennial meeting of the Baptist General Convention for Missionary Purposes, New York. 65846

Proceedings of the fifty-sixth anniversary of the settlement of Hudson (0.). 33505

Proceedings of the first anniversary of the General Convention of Western Baptists. 102971

Proceedings of the first anniversary of the University Convention of the State of New York. 65847

Proceedings of the first annual commencement [of the Buffalo Female Academy.] 9063

Proceedings of the first annual convention of the American Normal School Association. 1167

Proceedings of the first annual meeting . . . and charter . . . with the reports of the committees. 60068

Proceedings of the first annual meeting, held at Louisville, Ky. 34466

Proceedings of the first annual meeting, . . . in Trenton, . . . January, 1850. 53186

Proceedings of the first annual meeting of the Minnesota Horticultural Society. 49276

Proceedings of the first annual meeting of the National Association of Cotton Manufactures and Planters. (51931)

Proceedings of the first annual meeting . . . [of the National Board of Trade] held in Cincinnati, December, 1868. 51941

Proceedings of the first annual meeting of the New Jersey Colonization Society. 53172

Proceedings of the first annual meeting of the New-York State Anti-slavery Society. 53801

Proceedings of the first annual meeting of the New-York State Lyceum. 53832

Proceedings of the first annual meeting of the Protestant Episcopal Historical Society. 66195

Proceedings of the first annual meeting of the stockholders of the Mobile and Ohio Railroad Company. 49783

Proceedings of the first annual meeting of the stockholders of the Richmond and Danville Rail Road Company. 71196

Proceedings of the first annual session, . . . 1860 [of the New Brunswick Provincial Board of Agriculture.] 52551

Proceedings of the first annual session of the American Philological Association. (65818)

Proceedings of the first annual State Sunday-School Convention. 49631

Proceedings of the first Assembly of Virginia. 2d note before 99889

Proceedings of the first Cattle Show and Fair. (35945)

Proceedings of the First Congregational Church in Ludlow. 65848

Proceedings of the first Convention of Managers and Superintendents. 33179

Proceedings of the first Convention of the Colored Citizens of the State of Illinois. 34312

Proceedings of the first General Assembly of "the Incorporation of Providence Plantations." 65849, 70617, 90478

Proceedings of the first meeting of the General Committee appointed by the World's Temperance Convention. 65850

Proceedings of the first meeting of the National Board of Trade. 51941

Proceedings of the first National Convention of the Fenian Brotherhood. (24061)

Proceedings of the first New England Temperance Convention. 65951

Proceedings of the first semiannual session of the Massachusetts Grand Lodge. (45848)

Proceedings [of the first triennial meeting of the Society of the Alumni of Dartmouth College.] 8555

Proceedings of the first triennial meeting of the Southern Baptist Convention. 88308

Proceedings of the first ten years of the American Tract Society. (1248)

Proceedings of the first U. States Anti-masoni Convention. 50682, 97958

Proceedings, of the formation of the New-York State Colonization Society. 53816

Proceedings of the fortieth anniversary of the Presbyterian Church of Mt. Gilead. (65852)

Proceedings of the fourth annual convention of the Sabbath School Teachers of Massachusetts. (46119)

Proceedings of the fourth annual meeting [of the Indiana State Medical Society], 1853. 93975

Proceedings of the fourth annual meeting of the stockholders [of the Sunbury & Erie Rail Road Company.] 93733

Proceedings of the fourth annual session of the Grand Commandery of Knights Templar. 60184

Proceedings of the fourth Convention of Merchants and Others. 12070

Proceedings of the fourth National Temperance Convention. 1240

Proceedings of the Franklin Institute. 25656

Proceedings of the Fredonia Academy Re-union. 25698

Proceedings of the Free Convention, held at Rutland, Vt. 65853

Proceedings of the Free-Will Baptist Elders' Conference. 65665

Proceedings of the Friends of a National Bank. 3181

Proceedings of the Friends of a Railroad to San Francisco. 19303, 58089, (65854), (76066)

Proceedings of the friends of Gen. Jackson at Louisville. 42339

Proceedings of the general and state societies [of the Cincinnati.] 13126

Proceedings of the General Anti-slavery Convention. 8084, note after (65854)

Proceedings of the General Assembly, and the Council of . . . Massachusetts-Bay. (45945)

Proceedings of the General Assembly of North Carolina of [sic] the subject of international exchanges. 55665

Proceedings of the General Association of Connecticut, for the year 1801. 15803

Proceedings of the General Association of Connecticut, June, 1812. 15822

Proceedings of the General Association of Connecticut relative to Rev. Abiel Abbot. 16

Proceedings of the General Association of New-Hampshire. 52895

Proceedings of the General Association of New-Hampshire, at Keene. 52824

Proceedings of the General Convention of Congregational Ministers and Delegates in the United States. (65855)

Proceedings of the General Convention of Delegates Representing the Citizens and Inhabitants of Texas. 94950

Proceedings of the general court martial convened for the trial of Commodore James Barron. 3644

Proceedings of the general court-martial in the trial of Major John Gordon. 27982

Proceedings of the General Grand Chapter, at a meeting held in the city of New York. 53680

Proceedings of the General Grand Chapter of the United States. 25813

Proceedings of the General Grand Encampment of the Knights Templar. (38134)

Proceedings of the General Society of the Cincinnati. 13125, 13131

Proceedings of the General Society of the Cincinnati, at the triennial general meeting of 1799. 86105

Proceedings of the general town meeting held in the State-House Yard. 62086

Proceedings of the government and citizens of Philadelphia. 62087

Proceedings of the government of the United States, in maintaining the public right to the beach of the Misisipi [sic]. 35912

Proceedings of the graduates of Union College. 97784

Proceedings of the Grand Caucus. (55472)

Proceedings of the Grand Chapter of . . . New York. 53690

Proceedings of the Grand Chapter of the state of Vermont. 99180

Proceedings of the Grand Chapter of the state of Vermont, at its annual communication June, 5825. 99179

Proceedings of the Grand Commandery of Knights Templar in . . . New-Hampshire. 52895

Proceedings of the Grand Commandery of Knights Templars, of . . . Ohio. 57022

Proceedings of the Grand Convention of the Mechanics' Mutual Protection of the U. S. A. 65856

Proceedings of the Grand Convocation and Supreme Grand Council of the I. O. S. M. 86990

Proceedings of the Grand Convocation and Supreme Grand Lodge of Virginia, I. O. S. M. 86996

Proceedings of the Grand Council of Royal and Select Masters, of the state of Indiana. 34552

Proceedings of the Grand Council of Royal and Select Masters of the state of Michigan. (48765)

Proceedings of the Grand Democratic Republican Meeting. 54605

Proceedings of the Grand Division of New Jersey. 87055

Proceedings of the Grand Division of the Sons of Temperance of Canada West. 87021

Proceedings of the Grand Division, of the Sons of Temperance, of Eastern New-York. 87062

Proceedings of the Grand Division of the Sons of Temperance of . . . Indiana. 34569

Proceedings of the Grand Division of the Sons of Temperance of Western New-York. 87063

Proceedings of the Grand Division of the State of Maryland. 87030

Proceedings of the Grand Division, Sons of Temperance, of Pennsylvania. 87074

Proceedings of the Grand Division, S. of T., of the state of Connecticut. 87022

Proceedings of the Grand Encampment of Knights Templar of the state of Connecticut. 65857

Proceedings of the Grand Encampment, of . . . Ohio. 57023

Proceedings of the Grand Lodge . . . at Philadelphia. 60129

Proceedings of the Grand Lodge in June, A. L. 5827. (53692)

Proceedings of the Grand Lodge of Ancient Free and Accepted Masons of Minnesota. 49299

Proceedings of the Grand Lodge of Ancient Free-Masons of South-Carolina. 87834

Proceedings of the Grand Lodge of Ancient York Masons of North Carolina. 55622

Proceedings of the Grand Lodge of Free and Accepted Masons of Maryland. 45159

Proceedings [of the Grand Lodge of F. and A. M. of New Jersey.] 83526

Proceedings of the Grand Lodge of Free and Accepted Masons, of . . . Ohio. 57024

Proceedings of the Grand Lodge of Idaho, A. F. & A. M. (34169)

Proceedings of the Grand Lodge of Iowa. 35022

Proceedings of the Grand Lodge of Kentucky. 37542

Proceedings of the Grand Lodge of Louisiana. 42259

Proceedings of the . . . Grand Lodge of . . . Masons, of . . . Oregon. (57568)

Proceedings of the Grand Lodge of Missouri. 49596

Proceedings of the Grand Lodge of New Hampshire. 52835

Proceedings of the Grand Lodge of New Hampshire, at its annual meeting. 52835

Proceedings of the Grand Lodge of New-Hampshire, from July 8, 5789. 52835

Proceedings of the Grand Lodge, of . . . New York. (53692)

Proceedings of the . . . Grand Lodge of . . . New-York, and of the . . . Grand Stewards' Lodge. (53692)

Proceedings of the Grand Lodge of North Carolina and Tennessee. (55623)

Proceedings of the Grand Lodge of . . . Odd Fellows of . . . Connecticut. 65858

Proceedings of the Grand Lodge of . . . Ohio. 57024

Proceedings of the Grand Lodge of Pennsylvania for] A. D. 1862, A. L. 5862.

Proceedings of the Grand Lodge of Pennsylvania for 1853. 60128

Proceedings of the Grand Lodge of . . . Rhode Island. 70584

Proceedings of the Grand Lodge of South-Carolina. 87846

Proceedings of the Grand Lodge of Tennessee. 94798

Proceedings of the Grand Lodge of Texas, at its sixth annual communication. 95085

Proceedings of the Grand Lodge of Texas from its organization. 74462

Proceedings of the Grand Lodge of the state of Indiana. 34553

Proceedings of the Grand Lodge of the state of Maine. (43992)

Proceedings of the Grand Lodge of the state of Vermont. At their annual communication A. L. 5818-5819. 99189

Proceedings of the Grand Lodge of the state of Vermont. At their annual communication A. L. 5816 & 5817. 99189

Proceedings of the . . . Grand Lodge of the United States. (56696)

Proceedings of the Grand Lodge of Vermont. 99187

Proceedings [of the Grand Lodge of Virginia.] 100475

Proceedings of the Grand Lodge of Virginia; held at Mason's Hall. 100475

Proceedings of the grand mass meeting of the citizens of San Francisco. 76067

Proceedings of the grand reception extended by the pupils. (54604)

Proceedings of the Grand Royal Arch Chapter of Kentucky. 37543

Proceedings of the Grand Royal Arch Chapter of Missouri. 49596

[Proceedings] of the Grand Royal Arch Chapter of New-Hampshire. 52835

Proceedings of the Grand Royal Arch Chapter of South Carolina. 87832

Proceedings of the Grand Royal Arch Chapter of Tennessee. 94796

Proceedings of the Grand Royal Arch Chapter of the state of Georgia. 65859

Proceedings of the Grand Royal Arch Chapter of the state of Vermont. 99178

Proceedings of the Grand Royal Arch Chapter of Virginia. 100470

Proceedings of the great mass meeting in favor of the union. 76068

Proceedings of the great meeting of the Friends of Civil and Religious Liberty. 45289

Proceedings of the Great Peace Convention, held in the city of New York. (65860)

Proceedings of the Great Southern Co-operation and Anti-secession Meeting, held in Charleston. 88476

Proceedings of the Great Union Meeting held in . . . Philadelphia. 62088

Proceedings of the Greene County Agricultural Society. 28622

Proceedings of the Grenada Agricultural Society. 28761

Proceedings of the Harbor and River Convention. 12634

Proceedings [of the Herkimer County Agricultural Society.] 31490

Proceedings of the High Court of Impeachment. 25694

Proceedings of the High Court of Vice-Admiralty in Charleston, South-Carolina. 39927

Proceedings of the High Court of Vice-Admiralty in Charlestown, [sic] South Carolina. 39926, 1st note after 87356, note after 87824

Proceedings of the [Historic-Genealogical] Society. 52688

Proceedings of the Historical Society [of Pennsylvania.] 60144

Proceedings of the Homoeopathic Medical Society. (53695)

Proceedings of the Honourable House of Assembly of Jamaica, in relation to those which took place in the British House of Commons. 35663

Proceedings of the Hon. House of Assembly of Jamaica, on the sugar and slave-trade. 35651

Proceedings of the Honourable House of Assembly relative to the Maroons. (21908)

Proceedings of the Horticultural Association of Monroe, Michigan. 50032

Proceedings of the House of Assembly of Maryland. 45290

Proceedings of the House of Assembly of the state of New York. 35783

Proceedings of the House of Burgesses of Virginia. 99927

Proceedings of the House of Commons on the slave trade. 65861

Proceedings of the House of Lords in relation to the late Directors of the South-Sea Company. 65862, 88190

Proceedings of the House of Representatives of South Carolina. (71070)

Proceedings of the House of Representatives of the United States. 67796

Proceedings of the House of Representatives, Thursday, February 20, 1851. 65863

Proceedings of the Humane Society of Massachusetts. 30510

Proceedings of the meetings of the Washington City Bible Society. 101959

Proceedings of the Merchants Great Democrati Meeting at the New York Exchange. (54609)

Proceedings of the Middlesex Convention for Suppressing Violations of the Lord's Day. 48845

Proceedings of the Military Convention . . . Harrisburg. 60420

Proceedings of the Military Court of Inquiry. 78421

Proceedings of the Mississippi River Improvement Convention. 49552

Proceedings of the Montpelier Congregational Association. 50218

Proceedings of the Most Worshiful Grand Lodge of Ancient Freemasons. 87843

Proceedings of the M. W. Grand Lodge of Connt. (65871)

Proceedings of the M. W. Grand Lodge of Free and Accepted Masons. 65872

Proceedings of the M. W. Grand Lodge . . . of . . . Rhode Island. 70584

Proceedings of the M. W. Grand Lodge of Vermont. 99188

Proceedings of the National Association of Knit Goods Manufacturers. 51932

Proceedings of the . . . National Association of Local Preachers. (65873)

Proceedings of the National Association of School Superintendents. (51933)

Proceedings of the National Bank Convention held in New York City, . . . 1869. 51936

Proceedings of the National Bank Convention held in New York City, . . . October 19, 1864. (65874)

Proceedings of the National Baptist Educational Convention. 51939

Proceedings of the . . . [National Commercial] Convention, held in Boston. 51950

Proceedings of the National Congress on Uniform Divorce Laws. 84513

Proceedings of the National Convention for the Promotion of Education in the United States. (65875)

Proceedings of the National Convention for the Protection of American Interests. 65876

Proceedings of the National Convention of Artists. 65877

Proceedings of the . . . [National Convention] of Business Men. 61856

Proceedings of the National Convention of Farmers, Gardeners and Silk Culturists. 64878

Proceedings of the National Convention of Fruit Growers. (65879)

Proceedings of the National Convention of Jurneymen Printers. 65880

Proceedings of the National Convention of Manufacturers. 65881

Proceedings of the National Convention of Silk Growers. 65882

Proceedings of the National Convention of the Colored Men . . . in Washington, D. C. 65883

Proceedings of the National Convention of the Colored Men, . . . Syracuse, N. Y. 65883

Proceedings of the National Convention of the Friends of Public Education. (51956)

Proceedings of the National Convention of the Soldiers of the War of 1812, held . . . in . . . Philadelphia, . . . 1854. 61857, 65884

Proceedings of the National Convention of the Soldiers of the War of 1812, held in the City of Washington. 65885

Proceedings of the National Democratic Convention, convened at Charleston, S. C. 19500

Proceedings of the National Democratic Convention, held at Baltimore. 65886

Proceedings of the National Democratic Convention, held in . . . Baltimore. 65886

Proceedings of the National Democratic Convention, held in Cincinnati. 13100

Proceedings of the National Division, S. of T. 87009

Proceedings of the National Emigration Convention of Colored People. (65887)

PRoceedings of the National Encampment of the Grand Army of the Republic. 65888

Proceedings of the National Institute, Washington, D. C. 51988

Proceedings of the National Liberty Convention held at Buffalo. 65890

Proceedings of the National Lord's Day Convention. 51998

Proceedings of the National Masonic Convention. (65891)

Proceedings of the National Medical Convention (65892)

Proceedings of the National Museum, Washington 84230

Proceedings of the National Musical Convention. 52011

Proceedings of the National Pharmacutical [sic] Convention. 65893

Proceedings of the National Republican Convention. 60421

Proceedings of the National Republican Convention held at Chicago. 65894

Proceedings of the National Republican Convention, held at Frankfort, Kentucky. 65895

Proceedings of the National Republican Convention of Young Men. (65896), note after 101943

Proceedings of the National Ship-Canal Convention. 12638

Proceedings of the . . . National Temperance Convention. 65897

Proceedings of the . . . National Temple of Honor of the United States. 65898

Proceedings of the National Theological Institu and University. 65899

Proceedings of the National Union Convention held in Baltimore. 51457

Proceedings of the National Union Republican Convention. 12662

Proceedings of the National Women's Rights Convention. 65901

Proceedings of the Native American State Convention, . . . Harrisburg. 60422

Proceedings of the Natural History Society of Montreal. 10637

Proceedings of the naval court martial in the case of Alexander Slidell Mackenzie. 16515, 43526

Proceedings of the naval general court martia in the case of Lieutenant C. H. McBlair (42957)

Proceedings of the New-England Anti-slavery Convention, held in Boston . . . May, 1834. 52655

Proceedings of the New England Anti-slavery Convention, . . . May 31 [1860.] 58768, 12th note after 96966

Proceedings of the New England Manufacturer Convention. 65902

Proceedings of the New General Association. 52768

Proceedings of the N. H. Anti-slavery Convention. (15149), 52856

Proceedings of the New Hampshire Medical Society. 83654

Proceedings of the New Hampshire Publishers, Editors and Printers' Association. 52882

Proceedings of the New Jersey Historical Society. 37786, (53177), 82980, 95396

Proceedings of the New-York Anti-secret Society Convention. (53800)

Proceedings of the New York Historical Society. 3747, 8174, 54476, (77850), 77875, 82845, 89993, 92154

Proceedings of the New York Historical Society on the death of Hon. Luther Bradish. (7271)

Proceedings of the New York Historical Society, upon the decease of Colonel William L. Stone. 92154

Proceedings of the . . . [New York Horticultural] Society. 54479

Proceedings of the New York Society of the Cincinnati. 13125

Proceedings of the . . . [New York State Agricultural] Society. 53811

Proceedings of the New-York State Convention for "Rescuing the Canals from the Ruin With Which They are Threatened." 65903

Proceedings of the New-York State Sabbath Convention. (53838)

Proceedings of the New York State Society, of the Cincinnati. 13119

Proceedings of the New York State Sunday School Teachers' Association. 53842

Proceedings of the New York Sunday-School Institute. 54547

Proceedings of the New York Young Men's State Convention. (54868)

Proceedings of the Newcastle County Agricultural Society and Institute. 54929

Proceedings of the ninth academic commencement. 74445

Proceedings of the Norfolk County Anti-slavery Convention. 55473

Proceedings of the North American Pomological Convention. 55559

Proceedings of the North and South Consociations of Litchfield County, Ct. 41472

Proceedings of the North Carolina Grand Lodge. 45666

Proceedings of the North Missouri Railroad Convention. 49554

Proceedings of the Northern Association of Universalists. 98013

Proceedings of the officers of the Thirty-Ninth Regiment of Maryland Militia. 45264

Proceedings of the Ohio Anti-slavery Convention. 57043

Proceedings of the Ohio State Christian Anti-slavery Convention. (57003)

Proceedings of the Ohio Women's Rights Convention. (57019)

Proceedings of the one hundred and fiftieth anniversary of the First Congregational Society. 88590

Proceedings of the Onondaga Teachers' Institute. 57362

Proceedings of the Onondaga Whig Convention. 57362

Proceedings of the opponents of the present administration. 98425, 101950

Proceedings of the Overseers of Harvard University relative to the late disturbances in that university. (30752)

Proceedings of the Overseers of Harvard University, the report accepted, and the resolutions adopted by them. (30752)

Proceedings of the Peace Convernece Convention. 59403

Proceedings of the Peace Convention, held at Boston. 65905

Proceedings of the Peace Convention, held in Boston. 65904

Proceedings of the Peace Convention held in Boston, Sept. 18, 19, 20, 1838. 59402

Proceedings of the Peace Convention on the death of J. C. Wright. 59403

Proceedings of the . . . [Pennsylvania Agricultural] Society. 60297

Proceedings of the Pennsylvania Canal Convention. (60423)

Proceedings of the Pennsylvania Convention Assembled to Organize a State Anti-slavery Society. 60424

Proceedings of the Pennsylvania Democratic State Convention. 60425

Proceedings of the Pennsylvania Society of the Cincinnati. 13130

Proceedings of the Pennsylvania State Convention, to Promote Common School Education. 60426

Proceedings of the Pennsylvania Yearly Meeting of Progressive Friends. (60386)

Proceedings of the People's League of the Old and New World. 60823

Proceedings of the . . . [Philadelphia] Society [for Promoting Agriculture.] 62036

Proceedings of the Philological Society for 1842-43 and 1843-44. (62549)

Proceedings of the Physico-Medical Society of New-Orleans. (53361)

Proceedings of the Portland Society of Natural History. 64369

Proceedings of the preference bondholders historically, legally and financially considered. 85419

Proceedings of the Presbyterian Reunion . . . Pittsburgh, Nov. 12, 1869. (65207)

Proceedings of the Presbytery of Philadelphia. 102637

Proceedings of the presentation meeting held in Boston. (6765), note after 97006

Proceedings of the President and Fellows of the Connecticut Medical Society. 15783

[Proceedings of the President and Fellows of the Connecticut Medical Society, in convention] May, 1837. 15783

Proceedings of the Printers' Festival, held . . . in Rochester. (24956)

Proceedings of the proprietors and of the vestry of Trinity Church. 6677

Proceedings of the Protestant Episcopal Society for the Promotion of Evangelical Knowledge. 66202

Proceedings of the Providence Franklin Society. 66326

Proceedings of the Provincial Conference of Committees. 60427

Proceedings of the public demonstration of sympathy with Pius IX. (63171)

Proceedings of the Railroad Convention, . . . Harrisburg. 60428

Proceedings of the Republican celebration, at Washington. 101949

Proceedings of the Republican Convention held in Suffolk. 100456

Proceedings of the Republican Convention, Monday, March 18, 1839. 70026, 100455

Proceedings of the Republican Meeting of the Citizens of Albany and Colonie. 626

Proceedings of the Republican National Convention, Chicago. 12661

Proceedings of the Republican National Convention, held at Chicago. 70035

Proceedings of the Republican State Convention, held at Milwaukee. 83675

Proceedings of the Rhode-Island Anti-masonic State Convention. (70618)

Proceedings of the Rhode-Island Anti-slavery Convention. 70619

[Proceedings of the Rhode Island Association for Freedmen.] 70709

Proceedings of the Rhode Island Historical Society. 70719, 104330

Proceedings of the Rhode Island State Temperance Society. 70737

Proceedings of the Rhode-Island State Total Abstinence Society. 70738

Proceedings of the Richmond Baptist Foreign and Domestic Missionary Society. 71201

Proceedings of the R. W. Grand Encampment of Patriarchs. 65906

Proceedings of the R. W. Grand Lodge of Pennsylvania, . . . April 13, 1858. 49703

Proceedings of the R. W. Grand Lodge of Pennsylvania, at a quarterly grand communication. 18320

Proceedings of the R. W. G. Lodge of the Independent Order of Odd Fellows. (53692)

Proceedings of the Right Worthy Grand Lodge of the Independent Order of Odd-Fellows. Of South-Carolina. 87908

Proceedings of the Right Worthy Grand Lodge of the Independent Order of Odd-Fellows of South-Carolina, from January 3, 1843. 87909

Proceedings of the River Improvement Convention. 65907

Proceedings of the Rockingham Convention. (72389)

Proceedings of the Royal Geographical Society. 73792

Proceedings of the Royal Geographical Society of London. 73792

Proceedings of the Sabbath Convention. 72350

Proceedings of the St. Louis Chamber of Commerce. 11792, 75341

Proceedings of the San Francisco Union Ratification Meeting. 76069

Proceedings of the Sangerfield Meeting. 65908

Proceedings of the Schenectady County Bible Society. 77605

Proceedings of the 2d and 3d conventions [of the National Convnetion of Artists.] 65877

Proceedings of the second annual meeting of the Convention of the Baptist Denomination. 49534

Proceedings of the second annual meeting of the Immigrants' Friend Society for the Valley of the Mississippi. 34365

Proceedings of the second annual meeting of the Iowa Soldiers' Orphans Home. 35030

Proceedings of the second annual meeting of the Minnesota Editorial Convention. (49272)

Proceedings of the second annual meeting [of the Southern Historical Society.] 88369

Proceedings of the second annual meeting of the stockholders of the Wilmington & Raleigh Rail-road Company. 104585

Proceedings of the second annual State Convention of the Young Men's Christian Association. 52940

Proceedings of the Second Church and Parish in Dorchester. 20622, (20626)

Proceedings of the second Convention for Bible Missions. (65832)

[Proceedings] of the second Convention [of Managers and Superintendents . . . in the United States . . . 1860.] 33179

Proceedings of the second session of the National Labor Union. 65889

Proceedings of the second session of the National Typographical Union. 65900

Proceedings of the second United States Anti-masonic Convention. 97960

Proceedings of the semi-annual meeting, . . . at Boston, July 18, 1866 [of the New England Cotton Manufacturers' Association.] 52669

Proceedings of the semiscentenary celebration of the Presbyterian Board of Education. 89260

Proceedings of the semi-centennial celebration of the Rensselaer Polytechnic Institute. 69641

Proceedings of the semi-centennial of the Washington Light Infantry. (12065), note after 88107

Proceedings of the Senate and House of Representatives of Massachusetts. (65250)

Proceedings of the Senate and House of Representatives of the Fenian Brotherhood. 24060

Proceedings of the Senate and House of Representatives, upon the petition of George N Withington and others. 11117, (45948)

Proceedings of the Senate sitting for the trial of Andrew Johnson. 36179

Proceedings of the Session of Broadway Tabernacle, against Lewis Tappan. (54136), 94370

Proceedings of the session of Congress, commencing November 3d, 1794. 10067

Proceedings of the seventh anniversary, Delph October, 1849. 34496

Proceedings of the seventh annual meeting [of the St. Lawrence and Atlantic Railroad.] (75309)

Proceedings of the several state boards of equalization. 57026

Proceedings of the sixty-ninth annual Convention of the Connecticut Medical Society. 15783

Proceedings of the Society for Educating the Poor of Newfoundland. 8950, 54987

Proceedings of the Society for the Advancement of General Education, in the Count of Bucks. 85871

Proceedings of the Society for the Encouragement of Arts, Manufactures, and Commerce established in Barbadoes. 34825

Proceedings of the Society for the Propagation of the Gospel in Foreign Parts. 78717, 90218-90218, 103964

Proceedings of the Society of United Irishmen of Dublin. 86176

Proceedings of the Soldiers and Sailors' Nati Convention. 86326

Proceedings of the Soldiers' & Sailors' State Convention. 86331

Proceedings of the Soldiers' and Sailors' Uni of the State of New York. 86332

Proceedings of the South Carolina Yazoo Company. 88054

Proceedings of the Southern and Western Commercial Convention. 88292

[Proceedings of the Southern and Western Railroad Convention.] 88299

Proceedings of the Southern and Western States Reform Medical Association. 88301

Proceedings of the Southern Baptist Convention. 3241, 88309

Proceedings of the Southern Commercial Convention at its annual session at Concinnati, Ohio, October, 1870. 88326

Proceedings of the Southern Commercial Convention, held in the city of New Orleans. 88327

Proceedings of the Southern Convention, held in Savannah, Geo. 88328

Proceedings of the Southern Historical Convention. 88369

Proceedings of the Southern Loyalists' Convention. 69942, 88394

Proceedings of the Southern Rail-Road Convention, of 1855. 88454

Proceedings of the Southern Rights Convention. 88481

Proceedings of the Southern States Convention of Colored Men. 88499

Proceedings of the Southern Vine-Growers' Convention. 88513

Proceedings of the Special Committee of the Legislative Assembly. 10502

Proceedings of the Special Committee of the Select and Common Councils. 62091

Proceedings of the Special Grand Communication of the M. W. Grand Lodge. (53692)

Proceedings of the special meeting of the Charleston Board of Trade. 87934

Proceedings of the State Agricultural Convention . . . at . . . Albany. 53810

Proceedings of the State Agricultural Society, of South Carolina. 88059

Proceedings of the State Board of Agriculture. (45949)

Proceedings of the State Board of Equalization at Springfield. 34315

Proceedings of the State Convention at Canton. 57027

Proceedings of the State Convention at Hallowell. 44004

Proceedings of the State Convention, held at Rochester. (53869)

Proceedings of the State Convention of Colored Men. 37567

Proceedings of the State Convention of Colored People. (53870)

Proceedings of the State Convention of Maryland to Frame a New Constitution. 45293

Proceedings of the State Convention, of Maryland, to Frame a New Constitution, commenced at Annapolis, May 8, 1867. (45294)

Proceedings of the State Convention of Mechanics, held at Utica. (65909)

Proceedings of the State Convention of National Republican Young Men. 15794

Proceedings of the State Convention of the National Democracy. 65910

Proceedings of the State Convention of the Southern Rights Party of Kentucky. 88482

Proceedings of the State Convention of the State Rights Democracy. 60429

Proceedings of the State Convention of the Whig Young Men of Massachusetts. 103274

Proceedings of the State Democratic Convention held at Columbia, S. C. 87816

Proceedings of the State Disunion Convention. (45950)

Proceedings of the State Medical Convention. (60430)

Proceedings of the State Military Convention held at Syracuse. 65911

Proceedings of the State Military Convention, held at Worcester. 45951

Proceedings of the State-Right Celebration at Charleston, S. C. 12072

Proceedings of the State Rights & Free Trade Convention. 65912, 88067

Proceedings of the State Rights Celebration, at Charleston, S. C. 88061

Proceedings of the State Rights' Meeting, in Columbia, S. C. 65913, 88062

Proceedings of the State Sabbath Convention, . . . Harrisburg. 60431

Proceedings of the State St. Church. 64379

Proceedings of the State Temperance Convention: . . . Harrisburg, Penn. 60432

Proceedings of the State Temperance Convention, held in Charleston, S. C. 80073

[Proceedings of the State Temperance Convention, S. C., 1845.] 80073

Proceedings of the State Treasurer of New Hampshire. 50395

Proceedings of the State U. C. of Ohio. 57028

Proceedings of the stockholders . . . at their . . . meeting. 59910

Proceedings of the stockholders . . . at their second meeting. 42325

Proceedings of the stockholders, . . . 1852. 55733

Proceedings of the stockholders of the Bank of the United States. 3189

Proceedings of the stockholders of the City Bank, Providence, R. I. 66295

Proceedings of the stockholders of the South-Carolina Rail-Road. 88023, 88027

Proceedings of the stockholders of the Union Bank of Maryland. 45081

Proceedings of the stockholders 28th October 1816. 3189

Proceedings of the Strafford Counference. 92668

Proceedings of the Suffolk Bar. 21568

Proceedings of the Suffolk County Temperance Society. 93435

Proceedings of the Supreme Court of Illinois. 41186

Proceedings of the Supreme Executive Council of the state of Pennsylvania. (2062), 60433

Proceedings of the Tax-Payers' Convention of South Carolina. 88077, 1st note after 94434

Proceedings of the Temperance Convention, held at Greenville, C. H. 88072

Proceedings of the Temperance Convention held in Boston. 6547

Proceedings of the Temperance Convention which met in Philo Hall. 94646

Proceedings of the Temperance Society of Columbia, S. C. 94653

Proceedings of the Temperance Union, D. C. 20311, note after 94656

Proceedings of the tenth annual convention of the Minnesota State Sabbath School Association. (49292)

Proceedings of the tenth annual meeting of the Baptist State Convention of North Carolina. 55667

Proceedings of the Territorial Delegate Convention. 37077

Proceedings of the third annual meeting of the American Indian Missionary Association. 65914

Proceedings of the third annual meeting of the Ohio State Phonetic Association. (57009)

Proceedings of the third Anti-slavery Convention of American Women. 82039

Proceedings of two ecclesiastical councils, in the town of Berkeley. [sic] 92834

Proceedings of two ecclesiastical councils, in the town of Berkley. 21820, 65920, 70221

Proceedings of two meetings, held in Boston, on the 7th & 14th July. 6548, 78422

Proceedings of two meetings of citizens of Philadelphia. 62092

Proceedings . . . on its first anniversary; . . . with an address to the public [by the New-York State Colonization Society.] 53816

Proceedings on . . . laying the corner stone . . . . Including the address by Geo. B. Wood, M. D. 60332

Proceedings on . . . laying the corner stone of a building. 45829

Proceedings on . . . laying the corner stone of the library edifice. 52467

Proceedings on occasion of the one hundredth anniversary of the ordination of the Rev. Joseph Lathrop. 89729

Proceedings . . . on occasion of the reception of Their Excellencies, Senor Joaquim Maria Nascentes de Azambuja. 53590

Proceedings on . . . opening the new . . . [Pennsylvania] Hospital . . . [for the Insane] at Philadelphia. 60332

Proceedings on the announcement of the death of Col. Francis S. Bartow. 15261

Proceedings on the announcement of the death of Hon. John Tyler. 15260

Proceedings on the . . . announcement of the death of the Hon. Samuel Prentice, of Vermont. 65097

Proceedings . . . on the announcement of the death of William Hickling Prescott. 54476

Proceedings . . . on the continued piracies of vessels. 53590

Proceedings . . . on the death of Hon. Benjamin F. Hopkins. (43745)

Proceedings on the death of Hon. Solomon Foot. 25011

Proceedings . . . on the . . . death of Luther Bradish. 54476

Proceedings . . . on the enlargement of the canals. 53590

PRoceedings on the impeachment of William Blount. 6002

Proceedings on the occasion of laying the corner stone of the city hall. 6684

Proceedings on the occasion of laying the corner-stone of the new hospital in Belmont, Philadelphia. 61535, 62093

Proceedings on the occasion of laying the corner-stone of the public library. 6759

Proceedings on the occasion of laying the corner-stone of the Sailor's Snug Harbor of Boston. 6771, 74976

Proceedings on the occasion of the death of John Anthon. 1679

Proceedings on the occasion of unveiling the monument. 88111

Proceedings [on the installation of the Second National Congress of Venezuela.] 6189

Proceedings on the presentation of a tea service of silver. 7052

Proceedings on the reception of H. E. Senhor D'Azambuja. 7591, 53586

Proceedings on the trail of Lieut. Col. Cockburne. 14092

Proceedings relating to the organization of the General Theological Seminary. 26911, (54291)

Proceedings relative to a canal from the lakes to the Mississippi. 65921

Proceedings relative to calling the conventions of 1776 and 1790. 60435, 80768

Proceedings relative to the Danish Brig Hope, and cargo. 96935

Proceedings relative to the erection of a monument. 65922

Proceedings relative to the establishment of a Presbyterian place of worship in Kingston. 37916

Proceedings relative to the formation of an Anti-slavery Church in . . . Philadelphia. (62094)

Proceedings relative to the Union of Free Masons in South Carolina. 87835

Proceedings, resolutions, &c., of the Board of Commissioners on the cases before them. 13196

Proceedings, speeches, &c. at the dinner . . . Washington, Jan. 7, 1852. 38269

Proceedings, statements and resolutions of a meeting of the Methodist Episcopal Church. (3062)

Proceedings . . . upon the convention, . . . between His Majesty and the United States. 56163

Proceedings upon the dedication of Plummer Hall. 63467

Proceedings upon the resignation of Capt. Wm. A. Courtenay. 88108

Proceedings . . . with account of the yellow fever, 1822. 54124

Proces de conspirateurs de Washington. 41229

Proces de David M'Lane pour haute trahison. 97902

Proces de Joseph Berube et de Cesaree Theriault. 65923

Proces de Joseph N. Cardinal, et autres. 93241

Proces de Marie-Galante (Guadeloupe) 77750

Proces . . . discute . . . 1775. 29240

Proces-verbal de la Commission d'Enquite formee a Lyon. 84478

Proces-verbal de la Peremiere Assemblee Tenue au Port-au-Prince. 85822

Proces-verbal de la seance de ll Mai 1876. 58503

Proces-verbal de l'Assemblee des Citoyens-Libres et Proprietaires de Couleur. (75118)

Proces verbal de l'excursion de la tribu des Pieds-en-Sueur. (65924)

Proces-verbal, N°. 345. 99254

Proces verbal of the ceremony of installation of President. 99273

Proces verbaux. 14717

Proces-verbaux des senaces de la Commission de Colonisation de la Guyane. (29189)

Proces-verbaux des seances, et journal des debats. (75180)

Proces-verbaux 1840-43. 14992

Proceso contra el Presidente de los Estados Unidos de Colombia. 51073

Proceso de Residencia instruido contra Nuno de Guzman. 67646

Procesco del Gen. Santa-Anna. 76745

Proceso del P. M. Fray Luis de Leon. 40079

Proceso formado de orden S. M. a las autoridades de Cuba. (29449)

Proceso instructivo formado por la seccion del Gran Jurado. 582, (65925)

Proceso instruido a los ex-ministros de estado, Senores . . . Luis Gonzaga Cuevas. 65926

Proclamation. Whereas His Most Excellent Majesty having received advice. 78202

Proclamation. Whereas it appears by the minutes of the Council. 98065C

Proclamation. Whereas it is represented to me, by His Excellency Thomas Mifflin. 100219

Proclamation, whereas Rip van Dam, Esq; 98436

Proclamation. Whereas several persons, inhabitants of the United States of America. 101696

Proclamation: whereas the enemy have invaded this state. 87535

Proclamation. Whereas the . . . exertions of the good people of this state. 90051

Proclamation. Whereas the General Court of the commonwealth of Massachusetts. 90058

Proclamation. Whereas the Legislature of ths this state, at their session in June last. 90054

Proclamation. Whereas sundry persons, inhabitants of this state. 90053

Proclamation: with plates. (31888), 63502, 100509

Proclamations, addresses, &c. 45290

Proclamations and other papers issued by the British Commanders. 95299, 102861

Proclamations for thanksgiving, issued by the Continental Congress. 33150

Proclamations of His Excellency B. F. Perry. 87445

Proclamations of the President, including treaties, conventions, etc. 95000

Procli De sphaera liber I. 65940-65941

Proclus, Lycius, surnamed Diadochus. 65940-65941

Procter, B. W. ed. 104511

Procter, George H. 65942

Procter, William. 65943-65944

Proctor, Charles Hayden. (65945)-65946

Proctor, Edna Dean. 4316

Proctor, Francis. 65947

Proctor, John J. 65948

Proctor, John W. 65949

Proctor, L. B. (65950), 91754

Proctor, Redfield. ed. 1st note after 98997

Proctor, Robert. 65951, 99366

Procuradores Generales de las Ordenes de Santo Domingo, S. Francisco, S. Agustin, y las demas religiones. 106408

Procuring cause, and a remedy proposed. 52760

Prodesse conamur. 31226

Prodigal daughter, or a strange and wonderful relation. 65952

Prodigal daughter; or the disobedient lady reclaimed. 65953

Prodigals, a play, in three acts. 83780

Prodigo milagroso del occidente. 98605

Prodigioso milagro por intercessio de la B. Rosa de Santa Maria. 73186

Prodigo avara. 63599, 75999

Prodrome d'un monographie des rosiers de l'Amerique Septentrionale. 67462

Prodome d'une monographie de turbionlies fossiles du Kentuki. 67462

Prodromus commentarii in xviii. cap. Esaiae. (63711)

Prodromus florae Bryologicae Surinamensis. 20802

Prodromus of the flora Philadelphia. 3859

Prodromus of the flora Columbiana. 7731

Prodromus plantarum Indiae Occidentalis. 30043

Produce Exchange, San Francisco. see San Francisco. Produce Exchange.

Producteur. (65954)

Production, distribution, and consumption of wealth. 77363

Production, export, manufacture, and consumption of cotton. 3313

Production historique des faits qui se sont passes. 65955

Production of iron and steel in its economic and social relations. 31637-31638

Production of wine in California. 67612

Productions by nature and art. 12470

Productions naturelles & les commodities du pais. 5115-5117, 2d note after 100478

Productions of Mrs. Maria W. Stewart. 91700

Productive geography. 83928

Productive grammar. English grammar on the productive system. note before 83906, 83917, 83919, 83922, 83927

Proemio. 1537, 106365

Proemio del viaggio fatto nell Etiopia per Don Francesco Alvarez. 67730

Proemio dell' avttore. (67737)

Proemio di Mattheo di Micheovo. 67738

Proemio [et navigationi] del nobel hvomo Messer Alvise da Ca da Mosto. 67730

Proeve eener handleiding om het Meger-Engelsch. 31263

Proeve eener Hollandsche spraakkunst. 48227, 66752

Proeve over de middelen die tot bescherming. 19800, 65956

Proeve over de natuurlyke geschiedenis van Guana. 3108

Proezas de Hernan-Cortes. 74025

Professing people directed. 59312

Profession de foi et considerations sur le systeme republicain. 26329

Profession of belief and plan of church government. 98010

Profession of faith, and constitutional plan of government. 102967

Profession of faith and covenant of the Second Congregational Church. (53263)

Profession of faith, by John Davenport. 52959

Profession of faith, made by . . . Mr. John Davenport. 17058

Profession of the faith of that Reverend and Worthy Divine Mr. J. D. 18709

Profession of their faith. 92825

Professional gentleman. pseud. comp. Laws of Grenada and the Grenadines. 28756

Professional morality. 36136

Professional papers, Corps of Engineers, no. 16. 27423

Professional planter. pseud. Practical rules. (64873)

Professional reputation. 27665

Professional scholarship demanded by the age. 79761

Professional years of John Henry Hobart, D. D. 43679

Professions and practice of Republican & Democratic statesmen contrasted. 16178

Professor at the breakfast-table. 32621

Professor Hale and Dartmouth College. 29615, 57202

Professor Henry D. Roger's address. (72654)

Prof. Henry's exposition before the New Jersey Historical Society. 31403

Prof. Hoornbeek's sorg en raad. (32437)

Professor John Addison Porter. 64277

Professor List's speech. 41427

Professor Lyell's lecture. 74632, (39857)

Professor Mitchell's farewell to the graduating class. 49725
Professor of mathematics, in Yale College. pseud. Connecticut almanack. see Strong, Nehemiah.
Professor Powell's report. 85048
Professor Risley's original gigantic moving panorama. 83010
Professor Silliman's report upon the oil property. 81054
Prof. Smyth's address at the meeting. 85218
Professor Sonntag's thrilling narrative. 86971
Prof. Stuart and slave catching. 60952, 93197
Professor Stuart's letters to Mr. Channing. 90713
Prof. Ville's new system of agriculture. 71271
Professors and Tutors of Harvard University. petitioners see Harvard University. Professors and Tutors. petitioners
Professors warn'd of their danger. 43293
Profest enemy of oppression, W. P. pseud. Truth rescued from imposture. see Penn, William, 1658-1716.
Profeta Jeremias nacido en Valladolid. 89418
Profezia di Dante. 64007-64008
Proffit, George H., 1807-1847. 65957
Profit and loss of Great Britain and Spain, from the commencement of the present war to this time. 65959
Profit and loss of Great Britain in the present war with Spain. From July 1739 to July 1741. 65958
Profit and loss of Great-Britain, in the present war with Spain, set in its true light. 31991
Profitable advice for rich and poor. (55502), note after 87925
Profits on manufactures at Lowell. 11219, note after 96512
Pro-forma sales and invoices of imports. 5532, (71467)
Progetto di navigazione sull' Amazone. 67909
Prognosticks of impending calamities. 104099
Program of the celebration of the Cape Cod Association at Provincetown. 10734
Programa de las materias cursadas en el Colegio de la Independencia Americana de Arequipa. 65960
Programa de un liberal. 75917
Programa del imperio. 46174
Programa propuesto en la 2ª catedra de derecho patrio. 94223
Programm testimonial benefit dendered to Rev. S. F. Smith. 84058
Programm und Statuten der Social-Demokratischen Arbeiter-Partei von N. Amerika. 85688
Programme, constitution, and proposed members. (1218)
Programme d'etude pour la formation d'une banque agricole nationale. 19113
Programme, etc. [of the Rensselaer Polytechnic Institute.] (69641)
Programme for a review of the THird Regiment of Connecticut. 68808
Programme for . . . 1862. 60326
Programme generale des examens de Lycee National du Port-au-Prince. 64181
[Programme of] Commencement week [at Bowdoin College.] 7035
Programme of "conflagratio conicorum," Trinity College. 65961
Programme of organization of the Smithsonian Institution. 85049
Programme of peace. 65962
Programme of the examination and exhibition, at St. Timothy's Hall. 75501

Programme of the fourth session . . . July 16th, 1860. (34934)
Programme of the order of exercises at the re-raising of the United States flag. (25167)
Progres de la colonie Icarienne etablie a Nauvo 9786
Progresista, periodico politico, cientifico y literario. 65963
Progreso del apostadero de Iquitos. 65964
Progress: a satire. (77345)
Progress: a satirical poem. 77344
Progress. An address before the Phi Beta Kappa Society. (58703)
Progress and principle of the temperance reformation. 9409
Progress and prospects of Christianity. 2791
Progress and prospects of the great struggle for freedom in America. 65965
Progress and results of emancipation in the English West Indies. 35846
Progress backwards. (44755)
Progress: considered with particular referenc to the Methodist Episcopal Church, South 77127
Progress in agriculture. 22085
Progress. Its grounds and possibilities. (7282)
Progress of America; a pocket companion. 65966
Progress of America, from the discovery by Columbus to . . . 1846. 43288
Progress of American journalism from 1840 t 1870. 46979
Progress of animal magnetism in New England (64852)
Progress of Baptist principles in the last four hundred years. 18067
Progress of Christianity retarded by its frienc 71062
Progress of civil liberty. 78399
Progress of colonial reform. 65967
Progress of coquetry, or the adventures of Miss Harriet Simper. 97238
Progress of discovery on the more northern coasts of America. 97657
Progress of dulness. 96234-97239B, 2d note after 105937
Progress of ethnology. 3747, 54476
Progress of fanaticism. 92146
Progress of freedom. 65968
Progress of freedom; and other poems. 8053
Progress of genius. 102716
Progress of ice islands from Greenland to Newfoundland. 6026
Progress of judicial usurpation. 36166
Progress of liberal opinions. 91593
Progress of liberty; a Pindaric ode. 17434
Progress of maritime discovery. (74967)
Progress of maritime discovery, from the earliest period. 13419
Progress of medicine during the first half of the nineteenth century. (8793)
Progress of nationality among the people and in the government. 65568
Progress of nations. 65969
Progress of naval architecture. 18908
Progress of Puseyism. 65970
Progress. Read before the Roxbury Mechanic Institute. 71822
Progress of refinement. 56722
Progress of religion traced round the world. 49468
Progress of religious ideas, through successiv ages. (12727)
Progress of Romanism since the revolutionary war. 55878

Progress of science. A poem. 19902
Progress of science, spoken by Samuel Dexter. 14648
Progress of society. 65971
Progress of statistics. 37433
Progress of the African race. 49730
Progress of the age, and the danger of the age. 31651
Progress of the Catholic Church in America. (46977)
Progress of the city of New-York, during the last fifty years. 37789
Progress of the college. 23679
Progress of the colony of Georgia. 27087
Progress of the common school system of Upper Canada. 32348
Progress of the false position. 36161
Progress of the French in their views of universal monarchy. (65972)
Progress of the nation, in its various social and economical relations. (64253)
Progress of the republic, . . . a full and comprehensive review of the progress. 37429
Progress of the ultra-democratic principle. (65973)
Progress of the United States. 88947
Progress of the United States in population and wealth. 97307
Progress of the United States of America. 24491
Progress pamphlets. Part I. 31949
Progress, resources and prospects of the city of Joliet. 36409
Progress, the law of the missionary work. 81643
Progress to the mines. (9721)
Progress; or, the south defended. 47120
Progressive annual for 1862. (65974)
Progressive democracy in religion. 65975
Progressive Friends. An account of the fourth annual meeting. 24512
Progressive Gardner's [sic] Society of Philadelphia. 62096
Progressive Spain. 84737
Progressus fidei Catholicae in Nouo Orbe. 67498, 96969
Prohemio. Al Excelentissimo Senor Don Fernando de Torres y Portugal. 32492, 100643
Prohemio ofte voorreeden totten leser. 41356
Prohemio primo, sopra il libro di Messer Marco Polo. 67736
Prohemio secondo, sopra il libro di M. Marco Polo. 67736
Prohiac de Fount de Pradt, Dominique Georges Frederic de Riom de. see Pradt, Dominique Georges Frederic de Riom de Prolhiac de Fourt de, Abp., 1759-1837.
Prohibicion del folleto titulado: la religion del dinera. 65976
Prohibicion que el Rey manda se haga del comercio. 65977
Prohibition does prohibit. 90903
Prohibition not a failure. 90903
Prohibition of Sunday travelling. 60358
Prohibition of the sale of intoxicating liquours impracticable. (13256)
Prohibitionist. (65978)
Prohibitory law and its workings. 17661
Prohibitory liquor law. 65979
Prohibitory liquor law for Upper Canada. 41386
Prohibitory liquor laws of Delaware. (19399)
Prohibitory liquor law: their . . . operation in the United States. 41309
Proissy, -------. 19366 see also France. Commission des Colonies.
Proisy, ---------, Chevalier de. (3305), 65980

Project for a tonal system. 56363
Project for the civilization of the Indians of North America. (13240)
Project for the emission of one hundred thousand pounds of province bills. 103902
Project of a law, for the commitment of the insane to custody. 84265B
Project of a national railroad from the Atlantic to the Pacific Ocean. 103999
Project of a new penal code for the state of Louisiana. (41612)
Project of the constitution for the republic of Bolivia. 6206
Project of the William Penn Market is wholly impracticable. 104159
Project to connect the Atlantic and Pacific by a canal. 51764
Projected ship canal to connect the Atlantic and Pacific Oceans. 97550
Projection for erecting a bank of credit in Boston. 6710
Projection or scheme of reasonable terms. 33163
Projecto apresentado a Camara dos Srs. Deputados em sessao de 6 de Agosto de 1870. 85652
Projecto apresentado a Camara dos Srs. Deputados na sessao de 19 de Julho de 1869. 85636
Projecto apresentado a Camara dos Srs. Deputados na sessao de 22 de Julho de 1870. 85656
Projecto da Commissao del Melhoramento do Commercio. (65981)
Projecto de constituicao para o imperio do Brasil. 7617
Projecto de reglamento de elecciones 1828. 76859
Projecto do codigo criminal por uma Commissao Composta de Visconde do Uruguay, Joao P. dos Santos Barretto e M. Felisardo de Souza e Mello. 85642
Projecto e memoria sobre o encanamento das aguas potaveis. 60990
Projecto elaborado pela Sociedade Democratica Constitucional Limeirense. 85773
Projecto para a suppressao de alguns impostos e amortisacao de parte da divida publica fundada. 88769
Projecto. Regulamento da Secretaria do Conselho Director do Imperio Instituto de Agricultura. 85630
Projector. pseud. Concise view of the inland navigation. see Merritt, W. H.
Projector. 78358, (78365), 78378-78379
Projector detected. 17729
Projector, teaching a direct, sure and ready way. 78358
Projector. Teaching a direct, svre, and ready way. 78368
Projectors . . . and empire travelling westward. 89187
Projectos de leyes sobre instruccion publica. 65982, 1st note after 98882
Projet de colonisation dans les deux Ameriques. 36064
Projet de colonisation pour la Guyane Francaise. 11642
Projet de l'establissement de navigation a vapeur. 59344
Projet de pacification generale. (65986)
Projet de reconstruction territoriale et dynastique. (65987)
Projet de societe. 29099
Projet de souscription pour un armement destine. (38427)

Projet d'amelioration coloniale. 21033
Projet d'establissement d'une ligne de paquebot
Projet d'etablissement d'une ligne de paquebot
  a vapeur. (65983)
Projet d'etablissement d'une sucrerie centrale.
  (4942)
Projet d'instruction sur une maladie convulsive.
  (63712), 65984
Projet d'un canal de jonction de l'Ocean
  Pacifique et de l'Ocean Atlantique. 26660
Projet d'un canal maritime sans ecluses entre
  l'Ocean Atlantique et l'Ocean Pacifique.
  37256
Projet d'un corps d'histoire du Nouveau Monde.
  12135
Projet d'un decret pour les subsistances de
  l'ile de Saint-Domingue. 14055
Projet d'une colonization agricole et industrielle.
  39602
Projet d'une constitution religieuse. (65985)
Projet pour tener la decouverte du Pole
  Gauche. 79173
Proklamation durch Andreas Jackson. 35355
Prolegomana and exercitations of Scriblerus.
  59272
Prolegomena. 99276
Prolegomenos del derecho. 23718
Prolix, Peregrine. pseud. Letters descriptive
  of the Virginia springs. see Nicklin,
  Philip Houlbrooke.
Prolix, Peregrine. pseud. Pleasant peregrina-
  tion. see Nicklin, Philip Houlbrooke.
Prologo al lector. 74953
Prologo al pio lector. 72811
Prologo critico biografico, por el Doctor Landa.
  63563
Prologo Galeato. 105733
Prologo ou elogio historico. 52217
Prologo. [Per Bartholomaeum Casaum con-
  scripta.] 11283, 11285
Prologo por D. Juan de Dios de la Rada y
  Delgado. 63306
Prologo. [Por Diego de Torres Rubio.] 96268
Prologo por el Doctor Don Antonio Hay de la
  Puente. 86227
Prologo por Francisco Sanchez del Arco. 63746
Prologo y un juicio critico por los eminentes
  escritores. 71636
Prologomeno a toda la historia de lo futuro.
  99525
Prologue. 97788
Prologue by John H. Hewitt. (7653)
Prologue [to California.] 94438
Prologus super constitutiones Fratruum Heremita-
  rum. (68936), 98913
Prolongatie van't octroy der West-Indische
  Compagnie. (66523), 102909
Prolusio academia in Divi Marci Limana Uni-
  versitate recitanda. (76317)
Prolusio academica pro studiorum inauguratione.
  73621
Prolusio academica, recitanda in D. Marci
  Limana Universitate. 67332
Promenade a travers l'Amerique du Sud. 26282
Promenade autour du monde. 1867
Promenade en Amerique. Etats-Unis, Cuba,
  Mexique. 1347
Promenade sentimentale en France et au Bresil.
  21162
Promenades d'un artiste parmi les Indiens.
  19428, 37009
Promethean tunnel in Nevada. 65988
Prometheus. pseud. Prometheus' diarial
  account. (65989)
Prometheus' diarial account. (65989)
Prometheus II. with other poems. 60869

Prominence of the atonement. (79299), 9227?
Prominent characteristics of the congrega-
  tional churches. (50293)
Prominent characters and incidents of our
  history. 97610
Prominent political acts of George Washington
  16111
Promis, Vicenzo. 65990
Promiscuous singing, no divine institution.
  30081
Promise-keeping a great duty. 104100
Promised seed. 16643
Promotion of American industry. 45441
Promotion of education. 66092
Promotion of medical science. 15625
Promotion of trade made easy, and lands
  advanced. 97286
Prompter. 102351, 102376, 102378-102394,
  102397
Prompter: a series of essays on civil and
  social duties. 65991
Prompter. A weekly miscellany devoted to
  public amusements. 65992
Prompter, or maxims and common sayings.
  (25598)
Prompter's whistle. 65993
Promtuario de la constitucion de la monarqui
  Espanola. 23587
Promptuario eleitoral. 24169
Promptuario manual Mexicana. 58575
Promptuario para los Alcaldes de Cuartel y
  Gefes de Manzana. 23575
Promyschleniki. 90063
Pronostico de la felicidad Americana. 98861
Pronostico funesto de inmensos males. 9618
Prontuario de agricultura general. 2611
Prontuario de ordenanza para el ejercito.
  (22892)
Prontuario de ordennanzas. 65994
Prontuario diplomatico y consular. 16973
Prontuario e instruccion de ordenandos dedic
  al Senor D. D. Pedro Jose de Guerra.
  65995
Prontuario general en cinco tarifas. 65996
Prontuario o manual y correspondencia de
  delitos y penas. 86225
Prontuario por materias y orden alfabetico.
  48630
Pronunicamento. 42303
Pronunciamiento de Perote por el General
  Antonio Lopez Sta. Anna. 65997
Pronunciamiento de Perote, y sucesos de su
  campana. 767646
Pronunciamiento y acta de organizacion de ur
  gobierno provisario. (65998)
Proof. American nuggets. 91509
Proof and procedure before the Arbiters on
  the Submission. 104487
Proof of Jesus Christ His being the ancient
  promised Messiah. 3470
Proof of the alliance between American whigs
  and British tories. 36676
Proof palpable of immorality. 76966
Proof sheet. 65999
Proof that black's white. note after 92624
Proof that Great-Britain must be injured by
  that act. (52213)
Proofs and demonstrations how much of the
  projected registry of colonial Negroes
  in unfounded and uncalled for. (81893),
  note after 102820
Proofs and demonstrations that the registry
  of colonial Negroes is uncalled for.
  11768
Proofs considered of the early settlement of
  Acadie by the Dutch. 19636

Proofs for working men of the monarchic and aristocratic designs. 66000

Proofs of a conspiracy against all the religions. 77242-72244

Proofs of a conspiracy, against Christianity. 5597

Proofs of error in the decision of the state of New York. 31595

Proofs of the being of satan and of evil spirits. 65496

Proofs of the corruption of Gen. James Wilkinson. (13265)

Proofs of the falsity of Conover's testimony. 66001

Proofs of the origin of the yellow fever. 62097

Proofs of the protozoic age of some of the altered rocks. 72746

Proofs of the real existence and dangerous tendency of illuminism. 59316

Proofs that credit as money . . . is . . . preferable to coin. (30369)

Proofs that Great Britain was successful against each of her numerous enemies before the late victory. 66002

Propaganda anti-esclavista. 85710, 85712

Propagateur Haiten. 29584

Propagation de la Foi. see Society for the Propagation of the Faith.

Propagation of the Faith. see Society for the Propagation of the Faith.

Propagation of the Gospel in the east. (66003)

Propagation of truth. 43275

Propemtion inaugurale quo ilustris Senatus Academicus Fautores et Civil Academici ad disputationem inauguralem. 89437

Proper and seasonable mirror for the present Americans. (72991)

Proper limits of the government's interference. 90099

Proper location for a national foundry. 25664

Proper mode of conducting missions to the heathen. 104913

Proper mode of observing a public fast. 11007

Proper objects of the present war with France and Spain considered. 66004

Proper reply to a late scurrilous libel. 66643

Proper sphere and influence of woman in Christian society. 78768

Proper supplement to the original papers relating to the expedition to Carthagena, Cuba, and Panama. 40541, 99245

Properties of plants and flowers. 45862

Propertius, Sextus Aurelius. 67730

Property Holders' Union of New Orleans. 90641

Property possessed by slaves in the Virgin Islands. 66005

Property qualification or no property qualification. 52302

Prophane schisme of the Brownists or Separatists. 72110

Prophane swearing condemn'd at the bar of reason. 24681

Prophecia do Novo-Mundo. 58588

Prophecies in verse, with notes and illustrations. 66006

Prophecies of the Reverend Christopher Love. 92714

Prophecies of Thomas the Rhymer, in verse. 95453

Prophecy: a tale of Detroit. 71041

Prophecy. A tale of the Canadas. 71041, 100881

Prophecy, a tragedy. 23908

Prophecy. An Indian tale. 71042-71044

Prophecy fulfilled. A tale of the late American war. 71036, 71039

Prophecy, lately discovered. (66007)

"Prophecy of Andree," a poem. (66008)

Prophecy of Andree: an ode written in the year 1780. 28593

Prophecy of the great rebellion. 78872

Prophecy of the Santon, and other poems. 94013

Prophecy of the scripture and truth which came to pass in the year 1851. 77223

Prophecy of the union; a narrative poem. (2392)

Prophecy, or, prophetical dissertation. (2393) (34142)

Prophecy; or, Wacousta: a romance of the Canadas. (71040)

Prophecy restored. 85540

Prophet. (54816)

Prophet! A full and accurate report. 46898

Prophet Elisha. 42538

Prophet Jeremiah's resolution to get him unto great men. 30167

Prophet Joseph Smith tells his own story. 83080

Prophet Joseph Smith's views on the powers and policy of the government of the United States. 83279

Prophet of the nineteenth century. 11478

Prophet of the Senecas. 13698

Prophet of the west. 25864

Prophet Stephen, son of Douglas. pseud. Book of the Prophet Stephen. 6362, 103445

Prophete; avenir du monde. 12264

Prophetic almanac, for 1846. (64958)

Prophetic catechism to lead to the study of the prophetic scriptures. (82540)

Prophetic conjectures on the French revolution. 101877

Prophetic controversy. 92685

Prophetic drama. 18031, 89487

Prophetic fragment of a future chronicle. 80055

Prophetic leaf. 66010

Prophetic letter. 79659

Prophetic messenger. 83735

Prophetic number of Daniel and John calculated. 13442, 86774

Prophetical dissertation. (34142)

Propheticall song of Moses. (66436), (66440)-(66441)

Prophetick discussion. 92686

Propheties sur l'Amerique. (36567)

Prophetische Muthmassungen uber die Franzoische Revolution. 101877

Prophetische Muthmassungen uber die Franzoische Staats-Veranderung. 101877

Prophets. 66001

Prophet's death lamented and improved. 14511

Prophets prophecy falsly. 31915

Propiac, Catherine Joseph Ferdinand Girard de, 1759-1822. 66012

Proportion of provisions needful for such as intend to plant themselves in New England. (66013)

Proportions of foreigners to natives. 23221

Proposal for a charter to build a railroad from Lake Michigan to the Pacific Ocean. 66014

Proposal for a national rail-road to the Pacific Ocean. 104000

Proposal for a reconciliation with the revolted colonies. 45417

Proposal for altering the eastern front of the city of Philadelphia. (4236)

Proposals for printing by subscription, a body
of sermons. 84678C

Proposals for printing by subscription, a body
of sermons, upon the most important
branches of practical Christianity.
84650, 84675A

Proposals for printing by subscription a dis-
sent from the Church of England. 99418

Proposals, for printing by subscription, a
general history of the lies. (66032)

Proposals, for printing by subscription, a
gazetteer of America. 50943

Proposals for printing by subscription a new
work for the benefit of a public institution. (32720)

Proposals for printing by subscription a poem,
on the "prospects of America." 47003,
47004

Proposals for printing by subscription, a treatise
on the diseases of Virginia and the neigh-
boring colonies. 94716

Proposals for printing by subscription the history
of Adjutant Trowel and Bluster. 102066

Proposals for printing by subscription, the
history of the public life and distinguished
actions. 3d note after 95765, 102067

Proposals for printing by subscription, the life
of the late Rev. John Wesley. 103664

Proposals for printing by subscription the
Pennsylvania mercury, and universal
advertiser. 92273

Proposals for printing by subscription, the
vision of Columbus. 100597

Proposals for promoting the same. 7473

Proposals for publishing a genealogical chart
of the descendants of the royal house of
Stuart. 85244

Proposals for publishing a genealogical chart
of the royal house of Stuart. 85246

Proposals for publishing a large and comprehensive map of the southern division of
the United States of America. 94410

Proposals . . . for publishing a new periodical
work. 103983A

Proposals for publishing a survey of the trade
of Great Britain and Ireland. (50807)

Proposals for publishing by subscription. A
complete history of Connecticut. 97190

Proposals for publishing, by subscription, a new
system of geography. 97654

Proposals for publishing by subscription the
works of George Washington. 88998

Proposals for publishing Rivington's New-York
gazetteer. (54420), 71691

Proposals for raising a new company, for carrying on the trades of Africa and the Spanish-
West-Indies. 66033, 86764A

Proposals for recovering America and saving
Great Britain. 11156

Proposals for restoring credit. 88194

Proposals for securing the friendship of the
Five Nations. 66034

Proposals for settling a colony in Florida.
66035

Proposals for steam navigation on the head
waters. 32912

Proposals for such changes as shall secure its
benefits without its evils. 68756

Proposals for the encouragement of all those
that are minded to settle there. 64857,
64858

Proposals for the establishment of a colony of
English. 5569

Proposals for the establishment of townships and
sale of lands. 8109

Proposals for the formation of a West India
Free Labor Company. (13282)

Proposals for the incouragement and promoting
of religion and learning. 66036

Proposals for the printing of a large Bible.
(66038)

Proposals for the propagation of the Christian
religion. 7472

Proposals for the propagation of the Christian
religion in the several provinces on the
continent of North America. 7479

Proposals for the publishing a digest of the
laws of Castile. 105480

Proposals for the revival of dying religion.
46482

Proposals for the preservation of religion in
the churches. 66037

Proposals for the speedy settlement of the
waste and unappropriated lands. 14410

Proposals for tobacco warehouses. 45295

Proposals for traffick and commerce, or
foreign trade in New-Jersey. 66039

Proposals for uniting the English colonies.
66040

Proposals for uniting the Virginia Foundry
Company. 96760

Proposals of Isaiah Thomas and Company.
95411

Proposals of Isaiah Thomas, Jun. 95416

Proposals of Isaiah Thomas, of Worcester.
95412

Proposals of Oliver Fairplay. 35913

Proposals of piety reasonably and seasonably
complyed with. 46424

Proposals of some things to be done. 32737

Proposals of the Maryland Institute. 45225

Proposals of the Massachusetts Hospital Life
Insurance Company. (45863)

Proposals of the Norwich Water Power Company.
55938

Proposals of the . . . [Pennsylvania] Company
. . . [for Insurances.] 60315

Proposals of the Phenix Mining Company.
61402

Proposals of the President and Managers of the
Trenton Delaware Falls Company. 96775

Proposals offered for the sugar planters redress.
(66041)

Proposals of the Trustees of Dartmouth College
to this state. 103220

Proposals relating to the education of youth
in Pennsylvania. (25575)

Proposals, reports, and documents. 33172

Proposals to all such people as are minded to
transport or concern themselves in the
island of Tobago. 64856

Proposals to amend and perfect the policy.
(66042)

Proposals to establish the American Homestead
Association. 1101A

Proposals to lawyers. 46469

Proposals to prevent scalping, &c. (66043)

Proposals, to prevent that great folly and
mischief. 46361

Proposals to such who desire to have any
property therein. 102942

Proposals to publish by subscription a selection
of the miscellaneous works of C. S.
Rafinesque. 67465

Proposals to the public, . . . to regain the important island of Minorca. 67513

Proposals touching the accomplishment of pro-
phesies humbly offered. 79447

Proposed act to consolidate the cities of Brooklyn
and Williamsburgh. 8312

Propositions made by the Five Nations of Indians. 66061

Propositions made by the Sachems of the Three Maquas Castles. 628, 66062

Propositions of Alexander Hamilton. 29974

Propositions of amendment to the constitution. 66063

Propositions presentees par Monsieur de Souza de Macedo. 88762

Propositions respectng baptism and consociation of churches. 57611, 63342

Propositions sur les preceptes d'hygiene navale. 20956

Propositions with my imperfect answers. 11120

Proposta do governo para operacoes de credito e emissao do papel-moeda. 85654

Proposta e relatorio apresentados a Assemblea Geral Legislativa. 21365

Proposta e relatorio do Ministero da Fazenda. 66064

Proprietaire d'esclaves. pseud. Abolition de l'esclavage. see Vitalis, Louis.

Proprietaire d'esclaves. pseud. Petition a MM. les membres de la Chambre des Deputes. see Vitalis, Louis. petitioner

Proprietaires de Saint-Domingue, Residans a Paris. petitioners (75037), 75176

Prop, tes privees des sujets belligerants sur mer. 30863

Proprietor. pseud. "Advertisement." 95799

Proprietor. pseud. Facts versus Lord Durham. 38750

Proprietor. pseud. Letter to the firends of Rev. F. T. Gray. see Pray, Lewis G.

Proprietor. pseud. Jamaica under the apprenticeship system. 35604

Proprietor. pseud. Observations on the system. 35642

Proprietor. pseud. Remarks upon the "Proceedings of the Trustees of the Greene Foundation." 69533

Proprietor of lands on the Scioto. pseud. Address to the inhabitants of Alexandria. 746, 66065

Proprietor of the authentic papers. pseud. Annals of administration. 1589, (26993)

Proprietor of the condensing cards. pseud. Statistics of the woollen manufactories. see Goulding, John. supposed author

Proprietor of the said company. pseud. Address to the proprietors of the South-Sea capital. 88169

Proprietor of said church. pseud. Letter to Rev. Frederick T. Gray. see Mussey, Benjamin B.

Proprietor of West-India property by inheritance. pseud. Letter to the Marquis of Chandos. 102846

Proprietors, and Owners of the Lands in the Narragansett Country, or Kings Province. petitioners see Proprietors of Lands in the Narragansett Country. petitioners

Proprietors meetings. High treason. 99096

Proprietors of Charles River Bridge. plaintiffs 6602, 12030-12031, 101499, 2d note after 101499

Proprietors of Charles River Bridge, in equity vs. the Proprietors of Warren Bridge. 12031

Proprietors of Charles-River Bridge vs. Proprietors of Warren Bridge et als. 6602

Proprietors of East New Jersey. see Board of Proprietors of the Eastern Division of New Jersey.

Proprietors of Gold and Silver Mines in Jamaica. respondents 105082

Proprietors of Huron, Mich. see Huron, Mich. Proprietors.

Proprietors of Indiana. 25595, 34579-34580, 63221, 99584, 1st note after 103107, note just before 103108

Proprietors of Lands in the Narraganset Country. petitioners 95937

Proprietors of Lands in the State of Pennsylvania. pseud. see Subscribers, Proprietors of Lands in the State of Pennsylvania. pseud.

Proprietors of Narraganset Township, No. 1, Maine. see Buxton, Me.

Proprietors of Neponset Bridge. 52336

Proprietors of Plantations in Nevis and St. Christophers. petitioners 33697, (61275)

Proprietors of Plantations in St. Christophers. petitioners see Proprietors of Plantations in Nevis and St. Christophers. petitioners

Proprietors of Plantations in the Islands of St. Nevis and St. Christophers. petitioners see Proprietors of Plantations in Nevis and St. Christophers. petitioners

Proprietors of Shares in the Gold and Silver Mines in Jamaica. respondents (11193)

Proprietors of Sundry Tracts of Land, Situate in the Province of Nova-Scotia, or Acadia. 103249

Proprietors of the Charles River Bridge, in equity vs. the Proprietors of the Warren Bridge. 101499

Proprietors of the Eastern Division of the Province of New Jersey. see Board of Proprietors of the Eastern Division of New Jersey.

Proprietors of the Kennebeck Purchase. see Plymouth Company, 1749-1816.

Proprietors of the Kennebec Purchase. A schedule of lands, &c., to be sold at auction January 22, 1816. 37386

Proprietors of the Locks and Canals on Merrimack River. (1814), 48015, 95943

Proprietors of the Locks and Canals on Merrimac River. Committee on a New Canal. 48016, 69832

Proprietors of the Locks and Canals on the said river having incorporated by the Legislature. 95943

Proprietors of the Middlesex Canal. 93536

Proprietors of the Mortgage-Lands. petitioners see Proprietors of Lands in the Narraganset Country. petitioners

Proprietors of the New Hampshire Grants. petitioners 61280, 2d note after 98997 see also New Hampshire Grants. and Vermont.

Proprietors of the New Hampshire Grants. Attorney. 61280, 2d note after 98997 see also Robinson, Samuel.

Proprietors of the New South Meeting-House in Dorchester, Mass. see Dorchester, Mass. New South Meeting-House. Proprietors.

Proprietors of the New York and Liverpool Line of American Steamers. petitioners see New York and Liverpool Line of American Steamers. Proprietors. petitioners

Proprietors of the Salem & Danvers Aqueduct. see Salem & Danvers Aqueduct.

Proprietors of the Second Turnpike Road in New-Hampshire. (52780)

Proprietors of the Society Library in Salem, Mass. see Society Library, Salem, Mass. Proprietors.

Prospectus and specimens of the new periodical publication. (66077)

Prospectus. Bibliographia Americana. 91519

Prospectus, by-laws, & charter, of the Transylvania Botanic-Garden Company. 96460

Prospectus, charter and by-laws of the Equitable Mining Company. 75347

Prospectus, charter and by-laws of the Stanton Copper Mining Company. 90448

Prospectus, charter, etc., of the Milwaukie [sic] & Superior R. R. Co. 49171

Prospectus. Compagnie de Wilmington. 104584

Prospectus de l'Academie Classique et Militaire de Mantua. 92099, 98402

Prospectus du Chemin de Fer de Montreal et Bytown. 50273

Prospectus d'un journal des revolutions de la Partie Franciase de Saint-Domingue. Exposition. 94307

Prospectus d'un journal sous le titre Mecure des Isles du Vent. 66078

Prospectus d'une maison d'education. 66079

Prospectus et reglements. 85797

Prospectus for a loan of £80,000 secured by a pledge of real estate. 66080

Prospectus for a statue to the late General Thos. J. "Stonewall" Jackson. 35470

Prospectus for printing by subscription. 21658

Prospectus for the formation of a mining company. (57371)

Prospectus for translating into English. 94947

Prospectus, geological survey and report of the Gregory Gold Mining Company. 66081

[Prospectus.] Mount Moriah Cemetery. 61848

Prospectus of a bibliographical and historical essay. 2185

Prospectus of a combined system of railways. 39012

Prospectus . . . of a . . . company, trading from Liverpool to . . . Mexico and Peru. 66073

Prospectus of a loan of £300,000 sterling. 64840

Prospectus of a national institution. 3429

Prospectus of a new and highly interesting work. 20654

Prospectus of a new and original periodical work. 104129

Prospectus of a permanent national vaccine institution. 82778

Prospectus of a plan of instruction. 32319

Prospectus of a school to be established. 14218

Prospectus of a series of lectures. 91694

Prospectus of a statistical and historical account. 101363

Prospectus of an American bibliographier's manual. 74692

Prospectus of an important work in three volumes. 28983

Prospectus [of Cooperstown Classical and Military Academy.] 16650

Prospectus of Herbert Hall, Highlands, Worcester, Mass. 75801

Prospectus of historical and geographical tracts on Louisiana. 18535

Prospectus of Joseph Emerson's Female Seminary. (22449)

Prospectus [of Lebanon Springs Railroad.] 39577

Prospectus of Messrs. Blanchard and Boker's intended aerial voyage. (65665)

Prospectus of national panzographia. 19358

Prospectus of one hundred thousand acres. 66082

Prospectus of Saint Ignatius College, S. J. San Francisco, Cal. 75236, (76087)

Prospectus of Saint Ignatius' College with a catalogue. 75236, 76086

Prospectus of St. Mary's Hall, Green Bank, Burlington, New Jersey. 20391

Prospectus of St. Timothy's Hall, Baltimore, Md. 75501

Prospectus of San Antonio Silver Mining Company. 75994

Prospectus of Santa Clara College. 76750

Prospectus of the American Classical and Military Academy at Mount Airy, near Germantown. 27161

Prospectus of the American Literary, Scientific and Military Academy, to be opened at Middletown, Ct. 48870

Prospectus of the American Literary, Scientifick, and Military Academy, Norwich, Vt. note after (58963)

Prospectus of the American Society for the Diffusion of Useful Knowledge. 66083

Prospectus of the Astor Mining Company. 2256

Prospectus of the Atlantic and Pacific Gold & Silver Mining Co. 66084

Prospectus of the Atlantic Dock Company. (8314)

Prospectus of the Atrato and San Juan Canal and Transportation Co. (2319)

Prospectus of the Atrato River Mining and Trading Company. (2320)

Prospectus [of the British and North American Mining Association.] 8087

Prospectus of the Building Society of the District of Dalhousie. 66085

Prospectus of the Cairo City and Canal Company. 9862

Prospectus [of the California and New York Steamship Company.] 9965

Prospectus of the Canada Landed Credit Company. 10556

Prospectus of the Canton Company. (10717)

Prospectus of the Chestatee Hydraulic Company. 5805, 12526

Prospectus of the collections of the Massachusetts Historical Society. (45858)

Prospectus of the Collegiate Institute, Louisville, Ky. 42340

Prospectus of the colonization of the county of Beauharnois. 66086

Prospectus of the Columbia Gold-Mining Company. (14846)

Prospectus of the Commercial Academy. (25200)

Prospectus of the course of instruction. 45831

Prospectus of the Dorchester Mining Company. (20628)

Prospectus of the Emporium of Arts and Sciences. 17285

Prospectus of the Episcopal School of North-Carolina. 55669

Prospectus of the European and North American Railway Company. 66087

Prospectus of the Farist Community. 23809

Prospectus of the Grahame Crystallized Rock Oil Company. 66088

Prospectus [of the Hartford Female Seminary.] (30661)

Prospectus of the Harvard Silver Mining Association. 30766

Prospectus of the Householders' Mutual Insurance Company. 54318

Prospectus of the Indian Creek and Jack's Knob Coal, Salt, Lead, Lumber, Oil and Manufacturing Company. (34463)

Prospectus of the Inexhaustible Petroleum Co., of New York. 66089

Prospectus of the Kip & Buell Gold Co. Colorado. 37951

Prospectus of the Lawrence Water-Cure. 7444

Prospectus of the Lexington Manual Labor Seminary. 40889

Prospectus of the Lyceum at Mount Airy. 27161

Prospectus of the Missouri Iron Company and Missouri and Iron Mountain cities. 49618

Prospectus of the Mutual Benefit Life Insurance Company. 51607

Prospectus of the Neff Petroleum Company. 52243

Prospectus of the Nekossa Lumbering Company. (52300)

Prospectus of the New York and African Exchange Company. 54722

Porspectus of the New-York Life Insurance and Trust Company. 54793

Prospectus of the North-Martinsburg Lead-Mining Company. (55719)

Prospectus of the Oakland Coal and Iron Co. 56391

Prospectus of the Ohio Petroleum Company. (56992)

Prospectus of the Oil Creek and Allegany Oil Co. (57073)

Prospectus of the Philadelphia Ocean Steamship Company. (62022)

Prospectus of the Philadelphia School of Design for Women. 62032

Prospectus of the plan and principles of a society. 85869

Prospectus of the Preparatory School. 9337

Prospectus of the proposed loan of the state of Indiana. 34561

Prospectus of the Quipola. 92882, 95532

Prospectus of the Rio de la Plata Agricultural Association. 39001

Prospectus of the Rock-Island Medical School. 72394

Prospectus of the Rossie Lead Mining & Smelting Company. 73422

Prospectus [of the Round Hill School, Northampton, Mass.] 55772

Prospectus of the St. Louis Bridge. 75364

Prospectus of the St. Mary's Copper Mining Company. 75426

Prospectus of the Samana Bay, San Domingo and Hayti Steamship Company. 75883

Prospectus of the Snow Fork Valley Railroad Company. 85573

Prospectus of the Society for the Extinction of the Slave Trade. 82040

[Prospectus of the South American and Colonial Gas Company.] 87320

[Prospectus of the South American Gem Company.] 97321

Prospectus of the South Baltimore Company. 3061, 87331

Prospectus of the Southern Academy. 88271

Prospectus of the Southern Gold Company. 88362

Prospectus of the Southern Minnesota Railroad, map and statistics. 88410

Prospectus of the spiritual telegraph. 89531

Prospectus of the Union Insurance Company. 97805

Prospectus of the University of South Carolina. 88098

Prospectus of the West Virginia Iron Mining and Manufacturing Company. 102948

Prospectus of two periodical works. (67448)

Prospectus of Walnut Grove School. 101141

Prospectus pour l'etablissement sur les Rivieres d'Ohio et de Scioto. (66090)

Prospectus pour placer a la tete de l'ouvrage 63911

Prospectus, rules, regulations, &c. of the San Francisco College. 76090

Prospectus. Southern Minnesota Rail Road Co 88409

Prospectus to the first volume of Gould's Stenographic reporter. 91226

Prospectus, with charter, land grants, maps, statistics, etc. 88411

Prosper, Tiro, Aquitanus, Saint. 23114

Prosperidades de la union y desastres del vico opuesto. 26577

Prosperity: its influence on man. 90430A

Prosperity of a church. 79793

Prosperity of the soul proposed and promoted 46570, note after 98363

Prosperous voyage of Mr. Thomas Candis. 20829, 105624

Prosser, E. S. (66091)

Prosser, William F. 66092

Prostitution in London. (74531)

Prostrate state. 62820

Proteaux, A. 66093

Protected copyright with free-trade competitic 83877-83878

Protecting Society, for New Bedford. 52475

Protecting system. 10889

Protection a boon to consumers. 31026

Protection and free trade compared. 33359

Protection and free trade. From the North American review. 66094

Protection and free trade. The question state and considered. 28492

Protection and freedom in Arizona. 2191

Protection in the family, in society, and in th state. 33271

"Protection," not "British free trade." 91008

Protection of home labor and home products necessary. 2782

Protection of life at the south. 64024

Protection of life, etc., at the south. 64024

Protection of majorities. 67273

Protection of our industry. 91015

Protection ou liberte: que veulent les colonie 64848

Protection tariff or free trade. 50791

Protection to American industry. 85868

Protection vs. free trade. Address . . . befo the Legislature of Michigan. 24287

Protection vs. free trade: or the practical development of our own resources. 660

Protection vs. free trade. Letters to Americ voters. 106060

Protectionist. 66096

Protective policy and the warehousing system 50780

Protective policy in literature. 14202

Protective question abroad. 31026

Protective system considered. 9305

Protective tariff, a benefit to the laboring ma 91004

Protective tariff. Necessary rights of labor. 10224

Protective tariff. Speech . . . February 24, 1859. (28280)

Protective War Claim and Pension Agency, Philadelphia. see United States Sanitar Commission. Protective War Claim and Pension Agency, Philadelphia.

Protective War Claim Association of the State of New-York. (66098)

Protector. 66099

Protector. A journal for the people. 66100
Protector del estado religioso. 72518
Protector nominal de los pueblos libres. 9030
Protectorado de Espana. 66101
Protest against American slavery. 81836
Protest against closing the River Schuylkill at South Street. 62100
Protest against expunging. 102302
Protest against political preaching. 23317
Protest against popery, &c. (36512)
Protest against proceedings of the First Church in Worcester. 2425
Protest against the aggressions of slavery. 67880
Protest against the appointment of Mr. Franklin. 25576-25577, (59888), 84586
Protest against the bill to repeal the American stamp act. 66103, 78739
Protest against the consecration of the Rev. Dr. Hawks. 66972
Protest against the convention of April 11, 1839. 75830
Protest against the exclusion of their delegates. 29890, 91524
Protest against the illegal election held in Trinity Church. (66104)
Protest against the installation of Rev. Charles Packard. 66105
Protest against the nomination of candidates for President and Vice-President. 23497
Protest against the present action of Fairfield West Association. (66106)
Protest against the proceedings of the Philadelphia Baptist Association. (32464)
Protest against the proposed repeal of the neutrality laws. 4626
Protest, against the result of an ecclesiastical council. 7664, 32317
Protest against the same, by a member of the said Council. 21967, 55771
Protest against the war. 58605
Protest and appeal of Bishop Doane. 20395
Protest and appeal of George Washington Doane. 20391
Protest and argument against a subscription. (67512)
Protest and argument against a subscription on the part of the state. 45296
Protest and declaration of the state of Rhode Island and Providence Plantations. 70621
Protest, and draft of a pastoral letter. 32929
Protest in Council. 84558
Protest of Deacons Wood, Kingsley and Johnson. 66107
Protest of General Jesus Gonzales Ortega. 57679
Protest, &c. [of John Champneys.] 11849
P rotests of Hart B. Holton. 32659
Protest of R. M. Whitney. 103779
Protest of some free men. 95069
Protest of southern senators against the passage of the California bill. 66108
Protest of the American A. S. Society. 14400
Protest of the American Anti Slavery Society. 5580
Protest of the American minister. 104130
Protest of the Bishop and Clergy of the Diocese of Pennsylvania. (32928)
Protest of the Cherokee Delegation laid before the Senate. 73391
Protest of the Columbia Typographical Society. 28516, 1st-2d notes after 101931, note after 101967
Protest [of the Deacons of the Church of the Puritans.] 54184
Protest of the friends of George Clinton. 13746

Protest of the General Assembly against the illegal arrest and imprisonment. 45297
Protest of the Humboldt Savings and Loan Society. 34912, 76050
Protest of the laity of Trinity Church. 6680
Protest of the Legislature of Rhode Island. 70622-70623
Protest of the Master against the seizure of the steamship "Star of the West." 66109
Protest of the minority [of the Ecclesiastical Council at Princeton, Mass., 1817.] 27695, 70109
Protest of the minority of the House of Representatives. 52949
Protest of the minority of the House of Representatives against the bill for dividing the state. 45954
Protest of the minority of the members of the Legislature of Rhode Island. 70622-70623
Protest of the minority of the Senate of Massachusetts. 45955
Protest of the Philadelphia clergy. 39789
Protest of the Philadelphia Home Missionary Society. 62003
Protest of the President of the United States. (35356)
Protest of the state of Louisiana to the Senate. 42285
Protest. Ofte scherp dreyghement. 66102
Protest or remonstrance of M. Field Fowler. 25312
Protest presented to the House of Assembly. 84586
Protesta. 85666
Protesta a favor de Sv Magestad. 105732
Protesta de Jose Urrea. 98153
Protesta de la Compania de Diligencias. 74745
Protesta de los Disputados de la Junta Preparatoria. 66111
Protesta del General Jose Maria Tornel y Mendivil. 96207
Protesta del General Pedro Alcantara Herran. 31536
Protesta del Ilmo Senor Arzobispo de Cesarea y Vicario Capitular. 66112
Protesta del Obispo de San Luis Potosi. 76150
Protesta del Presidente y Cabildo de la Iglesia Catedral de la Puebla. 66113
Protesta hecha por el Obispo de Michoacan. 59633
Protesta que en acuerdo pleno y con asociacion de los empleados publicos. 66114
Protesta que hizo contra varios articulos. 39282
Protestacion de quelques dissidents et repons du Citoyen Gabet. 9788
Protestant. pseud. Protestant Jesuitism. see Colton, Calvin.
Protestant. pseud. Protestant's resolution. 66212
Protestant. pseud. Sons of St. Dominick. 87004
Protestant. pseud. Statistics of the common schools. 90823
Protestant. Editor. pseud. see Editor of the Protestant. pseud.
Protestant and a native Philadelphia. pseud. Truth unveiled. 62346, note after 97268
Protestant armed from the tower of David. 46332, 46589
Protestant Association of Great Britain. 91598
Protestant Association of Rhode Island. see Rhode Island Protestant Association.
Protestant Christianity contrasted with Romanism. 77736

Protestant churchman. 4973, 82920, 82947, 83526, 2d note after 96984

Protestant dissenter of Old England. pseud. Claims of the Church of England seriously examined. (47141)

Protestant Episcopal Adult School Society, Philadelphia. see Protestant Episcopal Sunday and Adult School Society, Philadelphia.

Protestant Episcopal almanac for . . . 1854. 66187

Protestant Episcopal Association for the Promotion of Christianity Among the News. (66186)

Protestant Episcopal Book Society, Philadelphia. 86305

Protestant Episcopal Charity Foundation, Buffalo, N. Y. 9063

Protestant Episcopal Church, Southborough, Mass. see Southborough, Mass. Protestant Episcopal Church.

Protestant Episcopal church almanac for 1869. 66188

Protestant Episcopal Church Association of . . . New-York. (54611)

Protestant Episcopal Church catechism. 66190

Protestant Episcopal Church in the C. S. A. 15262, (57487)

Protestant Episcopal Church in the C. S. A. Book of Common Prayer. 6354-6355

Protestant Episcopal Church in the C. S. A. General Council, Augusta, Ga., 1862. 15277, 59016

Protestant Episcopal Church in the C. S. A. House of Bishops. 59016

Protestant, Episcopal Church in the U. S. A. 12891, (15009), (18299), 23413, 37199, 45299, 45301, 56627, 56752, 61054, 66121, 66128, (66131), 66134-66135, 66137, 66140, 66171, (66173)-66174, 66179-66180, 66187-66188, 66197, (66462), 72118, 75861, 79325, 84358-84362, 84365, 84694-84695, 91333, 100511A, note after 103462, 103463

Protestant Episcopal Church in the U. S. A. Bishops. see Protestant Episcopal Church in the U. S. A. House of Bishops.

Protestant Episcopal Church in the U. S. A. Board of Missions. 66132, (66141), 66240, 89482 see also Protestant Episcopal Church in the U. S. A. Domestic and Foreign Missionary Society.

Protestant Episcopal Church in the U. S. A. Board of Missions. Committee. (66127)

Protestant Episcopal Church in the U. S. A. Board of Missions. Domestic Committee. 6353, 66123, 66142-66143

Protestant Episcopal Church in the U. S. A. Board of Missions. Domestic Committee. Secretary and General Agent. (30491) see also Harris, N. S.

Protestant Episcopal Church in the U. S. A. Board of Missions. Foreign Committee. (66127)

Protestant Episcopal Church in the U. S. A. Board of Missions. Freedman's Commission. see Protestant Episcopal Freedman's Commission.

Protestant Episcopal Church in the U. S. A. Book of Common Prayer. 6349-6350, 6353, 9349, (15009), 18885, (41553), 49838, 57093, 57882, 65000, 69364, 83518, 84678C, 86305

Protestant Episcopal Church in the U. S. A. Canons. 20146, 32402, 32404

Protestant Episcopal Church in the U. S. A. Catechism. 66130, 66190, (80663)

Protestant Episcopal Church in the U. S. A. Church Congress, 1874. 66126

Protestant Episcopal Church in the U. S. A. Church Scholarship Society. (15815), 66125, 101999

Protestant Episcopal Church in the U. S. A. Clergy. 66197

Protestant Episcopal Church in the U. S. A. Commission. 47700, 70086

Protestant Episcopal Church in the U. S. A. Committee Appointed to Consider the Sentence Upon the Right Reverend Benjamin T. Onderdonk. 57309

Protestant Episcopal Church in the U. S. A. Committee on the Question of the Episcopate in Maryland. see Protestant Episcopal Church in the U. S. A. Maryland (Diocese) Committee on the Question of the Episcopate in Maryland.

Protestant Episcopal Church in the U. S. A. Committee on the State of the Church. Chairman. 45481 see also Mason, R. S.

Protestant Episcopal Church in the U. S. A. Committee to Digest the Canons. 66205

Protestant Episcopal Church in the U. S. A. Constitution. 20146

Protestant Episcopal Church in the U. S. A. Convention for Forming an American Constitution, 1786. see Protestant Episcopal Church in the U. S. A. General Convention, 1786.

Protestant Episcopal Church in the U. S. A. Convention of Delegates from the Dioceses of Mississippi and Alabama, and the Clergy and Churches of Louisiana, New Orleans, 1835. 99819

Protestant Episcopal Church in the U. S. A. Convention of the Mutual Benefit Societies or Brotherhoods, New York, 1853. see Convention of the Mutual Benefit Societies or Brotherhoods of the Protestant Episcopal Church in the United States, New York, 1853.

Protestant Episcopal Church in the U. S. A. Convention of the Trustees of a Proposed University for the Southern States, Atlanta, 1857. see Convention of the Trustees of a Proposed University for the Southern States, Under the Auspices of the Protestant Episcopal Church, Atlanta, 1857.

Protestant Episcopal Church in the U. S. A. Convention to Form a Liturgy, 1789. se Protestant Episcopal Church in the U. S. A. General Convention, 1789.

Protestant Episcopal Church in the U. S. A. Domestic and Foreign Missionary Society 49476, (66141) 66178, 66184 see also Protestant Episcopal Church in the U. S. A. Board of Missions.

Protestant Episcopal Church in the U. S. A. Domestic and Foreign Missionary Society Board of Missions. see Protestant Episcopal Church in the U. S. A. Board of Missions.

Protestant Episcopal Church in the U. S. A. Domestic and Foreign Missionary Society Secretary. ed. 66184

Protestant Episcopal Church in the U. S. A. Evangelical Educational Society. see Evangelical Educational Society of the Protestant Episcopal Church.

Protestant Episcopal Church in the U. S. A.
Freedman's Commission. see Protestant Episcopal Freedman's Commission.

Protestant Episcopal Church in the U. S. A.
General Convention. 61052, 66171-
(66173), 103461, note after 103462

Protestant Episcopal Church in the U. S. A.
General Convention, 1785. (60438),
66157, 84678C

Protestant Episcopal Church in the U. S. A.
General Convention, 1786. 3721, 66157

Protestant Episcopal Church in the U. S. A.
General Convention, 1789. 38183, 66157-
66158, 84675A, 85678C

Protestant Episcopal Church in the U. S. A.
General Convention, 1804. 84693

Protestant Episcopal Church in the U. S. A.
General Convention, 1808. (59025)

Protestant Episcopal Church in the U. S. A.
General Convention, 1811. 59013, note
after 103465

Protestant Episcopal Church in the U. S. A.
General Convention, 1814. (60438)

Protestant Episcopal Church in the U. S. A.
General Convention, 1820. 59024

Protestant Episcopal Church in the U. S. A.
General Convention, 1826. Joint Committee of the House of Bishops, and of
the House of Clerical and Lay Deputies,
on the General Theological Seminary.
26910

Protestant Episcopal Church in the U. S. A.
General Convention, 1831. Committee to
Revise the Canons. 66208

Protestant Episcopal Church in the U. S. A.
General Convention, 1859. 66140

Protestant Episcopal Church in the U. S. A.
General Convention, 1859. Lay Committee.
66119

Protestant Episcopal Church in the U. S. A.
General Convention, 1862. 66140

Protestant Episcopal Church in the U. S. A.
General Convention, 1865. 66137, 66140,
69942, 88394

Protestant Episcopal Church in the U. S. A.
General Convention, 1865. House of
Clerical and Lay Deputies. 66156

Protestant Episcopal Church in the U. S. A.
General Convention, 1865. House of
Clerical and Lay Deputies. Standing
Committee on Christian Education. 66151

Protestant Episcopal Church in the U. S. A.
General Convention, 1868. (66131), 66138

Protestant Episcopal Church in the U. S. A.
General Convention, 1871. Joint Committee on Theological Education. (66120)

Protestant Episcopal Church in the U. S. A.
General Convention of the Brotherhood.
see General Convention of the Brotherhood of the Protestant Episcopal Church.

Protestant Episcopal Church in the U. S. A.
General Theological Seminary, New York.
see New York (City) General Theological Seminary of the Protestant Episcopal
Church in the U. S.

Protestant Episcopal Church in the U. S. A.
Historical Society. see Protestant
Episcopal Historical Society.

Protestant Episcopal Church in the U. S. A.
Historiographer. 61054, (66173) see also
Perry, William Stevens.

Protestant Episcopal Church in the U. S. A.
House of Bishops. 43323, 57318, 59013,
59022-59023, 59024-(59025), 66171, 66182-
66183, 79325, 93704, note after 103462,
note after 103465

Protestant Episcopal Church in the U. S. A.
House of Bishops. Court for the Trial
of Benjamin T. Onderdonk, 1844-1845.
57309, 100681

Protestant Episcopal Church in the U. S. A.
House of Bishops. Court for the Trial
of Benjamin T. Onderdonk, 1844-1845.
Minority. 57309

Protestant Episcopal Church in the U. S. A.
House of Bishops. Court for the Trial
of George Washington Doane, Burlington,
N. J., 1852. (20385), 20394, 47243

Protestant Episcopal Church in the U. S. A.
Ladies' Domestic Missionary Relief
Association. 66175

Protestant Episcopal Church in the U. S. A.
Members. pseud. see Members of the
Protestant Episcopal Church. pseud.

Protestant Episcopal Church in the U. S. A.
Philadelphia Academy. see Academy
of the Protestant Episcopal Church,
Philadelphia.

Protestant Episcopal Church in the U. S. A.
Divinity School, Philadelphia. 83571

Protestant Episcopal Church in the U. S. A.
Presiding Bishop. 57318

Protestant Episcopal Church in the U. S. A.
Society for Educating Pious Young Men
for the Ministry. see Society for Educating Pious Young Men for the Ministry
of the Protestant Episcopal Church.

Protestant Episcopal Church in the U. S. A.
Society for Promoting Religion and
Learning in the State of New York. see
Protestant Episcopal Society for Pro-
moting Religion and Learning in the
State of New York.

Protestant Episcopal Church in the U. S. A.
Society for the Education of Pious Young
Men for the Ministry. see Society for
the Education of Pious Young Men for
the Ministry of the Protestant Episcopal
Church.

Protestant Episcopal Church in the U. S. A.
Society for the Promotion of Evangelical
Knowledge. see Protestant Episcopal
Society for the Promotion of Evangelical
Knowledge.

Protestant Episcopal Church in the U. S. A.
Special Committee of Nine on the Con-
dition of Our Church as Affected by the
Condition of Our Country. (69906)ᶜ

Protestant Episcopal Church in the U. S. A.
Sunday Presbyters. petitioners 23458,
51252, 66167 see also Muhlenberg,
William Augustus, 1796-1777. petitioner

Protestant Episcopal Church in the U. S. A.
Synod, 1844. 66148

Protestant Episcopal Church in the U. S. A.
Theological Education Society in the
State of New York. see Protestant
Episcopal Theological Education Society
in the State of New York.

Protestant Episcopal Church in the U. S. A.
Theological Seminary, Hartford, Conn.
see Theological Seminary of the Protestant Episcopal Church in the United
States, Hartford, Conn.

Protestant Episcopal Church in the U. S. A.
Alabama (Diocese) 66160 see also
Protestant Episcopal Church in the
U. S. A. Convention of Delegates from
the Diocese of Mississippi and Alabama,
and the Clergy and Churches of Louisiana, New Orleans, 1835.

Protestant Episcopal Church in the U. S. A.
Albany (Diocese) (53877)

Protestant Episcopal Church in the U. S. A.
California (Diocese) 10014, (66161)

Protestant Episcopal Church in the U. S. A.
Central New York (Diocese) 53875

Protestant Episcopal Church in the U. S. A.
Chicago (Diocese) 66165

Protestant Episcopal Church in the U. S. A.
Connecticut (Diocese) (15009), (15815),
30973, 66162, 75861, 78555-78556, 84693,
101999

Protestant Episcopal Church in the U. S. A.
Connecticut (Diocese) Clergy. (15654),
39529, 35801, 78555-78556

Protestant Epsicopal Church in the U. S. A.
Connecticut (Diocese) Convocation. Committee. 13028

Protestant Episcopal Church in the U. S. A.
Connecticut (Diocese) Theological Semi-
nary. see Theological Seminary of the
Protestant Episcopal Church in the United
States, Hartford, Conn.

Protestant Episcopal Church in the U. S. A.
Eastern Diocese. 20207, (28881), 66136,
66163

Protestant Episcopal Church in the U. S. A.
Georgia (Diocese) 66164

Protestant Episcopal Church in the U. S. A.
Illinois (Diocese) see Protestant Epis-
copal Church in the U. S. A. Chicago
(Diocese)

Protestant Episcopal Church in the U. S. A.
Indiana (Diocese) 34499, 66166

Protestant Episcopal Church in the U. S. A.
Kansas (Diocese) (37079), 66167

Protestant Episcopal Church in the U. S. A.
Kentucky (Diocese) 37569

Protestant Episcopal Church in the U. S. A.
Kentucky (Diocese) Theological Seminary,
Lexington. see Theological Seminary of
the Protestant Episcopal Church in Kentucky, Lexington.

Protestant Episcopal Church in the U. S. A.
Long Island (Diocese) 41892, 66168

Protestant Episcopal Church in the U. S. A.
Louisiana (Diocese) 99819 see also
Protestant Episcopal Church in the U. S. A.
Convention of Delegates from the Diocese
of Mississippi and Alabama, and the
Clergy and Churches of Louisiana, New
Orleans, 1835.

Protestant Episcopal Church in the U. S. A.
Maine (Diocese) 44005

Protestant Episcopal Church in the U. S. A.
Maryland (Diocese) 26743, 45127, 45180,
45299, (45302), 45304, (45306)-(45307),
84582

Protestant Episcopal Church in the U. S. A.
Maryland (Diocese) Clergy. petitioners
22337

Protestant Episcopal Church in the U. S. A.
Maryland (Diocese) Committee on the
Proposed Division of the Diocese. 45308

Protestant Episcopal Church in the U. S. A.
Maryland (Diocese) Committee on the
Question of the Episcopate in Maryland.
45309

Protestant Episcopal Church in the U. S. A.
Maryland (Diocese) Corporation for the
Relief of Widows and Children of the
Clergy. see Corporation for the Relief
of the Widows and Children of the Clergy
of the Protestant Episcopal Church in
Maryland.

Protestant Episcopal Church in the U. S. A.
Maryland (Diocese) Free Church Association. (45303)

Protestant Episcopal Church in the U. S. A.
Maryland (Diocese) Prayer Book and
Homily Society. 45305

Protestant Episcopal Church in the U. S. A.
Maryland (Diocese) Theological Seminary
see Protestant Episcopal Theological
Seminary of Maryland.

Protestant Episcopal Church in the U. S. A.
Massachusetts (Diocese) 45956-(45957),
65252, 66134, 66169

Protestant Episcopal Church in the U. S. A.
Massachusetts (Diocese) Board of Missions. 45677

Protestant Episcopal Church in the U. S. A.
Massachusetts (Diocese) Church Union.
2567

Protestant Episcopal Church in the U. S. A. Mas
chusetts (Diocese) Missionary Society. se
Massachusetts Episcopal Missionary Socie

Protestant Episcopal Church in the U. S. A.
Massachusetts (Diocese) Society for the
Religious Instruction of Freedmen. see
Massachusetts Episcopal Society for the
Religious Instruction of Freedmen.

Protestant Episcopal Church in the U. S. A.
Michigan (Diocese) 48779, 66170

Protestant Episcopal Church in the U. S. A.
Minnesota (Diocese) 49259

Protestant Episcopal Church in the U. S. A.
Mississippi (Diocese) 99819 see also
Protestant Episcopal Church in the
U. S. A. Convention of Delegates from
the Diocese of Mississippi and Alabama,
and the Clergy and Churches of Louisiana, New Orleans, 1835.

Protestant Episcopal Church in the U. S. A.
New England (Diocese) 52631

Protestant Episcopal Church in the U. S. A.
New Hampshire (Diocese) 52842

Protestant Episcopal Church in the U. S. A.
New Jersey (Diocese) (20385), 47243,
53110, 53198, 53208, 66185, 88253

Protestant Episcopal Church in the U. S. A.
New Jersey (Diocese) Committee. 4724?

Protestant Episcopal Church in the U. S. A.
New York (Diocese) 30972, 35837,
53673, (53874), 53876, 53878, (53880),
53881, 57309, 70085, 85946, 5th note
after 96966, 97630

Protestant Episcopal Church in the U. S. A.
New York (Diocese) Board of Clergy
Canonically Constituted for Trying the
Truth of Certain Charges Against the
Rev. John Ireland, of Brooklyn, 1810.
35054, 35055

Protestant Episcopal Church in the U. S. A.
New York (Diocese) Clerical Association
of the City of New York. see Protestant Episcopal Clerical Association of the
City of New York.

Protestant Episcopal Church in the U. S. A.
New York (Diocese) Corporation for the
Relief of Widows and Children of Clergy
men of the Protestant Episcopal Church
in . . . New York. see Corporation
for the Relief of Widows and Children
of Clergymen of the Protestant Episcopa
Church in . . . New York.

Protestant Episcopal Church in the U. S. A.
New York (Diocese) Corporation of the
New-York Protestant Episcopal Public
School. see Corporation of the New-
York Protestant Episcopal Public School.

Protestant Episcopal Church in the U. S. A.
New York (Diocese) Education and Missionary Society. see Education and Missionary Society of the Protestant Episcopal Church in the State of New York.

Protestant Episcopal Church in the U. S. A.
New York (Diocese) Lay Delegates from St. Peter's Church, Albany. see Albany. St. Peter's Church. Vestry. Lay Delegates to the Diocesan Convention, 1845. and Spencer, John Canfield.

Protestant Episcopal Church in the U. S. A.
New York (Diocese) Meeting of Episcopalians in the City of New York, 1812. see Meeting of Episcopalians in the City of New York, 1812.

Protestant Episcopal Church in the U. S. A.
New York (Diocese) Meeting of Episcopalians, New York, 1857. see New York (City) Meetings of Episcopalians, 1857.

Protestant Episcopal Church in the U. S. A.
New York (Diocese) Pastoral Aid Society. 53855, 66181

Protestant Episcopal Church in the U. S. A.
New York (Diocese) Press. see New York Protestant Episcopal Press.

Protestant Episcopal Church in the U. S. A.
New York (Diocese) Society for Promoting Religion and Learning. see Protestant Episcopal Society for Promoting Religion and Learning.

Protestant Episcopal Church in the U. S. A.
New York (Diocese) Society for the Promotion of Evangelical Knowledge. see Protestant Episcopal Society for the Promotion of Evangelical Knowledge, New York.

Protestant Episcopal Church in the U. S. A.
New York (Diocese) Standing Committee. 52516, 75464

Protestant Episcopal Church in the U. S. A.
New York (Diocese) Trustees of the Parochial Fund. (66207)

Protestant Episcopal Church in the U. S. A.
Ohio (Diocese) (56878), 56939, 57056, 102739

Protestant Episcopal Church in the U. S. A.
Ohio (Diocese) Agent. 102729 see also West, George Montgomery.

Protestant Episcopal Church in the U. S. A.
Pennsylvania (Diocese) (32928), 59901, (60438), 62101

Protestant Episcopal Church in the U. S. A.
Pennsylvania (Diocese) Board of Missions. (59921)

Protestant Episcopal Church in the U. S. A.
Pennsylvania (Diocese) Committee of Seven. (60438)

Protestant Episcopal Church in the U. S. A.
Pennsylvania (Diocese) Convocational Congress, Reading, 1867. 65838

Protestant Episcopal Church in the U. S. A.
Pennsylvania (Diocese) Corporation for the Relief of Widows and Children of Clergymen. see Corporation for the Relief of Widows and Children of Clergymen, of the Protestant Episcopal Church in Pennsylvania.

Protestant Episcopal Church in the U. S. A.
Pennsylvania (Diocese) Missionary Society. see Protestant Episcopal Missionary Society in Pennsylvania.

Protestant Episcopal Church in the U. S. A.
Pennsylvania (Diocese) Society for the Advancement of Christianity. see Society for the Advancement of Christianity.

Protestant Episcopal Church in the U. S. A.
Pennsylvania (Diocese) Sunday-School Society. see Protestant Episcopal Sunday-School Society of Pennsylvania.

Protestant Episcopal Church in the U. S. A.
Rhode Island (Diocese) 13385, 70624-70625

Protestant Episcopal Church in the U. S. A.
South Carolina (Diocese) (18299), 87928-87931, 90670

Protestant Episcopal Church in the U. S. A.
South Carolina (Diocese) Society for the Relief of the Widows and Orphans of the Clergy in the Diocese. see Society for the Relief of the Widows and Orphans of the Clergy of the Protestant Episcopal Church in South Carolina.

Protestant Episcopal Church in the U. S. A.
Tennessee (Diocese) 94804

Protestant Episcopal Church in the U. S. A.
Texas (Diocese) 24234, 28703

Protestant Episcopal Church in the U. S. A.
Vermont (Diocese) 99201-99204

Protestant Episcopal Church in the U. S. A.
Vermont (Diocese) Agent. 28230, 1st note after 99204 see also Graham, John A.

Protestant Episcopal Church in the U. S. A.
Virginia (Diocese) 30963, 30967, 1st note after 100494, 100511-100514

Protestant Episcopal Church in the U. S. A.
Virginia (Diocese) Society for the Relief of the Widows and Orphans of Deceased Clergymen. see Society for the Relief of the Widows and Orphans of Deceased Clergymen in the Diocese of Virginia.

Protestant Episcopal Church in the U. S. A.
Virginia (Diocese) Theological School. see Alexandria, Va. Protestant Episcopal Theological Seminary in Virginia.

Protestant Episcopal Church in the U. S. A.
Western New York (Diocese) (53879)

Protestant Episcopal Church in the U. S. A.
Western New York (Diocese) Society for Promoting Christian Knowledge. see Protestant Episcopal Society for Promoting Christian Knowledge in the Western District of the State of New York.

Protestant Episcopal Church in the U. S. A.
Western New York (Diocese) Society for the Promotion of Evangelical Knowledge. see Protestant Episcopal Society in Western New York for the Promotion of Evangelical Knowledge.

Protestant Episcopal Church Hospital, Philadelphia. see Philadelphia. Hospital of the Protestant Episcopal Church.

Protestant Episcopal Church Missionary Society for Seamen, New York. 54525

Protestant Episcopal Church Missionary Society for Seamen, New York. Board of Managers. 66191

Protestant Episcopal Church of the Evangelists, Southwark, Pa. see Southwark, Pa. Protestant Episcopal Church of the Evangelists.

Protestant Episcopal Church of the United Brethren. see United Brethren.

Protestant Episcopal Church Reading Room, Boston. see Boston. Church Reading Room.

Protestant Episcopal Church Scholarship Society. see Protestant Episcopal Church in the U. S. A. Church Scholarship Society.

Protestant Episcopal Church Union, Boston. 66133

Protestant Episcopal Church. What she has, what she lacks, and what her position with reference to other churches. 66189

Protestant Episcopal City Mission Society, New York. see New York Protestant Episcopal City Mission Society.

Protestant Episcopal Clerical Association of the City of New York. 7883, 13642, (32305), (54611), 66116, note after 97492, 99815

Protestant Episcopal Divinity School, Philadelphia. see Protestant Episcopal Church in the U. S. A. Divinity School, Philadelphia.

Protestant Episcopal Education Society of Pennsylvania. see Episcopal Education Society of Pennsylvania.

Protestant-Episcopal Freedman's Commission. (66150), 66192

Protestant Episcopal Freedman's Commission. Occasional paper. 66192

Protestant Episcopal Historical Society. 3720, 66193, 66194, 66195

Protestant Episcopal Historical Society. Executive Committee. 66193, 66195

Protestant Episcopal Historical Society. [Proceedings at a meeting.] 66195

Protestant Episcopal Mission Church of the Evangelists, Southwark, Pa. see Southwark, Pa. Protestant Episcopal Church of the Evangelists.

Protestant Episcopal Mission House, Philadelphia. see Philadelphia. Mission House of the Protestant Episcopal Church.

Protestant Episcopal Mission to Seamen, New York. 54260

Protestant Episcopal Missionary Association for the West. 22688, 66196

Protestant Episcopal Missionary Association for the West. Board of Managers. 22688, 66147

Protestant Episcopal Missionary Society, Charleston, S. C. 12092

Protestant Episcopal Missionary Society, New York. see New York Protestant Episcopal Missionary Society.

Protestant Episcopal Missionary Society of Pennsylvania. 60068

Protestant Episcopal Missionary Society of Pennsylvania. Charter. 60068

Protestant Episcopal Missionary Society of Pennsylvania. Committees. 60068

Protestant Episcopal Missionary Society of Pennsylvania. Committee on a General Missionary Soviety for Foreign and Domestic Missions. 60439

Protestant Episcopal Orphan Asylum of the City of Louisville, Ky. 42341

Protestant Episcopal Orphan Asylum of the City of Louisville, Ky. Board of Managers. 42341

Protestant Episcopal Orphan's Home, New York. see New York (City) Orphan's Home of the Protestant Episcopal Church in New York.

Protestant Episcopal Press, New York. see New York Protestant Episcopal Press.

Protestant Episcopal pulpit. 66197

Protestant Episcopal quarterly review, and church register. 66198

Protestant Episcopal School, New York. see New York (City) Trinity School.

Protestant Episcopal Society for Promoting Christian Knowledge in the Western District of the State of New York. 66200

Protestant Episcopal Society for Promoting Religion and Learning in the State of New York. 53882-53883, (66124), 85857

Protestant Episcopal Society for Promoting Religion and Learning in the State of New York. Board of Trustees. 85857

Protestant Episcopal Society for Promoting Religion and Learning in the State of New York. Charter. 85857

Protestant Episcopal Society for the Advancement of Christianity in South Carolina. 19310, 87932

Protestant Episcopal Society for the Advancement of Christianity in South Carolina. Trustees. 87933

Protestant Episcopal Society for the Increase of the Ministry. (66199)

Protestant Episcopal Soviety for the Increase of the Ministry. Annual Meeting, 15th, Baltimore, 1871. (66199)

Protestant Episcopal Society for the Promotion of Evangelical Knowledge, New York. 1490, 1793, 66202, 86276, 92074

Protestant Episcopal Society for the Promotion of Evangelical Knowledge, New York. Board of Directors. 66202

Protestant Episcopal Soviety in Western New York for the Promotion of Evangelical Knowledge. 66201

Protestant Episcopal Missionary Soviety of Philadelphia. see Philadelphia Episcopal Missionary Society.

Protestant Episcopal Public School, New York. see New York (City) Trinity School.

Protestant Episcopal Sunday and Adult School Society, Philadelphia. 62104-62105

Protestant Episcopal Sunday and Adult School Society, Philadelphia. Managers. 62104

Protestant Episcopal Sunday-School Society, New York. see New York Protestant Episcopal Sunday School Society.

Protestant Episcopal Sunday School Society, Philadelphia. see Protestant Episcopal Sunday and Adult School Society, Philadelphia.

Protestant Episcopal Sunday-School Society of Pennsylvania. 60069

Protestant Episcopal Sunday-School Union. Pennsylvania Auxiliary. see Protestant Episcopal Sunday-School Society of Pennsylvania.

Protestant Episcopal Sunday School Union, New York. see General Protestant Episcopal Sunday School Union, New York.

Protestant Episcopal Theological Education Society in the State of New York. 53884

Protestant Episcopal Theological Seminary in Virginia, Alexandria, Va. See Alexandria, Va. Protestant Episcopal Theological Seminary in Virginia.

Protestant Episcopal Theological Seminary of Maryland. Board of Trustees. 36155

Protestant Episcopal Tract Society. (66203), 86179

Protestant Episcopal Tract Society. Board of Trustees. (66203)

Protestant Episcopal Tract Society. Instituted in New-York, 1810. (66203)

Protestant Episcopal Tract Society, New York. see New York Protestant Episcopal Tract Society.

Protestant Episcopalian. pseud. Letters to the laity of the Protestant Episcopal Church. (40649)

Protestant Episcopalian. pseud. Reply to the review of Dr. Wyatt's sermon. see Weller, George.

Protestant Episcopalian. 13008, 102720, 103473
Protestant Episcopalian and church register. 66210
Protestant Half Orphan Asylum Society, New York. see Society for the Relief of Half Orphan and Destitute Children in the City of New York.
Protestant; or expositor of popery. 66115
Protestant Orphan Asylum, Montreal. see Montreal Protestant Orphan Asylum.
Protestant Orphan Asylum Society, San Francisco. (76071)
Protestant Pastors of France. pseud. Address. 8124, 37781
Protestant reformation in France. 44722
Protestant religion is a sure foundation. 90296-90297
Protestant t[utor?] for childr[en.] 66211
Protestantism of the Episcopal Church. 82947
Protestantism, the parent and guardian. (43541)
Protestant's danger, and the protestant's duty. 68201
Protestant's resolution. 66212
Protestation contre les Angloys. (32028)
Protestation contre tout la presse Francaise. 15459
Protestation des habitants de la Caroline du Nord. (55610), 79519
Protestation du peuple de St.-Pierre. 66213
Protestation. 1841. 38986
Protestation faite au nome des habitants de la Guadeloupe. 66214
Protestation gegen die Bestellung Herrn Benjamin Franklins. 5130, 25576, (66215), 84586
Protestation [of General Gage.] 51804
Protestation presented to the Synod of Philadelphia. 66216
Protestation presented to the Synod, of Philadelphia, June I. 1741. 17662, 62106, 94686, 94700
Protestations-Schreiben. 25576-25577, (59888), 84587
Protestatium fratrum suorum charissimorum. 95251
Protesten der Stad Amsterdam. 66217
Protesting Brethren. pseud. Two papers brought in. 95580
Protesto do Sr. Visconde de Jequitinhonha. 88737
Protests of the Delegates of the Creek, Cherokee, and Choctaw Nations. 73410
Proteus ecclesiasticus. 37220, 66740
Prothonotario de Lucena. pseud. Carta. 57714
Protocol for the settlement of the strife in North America. 66218
Protocolo de antiguedades. (66219)
Protocolo de las conferencias entre los Comisionados. (76208)
Protocolo de las conferencias y notas de las Comisiones. 21800, (66220)
Protokoll der Sitzung der Evangelisch-Lutherischen Synod von Maryland und Virginien. 66221
Protokoll der Versammlung die sie Entworfen. 29013
Proton, J. F. Perault. ed. 42512
Proud, John G. 66222
Proud, Joseph. 52575
Proud, Robert. 66223, 89175, 97288
Proud man fairly dealt with. 23711
Proud Miss Macbride. 77346

Proudfit, Alexander, Moncrief, 1770-1843. 25152, 66224-66228, 106169 see also New York Colonization Society. General Agent and Corresponding Secretary.
Proudfit, John. 66229
Proudfit, John Williams, 1803-1870. 25152
Proudfit, Robert. 66230
Proudhon, P. J. 66231
Prouesses Anglaises en Acadie, Canada, etc. 12610
Prousses Angloises en Acadie, Canada, etc. 18221
Prout, Timothy. 66232
Prouty, William. defendnat at court martial 96952, 102153
Prouvencal de Saint-Hilaire, Auguste Francois Cesar. see Saint-Hilaire, Auguste Francois Cesar Prouvencal de, 1779-1853.
Prouville, Alexandre de, Marquis de Tracy. 66233
Provancher, Leon A., 1820-1892. 52049, (66234)-66235
Provas da parte primeira. (81089)
Prove voer de middelen die tot bescherming. 19800, 65956
Proveido al memorial de justas quejas. 99789
Provence et presil. 5907
Proverbial philosophy of wit and humor. 79909
Proverbs of Solomon and the prohecies of Jeremiah. (75836)
Providence, R. I. 66239, (66246), (66260), 66277-66278, 66287, 66292, (66316)-(66317), 85495
Providence, R. I. African Union Meeting and School-House. (66365), 80636
Providence, R. I. American Institute of Instruction. see American Institute of Instruction.
Providence, R. I. Anti-masonic State Convention, 1830. see Anti-masonic State Convention of Rhode Island, Providence, 1830.
Providence, R. I. Anti-masonic State Convention, 1831. see Anti-masonic State Convention of Rhode Island, Providence, 1831.
Providence, R. I. Anti-masonic State Convention, 1835. see Anti-masonic State Convention of Rhode Island, Providence, 1835.
Providence, R. I. Art Gallery. see Providence, R. I. Free Public Library, Art-Gallery, and Museum.
Providence, R. I. Association of Mechanics and Manufacturers. see Providence Association of Mechanics and Manufacturers.
Providence, R. I. Athenaeum. (66307)-(66309)
Providence, R. I. Athenaeum. Charter. (66307), (66309)
Providence, R. I. Athenaeum. Directors. (66308)
Providence, R. I. Athenaeum. Library. (66309), (66330)-66331
Providence, R. I. Athenaeum. Library. Charter. 66331
Providence, R. I. Athenaeum. Meeting, 3d, 1838. (66309)
Providence, R. I. Atheneum. see Providence, R. I. Athenaeum.
Providence, R. I. Auxiliary Bible Society. see Providence Auxiliary Bible Society, Providence, R. I.

Providence, R. I. Auxiliary Unitarian Association. see Providence Auxiliary Unitarian Association.

Providence, R. I. Bank. see Providence Bank, Providence, R. I.

Providence, R. I. Benefit Street Central Congregational Society. Charter. 66241

Providence, R. I. Benevolent Congregational Society. 66242

Providence, R. I. Benevolent Congregational Society. Charter. 66242

Providence, R. I. Bible Mission. see Providence Bible Mission, Providence, R. I.

Providence, R. I. Boys' High School. English and Scientific Department. 70586

Providence, R. I. Brown University. see Brown University.

Providence, R. I. Butler Hospital for the Insane. 66243

Providence, R. I. Butler Hospital for the Insane. Charter. 66243

Providence, R. I. Butler Hospital for the Insane. Superintendent. 66243

Providence, R. I. Butler Hospital for the Insane. Trustees. 66243

Providence, R. I. Celebration for the Arrival of Washington, 1790. 101869

Providence, R. I. Celebration of the Two Hundred and Fiftieth Anniversary of Congregationalism in This Country, 1870. 62845

Providence, R. I. Census, 1855. 66245

Providence, R. I. Census, 1874. 66245

Providence, R. I. Certain Citizens. petitioners see Providence, R. I. Citizens. petitioners

Providence, R. I. Channing Division No. 5. see Sons of Temperance of North America. Rhode Island. Channing Division No. 5, Providence.

Providence, R. I. Charitable Baptist Society. see Charitable Baptist Society, Providence, R. I.

Providence, R. I. Charter. 66248-66250

Providence, R. I. Chief of Police. see Providence, R. I. Police. Chief.

Providence, R. I. Children's Friends' Society. see Children's Friends' Society, Providence, R. I.

Providence, R. I. Church Missionary Union. see Church Missionary Union of Providence, R. I.

Providence, R. I. Citizens. petitioners 33003, 66361, 97951

Providence, R. I. City Auditor. (66254), 66259

Providence, R. I. City Bank. see City Bank, Providence, R. I.

Providence, R. I. City Council. 66293

Providence, R. I. City Council. Committee on a House of Correction. 66353

Providence, R. I. City Council. Committee on the Introduction of Gas Light into the City. 66354

Providence, R. I. City Council. Committee on the Supply of Water. 66347

Providence, R. I. City Council. Committee to Collect the Statutes and Ordinances Relating to the City. 66250

Providence, R. I. City Council. Committee to Examine the Sources of Water Supply. 66346

Providence, R. I. City Council. Select Committee on House of Industry. Majority. 66279

Providence, R. I. City Council. Select Committee on House of Industry. Minority. 66279

Providence, R. I. City Council. Select Committee Upon the Subject of Relief to the Out-Door Poor. 66349

Providence, R. I. City Council. Common Council. (66294)

Providence, R. I. City Marshal. 66288

Providence, R. I. City Registrar. (66238), 66255 see also Snow, Edwin Miller, 1820-1888.

Providence, R. I. Committee in Behalf of Cotton Manufactures. petitioners see Cotton Manufacturers, of Providence, R. I. Committee. petitioners

Providence, R. I. Committee on Public Schools. 66363 see also Providence, R. I. School Committee.

Providence, R. I. Committee on the Providence and Bristol Railroad. see Committee Appointed by the Citizens of Providence, Warren and Bristol, [R. I.] on the Providence and Bristol Railroad.

Providence, R. I. Committee to Superintend the Erection of School Houses. 66355

Providence, R. I. Cotton Manufactures. Committee. petitioners see Cotton Manufactures, of Providence, R. I. Committee. petitioners

Providence, R. I. Court of Common Pleas. Grand Jury. 90477

Providence, R. I. Democratic State Convention, 1841. see Democratic Party. Rhode Island. Convention, Providence, 1841.

Providence, R. I. Democratic State Convention, 1845. see Democratic Party. Rhode Island. Convention, Providence, 1845.

Providence, R. I. Dexter Asylum. 19910

Providence, R. I. Dexter Asylum. Board of Attending and Consulting Physicians and Surgeons. 19911

Providence, R. I. Ecclesiastical Council, 1792-1793. see Congregational Churches in Rhode Island. Ecclesiastical Council, Providence, 1792-1793.

Providence, R. I. Ecclesiastical Council, 1832 see Congregational Churches in Rhode Island. Ecclesiastical Council, Providence, 1832.

Providence, R. I. Ecclesiastical Council, 1835. see Congregational Churches in Rhode Island. Ecclesiastical Council, Providence, 1835.

Providence, R. I. Employment Society. see Employment Society, Providence, R. I.

Providence, R. I. Exhibition of the Rhode Island Art Association, 1854. see Rhode Island Art Association. Exhibition, 1st, Providence, 1854.

Providence, R. I. Ex-parte Council, 1832. see Congregational Churches in Rhode Island. Ecclesiastical Council, Providence, 1832.

Providence, R. I. Female Domestic Missionary Society. Missionary. pseud. see Missionary of the Latter Society. pseud.

Providence, R. I. Fifth Congregational Church. (66269)

Providence, R. I. Fire Department. (66260)

Providence, R. I. First Baptist Church. 66261

Providence, R. I. First Baptist Church. Committee. 70197

Providence, R. I. First Light Infantry Company. see Rhode Island. Militia. First Light Infantry Company, Providence.

Providence, R. I. Fourth Congregational Church. 66262

Providence, R. I. 14th Rhode Island Baptist State Convention, 1854. see Baptists Rhode Island. State Convention, 14th, Providence, 1854.

Providence, R. I. Franklin Museum. Charter. 66263

Providence, R. I. Franklin Museum. Library. 66263

Providence, R. I. Franklin Society. see Providence Franklin Society, Providence, R. I.

Providence, R. I. Free Evangelical Congregational Church. 66264

Providence, R. I. Free Public Library, Art-Gallery, and Museum. 66265

Providence, R. I. Free Public Library, Art-Gallery, and Museum. Gallery of Paintings. 66244

Providence, R. I. Friends' Boarding School. see Friends' Boarding School, Providence, R. I.

Providence, R. I. Friends' School. see Friends' School, Providence, R. I.

Providence, R. I. Girls' High School. Senior Department. 27560

Providence, R. I. High Street Congregational Sabbath School. Superintendent. 66268

Providence, R. I. Home for Aged Women. see Home for Aged Women, Providence, R. I.

Providence, R. I. House of Reformation. 66272

Providence, R. I. Inspector of Milk. 66273

Providence, R. I. Kent Academy. see Kent Academy, Providence, R. I.

Providence, R. I. Ladies' Bethel Association. see Ladies' Bethel Association, Providence, R. I.

Providence, R. I. Library Company. see Providence, R. I. Athenaeum. Library.

Providence, R. I. Mayor, 1832. 66249

Providence, R. I. Mechanics' and Apprentices' Library. 66281

Providence, R. I. Mechanics' Festival of the Providence Association of Mechanics and Manufacturers, 1860. see Providence Association of Mechanics and Manufacturers. 71st Anniversary Celebration, 1860.

Providence, R. I. Meeting of Citizens on the Occasion of the Execution of John Brown, 1859. 3694, 8524, note after 89213

Providence, R. I. Meeting of the Citizens Friendly to the Promotion of Temperance, 1828. see Meeting of the Citizens of Providence, Friendly to the Promotion of Temperance, Providence, R. I., 1828.

Providence, R. I. Ministry at Large. 66283, 92046 see also Stone, Edwin Martin.

Providence, R. I. Museum. see Providence, R. I. Free Public Library, Art-Gallery, and Museum.

Providence, R. I. New-England Yearly Meeting Boarding School. see Friends' School, Providence, R. I.

Providence, R. I. Nursery. see Providence Nursery, Providence, R. I.

Providence, R. I. Ordinances, etc. 66250, 66286, 66369

Providence, R. I. Overseer of the Poor. 66288

Providence, R. I. Pacific Congregational Church. 58080

Providence, R. I. Peace Convention, 1866. see Peace Convention, Providence, R. I., 1866.

Providence, R. I. Pilgrim Jubilee, 1870. see Providence, R. I. Celebration of the Two Hundred and Fiftieth Anniversary of Congregationalism in This Country, 1870.

Providence, R. I. Pine Street Baptist Church. 66289

Providence, R. I. Police. Chief. 66251

Providence, R. I. Providence Aid Society. see Providence Aid Society, Providence, R. I.

Providence, R. I. Providence Dispensary. see Providence Dispensary, Providence, R. I.

Providence, R. I. Providence Division No. 2. see Sons of Temperance of North America. Rhode Island. Providence Division No. 2.

Providence, R. I. Provident Association for Friendless Females. see Provident Association for Friendless Females, Providence, R. I.

Providence, R. I. Public Library. Librarian. 66333

Providence, R. I. Public Meeting of the Citizens on the Outrage in the Senate upon Charles Sumner, 1856. 57964, 93647

Providence, R. I. Public Meeting to Protest Against Slavery in Nebraska, 1854. see Public Meeting to Protest Against Slavery in Nebraska, Providence, R. I., 1854.

Providence, R. I. Public Schools. 66363

Providence, R. I. Reform School. see Reform School, Providence, R. I.

Providence, R. I. Relief Committee. see Relief Committee for the Relief of the Families and Dependents of Volunteers and Drafted Soldiers, Providence, R. I.

Providence, R. I. Rhode Island Hospital. (70722)

Providence, R. I. Rhode Island Hospital. Executive Committee. (70722)

Providence, R. I. Rhode Island Hospital. Trustees. (70722)

Providence, R. I. Rhode Island Institute of Instruction annual meeting, 23, 1848. see Rhode Island Institute of Instruction. Annual Meeting, 23d, Providence, 1848.

Providence, R. I. Richmond Street Church. see Providence, R. I. Richmond Street Congregational Church.

Providence, R. I. Richmond Street Congregational Church. 66362, 70112

Providence, R. I. St. John's Church. United Society. 97899

Providence, R. I. St. John's Church. United Society. Charter. 97899

Providence, R. I. Schofield's Commercial College. see Schofield's Commercial College, Providence, R. I.

Providence, R. I. School Committee. 66363 see also Providence, R. I. Committee on Public Schools.

Providence, R. I. School Committee. Special Committee on Health in the Schools. 66267

Providence, R. I. Society for Abolishing the Slave-Trade. see Society for Abolishing the Slave-Trade, Providence, R. I.

Providence, R. I. Society of Moral Philanthropists. see Society of Moral Philanthropists, Providence, R. I.

Providence, R. I. Soldiers' Monument. 66291-66292, 70610

Providence, R. I. Sundry Citizens. petitioners see Providence, R. I. Citizens. petitioners

Providence, R. I. Superintendent of Health. (66350), 66357-66359, 66368, 66370 see also Snow, Edwin Miller, 1820-1888.

Providence, R. I. Superintendent of Lights. (66371)

Providence, R. I. Superintendent of Public Buildings. 66372

Providence, R. I. Superintendent of Public Schools. 66363

Providence, R. I. Superintendent of the Census. 66245 see also Snow, Edwin Miller, 1820-1888.

Providence, R. I. Surveyor of Highways. (66373)

Providence, R. I. Swan Point Cemetery. (66374), note after 94020

Providence, R. I. Swan Point Cemetery. Actuary. (66374), note after 94020

Providence, R. I. Swan Point Cemetery. Charter. (66374), note after 94020

Providence, R. I. Swan Point Cemetery. Owners. Committee. (66374)

Providence, R. I. Town Meeting. Committee on a Plan of City Government, 1828. (66290)

Providence, R. I. Trustees of Obadiah Brown's Benevolent Fund. see Trustees of Obadiah Brown's Benevolent Fund, Providence, R. I.

Providence, R. I. Union Congregational Anti-slavery Society. see Union Congregational Anti-slavery Society, Providence, R. I.

Providence, R. I. Union Congregational Church. 66375

Providence, R. I. Union for Christian Work. see Union for Christian Work, Providence, R. I.

Providence, R. I. United Society of St. John's Church. see Providence, R. I. St. John's Church. United Society.

Providence, R. I. University Grammar School. Exhibition, 1853. 66377

Providence, R. I. Uxbridge Female Seminary. see Uxbridge Female Seminary, Providence, R. I.

Providence, R. I. Washington Section, No. 2, Cadets of Temperance. see Cadets of Temperance. Rhode Island. Washington Section, No. 2, Providence.

Providence, R. I. Washington Total Abstinence Society. see Providence Washington Total Abstinence Society, Providence, R. I.

Providence, R. I. Water Commissioners. 66379

Providence, R. I. Water Works. Chief Engineer. 66338

Providence, R. I. Waterman Street Baptist Church. 66380

Providence, R. I. Westminster Church of Christ. 66381

Providence, R. I. Westminster Congregational Society. see Providence, R. I. Westminster Church of Christ.

Providence, R. I. Women's Christian Association. see Women's Christian Association, Providence, R. I.

Providence, R. I. Young Ladies' High School. Reunion, 1858. 66383

Providence County, R. I. Jail. 70544

Providence County, R. I. Temperance Society. see Providence County Temperance Society, R. I.

Providence Aid Society, Providence, R. I. 66297

Providence almanac and business directory, containing also a business directory for the city of Newport. 66298

Providence almanac and business directory for 1857. 66298

Providence almanac and business directory for . . . 1846. 66298

Providence almanac and business directory for the year 1845. 66298

Providence almanac and business directory, for . . . 1843. 66298

Providence American journal. see American journal.

Providence, an allegorical poem. (56840)

Providence and purpose of God in our national history. 36484

Providence and Stonington Railroad (Proposed) 54839

Providence and Worcester Canal (Proposed) Engineer. (66236)

Providence & Worcester Railroad Company. Directors. 66301

Providence & Worcester Railroad Company. Directors. 66301

Providence Anti-slavery Society. 66302, (81953)

Providence asserted and adored. 46470

Providence Association for the Benefit of Colored Orphans. (66303)

Providence Association for the Promotion of Temperance. Committee. (66304)

Providence Association for the Promotion of Temperance. Managers. (66304)

Providence Association of Mechanics and Manufacturers. 66305

Providence Association of Mechanics and Manufacturers. Charter. 66305

Providence Association of Mechanics and Manufacturers. Subscribers to the Funeral Fund. 66305

Providence Association of Mechanics and Manufacturers. 71st Anniversary Festival, 1860. 66305, 92046

Providence Association of the Friends of Moral Reform. Executive Committee. 66306

Providence Association, Salem, Mass. see Salem Providence Association.

Providence Athenaeum. see Providence, R. I. Athenaeum.

Providence Auxiliary Bible Society, Providence R. I. 66310

Providence Auxiliary Unitarian Association. 66311

Providence Bank, Providence, R. I. plaintiffs 66240

Providence Bank, Providence, R. I. Charter. (66312)

Providence Bank, Providence, R. I. Counsel. 66240 see also Hazard, Benjamin, 1770 1841.

Providence Baptist Association. see Baptists Rhode Island. Providence Baptist Association.

Providence Bible Mission, Providence, R. I. 66314

Providence Charitable Fire Society. 66315

Providence city documents, from June, 1865, to June, 1866. (66316)

Providence city manual. (66317)

Providence collection of psalm and hymn tunes 79951

Providence County Temperance Society. 66318

Providence daily journal. 85497

Providence directory, containing a general directory. (66319)

Providence directory; containing names of the inhabitants. (66319)

Providence directory, enlarged and improved. (66319)

Providence directory, enlarged and improved, for . . . 1856. (66319)

Providence Dispensary, Providence, R. I. 66320

Providence display'd. (79017)

Providence displayed. (35704), 79018

Providence Division No. 2, Sons of Temperance see Sons of Temperance of North America. Rhode Island. Providence Division No. 2.

Providence Domestic Missionary Society. 66321

Providence Evangelical Seamen's Friend Society. (66322)

Providence, Feb. 26, 1781. 100476

Providence Female Benevolent Society. Committee. 66323

Providence Female Society for the Relief of Indigent Women and Children. 66324

Providence Female Tract Society. 66325

Providence Franklin Society, Providence, R. I. 66326

Providence Franklin Society, Providence, R. I. Charter. 66326

Providence gazette. 79290, 91805

Providence gazette, and country journal. 66327

Providence, Hartford and Fishkill Railroad Co. (66328)

Providence Infant School Society. (66329)

Providence, January 1, 1783. 102203

Providence journal. 8538, 17125, 20403, 21618, (29885), 30058, 35313, 50806, 66283, 66364, 70510, (71146), 85496, 89941, 89973, 90476, 92046, 96905

Providence Library Company, Providence, R. I. see Providence, R. I. Athenaeum. Library.

Providence Nursery, Providence, R. I. (66332)

Providence of God displayed in the revolutions. 58800

Providence of God displayed in the rise and fall of nations. 103168

Providence of God in raising up under our republican institutions. 75963

Providence of God, in the settlement and protection of Georgia. 91579

Providence of God manifested in the events of the last year. 91660

Providence of law in distinction from that of truth. (13256)

Providence Plantations. see Rhode Island.

Providence post. 35313

Providence Reform School, Providence, R. I. 66334

Providence Reform School. Second annual report. 66334

Providence Republican herald. 2485

Providence Society for Abolishing the Slave Trade. petitioners 47745

Providence Society for the Encouragement of Faithful Domestic Servants. 66335

Providence theological magazine. 66336

Providence tribune. 35313

Providence Washington Total Abstinence Society, Providence, R. I. 66337

Providence Water Works. Report of the Chief Engineer. 66338

Providence Young Men's Bible Society, Providence, R. I. 66339

Providence Young Men's Christian Association. see Young Men's Christian Association, Providence, R. I.

Providence Young Men's Christian Union, Providence, R. I. 66341

Providence Young Men's Christian Union, Providence, R. I. Directors. 66341

Providence Young Men's Christian Union. Organized April 12, 1853. 66341

Providence Young Men's Temperance Society, Providence, R. I. (66342)

Providences of God in history. (58560)

Providencia, Josepha de la. see Josepha de la Providencia.

Provident Association for Friendless Females, Providence, R. I. 66343

Provident Association of Portland, Me. (64370)

Provident Society for the Employment of the Poor, Philadelphia. (62107)

Providence Society of New York. 54712

Providential aspect and salutary tendency of the existing crisis. 66384

Providential escape. 104175

Providential escape after a shipwreck. 82278

Providential escape and sufferings of Captain Boyce. 7099, 25368

Providential position of the evangelical churches. 89753

Province of Corrientes. 67126

Province de Quebec et l'emigration Europeene. 67037

Province of N. Scotia. Proceedings . . . upon the convention. 56163

Province of New York, ss. Whereas . . . 53672

Province of Ontario. 10436

Province of Ontario gazetteer and directory. 47364

Province of Quebec and European emigration. (67038)

Province of the American scholar. 90005

Provinces Argentines et Buenos-Ayres. 44343

Provinces de la Confederation Argentine et Buenos-Ayres. 66385

Provinces de la Plata erigee en monarchie. 86200

Provinces du Caucase, l'empire du Bresil. 93984

Provinces-Unies de l'Amerique du Sud. see Argentine Republic.

Provincetown, Mass. Church of the Redeemer, Universalist. 84234

Provincetown, Mass. Provincetown Seminary. see Provincetown Seminary, Provincetown, Mass.

Provincetown book. 83652

Provincetown Seminary, Provincetown, Mass. 83652

Provincia de Immaculado Conceicao, Brazil. see Immaculado Conceicao (Brazilian Province)

Provincia de los Doze Apostles de Peru. see Doze Apostles del Peru (Ecclesiastical Province)

Provincia Espanola de Santo Domingo. see Santo Domingo (Spanish Colony)

Provincial. 66388

Provincial Agricultural and Industrial Exhibition of Nova Scotia, 1868. see Nova Scotia. Provincial Agricultural and Industrial Exhibition, 1868.

Provincial Agricultural Association's prize list. 66389

Provincial Agricultural Society, Halifax, Nova Scotia. see Society for Promoting Agriculture in the Province of Nova-Scotia, Halifax.

Provincial and state papers [of New Hampshire.] 52791, 61280, 66514, 1st-2d notes after 98997, note after 98998, 1st note after 99003, 103894

Provincial Assembly of Presbyterian Ministers, London, 1649. 99805, 103400

Provincial Board of Agriculture. . . . Abstract of the proceedings. 52551

Provincial Conference of Committees, Philadelphia, 1776. see Pennsylvania (Colony) Provincial Conference, 1776.

Provincial courts of New Jersey. 24291

Provincial del Carmen. 26484

Provincial Exhibition of the New Brunswick Society for the Encouragement of Agriculture, Home Manufacturers and Commerce, 1852. see New Brunswick

Proyecto sobre un establecimiento de papel moneda. 66409, 2d note after 94147

Proyectos contra la Iglesia publicados en Vera Cruz. 26719

Proyectos de arreglo de los gastos de la hacienda publica. 59303

Proyectos de colonization presentados por la Junta Directiva. (48632)

Proyectos de tratados sobre principios de derecho internacional. 61158

Pr-t-st of the m—ch—ts of G——t B——n. (66110)

Prudden, Nehemiah. 66410, 97178

Prudent advice to young tradesmen and dealers. 24459

Prudent voyageur. 22192, 47073

Prudential maxims for statesmen and courtiers. 67599

Prudentij opera que in hoc libro continentur. Cathemorion. (66411)

Prudentius, Antonius. (66411)

Prudentius, Americanus Aurelius. pseud. Sacred minister. see Mather, Samuel, 1706-1785.

Prudhomme, Louis. 66412, 1st note after 100802 100802

Pruna, Manuel de Lebrixa y. see Lebrixa y Pruna, Manuel de.

Prussia. 34100-34107

Prussia. Sovereigns, etc., 1740-1786 (Friedrich II) 100667 see also Friedrich II, King of Prussia, 1712-1786.

Prussia. Treaties, etc. 15493, 96570-96571, 96590

Prussian evolutions in actual engagements. 30275

Prussian method of teaching the elements of the Latin language. 78632

Prussian mission of the Church of Jesus Christ of Latter-Day Saints. 89373

Prussian officer in the Confederate service. pseud. Army of the Potomac. 2052A, 19241

Prussian system of public instruction. 92389

Pruvonena, P. pseud. Memorias y documentos. see Riva Aguero, Jose de la.

Pruyn, Anna Fenn (Parker) 1840- 66415

Pruyn, John Van Schaick Lansing, 1811-1877. (66414), 69699

Pruyn, Mrs. John Van Schaick Lansing. see Pruyn, Anna Fenn (Parker) 1840-

Pryne, Arbam. 66416

Prynne, --------, fl. 1840. 51373

Prynne, Arthur. tr. 19982

Prynne, William, 1600-1669. 10199, (66417), 103441

Prynne's almanac for 1841. 51373

Pryor, Abraham. 66418

Pryor, J. P. 36654

Pryor, Roger Atkinson, 1828-1919. 66419-66420

Pryor, William. 66421

Przewodowski, Andre. 66422

Przybylskiego, Waclawa. 92597

Psalm-boek voor die tot die evangelische Broeer-Kerk. 66423

Psalm C to be sung at a tea party. 51906

Psalm of thanksgiving. (66424)

Psalm singer's amusement. 5418

Psalm-singer's assistant. 4050

Psalm wowapi. 71342

Psalmen Davids. 52363, 60271

Psalmes hymns and spiritual songs. 66432

Psalmist. 84062, 92375

Psalmodia Christiana. 74953

Psalmodia Germanica. 66456

Psalms and hymns. [By Dr. Watts.] 71539

Psalms and hymns, selected from the most approved versions. 66425

Psalms and hymns, with the catechism. 66426

Psalms, carefully suited to the Christian worship. 66427

[Psalms,] hymns, and [spiritual songs,] also the catechism. 66443

Psalms, hymns, and spiritual songs of the Old and New Testament. (66441)-(66442)

Psalms, hymns, and spirigual songs: selected and designed for the use of the church universal. 70925

Psalms, hymns, and spiritual songs: selected and original. 66444

Psalms in metre in the Indian language. 66445

Psalms of David. 6350, 7315, (41553), 52737, 64998-65000, note after 65546, (66459), 66460, 66461, (66463)

Psalms of David, designed for standing use. 86859

Psalms of David. In meeter. Newly translated. 66446

Psalms of David in metre. According to the Church of Scotland. 66447

Psalms of David, pointed as they are to be sung. (66462)

Psalms of David, with the Gospel according to John. 45537

Psalms of David, with the Ten Commandemnts. 66448

Psalms of freedom. 39505

Psalter. 6354, 66458

Psalter Davids. 66464

Psalter des Koenigs und Propheten Davids. 66467

Psalter des Konigs und Propheten Davids. 42728, (66465)

Psalter des Konigs und Propheten Davids, verteutscht von D. Martin Luther. 66466

Psalter for children. 66457

Psalter, or psalms of David. 6350, (41553), 64998-65000, (66459), 66461

Psalter or psalms of David, pointed as they are to be sung. (66462)

Psalter, or psalms of David, with the proverbs of Solomon. 66460

Psalterium Americanum. 46471

Psalterium, Hebreum, Grecu, Arabicu, & Chaldeu. (66468)

Psi Upsilon Fraternity. 86939

Psi Upsilon Fraternity, New York University. see New York University. Psi Upsilon Fraternity.

Psycomachia. (66411)

Psychomancy. (58146)

Psychopathick Hospital of the future. 21628

Pterigraphia Americana icones. 61288

Ptolomaei Antiqui orbis tabulae xxvii. 43822

Ptolomaei Geographicae enarrationis libri viii. 43822

Ptolemaeus, Claudius. 34100, 43822, 63016, 66469-66508, (66890), 73198, (73890), 76838, 76897, 91866-91868, 99374, 104696-104698, 106294, 1036330-106331

Ptolemaevs acvtvs restitivtvs. Emacvlatvs. (66480)

Ptolomei Tabulae geographicae com Eanduai [sic] annotationibus. 66508

Ptolemeo La geografia di Clavdio Ptolemeo. (66502)

Ptolemy, Claudio. see Ptolemaeus, Claudius.

Ptolemy. 5014

Pu, Piang. pseud. see Piang Pu. pseud.

Puberiano y Popayanez. pseud. Lamentacion. 38753

Publick Academy, Philadelphia. see Pennsylvania. University.

Public accounts of the province of Canada, for 1857 and 1858. 10452, (10557)

Publick accounts kept during the revolutionary war. 101724

Public acts in force. 3280

Public acts of the General Assembly of North-Carolina and Tennessee. 94780

Public acts [of Upper Canada.] 10499

Public acts, passed by the General Assembly. (15772)

Public acts relating to common schools. 15729

Public acts relating to elections. 15827

Public acts relating to elections, and the admission of electors. (15773)

Public address delivered in the . . . Massachusetts House of Representatives. 33964

Public addresses. 103173

Public advertiser, London. 25580, 26123, 62700, 67676, 97362

Public and domestic life of His late most Gracious Majesty, George the Third. 32646

Public and domestic life of the Rt. Hon. Edmund Burke. 9312

Public and general laws of the commonwealth of Massachusetts. 45958

Public and general statutes passed by the Congress of the United States of America. 15586, 92320

Public and private acts of the General Assembly of Connecticut. 15771

Public and private economy. 78836-(78837)

Public and private history of Napoleon the Third. 85170

Public and private history of Napoleon III. 85156-85157

Public and private instructions to Col. Clark. (13287)

Public and private life of George the Third. (33629)

Public and statute laws of the state of Illinois. 34285

Public answer of Hon. Gershom B. Weston. 21492, 103045

Public are . . . informed, that this company will make insurance. 61674

Public auction,—at Worcester. 105369

Public Breakfast Held in Honour of William Lloyd Garrison, London, 1867. 26711

Public buildings and architectural ornaments of the capitol. 101951

Public buildings and statuary of the government. 101951

Public causes for gratitude. 3794

Public cemetery. 73668

Public ceremonies of the Order of the Sons of Temperance. 87016

Public characters, for 1802. 7083

Public characters, or contemporary biography. 66511

Public credit—gold contracts. (77580)

Public credit. Speech . . . in the House of Representatives. 15630

Public credit. Speech . . . on the bill of strengthen the public credit. 18818

Public Creditors, Citizens of . . . New Jersey. petitioners see New Jersey (Colony) Public Creditors. petitioners

Public Creditors of Pennsylvania. petitioners see Pennsylvania. Public Creditors. petitioners

Public Creditors, Who are Citizens of the Commonwealth of Pennsylvania. petitioners see Pennsylvania. Public Creditors. petitioners

Public debt and currency. Speech . . . February 11, 1869. 50791

Public debt and currency. Speech of Hon. John Sherman. (80379)

Public debt . . . and finance of the United States. 26403

Public debt and internal improvements. 41059

Public debt and lands of Texas. 33883

Public debt and taxation of South Carolina. 87934

Public debt of the United States. 27290

Public debt.—The act of confederation defective. 97439

Public debt, the currency, specie payment, and national banks. 32335

Public debt, the new national banks. 8348

Public debt: what to do with it. 68549

Public debts and the public credit of the United States. (66512)

Public defaulters brought to light. 27376, 66513

Public defence of the rights of the New-Hampshire Grants. 66514, 1st note after 99003

Public Deliberative Meeting of the American Tract Society, New York, 1848. see American Tract Society, New York. Public Deliberative Meeting, 1848.

Public Demonstration of Sympathy with Pius IX, New York, 1847. see New York (City) Public Demonstration of Sympathy with Pius IX, 1847.

Public dinner, given in honor of the Chickasaw and Choctaw treaties. 101068

Public Dinner Given to Mr. William C. Rives, Albemarle County, Va., 1834. see Albemarle County, Va. Public Dinner Given to Mr. William C. Rives, 1834.

Public dinner in Honor of the Centennial Anniversary of Washington, Washington, D. C. 1832. 89200, 6th note after 101885

Public discourse in commemoration of Peter S. Du Ponceau. (21278)

Public documents concerning the Ohio canals. 37751, (57029), (66515)

Public documents, containing proceedings of the Hartford Convention. 45959

Public documents of . . . Kansas for . . . 1862. 37078

Public documents of the city of New York, 1868. 54613

Public documents of the first fourteen Congresses. 83310, 83991

Public documents of the House of Delegates. 45167

Public documents of the Legislature of Connecticut. 15796

Public documents of the Legislature of Massachusetts. (45960)

Public documents of various subjects. 65639

Public documents relating to Lord Aylmer's administration. 2519, (10557A), 4th note after 42522

Public documents relating to the New York Canals. 29551

Public duty of a private citizen. 29699

Public economy for the United States. 14781

Public education in Baltimore. 49998

Public education in the city of New York. 54614, 66516

Public education of the people. note after (58767)

Public exercises at the inauguration of President S. G. Brown. 30064

Public exercises at the inauguration of Rev. Samuel Ware Fisher. 24502, 30063

Public exercises at the laying of the corner stone of the People's College. (30868)

Public expenditure from 1824 to 1838. 103265
Public expenditures . . . Speech . . . January 23, 1862. 26664
Public expenditures. Speech . . . in reply to Mr. Voorhees. 18918
Public expressions of grief for the death of General Washington at Dorchester. 20623, 101594, 101810, 1st note after 101877
Public faith. 60440
Public finances—the new tax bill. 65675
Public general laws. 45207
Public good, being an examination into the claim of Virginia. 58237-(58238), 1st note after 100516
Publick good without private interests. 26760, 2d note after 100516
Public grounds of Chicago. (13667)
Public health of the city of New York. 23317
Public health papers and reports. 84252, 84260
Public health. The basis of sanitary reform. (54188)
Public honors to Lieutenant-General Grant. 28317
Public interest and private monopoly. 67269
Public journal. 21928
Public lands. 14775
Public lands in New Hampshire. 52950
Public lands. Speech . . . January 29, 1851. 36885
Public Latin School, Boston. see Boston. Public Latin School.
Public laws. 61208
Public laws and acts of the state of Connecticut. 15770
Public laws . . . from January 1857, to January, 1859, inclusive. 70700
Public laws . . . from January 1857, to January, 1859, inclusive. 2d [-8th] supplement. 70700
Public laws of Georgia. (27088)
Public laws of . . . New-Hampshire. 52898
Public laws of . . . North-Carolina, passed by the General Assembly, at its adjourned session of 1864. 55673
Public laws of . . . North-Carolina, passed by the General Assembly, at its adjourned session of 1863. 55673
Public laws of . . . North-Carolina, passed by the General Assembly, at its adjourned session of 1862-'63. 55673
Public laws of . . . North-Carolina, passed by the General Assembly, at its called session of 1863. 55673
Public laws of . . . North-Carolina, passed by the General Assembly, at its second extra session, 1861. 55672
Public laws of . . . North-Carolina, passed by the General Assembly, at its session of 1856-'57. 55671
Public laws of . . . North Carolina, passed by the General Assembly . . . 1866-'67. (55674)
Public laws [of South Carolina.] note before 87563
Public laws of the Confederate States of America, passed at the first session of the first Congress, 1862. (15342), 15416
Public laws of the Confederate States of America, passed at the fourth session of the first Congress; 1863-4. 15346
Public laws of the Confederate States of America, passed at the second session of the first Congress; 1862. 15343
Public laws of the Confederate States of America, passed at the third session of the first Congress; 1863. 15345

Public laws of the General Assembly of North Carolina. (55670)
Public laws of the state of Rhode-Island and Providence Plantations. 70628
Public laws of the state of Rhode-Island and Providence Plantations, as revised by a committee, and finally enacted by the Honourable General Assembly, at their session in January, 1822. 70627
Public laws of the state of Rhode-Island and Providence Plantations, as revised by a committee, and finally enacted by the Honorable General Assembly, at their session in January, 1798. 70626
Public laws of the state of Rhode-Island and Providence Plantations, passed at the sessions of the General Assembly. 70700
Public laws of the state of Rhode-Island . . . passed since the session of the General Assembly, in January, . . . 1798. 70626
Public laws of the state of South-Carolina. 87706
Public laws of the United States of America, passed at the first session of the thirty-seventh Congress. 61208, 66517
Public laws of the United States of America, passed at the first session of the twenty-ninth Congress. 49318
Public laws of Vermont. note before 99008, note after 99131
Public laws of Vermont adopted in 1833. note before 99075
Public laws of Vermont of 1933. note before 99131
Public laws passed at the first session of the second Congress. 15344
Public laws passed by the General Assembly of the state of Georgia. 27089
Public lecture, Boston. (47125), 58895, 58602, 59604, 65587, 65597, 65611, 65614, 79418
Public lecture in Harvard College. 103910
Public lecture, occasioned by the death of the Rev. Joseph Willard. 59442
Publick lecture in Harvard-College, June 24th. 1755. 103906
Public ledger (Annapolis) 45069
Public ledger (Boston) (47405)
Public ledger (London) 80040, 98690
Public ledger almanac. (66518)
Public Ledger Building, Philadelphia. 62109
Public Ledger Building, Philadelphia. With an account of the proceedings. (62110)
Public letter . . . to the people of Missouri. 8453
Public libraries and common schools attacked and defended. 74551
Public libraries of the United States. 89555
Public Library, Beverley, Mass. see Beverley, Mass. Public Library.
Public Library, Boston. see Boston. Public Library.
Public Library, Cincinnati. see Cincinnati. Public Library.
Public Library, New York. see New York (City) Public Library.
Public Library of Cincinnati. 1867. Rules, by-laws, and other items. 13093
Public life in Washington. 4572
Public life of Capt. John Brown. 68528
Public man. 850
Public Meeting, St. Louis, 1860. see St. Louis. Public Meeting, August 18th, 1860.
Public Meeting, Shocco Springs, N. C. see Shocco Springs, N. C. Public Meeting.

Public Meeting, Staunton, Va., 1793. see Staunton, Va. Public Meeting, 1793.

Public meeting. 96770

Public Meeting Against Closing the Canal Locks and Stopping the Mails on Sunday, Buffalo, 1858. see Buffalo. Public Meetings Against Closing the Canal Locks and Stopping the Mails on Sunday, 1858.

Public meeting. At a meeting held by public notice at the house of Wm. H. Alexander. 105693A

Public Meeting at York, [i. e. Toronto,] 1830. see Toronto, Canada. Public Meeting, 1830.

Public Meeting Composed of Twenty-five Clergymen, Chicago, 1854. 20693

Public Meeting Concerning the Protestant Episcopal Diocese of Ohio, Dublin, 1828. see Dublin. Public Meeting Concerning the Protestant Episcopal Diocese of Ohio, 1828.

Public Meeting, Faneuil Hall, Boston, 1846. see Boston. Public Meeting, Faneuil Hall, Sept. 24, 1846.

Public Meeting for the Relief of the Greeks, Boston, 1823. see Boston. Public Meeting for the Relief of the Greeks, 1823.

Public Meeting Held at Finsbury Chapel, to Receive Frederick Douglass, Moorfields, England, 1846. 20716

Public Meeting Held in Boston, December 19, 1823, for the Relief of the Greeks. see Boston. Public Meeting for the Relief of the Greeks, 1823.

Public Meeting in Behalf of the Society for the Promotion of Collegiate and Theological Education at the West, Boston, 1845. 85922

Public meeting in Faneuil Hall. 69657

Public Meeting in Favor of an Out-let Canal at Well's Galls, New Hope, Pa., 1846. see New Hope, Pa. Public Meeting in Favor of an Out-let Lock at Well's Falls, 1846.

Public Meeting in the Pine-Street Church, Boston, 1851. see South End Provident Association, Boston. Public Meeting, 1851.

Public Meeting of Anti-slavery Citizens of Chester County, Pa., 1835. see Chester County, Pa. Public Meeting of Anti-slavery Citizens, 1835.

Public Meeting of Citizens of Minnesota, in Favor of a Semi-weekly Overland Mail from Saint Paul to Puget Sound, St. Paul, 1850. (49297)

Public Meeting of Persons Interested in the Preservation of the British West India Colonies, London, 1833. 102859

Public Meeting of the Citizens of Franklin County, Favorable to the Election of Andrew Jackson, Columbis, O., 1827. see Democratic Party. Ohio. Franklin County.

Public Meeting of the Citizens of Providence, on the Outrage in the Senate Upon Charles Sumner, 1856. see Providence, R. I. Public Meeting of the Citizens on the Outrage in the Senate Upon Charles Sumner, 1856.

Public Meeting of the Citizens of Richmond County, Ga., 1860. see Richmond County, Ga. Public Meeting, 1860.

Public Meeting of the Citizens of Richmond County, Monday, December 24th, 1860. Address of Hon. Chas. J. Jenckins. 71214

Public Meeting of the Colored Citizens of Oberlin, O. (56418)

Public Meeting of the Friends of African Colonization, Baltimore, 1827. see Friends of African Colonization. Meeting Baltimore, 1827.

Public Meeting of the Friends of the Union, Baltimore, 1861. see Baltimore. Public Meeting of the Friends of the Union, 1861.

Public Meeting on Occasion of the Arrival of the Tea Ship, Philadelphia, 1773. see Philadelphia. Public Meeting on Occasion of the Arrival of the Tea Ship, 1773.

Public Meeting on Postal Reform, New York, 1856. (64518)

Public Meeting on the Subject of a National Western Armory, Cincinnati, 1841. see Cincinnati. Public Meeting on the Subject of a National Western Armory, 1841

Public Meeting Respecting St. Ann's Church for Deaf-Mutes, New York, 1853. see New York (City) Public Meeting Respecting St. Ann's Church for Deaf-Mutes, 1853.

Public meeting . . . to commemorate the four anniversary of John Brown's death, London, 2d December, 1863. 8523

Public Meeting to Consider the Condition of the Public Schools, Rochester, 1838. se Rochester, N. Y. Public Meeting to Consider the Condition of the Public Schools, 1838.

Public Meeting to Consider the Recent Case of Kidnapping from Our Soil, Boston, 1846. see Boston. Citizens.

Public Meeting to Protest Against Slavery in Nebraska, Providence, R. I., 1854. 6580

Public Meetings Held by the Opponents of the Present Administration, Washington, D. 1840. see Whig Party. Washington, D. C.

Public men and events. 77029

Public men, and public institutions of the chur 5824

Public men of the revolution. 93559

Public morals; or the true glory of a state. 761

Publick news letter. 46723, 1st note after 65324

Publick occurences both foreign and domestick 66526

Public oration delivered before the Phi Alpha Theta Society. 20812

Public parks and the enlargement of towns. 57245

Public parks: their effects upon the moral, phusical and sanitary condition. 67968

Public policy. 83965

Public press and the actions of Councils. 62111

Public press as the advocate of human rights. 84790

Public printing. A sketch of the debates in Congress. 71575

Public printing. Statements of John M. M'Cal 32337

Public proceedings on the removal of De Witt Clinton. 13735

Public record: including speeches, messages, proclamations. 16293, 79652

Public Record Office, London. see Great Britain. Public Record Office, London.

Public records of the colony of Connecticut. 1521, 15797, 15801, 24588, 66519, note after 68296, note after 68297, 93936

Public regulations for the establishment of pea and good order. (66983)

Public revenue and the tariff. 55133
Public sale, at Brunswick, Georgia. (8763)
Public School Library, St. Louis. see St. Louis. Public School Library.
Public School Library Society of St. Louis. 75370-75371
Public School Library Society of St. Louis. Charter. 75371
Public School Library Society of St. Louis. Library. 75371
Public School Library Society of St. Louis. Incorporated Fev. 1865. 75370
Public School Society, New York. 54121, 54615
Public School Society, New York. Trustees. 54615
Public School Society of New York. 54371
Public school system of New York City. 7334
Public school system of the town of Pittsfield. 83333
Public schools and the Berkshire Athenaeum. 83333
Public schools——city of Cleveland. 13680
Public schools of Albany. 629
Public schools of Marietta. 44567
Public schools of the city of Rochester. 72366
Public schools of Washington. (11866)
Public sins a cause for humiliation. 97370
Public slander. 104234
Public speculation unfolded. 19001
Public speeches and despatches of the governors. 81986
Public spirit: a monthly magazine of choice literature. 66520
Public spirit and mobs. 81161
Publick spirit described & recommended. 103790
Publick spirit, illustrated in the life and designs of the Reverend Thomas Bray. 7484, 83976-83977
Publick spirit, in the private citizen. (81592)
Public statute law of the state of Connecticut. 15774
Public statute laws of the state of Connecticut. 15775
Public statute laws of the state of Connecticut, passed subsequent to the revision of 1821. 105844
Public statutes at large of . . . Ohio. (57030)
Public statutes at large of the United States of America. 61208, 65725, 66517
Public statutes of the state of Minnesota. 49300
Public statutes of the state of Rhode Island and Providence Plantations. 70700
Public thanksgiving. A sermon, . . . in . . . Elizabeth, N. J. (43820)
Public tranquillity the object of every individual's concern. (60802)
Publick tryal of the Quakers in Barmudas upon the first day of May, 1678. 6285, (23054)
Public universal friend. 104031
Public works of the United States of America. 92814
Public worship a universal duty. 37976
Public worship considered and recommended. 92108, 97741
Publica -se nas quartas- feiras e sabbados. 46737
Publica vindicacion del Ilustre Ayuntamiento de Santa Fe de Guanaxuato. (31729), (66521)
Publicacao mensal. 47730
Publicacion de los principales documentos. 66522
Publicacion oficial. 9019, (39845)
Publicaciones de la Sociedad Democratica de los Amigos de America. 85739

Publicacions officielles de la Commission Belge. (79351)
Publicacon, by His Maiesties Councell of Virginea touchinge the deferringe of the lotterye. 99869
Publicacon of the lotary for Virginia. 99868
Publicans of New-England. pseud. Humble address. (33688)
Publicas demonstraciones de celebriad y jubilo. 22059
Publicatie. De Staten Generael der Vereenighde Nederlanden. 66513, (66523), 102909-102910
Publicatie: prolongatie van't octroy der West-Indische Compagnie. (66523), 102909
Publicatie van Bewinthebberen der West-Indische Compagnie. 66524
Publication by the Counsell of Virginea, touching the plantation there. 99858
Publication de la Societe d'Etudes Pour la Colonisation de la Guyane. 29191, 39637
Publication du journal Le siecle. 92536, 93411
Publication fund series [of the Historical Society of Pennsylvania.] 60143
Publication fund series of the New York Historical Society. 54474, 84566, 86744, note after 95562, 1st note after 98997, 99325
Publication mensuelle. 70358
Publication no. 88 [of the Loyal Publication Society.] 47704, note after 95516
Publication no. 11 [of the Young Men's Anti-masonic Association for the Diffusion of Truth.] 50682, 97958
Publication no. 5 [of the Maryland Historical Society.] 37409
Publication no. 19 [of the Bureau of Science of the Department of Agriculture and Natural Resources of the Philippine Islands.] 84529
Publication no. I [of the Tennessee Department of Education.] 94750
Publication no. 644 [of the American Academy of Political and Social Science.] 84514
Publication no. 322 [of the American Academy of Political and Social Science.] 83383
Publication no. 2 [of the South Carolina Society for the Advancement of Learning.] 30446, 88041
Publication no. II [of the Young Men's Anti-masonic Association for the Diffusion of Truth, Boston.] 50682, 97958
Publication of Gviana's plantation. 29190
Publication of Rationalis [pseud.] 84642
Publication of Rev. Josiah Moore. 21492, 103045
Publication of the Associate Alumni [of the General Theological Seminary.] (54291)
Publication of the Associate Alumni of the General Theological Seminary of the Protestant Episcopal Church in the United States. 89342
Publication of the Associate Alumni of the General Theological Seminary of the Protestant Episcopal Church in the United States, for the year of Our Lord MDCCCXLII. 89107
Publication of the United States Sanitary Commission, no. 70. (12061)
Publication under the signature of Vindex. 32777), note after 99774
Publications [de la Societe d'Etudes Pour la Colonisation de la Guyane Francaise.] 29191, 39637, 94849
Publications du journal Le siecle. 14935, 14938

Pue, Hugh A. 66543

Puebla, Mex. (Archdiocese) (23592)-(23593), 66544, 66551, (66554)

Puebla, Mex. (Archdiocese) defendants 56403

Puebla, Mex. (Archdiocese) plaintiffs 99441

Puebla, Mex. (Archdiocese) Bishop [ca. 1826] 66567

Puebla, Mex. (Archdiocese) Bishop [ca. 1827] (56445)

Puebla, Mex. (Archdiocese) Bishop [ca. 1847] 66553

Puebla, Mex. (Archdiocese) Bishop [ca. 1864] 47034

Puebla, Mex. (Archdiocese) Bishop (Escobar y Llamas) 66573 see also Escobar y Llamas, Diego Osorio de, Bp.

Peubla, Mex. (Archdiocese) Bishop (Escobar y Llamas) plaintiff 35266 see also Escobar y Llamas, Diego Osorio de, Bp. plaintiff

Puebla, Mex. (Archdiocese) Bishop (Escobar y Llamas) defendant 66561, (66574) see also Escobar y Llamas, Diego Osorio de Bp.

Puebla, Mex. (Archdiocese) Bishop (Fabian y Fuero) (23592)-(23593), 66551 see also Fabian y Fuero, Francisco, Bp.

Puebla, Mex. (Archdiocese) Bishop (Gonzalez del Campillo) 10312, 34190, 66555, 66562 see also Gonzalez del Campillo, Manuel Ignacio, Bp., 1740-1813.

Puebla, Mex. (Archdiocese) Bishop (Gonzalo) 27826 see also (Gonzalo, Victoriano Lopez, Bp.

Puelba, Mex. (Archdiocese) Bishop (Palafox y Mendoza) (36797), 56265, 57540, (77142), 94275 see also Palafox y Mendoza, Juan de, Abp., 1600-1659.

Peubla, Mex. (Archdiocese) Bishop (Palafox y Mendoza) defendant 98804 see also Palafox y Mendoza, Juan de, Abp., 1600-1659. defendant

Puebla, Mex. (Archdiocese) Bishop (Palafox y Mendoza) plaintiff 98804 see also Palafox y Mendoza, Juan de, Abp., 1600-1659. plaintiff

Puebla, Mex. (Archdiocese) Bishop (Vazquez) (49770)-(49772), 98716 see also Vazquez, Francisco Pablo, Bp.

Puebla, Mex. (Archdiocese) Cabildo. 66567

Puebla, Mex. (Archdiocese) Comision de Curas. (49770), 47992, 98716

Puebla, Mex. (Archdiocese) Comision Unida de Curas de la Mistexa Baja y Montanez. trs. (49771), 98716

Puebla, Mex. (Archdiocese) Promotor Fiscal. plaintiff 94348

Puebla, Mex. (Archdiocese) Representante de la Mitra. petitioner 49518 see also Serrano, Francisco. petitioner

Puebla, Mex. (Archdiocese) Sacerdote. pseud. see Sacerdote del Obispado de la Puebla de los Angeles. pseud.

Puebla, Mex. (City) 47032, 56014, 66549

Puebla, Mex. (City) Academia Medico Quirurgica. see Academia Medico Quirurgica, Puebla, Mex.

Peubla, Mex. (City) Alcalde. 66564

Puebla, Mex. (City) Alcalde Mayor. 35266, 66573 see also Izeqvierdo, Pedro Saenz.

Puebla, Mex. (City) Ayuntamiento. 66546, 66576

Puebla, Mex. (City) Basilica. defendants 86420

Puebla, Mex. (City) Basilica. Cabildo. (56445), 58279, 66113

Puebla, Mex. (City) Basilica. Canoniga Lectoral. 86862

Puebla, Mex. (City) Basilica. Choro. (66575)

Puebla, Mex. (City) Basilica. Dean y Cabildo. 58279, 72777, (73620)

Puebla, Mex. (City) Basilica. Dean y Cabildo. petitioners 72777, (73620)

Puebla, Mex. (City) Basilica. Dean y Cabildo. plaintiffs 93332

Puebla, Mex. (City) Catedral. see Puebla, Mex. (City) Basilica.

Puebla, Mex. (City) Colegio de Abogados. see Colegio de Abogados de Puebla.

Puebla, Mex. (City) Real Colegio de S. Ignacio de la Compania de Jesus. see Real Colegio de S. Ignacio de la Compania de Jesus, Puebla, Mex.

Puebla, Mex. (City) Convento de la Santissima Trinidad. 66551, 68847-68848

Puebla, Mex. (City) Convento de la Purisima Concepcion. 66551

Puebla, Mex. (City) Convento de N. P. S. Domingo. 66568

Puebla, Mex. (City) Convento de Nuestra Senora de la Concepcion. 68847-68848

Puebla, Mex. (City) Convento de San Geronimo (Augustinian) 24150, 66551, 68846

Puebla, Mex. (City) Convento de Santa Catarina de Sena. 66551

Puebla, Mex. (City) Convento de Santa Ines de Monte Policiano. 66551

Puebla, Mex. (City) Convento del Glorioso Padre San Geronimo. see Puebla, Mex. (City) Convento de San Feronimo (Augustinian)

Puebla, Mex. (City) Gremio de Plateros. see Gremio de Plateros, Puebla, Mex.

Puebla, Mex, (City) Iglesia Catedral. see Puebla, Mex. (City) Basilica.

Puebla, Mex. (City) Ordinances, etc. 66570

Puebla, Mex. (City) Santa Iglesia Catedral. see Puebla, Mex. (City) Basilica.

Puebla, Mex. (City) Senadores Eclesiasticos. 66569

Puebla, Mex. (City) Sindico. 66564

Puebla, Mex. (City) Sociedad Bienhechora, Puebla, Mex.

Puebla, Mex. (Departamento) see Puebla, Mex. (State)

Puebla, Mex. (State) Congreso. 66553

Puebla, Mex. (State) Congreso Constituyente. 66550, 66552, 66572

Puebla, Mex. (State) Constitution. 66552

Puebla, Mex. (State) Gobernador (Ibarra) 66556 see also Ibarra, Francisco.

Puebla, Mex. (State) Junta. 69982

Puebla, Mex. (State) Junta de Industria. 66577

Puebla, Mex. (State) Laws, statutes, etc. 66550, 66552, 66558, 66572

Puebla, Mex. (State) Secretario del Despacho de Gobierno. 66565

Puebla, Mex. (State) Tribunal Superior. (66545)

Puebla, par Louis Noir. (55409)

Puebla sagrada y profana. 99620

Puebla de los Angeles, Mexico. see Puebla, Mexico.

Pueblo Colony, South Pueblo, Colorado. firm 88158

Pueblo colony of southern Colorado. 88158

"Pueblo question" solved in a plain statement of facts and law. (36629)

Puego, Sylvestri. ed. 530

Pueirredon, Juan Martin de. see Pueyrredon, Juan Martin de.

Puella quaedam sectae Anglicanae. pseud. Epistola alia. see Pitt, Miss ---------.

Puelles, Jose Maria de Jesus. 95094

Puenta, Juan Gonzalez de la. see Gonzalez de la Puenta, Juan.